Oxford Dictionary of
National Biography

Volume 50

Oxford Dictionary of National Biography

IN ASSOCIATION WITH
The British Academy

From the earliest times to the year 2000

Edited by
H. C. G. Matthew
and
Brian Harrison

Volume 50
Sharp–Smiles

OXFORD
UNIVERSITY PRESS

OXFORD
UNIVERSITY PRESS

Great Clarendon Street, Oxford OX2 6DP

Oxford University Press is a department of the University of Oxford.
It furthers the University's objective of excellence in research, scholarship,
and education by publishing worldwide in

Oxford New York

Auckland Bangkok Buenos Aires Cape Town
Chennai Dar es Salaam Delhi Hong Kong Istanbul Karachi
Kolkata Kuala Lumpur Madrid Melbourne Mexico City Mumbai Nairobi
São Paulo Shanghai Taipei Tokyo Toronto

Oxford is a registered trade mark of Oxford University Press
in the UK and in certain other countries

Published in the United States
by Oxford University Press Inc., New York

British Library Cataloguing in Publication Data
Data available

Library of Congress Cataloging in Publication Data
Data available: for details see volume 1, p. iv

ISBN 0-19-861400-4 (this volume)
ISBN 0-19-861411-X (set of sixty volumes)

Text captured by Alliance Phototypesetters, Pondicherry
Illustrations reproduced and archived by
Alliance Graphics Ltd, UK
Typeset in OUP Swift by Interactive Sciences Limited, Gloucester
Printed in Great Britain on acid-free paper by
Butler and Tanner Ltd,
Frome, Somerset

LIST OF ABBREVIATIONS

1 General abbreviations

AB	bachelor of arts
ABC	Australian Broadcasting Corporation
ABC TV	ABC Television
act.	active
A$	Australian dollar
AD	*anno domini*
AFC	Air Force Cross
AIDS	acquired immune deficiency syndrome
AK	Alaska
AL	Alabama
A level	advanced level [examination]
ALS	associate of the Linnean Society
AM	master of arts
AMICE	associate member of the Institution of Civil Engineers
ANZAC	Australian and New Zealand Army Corps
appx *pl.* appxs	appendix(es)
AR	Arkansas
ARA	associate of the Royal Academy
ARCA	associate of the Royal College of Art
ARCM	associate of the Royal College of Music
ARCO	associate of the Royal College of Organists
ARIBA	associate of the Royal Institute of British Architects
ARP	air-raid precautions
ARRC	associate of the Royal Red Cross
ARSA	associate of the Royal Scottish Academy
art.	article / item
ASC	Army Service Corps
Asch	Austrian Schilling
ASDIC	Antisubmarine Detection Investigation Committee
ATS	Auxiliary Territorial Service
ATV	Associated Television
Aug	August
AZ	Arizona
b.	born
BA	bachelor of arts
BA (Admin.)	bachelor of arts (administration)
BAFTA	British Academy of Film and Television Arts
BAO	bachelor of arts in obstetrics
bap.	baptized
BBC	British Broadcasting Corporation / Company
BC	before Christ
BCE	before the common (*or* Christian) era
BCE	bachelor of civil engineering
BCG	bacillus of Calmette and Guérin [inoculation against tuberculosis]
BCh	bachelor of surgery
BChir	bachelor of surgery
BCL	bachelor of civil law
BCnL	bachelor of canon law
BCom	bachelor of commerce
BD	bachelor of divinity
BEd	bachelor of education
BEng	bachelor of engineering
bk *pl.* bks	book(s)
BL	bachelor of law / letters / literature
BLitt	bachelor of letters
BM	bachelor of medicine
BMus	bachelor of music
BP	before present
BP	British Petroleum
Bros.	Brothers
BS	(1) bachelor of science; (2) bachelor of surgery; (3) British standard
BSc	bachelor of science
BSc (Econ.)	bachelor of science (economics)
BSc (Eng.)	bachelor of science (engineering)
bt	baronet
BTh	bachelor of theology
bur.	buried
C.	command [identifier for published parliamentary papers]
c.	*circa*
c.	*capitulum pl. capitula*: chapter(s)
CA	California
Cantab.	Cantabrigiensis
cap.	*capitulum pl. capitula*: chapter(s)
CB	companion of the Bath
CBE	commander of the Order of the British Empire
CBS	Columbia Broadcasting System
cc	cubic centimetres
C$	Canadian dollar
CD	compact disc
Cd	command [identifier for published parliamentary papers]
CE	Common (*or* Christian) Era
cent.	century
cf.	compare
CH	Companion of Honour
chap.	chapter
ChB	bachelor of surgery
CI	Imperial Order of the Crown of India
CIA	Central Intelligence Agency
CID	Criminal Investigation Department
CIE	companion of the Order of the Indian Empire
Cie	Compagnie
CLit	companion of literature
CM	master of surgery
cm	centimetre(s)

Cmd	command [identifier for published parliamentary papers]
CMG	companion of the Order of St Michael and St George
Cmnd	command [identifier for published parliamentary papers]
CO	Colorado
Co.	company
co.	county
col. *pl.* cols.	column(s)
Corp.	corporation
CSE	certificate of secondary education
CSI	companion of the Order of the Star of India
CT	Connecticut
CVO	commander of the Royal Victorian Order
cwt	hundredweight
$	(American) dollar
d.	(1) penny (pence); (2) died
DBE	dame commander of the Order of the British Empire
DCH	diploma in child health
DCh	doctor of surgery
DCL	doctor of civil law
DCnL	doctor of canon law
DCVO	dame commander of the Royal Victorian Order
DD	doctor of divinity
DE	Delaware
Dec	December
dem.	demolished
DEng	doctor of engineering
des.	destroyed
DFC	Distinguished Flying Cross
DipEd	diploma in education
DipPsych	diploma in psychiatry
diss.	dissertation
DL	deputy lieutenant
DLitt	doctor of letters
DLittCelt	doctor of Celtic letters
DM	(1) Deutschmark; (2) doctor of medicine; (3) doctor of musical arts
DMus	doctor of music
DNA	dioxyribonucleic acid
doc.	document
DOL	doctor of oriental learning
DPH	diploma in public health
DPhil	doctor of philosophy
DPM	diploma in psychological medicine
DSC	Distinguished Service Cross
DSc	doctor of science
DSc (Econ.)	doctor of science (economics)
DSc (Eng.)	doctor of science (engineering)
DSM	Distinguished Service Medal
DSO	companion of the Distinguished Service Order
DSocSc	doctor of social science
DTech	doctor of technology
DTh	doctor of theology
DTM	diploma in tropical medicine
DTMH	diploma in tropical medicine and hygiene
DU	doctor of the university
DUniv	doctor of the university
dwt	pennyweight
EC	European Community
ed. *pl.* eds.	edited / edited by / editor(s)
Edin.	Edinburgh
edn	edition
EEC	European Economic Community
EFTA	European Free Trade Association
EICS	East India Company Service
EMI	Electrical and Musical Industries (Ltd)
Eng.	English
enl.	enlarged
ENSA	Entertainments National Service Association
ep. *pl.* epp.	*epistola(e)*
ESP	extra-sensory perception
esp.	especially
esq.	esquire
est.	estimate / estimated
EU	European Union
ex	sold by (*lit.* out of)
excl.	excludes / excluding
exh.	exhibited
exh. cat.	exhibition catalogue
f. *pl.* ff.	following [pages]
FA	Football Association
FACP	fellow of the American College of Physicians
facs.	facsimile
FANY	First Aid Nursing Yeomanry
FBA	fellow of the British Academy
FBI	Federation of British Industries
FCS	fellow of the Chemical Society
Feb	February
FEng	fellow of the Fellowship of Engineering
FFCM	fellow of the Faculty of Community Medicine
FGS	fellow of the Geological Society
fig.	figure
FIMechE	fellow of the Institution of Mechanical Engineers
FL	Florida
fl.	*floruit*
FLS	fellow of the Linnean Society
FM	frequency modulation
fol. *pl.* fols.	folio(s)
Fr	French francs
Fr.	French
FRAeS	fellow of the Royal Aeronautical Society
FRAI	fellow of the Royal Anthropological Institute
FRAM	fellow of the Royal Academy of Music
FRAS	(1) fellow of the Royal Asiatic Society; (2) fellow of the Royal Astronomical Society
FRCM	fellow of the Royal College of Music
FRCO	fellow of the Royal College of Organists
FRCOG	fellow of the Royal College of Obstetricians and Gynaecologists
FRCP(C)	fellow of the Royal College of Physicians of Canada
FRCP (Edin.)	fellow of the Royal College of Physicians of Edinburgh
FRCP (Lond.)	fellow of the Royal College of Physicians of London
FRCPath	fellow of the Royal College of Pathologists
FRCPsych	fellow of the Royal College of Psychiatrists
FRCS	fellow of the Royal College of Surgeons
FRGS	fellow of the Royal Geographical Society
FRIBA	fellow of the Royal Institute of British Architects
FRICS	fellow of the Royal Institute of Chartered Surveyors
FRS	fellow of the Royal Society
FRSA	fellow of the Royal Society of Arts

FRSCM	fellow of the Royal School of Church Music	ISO	companion of the Imperial Service Order
FRSE	fellow of the Royal Society of Edinburgh	It.	Italian
FRSL	fellow of the Royal Society of Literature	ITA	Independent Television Authority
FSA	fellow of the Society of Antiquaries	ITV	Independent Television
ft	foot *pl.* feet	Jan	January
FTCL	fellow of Trinity College of Music, London	JP	justice of the peace
ft-lb per min.	foot-pounds per minute [unit of horsepower]	jun.	junior
FZS	fellow of the Zoological Society	KB	knight of the Order of the Bath
GA	Georgia	KBE	knight commander of the Order of the British Empire
GBE	knight or dame grand cross of the Order of the British Empire	KC	king's counsel
GCB	knight grand cross of the Order of the Bath	kcal	kilocalorie
GCE	general certificate of education	KCB	knight commander of the Order of the Bath
GCH	knight grand cross of the Royal Guelphic Order	KCH	knight commander of the Royal Guelphic Order
GCHQ	government communications headquarters	KCIE	knight commander of the Order of the Indian Empire
GCIE	knight grand commander of the Order of the Indian Empire	KCMG	knight commander of the Order of St Michael and St George
GCMG	knight or dame grand cross of the Order of St Michael and St George	KCSI	knight commander of the Order of the Star of India
GCSE	general certificate of secondary education	KCVO	knight commander of the Royal Victorian Order
GCSI	knight grand commander of the Order of the Star of India	keV	kilo-electron-volt
GCStJ	bailiff or dame grand cross of the order of St John of Jerusalem	KG	knight of the Order of the Garter
		KGB	[Soviet committee of state security]
GCVO	knight or dame grand cross of the Royal Victorian Order	KH	knight of the Royal Guelphic Order
		KLM	Koninklijke Luchtvaart Maatschappij (Royal Dutch Air Lines)
GEC	General Electric Company	km	kilometre(s)
Ger.	German	KP	knight of the Order of St Patrick
GI	government (*or* general) issue	KS	Kansas
GMT	Greenwich mean time	KT	knight of the Order of the Thistle
GP	general practitioner	kt	knight
GPU	[Soviet special police unit]	KY	Kentucky
GSO	general staff officer	£	pound(s) sterling
Heb.	Hebrew	£E	Egyptian pound
HEICS	Honourable East India Company Service	L	lira *pl.* lire
HI	Hawaii	l. *pl.* ll.	line(s)
HIV	human immunodeficiency virus	LA	Lousiana
HK$	Hong Kong dollar	LAA	light anti-aircraft
HM	his / her majesty('s)	LAH	licentiate of the Apothecaries' Hall, Dublin
HMAS	his / her majesty's Australian ship	Lat.	Latin
HMNZS	his / her majesty's New Zealand ship	lb	pound(s), unit of weight
HMS	his / her majesty's ship	LDS	licence in dental surgery
HMSO	His / Her Majesty's Stationery Office	*lit.*	literally
HMV	His Master's Voice	LittB	bachelor of letters
Hon.	Honourable	LittD	doctor of letters
hp	horsepower	LKQCPI	licentiate of the King and Queen's College of Physicians, Ireland
hr	hour(s)	LLA	lady literate in arts
HRH	his / her royal highness	LLB	bachelor of laws
HTV	Harlech Television	LLD	doctor of laws
IA	Iowa	LLM	master of laws
ibid.	*ibidem*: in the same place	LM	licentiate in midwifery
ICI	Imperial Chemical Industries (Ltd)	LP	long-playing record
ID	Idaho	LRAM	licentiate of the Royal Academy of Music
IL	Illinois	LRCP	licentiate of the Royal College of Physicians
illus.	illustration	LRCPS (Glasgow)	licentiate of the Royal College of Physicians and Surgeons of Glasgow
illustr.	illustrated		
IN	Indiana	LRCS	licentiate of the Royal College of Surgeons
in.	inch(es)	LSA	licentiate of the Society of Apothecaries
Inc.	Incorporated	LSD	lysergic acid diethylamide
incl.	includes / including	LVO	lieutenant of the Royal Victorian Order
IOU	I owe you	M. *pl.* MM.	Monsieur *pl.* Messieurs
IQ	intelligence quotient	m	metre(s)
Ir£	Irish pound		
IRA	Irish Republican Army		

m. *pl.* mm.	membrane(s)		ND	North Dakota
MA	(1) Massachusetts; (2) master of arts		n.d.	no date
MAI	master of engineering		NE	Nebraska
MB	bachelor of medicine		*nem. con.*	*nemine contradicente*: unanimously
MBA	master of business administration		new ser.	new series
MBE	member of the Order of the British Empire		NH	New Hampshire
MC	Military Cross		NHS	National Health Service
MCC	Marylebone Cricket Club		NJ	New Jersey
MCh	master of surgery		NKVD	[Soviet people's commissariat for internal affairs]
MChir	master of surgery		NM	New Mexico
MCom	master of commerce		nm	nanometre(s)
MD	(1) doctor of medicine; (2) Maryland		no. *pl.* nos.	number(s)
MDMA	methylenedioxymethamphetamine		Nov	November
ME	Maine		n.p.	no place [of publication]
MEd	master of education		NS	new style
MEng	master of engineering		NV	Nevada
MEP	member of the European parliament		NY	New York
MG	Morris Garages		NZBS	New Zealand Broadcasting Service
MGM	Metro-Goldwyn-Mayer		OBE	officer of the Order of the British Empire
Mgr	Monsignor		obit.	obituary
MI	(1) Michigan; (2) military intelligence		Oct	October
MI1c	[secret intelligence department]		OCTU	officer cadets training unit
MI5	[military intelligence department]		OECD	Organization for Economic Co-operation and Development
MI6	[secret intelligence department]		OEEC	Organization for European Economic Co-operation
MI9	[secret escape service]			
MICE	member of the Institution of Civil Engineers		OFM	order of Friars Minor [Franciscans]
MIEE	member of the Institution of Electrical Engineers		OFMCap	Ordine Frati Minori Cappucini: member of the Capuchin order
min.	minute(s)		OH	Ohio
Mk	mark		OK	Oklahoma
ML	(1) licentiate of medicine; (2) master of laws		O level	ordinary level [examination]
MLitt	master of letters		OM	Order of Merit
Mlle	Mademoiselle		OP	order of Preachers [Dominicans]
mm	millimetre(s)		op. *pl.* opp.	opus *pl.* opera
Mme	Madame		OPEC	Organization of Petroleum Exporting Countries
MN	Minnesota		OR	Oregon
MO	Missouri		orig.	original
MOH	medical officer of health		OS	old style
MP	member of parliament		OSB	Order of St Benedict
m.p.h.	miles per hour		OTC	Officers' Training Corps
MPhil	master of philosophy		OWS	Old Watercolour Society
MRCP	member of the Royal College of Physicians		Oxon.	Oxoniensis
MRCS	member of the Royal College of Surgeons		p. *pl.* pp.	page(s)
MRCVS	member of the Royal College of Veterinary Surgeons		PA	Pennsylvania
MRIA	member of the Royal Irish Academy		p.a.	per annum
MS	(1) master of science; (2) Mississippi		para.	paragraph
MS *pl.* MSS	manuscript(s)		PAYE	pay as you earn
MSc	master of science		pbk *pl.* pbks	paperback(s)
MSc (Econ.)	master of science (economics)		*per.*	[during the] period
MT	Montana		PhD	doctor of philosophy
MusB	bachelor of music		pl.	(1) plate(s); (2) plural
MusBac	bachelor of music		priv. coll.	private collection
MusD	doctor of music		pt *pl.* pts	part(s)
MV	motor vessel		pubd	published
MVO	member of the Royal Victorian Order		PVC	polyvinyl chloride
n. *pl.* nn.	note(s)		q. *pl.* qq.	(1) question(s); (2) quire(s)
NAAFI	Navy, Army, and Air Force Institutes		QC	queen's counsel
NASA	National Aeronautics and Space Administration		R	rand
NATO	North Atlantic Treaty Organization		R.	Rex / Regina
NBC	National Broadcasting Corporation		*r*	recto
NC	North Carolina		r.	reigned / ruled
NCO	non-commissioned officer		RA	Royal Academy / Royal Academician

RAC	Royal Automobile Club
RAF	Royal Air Force
RAFVR	Royal Air Force Volunteer Reserve
RAM	[member of the] Royal Academy of Music
RAMC	Royal Army Medical Corps
RCA	Royal College of Art
RCNC	Royal Corps of Naval Constructors
RCOG	Royal College of Obstetricians and Gynaecologists
RDI	royal designer for industry
RE	Royal Engineers
repr. *pl.* reprs.	reprint(s) / reprinted
repro.	reproduced
rev.	revised / revised by / reviser / revision
Revd	Reverend
RHA	Royal Hibernian Academy
RI	(1) Rhode Island; (2) Royal Institute of Painters in Water-Colours
RIBA	Royal Institute of British Architects
RIN	Royal Indian Navy
RM	Reichsmark
RMS	Royal Mail steamer
RN	Royal Navy
RNA	ribonucleic acid
RNAS	Royal Naval Air Service
RNR	Royal Naval Reserve
RNVR	Royal Naval Volunteer Reserve
RO	Record Office
r.p.m.	revolutions per minute
RRS	royal research ship
Rs	rupees
RSA	(1) Royal Scottish Academician; (2) Royal Society of Arts
RSPCA	Royal Society for the Prevention of Cruelty to Animals
Rt Hon.	Right Honourable
Rt Revd	Right Reverend
RUC	Royal Ulster Constabulary
Russ.	Russian
RWS	Royal Watercolour Society
S4C	Sianel Pedwar Cymru
s.	shilling(s)
s.a.	*sub anno*: under the year
SABC	South African Broadcasting Corporation
SAS	Special Air Service
SC	South Carolina
ScD	doctor of science
S$	Singapore dollar
SD	South Dakota
sec.	second(s)
sel.	selected
sen.	senior
Sept	September
ser.	series
SHAPE	supreme headquarters allied powers, Europe
SIDRO	Société Internationale d'Énergie Hydro-Électrique
sig. *pl.* sigs.	signature(s)
sing.	singular
SIS	Secret Intelligence Service
SJ	Society of Jesus

Skr	Swedish krona
Span.	Spanish
SPCK	Society for Promoting Christian Knowledge
SS	(1) Santissimi; (2) Schutzstaffel; (3) steam ship
STB	bachelor of theology
STD	doctor of theology
STM	master of theology
STP	doctor of theology
supp.	supposedly
suppl. *pl.* suppls.	supplement(s)
s.v.	*sub verbo* / *sub voce*: under the word / heading
SY	steam yacht
TA	Territorial Army
TASS	[Soviet news agency]
TB	tuberculosis (*lit.* tubercle bacillus)
TD	(1) *teachtaí dála* (member of the Dáil); (2) territorial decoration
TN	Tennessee
TNT	trinitrotoluene
trans.	translated / translated by / translation / translator
TT	tourist trophy
TUC	Trades Union Congress
TX	Texas
U-boat	*Unterseeboot*: submarine
Ufa	Universum-Film AG
UMIST	University of Manchester Institute of Science and Technology
UN	United Nations
UNESCO	United Nations Educational, Scientific, and Cultural Organization
UNICEF	United Nations International Children's Emergency Fund
unpubd	unpublished
USS	United States ship
UT	Utah
v	verso
v.	versus
VA	Virginia
VAD	Voluntary Aid Detachment
VC	Victoria Cross
VE-day	victory in Europe day
Ven.	Venerable
VJ-day	victory over Japan day
vol. *pl.* vols.	volume(s)
VT	Vermont
WA	Washington [state]
WAAC	Women's Auxiliary Army Corps
WAAF	Women's Auxiliary Air Force
WEA	Workers' Educational Association
WHO	World Health Organization
WI	Wisconsin
WRAF	Women's Royal Air Force
WRNS	Women's Royal Naval Service
WV	West Virginia
WVS	Women's Voluntary Service
WY	Wyoming
¥	yen
YMCA	Young Men's Christian Association
YWCA	Young Women's Christian Association

2 Institution abbreviations

All Souls Oxf.	All Souls College, Oxford
AM Oxf.	Ashmolean Museum, Oxford
Balliol Oxf.	Balliol College, Oxford
BBC WAC	BBC Written Archives Centre, Reading
Beds. & Luton ARS	Bedfordshire and Luton Archives and Record Service, Bedford
Berks. RO	Berkshire Record Office, Reading
BFI	British Film Institute, London
BFI NFTVA	British Film Institute, London, National Film and Television Archive
BGS	British Geological Survey, Keyworth, Nottingham
Birm. CA	Birmingham Central Library, Birmingham City Archives
Birm. CL	Birmingham Central Library
BL	British Library, London
BL NSA	British Library, London, National Sound Archive
BL OIOC	British Library, London, Oriental and India Office Collections
BLPES	London School of Economics and Political Science, British Library of Political and Economic Science
BM	British Museum, London
Bodl. Oxf.	Bodleian Library, Oxford
Bodl. RH	Bodleian Library of Commonwealth and African Studies at Rhodes House, Oxford
Borth. Inst.	Borthwick Institute of Historical Research, University of York
Boston PL	Boston Public Library, Massachusetts
Bristol RO	Bristol Record Office
Bucks. RLSS	Buckinghamshire Records and Local Studies Service, Aylesbury
CAC Cam.	Churchill College, Cambridge, Churchill Archives Centre
Cambs. AS	Cambridgeshire Archive Service
CCC Cam.	Corpus Christi College, Cambridge
CCC Oxf.	Corpus Christi College, Oxford
Ches. & Chester ALSS	Cheshire and Chester Archives and Local Studies Service
Christ Church Oxf.	Christ Church, Oxford
Christies	Christies, London
City Westm. AC	City of Westminster Archives Centre, London
CKS	Centre for Kentish Studies, Maidstone
CLRO	Corporation of London Records Office
Coll. Arms	College of Arms, London
Col. U.	Columbia University, New York
Cornwall RO	Cornwall Record Office, Truro
Courtauld Inst.	Courtauld Institute of Art, London
CUL	Cambridge University Library
Cumbria AS	Cumbria Archive Service
Derbys. RO	Derbyshire Record Office, Matlock
Devon RO	Devon Record Office, Exeter
Dorset RO	Dorset Record Office, Dorchester
Duke U.	Duke University, Durham, North Carolina
Duke U., Perkins L.	Duke University, Durham, North Carolina, William R. Perkins Library
Durham Cath. CL	Durham Cathedral, chapter library
Durham RO	Durham Record Office
DWL	Dr Williams's Library, London
Essex RO	Essex Record Office
E. Sussex RO	East Sussex Record Office, Lewes
Eton	Eton College, Berkshire
FM Cam.	Fitzwilliam Museum, Cambridge
Folger	Folger Shakespeare Library, Washington, DC
Garr. Club	Garrick Club, London
Girton Cam.	Girton College, Cambridge
GL	Guildhall Library, London
Glos. RO	Gloucestershire Record Office, Gloucester
Gon. & Caius Cam.	Gonville and Caius College, Cambridge
Gov. Art Coll.	Government Art Collection
GS Lond.	Geological Society of London
Hants. RO	Hampshire Record Office, Winchester
Harris Man. Oxf.	Harris Manchester College, Oxford
Harvard TC	Harvard Theatre Collection, Harvard University, Cambridge, Massachusetts, Nathan Marsh Pusey Library
Harvard U.	Harvard University, Cambridge, Massachusetts
Harvard U., Houghton L.	Harvard University, Cambridge, Massachusetts, Houghton Library
Herefs. RO	Herefordshire Record Office, Hereford
Herts. ALS	Hertfordshire Archives and Local Studies, Hertford
Hist. Soc. Penn.	Historical Society of Pennsylvania, Philadelphia
HLRO	House of Lords Record Office, London
Hult. Arch.	Hulton Archive, London and New York
Hunt. L.	Huntington Library, San Marino, California
ICL	Imperial College, London
Inst. CE	Institution of Civil Engineers, London
Inst. EE	Institution of Electrical Engineers, London
IWM	Imperial War Museum, London
IWM FVA	Imperial War Museum, London, Film and Video Archive
IWM SA	Imperial War Museum, London, Sound Archive
JRL	John Rylands University Library of Manchester
King's AC Cam.	King's College Archives Centre, Cambridge
King's Cam.	King's College, Cambridge
King's Lond.	King's College, London
King's Lond., Liddell Hart C.	King's College, London, Liddell Hart Centre for Military Archives
Lancs. RO	Lancashire Record Office, Preston
L. Cong.	Library of Congress, Washington, DC
Leics. RO	Leicestershire, Leicester, and Rutland Record Office, Leicester
Lincs. Arch.	Lincolnshire Archives, Lincoln
Linn. Soc.	Linnean Society of London
LMA	London Metropolitan Archives
LPL	Lambeth Palace, London
Lpool RO	Liverpool Record Office and Local Studies Service
LUL	London University Library
Magd. Cam.	Magdalene College, Cambridge
Magd. Oxf.	Magdalen College, Oxford
Man. City Gall.	Manchester City Galleries
Man. CL	Manchester Central Library
Mass. Hist. Soc.	Massachusetts Historical Society, Boston
Merton Oxf.	Merton College, Oxford
MHS Oxf.	Museum of the History of Science, Oxford
Mitchell L., Glas.	Mitchell Library, Glasgow
Mitchell L., NSW	State Library of New South Wales, Sydney, Mitchell Library
Morgan L.	Pierpont Morgan Library, New York
NA Canada	National Archives of Canada, Ottawa
NA Ire.	National Archives of Ireland, Dublin
NAM	National Army Museum, London
NA Scot.	National Archives of Scotland, Edinburgh
News Int. RO	News International Record Office, London
NG Ire.	National Gallery of Ireland, Dublin

NG Scot.	National Gallery of Scotland, Edinburgh
NHM	Natural History Museum, London
NL Aus.	National Library of Australia, Canberra
NL Ire.	National Library of Ireland, Dublin
NL NZ	National Library of New Zealand, Wellington
NL NZ, Turnbull L.	National Library of New Zealand, Wellington, Alexander Turnbull Library
NL Scot.	National Library of Scotland, Edinburgh
NL Wales	National Library of Wales, Aberystwyth
NMG Wales	National Museum and Gallery of Wales, Cardiff
NMM	National Maritime Museum, London
Norfolk RO	Norfolk Record Office, Norwich
Northants. RO	Northamptonshire Record Office, Northampton
Northumbd RO	Northumberland Record Office
Notts. Arch.	Nottinghamshire Archives, Nottingham
NPG	National Portrait Gallery, London
NRA	National Archives, London, Historical Manuscripts Commission, National Register of Archives
Nuffield Oxf.	Nuffield College, Oxford
N. Yorks. CRO	North Yorkshire County Record Office, Northallerton
NYPL	New York Public Library
Oxf. UA	Oxford University Archives
Oxf. U. Mus. NH	Oxford University Museum of Natural History
Oxon. RO	Oxfordshire Record Office, Oxford
Pembroke Cam.	Pembroke College, Cambridge
PRO	National Archives, London, Public Record Office
PRO NIre.	Public Record Office for Northern Ireland, Belfast
Pusey Oxf.	Pusey House, Oxford
RA	Royal Academy of Arts, London
Ransom HRC	Harry Ransom Humanities Research Center, University of Texas, Austin
RAS	Royal Astronomical Society, London
RBG Kew	Royal Botanic Gardens, Kew, London
RCP Lond.	Royal College of Physicians of London
RCS Eng.	Royal College of Surgeons of England, London
RGS	Royal Geographical Society, London
RIBA	Royal Institute of British Architects, London
RIBA BAL	Royal Institute of British Architects, London, British Architectural Library
Royal Arch.	Royal Archives, Windsor Castle, Berkshire [by gracious permission of her majesty the queen]
Royal Irish Acad.	Royal Irish Academy, Dublin
Royal Scot. Acad.	Royal Scottish Academy, Edinburgh
RS	Royal Society, London
RSA	Royal Society of Arts, London
RS Friends, Lond.	Religious Society of Friends, London
St Ant. Oxf.	St Antony's College, Oxford
St John Cam.	St John's College, Cambridge
S. Antiquaries, Lond.	Society of Antiquaries of London
Sci. Mus.	Science Museum, London
Scot. NPG	Scottish National Portrait Gallery, Edinburgh
Scott Polar RI	University of Cambridge, Scott Polar Research Institute
Sheff. Arch.	Sheffield Archives
Shrops. RRC	Shropshire Records and Research Centre, Shrewsbury
SOAS	School of Oriental and African Studies, London
Som. ARS	Somerset Archive and Record Service, Taunton
Staffs. RO	Staffordshire Record Office, Stafford

Suffolk RO	Suffolk Record Office
Surrey HC	Surrey History Centre, Woking
TCD	Trinity College, Dublin
Trinity Cam.	Trinity College, Cambridge
U. Aberdeen	University of Aberdeen
U. Birm.	University of Birmingham
U. Birm. L.	University of Birmingham Library
U. Cal.	University of California
U. Cam.	University of Cambridge
UCL	University College, London
U. Durham	University of Durham
U. Durham L.	University of Durham Library
U. Edin.	University of Edinburgh
U. Edin., New Coll.	University of Edinburgh, New College
U. Edin., New Coll. L.	University of Edinburgh, New College Library
U. Edin. L.	University of Edinburgh Library
U. Glas.	University of Glasgow
U. Glas. L.	University of Glasgow Library
U. Hull	University of Hull
U. Hull, Brynmor Jones L.	University of Hull, Brynmor Jones Library
U. Leeds	University of Leeds
U. Leeds, Brotherton L.	University of Leeds, Brotherton Library
U. Lond.	University of London
U. Lpool	University of Liverpool
U. Lpool L.	University of Liverpool Library
U. Mich.	University of Michigan, Ann Arbor
U. Mich., Clements L.	University of Michigan, Ann Arbor, William L. Clements Library
U. Newcastle	University of Newcastle upon Tyne
U. Newcastle, Robinson L.	University of Newcastle upon Tyne, Robinson Library
U. Nott.	University of Nottingham
U. Nott. L.	University of Nottingham Library
U. Oxf.	University of Oxford
U. Reading	University of Reading
U. Reading L.	University of Reading Library
U. St Andr.	University of St Andrews
U. St Andr. L.	University of St Andrews Library
U. Southampton	University of Southampton
U. Southampton L.	University of Southampton Library
U. Sussex	University of Sussex, Brighton
U. Texas	University of Texas, Austin
U. Wales	University of Wales
U. Warwick Mod. RC	University of Warwick, Coventry, Modern Records Centre
V&A	Victoria and Albert Museum, London
V&A NAL	Victoria and Albert Museum, London, National Art Library
Warks. CRO	Warwickshire County Record Office, Warwick
Wellcome L.	Wellcome Library for the History and Understanding of Medicine, London
Westm. DA	Westminster Diocesan Archives, London
Wilts. & Swindon RO	Wiltshire and Swindon Record Office, Trowbridge
Worcs. RO	Worcestershire Record Office, Worcester
W. Sussex RO	West Sussex Record Office, Chichester
W. Yorks. AS	West Yorkshire Archive Service
Yale U.	Yale University, New Haven, Connecticut
Yale U., Beinecke L.	Yale University, New Haven, Connecticut, Beinecke Rare Book and Manuscript Library
Yale U. CBA	Yale University, New Haven, Connecticut, Yale Center for British Art

3 Bibliographic abbreviations

Adams, *Drama* W. D. Adams, *A dictionary of the drama*, 1: *A–G* (1904); 2: *H–Z* (1956) [vol. 2 microfilm only]

AFM J O'Donovan, ed. and trans., *Annala rioghachta Eireann / Annals of the kingdom of Ireland by the four masters*, 7 vols. (1848–51); 2nd edn (1856); 3rd edn (1990)

Allibone, *Dict.* S. A. Allibone, *A critical dictionary of English literature and British and American authors*, 3 vols. (1859–71); suppl. by J. F. Kirk, 2 vols. (1891)

ANB J. A. Garraty and M. C. Carnes, eds., *American national biography*, 24 vols. (1999)

Anderson, *Scot. nat.* W. Anderson, *The Scottish nation, or, The surnames, families, literature, honours, and biographical history of the people of Scotland*, 3 vols. (1859–63)

Ann. mon. H. R. Luard, ed., *Annales monastici*, 5 vols., Rolls Series, 36 (1864–9)

Ann. Ulster S. Mac Airt and G. Mac Niocaill, eds., *Annals of Ulster (to AD 1131)* (1983)

APC *Acts of the privy council of England*, new ser., 46 vols. (1890–1964)

APS *The acts of the parliaments of Scotland*, 12 vols. in 13 (1814–75)

Arber, *Regs. Stationers* F. Arber, ed., *A transcript of the registers of the Company of Stationers of London, 1554–1640 AD*, 5 vols. (1875–94)

ArchR *Architectural Review*

ASC D. Whitelock, D. C. Douglas, and S. I. Tucker, ed. and trans., *The Anglo-Saxon Chronicle: a revised translation* (1961)

AS chart. P. H. Sawyer, *Anglo-Saxon charters: an annotated list and bibliography*, Royal Historical Society Guides and Handbooks (1968)

AusDB D. Pike and others, eds., *Australian dictionary of biography*, 16 vols. (1966–2002)

Baker, *Serjeants* J. H. Baker, *The order of serjeants at law*, SeldS, suppl. ser., 5 (1984)

Bale, *Cat.* J. Bale, *Scriptorum illustrium Maioris Brytannie, quam nunc Angliam et Scotiam vocant: catalogus*, 2 vols. in 1 (Basel, 1557–9); facs. edn (1971)

Bale, *Index* J. Bale, *Index Britanniae scriptorum*, ed. R. L. Poole and M. Bateson (1902); facs. edn (1990)

BBCS *Bulletin of the Board of Celtic Studies*

BDMBR J. O. Baylen and N. J. Gossman, eds., *Biographical dictionary of modern British radicals*, 3 vols. in 4 (1979–88)

Bede, *Hist. eccl.* *Bede's Ecclesiastical history of the English people*, ed. and trans. B. Colgrave and R. A. B. Mynors, OMT (1969); repr. (1991)

Bénézit, *Dict.* E. Bénézit, *Dictionnaire critique et documentaire des peintres, sculpteurs, dessinateurs et graveurs*, 3 vols. (Paris, 1911–23); new edn, 8 vols. (1948–66), repr. (1966); 3rd edn, rev. and enl., 10 vols. (1976); 4th edn, 14 vols. (1999)

BIHR *Bulletin of the Institute of Historical Research*

Birch, *Seals* W. de Birch, *Catalogue of seals in the department of manuscripts in the British Museum*, 6 vols. (1887–1900)

Bishop Burnet's History *Bishop Burnet's History of his own time*, ed. M. J. Routh, 2nd edn, 6 vols. (1833)

Blackwood *Blackwood's [Edinburgh] Magazine*, 328 vols. (1817–1980)

Blain, Clements & Grundy, *Feminist comp.* V. Blain, P. Clements, and I. Grundy, eds., *The feminist companion to literature in English* (1990)

BL cat. *The British Library general catalogue of printed books* [in 360 vols. with suppls., also CD-ROM and online]

BMJ *British Medical Journal*

Boase & Courtney, *Bibl. Corn.* G. C. Boase and W. P. Courtney, *Bibliotheca Cornubiensis: a catalogue of the writings … of Cornishmen*, 3 vols. (1874–82)

Boase, *Mod. Eng. biog.* F. Boase, *Modern English biography: containing many thousand concise memoirs of persons who have died since the year 1850*, 6 vols. (privately printed, Truro, 1892–1921); repr. (1965)

Boswell, *Life* *Boswell's Life of Johnson: together with Journal of a tour to the Hebrides and Johnson's Diary of a journey into north Wales*, ed. G. B. Hill, enl. edn, rev. L. F. Powell, 6 vols. (1934–50); 2nd edn (1964); repr. (1971)

Brown & Stratton, *Brit. mus.* J. D. Brown and S. S. Stratton, *British musical biography* (1897)

Bryan, *Painters* M. Bryan, *A biographical and critical dictionary of painters and engravers*, 2 vols. (1816); new edn, ed. G. Stanley (1849); new edn, ed. R. E. Graves and W. Armstrong, 2 vols. (1886–9); [4th edn], ed. G. C. Williamson, 5 vols. (1903–5) [various reprs.]

Burke, *Gen. GB* J. Burke, *A genealogical and heraldic history of the commoners of Great Britain and Ireland*, 4 vols. (1833–8); new edn as *A genealogical and heraldic dictionary of the landed gentry of Great Britain and Ireland*, 3 vols. [1843–9] [many later edns]

Burke, *Gen. Ire.* J. B. Burke, *A genealogical and heraldic history of the landed gentry of Ireland* (1899); 2nd edn (1904); 3rd edn (1912); 4th edn (1958); 5th edn as *Burke's Irish family records* (1976)

Burke, *Peerage* J. Burke, *A general [later edns A genealogical] and heraldic dictionary of the peerage and baronetage of the United Kingdom* [later edns *the British empire*] (1829–)

Burney, *Hist. mus.* C. Burney, *A general history of music, from the earliest ages to the present period*, 4 vols. (1776–89)

Burtchaell & Sadleir, *Alum. Dubl.* G. D. Burtchaell and T. U. Sadleir, *Alumni Dublinenses: a register of the students, graduates, and provosts of Trinity College* (1924); [2nd edn], with suppl., in 2 pts (1935)

Calamy rev. A. G. Matthews, *Calamy revised* (1934); repr. (1988)

CCI *Calendar of confirmations and inventories granted and given up in the several commissariots of Scotland* (1876–)

CClR *Calendar of the close rolls preserved in the Public Record Office*, 47 vols. (1892–1963)

CDS J. Bain, ed., *Calendar of documents relating to Scotland*, 4 vols., PRO (1881–8); suppl. vol. 5, ed. G. G. Simpson and J. D. Galbraith [1986]

CEPR letters W. H. Bliss, C. Johnson, and J. Twemlow, eds., *Calendar of entries in the papal registers relating to Great Britain and Ireland: papal letters* (1893–)

CGPLA *Calendars of the grants of probate and letters of administration* [in 4 ser.: England & Wales, Northern Ireland, Ireland, and Éire]

Chambers, *Scots.* R. Chambers, ed., *A biographical dictionary of eminent Scotsmen*, 4 vols. (1832–5)

Chancery records chancery records pubd by the PRO

Chancery records (RC) chancery records pubd by the Record Commissions

CIPM	*Calendar of inquisitions post mortem*, [20 vols.], PRO (1904–); also *Henry VII*, 3 vols. (1898–1955)
Clarendon, *Hist. rebellion*	E. Hyde, earl of Clarendon, *The history of the rebellion and civil wars in England*, 6 vols. (1888); repr. (1958) and (1992)
Cobbett, *Parl. hist.*	W. Cobbett and J. Wright, eds., *Cobbett's Parliamentary history of England*, 36 vols. (1806–1820)
Colvin, *Archs.*	H. Colvin, *A biographical dictionary of British architects, 1600–1840*, 3rd edn (1995)
Cooper, *Ath. Cantab.*	C. H. Cooper and T. Cooper, *Athenae Cantabrigienses*, 3 vols. (1858–1913); repr. (1967)
CPR	*Calendar of the patent rolls preserved in the Public Record Office* (1891–)
Crockford	*Crockford's Clerical Directory*
CS	Camden Society
CSP	*Calendar of state papers* [in 11 ser.: *domestic, Scotland, Scottish series, Ireland, colonial, Commonwealth, foreign, Spain* [at Simancas], *Rome, Milan*, and *Venice*]
CYS	Canterbury and York Society
DAB	*Dictionary of American biography*, 21 vols. (1928–36), repr. in 11 vols. (1964); 10 suppls. (1944–96)
DBB	D. J. Jeremy, ed., *Dictionary of business biography*, 5 vols. (1984–6)
DCB	G. W. Brown and others, *Dictionary of Canadian biography*, [14 vols.] (1966–)
Debrett's Peerage	*Debrett's Peerage* (1803–) [sometimes *Debrett's Illustrated peerage*]
Desmond, *Botanists*	R. Desmond, *Dictionary of British and Irish botanists and horticulturists* (1977); rev. edn (1994)
Dir. Brit. archs.	A. Felstead, J. Franklin, and L. Pinfield, eds., *Directory of British architects, 1834–1900* (1993); 2nd edn, ed. A. Brodie and others, 2 vols. (2001)
DLB	J. M. Bellamy and J. Saville, eds., *Dictionary of labour biography*, [10 vols.] (1972–)
DLitB	Dictionary of Literary Biography
DNB	*Dictionary of national biography*, 63 vols. (1885–1900), suppl., 3 vols. (1901); repr. in 22 vols. (1908–9); 10 further suppls. (1912–96); *Missing persons* (1993)
DNZB	W. H. Oliver and C. Orange, eds., *The dictionary of New Zealand biography*, 5 vols. (1990–2000)
DSAB	W. J. de Kock and others, eds., *Dictionary of South African biography*, 5 vols. (1968–87)
DSB	C. C. Gillispie and F. L. Holmes, eds., *Dictionary of scientific biography*, 16 vols. (1970–80); repr. in 8 vols. (1981); 2 vol. suppl. (1990)
DSBB	A. Slaven and S. Checkland, eds., *Dictionary of Scottish business biography, 1860–1960*, 2 vols. (1986–90)
DSCHT	N. M. de S. Cameron and others, eds., *Dictionary of Scottish church history and theology* (1993)
Dugdale, *Monasticon*	W. Dugdale, *Monasticon Anglicanum*, 3 vols. (1655–72); 2nd edn, 3 vols. (1661–82); new edn, ed. J. Caley, J. Ellis, and B. Bandinel, 6 vols. in 8 pts (1817–30); repr. (1846) and (1970)
DWB	J. E. Lloyd and others, eds., *Dictionary of Welsh biography down to 1940* (1959) [Eng. trans. of *Y bywgraffiadur Cymreig hyd 1940*, 2nd edn (1954)]
EdinR	*Edinburgh Review, or, Critical Journal*
EETS	Early English Text Society
Emden, *Cam.*	A. B. Emden, *A biographical register of the University of Cambridge to 1500* (1963)
Emden, *Oxf.*	A. B. Emden, *A biographical register of the University of Oxford to AD 1500*, 3 vols. (1957–9); also *A biographical register of the University of Oxford, AD 1501 to 1540* (1974)
EngHR	*English Historical Review*
Engraved Brit. ports.	F. M. O'Donoghue and H. M. Hake, *Catalogue of engraved British portraits preserved in the department of prints and drawings in the British Museum*, 6 vols. (1908–25)
ER	The English Reports, 178 vols. (1900–32)
ESTC	*English short title catalogue, 1475–1800* [CD-ROM and online]
Evelyn, *Diary*	*The diary of John Evelyn*, ed. E. S. De Beer, 6 vols. (1955); repr. (2000)
Farington, *Diary*	*The diary of Joseph Farington*, ed. K. Garlick and others, 17 vols. (1978–98)
Fasti Angl. (Hardy)	J. Le Neve, *Fasti ecclesiae Anglicanae*, ed. T. D. Hardy, 3 vols. (1854)
Fasti Angl., 1066–1300	[J. Le Neve], *Fasti ecclesiae Anglicanae, 1066–1300*, ed. D. E. Greenway and J. S. Barrow, [8 vols.] (1968–)
Fasti Angl., 1300–1541	[J. Le Neve], *Fasti ecclesiae Anglicanae, 1300–1541*, 12 vols. (1962–7)
Fasti Angl., 1541–1857	[J. Le Neve], *Fasti ecclesiae Anglicanae, 1541–1857*, ed. J. M. Horn, D. M. Smith, and D. S. Bailey, [9 vols.] (1969–)
Fasti Scot.	H. Scott, *Fasti ecclesiae Scoticanae*, 3 vols. in 6 (1871); new edn, [11 vols.] (1915–)
FO List	*Foreign Office List*
Fortescue, *Brit. army*	J. W. Fortescue, *A history of the British army*, 13 vols. (1899–1930)
Foss, *Judges*	E. Foss, *The judges of England*, 9 vols. (1848–64); repr. (1966)
Foster, *Alum. Oxon.*	J. Foster, ed., *Alumni Oxonienses: the members of the University of Oxford, 1715–1886*, 4 vols. (1887–8); later edn (1891); also *Alumni Oxonienses … 1500–1714*, 4 vols. (1891–2); 8 vol. repr. (1968) and (2000)
Fuller, *Worthies*	T. Fuller, *The history of the worthies of England*, 4 pts (1662); new edn, 2 vols., ed. J. Nichols (1811); new edn, 3 vols., ed. P. A. Nuttall (1840); repr. (1965)
GEC, *Baronetage*	G. E. Cokayne, *Complete baronetage*, 6 vols. (1900–09); repr. (1983) [microprint]
GEC, *Peerage*	G. E. C. [G. E. Cokayne], *The complete peerage of England, Scotland, Ireland, Great Britain, and the United Kingdom*, 8 vols. (1887–98); new edn, ed. V. Gibbs and others, 14 vols. in 15 (1910–98); microprint repr. (1982) and (1987)
Genest, *Eng. stage*	J. Genest, *Some account of the English stage from the Restoration in 1660 to 1830*, 10 vols. (1832); repr. [New York, 1965]
Gillow, *Lit. biog. hist.*	J. Gillow, *A literary and biographical history or bibliographical dictionary of the English Catholics, from the breach with Rome, in 1534, to the present time*, 5 vols. [1885–1902]; repr. (1961); repr. with preface by C. Gillow (1999)
Gir. Camb. opera	*Giraldi Cambrensis opera*, ed. J. S. Brewer, J. F. Dimock, and G. F. Warner, 8 vols., Rolls Series, 21 (1861–91)
GJ	*Geographical Journal*

Gladstone, *Diaries* — *The Gladstone diaries: with cabinet minutes and prime-ministerial correspondence*, ed. M. R. D. Foot and H. C. G. Matthew, 14 vols. (1968–94)

GM — *Gentleman's Magazine*

Graves, *Artists* — A. Graves, ed., *A dictionary of artists who have exhibited works in the principal London exhibitions of oil paintings from 1760 to 1880* (1884); new edn (1895); 3rd edn (1901); facs. edn (1969); repr. [1970], (1973), and (1984)

Graves, *Brit. Inst.* — A. Graves, *The British Institution, 1806–1867: a complete dictionary of contributors and their work from the foundation of the institution* (1875); facs. edn (1908); repr. (1969)

Graves, *RA exhibitors* — A. Graves, *The Royal Academy of Arts: a complete dictionary of contributors and their work from its foundation in 1769 to 1904*, 8 vols. (1905–6); repr. in 4 vols. (1970) and (1972)

Graves, *Soc. Artists* — A. Graves, *The Society of Artists of Great Britain, 1760–1791, the Free Society of Artists, 1761–1783: a complete dictionary* (1907); facs. edn (1969)

Greaves & Zaller, *BDBR* — R. L. Greaves and R. Zaller, eds., *Biographical dictionary of British radicals in the seventeenth century*, 3 vols. (1982–4)

Grove, *Dict. mus.* — G. Grove, ed., *A dictionary of music and musicians*, 5 vols. (1878–90); 2nd edn, ed. J. A. Fuller Maitland (1904–10); 3rd edn, ed. H. C. Colles (1927); 4th edn with suppl. (1940); 5th edn, ed. E. Blom, 9 vols. (1954); suppl. (1961) [see also *New Grove*]

Hall, *Dramatic ports.* — L. A. Hall, *Catalogue of dramatic portraits in the theatre collection of the Harvard College library*, 4 vols. (1930–34)

Hansard — *Hansard's parliamentary debates*, ser. 1–5 (1803–)

Highfill, Burnim & Langhans, *BDA* — P. H. Highfill, K. A. Burnim, and E. A. Langhans, *A biographical dictionary of actors, actresses, musicians, dancers, managers, and other stage personnel in London, 1660–1800*, 16 vols. (1973–93)

Hist. U. Oxf. — T. H. Aston, ed., *The history of the University of Oxford*, 8 vols. (1984–2000) [1: *The early Oxford schools*, ed. J. I. Catto (1984); 2: *Late medieval Oxford*, ed. J. I. Catto and R. Evans (1992); 3: *The collegiate university*, ed. J. McConica (1986); 4: *Seventeenth-century Oxford*, ed. N. Tyacke (1997); 5: *The eighteenth century*, ed. L. S. Sutherland and L. G. Mitchell (1986); 6–7: *Nineteenth-century Oxford*, ed. M. G. Brock and M. C. Curthoys (1997–2000); 8: *The twentieth century*, ed. B. Harrison (2000)]

HJ — *Historical Journal*

HMC — Historical Manuscripts Commission

Holdsworth, *Eng. law* — W. S. Holdsworth, *A history of English law*, ed. A. L. Goodhart and H. L. Hanbury, 17 vols. (1903–72)

HoP, Commons — *The history of parliament: the House of Commons* [1386–1421, ed. J. S. Roskell, L. Clark, and C. Rawcliffe, 4 vols. (1992); 1509–1558, ed. S. T. Bindoff, 3 vols. (1982); 1558–1603, ed. P. W. Hasler, 3 vols. (1981); 1660–1690, ed. B. D. Henning, 3 vols. (1983); 1690–1715, ed. D. W. Hayton, E. Cruickshanks, and S. Handley, 5 vols. (2002); 1715–1754, ed. R. Sedgwick, 2 vols. (1970); 1754–1790, ed. L. Namier and J. Brooke, 3 vols. (1964), repr. (1985); 1790–1820, ed. R. G. Thorne, 5 vols. (1986); in draft (used with permission): 1422–1504, 1604–1629, 1640–1660, and 1820–1832]

IGI — *International Genealogical Index*, Church of Jesus Christ of the Latterday Saints

ILN — *Illustrated London News*

IMC — Irish Manuscripts Commission

Irving, *Scots.* — J. Irving, ed., *The book of Scotsmen eminent for achievements in arms and arts, church and state, law, legislation and literature, commerce, science, travel and philanthropy* (1881)

JCS — *Journal of the Chemical Society*

JHC — *Journals of the House of Commons*

JHL — *Journals of the House of Lords*

John of Worcester, *Chron.* — *The chronicle of John of Worcester*, ed. R. R. Darlington and P. McGurk, trans. J. Bray and P. McGurk, 3 vols., OMT (1995–) [vol. 1 forthcoming]

Keeler, *Long Parliament* — M. F. Keeler, *The Long Parliament, 1640–1641: a biographical study of its members* (1954)

Kelly, *Handbk* — *The upper ten thousand: an alphabetical list of all members of noble families*, 3 vols. (1875–7); continued as *Kelly's handbook of the upper ten thousand for 1878* [1879], 2 vols. (1878–9); continued as *Kelly's handbook to the titled, landed and official classes*, 94 vols. (1880–1973)

LondG — *London Gazette*

LP Henry VIII — J. S. Brewer, J. Gairdner, and R. H. Brodie, eds., *Letters and papers, foreign and domestic, of the reign of Henry VIII*, 23 vols. in 38 (1862–1932); repr. (1965)

Mallalieu, *Watercolour artists* — H. L. Mallalieu, *The dictionary of British watercolour artists up to 1820*, 3 vols. (1976–90); vol. 1, 2nd edn (1986)

Memoirs FRS — *Biographical Memoirs of Fellows of the Royal Society*

MGH — Monumenta Germaniae Historica

MT — *Musical Times*

Munk, *Roll* — W. Munk, *The roll of the Royal College of Physicians of London*, 2 vols. (1861); 2nd edn, 3 vols. (1878)

N&Q — *Notes and Queries*

New Grove — S. Sadie, ed., *The new Grove dictionary of music and musicians*, 20 vols. (1980); 2nd edn, 29 vols. (2001) [also online edn; see also Grove, *Dict. mus.*]

Nichols, *Illustrations* — J. Nichols and J. B. Nichols, *Illustrations of the literary history of the eighteenth century*, 8 vols. (1817–58)

Nichols, *Lit. anecdotes* — J. Nichols, *Literary anecdotes of the eighteenth century*, 9 vols. (1812–16); facs. edn (1966)

Obits. FRS — *Obituary Notices of Fellows of the Royal Society*

O'Byrne, *Naval biog. dict.* — W. R. O'Byrne, *A naval biographical dictionary* (1849); repr. (1990); [2nd edn], 2 vols. (1861)

OHS — Oxford Historical Society

Old Westminsters — *The record of Old Westminsters*, 1–2, ed. G. F. R. Barker and A. H. Stenning (1928); suppl. 1, ed. J. B. Whitmore and G. R. Y. Radcliffe [1938]; 3, ed. J. B. Whitmore, G. R. Y. Radcliffe, and D. C. Simpson (1963); suppl. 2, ed. F. E. Pagan (1978); 4, ed. F. E. Pagan and H. E. Pagan (1992)

OMT — Oxford Medieval Texts

Ordericus Vitalis, *Eccl. hist.* — *The ecclesiastical history of Orderic Vitalis*, ed. and trans. M. Chibnall, 6 vols., OMT (1969–80); repr. (1990)

Paris, *Chron.* — *Matthaei Parisiensis, monachi sancti Albani, chronica majora*, ed. H. R. Luard, Rolls Series, 7 vols. (1872–83)

Parl. papers — *Parliamentary papers* (1801–)

PBA — *Proceedings of the British Academy*

Pepys, *Diary* The diary of Samuel Pepys, ed. R. Latham and W. Matthews, 11 vols. (1970–83); repr. (1995) and (2000)

Pevsner N. Pevsner and others, Buildings of England series

PICE *Proceedings of the Institution of Civil Engineers*

Pipe rolls *The great roll of the pipe for . . ., PRSoc. (1884–)*

PRO Public Record Office

PRS *Proceedings of the Royal Society of London*

PRSoc. Pipe Roll Society

PTRS *Philosophical Transactions of the Royal Society*

QR *Quarterly Review*

RC Record Commissions

Redgrave, *Artists* S. Redgrave, A dictionary of artists of the English school (1874); rev. edn (1878); repr. (1970)

Reg. Oxf. C. W. Boase and A. Clark, eds., *Register of the University of Oxford*, 5 vols., OHS, 1, 10–12, 14 (1885–9)

Reg. PCS J. H. Burton and others, eds., *The register of the privy council of Scotland*, 1st ser., 14 vols. (1877–98); 2nd ser., 8 vols. (1899–1908); 3rd ser., [16 vols.] (1908–70)

Reg. RAN H. W. C. Davis and others, eds., *Regesta regum Anglo-Normannorum, 1066–1154*, 4 vols. (1913–69)

RIBA Journal *Journal of the Royal Institute of British Architects* [later *RIBA Journal*]

RotP J. Strachey, ed., *Rotuli parliamentorum ut et petitiones, et placita in parliamento*, 6 vols. (1767–77)

RotS D. Macpherson, J. Caley, and W. Illingworth, eds., *Rotuli Scotiae in Turri Londinensi et in domo capitulari Westmonasteriensi asservati*, 2 vols., RC, 14 (1814–19)

RS Record(s) Society

Rymer, *Foedera* T. Rymer and R. Sanderson, eds., *Foedera, conventiones, literae et cuiuscunque generis acta publica inter reges Angliae et alios quosvis imperatores, reges, pontifices, principes, vel communitates*, 20 vols. (1704–35); 2nd edn, 20 vols. (1726–35); 3rd edn, 10 vols. (1739–45); facs. edn (1967); new edn, ed. A. Clarke, J. Caley, and F. Holbrooke, 4 vols., RC, 50 (1816–30)

Sainty, *Judges* J. Sainty, ed., *The judges of England, 1272–1990*, SeldS, suppl. ser., 10 (1993)

Sainty, *King's counsel* J. Sainty, ed., *A list of English law officers and king's counsel*, SeldS, suppl. ser., 7 (1987)

SCH Studies in Church History

Scots peerage J. B. Paul, ed. *The Scots peerage, founded on Wood's edition of Sir Robert Douglas's Peerage of Scotland, containing an historical and genealogical account of the nobility of that kingdom*, 9 vols. (1904–14)

SeldS Selden Society

SHR *Scottish Historical Review*

State trials T. B. Howell and T. J. Howell, eds., *Cobbett's Complete collection of state trials*, 34 vols. (1809–28)

STC, 1475–1640 A. W. Pollard, G. R. Redgrave, and others, eds., *A short-title catalogue of … English books … 1475–1640* (1926); 2nd edn, ed. W. A. Jackson, F. S. Ferguson, and K. F. Pantzer, 3 vols. (1976–91) [see also Wing, *STC*]

STS Scottish Text Society

SurtS Surtees Society

Symeon of Durham, *Opera* Symeonis monachi opera omnia, ed. T. Arnold, 2 vols., Rolls Series, 75 (1882–5); repr. (1965)

Tanner, *Bibl. Brit.-Hib.* T. Tanner, *Bibliotheca Britannico-Hibernica*, ed. D. Wilkins (1748); repr. (1963)

Thieme & Becker, *Allgemeines Lexikon* U. Thieme, F. Becker, and H. Vollmer, eds., *Allgemeines Lexikon der bildenden Künstler von der Antike bis zur Gegenwart*, 37 vols. (Leipzig, 1907–50); repr. (1961–5), (1983), and (1992)

Thurloe, *State papers* A collection of the state papers of John Thurloe, ed. T. Birch, 7 vols. (1742)

TLS *Times Literary Supplement*

Tout, *Admin. hist.* T. F. Tout, *Chapters in the administrative history of mediaeval England: the wardrobe, the chamber, and the small seals*, 6 vols. (1920–33); repr. (1967)

TRHS Transactions of the Royal Historical Society

VCH H. A. Doubleday and others, eds., *The Victoria history of the counties of England*, [88 vols.] (1900–)

Venn, *Alum. Cant.* J. Venn and J. A. Venn, *Alumni Cantabrigienses: a biographical list of all known students, graduates, and holders of office at the University of Cambridge, from the earliest times to 1900*, 10 vols. (1922–54); repr. in 2 vols. (1974–8)

Vertue, *Note books* [G. Vertue], *Note books*, ed. K. Esdaile, earl of Ilchester, and H. M. Hake, 6 vols., Walpole Society, 18, 20, 22, 24, 26, 30 (1930–55)

VF *Vanity Fair*

Walford, *County families* E. Walford, *The county families of the United Kingdom, or, Royal manual of the titled and untitled aristocracy of Great Britain and Ireland* (1860)

Walker rev. A. G. Matthews, *Walker revised: being a revision of John Walker's Sufferings of the clergy during the grand rebellion, 1642–60* (1948); repr. (1988)

Walpole, *Corr.* The Yale edition of Horace Walpole's correspondence, ed. W. S. Lewis, 48 vols. (1937–83)

Ward, *Men of the reign* T. H. Ward, ed., *Men of the reign: a biographical dictionary of eminent persons of British and colonial birth who have died during the reign of Queen Victoria* (1885); repr. (Graz, 1968)

Waterhouse, *18c painters* E. Waterhouse, *The dictionary of 18th century painters in oils and crayons* (1981); repr. as *British 18th century painters in oils and crayons* (1991), vol. 2 of *Dictionary of British art*

Watt, *Bibl. Brit.* R. Watt, *Bibliotheca Britannica, or, A general index to British and foreign literature*, 4 vols. (1824) [many reprs.]

Wellesley index W. E. Houghton, ed., *The Wellesley index to Victorian periodicals, 1824–1900*, 5 vols. (1966–89); new edn (1999) [CD-ROM]

Wing, *STC* D. Wing, ed., *Short-title catalogue of … English books … 1641–1700*, 3 vols. (1945–51); 2nd edn (1972–88); rev. and enl. edn, ed. J. J. Morrison, C. W. Nelson, and M. Seccombe, 4 vols. (1994–8) [see also *STC, 1475–1640*]

Wisden John Wisden's Cricketer's Almanack

Wood, *Ath. Oxon.* A. Wood, *Athenae Oxonienses … to which are added the Fasti*, 2 vols. (1691–2); 2nd edn (1721); new edn, 4 vols., ed. P. Bliss (1813–20); repr. (1967) and (1969)

Wood, *Vic. painters* C. Wood, *Dictionary of Victorian painters* (1971); 2nd edn (1978); 3rd edn as *Victorian painters*, 2 vols. (1995), vol. 4 of *Dictionary of British art*

WW Who's who (1849–)

WWBMP M. Stenton and S. Lees, eds., *Who's who of British members of parliament*, 4 vols. (1976–81)

WWW Who was who (1929–)

Sharp. *See also* Sharpe.

Sharp, Abraham (*bap.* **1653**, *d.* **1742**), mathematician and scientific instrument maker, was born at Horton Hall, Little Horton, near Bradford, and baptized at Bradford, Yorkshire, on 1 June 1653, the ninth child and sixth son of John Sharp of Little Horton, and his wife, Mary, the daughter of Robert Clarkson of Bradford. His nineteenth-century biographer, William Cudworth, believed that he was born in 1653 and that the monumental inscription stating that he died in his ninety-first year is incorrect; evidence to support this appears in a letter of November 1715, where Sharp says he is 'now in my grand Clymacterick', or sixty-third year (Royal Greenwich Observatory Archives, CUL, RGO 1/34, fol. 125*r*).

John Sharp prospered as a farmer, clothier, and merchant; during the civil war period he took the side of parliament and served as financial secretary to General Sir Thomas Fairfax; he later became a collector of Commonwealth taxes. He gave his sons a good education, sending two to university and placing the rest in respectable trades. Abraham went on from a village school to Bradford grammar school and in May 1669 was apprenticed to a York mercer. He probably learned some mathematics as a schoolboy, and as an apprentice must have studied its practical applications. Some accounts assert that he left his master prematurely and moved to Liverpool, where he taught writing and commercial arithmetic; this is not implausible, as a legacy of £160 on his father's death in 1672 may have prompted or assisted the move.

Nothing more is known of Sharp's activities until the spring of 1684, when he was in London, using the Hen and Chickens in the Strand as a correspondence address, and began to assist the astronomer royal, John Flamsteed, at the Royal Observatory at Greenwich. He was employed there for some months during 1684–5 and from August 1688 to the autumn of 1690. In the intervening period he lived in London but remained in close touch with Flamsteed. During his second stay at the observatory he helped complete the great mural arc, 6 feet 9 inches in radius, which was to serve as Flamsteed's principal instrument for three decades and set a new standard for the observatories of Europe. In this connection Flamsteed described Sharp as:

> the fittest for my purpose, that could be[,] a curious
> Mechanick and An excellent Geometrician, who screwd the
> limbe, wrought the Index and after I had fixed the point for
> the beginning of the divisions inscribed them and engraved
> the Numbers both for the diagonalls and revolves so
> curiously that I thinke I may say … tis the neatest limbe that
> ever was made of the same bignesse. (*Correspondence of John
> Flamsteed*, 2.449)

In carrying on the everyday business of astronomy, however, Sharp sometimes seemed 'as uselesse to me as any that can but write well could be, or rather lesse' (ibid., 2.451), so his departure was not much regretted.

On leaving the Greenwich observatory in November 1690, Sharp lodged with William Court at the Mariner and Anchor on Little Tower Hill, where mathematical books and instruments were sold; he possibly succeeded his

Abraham Sharp (*bap.* 1653, *d.* 1742), by George Vertue, 1744

acquaintance Marmaduke Hodgeson as Court's resident teacher of mathematics. Soon afterwards he was offered a clerkship in the king's shipyard at Portsmouth and overcame a reluctance to accept it: one of his notebooks reveals that he moved to Portsmouth in February 1691 and had some connection with the dockyard, though his presence seems to have left no trace in its official records. He also received occasional sums for teaching and a salary of £10 a year from a Mr Graham, perhaps as an instrument maker. The interlude was a brief one: on the death of his eldest brother in 1693, his widowed sister-in-law asked him to return to Little Horton. He did so early in 1694 and lived there for the rest of his life. His principal importance in the locality was as a promoter and generous patron of the first Presbyterian chapel in Bradford.

Horton Hall was demolished in the 1960s, but is known to have been a stone-built house in a style characteristic of the area; Sharp is believed to have adapted its central tower to create an observing platform. His continuing interest in mathematics, astronomy, and instrument making is reflected in surviving notebooks and in correspondence with local and London friends. He sold an odometer to his distant relative John Sharp, archbishop of York, and corresponded occasionally with the antiquary Ralph

Thoresby, who lists 'a declining Dial for the Library Window, by the celebrated Mr. Abr. Sharp' among his collection of 'Rarities' (Thoresby, 475). Sharp was also in touch with the elder and younger Euclid Speidell, Joseph Raphson, Henry Sherwin, Edmond Halley, the optical instrument maker John Yarwell, and the publisher Richard Mount; their letters reflect Sharp's endeavours to obtain books and instruments and to secure publication of mathematical works. His *Geometry Improv'd*, containing elaborate tables and a treatise on polyhedra, appeared in 1717; Sherwin's *Mathematical Tables* (1710 and many later editions) also included a substantial contribution from:

> the ingenious and unwearied Mr. Abr. Sharp, with his Table of Logarithms to above fifty Figures ... the Construction of the Sines, Tangents and Secants; with the whole Process of the Quadrature of the Circle to 72 Figures: Which Quadrature was invented ... by Mr. Halley. (Sherwin, preface)

Sharp claimed that his earlier paper on this last subject, fruitlessly submitted to the Royal Society, had pre-dated and informed Halley's work.

From February 1702 until his death at the end of 1719, Flamsteed was Sharp's principal correspondent. Virtually all the letters they exchanged survive, and many of them reveal details of Sharp's activities. By 1702 he had 'made a small Instrument to which I have adapted a Six ft Telescope in the nature of sights; hereby both the altitude and azimuth may be had at the same instant' (*Correspondence of John Flamsteed*, 2.908), had improved his lathe by devising 'Engines, one for Rose and Crown work, the other for Ovall and Rose work, and likewise ... an Engine for cutting Wheels' (ibid., 2.909), and had 'made a large brasse Sphaere or Armilla of a peculiar contrivance, which with much ease ... represents any sphaericall Triangle that can be proposed' (ibid., 2.932). This last may be the instrument depicted on his tombstone and in a portrait engraving by George Vertue (1744).

Sharp went on to assist his former employer in a variety of ways: he made him a micrometer (1704); calculated places of the moon and planets and extensive subsidiary tables for the planned *Historia coelestis*; produced tables of the predicted eclipses of Jupiter's satellites annually from 1707 to 1719 (for 1708 to 1720); attempted to observe some of these and other eclipses, rarely with success; and systematically collected barometric observations. After Flamsteed's death he corresponded with the Greenwich assistant Joseph Crosthwait and helped prepare the revised *Historia coelestis Britannica* (1725) for publication; in particular he produced an updated version of Halley's catalogue of the southern stars. He also worked on star charts for the *Atlas coelestis* (1729).

Sharp died at Horton Hall on 18 July 1742, and was buried on 21 July in St Peter's, Bradford (now Bradford Cathedral), where a monument was later erected. His instruments and tools were dispersed; those few that survive are at Bolling Hall Museum, Bradford, the National Maritime Museum, and the Science Museum.

FRANCES WILLMOTH

Sources W. Cudworth, *The life and correspondence of Abraham Sharp* (1889) • W. Yorks. AS, Bradford, Bardsley-Powell family papers • *The correspondence of John Flamsteed, the first astronomer royal*, ed. E. G. Forbes and others, 3 vols. (1995–2001) • F. Baily, *An account of the Revd John Flamsteed, the first astronomer-royal* (1835); repr. (1966) • W. T. Lancaster, ed., *Letters addressed to Ralph Thoresby FRS*, Thoresby Society, 21 (1912), 11–12, 188–9 • R. Thoresby, *Ducatus Leodiensis, or, The topography of ... Leedes* (1715), 475, 497, 548 • M. Holbrook, R. G. W. Anderson, and D. J. Bryden, *Science preserved: a directory of scientific instruments in collections in the United Kingdom and Eire* (1992), 98–9 • N. S. Heineken, 'Relics of the mechanical productions of Abraham Sharp, the assistant of Flamsteed', *London, Edinburgh, and Dublin Philosophical Magazine*, 3rd ser., 30 (1847), 25–7 • S. Melmore, 'Abraham Sharp's universal instrument', *The Observatory*, 61 (1938), 248–50 • H. Sherwin, *Mathematical tables* (1710) • GM, 1st ser., 12 (1742), 387 • CUL, Royal Greenwich Observatory papers, RGO 1/34, fol. 125r

Archives Bolling Hall Museum, Bradford, instruments • CUL, Royal Greenwich Observatory archives, MSS • NMM, instruments • RS, MSS • Sci. Mus., instruments • York Minster Library, York Minster Archives, account and memo books, notes, and tables | W. Yorks. AS, Bradford, Bardsley-Powell MSS, corresp. and papers

Likenesses G. Vertue, engraving, 1744, AM Oxf., NMM [*see illus.*] • portrait, priv. coll.; repro. in Cudworth, *Life and correspondence*, facing p. 157

Wealth at death over £1250; plus lands: will, Cudworth, *Life and correspondence*, 201–2

Sharp, Anthony (1643–1707), Quaker leader, was born in January 1643 at Tetbury, Gloucestershire, the son of Thomas Sharp, woollen manufacturer, and his wife, Elizabeth. Sharp probably studied at the grammar school in Tetbury before his parents apprenticed him to an attorney at Marlborough, Wiltshire, but he opted not to pursue a legal career. While serving as a journeyman wool-comber in his father's employ, Sharp saved enough money to go into the wool trade on his own, aided by family funds. On 27 March 1663 he married Esther Curtis (1643–1672), daughter of the woollen draper Thomas Curtis of Tetbury, with whom he had four children, all of whom died in infancy. At the invitation of a Quaker employee, Roger Gillet, Sharp visited incarcerated Friends in Warwickshire, including William Dewsbury, who persuaded him to become a Quaker.

In the late summer or early autumn of 1669 Sharp moved his family to Dublin, which he had visited during his legal apprenticeship, to pursue the woollen trade. They joined the Quaker meeting in Dublin and shortly thereafter Sharp welcomed William Penn on his visit to the city. By 1671 Esther had been stricken with tuberculosis; she died on 24 October 1672, after which Sharp likened himself to a dove that had lost its mate. The previous month the Dublin assembly had granted him and three fellow Quakers—Samuel Clarridge, Robert Turner, and William Maine—the freedom of the city, enabling them to trade on the same terms as other freemen and vote in municipal elections. In lieu of the usual oath, each paid an entry fine of £3, plus 5s. per annum. Sharp acquired property within and beyond the city walls, founded a woollen manufactory that employed approximately 500 workers by 1680, some of whom were Catholics, and exported wool to England. Occasionally he incurred substantial losses at sea, including in 1674–5 wares estimated at £2000.

Longing for female companionship, Sharp wrote to Thomas Crabb, a wool-stapler in Marlborough, in February 1674, seeking approval to marry one of his daughters. After accepting Crabb's invitation to meet his daughter Ann (c.1652–1702), Sharp fell in love with her, and the couple were wed with the approval of their Quaker meetings on 17 August at Marlborough. During their 28-year marriage, they had nine sons and seven daughters, of whom ten or eleven died in infancy. The Sharps sent two of their sons, Jonathan and Daniel, to study with the Quaker schoolmaster Gilbert Thompson at Penketh, Lancashire. The death of the pious Jonathan at the age of fourteen in 1702 was an emotional blow to his parents, as was the immoral life of Joseph. The other surviving son, Isaac, in 1700 emigrated to America, where Sharp had invested in West and East Jersey in 1677 and 1682 respectively. In 1681 Sharp and Turner financed an expedition to West Jersey led by Thomas Sharp, Anthony's nephew, which established a settlement at Newton Creek, across the Delaware River from Philadelphia. Sharp also acquired 5834 acres in East Jersey, but he declined Penn's invitation to purchase property in Pennsylvania as well as an opportunity to buy Susquehanna Manor on Octoraro Creek from Maryland's surveyor-general, George Talbot. Apart from helping to support Quaker havens in America, Sharp was primarily interested in land speculation rather than transatlantic commerce.

In Dublin, Sharp became active in the weavers' guild, receiving permission to attend its meetings in 1672 and becoming a quarter-brother in 1678–9. When James II implemented a policy of toleration, Sharp became a free brother in the guild on 2 May 1687. A year later he was elected to the mastership, though he apparently did not take up the post until July. During his mastership the guild agreed to accept a new charter from James. By the time Sharp stepped down in the autumn of 1689 he had been master at least sixteen months, the second longest tenure of any master during his years in the guild. In addition to serving as the weavers' master, Sharp, like Clarridge, was appointed an alderman in the new city charter issued in November 1687, a position he apparently retained until the spring or early summer of 1690. It was probably during his aldermanic tenure that he wrote a proposal to deal with the problem of the city's poor, including a reduction in the number of beggars. Because of his financial expertise he was appointed to the committee that audited the municipal accounts. The substantial respect Sharp enjoyed beyond Quaker circles is reflected in the lord mayor-elect's solicitation in 1700 of his advice on how to govern Dublin.

Arguably the most influential member of the Dublin Quaker community, and second in stature among Irish Friends only to William Edmundson, Sharp served the movement in numerous ways, including intervention on behalf of imprisoned Quakers with government and ecclesiastical officials, sometimes by petition, sometimes in person. Commencing in 1674 he served as a public Friend—a minister in 'truth's service'—whose travels took him frequently throughout Ireland and to England (in 1695, 1696, and probably 1699), the Netherlands and Schleswig (1695), and Scotland (1696). A leading member of the Dublin men's meeting, the Leinster provincial meeting, and the six-months' national meeting, he helped manage finances, negotiate leases, collect funds to relieve the needy and ransom Friends captured by North African pirates, record the meetings' business, communicate with other Quaker groups, maintain accounts of the Friends' suffering, aid refugees, and oversee the construction and maintenance of meeting-houses and burial-grounds. For the most part he was generous with his money as well as his time, donating more than any other Friend to the new Meath Street meeting-house in Dublin and the burial-ground at Dolphin's Barn, south-west of the city centre, yet he was less than munificent in giving to the indigent. Sharp also helped manage the Quaker school in Dublin (founded in 1680), negotiating with schoolmasters and monitoring the curriculum, and arranged the terms of apprenticeships and mediated quarrels between masters and apprentices. As Irish Quakers became increasingly involved in the publication of religious literature, Sharp negotiated contracts with printers, supervised the distribution of books, saw works through the press, reviewed manuscripts to determine their fitness for publication, and, at the national meeting's behest, wrote a postscript to William Morris's *Tithes No Gospel-Ordinance*. From 1692 to 1705 Sharp was a member of the committee that monitored and attempted to influence parliamentary proceedings that had a major impact on the Friends, including a bill that would have permitted Quakers to make an affirmation (opposed by Sharp because it mentioned God's name) in lieu of an oath.

Sharp devoted substantial effort to shaping and overseeing Quaker conduct, including the development of standards of attire more rigorous than those that prevailed among English Friends. The formulation of a detailed dress code occurred primarily in the mid- and late 1690s following Ireland's time of troubles when some Friends began assimilating worldly ways. Sensitive to the fact that outsiders judged the Friends by their conduct, Sharp and his colleagues countered with a system of home and shop visitations designed to enforce strict Quaker standards. Proper behaviour included the refusal to render oaths, pay tithes, or have others remit them on one's behalf. Sharp was never imprisoned for refusing to pay tithes and church rates, though church officials distrained his goods many times. In fact, only once did he go to gaol, from 5 to 7 August 1683 for having attended an illegal religious meeting. A disciplinarian, Sharp had little sympathy for wilful transgressors, including Clarridge, whose impregnation of a maid and haughty behaviour infuriated him.

Sharp found time to engage in the 'Lamb's War' against evil as a polemicist and apologist. Most of his disputing was done in person or through correspondence, though he wrote a number of works between February 1677 and December 1700, of which only two were published: *Gospel-*

Truths (1698), written by Penn with the assistance of Sharp, Thomas Story, and George Rooke, refuting the General Baptist John Plimpton's *Ten Charges Against the People called Quakers*; and *Dirt Wip'd off* (1698), defending Penn against Plimpton. Sharp disputed with the Catholics Thomas Gormagan, Father Nicholas Nugent, and William Joseph, and the congregational minister James Barry. Following a debate with the protestant Thomas Adams at Coleraine in January 1693, Sharp wrote a pamphlet that defended the Quaker belief in continuing revelation and the doctrine of perfection. In another unpublished pamphlet he attacked the Church of Ireland minister Charles Whittingham, dealing with such topics as the sacraments, tithes, and immediate revelation. Sharp also refuted lapsed Quakers and Muggletonians. His writings indicate that he read not only other Quaker authors but John Foxe's *Actes and Monuments*, the Westminster confession, the larger catechism, and the Book of Common Prayer. His writings also include an unpublished account of the time of troubles.

Following Ann Sharp's death on 8 June 1702, Anthony Sharp remained active in the Quaker movement until his own demise in Dublin on 13 January 1707. The Sharps were interred in the Quaker burial-ground adjacent to St Stephen's Green, Dublin; a large crowd accompanied Anthony's body to the grave site. His will, signed on 4 October 1706 (with four codicils in October 1706 and January 1707), bequeathed to Isaac extensive lands in Queen's county, property in West Jersey, half his holdings in East Jersey, plate, £200, and a jointure for Isaac's wife. To Joseph went property in Wiltshire, a quarter of Anthony's land in East Jersey, plate, and money, while Daniel received the remaining property in East Jersey, land in Queen's county, approximately two dozen houses in Dublin, plate, money, and household goods. Sharp's only surviving daughter, Rachel, inherited land in King's county, six houses in Dublin, plate, money, and household goods. Others, including indigent Quakers, received only token benefactions. Through his tireless endeavours and spiritual leadership Sharp did much to help Irish Quakers establish an organizational structure that enabled them to survive and even prosper in the eighteenth century.

RICHARD L. GREAVES

Sources Historical Library of the Society of Friends in Ireland, Dublin, Sharp MSS · minutes of the Dublin men's meeting, 1677–84, 1684–91, 1691–1701, 1701–10, Historical Library of the Society of Friends in Ireland, Dublin · minutes of the half-yearly national meeting, 1671–88, 1689–1706, Historical Library of the Society of Friends in Ireland, Dublin · minutes of the Leinster province meeting, 1670–1706, Historical Library of the Society of Friends in Ireland, Dublin · R. L. Greaves, *Dublin's merchant-Quaker: Anthony Sharp and the community of Friends, 1643–1707* (1998) · parliamentary committee minutes, 1698–1731, Historical Library of the Society of Friends in Ireland, Dublin · sufferings, Dublin monthly meeting, 1660–1780, Historical Library of the Society of Friends in Ireland, Dublin · transcript of the will of Anthony Sharp, NA Ire., MS TA6899 · 'A book generall from 1676 to 1702 for the Corporation of Weavers', Royal Society of Antiquaries in Ireland, Dublin · testimonies against tithes, Historical Library of the Society of Friends in Ireland, Dublin · J. T. Gilbert, R. M. Gilbert, and J. F. Weldrick, eds., *Calendar of the ancient records of Dublin*, 18 vols. (1889–1922), vols. 4–5 · D. Goodbody, 'Anthony Sharp: a Quaker merchant of the Liberties', *Dublin Historical Record*, 14/1 (1955–8), 12–19

Archives Religious Society of Friends, Dublin, MSS | Religious Society of Friends, Dublin, minutes of the Dublin men's meeting · Religious Society of Friends, Dublin, minutes of the half-yearly meeting · Religious Society of Friends, Dublin, minutes of the Leinster province meeting · Religious Society of Friends, Dublin, parliamentary committee minutes
Wealth at death very wealthy: transcript of the will of Anthony Sharp, NA Ire., MS TA6899

Sharp, Cecil James (1859–1924), collector of English folksongs and dances, was born on 22 November 1859 at Denmark Hill, London, the eldest son and third of the eleven children of John James Sharp (1827–1903), a slate merchant, and his wife, Jane (1829?–1915), the daughter of Joseph Bloyd, a lead merchant.

Early life Sharp attended a private school in Brighton from 1867, then in 1869 went to Uppingham School, where his musical abilities, fostered by his family, flourished. From 1874 he attended a coaching school in Weston-super-Mare run by George Heppel, an old family friend. Here he performed well enough in mathematics to enter Clare College, Cambridge, in 1879. But he concentrated more on music than on mathematics, and left with a third-class degree in 1882.

Sharp's family now sent him to Australia, whither he sailed in October 1882. The reasons are unclear; Sharp hinted that his family made him agree not to pursue a musical career for several years. Clerical work in the Commercial Bank of Australia was followed by a period in legal chambers; in April 1884 he became assistant to the chief justice of South Australia. He pursued amateur musical interests, joining the Adelaide String Quartet Club, and was its musical director in 1883. He also became conductor of the Philharmonic Society, taught violin and piano, and undertook other occasional musical duties.

Sharp returned to England in 1886 to convalesce at his parents' home after an attack of typhoid, the effects of which dogged him through life. Since he failed to find professional musical employment in London, he returned to Adelaide. Here he enrolled for the music degree course at the university to obtain a certificate of competency, but apparently did not complete it.

In January 1889 Sharp resigned from the office of the chief justice and embarked on a career as a professional musician, joining Immanuel Reimann as co-director of the Adelaide College of Music. He also composed operettas in collaboration with Guy Boothby. The second of these, *Sylvia*, was well received, and in January 1891 Sharp went to London, hoping to have it staged there. Having met with no success, he returned to Adelaide in April. He and Reimann increasingly disagreed about the college, and dissolved their partnership. Sharp decided to return to England, and arrived in January 1892.

Sharp now sought employment to support his chief aim of composing. He had written several works by 1900, without making any significant impression. He took various posts in music, including those of music master at Ludgrove preparatory school from January 1893 until 1910 and principal of the Hampstead Conservatoire from 1896 to July 1905 (a half-time post which provided a house). He

Cecil James Sharp (1859–1924), by Esther Blaikie Mackinnon, 1921

was conductor of the Finsbury Choral Association from June 1893 until July 1897, but resigned after a dispute involving its committee and Hubert Parry.

At Clevedon, on 22 August 1893, Sharp married Constance Dorothea Birch (d. 1928), whom he had known since his holidays with the Heppels in 1874. Three daughters and a son followed over the next decade. The pair were married by Charles Latimer Marson, whom Sharp had met in Adelaide and who played a significant role in Sharp's later life. Marson was a Fabian, like Sharp, and awakened in him for a time a greater interest in the established faith; Sharp also dabbled in Christian Science and spiritualism.

Folk-music The defining events in Sharp's life were his initial encounter with English folk-music in 1899 and his first success as a collector in 1903. On Boxing day 1899 he was staying with his mother-in-law in Headington, near Oxford, when nine men walked up the drive. One began to play the concertina while six of the others danced a series of morris dances. Sharp was fascinated. He asked the musician, William Kimber, to return the following day, when he noted five tunes from him. The full consequences of this encounter only became manifest later, but it awakened in Sharp an interest in folk-music in the context of the debate on the need for an English national music. In 1902 he published *A Book of British Song for Home and School*, a mixture of 'national' and 'traditional' songs, the latter mainly from the collections of Baring-Gould, Fuller Maitland, and Broadwood. While searching for suitable songs for his Ludgrove pupils, he decided to collect traditional songs himself, and wrote to Marson in Hambridge, Somerset, to enquire whether the district might yield such material. Marson was doubtful, but Sharp visited and began his search. It is usually said that he overheard Marson's gardener, John England, singing 'The Seeds of Love' in September 1903. In reality, the encounter happened on 22 August and was not accidental: Marson told Sharp that England knew the song, and 'with the aid of a pipe full of tobacco I [Sharp] extracted [it] from him' (Sharp, lecture notes, November 1903). He collected forty-one further songs during that visit.

Sharp presented his results almost immediately, giving his first lecture on folk-song at the Hampstead Conservatoire on 26 November 1903. He now flung himself into collecting, amassing more than 1500 tunes in the next four years, and into promoting the cause of folk-music. He was elected to the committee of a revivified Folk-Song Society (founded 1898) in February 1904, but in 1905 became embroiled in the debate about the role of folk-music in schools, and attacked the society for endorsing the Board of Education's new list of 'national or folk-songs' for school use. The content was much as in Sharp's 1902 book, but he now strenuously rejected this mixture, insisting that only pure folk-songs were suitable for schools. His argument was based on a cultural Darwinism, combining the survival of the fittest—which justified their suitability—with an analogy between racial and cultural purity, which explained their demise outside rural pockets isolated from the mainstream of music and culture in England.

This contradictory analysis was propounded in *English Folk Song: some Conclusions* (1907), and was accompanied by a collection, *English Folk-Songs for Schools* (with Baring-Gould, 1906). The latter was dedicated to the princes Edward and Albert (to whom Sharp was music tutor from 1904 to 1907), a move presaging Sharp's later adroitness in capitalizing on his connections. In 1909 he persuaded E. G. A. Holmes, chief inspector of elementary schools, to his view; later (probably through the intercession of Fisher's brother-in-law Vaughan Williams) he won the support of H. A. L. Fisher, president of the Board of Education (1916–22). Between 1908 and 1922 Sharp edited the Novello series *Folk-Songs for Schools*, which helped to disseminate the material widely. In championing the use of folk-songs in schools he was radical, but his pedagogical methods were reactionary; he advocated learning by rote, as a naturalistic method, and in keeping with his ideas on cultural evolution.

Sharp constantly emphasized the purity of folk-song and the need to respect it. In his school collections, however, he was forced to censor 'unsuitable' words; and he justified setting songs to piano accompaniment as being necessary for public acceptance. The first volumes of *Folk Songs from Somerset* (1904–19) were edited jointly with Marson, but in 1906 they quarrelled and the final volumes appeared under Sharp's name alone. This dispute, too, may have involved faithfulness to the originals, but certainly also entailed a personal disagreement.

In July 1905 Sharp had resigned from the Hampstead

Conservatoire after a prolonged dispute about payment and his right to take on students for extra tuition. He had to leave the principal's house, and apart from his post at Ludgrove his income was henceforth derived largely from lecturing and publishing on folk-music.

Folk-dance While Sharp was in the throes of leaving the conservatoire, the social worker Mary Neal came to ask him for folk-songs suitable for her Espérance Girls' Club. The songs he supplied were very successful, and Neal returned to him for folk-dances. Sharp told her of his meeting with Kimber. She went to Headington Quarry, found Kimber, and brought him to London to teach the dances. Initial demonstrations culminated in a public performance on 3 April 1906, at which Sharp lectured on folk-song; thereafter the club girls began teaching throughout the country. The demand for teaching materials led to the publication in April 1907 of part 1 of *The Morris Book* by Sharp and Herbert MacIlwaine, Espérance's musical director. Although Sharp was later credited with inventing the dance notation, this was MacIlwaine's work; Sharp contributed the music and the history. Sharp collected three tunes from Kimber in May 1906, and eight from the Bidford Morris in June, with only the barest indications of dance notation.

Morris dances became immensely popular, and in November 1907 the Association for the Revival and Practice of Folk Music was founded, with Neal a driving force. During this period Sharp was embroiled in, and losing, his battles in the Folk-Song Society. Issues of accuracy, authority, and control had arisen in that dispute, and were also to be the focus of folk-dance disputes over the next five years. Sharp saw that Neal was being acknowledged as the movement's leader, and that she valued enthusiasm and mass participation above accuracy and artistic value. Although his field experience was still limited, he believed that his role as collector was being overshadowed. Neal was finding and learning from other dancers, and revealing variability in the dances and inconsistency among the dancers. Sharp's description of the dances had been mediated by overgeneralization from limited evidence and by his sociocultural theories about 'the folk'. After his first true notation of dances collected, from Winster, Derbyshire, in June 1908 and Sherborne, Gloucestershire, in July, he began to dissociate himself from the association, and last spoke at an association concert in January 1909. Part 2 of *The Morris Book* (July 1909) omitted mention of Espérance. Throughout 1909 he and Neal exchanged increasingly bitter letters, and during the year he made moves to establish his own group of dancers for demonstrations and lectures. An encounter with E. G. A. Holmes in 1909 enabled him to have morris dances recognized by the Board of Education. Meanwhile he continued to collect, and met William Wells of Bampton, a major source. By May 1910 he had also contacted dancers from Eynsham, Brackley, Abingdon, and Chipping Campden.

In April 1910 the dispute with Neal became public when *The Espérance Morris Book* was published, in some respects contradicting Sharp's books. A series of acrimonious articles and letters appeared over the following months, many in the *Morning Post* and *Daily Mail*. At this stage Sharp was under pressure: Neal had more dancers, a strong organization, and a body of knowledge which brought into question his ideas on the true nature of the morris dance. Moreover, those dancers he had now met danced in styles markedly different from that which he had published as correct. However, he had influential supporters and was collecting new material to an extent not matched by Neal. Fortunately, the dancers he next came across, from Leafield and elsewhere, strengthened his case for morris style and showed him dances exhibiting great artistry and skill. In June 1910 he encountered sword dances after meeting D'Arcy de Ferrars, who had used them in the Ripon millenary celebrations; but that meeting revealed to him that the Bidford dances published in part 1 of *The Morris Book* were also heavily influenced by de Ferrars.

In 1911 the tide turned in Sharp's favour. He won musical control of the prestigious Stratford upon Avon festival from Neal, his standing was enhanced by the award of a civil-list pension, and in part 4 of *The Morris Book* he changed his characterization of dance style from total uniformity—which was untenable—to uniformity within a place but variation between places, so initiating the enduring concept of the village-based tradition. He went on (1912–24) to revise parts 1 to 3 to reflect the changed analysis. He found a rich vein of country-dance material in the successive editions of John Playford's seventeenth-century work *The English Dancing Master*. This formed the basis for part 2 and subsequent parts of *The Country Dance Book* (1911), the first part of which (1909) had consisted of dances collected by Sharp himself. On 6 December 1911 the English Folk Dance Society was founded, giving Sharp the organizational base he had lacked.

The new society quickly spread: within thirty months it had nineteen branches nationwide and an extensive network of teachers and certification. Sharp was now more concerned with dissemination of dances than with collecting; the final parts of both *The Morris Book* and *The Sword-Dance Book* were published in 1913 (though the former was subsequently revised), while *The Country Dance Book* used early printed sources. Folk-songs predominated in his subsequent collecting expeditions in England.

America In February 1914 the theatre producer Harley Granville Barker asked Sharp to arrange the music and dances for *A Midsummer Night's Dream* at the Savoy, and in December invited him to assist with the New York production. Sharp realized that conditions in wartime England were not propitious for the lecturing, demonstrating, and teaching on which his income depended, so he accepted the invitation, hoping to augment his income there in like manner. One of his dancers, Claud Wright, had taught in the United States in 1913 and 1914 and laid the groundwork for classes and summer schools, but Sharp dissuaded his American contacts from using Wright's services further and developed anew the structure he found. He visited England in April 1915; when he returned to America in June, Olive Dame Campbell showed him songs collected by her in the Appalachians. He sailed yet again for England to direct the Stratford upon Avon festival in July, then worked on *One Hundred English Folk Songs* for American publication (1916).

Sharp returned to America in February 1916 and organized a full schedule of classes and lectures. Maud *Karpeles, who had been his amanuensis since he had suffered an attack of neuritis in his right arm in 1913, and who from then on had lived with the Sharp family, joined him in April. The pair spent the rest of Sharp's time in America together. Encouraged by Campbell, they spent two months in summer collecting in the Appalachians before lecturing in various cities in the United States and Canada. In December they sailed to England, where Sharp's son was in hospital after being wounded in France, but in February 1917 returned to America, where they remained until December 1918. Most of the period from April to October in both years was spent in the Appalachians, where in addition to folk-songs they noted the 'Running Set' dance, later published in part 5 of *The Country Dance Book*.

Sharp collected more than 1500 songs in the Appalachians, often enduring physical hardship and illness. He found that music-hall and other contemporary songs were not generally known as they were in England, and believed that the Appalachian people maintained an unspoilt culture which had preserved the musical traditions found only in isolated pockets and under stress in England.

Last years and death Sharp and Karpeles decided 'after much heart-searching' (Karpeles, MS autobiography) to return to England in December 1918. In April 1919 Sharp was appointed occasional inspector of training colleges in folk-song and dancing by the Board of Education, and from December accepted a salary for the office of director of the English Folk Dance Society, whose aims he prosecuted with much success through a proliferation of local branches—they almost doubled in number in the five years to 1924—and vacation schools. In 1923 alone four schools were held, teaching 1830 pupils. In the same year he was awarded the honorary degree of master of music by Cambridge University.

As director Sharp had little time for collecting; his last tune came, like the first, from Headington, on 13 September 1923. He suffered frequently from fevers and asthma, and took several short breaks. On one such in Montreux in 1923 his fever was diagnosed as malaria and improved under treatment. During 1924 he undertook a strenuous tour of England, lecturing and judging folk-dance competitions. On 28 May he fell ill, and travelled home to Hampstead on 3 June, very weak. An X-ray showed a malignant tumour in the chest, beyond hope of recovery. It was described on his death certificate as a sarcoma of the mediastinum, but this unlikely diagnosis was not confirmed by any post-mortem. Sharp died at his home, 4 Maresfield Gardens, in the early hours of 23 June 1924. He was cremated at Golders Green crematorium on 25 June; a memorial service was held at St Martin-in-the-Fields, London, on 27 June.

Assessment Sharp's physical monument is the English Folk Dance and Song Society's headquarters, Cecil Sharp House, in Camden Town, London, but his true monument is the corpus of song and dance he collected and transmitted through his publications and the society. He was not the first in either field, but brought to the task a dedication and tenacity which enabled him to transcend hardship and rebuff. He had a major influence on the English musical renaissance, on music and movement education, and on the cultural awareness of the English. In pursuing his goals he insisted that his authority should prevail, and crossed many—both friends and adversaries—in doing so. He was quick to take offence and difficult to placate. (The ease with which his clear-cut features reddened in debate earned him the nickname 'Punch' at Cambridge.) The positive aspect of this temperament was the enthusiasm and inspiration which he communicated in his lecturing and teaching; many commented on his ability to lift dancers by the expression and sense of rhythm of his piano accompaniments.

When collecting, Sharp was a model of patience, though his disregard of informants as rounded persons may now be regretted: he neglected the songs in their repertory which he thought not 'traditional' and failed to record their background and circumstances. His views on traditional music and dance were coloured by preconception and misconception: he collected neither the elaborate morris dances of the industrial north-west—because their background did not match his idea of 'the folk'—nor any of the widespread step-dances. His collecting was concentrated on rural areas: the west country for songs and the Cotswolds for dances. At the same time he encouraged the view that only he could successfully collect the material. During his last illness, Cambridge morris men visited him en route to the Cotswolds to perform in their villages the dances Sharp had collected and to meet the dancers. They were seeking his blessing, but Sharp 'felt like a suspected person' (Kennedy). Since his death folk-music and dance have undergone many metamorphoses, in some of which his work has been denigrated; but his heritage is that all work since has defined its identity by reference to his achievement.　　　　　　　　MICHAEL HEANEY

Sources A. H. Fox-Strangways and M. Karpeles, *Cecil Sharp* (1933); 2nd edn (1955) · M. Karpeles and A. H. Fox-Strangways, *Cecil Sharp: his life and work*, rev. edn (1967) · R. Judge, 'Mary Neal and the Espérance morris', *Folk Music Journal*, 5 (1985–9), 545–91 · A. D. Townsend, 'Cecil James Sharp as collector and editor of traditional dance', *Traditional Dance*, 5/6 (1988), 53–76 · *E.F.D.S. News*, 8 (1924) · *The Times* (24 June 1924) · H. Anderson, 'Virtue in a wilderness: Cecil Sharp's Australian sojourn', *Folk Music Journal*, 6 (1990–94), 617–52 · R. Judge, 'Cecil Sharp and Morris, 1906–1909', *Folk Music Journal*, 8 (2001–5), 195–228 · E. C. Cawte, 'Watching Cecil Sharp at work', *Folk Music Journal*, 8 (2001–5), 282–313 · *Journal of the English Folk Dance and Song Society*, 8/4 (1959) · M. Karpeles, autobiography, c.1970, DWL · D. Harker, *Fakesong* (1985) · C. J. Sharp, Lecture, Hampstead, Nov 1903, Vaughan Williams Memorial Library, Sharp corresp., Box 1 · D. Kennedy, 'Folk dance revival', *Folk Music Journal*, 2 (1970–74), 80–90 · J. C. Brickwedde, 'A. Claud Wright: Cecil Sharp's forgotten dancer', *Folk Music Journal*, 6 (1990–94), 5–36 ·

A. H. Fox-Strangways, 'Our folk dances', *Music and Letters*, 4 (1923), 321–33 · G. Boyes, *The imagined village* (1993) · G. Cox, *A history of music education in England, 1872–1928* (1993) · R. Stradling and M. Hughes, *The English musical renaissance, 1860–1940* (1993) **Archives** Clare College, Cambridge · Vaughan Williams Memorial Library **Likenesses** J. Davies, photograph, *c.*1875, English Folk Dance and Song Society, London, Vaughan William Memorial Library; repro. in Fox-Strangways and Karpeles, *Cecil Sharp* [pl. 1] · photographs, 1875–1917, English Folk Dance and Song Society, London, Vaughan Williams Memorial Library; repro. in Fox-Strangways and Karpeles, *Cecil Sharp* [pl. 3] · L. Connell, photograph, *c.*1900, English Folk Dance and Song Society, London, Vaughan Williams Memorial Library; repro. in Fox-Strangways and Karpeles, *Cecil Sharp* [pl. 2] · four photographs, *c.*1912–1917, English Folk Dance and Song Society, London, Vaughan Williams Memorial Library; repro. in Fox-Strangways and Karpeles, *Cecil Sharp* [pls. 4(a), 4(b), 18(a), 18(b)] · W. Rothenstein, crayon drawing, 1920, Cecil Sharp House, London · E. B. Mackinnon, chalk drawing, 1921, NPG [*see illus.*] · E. B. Mackinnon, pencil drawing, 1921, NPG · Debenhams, Longman & Co., photograph, 1922, English Folk Dance and Song Society, London, Vaughan Williams Memorial Library; repro. in Fox-Strangways and Karpeles, *Cecil Sharp* [pl. 5] · W Rothenstein, oils, English Folk Dance and Song Society, London; repro. in Fox-Strangways and Karpeles, *Cecil Sharp* (1933), frontispiece [with the title 'Cecil J. Sharp'] **Wealth at death** £6273 15s.: probate, 4 Sept 1924, *CGPLA Eng. & Wales*

Clifford Dyce Sharp (1883–1935), by unknown photographer

Sharp, Clifford Dyce (1883–1935), journalist and journal editor, was born on 21 October 1883 at White Post House, Redhill, Surrey, the son of William Sharp, a solicitor, and his wife, Harriot Luisa Dyce. He had a stern nonconformist upbringing, and after attending St Lawrence College at Ramsgate submitted to his parents' wishes that he study engineering at University College, London, and then join his father's practice after graduation. As an articled attorney he found the law as tedious as applied science, and looked to Fleet Street for his eventual career. Not only could he write quickly and to order, but his legal training and engineering background had left him uniquely skilled to embrace the technical side of editing. A. R. Orage of *New Age* introduced the tiro editor to the finer points of newspaper composition and production. With his innovative ideas in layout and typography Sharp soon pioneered a fresh approach to weekly journalism.

Sharp was employed by Sidney and Beatrice Webb to help run the National Committee for the Prevention of Destitution (NCPD), their singularly unsuccessful attempt to promote the minority report of the poor law commission. Between 1910 and 1913 he transformed the NCPD's *Crusade* from a rather amateurish 12-page campaign newsletter into a polished if ponderous 35-page monthly magazine. The Fabian technician *par excellence*, the dour but ambitious Sharp had since joining the Society in 1900 assiduously cultivated the 'old gang' of Hubert *Bland, George Bernard Shaw, and the Webbs. When in 1906 younger members established a 'Fabian nursery' he was duly elected treasurer; the secretary was Bland's (and his wife Edith *Nesbit's) daughter, Rosamund Edith Nesbit Bland (*b.* 1886/7). Paternal intervention and the threat of a public scandal ended her romance with H. G. Wells, and

on 16 October 1909 a heartbroken Rosamund reluctantly married Sharp. The couple had no children.

Despite his debt to Orage, Sharp in April 1913 had the guild socialist *New Age* firmly in his sights when launching the Webbs' last great propagandist initiative, the *New Statesman*, which embodied an unashamedly top-down Fabian collectivism. As its first editor, he swiftly established the *New Statesman* as a weekly flagship of progressive opinion and an influential literary review, with a metropolitan influence which far exceeded its modest circulation. He relied heavily on the reputation of George Bernard Shaw, even though the relationship between the two men was stormy. The editor's increasing reluctance to tolerate his principal contributor's idiosyncrasies and eccentric opinions culminated in Shaw's resigning from the *New Statesman* board in October 1916. Sharp tolerated Shaw, but genuinely loathed David Lloyd George. The prime minister reciprocated by orchestrating Sharp's conscription into the Royal Artillery early in 1917.

Ironically, Sharp was infuriated when the Foreign Office soon secured the trainee subaltern's release. Posing as a freelance journalist, Sharp canvassed opinion among social democrats at the Stockholm conference. He became head of the British embassy's information service in Sweden, and late in 1918 commenced clandestine work for the Foreign Office's political information department as the author of fiercely anti-Bolshevik reports. Yet, when the articles finally appeared in the *New Statesman*, following Sharp's return to London in March 1919, they unequivocally condemned counter-revolutionary excesses in Finland and northern Russia.

Sharp quickly discovered that the *New Statesman* had moved decisively to the left during his absence. He endeavoured in vain to bring his creation within the orbit of Asquith's circle, with whom he desperately sought to ingratiate himself. Rejecting the opportunity to edit one of London's evening newspapers, the Liberal *Westminster*

Gazette, Sharp battled with the bottle and with his board. His erstwhile colleagues were convinced that politically and commercially the *New Statesman*'s best course was to remain an independent and if necessary deeply critical supporter of a Labour Party which in the 1920s was making significant electoral gains at the expense of the Liberals. In 1924 Sharp survived dismissal and reinstatement, but his alcoholism became so chronic that five years later the directors funded a lengthy visit for him to New York in order to dry out. After his return in 1930 the unrepentant inebriate was duly dismissed. The *New Statesman* had suffered deep wounds as a consequence of prolonged inertia and the absence of a clear editorial policy. Yet Sharp's creation was resilient enough in 1931 to absorb the moribund Liberal weekly *Nation*, and then embark upon a golden age of high sales and high politics under Kingsley Martin as editor.

Sharp never wholly adjusted to his new circumstances, and his drinking prevented him from successfully completing any subsequent commissions. He was forced to live off his wife, despite their brief separation in the winter of 1932–3. In the final year of his life Sharp desperately tried to stop drinking, but on 11 February 1935 he died of a heart attack at Farnborough Hospital, Farnborough, Kent. Although Beatrice Webb was quick to acknowledge her protégé's accomplishments as an editor, Clifford Sharp soon became the forgotten man of Fleet Street, his reputation as the chief architect of the *New Statesman* eclipsed by the high profile of his successor.   ADRIAN SMITH

Sources A. Smith, *The 'New Statesman': portrait of a political weekly, 1913–1931* (1996) • A. Smith, 'Heart to the right, brain to the left', *New Statesman* (8 Jan 1988) • E. Hyams, *The 'New Statesman': the history of the first fifty years, 1913–1963* (1963) • *The diary of Beatrice Webb*, ed. N. MacKenzie and J. MacKenzie, 4 vols. (1982–5), vols. 3–4 • M. Holroyd, *Bernard Shaw*, 2 (1989) • b. cert. • m. cert. • d. cert. • *WWW*
Archives BL, Bernard Shaw papers • BLPES, Passfield papers • University of Illinois, Urbana–Champaign, H. G. Wells archive
Likenesses photograph, *New Statesman* offices, London [*see illus.*]
Wealth at death £622 12*s.* 6*d.*: probate, 12 March 1935, *CGPLA Eng. & Wales*

Sharp, Sir Cuthbert (1781–1849), historian, was born at Hartlepool, co. Durham, the son of Cuthbert Sharp, a shipowner, and his wife, Susannah (d. 1794), the daughter of Hercules Crosby of Stockton. His mother was the sister of Brass Crosby, the controversial lord mayor of London and an important figure in political history, especially in connection with the publication of parliamentary debates. Sharp was educated at Greenwich in the school of the eminent Greek scholar Dr Charles Burney. When he was about eighteen he took a commission in the Essex fencibles, a cavalry force introduced by the government for the defence of the kingdom. He saw action in Ireland and, having studied briefly at Edinburgh University, became one of the first Britons to visit Paris after the peace of Amiens of 1801. When the treaty broke down he was taken as a prisoner of war but used influence to stay on parole in the French capital. While there he made himself an expert in the language and customs of France. After being

a prisoner 'for some years' (Brockie, 143) he returned to England via the Netherlands. In 1811 he eloped with Elizabeth, the daughter of Thomas Croudace of Bishopwearmouth, Sunderland. Two marriage ceremonies were performed, the first at Coldstream on 15 October and the second at the English church, Edinburgh, on 22 October. There appears to have been one child from the marriage—a daughter, Louise Laura.

Sources agree that the main focus of Sharp's life thereafter became literary, and three publications, in particular, are worthy of reference. His *Bishoprick Garland* (1834), a mixture of scraps of north-eastern songs and traditional nursery rhymes, was reprinted at the end of the twentieth century and used by researchers into cultural history. His *History of Hartlepool* (1816), reprinted in 1851 with an appendix by the publisher and historian John Proctor, still stands as the standard history of the ancient port and borough of Hartlepool. His *Memorials of the Rebellion of 1569*, culled from primary sources, was highly rated by nineteenth-century biographers. He also composed a large number of tracts and Durham family trees, many of which have since been proved inaccurate.

Although he was registered as 'retired' and devoted himself to 'literary pursuits' (Brockie, 143) possibly from his twenties, Sharp also led an active public life. Living in Hartlepool after his return from France, he served as mayor in 1813, 1816, and 1824 and was knighted in 1814 'on presenting an address to the Prince Regent' (Latimer, 265). Between 1823 and 1845 his main residence was in Sunderland, where he was collector of customs for twenty-two years. From 1845 to 1849 he filled a similar position at the larger port of Newcastle upon Tyne. He was heavily involved in freemasonry, and rose from minor office in the Sunderland branch in the 1820s to the position of deputy provincial grand master of the province of Durham from 1832. He was also a fellow of the Society of Antiquaries, having been recommended by Burney, among others, in 1810. He resigned in 1825 on account of financial problems.

Brief nineteenth-century biographies afford some small insight into both Sharp's looks and character. Local legend in Sunderland held that Queen Victoria had once described him as 'the ugliest man that has come to my court' (Corder, MSS 33–4). Despite his apparent popularity at school and even as customs collector, he had family problems and feuded with his daughter, though they were reconciled late in his life. He had friends of consequence, including Robert Surtees, whom he helped with his *History of Durham*, and, through Surtees, Sir Walter Scott, who corresponded with Sharp in verse on antiquarian matters.

Sharp was in poor health when he took up his new post in Newcastle in 1845. He was about to tender his resignation as customs collector when he died there, at his house in Northumberland Street, on 17 August 1849.

KEITH GREGSON

Sources B. R. Hill, *A sketch of the life of Sir Cuthbert Sharp* (1910) • W. Brockie, *Sunderland notables: natives, residents, and visitors* (1894) •

Sunderland pedigrees and family records, Sunderland local studies library, Corder MSS, no. 16 vol. 2 · *History, topography, and directory of the county palatine of Durham*, F. Whellan & Co., 2nd edn (1894) · J. Latimer, *Local records, or, Historical register of remarkable events which have occurred in Northumberland and Durham … 1832–57* (1857) · *Sunderland Herald* (2 May 1845) · *Sunderland Herald* (20 June 1845) · *Sunderland Herald* (24 Aug 1849) · *DNB* · d. cert.

Archives BL, MSS, Add. MSS 34208, 34556 · Durham Cath. CL, antiquarian MSS · Durham RO, MSS relating to Bowes family of Streatlam · U. Durham, lists compiled by him of Durham grand juries · W. Yorks. AS, Leeds, extracts from parish registers; notes relating to Pilgrimage of Grace | BL, letters to Joseph Hunter, Add. MS 24875 · Bodl. Oxf., corresp. with Sir Thomas Phillipps · Durham RO, corresp. relating to construction of Seaham harbour · Lambton Park, Chester-le-Street, co. Durham, letters to first earl of Durham · NRA, priv. coll., corresp., mainly to his mother and brother, Hercules · NRA, priv. coll., letters to Henry Howard · Sunderland Library, local studies section, Corder MSS · U. Durham, corresp., mainly with first earl of Durham

Likenesses T. L. Busby, engraving (after W. Foster), repro. in Hill, *Sketch of the life* · miniature, priv. coll.; repro. in Hill, *Sketch of the life*

Sharp, David (1840–1922), entomologist, was born on 15 October 1840 at Towcester, Northamptonshire, the only son (there were also three daughters) of William Sharp, currier, and his wife, Sarah Pepler. He spent his childhood in Stony Stratford and, from 1851, in London. After attending several preparatory schools, he entered St John's foundation school, Kilburn, before working for his father from the age of seventeen. During the next few years he took up entomology in earnest, his favourite haunts being Ken Wood, the Hammersmith marshes, and the shores of Deal and Dover. Fearing an inherited chronic melancholy, Sharp's father cultivated a lively household. Consequently, Malvern House, 13 Loudoun Road, St John's Wood, was also home to four boarders. Among the latter, in 1857–8, was Herbert Spencer (1820–1903). Spencer later speculated that his tenancy was terminated because William Sharp feared that his son was imbibing dangerous doctrines from Spencer.

In 1862 Sharp began medical studies at St Bartholomew's Hospital and became a member of the Entomological Society of London. Two years later he proceeded to the University of Edinburgh, where he graduated as bachelor of medicine in 1866. By this time he had also amassed a collection of approximately 2000 named British species of Coleoptera. He returned to London to work under the Sharp family doctor, and to assume the secretaryship of the Entomological Society for 1867. By the end of the year, however, he again departed for Scotland to become a medical officer in the Crichton Asylum at Dumfries. Shortly thereafter, he took charge of a private patient at Thornhill, Dumfriesshire.

On 1 February 1876, at Eccles, Dumfries, Sharp married 27-year-old housemaid Jessie Murdoch, daughter of James Murdoch, coachman, and his wife, Isabella Pagan; they had five daughters and two sons. In 1876, Sharp joined the Dumfriesshire and Galloway Scientific, Natural History, and Antiquarian Society. In January of the same year he had made an unsuccessful bid to become curator of the City of Glasgow Industrial Museum. Clearly desirous of quitting medicine, he made the leap after the death of his

private patient about 1884. Sharp and his family moved to Southampton, relocating to Wilmington, near Dartford, Kent, in 1888. From 1884 Sharp rapidly became an active participant in London's scientific circles. In 1885 he became recorder of insects for the *Zoological Record*. The following year, he was elected a fellow of the Zoological Society (subsequently serving on its council from 1901 to 1905); elections to fellowship of the Linnean Society (1888) and the Royal Society (1890) followed. Nevertheless, he was most active in the Entomological Society, serving as president (1887–8), vice-president (1889, 1891–2, 1896, and 1902–3) and as a member of council (1893–5 and 1902–04). In 1921 he was made a special life fellow.

In 1890, a year after moving to Cambridge, Sharp was appointed curator of the MacAndrew collection at the University Museum. 'The arrival of so eminent an entomologist in Cambridge', observed A. E. Shipley, 'gave a great impetus to the Study of Insects' (Shipley, 288). A special room in the museum was set aside as the 'Entomological Department', where Sharp held classes for the likes of A. D. Imms, H. M. Lefroy, and J. F. C. Fryer. He took on the additional burden of editor of the *Zoological Record* in 1891.

Sharp was eulogized by *The Times* as 'the most learned of British entomologists'. By the time of his death he had produced some 300 publications. The majority of his published papers dealt with insect nomenclature and classification, with a special emphasis on Coleoptera, or beetles. A devoted collector throughout his life, he accompanied friends on excursions throughout Britain, France, and Spain, and, through correspondence networks, he cast his net wider still. However, although extraordinarily assiduous and productive, he was not a rigorous thinker and often ended up muddying waters when his intent was clarification. In late 1866, for instance, he became embroiled with J. O. Westwood, H. W. Bates, and A. R. Wallace in a minor discussion about Darwinian explanations of insect mimicry. Sharp concluded that Darwinism could not explain similarities because it was principally about differentiation. His *Object and Method of Zoological Nomenclature* (1873) attempted to separate nomenclature from classification, by declaring that the first published binomial for each specimen should be its permanent species name. His adherence to this nomenclature, immediately rejected by his colleagues, meant that his Coleoptera part of the Entomological Society's *Catalogue of British Insects* (1870–73) was never published. Undoubtedly emboldened by the extent of his scientific reputation, he published his timely *Scheme for a National System of Rest-Funds (or Pensions) for Working People* in 1892. Perhaps unsurprisingly, it was a curious mixture of old and new Liberalism. He proposed a contributory scheme in order to reduce demands on poor-law funds, and to dissuade the working classes from falling into anarchism and socialism. But his *magnum opus* was his two-volume *Insects*, contributed to the Cambridge Natural History series in 1895 and 1899. These volumes passed through four reprintings by 1922 and a Russian translation in 1910; they constituted the standard text on the subject at the turn of the century, and earned Sharp an enduring place in the history of entomology.

After a productive career at Cambridge, Sharp retired to Brockenhurst, in the New Forest, in 1909, where he built a house, Lawnside, facing the heath of Black Knowl. Here he remained until his death at home on 27 August 1922. Described as a 'slight and delicate-looking man' (*The Times*, 31 Aug 1922, 9, col. c), only several months before his death, 'he might be recognised by his rapid stride, slight stoop, and long white beard, as he took his almost daily walk into the Forest he loved so well' (*The Entomologist*, 55, 1922, 221). He was buried at the Brockenhurst parish churchyard, overlooking the forest, on 31 August 1922.

J. F. M. CLARK

Sources *The Entomologist*, 55 (1922) · *Entomologist's Record*, 34 (1922) · *The Times* (31 Aug 1922) · Venn, *Alum. Cant.* · H. Spencer, *An autobiography*, 2 (1904) · D. Duncan, *The life and letters of Herbert Spencer* [1908]; repr. (1911) · S. A. Neave, *The centenary history of the Entomological Society of London, 1833–1933* (1933) · A. E. Shipley, '*J.': a memoir of John Willis Clark, registrary of the University of Cambridge and sometime fellow of Trinity College* (1913) · review of *The object and method of zoological nomenclature* by David Sharp, *Entomologist's Monthly Magazine*, 10 (1874), 215 · P. Chalmers Mitchell, *Centenary history of the Zoological Society of London* (1929) · H. Scherren, *The Zoological Society of London: a sketch of its foundation and development* (1905) · b. cert. · m. cert. · d. cert.

Archives Royal Entomological Society of London, autograph album, corresp., MSS, scrapbook · U. Cam., Museum of Zoology, catalogues | NHM, letters to Thomas Bell · Oxf. U. Mus. NH, mainly letters to Sir E. B. Poulton

Likenesses W. J. Lucas, photograph, repro. in *The Entomologist*, pl. III, facing p. 217

Wealth at death £9786 13s.: probate, 9 Dec 1922, *CGPLA Eng. & Wales*

Sharp, Eric, **Baron Sharp of Grimsdyke** (1916–1994), businessman, was born on 17 August 1916 at 20 Oxford Street, Whitechapel, London, the last of four children of Isaac Sharp (1879–1965), trade union secretary and local councillor, and his wife, Martha, *née* Belinsky (1881–1967). His parents were both Jewish immigrants from Russia. His birth was itself quite an event. Conceived eleven years after his youngest sister, his mother tried several methods to end her pregnancy naturally but the baby's will proved the stronger. Once born, he became the darling of his mother and two sisters, and enjoyed rare emotional security in poor family circumstances. His father, an idealist and committed socialist, was a founder of the Jewish Bakers' Union and a Labour councillor for Poplar, and stood as an independent candidate for parliament. Working actively for the good of humanity, he was rarely at home. Martha was, therefore, left to bring up the children very much on her own. She took in lodgers and went out to work in order to help her youngest son obtain the best local education, which included violin lessons, until he won a violin scholarship to the Guildhall School of Music.

From the ages of thirteen to eighteen Sharp attended Raines grammar school in the East End of London. Growing up through the depression, with a father active in left-wing politics, it was almost natural for him to volunteer for the Spanish Civil War. He was not called. Instead he won a scholarship to the London School of Economics, where he read statistics and economics. Graduating in 1940, he volunteered for the army, becoming a staff captain in southern command in 1944. As with so many of his generation, the Second World War marked a turning point. His army service brought him more into the mainstream of British life. Involved in the planning of the Normandy landings, he gained a lively sense of participation in the making of history, turning the seemingly impossible into a telling success. He never lost this sense, and there was always a smack of the Churchillian in his later business life.

In 1945 Sharp spoke on Labour platforms and in 1946 he joined the Board of Trade. In 1948 he moved to the Ministry of Fuel and Power as a principal and served as the UK delegate to the coal and petroleum committee of the Organization for European Economic Co-operation, and from 1951 to 1954 he served as vice-chairman of its electricity committee. This was the ideal background for his last post in the civil service, as secretary to the Herbert committee of inquiry into the electricity supply industry, from 1956 to 1957. His civil service career proved an invaluable training ground and gave him permanent confidence in handling government–industry relations. More important in terms of his own development was his marriage, at the New West End Synagogue, Paddington, on 22 October 1950, to Marion, daughter of Jack Freedman, merchant, of Edgware, Middlesex. Marion married much to the disappointment of her parents, who were not content with Eric's provenance and prospects. For her, however, Eric was 'something special' (private information). In their tight circumstances, and with Eric often absent in Paris, the couple had three children by 1956, Nicola (*b.* 1954), whose tragic death in 1987 he found hard to bear, and Richard and Victoria, twins born in 1956.

Aged forty and with growing family responsibilities and a sense that his progress in the civil service was blighted by his own Russian family background in the wake of the Burgess and Maclean affair, Sharp decided to leave the civil service for the private sector. At British Nylon Spinners Ltd (BNS), from 1957 to 1964, he found ample scope for his leadership and creative talents: with the ending of the nylon monopoly, he was thrown into the fray as marketing manager. With a large and happy team, he fought hard to hold market share until ICI Fibres took over in 1964. He was one of only two BNS directors to be retained by ICI, but was unable to enjoy the freedom he needed to give of his best. After a transitional hiatus of a few months, he joined the American-owned chemicals company Monsanto Ltd in 1969, and was sent to the USA to turn around Monsanto's main fibre division. This he did, successfully overcoming American resentment that a Briton was telling them how to run their company. Monsanto recognized his leadership qualities and he was deputy chairman of Monsanto Ltd from 1973 to 1974 and then chairman from 1975 to 1981. He was president of the British Chemicals Industry Association in 1979 and 1980, and earned his CBE in 1980 for the sensitive handling of a major plant closure in Scotland.

Plucked out of almost certain retirement by Sir Keith Joseph, then secretary of state for industry, to become part-time chairman of Cable and Wireless in 1980, and then full-time chairman and chief executive from 1981 to 1990, Sharp responded to the challenge of privatizing and transforming 'a relic of empire' into a world-class telecommunications company with youthful zest and utter determination. In a brief ten-year span he gained world fame in an industry completely new to him. At a time when almost all public telecommunications operators were content with their inherited monopoly positions, he carved out a new path for Cable and Wireless, and in the process enabled the company to record a notable series of firsts: the first telephone company to be privatized (1981), the first to make a new market entry in the UK (with Mercury, in 1982), the first to make a major acquisition (the Hong Kong Telephone Company, in 1983), the first to build a private sector cable across the Atlantic (1984–9), the first to link Japan to mainland USA by cable (1986–91), the first foreign company to enter the heart of Japanese telecommunications (with the formation of IDC in 1987), the first to link Korea, Japan, and Hong Kong by fibre optic cable (1990), the first to introduce Cellular Wireless at 1800 gigahertz (1991), the first to break into the market in Sweden (1991) and Australia (1991), the first to establish a joint venture in Russia (1991), and the first to conceive and implement a global digital highway, linking the shores of Asia to the shores of Europe via the USA.

Sharp shook the old telecommunications order and in effect was a pioneer of the new information era. He led from the front, fearless in confronting those who blocked his way, however high they stood in political or regulatory circles, and tireless in courting those whose support he needed. While a habitual communicator with ministers and heads of government, he was equally interested in anyone, however humble in status, who could contribute to the Cable and Wireless cause. This rare human quality won him much affection and admiration throughout the company and beyond, particularly in the countries he cultivated hardest—China, Japan, and the United States. President of the Sino-British Trade Council from 1985 to 1990, his special relationship with China was the pillar of his business life after Cable and Wireless, as non-executive director at Carlton Communications and Stanhope Properties.

From humble beginnings Sharp became a world figure, constantly moving with the times. A socialist in 1945, he became one of Margaret Thatcher's favourite businessmen, earning a knighthood in 1984 and a peerage, as Baron Sharp of Grimsdyke, in 1989. A civil servant expert on nationalized industries in the late 1940s and early 1950s, he became a leading private-sector protagonist and practitioner of privatization in the 1980s and 1990s. His greatest strengths were his financial ingenuity, powerful intellect, rare intuition, and vigorous energy, which he combined with a sensitivity to human vulnerabilities, derived from his own experience. He died from a heart attack in London, shortly after returning from a business trip to China, on 2 May 1994. He was survived by his wife. He was cremated at Golders Green on 6 May; a memorial service was held at St John's, Smith Square.

JONATHAN SOLOMON

Sources *The Independent* (7 May 1994) · *The Times* (5 May 1994) · *Sunday Telegraph* (4 May 1994) · Cable and Wireless press notices · *Recorder* [Cable and Wireless Group] · private information (2004) · b. cert. · d. cert.
Likenesses C. Thornton-Jones, portrait, 1984, priv. coll. · photograph, repro. in *The Times* · photograph, repro. in *The Independent*
Wealth at death £949,577: probate, 15 Feb 1995, *CGPLA Eng. & Wales*

Sharp, Evelyn Adelaide, Baroness Sharp (1903–1985), civil servant, was born on 25 May 1903 at Ealing, Middlesex, the daughter of the Revd Charles James Sharp, vicar of Ealing, and his wife, Mary Frances Musgrove Harvey. The third child in a family of five, she had two elder sisters, and a younger sister and brother. Her father was a very 'modern' vicar, one who questioned the virgin birth, wanted his daughters to have careers, and who was a radical Liberal, active in local politics in London. At St Paul's Girls' School in London and then at Somerville College, Oxford, she was sporty rather than intellectual, and was a rebel, even at school clashing with the authorities. After taking a second-class history degree at Oxford in 1925 she entered the administrative class of the home civil service in 1926. This was only the second year in which the relevant examinations were open to women.

Sharp's first post was in the Board of Trade, but after eighteen months she was transferred to the Ministry of Health, the government department then dealing with housing and local government matters. Promotion was slow in inter-war Whitehall: only in 1935 did she become an acting principal (a full principal a year later), making the assistant secretary grade in 1940. She spent four years during the Second World War at the Treasury, working on the establishments side of that department, a great deal of her time being occupied with plans for the post-war organization of the civil service. In 1945 she returned to the Ministry of Health as an under-secretary, working on the post-war rehousing programme. She was deputy secretary in the Ministry of Town and Country Planning, 1946–50, and then in the Ministry of Housing and Local Government, 1951–5, her arrival among the élite of the civil service being recognized with her appointment as a DBE in 1948. Women in the civil service did not get equal pay with men until the 1950s, but an exception was made for Evelyn Sharp when she became a deputy secretary: she thus got equal pay ten years before other women in the civil service. She became the ministry's permanent secretary in October 1955, the first woman ever to become a permanent secretary.

Evelyn Sharp was widely recognized as one of the most formidable and outstanding Whitehall officials of her day, marked out by her professional abilities as a civil servant; her unique specialist knowledge and experience born of a virtual career-long association with the field of local government, housing, and planning; and her forthright and strong-willed manner. She was a 'can-do' civil servant,

Evelyn Adelaide Sharp, Baroness Sharp (1903–1985), by Madame Yevonde

concerned to bring solutions to ministers rather than just to point out problems. Her approach was tough-minded, direct, and decisive. She was invariably inventive, resourceful, and committed to achieving results and positive action. Ministers from both main parties—including Hugh Dalton, Harold Macmillan, Enoch Powell, and Charles Hill—testified to her power and brilliance as an administrator and adviser. Richard Crossman's *Diaries of a Cabinet Minister* gave a vivid (sometimes acute and sometimes unfair) account of her late in her career. She was never one to mince words, but while there might be fierce arguments with her minister, there would always be loyal acceptance of his decision—though she once talked in an interview of a permanent secretary producing initiatives of her own and on occasion being a brake to the minister, she was clear that in the end it was not a civil servant's job to override his or her minister (*The Guardian*, 11 March 1966). Within the Ministry of Housing and Local Government she exerted a massive dominance, and she always fought her department's corner hard in Whitehall's interdepartmental battles, particularly when it came to taking on the Treasury. A critic of what she saw as the iniquities of traditional 'Treasury control', she was one of the senior civil servants who sat as 'assessors' on the Plowden committee on the control of public expenditure (1959–61).

Sharp was centrally involved with the important planning developments of the 1940s and early 1950s, playing a major role in the framing of the 1947 Town and Country Planning Act and having special responsibility for the planning problems of Greater London (including the dispersal of population). She was also a driving force behind the new towns programme. In the late 1940s she fought and won an internal Whitehall battle to have planning, local government, and housing responsibilities combined in one department (she had seen the problems caused by separating these interrelated functions and later, in 1964, successfully fought to save planning for her ministry when the new Labour government created the short-lived Ministry of Land and Natural Resources). Pre-war planning had been negative and concerned chiefly with urban sprawl; the post-war aim was for planning to be positive, constructive, and comprehensive, the new approach being in tune with Evelyn Sharp's own philosophy and temperament. She had strong views about 'the urgency of the urban problem' (*Hansard 5L*, col. 185, 1 Aug 1972), and made no secret of her belief in the beneficent role of government, seeing the civil service as an instrument for making life better for ordinary people. She went along with the conventional wisdom of the time in backing high-rise flats—something she later regretted.

Probably Sharp's single greatest personal achievement was in the maintenance of a close working relationship between local government and central government. Throughout her career she was always very active in getting out of her office and visiting local councils up and down the country, and she built up an extensive network of contacts throughout the local government world. She was a great champion of local government. But she was aware of the need for reform—for higher-calibre councillors and staff, fewer and bigger authorities, bringing town and country together—to strengthen local government's independence, influence, and capacity for initiative. Indeed, after her retirement from the civil service in 1966 she was one of the dominant figures on the royal commission on local government in England (1966–9) and a key influence shaping the commission's proposal for unitary authorities. The centralization of the 1980s and the Thatcher government's abolition of the Greater London council and the metropolitan county councils appalled her.

Her DBE having been raised to GBE in 1961, Evelyn Sharp was made a life peer in 1966. She was a member of the Independent Television Authority (1966–73), a director of Bovis, and president of the London and Quadrant Housing Trust. She conducted several inquiries for the government: the manpower needs of urban transport planning, the mobility of the physically disabled, and army training on Dartmoor. In the late 1960s she chaired a small group of former senior officials asked by the then leader of the opposition, Edward Heath, to give him private advice on the reform of the machinery of government. Made an honorary fellow of Somerville in 1955, she was granted an honorary DCL at Oxford (1960), and honorary LLDs at Cambridge (1962), Manchester (1967), and Sussex (1969).

Evelyn Sharp was never a faceless bureaucrat—she was a warm, unstuffy, impulsive, and tremendously energetic person. She never married. Looking back in a 1966 interview she was to admit that she regretted never having had a family: 'I should prefer to have been a man: then I could have had a career and marriage too' (*The Times*, 18 Feb 1966). Her twenty-year-long relationship (starting in the 1950s) with another very senior civil servant was a semi-open secret at the top of Whitehall. Over the years, a Jewish refugee from Nazi Austria, a Hungarian fleeing the 1956 Soviet invasion, and (in Evelyn's old age) the grand-daughter of an old friend were each taken under her wing, striking examples of her kindness and generosity. As her oldest friend, Dame Alix Meynell, put it in her memorial address: 'she was a very human person; the truest of friends and the best of companions; a great appreciator and giver of enjoyment; in her company there was always laughter' (Meynell). She died at Lavenham, Suffolk, on 1 September 1985.   KEVIN THEAKSTON

Sources K. Theakston, *Leadership in Whitehall* (1999), chap. 6 · memorial address by Lady Meynell, 9 Sept 1985, priv. coll. · *The Times* (4 Sept 1985) · R. H. S. Crossman, *The diaries of a cabinet minister*, 1 (1975) · private information (2004) · *DNB · CGPLA Eng. & Wales* (1985)
Archives Strathclyde University, Pepler MSS, correspondence with G. L. Pepler | FILM BFI NFTVA, current affairs footage · BFI NFTVA, documentary footage | SOUND BL NSA, Bow dialogues, 15 July 1969, C812/22/C14 · BL NSA, current affairs recordings
Likenesses Madame Yevonde, photograph, NPG [*see illus.*] · photograph, repro. in *The Times*
Wealth at death £87,955: probate, 23 Oct 1985, *CGPLA Eng. & Wales*

Sharp [married name Nevinson], **Evelyn Jane** (1869–1955), children's writer and suffragette, was born in Denmark Hill, London, on 4 August 1869, the ninth of eleven children, nine of whom survived beyond childhood, of Jane (née Bloyd) (1829?–1915) and John James Sharp (c.1827–1903), slate merchant. Her brother Cecil *Sharp was the folk song and dance expert. In 1928 Evelyn wrote a book on the origin of dance, *Here we go round*.

The youngest of the four girls, Evelyn Sharp was taught by sisters until she was about twelve, then attended school in London for three years; she studied at the Collège de France, Paris from 1890. Many of her children's stories from *The Youngest Girl in the School* (1901) onwards reflect her own happy schooldays as a boarder. Her family discouraged her wish to go to university. Neither did they approve of this clever young woman with big, expressive brown eyes earning her own living in London. In 1894 she taught, writing stories at night in her London hostel—perhaps similar to the one depicted in her novel *The Making of a Prig* (1897). She had already written one novel at home. In 1895 John Lane published *At the Relton Arms*, its jacket designed by Beardsley, and the first of six short stories appeared in the *Yellow Book*. Evelyn joined the group of writers associated with these infamous volumes.

Evelyn Sharp's first publication had been a non-fictional defence of fairy tales. Her appeal to children's imaginations, to 'the marvellous in their minds' (E. Sharp, *Fairy Tales as they are, as they were and as they should be*, 1889, 2) lay behind much of her subsequent success. *Wymps and other Fairy Tales* (1896) was the first of over twenty books and hundreds of short stories which treated children as creative, intelligent beings. Despite (or perhaps because of)

the fact that Evelyn never had children of her own, she appeared to possess empathy with the child's perception of the world, depicting 'grown ups' as the mysterious, irrational ones. Her fairy stories and schoolgirl tales were neither patronizing nor moralistic though they reflect her own increasingly progressive views on gender, class, internationalism, and peace. In the 1920s she wrote an account of educational opportunities for London children and in 1931 reported on the International Conference on African Children in Geneva run by Save the Children International Union. Evelyn became a prolific journalist, writing for papers such as the *Manchester Guardian* (as its first regular women's page writer), *Daily Herald* (on their staff between 1915 and 1923), and *Daily Chronicle* (supplying daily features and stories for children in the 1930s). She became a fellow of the Royal Society of Literature. Her stories combined a strong social purpose with a persistent sense of humour.

Evelyn Sharp had been converted to women's suffrage in 1906 after a speech given by the writer and former actress Elizabeth Robins. She now found that 'freedom, directly you discover you haven't got it, will not wait another minute' (Sharp, *Unfinished Adventure*, 128). From the non-militants she graduated to the Women's Social and Political Union, lectured for them in Denmark and became secretary of the Kensington branch. She was briefly imprisoned in 1911 and 1913, recuperating from forcible feeding with the physicist Dr Hertha Ayrton. In 1926 she published a 300-page memoir of Dr Ayrton at the request of her daughter Barbara Gould. Barbara, along with Dr Louisa Garrett Anderson, was one of many friends Evelyn gained in the suffrage years: she carefully included friendships among her list of recreations. She worked with Barbara Gould in the United Suffragists which played a pivotal part in securing the partial victory of votes for some women in 1918.

During the war Evelyn Sharp edited the women's suffrage journal *Votes for Women*. She also refused to pay taxes. Her furniture was distrained. She was only discharged from bankruptcy in 1918 once she was assured of taxation *with* representation. She also joined the Labour Party. She had been refused permission to go to the Women's International Congress at The Hague (1915) but attended the second congress of the International Committee of Women for Permanent Peace at Zürich in 1919. The war had confirmed her pacifist tendencies. Although she never joined the Society of Friends, she worked for them in war-ravaged Germany in 1921, also visiting famine areas of Russia in the 1920s with their relief committee.

Since the early 1900s Evelyn Sharp had enjoyed a close relationship with her fellow journalist and lover of social justice and travel Henry Woodd *Nevinson (1856–1941). Whether on excursions organized by their Saturday walking club, urging women's suffrage, denouncing the excesses of the Black and Tans in Ireland or reporting from Germany in 1923 on the French occupation of the Ruhr, they were constant companions. Continually confounding expectations, Evelyn ended her autobiography, written in her sixties, with the observation that she might now be expected to 'put on a cap and settle down to enjoy a spinster's twilight'. Instead, on 18 January 1933, the day she completed this book, she married the seventy-five-year-old Henry who had recently been widowed. They spent seven years together in Hampstead before bombs drove them to the Cotswolds where Henry died in 1941. Evelyn returned to living alone in London flats as she had done for most of her adult life. Depression and failing eye sight made her final years tough ones. She died in Methuen Nursing Home, 13 Gunnersbury Avenue, Ealing, London, on 17 June 1955.   ANGELA V. JOHN

Sources Bodl. Oxf., MSS Evelyn Sharp Nevinson · E. Sharp, *Unfinished adventure* (1933) · H. W. Nevinson, diaries, Bodl. Oxf. · H. W. Nevinson, *Changes and chances* (1923) · H. W. Nevinson, *More changes and chances* (1925) · H. W. Nevinson, *Last changes, last chances* (1928) · J. Alberti, *Beyond suffrage: feminists in war and peace, 1914–1928* (1989) · J. E. Miller, *Rebel women* (1994) · K. L. Mix, *A study in yellow: the Yellow Book and its contributors* (1960) · *The Times* (21 June 1955) · *Manchester Guardian* (20 June 1955) · M. Stott, ed., *Women talking: an anthology from the Guardian women's page* (1957) · A. V. John, '"Behind the locked door": Evelyn Sharp, suffragette and rebel journalist', *Women's History Review*, 12/1 (2003), 5–13 · W. Harris, 'H. W. Nevinson, Margaret Nevinson, Evelyn Sharp: little-known crusaders', *English Literature in Transition, 1880–1920*, 45 (2002), 280–305 · *CGPLA Eng. & Wales* (1955)
Archives Bodl. Oxf., corresp. and papers, incl. diaries and journals · Women's Library, London, letters | BL, Society of Authors MSS, Add. MS 56804 · JRL, letters to the *Manchester Guardian* · Ransom HRC, letters to Elizabeth Robins · U. Reading, letters to the Bodley Head Ltd · U. Reading, letters to Macmillan, MS 1089
Likenesses photographs, 1879–c.1933, Bodl. Oxf.; repro. in Sharp, *Unfinished adventure* · W. Rothenstein, pencil drawing, 1933, NPG; repro. in Sharp, *Unfinished adventure*
Wealth at death £7641 4s. 9d.: administration with will, 6 Oct 1955, *CGPLA Eng. & Wales*

Sharp, Granville (1735–1813), author and slavery abolitionist, was born at Durham on 10 November 1735. He was the scion of a clerical family, the ninth and youngest son of Thomas *Sharp (1693–1758), archdeacon of Northumberland, and his wife, Judith Wheler (d. 1757). His grandfather was John *Sharp, archbishop of York; two of his brothers became Anglican clergymen. According to Prince Hoare, his first biographer, Granville:

> was at a very early age withdrawn from the public grammar-school at Durham, before he had gained more than the first rudiments of the learned languages, and was sent to a smaller school, to be instructed more particularly in writing and arithmetic. (Hoare, 27)

His father's straitened financial circumstances led to his being apprenticed in May 1750 to a Quaker linen draper named Halsey, of Tower Hill, London. On Halsey's death in 1753 he continued to serve his family and, in his own words, 'was turned over to a Presbyterian, or rather, as he was more properly called, an Independent. I afterwards lived some time with an Irish Papist, and also with another person, who, I believe, had no religion at all' (ibid., 28). These contacts encouraged Sharp to engage in theological disputation, and he used his leisure to acquire that largely self-taught knowledge of Greek and Hebrew which formed an important basis for his career as a writer. In 1757 he completed his apprenticeship and became a

Granville Sharp (1735–1813), by George Dance, 1794

freeman of the City of London as a member of the Fishmongers' Company; the following year the failure of a linen business in which he was employed led him to accept a clerkship in the Ordnance office at the Tower. In 1764 he received promotion to the minuting branch as a clerk-in-ordinary.

During this period Sharp's intellectual interests, particularly in the realms of biblical scholarship, linguistics, and antiquarianism, deepened. He researched into the claim of his former master, Henry Willoughby, to the barony of Willoughby of Parham; he published a reply to Benjamin Kennicott's *Catalogue of the Sacred Vessels Restored by Cyrus* (1765), wrote *A Short Treatise on the English Tongue* (1767), and completed a book on scriptural prophecies in 1768. Each of these works went into at least two editions, and it was largely on the strength of them that his maternal uncle Granville Wheler offered him a benefice at Great Leek, Nottinghamshire. Wheler was married to the sister of the ninth earl of Huntingdon, whose wife was the celebrated evangelical countess. The connection with evangelicalism remained with Sharp all his life. However, he declined both the offer and the suggestion that he take holy orders.

In the mid-1760s Sharp became seriously interested in the abolition of slavery. His concern seems to have been occasioned in 1765 by his fortuitous encounter at the house of his brother William with a slave, Jonathan Strong. William Sharp had medical knowledge, and Strong was seeking treatment after sustaining injuries inflicted by his owner, David Lisle. Granville Sharp took up Strong's case, secured his release from prison when Lisle obtained his arrest as an escaped slave, and fought off a legal challenge which accused him of violating the owner's property rights. Thereafter Sharp, with characteristic devotion to research, applied himself to a detailed study of the legal status of slaves in Britain, as distinct from the colonies, and of the laws of civil liberty in Britain itself. An early result was *A Representation of the Injustice and Dangerous Tendency of Tolerating Slavery* (1769). He began to correspond and collaborate with the Quaker abolitionist Anthony Benezet and (from 1773) the Philadelphia abolitionist Benjamin Rush. Soon he took up the cases of other slaves in England, such as Thomas Lewis. His efforts reached a climax with Lord Mansfield's celebrated judgment in the case of James Somerset (1772), which, although much debated subsequently, was widely interpreted as stating that any slave setting foot in England immediately became free. At all events, it was a massive propaganda victory for abolitionists, and Sharp was set on what became the most notable feature of his career. In 1776 he published several anti-slavery works including *The Law of Liberty*.

During these years Sharp followed closely the deterioration in the relations between Britain and her North American colonies. Strongly sympathetic to the colonial grievances, he associated himself with traditional whig and Commonwealth libertarian ideas, as espoused by such as Richard Price and John Cartwright. In his *Declaration of the People's Natural Right to a Share in the Legislature* (1774) he argued for American representation in the Westminster parliament, claiming that such representation was consistent both with natural rights and with historic English liberties as enshrined in Magna Carta. But, since he was 'patriot as well as a radical' (Bonwick, 74), he also deplored the idea of rebellion or American separation, and believed that appropriate reforms, such as the abandonment of parliamentary taxation, could preserve the unity of the empire. In particular he urged that 'we should strictly maintain our *Loyalty* to the *Crown*, at the same time that we steadily assert our legal and constitutional Rights' (G. Sharp, *Declaration*, 1774, 42). He believed that those 'rights' were best safeguarded by measures of constitutional reform, and he argued strongly in favour of annual parliaments.

In 1776 Sharp's opposition to the American War of Independence led him to resign from the Ordnance office. Thereafter he followed no formal profession and was supported by the generosity of his brothers William and James, together with the proceeds from his published works, of which sixty-one are listed in Hoare's biography. The onset of war gave Sharp a further cause to champion: opposition to the use of the press-gang for naval recruitment. In collaboration with James Oglethorpe, to whose *Sailor's Advocate* he contributed an introduction, Sharp drew on his libertarian ideology and legal researches to take up an issue which drew widespread support. He was a persistent critic of the colonial and domestic policies of Lord North's administration, which he condemned in his *Address to the People* (1778) as arbitrary and corrupt. He became one of the earliest members of the Society for Constitutional Information, founded in 1780; he corresponded with Christopher Wyvill, John Jebb, and other reformers; he wrote strongly against triennial parliaments as an insufficient measure; and he supported the legislative independence of the Irish parliament. In the belief that the ancient constitution represented people rather than property, and as an alternative to the universal suffrage for which he was not an enthusiast, Sharp advocated a revival of the Anglo-Saxon system of frankpledge. It would involve a system of administration from tithing courts to parliament, which would secure the involvement in government, and the preservation of the rights, of an active citizenry. He formulated these ideas in his *Account of the Constitutional Polity of Congregational Courts* (1786). Parliamentary reform sat easily with Sharp's anti-slavery convictions; the Society for Constitutional Information supported a Quaker petition against the slave trade in 1783 and reprinted anti-slavery tracts.

Throughout his life Sharp remained a member of the Church of England. Though he did not live in Clapham and was rather more radical than some members of the evangelical Clapham Sect, he was none the less associated with it, shared many of its moral priorities, and has been seen by historians of anti-slavery as 'a member of the Evangelical core group' (Anstey, 158) of abolitionists. After the British recognition of American independence in 1783 Sharp's Anglican commitment led him to campaign for the restoration of the episcopalian church in the former colonies. So anxious was he that there be no doubt about the legitimacy of a 'true episcopal succession' in America that he insisted, as he told Benjamin Rush, 'the first *American Bishops* should rather receive their consecration from the hands of 3 or 4 of our *English Bishops* than from the *Nonjurors* of Scotland' (Woods, 27), as had happened with Samuel Seabury. His efforts were rewarded with the consecration of the bishops of New York and Pennsylvania in 1787. The *Dictionary of National Biography* is incorrect in stating that Sharp was aided in this process by Archbishop Thomas Secker; Secker died in 1768.

In common with many radicals Sharp compared the state of slavery to that of political reformers allegedly repressed by an unjust government in his own country. Like them, too, he was more concerned with constitutional issues than with the social grievances of the poor in Britain. The latter were not the legal property of others and, as he wrote to Bishop Porteus in 1795, 'the English labourer is protected at least from all personal ill usage and outrage by equal laws' (Anstey, 242–3) and could seek parish relief. From 1776 Sharp began to publish tracts on slavery and corresponded energetically with many leading members, lay and clerical, of the political establishment. He tried, unsuccessfully, to institute a private prosecution for murder after the infamous *Zong* incident in 1783, when over a hundred African slaves were thrown overboard from this slave ship in an effort to defraud the underwriters. When the anti-slavery movement began to organize nationwide petitioning campaigns, Sharp was at the forefront. The Society for the Abolition of the Slave Trade was founded in 1787. When its London committee was set up on 22 May 1787 he was one of its twelve founding members—and one of only three who were not Quakers. Sharp urged the movement to campaign for the immediate abolition of slavery itself as well as the trade, but was in a minority of one. He none the less gave his full endorsement to the motions for the abolition of the British slave trade introduced in the House of Commons by William Wilberforce. Sharp, together with Thomas Clarkson, provided much of the essential information for the abolitionist campaign. He met William Pitt to discuss the matter, and on the outbreak of the French Revolution he corresponded with several French sympathizers in the national assembly. With Clarkson and Wilberforce he helped to sponsor the establishment of a colony for freed slaves at Sierra Leone and published a *Short Sketch* for its government in 1786. Sharp was also one of the first directors of the St George's Company, which managed the settlement until it was ceded to the crown in 1808, and he became one of the first directors of the African Institution in 1807.

A combination of mobilization and a change in the religious and intellectual climate had brought much public support to abolitionism since 1788, the year of the first major petitioning movement. In 1792 the House of Commons passed a motion for gradual abolition which faded away in House of Lords committees. The rearguard resistance of the West Indian interest, and fear of the dangers of reform in an atmosphere of potential revolution, inhibited the cause in the later 1790s. Sharp continued to write on the subject, notably in his *Serious Reflections on the Slave Trade and Slavery Wrote in March 1797*, published in 1805. He also remained vigorous in the cause of parliamentary reform during that decade. In 1802 he was 'almost alone' in protesting against the re-enslavement of free blacks in the conquered French Caribbean islands (Drescher, 105).

The suggestion that Sharp was not a 'real evangelical' (Cooper, 435) is undermined by his missionary zeal, some of which found expression through his membership of the Society for the Propagation of the Gospel and his contribution to the foundation of the British and Foreign Bible Society, of which he became the first chairman in 1804. He shared some of the anti-Roman Catholicism espoused by many evangelicals, and in 1813 served as the first chairman of the Protestant Union, a body which existed to oppose Catholic emancipation. His defenders insisted that for all his anti-Catholicism, he 'lived in habits of friendship and intimacy' with individual Catholics (Hoare, 478). Sharp used his biblical researches to take part in a significant theological debate. His *Remarks on the Uses of the Definitive Article in the Greek Text of the New Testament* (1798; 3rd edn, 1803) argued strongly for the divinity of Christ and struck a blow against the Socinian position; Benjamin Rush credited the work with the conversion of a (previously) anti-Trinitarian clergyman near Philadelphia (Woods, 36). As a memoirist in the *Gentleman's Magazine* put it, Sharp:

was sensible that the religion of the divine Saviour and Redeemer of the world requires something more than a cold and indolent assent of the understanding; that it imperiously calls for an entire change in the dispositions of the heart. (*GM*, 88, 1818, 491)

Music was important in Sharp's social life. He himself played a harp of his own design, and his family formed an orchestra which delighted in musical trips by boat on the Thames, during which they entertained royalty and were charmingly portrayed by J. J. Zoffany. In 1767 Sharp found time to write *A Short Introduction to Vocal Music*; it went into a second edition ten years later. His other interests reflected his energy as well as his eccentricity. They included an idea for issuing bales of wool to protect British soldiers in the Peninsular War; a plan to extend London parish relief to all the poor, irrespective of their origin; an insistence that Napoleon was the 'little horn' of the book of Daniel; and more than a passing interest in the sense of the imminence of the apocalypse, widespread in intellectual as well as popular circles at this time. He lived mainly in Garden Court, Temple, London, until the death of his brother William, when he resided with the latter's widow at Fulham. After a gradual physical and mental decline he died there, unmarried, on 6 July 1813 and was buried in Fulham churchyard on 13 July.

Although Sharp was never a popular or even accessible writer, his work was of immense importance to the antislavery movement in Britain. It was partly through his efforts that it gained public attention and sympathy and that it transformed itself from a benign climate of opinion to a highly organized campaign. Thomas Clarkson regarded him as a founder of the movement; according to the whig Francis Horner, he was one of those who had started it. He was predictably criticized in West Indian circles, which questioned his motivation; they accused him, for instance, of proposing to withhold charity from the black poor in London to force them to leave for Sierra Leone (Drescher, 258, n. 74). None the less, he attracted remarkably few personal enemies. Sharp had an exceptionally wide circle of friends, and could win affection as well as respect. James Stephen credited him with 'the most inflexible of human wills united to the gentlest of human hearts' and opined that his life was evidence that 'it was too soon to proclaim that the age of chivalry was gone' (Stephen, 2.314).   G. M. DITCHFIELD

Sources DNB · P. Hoare, *Memoirs of Granville Sharpe, esq.* (1820) · E. C. P. Lascelles, *Granville Sharp and the freedom of the slaves in England* (1928) · J. Stephen, *Essays in ecclesiastical biography*, 2 vols. (1849), vol. 1, pp. 312–22, vol. 2, pp. 287–383 · GM, 1st ser., 83/2 (1813), 89–90 · R. A. Cooper, 'Sharp, Granville', *BDMBR*, vol. 1 · R. Anstey, *The Atlantic slave trade and British abolition, 1760–1810* (1975) · D. B. Davis, *The problem of slavery in western culture* (1966) · J. R. Oldfield, *Popular politics and British anti-slavery: the mobilisation of public opinion against the slave trade, 1787–1807* (1995) · T. Clarkson, *The history of the rise, progress and accomplishment of the abolition of the African slave trade by the British parliament* (1808) · S. Drescher, *Capitalism and antislavery: British mobilization in comparative perspective* (1986) · C. Bonwick, *British radicals and the American revolution* (1977) · J. Woods, 'The correspondence of Benjamin Rush and Granville Sharp', *Journal of American Studies*, 1 (1967), 1–38 · J. Oldham, *The Mansfield manuscripts and the growth of English law in the eighteenth century*, 2 vols. (1992) ·

J. Oldham, 'New light on Mansfield and slavery', *Journal of British Studies*, 27 (1988), 45–68 · F. O. Shyllon, *Black slaves in Britain* (1974) **Archives** Glos. RO, corresp. and papers; diary · Hunt. L., letters · New York Historical Society, papers | Boston PL, MSS and letters · Glos. RO, letters to Samuel Viner · LPL, letters relating to America; corresp. relating to Society for the Propagation of the Gospel · N. Yorks. CRO, Wyvill MSS · U. Southampton L., corresp. with Charles Spalding [copies] · York Minster Library, letter-book, mainly relating to abolition of slavery · York Minster Library, letters and papers relating to Archbishop Sharp and Prussian church **Likenesses** J. Zoffany, group portrait, oils, 1779–81 (*The Sharp Family*), NPG · G. Dance, pencil drawing, 1794, NPG [*see illus.*] · H. Mayer, engraving, 1794 (after G. Dance, 1794), repro. in Hoare, *Memoirs*, frontispiece · C. Andras, portrait, 1809, priv. coll. · T. Blood, engraving, 1817 (after G. Dance) · S. Cousins, mezzotint, pubd 1827 (after bust by F. Chantrey), BM · G. Adcock, stipple, pubd 1833 (after unknown artist), NPG · M. Brown, portrait, priv. coll. · F. Chantrey, bust, Guildhall · F. Chantrey, bust, AM Oxf. · J. Hayller, oils, V&A; on loan to Wilberforce House, Hull · C. Turner, mezzotint (after L. F. Abbott), BM; repro. in *The claims of the people of England* (1805) · Zoffany, group portrait (*Music Party*), RA · plaster medallion (after C. Andras), Scot. NPG · portrait medallion, Westminster Abbey · silhouette, repro. in *GM*, 88 (1818), facing p. 489 **Wealth at death** under £7500: administration, Oct 1813, PRO, PROB 6/189, fol. 304*v*

Sharp, Isaac (1806–1897), missionary, elder son of Isaac Sharp of Brighton, Sussex, and his first wife, Mary Likeman, was born in Brighton on 4 July 1806. His father had joined the Society of Friends upon his marriage, and at eleven the son was sent to a Quaker school at Earl's Colne, Essex. At twenty-four he went to Darlington as private secretary to Joseph Pease, succeeding afterwards to the management of the Pease estate near Middlesbrough. In February 1839, he married Hannah Procter; they had two daughters before her death, four years after the marriage.

Sharp first began to preach about 1832, and in 1843 was 'recorded' a minister by Darlington monthly meeting. From this body he afterwards received on forty-five separate occasions certificates or credentials for gospel travel at home and abroad. He began his journeys in 1846 by visits to Norway, Orkney and Shetland, and Iceland, the Faeroes, Denmark, Greenland, and Labrador. But it was not until he was past sixty that he embarked upon the wider range of sustained missionary activity, to which the remaining years of his life were devoted.

In 1877 Sharp started for the southern hemisphere. He was welcomed at Cape Town by members of all denominations, including Sir David Tennant and Lady Frere, in the absence of her husband, Sir Henry Bartle Edward Frere, then governor of Cape Colony. Sharp travelled in a cape cart northward to Shoshong, visited King Khama, and was at Kuruman shortly before the outbreak of the Anglo-Zulu War. Reaching Kimberley in September 1878 he was invited to take up his quarters at Government House. After visiting the French missions in Basutoland, he left for Madagascar, where an important station had been founded by the Society of Friends. He next travelled to Sydney, Melbourne, and other Australian towns, then to

Stewart Island and New Zealand, and thence to San Francisco, the United States, and Mexico. On his way eastward he made contact with the American Quaker poet John Greenleaf Whittier. Sharp finally returned to England, after seven years' absence, in March 1884.

In 1891, when in his eighty-fifth year, and in spite of a complaint which at times made him dependent upon surgical aid and skilled nursing, his buoyant faith and spirits induced him to set out on another long voyage. In the face of much opposition, medical and otherwise, and a severe illness in Paris, he started for the East, and was able to carry out a long-cherished plan of visiting Constantinople, India, Japan, and the interior of China.

A fortnight after his return to England Sharp set out on his eighth visit to Norway. Some weeks spent in Syria during the autumn of 1895 proved to be his final evangelical tour. On nearly the last day of 1896 he lectured to a large audience at Devonshire House, Bishopsgate, on his foreign experiences as a missionary, but on returning home he caught a cold. He died on 21 March 1897, aged ninety, at his home, the Coffee House, Ettington, Warwickshire, and was buried on 26 March in the Quaker burial-ground close by.

Isaac Sharp's short robust figure, twinkling eyes, and alert manner, to the last utterly belied his years. Possessed of a peculiarly musical voice, his preaching, like himself, exhaled love. A ready fund of anecdote and humour endeared him to the inmates of lonely mission stations and isolated dwellings from the northern to the southern polar circle, no less than to all in England. An excellent correspondent, he expressed himself as readily in verse as in prose.

CHARLOTTE FELL-SMITH, rev. H. C. G. MATTHEW

Sources F. A. Budge, *Isaac Sharp: an apostle of the nineteenth century* (1898) · private information (1901) · *CGPLA Eng. & Wales* (1897) **Archives** RS Friends, Lond. **Wealth at death** £2543 8s. 5d.: probate, 23 June 1897, *CGPLA Eng. & Wales*

Sharp, Jack, of Wigmoreland. *See* Perkins, William (*d.* 1431).

Sharp, James [*alias* Francis Pollard] (1576–1630), Jesuit, was born in Bradford in the West Riding of Yorkshire on 26 September 1576. He matriculated from Oriel College, Oxford, on 20 March 1593, graduated BA at Trinity College in 1597, and proceeded MA in 1600. He became a convert to Roman Catholicism and, entering St Alban's College at Valladolid on 21 June 1602, was ordained priest on 14 April 1604. He taught at the English College, Douai, from 1606 to 1607 and then went to England, where he was admitted a member of the Society of Jesus in 1607–8 and was professed in 1622. For a time he was professor of sacred scripture and Hebrew at the English Jesuit college at Louvain. In 1611 he had been sent to England, where he made it his first endeavour to bring about the conversion of his parents. They, however, refused to listen to him, and kept him in strict confinement, seeking to reconvert him to protestantism. He obtained his liberty by proclaiming himself a priest, but thereby incurred the penalty of banishment. After a brief sojourn in the Spanish Netherlands he returned to England under the name of Francis Pollard, and was serving in the Yorkshire district in 1621 and then in Staffordshire. In 1625 he was labouring in Lincolnshire, and in 1628 had removed to Leicestershire. He was the author of *The triall of the protestant private spirit, wherein their doctrine making the sayd spirit the sole ground and meanes of their beliefe is confuted … the second part, which is doctrinall,* published at the English College press at St Omer in 1630. Part one was apparently not published. He also composed a manuscript endorsed 'Annals of F. Polla[rd]. Divers examples of cruelty and persecution in England, especially about York, and of the constancy of the Catholics in the time of King James, 1610, 14 Oct.', held at Stonyhurst College, and later printed in J. Morris's *Troubles of our Catholic Forefathers* (1877). He died in Lincoln at the residence of St Dominic on 11 November 1630.

E. I. CARLYLE, *rev.* G. BRADLEY

Sources T. M. McCoog, *English and Welsh Jesuits, 1555–1650*, 2 vols., Catholic RS, 74–5 (1994–5) · G. Anstruther, *The seminary priests*, 2 (1975) · J. Morris, ed., *The troubles of our Catholic forefathers related by themselves*, 3 (1877) [Stonyhurst MSS, Ang., p. 100] · H. Foley, ed., *Records of the English province of the Society of Jesus*, 2 (1875), 617–25; 3 (1878), 138, 189, 202, 205; 5 (1879), 767; 7 (1882–3), 702 · H. More, *Historia missionis Anglicanae Societatis Iesu* (St Omer, 1660) · E. Henson, ed., *The registers of the English College at Valladolid, 1589–1862*, Catholic RS, 30 (1930) · E. H. Burton and T. L. Williams, eds., *The Douay College diaries, third, fourth and fifth, 1598–1654*, 1–2, Catholic RS, 10–11 (1911) · Foster, *Alum. Oxon.* · A. F. Allison and D. M. Rogers, eds., *A catalogue of Catholic books in English printed abroad or secretly in England, 1558–1640*, 2 vols. (1956) · Archivum Romanum Societatis Iesu, Rome, Fl Belg 10

Archives Stonyhurst College, Lancashire, Stonyhurst MSS, Anglia vol. 3. 100

Sharp, James (1618–1679), archbishop of St Andrews, was born at Banff Castle on 4 May 1618, one of three sons of William Sharp (*d.* 1638), sheriff clerk of Banff (1617), and Isobel Lesley, daughter of the laird of Kinninvy.

Education and early career Sharp's father was a servant of the earl of Buchan, and beneficiary of the patronage of the earl of Findlater, whom he had served earlier; he was also elder in the Banff parish. *A True and Impartial Account of the Life of … Sharp* (1723) gives William a pedigree among the landed classes: his father was an Aberdeen merchant born to a 'gentleman in Perthshire'; his maternal grandmother belonged to a lairdly family from Forfarshire. James went to the new (1620) grammar school in Banff. In 1633 he entered King's College, Aberdeen, where he studied under John Forbes of Corse, professor of theology at the college. There he imbibed its tradition of ecclesiastical moderation, upheld by the Aberdeen doctors, who were Augustinians in theology, shared a wide commitment to patristic learning, and were willing to embrace ceremony in worship, a moderate episcopacy generally without notions of the *jus divinum* in polity, and royal supremacy over the church.

James Sharp (1618–1679), after Sir Peter Lely

In 1638—perhaps following the introduction in February of the national covenant—Sharp journeyed to England, intending to obtain preferment in the English church. He visited both universities, but there is no evidence that he did in fact find a position in England, and early in 1642 he was a regent at St Andrews University. Clearly he had by then set aside possible scruples and subscribed the national covenant; it may have been with the help of Alexander Henderson, the clerical leader of the covenanting movement, and also John Leslie, seventh earl of Rothes, an aristocratic insider in the movement and Sharp's kinsman on his mother's side, that he obtained this position. The *Life of Mr James Sharp* (1719) states that while at St Andrews, Sharp fathered and murdered an illegitimate child, but the allegation is entirely lacking in credibility; more credence may be given to a story which has him involved in a fight at the table with another regent, John Sinclair. In 1648 the earl of Crawford presented Sharp to the parish of Crail, a royal burgh in Fife, and within the presbytery of St Andrews.

Sharp was appointed a synod delegate from the presbytery, then a member of a search committee for faculty at St Andrews. In 1649, and again in 1650, he was sought as pastor for Edinburgh. On the second occasion the general assembly permitted his transfer, but Cromwell's intervention in the country meant that nothing came of the project. In April 1653 Sharp married Helen Moncrieff, daughter of the laird of Randerston. They had seven children: Sir William, who succeeded his father in the barony of Scotscraig; John; Isabella, who married John Cunningham of Barns; Catherine; Margaret, who married William, Lord

Saltoun; and another daughter who married Erskine of Cambo.

Mediator in the 1650s Sharp's career in the 1650s was defined by the rupture of the kirk between the radical protesters or remonstrants and the resolutioners, the more moderate group with which Sharp identified. He was elected a member of the commission of the general assembly in 1650, and first attended its sessions on 13 September 1650, ten days after Oliver Cromwell defeated the Scottish army at Dunbar. There he began his work of mediation between the two parties, seeking to avoid a lasting split, although this occurred in July 1651. Following the disaster at Worcester in August 1651 Sharp and others were detained by Cromwell and he spent nearly a year in London, though in April 1652 he was bailed from the Tower, perhaps because he was then only a minor player. He returned to his parish by August, and in January 1653 was a resolutioner representative to a unity conference. In October 1654 he was moderator of the provincial synod which declared itself against Gillespie's charter, a compromise with Cromwellian governance of the church. Still, Sharp showed himself a willing negotiator, trying always to avoid breakdowns in communication and rigid positions; thus he was willing to bargain away public prayers for the king in exchange for various freedoms.

When the protesters prepared to send a delegation to London to advance their own cause the resolutioners countered with Sharp, who went south late in 1656 in the company of Lord Broghill; it was during this trip that he saw a resolutioner apology through the press, *A true representation of the rise, progress, and state of the present division in the Church of Scotland*. Sharp built support among the local church leaders in London and succeeded in blocking the protesters' plans before returning to Scotland towards the end of 1657. In February 1659 he returned to London to treat with Richard Cromwell, but the army's intervention leading to Cromwell's abdication left Sharp exposed as a royalist and he was interrogated before the council. He was ordered to return to Scotland on 29 June, having achieved but little. In December he wrote an explanatory document for General George Monck, who was about to enter England to effect the restoration of the house of Stewart. The 'Declaration of his intentions in marching into England with his army' denounced usurpation by the current English regime and identified the army's goal as 'the recovery of the just liberties and freedoms of the people' (Buckroyd, 45). Sharp returned to his diplomatic duties in London in February 1660. During this time the resolutioner party finally achieved ascendancy over the protesters, and Sharp attempted to defend the loyalty of the resolutioners and make them acceptable to the king. He sailed for Breda on 4 May and returned to England with the court, arriving on 25 May. He was under pressure from Scotland to remind the king of the covenant, but this notion of the direction of events was far from reality, though the king did utter affectionate words about Scotland and promised to call a general assembly of the church. Sharp arrived in Scotland on 31 August 1660.

Thereafter he wrote of his confident expectation of a presbyterian future at least for Scotland, though it is also clear that already some were beginning to suspect that he was conspiring to effect a change, which he vigorously denied—'I am a Scot and a Presbyter' (Airy, 1.52)—and ridiculed alleged ambition in the light of the reception one might hope for as a bishop in Scotland. He did, however, make clear his belief that the church must be so ordered as to remove any conflicts with 'the king's interest', but the king had smiled at this and told Sharp that 'you will be counted a malignant when you come home' (ibid., 1.48).

Convert to episcopalianism Sharp was under pressure to leave Crail for Edinburgh, but in fact on 16 January 1661 he moved back to St Andrews, becoming third master at St Mary's College and professor of divinity—much against Samuel Rutherford's wishes. He also assumed duties as king's chaplain in Scotland. Sharp's confidence in the presbyterian future of Scotland was soon eclipsed by the actions of the Scottish parliament. The Act Rescissory and the Act Concerning Religion and Church Government on 28 March did not end presbytery, but the language was ambiguous and imposed the royal supremacy in the determination of church polity. The drift of events cast Sharp's actions and his policy of moderation in a bad light—Robert Baillie expressed a mild concern in a letter to the earl of Lauderdale on 18 April.

In late April Sharp departed for London again to negotiate about, but not for, the church, in that his appointment was from the parliamentary commissioner, John Middleton, first earl of Middleton, and not the church. He was willing to give up certain elements of presbytery, permitting the institution of constant moderators in the presbyteries; he hoped thereby to avoid worse infringements. The episcopal party, led by Middleton, was in power, and it was clear that without the establishment of episcopacy Scotland would remain an occupied country. Sharp was confronted with a choice, whereby he could hold to his presbyterianism and lose all, 'or he could resign himself to the inevitable, go along with the change and try to ensure that it conformed at least to some extent with the desires of Scots churchmen' (Buckroyd, 71). Given both his personality and his moderate opinions on church government, he submitted to the inevitable. On 6 August Alexander Brodie of Brodie recorded in his diary that in London he had met Sharp, who related 'what conflicts he had heir to hold out unworthi men from being Bishops' (*Diary*, ed. Laing, 201) and to withstand the attempts of English bishops to force their own choices on Scotland. On 6 September a proclamation concerning episcopacy was read in Edinburgh, and Sharp, now back in Scotland, became an agent for the new scheme; Baillie said he was poisoned by Gilbert Sheldon, then bishop of London, and George Morley, bishop of Winchester, and sought to recruit resolutioners to serve as bishops, an attempt which miscarried entirely. He returned to London on 15 October. On 14 November he was nominated to the archiepiscopal see of St Andrews, and on 15 December was consecrated in Westminster Abbey by Sheldon and Morley, using the prayer book, 'but without prejudice to the privileges of the Church of Scotland' (*CSP dom.*, 1661–2, 171). With him three others were also consecrated: Andrew Fairfoul for Glasgow, Robert Leighton for Dunblane, and James Hamilton for Galloway. Sharp and Leighton were compelled to re-enter orders as deacons then as priests since their presbyterian ordinations were invalidated, though Sharp initially opposed this demand. Such a policy was not, however, generally pursued back in Scotland with regard to the parochial clergy.

Archbishop Archbishop Sharp returned, in the splendour of a new coach bought in London, complete with 'two lakqueys in purple', to Edinburgh on 8 April 1662, with Fairfoul and Hamilton, while Leighton boycotted the pomp and ceremony. On the 15th and 16th he journeyed through Fife to his see, and on the 17th he preached on 1 Corinthians 2: 2, in which he justified his actions, claiming 'that he was ever in his judgment for Episcopacy and the ceremonies' (*Life of Robert Blair*, 405). On 7 May he participated in the consecration, performed with great ceremony and using the prayer book, of another six bishops in Edinburgh, and on 8 May the bishops returned to parliament as the traditional ecclesiastical estate. On 17 May parliament passed an act restoring episcopal government. With two more consecrations in St Andrews on 3 June the Scottish episcopate had been resuscitated. Beginning in late September the government began its harassment of nonconforming ministers, and Sharp evinced concern about the direction of policy. But by now he had allied himself with the government and against the presbyterians, and already his policy of moderation leading to unity was under strain. He again visited London in early 1663, and upon his return in June he and Fairfoul were brought into the privy council, where his accession to more rigorous action became apparent, as in the instance of Andrew Donaldson, minister of Dalgetty, whom he forced out against the wishes of the earl of Dunfermline, lord privy seal. Another trip — of which a detailed financial account survives in the archbishop's household book (pp. 37–59)— to London in December lasted until February 1664, and his achievement this time was the church commission which assumed the privy council's work in combating nonconformity. In 1664 he went to London to lobby for appointment to the chancellor's post. This attempt failed, but until 1666 Sharp and his old ally, John Leslie, earl of Rothes, were supreme in Scotland. However, the Scottish political nation grew discontent with Sharp's apparent usurpation of the political power it coveted—Sir John Lauder of Fountainhall stated that John Cunningham, earl of Glencairn, and even Rothes, as chancellors, would never grant Sharp the precedency he was supposed to receive—and by late 1666 his rising star began to pale. The Pentland rising in November was suppressed and a defeat inflicted on the rebels at Rullion Green on 28 November. His efficient direction of the suppression became the pretext for his disgrace, and from 1 February 1667 until 4 July he was absent from the privy council; he came close to losing his position, and for some months attended only to diocesan duties.

Sharp was now clearly subordinated to the regime headed by John Maitland, earl of Lauderdale, so that his vision for an independent church governed by a moderate episcopacy was in ruins, the archbishop was regarded with suspicion by the landed classes and government, and he was alienated from a vocal part of the church. The extremity of the situation was manifested when James Mitchell made an attempt on his life on 11 July 1668, in Edinburgh. Sharp was uninjured, but Andrew Honeyman, bishop of Orkney, was wounded in the arm. Burnet claimed that 'Sharp was so universally hated, that, tho' this was done in the full day light, and on the high street, yet no body offered to seize the assassin' (*Bishop Burnet's History*). This episode notwithstanding, the policy of repression which Sharp had come to advocate was now superseded by Bishop Robert Leighton's accommodation, supported by the Lauderdale administration; Sharp's co-operation was secured while he visited London in the months August to November. Leighton's episcopal policies trod lightly on the unwilling, giving more power to the rank and file of clergy in synods, recalling Bishop William Cowper's programme of bishop-in-presbytery during the Jacobean era. On 7 June 1669 was issued the first indulgence, whereby forty-two presbyterians were allowed back to their parishes under restrictions, but without any demand for acceptance of episcopacy. Sharp disliked the reversal but was powerless to stop it. His colleague in the see of Glasgow, Alexander Burnet, also ran afoul of the political class and in late 1669 was forced to resign. On 16 November parliament passed the Act of Supremacy—much against Sharp's judgement—whereby the king gained 'Supream Authority and Supremacie over all persons and in all causes ecclesiasticall within this kingdom' (Dickinson, Croft, and Donaldson, 3.160). Sharp therefore had no choice but to participate in Leighton's transfer to Glasgow, which took place, against Leighton's first wishes, in April 1670.

Eclipse In fact Sharp was very nearly a cipher in these years—he was not even consulted about the vacant see of Edinburgh, and the 1672 indulgence went ahead without his concurrence. But another change came when the accommodation scheme failed to bring in the determined radical presbyterians. In spring 1674 the synod of Fife expressed its discontent with the confusion aroused by the radicals and Sharp took the message to Lauderdale. The church was now on the verge of schism between hardline episcopalians and moderates who supported Leighton, whose resignation was ultimately accepted in August 1674. Now a political struggle broke out pitting Lauderdale against William Douglas-Hamilton, duke of Hamilton, and this encouraged a reconciliation between Sharp and Lauderdale. If he was subjected to public intimidation in Edinburgh in June 1674, his political position was bolstered by the restoration of Burnet to the see of Glasgow in September 1674, while an episcopal opponent, James Ramsey of Dunblane, was suspended. Sharp was in London from August 1674 to August 1675, and when he returned he was once again the master of the church and went ahead with a strident programme against nonconformity, including the Highland Host. In his final years his moral stature was much diminished by his defence of the dubious judicial proceedings against the presbyterian James Kirkton and then his role in the sordid affair which led to the execution of James Mitchell, who had attempted to assassinate him in 1668. Sharp perjured himself in order to disoblige the government of promises of leniency. He was now a hostage to the fortune of the sometimes beleaguered Lauderdale. There were also rumours to the effect that the archbishop and his wife were at odds with each other, 'objecting, adulteri and incest the one, and witchcraft the other' (*Diary*, ed. Laing, 350). While almost certainly false, these allegations hint at the archbishop's reputation among his foes.

The end came quickly on 3 May 1679. A band of nine conventiclers in Fife, two lairds, a weaver, and six tenant farmers, had plotted mischief against the local sheriff depute, but when they heard that Sharp was driving home to St Andrews they changed their target and chased down the carriage on Magus Moor near St Andrews; they shot and stabbed the archbishop to death before his daughter Isabella's eyes. A somewhat muddled investigation followed, leading to the executions of David Hackstone of Rathillet and Andrew Guillan, a weaver. William Dingwall perished at Drumclog a month after the murder; the other six escaped. Sharp's funeral was conducted at Holy Trinity Church, St Andrews, on 17 May. Among the bequests made from his estate was a gift of 1000 marks to aid the poor of Banff (Foster, 63).

Reputation The presbyterian tradition has been merciless to Sharp. Before his 'treachery', Robert Baillie had written: 'You were the most wise, honest, diligent, and successfull agent of the nation in the late dangers of our Church in Cromwell's tyme. ... Since first acquaintance yow have ever been very faithfull and loving to myself in all occasions' (*Letters and Journals of Robert Baillie*, 3.473). After his consecration he was regarded as a traitor. One contemporary poem was entitled 'Misanthrōpos, Judas, Scoto-Brittanus his Lyfe, Lamentation and Legacie'. The seventieth stanza has Sharp confess:

My master Judas was more stout
Then I his schollar faint
and the more honest was in that
he shooner did recant.
(NL Scot., Wodrow MSS, Octavo xxix, no. 11, 113r–128v; stanza 70, pt 1, 119v)

James Kirkton, who had reason to hold a grudge, wrote that Sharp's

great gift was his prudence, dissimulation, and industry, which qualified him well for his terrible undertakings. He was by all that knew him taken to be no better than a state atheist; he used no private prayers, and once in a month served his family: yea, he was known to be a man of flagitious life, and not only a debauched pailliard, but a cruel murtherer. (Kirkton, 83)

His modern biographer believes that Sharp's interpreters have commonly 'ante-dated his corruption' (Buckroyd, 118), but even if one is generous in dating the fall, Sharp's final years left ample opportunity for him to stain his historical record, beyond the mere fact of a realist inclined to make strategic retreats by clutching to position, if not

power, at all costs. As happened over the previous century, the episcopate all too frequently was episcopalianism's worst enemy. DAVID GEORGE MULLAN

Sources J. Buckroyd, *The life of James Sharp, archbishop of St Andrews, 1618–1679: a political biography* (1987) · F. D. Dow, *Cromwellian Scotland, 1651–1660* (1979) · *The letters and journals of Robert Baillie*, ed. D. Laing, 3 vols. (1841–2) · *The Lauderdale papers*, ed. O. Airy, 3 vols., CS, new ser., 34, 36, 38 (1884–5) [repr. New York, 1965] · *The diary of Alexander Brodie of Brodie, 1652–1680* (1863) · I. B. Cowan, *The Scottish covenanters, 1660–1688* (1976) · J. Kirkton, *The secret and true history of the Church of Scotland*, ed. C. K. Sharpe (1817) · W. R. Foster, *Bishop and presbytery: the Church of Scotland, 1661–1688* (1958) · W. C. Dickinson, W. Croft, and G. Donaldson, eds., *A source book of Scottish history*, 2nd edn, 3 vols. (1958–61) · *The life of Mr Robert Blair ... containing his autobiography*, ed. T. M'Crie, Wodrow Society, 11 (1848) · J. Lauder, *Historical observes of memorable occurrents in church and state, from October 1680 to April 1686*, ed. A. Urquhart and D. Laing, Bannatyne Club, 66 (1840) · *Historical notices of Scotish affairs, selected from the manuscripts of Sir John Lauder of Fountainhall*, ed. D. Laing, 2 vols., Bannatyne Club, 87 (1848) · 'The household book of James Sharp, lord archbishop of St. Andrews, 1663–1666', J. Stirton, *Leaves from my manuscript portfolio* (1929) · [D. Symson], *A true and impartial account of the life of the most reverend father in God, Dr. James Sharp* (1723) · *Life of James Sharp, archbishop of St. Andrews* (1719) [first published 1719; attributed date of 1678 is incorrect] · *Bishop Burnet's History*
Archives Buckminster Park, Lincolnshire, corresp. and papers | BL, corresp. with Lauderdale and others, Add. MSS 23114–23138, 23242–23243 · NA Scot., letters to the laird of Wormiston · NL Scot., letters to duke of Lauderdale · NL Scot., Wodrow MSS
Likenesses G. Vertue, line engraving, 1710, BM, NPG · after P. Lely, oils, Scot. NPG; repro. in Buckroyd, *Life*, jacket · after P. Lely, oils, priv. coll. [see illus.] · D. Loggan, line engraving (*ad vivum*), BM, NPG

Sharp, Jane (*fl.* 1641–1671), midwife, was the author of the best-known seventeenth-century textbook on midwifery in English written by a woman. Nothing is known about her life, except that she describes herself as a 'practitioner in the art of midwifery above thirty years' in the preface to her book, *The midwives book, or, The whole art of midwifery discovered, directing childbearing women how to behave themselves in their conception, bearing and nursing of children* (1671). It has been widely assumed that Sharp was a London practitioner, but no record of either her life or her practice has been found in London, despite extensive searches. Her use of the west-country phrase 'by odds' and the book's dedication to Lady Elleanour Talbutt, who, as an unmarried sister of the tenth earl of Shrewsbury, was probably living in Shropshire or Gloucestershire, suggest that Sharp may not have been from London at all. It has been speculated that she may have had a daughter, or more probably a daughter-in-law, to whom she passed on her skills, since a midwife named Sarah Sharpe is mentioned in the will of Anne Parrott, midwife in St Clement Danes, London. As other historical evidence is lacking, Sharp's existence has sometimes been denied. Late twentieth-century feminist scholars have sought to correct this view, drawing attention to the difficulties of establishing women's identity in the early modern period.

Published as a small octavo, *The Midwives Book* was a lengthy text of 95,000 words. It sold, bound, for 2*s.* 6*d.*, and achieved four editions by 1725; the third and fourth editions, published by John Marshall in 1724 and 1725, appeared after Sharp's death with the title *The Compleat Midwife's Companion*.

In the introduction to *The Midwives Book* Sharp addressed herself to her 'sisters, the Midwives of England' and gave her reasons for writing the book. She claimed that her distress at 'the many miseries women endure in the hands of unskilful midwives' who practised only for 'lucre's sake' had prompted her work (Sharp, introduction). However, her educational purpose cannot be taken at face value. Printed textbooks were largely irrelevant to the education of seventeenth-century midwives, who were trained by apprenticeship, and the full title of the book suggests that Sharp had a wider audience in mind. It seems likely that the book, like other midwifery manuals, was intended for both lay and medical readers; indeed in her introduction Sharp anticipated that her readership would include young men and women anxious to learn about sexuality and reproduction.

Divided into six sections, *The Midwives Book* explored the full range of topics then thought to be relevant to human reproduction. It discussed conception and the promotion of fertility; the signs of pregnancy and the care of pregnant women; the management of both normal deliveries and malpresentations; the treatment of venereal disease; and the post-natal care of both mother and baby. The book also included information about the anatomy of the male and female sexual organs, and a short section on the diseases of children. Sharp has been criticized for her seeming unawareness of podalic version (turning the foetus so that the feet present), but this shortcoming was common to other contemporary medical writers.

Sharp claimed that the manual was the product of her own experience and the study of foreign authors, but she was very dependent on the work of Nicholas Culpeper, the seventeenth-century radical. Many of the stories, remedies, and descriptions that Sharp uses in books 1, 5, and 6 are based on Culpeper's translation of David Sennert's *Practical Physick* (1664). Sharp also borrowed extensively from Culpeper's *Dictionary* and his *Bartholinus Anatomy*, translated from Bartholinus, and from Helkiah Crooke's *Microcosmographia*, a manual of anatomy first published in 1615. However, *The Midwives Book* was not merely a patchwork of earlier works. Sharp demonstrated her originality by reworking her sources, adding material of her own, and rewording anatomical definitions from a woman's point of view. On the whole *The Midwives Book* contained much good sense, though it was not in the same league as some contemporary works by continental midwives.

Sharp's work is important for its defence of the traditional role played by women as birth attendants. In the seventeenth century male practitioners were beginning to encroach upon the professional territory of the midwife, and Sharp felt the need to emphasize the value of the midwife's expertise. Man-midwifery, she argued, was a frivolous fashion, since country folk who could not afford the fees of a male practitioner fared as well in childbirth as the greatest ladies of the land. Sharp did recognize that unskilled midwifery could cause misery, but unlike male critics of midwifery practice she did not represent this as a result of the limited intellectual capacities of women. In her introduction Sharp explained:

> It is not hard words that perform the work, as if none understood the Art, that cannot understand Greek. Words are but the shell that we ofttimes break our Teeth with them to come at the kernel, I mean our brains to know what is the meaning of them; but to have the same in our mother tongue would save us a great deal of labour.   (Sharp, 3–4)

Although men alone could study anatomy at the universities, Sharp added, women could learn from each other and from 'long and diligent practice'. Sharp may have been aware of the proposals for a college of midwives, controlled by medical practitioners, repeatedly put forward by the Chamberlen family in the first half of the seventeenth century. Within this context, her acceptance of Culpeper as an authority may be significant. An arch-critic of 'closed shops' and professional monopolies, Culpeper was especially popular among mid-seventeenth-century London midwives, who faced the most serious challenge to their status and professional independence. His anti-establishment stance may have had some appeal for Sharp too, as she sought to defend the midwife's time-honoured claim to the practice of midwifery.

ORNELLA MOSCUCCI

Sources J. Sharp, *The midwives book, or, The whole art of midwifry discovered*, ed. E. Hobby (1999) • E. Hobby, '"The head of this counterfeit yard is called *Tertigo*", or, "It is not hard words that *perform the work*": recovering early-modern women's writing', *Women writing, 1550–1750*, ed. P. Salzman and J. Wallwork (2001), 13–23 • E. Hobby, 'Yarhound, Horrion, and the horse-headed Tartar: editing Jane Sharp's *The midwives book* (1671)', *Women and literary history: 'For there she was'*, ed. K. Binhammer and J. Wood (2002) • H. King, '"As if none understood the art that cannot understand Greek": the education of midwives in seventeenth-century England', *The history of medical education in Britain*, ed. V. Nutton and R. Porter (1995), 184–98 • E. Keller, 'Mrs Jane Sharp: midwifery and the critique of medical knowledge in seventeenth-century England', *Women's Writing*, 2 (1995), 101–11 • R. A. Erickson, '"The books of generation": some observations on the style of the English midwife book, 1671–1764', *Sexuality in eighteenth-century Britain*, ed. P.-G. Boucé (1982), 74–94 • D. Evenden, *The midwives of seventeenth-century London* (2000) • J. Donnison, *Midwives and medical men: a history of inter-professional rivalries and women's rights* (1977) • A. Wilson, *The making of man-midwifery: childbirth in England, 1660–1770* (1995)

Sharp, John (1572–1647), Church of Scotland minister and theologian, was born in Edinburgh, of unknown parentage. Educated at the University of St Andrews, he graduated MA in 1592. A theologian of considerable renown, his first work, *Theses theologicae de peccato*, was published at Edinburgh in 1600. In 1601 Sharp became minister of Kilmany in Fife. A staunch presbyterian he was appointed clerk to the general assembly of 1605 which met in Aberdeen in defiance of the command of James VI. Ordered before the privy council to explain his conduct, Sharp, along with five other ministers, declined the authority of the court as incompetent to judge a purely ecclesiastical question. The six ministers were subsequently confined in Blackness Castle and charged with treason. The case was heard before a packed jury at Linlithgow in January 1606, and Sharp, together with his five colleagues, was banished for life.

Sharp went to France, and in 1608 he was appointed professor of theology in the college of Die in Dauphiné. He was a prolific author, whose writings included the *Tractatus de justificatione hominis coram Deo* (Geneva, 1609); *Tractatus de misero hominis satu sub peccato* (Geneva, 1610); and *Symphonia prophetarum et apostolorum* (Geneva, 1625). Sharp's support for a restoration of presbyterianism in Scotland remained constant throughout his time in exile.

In 1618 John Spottiswood, archbishop of St Andrews, indicated that Sharp's recall was imminent and the minister dedicated his *Cursus theologicus* to James in the hope of a reconciliation. Negotiations collapsed, however, on Sharp's refusal to submit to the episcopalian regime. The minister remained at Die for a further twelve years until his protestant teachings brought him into conflict with the French government. Taking advantage of Charles I's moratorium on the prosecution of dissident ministers Sharp returned to London in 1630, where 'the town council of Edinburgh, hearing that Mr John Sharp … was by Cardinal Richelieu's procurement thrust out of France … thought fit to give him a call to the professor of Divinity in [the latter] Colledge' (Craufurd, 117). He took up the post in November that year.

Probably after 1630 Sharp married Agnes Davidson. The couple had a daughter, Marie, baptized on 18 August 1640, and a son, John, baptized on 8 August 1641. In 1637 Sharp sided with the covenanting party, and, in that year, signed the supplication against the prayer book raised by the presbytery of Edinburgh. He died, probably at Edinburgh, in 1647. VAUGHAN T. WELLS

Sources D. Calderwood, *The history of the Kirk of Scotland*, ed. T. Thomson and D. Laing, 8 vols., Wodrow Society, 7 (1842–9), vol. 6 · *Reg. PCS*, 1st ser., vol. 7 · *Fasti Scot.*, new edn, vol. 5 · T. Craufurd, *History of the University of Edinburgh from 1580 to 1646* (1808) · *The letters and journals of Robert Baillie*, ed. D. Laing, 1 (1841) · *STC, 1475–1640*

Sharp, John (1645?–1714), archbishop of York, was born at Ivegate, Bradford, probably on 16 February 1645, the eldest of five children. His father was Thomas Sharp, a wet and dry salter; his mother, Dorothy, *née* Weddal, was the eldest daughter of John Weddal of Widdington, Yorkshire. The Sharps were a well-established Yorkshire family, mainly clothiers and farmers on a small scale. Sharp was baptized in Bradford parish church by an episcopally ordained minister, a fact which gave him great satisfaction in later life: by that time in the civil war the officiant might not have received episcopal ordination, and so would have been regarded by Sharp as a layman. Sharp's father was a devout puritan and a parliamentarian follower of Sir Thomas Fairfax and his mother an Anglican and royalist. Sharp admired his father's piety but was more influenced by his mother's devotion to the prayer book. He was educated at Bradford grammar school and in 1660 entered Christ's College, Cambridge. In 1663 he graduated BA and thereupon concentrated on the study of divinity; he proceeded MA in 1667, though he failed to gain a fellowship.

Rector of St Giles-in-the-Fields and dean of Norwich That year Sharp was ordained deacon and priest at the same service

John Sharp (1645?–1714), attrib. Sir Godfrey Kneller, c.1691

by special dispensation. At Cambridge he had been influenced by Henry More, who recommended him as chaplain and tutor to Sir Heneage Finch, then solicitor-general and later lord chancellor. Finch gained Sharp promotion to the archdeaconry of Berkshire in 1673 and, in 1675, to a prebend in Norwich and to the London parish of St Giles-in-the-Fields. In this important cure he was to remain for sixteen years, until he became archbishop of York. In April 1676 Sharp married Elizabeth Palmer of a well-known Lincolnshire family, the ceremony being performed by his friend and neighbour at St Lawrence Jewry, John Tillotson. In common with other rising London clergymen, Sharp now devoted himself to the hard-working life of a model parish priest. He fully shared the parochial visiting in this mainly poor and malodorous area with his two or three curates; about his preaching he took immense pains, preparing 'the diction as well as the matter', to avoid, as Gilbert Burnet (who reckoned him a good preacher) said, any danger of 'flatness' (Sharp, *Life*, 1.39–40). His son and biographer said of his preaching that 'his great excellence lay in representing the truths of religion with such plainness and unaffected simplicity as was … very persuasive and affecting' (ibid., 1.24). With preaching went catechizing, in which he excelled owing to his 'very kind, warm way of talking' on religious matters (ibid., 1.45). In 1681 Sharp was nominated to the deanery of Norwich, which he held in tandem with his London rectory. He instituted an inquiry into the revenues of the cathedral, but seems mainly to have seen Norwich as providing the opportunity 'of improving in his spiritual life through the advantages of retirement and disengagement from company and business which Norwich afforded him' (ibid., 1.51).

Back in London, Sharp fell foul of the new Roman Catholic king. In common with many others he was concerned to refute Roman Catholicism. For him this took the form of a series of sermons at St Giles's starting in May 1686. The king commanded Henry Compton, the bishop of London, to suspend him from preaching. This Compton felt he could not do, because Sharp had not been properly tried for his offence; but he 'advised him to forbear the pulpit' (*King James's Ecclesiastical Commission*, 20). Compton was summoned before the recently created ecclesiastical commission and, when he insisted that the king could not command something which was unlawful, he was suspended and the diocese put into commission. Compton had proved himself a thorn in the royal flesh on several occasions, and it is clear that the king used the Sharp incident to engineer his downfall. In 1687 Sharp continued with his series of sermons without hindrance, demonstrating that he had been a pawn in a higher game.

Sharp also engaged himself in controversy at the other end of the ecclesiastical spectrum. In 1684 he produced his only written work. This was a pamphlet, *A Discourse Concerning Conscience*, which in 1686 was incorporated into a two-volume *Collection of cases … written to recover dissenters to the communion of the Church of England*, contributed by leading Anglicans. After a casuistical examination of the nature of conscience Sharp applies his findings to the separation of dissenters from the church. Here he takes a typical high-church standpoint, emphasizing the seriousness of separation and schism. If a dissenter feels it would actually be sinful for him to join the established church, then continued separation is permissible; but there are other reasons for separation, such as education, friendship, or force of habit, which are not excusable. Those who practise occasional conformity but remain outside the church are doing so for worldly reasons: 'with what conscience dare they do it at all?' (*Discourse*, 40). Sharp makes a powerful case and one which was obviously heartfelt. His thinking was not Erastian, but rather based on Augustine and Aquinas. The former had believed that schismatics should be 'compelled to enter' the church, a tactic which many high-churchmen after the Restoration favoured; the latter, closely followed by Sharp, had differentiated between various operations of conscience. In Sharp 'a high church sensibility, authoritarian yet plainly pastoral, prevailed over erastian arguments' (Goldie, 'The theory of religious intolerance', 358).

Sharp took no immediate part in the invitation to William to come to England, but in January 1689 he was involved in London meetings to discuss the complicated permutations of the constitutional settlement. On 30 January 1689 he preached before the House of Commons and prayed for King James, which was legally correct. Two days earlier the Commons had passed the bill pronouncing the abdication of James and the consequent vacancy of the throne, but the bill had not yet gone through the Lords. Nevertheless, it was a courageous act on Sharp's part, and the Commons were duly—though temporarily—incensed. At this time of dynastic confusion the state prayers were something of a litmus test for the clergy, and it may have been that, in praying for James, Sharp was intending to reserve his position for as long as possible.

Two issues important for the constitution of the established church were debated in the revolution settlement—comprehension in the church to encourage dissenters to enter its fold, and toleration for those who continued to refuse. Moves to comprehension suffered an early blow when, after a disastrously tactless speech from the throne from William, who did not understand the English ecclesiastical scene, parliament threw out the proposals in March 1689. But a commission was appointed to prepare proposals for comprehension to be presented to convocation. Sharp was one of ten bishops and twenty dignitaries appointed to this commission. The preamble to its instructions struck an eirenic note, granting that in matters 'indifferent' in church affairs 'changes and alterations should be made therein, as to those that are in place and authority, should from time to time seem either necessary or expedient' (T. Birch, *Tillotson*, 1783, 180). That said, the nonconformists were to be presented with an Anglican *fait accompli*, rather than being involved in the discussions. These centred mainly on the alterations to the liturgy, rather than on the review of the canons and the reform of the church courts. There was evidently no discussion of the thorny issue of nonconformist ordinations. However, the plans were scotched by the high-churchmen in convocation after Sharp had failed to engineer the election of Tillotson as prolocutor. William immediately adjourned convocation, which did not meet again for ten years. Although some high-churchmen at the time were averse to any scheme of comprehension which involved compromise—as introducing schism into the church itself—it may be assumed, because of his efforts in convocation, that Sharp approved the plans.

This left the Toleration Bill which had been proceeding through parliament. When it passed it was not as 'liberal' as some might have hoped, partly because it had originally been drafted to deal with hard-core dissenters who had refused the comprehension offer. Sharp may not have regretted this. In 1694 when Archbishop Tenison tried briefly to revive the comprehension issue he asked Sharp for his copy of the earl of Nottingham's 1689 papers—the Finch connection again.

Archbishop of York Sharp was one of the seven senior clergymen recommended by Burnet, William's chief ecclesiastical adviser, for early promotion to bishoprics. However, because of his refusal to take a see made vacant by a nonjuror (Norwich was the obvious suggestion, but he would not fill the shoes of his friend the nonjuring Bishop William Lloyd) this promotion was delayed. Instead, in September 1689 he became dean of Canterbury, John Tillotson having become archbishop. But when Archbishop Thomas Lamplugh of York died, the way was open for Sharp, and on 5 July 1691 he was consecrated archbishop by Tillotson. While his friend was at Canterbury the two archbishops worked harmoniously together. For example in 1692 when Tillotson launched a programme of clerical reform Sharp was included in the consultation. Once in York, Sharp set about his work in a typically thorough manner, starting with the compilation of a four-volume survey of the diocese. A feature of his long reign of twenty-two years was that with two exceptions, unlike other bishops, he steadily refused to grant lucrative offices to well-connected suitors; rather, he promoted worthy clergymen from within the diocese to prebendal stalls or to the major parishes at his disposal. The exceptions were his two former pupils, the sons of his patron, now Lord Nottingham. Henry Finch was appointed in 1695 to the richest prebendal stall in the minster. Sharp hoped to promote him to the deanery but was twice thwarted by the king. Finally, in 1704 Henry achieved the deanery, to be succeeded in his stall by his brother, Edward. Sharp refused to become involved in parliamentary elections, and would give no guidance in the matter to his clergy. Instead he concentrated on the pastoral and administrative aspects of his work. Lamplugh had been seventy-six when he died, and consequently the diocese was not in very good shape when Sharp succeeded.

The keystone to more vigorous administration was Sharp's use of his triennial visitations, following in the footsteps of the annual visitations of the archdeacons. He could also mount metropolitan visitations in the three dioceses of the province, especially when these were *sede vacante*. Sharp was as punctilious as possible in this work, though weakness in his later years made it difficult; also, it was confined to the six months in which he was resident in the diocese, roughly from Easter to the early autumn when his parliamentary and other duties called him back to London. In May 1693 Sharp undertook a visitation of the collegiate church of Southwell, where it was clear that discipline and administration had become very slack. He asked a detailed and searching set of questions and received evasive answers. In March 1694 he returned with a fierce set of injunctions, especially concerning absenteeism and the dilapidations on the chapter property. These were not popular but were obeyed and continued in force. A set of visitation articles for the diocese of Chester *sede vacante* show Sharp at his best: they follow much the same lines as those in other dioceses but are more detailed and specific, especially on the questions concerning property and residence. Moreover the preliminary 'Advertisement' is unusual: the parson and churchwardens are to meet 'divers times to deliberate and confer about' the articles and to answer 'particularly, advisedly and truly according to their consciences' (Borth. Inst., V.1707/visitation papers). Thus Sharp turned an inquisition into a pastoral opportunity.

In other aspects of his episcopal ministry Sharp 'set a signal example of personal care and devotion to public duty' (N. Sykes, *Church and State in the Eighteenth Century*, 1934, 105). He was concerned to make ordination a properly solemn ceremony and to ensure that no one unsuitable was admitted to orders. He fought against pluralism and non-residence; he exercised his own patronage with great care, and set his face against simony. Once his clergy

were in post Sharp showed much concern about their problems and performance, as witness hundreds of surviving letters dispensing advice, encouragement, and patient reprimand. He was particularly concerned about the further education of the clergy and often made small grants from his own pocket for the purchase of books, typical of his many acts of generosity, which centred on the hospitality he provided at Bishopthorpe. He was a frequent weekday attender at his own cathedral and also set up and attended weekly sermons in York which were given by clergy from all over the diocese; the preacher was asked to dinner at Bishopthorpe afterwards and submitted to a tutorial from his archbishop. He found that the administration of confirmation in the diocese had been particularly neglected and set about redressing this, at the same time encouraging the bishops in the three other dioceses to follow his example. He was also concerned with the oversight of schools, taking pains over the appointment of schoolmasters, monitoring statutes, and giving sensible advice about the regime for pupils.

Sharp envisaged a larger role for the rural deans than would have obtained in most dioceses. In 1705 he issued rules and orders for them. They were to have a supervisory function in their deaneries, granting matrimonial licenses, reporting vacancies and dilapidations, annually collecting and returning parish registers, and notifying the church courts of scandalous offenders who had escaped being presented. In many ways this would have added a local tier to diocesan administration.

However, in the end it was the church courts which were responsible for enforcing discipline and good order in the diocese. They had not been reformed at the Restoration or again in 1689. Sharp had had a ringside view of this failure, which evidently continued to rankle with him. He believed that the Church of England was the best church in Christendom, but recognized its weakness in the field of discipline, 'which had never been effectually provided for' (Sharp, *Life*, 2.355). He had long been troubled about his own courts: he tried to stop the practice of commuting penances, and he issued instructions that the sentence of excommunication was to be delayed as long as possible. Matters came to a head in 1698 when serious accusations of malpractice were made against the deputy register of the exchequer (testamentary) court. This led Sharp to mount a visitation of his courts, probably the only one in the Church of England after the Restoration. He issued cautious articles of inquiry; only the close examination of the practice of deputy registers, who could also be busy proctors in other diocesan courts, revealed the fact that he was seeking the root of corruption. When they came in, the replies from the court officers—from the chancellor, Henry Watkinson, downwards—were vague and evasive. One thing they seem to show is the inbred conservatism of the courts. Sharp continued to have meetings with Watkinson and others until 1705, but in the end he had to admit defeat. It was no doubt this bruising experience which in 1710 led him to propose various reforms for the Canterbury convocation to consider, all to no avail. The decline of the courts in the period before the revolution, capped by the Toleration Act legitimizing the practice of dissent, meant that the Church of England could no longer pretend to exercise spiritual discipline across the country.

This was the context for the societies for the reformation of manners. Founded by a layman, these societies embraced churchmen and dissenters. Through lectures and by direct action against vice in the church and secular courts, the societies sought to roll back the tide, as they saw it, of vice. The movement was endorsed by both William and Mary and received the support of Tenison and most of the 'whig' bishops. Not so Sharp: 'he always disliked and discouraged … the Societies for the Reformation of Manners' (Sharp, *Life*, 1.170). He felt that the presence of dissenters in the meetings was in danger of turning them into illegal conventicles, and he disliked the element of witch-hunting in place of genuine reformation of character. When a society was established by Nottinghamshire clergy he moved at once to control it, insisting that it must be 'modest, prudent and inoffensive' in its work (ibid., 1.173). But he tolerated other societies in the diocese where they were composed only of churchmen.

In 1702 William Nicolson became the bishop of Carlisle, and this led in time to the most difficult confrontation between the archbishop and one of his three suffragans that Sharp had to deal with. Nicolson had started life as a tory but at Carlisle became more of a whig. When the high-flying tory gadfly Francis Atterbury was appointed dean of Carlisle in 1704, the sparks were set to fly. Nicolson and Atterbury were old enemies, Nicolson having written against Atterbury's position on the powers of convocation. Nicolson now refused to institute Atterbury 'unless he first revoked certain propositions relating to the royal supremacy, which might seem to be deducible from his convocation book' (N. Sykes, *Edmund Gibson*, 1926, 58). Tenison backed Nicolson, but the tory bishops, including Sharp, by this time clearly on the tory side, were behind Atterbury. Nicolson continued to refuse to institute Atterbury, deducing from the Carlisle statutes that he had the same power over the dean (on institution) as over 'the meanest vicar in my diocese' (Glos. RO, L-B-S MSS, box 4, bundle V.1). Sharp, to save Nicolson's face, offered to institute Atterbury himself under commission from Nicolson. Nicolson refused and summoned Atterbury to Carlisle from Bishopthorpe to discuss the matter. Sharp now tried to get Sir Robert Harley to persuade Anne to intervene. When she did so Nicolson had to institute Atterbury. The vice-dean, Hugh Todd, had been Atterbury's supporter in Carlisle, and this led to further trouble for Sharp. Todd was in dispute with Nicolson and was not slow to involve Sharp over his bishop's head. By his patient intervention and eventual strictness with Todd, Sharp calmed the troubled waters. Meanwhile Atterbury had made himself obnoxious in Carlisle, and the chapter urged Nicolson to visit the cathedral. Atterbury retorted that, as Carlisle was a royal foundation at the Reformation, the bishop had no right of visitation. Tenison rightly saw that this was a matter of national importance, and when Nicolson introduced a bill to declare Henry VIII's statutes valid the whig

bishops supported it. Sharp did not feel he could do so and there was a heated debate in the Lords in January 1708 which Nicolson won. On 28 March Nicolson, who was afraid Sharp had been seeing Todd, called on his archbishop: he 'received me very kindly desiring that our warmth in the House of Lords might be mutually forgotten' (*Diary*, 19, 28). Thus, in a typical act of magnanimity, ended a struggle which must have caused Sharp much pain, and in which he had to admit defeat.

The archbishop and the nation Sharp was the only one of the seven churchmen recommended by Burnet to William for bishoprics who was consistently a high-churchman and usually on the side of the tories in parliament. But in the early years of William's reign he was able to work with his brother bishops. In 1694 he was appointed to a new commission to oversee church affairs, especially episcopal promotions. He was however moving away from his colleagues, typically when he refused to support William's desire for the attainder and execution of the Jacobite Sir John Fenwick. After this 'he virtually ceased lending his support to the ecclesiastical commission', though Tenison continued to send him the papers (Bennett, 'King William III and the episcopate', 127). With the accession of Anne everything changed. It was soon clear that Sharp was her favourite cleric. At her insistence, and despite illness, Sharp preached her coronation sermon, taking the classic text 'kings shall be thy nursing fathers and their queens thy nursing mothers' (J. Sharp, *A Sermon Preach'd at the Coronation of Queen Anne*, 1702, 1). Anne 'leaned upon the spiritual counsel and friendship of … Sharp and in his Caroline piety she found much comfort' (Bennett, *White Kennett*, 113). From her side Anne expressed the relationship as that 'I should be her confessor and she would be mine' (Sharp, *Life*, 1.300). This hardly makes Sharp her 'confessor' in the technical sense, but he was certainly at her side as she prepared for the sacrament. Anne took her duties as head of the church very seriously and felt that the high-flyers' cry of 'the church in danger' was a personal insult. However, this sense of duty carried with it obligations for Sharp. She expected him and others not to vote against her interests in the Lords:

> she pressed me earnestly to be on her side on all matters that came before parliament relating to the prerogative … she desired that I would never promise my vote, till I had acquainted her with my objection … but if she could not satisfy me, then I should vote as I pleased. (ibid., 1.300)

This undertaking Sharp was glad to give.

The most serious clash between Sharp and his queen came over the Act of Union. Churchmen saw that the union between England and Scotland raised potential problems for the Church of England as the established church in England. In 1702 Tenison and Sharp were appointed to a commission to think this through, though in the event Sharp never attended. Tenison brought in a bill 'for the security of the Church of England' guaranteeing its traditional constitutional place (Carpenter, 393). Sharp felt the bill was not sufficient protection because the Act of Union pronounced that 'Scottish religion is the true protestant religion and the presbyterian government is necessary', so that it 'cut off all the hopes of the episcopal clergy' (Sharp, *Life*, 1.393). Anne, who was set on the union, urged Sharp to drop his opposition, but he, with the tory bishops, refused. However, it passed. Sharp had also been concerned about individual episcopalian clergymen in Scotland and from 1704 was distressed to hear of actual persecution in Edinburgh and elsewhere. Accordingly he did his best to forward the cause of toleration in Scotland. The close alliance between Anne and Sharp was most clearly expressed in ecclesiastical appointments; for much of the time of their partnership they worked with Harley, the great parliamentary fixer, though Harley's position varied according to the ministerial permutations of the time. The candidates were mainly Sharp's, but on occasions Anne did not hesitate to exercise her prerogative. Sharp's appointments were mainly moderate high-churchmen. But the triumvirate did not have it all their own way, and Godolphin, the lord treasurer, often opposed them on behalf of the whigs, in 1705, for instance, getting William Wake to Lincoln against Sharp's candidate, Sir William Dawes. Matters came to a head in 1706 with the so-called 'bishoprics crisis'. Exeter and Chester were vacant, and Sharp had his candidates accepted. Godolphin was furious, and threatened that the whigs would withdraw from the ministry if Anne did not change her mind. Face was saved by a vacancy at Ely to which John Moore, a whig, was appointed. Lord Somers blamed these defeats on Tenison: 'the Archbishop is principally at fault, who does not speak plainly and fully to the Queen, when the Archbishop of York never suffers her to rest' (Bennett, 'Bishoprics crisis', 738). In the fluid politics of the time the episcopal vote in the Lords was important, and Godolphin lost patience, writing to Anne:

> what reflection will it not cause in the world that all these weighty things (of state) together cannot stand in the balance with the single point of whether Dr Blackall at this time be made a bishop, or a dean or a prebend.   (Gregg, 249)

One earlier outcome of struggles between church and state had been the foundation of Queen Anne's Bounty in 1704. The original idea had been Burnet's, but the actual proposal had been Harley's, to regain favour with the clergy after the failure of the high-church Occasional Conformity Bill. By it the crown was to surrender the proceeds of tenths and first-fruits on ecclesiastical appointments to create a fund to augment poor livings, something which would be dear to Sharp's heart: 'I find the Archbishop of York is highly transported with your notion about the firstfruits', wrote Godolphin to Harley (Longleat, miscellaneous vol., fol. 84). In due time Sharp, who had been involved in the plan since its inception, threw his weight behind the bill, against whig opposition, and for once carried all the bishops with him.

A recurrent issue on which Sharp differed from his low-church brethren was that of occasional conformity. Sharp disliked the practice of occasional conformity, considering it dishonest when it was used to procure advancement in political life, though tolerable when it expressed Christian charity, as when Richard Baxter communicated at St Giles's. But in 1704 the tories attempted to steer their bill

banning the practice through the Lords by tacking it to a finance bill after it had twice been defeated by the whig peers; Sharp felt this was a shabby manoeuvre and used all his influence to get it defeated in the Commons. The matter was again revived—this time with his support—in 1711 when the bill against occasional conformity was passed.

All this time relations between Sharp and Tenison, who was painfully shy and suffering from gout, deteriorated steadily. Matters came openly to a head in 1712 over the question of lay baptism. High-flying clergy, including Henry Dodwell, had attacked the validity of baptism by a layman. Tenison informally gathered together some bishops, including Sharp, who issued a declaration that lay baptism was to be discouraged but was not invalid— the classic 'Catholic' doctrine. Tenison then went further and drew up an instruction to the clergy that they should not rebaptize. This he sent to Sharp for approval. Sharp, with his high-church episcopal colleagues William Dawes of Chester, Offspring Blackall of Exeter, and Philip Bisse of St David's, demurred and replied to Tenison:

> I can by no means come into that proposal your grace has now made in your letter … for I am afraid that it would be too great an encouragement to the Dissenters to go on their way of irregular uncanonical baptisms.   (Sharp, *Life*, 1.376)

Burnet says that Sharp was 'prevailed on to change his mind' (*Bishop Burnet's History*, 2.605). But it was one thing for some bishops to assent to an informal declaration and another to take it forward to a formal instruction to all the clergy. The incident also demonstrates that towards the end of his life Sharp was hardening in his attitude to dissenters, though he disapproved of their being 'vilified' in Anglican pulpits (Sharp, *Life*, 1.357).

Nevertheless Sharp did not fail to respond to appeals from foreign protestants distressed by the fortunes of war, such as the Vaudois clergy and those of the Palatinate. But his most regular foreign contacts were with the Lutherans in Prussia and Hanover. In 1711 he worked with George Smalridge, a friend and protégé who later wrote his Latin epitaph in York Minster, to get the English liturgy used at the court of Hanover. But despite the potential importance of the move it came to nothing. In Prussia Daniel Ernst Jablonski hoped to introduce a translated English liturgy into the court chapel of Frederick I. He sought to interest Tenison in the plans, but for some reason Tenison failed to respond. Jablonski persisted and embarked on a lengthy correspondence with Sharp through the good offices of Smalridge. Sharp was always concerned to move the thinking forward from the use of the Anglican liturgy to questions of order, that is, episcopacy. This Jablonski espoused in a treatise on episcopacy in 1711. Despite correspondence the scheme ran into the sands in 1712.

Sharp's last illness began in December 1713. A visit to Bath did nothing to revive him and he died there on 2 February 1714; his wife survived him. He was buried in his cathedral at York, in St Mary's Chapel, where he had been archbishop for twenty-two years. Sharp and his wife had fourteen children, seven of each sex, of whom only two sons and two daughters survived him. The elder son, John

*Sharp, became MP for Ripon and was a high-flying tory. The younger, Thomas *Sharp, was ordained and became successively chaplain to Archbishop Dawes at York and archdeacon of Northumberland; he was his father's biographer, having access to his diaries which were subsequently lost. Sharp's chief recreation was as a numismatist. As such he was friendly with the York antiquary Ralph Thoresby, to whom he left his coin collection. Sharp was largely responsible for Thoresby's conversion from dissent. He was also very interested in his gardens at Bishopthorpe, where latterly he spent much time in prayer, calling them his 'Temple of Praise' (Sharp, *Life*, 2.65). Sharp was undoubtedly a man of deep personal piety. Besides his daily devotions he regularly dedicated 24 June, which he reckoned his spiritual birthday, to solemn prayer and self-examination. This custom went back to 1688 about which his diary reads: 'I began to apply myself more diligently to the work of religion and spent the summer well. And I thank God most heartily that I have never relapsed' (ibid., 2.65). These strenuous days of devotion (together with his birthday and new year's day) continued until 1713, when his health began to fail.   BARRY TILL

Sources A. Tindel Hart, *The life and times of John Sharp* (1949) · T. Sharp, *The life of John Sharp, D.D.*, ed. T. Newcome, 2 vols. (1825) · B. D. Till, 'The ecclesiastical courts of York, 1660–1683' (typescript), 1964, Borth. Inst. · E. Gregg, *Queen Anne* (1980) · E. Carpenter, *Thomas Tenison, archbishop of Canterbury* (1948) · *The works of the Most Rev Dr John Sharp*, 7 vols. (1754) · J. Sharp, *A discourse concerning conscience* (1684) · *A history of King James's ecclesiastical commission* (1711), 5.17.32 · *The diary of William Nicolson*, Cumberland and Westmorland Antiquarian and Archaeological Society, new ser., 4 (1904) · G. V. Bennett, *The tory crisis in church and state: the career of Francis Atterbury, bishop of Rochester* (1975) · T. Claydon, *William III and the godly revolution* (1996) · R. Beddard, 'The unexpected whig revolution of 1688', *The revolutions of 1688*, ed. R. Beddard (1991), 11–101 · M. Goldie, 'The political thought of the Anglican revolution', *The revolutions of 1688*, ed. R. Beddard (1991), 102–36 · G. V. Bennett, *White Kennett, 1660–1728, bishop of Peterborough* (1957) · J. Israel, 'William III and toleration', *From persecution to toleration: the Glorious Revolution and religion in England*, ed. O. P. Grell, J. Israel, and N. Tyacke (1991), 129–70 · M. Goldie, 'The theory of religious intolerance in Restoration England', *From persecution to toleration: the Glorious Revolution and religion in England*, ed. O. P. Grell, J. Israel, and N. Tyacke (1991), 331–68 · G. V. Bennett, 'King William III and the episcopate', *Essays in modern English church history: in memory of Norman Sykes*, ed. G. V. Bennett and J. Walsh (1966), 104–31 · J. Spurr, 'The Church of England, comprehension and the Toleration Act of 1689', *EngHR*, 104 (1989), 927–46 · T. Isaacs, 'The Anglican hierarchy and the reformation of manners, 1688–1738', *Journal of Ecclesiastical History*, 33 (1982), 391–411 · N. Sykes, 'Queen Anne and the episcopate', *EngHR*, 50 (1935), 433–64 · G. V. Bennett, 'Robert Harley, the Godolphin ministry, and the bishoprics crisis of 1707', *EngHR*, 82 (1967), 726–46 · N. Sykes, *Daniel Ernst Jablonski and the Church of England* (1950) · *DNB*

Archives Bishopthorpe Palace, York, Archbishop Sharp's MS books, vols. 1–2 · Borth Inst., official corresp. and papers · Glos. RO, corresp. and papers relating to library and coin collection · LUL, MS of treatises on the coins of England · York Minster Library, York Minster archives, papers | BL, letters to J. Killingbeck, Add. MS 4274 · York Minster Library, York Minster archives, Torr papers

Likenesses attrib. G. Kneller, oils, c.1691, Bishopthorpe Palace, York · attrib. G. Kneller, oils, c.1691, St Giles-in-the-Fields, London [see illus.] · F. Bird, tomb effigy sculpture, 1714, York Minster · attrib. G. Kneller, oils, Canterbury Cathedral, deanery · R. White, engraving, BM, NPG, Bishopthorpe Palace, York · R. White, pencil sketch, Christ's College, Cambridge · oils (after R. White), Bishopthorpe Palace, York; version, deanery, Canterbury Cathedral

Sharp, John (1678–1727), politician, was born on 18 June 1678 in London, the elder of the two sons of John *Sharp (1645?–1714), archbishop of York, and his wife, Elizabeth, the daughter of William Palmer of Winthorp, Lincolnshire. He attended Coneyhatch School near Highgate (c.1680–1693), was a fellow commoner at Christ's College, Cambridge, in 1693, and received his MA in 1695. He was admitted at the Inner Temple in 1698 and was called to the bar in 1703.

Sharp was elected to parliament for Ripon in 1701 (having been nominated by his father, who was its lord of the manor), and he lived in his father's London house in Petty France. Robert Harley classed him as a tory. He was a prominent supporter of the Occasional Conformity Bill, and on 10 December 1702 was appointed to the committee considering the amendments to the bill by the Lords—his father being one of the few bishops not opposing it. During the spring of 1710 he voted against a motion that Dr Sacheverell's sermon should be burnt by the common hangman and against his impeachment.

On 15 August 1710 Sharp married Anne Maria, the daughter of Charles Hosier of Wicken Park, Northamptonshire. Estates in Leeds and Bradford and the Yorkshire village of Wistow were settled on him, besides other lands valued at £6000 altogether.

The general election in the autumn of 1710, which resulted in a large tory majority and Harley's administration, brought Sharp prominence and power. Being among the tory 'patriots' opposed to the War of the Spanish Succession, he joined the extremists of the October Club, who, dining together over October ale, demanded less moderation and toleration from Harley. He was appointed to the committee on the address on 29 November 1710 and to the Irish revenue commission in July 1712, for which his father thanked Harley: 'I may be bold to say on his behalf that, if honest principles and true love to the Queen and the Church can recommend him, he is a just object in your favour' (HoP, *Commons*). In June he was ordered to introduce a bill to examine the previous administration's army and navy debts and was a teller against a motion censuring the writings of William Fleetwood, bishop of St Asaph. From 1711 he subscribed to every lottery, and through John Aislabie, his relative and fellow member for Ripon, invested considerably in South Sea Company stock. He acquired also eleven burgages at Ripon.

Sharp was among the 'October' members promoted when he was made a commissioner of the Board of Trade and Plantations in February 1713, at an annual salary of £1000. He voted for the bill confirming the eighth and ninth articles of the commercial treaty with France on 18 June 1713, and was appointed five days later to the committee to compose the address thanking the queen for the treaties of peace and commerce with France and on 1 July to that on the address urging the Pretender's removal from Lorraine. That summer he was involved with two other commissioners of trade when he successfully defended before the Lords Arthur Moore, whom Robert Monckton accused of being bribed by the Spanish king in the negotiations over the commercial treaty with Spain and the Asiento.

George I's accession resulted in Sharp losing office in December 1714, and being defeated at Ripon by a whig supporter of Aislabie. He retired from politics and sold his burgages to Aislabie, who in return enabled him to survive the South Sea Bubble in 1720. He died at his home, Grafton Park, Northamptonshire, on 9 March 1727 and was buried at Wicken. His brother, Thomas Sharp, archdeacon of Northumberland, declared him 'a polite scholar, an accomplished gentleman, a most affectionate husband and father, a true friend and desirable companion, beloved and esteemed by all who knew him' (Sharp MSS). LEONARD W. COWIE

Sources 'Sharp, John', HoP, *Commons* · A. H. Basyre, *The lords commissioners of trade and plantations* (1925) · M. A. Thomson, *The secretaries of state, 1681–1782* (1968) · B. Hill, *The growth of parliamentary politics, 1689–1742* (1976) · A. Newman, ed., *The parliamentary lists of the early eighteenth century: their compilation and use* (1993) · W. A. Speck, *Tory and whig: the struggle in the constituencies, 1701–1715* (1970) · J. Peile, *Biographical register of Christ's College, 1505–1905, and of the earlier foundation, God's House, 1448–1505*, ed. [J. A. Venn], 1 (1910) · G. Baker, *The history and antiquities of the county of Northampton*, 2 (1836–41) · Venn, *Alum. Cant.* · British Record Society, Faculty office marriage licences · Glos. RO, Sharp MSS
Archives Bodl. Oxf., Ballard MSS · Glos. RO, Hardwicke Court MSS, Sharp MSS · Leeds Public Library, Vyner MSS
Likenesses monument, Wicken church, Northamptonshire

Sharp, John (1723–1792), Church of England clergyman and charity administrator, was born at Rothbury, Northumberland, and baptized there on 2 April 1723, the eldest son of Thomas *Sharp (1693–1758), also a clergyman and then newly appointed archdeacon of Northumberland, and his wife, Judith Wheler (d. 1757). He was born into an eminent ecclesiastical family: his paternal grandfather, also John *Sharp (1645?–1714), had become archbishop of York soon after the revolution of 1688, and his maternal grandfather, George Wheeler, had also been prebendary at Durham. John Sharp matriculated in 1740 as a pensioner at Trinity College, Cambridge, graduated BA in 1744, MA in 1747, and DD in 1759. He received deacon's orders in 1748. In the following year he was admitted to the priesthood, and promptly presented with the living of Hartburn in Northumberland, thus beginning what was to be a forty-three-year ministry in the diocese of Durham. Granville *Sharp (1735–1813), who worked to abolish the slave trade, was a younger brother. In 1752 John Sharp married Mary Dering (1721–1798), daughter of Heneage Dering, dean of Ripon; they had a daughter, born about 1762.

In 1751 Sharp was made chaplain to Bishop Joseph Butler. There is evidence that he might have had an opportunity to exercise this office during Butler's brief episcopate. On Richard Trevor's translation to the see of Durham in 1752, John Sharp was approved as official to the archdeaconry of Northumberland, and thereafter assisted his father in this jurisdiction. After the latter's death in 1758 John Sharp was himself raised to the archdeaconry of

Northumberland, in which he was to remain for thirty years. It was not long until he added a prebend to his list of benefices. In 1768 Bishop Trevor collated him to the ninth stall of Durham Cathedral. Furthermore, when his younger brother Thomas, who had been the incumbent at Bamburgh, died in 1772, John Sharp took personal charge of Bamburgh Castle and Bamburgh church as senior trustee on behalf of the Lord Crewe's trust, where Thomas had succeeded their father in 1758. It is probably the task for which he is best remembered in the area. For twenty years he devoted himself to 'improving' Bamburgh Castle (*GM*), and practised the charity that he preached. Using the surplus revenues of the trust's Bamburgh and Blanchland estates he devised a plan of practical benevolence. Part of the castle was converted to a residence for the senior trustee, and with seemingly indefatigable energy, he set up several philanthropic establishments, including an asylum providing accommodation for shipwrecked mariners.

In 1791 the new bishop of Durham, Shute Barrington, bestowed the eleventh stall on Dr Sharp, who was not to enjoy that last preferment for very long, since he died on 28 April 1792, soon after his sixty-ninth birthday. He was buried in the Galilee chapel of Durham Cathedral; his body was placed beside the remains of his father, Thomas, who had influenced him so much. A marble monument in the cathedral cloisters pays tribute to their ministry. The hatchment that was designed in his memory, incorporating the armorial bearings of his wife's family, Dering, with the Sharp coat of arms, was subsequently moved to the cathedral Treasury.

On his death the balance of Dr Sharp's personal estate, which amounted to 'about £2,550', was equally divided between his widow and his unmarried daughter, Jemima. In his will the archdeacon also bequeathed most of his library, which contained the most valuable part of his grandfather's comprehensive collection of books, subsequently increased by his father and younger brother Thomas, to the Lord Crewe's charity trustees, provided it be kept in Bamburgh Castle. Indeed, it remained there until 1958, when it was deposited with the university library in Durham. The more recent part of the library, named after Archdeacon Sharp, is administered by the trustees and the University of Durham.

The key to John Sharp's personality lies in a collection of approximately forty-five manuscript sermons, composed from 1748 to 1761 (now in the Durham Chapter Library), only one of which ever came to be published: *A sermon preached at St Nicholas's Church in Newcastle, before the governors of the infirmary, for the counties of Durham, Newcastle, and Northumberland, on Wednesday June 24, 1752* (1752). For more than thirty years until his death the preacher kept reusing and amending his collection of sermons. These conveyed a typically latitudinarian world view, with particular emphasis on practical religion and a moral sense of duty. FRANÇOISE DECONINCK-BROSSARD

Sources F. Deconinck-Brossard, *Dr. John Sharp: an eighteenth-century Northumbrian preacher* (1997) [University of Durham: St Mary's College Fellowship Lecture 1995] · pedigree, Glos. RO,

D3549, 1/2/4 · correspondence, Northumbd RO, Newcastle upon Tyne, 452/C3/33 · J. C. Shuler, 'The pastoral and ecclesiastical administration of the diocese of Durham, 1721–1771: with particular reference to the archdeaconry of Northumberland', PhD diss., U. Durham, 1975 · *GM*, 1st ser., 61 (1791), 889 · R. Welford, *Men of mark 'twixt Tyne and Tweed*, 3 (1895) · Venn, *Alum. Cant.*
Archives Durham Cath. CL, MS sermons · U. Durham, MS catalogue of books belonging to Sharp in Bamburgh Castle | Glos. RO, D3549, 9/1/1–16 · Newcastle RO, 452/C3/33
Likenesses J. Zoffany, group portrait, 1779–81, NPG · [M. A.] Knight, oils (after J. Zoffany), priv. coll. · H. Schmirchen, portrait, Bamburgh Castle, Northumberland · pencil and watercolour drawing, priv. coll.
Wealth at death approx. £2550: Glos. RO, D3549, 9/1/12

Sharp, Leonel. *See* Sharpe, Leonell (*bap.* 1560, *d.* 1631).

Sharp, Michael William (1776/7–1840), portrait and subject painter, was born in the parish of St Paul's, Covent Garden, London, the son of Michael Sharp (1750/51–1800), a principal oboe player at the Theatre Royal, Covent Garden, and music master, and his wife, an actress. He was almost certainly the Michael William Sharp who was baptized on 9 May 1779 at St Paul's, Covent Garden, the son of Michael Sharp and Elizabeth. The family moved to Norwich about 1783 or 1784. Sharp originally studied music with his father, but showed a talent for painting and may have taken lessons from the Norwich school artist, John Crome. At the age of twenty he went to London where he entered the Royal Academy Schools on 21 October 1797. By 1799 he was studying with William Beechey, whom he accompanied to Windsor Castle when Beechey was commissioned to paint portraits of the royal family. Here Sharp came to the attention of George III, who is reported to have requested many of the nobility to sit to Sharp, and 'The consequence was that Mr Sharp is said in a few days to have orders for 140 Pictures of Persons of the Highest Rank' (*Norwich Mercury*, 1 May 1802). These included members of the royal family.

Sharp first exhibited at the Royal Academy in 1801 from a London address, and continued to exhibit there until 1836. He appears to have married by 1805 when he exhibited a portrait entitled *Mrs Sharp* at the Royal Academy. He also exhibited from 1806 to 1830 with the British Institution, gaining the premium in the familiar life class for his painting *The Music-Master* in 1809. In 1808 he joined the Society for the Study of Epic and Pastoral Design (formerly the Sketching Society), whose members included the brothers John James Chalon and Alfred Edward Chalon, Francis Stevens, and Cornelius Varley. He remained with the society for a year. Sharp retained his links with Norwich and with Crome, and in 1813 he exhibited for the first time with the Norwich Society of Artists. In the same year he probably painted the portraits in Norwich Castle Museum and Art Gallery of Crome and his wife, Phoebe (exh. 1814; Norwich Society of Artists), whose youngest son (*b.* 1813) was named after him. Sharp continued to exhibit with the Norwich Society until 1821, becoming vice-president in 1816 and president in 1817, the year of his wife's death. During his visits to Norwich he stayed at Crome's home and rented a studio at the Assembly House, where he carried out commissions for portraits.

Probably because of his family background, many of Sharp's paintings have theatrical or musical themes and include portraits of performers. An example is his exhibit with the Royal Academy in 1823, *Shakespeare's jubilee, with portraits of the performers of the Theatre Royal, Drury Lane, Covent Garden*, 'with the exception of Mr Macready, who declined sitting' (*Norwich Mercury*, 24 May 1823). The subject paintings and portraits, usually painted on a small scale, often have humorous overtones. When he signed his work he used initials, MWS, or M. W. Sharp. His paintings were very popular in his day and he found a ready market for them. Many were engraved, including *Sunday Morning* (engraved by Charles Heath in 1820) and his portrait of the duke of Wellington (engraved in mezzotint by William Say in 1828). In 1820 he delivered a lecture to the Philosophical Society of Norwich which was published as 'An essay on gesture' in James Elmes's *Annals of the Fine Arts*, volumes 4 and 5. He exhibited with the Society of British Artists in 1825 and 1826. Little is known of his last years. He died in France at Boulogne in 1840.

NORMA WATT

Sources [J. Chambers], *A general history of the county of Norfolk*, 2 (1829), 1118 · *Norwich Mercury* (1 May 1802) · Rajnai Norwich Artists archive · IGI · S. C. Hutchison, 'The Royal Academy Schools, 1768–1830', *Walpole Society*, 38 (1960–62), 123–91, esp. 157 · DNB

Sharp, Patrick (*d.* **1615**), theologian, was apparently related to the Sharps of Houstoun. He is first recorded in 1574, when he was made master of Glasgow grammar school. His previous education is unknown, but he may have been qualified in theology already. While in this position he was brought into frequent contact with Andrew Melville, to whom he subsequently acknowledged himself greatly indebted. Soon after 1575 he was appointed one of a commission of classical scholars to draw up a new Latin grammar for use in the Scottish schools. He demitted the schoolmastership in November 1582 and became a university regent, being recorded as minister of Paisley in 1584. In 1585 James VI appointed him principal of the University of Glasgow, and many French protestant refugees studied divinity under him, as well as the future principal John Cameron.

From this time Sharp took an important part in the affairs of the Scottish church. He seems to have wished to preserve a position of neutrality between the two parties dividing the kirk, but gradually inclined to the king's side. In 1586 he was placed on a commission charged by the general assembly to control the proceedings of the bishops and in 1596 the general assembly appointed him and fifteen others to organize the church in opposition to the government. As a result the privy council ordered him to return to Glasgow. But in the following year he took part in the general assembly at Perth at which the king recovered the initiative, and subsequently joined the commission to whom were delegated the powers of the general assembly when that body was not in session, and whose appointment paved the way for the re-establishment of bishops. About 1602 he supervised some university reforms and assured its autonomy relative to the town. In 1606 Sharp was summoned to Hampton Court, with seven other divines, to support the king's side in a debate with Andrew Melville and seven ultrapresbyterians on the general questions at issue between king and kirk. That year he was also appointed constant moderator to the Glasgow presbytery in the absence of the bishop, and met so much opposition that the privy council had to order the presbytery to receive him or face the penalties of rebellion. Yet in the following year he was rebuked for endeavouring to extend the jurisdiction of the presbytery to cover criminal cases. In June 1608 Sharp took part in the Falkland Conference, which was intended to make matters easy for the bishops at the next general assembly. He was appointed to the newly instituted Scottish high commission on 15 May 1610 and continued to serve until 11 August 1614. In December 1613 a royal visitation of the university was set up in response to 'enormiteis'. Sharp's theology may have seemed oldfashioned, and an up-to-date replacement was available in Robert Boyd. Sharp anticipated deposition by resigning his principalship. Among his achievements had been the recovery of the university's medieval silver mace, removed at the Reformation by the principal of the time.

Sharp died in May 1615 in Glasgow, leaving an estate valued at £1362 Scots. He was three times married. He and his first wife, Agnes Cairns (d. in or before 1593), had two sons, David and James. On 1 September 1593 he married Mary Fowlis, widow of John Haldane of Balwill, with whom he had one son, Christian, and two daughters. His third wife, whom he married some time after 1600, was Elizabeth, daughter of Thomas Jack of Eastwood and widow of Walter Maxwell of Pollok. Sharp was a distinguished scholar, but only one of his works survives, *Doctrinae Christianae brevis explicatio*, printed by Robert Waldegrave at Edinburgh in 1599. A work of exegesis, it is simplified on Ramist lines (it speaks of the 'use of doctrine'), quotes 'aphorisms' as memory aids, transliterates its Greek and Hebrew citations, and cites some of the fathers.

E. I. CARLYLE, rev. JOHN DURKAN

Sources J. Durkan and J. Kirk, *The University of Glasgow, 1451–1577* (1977) · T. Thomson, ed., *Acts and proceedings of the general assemblies of the Kirk of Scotland*, 3 pts, Bannatyne Club, 81 (1839–45), esp. pt 3 · *The autobiography and diary of Mr James Melvill*, ed. R. Pitcairn, Wodrow Society (1842) · R. Renwick, ed., *Abstracts of the protocols of the town clerks of Glasgow*, 11 vols. (1894–1900), vols. 8–11 · J. D. Marwick, ed., *Extracts from the records of the burgh of Glasgow, AD 1573–1642*, 1, Scottish Burgh RS, 11 (1876) · C. Innes, ed., *Munimenta alme Universitatis Glasguensis / Records of the University of Glasgow from its foundation till 1727*, 4 vols., Maitland Club, 72 (1854) · W. Fraser, ed., *Memoirs of the Maxwells of Pollok*, 2 vols. (privately printed, Edinburgh, 1863) · R. Wodrow, *Collections upon the lives of the reformers and most eminent ministers of the Church of Scotland*, ed. W. J. Duncan, 2/1, Maitland Club, 32 (1848), 116–17 · NA Scot., CC9/7/11, fols. 113–14 · H. M. B. Reid, *The divinity principals in the University of Glasgow, 1545–1654* (1917) · D. Calderwood, *The history of the Kirk of Scotland*, ed. T. Thomson and D. Laing, 8 vols., Wodrow Society, 7 (1842–9) · *Reg. PCS*, 1st ser., vols. 2, 5, 7–8

Wealth at death £1362 Scots: Durkan and Kirk, *University of Glasgow*, 352; will, NA Scot., CC9/7/11, fols. 113–14

Sharp, Sir Percival (1867–1953), schoolteacher and educational administrator, was born on 12 September 1867, at Bishop Auckland, co. Durham, the son of Henry Sharp, a grocer, and his wife, Catherine. He attended Edward Walton's endowed (public elementary) school, Bishop Auckland, and at the age of thirteen was apprenticed as a pupil teacher. He moved on to Homerton College, Cambridge, where he was top student of his year. On 28 March 1891 he married Janet (b. 1867/8), daughter of Thomas Henderson McLaren, with whom he had three sons. As a certificated teacher he held posts in West Hartlepool, Croydon, and Hull where he taught at the central higher grade school. After a short period of headship in Hull, he became headmaster of Bowerham School, Lancaster's first board school.

In 1903 Sharp was appointed inspector of schools in St Helens and subsequently director of education and in 1914 moved to Newcastle in a similar capacity. In 1919 he was invited to become Sheffield's first director of education, a post which he held until 1932. He was first elected to the executive committee of the Association of Education Committees (AEC) in 1911, and, except for a two-year break, was an active member of the executive for the rest of his life. The Association of Education Committees was set up in 1904 to represent the interests of the newly created education committees to government, and both chairs of committees and directors of education were normally in membership of the association. In its early years most of the education committees in the boroughs and urban districts joined the association, but it was not until the late 1940s that county education committees came in. The reorganization of local government in 1974 led directly to the association's demise in 1977. Sharp was the honorary secretary of the association from 1925 to 1932, when he was appointed as the association's first full-time secretary, a position he held until the end of 1944.

Sharp's long life was devoted to the state education service, and particularly to enhancing the role of the local education authorities within it. After the passing of the 1902 Education Act, the Board of Education under Sir Robert Morant's leadership, tried to keep the newly created local education authorities (LEAs) firmly under its own control. Several of the directors of education in the large industrial cities resisted and were determined to raise the status of the chief officers of LEAs. Spurley Hey (Manchester), James Graham (Leeds), and Sharp, affectionately termed the Three Musketeers by contemporaries, took a leading part in this and by the end of the 1920s had largely succeeded in their objective. Later, board officials complained that in the 1920s the balance of power had passed to the LEAs and that the department's own position had been belittled (Cooke and Gosden, 50).

For about twenty years Sharp was at the helm at the AEC, and was effectively the voice of the LEAs. He was the driving force behind the setting up of a national office in London, and he also conducted the negotiations which brought the journal, *Education*, under the association's control. He had a formidable reputation as an organizer, a forceful speaker, and writer, although some saw his manner as dictatorial. Lord Eustace Percy, a former president of the Board of Education, referred to him as the AEC's 'chief professional henchman' who was 'a little combative bull-terrier of a man' (Percy, 122). His successor as secretary to the AEC, Bill Alexander, pointed out that 'he loved a fight and no one can deny he was a bonny fighter' (*Education*, 13 Feb 1953, 261). Sharp was also described as 'a pedagogic gnat on the loins of the minister of education' (*Education*, 24 Nov 1944, 643). In 1944 Sharp recalled 'the time when to approach the board of education was like laying a profane hand on the Ark of the Covenant', but took pride in the fact that 'now the association's advice was not only welcomed but sought' (ibid., 643). At times Sharp irritated the board's officials, acquiring a reputation for making public material they regarded as confidential, and he never enjoyed the same measure of confidence among them as Alexander did after the war.

Throughout his career Sharp took a strong interest in teachers' pay. In his early days as a teacher he negotiated with Croydon school board for a pay rise for his colleagues. He was involved with the Burnham committee from its inception in 1919, serving as secretary to the local authorities' panel on that body from 1925 to 1944. He helped to frame the original Burnham pay scales, and later expressed the view that the work of this committee 'had revolutionised the economic condition of vast numbers of teachers' (*Education*, 5 Jan 1945, 14). In 1949 he resigned in protest from Burnham when the committee was forced by government to reject a pay rise for teachers which he believed was merited.

During the Second World War, Sharp was involved in the negotiations which led up to the 1944 Education Act. He had little option but to fight for the continued existence of part 3 education authorities which had been set up by the Education Act of 1902 as authorities for elementary education in non-county boroughs with populations over 10,000 and in urban districts with populations over 20,000. The AEC stood to lose a large number of members if they were abolished. There was, by this time, widespread agreement that these authorities had outlived their usefulness and Sharp lost this battle. At this time, Sharp also served on the Norwood committee which reported to the Board of Education on the curriculum and examinations in secondary schools. The committee provided much of the rationale for the post-war tripartite system of secondary schooling. There is no evidence to suggest that Sharp played a leading role on the Norwood committee, and he was quite content to subscribe to the prevailing view that there should be differentiation between types of secondary schools. His main interest was to ensure that local education authorities retained control of the proposed new secondary modern schools which he tended to see as former senior elementary schools (PRO, Ed. 136/378, note of meeting, 11 Aug 1943). He saw no reason why these schools, even if they were secondary in name, should be given the same kind of independence afforded to the grammar schools.

In 1938 Sharp was knighted for his services to education. From humble origins he came 'to the top the hard way' and tended, at least in his later years, 'to look at education always rather from the extinct pupil-teacher point of view' (Percy, 122). He was invariably a forceful negotiator, and 'a tough nut' which is well illustrated by the fact that he travelled from Falmouth to London for AEC executive meetings when he was in his eighties. He attended his last executive on 30 January and died at his home, Kinbrae, Gyllyngvase Road, Falmouth, Cornwall, on 8 February 1953.   PAUL SHARP

Sources *The Times* (11 Feb 1953) · *Education* (13 Feb 1953), 259–61 · *Education* (5 Jan 1945), 5–9, 14 · *Education* (24 Nov 1944), 642–3 · G. Cooke and P. Gosden, *Education committees* (1986) · E. Percy, *Some memories* (1958) · P. H. J. H. Gosden, *Education in the Second World War: a study in policy and administration* (1976) · M. Barber, *The making of the 1944 Education Act* (1994) · m. cert.
Archives U. Leeds, Brotherton L., Association of Education Committees archive
Likenesses photograph, repro. in *The Times*, 10 · photographs, repro. in *Education* (5 Jan 1945)
Wealth at death £1005 18s. 7d.: probate, 3 July 1953, CGPLA Eng. & Wales

Sharp, Richard [called Conversation Sharp] (1759–1835), politician and wit, was born in the garrison of St John's, Newfoundland, the elder son of Richard Sharp (1737–1765), a British army officer, and Elizabeth Adams (1739–1799), a citizen of St John's. He was related to the Sharps of Romsey, Hampshire, a well-known family of successful merchants. The family returned to London from Newfoundland in the early 1760s, and as a member of a staunchly nonconformist family the young Sharp was educated by the classical scholar the Revd Dr John Fell, Independent minister for Thaxted, Essex. Having been 'bred to trade from infancy' (Wilson, 133), Sharp successfully completed his apprenticeship before taking over the hatter's business which had been started by his grandfather on Fish Street Hill, London. In recent times Sharp has been credited with having been 'the world's first truly famous hatter' (McDowell, *Hats: Status, Style and Glamour*, 1992, 54). About 1798 his business interests moved to 17 Mark Lane where, as a partner in the West India firm of Boddington, Philips, Sharp & Co., he prospered to become one of London's most prominent merchants. He subsequently lived briefly at Mansion House Place before purchasing in 1808 23 Park Lane, where portraits by Reynolds—of Burke, Johnson, and of Reynolds himself—adorned his drawing-room.

At both Park Lane and his much loved country retreat at Fredley Farm in Mickleham, Surrey, Sharp received and entertained many of the most able and cultured minds of the day, including Babbage, Faraday, Walter Scott, Grattan, Brougham, Horner, Romilly, John Russell, Chantrey, Porson, Hallam, Macaulay, Rogers, and Horne Tooke. Sydney Smith was such a frequent visitor to Fredley that he was nicknamed the Bishop of Mickleham and following the French Revolution other visitors included Talleyrand, D'Arblay, and Mme de Staël. According to Clayden, Sharp was possibly the most popular person in London society during this period, his gifted eloquence and kindly good nature making him 'universally welcome' (Clayden, *The Early Life of Samuel Rogers*, 280). Such tributes to Sharp's personal qualities were widespread: Sir James Mackintosh the respected lawyer, historian, and metaphysician, described Sharp as the best critic that he had ever known and someone who had 'produced more effect on my character than any other man' (Hills, 43). Macaulay was impressed that Sharp never gossiped or spoke badly of anyone: 'if he can say nothing good of a man he holds his tongue' (ibid., 66). Among the poets, Samuel Rogers, who was later offered the laureateship, owed much to his close and lifelong friendship with Sharp, and others who benefited from his advice and beneficence included Wordsworth, Coleridge, Hazlitt, and Sheridan. The extraordinary social impact which Sharp made during his lifetime is summarized by Kegan Paul who wrote that 'both in Parliament and in Society he had a power quite out of proportion to that which most other persons in his seeming position would have wielded' (Paul, 12).

Sharp was a frequent and welcome guest at Holland House and he belonged to many London clubs including Brooks's, Eumelean, the Unincreasable, Clifford Street, and the exclusive King of Clubs of which—with Mackintosh, Robert (Bobus) Smith, Rogers, Scarlett, and Allen—he had been a founder member. Sharp was elected FSA on 19 April 1787. In 1806 he was one of the first members of the Literary Society and on 12 June that year he was elected FRS. He played a leading role in establishing the London Institution for the Improvement of Science and Literature and, having joined the Fishmongers' Company at the age of twenty-one, he was elected their prime warden for the years 1810–12.

Politically Sharp represented the pocket borough of Castle Rising, Norfolk, in 1806–12 as a staunch whig and one of very few dissenters to be returned and he was appointed to the finance committee of the House of Commons because of his experience in banking and commerce. In this position, and later as a member of Horner's bullion committee, he met with success and he was complimented by Henry Bankes for his contribution to the house. In 1808 Sharp made his Copenhagen speech, fiercely criticizing the government for the unprovoked attack on the Danish fleet. Although this was received with the 'utmost applause and favour' (Clayden, *Rogers and his Contemporaries*, 1.44) Sharp thereafter preferred, much to the disappointment of his friends, to exert his influence less overtly. At the by-election of 1816 he was returned for the Irish constituency of Portarlington which he retained at the general election of 1818 but from which he resigned in 1819 in order to make way for his friend David Ricardo.

As a dissenting whig Sharp pressed hard for greater civil and religious liberties. He served as a 'deputy' among London's dissenters and in 1790 wrote his stirring keynote letter to the public meeting of the friends to the repeal of the Test and Corporation Acts. Sharp was a member of the Society for Constitutional Information and in 1791–2 he, Rogers, and others initiated the Friends of the People group which agitated for political reform. In the cause of greater personal freedom Sharp stressed the importance of education, holding strong views on the subject of the English language. He wrote the preface to Fell's *Grammar* (1784), addressed the Manchester Society on 'The nature and utility of eloquence' (1787), and advocated—in reaction to 'Johnsonism'—the common use of a purer, less pedantic form of English language which might owe less to Latin and other languages. His wit, wisdom, and interesting views on many subjects are contained in *Letters and Essays in Poetry and Prose*, published anonymously and to wide acclaim in 1834. This was his only significant publication although he corresponded with his friend John Adams, the future president of the United States, about writing an account of the establishment of American independence.

Sharp did not marry and for the earlier part of his life, following his father's premature death, he remained at Fish Street Hill with his grandfather, mother, brother, step-father (Thomas Cable Davis), and a number of step-siblings. Later, about 1813, Maria Kinnaird became the much loved ward and adopted daughter of Richard and his brother William, and they, with William's wife Anna, lived together at their Park Lane address. When Richard Sharp died Maria inherited the bulk of his £250,000 estate and she married Thomas Drummond shortly afterwards.

Throughout his life but increasingly from 1815 onwards Sharp delighted in travel, particularly in France, Switzerland, Italy, Scotland, and the Lake District, and became such an expert on itineraries that many were grateful for his advice. According to Wordsworth, Sharp knew Italy better than anyone he had ever met (Knight, 3.250–51). For much of his life Sharp suffered from a bad chest and a persistent 'winter cough' so his trips were partly motivated by concern for his health and from about 1832, when his condition worsened, increasing periods of time were spent at his house on Higher Terrace, Torquay. He died at Dorchester, Dorset, on 30 March 1835 at the age of seventy-six while returning to London from Torquay and he was buried on 4 April alongside other members of his family in the dissenters' burial-ground of Bunhill Fields, London. Sharp was an accomplished businessman, politician, philosopher, and author but he achieved distinction as Conversation Sharp, a highly acclaimed critic and popular conversationalist, whose opinions and advice on a wide range of issues were sought by many of the cleverest people of his day. He is believed to have been the inspiration for Dickens's Conversation Kenge in *Bleak House*.

DAVID KNAPMAN

Sources Mrs E. Hills, 'Conversation Sharp (1759–1835) and his friends', Bodl. Oxf., MS Eng. misc. d. 464 · P. W. Clayden, *The early life of Samuel Rogers* (1887) · P. W. Clayden, *Rogers and his contemporaries*, 2 vols. (1889) · R. G. Thorne, 'Sharp, Richard', HoP, *Commons, 1790–1820* · J. Wilson, ed., *A biographical index to the present House of Commons* (1808), 133 · [R. Sharp], *Letters and essays in prose and verse* (1834) · *Memoirs of the life of the Right Honourable Sir James Mackintosh*, ed. R. J. Mackintosh, 2nd edn, 2 vols. (1836), vol. 1, p. 197 · *DNB* · C. K. Paul, *Maria Drummond* (1891) · W. A. Knight, *The life of William Wordsworth*, 3 vols. (1889), 3.250–51 · R. W. Frazer, *Notes on the history of the London Institution* (1905) · R. Sharp, Letter to the public meeting of the friends to the repeal of the Test and Corporation Acts: at the

London Tavern on February 13th 1790 from a lay dissenter, 1790, BL, Add. MS 37296 · J. Fell, *An essay towards an English grammar* (1784) · private information (2004)
Archives BL, corresp. with Lord Holland and Lady Holland, Add. MS 51593 · BL, corresp. with Sir James Mackintosh, Add. MS 5241A
Likenesses pencil and chalk drawing, *c.*1810, Bodl. Oxf.
Wealth at death £250,000: Hills, 'Conversation Sharp'; Thorne, 'Sharp, Richard'; *GM* (July 1835)

Sharp, Robert (1773–1843), diarist and schoolmaster, was born on 22 September 1773 at Barmston in the East Riding of Yorkshire, the eldest of the four children of John Sharp (*bap.* 1742, *d.* 1825), shepherd, and his wife, Elizabeth, *née* Harrison (*bap.* 1744, *d.* 1832). He attended the village school until the age of thirteen, when he moved to the nearby town of Bridlington, where he was probably apprenticed to a shoemaker, since he was recorded as following that occupation in 1803. He married Ann Read (*bap.* 1775, *d.* 1868) at Bridlington on 5 May 1795. They had six children, of whom only two, William (1798–1870) and Elizabeth (1806–1866), survived to adulthood. In 1804 Sharp was appointed master of the parish school at South Cave, near Beverley, in the East Riding of Yorkshire, where he remained until his death.

Robert Sharp is noted for his letters and diary (1812–37), which have survived in manuscript as a bound volume, deposited with the East Riding of Yorkshire Archives Service at Beverley, and which have been published (1997). The diary, from 1826 to 1837, was sent in instalments by Sharp to his son, William, who worked for the London publishing firm of Longman's; between 1812 and 1825 he had also sent William a series of letters. Together the diary and letters provide a detailed picture of rural life and village administration. Sharp was well placed to chronicle the life of the village, since he was himself a villager, on the same social level as most of those whom he described, and took an active part in village affairs as its schoolmaster and also as a tax assessor and collector, deputy constable, clerk to the local friendly society, measuring surveyor, shopkeeper, and general scribe to his neighbours. He was an acute and wryly sympathetic observer of the lives of his fellow villagers, whose conversations he often quoted verbatim.

Officially Anglican, Sharp had strong leanings towards Congregationalism. His own views and political beliefs, which were broadly liberal, are reflected in his writings. As a regular reader of *The Times* and Cobbett's *Weekly Political Register*, he was well informed on national politics and events, and commented on all the most important issues, such as parliamentary reform, the corn laws, Catholic emancipation, the new poor law, the abolition of slavery, and the social effects of industrialization. His diary is especially valuable in that it shows how major reforms and changes were reflected at local level, how they were perceived by the villagers, and the extent to which their lives were affected. Although largely self-educated, Sharp was well-read and had a good knowledge of English literature. His own literary style, combined with his dry sense of humour and close observation, make his diary and letters a pleasure to read. Sharp died of bronchitis at Market Cross schoolhouse, South Cave, East Riding of Yorkshire, on 5 May 1843 and was buried at South Cave churchyard on 7 May.   PETER A. CROWTHER

Sources Manuscript diary and letters of Robert Sharp, East Riding of Yorkshire Archives Service, Beverley, DDX/216/4 · J. E. Crowther and P. A. Crowther, eds., *Diary of Robert Sharp of South Cave: life in a Yorkshire village, 1812–1837* (1997) · baptismal register of the Zion Independent Chapel at Bridlington, East Riding of Yorkshire Archives Service, Beverley, Mf 2 [3020] · parish registers of Barmston, Beeford, Bempton, Bridlington, Kirk Ella, Reighton and South Cave · d. cert. · will, proved, 18 July 1843
Archives East Riding of Yorkshire Archives Service, Beverley, diary and correspondence
Wealth at death under £300: will, proved 18 July 1843

Sharp, Samuel (*bap.* **1709**, *d.* **1778**), surgeon, son of Henry Sharp, brazier, and his wife, Hannah *née* Puller of London, was baptized at St Peter's, Cornhill, London, on 17 June 1709. The fortunate apprentice of William Cheselden, senior surgeon at St Thomas's Hospital, he was indentured in 1724 for a fee of £300 paid by Elizabeth Sale, a widowed aunt living at Hertford. Her father, Sharp's maternal grandfather, was Isaac Puller MP, a former mayor of Hertford. Nothing is known of Sharp's early schooling. During his apprenticeship he met S.-F. Morand, a French surgeon dispatched to study Cheselden's lithotomy technique, and in 1729 or 1730 he became Morand's pupil in Paris. In 1732 he obtained the diploma of the Barber–Surgeons' Company and in 1733 he was elected surgeon to Guy's Hospital. In the same year Cheselden published his monumental *Osteographia, or, The Anatomy of the Bones*, towards which Sharp assisted; a vignette on the title-page shows Cheselden drawing with two apprentices said to be John Belchier and Sharp; no other certain likeness is known. Sharp rapidly acquired an extensive practice, and in 1739 published *A Treatise on the Operations of Surgery*, illustrated with fourteen plates of instruments; it was the first monograph in English on the subject and achieved eleven editions, and translations into French, Portuguese, Dutch, Spanish, and Italian. In July 1740 Sharp married Eleanor Baynes of Hatton Garden, daughter of Richard Baynes, alderman of York; they had three daughters and a son who took the name Samuel Sharpe Pocklington on marriage.

In 1746 Sharp relinquished to William Hunter the 'course of anatomical lectures, to which were added the operations of surgery, with the application of bandages', delivered in Covent Garden on winter afternoons to naval surgeons. In 1749 Sharp became a fellow of the Royal Society of London and on a second visit to Paris was elected a foreign member of the Royal Academy of Surgery. Two papers in *Philosophical Transactions* concerned cataract extraction and in 1751 he couched the composer G. F. Handel, being as unsuccessful as two later practitioners. In 1750 he published *A Critical Enquiry into the Present State of Surgery*, which achieved four editions, and translations into French, Dutch, Spanish, German, and Italian. This influential work focused on controversial surgical issues including hernia, cerebral concussion, lithotomy, tonsillectomy, and amputation.

Sharp resigned from Guy's Hospital in 1757 on the

grounds of ill health, probably asthma, but he continued in private practice until 1765, when he set out on a winter tour through Italy. The results were published in his forthright *Letters from Italy*, of 1766; these included an account of a visit to Geneva to see Voltaire again, Sharp having met him previously in London and Paris. Of his letters, Dr Johnson thought 'there was a great deal of matter in them' (Boswell, *Life*, 755). The publication of a second edition in 1767 produced Giuseppe Baretti's *Account of the Manners and Customs of Italy*, an acrid criticism of Sharp's views. It was answered by Sharp in *A view of the customs, manners, drama, &c., of Italy, as they are described in the 'Frusta litteraria'*, of Baretti in which, happily for Sharp, were recorded similar censures to the *Letters from Italy*.

Sharp proved an innovative surgical practitioner and communicator as the many editions of his books in seven European languages indicate. Nineteenth-century surgeons admired his forthrightness and skills. Louis Bégin, a French practitioner, assessed Sharp in 1825 as

one of those surgeons whose works show in the highest degree the impress of an observing mind, hostile to all authority and routine. There are few diseases on which he did not put forward new ideas, few operations whose instruments or procedures he did not improve. His writings contain many things in few pages, and we find in them both an originality and an independence of thought which charm the reader and always secure his attention. (Kirkup, 1)

James Paget said he

was a thoroughly informed surgeon, well read, observant, judicious, a lover of simplicity, wisely doubtful. I think, too, he must have been an eminently safe man, who might be relied on for knowing or doing whatever, in his time, could be known or done for the good of his patients. (Paget, 53)

In England Sharp was the immediate link between Cheselden and both Percivall Pott and John Hunter. Sharp cultivated anatomical and operative precision, introducing numerous improvements in techniques and instruments. In place of the usual chair for amputation, he advised a table and specified the table's height, both for this and for herniotomy and lithotomy. He promoted the cylindrical, as opposed to the conical, cranial trephine saw and modified its controlling handle; he designed a cataract knife and made cogent observations on the manufacture of scalpels and suture needles. Indeed, in the reconstruction of surgical perceptions of this period, Samuel Sharp's contributions remain unique and invaluable sources.

In 1766 Sharp retired to Bath, where he died at his home in the Circus on 24 March 1778 after a lingering illness; he was buried in Bath Abbey. JOHN KIRKUP

Sources S. Wilks and G. T. Bettany, *A biographical history of Guy's Hospital* (1892) · J. Kirkup, 'Samuel Sharp and the *Operations of surgery*', *Journal of Medical Biography*, 4 (1996), 1–7 · GL, MS 8820 · A. St Hill, letter, 28 April 1936, RCS Eng., 42.e.1 · *GM*, 1st ser., 10 (1740) · *GM*, 1st ser., 48 (1778) · will, 4 April 1778, PRO, PROB 11/1041 · M. Keynes, 'Handel's illnesses', *The Lancet* (20–27 Dec 1980), 1354–5 · C. P. Russel, 'Inscriptions on flat gravestones in Bath Abbey', Bath Reference Library · J. Paget, *The Hunterian oration 1877* (1877), 53 · *Bath Chronicle* (26 March 1778) · Bath rate book, no. 1, 1766, City of Bath RO · Bath rate book, no. 22, 1776, City of Bath RO · *DNB* · Boswell, *Life*

Archives Guy's Hospital, London, Wills Library, 'A treatise on the operations of surgery'
Likenesses G. Vandergucht?, engraving (with W. Cheselden), repro. in W. Cheselden, *Osteographia, or, The anatomy of the bones* (1733), title-page · engraving, Guy's Hospital, London, Gordon Museum
Wealth at death property in England and France, incl. house in the Circus, Bath; legacies; annuities; books: will, PRO, PROB 11/1041, sig. 172

Sharp, Samuel (1814–1882), geologist and antiquary, was born on 18 July 1814 at Romsey, Hampshire, the son of Stephen Sharp (*bap.* 1791) and his wife, Anna Maria Bloor (*bap.* 1784), formerly of Uppingham. His father died while he was a child and his mother married the proprietor and editor of the *Stamford Mercury*. Samuel, after schooling at Southsea, moved to Stamford, where he assisted in managing and editing the newspaper. He had an early interest in astronomy and chemistry but took up geology after attending a lecture at Stamford by George Fleming Richardson (1796–1848) in 1842. Together with John Morris (1810–1866), Sharp studied the geology of the local area, making use of sections newly exposed by railway construction.

In 1846 Sharp married Caroline Ann Weldon and in 1857 they moved to Dallington Hall, near Northampton, where Caroline Sharp soon opened a new girls' boarding-school. Here Sharp's geological collecting continued, aided by the superintendent at the extensive open-cast Ironstone mine at Duston. As might be expected from someone connected with a school, Sharp gave constant assistance to naturalists of the younger generation in Northamptonshire. He also 'laboured energetically to found a good provincial museum' in Northampton, placing there from 1869, 'valuable contributions from his own large geological and antiquarian collections' (Judd 1883, 72). Over 1500 of his fossils were purchased by the British Museum in 1876; they included examples of a number of fossil species named after him. The residue of his collection went to Mason College, Birmingham. Sharp was fellow of the Geological Society from 1862 and published important papers on the oolites of Northamptonshire in 1870 and 1873, and on an uninformed search for coal near Northampton in 1871. His text book *Rudiments of Geology* followed in 1875 (2nd edn, 1876).

Sharp was also active as an antiquary. Long a fellow of the Society of Antiquaries, Sharp published papers on architecture and local history, as well as one against cruelty to animals. A member of the Numismatic Society, Sharp also formed an unrivalled collection of the productions of the Stamford mint, on which he published in 1869 and 1880. He died on 28 January 1882 at his home, Great Harrowden Hall, near Wellingborough. The fossil brachiopod *Kallirhynchia sharpi*, named after him in 1938, now marks the long-distance Jurassic way footpath through both his adopted counties. H. S. TORRENS

Sources J. W. J[udd], 'Obituary and bibliography', *Journal of the Northamptonshire Natural History Society and Field Club*, 2 (1883), 71–3 · [J. W. Judd], *Quarterly Journal of the Geological Society*, 38 (1882), 53–4 · *Nature*, 25 (1881–2), 319 · 'Midland Union of Naturalist History Societies', *Midland Naturalist*, 3 (1880), 182–6 · R. Le Schorix, 'Notes on

archaeology in provincial museums: no. 36, Northampton', *Antiquary*, 33 (1894), 100–107 • accessions books, MSS, 1866–84, Northampton Central Museum • *CGPLA Eng. & Wales* (1882) • IGI
Archives Northampton Central Library, B. Thompson archive • UCL, letters to Edwin Chadwick
Likenesses photograph, 1868, repro. in B. Thompson, *The Northampton sand of Northamptonshire* (1928), facing p. 1
Wealth at death £1838 8s. 4d.: probate, 5 Sept 1882, *CGPLA Eng. & Wales*

Sharp, Thomas (1693–1758), Church of England clergyman and theological writer, was born on 12 December 1693, the younger son of John *Sharp (1645?–1714), archbishop of York, and his wife, Elizabeth Palmer (*fl.* 1660–1715), of Winthorpe in Lincolnshire. He was educated at first privately, by a Mr Ellis, then at Leeds grammar school, and later at St Paul's School, London. Admitted at Trinity College, Cambridge, on 25 April 1709, where he was tutored by Nicholas Clagett, college librarian, he became a Jermyn scholar in the following year. A commonplace book survives from his period as an undergraduate detailing his reading in theology, trigonometry, optics, and hydrostatics. He graduated BA in 1713 as a wrangler, was elected to a fellowship in 1715, and proceeded MA in 1716. He was ordained deacon in the diocese of London on 16 June 1716 and priested at York in February 1718. He became chaplain to Archbishop Dawes, prebendary of Southwell in Nottinghamshire, and a member of the Gentlemen's Society at Spalding. He was installed as prebendary of Wistow in the diocese of York on 8 May 1719, an office he held until his death in 1758. He was presented to the living of Ormsby, Yorkshire, in 1719, then on 27 February 1723 to the living of Rothbury in Northumberland, the second most valuable in the county. At the same time he was appointed archdeacon of Northumberland. He was created DD at Cambridge in 1729. On 1 December 1732 he was installed in the tenth prebend of Durham Cathedral, in 1755 succeeding Dr Mangey as official to the dean and chapter there. Although this excessive plurality must have been lucrative for Sharp, he appears to have been a conscientious and tireless pastor, as well as an efficient ecclesiastical administrator.

Sharp married Judith (d. 1757), daughter of Sir George Wheler (1651–1723), traveller, and Grace Higgons, on 19 June 1722 at Houghton-le-Spring, co. Durham; between 1723 and 1738, they had fourteen children, to whom he remained devoted throughout his life. He engaged in a voluminous correspondence with many of them. Much of his wealth was spent on the education of his two eldest sons, John *Sharp and Thomas, both of whom followed him to Trinity College, Cambridge. John became, like his father, prebendary of Durham, and Thomas, fellow of Trinity, became curate at Bamburgh. Of his other children, Granville *Sharp became a noted abolitionist, and William surgeon to George III. The Sharp family remained closely knit, bound together partly by religion, partly by a love of music. Many of his children were depicted playing music together on the family barge on the Thames by Zoffany in his painting *The Sharp Family*, now in the National Portrait Gallery.

Sharp was a considerable book collector and owned a large library, in part inherited from his father. It was divided between his homes at Rothbury and Durham, and contained a substantial collection of early book auction catalogues. His books eventually became part of the library of Bamburgh Castle, one of Lord Crewe's charities, and are now on deposit in Durham University Library. Sharp was, like his sons, closely associated with the Corporation of the Sons of the Clergy, his first publication being a printed edition of a sermon he delivered to the corporation in York in 1721, *A Charity-Sermon for the Relief of Poor Widows and Children of Clergymen* (1721). Many of the sermons he preached in Durham, Newcastle, York, Cambridge, and London were printed, together with a number of theological works. The first and most frequently reprinted of these was *The Necessary Knowledge of the Lord's Supper* (1727), reprinted six times in the eighteenth century alone. He regularly engaged in theological controversy; his *Enquiry about the Lawfulness of Eating Blood* (1733) was quickly followed by a *Defence of the Enquiry about the Lawfulness of Eating Blood* (1734), and he published a *Reply to a Pamphlet Entitled, 'The Protestant Flair'* (1735). His *Two dissertations concerning the etymology and scripture-meaning of the Hebrew words Elohim and Berith* (1751) was written with the advice of Thomas Birch, who also saw it through the press for him. Sharp was forced to publish *A review and defence of two dissertations concerning the etymology and scripture-meaning of the Hebrew words Elohim and Berith* in 1754 and 1755. A related work, *Discourses Touching the Antiquity of the Hebrew Tongue and Character*, was published in 1755. His lengthy correspondence with Catherine Cockburn on moral virtue and moral obligation, published in volume 2 of Cockburn's *Works* (1751), survives in manuscript. It was recommended by Richard Price in the first edition (1758) of his influential *Review of the Principal Questions and Difficulties in Morals*. Sharp's *Collected Works* were published in six volumes in 1763. He died at Durham on 16 March 1758 and on 23 March was buried in the galilee chapel in Durham Cathedral.   RICHARD OVENDEN

Sources A. T. Hart, *The life and times of John Sharp, archbishop of York* (1949) • admissions registers, 1635–1740, Trinity Cam., muniment room • J. R. Tanner, ed., *Historical register of the University of Cambridge … to the year 1910* (1917) • 'Thomas Sharp's commonplace book', Glos. RO, D.3549, box 37b • Index to Thomas Sharp's library, Glos. RO, D.3549, box 37b • P. Hoare, *Memoirs of Granville Sharpe, esq.* (1820) • R. Ovenden, 'Thomas Sharp's library at Cambridge, c.1748', MA diss., U. Lond., 1987 • R. Ovenden, 'The early use of sale catalogues', *Factotum: Newsletter of the XVIIIth-Century Short Title Catalogue*, 26 (1987), 10–14 • J. C. Shuler, 'The pastoral and ecclesiastical administration of the diocese of Durham, 1721–1771: with particular reference to the archdeaconry of Northumberland', PhD diss., U. Durham, 1975 • C. J. Stranks, *The charities of Nathaniel Lord Crewe and Dr John Sharp, 1921–1976* (1976) • DNB • IGI • M. McDonnell, ed., *The registers of St Paul's School, 1509–1748* (privately printed, London, 1977) • P. Mussett, *List of deans and major canons of Durham* (1974)
Archives Glos. RO, corresp. • York Minster Library, York Minster archives, list of Durham Cathedral office-holders, MS of his life of Archbishop Sharp; sacred poems | BL, corresp. with T. Birch, Add. MS 4318 • BL, corresp. with C. Cockburn, Add. MSS 4264, 4266 • Bodl. Oxf., letters to Gregory Sharp relating to Latin • U. Durham, Bamburgh Castle Library deposit

Likenesses T. Hudson, oils, 1757, Man. City Gall. · stipple, 1825, NPG · engraving, repro. in *The works of Thomas Sharp* (1763), frontispiece

Sharp, Thomas (1770–1841), antiquary, only son of Thomas Sharp of Coventry, hatter, was born on 7 November 1770, in a house in Smithford Street, Coventry, which bore the effigy of 'Peeping Tom'. He was educated at the free grammar school in Coventry and on his father's death, in 1784, he joined the family business. He married, in 1804, Charlotte Turland of Barnwell, Cambridgeshire; they had nine children, of whom seven survived him.

From youth Sharp devoted himself to the study of local antiquities and the Coventry city muniments. About 1798 Sharp, with two friends, George Howletts and George Nickson, commissioned views of all the buildings of interest in the county, to be engraved and inserted in their copies of William Dugdale's *Warwickshire*. In 1820 Sharp procured rubbings of all the brasses in the county for insertion in the same work. In 1804 he retired from the retail trade to become a wholesaler, and devoted his additional leisure to antiquarian research, producing many pamphlets and articles, and in 1824 a *Guide to Coventry*. His chief work, *A dissertation on the pageants, or dramatic mysteries, anciently performed at Coventry by the trading companies of that city*, was published at Coventry in a small edition in 1825. It was praised by Sir Walter Scott for its 'carefulness and extent of research' (*Letters*, 9.444). It remains indispensable, especially because of the loss by enemy action in 1940 of the guild records which Sharp—here anticipating the course of later research—had used to provide the plays with a context. He was in error in believing *Ludus Coventriae* to be a genuine Coventry play; it is now regarded by scholars as an 'N-Town play'. Sharp proposed to publish an edition of 125 copies of the Coventry Corpus Christi plays, but failed to secure sufficient signatures. (The compilation was published by the Shakespeare Society in 1841.)

In 1834 Sharp relinquished his declining business altogether and moved to Leamington, where he continued his frequent communication with fellow antiquaries such as Sir Francis Palgrave, Dawson Turner, Francis Douce, William Salt, and John Britton. In 1831 he acted as executor of William Hamper, whose friend and correspondent he had been. Always active in promoting municipal welfare, in 1837 Sharp took a principal part in founding the Coventry and Warwick Hospital. He died on 12 August 1841 at Leamington and was interred at St Michael's burial-ground, Coventry.

At the time of his death Sharp was engaged on a history of Coventry, which appeared posthumously and incomplete as *A Concise History of Coventry*. His *Illustrative Papers on the History and Antiquities of the City of Coventry* was published in 1871, with a memoir by William George Fretton.

Apart from his topographical collections relating to Warwickshire (the majority of which, like the extra-illustrated Dugdale, were purchased in 1834 by William Staunton of Longbridge House, near Warwick), Sharp was an assiduous collector of coins, and he was an authority on provincial coins and tokens. In 1834 he published a detailed catalogue of the Chetwynd collection at Grendon Hall. One of Sharp's own coins, a gold half-florin of Edward III, of which only two specimens were known, is now in the British Museum. Part of Sharp's library was sold in London by Sotheby and Wilkinson on 23 July 1858. The bulk of his collections of Warwickshire manuscripts was destroyed in a fire at the Birmingham Free Reference Library in 1879, but an annotated copy of his *Dissertation on the Dramatic Mysteries* and a volume of his Coventry tracts, also annotated, survive in the British Library (Add. MSS 43645 and 44932).   E. I. CARLYLE, *rev.* ALAN BELL

Sources W. G. Fretton, 'Memoir', in T. Sharp, *Illustrative papers on the history and antiquities of the city of Coventry* (1871) · *GM*, 1st ser., 70 (1800), 945 · *GM*, 2nd ser., 16 (1841), 436–8 · R. Beadle, *Cambridge companion to the medieval English theatre* (1994) · F. L. Colvile, *The worthies of Warwickshire who lived between 1500 and 1800* [1870], 676–9 · *The letters of Sir Walter Scott*, ed. H. J. C. Grierson and others, centenary edn, 12 vols. (1932–79)

Archives BL, Add. MSS 43645, 44932 · Coventry City RO

Likenesses J. S. Cotman, drawing, 1823, repro. in Fretton, 'Memoir', frontispiece · D. Turner, etching (after J. S. Cotman), BM

Sharp, Thomas Wilfred (1901–1978), town planner and writer, was born on 12 April 1901 at Bishop Auckland, co. Durham, the only son and second of three children of Francis Sharp, insurance agent, and his wife, Margaret Ann Beresford, of Salatyn, Shropshire: both were from mining families. Sharp was educated at Bishop Auckland grammar school, which he left in 1918 to become a trainee surveyor with the town's borough surveyor. Four years later he moved to Margate to help with the preparation of a development plan. From there he went to Canterbury and then to London, to the offices of town planning consultants Thomas Adams and Longstreth Thompson. Following this, an important post as regional planning assistant to the south-west Lancashire regional advisory group should have promised much for Sharp's career. But when credit for his mammoth report on the area in 1930 was given, as tradition demanded, to the honorary surveyor, he resigned in anger, setting a precedent he was to follow more than once. He was unable to find a job for two years.

Turning misfortune to good purpose, Sharp wrote his first book, *Town and Countryside* (1932), an angry polemic which established his reputation as an eloquent writer who was not afraid to be controversial. His argument rested on the separate, individual qualities of town and countryside: he thus challenged the popular garden city movement which sought to unite them, and which he felt had been bastardized in the suburb. The book was finished at the family home in co. Durham: the area's squalid mining inheritance and its magnificent cathedral were to provide inspiration for much of Sharp's writing, and he spent years as a consultant protecting Durham city from adverse development.

Sharp regarded the man-made English landscape as one of the most beautiful in the world, and the English village as the perfection of the village idea. He also loved the beauty of formal street architecture of Renaissance towns, although over the years he came to prefer the less predictable richness of medieval streets. These ideas were expressed in *English Panorama* (1936), written after an unplanned move took him into the academic world, as a lecturer (from 1937) and later as reader, in Durham University's architecture department at Newcastle. Here he wrote *Town Planning* (1940), a paperback which popularized his ideas among a war-torn populace. It sold a quarter of a million copies.

Sharp spent part of the Second World War in London, as a senior research officer from 1941 to 1943 in the planning section of the Ministry of Works and Planning set up by Lord Reith. He contributed substantially to the influential Scott report on land utilization in rural areas, which laid the foundations for post-war legislation to protect the countryside. He also produced *The Anatomy of the Village* (1946), which became a classic on the subject of village design, despite almost being suppressed by the ministry. In it Sharp for the first time consciously developed the concept of townscape, then almost unknown and still widely misunderstood, as a counterpart to landscape. It was a dramatic vision of the quality of urban space which he perfected, in outstanding analyses of historic towns, in his post-war plans—notably those for Durham, Oxford, Exeter, Salisbury, and Chichester, between 1943 and 1949. This work followed a brief return to Durham University in 1941. Here he devised the first undergraduate planning course in the country before leaving to concentrate on his own planning consultancy in Oxford, after it was made clear that there would be no immediate establishment of a chair in the new subject. Soon after he left, however, a chair in town planning was created, leaving Sharp extremely bitter.

Sharp was made DLitt of Durham University in 1948 (he had obtained his Durham MA in 1940) and held office as president of the Town Planning Institute in 1945–6 and of the Institute of Landscape Architects in 1949–51. In 1951 he was appointed CBE, and he became FRIBA in 1961. But after his decade of achievement in the 1940s the remaining years were ones of frustration and disillusionment as changes in the profession and his own inability to compromise made work hard to find. Post-war legislation created more local authority planning departments, and even when consultants came briefly back into the limelight in the 1960s building boom, Sharp chose to remain an offstage critic of his profession. He took occasional commissions, fought for a road across Christ Church meadow as the only way of saving Oxford's peerless High Street from traffic, and wrote poems and novels which, to his disappointment, remained largely unpublished. His last planning book was *Town and Townscape* (1968).

These years were brightened by Sharp's marriage on 16 February 1963 to Rachel Dorothy Morrison (*b.* 1906/7), whom he had known for many years: she was the daughter of his old friend Cameron Morrison, principal of Newington College, Madras, and later a lecturer at St Andrews University. They had no children. Their home, 1 Farndon Road, Oxford, was constantly visited by friends and admirers, and Sharp's refuge was his study, lined with his collection of books, in which he took great delight until his death in hospital at Oxford on 27 January 1978; his remains were cremated in Oxford. His wife survived him.

K. M. Stansfield, *rev.*

Sources K. M. Stansfield, 'The poetry of planning', MA diss., Manchester University, 1974 · G. E. Cherry, ed., *Pioneers in British planning* (1981) · G. Dix, 'Thomas Sharp', *RIBA Journal*, 85 (1978), 153–4 · private information (1986) · m. cert.
Archives U. Newcastle, School of Architecture, Planning and Landscape | Welwyn Garden City Central Library, correspondence with Frederic Osborn
Likenesses photograph, 1945–6, repro. in Stansfield, 'The poetry of planning'
Wealth at death £14,414: probate, 28 June 1978, *CGPLA Eng. & Wales*

Sharp, William (1749–1824), engraver, was born on 29 January 1749 at Haydon Yard, Minories, London, the address of his father, a gunmaker. Having been apprenticed to Barak Longmate, a bright engraver skilled in heraldry, he later claimed that his first engravings were made upon a publican's pewter pot, but from 1771 he extended his experience as a pupil in the Royal Academy Schools. He commenced his career as a writing engraver in Bartholomew Lane, and gave his first demonstration of greater powers in 1775 with a small quarto engraving, *Hector*, of an old lion in the Tower of London. Plates for the *Novelist's Magazine* after designs by Stothard revealed his skills to a wider audience, and by 1782 he had moved to Vauxhall, where he worked on more substantial plates. The engraving *Alfred the Great Dividing his Loaf with the Pilgrim*, after Benjamin West and published by Boydell in 1782, made his reputation. After inheriting a legacy from a brother who had died at Gibraltar, Sharp moved from Vauxhall to a house in Charles Street, near the Middlesex Hospital, and later, successively, to Titchfield Street, to Acton, and to Chiswick.

Sharp was soon recognized as a very important contributor to the revival of the classical style of line engraving in England, following Sir Robert Strange and William Woollett, and in 1789 he completed the engraving *King Charles II Landing at Dover*, after West, a work that Woollett had left unfinished at his death in 1785. In the twentieth century he was still seen as:

> one of the most accomplished of all the reproductive line-engravers of the eighteenth century … in his portraits, in particular, he showed a wonderful power of interpreting his originals … *Richard Hart Davis, John Hunter, Porson* (1810) and *Dr Raine* (1815) exhibit a command of gradations of tone seldom outside mezzotint. (Hind, 205)

Sharp's contemporaries considered his best engravings to be *The Doctors of the Church*, after Guido; *John Hunter*, after Reynolds, and *King Lear in the Storm*, after West. He was also noted for two large plates of scenes from the siege and relief of Gibraltar (1781): *The Sortie*, after Trumbull, published in 1799, and *The Destruction of the Floating Battery*, after Copley, published with a keyplate in 1810, and for his involvement with the most prestigious serial publications of the time. He engraved three plates for Macklin's series of Bible illustrations, including *The Holy Family* after Reynolds (1792), for which Macklin had paid Reynolds 500 guineas; three plates for Robert Bowyer's series of illustrations to Hume's *History of England*, and three more, including *King Lear in the Storm*, for John Boydell's *Shakspeare Gallery* (1791–1802).

Despite his fame and reputation Sharp regarded the established structure of artistic patronage with suspicion. Like Strange and Woollett before him, he refused to accept membership of the Royal Academy on the inferior associate basis offered to engravers: this decision is said to have alienated him from the president, Sir Joshua Reynolds. However, he accepted honorary membership of the Imperial Academy of Vienna and of the Royal Academy of Munich. His political sympathies were with those who criticized the established order and with the revolutionary forces in America and France. The theme of liberty was celebrated in two of his earliest historical engravings, *Boadicea Haranguing the Britons* and *The Declaration of Rights*, both after Thomas Stothard; the second print, engraved in 1782, was dedicated to the Society for Constitutional Information, of which Sharp was a member. He engraved and published fine portraits of Thomas Paine, the author of *The Rights of Man*, after Romney in 1793, and of the populist reformer Sir Francis Burdett, after Northcote in 1811. In 1794 he was examined on treasonable charges before the privy council, but his good-natured attempt to use the occasion to solicit subscriptions for his engraving of General Kościuszko, after West, ensured his early acquittal. Contemporaries agreed that Sharp was 'by no means qualified to be a conspirator; he was fond of good cheer, grew corpulent from indulging in it, and had the gout' (Bryan, *Painters*, 733).

Sharp's eccentricity was marked in other ways. He had great faith in the study of physiognomy—'Cobbett's profile he likened to that of a bull-dog. ... he often eulogised Mr Vansittart and Lord Sidmouth' (*GM*, 1st ser., 94/2, 1824, 471)—but this was thought extravagant. His religious convictions were yet more peculiar, even by the common standards of radical heterodoxy. Having been influenced by the notions of Mesmer and Swedenborg, he became a follower of the enthusiast Richard Brothers, whose portrait he engraved in 1795 as *The Man whom God has Appointed*. However, on Brothers's confinement as a lunatic later that year, Sharp transferred his allegiance to the fanatic Joanna Southcott, who in 1806 defaced with red paint a thousand copies of his print of Brothers. In 1812 Sharp engraved a portrait of Southcott, towards the cost of whose journey from Exeter and residence in London he had contributed very substantially, and he never lost faith in her pretended divine mission, even after her death in 1814.

Sharp resided on Chiswick Mall, Chiswick, where he died on 25 July 1824, epitomized, justly, as 'an extraordinary compound of high professional talent, good moral intentions and egregious credulity' (ibid.). He was buried on 29 July in the churchyard of St Nicholas, Chiswick, close to William Hogarth, 'whom he esteemed the most extraordinary painter who had ever existed' (ibid.).

RICHARD SHARP

Sources W. S. Baker, *William Sharp, engraver, with a descriptive catalogue of his works* (1875) · *GM*, 1st ser., 94/2 (1824), 469–72 · Bryan, *Painters* (1849) · T. Clayton, *The English print, 1688–1802* (1997) · A. M. Hind, *A history of engraving and etching*, 3rd edn (1923); repr. (1963) · D. Alexander, 'Sharp, William', *The dictionary of art*, ed. J. Turner (1996) · Thieme & Becker, *Allgemeines Lexikon* · *Engraved Brit. ports.* · *DNB* · bishop's transcripts, St Nicholas, Chiswick, LMA

Likenesses W. Sharp, line engraving, pubd 1817 (after G. F. Joseph), BM, NPG; repro. in *Engraved Brit. ports.* · attrib. M. Brown, chalk drawing, Scot. NPG · F. Chantrey, bust, AM Oxf. · B. R. Haydon, drawing, BM · J. Lonsdale, oils, NPG · M. A. Shee, oils, Petworth House, West Sussex · Miss Turner, lithograph (after drawing by B. R. Haydon), BM

Sharp, William (1805–1896), physician and homoeopathist, third son and fifth child of Richard Sharp, merchant, and his wife, Mary Turton, was born at Armley, near Leeds, on 21 January 1805. His family had lived in that neighbourhood and at Horton, near Bradford, for several generations. One relation was John Sharp (1645?–1714), archbishop of York; another was Abraham Sharp (*bap.* 1653, *d.* 1742), the astronomer and mathematician. William Sharp was educated at Wakefield grammar school from 1813 to 1816, and at Westminster School, London, from 1817 to 1820.

Originally destined for the church, Sharp was articled in 1821 to his uncle, William Sharp, a leading surgeon in Bradford. He subsequently served a part of his apprenticeship with his uncle's cousin, William Hey of Leeds. Sharp went to London to complete his training at Guy's and St Thomas's hospitals. In 1826 he obtained the licence of the Society of Apothecaries, and in 1827 he was admitted a member of the Royal College of Surgeons. He spent a year in Paris at the Sorbonne before returning to Bradford to assist his uncle, to whose practice he succeeded in 1833. Sharp was elected a surgeon to the Bradford Infirmary in 1829, and became its senior surgeon in 1837; for many years he also had the largest general practice in the West Riding of Yorkshire. In 1856 the degree of MD was conferred upon him by the archbishop of Canterbury.

During the winter of 1838–9 Sharp gave a course of scientific lectures, which were so successful that he proposed the revival of the Bradford Philosophical Society, originally formed by Joseph Priestley. He was elected as the first president of the new society, whose principal aim was the formation of a local museum, a subject in which Sharp had a particular interest. The museum which was eventually opened in Bradford was the first of its kind in the country. A paper read to the Birmingham meeting of the British Association on the subject of local museums led to Sharp's election as FRS on 7 May 1840.

In 1843 Sharp left Bradford for Hull, where he lived until 1847. He then moved to Rugby so that his sons could attend Rugby School. Sharp convinced Dr Tait, the headmaster, of the value of the teaching of natural science. As a result he was appointed as the school's first 'reader in natural philosophy'. He thus became the first teacher of science in a public school, setting the example which other schools followed. He resigned the post in 1850, to devote himself more exclusively to medical research.

At the suggestion of his friend Dr Ramsbotham of Leeds,

Sharp next studied homoeopathy, and two years later adopted its methods. While he accepted the basic principle of 'like cures like' he had little time for Samuel Hahnemann, the founder of homoeopathy. Many of his contemporaries were unable to accept Hahnemann's explanatory theories but Sharp went much farther. In his *Letter to Sir Benjamin Brodie* (1861) he described Hahnemann as 'a visionary, unscientific mind', and in his essay entitled *Organopathy* (1867) he stated that 'Homoeopathy, as represented by Hahnemann, is vague, indefinite and unproved'. For Sharp, disease was local. He rejected Hahnemann's proposal that most disease was a general condition and concluded that Hahnemann's drug provings had accumulated numerous unnecessary symptoms. According to Sharp, drugs must affect the same organs as the disease affects. This, he said, was 'organopathy'. His alleged discovery that drugs in different doses caused different therapeutic effects gave rise to the allied method of 'antipraxy'. Both these systems were described in Sharp's *Essays on Medicine* (1874–80). In 1873 Sharp presided at the British Homoeopathic Congress, but his address, which focused on his own ideas, was virulently criticized when reported in the *British Journal of Homoeopathy*.

By his own account Sharp played an important part in preventing the inclusion, in the Medical Act of 1858, of proposals that would have prevented the registration of homoeopathic doctors. He wrote brilliantly in defence of homoeopathy but could not avoid including in that defence his own personal theories. Whether by accident or by design, he ignored the work of most homoeopaths who had practised before him. He seemed to regard himself as the saviour of homoeopathy, as if nothing significant had happened before his arrival in 1852.

Sharp retired from practice in 1877. He continued to write tracts on homoeopathy, which finally totalled sixty-three works, the first twenty-four of which were collected and published in his *Essays on Medicine*. He also learned Hebrew in order to study the Bible in its original. When the Revised Version was published he submitted several criticisms which were accepted by the editors.

Sharp was married in 1833 to Anne (1811–1834), daughter of the botanist Samuel *Hailstone (1767–1851). After her death he married on 10 March 1836 Emma, sixth daughter of John *Scott, vicar of St Mary's, Hull [*see under* Scott, Thomas]. Sharp died at 4 South Parade, Llandudno, Wales, while on a visit to Llandudno, on 10 April 1896, and was buried at Llan-rhos cemetery.

Sharp's claim to recognition rests on his encouragement of the teaching of science in schools and for the establishment of local museums. His medical theories were not accepted by the homoeopathic medical community of his time and have passed into oblivion. His apparent view of himself as the saviour of homoeopathy, and indeed of medicine, appears to reflect a personality similar to that which he criticized in Hahnemann. It is regrettable that the energies of one who had so much to contribute were sometimes so sadly misdirected.

Bernard Leary

Sources *The Times* (12 April 1896) · *Bradford Observer* (11 April 1896) · *Homoeopathic World* (1 May 1896) · *Meteor* (1896) [Rugby School magazine] · *British Journal of Homoeopathy*, 9–13 (1851–5) · private information (1997) [the prebendary, Bradford Cathedral] · W. Cudworth, *Bradford Infirmary: a sketch of the history of the institution* (1880) · W. Scruton, *Report of the Bradford Philosophical Society*, 25 (1889–1900) · J. A. R. Bickford and M. E. Bickford, *The medical profession in Hull* (1983) · E. Edwards, *Report of Rugby School Natural History Society* [n.d.] · J. James, *The history and topography of Bradford* (1841) · S. C. Scott, *Things that were* (1923) · W. Cudworth, *Rambles round Horton* (1886) · *DNB*
Archives BL · Glasgow Homoeopathic Hospital, Faculty of Homoeopathy Library
Likenesses T. Richmond, oils, 1840; formerly in possession of Mrs Sharp, 1897 · W. Daniell, etching (after G. Dance), Wellcome L.
Wealth at death £54,811 11s. 1d.: probate, 30 April 1896, *CGPLA Eng. & Wales*

Sharp, William [*pseud.* Fiona MacLeod] (1855–1905), novelist and mystic, was born at Paisley on 12 September 1855, the eldest child of David Galbraith Sharp (d. 1876), textile manufacturer, and his wife, Katherine, daughter of William Brooks, Swedish vice-consul at Glasgow (her family was of Swedish descent). Sharp was from the beginning an unusual and distinctive child, sharing from an early age his father's love of the west highlands: in the early 1870s Sharp claimed to have 'sailed up every loch, fjord and inlet in the Western Highlands and Isles' (Alaya, 19). He was educated at Blair Lodge Academy, Polmont, and from 1867 at Glasgow Academy. Gifted at languages, in 1871 he entered Glasgow University, where he came under the influence of the charismatic professor of English, John Nichol. Sharp stayed at Glasgow for only two years, however, and in 1874 was apprenticed to a lawyer's office in the city, shortly after an interlude of three months' travelling with a troupe of Gypsies.

The death of his father in August 1876 precipitated a breakdown in Sharp's health, and he was sent to Australia to recuperate. This was to prove an imaginatively fruitful period. After his return from Australia, Sharp went to London in 1878 to work for the Melbourne Bank, but his irregular attendance helped to curtail his banking career, which ended in 1881. In the same year he gained an introduction to Dante Gabriel Rossetti from Sir Noël Paton, who had once been a pattern designer in the Sharp family firm in Paisley. Sharp was able to gain a temporary post at the Fine Art Society's gallery in Bond Street, but when this ended he was in difficulties. In 1882 he published three books, *Dante Gabriel Rossetti: a Record and a Study*, *Pictorialism in Verse*, and his first volume of poetry, *The Human Inheritance*. Though these attracted some notice, Sharp none the less remained in financial difficulties, and was saved from a fantasy of enlisting in the army by a combination of £40 from *Harper's Magazine* and a gift of £200 from a friend of his grandfather's, given on the recommendation of Sir Noël Paton (this latter enabled him to visit Italy for five months). The quality of Sharp's character was also important to his eventual success: his pluck, presence, and sense of address, combined with his blonde hair and (later) beard and height of more than 6 feet, won him an entrance at many editorial offices.

William Sharp [Fiona MacLeod] (1855–1905), by Frederick Hollyer

By 1883 Sharp had been appointed London art critic of the *Glasgow Herald*, and his rise into the literary coterie of London continued: in these years he made the acquaintance of Swinburne, Morris, Pater, Browning, Meredith, William Bell Scott, Ford Madox Brown, and Holman Hunt. A decade of rewarding literary hack work began. By 1885 Sharp was employed by Eric Robertson of the Great Writers series to work on biographies of Shelley, Heine, and Browning. Sharp was also a contributor to Ernest Rhys's Camelot Classics, the art critic for the *Art Journal* as well as the *Herald*, and an editor in the Canterbury Poets series (he edited about a dozen volumes in this and the Camelot series). Under the burdens of such success he began to suffer from the strain inherent in suppressing his visionary, fantastic self. In the 1890s, as the direction of his life changed, Sharp passed on some of his critical work to his wife.

After a nine-year relationship Sharp married his first cousin, Elizabeth Amelia Sharp (1856–1932), in 1884. They had no children. A writer herself, Elizabeth Sharp published books on art and music history, translated Heine, and was the editor of *Women Poets of the Victorian Era* (1890). She was the daughter of Sharp's father's elder brother Thomas, and Agnes Farquharson, daughter of Robert Farquharson, sometime provost of Paisley. Husband and wife collaborated to some extent, most notably on *Lyra Celtica* (1896). Sharp continued to suffer from ill health, although ill health had a tendency to stimulate his imagination:

while bedridden in 1886 he had a 'psychic experience'. Always a sufferer from nerves in public, in 1889 he withdrew his application for a chair in literature at University College, London, on medical advice.

In 1890 Sharp took a trip through Europe and developed or completed a feeling of deep dislike towards city living. He had visited Italy before, but it was his experience on this visit which deeply changed his perception: it seems almost to have been a Forsterian awakening, and was undoubtedly connected with a woman whom he met in Italy, Mrs Edith Wingate Rinder, a Celticist and translator of Breton folk tales, who spent three weeks with the Sharps at Rome. Sharp seems to have become at least emotionally involved with her, and she appears to have been the wellspring for the emergence of Fiona MacLeod, who began to take form in his mind in 1891. Sharp stayed in Rome from December 1890 to March 1891, and after his stay produced a book of poetry, *Sospiri di Roma*, which was privately printed at Anzio in 1891. Its free verse and free themes marked a new departure for Sharp: in point of verse form, in fact, it was pioneering work, cited alongside Walt Whitman and W. E. Henley by Richard Burton in 1894. One of its most frequently anthologized pieces, 'The White Peacock', probably gave D. H. Lawrence the title for his first novel, and it is possible that Sharp's free verse was also an influence on Lawrence.

By the end of 1891 Sharp was back in London, but his personal as well as his literary mode had changed: the Sharps moved to Phenice Croft at Rudgwick in Sussex in 1892, and although they only used this cottage for two years, Sharp was never again regularly resident in London, resuming instead a wandering life which in the next four years took him to the USA (where in 1892 he met Walt Whitman), Paris (where he made the acquaintance of many of the *décadents* and *symbolistes*), Algeria, Tunisia, Iona, Edinburgh, and Venice. In 1892, he edited (and indeed entirely composed under a variety of pseudonyms) *The Pagan Review*, one of the chief texts of the 'new paganism' of the 1890s. Its cover bore the motto '*Sic transit gloria Grundi*', and in it Sharp called for 'a new inwardness to withdraw from life the approved veils of convention'. Within a year, this 'new inwardness' had risen to the surface.

In *The Pagan Review* Sharp argued against discriminating between men and women, in language suggestive of the fraying of the boundaries of sex themselves. Sharp himself was shortly to attempt to prove the presence of a woman within by developing the persona of Fiona MacLeod, who in large part took over his imaginative life from 1893 on. Her surname may derive from Seamus Macleod, an old fisherman Sharp had known as a boy, while her first name was the feminized form of Fionn/Fingal/Finn, the ancient Gaelic 'sleeping hero' of whom it was reputed in some traditions that he would, like Arthur, wake again to save his people. The feminization of this figure was symbolically appropriate to the 'Celtic twilight' vision of the Gaeltacht which Sharp sought to create, where the highlands were the repository of an ancient but fading wisdom, both beautiful and supine, a vision he shared with

Matthew Arnold, but which was vigorously rebutted by W. B. Yeats. Sharp's own view in *Lyra Celtica* that Yeats was too 'clear-sighted' to be Irish 'at the expense of being English in the high and best sense of the word' (p. 51), clearly indicates the gap between them. Sharp's first production as Fiona MacLeod was the novel *Pharais*, which appeared in 1894 and was dedicated to Edith Wingate Rinder. The production of the female persona of Fiona seems to have caused Sharp frequent ill health, culminating in a near total breakdown in 1897–8; moreover, he had a feeling of being haunted by past lives. The Jungian doctrines of archetype and the collective unconscious suggest themselves in examining Sharp's imagination, particularly the powerful anima of Fiona which emerged in his consciousness in the 1890s, peaking in 1894–6, and which he projected onto the scenes and interests of his childhood. His wife developed an understanding of Sharp's creative duality, which she defended elaborately in her 1910 biography of the poet: her pet name for him was Wilfion.

Fiona MacLeod's début was succeeded by a spate of activity. In the autumn of 1894 Sharp went to Edinburgh, where he collapsed after delivering the first of a series of lectures at the university but none the less made his influence felt. Together with Patrick Geddes he headed the *Evergreen* circle which was, among other things, concerned with developing a distinctive and renewed Scottish Celticism in the context of recapturing Edinburgh's status as a metropolis of European stature. Two Fiona MacLeod novels, *The Mountain Lovers* and *The Sin Eater*, appeared in 1895, the latter being published by Patrick Geddes and Colleagues, a firm established to publish literature in support of the Celtic revival; Sharp was its literary adviser. In 1896 Sharp further contributed to this renewal by publishing an edition of Macpherson's *Ossian*, and on a visit to Ireland in 1897 met George Russell, Lady Gregory, Standish O'Grady, Edward Martin, and Douglas Hyde. By this stage Yeats, initially hostile but afterwards friendly, was becoming irritated by the Scottish writer's verbiage and vagueness; in *Autobiographies* he commented that Sharp 'never told one anything that was true; the facts of life disturbed him and were forgotten' (p. 341). Perhaps, as hinted in a letter of Sharp's of 30 April 1898, Yeats also guessed at the Fiona Macleod deception. The fact that Fiona Macleod declined to lend her name to the political side of the Celtic movement was also irritating to the Irish writers.

Sharp continued to write productively under his own name; he needed the money, for his wife was unable to earn anything from her art criticism while on their frequent travels. In 1898 Sharp suffered a total nervous collapse, and thenceforward made frequent visits to the Mediterranean to recuperate. The struggle of the 1880s which had imposed the literary opportunist on the passive visionary was now succeeded by a mental struggle to maintain both the Sharp and MacLeod identities. Sharp constructed an elaborate series of deceptions, implicit and explicit, to maintain his secret: he even contributed a fictional entry for Fiona MacLeod to *Who's Who*. On 28 January 1899 an unsigned article in the *Daily Chronicle* suggested that Sharp and MacLeod were one and the same. Sharp wrote a disclaimer, but a further embarrassment arose in 1902, when he had to decline being put forward for a civil-list pension on the basis of Fiona MacLeod's work. Fortunately for Sharp the prime minister, Arthur Balfour, accepted a verbal assurance from Sharp, which obviated the need for the identity of Fiona to be made public.

Sharp's health continued to fail, and he died in Alcantara, Sicily, at Castle Maniace, the home of his friend the duke of Bronte, on 12 December 1905. His wife survived him. He left a letter to his friends disclosing his identity as Fiona Macleod. Sharp was buried in a woodland cemetery on the hillside at Alcantara two days later. 'An Iona cross, carved in lava' (Sharp, 419), was set above the grave with an inscription of the writer's own choosing.

Sharp wrote or edited almost forty books in his own name, as well as more than ten as Fiona MacLeod. As Sharp his work is all but forgotten, though the free verse is of recognized 'literary-historical importance' (Fletcher, 485). As Fiona MacLeod he created an especially intense vision of a doomed and marginal Celticism, which not only has an appeal by virtue of its distinctive prose and visionary emotionalism, but also through its influence on the twentieth-century Scottish novel, notably the work of Neil Gunn.   MURRAY G. H. PITTOCK

Sources E. A. Sharp, *William Sharp (Fiona MacLeod): a memoir* (1910) · F. Alaya, *William Sharp—'Fiona MacLeod', 1855–1905* (1970) · W. B. Yeats, *Memoirs*, ed. D. Donoghue (1972) · K. Hopkins and R. van Roekel, *William Sharp/Fiona MacLeod: a biographical sketch* (1977) · C. Manlove, *Scottish fantasy literature* (1994) · R. J. Finneran and others, eds., *Letters to W. B. Yeats*, 1 (1977) · W. B. Yeats, *Uncollected prose*, ed. J. P. Frayne, 2 vols. (1970–75), vol. 1 · M. G. H. Pittock, *Spectrum of decadence: the literature of the 1890s* (1993) · I. Fletcher, ed., *British poetry and prose, 1870–1905* (1987) · W. B. Yeats, *Autobiographies* (1956) · *The collected letters of W. B. Yeats*, 1, ed. J. Kelly and E. Domville (1986)

Archives Hunt. L., letters and literary MSS · Morgan L., literary papers · NL Scot., corresp. and literary papers · U. Cal., Berkeley, papers | NL Scot., letters to Patrick Geddes · NL Scot., collected letters, mainly to John Macleay · TCD, letters to Edwin Dowden · U. Leeds, Brotherton L., letters to Theodore Watts-Dunton · U. Reading L., letters to George Bell and Sons

Likenesses photograph, 1883, repro. in Sharp, *William Sharp* · C. Ross, pastel drawing, 1891, repro. in Sharp, *William Sharp* · W. Strangard, etching, 1896, Renfrew District Museums; repro. in Sharp, *William Sharp* · D. A. Wehrschmidt, oils, 1898, Scot. NPG · A. N. Hood, photograph, 1903, repro. in Sharp, *William Sharp*, 358 · F. Hollyer, photograph, Royal Photographic Society, Bath [*see illus.*] · W. Strang, etching, BM · W. Strang, metalpoint drawing, BM, NPG

Wealth at death £378: probate, 5 March 1906, *CGPLA Eng. & Wales*

Sharpe, Bartholomew (*b. c.*1652), buccaneer, born in Wapping of unknown parents, gave his age in 1682 as about thirty. He claimed to have served under Henry Morgan in the sacking of Panama in 1671. He seems also to have been among those who destroyed Porto Bello in 1679. In an attempt to repeat Morgan's earlier feat, Sharpe and some 330 buccaneers landed on the coast of Darien on 5 April 1680 with the aim of crossing the isthmus and sacking

Panama for a second time. This small army included what might now be described as a 'press corps': Basil Ringrose, whose journal was printed as the second volume of Exquemelin's *Bucaniers of America* (1685), William Dampier, author of *New Voyage Round the World* (1697), and Lionel Wafer, surgeon and author of *A New Voyage and Description of the Isthmus of America* (1699). Two lesser figures also left eyewitness narrative accounts relating to the expedition.

The Indians who led the buccaneers through the forest persuaded them to undertake a preliminary attack on the Spanish settlement at Santa Maria, where great quantities of gold were reputed to be stockpiled. After the attack on Santa Maria on 15 April, which yielded no gold, the buccaneers made their own way, on foot and in canoes, to the port of Panama. On 25 April they surprised a fleet of three ships and 280 Spaniards and took possession of several armed vessels, a coup which offered scope to conduct unlimited operations. After two large-scale defections, Sharpe was elected overall commander on 28 May. With a force reduced to 140 men, and on board a single vessel, the *Trinity*, Sharpe spent the next eighteen months scouring the coast for prizes. On 28 October he attempted an opposed landing on the Chilean coast at Port Ilo, near Arica, before sailing southwards as far as the 30th parallel. On 3 December a raid ashore was repelled by a large force of about 250 Spanish cavalry. On 4 December, despite stiff opposition, the buccaneers entered the town of Coquimbo where an attempt to extort 100,000 pieces of eight from the governor failed, forcing them to withdraw.

Sharpe now made for Juan Fernandez to resupply before attempting a voyage home through the Strait of Magellan, but the decision to return caused a mutiny and Sharpe was put in irons. On 28 January the *Trinity* loomed off Arica for a second time and a hundred men disembarked to attack the town. This time the buccaneers were repulsed by a force of more than 600. After the battle twenty-seven buccaneers lay dead and the remainder withdrew to the *Trinity's* waiting boats. Sharpe was quickly reinstalled as commander. On 28 July 1681, in what are now Equadorian waters, Sharpe overhauled the Spanish vessel *Rosario*. During the struggle Sharpe shot the captain, John Lopez, and seized a book which the Spaniards were about to heave overboard. On examination the book was found to be a *derrotero*, or waggoner; a secret collection of charts and pilotage directions detailing coastal features and all the anchorages from California to Cape Horn. The *Rosario* also carried another treasure: she was smuggling a large quantity of silver, coated in tin to avoid duty. Sharpe's subsequent claim that he was unable to persuade his crew to transfer the contraband into the *Trinity* seems unlikely. He and his crew were probably just ignorant of what lay in the hold. Accordingly, they cut the vessel and her silver adrift. Their error was discovered only when one of the bars, taken as a souvenir, was examined in England.

The *Trinity* now remained at sea almost continuously until the second week of October when, after days of heavy storms, Sharpe sighted the mountains of southern Chile and sheltered in a coastal inlet. On 6 November he sailed for the straits but a great storm on the 12th pushed him far south of his intended track. He had no option but to weather the Horn instead, becoming the first English captain to do so in an easterly direction. On 20 November the *Trinity* reached her most southerly position, 57°40′ S, where she steered among icebergs. In sailing so far south Sharpe was able to prove that *terra australis incognito* was a fiction and this constitutes his greatest achievement. In one manuscript copy of his journal the entry for 28 November 1681 reads:

> in this my passage about Terra del Fuogo I sailed in near 60 degrees south lattitude therefore doe find by experience that there is no such a tract of land as the dutch call Terra australis incognito and that which lies to the eastward of the straghts of Le maire which the Dutch call staten land I found to be an Isle the which I named Albemarle Island & I being the first that ever sailed about all this way doe call the passage after my own name. (Sharpe's journal, Pierpont Morgan Library, MA 3310)

By 26 January 1682 favourable winds allowed the ship to cover distances of up to 132 miles a day. Barbados was sighted on 28 January but the presence of the English warship *Richmond* forced the buccaneers to steer for Nevis. From here, most of the crew took passage to England, Sharpe arriving in Plymouth on or about 24 March.

On 10 June 1682 Sharpe and two of his crew were indicted on charges of piracy and murder in the high court of Admiralty. The charges were instigated by the Spanish ambassador to London, Don Pedro Ronquillo, who also acted as chief prosecutor. Evidence that Charles II tampered with the trial in order to obtain an illicit copy of the *derrotero* and to spare Sharpe's life probably explains the court's decision to acquit the defendants on a technicality. The verdict caused a minor diplomatic incident with Spain.

After his trial Sharpe was appointed captain of his majesty's sloop *Bonetta* by the Admiralty. He never took up his command. According to one source he bought a leaky vessel moored in the Thames which he used to board a French vessel near the Downs. In this prize he returned to the Caribbean, appearing in the Leeward Islands with a commission to hunt down pirates in January 1684, and later in Bermuda, where he ingratiated himself with the governor, Richard Coney. In July 1686 the governor of Nevis sent the frigate *Dartmouth* to Bermuda to bring Sharpe to justice for acts of piracy in Jamaica (1684) and Campeachy (1686). Sharpe stood trial in Nevis on 30 December, and again on 12 February 1687, but he wriggled free both times. In 1688 he appeared in Anguilla, having declared himself governor.

By 1696 Sharpe had settled on the island of St Thomas, acquiring a smallholding and seven slaves. He seems to have married, and to have had a son. By 1698 he was heavily in debt and, in an attempt to evade his creditors, Sharpe made an arrangement with Captain Garwey, commander of a visiting English vessel, to leave the island secretly. Tipped off by the slaves, the Danish authorities arrested Sharpe on the night of 10 May 1698 as he loaded his chattels into the launch sent to meet him. Swearing to avenge himself upon the island as a whole Sharpe was sentenced to life imprisonment. His wife and son were held in custody in the fort. The governor, J. Lorentz, tried to have Sharpe transferred to Bremerholm prison in Copenhagen but permission was denied. Sharpe's wife died on 30 October 1698, and the boy died on 12 December. Sharpe was still captive in the fort on St Thomas in 1699. About this time he was described as being lame, and without the use of his hands.   JAMES WILLIAM KELLY

Sources copy of Bartholomew Sharpe's journal (possibly holograph), 1683, priv. coll. [formerly known as lot 245 in Christies sale, 13–14 June 1979] • a copy of Sharpe's journal, c.1685, BL, Sloane MS 46A • a copy of Sharpe's journal, 1683, BL, Sloane MS 46B • a copy of Sharpe's journal, c.1684, Pepys Library, Cambridge, MS 2610 • a copy of Sharpe's journal, c.1684–6, Pepys Library, Cambridge, MS 2874 • B. Sharpe, copy of journal, c.1695, Morgan L., MA 3310 • a copy of Sharpe's journal, c.1698, Naval History Library, Taunton, MS 4 • W. Hack, presentation copy of *derrotero* for Charles II, BL, K. Mar. VIII 15 (7 TAB 123) • B. Ringrose, 'South sea waggoner', [n.d., in or before 1682–1683], NMM, P.32 • B. Ringrose, 'Journal', holograph, [n.d., in or before 1683], BL, Sloane 3820 • indictments against Sharpe, PRO, HCA 1/11, 102, 102 • verdicts, PRO, HCA 1/11, 103 • Sharpe's evidence before the Admiralty Court, PRO, HCA 1/5, fols. 183–4 • report from J. Lorentz to the managing board of the West Indian Guinea Company, 24 June 1698, Danish National Archives, Vestindisk-Guinesisk Kompani, V-gK. 89–90 • notices 1698–1702; notes by the commandant of Christian's fort dated 30/10/1698 and 12/12/1698, Danish National Archives, V-gK. 501 • *The voyages and adventures of Capt. Barth. Sharpe and others in the south sea* (1684) • W. Dampier, *A new voyage round the world* (1697) • B. Ringrose, *Bucaniers of America: the second volume, containing the dangerous voyage and bold attempts of Captain Bartholomew Sharp and others* (1685) • W. Hacke, ed., *A collection of original voyages* (1699) • L. Wafer, *A new voyage and description of the isthmus of America* (1699) • unpublished biographical description of a Spanish *derrotero* sold at auction at Christies, 13–14 June 1979, as lot 175 (possibly the original document taken by Sharpe from the *Rosario*) • parish records, St Dunstan and All Saints', Stepney, LMA, P93/DUN/257 • D. Howse and N. J. W. Thrower, eds., *A buccaneer's atlas: Basil Ringrose's atlas, Basil Ringrose's South Sea waggoner* (Berkeley, CA, 1992) • G. Williams, *The great South Sea: English voyages and encounters, 1570–1750* (1997) • C. Lloyd, 'Bartholomew Sharpe, buccaneer', *Mariner's Mirror*, 42 (1956), 291–301 • P. T. Bradley, 'Sharp and company: the first of the buccaneers, 1679–82', *The lure of Peru: maritime intrusion into the south sea, 1598–1701* (1989), 103–28 • E. Lynham, 'William Hack and the south sea buccaneers', *The mapmaker's art: essays on the history of maps* (1953) • T. R. Adams, 'William Hack's manuscript atlases of "The great south sea of America"', *Annual Report* [John Carter Brown Library] (1965–6), 45–52 • A. Campbell, 'The Drapers' Company and its school of seventeenth-century chart-makers', *My head is a map: essays and memoirs in honour of R. V. Tooley*, ed. H. Wallis and S. Tyacke (1973), 81–99 • G. Williams, '"The inexhaustible fountain of gold": English projects and ventures in the south seas, 1670–1750', *Perspectives of empire: essays presented to Gerald S. Graham*, ed. J. E. Flint and G. Williams (1973), 27–52

Archives BL, journals, Sloane MSS 46A, 46B [copies] • Magd. Cam., MSS 2610, 2874 • Morgan L., MA 3310 • Naval History Library, Taunton, MS 4

Wealth at death one slave: archives of Danish colonial administration on St Thomas; *Dansk Vestindien indtil 1755* (Copenhagen, 1966), vol. 1 of *Vore gamle tropekolonier*, ed. J. Brøndsted, 2nd edn, 156–7

Sharpe, Charles Kirkpatrick (1781–1851), antiquary and collector, was born at Hoddam (or Hoddom) near Dumfries on 15 May 1781, the third son and seventh child of Charles Sharpe of Hoddam (c.1738–1813) and Eleanora

Charles Kirkpatrick Sharpe (1781–1851), by David Octavius Hill and Robert Adamson [seated, with an unknown companion]

Renton (1748–1836), daughter of John Renton of Lammerton. In February 1796 he went to Edinburgh for his education, and from October in that year he attended Professor John Robison's class at the university. He left Edinburgh in May 1798, and after a short period at home, went up to Christ Church, Oxford, where he matriculated on 22 November, before graduating BA on 17 June 1802, and proceeding MA on 28 January 1806. Sharpe's education was to have fitted him for a living in the Church of England, but he seems never to have pursued this line with enthusiasm, perhaps because his high-pitched voice was unsuited to the pulpit. After graduation he divided his time between London, Oxford, and Hoddam, but after the death of his father in 1813 he settled with his mother at the family's house at 93 Princes Street, Edinburgh. After her death in August 1836 he lived for a while at 19 West Nicolson Street until, on his eldest brother's death in February 1845, he succeeded to Hoddam, and moved to 28 Drummond Place. He never married, and does not appear to have left Edinburgh or its immediate vicinity between 1813 and his death at home in Drummond Place on 17 March 1851. He was buried at Hoddam.

Sharpe's significance lies in his antiquarian and other intellectual pursuits. As a child he had listened to ballads and songs in Dumfriesshire. His father had known Burns, though Sharpe's acquaintance seems to have been limited to seeing him at a theatre in Dumfries in October 1792. When Walter Scott's *Minstrelsy of the Scottish Border* appeared in 1802, Sharpe immediately sent him copies of 'The Twa Corbies' and 'The Douglas Tragedy'. Scott visited Sharpe in Oxford that year, and though each man was alive to the other's weaknesses (and Sharpe could be extremely unkind about those who tried to help him), they remained on good terms until Scott's death. Scott invited him to collaborate in the *Edinburgh Review*, but he refused 'not only on account of my profound ignorance respecting modern political transactions, but because my style is at least one hundred good years behind that of most people both in strength and eloquence' (NL Scot., MS 3876, fol. 155). However he wrote some poetry, and published *Metrical Legends and other Poems* in 1807—though, in Scott's words in his *Journal*, 'as a poet he has not a very strong touch'—and he edited ballads. *A Ballad Book* appeared in 1823 and *Surgundo, or, The Valiant Christian* in 1837.

In prose Sharpe preferred Richardson and Fielding to Scott, whose writing he criticized on both literary and antiquarian grounds, though later in life he both admired and encouraged Harrison Ainsworth. In 1808 he wrote a play of which Scott approved, and 'will certainly endeavour to get it acted', he wrote to his sister Isabella, 'but do not whisper one word of it to any mortal, for if it be damned I must never confess myself the author' (Bodl. Oxf., MS Eng. misc. c. 38, fol. 151). He felt himself secure only on antiquarian subjects, and this is where his literary reputation rests. He edited James Kirkton's *Secret and True History of the Church of Scotland* in 1817, with elaborate notes. His introduction to Robert Law's *Memorials* (1818), written at Scott's suggestion and with the use of his library, remains to this day a standard history of witchcraft in Scotland. His editorial work for the Bannatyne Club is of a high quality. His historical interests led him into a number of byways. Witchcraft, female criminality, and historical gossip were supported by an exceptional knowledge of the sixteenth- and seventeenth-century sources. In his copy of Douglas's *Peerage* (1764), now at the Royal Library, Windsor, more than half the entries are corrected or expanded by his annotations. Occasionally these are coloured by his high-tory views and his taste for marital scandal, but for the most part he gives authority for what he says. As a display of learning it is astonishing. This learning was available to anyone who asked for it, including Robert Chambers, for whose *Traditions of Edinburgh* (1824–5) he was extremely helpful. He also collaborated with the antiquaries Thomas Thomson and David Laing.

Sharpe was a draughtsman and painter of more than amateur skill. While at Oxford he produced portraits of his contemporaries (mostly in seventeenth-century dress); his drawing of 'Queen Elizabeth dancing before Melville' caused 'inextinguishable laughter' (J. G. Lockhart, *Life of Scott*, 1882, 3.163) when it was received by Scott in December 1808; and his caricature of Madame de Staël, whom he met in London in 1813, is unflatteringly accurate. He subsequently illustrated several Bannatyne Club publications as well as some of his own work. Scott tried unsuccessfully to have him appointed king's limner in Scotland.

Sharpe was also a musician. Like his father, he played the fiddle, and at Oxford took piano lessons. His musical library included early printed works, with material he had inherited from his father, acquired from the Edinburgh Musical Society (including the catalogue of its library of orchestral works), or bought. The emphasis is on Handel and the early eighteenth century, and the collection includes Mrs Crokat's music book (1709) (recorded in Grove's *Dictionary* as long untraced) and music by the earl of Kellie, a selection of whose *Minuets* he published in 1836. He was also a noted collector. While still at Oxford he was given Lely's portrait of the duchess of Portsmouth. In 1802 he told his mother that he must leave his college lodgings. 'I shall begin then to pack off my knick knacks for Scotland. … You will be overwhelmed with swinging great boxes and charmed with my Nell Gwynn and Lady Aston' (Bodl. Oxf., MS Eng. misc. c. 38, fol. 25). At his death he owned a very considerable number of portraits, including *Margaret Tudor* by Holbein, Hogarth's *Sarah Malcolm*, Kneller's *Duchess of Marlborough*, and twelve previously in Kellie Castle. He also owned pictures by Breughel, Cranach, Van Eyck, Giorgione, Raeburn, Rembrandt, Reynolds, and Rosa. He acquired, from the hoard of twelfth-century ivory chessmen found around 1830 on Lewis, the eleven pieces now in the Royal Museums of Scotland. He was never a rich man, but he bought with care, and his known taste for historical objects ensured that much was offered to him. His collection was dispersed at his death, either in two sales which lasted in total nearly a fortnight, or to various beneficiaries under his will. It was one of the great private collections of nineteenth-century Scotland, but while it was similar in nature to Scott's, Sharpe's exceptional connoisseurship ensured that the quality of the individual pieces he had gathered was greatly superior.

Sharpe lived in and for the past. His clothing throughout his life was that of the Oxford undergraduate of the early nineteenth century; his tastes in music, literature, and gossip remained firmly in the mid-eighteenth; and his relationships with others were conducted in a style long outmoded. But his scholarship was real. In the words of his obituarist in *The Scotsman*, his knowledge was like his taste, 'a thing perfect in itself. Whatever might be its limits it was complete and faultless within them' (NL Scot., MS 2511, fol. 3). PATRICK CADELL

Sources C. K. Sharpe, letters and papers, Bodl. Oxf., MS Eng. misc. c. 38 • NL Scot., Sharpe MSS • NL Scot., MS 2511, fol. 3 • *The Scotsman* (1851) • W. K. R. Bedford, introduction, in *Letters from and to Charles Kirkpatrick Sharpe*, ed. A. Allardyce, 2 vols. (1888) • *Catalogue of the collection … of objects of virtu, prints, etchings, and drawings, of … Charles Kirkpatrick Sharpe* (1851) [sale catalogue, C. B. Tait and T. Nisbet, Edinburgh, 12 June 1851] • *GM*, 2nd ser., 35 (1851), 557 • *The journal of Sir Walter Scott*, ed. W. E. K. Anderson (1972)
Archives Bodl. Oxf., corresp. and literary papers • Edinburgh Central Reference Library, notes on portraits in Scottish houses • Mitchell L., Glas., genealogical notes • NA Scot., corresp. • NA Scot., notebook • NL Scot., corresp. and papers | Edinburgh Central Reference Library, papers relating to Burke and Hare • NL Scot., corresp. with Blackwoods • NL Scot., letters to Robert Chambers • NL Scot., letters to Sir Walter Scott • Northants. RO, Sharpe Music

Collection, Boughton House music 1–115 · U. Edin., letters to David Laing
Likenesses T. Fraser, oils, *c*.1805, Scot. NPG · C. K. Sharpe, wash drawing, *c*.1805 (after T. Fraser), Scot. NPG · C. K. Sharpe, self-portrait, caricature, drawing, 1831, repro. in C. K. Sharpe, *Etchings* (1869) · D. O. Hill, calotype, *c*.1843, repro. in C. K. Sharpe, *Etchings* (1869) · D. O. Hill and R. Adamson, photograph, NPG [*see illus.*] · J. Irvine, oils, Scot. NPG
Wealth at death £1533 6*s*. 11*d*.—heavily encumbered estate at Hoddam; house in Edinburgh; collection of antiquities: inventory, 30 May 1851, NA Scot., SC 70/1, vol. 72, p. 888

Sharpe, Charlotte (*c*.**1793–1849**). *See under* Sharpe, Louisa (*bap.* 1798, *d.* 1843).

Sharpe, Daniel (**1806–1856**), geologist and philologist, was born on 6 April 1806 at Nottingham Place, Marylebone, Middlesex, the youngest son of Sutton Sharpe (1756–1806), brewer, and his second wife, Maria (*d.* 1806), sister of the poet Samuel Rogers (1783–1855). Orphaned before his first birthday (his mother died on 22 April 1806, his father on 26 September), he was looked after in Stoke Newington by a half-sister, who also took in a sister and four brothers.

Sharpe was educated for two years at a school in Stoke Newington, and from the age of twelve at Mr Cogan's school in Walthamstow, where he obtained a knowledge of the classics. At sixteen he became a clerk in the counting-house of Van Zeller, a Portuguese merchant in London. When he was twenty-five, Sharpe entered into a partnership with his brother Henry at Pinner's Hall, Broad Street, which became the leading London house in the trade with Portugal. For a year about 1830 and from 1835 to 1838, Sharpe lived in Portugal, which he visited frequently on business.

Sharpe had a long-standing interest in natural history, and joined the Geological Society of London in 1827. Papers read before the Society from 1832 made use of his travels by describing Portuguese geology, which had hitherto been little known. In the 1840s he turned to the Lake District and north Wales, regions where the older rocks had already become the subject of controversy. Sharpe argued that all of the strata originally identified as belonging to Adam Sedgwick's 'Cambrian' were of the same age as Roderick Murchison's 'Silurian'. This had been suspected for some time on fossil grounds, but Sharpe's structural evidence for an equivalence was new. His brash self-confidence in trespassing on Sedgwick's territory led to puns about a 'sharp move' and the 'Sharp fellow', clear references to the fact that Sharpe spent his days in a counting-house.

During his research on the older rocks, Sharpe became involved in debates about slaty cleavage, which (as Sedgwick had shown) had to be distinguished from ordinary stratification. Sharpe proposed that this structure resulted, neither from crystallization nor from the force of upheaval, but from lateral pressure. He applied this theory in 1854 to some of the most vexed problems in alpine geology, particularly at Mont Blanc and the valley of Chamonix, where semi-crystalline schists appeared to alternate with younger Jurassic strata. In papers for the Royal Society and the Geological Society, he also tackled

Daniel Sharpe (**1806–1856**), by Maull & Polyblank, 1855

the complex geology of the Scottish highlands, and with George Bellas Greenough constructed a revised geological map of Scotland in 1852.

Sharpe's last paper was his most speculative. It argued that the Alps had been until fairly recently covered by the sea, which had left marks of its presence at a height of some 9000 feet. Sharpe thus ascribed to wave action most of the erosion that other geologists (following Louis Agassiz) attributed to glaciers. However, this bold extension of Robert Chambers's theory of ancient sea terraces won little support.

Unlike many geologists of the period, Sharpe identified his own fossils rather than sending them out to specialists. His first paper for the Geological Society in 1827 described a new species of ichthyosaurus, and he later became especially interested in invertebrate palaeontology. In 1846, together with John Morris, he identified shells collected from the Falkland Islands by Charles Darwin, and in 1848 he did the same for specimens collected by Charles Lyell during his travels in North America. In both cases Sharpe's results provided strong support for Murchison's concept of a globally valid Silurian fauna. At his death Sharpe was engaged in a monograph for the Palaeontographical Society on the fossil cephalopoda of the English Chalk.

Sharpe, who never married, became a familiar figure within metropolitan intellectual circles, especially through connections with his uncle Samuel Rogers and friendships made at the Geological Society. Known for his sarcastic wit, love of controversy, and philanthropic benevolence, for many years he served as secretary of the school for the poor in Harp Alley, Fleet Market. A keen student of ancient philology, Sharpe published an appendix on Lycian inscriptions and coins in Sir Charles Fellows's second account of his discoveries at Xanthus. Sharpe was elected a fellow of the Royal Society in 1850, and became Geological Society president in February 1856. He died a few months later on 31 May 1856 in his lodgings in Soho Square, having fractured his skull in a riding accident. He was buried at St John's Church, Hampstead.

J. A. SECORD

Sources J. E. Portlock, *Quarterly Journal of the Geological Society*, 13 (1857), xlv–lxiv • *PRS*, 8 (1856–7), 275–9 • *Literary Gazette* (7 June 1856), 351–2 • J. A. Secord, *Controversy in Victorian geology: the Cambrian–Silurian dispute* (1986) • *DNB*
Archives BGS, notebook • GS Lond., maps
Likenesses Maull & Polyblank, photograph, 1855, NPG [*see illus.*] • print (after photograph), BM

Sharpe, Edmund (1809–1877), architect and engineer, was born on 31 October 1809 at Brook Cottage, Brook Street, Knutsford, Cheshire, the only son of Francis and Martha Sharpe. He was educated locally, then at Dr Burney's school at Greenwich, Sedbergh School, and St John's College, Cambridge, where he graduated BA in 1833 and proceeded MA in 1836. In 1832 he was awarded a Worts travelling fellowship, which he devoted to the study of architecture, mainly in France and Germany, with a particular interest in Romanesque and early Gothic work. In 1835 he settled in Lancaster and practised as an architect for fifteen years. On 27 July 1843 he married Elizabeth Fletcher (*d.* 1876), sister of John Fletcher. They had three sons and two daughters.

Sharpe, along with his partner from 1845 (and former pupil), E. G. Paley, erected nearly forty new churches. Early on he often favoured a simplified Romanesque style, but the most famous works are a pair of all-terracotta Gothic churches at Lever Bridge, Bolton (1842–5), commissioned by his father-in-law, and Rusholme, Manchester (1845–6). He also undertook secular buildings, the most ambitious being Capernwray Hall, Lancashire (1844–7), the remodelling of Hornby Castle, Lancashire (1847–8), and Ince Hall, Cheshire (1847–9).

Sharpe's vigorous involvement in civic improvements established his reputation far beyond architecture: 'our excellent friend and fellow townsman' the *Lancaster Gazette* called him as early as 1840 (17 October 1840). A lifelong tory, he was elected to Lancaster council in 1841 and served as mayor for the year 1848–9, when he led the way for major sanitary improvements. In 1850 he purchased the Phoenix foundry in Lancaster and in 1851 withdrew from architecture, although the name Sharpe and Paley was retained by Paley until early 1856. From the 1830s he had been active in promoting railways and in 1856 he went to live at Coed-y-Celyn, near Betws-y-coed, Caernarvonshire, where he organized the building of the Conwy–Llanrwst Railway. In 1859 he was appointed JP for Lancashire, and for Denbighshire. From 1863, when the Conwy valley line opened, until 1866 Sharpe lived abroad, constructing a horse-drawn tramway in Geneva and the Perpignan–Prades railway in south-west France. Although he acquired iron mines and property there, in 1867 he returned to Lancaster.

Throughout his life Sharpe was an enthusiastic and profound student of medieval architecture, and he published several works on the subject, of which the first was *Architectural parallels, or, The progress of ecclesiastical architecture in England during the twelfth and thirteenth centuries* (1848). This was followed by: *Decorated Windows: a Series of Illustrations of the Window Tracery of the Decorated Style* (1849); *The Seven Periods of Architecture* (1851), in which he advocated a new system of nomenclature for the successive styles of medieval work; *The Mouldings of the Six Periods of British Architecture* (1874); *The Architecture of the Cistercians* (1874); and several others. His minor publications were numerous. In 1875 Sharpe received the gold medal of the Royal Institute of British Architects (he became a fellow in 1848) for his architectural writings. He was also a member of the Archaeological Institute of Great Britain and Ireland and contributed many papers to the proceedings of both organizations. In 1869 he joined the Architectural Association, which, during the next few years at his suggestion and under his guidance, made annual excursions for the study of Gothic architecture in Britain and France. An account of the last of these, *A Visit to the Domed Churches of Charente … in 1875*, with a memoir of Sharpe and a complete list of his publications, was drawn up and printed by the association in 1884 as a memorial. While collecting material for further writings, Sharpe died at Milan, after a brief illness, on 8 May 1877; he was buried at Lancaster cemetery.

F. M. O'DONOGHUE, *rev.* GEOFFREY K. BRANDWOOD

Sources R. Jolley, 'Edmund Sharpe (1809–77): a study of a Victorian architect', MA diss., U. Lpool, 1966 • 'Mr Edmund Sharpe', *Lancaster Guardian* (3 Jan 1910) • 'Memoir', *A visit to the domed churches of Charente, France, by the Architectural Association in the year 1875 …* (1884), i–xiv • [Lancaster newspapers] (1836–1914) • Venn, *Alum. Cant.* • *CGPLA Eng. & Wales* (1877) • private information (2004) [John M. Hughes]
Likenesses likeness, repro. in *Lancaster Guardian* • woodcut, repro. in *The Builder* (1870), 1026
Wealth at death under £14,000: probate, 22 Aug 1877, *CGPLA Eng. & Wales*

Sharpe, Eliza (1796–1874). *See under* Sharpe, Louisa (*bap.* 1798, *d.* 1843).

Sharpe, Ella Agnes Freeman (1875–1947), psychoanalyst and schoolteacher, was born on 23 February 1875 at Garden Place, Cross Street, Sudbury, Suffolk, the daughter of Frank Sharpe, silk weaver, and Mary Ann Freeman. Owing to the premature death of her father, Ella Sharpe took on the responsibilities of an eldest son, forgoing the chance to study at Oxford in order to provide for her mother and sisters. She did, however, attend Nottingham University for three years, becoming an English teacher and co-head of Hucknall Pupil Teachers' Training Centre for boys and girls aged fifteen to eighteen. She held this post from 1904 to 1916, where she exhibited a profound skill in empathizing with and assessing the difficulties of adolescence.

Sharpe gave up formal teaching in 1917 to study psychoanalysis at the Medico-Psychological Clinic at Brunswick Square, London. She entered the clinic as a patient and was later trained to be a psychoanalyst under James Glover. Like Glover, Sharpe went to Berlin in 1920, where she was in analysis with and trained by Hanns Sachs; analysis continued with Sachs over several years during the summer months. In 1921 she was elected associate member of the British Psycho-Analytical Society, and as a member in 1923. For Sharpe psychoanalysis was an adjunct to education, and she brought to it all the proficiency in understanding human behaviour she had developed while in Nottingham. One of the large group of women coming to prominence in psychoanalysis in the 1920s, Sharpe negotiated her own position between object relations theorist Melanie Klein, an early influence (she analysed Klein's daughter Melitta Schmideberg in 1934), and Anna Freud, whom she later supported.

Disputes raged over the status of child analysis, and Sharpe was initially encouraged by Klein to treat children's play as the equivalent to the free associations of adults, finding Klein's conceptual tools useful in her own theories of pure art. In the 1940s debates continued between Freud and Klein (over the latter's interpretation of Freud's concept of the death instinct, for example), and Sharpe was an important voice in those discussions, taking issue with Klein over the depressive phase and the introjected love object. In the inter-war years she became an influential and highly respected training analyst, and a distinguished professional in the field of child development. Sharpe's prime contribution to this field was the recognition that imitation and play were symbolic activities structured according to 'interpersonal identifications' (Rayner, 50). In her work as a training analyst she was an inspiration to her students and was part of the movement to advocate the self-awareness of the analyst in the relationship with the analysand. Eschewing the path taken by the scientist, she preferred the more subjective route chosen by those 'who find obstinate problems within themselves for which they seek understanding and solution' (E. A. F. Sharpe, *Collected Papers*, 1950, 109).

Like Sigmund Freud and Ernest Jones, Ella Sharpe believed that humanistic studies, rather than pure science, were vital to the development of both the analyst and psychoanalysis. For Sharpe, the 'dawn of civilization is the dawn of art' (E. A. F. Sharpe, *Collected Papers*, 1950, 126) and she urged would-be analysts to remember that '[o]utside the consulting-room we need to see life whole and to remember that our culture is inseparable from our conflicts' (ibid., 21). Sharpe's most original work lay in her psychoanalytic interpretation of literature, notably her essays on the religious poet Francis Thompson and Shakespeare's tragedies, in which she reconstructed Shakespeare's emotional life from the psychoanalytic evidence of the plays, and argued for the 'regressive movement of the libido' in Hamlet. Her skills as a literary theorist are attested to in her essay on metaphor and bodily discharge, 'Psycho-physical problems revealed in language: an examination of metaphor'. In *Dream Analysis* (1937) Sharpe elaborated on the analogousness of poetic metaphor and the process of the dream work, originated by Freud and pioneered by F. C. Prescott in *The Poetic Mind*. Sharpe was an innovator in theorizing the creative

aspects of dreams, specifically the correspondences between dreams and metaphor. In Rayner's opinion her graceful prose 'succeeded in giving probably the best exposition of classical theory on dreams after Freud himself' (Rayner, 84). Sharpe was a forerunner of the psychoanalytic exploration of language developed by Jacques Lacan in the 1950s.

Sharpe, with M. N. Searl, Mary Chadwick, and M. G. Lewis, was one of the 'ladies' of the 'Gordon Street ménage'—so called by James Strachey because the women shared both lodgings and a certain position on psychoanalysis (*Bloomsbury Freud*, 43). She was referred to by James Strachey as 'the Sharpe', a remark elicited due to a wrangle over the logistics of an impending visit to London by Melanie Klein (*Bloomsbury Freud*, 272). This use of her name also throws light on her skills as a debater which is borne out by a reading of the proceedings of the Extraordinary Business Meetings of the British Psycho-Analytical Society, in which Sharpe pointedly defends her ground and challenges her detractors. She is remembered vividly by Sylvia Payne for her dramatic performances in her lectures and seminars—her audiences were often 'disturbed' by the physical nature of Sharpe's delivery in which both mind and body were fully operational (*International Journal of Psycho-Analysis*, 55)—most notably her reading of 'Sublimation and delusion' at the Oxford congress in 1928. Payne paints a sensuous and lively portrait of Sharpe, all deep rich tones, colourful dress, and mobile gestures.

Sharpe embarked on many projects in the last few years of her life, including a manual on the training of analysts and a novel, and exhibited no signs of a waning in her intellectual energy. But the disturbances of war wreaked havoc on her physical health and she died from cardiac failure on 1 June 1947 at St Bartholomew's Hospital, London. Her *Collected Papers*, edited by Marjorie Brierley, were published in 1950.   CLARE L. TAYLOR

Sources *International Journal of Psycho-Analysis*, 28 (1947), 54–6 · E. Rayner, *The independent mind in British psychoanalysis* (1990) · *Bloomsbury Freud: the letters of James and Alix Strachey, 1924–1925*, ed. P. Meisel and W. Kendrick (1985) · P. King and R. Steiner, eds., *The Freud–Klein controversies, 1941–1945* (1991) · P. Grosskurth, *Melanie Klein: her world and her work* (1985) · L. Appignanesi and J. Forrester, *Freud's women* (1992) · b. cert. · d. cert. · *CGPLA Eng. & Wales* (1947)
Likenesses photograph, repro. in Rayner, *Independent mind*, cover
Wealth at death £3396 11s. 10d.: probate, 15 Oct 1947, *CGPLA Eng. & Wales*

Sharpe, Gregory (1713–1771), Church of England clergyman and author, was born in Yorkshire, the son of John Sharpe, solicitor to the Treasury, and his wife. He was educated at Hull grammar school, and later at Westminster School under Dr Robert Freind. At Westminster he committed some irregularity, and from the summer of 1731 he lived for four years at Aberdeen with the classical scholar Thomas Blackwell. During this time, he may have gained an MA from Aberdeen University. On 2 June 1735 he was admitted fellow commoner at Trinity College, Cambridge, and graduated LLB in 1738. He returned to Trinity College on 8 June 1747, and proceeded LLD. On 4 July 1751 he was incorporated at Oxford.

Sharpe was ordained deacon at Bristol in 1737, and priest at Westminster on 20 January 1739, and served for some time as minister of Broadway Chapel, Westminster. From 1743 to 1756 he was vicar of All Saints, Birling, near Maidstone. He became prebendary of Yetminster secunda in Salisbury Cathedral on 18 March 1757, and vicar of Purton, Wiltshire, in 1761; he held these posts until his death. Sharpe was chaplain to Frederick, prince of Wales, until 1751, and to George III from 1762 to 1771. He gave the fast-day sermons for 1757–9, and gave charity sermons for the London Maternity Hospital for Married Women in 1759, Westminster Hospital in 1764, and the London Asylum for Orphan Girls in 1770. On the death of Samuel Nicolls in 1763 he was elected to the mastership of the Temple, where William Maxwell was his assistant.

In addition to his sermons Sharpe published widely on religious and classical subjects. He wrote several defences of Christianity, and his *Rise and Fall of the Holy City and Temple of Jerusalem* (1765) went into a second edition in 1766. He defended the rationalist philosophers Samuel Clarke and Gottfried Wilhelm Leibniz against Lewis Philip Thummig (1774), and in 1769 contributed a pamphlet to the debate about James Merrick's version of the Psalms. He also published pieces in the *Monthly Review*. A posthumous collection of his sermons, edited by Joseph Robertson, appeared in 1772.

Sharpe took a scholarly interest in systems for learning languages. In 1751 he published *A dissertation upon the origin and structure of the Latin tongue, containing a rational and compendious method of learning Latin*, and in the same year brought out a second edition of his *Seven Letters Containing a New and Easy Method of Learning the Hebrew Language*. He also wrote about Greek, and his *Origin and Structure of the Greek Tongue* (1767) was reissued in 1777. He contributed the translation of Aristophanes' *Frogs* to Charlotte Lennox's 1759 edition of *The Greek Theatre of Father Brumoy*, and, with the fourth earl of Shaftesbury, he published in 1766 John Locke's *Observations upon the Growth and Culture of Vines and Olives*, from the original manuscript. In the same year he revised Benjamin Martyn's biography of the first earl of Shaftesbury, later edited by Andrew Kippis (1771) and published about 1790. In 1767 he collected and edited the dissertations of Thomas Hyde.

Sharpe was elected FRS on 9 May 1754 and was fellow and the director of the Society of Antiquaries when he died, at the master's house in the Temple, on 8 January 1771. He had collected an impressive library, which was sold on 8 April 1778 and over the next ten days. A catalogue was published, listing his fine collection of oriental manuscripts and many valuable prints and drawings in addition to his books, and the library sold for over £577.

W. P. COURTNEY, rev. EMMA MAJOR

Sources Venn, *Alum. Cant.* · ESTC · J. Boswell, *Life of Johnson*, ed. R. W. Chapman, rev. J. D. Fleeman, new edn (1970); repr. with introduction by P. Rogers (1980), 446 · *GM*, 1st ser., 41 (1771), 47 · Watt, *Bibl. Brit.* · *Fasti Angl.* (Hardy) · Foster, *Alum. Oxon.* · private information (1897) · Nichols, *Lit. anecdotes*, 3.501 · C. Fielding, *Memories of Malling* (1893), 164 · W. H. Cooke, ed., *Students admitted to the Inner Temple, 1547–1660* [1878], 136
Archives Bodl. Oxf., corresp., MSS Eng. lett. d 145–146 | BL, letters to Lord Hardwicke, etc., Add. MSS 25412–36137
Likenesses V. Green, mezzotint, pubd 1770 (after R. Crosse), BM, NPG
Wealth at death library fetched £577 14s.

Sharpe, Horatio (1718–1790), army officer and colonial governor, was born on 15 November 1718 in Yorkshire, near Hull, the youngest son of William Sharpe (c.1664–1733) and his wife, Margaret, daughter of Thomas Beake of London, principal secretary of Maryland from 1714 to 1733. Sharpe was one of sixteen children, of whom nine sons and four daughters survived to adulthood. Of Sharpe's brothers, John (d. 1756), barrister and MP, was guardian to Frederick Calvert, sixth Baron Baltimore, from 1751 to 1756; William (1696–1767) was first clerk of the privy council; Joshua (1707–1786) was a solicitor and colonial agent; Gregory (1713–1771) was chaplain to George III; Philip (1716–1772) succeeded William as privy council clerk; and James was also a colonial agent.

Sharpe spent his early years as a career military officer, serving in the 20th regiment in Scotland under the celebrated general James Wolfe, achieving the rank of captain in the Royal Marines by 1745, and being commissioned in July 1754 as a lieutenant-colonel in the regiment of foot in the West Indies and appointed 'to Command of the Combined Forces that shall be Assembled in America to oppose the Hostile Attempts Committed by the French' (Browne, 31.52).

Viewed by historians as the 'most qualified and best-connected' (Rockefeller, 21) of Maryland's governors, Sharpe arrived to take up his post in August 1753. He undoubtedly owed his appointment both to the useful connections of his older brothers and to 'the obvious expediency of placing a military man in office on the eve of a threatened attack by the French' (Lonn, 26). Sharpe used his military experience to good advantage during the ensuing French and Indian War, but his tenure as the colony's longest-serving governor owed more to his skill in balancing the competing interests of proprietor, crown, and colonists.

As commander-in-chief of the British forces in America prior to the Earl General Edward Braddock's arrival in the summer of 1755, Sharpe in January 1755 travelled to western Maryland, where George Washington, as a colonel in the Virginia militia, had begun construction of Fort Cumberland, to reconnoitre the likely area of future fighting. Sharpe made the mid-winter return trip of 250 miles by canoe down the Potomac River, purchasing supplies and forage for future use as he progressed.

The governor's more serious challenges lay in persuading the Maryland assembly's lower house to vote money for the war effort without compromising his proprietary instructions. Delegates had learned in previous wars to use the need for appropriations as a wedge to extract proprietary concessions and tried the same tactics in the new conflict. Sharpe carefully weighed the manifest benefits of funding against the limited precedents set by the concessions he made. To obtain passage of the first money bill in 1754, Sharpe accepted designation of ordinary licence fees as part of the military support, despite Baltimore's instruction to reserve the income for his own private use. The second funding bill passed in 1756 with the inclusion of only two measures that violated Sharpe's instructions from Britain: a levy on all leased proprietary manors and a double tax on Roman Catholic landholders. Disallowance of the assembly's acts at a time of crisis would have been an impolitic move for the proprietor, Lord Baltimore, but governor and council nevertheless received orders to stand firm in the future. As neither side would yield, the bill of 1756 represented the Maryland assembly's last appropriation of funds.

Sharpe continued to assist the military effort by other means, relying on prerogative powers to call up the militia and rotating the counties' short-term commitments to ensure a regular supply of men. He personally visited soldiers in the field to encourage their efforts and led troops on one occasion. Sharpe also raised units by private subscription and encouragement of volunteers. His efforts, 'although purely defensive, severely limited, and by no means' personally satisfactory, 'adequately met the limited threats to his colony' (Rockefeller, 279, 286).

Sharpe met with mixed success in other administrative areas. He ably settled the thorny question of ordinary licence fees by persuading the council, composed of proprietary appointees, to approve legislation for the public's benefit, allocating the money to support schools. His efforts to supervise the proprietary bureaucracy, particularly to weed out incompetent or corrupt officials, met with less success because of meddling by both the proprietor and the provincial secretary (Lord Baltimore's uncle), to whom Sharpe's targets could appeal on their own behalf. Sharpe skilfully threaded his way through the Stamp Act crisis of 1765 over British taxation of internal colonial trade, relying on his expectation that the act would soon be repealed to refrain from taking measures that would antagonize the populace. He thus avoided the animosity experienced by governors in royal colonies. On the other hand, the proprietor's penchant for awarding government offices in Maryland to unsuitable favourites, particularly the Revd Bennett Allen and agent John Morton Jordan, compromised Sharpe's ability to win support for proprietary interests from powerful local leaders.

In August 1768 Sharpe's brother Joshua wrote to him of his impending replacement as governor:

> Capt Eden that married his Lordship's sister had by extravagant living & gaming run himself into such streights & difficulties that he could not well continue longer here, & … they had no other means of providing for him but by appointing him Governor of Maryland. (Ridout MSS, SC 373.184)

Proprietary kinship apparently counted for more than a record of able and loyal service.

Sharpe retired to Whitehall, his plantation across the Severn River from Annapolis, where his farm and garden had 'now become my principal Amusement' (Papenfuse,

2.727). He became an honorary member of the Homony Club, a social gathering of the Annapolis élite and their guests, and continued his interest in horse-racing, serving as steward of the Annapolis Jockey Club, which he had helped to found, and racing his own thoroughbreds.

Sharpe returned to England in 1773 on family matters, and remained there as the outbreak of the American War of Independence prevented a return to Maryland. He lived near London, in Middlesex, first in St Pancras parish, and then in Hampstead, where he died on 9 November 1790. Sharpe left his large estate to various friends and relations, having never married. He was buried in the family vault at Elstree in Hertfordshire.   JEAN B. RUSSO

Sources E. C. Papenfuse and others, eds., *A biographical dictionary of the Maryland legislature, 1635–1789*, 2 (1985) · R. J. Rockefeller, 'Their magistrates and officers—executive government in eighteenth century Maryland', PhD diss., University of Maryland, 1988 · A. C. Land, *Colonial Maryland: a history* (1981) · E. Lonn, 'Sharpe, Horatio', *DAB* · 'Correspondence of Governor Horatio Sharpe, 1753–1757', ed. W. H. Browne, *Archives of Maryland*, 6, 9, 14, 31 (1888–95) · A. C. Land, 'The familiar letters of governor Horatio Sharpe', *Maryland Historical Magazine*, 61 (1966), 189–209 · P. H. Giddens, 'Governor Sharpe and his Maryland government', *Maryland Historical Magazine*, 31 (1937), 156–74 · P. H. Giddens, 'Governor Horatio Sharpe retires', *Maryland Historical Magazine*, 30 (1936), 215–25 · W. H. Browne, ed., 'Proceedings of the council of Maryland … letters to Governor Horatio Sharpe, 1754–1765', *Archives of Maryland*, 31 (1911)
Archives Washington, DC, personal MSS | BL, Add. MSS 154–189 · BL, Newcastle MSS, Add. MS 32858 · Maryland State Archives, Annapolis, Ridout MSS, SC 371, 373, 504
Likenesses G. Hamilton, group portrait, oils, *c.*1753 (*The Sharpe family*), Maryland State Archives, Annapolis Collection, MCA SC 1545–1212; [on display at Government House, Annapolis, Maryland] · J. Hesselius, oils, *c.*1760, Johns Hopkins University, Baltimore
Wealth at death debts due on bonds held in America (£3341 3s. 11d. sterling and £725 4s. 9d. Maryland currency); English assets incl. Hampstead residence, one-sixth part of two freehold leases in Pall Mall, copyhold leases in Middlesex, leasehold tenement, and former woodyard developed by several tenements (both in Piccadilly); house in Westminster; £40,669 in three per cent consolidated bank annuities; £11,467 in liquid funds; also 'household goods, wines, plate, linen, china, books, jewels, furniture, and pictures': Papenfuse and others, eds., *Biographical Dictionary*, 2.728

Sharpe [Sharp], **Leonell** (*bap.* 1560, *d.* 1631), Church of England clergyman and author, the second son of Robert Sharpe, a successful member of the Mercers' Company of London, and Juliann Mallory, eldest daughter of Sir Richard Mallory, mercer and lord mayor of London, was baptized on 28 February 1560 at St Michael Bassishaw, London. Schooled at Eton College, he entered King's College, Cambridge, in August 1576 and graduated BA in 1581, MA in 1584, and DTh in 1597. He was a fellow of King's (1579–89) and was ordained deacon and priest in September 1587. At Cambridge, Sharpe met and cultivated Robert Devereux, second earl of Essex, perhaps a distant relative by marriage, who was a student at Trinity College (1577–81). Sharpe later claimed that Essex introduced him to Robert Dudley, earl of Leicester, who sent him to plead with Archbishop Whitgift on behalf of the presbyterians Thomas Cartwright, Dudley Fenner, and Humphrey Fen (*d*. 1587). Essex also later employed him to lobby Whitgift on behalf of other leading radicals.

Sharpe was present with Leicester and Essex when Queen Elizabeth visited the army at Tilbury in August 1588—he was employed to read out to the troops information about Spanish plans for crushing protestantism in England, and then to repeat the queen's speech to the army, of which he thus obtained the only copy. Despite his apparent lack of stature (he was often called 'Little Dr Sharpe'), both tasks attest his skill as an orator. He became a chaplain of Essex no later than 1589, when he attended the earl on the Portugal expedition. He subsequently accompanied him abroad to Normandy in 1591 and Cadiz in 1596.

In April 1590 Sharpe was presented by the crown, presumably at Essex's behest, to the rectory of Malpas in Cheshire, but probably spent little time in this strongly recusant parish, since he served Essex as both household chaplain (he baptized the earl's son Henry in April 1595) and man of business in academic matters relating to Cambridge. He helped John Coke to leave Cambridge and enter service with Essex's friend Fulke Greville (*c*.1590), conveyed a message from Essex to the bishop of Winchester about the disposition of William Whitaker's fellowship at Eton in December 1595, and acted as a liaison between Cambridge and Essex after the earl became chancellor of the university in August 1598. An eighteenth-century chronicler of King's College claimed that Sharpe showed himself 'too obsequious' to Essex, 'in prejudice to our revenue' (Allen, 2.931). Essex repaid such service by arranging for Sharpe to preach Lenten sermons at court in 1595, 1596, and 1598, and by urging Cambridge to allow him to proceed DTh without performing the usual exercises. This request failed, but Whitgift helped to secure Sharpe's doctorate in April 1597. In the same year, having presumably resigned Malpas, Sharpe was presented to the livings of Tiverton (Pitt portion) and Stokinteignhead in Devon. Difficulties with the latter presentation apparently prevented Sharpe from accompanying the earl on the Azores expedition that summer.

In 1602 Sharpe was listed as a supernumerary chaplain to the queen, an appointment that probably dates from 1598 or early 1599, before Essex lost influence over such promotions. Despite his entry into royal service, Sharpe was summoned to attend Essex on his sickbed in December 1599. His involvement (if any) in Essex's rising of February 1601 is unclear, but Sir Robert Cecil ordered him not to leave his Devon parishes for a period. He responded by seeking to distance himself from Essex's actions and cultivating Cecil's support. By April 1601 he had married Anne (*b*. 1578), second daughter of John Chichester of Hall, Devon. Sharpe was back at Cambridge in March 1603, where he preached a sermon praising the accession of James I. Along with a similarly laudatory tract, *Dialogus inter Angliam et Scotiam*, it was speedily published by the university printer.

These efforts to curry favour with the new regime proved successful. Sharpe was appointed a royal chaplain by 1604, regularly attending princes Henry and Charles,

but found himself in trouble in June that year, when he was sent to the Tower for privately organizing various gentlemen to defend the king against an alleged conspiracy which might have involved bloodshed between English and Scots. Coming at a time when James's efforts to create a formal union of England and Scotland were facing strong opposition in parliament, this action was regarded as extremely provocative, but Sharpe's profuse claims of loyalty to the king and pleas to Cecil soon secured his release. He was appointed a chaplain to Prince Henry by the end of 1605 and archdeacon of Berkshire in November 1605.

By the time of Cecil's death in 1612 Sharpe had pinned his hopes of advancement on Prince Henry and Henry Howard, earl of Northampton. In that year Henry (energetically) and Northampton (with little enthusiasm) tried unsuccessfully to secure Sharpe's appointment as provost of King's. It is probably no coincidence that this year also witnessed Sharpe's return to print, this time as a writer of violently anti-papal tracts: his *Novum fidei symbolum* included a polemic later translated (by his older brother, Edward) as *A looking-glasse for the pope, wherein he may see his owne face, the expresse image of Antichrist* (1616). The king declined to receive the dedication to this work; another tract of about this period, on salvation and the gospel, remained unprinted. In November 1612 his hopes were even more severely dented by the death of Prince Henry, for whom Sharpe published a funeral sermon which included verses by his brothers Andrew, William, and Edward. Rumours in late 1613 that Sharpe would be appointed bishop of Rochester (presumably by the efforts of his patron, Northampton) came to nothing.

In June 1614 Sharpe and Sir Charles Cornwallis were interrogated by the privy council and sent to the Tower for inciting John Hoskyns to deliver an incendiary speech in parliament that threatened an English version of the 'Sicilian vespers' if Scottish courtiers were not expelled from court. Northampton's death a few days later left them fully exposed to the king's anger. It emerged that Sharpe had chosen Hoskyns to give the speech and had suggested the reference to the massacre of foreigners in thirteenth-century Sicily, while Cornwallis had allegedly paid Hoskyns for undertaking the task. They were held in the Tower for a full year and Sharpe was subsequently banished to his Devon parishes until the following spring. He sought to regain royal favour by publishing an English version of his *Looking-Glasse* in 1616 and by allegedly ghost-writing Sir Lewis Stukeley's defence of his actions against Sir Walter Ralegh in 1618. By the 1620s, like Hoskyns, Sharpe had attached himself to George Villiers, from May 1623 duke of Buckingham. He sent advice to the duke about policies during the reign of Elizabeth and sermonized in defence of Buckingham's reputation after the defeat at the Île de Ré.

Buckingham's assassination in August 1628 removed the fifth and final major patron of Sharpe's career. Despite his apparently excellent Calvinist credentials as a chaplain to both Essex and Prince Henry, Sharpe adopted an increasingly anti-puritan tone by the 1610s. Towards the end of his life he even refused to pay his visitation fees to the new bishop of Exeter, the Calvinist Joseph Hall. Sharpe apparently spent Christmas 1629 with Sir Henry Wotton, provost of Eton and formerly Essex's secretary. He died on 1 January 1631 at Wotton's family home at Boughton Malherb, Kent, and was buried in the church there.   PAUL E. J. HAMMER

Sources state papers domestic, Elizabeth I–Charles I, PRO, SP 12, 14, 15, 16 · Hatfield House, Cecil MSS 54, 105, 109, 136, P.51 · BL, Lansdowne MSS 61, 79, 108, 444, 984 · exchequer, first fruits and tenths office, composition books, PRO, E 334/12, 14 · Westminster Abbey, muniment book 15 · Venn, *Alum. Cant.*, 1/4.50 · *Calendar of the manuscripts of the most hon. the marquis of Salisbury*, 24 vols., HMC, 9 (1883–1976) · R. Cooke, *Visitation of London, 1568*, ed. H. Stanford London and S. W. Rawlins, [new edn], 2 vols. in one, Harleian Society, 109–10 (1963) · F. T. Colby, ed., *The visitation of the county of Devon in the year 1620*, Harleian Society, 6 (1872) · *Cabala, sive, Scrinia sacra: mysteries of state and government in letters of illustrious persons*, 3rd edn (1691) · *The letters of John Chamberlain*, ed. N. E. McClure, 2 vols. (1939) · P. E. J. Hammer, 'The earl of Essex, Fulke Greville and the employment of scholars', *Studies in Philology*, 91 (1994), 167–80 · E. S. Chalk, *A history of the church of S. Peter, Tiverton, in the diocese of Exeter* (1905) · CUL, MS Mm.1.35 · *Report on the manuscripts of the family of Gawdy, formerly of Norfolk*, HMC, 11 (1885) · *Report on the manuscripts of the marquis of Downshire*, 6 vols. in 7, HMC, 75 (1924–95), vol. 6 · *The life and letters of Sir Henry Wotton*, ed. L. P. Smith, 2 vols. (1907) · W. Sterry, ed., *The Eton College register, 1441–1698* (1943) · A. Allen, 'Skeleton Collegii Regalis Cantab.', King's Cam. · chancery, dispensation rolls, PRO, C 58/3 · W. B. Bannerman, ed., *The registers of St Olave, Hart Street, London, 1563–1700*, Harleian Society, register section, 46 (1916) · monument, parish church, Boughton Malherb, Kent · IGI

Archives BL, letters, Add. MS 6178, fol. 130r · BL, MS 'Of the right preparation of the soule by the ghosple to receave our eternall salvation and blessednes in Christe: the second booke', Royal MS 18.B.XXIV, fols. 1r–46v · CUL, letters, Collect. Admin. 5, fol. 220r | BL, Lansdowne MSS, letters · Hatfield House, Hertfordshire, Cecil MSS · PRO, letters, state papers, Elizabeth I–Charles I, SP 12, 14, 15, 16

Sharpe, Lewis (*fl.* 1640), playwright, is unknown except as the author of *The Noble Stranger*, a comedy which was first acted 'at the Private House in Salisbury Court, by Her Majestie's servants' some time between 1638 and 1640, the year in which it was published. It is dedicated to 'the Worthy Knight, Sir Edmund Williams' and is prefaced with eulogistic verses by Richard Woolfall. From these it appears to have been a popular piece and frequently acted.

A contemporary, **Roger Sharpe** (*fl.* 1610), poet, is known only as the author of *More Fooles Yet, Written by R. S.*, a collection of epigrams published in 1610; an address to the reader is signed Roger Sharpe.

E. I. CARLYLE, *rev.* MATTHEW STEGGLE

Sources G. E. Bentley, *The Jacobean and Caroline stage*, 7 vols. (1941–68) · STC, 1475–1640

Sharpe [*married name* Seyffarth], **Louisa** (*bap.* 1798, *d.* 1843), miniature and watercolour painter, was born in Birmingham and baptized on 21 August 1798 at St Phillip's, Birmingham, the third of the four daughters of William Sharpe (1749–1824), engraver, and his wife, Susanna, whose maiden name may have been Fairhead. All four sisters were artists and presumably taught at home by their father although their principal studies were said to have

been carried out in French and German galleries. About 1816 the family moved to London and from the following year, when their address was 13 King Street in Covent Garden, Louisa and her sisters Charlotte and Eliza [*see below*] exhibited miniature portraits at the Royal Academy. Frederick, duke of York, was their first patron. Louisa Sharpe was represented by a total of twenty-nine works at the Royal Academy (1817–29), several of these being of actresses and figures connected with the nearby theatrical world. After her election as a member of the Old Watercolour Society on 9 February 1829, she devoted herself to larger subject compositions or costume pieces in watercolour which she also exhibited at the Liverpool Academy (1832–42). Of her thirty-nine exhibits (1829–42) at the society the majority were dramatic, literary scenes evincing pathos or humour. She drew subjects from the works of Sir Walter Scott, Thomas Moore, George Crabbe, Lord Byron, William Harrison Ainsworth, Oliver Goldsmith, Joseph Addison and Sir Richard Steele, and from contemporary periodical literature. A principal attraction at the gallery, where they sold readily, her pictures were noted for their 'high degree of finish' (Roget, 2.43) and for an innovative 'bold style of watercolour drawing' (Clayton, 1.380). Her most detailed and elaborate subjects were priced at 100 guineas. Between 1829 and 1839 Louisa Sharpe's work was widely engraved to illustrate literature in contemporary annuals such as *The Forget-me-Not* (1829, 1831, 1836), *The Keepsake* (1831–3, 1835, 1837), *Portraits of the Principal Female Characters in the Waverley Novels* (1832–4), *Heath's Book of Beauty* (1833–7), *Fisher's Drawing-Room Scrap-Book* (1839), and *Heath's Gallery of British Engravings* (1836, 1838). In 1824 Eliza, Louisa and Mary Anne Sharpe moved to 44 Upper Charlotte Street and subsequently shared several addresses in central London. After her marriage, in 1834, to Dr Woldemar Seyffarth (a professor and author who later, after his wife's death, was commissioner from the king of Saxony to the London International Exhibitions in 1851 and 1862), Louisa Seyffarth lived in Dresden. She had two children, one of whom, Agnes Seyffarth (*fl.* 1850–1859), was also a painter. She died in Dresden, 'of a painful disorder', on 28 January 1843.

Charlotte Sharpe (*c.*1793–1849), miniature painter, was the eldest daughter, and was baptized on 2 July 1793 at St Phillip's, Birmingham. She exhibited nineteen miniature portraits at the Royal Academy between 1817 and 1841, from various London addresses. After her marriage to Captain T. Best Morris in 1821 there was a six-year hiatus in her exhibiting career (1824–9) after which she resumed painting to support her family. The artist Charlotte B. Morris (*fl.* 1828–1867) is thought to have been her daughter. A son, J. B. Morris, died in childhood. Charlotte Morris died in 1849.

Eliza Sharpe (1796–1874), miniature and subject painter, was the second eldest daughter. She was born in August 1796 in Birmingham and baptized on 21 August 1798 at St Phillip's, Birmingham. She exhibited forty-eight works, primarily portrait miniatures, at the Royal Academy (1817–67). At the Old Watercolour Society—of which she became a member in 1829 and subsequently secretary—she showed eighty-four paintings (1829–70), the majority being costume pieces illustrating scenes from literature, although from 1836 her most highly priced (and, it appears, least popular) works were on biblical themes. She was also represented at exhibitions in Liverpool (1838–61) and at the Royal Manchester Instition (1841–53). Between 1831 and 1840 her paintings were often engraved for contemporary annuals. Towards the end of her life she was successful as a copyist of paintings at the South Kensington Museum; five of her nine exhibits at the Society of Female Artists (1860–74) were copies. Although less talented than her sister Louisa, by the 1870s Eliza Sharpe had earned 'a modest little fortune' (Roget, 2.207). She had also achieved a reputation for 'unusually original marked character', frequently manifest in acts of 'enthusiastic benevolence' (Clayton, 1.380). Having occupied at least twelve addresses in London, Eliza Sharpe died, unmarried, on 11 June 1874 at Woodside Poyle, Burnham Beeches, Buckinghamshire, the house of her nephew Mr C. W. Sharpe, the engraver. She was buried in Willesden cemetery.

Mary Anne Sharpe (1802–1867), miniature and subject painter, was born in Birmingham, and baptized on 31 December 1802 at St Martin's, Birmingham. She exhibited from the same London addresses as her sister Eliza. She was represented by nineteen works at the Royal Academy (1819–63), twenty-five at the Society of British Artists (1826–64) of which she was elected an honorary member in 1830, ten at exhibitions in Liverpool (1831–59), two at the Royal Manchester Institution (1847–52), and six at the Society of Female Artists (1860–65). She died in 1867.

CHARLOTTE YELDHAM

Sources J. L. Roget, *A history of the 'Old Water-Colour' Society*, 2 vols. (1891) • E. C. Clayton, *English female artists*, 2 vols. (1876) • *The Royal Watercolour Society: the first fifty years, 1805–1855* (1992) • D. Foskett, *A dictionary of British miniature painters*, 2 vols. (1972) • B. Stewart and M. Cutten, *The dictionary of portrait painters in Britain up to 1920* (1997) • Graves, *RA exhibitors* • J. Johnson, ed., *Works exhibited at the Royal Society of British Artists, 1824–1893, and the New English Art Club, 1888–1917*, 2 vols. (1975) • E. Morris and E. Roberts, *The Liverpool Academy and other exhibitions of contemporary art in Liverpool, 1774–1867* (1998) • exhibition catalogues (1841); (1847); (1852–3) [Royal Manchester Institution] • IGI • d. cert. [Eliza Sharpe] • CGPLA Eng. & Wales (1874)

Wealth at death under £2000—Eliza Sharpe: probate, 8 July 1874, CGPLA Eng. & Wales • under £100—Mary Anne Sharpe: administration, 20 June 1867, CGPLA Eng. & Wales

Sharpe, Mary Anne (1802–1867). *See under* Sharpe, Louisa (*bap.* 1798, *d.* 1843).

Sharpe, Matilda (1830–1916), headmistress, was born at 38 Canonbury Place, London, on 4 April 1830, the second of six children of Samuel *Sharpe (1799–1881), the banker and Egyptologist, and his wife, Sarah Sharpe (1796–1851), Samuel's cousin and an artist of some talent. From her strongly Unitarian, wealthy home in Highgate, Middlesex, Matilda gained a passion for educational and social concerns and a conviction that education was the key to freedom. She was educated at home by her parents in a stimulating milieu with constant visits from eminent scholars and scientists. 'Much drawing' with her mother, and classics, biblical Unitarianism, and Egyptology with her father, inspired Matilda with a love of these for life. Astronomy, botany, and electricity were pastimes and Matilda taught herself to sing with a tuning fork. She and her elder sister, Emily (1828–1914), the only surviving members of the family after 1881, were scholars to the end, travelling to Italy when over seventy to improve their accents.

Matilda Sharpe was a gifted painter who exhibited at the Royal Academy (two of her many portraits are in the National Portrait Gallery), but she devoted much of her life to teaching. Beginning at Newington Green Chapel Sunday school she went on to teach painting, Latin, and French to working-class students in night schools and at Harp Alley, Blackfriars, Islington, and Kentish Town day schools, the last three being attached to Unitarian chapels. From the early 1870s until the advent of free schooling she took over the management and expenses of these four day schools so that Latin and French could be taught in them, deeply believing that all children should have access to the best in education both for their own benefit and for that of the nation. She developed methods of teaching Latin by rote in large classes of eighty, including the kindergarten. In 1915 W. A. Holman, attorney-general and premier of New South Wales, Australia, attributed his rise in life and his love of learning to her lessons. Sure that God was known through the good and beautiful, she wanted every child to have the best of books, pictures, music, and drama.

In 1881 Matilda Sharpe was much influenced by the Revd Robert Spears to establish a boarding-school for the daughters of Unitarian ministers and other Unitarians that would provide the best education possible at the lowest possible cost, enabling its pupils to go on to university or any of the professions open to women if they wished. With Spears's help she opened Channing House School on Highgate Hill in January 1885 (and also founded Highgate Unitarian Chapel near the school). Unusual for being designated Unitarian, the school had unsectarian religious teaching, except for special instruction for boarders, and was open to all. Day scholars were also admitted and a kindergarten was later established for boys and girls under eight. The school soon attracted about sixty pupils a year, many of them from other countries, especially Hungary and Ireland. The broad education included all forms of science (astronomy as well) and appropriate domestic subjects, scientifically taught; art was encouraged and shorthand and typing available. Pupils were prepared for the matriculation, intermediate examinations, and external degrees of London University. A good academic standard was quickly established with visiting masters used in the higher classes until there were sufficient qualified women. As in many of the new public high schools for girls, games such as cricket and hockey were fostered and tight-lacing and female frailty discouraged, this helped by the fact that Highgate was one of the healthiest spots in London. In other ways Miss Sharpe was less radical, fearing any contact between her girls and boys or young men, even disliking the amount of 'love' in tennis (in which she also forbade the use of the term 'deuce').

Miss Sharpe lavished her money and time on the school and soon took sole responsibility for its management, retaining a deep interest in it even after 1899, when the school was incorporated, and 1903, when it was first inspected by the Board of Education inspectorate. Eccentric, enthusiastic, encouraging, very humorous and kind, she developed a school noted for its homely atmosphere, yet able to become a highly rated, non-sectarian, independent day school which gave middle-class girls every chance to take advantage of new opportunities.

Miss Sharpe published an anthology of poetry, *Old Favourites from the Elder Poets*, in 1881 and 1912, in which she included nine women poets, particularly the Unitarian Anna Laetitia Barbauld. She also wrote four idiosyncratic books of proverbs, moral maxims, and poetical comments on modern times, emphasizing her love of learning and travel, her dislike of smoking, alcohol, and fripperies, and her ardent support for education for all, 'unselfish' free trade, Liberalism, Asquith's 'Great Reform' of 1911, and any government which would 'treble tax the rich'. Her favourite, *Never Forget* (1915), dedicated to Channing girls and running to thirty-two editions, she gave away to any stranger she thought might appreciate it. Somewhat sentimental in her views on motherhood, nevertheless she wanted greater opportunities for women, including preaching, but there is no mention of the suffrage in her writings, although many pupils became suffragists. Small and entirely indifferent to fashion, she was always 'brimming over with some new invention for reforming the world, the parlour grate, or the British army' (Sharpe, 20). She satisfied a hankering after colour, music, gaiety, and crowds by much travel both abroad and around London, revelling in the use of the public omnibus for her constant visiting of art galleries and refreshment rooms. Matilda Sharpe died peacefully at her home, 32 Highbury Place, London, on 30 April 1916.   RUTH WATTS

Sources L. Sharpe, *Memorials of Matilda Sharpe, 1830–1916* (1916) · *The Inquirer* (13 May 1916) · *Christian Life* (16 May 1916) · *The Inquirer* (24 May 1930) [memorial] · M. Rowe and R. Roberts, eds., *Matilda Sharpe centenary, 1930* (1930) · T. E. Dalton, *Channing School, 1885–1960* (1960) · E. M. Saunders, *A progress: Channing School, 1885–1985* (1984) · *Channing House Magazine* [Channing School, Highgate, London], 1/1–10 (1906–10) · Channing House, *School prospectus* (1908) [Channing School, Highgate, London] · *The Inquirer* (20 July 1878) · *The Inquirer* (6 Aug 1881) [obit. of Samuel Sharpe] · *The Inquirer* (24 Oct 1914) [obit. of Emily Sharpe] · d. cert.
Archives Channing School archives, printed and visual materials incl. paintings by Matilda Sharpe
Likenesses S. Sharpe, oils, 1842, Channing School, Highgate, London · M. Sharpe, self-portrait, 1860, Channing School, Highgate, London · drawing, 1887 (by a pupil), Channing School, Highgate, London · photograph, 1910, Channing School, Highgate, London · photographs, Channing School, Highgate, London
Wealth at death £19,488 7s. 9d.: probate, 6 June 1916, CGPLA Eng. & Wales

Sharpe, Richard Bowdler

Sharpe, Richard Bowdler (1847–1909), ornithologist and museum curator, was born on 22 November 1847 at 1 Skinner Street, Snow Hill, London, the son of Thomas Bowdler Sharpe who edited and published *Sharpe's London Magazine*, and his wife, Elizabeth. He began his education under an aunt who ran a preparatory school in Brighton. About

Richard Bowdler Sharpe (1847–1909), by Maull & Fox

1856 he went to Peterborough grammar school, where his cousin the Revd James Wallace was a master. He subsequently moved to Loughborough grammar school when his cousin was appointed master there. At Peterborough Sharpe won a king's scholarship and was a choirboy in the cathedral but, although he was a brilliant scholar, his enthusiasm for observing and collecting birds precluded any designs by his father for an academic career.

In 1863 Sharpe's father gave him a sovereign and sent him to London with a letter which led to his engagement as a clerk with W. H. Smith. He spent 1865–6 with another bookseller, Bernard Quaritch. There his interest in birds was encouraged by the quality bird books in Quaritch's natural history department. During this period Sharpe spent his leisure time pursuing birds. His father had moved to Cookham, Berkshire, about 1860 and Sharpe wrote of 'careering about the neighbourhood of Cookham in search of birds' (Sharpe, xxi), and while doing so became acquainted with John Gould who went fishing there.

At Cookham in 1867 Sharpe married Emily Eliza Burrows (1842/3–1928). The couple went to live in Camden Town, where the first six of their ten daughters were born between the years 1869 and 1875.

In the year of his marriage Sharpe was appointed the first librarian of the Zoological Society of London. During a forty-year period from 1868 to 1909, he wrote or edited scholarly ornithological treatises, described birds collected from others' voyages across the world, supplied the ornithological section of the *Zoological Record*, founded the British Ornithologists' Club in 1892 (and for some years edited its *Bulletin*), and lectured. Sharpe was a congenial companion, who had a keen sense of humour and was a familiar figure at the Savage and Whitefriars clubs.

Sharpe began to write the book which launched his career, the *Monograph of the Kingfishers*, about 1864 and published it between 1868 and 1871, with 125 colour plates by John Gerard Keulemans (1842–1912). Keulemans was frequently employed to work on Sharpe's bird books, and he also instructed several of Sharpe's daughters in the colouring of bird book illustrations. (Four daughters later coloured the plates in Sharpe and Claude Wyatt's *Monograph of the Hirundinidae*, 1885–94.)

In September 1872 Sharpe was appointed a senior assistant at the British Museum. He was promoted to assistant keeper of zoology in 1895. In charge of the bird collections, he became heavily involved in the production of the *British Museum Catalogue of Birds*: he wrote eleven volumes, parts of two other volumes, and was the chief editor of the twenty-seven volumes published between 1874 and 1898. During his time at the museum, the number of bird specimens increased from 35,000 to over half a million and established the British Museum's collection as pre-eminent in this field. Among these specimens were some 82,000 collected in India by Allen Hume, which Sharpe went to Simla to pack and transport to the museum in 1886.

In 1891 Sharpe published a catalogue of the osteological specimens in the College of Surgeons museum, was awarded an honorary LLD by the University of Aberdeen, and addressed the second International Ornithological Congress at Budapest. Following his address to the congress on the classification of birds, the Austrian emperor conferred on him the Austrian gold medal for art and science. Sharpe was president of section A at the third Ornithological Congress, held in Paris in 1900, and president of the fourth Ornithological Congress in London in 1905. By this time, he was either a foreign or an honorary member of all the principal ornithological societies in the world.

When fellow ornithologist John Gould died in 1881 he left several books unfinished. Sharpe completed Gould's *The Birds of Asia*, *The Birds of New Guinea*, and a supplement to *A Monograph of the Trochilidae*. Sharpe had known and collaborated with Gould for many years, and in 1893 published *An Analytical Index to the Works of the Late John Gould*, adding a biography which has remained the main source of information about Gould's life and work.

African birds were Sharpe's favourite subject. He completely revised Edgar Leopold Layard's text of *Birds of South Africa* between 1875 and 1884. After the death of Henry Seebohm in 1895, Sharpe edited both Seebohm's *A Monograph of the Turdidae* (1898–1902) and the colour plates of the eggs to complete Seebohm's *A History of British Birds* (1896).

While preparing his (1900) edition of Gilbert White's *The Natural History and Antiquities of Selborne and a Garden Kalendar* (first published in 1789), Sharpe spent much of his spare time in Selborne. He was vice-president of the Selborne Society for several years and demonstrated some of his minutely detailed knowledge of Gilbert White and Selborne in lantern lectures. In 1901 he joined in the excavations at Selborne Priory. In order to facilitate these activities, Sharpe purchased a new bungalow in Selborne in 1905–6, built on a piece of land called Sparrow's Hanger which had been owned by Gilbert White.

Sharpe died at Lyndhurst, 4 Barrowgate Road, Chiswick, on 25 December 1909. He was buried, following cremation, in the family grave at Highgate. In 1910 his widow and three of his daughters were awarded a civil-list pension of £90.   CHRISTINE E. JACKSON

Sources W. H. Mullens and H. K. Swann, *A bibliography of British ornithology from the earliest times to the end of 1912* (1917) · *British Birds*, 3 (1910), 273–88 [obituary] · *Selborne Magazine*, 21 (1910), 127 [obituary] · *The Auk*, 27 (1910), 124–9 · *The Ibis*, 9th ser., 2 (1908), 198–201 · *WWW* · 10 letters to R. B. Sharpe and his daughter, Emily, 1874–1916, BL, Add. MS 42181 · Keeper's correspondence, NHM, department of entomology, archives · Keeper's correspondence, NHM, department of zoology, archives, 1900 onwards · R. B. Sharpe, *An analytical index to the works of the late John Gould* (1893) · C. E. Jackson, 'Richard Bowdler Sharpe and his ten daughters', *Archives of Natural History*, 21 (1994), 261–9

Archives BL, corresp., Add. MS 42181 · NHM, vertebrata · NHM, papers relating to Royal Society expedition to Kerguelen's Land · NL Aus., notes and papers | NHM, letters, mainly to A. Hay, ninth marquess of Tweeddale, about birds

Likenesses Maull & Fox, photograph, Linn. Soc. [see illus.] · portrait, repro. in *British Birds*, pl. 13

Wealth at death £1024 8s. 8d.: probate, 17 Feb 1910, CGPLA Eng. & Wales

Sharpe, Roger (*fl.* 1610). *See under* Sharpe, Lewis (*fl.* 1640).

Sharpe, Sam (d. 1832), rebel slave leader, was born in Jamaica. He officially belonged to Croydon estate in St James parish, but worked as a domestic slave in Montego Bay, the second largest town in the island. Literate and intelligent, he was also a passionate and charismatic speaker. Sharpe became a class leader in the Montego Bay Baptist Church; his duties included helping the British missionary Thomas Burchell with the supervision of membership classes. At the same time, Sharpe was a 'Daddy' or 'ruler' among the independent black-led Native Baptists.

From his reading of the Bible, Sharpe became convinced that slavery was morally wrong. He helped to spread the view that the crown had already freed the slaves and that the local white people were withholding that freedom. Accordingly, Sharpe planned a campaign of passive resistance for the period just after Christmas in 1831: the slaves would simply cease work until their owners paid their wages and thereby conceded that the slaves were free. However, Sharpe developed an alternative strategy of armed rebellion in case passive resistance failed. His chief allies included other élite slaves, many of whom were also Baptists and Native Baptists.

The rebellion which broke out on 27 December 1831 was massive: it involved 20,000 slaves and spread over 750 square miles of the richest sugar-growing area of Jamaica.

Although the slaves enjoyed some initial successes, the rebellion was quickly and ferociously suppressed. At least 540 slaves were killed, while fourteen white inhabitants lost their lives. By the end of January 1832 Sharpe was in custody; he was tried on 19 April and hanged on 23 May. A missionary who interviewed him in gaol described Sharpe as 'certainly the most intelligent and most remarkable slave [he] ever met with' (Bleby, 115). Before his death Sharpe declared that he 'would rather die upon yonder gallows than live in slavery' (ibid., 116). Although Sharpe did not live to see the end of slavery, the rebellion had a significant effect in promoting the cause of emancipation. One week after Sharpe's death, the House of Commons established a committee to look into the best means of abolishing slavery.   GAD HEUMAN

Sources M. Turner, *Slaves and missionaries: the disintegration of Jamaican slave society, 1787–1834* (1982) • M. Reckord, 'The Jamaica slave rebellion of 1830', *Past and Present*, 40 (1968), 108–25 • M. Craton, *Testing the chains: resistance to slavery in the British West Indies* (1982) • G. Heuman, 'The killing time': the Morant Bay rebellion in Jamaica (1994) • H. Bleby, *Death struggles of slavery: being a narrative of facts and incidents which occurred in a British colony during the two years immediately preceding negro emancipation* (1853) • E. K. Brathwaite, 'The slave rebellion in the great river valley of St James, 1831–1832', *Jamaica Historical Review*, 13 (1982), 11–30

Sharpe, Samuel (1799–1881), Egyptologist and biblical scholar, second of the six children of Sutton Sharpe (1756–1806), brewer of King Street and of 10 Nottingham Place, Marylebone, Middlesex, and his second wife, Maria (d. 1806), third daughter of Thomas Rogers, banker, was born in King Street, Golden Square, London, on 8 March 1799, and baptized at St James's, Piccadilly, on 13 April. His mother, a descendant of Philip Henry, was sister of Samuel Rogers the poet; Daniel *Sharpe was Samuel's younger brother. After the death of his mother and then his father's bankruptcy and death, Samuel was cared for by his half-sister Catherine; the family moved to Paradise Row, Stoke Newington. In summer 1807, Samuel became a boarder in the school of Eliezer Cogan at Higham Hill, Walthamstow. At Christmas 1814 he was taken into the banking house of his uncles, Samuel and Henry Rogers, at 29 Clement's Lane, Lombard Street, and remained connected with the firm until 1861, having been made partner in 1824. Methodical, punctual, and cautious, Sharpe proved a successful businessman. In 1821 the Sharpe family moved to 12 New Ormond Street, as his brothers needed to reside closer to their places of business.

Brought up in the Church of England, Sharpe came gradually to adopt the unitarian views held by his mother's family, after extensive reading, notably of the New Testament in Greek, and personal reflection; in 1821 he joined the congregation of William Johnson Fox at South Place, Finsbury. For many years Sharpe and his brothers taught classes, before office hours, in the Lancasterian School in Harp Alley, Farringdon Street. Sharpe was elected a fellow of the Geological Society on 1 June 1827 but took a greater interest in mathematics and archaeological research, as shown by contributions between 1828 and 1831 to the *Philosophical Magazine*. He married at Tottenham, on 30 July 1827, his cousin Sarah (1796–1851),

daughter of Joseph Sharpe; they had six children, of whom two daughters survived him. The younger of their surviving daughters was Matilda *Sharpe. The couple settled in 4 Canonbury Place, Islington and stayed there until 1840, when they moved to nearby 32 Highbury Place.

Sharpe's interest in Egyptology was aroused by the research of Thomas Young (1773–1829). He read the works of J. F. Champollion and John Gardner Wilkinson, learned Coptic, and formed a hieroglyphic vocabulary. Before publishing his first book, *The Early History of Egypt* (1836), he consulted his uncle, Samuel Rogers, who said, 'Why, surely you can do it if Wilkinson can; his only thought is where to buy his kid gloves' (Clayden, 65). The first part of his *Egyptian Inscriptions*, published in the spring of 1837, contained the largest collection of hieroglyphical writing yet published, and it was followed by a second part in 1841 and a second series in 1855. His *Rudiments of a Vocabulary of Egyptian Hieroglyphics* was published in the autumn of 1837; in the introduction he stated his general method of investigation, which involved deducing the meaning of a word from its context in a phrase including other known ciphers. He allowed that the results were often tentative. Sharpe had a natural gift for decipherment, often amusing his friends by the facility with which he would read off a difficult cryptogram. In the autumn of 1838 his *History of Egypt under the Ptolemies* appeared and in 1842 his *History of Egypt under the Romans*; these two works were incorporated with the *Early History* in *The History of Egypt* (1846). Sharpe collaborated with Joseph Bonomi, a personal friend, in several publications and articles, notably *The Chronology and Geography of Ancient Egypt* (1849), *The Triple Mummy Case of Aro Eri-Ao* (1858), *Egypt, Nubia, and Ethiopia* (1862), and *The Alabaster Sarcophagus of Oimenepthah I* (1864). He was also involved with Bonomi and Owen Jones in the preparation of the Egyptian courts in the Crystal Palace exhibitions of 1854. He dated the monuments, composed the hieroglyphic inscriptions to Queen Victoria, and contributed to the publication *Description of the Egyptian Courts in the Crystal Palace* (1854).

Sharpe was on friendly terms with Samuel Birch of the British Museum, but he was annoyed when the institution's trustees refused to buy the fine statue of Prince Khaemwese, son of Rameses II, in 1866. He himself purchased the statue for about £500 and presented it to the museum. His later Egyptological publications included *Egyptian Hieroglyphics* (1861), *Egyptian Antiquities in the British Museum* (1862), *Egyptian Mythology and Egyptian Christianity* (1863), *The Decree of Canopus* (1870), and *The Rosetta Stone* (1871). The pains and skill of his workmanship were unquestioned; but he worked very independently, and on many points his conclusions were not accepted by contemporary scholars of Egyptology. He said of himself, 'I am a heretic in everything, even among Unitarians' (Clayden, 72). His research has since been superseded by later scholarship. Sharpe's contribution to Egyptology lay in his publications of accurate copies of hieroglyphic inscriptions which made these widely available to scholars and which still remain a useful reference source. Together with Wilkinson he was instrumental in exciting interest in Egyptology among the general public through popular works.

Sharpe's work as a translator of the Bible began with *The New Testament Translated* (1840), a revision of the Authorized Version of the New Testament. His Greek text was that of the German New Testament scholar J. J. Griesbach, and to this he always adhered, taking little interest in the progress of purely textual studies. His revision of the Authorized Version of the Old Testament, *The Hebrew Scriptures, Translated*, was first issued in 1865. In eight editions of his New Testament, and four of his old, he devoted great care to the improvement of his work. As a translator he was unoriginal but showed sound judgement; he was successful beyond others of his time in the difficult experiment of removing the archaisms without destroying the stylistic beauty of the English Bible. Among the last advocates of unpointed Hebrew, he published manuals for instruction in this system, notably *A Short Hebrew Grammar without Points* in 1877; his plan of printing his Hebrew extracts with capital letters, for the proper names and the beginnings of sentences, was unique. Apart from several exegetical works, he published *History of the Hebrew Nation and its Literature* (1869), and, combining his interest in archaeology and biblical studies, *Texts from the Bible Explained by ... Ancient Monuments* (1866), *Hebrew Inscriptions from the Valleys between Egypt and Mount Sinai* (1875), and *An Inquiry into the Age of the Moabite Stone* (1879). As with his Egyptian works, he proved a popularizer of biblical studies, linking archaeology and the Bible within the limits of the scholarship of his day. When, in 1870, the project of a revised version of the New Testament was undertaken by the convocation of Canterbury, Sharpe was one of four scholars of his denomination invited to select a member of their body to co-operate with the New Testament Revision Company.

In purely theological controversies Sharpe took little part, though he was a zealous propagandist for religious and educational causes of which he approved. His various benefactions to University College School and to University College, in London, exceeded £15,000, and he was a great benefactor of the Unitarian church. He wrote constantly for some years for the unitarian paper *The Inquirer*, founded in 1842 by Edward Hill, though he thought newspaper writing 'a bad employment' (Clayden, 112). He resumed it, however, in 1876, when the *Christian Life* was started by his friend Robert Spears, and wrote a weekly article until his death. He had contributed papers, chiefly biblical, to the *Christian Reformer*, between 1834 and 1863, and to many minor periodicals. He also wrote a memoir of his uncle, *Some Particulars of the Life of Samuel Rogers* (1859). He was a trustee of Dr Daniel Williams's foundations between 1853 and 1857; a member of the committee of management of University College, London, from 1866; president of the British and Foreign Unitarian Association in 1869–70; and president of Manchester College (later at Oxford) in 1876–8.

Sharpe spent his later years in retirement, though his house was still the resort of literary friends and young disciples. He suffered from progressive paralysis from April 1881, probably caused by a series of small strokes. He died at 32 Highbury Place, London, on 28 July 1881, and was buried at Abney Park cemetery on 3 August.

ALEXANDER GORDON, *rev.* M. L. BIERBRIER

Sources P. W. Clayden, *Samuel Sharpe* (1883) · *Christian Life* (7 Oct 1876) · *Christian Life* (13 Aug 1881) · *The Athenaeum* (6 Aug 1881), 175 · Parish register, St James's, Piccadilly, 13 April 1799, City Westm. AC [baptism] · Marylebone rate books, City Westm. AC · Tottenham parish register, LMA [marriage] · GS Lond. · BM · S. Lawrence, *Descendants of Philip Henry* (1844), 51 · W. D. Jeremy, *The Presbyterian Fund and Dr Daniel Williams's Trust* (1885), 213
Archives UCL, Rogers MSS
Likenesses M. Sharpe, oils, 1868, NPG
Wealth at death £63,244 7s. 5d.: probate, 14 Sept 1881, *CGPLA Eng. & Wales*

Sharpeigh, Alexander (*d.* 1613), merchant and sea captain, from Biddenden, Kent, was in 1608 and 1609 the commander of the East India Company's fourth voyage to Aden, Surat, and Bantam. In his youth he served as an apprentice to a member of the Levant Company and was, in that capacity, a factor in Constantinople. It is known from his will that he then became the captain of a merchant ship, the *Adventure*, and accrued capital of at least £500 trading in the Mediterranean for, among other commodities, grogram yarn and Venetian glass.

The chief aim of the fourth voyage was to establish trade with Aden and Surat. Fifty-six subscribers between them invested £33,000 in shares each worth £550 (parts of which might in turn be privately sold to under-subscribers). Of this capital the company spent nearly £1750 on purchasing two ships, the *Ascension* and *Union*, £14,600 on operating costs such as victuals and wages, £3400 on goods such as cloth, iron, and tin, and £15,000 in specie, chiefly Spanish reales. Sharpeigh himself bought one share in the voyage, and sold a quarter of this share to Sir Henry Lello and a quarter to a merchant, Stephen Harvey. To further his own trading prospects on the voyage Sharpeigh carried with him £100 worth of specie, and other commodities such as tobacco and gilded ornaments in partnership with other merchants. Whatever hopes the subscribers and Sharpeigh himself may have had for the voyage, the amount they recovered was to be no greater than 3 shillings and 6 pence in the pound, or 17.5 per cent of the original investment. Shipwrecks of both ships were to claim most of the capital the investors subscribed.

Sharpeigh, in command of the *Ascension* and *Union*, departed in April 1608 but misfortune beset the voyage, on more than one occasion caused by bad judgement. A day after setting sail from the Cape of Good Hope, a storm caused the ships to be separated. Proceeding to Aden in the *Ascension*, in April 1609 Sharpeigh handled negotiations with the Ottoman beylerbeyi with prudent caution, trading a few goods in a spirit of mutual mistrust. Unable to establish a factory, he then sailed for Surat. In September he reached landfall at Mahuwa, where local mariners warned him of the dangerous shoals in the Gulf of Cambay. The master of the ship, Philip de Grave, according to John Jourdain (114), 'stormed very much that he had brought the ship so far and now must have a pilot to carry him 20 leagues'. Sharpeigh deferred to Grave, and on the approach to Surat, without a pilot, the *Ascension* ran aground. The crew made a landing near Surat, but the goods were lost.

The fate of shipwreck was also to befall the *Union*, under the captaincy of Richard Rowles. Not finding Sharpeigh at Madagascar or Socotra, Rowles sailed for Bantam, where he traded for spices. Members of the crew successively succumbed to illness, however, and on the return voyage to England, only four weakened survivors remained when the ship drifted uncontrolled onto the coast of Brittany. The 25,000 reales left behind at Bantam, and invested for subsequent ladings to England, was the only capital which yielded a return for subscribers to the fourth voyage.

Sharpeigh spent the next three years accompanying Sir William Hawkins and Sir Henry Middleton. Denied entry into Surat by the governor (a position encouraged by the Portuguese), Sharpeigh and his crew joined Hawkins at Agra and the court of the Mughal emperor, Jahangir (*c.*1570–1627); he spent upwards of twenty months there. Reports that the sixth voyage under the command of Middleton would be arriving soon and anxiety about the weakening position of the English at the Mughal court prompted Sharpeigh in July 1611 to meet the fleet near Surat. According to Nicholas Downton, Middleton came to rely on Sharpeigh almost exclusively for advice. When they sailed to Bantam, however, Middleton was unsuccessful in his bid to secure the position of chief merchant of the factory for Sharpeigh, who, instead of remaining with Middleton or holding a lesser position, in December 1612 led an expedition to Sukadana in south-western Borneo, known for its diamond mines. Soon thereafter Sharpeigh disappeared, and he died either in Batavia or on the second leg of the voyage.

Sharpeigh's will was proved on 11 June 1620, seven years after his family received letters informing them of his disappearance. John Eldred, the well-known traveller and merchant, was to oversee any commercial transactions that needed to be completed. Sharpeigh made several small bequests to his mother, his sisters, and their children, the remainder to be divided between his brothers, John and Richard. Five merchants were to divide his much devalued East India Company stock. Sharpeigh did not marry but was enamoured of Ruth Percy (*d.* 1608) of Plymouth, leaving her £30 for 'the interchangeable love and entire affection between us'. He also made a charitable bequest to the poor of Biddenden, Kent.

J. K. LAUGHTON, *rev.* TREVOR DICKIE

Sources *The journal of John Jourdain, 1608–1617*, ed. W. Foster, Hakluyt Society, 2nd ser., 16 (1905), xvii–xlvii, 114 · will, PRO, PROB 11/135, sig. 64 · S. Purchas, *Hakluytus Posthumus, or, Purchas his pilgrimes*, bk 3 (1625); repr. Hakluyt Society, extra ser., 16 (1905), 12, 17, 26–7, 61–74 · F. C. Danvers and W. Foster, eds., *Letters received by the East India Company from its servants in the east*, 6 vols. (1896–1902), vol. 1, pp. 45, 138–9, 213–14, 230–32, 251, 259 · W. Foster, *England's quest of Eastern trade* (1933), 189, 249
Wealth at death approx. £250; incl. East India Company stock: PRO, PROB 11/135, sig. 64, fols. 510r–512v

Sharpey, William (1802–1880), physiologist, was born at Arbroath, Forfarshire, on 1 April 1802. He was the youngest of five children of Henry Sharpey (1758–1801), a shipping agent from Folkestone, Kent, who died before William was born, and his wife, Mary Balfour (1774–1836), from a well-known Arbroath family. Two other sons died in infancy; two daughters subsequently married. Sharpey's mother married, in 1806, William Arrott, a medical practitioner in the town, raising two daughters and four sons, three of whom became doctors.

Sharpey was educated at his local school and entered the University of Edinburgh in November 1817 to study the humanities and natural philosophy. He commenced medical studies in 1818, learning anatomy from John Barclay at the extramural school; he obtained the diploma of the College of Surgeons of Edinburgh in 1821. Rather than take up medical practice he sought further education and spent some months at the Brookes school of anatomy in London before going to Paris for a year, learning anatomy and surgery. Here he met James Syme, the famous Edinburgh surgeon, with whom he maintained a close friendship for the rest of his life. In August 1823 Sharpey graduated MD at Edinburgh with a thesis on stomach cancer and then returned to Paris for the greater part of 1824. He went home to Arbroath, where he assisted in his stepfather's practice, but he soon decided to devote himself entirely to anatomical and physiological pursuits.

Sharpey therefore returned to the continent in 1827, spending time with Panizza in Pavia, Rudolphi in Berlin, and Tiedemann in Heidelberg, among others. Back in Edinburgh by 1829 he prepared a thesis, 'On the pathology and treatment of false joints', which obtained for him the fellowship of the College of Surgeons of Edinburgh in 1830 and his recognition by the college as an extramural teacher. He gave his first course of lectures at the extra-academical school in 1831–2 in association with Allen Thomson, who became his lifelong friend and correspondent. Sharpey was successful as a teacher; the numbers in his class rose in each of the five years he was in Edinburgh.

During this time Sharpey undertook his only piece of research, on ciliary movement, which gained him election to the Royal Society of Edinburgh in 1834. Although not the first to recognize cilia, he made an original contribution in the *Edinburgh Medical and Surgical Journal* in 1830, well before the classical paper of Purkinje and Valentin (1834), which he translated into English. He also wrote a scholarly review of the subject for Todd's *Cyclopaedia of Anatomy and Physiology* (1836). In the summer of 1836, at the suggestion of Richard Quain, he successfully applied for the new chair of anatomy and physiology at University College, London, which he held until he retired in 1874. There he taught, for the first time in England, a course of systematic physiology; previously this subject had been treated only as an appendage to anatomy. Almost unwittingly he acquired the reputation for which he is now chiefly remembered: the father of modern physiology in Britain. This is a somewhat paradoxical title since he was neither a laboratory physiologist nor the founder of a notable school of physiology. Nor did he write a textbook on the subject, although he often complained of the lack of a suitable one for his students. His only writing during his professorship was as a joint author of several editions of Quain's *Elements of Anatomy*.

Nevertheless, Sharpey had a considerable personal influence which motivated a number of distinguished physiologists of the next generation. In part this was due to his position as a secretary of the Royal Society which he held from 1854 to 1872, concurrently with his professorship; he had been elected FRS in 1839 and was a member of its council from 1844. During this time he communicated many valuable papers by non-fellows to meetings of the society and he refereed over sixty manuscripts submitted for publication in its *Transactions*. A significant example of the latter was his report on the classical paper by A. V. Waller on degeneration in nerve (1850). From his extensive knowledge of continental work Sharpey was able to refer to earlier papers on this subject which Waller had missed but he also recognized the importance of the new work and recommended its publication.

It was through his teaching at University College that Sharpey's influence was strongest. His lectures stimulated the interest of John Marshall, the anatomist, who wrote a textbook of physiology (1867) based on Sharpey's course, and Joseph Lister, who published some valuable physiological papers on vasomotor nerves and inflammation before taking up his surgical career. However, the single most important event which led to the re-establishment of British physiology was the foundation, on Sharpey's recommendation, of a lectureship in practical physiology at University College in 1855. The first holder, J. B. Hayes, a Sharpey pupil, left after giving only one course; he was succeeded in turn by George Harley, Michael Foster, Edward Schafer, who later took the name Sharpey-Schafer as a mark of his profound admiration for his teacher, and John Burdon Sanderson. These former students and colleagues were directly responsible for the development of physiology as an independent discipline based at first on University College, London, but extending to the establishment of distinguished schools of physiology at Cambridge, Oxford, and Edinburgh. They all acknowledged their gratitude and their affection for their teacher. His strong support for physiology was shown by his evidence to the 1875 royal commission on the use of animals in experiments and also as a founder member of the Physiological Society the following year. He and Charles Darwin were immediately elected honorary members. Other distinctions included membership of the General Medical Council, a trustee of the Hunterian Museum and, in 1860, an honorary LLD from Edinburgh University.

In 1871 a Sharpey scholarship in physiology was established in his honour by his colleagues at University College, to which he subsequently bequeathed the greater part of his modest estate. His former students and his obituarists wrote warmly of Sharpey's personal qualities as a teacher and friend. His letters to Allen Thomson over a period of forty years show him to be shrewd, witty, observant, and greatly interested in the activities of all those who shared his academic world. He displayed a lack of financial ambition and showed no animosity to those with whom he disagreed. He had the power of attaching his pupils by ties of personal affection as well as those of common scientific interest. Sharpey's knowledge was wide, accurate, and up to date, and included the works of French and German authors. His loyalty to the two institutions which he served, University College and the Royal Society, never wavered, even when he was offered the prospect of the chair of anatomy at Edinburgh. He enjoyed visiting Scotland, travelling by sea to Dundee before the railway line opened in the 1840s.

Of the few anecdotes about Sharpey on record, one which shows his self-deprecating humour was his remark, to George Harley, that, as he was now an old man he should find a young wife since, in anticipation of marriage, he had contributed for fifty years to a Scottish Widows Fund which now refused to pay out unless there was a widow.

Sharpey never married, however. In London he lived mainly in the Russell Square area and Hampstead, where he was looked after by his niece Mary Colvill, daughter of his sister Elizabeth. She died in 1878 and he took lodgings at 50 Torrington Square, where he died on 11 April 1880 after an attack of bronchitis. He was buried on 17 April in the family plot in the abbey graveyard at Arbroath, the home town which he always remembered with affection.

A. H. SYKES

Sources D. W. Taylor, 'The life and teaching of William Sharpey, "father of modern physiology" in Britain', *Medical History*, 15 (1971), 126–53, 241–59 · L. S. Jacyna, ed., 'A tale of three cities: the correspondence of William Sharpey and Allen Thomson', *Medical History*, suppl. 9 (1989) [whole issue] · *DNB* · *PRS*, 31 (1880–81), x–xix · correspondence relating to the Royal Society, UCL, MS Add. 227 · lecture notes by W. Sharpey, UCL, MSS Add. 278–284 · W. Sharpey, reports, RS · U. Glas., Allen Thomson MSS · Wellcome L., Sharpey-Schafer MSS · E. Sharpey-Schafer, *History of the Physiological Society* (1927) · U. Edin. L., special collections division, letters and theses of William Sharpey · H. H. Bellot, *University College, London, 1826–1926* (1929) · *BMJ* (24 April 1880), 606 · G. L. Geison, *Michael Foster and the Cambridge school of physiology: the scientific enterprise in late Victorian society* (1978) · bap. reg. Scot.

Archives Arbroath Museum, letter-book used as secretary of the Royal Society; academic certificates · RS, corresp. · U. Edin., corresp. and papers · UCL, corresp. relating to Royal Society · UCL, lecture notes · Wellcome L., corresp. and MSS | CUL, corresp. with Sir George Stokes, etc. · NHM, corresp. with Sir Richard Owen and William Clift · U. Glas. L., corresp. with Allen Thomson

Likenesses Maull & Polyblank, photograph, 1855, NPG · W. H. Thornycroft, marble bust, exh. RA 1872, University College Hospital, London; reduced plaster model, University Museum, Oxford · photograph, 1874, Wellcome L. · Beynon & Co., colour lithograph, Wellcome L. · photograph, Wellcome L.

Wealth at death £8000—effects in England: probate, 21 May 1880, *CGPLA Eng. & Wales*

Sharpham, Edward (*bap.* 1576, *d.* 1608), playwright and pamphleteer, was baptized on 22 July 1576 at Colehanger, East Allington, Devon, the third of five children of Richard Sharpham (*d.* 1581) and Mary Pomeroy (*b.* 1548). His father died when he was five; his mother later married Alexander Hext (*d.* 1588), with whom she had three more children, and Charles Barnaby (*d.* 1596) of Clement's Inn. In 1592 she sued Thomas Fortescue for allegedly using witchcraft to kill her first husband and make her fall in love with Fortescue. In February 1596 Sharpham sued Fortescue and William Bastard of the Middle Temple for allegedly tampering with evidence related to the case (Eccles, 120).

Sharpham undoubtedly attended grammar school in Devon, possibly at Plymouth under the pedagogue William Kemp. On 9 October 1594 he was admitted to the Middle Temple. Although he never had chambers there and was never called to the bar, he was associated with the Middle Temple to the end of his life, and his plays show the influence of inns of court revels. In 1597 he published a cony-catching pamphlet entitled *The Discoverie of the Knights of the Poste*, a picaresque first-person account of rogues and criminals on the road between London and Exeter. This work was attributed only to 'E. S.', but Petter summarizes the strong evidence for Sharpham's authorship (Petter, 72–9).

For the next decade Sharpham must have associated with inns of court literary circles, but documentary evidence of his activities is lacking. Ben Jonson called Sharpham a 'rogue' (*Ben Jonson*, 1.133), but he may still be the 'E. S.' who wrote a commendatory poem for Jonson's *Volpone* (1607). His authorship of two plays printed in 1607, *The Fleire* and *Cupid's Whirligig*, is more certain. *The Fleire* was written for the Blackfriars Boys between late 1605 and its entry in the Stationers' register on 13 May 1606. The play is a cynical, thinly veiled satire of King James's court, modelled on John Marston's *The Malcontent* and *The Fawne* with elements of the Gunpowder Plot thrown in. It was apparently quite popular, being printed in editions of 1607, 1610, 1615, and 1631.

Cupid's Whirligig was written in early 1607 for the Children of the King's Revels at the Whitefriars, and probably produced that spring. On 30 August Sharpham was in debt to Richard Edwards for four felt hats he had borrowed earlier, possibly for this production. The play is another satire, parodying Lyly and again influenced by Marston, but it shows signs of hasty construction. The character of Nucome may have been a jab at King James's favourite Robert Carr, and Leech shows that the text was altered to remove satiric references to the Scots. The play was printed later in 1607 with a dedication to fellow Devonian Robert Hayman, and was reprinted in 1611, 1616, and 1630. On 22 April 1608, ill with the plague, Sharpham made a will which divided up his colourful wardrobe among friends and relatives. The next day he was buried in St Margaret's, Westminster.   DAVID KATHMAN

Sources C. G. Petter, *A critical old spelling edition of the works of Edward Sharpham* (1986) · M. Eccles, *Brief lives: Tudor and Stuart authors* (1982), 119–21 · C. Leech, 'The plays of Edward Sharpham: alterations accomplished and projected', *Review of English Studies*, 11 (1935), 69–74 · *Ben Jonson*, ed. C. H. Herford, P. Simpson, and E. M. Simpson, 11 vols. (1925–52), vol. 8

Wealth at death apparently in debt: Petter, *Critical old spelling edition*, 45

Sharples, Ellen (1769–1849). *See under* Sharples, Rolinda (1793–1838).

Sharples, James (1751/2–1811), portrait painter, was born into a Roman Catholic family in Lancashire. His brother, Henry, became a timber merchant in Liverpool and a half-sister, Mrs Talbot, was subprioress in a Catholic school. His parents sent him to study for the priesthood in France, but he decided instead to become an artist. A bequest from an uncle possibly assisted him in this decision. He may have studied with George Romney, and in 1774 he exhibited a portrait and two miniatures at the first exhibition of the Liverpool Society of Artists, when his address was given as Duke Street, Liverpool. From 1779 to 1785 he occasionally exhibited portraits at the Royal Academy. In 1781 he advertised himself as a 'Portrait Painter in Oil and Crayons' in the *Bristol Advertizer* (28 July 1781), and exhibited in Bristol 'upwards of one hundred specimens of known characters' (Miles, 725). By 1785 he had moved to London and married twice. The sons of his first and second marriages, George and Felix Thomas (1786–1832x49), both became artists. After his second wife's death Sharples returned to Liverpool, where about 1787 he married Ellen Wallace (1769–1849) [*see under* Sharples, Rolinda], a Quaker. She had been his pupil in Bath. Their two children, James junior (*c.*1788–1839) and Rolinda *Sharples (1793–1838) both became artists.

In 1793 Sharples set out with his young family for the United States of America. After a delay of seven months, when their ship was interned at Brest after being captured by a privateer, they arrived in New York. They settled in Philadelphia, where Sharples executed small profile portraits, mostly in pastels. The American painter William Dunlap recorded that Sharples carried letters of introduction to

> persons distinguished, either military, civil or literary, with a request to paint their portraits for his collection. This being granted, and the portrait finished in about two hours, the likeness generally induced an order for a copy, and brought as sitters all who saw it. His price for the profile was $15; and for the full-face (never so good) $20.   (Miles, 725)

Ellen Miles notes that:

> The portraits were on thick, textured, gray paper measuring about nine by seven inches. The outlines of the bust-length portraits were apparently drawn with a mechanical instrument to ensure physiognomic accuracy. The powdered colors, applied with a fine brush, were predominantly black, gray, and white, with flesh tones for the faces and blue for the backgrounds.   (ibid.)

His earliest recorded commissions were from George Washington in 1796. These included portraits of Washington himself (National Portrait Gallery, Smithsonian Institution; City of Bristol Museum; two pastel copies after Sharples, NPG; a copy by Ellen Sharples, Yale University Art Gallery); Motier Lafayette, the son of the marquis de Lafayette; and the president's wife, Martha, and adopted grandson, George Washington Parke Custis. Other sitters included Alexander Hamilton (1755/7–1804), Gouverneur

Morris (1752–1816), and the chemist Joseph Priestley (all National Portrait Gallery, Smithsonian Institution). James and Dolley Madison and Thomas Jefferson also sat to Sharples in Philadelphia. In her diary Ellen Sharples noted that 'copies were frequently required; these I undertook and was so far successful as to have as many commissions as I could execute; they were thought equal to the originals, price the same' (ibid.). Her long-continued practice of making replicas has sometimes confused attempts to attribute individual works to Sharples.

After working in New York from October 1797 to 1801, when his name sometimes appears in trade directories as Sharpless, concern about the possibility of war between England and France led Sharples to return with his family to England. He continued to take likenesses and to exhibit his American portraits. His sons James and Felix returned to America in 1806 and worked as pastel portraitists in New York state and in Virginia. Sharples returned with his wife and daughter in 1809, settling in New York. He made working visits to Niagara Falls and Philadelphia but his health deteriorated, and he died in New York as a result of a heart attack on 26 February 1811, and was buried in St Peter's Roman Catholic Church in the city. Ellen offered for sale his collection of portraits of distinguished Americans in the New York *Public Advertizer* (6 April–10 July 1811) and returned to England with Rolinda and James junior. Felix Sharples remained in the United States and had died by 1849 in North Carolina. His collection of his father's unsold portraits is now at Independence National Historical Park, Philadelphia. The portraits retained by Ellen Sharples went first to the Bristol Fine Arts Academy and are now in Bristol City Art Gallery. These include portraits of Sir Humphrey Davy, Sir William Herschel, William Godwin, and Robert Southey. Further examples of his work are in the Metropolitan Museum of Art, New York, and Boston Museum.

Dunlap, who sat to Sharples, thought his works 'strikingly like' and described him as 'a plain, well-disposed man [who] accumulated property by honest industry, and uncommon facility with his materials' (Miles, 726). His interest in the application of mechanical aids to his art also led him to take out patents in England on three designs for machinery in 1791, 1802, and 1804. He also designed a special carriage to carry his family and working materials in America. His portraits of American sitters continue to be appreciated not only for their strikingly accurate likenesses, but for recording prominent figures of historical importance, particularly leaders of the American War of Independence.

L. H. CUST, *rev.* ANNETTE PEACH

Sources E. Miles, 'Sharples, James', *ANB* · private information (2004) [Francis Greenacre] · R. Walker, *National Portrait Gallery: Regency portraits*, 2 vols. (1985) · www.npg.si.edu, 23 April 2002 · *The Sharples collection: family and legal papers (1794–1854)* (2001) [microfilm; intro. by D. Waggoner] · D. Foskett, *Miniatures: dictionary and guide* (1987)
Archives Bristol RO, corresp. and papers

Sharples, James (1825–1893), blacksmith and artist, was born on 4 September 1825 in Wakefield, Yorkshire, one of

the thirteen children of James Sharples (*c*.1793–1855), blacksmith and wrought iron worker, and his wife, Margaret (*c*.1797–1854). Both Sharples's grandfathers were blacksmiths, and Sharples himself entered the trade as a smithy boy, working in a foundry at the age of ten. He was later set to work in an engine shop where he heated and carried rivets for the boilermakers. It is said that he expressed his early aptitude for art by drawing boiler designs in chalk on his mother's kitchen floor, and it was with her support and that of an elder brother that he was encouraged to pursue his talent. At sixteen he attended weekly art classes at Bury Mechanics' Institute and he spent what little spare time he had outside the foundry in making copies of drawings, and in improving his reading so that he could better understand the principles of art.

Having made his own easel, palette, and canvas, Sharples taught himself oil painting from a shilling guide and after initial disappointments produced a copy of an engraving, *Sheep-Shearing*, which he sold for a half-crown. This gave him the confidence to attempt a more ambitious work and he began making sketches while working in the foundry, where he opted for the heavier kind of iron work, allowing him more time to draw while waiting for the metal to heat. He learned perspective from Brook Taylor's *Principles* and techniques for depicting the human form from Flaxman's *Anatomical Studies*.

The result of this endeavour was a large painting called *The Forge*, completed about 1849. The artistic merits of this painting, which was solid in its conception and execution, were less impressive than the trials that had been undergone to produce it, and Sharples was justly celebrated for his achievement. Samuel Smiles used him as one of the 'illustrations of character and conduct' in *Self-Help* (1860) and the success of the picture encouraged Sharples to consider full-time painting. But, as Smiles noted, 'not obtaining sufficient employment at portraits to occupy his time, or give him the prospect of a steady income, he had the good sense to resume his leather apron, and go on working at his honest trade' (Smiles, 135). He painted one other large work, *The Smithy*, and in 1851 won a prize for an emblematical design offered by the Amalgamated Society of Engineers, of which he was a member.

The suggestion that *The Forge* would make an admirable reproduction prompted Sharples next to learn the art of steel-engraving, and in 1859, after many years of Labour, he completed a work that was as remarkable in its way as the original. The quality of his etching, part line engraving and part mezzotint, was noted in the London art journals and copies were widely sold. But a combination of bad luck and naïvety deprived Sharples of most of the profit from this venture and to the end he was reliant upon the foundry for an income.

Sharples married on 7 April 1852 Sarah Moore (1832–1861), with whom he had one son and a daughter, who died in infancy; after his first wife's death he married Sarah Ford on 20 June 1863, with whom he also had a son and a daughter. Sharples died in Blackburn, where he had settled, on 13 June 1893 and was buried at the town's cemetery four days later. Of *The Forge*, which defined him as an artist and as a man, and serves as his epitaph, Sharples wrote: 'The picture simply represents the interior of a large workshop such as I have been accustomed to work in' (Smiles, 227).   L. H. CUST, *rev.* MARK POTTLE

Sources Mallalieu, *Watercolour artists* · J. Baron, *James Sharples, blacksmith and artist* (1893) · Bryan, *Painters* (1903–5), vol. 5 · S. Smiles, *Self-help: with illustrations of character and conduct*, rev. edn (1860); another edn (1910) ['one shilling edition'] · *The Times* (15 June 1893) · *The Sharples collection: family and legal papers* (1794–1854) (2001) [microfilm; intro. by D. Waggoner]

Sharples, Rolinda (1793–1838), portrait and genre painter, was born on 3 September 1793, probably in Bath, the second child and only daughter of James *Sharples (1751/2–1811) and of his third wife, **Ellen Sharples** [*née* Wallace] (1769–1849). Both Rolinda's parents were professional artists, James being a very talented if not outstanding painter of portraits in pastel. Rolinda's half-brother Felix Sharples (1786–*c*.1832) and her brother James (*c*.1788–1839) also became professional artists. Together with his family, James Sharples senior took his portrait practice to the United States, setting out in 1793 but being delayed by seven months' internment in Brest, after being captured by a French privateer. James Sharples drew many of the most prominent Americans, including George Washington, before the family returned to Bath in 1801. They all set out again from Bristol in 1806, but this time their vessel ran aground on the muddy banks of the Avon. Felix and James junior continued to the United States but their parents and Rolinda remained in Bristol until 1809. In February 1811 her father died in New York and in June, Ellen, James junior, and Rolinda returned to Bristol. Before her marriage about 1787 Ellen had been a pupil of James Sharples, learning drawing 'as an ornamental art for amusement' as she later wrote in her diary (Ellen Sharples's diary, summary of events, May 1806–Jan 1808). However, she made many excellent and indistinguishable copies of her husband's pastels and a small number of original portraits. Now, settled in the elegant and fast-expanding village of Clifton (then just outside Bristol), she devoted herself principally to her daughter's education and career.

Rolinda first decided to be a professional artist at the age of thirteen. She initially concentrated on portrait painting, mostly in oil and often of her Clifton acquaintances. Many of her friends were depicted in her first major work, *The Cloak Room, Clifton Assembly Rooms*, completed in 1818 (Bristol Museum and Art Gallery). This charming picture of Bristol's social scene has aptly illustrated the corus of more than one novel by Jane Austen. The perspective and scale are uncertain and the poles are contrived and a little stiff, for the observation of the thirty-one gentlefolk there depicted is acute, friendly, and even witty. Rolinda depicted an event at which she would have been at ease. Much larger and more ambitious scenes of Bristol life followed: *The Market* and *Rownham Ferry* (Sothebys, 15 July 1992, lot 15) were shown at the Royal Academy in 1820 and 1822, respectively, and *St James's Fair* (priv. coll.) and *The Stoppage of the Bank* (Bristol Museum and Art Gallery) were exhibited at the Society of British Artists in 1825 and 1827. The subject of the last painting had been suggested by the

Rolinda Sharples (1793–1838), self-portrait, *c*.1816 [with her mother, Ellen Sharples]

failure of a Bristol bank in 1822 and was chosen by Rolinda because it was 'well suited to a great variety of expression' (diaries of Ellen and Rolinda Sharples, 'Reminiscences'). The artist's apparently uncritical detachment from the human tragedies she was depicting is still more apparent in *The Trial of Colonel Brereton* (1832–4; Bristol Museum and Art Gallery). Brereton was tried for negligence in the handling of the Bristol riots of October 1831. After only two days of the trial, which Rolinda attended, he committed suicide. While the artist's diary suggests a genuine sympathy for 'the poor and much pitied Col. Brereton' (Rolinda Sharples's diary, 1832), the printing is a laborious social almanac including over a hundred portraits, many of persons who did not even attend the trial. More successful was her last large Bristol scene, *Clifton Race Course* (Bristol Museum and Art Gallery), completed in 1836. Rolinda died of breast cancer on 10 February 1838 at 3 St Vincent Parade, Holwells, Bristol, whither she and her mother had moved from 2 Lower Harley Place, Clifton, in 1831. She was buried in St Andrew's churchyard, Clifton. Her mother gave £2000 to the nascent Bristol Academy of Fine Arts, and bequeathed to it a further £3465 and her large collection of works by members of her family on her death in 1849. Today she is acknowledged as the founder of what is now the Royal West of England Academy.

Rolinda Sharples was born into a family of professional artists with a modest income from property and capital investments. She had little social contact with her fellow Bristol artists perhaps as much because of her social status as her gender. Her formal training was limited to a series of lessons from Philip Reinagle in London in 1814 and 1820. The principal influences upon her work, however, were the paintings of the Bristol artist Edward Bird RA (1772–1819). Her genre or narrative paintings, most notably *The Stoppage of the Bank*, are also closely comparable to other works of the 1820s by Bristol artists such as E. V. Rippingille (1798–1859) and Samuel Colman (1780–1845) and she was undoubtedly a significant member of the Bristol school.   FRANCIS GREENACRE

Sources K. Metz, 'Ellen and Rolinda Sharples, mother and daughter painters', *Women's Art Journal*, 16/1 (1995), 3–11 • K. M. Knox, *The Sharples: their portraits of George Washington and his contemporaries* (1930); repr. (1972) • MS diaries of Ellen and Rolinda Sharples, 1803–36, Bristol reference library [typescripts in Bristol City Museum and Art Gallery, and Frick Art Reference Library, New York] • F. Greenacre, *The Bristol school of artists: Francis Danby and painting in Bristol, 1810–1840* [1973], 211–17 [exhibition catalogue, City Museum and Art Gallery, Bristol, 4 Sept – 10 Nov 1973] • A. Wilson, 'Rolinda Sharples and her family', *Country Life*, 143 (1968), 26–8 • A. Wilson, 'The Sharples family of painters', *Antiques* (Nov 1971), 740–43 • K. Metz, 'Ellen and Rolinda Sharples', *Dictionary of women artists*, ed. D. Gaze (1997), 1262–5 • A. E. A. Hunt, 'Notes on Felix Thomas Sharples', *Virginia Magazine of History and Biography*, 59 (1951), 216–19 • *Matthews' Bristol Directories* (1793–1870) • tombstone • *The Sharples collection: family and legal papers* (1794–1854) (2001) [microfilm; intro. by D. Waggoner]
Archives Bristol City Museum and Art Gallery • Bristol Reference Library, MSS, diaries
Likenesses R. Sharples, self-portrait, oil on panel, *c.*1816, City Museum and Art Gallery, Bristol [*see illus.*] • J. Sharples, oils, exh. AM Oxf. *c.*1998 (Ellen Wallace)

Sharrock, Robert (*bap.* 1630, *d.* 1684), Church of England clergyman and natural historian, was baptized at Drayton Parslow, Buckinghamshire, on 29 June 1630, one of the four sons and two daughters of Robert Sharrock (*d.* 1671) and his wife, Judith. His father was rector of Drayton Parslow from 1639 to 1642 and subsequently of Adstock, in the same county. In 1643 he went to Winchester School as a scholar, and in March 1649 the parliamentary visitors elected him perpetual fellow of New College, Oxford. He matriculated in November 1650, graduating BCL in October 1654 and proceeding DCL in May 1661.

At Oxford, Sharrock was one of those active around the university's botanic garden and in the circle of scientifically minded people who met in the Oxford lodgings of the Hon. Robert Boyle. These meetings, which preceded the foundation of the Royal Society in 1662, included several who went on to be its founding fellows, their discussions embracing chemistry, physics, and medicine. By 1660, when his own illness and an outbreak of smallpox in the university drove him to the family home at Adstock, and Boyle was living in London, Sharrock was overseeing Boyle's publications through the press at Oxford; as he wrote to Boyle on 9 April:

I shall willingly promise that except only some studies altogether necessary for mee, wch will not take up one halfe of my studyeing time, I shall doe no other business but yours in this overlooking of Copy, the Presse, and rendering from Latine. (RS, Boyle letters, 5, no. 88)

This referred to Boyle's *New Experiments Physico-Mechanical*, written by Boyle in English, which Sharrock and his junior helpers were translating into Latin for simultaneous publication in both languages. In December Sharrock's father settled on him the rent of a small property in Northampton, to augment his fellowship, as he had given up a bursarship and tutorships 'in change for study whch is a better employment' (ibid., 5, no. 92), and in the hope that this income would equal the cost of maintaining his laboratory, where from time to time he copied experiments described by Boyle. He also contributed prefaces for Boyle's other treatises which were issued during this period.

At the same time, with Boyle's encouragement, Sharrock had been writing his own book, *The History of the Propagation and Improvement of Vegetables*, published in Oxford, probably with Boyle's financial assistance, in 1660, with later editions in 1666 and 1672. 'Written according to observations made from Experience and Practice' (title-page) and intended as a practical text for husbandmen and gardeners, it included some perceptive remarks on the germination of seeds, on the external morphology of seedlings, and on the different ways of propagating, by offshoots, layering, grafting, and the taking of cuttings. Sharrock mused on the similarity of some plant forms and their possible relationship, and on the mathematical symmetry in the arrangement of bud and leaf, and the possibility of finding some natural law which controlled their growth: 'even in the wayes of Propagation that are most artificial, there is more of Nature than of Art ... it is the great Art of Man to find out the Arts of Nature' (p. 4).

While still at Oxford, Sharrock also published *De officiis secundum naturae jus* (1660), a hypothesis of the law of nature (a concept derived from classical Greece), in which he contested Hobbes's views of ethics and politics, and *Judicia (seu legum censurae) de variis incontinentiae speciebus* (1662), with definitions and penalties for adultery, polygamy, fornication, rape, sins against nature, and incest. His *Provinciale vetus provinciae Cantuariensis* (1663, 1664), a collection of constitutions and statutes of the archbishops of Canterbury from 1222 to 1415 and of the cardinal legates Otho and Othobonus, seems to have been the revision of an earlier work.

In the summer of 1665 Sharrock took up the rectorate of Great Horwood, Buckinghamshire, and later in that year he was installed prebendary of Winchester. In 1668 he exchanged Horwood for the rectory of East Woodhay, Hampshire, succeeding his younger brother Edmund (1635–1689), and about this time he married Frances (*d.* 1692), daughter of Edmund West. Their daughters Anne (*bap.* 1669 or 1670) and Frances (*bap.* 1672) were followed by a son, Robert (*b.* 1677 or 1678, *d.* 1708), who later entered the Inner Temple. Sharrock became rector of Bishop's Waltham, Hampshire, in 1669 and archdeacon of Winchester in April 1684. He maintained his interest in natural laws, publishing *De finibus virtutis Christianae* (1673) and *Royal Table of the Laws of Human Nature* (1682), which was an outline of his earlier *Naturae jus*. Sharrock's books were recommended for the study of natural law in Oxford University, while *Naturae jus* and *Judicia* were reprinted on the continent in 1667 and 1668 respectively. Sharrock died on 11 July 1684, presumably at Bishop's Waltham, and was buried at Bishop's Waltham. His library passed to his son, who doubtless amplified it; at its sale on 11 February 1711 the Bibliotheca Sharrockiana consisted of more than 2000 volumes in several languages, encompassing divinity, history, natural sciences, medicine, and law.

ANITA McCONNELL

Sources A. Arber, 'Robert Sharrock (1630–1684): a precursor of Nehemiah Grew (1641–1712) and an exponent of "natural law" in the plant world', *Isis*, 51 (1960), 3–8 · *DSB*, 12.357 · Wood, *Ath. Oxon.*, new edn, 4.147–8 · *VCH Buckinghamshire*, 4.144 · T. F. Kirby, *Winchester scholars: a list of the wardens, fellows, and scholars of … Winchester College* (1888) · *Hist. U. Oxf. 4: 17th-cent. Oxf.* · RS, Boyle letters, vol. 5 · parish register, Drayton Parslow, Bucks. RLSS, 29 June 1630 [baptism] · Foster, *Alum. Oxon.* · *Fasti Angl., 1541–1857*, [Canterbury] · IGI · *The works of Robert Boyle*, ed. M. Hunter and E. Davies, 14 vols. (1999–2000), vols. 1, 2, 3, 6

Shastri, Lal Bahadur (1904–1966), prime minister of India, was born on 2 October 1904 at Mughal Sarai, Benares district, United Provinces, the second of three children of Sharda Prasad, teacher, and his wife, Ramdulari Devi, daughter of Hazarilal of Mirzapur. He had two sisters. His father died during his infancy in 1906, leaving the family with few resources. Lal Bahadur, a member of the Kayastha caste, lived ever after—in later life by choice rather than necessity—in simplicity, eschewing modern comforts and amenities, and at times even limiting consumption of basic necessities for himself and his family. He married Lalita Devi, *née* Lalmani, daughter of Ganesh Prasad, on 16 May 1928; they had six children. He was educated at Harish Chandra high school and Kashi Vidyapith, Benares, the nationalist university, where he was among the first students admitted and from where he received his degree of Shastri, which he used ever after as his surname. He joined the Servants of the People Society upon his graduation and remained a member of it—ultimately becoming its president—for the rest of his life, which was otherwise devoted exclusively to political activity.

Lal Bahadur Shastri was a Gandhian, who lived simply and sought to work for the benefit of the poor and common people. He participated in all the major movements for independence, from the non-co-operation movement of 1921 to the movement of individual *satyagraha* in 1941, as a consequence of which he spent more than nine years in gaol in numerous terms of imprisonment. His political patrons included Purushottam Das Tandon, Jawaharlal Nehru, and Pandit Govind Ballabh Pant. He worked in Allahabad, after moving there in 1929, under Tandon in the Servants of the People Society and as secretary of the District Congress Committee, Allahabad, in both of which organizations Tandon was the president. At Allahabad Shastri became close to Nehru as well. From the 1930s on he progressed upward politically both in the party organization of the Indian National Congress and in legislative and governmental positions. Just before independence he became a trusted member of the government of Pandit Pant in United Provinces, where he served first as his parliamentary secretary, then as home minister from 1947 until 1951.

Shastri's move to Delhi occurred in 1951 as a consequence of the rift between two of his former patrons,

Lal Bahadur Shastri (1904–1966), by Terry Fincher, 1965

Tandon and Nehru, which led to the displacement of Tandon by Nehru as president of the Indian National Congress. Nehru, who was also prime minister at the time, called Shastri to Delhi to become general secretary and to organize the party's first general election campaign in 1952. After the overwhelming victory of the Congress in the 1952 elections Shastri successfully contested election to the Rajya Sabha, the Indian upper house, after which he was taken into the government as minister for railways and transport. In a demonstration, rare in post-independence Indian politics, of strict responsibility and accountability for his performance, he resigned from his post in 1956 after a major railway accident in Madras, involving considerable loss of life. However, Nehru did not allow him to remain idle and assigned him the task of co-ordinating the election campaign of 1957. He was again taken into the council of ministers in 1957. In April 1961 he replaced Pandit Pant as home minister of the government of India. In 1963 he resigned from government once again under the Kamaraj plan, a major strategic political move which was ostensibly designed to improve the functioning of the Congress organizations and governments throughout the country, but which also laid the basis for the succession to Pandit Nehru, who became gravely ill in January 1964.

Shortly after Nehru's stroke Shastri, Nehru's chosen heir, was called to rejoin the cabinet as minister without portfolio. Upon Nehru's death he was selected unanimously, though not without some discontent among rival contenders, as the second prime minister of India. He was installed on 9 June 1964.

In his brief tenure as prime minister Shastri introduced economic policies in favour of agriculture and private investment which deviated from those of Nehru. However, his major contribution to Indian politics was as a 'troubleshooter' for others and a peacemaker while in office, who worked to settle disputes in the party, the country, and international relations in several crises concerning Assam, Punjab, Kashmir, the official language issue, and relations between India and Ceylon, Nepal, and Pakistan. Ironically, though peace and conciliation were his hallmarks, his greatest accomplishment is often considered to be India's victory during his prime ministership in the Second Indo-Pakistan War. He died in Tashkent, Uzbekistan, on 11 January 1966, of heart failure, on the evening after signing the peace agreement there restoring the *status quo ante bellum*. Shastri, a Hindu, was cremated, the final irony being the naming of his cremation site, a national memorial in Delhi, as Vijaya Ghat, commemorating India's victory in the war against Pakistan. He was survived by his wife.   PAUL R. BRASS

Sources D. R. Mankekar, *Lal Bahadur Shastri* (1973) · R. Prasad, *Days with Lal Bahadur Shastri: glimpses from the last seven years* (1991) · M. Brecher, *Nehru's mantle: the politics of succession in India* (1966) · K. C. Saxena and others, eds., *Saga of Lal Bahadur Shastri* (1989) · *Selected speeches of Lal Bahadur Shastri (June 11, 1964, to January 10, 1966)* (1974) · F. R. Frankel, *India's political economy, 1947–1977: the gradual revolution* (1978)
Archives FILM BFI NFTVA, documentary footage · BFI NFTVA, news footage
Likenesses photographs, 1964–5, Hult. Arch. · T. Fincher, photograph, 1965, Hult. Arch. [*see illus.*]

Shattock [*formerly* Betty], **Samuel George** (1852–1924), pathologist, was born on 3 November 1852 in Mornington Street, Regent's Park, London, the son of Samuel Chapman Betty, chemist, and his wife, Jane *née* Brown. Some thirty years later he changed his name to Shattock. He was educated at University College, London, first at the boys' school and afterwards as a medical student, and qualified in 1874. After a few years as curator of the museum at his own school, he moved to St Thomas's Hospital, where he rearranged the museum and taught pathology. His connection with the Royal College of Surgeons began informally soon after he graduated. In 1897 Shattock became curator of its pathological museum and reorganized the whole collection. He held this post for twenty-seven years. From 1880 onwards he was one of the mainstays of the Pathological Society of London and its successor, the section of pathology of the Royal Society of Medicine, editing its *Transactions* and *Proceedings* for many years and contributing about 150 papers. He was elected a fellow of University College in 1910 and a fellow of the Royal Society in 1917, the reward for years of high-quality research rather than any single outstanding discovery.

For forty years Shattock was one of the chief influences in London on the transformation of pathology. In the 1880s, pathology was remade as a science with its own methods and results rather than left as a casual interest of medical practitioners. Its scope was also greatly enlarged by the development of bacteriology and by the appreciation of the importance of experimental and chemical methods of investigation. Shattock was one of the first holders of a full-time post in pathology and he played an important part in this revolution of outlook. He was a devoted and industrious student who became the most erudite pathologist of his time. He had a broad conception of the content of pathology: he was an acknowledged authority on morbid anatomy, and he investigated the virulence of bacteria, the healing of wounds in plants, the microbic origin of cancer, and secondary sexual characters. His teaching was clear and dramatic, and 'Ask Shattock' was a common response in metropolitan medical circles to difficult questions in pathology for nearly half a century. While never a public scientist, the respect that Shattock enjoyed allowed him to provide leadership and service behind the scenes to many ventures, including the

Lister Institute, the University of London, and the *British Medical Journal*.

Shattock was a shy and very reserved man, though he would readily share his considerable knowledge with colleagues and students. His expertise extended across the sciences and on to an encyclopaedic knowledge of certain sports, especially Derby winners and cricket scores. He was a devout Roman Catholic and the posthumous publication of his *Thoughts on Religion* (1926) revealed an aspect of his life of which few of his colleagues had been aware. Shattock died at his home, Prior Park Lodge, 4 Crescent Road, Wimbledon, on 11 May 1924. He left a wife, Emily Lucy *née* Wood, with whom he had three sons and a daughter.   A. E. BOYCOTT, *rev.* MICHAEL WORBOYS

Sources *The Lancet* (17 May 1924), 1028 · *BMJ* (17 May 1924), 889 · *PRS*, 96B (1924), xxx–xxxii · 'Samuel George Shattock', *Journal of Pathology and Bacteriology*, 27 (1924) · S. G. Shattock, *Thoughts on religion* (1926) · personal knowledge (1937) · *CGPLA Eng. & Wales* (1924)
Archives RS | RCS Eng., pathological specimens
Likenesses photograph, repro. in *The Lancet* · photograph, repro. in *BMJ* · photograph, repro. in 'Samuel George Shattock', *Journal of Pathology and Bacteriology*, xxvii
Wealth at death £8730 5s. 5d.: probate, 12 July 1924, *CGPLA Eng. & Wales*

Shaughnessy, Thomas George, first Baron Shaughnessy (1853–1923), railway executive in Canada, was born on 6 October 1853 at Milwaukee, Wisconsin, USA. He was the son of Thomas Shaughnessy, an officer in the Milwaukee detective police, a native of Ashford, co. Limerick. His mother was also of Irish birth. He was educated in the public and Catholic schools of Milwaukee, where he showed a special aptitude for mathematics, and spent several months in 1869 at the Spencerian Business College in the same town.

In 1869 Shaughnessy joined the purchasing department of the Milwaukee and St Paul Railway. For some time he participated in local city politics, and studied law privately, hoping to escape his mundane work; but as his energy, and enterprise, gained him promotion, he became reconciled to his calling. He attracted the very favourable notice of William Cornelius Van Horne, the general superintendent of the railway company, at whose instance he was in 1879 appointed its general storekeeper. In 1882, however, Van Horne, now general manager of the newly formed Canadian Pacific Railway (CPR), persuaded Shaughnessy to become the CPR's general purchasing agent. Shaughnessy moved to Montreal, where he would end up residing for the rest of his life.

During Shaughnessy's first years in Canada the financial situation of the Canadian Pacific Railway was often extremely precarious, and he proved masterful in placating and warding off alarmed and importunate creditors. He also exhibited great skill in squeezing the highest value possible from each dollar spent by the railway, and pushing the CPR, and Van Horne, to begin reducing the railway's enormous debt load. Van Horne's biographer, Walter Vaughan, goes so far as to say that in the early months of 1885, when the very difficult section of the line along Lake Superior was being built 'on faith and credit', 'the one bright spot in the darkness was the success of the indefatigable and resourceful Shaughnessy'. In 1885 he was appointed assistant general manager, and the assistant to president Van Horne four years later. In 1891 he became vice-president, and in 1899 president succeeding Van Horne, who had relied so heavily on his business acumen and organizing ability.

Although Shaughnessy remained permanently grateful for Van Horne's friendship and assistance, he was a tireless critic of his predecessor's lack of systematic organization and management. Upon taking the presidency, he centralized financial operations in the Montreal head office, including control over budget, earnings, and allocations, while decentralizing managerial control in the field, ensuring that divisional heads had both the clear responsibility and the ability to run their affairs on behalf of the CPR as efficiently as possible. The period of Shaughnessy's presidency saw the Canadian Pacific at the height of its prosperity and renown, a product of the great Laurier boom—when Canada's growth rate exceeded that of every country in the world—and his own abilities as a railways manager. During this golden era, the CPR's network of mileage in western Canada was almost doubled. At the same time, Shaughnessy diversified the railway company's operations by building grand hotels throughout the country, establishing a mining and smelting operation in British Columbia, and by entering the freight and passenger shipping business on both coasts.

Perhaps his most notable achievement was the creation, partly by purchase, partly by new construction, of the company's Atlantic Fleet, which for the first time attracted large numbers of both immigrant and well-to-do passengers to the St Lawrence route to North America. On the collapse of the Laurier boom in 1913—a misfortune soon aggravated by the outbreak of the First World War—Shaughnessy showed that his old resourcefulness had not left him, and his shrewd and daring financial measures enabled the company to weather the crisis and, alone among the important railways of Canada, to continue as a private undertaking. His reputation still intact, he resigned the presidency in 1918, becoming chairman of Canadian Pacific's board of directors.

Shaughnessy was knighted on 21 September 1901 and created KCVO in 1907. In 1916 he was raised to the peerage of the United Kingdom. In 1911 he received the honorary degree of DCL from Trinity College, Dublin. These public honours were a recognition of his contribution to the economic development of Canada as manager of the country's largest business enterprise. Soon after he joined the staff of the Canadian Pacific Railway he was naturalized as a British subject.

Like many in the Canadian corporate élite, including ex-Americans like Van Horne, Shaughnessy opposed the Liberal government's proposed policy of reciprocal free trade with the United States, and threw the CPR's considerable might behind the Conservative opposition in the 1911 election. When he cried, 'Fix the channels of Canadian trade eastward and westward,' his critics naturally pointed out that such advice was in striking accord with the interests of his railway. During the First World War,

Shaughnessy turned his experience and energy to the promotion of his country's cause: he was freely consulted by both the Canadian and the British governments; in particular, he acted as a very useful financial intermediary between Lloyd George's government, and the American investment banks, raising money for the war effort.

On 12 January 1880 Shaughnessy married Elizabeth Bridget Nagle (*b*. 1850), of Milwaukee, with whom he had two sons and three daughters. He died at Montreal on 10 December 1923 after a heart attack. He was succeeded as second baron by his elder son, William James (*b*. 1883). His younger son was killed in the First World War. Much of Shaughnessy's success may have been due to his faculty of detaching his mind from his work, when business hours were over. For many years he habitually drank a pint of champagne with his dinner; he was fond of billiards and bridge; for some time he owned one or two racehorses; but he took no exercise whatever until, when quite elderly, he became interested in golf.

W. T. Waugh, *rev.* Gregory P. Marchildon

Sources J. A. Eagle, *The Canadian Pacific Railway and the development of western Canada, 1896–1914* (1989) · D. Cruise and A. Griffiths, *Lords of the line: the men who built the CPR* (1988) · W. K. Lamb, *History of the Canadian Pacific Railway* (1977) · 'Shaughnessy, Thomas George', *The Canadian Encyclopedia*, 2nd edn (1988) · G. D. Taylor and P. A. Baskerville, *A concise history of business in Canada* (1994)
Archives NA Canada | CPR Archives, Montreal, CPR MSS [particularly Shaughnessy letter books] · NA Canada, Canadian Pacific railway MSS
Likenesses W. Stoneman, photograph, 1919, NPG · Spy [L. Ward], caricature, NPG; repro. in *VF* (26 Aug 1908) · photograph, NA Canada; repro. in Eagle, *Canadian Pacific railway*, centrepiece · photographs, repro. in Cruise and Griffiths, *Lords of the line*

Shaw. *See also* Shawe, Schaw.

Shaw, Alexander (1804–1890), surgeon, was born in Scotland on 6 February 1804, the sixth son of Charles Shaw, clerk of the county of Ayr, and Barbara Wright, his wife, daughter of a customs official at Greenock. John *Shaw (1792–1827), Sir Charles *Shaw (1795–1871), and Patrick *Shaw were his elder brothers. One sister, Marion, married Sir Charles Bell, and another sister married Bell's brother, Professor George Joseph Bell. Alexander Shaw was educated at Edinburgh high school, and afterwards went to the University of Glasgow, where he matriculated in 1819 and graduated MA on 11 April 1822. Shaw was connected with the Middlesex Hospital, London, for more than half a century. He entered there as a pupil in 1822; was made assistant surgeon in 1836; and became surgeon in 1842. Sir Charles Bell lectured at the hospital between 1812 and 1836. On his retirement in 1872 Shaw was appointed consulting surgeon. He joined the medical school of the hospital on its formation, and at the time of his death he was the sole survivor of the original members of staff. With the idea of obtaining an MD degree, Shaw was admitted as a pensioner at Downing College, Cambridge, on 28 June 1826, but on the death of his brother John in 1827 he left Cambridge to take up his work at the Great Windmill Street School. From this time he devoted all his energies to his professional work, and he abandoned the idea of taking his Cambridge degree. He obtained the licence of the Society of Apothecaries in 1827, and in the following year gained membership of the Royal College of Surgeons. On the institution of the fellowship of the college, Shaw was elected one of the first fellows on 11 December 1843. He served on the college council from 1858 to 1865.

Shaw took an active part in the work of the London medical societies. At the Royal Medical and Chirurgical Society he served the offices of honorary secretary, vice-president, and treasurer, and in the *Transactions* of that society he published some valuable papers on rickets. In 1839 he published *A Narrative of the Discoveries of Sir Charles Bell in the Nervous System*. After Bell's death in 1842 Lady Bell lived with her brother, and their house became a centre for the literary and scientific society of the period. In 1856 Shaw married Susan, *née* Turner (*d.* 1891), the widow of Mr J. Randall; they had a son who died in infancy. In 1869 Shaw republished Bell's *New Idea of the Anatomy of the Brain* (originally published in a limited edition in 1811) with additions, consisting chiefly of selected passages bearing on the same subject and written by Bell before the publication of the *New Idea* (see *Journal of Anatomy and Physiology*, 3, 1869, 147). Shaw also edited Bell's *Anatomy and Philosophy of Expression* (3rd edn, 1844), to which he added a contribution on the nervous system, and *The Hand* (6th edn, 1860). In his own right he published work on diseases of the spine.

Shaw was a surgeon of repute, and, though incapacitated for work for some years before his death, he never lost interest in his profession. He died in London at his home, 136 Abbey Road, Kilburn, on 18 January 1890; his wife died the following year.

J. B. BAILEY, *rev.* B. A. BRYAN

Sources *BMJ* (15 Feb 1890), 393 · *The Lancet* (8 Feb 1890), 327 · *Medico-Chirurgical Transactions*, 73 (1890), 23–4 · *The Times* (22 Jan 1890), 7
Archives Wellcome L.
Wealth at death £1863 16s. 6d.: resworn probate, May 1890, *CGPLA Eng. & Wales*

Shaw, Alexander, second Baron Craigmyle (1883–1944). *See under* Shaw, Thomas, first Baron Craigmyle (1850–1937).

Shaw, Alfred (1842–1907), cricketer, born at Burton Joyce, near Nottingham, on 28 August 1842, was the youngest of thirteen children of William Shaw, a frame-work knitter, and his wife, Mary Goodwin. On his mother's death in 1852 he left school to work on a farm scaring crows. Dismissed for playing cricket instead, he became apprenticed to a hand-frame stocking knitter. The system of piece-work then prevailing gave him more time to develop his aptitude for cricket, and in 1862 he succeeded his brother Arthur (1834–1874) as professional to the Grantham cricket club.

Playing for Nottinghamshire Colts against the county side in 1863, Shaw first displayed his skill as a bowler by taking 7 wickets, and helping to dismiss the county for 41 runs. In 1864, on his first appearance at Lord's for the Colts of England against the MCC, he took 13 wickets for 63 runs in the match. He was immediately appointed to the

Alfred Shaw (1842–1907), by unknown photographer, pubd 1908

ground staff at Lord's, a post he held almost continuously until 1882. For several seasons he was the club's leading bowler. In a minor match for the MCC against Thordon Hall in 1870 he took 18 wickets for 52, while against the North of England in 1874 he took all 10 wickets in an innings for 73. In the famous match in 1878 in which the Australians beat the MCC in one day, Shaw secured 6 wickets for 14 in 166 balls. But it was as a professional for Nottinghamshire that he was mainly employed from 1864 onwards. For the county against the MCC in 1875 also in 166 balls, he took 7 wickets, including those of W. G. Grace and Lord Harris, for 7 runs. Against Gloucestershire in 1884, in taking 14 wickets for 65, he claimed a hat-trick in each innings.

Shaw first appeared for the Players against the Gentlemen in 1865, and during his career he played in twenty-eight of these matches. At the Oval in 1880 he dismissed 7 of the Gentlemen for 17 runs, and in 1881, at Brighton, he took 6 for 19. In September 1880 he played for England against Australia at the Oval in the first test match in this country, having previously played at Melbourne in 1877 in the first test in Australia. He had gone to Australia as a member of James Lillywhite's team in 1876–7. He returned on four further occasions as captain (1881–2) and as joint manager (1881–2, 1884–5, 1886–7, 1887–8) with Lillywhite and Arthur Shrewsbury. While the first three enterprises made a profit, the last one cost him and

Shrewsbury £2400, and a rugby football tour to New Zealand which they organized in 1888 cost them a further £800. The two men had also established an athletics outfitter's business in Nottingham. As a player, Shaw achieved little in his Australian visits. He made a sixth and final trip there in 1891–2, acting as the manager for the tour financed by the third earl of Sheffield. He also made two visits to America—with Edgar Willsher's team in 1868, and with that of Richard Daft in 1879, when he had the outstanding record of 178 wickets for 426 runs.

From 1883 to 1895 Shaw was employed by Lord Sheffield in Sussex; during that period he coached and in 1894–5 also played for the county. He accompanied Sheffield on a tour to Norway, taking part in a match on board the latter's yacht, the *Lusitania*, by the light of the midnight sun at Spitsbergen on 12 August 1894. After his retirement he umpired in first-class matches (1898–1905).

Shaw, called by Daft 'the Emperor of Bowlers', began his career as a medium-pace bowler, later becoming a slow one able to turn the ball both ways. He was the most accurate and economical bowler of his day, more than half the overs he bowled being maidens. He took 100 wickets in a season on eight occasions (including 201 at an average of 10.96 in 1878) and 2026 (at 12.13) in his first-class career. He was a lower-order batsman, and a sound fielder in the slips. It was also his idea, in the 1860s, to have the batsman's crease whitewashed onto the pitch rather than cut into the turf.

Apart from his cricketing activities, Shaw was landlord of the Lord Nelson inn in his native village from 1869 to 1878, when he went to Kilburn, London, to take charge of the Prince of Wales inn. In 1881 he left Kilburn to become landlord of The Belvoir inn, Nottingham. He died on 16 January 1907, after a long illness, at Gedling, near Nottingham, where he was buried.

W. B. OWEN, *rev.* GERALD M. D. HOWAT

Sources A. W. Pullin, *Alfred Shaw* (1902) · A. Haygarth, *Marylebone club cricket scores and biographies*, 8 (1877) · *The Times* (17 Jan 1907) · *The Times* (21 Jan 1907) · *Cricket* (11 Jan 1883) · *Cricket* (31 Jan 1907) · *Wisden* (1879) · *Wisden* (1908) · A. Shaw and A. Shrewsbury, *Shaw and Shrewsbury's team in Australia* (1885) · A. Shaw, *Jottings on bowling* (1883)
Likenesses photograph, *c*.1870, Marylebone Cricket Club, Lord's, London, ref. 170 · photograph, *c*.1870, repro. in W. G. Grace, *Cricket* (1891) · Simons, photograph, 1884, repro. in Shaw and Shrewsbury, *Shaw and Shrewsbury's team* · Hawkins, photograph, 1894, repro. in Pullin, *Alfred Shaw* · Blomfield, photograph, 1901, repro. in Pullin, *Alfred Shaw* · photograph, pubd 1908, NPG [*see illus.*]
Wealth at death £2462 9s. 5d.: probate, 26 Feb 1907, CGPLA Eng. & Wales

Shaw, Benjamin (1772–1841), mechanic and autobiographer, was born on 23 December 1772 at Hallbank, near Dent in the West Riding of Yorkshire, the eldest child of Joseph Shaw (1748–1823), a weaver and mechanic, and his wife, Isabel (*bap.* 1751, *d.* 1798), daughter of George and Margaret Noddle of Garsdale. He received no formal education but at the age of four, like many children in Dentdale, he went to a 'knitting school', the knitting of stockings being one of the main trades of the valley. He learned to read a little, but not to write, and as he grew up he also worked alongside his father as a jobbing mechanic. In 1791 the Shaw family left Dent and found work in the new water-powered worsted mill at Dolphinholme, on the River Wyre near Lancaster.

There Benjamin was apprenticed as a mechanic and formed an attachment to a mill girl, Betty Leeming (*bap.* 1773, *d.* 1828). The pair constantly quarrelled and in the autumn of 1792 she moved to Preston. However, she wrote to Benjamin and in order to understand her letters and send replies he taught himself to read and write, opening up a world of learning which was thenceforth his greatest pleasure. In February 1793 he stayed the night with her in Preston and shortly afterwards she told him of her pregnancy. They married on 23 September 1793 and in March 1795, the mill at Dolphinholme having closed, they moved to Preston, where they lived for the rest of their lives. Marriage, far from ending their quarrelling, exacerbated it, for almost without a break until Betty's death from consumption in February 1828 they argued and disagreed. While Benjamin was cautious with money to the point of meanness, Betty was, he felt, feckless and extravagant: 'there never [were] two persons, I think, more at varience in our plans, of conducting household affairs, than we were' (Shaw, 34). Yet despite the extreme disharmony of their characters the couple were physically very compatible, and during the twenty years from 1793 they produced eight children, all but one of whom reached adulthood.

At Preston, Shaw worked as a mill mechanic. He was one of the army of men who laboured to make by hand the machinery for the new steam-powered cotton spinning mills. In 1810 he had a leg amputated—it had become ulcerous as a result of an injury in 1793—and during the long months of recovery and before he returned to work in 1815 he studied voraciously, extending his education, reading newspapers, writing verses and aphorisms, making notes, and collecting information about his own life and times. In May 1826, perhaps distressed by the recent death of his daughter Hannah and the deplorable behaviour of his other children, and as his wife entered the early stages of her last lingering illness, he began work on what he called his 'Family records', comprising his own autobiography and shorter biographies of thirty other members of his family. The book was finished in August 1826 but then updated at intervals until Betty's death two years later. In 1829 he began a second volume, in the form of a review of the year, which was maintained until 1836. Benjamin was by then exhausted by ill health, old age, and a seemingly endless succession of family tragedies, and he wrote almost nothing more after that date. He died at Park Lane, Preston, on 7 June 1841 and was buried at St Paul's Church, Preston, two days later.

In his progress from a childhood in a beautiful Pennine valley, via apprenticeship at one of the earliest large mechanized textile mills, to long years lived in the shadow of John Horrocks's cotton factory in Preston, Shaw's life mirrored the experience of the English industrial revolution, and comparable paths were trodden by many hundreds and thousands of others. But in one crucial sense Benjamin Shaw was quite exceptional, for using his self-taught skills in reading and writing he produced one of the greatest of all nineteenth-century working-class autobiographies. Written in an understated but powerful and often moving fashion, 'Family records' examines courtship and marriage among the poor, illegitimacy, ill health and disease, child labour, infant mortality, working conditions, the effect of the Napoleonic wars, the process of migration and its emotional impact, the workings of the domestic economy, the vagaries of the poor law, and the nature of family life. Now recognized as a major source for social and economic history, it provides a real insight into the life not only of Benjamin Shaw, but also of the English working class in that crucial period.

ALAN G. CROSBY

Sources B. Shaw, *The family records of Benjamin Shaw, mechanic of Dent, Dolphinholme and Preston, 1772–1841*, ed. A. G. Crosby (1991) · d. cert. · parish register, Preston, St Paul, 9 June 1841, 9 June 1841 [burial] · parish register, Dent, West Ridin of Yorkshire, 23 Dec 1772 [baptism]
Archives Lancs. RO, papers, DDX 1554
Wealth at death under £300: administration, Lancs. RO, WRW(A)

Shaw, Benjamin Howard (1865–1942), politician, was born on 27 July 1865 in Huddersfield, Yorkshire, the third of four sons of George Shaw, cotton-mill owner, and his wife, Mary Wilson. He was educated at an elementary school in his native village of Longwood, a suburb of industrial Huddersfield, and briefly, at the age of eighteen, attended Huddersfield Technical College. In accordance with his father's wishes, he entered the family business. Perhaps as a reaction to his father's domineering ways, or simply from his profound sympathy for the less fortunate, he developed an interest in labour affairs and to this end began corresponding with Keir Hardie. His practical entry into Labour politics began in January 1892 when Shaw joined the Colne Valley Labour Union. Although the Colne valley was not as important a centre for the development of Labour politics in Britain as Bradford and Glasgow were, it played a significant part in the building of the Independent Labour Party (ILP), of which he was a founder member. He also became secretary of the Labour Church in Longwood and helped to establish a labour club there.

In 1894 Keir Hardie offered Shaw a job in Glasgow with the weekly ILP paper, *Labour Leader*. Four months later Shaw found work with another publisher, the Civic Press Limited, which specialized in printing work for the labour movement, and was its secretary for many years. Shaw also edited another radical paper in the 1890s, the *Commonweal*, which coincidentally led to his first marriage. An article on sweated female labour in the tailoring trade brought him into contact with the writer, Joanna Bruce, and they were married in Glasgow's North Woodside Free Church on 28 June 1900. They had a daughter. Shaw was secretary of the Glasgow Central branch of the ILP from 1903 to 1906, and stood (unsuccessfully) in the municipal elections of November 1905 in Glasgow as ILP candidate for the city's Townhead Ward.

Outside journalism Shaw was employed in a series of clerical posts within the trade union movement, particularly with the Scottish Horse and Motormen's Association. This connection provided links with the Scottish Trades Union Congress (STUC) and he was appointed vice-chairman in 1909. His increasingly high profile within the labour movement in Scotland led to his election as first secretary of the Scottish Advisory Council (SAC) of the Labour Party in March 1914. As secretary he saw his task as improving and strengthening the internal organization of the party in Scotland, as well as building stronger links with the trade unions. This was an immense task, as the Liberal Party was then the dominant electoral force in Scotland. Moreover, the ILP had become the political voice of Labour north of the border, with the official Labour Party somewhat on the sidelines. He failed to dent the predominance of the ILP, and the official party continued on the periphery in Scotland until the ILP disaffiliated from it in 1932. However, the hegemony of the Liberals in Scotland was broken following the end of the First World War.

During the war, Shaw's leading position within the SAC brought his involvement with anti-war protesters, although his own position on the war is not known. Along with the executive of the SAC and the parliamentary committee of the STUC, he played a key role in securing the release of John Maclean, first Bolshevik consul in Britain, from Perth gaol in 1918 and again in 1922. Throughout the 1920s he kept up his prodigious efforts on behalf of the Labour Party, until in 1932, at the age of sixty-seven, he retired from his post as secretary of the Scottish Labour Party. In the same year he resigned from the ILP because of its disaffiliation from the Labour Party.

Shaw was a modest man and keen advocate of temperance. His shy and retiring personality probably damaged his chances of becoming an MP. As he put it: 'My job is to get other people into Parliament, not to get there myself' (B. Shaw to M. Shaw). To this end he took part in every by-election campaign in Scotland which involved a Labour candidate. At the same time he was a respected figure in the party and was viewed as a shrewd negotiator in dealing with internal disputes.

Shaw's first wife, Joanna, died in 1916 from cancer. He married Clarice Marion (1883–1946) [see Shaw, Clarice Marion], the daughter of Thomas Charles McNab, cloth weaver, and Mary (née Fraser), whom he had met while she was serving as a member of the Women's Labour League, on 3 July 1918 in St Giles's Cathedral, Edinburgh. Shaw died at his home, 1 Portland Terrace, Troon, Ayrshire, on 27 October 1942 and was cremated at Glasgow crematorium. His widow, Clarice, who was a Labour councillor for Troon in the 1920s and 1930s, was elected MP for Kilmarnock in 1945, but failed to take her seat in the Commons owing to a long illness, and died on 27 October 1946.

W. W. J. KNOX

Sources *Daily Herald* (28 Oct 1942) · *Glasgow Herald* (28 Oct 1942) · *The Scotsman* (28 Oct 1942) · H. Corr, 'Shaw, Benjamin Howard', *Scottish labour leaders, 1918–39: a biographical dictionary*, ed. W. Knox (1984) · B. Shaw, letter to M. Shaw, NL Scot., Shaw MSS Acc. 6471 · D. Clark, *Colne Valley: radicalism to socialism* (1981) · R. McKibbin, *The*

evolution of the labour party, 1910–1924 (1974) • A. McKinlay and R. J. Morris, eds., *The ILP on Clydeside, 1893–1932* (1991) • I. Donnachie, C. Harvie, and I. S. Wood, *Forward! Labour politics in Scotland, 1888–1988* (1989) • Labour party, minutes of the executive committee, Labour party archives • m. cert.
Archives NL Scot., MSS, Acc. 6471
Wealth at death £2706 10s. 9d.: confirmation, 18 Jan 1943, *CCI*

Shaw, Brian Duncan (1898–1999), chemist and army officer, was born on 10 February 1898 at Fern's Hollow, Station Road, in Ilkeston, Derbyshire, the youngest child of Samuel Shaw (1862–1941), a brick manufacturer, and his wife, Lydia Emma *née* Evans (1864–1931), who had been a teacher. Shaw attended Ilkeston county secondary school, leaving in 1914 to become first an apprentice pharmacist with Boots and later a student teacher. A month before his eighteenth birthday he enlisted in the Sherwood Foresters. He was transferred to the 2/5 battalion of the South Staffordshire regiment and served with them during the Easter rising in Ireland. Back in Nottingham, on 4 May 1916, he married Margaret Elsie Wheldon (1897–1990). Their only child, Samuel, was born in September 1916, but died four months later.

Shaw's regiment was sent to France early in 1917. He saw action on the Somme, near Ypres, and in the battle of Cambrai. He was awarded the Military Medal in July 1917 at Equancourt, north of Péronne. Shaw and another lance-corporal volunteered to find a missing patrol in no man's land. In broad daylight, and in full view of the enemy, they located the missing men and brought back, under fire, the only survivor. In January 1918 Shaw was commissioned 2nd lieutenant in the Lincolnshire regiment.

After the war Shaw returned to Nottingham to study chemistry at the University College. He graduated BSc with first-class honours in 1922, stayed on to work under Professor F. S. Kipping, and completed his PhD in 1927. In January 1924, after one term at East London College, Shaw was appointed to a teaching post in Nottingham. During the 1920s and 1930s he was an active member of Kipping's research group, working in the field of heterocyclic chemistry. He published eleven articles on pyridines, some together with colleagues and research students, and all but one in the *Journal of the Chemical Society*. It was, however, for his lecture on explosives that he became famous. Kipping, according to Shaw, was concerned by declining attendances at the department's public lectures, and asked him to give a talk that would 'bring a crowd in' (Holloway, 95). Shaw's lecture on explosives revealed his talent for dramatic presentation and was to be repeated many times.

Shaw rejoined the Officers' Training Corps (OTC) after the war and the Territorial Army (TA) in 1922. In 1939 he was sent with his battalion of the Sherwood Foresters to Normandy. In May 1940, due to the temporary absence of the commanding officer, Shaw—now a major—commanded the battalion during their defence of the River Bresle. As the battalion fell back towards Le Havre, Shaw became separated and was reported missing. After hiding on a farm during the summer he set off for Spain on a bicycle and had reached Poitiers before he was captured.

Transferred to Germany, he spent the rest of the war in POW camps, principally at Spangenburg bei Kassel. On his release in 1945 he was promoted lieutenant-colonel.

In 1945 Shaw returned to the chemistry department in Nottingham where he spent the rest of his career. An enthusiastic and popular teacher, he was promoted senior lecturer in 1959. He also remained active in the TA and in the OTC. He was an excellent marksman and successfully trained the award-winning university shooting team. He also shot for the English national team for several years, was captain for three, and won the king's medal at Bisley in 1950. Shaw was a council member of the National Rifle Association for twenty-one years.

After his retirement in 1965 Shaw continued to work as a consultant. He was an expert witness for the defence at a number of high-profile trials, including that of the Angry Brigade in 1972. But it is for his lecture on explosives that he will chiefly be remembered. Shaw gave it over 1500 times, continuing well into his nineties. Photographs published with his lecture at the Royal Institution in 1965 give some sense of its drama (Shaw). In 1969 the lecture was broadcast by the BBC on *Horizon*, attracting over a million viewers.

Shaw's achievement in bringing science to a wider public won him wide recognition. He was awarded an honorary DSc by Nottingham in 1979, and in 1988 the university endowed the Shaw medal and lecture for demonstration lectures. Three years earlier the Royal Society of Chemistry had presented him with a special award for his work in popularizing chemistry. Shaw's military career was also remembered. In 1998, as one of the last British survivors of the First World War, he received the Légion d'honneur.

After the death of his first wife in 1990 Shaw married, on 5 June that year, Alice Maud, *née* Eyre (1900–1998). Throughout his retirement Shaw lived in Beeston, Nottingham. He died at the Silverwood Nursing Home, Imperial Road, on 7 November 1999, aged 101.

ROBIN MACKIE

Sources *The Times* (10 Dec 1999) • J. H. Holloway, 'Brian Shaw, the incendiary colonel', *Chemistry in Britain* (Feb 1986), 95 • *Chemistry in Britain* (April 2000), 60–61 • www.nottingham.ac.uk/b.d.shaw.centenary/ • C. Housley, *British gallantry awards, 45th and 95th foot, Sherwood foresters, 1854–1970* [n.d.] • C. N. Barclay, *The history of the Sherwood foresters (Nottinghamshire & Derbyshire regiment), 1919–57* (1959) • J. P. Jones, *A history of the south Staffordshire regiment, 1705–1923* (1923) • W. L. Vane, *History of the south Staffordshire regiment* (1969) • B. D. Shaw, 'Explosives', *Proceedings of the Royal Institution of Great Britain*, 40/186 (1965), 446–54 • private information (2004) • b. cert. • m. certs. • d. cert. • D. Jones, 'Still going down like a bomb', *New Scientist* (28 Nov 1985), 62–3 • 'Address by Professor King', *University of Nottingham Gazette*, 99 (1979), 2325
Likenesses photographs, News Int. RO, *The Times* archive • photographs, U. Nott. • photographs, Royal Society of Chemistry, London • photographs, repro. in Shaw, 'Explosives'
Wealth at death £408,373—gross; £403,353—net: probate, 2 Aug 2000, *CGPLA Eng. & Wales*

Shaw, (John) Byam Liston (1872–1919), painter and illustrator, was born on 13 November 1872 at Ferndale, Madras, India, the youngest of the three children of John Shaw (*d.* 1887) and Sophia Alicia Byam, daughter of John Houlton Gunthorpe. Byam Shaw—as he was known throughout his life—lived in India until his father abandoned the position of registrar of the High Court, Madras, in favour of a solicitor's practice in London, in 1878. After a period in Bath (1878–9) he was educated privately by his mother and a governess in the family home at 103 Holland Road, Kensington. His early artistic promise was encouraged by his parents, and on the advice of Sir John Everett Millais he was enrolled in 1887 at St John's Wood Art Schools. The schools, under the direction of Abelardo Alvarez Calderon and Bernard Evans Ward, specialized in preparing students for entry into the Royal Academy Schools, through a strict course of drawing from the antique and from life. Shaw duly entered the Academy Schools in 1890, where the visitors, or tutors, included leading members and associates of the Royal Academy, such as its president, Sir Frederic Leighton.

Shaw shared a studio with his friend Gerald Metcalfe from 1893 (the year he first exhibited at the Royal Academy) and produced a series of elaborate allegorical compositions which marked the development of his distinctive artistic personality. Among his most ambitious early productions was the decorative painting *Love the Conqueror* (exh. RA, 1899; priv. coll.; reproduced Taylor), a 10 foot canvas featuring almost a hundred literary and historical figures of great lovers. Controversial at the time, when it was attacked as vulgar and overblown, the painting displays Shaw at his most overwhelmingly eclectic. *Whither?* (exh. RA, 1896; reproduced Cole, 47), demonstrating an awareness of European symbolism, is a brilliantly coloured decorative composition in which two lovers are drawn across the sea of life by nude allegorical figures of Birth, Maturity, and Death; bubbles rising from the sea contain visions of the past and future life of the protagonists. *The Blessed Damozel* (exh. RA, 1895; Guildhall Art Gallery, London) pays tribute, both in subject and pictorial treatment, to the work of Dante Gabriel Rossetti. In 1899 Shaw married the miniature painter and teacher (Caroline) Evelyn Eunice Pyke-Nott (1870–1959). Their household some years later is recorded in the elegant pastel *My Wife, my Bairns and my Wee Dog John* (1903, Ferens Art Gallery, Hull), in which the artist's face appears in the mirror. Of their five children, James Byam *Shaw (1903–1992) and Glencairn Byam *Shaw (1904–1986) attained eminence as, respectively, a leading connoisseur and an actor and theatre director.

Working closely with the artist Eleanor Fortescue-Brickdale, Shaw increasingly became identified as a late follower of the Pre-Raphaelite Brotherhood (founded in 1848), notably in *Boer War, 1900* (exh. RA, 1901; City of Birmingham Museum and Art Gallery), which recalls the naturalism of Millais, thus tacitly rejecting the influence of French impressionism which was dominant among Shaw's contemporaries. Heightened colour and brilliant detail remained hallmarks of Shaw's style throughout his career.

Shaw excelled as a painter of genre scenes of historical and modern subjects. He exhibited thirty-nine such paintings, 'Thoughts Suggested by some Passages from British Poets', at Dowdeswell Galleries (160 New Bond Street), London, in 1899. A further exhibition, 'Sermons in stones and good in everything: suggested by the book of Ecclesiastes', followed in 1902 at the same gallery. As a book illustrator he ranged widely from the classics, for example, *The Chiswick Shakespeare* (1899), to contemporary and orientalist subjects such as *The Garden of the Kama* (1914). During the First World War his graphic skills were harnessed in the preparation of cartoons and propagandistic illustrations. He also explored other decorative media, notably in a large fresco, *Mary's Entry into London as Queen, AD 1553*, for the palace of Westminster, and a design for the act drop at the London Coliseum (exh. RA, 1914; English National Opera, London).

In 1904 Shaw joined his friend and future biographer, the landscape painter Rex Vicat Cole, on the teaching staff of the women's department of King's College, London. In 1910 they founded the Byam Shaw and Vicat Cole School of Art at 70 Campden Street, Kensington. Offering a traditional grounding in drawing from the antique and from life, the school added pen-and-ink illustration, miniature painting, landscape, and other elements to the curriculum. Renamed the Byam Shaw School of Art on Cole's retirement in 1926, it has continued to flourish.

An academic artist who never fulfilled his ambition of election to membership of the Royal Academy, Shaw was a dedicated member of the Royal Institute of Painters in Water Colours, to which he was elected in 1898; he also became an associate of the Royal Society of Painters in Water Colours in 1913. He emphatically rejected the idea of the artist as a bohemian: a contemporary recalled that he 'often appeared in a suit of loud checks, looking more like a bookie on a race-course than an art master' (Cole, 135). Content throughout his life to conform to the norms of the upper-middle-class professional circles in which he moved, Shaw was a committed tory imperialist. His character, combining shyness with a fondness for japery and an enjoyment of the camaraderie of his students, emerges very clearly from Rex Vicat Cole's affectionate memoir of 1932.

Shaw died on 26 January 1919, at 40 Grove End Road, St John's Wood, London; he was buried at St Barnabas's, Addison Road, London. By the time of his death his work had come to seem dated and irrelevant. As Frank Rutter noted in his obituary, 'he was not a "modern" as the word is now understood … [but rather] a decorative painter who was born a little too late to find his just milieu' (*Sunday Times*, 23 March 1919). Recent reappraisals of Byam Shaw's work have been more enthusiastic in their assessment of his merits: the opulent and eclectic quality of his productions finds more favour with post-modernist than with modernist critics.   TIM BARRINGER

Sources R. V. Cole, *The art and life of Byam Shaw* (1932) · T. Barringer, 'Not a "modern" as the word is now understood: John Byam Liston Shaw (1872–1919)', *English art, 1860–1914: modernities and identities*, ed. D. P. Corbett and L. Perry (2000) · G. Taylor, *Byam Shaw, 1872–1919* (1986) [exhibition catalogue, AM Oxf.] · P. Skipwith, 'Byam Shaw: a pictorial story teller', *The Connoisseur*, 191 (1976), 189–97 · J. Christian, ed., *The last Romantics: the romantic tradition in British art* (1989) [exhibition catalogue, Barbican Art Gallery, London, 9 Feb – 9 April 1989] · A. L. Baldry, 'Our rising artists: Mr Byam Shaw', *Magazine of Art*, 22 (1897–8), 633–42 · *CGPLA Eng. & Wales*

(1919) • F. Rutter, *Sunday Times* (23 March 1919) • Graves, *RA exhibitors* • G. Taylor, 'Shaw, Byam', *The dictionary of art*, ed. J. Turner (1996)
Likenesses G. Metcalfe, drawing, 1896, repro. in Cole, *Art and life of Byam Shaw*, frontispiece • J. B. L. Shaw, self-portraits, repro. in Cole, *Art and life of Byam Shaw* • photographs, repro. in Cole, *Art and life of Byam Shaw*
Wealth at death £4184 17s. 5d.: administration, 2 April 1919, CGPLA Eng. & Wales

Shaw, Sir Charles (1795–1871), army officer, third son of Charles Shaw, clerk of the county of Ayr, and his wife, Barbara Wright, daughter of a customs official at Greenock, was born at Ayr. Alexander *Shaw (1804–1890), John *Shaw (1792–1827), and Patrick *Shaw (1796–1872) were his brothers. He was educated in Ayr, and at the universities of St Andrews and Edinburgh. He entered the army by purchase as ensign in the 52nd light infantry on 23 January 1813, and joined the 2nd battalion at Shorncliffe in March. From Shorncliffe, Shaw went to Hythe, and at the end of November he accompanied his regiment to Ramsgate, where they embarked for the Netherlands, landing at Tholen on 19 December. He was engaged in the capture of the village of Merxem, near Antwerp, on 31 January 1814, and, after serving through the campaign, was employed with his regiment in garrison duty at Antwerp. On the escape of Napoleon from Elba, Shaw was sent to Courtrai towards the end of March and to Ath in April, in the middle of which month he was drafted into the 1st battalion, commanded by Sir John Colborne. During the battle of Waterloo Shaw was on baggage-guard duty at Brussels. He took part in the subsequent march to and occupation of Paris.

In March 1816 Shaw joined the 2nd battalion at Canterbury, and on its disbandment in July was placed on half pay. After six months in Scotland, he travelled in the Netherlands in 1817. In July he was brought back to full pay in the 90th light infantry. On obtaining leave of absence, he made a tour in the Hartz Mountains, and in September entered as a student in the military department of the Carolinum College at Brunswick to improve his qualifications for a military career. He left Brunswick in January 1818 for Berlin to see something of the Prussian army, and, after a tour in Prussia, joined the 90th at Plymouth on 10 March 1818. From Plymouth the regiment went to Chatham, and, on a reduction of the army taking place shortly after, Shaw was again placed on half pay.

After attending a course of lectures at Edinburgh University, Shaw accepted an offer of partnership in an old-established wine business in Leith. He became captain and commander of the volunteer corps of Leith sharpshooters, and brought them to a high state of efficiency. On the disbandment of this corps Shaw was presented by its members, on 19 July 1822, with a handsome piece of plate. He established the first military club in Edinburgh, called the Caledonian United Service Club, for which he acted as honorary secretary until 1830. In that year, disliking commerce, he sold his business and travelled on the continent, returning to England in September 1831.

In November 1831 Shaw was appointed captain of a light company of marines in the liberating army of Portugal against Dom Miguel, the heir to the throne. He embarked with recruits on 15 December, joined the fleet of Admiral George Sartorius at Belle Île, arrived at the rendezvous at Terceira in the Azores towards the end of February 1832, and in May proceeded to Fayal and St Michael's. In June the expedition left the Azores for Portugal, and disembarked on the morning of 5 July at Mindella, about 10 miles from Oporto, which city was entered the same afternoon, the Miguelites having evacuated it.

Shaw, who in August 1832 was made a major of one of the battalions of British volunteers, saw much fighting around Oporto, and was in every action and sortie during the siege of the city by Dom Miguel. He was twice wounded in the attack on his position on 29 September, when after a severe fight the Miguelites were repulsed. He was also severely wounded in the sortie of 17 November, and was subsequently made a knight of the Tower and Sword of Portugal.

In 1833 Shaw commanded the Scottish contingent at Lordello, an outpost of the defences of Oporto. In July 1833 he was appointed colonel and given the command of an English battalion, which he led in the repulse of Bourmont's attack on 25 July. At the end of September he embarked with his battalion for Lisbon, landing at São Martinho and marching from there to Torres Vedras to operate on the rear of the Miguelite army on its withdrawal from the attack on Lisbon. He and his battalion did much marching during the next eight months, but not much fighting. On 26 May 1834, two days after Shaw entered Estremez, the war ended.

On 1 June 1834 Shaw marched to Lisbon in command of a brigade of 2500 men, which he there handed over to a Portuguese officer. From this time until February 1835 Shaw's time was mainly occupied in attempts to effect a financial settlement between the officers and men of the British contingent under his command and the Portuguese government in accordance with the terms of engagement, but he was only partially successful. He left Portugal in June 1835 and arrived at Falmouth on 12 July.

On 17 July Shaw was gazetted a brigadier-general to command a Scottish brigade of the auxiliary legion then being raised in England by Sir George de Lacy Evans for service in Spain against the Carlists, and at once went to Glasgow to assist in raising recruits. He went to Spain in September 1835, landing on the 10th at Santander and marching with some 1600 men, whom he brought out with him, to Portugalete. Here he found that his rank would be only that of colonel in command of a small brigade of two regiments. In February 1836 he was given command of a brigade of three fine Irish regiments, but not the rank of brigadier-general. Until April 1836 he was quartered principally in Vitoria and the surrounding area. On 13 April his brigade embarked at Santander and arrived on the 24th at San Sebastian, which was besieged by Don Carlos. On 5 May an attack was made on the Carlist position on the heights above San Sebastian, and after a protracted fight the day was won. Shaw was struck by a spent ball, and another struck his watch. He was made a brigadier-general and decorated with the third class of the order of San Fernando. On 31 May Shaw skilfully repulsed an attack on his lines; at the end of August, owing to an unfortunate and avoidable quarrel with Evans, Shaw sent in his resignation, which Evans accepted with great regret at the loss of so gallant an officer.

Shaw arrived in England at the end of September 1836, and for a time resided at Richmond, Surrey. In 1837 he published his rambling and egotistical *Personal memoirs and correspondence … Comprising a narrative of the war for constitutional liberty in Portugal and in Spain from its commencement in 1831 to the dissolution of the British legion in 1837.* He was appointed in September 1839 chief commissioner of police at Manchester, a post that he held until September 1842.

Shaw married, in 1841, Louisa Hannah, only daughter of Major Martin Curry of the 67th regiment; they had a son, Charles Martin, who, with his mother, survived Shaw. During the latter part of his life Shaw lived at Homburg-von-der-Hohe, where he died in February 1871 and was buried with military honours.

R. H. VETCH, *rev.* JAMES FALKNER

Sources Army List · *The Times* (28 Feb 1871) · *Hart's Army List* · *Annual Register* (1871) · J. H. Humfrey, *A concise review of the campaigns of the British legion in Spain* (1838) · E. Holt, *The Carlist wars in Spain* (1967) · G. de Lacy Evans, *Memoranda of the contest in Spain* (1840) · Boase, *Mod. Eng. biog.* · C. Shaw, *Personal memoirs and correspondence of Col. C. Shaw … 1831 to … 1837*, 2 vols. (1837)
Archives UCL, corresp. with E. Chadwick

Shaw, Charles (1832–1906), potter and autobiographer, was born in Tunstall, Staffordshire, the third son and fifth of eight children of Enoch Shaw (*b.* 1792/3), pottery painter and gilder, and his wife, Ann Mawdesley (*b.* 1796/7). The Shaw family lived in a small terrace house in Piccadilly Street.

From 1835/6 until 1839 Shaw attended Betty Wedgwood's dame-school where he learned to read. He also attended the local Wesleyan Methodist Sunday school. At seven he started work as a mould-runner in the pottery factory of Enoch Wood & Sons in Burslem. He earned a shilling a week, worked about fourteen hours a day, and suffered from exhaustion, hunger, beatings, and extremes of temperature. After a year he became a handle-maker in Samuel Alcock's Hill Pottery, also in Burslem. Here he worked in damp, stuffy cellars, rarely seeing daylight, horrified by scenes of drunken debauchery, and exhausted by overwork.

Shaw's father was involved in an unsuccessful strike at Davenport's works in late 1841. As a result Shaw and his family were driven into the workhouse for four or five weeks. He and his father eventually found work at George Hood's small 'toy' works, making pottery portrait figures. Derided at the Wesleyan Sunday school when he appeared in workhouse clothes, Shaw transferred his allegiance to the New Connexion Methodist Sunday school. He began to take an interest in public affairs, greatly admired his elderly neighbour Joseph Capper the Chartist, and witnessed the Burslem riots of August 1842. In the late 1840s

he was taught to write and do simple arithmetic by a shoemaker. In the early 1850s he joined the Tunstall Young Men's Mutual Improvement Society. In 1853 he became a lay preacher, in 1854 a full-time minister, and he left north Staffordshire.

Shaw began his ministry in Oldham, officiating at Zion Chapel, Lees. He was briefly stationed in Sheffield, Mansfield, and Huddersfield before his marriage in 1858 to Jane Halliwell of Springhead, near Oldham. From 1859 he was stationed in Ashton under Lyne and undertook part-time study at Owens College, Manchester. A nervous breakdown followed, and in 1861 he resigned from the ministry and entered his father-in-law's cotton-spinning business.

Shaw and his wife had three children before her death in the late 1860s. In 1870 he married Maria Arthington (1839–1927) from Huddersfield, with whom he had three more children. By the early 1870s he was a partner in Radcliffe Mill, Springhead. In the 1880s the firm became Charles Shaw & Son, employing in 1881, forty-eight men and thirty-eight women. Remaining an active layman at Zion Chapel, Lees, for many years he wrote leaders for the radical Liberal *Oldham Express* and also contributed to the *Methodist New Connexion Magazine*. The New Connexion published his *Life of Henry Atherton of Lees*, a chapel stalwart (*c.*1890).

In the 1890s the mill failed and Shaw re-entered the ministry. He served in Douglas, Isle of Man, from 1897 to 1900, and in Bangor, co. Down, from 1900 until 1905, when old age at last compelled him to retire. Shaw died from heart failure at his home—Spring Cottage, Walker's Lane, Springhead, Oldham, Lancashire—on 5 March 1906. The funeral was held at Zion Chapel, Lees, and he was buried in Hey church cemetery, Oldham, on 8 March.

In 1892–3 Shaw had contributed a series of anonymous articles on his childhood memories to the *Staffordshire Sentinel*. These reminiscences, considerably expanded, were published by Methuen in March 1903 as *When I was a Child*, by 'An Old Potter'. Shaw, as a staunch Liberal and freetrader, evidently intended his account of the trials of his childhood and youth in the Potteries as, in part, a contribution to contemporary political debate, and in particular a warning of the dangers of a return to protectionism. The eminent Liberal Robert Spence Watson wrote an introduction stressing the book's importance as a reminder of the exploitation of child labour in the 1840s, and as a spur to further improvement in the condition of children generally. He also helped to finance the publication of an edition of 1500 copies. But Shaw's memoir attracted little interest and did not sell well.

Arnold Bennett relied closely upon *When I was a Child* as a source for the early chapters of *Clayhanger* (1910). Otherwise the book, though known to those with a special interest in Potteries history, was not widely read until it was republished in 1969. Since then it has been almost continuously in print. Shaw's autobiography of his early life is now valued both as a moving firsthand account of child labour in the pottery industry, and as a narrative of his 'pursuit of knowledge under difficulties', inspired by the values of self-help and his religious faith, which enabled him to escape from a life of manual labour. The book vividly illuminates many aspects of Potteries social history, such as popular recreations, life in the workhouse, and the riots of 1842, in a way unequalled by any other source. The popularity of 'history from below', and academic interest in working-class autobiographies, have established *When I was a Child* as not only an essential source for Potteries history, but also a classic of its kind and a memorial to its otherwise obscure author.

ROBERT FYSON

Sources C. Shaw, *When I was a child* (1903); repr. (1969) · W. Walker, *Builders of Zion* [n.d., 1919?] · W. H. Chaloner, '*When I was a child* by "An Old Potter" (1903)', *Proceedings of the Wesley Historical Society*, 40 (1975–6) · O. A. Beckerlegge, *United Methodist ministers and their circuits* (1968) · D. Stuart, ed., *People of the Potteries* (1989) · Shaw family genealogical notes by Muriel Barritt, Chapel Museum, Mow Cop [Muriel Barritt was Charles Shaw's great-granddaughter] · letter from Associated Book Publishers to Stoke-on-Trent city librarian, 12 Sept 1968, Stoke-on-Trent City Archives · A. Wood, 'Eightieth birthday', *BBC Radio Stoke Magazine* (summer 1983) · Tunstall Wesleyan Sunday school admittance register, 1836, Chapel Museum, Mow Cop · census returns for Tunstall, 1841, 1851 · census returns for Springhead, Saddleworth parish, 1881 · *Staffordshire Potteries Telegraph* (24 June 1854) · *Staffordshire Sentinel* (9–10 Dec 1892) · *Staffordshire Sentinel* (17 Dec 1892) · *Staffordshire Sentinel* (24 Dec 1892) · *Staffordshire Sentinel* (31 Dec 1892) · *Staffordshire Sentinel* (7 Jan 1893) · *Staffordshire Sentinel* (14 Jan 1893) · *Staffordshire Sentinel* (21 Jan 1893) · *Staffordshire Sentinel* (28 Jan 1893) · *Staffordshire Sentinel* (4 Feb 1893) · *Staffordshire Sentinel* (11 Feb 1893) · *Staffordshire Sentinel* (18 Feb 1893) · *Staffordshire Sentinel* (25 Feb 1893) · *Staffordshire Sentinel* (11 March 1893) · *Staffordshire Sentinel* (18 March 1893) · *Staffordshire Sentinel* (1 April 1893) · *Staffordshire Sentinel* (8 April 1893) · *Staffordshire Sentinel* (15 April 1893) · *Staffordshire Sentinel* (13 May 1893) · *Daily Despatch* (9 March 1906) · *Oldham Chronicle* (10 March 1906) · *Methodist New Connexion Magazine* (1906) · *Methodist New Connexion Conference Minutes* (1906) · L. Tillier, *Studies in the sources of Arnold Bennett's novels* (1969) · D. Gurr and J. Hunt, *The cotton mills of Oldham* (1998) · B. Barnes, 'Mills in Saddleworth: notes vol. III', Oldham Public Library · private information (2004) [John Anderson, Chapel Museum, Mow Cop; Oldham Local Studies Library; Stoke-on-Trent City Archives]

Archives Associated Book Publishers, Andover, Methuen archives, Methuen publishers' corresp. with Shaw and Robert Spence Watson concerning publication and sales of *When I was a child*

Likenesses photograph, repro. in *Daily Despatch*

Wealth at death 'poor' in 1905: Associated Book Publishers, Methuen archives

Shaw, Charles James Dalrymple, Baron Kilbrandon

(1906–1989), judge, was born on 15 August 1906 in Martnaham, near Maybole, Ayrshire, the only son and second of three children of James Edward Shaw, of High Greenan by Ayr, solicitor and county clerk of Ayrshire, and his wife, Gladys Elizabeth, *née* Lester. He was educated at Charterhouse School, Balliol College, Oxford, and Edinburgh University. He obtained a second class in philosophy, politics, and economics at Oxford (1928) and an LLB at Edinburgh (1932).

Shaw was called to the Scottish bar in 1932. In 1937 he married (Ruth) Caroline, youngest daughter of Frank Morrison Seafield Grant, landowner, of Knockie, Whitebridge, Inverness; they had two sons and three daughters. By 1939 he had a substantial junior practice, had been commissioned as a territorial officer in the Royal Artillery, and had sustained a knee injury while skiing, which made

Charles James Dalrymple Shaw, Baron Kilbrandon (1906–1989), by Walter Bird, 1966

him lame for the rest of his life. In 1939 he was mobilized and served in the Royal Artillery, mostly on the staff in the rank of major (from 1941), until the end of the Second World War in 1945. On his return to the bar his practice rapidly increased. He took silk in 1949. It then became clear that, despite a tendency to be unbusinesslike and absent-minded, he was destined for the highest appointments. (He was liable to be found in Kilbrandon on the coast of Argyll, having forgotten a professional engagement in Edinburgh. The unaccountably missing brief would be found among his much-loved music.)

In 1957 Shaw was elected dean of the Faculty of Advocates, the highest honour which can be conferred on a member of the Scots bar. As dean, he was an anxious guardian of the faculty's traditions. In May 1959 he was appointed to the bench of the Court of Session, taking the judicial title of Lord Kilbrandon. From the outset he displayed the highest judicial qualities—complete impartiality, patience and courtesy, legal scholarship, and a determination not to be prevented from doing justice by any rules of mere procedural law. His judicial career in Scotland ended with his appointment in 1965 as chairman of the Scottish Law Commission, for he retained that office until his elevation to the House of Lords in 1971, as a life peer, privy councillor, and lord of appeal in ordinary. As chairman he found in Sir Leslie Scarman, the first chairman of the English Law Commission, a kindred spirit. Kilbrandon was also a member of the royal commission on the constitution from 1969 to 1972 and its chairman in

1972–3. The commission's report was a major contribution to the contemporary debate on devolution. In 1969 he was elected an honorary fellow of Balliol, a distinction which he particularly cherished, and in 1974 he was elected visitor, a position he held until 1986. He became an honorary LLD of Aberdeen (1965) and an honorary DSc of Edinburgh (1970).

Kilbrandon's elevation to the Lords was predictable. For three years he sat as the junior Scottish colleague on the judicial committee of the octogenarian Baron Reid. In an apt obituary of Reid, Kilbrandon wrote: 'Counsel found him a formidable figure, and so did I'. Kilbrandon, on the other hand, did not have it in him to be what Ronald Knox called an 'awful presence', unless dealing with someone whose conduct gave him no option. In a line of Scots who have become lords of appeal in ordinary, Kilbrandon was *sui generis*. Large of frame, heart, and mind, he had the traditional Scottish regard for legal principles but he had more. He had the breadth of outlook, culture, and philosophical learning of James Dalrymple, first Viscount Stair, the father of Scots law. Endowed with a verbal dexterity, analogous to the cartoonist's art, he was able to compress profound and novel ideas into a synoptic phrase. In his Hamlyn lectures (1966) he derided the civil jury as a mere 'bingo session'. His observation in *Customs and Excise* v. *Thorn Electrical* (1975), that 'a modern Hampden would in many quarters be pilloried as a tax evader', was worthy of F. X. J. Russell, Baron Russell of Killowen. Kilbrandon's most lasting memorial may be the Social Work (Scotland) Act (1968), which arose from his report for the departmental committee on the treatment of children and young persons in Scotland (1964). Kilbrandon retired as a lord of appeal in ordinary in 1976.

Kilbrandon was an outstandingly handsome man. Over 6 feet in height, he was a striking figure in his Inverness cape, limping at a smart pace from Westminster to Gray's Inn, where he lived during term. He was elected an honorary bencher in 1971. Until almost seventy he retained a boyish appearance enhanced by his thick, wavy hair. In old age he enjoyed a peaceful retirement in the beautiful setting of Kilbrandon House on the island of Seil in Argyll. The essential Kilbrandon was the man of religion whose faith pervaded his life and outlook. He liked to speak of himself as a Catholic although he was, denominationally, a Scottish Episcopalian of high-church outlook. One who knew him well described him as 'a practising Christian'. This was apt. His amiability, sweetness of character, freedom from prejudice, and kindness were all exceptional. He died from heart disease in Kilbrandon House, Balvicar, by Oban, Argyll, on 10 September 1989.

D. W. R. BRAND, *rev.*

Sources *The Times* (12 Sept 1989) · *The Independent* (14 Sept 1989) · *WWW* · private information (1996) · personal knowledge (1996)
Likenesses W. Bird, photograph, 1966, NPG [*see illus.*]

Shaw [*née* McNab], **Clarice Marion** (1883–1946), social reformer and politician, was born at 10 Morton Street, Leith, near Edinburgh, on 22 October 1883, the eldest daughter of Thomas Charles McNab, a wire-cloth weaver, and his wife, Mary Deas Fraser. Her father was a high-profile figure in local politics, including being a director of Leith's co-operative association, and played a large part in moulding Clarice's radical and political beliefs in Labour politics.

Clarice combined an interest in education and socialism from an early stage. Inspired by Keir Hardie's published views on religious education, she was a founder member of the Glasgow Socialist Sunday School in the 1890s. After training as a music teacher, at about the age of twenty she began teaching in an elementary school in Leith and became an advocate of the state provision for improved medical and welfare services for schoolchildren. Her election to the Leith school board in April 1922 indicated her ambitions in local government, which were enhanced by her activities in the Women's Labour League—an organization focusing on the employment and pay of female workers. Her radical approach towards women's rights, which included campaigning for the extension of job opportunities for girls after school, broadened into urging the abolition of children's employment and raising the school leaving age to sixteen.

Unlike many of her peers Clarice displayed clear political ambitions. By 1913 she had joined the Labour Party, partly out of support for socialist principles, but also as a route into local politics. In November 1913 she was elected to Leith town council, giving her the distinction of being the first Labour female member of a town council in Scotland. As a councillor she took a personal interest in medical and child welfare issues. In 1916 she was appointed as the Women's Labour League representative to attend meetings of the Scottish executive committee of the Labour Party. There she met, worked with, and eventually married in Edinburgh in July 1918, the widower Benjamin Howard *Shaw (1865–1942), first secretary of the Scottish Labour Party. The couple complemented each other in terms of political ideas and tastes, teetotalism, and temperance reform. Both she and Ben Shaw were also closely associated with the Glasgow Socialist Sunday School, of which Clarice was the national president for twenty-five years. The marriage did not produce any children.

Clarice Shaw enjoyed an unusual period of relative inactivity in public life after the couple's move to Glasgow in 1918, but this came to a close in 1921 following their move in that year to Troon, Ayrshire. She was subsequently a member of Troon town council and Ayrshire county council, and during the next twenty years she fulfilled a number of roles in civic administration, continuing her educational campaign and serving as a JP. She was appointed a member of the Scottish Food Council, the price regulation committee for Scotland, and the 1928 royal commission on educational endowments in Scotland. Twice—in 1929 and 1931—she unsuccessfully fought Ayr burghs at the general election. When international tensions began to develop in the 1930s, Clarice initially held to her pacifist principles. She appeared at various peace assemblies and in 1935 was one of the key speakers at a women's peace conference in the Keir Hardie Institute alongside Agnes Dollan. As the fascist threat grew more acute, however, she appears to have modified her views.

Although she abhorred the many side effects of the Second World War, such as the lowering of educational standards, by 1945 she was demanding total victory and the crushing of German power.

Clarice Shaw's activities during the war represented the height of her manifold achievements. She was chairman of the Scottish Labour Party, a Labour councillor, and a member of the Scottish Committee of Co-operative, Labour and Trade Union Women, founded—partly by her—in 1934. She had close links with the Scottish Trades Union Congress and the Women's Co-operative Guild in England. When her husband died in October 1942, she committed even more time and energy to the Labour Party. At the general election in July 1945 she was rewarded with a 7537 majority over the only other candidate, the Conservative Lieutenant-Colonel George E. Walker, in Kilmarnock. Moreover, her services to the Labour Party were recognized by her being chosen as the secretary of the Scottish parliamentary group. Having fulfilled her major ambition, however, Clarice was then struck down by a serious illness shortly afterwards which rendered her incapable of ever attending the sessions in the House of Commons. She continued to deal with her parliamentary correspondence until she was forced to resign her seat in September 1946.

Ben and Clarice Shaw were remembered as one of the most successful and popular partnerships in the Scottish Labour Party. While Ben was introverted, Clarice's oratorical skills gave her the ability to command large audiences, despite her plump and matronly appearance. She was equally adept at handling the affairs of several prestigious governmental committees and commissions. She died on 27 October 1946 at 36 Titchfield Road, Troon, and was buried at Troon.   HELEN CORR

Sources H. Corr, 'Shaw, Clarice Marion McNab', *Scottish labour leaders, 1918–39: a biographical dictionary*, ed. W. Knox (1984) · b. cert. · d. cert.

Wealth at death £7765 15s. 3d.: confirmation, 10 Jan 1947, *CCI*

Shaw, Cuthbert (1738/9–1771), poet, was born at Ravensworth, near Richmond, Yorkshire, the son of Cuthbert Shaw (*bap.* 1711), shoemaker, and his wife, Ann, *née* Neeson. After schooling at Kirby Hill and Scorton, both near Richmond, he became a school usher, first at Scorton, then at Darlington grammar school. At Scorton he was befriended by George Allan (1736–1800), the antiquary; at Darlington he published his first poem, *Liberty* (1756), inscribed to Henry Vane, first earl of Darlington. The poem was thoroughly damned in the *Monthly Review*, 14 (1756), 575–6.

Obliged to leave Darlington on account of some unspecified imprudence, Shaw found irregular work as an actor between 1758 and 1762 in Norwich, Ireland, and London. He also published *Odes on the Four Seasons* under the pen-name W. Seymour at Bury St Edmunds (1760). His only stage success was a run of thirty-five performances as Sir George Wealthy in Samuel Foote's comedy *The Minor* at the Haymarket from June 1760. His last appearance was at Covent Garden, as Pierre in Otway's *Venice Preserv'd* on 14 May 1762 for his own benefit. Then, 'partly losing his nose

[from syphilis], he withdrew from the world, and employed himself wholly in a literary capacity' (Highfill, Burnim & Langhans, *BDA*, 13.290).

Shaw settled in Marylebone, Middlesex, and subsisted by writing paragraphs for newspapers and verse satires, the first of which, *The Four Farthing-Candles* (1762), attacks Charles Churchill, Robert Lloyd, George Colman, and the dramatist William Shirley. His *The Race* (1765), by 'Mercurius Spur', with mock pedantic notes by 'Faustinus Scriblerus', is a more substantial work; it is modelled on the booksellers' race in Pope's *Dunciad* and attacks Smollett, Mallet, Murphy, and many lesser figures, though Churchill is now praised. Of Shaw's portrait of Johnson, quoted in Boswell's *Life*, Johnson reportedly said, 'the Author bore no ill-will, he has paid me a great compliment and I am obliged to him' (Boswell, *Life*, 2.480). A revised, enlarged edition of *The Race* appeared in 1766.

In May 1765 Shaw's neighbour in Marylebone, who kept a boarding-school attended by the fourth earl of Chesterfield's nine-year-old godson and heir, recommended Shaw as a man of sound classical learning who had been 'headmaster to a great school' (*Letters*, ed. Dobré, 2652). Consequently the boy was sent to Shaw for tuition: two hours each morning and evening for four months until William Dodd (another master of misrepresentation) became his tutor. On 5 November 1765 at St Mary's Church, Marylebone, Shaw married Ann Rivers, of a good family, against the wishes of her friends. Her early death in childbirth prompted Shaw's best-known poem, *A Monody to the Memory of a Young Lady* (1768). This work brought him to the attention of George Lyttelton (author of a similarly affecting poem on the death of his own wife) and John Wilkes; the second edition (1769) was dedicated to Lyttelton. To the third edition (1770) was added *An Evening Address to a Nightingale*, Shaw's elegy on the three-year-old daughter whose birth had cost her mother's life.

Meanwhile Shaw had involved himself in opposition politics. His verse satire *Corruption*, inscribed to Richard Grenville, Earl Temple, appeared in December 1768. In August 1769 he became editor of *The Middlesex Journal, or, The Chronicle of Liberty*, and asked Wilkes, who was then in prison, and other friends of freedom to write in its support (BL, Add. MS 30870, fol. 186). Later that year he was writing caustic political pieces in the pro-Wilkes *Freeholder's Magazine, or, Monthly Chronicle of Liberty*, where, in April and May 1770, also appeared long extracts from his unpublished poem 'Resignation'. He wrote an elegy on Charles Yorke, lord chancellor, who died on 20 January 1770, but Yorke's family paid to have it suppressed, perhaps because of Shaw's politics or bad character.

Shaw suffered from poor health, dissipation, and poverty. Mention of the 'Theban drug' in the *Monody* refers to his opium habit, and a letter to George Allan in 1769 tells of pawned property and 'the vast expense of physic and asses' milk which I am obliged constantly to use' (Longstaffe, 256n.). Near the end of his life his uncertain literary income was augmented by profits from his part-ownership, with Francis Newbery (1743–1818), of some patent medicines, including the once celebrated 'Beaume de vie', on the virtues of which he wrote an untraced *Account*. This nostrum may be identical with one of the same name on sale a decade earlier in Paris and composed of aloes, gentian, rhubarb, myrrh, agaric, saffron, and zedoary, helped down by treacle, sugar, and proof spirit; it was said to restore and fortify the stomach. At least it was effective in making Shaw 'able to set up his equipage, house, servants, &c.' (ibid.). He had already distanced himself from his one-time acquaintance, and perhaps drinking companion, the poet Christopher Smart.

Shaw died intestate, in debt, and, it was said, 'overwhelmed with complicated distress', on 1 September 1771 at his house in Titchfield Street, Oxford Market, London (*London Magazine*, 1771, 472). In view of the profitability of patent medicines his own distress was probably due to mismanagement, but, as his patents had another fifty years to run, they perhaps enriched his next of kin (two uncles in Yorkshire) and their descendants.

JAMES SAMBROOK

Sources *European Magazine and London Review*, 9 (1786), 14–16 • R. Anderson, *A complete edition of the poets of Great Britain*, 13 vols. (1792–5), vol. 11, pp. 557–60 • Highfill, Burnim & Langhans, *BDA*, 13.290 • W. H. D. Longstaffe, *The history and antiquities of the parish of Darlington*, new edn (1909), 255–6 • *The letters of Philip Dormer Stanhope, fourth earl of Chesterfield*, ed. B. Dobrée, 6 vols. (1932), vol. 6, pp. 2652–6, 2663 • Boswell, *Life*, 2.31–2, 480 • G. W. Stone, ed., *The London stage, 1660–1800*, pt 4: 1747–1776 (1962) • A. C. Wootton, *Chronicles of pharmacy*, 2 (1910), 176 • *GM*, 1st ser., 38 (1768), 40, 48 • *GM*, 1st ser., 41 (1771), 426 • C. Welsh, *A bookseller of the last century, being some account of the life of John Newbery* (1885), 22 • D. E. Baker, *Biographia dramatica, or, A companion to the playhouse*, rev. I. Reed, new edn, rev. S. Jones, 3 (1812), 44 • Nichols, *Lit. anecdotes*, 8.346n. • P. G. D. Thomas, 'The beginning of parliamentary reporting in newspapers, 1768–1774', *EngHR*, 74 (1959), 623–36 • E. Partridge, ed., *The poems of Cuthbert Shaw and Thomas Russell* (1925) • A. Sherbo, *Christopher Smart, scholar of the university* (1967), 253–4
Archives BL, letters to John Wilkes, Add. MS 30870, fols. 186, 215
Wealth at death in debt, but indentures for patent medicine said to 'run good for fifty years to come' and likely to benefit executors and assigns [his uncles]: Longstaffe, *History and antiquities*, 256n.; Highfill, Burnim & Langhans, *BDA*

Shaw, Duncan (1727–1794), Church of Scotland minister, was born at Inverness, on 15 December 1727, the eldest of eight children of Lachlan *Shaw (1686?–1777), Church of Scotland minister and historian, and his second wife, Anne Grant (*d.* 1783). He was educated at Elgin Academy and at King's College, Aberdeen, where he graduated MA in 1747 before studying divinity at Edinburgh University (*c*.1749–*c*.1752). Shaw was licensed by the presbytery of Elgin on 14 November 1752, and was ordained minister of the parish of Rafford, Morayshire (10 May 1753). On 10 January 1754 he married Jean (*d.* 1795), daughter of George Gordon, minister of Alves, with whom he had four daughters and three sons. Early in his long ministry in Rafford, Shaw assisted Alexander Adam with a letter of recommendation at the outset of a career which ended with the rectorship of the high school of Edinburgh. Shaw was later remembered as 'a man of cultivated mind, and of pleasing manners, possessing in no ordinary degree the affections of the people' (*New Statistical Account of Scotland*, 245). In

1774 Shaw received the degree of DD from Marischal College, Aberdeen. He was translated and admitted to the third charge of St Nicholas's Church, Aberdeen, on 13 November 1783. In 1786 he served as moderator of the general assembly of the Church of Scotland. Described by Thomas Christie as 'a sensible and learned man' (Nichols, 4.823), Shaw published, in two volumes, *A Comparative View of the Several Methods of Promoting Religious Instruction* (1776); *The History and Philosophy of Judaism* (1787), designed in part as a refutation of David Hume's views; and *The Centurion* (1793). He died on 23 June 1794 and was buried in St Nicholas's churchyard, Aberdeen.

LIONEL ALEXANDER RITCHIE

Sources DNB • *Fasti Scot.*, new edn, 6.15 • *Scottish Notes and Queries*, 4 (1890–91), 65–6 • Nichols, *Illustrations*, 4.823 • *The new statistical account of Scotland*, 13 (1845) • W. Steven, *The history of the high school of Edinburgh* (1849), 109 • bap. reg. Scot.

Shaw [Shaa], **Sir Edmund** (*d.* 1488), goldsmith and mayor of London, was the son of John Shaa of Dukinfield in Cheshire. He was apprenticed in 1450 to a London goldsmith, probably Robert Butler, and completed his apprenticeship in 1458. Shortly after, in early 1462, he received a life grant of the office of engraver to the Tower of London and other English and Calais mints, which he held for twenty years. A successful member of his craft, he seems to have been primarily a working goldsmith all his life, referring to his shop, warehouse, and working houses in his testament. There is no evidence that he traded regularly overseas, and the small number of debts for which he sued indicates that he probably did not often act as a moneylender or mortgagee.

Like almost every other contemporary Londoner of note, however, Shaw lent money to Edward IV as part of an orchestrated loan in 1468, and subsequently he made several private loans, suggesting that his dealings with a fellow goldsmith, Hugh Brice, had brought him into closer association with the king. In addition to the craft connection between them, Brice had been appointed keeper of the Tower mint at about the same time as Shaw was made engraver, and in early 1469 Shaw was one of eight friends whom Brice persuaded to make further large loans to the king. Later that year Shaw lent £240 by himself, and he continued to have both financial and commercial dealings with Edward IV thereafter.

According to Sir Thomas More (a biased source) Shaw was a proud and ambitious man. After two unsuccessful nominations for the London aldermanry, in September 1470 and June 1471, he was eventually elected alderman of Cripplegate ward in July 1473, and he became sheriff the following year. A member of the fraternity of St Giles, Cripplegate ward, he probably lived in that ward for most of his later life (as did his brother Ralph [*see below*]). None the less in 1485 he transferred to Cheap ward on the death of Sir Thomas Hill, whose testament he supervised. In 1482, having been the unsuccessful mayoral candidate the previous year, Shaw was elected mayor, and was therefore serving both when Edward IV died and throughout the tumultuous period leading up to the usurpation of Richard III.

It is for his role and assumed political attitude during this time that Shaw is mainly remembered. According to Sir Thomas More (writing in the years around 1515) and the sixteenth-century London chroniclers it was his brother **Ralph Shaw** (d. 1484), a Cambridge graduate, doctor of theology, and a canon of St Paul's, who preached a sermon at Paul's Cross, claiming that the then duke of Gloucester was the only lawful claimant to the throne. Reportedly he had formerly been a popular preacher, but so hostile was Dr Shaw's audience on this occasion that his death in the following year was said to have been due to chagrin at the cold reception accorded to his sermon. Edmund Shaw himself, as mayor, was extensively involved in the ceremonies surrounding the coronation of Richard III, and he was subsequently knighted and sworn of the privy council. The value of his commercial dealings with Richard and of the grants he received suggests that, at the very least, the king was keen to secure his support. Shaw survived Richard's downfall without apparent difficulty, however, and made no specific mention of or spiritual provision for his brother when he drew up his testament in March 1488.

Edmund Shaw died on 20 April 1488. One of his executors was his 'cousin' John Shaw, also a goldsmith and a future mayor of London; another was his 'right especiall and tender loving Frende', Henry VII's close adviser Sir Reynold Bray (PRO, PROB 11/8/12). Shaw was buried in the mercers' chapel, St Thomas of Acon, but left numerous legacies both to his parish church, St Peter's, Westcheap, and to the inhabitants of Cripplegate ward, including a sum for the rebuilding of Cripplegate itself. Another legacy was intended to establish a grammar school in Stockport, Cheshire, where his parents were buried. Among those for whom he made arrangements for prayers to be said were Edward IV, Edward's sister Anne, duchess of Exeter, and Lord Herbert. Shaw held Essex properties worth over £50 per annum at his death, equating to a purchase price of perhaps £750–£1000, and bequeathed over £4000 in cash and plate as well as personal and household effects. He was survived by his wife, Juliana, a son, Hugh, who died childless a few years later, daughters Margaret (married to a mercer, Thomas Rich) and Katherine (who later married William Brown, another mercer), as well as four sisters.   P. Tucker

Sources A. B. Beaven, ed., *The aldermen of the City of London, temp. Henry III–[1912]*, 2 (1913) • T. F. Reddaway, *The early history of the Goldsmiths' Company, 1327–1509*, ed. L. E. M. Walker (1975) • L. E. M. Walker, ed., *The book of ordinances, 1478–83* (1975) • will, PRO, PROB 11/8, sig. 12 • will, PRO, PROB 11/7, sig. 17 [Sir Thomas Hill] • journals, CLRO, 6–7 • *CIPM, Henry VII*, 1 • St Thomas More, *The history of King Richard III*, ed. R. S. Sylvester (1963), vol. 2 of *The Yale edition of the complete works of St Thomas More* • R. Horrox and P. W. Hammond, eds., *British Library Harleian manuscript 433*, 1 (1979) • *CPR, 1461–7* • A. F. Sutton and P. W. Hammond, eds., *The coronation of Richard III: the extant documents* (1983) • PRO, Exchequer, Queen's Remembrancer, customers' accounts, E 122 • PRO, Court of Common Pleas plea rolls, CP40 • A. H. Thomas and I. D. Thornley, eds., *The great chronicle of London* (1938) • Emden, *Cam.* • J. Stow, *A survey of the cities of London and Westminster and the borough of Southwark*, ed. J. Strype, new edn, 2 vols. (1720) • S. L. Thrupp, *The merchant class of medieval London, 1300–1500*, pbk edn (1962)

Wealth at death over £4000 in cash and plate, plus household effects; lands worth *c*.£750–£1000: will, PRO, PROB 11/8, sig. 12; *CIPM, Henry VII*, 1

Shaw, Sir Eyre Massey (1828–1908), fire officer, was born on 17 January 1828 (though in later life he allowed the date to be given as 1830), probably at Glenmore Cottage, Ballymore, Cobh, co. Cork, the third son of Bernard Robert Shaw (b. 1801), a merchant, who later leased Monkstown Castle, co. Cork, and his first wife, Rebecca, daughter of Edward Hoare Reeves of Castle Kelvin and Ballyglissane, co. Cork. He was educated at Dr Coghlan's school, Queenstown, before matriculating in 1843 at Trinity College, Dublin, where he graduated BA in 1848 and MA in 1854. He was intended for the church, but immediately after taking his degree examinations in the summer of 1847 decided that he was unsuited to the clerical vocation. He fled to sea, joining the crews of timber vessels trading between Cork and Quebec. The details of these years are sketchy, but he spent much time in America before, in 1854, his family obtained a commission for him in the North Cork Rifles. On 27 January 1855, at Torquay, he married Anna Maria (1827/8–1897), daughter of Mordecai Dove of Lisbon, Portugual, with whom he had two sons and four daughters.

Though promoted to captain, Shaw had an undistinguished military career and saw no action other than a rampage by his men through Sheerness, Kent, where they were stationed in October 1858. His regiment was disembodied in February 1860 and on 10 May 1860 he was appointed superintendent of the police and fire services of Belfast. He later gave an account of his success in suppressing sectarian disturbances and his reputation for impartiality between the Orange and Catholic factions. He was energetic in raising the efficiency of the fire brigade and this led to his appointment on 19 August 1861 as superintendent of the London Fire Engine Establishment following the death of James Braidwood. He gave evidence to the parliamentary select committee on fires in the metropolis (1862), whose findings led in 1866 to the formation of the Metropolitan Fire Brigade, a publicly funded force under the direction of the Metropolitan Board of Works.

A vigorous organizer, Shaw successfully got the new service off the ground. He confidently fended off attacks against his force from the voluntary fire brigades, the water companies, and insurance companies. Socially well connected, and with a military bearing, he stood firm in his appearances before parliamentary select committees in 1867 and 1876/7, the latter following a series of disastrous London fires. He repelled interference with his brigade, adopting a peremptory manner with committees of local politicians. Determined to make the London fire service the best in the world, he prided himself on the growth in its resources and personnel which he achieved despite the limited funding yielded by the statutory halfpenny rate. He expanded the use of steam fire engines and introduced telegraph communication. Until 1881 he had no deputy. In 1878 a new headquarters was acquired in

Sir Eyre Massey Shaw (1828–1908), by Barraud, pubd 1890

Southwark Bridge Road with a spacious adjoining residence, Winchester House, where the Shaws lived and entertained visiting dignitaries.

The Skipper, as Shaw was known, never shirked danger, and was almost reckless in his daring. He was several times badly injured, on two occasions severely, and gained a heroic status in late Victorian London. Yet his achievements were tinged with a gift for self-advertisement. Informed contemporaries observed that his handbook, *A complete manual of the organisation, machinery, discipline and general working of the fire brigade of London* (1876; rev. edn, 1890), made exaggerated claims for the novelty of his practices. In technical knowledge and firemanship he was not considered the equal of his predecessor. His treatise on *Fires in Theatres* (1876; 2nd edn, 1889) was reckoned unduly sensational, though it was a prelude to his massive report on fire safety in London theatres and music-halls (1882). He set great store by what would later be called public relations. Fond of ceremonies and gallops-past, he put on daytime drills for the benefit of spectators. Continental 'fact-finding' missions frequently took him away from London; one of his first actions in 1866 was to introduce brass helmets modelled on the Parisian *sapeurs-pompiers* (though these later had to be replaced because of the risk of electrocution). He was careful to cultivate good relations with journalists, but was rather less popular with his own men, who found him an autocratic disciplinarian.

Shaw moved easily in London's aristocratic clubland (he belonged to the St James's, Carlton, and Marlborough clubs) and was honoured by royalty, indulging the prince of Wales's taste for attending fires in fireman's uniform. He sported a longish goatee beard, which greyed with age, and was described as a handsome figure. 'Tall, lithe, active, without an unnecessary ounce of flesh on his body' (While, 44), he was frequently in the company of titled ladies on his inspections of fire stations; his celebrity in this regard was confirmed by the love-sick fairy queen's air 'Oh Captain Shaw' in Gilbert and Sullivan's *Iolanthe* (1882). His intimacy with Lady Colin Campbell led to his being named as one of the three co-respondents in her sensational divorce trial at the end of 1886, though no charge was proved. The case did not harm his reputation. In the following year *Punch* depicted him as 'Shaw the Lifeguard Man', with hosepipe at the ready vanquishing the fire fiend.

Shaw, who was accustomed to getting his own way, was never comfortable working under the London county council (LCC), the new public authority for London elected with a Progressive majority in 1889. On 26 June 1891 he gave notice of his resignation. The council's resolution that he reconsider was not unanimous (26 June 1891), and he formally retired on 31 October 1891, handing in a report listing his achievements over the previous thirty years. On that day it was announced that he was to receive a knighthood (KCB) in what was seen as a snub to the LCC by Shaw's patrons in the Conservative government and at court. Press comment on his resignation divided sharply on party lines. He became managing director of the Palatine Insurance Company, chairman of the Metropolitan Electric Supply Company, and a deputy lieutenant for Middlesex. After an attack of thrombosis in 1898 he suffered the amputation of both legs, and was looked after by his unmarried daughter. Shaw died at the Grand Hotel, Folkestone, Kent, on 25 August 1908, and was buried at Highgate cemetery on 29 August. His helmet, axe, and uniform belt were presented to the London Fire Brigade.

M. C. CURTHOYS

Sources G. V. Blackstone, *A history of the British fire service* (1957) · R. Cox, *Oh, Captain Shaw*, 2nd edn (1988) · J. While, *Fifty years of fire fighting in London* (1931) · A. T. C. Pratt, ed., *People of the period: being a collection of the biographies of upwards of six thousand living celebrities*, 2 vols. (1897) · *Men and women of the time* (1899) · *The Gallery of Celebrities* (1891) · Burtchaell & Sadleir, *Alum. Dubl.* · G. H. Fleming, *Victorian 'sex goddess': Lady Colin Campbell*, pbk edn (1990)
Likenesses Count Gleichen, statuette, 1870 · H. Weigall, oils, 1871, London Fire Brigade · engraving, 1879, repro. in Cox, *Oh, Captain Shaw*, facing p. 87 · photograph, 1891, London Fire Brigade Library; repro. in Cox, *Oh, Captain Shaw* · Ape [C. Pellegrini], chromolithograph caricature, NPG; repro. in *VF* (3 June 1871) · Barraud, photograph, NPG; repro. in *Men and Women of the Day*, 3 (1890) [see illus.] · photograph (in uniform), repro. in Blackstone, *History of the British fire service*, facing p. 209 · photograph, Royal Collection
Wealth at death £9042 12s. 5d.: administration with will, 1 Oct 1908, *CGPLA Eng. & Wales*

Shaw, Ferdinando (*bap.* 1674, *d.* 1745), Presbyterian minister and religious controversialist, was baptized on 10 January 1674 at St Helen's parish, Ashby-de-la-Zouch, Leicestershire, the son of Samuel *Shaw (1634/5–1696), the former rector of Long Whatton, Leicestershire, who refused to conform in 1662, and his wife, Jane, daughter of Ferdinando Poole, another ejected minister. Ferdinando was named after his grandfather. He probably received his early education from his father, master of the Ashby grammar school, and was educated for the nonconformist ministry at John Woodhouse's academy at Sheriffhales, Shropshire. By his own statement he began his MA in 1693, presumably at a Scottish university. He was ordained in April 1698.

Shaw began his ministry at Bromsgrove, Worcestershire, where he married his first wife, whose surname was Harris. In March 1699 he accepted a call to be assistant minister at the Presbyterian meeting in Friar Gate, Derby, in succession to William Cross (d. 1697), his uncle. At St Werburgh's, Derby, he married his second wife, Mary Simmons, a widow, on 26 March 1702. As the junior minister he appears to have served the parishes around Derby, but in 1704, on the death of Robert Moore, the senior minister, he became the sole minister on a stipend of £45. Ill health led to the appointment of Josiah Rogerson as joint pastor in August 1724. On 4 August 1708 at St Werburgh's Shaw married his third wife, Elizabeth Eyre (d. 1740), third daughter of William Eyre of Holme, Derbyshire, and the granddaughter of Sir John Gell, second baronet, of Hopton.

Shaw came to prominence following the refusal of the vicar of St Alkmund's, Henry Cantrell, and the rest of the clergy in Derby to bury children baptized by dissenting ministers. Shaw preached a sermon to his congregation on 22 March 1713, subsequently published as *The validity of baptism administ'red by dissenting ministers: and the unreasonableness of refusing burial to children so baptiz'd* (1713). The work provoked a major controversy and nearly twenty titles were published locally. Shaw claimed that the whole of the first impression of 750 copies was taken off in three or four weeks, mainly by the neighbouring counties. Shaw's decision to show only that 'many eminent Writers of the Church were for the Validity of lay-Baptism', and therefore that 'Baptism administered by dissenting ministers is valid in the judgement of the Church of England', rather than to demonstrate the right of Presbyterian ministers to baptize was a misjudgement (F. Shaw, *Reflections on the Layman's Vindication of his Answer*, 1715, 4). His high-church critics dismissed his arguments: 'this Author had not prov'd Lay-Baptism, or that Administered by Dissenting Teachers to be Valid' (Lay-man, *An Answer to a Late Pamphlet*, 1713, 25–6). It took John Hartley, the Presbyterian minister at Ashby-de-la-Zouch, to provide a reasoned defence of Presbyterian ordination in his *Vindication of Presbyterian Ordination* (1714). Shaw did expose the inconsistency of the high-church position in denying burial only to infant and not adult dissenters by emphasizing their lack of charity and, embarrassingly, pointing out that the martyred Charles I might not have received baptism from an episcopal minister. Between 1714 and 1716 he published a further four works answering his critics.

Like many dissenters, Shaw actively supported the Hanoverian succession, publishing two sermons, *Condolence and Congratulation* and *The Crown Shall Flourish*, to mark George I's accession and coronation. They provoked the anonymous Well-Wisher to publish some *Remarks* in 1714. Shaw published a further sermon in 1730 to mark the birthday of the prince of Wales. Although most of his publications were controversial, he also published on practical and devotional subjects, particularly in later years when his health was failing: 'I hope I have quit myself of Controversies, for the remainder of my Life' (F. Shaw, *A Summary of the Bible*, 1730, iii). They included a *Catholick Catechism* (1716; 3rd edn, 1724) and *A Summary of the Bible* (1730).

Shaw died on 26 January 1745 in Derby and was buried in St Werburgh's on 31 January. His wife had died five years earlier on 11 October 1740. His eldest son by his first marriage, Samuel Shaw (1699–1748), also became a Presbyterian minister. Unusually for a nonconformist minister, Ferdinando Shaw was the subject of a poetic tribute in the *Gentleman's Magazine*.   DAVID L. WYKES

Sources account and minute book for Friar Gate Unitarian Chapel, Derby, 1697–1819, Derbys. RO, 1312D/A1, fols. 5a, 6 · register of Friar Gate, Derby, baptisms, 1698–1743, PRO, RG 4/5 · C. E. Surman, 'Eighteenth century sidelights on Derbyshire nonconformity: extracts from the *Derby Mercury*', *Transactions of the Congregational Historical Society*, 15 (1945–8), 88–92 · J. Hunter, *Familiae minorum gentium*, ed. J. W. Clay, 1, Harleian Society, 37 (1894), 377 · *Calamy rev.*, 353–4, 394, 435 · will, Leics. RO, will 1695/48 [Revd Samuel Shaw of Ashby-de-la-Zouch, schoolmaster] · J. Toulmin, *An historical view of the state of the protestant dissenters in England* (1814), 563 · J. Evans, 'List of dissenting congregations and ministers in England and Wales, 1715–1729', DWL, MS 38.4, 22 · J. Rogerson and F. Shaw, *The Christian course finished with joy: a funeral sermon, preach'd at … the interment of Mrs Elizabeth Shaw, wife of the Reverend Ferdinando* (1740) · 'Poetic tribute to Mr Ferdinand Shaw', *GM*, 1st ser., 15 (1745), 104 · parish register, Ashby-de-la-Zouch, St Helen, Leics. RO, DE 1013/1 [baptism] · *Drewry's Derby Mercury* (1 Feb 1745)
Archives Shrops. RRC, Astley MSS, pedigree of Shaw family, 6000/1601

Shaw, Dame Flora Louise. *See* Lugard, Dame Flora Louise, Lady Lugard (1852–1929).

Shaw, Sir Frederick, third baronet (1799–1876), politician, born at Bushy Park, co. Dublin, on 11 December 1799, was the second son of Sir Robert Shaw (1774–1849), and his first wife, Maria (d. 1831), daughter and heir of Abraham Wilkinson of Bushy Park. The father, a Dublin banker, sat in the Irish parliament (1798–1800) for Bannow borough, co. Wexford; after voting against the union he was for twenty-two years (1804–26) member for Dublin city in the Westminster parliament. He also served as lord mayor of Dublin, and was created a baronet in 1821.

Shaw entered Trinity College, Dublin, in 1816, but shortly afterwards moved to Brasenose College, Oxford, where he graduated BA in 1819. In 1822 he was called to the Irish bar and quickly attained a considerable practice. In 1826 he was appointed recorder of Dundalk, an office that he vacated two years later on his nomination to the recordership of Dublin. Shaw married, on 16 March 1819, Thomasine Emily (d. 1859), sixth daughter of the Hon. George Jocelyn, and granddaughter of Robert, first earl of Roden; they had five sons and three daughters.

His father's influence, combined with his own abilities,

soon led to Shaw's selection as one of the tory candidates for the representation of Dublin. In 1830 he successfully contested the city, defeating Henry Grattan's son. At the general election of 1831 he was unsuccessful, but was awarded the seat on petition, and held it for the brief remainder of the unreformed parliament. Each of his elections for the unreformed constituency of Dublin cost him £10,000. After the Reform Act, O'Connell had hopes that Shaw might be persuaded to stand as a conservative repealer, but was soon disabused of this notion. At the election of 1832, Shaw was returned with Serjeant Lefroy for the University of Dublin; he was subsequently re-elected four times for the same constituency.

In the House of Commons Shaw rapidly acquired a reputation. He possessed debating talents of a high order, and became the recognized leader of the Irish Conservatives. He was regarded as the most capable opponent of O'Connell, though he did not take the extreme tory view of any question, and had been a supporter of Catholic emancipation before that measure was passed. His moderation was unrepresentative of the Irish tory rank and file, and distanced him from the Lords' leaders Roden and Enniskillen. His most considerable parliamentary achievement was in the debate on the charges brought by O'Connell against Sir William Cusack Smith, an Irish judge. O'Connell had on 13 February 1834 carried by a majority of ninety-three a motion for the appointment of a select committee to inquire into the conduct of Baron Smith in introducing political topics in his judicial charges. A week later a motion to rescind this resolution was carried, notwithstanding ministerial opposition, as a result mainly of Shaw's eloquent defence of the accused judge.

When Peel formed his government in 1834, Shaw declined on professional grounds all preferment beyond a seat in the Irish privy council. During this short administration he was, however, the chief adviser of Lord Haddington's Irish government, which was called by opponents the 'Shaw viceroyalty'. On the return of the whigs to office, Shaw became one of Peel's most active colleagues in opposition. He took an active but not extreme part in the opposition to Lord John Russell's Irish Municipal Corporations Bill of 1835, and proposed a successful amendment to the 1838 Tithe Bill. He favoured an extensive poor-relief measure. Although he had entered parliament as a representative of Conservative and protestant principles, Shaw's opinion and conduct had by 1847 become too liberal for some of his old supporters, particularly after he followed Peel in voting for repeal of the corn laws in 1846. At the elections of 1847 he retained his seat for the university only after a very severe contest with Sir Joseph Napier, later Irish lord chancellor.

In 1848 poor health obliged Shaw to resign his seat and retire from political life. On the death, unmarried, of his elder brother, Robert, on 19 February 1869, he succeeded to the baronetcy. Early in 1876 he resigned his office of recorder of Dublin, receiving an address from the bar. He had been made a bencher of the King's Inns in 1835. He

died on 30 June 1876 at his home, Terenure Manor (formerly known as Kimmage House), Crumlin, co. Dublin, and was buried at Mount Jerome cemetery.

C. L. FALKINER, rev. PETER GRAY

Sources WWBMP · A. D. Macintyre, *The Liberator: Daniel O'Connell and the Irish party, 1830–1847* (1965) · O. MacDonagh, *The emancipist: Daniel O'Connell, 1830–47* (1989) · Boase, *Mod. Eng. biog.* · Burke, *Peerage* · CGPLA Ire. (1876)
Archives BL, corresp. with Sir Robert Peel, Add. MSS 40407–40541
Likenesses J. H. Lynch, lithograph, pubd after 1832 (after B. R. Green), NG Ire. · J. Doyle, pen and pencil drawing, 1840, BM · G. Hayter, group portrait, oils (*The House of Commons, 1833*), NPG · F. Reynolds, oils, King's Inns, Dublin · E. Scriven, stipple (after F. Cruikshank), BM, NPG; repro. in H. T. Ryall, *Portraits of eminent conservatives and statesmen* [1836] · engraving, repro. in *ILN* (1844)
Wealth at death under £3000: probate, 27 July 1876, CGPLA Ire.

Shaw, Frederick John [*pseud.* Brougham Villiers] (1863–1939), socialist and author, was born on 15 November 1863 at 1 Hawthorn Terrace, Newcastle upon Tyne, the eldest child of Frederick Shaw, merchant, and his wife, Elizabeth Foster. He had four sisters, and two of his cousins also lived with the family. His grandfather Thomas Shaw and his father had done well as seed cutters with the colour manufacturers Hoyle and Robson, and the family was comfortably off (it employed several servants throughout Shaw's childhood). Until 1908 he was engaged in business, except for an interval as joint editor of the *Newcastle Evening News* and *Morning Mail*. He moved around the north-east, and lived in South Shields, Gateshead, and then Heaton. During this time he wrote a volume of poems, *Past and Future*, published locally in 1898.

Shaw joined the Fabian Society in 1890 and the Independent Labour Party in 1894, and he played an active role with his wife, Margaret Dorothy Shaw, in promoting the socialist and labour movements in the north-east. He wrote penny tracts on *Canny Newcastle and her Corporations* and *Socialism for the North* for local branches of the Independent Labour Party. At the turn of the century he joined the Newcastle and district Labour Representation Committee, for whom he again wrote a tract, this time on *Facts for Newcastle*. In 1907 he accepted a post with the Free Trade Union which took him first to Bradford and then to Glasgow. In 1912 he moved to London on being appointed secretary of the Cobden Club, and soon afterwards also became secretary of the international committee to promote universal free trade. It was in the former capacity that he collaborated with Cobden's daughter to produce *The Land Hunger* as a tribute to her father.

Shaw wrote a number of studies of the Liberal, socialist, and suffrage movements in Britain, almost always using the pseudonym Brougham Villiers. His main ideas remained fairly constant, though the First World War, not surprisingly, altered his view of the immediate tasks before society. Before the war his main works were *The Opportunity of Liberalism* (1904), *The Socialist Movement in England* (1908), and *Modern Democracy* (1912). He adopted a sociological approach rather than a more ethical or polemical one, arguing that the viability of a policy depends less on ideas than social and economic forces, but he readily drew political conclusions from his sociology. He thought the mutual dependence of humans implies that society necessarily evolves towards ever greater solidarity, with a reasoned organization replacing an instinctive individualism. The new Liberalism and socialism were manifestations of this evolutionary process; they represented the moment of democracy conceived as the will of the average person. The way to discover the implications of this democratic moment is not to listen to politicians but to investigate the concerns of the average. Because the average constantly face the threat of poverty, the social question will dominate; because they meet this threat with trade unions and the co-operative movement, the state will respond by promoting co-operation to provide a minimum standard of life; and because they deal with poverty as a practical problem, the state will introduce this minimum standard by rule of thumb methods.

Shaw supported the suffragettes out of principle—he edited *The Case for Women's Suffrage* (1907)—but also because of the effect votes for women would have on national politics. Women would not stand for tariffs on foodstuffs, while their caring role made their political participation especially necessary at a time when the state was taking on welfare functions. After 1914 Shaw's main works were *Britain after the Peace* (1918) and *England and the New Era* (1920), the latter being his last important work. He argued the war had entailed a high level of expenditure, much geographical displacement of people, and other social changes, all of which inaugurated a revolutionary era. Whereas collectivists of the 1890s had championed an evolutionary approach to change, they now had to concentrate on the peaceful, orderly management of a revolution. In particular, he advocated a capital levy so as to restore the finances of the state, and a League of Nations overseeing demilitarization and free trade so as to ensure peace. Shaw died at his home, 18 Sudbury Court Drive, Wembley, Middlesex, on 26 June 1939; his wife survived him. MARK BEVIR

Sources H. B. Lees-Smith, ed., *The encyclopaedia of the labour movement* (1928) · *The Labour who's who* (1927) · *Ward's north of England directory* · census returns · b. cert. · Nuffield Oxf., Fabian MSS · CGPLA Eng. & Wales (1939) · d. cert.
Wealth at death £126 10s. 0d.: probate, 11 Aug 1939, CGPLA Eng. & Wales

Shaw, George (1751–1813), natural historian, was born on 10 December 1751 at Bierton, Buckinghamshire, the younger of two sons of the Revd Timothy Shaw, vicar of Bierton. He was educated at home by his father until 1765, with a strong interest in natural history, then entered Magdalen Hall, Oxford, graduating BA on 24 May 1769, and MA three years later. He was ordained deacon in 1774 to assist his father. His continuing interest in natural history led him after a few years to abandon the church as a profession and to study medicine in Edinburgh, then at its peak as a centre for natural history and medical education. On his return to Oxford he was appointed deputy botanical lecturer. On 17 October 1787 he was admitted to the degrees of bachelor and doctor of medicine. He was unable to succeed to the botany professorship because of the conditions of its establishment, so left for London to make a career in medical practice. He rapidly became a member of the group of naturalists led by James Edward Smith, and joined with them in founding the Linnean Society in 1788. Six years later he was elected its vice-president.

Shaw was elected a fellow of the Royal Society in 1789. In 1791 he was appointed assistant keeper of the natural history section of the British Museum, and was promoted to keeper in 1807. He was responsible for organizing its collections at a time when budgetary limitations and lack of space led to their continuing deterioration. His annual burnings of those which time, insects, and rot were destroying became part of the folklore of the museum's early history. He retained the post until his death.

Shaw had a tenacious memory, wrote Latin with facility, elegance, and purity, and sometimes lapsed into poetry. He delivered a series of twelve popular lectures on zoology at the Royal Institution in 1806 and 1807 (published in 1809). He was an indefatigable worker, and in his *Philosophical Transactions Abridged* (18 vols., 1809) dealt with all the papers on natural history, nearly 1500 in number, inserting the Linnaean names of the species and adding references to later works.

Shaw was more a popularizer than a naturalist. Subscribing to the Linnaean method of classification, he brought to the attention of an expanding lay audience for natural history the more remarkable novelties not only in such collections as the Leverian Museum, with which he had a working association, but also from the recently settled Australia with which he became familiar as the editor of the natural history appendix to J. White's *Journal of a Voyage to New South Wales* (1790); in the latter he provided the first systematic description of the natural wonders of the new continent. His most important contribution to natural history was his *Naturalist's Miscellany* whose twenty-four volumes from 1789 until his death in 1813 consisted of a monthly series of coloured illustrations and Latin and English classificatory descriptions of the more interesting botanical and zoological novelties, such as the remarkable black swan and the egg-laying mammalian spiny anteater (echidna) and the duck-billed platypus. The materials of the *Miscellany* served as the basis for the multi-volumed *General Zoology*, begun in 1800 but left unfinished at his death. His publications were well illustrated, providing for the non-professional naturalist the description of rare specimens available in the original only to the wealthiest collector or museum. Shaw died at his residence in the British Museum on 22 July 1813.

B. B. WOODWARD, rev. JACOB W. GRUBER

Sources GM, 1st ser., 83/2 (1813), 290–92 · A. E. Gunther, *The founders of science at the British Museum, 1753–1900* (1980)
Archives McGill University, Montreal · NHM
Likenesses W. Holl, stipple (after J. Russell), BM, NPG; repro. in R. J. Thornton, *A new illustration of the sexual system of Linnaeus* (1803) · engraving (after J. Russell), RS · engraving, RS

Shaw, George Bernard (1856–1950), playwright and polemicist, was born on 26 July 1856 at 3 Upper Synge

George Bernard Shaw (1856–1950), by Augustus John, 1915

Street (later 33 Synge Street), Dublin. He was the third and youngest child, and only son, of George Carr Shaw (1815–1885), a pensioned law-court clerk and failing corn merchant, and Lucinda Elizabeth, *née* Gurly (1830–1913), daughter of Walter Bagnall Gurly, an impoverished country gentleman of co. Carlow. On his father's side Sonny, as Shaw was known as a child, came from the fading protestant ascendancy, landed gentry who had crossed the Irish Sea, after Cromwell, from Scotland and England. His grandfather, an earlier Bernard Shaw, had eleven children who survived into maturity, most of them what his grandson called 'downstarts'. The 'Shaw family of dipsomaniacs', as Shaw described them in a note in his diary in 1882, were on the male side 'unconvivial dramdrinkers'. His father was a furtive drinker when he married the much younger Bessie Gurly on 17 June 1852. Eager to escape her dour, hunchbacked aunt, Ellen Whitcroft, who had brought her up, Bessie chanced life with an unpleasant, quirky Dubliner who had squandered his income; by marriage Bessie lost her own assets to her widowed father, who had remarried a month earlier to legalize a natural infant daughter. On Bessie's honeymoon with George Shaw in Liverpool she discovered that he was an advanced alcoholic. She had nowhere to go, remaining in what her son described as the 'hell' of 'shabby-genteel poverty with a drunken husband' (*Autobiography*, 22).

Early years and education With his sisters Lucinda Frances (*b.* 1853) and (Elinor) Agnes (*b.* 1855), George Bernard (he dropped the George when he left home) endured a middle-class impecuniosity which seemed even more humiliating than to have been born poor and to have pretensions to nothing more. After being tutored by an 'ill-tempered, but quite sober' clerical uncle (*Diaries*, 1.29), he attended, briefly, Dublin day schools. His first was the Wesleyan connexional, nearby at 79 St Stephen's Green, which he entered at nine in the summer term of 1865, and where he was taught—badly, he later thought—Homer, Caesar, Virgil, and scripture. After three months he was removed, returning in August 1867 for another three months; in February 1868 he was readmitted. In one of the interstices he attended, briefly, a lower-class school at 23–4 Sandycove Road, near Dalkey.

Bessie Shaw, who had an attractive mezzo-soprano voice and some talent at the piano, had begun offering lessons in her home to eke out her husband's diminishing income, and she was already a member of George John Lee's Amateur Musical Society. A mesmeric figure in Dublin musical circles, Lee proposed, after the death of his invalid younger brother in 1862, a joint household in which he and Mrs Shaw could share larger rooms for lessons and rehearsals. When George Carr Shaw, a cipher in the arrangement, ignored by his increasingly cold and independent wife, offered no objections, the move to the more upscale 1 Hatch Street house created a *ménage à trois* that gave Sonny, in effect, an additional and more admirable father figure.

Whether Lee was also Shaw's biological father—he had been close to Bessie long enough for that possibility—obsessed Shaw all his life. Mrs Shaw had turned to music, and to Lee, for consolation. Lee's former residence in Harrington Street, a short stroll from Synge Street, had been a magnet for women eager to acquire the 'method' ministered by the Svengali-like voice coach who turned modest voices like Bessie's into concert-quality, conducted female choruses, and basked in the attentions of the fair sex. Yet Shaw noted in later years that Lee, who was his mother's age, seemed at the time to have had no dalliances with women, and he characterized his mother as a fiercely chaste dragon. Shaw also defensively maintained that he resembled the bearded George Carr Shaw, pointing to Lee's socially impossible Roman Catholicism, his lame leg, and his puny stature. It may be an index to his anxieties, however, that he peopled his plays from the start with orphans, natural children, children with multiple parents, children who did not know the identities of their parents, and other genetic mysteries not far removed from the plot staples of Victorian fiction and melodrama. None the less he was legally George Shaw's son, and Lee's 'method' appears to have been limited to the larynx.

Lee not only made music with Mrs Shaw at Hatch Street but for the months of milder weather leased Torca Cottage on Dalkey Hill, overlooking Killiney Bay from the steeply sloped front garden. At seventy-five Shaw recalled his days there as a ten-year-old as the happiest of his life, where, under the 'canopied skies', he could be 'a prince in a world of my own imagination' (Holroyd, 1.28). Resorting to his inner self was essential, as his father, having no occupation beyond the unrewarding mill but his bibulousness, had even less interest in Sonny than did Bessie. Inexperienced with children, Lee offered him, on occasion, some of the rudiments of music, especially opera. The boy was enchanted. Later Shaw claimed the boon of three fathers, as dramatized in *Misalliance* (1909) in the experience of Joey Percival, who has 'the regulation natural chap', 'a tame philosopher', and 'an Italian priest' (*Plays*, 4.166):

> [the trio] took charge of Joey's conscience. … You see, the philosopher was a freethinker, and always believed the latest thing. The priest didn't believe anything. … And the natural father kept an open mind and believed whatever paid him best. Between the lot of them Joey got cultivated no end. (ibid.)

In Sonny's own case the philosophical father figure was his 'Rabelaisian' uncle, Walter Gurly, a ship's doctor who visited between voyages. Uncle Walter destroyed, Shaw recalled, 'all my inculcated childish reverence for the verbiage of religion, for its legends and personifications and parables' (*Autobiography*, 1.37). The non-believing priest suggests Lee, who ministered to his special flock with his 'method', its holy book, and professed a nominal Catholicism. In February 1869 Shaw was withdrawn from the Wesleyan connexional school for failure to learn, and transferred to the Central Model School in Marlborough Street, a less genteel, non-denominational institution that included Roman Catholic boys. Shaw, who attended this school for seven months, at ninety recalled his 'shame and wounded snobbery' (Shaw, *Self Sketches*, 39). At thirteen he was enrolled in the Dublin English Scientific and Commercial Day School, a protestant academy in Aungier and Whitefriars streets that substituted business training for Latin and Greek. He remained for two years, accepting his incarceration as a final prison term. Shaw claimed to have learned little there, waiting out each day until he and a friend, Matthew Edward McNulty, could go off to afternoon classes at the Royal Dublin Society's Schools of Art, or visit the National Gallery.

Shaw's employment began on 26 October 1871, when he was fifteen, as a junior clerk in a Dublin estate agency run by two brothers, Charles Uniacke and Thomas Courtney Townshend, at a salary of £18 a year. From nine to six, as Shaw relived the experience through the character of Julius Baker in *Misalliance*, he sat in 'a stuffy little den counting another man's money. … I enter and enter, and add and add, and take money and give change, and fill cheques and stamp receipts'. He also copied business letters and filed them, and ran petty errands which at the least released him into the outside world. It was, he thought, a 'damnable waste of human life' (*Plays*, 4.214–15). While he performed his drudgery so conscientiously over fifteen months that his wages rose to £24, his family situation had altered. His musical 'father', who had intimated grander aspirations by renaming himself G. J. Vandeleur Lee, had begun producing Italian opera, exploiting the talents of his flock. In January 1872 he also founded a

New Philharmonic Society as a rival to the existing Dublin orchestra. At Hatch Street Bessie Shaw was his adjutant. By early 1873 Lee was conductor of the annual Dublin Musical Festival, but his ambitions now could not be contained by Ireland. At the beginning of June, cancelling his next advertised concert, Lee embarked for London.

On 17 June 1873, in a move planned well in advance, Mrs Shaw, with Agnes (Lucy followed later) also left for London. Whether or not she intended the symbolism, it was her twenty-first wedding anniversary. George Carr Shaw remained behind with their son. Abandoned with the furniture was the piano. With the music stopped, young Shaw purchased a manual, began teaching himself the keyboard, and laboriously learned the fingering for his mother's vocal score of *Don Giovanni*.

In February 1873, just before the Hatch Street ménage broke up, the head cashier at Townshends abruptly departed. Shaw substituted so efficiently that he was given the job at double his wages. At £48 a year he could even afford the necessary uniform of a tailcoat. Tabulating rental payments, especially those of the poor, and going out each Tuesday to collect some of them, was an early confrontation with economic injustice and inequality of opportunity. Books as well as music—after working hours—compensated for office tedium. There were few books at home because no adult at Hatch Street valued reading; however, most protestant families displayed Bunyan and the Bible, and such periodicals as *Household Words*. Shaw discovered Blake, Byron, and Shelley—all rebels to be read somewhat furtively. Although Dublin productions were largely adaptations of French melodrama and watered-down Shakespeare, theatre was an affordable joy.

First years in London While Shaw served his time, his mother and sisters had settled at 13 Victoria Grove, a house off the Fulham Road, London. Lee was a half-hour's walk away, at 13 Park Lane, an appropriately posh address for his ambitions. Bessie returned to Dublin in March 1874 to sell her furniture and move her abandoned husband and son to cheaper rooms at 61 Harcourt Street. Since George Carr Shaw remained legally responsible for his wife, he agreed to send her £1 a week. They never lived under the same roof again.

At Harcourt Street the elder Shaw spent his evenings over a newspaper or the dismal mill accounts. He and his son seldom spoke to each other. But early in 1876 young George learned from his mother that Yuppy, as Agnes was known, had been moved to a sanatorium to finish out her days. She had long suffered from tuberculosis. Claiming family feeling, he had an excuse to leave his post, now paying him £84 a year. In any case he had been peeved that the Townshends were proposing to place a relative in the cashier's chair. Refusing an insignificant job at a higher salary, he resigned on 29 February. He was still working out his month's notice when Agnes died on 27 March.

Although Shaw left almost immediately on the North Wall boat to London, travelling from there with his mother and Lucy to Agnes's funeral at Ventnor, and intending never to return to Dublin, at nearly twenty his only vocational skill was in a role he had rejected. In London now to stay, he found no work but ghost-writing, for Lee, unsigned musical notices in *The Hornet*, a satirical weekly. The subterfuge lasted for ten months, after which the faltering paper, which expired early the next year, was unable to pay for further reviews.

Lucy and her mother were now only 'frostily civil' to Lee (Holroyd, 1.62) because of his unwanted attentions to Lucy. Mrs Shaw began taking voice pupils herself, and Lucy, who was pretty and talented, sought singing roles. Since Shaw needed some source of income, he kept close to Lee even after the ghosting ended, helping at the piano when Lee held rehearsals, but Lee's vogue was proving short-lived. Shaw drafted a third edition of Lee's 'method' pamphlet, *The Voice*, that was never published. Moneyless and forgotten, Lee died of heart disease in November 1886.

Filling empty days while waiting for responses to job applications, Shaw procured a reader's ticket to the British Museum and spent most weekdays at a desk in the spacious round reading room under the newly gaslit dome. It became his informal university, and because it was home to radical intellectuals of both sexes who also needed such a venue the reading room further became Shaw's informal club. He tried writing short fiction and drama, even beginning in February 1878 a blank-verse satire about the home life of Jesus, with Mary as a termagant mother and Judas, favourably, as a young man 'unblinded' by 'self-delusion' (*Plays*, 7.508). After 1260 lines he abandoned the effort in the second act. (It was published posthumously as *Passion Play*.) Also in February 1878 he wrote a satire, *My Dear Dorothea*, subtitled, eighteenth-century style, 'A practical system of moral education for females embodied in a letter to a young person of that sex'. (It was also published posthumously.) Later that year he began a novel as 'The Legg Papers'. A survival from it may be the short story 'The Miraculous Revenge', about a wandering graveyard. W. B. Yeats, offered it in 1906, published it in his miscellany *The Shanachie*.

In his neat clerical hand Shaw began a more ambitious effort on 5 March 1879, an autobiographical novel he titled, 'with merciless fitness' (Holroyd, 1.73), *Immaturity*. In the reading room he attempted at least five pages a day about the adventures of a diffident young clerk who comes to London from the provinces at twenty to seek a more interesting life but fails to grow up. It was Shaw's own *David Copperfield*, with a flavour both reminiscent of Dickens and, in its grimy realism, anticipatory of Gissing. Its sometimes sober, often satirical, evocation of mid-Victorian England, crowded with closely realized characters and scenes, put off every publisher in London. It emerged only as the first volume of Shaw's collected edition of 1930–31.

Unhopeful as he completed revisions on 5 November 1879, Shaw began anew to seek employment. Writing with scrupulous honesty to the manager of the Edison Telephone Company, new in London, he confessed, 'I know how to wait for success in literature, but I do not know how to live on air in the interim' (*Letters*, 1.23). He was placed in the way-leave department to persuade East End residents to allow wires and other telephone paraphernalia to cross their properties. Hired on 14 November 1879, he was running the unit by February 1880, his annual salary rising from £48 to £80. Still, when the company merged with a rival as the United Telephone Company, he chose not to go with it. On the same day he began *The Irrational Knot*, his second novel, its protagonist an American electrical engineer of the breezy, confident sort imported for telephone work. Together with Shaw's three novels that followed, similarly turned down on completion, it padded out propagandist magazines sponsored by Shaw's socialist friends. *The Irrational Knot*, its title a sneer at conventional marriage, was completed on 1 December 1880, serialized in 1886–7 in Annie Besant's *Our Corner*, and not published in book form until 1905. Shaw later pronounced the novel a forerunner of Ibsen, of whom he had not yet heard, because one spouse—in Shaw's case the husband—walks out on the other at the close. Shaw's characters, several hardly more than animated theories, were endowed with what he described as an 'original morality' (preface, *The Irrational Knot*, 1905 American edition, xxii, xviii) which publishers found crude, disagreeable, and even perverse.

With half-hearted job-hunting still fruitless, Shaw began *Love among the Artists* on 19 May 1881. By then he had adopted vegetarianism—inspired by Shelley, by poverty, and because it was the choice of the radical friends he joined for meals (his mother ignored him). Before he was very far into his daily routine of five pages he came down with smallpox, then prevalent in London, and was confined to lodgings at 37 Fitzroy Street, where he, with his breadwinning mother and occasionally his sister, had moved the previous December. Now retired from his seafaring practice and living in Leyton, Uncle Walter took him in. Shaw had continued with his novel, finishing it in January 1882, and also using his sickbed isolation to teach himself Pitman shorthand. When he returned to his Bloomsbury haunts, friends suggested that for a change of scene after his long illness, as well as for greater opportunities, he emigrate to America. Instead, Shaw sent *The Irrational Knot* across the Atlantic, but it was turned down on moral grounds.

In mid-April 1882, just before Shaw and his mother (Lucy was engaged in small roles with travelling operetta companies) moved once more, to 36 Osnaburgh Street, near Regent's Park, he began a new novel in which the hero is a prize-fighter. With a friend, Pakenham Beatty, as sparring partner, he had taken up amateur boxing the year before. Further illness intervened, this time scarlet fever, which sent him back to Leyton, and before he resumed work on the boxing novel he wrote another short story, 'The Serenade', published after several rejections in the *Magazine of Music* in November 1885. Interruptions in his routine are not evident in the 324 pages of the manuscript novel, which he finished on 6 February 1883. The writing is exuberant. Serialized in 1885–6 and published in book form from the magazine plates in 1886, *Cashel Byron's Profession* examined the 'immoral' and 'retrograde' professions (in the words of the heroine, the millionairess Lydia Carew) of prize-fighting and the wagering on the outcome. As an indictment of society it anticipated such early plays of his as *Mrs Warren's Profession*. In 1901 Shaw satirized his own novel, which had sold out its 1s. original run of 2500 copies, in a burlesque Elizabethan blank-verse play, *The Admirable Bashville*.

The socialism in *Cashel Byron* had been an afterthought, some of it inserted for its appearance in *To-Day* after he had been converted by attending a lecture by Henry George, a socialist and political economist. Shaw was spurred to reading Marx, whose gospel became the springboard for his final complete novel, *An Unsocial Socialist* (originally entitled 'The Heartless Man' when he began it in March 1883). With his self-taught shorthand he drafted it with new efficiency, then made a copy in his clerical copperplate. It was finished, largely by abbreviating the adventures of his hero, on 15 December 1883, serialized in the socialist *To-Day* in 1884, and published in book form after many rejections in 1887. *An Unsocial Socialist* was, at the very least, different. Intended as 'a gigantic grapple with the whole social problem' (*Autobiography*, 1.104), it broke down under the weight of its incongruities, which included a runaway husband, a finishing school for girls, and ponderous paraphrases from Marx's *Capital*, among sparkling passages of Shavian dialogue that foreshadowed his later work. Sidney Trefusis, the socialist agitator as handsome hero, is a prototype of John Tanner of *Man and Superman*.

A fragment written in 1887–8 and posthumously published in 1958 as *An Unfinished Novel* was Shaw's final false start in fiction, with an abortive plot that anticipates both *Candida* and *The Doctor's Dilemma*. However, he was by then deep in more rewarding pursuits, for despite his failures in fiction the 1880s was the decade in which Shaw found himself personally and professionally. Even the abandoned novel was evidence of that, for its hero is pursued by two desirable women, both of them married; Shaw, lean and just above 6 feet in height, with an auburn beard cultivated to conceal the scars of smallpox, had discovered that he was extremely attractive to women. He showed interest in several he had met at political evenings, or encountered as his mother's voice students, but an older woman, the widowed Jane (Jenny) Patterson (1839–1924), had designs upon him. In his diary in July 1885 he noted that he 'celebrated my birthday with a new experience': the willing loss of his virginity, at which she had assisted. Too poor to maintain a wife, he had evaded, he later claimed, sexual ties which might have required marriage, and hence giving up the struggle to become a writer. His first mistresses were married, or once married, women.

Journalism and politics In the mid-1880s Shaw became a socialist, a polemicist, a journalist, a spellbinding speaker, a critic of the arts—even, tentatively, a playwright. He emerged as the force behind the Fabian Society, newly founded in 1884, a middle-class socialist group which aimed to transform Britain not through radicalism or revolution but through 'permeation' (Sidney Webb's term) of the nation's intellectual and political life. Adept at committee work and at anything involving writing skills, Shaw involved himself in every aspect of Fabian activities, most visibly at the start in editing a landmark of modern British politics, *Fabian Essays in Socialism* (1889), to which he also contributed.

A shy young man on his arrival in London in 1876, and also impecunious, Shaw found that the cheapest, and the most stimulating, entertainment could be found in the many meeting rooms in which speech making and debating on political, social, and religious issues took place. Soon he was drawn into them, and the subjects focused his reading, which in turn gave him confidence to rise and offer his own opinions. The most significant lecture he attended may have been that of Henry George, who expounded upon his influential *Progress and Poverty* (1879). Shaw became convinced that there was an economic basis to humane living which required more equality of opportunity to reap the rewards of work. Becoming a socialist, he came to believe that through social change human aspiration to be better and live better would become realistic and attainable. As his pragmatic yet idealistic industrialist, Andrew Undershaft, put it in *Major Barbara* (1905), in what represents the kernel of Shaw's philosophy, the 'deadly sins' responsible for the social 'crime' of poverty were 'Food, clothing, firing, rent, taxes, respectability and children'. Almost all his writings, directly or indirectly, concerned how society might be better organized to eliminate the 'millstones' to human progress (*Plays*, 3.171–2).

Through the Fabians Shaw assisted at the formation of the Independent Labour Party in 1893, and spoke on behalf of Fabian-endorsed candidates regardless of party. Before the consolidation of London local government he was himself a vestryman and borough councillor for St Pancras (1897–1903), which led to his promoting the municipalization of utilities and transport in *The Common Sense of Municipal Trading* (1904). After losing an election for London county council he turned down appeals that he run for parliamentary seats.

A pamphleteer and speaker of rare dialectical skill, Shaw harangued audiences of any size, from a handful in a back room to outdoor crowds of thousands—often as frequently as three times a week, and always without fee. The experience forged the forceful prose of what he called his missionary books, which included *The Quintessence of Ibsenism* (1891, enlarged 1913); *The Perfect Wagnerite* (1898); and *The Sanity of Art* (written as a lengthy review in 1895, enlarged into book form in 1908). In the same spirit were the challenging prefaces to, and debating dialogue of, many of his plays.

Shaw's journalism had dried up after the *Hornet* experience, but for a few minor pieces in the early 1880s—until he met a young drama critic, William Archer, in the British Museum in 1883. Through Archer, a translator of Ibsen, Shaw secured some play-reviewing assignments and then a regular post as art critic for *The World*. His first unsigned art column appeared on 10 February 1886. Until

1891 he walked the Bond Street galleries and the Royal Academy shows in Piccadilly, writing about pictures also for the afternoon *Star* and the weekly *Truth*. Encounters with the visual and plastic arts convinced him that they could be used to promote social progress, and that art could be exploited in the dialogue, design, settings, and symbolism of his plays. These began in earnest in the early 1890s.

Shaw also contributed unsigned book reviews to the *Pall Mall Gazette*, his first appearing on 16 May 1885 and the last, after which his reviewing became only occasional, on 26 December 1888. Meanwhile, on the sudden departure of the *Star*'s music critic, he initiated what became six years of brilliant, if sometimes brilliantly digressive, musical columns, first from 1888 to 1889 as Corno di Bassetto (basset horn), afterwards, for *The World* (1890–94), as G.B.S.— initials that became recognized worldwide as his signature. His intention, he explained, was to write such readable copy that even 'deaf stockbrokers' would read his columns. They were more than entertainments, however: 'it is the capacity for making good or bad art a personal matter', he claimed, 'that makes a man a critic'. He explained, further:

> I am always electioneering. … I desire certain reforms, and in order to get them, I make every notable performance an example of the want of them [elsewhere]. … Never in my life have I penned an impartial criticism; and I hope I never may. (*The World*, 6 July 1892)

Years later, when collecting his music reviews for book publication, Shaw confessed that he had been too quick to undervalue Mendelssohn as sentimental treacle and Brahms as secondhand Beethoven. He had also promoted some composers who did not last, hoping to revive a school of 'English' music that went beyond faddish oratorios and lightweight operettas (his view of Gilbert and Sullivan). He saw Edward Elgar as being in the English vanguard—a zeal that eventually caused Elgar to dedicate the *Severn Suite* (1930) to him. Shaw was Wagner's staunchest advocate in Britain, a keen exponent of the early Puccini and Mascagni, seeing Italian opera 'born again', and a missionary for the rehabilitation of Mozart, Haydn, Gluck, and Weber.

Recruited by Frank Harris as a theatre critic for the *Saturday Review*, again as G.B.S., Shaw campaigned in its columns from January 1895 to May 1898 to displace the artificialities and hypocrisies of the Victorian stage (which he labelled, collectively, 'Sardoodledom'—*Saturday Review*, 1 June 1895) with a theatre of vital ideas embodied in vital characters. With the talk about a 'New Drama' threatening to end, in England at least, as 'only a figment of the revolutionary imagination', Shaw had already determined that the stagnation in the West End was unacceptable: 'I had rashly taken up the case; and rather than let it collapse I manufactured the evidence' (*Autobiography*, 1.281). Even before he had become the leading play critic in London, however, he had become a playwright.

Early plays Shaw had been experimenting with drama since his early twenties, but not until William Archer in 1884 suggested a collaboration (he to supply the plot,

Shaw the dialogue) did G.B.S. work seriously with the stage in mind. Even then their project was abandoned after Shaw, Archer claimed, used up all the projected plot (a variation on Wagner's *Rheingold* motif). Eight years later, in 1892, Shaw returned to the script, completing it on his own for J. T. Grein's new Independent Theatre Society. As *Widowers' Houses* it created a newspaper sensation disproportionate to its two performances in December 1892: the press, goaded by Shaw's self-promotion, saw it as a dramatized socialist tract, although he had lightened it through what he had learned about ironic comedy from Ibsen and Dickens. The romantic predicament of the lovers (who discover that both their incomes derive from exploiting the poor) becomes an economic one. The 'happy ending' in which the betrothed pair embrace a comfortable immorality as well as each other, displeased audiences expecting maudlin conventions exploited even by the most daring contemporary playwrights. Shaw had to publish the play (in 1893) to make it accessible.

Unafraid to satirize himself, or even the new movements he championed, Shaw next invented an 'Ibsen Club' and ironically portrayed the New Woman types likely to be its members in *The Philanderer* (completed on 11 July 1893). In the autobiographical anti-hero, Leonard Charteris, Shaw created a charming cynic over whom even advanced women lost their self-respect. Concern that the comedy could not be performed, and the anticipated red-pencilling by the censor, kept it from production until 1905. Undeterred, Shaw completed on 2 November 1893 a third play, *Mrs Warren's Profession*, on the heels of the second. Refused a licence on grounds of immorality (there was a suggestion of incest), it sinned more by being unconventional in ironically justifying the 'oldest profession'. Commercial prostitution was treated without the titillation afforded by fashionable dramas about 'fallen women' long popular in the West End. To make that distinction certain, Shaw drew his Kitty Warren as a vulgarly flashy woman who found that being proprietor of her own body was more advantageous than sweating for a pittance in a factory or pub, and who turned that perception into a chain of profitable brothels financed by outwardly respectable gentlemen. Her daughter, Vivie, whose discovery of how her élite Newnham College education in Cambridge had been financed brings the problem into focus, is an apparently cold-blooded creature unlikely to look sentimentally at daughterly duty. The result is a sardonic high comedy built upon a paradox: her mother's profession is meant to symbolize not only the social and economic guilt responsible for it but all the ways in which people prostitute themselves for gain. Produced privately (beyond the censor's powers) in 1902, it was not licensed for the public stage in England until 1925, when it was already world-famous.

Labelling as 'unpleasant' the first three works in his *Plays: Pleasant and Unpleasant* (1898), Shaw explained that 'their dramatic power is being used to force the spectator to face unpleasant facts. No doubt all plays which deal sincerely with humanity must wound the monstrous conceit which it is the business of romance to flatter'. The 'pleasant' plays of the companion volume were Shaw's attempts to find the producers and the audiences which his mordant comedies put off. 'To me', he contended in his preface,

> [both] the tragedy and the comedy of life lie in the consequences, sometimes terrible, sometimes ludicrous, of our persistent attempts to found our institutions on the ideals suggested to our imaginations by our half-satisfied passions, instead of on a genuinely scientific natural history. (*Plays*, 1.2)

Arms and the Man, written between 26 November 1893 and 30 March 1894 (presented on 21 April 1894) satirizes, in a spoof-Balkan setting, romantic falsifications of love, war, and upward mobility, and was itself romanticized (although unauthorized by Shaw) in the Oscar Straus operetta *The Chocolate Soldier* (1909). The producer and second female lead, playing the wily and sexy servant, Louka, was Shaw's mistress since 1891 (in parallel with the tenacious Jenny Patterson), Florence Farr (1860–1917). The 'pleasant' *Candida*, written between 2 October and 7 December 1894 and first performed on 30 July 1897, seemed to be a conventional comedic melodrama about husband, wife, and young interloper, complete to happy ending in which the sanctity of marriage is upheld and the trouble-maker ejected into the night. Beneath its surface, however, the wife—who represents herself in a tense 'auction' scene as being forced to decide between her clergyman husband (a heretofore smug Christian socialist) and a hysterical and immature budding poet—chooses the best of all possible worlds for herself. Perceiving the charade, the poet renounces what Shaw later described as 'the small beer of domestic comfort' for the larger purposes he senses within himself.

The attractive interloper was a role which Shaw had already played in real life at least twice. William Morris's second daughter, May, six years younger than G.B.S., had waited hopelessly for his proposal, then settled for a mediocre match with H. H. Sparling, whereupon Shaw, ill again late in 1892 and needing a home in which to be cared for, moved in with the newly weds, destroying the marriage. Candida, played by Janet Achurch, for whom Shaw had created the role, had been Nora in the first English production of *A Doll's House* in 1889. The actress was the object of his infatuation for years, and was conveniently married to a complaisant husband. 'As an Irishman, an irregular artistic person, an anarchist in conduct', G.B.S. confessed to her, he was 'creator of an atmosphere subtly disintegrative of households' (Peters, 173). When she died at fifty-two in 1916, Shaw, whose cheques had kept the bailiffs away during her decline, paid the funeral expenses.

The 'pleasant' one-act *The Man of Destiny*, written between May and August 1895 and first performed in July 1897, was written for Henry Irving, the leading actor–manager of his day, but the autocratic Irving spurned it. Shaw intended 'a bravura piece' (*Plays*, 1.375) to display the virtuosity of the two major performers (of the cast of four), the other to have been the company's leading lady, Ellen Terry. His antidote to the 'older, coarser Napoleon'

(ibid., 1.664) of previous plays in his time, it was his first study in greatness. Fourth of the 'pleasant' series, *You Never Can Tell*, written between July 1895 and May 1896 (first performed on 26 November 1899), was almost unique in its century in having a dentist as romantic hero, and a tooth extraction performed on stage. In light-hearted fashion it probed parent–child relationships, the equality of women in society, and the power of the sex instinct ('chemistry')—the duel of sex bringing together an amorist of uncertain confidence and an impregnably rational New Woman.

Once Oscar Wilde was disgraced in 1895, Shaw had no rival as comic dramatist. He considered none of his plays, however, as anything less than springboards for the conflict of ideas. 'Every jest', his Father Keegan observes in *John Bull's Other Island* (1904), 'is an earnest in the womb of time'. And many of his works for the stage, whatever their comic texture, possess a high purpose and a prose elegance unmatched by his theatre contemporaries.

Three Plays for Puritans (1901) packaged Shaw's continuing output, again with what became the expected Shavian preface—an introductory essay in lively prose, dealing as much with the ideas suggested by the plays as with the plays themselves. *Three Plays* made Shaw available to a wider public to whom his plays were generally inaccessible even when produced. The texts included stage directions and scene descriptions in narrative form rather than in brief directorial jargon (this Shaw practice later became a publishing norm). The title suggested, as Shaw declared in his preface, that the theatre had to reach beyond 'pleasure' to dramatize principle: 'The cart and trumpet for me' (*Plays*, 2.30).

Both the cart and the trumpet had kept Shaw's early plays from the stage and impelled his publication of them. He joked wryly in an interview in 1897: 'My reputation as a dramatist grows with every play of mine that is *not* performed' (*Daily Mail*, 15 May 1897). Two of his first three plays had trouble with the censor; most of his other early plays were deemed unpleasant and uncommercial by producers for the commercial theatre who thrived on what he derided as 'shallow amusement' and 'unwholesome confectionery'. Plays that might have been conventionally sentimental in other hands had been up-ended by Shaw; plays that suggested the usual dramatic turns underwent reversals. It took much of his first decade as a playwright to become a successful missionary for his new drama in the face of critical and commercial opposition to 'intellectual seriousness' on stage. To do so he created new theatregoers and converted traditional ones. To make that possible, he later explained, he had to employ a paradox and 'cut cerebral capers' once the curtain rose (*Plays*, 5.338–9).

Shaw's first 'puritan' play, *The Devil's Disciple*, written from September to December 1896 and first performed (in New York) in October 1897, was set in New Hampshire during the American War of Independence. Shaw's New England was as unrealistic a venue as the Bulgaria of *Arms and the Man*, and was written as an inversion of popular Adelphi Theatre melodrama. Audiences everywhere accepted the play as conventional, if witty, melodrama because their opening expectations are fulfilled almost without exception. Dick Dudgeon, however, the black sheep of his family because he despises puritan masochism and hypocrisy, is represented as heroically taking the place of a rebel minister whom the English condemn to the gallows in the style of *Tale of Two Cities*. Yet the characteristically contrary Dudgeon does the right things for the wrong reasons. He acts, not in Sydney Carton fashion (Shaw's Dickensian inspiration for the scene), out of love for the patriotic Anthony Anderson's young wife, as she supposes, but spontaneously, out of some instinctive imperative. As with Caesar and other crucial Shavian protagonists to come, virtue is a quality rather than an achievement.

Shaw's ambitious *Caesar and Cleopatra* was an attempt to write a play of Shakespearian scope for a heroic actor (Sir Johnston Forbes-Robertson). Begun in April 1898 and completed that December, it was first performed by Forbes-Robertson's company in New York on 30 October 1906. (It had opened in Berlin in a production by Max Reinhardt on 31 March 1906.) He creates in his 'History' (as it was subtitled) a sixteen-year-old Cleopatra prior to her meeting Antony, and a Caesar not yet enticed back to Rome, and the demagoguery against which Brutus reacts. Shaw therefore eludes, by evading the Bard's Roman plays, the 'Better than Shakespear?' challenge seemingly raised in his preface. His feline Cleopatra, however, is a persuasive younger version of Shakespeare's cunning and more mature heroine; and his Caesar, as much philosopher as militarist in this mentor–disciple play, is meant to be a study in magnanimity and in 'original morality' rather than a larger-than-life figure on a stage pedestal: in Shaw's words, a hero 'in whom we can recognize our own humanity' (Shaw to B. W. Findon, *Play Pictorial*, Oct 1907).

The volume closed with *Captain Brassbound's Conversion*. Written from May to July 1899 and performed in London on 16 December 1900, it appeared to be little more than a north African encounter of the Mary Kingsley sort. Composed with Ellen Terry in mind, it featured a fearless Englishwoman among Gilbert-and-Sullivanesque brigands in turn-of-the-century Morocco. Serious themes, however, emerged from its musical-comedy plot, particularly that of revenge as twisted justice.

Marriage and its impact In 1898 Shaw's multifarious activities were briefly curtailed by medicine. In the conditions of non-care in which he lived at 29 Fitzroy Square with his mother (the Shaws had moved again on 5 March 1887), an unhealed foot injury required Shaw's hospitalization. On 1 June 1898, while on crutches and recuperating from surgery for necrosis of the bone, Shaw married his informal nurse, Charlotte Frances Payne-Townshend, at the office of the registrar at 15 Henrietta Street, Covent Garden. He was nearly forty-two; the bride, a wealthy Irishwoman born at Londonderry on 20 January 1857, thus a half-year younger than her husband, resided in some style at 10 Adelphi Terrace, London, overlooking the Embankment.

A friend of Sidney and Beatrice Webb and a Fabian, she had met Shaw on 29 January 1896. The Webbs had been trying to match her with the historian Graham Wallas,

who was handsome and sophisticated, to link her further to the Fabians; however it was the bohemian Shaw who became her constant companion, yet never in the most intimate sexual sense, even after their marriage and his move to Adelphi Terrace. At Charlotte's insistence, there was no consummation, although G.B.S. may have assumed that, given his success with women, her anxieties would be overcome in time. In any case, he was not in a condition to be persistent, and matters became worse. As he told Wilfrid Scawen Blunt in 1906, with typical hyperbole:

> I thought I was dead, for it would not heal, and Charlotte had me at her mercy. I should never have married if I had thought I should get well. Then I tumbled again, this time downstairs from top to bottom. When I found myself on the floor of the hall with every bone broken I felt satisfied. (Blunt, 136)

Although Shaw moved in with Charlotte after a less-than-passionate honeymoon at Hindhead which he spent as an invalid in a wheelchair, he maintained a legal address at Fitzroy Square as long as he continued to be vestryman for St Pancras. That their union remained childless at her choice may be attributed to Charlotte's concerns about her age as well as other emotional factors. That it remained unconsummated is suggested by internal evidences in Shaw's plays that corroborate his explanations after her death that she wanted it that way. Strikingly, in his early plays, sexual passion is dramatized as overtly as contemporary censorship of the stage would have permitted. In fact, two of his first three plays went unperformed publicly for years because the censor's cuts would have gutted them. However, in *Caesar and Cleopatra*, the play Shaw began just before the marriage, he rewrote history by having Caesar eschew any sexual interest in Cleopatra (with whom in reality he had a son). Thereafter the erotic element in his plays diminishes to nearly nothing, almost as if he were denying its necessity, rationalizing an altered lifestyle which precluded sex. Yet in his private life a sexual itch, whether or not physically satisfied, persisted into his seventies. Although Shaw's friendships with women were largely epistolary, the sultry Stella, Mrs Patrick Campbell (1865–1940)—the Eliza Doolittle of his *Pygmalion* in 1914, and the actress for whom he had written his Cleopatra—nearly wrecked his marriage. As late as August 1913 he had planned to run off with her, whatever the cost to their careers. Realizing finally the price she would pay, 'Mrs Pat' ducked their assignation at Sandwich. 'Farewell, wretch that I loved', Shaw scolded (*Letters*, 3.195).

In Shaw's futuristic later plays, sexual reproduction becomes obsolete, and sexually prompted orgasm is replaced by intellectual passion and thought-inspired ecstasy. As he wrote in the preface to a volume of his correspondence with Ellen Terry in 1931, 'Only on paper has mankind ever yet achieved glory, beauty, truth, knowledge, virtue and abiding love' (*Ellen Terry and Bernard Shaw: a Correspondence*, xviii).

The Royal Court Theatre plays As the new century opened, G.B.S. possessed the best-known initials in England; his physical form, always striking, had matured into the characteristic appearance by which the public came to know him: white hair and a long, full white beard. 'I have advertized myself so well', he claimed, 'that I find myself, whilst still in middle life, almost as legendary a person as the Flying Dutchman' (Plays, 2.32). With that licence he began, in July 1901, Man and Superman, a play which he completed in June 1902 and which encapsulated all his professional interests since he had begun writing. He 'took the legend of Don Juan in its Mozartean form', he explained:

> and made it a dramatic parable of Creative Evolution. But being then at the height of my invention and comedic talent, I decorated it too lavishly. I surrounded it with a comedy of which it formed only one act, and that act [his Don Juan in Hell] was so episodical (it was a dream that did not affect the action of the piece) that the comedy could be detached and played by itself. (Plays, 2.338)

Also, he supplemented the published play (1903) 'with an imposing framework consisting of a preface, an appendix called The Revolutionist's Handbook, and a final display of aphoristic fireworks'. Shaw had so crowded his shop window 'that nobody noticed the new religion in the centre of the intellectual whirlpool' (ibid., 2.338–9). Seemingly too difficult to produce, it was first performed at the Royal Court Theatre after the success of his next play, John Bull's Other Island.

In Man and Superman Shaw introduced his term 'life force' to characterize the energy impelling 'creative evolution'. Although he was an outspoken atheist in his twenties, Shaw moved thereafter into agnosticism and then into a personal mysticism inspired by the feeling that the universe had purpose behind it, rather than randomness: 'Has the colossal mechanism no purpose?' Don Juan challenges in the hell scene (Plays, 2.684). Shaw's own religious ideas—which remained firm despite his self-mockery of them in an urge always to turn drama into debate, and debate into drama—involved the centrality of a life force, or impersonal and amoral will, which worked through creative evolution (energized through eugenic procreation), to strive toward a superman (unrealizable pure intellect), and toward God (divine perfection). Although there are philosophical affinities with Henri Bergson's L'évolution créatrice (1907), Shaw's 'comedy and a philosophy'—his subtitle for his play—preceded Bergson (Pharand, 243–4). The two seem not to have known about each other until 1911, when the French treatise was translated into English and the parallels became apparent. In Shaw's preface and play-within-the-play, creative evolution was a purposeful and eternal movement to ever higher organisms which Shaw proposed as a more satisfactory explanation of the nature of life than 'blind' Darwinian evolution, and which, besides, restored intimations of divinity to the universe.

Subtitled 'A comedy and a philosophy', Man and Superman is a comedy of manners in which a resourceful young woman, Ann Whitefield, determines to capture the reluctant John Tanner, a social philosopher and socialist propagandist. The action incorporates interlocking debates and discussions in which Shaw explores the intellectual climate at the beginning of the new century. The ironic romance provides, too, the frame for the non-realistic third act dream interlude, often performed separately and independently, in which mythic counterparts to four characters in the comedy—Don Juan Tenorio, Doña Ana, the Commander (Doña Ana's late father, now a memorial statue), and the Devil—play out a dramatic quartet that is spoken theatre at its most operatic. Shaw often cast his plays according to the timbre of voice needed, and shaped his scenes into recitatives, arias, and vocal ensembles. In the duets and arias of Don Juan and the Devil, twentieth-century writing for the stage reached a peak, in its first years, that it would seldom touch again.

Shaw's next play, John Bull's Other Island (written and performed in 1904), was commissioned by W. B. Yeats for Dublin's Abbey Theatre, but its directors (Yeats included), uneasy about audience reaction to the unsentimental honesty of Shaw's depiction of Ireland, used the excuse of casting difficulties to evade its production. Yet Shaw had made the central figure in his play about Anglo-Irish misunderstanding and smug colonialist exploitation a pompous Englishman as absurd as the comic Irishman common to the English stage. (Thomas Broadbent may be a genial caricature of an ambitious young MP, Winston Churchill.) Recognizing its political insights, Beatrice and Sidney Webb brought the prime minister, Arthur Balfour, who soon returned with two leaders of the opposition, prompting Edward VII to complain that the play, in repertory at the Royal Court Theatre since 1 November 1904, had closed before he saw it. A special performance was arranged for 11 March 1905, during which the king laughed so heartily that he broke the royal chair hired for the occasion. A Shaw boom arose that lasted into the First World War.

In the secondary but exquisitely drawn character of the unfrocked priest, Father Keegan, is Shaw's earliest exploration of the religious rebel as saint. Unlike the confident Englishman, Broadbent, Keegan confesses (in act IV) to not feeling 'at home in the world', which he sees as

> a place of torment and penance; a place where the fool flourishes and the good and wise are hated and persecuted … Now, sir, there is only one place of horror and torment known to my religion; and that place is hell. Therefore it is plain to me that this earth of ours must be hell.

But Broadbent finds it 'rather a jolly place, in fact', and recommends 'phosphorus pills. I always take them when my brain is overworked'.

Although performances of Shaw's earlier plays on the continent had already begun to establish him there as a major dramatist, it was the John Vedrenne–Harley Granville Barker production of John Bull in London which confirmed Shaw's stage reputation in England. He had begun backing the Royal Court Theatre management, unfashionably distant from the West End in Sloane Square, not only with his own capital but with his plays. The years of their association at the Royal Court (1904–7), with Barker performing in, as well as directing, a versatile company, afforded Shavian drama some of its finest moments.

It was at Shaw's as well as Barker's desire that the Royal Court seasons showcased new playwrights, and others new to London, and Shaw also encouraged his literary peers to attempt the stage with the prospect of Royal Court performances. Galsworthy, Masefield, and Hewlett responded with plays as did, among the younger generation, St John Hankin as well as Barker himself and the feminist Elizabeth Robins. Shaw also solicited Yeats, Wells, Kipling, Laurence Housman, Conrad, and G. K. Chesterton—even drafting a scenario to tempt G.K.C. From the continent came works by Ibsen, Hauptmann, Schnitzler, and Maeterlinck. Also, Shaw encouraged Gilbert Murray's verse adaptations of Euripides. He did not want the Royal Court to be a one-man show—himself.

In a public appeal for a national theatre that followed the Royal Court seasons, Shaw pointed to its critical success as showing the way 'for the public good' toward an endowed repertory theatre. G.B.S. also promoted an endowed Shakespeare theatre, and wrote a play, *The Dark Lady of the Sonnets* (written 17–20 June 1910, produced 24 November 1910), on behalf of the Shakespeare Memorial National Theatre.

In *Major Barbara*, written from March to September 1905 and first presented (at the Royal Court Theatre) on 28 November, Shaw continued through high comedy to explore the religious consciousness as well as to probe society's complicity in its own evils. During the play Barbara Undershaft, a major in the Salvation Army, discovers that her father, a millionaire munitions manufacturer estranged from his family by his ultra-conventional wife, an earl's daughter, is an unconventional dealer in death. His principles, if not his business practice, are religious in the highest sense, while the Salvation Army, despite its good works and unassailable ideals, requires the hypocrisies of false public confession by the poor, and self-serving donations by the wealthy distillers and armaments dealers against whom it inveighs. (The Salvation Army, whose ameliorating efforts Shaw nevertheless praised, helped to mount the production.)

Indebted to Plato (*The Republic*) and Euripides (*The Bacchae*) and the lives of such contemporary armourers as Alfred Nobel, Basil Zaharoff, and Alfred Krupp, *Major Barbara* is one of Shaw's most complex plays. Nevertheless it is also one of his most moving, particularly in its Dickensian shelter scene in which a distraught Barbara recants her 'bribe of bread' evangelism. *Major Barbara* remains as universal as faith and war.

Between full-length plays, Shaw had been writing one-act experimental pieces, some as vehicles for favourite players, some as political thrusts, others to challenge the orthodoxies and proprieties of the stage. Several foreshadow the 'theatre of the absurd': while Shaw was working on *Major Barbara*, one such playlet—*Passion, Poison and Petrifaction*—was being performed in July 1905, anticipating by forty-five years Eugene Ionesco's *The Bald Soprano* (with its English clock striking seventeen English strokes). Much in Shaw's farce is 'absurd'—as were the dialogue

and action in other short works which he christened 'tomfooleries'. In these precursors of the radical theatre that followed both world wars, it was not that the stage encompassed all the world but rather that all the world is the stage.

Challenged to prove his mettle as a serious dramatist by writing a death scene, Shaw produced, in *The Doctor's Dilemma*, written and performed in 1906, a comedy with a serio-comic on-stage death. A multifaceted satire, it focused upon the medical profession (representing the self-protectiveness of professions in general) and upon the artistic temperament, as well as upon the failure of the public to separate personality from artistic quality. If, in the dying and double-dealing painter Louis Dubedat, Shaw did not portray a convincing artistic genius, it was not that he was unable to create one, but that he targeted self-advertising charlatans who duped the unsophisticated in art.

Pre-war and wartime plays Other significant plays of the pre-war period ranged from alleged potboilers (although some were Shaw's opportunities to experiment), to attempts to create a discussion drama best described as serious farce. *Getting Married* (written in 1907–8, performed in 1908), *Misalliance* (written in 1909, performed in 1910), and *Fanny's First Play*, his greatest first-run success with 622 performances (written in 1910–11, opened in 1911), are early examples of the genre. Each exploited artificiality and absurdity in setting, plot, and dialogue. *Misalliance* even had, in the early days of aviation, a shattering air crash just off-stage; *Getting Married* included a lady mayoress in a clairvoyant trance; *Fanny's First Play* set a suffragette comedy within an artificial frame-play, and identified the author as 'Xxxxxxx Xxxx'. Within were debates on parents and children, women's rights, marriage, and other issues then on the cutting edge for London audiences. *The Shewing-up of Blanco Posnet* (written in 1909) was set in an improbable American Wild West, parodying Bret Harte and aptly subtitled 'A sermon in crude melodrama'. The central action involves the conversion of a grimy horse thief who offers an impromptu preachment in a seedy saloon. When the lord chamberlain's censor of plays banned it on grounds of heresy, Shaw took the play to Dublin, where it played at the Abbey Theatre in August 1909 to capacity audiences who considered attendance as comeuppance to the British. When *Blanco Posnet* was published in 1911, Shaw included a long preface which incorporated a statement he had offered to a parliamentary hearing on stage censorship: 'I am not an ordinary playwright in general practice', he declared. 'I am a specialist in immoral and heretical plays. My reputation has been gained by my persistent struggle to force the public to reconsider its morals'. *Androcles and the Lion* (written and performed in 1912) treated true and false religious exaltation less heretically than did *Blanco Posnet*. Combining the medieval traditions of the miracle play with the nineteenth-century Christmas pantomime, Shaw transformed the fable of the Greek slave and the Roman lions into a philosophical farce about early Christianity. Its central theme—that one must have something worth dying for, an end beyond the self, to make life worth living—is recurrent in Shaw. Lavinia, its heroine, is, like Keegan and Barbara before her, a step toward Shaw's Joan of Arc.

Transforming another familiar myth, Shaw turned to the Greek romance of Pygmalion and Galatea. His *Pygmalion*, written from March to June 1912, was performed in German in Vienna in October 1913 as translated by Siegfried Trebitsch, whose inadequate redactions were endured by Shaw complainingly but loyally all his life. The London opening occurred in April 1914, Shaw waiting for Mrs Patrick Campbell to become available despite her rebuff the year before, and the uncertainty that at forty-eight she could suggest a girl of eighteen. English audiences, however, preferred star quality to verisimilitude. Although Shaw claimed that he had written a didactic play about phonetics, and its anti-heroic protagonist, Henry Higgins, is indeed a speech professional, what play-goers saw was a high comedy about love and class, about a cockney flower-girl from Covent Garden educated to pass as a lady, and the repercussions of the experiment. Possibly Shaw's comedic masterpiece, the film adaptation (1938) earned him an Academy award for his screenplay, and further worldwide success was won by the Alan Jay Lerner–Frederick Loewe musical adaptation, *My Fair Lady* (1956).

The First World War began as *Pygmalion* was nearing its hundredth sell-out performance, and gave Shaw an excuse to wind down the production. Feeling that plays were futile in wartime, he turned out a lengthy Swiftian pamphlet, *Common Sense about the War*, which appeared on 14 November 1914 as a supplement to the *New Statesman*. His readership, predictably jingoistic at the start of the war, proved largely hostile to the idea of negotiation and peace, especially as Shaw held Britain and its allies equally culpable with the Germans and Austrians. It sold more than 75,000 copies before the end of the year and made him internationally notorious. Despite what he called its 'relative sanity', it 'grew monstrously in the public patriotic imagination' for what was perceived to be its 'passionate pro-Germanism, Defeatism and Pacifism' (Shaw, *What I Really Wrote about the War*, 1930, 116). Unreason reigned (some of his anti-war speeches were banned from the newspapers), and he was ejected from the Dramatists' Club, although he was its most distinguished member.

Unrepentant, Shaw badgered the government with farces about the war. *The Inca of Perusalem*, written in the first week of August 1915 and produced in Birmingham on 7 October 1916, was intended to make fun of Junker pomposity (the title figure was an absurd Kaiser Wilhelm II). Instead it revealed the pompous blindness of the British authorities. Shaw sent the text to the censor, assuming that the arch-enemy in war propaganda was a reasonable subject for satire. Doing business as usual, the lord chamberlain's office mandated a number of strictures, and banned German uniforms, adding, 'Would you also kindly see that the make-up of the Inca does not too closely resemble the German Emperor' (Weintraub, *Journey to Heartbreak*, 130).

Even earlier, on 23 July 1915, Shaw had begun a playlet satirizing British ineptitude in recruiting Irishmen. The process had been bungled in every way, in many cases deliberately, by officials wary of having young men they considered heretics and rebels trained to use firearms. After abandoning his manuscript Shaw began again on 3 September 1915, completing *O'Flaherty, V.C.* on the 14th. With a tongue-in-cheek subtitle, 'A recruiting pamphlet', it was first performed beyond the censor's purview—at the headquarters of 40 squadron, the Royal Flying Corps, Treziennes, Belgium—on 17 February 1917, because the commanding general of the Dublin district, although legally outside the censor's jurisdiction, had intimidated the Abbey Theatre management into cancelling its première.

A third wartime playlet, *Augustus Does his Bit*, begun on 12 August 1916 and completed eleven days later, appeared safe enough to be performed at the Royal Court Theatre on 21 January 1917, just before G.B.S., khaki-clad for the first time in his life, crossed to Boulogne on his way to Flanders. The farce caricatured the conscientious but obtuse and egotistic home-front bureaucrat, here Lord Augustus Highcastle, who was, according to Shaw's preface of 1919, 'well-meaning, brave, patriotic, but obstructively fussy, self-important, imbecile and dangerous'. The play, and press accounts of it, opened the hearts of military officialdom to Shaw. As the tide of public opinion shifted, the government's estimate of Shaw's usefulness altered as well, and early in 1917 he was even invited to report from the front for the London press. His accounts appeared in the issues for 6–8 March of the *Daily Sketch*, and were reprinted in *What I Really Wrote about the War* (1930, 1931). G.B.S. was once more respectable. T. S. Eliot remarked later:

> It might have been predicted that what he said then would not seem so subversive or blasphemous now. The public has accepted Mr Shaw not by recognising the intelligence of what he said then, but by forgetting it; we must not forget that Shaw was a very unpopular man. He is no longer the gadfly.   ('London Letter', *The Dial*, Oct 1921, 253–4)

The unforgetful Shaw adapted his experience of 1914–18 into a dozen plays, sometimes defiantly, sometimes unobtrusively. *Heartbreak House*, written in 1916–17 and performed in 1920, became the classic Shavian presentation of the spiritual bankruptcy of the generation responsible for the war. He combined in it high discursive comedy with a new symbolism, creating a sombre vision owing its mood to Chekhov's *The Cherry Orchard*, while its elderly leading figure, and much else, recalled Shakespeare's *King Lear*. Captain Shotover is eighty-eight and half-mad; and although he tries to draw the play's *ingénue* back from a cynical despair induced by discovering the falsity of all her values, his own sense of foreboding (he warns of the need to 'learn navigation') is expressed in his having turned his ingenuity as an inventor to military uses. At the end, a night air raid causes casualties and destruction, yet the drama's culminating horror lies not in exploding bombs, but in the lines of two women at the curtain. One exclaims, 'What a glorious experience! I hope they'll come again tomorrow night.' The other ('radiant at the prospect' in Shaw's stage directions) agrees, 'Oh, I hope so.' Thanatos has replaced Eros.

Between the wars *Back to Methuselah*, written in 1918–20 and performed in 1922, was Shaw's attempt to fend off 'the bottomless pit of an utterly discouraging pessimism'. A cycle of five linked plays (*In the Beginning*, *The Gospel of the Brothers Barnabas*, *The Thing Happens*, *The Tragedy of an Elderly Gentleman*, *As Far as Thought can Reach*), it created a parable of creative evolution from the Garden of Eden to AD 31920. His 'Metabiological Pentateuch', it drew imaginatively upon Genesis, Plato, Swift, and even from the war in progress when he began, with the aim of creating a work on the scale of Wagner's *Ring* cycle.

The first play, through Adam and Eve (and the Serpent), and Cain and the murdered Abel, dramatizes the need to overcome death by the renewal of birth, and the need to nurture aspirations beyond mere subsistence. The second occurs in the years just after the First World War and is an indictment of the generation which made the war: Burge is Lloyd George while Lubin is Asquith. Conrad Barnabas discovers that sufficient longevity to learn from experience—perhaps 300 years—might be (in non-Darwinian fashion) willed. Here the Shavian superman is no longer thought of as, according to Shaw's earlier thesis, attainable soon enough through eugenic breeding. Rather he arrives with a leap in the third play, where two undistinguished characters from *Barnabas* are still alive in AD 2170. Longevity has brought them wisdom.

In the fourth play, set in AD 3000, a visitor from the dwindling race of the short-lived confronts the passionless and ascetic long-lived, who possess extraordinary powers but no evidence of soul. In the fifth play, far into the future, humans are born, fully developed, from eggs, and enjoy a contemplative ecstasy achieved after an adolescent phase of physical pleasure that quickly palls. In satire that ranges from bright to bleak, Shaw speculates through his futuristic characters about the pros and cons of escaping from 'this machinery of flesh and blood'. *Back to Methuselah* is dated as well as enlarged by the topical allusions in the less successful middle plays. Ennobling in vision, it proves awkward, however, as a total theatre experience.

As had been Shaw's practice for years, he had written the plays in Pitman shorthand, and had a secretary type out a draft which he would then revise. Since 1920 she had been Blanche Patch, who remained with him the rest of his life. He continued his revisions through whatever proofs were needed, as he had assumed the expenses of publication himself. Archibald Constable, his publisher since 1903, was only his distributor on commission.

Assuming that the long cycle had exhausted his creative energies, Shaw anticipated, at sixty-seven, that he was finished as a playwright. The canonization of Joan of Arc in 1920, however, reawakened ideas for a chronicle play which had never quite been dormant. The maid's sharp-tongued responses at her trial, he discovered, were in places almost Shavian (he used some of Joan's words nearly verbatim).

For Shaw it was insufficient to depict Joan as a sentimental heroine arrayed against melodramatic villains. Also, neither the militant nor the martyr in Joan appealed to him as much as did her symbolizing the possibilities of the race. The maid became Shavian saint and martyr as well as Catholic saint and martyr, an amalgam of practical mystic, heretical saint, and inspired genius. To make Joan's greatness of soul credible on-stage he made her adversaries credible, rehabilitating Bishop Peter Cauchon and his clerical colleagues who convicted her of heresy five centuries earlier. Since classic tragedy seemed inadequate, Shaw wrote an epilogue in which a newly canonized Joan is again rejected.

Acclaim for the play, written between 29 April and 24 August 1923, began with its première in New York on 28 December. Even the Nobel prize committee could no longer ignore Shaw after *Saint Joan*, offering him the prize for 1925. To the consternation of the Royal Swedish Academy he wrote that he wished

> to discriminate between the award and the prize. For the award I have nothing but my best thanks. But … I cannot persuade myself to accept the money. My readers and my audiences provide me with more than sufficient money for my needs; and as to my renown it is greater than is good for my spiritual health.

At his request an Anglo-Scandinavian Literary Foundation was funded with the prize money, 'to encourage intercourse and understanding in literature and art between Sweden and the British Isles' (*Letters*, 4.34).

During his six-year theatrical hiatus after *Saint Joan*, Shaw continued to speak out, and to utilize, with artistry and verve, the new medium of radio as a frequent BBC speaker from the middle 1920s into the early 1940s, accepting no fee. As early as 20 November 1924 he read *O'Flaherty, V.C.* on the air, and he said his goodbye to the broadcast medium on his ninetieth birthday via BBC television. He also worked on his collected edition of more than thirty volumes and his political summa, *The Intelligent Woman's Guide to Capitalism and Socialism* (1928).

Shaw's Platonic 'political extravaganza' *The Apple Cart* (written in November and December 1928) was first performed, in Polish in Warsaw, on 14 June 1929. A futuristic high comedy, it revealed Shavian inner conflicts between his lifetime of radical politics and his essentially conservative mistrust of the common man's ability to govern himself. His dream epilogue to *Saint Joan* had continued his explorations into non-realism and symbolism, yet the new play included a threatened royal abdication that prefigured a real one in December 1936. Most of his succeeding plays employed broad caricatures and other extravagances designed to eliminate Ibsenite actuality by reminding audiences that they were experiencing performances on a stage rather than life in a three-walled room or realistic exterior. Shaw also employed apocalyptic imagery, warning that 1914–18 was about to be repeated. The deliberately absurd *Too True to be Good*, written from March to June 1931 and premièred in Boston on 29 February 1932, was a dream-fantasy, including a Bunyanesque prophet, an affectionate Lawrence of Arabia burlesque, and a burglar-turned-preacher (a disillusioned officer in the late war) who suggests at the curtain Shaw confronting his own obsolescence. He was seventy-five.

On the Rocks, written from February to July 1933 and performed in London on 25 November, predicted, despite its comedic texture, the collapse of parliamentary government in a proto-fascist, depression-blighted England. *The Simpleton of the Unexpected Isles*, written from February to April 1934 and first staged in New York on 18 February 1935 to Shaw's most derogatory reviews in decades, utilized a futuristic setting to satirize eugenic solutions to human problems—which Shaw himself had preached—and ends with a farcical yet mordant day of judgement.

It was the most travel-orientated work of many which were inspired or fleshed out by Shaw's experiences abroad. A Wagner pilgrimage to Bayreuth in 1889 had reinforced his zeal for the composer and led to *The Perfect Wagnerite*. His Italian tours with the Art Workers' Guild in 1891 and 1894 are recalled in his 'Virgin Mother' play *Candida*. Visiting north Africa had inspired *Captain Brassbound's Conversion*, and also the unseen but plot-crucial automobile race to Biskra in Algeria in *Man and Superman*. His visits to fascist Italy and a mid-1931 junket to Soviet Russia reinforced his convictions about the efficiency of dictatorial regimes, the subject of several late plays. A voyage to South Africa in 1932 resulted in his writing, while in Knysna, the novella *The Adventures of the Black Girl in Her Search for God*. *The Six of Calais*, a short play written at sea in 1935, recalled Rodin's *Les bourgeois de Calais* sculpture group, while the brief *Village Wooing*, written from January to July 1933, was a response to his attempting to ply his craft while on board ship. *The Simpleton* drew upon Shaw's visiting islands in the south Pacific, and Jain temples and the Elephanta caves near Bombay, while on a round-the-world voyage. A stop on the voyage at Hong Kong, where he visited an elaborate home with a Buddhist shrine, led to a scene in *Buoyant Billions*, which he began on 17 February 1936 but put aside until 1945. The play also includes a Panama Canal episode drawn from a voyage in the 1930s. A second world war, and old age, put an end to the Shaws' journeyings.

The Millionairess, written in a two-week spurt from 27 April to 10 May 1934 and first performed in German translation in Vienna on 4 January 1936, was subtitled 'A Jonsonian comedy'. A knockabout farce, it examines the 'born boss', here an energetic exaggeration of Beatrice Webb. *Geneva*, written from February to April 1936 and first staged in Warsaw on 25 July 1938, had to be revised to fit changing events once it opened in England on 1 August that year. Lampooning the futile League of Nations, which signatory nations failed to support, it caricatured the dictators Hitler, Mussolini, and Franco, on-stage in nearly invisible disguises. That the despots were treated so lightly, downplayed as braggarts on the eve of inevitable war, suggests that Shaw's flirtation with authoritarian inter-war regimes and his disillusion with flaccid inter-war democracies were slow in fading. His confidence in Stalinism, which seemed in his last years merely a façade

he could not relinquish after a lifetime of radical activism, lasted to the end.

In Good King Charles's Golden Days (written from November 1938 to May 1939, performed on 11 August 1939) looked at authoritarianism more genially. His last pre-Second World War play, it echoed the mood of *The Apple Cart*, and was a warm, discursive high comedy set in the past rather than the future (it was subtitled 'A true history that never happened'). Witty and often moving, it dwells autumnally with the major preoccupations of Shaw's long life: 'The riddle of how to choose a ruler is still unanswered', says Charles, 'and it is the riddle of civilization.'

Shaw's serenely managerial queen in the play, Catherine of Braganza, is a late tribute to Charlotte Shaw, who endured her husband's genius and, while her health lasted, oversaw their households in the country and in London. Their marriage lasted their lives. Childless, they indulged in surrogate sons and daughters whose children often went to school on quiet Shavian largesse. Granville Barker and Lillah McCarthy had their Royal Court and Savoy seasons underwritten by G.B.S., who lost, unconcernedly, all his investment. On leaving the theatre to join the Royal Flying Corps in 1914, Robert Loraine listed the Shaws as his next of kin. T. E. Lawrence, a friend since 1922, even took the name Shaw by deed poll in 1927, and had his own upstairs room at Ayot St Lawrence for visits on his explosive Brough motorcycle. At least one machine was unobtrusively paid for by the Shaws, and when Lawrence died in a motorcycle crash on its trade-in successor in 1935, G.B.S. and Charlotte, then away in South Africa, were doubly grieved.

Wartime and last works The German blitz left 1940s London intolerable for the elderly Shaws, now in their middle eighties. They spent most months in the country, with G.B.S. keeping informed through the BBC and the newspapers. He wrote little at length except a vigorous tract of nearly 400 pages, *Everybody's Political What's What?* (1944). The need for a better world, he contended, 'has not the faintest chance of being supplied by our generations of Yahoos, now busy slaughtering and murdering each other in a war which is fundamentally not merely maniacal but nonsensical'. Unfettered capitalism was 'not an orgy of human villainy' but 'a Utopia that has dazzled and misled very amiable and public spirited men' (p. 2).

Shaw's film script of *Major Barbara* had gone before the cameras between air raids in 1940, followed by, later in the war, *Caesar and Cleopatra*, like *Pygmalion* and *Major Barbara*, directed by Gabriel Pascal. Filming from Shaw's screenplay began in June 1944 in Egypt and England under wartime logistical and financial constraints and largely beyond the oversight of its author, nearly ninety. It opened in London on 13 December 1945, in the first months of peace, to mixed notices. *Buoyant Billions*, begun in 1936–7, was completed in 1947, just before Shaw's ninety-first birthday. First presented in Zürich, in Siegfried Trebitsch's translation, on 21 August 1948, as *Zu viel Geld*, and subtitled in English 'A comedy of no manners', it dramatized the travels of Junius Smith, a self-styled 'world betterer'. *Farfetched Fables*, written in July and

August 1948 and presented on 6 September 1950, was a farce in six short scenes in which Shaw attempted to peer into a timeless future. In his post-atomic outlook, it seemed much different and more absurd than he had envisioned in 1920 in *As Far as Thought can Reach*.

Even briefer was an elegiac yet comic puppet play, written in four days beginning on 20 January 1949. After a life in the shadow of Shakespeare, Shaw, in *Shakes versus Shav*, has the two playwrights confront each other and, in blank verse, challenge each other's greatness. Closing, Shav reaffirms his once-shaken evolutionary optimism in the face of the *Lear*-like pessimism of Shakes, and adds,

> For a moment suffer
> My glimmering light to shine.
> (*Plays*, 7.477)

A last playlet, *Why She Would Not*, begun on 17 July 1950 and noted as completed on 23 July, three days before Shaw's ninety-fourth birthday, was first performed in New York on 21 January 1957. A fantasy with flashes of the earlier G.B.S. in evidence, it combines the 'born boss' theme with the duel of sex, but has more historic than dramatic interest. As Shaw had written in his preface to *Buoyant Billions*, 'As long as I live I must write' (ibid., 7.307).

When Charlotte, crippled by osteitis deformans, died aged eighty-six on 12 September 1943, G.B.S., frail and feeling the effects of Second World War austerities, made permanent his retreat from the Whitehall Court flat where they had moved from Adelphi Terrace in October 1927. (He had been living at the former rectory in Ayot St Lawrence in Hertfordshire that had been their country home since 1906.) A fall on 10 September 1950, while pruning trees, fractured his hip. Bedridden, he developed kidney failure. With hospitalization useless, he asked to be returned home, where he died on 2 November. Charlotte's ashes had been stored since her cremation at Golders Green awaiting G.B.S.'s own. After his cremation the next day—at which Sydney Cockerell read the final passage of Mr Valiant for Truth from *The Pilgrim's Progress*, to which Shaw had long contended that he owed much of his writing style—his ashes were mixed with Charlotte's. On 23 November 1950, supervised by representatives of the public trustee, the joint remains were emptied into flower beds at Ayot St Lawrence. There was no ceremony.

Shaw's last major work was his lengthy last will and testament, prepared that July. By his bequest the National Trust would acquire the house, Shaw's Corner, at Ayot. After instructing the public trustee to license his publications only under the name Bernard Shaw (eliminating, he hoped, the George from authorized editions of his writings), and distributing small legacies, he directed that his assets form a charitable trust to revamp the unwieldy English alphabet into a phonetic one of forty letters. Since the estate at his death was estimated as amounting to £367,233, and was expanding with accruing royalty income, the residuary legatees (the British Museum, recipient of his papers, the Royal Academy of Dramatic Art, and the National Gallery of Ireland) sued in Chancery to invalidate the trust on grounds of national interest. In December 1957 a settlement gave only token recognition

to alphabet reform by setting aside a small sum (£8300) for a competition for a new alphabet in which an edition of *Androcles and the Lion* was printed (1962). The balance remained with the residuary legatees to share as long as Shaw's copyrights remained in force.

Shaw left no school of playwrights although much of the drama of his time and after was indirectly in his debt. His creation of a drama of moral passion and of intellectual conflict and debate, his revivifying the comedy of manners, his ventures into symbolic farce and into a drama of disbelief, all helped to shape the theatre of his time and after, while his bringing of a bold new critical intelligence to his many other areas of interest helped to mould the political, economic, and social thought of three generations.

For decades after Shaw's death in 1950 reprints of his works and new stagings of his plays were inhibited in copyright-adhering nations by the paucity of his works in free public domain. Royalties had to be paid to the public trustee (Society of Authors) for performances and publications still in copyright. Directors in a new theatrical era where audiences craved not a plethora of words but a quicker exit could not legally cut back long speeches or make other condensations. While there has never been any slackening in biographies and critical studies, and while publication of Shaw's letters, diaries, journalism, and other writings has enlarged the body of his work for study, the fading of copyright has begun to enhance Shaw's posthumous reputation through an acceleration of translations, revivals, and reprints. A significant factor in sustaining Shaw's posthumous reputation has been the Shaw Festival Theatre in Niagara on the Lake, Canada, which has grown into a nearly year-round operation with three theatres, imaginative direction, superbly trained casts, and an international clientele. In 1921 Shaw concluded the preface to a play:

> It is my hope that a hundred parables by younger hands will soon leave mine as far behind as the religious pictures of the fifteenth century left behind the first attempts of the early Christians at iconography. In that hope I withdraw and ring up the curtain.

While Shaw has been left behind as he indeed wished, his writings live.　　STANLEY WEINTRAUB

Sources D. H. Laurence, *Bernard Shaw: a bibliography*, 2 vols. (1983) · D. H. Laurence and M. K. Crawford, eds., 'Bibliographical Shaw', *Shaw. The Annual of Bernard Shaw Studies*, 20 (2000), viii–128 · *Collected letters: Bernard Shaw*, ed. D. H. Laurence, 4 vols. (1965–88) · B. C. Rosset, *Shaw of Dublin: the formative years* (1964) · A. Henderson, *George Bernard Shaw: his life and works* (1911) · St J. Ervine, *Bernard Shaw: his life, work and friends* (1956) · M. Holroyd, *Bernard Shaw*, 4 vols. (1988–93) · R. Mander and J. Mitchenson, *Theatrical companion to Shaw* (1955) · R. Weintraub, ed., 'Shaw abroad', *Shaw. The Annual of Bernard Shaw Studies*, 5 (1985) · S. Weintraub, *Journey to heartbreak: the crucible years of Bernard Shaw, 1914–1918* (1971) · *Shaw: an autobiography*, ed. S. Weintraub, 2 vols. (1969–70) · A. M. Gibbs, ed., *Shaw: interviews and recollections* (1990) · S. Weintraub, *Bernard Shaw: a guide to research* (1992) · *Bernard Shaw: the diaries, 1885–1897*, ed. S. Weintraub, 2 vols. (1986) · *The Bodley Head Bernard Shaw: collected plays with their prefaces*, 7 vols. (1970–74) · G. B. Shaw, *Sixteen self sketches* (1948) · W. S. Blunt, *My diaries: a personal narrative of events, 1888–1914* (1921) · *Ellen Terry and Bernard Shaw: a correspondence*

(1931) • M. Peters, *Bernard Shaw and the actresses* (1980) • M. W. Pharand, *Bernard Shaw and the French* (2001) • d. cert.

Archives BL, corresp., etc., Add. MS 63728 • BL, corresp. and papers, Add. MSS 50508–50743, 63179–63187 • BLPES, business corresp. and papers, incl. engagement diaries • BLPES, corresp. and papers given to Fabian Society • BLPES, diaries • Boston University, letters • Brown University, Sidney Albert collection, letters and MSS • Camden Local Studies and Archives Centre, London, letters • Col. U., Rare Book and Manuscript Library, corresp. and papers relating to 'Political science in America' lecture • Colby College, Waterville, Maine, papers • Cornell University, Ithaca, New York, papers, incl. literary MSS • Free Library of Philadelphia, papers • Harvard U., Houghton L., corresp., literary MSS, and papers • Hunt. L., letters, literary MSS • Leo Baeck Institute, New York, archives division, papers • NL Ire., papers • NRA, corresp. and literary papers • NYPL, papers • NYPL, Henry W. and Albert A. Berg Collection of English and American Literature, papers • Ransom HRC, corresp. and papers • Theatre Museum, London, letters • University of Guelph, Ontario, Dan H. Laurence Shaw collection • University of Victoria, British Columbia, McPherson Library, corresp. and literary MSS • V&A NAL, letters, literary MSS, and rehearsal notes | BBC WAC, letters to Lord Reith • Birm. CA, corresp. with Sir Barry Jackson • BL, letters to Lady Aberconway, Add. MS 52556 • BL, corresp. with William Archer, Add. MS 45296 • BL, corresp. with John Burns, Add. MS 59784 • BL, corresp. with G. K. Chesterton and F. A. Chesterton, and others, Add. MS 73198, fols. 1–120 • BL, letters to Henry Havelock Ellis, Add. MS 61891 • BL, letters to Sir J. Forbes-Robertson and family, Add. MS 61998 • BL, letters to Holbrook Jackson, Add. MS 62992 • BL, letters to Edward Pease, Add. MS 59784 • BL, corresp. with Society of Authors, etc., Add. MSS 56627–56637 • BL, corresp. with Marie Stopes, Add. MS 58493 • BL, corresp. with Ellen Terry, Add. MSS 43800–43802, 46172g, MS Facs. 496 • BL, letters to his wife, Add. MSS 46505–46507 • BL, lord chamberlain's papers • BLPES, letters to A. G. Gardiner • BLPES, corresp. with the independent labour party • BLPES, letters to Graham Wallas • BLPES, letters to Sidney Webb and Beatrice Webb • British Theatre Association Library, London, corresp. with Gilbert Murray • CAC Cam., letters to E. Lyttelton [incl. copies] • CUL, letters to Lady Kennet • Elgar Birthplace Museum, corresp. with Sir Edward Elgar and family • Herts. ALS, letters to St Albans Rural District Council • HLRO, letters to Herbert Samuel • Internationaal Instituut voor Sociale Geschiedenis, Amsterdam, corresp. with Dora Russell • Internationaal Instituut voor Sociale Geschiedenis, Amsterdam, corresp. with Andreas Scheu • JRL, letters to the *Manchester Guardian* • King's AC Cam., letters to John Maynard Keynes • King's AC Cam., letters to Gertrude Kingston • King's Lond., Liddell Hart C., corresp. with Sir B. H. Liddell Hart • NL Scot., letters to R. & R. Clark Ltd • NL Wales, letters to his aunt Georgina • NL Wales, corresp. with Thomas Jones • Plunkett Foundation, Long Hanborough, Oxfordshire, corresp. with Sir Horace Plunkett • PRO NIre., letters to Lady Londonderry • Stanbrook Abbey, Worcestershire, letters to Dame Laurentia McLachlan • TCD, corresp. with Thomas Bodkin • TCD, corresp. with Sir Almroth Wright • Theatre Museum, London, corresp. with Ernest Thesiger • U. Edin. L., corresp. with Charles Sarolea • U. Hull, Brynmor Jones L., corresp. with R. Page Arnot • U. Hull, Brynmor Jones L., corresp. with J. H. Lloyd • U. Reading L., corresp. with Nancy Astor • U. Reading L., corresp. with Keith Read • U. Sussex, corresp. with Kingsley Martin • UCL, corresp. with Karl Pearson • University of North Carolina, Chapel Hill, corresp. with Constable & Co. | FILM BFI NFTVA, 'Bernard Shaw', 1957 • BFI NFTVA, actuality footage • BFI NFTVA, current affairs footage • BFI NFTVA, documentary footage • BFI NFTVA, home footage • BFI NFTVA, other footage | SOUND BBC Sound Archives • BL NSA

Likenesses E. Walker, photographs, 1888, NPG • H. Furniss, caricatures, pen-and-ink sketches, c.1890–1900, NPG • A. Ludovici, pencil and watercolour drawing, 1892, BM • B. Partridge, watercolour, 1894, Jerwood Library of Performing Arts, London, Mander and Mitchenson collection • B. Partridge, caricatures, watercolours, 1894–c.1925, NPG • F. H. Evans, photograph, 1896, NPG • E. J. Steichen, photograph, c.1902, National Museum of Photography, Film and Television, Bradford, Royal Photographic Society collection • A. L. Coburn, photogravure, 1904, NPG; repro. in T. Cooper, *Men of mark: a gallery of contemporary portraits* • F. H. Evans, photograph, 1905, BL, Shaw papers • A. L. Coburn, photograph, 1906, George Eastman House, Rochester, New York • A. Rodin, bronze bust, 1906, Rodin Museum, Philadelphia • A. Rodin, marble head, 1906, Musée Rodin, Paris • A. P. Barney, pastel drawing, 1908, National Collection of Fine Arts, Washington, DC • A. L. Coburn, photograph, 1908, National Museum of Photography, Film and Television, Bradford, Royal Photographic Society collection • Elliott & Fry, photograph, 1910, repro. in *Shaw: an autobiography*, ed. Weintraub, vol. 2; priv. coll. • C. Townshend, stained-glass window, 1910, Beatrice Webb House, Leith Hill, Surrey • A. John, oils, 1915, FM Cam. [see illus.] • A. John, oils, 1915, Royal Collection • A. John, oils, 1915, Shaw's Corner, Hertfordshire • W. Rothenstein, pencil drawing, 1916, Man. City Gall. • W. Rothenstein, etching, 1920, NPG • H. Lavery, oils, 1925, Man. City Gall. • P. Troubetzkoy, bronze sculpture, 1926, Tate collection • J. Collier, oils, 1927, NG Ire. • P. Troubetzkoy, bronze statue, 1927, NG Ire. • W. Rothenstein, crayon drawing, 1928, U. Texas • J. Davidson, bronze sculpture, 1929, U. Texas • E. Kapp, drawing, 1930, Barber Institute of Fine Arts, Birmingham • J. Coplans, bronze sculpture, 1932, NG Ire. • J. Farleigh, woodblock print, 1932, repro. in G. B. Shaw, *The adventures of the black girl in her search for God* (1932) • L. Knight, oils, exh. RA 1933, Hertford Art Gallery • J. Epstein, bronze bust, 1934, Birmingham Museums and Art Gallery • J. Epstein, bronze bust, 1934, Metropolitan Museum of Art, New York • J. Epstein, bronze bust, 1934, National Gallery of Canada, Ottawa • J. Epstein, bronze head, 1934, NPG • J. Epstein, bronze bust, 1934, U. Texas • F. Topolski, oils, 1939, Art Gallery and Museum, Glasgow • Y. Karsh, photograph, 1943, NPG, Karsh of Ottawa, Canada • F. Topolski, oils, 1943, U. Texas • C. Winsten, oils, 1945, U. Texas • C. Winsten, bronze sculpture, 1946, U. Texas • M. Beerbohm, caricature, drawing, NYPL • M. Beerbohm, caricature, drawing, Yale U. • M. Beerbohm, caricature, drawing, U. Texas • M. Beerbohm, caricature, drawing, BM • M. Beerbohm, caricature, drawing, U. Cal., Los Angeles • M. Beerbohm, caricature, drawing, FM Cam. • M. Beerbohm, caricature, drawing, Cornell University Library, Ithaca • H. Brodzky, caricature, coloured print, V&A • A. L. Coburn, photograph, International Museum of Photography, Rochester, New York • J. Coplans, sculpture, National Book League, London • F. Hollyer, photographs (in middle age), V&A • Kathleen, Lady Kennet, bronze bust, Russell-Cotes Art Gallery, Bournemouth • L. Knight, drawing, Castle Museum, Nottingham • J. Lavery, oils, Hugh Lane Municipal Gallery of Modern Art, Dublin • E. Nerman, caricature, pen and ink?, V&A • B. Partridge, caricature, watercolour, Hugh Lane Gallery of Modern Art, Dublin • A. P. F. Ritchie, caricature, lithograph, NPG; repro. in *VF* (16 Aug 1911) • W. Rothenstein, chalk drawing, Abbey Theatre, Dublin • Ruth [M. Beerbohm], caricature, NPG; repro. in *VF* (28 Dec 1905) • R. S. Sherriffs, group portraits, caricatures, sketches (with the Sitwells), NPG; repro. in *The Sketch* (12 Aug 1936) • W. Strang, etching, NPG • F. Topolski, ink drawing, Royal Academy of Dramatic Art, London • P. Troubetzkoy, plaster statuette, Shaw's Corner, Hertfordshire • photographs, National Theatre, London • photographs, Royal Academy of Dramatic Arts, London • photographs, BL, NPG, V&A

Wealth at death £367,233 13s.: probate, 20 March 1951, *CGPLA Eng. & Wales*

Shaw, Gilbert Shuldham (1886–1967), Church of England clergyman and spiritual director, was born on 10 July 1886 in Dublin, the first of two children of Joseph Shaw QC (d. 1933), a parliamentary advocate, and his wife, Charlotte Blanche (d. 1897), daughter of Sir Philip Crampton *Smyly, honorary physician to Queen Victoria. His mother was the niece of William Conyngham Plunket, archbishop of Dublin, who baptized him.

Brought up in London, Shaw entered Eton College in 1900 before going up to Trinity College, Cambridge, in 1906 to read history. After Cambridge he read for the bar and was called as a member of the Inner Temple in 1913. On 22 July 1913 he married Sylvia Mary Smyly (1891–1974) (a distant relative), daughter of William Cecil Smyly, a county court judge. They had three children, the daughter, Patricia, marrying Burke Frederick St John *Trend, later Baron Trend (1914–1987).

On the outbreak of the First World War Shaw secured a commission in an artillery regiment but was invalided out following a fall from a horse. Abandoning the law he worked instead as a farmer and lay evangelist in the diocese of Oxford. Despite considerable opposition from his family Shaw now sought ordination and in 1924 he left his wife and children and moved to Lincolnshire as vice-principal of St Paul's Missionary College, Burgh. For the remainder of his life he mostly lived apart from his family.

Having already established a reputation as a spiritual director and confessor, in 1928 Shaw was appointed head of the Association for Promoting Retreats. In 1932 he left the association and moved into a disused beer house in Poplar, 'The Sydney', where for the next eight years he gave himself to serving the poor. Unlike other well-known priests in the East End he held no office and had no church. His financial support came mostly from wealthy supporters and he proved himself a doughty fighter on behalf of those most in need. His work became well-known and widely respected by, among others, the social thinker and lay theologian J. H. Oldham, who invited Shaw to be a member of The Moot, a group which met throughout the war years led by Karl Mannheim and T. S. Eliot.

Shaw's work in Poplar ended in 1940 but his reputation led to an appointment as warden of St Anne's, Soho, a pioneering work aimed at the intelligentsia of London. It was to be an unhappy move for Shaw. The people of St Anne's, among them Dorothy L. Sayers, disliked his austere style and he found their 'sitting room' spirituality wholly foreign to his deepest instincts. Equally unsatisfactory were his six years from 1947 as chairman of G. J. Palmer & Sons, parent company of the *Church Times*. His strident theology sought a deeper editorial expression than the editor could countenance and relationships were often stormy.

After Soho Shaw took a room in Southwark which he used as a base for extending his work of giving retreats and spiritual direction (and he ministered to many hundreds of individuals and religious communities in these years), developing contacts with members of the Eastern Orthodox churches (with whom he enjoyed the closest rapport), and (controversially) in a sustained involvement with the occult. He acquired a widespread reputation (or notoriety) as an exorcist: his writings have been highly influential in shaping subsequent thinking on the subject within the churches. Believing himself since undergraduate days possessed of unusual psychic gifts he maintained that he could use them to neutralize those being abused by others.

From 1957 Shaw became closely involved with the Sisters of the Love of God, an enclosed community for women at Fairacres in Oxford, eventually becoming their warden and making his home at the convent. His voluminous teachings helped to re-shape the life of the community by focusing upon the work of St Teresa of Avila and St John of the Cross, together with teaching from Eastern Orthodoxy, as normative for its spiritual life. He also helped to establish a house given over to providing opportunities for sisters to live as hermits, winning support for it from Archbishop Michael Ramsey. He played a similar role in the founding and development of the Community of the Servants of the Will of God, an enclosed community for men in Sussex, which has purpose-built hermitages in the forest surrounding the monastery. The subsequent recovery of the eremitical life in Britain owes a great deal to the pioneering work of Shaw.

'Father Gilbert' was looked upon with considerable suspicion by many within his own church. Others thought him harsh, but to those who knew him well he was a warm and genial companion who inspired much affection. He was always first and foremost a priest led (or driven) to live out a demanding faith to the full. His published writings (*A Pilgrim's Book of Prayers*, 1945, and *The Face of Love*, 1959) are collections of prayers and meditations mostly drawn from the early part of his life. Unpublished are the more significant works, homilies and addresses belonging to his later years which continue to underlie significant developments in spiritual and social thinking within the churches. He died at the Convent of the Incarnation in Oxford on 18 August 1967, and was buried in Oxford.   R. D. HACKING

Sources R. D. Hacking, *Such a long journey: a biography of Gilbert Shaw, priest* (1988) · b. cert. · d. cert. · private information (2004) · L. Lang-Sims, *A time to be born: volume one of an autobiography* (1971) · *CGPLA Eng. & Wales* (1968)

Archives Convent of the Incarnation, Fairacres, Oxford, letters, papers, and sermons · Monastery of the Holy Trinity, Crawley Down, Sussex, letters and sermons

Likenesses photograph, 1967, repro. in Hacking, *Such a long journey*, facing p. 71

Wealth at death £39,932: probate, 2 Jan 1968, *CGPLA Eng. & Wales*

Shaw, Glencairn Alexander [Glen] **Byam** (1904–1986), actor and stage director, was born on 13 December 1904 at Addison Road, London, the fourth in the family of four sons and one daughter of John Byam Liston *Shaw (1872–1919), artist, and his wife, (Caroline) Evelyn Eunice Pyke-Nott (1870–1959), miniaturist. He went to Westminster School as a day-boy during the First World War and his contemporaries included his elder brother James Byam *Shaw who became a distinguished art historian, and John Gielgud, a lifelong friend and colleague.

Byam Shaw next surfaced on 1 August 1923 as an apparently untrained professional actor in *At Mrs Beam's* at the Pavilion Theatre, Torquay. In the era of the matinée idol,

Glencairn Alexander Byam Shaw (1904–1986), by Thomas F. Holte

Byam Shaw's dazzling and lifelong good looks, together with the reported encouragement of his cousin May Ward, a close friend of Ellen Terry, may have been enough to make him take the plunge into acting. His first London appearance in 1925 was as Yasha in *The Cherry Orchard* (John Gielgud was Trofimov), and in the next four years he had the good fortune to appear in three more Chekhov plays.

In 1929 Shaw married the actress (Madeleine) Angela Clinton Baddeley, the elder sister of Hermione Baddeley. Their father, William Herman Clinton-Baddeley, was an unsuccessful composer. The Byam Shaw marriage was a supremely happy one, both domestically and professionally, until Angela's death in 1976. They had a son and a daughter.

After a tour together to South Africa in 1931 Byam Shaw appeared memorably at the Lyceum in 1932 in Max Reinhardt's mime play *The Miracle*, with Lady Diana Cooper as the Madonna. In 1933 the long and mutually rewarding association with John Gielgud began when Byam Shaw took over the Gielgud part in the long-running *Richard of Bordeaux* by Gordon Daviot (that is, Elizabeth MacKintosh, whose other pseudonym was Josephine Tey). In 1934 he was Darnley in Daviot's *Queen of Scots*, and later Laertes in Gielgud's longest running *Hamlet*, each time directed by Gielgud. In 1935 he played Benvolio in the famous *Romeo and Juliet* with Laurence Olivier, Edith Evans, and Peggy Ashcroft. During the play's run there was the beginning of a sea change in Byam Shaw's career. He assisted Gielgud in directing *Richard II* for the Oxford University Dramatic Society—Vivien Leigh was the Queen and Michael Denison played three small parts—and he was as stimulating, firm, and courteous to his undergraduate cast as he was always to be to professional companies. He had now found his true métier; he had never enjoyed acting. Until the Second World War, however, he continued to act, mostly in supporting parts in prestigious Gielgud productions, but also, importantly for the future, with Michael Redgrave, George Devine, and Peggy Ashcroft in Michel Saint-Denis's short season at the Phoenix. But he was now directing too, and in 1938 was engaged to direct Gielgud in Dodie Smith's *Dear Octopus*.

Byam Shaw had joined the emergency reserve of officers before the war and with his brother James was commissioned into the Royal Scots in 1940. They both served in Burma from 1942 and were both wounded. Byam Shaw ended his service in 1945 as a major making training films in India. By 1946 he had joined Saint-Denis and Devine in running the Old Vic Centre, which combined a school of acting, an experimental project, and the Young Vic Company. Byam Shaw also found time to direct *The Winslow Boy* by Terence Rattigan (with Angela in a key role)—the start of another rewarding association—and also three Shakespeare plays at the Vic. Despite much success in all fields the three partners fell foul of the Vic governors and of the theatre's top-heavy and largely hostile administration and resigned in 1951.

Fortunately for Byam Shaw and the British theatre there followed his great work at Stratford, first as co-director with Anthony Quayle (1952–6) and then on his own, until handing over to his chosen successor Peter Hall in 1959. Byam Shaw directed fourteen plays at Stratford, notably *Antony and Cleopatra* (Redgrave and Ashcroft), *Macbeth* (Olivier and Leigh), *As You Like It* (Ashcroft), *Othello* (Harry Andrews and Emlyn Williams), and *King Lear* (Charles Laughton and Albert Finney), and chose companies which were a magnet to directors of the calibre of Hall, Peter Brook, and Gielgud. He helped transform Stratford from a worthy tourist trap into the country's theatrical capital. Ironically the company became 'Royal' only after he left.

As a freelance director in the 1960s Byam Shaw was much in demand. Then suddenly, though self-confessedly tone deaf, he turned to opera; and, unencumbered by musical considerations, brought his special gift for clarifying texts to the service of outrageous operatic story-lines, inculcating in principals and chorus his passion for theatrical truth. From *The Rake's Progress* at Sadler's Wells (1962) to Wagner's *Ring* at the Coliseum (1973), in all he directed fifteen operas, sweeping the stage before first nights 'to calm his nerves'. The decoration of the Coliseum's safety curtain was taken from a painting by his father.

Byam Shaw was slim, neatly and untheatrically dressed, with shoes always highly polished; his white hair, ruddy complexion, and searching brown eyes were those of the archetypal senior officer. Even his quiet voice and beautiful manners cloaked a steely authority. He did not aspire to be a virtuoso director, manipulating the playwright's intentions to conform to a subjective vision. He was content to be an interpreter, but he brought to that characteristically modest role the highest level of research, intuition, and love of the theatre and its workers.

Byam Shaw was appointed CBE in 1954 and was given an honorary DLitt by Birmingham University in 1959. He died in a nursing home in Goring-on-Thames on 29 April 1986, not far from his house at Wargrave.

MICHAEL DENISON, *rev.*

Sources *The Times* (1 May 1986) · M. Billington, *Peggy Ashcroft* (1988) · M. Denison, *Double act* (1985) · *WWW* · *CGPLA Eng. & Wales* (1986)
Archives CUL, letters to Siegfried Sassoon · U. Birm. L., Eden MSS, corresp. with Lord Avon
Likenesses T. F. Holte, photograph, NPG [*see illus.*]
Wealth at death £352,612: probate, 21 July 1986, *CGPLA Eng. & Wales*

Shaw [*née* Graham], **Helen Brown** (1879–1964), politician, was born on 2 June 1879 at 95 Finlay Drive, Dennistoun, Glasgow, the eldest of a large family. Her parents were David Graham (*c*.1852–1919), a Glasgow-born wine merchant, and his wife, Annie Gillespie (*b. c*.1860), who originally came from Dumbarton. Robert Graham & Sons was a long-established and successful business, and by 1888 the family had become sufficiently prosperous to move away from Dennistoun, a middle-class district rather too close to the industrial pollution of Glasgow's east end. The Grahams settled in Uddingston, a Lanarkshire village to the east of Glasgow, which was in the midst of a villa-building boom. For the rest of her life Helen Graham's home was in Uddingston. She was educated privately.

Marriage, family, and community life preoccupied Helen Graham up to the First World War. On 18 September 1902 she married David Perston Shaw (1875/6–1915), with whom she had a son and a daughter. The Shaws were close neighbours of the Graham family in Uddingston and were similarly engaged in the drinks' trade. David Perston Shaw belonged to the Glasgow firm of Anderson and Shaw Ltd, wholesale tea, wine, and whisky suppliers. He enlisted at the outbreak of war in 1914, serving as a major in the 6th Scottish Rifles, a distinctively Lanarkshire battalion of the Cameronians, and was killed in action in France on 16 June 1915.

Even before her husband's death Helen Shaw took an organizational role in the war effort. In 1914 she inaugurated the Bothwell branch of the Soldiers' and Sailors' Families Association, and served prominently on various local and county committees relating to war pensions, prisoners of war, and food control. In 1920 she was made an MBE for patriotic services. During the 1920s she consolidated her record of public service, taking a particular interest in the welfare of young people. From 1919 she was district commissioner for the Lanarkshire Girl Guides, from 1920 she represented Uddingston on Lanarkshire education authority, and in 1930, after schooling provision was transferred to the Scottish county councils, she was co-opted as the first woman to serve on Lanarkshire county council.

The growing electoral success of the left in Lanarkshire

Helen Brown Shaw (1879–1964), by Bassano, 1931

also encouraged the avowedly anti-socialist Shaw to become active within the Unionist Party, as the Conservatives were then known in Scotland. Uddingston was in the Bothwell parliamentary constituency, and in 1919 John Robertson had taken the seat for Labour in a by-election. The weight of the Lanarkshire Miners' Union had been behind him, notably in populous coal- and steel-producing communities such as Bellshill, Mossend, and Carfin. Shaw first stood as the Unionist candidate for Bothwell in the 1924 general election and, although defeated, acquitted herself well, taking almost 44 per cent of the total vote. She stood again in 1929, and took nearly 40 per cent of the vote in a three-way contest with Labour, who retained the seat, and the Communists. For all that three-quarters of the electorate was estimated to be from mining areas, there was a solid base of Unionist support in the constituency.

This underpinned Shaw's victory in the general election of 1931. Her Labour opponent on this occasion was Joseph Sullivan, Robertson's successor as MP. Sullivan was a Roman Catholic, an allegiance that caused leaders of Lanarkshire's influential Orange order to declare in favour of Shaw, who was staunchly Church of Scotland. However, Sullivan seemed to be more anxious about the loss of Labour votes to the Communist candidate, and urged electors who were disenchanted with Labour to support Shaw, the National Unionist, rather than the Communist (*The Scotsman*, 24 Oct 1931). Communist intervention tipped the election in Shaw's favour, but her achievement in Bothwell, winning by a majority of 2148, was the outcome of far more than the divided left-wing vote.

Shaw's record of public service, her campaigning emphasis on health, education, and welfare issues, and her status as a war widow all made her an attractive candidate for the Unionists. Yet during her four years at Westminster Shaw was less at ease with her role as MP. The depression hit Lanarkshire hard, and in 1933 the wholesale transfer of the Mossend steel plant of Stewarts and Lloyds to Corby in Northamptonshire, as part of industrial rationalization, proved to be bitterly controversial. Shaw was initially uncomfortable about the impact on her constituents, but came round to accepting the need for such drastic measures as a means of stimulating national regeneration. The social effect of the economic crisis was a recurring theme in her contributions to parliamentary debate, but she was an infrequent speaker, and most confident on the topic of education.

The Labour candidate had a clear run against Shaw in the general election of 1935, and—as was expected—Shaw lost the Bothwell seat. Thereafter she returned to voluntary and public service. From 1938 she was particularly active in the Women's Voluntary Services, and took a leading organizational role in Scotland during the Second World War. In the general election of 1945 she stood again for the Unionists in Bothwell, but by this time there was little realistic prospect that she could win, and her Labour opponent secured a large majority. Although still well known in Uddingston, her public profile thereafter became less prominent. She died on 20 April 1964 in Bon Secours Nursing Home, 36 Mansionhouse Road, Langside, Glasgow, and was cremated at Daldowie crematorium, Uddingston, on 22 April.

Tall and impeccably groomed, Shaw identified strongly with her community and was motivated by a deep sense of public duty. While holding forthright views about the need for women to cultivate domestic skills to enhance their family role, she demonstrated her personal flair for organization in the public sphere. Her daughter, Anne Gillespie Shaw (1904–1982), redirected these abilities to become a noted businesswoman and authority on scientific management.   IRENE MAVER

Sources *Glasgow Herald* (21 April 1964) · *Glasgow Herald* (29 Oct 1931); (12 Nov 1935); (28 June 1945) · *Hamilton Advertiser* (18 Oct 1924); (6 Dec 1930); (24 Oct 1931); (31 Oct 1931); (9 Nov 1935); (16 Nov 1935); (30 June 1945) · *The Scotsman* (19 Oct 1931); (20 Oct 1931); (24 Oct 1931); (29 Oct 1931) · *Hansard 5C* (1932), 268.992; (1934), 293.2065–8 · *Scottish biographies* (1938) · *WWW, 1971–80* · *WWBMP*, vol. 3 · b. cert. · m. cert. · d. cert. · D. Jamieson, *Uddingston, the village: a history of Uddingston and district*, 5 vols. [n.d., *c*.1975–*c*.1979] · *Hamilton Advertiser* (20 Sept 1902) · *Uddingston Standard* (26 June 1915) · *The Bailie* (23 Sept 1908) · *Hamilton Advertiser* (8 March 1919) · *WWW, 1991–5* [Anne Gillespie Shaw, daughter] · C. Burgess, 'The long slow march of Scottish women MPs, 1918–1945', *Out of bounds: women in Scottish society, 1800–1945*, ed. E. Breitenbach and E. Gordon (1992), 151–73 · B. Harrison, 'Women in a men's house: the women MPs, 1919–45', *HJ*, 29 (1986), 623–54 · *CCI* (1964)
Archives NRA, papers
Likenesses Bassano, vintage print, 1931, NPG [*see illus.*] · photograph, *c*.1935, repro. in Jamieson, *Uddingston, the village*, vol. 5,

suppl., p. 40 · photograph, repro. in *Hamilton Advertiser* (31 Oct 1931) · photograph, repro. in *Hamilton Advertiser* (30 June 1945)
Wealth at death £5109 15*s*.: NA Scot., SC 37/42/162, pp. 643–6

Shaw, Henry (1800–1873), antiquary and illuminator, was born in London on 4 July 1800; nothing is known of his family or education. A precocious architectural draughtsman, he published details of ornament from English medieval churches in 1823 (*A Series of Details of Gothic Architecture*) and supplied John Britton with drawings of Wells Cathedral for plates dated 1824 and 1825 included in the fourth volume of *Cathedral Antiquities*, eventually published as a series in 1836; Shaw's view of the interior was remembered as 'one of the best plates' (Britton, 2.134). He contributed to a number of de luxe publications promoted by antiquarian enthusiasts, among them *The History and Antiquities of the Chapel at Luton Park, a Seat of the … Marquess of Bute* (1829–30), *The history and illustrations of a house in the Elizabethan style of architecture, the property of John Danby Palmer* (1838), Thomas Alcock Beck's *A Description of Furness Abbey* (1845), and, most impressively, William Sidney Gibson's *History of the Monastery Founded at Tynemouth* (1846–7).

Shaw marketed prints from these publications from at least June 1830. His prints of details of illuminated manuscripts, artefacts, and ornament of the middle ages and later periods were published by William Pickering. Sets of prints were published as books, the first as *Illuminated ornaments selected from manuscripts and early printed books from the sixth to the seventeenth centuries* (1833), with an introduction by Frederic Madden. A similar publishing formula was adopted for other categories of artefact: works on Elizabethan architectural decoration appeared in 1834–5, on medieval furniture in 1836, on ornamental metalwork in 1836, on dresses and decorations of the middle ages in 1843, on alphabets in 1843, and on the medieval decorative arts in general in 1850. Plates were engraved for Shaw and mostly finished with hand-colouring, for which he employed assistants, especially after about 1840. Shaw designed initial letters based on medieval forms that were used in the printing trade. He provided initials and ornament for the prestigious New Testament published by Longman in 1864 with engravings of works by artists from Fra Angelico to Raphael.

Shaw was elected a fellow of the Society of Antiquaries of London in 1833. His reproductions of medieval and Renaissance artefacts and manuscripts established standards of finish, colour, and form that the originals themselves had to match to satisfy Victorian taste. By 1845 he had assistants making facsimiles in the British Museum Library under his supervision for sale. John Ruskin was among his customers. In 1866 he organized an exhibition of illuminated drawings, facsimiles of famous illuminated manuscripts dating from the ninth to the sixteenth centuries; the works were sold at Christies on 6 June of that year, prices ranging from £4 to over £90. The South Kensington Museum ordered further copies of works in this sale for its own collections. A review of Shaw's *Handbook of the Art of Illumination* (1866) described him as 'an authority on a peculiar and most beautiful department of the Arts of the Middle Ages' (*Art Journal*, 28, 1866, 342), one of a group who had brought this art to the attention of the educated public. Shaw justified use of wood-engravings in his *Handbook* by its cheapness: he had employed chromo-lithography in earlier publications, but considered hand-colouring alone capable of faithful reproduction. He is reported to have supplied to order illuminated addresses, documents produced for ceremonial purposes that from the 1860s were offered to honoured persons on public occasions, to celebrate coming of age, marriage, retirement, or official visits.

Shaw's mission was educational as well as antiquarian. His *Encyclopedia of Ornament* (1842) aimed to provide models for 'artist or manufacturer' and to encourage 'enlargement of correct taste'. Though lacking a theoretical or systematic approach, this was a precursor of Owen Jones's *Grammar of Ornament* (1856), a work that under-pinned the national system of design education elaborated by Henry Cole and the South Kensington Museum. In the *Catalogue of the Museum of Medieval Art Collected by the Late L. N. Cottingham, FSA, Architect* (1850), Shaw expressed the hope that the government might acquire Cottingham's copies either for the School of Design or as the nucleus of a national and medieval museum as a means of improving the education of workmen and designers. The catalogue of his 1866 exhibition states that, 'for purposes of instruction, [facsimiles of illuminated manuscripts] … may … be considered more satisfactory than the original drawings' (*Catalogue of Illuminated Drawings*, 3–4), a point he made to the South Kensington Museum in 1864 when asked to evaluate its collection of 'illuminations'.

Shaw died on 12 June 1873 at Broxbourne, Hertfordshire. The executors of his will were Alfred Maples Jeaffreson and Edward Warren, the son of his niece and an assistant at the British Museum respectively. The estate was valued at nearly £3000, the chief beneficiaries being Shaw's nieces Mary Warren, Eliza Westropp, Louisa Gray Compton, and Blanche Jeaffreson (the wife of Alfred Jeaffreson and the youngest daughter of Louisa Compton).

ROWAN WATSON

Sources F. Madden, correspondence, BL, Egerton MS 2844, vol.8 · Chiswick Press MSS, BL, Add. MS 43986, vol.108 · manuscript collection, Edinburgh City Library, BRS/qwN 45 · papers, S. Antiquaries, Lond. · R. Watson, 'Educators, collectors, fragments, and the 'Illuminations' collection at the Victoria and Albert Museum in the nineteenth century', *Interpreting and collecting fragments of medieval books*, ed. L. L. Brownrigg and M. M. Smith (2000), 21–46 · S. Hindman, 'Facsimiles as originals: an unknown manuscript by Henry Shaw', *Journal of the Walters Art Gallery*, 54 (1996), 225–32 · *Art Journal*, 35 (1873), 231 · *The Athenaeum* (21 June 1873), 798 · J. Myles, *L. N. Cottingham, 1787–1847, architect of the Gothic revival* (1996) · R. Strong, *And when did you last see your father? The Victorian painter and British history* (1978) · J. Britton, *The autobiography of John Britton*, 3 vols. in 2 (privately printed, London, 1849–50), vol. 2 · *Art Journal*, 28 (1866), 342 · *A catalogue of illuminated drawings by Henry Shaw* (1866) · d. cert.

Archives GL, account books and corresp. · S. Antiquaries, Lond., MSS

Wealth at death under £3000: probate, 29 June 1873, *CGPLA Eng. & Wales*

Shaw, Henry Selby Hele- (1854–1941), mechanical and automobile engineer, was born at Billericay, Essex, on 29 July 1854, the eldest of the thirteen children of Henry Shaw, a solicitor, and his wife, Marion, daughter of Henry Selby Hele, vicar of Grays, Essex. He was the first in his family to manifest a scientific and inventive genius, though his younger brother, Philip Egerton Shaw, became professor of physics at Nottingham. Shaw added his mother's maiden name to his own surname in his early twenties. Shaw was privately educated, and at the age of seventeen was apprenticed at the Mardyke engineering works of Rouch and Leaker in Bristol. In 1876 he obtained the first of a number of Whitworth prizes, enabling him to become a student at University College, Bristol. He repeated and improved on this performance in each of his three years as a student. When the time came for his final examination he was found to be suffering from congestion of the lungs but, having attended the examination wrapped up in blankets, he was placed first on the list. In addition he was, in 1880, awarded the Miller scholarship from the Institution of Civil Engineers for a paper entitled 'Small motive power'.

On obtaining his degree in 1880, Hele-Shaw was appointed lecturer in mathematics and engineering in his own college at Bristol, and in 1881 he became the first professor of engineering there. He was then only twenty-seven. In 1885 he became the first occupant of the chair of engineering at the University College of Liverpool. Hele-Shaw married, in 1890, Ella Marion (*d.* 1947), daughter of Samuel Greg Rathbone, of the famous Liverpool family. They had one son, who was killed in the First World War, and one daughter.

In 1904 Hele-Shaw accepted an invitation to initiate a college of engineering at the Transvaal Technical Institute, of which he became principal within a year. This was at a time when the importance of engineering science as a university subject was becoming recognized and a number of new colleges were coming into existence, but even so, Hele-Shaw's record in founding three such important departments is probably unique. He remained in South Africa for only two years, and after his return to England in 1906 he never again held an academic appointment, although he retained his interest in education to the end of his life. He had no difficulty in holding the attention and interest of his students. On his own subject of kinematics he was a fine lecturer, making use of frequent demonstrations which his inventiveness suggested to him. His geniality and his undoubted pre-eminence as a practical engineer earned him the affection and respect of his students.

It is, however, mainly as an inventor and research worker that Hele-Shaw is remembered. His inventions cover a wide range, beginning in 1881 with several instruments for the measurement and recording of wind velocities, and proceeding next by a logical development to the field of integrating machines. For his paper to the Institution of Civil Engineers 'Mechanical integrators' in 1885 he received the Watt gold medal and Telford premium. Similarly, his main contributions to science arose from the facility with which he designed new apparatus for experiment. A good example of this may be found in his demonstration of the nature of streamline flow, of which a theoretical exposition was provided at the time by Sir George Stokes. The scientific significance of this work was great, since not only were the hydrodynamic equations involved considered to be insoluble, except in a few cases, but hydrodynamics as a whole was regarded as a purely mathematical subject with little application to real fluids. His work drew severe criticism from Osborne Reynolds, who, in *Nature*, on 15 September 1898, both disputed the conclusions reached and implied that he himself had anticipated many of the results in earlier work of his own. Hele-Shaw defended himself stoutly against his great antagonist, and his election as FRS the next year (1899) in recognition of this work shows that even at the time it was clear that Reynolds had underestimated both the value of the investigation and the extent of Hele-Shaw's contribution. In his whole career Hele-Shaw contributed more than a hundred papers, many of them of great importance, to various learned societies. He was awarded honorary degrees by the universities of St Andrews (LLD, 1897), Bristol (DSc in engineering, 1912), and Liverpool (DEng, 1931).

Even when most absorbed in research Hele-Shaw took an interest in practical engineering progress. In 1896 the Locomotives on Highways Act opened an entirely new field to British engineering, and in the early years of the motor industry he was in touch with every problem that arose. He acted as judge in almost every trial, and the famous Liverpool trials on commercial motor vehicles in 1897 were organized by him. He invented a number of important devices, including a friction clutch which at one time was fitted to the majority of motor vehicles. Hele-Shaw drove his own Benz car in the days before the act of 1896, when it was obligatory for motorists to be preceded by someone walking before, carrying a red flag. Among Hele-Shaw's inventions in the field of hydraulics were his streamline filter, his hydraulic transmission gear—the first of a type which has since become very important— and his hydraulic steering gear for ships, together with several pumps and hydraulic motors.

For the last thirty years of his life Hele-Shaw was engaged entirely as a consulting engineer, in invention, and in the exploitation of previous inventions. He had a flair for the commercial exploitation of his discoveries, some of which enjoyed a long life. With T. E. Beacham he introduced, in 1924, the first practical automatic variable pitch airscrew. At that time little advantage was obtainable from this device, but twenty years later it was essential for almost all fast aircraft.

In later life Hele-Shaw took an increasing interest in the professional engineering institutions. He was president of the Institution of Automobile Engineers in 1909 and of the Institution of Mechanical Engineers in 1922. It may well be that his most important service to British engineering was his influence in introducing the national certificate scheme in 1920, which was organized jointly by the Board of Education and the Institution of Mechanical

Engineers, through which a very large number of engineers were trained.

Hele-Shaw recovered from his illness at university to enjoy robust health. He was a keen sportsman, a first-class player at golf and lacrosse, and a good mountaineer and yachtsman. He was a lively and humorous conversationalist, and an excellent speaker. He grew up in an age of vigorous scientific controversy, and he enjoyed it. In his old age he was sometimes thought to be intolerant of opinions which differed from his own, but he never failed in kindliness towards his juniors. Hele-Shaw retired to Ross-on-Wye in Herefordshire at the age of eighty-five and died there, at the Cottage Hospital, on 30 January 1941. He was survived by his wife.   D. G. CHRISTOPHERSON, *rev.*

Sources H. L. Guy, *Obits. FRS*, 3 (1939–41), 791–811 · *Institution of Mechanical Engineers: Proceedings*, 145 (1941) · *The Engineer* (7 Feb 1941) · *Engineering* (7 Feb 1941) · private information (1959) · *CGPLA Eng. & Wales* (1941)
Archives CUL, letters to Sir George Stokes
Likenesses W. Stoneman, photograph, 1917, NPG · H. Speed, oils, Institution of Mechanical Engineers, London · photograph, repro. in Guy, *Obits. FRS*, 3 (1941)
Wealth at death £26,727 1s. 7d.: probate, 26 June 1941, *CGPLA Eng. & Wales*

Shaw [*née* Essex], **Hester** (*bap.* 1586?, *d.* 1660), midwife, was probably baptized in Allhallows parish, London, on 11 April 1586, the only recorded daughter of Nicholas Essex, gentleman. She began practising midwifery in London about 1610 and was licensed by the bishop of London before 1634. In that year Mrs Shaw and Mrs Whipp led a petition of sixty midwives of the City in opposition to Peter Chamberlen the elder, a man-midwife who planned to incorporate the midwives under his governorship. The petition, which was presented both to the king and to the College of Physicians and referred to the archbishop of Canterbury, alleged that Chamberlen had pecuniary interests in keeping midwives ignorant so that he could take on their difficult cases. The petition was successful in aborting Chamberlen's scheme; however, it did not result in an improvement of the ecclesiastical licensing system, as the midwives had hoped.

In January 1650 Hester Shaw's house in Tower Street was destroyed by a gunpowder explosion while she was attending a childbirth. Sixty-seven people were killed, including her son-in-law and three grandchildren. Shaw claimed to have lost all her midwifery earnings in the explosion, and a total of over £3000. She also claimed that her minister, Thomas Clendon, had attempted to confiscate three bags of her money, worth £953 6s. 8d. These had been blown out of her house and taken into his for safe keeping. She explained the minister's ill treatment of her as revenge for her withdrawal of an annual gift of £8 to the parish church when she found out that he had attempted to publish her charity. In 1653 Clendon complained of her allegations in his pamphlet *Justification Justified* and she returned with *A Plaine Relation of my Sufferings* and *Mrs. Shaw's Innocency Restored*. Affidavits taken before the lord mayor, a personal friend of hers, indicate that public opinion was on her side. She was described by Clendon as a woman 'by many reputed Religious, having by her good education, and volubility of tongue, and natural boldness, and confidence, attained some ability in prayer, and in speaking of matters of Religion'.

Hester was married to John Shaw, the churchwarden of Allhallows parish, before 1 April 1610, when their daughter Elizabeth was born. Elizabeth became Dame Bludden, and Hester had at least one other daughter, who married George Farrington. John Shaw died before 1643. Hester Shaw was buried in Allhallows parish on 18 June 1660.

ANN GIARDINA HESS, *rev.*

Sources J. H. Aveling, *The Chamberlens and the midwifery forceps* (1882) · J. Donnison, *Midwives and medical men: a history of interprofessional rivalries and women's rights* (1977) · H. Shaw, *A plaine relation of my sufferings* (1653) · H. Shaw, *Mrs. Shaw's innocency restored* (1653) · H. Shaw, *Death's master-peece* (1649) · parish register (baptism), Allhallows, London · parish register (burial), Allhallows, London

Shaw, (George William) Hudson (1859–1944), Church of England clergyman and public lecturer, was born on 6 August 1859 at 2 Spencer Villas, Francis Street, Potter Newton, Leeds, first child of Edward Walker Shaw (1824–1871), civil engineer, and Margaret Helen Hudson (1833–1913). Shaw's father died young, leaving the family in difficulties. When his mother, now remarried, emigrated to Australia, a wealthy aunt became his guardian and sent him to Bradford grammar school and then to university. He went up to Oxford in 1879 under the non-collegiate scheme, and was soon captured by Balliol. He won the Stanhope prize (1882), was president of the union (Hilary term 1883), and enjoyed sports, but failed to shine in his modern history final examinations.

After graduation Shaw was again saved from Australia, this time by an anonymous benefactor (later revealed to be Bolton King), whose support allowed him to undertake ordination in the Church of England. He began to prepare for ordination in 1884, and he also impetuously married Edith Emma Hirst on 1 January; a son was born that year. In some poverty himself, Shaw was burning to serve the urban poor. In 1886 Michael Sadler persuaded him that a travelling lectureship under the Oxford University extension scheme would satisfy his vocation. For much of his twenty-five years with the extension scheme he would combine lecturing with the charge of small parishes.

The Revd Hudson Shaw was a short, stocky man, forthright in expressing himself. A compelling orator, he spoke with a somewhat harsh and identifiably northern accent. As a history lecturer he was popular everywhere, but his special value to Oxford was his appeal to working men. They flocked to follow even such topics as the history of Florence and Venice; lecture courses on his favourite English social reformers, above all John Ruskin, brought him what Sadler called an 'almost mystical' reputation in the industrial north (Royden, 34). Shaw had a special feeling for south Lancashire; his commitment to extension work at centres such as those in Ancoats (which he called Ancoats University), Bolton, and Oldham was repaid in the adulation of his student followers.

In 1890 Balliol elected Shaw to a fellowship in recognition of his services as a public lecturer. Three years later

(George William) Hudson Shaw (1859–1944), by unknown photographer

came the first of several highly acclaimed tours in the eastern United States. Beneath this outward success private problems multiplied. On 21 April 1890, after the untimely death of his first wife in 1888, he had married a withdrawn and unworldly cousin, Agnes Josephine (Effie) Ringrose. It was another impulsive act, intended to give Effie and her widowed mother some security. After three years Effie bore a son and the unwanted experience plunged her into mental invalidism. Shaw's own vulnerability had been evident for some years: he suffered from mysterious physical complaints and often after the end of the lecture season succumbed to severe depression. In 1901 he met the much younger Maude *Royden (1876–1956); their relationship, initially a pastoral prop to her career in social work, soon turned into a chaste love affair and contributed its own rewards and difficulties. In 1905 Shaw's elder son abandoned an Oxford education and fled to America; there the wayward Arnold became agent to J. C. Powys, lecturer and author, and predeceased his father. Arnold's less mercurial half-brother, Bernard, qualified as an engineer, but was killed in the First World War.

The success of the Workers' Educational Association (WEA) was the turning point of Shaw's public career. Originating in 1903 within the extension movement, it embraced him as its first chairman; by 1908, however, it had assumed a stance of virtual opposition under a younger and more politically acute leadership. Shaw preached that the fate of democracy lay not with working-class assertiveness, but with religion and education, church and university, but his somewhat moralizing and patriarchal liberalism seemed outmoded; he was no longer honoured as a prophet. He did subsequently support the WEA, but off the record continued to insist that it should have remained a subordinate part of the extension system.

Perhaps it was no coincidence that in 1909 Shaw suffered his worst breakdown. He never properly resumed lecturing. In 1912, at a ceremony marking his final departure from Oxford, Sadler recalled building up the extension scheme and his friend's place as 'the keystone to the arch' (*University Extension Bulletin* 13, 4–5). Out of sheer loyalty Shaw had previously refused offers of more lucrative or sedate employment elsewhere; now influential friends settled the matter by obtaining for him the crown living of St Botolph without Bishopgate in the City of London. At St Botolph, Shaw did not serve quietly; seemingly he could not help taking a combative stand in the diocese, and his efforts to have Maude Royden preach from his pulpit led to unseemly confrontations with the bishop of London. Eventually he turned to less provocative causes, particularly Albert Schweitzer's hospital at Lambarene, but, sick and isolated from fellow clergy, he was becoming an absentee rector. He retired in 1935.

Effie Shaw died in February 1944. On 2 October of that year Hudson Shaw was married to Maude Royden; on 30 November, at their home, the Old Cottage, Bayley's Hill, Sevenoaks, Kent, he too died. He was buried in the Weald churchyard, Sevenoaks on 4 December. He had long outlived his own reputation. There was a brief posthumous revival of celebrity with the publication of *A Threefold Cord* (1947), Royden's candid portrayal of her relationship with the Shaws.

Shaw's publications were scanty and always incidental to some other purpose. His Stanhope prize essay was published. The syllabuses he wrote were routinely issued by Oxford and the American Society for Extension of University Teaching. His syllabus on Ruskin, written in a blaze of energy shortly after the master's death, assumed the proportions of a small textbook. The occasional sermon or lecture delivered at extension summer meetings, invariably revealing of the author's passions, appeared in print. STUART MARRIOTT

Sources extension committee/extension delegacy minutes, papers, reports; printed syllabuses of lecture courses, Oxf. UA, DES class · M. Royden, *A threefold cord* (1947) · private information (2004) · S. Fletcher, *Maude Royden: a life* (1989) · *Oxford University Extension Gazette* · *University Extension Journal* · *University Extension* [Philadelphia] · *University Extension Bulletin*, 13, 4–5 · Women's Library, London, Royden MSS, boxes 220–22 · I. Elliott, ed., *The Balliol College register, 1900–1950*, 3rd edn (privately printed, Oxford, 1953) · minutes of Balliol College governing body, Balliol Oxf. · M. Sadleir, *Michael Ernest Sadler … 1861–1943: a memoir by his son* (1949) · m. cert. · *CGPLA Eng. & Wales* (1945) · parish register (marriage), 21 April 1890, Thornthwaite

Archives Women's Library, London, Royden MSS, boxes 220–22
Likenesses group portrait (with extension lecturers), repro. in L. Goldman, *Dons and workers* (1995), pl. 11 · group portrait (with Workers' Educational Association delegates), repro. in A. Mansbridge, *An adventure in working-class education* (1920), facing p. 23 · photograph, priv. coll. [*see illus.*]
Wealth at death £9556 14s. 9d.: probate, 1 March 1945, *CGPLA Eng. & Wales*

Shaw, Sir James, first baronet (1764–1843), lord mayor of London, son of John Shaw, an Ayrshire farmer, whose ancestors had occupied the property of Mosshead for three centuries, and of Helen, daughter of David Sellars of the Mains, Craigie, Ayrshire, was born at Mosshead in the parish of Riccarton on 26 August 1764. On his father's death, about five years later, the family moved to Kilmarnock, where James Shaw was educated at the grammar school. When seventeen years old he went to America to join his brother David, who held a position in the commissariat service, and by his influence was placed in the commercial house of Messrs George and Samuel Douglass at New York. Three years later he returned to Britain, and was made a junior member of the firm in London, eventually becoming a full partner. In 1798 he was elected alderman for the ward of Portsoken, in 1803 became sheriff of London and Middlesex, and was lord mayor in 1805–6. He distinguished himself in this office by reviving the right of the city to precedence on public occasions, and exercised his privilege at the funeral of Lord Nelson, when many of the royal family took part in the procession.

From 1806 to 1818 Shaw was MP for the City of London, normally supporting the government, though after 1815 he took a more independent line. He sought and obtained a baronetcy in 1809 from the duke of Portland and continued an alderman until 1831, when he was elected chamberlain of London. In this position he was threatened with a serious misfortune. He inadvertently invested £40,000 held by him as banker to the corporation in the spurious exchequer bills with which the market at that time was flooded. On discovering his error he made immediate preparations to sacrifice almost his entire private fortune to make good the loss. A government commission, however, completely exonerated him, and he was repaid the full amount. In May 1843 he resigned the office of chamberlain, and on 22 October of the same year he died, unmarried, at his house in America Square.

Shaw was known for his energy as a patron. Among other kindnesses he succeeded in procuring a provision for the widow of Robert Burns and commissions for her sons. In 1848 a statue of him, by Fillans, was erected at the Kilmarnock Cross; and a portrait by James Tannock was presented to the borough. The baronetcy, by a special patent granted in 1813, descended to his sister's son, John MacGee, who took the name of Shaw. On his death, childless, in November 1868, it became extinct.

E. I. CARLYLE, rev. H. C. G. MATTHEW

Sources *GM*, 2nd ser., 20 (1843), 654–6 · *The Times* (25 Oct 1843) · HoP, *Commons* · A. McKay, *A history of Kilmarnock, including biographical notices* (1848)
Likenesses H. Meyer, mezzotint, pubd 1806 (after J. Hoppner), BM · J. Tannock, oils, 1817, Kilmarnock town hall · R. Dighton,

etching, 1819, NPG · J. Fillans, statue, 1848, Elmbank Avenue, Kilmarnock · Mrs. C. Pearson, oils, corporation of London · Ridley and Holl, stipple (after S. Drummond), BM, NPG; repro. in *European Magazine* (1806)

Shaw, (John) James Byam (1903–1992), art historian and art dealer, was born on 12 January 1903 in London, one of five children of the painter (John) Byam Liston *Shaw (1872–1919) and his wife, (Caroline) Evelyn Eunice Pyke-Nott (1870–1959), also a painter. James, known always as Jim, was the elder surviving son; his younger brother was the actor and director Glencairn Alexander Byam *Shaw. He was educated at Westminster School and Christ Church, Oxford. After graduating with a second-class degree in *literae humaniores* in 1925, he spent until 1933 travelling throughout Europe, studying independently, as he liked to stress, in the print rooms of the principal museums. His eye was naturally keen, and he acquired an extensive knowledge of graphic art, of prints no less than of drawings, recording his observations in notebooks now in the Ashmolean Museum, Oxford. On 10 April 1929 he married Eveline Margaret Grose Dodgson, daughter of Captain Arthur Dodgson RN. There were no children of the marriage.

It had been agreed that after his years of travel Byam Shaw would join the London firm of P. & D. Colnaghi, with which he had family connections. He joined it in 1934, having already served briefly as lecturer and as assistant to the director at the newly founded Courtauld Institute of Art. In 1937 he became a director of Colnaghis, remaining one until his retirement in 1968. His strong business acumen was complemented by a flair for making significant discoveries in the saleroom. He was always generous in allowing museums to benefit from his expertise, and as a result of his close friendship with Arthur Ewart Popham at the British Museum and particularly with Sir Karl Parker at the Ashmolean Museum, both collections gained greatly. During the Second World War, Byam Shaw served with the Royal Scots in India and Burma, was wounded, and was finally promoted to the rank of major. Having been divorced from his first wife in 1938, in 1945 he married Margaret Saunders, daughter of Arthur Saunders, veterinary surgeon. They adopted a son.

In the decades after 1950 Byam Shaw's high reputation as scholar, connoisseur, and dealer was consolidated internationally, adding significant lustre to the standing of Colnaghis. As early as 1927 he had published an article in *Old Master Drawings*, and he became an assiduous contributor to it, as also to the *Burlington Magazine*. Publication in 1951 of his first book, *The Drawings of Francesco Guardi*, revealed his gift for writing cogent, graceful prose. Still more felicitous, and on a less studied artist, was a comparable book, *The Drawings of Domenico Tiepolo*, published in 1962. In 1967 he published a catalogue of the paintings belonging to his old college, Christ Church, to which he was devoted. It was followed in 1976 by his two-volume catalogue of its large drawings collection. In the same year the college made him an honorary student. He was appointed CBE in 1972.

The later period of Byam Shaw's life was the most productive and, in personal terms, probably the happiest. His second wife died in 1965, but on 12 January 1967 he married Christina Pamela Gibson (*b.* 1914/15), widow of his friend William Pettigrew Gibson, who had been keeper of the National Gallery, London, and youngest daughter of Francis John Longley Ogilvy, stockbroker. In handsome appearance and lively intelligence they seemed a couple ideally matched. In 1983, at the age of eighty, Byam Shaw published a catalogue of the Italian drawings in the Lugt collection of the Institut Néerlandais, Paris. His catalogue of the Italian eighteenth-century drawings in the Robert Lehman collection of the Metropolitan Museum, New York, written in collaboration with George Knox, was published in 1987. His final publication was a letter in the *Burlington Magazine* in 1991. He died on 18 March 1992, and was survived by his third wife. A memorial service was held at Christ Church Cathedral, Oxford, on 16 May 1992.

Byam Shaw's scholarship was essentially a matter of discriminating, practical connoisseurship, and although he came to be associated specifically with Venetian eighteenth-century art, he possessed very much wider knowledge and interests. But he never concerned himself with interpretation of artistic styles, still less with artistic theory, and he had an innate distaste for extreme views of any kind. Urbanity, modesty, and a gentle though not uncritical humour pervaded his work and his whole outlook, making him as much liked as respected. Tall, trim, rubicund, dressed always with unobtrusive elegance, he remained into old age a figure upright and distinguished, exuding a mellow charm which truly reflected his character.   MICHAEL LEVEY

Sources *WWW*, 1991–5 · C. J. White, 'Per James B. Shaw', *Saggi e Memorie di Storia dell'Arte*, 19 (1994), 7–20 · C. White, *Burlington Magazine*, 134 (1992), 444–5 · *The Times* (21 March 1992) · *The Guardian* (30 March 1992) · *The Independent* (8 April 1992) · *WWW*, 1916–28 · m. certs.
Archives AM Oxf. · Institut Néerlandais, Paris, Fondation Custodia, F. Lugt collection | P. & D. Colnaghi, 14 Old Bond Street, London
Likenesses photograph, *c.*1970, repro. in *The Times*
Wealth at death £603,939: probate, 27 July 1992, *CGPLA Eng. & Wales*

Shaw, James Johnston (1845–1910), economist and judge, was born at Kirkcubbin, co. Down, on 4 January 1845, the second son of John Maxwell Shaw (*d.* 1852), a merchant and farmer of Kirkcubbin, and his wife, Anne, daughter of Adam Johnston. He was taught locally, first at the national school, and later by James Rowan, Presbyterian minister of Kirkcubbin. In 1858 he was sent to the Royal Belfast Academy, where apparently he became a favourite pupil of the principal, the Revd Reuben John Bryce LLD. In 1861 he entered Queen's College, Belfast, gaining the highest entrance scholarship in classics. After changing disciplines to the study of mental science and political economy, he graduated BA in 1865 and MA in 1866 in the Queen's University of Ireland, with first-class honours. In 1882 the university conferred on him the honorary degree of LLD.

Shaw went on to study theology at the Presbyterian

general assembly's college in Belfast and also at the University of Edinburgh. He was licensed to preach in 1869, by the presbytery of Ards, and was appointed in the same year by the general assembly to be the professor of metaphysics and ethics at Magee College, Londonderry. In 1870 Shaw married Mary Elizabeth, *née* Maxwell (*d.* 1908). They had one daughter and two sons.

In 1878 Shaw resigned his chair and was called to the Irish bar, where he quickly developed a successful practice. He also held the position of Whately professor of political economy at Trinity College, Dublin, from 1876 to 1891, publishing several papers which were read at meetings of the Statistical and Social Inquiry Society of Ireland, the British Association, the Social Science Congress, and elsewhere. He became president of the Statistical Society in 1901.

In 1886 Shaw was made a member of the senate of the Royal University of Ireland; he took silk in 1889 and in 1891 he became a commissioner of national education. In the following year he was made a county court judge of Kerry, a position which gave him more time to devote to other work. In 1902 he joined the council of trustees of the National Library of Ireland, and in 1908 he was chairman of a vice-regal commission of inquiry into the mysterious disappearance of the crown jewels from Dublin Castle. When the Queen's University of Belfast was founded by royal charter in 1908 he was appointed to frame the statutes of the university. He was also a member of the governing body of the university and in 1909 became pro-chancellor. In 1909 he was created recorder of Belfast, and county court judge of Antrim.

A clear writer and principled administrator, Shaw died at home, 69 Pembroke Road, Dublin, on 27 April 1910, and was buried in the city's Mount Jerome cemetery. A Shaw prize in economics was founded in his memory at the Queen's University of Belfast. After his death, his daughter collected and edited a number of his papers, in *Occasional Papers* (1910).

THOMAS HAMILTON, *rev.* SINÉAD AGNEW

Sources J. S. Crone, *A concise dictionary of Irish biography*, rev. edn (1937), 229 · T. W. Moody and J. C. Beckett, *Queen's, Belfast, 1845–1949: the history of a university*, 2 vols. (1959), vol. 1, pp. 204, 209, 388, 392, 413; vol. 2, pp. 787, 804 · *The Times* (28 April 1910), 13
Likenesses S. Rowley, oils, *c.*1911, Queen's University, Belfast · memorial brass (after S. Rowley), Queen's University, Belfast
Wealth at death £8242 7*s.* 10*d.*: administration, 20 July 1910, *CGPLA Ire.* · £2639: Irish administration sealed in London, 20 Aug 1910, *CGPLA Eng. & Wales*

Shaw, John (1558/9–1625), Church of England clergyman and religious writer, was born in Westmorland and attended school there. He matriculated from Queen's College, Oxford, on 17 November 1581, aged twenty-two, and graduated BA on 29 February 1584. He was instituted vicar of Woking, Surrey, on 11 September 1588. He probably married soon afterwards, but his wife's name is unknown. Their son Tobias was born in 1589 or 1590: he matriculated from Queen's College on 6 July 1604, aged fourteen. Shaw was deprived in 1596 for nonconformity, but appears to have been reinstituted, probably by the time of Tobias's

matriculation. His book *The Blessedness of Marie, the Mother of Jesus* (1618) contains a preface to Lady Dorothy Zouch, wife of Sir Edward Zouch, at Woking, which celebrates her 'coming in among us', her 'hearty love to true religion', and her 'comfort in the ministry and public worship of God established'; a distich in the church, now destroyed, likewise suggests that Shaw had been received back into the ministry. His *Bibliorum summula* (1621) was also signed from Woking. According to its translator, Simon *Wastell, who had been at school with Shaw, this work was 'much applauded of the godly learned ministers and of many other scholars' (Wastell, 2nd preface). Among the commendatory verses prefixed to the original book was one by Daniel Featley of Lambeth. Shaw lived at Woking until his death in 1625, and was buried there on 15 September. Tobias, who had graduated BA in 1611 and proceeded MA in 1614, became rector of Blendworth, Hampshire, in 1619.

CHARLOTTE FELL-SMITH, *rev.* STEPHEN WRIGHT

Sources Foster, *Alum. Oxon.* · Wood, *Ath. Oxon.*, 2.354–5 · S. Wastell, trans., *The divine art of memory, or, The sum of holy scriptures delivered in acrostic verses* (1683) · J. Shaw, *The blessedness of Marie, the mother of Jesus* (1618) · O. Manning and W. Bray, *The history and antiquities of the county of Surrey*, 1 (1804)

Shaw, John. *See* Shawe, John (1608–1672).

Shaw, John (1612/13–1689), Church of England clergyman, was born at Bedlington, co. Durham, the son of a clergyman, probably of John Shaw (*d.* 1637), curate of St John's, Newcastle upon Tyne, and his wife, Elizabeth (*d.* 1621). Shaw was educated by Thomas Ingmethorp, the rector of Great Stainton, Durham, before he matriculated at Queen's College, Oxford, on 21 November 1628, aged fifteen. He moved to Brasenose College on 2 April 1629, where he graduated BA on 24 March 1632. Returning to the north he was vicar of Alnham, Northumberland, from 1636, and appointed afternoon lecturer at All Saints, Newcastle, in December 1643. Ejected from both these posts by the Scots he was instituted rector of Whalton, Northumberland, in 1645. Unlike his parliamentarian namesake the vicar of Rotherham (with whom he has been confused), John Shaw was a royalist sympathizer, for which he was prevented from taking up his living at Whalton, and was allegedly imprisoned for four years. In the 1650s he settled in the poorer living of Bolton in Craven, in the West Riding of Yorkshire, which yielded him £50 per annum. In 1652 he wrote *The pourtraicture of the primitive saints in their actings and sufferings, according to St Paul's canon.*

In 1661 Shaw recovered the rectory of Whalton and he replaced the ejected presbyterian, Henry Lever, as lecturer at St John's Church, Newcastle, on 27 August 1662. Appointed to preach forenoon and afternoon sermons at St John's for £60 per annum he was also paid £10 per annum for his Thursday lecture at St Nicholas's Church, Newcastle. He was active suppressing Newcastle's dissenters, and personally broke open the doors of the conventicle at Richard Gilpin's house on 22 July 1669. About 1661, and again in 1679, he was chosen as a member of convocation for Yorkshire, and he also served as *procurator cleri* for the archdeaconry of Northumberland. In 1677 he wrote *Origo protestantium, or, An answer to a popish manuscript … wherein protestancy is demonstrated to be elder than popery*.

The corporation of Newcastle published some of Shaw's writings against popery at its own expense, but his work of 1685, entitled 'No reformation of the established Reformation', condemned Roman Catholics and dissenters alike with equal vehemence for undermining the church. He was 'a strict observer of the orders of the church' and 'somewhat warm in his temper' (*Ambrose Barnes*, 436). After suffering for several years with gout he died on 22 May 1689, 'a loyal, religious and learned Person' (Wood, *Ath. Oxon.*, 2.832), and was buried just before the altar in St John's Church, Newcastle. His monumental inscription, written by his son, reads 'Deo, ecclesiae, patriae, regi, pie fidelis' ('religiously loyal to God, church, country, king'; *Ambrose Barnes*, 436).

ANDREW J. HOPPER

Sources Memoirs of the life of Mr Ambrose Barnes, ed. [W. H. D. Longstaffe], SurtS, 50 (1867) • Foster, *Alum. Oxon.*, 1500–1714, vol. 4 • Wood, *Ath. Oxon.*, 2nd edn, vol. 2 • R. Howell, *Newcastle upon Tyne and the puritan revolution: a study of the civil war in north England* (1967) • R. Welford, ed., *History of Newcastle and Gateshead*, 3: Sixteenth and seventeenth centuries (1887) • DNB • [H. M. Wood], ed., *Wills and inventories from the registry at Durham*, 4, SurtS, 142 (1929)

Shaw, Sir John, first baronet (*c.*1615–1680), customs farmer, was the second in the family of three sons and two daughters of Robert Shaw, wine merchant, of Southwark, Surrey, and his wife, Elizabeth, daughter of John Domelawe, wine merchant, of London. His father, who was descended from an armigerous Cheshire family, was ruined by taking a share in the wine-licensing patent of 1631. Shaw settled in Antwerp before the civil war as factor to the great Somerset clothier John Ashe of Freshford, whose daughter he married before 1654. Ashe was a prominent parliamentarian; but Shaw advanced £1810 for the purchase of arms for the king's army, and during the interregnum he provided the principal channel of communication between the English royalists and the exiled court. According to Edward Hyde, earl of Clarendon, without him the king at one time could not have got bread.

After returning to England at the Restoration, Shaw became MP for Lyme Regis and one of Clarendon's chief business advisers. He held such a multiplicity of posts that Sir William Coventry described him sarcastically as 'a miracle of a man' (Pepys, 8.398). He was a commissioner of customs, trade, and plantations, and joint paymaster of the Dunkirk garrison until 1662, when he took a share in the great farm of the customs. On obtaining a lease of the crown manor of Eltham, Kent, in 1663, he employed Hugh May to build him a house. He was fortunate to have been accepted as a member of the new customs syndicate in 1667 before Clarendon's fall deprived him of his patron; but the lease was cancelled four years later, when the farmers sought guarantees against the heavy defalcations

to be expected in the imminent Dutch war. Thenceforth Shaw held only minor offices, but was still reckoned a government supporter, though 'apt to make the gout his excuse' (Browning, 3.104) for absence from the House of Commons.

Shaw was knighted in 1660 and created a baronet, with three of his partners, in 1665. He and his first wife, Sarah Ashe, who died in 1662, had a son, who succeeded to the baronetcy, and a daughter. On 24 December 1663 he married Bridget, daughter of Sir William Drury of Besthorpe, Norfolk, and widow of a Cheshire landowner, Charles, fourth Viscount Kilmorey; they had two sons and another daughter. He died in his town house in Bloomsbury Square on 1 March 1680, and was buried at Eltham. His younger children were well provided for, and his heirs retained the lease of Eltham until 1839. His widow married as her third husband the royal physician, Sir John Baber.

JOHN FERRIS, *rev.*

Sources HoP, Commons • G. J. Armytage, ed., *A visitation of the county of Surrey, begun … 1662, finished … 1668*, Harleian Society, 60 (1910), 101 • Hasted's history of Kent: corrected, enlarged, and continued to the present time, ed. H. H. Drake (1886), 183 • A. Browning, *Thomas Osborne, earl of Danby and duke of Leeds, 1632–1712*, 3 vols. (1944–51) • T. Wotton, *The baronetage of England*, ed. E. Kimber and R. Johnson, 3 vols. (1771) • GEC, *Baronetage*, vol. 4 • Pepys, *Diary* • will, PRO, PROB 11/362, sig. 41

Archives BL, corresp. and papers, Add. MS 23199 • Bodl. Oxf., corresp. [copies]

Wealth at death £5400; plus property in city: HoP, Commons, 1660–90, 430

Shaw, John (1776–1832), architect, was born on 10 March 1776 at Bexley, Kent, the son of John Shaw and his wife, Elizabeth. He was apprenticed for seven years to George Gwilt the elder in 1790, and began to practise independently in 1798. With his wife, Elizabeth Hester Whitfield (*bap.* 1776, *d.* 1864), who was the daughter of his uncle Francis Whitfield and his wife, Elizabeth, Shaw had seven sons and two daughters. The eldest son was John Shaw junior [see below]; the seventh son was Thomas Budd *Shaw.

From 1799 until 1831 Shaw was a regular exhibitor at the Royal Academy. In 1803, following his appointment to the post of surveyor of the Eyre estate in St John's Wood, he exhibited at the academy ambitious plans for a 'British circus' consisting of detached and semi-detached houses arranged in two circles on either side of a circular road. Although not the originator of this scheme, which was not carried into effect, Shaw and his eldest son were to become pioneers in the development of semi-detached houses in irregularly designed roads, as opposed to grid-plan terraced streets. In 1816 he was appointed architect and surveyor of Christ's Hospital school in Newgate Street, London, to which he made extensive additions: between 1820 and 1822 he built the infirmary; the west side of the quadrangle followed between 1825 and 1829, and the mathematics and grammar schools in 1832. These were built in the Gothic style, which Shaw later used to sympathetic effect in his additions to Newstead Abbey,

Linby, Nottinghamshire (1818–*c*.1830), for Colonel Wild-man, who had purchased the abbey from Lord Byron. Other examples of his work in this style are the church of St Dunstan, Fleet Street (1831–3; eventually completed by his son), and Ilam Hall, Staffordshire (1821–6).

Shaw made extensive valuations of property in London, and was architect to the Phoenix Fire Assurance Company. In addition to the projects mentioned above, he built many country houses, including Blendon Hall, Kent (*c*.1815; destr. 1834) and Rooks' Nest (later Croome House), Surrey (*c*.1818). He was a member of the Architects' Club and a fellow of the Royal and Linnean societies and of the Society of Antiquaries.

As architect to the trustees of Ramsgate harbour, Shaw designed the clock house, the steps known as Jacob's Ladder, and the obelisk erected to commemorate a visit by George IV on his way to Hanover. He died suddenly on 30 July 1832 at the age of fifty-six, while working at Ramsgate harbour, and was buried at Bexley, Kent.

John Shaw junior (1803–1870), architect, was born on 17 May 1803 at 25 Great James Street, Bedford Row, Holborn, London. He was a pupil of his father, whom he succeeded as architect to Christ's Hospital. About 1825 he became surveyor to Eton College, for which he designed the Tudor Gothic buildings in Weston's Yard at Eton, and developed the Chalcots estate near Chalk Farm in Hampstead, building semi-detached villas (1840–50). His designs for the hall, schools, dormitories, and chapel at Eton were exhibited at the Royal Academy between 1825 and 1846, together with designs for a marine villa at Bognor, the Law Life Assurance Company, and the Royal Naval School at Deptford (later Goldsmiths' College), built in 1843–4. He built Holy Trinity Church, Great New Street, Fetter Lane, in 1838, following which he published *A letter on ecclesiastical architecture as applicable to modern churches: addressed to the lord bishop of London* (1839), in which he advocated the use of the Romanesque style for that purpose. His last design, in the style of Wren, was Wellington College, Sandhurst, Berkshire (1855–9).

Shaw was one of the official referees of metropolitan buildings from 1844 to 1855, when the duties of that office were transferred to the Metropolitan Board of Works. Described as early as 1843 in *The Builder* as a designer in the manner of Wren, a recent commentator noted further that 'it was as a designer of buildings in a revived "Renaissance" style that Shaw was most successful and original' (Colvin, *Archs.*). Shaw was a fellow of the Royal Institute of British Architects. He died on 9 July 1870, at his home, 10 Sheffield Gardens, Kensington, London, and was buried in Kensal Green cemetery. He left a widow, Jane, and a son, William Francis Shaw. ANNETTE PEACH

Sources Colvin, *Archs.* · *GM*, 1st ser., 102/2 (1832), 285 · *IGI* · [W. Papworth], ed., *The dictionary of architecture*, 11 vols. (1853–92) · Graves, *RA exhibitors* · J. Summerson, *Georgian London* (1945), 158–9 · H. R. Hitchcock, *Early Victorian architecture in Britain*, 2 vols. (1954) · R. H. Harper, *Victorian architectural competitions: an index to British and Irish architectural competitions in The Builder, 1843–1900* (1983) · d. cert. [John Shaw junior] · *CGPLA Eng. & Wales* (1870) [John Shaw jun.] · will [John Shaw jun.]

Wealth at death under £45,000—John Shaw jun.: will, 1870

Shaw, John [Jack] (**1789–1815**), pugilist and soldier, was born on a farm between the villages of Cossall and Wollaton in Nottinghamshire, the son of William Shaw, farmer. Educated at Trowell Moor school, he was a delicate child, but grew to be a powerfully built young man. After being apprenticed to a wheelwright in Radford, Nottinghamshire, in 1802, he then became a carpenter at Wollaton Hall, home of Lord Middleton. He achieved fame as a boxer, and fought one match at which Jem Belcher, the veteran prize-fighter, was present, before enlisting in the 2nd Life Guards at Nottingham goose fair on 16 October 1807. Shaw showed particular aptitude as a soldier and gained a certain notoriety in his regiment by engaging in a street brawl near Portman Square, London, in which he defeated three toughs who taunted him for his red coat. After subsequently being introduced by his officers to the prize-fighting élite at the fives court in Little St Martin Lane, London, and to Jackson's Rooms, a fashionable club and boxing school in Bond Street, Shaw fought and defeated James Molyneaux, the American boxer, in a 'friendly' match (with gloves). Soon afterwards he outpaced and beat Captain Robert Barclay of the 23rd regiment, known for his devastating punches.

Jack Shaw's reputation as a fighter was established, despite a defeat by Tom Belcher, brother of Jem, and in July 1812 he outfought a Mr Burrows in his first bare-knuckle contest, in which he forced his opponent to retire in less than seventeen minutes. In April 1815, having issued a challenge to all England, he was matched against Ned Painter, whose second was the famed boxer Tom Cribb, on Hounslow Heath and beat his opponent ruthlessly with ten successive knock-down blows in twenty-eight minutes. Shaw apparently intended to challenge Cribb for the England championship title but before this happened the 2nd Life Guards were ordered to join Wellington's army in the south Netherlands as the crisis deepened following Napoleon's escape from Elba.

Now a corporal, Shaw was in charge of a foraging party early in the morning of 18 June 1815, when his troop was recalled to take its place with the regiment on the slopes above La Haye-Sainte at Waterloo. He took a conspicuous part in the numerous charges the 2nd Life Guards made that day as a part of the household brigade under Lord Edward Somerset, and was seen powerfully striking with his sword, causing terrible carnage among the French cavalrymen with whom he engaged. His energy and bravery were of the highest order, although reports that he captured a French eagle standard are contradictory and may be an exaggeration. Tom Morris of the 73rd regiment, who watched Shaw in action, noted that he had been drinking gin before the action began, and felt that he would have done better to attend more closely to the ordering of his troop. At last, venturing forward to the aid of Captain Edward Kelly of his regiment, Shaw was isolated from his comrades by French cuirassiers and his sword broke in his hand. Striking fiercely about him with his helmet, he was eventually unhorsed and cut down by his opponents, receiving numerous wounds. Shaw was seen later that night, lying dreadfully injured on a midden near La Haye-

Sainte, and in the morning his lifeless body was buried nearby; Sergeant-Major Edward Cotton, later proprietor of the Waterloo Museum, was one of the burial party.

Shaw's body was later exhumed and returned to Britain at the instigation of Sir Walter Scott, who had met him in the studio of the artist Benjamin Haydon, where Shaw posed as a model. A cast of his skull is in the Household Cavalry Museum in Windsor. Jack Shaw was a tall man, said to be 6 feet ½ inch tall and weighing 15 stone on entering the army. Noted for his very powerful physique and great strength, he was a brave and pugnacious boxer, and a skilful rider and swordsman. Although his fame faded after Waterloo, a memorial to those men of the village of Cossall who fought in the battle, including Shaw, was erected in 1877 in the parish churchyard.

JAMES FALKNER

Sources Major Knollys, *Shaw: the life guardsman*, ed. J. Potter Briscoe, 4th edn (1885) · *DNB* · R. H. Gronow, *Recollections and anecdotes of the camp, the court, and the clubs, at the close of the last war with France*, new edn (1864) · P. Haythornthwaite, 'John Shaw', *Military Illustrated*, 47 (April 1992), 49–51 · T. Morris, *Recollections of Sergeant Morris*, ed. J. Selby (1967) · E. Longford [E. H. Pakenham, countess of Longford], *Wellington*, 1: *The years of the sword* (1969) · C. Kelly, *The memorable battle of Waterloo* (1817) · W. Giborne, *History of the war in France and Belgium in 1815* (1844)
Likenesses engraving (in combat), repro. in Kelly, *Memorable battle of Waterloo*
Wealth at death under £50: administration

Shaw, John (1792–1827), surgeon and anatomist, born, probably in Ayr, on 2 April 1792, was the son of Charles Shaw, clerk of the county of Ayr, and his wife, Barbara Wright, daughter of a customs official at Greenock; he was the grandson of David Shaw, moderator of the general assembly of the Church of Scotland in 1775. His three brothers were the legal writer Patrick *Shaw, the surgeon and anatomist Alexander *Shaw (1804–1890), and the soldier Sir Charles *Shaw (1795–1871). One of his sisters, Marion, married Charles Bell; Shaw apparently lived with them after their marriage in 1811 until his death. Shaw's other sister, Barbara, married Charles Bell's brother, the eminent advocate George Joseph Bell.

Shaw was sent to London at the age of fifteen to study anatomy and surgery with Charles Bell at the Great Windmill Street School. As an anatomist Shaw is said to have made important additions to the school's collection of anatomical specimens. He was surgeon to the Middlesex Hospital from 1825 until his death in 1827. He published two surgical works concerned with distortions of the spine and chest; both works were published in the 1820s not only in England but also in Weimar, in German translation. Shaw's work as a demonstrator at the Great Windmill Street School led to his *Manual for the Student of Anatomy* (1821), which was republished twice in London in 1822 and published in German translation in Weimar in 1823. It was also published in the United States.

Shaw and his brother Alexander were drawn into the campaign carried out by their brother-in-law, Charles Bell, in support of Bell's claim that he had preceded François Magendie in the discovery that the roots of the spinal nerves differ in their functions, one being concerned with

sensation and the other with motion. Facsimile reproductions of some of the contributions by Bell and by the Shaws to that priority dispute are found in P. F. Cranefield's *The Way In and the Way Out* (1974). The latter also includes a facsimile reproduction of an article by A. D. Waller, published in *Science Progress* in 1911, in which Waller refers to the claim that Bell was greater than William Harvey as a 'family compact'. Shaw had extensive family connections to important and successful persons; it seems likely that both he and his brother were not only willing to join in a 'family compact' but were possibly anxious to secure a place in history for themselves and Charles Bell.

Shaw accomplished a great deal in his short life and the republication of his books in Germany and the United States shows that he had a good reputation in his day. Nevertheless, he is now remembered more for his connection with the Bell–Magendie controversy than for any major contribution to anatomy, physiology, or surgery. Shaw died at home, in London, on 19 July 1827, apparently from scarlet fever.   PAUL F. CRANEFIELD

Sources P. F. Cranefield, *The way in and the way out: François Magendie, Charles Bell and the roots of the spinal nerves* (1974) · G. Gordon-Taylor and E. W. Walls, *Sir Charles Bell: his life and times* (1958) · A. D. Waller, 'The part played by Sir Charles Bell in the discovery of the functions of motor and sensory nerves', *Science Progress*, 6 (1911–12), 78–106

Shaw, John, junior (1803–1870). *See under* Shaw, John (1776–1832).

Shaw, Joseph (1671–1733), legal writer, was the son of John Shaw, gentleman, of All Hallows, Stayning, London. He matriculated from Trinity College, Oxford, on 10 June 1687, was admitted to the Middle Temple on 15 April 1687, and was called to the bar on 3 May 1695. About 1700 he made a tour through the Netherlands, Flanders, and part of France, and embodied his observations in *Letters to a Nobleman*. These were addressed to Anthony Ashley Cooper, third earl of Shaftesbury, whose friendship and patronage he enjoyed. The letters were published in 1709. They are full of interesting details of the state of those countries during the brief interval of peace which followed the treaty of Ryswick.

In later life Shaw settled at Epsom in Surrey, and devoted himself to legal study. In 1728 he published *The Practical Justice of the Peace* (6th edn., 1756). Shortly before his death he published a companion volume entitled *Parish Law*, dedicated to his friend Sir John Fortescue Aland, justice of common pleas. The manual presented the law relevant to the parish's secular responsibilities and to its responsibilities for maintenance of both church and minister. In the nineteenth century, this manual was republished in conjunction with J. F. Archbold's *Parish Officer*. The fourth and last edition of this conjoint publication appeared in 1895. Shaw died at Lambeth, Surrey, on 24 October 1733, leaving a son, Joseph, who afterwards resided at Epsom.   E. I. CARLYLE, *rev.* NORMA LANDAU

Sources H. A. C. Sturgess, ed., *Register of admissions to the Honourable Society of the Middle Temple, from the fifteenth century to the year 1944*, 1 (1949), 220 · Foster, *Alum. Oxon.* · *GM*, 1st ser., 3 (1733), 550 · Allibone, *Dict.* · *GM*, 1st ser., 76 (1806), 672–3 · Holdsworth, *Eng. law*,

12.338 • J. Hutchinson, ed., *A catalogue of notable Middle Templars: with brief biographical notices* (1902)

Shaw, Lachlan (1686?–1777), Church of Scotland minister and historian, was the son of Donald Shaw, a farmer at Rothiemurchus, Inverness-shire. He was educated at Ruthven and then at King's College, Aberdeen, where he graduated MA on 2 May 1711. In the following year he was employed as a schoolteacher at Abernethy in Perthshire, and was presented a divinity bursary for the next two years. After studying theology at Edinburgh University he was licensed on 24 April 1716 by the presbytery of Haddington, and was appointed to the parish of Kingussie on 20 September. He transferred to Cawdor on 19 November 1719 with Helen, daughter of David Stuart, a collector of excise at Inverness, whom he had married on 1 October; the couple had one daughter and one son. Following Helen's death he married, on 14 March 1727, Anna (*d.* in or after 1777), daughter of Duncan Grant, a bailie of Inverness, with whom he had a further eleven children, among them Duncan *Shaw. On 9 May 1734 Shaw transferred to a post at Elgin, Moray, and remained there until his retirement in April 1774.

In addition to his work in the church, Shaw was a respected local historian who corresponded with many eminent figures, among them the judge and antiquary Sir David Dalrymple, Lord Hailes, and the naturalist Thomas Pennant, who visited him at Elgin in 1769. He wrote the account 'Of Elgin and the shire of Murray' in Pennant's *Tour of Scotland in 1769*, which appeared in 1771. Shaw was chiefly known for his *History of the Province of Moray*, published in 1775 and posthumously revised and republished in 1827 and 1882. During the early 1750s he also continued *A Genealogical Dedication of the Family of Rose of Kilravock*, written by Hew Rose in 1683–4 and printed in 1848. His 'Account of the family of Mackintosh', written in 1758, remained unpublished. Shaw died on 23 February 1777 and was buried near the high altar of Elgin Cathedral, where a memorial slab and window were dedicated to him in 1868.   J. R. MacDONALD, *rev.* SARAH COUPER

Sources *Fasti Scot.*, new edn, 5.365, 390, 439 • J. F. S. Gordon, preface, in L. Shaw, *The history of the province of Moray*, 3 vols. (1882), vol. 1, pp. ix–xvi • Watt, *Bibl. Brit.*, 2.849–50 • IGI

Shaw, Mabel (1888–1973), missionary and educationist, was born on 3 December 1888 at Prestwood Road, Heath Town, Willenhall, Wolverhampton, the eldest of three boys and two girls of Matthew Shaw, a tea-shop manager, and his wife, Elizabeth Anne, *née* Purchase. Between the ages of five and ten she lived with her grandmother in the Berkshire countryside and there, and later at her boarding-school in the Isle of Wight, she became a convinced Christian. On leaving school she went to study for four years in Edinburgh at St Colm's ecumenical Women's Missionary Training College, which had been founded by the remarkable Ann Hunter Small, who had herself been a missionary and educationist in India. At St Colm's, Shaw imbibed an informed respect for non-Christian religious traditions and beliefs, as well as a critical understanding of the New Testament. She was not forced into one religious pattern but was encouraged to find and 'follow her own bent, but without exclusiveness towards other points of view' (Wyon, 72).

Armed with Miss Small's injunction 'to understand and sympathise with the inner character and thought of the peoples of Asia and Africa' (A. Small, preface to *Missionary College Hymns*, 1914) Mabel Shaw accepted the London Missionary Society's call to go out to central Africa to start the Christian education of girls, and sailed for Cape Town in 1915. After a week's train journey to Broken Hill she was carried by bearers for a month overland—across plains, forests, and rivers, camping out in the open and learning as much as she could of her porters' language, until she reached Mbereshi in what is now Zambia. She then spent the first year learning to understand and speak Cibemba and acquainting herself with the local African traditions, especially with the traditional upbringing of girls. However initially shocked and alienated she was by some of the tribal customs concerning women, she knew it would be presumptuous to condemn everything out of hand. Instead she decided to build her own school village on traditional African foundations, growing communal crops, learning crafts such as pottery, and respecting the spirituality of the Africans' animist beliefs while having Christ as their chief.

Over the next twenty-five years Mabel Shaw grew to have immense faith in her girl pupils—among whom was the future wife of Kenneth Kaunda—and she described her activities in a number of articles and books in the 1920s and 1930s. These included *Children of the Chief* (1921), *Dawn in Africa: Stories of Girl Life* (1927), and also *God's Candlelights: an Educational Venture in Northern Rhodesia* (1932). What grieved her was the threat of destabilization and degradation resulting from European exploitation of the copperbelt with its shanty towns, alcohol, gambling, and prostitution. She was also appalled by the racist superiority complex of the white colonial settlers.

After laying the foundations for girls' primary education, teacher training, and nursing, and exercising a permanent influence on government and missionary educational policy in Africa, Mabel Shaw retired to Britain in 1940. However, she continued to publicize the cause of African women's education in Britain. She spoke in churches, schools, and colleges (and also on the BBC) making common cause with the anti-colonialist Dr Norman Leys in passionately opposing the British colonial education policy that restricted, via grossly unequal funding, the African child's educational aspirations to what a white child was expected to know by the age of ten.

After long years of crippling arthritis Mabel Shaw died on 25 April 1973 in the Royal Surrey County Hospital, Guildford, Surrey, almost destitute and apparently forgotten. Her great sorrow was that in her last years she had nothing to give those of 'her' African girls who had succeeded in reaching Britain for further education and training. But after she had been cremated her ashes were flown out to Mbereshi where there was a huge memorial service and Mama Shaw could be buried in the chapel grounds of the school she had founded more than half a century before.   SYBIL OLDFIELD

Sources SOAS, Shaw MSS · M. Shaw, 'A school village in Northern Rhodesia', *International Review of Missions* (Oct 1925), 523–36 · O. Wyon, *The three windows: the story of Ann Hunter Small* (1953) · b. cert. · d. cert. · T. Ranger and J. C. Weller, eds., *Themes in the Christian history of central Africa* (1975) · CGPLA Eng. & Wales (1973)
Archives SOAS, corresp. and papers |SOUND BBC WAC
Likenesses photograph, repro. in M. Shaw, *Dawn in Africa* (1927)
Wealth at death £14,903: probate, 4 June 1973, CGPLA Eng. & Wales

Shaw, Martin Edward Fallas (1875–1958), composer, was born on 9 March 1875 at 3 High Street, Kennington, London, the eldest of the nine children of James Shaw (1842–1907), church organist, and his wife, Charlotte Elizabeth James, who had trained as a pianist. A startling birthmark on the left of his face did not make him shy. Brought up in Belsize Park, where he attended a local private school, Martin became organist at Emmanuel Church, Hampstead, in 1895 and entered the Royal College of Music. He liked his tutor, C. V. Stanford, but lacked application and dropped out after two years.

Shaw made friends with the theatre reformer Edward Gordon Craig in 1897. Together they mounted an innovative production of *Dido and Aeneas* for the Purcell Operatic Society in 1900, yet the professional theatre was slow to engage them. Writing incidental music for occasional plays generated very little income for Shaw, who lost his church job in 1903. Though gruff with strangers, he was exuberant among fellow bohemians in Chelsea, where he sported a sombrero, sandals, and cloak. Ralph Vaughan Williams gave him casual work researching old tunes for the *English Hymnal* (1906). Then he conducted for Isadora Duncan, the American dance pioneer (and lover of Craig), on two European tours.

In 1908 Shaw took to the organ loft of St Mary the Virgin, Primrose Hill. Plainsong and chanting suited Percy Dearmer, the unconventional high-church vicar there, who decried sentimental nineteenth-century music. Shaw agreed, sometimes likening the popular hymns of Sir John Stainer, Joseph Barnby, and J. B. Dykes to overripe bananas. The two men sought to revive the purity of earlier sacred song, compiling *The English Carol Book* in 1913; in the same year Shaw co-founded the Summer School of Church Music. He also collaborated with Mabel Dearmer on musical plays for children, including *Brer Rabbit*.

Shaw joined the army in 1914 but was soon discharged owing to bouts of near blindness indirectly caused by diabetes. Fervently patriotic, he campaigned against performances of German music and secured his commercial breakthrough with *Six Songs of War* (1914). His marriage on 24 July 1916 further revitalized him. His wife, Joan Lindley Cobbold (*b*. 1890), was a music teacher from a Suffolk county family. He happily let her manage their lives and turn him into a countryman: a spare, clean-shaven figure in tweed suit and gaiters whose non-musical passions were woodcutting, riding, and farm work (an activity then still possible in Hampstead). Their three children, John,

Diccon, and (Mary) Elizabeth, were born between 1917 and 1923.

Shaw emerged as an artistic crusader: England had to free herself from the musical despotism of Germany. German composers after Bach had taken the path that ended in hysterical emotionalism, and all Europe had followed in the nineteenth-century. But good English music could grow only from wholesome English roots: folk-song and the Elizabethan masters. Vaughan Williams and Holst led the way. Shaw aimed to take English 'national' music to ordinary English people in theatres, schools, and churches, so that they could learn to prefer it. He started by launching the League of Arts in 1918 to provide music for victory celebrations.

Inspired by *The Beggar's Opera*, Shaw composed stage works in ballad opera style with lyrics by Clifford Bax. *Mr Pepys* ran for five weeks at the Royalty Theatre, Soho, in 1926. *The Thorn of Avalon* (1931) mixed Glastonbury legends with May day revels. His final offering, the wistful *Philomel*, flopped in 1932.

More rewarding was Shaw's career as a prolific arranger of choral music for schools. It helped that his brother Geoffrey Shaw (1879–1943), himself a composer, worked for the Board of Education as an inspector of music classes. *The Motherland Song Book*, *Songs of Britain*, and *Girl Guide Hymns and Tunes* contained traditional airs such as 'A frog he would a-wooing go' and 'My bonny cuckoo'. If the settings sounded bland, it had to be conceded that Shaw was catering for amateurs. His artistry is clearer in recital ballads like 'Song of the Palanquin Bearers'.

Shaw made his greatest impact on church music. From 1920 to 1924 he was organist at St Martin-in-the-Fields, London, and he directed the music for Maude Royden's fellowship services until 1936. Two classic publications disseminated his repertory. *Songs of Praise* (1925), edited by Shaw, Vaughan Williams, and Dearmer, replaced Victorian hymns with Tudor and folk-based ones. *The Oxford Book of Carols* (1928) consisted of the trio's choice of traditional religious songs plus new carols by English composers.

With missionary zeal Shaw toured the country, explaining the superiority of *Songs of Praise* to *Hymns Ancient and Modern*. He also composed a stream of anthems and services. Whereas the Victorians favoured triple time and lush chromatic harmonies, Shaw employed quadruple time or irregular groupings and stark quasi-modal harmonies. His works were easy enough for average congregations to sing yet 'progressive' enough to satisfy the fastidious. The growth of Anglo-Catholicism increased demand for liturgical music, and his *Anglican Folk Mass* (1918) spread far and wide.

The archbishop of Canterbury awarded Shaw (and his brother) the Lambeth doctorate of music in 1932. The diocese of Chelmsford employed him as its director of music from 1935 to 1944. A pillar of the church music establishment, he remained too dogmatic about 'Englishness' to get on well with his counterparts Walford Davies and Sydney Nicholson. To 'cultured' Anglicans between the wars, he was a saviour of hymnody and arbiter of taste.

Shaw's activities grew more localized after he left London for Essex in 1936. Half a dozen new choral pieces still appeared each year, notably *The Redeemer* (1944) and *God's Grandeur* (1948). He retired to Suffolk in 1946, became an OBE in 1955, and was elected a fellow of the Royal College of Music shortly before he died at his home, Long Island House, Southwold, on 24 October 1958. After cremation his ashes were interred at Southwold. His wife survived him.

By the end of the twentieth century, the music of Martin Shaw was not much prized. His foes in the cosmopolitan camp had always disparaged it, while even enthusiasts for 'English pastoralism' tended to assume that anything Shaw did, Vaughan Williams could have done better. They preferred to honour him for making the church a haven for other composers of broadly the same school until the 1970s. Certain parishes continued to sing his services, and many more the hymn tunes 'Little Cornard' and 'Marching'. His secular solo songs—the least didactic of his works—retained most critical esteem.   JASON TOMES

Sources E. Routley, *Martin Shaw: a centenary appreciation* (1975) · M. Shaw, *Up to now* (1929) · E. Montgomery Campbell, 'Martin Shaw, OBE, DMus, FRCM, 1875–1958: a personal recollection by his daughter', *English Church Music* (1975), 11–22 · *MT*, 99 (1958), 676–7 · E. A. Craig, *Gordon Craig: the story of his life* (1968) · N. Dearmer, *The life of Percy Dearmer* (1940) · M. Shaw, *The principles of English church music composition* (1921) · M. Shaw, 'Size and colour: a plea for the adjustment of musical values', *MT*, 58 (1917), 203–4 · N. Temperley, *The music of the English parish church*, 2 vols. (1979) · K. R. Long, *The music of the English church* (1972) · E. Routley, *Twentieth century church music* (1964) · b. cert. · m. cert. · d. cert.
Archives BL, letters to G. Parker, Add. MS 69458 · BL, corresp. with Society of Authors, Add. MS 56805
Likenesses photograph, repro. in Shaw, *Up to now*, frontispiece

Shaw [*née* Postans; *other married name* Robinson], **Mary** (1814–1876), singer, the daughter of Thomas Postans, a steward of the officers' mess at St James's Palace, was born at Lea in Kent. From September 1828 to June 1831 she was a student at the Royal Academy of Music, and afterwards became a pupil of Sir George Smart. She made her first appearance in public as a contralto in 1834. At the amateur music festival at Exeter Hall in the November of that year she attracted attention, and in 1835 she sang at the York festival. About the end of the year she married Alfred Shaw, an artist. In 1836 she sang at the Norwich and Liverpool festivals, and at the latter took the contralto part in Mendelssohn's *St Paul* on its first performance in England. After singing at the Gloucester festival in 1838 she took part in the Gewandhaus concerts at Leipzig under Mendelssohn's direction. In a letter to the directors of the Philharmonic Society, dated 19 January 1839, Mendelssohn described Clara Novello and Mrs Shaw as 'the best concert singers we have had in this country for a long time'. Mary Shaw next appeared at La Scala, Milan, on 17 November 1839, in the first performance of Verdi's *Oberto*. In 1842 she returned to England and made her London operatic début at Covent Garden with Adelaide Kemble: she had much success in *Il matrimonio segreto* and *Semiramide*. In 1843 she sang at the Sacred Harmonic Society with Clara Novello and at the Birmingham festival.

Soon afterwards her husband became insane, and her distress affected her voice. She retired from the stage and for three or four years resorted to teaching, appearing in public only at an annual benefit concert. Her husband died in 1847 and eventually she married John Frederick Robinson, a country solicitor, when she finally retired. She died from breast cancer on 9 September 1876 at her husband's residence, Hadleigh Hall, Suffolk.

E. I. CARLYLE, *rev.* J. GILLILAND

Sources Mrs C. Baron-Wilson, *Our actresses*, 2 (1844), 235–8 · J. N. Ireland, *Records of the New York stage, from 1750 to 1860*, 2 (1867), 144–5 · Boase, *Mod. Eng. biog.* · private information (2004) · H. S. Wyndham, *The annals of the Covent Garden Theatre: from 1732 to 1897*, 2 vols. (1906) · *New Grove* · *The Athenaeum* (23 Sept 1876), 411 · D. Hyde, *New-found voices: women in nineteenth-century English music* (1984) · Brown & Stratton, *Brit. mus.* · L. J. De Bekker, *Black's dictionary of music and musicians* (1924)
Likenesses portrait, repro. in *ILN*, 2 (1843), 117 · prints, Harvard TC · woodcut (as Roxy), repro. in *Harper's*, 39 (1895), 590

Shaw, Sir (William) Napier (1854–1945), meteorologist, was born at 84 Vyse Street, Birmingham, on 4 March 1854, third son in a nonconformist family of four brothers and four sisters of Charles Thomas Shaw, manufacturing goldsmith and jeweller, and his wife, Kezia, daughter of Thomas Lawden, gold chain maker, of Birmingham. From King Edward VI School, Birmingham (1862–72), he went as scholar in mathematics to Emmanuel College, Cambridge. In 1876 Shaw was sixteenth wrangler and achieved first class in the natural sciences tripos. The following year he was elected a fellow of his college and started work under Clerk Maxwell at the Cavendish Laboratory. After a period at Freiburg and Berlin universities under Warburg and von Helmholz he returned to Cambridge, becoming joint demonstrator at the Cavendish (with Richard Glazebrook) and eventually assistant director. In 1885 Shaw and Glazebrook's seminal textbook *Practical Physics* was published, and Shaw married Sarah Jane Dugdale, daughter of Thomas Harland MD, of Salford. His wife, a lecturer in mathematics at Newnham College, was a pioneer of colour photography.

Meanwhile, in 1877, the newly formed meteorological council instigated a programme of researches. Among topics chosen was the determination by chemical means of the moisture content of air, and its comparison with readings of conventional instruments. At Maxwell's suggestion this work was passed to Shaw, whose final report was published in *Philosophical Transactions of the Royal Society*, 1888. This was Shaw's earliest involvement with meteorology. It led to his appointment to the Kew committee of the Royal Society in 1894 and the meteorological council in 1897. Three years later he succeeded R. H. Scott as council secretary, a post involving executive control of the Meteorological Office which, at this time, was essentially a clerical organization and practically devoid of science. Shaw, at some financial loss to himself, resigned his Cambridge appointments and set about recruiting staff with professional training in physics, so that the office might become a centre of scientific meteorology.

Following a reorganization in 1905 Shaw acquired the title of director, with enhanced powers. He was also

Sir (William) Napier Shaw (1854–1945), by Bassano, 1911

appointed reader in meteorology at the University of London in 1907. Shaw encouraged study of the upper atmosphere by W. H. Dines and C. J. P. Cave, using kites and balloons. The results of investigations into airflow around north Atlantic pressure systems by Shaw himself and R. G. K. Lempfert were published in their *The Life History of Surface Air Currents* (1906) and formed an important section of Shaw's *Forecasting Weather* (1911). Shaw noted that airflow discontinuities around surface depressions were frequently associated with weather changes and proposed a model incorporating these relationships. But his upper-air studies had convinced him that surface pressure patterns were dictated by happenings at the 9 km level, a hypothesis suggested by Dines, and Shaw never made the step that led the Norwegian, Vilhelm Bjerknes, towards his polar front theory. Shaw supported the pioneering work on numerical methods by L. F. Richardson while another contribution was the Tφ-gram, a thermodynamic diagram with co-ordinates of temperature and entropy still in routine use at the end of the twentieth century. He also showed the importance of meteorology to agriculture and was concerned with investigations into atmospheric pollution. Shaw's vision recognized the international nature of meteorology. He worked hard within the International Meteorological Organization, where his gift for diplomacy proved invaluable. He was president 1907–23 and chaired various committees until 1930— obtaining agreement as to the organization's *modus operandi*, supporting the *Réseau mondiale*, and, with Bjerknes,

achieving international recognition for the millibar as a unit of pressure.

During the First World War the Meteorological Office became heavily involved in the war effort, and for eleven months during 1918–19 Shaw was relieved of routine administration by Colonel H. G. Lyons. A meteorological textbook was needed urgently to train forecasters for operational work with the armed forces, and Shaw spent much of this period in its preparation (*Manual of Meteorology*, pt 4, first edn, 1919). On Shaw's return the future of the office came into question. Shaw fought for it to be placed under the aegis of the Department of Scientific and Industrial Research, and evidence presented to the relevant cabinet committee supported his views. But Winston Churchill, then secretary for war and air, tabled a strong minute stressing the importance of meteorology to the RAF, and the office was eventually absorbed into the Air Ministry. However, Shaw delayed his retirement and succeeded in retaining as great a degree of independence for it as circumstances permitted. He retired from the office in 1920, but from 1920 to 1924 occupied a new chair of meteorology at Imperial College. A source of sadness was the loss of his wife, who died childless in 1923, but his crowning work was to follow in the completion of his *Manual of Meteorology* (4 vols., 1926–31). This work, in which he was assisted by Miss E. E. Austin, was the most comprehensive treatment of meteorology in English at that time. It was followed by a more popular and somewhat idiosyncratic book, *The Drama of Weather* (1933).

The later Shaw was a courteous man of distinguished appearance, with penetrating blue eyes and outstanding eyebrows. He contributed some 381 publications to the literature and received many honours, both at home and abroad. He was knighted in 1915, was president of the Royal Meteorological Society in 1918–19, of the mathematics and physics section of the British Association in 1908, of its educational science section in 1919, and chairman of the advisory committee on atmospheric pollution in 1917–25. Shaw was elected FRS in 1891, made commander of the order of St Iago da Espada (Portugal) in 1921, and awarded a royal medal in 1923. He received honorary degrees from the universities of Aberdeen, Edinburgh, Manchester, Dublin, Athens, and Harvard, was Halley lecturer at Oxford in 1918, Rede lecturer at Cambridge in 1921, and was elected an honorary foreign member of the American Academy of Arts and Sciences, the Accademia dei Lincei, and other learned societies. Shaw died at his home, 171 Old Brompton Road, Kensington, London, on 23 March 1945, and was buried at Key Hill cemetery, Birmingham.   JIM BURTON

Sources E. Gold, *Obits. FRS*, 5 (1945–8), 203–30 · R. Corless and E. Gold, *Quarterly Journal of the Royal Meteorological Society*, 71 (1945), 187–94 · R. G. K. Lempfert, *Nature*, 155 (1945), 688–91 · D. Brunt, *Monthly Notices of the Royal Astronomical Society*, 106 (1946), 35–7 · O. M. Ashford, *Prophet—or professor: the life and work of Lewis Fry Richardson* (1985) · R. M. Friedman, *Appropriating the weather* (1989) · CUL, Shaw MSS, Add. MSS 8124 and 8434 · Shaw correspondence, RS · N. Shaw, 'The march of meteorology', *Quarterly Journal of the Royal Meteorological Society*, 60 (1934), 99–124 · Catalogue of Emmanuel College portraits [by permission of the master, fellows, and scholars of Emmanuel College] • D.-W. Kim, 'J. J. Thomson and the emergence of the Cavendish school, 1885–1900', *British Journal for the History of Science*, 28 (1995), 191–226 • private information (2004) • d. cert.

Archives CUL, corresp. and papers; lecture notebook and corrected proofs of *The air and its ways* • RS

Likenesses Bassano, vintage print, 1911, NPG [*see illus.*] • W. Stoneman, photograph, 1917, NPG • W. Russell, oils, 1920, Emmanuel College, Cambridge; copy of original, the latter formerly in possession of meteorological office • memorial plaque, U. Cam., Rayleigh Library • oils, World Meteorological Organization, Geneva, Switzerland • photograph, U. Cam., Rayleigh Library

Wealth at death £33,005 17s. 4d.: probate, 27 July 1945, *CGPLA Eng. & Wales*

Shaw, Patrick (1796–1872), legal writer, was born at Ayr, the son of Charles Shaw, clerk of the county of Ayr, and his wife, Barbara Wright, the daughter of a customs official at Greenock. His grandfather was David Shaw DD, moderator of the general assembly of the Church of Scotland in 1775, who is referred to by Burns in the 'Twa Herds' (Burns, *Poetical Works*, ed. Chambers, 1836, 56). Alexander *Shaw, Sir Charles *Shaw (1795–1871), and John *Shaw (1792–1827) were his brothers. In boyhood Patrick lost a leg through an accident.

In 1819 Shaw was called to the Scottish bar, and in 1821 he commenced with his friend James Ballantine, and afterwards with Alexander Dunlop, a series of reports entitled *Cases Decided in the Court of Session*. In 1824 he commenced a similar series of reports of decisions in the House of Lords on appeal from the Scottish courts. These reports and others, covering other Scottish courts, remain valuable as historical records of precedent, and Shaw enhanced their contemporary usefulness by publishing supplementary digests of the decisions.

In 1848 Shaw was appointed sheriff of chancery, and he held the post until 1869, when he resigned owing to failing health. On 12 January 1860 he married Susan Khanim, the fourth daughter of William Fullarton of Skeldon, Ayrshire. Shaw died at his home, 36 Charlotte Square, Edinburgh, on 12 February 1872. He was survived by his wife.

E. I. CARLYLE, *rev.* H. J. SPENCER

Sources *The Scotsman* (16 Feb 1872) • *Fasti Scot.* • Allibone, *Dict.* • IGI • NA Scot., SC 70/1/156/911

Wealth at death £17,919 15s. 7d.: Scottish inventory resealed in England, 5 April 1872, *CGPLA Eng. & Wales*; NA Scot., SC 70/1/156/911

Shaw, Percy (1890–1976), manufacturer and inventor of the catseye road stud, was born on 15 April 1890 at Heginbottom Fold, 32 Ovenden Road, Halifax, the second son of James Shaw (1843–1929), a Halifax dyer's labourer, and his second wife, Esther Hannah Morrell (1856–1922), daughter of Joseph and Grace Morrell of Shelf, near Halifax. In 1891 nine of the fourteen children of his father's two marriages were living at home, and in the following year the family moved to 1 Mill Lane, Boothtown, Halifax, which remained Percy Shaw's home for the rest of his life.

From childhood, Shaw demonstrated a spirit of

Percy Shaw (1890–1976), by Peter Laurie, 1958

resourcefulness, contributing to the family budget by hawking home-produced fruit, herbs, and vegetables around the neighbourhood. He received his earliest education at Boothtown board school, leaving at the age of thirteen to commence work as a labourer at a blanket mill, but later attending evening classes in shorthand and bookkeeping. Low wages compelled him to abandon an apprenticeship with a Halifax wire manufacturer, and after a succession of jobs in welding, boilermaking, and machine tool construction, he went into partnership with his father in a small business specializing in the repair of mangle rollers, which supplied government contracts for cartridge cases, shell noses, and heddle wire during the First World War. After his father's death, Shaw built up a flourishing business constructing macadamized paths and drives, for which he developed a miniature motorized roller.

An early motoring enthusiast, Shaw's experience of negotiating the hazardous descent from Queensbury to Halifax after the removal of the tramlines, which had guided the motorist at night and in fog, induced a concern to improve road safety. Whether it was the reflection of his car headlamps on a reflective roadsign, as Shaw insisted in 1968, or his brother Cecil's perhaps apocryphal story of a cat's eyes transfixed in a beam of light, he realized by 1934 the need for reflecting studs set into the road surface as markers on unlit roads. A patent for a prototype road stud, in the shape of a Maltese cross, was approved in 1935 and a company formed, with the catseye as its registered trademark, and Percy Shaw as managing director. Initially, luminous glass lenses were obtained from Czechoslovakia and rubber pads from Manchester, but subsequently all components were manufactured and assembled on a 20 acre site at Boothtown, adjacent to Shaw's home. A series of further patents modified the original design, including the incorporation of a self-wiping mechanism, but orders were slow until Ministry of Transport backing, and the Second World War blackout, provided a major boost to production. Widening markets after the war ensured continuing expansion. In 1965 Shaw was appointed OBE for services to exports, and by the time of his death in 1976 some 15 million catseyes had been manufactured.

The broadcasters Richard Dimbleby and Alan Whicker travelled to Halifax in 1952 and 1968 respectively to interview Shaw—by now a celebrity—whose invention Whicker succinctly described as 'a blinking marvel' ('The world of Whicker: Whicker with the catseyes man on the road from Rose Linda's', Yorkshire Television, 1968). Photographic and film archive reveals Shaw in later life as an engagingly eccentric Yorkshireman, short-statured, with Churchillian features, a droll sense of humour, and a penchant for straw hats.

It was widely, if inaccurately, assumed that Shaw's invention had made him a multi-millionaire. While Shaw himself often joked about his high tax liability, rumours of a £17 million personal fortune were repeatedly denied, and probate records reveal a relatively modest personal estate of £193,500. Apart from the luxury of a customized Rolls-Royce and a profusion of television sets, Shaw's lifestyle was essentially unostentatious. He owned only two suits and often appeared attired in worn, moth-eaten pullovers. Alan Whicker compared the spartan atmosphere of the living-room at his home at Boothtown to a railway station waiting-room. Shaw rejected conventional domestic adornments such as curtains or carpets, cooked all his own meals, and stacked crockery and cutlery on open shelves, thus dispensing with the need for cupboards. Indeed, he was a somewhat reclusive figure in later years, rarely visiting his factory, except when it was closed, or leaving his home, except to play a round of golf. He died on 1 September 1976, a bachelor, at the age of eighty-six, from cancer and heart disease. An agnostic, towards the end of his life Shaw developed a close personal friendship with a local Methodist minister, who conducted his funeral service at Boothtown Methodist Church and cremation at Park Wood, Elland, on 6 September 1976.

JOHN A. HARGREAVES

Sources J. A. Hargreaves, 'The catseye man: Percy Shaw of Halifax, road stud manufacturer, 1890–1976', *Transactions of the Halifax Antiquarian Society*, new ser., 4 (1996), 126–34 · F. Edwards, *Cats eyes* (1972) · *Evening Courier* [Halifax] (2 Sept 1976) · *The Times* (3 Sept 1976) · private information (2004) · b. cert. · d. cert. · patents, 1935–52 · newspaper cuttings file, Halifax Courier Library · J. J. Mulroy, ed., *The story of the town that bred us* (1948) · L. Wells, 'A million eyes lead you home', *Highway Times* (Feb 1960), 8 · F. Edwards, 'The cats-eye man', *Yorkshire Life* (Dec 1967) · census returns, 1891, PRO, RG 12/3603/ED4, p. 26, fol. 72 · admissions register, Boothtown board school, 1893–1903, W. Yorks. AS, Calderdale, OR/ED 256 iii [microfilm] · *News Chronicle* (28 Nov 1939) · newspaper cuttings file, Calderdale Central Library

Archives FILM 'The world of Whicker: Whicker with the catseyes man on the road from Rose Linda's' [Yorkshire Television documentary, 1968] | SOUND 'Halifax down your way' [BBC radio broadcast, 28 Nov 1952]

Likenesses photograph, 1913, Boothtown Mansion, 1 Mill Lane, Boothtown, Halifax · double portrait, photograph, 1949 (with HRH Princess Elizabeth), Studio Lambert · double portrait, photograph, 1952 (with Richard Dimbleby), Kemsley Newspapers · P. Laurie, photograph, 1958, Hult. Arch. [see *illus.*] · J. Van Dalen, oils, 1960, Boothtown Mansion, 1 Mill Lane, Boothtown, Halifax · three photographs, 1967, repro. in *She* · double portrait, photograph, 1968 (with Alan Whicker), Yorkshire Television Ltd · double portrait, photograph, 1972 (with Florence Edwards), repro. in *Halifax Courier*

Wealth at death £193,500: probate, 3 Dec 1976, *CGPLA Eng. & Wales*

Shaw, Peter (1694–1763), physician and author, was born in March 1694 in Lichfield, Staffordshire, the youngest of the four children of Robert Shaw (c.1650–1704), master of Lichfield grammar school, and his wife, Ann (b. c.1658). He was baptized in St Mary's Church, Lichfield, on 9 April 1694. Nothing is known of his education, though he evidently acquired competence in Latin and studied medicine, perhaps at a foreign university. When in the early 1720s he embarked on a career in London as an author and translator of medical works, he styled himself MD.

Shaw's first two publications, both of which appeared in 1723, were *A Treatise of Incurable Diseases* and an edition of the *Praelectiones pharmaceuticae* by the apothecary John Quincy. The following year, the anonymous work *The Juice of the Grape* was ascribed to him. His *New Practice of Physic* (1726) comprised a catalogue of diseases with diagnostic signs, prognoses, and the appropriate regimen for each, said to be drawn from the practice of the leading physicians of London; the book was remarkably successful, reaching a seventh edition in 1753. Shaw also turned his talents to editing and translating the works of prominent scientific writers. He produced an abridged and 'methodized' edition of *The Philosophical Works of the Honourable Robert Boyle* (3 vols., 1725), and, later, *The Philosophical Works of Francis Bacon* (3 vols., 1733). He pioneered the introduction into England of continental works on chemistry, collaborating with the encyclopaedia writer Ephraim Chambers to bring out *New Method of Chemistry* (1727), a translation of a work by Herman Boerhaave. This translation was prepared from a French edition, unauthorized by the author, and from student notes of Boerhaave's lectures at Leiden. Shaw added extensive footnotes, comparing Boerhaave's doctrines with those of Newton and his English followers. In 1730 he produced a digest of the Jena lectures of Georg Ernst Stahl, *Philosophical Principles of Universal Chemistry*.

Shaw followed these publications with works of his own, designed to encourage the development of chemistry as a science of potentially widespread utility. His *Three Essays in Artificial Philosophy or Universal Chemistry* (1731) directed attention particularly to the distillation and fermentation of liquors. With the instrument maker Francis Hauksbee the younger, Shaw published, in 1731, *Proposals for a Course of Chemical Experiments* and *An Essay for Introducing a Portable Laboratory*. The latter was accompanied by the offer for sale of a new design for a portable chemical furnace. The same year, Shaw embarked on a series of lectures on chemistry and its applications, delivered in London in 1731 and 1732, and in Scarborough the following year. His *Chemical Lectures* was published in 1734.

In 1733 Shaw moved from London to Scarborough, where he found a fashionable audience for his lectures among visitors to the spa. He entered into collaboration with a Scarborough apothecary, Culmer Cockerill, and the London booksellers Ward and Chandler, to promote the medical benefits of the waters. Having already published *New Experiments and Observations upon Mineral Waters* (1731), a translation of a work by Friedrich Hoffman, Shaw followed up with his own *Inquiry into the Contents, Virtues, and Uses of the Scarborough Spaw-Waters* (1734), and the anonymous *Dissertation on the Contents, Virtues, and Uses of Cold and Hot Mineral Springs* (1735). About this time, he married Frances Tidmarsh (1700–1768), the widow of Richard Tidmarsh and daughter of John Hyde of Sundridge, Kent. The couple had four children, Jane, Peter, Elizabeth, who married the physician Richard Warren, and Margaret.

Shaw's popularity among the fashionable nobility and gentry in Scarborough enabled him to develop a successful career in medical practice, which displaced authorship as his primary occupation. He benefited from a growing reputation as a doctor, and his connections with prominent society figures and physicians proved valuable when he moved back to London in 1738. The same year, he defended the controversial claims of Joanna Stephens to have discovered an effective medicine for dissolving urinary calculi. Shaw published an *Examination of the Reasons for and Against the Subscription for a Medicament for the Stone* and *Inquiries on the Nature of Miss Stephens's Medicaments*, both in 1738. Having been summoned in 1739 by the censor's board of the Royal College of Physicians for practising without a licence in the capital, Shaw became a licentiate of the college in 1740, and subsequently (in 1754) a fellow. The patronage of Sir Edward Hulse, a court physician, and later physician to the duke of Newcastle, aided Shaw's rise to a prominent position in the medical profession. In 1751 he was granted an MD degree from Cambridge University by royal mandate, and he became a fellow of the Royal Society the following year. In 1753 he was appointed physician-extraordinary and later physician-in-ordinary to George II, and regularly accompanied the king on his visits to Hanover. He also attended the duke of Newcastle and his family, and the duke of Grafton. On the accession of George III, in 1760, he was confirmed as physician-in-ordinary to the new monarch.

Shaw died in London on 15 March 1763. His wife survived him. He was buried in the nave of Wimbledon church, where there is an inscription to his memory. Shaw's son-in-law, Richard Warren, spoke warmly of him in his Harveian oration of 1768.   JAN GOLINSKI

Sources F. W. Gibbs, 'Peter Shaw and the revival of chemistry', *Annals of Science*, 7 (1951), 211–37 · J. Golinski, 'Peter Shaw: chemistry and communication in Augustan England', *Ambix*, 30 (1983), 19–29 · Munk, *Roll*
Archives Suffolk RO, Bury St Edmunds, papers mainly relating to Commons petition | Wellcome L., letter to T. Robinson
Likenesses oils, *c*.1740, RCP Lond. · oils, *c*.1740–1750, RCP Lond. · portraits, RCP Lond.
Wealth at death see will, Suffolk RO

Shaw, Ralph (*d.* 1484). *See under* Shaw, Sir Edmund (*d.* 1488).

Shaw, Richard Norman (1831–1912), architect, was born in Edinburgh on 7 May 1831. His father, William Shaw (*c*.1779–1833), was an Irish protestant, the son of a Dublin coach builder; at the time of the child's birth, he was an

Richard Norman Shaw (1831–1912), by Ralph W. Robinson, 1889

Edinburgh lace merchant in impoverished circumstances, and he died less than two years later. Norman was the surname of the boy's paternal grandmother, who came from co. Meath, Ireland. His mother, Elizabeth Brown (1785–1883), was the daughter of an Edinburgh notary. There were six children, of whom only three survived to full adulthood. Richard, the youngest, went to school at the Hill Street Academy, Edinburgh, and afterwards for a year at Newcastle; but his education was chiefly imparted by his sister Janet (1818–1902).

Education Shaw's elder brother Robert Ewart Shaw (1823–1864) moved south to London in the 1840s and joined a firm of shipping agents; in 1858 he was to become a co-founder of the successful Shaw Savill Line, running steamers to and from New Zealand. A cousin, James William Temple (1821–1898), was closely associated in shipping with Robert Shaw, directed the Shaw Savill Line after his early death, and was to be an important client of his brother's. To London, therefore, Elizabeth Shaw took her other two children about 1846, to live at first in Dalston, and later near Swiss Cottage. After a period in an unknown architect's office, Richard Shaw took articles in the Piccadilly office of a fellow Scot, William Burn, between 1849 and 1854. Burn was then in the full tide of his career. In 1844 he had transferred his practice from Edinburgh to London, and was designing mansions for territorial magnates in all parts of Great Britain and Ireland. Under Burn, Shaw was well schooled in the art of planning country houses, and acquired a clean, clear style of draughtsmanship. Here he also met the equally promising but more privileged William Eden Nesfield, his future partner. The two soon became fervent Goths, sketched details of the Palace of Westminster, and even went to Pugin's funeral in 1852.

Shaw also attended the Royal Academy's architecture school, then under the direction of the classicist C. R. Cockerell, whom he later revered. Here he drew notice by winning the silver medal (1852), the gold medal (1853), and the travelling studentship (1854). For much of 1854–6 Shaw was on the continent, sometimes alone, sometimes with Nesfield or other young architects, sometimes with his mother and sister, who settled for a time outside Stuttgart. Chiefly he drew Gothic churches in France, Germany, Italy, and the Low Countries. The fruit of these tours was his *Architectural Sketches from the Continent* (1858), a picturesque compilation of the then fashionable continental Gothic. The sheets for the book were mostly lithographed by Shaw himself from his drawings.

In 1856–8 Shaw worked in the office of Nesfield's uncle Anthony Salvin, but in 1858 he joined the avant-garde of the Gothic revival by taking over from Philip Webb as chief assistant to George Edmund Street, the church architect. Street was then in the most creative phase of his career. He imbued all his assistants (among them at this time the brothers J. D. and Edmund Sedding) with the conscience of the building artist. This personal sense of aesthetic creation was to remain as clear in Shaw's Gothic churches as in his 'free classic' or 'Queen Anne' buildings. But Street, a rapid designer, would never let his staff even design a keyhole, so Shaw recollected. He was obliged to bide his time and limit his creativity largely to drawings for exhibition and a striking bookcase-cum-desk (1861), now in the Victoria and Albert Museum.

Early career In 1862 Shaw at last began practice and next year took an office with Nesfield at 30 Argyll Street, near Oxford Circus. There was a partnership between 1866 and 1869 but they mainly looked after each other's jobs, and never worked jointly on a design. Most of Shaw's early commissions were domestic. For these, following a tour looking at cottages and farmhouses in the Sussex weald made with Nesfield in September 1862, he evolved his 'Old English' or, as he himself called it, 'Old Sussex' style. This took as a basis the type of informal house planning latterly favoured by Burn, but Shaw's houses were smaller in scale, suppler, and prettier. Picturesque details such as tile-hanging, half-timbering, and tall chimneys were partly suggested by the cottages of George Devey, but pulled together with a discipline learned from the domestic work of Street and William Butterfield.

The first such important commissions were the extensions to Willesley outside Cranbrook (1864–5) for the artist John Callcott Horsley RA, through whose friendship Shaw met later clients, including many academician painters. Two houses at Groombridge, Sussex—Glen Andred (1866–8) for the painter E. W. Cooke and Leyswood (1868–70) for J. W. Temple, who was prospering as director of the Shaw Savill Line—brought the Old English style to maturity and a certain suavity. Leyswood was the first of Shaw's

houses to be illustrated by seductive perspectives at the Royal Academy exhibition; reproduced in the *Building News*, they were to make Shaw internationally known. By 1870, when he began extending Cragside, Northumberland, for Sir William Armstrong, he had risen to join the ranks of the country's leading architects. That reputation was confirmed by his first conspicuous effort in London, the Shaw Savill Line's New Zealand Chambers of 1871–3, whose projecting bays and Jacobean glazings offered spectacular protest against humdrum city classicalities.

Alongside their Old English country and suburban houses, Nesfield and Shaw were meanwhile exploring the new Queen Anne vocabulary of red-brick walls, tiled roofs, and white sash-barred windows informally disposed, as pioneered by such architects as Philip Webb, J. J. Stevenson, and E. R. Robson. During the 1870s this became the favoured medium for Shaw's London houses, and gave a new sense of building to dwellers in square, blank-windowed rooms and monotonous, drab streets. Lowther Lodge, Kensington Gore (later the Royal Geographical Society), is the most expansive early example of this approach—a town house standing in its own grounds and having style in the practical sense of its needs. A leaner, more playful, and more flexible mood is manifest in Shaw's many Queen Anne studio houses built for painters in Kensington and Hampstead. They include the pair for Luke Fildes and Marcus Stone in Melbury Road, Kensington, and two successive homes in Hampstead for Edwin Long, of which the second and more restrained one, 42 Netherhall Gardens (1887–8), has been demolished. To the same genre belongs the tall, almost gaunt house Shaw built for himself and his family at 6 Ellerdale Road, Hampstead (1874–6). He had married Agnes Haswell Wood (1847–1932), an Australian by birth, in 1867. They began life together next door to his mother's house near Swiss Cottage. The first drawings for Ellerdale Road were made on the day their third and last child was born.

Major commissions In 1876 Shaw finally parted company from Nesfield and took a larger office at 29 Bloomsbury Square. He was soon busy with a plethora of commissions, ranging from a church at Ilkley to grand stone mansions at Adcote, Shropshire, and Flete, Devon, several Queen Anne and Old English houses, the restyling of flats at Albert Hall Mansions, and the rescue after its slow start of the aesthetic suburb projected by Jonathan Carr at Bedford Park. Here Shaw designed not the layout but a variety of house types, the group of church, stores, and inn, a club, and a personal house for Carr, before handing over this radical but unremunerative job to assistants and followers. At about this time his health began to give way. It remained unreliable until the autumn of 1881, when Shaw much improved after a visit to Aix-les-Bains. During this period he learned to delegate work and offer generous leeway in detailing (and sometimes even elevating, though never in planning) to his assistants. Many were to become well-known architects, among them Ernest Newton, E. S. Prior, Mervyn Macartney, Gerald Horsley, R. W. Schultz, and W. R. Lethaby.

Later years During the 1880s Shaw moved towards a quieter style, in which he held ingenious planning, sound building, and English tradition dearer than originality. His domestic jobs consisted more often of extensions in a manner akin to the original building (as at The Rookery, Bromley Common; Walhampton, Hampshire; Moor Place, Much Hadham, Hertfordshire; Shavington Hall, Shropshire; Didlington, Norfolk) or of town houses in an outright neo-Georgian style (Bolney House, Ennismore Gardens, and 170 Queen's Gate). He could still be dynamic, as in his flamboyant offices in the 'Franco-Flemish' manner for the Alliance Assurance Company at the bottom of St James's Street, and would design houses in his former styles for clients who asked for that, but his heart was less in them. He preferred to rely on good builders, troubled much about technicalities such as foundations, boilers, drains, and plumbing, and took a conservative view of interior design, in which he favoured a simple richness. Shaw's first and only complete public building, the original portion of New Scotland Yard (now Norman Shaw North), constructed in 1887–90 for the Metropolitan Police, displays the strength, energy, good craftsmanship, wise planning, and preference for character rather than style which prevailed in his thinking at this time.

After Queen Victoria's golden jubilee Shaw was increasingly drawn to a full-blooded classical or imperial architecture, of which the entrance to New Scotland Yard was an early symptom. In this last phase of his career he repented of Gothic (except for churches) and yearned for the spirit of Jones, Wren, and Cockerell. Important houses he designed in this manner were the severely symmetrical Bryanston, Dorset (1889–94)—ingenious in plan but ponderous, and proof perhaps that mansions for the aristocracy were not Shaw's forte—and large extensions at Chesters and Haggerston Castle, both in Northumberland. But his chief contribution to the so-called Edwardian baroque style came after his official retirement in 1896. By then Shaw was widely regarded as the doyen of British architects. He was much in demand as a consultant to contribute street elevations, assess competitions, and otherwise influence a number of major planning schemes and buildings in London and Liverpool. To his advice for the London county council and other bodies were owed several attempts to endow the capital with imperial dignity. As with Wren, so with Shaw, his attempts to straighten out the haphazard muddle of London were mostly blocked. The most consequential of such projects was the rebuilding of the Regent Street quadrant and Piccadilly Circus, for which Shaw acted as consultant to the crown estate commissioners. His costly and weighty elevations for the Piccadilly Hotel were built, but the rest of his ambitious scheme fell into a slough of mixed opinions and vested interests from which it could not be extricated. He resigned in disappointment eight months before his death, which occurred at his home at 6 Ellerdale Road, Hampstead, on 17 November 1912. He was buried on 21 November at Hampstead church, where there is a tomb designed by Ernest Newton, leaving an estate valued for probate at over £100,000.

Though a private personality and something of an innocent abroad in public life, Shaw had firm loyalties. Chief among these was his adherence to the Royal Academy, which elected him an associate in 1872 and Royal Academician in 1877. He was assiduous at the academy's evening classes in architecture, where his encouragement and banter were appreciated by the students; he regularly helped choose and hang the annual exhibitions, and he made important alterations to Burlington House. Conversely, Shaw disliked the Royal Institute of British Architects (RIBA), which he looked upon as a mere trade union. It was he more than others who picked the quarrel with the RIBA that gave rise to the essays published in *Architecture: a Profession or an Art*, which he edited in 1891 with T. G. Jackson. Shaw's contribution to this volume, upholding the view that architecture is first and foremost an art, is his only published essay of substance. Yet he wrote perceptive and witty letters to clients and other correspondents of all sorts.

In 1884 the Art Workers' Guild was founded mainly by assistants of Shaw, with their master's blessing. But he took only a distant and benevolent interest in its work, and though he intermittently designed some very fine furniture and fittings before 1880 he cannot really be called an arts and crafts architect. Shaw loved the art of Burne-Jones but was averse to William Morris's socialism and felt that Philip Webb's architecture, though fine, manifested a 'liking for the ugly'. While trusting, admiring, and promoting his intellectual chief assistant, Lethaby, he admitted to not understanding him. It is symptomatic of his changing tastes that his assortment of blue and white Nanking porcelain, representing the avant-garde taste of the 1860s, was largely superseded in later life by a collection of clocks and clockwork mechanisms.

Norman Shaw (as he was latterly called) was one of the most fertile of all British architects, comparable in breadth of invention perhaps only to John Nash and Edwin Lutyens (who much admired Shaw in his early years). In power of design he was consistently ingenious, to the point of restlessness. His approach to style was intuitive and does not respond well to the weight of rational or progressivist analysis. Nevertheless there is a sense of discipline, power, balance, and breadth in most of his architecture. He cared more about planning and composition than refinement of detail. An able and solid constructor, he was at perfect ease with modern materials such as iron beams and mass or reinforced concrete. But he saw them as devices on which he could play the tunes he wanted, not instruments with a destiny of their own. Puritanical critics at the time and since have found Shaw's pragmatic indifference to structural 'truth' shocking.

The respective contributions of Shaw and Nesfield to the new ease and freshness of English domestic architecture in the 1860s and 1870s are hard to disentangle. Nesfield had the earlier big opportunities and the loftier connections. He more often chose the Queen Anne style when building in the countryside, and was the abler draughtsman, ornamentalist, and interior designer, but he was a less amenable personality and in due course lost ambition. Shaw devoted more of his time to creating a gamut of styles for bourgeois houses in town and country that were reliable, flexible, alert to character and context, and expertly planned. Theirs was a shared and equal venture; but Shaw proved in the end to have the more equable temperament and the stronger appetite for work.

Both as a stylist and as a person of charm, vitality, reliability, generosity, modesty, and honour, Shaw had a powerful effect upon British architecture up to the First World War. The influence of his Old English houses was most fully felt outside Britain in Australia and America, but penetrated into non-English-speaking parts of the world. Nevertheless the admiring picture drawn in Hermann Muthesius's book *Das englische Haus* of Shaw as the founder of a school of domestic architecture is one which its individualistic subject would have found impossible to recognize.

Shaw was a tall, handsome man, with fair hair, a slight drawl, a genial personality, and a developed sense of the ludicrous. He was always subject to ill health from mid-life onwards. The home life of the Shaws was harmonious and quiet, since his wife was not sociable. Despite his Presbyterian mother, Shaw himself was a committed high-church Anglican who worshipped at St Mary Magdalene, Munster Square. His daughter Elizabeth Helen (1868–1952) became an Anglican nun with the Sisters of Bethany, for whom in the 1870s Shaw had designed an inventive convent building at Boscombe, Hampshire, using concrete. Though principally known as a domestic architect—'You know I am not a Church man, I am a house man', he wrote to J. D. Sedding, 'and soil pipes are my speciality' (Saint, *Richard Norman Shaw*, 274)—Shaw restored several Anglican churches and built no fewer than sixteen new ones, never departing far from the Gothic style which had been his youthful enthusiasm. The finest of these, such as Holy Trinity, Bingley, Yorkshire (1866–8; dem.), All Saints', Leek, Staffordshire (1884–6), and All Saints', Richards Castle, Shropshire (1891–3), can stand comparison with the best churches by Street or G. F. Bodley, whom Shaw latterly regarded as Britain's foremost church architect.   ANDREW SAINT

Sources A. Saint, *Richard Norman Shaw* (1976) · R. Blomfield, *Richard Norman Shaw R.A.* (1940) · Robert Shaw's notes on his father, 1930–39, RIBA BAL · H. Muthesius, *Das englische Haus*, 3 vols. (Berlin, 1904–5), vol. 1, pp. 109–33 · A. Saint, 'Norman Shaw's letters: a selection', *Architectural History*, 18 (1975), 60–85 · P. Ferriday, ed., *Victorian architecture* (1963), 237–46 · CGPLA Eng. & Wales (1912)
Archives RIBA, family corresp. and accounts | BL, letters to G. L. Craik and D. M. Craik, Add. MS 61896 · RA, letters to Royal Academy · RIBA, letters to Arthur Keen
Likenesses J. C. Horsley, portrait, oils, exh. RA 1886, Aberdeen Art Gallery, MacDonald Collection · R. W. Robinson, photograph, 1889, NPG [*see illus.*] · J. C. Horsley, oils; known to be in priv. coll. in 1970 · Lock & Whitfield, woodburytype photograph, NPG; repro. in T. Cooper, *Men of mark: a gallery of contemporary portraits* (1883) · W. H. Thornycroft, plaque, New Scotland Yard, London, Norman Shaw North Building
Wealth at death £105,185 16s. 4d.: resworn probate, 13 Dec 1912, CGPLA Eng. & Wales

Shaw, Robert Archibald (1927–1978), actor and writer, was born on 9 August 1927 at 51 King Street, Westhoughton, Lancashire, the son of Thomas Shaw (d. 1939), a general practitioner, and his wife, Doreen Avery, a nurse from Pigg's Peak, Swaziland. In 1933 his father relocated to Stromness in the Orkneys, where the proud, precocious boy developed a lifelong sense of being an outsider.

Following a move to Somerset, Dr Shaw succumbed to recurrent bouts of alcoholism and depression, and committed suicide in 1939. His death had a profound effect on his son, who became increasingly self-reliant, competitive, moody, and sentimental while boarding at Truro School (1939–45). Here he proved so proficient at sport that he was offered a trial by Wigan rugby league club.

But it was acting that had captured his imagination, and Shaw enrolled at the Royal Academy of Dramatic Art in September 1946. Despite an initial rebellion against the system, he proved a dedicated student and, on graduating, took a diploma in drama at London University.

He joined the Shakespeare Memorial Theatre at Stratford in 1949, making his professional début as Angus in *Macbeth*. Having toured Australia with the company (1949–50), he fell out with its artistic director, John Gielgud, and was 'discovered' by Alec Guinness, who secured him a part in the film of *The Lavender Hill Mob* (1951), although most of his performance ended on the cutting-room floor. Later that year he was recruited for the Old Vic by Tyrone Guthrie. While on tour in 1952, he met and married Jennifer Bourke in Bulawayo, Rhodesia. The couple had four daughters, but the marriage ended in divorce.

Shaw's professional prospects had begun to look increasingly grim, and he turned to book reviewing to supplement his income from occasional stage and BBC assignments and minor supporting roles in films like *The Dambusters* (1954). Indeed, he was contemplating a job in a Heinz beans factory when he was offered the part of Dan Tempest in the CBS television series *The Buccaneers*, which ran for thirty-nine episodes from September 1956. The show helped to make Shaw's name in the United States, but it also engendered a 'can do' brashness that cost him the respect of the British theatrical establishment.

Denied work, Shaw wrote *Off the Mainland*, only for it to close after just six weeks at the Arts Theatre in the summer of 1956. However, he was rescued by George Devine, who cast him in *Live Like Pigs* at the Royal Court in January 1958. Acclaimed performances followed in Willis Hall's *The Long and the Short and the Tall* (1959) and Harold Pinter's *The Caretaker* on Broadway in October 1961.

Shaw's literary career had also taken off. He once claimed he would 'rather go down as having written one good novel than be acclaimed as a great actor' (Carmean and Gaston, 131) and, following his respectable début, *The Hiding Place* (1959), he won the Hawthornden prize with *The Sun Doctor* (1961). His later works, *The Flag* (1965), *The Man in the Glass Booth* (1967), and *A Card from Morocco* (1969), were worthy but less admired.

In the autumn of 1961, Shaw fathered two children—his fourth daughter, Katherine, with Jennifer, and a son, Colin, with the actress Mary Ure (1933–1975), whom he

Robert Archibald Shaw (1927–1978), by Bob Collins, c.1958

had met in New York. They married on 13 April 1963, just two weeks before the birth of a daughter, Elizabeth, the second of their four children. Meanwhile, Shaw had excelled as SPECTRE agent Red Grant in the film of Ian Fleming's James Bond blockbuster *From Russia with Love* (1963). He also impressed as Claudius in a 400th anniversary production of *Hamlet*, the first to be recorded at Elsinore. But fame and fortune still eluded him. Plans for screen adaptations of Len Deighton's *The Ipcress File* and Thomas Hardy's *The Mayor of Casterbridge* foundered, and he came to resent the success of 'angry young men' such as Richard Harris and Albert Finney.

Shaw finally landed his first lead in *The Luck of Ginger Coffey* (1964), one of the earliest Canadian feature films to make an international impact. Wealth came through a profits percentage in *A Man for All Seasons* (1965), directed by Fred Zinnemann, in which he gave an Oscar-nominated performance as Henry VIII. But stardom continued to elude him, following the cool receptions accorded *Custer of the West* (1967), *The Birthday Party* (1968), and *Figures in a Landscape* (1971), for which he also wrote the screenplay. He fared only marginally better as Lord Randolph Churchill in *Young Winston* (1972) and as a subway hijacker in *The Taking of Pelham 123* (1974).

Shaw's stage fortunes were similarly mixed. The Broadway musical *Gantry* (1970) closed after only four performances, while *Cato Street* (1971), which he wrote for Sir Laurence Olivier, also flopped. His personal life was equally traumatic, as he became increasingly dependent on alcohol after Mary Ure's fatal overdose on 3 April 1975. The following July, however, he married the family nanny, Virginia (Jay) Jansen, with whom he had his ninth child, Thomas, in December 1976.

Having become a tax exile in Tourmakeady in the Republic of Ireland, Shaw finally struck Hollywood gold with the 1930s crime caper *The Sting* (1973) and the killer shark adventure *Jaws* (1975). 'The only place for me is the top', he declared in an interview, 'because I'd be a lump of jelly elsewhere' (Carmean and Gaston, 240). His later films, however, including *Swashbuckler* (1976), *The Deep* (1977), and *Force Ten from Navarone* (1978), all proved critical and commercial disappointments.

Shaw died from coronary thrombosis on 10 August 1978, at his Irish home, Drumbawn House, Tourmakeady, leaving a novel, *The Ice Floe*, unfinished. His remains were cremated and his ashes scattered at an unknown location in England.   DAVID PARKINSON

Sources K. Carmean and G. Gaston, *Robert Shaw: more than a life* (1994) • D. Thomson, *A biographical dictionary of film*, 3rd edn (1994) • J. McBride, *Steven Spielberg* (1997)
Archives U. Hull, Brynmor Jones L., corresp. and literary papers | BFI, corresp. with Joseph Losey
Likenesses B. Collins, photograph, c.1958, NPG [*see illus.*] • photographs, Hult. Arch.

Shaw, Robert Barkley (1839–1879), explorer and government agent, son of Robert Grant Shaw, of Box, Wiltshire, and his wife, Martha Barkley, was born at Upper Clapton, London, on 12 July 1839. His sister Anna married Robert Younghusband. He was educated at schools on the continent, at Marlborough College, and at Trinity College, Cambridge, where he matriculated in 1859 but did not take a degree. The effects of rheumatic fever forced him to give up the idea of entering the army, and in 1859 he went to Kunyara in the Himalayas, where he settled as a tea planter.

Eager for adventure, he decided to explore the country north of the Karakoram; and, after one or two tentative excursions, he started in May 1868 for eastern Turkestan, travelling as a merchant, and taking with him trading goods, a prismatic compass, and a translation of Herodotus's *History*. He reached Yarkand on 8 December, and Kashgar on 11 January 1869, being the first Englishman to visit those places. At Kashgar, though not allowed to enter the city, he was treated graciously by Yakub Beg, the ruler of the country, who, mainly in consequence of the advice given him by Shaw, dispatched an envoy to India asking that a British officer be sent to arrange a treaty. Shaw returned by the Karakoram Pass, and proceeded to England. His *Visit to High Tartary, Yarkand and Kashgar* appeared in 1871, but while preparing it for the press he heard that Lord Mayo had decided to send an official mission to eastern Turkestan and at once telegraphed an offer of his services; this was accepted, and he accompanied Douglas Forsyth on his first mission. Yakub Beg was far from Yarkand when they arrived there on 3 August 1870, and the mission came back with its principal object unachieved. Shaw returned to England, where in 1872 the Royal Geographical Society awarded him the patron's gold medal for his explorations in eastern Turkestan and especially for his valuable astronomical observations, which fixed the position of Yarkand, Kashgar, and other places.

In recognition of his service to the government, Lord Mayo appointed Shaw to the political department, and he was made British joint commissioner in Ladakh. In 1875 he went to Yarkand in charge of the ratified treaty made by Sir Douglas Forsyth in 1874. He continued to write, publishing on the Eastern Turkish language in 1875 and the Ghalchah languages in 1876. He also contributed to the Royal Geographical and Royal Asiatic societies' publications. In 1878 he was appointed resident at Mandalay in Upper Burma. During the troubles which followed the death of King Mengdun in October 1878, his position at the residency was one of great danger; but throughout the crisis he acted with courage and discretion. He wrote to King Thibaw, who was massacring kinsfolk and rivals wholesale, that if any further murders took place he should, without waiting for orders from Calcutta, at once haul down the British flag; and he sent at the same time his assistant to explain the consequences such a measure would involve. He was made CSI and died at Mandalay on 15 June 1879. He was unmarried.

STEPHEN WHEELER, *rev.* ELIZABETH BAIGENT

Sources *Proceedings* [Royal Geographical Society], new ser., 1 (1879), 523–5 · *Parl. papers* (1886) [Burma] · H. R. Mill, *The record of the Royal Geographical Society, 1830–1930* (1930) · private information (1897) · *CGPLA Eng. & Wales* (1880) · Venn, *Alum. Cant.* · *The Times* (19 June 1879), 12 · *The Times* (23 June 1879), 7
Archives BL OIOC, corresp. with Sir Alfred Lyall, MS Eur. F 132
Wealth at death under £300: administration with will, 8 Dec 1880, *CGPLA Eng. & Wales*

Shaw, Samuel (1634/5–1696), clergyman, was born at Repton, Derbyshire, the son of Thomas Shaw, blacksmith. Educated at Repton School, he was admitted as a sizar, aged fifteen, to St John's College, Cambridge, on 23 December 1650. After graduating BA in 1656 he became master of the grammar school at Tamworth, Staffordshire; there he assisted the puritan vicar, Thomas Blake, at whose funeral he delivered an oration that was printed in Blake's posthumous *Vindiciae foederis* (1658). In January 1658 Shaw was ordained by the Wirksworth (Derbyshire) classis, having been invited the previous August to the curacy of Moseley, Bromsgrove, Worcestershire, by Richard Grevis. There he worked closely with Thomas Hall, the presbyterian curate of King's Norton. Through the influence of Captain Gervas Pigot of Thrumpton, Nottinghamshire, he received the protector's presentation to the sequestered rectory of Long Whatton, Leicestershire, of which he took possession on 5 June 1658. But, though the crown confirmed Shaw's title in September 1660, the opposition of Sir John Pretyman, MP for Leicester, forced his removal the following year, and he retired to Cotes, near Loughborough, Leicestershire. About this time he married Jane, daughter of Ferdinando Poole, the ejected vicar of Thrumpton.

In 1665 relatives from London carried the plague to Shaw's house. He lost 'two tender babes' and a sister during three months' confinement. The 'senseless aspersions' of Shaw's neighbours, some of whom blamed him for introducing the plague into their community, compounded his grief (Shaw, *Voice of One Crying*, foreword). Yet his experience of God's love in the midst of these afflictions inspired him to write the two books for which he is best known—*The Voice of one Crying in a Wilderness* (1666) and *Immanuel* (1667). Both sought to wean men from their 'false notions' of religion. This meant criticizing even his fellow nonconformists, those 'pretenders to religion', who still complain of 'persecution, [whose] cry is all for liberty'. Such complaints betrayed a 'mere selfish carnal principle'. For Shaw, true religion consisted not in performing duties, reforming worship, or 'raging against … Antichrist' (*Immanuel*, preface), but in God's 'changing the hearts, and as it were deifying the souls of men' (*Immanuel*, 18). Frequently reprinted, *Immanuel* has remained popular.

At the end of 1666 Shaw left Cotes for Ashby-de-la-Zouch, where in January 1668 he was appointed master of the free school. His reputation for moderation earned him the respect of prominent Anglicans, who were willing to wink at his nonconformity. Thus, in December 1670, Lord Conway persuaded Archbishop Sheldon to grant Shaw a licence to teach without requiring full subscription; Bishop Fuller of Lincoln, 'glad to have so worthy a man in his diocese', did likewise. 'Pleasant and facetious', the new schoolmaster had 'great skill … suiting himself to the temper of boys' (Calamy, *Abridgement*, 2.429–30). During Shaw's tenure Ashby School regained the prestige it had had at the beginning of the century under John Brinsley, and soon attracted scholars from as far away as London, many of whom went on to careers in the established church. Shaw's efforts to revive the school involved him in a long-running quarrel over rents with the feoffees, whom he regarded as 'enemies to learning' (Hunt. L., Hastings MSS, HA 10776). Fortunately he enjoyed the backing of local gentry, including Sir Edward Abney, and the town's clergymen, the godly conformists Alexander Jones and Ithiel Smart the younger.

Of Shaw's lesser-known works, his *A Receipt for the State-Palsie* (1660) attributed England's political troubles to the fact that 'every man is left to the free choice of … his own religion', and called upon magistrates to wield the sword for 'the terror of evil doers' (p. 18). A few months later, however, a more subdued Shaw commended repentance and resignation in a sermon dedicated to the presbyterian MP Sir John Swynfen (*Samuel in Sackcloth*, 1660). In addition to a treatise against usury, *The True Christian's Test* (1682), much admired by Bishop Thomas Barlow, Shaw published *Adam Abel … a Discourse … for Funeral Occasions* (1692), and an English translation of *An Apologie for the Ministry* (1660) by his friend Thomas Hall. He also published three guides to grammar and two of the comedies he wrote for his students to perform at Christmas time—*Words Made Visible* (1679) and *The Different Humours of Men* (1692).

Shaw died at Ashby on 22 January 1696, and was buried there two days later on 24 January. His brother-in-law, William Cross, ejected vicar of Beeston, Nottinghamshire, preached his funeral sermon. Shaw was survived by his wife, Jane, two married daughters, Frances Bragg and Jane Warner, and two sons, Samuel and Ferdinando *Shaw (*bap.* 1674, *d.* 1745). The latter published several works as minister of Friar Gate Presbyterian meeting, Derby, from 1699 until his death in 1745.   JIM BENEDICT

Sources E. Calamy, ed., *An abridgement of Mr. Baxter's history of his life and times, with an account of the ministers, &c., who were ejected after the Restauration of King Charles II*, 2nd edn, 2 vols. (1713), vol. 2, pp. 426–36 · E. Calamy, *A continuation of the account of the ministers … who were ejected and silenced after the Restoration in 1660*, 2 vols. (1727), vol. 2, pp. 592–3 · *Calamy rev.*, 435 · L. Fox, *A country grammar school* (1967) · A. Gordon, ed., *Freedom after ejection: a review (1690–1692) of presbyterian and congregational nonconformity in England and Wales* (1917), 67, 349 · correspondence with T. Hastings, Hunt. L., Hastings papers, HA 10774–10778, HAM Box 2, folder 13 · J. C. Cox, ed., *Minute book of the Wirksworth classis, 1651–58* (1880), 211–20 · *Calendar of the correspondence of Richard Baxter*, ed. N. H. Keeble and G. F. Nuttall, 2 (1991), 238 · J. Hunter, *Familiae minorum gentium*, ed. J. W. Clay, 1, Harleian Society, 37 (1894), 3777 · W. A. Shaw, *A history of the English church during the civil wars and under the Commonwealth, 1640–1660*, 2 (1900), 598 · L. Hutchinson, *Memoirs of the life of Colonel Hutchinson*, ed. N. H. Keeble (1995), 98, 358 · J. H. Pruett, *The parish clergy under the later Stuarts: the Leicestershire experience* (1978), 24 · *The nonconformist's memorial … originally written by … Edmund Calamy*, ed. S. Palmer, [3rd edn], 2 (1802), 404–11 · J. Nichols, *The history and antiquities of the county of Leicester*, 3 (1800–04), 1110 · Venn, *Alum. Cant.* · S. S. [S. Shaw], *The voice of one crying in a wilderness* (1674) · S. S. [S. Shaw], *A receipt for the state-palsie* (1660)

Archives Hunt. L., corresp. with T. Hastings, HA 10774–10778, HAM Box 2, folder 13

Likenesses J. Scott, engraving, repro. in S. S. [S. Shaw], *Emmanuel*, ed. R. Gordon, Glasgow edn (1829) · engraving (after unknown artist, NPG), repro. in Nichols, *History and antiquities*, vol. 2, part 2, p. 1106

Wealth at death property at Ashby and Repton; £5 p.a.: *Calamy rev.*; Gordon, *Freedom*, 67

Shaw, Stebbing

Shaw, Stebbing (1762–1802), historian, was born about the spring of 1762, apparently at or near Stone, Staffordshire. His father, also named Stebbing (1736/7–1799), was the son of John Stebbing Shaw of Stone, and was rector of Hartshorne, Derbyshire, from 1769 and also of Seckington, Warwickshire, from 1785. The elder Stebbing's first wife was evidently the daughter and heir of John Hyatt of Stallington in Stone parish, and the younger Stebbing was their only child. His father had another son and two daughters by a second marriage.

Shaw was educated at Repton School, Derbyshire, where he acquired a taste for literature and a lifelong enthusiasm for the violin. He was admitted pensioner at Queens' College, Cambridge, in 1780 and graduated BA in 1784, MA in 1787, and BD in 1796. He was elected scholar in 1784 and fellow in 1786, in which year he was also ordained. Probably in 1785 he went to live at the home of Sir Robert Burdett, a family friend, at Ealing as tutor to Sir Robert's grandson Francis. In 1788 he published an account of a tour the previous year to the western highlands of Scotland and in 1789 an account of a tour in 1788 to the west of England. Also in 1789 he was admitted to the reading-room of the British Museum. Between that year and 1792 he and his friend Samuel Egerton Brydges produced four volumes of a periodical called *The Topographer*; in 1792 there were seven numbers of a continuation, *Topographical Miscellanies*. Shaw later stated that it was Brydges's enthusiasm for antiquarian pursuits since their time together at Queens' which inspired his own efforts.

In the summer of 1791 he went to live with his father at Hartshorne, and in the autumn he began work on the history of the neighbouring county of Staffordshire. That was to be his main occupation for the rest of his life.

Shaw was indefatigable in his research. His former headmaster at Repton, William Bagshaw Stevens, dined at Hartshorne in October 1792 and found Shaw 'busily immersed in Topography'; the following August Stevens described him as 'pregnant with Topography' (*Journal of the Revd William Bagshaw Stevens*, ed. G. Galbraith, 52, 93). Shaw made many tours of Staffordshire, working in the muniment rooms and libraries of the nobility and gentry and also making numerous drawings. He spent much of the year in London, where he lodged near the British Museum. He acquired large collections of manuscripts, by purchase, gift, or loan, and secured extensive help from scholars and other experts. In 1795 he was elected a fellow of the Society of Antiquaries, and in 1799 the British Museum accepted his offer of work on the Harleian collection, which was being catalogued. Also in 1799 he succeeded his father as rector of Hartshorne.

The first of Shaw's three projected volumes entitled *The History and Antiquities of Staffordshire* was published in 1798. It covered part of Offlow hundred (south-east Staffordshire) and the city of Lichfield, with introductory sections on the county as a whole. Volume 2 followed in 1801, covering the rest of Offlow hundred and all of Seisdon hundred (south-west Staffordshire, including Wolverhampton). Shaw had originally intended to include Cuttlestone hundred (the area to the north) but decided to hold it over; corrected proofs of part of that section existed by the time of his death. His diligence was not matched by his execution, which was unsystematic and hurried, and Lord Bagot's terse comment some years later is a fair judgement: 'What he did publish is full of *curious matter*, miserably ill arranged' (William Salt L, Stafford, S. MS. 478, Bagot). On the other hand Shaw's work was the first attempt at a large-scale history of Staffordshire, based on a wide range of sources and generously illustrated. At the least it has proved, along with his unpublished collections, a valuable quarry for later historians.

Shaw, who remained unmarried, was of a quiet disposition. His health was poor, and overwork combined with financial worry and sensitivity to criticism led finally to mental breakdown. In 1799 he confessed to his friend Samuel Pipe Wolferstan, the antiquarian squire of Statfold, near Tamworth, that 'he did not feel all his former alacrity for excursions' (Staffs. RO, D. 1527/24, 22 July). Such excursions during hot weather in 1800 brought on a fever and sleeplessness. In October 1801 he suffered a worse attack, during which he was totally deranged. As a result of another attack in London in the spring of 1802 he was removed for a time from the care of his half-sister Elizabeth into the keeping of a Dr Willis. In October he had a violent attack at Hartshorne and was taken for medical advice to London, where he died on 28 October. He was buried at Hartshorne on 6 November 1802.

Shaw's collections, including the printed stock, passed to his half-sister Elizabeth as his heir. In 1810 she sold the manuscripts to Samuel Pipe Wolferstan, who in turn sold them to his friend William Hamper in 1813. The same year Hamper bought Shaw's printed stock along with his copper plates and drawings from Elizabeth's husband John Gillam. After Hamper's death in 1831 his Staffordshire collections were sold to William Salt and are now in the William Salt Library at Stafford. The rest of Hamper's library was sold to the bibliophile Sir Thomas Phillipps. It included Shaw's own copy of *Staffordshire* with a set of the corrected proof sheets for the continuation of volume 2 bound in. This later passed into the ownership of Sheffield City Library in 1961.   M. W. GREENSLADE

Sources M. W. Greenslade, *The Staffordshire historians*, Staffordshire RS, 4th ser., 11 (1982) · *GM*, 1st ser., 73 (1803), 9–11 · Venn, *Alum. Cant.*
Archives Sheffield Central Library · William Salt Library, Stafford
Likenesses T. Donaldson, engraving, 1801 (after earlier drawing), William Salt Library, Stafford · line engraving, pubd 1844, BM, NPG

Shaw, Thomas (1694–1751), traveller, son of Gabriel Shaw, shearman-dyer of Kendal, Westmorland, and his wife, who was probably called Agnes, was born on 4 June 1694 at Kendal and baptized there on 18 June. Having attended Kendal grammar school, he matriculated from Queen's College, Oxford, on 5 December 1711, graduating BA in 1716 and MA on 16 January 1720. Later that year he was appointed chaplain to the English factory at Algiers at a salary of £100 per annum. During his time there he travelled widely, to Egypt, Sinai, Cyprus, and the Holy Land in 1721–2 and to Tunis and Carthage in 1727, as well as making various excursions into the interior of Barbary (Algiers, Tripoli, and Morocco). In Barbary travel was comparatively safe, but in 'Aqabah he was stripped naked by robbers, and while travelling with 6000 pilgrims to Jerusalem he was seized and held to ransom. However, with 'a body capable of bearing the fatigues of travelling united to a mind rich in most kinds of human learning' (*European Magazine*, 19, 1791, 83), in all these regions he made careful observations of the geography, natural history, customs, and antiquities. In 1733, having married Joanna, the widow of his friend and benefactor, Edward Holden, consul at Algiers, Shaw returned to England. Elected a fellow of Queen's in 1727, he became doctor of divinity in 1734 and was presented to the vicarage of Godshill, Isle of Wight. He was also elected a fellow of the Royal Society on 13 June 1734, having contributed to their *Philosophical Transactions* of 1729, through Sir Hans Sloane, with 'A geographical description of the kingdom of Tunis'.

Four years later Shaw published *Travels, or, Observations Relating to Several Parts of Barbary and the Levant* (1738), which included maps, plates, lists of animals, plants (about 640 species), fossils, coins, and inscriptions, and a copious index. He had engaged the botanist Johann Jakob Dillenius to catalogue his flora. Dedicated to George II, the book also acknowledged the generous patronage of Queen Caroline. The bibliophile Thomas Dibdin called the work 'a safe inmate' of a well-chosen collection and exhorted 'Fly, fly, to secure it' (*Library Companion*, 1824,

2.48). It was especially admired for the illustrations of natural history, of classical authors, and of the scriptures. Gibbon honourably excepts him from the crowd of 'blind' travellers (E. Gibbon, *The Decline and Fall of the Roman Empire*, chap. 24), while his scrupulous veracity was vindicated by James Bruce and later African explorers.

Academic acrimony, however, arose when Richard Pococke, in his *Description of the East* (2 vols., 1743–5) took issue with Shaw on some, mainly geographical, statements. From his observations in Egypt, Shaw theorized that originally the delta of the Nile was part of the sea, while to the south was a valley bounded by mountains. Gradually over the centuries the soil brought down by the inundations had built up the banks until, while the delta became cultivable, the land to the far south was raised too high to be flooded, causing it to become barren. Pococke disagreed (1.39), believing the channel of the Nile was always augmented in proportion to its banks, and therefore nothing changed. Shaw's explanation is interesting in that it is based on firsthand observation and in that it admits of the possibility of landscape change through the operation in the past of presently observed processes. Elsewhere in his work, however, with references to 'the deluge', Shaw shows his adherence to traditional views of the earth's history.

Wounded over the Nile disagreement by being 'in so unexpected a Manner … drawn into a Controversy' (Shaw, 15) by a man he considered a friend, Shaw issued a supplement to his *Travels* in 1746, 'wherein some objections lately made are fully considered and answered', and in 1747 *A Further Vindication in a Letter to R. Clayton, Bishop of Clogher*. Both supplements were incorporated into the second and most valued edition of Shaw's *Travels* (1757), which, although published after his death, had been prepared by himself. A third edition, in two volumes, was published in 1808. The work was translated into German, Dutch, and French.

When on 18 August 1740 Shaw became principal of St Edmund Hall, Oxford, he found 'every Part of it in Ruins, and without an Inhabitant' and immediately set about repairs. He restored the eastern end of the north range of the front quadrangle in 1741, paying for this with 'the whole Profits I received from my Book of Travels', about £400 (Shaw to Robert Tomlinson, letter 3d; Cowdrey, 58). Through a fund-raising appeal, he was able to restore the western half of the range in 1746–7.

Shaw was appointed regius professor of Greek in 1741 and presented by Queen's College to the vicarage of Bramley, Hampshire, in 1742. He died there on 15 August 1751 'in high reputation for knowledge, probity, and pleasantry' (Nicholson, 429). He was buried at Bramley in September, where a memorial monument was erected in the church by his widow; a commemorative tablet was also placed in the English church at Algiers. He left to the university the manuscripts of his travels, with other papers, his collection of natural curiosities, and some antique coins and busts, three of which were engraved in *Marmoria Oxoniensa*. Forster named a botanical species *Shawia* in his honour. Portraits of him at St Edmund Hall and Queen's College show 'a stout and fierce, but not ill-tempered looking man' (note from Provost Magrath, *DNB*) with a countenance 'grotesque, but marked most strongly with jocularity and good humour'. An etching from a portrait then belonging to Sir William Musgrave, bt, prefixes an article in the *European Magazine* which bears the appearance of authorship by someone who knew him. He was, it says:

> Good, humane, temperate, sociable and cheerful to the highest degree, as long as any of his contemporaries exist, the infinite humor of his conversation will never be forgotten; which was heightened by a peculiarity of figure and countenance … his humor was chiefly exerted in the innocent conviviality of the Common Room, where his wit was provoked and sharpened by the raillery of his surrounding friends. (19, Feb 1791, 85)

PETA RÉE

Sources 'The life of Thomas Shaw, principal of St. Edmund's Hall, Oxford', *European Magazine and London Review*, 19 (1791), 83–6 • T. Shaw, *A supplement to a book entitled 'Travels', or, Observations relating to several parts of Barbary and the Levant and wherein some objections lately made are fully considered and answered* (1746) • C. Nicholson, *The annals of Kendal* (1832), 246–8 • Nichols, *Lit. anecdotes*, 2.287 • Foster, *Alum. Oxon.* • [Clarke], *The Georgian era: memoirs of the most eminent persons*, 3 (1834), 13–15 • A. Chalmers, ed., *The general biographical dictionary*, new edn, 28 (1816), 428–30 • T. Thomson, *History of the Royal Society from its institution to the end of the eighteenth century* (1812) • W. D. Macray, *Annals of the Bodleian Library, Oxford*, 2nd edn (1890), 224 • J. Aikin and others, *General biography, or, Lives, critical and historical of the most eminent persons*, 10 vols. (1799–1815) • Allibone, *Dict.* • J. Kitto, *Palestine: the physical geography and natural history of the Holy Land* (1841), xvii • J. N. D. Kelly, *St Edmund Hall: almost seven hundred years* (1989) • H. E. J. Cowdrey, 'Building work on the north range of the front quadrangle of St Edmund Hall, 1741–8', *Oxoniensia*, 58 (1993), 287–304 • *DNB* • monument, Bramley church, Hampshire

Archives Bodl. Oxf., charts, drawings, journals, and maps, Add. MSS D27 and 202763; descriptions of fossils, M Lat. misc. 376 • RBG Kew, list of plants | BL, Sloane MSS, essays on Algiers and Tunis, etc.; letters to Sir Hans Sloane

Likenesses J. Green, line engraving, BM, NPG • etching, repro. in 'The life of Thomas Shaw' • oils, St Edmund Hall, Oxford • oils, Queen's College, Oxford • portrait, repro. in Kelly, *St Edmund Hall*, 60

Wealth at death collection of manuscripts left to University of Oxford

Shaw, Thomas, first Baron Craigmyle (1850–1937), lawyer and politician, the only son of Alexander Shaw of Dunfermline and his wife, Isabella, *née* Wishart, was born there on 23 May 1850. His father, who was of highland origin, and was in business as a baker, died when Thomas was in his sixth year, and thereafter his upbringing was in the hands of one of those inestimable and self-sacrificing Scottish mothers who know so well how to combine for their sons affection with ambition. He attended Dunfermline high school, of which he became dux, and on leaving it was apprenticed to a local solicitor. He decided on advocacy at the Scottish bar and proceeded to the University of Edinburgh, where he pursued his studies in the faculties of arts and law with ardour and distinction. He was awarded the Hamilton fellowship in mental philosophy and the lord rector's historical prize, and for a time acted

Thomas Shaw, first Baron Craigmyle (1850–1937), by Sir Benjamin Stone, 1897

as assistant to Professor Henry Calderwood in the class of moral philosophy. In 1875 he was admitted a member of the Faculty of Advocates. In 1879 he married Elsie Stephen (*d.* 1939), daughter of George Forrest of Ludquharm, Aberdeenshire; they had a son and three daughters.

The generous and democratic fraternity of the Parliament House is always ready to extend a welcome to ability, however humble in origin, but at the price of conformity with its high professional standards. This price Shaw was not invariably disposed to pay. He early recognized that for him the path of advancement lay in politics. He did not, however, neglect the law and soon acquired a considerable practice, especially in jury trials, civil and criminal, which provided a more congenial sphere for the exercise of his gifts of advocacy than the more exacting tasks of legal argument. He first entered parliament in 1892 as Liberal member for the Hawick district of the border burghs, a seat which he held until 1909. He was a home-ruler, an opponent of the Second South African War, an ardent land law reformer, and in church connection an irreconcilable dissenter. Tommy Shaw's highly effective gifts as a political orator rendered him a valuable asset to the advanced wing of the Liberal Party in Scotland. In 1886 he was appointed an advocate-depute in the crown office, and from 1894 to 1895 he was solicitor-general in succession to Alexander Asher, and became a QC in the former year. In December 1905 his political services were rewarded by his appointment as lord advocate in the government of Sir Henry Campbell-Bannerman; he was sworn of the privy council in January 1906.

In 1909 Shaw was appointed on the nomination of Asquith a lord of appeal in ordinary and a life peer with the title of Baron Shaw of Dunfermline. Among other distinctions he was an honorary bencher of the Middle Temple (1910) and he received the honorary degree of LLD from the universities of St Andrews (1902), Aberdeen (1906), Edinburgh (1908), and Pennsylvania.

From 1909 to 1929, when he resigned, Shaw discharged his judicial duties in the House of Lords and the privy council with competent assiduity. The judgments which he delivered have literary style and lucidity, but it cannot be said that he made any distinctive contribution to the law. His best-known effort was his dissent from all his colleagues and all the judges below in *R. v. Halliday* (1917), in which with much vigour he condemned as illegal a defence of the realm regulation authorizing internment made during the First World War. So far as the treatment of Scottish appeals is concerned he was from 1913 onwards overshadowed by the presence and authority of Lord Dunedin.

On several occasions Shaw rendered useful service by presiding over public inquiries, notably the royal commission on the importation of arms into the Dublin district (1914), the Scottish committee on the state purchase of the liquor trade (1917), and a court of inquiry concerning the wages and conditions of employment of dock labour in the United Kingdom (1920). In an article which he contributed to the *Fortnightly Review* in 1900, 'The Scottish university crisis', he made a strong plea for extending free education in Scotland to the universities by the abolition of class fees. This article attracted the attention of Andrew Carnegie, a fellow native of Dunfermline, and greatly influenced him in founding (1901) the Carnegie Trust for the Universities of Scotland.

Shaw always retained his early interest in literature and was himself the author of a number of books. The best known is his *Letters to Isabel* (1921), an unconventional autobiography in the guise of a series of letters written to one of his daughters, in which he describes the leading features of his career as he wished it to be appreciated by posterity. So far as it purports to narrate facts and to convey impressions it must be read with considerable reservations. A sequel in similar vein, entitled *The other Bundle*, appeared in 1927. In 1911 he published a lecture under the title *Legislature and Judiciary*, which he had given at University College, London; an account of his visits to the annual meetings of the American and Canadian bar associations in 1922 and the addresses which he there delivered are to be found in a volume entitled *The Law of the Kinsmen* (1923). In 1928 he published a short study, *The Trial of Jesus Christ*, and in 1933 *John Marshall in Diplomacy and in Law*, a sketch of the life of Chief Justice Marshall of the United States supreme court. Plays in verse, *Darnley* (1925) and *Leicester* (1931), further testify to his versatility, as do his contributions on Scottish biography and history to the *Encyclopaedia Britannica* (9th edn).

On his resignation in 1929 Lord Shaw's life peerage was converted into an ordinary barony, and, taking his new title from the estate which he had bought in Aberdeenshire, he was thenceforth known as Lord Craigmyle. However much controversy attended his public career Craigmyle was singularly happy in his domestic life, where he was assured of admiration and affection. He died at Glasgow on 28 June 1937, and was buried on 2 July at Torphins cemetery, Aberdeenshire. He was succeeded as second baron by his son, **Alexander Shaw** (1883–1944), who was president of the Oxford Union Society in 1905 while attending Trinity College, Oxford, and was Liberal MP for Kilmarnock boroughs (1915–18) and for the Kilmarnock division of Ayrshire (1918–23). He was a member of several wartime bodies, including, as chairman, the special arbitration tribunal of female munition workers' wages. In 1913 he married Margaret Cargill, daughter of James Lyle *Mackay, first earl of Inchcape, the shipping magnate, and was himself director of several shipping companies. He died in 1944. MACMILLAN, *rev.* H. C. G. MATTHEW

Sources *The Times* (30 June 1937) · *The Scotsman* (15 Feb 1909) · A. Shaw, *Thomas Shaw (First Lord Craigmyle)* (1937) · Lord Shaw [T. Shaw], *Letters to Isabel* (1921) · Lord Shaw [T. Shaw], *The other bundle* (1927) · Burke, *Peerage* (1959) · GEC, *Peerage* · WWW
Archives BL, corresp. with Sir Henry Campbell-Bannerman, Add. MS 41227 · BL, corresp. with Lord Pentland, Add. MS 41230
Likenesses B. Stone, five photographs, 1897–1908, NPG [*see illus.*] · G. F. Watt, oils, Scot. NPG
Wealth at death £40,841 3*s*. 3*d*.: confirmation, 4 Sept 1937, CCI

Shaw, Thomas (1872–1938), trade unionist and politician, known as Tom Shaw, was born at Waterside, Colne, Lancashire, on 9 April 1872, the eldest son of Ellis Shaw, miner, and his wife, Sarah Ann Wilkinson. Shaw was educated at St James's elementary school at Waterside, and when ten years old entered a textile factory as a half-time worker: he left school finally at the age of twelve. He later took evening and technical classes to improve his education and developed a particular skill in languages. His command of French and German served him greatly in later life. In 1893 Shaw married Susannah Whitaker Sterne Ryan, daughter of Charles Woodhead, tackler. They had four daughters, two of whom predeceased their father.

Shaw joined the Colne Weavers' Association, and subsequently became its secretary. He also promoted the formation of the Northern Counties' Textile Federation, which embraced all the main sections of the cotton trade unions, and he was its first secretary. From 1911 to 1929, and again from 1931 until his death, he was secretary of the International Federation of Textile Workers and in this post visited almost every country in Europe, combining an intimate knowledge of the technicalities of the industry with a grasp of industrial politics both at home and abroad. During the First World War he was director of national service for the west midland region. He was appointed CBE in 1919.

An early and enthusiastic supporter of the Labour Party, Shaw was returned as the Labour member of parliament for Preston in 1918 and held the seat until his defeat in 1931. He was junior Labour whip in 1919, minister of labour in the first Labour government (January–October 1924), and secretary of state for war in the second Labour union movement in its efforts to prevent British intervention in the Russo–Polish conflict in 1921.

With a robust constitution and a plain, blunt manner of speech, Shaw was a popular figure in his local area and more broadly. Devoting his time to his union and political causes, he had no particular hobby beyond the collection of 'tacklers' tales'—unique examples of Lancashire factory humour—which he told and retold with unfailing and infectious enjoyment. While attending an International Federation of Textile Workers congress in Brussels in 1938, Shaw was suddenly taken ill. He returned to London and died at the Middlesex Hospital on 26 September 1938.   J. S. MIDDLETON, *rev.* MARC BRODIE

Sources *The Times* (27 Sept 1938), 14d · *Colne Times* (30 Sept 1938) · personal knowledge (1949) · private information (1949) · private information (2004) · *WWBMP* · *CGPLA Eng. & Wales* (1938)
Archives PRO, corresp. with Ramsay Macdonald, PRO 30/69/1/204
Likenesses W. Stoneman, photograph, 1924, NPG [*see illus.*] · photograph, repro. in *The Times*
Wealth at death £3029 16s. 1d.: probate, 11 Nov 1938, *CGPLA Eng. & Wales*

Thomas Shaw (1872–1938), by Walter Stoneman, 1924

administration (1929–31). As minister of labour he introduced measures which enhanced the benefits of the Unemployment Insurance Acts. He became a privy councillor in 1924.

On the reconstruction of the Labour and Socialist International at Hamburg in 1923, when Arthur Henderson (1863–1935) was appointed chairman, Shaw was elected joint secretary, sharing the post with Friedrich Adler, the Austrian socialist, until 1925. In this role he visited the Ruhr and reported against its continued occupation by French troops. He stressed the impossibility of enforcing the German reparations laid down in the treaty of Versailles, and forecast the probability of another war in twenty years' time.

In 1926 Shaw headed a delegation to investigate conditions in the Indian textile industry. He was a member of the Holman Gregory commission on workmen's compensation from 1917 to 1920. A convinced champion of the League of Nations and the International Labour Organization, he actively promoted the Washington convention for a forty-eight hour working week (1919) and was highly critical when in 1923 the British government declined to follow the lead of France, Belgium, and Holland in ratifying the proposal. A bill in Shaw's name for implementing the convention was before parliament in 1924, when the Labour government fell.

While disagreeing fundamentally with communist principles and the Russian Soviet system, Shaw favoured friendly political and trade relations with Russia and supported the council of action representing the British trade

Shaw, Thomas Budd (1813–1862), translator and literary scholar, was born on 12 October 1813 at 28 Gower Street, London, the youngest of the nine children of the architect John *Shaw (1776–1832), and his wife, Elizabeth Hester, *née* Whitfield (*bap.* 1776, *d.* 1864). He was frail and myopic, but in 1822 his uncle the Revd Francis Whitfield took him to the warmer climate of Berbice (in modern Guyana), where his health improved. In 1826 he was enrolled at Shrewsbury School, where he demonstrated a voracious appetite for classical and modern literature. In 1833 he took up residence at St John's College, Cambridge, and kept eleven terms over the next six years. Open-handed and convivial, he frequented alehouses and the billiards room of the Dramatic Club; his rolling gait made him a familiar figure in the town. In 1836 he published anonymously *Theophrastus in Cambridge*, a fresh and witty treatment of young men's vices and follies, and then edited *The Fellow* and *The Individual*, ephemeral but entertaining weekly miscellanies for undergraduates. To these and to national journals he contributed original poems and essays, as well as verse translations from Latin, Italian, and German.

Before graduating BA in 1839 Shaw already lived partly in London and earned what he could by tutoring the sons of businessmen, but he shifted from address to cheap address, and on 26 June 1840 was declared an insolvent debtor; he left immediately for Russia. After examinations at St Petersburg University in Latin, Greek, arithmetic, and English literature, he was issued on 8 October with a licence to teach these subjects and until the end of 1841 served as tutor in the household of A. V. Vasilchikov in Moscow, surprising people as much by his Cambridge cap and gown as by his ability to read the New Testament in Greek.

Back in St Petersburg in 1842, Shaw became friendly with Samuel Warrand (1792–*c*.1855), English tutor to the imperial family and professor at the university, who had just established an *English Review of Literature*. Shaw edited this until it ceased publication in July 1843. As well as reprinting extracts from the British press on a multitude of topics, and introducing literary works such as Dickens's *Barnaby Rudge*, it carried verse and prose by Shaw, including articles on Wordsworth and Defoe. Also thanks to Warrand, whose daughter Annette Frances he married on 15 October 1842, Shaw became adjunct professor of English literature at Pushkin's old school, the Imperial Alexander Lyceum at Tsarskoye Selo. He proved a most successful teacher and was commissioned to write a textbook, which, first published in Russia in 1846, was greatly expanded as *Outlines of English Literature* and reprinted in London and Philadelphia in 1849.

From 1843 Shaw began to translate Russian literature. In addition to translating popular novels such as Bestuzhev-Marlinsky's *Ammalat-Bek* and Lazhechnikov's *The Heretic*, he abridged Gogol's story 'The Portrait' and produced a remarkably vigorous yet faithful version of 'The gifts of Terek', the first significant English translation from the poetry of Lermontov. Most importantly, he promoted Pushkin's English reputation, translating 'The Coffin-Maker' and 'Kirdjali' and publishing an informative biography in *Blackwood's Magazine* (June–August 1845). This included copious translated excerpts from Pushkin and drew on knowledge gained from friends of the poet such as P. A. Pletnyov (in whose household Shaw was tutor at one time). Writing as he did in the Russia of Nicholas I, Shaw was unable to discuss Pushkin's political views, but his study proved otherwise reliable and authoritative.

In 1851 Shaw took his MA degree in Cambridge, and, despite stiff competition, succeeded his father-in-law as professor of English at the University of St Petersburg. Afterwards he also became tutor to the young dukes Nikolay and Yevgeny of Leuchtenberg, and to the little grand dukes Vladimir and Aleksey, third and fourth sons of Alexander II. He had some influence on the course of literature both as censor of English books and by his encouragement of the critic Druzhinin, who profited from Shaw's *Outlines*. Shaw himself still published, contributing the entry 'Petersburg' to the *Encyclopaedia Britannica* and writing about Chaucer for *Biblioteka dlya chteniya*, but he chiefly devoted himself to a revision of the *Outlines* and to a companion volume, *Choice Specimens of English Literature*; both were edited after his death by Dr William Smith, and the newly named *History of English Literature* remained in print until the end of the century.

Shaw, who for some years had been obese, contracted severe chest pains and died of an aneurysm at St Petersburg on 26 November 1862. His funeral was held five days later at the chapel of the British factory. A monument was erected at the lyceum to this fine scholar who spanned two literary worlds, uniquely able to interpret each through the eyes of both. PATRICK WADDINGTON

Sources W. Smith, 'A brief memoir of the author', in T. B. Shaw, *History of English literature* (1864) · L. M. Arinshteyn, 'Tomas Shou — angliyskiy perevodchik Pushkina', *Sravnitel'noye izucheniye literatur, Sbornik statey k 80-letiyu akademika M. P. Alekseyeva* (1976), 117–24 · M. P. Alekseyev and Y. D. Levin, 'Tri angliyskikh zhurnala v Rossii' [Three English journals in Russia], *Russkaya Literatura*, 3 (1994), 3–32 · J. Brown, *Sixty years' gleanings from life's harvest: a genuine autobiography* (1858) · St John Cam., Biographical archive · Shrewsbury School Register · *GM*, 3rd ser., 14 (1863), 129 · *Cambridge Chronicle and Journal* (30 May 1840), 1 · F. Bodenshtedt, 'Vospominaniya o prebyvanii v Rossii v 1841–1845 gg.' [Recollections of a period spent in Russia, 1841–1845], *Russkaya Starina*, 5 (1887), 437–8 · A. A. Polovtsov, ed., *Russkii biograficheskii slovar'* [Russian biographical dictionary], 22 (1905)

Shaw, William (1749–1831), Gaelic grammarian and lexicographer, was born on 3 February 1749 at Clachaig on the island of Arran. He received his early education in Ayr and, from about 1768, at the University of Glasgow, where he was awarded the degree of MA, apparently in 1772, though one source gives 1777 as the date of his graduation. While a student he taught at a grammar school in Glenorchy, Argyll, leaving the post under something of a cloud.

Shaw has come to prominence partly through his friendship with Samuel Johnson, to whom he was introduced in London in 1774. Johnson encouraged him to publish *An Analysis of the Gaelic Language*, having seen the material in manuscript. Two editions were published in Edinburgh in 1778. The book has been described by a modern Gaelic scholar as 'a rudimentary grammar, with no claim to distinction beyond its being the first published work of its kind' (MacDonald, 4). With the publication of Stewart's *Elements of Gaelic Grammar* in 1801, Shaw's work was superseded.

In June 1779 William Shaw was presented by the duke of Gordon to the parish of Ardclach in the presbytery of Nairn. His short ministry in the Church of Scotland was to begin and end in controversy. Before his ordination and induction to the charge, which took place on 14 October 1779, a paper signed by over sixty parishioners, objecting to the morals of their prospective minister and accusing him of preaching unsound doctrine, was submitted to the presbytery. Shaw's ordination went ahead, but after his settlement few attended his services and he was so unpopular that he was even threatened with stoning. One of the objections from parishioners was that they had difficulty in understanding his Arran Gaelic dialect. His opponents also appear to have been protesting against the system of patronage within the church, by which Shaw had been elected.

By May 1780 the synod of Moray heard complaints of absences from the parish against the minister of Ardclach, but before action could be taken the situation was resolved in August by Shaw's demission of his charge. The rest of his life was to be spent in England, where a new phase in his activities brought him a measure of fame as a writer.

In 1780 William Shaw published *A Galic and English Dictionary* in two volumes, and claimed to have travelled 3000 miles in Scotland and Ireland collecting material for it. Once again he became involved in a public dispute. Disappointed with the quality of the finished product, some of the subscribers refused to make the payment they had guaranteed. In the litigation that followed the lexicographer won his case, though, again, modern critics have not been favourable to the work. Shaw's dictionary has been dismissed as 'a bare list of words and equivalents, at least as many Irish as Scottish Gaelic among them, and as many obsolete as contemporary' (MacDonald, 14).

Shaw was also involved in the heated controversy regarding the authenticity of James Macpherson's 'Ossianic' poems. He shared the scepticism of Samuel Johnson in questioning the genuineness of the material published by Macpherson, and issued in 1781 *An Enquiry into the Authenticity of the Poems Ascribed to Ossian*. John Clark wrote a reply to Shaw's *Enquiry*. This resulted in a rejoinder from Shaw. According to James Boswell, 'Johnson took Mr. Shaw under his protection, and gave him his assistance in writing a reply, which has been admired by the best judges, and by many considered as conclusive' (Fitzgerald, 458).

Having withdrawn from the Church of Scotland, William Shaw in course of time became an Anglican clergyman, apparently at Johnson's suggestion. (Shaw had published, anonymously, in 1785, *Memoirs of the Life and Writings of the late Dr Samuel Johnson*.) He enrolled at Emmanuel College, Cambridge, in 1787, and was eventually awarded the degree of bachelor of divinity in 1800. From 1795 to 1831 he served as rector of Chelvey in Somerset.

Shaw continued to be embroiled in controversy, and in 1801 used his pen to publish a pamphlet attacking Hannah More's proposals for establishing Sunday schools. In 1802, using the pseudonym the Revd Sir Archibald MacSarcasm, Bart., he published the *Life of Hannah More, with a Critical Review of her Writings*. The long life of this colourful and controversial clergyman came to an end at the rectory, Chelvey, on 16 September 1831.   RODERICK MACLEOD

Sources *DNB* · K. D. Macdonald, 'The Rev. William Shaw: pioneer Gaelic lexicographer', *Transactions of the Gaelic Society of Inverness*, 50 (1976–8), 1–19 · *Fasti Scot.*, new edn, 6.431 · P. Fitzgerald, *The life of Samuel Johnson LL.D* (1897) · J. Reid, *Bibliotheca Scoto-Celtica, or, An account of all the books which have been printed in the Gaelic language* (1832) · [W. Shaw], *Memoirs of the life and writings of the late Dr Samuel Johnson, containing many valuable original letters, and several interesting anecdotes* (1785) · T. Costey, 'Johnson's last word on Ossian: ghost-writing for William Shaw', *Aberdeen and the Enlightenment*, ed. J. J. Carter and J. H. Pittock (1987), 375–431 · R. Sher, 'Percy, Shaw, and the Ferguson "cheat": national prejudice in the Ossian wars', *Ossian revisited*, ed. H. Gaskill (1991), 207–45

Shaw, William (1797–1853), agricultural editor, eldest son of John Shaw of Bath, was born in Bath and spent two years (1813–15) at Wadham College, Oxford; he was admitted to the Inner Temple on 20 June 1828 and called to the bar on 22 November 1833. He also farmed for a time in Wiltshire. He was married, but for many years separated from his wife.

In 1832 Shaw helped to found (with his lifelong friend, Cuthbert Johnson, as well as John and Joseph Rogerson, and Dr Blackstone) a new weekly agricultural newspaper, the *Mark Lane Express and Agricultural Journal*; he edited this paper, together with the associated monthly *Farmer's Magazine*, until his departure from England in 1852. In 1838 he began *Johnson and Shaw's Farmer's Almanack and Calendar*, which was issued under that title until 1872 and had a wide circulation. Also with Johnson, in 1844 he produced

Principles of Agriculture, an English edition of Von Thaer's original work. Under Shaw's editorship the *Mark Lane Express* gave comprehensive coverage of agricultural markets and technical innovation in farming. His concern to effect an improved flow of agricultural information was particularly evident in his promotion of agricultural societies. From 1834 he persistently advocated a national, non-political agricultural society for England, and the Royal Agricultural Society of England, which was established in 1838 (initially as the English Agricultural Society), was largely his creation. It was Shaw who personally persuaded John Charles, third Earl Spencer, to propose the formation of the society at the pre-Christmas meeting of the Smithfield Club in 1837. Shaw was the society's first secretary, being succeeded by James Hudson in 1840.

Shaw also founded the London Farmers' Club in 1843 and gave great encouragement to the formation of local farmers' clubs during the early 1840s for the purpose of non-political agricultural discussion. Shaw was a strenuous advocate of a reformed system of tenant right and, with Henry Corbet (who succeeded him as editor of the *Mark Lane Express*), produced a digest of the evidence on tenant right that had been given to Phillip Pusey's select committee on the question; this became a standard reference work. Shaw's support of tenant farmers' interests was recognized by a presentation of a service of silver plate on 1 April 1850, when he was described as 'the Cobden of Agriculture'; the previous year he had stood for parliament as a tenant-farmers' candidate in the northern division of Hampshire and, although not elected, achieved a highly creditable vote.

'Shaw of the Strand' (as he was known at the Farmers' Club) also had a number of business interests, and he was one of the chief founders (1840) and the managing director of the Farmers' Insurance Company. He was also managing director of the Farmers' and Graziers' Mutual Cattle Insurance Association, which was founded in 1844 but fell into financial difficulties in 1849. Soon afterwards Shaw sustained heavy financial losses in connection with his support for a project to relocate the Metropolitan Cattle Market at Islington instead of Smithfield, and it was these losses which caused him to flee to Australia in November 1852. After a period of extreme adversity in Melbourne he died penniless in a remote gold-prospecting area on 5 May 1853. His demise was largely ignored by his contemporaries, and for this reason Shaw never received the historical recognition as a leader of early Victorian agricultural opinion that his achievements merited.

ERNEST CLARKE, rev. NICHOLAS GODDARD

Sources *GM*, 2nd ser., 40 (1853), 422 · *Mark Lane Express* (31 March 1902) [70th birthday suppl.] · *Mark Lane Express and Agricultural Journal* (1832–52) · *Farmer's Magazine* (1832–52) · B. H. T. Gibbs, *The Smithfield club: a short history of its origin and progress* (1857), 14 · N. Goddard, 'William Shaw "of the Strand" and the formation of the Royal Agricultural Society of England', *Journal of the Royal Agricultural Society of England*, 143 (1982), 98–104
Archives U. Reading, Rural History Centre, records of the Royal Agricultural Society of England

Likenesses R. D. Ansdell, study, 1842, Royal Agricultural Society of England, London

Shaw, William (1823–1895), politician and businessman, was born on 4 May 1823 in Moy, co. Tyrone. His father, Samuel Shaw, was a Congregational minister. He was educated privately and then spent some time at Trinity College, Dublin, but did not take a degree. Being intended for the Congregational ministry, he studied at Highbury College, Middlesex, a theological seminary, and then served as the minister for an independent church in George's Street, Cork, between 1846 and 1850. Following his marriage in 1850 to Charlotte Clear, daughter of a wealthy corn merchant in Cork, he abandoned the clerical profession for a mercantile career.

Shaw initially attempted to enter parliament at the Bandon by-election on 14 February 1865, when he stood as a Liberal candidate but was defeated by 101 votes to 67. He next contested a parliamentary seat as a Liberal at Bandon at the general election in July 1865, which he narrowly lost. He then had his first success at Bandon, which he won by four votes at the general election of November 1868, when he campaigned as an independent Liberal. He represented this constituency until the dissolution in 1874, during which time he supported Gladstone's church and land bills.

Shaw had had a connection with the Young Ireland movement as a young man and, with the founding of the Home Government Association to advocate Isaac Butt's federalist ideas in 1870, he aligned himself with the new organization. His involvement was so conspicuous that he was selected to preside at the national conference called to found the Home Rule League held at the Rotunda in November 1873. At the general election of 1874 he was returned unopposed as a home-ruler for co. Cork. He then joined the new Home Rule Party formed after the election. Along with Mitchell Henry, he often deputized for the Home Rule Party chairman, replacing Isaac Butt during his frequent absences from Westminster and acting, in 1877, as the spokesman on a motion for a select committee of the House of Commons to inquire into the demand for an Irish parliament. Shaw remained steadfast in his loyalty to Butt during the increasingly bitter disputes that erupted from 1877 over 'obstruction' and, after Butt's death in May 1879, was chosen party chairman.

Shaw's determined support of Butt made him suspect to the growing body of MPs who gathered around Charles Stewart Parnell. Although Shaw was once again successful for co. Cork in the general election of 1880, when he came top of the poll, Parnell decided to challenge him for the sessional chairmanship—the first and only occasion upon which the office was contested until December 1890. At the party meeting held in Dublin on 17 May, Parnell won by twenty-three votes to eighteen. Thereafter Shaw increasingly became alienated from Parnellite militancy. He declined to follow the Irish party across the floor of the House of Commons and sat on the Liberal benches throughout the 1880–85 parliament.

In 1880 the Liberal government nominated Shaw to sit on the Bessborough commission, which was appointed to examine Irish land tenure. He refused to be identified with the Land League agitation and, along with fellow dissidents, formally ceased to act with the Irish party from 12 January 1881. During the debates on the Land Bill of 1881 he supported the government and voted for the measure on the second reading, when the majority of Parnellites abstained. Thereafter he and his friends gave general support to the Liberal administration, earning Gladstone's unguarded characterization of them as 'nominal home rulers', a label eagerly seized upon by militants anxious to discredit the moderates. Shaw resigned from the moribund Home Rule League in December 1881 and, after 1882, like most of the 'nominal home rulers', was often missing from the parliamentary forum. He did not again seek election and retired from active politics in 1885.

Although Shaw had a reputation for prudence and judgement that in political life earned him the sobriquet Sensible Shaw, his later commercial dealings proved disastrous. In 1885 the Munster Bank, of which he was the principal founder and chairman, folded. Unable to meet his personal liabilities he was declared a bankrupt on 12 January 1886. Subsequently, he lived mainly in London and was connected with several industrial and financial newspapers. He died on 19 September 1895 at his sister's home, Lislee, Enniskerry, co. Wicklow.

C. L. FALKINER, *rev.* ALAN O'DAY

Sources *The Constitution* [Cork] (21 Sept 1895) · *Freeman's Journal* [Dublin] (21 Sept 1895) · *The Times* (24 Sept 1895) · WWBMP · D. Thornley, *Isaac Butt and home rule* (1964) · C. C. O'Brien, *Parnell and his party, 1880–90* (1957) · H. W. Lucy, *A diary of two parliaments*, 2 vols. (1885–6) · *Dod's Parliamentary Companion* · J. L. Hammond, *Gladstone and the Irish nation* (1938) · A. M. Sullivan, *New Ireland*, [new edn] (1882) · M. MacDonagh, *The home rule movement* (1920) · A. O'Day, *The English face of Irish nationalism* (1977)
Archives NL Ire., Isaac Butt MSS

Shaw, William Arthur (1865–1943), archivist and historian, was born at Hooley Hill, Ashton under Lyne, Lancashire, on 19 April 1865, the younger son of James Shaw, manufacturer, and his wife, Sarah Ann Hampshire. He was educated at the Owens College, Manchester, where he was awarded the Cobden Club prize and the Bradford history scholarship (1883), the Shuttleworth political economy scholarship (1884), and was appointed a Berkeley fellow (1886). He graduated BA in 1883, MA in 1886, and LittD in 1892.

Shaw initially undertook editorial work for the Chetham Society, and his frequent visits to the Public Record Office led in 1894 to an offer to work for the office on the calendar of Elizabethan foreign state papers. When it was decided not to proceed with this work, he was employed on the *Calendar of Treasury Papers* (then completed to 1728). The scope of this project was significantly expanded on Shaw's initiative. As it progressed, Shaw moved away from the dry, usually descriptive nature found before in the introductions to such collections towards a livelier and more analytical style, placing the documents within a broader historical context and often triggering a telling reassessment of individuals and period. He was regarded by a contemporary as having 'opened the gateway into

Treasury Records not merely for the specialists but for any intelligent person' (Clapham, 350).

Shaw was twice married: first, to Clara Edith (*d*. 1919), associate of the Royal Academy of Music and the Royal Philharmonic Society, daughter of Thomas William John Goldsbrough MD, of West Square, London; and second, from 1924, to Mabel Elizabeth, daughter of Angus Grant, retired police officer of Rothiemurchus, Inverness-shire. She survived him. They had one daughter.

Besides his official work Shaw wrote many other scholarly articles and publications, chiefly on economics and on the history of the seventeenth century. These included *The History of Currency* (1895), *A History of the English Church during the Civil Wars and under the Commonwealth* (2 vols., 1900), *The Knights of England* (2 vols., 1906), and *Three Inventories of Pictures in the Collections of Henry VIII and Edward VI* (1937). He also wrote reports on the Sidney papers for the Historical Manuscripts Commission. Through his work, Shaw changed the way in which developments in public finance were viewed historically. His analysis of the breakdown of the medieval theory that 'the King should live of his own' and of the gradual change to more modern ideas of parliamentary control of expenditure was an important step in historical understanding in this field. Shaw's views were often contentious, and his own combative responses in historical debates could display elements of what one acquaintance suspected was 'a violent nature deep down somewhere' (Clapham, 349).

Shaw was elected FBA in 1940. He died at Chase Farm Hospital, Enfield, Middlesex, on 15 April 1943.

F. H. SLINGSBY, *rev.* MARC BRODIE

Sources J. H. Clapham, 'William Arthur Shaw, 1865–1943', *PBA*, 29 (1943), 349–55 · *The Times* (19 April 1943) · personal knowledge (1959) · *WWW* · J. D. Cantwell, *The Public Record Office, 1838–1958* (1991) · *CGPLA Eng. & Wales* (1943)
Archives JRL, notes, papers, and transcripts
Likenesses photograph, 1948, NPG · photograph, repro. in Clapham, 'William Arthur Shaw', facing p. 349
Wealth at death £1004 18*s*. 4*d*.: probate, 25 May 1943, *CGPLA Eng. & Wales*

Shaw, Sir William Fletcher (1878–1961), obstetric physician and gynaecologist, was born on 13 April 1878 at Richmond Terrace, Clayton, Manchester, the son of David Shaw, an oil distiller, and his wife, Zillah Fletcher, daughter of a Lancashire woollen manufacturer. He started his education as a pupil at Manchester grammar school, from where he went to Owens College to study medicine. He qualified MB BCh in 1903, the year in which Owens College became the Victoria University of Manchester, and graduated MD in 1906 with a thesis on chronic metritis, which earned him a gold medal. While an undergraduate he became president of the Medical Students' Debating Society and grew an impressive handlebar moustache, on account of which he was nicknamed Hairy Bill; this nickname stayed with him for the rest of his days, despite the fact that he was clean-shaven in later life. After qualifying Shaw filled resident appointments first at the Manchester Royal Infirmary and then at St Mary's Hospital; there he worked for many years, becoming in turn assistant to the out-patient department, pathologist in the first pathological laboratory to be set up at St Mary's, and, in 1912, assistant surgeon. In 1912 he was elected honorary gynaecologist to the Christie Hospital and assistant lecturer in obstetrics and gynaecology in the University of Manchester; in 1919 he joined the staff of the Manchester Royal Infirmary. He became professor of systematic obstetrics and gynaecology in the university in 1920 and five years later was elected professor of clinical obstetrics and gynaecology.

A gynaecologist of great distinction, Shaw was an enthusiastic and able teacher who published widely, particularly on the subject of chronic metritis and uterine prolapse. He popularized the operation for prolapse developed by the Manchester obstetricians Archibald Donald and William Fothergill, which he liked to be called the 'Manchester operation'; he was also renowned as one of the few gynaecologists in Manchester who performed vaginal hysterectomy. As a founder member of one of the first medical travelling clubs in Britain, the Gynaecological Visiting Society, he travelled to most of the schools of medicine in Europe. His favourite centre before the First World War was Vienna, where he got to know such well-known figures of European gynaecology as Ernst Wertheim and Friedrich Schauta.

Shaw's greatest contribution to obstetrics and gynaecology, however, was in connection with the foundation of the Royal College of Obstetricians and Gynaecologists at a time when gynaecology was in danger of being separated from obstetrics and brought under the control of the Royal College of Surgeons. Although the idea of combining the two specialities under the aegis of a new college was not original to Shaw, it was he who took the lead in 1924 in converting a concept into reality when he suggested it to the Liverpool obstetrician William Blair Bell. The hard work and tact that Shaw brought to bear on this ambitious project resulted in the establishment of the British (later Royal) College of Obstetricians and Gynaecologists in 1929, with Blair Bell as its first president. Shaw was honorary secretary from 1929 to 1938, and president from 1938 to 1943. He was knighted in 1942, the first president to be thus honoured, and received the honorary fellowship of the college at a special meeting in 1948. After retiring in 1943, Shaw continued to take a keen interest in college affairs, visiting Canada, Australia, New Zealand, and South Africa, and bravely writing at short notice *Twenty-five years: the story of the Royal College of Obstetricians and Gynaecologists, 1929–1954* (1954), a work which, much to his regret, could not be as frank as he would have wished it to be.

During his long career Shaw held numerous appointments and offices. He was president of the North of England Obstetrical and Gynaecological Society, of the section of obstetrics and gynaecology of the Royal Society of Medicine, and of the Manchester Medical Society. He was also examiner in his speciality for the universities of Liverpool, Leeds, Wales, Edinburgh, and Cambridge, and, with the advent of the National Health Service in 1948, he was appointed consultant adviser in gynaecology to the north-west region. In recognition of his work, in 1936 he was elected honorary fellow of the American College of Surgeons and in 1939 a fellow of the Royal College of Physicians. In 1947 the Society of Apothecaries conferred on him an honorary mastership of midwifery and the following year he received the honorary degree of LLD from Queen's University, Belfast.

Shaw was famed for his diplomacy and tact, though critics noted his lack of warmth and his rather Olympian manner when dealing with his juniors. He was interested in the training of young gynaecologists and was always ready to advise, but he appeared austere and remote and some found him slightly forbidding and difficult to know. Shaw was twice married: his first wife, Norah, daughter of David Meredith Jones, died in 1934, and he then married on 24 May 1939 Mabel Mary Stevenson (1876/7–1947), a widow, daughter of Richard Beaty, a merchant tailor. By his first marriage he had three sons and one daughter. The daughter died as an infant; the second son, William, was killed in Normandy in 1944 and is commemorated at the Royal College of Obstetricians and Gynaecologists by the William Meredith Fletcher Shaw lecture. There were no children of the second marriage. Shaw died of leukaemia in the Royal Infirmary Private Patients' Home, Manchester, on 14 November 1961. ORNELLA MOSCUCCI

Sources *BMJ* (25 Nov 1961), 1437–8 · *The Lancet* (25 Nov 1961), 1208–9 · R. W. Burslem, 'Sir William Fletcher Shaw, 1878–1961', *Some Manchester doctors: a biographical collection to mark the 150th anniversary of the Manchester Medical Society, 1834–1984*, ed. W. J. Elwood and A. F. Tuxford (1984), 140–46 · b. cert. · m. cert. · d. cert. · *WW* (1935) · *CGPLA Eng. & Wales* (1962)

Archives Royal College of Obstetricians and Gynaecologists, London, corresp. and papers; leaflet

Likenesses Lafayette studio, photograph, 1920, Royal College of Obstetricians and Gynaecologists, London · J. B. Souter, oils, 1933, Royal College of Obstetricians and Gynaecologists, London

Wealth at death £46,569 8s.: probate, 28 March 1962, *CGPLA Eng. & Wales*

Shawe, John (1608–1672), nonconformist minister, was born on 22 June 1608 at Sykehouse in the parish of Bradfield, Yorkshire, the only son of John Shawe (*d.* 1634) and his second wife, Emote Steade (*d.* 1652). He went to school at Darwen and Rotherham and in 1623 entered Christ's College, Cambridge, where he was tutored by William Chappell, later bishop of Cork. As a result of hearing sermons in a nearby village preached by Thomas Weld, Shawe determined on a ministerial career and was ordained priest at Peterborough on 28 December 1629, taking his MA degree the following year. He was appointed lecturer at Brampton in Derbyshire in 1630 and given a licence by the bishop, Thomas Morton, to preach throughout the diocese without being required to subscribe to the Articles. While there Shawe married Dorothy (*d.* 1657), daughter of George Heathcote, gentleman, of Cutthorpe Hall, Brampton, on 10 December 1632 in the church of Holy Trinity, Micklegate, in York, a city in whose religious life he was later to play a prominent part. More immediately, however, Shawe was invited by the feoffees of impropriations to a lectureship at Chulmleigh in Devon for a period of three years, having been heard preaching

in London by a group of merchants with connections to Devon. He moved there in 1633, by which time he had also been appointed chaplain to Philip Herbert, earl of Montgomery and Pembroke. His ministry at Chulmleigh was brought to an end in 1636 as a result of complaints against his churchmanship, probably instigated by Archbishop Laud. Shawe then withdrew to his estate at Sykehouse (his father having died in 1634) but was soon called to be one of the civic preachers at York by the puritan mayor, Alderman Vaux. He took up his post at All Saints, Pavement, but immediately fell foul of Archbishop Neile as a result of his first sermon in the city. Neile thought him the leader of the puritan party at York but refrained from further action against him when he discovered that Shawe was Pembroke's chaplain. For the next three years Shawe played a prominent role, along with Edward Bowles, in the religious life of the city.

On 17 April 1639 Shawe was instituted to the valuable living of Rotherham, Yorkshire, on Pembroke's presentation, and soon after accompanied him and the royal entourage to the siege of Berwick. While there he established a friendship with Alexander Henderson, which was renewed the following year when Shawe was chaplain to the English commissioners appointed to settle the grievances of the Scots, whom Henderson represented as a commissioner. Shawe's involvement with Scottish affairs at this time continued through his work as chaplain to Henry Rich, earl of Holland, and he also retained close links with the city of York, preaching a sermon critical of the king in one of the parish churches on the occasion of the royal arrival there in the spring of 1642.

After the king left York, Shawe moved to Hull, but was excluded by the governor, Sir John Hotham, as a result of his first sermon in the town. He then withdrew to Beverley where he preached a sermon, dedicated to the mayor and aldermen of Hull, and published as *A Broken Heart*, in which he defended his actions and likened the cause of the royalist armies to that of the northern earls of 1569. After returning to Rotherham, Shawe was asked to preach before Lord Fairfax and his army, then camped at Selby, on a special fast day called for 5 February 1643, a sermon subsequently published as *Two Clean Birds*. He was not long at Rotherham; apparently on account of his support for parliament, with three other leading townsmen, he was fined £1000; although his wife was made prisoner when the town was taken on 4 May 1643, Shawe escaped to Manchester. There he joined other puritan ministers in providing regular sermons, preaching every Friday in the town, continuing to live there after he accepted the rectory of nearby Lyme from Sir William Brereton later that year. In the spring of 1644 Shawe was invited to make a two-month missionary visit to Cartmel, Lancashire, where puritan preaching had been little heard before, and this experience of unreformed religion made a strong impression on him. In June 1644, on hearing of the arrival of Prince Rupert and his forces, he was once again on his travels, back across the Pennines this time, and he re-emerged in York immediately after the relief of the city and the parliamentarian victory at Marston Moor. He was appointed chaplain to the standing committee for the government of the northern counties on 16 July 1644 and on 20 September preached the sermon in York Minster on the occasion of the taking of the solemn league and covenant by Fairfax and others.

Throughout the upheavals of the 1640s and in subsequent years, Shawe remained firm in his commitment to a presbyterian form of church order (although he was not over-zealous in this respect) and influenced the religious policy of the interregnum both locally and nationally. He became secretary to the committee for scandalous ministers and was appointed to the wealthy living of Scrayingham by Fairfax. In 1645 he accepted an invitation to return to Hull, first as lecturer at St Mary's and later at the main church of Holy Trinity, and he remained in these posts until the Restoration. In addition, in 1651, after some litigation with the then incumbent, Shawe was made master of the Hull Charterhouse; he thereafter made this his home, spending considerable sums on the property both for his benefit and that of the poor inmates. Shawe preached in the town on Wednesdays and Thursdays and set up a godly discipline for the administration of the Lord's supper on presbyterian lines, which did not find favour among all members of the corporation, including some congregationalists. Relations with the corporation were also often strained over disputes about salary and the administration of the Charterhouse. During these years he played an active role on a wider stage; he was chaplain to the parliamentary commissioners negotiating with the king at Newcastle in 1646 and under the protectorate he preached often at both Whitehall and Hampton Court, receiving a pension of £100 per annum from Cromwell.

Shawe's first wife, Dorothy, died on 10 December 1657, and he published a memoir of her life the following year. On 19 December 1659 he married Margaret (d. 1693), daughter of John Stillington, esquire, of Kelfield, and it was for his young son of that marriage that Shawe subsequently wrote his autobiography. Despite his high profile under the protectorate, on 25 July 1660 he was appointed a royal chaplain. He was present at the coronation the following April, but by the end of 1660 his position at Hull was under threat from the officers of the garrison there. On 9 June 1661 a royal mandate inhibited him from preaching at Holy Trinity but, after a personal interview with the king, Shawe was allowed to retain the Charterhouse and his position as a royal chaplain. Although he initially returned to Hull, preaching at the Charterhouse to considerable crowds despite the opposition of the garrison, following the Act of Uniformity he resigned his post there, returning to Rotherham on 20 June 1662. During that summer he shared the pulpit at Rotherham with the vicar, but after St Bartholomew's day, and for the remainder of his life, preached only in private houses. He died on 19 April 1672, and was buried at Rotherham two days later. Despite his conflicts with Hull corporation over salary he had remained comfortably off, providing substantial marriage portions for his six daughters and leaving lands in

Penistone. By his will he bequeathed sixty bibles to be distributed to the poor, as well as other charitable bequests to Hull and elsewhere. His reputation for learning was recalled in the funeral inscription formerly in Rotherham parish which described him as a Barnabas or Boanerges.

WILLIAM JOSEPH SHEILS

Sources C. Jackson, ed., *Yorkshire diaries and autobiographies*, [1], SurtS, 65 (1877) [incl. Shawe's autobiography] · Venn, *Alum. Cant.* · Greaves & Zaller, *BDBR* · R. Marchant, *The puritans and the church courts in the diocese of York, 1560–1642* (1960) · *VCH Yorkshire East Riding*, vol. 1 · W. J. Sheils, 'Provincial preaching on the eve of the civil wars', *Religion, culture and society in early modern Britain*, ed. A. Fletcher and P. Roberts (1994)
Archives Otley Museum, West Yorkshire, Phillipps MSS, MS notes of sermon preached at York in Otley parish records, P83/102 [copy]
Wealth at death 'comfortably off'

Shaxton, Nicholas (*c*.1485–1556), bishop of Salisbury, was a native of Norfolk and studied at Cambridge, where he proceeded BA in 1506 or 1507, MA in 1510, BTh in 1521, and DTh in 1531. He became a fellow of Gonville Hall. In 1520, before he took up controversial views, he became a university preacher and was licensed to preach anywhere in the British Isles.

Cambridge evangelical In the 1520s many members of Gonville Hall became deeply involved in the theological ferment developing at Cambridge. Certainly it was more likely that Shaxton's early interest in Lutheran ideas was spurred inside his own college rather than at any informal meetings that might have taken place at the White Horse tavern, whose importance has been overrated. Gonville Hall, with Pembroke and Peterhouse, had among its members men whom John Foxe termed 'the godly learned in Christ' (*Acts and Monuments*, 5.415), including Edward Crome (who was a fellow with Shaxton) and John Skip (later chaplain to Anne Boleyn). The royal physician William Butts (an influential advocate of reform at court) was also a Gonville man. Shaxton's devotion to his college remained a great constant throughout his life.

Shaxton was a prompt supporter of Henry VIII's divorce from Katherine of Aragon, and was one of Anne Boleyn's most important protégés. In early 1530 Bishop Richard Nix of Norwich began to raise a new alarm about the growing availability of erroneous books, and in particular he complained of Gonville men who gave every appearance of holiness but in actuality savoured of heresy. Working in partnership with Archbishop William Warham and other conservative bishops Nix moved to suppress unorthodox preaching. Crome was among the first troubled in early 1531, but he was saved through Anne's influence, and by his own sophisticated aptitude for equivocating when tightly cornered, an ability Shaxton and many other reformers also cultivated. In August, Nix burnt Thomas Bilney (who had converted Hugh Latimer as well as many others at the university). His suspicions had also been aroused by Shaxton, who had been 'very sore suspected of many men' for his sermons and possession of heretical books (*Acts and Monuments*, 4.680).

None of Shaxton's sermon notes survive, and for much of his career it is possible only to make inferences about the nature of his opinions. Certainly he stood with many of the early reformers in supporting the primacy of scripture, and in impugning traditional tenets including purgatory, and eventually transubstantiation. According to Nix's hostile description, Shaxton had preached *ad clerum* in Cambridge on Ash Wednesday 1531 that it was wrong to assert publicly that there was no purgatory, but not damnable to think so privately. Aghast, Nix (according to Foxe) is supposed to have said: 'Christ's Mother! I fear I have burnt Abel, and let Cain go!' (*Acts and Monuments*, 4.650). But Bilney's execution had shocked the university and its officers strove to prevent any further burnings. Vice-chancellor John Watson and his assistants were willing to argue Shaxton into compliance, and they had 'much ado to bring him to forsake' his views. To avoid the scandal of an open abjuration Watson prepared a special oath for him and all candidates in theology to take, that they would never maintain or defend any errors by Wycliffe, Hus, or Luther (*Acts and Monuments*, 4.680). Eventually a panel of divines attested that they found Shaxton to be 'a good catholyke man' (*Acts and Monuments*, 5, appx 17, no. 1). The following year, without too much publicity, Latimer also had to retract some of the positions he had preached.

Court preacher and bishop In the fluid circumstances of these early years of doctrinal experimentation Shaxton's troubles only enhanced his reputation among other reformers, and by the beginning of 1534 he had risen to become Queen Anne's almoner. The court had rapidly become a testing ground for doctrinal change with Henry's supremacy over the English church. In Anne's evangelical household religious discussion was a fixture, especially at dinners, and the supreme head himself sometimes engaged in debates and arguments. During Lent 1534 Archbishop Thomas Cranmer introduced Shaxton (whom he accounted 'my old acquainted friend') and Latimer onto the court's preaching schedule, which may have been Shaxton's first formal speaking essay under the king's eye (*Miscellaneous Writings*, 309). Some time later, teamed with Latimer, Shaxton entered into a debate against the king and Sir James Boleyn (the queen's uncle) on a question of scripture (possibly on purgatory) which was so spirited that Henry later wrote out 'dyverse epistelles' on the matter ('William Latymer's chronicklle', 62).

Through Anne's influence Shaxton gained a series of ecclesiastical preferments, including a canonry in St Stephen's Chapel, Westminster. Early in 1535 he was made bishop of Salisbury (royal assent 5 March, temporalities restored 1 April, consecration 11 April), and Latimer was raised to Worcester when their Italian predecessors were deprived. Anne lent each of them £200 to pay for their first fruits and tenths, which was still owed at her execution the following year. In May 1536, a few days after her death, Shaxton wrote to Thomas Cromwell in desperation, pleading with him to continue her work in advancing the honour of God and his holy word. Within his new diocese he was active in promoting the reading of the Bible in the vernacular, and was also a strong advocate of preaching. In Holbein's title-page for Coverdale's Bible of 1535, as

well as the elaborate woodcut that graces the title-page of the Great Bible of 1539, Shaxton is portrayed standing shoulder to shoulder with his brother bishops Cranmer and Latimer as they receive holy scripture from the hand of the king.

Shaxton's reputation for advancing reform spread far beyond his own diocese. During the northern risings of the autumn of 1536 rebels cited him with the other bishops of recent promotion as having subverted the faith of Christ. The political realities of the later 1530s kept him (and all bishops) highly dependent upon the goodwill of Cromwell (especially in his capacity as vicegerent for spiritual matters), and ultimately, upon the king. But Shaxton's relations with Cromwell were continually strained. His letters never shared the confidence with which Latimer approached Cromwell, and his tenure as bishop was contentious even for a reformer, and probably high-handed. He quarrelled with the inhabitants of Salisbury as he tried to impose his authority over them, exacerbating long-term disagreements concerning episcopal influence over civic jurisdiction. They countered by calling him a heretic they trusted to see hanged. Eventually Cromwell complained that Shaxton had a stomach more meet for an emperor than a bishop. He had little credit left at court in 1539 when he proved unwilling to work for the passage of the six articles through parliament, in that dangerous period as Henry's tolerance for doctrinal innovation waned.

Marriage, resignation, and seclusion The cornerstone of the six articles was the act's defence of the mass and the real presence, and its tacit assumption that private masses assisted the departed in purgatory. Its promotion by the king was a setback for reformers. In addition Shaxton's reluctance to support the measure was probably dominated by an urgent personal factor, for some time before 1539 he had married. The act also prohibited clerical marriage and upheld vows of chastity, and lapses were considered felonies, punishable by death. As in the case of Cranmer, the details of Shaxton's marriage are almost completely shrouded in the obscurity that made the match possible. In his Ash Wednesday sermon of 1531 he had tested the issue of clerical celibacy by arguing that no man could maintain chastity only by prayer and fasting without God's help. In 1538 he tried to promote a married man as divinity lecturer at Reading Abbey, over the strenuous objections of the abbot. Although many reformers prompted Cromwell to permit clerical marriage, or secretly took wives, the issue remained clouded. Shaxton's marriage therefore had always represented a calculated risk, and from the passage of the Act of Six Articles in 1539 it was a positive danger.

Shaxton and Latimer resigned their sees in July 1539. So shocking and unfamiliar did it seem for bishops to relinquish their dioceses that Shaxton had to ask Cromwell if he should still dress like a bishop, and Crome had to defend them in his London sermons against the hostile popular conclusion that they had surrendered their honour with their dignities. On the continent Melanchthon wrote to Henry in protest against the six articles and praised their bravery. For some months Shaxton was held in ward at Chew by Bishop John Clerk of Bath and Wells. In December he and Latimer were each granted an annuity of 100 marks.

Following his resignation Shaxton's career entered an almost complete eclipse. Initially his movements were restricted, and his preaching prohibited. By 1542, due to the good auspices of Cranmer, he obtained a haven at Hadleigh in Suffolk, an ecclesiastical peculiar belonging to the diocese of Canterbury. Foxe referred to Hadleigh as seeming more like 'a university of the learned' than the clothmaking town it was in actuality (*Acts and Monuments*, 6.677), due in no small measure to the energy and effectiveness of its spiritual leaders, who included Bilney (who had preached there), Thomas Rose, and especially its rector, Rowland Taylor. In all likelihood Hadleigh's real circumstances may have been less glowing than Foxe would have his readers believe, for (as elsewhere) those townspeople sympathetic to reform probably constituted only a committed core among the rest. Nevertheless Shaxton could count upon those with connections to the archbishop's household, and Hadleigh provided an astonishing measure of security for his family. In 1539 Cranmer had very sensibly sent his wife, Margaret, for safety to her relatives on the continent, but neither Shaxton nor Taylor (who had also married before 1539 and served in Cranmer's employ) seem to have followed his example. Shaxton and his wife had at least three children.

Recantation Shaxton's next crisis occurred in 1546, when intense new struggles over doctrine developed in the waning months of the king's life. In April, Crome embarked on a series of London sermons that implicitly attacked the six articles by impugning the efficacy of votive masses, which could not, he argued, relieve the souls of the dead. As Crome came under heavy pressure to recant Shaxton and Latimer came to his aid, urging him not to retract his opinions. And Shaxton backed Crome with a sermon of his own in London at the beginning of June, denying the presence of Christ's body in the sacrament of the altar. Conservative opponents used this controversy to initiate a purge of reformers at court and in many parts of the country.

Shaxton was arrested and condemned to be burnt. Then a panel of theologians was sent to persuade him, with even greater success than in 1531. He accepted the six articles with no further reservations, and wrote an abject letter of apology to the king. As part of his submission he was sent to persuade Anne Askew, who had similarly denied the real presence. She told him that 'it had been good for him never to have been born' (*Acts and Monuments*, 5.547), and he presided when she was burnt with three others in Smithfield on 16 July. Two weeks later he appeared at Paul's Cross to recant formally, weeping copiously for his errors. It was about this time that he put away his wife. In November his reconciliation to the regime became complete when the king gave him a new licence to preach.

From 1546 Shaxton's alienation from reform was total.

He never retracted this recantation, he never apologized to his former allies, he was not reconciled with his wife, and he remained conservative in opinion for the rest of his life. Under Edward VI he seemed like a dangerous backslider to the new protestant regime, and he was the focus of many vituperative printed attacks, by John Bale (who said he fell from Christ) among others. The most damaging one, edited by Robert Crowley, carried an anonymous letter of criticism by Taylor, and even the simple rhyming admonition against sexual incontinence that Shaxton had written to his wife when he had separated from her.

> Voyde euil thoughtes, studie in scripture
> Kepe thine eye, ill company eschue
> Least delite and desire them do ensue.
> (Crowley, sig. A4r)

Last years and death Under Mary, Shaxton's position improved. In 1555 he received a pardon from Cardinal Reginald Pole for his illicit marriage and the heresies he had encouraged under Henry VIII. In the same year he became suffragan to Bishop Thomas Thirlby of Ely. Again he acted as examiner, and tried to persuade others to follow his example. 'Good brethren', he counselled William Wolsey and Robert Pygot of Wisbech in a futile effort to keep them from the stake, 'remember yourselves, and become new men, for I myself was in this fond opinion that you are now in, but I am now become a new man' (*Acts and Monuments*, 7.404). At Cambridge the university's habitual protectiveness ensured that there was only one execution there, at Easter 1556 of John Hullier, whose examination Shaxton led at Great St Mary's Church. To protestants these martyrdoms amplified the irony of Shaxton's apostasy.

Gonville Hall figured large in Shaxton's will of 5 August 1556, along with a weighty secret. His final benefactions to the college included his books, the hangings of green say in his chamber, and a house in Cambridge that he was in the midst of buying at the time of his death. Its income he wanted used 'to solace the compagnie at home' each Christmas. And he instructed his Hadleigh servant Thomas Alabaster to ensure that the residue of his estate was to go to one Thomas Dartsab, the curious name (bastard spelled backwards) hinting at the desperate and even poignant contrivances necessary to cope with the embarrassing fact that the one-time bishop had a son. His two daughters, perhaps already married to Hadleigh men and provided for, were not mentioned. Shaxton had died by 9 August, when his will was proved, and according to his wishes his body was interred in the chapel of Gonville Hall. In modern times the college has reinvigorated his bequest in the form of a holiday dinner for the fellows and their spouses.

SUSAN WABUDA

Sources will, 9 Aug 1556, CUL, department of manuscripts and university archives, wills I, fol. 100r · Reginald Pole's register, Bibliothèque Municipale, Douai, MS 922, vol. 2, fols. 49r–50v · [R. Crowley], *The confutation of. xiii, articles, whereunto Nicholas Shaxton … subscribed and caused to be set forth in print* [1548] · *The acts and monuments of John Foxe*, new edn, ed. G. Townsend, 8 vols. (1843–9) ·

Miscellaneous writings and letters of Thomas Cranmer, ed. J. E. Cox, Parker Society, [18] (1846) • 'William Latymer's chronicklle of Anne Bulleyne', ed. M. Dowling, *Camden miscellany, XXX*, CS, 4th ser., 39 (1990), 23–86 • J. Craig, 'Reformers, conflict, and revisionism: the Reformation in sixteenth-century Hadleigh', *HJ*, 42 (1999), 1–23 • J. S. Craig, 'The marginalia of Dr Rowland Taylor', *Historical Research*, 64 (1991), 411–20 • M. Dowling, 'Anne Boleyn and reform', *Journal of Ecclesiastical History*, 35 (1984), 30–46 • J. Fines, 'A biographical register of early English protestants' (typescript), CUL [also in U. Lond., Institute of Historical Research] • G. R. Elton, *Policy and police: the enforcement of the Reformation in the age of Thomas Cromwell* (1972), 100–07 • S. Wabuda, 'Equivocation and recantation during the English Reformation: the "subtle shadows" of Dr Edward Crome', *Journal of Ecclesiastical History*, 44 (1993), 224–42 • A. Brown, *Popular piety in late medieval England: the diocese of Salisbury, 1520–1550* (1995) • Venn, *Alum. Cant.*, 1/4.54 • LMA, DL/C/331, fol. 7*r*

Archives PRO, letters to Thomas Cromwell, SP 1 • Wilts. & Swindon RO, episcopal register

Shea, David [Daniel] (1777–1836), orientalist, son of Daniel Shea, a farmer, was born in co. Limerick. Shea, whose forename is given in some sources as Daniel, entered Trinity College, Dublin, on 3 June 1793, and in 1797 obtained a scholarship in classics. While at university he joined the Society of United Irishmen. In April 1797 Lord Clare, vicechancellor of the university, held a visitation, at which he required the students to take an oath that they would inform against any whom they knew to be connected with the society. Shea refused to comply and was expelled from the university.

Shea went to England, and obtained a mastership in a private school. His knowledge of Italian soon obtained for him the post of chief clerk in a large mercantile establishment at Malta. While there he mastered Arabic, acquiring a knowledge not only of the classical language but also of the chief current dialects. A project on the part of his employers to open a factory on the east coast of the Black Sea led him also to study Persian. When the firm was compelled to withdraw altogether from the Levant he was recalled to England. There he made the acquaintance of Adam Clarke, who found him employment as a private tutor in the house of a Dr Laurell, and afterwards procured for him an assistant professorship in the oriental department of the East India College at Haileybury.

Shea was made a member of the committee of the newly formed Oriental Translation Fund. He translated two books from Persian. The first was Mirkhond's work under the title *History of the Early Kings of Persia*, published in London in 1832. The second, *The Dabistān, or, School of manners*, was unfinished at the time of his death, and was completed by Anthony Troyer. Shea died at the East India College on 11 May 1836.

E. I. Carlyle, *rev.* Parvin Loloi

Sources private information (1897) • *The Athenaeum* (14 May 1836), 346 • A. Troyer, 'Introduction', *The Dabistán, or, School of manners*, trans. D. Shea and A. Troyer (1843), 91 • *Journal of the Royal Asiatic Society of Great Britain and Ireland*, 4 (1837), xviii–xix • A. J. Webb, *A compendium of Irish biography* (1878), 470 • Burtchaell & Sadleir, *Alum. Dubl.* • F. C. Danvers and others, *Memorials of old Haileybury College* (1894) • J. S. Crone, *A concise dictionary of Irish biography*, rev. edn (1937) • Allibone, *Dict.* • S. Maunder, *The biographical treasury*, new edn, rev. W. L. R. Cates (1870) • H. J. Rose, *A new general biographical dictionary*, ed. H. J. Rose and T. Wright, 12 vols. (1853)

Shea, Patrick [Paddy] (1908–1986), public servant and author, was born on 27 April 1908 at Delvin, co. Westmeath, Ireland, the second of the family of four sons and one daughter of Patrick Shea (d. 1952) and his wife, Mary Catherine McLaughlin. Shea's father was a member of the Royal Irish Constabulary (RIC) and came from an Irish-speaking family in co. Kerry. The next generation were brought up in police quarters at Athlone between 1908 and 1920, and then at Rathfriland and Clones, before settling at Newry, co. Down. Shea's father, who had reached the rank of head constable in the now disbanded RIC, became clerk of petty sessions there. Shea's autobiography is partly an affectionate tribute to the rank-and-file members of the RIC whom he had known so well as a child.

Between 1922 and 1926 Shea attended the Abbey School, Newry, which was run by the Christian Brothers. The Shea family, like all their RIC friends, had suffered from Irish republicanism; they were living in the hard-pressed 1920s, and they had no ideological objections to working for the new Northern Ireland government at Stormont, or directly for the UK government. All three surviving brothers did so with success.

In 1926 Shea became a clerk in the Stormont ministry of labour and moved to Belfast. He had dash and intelligence, made many rugby-playing and golfing friends, and discovered a lifelong love of the theatre. In 1939 he gained accelerated promotion to the post of assistant principal in the ministry of finance, where Sir Wilfred Spender was permanent secretary. Shea served there successfully, and on 17 September 1941 he married Annie (Eithne; d. 2000), daughter of Michael McHugh, a commercial traveller. They had a daughter and two sons.

Promoted to principal, Shea served in the Ministry of Education between 1947 and 1959, and took part in the large-scale post-war reconstruction of Northern Ireland education. During this period he wrote plays, short stories, and variety shows, several of which were broadcast by BBC Northern Ireland and Radio Éireann. Many were written in partnership with Kevin Maguire—they used the pseudonyms P. S. Laughlin and John Kevin—and they included a very successful radio series about Ned Kelly, the Australian bush ranger. His own three-act play *Waiting Night* was produced, though briefly, at the Abbey Theatre, Dublin. This literary work gave him great satisfaction at a time when very few people—all of them graduate former inspectors of schools—were promoted to senior posts in the ministry.

Shea, like others who were unpromoted, left the Ministry of Education, and he joined the works department of the ministry of finance, where he became assistant secretary in 1963, and later senior assistant secretary. Then in 1969 he returned to the Ministry of Education as permanent secretary. He held this post until 1973, when he retired from the civil service.

The following years were extremely active. Between

1973 and 1979 Shea chaired Enterprise Ulster, a new publicly funded body which organized hundreds of work projects in Northern Ireland. It relied heavily on Shea's knowledge of the construction industry and local government, on his capacity to encourage and relate to all kinds of people, and on his pleasure at being personally responsible for an undertaking, which ultimately provided work for 2000 people who needed it.

When that appointment ended Shea wrote his autobiography: *Voices and the Sound of Drums*, published in 1981 by the Blackstaff Press, Belfast. It filled a gap in twentieth-century Irish historiography and literature because it was written by a Roman Catholic who had worked very successfully at Stormont. Shea believed that his career had been impeded because he was a Roman Catholic, and yet that his success in it made him suspect to the church in Belfast and to some of his own faith. Neither of these convictions embittered him. He had wonderful tolerance and comprehension. The autobiography is a minor Irish classic.

Paddy Shea died on 31 May 1986 at his home, 1A Adelaide Park, Belfast, and was buried at St Mary's cemetery, Newry, on 2 June. He had been made an OBE in 1961 and a CB in 1972. Appointed an honorary member of the Royal Society of Ulster Architects in 1971, he was made a fellow of the Royal Society of Arts in 1977. For many years he was prominent in the Ulster Arts Club. Eithne Shea survived him, and died on 26 December 2000.   ARTHUR GREEN

Sources P. Shea, *Voices and the sound of drums* (1981) [autobiography] · *Belfast Telegraph* (2 June 1986) · *The Times* (19 June 1986) · *Belfast Telegraph* (28 March 1979) · WWW · private information (2004) [Mrs J. Lynch, daughter; A. Tannahill] · personal knowledge (2004) · b. cert. · m. cert. · d. cert.
Likenesses C. Mulholland, bust, Ulster Arts Club · photograph, repro. in *Belfast Telegraph* (28 March 1979)
Wealth at death £47,133: probate, 10 Sept 1986, *CGPLA NIre.*

Sheaffe, Sir Roger Hale, baronet (1763–1851), army officer, born at Boston, Massachusetts, on 15 July 1763, was the third son of William Sheaffe, deputy collector of HM customs at Boston, and his wife, Susannah, eldest daughter of Thomas Child of Boston. As a boy, Sheaffe became the protégé of Hugh Percy, Earl Percy (later second duke of Northumberland), who during the American War of Independence had his headquarters in Boston in the boarding house run by Sheaffe's widowed mother. Percy sent Sheaffe to sea, then transferred him to Lochée's military academy, Chelsea, and subsequently bought most of Sheaffe's commissions. On 1 May 1778, through Percy's influence, Sheaffe received an ensigncy, and on 27 December 1780 a lieutenancy in the 5th foot, of which Percy was colonel. He served in Ireland from January 1781 to May 1787, and in Canada from July 1787 to September 1797. Under orders from Guy Carleton, first Baron Dorchester, who had been instructed by Lieutenant-Governor John Graves Simcoe, he was sent in 1794 to protest against certain settlements made by the Americans on Indian land on the south shore of Lake Ontario. On 5 May 1795 he obtained his company in the 5th foot and on 13 December 1797 a majority in the 81st; on 22 March 1798 he became

lieutenant-colonel in the 49th, but he seems to have become unpopular with the men. He served in the Netherlands from August to November 1799, in the expedition to the Baltic from March to July 1801, and in Canada from September 1802 to October 1811. He was promoted brevet colonel on 25 April 1808, and major-general on 4 June 1811. He married, on 29 January 1810, Margaret, daughter of John Coffin of Quebec, and cousin of Admiral Sir Isaac Coffin, bt. They had two sons and four daughters, all of whom predeceased Sheaffe. His wife died at Bath on 1 May 1855. He again served in Canada from 29 July 1812 to November 1813. On 13 October 1812 United States troops took Queenstown on the Niagara, but on the same day Sheaffe, on the death of General Sir Isaac Brock, assuming command of the British forces, recaptured the town, the Americans losing heavily. On 27 April 1813 he defended the town of York (later Toronto), when the losses of the Americans in taking the place exceeded the total numbers of those opposed to them. Heavily outnumbered, Sheaffe withdrew his force; probably a sound decision, but much criticized. He continued to command in the upper province, cautiously declining to take risks, and to administer its government until June 1813 (when he was replaced by Major-General Francis de Rottenburg), and on retirement was praised by the executive council. He had lost the confidence of his superior officer, Lieutenant-General Sir George Prevost, and so was recalled to England, leaving in November 1813.

On 16 January 1813 Sheaffe was made a baronet for his victory at Queenstown, and further rewarded by being made colonel of the 36th on 20 December 1829, and promoted to general on 28 June 1838. He had a residence at Edswale, co. Clare, but from 1817 lived largely in Edinburgh, where he died on 17 July 1851, when his title became extinct.   G. C. BOASE, *rev.* ROGER T. STEARN

Sources C. M. Whitfield and W. B. Turner, 'Sheaffe, Sir Roger Hale', *DCB*, vol. 8 · J. Philippart, ed., *The royal military calendar*, 3rd edn, 5 vols. (1820) · *Dod's Peerage* (1851) · *GM*, 2nd ser., 43 (1855) · *Annual Register* (1812) · *Annual Register* (1813) · J. G. Wilson and J. Fiske, eds., *Appleton's cyclopaedia of American biography*, 5 (1888) · J. B. Brebner, *Canada: a modern history* [1960] · Boase, *Mod. Eng. biog.*
Likenesses M. Brown, oils, Albury Park, Surrey

Shearer [*née* Downing]**, Helena Paulina** (1839×47–1885), socialist and suffragist, was born in Dublin, the daughter of Washington Downing, journalist, and his wife, Mary Frances, *née* McCarthy; she was the niece of McCarthy Downing, MP for County Cork. Nothing further is known of her early life or education, but her family settled in London, where a sister was born in 1848 and a brother in 1850. An experienced suffrage lecturer with a special interest in factory legislation and the employment of women, from 1875 she served on the committees of the Women's Protective and Provident League (formed by Emma Paterson in 1874 to encourage the organization of women into trade unions) and the Vigilance Association for the Defence of Personal Rights and for the Amendment of the Law in points wherein it is Injurious to Women. Formed to fight the Contagious Diseases Act in 1871, the Vigilance Association was a women's rights organization made up primarily of middle-class egalitarian feminists and libertarians, who also opposed the introduction of further factory legislation specific to women.

Much later, in his 1923 memoir of a life in the organized labour movement, Francis Soutter recalled that Helena Downing also helped keep *The Radical* (the organ of the Anti-Coercion Society) financially solvent in its early days. In particular, he paid tribute to her reputation as a speaker at a time when the practised woman orator was a rarity. Looking back, he attributed her success to the fact that she always understood her audiences and paid careful attention to their composition when considering questions of style and delivery, all of which effectively ensured that her ideas were accessible to all her listeners. As a consequence he suggested Helena Downing was always 'at home' with her audience, even when they did not share her views: 'This happy faculty, in conjunction with the most charming Irish brogue, made her one of the most successful speakers I have ever met' (Soutter, 123–4).

In the autumn of 1879 Helena contested the division of Tower Hamlets in the third triennial elections for the London school board. Standing on a programme of free secular education and greater democratic control of the board schools, her electoral address included a pledge to secure 'a fair proportion of working men and women on the local school management committees' (*Englishwoman's Review*, 15 Oct 1879, 444). At the time her most prominent supporters were Herbert Burrows (a trade unionist and leading member of the Social Democratic Federation, who contested Tower Hamlets six years later) and Helen Taylor (the socialist and feminist, who represented Southwark in 1876–85), both of whom campaigned vigorously on her behalf. None the less, Helena Downing finished bottom of the poll, and the feminist press attributed this unexpected defeat to over-confidence among her friends, who split their votes rather than casting them as a block as they were entitled to do. On 24 November 1881 she married John Ronald Shearer, a 32-year-old accountant. It seems likely that she was the Mrs Shearer who in 1881–2 served as an executive committee member of the Married Women's Property Committee. Undeterred by her failure at Tower Hamlets she turned her attention to the administration of the poor law, and in 1884 was returned as a guardian of the poor in Islington. However, her success was short-lived because she was disqualified from serving. Conscious of the fact that poor-law guardians had to be ratepayers, the couple placed their London home in Helena's name, but when she tried to pay the rates they were refused, and her election was disallowed. Less than a year later she died of consumption at Cold Blow, Queen Elizabeth's Walk, Stoke Newington, on 8 March 1885. Her death certificate gave her age as forty-five; on her marriage in 1881 she had given her age as thirty-four.

JANE MARTIN

Sources F. W. Soutter, *Recollections of a labour pioneer* (1923) · *Englishwoman's Review* (15 Sept 1879) · *Englishwoman's Review* (15 Oct 1879), 444 · *Englishwoman's Review* (15 Nov 1879) · *Englishwoman's Review* (15 Dec 1879), 561 · m. cert. · d. cert. · P. Hollis, *Ladies elect: women in English local government, 1865–1914* (1987) · L. Holcombe, *Wives and property: reform of married women's property law in nineteenth-century England* (1983) · census returns, 1881 · b. cert. [Washington Downing]

Archives BLPES, Mill-Taylor MSS

Sheares, Henry (1753–1798). *See under* Sheares, John (1766–1798).

Sheares, John (1766–1798), Irish nationalist, was born at Goldenbush, co. Cork, the fourth son of Henry Sheares (*d.* 1776), banker and MP, and Jane Anne Bettesworth (*d.* 1803) of Glasheen, co. Cork. He spent his early years at Glasheen and almost died in a swimming accident that claimed the life of his elder brother Robert, a tragedy for which he felt responsible. Two other brothers, Richard and Christopher, died in the 1770s when serving with the military in the West Indies. John Sheares was educated at home as a boy and then by the Revd G. Lee of Cork, who prepared him to enter Trinity College, Dublin. His eldest brother, **Henry Sheares** (1753–1798), Irish nationalist, was also tutored at Glasheen before enrolling in Trinity in November 1773. Henry Sheares inherited the bulk of the family estate in May 1776 and resigned his commission in the 51st foot on half pay after three years' service.

John Sheares inherited £3000 from his father but did not manage the cash well. His mother's will records an advance of £500 to her 'late dear unfortunate son, John Sheares, as part of his provision when he came of age upon his being under some difficulties' (Madden, 3.199). He attended Trinity as a sixteen-year-old in 1783, graduated BA in 1787, and was called in 1788 to the Irish bar, where he was joined within a year by Henry. The brothers lodged in Dublin on Ormond Quay, along with Alicia Swete (1757–1791), with whom Henry Sheares had eloped in August 1782, and their four children. Their marriage allegedly incensed rival suitor John FitzGibbon, earl of Clare. R. R. Madden ascertained that John Sheares's affair with a Mrs White in 1791 produced a daughter, Louisa, who was adopted by her relatives.

The death of Alicia Sheares on 11 December 1791 occasioned the removal of three of her children to France by their maternal grandmother. The Sheares brothers consequently visited Paris in 1792, where they engaged in political debates and met leading revolutionaries such as Brissot and Roland. In November 1792 Henry and John Sheares signed a document which called for close co-operation between the governments of Ireland, Britain, and France. The reputation of John Sheares later proved vulnerable to allegations that he was a fanatical Francophile who had taken a lugubrious interest in the revolutionary experience. Daniel O'Connell claimed that Sheares had once brandished a handkerchief said to have been stained with the blood of Louis XVI. Factual errors in O'Connell's anecdote were highlighted by Madden while other admirers insisted that John Sheares was deeply moved by the fate of Marie Antoinette and wept at Louis's trial. There is little doubt, however, but that the brothers were fervent supporters of the ideals of the French Revolution and attended the execution of the king on 21 January 1793 just days before leaving Calais for home.

John Sheares (1766–1798), attrib. Charles Robertson

After returning to Dublin John Sheares moved into 128 Baggot Street, a house leased by his brother in March 1792. Prior to the French sojourn the only overt signs of the radicalism for which John Sheares became notorious were several patriotic poems written when a teenager. This changed about June 1793 when the brothers joined the Society of United Irishmen to campaign for Catholic emancipation and other far-reaching democratic reforms. Both quickly attained prominence in the élite Dublin society and chaired meetings in 1793–4, profiles indicative of prior acquaintance with the leaders of what remained a small, legal, middle-class organization. Many of the most determined United Irishmen were barristers and the legal practice of John Sheares suffered more than most once his political inclinations were revealed. The principal reason for this seems to have been the extreme hostility of Clare, a formidable opponent who freely used the powers invested in his office as lord chancellor to combat the United Irishmen.

Clare set his sights on the Sheares brothers on 18 July 1793 when he alluded to them in the Irish House of Lords as 'two persons who were members of the French Jacobin Club … in the pay of that society, to foment sedition' (Kavanaugh, 288). Henry Sheares penned a robust handbill refutation of this attack and the ill will arising from the exchange had not diminished when John Sheares came close to locking horns with Clare in a controversy centred on Simon Butler. On 16 August 1793 John Sheares chaired the meeting which voted an address to Butler and Oliver Bond on their release from prison. He was angered by the chancellor's reiterated views on Butler's disloyalty

and offered to deliver a verbal demand for either an apology or a duel. Fortunately for Sheares, the impropriety of engaging him on this errand led to his substitution by the more tactful Archibald Hamilton Rowan in early October. John Sheares had already acted as second to his barrister colleague and fellow United Irishman Leonard McNally in a politically motivated duel with Sir Jonah Barrington in April 1793.

In 1794 John Sheares became romantically linked to a Maria Steele of Merrion Square, daughter of the deceased Sir R. Parker Steele. This remained a secret from her mother until 1798 when Lady Steele registered her opposition to marriage owing to John's irreligiousness. His gravitation towards the more militant faction of United Irishmen may be inferred from his presence at the funeral of the Revd William Jackson in May 1795. Jackson's offer of French military aid to the United Irishmen had resulted in the banning of the society in May 1794 and the resignation of most moderates. John Sheares, though probably not a member of the inner circle of senior activists who transformed the movement into an underground, paramilitary organization, was privy to their general plans. Henry Sheares also remained active and, as William Drennan noted in October 1794, devised the scheme to reorganize the United Irishmen as a secret, cellular body. In late 1794 or early 1795 Henry Sheares met Sarah Neville of Mary Mount, Kilkenny (sister of Sir Robert Hudson), whom he married; they had two children prior to 1798. He may then have distanced himself from the day-to-day affairs of the Dublin organization but by March 1798 was once again conspiring with his more radical brother.

The supposed weakness of the conspiracy in the Cork region in 1798 has been attributed to the incompetence of the Sheares brothers, but recent scholarship indicates that the region failed to revolt for reasons that arose after their arrest. The main role fulfilled by John Sheares after October 1797 was to contribute articles to the radical *Press* newspaper using the pen-name Dion. Edited by Cork republican Arthur O'Connor, the paper became the main organ of the United Irishmen until its suppression in March 1798. John Sheares proved a skilled propagandist and may have authored several seditious documents in the advent of the 1798 rising. He reputedly considered going to France as an emissary in 1797 but this offer was rejected if ever made. The theory that his youth was at issue is highly unlikely, as is the story that professional hardship arising from Clare's persecution disposed him to contemplate emigration in December 1797. Extant evidence points to John Sheares's deepening ideological commitment and increasing influence within the movement. In the early months of 1798 the brothers joined William Lawless in subverting Irish militiamen based at Lehaunstown, co. Dublin. Neutralizing this reserve camp became more important during the spring when coercion made deep inroads into United Irish arms stocks and personnel.

The arrest of most of the United Irish leadership at Oliver Bond's on 12 March 1798 thrust John Sheares into the first echelon of the revolutionary leadership. He was not entirely trusted by the tight-knit coterie headed by Lord Edward Fitzgerald and Samuel Neilson but was a *de facto* member of the new directory. His presence in Cork on seditious business was in April 1798 made known to the authorities, who neglected to act at that time. He also attended spring assizes at Wexford and Kildare where he conferred with senior United Irishmen under the cover of legal affairs. On 10 May John Sheares was introduced to Captain John Warneford Armstrong of the King's county militia in the Grafton Street premises of radical bookseller Patrick Byrne. Armstrong feigned disloyalty during this chance encounter and aroused the interest of Sheares, who was anxious to strengthen the United Irish grip on his regiment. Mass defections from the military then featured strongly in United Irish strategy as it offered an alternative to French assistance. John Sheares hoped that republican soldiers would spearhead an irresistible *coup d'état* in the capital and obviate the need for the more risky national insurrection favoured by Neilson. Such tactical arguments led to a fissure between John Sheares and Neilson in early May and his isolation from the leadership. When John Sheares called to visit Lawless on 21 May he was arrested by Town Major Henry Charles Sirr, who had been searching the house on the basis of information supplied by Armstrong. Henry Sheares was then seized in Baggot Street by Alderman Alexander just two days before the planned uprising.

The brothers were questioned in Dublin Castle by their unsympathetic relative Lord Shannon, who noted that they 'would confess nothing but were much frightened' (*Lord Shannon's Letters*, 98). They were committed to Kilmainham prison until 4 July, when they were both arraigned on charges of high treason before Chief Justice Carleton. McNally, a government double agent when ostensibly Henry Sheares's friend and defence lawyer, helped ensure the conviction of his client on 12–13 July by insisting that he be tried alongside the more incriminated John. The younger Sheares anticipated capital conviction and prepared farewell letters ahead of the trial. Armstrong's willingness to prosecute gave the government a strong case, as did their possession of an inflammatory document attributed to John Sheares which had been intended for distribution after the insurrection commenced. He privately acknowledged authorship on the eve of his death but it is unclear whether the proclamation had been sanctioned by the directory. John Philpot Curran, the main defence lawyer, could do little to undermine such clear-cut evidence and his motion to adjourn was dismissed by Attorney-General John Toler.

The brothers were found guilty on the morning of 13 July and committed to Newgate prison to await execution the following day. The capital conviction of Henry Sheares surprised many and it was held that an appeal might well succeed. Nothing came of this as there was insufficient time to prepare a case between sentencing and the prompt execution date of the following afternoon. Barrington acknowledged receiving an overdue letter from Henry at 11 a.m. on 14 July and, as directed by his desperate college friend, showed it to Clare. Assent was received that Henry's life would be spared if he co-operated with the authorities but Barrington reached Newgate too late to furnish the stay of execution. It is extremely doubtful whether Sheares would have accepted such terms and he presumably hoped to delay proceedings long enough for the verdict to be challenged on a point of law.

John and Henry Sheares appeared dressed in black at about three o'clock on 14 July and advanced hand in hand to the public gallows outside Newgate. Their heads were removed after death and, in a rare gesture for the period, the bodies were surrendered to a family member, Brent Neville, to be laid out in St Michan's crypt, Dublin, the same day. John Sheares was survived by his daughter, Louisa, Henry by his widow and six children, Henry, Richard Benjamin, Alicia, Jane, Garrett, and Mary.

RUÁN O'DONNELL

Sources N. J. Curtin, *The United Irishmen: popular politics in Ulster and Dublin, 1791–1798* (1994) · R. R. Madden, *The United Irishmen: their lives and times*, 2nd edn, 4 vols. (1857–60) · J. Barrington, *Rise and fall of the Irish nation* (1843) · W. J. Fitzpatrick, *Secret service under Pitt*, 2nd edn (1892) · T. Graham, 'An union of power? The United Irish organization', *The United Irishmen, republicanism, radicalism and rebellion*, ed. D. Dickson, D. Keogh, and K. Whelan (1993), 244–55 · A. C. Kavanaugh, *John Fitzgibbon, earl of Clare* (1997), 288 · R. B. McDowell, *Ireland in the age of imperialism and revolution, 1760–1801* (1979) · R. Musgrave, *Memoirs of the Irish rebellion of 1798*, ed. S. W. Myers and D. E. McKnight, 4th edn (1995) · J. O'Connell, ed., *The life and speeches of Daniel O'Connell, M.P.*, 1 (1846) · *Lord Shannon's letters to his son: a calendar of the letters written by the 2nd earl of Shannon to his son, Viscount Boyle, 1790–1802*, ed. E. Hewitt (1982) · *Public Register, or, Freeman's Journal* (23 July 1798) · *Cork Gazette* (31 Oct 1795) · C. O'Keefe, *Life and times of Daniel O'Connell*, 2 vols. (1863–4)

Likenesses J. Comerford, watercolour on ivory (Henry Sheares), NG Ire.; repro. in Madden, *United Irishmen* · attrib. Comerford, watercolour on ivory (Henry Sheares?), NG Ire. · T. W. Huffam, mezzotint (Henry Sheares; after unknown artist), NPG · T. W. Huffam, mezzotint (after A. Buck), NPG · attrib. C. Robertson, miniature watercolour on ivory, NG Ire. [*see illus.*] · Irish school, watercolour on ivory (John Sheares?), NG Ire.

Wealth at death moderate: Madden, *United Irishmen* · substantial—Henry Sheares: Madden, *United Irishmen*

Shearman, Sir Montague (1857–1930), judge, was born on 7 April 1857 at Wimbledon, the second son of Montagu Shearman, solicitor, of Wimbledon, and his wife, Mary, daughter of Frederic Adam Catty, whose father, a royalist refugee from France, was French master at the Royal Military Academy, Woolwich. He attended Merchant Taylors' School (1869–75) where he was head monitor and captain of the rugby football fifteen in 1874–5, then went with a scholarship to St John's College, Oxford. At university he was distinguished both as a scholar and as an athlete. He obtained first classes in classical moderations (1877) and in *literae humaniores* (1879) and played in the university rugby football fifteen as both forward and three-quarter. He was president of the university athletic club in 1878 and represented the university between 1876 and 1879 in the hundred yards, the quarter-mile, and putting the weight. In addition, he was a good long jumper and rowed in his college eight. Shearman was also amateur champion for the hundred yards (1876) and the quarter-mile (1880), played rugby football for the south of England, and twice was 'reserve' for England. In 1881 he even swam the Niagara River below the falls.

But it is his role as a co-founder of the Amateur Athletic Association for which Shearman is best remembered within athletics circles. Together with Bernhard Wise, later attorney-general for New South Wales, and Clement Jackson, a tutor at Hertford College, Oxford, Shearman believed that amateur athletics should be rescued from the organizational chaos reflected in rival national championship meetings and élitist prohibition on the participation of 'mechanics, artisans and labourers' in the Amateur Athletic Club and in other 'gentlemen's' athletic clubs. By skilful canvassing and planning, Shearman, Wise, and Jackson secured support for the creation of a national Amateur Athletic Association (AAA) on 28 April 1880. It enabled organized amateur athletics to become open to working-class participation. This shift in the field of athletics from control by a closed, self-perpetuating, aristocratic élite to control by meritocratic élites mirrored broad trends in later Victorian liberal society and public administration.

Shearman became honorary secretary of the AAA from 1880 to 1883, then vice-president, and from 1910 president in succession to another judge, Viscount Alverstone. He was joint author with J. E. Vincent of *Football: its History for Five Centuries* (1885), and author of *Athletics and Football* (Badminton Library, 1887). The latter, running to five editions, stood the test of time for its comprehensiveness and for the quality of its writing.

Called to the bar (Inner Temple) in 1881, Shearman appeared in London, on the midland circuit, and at the Birmingham sessions where he impressed with his fluency, equanimity, skilful advocacy, fact, and common sense. In 1884 he married Mary Louise, daughter of Job Long of New York; they had two sons, the younger of whom died from wounds received in the First World War. Unofficial standing counsel to leading moneylenders' firms, Shearman took silk in 1903.

On the retirement of Lord Justice Vaughan Williams and Mr Justice Channell in 1914, Lord Haldane chose Shearman to fill one of the vacant judgeships in the King's Bench Division, and he was knighted. Although not a profound jurist, his wide experience in the courts made him a useful judge of first instance. An early case over which he presided was the trial for high treason of Nicolaus Ahlers, the German consul at Sunderland who had assisted German subjects to return home the day after Britain had declared war. The conviction, about which Shearman had reservations, was quashed on the ground of misdirection. A later misdirection to the jury in the trial of Dr Bateman for the manslaughter of a patient who had died in childbirth also led to an important clarification by the appeal judges in the law concerning the criminal liability of medical practitioners. Shearman was the judge of assize at Carmarthen in November 1920 when Harold Greenwood, after a seven days' trial, was acquitted on a charge of having poisoned his wife; in 1922, at the central criminal court, he tried Frederick Bywaters and Mrs Edith Thompson, who were convicted of the murder of Mrs Thompson's husband after a summing-up which, in respect to Mrs Thompson, some believe failed adequately to guide the jury on the distinction between moral outrage and evidence of guilt. After an unsuccessful appeal both were hanged. During the same year he tried at the central criminal court and sentenced to death the murderers of Field Marshal Sir Henry Wilson.

Shearman also served with Lord Hardinge of Penshurst and Sir Mackenzie Chalmers on the royal commission appointed in 1916 to inquire into the origin and causes of the Easter rebellion in Ireland. As he was identified with no political party, his appointment attracted no adverse criticism in the Commons. The report itself blamed the cause of the rebellion on the 'lawlessness' which the government had permitted to grow unchecked for several years and for which the chief secretary, Augustine Birrell, had to assume primary responsibility. Birrell, in reply, declared that the 'Three Good Men' who constituted the Hardinge Commission were 'engaged in the pursuit of the unknowable' and hence would find his behaviour inexplicable and blameworthy.

An operation necessitated by an old injury in the football field gravely impaired Shearman's powers of speech, and he struggled against this disability for some two years before his retirement in October 1929. He died at his London home, Leigh House, 6 Eaton Gate, on 6 January 1930.

THEOBALD MATHEW, *rev.* G. R. RUBIN

Sources *The Times* (7 Jan 1930) · *Law Journal* (11 Jan 1930) · P. Lovesey, *The official centenary history of the Amateur Athletics Association* (1979) · R. Jackson, *The chief: the biography of Gordon Hewart, lord chief justice of England, 1922–40* (1959) · D. G. Browne, *Sir Travers Humphreys: a biography* (1960) · L. Ó Broin, *The chief secretary: Augustine Birrell in Ireland* (1969) · CGPLA Eng. & Wales (1930)
Archives CUL, corresp. with Lord Hardinge
Likenesses M. Clifford, oils; known to be in family possession in 1937 · WAG, chromolithograph caricature, NPG; repro. in *VF* (4 July 1895) · photographs, repro. in Lovesey, *Official centenary history*, 25, 29, 80
Wealth at death £98,335 15s. 4d.: resworn probate, 28 Feb 1930, CGPLA Eng. & Wales

Shearman, William (1767–1861), physician and medical writer, born at Harwich in January 1767, graduated MD at Edinburgh on 12 September 1807 (with a dissertation on pneumonia), and was admitted a licentiate of the Royal College of Physicians, London, on 11 April 1808. In 1799 he had been appointed one of the staff of a periodical called *The New Medical and Physical Journal, or, Annals of Medicine, Natural History, and Chemistry*, and from 1810 to 1812 he was its editor. He continued his connection with the publication until 1815. Shearman contributed articles on a variety of topics to *Medical Reports* in 1824 and also published independently.

Shearman commenced practice as a physician in London, and then worked for a while in Maidstone before returning to London in 1813. He practised for many years in Northampton Square, Clerkenwell, and subsequently, until his death, at 17 Canonbury Villas, Islington. He was physician to the London Dispensary from 1813 to 1824, to the Infirmary for Children in Waterloo Road from 1816, and to the West London Infirmary and Lying-in Institution in Villiers Street from 1821. He was the senior member of the medical staff when the institution in Villiers Street became the Charing Cross Hospital, and he retained his position in the new hospital until 1852, when he became consulting physician. He gave annual lectures on the theory and practice of medicine at the Charing Cross Hospital school of medicine.

For several years Shearman was treasurer to the Medical Society of London. In 1824 he was president of the society, and in 1834 he published an oration delivered before it. Shearman was survived by at least two daughters, but the identity of his wife and any other family is not known. He died at his home on 21 November 1861, at the age of ninety-four, and was buried at Highgate cemetery in north London. Described by an obituarist as 'quite one of the old school of physicians [who] set his face strongly against the "new-fangled doctrines" of modern times' (*Lancet*, 536), he was nevertheless so respected that all lectures and teaching at Charing Cross medical school were suspended on 29 November, the day of his funeral.

W. W. WEBB, *rev.* ANITA MCCONNELL

Sources Munk, *Roll* · *List of the graduates in medicine in the University of Edinburgh from MDCCV to MDCCCLXVI* (1867), 39 · *The Lancet* (30 Nov 1861), 536 · *CGPLA Eng. & Wales* (1861) · d. cert.
Wealth at death under £6000: probate, 10 Dec 1861, *CGPLA Eng. & Wales*

Sheavyn, Phoebe Ann Beale (1865–1968), university teacher and feminist, was born on 16 September 1865 at Long Street, Atherstone, in Warwickshire. Her birth was registered nearly six weeks later by her mother, Jane Elizabeth Sheavyn, *née* Farmer. Her father, William Sale Sheavyn, was a draper in Long Street, Atherstone, and the family lived over the shop. As happens in folklore, the youngest child was in the end the luckiest. In old age Phoebe would affirm angrily that the early death of an elder sister was due to the conditions she had suffered as a living-in assistant at another draper's shop.

Phoebe was to be a school teacher. After a male inspector had examined her needlework through a magnifying glass she was set on the lowest rung of the pedagogical ladder, as an uncertificated teacher in a board school. Soon she failed to satisfy another inspector: she was thrown out, to make what living she could, at first exploited in a series of private schools. At last she found a post as governess to the children of an architect. Noticing her talent for drawing, he gave her lessons and advised her how to sit for the Cambridge local examinations. A scholarship to the University College of Aberystwyth followed. At the age of twenty-four she had a London BA and was teaching English in Haberdashers' Aske's School for Girls, Hatcham, where she remained from 1889 to 1892. She crossed the Atlantic to become a fellow and reader in English at Bryn Mawr College, Pennsylvania in 1892, returning to England in 1894. She held a post in Oxford working with the philologist Joseph Wright on the *English Dialect Dictionary* before being appointed in 1897 as the first resident tutor in English at Somerville College, Oxford.

Miss Maitland, then principal of Somerville, had seen the necessity to appoint a body of resident women tutors in order to change Somerville from a hall of residence into a college. In appointing Phoebe Sheavyn the college for the first time ventured outside Oxford or Cambridge. Phoebe admitted in later life that she had been 'prickly' at Oxford. At Aberystwyth she had learned that women could not only sit beside men as students but could also teach men. In the USA she had seen the generous provision for women's education. The position of women at Oxford dismayed her. There was compensation in the daily companionship of young, brilliant, forward-looking women, some of whom became lifelong friends. At Oxford she must have done most of her research for her book *The Literary Profession in the Elizabethan Age*, published by Manchester University Press in 1909. London University awarded her a DLitt in 1910.

Miss Sheavyn stayed for ten years before moving into the bracing academic air of Manchester University as university lecturer, tutor to women students, and from 1910 warden of Ashburne Hall, the hall of residence for women students, opened that year by Miss Penrose, principal of Somerville. A few months before Phoebe arrived, a group of seventeen women had met in Manchester to form the Federation of University Women. By 1909 the federation was ready to widen its field: a conference was held in Manchester for delegates from universities and colleges in England and Wales. The two Manchester delegates were Ida Smedley DSc, the virtual founder, and Phoebe Sheavyn. When in 1922 the federation became international, Sheavyn was again a delegate to a conference in Paris. In the same year she produced a pamphlet for the International Federation of University Women (since reorganized in the UK as the British Federation of Women Graduates). After a rather sketchy history of women's education, she surveyed the educational provision and the career opportunities open to girls and women in 1922. Sheavyn regretted that the apparent opening of spheres of work for women in the 1914–18 war had not proved permanent. She also observed that the recognition given to women as wardens of university hostels was 'not always entirely satisfactory' (P. Sheavyn, *Higher Education for Women in Great Britain*, 1922, 17), and reflected that the position of women university teachers was one of 'comparative subordination'.

Phoebe Sheavyn had already, in April 1917, resigned her wardenship, though she remained tutor to women students. Although illness played a part in her decision not to continue in both posts, there was also an element of frustration at the obstacles to improving the position of women in the university. The promoters of Ashburne Hall had hoped that it would become a college but it had remained a hall of residence. Sheavyn had been made a member of the university senate in 1912 'for administrative reasons' (Tylecote, 97): this position was not offered to her successor. Some feared that the fierceness of her feminism would not in the end benefit women (ibid., 139), though it was admitted that she had charm, and her Somerville friend Margery Fry spoke of her 'endless kindness'.

In a paper, 'Professional women', which she contributed to a collection entitled *The Position of Woman: Actual and Real* (1911), Sheavyn argued the case for utilizing women's capacities in all areas of professional employment, and suggested the creation of residential halls where 'disengaged' women (those without maternal responsibilities) could live together independently.

In 1923 Phoebe Sheavyn entered on what proved to be forty-five years of retirement. How she occupied this is something of a mystery. Margery Fry equipped her for oil painting and handed on techniques she had learned from her brother Roger. In her seventies Phoebe was exhibiting and selling landscapes and flower pieces. In later old age Margery introduced her to the new game of Scrabble. When Margery was in hospital in London in 1957, Phoebe, then ninety-two and nine years Margery's senior, was able to visit her. At that time Phoebe expressed something of her religious belief: she had never had a religious 'experience' but was convinced that her being 'did not need her body'. She could not, however, believe that old friends would meet again.

The great event of Phoebe's old age was the republication of her book by Manchester University Press in 1967. As its sensitive editor, J. S. Saunders, pointed out, she had, by excluding controversial writers, excluded the true professionals, the best-sellers of the Elizabethan age; but her book had been in 1909 one of the earliest works of contextual literary study. Phoebe Sheavyn's meticulous scholarship had not been superseded and her forthright, simple style was still readable. She herself conducted the correspondence about the publication. The proofs came to her in her retirement home, Bryony House, Selly Oak, Birmingham. She died there a few months after the publication, on 7 January 1968, in her 103rd year.

ENID HUWS JONES

Sources *Somerville College register, 1879–1971* [1972] • J. H. Sondheimer, *History of the British Federation of University Women, 1907–1957* (1958) • M. Tylecote, *The education of women at Manchester University, 1883–1933* (1941) • *The Times* (11 Jan 1968) • personal knowledge (2004) • C. Dyhouse, *No distinction of sex? Women in British universities, 1870–1939* (1995) • b. cert.

Likenesses portrait, Somerville College, Oxford

Wealth at death £4330: probate, 13 March 1968, *CGPLA Eng. & Wales*

Shebbeare, John (1709–1788), physician and political writer, was the eldest son of an attorney and corn-factor of Bideford, Devon. Unfortunately very little is known of his family history, parents, and early career, although the Shebbeares had once been modest landowners in the south of the county.

Education and early writing Shebbeare was educated at the free school at Exeter under the tuition of Zachariah Mudge, and at fifteen or sixteen he was apprenticed to an Exeter surgeon. Shebbeare's father died soon after, leaving the family in very poor circumstances. Friends assisted his mother in maintaining the corn-factoring business for some time, but it failed, and she was removed to the king's bench prison, where she died. During his apprenticeship, Shebbeare specialized in obstetrics and

developed a keen interest in chemistry, but perhaps because of financial necessity he did not wait to take a medical degree before attempting to establish a practice of his own, probably in Exeter. Shebbeare was married young, possibly in 1733, to a woman of a genteel background but with little fortune. They had three children, a boy and two girls. His wife, whose name is unknown, died on 25 November 1779. Shebbeare inherited little from his father, and his medical practice did not prosper. It was reported that Shebbeare's declining fortune was caused by the alienation of his former master and of many of the citizens, corporation, and magistrates of Exeter, who were the victims of his vindictive temper and predilection for literary satire, and by futile alchemical experiments.

In 1736 Shebbeare moved to Bristol and went into partnership with a chemist. Virtually nothing is known of his life in Bristol, although he probably attempted to continue with his medical career or worked as an apothecary. In 1740 he printed a treatise upon the medicinal properties of the Bristol waters. It was during this period that Shebbeare's close involvement in politics began, and the forging of connections with the tory-patriots of the city is suggested by the publication of an epitaph on the Bristol MP Thomas Coster, who died in 1739. It appears that Shebbeare moved to London about 1750, and briefly visited Paris during 1752, where he claimed to have earned a medical degree and to have been elected to the French Academy of Sciences.

Shebbeare's career as a writer commenced with a work inspired by the passage of the Marriage Act in 1753. The legislation, promoted by the whig lord chancellor, the earl of Hardwicke, had been drafted to prevent clandestine marriages by requiring that persons below the legal age of consent obtain the permission of their parents or legal guardians before marrying. In 1754 Shebbeare published *The Marriage Act*, a novel which inveighed against Hardwicke's reforms by dramatizing their pernicious impact upon the lives of aspiring young lovers whose passions had been sanctioned by God but were frustrated by tyrannical, acquisitive parents, guardians, and their legal minions, who coerced them into marrying for the social and financial aggrandizement of their families. In condemning the moral and social consequences of the act, Shebbeare also accused the whig ministry of blatantly espousing the class interests of the élite in attempting to prohibit marriages between members of unequal social stations. The ministry was angered by Shebbeare's criticism, and several days after the novel's appearance he was arrested for the aspersions he had cast upon parliament. Shebbeare was released soon after, upon condition that he appear before the courts at certain intervals as a guarantee of future good behaviour.

In 1755 Shebbeare published a second novel, *Lydia*, a sentimental tale of the sufferings of a virtuous young woman who endures poverty and persecution before marrying her lover and retiring to a life of piety and philanthropy. The novel is perhaps most memorable for its depiction of an Iroquois chief, who travels from New York to London to discover whether the inhabitants of England are as degenerate as the British American colonists who oppress his people. Shebbeare's Cannassatego, the courageous, honourable warrior-chief, reflects the era's fascination with romantic primitivism and represents one of the most positive portrayals of the native North American in eighteenth-century fiction. Although it is not a political novel, hostility towards the whig administration emerges throughout the narrative, most clearly in the figure of Cannassatego, an ostensibly objective observer, whose bitter disillusionment with the selfish materialism and political venality of Hanoverian England echoes the views of his creator. The composition of *Lydia* coincided with the escalation of territorial conflict between Britain and France in North America during 1754–5, and Shebbeare employed the novel to denounce the prime minister, the duke of Newcastle, for failing to defend British imperial interests from French aggression.

Civic satirist Shebbeare's growing engagement with politics during the 1750s was emphasized by a work of social and political satire also published in 1755. *Letters on the English Nation* was an epistolary fiction allegedly written by an Anglicized Italian Jesuit, whose long residence in England and analytical nature had endowed him with the insight and neutrality to develop a sweeping analysis of the decline of the English constitution, morals, manners, and culture under the corrupt rule of the whigs. The selection of a Jesuit as a narrative persona encouraged allegations that Shebbeare was a Jacobite at heart, prompting the whig antiquary Thomas Birch to revile the *Letters* as 'a Book, which an Englishman and a Protestant must detest' (BL, Add. MS 35398, fol. 255).

As the international crisis of 1755–6 developed into war between Britain and France, Shebbeare's political commitment increased, inspiring the composition of a series of pamphlets condemning the Newcastle ministry's management of the conflict, beginning with *A Letter to the People of England*, published in the autumn of 1755. Shebbeare accused the ministry of sacrificing British maritime and colonial interests in North America by slavishly pandering to the Hanoverian partialities of George II. He developed this theme in his later *Letters*, reinforcing his charges with a historical survey stretching back to the reign of William III to illustrate the damage inflicted upon Britain by the predilection of alien monarchs for their homelands. Moreover, Shebbeare charged that the whigs had connived in the bloody, expensive continental wars of William III and George II as a means of establishing their grasp upon political power.

Admiral John Byng's failure to save the Mediterranean island of Minorca from capture by the French in July 1756 precipitated an intense political controversy over the responsibility for the defeat. Shebbeare's *Fourth Letter*, published in August, formulated a scathing review of the Newcastle administration's European diplomacy and conduct of the war in North America, and blamed the loss of Minorca upon the neglect and incompetence of the ministers. Shebbeare may also have written several pamphlets in defence of Byng, denouncing the ministry for attempting to conceal its blunders by scapegoating the admiral.

Shebbeare's political journalism received stinging criticism from the era's leading literary reviewers, who disapproved of the violence of his anti-ministerial attacks. Shebbeare's feud with Ralph Griffiths, the editor of the *Monthly Review*, had begun in 1755, when Griffiths printed a critical account of a treatise Shebbeare had written describing the discoveries of his years of medical research. The article dismissed Shebbeare's study for its arrogance, plagiarism, and ignorance, and openly questioned his claim to a medical degree. Of a combative temper and sensitive to any criticism, Shebbeare had retaliated by satirizing Griffiths in *Lydia*, and the quarrel continued with the *Monthly*'s censure of the *Letters*. In commenting upon Shebbeare's pamphlets, Tobias Smollett, the editor of the *Critical Review*, was especially incensed by what he saw as their author's irresponsible fomenting of mob violence and civil dissension for pecuniary motives at a time when all Britons should unite against the common enemy. He denounced Shebbeare as a desperate incendiary without principles, talent, or common discretion. Shebbeare replied to his new adversary in May 1757 with *The Occasional Critic*, containing virulent abuse of Smollett's character and writings. The clash between the two authors degenerated into one of the eighteenth century's most bitter and brutally fought literary quarrels. Shebbeare was caricatured by Smollett in the novel *Sir Lancelot Greaves* (1760) as the misanthropic Ferret, an unscrupulous, self-serving political agitator and quack doctor who represents one of the most memorable minor characters in Smollett's fiction.

The pillory and imprisonment Shebbeare published a *Sixth Letter* in late 1757. It comprised one of his most blatant and extreme expressions of the malignant effects of the Hanoverian succession. Its notorious motto, alluding to the white horse of the Hanoverian coat of arms, was taken from Revelation 6:8, 'And I looked, and beheld a pale Horse: and his name that sat upon him was Death, and Hell followed him'. In 1756–7 the vulnerability of Hanover to French attacks had compelled the government to establish an alliance with Prussia and to finance the formation of an army for its defence. Now the ministry feared that Shebbeare's anti-Hanoverianism would increase the unpopularity of such controversial measures. Eager to stifle Shebbeare's persistent criticism, the ministry issued a general warrant for his arrest in January 1758. Shebbeare was taken into custody, and a seventh letter, which was being prepared for publication, was suppressed. Shebbeare was tried before the court of king's bench, and on 17 June 1758 he was convicted of seditious libel. The chief justice, Lord Mansfield, presided over the trial and, in interpreting the laws governing the press, ruled that satires upon dead kings were libellous. Mansfield's severe judgment offended many advocates of the liberty of the press, and prompted Horace Walpole's condemnation that it amounted to the censorship of history. On 28 November, Shebbeare was sentenced to pay a £5 fine, to serve a term of three years' imprisonment, to provide securities of good behaviour for seven years amounting to £1000, and to stand in the pillory at Charing Cross. The defiance Shebbeare exhibited during the execution of the last part of his punishment, aided and abetted by a tory political ally, the under-sheriff of Middlesex, Arthur Beardmore, provoked a political scandal. Shebbeare's allies had distributed a handbill around London 'inviting the friends of the liberty of the press, and of Old England … to see the British champion' (Walpole, *Memoirs*, 3.40). Shebbeare drove into Charing Cross on 5 December 1758 not in a prisoner's cart but in an elegant coach, and was greeted with three cheers by a large crowd of spectators. Rather than submit to the indignity of having his head, arms, and legs confined within the pillory, Shebbeare stood at his ease, while an Irish chairman held an umbrella over his head to shield him from the sun. Occasionally, when tired, he put his hands upon the holes of the pillory in order to rest.

William Hogarth recorded the disapproval of many contemporaries towards the extravagant virulence of Shebbeare's political polemic, his twisting of the facts, and the inflammatory nature of his rhetoric. In *The Polling* (1758), the third plate of Hogarth's Election series, Shebbeare, in leg irons, is depicted whispering seditious nonsense into the ear of an idiot, who is being sworn in as a voter. Shebbeare's enemies poured scorn upon his pretensions to political popularity and his attempt to transform the disgrace of his pillorying into a triumph. In *The Author* (1763) the whig poet Charles Churchill wrote:

> Where is SHEBBEARE? O, let not foul reproach,
> Travelling thither in a City-Coach,
> The Pill'ry dare to name; the whole intent
> Of that Parade was Fame, not Punishment,
> And that old, staunch Whig BEARDMORE standing by,
> Can in full Court give the report the lye.
> (p. 15)

Shebbeare served the full term of his sentence, and the financial strain it caused inflicted considerable hardship upon his family. He fell into debt and felt deserted by his political allies. At one time he became seriously ill. Shebbeare felt particularly resentful towards William Pitt, whom he had eulogized in *The Third Letter* for his patriotic opposition to Newcastle's diplomatic efforts to secure the safety of Hanover during 1755–6. Pitt was in coalition with Newcastle when Shebbeare was prosecuted, and the doctor blamed Pitt for failing to shield him from punishment despite having, as he claimed, 'contributed not a little towards creating the popularity, and thereby to the elevation of Lord Chatham to the seat of prime minister' (Shebbeare, 36). Shebbeare's difficult term in the king's bench cannot have been improved by the arrival of his adversary Smollett in 1760, who was himself imprisoned for libel.

Later writing and support for George III While in prison Shebbeare continued to support himself by his writings. He accepted subscriptions for an ambitious but unpublished history of England. He appears to have been the author of several pamphlets in defence of Lord George Sackville, who was accused of cowardice for his behaviour during the battle of Minden in 1759. Shebbeare continued

to follow politics and the progress of the war closely, and after his disillusionment with Pitt he became a supporter of the prince of Wales, later George III, and Lord Bute, who shared his opposition to British participation in the German war and advocacy of peace. During this time Shebbeare worked upon the composition of his most elaborate work, an allegorical history of Britain since the revolution of 1688, documenting the subversion of the constitution and the decadence of English society and culture under the tyranny of William III, the Hanoverians, and the whigs. *The History of the Sumatrans*, first published in 1760, concluded with a glowing panegyric upon George III and Bute, who were celebrated for restoring their people's political rights and liberties. True religion, moral virtue, artistic excellence, and economic prosperity are nourished by the beneficent reign of the young king and his adviser. Shebbeare's support was appreciated by the court, and he was rewarded with a pension of £200 in 1764 when the tory Sir John Philips applied to George III upon his behalf. When granting the request, it was reported that the king 'was pleased to speak of him in very favourable terms' (*European Magazine*, 13.87). From that time, Shebbeare distinguished himself as a loyal and energetic supporter of George III and his ministers in pamphlets and newspaper articles, replying to John Wilkes and defending Lord North's American policy from the criticisms of Edmund Burke. One of Shebbeare's most significant later social and political works, *An Essay on the Origin, Progress, and Establishment of National Society* (1776), was a reply to the writings of the nonconformist minister Richard Price, who supported the cause of the American revolutionaries.

Shebbeare's political and literary opponents sneered at his support for the court and his acceptance of a pension, denouncing him as an opportunistic hypocrite. The poet William Mason ridiculed him in *An Epistle to Dr. Shebbeare* (1777) as:

> The same abusive, base, abandon'd thing,
> When pilloried, or pension'd by a king
> (p. 9)

Samuel Johnson was also offered a pension by George III, and the two tory writers' names were joined together by the ministry's whig opponents in parliament. It was claimed that the administration had pensioned a He-bear and a She-bear. The boast, perhaps apocryphal, that he had embarked upon his career as a political journalist vowing 'to write himself into a place or the pillory' was frequently attributed to Shebbeare (Walpole, *Memoirs*, 3.39). His support for George III, however, the patriot-king who proudly proclaimed himself to be a Briton and the son of a Briton, was consistent with the tory-patriot political ideology he had expounded throughout his life. Although Shebbeare took advantage of the new reign to press his case for preferment, in accepting it he did not compromise his political principles.

Character and reputation Unfortunately for Shebbeare, assessments of his character, writings, and political opinions were transmitted to posterity primarily by his literary and political enemies. The fact that he appears to have made few friends emerges as a telling commentary. It has been suggested that Smollett later relented in his hostility towards Shebbeare, but this seems unlikely. The evidence appears to lie in a seemingly sympathetic account of Shebbeare's prosecution and imprisonment for the *Sixth Letter* in an edition of Smollett's *History of England*. The inconsistency most probably was caused by the corruption of the text, and should not be taken as an indication of a change of heart on the part of its author. The passage should also not be taken out of context, in which Shebbeare's punishment is employed by the tory Smollett as an example of the severity and arbitrary nature of whig justice.

One biographer who knew Shebbeare personally warned against the danger of judging his character from the tone of his political writings, praising him as a son, brother, husband, and father; but even he confesses that Shebbeare was quick-tempered, stubborn, immoderate, and intolerant of others' opinions. Shebbeare's marriage was apparently an unhappy one. The novelist Fanny Burney, who met Shebbeare in 1774, recorded him as declaring 'I think I have been yoked for one and forty years, and I have wished my wife under the ground any time since' (*Early Diary*, 1.275). She also accused him of misogyny. Shebbeare's troubled domestic situation may be reflected in the often ambiguous attitude towards women revealed in his fiction, where the idealization of virtuous young heroines appears beside strong condemnation of female vice and folly. In addition to his political intolerance, Shebbeare was also an uncompromising high-church tory and English nationalist, his works being riddled with abuse of Quakers, Presbyterians, other dissenters, Jews, and the Scots. An egoist, Shebbeare appeared to be perpetually at war with a world which he felt did not recognize his worth as a medical man, novelist, and political commentator. The poverty and obscurity of his early life may have contributed to his sensitivity and aggressive self-assertiveness.

Shebbeare's written works suffered from a lack of originality and the haste with which they were composed. His novels, modelled upon those of Henry Fielding, reveal these flaws in their diffuse style, rambling narratives, conventional plots, and poor construction. As a political writer, Shebbeare was also deeply indebted to others, most notably to Lord Bolingbroke, for the content of his political ideology and the form of its expression. His social satire and political commentary, however, could be energetic, cogent, and effective, as James Boswell recognized when claiming that 'whatever objections were made to him', he 'had knowledge and abilities much above the class of ordinary writers, and deserves to be remembered as a respectable name in literature, were it only for his admirable *Letters on the English Nation*' (Boswell, *Life*, 1151). During the Seven Years' War, Shebbeare's *Letters to the People of England* were widely read and politically influential. His emotionally charged, powerfully written patriot rhetoric contributed to the development of political discontent with the Newcastle ministry after the fall of Minorca, and encouraged the extra-parliamentary protests which helped to bring about its collapse in November

1756. There was also some foundation to Shebbeare's claim, however typically exaggerated, that he had assisted Pitt in his attempts to mobilize popular patriot support, especially among the tories. Shebbeare died in Eaton Street, Pimlico, on 1 August 1788.

M. JOHN CARDWELL

Sources *DNB* · 'An account of the life and writings of Dr John Shebbeare', *European Magazine and London Review*, 14 (1788), 83–7, 166–8, 244–5 · Walpole, *Corr.*, 21.38–9; 28.40–41, 325 · H. Walpole, *Memoirs of King George II*, ed. J. Brooke, 3 (1985), 39–40 · BL, Hardwicke MSS, Add. MSS 35397–35401 · Boswell, *Life* (1953) · *The early diary of Frances Burney, 1768–1778*, ed. A. R. Ellis, 2 vols. (1889) · J. Shebbeare, *An answer to the queries contained in a letter … in the public ledger* (1775) · G. G. Cunningham, ed., *Lives of eminent and illustrious Englishmen*, 5/2 (1836), 389–94 · Allibone, *Dict.* · *GM*, 1st ser., 58 (1788), 753 · J. R. Foster, 'Smollett's pamphleteering foe Shebbeare', *Publications of the Modern Language Association of America*, 57 (1942), 1053–100
Archives BL, Hardwicke MSS, Add. MSS 35397–35401
Likenesses W. Bromley, line engraving, BM, NPG; repro. in *European Magazine*, 13 (1788), 82

Shee, George Archer- (1895–1914), literary prototype, was born on 6 May 1895 at the Bank of England, Broad Street, Bristol, the elder child and only son of Martin Archer-Shee (1846–1913), banker, and his second wife, Helen Treloar. By his father's first marriage, to Elizabeth Edith Dennistoun Pell, George Archer-Shee had a half-brother, Martin Archer-Shee, who entered parliament in 1910 as MP for Central Finsbury, and two half-sisters, both of whom became nuns. George Archer-Shee achieved notoriety as a cadet at the Royal Naval College, Osborne, fame on his acquittal on charges of theft and forgery, and immortality as Ronnie Winslow in Terence Rattigan's 1946 play *The Winslow Boy*, which was made into a film two years later, directed by Anthony Asquith.

Descended from an Irish Catholic family, Archer-Shee was educated at Stonyhurst College before entering the Royal Naval College, Osborne. In 1908, at the age of thirteen, he was accused by the college authorities of stealing a 5s. postal order from another cadet, Terence Back, forging Back's signature, and cashing the order at the local post office. He was summarily dismissed from the service. However, Archer-Shee's father never doubted his son's innocence, and sought the advice of his elder son, since 1900 a holder of the DSO and an interested upholder of the family's honour; he thought his half-brother's treatment at the hands of the navy so iniquitous that the affair should be investigated by Sir Edward Carson. Carson was not only a great advocate but also a great humanitarian, and the drama that ensued became a battle for human rights fought by Carson against the forces of reaction, led by the solicitor-general, Sir Rufus Isaacs.

The undisputed facts were that only two boys had been given permission to go to the post office on 7 October 1908, the date of the theft, Archer-Shee and a cadet called Arbuthnot; that Archer-Shee, with savings of £5 10s. 11d., had purchased a postal order for 15s. 6d. with which to buy a model steam engine; and that Back's 5s. postal order had been cashed. The postmistress told the chief petty officer deputed to investigate, whom she later described in court as 'almost raving', that it was Archer-Shee who had cashed the 5s. postal order. Several cadets were paraded but the postmistress failed to identify either Archer-Shee or Arbuthnot, and at Archer-Shee's subsequent trial she admitted she could not recall any other transaction or conversation on the day in question. A leading handwriting expert gave it as his opinion that the endorsement was in Archer-Shee's hand, but at two judicial inquiries legal representation was denied to Archer-Shee, and there was therefore no cross-examination of witnesses brought against him. Archer-Shee returned to Stonyhurst to finish his education, where he was received 'with open arms' (Hyde, 266) by the rector.

As a cadet, Archer-Shee was not permitted to demand a court martial, and the director of prosecutions blocked a trial by jury by declining to prosecute. Nearly two years after the alleged offences Carson was left with no alternative but to argue in the High Court for a petition of rights. Contrary to precedent, the solicitor-general refused to give way and the judge found for the crown. But Carson managed to lodge a successful appeal. When the case came to trial, on 12 July 1910, George Archer-Shee was subjected to two days of gruelling cross-examination by Sir Rufus Isaacs. He never flinched, having protested his innocence from the start. The final outcome turned on a brilliant cross-examination of the postmistress by Carson, who enabled her to retain her reputation for honesty while admitting to a fallible memory.

The case suddenly collapsed on the fourth day of the trial, when the solicitor-general exonerated Archer-Shee on every charge and declined to proceed any further. The Admiralty had long strained to avoid a test of the facts at law, but when a trial was forced upon them they had to back down to forestall the humiliation of a jury's verdict against them. None of the crown's witnesses withdrew, and none of the evidence was changed, but the Admiralty knew that the boy's guilt could not be proved. Even then no offer came from the Admiralty to reinstate Archer-Shee, nor from the Treasury to recompense his father. Only after the matter had been raised in the House of Commons was Mr Martin Archer-Shee awarded £7120 by way of compensation and costs. The Archer-Shees' Roman Catholicism was probably a contributory cause of their prejudicial treatment. Shortly before the outbreak of war George Archer-Shee was commissioned in the South Staffordshire regiment. He went missing in action at Ypres on 31 October 1914. His name was inscribed on the Menin gate.   MICHAEL DE-LA-NOY

Sources H. M. Hyde, *Carson: the life of Sir Edward Carson, Lord Carson of Duncairn* (1953) • b. cert. • d. cert. • 'The naval cadet case', *The Spectator* (6 Aug 1910), 195–6 • *The Times* (28 March 1913) • Burke, *Gen. GB*

Shee, George Darell (1843–1894). *See under* Shee, Sir William (1804–1868).

Shee, Sir Martin Archer (1769–1850), portrait painter and writer, was born in Dublin on 20 December 1769, the

Sir Martin Archer Shee (1769–1850), by John Jackson, *c*.1815

younger surviving son of Martin Shee (1719/20–1783), merchant, and his wife, Mary (*d*. 1771), elder daughter of John Archer of Dublin. His grandfather, George Shee of Castlebar, co. Mayo, belonged to an Irish Roman Catholic family claiming kinship with the old family of O'Shea. True or not, genealogical vanity was a trait both of Martin Shee and of the future Sir Martin Archer Shee, as was a taste for turning more or less whimsical verses, which resulted, in the case of the painter, in several tedious volumes on art in rhyming couplets.

Education Shortly after the death of Shee's mother in 1771 his father left Dublin for Cookstown, co. Wicklow, where the boy and his brother George were looked after by their mother's widowed sister, Mrs McEvoy, who was already living with the family. Shee's father, who had gone blind some time before his marriage, provided his son with his early classical education. When Mrs McEvoy remarried (to a Mr Dillon) and moved to Dublin in 1781, Shee's father also moved back there. After his father's death in 1783 Shee was brought up in the Dillon household. He had by now received a year's classical education in Dublin with the Dominicans and had begun to study under Francis Robert West at the drawing academy of the Royal Dublin Society, where he won most of the premiums available and was awarded a silver palette. His dependent position persuaded him to leave home abruptly at fifteen and set up successfully as a portrait painter in crayon (pastel). By 1786 he was painting life-size portraits in oil and enjoying fashionable patronage. At this time he also developed a taste for the theatre, which he retained. In 1788, encouraged by Gilbert Stuart, Shee went to London, arriving on 29 June, and lodged in Southampton Street, Covent Garden.

Shee was armed with recommendations to the likes of James Barry, Edmund Burke, Sir Joshua Reynolds, Benjamin West, George Romney, and John Opie, but they proved optimistic. After his death some of these introductions, his son tells us, were found undelivered among his papers, but he had made use of some, and wrote accounts of several fruitless meetings. They include a revealing description of Barry, who was discovered in considerable 'déshabille' amid the chaos of his dining-room, where he was working upon an etching after one of his own designs:

> The walls were perfectly concealed by … little statues, busts, and old pictures, besides casts of legs, arms, skulls, bones, hands, feet, sketches, prints, drawings, palettes, pencils, colours, canvases, frames … disposed in all the confusion and disorder of the most negligent carelessness. (Shee, 1.83–4)

Nothing came of this, nor of a meeting with Reynolds, who, Shee suspected, had no knowledge of the provider of his introduction.

Shee was not in difficulties, however. He expressed his determination not to return to working in crayon, and evidently gained sufficient work as a portraitist. Indeed, he moved to larger lodgings in Craven Street, the Strand, in the autumn of 1788, and in the following spring had two portraits accepted for the Royal Academy exhibition. By this date he had already become friends with the young Thomas Lawrence, and expressed his admiration for him in letters to his brother. During this period he was befriended by the actor Alexander Pope, and also gained employment creating copies in oils which the publisher Thomas Macklin needed to engrave for his *Gallery of the British Poets*. He was able to earn as much as 12 guineas for each of these copies at a time when Lawrence was charging 10 guineas for a portrait head. His own portraits were admired by the publisher John Boydell.

After two years Shee's career took a decisive step forward when he got to know his cousin, Sir George Shee, an Indian nabob, who showed some of his pictures to a distinguished company at dinner in February 1790. As a result Shee obtained a second and more successful introduction to Burke and thus to Reynolds. He suffered a temporary setback when four pictures were accepted for the Royal Academy exhibition in 1790 but were not hung. In November that year, however, he entered the Royal Academy Schools and, to quote his son, 'the course of Mr. Shee's life, during the next four or five years, offers but few events of interest to the pen of the biographer' (Shee, 1.142). Shortly after he entered the schools Shee moved into an apartment in Jermyn Street previously occupied by Lawrence, whom he was eventually to succeed as president of the Royal Academy. Shee not only tended generally to follow in Lawrence's footsteps, but has also been overshadowed by his more brilliant gifts.

Established career Shee had no fewer than seven portraits at the Royal Academy in 1792, including *Anthony Pasquin* and two actors, *Alexander Pope* and *W. T. ['Gentleman'] Lewis*, who is seen in Vandyke costume as the marquess in Mrs Inchbald's *The Midnight Hour* (National Gallery, London).

He continued to exhibit thereafter at the academy, almost exclusively showing portraits, until 1845, missing only one or two years, with only an occasional foray into fancy or history pictures. It was upon portrait painting that his rapidly growing reputation rested and his exhibits in 1795 made a particularly strong impression, including his *Self-Portrait* (NPG), a work which suggests the influence of Hoppner. Indeed, Hoppner expressed his admiration of Shee at this time and the likelihood of Shee's soon becoming an associate of the Royal Academy. That election took place in November 1798. In autumn 1796 Shee had moved to a large house on the south side of Golden Square at the corner of Sherard Street, and on 19 December that year he married (in Paddington church) a Roman Catholic, Mary (d. 1846), eldest daughter of James Power of Youghall, co. Cork. Her ancestry, like Shee's, could be made to sound suitably grand but was similarly impoverished, and so the marriage was opposed on both sides (including, briefly, by Mrs Dillon), but was evidently happy.

In January 1799 Shee moved again, to the house in Cavendish Square previously occupied by Romney. He initially took the nineteen-year remainder of Romney's lease, but kept the house until the end of his life. Partly because a vacancy occurred among the academicians at Barry's expulsion, Shee was swiftly elected Royal Academician in February 1800 and submitted as his diploma picture *Belisarius* (RA). He was then commissioned to paint the duke of Clarence (afterwards William IV) for the Liverpool chamber of commerce (Walker Art Gallery, Liverpool), and from this date there was a marked increase in the number of his aristocratic and grander professional sitters.

In September 1802, after the treaty of Amiens, Shee, like so many artists, visited Paris to see the works of art looted by Napoleon then gathered in the Louvre. Having met the father of Prosper Mérimée, he was given the opportunity of studying Napoleon close to and at length, and was impressed; the extracts of his daily journal and his letters home are of interest, not least because Shee had fluent French. In the next couple of years, however, the threat of French invasion from his admired Napoleon led Shee to the surprising attempt to raise from among the ranks of the Royal Academy a volunteer force to oppose him. There were few takers.

Authorship It was shortly after this that Shee emerged as a poet, and *Rhymes on Art, or, The Remonstrance of a Painter* was published to favourable notices in 1805. It ran to three editions, and influenced the founding of the British Institution in 1807. Shee was much involved in the British Institution and exhibited there for many years after 1807, showing exclusively fancy and history pictures, in contrast with the Royal Academy, where he tended to show portraits. Shee next published *Elements of Art*, a poem in six cantos (1809), which did not do so well. It includes the following in its introductory lines:

> Yet, may the Muse, tho' still her course she trace
> In technic trammels, and didactic pace,
> Collect some flow'rets as she plods along,
> Should Taste propitious smile upon the song.

The laboured rhetorical modesty which these lines typify soon leads the author to identify his lines as 'rough sententious rhyme', a characterization with which it is hard to disagree. Shee went on, however, to publish *Commemoration of Reynolds, and other Poems* in 1814, followed by two novels: *Oldcourt* (1829), in which scenes of his childhood are described, and *Cecil Hyde* (1834); and a tragedy, *Alasco*, based on the unpromising topic of the partition of Poland. Charles Kemble put the play into rehearsal in 1823 but it was withdrawn when the licenser of plays, George Colman the younger, demanded alterations, although it was published in 1824.

Royal Academy administration In 1805 Shee first publicly appeared in the role in which he was to be more influential than as painter, poet, novelist, or dramatist: as a tireless politician within the Royal Academy especially and in the art world at large. His first target was Joseph Farington's conduct of the hanging committee of the academy. The matter is neatly summarized by W. T. Whitley (Whitley, 1.90–91, 95–7), who also provides insight into the many dissensions within the academy during this time. Shee's long-standing friendship with Hoppner had continued until this date, and was to endure, despite their professional rivalry: Shee's pursuit of Farington was founded upon the unfair exclusion from exhibition of a picture by Hoppner on the grounds of late submission to the academy. Hoppner had clearly been too ill to submit within the deadline, but at the same time Farington's committee had allowed a late picture by Northcote, although there was no such excuse in his case.

The long-standing result of these machinations was that Shee gained, and retained until the end of his life, the trust of his fellow academicians. Upon Lawrence's death in 1830 Shee was elected president, by eighteen votes to six for Beechey, and he was knighted in the same year. 'We expect much from Shee's self-devotion and chivalrous sense of honour', wrote Constable in a letter to a friend (Whitley, 2.185). In this curious phrase Constable seems to identify that mixture of egotism and desire 'to serve' that characterizes so many volunteer bureaucrats in British public life. It is certainly not hypocrisy; but nor is it quite selflessness. Shee was perfectly suited to running the Royal Academy. When he offered his resignation in 1845 his fellow academicians re-elected him, awarding him £300 p.a. from their funds. An annual pension in the civil list of £200 in recognition of Shee's 'merits and services' was also awarded to Lady Archer Shee, and was re-granted to their three daughters on her death on 4 May 1846. She died in Brighton, where in June 1845 Shee had effectively retired for the sake of his health, living in Pavilion Colonnade.

After his election as president Shee defended the Royal Academy in the face of many public attacks upon it. Among them were those of Benjamin Robert Haydon, who described Shee with some exaggeration as 'the most impotent painter in the solar system' and characterized him as 'the great founder of the tip-toe school' (*Diary*, ed. Pope, 2.477). These culminated in a parliamentary inquiry into the arts and principles of design, and especially into academies, by which was meant above all the Royal Academy. The evidence of Haydon and Shee, together with an extract from the select committee's report, is reprinted in Shee's *Life* (vol. 2, pp. 413 ff.). When it became necessary for the Royal Academy to move out of Somerset House in 1837, Shee directed its removal to the National Gallery, where in 1845 he escorted the young Queen Victoria on a visit. In 1826 he had become an honorary member of the Royal Hibernian Academy, having lobbied for its charter and foundation a few years earlier.

Later years Shee painted a portrait of Queen Victoria in 1842 (RA) although she preferred Hayter, and it is a rather unsatisfactory picture. Shee had performed much better in his portraits *William IV* and *Queen Adelaide* in 1834 (both Royal Collection). These full lengths of two royal sitters show that Shee could work on a grand scale in a manner suitable for state portraiture, indeed more so than any contemporary British artist other than Lawrence. He was excellent at portraying bishops, for example, a subject which has foiled countless British painters. A fine example is one of his portraits of a friend, *Edward Copplestone, Bishop of Llandaff* (priv. coll.), with its image of the west front of Llandaff Cathedral in the distance; Copplestone was Shee's professor of ancient literature at the Royal Academy. Shee could even do lawyers with grandeur and something approaching panache (see, for example, *Lord Campbell*; priv. coll.). Another example of his formal portraiture is *John B. Sawrey Morritt with the Toledo of Archmaster* (Society of Dilettanti, London). Such excellence chiefly in unsympathetic official portraiture means that it remains hard to think of Shee's professional achievement as anything other than one of passionless accomplishment. His male heads, however, are usually acutely defined, and he could sometimes strike an especially happy note. One such example is his *Annesley Children* (exh. RA, 1793), which has rare charm, and another, from his mature years, is the outstanding *Self-Portrait with Andrew Ellis Ellis* (ex Sothebys, London, 10 July 1991, lot 44), which may be considered his masterpiece.

Shee died in Brighton on 19 August 1850, after a prolonged illness characterized by sudden giddiness and vomiting, often brought on by reading or writing. The offer of the Royal Academy council to organize a funeral in St Paul's Cathedral was rejected by the family in favour of a private interment in Brighton cemetery (27 August 1850), after the Roman rites had been read over his coffin and those of the Anglican church in the church near the cemetery. He was survived by three sons and three daughters. Many details of his life are recorded in a remarkably pompous biography by his middle son (Martin Archer Shee, *The Life of Sir Martin Archer Shee*, 2 vols., London, 1860).   ROBIN SIMON

Sources M. A. Shee, *The life of Sir Martin Archer Shee*, 2 vols. (1860) · W. G. Strickland, *A dictionary of Irish artists*, 2 vols. (1913); facs. edn with introduction by T. J. Snoddy (1969) · W. T. Whitley, *Artists and their friends in England, 1800–1820*, 2 vols. (1928–30); repr. (1973) · DNB · *The autobiography and memoirs of Benjamin Robert Haydon (1786–1846) edited from his journals by Tom Taylor* (1926) [introduction by A. Huxley]

Archives FM Cam., corresp. · RA, letters | BL, corresp. with Sir Robert Peel, Add. MSS 40409–40598, *passim* · Bodl. Oxf., corresp. with Isaac Disraeli · NL Scot., letters to Sir David Wilkie and Sir George Reid · UCL, letters to Society for the Diffusion of Useful Knowledge
Likenesses M. A. Shee, self-portrait, oils, *c.*1794, NPG · J. Jackson, black chalk and watercolour drawing, *c.*1815, NPG, RA [*see illus.*] · T. Bridgford, drawing, *c.*1841, NG Ire. · H. Griffiths, stipple, pubd 1846, NPG · M. A. Shee, double portrait, self-portrait, oils (with Andrew Ellis Ellis); Sothebys, 10 July 1991, lot 44 · C. Vogel, drawing, Staatliche Kunstsammlungen, Dresden, Küpferstichkabinett · etching, BM, NPG; repro. in *Magazine of Fine Arts* (1834)

Shee, Sir William (1804–1868), judge, was born in Finchley, Middlesex, on 24 June 1804, the eldest son of Joseph Shee, a merchant of Thomastown, co. Kilkenny, and Laurence Pountney Place in the City of London, and his wife, Teresa, daughter of John Darell of Scotney Castle, Kent. He was educated at a French school in Somers Town run by Abbé Carron, an associate of the religious and political writer Félicité Robert de Lamennais. In 1818 he went to St Cuthbert's College, Ushaw, near Durham, where his cousin Nicholas Wiseman (afterwards the first cardinal archbishop of the restored English Catholic hierarchy) was a student. Later he also attended lectures at the University of Edinburgh, and became a member of the discussion group known as the Speculative Society. On 31 May 1823 he became a student at Lincoln's Inn, where he studied law in the chambers of Thomas Chitty, a well-known special pleader and legal writer. He was called to the bar on 19 June 1828.

Shee gradually built up an extensive legal practice and worked on the Maidstone sessions, becoming serjeant-at-law on 19 February 1840. He received a patent of precedence in Trinity vacation 1845, and was appointed queen's serjeant in 1857. On 26 December 1837 he married Mary (*d.* 1861), second daughter of Sir James Gordon, bt, of Gordonstown and Letterfourie, Banffshire. They had several children, including George Darell Shee [*see below*] and Henry Gordon Shee QC, recorder of Burnley and judge of the Salford Hundred court of record.

Shee was a moderate and consistent Liberal throughout his life. Soon after his call to the bar he spoke eloquently in favour of Catholic emancipation at a great protestant gathering which was held on Pennenden Heath, near Maidstone, on 24 November 1828. At the general election of July 1847 he stood unsuccessfully for parliament for Marylebone. In July 1852, however, he entered the House of Commons for co. Kilkenny, which he represented until parliament was dissolved in March 1857. Shee spoke for the first time on 12 November 1852, during the debate on the report on the address (*Hansard 3*, 123, 1852, 139–41). In the absence of the Irish land reformer and radical politician William Sharman Crawford, Shee took charge of the Tenant Right Bill, which he reintroduced on 25 November 1852. On 7 December he made a long speech on Sir Joseph Napier's Tenants' Improvement Compensation Bill. On the same day the Tenant Right Bill was read a second time, but it was subsequently condemned by the select committee, to which it and Napier's scheme of Irish land reform had been referred. On 16 February 1854 Shee brought in a

bill which, with the exception of three clauses, was the exact counterpart of Sharman Crawford's bill of the previous session, but it met with little encouragement. On 13 June 1854 he moved for leave to bring in a bill to amend the laws relating to the temporalities of the Church of Ireland, and to increase the funds for religious education and church buildings in Ireland. This motion was rejected, however, after a debate of three nights, by a majority of eighty-six votes. Convinced of the impossibility of carrying Sharman Crawford's bill through parliament, and with his blessing, on 20 February 1855 Shee brought in a Tenants' Improvement Compensation Bill, founded on two of Napier's bills as amended by the select committee of 1853. This bill was equally unpopular, however, and was eventually dropped. Because he was seen to have abandoned Sharman Crawford's measure, Shee lost his seat as MP for Kilkenny in the general election in April 1857, and was again defeated there at the general election in May 1859. In 1860 he refused the offer of the chief-justiceship of Madras and in September 1862 was nominated as a candidate at the by-election for Stoke-on-Trent, but received only thirty-two votes.

Shee was an earnest and conscientious advocate, and an able, if occasionally ponderous, speaker. His breadth of legal knowledge and common-sense approach won the approval of his fellow lawyers and he acted as counsel in many famous trials of the day, such as the *Roupell case*. He conducted the defence of William Palmer (1824–1856) and was criticized for saying in his speech that he believed Palmer to be innocent.

On 19 December 1863 Shee was appointed by Lord Westbury a justice of the court of queen's bench in the place of Sir William Wightman, and on 10 June 1864 he was knighted (*London Gazette*, 22 Dec 1863, 6645; *London Gazette*, 14 June 1864, 3072). He was the first Roman Catholic to be promoted to the English bench since the revolution of 1688.

Shee edited several editions of Lord Tenterden's *Treatise of the Law Relative to Merchant Ships and Seamen* and Samuel Marshall's *Treatise on the Law of Insurance*. He also wrote *Reflections on the Trial of the Prince de Polignac* (1836), *The Act for the more effectual Application of Charitable Donations and Bequests in Ireland* (7 & 8 Vict. c. xcvii. (1845), and a number of other works, including pamphlets on church appropriations and endowments (1849), *The Irish church: being a digest of the returns of the prelates, dignitaries, and beneficed clergy* (1852; 2nd edn, 1863 or 1864), a work on the Merchant Shipping Acts of 1854, and *Papers and letters on subjects of literary, historical, and political interest, and speeches at public meetings, in parliament, and at the bar*, (vol. 1, 1862, privately printed) and *Papers, letters, and speeches in the House of Commons on the Irish land question with a summary of its parliamentary history from the general election of 1852 to the close of the session of 1863* (1863). The last was, in effect, the second volume of Shee's *Papers and letters*, but though 'vol ii' appears on the original cloth cover, it is absent from the title-page.

After sitting on the bench for little more than four years, Shee died from an attack of apoplexy on 19 February 1868 at his residence, 5 Sussex Place, Hyde Park Gardens, London. His wife predeceased him on 11 October 1861, aged forty-five.

Their eldest son, **George Darell Shee** (1843–1894), born in London on 12 July 1843, was educated at Trinity Hall, Cambridge, where he graduated LLB in 1866. He was admitted to the Middle Temple on 6 November 1862, and was called to the bar on 30 April 1867. He joined the southeastern circuit, became district probate registrar for East Suffolk, and in July 1883 was appointed recorder of Hythe. He was the author of *A Remonstrance* (1886), which was addressed to Sir Charles Gavan Duffy, in reply to his attack on Sir William Shee in a book entitled *The League of the North and South*. On 14 October 1873 he married Jane, eldest daughter of Harry Innes of Thomastown. He died at his home, Landguard Lodge, Felixstowe, Suffolk, on 15 December 1894; his wife survived him.

G. F. R. BARKER, rev. HUGH MOONEY

Sources *Solicitors' Journal*, 8 (1863–4), 121–2 · *Solicitors' Journal*, 8 (1863–4), 247 · *Solicitors' Journal*, 12 (1867–8), 344–5 · *Law Times* (22 Feb 1868), 303, 317–18 · *Law Times* (22 Dec 1894), 192 [obit. of G. D. Shee] · E. Foss, *Biographia juridica: a biographical dictionary of the judges of England … 1066–1870* (1870) · J. Haydn, *The book of dignities: containing rolls of the official personages of the British empire* (1851) · W. Ballantine, *Some experiences of a barrister's life*, 7th edn (1883), 171 · Serjeant Robinson [B. C. Robinson], *Bench and bar: reminiscences of one of the last of an ancient race*, 2nd edn (1889) · *Annual Register* (1868) · *Law Journal* (21 Feb 1868), 139 · J. Foster, *Men-at-the-bar: a biographical hand-list of the members of the various inns of court*, 2nd edn (1885), 422 · *CGPLA Eng. & Wales* (1868) · *CGPLA Eng. & Wales* (1895) [George Darell Shee]
Likenesses D. J. Pound, stipple and line engraving (after photograph by Mayall), NPG; repro. in D. J. Pound, *Drawing room portrait gallery of eminent personages* (1859–60) · wood-engraving (after photograph by J. and C. Watkins), NPG; repro. in *ILN* (2 Jan 1864)
Wealth at death under £10,000: administration, 14 March 1868, *CGPLA Eng. & Wales* · £1458 1s. 4d.—George Darell Shee: probate, 9 Feb 1895, *CGPLA Eng. & Wales*

Sheed, Francis Joseph [Frank] (1897–1981), publisher and author, was born on 20 March 1897 in Sydney, Australia, the first of two children of John (Jack) Sheed (1865–1942), draughtsman and civil servant, and his wife, Mary (Min) Maloney (1867–1953). With his father an aggressive Marxist Scot, his mother a tenacious Irish Catholic, and his grandmother a hostile Presbyterian, he nevertheless emerged from his Methodist Sunday school a lifelong unswerving Roman Catholic. He became the personification of the missionary apologetic of English Catholicism, played a key role in the Catholic intellectual and literary revival of the 1920s and 1930s, and was the driving force behind the study by lay Catholics of serious theology.

From 1910 Sheed attended Sydney high school. In 1914 he began studies at Sydney University, and graduated BA in 1917. He became a student at Sydney University law school the following year. In 1920 he decided to take a year off in Europe. In London, Sheed accidentally discovered the recently formed Catholic Evidence Guild, devoted to out-of-doors speaking to explain the teaching of the Roman Catholic church. Startled by the discovery of his own theological ignorance, and bowled over by the excitement and immensity of the guild's task, he joined. There

he met Mary Josephine *Ward (1889–1975). Known always as Maisie, she was the daughter of Wilfrid Ward and granddaughter of Oxford Movement convert William Ward. He fell in love and proposed marriage. She dithered and he returned to Sydney in 1924 to complete his law qualifications. But she eventually accepted and, armed with his LLB, he returned to marriage (27 April 1926) and the guild, both of which had their lifelong commitment.

The early guild speakers were aggressive; the crowds were lively. Once Sheed was interrupted by the explosion of fireworks placed under his shoes. The need for change was signalled when Sheed got off the platform after what he had viewed as a very effective verbal punch-up, and a listener said: 'I feel bruised all over' (private information). Recognizing with horror what he had done, Sheed and Ward set formidable standards for each other and for the guild to change the atmosphere to a mutually respecting relationship in which a speaker with real understanding explained a doctrine to an intellectually interested audience. Sheed constantly emphasized that one must be able to state one's opponent's case better than one's own. Thus he wrote *Communism and Man* (1938), of which the first half was a statement of Marxism, the second a refutation. It delighted him that the first half became a textbook in communist training courses. For Sheed the outdoor crowd was a school of theology where the methodology of exposition replaced that of argument. He saw the speaker as 'making love to the audience' and at this he was expert.

Listeners converted must have been few, despite the commitment of guild members in half a dozen cities; more important was the production of a Catholic public viewing theology as an area of interest and consequence. The material for this was provided by Sheed and Ward, the publishing firm founded by the Sheeds in 1926 after their marriage. Sheed was a prolific writer, sometimes on specific issues, such as *Nullity of Marriage* (1932), more frequently on general works related to platform speaking: *Catholic Evidence Training Outlines* (1925, with Maisie Ward; many editions); *Map of Life* (1933); *Theology and Sanity* (1946), this latter a milestone in developing a thinking laity; and *Society and Sanity* (1953). In all he wrote sixteen books (and numerous smaller works), edited half a dozen, and contributed to several; translations included particularly *The Confessions of St. Augustine*.

Sheed and Ward welcomed convert authors, encouraged new authors, and introduced continental writers and developments. The British market being financially too small, in 1933 Sheed opened an office in New York, through which Sheed and Ward became the most influential Catholic publisher in the English-speaking world. In 1940, with the war in full spate, the family base, with daughter Rosemary (b. 1927) and son Wilfrid (b. 1930), became New York. Sheed returned to London whenever necessary. In December 1940 the London office of Sheed and Ward was totally destroyed in a night; Sheed produced a new organization within two months. He and Maisie Ward became involved in the USA with the *Catholic Worker*, the houses of hospitality, Friendship House, and scattered guild groups; they were also involved in lecturing widely. In 1946 the family returned to England, though the New York operation still demanded considerable attention.

Sheed received increasing recognition of his intellectual contribution through numerous honorary degrees at Roman Catholic universities. In 1956, in recognition of his theological contribution, the Vatican awarded him a pontifical doctorate in theology; he joked that he should be known as 'The Alfresco Doctor'. Sheed happily contributed to the preparation of the English-speaking Catholic community for Vatican II through the publication of influential continental theologians. In the crisis after the council he was not so comfortable, as evidenced by titles of later books: *Is it the same Church?* (1968); *Christ in Eclipse* (1978). Nevertheless, as he stated in *The Church and I* (1974), his faith in Christ and in the church never wavered. During the early 1960s Sheed gave up control of the firm, but with disastrous results, compelling his return to management and the sale of the New York office in 1973. His wife died soon after, on 28 January 1975. Sheed nevertheless continued lecturing and writing. He died of a stroke on 20 November 1981 at 7 Tonnele Avenue, Jersey City, New Jersey, USA, and was buried at Jersey City five days later.

PETER HASTINGS

Sources F. Sheed, *The church and I* (Garden City, NY, 1974) · D. Greene, *The living of Maisie Ward* (1997) · W. Sheed, *Frank and Maisie: a memoir with parents* (1986) · T. Burns, 'Tribute to Frank Sheed', *The Tablet* (28 Nov 1981) · *The Tablet* (5 Dec 1981) · private information (2004) [Mrs Rosemary Middleton, daughter]
Archives University of Notre Dame, Indiana, archives, corresp. and papers | BL, corresp. with D. E. Collins, former secretary of G. K. Chesterton, Add. MSS 73231A; 73231B; 73231C; 73475A; 73475; 73482

Sheed, Mary Josephine. *See* Ward, Mary Josephine (1889–1975).

Sheehan, Harold Leeming (1900–1988), pathologist, was born on 4 August 1900 in Carlisle, Cumberland, the second of six sons and second of thirteen children of Patrick Sheehan, general medical practitioner, and his wife, Eliza, daughter of Francis Leeming, a businessman in the cotton trade. He was educated at Carlisle grammar school and the University of Manchester, where he graduated MB, ChB with second-class honours in 1921. His father died in 1919 and as soon as Harold qualified he went back to Carlisle to assist his elder brother in the family medical practice for the next six years.

In 1927 Sheehan returned to Manchester University as a demonstrator, and later as a lecturer, in the department of pathology, where his researches into renal function earned him the degrees of MD, with a gold medal, in 1931 and MSc in 1932. He gained a Rockefeller medical fellowship in 1934 and spent a year on further studies of the kidney in the department of pharmacology at the Johns Hopkins medical school in Baltimore, Maryland, USA, after which he was appointed director of research at Glasgow Royal Maternity Hospital (1935–46). During the next five years he established himself as an international expert on the pathology of pregnancy by making important contributions on disease of the liver, brain, heart, and kidneys in pregnancy and, in particular, on the importance of shock and haemorrhage in causing necrosis of the anterior lobe of the pituitary gland.

Since he was a Territorial Army officer, on the declaration of war in 1939 Sheehan was mobilized and graded as a specialist in pathology, with the rank of major, in the Royal Army Medical Corps. He served in Britain until January 1944 and was then posted to Italy, with the rank of lieutenant-colonel. In January 1945 he became a full colonel and was director of pathology to the central Mediterranean forces until the end of the war. He was mentioned in dispatches.

In 1946 Sheehan was appointed to the chair of pathology in the University of Liverpool. Students found him informative, entertaining, and memorable; he challenged much accepted dogma. His well-deserved reputation as an exacting examiner, however, made him respected rather than popular. He continued his researches and accepted many invitations to lecture abroad. Gradually the effects of post-partum necrosis of the pituitary gland came to be known as Sheehan's syndrome. After his retirement Sheehan produced two books, *Pathology of Toxaemia of Pregnancy* (with J. B. Lynch, 1973) and *Post-partum hypopituitarism* (with J. C. Davis, 1982).

In 1940 Sheehan became a DSc of Manchester University. In 1941 he gained membership of the Royal College of Physicians of London and he was promoted to fellowship in 1947. He became a fellow of the Royal College of Obstetricians and Gynaecologists (1949) and a founder fellow of the Royal College of Pathologists (1964). His foreign honours included an honorary MD degree from the University of Szeged, Hungary, in 1982. He was an honorary member of endocrinological societies in Argentina, Chile, Romania, and Hungary. He was also an honorary fellow of the Obstetrical and Gynaecological societies of America and of Belgium, while in France he was a foreign associate of the National Academy of Medicine.

Physically, though not obese, Sheehan looked portly and stooped slightly. He wore formal suits, even at informal times, but never looked smart. His hair became white at an early age, but his eyebrows remained black until he was old. When he was excited or emphatic his eyes would bulge slightly. He was enthusiastic, talkative, argumentative, and self-confident. He smoked his pipe while he worked—even in the autopsy room. He ate and drank with discrimination and was an excellent host. He was a strong swimmer and a successful gardener. His secrecy about his personal affairs was notorious, but he was certainly affluent when his position had become established and he left a substantial sum at death.

In 1934 Sheehan married Eve Suzette Gertrude (d. 1986), daughter of (Martin) Henry Potter, theatre manager. She was a good linguist, assisted in the preparation of Sheehan's publications, and travelled abroad with him. She was rather reserved, but her penetrating remarks gave balance to her husband's exuberance. They had no children. Sheehan died in Kendal, Westmorland, on 25

October 1988, having become immobile following a fracture of his hip in January of that year. He was buried at Allerton cemetery, Woolton Road, Liverpool, on 4 November 1988.   A. H. CRUICKSHANK, *rev.*

Sources *The Independent* (3 Nov 1988) · personal knowledge (1996) · private information (1996) [Mrs Mary Bewlay, niece] · *CGPLA Eng. & Wales* (1989) · *WW* (1988) · *BMJ* (3 Dec 1988) · H. Orthner, 'Über das Sheehan-Syndrom', *Der Pathologe*, 12 (1991), 113–14 · Munk, *Roll*
Likenesses photograph, repro. in *Der Pathologe* · photographs, U. Lpool, department of pathology
Wealth at death £525,752: probate, 10 Feb 1989, *CGPLA Eng. & Wales*

Sheehan, John (1809–1882), journalist, was the son of Thomas Sheehan, a grazier, and Alicia Dunn of Celbridge, co. Kildare. He was educated at Clongowes Wood College, where he was taught by Francis Sylvester Mahony, better known as Father Prout. In October 1829 he entered Trinity College, Dublin, but he did not graduate. In 1830 he joined the Comet Club, a literary society with members including Samuel Lover, Joseph Stirling Coyne, Robert Knox, subsequently editor of the *Morning Post*, and Maurice O'Connell, son of Daniel O'Connell. At first its members prepared and issued pamphlets attacking the tithe system; the first, *The Parson's Horn Book*, which appeared in two parts with etchings by Lover, met with extraordinary success. According to Sheehan it had a greater circulation and caused more sensation than any book issued in Ireland since the days of Swift. The club then issued *The Comet*, a satirical weekly paper which attacked the Church of Ireland, the first number appearing on 1 May 1831. Sheehan was appointed sub-editor. In a few weeks it had reached a circulation of many thousand copies, and until it ceased at the end of 1833 exercised considerable influence. In the autumn of 1833 the government ordered the arrest of the editor, Thomas Browne, and Sheehan for libel. They were defended by Daniel O'Connell and Robert Holmes, but were each sentenced to twelve months' imprisonment and ordered to pay a fine of £100. The fine was, however, remitted, and the term of imprisonment was only partly served.

Sheehan, on his release, studied for the Irish bar, to which he was called in 1835. He shortly afterwards came to London, where he became a journalist, and in 1836 he was in Paris and Madrid as representative of *The Constitutional* newspaper. He next became parliamentary reporter of the *Morning Herald*, and contributed poems and sketches to *Bentley's Miscellany* and other magazines. In March 1839 he was admitted to Trinity College, Cambridge, but he did not graduate. He was admitted to the Inner Temple in 1841 and called to the English bar in 1846. He had been admitted to the King's Inns in 1843, but seems never to have practised. In 1852 he was proprietor and editor of *The Independent*, published in London and Cambridge. As a young man in Paris in the 1830s Thackeray knew Sheehan well, and he is believed to be the original of Captain Shandon in *Pendennis*.

Shortly after 1868 Sheehan married the widow of Colonel Shubrick, a wealthy Anglo-Indian officer, and spent some years in travelling about the continent. He eventually retired to the Charterhouse, where he died on 29 May 1882.   D. J. O'DONOGHUE, *rev.* MARIE-LOUISE LEGG

Sources B. Inglis, *The freedom of the press in Ireland, 1784–1841* (1954) · D. J. O'Donoghue, *The poets of Ireland: a biographical dictionary with bibliographical particulars*, 1 vol. in 3 pts (1892–3) · E. Keane, P. Beryl Phair, and T. U. Sadleir, eds., *King's Inns admission papers, 1607–1867*, IMC (1982) · Venn, *Alum. Cant.* · Burtchaell & Sadleir, *Alum. Dubl.* · The letters and private papers of William Makepeace Thackeray, ed. G. N. Ray, 1 (1945)

Sheehan, Patrick Augustine [P. A. S.] (1852–1913), Roman Catholic priest and novelist, was born and baptized in Mallow, co. Cork, Ireland, on 17 March 1852, the third of five children of Patrick Sheehan (*d.* 1863/4), owner of a small business, and Joanna Regan. He attended the local national school and received his secondary education at St Coleman's in Fermoy. In 1869 he began training for the priesthood at St Patrick's College, Maynooth, the national seminary. He was ordained in 1875. Sheehan was first assigned to the English mission and served in Plymouth and Exeter before returning to Ireland in 1877. He was sent to Mallow as curate; later he was called to the cathedral at Queenstown (Cobh), co. Cork, where he served until 1888. After another assignment in Mallow, he was appointed parish priest in Doneraile, co. Cork, in 1895. He was named doctor of divinity in 1902 and canon in 1903.

Sheehan's literary career began in 1881 as the essayist P. A. S. His observations in literary and religious magazines on issues related to education, philosophy, and clerical life attracted attention in Ireland, England, the continent, and the United States. In the 1880s he wrote a number of children's stories that were later published by the Catholic Truth Society of Ireland. His poetry, published under the title *Cithara mea* (1900), tried to solve everyday problems through a mystical appeal to faith. His sermons were printed under the title *Mariae corona* (1900), and his collected essays, *Under the Cedars and the Stars*, were published in 1903.

Sheehan is best remembered as a novelist. Many of his novels were originally serialized in religious magazines, including the *American Ecclesiastical Review*. Among his works are *Geoffrey Austin, Student* (1895) (his first novel), the immensely popular *My New Curate* (1899), *Glenanaar* (1905), *Lisheen* (1907), *The Intellectuals* (1911), and the posthumous *The Graves of Kilmorna* (1915). Drawing upon his life experiences, Sheehan's descriptions of the clergy and people of rural Ireland successfully mixed humour and pathos with melodrama. His novels portrayed traditional Irish life as simple, moral, and self-sacrificing. Reviewers admired his ability to criticize Irish social conventions and institutions without ridiculing his characters' foibles. Sheehan saved his scathing passages for the evils of modern life and English absentee landlords who neglected their Irish tenants.

The Intellectuals offered Sheehan's vision of a reorganized society that he hoped would take shape in an independent Ireland. His nationalism was neither exclusively Gaelic nor Catholic. The novel's archetypical characters, who included Catholic and protestant men and women from

Ireland, England, and Scotland, form a club to discuss current issues of the day. In the preface Sheehan explained his object: 'To show that there are really no invincible antagonisms amongst the peoples who make up the commonwealth of Ireland, no mutual repugnances that may not be removed by a freer and kindlier intercourse with each other' (*The Intellectuals*, p. v).

Three of Sheehan's best-known novels were works of historical fiction. *Glenanaar*, a story of the suspicion that clings to the descendants of an alleged political informer, was based on the Doneraile conspiracy trial of 1829. *The Queen's Fillet* (1911), set during the French Revolution, warned the Irish people of the dangers of demagoguery and the excesses caused by political uprisings. Sheehan's last novel, *The Graves of Kilmorna*, reflected a dramatic change in his outlook. Like many Irish nationalists of the period, Sheehan was disillusioned by the failure of constitutional methods to secure home rule for Ireland. The novel begins with Irish workers preparing for military action in the Fenian rising of 1867. One of the two heroes dies in battle—a martyr patriot. The novel then follows the remainder of the other hero's life: from Dartmoor prison to his death in Ireland at the hands of a drunken election-eve mob during his only engagement in constitutional activity.

Sheehan was diagnosed with a fatal illness in 1910 but refused to undergo surgery. Instead, he carried out his duties as parish priest until his death (from cancer) on 5 October 1913 at Doneraile. He was buried at the entrance to his parish church.   LAWRENCE W. McBRIDE

Sources H. Heuser, *Canon Sheehan of Doneraile: the story of an Irish parish priest as told chiefly by himself in books, personal memoirs and letters* (1917) · C. Candy, 'Canon Sheehan: the conflicts of the priest-author', *Religion, conflict, and coexistence in Ireland: essays presented to Monsignor Patrick J. Corish*, ed. R. V. Comerford and others (1990), 252–77 · B. Clifford, *Canon Sheehan: a turbulent priest* (1990) · L. McBride, 'A literary life of a socially and politically engaged priest: Canon Patrick Augustine Sheehan (1852–1913)', *Radical Irish priests, 1660–1970*, ed. G. Moran (Dublin, 1998), 131–48
Likenesses photographs, repro. in Heuser, *Canon Sheehan of Doneraile*
Wealth at death £2940 14s. 2d.: probate, 12 Feb 1914, CGPLA Eng. & Wales

Sheehy, Nicholas (1728/9–1766), Roman Catholic priest, was born near Fethard, co. Tipperary, Ireland. Little is known about his parents except that his mother's maiden name was Power. He was educated in Louvain, Belgium, and ordained in Rome in 1752, and upon his return to Ireland he became curate of Newcastle, co. Tipperary, and later parish priest of a group of parishes centring on Clogheen, co. Tipperary. Clogheen became the centre of serious agrarian disturbances, led by the Whiteboys, in the early 1760s. Their chief grievances were the enclosure of commons and the high rent for potato ground, both of which resulted in the displacement of settlements. As the latter were the source of income for Catholic priests such as Sheehy, they were now left with little or nothing. These circumstances may have predisposed Sheehy to concur with Whiteboy aims. He encouraged resistance to the collection of 5s. for every marriage celebrated in the area

around Ballyporeen, co. Tipperary, a novel claim advanced by a tithe farmer in 1762. He opposed the collection of church rates and tithes in the Newcastle area. R. R. Madden suggested that Sheehy collected money for the defence of those of his parishioners accused of Whiteboy crimes, and thus their acquittal was attributed to him. His apparent encouragement of this agitation was to mark him out as an enemy of the government and protestant gentry.

The 1760s saw the coincidence in time and place of a unique set of circumstances which caused protestants in the region to feel insecure in the face of, as they perceived it, a new assertiveness on the part of Catholics. Sheehy was seen by the county gentry as a ringleader in raising a rebellion to undo the land settlement, reverse the penal laws, and unite with the French. Multiple expressions of Catholic assertiveness, compounded by their inability to obtain convictions for Whiteboy offences, broke the nerve of the local gentry and unleashed a sectarian campaign, one victim of which was Sheehy.

Sheehy was presented by the grand jury at the summer assizes of 1762 for being an unregistered priest. This invoked a statute which had fallen into disuse, but nothing apparently came of the charge. In May 1763 he was indicted for forcing people not to inform against the Whiteboys, but the charge appears to have been dropped. Indictments for high treason, rebellion, and assault followed in 1764, but no convictions ensued. Frustrated at this, the local gentry influenced the government to issue a proclamation in February 1765 offering £300 for Sheehy's capture. Shortly after he surrendered voluntarily, and the government conceded to his wish to stand trial in Dublin rather than in Tipperary, where justice was likely to be more partial. Although he was bailed in June 1765 to the amount of £4000, it took eleven months before he stood trial in February 1766, largely because of questionable delays in assembling the prosecution case. At his trial he was acquitted as the prosecution witnesses proved unreliable, an outcome not entirely unforeseen by his prosecutors, who now brought forward a murder charge for which Sheehy was to be tried in Tipperary rather than Dublin, a concession which reneged on the original government assurance. The charge related to the disappearance in late 1764 of John Bridge, a key informant against Sheehy. The defence case rested on the unreliability of the prosecution witnesses, on an alibi for Sheehy's location on the night of the supposed murder, and on the lack of evidence that the victim had actually been murdered, since the body was never located and, in fact, Bridge was later rumoured to have gone to Newfoundland. None the less, on 12 March 1766 Sheehy was convicted and sentenced to death by hanging, which followed in Clonmel on 15 March. Prior to his execution, Sheehy, in a letter to Major Joseph Sirr, suggested that the real murderers of Bridge had been revealed to him in the confessional but, by virtue of his clerical office, he could not use this information in his own defence. He was buried in Shanrahan graveyard.

Most believed the murder charge to be spurious. Popular reaction among Catholics was exemplified in the stoning to death of Sheehy's executioner in 1770. Protestants outside the region did not view the charges as credible. Such were the proceedings against Sheehy regarded that the term 'Sheehy's jury' became a derogatory one applied to any jury which acted in an arbitrary fashion. Of the members of the grand jury that condemned Sheehy, the majority reportedly came to sad and sudden ends, which has been interpreted as divine retribution for their action. Within a short time Sheehy was accorded the status of martyr, and there were regular and well-attended pilgrimages to his grave. He became the subject of a number of poems and laments. Sheehy's memory was perpetuated in the context of the land war of the 1880s when he was cited as an exemplar of priestly leadership and collective action. The centenary celebrations of the 1798 rebellion in 1898 saw the erection of a memorial tablet on his grave site.

Sheehy's execution was one of the most significant events in eighteenth-century Ireland. It exemplified intense sectarian animosities and it cast the government, the local gentry, and the Catholic hierarchy in an unfavourable light.   THOMAS P. POWER

Sources W. P. Burke, *History of Clonmel* (1907) · R. R. Madden, *The United Irishmen: their lives and times*, 2nd edn, 4 vols. (1857–60) · J. Curry, *A parallel between the pretended plot in 1762 and the forgery of Titus Oates in 1679* (1767) · A. Griffith, *A letter to Daniel Toler, esq., relative to the death of Rev. Nicholas Sheehy* (1788) · T. P. Power, *Land, politics, and society in eighteenth-century Tipperary* (1993) · P. O'Connell, 'The plot against Father Nicholas Sheehy', *Irish Ecclesiastical Record*, 5th ser., 108 (1967), 372–84 · Mount Melleray Abbey, co. Waterford, W. P. Burke MSS · TCD, Sirr MSS · T. Power, 'Father Nicholas Sheehy (c.1728–1766)', *Radical Irish priests, 1660–1970*, ed. G. Moran (Dublin, 1998), 62–78 · *DNB* · J. Begley, *The diocese of Limerick from 1691 to the present time* (1938), 72–3 · P. Power, *Waterford and Lismore: a compendious history of the united dioceses* (1937), 134
Archives NL IRe., MSS G 582, 723 · St Patrick's College, Maynooth, MS C.25 | Mount Melleray Abbey, co. Waterford, W. P. Burke MSS · TCD, Sirr MSS

Sheepshanks, Anne (1789–1876). *See under* Sheepshanks, Richard (1794–1855).

Sheepshanks, John (1787–1863), art collector and patron, was born in Leeds, where his father, Joseph Sheepshanks, was a wealthy cloth manufacturer. His mother was Anne Wilson of a Westmorland family; Richard *Sheepshanks (1794–1855), the well-known astronomer, was his younger brother. John Sheepshanks retired before the age of forty, until which time he was a partner in his father's firm of York and Sheepshanks.

While still in business, Sheepshanks had developed a taste for collecting. He started by acquiring books and Flemish and Dutch prints, and proceeded to collecting copies of Italian old masters. Moving to London on his retirement, he turned his attention to promoting and encouraging contemporary British artists. Generally commissioning directly from artists, he built up a collection, largely of genre paintings: among the artists represented were Turner, Constable, Edwin Landseer, John Linnell, William Mulready, C. R. Leslie, David Roberts, Clarkson

Stanfield, David Wilkie, Thomas Creswick, R. P. Bonington, John Crome, and Alexander Nasmyth. Sheepshanks's collection was unique at the time, the only other large-scale collection of contemporary British art being that of Robert Vernon (who, however, also bought British old masters such as Reynolds and Gainsborough).

Vernon's collection had been given to the nation in 1847, and in 1857 Sheepshanks followed suit, offering his 233 paintings in oil and 289 drawings and sketches as a gift to form the nucleus of a national gallery of British art. The deed of gift was framed with a view to rendering the pictures a source of education to the rising generation of artists, and with this intention they were placed with the South Kensington Museum. The galleries built to house them—which opened on 20 June 1857—were the first permanent buildings on this site. In a truly altruistic spirit, Sheepshanks stated that it was not his desire that his collection 'be kept apart or bear his name as such'; however, the paintings have generally remained together and the collection has always been distinguished by the name of the donor. Sheepshanks added a notable proviso to his deed of gift, calling for Sunday afternoon openings as soon as possible. This provision was first carried out in 1896.

Sheepshanks moved to Hastings about 1833, and then to Blackheath, where he devoted himself to horticulture, becoming a fellow of the Royal Horticultural Society. He was of a retiring and unostentatious disposition, but his house was the resort of artists and literary figures. He died, unmarried, on 5 October 1863, at 24 Rutland Gate, London, where he had lived since 1842.

G. S. LAYARD, *rev.* SHARON E. FERMOR

Sources D. S. Macleod, *Art and the Victorian middle class: money and the making of cultural identity* (1996) · R. Redgrave, *On the gift of the Sheepshanks collection: with a view to the formation of a national gallery of British art* (1857) · *Art Journal*, 25 (1863), 241 · *Art Journal*, 19 (1857), 239 · letters to Mulready and Dyce, V&A NAL, Sheepshanks papers · C. H. Cope, *Reminiscences of Charles West Cope* (1891) · J. Physick, *The Victoria and Albert Museum: the history of its building* (1982) · private information (1897) [Revd Thomas Sheepshanks] · d. cert.
Archives U. Leeds, Brotherton L., letters to William Gott
Likenesses A. Geddes, oils, Winsley Hurst, Yorkshire · W. Mulready, double portrait, oils (with housekeeper), V&A · W. Mulready, double portrait, oils (with Thomas Sheepshanks) · pen-and-wash study (after oils by W. Mulready), BM
Wealth at death under £45,000: probate, 2 Dec 1863, *CGPLA Eng. & Wales*

Sheepshanks, Mary Ryott (1872–1960), educationist, feminist, and internationalist, was born on 25 October 1872 at Bilton vicarage, near Harrogate, Yorkshire, the second of the thirteen surviving children of John Sheepshanks (1834–1912), later bishop of Norwich, and his wife, Margaret Ryott, a descendant of Oliver Cromwell. Mary Sheepshanks experienced her childhood home in Anfield vicarage, Liverpool, as austere and joyless—she felt isolated and uncherished, causing her lifelong opposition to large families and total alienation from religion. The educational and other privileges granted her seven brothers fed into her feminism. At fourteen Mary was permitted to attend one of the first Girls' Public Day School Company high schools—Liverpool High School for Girls (later the Belvedere School)—where she distinguished herself in modern languages and literature. Her brilliant young teacher Lucy Silcox, later headmistress of St Felix School, Southwold, 'gave and inspired love' (Sheepshanks). Mary Sheepshanks read medieval and modern languages at Newnham College, Cambridge, discovering too late that her real bent was for moral sciences, psychology, and economics. While at Cambridge (1891–5) she began her commitment to social intervention, teaching adult literacy classes in the town. In October 1895, having been cut off by her family for her 'advanced views', Mary joined the Women's University Settlement, later the Blackfriars Settlement, in Southwark, the worst poverty blackspot in London. There, and later in Stepney, she became a pioneer social worker.

In 1897 Mary was appointed vice-principal—but *de facto* principal—of Morley College for Working Men and Women, becoming also a pioneer woman educational administrator. 'She possessed exceptional breadth of culture and determination of character' (Richards, 142). Mary Sheepshanks expressed her feminism at Morley by giving support to the tired working-class women students there, perceiving that they lacked the intellectual and social confidence of the men. She encouraged women's gymnastics, women's cycling, and debating clubs, enlisting Virginia Woolf (then Virginia Stephen) to teach history evening classes, and she also set up single inspirational lectures on Charlotte Brontë, the Women's Co-operative Guild, and heroines.

Mary Sheepshanks's (leased) home during 1899–1919 was 1 Barton Street, Westminster, which she shared with a succession of women friends, including the Quakers Dr Hilda Clark and Alice Clark, Catherine Marshall, and Irene Cooper, all suffragists. She herself became a prominent suffragist speaker 1908–13 and invited Christabel Pankhurst and Amber Reeves to speak at Morley. Mary Sheepshanks's attitude to the suffragettes was ambivalent—alienated by their violence, yet greatly admiring of their courage. In 1913 she was invited to go on a suffrage lecture tour that included visits to Brussels, Paris, Vienna, Munich, Berlin, Prague, Cracow, Warsaw, and Budapest, speaking in French or German on women and local government, industry, temperance, and education. Her letters to Bertrand Russell concerning the women's movement in Europe at this time are most illuminating (see Oldfield, 154–9). In June 1913 Jane Addams urged her to become secretary of the International Women's Suffrage Alliance and editor of its monthly paper, *Ius Suffragii*. Mary Sheepshanks's feminism was inspired both by outrage at the brutal injustice suffered by women and by faith that emancipated, enfranchised women could help to humanize the world.

When Europe descended into its competition in inhumanity in 1914, Mary helped draft an international manifesto of women protesting against the imminent catastrophe. In October 1914 her signed editorial in *Ius Suffragii*, 'Patriotism or internationalism', prophesied: '[The] world is relapsing into a worse, because a more scientific, barbarism than that from which it sprang' (*Ius Suffragii*, 9, 1914, 184), and in November 1914 she already looked ahead to what must be done after the war: 'Armaments must be drastically reduced and abolished, and their place taken by an international police force. … Peace must be on generous, unvindictive lines, … only so can it be permanent.' Simultaneously she was organizing refugee relief on a massive scale, agitating for the admission of hundreds of thousands of Belgians into Britain 'for the duration', while also arranging relief and travel permits for 'enemy' German women stranded in Britain. She continued throughout the war to bring out the international and internationalist *Ius Suffragii*, obtaining and disseminating humanist feminist news across enemy frontiers via neutrals. In April 1915 Mary Sheepshanks was one of the pacifist suffragists who broke with Mrs Fawcett by supporting the Women's International Congress at The Hague, which founded the Women's International League for Peace and Freedom.

At the end of the First World War, Mary, now based in Hampstead, was appointed secretary of the Fight the Famine Council, recently founded by Gilbert Murray, R. H. Tawney, Leonard Woolf, Maynard Keynes, Olive Schreiner, and others to educate public opinion concerning the need for a new, just economic order in Europe and to relieve the hunger consequent upon the allied blockade (one off-shoot of the council was to be the Save the Children Fund). In 1920 Mary, as representative of the council, lobbied the League of Nations unsuccessfully for the immediate admission of Germany and the revision of the punitive reparations clauses of the treaty of Versailles. In 1923 she spoke on international conciliation in Berlin, Einstein calling her speech 'masterly'; in Munich she needed socialist bodyguards at her speaking engagements because of Hitler's Bierkeller toughs. In 1927 Mary became international secretary of the Women's International League (WIL), based in Geneva, editing its monthly paper *Pax International*. In September 1928 she headed another unsuccessful deputation to the League of Nations to present an urgent memorandum calling for a world disarmament conference. In 1929 she organized the first scientific conference on modern methods of warfare and the civilian population in Frankfurt, and in 1930 the first Conference on Statelessness in Europe (held in Geneva). Feeling increasingly isolated on the WIL international executive among its French or German 'left-extremists', however, she resigned in 1931. She then went on an undercover fact-finding mission to the Ukrainians of Galicia, whose brutal oppression by the Polish regime of Marshal Pilsudski she proceeded to publicize. Twenty years later, she was told that there were 300,000 Ukranian migrants now settled in Canada who loved her.

During the late 1930s Mary Sheepshanks gave shelter in her own home to a succession of Trotskyist exiles, to Sudetenland socialists, and, increasingly, to German and Austrian Jews. Finally, in 1939, she had to renounce her lifelong pacifism and back the war against Nazi Germany. In 1945, however, she was deeply opposed to the dropping of the atom bomb. On 21 January 1960, confined by arthritis to a chair and faced with compulsory institutionalization, she took her own life, dying at her home, 15 Thurlow Road, Hampstead, London.

Mary Sheepshanks was a tall, upright woman with bespectacled, brilliantly blue eyes and a brusque manner. Incomparably articulate, her exceptional intellectual competence masked deep personal insecurity; she found it difficult to believe she was liked. But the many colleagues who crossed swords with her never doubted her prescience, her altruism, or her integrity.

SYBIL OLDFIELD

Sources S. Oldfield, *Spinsters of this parish* (1984) · G. Bussey and M. Tims, *Pioneers for peace: Women's International League for Peace and Freedom, 1915-1965*, [2nd edn] (1980) · A. Wiltsher, *Most dangerous women: feminist peace campaigners of the First World War* (1985) · D. Richards, *Offspring of the Vic: a history of Morley College* (1958) · J. Alberti, *Beyond suffrage: feminists in war and peace, 1914–1928* (1989) · D. E. S. Muir, *Lift the curtain* (1955) · *Pax International* (1920–30) [Eng. edn] · *Pax et Libertas* (1920–30) [Eng. edn] · d. cert. · b. cert. · private information (2004) · M. Sheepshanks, 'The long day ended', Women's Library, London
Archives Women's Library, London, memoirs, 'The long day ended' [typescript] | BLPES, *Pax International* · Swarthmore College, Swarthmore, Pennsylvania, Women's International League for Peace and Freedom MSS
Likenesses photographs, repro. in Oldfield, *Spinsters*
Wealth at death £6609 3s. 2d.: probate, 16 Sept 1960, *CGPLA Eng. & Wales*

Sheepshanks, Richard (1794-1855), astronomer, was born at Leeds on 30 July 1794, the fourth son and sixth child of Joseph Sheepshanks, a cloth manufacturer, and his wife, Anne, daughter of Richard Wilson of Kendal. John *Sheepshanks was his brother. Educated at Richmond School, Yorkshire, Sheepshanks entered Trinity College, Cambridge, in 1812, graduated in mathematics as tenth wrangler in 1816, and took his MA in 1819. At Cambridge he formed, with William Whewell, Adam Sedgwick, Connop Thirlwall, and others, the brilliant group later known as the 'Northern Lights'.

Sheepshanks was elected fellow of Trinity in 1817, and, as he never married, he retained the fellowship for life. He was called to the bar in 1825, and took orders in the church of England on 18 June 1826, but the comparative affluence in which his father's death left him permitted him to follow instead his scientific vocation. He joined the Astronomical Society on 14 January 1825 and, as its secretary from 1829 onwards, edited for many years and greatly improved its *Monthly Notices*. In 1830 the Royal Society elected him a fellow, and two years later he became a member of its council. He took part in 1828 in George Airy's pendulum operations in Dolcoath mine, Cornwall, though these were abandoned following subterranean flooding, and about the same time he actively promoted the establishment of the Cambridge observatory. Appointed in 1831 a commissioner for revising borough boundaries under the Reform Act, he visited and determined most of those between the Thames and Humber. He also occasionally acted as an adviser to the government on routine astronomical matters.

When he became secretary of the Astronomical Society,

Sheepshanks quickly came into conflict with its president, James South. Late in 1829 South purchased a French telescopic object-glass of exceptional size and quality, and he commissioned the venerable instrument maker Edward Troughton to mount it. South, however, was dissatisfied with the result and refused to pay Troughton, whereupon Troughton, with the strong encouragement of Sheepshanks, took South to court. The case lasted from 1834 to 1838, with Sheepshanks taking a prominent role, and eventually South was forced to pay. The dispute had something of class character to it, with South, who was knighted in 1830, and was a wealthy scientific amateur, seeking to pit his expertise against the expert tradesman Troughton and the paid astronomer Airy. South and his ally, Charles Babbage, were able to take their revenge in 1852, most notably through a letter from South published in the *Mechanics' Magazine* for 24 January publicizing an incident in 1823 when Sheepshanks, to avoid paying duty on the importation of a French instrument, had had the instrument engraved with Troughton's name to make it appear of British manufacture. Babbage sent copies to the Royal Society and the Royal Astronomical Society, 'as a sort of impeachment', and even brought the matter before the board of visitors of the Royal Observatory, to which Sheepshanks belonged. Sheepshanks defended himself, admitting and regretting the deception, but denying the alleged aggravating circumstances, in a lengthy and abusive *Letter in Reply to the Calumnies of Mr. Babbage* (1854). This was one of several 'piquant pamphlets' (De Morgan, 562–3) with which he enlivened the scientific scene around the mid-century. Another dealt with the award of the Neptune medal, and a third, in 1845, with the affairs of the Liverpool observatory. Sheepshanks, as a gentleman of leisure himself, appears to have regarded it as his duty to attack what he saw as injustices committed by others of his standing.

Sheepshanks was a member of the royal commissions on weights and measures in 1838 and 1843, and was entrusted in 1844, after the death of Francis Baily, with the reconstruction of the standard of length. The work, for which he accepted no payment, occupied eleven laborious years. It was carried on in a cellar beneath the Royal Astronomical Society's rooms in Somerset House, and involved the registration of nearly 90,000 micrometrical readings. In order to ensure their accuracy he constructed his own standard thermometers by a process he communicated to the society in June 1851. His succinct account of the whole series of operations was embodied in the report of the commissioners presented to parliament in 1854. Their result was of first-class excellence, and the new standard, with certain authorized copies, was legalized by a bill that received the royal assent on 30 July 1855.

Sheepshanks presented in 1838 to the Royal Observatory, Greenwich, an 8 foot equatorial telescope, with an object-glass, by Cauchoix, of nearly 7 inches aperture. In the same year he determined the longitudes of Antwerp and Brussels, and in 1844 those of Valentia, Kingstown, and Liverpool. He lavished time and money on astronomical instruments, though he was often more concerned with the instruments for their own sake than for what he might achieve with them. In particular, he originated an effective and easy method of driving an equatorial by clockwork. He lived at Woburn Place, London, from 1824 to 1841 and at Reading from 1841 until his death. A small observatory was attached to each house.

On 29 July 1855 Sheepshanks was struck with paralysis, and died on 4 August 1855 at Reading. Sometimes described as the 'radical parson', Sheepshanks inspired both irritation and affection in his scientific circles. His biting satirical language and fighting spirit were hallowed by an earnest commitment to justice and a sociable nature.

Anne Sheepshanks (1789–1876), patron of science, was Richard Sheepshanks's elder sister. She lived with him from the time he left college and was his sole heir. In 1858 she presented £10,000 to the University of Cambridge for the promotion of research in astronomy, terrestrial magnetism, and meteorology at the observatory, as well as for the foundation of an exhibition in astronomy bearing her brother's name. To this she added in 1860 £2000 for the purchase of a transit circle. To the Royal Astronomical Society she made, in 1857, a donation of Sheepshanks's extensive and valuable collection of instruments, and was elected in return to honorary membership on 14 February 1862. She died at London Road, Reading, on 8 February 1876. A. M. CLERKE, rev. MICHAEL HOSKIN

Sources Monthly Notices of the Royal Astronomical Society, 16 (1855–6), 90–97 · M. Hoskin, 'Astronomers at war: South v. Sheepshanks', Journal for the History of Astronomy, 20 (1989), 175–212 · A. De Morgan, The Examiner (8 Sept 1855), 562–3 · PRS, 7 (1854–5), 612–13 · Venn, Alum. Cant.
Archives CUL, corresp. and papers · RAS, corresp. and papers · Trinity Cam., letters to William Whewell · UCL, letters to Society for the Diffusion of Useful Knowledge | BL, corresp. with Charles Babbage, Add. MS 37195 · Ransom HRC, letters to Sir John Herschel · RAS, letters to Augustus De Morgan · RS, corresp. with Sir John Herschel · RS, letters to Sir John Lubbock
Likenesses J. H. Foley, bust on monument (posthumous), Trinity Cam. · J. Jackson, portrait (in early life) · L. Stocks, line print, BM · engraving, repro. in R. Sheepshanks, A letter to the board of visitors of the Royal Greenwich Observatory (1856), frontispiece
Wealth at death over £12,000

Sheepshanks, Sir Thomas Herbert (1895–1964), civil servant, was born in the bishop's palace, Norwich, on 10 January 1895, the youngest of the twelve surviving children of John Sheepshanks (1834–1912), bishop of Norwich, and his wife, Margaret, daughter of William Hall Ryott MD. Mary Ryott *Sheepshanks was his elder sister. The austere domestic life imposed by their father, who as a young man had undergone privations as a missionary in British Columbia, was later described by one of the daughters, Dorothy Muir, in Lift the Curtain (1955). Like three of his five brothers, Thomas Sheepshanks held a scholarship at Winchester College, from where he entered Trinity College, Oxford, as a scholar in 1913. At the outbreak of war he joined the Norfolk regiment and served in France attached to the Suffolk regiment, reaching the rank of captain.

Sheepshanks did not return to university after the war, but in 1919 successfully took the examination for entry to the civil service and was assigned to the newly created Ministry of Health, where he joined a team of outstanding young civil servants. In 1921 he married Elizabeth Creemer (d. 1977), younger daughter of James Calvert JP; they had two sons and a daughter. Promotion within the Ministry of Health was slow in coming, despite his abilities, and it was not until 1936 that he became an assistant secretary.

Sheepshanks's major break came in 1937 when he was seconded to the air raid precautions department of the Home Office. Local authorities had been given responsibility for the implementation of policy and they demanded funding from central government. No one in the Home Office had the requisite negotiating skills, whereas Sheepshanks, with his wide experience at the Ministry of Health, which had been the principal point of contact between central and local government in the interwar period, had both the expertise and the contacts. He also revealed an ability to draft political briefs for ministers who were faced with a series of public and parliamentary crises over a policy which many regarded to be excessively secretive and amateurish. When, as lord privy seal, Sir John Anderson was given responsibility for the Civil Defence Bill in 1939, Sheepshanks became his right-hand man.

On the outbreak of the Second World War, Sheepshanks was made principal assistant secretary at the Ministry of Home Security, becoming deputy secretary in 1942. He played a major role in establishing the new ministry and developing a working relationship with the strong characters who had become regional commissioners in 1939. In 1943 he was seconded with Sir Thomas Phillips to the minister of reconstruction, Lord Woolton, to plan the implementation of Sir William Beveridge's report on social insurance and allied services. Sheepshanks was the main draftsman of the resultant government white paper on social security. This involvement led to his appointment in 1944 as deputy secretary of the newly established Ministry of National Insurance. He then spent 1945–6 in the Treasury as an under-secretary before moving to the Ministry of Town and Country Planning, where he became permanent secretary. He was heavily involved in the passage of the New Towns Act (1946) and the Town and Country Planning Act (1947). From 1951 until his retirement in 1955 he was permanent secretary of the Ministry of Local Government and Planning (later renamed housing and local government). He was appointed CB in 1941, KBE in 1944, and KCB in 1948.

Sheepshanks in many ways epitomized the strengths and weaknesses of the generalist, interwar civil servant. He had a strong character, a good mind, and integrity. He was an excellent organizer who drove his officials hard but won their respect through his own hard work and consideration. He could be relied upon in a crisis. He was also an able negotiator although he could be explosive in speech. The contrast between the extreme caution with which he handled politically sensitive material and the austerity with which he expressed himself on paper, and his occasional verbal outbursts, surprised those who did not know him well. For all these reasons, one of his ministers, Hugh Dalton, described Sheepshanks as a 'man who will never drop a catch'. But he then added that he would never 'hit a six' (Pimlott, 578). This was because Sheepshanks's definition of the 'public interest' was the minimization of government and a rigid control of public expenditure which were at odds with both wartime needs and the political imperatives of the post-war period. His secondment to draft the social security white paper was a typical Treasury appointment since he had been heard in private to argue that 'the Beveridge proposals could be called a fraud' (Harris, 426). Having given Dalton three good reasons why the minister could not do something, he also had to be instructed to 'go away and bring me one reason why I should' (Pimlott, 578). Most seriously of all, the 1951 electoral commitment of the Conservative Party to build 300,000 houses a year led Harold Macmillan as minister for housing and local government to declare it a 'war job' which had to be tackled 'in the spirit of 1940'. Macmillan's appointment of Sir Percy Mills as director-general to oversee the programme effectively sidelined Sheepshanks as permanent secretary. He appealed to the head of the civil service, from whom he received much sympathy but no redress.

Sheepshanks died at St Thomas Home, Lambeth, London, on 1 February 1964, survived by his wife and younger son; his elder son and daughter predeceased him.

RODNEY LOWE

Sources DNB · *The Times* (4 Feb 1964) · D. E. Muir, *Lift the curtain* (1955) · B. Pimlott, *Hugh Dalton* (1985) · J. Harris, *William Beveridge*, 2nd edn (1997) · E. Bridges, 'housing, 1951–2', PRO, T 273/191 · H. Macmillan, *Tides of fortune, 1945–1955* (1969), chap. 13 [vol. 3 of autobiography] · *CGPLA Eng. & Wales* (1964)
Likenesses W. Stoneman, photograph, 1948, NPG
Wealth at death £49,580: probate, 8 April 1964, *CGPLA Eng. & Wales*

Sheeres, Sir Henry. *See* Sheres, Sir Henry (*bap.* 1641, *d.* 1710).

Sheffield. For this title name *see* individual entries under Sheffield; *see also* Holroyd, John Baker, first earl of Sheffield (1741–1821); Holroyd, Henry North, third earl of Sheffield (1832–1909); Stanley, Edward Lyulph, fourth Baron Sheffield, fourth Baron Stanley of Alderley, and third Baron Eddisbury (1839–1925).

Sheffield [*née* Howard], **Douglas**, Lady Sheffield (1542/3–1608), noblewoman, was born in 1542 or 1543 (she was seventeen when she married in 1560), the eldest of the three daughters of William *Howard, first Baron Howard of Effingham (*c*.1510–1573), naval commander, and his second wife, Margaret (*d.* 1581), third daughter of Sir Thomas Gamage of Coety, Glamorgan, and his wife, Margaret. Her elder brother was Charles *Howard, second Baron Howard of Effingham and first earl of Nottingham (1536–1624). The best explanation for her unusual Christian name is that her godmother was probably Margaret Stewart, *née* Douglas, countess of Lennox.

Early years and relationship with Leicester, 1542/3–1579 In the absence of any family papers the circumstances of

Douglas Howard's childhood are unknown, but although she has left no other evidence of serious intellectual pursuits (there were only four books dedicated to her), she spoke and wrote French with some fluency. Her father protected her cousin *Elizabeth I (1533–1603) in 1554–5, despite being lord high admiral to Mary I. For this service he was appointed lord chamberlain of the household at Elizabeth's accession, and Douglas Howard and her sister Mary (*d.* 1600) maids of honour by the time of her coronation. In autumn 1560, however, she vacated her place on her marriage to John Sheffield, second Baron Sheffield (*c*.1538–1568), nobleman, of Butterwick, Lincolnshire, only son and heir of Edmund Sheffield, first Baron Sheffield, and his wife, Anne. According to Robert Kenny, her dowry amounted to a miserly £800. The queen, however, provided a wedding gift on 27 October 1560 (BL, Add. MS 5751A, fol. 57r). The couple had two surviving children, Edmund *Sheffield, third Baron Sheffield and first earl of Mulgrave (1565–1646), and Elizabeth (*d.* 1600), who married Thomas *Butler, tenth earl of Ormond (1531–1614), in 1583. Lord Sheffield died on 10 December 1568 and his widow returned to court as an extraordinary gentlewoman of the privy chamber.

In the early 1570s Douglas Sheffield began an affair with Robert *Dudley, earl of Leicester (1532/3–1588), courtier and magnate, the fifth son of John Dudley, duke of Northumberland, and his wife, Jane, that came to dominate the rest of her life. There is only one item of reliable evidence for the affair, apart from the circumstances of the birth of their son, Sir Robert *Dudley (1574–1649), on 7 August 1574, and gossip at court in May 1573 that Sheffield and her sister Frances (1553/4–1598) were both 'very far in love' with Leicester (LPL, MS 3197, fol. 79). This is the long undated letter Leicester wrote to her at some point before 1574, defending his refusal to marry for fear of Elizabeth's displeasure ('Letter … to a lady', 14–26). However, in 1584–5 the tract *Leicester's Commonwealth* broadcast round Europe details of what had been the discreet knowledge of the court. More controversial still were the two depositions Sheffield supplied on 6–7 June 1604 in 'the great cause of Sir Robert Dudley', the court of Star Chamber case arising from his claim to be Leicester's legitimate son, in which she declared under oath that Leicester had formally married her (CKS, U 1475/L 2/3, items 12–13).

The story originating in *Leicester's Commonwealth* and embellished in the seventeenth century that their affair began at Belvoir Castle, Leicestershire, during the royal progress in 1568 and that Leicester had Lord Sheffield poisoned to expedite their adultery is a myth, not least because Elizabeth never visited Belvoir. In his letter Leicester specifically mentions that his relationship with Douglas Sheffield began 'after yor wydowed beganne uppon the first occasione of my cominge to you' ('Letter … to a lady', 21). According to *Leicester's Commonwealth*, she gave birth to a daughter by Leicester about 1572 at Dudley Castle, Staffordshire, the home of her sister Mary, who married Edward Sutton (known as Dudley), fourth Baron Dudley, in early 1571, but the child was stillborn and buried secretly.

In 1604 Sheffield vehemently denied she had any children by Leicester other than Robert Dudley. She claimed that she married Leicester at her family's house at Esher, Surrey, between 11 November and 25 December 1573, having persuaded him to agree to a contract of marriage in 1571 because she believed then that she was pregnant. Although her testimony was central to her son's case, she could supply no supporting evidence and claimed that servants had stolen all the records of her marriage, apparently at Leicester's behest. She did, however, state that the principal mover of the marriage was her cousin Thomas *Howard, fourth duke of Norfolk (1538–1572), and it is possible that he encouraged the affair to solidify an alliance with Leicester for his own rehabilitation in 1570–71. Equally obscure are the circumstances under which Leicester abandoned her. She deposed that at some point before his marriage to Lettice Devereux, dowager countess of Essex, in 1578, he offered her £700 a year for life to disclaim their marriage. When she refused, 'he departed from her with protestation not to come any more to her' (CKS, U 1475/L 2/3, item 13, fol. 12).

Marriage to Sir Edward Stafford, 1579–1584 On 28 November 1579 Sheffield secretly married at her house at Blackfriars, London, the gentleman pensioner Edward *Stafford (1552–1605), diplomat, of London, first son of Sir William Stafford of Chebsey, Staffordshire, and his second wife, Dorothy. This marriage was in its own way as controversial as her affair with Leicester. Most of what is known of the circumstances comes from Stafford's own lengthy deposition in 1604, which was testimony against Sheffield, for if she had been married to Leicester she had committed bigamy in marrying him (CKS, U 1475/L/2/4, item 3). Stafford stated that he had courted her in the summer of 1579 after his first wife died. On 1 November 1579 Sheffield agreed to marry him and told him then that she had contracted marriage with Leicester and had borne him a son.

Immediately after his marriage, Stafford left for France as Elizabeth's envoy to François, duc d'Anjou. He finally returned to England on 16 February 1580, when he was summoned to a dramatic interview with the queen. After forcing him to admit that he had married Sheffield, Elizabeth claimed to have evidence that she was already married to Leicester. With a mixture of bribery and cajolery she tried through Stafford and others to persuade Sheffield to testify to this effect. Sheffield—almost hysterical—refused to concede any more than breach of contract. Her refusal, Stafford considered, was crucial evidence against the marriage. There is some external confirmation of this phase of the saga. On 8 February the French ambassador, Castelnau de Mauvissière, reported that Elizabeth was angry because Stafford had secretly married a cousin of hers.

When the discrepancy between her testimony and her husband's was put to Sheffield in 1604 she claimed that she had believed that since Leicester had remarried she was free to do so as well. Thanks to intimidation by Leicester—and after his death by his widow and her son, Robert Devereux, second earl of Essex—she had been afraid ever to mention their marriage again. This, however, is not the only unresolved question. How did Elizabeth find out about Sheffield's marriages? It is possible that the famous revelation to her by Jean de Simier, Anjou's agent, was not just that Leicester was married to the dowager countess of Essex, but that he was already married to Sheffield as well. A second issue is whether Leicester actually arranged Sheffield's marriage to Stafford, as Mauvissière was informed. She and Stafford vehemently denied this and made much of their hatred of Leicester when questioned at length on the subject in 1604. In his opening statement Sir Robert Dudley described Stafford as 'a man very adverse' to Leicester (Hawarde, 199). Yet Stafford and Leicester were on good terms before 1579. Last there is the issue of the young Robert Dudley himself. Sheffield deposed in 1604 that Leicester offered her £1000 for the custody of their son, but she refused. In fact custody appears to have been settled quite amicably. By 1580 Robert Dudley was 'being then brought upp at the Lord Northes'—with Leicester's close friend Roger North, second Baron North—yet he also had 'leave to see the said ladie [Sheffield]' (CKS, U 1475/L/2/4, item 3, fol. 36).

By autumn 1580 Sheffield was 'great with child' and ultimately she and Stafford had two sons, but both predeceased their parents and little is known about them (CKS, U 1475/L2/4. item 3, fol. 33). Marriage brought her no financial advantages, for Stafford was notoriously poor and admitted in 1583 that he was dependent on her jointure income from the Sheffield estate. In October of that year he was appointed ambassador to the French court and she accompanied him. Thanks to her place at Elizabeth's court and her command of French, Sheffield was the most socially successful of all the wives of the Elizabethan ambassadors in France. Not only did she get on famously with Catherine de' Medici, but she also made a significant contribution to the administration of the Valois court. At the beginning of 1585 Henri III promulgated a new series of household ordinances intended to give him greater privacy. These, Jacques de Thou later recorded, were based on discussions he had had with Sheffield about Elizabeth's practice.

Leicester's Commonwealth, 1584–1588 Sheffield was equally involved in the more controversial aspects of Stafford's embassy. In December 1583 her cousin Charles Arundel arrived in Paris following his implication in the Throckmorton plot, and she and Stafford entertained him, unaware (so they said) of the reasons for his departure from England. At the same time Stafford proposed that his wife should disguise herself as a Catholic in order to gain greater access to the French court and penetrate the English exile circles. This plan was firmly quashed. During spring and summer 1584 Arundel and his friends compiled *Leicester's Commonwealth*, and Sheffield's affair with Leicester was high among its juicier contents. Stafford was relatively relaxed about the publication of the first (English) edition in the autumn of 1584, but was seriously alarmed by the preparation of a French edition with an 'addition' supplied from England in the spring of 1585. He then reported that embarrassment caused by the first edition had made his wife ill and he was worried about the possible effects of the new one. She may have contemplated retiring to England at this point, but he persuaded her to 'pluck up a good heart' and stay with him (*CSP for.*, 1584–5, 400).

What is particularly interesting is that while Sheffield was identified in the first edition, Stafford was sufficiently close to the compilers to be assured by them that she would not be in the French edition. This was in fact the case, but the 'addition' was another matter. It included a deliberately obscene libel, the story that Leicester tried to seduce a lady of honour with an aphrodisiac containing his own semen. Although the lady was not identified, the fact that she was described as still living made Sheffield an obvious candidate. The extent of Stafford and Sheffield's involvement with the compilers of *Leicester's Commonwealth* remains a perplexing issue. Neither of them would appear to have wanted her personal affairs exposed in this manner, but they were close to Arundel and how else could the work have contained so much detail? The editor of the modern edition leaves the question open, but then he does not consider the references to Sheffield to be more than a 'jest or two', which is undoubtedly an understatement (Peck, 29–31). The case against her involvement rests primarily on her later denial of the stillborn daughter.

Even more puzzling is the fact that the publication of *Leicester's Commonwealth* did not terminate Stafford and Sheffield's relations with Arundel. Arundel advised the Spanish agent in Paris in 1584 that Stafford could be bribed, and he was the intermediary between Stafford and Bernardino de Mendoza when Stafford's 'treason' began in earnest in 1587. The extent of Sheffield's involvement in this is unknown, but one of Stafford's attractions to the Spaniards was that her brother was lord high admiral and Arundel's friends claimed to have received political information from her.

Final years, 1588–1608 Stafford remained as ambassador in France until 1591, but he sent his wife home in August 1588 for her own protection. Sheffield arrived at Dover the day Leicester died (4 September), and was gratified to learn that he had named her son heir to his estates after his brother Ambrose Dudley, earl of Warwick, and that 'the Queen had assured her that shee would take great care of him'. To this Stafford replied 'with his acustomed humour … that whensoever that the Queene did the said Sir Robert good the next newes the said Lady Sheffield should heare would be that he [Stafford] was chosen Pope' (CKS, U 1475/L/2/4, item 3, fols. 76–9). Sheffield returned to service at court during the next decade, although there are only a few references to her. She was certainly there in July 1592, when she participated in a scheme to persuade Henri of Navarre to retain a portrait that Elizabeth was sending to his sister, Catherine of Bourbon. Her letter to the French ambassador, Beauvoir la Nocle, is the one known example of her French composition. It includes an apology for her 'movez escritur, qui est desaprins [*sic*] depuis que suis en Engleterre' (Egerton, 415).

Sheffield's involvement in Sir Robert Dudley's case is the final mystery of her life. Dudley filed suit for defamation over his bastardy at the commissary court at Lichfield, Staffordshire, in September 1603. Stafford heard about the suit shortly afterwards and was 'as much amased as ever he was at any thinge in his life'. Angry at having his own marriage called into question, he went to see his wife at Sudeley Castle, Gloucestershire. After a stormy encounter he was convinced that she had been browbeaten by her son into supporting his case, though only under the condition that Dudley would not use her evidence until she was dead. Stafford claimed he had persuaded her not to 'medle nor entre with the matter any more', but, after he left, Dudley came to see her and 'did so terrifye her … tellinge her that shee was soe far gone that theare was noe torninge back' (CKS, U 1475/L/2/4, item 3, fols. 44, 55, 58, 64). Sheffield claimed that she was not involved in the Lichfield case and only agreed to acknowledge her marriage to Leicester after it, 'althogh she hath been often moved by her son for such purpose' (CKS, U 1475/L 2/3, item 13, fol. 1). She denied she had delayed in order to ensure that her testimony confirmed that of her son's other witnesses. Yet, however important her depositions were to her son's case, they were ignored in the Star Chamber judgment, which was concerned specifically with the 'conspiracy' behind the Lichfield suit. Many, both at the time and since, have noted that the substantive issue of her marriage to Leicester was never addressed at the trial, let alone resolved, but the inconclusive result also saved her from a possible charge of perjury.

Sheffield tried to maintain contact with Dudley in his self-imposed exile in Florence through the Tuscan agent in London, but in her last years she drew closer to her elder son, Lord Sheffield. She made her will on 14 September 1608, though still 'in health of body and mind'. She requested burial either in Reigate, Surrey, with her parents or in St Margaret's, Westminster, 'by my sister', Lady Dudley, not mentioning that Stafford, who had died on 5 February 1605, was buried there as well (Greenfield, 368–70). Her executor was 'my friend' William Crashaw, a puritan preacher then closely associated with Lord Sheffield (Adams, 'Protestant cause', 434). She died in Westminster at the beginning of December 1608, and was buried in St Margaret's on the 11th. No monument to her or to Stafford was erected.

Sheffield has either attracted sympathy as a betrayed woman or been dismissed as insubstantial. Neither verdict is justified. It should not be forgotten that her sister Frances, who became first the mistress and then the second wife of Edward *Seymour, first earl of Hertford (1539?–1621), enjoyed almost as colourful a love life as she did. She was clearly a woman of intelligence, though also of stormy temper and powerful mood swings. For all Stafford's claims of a happy marriage, there were frictions there as well: he referred to jars with his wife in 1586, and admitted that she was annoyed by his joke about the queen in 1588. Sheffield's claim in 1604 that she had been married to Leicester can no longer be credited, for there are simply too many discrepancies in her account. The Tuscan agent, who investigated her son's claims in 1621, neatly put his finger on it: 'his friends maintain that his father married Lady Sheffield, but they are unable to account for her marriage during his lifetime, an act so injurious to the alleged legitimacy of her son' (*Skrine MSS*, 183).   SIMON ADAMS

Sources exchequer wardrobe account, coronation of Elizabeth, PRO, E 101/429/3 · BL, Add. MS 5751A [miscellaneous warrants] · R. W. Kenny, *Elizabeth's admiral: the political career of Charles Howard, earl of Nottingham, 1536–1624* (Baltimore, MD, 1970) · *The manuscripts of his grace the duke of Rutland*, 4 vols., HMC, 24 (1888–1905), vol. 1 · 'A letter from Robert, earl of Leicester, to a lady', ed. C. Read, *Huntington Library Bulletin*, 9 (1936), 14–26 · CKS, Penshurst papers, U1475 · D. C. Peck, ed., *Leicester's commonwealth: the copy of a letter written by a master of art of Cambridge (1584) and related documents* (1985) · G. Holles, *Memorials of the Holles family, 1493–1656*, ed. A. C. Wood, CS, 3rd ser., 55 (1937) · *Les reportes del cases in camera stellata, 1593 to 1609, from the original ms. of John Hawarde*, ed. W. P. Baildon (privately printed, London, 1894) · S. Adams, 'The papers of Robert Dudley, earl of Leicester, pt 3, the countess of Leicester's collection', *Archives*, 22 (1996), 1–26 · Shrewsbury papers, LPL · *Calendar of the manuscripts of the most hon. the marquis of Salisbury*, 24 vols., HMC, 9 (1883–1976) · Bibliothèque Nationale de France, Paris, MS français 15793, registre de Michel de Castelnau, seigneur de Mauvissière, 1578–81 · D. Wilson, *Sweet Robin: a biography of Robert Dudley, earl of Leicester, 1533–1588* (1981) · A. M. Mimardière, 'Stafford, Edward II', HoP, *Commons, 1558–1603*, 3.430–32 · *CSP for., 1558–89* · A. Chéruel, *Marie Stuart et Catherine de Médicis* (Paris, 1858) · BL, Cotton MS Galba E. vi [Stafford correspondence] · D. Potter and P. R. Roberts, 'An Englishman's view of the court of Henri III, 1584–5: Richard Cook's "Description of the court of France"', *French History* (1988), 312–44 · M. Leimon and G. Parker, 'Treason and plot in Elizabethan diplomacy: the "fame of Sir Edward Stafford" reconsidered', *EngHR*, 111 (1996), 1134–58 · L. Hicks, *An Elizabethan problem: some aspects of the careers of two exile adventurers* (1964) · J. K. Laughton, ed., *State papers relating to the defeat of the Spanish Armada, anno 1588*, 2 vols., Navy RS, 1–2 (1894); facs. edn (1987) · F. H. Egerton, *The life of Thomas Egerton, lord chancellor of England* (Paris, 1828) · R. B. Wernham, ed., *List and analysis of state papers, foreign series, Elizabeth I*, 7 vols. (1964–2000) · R. Strong, *The portraits of Queen Elizabeth I* (1963) · J. Temple-Leader, *Life of Sir Robert Dudley* (Florence, 1895); repr. (Amsterdam, 1977) · [B. W. Greenfield], 'Abstract of the last will of Lady Douglas Sheffield, the repudiated wife of Robert Dudley, earl of Leicester', *Miscellanea Genealogica et Heraldica*, new ser., 3 (1880), 368–70 · A. Gould Lee, *The son of Leicester: the story of Sir Robert Dudley* (1964) · S. L. Adams, 'The protestant cause: religious alliance with the west European Calvinist communities as a political issue in England, 1585–1630', DPhil diss., U. Oxf., 1973 · A. Somerset, *Elizabeth I* (1991) · *The manuscripts of Henry Duncan Skrine, esq. Salvetti correspondence*, HMC, 16 (1887) · GEC, *Peerage*

Likenesses portrait, 18th cent. · engraving (after unknown artist), repro. in V. Thomas, *The Italian biography of Sir Robert Dudley* (privately printed, Oxford, 1849), facing p. 55 · portraits; known to be at Leicester House in 1580–82

Sheffield, Edmund, first Baron Sheffield (1521–1549),

nobleman, was born on 21 November 1521, the elder son of Sir Robert Sheffield (*d.* 1531), of West Butterwick, Lincolnshire, and his first wife, Jane Stanley, a second cousin of Henry VIII. His family had prospered in recent generations, mainly through legal practice, and Edmund, who had a younger brother, David, and a sister, Eleanor, was heir to a substantial estate in the north midlands and Lincolnshire. Following his father's death on 15 November 1531, on 28 April 1533 Edmund's wardship was granted to George Boleyn, Viscount Rochford. Rochford was executed on 17 May 1536, and on 2 January 1538 the wardship

and marriage were granted to John de Vere, fifteenth earl of Oxford; the grant probably confirmed an existing situation, for by the end of that month Sheffield was married to Oxford's daughter Anne, and the earl was asking Thomas Cromwell to be good lord to his son-in-law. About this time Sheffield was duly numbered among the 'Gentlemen of my lord Privy Seal's mete to be preferred unto the King's Majesty's service' (*LP Henry VIII*, 13/2, no. 1184).

Cromwell's services to his young protégé were not confined to such presumed patronage. Predeceased by his first wife, Sir Robert Sheffield had later married Margaret Zouche. Following Sir Robert's death his widow herself remarried, her second husband being John Cavendish. About 1538 Edmund Sheffield quarrelled with Cavendish and sent him rude letters which came into Cromwell's hands. Sheffield now wrote to the secretary in Latin, addressing him as a fellow evangelical—'most vigilant patron ["Maecenas"] of holy scripture'—and begging for his intercession. This lengthy epistle, which apologizes for literary incompetence while exuding all the self-confidence of a clever young man, may well have amused Cromwell, who had it endorsed 'Edmund Sheffelde Scholasticall Letter' (PRO, SP 1/134 fol. 202r–v). Another quarrel about this time put Sheffield in prison, whence he sent Cavendish (now apparently on good terms with him) a letter in English, full of scriptural references and asking for a visit and also for an appeal to Cromwell on his behalf. Neither episode did Sheffield any harm. Having attained his majority at the end of 1542, he had livery of his lands on 7 February 1543. In 1544 he went with the army to France. Before he left, on 20 May, he made his will, which reveals that by this time he had a son, John, and two daughters, Frances and Eleanor. On the same day he conveyed his estates in Nottinghamshire, Staffordshire, and Derbyshire to trustees headed by Henry Howard, earl of Surrey. Two years later he accompanied Viscount Lisle's embassy to France.

At the end of 1546 Sheffield was one of ten men considered by Henry VIII for promotion to the baronage, and one of only four to be eventually ennobled: his charter of creation was given on 16 February 1547. His qualifications in terms of past services are hardly conspicuous. He was a wealthy man, however, able in his will to order the payment of debts and bequests totalling some £3000, and with lands assessed at £400 per annum in 1547, and it may have been hoped that he and Sir William Willoughby of Parham, likewise made a baron, would fill a gap left in the structure of authority in Lincolnshire in 1545 by the death of the county's greatest lord, Charles Brandon, duke of Suffolk, leaving a nine-year-old heir. He may also have owed his ennoblement to his personal qualities: loyal, brave, cultivated—Thomas Fuller later wrote of him, 'Great his skill in music, who wrote a book of sonnets after the Italian fashion' (Fuller, 2.291)—and with reformist leanings in religion, perhaps he was simply the sort of promising young man the old king liked and wished to advance.

Later in 1547 Sheffield was appointed to the Lincolnshire peace commission (though not to the quorum), but was arguably still too young for a role in government. He never had the chance to take such a part. In 1549 he joined the royal army confronting Kett's rising in Norfolk, and was a member of the force with which the marquess of Northampton tried to occupy Norwich on 31 July. The incursion came to grief in the city streets, and Sheffield fell into a ditch while wheeling his horse and was killed by the rebels, pleading in vain for his life—a butcher named Fulke is said to have struck the fatal blow. He was buried next day in St Martin's at the Palace, Norwich. Sheffield's death prompted grief at the loss of a gifted young man, and also outrage at the killing of a nobleman by his social inferiors. Barnabe Googe, only nine at the time but a native of Lincolnshire, later addressed an epitaph to Sheffield as 'good Lord whom deare I loved', and denounced the 'crabbed Clowns' and 'Dunghyll Dogs' who slew him (Googe, 69–70), while Sir John Cheke paid warm tribute to his virtues, describing him as 'both fit for counsell in peace, and for conduct in war … being loved of everie man, and hated of no man …' (Holinshed, 3.1046). In 1551 his son John, in compensation for his father's expenses two years earlier, was granted from his inheritance an annuity first of £20 and then of nearly £50, and also his own marriage. His widow, who later married John Brock of Colchester, died early in 1572.

HENRY SUMMERSON

Sources GEC, *Peerage*, 11.661–2 · state papers, general series Henry VIII, PRO, SP 1/134, fols. 202r–203v · chancery, inquisitions post mortem series II, PRO, C 142/53, nos. 6, 20; 54, nos. 85, 89; 56, nos. 96, 108 · court of wards, inquisitions post mortem, PRO, WARD 7/5, nos. 65, 90, 94 · exchequer, king's remembrancer, lay subsidy rolls, PRO, E 179/69/51 · will, PRO, PROB 11/33, fols. 48v–49v · *LP Henry VIII*, vols. 13/1–21/2 · *CSP dom.*, 1547–53 · *CPR*, 1547–53 · *APC*, 1550–52 · R. Holinshed and others, eds., *The third volume of chronicles, beginning at Duke William the Norman*, ed. J. Hooker (1587) · J. Hayward, *The life and raigne of King Edward the Sixth*, ed. B. L. Beer (1993) · J. Strype, *Ecclesiastical memorials*, 3 vols. (1822), vol. 2/1 · Fuller, *Worthies* (1840), 2. 290–91 · B. Googe, *Eglogs, epytaphes & sonettes, 1563*, ed. E. Arber (1871) · H. Miller, 'Henry VIII's unwritten will: grants of lands and honours in 1547', *Wealth and power in Tudor England: essays presented to S. T. Bindoff*, ed. E. W. Ives, R. J. Knecht, and J. J. Scarisbrick (1978), 87–105

Wealth at death In 1543 able to dispose of over £3000 cash; 1547 lands assessed for subsidy at £400: will, PRO, PROB 11/33, fols. 48v–49v; E 179/69/51

Sheffield, Edmund, first earl of Mulgrave (1565–1646), politician, was born on 7 December 1565, the only son of John, second Baron Sheffield (*c*.1538–1568), of Butterwick, Lincolnshire, and his wife, Douglas *Sheffield, Lady Sheffield (1542/3–1608), daughter of William Howard, first Lord Howard of Effingham. He inherited his father's title on 10 December 1568. Shortly after his father's death, his mother embarked upon a liaison with the earl of Leicester. She later claimed that a secret marriage occurred about 1571 and, although the evidence for this union is inconclusive, she did bear Leicester a son. In any event Leicester denied the existence of the bond when he married Lettice, countess of Essex, in 1578. Sheffield was educated at Christ Church, Oxford (1574–9), and in 1582

Edmund Sheffield, first earl of Mulgrave (1565–1646), by Renold Elstrack

Queen Elizabeth commanded him to accompany the duke of Anjou on his return voyage to the continent. In 1585 he served as a volunteer in the Netherlands. The approach of the Spanish Armada offered him further opportunities and he served as captain of three ships in the campaign: the *Victory, Dreadnaught*, and *White Bear*. His uncle Lord Admiral Howard knighted him for his service on 26 July 1588, and praised him in reports to the council.

Despite his heroics at sea and in the Netherlands, however, Sheffield's standing with the queen was threatened by suspicions about his religion. His wife, Ursula Tyrwhitt, of Kettleby, Lincolnshire, was a devout Catholic, and the two were married according to the Catholic rite some time before 13 November 1581. Success at court came only slowly. In 1591 the crown granted him the manor of Mulgrave in Yorkshire, and thereafter Sheffield gradually transferred his interests northward from Lincolnshire. In 1594 Sir Robert Carey reported that the queen refused to grant him the presidency of the Welsh marches because of his wife's religion. He demonstrated his allegiance by strenuously persecuting Catholics in his neighbourhood, winning praise from local authorities: 'My lord took great pains to give such testimony of his affection to religion as none of his coat have done' (*CSP dom.*, 1598–1601, 232). Catholics denounced him for his harshness and claimed that the untimely deaths of all six of his sons with Ursula was a divine judgment. Elizabeth honoured him with the Garter in April 1593, and in January 1599, after vigorous lobbying on his part, she appointed him governor of Brill in the Netherlands, a post he apparently never took up.

It was not until the accession of James I that Sheffield received the post he coveted most, the presidency of the council of the north; he had asked for the job as early as 1595 but Elizabeth had denied him. As a prelude James named him lord lieutenant of Yorkshire on 1 August 1603, and added the presidency on 19 September. Sheffield's good fortune did not satisfy him, however. The expenses of his office were high, and he had nine daughters to provide for. In 1604 he complained bitterly of his plight. In an audience with the king he lamented that James had 'repaired the ruins of every nobleman's estate in England except his'. The king, irritated by Sheffield's petulance, offered him an annual pension of £1000 which Sheffield said 'would do him no good', but James held firm, telling his suitor that 'my liberality ought not to be measured by his want, for I was bound to be no man's banker' (Akrigg, 242–5). Eventually James relented and, before 1609, Sheffield received an interest in the Yorkshire alum mines, from which over the years he drew a substantial—though always insufficient—amount of money.

As lord president and, from 1616, vice-admiral of Yorkshire, Sheffield actively enforced the laws against recusants. In 1604 he presided over the indictment of 900 recusants at York assizes, and in later years was vigilant against what he perceived as the Catholic threat in the north. He did not always get along with his colleagues on the council; in 1609 charges were laid against him for 'arbitrary conduct and not consulting the other commissioners', though these seem to have come to nothing (CSP dom., 1603–10, 577). In any event, the heavy expenses of his office and his weak estate encouraged him to seek a buyer for the office by 1614. His tottering fortune was briefly shored up by the king's favour in 1615 when he collected the £10,000 Sir Robert Dormer paid for his barony. He finally sold the lord presidency of the north to Lord Scrope in 1619, although he retained his vice-admiralty. He left office under a cloud, for the Spanish ambassador had complained about Sheffield's execution of a Catholic priest, though it seems likely that his money problems were a more important factor.

Sheffield's financial troubles were exacerbated by his colonial speculations; he was an early member of the Virginia Company and in succeeding years worked diligently to advance its fortunes, though with little success. He also invested in the New England Company, with similar results. Ursula had died some time before 4 August 1618 and after a fruitless search for a rich wife, in 1619, when he was sixty-four, Sheffield settled on Mariana (c.1603–c.1676), the sixteen-year-old daughter of Sir William Irwin, a Scot maliciously (and inaccurately) described by John Chamberlain as 'a kind of dancing tutor to Prince Henry' (CSP dom., 1619–23, 21). They were married on 4 March 1619. Although Irwin was a gentleman of Prince Henry's privy chamber, Anne Clifford described the match as 'very mean and … indiscreet' (Diary, 102). Indiscreet or not, the couple had five children, further adding to Sheffield's financial woes. The alum monopoly which provided a large portion of his income was an unreliable source, and after 1620 he received little of the profits of office. He was estranged from the duke of Buckingham in the 1620s, but after his accession Charles I, on 5 February 1626, promoted him to earl of Mulgrave, possibly as a reward for his staunch support of the war against Spain.

Mulgrave grew increasingly alienated from the king, despite his new rank. In 1640 he refused to contribute an assessment of £1 to the war effort against the Scots, alleging poverty. His financial situation was certainly grim, but his call for a parliament in August 1640 suggests that his resistance was founded on other grounds. When the civil war came he and his family sided with parliament; two of his sons served in parliament's army, and two daughters married into the family of the parliamentarian general Lord Fairfax. Because most of his property in the north remained in royalist hands throughout the war, from March 1645 parliament paid Mulgrave a weekly pension of £50. His advanced age kept him from constant attendance in the House of Lords, but his proxy was a valuable commodity in the thinly attended chamber. Although at first in the hands of Lord Saye and Sele, in May 1646 he switched his allegiance to the presbyterian Essex, who held the earl's proxy thereafter. This was Mulgrave's final significant political act; he died at his home in Hammersmith, Middlesex, in October 1646, aged eighty-one, and was buried in the church he had founded there. He was succeeded by his grandson, Edmund *Sheffield, second earl of Mulgrave. VICTOR STATER

Sources GEC, Peerage · Calendar of the manuscripts of the most hon. the marquess of Salisbury, 15–21, HMC, 9 (1930–70) · CSP dom., 1581–1625 · J. K. Laughton, ed., State papers relating to the defeat of the Spanish Armada, anno 1588, 2 vols., Navy RS, 1–2 (1894) · M. Prestwich, Cranfield: politics and profits under the early Stuarts (1966) · A. F. Upton, Sir Arthur Ingram, c.1565–1642: a study in the origins of an English landed family (1961) · Letters of King James VI & I, ed. G. P. V. Akrigg (1984), 242–5 · S. R. Gardiner, History of England from the accession of James I to the outbreak of the civil war, 10 vols. (1883–4); repr. (1965) · S. R. Gardiner, History of the great civil war, 1642–1649, new edn, 4 vols. (1901–5) · R. Lockyer, Buckingham: the life and political career of George Villiers, first duke of Buckingham, 1592–1628 (1981), 96, 304 · S. M. Kingsbury, ed., The records of the Virginia Company of London, 3 (1933) · C. Russell, The fall of the British monarchies, 1637–1642 (1991), 134 · J. P. Cooper, ed., Wentworth papers, 1597–1628, CS, 4th ser., 12 (1973) · C. Russell, Parliaments and English politics, 1621–1629 (1979), 163–4 · The diary of Anne Clifford, 1616–1619, ed. K. Acheson (1995) · M. Strachan, Sir Thomas Roe, 1581–1644: a life (1989), 17, 50

Archives CKS, letters to Lionel Cranfield

Likenesses R. Elstrack, line engraving (when Lord Sheffield), BM, NPG, V&A [see illus.]

Sheffield, Edmund, second earl of Mulgrave (1611–1658), parliamentarian nobleman, was born about December 1611, the grandson of Edmund *Sheffield, first earl of Mulgrave (1565–1646). His father, Sir John Sheffield, who drowned in the Humber in 1614, had married Grizel, daughter of Sir Edmund Anderson, chief justice of the common pleas. In May 1617 Edmund was not expected to survive head injuries received after falling downstairs. He married Elizabeth Cranfield (1607/8–1672), daughter of the financier Lionel Cranfield, earl of Middlesex, by licence dated April 1631, with a dowry of £2000. Difficulties over money long soured his relationship with his father-in-law. His unorthodox religious beliefs are indicated by the fact that at some date in the 1630s the dean of the arches, Dr John Lambe, cited him for commissioning a translation of 'that cursed book', the medieval spiritual work *Theologia Germanica*. The effort and risk involved implies intense interest in or sympathy with its mysticism. Lord Sheffield since his grandfather assumed the earldom in 1626, he succeeded as second earl of Mulgrave on 6 October 1646 and took his seat in the House of Lords on 20 October.

Acquiring a London residence, the sequestrated Kirke House in Spring Gardens, for £50 rent in October 1645, Mulgrave was appointed vice-admiral of Yorkshire in succession to his grandfather (13 November 1646) by the Long Parliament. In August 1647 he signed the engagement to stand by Fairfax and the army for the restoration of the freedom of parliament. He was named as one of the commissioners for compounding on 8 February 1647 and for the navy and customs on 17 December 1647, and on 1 June 1648 he was added to the parliamentarian executive Derby House committee. He also appealed successfully to the Lords to cancel the monopoly on the manufacture and sale of alum granted to Sir John Gibson, in order to utilize the alum works he owned in Yorkshire. On 14 February 1649 he was appointed a member of the council of state of the Commonwealth, but declined to accept the post from dissatisfaction at the execution of the king and the abolition of the House of Lords. In August 1649 he accepted John Lisle's invitation to lodge with him and Bulstrode Whitelocke at Sion House, Middlesex, unaware that Whitelocke had invited Lisle alone. In February 1653 Mulgrave petitioned the council of state for compensation for parliament's partial demolition of Mulgrave Castle in 1647. The recommendation of the Irish and Scots affairs committee for the payment of £1200 was not implemented due to the dissolution of the Rump Parliament, but on 3 February 1654 Cromwell agreed to take the matter on. His council voted £1000 to Mulgrave though the order for payment by the exchequer had to be transferred to the treasury commissioners in March 1655.

Mulgrave had been considered reliable enough to be recommended to Cromwell as an additional councillor on 19 June 1654. He took his place on the protectorate council on 30 June and was in regular attendance for some years. He took particular responsibility for the preservation of game in the former royal forests in Lincolnshire, but his attendance at the council declined, possibly owing to poor health; in 1656 he was absent from 22 May until 16 September and only then returned on orders. In December 1657 the protector summoned him to his new House of Lords, but Mulgrave never took his seat; disapproval is less likely than illness. He died 'by the way' on 24 August 1658

en route for London in response to a summons to attend the upper house, and was buried at Normanby church, Yorkshire. One of the few peers to have adhered to Cromwell, he was succeeded by his son John *Sheffield, afterwards first duke of Buckingham and Normanby.

C. H. FIRTH, *rev.* TIMOTHY VENNING

Sources J. E. Doyle, *The official baronage of England*, 2 (1886) • GEC, *Peerage*, new edn, 9.390–91 • *VCH Yorkshire East Riding*, vol. 2 • *CSP dom.*, 1648–9; 1651–5 • G. H. Gater and E. P. Wheeler, *The parish of St Martin-in-the-Fields*, 1: *Charing Cross*, Survey of London, 16 (1935) • *The diary of Bulstrode Whitelocke, 1605–1675*, ed. R. Spalding, British Academy, Records of Social and Economic History, new ser., 13 (1990) • *The writings and speeches of Oliver Cromwell*, ed. W. C. Abbott and C. D. Crane, 3–4 (1945–7) • C. Hill, *The world turned upside down: radical ideas during the English revolution* (1972)
Archives HLRO, legal cases involving Mulgrave before the House of Lords
Likenesses R. Grave, line engraving, NPG
Wealth at death manors of Hutton Mulgrave and Newton Mulgrave, Yorkshire (East Riding), with Mulgrave Castle; Kirke House, Spring Gardens, London: *VCH Yorkshire, East Riding*, vol. 2

Sheffield, George (1838–1892), marine and landscape painter, was born on 1 January 1838 at High Street, Wigton, Cumberland, the son of Thomas Sheffield, a draper, and his wife, Jane Johnston. His uncle, George Sheffield (1800–1852), had been a student at the Royal Academy, and had a considerable local reputation as a portrait painter. From him and from Henry Hoodless, also a Wigton resident, Sheffield obtained help in his youthful studies. While still very young he moved with his father to Warrington, where he received his first art teaching from the portrait and genre painter Samuel Luke Fildes RA in the art school of that town. At first Sheffield adopted the sea as a profession, sailing across the Atlantic and to Holland, but after a few years' experience of this life he settled at Manchester, studying in the school of art and becoming a pattern designer with a firm of calico printers. He soon turned his attention to landscape painting, producing with great facility, truth, and beauty, seascapes, coast scenes, and landscapes. Like other Manchester-based artists he spent time painting around Conwy Falls in north Wales.

Sheffield worked in oil and watercolour, and produced some fine works in both mediums, but undoubtedly his forte was the use of monochrome. His drawings in sepia and black and white are remarkable for their variety and delicate beauty of atmospheric effect. He worked with great speed, and produced a vast number of drawings. In 1869 he was elected an associate of the Manchester Academy and a full member in 1871. From 1868 he was a regular exhibitor at all the Manchester and other local exhibitions, and between 1872 and 1890 he showed six pictures at the Royal Academy, including *Lindon Common* and *View in the Island of Sark*, and eleven at other London exhibitions. Nearly all his best pictures were acquired by Lancashire collectors, including Robert H. Edmondson. There are in Manchester City Galleries two works by Sheffield— an oil painting, *A Hundred Years Ago*, and a number of watercolours, including *The Trough of the Sea*. Sheffield died in Ancoats Hospital, Mill Street, Manchester, on 2 October 1892. His wife predeceased him; eight children survived him. ALBERT NICHOLSON, *rev.* MARK POTTLE

Sources Mallalieu, *Watercolour artists*, vol. 1 · J. Johnson and A. Greutzner, *The dictionary of British artists, 1880–1940* (1976), vol. 5 of *Dictionary of British art* · B. Stewart and M. Cutten, *The dictionary of portrait painters in Britain up to 1920* (1997) · Wood, *Vic. painters*, 3rd edn · Boase, *Mod. Eng. biog.* · *Art Journal*, new ser., 12–13 (1892–3) · private information (2004) · b. cert. · d. cert.

Likenesses portrait, repro. in *Momus* (26 Aug 1880)

Sheffield [Sheffeild], **John** (*d.* 1680), clergyman and ejected minister, came from Northamptonshire. His parents' names are not known, though Sheffield (or Sheffeild, the spelling under which his books were published) seems to have come from a junior branch of the family of the Sheffields, earls of Mulgrave and lords Sheffield of Butterwick. In the dedication to a book he published in 1650 he saluted Edmund, the second earl, as 'head of a great family, and the highest branch of a numerous name, all whose sheaves do willingly bow to your Lordship's sheaf as gladly and wilingly as Joseph's brethren did to him' (Sheffeild, *A Good Conscience the Strongest Hold*, sig. A4).

Sheffield matriculated from Peterhouse, Cambridge, in 1618, where he was listed as a poor scholar on 5 December of that year. He graduated BA in 1622 and proceeded MA in 1625. Ordained a deacon in the diocese of Peterborough on 22 December 1622 he became curate of Felmersham, Bedfordshire, in the following year while still at Cambridge, but his ordination as a priest (also at Peterborough) was delayed until 22 September 1628. On 4 May 1629 he was instituted as rector of Careby, Lincolnshire, and it was probably about this time that he married his wife, Elizabeth; they may well have been the John Sheffield and Elizabeth Eastwicke who married at Boston, Lincolnshire, on 2 October 1628. Their eldest son, John, who was at Tonbridge School in 1646 and was admitted to St John's College in May of that year, was born in 1629 or 1630. A daughter, Katherine, and a son, Stephen, were baptized at Careby in 1632 and 1634 respectively; the latter was admitted to Merchant Taylors' School in 1648. It is uncertain whether John's two younger sons, Timothy (*bap.* 1654/5) and Nathaniel (*bap.* 1662), were the children of his first wife, Elizabeth, or his second, Barbara (*d.* 1684), whose former name was probably Smith.

It may be that John Sheffield arrived with his family to take up the ministry at Tonbridge, Kent, following the sequestration in 1643 of Edward Ashburnham, the rector there and a prebendary of Chichester Cathedral, though there is no certain confirmation of his ministering there until July 1647. Soon afterwards, however, Sheffield moved to the parish of St Swithin London Stone, London, where on 7 November 1647 he was elected minister at a meeting of the vestry. He was a signatory on 14 December 1647 of *A Testimony to the Truth of Jesus Christ, and to our Solemn League and Covenant*, and in January 1649 signed as minister of St Swithin *A Vindication of the Ministers of the Gospel*, which deplored the proceedings against Charles I. As all this may suggest, Sheffield was a presbyterian by persuasion. In 1650 he published *A Good Conscience the Strongest Hold*. The preface, addressed 'To the conscientious reader' advised: 'Conscience is the book of books, the ancientest piece of scripture in the world', lamenting that 'these times of our have been too fruitful in disputes and controversies; in dealing with which there is no end'. A report dated 29 April 1652, which included the information that one minister and three ruling elders were in place at St Swithin, was signed by Sheffield as moderator of the third London classis. But he was formally presented by the Salters' Company to the rectory of St Swithin only on 12 May 1657, signing a grateful preface to the master and officials of the company in his *The Sinfulness of Evil Thoughts* (1659). In *The Rising Sun, or, The Sun of Righteousness* (1654) something of the flavour of his ministry at St Swithin is suggested by a preface to his friends there, who 'have had the sum of this discourse preached among you, and divers of you have it written in your note books and repeated in your families'. Sheffield served as an assistant to the London commission for scandalous ministers under the ordinance of 28 August 1654, and was appointed as a commissioner for the approbation of ministers in March 1660.

In 1660 Sheffield was ejected from St Swithin upon the return of the sequestrated minister. He did not immediately leave the parish, where his son Nathaniel was baptized on 27 March 1662. However, probably shortly afterwards he settled at Enfield, Middlesex. He took the Oxford oath in 1666, and on 15 April 1672 was granted a licence under the declaration of indulgence to teach at his own and two other houses in Enfield. Although, according to Calamy, 'from his youth up was addicted to piety and seriousness', Sheffield 'was one that formed his sermons not from monastic contemplations in his cell, but took for a ground work such things as did occur' in the world around him; perhaps as a result 'a briskness appears in all his writings' (Calamy, *Abridgement*, 2.38–9). John Sheffield was buried at Enfield on 3 August 1680. In his will, dated from there on 26 May 1680 and proved on 17 August 1680, he left property at Enfield and elsewhere to his second wife, Barbara, who died in 1684. STEPHEN WRIGHT

Sources J. Whitebrook, 'Two John Sheffields', *Transactions of the Congregational Historical Society*, 11 (1930–32) · *Calamy rev.* · Venn, *Alum. Cant.* · *Walker rev.* · T. A. Walker, *A biographical register of Peterhouse men*, 2 (1930) · G. Hennessy, *Novum repertorium ecclesiasticum parochiale Londinense, or, London diocesan clergy succession from the earliest time to the year 1898* (1898) · E. Calamy, ed., *An abridgement of Mr. Baxter's history of his life and times, with an account of the ministers, &c., who were ejected after the Restauration of King Charles II*, 2nd edn, 2 vols. (1713) · W. A. Shaw, *A history of the English church during the civil wars and under the Commonwealth, 1640–1660*, 2 vols. (1900) · will, PRO, PROB 11/363, fols. 396v–397v

Sheffield, John, first duke of Buckingham and Normanby (1647–1721), politician and author, was born on 8 September 1647, the only son of Edmund *Sheffield, second earl of Mulgrave (1611–1658), one of Oliver Cromwell's councillors and one of the peers called to the protector's upper house, and Elizabeth Cranfield (1607/8–1672), daughter of Lionel *Cranfield, first earl of Middlesex. On his father's death, he succeeded as third earl of Mulgrave. In 1661 his mother married Sir John Bennet,

John Sheffield, first duke of Buckingham and Normanby
(1647–1721), by Sir Godfrey Kneller, c.1685–8

and Mulgrave was sent to France in the care of a private tutor, who took care that he was not caught up in Catholic practices, on one occasion preventing him from kneeling in the street as a procession carrying the host passed by. On his return to England, and to the court, in 1665 Mulgrave undertook a programme of self-education, learning Latin well enough to translate Epicurus and write a commentary on the letters of Cicero.

In the service of Charles II In 1666 Mulgrave joined the navy as a volunteer, serving on the flagship of Prince Rupert against the Dutch. On 13 June 1667, with the Dutch threatening to invade England, Mulgrave was made captain of a troop of horse. In November 1669 he challenged John Wilmot, second earl of Rochester, to a duel, believing Rochester had written a satire about him, but Rochester treated the challenge as a joke, arriving at the duel to claim that he was not in good health and unable to proceed. Mulgrave was deeply offended and subsequently held Rochester to be an enemy, although Rochester was probably obeying an order from Charles II not to carry out the duel. Mulgrave served as a volunteer with the fleet at the battle of Solebay on 28 May 1672. He continued to be promoted, becoming a gentleman of the bedchamber, and was appointed commander of the *Captain*, one of the best second-rate vessels in the fleet, in 1673. His army commission was raised to colonel of the 3rd foot, or Old Holland regiment, the same year, and he was nominated knight of the Garter on 23 April 1674, being invested on 28 May. He continued his military education by serving under Marshal Turenne in France.

Despite these successes, Mulgrave deeply resented that

James Scott, duke of Monmouth, eldest illegitimate son of Charles II and from April 1678 captain-general of land forces, opposed his wish to command the 1st troop of Horse Guards. In revenge Mulgrave encouraged the animosity between Monmouth and James, duke of York, the king's brother, suggesting that Monmouth was planning a coup to seize the throne and was manoeuvring himself into a position to accomplish it, while intimating to Monmouth that York had sexual designs on Monmouth's wife. When York and Monmouth fell out Mulgrave benefited handsomely, accepting the positions of governor of Hull and lord lieutenant of the East Riding of Yorkshire that had been stripped from Monmouth.

The development of Mulgrave's career at court was accompanied by the expansion of his literary interests. He wrote a prologue to a performance at court of Elkanah Settle's *The Empress of Morocco* in July 1673, alongside another by his rival Rochester. He established a friendly relationship with John Dryden, combining the roles of patron and collaborator. Dryden benefited from Mulgrave's access to Charles II and the duke of York, as well as from financial support. Mulgrave had his attempts at verse corrected by Dryden. In 1676 Mulgrave was the dedicatee of Dryden's *Aureng-Zebe*, a play whose protagonist was a dispossessed prince; the dedication implicitly praised Mulgrave for his loyal partisanship of the duke of York's right to succeed Charles II. Subsequently, in March 1679, Mulgrave collaborated with Dryden on the translation of Ovid's letter from Helen to Paris for Dryden's *Ovid's Epistles*. Mulgrave was probably the author of the 'Essay on satire' which circulated in manuscript in 1679 and attacked prominent figures at court including the king and Rochester; Dryden was blamed and physically assaulted, but the friendship between patron and poet survived.

Mulgrave continued to support the court during the exclusion crisis, winning further literary endorsement from Dryden, and consistently voted against attempts to remove the duke of York from the succession in the Lords. In 1680 he commanded a relief expedition to the English garrison at Tangier, but the mission was poorly planned and so badly supplied that it accomplished little. He incurred the king's displeasure by refusing to drink healths to Charles until he and his men were safely landed in a rotting boat they had been assigned, but redeemed himself with a carefully drawn report on the fortifications of Tangier. In 1682 he published the first edition of his *An Essay upon Poetry*, imitating Horace's *Ars poetica*; it went through several subsequent revised editions during Mulgrave's lifetime. He remained in the king's favour until November 1682, when he was banned from court after gossip circulated that he had seduced the duke of York's daughter Anne. He claimed that it was a harmless flirtation and that he was 'only ogling' her (Gregg, 27), but he was stripped of his offices and remained without employment until 1684, when he was restored to the Holland regiment.

James II and the revolution The accession of James II brought Mulgrave back into full royal favour. In May 1685 he was appointed a gentleman of the bedchamber, on 24

July he joined the privy council, and in October was promoted to lord chamberlain of the household. After a long bachelorhood Mulgrave married at Littlecote Chapel, Ramsbury, Wiltshire, on 18 March 1686; his wife was Ursula (d. 1697), widow of Edward Conway, earl of Conway, eldest daughter of George Stawell and Ursula, née Austen. Her grandfather was the royalist army officer Sir John Stawell. They had no children. James made Mulgrave an ecclesiastical commissioner on 22 November 1686, replacing Laurence Hyde, earl of Rochester, and Mulgrave became closely associated with James's religious policies. He attended mass with the king, but never converted to Catholicism nor took communion. In 1687 he was reappointed lord lieutenant of the East Riding of Yorkshire and also became vice-admiral for Yorkshire and Northumberland. Later Mulgrave excused his accepting a seat on the ecclesiastical commission by claiming that he had no idea the commission was illegal, nor had he intended to take the lieutenancy of the East Riding from Charles Seymour, sixth duke of Somerset, whom James had removed for not introducing the papal nuncio at court.

In 1688 Mulgrave witnessed the birth of the king's son James Francis Edward, and remained at the king's side in London until James II fled on 11 December 1688. He was one of the peers who met at the Guildhall in London that day and formed the provisional government. He received praise from all sides when he rescued the Spanish ambassador from an anti-Catholic mob and saved the ambassador's house from destruction, thereby preserving England's relationship with Spain, which was sympathetic to William's invasion. He was initially loyal to James, and on learning of James's capture at Faversham led moves for his rescue. When James returned to Whitehall, Mulgrave requested a marquessate, but was rejected. Mulgrave, slighted, abandoned James, supported moves to establish the convention, and in February 1689 voted to accept William and Mary as joint sovereigns. That year he wrote an essay, 'Humanum est errare, or, False steps on both sides', which reflected badly on the conduct of both James and William, but it was never published; the manuscript survives in the British Library. Another essay of this period was 'The character of a tory, in answer to that of a trimmer', replying to the pamphlet by George Savile, marquess of Halifax.

The 1690s Mulgrave was not trusted by the new regime. He was not included in the new monarchs' privy council, although in 1691 the lord president, Thomas Osborne, marquess of Carmarthen (formerly earl of Danby), included Mulgrave on a list of candidates for the post of lord lieutenant of Ireland that was sent to William. None the less he drifted into opposition as a non-government tory. In January 1693 he supported the claim of the lords to be allowed to assess their own estates for the land tax. However later that year he opposed the Triennial Bill, thereby aligning himself with William, but also protested with the whig leaders Halifax and Charles Talbot, twelfth earl of Shrewsbury, against the renewal of press censorship. As part of the reconstruction of the government to

accommodate Shrewsbury in spring 1694, on 3 May he was made a privy councillor, with an annual pension of £3000, and on 10 May was created marquess of Normanby. He attended the cabinet and in November 1694 acted as speaker of the House of Lords during the illness of the lord keeper, Sir John Somers. On 25 January 1695 he replied for the government in the Lords against the speech of the former secretary of state Daniel Finch, second earl of Nottingham. However, following the uncovering of the Jacobite plot to assassinate William in 1696, Normanby refused to sign the association recognizing William as rightful and lawful king, and on 12 March 1696 was struck off the list of privy councillors by William's own hand.

Normanby's refusal to abjure James by signing the association won him the praise of Dryden in the *Dedication of the Aeneis*, but he was again out of office with little prospect of return. He emphasized that he was not a supporter of Catholic hegemony in England by publishing in 1696 *The Character of Charles II, King of England, with a Short Account of his being Poyson'd*, which insinuated that Charles had been murdered by Catholics in order to ensure the accession of the allegedly more pliant James II. In November 1696 he joined the duke of Leeds (formerly Carmarthen) in opposing the government proposal to extend the privileges of the Bank of England, and opposed the attainder of the Jacobite conspirator Sir John Fenwick. On 12 March 1699 he married his second wife, Katherine (d. 1704), widow of Wriothesley Noel, second earl of Gainsborough, and daughter of Fulke Greville, fifth Baron Brooke of Beauchamp's Court, and Sarah, née Dashwood. This marriage was also childless. Normanby opposed settling the English succession on the house of Hanover, and in debates on the Act of Settlement in 1701 suggested that Prince George of Denmark should have preference over the Hanoverians in inheriting the throne. Although frequently criticized for switching sides from James II to William and Mary, Normanby's course during the 1690s rarely led him to power and he seems to have genuinely followed his conscience, frequently to his detriment.

Office and opposition under Anne Normanby's allies in opposition were defenders of the high-church position, and with them he moved closer to William III following the decision of Louis XIV to recognize the son of James II as James III following the dethroned monarch's death in 1701. On 2 January 1702 Normanby proposed the Lords' address of thanks to William III, which expressed the peers' hostility to Louis. Following the accession of Queen Anne, who remembered her former admirer fondly, as well as his courtesy towards her husband, he was reappointed to the privy council on 21 April 1702, and became lord privy seal on 2 May. He also became lord lieutenant of the North Riding of Yorkshire. In cabinet he argued against Anne's orders that the Electress Sophia of Hanover be included in prayers for the royal family, and thought that England should be an auxiliary member of the grand alliance and use the war against France to improve her colonial position and avoid a lengthy entanglement on land. Nevertheless, he survived the removal of Rochester from office in February 1703, and Anne showed her continued support for him by creating him duke of Buckingham and Normanby on 23 March 1703. As the letters patent specified that he was to be 'duke of the county of Buckingham', he was sometimes referred to as duke of Buckinghamshire.

Buckingham's promotion may have been intended to show the high-church interest that they were still regarded highly by the queen, but it was seen as an inconvenience by the lord treasurer, Sidney Godolphin, first earl of Godolphin, who wanted to secure the ministry by making it more acceptable to the whigs. Sarah Churchill, duchess of Marlborough, the keeper of the queen's privy purse, also resented Buckingham's influence over court administration and the permission the queen had given him to build a town residence, Buckingham House, on the western edge of St James's Park. Buckingham was gradually forced from office during 1704; his pension ceased to be paid, rumours spread that he was intriguing with the tory opposition, and on 23 March 1705 he was dismissed from his offices. His removal was criticized in a pamphlet, *The Memorial of the Church of England* (1705), which portrayed Buckingham as a friend of the church, wronged by Anne, whose dismissal left the church open to attack from the duke of Marlborough, Godolphin, and their whig allies. It was cited in an acrimonious debate in the Lords that December, when Buckingham and Rochester were attacked as responsible for it as part of a campaign to discredit the queen and her whig ministers. In November 1705 he was one of the ringleaders of the tory scheme to embarrass the queen and ministry by inviting the Electress Sophia to reside in England. On 20 May 1707 he was removed from the privy council. Later that year Robert Harley and Godolphin planned to include him in an abortive ministerial reconstruction that would have freed the ministry from reliance on the junto whigs.

Buckingham's interests outside politics at this time included the construction of Buckingham House from a design executed (but perhaps not originated) by William Winde. The house was built between 1703 and 1705 and led Buckingham's enemy at court, the duchess of Marlborough, to invite him to advise on the construction of Marlborough House, also in St James's Park, in 1709. He also became a patron of the poet Alexander Pope. On 16 March 1706, at St Martin-in-the-Fields, Westminster, he married Catherine (1681/2–1743), widow of James Annesley, third earl of Anglesey, and previously Lady Catherine Darnley, illegitimate daughter of *James II and Catharine *Sedley, *suo jure* countess of Dorchester. The new duchess was a Jacobite sympathizer, and the marriage served to identify Buckingham further with high toryism. They had three sons, only one of whom, Edmund (1716–1735), survived to adulthood. Buckingham already had at least two children out of wedlock. A relationship with Frances Stewart, wife of Oliver Lambart, younger son of Charles, third earl of Cavan, resulted in the birth of a son, Charles Herbert,

later Sir Charles Sheffield, first baronet (*c*.1706–1774), who eventually inherited the Normanby estate in Lincolnshire. An illegitimate daughter from an earlier relationship, Mary Sheffield (*d*. 1729), married Arthur Annesley, fourth Baron Althan (1688/9–1727), and may have been the mother of the peerage claimant James Annesley.

Buckingham had connections with financiers in the City of London—he was a proprietor in the East India Company—and Harley made use of these to secure city support for a future Harley-led ministry. Buckingham returned to office when Harley formed a tory-based ministry in 1710, becoming a privy councillor once more and lord steward of the household; in June 1711 he was promoted to lord president of the council, and also that year recovered the lord lieutenancies of the north and east ridings of Yorkshire, as well as gaining that of Middlesex. He was also appointed one of the lords justices, who were to carry out administration between the queen's death and the arrival of her successor from Hanover. Following the accession of George I he was removed from all his offices, including his place on the privy council, despite his long correspondence with the Hanoverian court.

Retirement and death Buckingham devoted the rest of his life to literary pursuits. He supported Pope's *Iliad* and in 1717 contributed verse to *Poems on Several Occasions* alongside Pope and Anne Finch, countess of Winchilsea. He also restructured Shakespeare's *Julius Caesar* in accordance with early eighteenth-century tastes, dividing it into two independent works, *The Tragedy of Julius Caesar* and *The Death of Marcus Brutus*, introducing new characters and inserting love scenes, and scaling back the importance of the Roman citizenry. Pope contributed two of the choruses placed between the acts. Buckingham's poetry was witty and cynical, as in his derisive commentary on the morals, manners, and personal hygiene of the Parisians.

Buckingham died at Buckingham House on 24 February 1721, and was buried in Westminster Abbey on 25 March 1721. He was succeeded as second duke of Buckingham and Normanby by his son, Edmund, upon whose death all his titles became extinct. At the request of the duchess Pope edited Buckingham's works for publication, but before Pope's edition could be published an unauthorized collection was released in 1721 by Edmund Curll. Pope's version appeared on 24 January 1723, but the books were seized by the government as 'in some Part of these Volumes great Reflections are cast upon the late happy Revolution' (Mack, 396), forcing the excision of 'Some account of the revolution', where Buckingham had insinuated that William III had come to England with the deliberate intention of seizing the throne, and 'A feast of the gods', where Buckingham commented that the Dutch were 'remarkable for industry, and for having no one good quality besides' (ibid.). The two essays were published separately—in London as *The Castrations* in 1723 and in The Hague as *Buckingham Restor'd* in 1727—and included in the fourth edition of Buckingham's works in 1740. Samuel Johnson wrote of him that 'His verses are often insipid, but his memoirs are lively and agreeable; he had the perspicuity and elegance of an historian, but not the fire and fancy of a poet' (Johnson).   MARGARET D. SANKEY

Sources *Works of John Sheffield*, 2 vols. (1726) · V. de Sola Pinto, *Restoration carnival* (1954) · J. Doyle, *Official baronage of England*, 5 vols. (1885) · GEC, *Peerage* · DNB · E. Gregg, *Queen Anne* (1980) · H. Horwitz, *Revolution politicks: the career of Daniel Finch, second earl of Nottingham, 1647–1730* (1968) · G. S. Holmes, *British politics in the age of Anne*, rev. edn (1987) · W. A. Speck, *The birth of Britain: a new nation, 1700–1710* (1994) · J. A. Winn, *John Dryden and his world* (1987) · M. Mack, *Alexander Pope: a life* (1985) · R. Beddard, ed., *A kingdom without a king: the journal of the provisional government in the revolution of 1688* (1988) · F. Harris, *A passion for government: the life of Sarah, duchess of Marlborough* (1991) · A. Browning, *Thomas Osborne, earl of Danby and duke of Leeds, 1632–1712*, 3 vols. (1944–51) · C. E. Ward, *The life of John Dryden* (1961) · D. Bywaters, *Dryden in revolutionary England* (1991) · Burke, *Peerage* (1999) · S. Johnson, 'The life of John Sheffield', ed. K. N. Kemmerer, www.hn.psu.edu/faculty/kkemmerer/poets/sheffield/default.html [the Penn State Archive of Samuel Johnson's *Lives of the Poets*], 28 April 2002
Archives Balliol Oxf., personal papers of duke of Buckingham and Catherine (his third wife) · LUL, memorandum book · PRO, accounts of the duke of Buckingham and dowager duchess of Buckingham, C105/20 | BL, letters to George, elector of Hanover, and electress Sophia of Hanover, Stowe MSS 222–224, 241, *passim* · BL, letters to Lord Nottingham, Add. MS 29588, fols. 356–62 · CKS, corresp. with Alexander Stanhope · U. Nott. L., letters to Lord Portland · Warks. CRO, letters to Everard de Weede, baron de Dyckvelt
Likenesses G. Kneller, oils, second version, c.1685–1686, NPG · G. Kneller, oils, c.1685–1688, NMM [*see illus.*] · S. Dubois, oils, 1696, Hughenden Manor, Buckinghamshire · J. Richardson, oils, c.1703–1705, Examination Schools, Oxford · L. Delvaux, D. Plumier, and P. Scheemakers, effigy on monument, c.1721, Westminster Abbey · G. Vertue, line engraving, 1722 (after G. Kneller), BM, NPG; repro. in *The works of John Sheffield*, 2 vols. (1723) · J. Smith, mezzotint (after G. Kneller), BM, NPG
Wealth at death very wealthy; Buckingham House inherited by his son Edmund (d. 1735)

Sheffield, John (1653/4–1726), Presbyterian minister, was born at Ibstock, Leicestershire, the son of William Sheffield (d. 1673), who was rector at Ibstock from 1644 to 1662. After attending Kibworth grammar school John Sheffield was sent to learn a trade, but he was eager to enter the ministry and began to study under John Shuttlewood, ejected clergyman and in the 1660s an itinerant preacher in Leicestershire, accompanying him from one hiding place to the next. In December 1668 Shuttlewood, Sheffield, and others were surprised at a conventicle. The next day Sheffield was required by the local magistrate to state 'when he had been at his parish church to hear Divine Service' and whether he would go next Sunday, but 'answered that he did not know how Divine Providence might dispose of him before that time' (Pearse, 79). He was sent to Leicester gaol in the custody of Charles Gibbons, quartermaster of the trained bands. In 1672 an attempt was made to distrain his goods, despite his possession of a licence. In 1674 Sheffield was living at Lubenham, Leicestershire, where he was visited by his old friend Gibbons, 'roaring into his congregation after his wonted manner'; a warrant was secured 'to distrain upon Mr Sh for forty pounds: And the officers took away seven milch cows of Mr Sheffields' which were sold for £7 and the proceeds paid to the justices (ibid., 81). Eventually Sheffield found a

position as chaplain to Mrs Palmer at Temple Hall, in the parish of Sibson, Leicestershire. There he married; although his wife's name is unknown, they had at least two daughters, Letitia and Lydia, and two sons, Nathaniel, a lawyer, and the eldest child, William, born in 1682, who became a dissenting minister at Buckingham, Windsor, and later Haverhill, Suffolk.

On 27 September 1682 Sheffield was ordained by Shuttlewood and three other ejected ministers. Two meeting-houses were built for him, probably in 1689, at Temple Hall and at Atherstone, Warwickshire, where he had also begun preaching. In the early 1690s he was granted £4 a year for his pastoral work at Appleby, Leicestershire, by the managers of the Common Fund of Presbyterian and Independent ministers, and continued to receive this support until 1703. He himself was elected to serve as a fund manager in 1697. Also in that year, he succeeded as minister of the Presbyterian congregation in St Thomas Street, Southwark. He was a friend of the philosopher John Locke, whom he visited at Oates, near High Laver. In the Salters' Hall debates of 1719 he sided with the non-subscribers. In March 1720, when his son Nathaniel was admitted as a student of the Middle Temple, John Sheffield was given as resident of Queen Street, Southwark. Despite his earlier stormy relationships with the authorities, Sheffield has been described as akin to Richard Baxter in his views. According to Calamy:

> He was much for catholic Christianity: and therefore did he the less relish the National Establishment, and therefore was he the more contented to renounce the emoluments of it, because he thought it set up such a sort of uniformity as hindered unity, and turned the national church into a mere party. (Calamy, 37)

Judging from Calamy's gruesome account of the results of the autopsy, Sheffield must have spent his last years in agony, eventually succumbing to stone of the bladder and kidneys on 24 January 1726, aged seventy-two. He probably died in Southwark.

ALEXANDER GORDON, rev. STEPHEN WRIGHT

Sources J. C. Whitebrook, 'Two John Sheffields', *Transactions of the Congregational Historical Society*, 11 (1930–32); repr. in J. C. Whitebrook, *Two John Sheffields* (1932) · A. Gordon, ed., *Freedom after ejection: a review (1690–1692) of presbyterian and congregational nonconformity in England and Wales* (1917) · W. Wilson, *The history and antiquities of the dissenting churches and meeting houses in London, Westminster and Southwark*, 4 vols. (1808–14), vol. 4, p. 307 · will, PRO, PROB 11/607, sig. 34 · E. Calamy, *A funeral sermon for the late Reverend Mr John Sheffield, minister of the gospel in Southwark, who departed this life Jan 24 1726, an aetat 73* (1726) · E. P. [E. Pearse], *The conformist's fourth plea for the nonconformists, wherein several considerations are offered for Christian forbearance* (1683)

Sheffield, Sir Robert (b. before 1462, d. 1518), lawyer and speaker of the House of Commons, was the son of Robert Sheffield (c.1430–1502), a lawyer and administrator of South Cave, Yorkshire, and his wife, Jane Lounde. It was through his mother that the younger Robert Sheffield became lord of West Butterwick, Lincolnshire. Trained in the Inner Temple, of which he became a governor in 1511, he had become recorder of London by 21 September 1495, and served in that office until April 1508. Consequently he was *ex officio* an MP for London in 1495, 1497, and 1504. Knighted by Henry VII after the battle of Blackheath (17 June 1497), by way of thanking the city for its loyalty, in 1504 Sheffield attracted some odium for failing to defend its corporate privileges. In 1497 Giles, Lord Daubeney (*d.* 1508), tried to buy Sheffield the speakership, but was outbid. From about 1508–9, by now 'of counsel' to the king, Sheffield largely retired to his county, receiving royal grants of several stewardships around Lincoln; by 1516 he was Lindsey's *custos rotulorum*. He probably represented Lincolnshire in the parliaments of 1512 and 1515, but London still paid him an annuity to be mindful of its interests. In February 1512 he was 'elected' speaker, the crown paying him £300 for the three sessions held between then and 4 March 1514—an inflated rate.

In 1515 Sheffield helped Thomas Wolsey (*d.* 1530) to pilot his resumption bill through parliament. However, in the same parliament Sheffield's support for the renewal of an act of 1512, denying benefit of clergy to men not in holy orders, appears to have aroused Wolsey's hostility, and in the following year he was arraigned in Star Chamber, charged with negligence as a JP. He had to give recognizances for 8000 marks, and was dismissed from the county bench. He obtained a pardon in November 1516, but his complaints to the king against the cardinal caused Wolsey to have Sheffield imprisoned in the Tower of London, before bringing him back into Star Chamber, accused of obtaining his pardon without licence and also of harbouring a killer (on which there may have been a real case to answer). Returned to the Tower, he may have died there, on 10 August 1518, though the church of the Austin friars, in which he chose to be buried, adjoined not only the Tower but probably also Sheffield's own house— his first wife, Ellen, the daughter of Sir John Delves of Doddington, Cheshire, was buried in the friary church. Ellen died in or after 1509, and Sheffield later married Anne (surname unknown), who outlived him. His son and heir, Robert, the child of his first marriage, married Jane Stanley, sister of Thomas Stanley, second earl of Derby; their son Edmund *Sheffield became first Baron Sheffield in 1547.   JULIAN LOCK

Sources A. D. K. Hawkyard, 'Sheffield, Sir Robert', HoP, *Commons, 1509–58*, 3.304–5 • P. Gwyn, *The king's cardinal: the rise and fall of Thomas Wolsey* (1990) • J. A. Guy, *The cardinal's court: the impact of Thomas Wolsey in star chamber* (1977) • H. Miller, 'London and parliament in the reign of Henry VIII', *BIHR*, 35 (1962), 128–49; repr. in *Historical studies of the English parliament*, ed. E. B. Fryde and E. Miller, 2 (1970), 125–46 • M. M. Condon, 'Ruling elites in the reign of Henry VII', *Patronage, pedigree and power in later medieval England*, ed. C. D. Ross (1979), 109–42 • N. H. Nicolas, ed., *Testamenta vetusta: being illustrations from wills*, 2 (1826), 555–7 • *LP Henry VIII* • J. S. Roskell, *The Commons and their speakers in English parliaments, 1376–1523* (1965) • A. F. Pollard, *Wolsey*, rev. edn (1953); repr. (1965) • J. C. Wedgwood and A. D. Holt, *History of parliament*, 1: *Biographies of the members of the Commons house, 1439–1509* (1936) • S. J. Gunn, 'The Act of Resumption of 1515', *Early Tudor England* [Harlaxton 1987], ed. D. Williams (1989), 87–106 • E. W. Ives, *The common lawyers of pre-Reformation England* (1983)
Wealth at death £533 to daughters; £67 to wife; real estate to son; fines and debts to crown: will, Nicolas, ed., *Testamenta vetusta*, 2.555–7

Sheil, Sir Justin (1803–1871), army officer in the East India Company and diplomatist, son of Edward Sheil, merchant, and his wife, Catherine (*née* MacCarthy), of Spring House, co. Tipperary, and brother of Richard Lalor *Sheil, was born at Rathpatrick, co. Kilkenny, on 2 December 1803. Educated at Stonyhurst College, he was nominated to an East India cadetship. On arriving in India he was posted as ensign to the 3rd Bengal infantry (4 March 1820). Exchanged to the 35th Bengal infantry, of which he became adjutant, he was present at the siege of Bharatpur (1826). He became a captain on 13 April 1830, and on 4 July 1833 was appointed second in command of the disciplined troops in Persia under Colonel Pasmore, who had specially recommended him to Lord W. Bentinck for this service. Pasmore wrote that he was sensible, well-informed, and conciliatory. On 16 February 1836 he was appointed secretary to the British legation in Persia, and in 1844 he succeeded Sir John McNeill as envoy and minister at the shah's court, and continued such until he retired in 1854. He married in 1847, Mary Leonora (*d.* 1869), only daughter of the Rt Hon. Stephen Woulfe, chief baron of the Irish exchequer. He contributed to his wife's book, *Glimpses of Life and Manners in Persia* (1856), and two articles in the journal of the Royal Geographical Society. He had been promoted to the rank of major on 17 February 1841, and became a major-general in 1859. In 1848 he was created a CB, and in 1855 a KCB. He died at 13 Eaton Place, London, on 17 April 1871.   STEPHEN WHEELER, *rev.* JAMES LUNT

Sources *The Times* (21 April 1871) • BL OIOC • V. C. P. Hodson, *List of officers of the Bengal army, 1758–1834*, 4 (1947) • C. E. Buckland, *Dictionary of Indian biography* (1906) • Boase, *Mod. Eng. biog.*
Archives BL OIOC, corresp. with George D'Arcy, MS Eur. D 645 • NA Scot., corresp. with Sir John McNeill • PRO, corresp. with Stratford Canning, FO 352 • U. Durham L., letters to Viscount Ponsonby
Wealth at death under £50,000: probate, 21 Oct 1874, *CGPLA Ire.*

Sheil, Richard Lalor (1791–1851), playwright and politician, was born on 17 August 1791 at Drumdowney, co. Kilkenny, the eldest of the four sons of Edward Sheil and Catherine McCarthy of Spring House, co. Tipperary. Edward Sheil was one of a burgeoning and successful Irish Catholic mercantile middle class. He purchased an estate and married into a family with aristocratic connections. For his eldest son he planned a professional career. As Richard Sheil later explained, in an autobiographical aside to a parliamentary committee, a Catholic who made money in trade considered it a feather in his own cap if he made his son a barrister, for the bar in Ireland enjoyed more station than in England because of the absence in the former country of persons of real rank. Educated initially by a resident tutor in the person of a refugee French priest, he was then dispatched to a school in Kensington run by French Jesuits settled in England. Its émigré character and the language of much of the instruction ensured that precious little sense of Britishness was inculcated here. However, he was transferred to the intensely English Roman Catholic environment of Stonyhurst College in Lancashire in October 1804. He found a role model

Richard Lalor Sheil (1791–1851), by Joseph Haverty

among the members of staff—a mind steeped in classical knowledge, with highly polished manners and great eloquence—and was taught to be loyal to the constitution and liberties of Britain despite the religious discrimination to which Catholics were subjected. As much as Sheil resented those remaining disabilities which threatened to restrict the reach of his ambition, he emerged from Stonyhurst not only with an understanding of English Catholic opinion—which was invariably more moderate than Irish—but also well indoctrinated in the glories of the British nation. Hence his later claim that he was 'as devoted to the maintenance of the glory, the honour, and the power of this great country' as any native born Englishman (MacNevin, 202).

The bar, marriage, and London life Admitted to Trinity College, Dublin, in November 1807, Sheil graduated in July 1811 and subsequently kept terms at Lincoln's Inn for the requisite two years before being called to the Irish bar. These years brought the first crisis in his life, when his father was reduced to virtual bankruptcy. He completed his university education with the assistance of a small allowance from a member of his mother's family, and sought to cover the costs of setting up and establishing himself in his profession through playwriting. His interest in literature and drama—first awakened at Stonyhurst—had developed at Trinity. Beginning in 1814, and over a period of a decade, he earned a modest but useful income with a succession of plays, eight in all, which made him something of a favourite of contemporary literary critics. His taste was for sentimentality and horrors,

perhaps a reflection of a desire more to dazzle the audience with staging than dramatic content, hence his anxiety to secure Eliza O'Neill (1791–1872), one of the most celebrated actresses of the day, for starring roles. His one enduring success was *Evadne, or, The Statue*, which reworked Shirley's *The Traitor* (1635) and has been described as an illustration of the nineteenth-century mind at work on Jacobean drama. The heavy emphasis on infidelity and sin is lightened by a resolution which sees a happier triumph of Sheil's heroine than Shirley's. Performed some thirty times at Covent Garden during its first season, it was staged again as late as 1881.

Sheil's choice of a bride in 1816 may have been influenced not merely by her physical attractions but also by her connections. She was the niece of the master of the rolls, William McMahon, who had the ability to promote a legal career. However, Sheil's increasingly conspicuous participation in the agitation for Catholic relief saw him shunned by his wife's cautious relative, who had been born into a Catholic family but conformed to the established church. All the master ever gave him was breakfast, he later joked. Nevertheless, his practice did slowly prosper despite his refusal to give it his full attention. And when, shortly after the birth of his only son on 9 January 1822, his wife died, Sheil found solace not at the bar but in popular literature. He began to publish a series of sketches of his contemporaries in the profession. First appearing in the *New Monthly Magazine*, but subsequently expanded to embrace political figures and events, and republished in book form, they were characterized by grace, wit, and generosity. They won a wide and admiring readership and even helped to facilitate a reconciliation with Daniel O'Connell, with whom he clashed over political strategy. Many of the articles, including that on O'Connell, were in fact the work of his friend and collaborator William Henry Curran. But O'Connell assumed, as did most contemporaries, that they all came from Sheil's pen (*Sketches of the Irish Bar*) and was surprised by its tone given the bitter nature of their dispute.

A rigorous training in rhetoric at Stonyhurst, membership of the Trinity College Historical Society, and of the Eccentrics debating club during his terms at Lincoln's Inn, provided Sheil with a firm grounding in public speaking and the confidence to seek to master his natural defects as an orator. Painfully self-conscious about his diminutive size, and struggling always to modulate his high-pitched voice, Sheil quickly concluded that passion was his key to capturing and holding the attention of an audience. He cultivated the arts of the demagogue. He was blessed with 'as fine a pair of eyes as ever graced a human head—large, deeply set, dark, liquid, flasing like gems'—which fixed listeners 'like a basilisk' and helped them to forget all else about his appearance (*Blackwood's Magazine*, 30 (1831), 411). When he spoke he deliberately sought to sweep his listeners away with passages of poetic beauty, savage satire, and unrestrained emotion. 'Sheil possesses in eminent degree the surprising faculty of exciting himself to the verge of delirium without once losing his complete self-possession', commented a French listener. 'I was seduced,

I was dazzled, and together with me, the whole assembly' (McCullagh, *Memoirs of Sheil*, 1.310–11). These were the emerging skills he put, while still an undergraduate, at the service of Catholic emancipation, and one of that cause's leading lights admiringly observed that he had seldom seen a youth from college quite so well informed.

Relations with O'Connell Yet Roman Catholics were far from united, either by rank or in strategy. Those of the highest social rank, together with a more substantial number of professional men and merchants, and English Catholics, were willing to try to facilitate emancipation through concessions to liberal protestant opinion, such as a crown veto over Catholic episcopal appointments. His education at Stonyhurst, his political pragmatism, his rank, his personal desire for full and equal citizenship in the British nation, made Sheil a natural vetoist. This was the issue which eventually brought him into acrimonious conflict with Daniel *O'Connell, the uncompromising leader of the anti-vetoists. Convinced that an obdurate O'Connell was delaying emancipation, he launched a stinging personal attack on his adversary in 1821. Not that Sheil was a match for O'Connell in the art of personal abuse. The latter savagely ridiculed the younger man's pretensions as a dramatist and style as a speaker. Only with great difficulty were friends able to dissuade Sheil from completing the breach in Catholic ranks by challenging O'Connell to a duel. The two men did combine early in 1822 on an address of welcome to a new viceroy, Richard Wellesley, whose appointment they both unwisely regarded as the harbinger of emancipation, and were formally reconciled at a dinner party on 8 February 1823, at which the decision was taken to reinvigorate the emancipation agitation through the agency of a new Catholic Association.

Sheil's contribution to the successful launch of this powerful instrument of extra-parliamentary popular pressure was widely recognized as second only to that of O'Connell. Suppressing his initial doubts about the mobilization of the lower orders, he loyally supported the decisions to embrace the entire range of peasant grievances and to offer inexpensive associate memberships as means of binding the masses more closely to the cause while filling association coffers. He tirelessly toured the provinces delivering inspirational harangues, and was paired with O'Connell in the deputation dispatched to London early in 1825 in an unavailing effort to defend the association from suppression and advance emancipation. They testified before parliamentary committees, with Sheil developing the familiar themes of a justice system blighted by aristocratic and religious bias. Further, he avowed that removal of the impediments to advancement in his profession would lead him to retire from politics. It may have been this assurance which prompted O'Connell privately to describe his examination as 'most comical'. Sheil also renounced his support of the veto, insisted that emancipation would remove priests from politics and that Roman Catholics would accept higher franchise qualifications in return for relief, and declared that those who still qualified as voters would not show a partiality in elections for their fellow religionists. However, the impact of his evidence was lessened by his interrogators' scepticism that the lower orders would long be content with a measure which directly benefited only their betters. Similarly, his credibility was damaged by his past demagogic excesses.

Bitterly disappointed by the failure of emancipation to soar even with a pair of protestant 'wings', Sheil was in the vanguard of the new association and its more aggressive politicization of the enfranchised lower orders. Like O'Connell, he publicly expressed regret for his earlier willingness to sacrifice their voting rights on the altar of relief. He also retreated from his earlier opposition to any concession of a special position to priests in the struggle for emancipation. They clearly had a vital role to play in the staging of freeholder uprisings against landlord electoral domination. He played his part in the limited uprising of 1826, which to his mind amounted to a political revolution because the people had at last been taught to know their rights. Sheil it was who interested the French press in the Irish problem, much to the embarrassment of the government, and he proposed a series of imaginative measures, such as a Catholic census and simultaneous parish meetings, to re-emphasize the numerical supremacy of Catholics in Ireland and their wholehearted commitment to the cause. Indeed, he consistently encouraged his fellow religionists to recognize the power their number gave them to intimidate and extract concessions without a resort to violence. And when O'Connell made the fateful decision to contest the by-election in County Clare in 1828, Sheil served as his counsel and campaigned on his behalf.

Sheil as MP Sheil's personal ambition following emancipation in 1829 was to make the difficult transition from agitator to politician, and even to statesman. He was assisted by his marriage on 20 July 1830 to Anastasia Power (*née* Lalor), a wealthy widow, for he was at last ensured of financial security. But his years of demagoguery, and not least a pitiless attack on the character of the duke of York in 1826, had made him powerful enemies. Indeed, he had been saved from prosecution in 1827 only by the formation of the brief Canning administration. A proposal originating with a viceroy that he be put into parliament was resisted by prime minister Wellington, even though many tories were keen to exploit the differences which were re-emerging between Sheil and O'Connell over the latter's turning to the issue of repeal of the union: Sheil was still willing to reconcile himself to the status of a west Briton. He was called to the inner bar in 1830, while O'Connell continued to be denied a silk gown and was left to fume at this studied insult. Sheil did dicker with the tories for a parliamentary seat, but remained unacceptable to Wellington, whose distrust of him extended to the issue of parliamentary reform. The formation of a whig government in 1830 appeared to enhance his prospects, for even those leading lights who visited Ireland and left scornful of its people and scenery were impressed with Sheil. Moreover, he proffered his services as a parliamentary counterweight to O'Connell. Indeed, the Liberator's suspicion that Sheil was provided with a seat for the purpose of 'abusing' him was not entirely unfounded. Temporarily accommodated with the rotten borough of Milbourne Port, Sheil entered the Commons on 8 March 1831. The dissolution two months later saw him returned for co. Louth, having unsuccessfully contested it in 1830, but this time he had the backing of the viceroy's extensive local interest. Nevertheless, disillusionment with whig policy in Ireland, a visceral dislike of Edward Stanley, the Conservative chief secretary, and the apparent unwillingness of ministers to reward him with office, led him to make his peace with O'Connell and secure election for co. Tipperary as a repealer in 1833. This prompted accusations that he was a mere 'mercenary' whose loyalty could only be purchased with favours, and his reputation was further sullied early in 1834 when he found himself at the centre of an ugly controversy over the English complaint that Irish members were 'perfect swindlers' who privately supported legislation which publicly they opposed. He weathered the crisis with the staunch support of O'Connell, and warmly advocated the latter's informal arrangement with the whigs which restored them to office under Melbourne in 1835, following a brief tory hiatus.

Sheil rebuilt his parliamentary career and reputation on the strength of his oratory. Careful not to speak too often and coldly calculating in the timing of his interventions, he devoted days to the preparation of his speeches and on occasion took rooms so as to be able to rehearse at full volume. He was equally careful to ensure their publication, making an arrangement with the *Morning Chronicle* in 1835. Alternately employing the stiletto of irony and the cudgel of sarcasm, he made repeated appeals for religious and political equality in Ireland, though even to sympathetic listeners he appeared to undervalue the importance of social grievances as sources of discontent; he memorably castigated the former, and future, tory lord chancellor, Lyndhurst, for his offensive dismissal of the Irish as aliens in blood, language, and religion; eloquently defended the whig commitment to conciliation of Ireland, as distinct from tory coercion; evoked the historic memory of centuries of misgovernment to explain Irish lawlessness; and distanced himself from O'Connell's resurrection during the late 1830s of repeal. All of this time he was assiduously pursuing office. In 1836 he requested the vice-treasurership of Ireland, only now to learn of the insuperable opposition of William IV who had neither forgotten nor forgiven the attack a decade earlier on his brother. In 1838, following the accession of Victoria, he received a demeaning offer of the clerkship of the ordnance, which he naturally declined. He did subsequently accept the commissionership of Greenwich Hospital. Senior whigs objected to a more senior post because of his commitment to the (secret) ballot, which he believed would provide Irish tenants with greater protection from the political tyranny of landlords. Not that he was long content, and within a few months he was soliciting closer connection with the government on the grounds that this alone could help him justify to his constituents his refusal to stand with O'Connell. In 1839 he sought the vacant vice-presidency of the Board of Trade, explaining beseechingly that his 'great object' was to hold such an office if only for a short period. A fragile ministry desperate to bolster its support in the Commons duly appeased him. And when Melbourne undertook a last minute reconstruction of his government in 1841, he finally appointed Sheil to the position he had long sought, that of judge advocate. Melbourne's earlier objection to this promotion had been the fact that it would give an Irish Roman Catholic and an 'agitator' frequent access to the queen as well as control of the discipline of the army. However, now asked whether the appointment would be disliked, she surprisingly replied that she would not object because she had a 'high opinion' of Sheil.

The 1841 general election, a tory triumph, found Sheil sitting for the less taxing constituency of Dungarvan. Throughout the Peel administration he continued to make his mark as a trenchant critic of the government. At the same time, he spoke as one of a handful of Irish Liberal Unionists who continued to urge the conciliation of their native land as an alternative to O'Connell's ever more popular demand for repeal. Nevertheless, perhaps to retain his credibility in Ireland, he served in 1844 as counsel to one of the traversers, John O'Connell, in the trials which followed the suppression of the monster repeal meetings. In a long and powerful opening address, whose wide publicity he had thoughtfully arranged before leaving London, he restated his conviction that Ireland's grievances were rooted in the colonial attitude of Britain. 'The union has never been carried into effect', he protested, having long since warned that to draw 'odious distinctions' between England and Ireland, to insist that they required different laws, was to provide repealers with a more 'plausible pretence' that they also required different lawgivers (MacNevin, 291). The year 1845 was largely devoted to desperate attempts to halt the deterioration in the health of his son, only for him to die on the island of Madeira in November. Sheil was on hand the following spring, however, to participate in the ousting of Peel and receive a reward. He was appointed master of the Royal Mint, which he flattered himself was an office just below cabinet rank. The last politician to occupy the position, but the first Roman Catholic to be sworn a member of the privy council since the reign of James II, it fell to him to announce the government's compromise with the demands for decimalization by minting a florin at one-tenth of a pound. Unfortunately, the omission of the traditional Latin contractions for 'By grace of God defender of the faith' from the side bearing the queen's image was regarded in some quarters as a sinister manifestation of the master's religion. Instead, the simplified inscription had been suggested by Prince Albert, but Sheil was obliged to apologize for the change, which was corrected on the second issue of the coin in 1851. He was more successful in the appointment in February 1848 of a royal commission, with himself in the chair, to examine the structure and expenses of the mint, but resigned the mastership before any of its recommendations could be implemented.

During these years Sheil spoke infrequently, and rarely at length, in the house. He did pay a short tribute to O'Connell following the Liberator's death in May 1847 and took this opportunity briefly to discuss the famine. He denied that it was merely a provincial problem, acknowledged that some men had permitted 'national kindness' to be overcome 'by their austere political economy' and observed that Britain would happily spend a fortune on a war. Irish gratitude for assistance, he added, would be commensurate with English generosity (*Hansard 3*, 93.1013–16).

Final years By 1850 Sheil was anxious to retire from the political fray, having long suffered painfully from gout and having become alarmingly dependent on an opiate which friends feared was far from safe. Further, the 'infamous ingratitude of this vile populace' made his return for Dungarvan increasingly problematic (Sheil to Hope, 6 Aug 1847, NL Ire., Wyse MS 15026). In 1848 Russell had seriously considered dispatching him to Greece as minister there. On 4 November 1850 he did nominate him minister to Tuscany. The allure of Italy was its history and gentler climate, while Florence had been the scene of Shirley's play which had been the basis of his greatest success as a dramatist. However, in departing a Britain convulsed by a frenzy of anti-Catholicism released by the pope's announcement of the restoration of a Catholic hierarchy in England, and Russell's unfortunate Durham letter, Sheil entertained hopes of being the instrument of reconciliation between faith and nation, hence his determined assertion of his authority over the resident British agent in Rome. But he was denied the time in which to achieve anything of substance. He arrived in Florence on 26 January 1851 and died suddenly, probably of a heart attack, on the morning of Sunday 25 May, only two days after he and his wife received the tragic news of her son's death in Ireland. Following an impressive funeral at the church of San Michelino, attended by Tuscan ministers and the entire diplomatic corps, Mrs Sheil requested as a final mark of respect that the body be transported home to Ireland aboard a naval vessel. Only after much dithering was this done. Sheil's remains were delivered to Dublin on 24 February 1852, and interred at his home, Long Orchard, co. Tipperary.

If Sheil's career, and life, expired in the relative diplomatic obscurity of the Tuscany mission, this was a fate he had invited. Indeed, the sense of anticlimax had long been palpable. His fame had been won at a very young age, first as a dramatist and then as a demagogue. Yet few of his plays had enjoyed more than transitory success, and his reputation as a dramatist was to suffer because of their lack of realism. His powers of speech did see him make the transition from agitator to orator. Giants on the parliamentary stage, such as Gladstone and Disraeli, singled him out for praise, yet within two generations of his death Justin McCarthy could write that he was nothing more than an orator, that he had failed to leave a mark on parliament or politics and had allowed his career to fade away into 'second class ministerial office'. There is a large measure of truth in the last accusation. Nevertheless, Lecky did

embrace him as one of the *Leaders of Public Opinion in Ireland* and acknowledged that his speeches met Burke's test of perfect oratory—'half poetry, half prose'—but was critical of the profusion of ornaments and the paucity of spontaneity. There have been modern echoes of this criticism, with both his literary style and his public speaking dismissed as 'stilted'.

Such cavils do less than justice to Sheil. Fashions in oratory inevitably change over time, but in his day Sheil captivated members of parliament just as earlier he had swept away throngs of Irishmen. Moreover, there was a consistent and modernist theme to his many well-constructed and carefully crafted speeches on Ireland. He argued that inequalities—economic, social, sectarian, and political—were breeders of discontent and violence. 'If something not be done by those who ought to derive a warning from the past', he repeatedly cautioned, if they

> do not in time adopt the measures requisite to correct abuses proved and indisputable, the next requisition for change, which shall be made, perhaps by an excited people, will be far more formidable than that which we propose, and may lead to consequences by which the worst prognostications may be realized. (MacNevin, 254)

He voiced the fear that 'the spirit of eminence and masterdom' was 'so fixedly settled' in the English that they could never bring themselves to regard Irishmen as their equals (*Hansard 3*, 87.1013).

That Sheil placed the greatest emphasis on existing political inequalities reflected his personal ambition for advancement and desire for full integration within the United Kingdom. No doubt his political reputation has suffered because he was found, eventually, on the wrong side of history. Persuaded that repeal was a dead end, he accepted the status of a west Briton. Unlike O'Connell, he never spoke of his 'hatred' of Britain. However, he has received his due from modern historians of Catholic emancipation. His alliance with O'Connell has been described as 'absolutely crucial' to the successful launching of the Catholic Association (O'Ferrall, 31); James Reynolds has pointed out that the two men shared national popularity, while the Liberator's most recent biographer has acknowledged him as 'the foremost observer and delineator of the immediate in the Association' (Macdonagh, *The Hereditary Bondsman*, 244). Brian Jenkins

Sources W. T. McCullagh, *Memoirs of the Right Honourable Richard Lalor Sheil*, 2 vols. (1855) · T. MacNevin, ed., *Speeches of the Rt. Hon. Richard Lalor Sheil, with memoir* (1847) · *Sketches of the Irish bar by the Rt. Hon. Richard Lalor Sheil*, ed. R. S. MacKenzie, 2 vols. (1856) · 'Select committee on the state of Ireland: first report', *Parl. papers* (1825), 8.85–107, no. 129 [minutes of evidence] · *The correspondence of Daniel O'Connell*, ed. M. R. O'Connell, 8 vols. (1972–80) · Royal Arch., Melbourne papers, 35/104; 46/72, 74–5; 50/81; 50/83–4; 52/70–73 · Queen Victoria, journal, Jan–June 1841, Royal Arch. · Foreign Office, Tuscany, PRO, 79/147, 149, 150 · J. A. Reynolds, *The Catholic emancipation in Ireland, 1823–1829*, repr. edn (1970) · F. O'Ferrall, *Catholic emancipation: Daniel O'Connell and the birth of Irish democracy, 1820–30* (1985) · B. C. MacDermot, ed., *The Catholic question in Ireland and England, 1798–1822: the papers of Denys Scully* (1988) · A. Aspinall, ed., *Three early nineteenth-century diaries* (1952) [extracts from Le Marchant, E. J. Littleton, Baron Hatherton, and E. Law, earl of Ellenborough] · A. D. Kriegel, ed., *The Holland House diaries, 1831–1840* (1977) · D. D. Olien, *Morpeth: a Victorian public career* (1983) · W. E. H.

Lecky, *Leaders of public opinion in Ireland*, 2 vols. (1903) • W. T. McCullagh, *Memoirs of the Right Honourable Richard Lalor Sheil*, 2 vols. (1855) • J. Craig, *The mint: a history of the London mint from AD 287 to 1948* (1953) • R. Sloan, 'O'Connell's liberal rivals in 1843', *Irish Historical Studies*, 30 (1996–7), 47–65 • A. Nicoll, *Early nineteenth-century drama, 1800–1850*, 2nd edn (1966), vol. 4 of *A history of English drama* • J. W. Donohue, jun., *Dramatic character in the English romantic age* (1970) • O. Macdonagh, *The hereditary bondsman: Daniel O'Connell, 1775–1829* (1988) • O. Macdonagh, *The emancipist: Daniel O'Connell, 1830–1847* (1989) • B. Jenkins, *Era of emancipation: British government of Ireland, 1812–1830* (1988)

Archives University College, Dublin, political and personal corresp. | NL Ire., letters to his wife • U. Southampton L., corresp. with Lord Palmerston

Likenesses R. Cooper, stipple, pubd 1825 (after J. C. Smith), BM, NPG • C. Moore, marble bust, 1847, NG Ire. • W. Bewick, chalk drawing, Scot. NPG • T. Farrell, plaster bust, NG Ire. • J. Haverty, oils, NG Ire. [*see illus.*] • G. Hayter, group portrait, oils (*The House of Commons, 1833*), NPG • D. Maclise, caricature, lithograph, repro. in *Fraser's Magazine* (1834) • D. Maclise, preliminary sketch, V&A • engraving (after C. Moore), repro. in McCullagh, *Memoirs of … Richard Lalor Sheil*

Sheilds, Alexander (1659/60–1700), Presbyterian minister, was born at Haughhead, Earlston, Berwickshire, the son of a farmer, James Shields. Alexander attended Edinburgh University, graduating MA on 7 April 1675 'with no small applause'. After graduation he remained to study theology at Edinburgh under the tutelage of Lawrence Charteris, the son of Principal Henry Charteris, who like his father taught divinity at the university until he resigned because of the Test Act which forced many covenanters from office. In 1679 Sheild's own covenanting convictions led him, along with others, to flee Scotland for the Netherlands where, in 1680, he continued his theological studies at Utrecht.

After returning to Scotland he went to London, where he served as amanuensis to John Owen, the puritan theologian. Sheilds was licensed to preach by Scottish Presbyterians in London on the persuasion of Nicholas Blaikie, the minister of the Scottish church at Founder's Hall, Lothbury. However, Sheilds's unwillingness as a covenanter to take the oath of allegiance, and his preaching against such an oath, brought him to the attention of authorities who after 1684 sought strict enforcement of the oath. His name became linked in November 1684 to that of James Renwick initially through Sheilds's adherence to the 'Apologetical declaration' issued by the United Societies, an affiliation of covenanters to which Renwick belonged.

Sheilds was arrested by the city marshal at an illegal conventicle at Embroiderers' Hall, Gutter Lane, in Cheapside, on 11 January 1685, along with seven others. He was granted bail to appear at the Guildhall on 14 January. Sheilds failed to appear before the court and consequently forfeited his bail. He did appear on 20 January, but gave no account of his views and was committed to Newgate until the next quarter sessions, which were to be held on 23 February. Following Charles II's death on 6 February the decision was made to remit Sheilds and his compatriots to Scotland's judgment on 5 March, without benefit of an English trial. He was examined by the Scottish privy council on 14

March and subsequently (23 and 25 March) also by the lords justices. In all of these appearances Sheilds reportedly declined 'direct answers'. Finally, on 26 March, he was forced on pain of torture to sign the statement he described as his 'fatal fall', renouncing all activities in which he engaged 'in so far as they declare war against the king'. Unfortunately for him, a letter to his friend John Balfour of Kinloch, in which he expressed his regret at having falsely signed this statement, was intercepted by officials who sent archbishops Arthur Ross and Alexander Cairncross and Bishop Andrew Bruce to question Sheilds. On 6 August Sheilds was again brought before the lords justices who sentenced him to imprisonment on the Bass Rock. After fourteen months' imprisonment he escaped in November 1686 disguised as a woman and sought out James Renwick.

Despite Sheilds's defection and 'fall' Renwick accepted him back into the covenanters' fold and helped him to regain the trust of members of the societies. Sheilds assisted in revising the 'Informatory vindication', the classic apologetical text of the Cameronians or Society people. Sheilds's own book, *A Hind Let Loose*, also written at this time, offers a historical defence of the position he and Renwick took. Sheilds reveals the depths of his own struggle with this position in his 22 December confession to a gathering of Renwick's followers of the guilt he suffered for 'owning the so-called authority of James VII'.

In 1687 Sheilds returned to Utrecht to seek the publication of both the 'Informatory vindication' and his own work, travelling back to Scotland when both books were at press (both were published in 1687). Upon publication, *A Hind Let Loose* was so feared by authorities in Edinburgh that copies were ordered to be destroyed. After Renwick was executed at the Grassmarket, Edinburgh, on 17 February 1688 on a charge of treason, Sheilds engaged in the same kind of open field preaching which had characterized Renwick's work. In April 1688 he denounced the execution at a gathering at Distinkhorn Hill in Galston parish, Kyle Stewart, and memorialized Renwick in *An Elegie upon the Death of Mr. James Renwick* (1688) and at greater length in the posthumously published *The Life and Death of Mr. James Renwick* (1724).

Sheilds became a vigorous apologist for the Cameronians and, with Thomas Lining and William Boyd, served as one of the societies' three ministers. He approved of the societies' 1688 insurrection under the leadership of Daniel Ker, in which ministers of churches in the west of Scotland were forcibly removed from their charges. He was present at a gathering at the cross of Douglas, Lanarkshire, where these activities were defended, and he provided a vindication of the position taken by the societies with regard to their refusal to adhere to the ministers who had taken the declarations of indulgence, whom they regarded as Erastian. Sheilds and the societies became champions of the cause of William of Orange, in support of whom the Cameronian regiment was raised to fight against James in the revolution of 1688. On 3 March 1689, along with Lining and Boyd, Sheilds took part in a renewal of the covenants at Borland Hill, Lanark-shire, of which he wrote *The Renovation of the Covenant at Boreland* (1689).

In 1690 Sheilds finally decided that he should become reconciled to the Church of Scotland: thus Sheilds, Lining, and Boyd presented two documents to the first general assembly under the Presbyterian settlement. The first consisted of a collection of grievances which the assembly refused to read publicly so as not 'to kindle contentions'. The second document set out terms of submission on the part of the societies' three ministers, marking their recognition that the reconstituted Church of Scotland was a true church and requesting that they be received into its fellowship. The submission was dated 22 October; it was accepted by the assembly three days later, when the assembly admonished Sheilds and his colleagues 'to walk orderly in time coming'.

Sheilds received an appointment on 4 February 1691 to serve as chaplain to the Cameronian regiment raised in 1689 by James, earl of Angus. On the same day he was called to serve with Thomas Forrester in the parish of St Andrews, though he was not admitted to this charge until 15 September 1697. This was Sheilds only charge to a parish ministry, and he remained there for just under two years before a commission of the general assembly authorized him to accompany three other ministers and a group of colonists to the Darien (or New Caledonia) Colony in Central America 'to labour among the heathen'. Sailing from Rothesay on 24 September the company, including Sheilds and his brother Michael, reached Darien on 30 November, but not before no less than 160 of their number had died at sea. In a letter to the moderator of the commission of the general assembly Sheilds reported that 'one hundred and thirty are sick on shore and forty or fifty are dead already'. The colonists 'do scandalise the natives', Sheilds continued, 'by stealing from them and by teaching them both to swear and drink'. The only people about whom Sheilds was able to report positively were the indigenous people themselves, whose hospitality and kindness particularly impressed him (Barr, 243). Sheilds's work as a missionary was cut short when, after only a few inland expeditions, he travelled to Jamaica with Francis Borland and there contracted a fever. He died on 14 June 1700 in the home of Isabel Murray, a fellow Scot, at Port Royal, Jamaica. By the time of his death at the age of forty, 'much lamented by all those who knew his worth and parts' (*Fasti Scot.*, 1.400), Sheilds had given up on the mission and was determined to return to Britain.

Among his other books to be published after his death were *Church Communion Enquired Into* (1706) and the autobiographical tract *True and Faithful Relation of the Sufferings of Alexander Shields* (1715).   MICHAEL JINKINS

Sources DNB · A. Shields, *A true and faithful relation of the sufferings of Alexander Shields* (1715) · P. Walker and A. Shields, *Biographia Presbyteriana*, ed. J. Stevenson, 2 vols. (1827) · H. Macpherson, *The covenanters under persecution* (1923) · H. Macpherson, *The Cameronian philosopher: Alexander Shields* (1932) · J. Barr, *The Scottish covenanters* (1947) · A. Smellie, *Men of the covenant* (1903) · I. B. Cowan, *The Scottish covenanters, 1660–1688* (1976) · J. H. Thomson, *The martyr graves of Scotland*, ed. M. Hutchinson (1903) · J. D. Douglas, *Light in the north: the story of the Scottish covenanters* (1964) · *Fasti Scot.*, 1.400

Wealth at death library at St Andrews valued at £1, and property at £6483 16s. 10d.: DNB

Shelburne. For this title name *see* Petty, William, second earl of Shelburne and first marquess of Lansdowne (1737–1805).

Sheldon, Dominic (*b.* in or before **1633**, *d.* **1721**), army officer, was the son of Edward *Sheldon (1599–1687), member of a cadet branch of the long-established Catholic Sheldon family of Beoley, Worcestershire, and Mary, daughter of Lionel Wake of Antwerp. In his youth he supported Charles II against Cromwell and first served abroad as a lieutenant in Sir Henry Jones's regiment of light horse in France. He saw action at Maastricht in 1673 and in the Rhineland campaign in the following year, at Sinsheim, Ensheim, and Mulhouse. He was promoted captain-lieutenant in the regiment, now commanded by the duke of Monmouth, on 5 October 1674, and served at Turckheim and Consarbrick in 1675, and in 1676 at the sieges of Condé, Bouchain, and Aire. He returned to England when his regiment was disbanded and was appointed captain-lieutenant of Monmouth's new regiment of horse, virtually reformed from his old unit, on 9 February 1678, but the subsequent purge of Catholic officers saw him re-enter French service for the years 1679–85. With the accession of James II he was appointed captain in the Irish foot guards and in 1686 lieutenant-colonel of the earl of Tyrconnell's regiment of horse. He accompanied Mary of Modena to France and was appointed a colonel of horse in James II's army in Ireland on 14 January 1689. He rose to the rank of brigadier-general later that year, and of major-general in 1690, and fought at the Boyne (1690) and at Aughrim (1691), where he commanded the left wing of the Jacobite cavalry. During the absence in France of Lord Deputy Tyrconnell in 1690–91 he served on the council assisting the duke of Berwick.

Following the treaty of Limerick, Sheldon commanded the first body of Irish soldiers shipped to France to form James's army in exile. In January 1692 he was appointed colonel of the first, the King's regiment of horse, and was promoted to mestre de camp de cavalerie on 11 February 1693 and brigadier on 3 March 1694. He fought in the French campaigns in Germany in 1694–6 and then served on the Meuse (1696) and on the Moselle (1697). After the peace of Ryswick the King's and Queen's regiments of horse were amalgamated as Sheldon's regiment of horse on 15 February 1698. With the outbreak of the War of the Spanish Succession he led his regiment on campaign in Germany and then in Italy, at Mantua, Cremona, and Santa Vittoria. He rose to maréchal de camp on 21 February 1702 and lieutenant-general on 26 October 1704, and served with his regiment until January 1706. Subsequently he was employed by James III (James Francis Edward Stuart), accompanying him to Scotland in 1708 and 1715. He died in France in 1721, having never married, and leaving no children.

Dominic Sheldon's brother **Ralph Sheldon** (1633–1723)

was born at Ditchford in 1633 and was appointed a lieutenant in the duke of Buckingham's regiment of foot in 1672. In the same year he joined his elder brother in Sir Henry Jones's regiment as a cornet, serving alongside Dominic Sheldon in France in 1674-6 and in the French service in 1679-85. Having returned to England in 1685, he was appointed lieutenant of an independent troop of horse, then equerry to James II. He sailed with James to France and remained with the Jacobite court until his death in 1723. He had married Elizabeth, daughter of Daniel Dunn of West Heath, Worcestershire, with whom he had a son, William, and a daughter, Christina, who married her father's uncle Arthur Dillon, colonel-proprietor of a family regiment in the Irish brigade in French service.

P. J. C. ELLIOT-WRIGHT

Sources J. C. O'Callaghan, *History of the Irish brigades in the service of France*, [new edn] (1870), 48, 152-3 · J. C. R. Childs, *Nobles, gentlemen and the profession of arms in Restoration Britain, 1660-1688: a biographical dictionary of British army officers on foreign service* (1987), 84 · T. B. Minney, 'The Sheldons of Beoley', *Worcestershire Recusant*, 5 (1965), 1-17 · T. R. Nash, *History and antiquities of Worcestershire*, 2 vols. and suppl. (1781-99), 1.62-73 · Gillow, *Lit. biog. hist.*, 5.499-500 · *CSP dom.*, 1673-5, 374, 587; 1687-9 · M. H. Massue de Ruvigny, ed., *The Jacobite peerage* (1904), 218-20, 223, 238, 243 · M. O'Conor, *Military history of the Irish nation* (1845), 240-41, 256, 269-70 · E. A. B. Barnard, *The Sheldons* (1936) · C. Dalton, ed., *English army lists and commission registers, 1661-1714*, 1 (1892), 120 · G. Duckett, ed., *Penal laws and Test Act*, 2 (1883), 88, 134

Sheldon, Edward (1599-1687), translator, was born on 23 April 1599 at Beoley, Worcestershire, the third of the six children of Edward Sheldon (*bap.* 1566, *d.* 1643) and his wife, Elizabeth (*c.*1565-1630), daughter of Thomas Markham of Ollerton, Nottinghamshire, and his wife, Mary Griffin. He became a gentleman commoner at Gloucester Hall, Oxford, about 1613, and was admitted to Gray's Inn, London, on 1 March 1620. He then returned to Oxford, matriculating as a member of University College on 19 November 1621. After travelling on the continent for several years, he returned to the family house at Stratton, near Cirencester, 'which at length he lost, or was forced to quit, for the cause of king Charles I and for his religion' (Wood, *Ath. Oxon.*, 4.206: 1). An Edward Sheldon was one of the garrison of Worcester when it surrendered in July 1646 after attempting to hold the city for Charles.

Sheldon's translations provide evidence of his committed Catholicism. His first published work was *The Holy Life of Monsr. Renty* (1658), which Wood describes as having been 'mangled by an Irish priest when it went to press' (Wood, *Ath. Oxon.*, 4.206: 2). He went on to publish *The Rule of Catholick Faith* (1660), an English version of François Véron's *Règle générale de la foy catholique*, and two later translations from French, *Christian Thoughts for every Day in the Month* and *Counsels of Wisdom*, were both published in London in 1680. Of these, his translation of Véron's work, later described as 'one of the most hazardous and difficult [tasks] a mere layman could have undertaken' (*Catholic Miscellany*), appears to have been most controversial; although it too was printed in London, in 1660, its title-page claims publication in Paris.

Sheldon married Mary, daughter of Lionel Wake, a merchant of Antwerp and of Pedington, Northamptonshire. His Catholic and royalist connections remained strong. Of their fifteen children, Bridget and Teresa became nuns, and another daughter, Mary, married the royalist Sir Samuel Tuke. Both Dominic *Sheldon and Ralph (*d.* 1723) served James II, while Lionel (*d.* 1678) was a Benedictine monk and chaplain to James's first wife, Anne. Ralph, his wife Elizabeth, and his brother Edward were among the Catholics who paid for the keep of Archbishop Plunket when he was imprisoned in London, and witnessed the removal of Plunket's head and arms as relics after his execution. Two other daughters, Frances and Katharine, were maids of honour and dressers to Charles II's wife, Catherine, to whom Sheldon dedicated his *Counsels of Wisdom*, 'Being desirous in these distracted times to offer something that is serious, and may invite People and direct them to the way of Virtue' (1680, sig. A2r). One of the copies in the Bodleian Library was given to Anthony Wood by Frances Sheldon. Sheldon died at his house in St James's Street, Westminster, on 27 March 1687, and was buried under the chapel at Somerset House.

THOMPSON COOPER, *rev.* JANE GRIFFITHS

Sources Wood, *Ath. Oxon.*, new edn · *The life and times of Anthony Wood*, ed. A. Clark, 5 vols., OHS, 19, 21, 26, 30, 40 (1891-1900) · H. Foley, ed., *Records of the English province of the Society of Jesus*, 5 (1879) · T. Nash, *Collections for the history of Worcestershire*, 1 (1781) · J. Humphreys, *Elizabethan Sheldon tapestries* (1929) · T. H. Clancy, *English Catholic books, 1641-1700: a bibliography* [1974] · Wing, *STC* · *Reg. Oxf.*, vol. 2/1-2 · Foster, *Alum. Oxon.* · J. Foster, *The register of admissions to Gray's Inn, 1521-1889, together with the register of marriages in Gray's Inn chapel, 1695-1754* (privately printed, London, 1889) · E. A. B. Barnard, *The Sheldons* (1936) · *IGI* · *Catholic Miscellany*, 6 (1826), 73

Sheldon, Gilbert (1598-1677), archbishop of Canterbury, was born, according to the autograph notes in his bible, on the morning of 19 June 1598 and baptized on 22 June at Stanton, Staffordshire. He was the youngest son of Roger Sheldon (*d.* 1635), member of an ancient and well-to-do family and bailiff to Gilbert Talbot, seventh earl of Shrewsbury, for whom he had 'speciall imployments and trusts'. The earl stood as godfather to Gilbert Sheldon, who was named after him; the other godfather was Robert Sanderson, father of the future bishop of the same name.

The University of Oxford Sheldon matriculated at Oxford on 1 July 1614, graduated BA from Trinity College on 27 November 1617, was incorporated at Cambridge in 1619, and proceeded MA on 28 June 1620. In November 1621 he was elected a probationer of All Souls and admitted as a fellow on 14 January 1623. On 23 May 1624 he was made deacon by the bishop of Oxford at Dorchester and was presumably ordained priest then or shortly afterwards. In the mid-1620s Sheldon became domestic chaplain to the lord keeper, Coventry, and served him as an examining chaplain. Charles I intended Sheldon to be master of the Savoy and dean of Westminster 'that he might better attend on his royal person' (Beddard, 'Memoir', 45). On 11 November 1628 Sheldon gained the degree of BD. This may well have been the occasion when he rattled the academic and theological dovecotes by denying that the pope was Antichrist:

Gilbert Sheldon (1598–1677), by Sir Peter Lely, c.1665–9

he was the first, according to the memory of Thomas Barlow, to voice this shocking denial of a fundamental axiom of the Calvinist establishment.

Sheldon's university career flourished. He was a sympathizer with and possibly a protégé of Archbishop William Laud, chancellor of the university. On 25 June 1634 he completed the academic exercises for the degree of DD by arguing against the propositions that the pope had the power to depose Christian princes and that clerics are exempted by God's law from obedience to secular rulers and by asserting that it was permissible to oblige Roman Catholics in England to swear allegiance. In March 1635 Sheldon was elected warden of All Souls. He served the university in various roles: in 1634 and 1640 he was pro-vice-chancellor; in 1638 he took part in the visitation of Merton College. Sheldon, perhaps characteristically, was stern in his denunciation of the warden, Nathanael Brent:

> if I were conscious of such carelessness of the main affairs of this college, or of such practising upon the company, for the wasting of the common stock and my own advantage, I should not have the face to endure a visitation, but should lay the key under the door and be gone. (Trevor-Roper, 356)

As was usual in the seventeenth century Sheldon's rise

within the university also brought with it preferment within the church: on 26 February 1632 he was installed as prebendary of Gloucester; in 1633 he became vicar of Hackney; in 1636 rector of Oddington, Oxfordshire, and Ickford, Buckinghamshire, and a royal chaplain; and in 1639 he became rector of Newington, Oxfordshire.

Accounts of Sheldon's early career have been coloured by Edward Hyde, earl of Clarendon's nostalgic memoir of the high-minded gatherings at Lord Falkland's country house at Great Tew in Oxfordshire. Sheldon, along with other luminaries of the University of Oxford and the wider world of politics and learning, attended and impressed his host, Hyde, and several others with his learning, gravity, and prudence. Clarendon's hindsight undoubtedly invested these social occasions with more significance than they originally possessed, indeed Tew stood as a symbol of what had been lost by civil wars and puritan revolution, but connections and friendships were established by Sheldon in these years which were to be sustained for decades. The close friendship which he established with Richard Newdigate of Arbury lasted for half a century: from Oxford, Sheldon kept the Newdigate family in touch with literary fashions, political news, and the most recent sermons; he visited them, lobbied on their behalf, and prayed by their bedsides.

The civil war When the regime of Charles I began to unravel in 1640 Sheldon was four-square behind his monarch and encouraged his friend Hyde's efforts to rally support for so-called constitutional royalism. Like several other heads of colleges Sheldon took the protestation oath of 1642 only with qualifications, which emphasized his obedience to royal authority. During the civil war Sheldon waited on Charles I at Oxford and elsewhere. About 1646 he was appointed clerk of the closet. He seems to have been trusted as a political as well as a spiritual adviser for he certainly participated in various peace negotiations. In February 1644 Sheldon took part in the talks for the treaty of Uxbridge but his strenuous arguments in defence of the Church of England may have alienated the other parties to the negotiations.

Sheldon's role did not diminish after the defeat of the royalists. In June 1647 Charles asked Sir Thomas Fairfax for his chaplains Sheldon and Henry Hammond and, despite the protests of MPs, the request was granted. Sheldon appears to have been with Charles at Hatfield and New-market in the summer of 1647. That summer he took extensive soundings from leading Anglican clergy such as Bishop Robert Skinner, Bishop Thomas Morton, and Archbishop James Ussher about the possibility of a religious toleration as the basis of a potential treaty between the king and his adversaries. In 1648 Charles once again sought the presence of Sheldon and Hammond, but although parliament acceded the two chaplains did not reach the Isle of Wight because they were under detention at Oxford.

During the war years Sheldon had remained active in university life at Oxford. There are glimpses of him pursuing the duties of a royal chaplain; lodging his friend Hyde in All Souls; seeking the signatures of academics to the royalist loyalty oath imposed in April 1645; and urging the university's rights in the negotiations for the surrender of Oxford in 1646. He took a leading part in the university's resistance to the parliamentary visitation of 1647, but to no avail. He was officially ejected from the wardenship of All Souls by the visitors on 30 March 1648 and when he refused to surrender his lodgings they ordered his forcible removal and detention. So many well-wishers visited him in prison that the authorities tried unsuccessfully to move him and Hammond to Wallingford Castle. It is unclear how long Sheldon remained incarcerated. A. G. Matthews claimed that entries in the parish register at Ickford indicated that Sheldon was there between 7 May 1648 and 27 December 1650—although he had been ejected from the benefice by November 1646. Other sources claim that Sheldon was released from prison or, more likely, house arrest in Oxford at the end of 1648 on condition that he did not go within 5 miles of Oxford or of the king's gaol in the Isle of Wight. A draft letter of 15 January 1649 survives, in which he describes himself as having been 'a stranger to the world for these nine months' but 'I now conceive myself as good as at liberty & intend about a week hence to make my first journye to our friends in the forrest' (Pocock, 15.182). Whether the 'forrest' was a real location or a metaphor for the refuge of a royalist in the darkest days of the Stuart cause is not clear. Sheldon was 'unresolved' about whether to join the royalist exiles on the continent. In the event he retired to the midlands, basing himself variously in Derbyshire, Leicestershire, Nottinghamshire, and Staffordshire. He spent long periods at Sir Robert Shirley's house at Staunton Harold, with his Okeover relatives at East Bridgford, Nottinghamshire, at his brother's house in Stanton, and visited the Pakingtons, Coventrys, and Yelvertons. Although he is recorded at Petersham Lodge in autumn 1658 Sheldon rarely ventured south despite the fact that many Anglican clergy lived unmolested in London throughout the 1650s.

The interregnum Sheldon's role in royalist and Anglican circles during the 1650s can be reconstructed in outline from his remarkable incoming correspondence, most of which seems to have been addressed to him care of his nephew Joseph Sheldon at the house of Mr Price, a woollen draper, at the Gold Key in St Paul's Churchyard. Although some of Sheldon's own letters survived and were later printed by Barwick, it is the letters to him from Hammond, Bishop Matthew Wren, Bishop Brian Duppa, Dr Robert Payne, and Dr John Barwick that reveal him as a trusted intermediary in the royalist cause and a man of wide and discriminating intellectual interests.

In 1649 Hyde had assured Sheldon that 'you are one of those few by whose advice and example I shall most absolutely guide myself, and upon whose friendship I have an entire and absolute dependence' (Bosher, 55). Nor was this mere formal compliment, for Hyde clearly used Sheldon as a channel for communicating with the remnants of the Church of England's leadership. In October 1651 Hammond wrote to Bishop Wren, the most senior of the bishops, who was imprisoned in the Tower, that Sheldon had urged him to exhort the surviving bishops 'to think of

doing somewhat to preserve a church amongst us, lest it perish with their order' (Pocock, 9.294). The continuation of the ministry by further consecrations to the episcopate and by episcopal ordination of ministers was an urgent problem for the Church of England. The other was the dilemma over whether to use the proscribed Book of Common Prayer or to find some way of compromising over the liturgy. Sheldon's own view of the resulting schism and confusion was dramatically expressed in a letter of January 1653:

> Amongst those that either are, or would be thought loyal subjects to the King and obedient sons of this Church, there is great diversity of opinion and practice about Prayer and the public worship of God; some believing themselves excused by the times, if they wholly omit it, some contriving the substance of it into a prayer of their own making; supposing they have done their duty, if they pray nothing against the old form; other retain part, some more, some less, according to their several judgment; and some again holding themselves obliged to use all, according to their former engagements; and not so much as to communicate with any that use it not (supposing them schismatical). (Barwick, 537)

The solutions which Sheldon seems to have proposed in schemes which John Barwick laid before Wren are revealing. Sheldon wanted the bishops to make a ruling which their scattered and harassed clergy could then follow. He seems to have contemplated a relaxation of the rule of absolute conformity to the prayer book with resignation if not equanimity. He argued that the bishops had authority to do this since they were reduced to the 'primitive' state of the early church 'under a civil authority, though not pagan, yet clearly antichristian, and such as endeavour to destroy the Church of God'. If they demurred the exiled king could be approached for a commission by which no more than three of the bishops could dispense with or temper 'the old laws' (ibid., 541).

In May 1654 a meeting of the leading Anglican bishops and clergy was called at Richmond, home of Bishop Duppa, to address these issues and in particular to stiffen the backbones of some of the Anglican clergy who seemed to be weakening—both Jeremy Taylor and Robert Sanderson were thought to be in danger of complying with the authorities to some degree. Judging by their letters Hammond, Duppa, and others regarded Sheldon as vital to this effort, yet he did not attend, the meeting fizzled out, and there were no more concerted attempts by the Anglican clergy to perpetuate their episcopate. Sheldon still remained prominent in Anglican circles in the later 1650s, when the churchmen were harassed in several ways: 'and yet we go on' as Taylor wrote to Sheldon in December 1657, 'and shall till we can go on no longer' (Bosher, 43). In May 1659 when Hyde once again mooted the idea that new bishops be consecrated in England, Sheldon's name was prominent on the list of his preferred candidates.

Sheldon's correspondence of the 1650s attests to the bookish interests of Sheldon and his circle during their enforced leisure. The virtuoso Robert Payne, ejected canon of Christ Church and an early admirer of Thomas

Hobbes, wrote to Sheldon with news and snippets from the works of Hobbes, Gassendi, and Athanasius Kircher. Sheldon asked George Morley to send him Catholic books of devotion from Antwerp. Hammond expected Sheldon's advice on his own writings: he asked for his views on Grotius's annotations of the scriptures, the Ignatian epistles and other patristic matters, but he also wanted to know whether Sheldon thought the time right to reply to the presbyterian critics of episcopacy. Sheldon was thought to have better political antennae and greater influence than most of his brethren, and he was encouraged to think so himself, as Hyde wrote to him in October 1659, 'when you meet, as meet you will, I think you will be satisfied with [the King], and nobody is like to do so much good upon him as you are, for sure he reverences nobody more' (Bosher, 136).

Restoration of monarchy and church, 1660–1663 The restoration of the monarchy was the work of presbyterian politicians and clergy. At first Anglicans like Sheldon could only watch and wait. Throughout the winter of 1659–60 the leaders of the Church of England began to gather in London: on 27 April 1660 Sheldon arrived in the capital and met Morley, the envoy of the exiled court; on 4 May a meeting of the clerical leaders, including Duppa, Wren, John Warner, Morley, and Barwick, took place and Sheldon was almost certainly also present. Charles Stuart landed at Dover on 25 May to be greeted by the presbyterians. At Canterbury the following evening he had a private meeting with Sheldon. Now that Charles and Hyde were back in England they responded to the realities on the ground and to circumstances rather than following a premeditated plan. Several interests and parties had to be placated and Sheldon and his brethren were only one group among many. Hyde, ennobled as earl of Clarendon, ensured that responsibilities and honours were spread widely. In mid-June Sheldon, John Earle, and Morley were entrusted with deciding on some of the many petitions for presentations to crown benefices. Sheldon became dean of the Chapel Royal and when he was called upon to preach before the king at Whitehall on 28 June 1660, a day set aside for thanksgiving for the return of the monarchy, he trod carefully so as not to alienate presbyterian and puritan feeling. In his sermon, published as *Davids Deliverance and Thanksgiving* (1660), he acknowledged 'the Registers of his Providence', and lamented the debauchery, the impiety, the ingratitude which reigned still among the impudent English—a safely uncontentious blanket charge (p. 13). In August 1660 Bishop Brian Duppa wrote to Sheldon: 'you are the only person about his majesty that I have confidence in and I persuade myself that as none hath his ear more, so none is likely to prevail on his heart more, and there was never more need of it' (Bodl. Oxf., MS Tanner 40, fol. 17). Others like William Nicholson wrote in equally flattering style of Sheldon's proximity to power. But there is a question mark over Sheldon's real influence on the king or political decision making. He certainly reaped the rewards of his loyal service: on 21 September 1660 he was nominated to the bishopric of London in succession to William Juxon. On 9 October he was elected;

this was confirmed on 23 October and on 28 October he was consecrated alongside Morley, Humphrey Henchman, George Griffith, and Sanderson in Henry VII's chapel at Westminster Abbey by Bishops Duppa, Accepted Frewen, Wren, Warner, and Henry King. John Sudbury's sermon was an unabashed paean to episcopacy. The service was followed by a feast at Haberdashers' Hall. There were, however, several individuals among the first round of appointments to the episcopate who would never have been nominated by Sheldon. Indeed he actually disapproved of some of the candidates, such as John Gauden.

Sheldon's influence at court is difficult to gauge. He quickly acquired the reputation of an *éminence grise*. He had been appointed master of the Savoy, where the 1661 Savoy Conference of 1661 between presbyterians and episcopalians was held, and although he rarely attended sessions it was widely believed that he knew more of the king's mind than any other. Whatever his personal sway Sheldon appreciated the need for political organization. In April 1661 he was a moving force behind the election of clerical representatives to convocation in an attempt to outflank the presbyterian party. When two presbyterians, Richard Baxter and Edmund Calamy, were elected by the London clergy Bishop Sheldon found a loophole which allowed him to 'excuse' them from service. After the failure of the Savoy conference, convocation devoted itself to revising the Book of Common Prayer so that it could be attached to an act of uniformity which was under consideration in parliament.

The Cavalier Parliament, which met in 1661, was of paramount importance to the future of the Church of England, and Sheldon proved to be a consummate parliamentary politician. He had to be, for two reasons. The first was that Charles and Clarendon contemplated a far more conciliatory and permissive religious settlement than suited Sheldon's view of the Church of England. Parliament, therefore, would have to be used as a lever on royal policy. The second reason was that contrary to widespread assumptions this assembly was not overwhelmingly Anglican, nor full of reactionary gentry determined to stamp out puritanism and drive every subject into the national church. It needed leadership and management if it was to protect the Church of England. Although sparsely documented Sheldon's role is apparent after November 1661 when the bishops had returned to the House of Lords and Sheldon kept up a steady pressure on his brethren to attend in person, to vote in the interests of the king and the church, and to send him their proxies. Sheldon's relations with the small group of MPs who were his allies in the Commons were less formal. Men such as Sir Job Charleton, Sir John Bramston, Sir Heneage Finch, Sir Thomas Fanshaw, Sir John Berkenhead, Sir Thomas Meres, Sir Henry Yelverton, and John Vaughan were committed to the Church of England and naturally deferred to its primate. These MPs were the workhorses behind the religious and ecclesiastical legislation of the period. They gave the lead which their backbench colleagues would follow. And they took their cue from Sheldon.

In politics Sheldon was adroit, pragmatic, and flexible,

but he had his limits. For example, in February 1662 Sheldon and other bishops allowed themselves to be persuaded by Clarendon to wreck a Commons measure which would turf presbyterian incumbents out of their livings. Why would Sheldon assist Clarendon to keep presbyterians within the church? He probably preferred another strategy to oust them. The failed measure was transferred to the Uniformity Bill which his allies in the Commons had produced. On 19 May 1662 Charles II gave his assent to the Act of Uniformity which brought together the revised prayer book, the clauses requiring presbyterian incumbents to accept episcopal ordination or leave their livings, and the other stipulations of total liturgical conformity and obedience to episcopal authority. But Sheldon's work was not at an end. There were real threats to the act. Nervous of its consequences Clarendon proposed its postponement or moderation. Sheldon took a stand and told the privy council that to suspend a law 'would not only render the parliament cheap, and have influence upon all other laws, but in truth let in a visible confusion upon Church and State' (Seaward, *Cavalier Parliament*, 180). He wrote angrily to Clarendon complaining of this 'great unkindness' in exposing him to the hatred of parliament or of 'that malicious party in whose jaws I must live' (Bodl. Oxf., MS Clarendon 77, fol. 319), and he took care that his views were known: Sir John Berkenhead's *Mercurius Publicus* published an account with the same phraseology as Sheldon's letter; and Yelverton wrote to friends of how 'the prudence and wisdom of my Lord of London' had foiled the presbyterians (Bodl. Oxf., MS Eng. lett. C 210, fol. 78).

Archbishop of Canterbury Sheldon's elevation to the archbishopric of Canterbury on the death of Juxon was a foregone conclusion. He had already been effectively deputizing for the frail and elderly archbishop, performing his role at Charles II's coronation, and receiving a commission in November 1661 to consecrate the new Scottish bishops. On 6 June 1663 the *congé d'élire* was issued for Sheldon's election as archbishop, the dean and chapter duly elected him on 11 August, and he was installed on 31 August.

Sheldon's government of the Church of England was concerned with uniformity, reform, and above all defence. He would contemplate no relaxation of uniformity to aid dissenters: as he told Ormond in 1663,

Tis only a resolute execution of the law that might cure this disease—all other remedies have and will increase it—and 'tis necessary that they who will not be governed as men by reason and persuasion, should be governed as beasts by power of force; all other courses will be ineffectual, ever hath been so, ever will be. (Bodl. Oxf., MS Carte 45, fol. 151)

He recognized that nonconformity drew strength from the partial conformity of some supposedly Anglican ministers, men like Mr Hart of Peterborough diocese who would not read the prayer book, wear the surplice, or respect the holy days, and who is 'rich & stubborne, & therefore the fitter to be made an Example' (Bodl. Oxf., MS Add. 308, fol. 76). If uniformity was to succeed it would require reform and greater discipline within the church.

Reform was a priority. As he told William Sancroft in 1662 when arranging to bring him south from Durham,

the moulding of new statutes for Cathedralls and some Colledges (when we have leasure for it) is like to be part of your burden when you come among us; my declining age stands in need of such assistants, and when I shall be able to put those that are best able to serve the church in the readyest way to do it I shall sing a Nunc Dimittis. (BL, Harley MS 3784, fol. 77)

Plans were indeed drafted. Clerical incomes, pluralism, and standards, all needed attention: Sheldon's *Orders Concerning Ordinations* (1665) wanted to exclude those who were 'to the Scandall of the Church and the dissatisfaction of good men' (Bodl. Oxf., MS Add. C 308, fol. 30). The church courts were another bugbear. The archbishop warned Sir Giles Sweit, dean of the arches, in March 1668, 'great clamours … are made against the ecclesiastical courts for delays of justice and other abuses'. He instructed Sweit to draw up reforms, 'nor can you be ignorant what a shock the church is at this time likely to undergo upon that account, if you mend not your ways' (Bodl. Oxf., MS Add. C 308, fol. 114). Good in itself, reform was also a defence of the church.

Sheldon defended the church against its main enemies by any means. He asserted its legal rights: conferring in 1671 with Dean Thomas Turner of Canterbury on the privileges enjoyed by that cathedral so as to strengthen the hand of the dean of Gloucester in a jurisdictional struggle with the mayor and corporation. He tacked the nonconformist problem with hard facts and blatant propaganda. In 1663 he instigated a survey of the distribution of dissenters in his diocese; in 1665 he sent out a questionnaire to all the bishops asking 'where and how and in what profession of life' the ejected ministers lived, and how they behaved 'in relation to the peace and quiet as well of the Church as of the State'. Simultaneously Lambeth Palace seems to have been behind a series of virulent and nakedly political tracts on the dangers of religious pluralism by clerical authors such as Thomas Tomkins, Samuel Parker, and George Stradling, many of them Sheldon's chaplains, which played on lay anxiety. The purpose of both the fact gathering and the pamphleteering was to smooth the way for the anti-dissenter legislation such as the Conventicle and Five Mile Acts which Sheldon's allies were promoting in the Commons.

Sheldon bound the fortunes of the church to parliament. In 1664 he surrendered the clergy's right to tax themselves in convocation in return for their right to vote in parliamentary elections. Convocation ceased to conduct business and atrophied. But the 1660s saw a steady stream of statutes designed to buttress the church and suppress its protestant rivals. Legislation needs, however, to be enforced. This was the weakest point in Sheldon's position. Neither the government not the local JPs were to be relied upon. In August 1669, for instance, Sheldon complained of the neglect of those who should assist the church by enforcing religious uniformity 'so that unless the Parliament when they meet will give us better remedies, we must (I think) yield up the cudgels' (BL, Harley MS

7377, fol. 4v). Yet such were the vacillations of royal policy that by May 1670 Sheldon found himself writing to every bishop with news of the new Conventicle Act. He urged them to ensure that it was widely publicized, especially in peculiar jurisdictions, to admonish their clergy to persuade nonconformists and to maintain exemplary lives and strict conformity to the prayer book. The Commons, Sheldon believed, were at the mercy of courtiers' machinations, 'for all the disorders have arisen from the King's family and servants' (Bodl. Oxf., MS Carte 45, fol. 212).

The personnel and mores of Charles II's court were antipathetic to Sheldon. Even worse the reputation of the archbishop and the church suffered by association with the court. Already unpopular in many quarters for their pretensions and their persecution of protestant dissenters the bishops were subject to scurrilous rumours. Pepys heard that Sheldon 'doth keep a wench' and Andrew Marvell's *Last Instructions to a Painter* alleged that he had several mistresses. At Easter 1668 a mob vented its grievances about the sexual licence of the court and religious persecution by attacking London's brothels: the supposed sexual peccadilloes of the archbishop figured prominently in the accompanying satires and rhetoric. In fact Sheldon was probably already out of royal favour as a consequence of Clarendon's fall from power in 1667. The earl of Lauderdale told Gilbert Burnet that when the king summoned Sheldon to tell him of Clarendon's dismissal the archbishop made no reply and, when pressed by the king, said 'Sir, I wish you would put away this woman that you keep' (*Burnet's History*, 1.453). The inference that Sheldon blamed Lady Castlemaine for Clarendon's fall is not borne out by Sheldon's private correspondence. Sheldon believed that the lord chancellor had long courted his own ruin 'since he that despiseth counsell must perish'. When the storm broke over Clarendon, Sheldon told the duke of Ormond plainly that 'God knows for these divers yeares I have had litle reason to be fond of him … I am sure we owe the confusion we are in to his ill management of our affayres, and of himself' (Bodl. Oxf., MS Carte 45, fols. 222, 232). In the coffee houses Sheldon was praised as 'a mighty stout man, and a man of a brave high spirit and cares not for this disfavour he is under at Court' (Pepys, *Diary*, 8.593). But it is likely that he felt the loss of influence keenly. He told one suitor for preferment in July 1670 that his 'advice is seldom asked of late in any promotions' (Bodl. Oxf., MS Tanner 44, fol. 215).

The 1672 declaration of indulgence was the nadir of Sheldon's archiepiscopate and church. Even after Charles's climb-down in 1673 confusion reigned about royal policy and the legal position of conventicles; but Sheldon resolutely told his diocesans that 'His Majestie's sence is no otherwise knowne than by his publique laws, and by them, therefore, wee are only to be guided in our dutyes' (BL, Harley MS 7377, fol. 55v). The elderly archbishop was increasingly sidelined. In 1674–5 the earl of Danby attempted to revive the 'Cavalier and Church' party and the bishops held meetings at Lambeth, but Sheldon did not figure in them and Bishop Morley seems to have provided the leadership. Meanwhile younger men, many of them promoted by Sheldon, such as Sancroft, John Dolben (who was married to Sheldon's niece), and Henry Compton, were coming to the fore. It was Compton, for example, who organized the most comprehensive national survey yet of religious affiliation in 1676. In December 1676 Sheldon was ageing and ailing, complaining of cataracts in both eyes.

Benefactions At the Restoration Sheldon's connections were renewed with Oxford. He was reinstated as warden of All Souls on the death of the interloper, but was never installed in office. Sheldon was involved from an early stage in the plans to build a university theatre—Christopher Wren displayed a model to the Royal Society in 1663—to complete Laud's scheme of relocating all the university's secular ceremonies away from the sacred space of St Mary's, the university church. Sheldon's initial gift of £1000 in 1664 was acknowledged by the university as worthy of 'that victim of piety, your noble predecessor' Laud (*Hist. U. Oxf. 4: 17th-cent. Oxf.*, 161), but it did not stimulate other benefactions and by September 1665 Sheldon undertook to fund the whole project. By the time the theatre had been built and equipped Sheldon had spent £12,239 and invested another £2000 to provide a maintenance fund. When Clarendon resigned as chancellor of the university, Dean John Fell of Christ Church secured the election of Sheldon as his successor. But Sheldon was unwilling to take up the position in the light of his other duties and perhaps of his lack of royal favour. He reigned in name only until he could resign in July 1669 in favour of the staunch Anglican James Butler, duke of Ormond.

The Sheldonian was the most public of Sheldon's many charitable benefactions. Sheldon's secretary, Miles Smyth, believed that he had spent £38,000 on good and charitable causes in the 1660s alone. This included the purchase of a City residence for the bishop of London, repairs to the palaces at Croydon, Fulham, and Lambeth (where he built 'the fayre librarie'), contributions to the rebuilding of St Paul's, sums to Trinity College, Oxford, and Trinity College, Cambridge, payments to the redemption of captives out of Algiers, payments to the king, and abatements of fines to tenants and purchasers of archiepiscopal lands.

Theology, piety, and churchmanship In his will Sheldon described himself as 'holding fast the true orthodox profession of the catholique faith of Christ … being a true member of His catholique church within the communion of a living part thereof, the present church of England' (*DNB*). An awareness of the catholicity of the church was an important aspect of Sheldon's outlook. It informed his views of the Roman Catholic church. As a young man Sheldon had been one of the first to break with the orthodoxy that the pope was the Antichrist. According to Burnet, Sheldon told the duke of York that it was not the doctrine of the Church of England that Roman Catholics were idolators. Another anecdote has it that when Anne Hyde, duchess of York, converted to Rome, Sheldon told her that he regretted the Church of England's abandonment of confession and prayer for the dead. Such attitudes may stem from his association with Laud in the 1630s and after the Restoration he was a defender of the Laudian heritage and mythology: he arranged for the publication of Laud's prayers as *A Summarie of Devotions* (Oxford, 1667); and after rescuing Laud's papers from the clutches of William Prynne he asked William Sancroft to prepare Laud's diary and the history of his trial for the press. However, Sheldon's only publication, the sermon of 28 June 1660, was utterly conventional in its denunciation of the nation's crying sins and its uncompromising assertion that 'gratitude [for divine mercies] is not the business of a day or a year, but of our whole life' (p. 49). Manuscript notes of sermons probably preached in the 1620s are also unexceptional in their appeal to reason and faith, and their assertion of the fundamentally miraculous events such as the resurrection at the heart of Christian faith. In terms of the great early seventeenth-century theological wars, Sheldon was no doubt an Arminian. But speculative theology was no longer the explosive issue it had once been. When Sheldon recommended Arminians like William Creed and Richard Allestree to the regius chair of divinity at Oxford he was doing as much to promote royalists and 'sufferers' as he was to balance the theological influence of Calvinist figures like Thomas Barlow, the Lady Margaret professor.

A liturgical and devotional conservative, a catholic with less hatred of popery than most, and an Arminian, Sheldon can still appear a tepid kind of Christian. His enemies and some of his friends were less than complimentary about his piety. Gilbert Burnet described Sheldon as seeming 'not to have a deep sense of religion, if any at all' and talking of religion 'most commonly as of an engine of government and a matter of policy'. Even his one-time chaplain, Samuel Parker, remarked that 'though he was very assiduous at prayers, yet he did not set so great a value on them as others did, nor regard so much worship as the use of worship, placing the chief point of religion in the practice of a good life' (*DNB*).

What seemed to ignite Sheldon's zeal was the safety of the church. He is said to have told the Cambridge Platonist Henry More that he was well disposed towards the new philosophy provided 'that the faith, the peace, and the institutions of the Church were not thereby menaced' (*Hist. U. Oxf.* 4: *17th-cent. Oxf.*, 423). Sheldon's was an authoritarian mentality and he put a premium on the discipline of the church. He preferred team players and could be harsh in his judgements on those like Barlow or Bishop John Wilkins who failed to abide by what he took to be the rules of the game. Even those whom posterity has sanctified were not beyond Sheldon's reproach. On news of Jeremy Taylor's death Sheldon was brutally frank:

> I am glad he left no more trouble behind him, he was of a dangerous temper apt to break out into extravagancies, and I have had, till of late years, much to do with him to keep him in order, and to find diversions for him—now those fears are at an end. (Bodl. Oxf., MS Carte 45, fol. 222)

Sheldon died at Lambeth Palace on 9 November 1677 and was privately buried on the south side of Croydon church near the tomb of Archbishop Whitgift 'according to his own special direction' on 16 November. His nephew and executor Sir Joseph Sheldon erected a monument to his memory in Croydon church. The white marble effigy of the archbishop with mitre and crozier was the work of Jasper Latham and bore a Latin inscription by Bishop John Dolben. Sheldon left £1500 in charitable legacies to All Souls, Canterbury Cathedral, the hospital of Herbaldown, Kent, and to indigent persons. The rest of his personal estate went to the five children of his older brother Ralph.

Sheldon played an important role in maintaining the identity and morale of the Church of England during the 1640s and 1650s. He took a central part in the manoeuvres which led to the restoration of the church with almost all of its rights and powers in 1662, and bears much of the responsibility for the penal laws of the 1660s. However, none of his efforts towards religious uniformity, ecclesiastical reform, or the defence of the church were marked with conspicuous success. The Church of England's pretensions to be the exclusive national church were never sustainable after the 1640s. Much of the undoubted support that the restored church enjoyed among the population was thanks to a younger generation of preachers and devotional writers or to the theologians among Sheldon's contemporaries. Nevertheless it was Sheldon's presence at the helm of the Church of England that ensured that it survived in its essentially sixteenth-century form into the later seventeenth century and beyond.   JOHN SPURR

Sources Bodl. Oxf., MSS Tanner · Bodl. Oxf., MSS Add. C. 303, 305, 308 · Bodl. Oxf., MS Eng. Bible 1648d3 · Bodl. Oxf., MS Clarendon C 70 · BL, Add. MS 4162 · BL, Harley MSS 3784, 3785, 6942, 7377 · P. Barwick, *The life and death of the Reverend Dr John Barwick* (1724) · N. Pocock, ed., 'Illustrations of the state of the church during the great rebellion', *The Theologican and Ecclesiastic*, 6–15 (1848–54) · R. A. Beddard, 'Sheldon and Anglican recovery', *HJ*, 19 (1976) · R. A. Beddard, 'The privileges of Christchurch, Canterbury: Archbishop Sheldon's enquiries of 1671', *Archaeologia Cantiana*, 87 (1972) · R. A. Beddard, 'An unpublished memoir of Archbishop Sheldon', *Bodleian Library Record*, 10 (1978–82) · R. S. Bosher, *The making of the Restoration settlement: the influence of the Laudians, 1649–1662* (1951); rev. edn (1957) · I. M. Green, *The re-establishment of the Church of England, 1660–1663* (1978) · V. Staley, *The life of Gilbert Sheldon* (1913) · *Burnet's History of my own time*, ed. O. Airy, new edn, 2 vols. (1897–1900) · H. R. Trevor-Roper, *Archbishop Laud, 1573–1645*, 2nd edn (1962) · J. W. Packer, *The transformation of Anglicanism, 1643–1660, with special reference to Henry Hammond* (1969) · P. Seaward, 'Gilbert Sheldon, the London vestries, and the defence of the church', *The politics of religion in Restoration England*, ed. T. Harris, P. Seaward, and M. Goldie (1991) · P. Seaward, *The Cavalier Parliament and the reconstruction of the old regime, 1661–1667* (1989) · N. Sykes, *From Sheldon to Secker: aspects of English church history, 1660–1768* (1959) · J. Gregory, *Restoration, reformation and reform, 1660–1828: archbishops of Canterbury and their diocese* (2000) · J. Spurr, *The Restoration Church of England, 1646–1689* (1991) · H. Cary, ed., *Memorials of the civil war*, 2 vols. · Pepys, *Diary* · *Calendar of the correspondence of Richard Baxter*, ed. N. H. Keeble and G. F. Nuttall, 2 vols. (1991) · *Calamy rev.* · *Walker rev.* · *Hist. U. Oxf.* 4: *17th-cent. Oxf.* · Wood, *Ath. Oxon.* · new edn · Wood, *Ath. Oxon.*: *Fasti* · Foster, *Alum. Oxon.* · Venn, *Alum. Cant.* · W. Kennett, *A register and chronicle ecclesiastical and civil* (1728) · *Fasti Angl.* (Hardy) · T. Harris, *London crowds in the reign of Charles II* (1987) · R. Dunning and J. Bickersteth, *The clerk of the closet* (1981), 109 · V. Larminie, *Wealth, kinship and culture: the seventeenth century Newdigates of Arbury and their world* (1995)

Archives BL, Add. MS 4162; Harley MSS 3784, 3785, 6942, 7377 · Bodl. Oxf., corresp. and papers, MSS Add. C 303, 305, 308 · Bodl. Oxf., letter-book and calendar · Bodl. Oxf., MS Eng. Bible 1648 d 3; Clarendon C 70 · LPL, corresp. · LPL, corresp. relating to Plague and Great Fire, also All Souls College Oxford
Likenesses studio of P. Lely, oils, c.1655, NPG; versions, Bodl. Oxf., LPL · P. Lely, oils, c.1665–1669, Sheldonian Theatre, Oxford [see illus.] · S. Cooper, watercolour miniature, 1667, Workers Art Gallery, Baltimore, Maryland · D. Loggan, line engraving, BM · Vertue, engraving · oils, All Souls Oxf. · portrait, Bothwell Castle, South Lanarkshire

Sheldon, Helen Maud (1859–1945), educationist, was born in Handsworth, Birmingham, on 15 October 1859, the second daughter of John Sheldon (1822?–1903), at that time vicar of St James's, Handsworth, and his wife, Anne *née* Sharp (1830?–1907). The family consisted of five daughters and two surviving sons. When at an early age Maud, as she was known in the family, decided that she wanted above everything to teach, her father undertook to give her the best education obtainable. The daughters attended Handsworth Ladies' College and three went on to Cambridge: Sheldon herself read mathematics at Girton, and one younger sister read science at Newnham, while another read classics, again at Girton. This was a considerable sibling achievement at a time when university education for women had barely begun: Sheldon actually took the tripos in 1881—the year before women were formally admitted to the final examination. She was unofficially ranked two-thirds of the way down the tripos list in mathematics (which contained six women and more than ninety men). Not until 1906 was she able to obtain the MA degree she had earned, from Trinity College, Dublin. After preliminary experience (1881–4) at a school run by the Girls' Public Day School Trust (GPDST) at Kensington, west London, Sheldon returned to Girton as resident lecturer in mathematics (1884–7). However, a contemporary reports her assertion that she 'did not know enough mathematics' (Smith), and her final career choice led to a working life spent entirely at GPDST schools. In 1888 she became a mathematics mistress at Blackheath high school in south-east London, under the headship of the remarkable Miss Gadesden, until her talent for leadership was acknowledged by an appointment as headmistress at Dover high school, Kent (1898–1901). Then she was rapidly promoted to headmistress of Sydenham high school, south-east London, where she had the opportunity to realize her wider potential. This school had been founded in 1887, and Sheldon was its second headmistress. She was responsible for introducing to GPDST schools the organization into houses and the prefect system (of proven success in boys' independent schools). Her generosity was legendary and occasionally inspired: it often took the form of supplying much-needed equipment—notably a retired tram for use as a sports pavilion. Having inherited money from her mother, she was able to indulge her munificent impulses by lending money interest-free in order to buy adjoining properties to enable the school to expand. The school orchestra was practically her creation.

A. H. H. Maclean, a long-serving secretary to the GPDST, apparently amused himself by inventing anonymous rhymes about some headmistresses he encountered. (The collection was privately printed as *H.M.'S.: Some of them* in 1932.) There is common consent that he was referring to Sheldon when he wrote:

> She had at times a grumpy way
> Of saying what she had to say.
> We didn't mind, because, behind,
> We knew that she was wise and kind.

The first couplet may have represented reaction to the abruptness of manner typical of a forthright woman. It is perhaps of greater significance that a former pupil—with hindsight of eighty years—remembers 'a lesson in integrity … even more important than learning' (private information). Another, from the Blackheath days, has mentioned the aptness of her initials' reinforcing her aura of authority, while recalling that 'she had an awfully nice face and a humorous twinkle' (Friends of the GPDST, 43).

Sheldon was headmistress at Sydenham from 1901 to 1917, and her retirement (aged fifty-seven) in the middle of the disruption due to the war was somewhat unexpected. She continued to live in the area, and was elected to the borough council of Lewisham, which included Sydenham. Her service as treasurer of the Association of Headmistresses from 1905 to 1909 was recognized by her being made an honorary life member. She retained her interest in mathematical education, having contributed to the ground-breaking 1916 report of the Mathematical Association, *Elementary Mathematics in Girls' Schools*. She served as a member of the council of Girton College in 1910–19. In the early 1920s she moved to central London and in 1931 to Richmond. She died on 16 May 1945 at the Royal Northern Hospital, Holloway, London. A. E. L. DAVIS

Sources K. T. Butler and H. I. McMorran, eds., *Girton College register, 1869–1946* (1948) · M. S. Smith, *Girton Review* (1945), 29–30 · Girton Cam. · M. C. Malim and H. C. Escreet, eds., *The book of the Blackheath High School* (1927) · L. Magnus, *The jubilee book of the Girls' Public Day School Trust, 1873–1923* (1923), 120–01 · M. D. Yardley, ed., *Sydenham High School GPDST, 1887–1987* (privately printed, [n.d.]) · *G.P.D.S.T., 1872–1972: a centenary review* (privately printed, 1972) · J. Kamm, *Indicative past: one hundred years of the Girls' Public Day School Trust* (1971), 105 · *Newsletter* [Friends of the G.P.D.S.T.] (1958), 43 · M. H. Price, *Mathematics for the multitude? A history of the Mathematical Association* (1994), 101–05, 286–7 · A. Maclean, *H.M.'S: some of them* (privately printed, 1932) · d. cert. · private information (2004) · parish register (birth), Handsworth, Birmingham, 15 Oct 1859 · parish register (baptism), Handsworth, Birmingham, 30 Nov 1859
Likenesses group portrait, photograph, 1919, repro. in Kamm, *Indicative past*
Wealth at death £19,868 12s. 6d.: probate, 4 Oct 1945, CGPLA Eng. & Wales

Sheldon, John (1752–1808), anatomist and surgeon, was born at his father's house in Tottenham Court Road, London, on 6 July 1752, the eldest son of John Sheldon, surgeon apothecary, formerly in the Royal Navy. He had a younger brother, Thomas, and two sisters, Mary Elizabeth and Anna Maria. Educated at Harrow School, where he was flogged for 'making a boat and floating it', he was then apprenticed to Henry Watson, professor of anatomy at the Company of Surgeons, whose school at Rathbone Place,

John Sheldon (1752–1808), by William Barnard (after John Keenan, exh. RA 1802)

London, was later wrecked by a mob. Sheldon trained also at the Westminster and the Lock hospitals. On William Hewson's death in 1774 he succeeded him as resident pupil to John Hunter, attending William Hunter's school of anatomy in Great Windmill Street. Sheldon's interest in embalming profited from the knowledge gained from both teachers. After receiving his diploma in 1775 from the Company of Surgeons he was appointed to the Lock Hospital, where he had been a pupil, continuing lecturing and research. There he was able to use his embalming skills in a case for which he became notorious. Sheldon had as a patient a young woman, dying of phthisis, to whom, he said, he became deeply attached. Acceding to her request for her body to be preserved after death and kept beside him, he removed it, embalmed and injected, to his own house, where it was displayed in a glass-topped cabinet. Later it was described with enthusiasm by Faujas-de-St-Fond. Twenty years later Sheldon's widow presented the mummy to the museum of the Royal College of Surgeons. Appointed lecturer in anatomy at William Hunter's school in 1776, Sheldon's success prompted him to open his own school in Great Queen Street, London, in 1777. Though still only twenty-five years of age, with William Hewson and Magnus Falconar now deceased he was the only outstanding teacher of his generation. He was appointed surgeon to the General Medical Asylum in Welbeck Street, and on 18 July 1783 succeeded William Hunter as professor of anatomy at the Royal Academy, earning, it is said, great respect. It is related how, having dissected a horse, he had casts made of it for the use of the students.

In 1779 Sheldon founded the Great Queen Street Medical Society, becoming its first president. At one time it had 150 members and issued diplomas. One rule required the president to 'wear his hat while in the chair'. On 29 April 1784 he was elected a fellow of the Royal Society, and on 20 April 1786 a member of the Royal Society of Medicine of Paris.

In 1781 Sheldon edited a catalogue of Petrus Camper's works, *Historiae literariae cultoribus*; the following year he edited four dissertations by J. N. Lieberkuehn, published in London. Sheldon's chief work, *The History of the Absorbent System, Part the First*, was published in 1784. In it he paid generous tribute to William Hewson, and to John Hunter, who had ingested madder to prove the pigment was absorbed and carried by the lymphatics. He described meticulously his own methods of injection and preservation, his cannula tip bevelled, as in a modern instrument, to facilitate penetration of the vessels. Antonio Scarpa, professor of anatomy at Pavia, was so impressed by his work that he prepared two illustrations for the book. Sheldon was widely praised because he made no secret of his methods. It was in fact a most learned treatise that corrected many errors of earlier writers on the subject.

Sheldon now became much involved with early efforts at ballooning, making calculations about the gravity of the atmosphere and investigating materials for construction. An attempt at making a balloon failed in 1784, but on 16 October that year Sheldon made his first ascent with J. P. Blanchard, who had already had several successes. Although the balloon travelled as far as Sunbury, where Sheldon alighted, a violent altercation had developed between them, and Blanchard proceeded alone to Romsey. About 1784 Sheldon married Rebecca (d. 1820), second daughter of the Revd William Palmer, vicar of Combe Raleigh in Devon; they had no children.

Sheldon was elected surgeon to Westminster Hospital on 20 April 1786. At the time he had become interested in studying the anatomy of whales. He devised a poisoned harpoon for this purpose, and in 1788 set out for Greenland. On the voyage he is said to have had an attack of brain fever and had to be transferred to a returning ship. He moved from London to Exeter in the same year, from then on subject to recurrent illness, probably a manic-depressive psychosis. His brother petitioned the queen for him to be allowed to continue the annual lectures at the Royal Academy, which he gave until his death. Sheldon's brother and sisters assisted in his nursing. His *Essay on the Fracture of the Patella*, already written, was published in 1789. During recovery, in 1796, he contributed 'An essay on the iris' to the volume *Essays, by a Society of Gentlemen at Exeter*.

In 1797 Sheldon was appointed a surgeon to the Royal Devon and Exeter Hospital. Highly regarded by his colleagues, it was recognized that his intellect became 'clouded at intervals' (Harris, 84, and also mentioned by *Farington Diary*, ed. Greig, 6.182). He died on 8 October 1808 at his cottage in Exeter by the Exe, and was buried in Combe Raleigh churchyard. An obituary notice in the *Monthly Mirror* spoke of him as 'humane, active in every intercourse of friendship and, though of so animated a character, mild, forbearing and affable ... There was nothing like envy in his composition' (Dobson, 83).

ALICK CAMERON

Sources J. Dobson, 'John Sheldon, MD, FRS', *The Practitioner*, 173 (1954), 77–83 • *DNB* • J. D. Harris, *History of the Royal Devon and Exeter Hospital* (1922) • N. Capener, 'John Sheldon, FRS, and the Exeter Medical School', *Proceedings of the Royal Society of Medicine*, 52 (1959), 231–8 • G. Oliver, 'Biography of Exonians, no. 35', collected newspaper articles, Devon and Exeter Institution, Exeter • B. Faujas-de-St-Fond, *Travels in England, Scotland, and the Hebrides* (1799), 1.38–47 • *The Farington diary*, ed. J. Greig, 6 (1926), 182

Likenesses G. Dance, pencil and crayon drawing, 1793, RCS Eng. • W. Barnard, mezzotint (after J. Keenan, exh. RA 1802), NPG, RCS Eng., Wellcome L. [*see illus.*] • W. Daniell, soft-ground etching (after G. Dance, 1793), NPG, RCS Eng., RS, Wellcome L. • S. Freeman, stipple engraving (after A. W. Devis, 1809), NPG; repro. in *Monthly Mirror* (1809) • S. Freeman, stipple engraving (after A. W. Devis), BM; repro. in *Monthly Mirror* (1809) • J. Keenan, oils, Devon and Exeter Hospital • P. Sandby, caricature

Sheldon, Ralph (1623–1684), antiquary, was born on 1 August 1623 at Beoley, Worcestershire, the eldest son of William Sheldon (1589–1659) of Beoley and Weston in Long Compton, Warwickshire, and Elizabeth (1592–1656), daughter of William, second Lord Petre. He was a nephew of Edward Sheldon the translator. The Sheldons were one of the wealthiest gentry families in the region, but their access to public life was limited by their Catholicism. Sheldon left England for France and Italy in 1642, returning shortly before his marriage in 1647 to Lady Henrietta Maria, daughter of John Savage, second Earl Rivers (*c.*1603–1654). In the civil war the house at Beoley was apparently burnt to prevent it falling to the parliamentarian forces and the estate was sequestrated. Following the Restoration Sheldon was nominated as a member of the contemplated order of the Royal Oak for his family's devotion to the royalist cause.

After his wife's death, childless, in 1663 Sheldon devoted himself to the study of genealogy, heraldry, and antiquities, drawing up a 'Catalogue of the nobility of England since the Norman Conquest' (CUL, Add. 8138). He created a fine library at Weston, catalogued by Anthony Wood; he also had a cabinet of curiosities. In 1667 he again travelled to Rome, where over three years he extended his collection. Described by Wood as 'a munificent favourer of learning and learned men' (Hamper, 434–5), he granted a pension to the antiquary John Vincent, from whom he purchased an important collection of manuscripts belonging to his father, the herald Augustine Vincent. On his own death he bequeathed this collection to the College of Arms. Despite his Catholicism, which led to his arrest in 1678, Sheldon was apparently popular locally and known as 'Great Sheldon' (Nash, 1.68). He died at Weston on 24 June 1684; 500 people viewed the body before its burial at the family chapel at Beoley.   JAN BROADWAY

Sources L. Campbell and F. Steer, *A catalogue of manuscripts in the College of Arms collections*, 1 (1988), 233–463 • T. Nash, *Collections for the history of Worcestershire*, 1 (1781), 64, 67–8 • *The life, diary, and correspondence of Sir William Dugdale*, ed. W. Hamper (1827), 434–5, 455–8 • J. T. Cliffe, *The world of the country house in seventeenth-century England*

(1999), 45, 163–4, 197 • J. Chambers, *Biographical illustrations of Worcestershire* (1820), 208–10 • *VCH Worcestershire*, 4.12–9 • Wood, *Ath. Oxon.*, new edn, 1.xcix–c • N. H. Nicolas, *Memoir of Augustine Vincent* (1827), 92–100 • E. O. Browne and J. R. Burton, *Worthies of Worcestershire* (1916) • E. A. B. Barnard and A. J. B. Wace, 'The Sheldon tapestry weavers and their work', *Archaeologia*, 78 (1928), 255–314 • GEC, *Peerage*

Archives BL, corresp. relating to his arrest, Add. MS 34730, fols. 30, 32 • Bodl. Oxf., collections and papers • CUL, catalogue of the nobility of England, Add. 8138 • Jesus College, Oxford, MSS collection | Bodl. Oxf., corresp. with Anthony Wood, fols. 5, 6, 11, 18, 44–5 • Coll. Arms, Vincent collection

Wealth at death estate valued at £2000 p.a. in 1660s; left Wood £100 towards printing the *Athenae*; £40 for sorting papers and delivering collection to College of Arms: Barnard and Wace, 'The Sheldon tapestry weavers'; Hamper, ed., *The life*; Chambers, *Biographical illustrations*; Nicolas, *Memoir*

Sheldon, Ralph (1633–1723). *See under* Sheldon, Dominic (*b.* in or before 1633, *d.* 1721).

Sheldon, Richard (1570?–1651?), Church of England convert and polemicist, was born in Wolverhampton, Staffordshire, almost certainly a relative of the Sheldons of Beoley, Worcestershire, and Weston, Warwickshire, and was raised a Roman Catholic. He became a student at the English College for training secular priests at Rheims, France, in January 1589, and was sent on to the English College at Rome, where he was admitted as a *metaphysicus* in October 1590. He describes himself as well reputed in learning, and was ordained subdeacon, deacon, and priest in 1593, but his observations of the higher clergy in Rome, when he had become zealous and willing for martyrdom, apparently left him very critical. About 1595 he was sent via Genoa to Alicante in Spain. Accompanied by Robert Persons, he had access to Cardinal Cajetan and the Jesuit general, Acquaviva, and was at Valladolid by April 1596, presumably to study further at St Alban's College there.

By November Sheldon had arrived in Flanders, and before the end of the year he began working in England, at least partly in Oxfordshire, moving, he states, in the best circles. He testifies to being zealous in exhorting and writing, and preaching diligently, on at least one occasion for an hour and a half. Even at this time he emphasized respect for civil authority and thus clashed with Jesuits. The Gunpowder Plot 'of the accursed Catesby' (Sheldon, *Certain General Reasons*, introduction) was a turning point for him, and was reinforced by the assassination of Henri IV of France in 1610. He felt vehemently that it was completely wrong to bring in the kingdom of God by subversion, and bitterly attacked the Jesuits for, in his view, advocating it. He surreptitiously attended Anglican services, and records how his views changed 'as God touched my heart'. Sung psalms and preaching immediately struck him by their simplicity and gravity, 'that I began to thinke ... perhaps God is among them', but when he discovered that most of the liturgy 'was composed out of the infallible word of God ... I resolved that the same must needs be good'. With the subsequent appreciation that 'the Preachers continually did inculcate ... integritie of conscience, and holinesse of conversation with the necessitie of good works to salvation: I well and clearly perceived how the Church of England was calumniated by the Roman Doctors'. He was also very impressed by the integration of mind and tongue in the liturgy, 'with their pious sounds to beate the gates of heaven, and begge mercie at his hands onely: who with the Father and the holy Ghost I saw onely worshipped' (Sheldon, *Motives*, 135–6).

Sheldon was at St Omer about the time of Henry Garnet's execution in 1606, perhaps because he was banished, but perhaps also because he was, as Benjamin Norton wrote to Geoffrey Pole, 'a broker for the Jesuites in getting monie for St O[mer], and rich Nunns for Bruxells' (Questier, 90–91). He returned to England, but was arrested and exiled in 1610, when he spent time in theological discussion at Louvain. As early as October that year, according to Norton, he may have taken the oath of allegiance to James I, but when he again arrived in England in April 1611 he was immediately captured, probably under the name Gervaise Sheldon. He was imprisoned in Newgate, one of the London gaols for people likely to be executed, and there he again reportedly took the oath of allegiance to James I. This doubtless led to his transfer to the Clink, which was much more lenient. There he was set to confer with secular priest Thomas Leek and persuade him to take the oath, and also wrote *Certain General Reasons, Proving the Lawfulness of the Oath of Allegiance* (1611), allegedly for a friend. This fell into the hands of the archbishop of Canterbury, who urged publication. Sheldon writes still as a Roman Catholic priest, but attacks the Jesuits for exalting papal authority, and denies the pope has power to depose rulers. He argues that they all receive their authority from God, the ultimate source of temporal power, and are irremovable. Such views show to his readers that he was moving to apostasy from Roman Catholicism: this gave the work special propaganda value in Archbishop Abbot's anti-popery campaign. Sheldon may in part have been making a shrewd bid for his patronage. By mid-December 1611 he was reported to have 'gone to church' (ibid., 134). His *Motives of Richard Sheldon … for his just, voluntary, and free renouncing of communion with the bishop of Rome*, published by authority in February 1612, argued that papal authority and other Roman Catholic doctrines were not scriptural nor existed in the early church. At this point he was released and pardoned by the king for activities deemed treasonable under the 1585 act against Jesuits and seminary priests; Bishop James Montague of Bath and Wells took him to kiss the king's hand. On 28 March he preached a sermon in St Martin-in-the-Fields, London, on Christ as the sole sacrifice for sin, and the following day seems to have delivered it again as his formal recantation sermon at Paul's Cross; it was subsequently published as *The First Sermon of R. Sheldon Priest* (1612).

Sheldon was then employed by James I to write with William Warmington, another former Catholic who had defended the oath of allegiance, a book against Vorstius, but Warmington subsequently reverted to Catholicism, and any resulting book was not published. Sheldon also served as a royal chaplain to James and later to Charles I. Archbishop Abbot presented him to the vicarage of Appledore-with-Ebony, Kent, in November 1612. In his *Motives* Sheldon had fulminated against clerical celibacy: clearly he found it hard. On 9 March 1613 he married in Hackney Ann (possibly also known as Agnes) Smyth, described in Catholic correspondence as 'a rich maiden or widow' (Questier, 230n.); they had six known children.

Sheldon's views had become more anti-Catholic by the time *A Survey of the Miracles of the Church of Rome* was published in 1616, since this identified the pope with Antichrist. Such views supported Archbishop Abbot's campaign against a Spanish match for Prince Charles, but led to a rift with James I. None the less, Sheldon not only preached before the king but also published his *Christ, on his Throne: not in Popish Secrets* (1622), albeit with an apologetic preface. In 1623 he preached a sermon at Paul's Cross, London, attacking the pope as the beast in Revelation, and his followers as damned, for which the king reprimanded him. However, this eventually appeared in print as *A Sermon … Laying Open the Beast, and his Marks* (1625) as a counterblast to Charles's marriage arrangements for Henrietta Maria of France, which included Roman Catholic toleration in her household and the suspension of the penal laws. Meanwhile Sheldon was not without patrons: he was created an honorary DD of Cambridge and was instituted to the vicarage of Bearstead, Kent, in November 1624. Under Charles I he sought favour by a treatise on the royal prerogative, but Archbishop Laud ignored it, and Sheldon petitioned for its return five years later.

Sheldon continued as vicar of both his benefices for the rest of his life. His parishioners at Appledore-with-Ebony responded to the 1640 Kentish petition against the clergy by recounting that Sheldon had left two competent curates undisturbed on his institution, in Ebony's case at the parishioners' request, had raised their salaries and those of their successors to as much as they and their parishioners wished, and had secured hard-working, preaching, men. At Bearstead, he constantly used the prayer book, and catechised with exposition each Sunday. Though he was summoned by the Commons on 4 April 1642 when they investigated Sir Edward Dering's petition supporting the prayer book and royal control of the militia, they let the case lapse. He describes himself as living in Bearstead and as minister of God's word in his will, finalized in September 1648. He was sufficiently well off to leave the equivalent of £300 to each of his three surviving sons, some of which was invested in the East India Company, to dower his two daughters for marriages with gentlemen, and to leave each a silver spoon. He probably died at Bearstead in 1651, his will being proved on 3 December that year by his widow and executrix.   ELIZABETH ALLEN

Sources G. Anstruther, *The seminary priests*, 1 (1969), 308 · R. Sheldon, *The motives of Richard Sheldon, priest, for his just, voluntary, and free renouncing of communion with the bishop of Rome* (1612), 4, 5, 135–6, 151, 154–9 [incl. Sheldon's *The … observation of the English pontifcians spirits*, see pp. 2–3, 11–12] · R. Sheldon, *A survey of the miracles of the Church of Rome* (1616), 25, 112–13, 272 · W. Kelly, ed., *Liber ruber venerabilis collegii Anglorum de urbe*, 1, Catholic RS, 37 (1940), 76 · R. S[heldon], *Certain general reasons, proving the lawfulness of the oath of allegiance* (1611), 2, 37 · PRO, PROB 11/219 · M. C. Questier, *Newsletters* *from the archpresbyterate of George Birkhead*, CS, 5th ser., 12 (1998) • register of Archbishop Abbot, LPL, 1, fol. 394v; 2, fol. 338 • H. Foley, ed., *Records of the English province of the Society of Jesus*, 7/2 (1883), 1018 • *Calendar of the manuscripts of the most hon. the marquess of Salisbury*, 21, HMC, 9 (1970), 329 • *CSP dom.*, *1611–18*, 119; *1640–41*, 374 • A. Milton, *Catholic and Reformed: the Roman and protestant churches in English protestant thought, 1600–1640* (1995) • parish register, Hackney, St John's (transcript), GL, 1612–13; 1622; 1624–5 • parish register, Bearstead, CKS [transcript], 1625–41 • Canterbury Cathedral Archives, DCb/BT1/5 • L. B. Larking, ed., *Proceedings principally in the county of Kent in connection with the parliaments called in 1640, and especially with the committee of religion appointed in that year*, CS, old ser., 80 (1862), 101–2 • *JHC*, 2 (1640–42), 502–3, 510, 517

Wealth at death £300 each to three sons: will, proved 3 Dec 1651, PRO, PROB 11/219

Sheldon, Sir Wilfrid Percy Henry (1901–1983), paediatrician, was born on 23 November 1901 at Woodford, Essex, the second of three sons and fourth of five children of John Joseph Sheldon, a bank clerk in the City of London, and his wife, Marion Squire, daughter of Henry Spring, a Lloyds' underwriter who insured sailing ships. He was educated at Bancroft's School, Woodford, and King's College, London, where he studied medicine. He qualified MRCS, LRCP in 1923 and graduated MB, BS (London) a year later with honours in anatomy and medicine. He held several resident appointments at his teaching hospital including a house physicianship to (George) Frederic Still, the well-known British paediatrician. In 1925 he became MRCP and MD (London), both by examination. In 1927 he married Mabel Winifred (Maithe), daughter of John Netherway, accountant to Allen and Hanburys Ltd; they had three daughters, the second of whom, Joanna Sheldon (*d.* 1985), became FRCP in 1975. Sheldon himself became FRCP in 1933.

After holding a medical registrarship at the Royal Free Hospital, Sheldon was appointed to a key post for an ambitious young paediatrician—that of medical registrar and pathologist to the Hospital for Sick Children, Great Ormond Street, thus beginning an association with that hospital which was to last until his retirement in 1967. He became a consultant there in 1947. He was concurrently consultant paediatrician at King's College Hospital. During the Second World War Sheldon worked in the Emergency Medical Service organizing the transfer and care of sick children from London to hospitals in Cuckfield and, later, Haywards Heath, Sussex. After the war he was responsible for the successful liaison between Great Ormond Street and Mulago Hospital, Kampala, which lasted until the regime of Idi Amin took control in Uganda.

Like most of his generation in paediatrics Sheldon had no training in the methodology of research and was thus no clinical scientist. But he was an outstanding clinical observer and diagnostician, who relied more on accurate history taking and physical examination than on laboratory findings. He quickly amassed a great store of recollected experience. As a young paediatrician Sheldon published many brief case reports of unusual cases, especially in the *Proceedings* of the Royal Society of Medicine. Later he published full-length papers on a variety of topics relating to child health or disease, but he made no great

discoveries or contributions of lasting importance. His *Diseases of Infancy and Childhood* was deservedly the most popular medium-sized textbook of paediatrics during his working life; the first edition appeared in 1936 and the eighth and last in 1962. In the 1940s Sheldon began to take a special interest in coeliac disease and Great Ormond Street became a referral centre for this uncommon but serious disorder. He was an early advocate of a starch-free diet, but he made the false assumption that a diet free of wheat flour was synonymous with this.

Sheldon enjoyed every aspect of his varied career in children's medicine but that which undoubtedly gave him the greatest satisfaction and pleasure was his appointment in 1952 as physician and paediatrician to Queen Elizabeth. He was the first royal doctor to be accorded that title, and he held the post until 1971. He possessed all the qualities of an ideal courtier: he was justifiably self-confident and self-assured, always within the limits of propriety; he was well-mannered and deferential, but never obsequious; he was interesting and amusing; and he was discreet, but not to the extent of hindering the escape of some entertaining stories from the royal nurseries. He was rewarded by the friendship of the royal family and his appointment in 1954 as CVO and in 1959 as KCVO. He was also one of the very few London-based paediatricians to make a financial success of private practice in Harley Street.

Sheldon was an inspiring teacher of nurses, medical students, and postgraduates. He was before his time in the importance he attached to effective communication with parents. Students were always present when he talked to parents and parents were always present when he dictated letters to GPs. Early in his career he was consultant paediatrist to the London county council. For many years he was adviser in child health to the Ministry of Health, and wielded much influence in this role. He was involved in a number of published government reports—for example, on welfare foods (1957), cerebral palsy (1960), congenital malformations (1963), child welfare centres (1967), and special care for babies (1971). Each of the two last named was known in its day as the Sheldon report, since he was chairman of the committee reporting. Sheldon was president of the British Paediatric Association (1963–4), and an honorary fellow of both the American Academy of Pediatrics and the Royal Society of Medicine. He became an honorary fellow of the Royal College of Obstetricians and Gynaecologists (1972) and honorary MMSA (1972), and was a corresponding member of the Portuguese Paediatric Society.

Sheldon was tall, well-built, handsome, and impressive. His appearance and behaviour could and did elicit awe and adoration—not as a rule simultaneously. He was usually kind and urbane in social intercourse, showing to his close friends a genuine and disarming humility. But if his customary equanimity was threatened—for instance by somebody presuming on a mere acquaintanceship—he could be disagreeably abrupt and arrogant. He was always kind and gentle to children, always thoughtful and considerate to parents, and always at pains to help and befriend a stranger, bewildered and ignored in unfamiliar surroundings. He was an expert, learned, and energetic gardener (his father was an FLS).

Sheldon died in a private nursing home near his home in Kingston upon Thames, Surrey, on 9 September 1983. He was survived by his wife. A memorial service was held for him at the church of St George the Martyr, Queen Square. PETER TIZARD, *rev.*

Sources *King's College Hospital Gazette*, 46 (1967), 172–4 · *The Times* (14 Sept 1983) · *The Times* (21 Sept 1983) · *The Lancet* (24 Sept 1983), 749 · *BMJ* (24 Sept 1983), 918; (1 Oct 1983), 992; (15 Oct 1983), 1146 · personal knowledge (1990) · private information (1990) · *CGPLA Eng. & Wales* (1984)

Wealth at death £82,444: probate, 28 March 1984, *CGPLA Eng. & Wales*

Sheldrake, Timothy (*bap.* 1691?, *d.* before 1759), botanist, was probably the son of Timothy Sheldrake (*d.* 1717), saddler, and his wife, Anne, baptized at St Gregory, Norwich, on 25 September 1691. In a biographical sketch given to Sir Hans Sloane in 1736 Sheldrake explained that as a youth his leisure had been spent in drawing and painting. He was not successful as a saddler, and, when unemployed, studied natural history. A series of letters written from Norwich to the gardener and botanist Thomas Fairchild (1667–1729) demonstrates his interest in botanical subjects, notably the cultivation of tropical fruit and nut-bearing trees. Needing an occupation, he took over a distilling office adjacent to his saddlery, and found himself required to study botany, chemistry, and the manufacture of drugs. At the same time, he gained a small knowledge of medicine, sometimes being improperly known as MD, and his affairs prospered.

By this time Sheldrake and his wife, Mary, had baptized two children at St Peter Mancroft, Norwich—Timothy on 8 February 1729 and Anne on 18 June 1732. When an act was passed in 1736 restricting the sale of distilled spirits, apothecaries were not affected, and Sheldrake wrote to Sloane seeking his advice, as he needed to keep his business going to support a young family. Shortly after, perhaps on Sloane's advice, he moved to Westminster and settled near the Strand.

Sheldrake's interest in tropical plants led him to send a letter on the causes of heat and cold in all climates, which was read to the Royal Society and published in 1756, and to draw up a large chart entitled *The gardener's best companion in a greenhouse, or, Tables showing the greatest heat and cold of all countries … measured upon the thermometer* (1756), dedicated to Sloane and stated to have the approval of Philip Miller. These tables were based on Sheldrake's naïve assumption that temperature at a particular place on the earth was directly related to its latitude. A posthumous work, *Botanicum Medicinale: an Herbal of Medicinal Plants on the College of Physicians' List* (1759), gave names in nine languages and was illustrated by 120 copper plates, mostly engraved by C. H. Hemerich, and said to be 'from the exquisite drawings of the late ingenious T. Sheldrake'. The work was issued at £3 plain and £6 coloured. A pamphlet by Sheldrake on the 'Norwich Gothic cross' was advertised in the *Gardener's Companion*. No details of his death are known.

Sheldrake's son Timothy (1729–1800), lived in the Strand, Westminster, and practised as a truss maker. Known as 'the elder', he and his common-law wife, Christian (*d.* 1813), had several children, of whom the eldest son, Timothy Sheldrake the younger (*b.* 1759), also practised as a truss maker, and was employed by the Westminster Hospital and Marylebone Infirmary. The younger Sheldrake was not medically qualified but the high cost of his appliances gained him a considerable reputation, and he travelled through Britain attending to children of the richer classes. He was latterly in partnership with Henry Bigg. His brother William (*b.* 1770) also practised orthopaedics, and treated Byron's club foot, though apparently without much success.

G. S. BOULGER, *rev.* ANITA MCCONNELL

Sources [T. Sheldrake], commonplace book, Wellcome L. · D. Le Vay, *The history of orthopaedics* (1990), 78–81, 495–6 · will, PRO, PROB 11/1336, sig. 64 [Timothy Sheldrake 'the elder'] · private information (2004) · T. Sheldrake, *Essay on the various causes and effects of the distorted spine* (1783)

Archives Wellcome L. | BL, Sloane MSS

Shelford, Leonard (1795–1864), legal writer, second son of Leonard Shelford BD (*d.* 1813), and his wife, Ellen, daughter of William Grigson of West Wretham, Norfolk, was born on 26 July 1795. His father, who was a fellow of Corpus Christi College, Cambridge, and rector of North Tuddenham, Norfolk, wanted him to become a solicitor, and he served his articles with William Repton of Aylsham, Norfolk. He then went to the office of Boodle & Co., London, but, deciding to become a barrister, he entered the Middle Temple, and was called to the bar in 1827. For nearly forty years he occupied chambers in the Temple, living the life of a recluse, and compiling a considerable number of legal works, which not only obtained a large circulation in England, but were also reprinted in America, often without the author's consent. Most of these works were legal handbooks but Shelford also prepared new editions of Herbert Broom's *Practice of the County Courts* (1857) and George Crabb's *The Conveyancer's Assistant* (1860). Shelford died, unmarried, in his chambers, at 3 Brick Court, Middle Temple, on 17 March 1864.

E. I. CARLYLE, *rev.* JONATHAN HARRIS

Sources *GM*, 3rd ser., 16 (1864), 542 · Boase, *Mod. Eng. biog.* · *Law Magazine*, new ser., 17 (1864), 196–7 · Allibone, *Dict.*

Wealth at death under £450: probate, 21 May 1864, *CGPLA Eng. & Wales*

Shelford, Robert (*c.*1563–1638/9), Church of England clergyman and religious writer, was possibly the son of John Shelford (*d.* 1595) of Great Wendon, Essex, who left a widow, Mary. On 30 April 1580 he was admitted sizar at Peterhouse, Cambridge. From 1581 to 1586 he was a scholar of the college, where, according to the Latin preface of his *Five Pious and Learned Discourses* (1635), he was also bible-clerk ('biblioclericum') and amanuensis to the master, Andrew Perne. He graduated BA early in 1584, proceeded MA in 1587, and was ordained deacon and priest in the diocese of Peterborough on 6 August 1587. In 1599 Sir

Thomas Egerton presented him to the rectory of Rings-field, Suffolk, where he remained until his death.

In 1596 Shelford published his first book, *Lectures or Readings upon the 6. Verse of the 22. Chapter of the Proverbs*. This was a treatise on the education of children, described on the title-page of the 1606 edition as a work 'very necessary for all parents in this corrupt and declining age of the world'. Shelford feared that the 'ancient discipline of parents' had fallen into disuse, 'as a lawe worne out of mind', and complained: 'such is the foolish love that many poore parents have towards their children, that rather than they will put their tenderlings to any laborious busines, they will do all themselves' (Shelford, *Lectures*, 1606, 35). He urged parents to teach their children 'good manners and civill behaviour', to place them in the service of 'godly and religious' masters, and to ensure that they learned a useful trade. The first edition of the *Lectures* (surviving in a single copy, now BL, C.193.a.53) was published anonymously, but the 1602 and 1606 editions contain the author's name, together with a dedicatory epistle to Sir Thomas Egerton in which Shelford described himself as 'a poore Minister beginning at low steps to ascend higher in religious duties' and attacked certain unnamed 'enemies in the flesh' who had accused him of being 'a vaine-glorious man' (Shelford, *Lectures*, 1606).

Some thirty years later Shelford published his second book, *Five Pious and Learned Discourses* (1635), a far more controversial work in which he made his Laudian sympathies very clear. In the first discourse, 'A sermon shewing how we ought to behave ourselves in God's house', he stressed the importance of reverent behaviour in church, including bowing to the altar and standing at the recitation of the creed and the gloria. Like other Laudian divines he was critical of what he saw as the puritan obsession with preaching, complaining that 'one beauty hath beat out another; the beauty of preaching (which is a beauty too) hath preacht away the beauty of holinesse' (Shelford, *Discourses*, 12). The book was published at Cambridge, with complimentary poems by a number of like-minded Cambridge divines including Richard Crashaw, fellow of Peterhouse (whose poem 'On a treatise of charity', beginning 'Rise then, immortall maid! Religion rise!' was printed here for the first time), Richard Drake, fellow of Pembroke (whose copy of the book is still preserved in Pembroke College Library), and Richard London, fellow of Gonville and Caius (to whom Shelford later bequeathed £10 'after his coming from travaile').

The most provocative section of the book was the final discourse, 'A treatise shewing the Antichrist not to be yet come', in which Shelford rejected the common identification of the pope with the Antichrist, and called for more friendly relations between protestants and Catholics:

> Let Protestants love the Papists, because they have kept the holy oracles and sacred mysteries for them; and let Papists love the Protestants, because they are descended from them, wear the badge of the covenant with them, and by a light and oblique dissent provoke them to better life and more refined learning. (Shelford, *Discourses*)

Archbishop James Ussher wrote to Samuel Ward on 15 September 1635 expressing astonishment at the publication of the book: 'how cometh it to pass that you in Cambridge do cast such stumbling blocks in our way? by publishing unto the world such rotten stuff as Shelford hath vented in his five discourses'. This, he observed, was just what one might expect from a disciple of Perne. 'The Jesuits of England' he continued:

> sent over the book hither to confirm our papists in their obstinacy, and to assure them that we are now coming home unto them as fast as we can; I pray God this sin be not deeply laid to their charge, who give an occasion to our blind thus to stumble. (Ussher, 16.9)

Much seventeenth-century woodwork for which Shelford was probably responsible survives in Ringsfield parish church, including an inscription over the south door: 'This is none other but the house of God, and this is the gate of Heaven. When thou seest God's house adorned, think of his greatness that oweth it, and render thy reverence accordingly'. On the north wall of the chancel is a memorial tablet, erected by Shelford during his lifetime, in which he describes himself as 'coelebs et sacerdos', an unmarried priest (echoing his self-description on the title-page of the *Discourses*, 'Robert Shelford, Priest'), and warns against any sacrilegious attempt to alienate the property of the church. Shelford drew up his will on 1 August 1638 and died, aged about sixty-four, some time before it was proved on 14 May 1639. He left 'my copes hanging in the kitchin' for the use of succeeding incumbents of Ringsfield, and gave instructions that his body was to be 'decently buried in the churchyard of Ringsfield right over against my monument in the church on the north side of it' (will).   ARNOLD HUNT

Sources R. Shelford, *Lectures or readings upon the 6. verse of the 22. chapter of the Proverbs* (1596); (1606) · R. Shelford, *Five pious and learned discourses* (1635) · *The whole works of … James Ussher*, ed. C. R. Elrington and J. H. Todd, 17 vols. (1847–64) · Venn, *Alum. Cant.* · will, PRO, PROB 11/180
Wealth at death over £100; incl. land in Suffolk: will, PRO, PROB 11/180

Shelford, Sir William (1834–1905), civil engineer, was born at Lavenham on 11 April 1834, the eldest son of the ten children of William Heard Shelford (d. 1854), rector of Preston St Mary, Suffolk, and Emily Frost, eldest daughter of Richard Snape, rector of Brent Eleigh parish. Despite a clerical tradition on both sides of his family, Shelford chose on leaving Marlborough College in the summer of 1852 to pursue a career in engineering. Throughout his childhood he had been interested in things mechanical and he persuaded his father to let him begin training as an engineer at Young & Co.'s works in Ayr.

In 1854 Shelford's father died, creating financial problems for the family. Shelford transferred his pupillage to William Gale, at that time a leading waterworks engineer based in Glasgow. This enabled him to attend lectures at Glasgow University. Such was his progress that after two years Shelford moved to London on Gale's advice in search of a salaried position. Initially unsuccessful, he finally obtained unpaid work in John Fowler's office. There he rapidly proved himself to Fowler who offered him a post on the Nene improvement works. Fowler gave him increasing responsibility, and in 1859 he returned to London to work on the first section of the Metropolitan Railway.

In the autumn of 1860 Shelford joined the staff of Frederick Thomas Turner (1812–1877), the engineer largely responsible for the London, Chatham, and Dover Railway, formerly the East Kent Railway, and its associated lines. The London extension of this line received parliamentary approval in 1860. In 1862 the Crystal Palace (high level) line received parliamentary approval, and Turner appointed Shelford resident engineer, making him responsible for its design. He also worked on the Greenwich extension to Blackheath.

Following his father's death Shelford had been troubled by financial problems and Turner allowed him to take a pupil, Frank Smith, and receive his premium. Like many of Fowler's staff, Shelford earned a high reputation for the training he provided. On 10 February 1863 he married Anna, the third daughter of Thomas *Sopwith FRS. They had eight children, not all of whom survived childhood. They had met through a choral society which Shelford had joined while a member of Christ Church choir, Lancaster Gate. His interest in music and local church affairs continued throughout his life.

In 1865 Shelford set up in partnership with Henry Robinson (1837–1915), who had previously been working at Sir W. G. Armstrong's Elswick works. Robinson brought knowledge and experience of hydraulic and steam power to the partnership. Over the next ten years they carried out all manner of engineering work—railways, waterworks, sewage works, mining engineering—both in the UK and overseas. In the wake of the Overend Gurney banking failure and the financial crash of 1866 work was scarce and Shelford leased out his London home for a time, during which the family lived at Kingsgate, Isle of Thanet. He visited Sicily to advise on the sulphur mines in 1869, and was made a chevalier of the order of the Corona d'Italia for his work in modernizing them. In 1875 the partnership with Robinson was dissolved. Shelford set up his offices at 35A Great George Street, where he remained until his death. Work was slow at first and in 1877 he suffered from depression. However, this was alleviated the following year when he became engineer to Truro waterworks and Boston tramways, the latter being the first of many similar appointments. By the 1880s he had over forty staff.

Shelford's third son, Frederick (1871–1943), joined him in 1892 and became his partner in 1899. At home his railway works included the Louth and East Coast Railway, the Burry Port and Gwendraeth Valley line, Downham and Stoke Ferry, and Brechin and Edgell railways. He was responsible for many waterworks including Louth and Chichester, and sewerage schemes at Crossness, Tottenham, and Southampton. He was engineer for the Hull, Barnsley, and West Riding Railway, built 1880–85, the largest capital project to come before parliament after the Great Northern Railway in 1845. The contractor, John Aird, was heavily involved and became his personal friend.

Although primarily a railway engineer, Shelford carried out some important investigations of rivers, and recorded the results of his studies of the Humber, Mersey, and Tiber, in papers to the Institution of Civil Engineers. He was also frequently called upon to act as arbitrator, and to give evidence on parliamentary bills, as was the case with his support for the Manchester Ship Canal.

Shelford was involved with many schemes abroad. He visited Canada in 1885, Italy (for the second time) in 1889, Argentina in 1890, and Spain in 1892. He was consultant with Sir Frederick Bramwell on the Winnipeg and Hudson Bay Railway. Most important was his association with the British colonies in west Africa, where he acted as consultant to the crown agents, at one time employing more than 1500 engineers and assistants. This project was his most significant public work, and in consequence he was made CMG in 1901 and KCMG in 1904.

Following surveys carried out in 1893 on his behalf by W. Bradford, Shelford designed a system of narrow gauge railways in Sierra Leone. The first section from Freetown to Songo Town was built in 1896–9, and by the time of his death it had reached Baiima, 220 miles from Freetown. In addition a short line of 6 miles was built in 1904 from Freetown, forming the Sierra Leone mountain Railway. In Ghana 168 miles of railway were built, initially (1898–1901) from Sekondi to Tarkwa, extended by October 1903 to Kumasi. Shelford's son Frederick acted as chief of the exploration party from Sekondi to Kumasi, and was the first European to explore the forest on the route. In Nigeria Frederick led the survey mission to Lagos of 1897. The 125 mile Lagos Government Railway to Ibadan was opened in 1901, and a series of road bridges, including the 2600 ft Carter Bridge, were designed to join Lagos to the mainland. Other surveys and reports were carried out at this time for government railways in Malta, in British Honduras and British Guiana, in Malaya, including Singapore harbour, in Egypt, and Cyprus. Shelford's work overseas was reflected in the paper he presented on girder bridges to the British Association in 1885, which drew British engineers' attention to the more economical forms of bridge construction being used in North America, which were better suited to colonial practice.

Shelford was a member of many learned societies, becoming a member of the Institution of Civil Engineers in 1866, a fellow of the Geological Society in 1869, and of the Statistical Society of London in 1875. Active in the British Association he was also a member of the Society of Arts and the Royal Geographical Society, and a founder member of the African Society. He was the author of many papers and reports, one of the most prescient of which was his 1877 pamphlet, written with R. Price Williams, which advocated the creation of a Metropolitan Water Board. Shelford's high reputation in the profession was reflected in his election to the council of the Institution of Civil Engineers in 1887. Only his retirement from the council due to ill health in 1897 prevented him becoming vice-president. He had been dogged by poor health throughout his career, and was frequently crippled by sciatica. Shelford retired in August 1904, and died on 3 October 1905 at his home, 49 Argyll Road, Kensington, London. He was survived by his wife.   MIKE CHRIMES

Sources A. E. Shelford, *The life of Sir William Shelford KCMG* (1909) · *PICE*, 143 (1900–01), 384–6 · *The Engineer* (6 Oct 1905) · *WWW, 1897–1915* [Leonard Edmund Shelford] · 'Frederick Shelford', *Who's who in engineering: a biographical dictionary of contemporaries, 1922–23* (1922) · 'Frederick Shelford', W. T. Pike, *Contemporary biographies* · F. T. Turner, *PICE*, 50 (1876–7), 181–4 · H. Robinson, *PICE*, 200 (1914–15), 471–2 · *CGPLA Eng. & Wales* (1905) · *DNB* · d. cert.
Archives Inst. CE · PRO, crown agent records; railway company records
Likenesses engraving, *c.*1904–1905 (after portrait by S. Lucas), Inst. CE
Wealth at death £16,571 17*s.* 4*d.*: probate, 24 Oct 1905, *CGPLA Eng. & Wales*

Shelley, George (*c.*1666–*c.*1736), writing-master, appears to have been born in London. Nothing is known of his early life or parentage except that his poverty is suggested by his education at Christ's Hospital, a charitable institution which primarily took care of London orphans. From these humble beginnings Shelley rose to become one of the preeminent and most prolific penmen of his day; indeed, he was described, posthumously, as a 'shining figure in the common-weal of English calligraphy' (Massey, 2.131).

By 1708 Shelley was living at the Hand and Pen in Warwick Lane where he kept a school. Prior to that he worked as a private tutor teaching penmanship to the children of the gentility. This is evident from *The Penman's Magazine* (1705), his first published copybook, which was dedicated to his former pupils Ann and Dorothy Sharpe, the daughters of the archbishop of Canterbury. From the outset of his publishing career Shelley's preference for the most decorative genres of penmanship is clear. He was an expert flourisher, writing texts in a variety of hands which were then ornamented with patterns and fantastic figures executed with one continuous stroke of the pen. He could also show more restraint when producing utilitarian texts in 'round hand', the writing style best suited to business transactions. Examples of his more practical penmanship can be found in *Natural Writing* (1709?) where the trading links were made clear in Shelley's artful and, most probably, uninvited dedication to the directors of the Bank of England. In the preface to this work Shelley went to great lengths to augment his reputation by insisting on the high regard in which he was held by other writing-masters. A certain vanity can also be detected, for instead of praising the engraver George Bickham, as writing-masters usually did, Shelley tried to deter any critics by complaining that 'his Imitation falls short of my originals' (Shelley, preface). His motivation for such unusually self-regarding assertions was probably linked to his application, in the same year, for the prestigious position of writing-master to Christ's Hospital; a fiercely contested post, which Shelley succeeded in winning over eight rival penmen. His sense of competition can also be discerned from the lengthy and public battle which, along with Charles Snell,

he waged against the writing-master John Clark. The subject of this debate was the comparative merits of 'sprigging'—the more artistic aspect of penmanship—and clear hands designed for the advancement of trade. Rather ironically, although Shelley was considered a master of round hand, he was also a virtuoso of the flourish and consequently he preferred to promote this less accessible aspect of his penmanship.

After selling up his Warwick Lane academy to John Clark, Shelley established himself at Christ's Hospital and his next published copybook, *Alphabets in All the Hands* (1710), sold for the benefit of the 'orphans of Christ's Hospital', reflects his pride in his new position. Throughout the remainder of Shelley's career he continued to publish various copybooks, some of which were more biased towards the ornamental hands and decorative texts than others. Despite his many published copybooks, Shelley appears to have led a somewhat dissolute life. In 1725 he was deeply in debt and he was forced to petition the court of Christ's Hospital to advance him £166 to pay his creditors. Matters obviously did not improve as, in 1726, a meeting of the Hospital's committee reported finding that Shelley had absented himself for days and sometimes weeks. Although he pleaded fear of persecution on account of his debts, the Hospital decided that they had been generous enough. Shelley was immediately discharged from his post at Christ's Hospital and was succeeded by Benjamin Durnford. Nothing is known of Shelley's last ten years but William Massey assumed that he died in 'low circumstances' about 1736.   LUCY PELTZ

Sources A. Heal, *The English writing-masters and their copy-books, 1570–1800* (1931) · I. D'Israeli, *Curiosities of literature*, 14th edn, 3 vols. (1849) · *A biographical history of England, from the revolution to the end of George I's reign: being a continuation of the Rev. J. Granger's work*, ed. M. Noble, 3 vols. (1806) · *Engraved Brit. ports.* · Thieme & Becker, *Allgemeines Lexikon* · W. Massey, *The origin and progress of letters: an essay in two parts* (1763) · *DNB* · G. Shelley, *Natural writing in all the hands, with variety of ornament* [1709]
Likenesses G. Bickham, engraving (after B. V. Lens), BM, NPG; repro. in G. Shelley, *The second part of natural writing* [1714] · G. Bickham, group portrait, engraving, repro. in *A Poem on writing* · G. Bickham, line engraving, BM, NPG, V&A; repro. in Shelley, *Natural writing*
Wealth at death impoverished: *Biographical history*, ed. Noble, vol. 2, p. 360

Shelley [*née* Godwin], **Mary Wollstonecraft** (1797–1851), writer, was born at 29 The Polygon, Somers Town, London, on 30 August 1797, the only daughter of William *Godwin (1756–1836), author and political philosopher, and the second daughter of Mary *Wollstonecraft (1759–1797), author and political philosopher. Wollstonecraft died of puerperal fever eleven days after Mary Godwin was born, and William Godwin undertook to raise their daughter as well as Fanny Imlay Godwin (1794–1816), Wollstonecraft's illegitimate daughter with Gilbert Imlay (1754–1828). Mary Jane *Godwin (*née* Vial; former married name Clairmont) (1768–1841), whom Godwin married in 1801, brought her two illegitimate children to the family: Charles Gaulis Clairmont (1795–1850) and Clara Mary Jane (Claire) *Clairmont (1798–1879). The birth of William

Mary Wollstonecraft Shelley (1797–1851), by Richard Rothwell, exh. RA 1840

*Godwin jun. (1803–1832) brought to five the siblings who were partially, or by law, related. Presided over by John Opie's portrait of Mary Wollstonecraft that hung in Godwin's study, this unconventional family, in which political idealism and financial distress were part of daily life, brought Mary Godwin an early apprenticeship in the largely unorthodox path she followed throughout her life.

Early years and education Mary Wollstonecraft Godwin's education as a child included attendance at a dame-school and a spell of seven months in 1811 at Miss Caroline Petman's school for the daughters of dissenters at Ramsgate, where she had been sent for sea-bathing to treat an infected arm. Unquestionably, however, she received her most important education at home. William Godwin set a high intellectual standard for the household, encouraging the children's aptitudes and imaginations, and instilling in Mary Godwin confidence in her own power and responsibility to effect change as an activist in a society in transition. Under his tutelage, she achieved a solid foundation in history (ancient and modern), mythology, literature, and the Bible; visiting instructors provided art and French lessons. She also studied Latin, an uncommon subject for girls, and attended adult theatre and lectures with her father and family. Mary Godwin adopted her father's deism, which she blended with a poetic pantheism. She also adopted his daily discipline of spending each morning in writing and study, and throughout the course of her life she continued to study widely and in depth. She was fluent in Italian and French, acquired Latin and Greek, and some Spanish.

The unusual circumstance of two parents whose works voiced and influenced the reformist politics of an age of political, social, and technological revolution developed in Mary Godwin from childhood a keen awareness of the socio-political issues of her era. Her introduction to the 1831 edition of *Frankenstein* provides a picture of her precocity and her early awareness of her parents' literary significance:

> It is not singular that, as the daughter of two persons of distinguished literary celebrity, I should very early in life have thought of writing. As a child I scribbled; and my favourite pastime, during the hours given me for recreation, was to 'write stories'. (p. v)

To this heritage, Mary Godwin's stepmother, with whom she had a difficult and strained relationship, none the less provided another untraditional role model as an occasional author and as proprietor of the family publishing firm, M. J. Godwin & Co. In addition, the Godwins' many friends and acquaintances included a spectrum of important authors, scientists, and political reformers of the day, who brought to the home a world of ideas and a level of discourse that few girls (or boys, for that matter) would have experienced. Some, like S. T. Coleridge and Charles and Mary Lamb, strongly influenced Mary Shelley's works.

In 1811 William Godwin described his daughter as 'singularly bold, somewhat imperious, and active of mind. Her desire of knowledge is great and her perseverance in everything she undertakes, almost invincible.' He also commented that she was 'very pretty' (Abinger MSS). Mary Godwin's contribution of a summary sketch for *Monsieur Nongtongpaw*, a comic poem published by M. J. Godwin & Co. in 1809 and often reprinted, demonstrates her precocious intellect, as does Aaron Burr's report of her 1812 'lecture', 'The influence of governments on the character of a people', orated by her brother (Burr, 1.307). Her father's opinion regarding her appearance was confirmed by most observers, who often noted her hazel eyes, light auburn hair, high forehead, and exceptionally fair complexion. R. Easton's posthumous miniature portrait (Bodleian) captures her younger appearance; R. Rothwell's 1840 portrait (National Portrait Gallery), her more mature.

Life and career, 1812–1816 In June 1812 Mary Godwin was sent to the home of William Baxter, one of Godwin's political admirers, again to treat her infected arm. On 10 November 1812 she and Christina Baxter arrived at the Godwins for a seven-month sojourn in London, and on the next day, Mary Godwin met Percy Bysshe *Shelley (1792–1822) and his wife, Harriet, at the Godwin home. In March 1814 Mary Godwin's stay with the Baxters in Dundee ended, and she returned home. In the interval, P. B. Shelley's intellectual pursuits as well as his commitment to provide Godwin with desperately needed financial assistance, had gained him the interest and admiration of the entire Godwin household. In early May, Mary Godwin encountered P. B. Shelley once again, and the pair, often meeting at Wollstonecraft's graveside in St Pancras churchyard, fell in love. Mary Shelley later described that period of her life as 'careless, fearless youth' (*Journals of*

Mary Shelley, 2.443) and P. B. Shelley praised her for 'The irresi[s]tible wildness & sublimity of her feelings' (*Letters of Percy Bysshe Shelley*, 1.402). They found in each other ideal mates: she, almost seventeen, Godwin's and Wollstonecraft's 'Child of love and light' (P. B. Shelley, *Revolt of Islam*, I.i.9), eager to study and write; he, five years older, already a published poet, and her parents' ardent disciple.

William Godwin failed in his attempts to convince both his daughter and P. B. Shelley to end the relationship, no doubt in part because of the very arguments against legal marriage advanced in his own and in Wollstonecraft's works. At 5 a.m. on the morning of 28 July, Mary Godwin, accompanied by her stepsister Claire Clairmont, met with P. B. Shelley at a waiting coach, and, with very little money, eloped to the continent. This marked the beginning of the couple's life together, which Mary Godwin described as 'very political as well as poetical' (*Letters of Mary Wollstonecraft Shelley*, 1.29), a hectic and passionate amalgam of love, study, creativity, social defiance, and financial skirmishes, which periodically caused her considerable distress. But she recognized her own affinity with that lifestyle, musing that 'The soul only enjoys' serenity 'in passing' but it 'constrains' the imagination 'too much, so that it always comes back to the state it finds more suitable, a state of agitation' (*Journals of Mary Shelley*, 2.514).

While on their unconventional walking tour through war-torn Europe during the lull between Napoleon's first and final defeat, Mary Godwin and P. B. Shelley kept a daily journal, which soon became principally hers, and which she continued to keep until 1844. Mary Shelley's revision of the elopement journal, along with four 1816 letters and P. B. Shelley's poem 'Mont Blanc', was published anonymously as *History of a Six Weeks' Tour of France, Switzerland, and Germany* (1817). It formed a narrative of the Romantic feelings and observations about nature, social mores, and politics. The elopement journey was the first of their many travels and collaborations, in which they encouraged and inspired each other's writing, at times worked on the same projects, and pursued their iconoclastic lifestyle. Mary Godwin was already pregnant when the elopers, penniless, returned to England in September 1814 and met with almost universal disapproval from family and friends. It was only later, after the loss of P. B. Shelley's protection and wealth, that she was painfully brought to the full realization of the effects of the severe and enduring societal censure placed on her as a result of what she termed 'the outset of my life' (*Letters of Mary Wollstonecraft Shelley*, 3.92).

The death of his grandfather in 1815 brought P. B. Shelley an annual income of £1000, which ended the couple's acute financial difficulties. From August 1815 until April 1816 P. B. Shelley and Mary Godwin made their home at Bishopgate, in Windsor Great Park, which later served as a setting for her third novel, *The Last Man* (1826). In January 1816 Mary Godwin gave birth to their son William, all the more rejoiced in, as the couple's first daughter, born in London on 22 February 1815, had died twelve days later.

The writing of *Frankenstein*, 1816 In May 1816 P. B. and Mary Shelley (as she was slowly becoming known, although they would not marry until later that year) travelled with their four-month-old son and Claire Clairmont to Geneva, Switzerland, with the hopes of remedying P. B. Shelley's poor health. They chose Geneva rather than Italy because Claire Clairmont, who had earlier initiated an affair with Lord Byron, was already pregnant and anxious to see him, in hope of a permanent liaison. For the Shelley–Byron colony of writers and would-be writers, the summer was a period of mutual inspiration and productivity. In her introduction to her 1831 revised edition, Mary Shelley recounted the story, itself part of literary history, of that stormy night in June in which a ghost-writing contest led to her novel *Frankenstein* (1818). From a 'waking dream' she created an instant myth that captured the public imagination. The story of the scientist and his creature rapidly permeated all levels of society, and became the material of theatrical productions, newspapers, political cartoons, parliamentary debate, translations, and countless inexpensive and/or pirated reprints.

Mary Shelley's first novel voices the concept of private politics as a mirror image of public politics, a tenet that would pervade all of her major works. She used the trappings of the Gothic novel to illustrate the destructiveness not of science, but of power protected by wealth and position. In the public mind, the nameless Creature has often been given his Creator's name, ironically supporting Mary Shelley's thesis that a corrupt political system equally victimizes the empowered and the disempowered. The best-known fiction of the Romantic era, *Frankenstein* is credited with introducing the science fiction genre into English literature.

Initially, critics believed *Frankenstein* was written by a man. Walter Scott proposed the author was P. B. Shelley, beginning a chain of criticism that has endured to the present. Analysis of the novel, whether favourable or not, was conducted in terms of its reformist political vision, which grappled with the social, scientific, industrial, and economic issues of the era. Once it was discovered that its author was a woman, however, critics seldom directly addressed the novel's politics, considered a 'male topic'. Like P. B. Shelley and other English Romantics, Mary Shelley utilized her own experiences to interpret society, revered nature as a source of renewal, and was committed to public and domestic reform based on democratic principles, education, and expansive love. But the traditional bias against intellectual women caused most contemporary reviewers to evaluate her novels largely as romances, although the fervent animus of some reviews may have resulted from the unspoken belief that her work would be dangerous to the *status quo*. The power and imagination of her writing was recognized by various commentators with the dubious compliment that she had a 'masculine mind'.

Married life with P. B. Shelley, 1816–1822 On the Shelleys' return to England in 1816, they first took lodgings in Bath to prevent William and Mary Jane Godwin from learning of Clairmont's pregnancy. That autumn two tragedies deeply affected the Shelley–Godwin circle. On 9 October Fanny Imlay Godwin committed suicide at Swansea. And on 9 November Harriet Shelley, in an advanced state of pregnancy, drowned herself in the Thames, her body not being discovered until 10 December. On 30 December, with the Godwins as witnesses, the Shelleys were married at St Mildred's Church, London, thus healing the breach between father and daughter. In March 1817 the Shelleys moved to Albion House, Marlow, where they remained until they left for the continent in March 1818. To both Shelleys' great disappointment, the court of chancery that spring refused P. B. Shelley's efforts to gain custody of Ianthe and Charles Shelley, his children with Harriet Shelley.

Mary Shelley's letters and journal express her eagerness to have children; she gave birth to her second daughter, Clara Everina Shelley, at Bishopgate on 2 September 1817. In March 1818 the Shelley entourage, including Claire Clairmont and her daughter Clara Allegra Byron, travelled to the warmer climate of Italy to treat P. B. Shelley's illness, which had been diagnosed as pulmonary disease (White, 1.538). In Italy they continued their intellectual practice of wide reading and writing, expanded their social circle, and frequently changed residences. At Leghorn Mary Shelley reintroduced herself to Maria (Reveley) Gisborne (who had cared for her during Wollstonecraft's final days), and her husband, John Gisborne, with whom she and P. B. Shelley formed a lifelong friendship.

From Leghorn, the Shelleys moved to the Casa Bertini in Bagni di Lucca, in the foothills of the Apennines, an area of Tuscany rich in the history of Castruccio Castracani, the subject of Mary Shelley's next novel. From there, they moved to Venice and Este, so that Claire Clairmont could visit her daughter Allegra, who was in Byron's custody. The infant Clara Shelley, already ill before the journey, died of dysentery at Venice on 24 September 1818. On that day, Mary Shelley noted: 'This is the Journal book of misfortunes' (*Journals of Mary Shelley*, 1.226). After wintering at Naples the Shelleys travelled to Rome in April 1819, where on 7 June William died of malaria, further devastating both Shelleys. Mary Shelley, already expecting her fourth child, suffered a severe depression, and, always of a more reserved nature, she withdrew further into herself and away from P. B. Shelley. The two tragedies caused considerable strain in the Shelleys' relationship, a strain, it has been suggested, which may also have been exacerbated by P. B. Shelley's attraction to other women. But the Shelleys' union, from its dramatic beginning, favoured the concept of expansive rather than exclusive love, as articulated in Mary Shelley's letters during her brief love experiment in 1814–15 with P. B. Shelley's friend Thomas Jefferson Hogg, and in P. B. Shelley's poem *Epipsychidion*. Nevertheless, Mary Shelley became impatient when she felt his inclusivity demanded too much attention, as it had with Claire Clairmont.

Perhaps as a means to return the Shelleys to their usual empathy, their next projects were written in close collaboration. While at Leghorn from June until October 1819, they borrowed a holograph transcription of the *Relazione della morte della famiglia Cenci seguita in Roma il di II Maggio 1599*, which Mary Shelley copied. Based on her copy, P. B. Shelley wrote his tragedy *The Cenci*, the story of the Cenci family's history of incest and murder, and Mary Shelley translated the story into English, which the Shelleys originally intended to publish with the play. During the same period, Mary Shelley wrote *Matilda*, a fictional account of a father's incestuous love for his daughter. William Godwin, and then Mary Shelley herself, withheld the novella from publication, fearing that a woman's writing on this taboo topic would provoke a scandal akin to those generated by Godwin's publication of Wollstonecraft's *Memoirs* and by the Shelleys' elopement. Not published until 1959, *Matilda* has often been construed in narrow biographical terms, but recent scholarship has reinterpreted it in terms of its literary complexity of character and narrative voice. As a result, *Matilda* is often placed among Mary Shelley's most accomplished works.

From Leghorn, the Shelleys went to Florence, where they resided at Palazzo Marini, via Valfonda 4395, where their fourth, and only surviving child, Percy Florence Shelley, was born on 12 November 1819. They intended to remain in Florence so that Mary Shelley could continue her research for the historical novel she had begun in Marlow in 1817, *Valperga, or, The Life and Death of Castruccio Castracani*, published in 1823 for her father's benefit. In January 1820, however, they moved to Pisa, their home for the following year and a half, where they formed an international circle of British, Greek, and Italian friends. In May 1822 the Shelleys and their friends the Williamses moved to Casa Magni at San Terenzo for the summer, where the next month, Mary Shelley suffered a near fatal miscarriage. Then, on 8 July, the Shelleys' life together came to a tragic close: P. B. Shelley and Edward Williams, returning from welcoming Leigh and Marianne Hunt to Italy, drowned in a squall in the gulf of Spezia.

Life and career, 1822–1844 Although deeply bereaved, Mary Shelley, almost immediately after P. B. Shelley's death, expressed her confidence in her ability to write and to raise her son. She was also determined to bring P. B. Shelley the widespread recognition that he had failed to receive in his lifetime, by editing and publishing his works. Within a year after P. B. Shelley's death, she published her own 'A Tale of the Passions', and two essays, 'Madame D'Houtetot', and 'Giovanni Villani', as well as P. B. Shelley's texts, in *The Liberal*.

Initially, Mary Shelley had planned to remain on the continent, which she found more conducive to her independent temperament. But Sir Timothy Shelley, P. B. Shelley's father, who refused ever to meet her, would not consider any support for Percy Florence unless he was raised in England. For her son's sake, she returned in August 1823 and spent most of the remainder of her life as an 'exile' in a conservative England that was inhospitable to her ambitions and her intellect. Sir Timothy granted a repayable allowance for Percy Florence that carried with it serious restrictions for Mary Shelley. After the publication of her edition of P. B. Shelley's *Posthumous Poems* (1824), Sir Timothy withdrew the allowance, demanded the volume be withdrawn, and prohibited Mary Shelley from publishing P. B. Shelley's works or bringing the Shelley name to public attention. Two years later, he temporarily withheld the allowance when a critic cited her name in a review of *The Last Man*, which had been published as 'by the author of *Frankenstein*'. Despite his power over her, Mary Shelley over the years found a number of ways to circumvent his restriction just as she persistently negotiated for additional funds as Percy Florence's educational needs increased.

Over the next two decades Mary Shelley published several dozen reviews, short-stories, and poems, as well as some of P. B. Shelley's works, in prominent London journals and the then popular annuals. Her own ambitions, however, went far beyond the periodical press. As she announced to Leigh Hunt on 9 February 1824, 'I am going to plunge into a novel, and hope that its clear water will wash off the … mud of the magazines' (*Letters of Mary Wollstonecraft Shelley*, 1.412). That novel was *The Last Man* (1826). Set in the twenty-first century, it focuses on six characters whose lives are dramatically interwoven with private and public issues of power when a cataclysmic plague seemingly destroys every person on earth except one, Lionel Verney, the narrator of the novel. This highly political work of fiction, with its graphic scenes of death and war, received almost universally scathing reviews. Dismissed as another end-of-the-world work of the kind then popular, with its fundamental thesis of the imagination as curative and its parable of personal and societal politics, the novel was alien to contemporary critics. Today, *The Last Man* is generally regarded as her second best novel.

Mary Shelley's next major work returned to the genre of the historical novel. *The Fortunes of Perkin Warbeck* (1830) is set in the fifteenth century, and presents a retelling of the events surrounding the struggles of Perkin Warbeck, who claimed to be Richard, duke of York, to wrest the English throne from Henry VII. Although it portrays Henry as ruthless and manipulative and Richard as seemingly idealistic and caring, the novel enunciates her philosophy that, in the end, there is little difference between men who destroy nations in the interest of their own power. *Lodore* (1835), her fifth novel, and *Falkner* (1837), her sixth and final novel, were to continue this theme, but differ from her earlier work in their shift away from supernatural or historical settings to contemporary stories in which private politics metaphorically critique the limitations of the conventional Victorian class and legal systems. Between 1832 and 1839, while she was completing *Lodore* and *Falkner*, Mary Shelley also contributed the vast majority of the essays comprising the five volumes of the Revd Dionysius Lardner's *Cabinet of biography: lives of the most eminent literary and scientific men of Italy, Spain and Portugal* (1835–7) and *Lives of the most Eminent Literary and Scientific Men of France* (1838–9). Drawing on her past readings and current research, the *Lives* astutely profile a wide spectrum of figures within their historical context while continuing to reflect her reformist vision.

Mary Shelley's determination to reprint her husband's works had not waned during this time, and in 1839 Edward Moxon published her carefully edited collections: *The Poetical Works of Percy Bysshe Shelley* (4 vols.), and *Essays, Letters from Abroad, Translations and Fragments by Percy Bysshe Shelley* (2 vols.). Her one-volume edition of his poetical works, also published by Moxon, is dated 1840. In order to circumvent Sir Timothy's restriction on biography, she included annotations that placed the works within their historical context. The edition is regarded as a turning point in the acceptance of P. B. Shelley as a major author, and despite their strategic reticence, her notes have proved an invaluable resource for future biographers and critics.

After her return to England in 1823, Mary Shelley had formed new friendships with a number of leading figures of the day, including Frances Wright, Prosper Mérimée, Thomas Moore, Lady Morgan, Caroline Norton, and John Howard Payne. She continued her friendship with the Lambs and Thomas Love Peacock and renewed her girlhood friendship with Isabella Baxter Booth. She also became a close friend of the Joshua Robinson and Beauclerk families, and played a major role in a transgender deception in which the writer Mary Diana Dods passed as 'Mr Sholto Douglas' and Isabella Robinson successfully passed as 'his wife' in an élite Anglo-French circle in Paris. Of her circle in Italy, she remained close friends only with Jane Williams and the Gisbornes. And almost until the end of her life, she and Claire Clairmont sparred, at times drawing together in mutual aid.

Although Mary Shelley at times found wanted comfort and companionship in male and female friendships, she never formed another relationship that approached the one she had shared with P. B. Shelley. She rejected offers of marriage from Payne and Edward John Trelawny, expressed interest in Washington Irving, and appears to have formed an intimacy with Aubrey Beauclerk, a Liberal MP, which ended in disappointment. As she wrote, 'I have always felt certain that I should never again change my name—& that is a comfort, it a pretty & a dear one' (*Letters of Mary Wollstonecraft Shelley*, 2.204).

Always pressed for funds, Mary Shelley moved frequently, residing mainly in the area of greater London, but from 1833 until 1836 at Harrow on the Hill, in order for Percy Florence Shelley to attend Harrow School. Later, she would see that he attended Trinity College, Cambridge, as well, fulfilling P. B. Shelley's and her own educational aspirations for their son. Despite her own financial restrictions, she habitually aided her father, her widowed stepmother, and many others in her circle.

Final years, 1840–1851 With the impetus to provide funds for an Italian expatriate who would later try to blackmail her, Mary Shelley wrote the two-volume *Rambles in Germany and Italy, in 1840, 1842, and 1843* (1844), her last full-length work, based on letters written during two journeys that she had taken with Percy Florence and several of his friends. Unlike most other works in the popular genre of travel memoirs, *Rambles* interpolates a strong Romantic reformist perspective through its commentaries on war, national manners, historical perspectives, and politics.

In 1844 Sir Timothy Shelley's death left the encumbered part of the estate to Mary and Percy Florence Shelley, who also inherited the title. For the first time since P. B. Shelley's death, she knew financial security. But it would only be four years later, with the marriage of Percy Florence Shelley and the widowed Jane Gibson St John, that Mary Shelley again had a domestic circle in which she felt genuine love and contentment. Throughout the last decade of her life, she suffered from periods of intense headaches, as well as pain and paralysis in her arm. Nevertheless, she travelled, made changes to her editions of P. B. Shelley, and as late as 1848 returned to work again on the biography of her husband that she had begun years earlier. But illness, first that of her daughter-in-law, then her own, put an end to that plan. On 1 February 1851, already in a coma, Mary Shelley died of a brain tumour at her home at 24 Chester Square, London. The younger Shelleys fulfilled her wish of burial with her parents by removing Wollstonecraft's and Godwin's remains from the St Pancras churchyard and burying all three on 8 February in St Peter's Church, Bournemouth, near Boscombe, the Shelleys' home.

Reputation During her lifetime, Mary Shelley was celebrated as the author of the extraordinary *Frankenstein* and otherwise generally regarded as a gifted writer of romances. Since that time, her own accomplishments were subsumed under P. B. Shelley's, even to the extent of wrongly crediting *Frankenstein* in large measure to him rather than to the actual author. Critics continued to ignore Mary Shelley's vision, which depicted the limitations of conventional values through her metaphoric use of public and domestic abuse of power, advocating instead an egalitarian, humane system based on reason and universal love. Her own family abetted the depoliticization and domestication of Mary Shelley's works, which was not an unusual development within the context of Victorian conventional presumptions of women's ambitions, intellect, and concerns. Whatever her frustrations and occasional ambivalence in her struggle as a single, independent, intellectual woman, however, she had always held to the belief that it was her 'fate' to be a writer (*Journals of Mary Shelley*, 2.431–2, *Letters of Mary Wollstonecraft Shelley*, 3.105).

Mary Shelley's unusual childhood prepared her for that destiny; her adult life fostered her aspiration with each major work to achieve more 'in the staircase I am climbing' (*Letters of Mary Wollstonecraft Shelley*, 1.361). Reassessment of her works in the mid- to later twentieth century initially often depicted her as a victim of conventional expectations for women. Readers, however, spurred by the women's movement, began to recognize her as a Romantic whose inherent independence of vision and political dissonance required further reconsideration. The impetus for this change in perspective originated in renewed interest in *Frankenstein*, as the ethical dilemmas posed by technological and medical advances increasingly resonated with the novel's prescient examination of power and responsibility. As a result, in the closing quarter of the twentieth century, new editions of Mary Shelley's novels, short stories, letters, and journals were published that provided a wide opportunity to read her works unfiltered by nineteenth-century mores. In this period, upwards of 500 books and scholarly articles as well as countless review articles appeared that discuss Mary Shelley and her works.

Frankenstein also holds an enduring place within popular culture, quickly becoming a common, often misunderstood, metaphor. In 1824 George Canning in parliamentary debate argued that freeing the West Indian slave 'in the manhood of his physical strength, in the maturity of his physical passion, but in the infancy of his uninstructed reason, would raise up a creature resembling the splendid fiction of a recent romance' (*Hansard 2*, 10, 16 March 1824, 1103). Charles Sumner, an American statesman, during the American Civil War equated 'the Southern Confederacy with the soulless monster of Frankenstein. The wretched creation of a mortal science without God; endowed with life and nothing else' (R. Florescu, *In Search of Frankenstein*, 1999, 14). Some decades later, Sir John Lubbock argued in parliament that it 'would be impossible to control the Frankensteins we have ourselves created', the Frankensteins in this case being liberal reforms (ibid.).

The story of the creature and the scientist has been drawn on as the basis of more than one hundred stage productions, beginning with Richard Brinsley Peake's 1823 *Presumption* in London, which inspired fourteen other dramatizations within three years in France and England (S. E. Forry, *Hideous Progenies*, ix). *Frankenstein*'s film history began with Thomas Edison's 1910 production, but indisputably the most influential screen production was the 1931 version directed by James Whale, and starring Boris Karloff as the creature, a role that he reprised in *The Bride of Frankenstein* (1935) and *Son of Frankenstein* (1939). Karloff's presentation of the creature, with its halting movements and its prominent scars, has remained imprinted on the popular consciousness, a pervasive cultural icon with which every subsequent cinematic interpretation has had to deal. The numerous serious film versions that followed have, to date, failed to capture the complexities of the novel, or replace the Karloff image in the popular imagination. Persistent cinematic interest has also spawned comedic versions which helped to contribute to the popular dissemination and distortion of the original work; Mel Brooks's *Young Frankenstein* (1974) is the most famous and enduring of these satires, but also influential in this regard was the 1960s television series *The Munsters*. The creature and the scientist, in various incarnations, also appear commonly in cartoons, advertisements, comic books, toys, records, CD-ROMs, and on the internet.

Notwithstanding these numerous popular interpretations and adaptations of *Frankenstein*, the novel and Mary Shelley's other texts are increasingly the focus of scholarly interest and literary investigation. As a result, large numbers of readers have come to appreciate the complexities of the original novel that Mary Shelley referred to as her 'defence of Polypheme' (*Letters of Mary Wollstonecraft*

Shelley, 1.91). Mary Shelley's international significance was demonstrated in 1997, as bicentennial conferences and exhibits in Australia, the United States, and Europe celebrating her birth explored the meaning of her works and her philosophy. The unusual attention given the discovery of her lost children's story *Maurice* and its 1998 publication represent another marker of the recognition of Mary Shelley's increased stature. Re-evaluation of Mary Shelley's literary achievements is currently very much in process, and her overall significance is yet to be recognized. More than 245 editions of *Frankenstein* have been published, including translations in Chinese, French, German, Hebrew, Italian, Japanese, Spanish, and Swedish. If she had created only *Frankenstein*, her significance in literary history would be secure; but a full understanding of the import of all of her major works may change our understanding of literary history as well.

BETTY T. BENNETT

Sources *The journals of Mary Shelley, 1814–1844*, ed. P. Feldman and D. Scott-Kilvert, 2 vols. (1987) · *The letters of Mary Wollstonecraft Shelley*, ed. B. T. Bennett, 3 vols. (1980–88) · MSS of the Shelley–Godwin circle, Bodl. Oxf., MSS Abinger [on deposit] · W. Godwin, journals, 6 April 1788–26 March 1836, Bodl. Oxf., MSS Abinger · NYPL, Humanities and Social Sciences Library, Pforzheimer collection · B. T. Bennett, *Mary Wollstonecraft Shelley: an introduction* (1998) · E. W. Sunstein, *Mary Shelley: romance and reality* (1989); repr. (1991) · *The letters of Percy Bysshe Shelley*, ed. F. L. Jones, 2 vols. (1964) · W. H. Lyles, *Mary Shelley: an annotated bibliography* (1975) · A. Burr, *The private journal of Aaron Burr*, ed. M. L. Davis, 2 vols. (1838) · *The novels and selected works of Mary Shelley*, ed. N. Crook, P. Clemit, and B. T. Bennett, 8 vols. (1996) · *The Clairmont correspondence: letters of Claire Clairmont, Charles Clairmont, and Fanny Imlay Godwin*, ed. M. K. Stocking, 2 vols. (1995) · K. N. Cameron, D. H. Reiman, and D. D. Fischer, eds., *Shelley and his circle, 1773–1822*, 10 vols. (1961–2002) · W. St Clair, *The Godwins and the Shelleys* (1989) · E. Dowden, *The life of Percy Bysshe Shelley*, 2 vols. (1886) · C. Kegan Paul, *William Godwin: his friends and contemporaries*, 2 vols. (1876) · R. G. Grylls, *Mary Shelley* (1938) · R. Ingpen, *Shelley in England* (1917) · J. Marshall, *The life and letters of Mary Wollstonecraft Shelley*, 2 vols. (1889) · *Mary Shelley: collected tales and stories*, ed. C. E. Robinson, 4 vols. (1891) · *Shelley and Mary*, 4 vols. (privately printed, 1882) · W. R. Thurman, 'Letters about Shelley from the Richard Garnett papers', PhD diss., U. Texas, [n.d.] · N. I. White, *Shelley*, 2 vols. (1940) · S. Curran, *Frankenstein: the Pennsylvania electronic edition* (1999) · b. cert. · m. cert. · d. cert.
Archives BL, MSS · Bodl. Oxf., corresp., literary MSS, and papers · Bodl. Oxf., corresp. and papers · Duke U., Perkins L., papers · Harvard U., Houghton L., letters · Hunt. L., letters · Keats Shelley Memorial Association, MSS · Mitchell L., NSW, papers · NL Scot., letters · NYPL, collection of Shelley and his circle, papers · NYPL, Berg collection, papers · Ransom HRC, MSS · University of Iowa Libraries, Iowa City, papers · Washington University, St Louis, Missouri, papers | BL, letters to Claire Clairmont, Ashley MSS 4020, 5023 · BL, corresp. with Leigh Hunt, Add. MSS 38523–38524 · BL, letters to Royal Literary Fund · Bodl. Oxf., Abinger MSS · Bodl. Oxf., letters to Mary Peacock · Keats House, Hampstead, London, letters to John Murray and Leigh Hunt · Trinity Cam., letters to Lord Houghton
Likenesses R. Rothwell, oils, exh. RA 1840, NPG [*see illus.*] · R. Easton, miniature, oils, 1851–93, Bodl. Oxf.
Wealth at death held funds and real estate in common with son

Shelley, Norman Francis

Shelley, Norman Francis (1903–1980), actor, was born on 16 February 1903 at 4 Milton Chambers, Chelsea, London, the son of Frank Shelley, a painter, and his wife, Alice Campbell, *née* Glover. He originally intended to become an aircraft designer, but took up stage acting on the advice of the actress and teacher Rosina Fillipi. His first appearance was at the Old Vic in 1919, and in the early 1920s he toured with the Charles Doran Shakespeare Company (which also boasted such actors as Ralph Richardson and Donald Wolfit), in such parts as Trebonius in *Julius Caesar* and Sebastian in *Twelfth Night*. During the 1920s and early 1930s he worked principally in London, where he was most associated with Peter Godfrey's experimental productions at the Gate Theatre Studio, including Eugene O'Neill's *The Hairy Ape* and *All God's Chillun* (both 1928), Constant Lambert's version of Oscar Wilde's *Salome* (1931), and Walter Hasenclever's *Murder* (1933).

Shelley first broadcast for the BBC in 1926, though he made his early radio reputation in Australia and New Zealand. He gradually shifted his interest from stage to radio (though he continued to make stage, film, and—later—television appearances throughout his career), and in the late 1930s he established his reputation as one of the most respected and versatile radio actors in Britain. On 16 April 1937 he married Monica Daphne (*b*. 1911/12), daughter of Harvey Edwin Brett; she was a fellow actor who left the stage on her marriage. They had a son, Anthony. During the Second World War he was an original member of the BBC's wartime repertory company, but left to serve as a ferry pilot in the Air Transport Auxiliary.

On stage Shelley was an intelligent and reliable supporting actor, often cast as a much older man. On radio, however, he was a leading man of remarkable versatility. In the 1930s and 1940s he was a *Children's Hour* regular, famous as Dennis the Dachsund in *Toytown*, and as Winnie-the-Pooh (his favourite radio role), whom he first played in 1939. He played Dr Watson to Carleton Hobbs's Sherlock Holmes over a twenty-five year period. In the 1950s his parts ranged from Prospero in *The Tempest*, Johnson in J. B. Priestley's *Johnson over Jordan*, and Horace Lamb in Ivy Compton-Burnett's *Manservant and Maidservant*. He was a regular reader in *Book at Bedtime*. Late in life he found new fame as the courteous retired military gentleman Colonel Danby in the long-running BBC radio serial *The Archers*. But perhaps his most celebrated performance was one that no one in Britain heard at the time: a recording of Winston Churchill's speech to the House of Commons of 4 June 1940 ('We will fight on the beaches …') in the manner of Churchill himself, made for the British Council to use as propaganda material in the USA. Churchill had refused to reread his speech for a recording and suggested they 'get someone else to do it'; according to Shelley, Churchill was highly pleased with the result, commenting with approval: 'He's even got my teeth.' Apparently many American listeners believed they were listening to Churchill himself.

Shelley continued to work on stage and radio until his death, demonstrating his versatility and range to the last. One of his first stage appearances had been with the legendary Ellen Terry; his last was in Tom Stoppard's *Dirty Linen* at the London Arts Theatre in 1979. He was still recording episodes of *The Archers* at the time of his death.

He collapsed suddenly at Finchley Road tube station, London, on 21 August 1980, and was declared dead in the Royal Free Hospital, Camden. His wife had predeceased him; he was buried near her at Long Hanborough, Oxfordshire, on 28 August.

After Shelley's death the story of his 'Churchill impersonation' took on a life of its own. There had always been some confusion about the details of the story: in the early 1970s one anecdotal history of the BBC had suggested that Shelley had reread Churchill's speech over the BBC European Service, although when Shelley himself recounted the story in the press in 1979 he specifically referred to a recording for the British Council. In 1983 the writer David Irving claimed that Shelley had told him he had impersonated Churchill on the domestic services of the BBC on 4 June 1940, and again on 18 June 1940 (the 'Finest hour' speech). Despite the fact that the 'We will fight on the beaches' speech was not broadcast at all on the BBC on 4 June, and that Churchill himself certainly broadcast in person on 18 June, the story that it was Shelley who had broadcast Churchill's most famous wartime speeches to the British people continues to re-emerge at intervals. In 2000 Shelley's son discovered among his father's effects a copy of the 'On the beaches' recording. This represented the first tangible proof of Shelley's original claim that he recorded the speech for the British Council. However, the discovery was again used by the popular press as an opportunity to spread the more fanciful version.

SIÂN NICHOLAS

Percy Bysshe Shelley (1792–1822), by Amelia Curran, 1819

Sources *Radio who's who*, 2nd edn (1947) · *Radio and television who's who*, 3rd edn (1954) · *The Guardian* (23 Aug 1980), 2, 11 · *The Times* (23 Aug 1980) · J. Snagge and M. Barsley, *Those vintage years of radio* (1972) · D. J. Wenden, 'Churchill, radio and cinema', *Churchill*, ed. R. Blake and W. R. Louis (1992) · *Sunday People* (30 Sept 1979) · b. cert. · m. cert. · d. cert.
Archives SOUND BBC Sound Archive
Likenesses D. Graves, photograph, repro. in *Sunday People*

Shelley, Percy Bysshe (1792–1822), poet, was born on 4 August 1792 at Field Place, near Horsham in Sussex, the eldest son of Timothy, afterwards Sir Timothy Shelley, baronet (1753–1844), and his wife, Elizabeth (1763–1846), daughter of Charles Pilfold. He was baptized at Warnham, Sussex, on 7 September 1792.

1792–1811: early years and education Shelley had four younger sisters and one younger brother: Elizabeth (1794–1831), to whom he was evidently close; Mary (1797–1884); Hellen (1799–1885), whose letters about Shelley's childhood, though written in the 1850s, are an invaluable mine of information (they are included in Hogg); Margaret (1801–1887); and John (1806–1866). The Shelley family had migrated to America in the person of the poet's great-grandfather Timothy (1700–1771). His son Sir Bysshe Shelley (1731–1815) returned to England, adding substantially to the family fortune and social status by two successive marriages, each involving elopement: the first with Mary Catherine Mitchell (1734–1760, married 1752); the second with Elizabeth Jane Sidney (1741–1781, married 1769).

Often Shelley is seen as something of a genetic mystery: where, it is asked, with his stolid background did he get his unique poetic genius? Perhaps his grandfather Sir Bysshe Shelley, a domineering figure, offers something of an answer. In a letter of 1812 Shelley wrote of him with distaste as 'a bad man' and 'a curse on society' for whom he 'never had respect' (*Letters of Percy Bysshe Shelley*, 1.239). Yet Shelley may have had more in common with his grandfather than he cared to notice. Edmund Blunden sees in a portrait of Sir Bysshe the depiction of 'a sort of mystic, who trusted in the discovery of truths less by system than by sudden light through the clouds' (Blunden, 18). Certainly Shelley inherited his intrepid courage and resoluteness.

The poet's father—well-meaning, decent, and utterly conventional—was a member of parliament for New Shoreham, a borough controlled by the duke of Norfolk, who was a supporter of the whig leader, Charles James Fox. Shelley grew up, therefore, in a climate sympathetic to whig notions of liberty, notions that had some influence on, even as they were outdone by, his mature political views; he assumed (as is witnessed by a letter he wrote to Leigh Hunt while at Oxford) that on attaining twenty-one he would enter public life, filling his father's seat (*Letters of Percy Bysshe Shelley*, 1.55). At the same time Shelley would have noticed, as Hunt points out in an incisive analysis of the 'Whig Aristocrats' to whom the poet's family belonged, the gap between 'professed demands of what is right and noble' and 'real inculcations of what is wrong and full of hypocrisy' (Holmes, 12–13).

Shelley's mother is usually treated as a peripheral presence in his life. But there is a growing recognition that she (and the family dynamics of which she and her son were a central part) may well provide a key to understanding the poet's complex personality. Shelley was largely silent about her, and yet his poetry shows a strong concern with the relations between mother and child, as well as between father and child. To judge from scattered anecdotes and the portrait of her by George Romney painted in May 1795, Elizabeth Shelley was an attractive, somewhat formidable woman who took pride in her son's cleverness; she liked to talk of his learning by heart, after one reading, Gray's 'Ode on the Death of a Favourite Cat'. Shelley grew up in a largely female household, much admired by his sisters. Elizabeth left no record of her memories, but Hellen remembered her considerably older brother as 'full of cheerful fun' if somewhat wild, telling his sisters stories of ghosts, alchemists, and the '"Great Tortoise" that lived in Warnham Pond', and given to nocturnal walks, flights of fancy, and experiments involving 'electricity' (Hogg, 1.25, 22, 25, 23). There is a sense in poems such as the rhapsodic *Epipsychidion* (1821) that Shelley tries to create in imagination some equivalent to the emotional harmony he had known as a boy, the centre of female attention.

At the age of six Shelley went daily to the school run by the curate at Warnham, the Revd Evan Edwards. Here he began to learn Latin and Greek, languages of great importance for his poetic development; his father, thinking to make Shelley 'a good and gentlemanly Scholar' (Blunden, 12), no doubt hoped that a grounding in the classics would help his son's political career. When Shelley was ten he transferred to Syon House Academy, Isleworth, with his older cousin Thomas Medwin. The school was run by the Revd Dr Greenlaw and was not enjoyed by Shelley, who 'passed among his schoolfellows', according to Medwin, 'as a strange and unsocial being' (Mullan, 145). There is a drawing, probably of Shelley at this age, by Antoine-Philippe, duc de Montpensier. It shows a sensitive but determined face, with a strong nose, firm mouth, and calm eyes. At Syon House Shelley was teased and bullied, yet he found refuge from the traumas of school in reading Gothic romances. Here he attended lectures by Adam Walker on nature and science, which fired his imagination; the final act of *Prometheus Unbound* (1820) is the fruit of his passion for a type of scientific enquiry appropriately described as 'speculative and imaginative' (Holmes, 16).

In 1804 Shelley went to Eton College. There he was tormented, as at Syon House, by his fellows, especially in his early years at the school. The headmaster until 1809 was Dr Goodall, a jovial figure; in 1809 he gave way to his assistant John Keate, a sterner disciplinarian. At Eton, Shelley showed a characteristic refusal to submit to authority (he disliked the practice of fagging) as well as a capacity for anger in the face of injustice which stayed with him, for both good and ill. The poet who flayed political oppression in *The Mask of Anarchy* (1819) was also the young man who wrote some singularly violent letters to his father and sharply recriminating letters to his deserted first wife. One schoolfellow, W. H. Merle, recalled his response to the 'practical jokes' to which he was subjected as 'a paroxysm

of anger which made his eyes flash like a tiger's' (Blunden, 27). During his time at Eton, Shelley excelled in composing Latin verse; he translated half of Pliny's *Natural History*, and came into contact with Dr James Lind, a scholar who served as something of a mentor and father figure for Shelley. Indeed, his final years at school seem to have been relatively happy. He enjoyed walking in the vicinity of the school, and a friend, Halliday, recalled 'the sparkling poetry of his mind' which 'shone out of his speaking eye, when he was dwelling on anything good or great' (ibid., 28). Shelley was still at Eton when he wrote and published a Gothic romance called *Zastrozzi* (Wilkie and Robinson, 1810). Like its successor *St Irvyne, or, The Rosicrucian* (published during Shelley's first term at Oxford by John Joseph Stockdale in December 1810, despite the 1811 date on its title-page), *Zastrozzi* attempts to cash in on the vogue for sensationalist fiction. But both novels warrant attention as looking ahead, in their concern with oppression, revolt, and subversion, to Shelley's more mature use of Gothic elements.

When Shelley went up to University College, Oxford, in 1810 he was already a published poet, the co-author with his sister Elizabeth of *Original Poetry by Victor and Cazire*, published by Stockdale in 1810 but withdrawn after the discovery that one poem had been plagiarized from Monk Lewis. (Shelley blamed Elizabeth for this.) Some lyrics addressed to Shelley's cousin Harriet Grove (1791–1867), with whom he was in love, have an ease and grace that look ahead to much finer work, and hint at the metrical command characteristic of his mature writing. The budding love affair with Harriet Grove was a casualty of Shelley's increasingly fervent opposition to Christianity, an opposition which culminated in his expulsion from University College on 25 March 1811 after refusing to disavow authorship of *The Necessity of Atheism* (printed in Worthing by C. and W. Phillips in 1811). This work was co-written with Thomas Jefferson Hogg, who was also expelled, after insisting that he share Shelley's punishment. According to Hogg, Shelley was presented at his interview with a sentence of expulsion that had already been 'drawn up in due form, under the seal of the college' (Hogg, 1.169). Hogg was a fellow student at University College, and Shelley's closest friend at Oxford. In his *Life* he has left a vivid if mischievous portrait of Shelley the undergraduate: a poetic genius, intellectually brilliant, and devoted to liberty in all forms, and yet the object of the biographer's worldly amusement. Hogg likes to present Shelley as wildly eccentric, snatching a baby from its mother's arms on Magdalen Bridge to see whether it would 'tell us anything about pre-existence' (ibid., 1.147), or falling asleep in front of a fire 'like a cat' (ibid., 1.59) before waking up and plunging straightaway into argument or reciting verse. These anecdotes, like so many told about Shelley, seem at once melodramatic and to contain a germ of truth. Hogg also praises Shelley's 'pure, entire, and perfect gentility' (ibid., 1.130). This quality, blended 'intimately with his entire nature', was commented on by many of Shelley's friends: according to Byron 'Never did a more finished gentleman than Shelley step across a drawing-room!' (ibid.); for him

Shelley was 'the most gentle, most amiable, and *least* worldly-minded person I ever met' (Cameron, 87).

Shelley found the university academically uninspiring, but he continued with his reading and scientific experiments. Hogg claims that he helped Shelley to compose the seemingly burlesque but covertly anti-establishment collection of poems, *Posthumous Fragments of Margaret Nicholson* (published by Munday in 1810), an early example of Shelley's ability to deploy humour for serious ends. If that work failed to stir suspicion, *The Necessity of Atheism* went out of its way to provoke: its nonchalant conclusion, 'Every reflecting mind must allow that there is no proof of the existence of a Deity. Q.E.D.' (*Prose Works of Percy Bysshe Shelley*, 5), was, in particular, designed to vex the bishops, heads of colleges, and clergymen to whom the authors sent their pamphlet, often under assumed names.

1811–1814: first marriage and youthful writings The expulsion from Oxford heralded a difficult period in Shelley's life. He moved to London, taking lodgings with Hogg at 15 Poland Street. His relations with his father deteriorated as he resisted Sir Timothy's attempts to make him forswear his atheism. At a loss to know how to manage his wayward son, Sir Timothy placed responsibility for dealing with Shelley with his solicitor William Whitton. Shelley, meanwhile, embarked on a period of restless wandering and growing involvement in political agitation. In August of this year he eloped with and married Harriet Westbrook (1795–1816), a fellow pupil of his sisters at a school in Clapham. Harriet was the sixteen-year-old daughter of the well-off owner of a coffee house. In an age of sharp social divisions she would have been regarded as beneath Shelley, and it cannot have been lost on her parents and her considerably older sister Eliza (*b.* 1782), who would become one of Shelley's bitterest enemies, that a match between her and the heir to Field Place would have its advantages. Unhappy at her school, Harriet wrote plaintively to Shelley, who had gone in July to Cwm Elan in Radnorshire, the estate of his cousin Thomas Grove, and who was maintaining an impressive if high-flown correspondence with Elizabeth Hitchener, a Sussex schoolteacher known to his uncle Captain Pilfold. The young poet described to Hogg the gist of Harriet's most significant letter thus: 'she would fly with me, & threw herself on my protection' (*Letters of Percy Bysshe Shelley*, 1.131). The couple eloped, arriving in Edinburgh on 28 August, where they were soon joined by Hogg, and, despite Shelley's objections to marriage as fettering free enquiry, were married the next day. It was to prove among the most fateful events in Shelley's life.

An immediate consequence was the breakdown of Shelley's relationship with his father, who cut off his allowance and ceased to communicate with his son. An indignant letter from Shelley to his father in October tells Sir Timothy, 'You have treated me *ill, vilely*' (*Letters of Percy Bysshe Shelley*, 1.149). Shelley had by this stage moved to 20 Coney Street, York. During this period his letters to his father oscillate between self-justification and an implicit desire for his father's approval. Late in October he visited

Cuckfield, staying with Captain Pilfold, and causing considerable turmoil, partly by accusing his mother of having an affair with Edward Graham, a music teacher and protégé of Shelley's parents. On his return to York, Shelley discovered that Hogg had taken his friend's anti-matrimonial beliefs with inappropriate literalness and had tried to seduce Harriet. Shelley's letters to Hogg from Keswick, to which he, Harriet, and Eliza Westbrook (who had joined Harriet in York during Shelley's absence) had now moved, declare love for and disapproval of Hogg in equal measure, and it is clear that he was devastated by the temporary breakdown of their friendship.

In Keswick, Shelley met and exchanged ideas with Robert Southey, who treated the young radical poet with sympathy and middle-aged scepticism: 'he has a very happy knack', Shelley wrote to Hitchener, 'when truth goes against him of saying, "Ah! when you are as old as I am you will think with me"' (*Letters of Percy Bysshe Shelley*, 1.223). Shelley grew disenchanted with Southey, but the encounter made a powerful impact on both men. Shelley quotes Southey's remark that the younger man was 'not an Atheist but a Pantheist' (ibid., 1.219), while Southey, on whom Shelley acted as his 'own ghost', put Shelley 'upon a course of Berkeley' (ibid.), which led ultimately to Shelley's formulation of his own 'intellectual philosophy' (Reiman and Powers, 477) in his essay 'On life' (1819). Southey appears to have discussed Wordsworth with Shelley, who sent off to Hitchener an early version of what ended up as 'A Tale of Society as it is, from Facts', a poem that shows Wordsworthian influence in its plain diction and sensitive rhythms. This poem was included in a collection of his early work transcribed in the so-called 'Esdaile Notebook', which Shelley tried but failed to have published in 1813.

In January 1812 Shelley began a significant correspondence with William Godwin, the author of *Enquiry Concerning Political Justice* (1793) and the poet's future father-in-law. *Political Justice*, which Shelley may have first read while still at Eton, exercised a durable influence over his mind: he told Godwin that it changed him from 'the votary of Romance' into someone aware he 'had duties to perform' (*Letters of Percy Bysshe Shelley*, 1.227–8). Godwin's belief that human beings must be guided by rational self-rule and his faith in perfectibility pervade much of Shelley's mature work. Tension, however, as much as devotion is apparent in their relationship, and Shelley's visit to Ireland (February–April 1812) in support of agitation to repeal the Act of Union and secure Catholic emancipation was frowned on by his mentor, who preferred a quieter way of working towards a better world. Shelley wrote two pamphlets on Irish affairs, *An Address, to the Irish People*, aimed at poor Irish Catholics and energetically distributed by the young aristocrat, who threw copies at likely passers-by from his balcony in Sackville Street, and *Proposals for an Association of Philanthropists*, which is especially notable for its analysis of what went wrong with the French Revolution and for its commitment to the Godwinian belief that 'We are in a state of continually progressive improvement' (*Prose Works of Percy Bysshe Shelley*, 52). Shelley's involvement in

Ireland's troubled politics was short-lived but more than merely farcical. At the very least, his efforts brought him up hard against the obdurate realities of specific political problems.

Finally responding to Godwin's objections, Shelley, Harriet, and Eliza departed from Dublin on 4 April to live in a variety of dwellings, first in Nantgwillt, Radnorshire, then, briefly, in June with the Groves at Cwm Elan where Shelley wrote 'The Retrospect', among his most accomplished and self-revealing earlier poems. By the end of June the party was living in Lynmouth in north Devon. Here Shelley completed and distributed his prose work *A Letter to Lord Ellenborough*, protesting against Lord Ellenborough's harsh sentencing (prison and pillory) of Daniel Isaac Eaton, a radical bookseller. With Elizabeth Hitchener, who joined the Shelley household in mid-July, he distributed copies of the revolutionary *A Declaration of Rights* and the broadsheet ballad 'The Devil's Walk' by various means, including bottles thrown into the sea and even home-made fire balloons. In August Daniel Healey, Shelley's Irish servant, was arrested in Barnstaple for posting copies of *A Declaration of Rights* and imprisoned for six months, an event which brought Shelley's radical activities to the attention of the Home Office. The decision was taken not to prosecute Shelley for his seditious behaviour, but to have him watched. In the meantime, however, Shelley, with his female companions, left Lynmouth, giving the authorities the slip, and virtually stumbled on the would-be model village of Tremadoc created by William Madocks out of land reclaimed from the sea. Shelley supported this project, but over the months he came into conflict with local interests, a conflict culminating in his forced departure from his rented house (Tan-yr-Allt) in February 1813, after supposedly grappling with and being shot at by (and possibly himself firing at) a nocturnal assailant. Traditionally dismissed in the words of Thomas Love Peacock as a 'sort of semi-delusion' (Mullan, 315), Shelley's account of the incident has recently received cautious endorsement.

Between late 1812 and July 1814 Shelley's personal life went through a phase of great turbulence. In October 1812 he first met Godwin and through him other figures such as the eccentric John Frank Newton, whose vegetarian and Zoroastrian ideas made a considerable impression on the poet; about this time, too, he met Peacock, a man different in temperament from Shelley, but sharing with him and, indeed, doing much to foster in the younger poet over the years a love of classical literature: a love with heterodox ideological implications. In November 1812 Elizabeth Hitchener, who had, in Harriet's words, turned out to be a 'great disappointment' (*Letters of Percy Bysshe Shelley*, 1.331), left Shelley's household in a manner that suggests she was virtually expelled. Shelley emerges somewhat tarnished from the affair. To Hogg he acknowledged the 'fatuity, inconsistency, and bad taste' apparent in his idealization of his former Platonic soulmate, now known as the 'Brown Demon' (ibid., 1.336), and he arranged to pay her a small stipend.

After leaving Tan-yr-Allt, Shelley spent a few weeks in Dublin and Killarney. From Dublin he wrote to the publisher Thomas Hookham of his new poem *Queen Mab*, which should, he instructed, be printed 'on fine paper & so as to catch the aristocrats' whose sons and daughters Shelley hoped to reach (*Letters of Percy Bysshe Shelley*, 1.361), revealing his abiding and often shrewd concern for audience. Breathing indignation against tyranny in fiercely denunciatory blank verse, and containing eloquent essay-like notes on such subjects as the evils of meat-eating and marriage, *Queen Mab* shows the youthful radical poet in quintessential form. Shelley decided against publication, but he distributed some seventy copies to individuals. Frequently pirated, the poem was easily the most widely read of Shelley's poems for many years and inspired the Chartists and others. Subtitled 'A Philosophical Poem', the poem displays the range of Shelley's early intellectual interests, and forms something of a compendium of Enlightenment ideas. *Queen Mab* is especially influenced by the materialism of the *philosophes*. Preferring the impersonal concept of Necessity to the Christian notion of God, it is pervaded by a vision of existence as dynamic and capable of endless betterment.

In 1813 Shelley's money problems, which dogged him throughout his life, were acute, involving him, in October, in taking out a 'post-obit' loan of £2000 for £500. A daughter, Eliza Ianthe, was born to Shelley and Harriet in June 1813, but the first evidence of rifts between husband and wife appear in this year, when Shelley writes to Hogg in November that 'I shall return to London alone' (*Letters of Percy Bysshe Shelley*, 1.379–80). In the same year Shelley came to know Mme de Boinville and her daughter Cornelia, with whom he appears to have been briefly in love; Mme de Boinville was the widow of a French soldier who died during the retreat from Moscow in February 1813, and as late as April 1819 Shelley expressed his retrospective admiration for her, partly because of her sympathy for recent French history, as 'the most admirable specimen of a human being I had ever seen' (ibid., 2.92). In 1814 Shelley turned for comfort to Mme de Boinville and Cornelia as his ties with Harriet began to unravel; the domestic unhappiness he was experiencing, especially with regard to the influence exercised by Eliza Westbrook, and the tug of the Boinville household underlie his affecting 'Stanzas.—April, 1814', a poem whose rhythmic pulse quickens and slows in expressive ways. At the same time his interest in theological polemic resurfaces in his cunningly organized dialogue *A Refutation of Deism*, anonymously published in 1814. Though he remarried Harriet in March to ensure her legal status as his wife, Shelley's emotional restlessness is apparent in his actions and in certain verses. He began to feel, so he later told Hogg, that his marriage had failed, 'as if a dead & living body had been linked together in loathsome & horrible communion' (ibid., 1.402), and in May and June of 1814 he formed a passionate relationship with Mary Wollstonecraft Godwin (1797–1851) [*see* Shelley, Mary Wollstonecraft], his mentor's daughter. After a period of some anguish and self-division, he chose and was chosen by Mary, both these creative geniuses embarking on the most significant relationship of their lives after Mary told Shelley of her love beside the grave of her illustrious mother, Mary Wollstonecraft, in St Pancras churchyard. Shelley spoke to Godwin of their feelings, but Godwin expressed disapproval of the relationship.

The upshot was Shelley's and Mary's secret elopement to the continent on 28 July. Mary's half-sister Jane (later Claire) *Clairmont (1798–1879) accompanied them at Shelley's last minute suggestion, refusing to turn back at Calais, despite the pleas of her mother, the second Mrs Godwin, who had pursued and caught up with the runaways. Thus was fostered a triangular relationship that grew increasingly troubled over the years, and caused Mary, in particular, much distress. However, Shelley developed with Claire an intimate friendship of great importance to him. The three escapees travelled through France (where they witnessed the recent devastation caused by the Napoleonic wars) to Switzerland, and then by river back to Rotterdam, before returning to London. Shelley began *The Assassins*, a fragment of a novel, of interest for its attempt to imagine an ideal community.

Harriet lamented that Shelley had been seduced by Godwin's daughter and ideas, and had ceased to be the man she loved. Despite Shelley's quixotic offer in a letter from Switzerland that she should still live under his protection, their relations deteriorated over the year. As Harriet struggled to negotiate with Shelley, she received a number of coldly offensive letters from him, best understood as showing on Shelley's part repressed guilt about his decision to abandon his wife and daughter. As in other crises in his life, where Shelley's need to think well of himself was threatened by the possibility that others might criticize his conduct, his response to Harriet was to assert an ideal self-image. But despite his declaration in September 1814 that 'You are plainly lost to me' (*Letters of Percy Bysshe Shelley*, 1.398), some measure of the messy intricacy of their relations is given by the fact that at the end of November their second child, Charles, was born. Shelley, Mary, and Claire spent the latter half of 1814 in a variety of London lodgings, including 56 Margaret Street, Cavendish Square, 5 Church Terrace, St Pancras, the Cross Keys inn in St John's Street, and 2 Nelson Square, Blackfriars Road. Often Shelley was on the run from bailiffs and creditors, able to meet the now pregnant Mary only intermittently.

1815–1816: poetry, travel, suicides Shelley's financial difficulties were temporarily solved after the death of his grandfather Sir Bysshe in January 1815. He immediately took a large apartment at Hans Place in London. Leaving Mary with Hogg, Shelley went with Claire to Field Place for the reading of the will, but he was not permitted to enter the house; he awaited the outcome of the will sitting on the front steps, where he read Milton's *Comus*. The resulting settlement with his father (finalized in May) gave Shelley a lump sum of £4500 as well as a sum of £2900 to settle outstanding debts (which Shelley did only to a limited extent: unpaid creditors included Thomas Charters, from whom Shelley had ordered a carriage in

1813, and the Nash brothers, moneylenders from whom Shelley borrowed a large sum, also in 1813). By the financial arrangement Shelley also received a yearly allowance of £1000, to be paid quarterly, of which he agreed to give £200 per year to Harriet; he also paid Harriet a sum of £200 to cope with immediate difficulties. Shelley gave Godwin £1000, though that did little to stop the older man's demands for money.

The opening months of 1815 are harder to reconstruct than most periods in Shelley's life because relevant sections of Mary's (and Shelley's) journals have been destroyed. These sections may have documented his efforts to set up a shared community of friends, in which, in addition to the central relationship between himself and Mary, there would be a close intimacy (possibly sexual) between Mary and Hogg, as well as a tutor–pupil relationship between himself and Claire. Mary's letters to Hogg during this period suggest a flirtation just stopping short of sexual intimacy, and it is to Hogg she wrote for consolation after the death on 6 March of her unnamed baby daughter, who had been born prematurely on 22 February. Mary's relationship with Hogg did not survive long. Her jealousy with regard to Shelley and Claire was longer-lasting and made for difficulties, as it would throughout Shelley's life. As a result Claire temporarily left the Shelley household in May; she returned in the spring of 1816 when she pursued Lord Byron, having a brief affair with him that led to the birth of their daughter, Allegra.

It is in 1815 that Shelley emerges as a major poet, composing by the end of the year the blank-verse poem *Alastor*, his enigmatic and haunting study of longing, desire, and what in the 'Preface' he calls 'self-centred seclusion' (Reiman and Powers, 69). The poem was partly inspired by a boat trip taken by Shelley, Mary, Peacock, and Charles Clairmont in August up the Thames from Windsor lock (Shelley had rented a house in Bishopsgate, at the edge of Windsor Great Park) to Lechlade, and back again. Shelley's atmospheric and sceptically hopeful lyric 'A Summer Evening Church-Yard' was written at Lechlade, and included in a volume entitled *Alastor, or, The Spirit of Solitude; and other Poems*, published by Baldwin, Cradock, and Joy in February 1816 after Shelley had offered the title poem to John Murray, Byron's publisher. The volume also contained much revised versions of the first two cantos of *Queen Mab*, published under the title 'The Daemon of the World', along with another revised section (entitled 'Superstition') from canto 6. In style and theme *Alastor* shows the influence of Wordsworth's *Excursion* (1814) and its portrait of the disillusioned Solitary. While Shelley disliked Wordsworth's reactionary politics (as he saw them), *Alastor* reveals that he now regarded the question of the poet's role as provoking dilemmas. Furnished with an epigraph from St Augustine about wanting to love while not finding what to love, the poem, in its brooding introspection, is a world away from the explicit radicalism of *Queen Mab*. *Alastor* is at some level an elegy for Shelley's failed marriage with Harriet. It gives readers access, however obliquely, to Shelley's deepest feelings about that failure, and its sources in his compulsion to idealize. It sold reasonably well, though the reviews were not especially favourable, giving Shelley his first taste of the relative critical neglect which his published poems encountered during his lifetime.

In January 1816 Mary and Shelley's son William was born at Bishopsgate. Over the next few months Shelley moved with his family (by now including Claire once more) into several lodging addresses in London: 13 Norfolk Street, 32 Norfolk Street, and 26 Marchmont Street. On 3 May they left for the continent, partly driven to do so by continuing financial problems arising out of the decision by chancery not to allow the arrangement agreed between Shelley and his father the previous year (whereby Shelley would sell to his father the rights of reversion granted him by his grandfather's will). Shelley's party arrived in Paris on 8 May, leaving two days later for Geneva so that Claire could be near Byron; they got there on 13 May, first staying in Secheron, at the Hôtel d'Angleterre, where Byron arrived with Dr Polidori in late May. The poets, introduced by Claire, began a major, if sometimes fraught, personal and poetic friendship. Polidori, a somewhat trying presence, found Shelley 'bashful, shy, consumptive' at first meeting, but soon came to view him as 'very clever' (Mullan, 418). Early in June Shelley moved to a small cottage close to Lake Geneva near Cologny, while a few days later Byron took up residence in the Villa Diodati, a rather grander house once lived in by Milton. Shelley and Byron talked and sailed together, making an extended trip round the lake towards the end of June, during which they visited various places made famous by Rousseau's *La nouvelle Héloïse*. Rousseau is the subject of ambivalent stanzas in canto 3 of Byron's *Childe Harold's Pilgrimage*, much of which was written in his stay at Geneva, and reflects the influence of Shelley and his advocacy of Wordsworth's poetry. Other works which resulted from this creative summer include Mary's *Frankenstein*, inspired, in part, by Shelley's and Byron's ideas: 'Many and long', she would later write, 'were the conversations between Lord Byron and Shelley to which I was a devout but nearly silent listener' (Holmes, 328). Shelley contributed to the composition of the novel (the manuscript shows substantial additions and corrections in his hand), and the helpfulness of his interventions has been a matter of controversy. Readers can now study the evidence in Charles E. Robinson's facsimile edition; on balance, it is clear that the novel's composition represents another example of the creative collaboration (sometimes involving differences of outlook) that did much to benefit the writing of both the Shelleys. Shelley also secured publication of the novel with Lackington (it appeared in 1818).

Shelley himself composed relatively little by comparison with Byron, whose productivity often seemed to inhibit his friend. However, he did write two major shorter poems, 'Hymn to Intellectual Beauty', drafted on his boat excursion with Byron, and 'Mont Blanc', written after his visit in late July to Chamonix, finished versions of which were probably left with Byron on Shelley's return to England at the end of August 1816, in a notebook which turned up in 1976 in a trunk belonging to Scrope Berdmore Davies, to whom the notebook was almost certainly entrusted by Byron. This notebook also contains two hitherto unknown sonnets which, to judge from internal evidence, are by Shelley: 'Upon the Wandering Winds that through the Sky' and 'To Laughter'. The versions by which the 'Hymn' and 'Mont Blanc' are usually known derive from their first printings in 1817: the 'Hymn' in *The Examiner* and 'Mont Blanc' in *History of a Six Weeks' Tour*, an account, largely written by Mary, of both their visits to the continent and containing vividly detailed letters by Shelley to Peacock, describing his experience of visiting Mont Blanc. The poems were Shelley's finest creations to date: the 'Hymn' creates its own secular alternative to traditional Christian worship, but it is alive to the fact that its own faith is built on hope and desire; refusing to find in the sublimity of the Alps evidence of a benevolent deity, 'Mont Blanc' explores the mind's 'imaginings' and the way they can free themselves from politically and spiritually crippling deference to absolutes. Both poems challenge through their style as well as through their meaning. The 'Hymn' is concerned with what lies beyond the senses, and employs an array of comparisons designed to suggest the unstable, fascinating lure of intellectual beauty; 'Mont Blanc' mimics the 'unremitting interchange' between the mind and the external world through an irregular rhyme scheme, purposefully ambiguous syntax, and the deliberate subversion of its own developing structures of understanding. Shelley's stylistic intricacy in many of his poems has been seen as confusion by his detractors; but it is best viewed as an appropriate vehicle for a poet who blends precision and intensity as he presses beyond appearances and seeks to capture dynamic processes of consciousness, history, and the cosmos. It is the style of a sophisticated, self-aware questioner and transformer of supposed reality, and, revealingly, during the visit to Chamonix, Shelley signed himself (in Greek) in the registers of several hotels as 'democrat, great lover of mankind, and atheist' (Bradley, 33), a declaration which, despite Byron's erasure of one such entry, would soon become notorious.

Shelley returned with his companions to England in September, after visiting Versailles. He had with him a copy of Byron's *Childe Harold*, canto 3, having been commissioned by the author to deliver the manuscript to and arrange terms with the publisher, John Murray, who refused to send proofs to Shelley. Claire, by now pregnant, took lodgings with Mary at 5 Abbey Churchyard, Bath. The rest of the year was shadowed by two suicides: that of Fanny Imlay, Mary's half-sister and daughter of Mary Wollstonecraft and Gilbert Imlay, and that of Harriet Shelley. Fanny Imlay, depressed at being left behind with the Godwins by Shelley, Mary, and Claire, as well as having recently learned that she was illegitimate, overdosed with opium on 9 October in the Mackworth Arms, Swansea. Shelley's 'Her voice did quiver as we parted' captures his distressed feelings about Fanny's death, the circumstances of which Godwin kept secret.

Tragedy came even closer to home in the next few

months. Harriet Shelley was found dead in the Serpentine on 10 December, 'far advanced in pregnancy', as *The Times* put it (Holmes, 352); she left a heart-rending note, probably written on 7 December, intended for Shelley, her parents, and her sister Eliza, in which she expressed her wish that Ianthe should be brought up by Eliza. Shelley's immediate response to Harriet's death was to deny responsibility and impute blame to the Westbrook family. He was determined to obtain custody of the children, and partly to achieve this end, married Mary on 30 December at St Mildred's Church, Bread Street, London, an event which caused Godwin and his wife much satisfaction, and brought about a reconciliation between Godwin and Shelley. Leigh Hunt, whom Shelley had just met before learning of Harriet's death, and who introduced the younger man to Horace Smith and John Keats, became possibly Shelley's closest friend, and certainly his principal literary ally, partly because of his support at this difficult time.

The long-term effect on Shelley of Harriet's death was considerable; its full, desolate impact can be felt in the central autobiographical passage of *Epipsychidion*. Much later, taking exception to W. M. Rossetti's attempts to whitewash Shelley, Claire Clairmont wrote that 'Harriet's suicide had a beneficial effect on Shelley—he became much less confident in himself and not so wild as he had been before' (Holmes, 356). Peacock, always an advocate of his friend's first wife, reported that Shelley's 'feeling for Harriet's death grew into a deep and abiding sorrow' (ibid., 358). From this time forward, however optimistic Shelley might wish to be, he frequently displayed in his writing an awareness of guilt, painful memory, and remorse that suggests first-hand knowledge.

1817–1818: from England to Italy Much of Shelley's energies in the months after Harriet's suicide went into the attempt to gain custody of their children. In this he was opposed by the Westbrook family, and the case came before Lord Eldon, the lord chancellor, who in a celebrated decision ruled on 27 March 1817 that neither Shelley nor the Westbrooks should have custody. Eldon decided against Shelley on the grounds that the latter's 'principles' would lead to the recommendation of 'conduct' that was 'immoral and vicious' (Blunden, 138). The children were put in the care of a Dr and Mrs Hume, at Shelley's suggestion. Shelley's bitterness at the decision finds its way into a number of poems, principally his complex cursing of Eldon in 'To the Lord Chancellor'. Children were a crucial part of Shelley's life in 1817. On 12 January Claire Clairmont gave birth to Allegra, and on 2 September he and Mary had a daughter, Clara Everina. Shelley's attempts over the next few years to provide for Claire and Allegra and to interest Byron in his daughter's welfare show him at his most tactful and prepossessing, even though they exposed him to scandal about his relations with Claire. Disaster ensued later in Italy after Shelley had returned Allegra to Byron in 1818; in 1822 the girl died of typhoid in a convent in Bagnacavallo.

Awaiting the chancery decision, Shelley and Mary spent much time with the Hunts at their house in Hampstead, where they met Hunt's circle. Only Horace Smith, a banker and writer of parodic verses, took a warm liking to Shelley, providing a vivid picture of Shelley's manner ('it was impossible to doubt even for a moment that you were gazing upon a *gentleman*' (Blunden, 145)). William Hazlitt found him 'sanguine-complexioned, and shrill-voiced' and thought him too much 'the philosophic fanatic' (ibid., 143). Keats, according to Hunt, 'did not take to Shelley as kindly as Shelley did to him' (ibid., 142), probably feeling that Smith's 'gentleman' was a little too persuaded of his social distinction. Benjamin Robert Haydon, the painter, quarrelled with Shelley when the poet began 'saying in the most feminine and gentle voice, "As to that detestable religion, the Christian …"' (ibid., 143).

Provoking as Shelley could no doubt be, his desire to change minds acted as a creative spur throughout a year of social unrest and clamour for political reform. In March, just before Shelley moved into Albion House in Marlow, Charles and James Ollier published his pamphlet *A Proposal for Putting Reform to the Vote throughout the Kingdom*. In this work Shelley seeks to promote a gradualist approach to 'beneficial innovations' such as reform of parliament, declaring 'Universal Suffrage' to be, at present, 'a measure fraught with peril' (*Prose Works of Percy Bysshe Shelley*, 175). Throughout Shelley's career, the tension between his radical visions and his readiness to support step-by-step reforms, along with his awareness of what elsewhere he calls 'the difficult and unbending realities of actual life' (Clark, 254), gave a satisfying complexity to his political utopianism. Later in the year, also using the pseudonym of the 'Hermit of Marlow', Shelley produced his most vigorous and sardonic piece of political prose, *An Address to the People on the Death of the Princess Charlotte*, in which he laments the death, not of the princess, but of Liberty as a result of the execution of three labourers involved in the abortive Pentridge revolution; the pamphlet, of which only a few copies were printed, concludes with an imagining of some 'glorious Phantom' (Liberty reborn) (*Prose Works of Percy Bysshe Shelley*, 239), which anticipates the close of a later response to political repression, the sonnet 'England in 1819'. Other major prose works probably written this year include fragments of the so-called 'Speculations on metaphysics' (first published by Mary Shelley in 1840) and the fascinating if unfinished *Essay on Christianity* (first published by Lady Shelley in her *Shelley Memorials* in 1859), altogether a more thoughtful and inward reading of that religion than is supplied by *Queen Mab*. Here Shelley offers a mainly, but not solely, humanist account of God, suggests that the notion of life after death is a delightful fiction, and praises the teachings of Christ, which are glossed in a way that sounds distinctly Shelleyan.

But the main project of 1817 was Shelley's latter-day epic poem, written in Spenserian stanzas, *Laon and Cythna*, published by Ollier, with Sherwood, Neely, and Jones, in December 1817. Retitled *The Revolt of Islam*, the work was republished the next month in censored form, after Shelley had reluctantly agreed to cut overtly anti-Christian phrases and references to an incestuous relation between the hero and heroine. Shelley described the poem in his 'Preface' as 'an experiment on the temper of the public mind' (T. Hutchinson, ed., *Shelley: Poetical Works*, corr. G. M. Matthews, 1970, 32). Yet, for all its beauty of versification and power of thought, the poem was too cloudily symbolic and abstractly anti-establishment to be popular. The *Quarterly Review* ran a particularly sharp and hostile piece on the poem. The reviewer was J. T. Coleridge, but Shelley suspected Southey, a suspicion which led in 1820 to a bitter exchange of letters between the two poets. *The Revolt of Islam* contains in its 'Preface' and its dedicatory stanzas to Mary passages of idealized poetic autobiography, in which Shelley presents himself as the mouthpiece for 'Truth's Deathless Voice'. Much of the poem concerns itself with replaying the French Revolution and depicting Laon and Cythna as heroic revolutionary figures. The fact that the two central figures go to a postmortal 'Temple of the Spirit' after the failure of the revolution indicates the poem's enriching awareness that its political and spiritual goals are hard to achieve.

On 11 March 1818 Shelley left England for Italy, never to return. His departure was motivated by financial and health problems (including a recent bout of ophthalmia, possibly the result of visiting the poor in Marlow), as well as by the wish to hand over Allegra to Byron, the fear that after Lord Eldon's judgment he might lose the children he had with Mary, and an increasing sense of alienation from English society and culture. His early response to 'the loveliness of the earth & the serenity of the sky' (*Letters of Percy Bysshe Shelley*, 2.3) gives a foretaste of how his poetic gifts flourished in response to the landscape and artistic heritage of Italy. At the Casa Bertini in the Bagni di Lucca, where Shelley and his party stayed from June to August, he translated Plato's *Symposium* in ten days. Shelley's gifts as a translator were remarkable, as *The Cyclops*, his expert version of Euripides' work, bears witness. His elegant translation of the *Symposium* indicates the growing importance of the Greek philosopher for Shelley's thinking; Plato's ideas and images pervade Shelley's Italian productions, though Shelley is too sceptical about ultimate truth ever to be a Platonist in any strict philosophical sense. About this time he wrote his brief but important essay 'On love' and his *Discourse on the Manners of the Antient Greeks Relative to the Subject of Love* (not published in full until 1931). In August he finished *Rosalind and Helen*, a poem begun the previous year, and published in the spring of 1819; it is a minor by-product of *Laon and Cythna*, most interesting for its presentation of the poet figure, Lionel.

Prompted, in part, by Claire's anxieties about Allegra, Shelley renewed his acquaintance with Byron in Venice in late August. Their conversations and disagreements about human destiny found their way into *Julian and Maddalo* (first published in 1824), which was finished in August 1819, another of Shelley's masterpieces that both incites and frustrates biographical speculation. The poem's couplets accommodate a range of inflections, and its two main characters, the optimistic Julian and the pessimistic Maddalo, overhear at the poem's centre a disturbed and disturbing speech by a Maniac who has been disappointed

in love. Shelley's marital problems may find covert expression in this section of the poem. It is likely that there was strain between him and Mary following the death of their daughter Clara in September 1818 after Mary had undertaken, at Shelley's instructions, a long journey in the Italian heat from Este to Padua. More anguish followed in June 1819, when their much-loved son William died, plunging Mary into profound melancholia and creating a distance and tension between her and Shelley which shadowed their marriage henceforth. In between these tragic deaths occurred the mysterious episode of Shelley's 'Neapolitan charge' (*Letters of Percy Bysshe Shelley*, 2.211). A girl, born on 27 December 1818, was registered as 'Elena Adelaide Shelley'. Despite the later blackmailing allegations of an Italian servant, Paolo Foggi, it is unlikely that Claire was the mother; the view that the Shelleys' Swiss servant Elise (later Foggi's wife, her maiden name is unknown) was the mother is sometimes expressed; some biographers see Shelley as the likely father, but there is no proof of this. The child was left in Naples with foster parents after Shelley left. She died in the summer of 1820, an event that produced in the poet a morbid sense that 'the destruction that is consuming me' was like 'an atmosphere which wrapt & infected everything connected with me' (ibid.). The pressures endured by Shelley at the close of 1818 are turned into lyric art in his 'Stanzas Written in Dejection'. Personal and political dejection also mark his fine *Lines Written among the Euganean Hills*, a reworking of the eighteenth-century prospect poem, begun at Este in October and included in the *Rosalind and Helen* volume; the poem records what Shelley in the volume's 'Advertisement' calls 'the sudden relief of a state of deep despondency' (T. Hutchinson, ed., *Shelley: Poetical Works*, corr. G. M. Matthews, 1970, 167), and it concludes with a brief imagining of happiness and peace.

1819–1820: Italian masterpieces Shelley's creative resilience in the face of personal suffering is remarkable. In 1819 he wrote many of the works by which he is best known. His responsiveness to Italian landscapes, history, and art, recorded in some majestic letters written to Peacock, is especially acute around this period. In January 1819 he visited Pompeii, in February Paestum, and in March he arrived in Rome, experiences which would leave deep impressions on his imagination. These impressions were not always radiant. In *Prometheus Unbound*, II. iv, Shelley seems to draw an image of the 'great chain' of evil from his sight in the square of St Peter's of '300 fettered criminals at work' (*Letters of Percy Bysshe Shelley*, 2.93). Indeed, 1819 is a year in which Shelley's career-long belief in the need to:

> hope, till Hope creates
> From its own wreck the thing it contemplates
> (*Prometheus Unbound*, IV. 573–4)

receives severe tests as well as eloquent reaffirmation. *Prometheus Unbound* was largely written in this year (it was begun at Este in 1818 and was published by Ollier with some shorter poems in August 1820).

The work represents, in its allusive sophistication,

multiplicity of imaginative suggestions, generic complexity (it is a 'lyrical drama'), and richness of invention, Shelley's most ambitious attempt to 'familiarise the highly refined imagination' of his readers 'with beautiful idealisms of moral excellence', as he puts it in his 'Preface' (Reiman and Powers, 135). But it is a mark of his readiness to take a full look at the worst that while or, in the case of 'Athanase', in the months before, he was working on the lyrical drama he also composed at least five substantial works exploring darker aspects of the human condition: in addition to *Julian and Maddalo* and *Lines Written among the Euganean Hills*, these works include 'Athanase' (first published in 1824), in which Shelley presents a condition of unexplained dejection; *The Cenci* (first published in 1819), a gripping drama that centres on the ethics of revenge, which was turned down by the major London theatres because of the incestuous rape at its heart; and *The Mask of Anarchy*, a satirical yet visionary ballad, written in response to the infamous Peterloo massacre that took place in Manchester in August. Like many of Shelley's most uncompromising works, *The Mask of Anarchy*, which settles scores with members of the Liverpool administration such as Castlereagh and Eldon, was published only after Shelley's death (in 1832 by Leigh Hunt, to whom it had been sent by Shelley, who hoped that his friend might publish the poem in his literary and political paper, *The Examiner*). *The Cenci* made it into a second edition (published in 1821), the only work of Shelley's to do so in his lifetime. Its relative popularity derived, in part, from its readiness to deal with believable characters in an austere blank verse unburdened by what in his 'Preface' Shelley says is 'commonly called mere poetry' (ibid., 241). John Scott's review of the work was reasonably typical: he disapproved of its 'radical foulness of moral complexion', but he complimented its 'uncommon force of poetical sentiment' (O'Neill, 97).

The year 1819, in many ways Shelley's *annus mirabilis*, saw him (and his party) moving round Italy. He stayed in Rome until just after the death of his son, then he moved to the Villa Valsovano between Leghorn and Monte Nero; in October he switched to the via Valfonda in Florence. While he was in Rome his portrait was painted by Amelia Curran, daughter of the Irish nationalist and acquaintance of Shelley John Philpott Curran. This portrait, the best-known picture of Shelley, was regarded as 'ill done' by the artist herself, who had been on the point of burning it when it was sent for by Mary Shelley after her husband's death (Holmes, 512). It offers a sentimentalized picture of the poet as a boyish angel, but, in fairness, Medwin could 'conceive of no one so difficult to pourtray' on account of Shelley's 'ever flitting and varied' expression (Woof, 92). Most contemporary descriptions note his height (5 feet 10 or 11 inches), slight stoop, prematurely grey hair (associated by Shelley, it would appear from a passage in *Epipsychidion*, with a bout of venereal disease), slimness, brilliant eyes, small nose, pointed chin, and fair complexion. Leigh Hunt remarks on 'the sensitiveness and tremulous firmness of the mouth' (ibid., 92).

While living in Florence, at the Palazzo Marini, 4395 via Valfonda, Shelley wrote his greatest shorter poem, 'Ode to the West Wind', in which prosodic brilliance (each section is a sonnet in *terza rima* with a concluding couplet), metaphorical daring, and poignant feeling combine to create an enduring record of his desire to 'scatter' his 'words among mankind'. During this time he also wrote *Peter Bell the Third* (not published until 1839), a poem that again demonstrates Shelley's underestimated capacity to write with penetrating and subtle wit as it mocks Wordsworth's 'dullness' yet shows admiration for his achievement. Shelley hoped to publish a series of '*popular songs* wholly political' (*Letters of Percy Bysshe Shelley*, 2.191) as a separate volume, but he could not persuade his publishing contacts in England (principally Leigh Hunt) to help these often inflammatory works into print at a time of increasing political repression. Also fated not to be published until many years after his death was a long, unfinished prose treatise, *A Philosophical View of Reform*, which he began in November 1819, a work which sets out in detail Shelley's mature political views, and illustrates both his awareness that change is a complicated process and that change for the better is unremittingly to be pursued. A further piece of political prose written about this time—and also unpublished during his life—is his letter to *The Examiner* protesting about the sentencing to three years' imprisonment of Richard Carlile on a charge of blasphemous libel. Here Shelley shows a capacity for witty polemic that is apparent, too, in his subsequent essay 'On the devil, and devils' (written between late 1819 and June 1820). In the midst of this furious literary activity Mary gave birth to a son, Percy Florence, on 12 November. Shelley and Mary were visited by Sophia Stacey, a ward of the poet's uncle Robert Parker, and a friendship briefly blossomed. Stacey had a good singing voice, and she was the recipient of a number of lyrics written for her by the poet, including 'Thou art fair, and few are fairer' and a version of the impassioned, virtuosic poem variously known as 'The Indian Serenade' and 'An Indian Girl's Song' (this poem may also have been given as a gift to Jane Williams, the common-law wife of Edward Ellerker Williams, in 1821).

Sophia Stacey left for Rome on 29 December, and the Shelleys themselves left for Pisa on 26 January 1820. As always, Shelley followed public events with keen interest: the stirrings of revolt in Spain in January prompted his 'Ode to Liberty', which sets the Spanish revolt in the context of the battle for freedom throughout history. Much of the poem, therefore, feels like a rhapsodic versifying of *A Philosophical View of Reform* and confirms Shelley's ease among poetic genres and modes, yet its intricacy extends beyond its syntax and rhyming; at the close, the prophetic 'song, its pinions disarrayed of might, / Drooped' is an example of Shelley's fondness for staging uncertainty that inspiration will last. Along with 'Ode to the West Wind', 'The Sensitive Plant', 'The Cloud', 'To a Sky-Lark', and some other lyrics, 'Ode to Liberty' was published in the *Prometheus Unbound* volume later in the year. The lyrical drama was the major work in the volume, but the accompanying pieces include some of Shelley's best work. 'The Sensitive Plant' is a subtle fable about beauty and transience. It hopes against hope that since our senses may play us false, our cherished ideals may be true. In 'The Cloud' celebration of the natural becomes, in the context of the volume, libertarian affirmation: 'I change, but I cannot die'. Unfortunately, despite Shelley's requests to Ollier that he be sent 'the *revised* sheets' (*Letters of Percy Bysshe Shelley*, 2.178), he did not receive proofs of the volume; the result was that the title-poem, in particular, was printed full of errors. Modern editors are still trying to track down how many. The volume received a perceptive though qualified review by John Lockhart in *Blackwood's*, but it did not sell well.

In 1820 the Shelleys were a good deal in contact with Maria and John Gisborne. Maria's son from an earlier marriage, Henry Reveley, was another of those to whom Shelley lent money he could ill afford: in this case, to build a steamboat to run between Leghorn, Genoa, and Marseilles. The scheme failed, but one positive result of the friendship was Shelley's affectionate, amusing, and revealing *Letter to Maria Gisborne* (first published in 1824), which he wrote in June after he had moved to Leghorn to live in the Gisbornes' house, the owners having gone to London for a few months. At the heart of this epistle are shrewd and thoughtful portraits of Godwin, Coleridge, Hunt, Hogg, and Peacock. Godwin, who had been badgering Shelley for money, is seen as 'fallen', and yet assured of fame 'Before the dread tribunal of *to come*'. In July Shelley translated the Homeric *Hymn to Mercury*, written in *ottava rima*, and, in its delight in the god's prankster-like high spirits, a dry run for *The Witch of Atlas*, composed in a few days in August after the Shelleys had moved to the Baths of San Giuliano, near Pisa. *The Witch of Atlas* displays a fine-spun, ethereal myth making and a tone of lawless shape changing. Avoiding polemic, it succeeds in opposing the authoritarian and orthodox less through statement than style. Yet, as often in Shelley's later work, 'a shadow tracks [its] flight of fire', to borrow a line from 'The Two Spirits: an Allegory', since the Witch's aloofness from human sorrow reminds the reader, by contrast, of what, in his 'Dedication' to *The Cenci*, Shelley calls 'sad reality' (Reiman and Powers, 237). About this time Shelley wrote *Swellfoot the Tyrant*, a mock-Aristophanic work that responds wittily to the Queen Caroline affair, exploiting the conventions of radical satire to indict the Liverpool government and envisage revolutionary change when Liberty makes common cause with Famine: the work was published by J. Johnston in December but immediately suppressed at the insistence of the Society for the Suppression of Vice. Another poem also responding to political turmoil is the impassioned if highly rhetorical 'Ode to Naples', written in the latter half of August.

The 'Ode' is typical of Shelley's later work in its occasional nature, as though, after various critical buffetings, he needed to be spurred into verse by some specific event or fact. Certainly some of his finest work from this time forward originates in its response to such stimuli, even as his letters begin to brood on his sense that he was, 'speaking literally, infirm of purpose' (*Letters of Percy Bysshe*

Shelley, 2.244). At the end of October Shelley moved back to Pisa; he met a beautiful, young woman, Teresa Viviani (1801–1836), who was being kept in a convent awaiting the outcome of marriage arrangements in which she played little part. Once again, Shelley was fired by the wish to save a young woman in distress, as he had been with his first wife; once again, disenchantment was the consequence.

1821–1822: late works Shelley's final year and a half show him writing at the height of his powers, though often out of the depth of tangled feelings. Some of his most evidently personal poetry is written in these months, including—and especially—a series of lyric poems composed for Jane Williams. Jane and Edward arrived in Pisa in January 1821, attracted by what they had heard about Shelley from Medwin, who had been staying with the Shelleys since October 1820. Shelley's feelings for Jane are hard to assess accurately. They lie somewhere between friendship and love, and are, indeed, the overt subject of exploration in poems remarkable for a note that many critics have recognized as new: a note at once serene and frustrated, saddened and accepting, submitting to, perhaps even glad of, constraint, yet constantly if undemonstratively lamenting the gap between the human lot and

> some world far from ours,
> Where music and moonlight and feeling
> Are one.

These poems, a late letter to John Gisborne ('I only feel the want of those who can feel, and understand me ... Mary does not' (*Letters of Percy Bysshe Shelley*, 2.435)), and the central section of *Epipsychidion* indicate the growing difficulties Shelley was experiencing in his marriage with Mary Shelley. It should be said, however, that the marriage also seems at its maturest and most real in these months. The bond that kept husband and wife together may have sometimes felt like a chain, as in 'The Magnetic Lady to her Patient', but it was forged in the fires of shared trials, suffering, and creative interaction.

Epipsychidion was the one major poem that Mary printed without an additional note in her great editions of 1839—and one can see why. In it, she plays a secondary role as 'The cold chaste Moon', forgotten altogether in the final 'invitation au voyage' addressed to Viviani. That in the poem itself, and subsequently, Shelley recognized the desirability and impossibility of his fantasized 'Italian platonics' (*Letters of Mary Wollstonecraft Shelley*, 1.223), as Mary called them, suggests the centrality of *Epipsychidion* in any account of him as a poet of idealist desire. Shelley adapts Plato's and Dante's accounts of love in the *Symposium* and the *Vita nuova*, respectively, to his own highly individual explorations; the result is a masterpiece that can still disconcert as its couplets waver unstably and yet valuably between the spiritual and the sexual, the allegorical and the literal, the erotic and the political, devotion to one figure and advocacy of free love. Shelley first suggested a printing of 100 copies for the 'esoteric few' (*Letters of Percy Bysshe Shelley*, 2.263), then asked Ollier to withdraw it from circulation.

In the aftermath of writing *Epipsychidion* Shelley composed *A Defence of Poetry*, his eloquent answer to Peacock's satirical 'Four ages of poetry'. *A Defence of Poetry*, sent to Ollier on 20 March though unpublished until Mary Shelley's *Essays, Letters from Abroad, Translations and Fragments* (1840 [1839]), contends that poetry is useful because it develops the imaginative powers of its readers. 'The great instrument of moral good', he writes, balancing the aesthetic and the ethical, 'is the imagination; and poetry administers to the effect by acting upon the cause' (Reiman and Powers, 488). As much a radiant prose-poem as critical treatise, the essay's implications are still being teased out by commentators. Typically, Shelley argues for an association between periods of political reform and great poetry, yet refrains from urging a causal link. The essay celebrates imaginative creativity above analytical reasoning, and reveals the poet's break with the Enlightenment reasoning on which his early work had depended. There are manifest links in phrasing and conceptualizing between *A Defence of Poetry*, *Epipsychidion*, and *Adonais*, Shelley's elegy for John Keats who had died in Rome in February 1821. In this work Shelley, who subscribed to the belief that Keats's fatal illness had been brought on by a bad review in the *Quarterly Review*, produced his most exalted vision of the significance of poets and poetry. Yet, giving poignancy to his praise for 'The splendours of the firmament of time' is his desire to leave behind 'the contagion of the world's slow stain'. Sometimes criticized as promoting an insipid image of Keats, *Adonais*, in fact, pays tribute to the achievement of a writer whose recent productions—especially *Hyperion*—were much admired by Shelley, always a perceptive and generous critic of his contemporaries. The elegy was printed in Pisa, so that Shelley could oversee the publishing process. A copy was sent to John Gisborne on 13 July, while others were given to Ollier for distribution. Ollier did distribute those copies Shelley sent to him, but he did not republish the poem; indeed, Ollier was irksomely unco-operative over the winter of 1821-2, leading Shelley to search, unsuccessfully, for an alternative publisher.

Over the last few months of his life Shelley was engaged in a number of projects, including a play, *Charles the First*, of which a good deal of drafted material remains. His notebooks of the period bear witness to his work on translations (especially Goethe's *Faust*), lyrics, and other projects, despite his increasingly insistent emphasis in letters on his loss of inspiration (accompanied by admiration for the prolific output of and success enjoyed by Byron, who had moved to Pisa in November 1821). Shelley's final published work *Hellas*, another 'lyrical drama', was composed in October 1821 and appeared in the first few months of 1822. It was sparked into being by Shelley's support for the Greeks in the War of Greek Independence which had broken out in April 1821; the poem, which Shelley called 'a mere improvise' ('Preface'), is dedicated to Prince Alexander Mavrocordato, later to become prime minister of Greece after independence, a friend of the Shelleys and the leading figure in a group of Greek exiles living in Pisa. Though the poem is partisan, it sets the struggle for Greek independence in vast historical and metaphysical contexts. Modelled on Aeschylus's *The Persians*, *Hellas* concentrates on the figure of a doomed tyrant, here Mahmoud, who, in dialogue with the sage Ahasuerus, is brought to a recognition of the futility of his power and of the supremacy of thought. The choral lyrics elaborate these ideas with musical sophistication.

Towards the end of April 1822 Shelley, anxious to move away from close proximity with Byron, moved with his family and that of Edward and Jane Williams to San Terenzo near Lerici in the Bay of Spezia, where the two families shared a house, the Casa Magni, a converted boathouse directly giving on to the sea. With Williams Shelley sailed in his new boat (which to his annoyance came from Genoa with the words *Don Juan* painted on the forward mainsail: Shelley insisted that the offending sections of sail be cut out and replaced). He also worked on his last major work, *The Triumph of Life*, which was left unfinished at his death, just after the poem's narrator has asked the question near the centre of Shelley's poetry: 'Then, what is Life?' Despite its incomplete, much cancelled state, *The Triumph of Life*, a Romantic reworking of Dante and Petrarch, shows a creative intensity, a precision, and an inventiveness that are at odds with the seeming pessimism of its content: a visionary depiction of the nightmare of history and the failure of idealistic hope. Its overall mood turns out to be less disillusioned than relentlessly questioning, in common with Shelley's assertion in a late letter, 'Let us see the truth whatever that may be' (*Letters of Percy Bysshe Shelley*, 2.442).

The last weeks of Shelley's life were a turbulent mixture of pleasure in the beauty of nature and the companionship of Jane Williams, domestic problems, including a near-fatal miscarriage suffered by Mary on 16 June (Shelley saved her life by making her sit in a hip-bath full of ice to stop the bleeding), hallucinations, and troubled dreams. In a letter written just after Shelley's death, Mary recounts a number of such dreams and hallucinations: they include Shelley's nightmare that 'the sea was rushing in' and that 'he saw the figure of himself strangling me [that is, Mary]', and a waking vision he experienced of meeting his double 'which met him as he walked on the terrace & said to him—"How long do you mean to be content?"' (*Letters of Mary Wollstonecraft Shelley*, 1.245). Together with the emotional and creative stresses Shelley was evidently experiencing in San Terenzo, he expresses an affecting reluctance to think too far ahead into the future, feeling, in his own words, as though he stood 'upon a precipice …, content if the heaven above me is calm for the passing moment' (*Letters of Percy Bysshe Shelley*, 2.436). One plan he did throw himself into was the setting up, with Leigh Hunt and Byron, of the anti-establishment journal *The Liberal*. Hunt came to Italy to participate in this venture. On 1 July Shelley and Williams sailed to Leghorn to meet Hunt and his family whom they accompanied to Pisa. On 8 July Shelley, Williams, and Charles Vivian (a young sailor) began their return voyage to San Terenzo. A squall arose; the *Don Juan* sank accidentally (the suicide theory occasionally proffered is dubious); Shelley and Williams drowned, Shelley's body being washed ashore on 18 July near Viareggio. A month later, on 16 August 1822, exhumed from the sands where they were buried in quicklime, the bodies of Shelley and Williams were cremated near Viareggio in a scene described by Edward John Trelawny, the lively biographer of Shelley's last months.

Trelawny's account (revised several times by him) of the discovery of Shelley's body (a 'volume of Sophocles in one pocket, and Keats's poems in the other, doubled back' (Hogg, 2.217)) and of its cremation in a 'furnace' he had obtained in Leghorn (ibid., 2.220) may not be wholly trustworthy in its details. Doubt has been cast on the assertion that the organ snatched by Trelawny from the pyre and later quarrelled over by Hunt and Mary before being stored lovingly by the latter really was the poet's heart; it might, so a Mr A. S. Bicknell suggested to *The Athenaeum* in 1885, have been the poet's liver, an organ more likely to resist fire than the heart. But Trelawny, who evokes the sickened response of Byron, renders memorably a quasi-symbolic collision between the imaginative (Shelley's 'spirit soaring over us') and the corporeal ('The corpse fell open and the heart was laid bare' (ibid., 2.223)). Trelawny collected the poet's ashes and subsequently placed them in 1823 in the protestant cemetery in Rome, where Keats and William Shelley were also buried.

Posthumous reputation In Pisa before his death Shelley told Marianne Hunt, 'If I die tomorrow I have lived to be older than my father, I am ninety years of age' (Barker-Benfield, 190). The remark suggests the amount of experience he got through in his short life. Above all, this experience includes an astonishing intensity of intellectual and poetic activity. It has taken generations of critics and scholars a long time to come close to defining satisfactorily his wide-ranging achievement. As Shelley himself asserted in *A Defence of Poetry*, probably with his own case in mind, 'the jury which sits in judgement upon a poet, belonging as he does to all time, must be composed of his peers: it must be impannelled from the selectest of the wise of many generations' (Reiman and Powers, 486).

In the face of opposition from Sir Timothy, Shelley's father, Mary Shelley worked heroically to bring his work to public attention, and all readers of the poet are indebted to her impressive, if inevitably imperfect, editorial and critical labours. In understandable reaction against those who derided Shelley's poetry because they disliked his atheism and unconventional private life, she offered a version of Shelley in her 'Notes' to her 1839 editions of the poems that is undeniably idealized. At the same time her comments on Shelley's poetic achievement in such works as *The Cenci* (a favourite of hers), and on his intellectual development, are always thought-provoking and often persuasive. The beginnings of a cult of Shelley are apparent in Mary's 'Notes', as well as in poetic tributes from the likes of Thomas Lovell Beddoes and Robert Browning (in *Pauline*, published in 1833); this cult took on more sentimental and full-blown form when custody of the poet's papers and reputation passed to Mary's son

Percy Florence and his wife, Jane, Lady Shelley, who created at Boscombe Manor a virtual shrine to the poet's memory. Potentially disagreeable aspects of or opinions about the poet's life could not be wholly suppressed, however, as Lady Shelley discovered when she inadvisedly commissioned Hogg to write his life of Shelley, still influential: the portrayal of Shelley in recent works such as Ken Russell's film *Geneva* as a frantic visionary owes much to the representations of Hogg and others.

Despite the setting up of a Shelley Society in 1886 and the transformation of the poet in the eyes of some into a martyr at the hands of an uncaring and philistine world (a view given iconic form in the grandiose sculpture of Shelley by Onslow Ford installed in 1893 in the Oxford college that had expelled him), dislike of Shelley, often focusing on his treatment of his first wife, was articulated throughout the nineteenth century and beyond. Matthew Arnold's response to Edward Dowden's biography (1886)—the first major attempt to see Shelley plain—was to exclaim in disgust, 'that set!' (Norman, 235): Shelley's capacity to induce moral revulsion was as strong posthumously as it had been during his life. Indeed, seeing Shelley steadily and seeing him whole has always been difficult—and, one is tempted to say, always will be. How to combine the political radical and the lyrical or imaginative poet has continually exercised readers of the poet. In their different ways, Mary Shelley and Leigh Hunt, two of the poet's most intelligent advocates, felt under pressure to represent Shelley's radicalism in terms that would be thought acceptable by the readership which they were seeking to create for the poetry. Certainly later Victorian critics (Francis Thompson is a notable example) concentrated on the lyric beauty of the poet's writing at the expense of his engagement with history and politics.

Nor, until recently, has Shelley's poetic reputation ever been secure. Early on, his idealism and figurative complexity earned the adverse criticism of Hazlitt. In 1881 Matthew Arnold dismissed him as a 'beautiful and ineffectual angel', 'beating in the void his luminous wings in vain' (Swinden, 69). In the first half of the twentieth century Shelley's reputation suffered a sharply downwards plunge, as his poetry fell foul of modernist tenets of figurative concreteness and impersonality. His writing received partial and unjust verdicts from T. S. Eliot, who found that the man—'humourless, pedantic, self-centred and sometimes almost a blackguard' (ibid., 71)—obtruded on the poetry, and F. R. Leavis, who excoriated a supposedly 'weak grasp upon the actual' (*Revaluation*, 1936, 194). In a period dominated by 'new criticism', with its attention to words on the page, Shelley's linguistic subtleties were largely—and bafflingly—ignored. Since the 1960s, however, Shelley's critical fortunes have soared thanks to rigorous attention to his intellectual complexity and poetic subtlety and integrity, and to the daunting task (spearheaded by scholars such as Donald H. Reiman, G. M. Matthews, Timothy Webb, E. B. Murray, and Kelvin Everest) of producing the best possible texts of his works. His concern with politics has received due and thoughtful recognition. That said, Shelley the political radical can be simplified and stereotyped as well as downplayed, and late-twentieth-century delight in a 'Red Shelley' (the phrase is Paul Foot's) can be as misleading as the Victorian image of him as transcending topical issues; recent literary treatment of Shelley, as in Howard Brenton's play, *Bloody Poetry* (1985), often seems close to caricature. But the quality of critical and editorial work on Shelley has reached a new pitch of understanding. Clearly, Shelley's best modern critics recognize the applicability to his own work of his view in *A Defence of Poetry* that 'All high poetry is infinite', 'the source', for succeeding generations of readers, 'of an unforeseen and an unconceived delight' (Reiman and Powers, 500).   MICHAEL O'NEILL

Sources T. J. Hogg, 'The life of Shelley', in T. J. Hogg and others, *The life of Percy Bysshe Shelley*, 2 vols. (1933) [introduction by H. Wolfe] • J. L. Bradley, *A Shelley chronology* (1993) • *The letters of Percy Bysshe Shelley*, ed. F. L. Jones, 2 vols. (1964) • E. Blunden, *Shelley: a life story* (1946) • R. Holmes, *Shelley: the pursuit* (1974) • D. H. Reiman and S. B. Powers, eds., *Shelley's poetry and prose* (1977); 2nd edn, ed. D. H. Reiman and N. Fraistat (2002) • *The prose works of Percy Bysshe Shelley*, ed. E. B. Murray (1993) • D. L. Clark, ed., *Shelley's prose* (1966) • K. N. Cameron, D. H. Reiman, and D. D. Fischer, eds., *Shelley and his circle, 1773–1822*, 10 vols. (1961–2002) • D. H. Reiman and others, eds., *The Bodleian Shelley manuscripts*, 23 vols. (1986–2002) • N. I. White, *Shelley*, 2 vols. (1947) • K. N. Cameron, *Shelley: the golden years* (1974) • M. O'Neill, *Percy Bysshe Shelley: a literary life* (1989) • R. Woof, *Shelley: an ineffectual angel?* (1992) • J. Mullan, ed., *Shelley* (1996), volume 1 of *Lives of the great romantics* • *The journals of Mary Shelley*, ed. P. R. Feldman and D. Scott-Kilvert, 2 vols. (1987) • D. H. Reiman, ed., *Shelley*, 9 vols. (1985–97), in *Manuscripts of younger romantics* • J. A. Notopoulos, *The Platonism of Shelley: a study of Platonism and the poetic mind* (1949) • *The letters of Mary Wollstonecraft Shelley*, ed. B. T. Bennett, 3 vols. (1980–88) • P. Swinden, ed., *Shelley: shorter poems and lyrics, a casebook* (1976) • S. Norman, *Flight of the skylark: the development of Shelley's reputation* (1954) • B. C. Barker-Benfield, *Shelley's guitar* (1992)

Archives BL, notebook, loan 70 • BL, notes amending E. E. Williams's *The promise*, Add. MS 43805 • BL, papers relating to death, Add. MS 52631 • Bodl. Oxf., corresp. and literary papers • Bodl. Oxf., journal [copy]; papers concerning his expulsion from university • Duke U., Perkins L., papers • Harvard U., Houghton L., poems and letters • Hunt. L., notebooks, and literary MSS • Keats House, Hampstead, London, MSS • Morgan L., papers • NYPL, Carl H. Pforzheimer Collection of Shelley and His Circle, papers • Ransom HRC, papers • U. Cal., Berkeley, papers • Washington University, St Louis, Missouri, papers | BL, corresp. with Elizabeth Hitchener, Add. MS 37496 • Bodl. Oxf., letters to T. J. Hogg and others • Bodl. Oxf., letters, mostly to Thomas Hookham • U. Nott. L., letters to J. T. T. Tisdall

Likenesses Duc de Montpensier, tinted drawing, 1802?–1804 (as a boy), Bodl. Oxf. • A. Curran, oils, 1819, NPG [*see illus.*] • A. Clint, oils, 1820–39 (after A. Curran), NPG • E. Elleker Williams, pencil drawing, 1821, repro. in Holmes, *Shelley* • attrib. M. L. Hunt, marble bust, Eton College • M. L. Hunt, plaster cast of medallion, NPG

Wealth at death nil: allowance ceased at death; did not insure his life

Shelley, Sir Richard (*c.*1513–1587), diplomat and prior of the hospital of St John of Jerusalem in England, was the second son of the judge Sir William *Shelley (1478/9–1549) and Alice Belknap (*d.* 1536), both of Sussex. Richard Shelley followed others of his family by joining the knights of St John (the hospitallers, or knights of Malta). In the mid-1530s he went to the continent to round off his education, and in 1539, wearied of study, took his first steps on a diplomatic career, accompanying the Venetian

Sir Richard Shelley (*c.*1513–1587), by Bernardo Rantvic, 1577

ambassador on a mission to the Turkish court in the hope of gaining firsthand knowledge to employ in Henry VIII's service. The expedition to Turkey was arduous, but the experience does seem to have helped equip him for his chosen career, and by at least January 1541, though he had protested against Henry VIII's suppression of the hospitallers in England in 1540, he was a recognized member of the diplomatic corps, receiving expenses in 1546 as a member of the English mission in France.

Shelley was now acquiring a reputation as a suave diplomat and able linguist, so much so that in October 1550 he was mentioned as a possible special commissioner to unblock deadlocked negotiations with the French over the boundaries of the recent English conquest at Boulogne. At some point Henry VIII seems to have employed him in Germany. In November 1551 he was chosen for the special task of escorting Mary of Guise, the widow of the Scottish king James V, through the English part of a journey from France to Scotland. In March the following year, 'an honest gentleman … who speaks several languages', though reputed to be 'of the new religion' (*CSP Spain*, 1550–52, 468, 494), Shelley was selected as ambassador at the court of the emperor Charles V, and in January 1554 he reported his interview in Vienna with Charles's brother, Ferdinand, king of the Romans, in which, shown signal marks of favour, he discussed Anglo-Habsburg friendship and royal marriage proposals.

Accomplished diplomat though he clearly was, Shelley must have needed to summon up all his skills as an emissary in July 1553, when he had to reassure Charles V, always highly protective of his family's welfare, of the safety of the emperor's cousin, Mary Tudor, briefly set aside in the succession to the throne by the accession of Lady Jane Grey. Following Mary's seizure of the throne in August, Shelley faced, in January 1554, the doubtless more agreeable task of formally announcing to the emperor the marriage to Charles's son Philip of 'the Queen, his mistress' (*CSP Spain*, 1553, 479). His role as a courtier-diplomat was fully evident late in 1555 when, as a gentleman of the household who in April had been granted an annual income of £50 for life, he was deputed to convey formally to the Portuguese royal family and the regent of Spain the news of the queen's confinement, paying his respects to the king of France *en route*.

In point of fact Shelley's ambassadorial career, clearly blossoming up to this point, was interrupted when Mary restored to him his membership of the knights of St John by re-establishing the hospitallers in England in April 1557. He was appointed turcopolier, or commander of the light infantry of the knights, a post traditionally reserved to Englishmen, and made commander of the preceptory (or religious house) of Slebech (Pembrokeshire) and Halston (Shropshire). Following Mary's death in November 1558 and her succession by the protestant Elizabeth, Shelley, who was on his way to Malta, the knights' headquarters, adopted an unmistakably Catholic stance. Though there was a possibility of his resuming his diplomatic career under Elizabeth, in the 1560s his fortunes became caught up with those of the knights, and in September 1561 he succeeded Thomas Tresham as grand prior. Now an exile in the world of Catholic Europe, Shelley, if he was to return to work as an envoy, would do so under the aegis of Philip II of Spain, who sent him on a mission to congratulate the new king of the Romans in 1562. It was from Madrid that Shelley wrote, in June 1565, to the secretary of state, William Cecil, advising the adoption of a moderate course in religion in England, giving notice of his own imminent departure for Malta, hoping to resume his services for his country, but otherwise resigning himself to a Catholic retirement with his 'Book & Beads' (*Catalogue of the Harleian Manuscripts in the British Museum*, 2.465, no. 6990, 31). His intention in July 1565 of playing his part in opposing the great, but ultimately unsuccessful, Turkish siege of Malta was stalled at Naples, though Shelley did eventually reach the island, even if disputes with the grand master led to his withdrawal at the end of the 1560s.

The final phase of Shelley's life now opened, in Venice, at the invitation of the government of that republic. There, in April 1574, he was noted by Philip Sidney as 'very much devoted to papist superstitions' (Pears, *Correspondence of Sir Philip Sidney*, 50). In July of the same year, though ill, he journeyed on to Prague and Hamburg, but by June 1575 he was evidently back in Venice. From there a long series of letters home, written in the 1570s and 1580s to the queen and to the secretary of state, Sir Francis Walsingham, shows that he acted as a semi-official, unpaid, commercial representative of English merchants' fiscal concerns. In this correspondence he vehemently protested both his loyalty to the queen (involving the refusal of a Spanish pension), and his unbudging Catholicism: in February 1576 he was in Rome, where he was identified as opposed to the militant Catholic strategy of Cardinal William Allen. Shelley grew increasingly desperate to return home and begged Walsingham to allow him to do so, to live as a private Catholic. He was hated by the émigré Catholic militants and strongly opposed the Jesuits. Memoranda of April 1582 and May 1583 reported him to be in the hands of the Inquisition, perhaps because of his political views, and he was also summoned to Rome in 1586 but refused to go—though he was referred to in July 1587 as a possible cardinal. Dark references in his correspondence to matters of national security that could not be broached in open letters strongly suggest that he was supplying Walsingham with information on Catholic subversives on the continent—'I have a meaning (and very good means) to discredit some' (*CSP for.*, 19.182)—but the involvement in 1584 in the alleged treason of his recusant nephew Richard Shelley, on whose behalf he bravely petitioned the queen and Walsingham, must have put paid to any expectations that such services as he provided might be rewarded with a passport home. Sick and poor, heavily in debt, and begging for the payment of the arrears of his salary granted in happier days by Mary, Shelley gave final expression to the strength of conviction of his dual position—'a Catholic, yet in his heart … a most dutiful subject' (Stern, 76)—by dying, probably of apoplexy, about 12 September 1587, following a heated dispute with Jesuits in Venice over their 'justifying of the English traitors executed in England' (Read, 3.282). The knights of St John quickly buried him, next day in Venice, and seized what property he had possessed.   MICHAEL MULLETT

Sources *LP Henry VIII*, vols. 13–16, 21 · *CSP for.*, 1547–58; 1581–8 · *CSP Spain*, 1550–53 · *CPR*, 1554–5, 1557–8 · H. Ellis and F. Douce, eds., *A catalogue of the Lansdowne manuscripts in the British Museum*, 2 (1819) · A. J. Loomie, *The Spanish Elizabethans* (1963) · *A catalogue of the Harleian manuscripts in the British Museum*, 1 (1808); repr. (1973) · C. Read, *Mr Secretary Walsingham and the policy of Queen Elizabeth*, 3 (1925); repr. (1967) · V. F. Stern, *Sir Stephen Powle: court and country memorabilia of a government agent for Queen Elizabeth I* (1992) · E. J. King, *The grand priory of the order of the hospital of St John of Jerusalem in England: a short history* (1924) · G. M. Bell, *A handlist of British diplomatic representatives, 1509–1688*, Royal Historical Society Guides and Handbooks, 16 (1990) · S. A. Pears, trans., *The correspondence of Sir Philip Sidney and Hubert Languet* (1845) · J. M. Osborn, *Young Philip Sidney* (1972)

Archives BL, letters and MSS, Harley MSS

Likenesses B. Rantvic, medal, 1577, BM [*see illus.*] · medal (*Grand prior of England 1561–1590*; after contemporary medal at St John's Gate), repro. in King, *Grand priory*, facing p. 100 · medals, BM

Wealth at death £1600 pension arrears, plus rents from London properties (remained unpaid): calendar of patent rolls; state papers

Shelley, Samuel (1756–1808), artist, was born in Whitechapel, London, in August 1756. He entered the Royal Academy Schools on 21 March 1774 (their records state that he was '17 last August') but he had first exhibited at the Society of Artists in 1773. He exhibited at the Royal Academy from 1774 to 1804, in that period missing only the 1775 exhibition. Through a judicious use of frames containing between five and ten miniature portraits Shelley exhibited well over 200 works. Initially he exhibited conventional miniature portraits but from 1780 he began exhibiting subject pictures.

Shelley was self-taught as a miniaturist but was greatly

influenced by the RA and its president, Sir Joshua Reynolds, who encouraged students towards history painting. Shelley aspired to be more than a painter of faces, hoping to demonstrate his invention and originality through painting subject pictures. He was probably equally encouraged by ventures such as the Shakspeare Gallery and Thomas Macklin's Poets' Gallery, which commissioned oil paintings based on subjects from Shakespeare and the great English poets. Reynolds contributed a painting, *Macbeth and the Witches*, which was the subject that Shelley chose for an exhibition piece at the RA in 1782 (V&A).

Shelley collaborated successfully with engravers such as Bartolozzi. A major project was the *Cabinet of Genius* (1787), a collection of poems by writers such as Gray, Pope, Thomson, and Goldsmith, each accompanied by an original design by Shelley. These were engraved by C. Taylor and W. Nutter in an oval format with a 'frame' in imitation of conventional oval portrait miniatures, and usually of a single figure, such as Sylvia from Pope's 'Summer'. The poems were published in batches of twelve but 'Gentlemen [could] bind any numbers together to make a volume, and in any order they please' (*Cabinet of Genius*, 1, 1787, ii), and its success led to a second volume. This was a massive undertaking and the sixty-six designs by Shelley are of variable quality.

Shelley worked prolifically on developing his ideas. The Royal Academy has the drawing *A Vestal Virgin Attending a Sacred Flame*, in pencil and watercolour. (Foskett refers to 'letters and drawings' held by the RA but only one drawing by Shelley and one brief letter from him, referring to and accompanying a drawing by another artist, are in the Royal Academy collection (Foskett, 1.504).) The Scottish National Gallery has sketches of symbolical figures in oil on paper and the Victoria and Albert Museum has sketchbooks in which Shelley worked out his compositional ideas. Shelley also belonged to an informal sketching society referred to by Farington in 1804: 'for four years past [they have] been accustomed to meet once a week during the winter season at each others houses … to sketch and converse upon Art' (Farington, *Diary*, 6.2271).

But while Shelley's studio contained evidence of serious study—in the form of Livy, Ripa, and others—Shelley's designs, especially those for the *Cabinet of Genius*, would rank more as pretty, 'fancy' pictures than as rigorous 'histories'. While his prints were successful his subject miniatures failed to find a market. The public was interested only in miniatures of loved ones and the famous. When Shelley died his studio contained many unsold subject miniatures.

Shelley was however a highly successful portraitist. He was employed at the court of George III and Queen Charlotte, although he was not accorded an official position there. He was ranked among the most well known and fashionable miniaturists of his time. The young miniaturist Andrew Robertson reported in a letter to his brother in 1802 that Shee had stated that if he pursued his ambition he would exceed Cosway and Shelley, the standard to be beaten. A number of Shelley's most beautiful and compositionally complex portraits are notable for their rich, heavily gummed colour in imitation of oil, such as *The Misses Annabella and Mary Crawford* (1782; V&A). But most of his miniatures found in public collections and in salerooms are conventional in size, composition, and colouring.

Farington reports that Shelley was very exercised about being chosen by the Royal Academicians as an associate (Farington, *Diary*, 3.1042). He was passed over on two occasions, which probably exacerbated his frustration with the lack of public interest in his 'histories' and his suspicion that his work was at a disadvantage next to the oil paintings which dominated the RA exhibitions. In 1804 Shelley and W. F. Wells encouraged seven other watercolour artists to found a watercolour society (subsequently known as the Old Watercolour Society) and at a meeting on 30 November 1804 he was made treasurer. The first exhibition opened on 22 April 1805, and in the period up to 1808 Shelley submitted sixty-three paintings. A large watercolour on paper, *Memory Gathering the Flowers Mowed Down by Time* (V&A), appeared at the first exhibition. Shelley was the only miniaturist to join the society and his fellow members were mostly landscape artists. Miniature painting had always had a place in the main exhibition room at the RA but landscape watercolours were relegated to small anterooms. Shelley's fellow watercolourists believed that in exhibiting portraits at the new society Shelley was not promoting the objectives of the society and so voted to exclude him from a share of the profits. Shelley resigned as treasurer in December 1806.

Shelley lived in London all his working life, at 7 Henrietta Street, Covent Garden, from 1784 to 1794 and at 6 George Street, Hanover Square, from 1794 until his death there on 22 December 1808. (Coincidentally the dowager Lady Shelley died on the same day, leading some writers to suggest that there is confusion over the date of Shelley's death.) Edward Nash and Alexander Robertson were his pupils. The sale catalogue of his collection of books, prints, drawings, and miniatures, organized by his friend the auctioneer Peter Coxe on 22 March 1809, pays tribute to him as 'Nobleman, Gentleman, Collector, Connoisseur and Artist', and states that he 'Leaves his best Image in his Works enshrined'. KATHERINE COOMBS

Sources G. Smith, *The Thackeray Gift: eighteenth-century watercolours in the Royal Academy of Arts library* (1998), 35, 44 • D. Foskett, *A dictionary of British miniature painters*, 2 vols. (1972) • *The letters and papers of Andrew Robertson*, ed. E. Robertson (1895) • P. Coxe, *Sale catalogue of miniatures by Samuel Shelley, and collection of paintings and effects* (London, 22–6 March 1809) • Farington, *Diary* • J. L. Roget, *A history of the 'Old Water-Colour' Society*, 2 vols. (1891) • B. S. Long, *British miniaturists* (1929) • RA, Royal Academy Schools • *DNB*

Shelley, Sir William (1478/9–1549), lawyer, was the son of John Shelley (1456–1527), a member of a family of London mercers and aldermen, and his wife, Elizabeth (1460–1513), the posthumous daughter of John Faulconer, otherwise Michelgrove, of Clapham in Sussex. The Shelleys were rumoured to be the abbot of Waltham's bondmen of a manor near Ware, Hertfordshire, and in 1467 Sir William's grandfather John Shelley, soon to be sheriff of London, broke the head of a fellow mercer who had called him a churl. Although later generations would claim a more elevated pedigree, the origins of the Shelleys should be sought among the Hertfordshire peasantry. In 1474 John Shelley joined the Sussex gentry by marriage to Elizabeth Michelgrove, a close relative of John Ernley, the future attorney-general. Probably a member of the Inner Temple, Shelley sat as MP for Horsham in 1491–2. William Shelley was admitted to the same inn at some point between 1500 and July 1502.

Probably about 1498 William Shelley married Alice (*b. c.*1481, *d.* in or before 1537), the daughter of Harry Belknap (*d.* 1488) of Knelle in Beckley near Rye in Sussex. He acquired as brothers-in-law the courtier and soldier Sir Edward Belknap (1470–1521) and John Caryll (*d.* 1523) of the Inner Temple, with whom he or his father shared chambers. In 1512 Shelley took his father's place on the Sussex bench. He failed to become solicitor to the Merchant Adventurers but was appointed recorder of Coventry, where Belknap had influence; his predecessor Anthony Fitzherbert described him as 'a gentleman of good conscience and well learned in the law' (HoP, *Commons, 1509–58*, 3.310). He joined Thomas More as an under-sheriff of London in June 1514 and resigned his office at Coventry the following year having found, like Fitzherbert before him, the residence requirement too onerous. As under-sheriff Shelley was a permanent legal official, advising the sheriffs and sitting as a judge in the weekly sheriffs' court. In 1520 Shelley succeeded Richard Broke as recorder, and represented the city in the parliament of 1523. He conducted delicate negotiations with the crown concerning city offices, loans, and the disarming of the Londoners following the execution in 1521 of the duke of Buckingham, who had been indicted before him at the Guildhall.

Plague forced the postponement of Shelley's reading in the autumn of 1517 until the following Lent. He was not included in the serjeants' call of December 1520, but in April received the king's letter to replace Baldwin Malet, who had used his influence to obtain a discharge. Shelley, too late to prepare his serjeant's reading, took the degree at Ely House on 29 or 30 June 1521. When in London, of which he remained recorder, Shelley lived in St Sepulchre, Holborn, where in 1523 he was assessed for £133 in goods; his lands, worth £140 a year, consisted largely of the fourth share of the Belknap estate which he had inherited in 1521. In January 1526 he was passed over as chief baron of the exchequer, an office for which the recordership was often a prelude, but by 17 November had been appointed to Fitzherbert's place as fourth justice of the court of common pleas; for the next seven years he rode the western assize circuit as junior justice to Sir John Fitzjames. Shelley succeeded to his father's estates in January 1527, at the age of forty-eight, and by 1534 had rebuilt Michelgrove as one of the finest houses in Sussex. He entertained the king, who subsequently told Shelley's son of the 'great cheer' he had had there. From 1529 until

his death he was personally summoned to parliament by writ of assistance; he remained an active member of the Sussex bench, which he chaired as *custos rotulorum* from before 1532.

Shelley's office of recorder of London involved frequent attendance on Thomas Wolsey, and it is clear that a friendship developed between the two men. Shelley advised Wolsey on the foundation of Cardinal College, and took the surrenders of several of the smaller houses dissolved for its creation in 1526. On Wolsey's fall, and perhaps as a test of his loyalty, Shelley was sent to Esher to receive possession of York Place, the archbishop's Westminster palace, for the king. According to George Cavendish, after an ironic interrogation of the judge on the conflict of law and conscience, the cardinal closed their interview by charging Shelley with the unenviable task of reminding Henry 'that there is both heaven and hell' (Cavendish, 119). York Place was to become Whitehall Palace, and Shelley was to be knighted there between 20 June and 24 November 1530. He seems to have respected Wolsey's subsequent entreaty 'for the old amity and love that hath been betwixt us and for that I have used your counsel therein to be good master' to his college (*LP Henry VIII*, 4, 6577), and the marriage of his heir, John Shelley, to the daughter of Wolsey's loyal treasurer William Fitzwilliam of Milton endorses the probability of his close involvement with the cardinal's circle.

While his wealth and landed estate grew, Shelley found himself increasingly out of sympathy with the political and religious changes of the 1530s. In December 1534 his remarks to Fitzherbert about heretical books, and condemnation of the *Supplication* of Dr Robert Barnes as 'a most detestable book of heresy' (Elton, 32–3) were reported to the king's council, and for the Lent assize of 1535 he was transferred to the home circuit under the watchful eye of his junior, the attorney-general Christopher Hales. Shelley was one of the quorum in the commissions of 23 April and 1 June for the trials of the Carthusians and of John Fisher, bishop of Rochester, but was omitted from that of 26 June for the trial of Sir Thomas More. He had been among the judges who upheld the will of Baron Dacre of the South early in the month but was absent, pleading sickness, at the crucial second meeting when the majority gave way to Thomas Cromwell and reversed their opinion in favour of the king's fiscal strategy. Shelley was dropped from the summer assize of 1535, when the judges were given specific instructions to publicize the supreme headship and the exemplary executions of Fisher and More; he was not commissioned again for almost a decade.

Richard Shelley remembered that in Cromwell's time his father had 'passed storms, and with great loss' (BL, Lansdowne MS 35, fol. 143), and there is evidence of the antagonism of the king's minister, although they had been on good terms before Wolsey's fall. Early in 1537 Cromwell proposed that the crown should purchase the timber on the manor of Knelle in Sussex, valued by Shelley at £2000, but began to treat the transaction as a sale of the lordship itself. 'Surely sir', wrote Sir William

Shelley 'there was never motion made to me of any sale of the manor but only of the woods and that was by your good lordship' (PRO, SP 1/117, fol. 141). The sale of timber went ahead, and four years later Shelley's woods were still being felled for the king's works at Calais and Camber. Although Cromwell's servants felt able to help themselves to hawks bred by Shelley at Michelgrove, Sir William was sufficiently confident in his own position to ask for several local manors in exchange for Knelle. No attempt was made to remove Shelley from the bench, either at Westminster or in Sussex, where he remained active as an instrument of government policy, investigating a riot by Sir Geoffrey Pole in 1536 and seeking the origin of rumours of the king's death in 1537, when Cromwell sent him to take the surrender of Titchfield Abbey in Hampshire.

According to Richard Shelley, the king finally made much of Sir William Shelley and in 1541, after Cromwell's fall, he was granted two of his manors in Essex; but he was to wait over three years for another assize commission, as the senior judge on the midland circuit. He acted as a receiver of petitions in the Lords in parliaments between 1539 and 1547 and, through the marriages of his son Thomas and daughter Elizabeth to members of the Copley family, seems to have shared effective control over the seat at Gatton in Surrey, of which the Copleys were the only electors. His servant Thomas Bishop of Henfield (who was to marry Edward Belknap's illegitimate daughter) represented the borough in 1542, his nephew Edward Bellingham in 1545, and his son Richard *Shelley (c.1513–1587) in 1547.

In 1544 Sir William Shelley may have accompanied the king to the siege of Boulogne, where his son Edward Shelley, a master of the household and gentleman of the privy chamber, was lieutenant of the horsemen. Edward was killed leading a cavalry charge at Pinkie in 1547. Sir William Shelley died, probably at Michelgrove, on 4 January 1549, and was buried at Clapham parish church in Sussex; a monument over his grave, depicting him in judicial robes with his wife, seven sons, and seven daughters, was still unfinished eighteen months later. His will, providing for the saying of 100 masses, is further evidence of his religious conservatism, which his descendants would maintain for many generations.

Shelley's judicial experience spanned thirty-three years, and he sat at Westminster for over twenty. But although he enjoyed a longevity that was denied to many of his fellows and remained a loyal servant of the crown, Shelley's less than wholehearted participation in the religious and political changes of the 1530s, his readiness to resist the king in *Lord Dacre's case* in 1535, and his continued maintenance of the old religion ensured that the highest prizes eluded him.   CHRISTOPHER WHITTICK

Sources HoP, *Commons, 1509–58*, 3.310–12 · A. S. Bevan, 'The role of the judiciary in Tudor government, 1509–1547', PhD diss., U. Cam., 1985 · Baker, *Serjeants*, 269, 536 · *The letters of Sir Richard Shelley* (1774) [some readings corrected from the originals in BL, Lansdowne MSS] · PRO, escheators' inquisitions, C140/2/17 [John Michelgrove] · PRO, escheators' inquisitions, C140/54/66 [proof of age of Elizabeth Michelgrove] · PRO, escheators' inquisitions,

C142/37/133 [Edward Belknap] · PRO, escheators' inquisitions, C142/46/14, 15, 40, 79, 92 [John Shelley] · PRO, escheators' inquisitions, C142/88/78 [William Shelley] · will of Henry Belknap, PRO, PROB 11/8 · will of Edward Belknap, PRO, PROB 11/20 · will of William Everard, PRO, PROB 11/21 · will of John Shelley, PRO, PROB 11/22 · will of John Everard, PRO, PROB 11/28 · will, PRO, PROB 11/32 · will of John Shelley, PRO, PROB 11/34 · will of Joan Everard, PRO, PROB 11/35 · G. Cavendish, *The life and death of Cardinal Wolsey*, ed. R. S. Sylvester, EETS, original ser., 243 (1959) · L. Lyell and F. D. Watney, eds., *Acts of court of the Mercers' Company, 1453–1527* (1936) · F. A. Inderwick and R. A. Roberts, eds., *A calendar of the Inner Temple records*, 1 (1896) · H. P. Scicluna, *The book of deliberations of the venerable tongue of England, 1523–1567* (1949) · *Sussex Archaeological Collections*, 26 (1875), 215 · *Sussex Archaeological Collections*, 77 (1936), 141–5 · T. W. Horsfield, *The history and antiquities of Lewes* (1827), vol. 2, pp. 174–7 · G. R. Elton, *Policy and police* (1972), 32–3 · VCH Sussex, 6/1.14, 225 · H. C. Andrews, 'The Shelley family in Herts', *Transactions of the East Hertfordshire Archaeological society*, 6 (1915–22), 241–55 · Sainty, *Judges*

Likenesses effigy on monument, Clapham church, West Sussex; repro. in *Sussex archaeological collections*, 26, 215

Shelton family (*per.* 1504–1558), gentry, took their name from the village of Shelton some 10 miles south of Norwich. They had been landowners in East Anglia since at least the beginning of the thirteenth century, before becoming briefly prominent under Henry VIII and his children. The change in their fortunes originated in a marriage. **Sir John Shelton** (1476/7–1539), who was the son of Ralph Shelton and Margaret Clere of Ormesby, was appointed sheriff of Norfolk and Suffolk in 1504, and was made a knight of the Bath at the coronation of Henry VIII. His wife, **Anne Shelton** [*née* Boleyn] (c.1483–1555), whom he had married by 1503, was the daughter of Sir William Boleyn of Blickling, Norfolk, and sister of Sir Thomas *Boleyn (1476/7–1539), the father of the future Queen *Anne (c.1500–1536). While Sir John played the role of courtier and crown servant, was reappointed sheriff in 1522, and was an active JP in Norfolk, at the end of 1533 his wife, probably through her niece's manoeuvring, was placed in charge of Princess Mary at Hatfield House, Hertfordshire. The purpose of her commission appears to have been that she should put pressure on Mary to recognize Anne as queen. Possibly at Anne's insistence Henry had his daughter more closely confined, but Lady Shelton, though occasionally exasperated by her charge's stubbornness, usually treated Mary with gentle consideration, much to the irritation of Anne's adherents.

By July 1536 Sir John Shelton had been appointed controller of the joint household established for Mary and her half-sister Elizabeth. On 22 November 1538 he was granted the site of the dissolved Benedictine nunnery of Carrow just outside Norwich, which became the family seat. He died on 21 December 1539, aged sixty-two, and was buried in the chancel of Shelton church. He had taken advice from three leading lawyers in drawing up a will which contravened the recently passed Statute of Uses. But his attempt to defraud the crown of its rights was soon detected, and in February 1540 his advisers were temporarily disgraced, while his 'crafty conveyances' were annulled by act of parliament (LP Henry VIII, 17, no. 28, C. 26). Lady Shelton outlived her husband, making her own will late in 1555; it was proved on 8 January 1556.

Sir John and Lady Shelton had at least six children. Their eldest son and heir, another **Sir John Shelton** (*b.* in or before 1503, *d.* 1558), was born at Shelton and was admitted to Lincoln's Inn on 1 March 1517. Like his father he was active in local government, as a JP for Norfolk from 1543 until his death, and as sheriff of Norfolk and Suffolk in 1554–5. He also served in the war with France in 1544 and was knighted in 1547 at Edward VI's coronation. In 1553 he was quick to commit himself to Mary's cause, being among the first to join her at Kenninghall in July; he was rewarded with an annuity of £60 and a seat on the council. In 1554 he was returned to parliament for Norfolk, but thereafter lived on his East Anglian estates. He made his will on 12 February 1558 and died in Norfolk on 15 November following; his heir was his elder son Ralph. Sir John had benefited from his mother's court contacts to make an advantageous marriage.

Sir John's wife, **Margaret Shelton** [*née* Parker] (*fl.* *c.*1530–1536), was the elder daughter of Henry *Parker, tenth Baron Morley (*d.* 1556); her younger sister Jane *Boleyn (*d.* 1542) was the wife of Queen Anne's brother George, Viscount Rochford. John and Margaret had two sons and three daughters, one of whom, as Mary Scudamore, was an influential figure at the court of Elizabeth I. It was not Margaret Shelton, however, who was briefly alleged to have become Henry VIII's mistress, as was once supposed. The lady in question was Mary *Shelton (1510x15–1570/71), a daughter of the elder and sister of the younger Sir John Shelton, who had become a maid of honour to her cousin Queen Anne. In February 1535 she was described by the imperial ambassador Chapuys as enjoying the king's favour. Her name was linked with the king's again early in 1538, and in the meantime her affections had been competed for by two leading courtiers, Henry Norris and Francis Weston. Mary survived these entanglements, and perhaps also one with the earl of Surrey, and married successively Sir Arthur Heveningham and Philip Appleyard. Her natal family continued to live at Carrow at least into the eighteenth century, but was not again of more than local consequence.   JOSEPH S. BLOCK

Sources F. Blomefield and C. Parkin, *An essay towards a topographical history of the county of Norfolk*, [2nd edn], 11 vols. (1805–10), vol. 5, pp. 263–70 · HoP, *Commons, 1509–58*, 3.312 · D. MacCulloch, *Suffolk and the Tudors: politics and religion in an English county, 1500–1600* (1986) · *LP Henry VIII* · P. Friedmann, *Anne Boleyn: a chapter of English history, 1527–1536*, 1 (1884) · R. Warwicke, *The rise and fall of Anne Boleyn* (1989) · J. Hurstfield, *The queen's wards* (1965) · E. W. Ives, *Anne Boleyn* (1986) · D. Loades, *Mary Tudor: a life* (1989) · W. Rye, ed., *The visitacion of Norffolk … 1563 … 1613*, Harleian Society, 32 (1891), 247 **Wealth at death** see HoP, *Commons, 1509–58*

Shelton, Anne, Lady Shelton (*c.*1483–1555). *See under* Shelton family (*per.* 1504–1558).

Shelton, Anne [*real name* Patricia Jacqueline Sibley] (1923–1994), singer, was born on 10 November 1923 at 39 Coleman Road, Camberwell, London, the daughter of William James Sibley, a commercial clerk, and his wife, Lammataina Bower. As a young girl she possessed a voice that sounded more mature than her years suggested, and she was first introduced, as Anne Shelton, to a radio audience

Anne Shelton (1923–1994), by Harry Hammond, 1956

at the age of sixteen by Ronnie Waldman on the BBC's *Monday Night at Eight*. One of those listening was the distinguished bandleader Bert Ambrose. He invited her to audition for him and offered her work with his band at London's Mayfair Hotel. She made the first of her many records with Ambrose (Cole Porter's 'Begin the Beguine') on 7 June 1940.

During the war years Anne Shelton became known as the 'forces' favourite'. The singer Vera Lynn, whom she had replaced with Ambrose's band, had already acquired the epithet 'forces' sweetheart'. Shelton's most famous wartime recording and the song that became her signature tune, 'Lili Marlene', was made at the suggestion of Winston Churchill to Cecil Madden, head of empire entertainment. It was an attempt to maintain morale after the discovery that the Desert Rats of the north African desert campaign had been tuning in to performances of this song by Lale Anderson on German radio. English words were provided by Tommie Connor. As it happened, one of her weekly radio programmes, *Introducing Anne*, was regularly broadcast to troops in the north African desert. Her other two regular programmes were *Monday Night at Eight* and *Calling Malta*. When Malta was under siege in 1942, the latter was the only link with British troops there. Her commitment to the fighting forces was also evident elsewhere: 'Coming in on a Wing and a Prayer' was one of several morale-boosting songs recorded for the Royal Air Force and Bomber Command, and she was the first to appear on *The Guinea Pig Show*, which was for pilots undergoing Archibald MacIndoe's innovative skin-graft surgery.

Shelton's reputation as a popular singer spread widely.

When Bing Crosby arrived in London in 1942, he asked her to appear with him at the Queensbury All-Services Club. In 1944 she sang in seven shows given in England by Glenn Miller. He gave her a gold bracelet as a tribute to her vocal talent and tried to persuade her to join him on what proved to be his fatal plane journey to perform at a French concert. She appeared on television, as well as in several films, which usually included the comedian Arthur Askey. In 1950 she appeared on television in the USA with Sophie Tucker, having had recent success in America with her records 'Be Mine' and 'Galway Bay'. In 1951 she undertook a major tour of the USA. In the 1950s she had big hits with 'My Yiddishe Momme', 'Arrivederci Darling', and 'Lay Down your Arms', but gradually began to be over-shadowed by newer singers like Alma Cogan, Ruby Murray, and Petula Clark. In 1963, however, she sang on the million-selling record *All-Star-Festival* produced by the United Nations high commissioner for refugees, and she continued to work in cabaret and to give concerts. One of her most important cabaret appearances was in 1978, the year 1200 American veterans returned to the Normandy beaches, scene of the D-day landings. Every year, one of her concerts would be for the Not Forgotten Association for disabled former servicemen. It was in recognition of her work as entertainments officer for this association that she was made an OBE in 1990.

That same year, Shelton's husband, David Reid, died. He was a naval lieutenant-commander whom she had met in her teens but not married until 1967. They had no children. Anne Shelton died on 31 July 1994 at Herstmonceaux, Sussex. A memorial service for her was held at Corpus Christi, Covent Garden, London, a Roman Catholic church. Her records still attract many admirers. She possessed a distinctive alto voice with a richly varied tonal palette, a polished technique, and wide dynamic range. She was one of the few British female singers of her time who were comfortable singing in a jazz or blues idiom, and her stylistic and rhythmic versatility allowed her to move easily from romantic ballads to up-tempo big-band numbers.

DEREK B. SCOTT

Sources *The Times* (1 Aug 1994) · *The Times* (11 Nov 1994) · C. Larkin, ed., *The Guinness encyclopedia of popular music*, 4 vols. (1992), 3751–2 · P. Gammond, *The Oxford companion to popular music* (1991); repr. with corrections (1993), 525 · J. Murrells, *Million selling records from the 1900s to the 1980s* (1984), 170 · *The Independent* (2 Aug 1994) · b. cert.
Archives FILM BFI NFTVA, performance footage | SOUND BL NSA, 'Anne Shelton: fifty years in showbusiness', B7561/01 · BL NSA, performance recording
Likenesses photographs, 1945–53, Hult. Arch. · H. Hammond, photograph, 1956, NPG [*see illus.*]
Wealth at death £315,535: probate, 1994, *CGPLA Eng. & Wales*

Shelton, Jerome (*c.*1500–1555×60), property speculator and royal official, was a younger son of Nicholas Shelton (*d.* 1515), resident in the parish of St Thomas of Acon, London, freeman and master of the Mercers' Company, and sheriff and alderman of London, and his second wife, Elizabeth, daughter of Richard Rawlins, a London mercer. Nicholas Shelton was a first-generation Londoner, a junior member of a prominent gentry family of Norfolk. At unknown dates, probably early in Jerome Shelton's career, he was admitted to the freedom of London in the right of his father, and admitted to membership of the Middle Temple. However, he does not appear to have carried on a settled trade, nor did he practise law. Instead, his career centred upon activities as a bondsman, moneylender, property speculator, and exchequer official. He was associated in many of his financial transactions with his three brothers from his father's second marriage, William, Thomas, and Robert, and, initially, his stepfather, Sir Humphrey Brown, serjeant-at-law and later a judge of common pleas.

As early as 1534 Shelton was speculating in property, at Westminster, with his brother William. In 1538 he secured his co-appointment for life with Brown as steward of all the property of Waltham Abbey in Essex, Hertfordshire, Bedfordshire, Berkshire, Cambridgeshire, Norfolk, and Surrey. This grant appears to have been sought as an investment in anticipation of the dissolution of the abbey, and in July 1540 Shelton and Brown surrendered their patent to the court of augmentations in return for a life pension of £20 p.a. In 1539 he leased land and secured an annuity of £26 13s. 4d. from the last prioress of St Helen's Priory outside Bishopsgate, London, the house in which his half-sister, Mary, was a nun; the grants were subsequently recognized by the crown. The Waltham Abbey enterprise ended in acrimony as Shelton and Brown fell out over the division of the pension and their 1546 administratorship of the sizeable estate of Shelton's uncle, William Rawlins, provost of Wells.

In 1539 Shelton also sub-let the former monastic property of Flitcham, Norfolk, from a family associate, Sir William Hollis, lord mayor of London, for thirty years. His efforts at rack-renting the manor produced political strife in the county and in 1541 led to the mediation of the Shelton family patron, Thomas Howard, third duke of Norfolk. Shelton withdrew with financial loss, but he soon thereafter did acquire the office of a tellership of the exchequer, on 18 January 1542, through Howard's patronage as lord treasurer of England. He held this office until 1555 and engaged in the practice of using his cash reserves of crown money for private speculation in the London money and commodities markets. He also, more controversially, exploited his office to avoid paying his own tax assessments, and he used his legal right as an exchequer official to be sued only in the exchequer of pleas to force litigants to contest cases on unfavourable ground. During the 1540s his speculations in the popular market in the lead stripped from the monastic houses led to significant debts owed to the crown. When he vacated his tellership in 1555, he owed another £2590 on his accounts. Most of this sum was never recovered by the state, and the debt wiped out any gains he enjoyed elsewhere, impoverishing his estate.

For much of his adult life Shelton resided in the parish of St Helen, London. His last years and death are obscure. Because he died intestate, his widow, identified only as Alice Hering, secured letters of administration on 28 February 1561. Already, on the preceding 28 May, the crown had excused her of all claims which it had on Shelton's estate. No record of children of the marriage has been located and the principal beneficiary of Shelton's tenure in the exchequer was a nephew, Humphrey Shelton, an Elizabethan officer of the receipt. Overall, Shelton's financial failures appear to have been the direct consequence of high-risk speculative investments, and loans. Ambitious, and one of the most litigious individuals of his generation, he alienated and exploited many members of his own immediate family, including his sister, Katherine Townshend. His career reveals the opportunities and liabilities of life as an unscrupulous mid-Tudor entrepreneur. Many individuals attempted to profit from the dissolution of the monasteries and a period of lax government administration. Shelton's misfortunes in this quest for material benefit can be attributed to his own overreaching ambition.   J. D. ALSOP

Sources J. Alsop, 'The financial enterprises of Jerome Shelton, a mid-Tudor London adventurer', *Guildhall Studies in London History*, 4 (1979–81), 33–50 · PRO, E 101/163/3, fol. 1v · PRO, PROB 6/1, FO 26 · H. A. C. Sturgess, ed., *Register of admissions to the Honourable Society of the Middle Temple, from the fifteenth century to the year 1944*, 1 (1949), 17 · CPR, 1558–60, 352 **Wealth at death** insolvent: PRO, E 163/13/26, fol. 123; SP 12/22, fol. 95; BL, Lansdowne MS 106, fol. 12

Shelton, Sir John (1476/7–1539). *See under* Shelton family (*per.* 1504–1558).

Shelton, Sir John (b. in or before **1503**, d. **1558**). *See under* Shelton family (*per.* 1504–1558).

Shelton, John (d. **1845**), army officer, was commissioned ensign in the 9th foot on 21 November 1805, became lieutenant on 26 August 1807, and captain on 17 June 1813. He served with the 9th in Portugal in 1808, being present at Roliça, Vimeiro, and Corunna; in the Walcheren expedition of 1809; and again in the Peninsula in 1812–13. He was at the siege and capture of Badajoz, at Salamanca, Burgos, Vitoria, and San Sebastian, where he lost his right arm. In 1814 he served in Canada. In 1817 he exchanged into the 44th foot (later 1st battalion, Essex regiment), which went to India in 1822, and was employed in Arakan during the First Anglo-Burmese War. He became regimental major on 6 February 1825, and lieutenant-colonel on 16 September 1827. For the next thirteen years he commanded the 44th in India, respected but not liked by the officers and men, for he was a harsh and imperious martinet, 'not a pleasant man on parade'.

At the end of 1840 Shelton was put in charge of a brigade, the 44th and two Indian regiments, to replace part of the force in Afghanistan. Colin Mackenzie, who accompanied the brigade, wrote that 'Shelton's gross want of arrangement and the unnecessary hardship he has exposed the men to … have caused much discontent' (Macrory, 137). He reached Jalalabad with his brigade in January 1841, made a punitive expedition into the Nazian valley in February, had to return through the Khyber to the Indus in May to open the road for Shah Shuja's family, and arrived at Kabul on 9 June. There, with the rank of brigadier-general, he was second in command to the ineffectual Elphinstone. Brave in battle but apparently stupid, Shelton was morose, cantankerous, churlish, badtempered, friendless, hated by officers and men, and openly contemptuous of Elphinstone, who disliked and distrusted him, and they failed to co-operate. Elphinstone wrote of Shelton, 'his manner was most contumacious … he … invariably found fault with all that was done' (Macrory, 169). George Lawrence considered him 'a great croaker and anxious to return to India' (Macrory, 157). However, as Sir John Fortescue wrote, 'it can never be known how far incessant physical pain, due to the rough surgery of those days, may have embittered his character' (Fortescue, *Brit. army*, 163).

Shelton was camped at Siah Sang, 2 miles east of the city, when the Afghan outbreak began, on 2 November 1841, with the murder of Sir Alexander Burnes. He was ordered to occupy the Bala Hissar (the Kabul citadel) with part of his brigade, to reinforce the shah's troops; but when he had been there a week he was summoned to the cantonments to assist Elphinstone and infuse some vigour into the defence. By then (9 November) the commissariat fort with vital supplies had been lost. The cantonments were commanded by the adjacent hills; their boundary was of no defensive strength, and nearly 2 miles long. There was only one British regiment, the 44th, and this, like others, was discouraged. Elphinstone, infirm and unstable, asked the advice of everyone, but would delegate authority to no one. Sir William Macnaghten, the envoy, energetic and self-confident, had much to say on military measures, and Shelton was ordered to carry out operations of which he disapproved. His own unyielding temper was ill suited to such a position. In this crisis he failed to provide decisive and effective leadership. At councils of war he ostentatiously slept or feigned sleep, and criticized Macnaghten in his absence. When Colin Mackenzie protested Shelton replied, 'Damn it, Mackenzie, I *will* sneer at him! I *like* to sneer at him!' (Macrory, 171).

On 10 November Shelton led an attack on the Rikabashee Fort, which was within 400 yards of the north-east angle of the cantonments. He had twice to rally his men before the fort was taken, and the 44th had nearly 100 men killed or wounded. He bungled his sortie to the Beymaroo hills (23 November), using unsuitable square formation and unnecessarily exposing his force to enemy fire and the resultant casualties; his force was routed and the survivors further discouraged. For 'this most disgraceful day' (Fortescue, *Brit. army*, 224) Shelton blamed the Sepoys, but contemporaries blamed Shelton.

Shelton favoured withdrawal from Kabul, but it was not until 11 December, when reportedly only one day's provisions remained, that Macnaghten met the Afghan chiefs in conference. He was treacherously shot by Akbar Khan on 23 December, and on 6 January 1842 the retreat from Kabul began.

During the retreat Shelton fought bravely with the rearguard. At Jagdalak on 11 January he was ordered to accompany Elphinstone to a meeting with Akbar Khan, and to remain with the latter as a hostage. He thus escaped the final massacre. He was well treated, quarrelled with his fellow captives, and was rescued with them by Sir Richmond Shakespeare and his cavalry on 17 September, after Sir George Pollock had reoccupied Kabul.

Elphinstone, whom Shelton blamed, had died and Shelton, the senior surviving officer, on 20 January 1843 was court-martialled at Ludhiana on four charges: ordering preparations to be made for retreat without authority; using disrespectful language to the general within hearing of the troops; entering into clandestine correspondence with Akbar Khan to obtain forage for his own horses while the envoy's negotiations were going on; suffering himself to be taken prisoner at Jagdalak by want of due precaution. He was acquitted on all charges except the third, and the court held that that had been duly censured at the time. They praised his 'personal gallantry of the highest kind, and … noble devotion as a soldier' (Macrory, 269).

Shelton returned to England and resumed command of the 44th, which had been practically raised afresh at its Colchester depot. He had become colonel in the army on 23 November 1841, and had had the local rank of major-general in India. On 10 May 1845, when the 44th was at Richmond barracks, Dublin, his horse bolted and threw him in the barrack square, inflicting such injuries on him that he died after three days' agony. Reportedly when the regiment heard of his death they turned out on the parade ground and gave three cheers. His remains were interred 'with unusual military pomp' (*GM*, 197) at St Peter's Church, Dublin. He left considerable property which passed to his nephew, Lieutenant William Shelton, 9th foot. He received no medals or decorations for his many campaigns, except Shah Shuja's discredited order of the Durrani empire. Sir John Fortescue later wrote of him: 'the brightest figure in the retreat from Kabul … to so gallant a spirit surely much may be forgiven' (Fortescue, *Brit. army*, 245). Maybe, but there was much to forgive.

E. M. LLOYD, rev. ROGER T. STEARN

Sources T. Carter, ed., *Historical record of the forty-fourth, or the east Essex regiment of foot* (1864) • *GM*, 2nd ser., 24 (1845) • J. H. Stocqueler, *Memoirs and correspondence of Major-General Sir William Nott*, 2 vols. (1854) • V. Eyre, *The military operations at Cabul*, 4th edn (1879) • J. W. Kaye, *History of the war in Afghanistan*, 2 vols. (1851) • *Naval and Military Gazette* (13 April 1843) • *Naval and Military Gazette* (17 June 1843) • P. Macrory, *Signal catastrophe: the story of a disastrous retreat from Kabul, 1842* (1966); repr. as *Kabul catastrophe* (1986) • Fortescue, *Brit. army*, vol. 12 • J. A. Norris, *The First Afghan War, 1838–1842* (1967) • M. E. Yapp, *Strategies of British India: Britain, Iran and Afghanistan, 1798–1850* (1980)
Archives NAM

Shelton, Margaret (*fl. c.*1530–1536). *See under* Shelton family (*per.* 1504–1558).

Shelton, Mary [married names Mary Heveningham, Lady Heveningham; Mary Appleyard] (1510×15–1570/71), contributor to manuscript miscellany, was the youngest daughter of Sir John *Shelton (1476/7–1539) of Norfolk [*see under* Shelton family], and his wife, Anne Boleyn (*d.* 1555) [*see* Shelton, Anne, *under* Shelton family], aunt of Queen

Anne Boleyn, who with her husband, from 1533 supervised the royal princesses. Mary attended on her cousin, the queen, playing a lively part in the amorous pastimes of the court. Queen Anne reportedly rebuked her for writing 'ydill poesies' in her prayerbook ('William Latymer's chricklle', 62) and in frantic 'confessions' before her execution, linked Mary, or her sister Margaret, with two of the queen's 'lovers' (Strype, 1, pt 1, 433). Rumour twice linked Mary amorously with Henry VIII (*LP Henry VIII*, 8, 263; 13, pt 1, 24). Mary contributed to the important 'Devonshire' album of Tudor courtly verse (BL, Add. MS 17492): she signs a sharp answer to a poem addressed to her, and her hand can be identified copying, and perhaps composing, fashionable balets into the album. Henry Howard, earl of Surrey, named Mary as the beloved of Sir Thomas Clere in the epitaph he composed to commemorate Clere's death on 14 April 1545. By 1546 she had married Sir Anthony Heveningham (1507–1557). The same year, the suggestion that 'menye secrettes' had passed between her and the earl of Surrey was noted for further investigation by a privy council suspicious of Surrey (*LP Henry VIII*, 21, pt 1, 1426). Mary and Sir Anthony had five children, the eldest being Arthur *Heveningham, and the youngest of whom, Abigail (who married Sir George Digby of Coleshill, Warwickshire), was in attendance on Queen Elizabeth in 1588. In 1558 Mary married Philip Appleyard (*b. c.*1528). A probable portrait of Mary by Hans Holbein is in the collection of Her Majesty the Queen at Windsor. Mary was buried in Heveningham church, Suffolk, on 8 January 1571.

ELIZABETH HEALE

Sources *LP Henry VIII*, 8.263; 13/1.24; 21/1.1426 • H. Baron, 'Mary (Howard) Fitzroy's hand in the Devonshire manuscript', *Review of English Studies*, new ser., 45 (1994), 318–35 • W. Rye, ed., *The visitacion of Norffolk … 1563 … 1613*, Harleian Society, 32 (1891), 247 • W. Harvey, *The visitation of Norfolk in the year 1563*, ed. G. H. Dashwood and others, 2 (1895), 346, 398 • parish register, Heveningham, Suffolk RO, burial Fc 68/D1/1, fiche 2 • 'William Latymer's chricklle of Anne Bulleyne', ed. M. Dowling, *Camden miscellany, XXX*, CS, 4th ser., 39 (1990), 23–65 • P. G. Remley, 'Mary Shelton and her Tudor literary milieu', *Rethinking the Henrician era: essays on early Tudor texts and contexts*, ed. P. C. Herman (1994), 40–77 • E. Heale, 'Women and the courtly love lyric: the Devonshire MS (BL, Additional 17492)', *Modern Language Review*, 90 (1995), 296–313 • J. Strype, *Ecclesiastical memorials*, 3 vols. (1822) • H. Howard [earl of Surrey], *Poems*, ed. E. Jones (1964), 34, no. 35 • HoP, *Commons, 1558–1603* • A. Hassell Smith, *County and court: government and politics in Norfolk, 1558–1603* (1974), 69, 148, 257 • F. Blomefield and C. Parkin, *An essay towards a topographical history of the county of Norfolk*, [2nd edn], 11 vols. (1805–10) • K. T. Parker, *The drawings of Hans Holbein in the collection of HM the king at Windsor Castle* (1945), pl. 26
Archives BL, the 'Devonshire MS', Add. MS 17492 • BL, MS genealogy drawn up by Sir Arthur Heveningham (son), Harley MS 4031, fol. 239 • BL, genealogy of Heveningham family drawn up in 1561 visitation of Suffolk, Harley MS 1560, pencil fols. 138–40
Likenesses H. Holbein, sketch

Shelton, Sir Richard (1578–1647), lawyer and politician, was born in Birmingham on 21 January 1578, the elder of two sons of John Shelton (*d.* 1601), a mercer there, and Barbara, the daughter and heir of Francis Stanley of West Bromwich. Shelton appears to have studied at Cambridge during the early or mid-1590s—he would also serve there as university counsel in 1625–31. He was at Clement's Inn and then proceeded to the Inner Temple in 1597, being called to the bar on 8 July 1606. During the late 1610s or early 1620s he joined the retinue of George Villiers, duke of Buckingham, and possibly because of this he gained a series of prestigious offices at the Temple, being called to the bench on 26 January 1623, serving as Lenten reader in 1625, and finally being appointed treasurer on 3 November 1628, an office he would hold until November 1634. In October 1625 the duke obtained for him the office of solicitor-general. It was customary for solicitors-general who had not been knighted to have that honour bestowed with their office, and he was knighted on 31 October 1625 by Charles I, at Hampton Court.

During the parliaments of 1626 and 1628–9 Shelton served in the Commons as a member from Bridgnorth, Shropshire (he was also elected, but did not sit, for Guildford in 1626). His performance in parliament was undistinguished, especially given that the solicitor-general was expected to be a major spokesman for the court. Although he served as chair of the committee of the whole on supply in 1628–9, was appointed to a number of committees, and carried out various directives of the house, these assignments may have reflected more a sense of his status than of his ability. He was only moderately active in debate and does not appear to have had much influence. In March 1628 his intrusion into a debate on the ramifications of the five knights' case seriously compromised court strategy, while prompting a response from John Selden which included sarcasm at Shelton's 'ingenuity' in searching out precedents for the case.

As solicitor-general Shelton was appointed to a commission to compound with recusants in November 1625 and in December 1633 to the reinforced high commission, which exercised ecclesiastical jurisdiction in England and Wales. During a Commons debate in February 1629 he defended the appointment of Richard Mountague, object of attack in the Commons, as bishop of Chichester. Neither his support for Mountague nor his presence on the commissions reveals his religious stance, since he was simply following crown initiatives. After the assassination of Buckingham in August 1628 Shelton does not appear to have had a major patron. When Sir Robert Heath was appointed chief justice of the common pleas in October 1631 it was not Shelton, but William Noy, who succeeded him as attorney-general, although the succession of the solicitor-general to the post would have followed the usual pattern. It is not known whether Shelton pushed his case for promotion; if he did, his failure may have been because he lacked a strong patron or ally at court.

In October 1634 Shelton was pressured into surrendering his patent as solicitor-general. Since he was not accused of misbehaviour, he could not simply be dismissed. Instead, he was able to negotiate a settlement that left him king's counsellor-at-large, with his former status and profits, and it appears that he could have opted for appointments as king's serjeant or puisne justice. In referring to his removal from office Edward Hyde, later earl of

Clarendon, described him as 'an old, illiterate, useless person' (Clarendon, *Hist. rebellion*, 2.110), but however fair this characterization may be it is unlikely that Shelton was forced out for sheer incompetence. Rather it appears that William Laud, archbishop of Canterbury, was cementing his power at court and wanted law officers in place who were loyal to him, as was Sir Edward Littleton, Shelton's successor.

Shelton does not seem to have been significantly involved with government business after he gave up his place as solicitor-general, although in March 1639 he joined other Inner Temple benchers in making a contribution to support the king's expedition against the Scots. By that time he was semi-retired, living on his manor at West Bromwich (a property that he had inherited from a cousin, William Stanley, in 1626) with his wife, Lettice (d. 1642), the daughter of Sir Robert Fisher of Packington. He contributed £150 to the Staffordshire parliamentarian county committee in 1644. He died in 1647 and was buried in West Bromwich on 7 December. The Sheltons left no children. West Bromwich passed to a nephew, John, who had also benefited from the family tie when in April 1629 he gained special admission to the Inner Temple at Shelton's behest.　　　A. F. POLLARD, *rev.* PAUL E. KOPPERMAN

Sources P. E. Kopperman, *Sir Robert Heath, 1575–1649: window on an age* (1989) · F. A. Inderwick and R. A. Roberts, eds., *A calendar of the Inner Temple records*, 2 (1898) · *IGI* · *CSP dom.*, 1625–6; 1634–5; 1638–9 · Venn, *Alum. Cant.*, 1/4 · Clarendon, *Hist. rebellion* · R. C. Johnson and others, eds., *Proceedings in parliament, 1628*, 1–4 (1977–8) · W. R. Prest, *The rise of the barristers: a social history of the English bar, 1590–1640* (1986) · parish register, Birmingham, St Martin [birth] · W. H. Cooke, ed., *Students admitted to the Inner Temple, 1547–1660* [1878]
Wealth at death left manor of West Bromwich to a nephew

Shelton, Thomas (*fl.* 1598–1629), translator, was probably the third of seven sons of Henry Shelton (d. c.1605), a Dublin merchant imprisoned in 1596 for refusing to take the oath of supremacy when he was elected sheriff, and his wife, Margaret, the sister of Peter Nangle, guardian of the Franciscan convent at Armagh, and thorn in the side of the authorities. Thomas may be the 'Thomas Shelton, Dublinensis' in the 1597 student list of the Irish college at Salamanca (Knowles, 174).

In late 1598 Thomas's elder brother, John, was involved in an abortive plot to seize Dublin Castle for Hugh O'Neill, earl of Tyrone, who had mounted a serious rebellion. John was hanged, and Thomas was sought as an accomplice (Knowles, 164). On 31 March 1600 a spy reported that he was at Tyrone's headquarters with Richard Nugent, a prominent Irish nobleman. A year later he offered his services to Florence MacCarthy, an equally obdurate rebel, in a letter which was intercepted and was added to a growing intelligence file. Nugent and Shelton arrived in Spain in June 1601 and Shelton went on to Flanders. He next turns up (as Thomas Skelton) in February 1604 at a capitular assembly at Douai presided over by Father Christopher Cusack, which suggests he was teaching at one of the English colleges.

Shelton was the first person to translate *Don Quixote* into

English, but his literary career began with an unremarkable piece in *Cynthia* (1604), a book of lyric verse published in London by Nugent, and an equally conventional verse, 'To his Deare Friend, M. Richard Verstegan', in Verstegan's *Restitution of Decayed Intelligence in Antiquities* (1605). Shelton's version of the first part of *Don Quixote* was published in London by Edward Blount in 1612. His original was the Velpius edition published in Brussels in 1607 (Knowles, 162). The signs of haste in the translation, which took Shelton only forty days, do not hide his verve, command of Spanish, and knowledge of Spain. Shelton published the second part of *Don Quixote* anonymously with Blount in 1620. James Fitzmaurice-Kelly's introduction to Shelton's translation claims that John Fletcher's *Knight of the Burning Pestle* was derived from Shelton, as was *Cardenio* (1613), a lost play by Shakespeare and Fletcher. But the book sold slowly, not being reprinted until 1652. It is dedicated to Theophilus Howard, Baron de Walden. Alexander Wright argues that Shelton and Howard were distantly related, which is not impossible despite the lack of evidence. But it is more likely that Howard, who had previously shown interest in contacting English exiles, met Shelton on a visit to the Low Countries in 1610. Shelton's past history would suggest that the 'deare friend' of the dedication was Verstegan, given that Verstegan was a Catholic refugee active in religious controversy.

In February 1612 Shelton, together with a Captain Rathfert, contacted William Trumbull, the English agent in Brussels, with authorization to negotiate the reconciliation of Tyrone with the crown. This seems to have prompted accusations that Shelton, Cusack, and John Roche, chaplain to Archbishop Bentivoglio, the nuncio to Brussels, were informers working for the English authorities. After questioning the accused, Bentivoglio wrote to the papal secretary, affirming that Shelton had lived in Flanders for several years and was of honourable reputation. He adds that Shelton's father had died after eight years in prison for his faith, and that his brother had been executed for the attempt on Dublin Castle.

By the summer of 1613 Shelton was short of money and ill. When he had recovered, he left for Paris with a letter of introduction from Trumbull to Sir Thomas Edmundes, the English ambassador. Trumbull disapproves of his religion, but attests to Shelton's knowledge of Irish affairs, to his skill in Spanish and French, and to his loyalty to his majesty, for which 'he is persecuted by the barbarous Irishe, as a malefactor. He is borne of honest and worthy parents, and allyed to sundry of the best familyes in the English Pale' (Knowles, 171). Once in Paris Shelton made contact with his cousin, Henry Stanihurst, and M. de Beaulieu, a friend of Trumbull's, and set about looking for work, but without success. His letter of 6 March 1614 to Trumbull, which is extremely abusive about the French, their promises, and their attitude to foreigners, raises the issue of a pardon and return to England: 'for I have great hope by my ld. of Walden's means, to get some advancement if I were there' (George, 157). This must be the dedicatee of *Don Quixote*. Shelton may have given his reasons for seeking a pardon in one of the letters he asked Trumbull to destroy.

Relations with Trumbull now began to cool. In his last letter to Trumbull (28 March 1614) Shelton says he was a messenger for somebody, had been asked to do something underhand, and had refused. Beaulieu reported to Trumbull that Shelton was desperately poor, but that he had acquired either a wife or a mistress. However, a letter written in Spanish (20 November 1629) by Father Thomas Strange, guardian of the Franciscans in Dublin, informs Father Luke Wadding that Strange had received Thomas Shelton of Dublin into the order and asks him to take Shelton into the Franciscan community in Rome (B. Jennings, *Wadding Papers*, 1953, 320). It is not known what happened to the wife or when Shelton died.   L. G. KELLY

Sources E. B. Knowles, 'Thomas Shelton, translator of *Don Quixote*', *Studies in the Renaissance*, 5 (1958), 160–75 · J. George, 'Thomas Shelton, translator, in 1612–1614', *Bulletin of Hispanic Studies*, 35 (1958), 157–64 · A. T. Wright, *Thomas Shelton, translator* (1898) · J. Fitzmaurice-Kelly, 'Introduction', in T. Shelton, *The history of Don Quixote of the Mancha* (1896), 1.ix–li · *DNB*
Archives PRO, State Papers Flanders, 77/10 I. 77 · PRO, Downshire MSS, V. 55

Shelton, Thomas (1600/01–1650?), stenographer, is believed to have been descended from the prominent Norfolk landowning Shelton family, although there is no firm evidence for his parentage or early life. Probably the most famous shorthand inventor of his day, he was teaching in London from the early 1620s until his death, probably in London some time early in 1650. In 1630 he was living in Cheapside, but by 1642 had moved to Old Fish Street and by 1645 to The Poultry. His wife may have been the Ann Shelton who was buried on 6 October 1650 at St Giles Cripplegate.

Shelton's earliest and most successful shorthand system, *Short-Writing*, was registered with the Stationers' Company on 17 April 1626; no copy of this edition appears to have survived. *Short-Writing* was reissued in 1630 and 1633. In 1635 an updated version, renamed *Tachygraphy*, was published in Cambridge, the first of several such editions to be produced by the university press there. *Tachygraphy* was first printed in London in 1639, with at least twenty-two further editions up to 1710, several of them pirated. Both *Short-Writing* and *Tachygraphy* incorporate many of the features of Edmond Willis's scheme of 1618 (*An Abreviation of Writing by Character*), as well as some elements of John Willis's earlier system (published anonymously as *The Art of Stenographie*, 1602). One of the most popular systems of its time, Shelton's tachygraphy was in use until at least the late eighteenth century, when it was employed by Thomas Jefferson. Among others known to have favoured his system are John Rushworth, Samuel Pepys, and the English civil war army secretary, Sir William Clarke.

In 1642 Shelton issued a companion volume, *A Tutor to Tachygraphy*, with two further editions in 1642. Both the *Tutor* and the 1647 edition of *Tachygraphy* were reprinted by the Augustan Reprint Society of Los Angeles in 1970. A Latin translation of *Tachygraphy*, *Tachy-Graphia*, appeared in 1660 and again in 1671. *Tachygraphy* was also translated into both French (Paris, 1681) and German (Leipzig, 1743). A new version of *Tachygraphy* by an anonymous author, combining it with some of the features of Jeremiah Rich's system, was produced in 1684 as *The Art of Short Writing According to Tachygraphy*, with, apparently, a further edition in 1705, of which no copy is known to have survived.

Late in 1649, just before he died, and perhaps because of the appearance of several illicit editions of *Tachygraphy*, Shelton completed a wholly new shorthand system entitled *Zeiglographia* (1650). Never as popular as the tachygraphy for which he is chiefly remembered, this was the first shorthand system ever to be advertised, both separately (BL, Harley MS 5921, fol. 29r) and in the newsbook *Mercurius Politicus* (no. 18, 3–10 October 1650, and subsequent issues).

Shelton's *Whole Book of Psalms in Meeter*, containing the metrical psalms of Sternhold and Hopkins, written in his system of tachygraphy and engraved by Thomas Cross, appeared posthumously, probably *c*.1660. Shelton was renowned for taking down in shorthand the sermons of leading puritan divines, and his record of twenty-three 'exercises before sermons', delivered by the radical Independent minister Walter Cradock, *Divine Drops Distilled*, was printed in 1650.

Shelton's own religious sympathies emerge clearly in *A Centurie of Similies* (1640), his only published work which was totally unconnected with shorthand. Vigorously puritanical in tone, it may account for Shelton's appearance, along with its printer Ralph Mabb, before the court of high commission in April–November 1640. Shelton also had connections with the radical MP Richard Knightley (*d.* 1639), to whom he dedicated *Short-Writing* and early issues of *Tachygraphy*; his own support for the parliamentarian side during the English civil wars is clear from his dedication of *Zeiglographia* (1650) to the newly established Commonwealth, to which he wished 'heavenly grace and earthly glory'.

The earliest known portrait of Shelton prefaces the 1647 edition of *Tachygraphy* (which gives his age as forty-six), with re-engraved versions appearing in *Zeiglographia* (1650), *The Whole Book of Psalmes* (1660?), and *Tachy-Graphia* (1660).   FRANCES HENDERSON

Sources A. T. Wright, *Thomas Shelton, tachygrapher* (1896) · W. J. Carlton, *Shorthand books, Bibliotheca Pepysiana*, 4 (1940), 29–46 · R. C. Alston, *A bibliography of the English language from the invention of printing to the year 1800*, rev. edn, 8: *Treatises on shorthand* (1974), 8–14, 18–19 · T. Shelton, *A tutor to tachygraphy, or, Short-writing* (1642): *Tachygraphy* (1647) (1970), i–x · Pepys, *Diary*, 1.xlviii–liv · *CSP dom.*, 1640, 408–29 · T. Shelton, *A centurie of similies* (1640) · S. West, *Arts improvement, or, Short and swifte writing* (1647), sig. A2v · F. Henderson, '"Posterity to judge"—John Rushworth and his "Historicall collections"', *Bodleian Library Record*, 15/4 (1996), 247–59 · 'A new art of short-writing, 1649', BL, Harley MS 5921, fol. 29r

Likenesses line engraving, 1650, NPG · T. Cross, line engraving, BM; repro. in T. Shelton, *The whole book of psalms in meeter* (1660?), frontispiece · line engraving (aged forty-six), NPG · portrait, repro. in T. Shelton, *Tachygraphy* (1647), frontispiece · portrait, repro. in T. Shelton, *Zeiglographia* (1650), frontispiece · portrait, repro. in T. Shelton, *Tachy-graphia* (1660), frontispiece

Shelvocke, George (1675–1742), privateer and author, was born in Deptford and entered the navy in 1690. On 25 April 1704 he was commissioned lieutenant in the *Scarborough*. He moved into the *Association*, then the *Britannia*, and soon afterwards was paid off. He found employment again only at the reduced rank of purser, in which he served aboard the *Monck* until 1713, when he was paid off once more before enduring five years of severe poverty. He applied for help to Edward Hughes, who had been purser in the *Scarborough* and was then partner in a plan to finance a privateering expedition to the South seas. Shelvocke was promised command of the larger of the two vessels, the *Success*. Letters of marque and reprisal were issued by the high court of Admiralty on 1 January 1719, authorizing Hughes and his associates 'to set upon by force of Arms, and to subdue and take the Men of War, Ships, and other Vessels whatsoever, as also the Goods, Monies and Merchandizes, belonging to the King of Spain, his vassals and Subjects' (PRO, HCA 26/29: 5). The 'Scheme of the Voyage' presented by the owners to the commanders was rather more specific, and instructed them to raid the town of Paita on the Peruvian coast, and to capture the treasure-ship plying between Lima and Panama. John Clipperton, who had sailed as chief mate with William Dampier in the *St George* (1703–4), was named commander of the *Success*, and Shelvocke was given the smaller ship, the *Speedwell*, a demotion resulting from excesses he committed with ship's stores while recruiting crew at Ostend. The expedition got under way on 13 February 1719. Very soon Shelvocke lost touch with Clipperton, and proceeded on his own into the Pacific Ocean where he raided Paita and headed for Juan Fernandez, the last point of rendezvous with Clipperton. There, on 25 May 1720, the *Speedwell* was wrecked in circumstances that left Shelvocke's management and motives open to doubt. For five months he and his crew were marooned on 'the Land of Robinson Crusoes' (Burney, 4.465), oddly perched between fact and fiction. Experiences of life on a deserted island was then a subject of public interest. Alexander Selkirk had become famous for the four years he spent in solitude on the island after he was left there by John Stradling of the *Cinque Ports*, Dampier's consort, in 1705. And in the same year Shelvocke set out for the South seas, Daniel Defoe published *The Life and Strange Surprizing Adventures of Robinson Crusoe*, loosely based on Selkirk's experiences. Indeed Shelvocke had been heard to say, 'It was not difficult living at Fernandes, if a man should accidentally be thrown there, since Mr Selkirk had continu'd upon it four years by himself' (Betagh, 172).

Shelvocke and his men built a 20 ton boat out of the wreck of the *Speedwell*, called her the *Recovery*, and put to sea in October. They transferred into their first prize, renamed the *Happy Return*, and resumed the cruise, several times encountering Clipperton in the *Success*. But when Clipperton discovered that the ship's articles in Shelvocke's vessel had been changed after the events on Juan Fernandez to resemble the 'Jamaica discipline' of the buccaneers, he refused to accompany it, and the owner's agent, James Hendry, and Thomas Dodd, lieutenant of marines, went aboard the *Success*. After transferring into a bigger prize, the 300 ton *Sacra Familia*, Shelvocke captured the *Concepcion de Recova*, heavily laden with sweetmeats and (according to an eyewitness) a large amount of silver which Shelvocke neglected to report. Suffering severely from thirst and scurvy, he and the survivors (a third of the original complement) made their way to Canton, where he sold his prize and took passage for England in the East Indiaman *Cadogan*; he arrived at Dover on 1 August 1722, and little more is heard of him after that.

In 1724 Shelvocke presented a journal of his 'Voyage to the South Sea to cruise on the Spaniards' to the lords of the Admiralty. In the expanded published version, *A Voyage Round the World by Way of the Great South Sea* (1726), he presciently discusses the economic possibilities of guano and whaling, as well as mentioning traces of gold on the coast of California. His narrative is best remembered for the solitary albatross shot by Simon Hatley as the *Speedwell* entered the Southern Ocean, an episode absent from the manuscript version but told in the book with such laconic emphasis that it found a passage to Wordsworth's heart, and thence to Coleridge's *The Rime of the Ancient Mariner* (1798). In 1726 Shelvocke wrote a memorial to the lords of the Admiralty, responding to a revival of interest in the scheme of establishing a British base off the coast of South America. He suggests Chiloe as 'the most weatherly & commodious place in every respect to curb the power of the Spaniards in South America' (BL, Add. MS 19034, fol. 84*v*).

It is clear from his journal and the *Voyage* that Shelvocke had enemies. He speaks scornfully of John Clipperton, whom he accuses of thwarting the expedition and of cheating the owners, and several times he recalls darkly how Clipperton stole Dampier's privateering commission fifteen years before, causing him to be imprisoned at Batavia on a charge of piracy, as if to draw a parallel between his case and Dampier's—'for I well remember'd how Dampier had been serv'd in these seas' (Shelvocke, 218). William Betagh, Edward Brooke, Samuel Randall, and Simon Hatley are accused of insubordination and mutiny, and Thomas Dodd and James Hendry are represented as periodically insane. The only one to respond publicly to these charges was William Betagh, who was captured by the Spanish before the *Speedwell* was lost. His testimony against Shelvocke is therefore largely hearsay, based on George Taylor's and Thomas Dodd's journals (no longer extant) for eyewitness reports of events which took place after his disappearance. In his *Voyage Round the World* (1728) Betagh tells a story of a captain of Machiavellian cunning, led on by revenge, greed, and love of power to construct a chain of seeming accidents designed to impugn the characters of his colleagues, to thin his crew, to force a change in the ship's articles, to defraud the owners of the bulk of the profit of the cruise, and to leave him—the perpetrator—looking like a helpless victim of misfortune and ill will. Specifically Betagh alleges that Shelvocke had no intention of accompanying Clipperton, and while still in the Atlantic took advantage of his independence by committing an act of piracy against a Portuguese ship. He goes on to say that covertly Shelvocke fomented two mutinies against his own command, first at St Catherine's in Brazil and then at Juan Fernandez, and that the latter plan included the deliberate wrecking of the *Speedwell*, an act performed on a serene day after various important items (including Shelvocke's commission and the ship's forge) had been sent ashore. Although Betagh suggests that this was done to exclude the owners from any interest in prizes taken in a new bottom, it seems more likely that Shelvocke aimed at two things—a revision of articles that would suit him while compromising the crew, and a situation sufficiently critical to cause some of them to remain on the island (eleven stayed behind), so increasing his dividend in another way. Betagh also accuses Shelvocke of drinking Jacobite toasts, and of celebrating the Pretender's birthday on Juan Fernandez with white cockades and volleys of musketry.

Although twentieth-century studies of the voyage have relied to a large extent on Betagh for important details, particularly concerning the legal aftermath, the lack of official corroboration has left him vulnerable. W. G. Perrin and Philip Edwards believe that his account of the St Catherine's mutiny is basically correct, yet Perrin inclines to the view that the bulk of his testimony is 'a rather incoherent jumble of accusations' (Perrin, 19). In the most authoritative recent discussion of these charges and counter-charges, Glyndwr Williams joins with O. H. K. Spate in believing it 'unprofitable to decide which was the more atrocious traducer' (Williams, 197; Spate, 383). Chancery records, however, have turned up an application for a writ of *ne exeat regnum* which supports to some degree Betagh's account of the voyage and of the legal entanglements following it. Betagh claims that Edward Hughes, disbelieving what Shelvocke told him when he finally got to London, had him placed first in the Wood Street compter and then in the king's bench while seeking a writ. Although no proof remains of Shelvocke's incarceration, the grant of the writ exists (PRO, C 33/339, pt 1, 7). In it Edward Hughes, John Gumley, Beake Winder, and Henry Neale (listed as owners in the letters of marque) are joined by five others (Alexander Strahan, Hinnfred Sharpe, Andrew Drummond, Richard Chichley, and George Middleton) to cite George Shelvocke, Blowfield Coldsea (master), Matthew Stewart (who organized the mutiny at St Catherine's), John Rainor (lieutenant of marines), George Shelvocke junior, and five more of the crew for breaking the articles of the cruise. The entry states:

> Shelvocke soon after setting sail with the ship Speedwell in Company with the Success being separated by a storm from her wilfully neglected joining with the said Ship Success again but proceeded … to voyage by himself & not only plundered … a vessel in Amity wt his Ma[jes]tie but also took severall Spanish Ships of considerable value & shared & divided up the prizes amongst himself & his Ships Company as by Affidt thereto annext.

The affidavits were supplied by William Betagh and Thomas Dodd, but the owners themselves affirmed that Shelvocke and his fellow defendants gave them no adequate account of prizes taken between July and

August 1721 (including the *Concepcion de Recova*), and the court found the evidence convincing enough to proceed. There seems little reason to doubt the estimate, based on Betagh's transcription of Stewart's account book, that Shelvocke emerged from the voyage with a sum adjacent to £7000, some of which he used to bribe himself out of trouble. For Betagh continues the story from the granting of writ:

> Shelvocke getting bail to the action at common law, contrived so with the marshal of the king's bench prison, that he escaped on a Sunday, and prevented the said writ in chancery being served upon him; and has ever since absconded. Mean time the bill in chancery was carry'd on, to which Shelvocke refusing to put in answer, a writ of rebellion was issued out: but a brother in law of Shelvocke apply'd to two of the owners, being complainants in the bill, and so prevailed with them, that they pretended they were about a composition with the defendant: so that a sudden stop was made to the prosecution. (Betagh, 230)

It is fair to add that it was not uncommon for privateering cruises to end in mutual recrimination and litigation. Depositions were taken accusing Dampier and Rogers of having secreted plunder; and there were bitter disputes between the crews of George Anson's squadron about the distribution of prize money. Perhaps the best state of the case against Shelvocke is given by John Harris (ed. John Campbell), upon whom John Callender and James Burney rely for their judgement of the voyage. Campbell believes that three aspects of Betagh's story deserve attention: Clipperton's refusal to cruise with him once he suspected him of piracy; the regular losses of ship's crew by capture, misadventure, and marooning; and the lading of the *Concepcion de Recova*. Although he does not spell it out, Harris finds 'a very extraordinary piece of secret history' linking the revision of the ship's articles (in which the Juan Fernandez episode seems to have been crucial) to the wastage of people meant to benefit from it, including those from whom Shelvocke had most to fear: Betagh, Hatley, Dodd, and Hendry, none of whom was allowed to keep a journal while under his command (Harris, 1.230; Betagh, 104). Clipperton might have given the most damning account of all, had he not died of alcoholism and a broken heart soon after reaching home. If Shelvocke were guilty of even half of what Betagh lays to his charge, then he proved a consummate exponent of the *tu quoque*, cleverly loading his enemies with the very guilt he deserved. The enigma of Shelvocke's voyage was current in maritime circles. Shortly before Captain Cheap shot and killed him on the coast of Patagonia, Henry Cozens (a midshipman on the *Wager* in Anson's expedition) shouted at him, 'That he was come into those Seas to pay Shelvocke's Debts; and also insolently added, Tho' Shelvocke was a Rogue, he was not a Fool; and by G— you are both' (Bulkeley, 40). Shelvocke's journal also reveals him to have been inclined to gout and corpulence, though even his enemies acknowledged his excellent seamanship. While capable of 'a winning address', he was 'not insensible of his own Merit' (Moore, 1.91). He died, according to a now destroyed memorial stone, in 1742, and was buried at St Nicholas's,

Deptford. Shelvocke's *Voyage* was reissued in 1757 by his son George, who was then secretary to the general Post Office.   JONATHAN LAMB

Sources *DNB* · W. Betagh, *A voyage round the world* (1728) · [J. Bulkeley], *A voyage to the South seas, 1740–44* (1745) · J. Burney, *A chronological history of the discoveries in the South Sea or Pacific Ocean*, 4 (1816), 465 · P. Edwards, *Sea-narratives in eighteenth-century England* (1994) · J. H. Moore, *A new and complete collection of voyages and travels*, 2 vols. (1785) · J. Harris, *Navigantium atque itinerantium bibliotheca, or, A complete collection of voyages and travels*, ed. J. Campbell, 2 vols. (1764) · W. G. Perrin, ed., *A voyage round the world* (1928) · G. Shelvocke, *A voyage round the world by way of the great South sea* (1726) · O. H. K. Spate, *The Pacific since Magellan: monopolists and freebooters* (1983), vol. 2 of *The Pacific since Magellan* · G. Williams, *The great South Sea: English voyages and encounters, 1570–1750* (1997) · PRO, HCA 26/29, 5 · BL, Add. MS 19034, fol. 84*v* · PRO, C 33/339, pt 1, 7

Archives Royal Naval Museum, Portsmouth, admiralty library and manuscript collection, journal, MSS, MS 18 | BL, Add. MS 19034, fol. 84 · PRO, pt 1, 7, C33/339 · PRO, 5, HCA 26/29

Wealth at death £7000: *DNB*; Williams, *The great South Sea*; Perrin, ed., *A voyage*

Shemza, Anwar Jalal (1928–1985), artist, was born on 14 July 1928 in Simla, India, the second of the four children of Khaja Mohammed Sadiq Butt (1896–1992), civil servant, and his wife, Iqbal Begum (*c*.1900–1965). His grandfather owned a family carpet-making and military embroidery business. The family home was at 71 Dinga Singh Buildings, Beadon Road (later Maulana Mohammed Ali Jauhar Road), Lahore. He was educated at mission schools in Simla, Ludhiana, and Lahore, but his religious affiliation was always to Islam. He studied Persian, Arabic, and philosophy at Punjab University from 1943. However, he gave up his BA studies and enrolled at the Mayo School of Art in Lahore in 1944. He obtained a diploma in commercial painting in 1947. He opened the Shemza Commercial Art Studio in Lahore in 1947, henceforth using the invented name Shemza in addition to his given name Anwar Jalal.

Through the late 1940s and early 1950s Shemza was a well-known writer as well as artist and designer in Pakistan. He wrote plays broadcast on Radio Pakistan and was the editor of *Ehsas*, a magazine of art and architecture. He published seven short novels in Urdu, including *Sotey jagtey* (1957), and poetry, including *Folk-tales and stories / Kissa kahani* (1954). He was part of a successful group of artists, influenced by cubism, modernism, and art brut, called the Lahore Art Circle. In 1956 he went to the Slade School of Fine Art in London; he gained a diploma in fine art from University College, London, in 1959 and a British Council scholarship to study printmaking for a further year with Anthony Gross. On 27 October 1958 he married Mary Katrina Taylor (*b*. 1937), artist, known as Mary Katrina, of Stafford, at St Pancras town hall. They had two daughters, Tasveer (*b*. 1959) and Hannah (*b*. 1981). Shemza returned to Pakistan to teach art in 1960, but settled in Stafford, England, in 1962. He lived at 116 Weston Road from 1962 to 1964 and at 77 Newport Road from 1964 until his death.

Shemza's experience during his early years as an unrecognized artist in London, confronted with the cultural prejudices around him, radically altered his perception of

Anwar Jalal Shemza (1928-1985), by unknown photographer, 1958

his own artistic inheritance. From this time a new direction emerged in his art. He combined Islamic motifs, themes, and underlying structures with elements and textures of European and American twentieth-century abstraction. He wrote: 'My work is based on the simplification of the three dimensional solid, architectural reality and the decorative element of calligraphy' (Shemza, 71). In 1958 he exhibited as part of the Pakistan Group London at the Woodstock Gallery in London. Acclaim followed and exhibitions were held at the New Vision Centre Gallery, London (1959), the Olde Soupe Kitchen, Stafford (1959), Gallery One, London (1960), the Gulbenkian Museum of Oriental Art and Archaeology, Durham (1963), the Commonwealth Institute, London (1966), the Arts Council galleries of Lahore (1967) and Karachi (1967), and the Ashmolean Museum, Oxford (1972).

Shemza worked in overlapping series, reworking themes year after year. Investigation of the interrelationships of squares and circles began in 1957. He constructed a visual calligraphy without verbal meaning that dominated the *Love Letters* series of the 1960s and *The Wall* of 1958. Arabic letters appeared as illegible pattern in the silk screen *The Page* (1984) or as mystical reverie inspired by the initial letter of the prophet Mohammed's name in the *Meem* series of the 1960s. The *Roots* series was begun in 1977; these small works on paper and canvas showed the separated parts of imaginary plants and their roots derived from Arabic script below. His techniques were original and varied. He was an internationally acclaimed printmaker, exhibiting at international print biennales. He paid particular attention to the board or paper supports for his work. One of his characteristic background surfaces was produced by dipping muslin in gouache, wringing out the muslin, laying it down with a newspaper on top of it, and stamping on it in flip-flops.

In addition to his work as a practising artist, Shemza was committed to art education for children. He taught at Lawrence College, Ghoragali, from 1954 to 1955, and at the cathedral school in Lahore from 1955 to 1956. He completed an art teacher's diploma with a thesis called 'Visual response of a black child in a white society' in 1972. After his return to England in 1962 he taught at Ounsdale high school, Wombourne, until 1979, and then Weston Road high school in Stafford as head of art and design until his death.

Shemza died following a heart attack in Stafford on 18 January 1985. He was buried at Stafford crematorium on 24 January 1985. He was survived by his wife and two daughters. His art works are included in the collections of Birmingham Museums and Art Gallery; the Ashmolean Museum, Oxford; Wolverhampton Art Gallery; the Gulbenkian Museum of Oriental Art and Archaeology, Durham; Cartwright Hall Art Gallery, Bradford; Somerville College, Oxford; Lahore Museum, Lahore; Peshawar Museum, Peshawar; the Pakistan National Art Council Collection, Islamabad; and Albertina im Akademiehof, Vienna. A posthumous exhibition of his *Roots* series toured Pakistan in 1985. The first retrospective of his work was held at Birmingham Museums and Art Gallery in 1997–8.   REYAHN KING

Sources M. Shemza, 'Anwar Jalal Shemza: search for cultural identity', *Third Text*, 8/9 (autumn–winter 1989), 65–78 • *Anwar Shemza* [exhibition catalogue, Birmingham Museums and Art Gallery, Birmingham, 12 Nov 1997 – 1 Feb 1998] • S. Hashimi, 'Shemza, Anwar Jalal', *The dictionary of art*, ed. J. Turner (1996) • P. Burnhill and M. Katrina, *Roots* [exhibition catalogue, Islamabad, Peshawar, Lahore, 1985] • private information (2004) [Mary Katrina Taylor, widow]

Archives priv. coll., MSS

Likenesses photograph, 1958, priv. coll. [*see illus.*] • photograph, 1959 • double portrait, photograph, 1960 (with Ayub Khon), priv. coll. • photograph, 1960, priv. coll. • photograph, 1985, priv. coll.

Wealth at death £31,210: administration, 26 March 1985, *CGPLA Eng. & Wales*

Shenstone, William (1714–1763), writer, was born on 18 November 1714 at The Leasowes, the family farm on Mucklow Hill, north-east of Halesowen, then part of Shropshire, and baptized at Halesowen church on 6 December, the elder of two sons of Thomas Shenstone (1685/6–1724), son of William Shenstone of Lapull, and his wife, Ann Penn (1692/3–1732), eldest daughter of William Penn of Harborough Hall, Hagley, part of which estate Shenstone later inherited. According to Johnson, Shenstone developed an early enthusiasm for reading, and pestered members of his family for new books every time they went to market: 'It is said that when his request had been neglected, his mother wrapped up a piece of wood of the same form, and pacified him for the night' (Johnson, 348). He was taught initially by Sarah Lloyd, later to be the model for his *School-Mistress*, and attended Halesowen grammar school briefly before being taught by the Revd

John Crompton at Solihull School. Here he met Richard Jago, a lifelong friend, correspondent, and fellow poet. Shenstone's father died in June 1724, aged thirty-eight, and his mother died in June 1732, aged thirty-nine; his grandmother managed the estate, but on her death he was placed under the guardianship of his uncle, the Revd Thomas Dolman of Broome, Staffordshire.

In May 1732 Shenstone was admitted commoner at Pembroke College, Oxford; Johnson had already left, but Shenstone formed lasting attachments with Anthony Whistler and the future novelist Richard Graves, both at Pembroke. Jago went to University College. Shenstone made a point of wearing his own hair rather than a wig, thus incurring 'ill-natured remarks' in the various clubs which he and Graves frequented (Graves, 178). He studied mathematics and after four years wore the gown of a student of civil law, but spent most of his energy on poetry. He left without a degree, though his name was on the register for ten years; a large mulberry tree in the fellows' garden was known as 'Shenstone's tree'. About 1733 he wrote a small mock-heroic poem, 'The Diamond', but his first published volume was the anonymous *Poems upon Various Occasions* (1737), which included an early version of *The School-Mistress*, the affectionate Spenserian parody for which Shenstone is chiefly remembered.

From Oxford Shenstone initially returned to Harborough Hall, where Richard Graves spent a pleasantly indolent month's visit. Shenstone visited London and Bath, contributed to the *Gentleman's Magazine*, went to the theatre, and flirted with literary society. In *The Judgement of Hercules* (1741), addressed to George Lyttleton, whom he supported at the Worcester election in 1740, he appears to choose the pursuit of active virtue and literary fame against the pleasures of slothful rural retirement, but most of the subsequent poetry reverses this decision. He revised *The School-Mistress* (1742), doubling the poem's size, adding detail to the portrait of the strict but sympathetic country teacher, and enhancing his appreciation of Spenser's 'peculiar tenderness of sentiment' ('Advertisement'). The poem did not receive the reception Shenstone thought its due, and gradually his work took on a more reclusive, melancholic, and occasionally Gothic tone: by 1748 he had written twenty-six elegies, many of them in praise of introspective retreat from society. His 'A Pastoral Ballad, in Four Parts', later set to music by Thomas Arne, laments parting from an early love (the sister of his friend Richard Graves), though it was later rewritten for another romance, curtailed by lack of funds. In the early 1740s he also wrote a large number of songs and ballads, and humorous pieces. This work was later published, sometimes without formal permission, in the last three volumes of his friend Dodsley's influential *Collection of Poems by Several Hands* (1748–58).

In 1744 Shenstone withdrew to The Leasowes, where he had sometimes boarded with the tenant. He now set about turning the estate into a landscape garden, or *ferme ornée*, 'which he did with such judgement and such fancy as made his little domain the envy of the great and the admiration of the skilful: a place to be visited by travellers, and copied by designers' (Johnson, 350). He continued to agonize about his decision to abandon literary society, and to revise *The School-Mistress*, but his main energies went into diverting streams to create waterfalls, and clearing undergrowth to display 'natural' beauties from advantageous viewpoints. Shenstone showed his many visitors round the serpentine walks and surprise vistas in a careful routine; the garden was popular enough to engender a certain rivalry with Lyttleton's much bigger park at Hagley, and Shenstone sometimes complained that Lyttleton showed people round his garden the wrong way on purpose. The garden was filled with seats, urns, temples, and obelisks, many with inscriptions, in the structured form of picturesque contemplation made popular by the designer Batty Langley. Among the buildings were some designed by Sanderson Miller, and a number of fashionable Gothic 'ruins', one of which was made habitable for a tenant.

Shenstone's mature years were saddened by ill health and the deaths of the poet James Thomson (1748), Shenstone's brother (1751), his cousin Mary Dolman (1754), Anthony Whistler (1754), and Lady Luxborough, the troubled sister of Viscount Bolingbroke with whom he had corresponded for many years (1756). He also found himself engaged in a lawsuit about the division of the Harborough property, which was eventually settled in 1758 after the intervention of Lord Stamford. Shenstone managed to establish new friendships with the printer John Baskerville, the critic Joseph Spence, and the industrialist Matthew Boulton. Otherwise he spent his time gardening, painting, playing music, and collecting *objets d'art*. He confined his literary efforts to letters and to the assistance of friends like his bookseller Robert Dodsley, and Thomas Percy, whose *Reliques of Ancient Poetry* owes much to Shenstone's literary taste. He also prepared an anthology of poems by his friends, which remained unpublished until 1952.

Graves describes Shenstone as having 'a dull heavy look, unless when his features were animated by any sprightly sentiment, which rendered them extremely pleasing. His favourite dress was a plain blue coat and a scarlet waistcoat with a broad gold lace' (Graves, 25). Carlyle met him in 1758 and described him as 'a large heavy fat man, dressed in white clothes and silver lace, with his gray hairs tied behind and much powdered, which, added to his shyness and reserve, was not at first prepossessing'; but Carlyle reports that once Shenstone's 'reserve and melancholy' abated, he 'became good company' (*Autobiography*, ed. Burton, 388). Richard Graves included a cameo of Shenstone in *The Spiritual Quixote* (1773), and the same author's *Columella* (1779) is partly based on Shenstone's character. Some of his contemporaries, such as Walpole and Gray, thought the pose of retirement was affected in order to elicit curiosity or sympathy.

Shenstone died at The Leasowes on 11 February 1763, 'of a putrid fever' (Johnson, 353), later rumoured to have been caused by sitting outside one night after an argument with his housekeeper (or mistress) Mary Cutler. The fever is more prosaically associated with Shenstone's return from a visit to Lord Stamford at Emville in connection with a government pension, for which Lord Loughborough had made application to Lord Bute. He was buried on 15 February in Halesowen churchyard, beside his brother Joseph (1722–1751), who had trained but never practised as an attorney; there is a memorial urn to him beside the north wall of the church with an inscription by Graves. Johnson suggests that the poet, whose income was about £300 a year, got himself into debt with extravagant works; he had perennial trouble in recovering his rents, and his 'The Progress of Taste' laments the disparity between his income and his ambitions. In his will Shenstone made provision for the payment of his debts by directing the sale of several small estates and houses. Dated a few days before he died, it bequeathes The Leasowes to his cousin John Hodgetts of Birmingham, for life, and thereafter to another cousin, Edward Cooke of Edinburgh, and his heirs, specifying that the property could be sold to friends such as the Hon. John Grey, son of Lord Stamford. Shenstone also left an estate at Quinton, Halesowen, and a house in Birmingham, to his cousin John Shenstone. There were several other sizeable bequests to relatives, friends, and servants. Mary Cutler received an annuity of £30. She later challenged the will on the grounds that back wages were unpaid, promises of recompense made by Shenstone had not been carried out, and the executors had failed to pay her specified legacies.

Shenstone's garden continued to attract visitors (Goldsmith wrote an essay on it in 1773), but it was not carefully maintained. The house had been rebuilt by 1781; it is now the clubhouse for Halesowen golf course, which partly covers the garden. The rest of the 58-hectare estate is managed by Dudley metropolitan borough council, and is being restored according to Shenstone's designs. Shenstone had been planning a subscription edition of his works, but in the event Dodsley immediately set about publishing Shenstone's *Works in Verse and Prose*. The poems constituted volume 1 (1764); *Essays on Men, Manners, and Things*, including influential essays on gardening, with a plan of The Leasowes and an enthusiastic description by Dodsley, appeared as volume 2 (1764); and a collection of Shenstone's letters to his friends made up volume 3 (1769). A scholarly edition of the letters was published by Marjorie Williams in 1939, but the poems, which were admired by Johnson, Burns, Hazlitt, and Ruskin, and reprinted many times into the nineteenth century, still lack a thorough modern edition.   PAUL BAINES

Sources M. Williams, *William Shenstone: a chapter in eighteenth-century taste* (1935) · A. R. Humphreys, *William Shenstone: an eighteenth-century portrait* (1937) · J. Tierney, 'William Shenstone', *Eighteenth-century British poets: first series*, ed. J. Sitter, DLitB, 95 (1990) · F. D. Burns, 'William Shenstone: a biographical and critical study', PhD diss., University of Sheffield, 1970 · E. M. Purkis, *William Shenstone: poet and landscape gardener* (1931) · M. Williams, *William Shenstone and his friends* (1933) · A. I. Hazeltine, *A study of William Shenstone and his critics* (1918) · R. Graves, *Recollections of some particulars in the life of the late William Shenstone* (1788) · S. Johnson, 'Shenstone', *Lives of the English poets*, ed. G. B. Hill, [new edn], 3 (1905), 348–60 · S. Grazebrook, *The family of Shenstone the poet* (1890?) · *The letters of William Shenstone*, ed. M. Williams (1939) · *Shenstone's miscellany*, ed. I. A. Gordon (1952) · *The autobiography of Dr Alexander Carlyle of Inveresk, 1722–1805*, ed. J. H. Burton (1910)

Archives Wellesley College, Massachusetts, corresp. and papers · Worcs. RO, legal documents · Yale U., Beinecke L., letters and papers relating to Leasowes estate | Birm. CA, letters to Matthew Boulton · BL, corresp. with Robert Dodsley, Add. MSS 28958–28959 · BL, letters to J. S. Hylton, Add. MS 27548 · BL, letters to Lady Luxborough, Add. MSS 28598–28599 · BL, corresp. with Thomas Percy, Add. MS 28221 · Bodl. Oxf., corresp. with Thomas Percy · Worcs. RO, letters to Edward Knight

Likenesses T. Ross, oils, 1738, NPG; replica or copy, Pembroke College, Oxford · E. Alcock, oils, 1760, NPG · engraving, c.1763, Hunt. L.; repro. in Tierney, 'William Shenstone' · J. Hall, line engraving, 1780, BM · etching on paper, 1780, Tate collection · attrib. E. Alcock, oils, Birmingham Museums and Art Gallery · line engraving, BM; repro. in Shenstone, *The works in verse and prose of William Shenstone*, ed. [R. Dodsley], 2 vols. (1764) · line engraving (after unknown artist), BM

Wealth at death The Leasowes; estate at Quinton; house in Birmingham; estate at Churchill, Romsley; houses in Halesowen; bequests of £100 or more: will, PRO, PROB 11/844, sig. 91

Shenstone, William Ashwell (1850–1908), chemist and schoolmaster, was born at Wells next the Sea, Norfolk, on 1 December 1850. He was the eldest son of James Burt Byron Shenstone, a pharmaceutical chemist in Colchester, and his wife, Jemima, daughter of James Chapman, of Wells next the Sea. His grandfather, Joseph Shenstone of Halesowen, was a cousin of the eighteenth-century poet, William Shenstone, after whom he was named.

Shenstone was educated at Colchester grammar school before he entered his father's business as an apprentice pharmacist. A serious fire in his father's shop left him lame and a permanent victim to physical pain for the rest of his life. In 1871 he was awarded a Bell scholarship to train as a pharmaceutical chemist at the school of the Pharmaceutical Society of Great Britain in London. On being awarded the Pereira medal in 1872 he was appointed demonstrator of practical chemistry in the school under Professor John Attfield (1835–1911). In the same year, Attfield's former colleague, William A. Tilden (1842–1926), was appointed senior science master at Clifton College, Bristol; Shenstone joined the college staff as his assistant in 1874. The following year he was appointed science master at Taunton School, and in 1877 science master at Exeter grammar school, where he built a cheap laboratory (Shenstone, *Nature*, 26 July 1878) that became a model for other public schools. He returned to Clifton College in 1880, succeeding Tilden as senior science master—a post he held until his death. On 27 December 1883 he married Jane Mildred, eldest daughter of Reginald N. Durrant, rector of Wootton, near Canterbury. There were two children, a son and a daughter.

While assistant to Tilden at Clifton, Shenstone collaborated with him in an investigation of the terpenes. Ambitious to be more than a secondary school teacher (though he took such duties extremely seriously) he sacrificed recreation, health, and holidays to the prosecution of chemical research. There were further joint researches with Tilden on the solubility of salts at high temperatures in the 1880s before Shenstone struck out on his own with research on the preparation of ozone and the curious properties of highly purified substances. A skilled glass-blower, he published an important practical manual on the subject in 1886 and introduced vitrified silica as a material for laboratory apparatus. In 1895 he published a valuable biography of the German chemist Justus von Liebig, who had been an inspiration to his own career. A series of popular essays on modern science that appeared in the *Cornhill Magazine* were collectively published as *The New Physics and Chemistry* in 1906 and reveal Shenstone's powers as a popular expositor and teacher.

Shenstone became a fellow of the Chemical Society in 1876 and a member of its council in 1893–5; he was a fellow of the Institute of Chemistry from its foundation in 1878, serving on the council in 1905–6. He was an original member of the Society of Chemical Industry. He was made a fellow of the Royal Society on 9 June 1898, one of only a handful of schoolteachers to achieve such an honour. Shenstone joined the Association of Public School Science Teachers on its formation in 1901. He died on 3 February 1908 at the Polurrian Hotel, Mullion, Cornwall, while on sick leave, and was buried in the village churchyard close by the sea. Devoted to his profession, Shenstone was highly successful both as a research chemist and as a teacher of chemistry, and generally influenced the introduction of practical methods of science teaching in schools.　　　　　　　　　　　　　　　W. H. BROCK

Sources W. A. T. [W. A. Tilden], *PRS*, 82A (1909), xxii–iv · W. A. T. [W. A. Tilden], *JCS*, 95 (1909), 2206–9 · T. I. Williams, 'Clifton and science', *Centenary essays on Clifton College*, ed. N. G. L. Hammond (1962), 195–212 · W. A. Shenstone, 'A school laboratory', *Nature*, 18 (1878), 347–8 · W. A. Shenstone, 'Vitrified quartz', *Notices of the Proceedings at the Meetings of the Members of the Royal Institution*, 16 (1899–1901), 525–31 · W. A. Shenstone, *The methods of glass blowing for the use of physical and chemical students*, 3rd edn (1894) · W. A. Shenstone, *Justus von Liebig: his life and work* (1895) · W. A. Shenstone, *The new physics and chemistry* (1906) · CGPLA Eng. & Wales (1908)
Likenesses photograph, Clifton College, Bristol · photograph, Clifton College, Bristol; repro. in E. J. Holmyard, *Physics for beginners* (1930), p. 124
Wealth at death £3026 13s. 8d.: probate, 24 March 1908, CGPLA Eng. & Wales

Shenton, Ellen Maria Nicholson (*bap.* 1828, *d.* 1859). *See under* Shenton, Henry Chawner (*bap.* 1803, *d.* 1866).

Shenton, Henry Chawner (*bap.* 1803, *d.* 1866), engraver, the son of John Shenton and his wife, Sarah, was baptized on 14 March 1803 at St Thomas's, Winchester, and moved to London in 1817. He became a pupil of Charles Warren, whose daughter Mary Ann he married on 9 March 1824. They had at least three children. Shenton was at first employed on small illustrations for books and annuals from designs by Thomas Stothard, Thomas Uwins, Richard Westall, Edward Corbould, and others, some of which he exhibited with the Society of British Artists between 1825 and 1832. For these early exhibits he is sometimes recorded as 'F. C. Shenton'. In 1825 he joined the Artists' Annuity Fund.

Shenton engraved some works after old masters: in 1833, *The Merry Fiddler*, after J. Berkheyden, and *A Jew Merchant*, after Rembrandt; in 1834, *Christ Reasoning with the Pharisees*, after Leonardo da Vinci, which appeared in Allan

Cunningham's *Cabinet Gallery* in 1836; and later, in 1861, *Death of Cleopatra*, after Guido Reni, completed by Herbert Bourne for the *Art Journal*. For the *Art Journal's* series of plates from the Vernon gallery he engraved *Country Cousins*, after Richard Redgrave, in 1854, also published in *The Vernon Gallery of British Art*, ed S. C. Hall (3 vols., 1854). His portraits included historical figures as well as those of contemporaries: *James V, King of Scotland*, after Solomon A. Hart, was published in 1834 by Charles Tilt; *William Allen*, after Henry P. Briggs, followed in 1845; and *The Earl of Zetland, M. W. Grand Master of English Freemasons*, unattributed, was exhibited at the Royal Academy in 1857. He executed some good plates on a larger scale, among them *The Stray Kitten*, after William Collins, and *The Hermit*, after Alexander Fraser. For *Finden's Royal Gallery of British Art* (1838–49), he engraved *A Day's Sport in the Highlands*, after Abraham Cooper, and *The Loan of a Bite*, after William Mulready, exhibited at the Royal Academy in 1858. He contributed one engraving, *Olden Hospitality*, after J. R. Robert, to Hall's *Gems of European Art* (1846). Shenton's best-known plates are the three published by the Art Union of London: *The Tired Huntsman*, after Charles Landseer (1840); *The Clemency of Coeur de Lion*, after John Cross (1856), a painting entered for the Westminster Hall competition; and *A Labour for Love*, after T. F. Dicksee (1863); this last was completed by C. H. Jeens after the failure of Shenton's eyesight. Shenton also executed for the Art Union a set of outlines of incidents in English history, from designs by various artists, issued in 1847. The *Art Journal* noted in 1866 that he was one of the last survivors of the able band of engravers in the pure line manner who had flourished during the first half of the century. Assessing Shenton's work, J. H. Slater later noted that 'their quality is … undoubted, and they should take a foremost place in any revival of interest in English line engraving of the period' (Engen, 177). He died suddenly at Camden Town on 15 September 1866.

Shenton's eldest son, **Henry Chawner Shenton** (*bap.* 1825, *d.* 1846), sculptor, was baptized at St Pancras Old Church, London, on 5 January 1825 and entered the Royal Academy Schools in 1843; he also studied in Rome. He was a pupil of the sculptor William Behnes. He exhibited at the Royal Academy in 1843 a group of Christ and Mary and in 1845 *The Penitent*, an alto relievo; in 1844, at the Westminster Hall competition, a colossal group of *The Burial of the Princes in the Tower*; and in 1845, also at Westminster Hall, a statue of Cranmer. Apparently Shenton worked under very difficult conditions, for his first group was:

> modelled in a stable with a roof so low that the ground had to be dug away to a depth of several feet, while the only light came through a narrow window in the wall, to the damps and chill of this fireless workroom his friends attribute the first insinuation of that disease which has laid the sculptor in an early grave.　(*The Athenaeum*, 1846, 72)

He died on 7 February 1846.

His brother, **William Kernot Shenton** (1836–1878), was born in June 1836. He also became a sculptor and exhibited medallion portraits, including *The Poet Schiller*, at the Royal Academy from 1857 to 1871. For a time he taught drawing and modelling in the art school at the Crystal Palace. He died on 19 April 1878.

Living at the same addresses in London in Camden Town and Regent's Park as Shenton and his two sons was his daughter **Ellen Maria Nicholson Shenton** (*bap.* 1828, *d.* 1859), also a sculptor. She exhibited Byronic, biblical, and Shakespearian subjects at the Royal Academy between 1850 and 1859.

F. M. O'DONOGHUE, *rev.* JOANNA DESMOND

Sources *Art Journal*, 28 (1866), 332 · B. Hunnisett, *An illustrated dictionary of British steel engravers*, new edn (1989), 118–19 · R. K. Engen, *Dictionary of Victorian engravers, print publishers and their works* (1979) · Graves, *RA exhibitors* · *Engraved Brit. ports.*, 6.683 · *IGI* · H. Guise, *Great Victorian engravings: a collector's guide* (1980), 13 · R. Gunnis, *Dictionary of British sculptors, 1660–1851* (1953) · J. Johnson, ed., *Works exhibited at the Royal Society of British Artists, 1824–1893, and the New English Art Club, 1888–1917*, 2 vols. (1975) · *The Athenaeum* (17 Jan 1846), 72 · *CGPLA Eng. & Wales* (1878) [William Kernot Shenton]
Wealth at death under £450—William Kernot Shenton: probate, 1878, *CGPLA Eng. & Wales*

Shenton, Henry Chawner (*bap.* **1825**, *d.* **1846**). *See under* Shenton, Henry Chawner (*bap.* 1803, *d.* 1866).

Shenton, William Kernot (1836–1878). *See under* Shenton, Henry Chawner (*bap.* 1803, *d.* 1866).

Shepard, Ernest Howard (1879–1976), painter and illustrator, was born in St John's Wood, London, on 10 December 1879, the second son and youngest of the three children of Henry Donkin Shepard, architect, and his wife, Jessie Harriet, daughter of William Lee, watercolour painter. Ernest's parents encouraged his talent for drawing, and some of his sketches drawn when he was only seven are remarkable for the lively accuracy of observation which became such a feature of his later work. His mother died when he was ten, after which his aunts helped to bring him up.

Shepard was educated at St Paul's School, Hammersmith, where his uncle was a senior master. At sixteen he went to Heatherley's Art School, from which, a year later, he gained a five-year studentship to the Royal Academy Schools. While at Heatherley's he received the nickname Kipper, by which he was known to his friends for the rest of his life. At the Royal Academy Schools he was taught by such academicians as John Singer Sargent, who, Shepard said, 'inspired us all'. Frank Dicksee, who was later president of the Royal Academy, was a family friend and a very early influence.

In 1899 Shepard won both the Landseer and the British Institution scholarships, and in the following year he was awarded a silver medal for figure painting and the third prize for figure drawing. While still studying Shepard was supplementing his meagre finances by selling drawings to magazines. He exhibited fairly regularly at the Royal Academy from 1901 until 1924, after which he only exhibited three times. Gradually his illustrative work took over more or less completely and he only painted in oils as a recreation. Among the books he illustrated before the First World War were *David Copperfield*, *Tom Brown's Schooldays*, *Aesop's Fables*, and *Henry Esmond*.

While at the Royal Academy Schools Shepard had met another gifted student, Florence Eleanor Chaplin (*d.* 1927), second daughter of James Hopper Chaplin, a gem expert and a member of Lloyds, and granddaughter of Ebenezer Landells, one of the founders of *Punch*. In 1904 they married; in 1907 their son Graham Shepard was born and in 1909 their daughter Mary *Shepard, who was to marry E. V. Knox. Graham died in 1943.

Ernest Howard Shepard (1879–1976), by Howard Coster, 1932

It was an ambition of Shepard to become a *Punch* artist but it was not until 1906 that his first drawings were accepted, and it was not until 1914 that he was having drawings regularly accepted. In 1915 he applied for a commission in the Royal Artillery; he always said he was fascinated by guns. He was in the battles of the Somme, Arras, and Ypres, and ended the war serving in Italy as Major Shepard MC. He managed to do a surprising amount of work during that period but suffered another blow when his beloved elder brother was killed. In 1921 he was invited to become a member of the staff of *Punch*, which meant that he had to produce at least one drawing a week and which provided him with the blessing of a regular income.

A. A. Milne had written a series of children's verses for *Punch* and Shepard was asked to illustrate them. This was a wonderful marriage of verse and vision. Shepard's delicately precise and fresh drawings had an instant appeal and were published, in 1924, as *When we were Very Young*. The success of this book led to a series: *Winnie the Pooh* (1926), *Now we are Six* (1927), *The House at Pooh Corner* (1928), and a number of others. It established both Milne and Shepard, though it was Christopher Robin and Pooh who became household names for generations of children and adults. Shepard was also commissioned by G. Bell & Sons to do sixty full-page drawings for *Everybody's Pepys* (1926), which was followed by *Everybody's Boswell* (1930) and *Everybody's Lamb* (1933). Florence died very suddenly, in 1927, and Shepard lost not only a wife but a valued critic.

During the 1930s Shepard buried himself in work, which included drawings for the 1931 edition of *The Wind in the Willows* by Kenneth Grahame, the 1932 edition of *Bevis* by Richard Jefferies, and *Victoria regina* (1934) by Laurence Housman. In 1935 he was appointed second cartoonist on the editorial staff of *Punch*, another landmark of success in his career. He carried on this responsible job through the Second World War until 1949, and finally left in 1953, when editorial changes were made. In 1944 he married, as his second wife, Norah, eldest daughter of J. C. Carroll of Australia; she was a nurse at St Mary's Hospital, Paddington.

After Shepard's dismissal from *Punch* he continued to illustrate books and began to lecture and broadcast. In 1957 he wrote *Drawn from Memory*, which is full of endearingly clear memories of his family and of himself as a little boy of eight. This was followed in 1961 by *Drawn from Life*, which takes the reader through his school and art student days to the time of his first marriage. His writing has the same observant and sympathetic charm that characterizes his drawings.

Shepard was fairly tall with penetrating, light blue eyes. His personality was warm and friendly and was allied to a shrewd mind and an immense capacity for work. 'A man for all men' was how fellow *Punch* cartoonist Leslie Illingworth described him. The enormous popularity of Winnie the Pooh, which grew through the years, meant that towards the end of Shepard's very long life he was constantly involved with new projects concerned with the A. A. Milne books, and particularly with coloured editions.

In 1972 he was appointed OBE. He managed to celebrate his ninety-sixth birthday, and died at Midhurst, Sussex, on 24 March 1976.   C. A. PARKER, *rev.*

Sources E. H. Shepard, *Drawn from memory* (1957) • E. H. Shepard, *Drawn from life* (1961) • R. Knox, ed., *The work of E. H. Shepard* (1979) • records, RA • personal knowledge (1986) • CGPLA Eng. & Wales (1976) • *The Times* (26 March 1976)
Archives University of Surrey, drawings, diaries, letters, and sketchbooks | BL, corresp. with Marie Stopes, Add. MS 58542 • Ransom HRC, corresp. with John Lane
Likenesses H. Coster, photographs, 1932, NPG [*see illus.*] • D. Montgomery, photograph, 1969, NPG • G. Morgan, photographs, NPG • Pathé News Pictorial, photograph, NPG
Wealth at death £68,948: probate, 22 July 1976, CGPLA Eng. & Wales

Shepard [*married name* Knox], **Mary Eleanor Jessy** (1909–2000), artist and illustrator, was born on 25 December 1909 at Red Cottage, Shamley Green, Wonersh, near Godalming, Surrey, the only daughter and younger child of Ernest Howard *Shepard (1879–1976), painter and illustrator, and his wife, Florence Eleanor Chaplin (d. 1927). She enjoyed a happy childhood at Red Cottage, attended St Monica's, Tadworth, near Epsom, Surrey, and was 'finished' at the Villa Ste Monique in Auteuil. In 1926 she and her brother Graham accompanied their father on his sketching trips to A. A. Milne's home in the Ashdown Forest, Sussex, and played with Christopher Robin. For her, he reacted as someone who had never known 'anyone older than himself actually playing games with him' (*The Independent*). She trained at the Slade, London, under Henry Tonks and Randolph Schwabe. She worked as an artist, had two exhibitions in London, and won a prize for etching in Paris.

Pamela Travers, an Australian then unknown, had her children's book, *Mary Poppins*, accepted by the publisher Gerald Howe and they hoped E. H. Shepard would illustrate it, but he had too much work. P. L. Travers saw a Christmas card designed by Mary Shepard, then aged twenty-three, and chose her to illustrate the book, published in 1934. P. L. Travers was demanding—she insisted that the pictorial Poppins resemble the peg doll she had as a child and 'have no figure' (*Daily Telegraph*)—and Mary Shepard's drawings defined the image of Mary Poppins and contributed much to the success of the book and its sequels, all of which she illustrated: the last was *Mary Poppins in Cherry Tree Lane* (1982). The illustration of Mr Banks was based on a family friend, Edmund George Valpy *Knox (1881–1971), editor of *Punch*, whom she married on 2 October 1937. She inherited her father's confident linework and feeling for the integration of drawing with the text, and she was meticulous in research. Her work of the 1930s indicates that she could have become a prominent book illustrator, but after her marriage she did little such work and became somewhat depreciatory of her talents as an illustrator. She had no children, but she was a second mother to her two step-children, Rawle Knox, journalist, and Penelope *Fitzgerald, the novelist. They lived at St John's Wood, London, and during the Second World War she served as an air-raid warden, kept chickens, and grew vegetables. After the war they moved to Hampstead, London, where Knox died in 1971 and where she continued to enjoy entertaining family and friends. Following a long illness she died on 4 September 2000 in Highgate Nursing Home, 12 Hornsey Lane, Islington, London.

ROGER T. STEARN

Sources The Times (20 Oct 2000) · The Independent (29 Sept 2000) · Daily Telegraph (26 Sept 2000) · A. Herne, The dictionary of 20th century book illustrators (1995) · b. cert. · m. cert. · d. cert.

Shepard, Thomas (1605–1649), minister in America, was born on 5 November 1605 at Towcester, Northamptonshire, the youngest child of William Shepard (d. 1615), a grocer originally from the village of Fossecut, who married the daughter of a merchant, a Mr Bland, from whom he learned his trade. When Thomas was about four his mother died, and his father subsequently married a woman who would not accept the child his mother had described as 'her youngest and best beloved' (Albro, xiv). Following their father's death Shepard's elder brother John eventually took charge of him and saw to it that he continued to receive an education at the free school of Towcester, which prepared him for admittance as a pensioner to Emmanuel College, Cambridge, on 10 February 1620. Shepard graduated BA in 1624.

Both disease and debauchery are said to have played roles in Shepard's spiritual awakening. At Cambridge he attended the preaching of several notable churchmen, and speaks with anguish of his dissolute behaviour and a lack of belief that caused him to veer from the contemplation of suicide to religious fervour. Under the preaching of John Preston, then master of Emmanuel College, Shepard entered into a profound religious conversion which led him finally to resolve to enter the ministry. Shepard describes his experience of hearing Preston preach:

> the Lord so bored my ears as that I understood what he spake and the secrets of my soul were laid upon [i.e., open] before me—the hypocrisy of all good things I thought I had in me—as if one had told him of all that ever I did, of all the turnings and deceits of my heart, insomuch as that I thought he was the most searching preacher in the world. And I began to love him much and to bless God I did see my frame and my hypocrisy and self and secret sins, although I found a hard heart and could not be affected with them.
> ('Autobiography', 44)

Anguish, and vacillation between assurance of salvation and fear of damnation, characterize Shepard's writings not only from this period but throughout a life troubled at the prospect that his beliefs and actions might ultimately prove unacceptable to God. He longed to know for certain whether he had won the eternal lottery, and this insecurity fired a lifetime of popular preaching and writing:

> It is a thousand to one if ever thou be one of that small number whom God hath picked out to escape this wrath to come. If thou dost not get the Lord Jesus to bear this wrath, farewell God, Christ, and God's mercy forever. ('The sincere convert', Works, 1.45)

From his time as a student at Cambridge, Shepard also struggled with the conflicting creeds of Calvinism, Arminianism, and a form of antinomianism known contemporaneously as Grindletonianism because of its association with Roger Brereley, minister in Grindleton, Yorkshire.

Probably at the suggestion of John Preston, Shepard left Cambridge in 1626 to enter the tutelage of Thomas Weld, the vicar at Terling, Essex. In a parochial apprenticeship characteristic of the development of godly ministry in the Jacobean period, he was given both pastoral formation and practical training, and was introduced to a network of potential mentors and colleagues. At Terling Shepard came under the influence of Thomas *Hooker, then preaching at Chelmsford. Both Weld and Hooker eventually preceded Shepard in emigrating to North America. Shepard's years at Terling proved to be formative and eventful; during them his vocation and theological identity were shaped as a member of the relatively close-knit circle of Essex ministers, often with ties to Emmanuel College, whose nonconformist sympathies shared at least a spiritual affinity with the Elizabethan puritan movement.

Shepard proceeded MA in 1627, took deacon's orders at Peterborough on 12 July the same year, and was ordained priest the following day. After considerable deliberation with Weld, Hooker, and other godly ministers and leading lay persons, he accepted the invitation of the people of Earls Colne, near Coggeshall, Essex, to serve as their minister in a three-year lectureship endowed by a Dr Wilson and originally intended for the town of Coggeshall. He served at Earls Colne from 1627 to 1630, after which the people of the town pledged the sum of £40 per year to underwrite his lectureship. The lecture provided by Dr Wilson was moved, in part because of Shepard's influence, to his home town of Towcester, where Samuel Stone, another graduate of Emmanuel College, took up the charge.

In the light of the affirmation of Earls Colne for his ministry, Shepard had determined to remain there. However, on 16 December 1630 he was summoned to London by Bishop William Laud, who silenced him and refused to allow him to exercise ministry in the diocese of London, according to Shepard, with the words, 'I will have no such fellows prate in my diocese' ('Autobiography', 51n.). Ironically, according to Shepard, until he was accused of nonconformity he had not made up his mind concerning the subject. Returning to Earls Colne, however, although he submitted to the bishop's injunction against teaching, Shepard came to 'see the evil of the English ceremonies, cross, surplice, and kneeling' (ibid., 52). When he appeared again before Bishop Laud the bishop instructed him to leave Earls Colne altogether.

Shepard says in his autobiography that it was at this time that he and Weld began to consider going to New England. Before doing so they hoped to preach in Ireland and Scotland, but after a third encounter with Bishop Laud, Shepard took flight to Yorkshire, where he had been offered a position in a prominent household sympathetic to the plight of ejected godly ministers. He became the chaplain to the family of Sir Richard Darley in Butter-crambe, Yorkshire, where he met a cousin of Sir Richard, Margaret Touteville; they were married on 23 July 1632. Shortly thereafter Shepard received a call from a church in the Northumbrian town of Heddon, near Newcastle, but Bishop Thomas Morton of Durham, at the direction of Archbishop Richard Neile of York, refused him permission to preach publicly there. Nevertheless, Shepard explains that he 'preached up and down in the country', and in at least one private home, belonging to Mr Fenwick, until John Cotton, Thomas Hooker, Thomas Weld, and Samuel Stone emigrated from England ('Autobiography', 56–7).

Under considerable official pressure, and without the support of these friends, Shepard decided also to sail for New England in October 1634. Following a failed Atlantic crossing, and (immediately after landfall) the death of their first child, Shepard and his wife remained in England for several more months, during which time a second child, Thomas *Shepard (1635–1677), was born. On 10 August 1635 they sailed again, arriving in New England on 3 October. Two days later Shepard and his travelling companions settled in the colonial village of Newtown. His wife soon died there of tuberculosis contracted on the journey.

Shepard made a significant contribution to the religious and educational life of the colonial settlement in Massachusetts. As minister of First Church, Newtown, perhaps in reaction to his own early temptations, he helped define puritan order and orthodoxy during the antinomian controversy of 1636–8, which eventually resulted in the expulsion from the colony of Anne Hutchinson, John Wheelwright, and their followers, and in the chastening of Shepard's old colleague, John Cotton. In contrast to Hutchinson's view that assurance of one's salvation cannot be obtained by contemplating one's own progress in righteousness, but is granted to the believer directly by the Holy Spirit, Shepard held that 'God made room for man's own striving within the larger framework of the divine initiative. God and man worked together in the process of salvation' (Hall, 18). As he wrote to Cotton, one cannot separate God's revelation in the Word (the Bible) from God's revelation in the Holy Spirit. Shepard worked out these themes in a series of sermons preached between 1636 and 1640, posthumously published in 1660 as *The Parable of the Ten Virgins*. Although he might, like the saints, boast of hope in Christ, men should not 'sluggishly put all on Christ', while it is true, he asserts, that 'the mighty working of Christ that must conquer thy lusts; but must this put you to neglect striving?' (*Works*, 2.250–51).

Shepard was also instrumental in founding Harvard College in 1636, at which time the name of Newtown was changed to Cambridge, and in establishing the colonial plan for Congregational church government, the *Cambridge Platform*, of 1647. In 1637 Shepard married Joanna, daughter of Thomas Hooker; together they had two sons, Samuel (*b.* 1639) and John (*b.* and *d.* 1646). Following Joanna's death in 1646, he married Margaret Boradel in 1647, with whom he had one son, Jeremiah, born in 1648.

Shepard died in Cambridge on 25 August 1649 and was buried there; his third wife survived him. His influence on religious thought in the New World remained considerable, not least through the eighteenth-century colonial theologian, Jonathan Edwards. MICHAEL JINKINS

Sources T. Shepard, 'Autobiography', *God's plot: puritan spirituality in Thomas Shepard's Cambridge*, ed. H. McGiffert, rev. edn (1994) • J. A. Albro, 'Life of Thomas Shepard', in *The works of Thomas Shepard*, 1 (1853); repr. (New York, 1967) • *The works of Thomas Shepard* (1853); repr. (New York, 1967) • T. Werge, *Thomas Shepard* (Boston, 1987) • M. Jinkins, 'John Cotton and the Antinomian controversy, 1636–1638', *Scottish Journal of Theology*, 43/3 (1990), 321–49 • A. Whyte, *Thomas Shepard: pilgrim father and founder of Harvard* (1909) • D. D. Hall, ed., *The antinomian controversy, 1636–1638: a documentary history* (1968) • W. K. B. Stoever, *'A faire and easie way to heaven': covenant theology and antinomianism in early Massachusetts* (Middletown, Connecticut, 1978) • P. Miller, *Errand into the wilderness* (1956) • P. Miller, *The New England mind*, 1 (1939) • C. Mather, *Magnalia Christi Americana*, 2 (1853) • T. J. Wertenbaker, *The puritan oligarchy: the founding of American civilization* (New York, 1947) • E. S. Morgan, *The puritan dilemma: the story of John Winthrop* (Boston, 1958) • P. Collinson, *The Elizabethan puritan movement* (1967) • T. Webster, *Godly clergy in early Stuart England: the Caroline puritan movement, c.1620–1643* (1997) • M. P. Winship, *Seers of God: puritan providentialism in the Restoration and early Enlightenment* (1996)

Shepard, Thomas (1635–1677), Congregational minister in America, was born in London on 5 April 1635, the second son, and first surviving child, of Thomas *Shepard (1605–1649) and his first wife, Margaret Touteville (*d.* 1636). He emigrated with his parents from England to the Massachusetts Bay colony on 10 August 1635. His mother died in February 1636, the same month as he was baptized—about 7 February—into the church at Newtown (later Cambridge) of which his father had just been appointed the first pastor. Shepard graduated BA from Harvard College in 1653, and was chosen as a fellow of the college on 27 November 1654. He retained this fellowship until 15 September 1673, when he resigned during a controversy over the appointment of Leonard Hoar as president of the college. Shepard took up his fellowship again on 15 March 1674, the day Hoar resigned.

Shepard married Hannah (or Anna; 1640–1709), daughter of William Tyng, a magistrate of the Massachusetts Bay colony, about 3 November 1656. They had two children: Thomas Shepard, born on 3 July 1658, who would succeed his father as a minister in the Charlestown, Massachusetts, church; and Anna, born on 13 September 1663. On 13 April 1659 Shepard was ordained a minister in the Charlestown church where he taught as a colleague of the Revd Zechariah Symmes. Shepard consistently represented what might be described as the conservative establishment interests in colonial religious politics. He was appointed a censor of the press on 19 October 1664. During the controversy over baptism in 1668, Shepard and Symmes stood with those who called for leaders among the Baptist congregations to be either exiled or imprisoned.

In the 1672 Massachusetts annual election sermon Shepard spoke eloquently for a balanced view of toleration, saying: 'To tolerate all things, and to tolerate nothing, (it's an old and true Maxime) both are intolerable: but 'tis

Satan's policy to plead for an indefinite and boundless toleration' (Sibley, 328). Shepard demonstrated his conception of a more appropriate toleration by praising an earlier generation of New England colonists for using their coercive powers to crush 'in the very Egg' the brood of 'poysonful, fiery, stinging Serpents' who threatened the religious purity of the church (Miller, *The New England Mind*, 132). As the historian Peter Carroll has observed: 'Thomas Shepard declared that the existence of doctrinal purity within the New England churches constituted a wall which separated … the saint from the sinner. By excluding the unregenerate, this shield defended the godly churches from the onslaught of disbelievers' (Carroll, 109). Toleration must, in Shepard's view, serve and be limited by the interests of ecclesiastical purity.

Shepard's most important literary product, *Eye-salve, or, A watch-word from our Lord Jesus Christ unto his churches: especially those within the colony of the Massachsets in New England, to take heed of apostacy* (1673), warned readers that God's protection of them in the perilous and isolated land of New England was jeopardized by the impurity of their faith. Building on his exposition of 'the Church of God' in the Old Testament, he writes:

> That the undeniable experience which the Covenant people of God have had of the Lord's being to them not a wilderness nor a land of Darkness, but the contrary, should caution them never to incur the guilt of so unreasonable a sin and dangerous folly, and provocation as to revolt from under the Lord, or to be unwilling to return again in case they have begun to decline from him. (*Eye-Salve*, 8)

The themes Shepard touched upon in this book were common among contemporaries in the second generation of New England religious leadership, such as John Higginson, William Stoughton, Urian Oakes, and Increase Mather, reflecting, as the great historian of New England puritanism Perry Miller wrote, 'a deep disquietude' a fear that 'something has gone wrong' with their holy social experiment (Miller, *Errand into the Wilderness*, 2).

Shepard, like his father, who took up the cause of the elders of the Massachusetts Bay colony against John Cotton and Anne Hutchinson in the antinomian controversy of 1636–8, was an energetic and courageous controversialist, praised posthumously by his friend Urian Oakes, in 'An Elegy upon the Death of the Reverend Mr. Thomas Shepard', as

> Our wrestling Israel, second unto none
> The man that stood i'th'gap, to keep the pass.
> (Miller and Johnson, 644)

Remembered primarily for his opposition to religious impurity, which he saw as a threat to the survival of the New England churches, Shepard died in Charlestown on 22 December 1677 at the age of forty-two, having contracted smallpox from a dying parishioner who had requested a pastoral visit. MICHAEL JINKINS

Sources J. L. Sibley, *Biographical sketches of graduates of Harvard University*, 1 (1873) · *God's plot: the paradoxes of puritan piety, being the autobiography and journal of Thomas Shepard*, ed. M. McGiffert (1972) · P. Miller and T. Johnson, eds., *The puritans*, 2 vols. (1938) · P. N. Carroll, *Puritanism and the wilderness: the intellectual significance of the New England frontier, 1629–1700* (1969) · P. Miller, *Errand into the wilderness* (1956) · P. Miller, *The New England mind*, 2 (1953) · F. J. Bremer, *The puritan experiment: New England society from Bradford to Edwards* (1976) · T. Shepard, *Eye-salve, or, A watch-word from our Lord Jesus Christ unto his churches* (Cambridge, MA, 1673)
Archives Harvard U., Harvard College corporation records · Mass. Hist. Soc.
Wealth at death £2386 4s. 0d.: Sibley, *Biographical sketches*

Shepesheved, William (*c*.1270–*c*.1325), chronicler and Cistercian monk, presumably took his name from Shepshed in Leicestershire. The fact that he was ordained priest on 26 February 1295 suggests that he was then at least twenty-four years old, and that he was born about 1270. His surname was that of several other monks of Croxden Abbey, Staffordshire, where William was professed on 11 September 1288, and it is likely that at least some of these, including perhaps the Richard who became abbot in 1329, were his kinsmen. But all that is known for certain of William's family is that his mother was named Millicent—he records her death in 1295.

Shepesheved was the author of a chronicle preserved in BL, Cotton MS Faustina B.vi, folios 69–94. Largely concerned with the history of his monastery, it concludes with a list of the monks, continued by later hands. But it starts in 1066, well before the foundation of Croxden in 1178, and refers throughout to events elsewhere in Britain and beyond—to the doings of English kings, to the crusades, and to the succession of popes. Consisting at first of little more than a series of notes, the chronicle becomes fuller as it approaches Shepesheved's own time. Though interesting in revealing that Shepesheved's political sympathies lay with Simon de Montfort and Thomas of Lancaster, the principal value of his chronicle lies in the light it sheds on the fortunes of Croxden, on the abbots and their deeds, particularly as builders, on relations with patrons, including a serious dispute with Thomas, Lord Furnival, in 1319, and on other aspects of monastic life. In 1313, for instance, Shepesheved tells how the monastery's great bell was accidentally broken, and how a founder from Lichfield failed expensively in his efforts to cast a replacement. He was also keenly interested in weather and meteorological phenomena, noting eclipses and other celestial apparitions, and also rainstorms, floods, and droughts, with their implications for harvests. In 1299 he observes that contrary to common expectations, heavy rain on St Swithun's day was followed by a beautiful summer. In the mid-1320s what is presumably Shepesheved's own hand is increasingly superseded by another, which is also responsible for a number of insertions on earlier folios. But although it may be assumed that Shepesheved died at about this time, the date is not recorded. Brief extracts from his chronicle were published by Dugdale in his *Monasticon Anglicanum*, more extensive ones by Frederic Madden in 1835. HENRY SUMMERSON

Sources BL, Cotton MS Faustina B.vi, fols. 69–94 · *VCH Staffordshire*, 3.226–30 · Dugdale, *Monasticon*, new edn, 5.661–2 · 'Extracts from the annals of Crokesden Abbey, co. Stafford', *Collectanea Topographica et Genealogica*, 2 (1835), 297–310
Archives BL, chronicle, Cotton MS Faustina B.iv, fols. 69–94

Shepey, John (d. 1412), diplomatist and ecclesiastic, came from a wealthy bourgeois family of Coventry, where he was born. His paternal grandfather, Lawrence Shepey, was a burgess who had endowed a chantry in St Michael's Church. His father, Jordan Shepey, was one of twelve Coventry merchants who had succeeded in wresting control of the town from the prior and monks of Coventry Cathedral and putting it in the hands of their class; he became second mayor of Coventry under its new charter of 1345.

As befitted the son of a wealthy local family who was heading for an ecclesiastical career, John Shepey became a canon of Lichfield Cathedral on 25 January 1363, and two months later chancellor. In the meantime, on 31 January, he was papally provided to a canonry in Wells Cathedral. By then his university career was well under way: Shepey was *licentiatus* in civil law at Oxford at the time of his appointment to Lichfield Cathedral. In 1364 and again in 1366 the pope granted him a *cum ex eo* licence to hold benefices *in absentia* while studying at university. Shepey was a doctor of civil law by 1367. Notes of lectures given by him in the canon-law school on fourteen titles of the *Decretals* have survived (BL, Royal MS 9 E.viii, fols. 156–66). He was soon active in the church courts: he was dispensed to be an advocate of the court of the arches on 16 October 1367, and became an official at Winchester in the following year.

Shepey's talents also brought him into the royal service. He served on a number of embassies: to Flanders in 1372, to the papal curia at Avignon in 1373 (being arrested by the French *en route* and released by papal intercession), again to Flanders in 1375, and, in later life, to the Scots in 1397. His service to the crown was rewarded in 1376 by an annual grant of £50 until he acquired a benefice of at least equal value. He had not long to wait. Later in the same year, on 22 December, Shepey became a canon of York Minster. His appointment by the pope to the deanship of Lincoln Cathedral in 1378 met with royal opposition, but, when the dust finally settled, John Shepey was dean of Lincoln and remained so until his death thirty-four years later.

The first in the line of three consecutive long-lived deans of Lincoln, who served for a total of 105 years, Shepey concentrated his energies during his deanship on the affairs of the cathedral and frequently became embroiled in controversy and, indeed, litigation with his chapter. In 1400, for example, Shepey claimed the right to visit the chapter with the power to correct and punish; he also claimed rights in the appointment and dismissal of the lower clergy of the cathedral. The assistance of both Henry IV and the pope, Boniface IX, was appealed to in this matter, until at length, in July 1404, Henry Beaufort, bishop of Lincoln and half-brother of the king, settled the dispute in favour of the chapter.

Shepey's career can be seen as representative of the churchman, who, born into urban wealth, followed a path that led from the study of canon law to service in the church courts, to diplomatic service for the crown, and then to a senior position in the ecclesiastical bureaucracy,

in his case the deanship of the cathedral church of England's largest diocese. He died, probably in Lincoln, in 1412: his will, dated 14 January of that year, was proved on 17 March. He left books to New College, Oxford, possibly his old college, and to the Franciscan friars of Stamford Priory in Lincolnshire, as well as a silver cross and a richly decorated vestment to Lincoln Cathedral, where his body is buried. He is to be distinguished from the Benedictine theologian and bishop of Rochester of the same name (d. 1360).   F. DONALD LOGAN

Sources Emden, *Oxf.*, 3.1683–4 · C. Lutgens, 'The canonists of BL Royal MS 9 E.viii and canon law in the fourteenth century', PhD diss., University of Toronto, 1979 · BL, Royal MS 9 E.viii, fols. 156–66 · A. H. Thompson, *The English clergy and their organization in the later middle ages* (1947) · Register of Thomas Arundel, archbishop of Canterbury, 2, LPL, fols. 150–52

Archives BL, Royal MS 9 E.viii, fols. 156–66

Shephard, Rupert Norman (1909–1992), painter and teacher, was born on 12 February 1909 at 53 Sotheby Road, Islington, London, the son of Quaker parents, William Henry Shephard, a mechanical and electrical engineer, and his wife, Alice Beck, a housewife and charity worker. Both parents were enthusiastic amateur artists, who encouraged Rupert and his elder sister, Stella, to paint. He was educated at Repton School (1922–6), and at the Slade School of Fine Art (1926–9) under the formidable Henry Tonks. Shephard flourished under Tonks's regime of strict academic draughtsmanship (later to stand him in good stead as a wartime industrial draughtsman) while taking in wider influences of continental painting to be found in West End galleries. Shephard was a tall and reserved man, whose years at the Slade were enlivened by visits to the bohemian homes of his fellow students Nicolette Macnamara, daughter of the Irish poet Francis Macnamara, at Blashford, and Vivien John, whose father, the celebrated painter Augustus John, presided over a chaotically stylish ménage at Fryern in Dorset. Shephard painted the Macnamara family members over the years, especially Nicolette's sister Caitlin and her husband, Dylan Thomas (informal but fine studies of whom are in the National Portrait Gallery).

On leaving the Slade, Shephard became a schoolmaster at Raynes Park County School, using his evenings to paint especially in music halls, theatres, and pubs. He joined the avant-garde Theatre Group which put on work by promising young writers such as W. H. Auden and Stephen Spender but, though he took on minor acting parts, he failed to secure the stage design job he had hoped for. He had exhibited his paintings since 1929 at such venues as the London Group, Wertheim Gallery, and Coolings Gallery. In 1937, the inaugural year of the Euston Road School of Drawing and Painting, he exhibited with the school's founder members William Coldstream, Claude Rogers, and Victor Pasmore at the Storran Gallery. His modernist, linear style of the early 1930s had by then developed into the subtle, soft-hued, painterly manner associated with the Euston Road School, and the next decade saw some of his finest work.

With the onset of the Second World War Shephard left

teaching to become a draughtsman in industry and later an official war artist, covering factories and the home front. On 31 July 1942 he married his first wife, Lorna Olive (1911–1962), daughter of Edward Frank Wilmott, a British-born businessman based in South Africa, and lived in London. Their three children, Murilla, Caroline, and Ben, were born in 1942, 1944, and 1948 respectively. Shephard applied himself energetically as always: exhibiting in the West End; undertaking portrait commissions, including several for ICI's ambitious *Portrait of an Industry*; lecturing at St Martin's School of Art and the Central School of Arts and Crafts; and painting local London scenes for *Recording Britain* (a project devised to record for posterity buildings deemed to be at risk from the blitz, though in reality it was later post-war development that destroyed many of them).

In 1948 Shephard took up the appointment of director at the Michaelis Art School at the University of Cape Town and moved to South Africa with his family. The brilliant colour and strong light of Africa had a profound and long-lasting effect on his painting, dissipating his low-toned palette and bringing vivid colour to his bold African native compositions. He had seven exhibitions in Cape Town and three in Johannesburg from 1948 to 1963 as well as showing in four international exhibitions. In 1954 he published *Capescapes*, a volume of verse illustrated with his own lino-cuts. His wife, a chronic asthmatic, died in 1962 and he decided to return to England with his children and to paint full-time.

On 24 April 1965 Shephard married Nicolette *Devas, *née* Macnamara (1911–1987), author and artist, whose husband, a fellow Slade student, Anthony Devas, had died in 1958. They lived at 68 Limerston Street, London, travelling often to France, when funds allowed. Shephard's work was underpinned by portrait commissions and exhibitions—mainly in London. In 1972 he was elected to the Royal Society of Portrait Painters. In 1966 and 1977 he published *The Passing Scene* (a portfolio of lino-cuts) and *Cockcrow and other Verses*. Despite the vigorous and hale persona that he presented to the world, his eyesight began to fail in the late eighties, forcing him to give up painting in 1990. He died of cancer on 16 March 1992 in London.

Examples of his work are in the National Portrait Gallery and Imperial War Museum, London.

SALLY HUNTER

Sources *The Independent* (17 March 1992) · *The Independent* (23 March 1992) · *The Times* (21 March 1992) · personal knowledge (2004) · private information (2004) · b. cert. · m. cert. [Lorna Wilmott] · m. cert. [Nicolette Devas] · d. cert. · *CGPLA Eng. & Wales* (1992)
Likenesses R. Shephard, self-portrait, oils, 1941 (*Self-portrait with chrysanthemums*), repro. in *The Independent* (17 March 1992)
Wealth at death £267,722: probate, 30 June 1992, *CGPLA Eng. & Wales*

Shepheard, Frances. See Ingram, Frances (1734?–1807).

Shepheard, George (1770–1842), watercolour painter and engraver, was born on 26 January 1770 in Guildford, Surrey. He was the second of the four sons and a daughter of George Shepheard (1747–1820) and Jane, daughter of John Baxter. The Shepheards were descended from a branch of the old Herefordshire family of Wallwyn or Walwyn, which had been seated at Hellens, Much Marcle, near Ledbury, since the reign of Henry V. On the evidence of a caricature drawing dated 1793, formerly in the Williams collection (Williams, 147), it would appear that George Shepheard's parents had connections with East Sheen in Surrey. On similar evidence it would seem that he was a pupil of 'Dickenson', perhaps the mezzotint engraver William Dickinson, along with a lifelong friend, the painter and engraver Matthew Haughton, son of the enamel and still-life painter Moses Haughton. He also studied at the Royal Academy Schools from 31 December 1786, winning a silver medal in 1790.

It is likely that another of Shepheard's friends from student days was John Field (1771–1841), the silhouettist, who may well have accompanied him when painting landscapes in Middlesex, Surrey, Kent, and Sussex. He probably visited Ireland about 1807 and Wales in the 1820s, and he was in France in April 1816. During the 1820s he also exhibited subjects from Somerset and Devon, Yorkshire, and Derbyshire. He exhibited at the Royal Academy from 1811 to the year of his death. The rustic figures that populate Shepheard's landscapes are good, as are his lively caricatures in pen and watercolour. As an engraver he produced mixed-media prints after Henry Bunbury and George Morland, and fifteen plates, *Lady Hamilton's Attitudes*, after Frederick Rehberg. In turn, George M. Brighty etched a set, *Vignette Designs*, after Shepheard's drawings. There is also a pencil portrait of James Northcote RA—again from the Williams Collection—in the National Portrait Gallery, London.

Shepheard was twice married, first, on 1 March 1800, to Caroline Alexandria Anderson and second to Amelia Anderson, whose elder sister Augusta had married his elder brother Captain Lewis Shepheard RN (d. 1838). There were three sons and three daughters of the first marriage and a son and daughter of the second. The eldest son, George [see below], and the third, Lewis Henry (b. 1816), became artists. The latter presumably had some hopes of succeeding to Hellens, since in 1881, along with several cousins, he took the surname of Wallwyn. George Shepheard died of dropsy on 7 September 1842 at 100 Guilford Street, London, his home since 1821.

George Wallwyn Shepheard (1804–1852), watercolour painter, travelled widely on the continent. In 1838 in Florence he married Laura Justina Parigi, with whom he had two children, Wallwyn Poyer Burnett Shepheard (b. 1840), a barrister, and Teresa Caroline (b. 1842). They each married a first cousin. G. W. Shepheard exhibited French and Italian views and free studies at the Royal Academy from 1837 to 1851 and lived in Bloomsbury. He died on 26 January 1852 at 5 Old Steyne, Brighton, of apoplexy and a diseased heart. His wife survived him.

HUON MALLALIEU

Sources I. O. Williams, *Early English watercolours and some cognate drawings by artists born not later than 1785* (1952), 147–8 · S. C. Hutchison, 'The Royal Academy Schools, 1768–1830', *Walpole Society*, 38 (1960–62), 123–91 · J. Duncumb and others, *Collections towards the*

history and antiquities of the county of Hereford, 3 (1882) • *The Times* (3 June 1881) • *The Times* (5 Aug 1881) • *The Times* (1 Sept 1881) • IGI • d. cert. • d. cert. [George Wallwyn Shepheard] • Graves, *RA exhibitors*
Likenesses M. Haughton, caricature • G. Shepheard, self-portrait, caricature

Shepheard, George Wallwyn (1804–1852). *See under* Shepheard, George (1770–1842).

Shepheard, Samuel (*c*.1648–1719), merchant and politician, about whose early life little is known, may have been the son of Joshua Shepheard, a London saddler. On 23 September 1673 he married Mary (*d*. 1723), daughter of Edward Chamberlayne of Princethorpe, Warwickshire. His considerable success as a merchant owed much to his initial involvement in first the wine and then the East India trade. During the mid-1690s he emerged as a prominent critic of the monopoly held by the old East India Company, and early in 1696, with Gilbert Heathcote, he represented the interests of Leeward Islands and East India traders in petitioning the House of Lords to introduce competition. Initially a keen supporter of the whig ministry, Shepheard—like Heathcote—became a government creditor in 1697, and a year later played an active role in establishing the new East India Company (to which he is said to have contributed £35,000) before being appointed a director. In January 1701 he was elected MP for Newport, his money also securing Andover for his eldest son, Francis, and Malmesbury for his second son, also Samuel [*see below*].

However, Shepheard's conduct during both elections was soon subject to parliamentary scrutiny and resulted in his being sent to the Tower, though he was not impeached. He was rehabilitated in political and business circles during the following year and, while his standing in the East India Company was undoubtedly affected, he campaigned, albeit unsuccessfully, for his son at Higham Ferrers in 1703. In May 1705 he himself stood for and won the seat for the City of London, becoming a supporter of the court during his three years in the Commons. During this period Shepheard maintained his trading connections, and in 1708 he was elected one of the first directors of the United East India Company.

Notwithstanding John Drummond's claim that Shepheard, though 'an excellent merchant for shipping and in foreign trade', was 'no banker' (*Portland MSS*, 4.559), he served as Robert Harley's financier and promoted tory interests in the City after 1710. Shepheard's last major financial activity centred on the formation of the South Sea Company, in which he invested heavily in 1711; he was appointed its deputy governor in 1713 and sub-governor in 1719. By then he had long since reverted to the whigs, having lost faith in Harley's commercial policy, and from 1714 he promoted whig interests in the City. Shepheard died on 4 January 1719 and left an estate worth £800,000 to his wife and sons.

The younger **Samuel Shepheard** (*c*.1676–1748), politician, having represented Malmesbury in 1701, was elected MP for Cambridge in 1708. Like his father and brother, Samuel favoured the tories during the Harley administration and became a close associate of the party leader in

Cambridgeshire, Sir John Hynde Cotton, and other prominent county politicians. However, Shepheard's friendship with Cotton foundered in 1714 during the split within the party over the succession of George I; his pro-Hanoverian position was subsequently challenged by tories in Cambridge at the election of 1715 and, though defeated at the polls, he retained his seat on petition until 1722 when he did not stand.

In 1724 Shepheard received the support of Robert Walpole to contest a by-election for the county seat of Cambridgeshire, in which he was successful and to which he was re-elected against Cotton in 1727; thereafter he sat, unchallenged, for the next twenty years. Relations with his former ally further deteriorated when Shepheard sought to revive a long-defunct right of the knights of the shire to claim money from the owners of the estate of Madingley, held by the Cotton family through marriage. His bid not only to reinstate the charge but also to demand substantive back payment provoked Cotton to brawl with his adversary during a meeting of the quarter sessions. Shepheard's persistent attempts to undermine Cotton's political stronghold of Cambridge, drawing heavily on the family's trading fortune, eventually forced Sir John, already unpopular with the local corporation, to quit the town for the safer seat of Marlborough. In 1747 Shepheard himself stood successfully for Cambridge, which he represented until his death, after an apoplectic stroke, at Hampton Court, Middlesex, on 24 April of the following year. In contrast with the colourful nature of his personal political rivalries, Shepheard proved a rather predictable parliamentarian who either voted with the opposition or abstained in the majority of divisions in the house. Though he died unmarried, he had lived for several years with a woman whom he had bought from her husband, a Mr Jenner, 'in form of conveyance' and whom he had left by February 1730 after she was discovered to have been 'familiar with [a] third person' (*Parliamentary Diary of Sir Edward Knatchbull*, 111). A somewhat unusual view of marriage and of personal relationships also inspired Shepheard's legacy to his natural daughter, Frances *Ingram, who was to receive his fortune on condition that she did not marry an Irishman, a Scot, or the son of a peer with the exception of that of his former political colleague, Henry Bromley, Lord Montfort. Combining family duty perhaps with the Shepheards' eye for an investment, she later married Charles Ingram, the nephew and heir of the eighth Viscount Irwin (Irvine).   PHILIP CARTER

Sources P. Gauci, 'Shepheard, Samuel', HoP, *Commons, 1690–1715* [draft] • R. R. Sedgwick, 'Shepheard, Samuel', HoP, *Commons, 1715–54*, 2.420 • *The parliamentary diary of Sir Edward Knatchbull, 1722–1730*, ed. A. N. Newman, CS, 3rd ser., 94 (1963) • *The manuscripts of his grace the duke of Portland*, 10 vols., HMC, 29 (1891–1931), vols. 5–10
Wealth at death £800,000: Gauci, 'Shepheard, Samuel'

Shepheard, Samuel (*c*.1676–1748). *See under* Shepheard, Samuel (*c*.1648–1719).

Shepheard, Samuel (1816–1866), hotel proprietor, was born on 21 January 1816 at Little Preston Manor, Preston Capes, Northamptonshire, the second son and third child of Richard Shepheard (*d*. 1820), farmer, and his wife, Jane

Berwick (d. 1817). Both parents died before he was four, and Samuel grew up in the family of his father's sister Esther and her husband, Joseph Stanley, the licensee of The Crown inn at Leamington. Family legend held that Samuel and a cousin, John Stanley, were sent away from home after minimal schooling to gain experience as farm-hands, and that Samuel was later apprenticed three times to pastry-cooks in Leamington. Breaking his indentures for the last time, he left to go to sea, and rose to become purser on one of the Peninsular and Oriental (P. & O.) Company's passenger and mail ships which plied between Bombay and Suez. Shortly after his twenty-sixth birthday, however, he was summarily put ashore at Suez, apparently following a mutiny of forecastle hands towards which he had shown himself to be sympathetic.

British interest in the condition of Egypt, from 1811 to 1848 the undisputed fief of the Albanian Mehmet Ali under the suzerainty of the Turkish Porte, centred on the overland route between Alexandria, Cairo, and Suez. In the late 1830s this ordeal by riverboat and camel had become the nexus between the two parts of the new, shorter sea-route from Europe to the East. Once Lieutenant Thomas Waghorn of the East India Company's fleet had established the viability of the route P. & O. gained a contract for the overland postal and passenger-carrying service, and remained in charge of the transit business from 1840 until the Egyptian government took control of it in 1846. Passengers from Europe landed at Alexandria, made an eighteen-hour journey by the Mahmudiyyah Canal and the Nile to Cairo, and rested, often at the British Hotel, until ready for the desert crossing eastwards to Suez. By the 1840s, visitors to Cairo included wealthy European and American tourists intent on seeing the pyramids and the upper Nile, as well as those bound on more serious business for India and further east.

Shepheard was taken on as an assistant at the British Hotel, became manager in 1844, and proprietor by 1846, renaming it Shepheard's Hotel. Two years later he moved the hotel from its cramped surroundings in the streets of the Frankish quarter to a row of buildings on the edge of the Esbekier, then a large, open, tree-lined square. By 1851 the hotel had become transformed and greatly enlarged by a grant of adjacent property from Mehmet Ali's grandson and heir, Abbas Pasha. In 1850 Shepheard was also granted a contract for the Suez Hotel. Two years later the traveller C. F. Andrews in Four Months' Tour in the East described him as having 'the cuisine of all the Nile steamers', and the provisioning of the desert rest-houses established by Arthur Anderson of the P. & O. Company (Bird, 171).

The cosmopolitanism and importance of its clientele and the determinedly entrepreneurial spirit of its proprietor made Shepheard's Hotel a household name among sophisticated travellers during the late 1840s and 1850s. Lord Stanley, the future prime minister and earl of Derby, stayed there on his way to visit India in 1852, and Lord Elphinstone, the new governor of Bombay, in 1853. In 1858, the novelist Anthony Trollope wrote much of Doctor Thorne in the newly re-extended Shepheard's Hotel while negotiating a treaty with the Egyptian ruler, Saʿid Pasha, about the conveyance of mails across Egypt by railway. According to Trollope, 'the English tongue in Egypt finds its centre in Shepheard's Hotel' (Bird, 160).

Events in the East during the 1850s brought additional profits to Shepheard as a provider of large-scale hospitality to officers and troops. On the outbreak of the Crimean War in 1854 he received a government contract to ease the passage of British detachments on their way to Sevastopol. This brought him £4500, part of which he obtained by pursuing defaulting officers as far as the Crimea. In 1857, by then the proprietor of the biggest hotel in the world, he was once again in demand to house and feed British soldiers before dispatching them on relays of donkeys to Suez, on their way to India to help quell the mutiny.

In 1859 the visit of Queen Victoria's son Prince Alfred on a training cruise to Egypt brought the entire Mediterranean Fleet to anchor off Alexandria, and many more visitors to Shepheard's Hotel. The opening of the Suez Railway in 1858 had removed many of the hazards previously associated with travel in Egypt, and Shepheard's enjoyed the peak of its international fame. In January 1860, however, having long planned retirement to England for health and family reasons, Shepheard sold the hotel to M. Zeck of Alexandria for £10,000.

In 1844 Shepheard had married a former hotel guest, Mary Rangecroft, whom he had met when she was on her way to India as a lady's companion, and who became an active partner in running the hotel. Of their two sons and six daughters, born between 1845 and 1856, four died of cholera and other illnesses at Cairo, one daughter died at the age of ten in England, and three other daughters lived to adulthood. Increasingly, Mary Shepheard spent long periods in England with her surviving small children. On a visit home on the strength of his Crimean War gains, Shepheard bought a farm at Radway, near Edgehill, Warwickshire; this he sold on a subsequent visit in 1857 and bought his eventual retirement home, Eathorpe Hall, near Leamington. Shepheard died at Eathorpe Hall on 12 June 1866, aged fifty. He was survived by his wife.

BRIGID ALLEN

Sources M. Bird, *Samuel Shepheard of Cairo* (1957) · *CGPLA Eng. & Wales* (1866)
Likenesses F. Goodall, oil sketch, 1859
Wealth at death under £8000: resworn probate, Feb 1868, *CGPLA Eng. & Wales* (1866)

Shepherd. *See also* Shepard, Shephard, Sheppard.

Shepherd, Anna [Nan] (1893–1981), author and college teacher, was born on 11 February 1893 at Westerton Cottage, East Peterculter, near Aberdeen, the second child of John Shepherd, a civil engineer, and Jane Smith Shepherd (*née* Kelly). Her paternal grandparents were farmers from Strachan and Drum; her mother's father was a well-known tailor in the city of Aberdeen, and her mother's uncle was the renowned local architect Dr William Kelly. Nan Shepherd had one elder brother, Frank, who became a civil engineer like his father, and died in South Africa, where he had gone to recuperate after serving in the First World War.

'I have had the same bedroom all my life', Shepherd once said. She lived in a house called Dunvegan, 503 North Deeside Road, in the village of Cults, 3 miles from Aberdeen; her family moved there a month after her birth. She attended Cults primary school (and went back in her eighties to tell enthralled pupils what it was like to be taught there at the turn of the century), then she proceeded to Aberdeen High School for Girls, then studied at the University of Aberdeen, graduating MA in 1915. Upon graduating she joined the staff of Aberdeen Training Centre for Teachers (later Aberdeen College of Education), becoming lecturer in English in 1919. She taught there until she retired in 1956, after which she edited the *Aberdeen University Review* from 1957 to 1963, writing essays on subjects such as Hugh MacDiarmid, the poet Charles Murray, and women in the university from 1892 to 1942. In 1964 the University of Aberdeen awarded her an honorary doctorate.

In 1928, when Shepherd was thirty-five, she published her first novel. *The Quarry Wood*, a novel which honours in its descriptions the university she loved so much, is the story of the emotional and intellectual education of its young heroine, Martha Ironside, who fights for the money and space for a school and university education, then comes to understand that the learning process involves the world beyond books too, a world of 'sharny boots and hacked hands seamed with dirt', that ideals are best tempered with reality, and that nature is a pretty good partner for intellect. Shepherd's next novel was *The Weatherhouse*, published in 1930, and her third and final novel, *A Pass in the Grampians*, was published in 1933. Both of these, like *The Quarry Wood*, deal with the clash between tradition and modernity, and are set lovingly in small communities in the north-east of Scotland, full of the rich, harsh speech of its people and the bleakness and the splendour of its mountains and weather. As Roderick Watson puts it: 'Nan Shepherd manages to invest the dourness of the Scottish land … with imagination and grace' (Watson, 'Introduction', *The Weatherhouse*). All three novels deal with the getting of wisdom and the challenging of convention; each one has its own lively, clever young woman trying to sort out self-knowledge from self-deception; each has a democratic layered narrative that builds up a picture not just of the individual but of the workings of community and communal responsibility; and each one has, in its tenacious narrator, the promise of a tolerant, humorous, intelligent, and ever open mind.

Shepherd's love for her native Aberdeenshire and the nearby Grampians is displayed throughout her work. She was an avid hill-walker and climber, and this is celebrated in her final two books. As a student she had published several poems in the student magazine, *Alma Mater*, which she also edited, but it was not until 1934 that she published *In the Cairngorms*, her slim volume of poems. Almost all of her poetry, from her early work to late unpublished pieces now in her archive at the National Library of Scotland, hymns the combination of nature and intellect, and *In the Cairngorms* is like the novels in its sense of 'the mind's own fineness' passionately engaged with the vastness, beauty, and ultimate indifference of rock, water, light, and air. The collection ends on a series of bruised and oblique love sonnets; 'very few people understand them,' she said once, 'which makes me feel better'.

Shepherd's final book, *The Living Mountain*, a series of meditations on the Cairngorm Mountains, was written in the 1940s and, after one publisher's 'courteous and negative' refusal, left unpublished in a drawer until 1977. 'It was written during the latter years of the Second War and those just after. In that disturbed and uncertain world it was my secret place of ease', she wrote in the foreword. This Zen-like 'pilgrimage to the mountain' is delightful, an enlightened fusion of philosophy and reportage on the forms and force of life everywhere in the beloved landscape:

> I can imagine the antiquity of rock, but the antiquity of a living flower—that is harder. It means that these toughs of the mountain top, with their angelic inflorescence and the devil in their roots, have had the cunning and the effrontery to cheat, not only a winter, but an Ice Age. (Shepherd, *The Living Mountain*)

Friends and former students remember a similar and joyful tenacity of spirit in Shepherd herself, as well as her sense of humour, her spellbinding teaching talent, and a feminist approach in her lectures years ahead of her time. A fellow member of staff at the college of education remembered how 'on my first morning I found a posy from her garden on my desk. That was typically Nan'. She was, friends recall, 'a lovely woman, with masses of auburn hair, and possessed of a fine speaking voice of a rare range', 'a tall slim figure with a halo of chestnut plaits'. Photographs of the young Nan Shepherd show a face full and open, likeably stubborn, a woman with beautiful hooded eyes that are at once determined and unsure, long luxurious hair, and an almost devil-may-care penchant for an arts-and-crafts style in clothes. In photos at the end of her life, her weather-lined face has lost none of its strength, and the eyes are still that mixture of sharp, direct, and self-protective.

Long friendships with Neil Gunn, Charles Murray, Agnes Mure Mackenzie, Willa Muir, Helena Shire, and many other writers, characterized Shepherd's life. When Lewis Grassic Gibbon died, she organized a trust fund for his bereaved wife and family; after the deaths of the poets J. C. Milne and Charles Murray she helped bring about publication of their last poems. But the most arresting story of her generosity and her bearing can be found in Jessie Kesson's warm recollection of the 'lady' Kesson fell over the feet of in a train carriage one dramatic day in 1941 when she was a milkmaid at an Aberdeenshire farm. Several weeks after the talkative train journey the lady wrote to tell her to write a story for a local competition, then offered to help, if necessary, with the entry fee of 7s. 6d. Kesson 'won the first prize of a Book Token, and learned the name of the Lady in the train', a good friend and helpful critic for the rest of her life. 'I was graced by Nan Shepherd', Kesson concludes (Kesson, 'Nan Shepherd in recollection').

Nan Shepherd seems to have valued her privacy highly, and was modest to the point of dismissiveness about her own fiction. In 1976 a local newspaper interviewed 'the forgotten authoress of Cults'. The journalist, caught off-balance by the old lady's intelligence, sat amazed as Shepherd, laughing, 'a twinkle in her eye', waved old reviews in the air that proclaimed her a writer of genius, saying, as if nothing could matter less, 'that's what you call a passing reputation'. She 'didn't really like writing', she said; and only wrote when she felt there was 'something which simply had to be written'. Then one day 'it just didn't come to me any more'. She once told Neil Gunn that she really wasn't a 'literary person': 'there's a great big bit of me detached and amused, and quite often cynical, that weighs the wind of the spirit with the weights of corn and potatoes and things' (F. R. Hart and J. B. Pick, *Neil M. Gunn: a Highland Life*, 1981). The pragmatic romanticism this comment (and all her work) reveals is right at the heart of twentieth-century Scottish fiction. Her complex and remarkable novels were forgotten after their publication, and Shepherd remembered as a prescient critic of Hugh MacDiarmid and a correspondent with Neil Gunn, until the reprinting of her work in the 1980s and 1990s showed her to be a forerunner of Lewis Grassic Gibbon, a quiet pioneer of narrative structure, and one of Scotland's finest novelists of the early twentieth century.

After years of teaching, encouraging, and tending others (her invalid mother died when Shepherd was sixty, after which she nursed their old housekeeper, Mamie Lawson, until she died in the early 1970s), Nan Shepherd became ill in her late eighties and lived for some time at the nursing home Annesley House, in Torphins. She died in Aberdeen at Woodend Hospital on 27 February 1981, at the age of eighty-eight. ALI SMITH

Sources R. Watson, 'Introduction', in N. Shepherd, *The Grampian quartet* (1996) · R. Watson, 'Introduction', in N. Shepherd, *The quarry wood* (1987) · R. Watson, 'Introduction', in N. Shepherd, *The weatherhouse* (1988) · J. Kesson, 'Nan Shepherd in recollection', *Aberdeen University Review*, 53 (1989–90), 187–91 · S. Hamilton, 'Writer of genius gave up', *Evening Express* (15 Dec 1976) · L. Donald, 'Nan Shepherd', *Leopard Magazine* (Oct 1977) · V. Forrest, 'In search of Nan Shepherd', *Leopard Magazine* (Dec 1986–Jan 1987) · H. MacPherson, 'Nan Shepherd', *Scottish Book Collector*, 4/2 (Dec 1993–Jan 1994) · b. cert.
Archives NL Scot.
Likenesses photograph, repro. in Forrest, 'In search of Nan Shepherd' · photograph, repro. in MacPherson, 'Nan Shepherd' · photographs, repro. in Donald, 'Nan Shepherd'
Wealth at death £88,519.78: confirmation, 7 Aug 1981, CCI

Shepherd, Anthony (1721?–1796), astronomer, was born at Kendal, Westmorland, the elder son of Arthur Shepherd. Following his schooling at Kendal under Mr Towers, he was admitted to St John's College, Cambridge, on 27 June 1740, at the age of nineteen. He received the degree of BA in 1744 and proceeded MA from Christ's College in

1747; he became a BD in 1761, and a DD in 1766. He was ordained in London on 23 February 1746 and held a long succession of livings—vicar of Croxton, Norfolk (1756–8), vicar of Bourn, Cambridgeshire (1758–63), rector of Barton Mills, Suffolk (1763–82), canon of Windsor (1777–96), rector of Eastling, Kent (1782–96), and rector of Hartley Wespall, Hampshire (1792–6)—while remaining throughout at Cambridge.

Shepherd was a fellow of Christ's College from 1747 to 1783 and a tutor from 1752 to 1777. Previous biographers have criticized his laziness, but other indications that he was not greatly esteemed by the fellows of Christ's may explain some of the animosity towards him. Shepherd involved the college in a lawsuit which began in 1765 and dragged on until 1805, linked to his lease of the tithes of Burnham Westgate. When he became canon of Windsor in 1777 the college requested that he resign his fellowship. He declined, and from 1777 to 1781 the college continually sought to have the fellowship declared vacant. Such a declaration was among the first accomplishments of John Barker after his election as master in 1780; Shepherd himself had been a candidate to head the college. Despite some objections, Shepherd's fellowship finally ceased on 22 November 1783.

Shepherd was elected Plumian professor of astronomy at the University of Cambridge in 1760 and FRS in 1763. In 1768 he was appointed master of mechanics to George III. He published several versions of *The Heads of a Course of Lectures in Experimental Philosophy Read at Christ's College*. As Plumian professor he was a commissioner of the board of longitude, which published *Tables for correcting the apparent distance of the moon and a star from the effects of refraction and parallax* (1772), to which he contributed a preface, including a brief history of the problem of determining longitude at sea; the tables themselves were calculated by others. In 1774 Captain Cook named a group of islands after his friend Shepherd.

Shepherd was known to have an interest both in wine and in music. He bequeathed a number of astronomical and musical instruments, some by important makers, but his taste was not above criticism. A member of Christ's who had been involved in the calculation of the astronomical tables, with whom Shepherd may not have been on the best of terms, suggested that 'the Doctor did not shine more in music than he did in astronomy; and that he was not qualified to play the second Cremona in a concert' (Nichols, 6.678). Fanny, the daughter of his musical friend Dr Charles Burney, described Shepherd as 'dullness itself', also noting that he was 'prodigiously tall and stout' (*Early Diary*, 1.284). His portrait, part of his bequest, is in the possession of the University of Cambridge. Shepherd, who never married, died at his house in Dean Street, Soho, London, on 15 June 1796. LIBA TAUB

Sources J. Peile, *Biographical register of Christ's College, 1505–1905, and of the earlier foundation, God's House, 1448–1505*, ed. [J. A. Venn], 2 (1913), 241 · J. Peile, *Christ's College* (1900), 262–4 · R. T. Gunter, *Early science in Cambridge* (1937), 80, 82, 168 · R. F. Scott, ed., *Admissions to the College of St John the Evangelist in the University of Cambridge*, 3: July

1715 – November 1767 (1903), 506–7 · Venn, *Alum. Cant.* · Nichols, *Illustrations*, 6.677–8 · *The early diary of Frances Burney, 1768–1778*, ed. A. R. Ellis, 1 (1889), 284 · W. Cole, notes for the *Athenae Cantabrigienses*, BL, Add. MS 5880, fol. 76 [renumbered 88 in pencil] · G. W. Meadley, *Memoirs of William Paley, DD* (1809), 29–30, 37–8 · *The works of William Paley, DD*, new edn, ed. E. Paley, 1 (1825), 80–81 · *A catalogue of the manuscripts preserved in the library of the University of Cambridge*, 4, ed. H. R. Luard (1861), item 47, fols. 120–37 · PRO, PROB 11/1276, sig. 331 · *Cambridge Chronicle and Journal* (28 May 1768) · J. Cook, *A voyage towards the south pole and round the world*, 2nd edn, 2 (1777), 39

Archives BL, letters to Dr J. Douglas, Eg. MSS 2180, 2186

Likenesses L. F. G. van der Puyl, oils, 1784, Old Schools, Cambridge · J. Bacon, marble bust, 1796, Trinity Cam.

Wealth at death £34,457 16s. 7d.: PRO, death duty registers, IR 26/1, no. 144

Shepherd, Augustin. *See* Crathorne, William (1670–1740).

Shepherd, Charles William Haimes (1917–1998), naval officer, was born on 10 December 1917 at 23 Richmond Street, Plymouth, Devon, the son of William Henry Haimes Shepherd, labourer in the naval dockyard, and his wife, Florence Ethel Hayter. He was a pupil at the Public Central School, Plymouth, and entered the Royal Navy in 1933 as an engineering artificer apprentice at HMS *Fisgard*, the naval school at Torpoint. On passing out top of his class he went to sea in the engine room of HMS *Repulse*.

Shepherd saw action at the second battle of Narvik on 13 April 1940 while temporarily assigned to HMS *Hero*. Commissioned a sub-lieutenant (E) in July 1940, he studied at the Royal Naval College, Greenwich, and qualified as an advanced engineer soon after his marriage to the 22-year-old Myra Betty Joan Major (1917/18–1988) on 9 November 1940. They had a son. Lieutenant Shepherd served in the battleship HMS *Royal Sovereign* (1941–4) and the cruiser HMS *Gambia* (1944–5) before joining the staff of the commander-in-chief, Pacific, in Sydney, Australia.

To his initial dismay, Shepherd was designated a project officer with research and development, guided weapons, at Farnborough in 1946. This determined the subsequent course of his career, apart from one last tour at sea as a lieutenant-commander with the 3rd training flotilla (1949–51). He learned much about solid fuel technology while working on the Sea Slug surface-to-air missile and, raised to commander (1952), was trials liaison officer on HMS *Girdle Ness*, the ship adapted to test it. Although an effective weapon, the Sea Slug came into service four years late in 1961, being so much larger than first planned that only eight purpose-built destroyers ever carried it. This experience left Shepherd with decided views about what to avoid when managing a weapons programme.

Promoted captain on 31 December 1960, Shepherd completed the senior officers' war course (1961–2) and became deputy director of naval intelligence (technical) at the Admiralty. Information exchange projects took him to the USA to study how the American navy was developing a new nuclear submarine armed with ballistic missiles (a craft known as the SSBN: submarine submersible ballistic nuclear). Consequently he well appreciated the implications of the unexpected upheaval in British nuclear

defence policy which occurred in December 1962. Hitherto Britain's nuclear deterrent had depended for its delivery on the V-bombers of the Royal Air Force. The Macmillan government, on abandoning Blue Streak (the proposed British medium-range missile), had arranged in 1960 to purchase Skybolt air-to-surface missiles from the USA to convey British nuclear warheads. Now, however, the USA was cancelling Skybolt, and the alternative—hastily secured by Macmillan via the Nassau agreement—was Polaris, a submarine-launched missile. Rather to its own consternation, the Royal Navy was required to procure SSBNs and assume full nuclear capability by 1968.

Shepherd accompanied the Begg–Zuckerman mission to Washington in January 1963 for the first round of Polaris planning talks. Then on 6 February he joined the technical directorate of the new Polaris executive as the deputy director, weapons (Polaris). This meant that he was working under the chief Polaris executive (Rear-Admiral Hugh (Rufus) Mackenzie) and the technical director, Polaris (Rowland Baker), and alongside the deputy director, naval construction (S. J. Palmer). While Palmer designed the submarines, Shepherd took responsibility for procuring, installing, proving, and servicing the Polaris weapon system (and torpedoes for self-defence). This was a challenging task, for, though the missiles would come from the USA, the warheads and re-entry system were to be made in Britain: technical integration had to be perfect. The navy, moreover, did not have experience of nuclear weapons, so a whole new training scheme was needed.

In his quest for suitable staff Captain Shepherd drew a large proportion of naval missile engineers and ordnance specialists into the technical directorate (Polaris) based at Bath—often to the chagrin of other divisions of the Admiralty. 'Turf wars' were inevitably a feature of the project; Shepherd fought them with zeal, asserting his claims against those of the director-general, weapons, and the Polaris project office attached to the Ministry of Aviation. A blunt-speaking man, not worried about making enemies, he compared these episodes to fisticuffs in the schoolyard and despised the 'great British compromise'. Whenever the five-year timetable 'Longcast 63' showed signs of slipping, his ire would descend on the Atomic Weapons Research Establishment, the Royal Ordnance Factory, Burghfield, and the civil contractors (Vickers, Cammell Laird, GEC, and the British Aircraft Corporation). The secret of punctual completion lay in keeping divergencies from the American system to a minimum. Shepherd prided himself on the suppression of 'WIBBIs': 'Wouldn't it be better if …?'

For seven years the deputy director, weapons (Polaris), took no leave. He often worked from 7.30 a.m. to 10 p.m. seven days a week and expected staff to follow his example, though bluff humour marginally tempered his regime. Shepherd saw this 'crackpot' dedication rewarded when the first British SSBN, HMS *Resolution*, test-fired an A3 Polaris missile off Florida at 11.15 hours on 15 February 1968 (as scheduled five years earlier). It amused him to grumble that the launch was fifteen thousandths of a second late; everyone else extolled a singular achievement: Polaris had been delivered on time and within budget. *Resolution* began operational patrols on 15 June 1968.

Shepherd, appointed CBE, led the technical directorate (Polaris) from 1968 to 1971 with the new title of director project teams (submarines) and deputy assistant controller, Polaris. He dealt with the commissioning of the fourth SSBN, HMS *Revenge*, and drew up the refit procedures for *Resolution*, *Repulse*, and *Renown*. His rank advanced to rear-admiral in 1970, before he assumed command of Britain's nuclear forces as the deputy controller of the navy, Polaris (1971–3). Thickset, bald, and bespectacled, he retired in 1974 and returned to Plymouth, where he lived at 5 Underhill Road, Stoke. Yachting and watching rugby were his hobbies.

Charles Shepherd, a key figure in the most successful British peacetime weapon procurement project of the century, died of a stroke on 24 February 1998 at Underhill House residential home, 12 Underhill Road, Stoke, Plymouth, Devon. JASON TOMES

Sources *Daily Telegraph* (13 March 1998) · *The Times* (20 March 1998) · C. Shepherd, 'The weapon system', *The impact of Polaris—the origins of Britain's seaborne nuclear deterrent*, ed. J. E. Moore (1999), 128–33 · P. Nailor, *The Nassau connection: the organisation and management of the British Polaris project* (1988) · H. Mackenzie, *The sword of Damocles* (1995) · J. Simpson, 'The Polaris executive: a case study of a unified hierarchy', *Public Administration*, 48 (1970), 379–90 · *Navy List* (1964) · m. cert. · d. cert. · b. cert. · *WW*
Likenesses photograph, repro. in *The Times*

Shepherd, Edward (*c*.1692–1747), building craftsman and architect, played a major part in the development of west London in the first half of the eighteenth century. Nothing is known of his antecedents and early life before his marriage on 14 May 1710 to Elizabeth Hill in St Marylebone parish church. He had a brother, John, a plasterer, with whom he often worked and who was once castigated by the duke of Chandos for having been 'drunk from morning to night and never minded the workmen' (Baker, 370), another brother, Joseph, and a sister, Frances. His wife's brother, George Hill, was a carver in wood and stone, who also worked on several of Shepherd's buildings.

Shepherd apparently trained as a plasterer, and gave this as his trade in 1718 when he took building leases of house plots in the vicinity of Hanover Square. Thereafter he extended his speculative building activities to other major developments in west London, such as on the Cavendish-Harley estate to the north of Oxford Street and the Grosvenor, Berkeley, and Curzon estates in Mayfair.

In the meantime, his career seems to have benefited from an association with one of the richest men in the country, James Brydges, first duke of Chandos, who had been paymaster-general to Marlborough's army. Chandos used his great wealth in various building enterprises, including the erection and subsequent embellishment of a large mansion at Canons, near Edgware, in Middlesex (since demolished), where work seems to have been almost continually in progress between about 1713 and 1725. Here Shepherd appears to have been employed initially as a building craftsman and later in a supervisory capacity. He also helped to supervise some of the duke's other building enterprises in Bridgwater and Bath, where he had some association with John Wood, the principal architect of Georgian Bath. For Chandos, Shepherd also built two houses on the north side of Cavendish Square and the rectory at Great Stanmore, near Canons (all demolished). He also remodelled the Great Lodge at Enfield Chase (demolished) and undertook alterations to Shaw House, Newbury, Berkshire.

From 1723 onwards Shepherd took several parcels of ground on the Grosvenor estate under building agreements and there he erected some of the finest Georgian houses in London. These include 66 Brook Street, which has an outstanding display of ornamental plasterwork in its principal rooms; 72 Brook Street, where Shepherd himself lived for a brief period and which, with its mixture of decorative plasterwork and woodcarving, may have been in the nature of a show house; 12 North Audley Street, where he provided a richly embellished gallery at the rear, possibly to the designs of the Irish Palladian architect Sir Edward Lovett Pearce; and 71 to 75 South Audley Street, where the interiors contain several examples of the fine plasterwork which became a trademark of his work. In 1728 he undertook to build on the north side of Grosvenor Square and erected three houses (since demolished) with a uniform palace-like facade which showed considerable maturity of design. The architectural writer Robert Morris claimed that Shepherd had provided a design for the whole of the north side of the square, but that it proved impossible to secure the agreement of the various owners of building plots to carry this out. Of the three houses which he did build, the centre one with a columned and pedimented facade was described in 1730 as 'the fine house in Grosvenor-Square built by Mr. Shepherd the famous Architect' (*St James's Evening Post*).

By this time Shepherd had acted as executant architect at 4 St James's Square, where Henry Grey, duke of Kent (1664–1740), built a grand town house, ostensibly of his own designing, and at Boreham House in Essex, where both James Gibbs and Henry Flitcroft appear to have been involved in the design. Indeed, Shepherd's rapid graduation from the status of a building craftsman to that of an architect who displayed an understanding of Palladian precedents, even if he frequently interpreted them in an individualistic way, suggests that he associated with the group of architects who were setting the standards of taste at that time, including Colin Campbell, who designed a house for himself on one of Shepherd's building plots in Brook Street and lived there as a near neighbour of Shepherd himself.

As an architect Shepherd also designed the Goodman's Fields Theatre in Whitechapel (subsequently demolished) and the first Covent Garden Theatre (burned down in 1808), undertook work at Hampden House, Buckinghamshire, and added wings at Petersham Lodge, Surrey (demolished). He was also responsible for the monuments in Flitton church, Bedfordshire, to the duke of Kent (signed 'Edw:d Shepherd Arch:t') and Lady Annabell de Grey. He almost certainly provided the design for the handsome Palladian house at 17 Bruton Street, Mayfair (subsequently the birthplace of Elizabeth II and since demolished), where the building lessee was his brother John. Other work which has been attributed to him on stylistic grounds includes Barnsley Park in Gloucestershire.

Throughout his career Shepherd continued to work as a speculative builder. In 1740–42, on the site of the notorious May fair, he built Shepherd Market (which was named after him) and other developments in the vicinity of Curzon Street. He erected a two-storey market house with butchers' shops on the ground floor and a large room for entertainments above (rebuilt in 1860), and several other buildings in the area. At the time of his death he was building yet another large town mansion on the north side of Curzon Street, but this house, which subsequently took the name of Crewe House, was much extended and altered by later owners.

Shepherd died on 21 October 1747, 'greatly lamented by all who had the Pleasure of his Acquaintance' (*Penny London Post*). His funeral was held in St George's Church, Hanover Square, where he had been a vestryman for several years. His widow continued to run his building business until her own death on 18 June 1761. They appear to have been childless, and the bulk of their estate, which included Shepherd Market and other property and was said to be very considerable, was left to a great-nephew. The estate was heavily mortgaged, however, and the complication of discharging the mortgages and family disputes in later generations led to a succession of Dickensian chancery cases which embroiled the estate for the best part of a century.   VICTOR BELCHER

Sources V. Belcher, 'The Grosvenor estate, I: the work of Edward Shepherd', *Country Life*, 162 (1977), 1362–5 · V. Belcher, 'The queen's birthplace: new light on a famous demolished house', *London Topographical Record*, 24 (1980), 81–92 · F. H. W. Sheppard, ed., *The Grosvenor estate in Mayfair*, 2 vols., Survey of London, 39–40 (1977–80) · C. H. C. Baker and M. I. Baker, *The life and circumstances of James Brydges, first duke of Chandos, patron of the liberal arts* (1949), 370 · Colvin, *Archs.* · PRO, PROB 11/757, fol. 266 [will of Edward Shepherd] · will of Elizabeth Shepherd, PRO, PROB 11/866, fol. 233 · *St James's Evening Post* (30 April–2 May 1730) · *Penny London Post* (23–6 Oct 1747) · parish register (marriages), London, St Marylebone, 14 May 1710 · parish register (burials), London, Hanover Square, St George's, 25 Oct 1747
Wealth at death very considerable estate: *Penny London Post*

Shepherd, George Robert, first Baron Shepherd (1881–1954), political organizer, was born at Spalding, Lincolnshire, on 19 August 1881, the son of George Robert Shepherd, a tailor, and his wife, Helena Sophia Hensman. He was educated at Spalding board school; the death of his father ended any hope of further education, and he began work in a shoe shop. Shepherd responded to the rigours of the retail trade by becoming active in the Shop Assistants' Union and continued his education by reading extensively on political and economic issues. His political ideas

might have been influenced by the accident of his employment in Bradford. This was a stronghold of the early Independent Labour Party (ILP), and socialist sentiments had become popular among some sections of the Bradford working class. Shepherd joined the ILP in 1901; he became an effective street-corner speaker and held office in the local party.

Shepherd's career as a full-time party worker began in 1908 as an organizer for the ILP's midland division. In the following year he moved to Dundee as registration agent for the sitting Labour member, Alexander Wilkie of the Shipwrights. Dundee was a two-member seat, Wilkie was the sole Labour candidate, and in both 1910 elections was successful in tandem with the only Liberal, Winston Churchill. Shepherd later insisted that this arrangement had taught him an important lesson. 'The guiding principle in everything that I have tried to do is independence in politics. That has been the making of our party' (*Labour Party Conference Report*, 1946, 135).

Shepherd moved to a similar post at Blackburn in 1913, where Liberal/Labour sharing of parliamentary representation also existed. The Labour beneficiary was Philip Snowden, a standard-bearer closer to Shepherd's own politics. On 4 August 1915 Shepherd married Ada (d. 1975), daughter of Alfred Newton, a gardener, and herself an organizer for the National Federation of Women Workers. They had a son and a daughter.

The First World War disrupted the basis of Blackburn Labour's electoral position. At the general election of 1918 Snowden and Shepherd faced a combination of the sitting Liberal and a Conservative, both of whom supported Lloyd George's coalition. For the first time Shepherd's organizational skills were not rewarded with electoral victory.

Labour's post-war ambitions involved developing a network of full-time district organizers. In 1920 Shepherd was appointed to head the London and southern district, and this was coupled with the role of assistant to the new national agent, Egerton Wake. Over the next few years, as Wake's health deteriorated, Shepherd became increasingly his effective replacement. In 1923 he became assistant national agent, and from April 1928, following Wake's breakdown, he ran the national agent's department in consultation with the party secretary, Arthur Henderson. Wake's death in March 1929 meant that Shepherd acted as national agent during the general election held in May 1929, when Labour became the largest parliamentary party for the first time. Shepherd's appointment as national agent was confirmed in June 1929.

The optimism of electoral victory was soon replaced by loss of support as the Labour government encountered rising unemployment. Shepherd faced discouraging municipal and by-election results and then the crisis and electoral disaster of 1931. He signed the letters conveying the national executive notice of expulsion to those who had joined or backed the National Government. Shepherd's qualities were evident in the difficult years that followed. Electoral recovery was limited; there was no real hope of a Labour government down to 1939. He worked assiduously to strengthen party organization; he blended an insistence on discipline with a willingness to listen sympathetically to the concerns of party members.

Shepherd perceived the popular shift to the left after 1940, but was concerned lest the Labour Party's involvement in the wartime coalition would mean a failure to benefit from this radicalization. The contribution of party organization to Labour's victory in 1945 is debatable. Under Shepherd's guidance the central organization was effectively directed towards a post-war election, but local parties had often been affected by wartime removals and dislocations. Nevertheless, when he retired in 1946 his years of commitment to the party could appear as a significant contribution to Labour's forward march. Clem Attlee characterized him as 'the Labour Carnot, the organiser of victory' (*Labour Party Conference Report*, 1946, 134).

In June 1946, after his retirement, Shepherd was created a peer, as Baron Shepherd, becoming the first Labour Party official to enter the House of Lords. There he reinforced the small Labour contingent and played his part in ensuring that the Attlee government's legislation passed through the predominantly Conservative Lords without serious confrontations. The reasonableness that had marked his career as national agent was equally evident in the Lords, where he became Labour chief whip in 1949.

Shepherd was a committed socialist whose loyalties had been formed before 1914. Having shared in the Labour optimism of the 1920s, he was marked by the trauma of 1931. A typical figure of Labour's second generation, he had much in common with his senior parliamentary colleagues, for whom the electoral victory of 1945 could seem both justification and fulfilment. Shepherd died in the General Hospital, Edgware, Middlesex, on 4 December 1954, and was cremated at Golders Green crematorium on 8 December. He was succeeded as second Baron Shepherd by his elder son, Malcolm Newton Shepherd (1918–2001), who became Labour chief whip in the House of Lords (1963–7), minister at the Foreign and Commonwealth Office (1967–70), and lord privy seal and leader of the House of Lords (1974–6).   DAVID HOWELL

Sources *DNB* · *The Times* (6 Dec 1954) · *The Times* (9 Dec 1954) · *The Labour who's who* (1927) · Burke, *Peerage* (2000) · *Labour party conference report, 1946* · *Labour party conference report, 1955* · *Labour party conference report, 1929* · S. Brooke, *Labour's war: the labour party during the Second World War* (1992) · *CGPLA Eng. & Wales* (1955)
Archives Bodl. Oxf., corresp. with Attlee
Wealth at death £1571 13s. 2d.: probate, 22 April 1955, *CGPLA Eng. & Wales*

Shepherd, George Sidney (1784–1862), draughtsman and watercolour painter, was born on 5 December 1784 in Old Street, Finsbury, London, the son of George Shepherd, a watchcase maker, and his wife, Nancy Hosmer. He was baptized on 22 March 1785 at his parish church of St Luke's, Old Street. Shepherd's dates and life have long been somewhat unclear. Until the late twentieth century George Shepherd—the present subject—was understood to be the father of George Sidney Shepherd, whose monogram G.S.S. first appears on two careful monochrome wash drawings of Highgate about 1810. It is now thought that George and George Sidney were not father and son but the same person. Even though reconciling the separate signatures remains problematic and despite the fact that there are significant stylistic differences between their work, conflating these two men helps to explain various biographical discrepancies. The full signature 'George Sidney Shepherd' first appears on a watercolour of Smithfield Market of 1824, the year in which he similarly baptized his son Algernon Sidney Shepherd. It was also the period when his style began to develop from delicate, small-scale, and precise *views* of places to larger-scale, more painterly, and impressionistic *scenes* of life, an evolution which can be understood in relationship to the changing taste for topography and genre. The possibility that George Shepherd changed his professional name in order to mark distinctions in his work is reinforced by the parish records which show that he continued as George when registering the baptism of his eight children.

Taking George Shepherd to be the youthful George Sidney helps to plot the events of this artist's career. Like his brother Thomas Hosmer [*see below*], who became a topographical draughtsman and drawing master, George showed talent early; by 1800 he had exhibited the first of many topographical views at the Royal Academy. During his late teens he also won silver palettes at the Society of Arts in 1803 and 1804 and may have mixed with other artists at Dr Cox Macro's sketching academy where there is a reference to a Mr Shepherd in 1806. Like the watercolour *Tottenham Court Church* (1800), Shepherd's earliest subjects were all within striking distance of his home, off the City Road in rural Islington. By 1807, however, he began to travel further afield, going to Cambridge and Northampton to produce sketches for John Britton's *Architectural Antiquities of Great Britain* in 1807. While his work for various publishers sent him to many areas of England, on 16 March 1812 Shepherd married Anna Sarah Lonnon (*b.* 1790, *d.* before 1831) of Bedfordshire and this explains his trips and watercolours of that region. Despite his reputation as a metropolitan topographer, Shepherd's marked sympathy with rural and natural landscapes can be seen in a number of his watercolours including *At East Acton* (1814) or his several scenes on the River Thames (*c.*1818–25). Doubtless Shepherd's greatest strength was in depicting the urban sphere and particularly London. He was an excellent topographical draughtsman who was able to express complicated perspectives and detailed architectural elevations in the many, deceptively simple, pen-and-wash drawings that he prepared for others to engrave. This can be seen to great effect in general works such as the *European Magazine* as well as in J. Booth's *Architectural Series of London Churches* (1818) or Robert Wilkinson's *Londina illustrata* (1825–34), which was published to fuel the increasing fashion for images which depicted the ancient roots of the modern metropolis.

Living on the outskirts of a bustling city, Shepherd evidently had an implicit understanding of urban life. Even in the most abbreviated lines he eloquently captured the humanity and humour that typified London life. This was consolidated in the second half of his career when he began to concentrate on these elements and seems to have sought recognition as a more painterly watercolour artist. Although he continued to favour scenes of London life, his views of Charing Cross, Hungerford Stairs, and demolition work near the Monument were executed in a larger format which gave him the opportunity to develop the genre and even caricature of these subjects. By the 1830s and 1840s he had expanded his palette and his technique; skies became more impressionistic and costumes more colourful.

In 1832 Shepherd began exhibiting at the Society of British Artists and was a founder subscriber to the New Society of Painters in Water Colours in 1834. Because he worked less frequently for publishers after the 1840s the minutes of that society give the best sense of Shepherd's activities during this time. Despite being fined for non-attendance at their meetings in 1840 he was evidently still active as he also owed them money for selling paintings at their exhibitions. By 1859 his name no longer appears on their list of members and a begging letter from his son, of 5 November 1860, records why the twice-widowed and ailing Shepherd was no longer heard from. After suffering a stroke in March 1858, Shepherd ceased working and became increasingly ill and impecunious until his death in 1862. He was supported by the New Society of Painters in Water Colours who made their final donation to his cause on 3 February 1861.

During his career Shepherd worked several times for the publishing magnate Rudolph Ackermann and it was under his auspices that he first collaborated with his younger brother **Thomas Hosmer Shepherd** (1793–1864) in 1813. Together they prepared a series of street views for Ackermann's *Repository of the Arts* where Thomas had already published his view of the East India House in 1809. Although the interests and skills of the two brothers certainly overlap, Thomas was less interested in antiquarian themes. In 1816 he designed a series of six London street scenes whose detail and vivacity characterized his *œuvre*. Despite a reputation built upon depicting a variety of modern, fashionable cities Thomas Hosmer showed a similar skill with nature. He made his first sketching tour aged seventeen and as the illustrations in Thomas Rose's *Westmorland* (1832) or William Gray Fearnside's *Views of the Rhine* (1832) demonstrate this was followed by several others. Due to the existence of a watercolour of the site of a former Napoleonic encampment at Boulogne it also appears that Thomas visited France in 1818 and it is thought that this was by way of a honeymoon with his new bride, Jane Maria (*b. c.*1797, *d.* in or after 1864). Perhaps the trip left the couple with especially fond memories; in June 1819 they named their first born, the artist, Frederick Napoleon Shepherd (1819–1878).

Although Thomas Shepherd had no problems finding work as a topographical draughtsman, his real break came in 1826 when Jones & Co. commissioned a series of views of London's newest buildings, streets, and squares for engraving on steel and issuing as a part work. With its text by the architect James Elmes, *Metropolitan Improvements* (1827) was principally received as a visual celebration of modern London. Such was the success of this publication that Jones & Co. capitalized on the formula with *Modern Athens* (1828), a similar volume on Edinburgh, and another called *Bath and Bristol … Displayed* (1829). Between 1826 and 1831 Jones & Co. 'appear to have monopolised Thomas Hosmer's pencil' (Phillips, *Shepherd's London*, 11) and during this time he produced about 450 plates by sketching on the spot, then working up finished wash drawings at home in his studio. However, as one surviving advertisement reveals, he also found time to offer his services as a drawing master, at his home in Chapman Street, Islington.

Work for Jones & Co. did eventually dry up but it was definitely the cornerstone to Thomas Shepherd's later career. He was able to rework or reduce many of these designs for his next (rather more modest) project, 400 drawings for Charles Frederick Partington's *Natural History and Views of London* (1835). Other London projects were soon forthcoming; Charles Knight commissioned thirty-four wood-engravings for his *London* (1841–4) and Ernest Gambart published twenty-two coloured lithographs after Shepherd in his *London in Miniature* (1854). The last major commission of his career was for sixteen drawings to illustrate *Mighty London* (1855) where a thronging, fashionable, and cosmopolitan London was proudly positioned at the very heart of the empire.

Although he found regular work providing topical and topographical images for the *Illustrated London News*, after 1842, Thomas Hosmer Shepherd was often drastically poor. Indeed, Thomas's lengthy relationship with Frederick Crace, the collector, was his saving. Between 1809 and 1859 Crace consistently commissioned him to make watercolours of specific London sites, buildings, and locations. Such was the renown of Crace's topographically organized, near-comprehensive, metropolitan collection that this led to further commissions for Shepherd. It is for this reason that many of his watercolours are known in multiple versions; the best version is usually in the Crace collection, now at the British Museum. Thomas's dependence on this patron is clear from the fact that his last dated drawing comes from five weeks before Crace's death on 18 September 1859. Five years later, on 4 July 1864, Thomas Hosmer Shepherd died in Islington. He was survived by two sons, Frederick Napoleon and Valentine Claude, who were both practising artists.   LUCY PELTZ

Sources J. R. Abbey, *Life in England in aquatint and lithography, 1770–1860* (privately printed, London, 1953); repr. (1972) · R. K. Engen, *Dictionary of Victorian engravers, print publishers and their works* (1979) · D. Bank and A. Esposito, eds., *British biographical archive*, 2nd series (1991) [microfiche] · Graves, *RA exhibitors* · S. C. Holliday, *Thomas Hosmer Shepherd, 1793–1864: a descriptive catalogue of watercolours and drawings in the local collections of Kensington and Chelsea libraries* (1973) · S. Houfe, *The dictionary of 19th century British book illustrators and caricaturists*, rev. edn (1996) · S. C. Hutchison, 'The Royal Academy Schools, 1768–1830', *Walpole Society*, 38 (1960–62), 123–91 · J. F. C. Phillips, *George Shepherd (1784–1862): a double career?* (1984) · J. F. C. Phillips, *Shepherd's London* (1976) · J. F. C. Phillips, *The Shepherds in a wider world: a supplement to 'Shepherd's London'* (1981) ·

E. Walford, 'The Crace collection of London prints', *Londoniana*, 1 (1879), 274–97 · Wood, *Vic. painters*, 3rd edn · Herts. ALS · *DNB*
Likenesses J. Stephanoff, oils, before 1830

Shepherd, Ian Douglas Dawson- (1915–1996), charity administrator, was born on 23 September 1915 at Port Said, Egypt, the second of four children of John Dawson-Shepherd, an agriculturist in the colonial service, and his wife, Margaret. He had an older brother, Hanbury, and two younger sisters, Pamela and Penelope. Dawson-Shepherd attended London University and in 1939 joined the army where he was commissioned in the King's regiment (Liverpool) and rose to the rank of captain. He was seriously wounded in north Africa and invalided out of the army in 1944. Married twice, he had three daughters with his first wife, Margaret Grigg: Rosemary Hope (1941–1986), Judith, and Andrea, and three with his second wife, Margaret Kathleen Johns: Anne, Sarah, and Deborah.

Dawson-Shepherd's first child, Rosemary, was born on 20 March 1941 with cerebral palsy. It was the family's experience of trying to care for Rosemary against the background of poor or non-existent services and hostile public attitudes to disability that led Dawson-Shepherd, together with two other parents, Alex Moria and Eric Hodgson, and a social worker, Jean Garwood, to found the National Spastics Society. Planning began in October 1951 when Dawson-Shepherd laid a £5 note on the table of the meeting as the starting capital and promised to raise a million pounds in five years, a promise he kept. At the time that he made this promise he privately doubted whether his own wartime injuries, which left him with a permanent impairment and needing to use callipers for a number of years, together with a pre-existing stammer, fitted him for a leadership role in a major national organization.

On 6 January 1952 the inaugural meeting of the National Spastics Society was held, attended by parents from across the country. The society's main aims were to establish a network of parents' groups and service centres to cater for the largely unmet needs of children and adults with cerebral palsy, to challenge attitudes towards disabled people, and to fund medical research into the cause of the disability.

Dawson-Shepherd pioneered the application of marketing and public relations techniques, which later became standard in the charity sector, to build the organization's income from £11,000 in its first year to £1,400,000 at his retirement from the chair in 1960. This remarkable growth was achieved by an astute mixture of campaigning, fundraising, and initiatives to raise public awareness. The marketing strategy focused on donations from ordinary people and culminated in the establishment of the Spastics football pools, an innovation that brought in over £2 million a year. This allowed the organization to expand rapidly in the late 1950s and early 1960s into the largest charity for physical disability in the country, with over thirty major services and a network of local parents' support groups being set up in less than ten years. Another innovation was the use of popular celebrities to attract

Ian Douglas Dawson-Shepherd (1915–1996), by unknown photographer

publicity and help with fund-raising. Together with Wilfred Pickles, then a major BBC radio star, in July 1955 Dawson-Shepherd founded a sister organization, Stars Organization for Spastics (now Stars Organisation Supporting Action for People with Cerebral Palsy). The founding members of the sister organization included such popular entertainers as Vera Lynn, Tommy Cooper, Thora Hird, Harry Secombe, and Peter Sellers. Advertising and fund-raising appeals focused on the needs of young disabled children as public sympathy was more easily aroused for children.

Dawson-Shepherd brought the needs of disabled people into strip cartoons, comics, and women's magazines. The award-winning *Jessie*, an adventure story for children featuring a child with cerebral palsy, which was based on an idea by Rosemary, and *Every Eight Hours*, a campaigning documentary, both reached wide audiences. The latter was one of the first attempts to combine news and documentary techniques to carry a public-education campaign on prime time television. Made for the BBC by his second wife, Margaret Johns, and personally scripted by Dawson-Shepherd, it was shown in 1960 to critical and popular acclaim. It featured Richard Dimbleby, at that time one of the best-known broadcasters in the country, and was repeated by the BBC because of demand from the public.

This populist approach was a defining hallmark of the charity in its early years, in a sector dominated by establishment charities. Dawson-Shepherd characterized the organization as 'working class Davids shouting at the state Goliath', and continually strove to position it as the 'ordinary man's charity' in a post-war world that had begun to tire of class distinctions (Dawson-Shepherd, 57).

Dawson-Shepherd also encouraged research into cerebral palsy. Advised by Dr Ronald MacKeith of the department of child health at Guy's Hospital, who had set up a pioneering clinic for children with cerebral palsy, he recruited Dr Paul Polani to develop a strategy for research into the causes of a number of neurological conditions. The pediatric research unit was established at Guy's in

1960 with a large grant from the organization. The association with MacKeith led to the establishment of the Mac Keith Press with support from the society in 1958. Its journal, *Cerebral Palsy Bulletin*, remained a pre-eminent source for worldwide medical research in pediatric neurology, helping to establish the field as a medical specialism.

Because of the pressures of his job as international marketing director for Aspro-Nicholas, Dawson-Shepherd resigned as chairman in 1960. It was also becoming clear to him that the skills and entrepreneurship needed in establishing a major charity were not necessarily those most suitable for sustaining it. There had been growing clashes with some members of the board and senior staff, who found his creative but sometimes maverick approach hard to cope with. He continued active involvement with the organization and made a series of films about disability. However, he became increasingly critical of the organization's financial performance, and of what he perceived to be its failure to build on the early public relations successes. He was fully supportive of the change of name to Scope in 1994 and saw this as a natural fulfilment of the organization's early aspirations, arguing eloquently for the adoption of the new name.

Dawson-Shepherd returned to the issues of medical prevention in 1990 when he used his considerable reputation within the medical establishment and his relationship with Professor Polani to found the Little Foundation, which aimed to reduce the incidence of disability at birth by research into the causes of neurological disorders. Despite his continued involvement and the support it received from some of the most renowned medical experts in the world, the foundation was not able to repeat his earlier fund-raising success. The funding environment had become more competitive and Dawson-Shepherd was still fund-raising for some of the major projects when he died of heart failure at Queen Mary's Hospital, London, on 8 January 1996. He was cremated and his ashes were buried at Girne (Kyrenia) in the old British cemetery in northern Cyprus, in the family plot and in the country where he had spent part of his childhood.

BRIAN LAMB

Sources I. Dawson-Shepherd, 'The revolutionary charity', unpublished · P. Polani, memorial service address, 16 April 1996 · *The Independent* (19 Jan 1996) · *The Guardian* (29 Jan 1996) · *Every eight hours*, 1960 [documentary film] · *Jessie*, 1959 [short film] · Scope council and AGM papers, 1954–66 · b. cert. [Rosemary Dawson, daughter]
Archives Spastics Society, council and annual general meeting papers, 1954–1986 · London, 'The revolutionary charity', unpublished history of the Spastics Society | FILM Scope Library, *Jessie*, *Every eight hours*
Likenesses photograph, Scope, London [*see illus.*]

Shepherd, John. *See* Sheppard, John (d. 1559?).

Shepherd, John (1759–1805), Church of England clergyman, son of Richard Shepherd of Goderthwaite, Cumberland, was born early in January 1759 in Beckermet in Cumberland, and baptized at St Bridget's Church there on 7 January. His parents both died when he was young and his upbringing was entrusted to a guardian, John Benson, of Egremont, Cumberland. In 1783 he was to marry his guardian's niece, Frances Benson. He went to school at Arthuret, near Longtown, and then to university at Queen's College, Oxford, where he matriculated in 1777, graduated BA in 1781, and proceeded MA in 1787. He took deacon's orders in 1782 and was ordained priest in 1783. In 1785 he was made perpetual curate of Paddington, Middlesex. There he made and renewed several scholarly connections, notably John Boucher, Dr Samuel Glasse, and the Bampton lecturer Dr William Barrow. One of Shepherd's concerns was the adequacy of the church building for, according to a memoir of Shepherd published by his daughter Eliza in 1817, 'the old church of Paddington was much too small for the accommodation of so populous a parish; and in a condition so ruinous as to endanger the lives of the few who could attend it' (Shepherd, 2). Some local opposition notwithstanding, the church was rebuilt through Shepherd's exertions between 1788 and 1791 and consecrated on completion by Beilby Porteus, bishop of London.

In 1797 Shepherd brought out the first volume of his *Critical and Practical Elucidation of the Book of Common Prayer*. It was favourably received; the first edition was exhausted before the second was ready for the press. He received many letters of congratulation, including one from George Pretyman Tomline, William Pitt's former tutor and bishop of Lincoln, to whom a later (1817) edition of the *Elucidation* was dedicated (the first had been dedicated to Porteus). They did not bring material fortune to the author of the *Elucidations*, however, as Shepherd's daughter Eliza noted in her memoir:

> The general expression of approbation that met his first appearance as Author was the chief if not the only reward of this labour. Habitual inattention to pecuniary concerns, and the too great liberality with which he gave away nearly as many copies as were sold, precluded the possibility of much emolument. (Shepherd, 3)

Shepherd had thirteen children and must have hoped for the incumbency of Paddington when it fell vacant with the death of Archdeacon Hayter in 1799; but it had already been promised elsewhere. In the summer of 1801 he was instead offered the curacy of Pattiswick in Essex and still in the London diocese of his patron Porteus, who indeed paid his removal expenses there. He resided nearby at Stisted. His health was not good and the atmosphere apparently not favourable. Two of his daughters predeceased him. His own self-remedial methods of dealing with a cold may have hastened his end. He died at Stisted on 2 May 1805. His body was taken to Paddington for burial in the new churchyard there. At the time of his death he was engaged on a third volume of the *Elucidation*, to cover the litany, but it was never published. A fifth edition of the first volume and a fourth of the second appeared in 1836.

ANDREW ROBINSON

Sources Foster, *Alum. Oxon.* · *GM*, 1st ser., 75 (1805), 491 · Portens MSS, vol. 35, f.150, LPL, Fulham MSS · E. Shepherd, 'Memoir of the author', in J. Shepherd, *Critical and practical elucidation of the Book of Common Prayer* (1817) · *IGI* · *DNB*

Archives LPL, Fulham MSS

Shepherd, Luke (*fl.* 1548), protestant propagandist, was born in Colchester, Essex. Personal details other than his birthplace, occupation, and London address are not known. John Bale called him 'Lucas Opilio' (a Latinized form of his name), considered him 'a most elegant poet, not at all inferior to Skelton', and declared his works 'full of suitable jests and exercises of wit' (Bale, *Cat.*, 2.109). Shepherd's anonymous works were printed in London in 1548, primarily by John Day, and include eight verse satires and one satiric prose tract. All except *Pathose, or, An Inward Passion of the Pope for the Losse of hys Daughter the Masse* are listed by Bale in his catalogue. Bale also ascribed a translation of the psalms, now lost, to Shepherd. Thomas Warton referred to these psalms and suggested that 'one or two of Shepherd's pieces in prose' were among Bishop Tanner's books at Oxford (Warton, 3.316). Subsequently, Joseph Ritson stated that Shepherd 'versify'd certain psalms' and wrote 'many other little things' (Ritson, 330–31). However, neither of these claims regarding additional texts can be substantiated. Andrew Maunsell listed several of Shepherd's satires anonymously in his bibliography.

Shepherd is identified by a contemporary, Edward Underhill, as his friend 'mr. Luke', a physician of Coleman Street and author of 'many proper bokes agaynst the papistes' (Nichols, 171–2) including the verse dialogue, *John Bon and Mast Person* which attacks the real presence and the feast of Corpus Christi. Underhill recounted the story of its printer, John Day, who was summonsed before the lord mayor of London, Sir John Gresham, to disclose the name of the anonymous author of this work which had been reported to him as seditious. Day avoided going to prison for printing this satire only because Underhill happened to be a dinner guest at Gresham's house when Day was sent for. Underhill had a copy of Shepherd's poem with him which he gave to the mayor, informing him it was in circulation and much admired at court. Gresham promptly 'reade a little off it, and laughed thereatt, as it was bothe pythye and mery', and subsequently dismissed Day without charge (Nichols, 172).

Shepherd was imprisoned in the Fleet for his anti-papist writings, according to both Underhill and John Strype, but their accounts do not provide any proof or particulars. No other contemporary details of Shepherd's life are known. It is possible he was recruited to write anti-Catholic satires by a protestant patron, but there is no evidence of such patronage or any other political connections. There is no indication as to when or where he died, and no will has been found.

Shepherd was one of the main writers of the polemical propaganda printed in London in the first two years of Edward VI's reign. His satires criticize the Roman church's pontiff, clergy, and ideology. *Pathose, A Pore Helpe,* and *The Upcheringe of the Messe* all attack the Catholic mass. *Antipus, The Comparison betwene the Antipus and the Antigraph,* and *John Bon and Mast Person* are concerned primarily with the doctrine of transubstantiation. *Doctour Doubble Ale* derides Catholic doctrines and clergy. *Phylogamus* denounces clerical celibacy and those writers who support its practice. *Cauteles Preservatory Concerning the Preservation of the Gods which are Kept in the Pixe* is a satiric prose work against the sacrament of the altar.

In addition to dealing with general issues of the Reformation, Shepherd also engaged in personal attacks on specific conservative figures, especially churchmen and writers. Contemporary subjects of Shepherd's satires include Bishop Stephen Gardiner, Henry George, Miles Hogarde, William Layton, Sir John Mason, and Dr Richard Smith.

JANICE DEVEREUX

Sources Bale, *Cat.* · Bale, *Index* · J. G. Nichols, ed., *Narratives of the days of the Reformation,* CS, old ser., 77 (1859), 171–2, 325–6 · J. Devereux, 'An edition of Luke Shepherd's satires', PhD diss., University of Otago, 1996 · *STC, 1475–1640* · J. Strype, *Ecclesiastical memorials,* 2/1 (1822), 181–2 · T. Warton, *The history of English poetry,* 4 vols. (1774–81), vol. 3, p. 316 · J. Ritson, *Bibliographia poetica* (1802), 330–31 · A. Maunsell, *The first part of the catalogue of English printed bookes* (1595) · *Holinshed's chronicles of England, Scotland and Ireland,* ed. H. Ellis, 4 (1808), 153 · F. Germann, *Luke Shepherd, ein Satirendichter der englischen Reformationszeit* (1911) · W. C. Hazlitt, ed., *Remains of the early popular poetry of England,* 4 vols. (1864–6), vols. 3 and 4

Shepherd [*née* Primrose], **Lady Mary** (1777–1847), philosopher, was born on 31 December 1777 at Barnbougle Castle, Linlithgowshire, the second of five children of Neil Primrose, third earl of Rosebery (1728–1814), and his second wife, Mary (1752–1823), daughter of Sir Francis Vincent of Stoke d'Abernon and Mary, *née* Howard. According to her eldest daughter, Mary Elizabeth, Lady Mary's upbringing was 'chiefly at Barnbougle (though sometimes in London at Holland House), on the old fashioned Scotch plan with a Dominie—one Mr. Pillans' (Brandreth, 25–6). She married Henry John Shepherd QC (1783?–1855), on 11 April 1808. Her father-in-law, Sir Samuel *Shepherd, was a well-known and widely respected lawyer, and a friend of Walter Scott. She had three children. Her son, Henry Primrose Shepherd, became an invalid in his youth, and her younger daughter, Maria Charlotte, lived only fifteen years.

Rosebery family papers describe Lady Mary as 'remarkable for her high attainments, humour and agreeable society'. At her 'salon', her 'humour seems to have been as well known as her logical powers, and occasional causticity' (Brandreth, 4). Above all, she was passionately interested in metaphysical debate. Both she and her husband corresponded over many years with Charles Babbage, the philosopher and mathematician, who encouraged her philosophical interests. He sent his *Essay on Induction* and other treatises in 1825. She, in return, often asked for his opinion of her latest theories and speculations.

Lady Mary's two metaphysical works, *An Essay upon the Relation of Cause and Effect* (1824) and *Essays on the Perception of an External Universe* (1827), challenged the conclusions of the philosophers George Berkeley and David Hume concerning ideas of the external world. These conclusions, she believed, could be used as a foundation for atheism.

She countered Hume's scepticism, arguing that reason, not 'fancy' or 'custom', leads to knowledge of cause and effect. In 'Lady Shepherd's metaphysics' (*Fraser's Magazine*, July 1832) she continued her criticism of Berkeley's philosophy that 'to be is to be perceived' (or that nothing exists outside the perception of mind). She admitted that her own views might appear at first sight to have much in common with his, since she too accepted the necessity of metaphysical reality as the ground of material or phenomenal reality. Berkeley's error, she argued, was a confusion of ideas with their external causes; ideas are incapable 'of the application of the definitions belonging to extension and to materiality' ('Lady Shepherd's metaphysics', *Fraser's Magazine*, July 1832, 698); this led Berkeley to deny the existence of objects that are independent of mind.

The power of Lady Mary's intellect and argument was respected among her contemporaries; for example, Robert Blakey discusses and praises the 'great acuteness and subtility' (Blakey, 40) of her work. Her criticisms of the conclusions of John Fearn, a retired naval officer with philosophical interests, were published in *Parriana* (1828), together with Fearn's inadequate and condescending reply: her article in *Fraser's Magazine* was a further response to Fearn and demonstrates the superiority of her intellectual grasp.

Samuel Taylor Coleridge records meeting Lady Mary at a gathering of British philosophers and scientists at Cambridge in November 1833. Also present were the astronomers Sir John Herschel and Sir George Biddell Airy. Having expressed admiration of the wives of these two men, Coleridge adds the following scribbled lines:

> Lady Mary Shepheard,
> As restless as a Leopard
> Tho' not so lithe and starry,
> Did wait on S. T. Coleridge
> To learn the extreme polar ridge
> Of Metaphysic Scholarship.
> (Coleridge, fol. 73)

The remainder of the comic verse suggests his admiration of Lady Mary's views, as opposed to the materialist positions of, for example, Herschel.

Her daughter's memoirs include an account of Lady Mary's friendship with Elizabeth Barrett Browning, and report that William Whewell 'made one of … [her] books a text book at Cambridge'. He, and Sir Charles Lyell, had spoken of Lady Mary as an 'unanswerable logician, in whose argument it was impossible to find loophole or flaw' (Brandreth, 29). She died on 7 January 1847 at Hyde Park Terrace, London. Her will contains a 'special Admonition' relating to the £10,000 settled on her at her marriage by her father.   MARY ANNE PERKINS

Sources letters to Charles Babbage, BL, Add. MSS 37183, 37201 · M. E. Brandreth, *Family and friendly recollections* (1884–5) · S. T. Coleridge, Notebook "Q", 1833, fol. 73 · R. Blakey, *A history of the philosophy of the mind: embracing all writers on mental science from the earliest period to the present time* (1850), 40 · M. Atherton, 'Lady Mary Shepherd's case against George Berkeley', *British Journal of the History of Philosophy*, 4 (1996), 347–66 · *GM*, 2nd ser., 28 (1847), 209 · 'Shepherd, Sir Samuel', *DNB*
Archives NA Scot., family MSS
Wealth at death £10,000—from father's settlement on her marriage: will, PRO, PROB 11/2055, sig. 361

Shepherd [Sheppard], **Nicholas** (1533–1587), college head, matriculated as a sizar from St John's College, Cambridge, in 1549, and was admitted a scholar there on the foundation of Sir Marmaduke Constable on 4 July, his native county being given as Westmorland. He was admitted at the command of the royal visitors. He graduated BA in 1553 and was elected a fellow on the foundation of William Fell on 25 March, but was ejected in 1554. Shepherd graduated MA in 1559, and was reinstated as a fellow in 1559–60. On 15 January 1561 he was elected a senior fellow. He served as junior bursar of the college in 1561–2, and on 4 July 1562 was elected a fellow of Trinity College. At Trinity Shepherd held office as junior dean (1562–3), senior bursar (1562–4), and vice-master (1564–9). He was university preacher in 1561 and 1566, and graduated BTh in 1568.

On 17 December 1569 Shepherd was elected master of St John's, 'with the great consent of the company' (Scott 1910, 299) according to Edmund Grindal, bishop of London, who wrote to William Cecil recommending Shepherd to his patronage. Grindal expressed the hope that he would restore the college to the 'antient fame it had in your days and mine'. This hope was to some extent vindicated by the election as fellows of the Hebraist Hugh Broughton, the Greek scholar Andrew Downes, Everard Digby, and others, for whose advancement Thomas Baker unequivocally gives Shepherd credit. Broughton himself states that Shepherd personally enforced his election in 1570, and tried to deter him from migrating to Christ's by persuading the seniors to join him in doubling the value of Broughton's fellowship out of their own allowances. According to Broughton, Shepherd, having failed, 'was sick for grief, as many did report' (*Works*, 360–61). Perhaps in complement to Broughton's work, a great Syriac Testament was bought by agreement of the master and seniors in 1570.

During September 1573 when the bishop of Ely carried out a visitation of St John's, some fellows indicted Shepherd on charges of peculation, insufficient residence, and opposition to the established church by fostering a puritan faction within the college. Shepherd responded to the charges, appealing to his patron Cecil, but in July the following year he vacated the mastership. His conduct, however well meaning, had been at times high-handed, as in the case of Broughton. He had been a prebendary of Peterborough since 1560 and of Lincoln since 1572, and retained these posts and the Lincolnshire rectory of Hougham until his death there between 10 and 16 July 1587, when he was buried at Hougham. His will mentions a wife, Rachel, as well as his mother, now named Anne Todd.   MALCOLM G. UNDERWOOD

Sources T. Baker, *History of the college of St John the Evangelist, Cambridge*, ed. J. E. B. Mayor, 1 (1869), 164–7 · Venn, *Alum. Cant.*, 1/4 · *The works of the great Albionean divine Hugh Broughton*, 4 vols. in 1 (1662),

1.360 · R. F. S. [R. F. Scott], 'Notes from the college records', *The Eagle*, 29 (1907–8), 29–33 · R. F. Scott, 'Notes from the college records', *The Eagle*, 31 (1909–10), 281–316 · *Fasti Angl., 1541–1857*, [Bristol], 122 · *Fasti Angl., 1541–1857*, [Lincoln], 116 · will, PRO, PROB 11/71 · register of admissions of fellows and scholars, St John Cam., Archives, C3.1 · biographical record sheet, St John Cam.

Shepherd [*née* Morgan], **Pamela** [*known as* Mother Shepherd] (1836–1930), evangelist, was born on 19 March 1836 in Tal-y-waun, near Newport, Monmouthshire. She was the eldest of the four surviving children of Benjamin Morgan (*b.* 1806), a blacksmith active in Chartist politics, and Margaret Evans (*b.* 1811), a Welsh Baptist and daughter of Hugh Evans, a Cardiganshire farmer. Her father's political activities made his position in south Wales increasingly difficult, and the family moved to London in 1845 as Benjamin Morgan sought work on the Great Western Railway. As the fortunes of Chartism waned Pamela's father took to drink, and her mother took in washing to support her family. Pamela Morgan married William (Bill) Shepherd, a carter, about 1860 and moved to Poplar. Her parents and siblings returned to Wales in 1861. Deprived of her close relations and faced with a feckless and irregular husband, Pamela Shepherd had to rely on the charity of her in-laws in the early years of her marriage to support herself and her young daughters. Although a self-confessed 'drunkard' she worked hard for her children, first as a laundress, then as a rag sorter. Conscious of her own lack of education (she admitted at the age of forty-two that she could read but not write), she arranged for her older daughters to receive some schooling.

Pamela Shepherd encountered the Salvation Army, or the Christian Mission as it was then known, in 1867 and was eventually converted by the preaching of James Dowdle. Dubbed the 'Hallelujah Washerwoman' she was soon employed on mission business, giving her testimony around London. In 1868 she was employed for a time in the household of William and Catherine Booth, the mission's founders, and from 1869 she assisted at the mission's Limehouse centre, a converted music-hall renamed the Penny Gaff. It was around this time that she became known as Mother Shepherd, the title which would remain with her for the rest of her life. A dedicated and enthusiastic worker, she was appointed hallkeeper and cook at the mission's Whitechapel headquarters in 1876.

In 1878 Mother Shepherd, as a native speaker of Welsh, was sent to begin work in Aberdâr, Glamorgan; her two eldest daughters served as her assistants. The period from 1878 to 1883 was one of unprecedented growth for the Salvation Army, and during that time Shepherd opened seven new stations. About 1883 she retired from full-time evangelism, but was later recalled to London by Florence Booth to superintend one of the army's rescue homes. Around 1891 she was given charge of the new Cardiff rescue home (housed in a building donated by Richard Cory). Aged fifty-seven, she retired from the Salvation Army, but continued to play an active part in Aberdâr philanthropic and moral reform causes. She was for fourteen years (1893–1907) a police court missionary, and after the introduction of the Probation of Offenders Act in 1907 she became the first probation officer in her area. Mother Shepherd was the founder and head of two missions: Cwm (*c.*1894–1908) and Pentwyn Bach at Trecynon (1908–25), which became known as Mother Shepherd's Mission. She died at her home, The Nook, at 7 East Avenue, Aberdâr, on 24 February 1930, and was buried on St David's day in Aberdâr old cemetery. She was accorded a public funeral, with members of the south Wales constabulary as her pallbearers, and Salvation Army officers and eminent Aberdâr ministers conducting the services.

L. E. LAUER

Sources C. Preece, *Woman of the valleys* (1988) · Salvation Army International Heritage Centre, London, Mother Shepherd files [includes MS Life of Mother Shepherd; local news clippings] · 'Disposition of Officers', 1883, Salvation Army International Heritage Centre, London · *War Cry* (23 April 1887), 5–6 · *War Cry* (30 April 1887), 1–2 · G. Horridge, *The Salvation Army: origins and early days, 1865–1900* (1993) · R. Sandall, *History of the Salvation Army*, 2, 1878–1886 (1950), chap. 2 · *CGPLA Eng. & Wales* (1930) · private information (2004) [C. Preece] · *Aberdare and Mountain Ash Express* (1 March 1930), 10
Likenesses portrait, exh. 1930; formerly at Aberdâr (now lost) · photographs, Salvation Army International Heritage Centre, London
Wealth at death £150: probate, 15 Sept 1930, *CGPLA Eng. & Wales*

Shepherd, Richard (1731/2–1809), Church of England clergyman and theological writer, was baptized on 10 October 1732 at Mareham-le-Fen, Lincolnshire, the son of Henry Shepherd (*d.* 1764), vicar of that parish, and his wife, Susanna. He matriculated from Corpus Christi College, Oxford, on 1 December 1749 at the age of seventeen. He graduated BA (1753), MA (1757), BD (1765), and DD (1788), and was elected probationary fellow of his college in 1760. After considering a military career he took orders in the Church of England and eventually was appointed chaplain to Thomas Thurlow, bishop of Lincoln and later of Durham; Thurlow's nomination gained Shepherd the archdeaconry of Bedford in July 1783. He was elected a fellow of the Royal Society in May 1781, and in 1788 he was Bampton lecturer at Oxford. In 1792 he was instituted to the rectory of Wetherden and Helmingham in Suffolk by Lord Chancellor Thurlow, brother of the bishop, and he held these preferments until his death.

Shepherd published a wide selection of writings, including poetry and drama, although he came to concentrate on theology. His poetry was not unsuccessful: his *Ode to Love* (1755?) was reprinted in 1760 and *The Nuptials* (1761) went into three editions. Most of his poetic and dramatic pieces were included in the two-volume *Miscellanies* (1776). Several of Shepherd's theological works went into two or more editions, including his response to Soame Jenyns in *The Review of a Free Enquiry* (1759), *The Requisition of Subscription to the Thirty-Nine Articles* (1771), and *Reflections on the Doctrine of Materialism* (1779), addressed to Joseph Priestley. Shepherd published regularly throughout his life; his last piece was *No False Alarm, or, A Sequel to Religious Union* (1808). He died at the parsonage at Wetherden on 3 January 1809. No details are known of his wife, with whom he had a son, Henry, born in 1792.

W. P. COURTNEY, *rev.* EMMA MAJOR

Sources Foster, *Alum. Oxon.* · *GM*, 1st ser., 79 (1809), 91–2 · *ESTC* · Allibone, *Dict.* · Nichols, *Lit. anecdotes*, 2.328–9, 361 · *IGI*
Archives NRA, corresp. with Sir Joseph Banks

Shepherd, Richard Herne (1840–1895), bibliographer, born at 20 Marlborough Square, Chelsea, on 5 April 1840, was a younger son of Samuel Shepherd FSA (1798/9–1856), and his wife, Ann, *née* Dyer. His grandfather Richard Herne Shepherd (1775–1850) was from 1818 to 1848 a well-known revivalist preacher at the Ranelagh Chapel, Chelsea, and published, besides sermons and devotional works, a volume of verse entitled *Gatherings of Fifty Years* (1843).

The younger Richard was educated largely at home, developed a taste for literature, and in 1858 published verses entitled *Annus moriens*. In 1861 he issued an essay on *The School of Pantagruel*, in which he traced 'Pantagruelism' in England from the earl of Rochester to Laurence Sterne. Subsequently he edited booksellers' editions of the classics, including Blake's *Poems* (1868 and 1874), Shelley's *Poems* (1871), Charles Lamb's *Poetry for Children* (1872 and 1878), Chapman's *Works* (1873), Lamb's *Works* (1875), Ebenezer Jones's *Poems* (1879), Poe's *Works* (1884), Dickens's *Speeches* (1870), Dickens's *Plays and Poems* (1885), and Shelley's *Prose Works* (1888). In 1869 he published *Translations from C. Baudelaire with a Few Original Poems* (reissued 1879); in 1873 he printed, with notes, Coleridge's forgotten *Osorio: a Tragedy*, and in 1875 'The Lover's Tale' (of 1833) and other early uncollected poems of Tennyson, unearthed from albums and periodicals. Fifty copies were privately printed in 1875, but the volume was suppressed by injunction in the court of chancery. In 1878 he published Elizabeth Barrett Browning's *Earlier Poems* without the assent of the writer's living representatives, who warmly resented his action. Continuing his career as a snapper-up of unconsidered trifles, he prepared editions in the same year of the juvenilia of H. W. Longfellow and Moore; and *Sultan Stork*, a volume of early pieces by W. M. Thackeray, in 1887. In 1878 there also appeared an agreeable confection of biographical and bibliographical gossip in his *Waltoniana*. The following year Shepherd obtained £150 damages from the *Athenaeum* newspaper for an 'injurious review' of his revised edition of Lamb's *Poetry for Children*. In 1881 he published a dull *Memoir of the Life and Writings of Thomas Carlyle*, some passages of which had to be cancelled.

Meanwhile Shepherd studied modern bibliography, preparing bibliographical accounts of Ruskin (1879), Dickens (1880; rev. edn, 1885), Thackeray (1881; rev. 1887 and appended to *Sultan Stork*), Carlyle (1881), Swinburne (1883, 1884, and 1887), and Tennyson; the last-named was published posthumously in 1896, as an expansion of Shepherd's earlier *Tennysoniana* (1866, and 1879). Some of these works were published by Shepherd's brother, who, under the name of Frank Hollings, ran a bookshop in Holborn.

Shepherd was a heavy drinker and lived for many years at the Bald-faced Stag, an inn in Putney. A vivid impression of him is given by W. Partington, who described him as:

a tall angular man, often shabbily dressed, with shoulders rounded from long nights of poring over books. He was

remarkable for the possession of a most beautiful voice and gentle manners. One of his idiosyncrasies was his persistence in walking always in the middle of the street—in defiance of the shouting and gesticulating jehus of London's cabs … (Partington, 200)

Shepherd died in Camberwell House Lunatic Asylum, London, on 15 July 1895. At the time of his death he was preparing a bibliography of Coleridge for *Notes and Queries*, to which he was a frequent contributor.

Shepherd's editorial work was extensive but more notable for dogged perseverance than discrimination. However, he never descended to forgery as was falsely alleged, long after his death, by T. J. Wise.   J. F. R. COLLINS

Sources W. Partington, *Thomas J. Wise in the original cloth* (1946) · W. D. Paden, 'Tennyson's *The lover's tale*', *Studies in Bibliography*, 18 (1965), 111–45 · R. Shepherd and S. Shepherd, *Memoir of the Rev. Richard Herne Shepherd* (1854) · 'Preface', R. H. Shepherd, *The bibliography of Tennyson* (1896) · *The Times* (30 July 1895) · b. cert. · d. cert.

Shepherd, Sir Samuel (1760–1840), lawyer and politician, was born on 6 April 1760, the son of Henry Shepherd, a jeweller and toy maker of 85 Cornhill, London, a friend of Garrick, and a dabbler in poetry. Shepherd attended the Merchant Taylors' School, London, from 1773 to 1774, and was then at a school at Chiswick, probably that of Dr William Rose. In July 1776 he was entered at the Inner Temple, where he became pupil of Serjeant Charles *Runnington, who married his sister Anna Maria in 1777. On 23 November 1781 he was called to the bar. On 1 January 1783 he married Elizabeth White (*d.* 1833), daughter of John White of Hick's Hall, St Sepulchre, Middlesex, who was pronounced 'fine and figety' by Sir Walter Scott.

Shepherd went the home circuit, and soon acquired a considerable practice both on circuit and in the court of common pleas. He earned the praise of lords Mansfield and Kenyon. Thomas Erskine became his travelling companion during the vacations. From about 1790 he began to suffer from progressive deafness. In 1793 he declined the dignity of king's counsel, but he was created serjeant-at-law in Easter term 1796, and in the following Trinity term became king's serjeant. On the death of Serjeant Cockell he rose to be king's ancient serjeant.

As regent, the prince of Wales made Shepherd his solicitor-general in June 1812, and in December 1813 he was appointed solicitor-general to the crown following a warm recommendation from Lord Ellenborough. He was knighted on 11 May 1814, and in the spring of 1817 was made attorney-general. From 11 April 1814 to June 1819 he sat for Dorchester in parliament, where he was effective in the transaction of legal business on behalf of Lord Liverpool's administration, and in rebuffing opposition attacks. In the law courts his chief cases were the prosecution of the radical publishers James Watson (in June 1817) and Richard Carlile, the latter for publishing Paine's *Age of Reason*.

By common consent Shepherd was a sound lawyer, who but for his deafness would have risen higher in his profession. He refused the two offices of chief justice of the king's bench and of the common pleas in 1818, partly owing to his deafness, and partly because he had made up

Sir Samuel Shepherd (1760–1840), by Sir Thomas Lawrence, c.1795

his mind not to accept a judicial office that involved the trial of prisoners. The objection did not apply to the post of lord chief baron of the court of exchequer in Scotland, which he held from June 1819 to February 1830. While in Scotland he sat on the bench with Scottish judges to assist them with the application of English law in treason trials arising out of the radical insurrection there in 1820. He was raised to the privy council on 23 July 1819.

After suffering some initial suspicions from Scottish lawyers, Shepherd became popular in Edinburgh society, and was a close friend of Sir Walter Scott, who said of him:

> There is a neatness and precision, a closeness and truth in the tone of his conversation, which shows perfect good humour … with a little warmth of temper on suitable occasions. His great deafness alone prevented him from being Lord Chief Justice. I never saw a man so patient under such a malady. (Lockhart, 8.152)

With his friend William Adam, lord chief commissioner of the jury court, Shepherd presented in 1834 to the Bannatyne Club, of which they were members, a volume of the ragman rolls (1291–6). Shepherd was also a member of the Blair-Adam Club, of which William Adam and Sir Walter Scott were leaders, and joined in the club's annual excursions. Scott once commented that Shepherd had 'too much English fidgettiness about him for rocks and precipices perpetually afraid that rocks would give way under his weight' (*Letters*, 6.466).

Ill health forced Shepherd to resign his post in 1830, when he retired, amid his own regrets and those of his Edinburgh friends, to a cottage at Streatley in Berkshire,

where he owned a small property. For the last three years of his life he was blind. He died at Streatley on 3 November 1840, and was buried in the churchyard there, where a monument was erected to his memory.

Shepherd's widow died at Hyde Park Terrace, London, on 24 March 1833, aged seventy-four. Their son Henry John Shepherd (1783?–1855), bencher of Lincoln's Inn (KC 1834), recorder of Abingdon, and commissioner of bankrupts, was author of *A Summary of the Law Relating to the Election of Members of Parliament* (1825; 3rd edn, 1836) and of *Pedro of Castile*, a poem (1838). He died at Caversham, near Reading, on 21 May 1845 (*GM*, 2nd ser., 44, 1855, 108). His wife, whom he married on 11 April 1808, was Lady Mary (1777–1847), the second daughter of Neil Primrose, third earl of Rosebery, and the author of three philosophical treatises [*see* Shepherd, Lady Mary (1777–1847)]. Sir Samuel's niece Sarah Garay Thomas was the first wife of his intimate friend John Singleton Copley (afterwards Lord Lyndhurst). W. P. COURTNEY, *rev.* ROBERT SHIELS

Sources R. G. Thorne, 'Shepherd, Samuel', HoP, *Commons, 1790–1820* · P. B. Ellis and S. Mac A'Ghobhainn, *The Scottish insurrection of 1820* (1970) · H. Shepherd, *Law Magazine*, 25 (1841), 289–310 · J. G. Lockhart, *The life of Sir Walter Scott*, [new edn], 10 vols. (1902) · *The letters of Sir Walter Scott*, ed. H. J. C. Grierson and others, centenary edn, 12 vols. (1932–79) · *GM*, 1st ser., 103/1 (1833), 378 · *GM*, 2nd ser., 15 (1841), 315 · H. W. Woolrych, *Lives of eminent serjeants-at-law of the English bar*, 2 vols. (1869)
Archives NA Canada, family corresp. | NA Scot., letters to Lord Melville
Likenesses T. Lawrence, painting, c.1795; Sothebys, 13 April 1994, lot 75 [*see illus.*] · portrait, pubd 1812 · J. R. Jackson, mezzotint, pubd 1846 (after T. Lawrence), BM, NPG · wax medallion, Scot. NPG

Shepherd, Thomas (*fl.* 1677–1694), merchant and conspirator, was active in the City of London from at least 1677. Nothing is known of Shepherd's origins or family. A liveryman of the Mercers' Company, he imported wine from Portugal and the Canary Islands, and linen and whale products from Hamburg.

Shepherd was an Independent in religion, probably a follower of the Independent divine Robert Ferguson. His signature on the May 1679 London petition on behalf of a protestant succession appeared adjacent to those of fellow Independent merchants George Boddington and Edward Bushell. By 1680–81 he was 'looked upon as a man of the greatest interest in the City' (*CSP dom., July–Sept 1683*, 327). His substantial residence in London's Abchurch Lane was a frequent whig meeting-place, and he also possessed a country seat at Bromley. Shepherd served on the common council for Candlewick ward in 1681, and in May of that year he offered to serve as sheriff of London and Middlesex. When the civic electorate chose other whig sheriffs for 1681–2, Shepherd was instead elected city bridgemaster. He was impanelled with whig colleagues for the London grand jury in August 1681, and he served on the special jury that rejected the government's treason case against the earl of Shaftesbury in November of that year.

When Shaftesbury and other leading whigs plotted

against Charles II in autumn 1682, they turned to Shepherd as their principal city agent. He may have been a relative of the earl's gentleman servant, Anthony Shepherd. He helped Shaftesbury find secret lodging when the earl went underground, and he was regarded as 'the only honest man in London to be entrusted with a bank of money' to finance a rebellion (*CSP dom.*, *1683–4*, 227). A critical meeting of the duke of Monmouth, Lord William Russell, Ford, Lord Grey, Sir Thomas Armstrong, Colonel John Rumsey, and Robert Ferguson took place at Shepherd's city house in early November 1682. According to Grey and Ferguson, those in attendance agreed to stage an insurrection on 19 November to check what they perceived as a drift towards arbitrary rule. Grey recalled that Shepherd was helpful in identifying places in the city that would need to be secured. During the evening Alderman Henry Cornish, a cloth factor with whom Shepherd regularly did business, made a brief appearance. These plans for revolt came to nothing, however, when a second gathering at Shepherd's house concluded that preparations could not be completed in time.

Shepherd remained a pivotal figure in the plotting that continued on the margins of the London whig movement until June 1683. He was in touch with Algernon Sidney and a group of whig grandees who conspired against Charles, beginning in January 1683. After receiving a letter from Shepherd, Robert Ferguson, who had fled with Shaftesbury to the Netherlands, returned to England and to plotting. Shepherd was intimate with attorney Robert West's conspiratorial cabal: they divulged to him their plan to assassinate Charles at the Rye House in Hertfordshire. Shepherd claimed to have discouraged this design out of respect for Monmouth, who may have desired the throne, but who did not desire his father's death. Shepherd also acted as intermediary between Monmouth and a group of disaffected Scotsmen, including the earl of Argyll, who hoped to organize a Scottish rebellion. They intended to lodge their funds with Shepherd, but Shepherd later denied having received any money from them. Lord Grey, on the other hand, subsequently suggested that Shepherd had received money from Russell that was intended for Argyll. Indeed, Grey thought Shepherd had raised money from Cornish and other citizens by threatening to accuse them unless they contributed.

After the disclosure of whig plotting to the government, Shepherd surrendered. He utilized his loyalist kinsman Sir Nathaniel Johnson to intercede for a pardon in exchange for his testimony, said to have been 'the most particular account' among the early confessions (*CSP dom.*, *Jan–June 1683*, 348). Shepherd gave evidence about Lord Russell's presence at his house during the plotting of November 1682. As a business acquaintance of Algernon Sidney, he was called upon to verify that the manuscript of the *Discourses Concerning Government* was in Sidney's hand. He also provided a deposition for the Scottish trial of Robert Baillie of Jerviswood.

Contemporary characterizations of Shepherd's role in the whig treason trials differ. Gilbert Burnet was highly critical of Shepherd's testimony about Lord Russell, and

Colonel Thomas Walcott blamed his capture and death on Shepherd. Roger North remembered that Shepherd had been rebuffed by Charles II in offering to spy on his former associates on condition that his co-operation with the government was kept secret (North, 383). On the other hand, Lord Grey, who may have been involved in a plan to silence Shepherd by having him murdered, also credited Shepherd with not fully divulging evidence against 'several of our best and ablest friends' (Grey, 74). In fact, the government suspected that Shepherd had not been fully forthcoming. He appeared on behalf of Henry Cornish in the alderman's 1685 trial and insisted, despite close questioning, that Cornish had been unaware of the plotting underway during his visit to Shepherd's house in November 1682.

Shepherd continued to trade after the whig treason trials, but he was much less visible in the city. He was confined with other leading London whigs and dissenters at the time of Monmouth's rebellion, but quickly released upon the order of James II. In 1689 he was among those London citizens who lent money to William of Orange, both before and after William's elevation to the English throne. He was probably the Thomas Shepherd who purchased £2000 of the original stock of the Bank of England in 1694 and who also owned some £4000 of East India Company stock. Shepherd is untraceable thereafter.

GARY S. DE KREY

Sources *CSP dom.*, *1680–81*, 328; *Jan–June 1683*, 13, 24, 347–8, 387; *1683*, 79, 128, 141, 145, 154, 164, 191, 214, 274, 327, 331, 337, 439; *1683–4*, 49, 163–4, 225–8, 257; *1684–5*, 48–9, 147–8 · [T. Sprat], *Copies of the informations and original papers relating to the proof of the horrid conspiracy against the late king, his present majesty and the government* (1685), 9–10, 17–18, 35, 41, 126, 131–3 · *State trials*, 9.372–4, 380–81, 397, 404, 484, 488–90, 600–01, 854; 10.686–701; 11.424, 442–8 · J. R. Woodhead, *The rulers of London, 1660–1689* (1965), 147 · R. L. Greaves, *Secrets of the kingdom: British radicals from the Popish Plot to the revolution of 1688–89* (1992), 112, 120–21, 123–4, 139–44, 162, 165, 167, 214–15, 247, 249, 254, 382n. · PRO, E190/102/1; E190/114/4; E190/131/1; E190/134/1; E190/142/1 · PRO, SP 29/417/112–14 · Ford, Lord Grey, *The secret history of the Rye-House plot: and of Monmouth's rebellion* (1754), 36, 43, 46, 73–5 · R. Ferguson, 'Concerning the Rye House business', in J. Ferguson, *Robert Ferguson the plotter: the secret of the Rye House conspiracy and the story of a strange career* (1887), 407–37, 427, 429, 431 · BL, Lansdowne MS 1152A, esp. fols. 247–8 · R. North, *Examen, or, An enquiry into the credit and veracity of a pretended complete history* (1740), 383 · Corporation of London Record Office, Alchin B/33/15 · Corporation of London Record Office, MS 40/35, 40/36 · *Burnet's History of my own time*, ed. O. Airy, new edn, 2 (1900), 350, 373 · T. Sprat, *A true account and declaration of the horrid conspiracy against the late king* (1685), 23, 36, 39, 78, 79–80, 113–14, 121–3, 131 · 26 May 1861, L. Cong., manuscript division, London newsletters collection, viii.196 · BL OIOC, Home Miscellaneous Series, vol. 2 · *The last speech and behaviour of William late Lord Russel* (1683), 3 · *The speeches of Captain Walcot, J. Rouse, and W. Hone* [1683], 3 · *A list of the names of all the subscribers to the Bank of England* [n.d., c.1694] · W. A. Shaw, ed., *Calendar of treasury books*, 9, PRO (1931), 1883 · [S. Lee], *A collection of the names of the merchants living in and about the City of London* (1677); repr. as *The London directory of 1677* (1878) [unpaginated, G7] · R. Ashcraft, *Revolutionary politics and Locke's two treatises of government* (1986), 356–8, 364–5 · J. Scott, *Algernon Sidney and the Restoration crisis, 1677–1683* (1991), 227, 297, 302, 304, 311, 313 · L. G. Schwoerer, *Lady Rachel Russell: 'One of the best of women'* (1988), 117 · G. Hampson, 'Johnson, Nathaniel', HoP, *Commons, 1660–90*, 2.655–6

Shepherd, Thomas Hosmer (1793–1864). *See under* Shepherd, George Sidney (1784–1862).

Shepherd, William (1768–1847), Unitarian minister and politician, was born in Liverpool on 11 October 1768, the son of William Shepherd (*d.* 1772), master cordwainer, and his wife, Elizabeth (*d.* 1787), daughter of Benjamin Mather (*d.* 1749), dissenting minister of Over Darwen. The older William Shepherd, a burgess and active politician, died in 1772. Elizabeth Shepherd's brother, Tatlock Mather (*d.* 1785), minister of a Unitarian congregation at Rainford, near Prescot, took over responsibility for the impoverished family. William was educated at Holden's academy near Rainford from 1776 to 1782, by the Revd Philip Holland (1721–1789) in Bolton in 1782–5, at the dissenting academy at Daventry from 1785 to 1788 under Thomas Belsham (1750–1829), and at New College, Hackney, from 1788 to 1790 under Belsham, Andrew Kippis (1725–1795), and Richard Price (1723–1791).

In 1790 Shepherd became tutor to the sons of the wealthy Revd John Yates (1755–1826) of Toxteth Park Chapel, Liverpool, and there made the acquaintance of William Roscoe (1753–1831), who greatly influenced his tastes and character. In 1791 he became minister of the Unitarian chapel at Gateacre, near Liverpool, and the next year, on marrying Frances (*d.* 1829), daughter of Robert Nicholson, merchant of Liverpool, moved to the old parsonage, The Nook, at Gateacre. There were no children. Shepherd opened a very successful school; some sense of the substance and method of his teaching can be gathered from *Systematic Education*, which he published in 1815 with two other prominent Unitarians, Lant Carpenter (1780–1840) and Jeremiah Joyce (1763–1816); it is a compendium of principles derived ultimately from David Hartley (1705–1757) and Joseph Priestley (1733–1804).

An enthusiast for civil and religious liberty, Shepherd went to London in May 1794 to visit Joyce, a friend from his years in Hackney, who had been committed to the Tower on a charge of treason. Five years later, when the Revd Gilbert Wakefield (1756–1801) was sentenced to two years' imprisonment, Shepherd visited him in Dorchester gaol and took charge of his son and eldest daughter. On 27 May 1796 he became a Liverpool burgess by inheritance; an eloquent speaker, he took an active part in municipal affairs as an advanced liberal. Although he had been critical of the *Edinburgh Review* in its early years, he became a close friend of one of its founders, the first Lord Brougham (1778–1868), and the extensive political correspondence between them is of considerable importance.

Meanwhile, Shepherd devoted himself to writing. His interest in Italian literature, aroused by Roscoe, led in 1803 to a *Life of Poggio Bracciolini*, which was well received and translated into French, German, and Italian. In 1807 he edited for private circulation Bracciolini's *Dialogus an seni sit uxor ducenda*. The published letters of his two visits to Paris in 1802 and 1814 are of interest, and a volume of original and translated poems appeared in 1829. On 10 July 1834 the University of Edinburgh conferred on him the degree of LLD. His pedagogical, political, and literary activity led to comparative neglect of the pulpit; he wrote few new sermons, choosing rather to preach those of others, with repetitions sufficiently well spaced to allow for congregational forgetfulness.

In 1801 Thomas De Quincey (1785–1859), then sixteen, was befriended by the Liverpool circle of whom Shepherd, Roscoe, and Dr James Currie (1756–1805), physician and editor of Robert Burns, were the most prominent members. A quarter of a century later, De Quincey contemptuously dismissed their literary accomplishments and their pretension (*Tait's Edinburgh Magazine*, 4, 1837, 70–73). While recognizing Shepherd's uprightness and patriotism, De Quincey deplored his 'coarseness' and his disrespectful wit, presumably shown in the attacks De Quincey remembered on Anglican churchmen and on Hannah More. Shepherd replied pointedly and with dignity (*Tait's*, 340) to this cruel elaboration of an old memory, which had given much offence in Liverpool. But, allowing for youthful priggishness, De Quincey's observations were not entirely without foundation. Shepherd had a rollicking sense of humour, which was readily turned on people and political positions he detested. Moreover, he had little sympathy for fashionable currents of thought towards the end of his long life: in 1834, in a letter to Brougham (10 Aug 1834; University College, London, Brougham MS 14831) he noted that 'that useless proser Coleridge is gathered to his fathers'; the young Coleridge had, of course, been an enthusiastic Unitarian, and the later Coleridge was simply incomprehensible to him.

After Frances Shepherd's death on 17 November 1829, the management of his household passed to his adopted child, Hannah, the youngest daughter of his old friend Jeremiah Joyce. Shepherd died at Gateacre on 21 July 1847, and was interred in the burial-ground of the chapel. His fine library was sold in Liverpool in December 1848. A marble tablet in the chapel, with an inscription by Lord Brougham, was erected in 1850, and is surmounted by a marble bust by Isaac Jackson of Liverpool.

ALBERT NICHOLSON, *rev.* R. K. WEBB

Sources F. Nicholson, *Memorials of the family of Nicholson*, ed. E. Axon (1928), 109–29 · H. Joyce, *Early letters of the Rev. William Shepherd* (privately printed) · *The Inquirer* (7 Aug 1847) · T. De Quincey, 'Autobiography of an English opium-eater', *Tait's Edinburgh Magazine*, new ser., 4 (1837), 70–73 · W. Shepherd, *Tait's Edinburgh Magazine*, new ser., 4 (1837), 337–40 · W. Shepherd, letter to Lord Brougham, 10 Aug 1834, UCL, Brougham MS 14831
Archives Cumbria AS, Barrow, journal of tour of the Lakes · DWL, student essays · Harris Man. Oxf., family and personal corresp. and papers · JRL, corresp. and papers | BL, letters to Sir A. Panizzi, Add. MSS 36714–36715, *passim* · UCL, letters to Society for the Diffusion of Useful Knowledge
Likenesses R. W. Sievier, stipple, pubd 1817 (after M. Haughton), NPG · J. Dickson, lithograph, pubd 1841, BM, NPG · I. Jackson, marble bust on memorial, 1850, Gateacre chapel, Liverpool · T. H. Illidge, oils, Walker Art Gallery, Liverpool · J. Thomson, stipple, BM, NPG; repro. in *Imperial Magazine* (1821)

Sheppard, Elizabeth Sara (1830–1862), novelist, was born in Blackheath, Kent, the daughter of John Sheppard, a graduate of St John's College, Oxford, and a Church of England clergyman who was of Jewish descent on his mother's side. Her father died young, without leaving provision for his family; upon his death, her mother opened a school. An accomplished linguist in Greek, Latin, Hebrew, French, and German, Sheppard was also a capable musician, and taught music in her mother's school.

At the age of sixteen Sheppard began her first novel, *Charles Auchester*. She sent the manuscript to Benjamin Disraeli, who forwarded it to his publisher and wrote to Sheppard: 'No greater book will ever be written upon music, and it will one day be recognised as the imaginative classic of that divine art' (*Atlantic Monthly*, Oct 1862, 499). It was published anonymously in 1853 in three volumes, with a dedication to the author of *Contarini Fleming*. Like Disraeli, Sheppard used real people as characters in her novels. In *Charles Auchester* Seraphael is supposed to be a portrait of Felix Mendelssohn. Another novel, *Counterparts, or, The Cross of Love*, published in three volumes in 1854, was dedicated to Mrs Disraeli. A second edition appeared in 1866.

Sheppard published three more novels, some poetry, and two collections of children's stories. She is said to have sometimes used the pseudonym E. Berger, a French rendering of her own surname. Critical response to her work was mixed; *The Athenaeum* described *Charles Auchester* as 'displaying … a passion for music rather than a knowledge of it', though acknowledging the 'spirit and eloquence' of her first two novels (Allibone, *Dict.*, 2075). Sheppard died, unmarried, in Brixton, London, on 13 March 1862.   ELIZABETH LEE, *rev.* MEGAN A. STEPHAN

Sources Allibone, *Dict.* · Blain, Clements & Grundy, *Feminist comp.* · J. A. Middleton, 'Introduction', in E. S. Sheppard, *Charles Auchester* (1911) · Foster, *Alum. Oxon.*

Sheppard, Sir Fleetwood

Sheppard, Sir Fleetwood (1634–1698), courtier and poet, born on 1 January 1634 and baptized on 20 January at Great Rollright, near Chipping Norton, Oxfordshire, was the second son of William Sheppard, esquire, of Great Rollright, and Maria (or Mary) Dormer, daughter of Sir Fleetwood Dormer of Grange, Buckinghamshire. His father (the son of William Sheppard and Dorothy Osborne, sister of Sir John Osborne, remembrancer of the exchequer) was in 1644 'slain by one of the king's soldiers', as the parish register has it. He was buried at Great Rollright on 2 October 1644, leaving his wife with seven children. She died in January 1647.

Fleetwood Sheppard matriculated at Oxford on 19 November 1650, and entered as a commoner at Magdalen Hall, but soon after migrated to Christ Church, where he was nominated to a studentship (fellowship), probably through the interest of the Carnarvon family, to whom he was doubly related: his mother's brother, Peter Dormer, married his father's sister, Ann Sheppard, on 17 May 1637.

Sheppard graduated BA on 10 May 1654, MA on 11 June 1657, and entered as a student at Gray's Inn on 14 October 1657, but seems not to have stood for the bar. At Christ Church Sheppard delivered a Latin oration in the divinity school on 27 July 1663 at the funeral of William Creed, regius professor of divinity. He was also said to be able to 'read Hebrew without the pricks' (Rymer, 142). In 1664, when all members of the chapter were required to be in

Sir Fleetwood Sheppard (1634–1698), attrib. Sir Godfrey Kneller, *c.*1694

full orders, the king instructed Henry Aldrich, dean of Christ Church, that 'Fleetwood Shepherd M.A. … has studied civil law, and is therefore not prepared to take orders, he being a person of much ability' (*CSP dom.*, 1664–5, 111).

Courtier 'After his majesty's restoration', Wood says, Sheppard 'retir'd to London, hang'd on the court, became a debauchee and atheist, a grand companion with Charles lord Buckhurst, afterwards earl of Dorset, Henry Savile, and others' (Wood, *Ath. Oxon.*, 4.627). Offsetting Wood's dyspeptic account there is a letter of recommendation from Ralph Montagu, ambassador to France, to secretary Sir Henry Bennet written before 25 April 1669:

> He is as witty and ingenious [a] man as ever I met with, and may be made very good use of [in the foreign service]. He is an excellent scholar; he left the University because he was too honest to be a divine. He is very modest, and so not likely to be troublesome to your Lordship.   (*Buccleuch MSS*, 1.421)

'The others' at court to whom Buckhurst introduced Sheppard were his sometime mistress, Nell Gwyn,

> Henry Killigrew … gro[o]me of the bed-chamber, Henry Savile sometime one of the gro[o]mes of the duke of York's bed-chamber, Hen. Guy cupbearer to his majesty, Baptist May keeper of the privy purse … Joh. Wilmot earl of Rochester, Joh. [Sheffield] earl of Mulgrave &c. All which were the king's companions at most suppers in the week, an[no] 1676, [16]77.

Sheppard soon 'became one of [the king's] companions in private to make him merry' (Wood, *Ath. Oxon.*, 4.627).

When Nell Gwyn's first child by the king, Charles Beauclerk, later duke of St Albans, was born in May 1670, Sheppard is said to have been appointed 'steward' of her household, managing her financial affairs and eventually tutoring her son. This claim, however, is not confirmed by other sources. What is certain is that on 16 October 1678 'Nell Gwyn with Fleetw. Shepard were entertained by certain scholars at Cambridge … and had verses presented to her' (*Life and Times of Anthony Wood*, 2.420).

Sheppard's familiarity with Charles II inevitably exposed him to such scurrilities as 'the best of all *Pimps*' (*Poems on Affairs of State*, 5.403) and 'less wit than clown' (Wilson, 94). But his rewards were modest: grants of £200 from the privy purse in 1680 and 1681.

Buckhurst, who succeeded as sixth earl of Dorset in December 1677, proved to be a more rewarding and more durable friend. In 1675–7 he would go to Great Rollright when Sheppard visited his brother, William Sheppard, who had inherited the estate. In September 1680 they travelled to Paris together to visit Henry Savile, now English ambassador (*CSP dom.*, 1680–81, 431). Sheppard's imaginative neighbour at Great Rollright, Ralph Sheldon of Weston, assured Anthony Wood that they entertained themselves 'talking blasphemy and atheisme, drinking, and perhaps that which is worse'. Wood also heard that 'Sheppard was either hanged or broke upon the wheele at Parys for some roguery that he had committed' (*Life and Times of Anthony Wood*, 2.359, 360). In earlier mishaps Sheppard was

> overturned in a coach att Matt Clifford's funerall and broake his head, and a little before was runn with a sword under the eye endeavouring to part [Henry] Bu[lkele]y [master of the King's household] and [George] Etheridge [the dramatist] squabbling in a Taverne. (*Bath MSS*, 2.160)

In the next reign, since James II could not conceal his dislike of him, Sheppard retired to Copt Hall, Dorset's estate in Epping Forest, north of London. After the revolution, however, Sheppard was returned to favour, or 'dwindled to flatter Dutchmen' (*Poems on Affairs of State*, 5.534), as one disgruntled tory put it. Promptly in 1689 William appointed Dorset chamberlain of the royal household (and a privy councillor *ex officio*), a post commanding vast patronage that Dorset voraciously exploited. Sheppard seems to have served Dorset much in the way that Jonathan Swift served Robert Harley, earl of Oxford—as dispenser of patronage. At least this is what Matthew Prior assumed when he asked Sheppard in 1689 to get him 'some little Place', like the laureateship, for which he had no pretensions whatever (*Literary Works of Matthew Prior*, 1.84). Dorset, however, was alleged to have 'Bequeath[ed] the Selling of Places to Shepherd' (BL, MS Harleian 7315, fol. 166v). Jonathan Swift said that 'Fleet. Shepherd … would often sell Places that were never in Being, and dispose of others … before they were vacant' (J. Swift, *A New Way of Selling Places at Court*, 1712, 5). One John Bearcroft, serjeant-at-arms to Charles II but now unemployed, petitioned the House of Commons on 2 June 1689 to require 'Fleet Sheppard [and others] … [to] give an Account of the many Thousand Guineas they have unjustly got from those now put in his Majesty's Service' (*JHC*, 10.192). No action was taken because the sale of offices was Dorset's perquisite as lord chamberlain of the household.

In 1690 Dorset appointed Sheppard a gentleman usher and daily waiter to the king, with lodgings in Whitehall Palace. Sheppard proved as successful in making 'The Queen … very merrey' (*Rutland MSS*, 2.137) as he had her uncle, Charles II. Indeed, it was not thought too much to say that he 'made himself and the World very merry' (Oldmixon, 72). On 26 April 1694 he was knighted and succeeded Sir Thomas Duppa as gentleman usher of the black rod, with responsibilities in the royal household, in the House of Lords, and in the Order of the Garter. In June 1696 Sheppard received his last post, keeper of his majesty's Little Park of Windsor. Prior's puzzling remark in a letter to Dorset of 12/22 June 1695, 'Sir Fleetwood … *went over to the other side*' (*Bath MSS*, 3.80), may be explained by the first of Tom Brown's *Letters from the Dead to the Living*, 'A letter of news from Mr. *Joseph Haines*, of merry memory, to his friends at Will's Coffee House in *Covent Garden*': 'Tony Lee [Anthony Leigh, another stage comedian] turn'd Presbyterian Parson upon his coming to these quarters … my Lord Warwick [a notorious Puritan] and Sir Fleetwood are his constant hearers' (Brown, 12).

In October 1696, after the House of Commons voted 'a Supply to be granted his Majesty, for carrying on the War against *France*' (*JHC*, 11.568), 'sir Fleetwood invited all the members to the kings cellar by his majesties command, where they drank the kings health' (Luttrell, 4.130).

Poet and critic Sheppard is said to have been the 'author of many poems' (Wood, *Ath. Oxon.*, 4.628), but since, like Rochester, he published none, only about fifteen have survived. These fifteen, however, spin a slender thread between the late metaphysicals and the early Augustans, between Andrew Marvell and Swift and Pope.

Sheppard began by translating Marvell's Latin verse into English, and ended by exchanging verse letters with Matthew Prior and subscribing to Dryden's translation of Virgil (1697). He witnessed three of the literary epiphanies of the late seventeenth century. He was there early in 1669 when Buckhurst bought from Thomas Helder's stall in Little Britain a remaindered copy of the first edition (1667) and 'discovered' *Paradise Lost*. In June 1675 an elaborate chronometer in the Privy Garden at Whitehall Palace was 'broken all to pieces (for they were of glass spheres) by the earl of Rochester, lord Buckhurst, Fleetwood Shephard, etc. coming in from their revells' (*Brief Lives*, 2.34). And although he is said to have known 'every tavern from Fish Street Hill to the Cockpit' (*Bath MSS*, 3.65), Sheppard's local was Arthur Prior's Rhenish wine house in Channel (later Cannon) Row. When Buckhurst came there looking for him, he found the proprietor's nephew, Matthew Prior, drawer and scullery boy, reading Horace at the bar and sent him back to school at Westminster under Richard Busby.

Sheppard's poems are satires, both social—'A description of a Hampton court life' (*Poems on Affairs of State*, 5.56), 'Upon an Old Affected Court Lady' (Buckingham, 182), and political—'Songs on the Duke of M[onmouth]' (Wilmot, 231), 'Epitaph on the French King' (*Literary Works of Matthew Prior*, 2.848) (Louis XIV was cut for an anal fistula in 1697 and declared 'past recovery' on 18 June 1698), 'The true and genuine explanation of one of King James's explanations' (1692) (Oldmixon, 72).

Since a satire, unlike a comedy, has no predetermined shape, it may take its shape from a dazzling array of subgenres. Sheppard adopted many of the same that Swift used later, such as: mock prophecy—'A prophecy, found under the foundation of Wallingford Chappel, ingraven in lead, discovered the 2nd of June 1694 and sent to the Lord Mayor by Thomas Povey to proclaime a fast immediately from four a clock to six a clock' (1694) (*Rutland MSS*, 2.326); mock petition—'The countess of Dorset's petition to the late Queen Mary for chocolate' (Harris, 154); mock epitaph—'An Epitaph on the d[uke] of G[rafton]' (1690) (*New Collection*, 272); and ballad—'The Ballad about the Person that was Kill'd at Newbury with Eating Custard' (*Remarks*, 5.105). Alexander Pope did not hesitate to appropriate some of Sheppard's best lines: 'And all in order on her Toylet Lay/Pray'r-Books and Patch Box, Sermon-Notes and Paint' (Buckingham, 83; cf. *Twickenham Edition*, 2.155). Sheppard also wrote 'A true and full account of a late conference between the wonderful speaking head [Thomas Tenison, later archbishop of Canterbury], and Father Godwyn, as 'twas related by the head's own mouth to Dr. Frasier' (*c*.1681) (*Poems on Affairs of State*, 1716, 3.121), an anticlerical satire in the tradition of Marvell's 'Fleckno, an English Priest of Rome'.

Besides his reputation as a poet, Sheppard was highly regarded as a critic. Rochester was content to have him 'And some few more … / Approve my sense' (Wilmot, 101). Three contemporary critics dedicated books to Sheppard: Thomas Rymer, *The Tragedies of the Last Age Consider'd and Examin'd by the Practice of the Ancients* (1678 for 1677); John Dennis, *Poems in Burlesque* (1692); and Charles Gildon, *Chorus poetarum* (1694). An anonymous writer opposing Thomas Shadwell's candidacy for the laureateship in 1690 bids 'Sheppard, arise! … / Thou judge of wit! Is not poor Shadwell weak?' (*Poems on Affairs of State*, 5.111). And Prior, who had reservations about Sheppard's verse: 'too much into Romance and Improbability' (Prior, *Dialogues of the Dead*, 186), had no doubt that Sheppard was 'the Muses Friend' (*Literary Works of Matthew Prior*, 1.73): 'All who write would fain please Sheppard' (Dennis, sig. A4*r*).

The deaths of Sir Fleetwood Sheppard Sheppard's last and best joke may have been his death, unmarried and without children, in 1698. In September 1694 Godolphin was informed that Sheppard was dead. Sir Fleetwood was able to deny this report himself, while 'confessing that he was afflicted with the stone for the last 12 or 14 years' (Redington, 385). In December 1697 he was again reported to be 'dead or dying' (*CSP dom.*, 1697, 538), but on 4 January 1698 the report was denied: 'Sir Fletw. Shepherd has deceived us, and still lives' (*CSP dom.*, 1698, 12). On 14/24 April Prior wrote to Keppel from Paris, 'The prints say poor Sir Fleetwood is worse, for which I am extremely sorry' (*Bath MSS*, 3.208). On 25 August/4 September 1698 Prior learned that his old friend '(who had for some time been in effect dead) marched off yesterday morning' (ibid., 3.261). Sheppard actually died at Copt Hall on 25 August 1698, and was buried in the chancel of Great Rollright chapel on 6 September. But this was apparently yet another false alarm, for

seventy years later it was discovered that 'There is now living, at his seat in Essex, Sir Fleetwood Sheppard … in perfect health, though at the age of 120 years' (*Annual Register*, September 1768, 175).

Tom Brown claimed, in a mock epitaph, that Sheppard 'defuncti Venere et Baccho' ('died in the service of Bacchus and Venus'; *Remarks*, 1.319). But Sheppard is no etiolated Rochester. He is very much his own man, famous for not answering letters, for failing to show up, for not keeping promises, and for 'Voluble' lies (*New Collection*, 439). But what the surviving evidence reveals is honesty: 'one virtue which I feare I have lost forever', he told Dorset, 'is humility' (*Bath MSS*, 2.172). And honesty is the quality that resonates in the Latin epitaph that he wrote for himself '*in my Lord* Dorset'*s Common Prayer-Book at* Copt-Hall' (*GM*, 600):

> O you who are sure of your salvation,
> pray for the soul
> of the abandoned sinner
> Fleetwood Shepheard,
> still among the living, and sinning wherever he find himself.
> Of meagre faith yet of hope unabashed,
> he wishes and awaits—without having earned it—a happy
>   resurrection.
> In the third year of the restoration of our religion and our
>   liberty,
> under the governance
> of William most brave and Mary most fair.
> (*Remarks*, 1.319, trans. M. Skulsky)

FRANK H. ELLIS

Sources *Calendar of the manuscripts of the marquis of Bath preserved at Longleat, Wiltshire*, 5 vols., HMC, 58 (1904–80) · Wood, *Ath. Oxon.*, new edn · N. Luttrell, *A brief historical relation of state affairs from September 1678 to April 1714*, 6 vols. (1857) · G. de F. Lord and others, eds., *Poems on affairs of state: Augustan satirical verse, 1660–1714*, 7 vols. (1963–75), vol. 5 · Foster, *Alum. Oxon.* · *The life and times of Anthony Wood*, ed. A. Clark, 5 vols., OHS, 19, 21, 26, 30, 40 (1891–1900) · *A new collection of poems relating to state affairs … by the greatest wits of the age* (1705) · *Remarks and collections of Thomas Hearne*, ed. C. E. Doble and others, 11 vols., OHS, 2, 7, 13, 34, 42–3, 48, 50, 65, 67, 72 (1885–1921) · *The literary works of Matthew Prior*, ed. H. B. Wright and M. K. Spears, 2 vols. (1959) · *GM*, 1st ser., 48 (1778) · B. Harris, *Charles Sackville, sixth earl of Dorset: patron and poet of the Restoration* (1940) · J. Oldmixon, *The history of England, during the reigns of King William and Queen Mary, Queen Anne, King George I* (1735) · G. Villiers, second duke of Buckingham, *Miscellaneous works* (1704) · *JHC*, 10–11 (1688–97) · *The manuscripts of his grace the duke of Rutland*, 4 vols., HMC, 24 (1888–1905) · *DNB* · J. Foster, *Men-at-the-bar: a biographical hand-list of the members of the various inns of court*, 2nd edn (1885) · T. Rymer, *The tragedies of the last age consider'd* (1678) · *CSP dom.*, 1660–1704 · *The manuscripts of his grace the duke of Buccleuch and Queensberry … preserved at Drumlanrig Castle*, 2 vols., HMC, 44 (1897–1903) · J. H. Wilson, *Court satires of the Restoration* (1976) · J. Y. Akerman, ed., *Moneys received and paid for secret services of Charles II and James II from 30th March 1679 to 25th December 1688*, CS, 52 (1851) · *The manuscripts of the House of Lords*, 4 vols., HMC, 17 (1887–94) · *The manuscripts of the House of Lords*, new ser., 12 vols. (1900–77) · W. A. Shaw, ed., *Calendar of treasury books*, [33 vols. in 64], PRO (1904–69) · T. Brown, *Letters from the dead to the living* (1705) · C. Gildon, *Chorus poetarum* (1694) · D. Masson, *The life of John Milton*, 7 vols. (1859–94); rev. edn [vol. 1 only] (1881); repr. [7 vols.] (1965) · *Brief lives, chiefly of contemporaries, set down by John Aubrey, between the years 1669 and 1696*, ed. A. Clark, 2 vols. (1898) · B. Lillywhite, *London coffee houses* (1963) · M. Prior, *Selected poems*, ed. A. Dobson (1889) · *The Twickenham edition of the poems of Alexander Pope*, ed. J. Butt and others, 11 vols. in 12 (1939–69) · *Poems on affairs of state … by the greatest wits of the age*, 6th edn, 4 vols. (1716) ·

J. Wilmot, second earl of Rochester, *The complete works*, ed. F. H. Ellis (1994) · M. Prior, *Dialogues of the dead and other works in prose and verse*, ed. A. R. Waller (1907) · J. Dennis, *Poems in burlesque* (1692) · J. Redington, ed., *Calendar of Treasury papers*, 6 vols., PRO (1868–89) · *Annual Register* (1759–1954) · J. Prinz, *John Wilmot earl of Rochester: his life and writings* (1927)

Likenesses attrib. G. Kneller, oils, c.1694, Knole, Kent [*see illus.*]

Sheppard, Hugh Richard Lawrie (1880–1937), dean of Canterbury, was born at 2 The Cloisters, Windsor, on 2 September 1880, the younger son of Edgar Sheppard (1845–1921), later subdean of the chapels royal and canon of St George's, Windsor, and his wife, Mary (*d.* 1926), daughter of Richard White of Instow, Devon. He was known as Dick Sheppard. His school days at Marlborough College were unhappy. In 1900 he volunteered for service in the Second South African War, but an accident on the way to the station prevented this and lamed him for life. After Trinity Hall, Cambridge (1901–4), he lived at Oxford House, Bethnal Green, and worked among the poor. He felt called to the priesthood. A year as secretary to the bishop of Stepney, Cosmo Gordon Lang, strengthened the call and created a lifelong friendship between the two men. At Cuddesdon College the eucharist and prayer became central for him. Having been ordained deacon in 1907 and priest in 1908, he returned to Oxford House, first as chaplain, then as head. His sacrificial ministry there led in 1910 to his breakdown and resignation. 'It was the nearest approximation to the love of Christ that any of us are likely to see on this side of the grave', commented Alan Don, later dean of Westminster, one of his colleagues (Roberts, 59). Lang, now archbishop of York, came to his rescue, and appointed him his secretary again. In 1911 he became curate-in-charge of St Mary's, Bourdon Street, London, and in 1913 he moved to Grosvenor Chapel, South Audley Street.

In August 1914 Sheppard accepted the living of St Martin-in-the-Fields, Trafalgar Square, but took only a half stipend. Before his induction he spent three months as a chaplain to a military hospital in France. He so completely identified himself with every dying soldier that he became utterly exhausted and had to be sent home. The eleven people who came through the fog to his induction in November heard him describe his vision of what he wanted St Martin's to become: a place where all kinds of people could drop in at any hour of the day or night because they felt it to be their home, where the Lord's supper was daily on the altar. The vision revealed Sheppard's devotion to Jesus in the needy and that romantic idealism which drew many to him, but made him impatient with the routine and the institutional. He opened the church all night for servicemen. He created a hostel for the destitute and turned the crypt into an air raid shelter. He did away with reserved pews, instituted a daily eucharist and a sung eucharist on Sundays and started a more informal people's service on Sunday afternoons. In a pageant about St Martin, written by Laurence Housman, he characteristically played the beggar. In 1916 he became a chaplain to the king.

On 5 June 1915 Sheppard married Alison Lennox, only daughter of William Oswald Carver JP, of Cranage Hall, Holmes Chapel, Cheshire. It was his ill health which initially brought them together: she nursed him during the two breakdowns which resulted from his war experiences. Later it was his recurrent illnesses, caused or aggravated by his persistent overwork, which were a major factor in driving them apart. They had two daughters.

In 1917 Sheppard proposed to William Temple, then at St James's, Piccadilly, the creation of a 'ginger group' which became known as Life and Liberty. It aimed to renew the Church of England through reforms and more self-government. One of its results, the church assembly, depressed Sheppard by its introversion and churchiness. He passionately wanted the church to be in touch with ordinary people. The first ever broadcast religious service came from St Martin's at Epiphany 1924. Subsequent monthly broadcast services spread its fame and that of its vicar throughout the country. But another breakdown in health that summer and the onset of serious asthma led to prolonged absences and eventually to his resignation in September 1926. At the end of his tether with himself and the church, he wrote *The Impatience of a Parson* (1927). He argued that the churches had misunderstood Jesus and complicated something that was essentially simple. 'I can more easily see our Lord sweeping the streets of London than issuing edicts from its cathedral' (156). It sold 100,000 copies. He longed for a non-institutionalized church held together mainly by spontaneous love.

Sheppard was made CH in 1927. In 1928 Lang became archbishop of Canterbury. The next year Sheppard was appointed dean of Canterbury. Soon thousands were coming to hear him preach or at least to catch a glimpse of him. After only eighteen months he had to resign because of illness. Despite his declared antipathy to institutional religion he visited Chartres Cathedral annually for reflection and prayer and also grew to love Canterbury Cathedral very deeply. He used to enter it regularly during the night and the watchman often found him kneeling in silence at one of the altars.

Sheppard announced his conversion to pacifism in 1927, but he had realized in 1914 as a chaplain that he was expecting servicemen to do what he could not do himself. The proposal that unarmed men and women should stand between the Chinese and Japanese armies in Shanghai in 1932 under Sheppard's leadership proved impracticable. But on 16 October 1934 the press published a letter from Sheppard calling on men to send him a postcard pledging that they would renounce war. At least fifty thousand did so, and the Peace Pledge Union (PPU) was formed in 1936. In order to attract the widest possible support he commended pacifism as both derived from Christian beliefs and as common-sense, rational politics. In the last years of his life, despite much illness, he travelled incessantly, addressing PPU meetings. Sheppard's sudden death in 1937 deprived the PPU of his charismatic leadership, which had held its members together.

Meanwhile in September 1934 Sheppard had accepted a canonry at St Paul's. But he soon felt stifled by its traditionalism, and contemplated resignation; in June 1937 his wife left him. But his election in October as rector of Glasgow University (which had given him an honorary DD degree in 1927) seemed a ringing endorsement of his pacifism. On 31 October 1937, the eve of All Saints' day, he died at 1 Amen Court, Paternoster Row, London. For two days and nights 100,000 people filed past the coffin at St Martin's. Crowds lined the route to St Paul's for the funeral. He was buried in the cloisters at Canterbury, and, in accordance with his surprising request, next to that cautious ecclesiastic Archbishop Davidson.   ALAN WILKINSON

Sources R. E. Roberts, *H. R. L. Sheppard* (1942) · C. Scott, *Dick Sheppard* (1977) · *DNB* · A. Wilkinson, *Dissent or conform? War, peace and the English churches, 1900–1945* (1986) · *Dick Sheppard by his friends* (1938) · C. S. Matthews, *Dick Sheppard: man of peace* (1948) · *WWW* · A. Hastings, *A history of English Christianity, 1920–1990*, 3rd edn (1991) · *CGPLA Eng. & Wales* (1937)
Archives LPL, corresp. and papers · NRA, priv. coll. | Bodl. Oxf., letters to Lord Ponsonby | FILM BFI NFTVA, documentary footage
Likenesses G. F. Kelly, oils, *c.*1923, 6 St Martin's Place, London · D. Low, pencil drawing, *c.*1927, NPG · H. Coster, photographs, 1937, NPG · photographs, 1937, Hult. Arch. · J. Ward, oils, deanery, Canterbury
Wealth at death £80,412 1*s.* 1*d.*: resworn probate, 26 Nov 1937, *CGPLA Eng. & Wales*

Sheppard, John (*d.* 1559?), composer, is of unknown parentage, family, education, and upbringing. At Michaelmas 1543 he was *informator choristarum* at Magdalen College, Oxford, in succession to Thomas Preston, and he remained in office there until some time between Michaelmas (29 September) and Christmas 1547. Although master of the choristers, he was not also organist; nor was he a fellow of the college, nor did he kidnap or imprison choirboys as some modern accounts have held. The college accounts for 1546–7 show a payment of £8 to Sheppard for his stipend as master of the choristers, and in the same year he was reimbursed for books, vestments, and organ repair (35*s.* 'pro duodecim libris, et eidem reparanti organorum vitia' and £3 'pro tribus cappis dalmaticis albis, per bursarios emptis ad festum Paschae'). He was paid 5*s.* for music books at the end of 1547, at which point he was succeeded by one Mr Games.

Sheppard became a member of the Chapel Royal between 1547 and 1553. Chapel Royal records list the gentlemen in order of joining, so his being the third of the twenty-three new members between 1547 and 1553 suggests that he entered earlier rather than later in this period, which would agree with his disappearance from the Magdalen records at the end of 1547. On 21 April 1554 he supplicated for the DMus degree of the University of Oxford, stating that he had studied music assiduously for twenty years and had composed much music; but this cannot have been granted, as he would undoubtedly have been given the title doctor in manuscript ascriptions of his music if so. At this time he also seems to have rekindled his contacts with Magdalen, being paid 20*s.* on 15 December 1554 'pro quibusdam canticis' ('for certain songs'; Macray, 2.121). He was certainly based at court by then as he was domiciled at Westminster; the Jane Sheppard who was buried in the churchyard of St Margaret's,

Westminster, on 9 April 1555 may have been his first wife. On new year's day 1557 he presented a roll of songs to the queen. Arrangements were made for livery for Mary's funeral (13 December 1558) and Elizabeth's coronation (17 January 1559) to be provided to him. However, during a severe visitation of epidemic disease in Westminster he had sketched an initial draft of his will on 1 December 1558, requesting burial in Westminster Abbey or, if leave were declined, in St Margaret's beside his first wife. His was a common name, and it is possible that he may be identified with the John Scheperde who was buried at St Margaret's, Westminster, on 21 December 1558. Yet this supposition is not consistent with the expectation that he would be present at Elizabeth's coronation, if it may be believed that the official who drew up the list had up-to-date knowledge of the gentlemen. It is more likely that he died about the middle of January 1559, for his will was presented for probate on 31 January 1559. His request for burial in Westminster Abbey would probably not have been made without some understanding that it would be granted, while his second choice of St Margaret's may reflect his anticipation that by the time of his death the abbot and convent of Westminster would no longer be in charge of the abbey. That they were makes it very feasible that he was indeed buried there.

Sheppard's draft will reveals that he had one child, Nathan, and a stepchild, Elizabeth; the former was old enough to assume certain financial responsibilities, while the latter was under age. She was the daughter of Sheppard's second wife, Elizabeth, whose first married name is thought to have been Clivigenne. Sheppard appointed Edmund Danyell as overseer of his will in respect of its provisions for his children. Danyell was subdean of the Chapel Royal and perhaps an Oxford colleague, having been at Merton College between 1540 and at least 1544. Nathan, sometimes appearing under the alias Chapman, later entered service as a schoolmaster with the Petre family of Ingatestone and Thorndon, Essex, a noted recusant family who also patronized William Byrd in the 1580s; he was still alive in 1611. Though not a rich man (his salary of £8 at Magdalen in 1547 compares unfavourably with the £10 paid some thirty years earlier to Thomas Ashwell at Durham), Sheppard was able to leave to Nathan an annuity out of which he was to pay his stepsister £4 and his stepmother £10 annually. To his wife Sheppard left the residue of his estate, and to his son the manor of Dean in the parish of St John, Margate, granted (in reversion) jointly to Sheppard and his Chapel Royal colleague Richard Edwards by Queen Mary on 13 July 1558.

Sheppard's early death is a profound loss to music, and the importance and brilliant quality of his compositions are now fully accepted. Most of his surviving music is for the pre-Reformation service and comes from the extensive collections copied mainly between 1575 and *c.*1581 by John Baldwin, a lay clerk at St George's, Windsor, from 1575 and later a gentleman of the Chapel Royal. The extreme familiarity shown by Baldwin towards Sheppard's name in his ascriptions (he sometimes simply calls him 'S') and the high proportion of works by Sheppard in these collections, made at least fifteen years after his death when there was no longer any liturgical occasion in the established church for their performance, suggest the esteem in which he was held by a fellow professional. Elsewhere, another indication of contemporary opinion appears against his gradual *Haec dies*, which is described in one partbook as 'a goode songe excellent good song fyne' (BL, Add. MS 30484, fol. 8) and in another as 'the best songe in England' (BL, Add. MS 30480, fol. 68v).

Sheppard's music is characterized by a punchy contrapuntal style in which simple points of imitation enter very quickly. For example, in the respond and prose *Gaude gaude gaude Maria virgo* all six voices enter within four beats, giving an impression of contrapuntal imitation even though not all of them are entirely imitative. The variety of sound is well illustrated in the prose section of this work, 'Inviolata', where he changes the texture by dropping alto and tenor and dividing both treble and mean voices, thus placing the emphasis on the higher part of his overall vocal range. His two settings of *Libera nos, salva nos* (strictly a matins antiphon for Trinity Sunday, but at Magdalen College this text was recited twice daily with the verse *Benedicamus patrem*, a usage that surely connects at least these works with Magdalen rather than the Chapel Royal) again highlight the treble voices, with intricate rippling counterpoint crowning the slow-moving plainsong, or faburden, in the bass. Elsewhere his contrapuntal technique is even more enterprising: at 'Media nocte' in another respond, *Audivi vocem de coelo*, the four voices enter on succeeding pitches of the scale, down a seventh or up a ninth from the previous entry, a technique rarely found and never, as here, based on the plainsong. When a voice breaks off before a new point of imitation it does so only briefly and resumes (again in close proximity to other entries) without more ado, and so, since all the voices are so quickly brought in, it follows that the sound is full and the urgency is marked. On the other hand, Sheppard uses a melismatic style at the ends of phrases, once most of the text has been declaimed. In his mass *Cantate* his assured handling of the six-part free contrapuntal texture, largely unconstrained by a *cantus firmus*, shows the new direction that Latin music might have taken.

Sheppard's hymns follow the normal layout of the time, with plainsong and complex polyphony alternating verse by verse. His flexibility of scoring is particularly noticeable here, for succeeding verses are occasionally set to quite different combinations. In *Sacris solemniis*, which is in up to eight parts, he sometimes divides the treble and the mean voices briefly into two, as if he is so bursting with potential contrapuntal entry points that he does not have enough voices for them all. In most of the hymns the tune is prominent at the top of the texture and there are distinct settings for each verse, which is an early example of variation, a technique just beginning to appear in England in the keyboard music of his fellow gentleman of the chapel Thomas Tallis.

Much of Sheppard's composition for the vernacular services of the Edwardian books of common prayer well illustrates the way in which composers at the beginning of the Reformation applied the values implicit in the so-called Lincoln Cathedral injunctions of April 1548; these reflect one of the chief aims of the English Reformation, to make the liturgy better understood, and state that composers should select and translate the best texts 'settyng therunto a playn and distincte note, for every sillable one'. His anthem 'I give you a new commandment' is typical, being written in syllabic style, though with imitative counterpoint, in a simple ABB form. Yet one of his most elaborate works for the English rite is his 'second' service (Magnificat and Nunc dimittis), which, especially towards the ends of phrases, has a complex and contrapuntal note for every syllable several, much like his Latin music. This sophisticated and confident work must date either from the early days of composition in English, before 1553, or from the beginning of Elizabeth's reign, when she anticipated restoring the 1549 prayer book. If the latter, however, it would need to have been written in little more than a month by a man who may have been mortally ill. The basic texture is in five parts, dropping to four when the two sides of the choir (decani and cantoris) alternate, but then Sheppard achieves up to eight real parts by considerable dovetailing as one side of the choir continues its phrase after the other has commenced the next. The assured word-setting, with its characteristic capture of the internal rhythms of the text, if necessary at the expense of the strong beats, is also indicative of the increasing confidence with which he and his generation approached the vernacular. Indeed, on many occasions in this work there are pre-echoes of Byrd's 'great' service in the rhythms, and even sometimes the shape, of the imitative points. While the beginning of the phrase at, for example, 'and to be the glory of thy people Israel' (Nunc dimittis) is plain, distinct, and syllabic, Sheppard treats the imitative point at length: there are no fewer than twelve entries of the point.

Only one significant example of Sheppard's secular work survives, 'O happy dames', in a keyboard arrangement with just the opening title, but the text by Henry Howard, earl of Surrey, can be fitted easily; sacred vernacular *contrafacta* also survive for this work, 'I will give thanks' and 'O happie man if thou repent', though the Howard poem is the more likely original.

In addition to Baldwin's approbation, Sheppard was known, at least by repute, to Thomas Morley, who in his *Plaine and Easie Introduction to Practicall Musicke* (1597) includes Sheppard with his peers as one of the 'famous Englishmen' skilled in composition. In the eighteenth century Burney and Hawkins both noticed him, but did not select his best works for discussion. Sheppard's music was little known during the early years of the twentieth century, although scholarly performers such as Alexander Ramsbotham, R. R. Terry, and H. B. Collins were discovering and performing it in the 1920s and 1930s. His work was to have been included in the second series of Tudor Church Music, which never appeared because of funding difficulties. In 1958 his music was particularly prominent in F. Ll. Harrison's important study *Music in Medieval Britain*, and in the 1960s scholars and performers of Sheppard's old Oxford college, Magdalen, led the way towards a thoroughgoing assessment of his work, both in print and in sound, establishing him without doubt as one of the major figures of the sixteenth century.

So it is for its exceptionally interesting sounds and concise counterpoint that Sheppard's music is valued today: he knew his choir and the effects it could achieve and he handled it perfectly and with subtlety. The beauty of the sound he creates is the result of contrapuntal skill, combined with great flexibility of scoring within the overall twenty-three-note compass characteristic of English choirs of this period. His works are among the outstanding masterpieces of sixteenth-century music.

ROGER BRAY

Sources *John Sheppard, 1: Responsorial music*, ed. D. Chadd, Early English Church Music, 17 (1977) · *John Sheppard, 2: Masses*, ed. N. Sandon, Early English Church Music, 18 (1976) · [J. Sheppard], *Office responds and varia*, ed. D. Wulstan (1978) · [J. Sheppard], *Hymns*, ed. R. Bray (1981) · D. Wulstan, 'New light on John Sheppard', *MT*, 135 (1994), 25–7 · draft of Sheppard's will, City Westm. AC, Bracey 146 [transcription of a lost original] · A. M. Burke, ed., *Memorials of St Margaret's Church, Westminster* (1914), 395, 401 · W. D. Macray, *A register of the members of St Mary Magdalen College, Oxford*, 8 vols. (1894–1915), vol. 2 · J. R. Bloxam, *A register of the presidents, fellows … of Saint Mary Magdalen College*, 8 vols. (1853–85), vol. 2, p. ii · D. Mateer, 'William Byrd, John Petre and Oxford, Bodleian MS Mus. Sch. e. 423', *Royal Musical Association Research Chronicle*, 29 (1996), 21–46 · J. Baldwin, collections of Sheppard's music, Christ Church Oxf., MSS 979–983 · BL, RM 24 d 2 [collections of Sheppard's music made by J. Baldwin]
Wealth at death see will, City Westm. AC, Bracey 146

Sheppard, John [Jack] (1702–1724), thief and prison-breaker, was born on 4 March 1702 in White Row, Spitalfields, London, the son of Thomas Sheppard (1672–*c*.1706), carpenter, and his wife, Mary. His father, reputedly an honest, industrious artisan, died young, leaving three children. John, known as Jack, together with an elder brother, Thomas (*b*. 1697), received a rudimentary education at Mr Garrett's school, near St Helen's, Bishopsgate. In or soon after 1714 Jack was employed as a servant by William Kneebone, a woollen draper, at the sign of the Angel on the north side of the Strand, opposite St Mary's Church. Kneebone was kind to the boy. He improved him in his writing and accounts and, on 2 April 1717, apprenticed him to Owen Wood, a carpenter in Drury Lane. Sheppard is said to have been a talented apprentice. However, in 1722 one Joseph Hayne, a button-mould maker who lived next door to Sheppard's master, gave up his trade to take the Black Lion alehouse in Lewkenor's Lane, hard by, and he encouraged Sheppard and other apprentices to patronize the house. It was at the Black Lion that Sheppard was introduced to 'a train of vices as before I was altogether a stranger to' (*Narrative*, 5–6). There he also met and became enamoured of Elizabeth *Lyon (*fl*. 1722–1726), a prostitute who became his mistress and induced him to steal.

Sheppard's first known theft was from the Rummer tavern, Charing Cross. Sent there to do a job for his master,

John [Jack] **Sheppard** (1702–1724), attrib. Sir James Thornhill, 1724

Sheppard stole two silver spoons. In August 1723, after further thefts, he absconded from his master and drifted into a life of professional crime. In February 1724 Sheppard was committing burglaries with his brother Thomas and Elizabeth Lyon. This partnership was short-lived. Thomas was apprehended at the beginning of April and informed against his accomplices. Shortly afterwards Jack himself was taken. He was lodged for the night in the parish roundhouse of St Giles-in-the-Fields, but within two hours had escaped by breaking a hole through the roof. It was the first of a series of daring and skilful escapes from captivity. On 25 May he effected a remarkable escape from New prison in Clerkenwell. Sheppard was held, together with Lyon, in the Newgate ward, said to be the strongest apartment in the gaol, but after he had sawed through his fetters and removed an oak muntin and an iron bar from the window the couple descended 25 feet to the yard below by means of a rope fashioned from a sheet, a blanket, and Lyon's gown and petticoat, and then surmounted a 22 foot perimeter wall. In the summer of 1724, with the footpad Joseph Blake (alias Blueskin), Sheppard experimented with highway robbery on the Hampstead Road. He also committed fresh burglaries, including one upon the house of his former benefactor William Kneebone on the night of 12–13 July. By this time, however, his activities had attracted the attention of the famous receiver and thief-taker Jonathan Wild, and his unwillingness to submit his booty to Wild's disposal had antagonized the thief-taker. Wild effected Sheppard's arrest in Rosemary Lane on 23 July and he was committed to Newgate prison in the City of London. He was brought to trial at the Old Bailey in August and, largely upon the strength of evidence procured by Wild, convicted of the Kneebone robbery and sentenced to death.

On 31 August, four days before the time appointed for his execution, Sheppard sawed through one of the iron spikes surmounting the door of the condemned hold in Newgate and, by squeezing through the gap in the remaining spikes, escaped from the hold into the Lodge, the prison's reception area. From thence, disguised in a nightgown and assisted by Elizabeth Lyon and another woman, he passed through the Lodge and out the main door. This exploit was the talk of London, but Sheppard's period of freedom was brief. Lyon was apprehended the day after the escape and remained in custody until after Sheppard's execution. Sheppard fled the capital, but after a brief sojourn in Warendon, Buckinghamshire, returned to London and was recaptured on Finchley Common on 10 September by a posse of Newgate turnkeys. Returned to the condemned hold, he immediately began to plan another escape. On 16 September, after a set of tools had been found concealed in the rushes of his chair, he was moved to a formidable fourth-storey apartment known as the Castle, where he was isolated from other prisoners and where visitors were carefully watched. He was also fettered and handcuffed, and his fetters were secured to an iron staple in the floor by a great horse padlock.

Despite these precautions, Sheppard accomplished his last and most spectacular escape on 15 October. After freeing himself from his handcuffs and breaking the chain of his fetters, he removed an iron bar from the chimney. Then, climbing up the chimney, he broke into the Red Room, directly above the Castle, and from thence, in a hugely impressive display of ingenuity, strength, and determination, worked his way to the upper leads, mastering the locks, bolts, and bars of six strong doors in his progress. He was now on the summit of the gaol, more than 60 feet above Newgate Street, but had to return to his cell for his blanket before letting himself down upon the house of William Bird, a turner, adjoining the prison. After entering Bird's house by a garret window, he stole down the stairs and left the house by the street door. The irons carried off by Sheppard were subsequently recovered at a lodging belonging to Catherine Cook (*fl.* 1717–1724), another of his mistresses, in Cranbourn Alley, Leicester Fields. On the night of 29–30 October Sheppard burgled a pawnbroker's shop in Drury Lane. It was his last robbery. Handsomely attired in some of the plundered finery, he was arrested, very drunk, in a Drury Lane brandy shop on 31 October. Crowds of people now flocked to Newgate to see him, among them Sir James Thornhill, serjeant-painter to the crown, who sketched portraits of him in the Middle Stone Room and the condemned hold. By 7 November the turnkeys were said to have earned more than £200 charging fees to visitors. On 10 November Sheppard was brought before the court of king's bench, Westminster, where a rule of court was ordered for his execution six days hence. He was watched day and night,

and on 16 November 1724 was executed at Tyburn before one of the largest crowds Londoners could then remember. He was buried the same day in the churchyard of St Martin-in-the-Fields. His brother Thomas was transported to Maryland in 1725.

Sheppard's exploits inspired pamphlets, ballads, engravings, and plays, and one clergyman is said to have exhorted his flock to emulate Sheppard in a spiritual sense by mounting the 'chimney of hope' to the 'leads of divine meditation' (*Select Trials*, 1.445–6). John Thurmond's *Harlequin Sheppard* played to 'vast applause' at Drury Lane in December 1724 (*Parker's London News*, 7 Dec 1724), and *The Prison-Breaker*, published in 1725 and intended for Lincoln's Inn Fields, was altered by Thomas Walker in 1728 and performed at Bartholomew fair as *The Quaker's Opera*. There is little reason to suppose that John Gay's Macheath was directly modelled upon Sheppard, but it is highly probable that the popular excitement generated by his escapes, and by the trial of Jonathan Wild in 1725, was a major factor in persuading Gay to develop Jonathan Swift's suggestion of a 'Newgate pastoral' into *The Beggar's Opera* (1728). Sheppard's fame was revived in 1839 by William Harrison Ainsworth's best-selling romance *Jack Sheppard*, illustrated by some of George Cruikshank's best cuts. Ainsworth's triumph inspired many imitative romances and innumerable stage plays and aroused 'respectable' fears that unwary youths might be led into crime by a desire to imitate Sheppard. 'Public morality and public decency', wrote John Forster, 'have rarely been more endangered than by the trumpeted exploits of Jack Sheppard' (*Examiner*, 3 Nov 1839). Moved by such considerations, successive lord chamberlains refused to license plays entitled *Jack Sheppard* for nearly forty years after 1840, but the ban was not strictly enforced outside London, and even there theatre managers frequently circumvented it by producing Sheppard plays under neutral titles like *The Idle Apprentice* and *Old London*. In 1886 the actress Nellie Farren enjoyed great success playing Jack in William Yardley and Henry Pottinger Stephens's burlesque, *Little Jack Sheppard*, staged at London's Gaiety Theatre, but thereafter Sheppard's popular fame, and hence the emotive power of his name, declined. During the twentieth century, nevertheless, his career continued to inspire writers and dramatists. Paramount's lavish but commercially unsuccessful *Where's Jack?* (1969), directed by James Clavell and starring Tommy Steele as Jack and Sir Stanley Baker as Jonathan Wild, was the last of three cinematic versions of the story.

The notice for Sheppard's arrest after his escape from the Castle described him as 'about 22 years old, about five foot four inches high, very slender, of a pale complexion, has an impediment or hesitation in his speech' (*Daily Journal*, 20 Oct 1724). Although Sheppard's talents as a prison-breaker were undoubtedly extraordinary his personal character has occasioned much dispute. The available evidence suggests that he was neither Ainsworth's dashing hero nor John Langbein's 'nasty thug' (*TLS*, 11 Oct 1991) but a mixture of worthy as well as unworthy qualities. His robberies were characterized by adroitness and skill rather than violence, and his courage, his loyalty to companions, and his cheery if impudent disposition lend some colour to popular portrayals of him as a likeable rogue. It cannot be said of him, on the other hand, that his crimes were prompted by necessity, and he became a persistent and—as the Kneebone robbery demonstrated—undiscriminating thief.   PHILIP SUGDEN

Sources The history of the remarkable life of John Sheppard (1724) · A narrative of all the robberies, escapes, … of John Sheppard (1724) · G. E., Authentic memoirs of the life and surprising adventures of John Sheppard, who was executed at Tyburn, November the 16th, 1724 (1724) · The proceedings on the king's commission of the peace (1723–4) [Old Bailey sessions papers, 8–10 July, 12–14 Aug, 14–21 Oct 1724]; (1724–5) [4–9 Dec 1724] · Middlesex gaol delivery rolls, LMA, MJ/GSR 2427, 2429, 2432, 2434 · Select trials … at the sessions house in the Old Bailey, 1 (1734), 432–53, 464–70 · Daily Journal (July–Nov 1724) · Daily Post [London] (July–Nov 1724) · Applebee's Original Weekly Journal (July–Nov 1724) · H. Bleackley and S. M. Ellis, Jack Sheppard (1933) [incl. detailed bibliography] · G. Howson, Thief-taker general: the rise and fall of Jonathan Wild (1970) · P. Rawlings, Drunks, whores and idle apprentices: criminal biographies of the eighteenth century (1992) · K. Hollingsworth, The Newgate novel, 1830–1847 (1963) · J. R. Stephens, 'Jack Sheppard and the licensers: the case against Newgate plays', Nineteenth-Century Theatre Research, 1 (1973), 1–13 · D. Forbes, 'Jack Sheppard plays and the influence of Cruikshank', Theatre Notebook, 54 (2000), 98–123 · parish register, St Dunstan's Stepney, LMA, 4 and 5 March 1702 [baptism] · Parker's London News (18 Nov 1724) · parish register (burials), 16 Nov 1724, St Martin-in-the-Fields, Westminster, London
Archives LMA, Middlesex sessions of the peace and gaol delivery rolls, MJ/GSR 2427, 2429, 2432, 2434
Likenesses attrib. J. Thornhill, chalk, pencil, and wash drawing, 1724, NPG · attrib. J. Thornhill, pen-and-wash drawing, 1724, Museum of London [see illus.] · lithograph, 1839 (after pen-and-ink drawing by J. Thornhill, 1724), BM · G. White, mezzotint (after J. Thornhill, 1724), BM · engraving (after portrait, 1724), BM · line engraving, BM · lithograph (after J. Thornhill), BM

Sheppard, John (1785–1879), religious writer, born on 15 October 1785 at Frome, Somerset (where his family had lived since the Restoration), was the son of John Sheppard and his wife, Mary Kelson, daughter of John Banger of Piddletown, Dorset. He left school in 1800 to enter the wool trade, in which most of his relatives worked. In 1806, after his father's death, he and his mother joined the Baptists, a body to which many of his family belonged. With John Foster (1770–1843), Baptist minister in Frome from 1804, Sheppard developed a lasting friendship. The death of his uncle, Walter Sheppard, who made him his heir, enabled him to give up his business. Deciding to study medicine, he matriculated at Edinburgh University in late 1812, but was soon diverted to the study of philosophy and Hebrew. During two years' residence at Edinburgh he formed friendships with Thomas Chalmers and with John Pinkerton, the antiquary. In 1816 and 1817 he made tours through France, Italy, Switzerland, and Germany, and studied for some months at the University of Göttingen. On his return he published *Letters on a Tour of France* (1817).

In 1823 Sheppard published his most successful work, *Thoughts Preparative or Persuasive to Private Devotion*, which went through five editions in as many years. From that period until his death he devoted himself to writing religious works, lay preaching, and foreign travel. His last work was *The Christian Harp* (1858). He died at Frome on 30

April 1879, and was buried in the dissenters' cemetery. He was twice married, and his second wife, Susan Anne Dawe, survived him.   E. I. CARLYLE, rev. MARI G. ELLIS

Sources T. G. Rooke, 'Memoir', in J. Sheppard, Thoughts chiefly designed … to private devotion, new edn (1881) · W. T. Lowndes, The bibliographer's manual of English literature, ed. H. G. Bohn, 8 [1857] · J. Julian, ed., A dictionary of hymnology, rev. edn (1907) · Life and correspondence of John Foster, ed. J. E. Ryland, 1 (1852) · CGPLA Eng. & Wales (1879)
Wealth at death under £20,000: probate, 16 June 1879, CGPLA Eng. & Wales

Sheppard, Sir John Tressider (1881–1968), classical scholar and college head, was born on 7 November 1881 in Peckham, London, the fourth of the five children (three sons and two daughters) of Alfred Henry Sheppard (d. 1930), a wool broker's clerk of Peckham, London, and his wife, Harriet Winifred, daughter of the Revd James Sears, a Baptist pastor and printer. He was educated at Dulwich College from 1895 to 1900 and was taught Greek there by A. C. Pearson who in 1921 was preferred to his pupil for the regius chair at Cambridge. Among his school friends were P. G. Wodehouse and Alic Halford Smith, later warden of New College, Oxford. When Sheppard was provost of King's he and Smith revived the *amicabilis concordia* between the two colleges.

After winning a scholarship in 1900 to King's College, Cambridge, Sheppard came under a brilliant scholar, Walter Headlam, and a born teacher, Nathaniel Wedd. But he often said that he owed as much to Oscar Browning, who had to get his Baptist parents' permission to take him to the theatre. He was an Apostle and a prizeman, though his zeal as president of the union condemned him to a second in part two (1904) after a first in part one (1902) of the classical tripos. In 1906 he won a fellowship at King's. The electors ignored a referee who wrote, 'Mr S. has an unfortunate lightness of touch. This might be cured by a year in a German seminar' (Morris, 62). In 1911 he published his book *Greek Tragedy*. His best work was his edition of the *Oedipus tyrannus* (1920) which won him a Manchester honorary LittD at the age of forty; and *The Pattern of the Iliad* (1922) was based on his Manchester lectures on Homer. He held the Brereton readership from 1931 to 1947.

When A. E. Housman went to Cambridge in 1911 he said to Sheppard, 'I hear your lectures are very well attended, so I know they must be bad' (Wilkinson, JTS: a Memoir, 21). They were in fact remarkable. Never using notes, he would sit on a table swinging his legs, his long underpants showing between his trousers and boots, or perch on a chair at an angle so perilous that disaster threatened. He became the characters in Homer or the tragedies, and made his audience feel they were seeing the drama as well as listening to an interpretation. More than any scholar of his generation (Gilbert Murray apart) he kept Greek literature alive at a time when it had ceased to be a compulsory subject in many schools. A school had only to ask and he would talk to the boys and girls, and dozens of boys went to King's because he had met them in a train or at school. He produced the triennial Greek plays eleven times and was made knight commander of the order of the

Sir John Tressider Sheppard (1881–1968), by Ramsey & Muspratt, *c*.1939

the verge of senility, tirelessly interested in people, helping them by stealth, histrionic in the highest degree, quick to spot the comic and to mock the pompous, the possessor of a gargantuan ego that was directed almost entirely to good ends, he was one of the most remarkable dons of his day. He died unmarried, of a cardiac arrest, at Northumberland House, 237 Ballards Lane, London, on 7 May 1968. His remains were cremated at Golders Green on 19 May 1968; on 10 February 1969 his ashes were placed in a vault of King's College chapel.   NOEL ANNAN

Sources *The Times* (8 May 1968) · L. P. Wilkinson, *John Tresidder Sheppard … a memoir* (privately printed, Cambridge, 1969) · D. Parry, *Lancelot Patrick Wilkinson, 1907–1985* (1985) · L. P. Wilkinson, *A century of King's* (1980) · C. Morris, *King's College: a short history* (privately printed for King's College, Cambridge, 1989) · personal knowledge (2004) · King's Cam.
Archives King's AC Cam., corresp., diaries, and papers | Bodl. Oxf., corresp. with Gilbert Murray · CUL, letters to G. E. Moore · King's AC Cam., letters to Oscar Browning · King's AC Cam., letters to John Maynard Keynes
Likenesses Ramsay & Muspratt, photograph, *c*.1939, NPG [*see illus.*] · H. Lamb, oils, 1944, King's Cam. · W. Stoneman, photograph, 1947, NPG · J. Crockford, oils, King's Cam. · J. Crockford, oils, King's Cam. · D. Grant, pencil drawing, King's Cam. · J. Horsley, oils, King's Cam.
Wealth at death £8622: probate, 3 July 1968, *CGPLA Eng. & Wales*

Redeemer by the Greek government. Peggy Ashcroft acted in his *Electra* and Joyce Carey in *Oedipus*. He was a mercurial producer and rehearsals were exhausting. 'First you are a flame, then you are a lily', he told the Cassandra of 1921, an Etonian athlete (Wilkinson, *A Century of King's*, 89). In 1950 he was knighted for his services to Greek (he had been appointed MBE in 1919).

Sheppard's other passion was King's. Like Oscar Browning he treated undergraduates as equals and Sheppard developed that tradition—and invented a good many others—steering many benefactions in their direction. He knew every undergraduate and undertook long postmortems on scholarship as well as tripos examination results. Elected vice-provost in 1929, he was a unanimous choice as provost in 1933; and such was the hold he established over the college that the fellows prolonged his tenure as provost for two years so that he retired in 1954.

Sheppard was an exacting colleague, and college meetings lasted for hours as he reminisced about the past; but it was his way of educating the fellows in the traditions of the college. He had no enthusiasm for the natural sciences, and as little for research. He wanted each branch of the humanities to fertilize the others. As a young don, the friend of J. Maynard Keynes, Bertrand Russell, G. Lytton Strachey, and Lady Ottoline Morrell, he had been an iconoclast, but as he grew older he preferred the company of the innocent to the clever. He was proud to be *ex officio* senior fellow of Eton and was much moved by the visit of George VI, Queen Elizabeth, and Princess Margaret to the college.

In later years Sheppard visited the four dominions, for each of which he established a graduate studentship; and Melbourne and New Zealand followed St Andrews in conferring honorary degrees. He created an *amicabilis concordia* with Queen Mary College, London (evacuated to King's during the war), and another with Berkeley College, Yale, where his contemporary at King's, Charles Seymour, was president.

Sheppard was a character. His mane of white hair brought him dignity which he masked with clowning. Shrewd yet naïve, tough yet appearing to be tottering on

Sheppard [*née* Malcolm], **Katherine Wilson** [Kate] (1847–1934), suffragist in New Zealand, was born probably on 10 March 1847 in Liverpool, the second of the five children of Andrew Wilson Malcolm (1819–1862), a clerk, and his wife, Jemima Crawford Souter (1821/2–1881). Although named Catherine at birth after her paternal grandmother, she called herself Katherine or Kate throughout her adult life. Her parents, both Scottish, were married on the Isle of Islay in the Hebrides in 1842. After Kate's birth the family shifted residence in England several times, as her father took a series of jobs. Following his death in 1862, the family separated for periods of time. Family tradition holds that Kate lived for a while in Nairn, Scotland, with an uncle who was a minister of the Free Church of Scotland and a Christian socialist, and who probably shaped her own adult political views. Nothing is known of her formal education, but her subsequent writings indicate wide reading, a fluent literary style, and an interest in the social issues of her day.

In 1869 Kate Malcolm emigrated to the city of Christchurch in New Zealand, with her mother, her sister Isabella, and two brothers, Frank and Robert. They joined Marie Beath, her elder sister, who had already settled in Christchurch and married a draper. Two years later, on 21 July 1871, Kate married Walter Allen Sheppard (1836–1915). Born in Bath, England, the son of a flour-miller, Walter Sheppard had established himself as a general merchant in Christchurch, where he became active in local government. The couple had one child, a son named Douglas, who was born in Christchurch on 8 October 1880.

Kate Sheppard and her husband were comfortably well off and built a pleasant home in the suburb of Riccarton. Fair-complexioned, and stylishly dressed, Kate was widely judged good looking. Her activities outside the domestic

Katherine Wilson Sheppard (1847–1934), by unknown photographer, 1896

circle were initially confined to parish work for the Trinity Congregational Church in Christchurch. She assisted in fund-raising, taught in Sunday school, and served as secretary of the ladies' association, which co-ordinated parish visiting. In the mid-1880s, however, her life changed dramatically when, with her sisters Marie Beath and Isabella May, she helped to form the Women's Christian Temperance Union in New Zealand. Under the leadership of Frances Willard, an advocate of women's emancipation and a Christian socialist, the parent body in the United States of America demanded a curb on men's excessive alcohol consumption, and an extension of women's civil rights. In New Zealand the union became an increasingly forceful campaigning group. From 1887 Kate Sheppard led the campaign for the union's central demand, namely women's attainment of full citizenship through parliamentary franchise. Drawing on theoretical and polemical literature from the United States and England, and attentive to the strategies of northern countries' campaigns, she shrewdly tailored New Zealand activism to the local demands of a small, rural, and relatively egalitarian white British colony. Just as Maori men had been enfranchised alongside European men, Kate Sheppard campaigned to enfranchise European and Maori women, although few Maori initially were members of the union.

Kate Sheppard's skilful direction of the fight for the vote marshalled the colony's Liberal and secular pro-suffrage forces to the women's banner alongside the temperance lobby. She herself became an able public speaker, newspaper columnist, and journalist, co-operated with sympathetic politicians of whatever political affiliation, and oversaw the presentation of well-supported petitions to the colonial legislature. In September 1893 suffrage for all women, European and Maori, twenty-one years of age and over, became law. Urged by Kate Sheppard to show their approval by voting in the forthcoming election, a large number of women registered and voted to return the Liberal government that had enfranchised them in November of the same year.

During the suffrage campaign Kate Sheppard had been in touch with many women reformers in northern countries and, following her success in New Zealand, she found herself in demand as a speaker at meetings and international conferences when she and her husband visited Britain in 1894–5 and again in 1903–4. While women throughout Europe and in all except a few western states of the United States of America remained voteless, Kate was distinctive and compelling on a public platform. Back in New Zealand she helped establish the National Council of Women and, drawing on international links through the International Council of Women, worked to further women's and children's legal and welfare reforms. She also edited the *White Ribbon* from 1895 to 1903, continued for several years as superintendent of franchise and legislative concerns for the Women's Christian Temperance Union, and worked on the committee of the Canterbury Women's Institute.

Kate Sheppard subsequently faced many personal sadnesses: her son died in 1910; her husband in 1915; her only grandchild also died at an early age. Her later years were clouded by ill health and the disapproval aroused by her unconventional relationship with a printer and suffrage supporter, William Sidney Lovell-Smith (1852–1929). Increasingly she withdrew from public life. She married Lovell-Smith on 15 August 1925 following the death of his wife the previous year, to be widowed once more four years later. She died of bronchitis at the Lovell-Smith home in Riccarton, Christchurch, on 13 July 1934, and was buried three days later in the city's Addington cemetery beside her mother, brother, sister, nephew, and niece.

PATRICIA GRIMSHAW

Sources P. Grimshaw, *Women's suffrage in New Zealand* (1972) · J. Devaliant, *Kate Sheppard: a biography* (1992) · D. Page, ed., *The suffragists: women who worked for the vote* (1993) · T. K. Malcolm, 'Sheppard, Katherine Wilson', *DNZB*, vol. 2 · d. cert.
Archives Canterbury Museum Library, Christchurch, New Zealand | General Assembly Library, Wellington, New Zealand, Hall MSS · priv. coll., Lovell-Smith collection
Likenesses photograph, 1896, NL NZ, Turnbull L. [*see illus.*] · photographs, priv. coll.

Sheppard, Nicholas. *See* Shepherd, Nicholas (1533–1587).

Sheppard, Oliver (1865–1941), sculptor, was born on 10 April 1865 in Cookstown, co. Tyrone, one of the five children of the sculptor Simpson Sheppard (*b.* 1836) of co. Tyrone, who specialized in marble inlaying of chimney-pieces, and his wife, Ellen White (*b.* 1842), who also came from co. Tyrone. About 1866 his father settled in Dublin, where he ran a marbleworks at Ormond Quay, and from 1869 at 72 Blessington Street. From 1884 to 1888 Oliver studied at the Dublin Metropolitan School of Art, where he was a fellow student with William Butler Yeats and George Russell, and from 1885 he also studied at the Royal Hibernian Academy (RHA) Schools. He first exhibited at the RHA in 1887 and was an annual exhibitor until his death. He proceeded on a scholarship to the National Art Training School, South Kensington, London, from the autumn of 1888 to June 1891, where he studied under Edward Lantéri and won silver and bronze medals. He received a travelling scholarship which enabled him to spend the academic year 1891–2 in Paris at the Académie Julian, after which he went to Italy with his friend the Irish sculptor John Hughes. In December 1892 he was appointed teacher of modelling at the Leicester School of Art, remaining there until July 1893. He worked as an assistant to Lantéri, probably in 1890–91. From September 1894 to June 1902 he was teacher of modelling at the Nottingham School of Art, where he was a close friend of the artists Harold and Laura Knight. Through Laura he met Rosalina (Rosie) Good (1868–1931), an amateur musician and the daughter of John Good, a wealthy local corn merchant, and married her on 16 July 1901; the couple had one daughter, Cathleen. During the 1890s he exhibited regularly at the RHA, showing subjects drawn mainly from Irish myth and legend, such as *The Training of Cuchulainn* (1897, National Museum of Ireland, Dublin) and *The Fate of the Children of Lir* (1901, National Gallery of Ireland, Dublin). He was commissioned by the Holbrook bequest to model a bust of the local poet Henry Kirke White (1902, Castle Museum, Nottingham).

In 1902 Sheppard returned to Ireland as instructor in modelling at the Dublin Metropolitan School of Art, a position secured partly through the good offices of William Butler Yeats and which he retained until his retirement in 1937. He had a great love of the poetry of the Irish cultural revival and was a leading figure in the Gaelic Society at the school. His mythological subjects culminated in *The Death of Cuchulainn* (1912, General Post Office, Dublin), adopted in 1935 as the national memorial to the Easter rising of 1916. He also modelled a number of free poetic pieces— mainly female nudes such as *La jeunesse* (1904, Hugh Lane Municipal Gallery of Modern Art, Dublin) and *In Mystery the Soul Abides* (1913, National Gallery of Ireland, Dublin). He established his reputation in public sculpture with his two memorials to the Irish rising of 1798 in Wexford (1904) and Enniscorthy (1907). He was employed by the state to model figures (c.1911) for the new Royal College of Science, Dublin; the barristers and solicitors commissioned him to supply war memorial reliefs there (1920, Four Courts and Incorporated Law Society).

Sheppard was popular with the Dublin medical profession as a portrait sculptor, beginning with a bust of Dr R. D. Purefoy (1904, Rotunda Hospital, Dublin). Other notable busts were of the Fenian patriot John O'Leary (1904, Hugh Lane Municipal Gallery of Modern Art), James Clarence Mangan (1909, St Stephen's Green), Professor John Joly (1932, Trinity College), Patrick Pearse (1937, Dáil

Éireann), and Sir Robert Woods (1939, Royal College of Surgeons in Ireland)—all in Dublin. Closely related to these were memorial portrait reliefs, such as those to James C. Culwick (1909, St Patrick's Cathedral, Dublin), Sir Henry Swanzy (1913, Royal Victoria Eye and Ear Hospital, Dublin), and the first Lord Iveagh (1929, the Guinness Brewery and Trinity College, both Dublin). He was employed to make prize medals incorporating commemorative portraits such as those of Sir John Banks (1900) and Professor George Fitzgerald (1912), both for Trinity College, Dublin. The Irish government commissioned from him the prize medal for the Tailteann festival in 1922.

Sheppard played an active role in the RHA, becoming a full member in 1901 and professor of sculpture in 1904. He was a highly influential and well-regarded teacher of modelling in Dublin. He had two homes: at 30 Pembroke Road, Dublin, where his studio was located, and Knockranny on Carrickbrack Road on the hill of Howth, co. Dublin, where he went at weekends and during the summers. His relaxation was to play golf. He was a warm-hearted man, full of jokes and anecdotes which endeared him to his students and friends. He died of heart failure at his home at Knockranny on 14 September 1941 and was buried on the 16th in St Fintan's cemetery, Sutton, co. Dublin. Sheppard was a sensitive and subtle modeller in clay. His style was based on the realist tradition of the British 'New Sculpture' and its French sources. Most of his work was intended to be cast in bronze, though he also carved some small pieces in marble.   JOHN TURPIN

Sources J. Turpin, 'The life of Oliver Sheppard, Dublin sculptor', *Dublin Historical Record*, 48 (1995), 55–78, 142–61 · T. Snoddy, *Dictionary of Irish artists: 20th century* (1996) · b. cert. · d. cert. · Dublin, register of births, 1865 · census returns for Ireland, 1901 · private information (2004) · m. cert. · *Dublin directory*, various edns · will, registry of wills, NA Ire.
Archives National College of Art and Design, Dublin, National Irish Visual Arts Library
Likenesses G. Russell, pencil drawing, c.1895, Hugh Lane Municipal Gallery of Modern Art, Dublin · W. Orpen, pencil drawing, 1907, NG Ire. · O. Sheppard, self-portrait, oils, c.1926, Hugh Lane Municipal Gallery of Modern Art, Dublin · photographs, National College of Art and Design, Dublin, National Irish Visual Arts Library, Sheppard MSS
Wealth at death £6086 13s. 7d.: will, NA Ire.

Sheppard, Philip Macdonald (1921–1976), geneticist, was born at Marlborough on 27 July 1921, the only child of George Sheppard (d. 1956), mathematics master at Bradfield College, and his wife, Alison, daughter of William Henry Macdonald. He was educated at Marlborough College. In 1939 he joined the Royal Air Force Volunteer Reserve, trained as an air crew member, and was posted to Bomber Command. He took part in the first thousand-bomber raid on Cologne in July 1942. However, his plane was damaged returning to England and was shot down by a German minesweeper over the North Sea. The crew was rescued by the Germans and Sheppard remained a prisoner for the rest of the war.

In 1946 Sheppard entered Worcester College, Oxford, to read honours zoology, obtaining second-class honours in 1948. He was an excellent shot and was captain of the

Oxford University rifle club in 1948, the year in which he also married Patricia Beatrice, the daughter of Reginald Harold Lee, master chef. (The couple later had three sons.) Following graduation Sheppard was attracted to the genetical theory of natural selection propounded by R. A. Fisher and, under the influence of E. B. Ford, he became interested in the genetics of the scarlet tiger moth, *Panaxia dominula*, and the snail *Cepaea nemoralis*. These formed the basis of his doctoral research during the time he held the Christopher Welch scholarship in genetics.

From 1951 (when he gained his DPhil) to 1956 Sheppard was junior research officer in zoology at Oxford. During this time he spent a year (1954–5) with Professor T. Dobzhansky at Columbia University, New York, on a Rockefeller fellowship, working on *Drosophila melanogaster*. In 1956 he went to Liverpool University as senior lecturer in genetics at the department of zoology. He became reader in the new sub-department of genetics in 1959 and the first professor in 1963.

The first of the four editions of Sheppard's *Natural Selection and Heredity* appeared in 1958. Its main purpose was to explain genetic principles and 'to avoid giving the impression that most problems concerned with natural selection are solved and that controversy no longer exists, an idea which elementary books often impart to their readers'.

Shortly after Sheppard's arrival at Liverpool the Nuffield Unit of Medical Genetics was set up in the medical school, financed by a £350,000 grant from the Nuffield Foundation. The director, Cyril A. Clarke, had previously worked with Sheppard. The unit's medical work stemmed from that on the Lepidoptera. After the tiger moth and snails it studied the evolution of mimicry in butterflies. For twenty-five years the unit worked on the three classical mimics, *Papilio dardanus* from Africa and *Papilio polytes* and *Papilio memnon* from south-east Asia. Results showed that a combination of only a few characters controlled the various wing patterns. This suggested that an apparent multiple allelomorphic series was really a supergene composed of alleles at several closely linked loci. Crossing over would occur within the supergene and explain some of the rarer forms.

The results obtained, combined with the observed genetic interactions in swallowtails, led Clarke and Sheppard to look for a corresponding situation in humans. They found it in the rhesus blood groups and their research led to a method of preventing rhesus haemolytic disease of the newborn by giving an injection of anti-rhesus antibody (anti-D) to Rh-negative mothers after they had been delivered of an Rh-positive baby. The preliminary work, which took about ten years, was carried out first on Rh-negative male volunteers and, when success was achieved, on mothers. Sheppard advised that the work should be carried out on women in a high risk group, who had experienced a considerable foeto-maternal haemorrhage. The trial was very successful; in 1970 the treatment was adopted by the National Health Service and became standard practice, leading to a great reduction of the disease.

Living near Liverpool, on the edge of one of Britain's worst polluted areas, Sheppard and Clarke were stimulated by H. B. D. Kettlewell to carry out a detailed local survey of the classical melanic moth *Biston betularia*. Perhaps the most interesting of the findings was the large decrease in the frequencies of the melanic form in smokeless zones and the beginning of the possible reversal of this extraordinary piece of evolution.

With the help of the Liverpool Tropical School Sheppard played a major part in studying population changes in mosquitoes in Bangkok. He also studied the mimetic Heliconius butterflies, worked on neural tube defects in man, and served on the Royal College of Physicians committee which reported in 1976 on the value of fluoridation of water supplies to prevent dental caries.

Sheppard was elected FRS in 1965. In 1974 he was awarded the Darwin medal of the Royal Society and in 1975 the gold medal of the Linnean Society. In 1975 he was made an honorary fellow of the Royal College of Physicians of London. He died of leukaemia on 17 October 1976 at the Liverpool Royal Infirmary.   CYRIL CLARKE, *rev.*

Sources C. A. Clarke, *Memoirs FRS*, 23 (1977), 465–500 • *The Times* (19 Oct 1976), 14f • personal knowledge (1986) • *WWW*, 1971–80 **Archives** American Philosophical Society Library, Philadelphia, MSS | Bodl. Oxf., corresp. with Edmund Brisco Ford • Rice University, Houston, Texas, corresp. with Sir Julian Huxley • Wolfson College, Oxford, corresp. with H. B. D. Kettlewell **Wealth at death** £35,895: probate, 22 Nov 1976, *CGPLA Eng. & Wales*

Sheppard, Sir Richard Herbert (1910–1982), architect, was born at 4 Longfield Avenue, Ashley, Bristol, on 2 July 1910, the eldest of three sons (there were no daughters) of William Herbert Sheppard, commercial traveller, and his wife, Hilda Mabel Hatton Evans. Sheppard was educated at Bristol grammar school, and had begun his professional training at the Royal West of England Academy when at the age of nineteen he was struck down by poliomyelitis. Athletic, extrovert, a born leader, he was hospitalized for two years and lost the use of his legs. Although he was now obliged to move about on crutches, his zest for life seemed undiminished and he moved to the Architectural Association (AA) School in London, qualifying as ARIBA in 1936. Here he met his first wife, Jean (1911/12–1974), daughter of Frank Shufflebotham, doctor of medicine: they were married on 21 July 1938 and had a son and a daughter. Both young architects taught at the evacuated AA School (Sheppard as vice-principal) during the Second World War. Thereafter, through Jean's friendship with Henry Morris and other educationists, the Sheppards became heavily involved in the post-war school building programme. In 1958 they took into partnership Geoffrey Robson (1918–1991), a former pupil, and the firm of Richard Sheppard, Robson & Partners was founded.

The firm built upwards of eighty schools, but Sheppard had no wish to become a specialist architect and was sceptical of the economy of prefabrication, the monotony of which he deplored. Indeed the first building to demonstrate his own unaffected integrity as a designer was not a school but some shipyard buildings for Swan Hunter on the River Tyne (1950). In the 1960s, like those of other leading architects, the practice was in demand for university and college buildings, notably at Loughborough (1961–6), Leicester, Brunel (1968–73), the City of London (1969–70), Durham, and Newcastle, as well as at Manchester Polytechnic and Imperial College, London. Sheppard's best-known work in this field—Churchill College, Cambridge (1974)—was won in competition in 1959. In later years the firm designed *inter alia* the major shopping centre at Wood Green, north London, some modest and distinguished office buildings in the City, and not least the delightful conversion of an old warehouse in Camden Town for its own offices. Some twenty buildings designed by the practice received architectural awards during Sheppard's years at its head.

Sheppard always disclaimed the existence of any 'house style': it was therefore a tribute to his meticulous yet relaxed leadership that three generations of his partners, each given his head on his own projects, produced work of such consistency. Like others of his generation, he was strongly influenced by Le Corbusier and by welfare-state idealism in his early work—for example in the sadly uncompleted square for Imperial College in Prince's Gardens, London, and in the Brunel University library. But to a person as sensitive as he was to the demands of economics and the nature of the site 'dessicated functionalism', as he called it, had no lasting appeal: he came to prefer warm brickwork, and traditional groupings for buildings such as the quad, seen at its best in the buildings at Manchester, Newcastle, and Durham, and to lament the decline of craftsmanship. The small house he built in his Hertfordshire garden when he could no longer manage the stairs of his Georgian rectory exemplified his easy mastery in its most appealing form.

Sheppard was a large man in presence and in spirit, who gave himself to the service of his profession and the support of his colleagues, serving on a variety of councils and committees into which he would struggle with a deprecatory grin. A bon viveur, he loved travelling with friends in Europe, was an enthusiastic if irreverent sightseer, and collected the work of painters and sculptors he admired (he described his recreation in *Who's Who* as 'looking at the work of others'). From 1954 Sheppard served for over two decades on the council of the Royal Institute of British Architects, latterly as vice-president, and was chairman of the Association of Consulting Architects until his death. He was appointed CBE in 1964, was elected ARA in 1966 and RA in 1972, and was knighted in 1981. He became an honorary DTech of Brunel in 1972.

Sheppard's wife, Jean, died in 1974. The following year, while on holiday, he fell and broke a leg, and was from 1976 frustratingly confined to a wheelchair. On 16 August 1976 he married the widow Marjorie Grace Head (*b.* 1919/20) who had been his companion through these trials. She was the daughter of Stanley Howe Hamilton, an engineer. Sheppard died in Hertford County Hospital on 18 December 1982. LIONEL ESHER

Sources A. Best and S. Hitchens, *Sheppard Robson: architects* (1983) · *The Times* (4 Jan 1983) · L. Esher, *A broken wave: the rebuilding of England, 1940–1980* (1981) · b. cert. · m. cert. · d. cert. · *WWW*, 1981–1990 · personal knowledge (2004)
Wealth at death £332,152: probate, 27 July 1983, *CGPLA Eng. & Wales*

Sheppard [Shepherd], **Robert** (*fl.* 1712–1740), engraver, remains a relatively obscure figure in the history of the eighteenth-century print world. It is said that he studied engraving under David Loggan (1634–1692), but if this is the case he must have worked with that engraver in his waning years, which were plagued by poverty and increasing blindness. In 1712 Sheppard's name appears on the list of members of the Great Queen Street Academy, founded by Sir Godfrey Kneller in the preceding year. Mixing there with more renowned engravers such as George Vertue, Gerard Vandergucht, and Nicolas Dorigny, he had the opportunity to hone his drawing skills through the study of antique casts and life models. Like those engravers, Sheppard (sometimes known as Shepherd) was also heavily involved in reproducing portraits of sovereigns and statesmen for the Knapton Brothers' enormously successful folio publication of Paul de Thoyras-Rapin's *History of England* (1732–7). With their characteristic sculptural ornamentation surrounding competently engraved portraits, these relatively standardized line engravings are usually signed 'R. Sheppard Sculp''. A few other portraits by Sheppard are known, including one of Edward Kidder, which formed the frontispiece to his *Receipts* of 1740. He also engraved three out of a set of six plates after Gérard Audran's *Battles of Alexander*; although these have been criticized as poor by Samuel Redgrave, it should be noted that they were worked up from some very cheap, and late, impressions and cannot therefore provide a true measure of Sheppard's capacity as an engraver. LUCY PELTZ

Sources T. Clayton, *The English print, 1688–1802* (1997) · L. Lippincott, *Selling art in Georgian London: the rise of Arthur Pond* (1983) · Redgrave, *Artists*, 2nd edn · Thieme & Becker, *Allgemeines Lexikon* · Vertue, *Note books*

Sheppard, Samuel (*c.*1624–1655?), writer, was the son of Harman Sheppard, physician, who died on 12 July 1639, aged ninety, and of Petronella (Parnell) Sheppard, who died on 10 September 1650. His parents married at Christ Church, London, on 10 April 1623, and all historical records relating to Samuel Sheppard situate him in London and its environs. No record of his education survives, though he appears to have been a presbyterian minister; John Hackluyt, a rival writer, called Sheppard a 'blasphemous Cleargy-spot' (*Metropolitan Nuncio*, 3, 6–13 June 1649, C.i.v). Sheppard's main activity, however, was as a writer, and from 1646 to 1654 he wrote copiously, in news weeklies, prose reports, essays, poetry, and drama, about the events of the civil war.

In *God and Mammon* (1646) and *The Yeare of Jubile* (1646), Sheppard supports Fairfax, Cromwell, and the parliamentarian reforms, but he also takes pains to represent King Charles as a noble man unfortunately surrounded by weak and corrupt counsellors, 'wicked *Incendiaries* … resident about the KING' (*God and Mammon*, title-page). In *The*

Famers Fam'd (1646) and *The False Alarm* (1646) Sheppard attacks John Lilburne, and in *The Times Displayed in Six Sestyads* (1646), Sheppard's first large poetic work, he satirizes a wide variety of religious denominations and appends an account of the best and worst in English poetry up to the death of Francis Quarles.

Although Sheppard had hitherto supported parliamentarian reforms from a presbyterian standpoint, he was greatly alarmed at the imprisonment of the king in 1646, and his subsequent writings aimed to support Charles and preserve his life. *The Committee-Man Curried*, a play in two parts (1647), depicts parliamentarians as corrupt and hypocritical while allowing a modicum of dignity and moral worth to the royalist character, Loyalty. From 1647 to 1649 Sheppard was active in the writing and editing of underground royalist mercuries and news weeklies, such as *Mercurius Melancholicus*, *Mercurius Pragmaticus*, *Mercurius Elencticus*, *Mercurius Aulicus*, *Mercurius Dogmaticus*, the *Parliament Kite*, and the *Royall Diurnall*. From late 1647-8 the newsbooks become openly hostile towards Fairfax and Cromwell, while Charles is idealized. In the context of bitter rivalry between news weeklies, persecution by parliamentary authorities, and the frequent imprisonment of editors and writers, Sheppard's activities cannot be determined precisely. The poet John Cleveland wrote *Mercurius Pragmaticus*, and Sheppard appears to have been connected with this journal at the outset (*Metropolitan Nuncio*, 3, 6–13 June 1649, C.i.v). In January 1648, probably while writing for *Mercurius Dogmaticus*, Sheppard was sought, and possibly imprisoned, by parliamentary authorities (*Mercurius Melancholicus*, 21, 15–22 Jan 1648, 120; *Mercurius Anti-Mercurius*, 1, 12–19 Sept 1648, 2–3). The revival of *Mercurius Aulicus* from early February to mid May 1648 has been attributed to Sheppard, chiefly because these editions bear his personal motto, 'Quis me impune lacessit'. In the spring of 1648 Sheppard became the chief writer of *Mercurius Elencticus* when its editor, George Wharton, was imprisoned (*Mercurius Anti-Mercurius*, 1, 12–19 Sept 1648, 1–2). In June 1648 Sheppard was imprisoned in Petre House, Aldersgate Street (*Mercurius Melancholicus*, 44, 19–26 June 1648, 265), and by the end of July he was at liberty and contributing to the *Royall Diurnall* and possibly the *Parliament Kite* as well as a counterfeit version of *Mercurius Melancholicus* (*Mercurius Melancholicus*, 51, 7–14 Aug 1648, title-page verso; the *Royall Diurnall*, 4, 14–22 Aug 1648, D.i.v).

On 16 April 1649 a warrant was issued for the arrest of Sheppard and William Wright, identified as writer and printer respectively of *Mercurius Elencticus* (*CSP dom.*, 1649–50, 529). Sheppard remained in prison until at least May 1650 (*CSP dom.*, 1650, 143), by which time Charles had been executed and Sheppard's cause lost; John Thurloe, secretary of state, appears to have supported Sheppard's release (Sheppard, *The Weepers*, 1652, 11). During this longest period of imprisonment, spent at Newgate and possibly also at Lollards' Tower, Lambeth, and again at Petre House, Sheppard completed his most interesting and ambitious work, *The Faerie King* (Sheppard, *Epigrams*, 1651,

6.16; 'Postscript', c.1654, to *Faerie King*). Unlike the preceding news weeklies, *The Faerie King*, existing in a single holograph MS (Bodl. Oxf., MS Rawl. Poet. 28) and unpublished until 1984, offers a richly ambivalent portrait of Charles and the nature of monarchy. The Spenserian title belies the originality and thoughtfulness of this verse epic.

After his release in 1650 Sheppard continued to publish in a variety of genres and managed to avoid further trouble with parliamentarian authorities: a prose romance, *Amandus and Sophronia* (1650); *The Joviall Crew* (1651), a play satirizing the ranters; *Epigrams Theological, Philosophical, and Romantick* (1651), which includes an epigram to Cromwell; *The Socratick Session* and *A Mausolean Monument*, both printed with *Epigrams* and the latter a tribute to his late parents, dedicated to his 'Kinsman' Christopher Clapham of Beamsley, Yorkshire, and also mentioning his wife, Mary; *Discoveries* (1652); the commendatory poem in Thomas Manley's *Veni; vidi; vici* (1652), a panegyric to Cromwell; possibly *Mercurius Mastix* (1652), a diatribe against news weeklies; *The Weepers* (1652), a darkly bitter work matching the mood of *Mercurius Mastix* and *The Faerie King* and hinting at Sheppard's continued respect for the king; *Merlinus Anonymous* (1653), a mock almanac, and probably *Good-Ale Monopolized* (1654), a satire on Robert Tichborne, both works published under the anagrammatic pseudonym Raphael Desmus. The last reference to Sheppard (which suggests he was still alive at the time of writing) is in William Winstanley's *The Muses Cabinet* (1655, 22), and he presumably died later in this year.

ANDREW KING

Sources H. E. Rollins, 'Samuel Sheppard and his praise of poets', *Studies in Philology*, 24 (1927), 509–55 · J. Frank, *The beginnings of the English newspaper, 1620–1660* (1961) · J. Raymond, *The invention of the newspaper: English newsbooks, 1641–1649* (1996) · C. Nelson and M. Seccombe, eds., *British newspapers and periodicals, 1641–1700: a short-title catalogue of serials printed in England, Scotland, Ireland, and British America* (1987) · *The Thomason tracts, 1640–1661: an index to the microfilm edition*, 2 vols. (1981) · S. Sheppard, *The faerie king (c.1650)*, ed. P. J. Klemp (1984) · [J. Hackluyt], *Metropolitan Nuncio*, 3 (6–13 June 1649) [C.i.v] · *Mercurius Melancholicus*, 21 (15–22 Jan 1648), 120 · *Mercurius Anti-Mercurius*, 1 (12–19 Sept 1648), 1–3 · *Mercurius Melancholicus*, 44 (19–26 June 1648), 265 · *Mercurius Melancholicus*, 51 (7–14 Aug 1648) [title-page verso] · *Royall Diurnall*, 4 (14–22 Aug 1648) [D.i.v] · *CSP dom.*, 1649–50, 529; 1650, 143 · DNB · S. Sheppard, *Epigrams theological, philosophical, and romantick* (1651) [incl. *A mausolean monument*]

Sheppard, Thomas (1876–1945), museum director and writer on geology, was born on 2 October 1876 in South Ferriby, Lincolnshire, but spent his entire life in east Yorkshire. He was the eldest of a family of ten born to Harvey Sheppard (1848–1912) of Wiltshire and his wife, Myra, *née* Havercroft (1854–1938), of South Ferriby. Both of his parents were teachers, the father successively holding headmasterships at three Hull schools from 1877 until his death. Thomas received only elementary-school education, his final year as a pupil teacher. On leaving school at the age of thirteen he worked as a clerk for eleven years, first in railway then dock offices at Hull. He took advantage of the free travel his position afforded to further his natural-history interests and improve his education, attending courses at South Kensington. There he gained certificates in a wide range of natural-history subjects and a first-class advanced-stage certificate in geology, which not only qualified him to teach, but also facilitated his appointment as the first city curator of the Hull Municipal Museum in 1901. In the same year he married, on 7 March, Mary Isobel Osbourn (1877/8–1947); the couple had one son, Thomas Harvey (b. 1902).

Over the eighteen-month period following his appointment, the museum was totally refurbished under Sheppard's direction. He abolished admission charges upon its reopening; thereafter the museum never had fewer than 2000 visitors per week. Over the years, Sheppard was responsible for establishing a further six museums in Hull: viz. the Natural History Museum (1910), Museum of Fisheries and Shipping (1912), Museum of Commerce and Transport (1925; the first of its kind in Britain), Wilberforce House Museum (1906), Mortimer Collection of Prehistoric Antiquities (1929), and the Railway Museum (1933), as well as the Tithe Barn Museum at Easington (1928; Britain's first open-air museum). The innovative 'Old Time' Street Museum, on which Sheppard had been working for much of his career, was destroyed by bombs in 1941 before its official opening. As director (a title conferred in 1926) of such a large number of successful museums Sheppard was highly influential locally and nationally, but his often ruthlessly acquisitive activities made him a decidedly controversial figure.

Sheppard was a prolific writer, being the author of numerous books, including *Geological Rambles in East Yorkshire* (1903), *The Making of East Yorkshire* (1906), *The Evolution of Kingston upon Hull* (1911), *The Lost Towns of the Yorkshire Coast* (1912), *Bibliography of Yorkshire Geology* (1915), *Yorkshire's Contribution to Science* (1916), and *William Smith; his Maps and Memoirs* (1920). He also contributed innumerable scientific and cultural papers to around 165 journals and magazines; he edited *The Naturalist* (1903–33), *Transactions of the East Riding Antiquarian Society* (1905–41), Hull Museum Publications (213 of which appeared during 1901–41, many under his authorship), and several other journals. He held presidencies, secretaryships, and other offices in many societies, such as the Yorkshire Naturalists' Union, Museums Association, and the Hull Geological Society. He received an honorary MSc from the University of Leeds (1915) in recognition of his scientific activities, more particularly his bibliographical work in geology; he also received several other honours including the Geological Society of London's Lyell award and the silver medal of the French Association for the Advancement of Science. He was elected ALS, FGS, FSA, FRGS, FZS, and FRAI, and had honorary memberships of at least sixteen societies.

About 1932 ill-health caused Sheppard to relinquish many activities, and overwork (and heavy drinking) resulted in the breakdown of his marriage. Nevertheless, through boundless energy and imagination, Sheppard amassed for his beloved Hull one of Britain's finest provincial museum collections. By doing so he not only put the city on the map but also gained a national reputation for himself and his collections. Tragically, many of the collections were destroyed by bombs and fire in 1941 and 1943—the destruction of these and many of his notes, his lifetime's work, contributed to the further decline in his health after his retirement in 1941. Financial pressures after this date forced the piecemeal sale of his extensive private library. His collection of local society journals was used to augment the British Museum (Natural History) holdings and his maps were acquired by the National Museum of Wales. He died at his home, 46 Anlaby Park Road, Hull, on 18 February 1945 and was cremated three days later. MARK SEAWARD

Sources B. J. Sitch, 'A critical assessment of Thomas Sheppard &c', MA diss., University of Leicester, 1992 · T. Schadla-Hall, *Tom Sheppard: Hull's great collector* (1989) · M. Horne, 'The history of the Hull Geological Society, 1888–1988', *Humberside Geologist*, 7 (1989), 1–40 · W. F. Walker, 'Thomas Sheppard, 1876–1945', *Transactions of the East Riding Antiquarian Society*, 29 (1949), 67–9 · M. Horne, 'Tom Sheppard "hyper scientist"', *Humberside Geologist*, 5 (1986), 5–6 · H. C. Versey, 'Thomas Sheppard, 1876–1945', *The Naturalist* (April–June 1945), 74–5 · B. J. Sitch, 'Thomas Sheppard and archaeological collecting', *East Riding Archaeological Society News*, 41 (1994), 5–13 · F. G. Tadman, ed., *Hull's who's who* (1935), 105–7 · A. Berry, 'The Hull Geological Society Medal, 1938', *Humberside Geologist*, 5 (1986), 7–11 · *WWW*, 1941–50 · S. Melmore, 'Obituary: Thomas Sheppard (1876–1945)', *North-Western Naturalist*, 20 (1945), 75–9 · 'Pen portrait no. 15: Mr Thomas Sheppard, FGS', *Yorkshire Notes and Queries* (1905), 65–6 · *Museum Journal*, 45 (1945), 11–12 · *Hull Times* (24 Feb 1945) · *Hull Daily Mail* (19 Feb 1945) · m. cert.

Archives GS Lond. · Hull Central Library · priv. coll. · U. Leeds, Brotherton L., draft of *Geological rambles around Hull* | Hull City Archives · NHM, letters to E. G. Bayford | FILM newsreel footage | SOUND BBC programmes

Likenesses V. Galloway, oils, 1932, Ferens Art Gallery, Kingston upon Hull; repro. in *The Naturalist* (1933), frontispiece · photograph, repro. in Schadla-Hall, *Tom Sheppard* · photograph, repro. in *The Naturalist*, 21 (1896), 336 · photograph, repro. in *The Naturalist*, 48 (1923), 310 · photograph, repro. in Versey, 'Thomas Sheppard', 74

Wealth at death £1532 3s. 11d.: probate, 20 March 1946, *CGPLA Eng. & Wales*

Sheppard, William (*bap.* 1595, *d.* 1674), barrister and legal writer, was baptized on 14 December 1595 at St Andrew's Church, Whitminster, near Frampton-on-Severn, Gloucestershire, the eldest of five children born to Philip Sheppard (*d.* 1623) and Elizabeth Tyrell. Two more sons and two daughters were born between 1597 and 1605 (Sarah, Rebecca, John, and Samuel), and in 1608 the family moved to Horsley in the Cotswold region south of Stroud.

Early years, education, and the civil war, 1595–1654 Horsley remained Sheppard's principal home until 1637. His first marriage, about 1617, to Mary of Wingfield, Wiltshire, brought them two children, John in 1618 and Mary in 1620; his wife apparently died soon after her daughter's birth. (John attended Wadham College, Oxford, and became a minister. Mary married John Clifford of Frampton.) In 1620 Sheppard was admitted to the Middle Temple where he was called to the bar in 1629. He retained the Temple lodgings he shared with William Hussey until 1631 when he returned to Horsley to establish a country law practice. In 1621 Sheppard married his second wife, Anne, daughter of George Worth of Buckington Manor, Wiltshire. Their children Elizabeth (*b.* 1623), Sarah (*b.* 1624), Samuel (*b.* 1627), and Anne (*b.* 1628) were baptized in Horsley.

Another son, William, was born during that decade, possibly to his third wife, the Widow Fisher. In August 1637 when he married his fourth wife, Alice Coney, Sheppard moved to Hempsted, a parish bordering Gloucester, where his daughter Rebecca was born in 1649. Apart from three years spent in Cromwell's service in London, Hempsted remained his home for the rest of his long life.

In his native county and neighbouring areas Sheppard practised as a conveyancer and served as steward on several manors, presiding over their courts. He was an attorney of Gloucester's local court, and attended the great sessions of Wales, the Oxford and western circuit assizes, and quarter sessions; the legal texts he published are filled with citations to cases heard in those courts. His undoubted expertise in conveyancing is apparent in The Touchstone of Common Assurances (1648, not 1641 as often given; English edns to 1826, Irish edn 1785, United States edns to 1840–41), a collection of twenty-three essays. Other early works reflecting his local country practice were several manuals for local law enforcement, The Offices and Duties of Constables (1641, rev. 1652, 1657), The Court-Keepers Guide (1649, 1650, 1654, 1656, 1662, posthumous edns in 1767 and 1791) for stewards of manor courts, and The Whole Office of the Country Justice of the Peace (1650, 1661, 1662). An Exact Collection of Choice Declarations (1653) by 'W. S.', one of the clerks of the upper bench office' (title-page) was incorrectly attributed to Sheppard by the Dictionary of National Biography. It was written by William Small, a clerk of the king's bench. Sheppard's initial effort to compile a legal encyclopaedia, the two-part The Faithfull Councellor, or, The Marrow of the Law in English (1651 and 1654), was the base for later works. In each of these books Sheppard presented in English an updated account of the law with clear and concise definitions and citations to recent cases. His goal from his first to his last publication was to clarify current law in the interest of accessibility to justice.

Sheppard's commitment to legal reform was mirrored by a passion for religious reform, and his call by Cromwell owes as much to his religious commitment as to his proven legal skills. His first two religious publications (both 1649) were a catechism dedicated to the people of Gloucester and an essay on salvation. His argument of 1652 advocating lay preaching identified Sheppard as a follower of John Owen and the Independents and was undoubtedly critical in bringing him to Cromwell's attention.

The protectorate years, 1654–1657 Sheppard was summoned to London in the spring of 1654 to advise Cromwell on legal matters and to create a law reform programme. There are strong inferential grounds that Sheppard drafted the chancery ordinance, a reform document issued in August 1654, and internal evidence—a determination to avoid delays, reduce costs, and eliminate corruption through regulating procedure—reflects Sheppard's approach to reform. Despite opposition, Cromwell implemented the ordinance in 1655 and it remained in effect until 1658.

Sheppard's outstanding achievement and the centrepiece of his contribution to the protectorate was England's Balme (1656, but 1657 on the title page). Dedicated to Cromwell 'and your council, by whose care it hath been brought forth', it was the fullest design for the reform of English law published in the seventeenth century. In it Sheppard gathered 'other men's grievances', including reforms advocated by earlier writers, and wove them into an original scheme, producing a plan notable for the comprehensiveness of its scope. A number of his recommendations were drafted as bills presented to the parliament of 1656, and the guiding principles and many particular reforms were adopted in the nineteenth century. A central tenet was the legal unification of England, with the fusion of law and equity in an integrated appellate judicial system, uniformity of process, abolition of special pleading and of benefit of clergy, reduction of capital crimes and abolition of imprisonment for debt, registration of title, simplified conveyancing, county courts for small claims, defendants in felony cases allowed counsel and sworn witnesses, and a number of social reforms. One jarring note in this package of essentially moderate reforms is a provision that 'godless and wicked men ... dangerous in their principles ... or notoriously wicked or scandalous ... so long as they continue so, be incapable of any office in the commonwealth' (W. Sheppard, England's Balme, 1656, 41–2). Predicated on Sheppard's belief that only godly men 'who declare the power of godliness in their lives' and a second rank of 'all sober and civil men' were fit to rule, his aim was to establish a new political order based upon a reformed law made more rational, simpler, and more humane (ibid.). Looking to the example of the Massachusetts Bay colony settlement for many of his ideas, he hoped to bring the laws and the governance of England into closer accord with the laws of God.

Sheppard prepared nine books to support the protector's agenda for reform during the three years he served as Cromwell's legal adviser (June 1654 – August 1657). To ensure support for a preaching ministry, The Parson's Guide providing guidance on tithe collection was issued three times in 1654. A handbook of warrants used by justices of the peace was published the same year (1654, updated edns 1660, 1672). In 1655 A View of All the Laws ... Concerning the Service of God or Religion set out the legal framework of the religious settlement that had been promulgated by ordinance in 1654. Published to serve immediate goals of the administration, these works were short-lived. In contrast, The President [Precedent] of Presidents (1655, edns to 1870) was issued in at least ten editions. A companion volume to his Touchstone (1648), it introduced standard forms to register land and was endorsed by the government newspaper as a conveyancing precedent 'of singular use and profit to all men' (Publick Intelligencer, 10 Feb 1656, 280). In April 1656 his A Survey of County Judicatures called for the reinvigoration of ancient courts to hear suits of small value, and the same month the fourth edition of his Court-Keepers Guide, also a review of local jurisdictions, was recommended in the government newspaper, the Publick

Intelligencer (21 April 1656, 509). Official approval of Sheppard's work was signalled by renewing his annual salary of £300 in January 1656, by the February appointment of a committee to consider his law reform proposals, and by the introduction of bills for both land registration and country courts to the second protectorate parliament in September. In May 1656 Sheppard's second legal encyclopaedia, *An Epitome of All the Common and Statute Laws of the Nation now in Force* (1656), was printed 'by his highness's special command' (title page). His last assignment under the protectorate provided material for his 1659 book, *Of Corporations, Fraternities, and Guilds*, the first book in English on the law of corporations which included the texts of five Cromwellian charters. In June 1656 the council of state assigned Sheppard to head a commission that prepared or revised at least fourteen corporation charters for boroughs throughout England and Wales.

The zenith of Sheppard's public career came in October 1656 when the government created him a serjeant-at-law just weeks after *England's Balme* was published. He continued working on borough charters until August 1657 when his employment under the protectorate government ended. Sheppard was paid some back salary owed him and he returned to his family and his country practice.

Later publications and the Restoration years, 1657–1674 Back in Hempsted and faced with financial hardship Sheppard petitioned Cromwell in November 1657 for 'some office or place to continue some part of [my] salary'. Finding that his association with the protectorate government was 'distasteful to many' and he had 'lost his law practice utterly in his country', the petition noted that he had five children of his own and the widow and three children of his son John, a minister, in his household, 'all as yet unprovided for' (PRO, SP 18/157/131, fol. 150). The council authorized an annual pension of £100, but no record of payments has been discovered. His final religious work, *Of the Foure Last and Greatest Things: Death, Judgement, Heaven and Hell*, was published in April 1658 in collaboration with Thomas Barlow, provost of Oxford's Queen's College. Sheppard, who returned to writing legal texts, heard no more from Westminster until September 1659, when he was called back into the political arena by the restored Rump Parliament and appointed to the Welsh bench and sworn as chief justice of the north Wales circuit. That autumn two works written during his service to Cromwell were published, *A New Survey of the Justice of Peace* (1659) and the more important *Of Corporations* (1659).

At the time of the Restoration, Sheppard was sixty-five years old, and in the remaining years of his life he published another seven books, principally dealing with local law enforcement and property law, topics that had long occupied his attention, but with two innovative studies, *Action upon the Case for Slander* (1662) and *Actions upon the Case for Deeds* (1663), both reprinted in the 1670s without the lengthy case illustrations. An entirely new handbook for magistrates, *A Sure Guide to his Majesties Justices of the Peace* (1662), bravely criticized the intolerance of the Restoration religious settlement, introducing legal arguments to soften persecution. A short manual, *Of the Office of the Clerk of the Market* (1665), illustrates Sheppard's indefatigable drive to define yet another local office. *The Practical Counsellor in the Law* (1671) and *The Law of Common Assurances* (1669) together constituted an enlargement on the *Touchstone*, but the added material did not improve upon the original. His final work, *A Grand Abridgment of the Common and Statute Law of England* (published posthumously in 1675), was a partly rewritten expansion of his two earlier encyclopaedias, *Faithfull Councellor*, 1 and 2 (1651, 1653) and *The Epitome* (1656).

Sheppard died on 26 March 1674 at Hempsted, Gloucestershire, and was buried in the nave of St Swithin's Church, Hempsted, four days later. His widow, Alice, died on 29 July 1693 and was buried with her husband.

Historical significance—changing interpretations of life and career Over a thirty-three-year writing career Sheppard produced forty-nine editions of his twenty-three books on the law and there is a fundamental consistency in the considerable contributions to legal literature of this formidably industrious and productive author. He broke new ground in the literature of actions on the case, the law of corporations, and standardized precedents for land records. His manuals for local officials updated and often improved on earlier efforts and are valuable for what they reveal about the way the law actually functioned in his generation. His three encyclopaedic compilations, which combined statutes, case law, and legal definitions, were the first published in English. They were, by the author's admission, incomplete, yet they demonstrate Sheppard's confidence that, with the right tools, the law could be made accessible and the legal system more efficient. The nine books he prepared for the protectorate typify the pragmatic reforms of Cromwell's administration and add an authoritative dimension to the evidence supporting Cromwell's reputation as an advocate of law reform. Sheppard's master-work of law reform proposals, *England's Balme*, the most comprehensive law reform document of this fruitful period, clearly places Sheppard in the historical continuum with Finch and other earlier reformers and the moderate lawyers who supported Cromwell. The failure of his programme can be partly explained by opposition from powerful forces within the legal establishment as well as challenges in the political realm, and the book was largely forgotten or ignored for more than a century. It is to Sheppard's credit that he never lost his confidence that the law could be made more rational and humane, and his tenacity in pursuing this goal is remarkable.

Sheppard's two most influential books endured for two centuries and served the profession well. In the *Touchstone* (1648, edns to 1840–41) and *The President* (1655, edns to 1870), he wrote clearly on the subject he knew best. The political discredit arising from his close association with Cromwell may have led to the allegation in 1760 that Sheppard plagiarized the *Touchstone*'s text from a manuscript found in John Doddridge's library. This charge was written by J. Booth of Lincoln's Inn on the title page of his copy, the story admittedly emanating from third-hand hearsay. Edward Hilliard, editor of the 1780 edition of the *Touchstone*, published the accusation as did later editors. Years later R. W. Bridgman in *A Short View of Legal Bibliography* (1807) and John Clarke in *Bibliotheca legum* (1810) disputed the allegation, noting that much of the text was grounded in material not available until the year of Doddridge's death (1628). Sheppard most certainly wrote the book himself, but the slur on his reputation persisted and was repeated by John Hutchinson in *A Catalogue of Notable Middle Templars* (1902), pages 223–4; W. R. Williams in *A History of the Great Sessions in Wales* (1899), page 60; P. H. Winfield in *The Chief Sources of English Legal History* (1925), pages 240–41; W. L. Holdsworth in *A History of English Law* (1923–37), volume 5, page 83, and by others. The evidence distinctly supports Sheppard's authorship and the *Touchstone* remained the best introduction to conveyancing in that 200-year period.   NANCY L. MATTHEWS

Sources N. L. Matthews, *William Sheppard, Cromwell's law reformer* (1984) • G. E. B. Eyre, ed., *A transcript of the registers of the Worshipful Company of Stationers from 1640 to 1708*, 3 vols. (1913–14) • E. Arber, ed., *The term catalogues, 1668–1709*, 3 vols. (privately printed, London, 1903–6) • *STC, 1475–1640*, 1st edn (1945–51) • [R. W. Bridgman], *A short view of legal bibliography* (1807) • J. Clarke, *Bibliotheca legum* (1810) • Allibone, *Dict.* • R. Bigland, *Historical, monumental and genealogical collections, relative to the county of Gloucester*, 2 vols. (1791–2) • T. F. Fenwick and W. C. Metcalfe, eds., *The visitation of the county of Gloucester* (privately printed, Exeter, 1884) • *Gloucestershire Notes and Queries*, 4 (1890) • C. H. Hopwood, ed., *Middle Temple records*, 2: 1603–1649 (1904) • *JHC*, 7 (1651–9), 719, 734, 744–5, 748–9 • H. A. C. Sturgess, ed., *Register of admissions to the Honourable Society of the Middle Temple, from the fifteenth century to the year 1944*, 1 (1949) • W. A. Sheppard, *A brief history of the Sheppard family … in the county of Gloucestershire, England* (1891) • J. Smyth, *Men and armour of Gloucestershire for 1608* (1902) • *Publick Intelligencer* (21 April 1656), 509 • PRO, SP 18/157/131 • private information (2004) [family] • Glos. RO, P 362 IN 1/1, fol. 6r • PRO, PROB 11/142, fol. 121 • Glos. RO, P 173, Acc. 3097, IN 1/1, fol. 43v

Archives Glos. RO, Gloucester city MSS; Gloucester diocesan MSS • Gloucester Public Library, Hockaday abstracts, typescript of parish records taken from MSS of the Gloucester consistory court by F. S. Hockaday • PRO, assizes, chancery, exchequer, probate, state papers • Worcester College, Oxford, Clarke MSS

Wealth at death plea to council of state for a pension for 'old age', November 1657: PRO, SP 18/157/131, fol. 150

Sheppard, William (*fl.* 1641–1660), portrait painter, makes his first appearance in historical records in February 1641, when 'Mr. Sheppard a Picture maker by Cree church [St Katharine Cree]' paid his admittance fee to the London Company of Painter–Stainers (Guildhall Library, MS 5667/1, fol. 157). It is also during this decade that Sheppard acquired his only recorded apprentice, Francis Barlow, who on arrival from Lincolnshire was 'put prentice to one Shepherd, a Face-Painter, with whom he lived but a few years because his Fancy did not lie that way' (Vertue, 2.135).

During the Commonwealth years Sheppard may have allied himself with the exiled royalists; he is referred to in the notebooks of Richard Symonds, the royalist diarist and antiquary, during the latter's stay in Rome from 1649

to 1651. Sheppard, then in Rome, informed Symonds of the price paid in London for *azzuro* (ultramarine). In Venice in 1650 Sheppard painted the portrait of the royalist Thomas Killigrew, who had been appointed Charles II's resident to the Venetian republic. This image, which is both a portrait of Killigrew and a mourning picture for Charles I, is the only painting by Sheppard known to survive; there are various versions, of which the principal belongs to the National Portrait Gallery, London. It was engraved by William Faithorne.

In 1651 'William Sheppard, an English limner' sailed from Italy to Constantinople. He was shipwrecked near Samos and was taken to Rhodes, where he was 'kept in restraint', and his wife in London had to solicit the Levant Company to obtain his release (*CSP dom.*, 50). Sheppard was back in London by the Restoration. Despite the lack of evidence, it seems that he enjoyed a good practice as in 1658 William Sanderson included him in his list of 'English modern masters': 'In the *Life*, *Walker*, *Zowst*, *Wright*, *Lillie*, *Hales*, *Shepheard*, *de Grange*, rare Artizans' (Sanderson, 20). The only work that may be attributed to William Sheppard apart from the portrait of Killigrew is a portrait of Sir Henry Terne (after 1660). It is only known from the engraving by William Faithorne.

George Vertue's information on Sheppard was brief:

Mr. Shephard face painter. who livd in K. Charles 2d time. Mr. Russel. when a boy knew him. he livd in London at that time. near the Royal exchange. was a pleasant Companion—afterwards retird into Yorkshire where he died. (Vertue, 4.64)

Horace Walpole transcribed Vertue's account in his *Anecdotes* but had nothing to add to it.

    CAROL BLACKETT-ORD

Sources Vertue, *Note books*, 2.135, 4.64 • 'Orders and constitutions', Painter–Stainers' Company, transcript of the court minute book, 1623–49, GL, MS 5667/1, fol. 157 • R. Symonds, 'Secrete intorno la pittura veduta e sentita dalla prattica dal Sig. Gio. Angelo Canini in Roma A°1650, 1651, 1652 etc.', BL, MS Egerton 1636, fol. 15 • *CSP dom.*, 1651–2 • W. Sanderson, *Graphice: the use of the pen and pensil, or, The most excellent art of painting* (1658), 20 • L. Fagan, *A descriptive catalogue of the engraved works of William Faithorne* (1888), 43, 63 • M. Rogers, '"Golden houses for shadows": some portraits of Thomas Killigrew and his family', *Art and patronage in the Caroline courts: essays in honour of Sir Oliver Millar*, ed. D. Howarth (1993), 220–42 • H. Walpole, *Anecdotes of painting in England: with some account of the principal artists*, ed. R. N. Wornum, new edn, 2 (1849); repr. (1862), 520

Sheppey, John (*c.*1300–1360), bishop of Rochester, presumably took his name from the Isle of Sheppey off the northern coast of Kent. Nothing is known of his family, except that he was survived by a sister, Alice, and her son, Peter, and may have been related to another John Sheppey, sub-sacrist at Rochester Priory. He was educated as a Benedictine at Rochester under the patronage of Bishop Hamo Hethe (*d.* 1352), and ordained deacon on 17 June 1318. He studied at Oxford and Hethe gave him permission to incept in theology in June 1332. On 12 August 1333 he was elected prior of Rochester. He was an able financial administrator, and enforced monastic observances said to have lapsed through negligence. Relations with Hethe were cordial, apart from a squabble during a visitation when Sheppey sided with a monk, John Hwytefelde, who, in a sermon, challenged Hethe's authority over the monks who had elected him. Sheppey's public duties drew him to the attention of government. In 1345 he was sent on a diplomatic mission to Castile to arrange Princess Joan's marriage, and he took this opportunity to visit the papal court at Avignon. He was a member of the king's council from 1345, and was one of the diplomats sent to Calais in 1349 to arrange a truce.

Following Hethe's resignation Sheppey was provided to the see of Rochester by papal letter dated 22 November 1352, and was consecrated in St Mary Overie, Southwark, by William Edington, bishop of Winchester (d. 1366), on 10 March 1353. His episcopal register survives only fragmentarily, but, as he himself declared in a sermon, he was vigorous in prosecuting the unchaste in his diocese. Secular duties multiplied, and from 28 November 1356 until his death he acted as treasurer of England. He died on 19 October 1360 at his manor of La Place, Lambeth, and was buried in Rochester Cathedral at the altar of St John the Baptist, where he had founded a chantry. His elaborately painted effigy still survives in the presbytery, where it was discovered walled up in 1825. His will was drawn up less than a month before his death; his legatees included his sister and nephew, the prior and convent of Rochester, William Whittlesey (d. 1374), who succeeded him as bishop, colleagues in the royal service, and his friend Edington, to whom he left a memorial ring.

Sheppey is best known as a preacher. His sermons—among the few fourteenth-century episcopal sermons extant—survive in his autograph collection in Oxford, New College, MS 92. The majority are dated between 1336 and 1354, and were preached principally in Rochester, though they include two preached at Paul's Cross, London; most of them are occasional sermons. Although they are recorded in Latin, Sheppey's own testimony, and the presence of many vernacular phrases, show that most were intended for English delivery. He also collected other sermons and theological material useful for preaching, which survive in Oxford, Merton College, MS 248, including what may be his own abridgement of the *Fabulae* of Odo of Cheriton (d. 1247). Three more books owned by him survive, principally of theology, but with some works of Aristotle.   H. L. SPENCER

Sources G. Mifsud, 'John Sheppey, bishop of Rochester, as preacher and collector of sermons', BLitt diss., U. Oxf., 1953 • Emden, *Oxf.* • F. M. Powicke, *The medieval books of Merton College* (1931) • A. G. Little and F. Pelster, *Oxford theology and theologians*, OHS, 96 (1934) • L. Hervieux, *Les fabulistes latins*, 5 vols. (Paris, 1893–9), vol. 4 • S. Cavanaugh, 'A study of books privately owned in England, 1300–1450', PhD diss., University of Pennsylvania, 1980 • W. H. St J. Hope, 'The architectural history of the cathedral church and monastery of St Andrew at Rochester', *Archaeologia Cantiana*, 23 (1898), 194–328, esp. 314–15 • A. J. Kempe, 'Description of the sepulchral effigy of John de Sheppey, bishop of Rochester, discovered in Rochester Cathedral, AD 1825 with illustrative drawings', *Archaeologia*, 25 (1834), 122–6 • Register of Simon Islip, LPL, fols. 169v–170 • [H. Wharton], ed., *Anglia sacra*, 1 (1691), 1 • *Chronica Johannis de Reading et anonymi Cantuariensis, 1346–1367*, ed. J. Tait (1914)

Archives BL, Royal MSS 10 C.xii; 12 D.xiv • Merton Oxf., MSS 243, 248 • New College, Oxford, MS 92
Likenesses effigy, Rochester Cathedral
Wealth at death see LPL, register of Simon Islip, fols. 169v–170

Shepreve, John (1509?–1542), classical scholar, was born in Sugworth, Berkshire; the Roman Catholic priest William Shepreve was his nephew. Having gained a scholarship to Corpus Christi College, Oxford, he was appointed a probationer fellow there in 1528. He graduated BA on 3 December 1529, and at an early age was held 'in great esteem for his sufficiencies in the Greek and Hebrew tongues' (Wood, *Ath. Oxon.: Fasti*, 1.81). Shepreve was made a full fellow in 1530, and incorporated MA three years later. The same year also saw his appointment as a supervisor of wine and, more significantly, as a college lecturer in Greek. In 1538 he was made a professor of Hebrew, a position he held concurrently with his college lectureship.

Shepreve was a gifted linguist and poet, much valued by his contemporaries. As a lecturer he sought to combine his devotion to the biblical languages with his conservative beliefs. While the evangelical party at his college claimed that in 1538 Shepreve had allegedly held the view that 'the studiying off the scriptures was subversion of goode order' (Milne, 30–31), in April 1542 he nevertheless petitioned the university authorities for a permission to read on the Hebrew text of Genesis. There can be no doubt that Shepreve abided by the decree that he should 'lecture in godly and catholic fashion' (Oxford University Archives, register I, fol. 81).

As a poet Shepreve was widely acclaimed; Wood claimed that it was 'an ordinary matter with him to compose 100 very good verses every day in his vacant hours' (Wood, *Ath. Oxon.*, 3rd edn, 1.135). His literary output not only was extraordinarily divergent but also offers a remarkable insight into his beliefs. In his authoritative biography in Latin hexameters of a former president of his college, John Claymond, he described pre-Reformation religious practice with so much genuine affection that a later Edwardian copyist added marginal notes warning the reader 'not to give credence' ('ne crede, lector') to some of the 'Papist' practices mentioned (Corpus Christi College, Oxford, MS 257, fol. 16v, fol. 244r). While Shepreve doubtlessly remained faithful to his conservative beliefs, his Hebrew hymn in praise of Henry VIII suggests that he probably subscribed to the royal supremacy.

Even Shepreve's literary publications are suffused by conservative beliefs. In a versified paraphrase of Ovid's *Phaedra*, he reminisced about traditional doctrines of justification and concluded that 'as piety is an ancient virtue, we should believe that former generations did good works' ('si vetus est pietas, tanto magis esse tenedam arbitrior antiquis multa fieri bona'; Corpus Christi College, Oxford, MS 266, fol. 29v). A few of his manuscript works were published posthumously by his admirers. His three mnemonic aids to the New Testament, composed for his students in Latin verse, were repeatedly incorporated in contemporary commentaries. Shepreve also built up a reputation as an accomplished translator. While his translations of Euripides' *Hecuba* into Latin, and Seneca's

Hercules furens into English are no longer extant, his Latin translation of Basil the Great's commentary on Isaiah remains in manuscript. He died in Amersham, Buckinghamshire, in July 1542.   J. ANDREAS LÖWE

Sources J. Caley and J. Hunter, eds., *Valor ecclesiasticus temp. Henrici VIII*, 6 vols., RC (1810–34), vol. 2, p. 249 · *Reg. Oxf.*, 1.154, 348 · J. Leland, *Cygnea cantio commentarii* (1554), 27 · J. G. Milne, *The early history of Corpus Christi College, Oxford* (1946), 30–31 · Wood, *Ath. Oxon.*, new edn, 1.134–6 · Wood, *Ath. Oxon.: Fasti* (1815), 81 · A. Wood, *The history and antiquities of the colleges and halls in the University of Oxford*, ed. J. Gutch, appx (1790), 233 · Foster, *Alum. Oxon.* · J. Pits, *Relationum historicarum de rebus Anglicis*, ed. [W. Bishop] (Paris, 1619), 730f.
Archives BL, Birch MS 4355; Royal MS 16. a. 2 · Bodl. Oxf., MS Wood F30; MS Rawl. misc. 335 · CCC Oxf., MS 257 (4), fols. 12–18; MS 266, fol. 235; MS 280 (27); MS 303 (2) · CCC Oxf., MS 266, fols. 202, 245

Shepreve [**Sheprey**], **William** (c.1540–1598), Roman Catholic priest and scholar, nephew of John Shepreve, was born near Abingdon, Berkshire, about 1540. On 16 February 1555 he was elected to a scholarship at Corpus Christi College, Oxford, 'aged fourteen or thereabouts' (Wood, *Ath. Oxon.*, 2.668). He was made a probationer of his college in November 1558 and graduated BA on 15 February 1560, 'which was the highest degree he took in this university' (ibid.).

A devoted Catholic, Shepreve left Oxford for the Low Countries. In 1574 he arrived at the English College in Douai and was ordained to the priesthood later that year. Soon after his arrival at Douai, Shepreve continued his studies and began to read for a BTh at the Catholic university there. He was examined on 20 November 1575 and admitted BTh on 23 December. On 5 May 1576 he was appointed principal of the College of Anchin, also in the diocese of Arras. He is recorded as one of the doctors who were admitted DTh at Douai.

Shepreve was sent to Rome on 9 November, intending to live in Italy and to help establish an English college there; he accompanied doctors Stapleton, White, and Martin. In Rome he was 'exhibited to' (maintained by) Gabriele Paleotti, cardinal archbishop of Bologna, whom he served as a chaplain. Two letters from Bologna to the rector of the English College, one by Paleotti and another by Shepreve, survive. A capable writer and biblical interpreter Shepreve devoted his skills to providing a thorough companion to the Marian office. His *Connexio literalis psalmorum in officio beatae Mariae virginis* (Rome, 1596) was the only work to be published. In manuscript, Shepreve left two minor glosses on the Pauline epistles and an exposition of the Marian office as well as an anthology of popular scriptural passages.

Shepreve died at St Severian's, Rome, in 1598, 'to the great reluctance of those who knew him' (Wood, *Ath. Oxon.*, 2.668).   J. ANDREAS LÖWE

Sources Foster, *Alum. Oxon.* · *Reg. Oxf.*, 1.241 · J. Pits, *Relationum historicarum de rebus Anglicis*, ed. [W. Bishop] (Paris, 1619), 859 · Tanner, *Bibl. Brit.-Hib.*, 667 · Wood, *Ath. Oxon.*, new edn, 2.668 · Wood, *Ath. Oxon.: Fasti* (1815), 156 · T. F. Knox and others, eds., *The first and second diaries of the English College, Douay* (1878) · E. H. Burton and T. L. Williams, eds., *The Douay College diaries, third, fourth and fifth, 1598–1654*, 1, Catholic RS, 10 (1911)

Shepstone, Sir Theophilus (1817–1893), politician in Natal, was born on 8 January 1817 at Westbury-on-Trym, on the outskirts of Bristol, Gloucestershire, the son of (John) William Shepstone (1796–1873), stonemason and Methodist missionary, and his wife, Elizabeth Brooks (1793–1833). In 1820 the Shepstone family joined one of the parties of English settlers recruited to establish farming settlements near the eastern frontier of Cape Colony in South Africa. For three years after landing with his family at Algoa Bay on 1 May 1820, William Shepstone was engaged in building work at Bathurst and Grahamstown. His abilities as a lay preacher attracted the attention of Methodist missionary superintendent William Shaw who was looking for men to establish stations beyond the Cape frontier. In 1823 William became assistant missionary at Wesleyville; from there he moved on to various missionary postings among the Xhosa. Theophilus was mainly educated at home, where he acquired from his African playmates a thorough colloquial knowledge of the Xhosa language, as well as his African name, Somtseu. As early as the age of ten he was already assisting missionary William Shrewsbury as an interpreter. By the age of fifteen he was collaborating with William Boyce in preparing the first Xhosa grammar and translations of religious materials.

After a brief period of formal schooling at Salem, Shepstone entered government service on his eighteenth birthday, as interpreter of native languages at Cape Town. At the outbreak of the Cape Frontier War of 1834–5 he was appointed to the military headquarters staff of Sir Benjamin D'Urban. After the war he was appointed clerk and general interpreter to the agent-general responsible for British resident officers beyond the frontier. From the middle of 1836 to the end of 1838 he lived mostly at Grahamstown where he met his future wife, Maria (1816–1893), whose father, Charles Palmer, was responsible for military transport. On 11 November 1838 the couple married at the Cape Town home of Colonel Harry Smith. Eight days later Shepstone sailed with Major Samuel Charters's expeditionary force to Port Natal, whose hinterland was then convulsed by warfare between Boer settlers and the Zulu kingdom. After returning to Grahamstown in February 1839, Theophilus took up an appointment as resident agent at Fort Peddie, charged with the oversight of local Xhosa chiefs and the reservation set aside for Mfengu refugees. He enjoyed his life as adviser to chiefs and would seek, unsuccessfully, on several later occasions to convince British authorities to appoint him to administer some African territory where he might rule as supreme chief over a host of lesser chiefs, raising revenue from hut taxes and dispensing justice according to customary law.

At the end of 1845 Shepstone moved to the new British colony of Natal, initially as diplomatic agent to natives, and subsequently secretary for native affairs. In this position for thirty years Shepstone wielded enormous power over the African population of the region. In the face of determined early opposition from officials and white settlers he succeeded in securing large reserved territories for exclusively African occupation. He also won Colonial

Sir Theophilus Shepstone (1817–1893), by Maull & Fox

Office approval for his policy of ruling the black population through their own chiefs in accordance with customary usages. In many ways his policy resembled the practice of 'indirect rule' by which much of British colonial Africa was governed in the first half of the twentieth century. Shepstone's first preference was for direct administration through magistrates with a solid grounding in Zulu language and culture. A shortage of resources forced him to make much greater use of chiefs than he had anticipated. His aim was gradually to supplant hereditary chiefs with appointed African officials whose positions would depend entirely on government preferment. Likewise, in relation to customary law, he hoped gradually to supplant African usages with European 'civilization'. Under his administration he elaborated a system of 'native law' to which virtually all Africans were subjected. His tolerance for polygamy and bride prices paid in cattle was condemned by most settlers and missionaries, but helped him, in the longer run, to acquire a reputation for tolerance motivated by a humane cultural relativism. The key to his early success was the raising of large sums through taxes and other charges levied on Africans. By the final years of his administration direct and indirect African contributions to the Natal treasury amounted to about three quarters of total government revenue. As an appointed member of the legislative council Shepstone was frequently attacked by white settler representatives who wanted to force more men into wage labour by reducing the land available for African occupation. Shepstone, however, could generally count on the support of large landowners who depended on rents paid by African tenants and by coastal sugar planters who looked to Shepstone to provide a steady flow of African migrant labourers from neighbouring territories. In his speeches to the legislative council Shepstone argued that any drastic reduction in African lands would inspire an armed rebellion that might quickly overwhelm the small white population.

Shepstone's fear of uprisings, perhaps born of his experiences on the strife-torn eastern Cape frontier, seems to have been entirely genuine. At the slightest hint of opposition he showed African chiefs the iron fist concealed beneath the velvet glove of cultural tolerance. In 1848, when Chief Fodo refused an order, he and his people were chased by government forces over the southern boundary of the colony. In 1857 Shepstone ruthlessly crushed opposition from chiefs Sidoi and Matshana. He created an African police force commanded by his *indunas*, men whose loyal service was rewarded by grants of cattle and women seized in battle. He believed that his system of administration, underpinned by his system of taxation, could be successfully applied to virtually any African territory. He longed to be given the opportunity to prove his claim, and was, for twenty years, supported in his ambitions by the bishop of Natal, John William Colenso. Shepstone's father had always regretted the Wesleyan break with the Church of England, so it was not so surprising that the son was confirmed in the Anglican faith in 1850 and began a lifelong involvement in church affairs. Colenso gave a theological underpinning to Shepstone's toleration of African customs, while Shepstone enthusiastically endorsed the liberal reading of scripture which caused Colenso to be tried for heresy. On at least three different occasions Colenso and Shepstone discussed going as a team into a neighbouring African territory to try out their missionary and administrative theories. Their plans were firmly squashed by the high commissioner, Sir George Grey, who said that the scheme was 'nothing else than that Great Britain should establish a new kingdom in South Africa—and make Mr. Shepstone the King of that country' (Gordon, 176). In 1868 Shepstone only narrowly failed to secure the annexation of Basutoland which would have vastly extended the scope of his administration.

During the 1850s Colenso and Shepstone schemed to make Mkungu, one of the younger sons of the Zulu king Mpande, heir to his father's throne. By 1861 they had decided to throw their support behind another son, Cetshwayo. In a risky expedition, Shepstone went into Zululand to confer official British recognition on Cetshwayo as heir apparent. After the old ruler died Shepstone led a large delegation to install Cetshwayo as king (August 1873), an event that marked the high-water mark of his influence in Zulu affairs. At the end of the same year the long-standing friendship with Colenso dissolved in rounds of bitter recriminations over Shepstone's role in the capture and trial of the Hlubi chief Langalibalele, who had defied orders to hand in unregistered guns and tried to flee over the Drakensberg Mountains. The bishop now pronounced Shepstone's administration to be a corrupt tyranny and returned to England in an attempt to marshal support from various philanthropic societies. Shepstone was sent on behalf of the Natal government to convey its version of events to the colonial secretary, H. H. M. *Herbert, fourth earl of Carnarvon. Although Carnarvon insisted on important reforms and sent Sir Garnet Wolseley to reform Natal's government, he was profoundly impressed by Shepstone's voluminous knowledge of African affairs both inside and outside the borders of the colonies. In 1876, when Shepstone travelled to England to participate in the conference Carnarvon had convened to promote the idea of federating the various states and colonies of southern Africa, he was promoted to the rank of KCMG (he had been made CMG in 1869), and designated to lead a delegation to the financially troubled Transvaal republic in January 1877. Invoking the secret commission he held to annex the territory if circumstances warranted, Shepstone raised the union flag on 18 April. For two tumultuous years he served as administrator of the Transvaal while recalcitrant Boers plotted to regain their independence, treasury officials complained that Shepstone's finances were a shambles, and his own misjudgement of African affairs sped on a military confrontation with neighbouring rulers. His advice to Carnarvon and the new high commissioner for South Africa, Sir Bartle Frere, was that the threat of a united rising of all the independent African polities must be countered by extending the mantle of British suzerainty over them all. He wrongly believed that Sekhukhuni's Pedi would crumble before an advance of British forces, and supported the impossible ultimatum Frere issued to the Zulu king in December 1878. Sekhukhuni's stalwart resistance and the catastrophic British defeat at the hands of Zulu forces at Isandlwana—where Shepstone's fourth son, George John Palmer, perished—called his judgement into question on precisely the ground on which he was supposed to be most capable. He relinquished his commission as administrator of the Transvaal in March 1879 and left the public service in 1880.

After the election of 1880 brought Gladstone's Liberal government to power on a platform of anti-imperialism, Shepstone's name and work lay under a cloud. An uprising in the Transvaal led to re-establishment of a Boer republic, and Zululand was carved up into thirteen independent chieftainships. Shepstone found a champion in H. Rider Haggard, who had served on his staff in the Transvaal and whose book *Cetewayo and his White Neighbours* (1882) argued for the wisdom of his old chief's policies. Haggard's subsequent novels, including *King Solomon's Mines* and *Allan Quatermain*, helped popularize Shepstone's notion of governing Africans in accordance with their own customs and traditions. When it was decided to restore Cetshwayo as Zulu king in 1883, Shepstone emerged briefly from retirement to supervise the re-installation of the monarch. In the remaining decade of his life he had the satisfaction of seeing many of his sons and other relatives occupying important posts in African administration. Colonial opinion gradually came to regard Shepstone's policy of separate lands, laws, and leaders for the African population as the best way of ensuring the peaceful maintenance of white supremacy and reliable labour supplies. Later scholarship endorsed the judgement that he had been one of the chief architects of segregationist policies used to govern Africans in colonies stretching from the Cape to Kenya. Some have even gone so far as to give him the dubious distinction of having erected key pillars of the apartheid system which dominated South Africa for much of the twentieth century.

Shepstone's wife died on 2 March 1893; he survived her by only a few months, succumbing to a respiratory illness on 23 June at Pietermaritzburg. He was buried two days later beside Maria in the old Anglican cemetery, Pietermaritzburg.   NORMAN ETHERINGTON

Sources R. E. Gordon, *Shepstone: the role of the family in the history of South Africa, 1820–1900* (1968) · N. Etherington, 'The "Shepstone system", in the colony of Natal and beyond the borders', *Natal and Zululand from earliest times to 1910*, ed. A. Duminy and B. Guest (1989), 170–205 · D. Welsh, *The roots of segregation: native policy in colonial Natal, 1845–1910* (1971) · C. F. Goodfellow, *Great Britain and South African confederation, 1870–1881* (1966) · J. Guy, *The heretic: a study of the life of John William Colenso* (1983) · J. Guy, *The destruction of the Zulu kingdom* (1982) · C. J. Uys, *In the era of Shepstone* (1933) · P. Delius, *The land belongs to us: the Pedi polity, the Boers and the British in the nineteenth-century Transvaal* (1983) · N. Etherington, 'Labour supply and the genesis of South African confederation in the 1870s', *Journal of African History*, 20 (1979), 235–53 · N. Etherington, *Preachers, peasants and politics in southeast Africa* (1978) · J. B. Wright and A. Manson, *The Hlubi chiefdom in Zululand-Natal: a history* (1983) · T. Cope, ed., *Izibongo: Zulu praise-poems*, trans. D. Malcolm (1968) · *DNB* · *Natal Witness* (26 June 1893)

Archives National Archives of South Africa, Pietermaritzburg, Natal Archives Depot, corresp., diaries, and papers · University of Natal, Durban, Killie Campbell Africana Library, corresp. and papers | Glos. RO, corresp. with Sir Michael Hicks Beach · LPL, corresp. with Edward Benson

Likenesses Maull & Fox, photograph, NPG [*see illus.*] · Niccoli of Carrara, marble effigy on monument, Pietermaritzburg, South Africa · photographs, Natal Archives Depot, Pietermaritzburg, South Africa · wood-engraving, NPG; repro. in *ILN* (30 June 1877)

Sherard, James (1666–1738), apothecary and botanist, and son of George Sherard or Sherwood of Bushby in Leicestershire, and Mary, his second wife, was born at Bushby on 1 July 1666. William *Sherard (1659–1728) was his brother. On 7 February 1682 he was apprenticed to Charles Watts, an apothecary, who was curator of the botanical gardens at Chelsea. Sherard worked hard as an apothecary, and by many years' practice in Mark Lane, London, accumulated an ample fortune. He retired from the business about 1720. By then, the gout from which Sherard suffered had already forced him to give up his pursuit of music, at which he was a gifted amateur. He had earlier composed twenty-four trio sonatas, which were published in two collections, in 1701 and 1711. The first of these was dedicated to the second duke of Bedford, for whose family Sherard's brother, William, had worked as a tutor. Sherard's sonatas are all of the *da chiesa* type, and owe much to Italian models. They were perhaps first performed by their composer, who was also an accomplished violinist.

On his retirement Sherard purchased the manors of Evington and Settle in Leicestershire, but he chiefly resided at Eltham in Kent, where he pursued the cultivation of valuable and rare plants and his garden, with its hothouses, became noted as among the finest in England. An illustrated catalogue of his collection was published by Dillenius in 1732 as *Hortus Elthamensis, sive, Plantarum rariorum quas in horto suo Elthami in Cantio collegit vir ornatissimus et praestantissimus Jac. Sherard, M.D., Reg. Soc. et Coll. Med. Lond. Soc. Catalogus.* Despite his election as a fellow of the Royal Society in 1706, Sherard was initially less well known as a botanist than his brother, William, as whose London agent he sometimes acted. By the 1720s, however, James Sherard's own reputation as a collector of rare plant specimens was established, and his discoveries of English plants had augmented those of Ray and others. He now travelled more widely in search of specimens, including trips to the continent, as well as keeping up correspondences and exchanges of plants with other botanists, notably Richard Richardson. During the 1730s, he also assisted with the management of the Chelsea gardens.

In 1728 Sherard was appointed as executor of his brother William's will. After initial disputes, he negotiated his brother's endowment of a professorship of botany in the University of Oxford, J. J. Dillenius being the first Sherardian professor. James Sherard's administration of the trust led the University of Oxford to confer upon him the degree of doctor of medicine, by diploma dated 2 July 1731, and the Royal College of Physicians to admit him on 30 September 1732 to its fellowship without examination and without the payment of fees. He died on 12 February 1738, leaving a fortune reputed to amount to £150,000. He had married Susanna (*b.* 1669), daughter of Richard Lockwood, but they had no children. He was buried at Evington parish church, where his widow erected a marble tablet to his memory. She died on 27 November 1741. W. W. WEBB, *rev.* SCOTT MANDELBROTE

Sources *GM*, 1st ser., 66 (1796), 810 · Munk, *Roll* · H. Field, *Memoirs of the botanic garden at Chelsea belonging to the Society of Apothecaries of London*, rev. R. H. Semple (1878), 43–8 · J. Sherard and R. Richardson, correspondence, Bodl. Oxf., Radcliffe Trust MSS c.3–9 · R. Pulteney, *Historical and biographical sketches of the progress of botany in England*, 2 (1790), 150–53 · W. L. Tjaden, 'William and James Sherard and John James Dillenius: some errors in their biographies', *Journal of the Society of the Bibliography of Natural History*, 8 (1976–8), 143–7 · M. Tilmouth, 'Sherard, James', *New Grove* · Foster, *Alum. Oxon.* · C. J. Robinson, ed., *A register of the scholars admitted into Merchant Taylors' School, from AD 1562 to 1874*, 2 vols. (1882–3)
Archives BL, notes on Asia Minor, Add. MS 10101 · NHM, papers · RS, corresp. and papers · U. Oxf., department of plant sciences, corresp. and papers | BL, journal of Bernard Mould of a journey in Asia Minor undertaken by him and Sherard, with later notes, Add. MSS 65142A–65142B · BL, Sloane MSS, letters to James Petiver · BL, Sloane MSS, letters to Sir Hans Sloane, 4041, fol. 165; 4042, fol. 65; 4063, fol. 57; 4064, fol. 125; 4052, fol. 227 · Bodl. Oxf., Radcliffe Trust MSS, letters to Richard Richardson, c.3, c.4, c.5, c.7, c.8, c.9

Wealth at death est. £70,000–£150,000; incl. bequests of more than £10,000; lands valued at more than £1200 p.a.: *GM*; will, PRO, PROB 11/668 sig. 76; Bodl. Oxf., MS Radcliffe Trust c. 3, fol. 37

Sherard, William (1659–1728), botanist, the second of six children and eldest son of a landowner, George Sherard (Sherwood), and Mary, his second wife, was born on 27 February 1659 at Bushby, a hamlet just outside Leicester. James *Sherard (1666–1738) was a younger brother. The family's social position is unclear, but it was sufficiently affluent for Sherard to attend Merchant Taylors' School in London in 1674–7, culminating in his being awarded in 1677 one of its coveted special fellowships at St John's College, Oxford, in theory reserved for poor scholars. These fellows were entitled to indefinite residence in the college as long as (*inter alia*) they did not marry. Sherard chose to read law and, after graduating BCL in December 1683, having scholarly inclinations and apparently under no pressure to seek a more remunerative livelihood, he decided to stay on.

Sherard early became captivated by the challenging diversity of the plant world and the need for a comprehensive system to impose order on this. While a student he had frequented the university's physic garden and there formed a lasting friendship with its new keeper, Jacob Bobart the younger, supplying plants and seeds to assist his task of completing Robert Morison's *Plantarum historiae universalis Oxoniensis.* It was probably at Bobart's instance that in December 1685 he obtained leave of absence, took up residence in Paris, and attended three of the renowned annual courses on botany given at the Jardin du Roi by Bobart's equivalent there, J. P. de Tournefort. Visiting the Netherlands, Sherard forged a strong link with the keeper of the Leiden Botanical Garden, Paul Hermann. The lists he compiled of the plants growing in these two outstandingly rich garden collections were rightly judged valuable enough to be turned into what was to be his only book, *Schola botanica*, published under the pseudonymous initials S. W. A. in 1689, the year of his return to England that November. Already, through his affability, unstinting helpfulness, and freedom to travel widely, his key role as a unifying agent in a badly fragmented European botanical community was starting to emerge.

Sherard's compulsive cataloguing extended to the countryside as well as to gardens. An appendix to Ray's *Synopsis* (1690) contains his plant records from across southern England; it also reveals that he had visited the Channel Islands, compiling the first published list of their plants.

With his college still indulgent over his absence, Sherard went to stay with a young Irish baronet, Sir Arthur Rawdon, on his estate at Moira in co. Down. It has been supposed that he went as tutor to Sir Rawdon's one surviving son, but the age of the boy makes that unlikely and probably he was invited as botanical adviser and companion to Rawdon, who was himself a sophisticated horticulturist. Life at Moira evidently proved seductive, for the stay extended to about three years, a sacrifice of time which in later years Sherard came to regret; even so it was by no means wasted, for on forays into the Ulster country-side he added several species to the little-known Irish flora. After a brief return to Oxford, where he progressed to DCL in June 1694, Sherard departed for the continent that autumn, as tutor to Charles, Lord Townshend, on the latter's grand tour. Though travelling with a young noble-man opened all doors, formal visits left him with frustrat-ingly little time for botany, much of which in any case had to be given over to completing Hermann's *Paradisus Batavus*, a catalogue of the plants growing in the Nether-lands, which with characteristic generosity he undertook for Hermann's widow following its author's sudden death.

No sooner was he back in England in November 1697 than Sherard left on a second grand tour, this time as tutor to the marquess of Tavistock, the young heir to the first duke of Bedford, and with the prospect of many months in Italy. They visited the chief cities, whose botanical gardens Sherard was able to examine with his customary thoroughness. It was during this trip that he apparently first seriously contemplated what was to be his central goal in life thereafter: a continuation of Bauhin's *Pinax* of 1623, a task suggested to him by Tournefort. This entailed updating that list of all the names given by botanical authors to each species of plant known up to that time, an encyclopaedic endeavour foreshadowing today's *Index Kewensis*. To this end he returned home with a large haul of rare books together with many herbarium specimens donated by leading Italian botanists.

Sherard was back in England by Christmas 1698 with his thirst for travel temporarily assuaged, and gave in to repeated requests from the dowager duchess of Beaufort to tutor her grandson Henry, an introduction he owed to Sloane. The duchess took justifiable pride in the rich gar-den she had built up at Badminton and doubtless really wanted him for his botanical knowledge. In the event the position proved uncongenial and it must have been a relief when it was terminated by the death of his pupil. Meanwhile Sherard was coming under pressure to take some part in the affairs of his college, and in November 1700 he returned to act as junior bursar. This experience seems to have killed any remaining taste for Oxford life, for soon he was seeking openings elsewhere. In May 1702 he was appointed to a short-term government commis-sion set up to ensure better care of French and Spanish prisoners, at a stipend of £300 per annum. Though this was patently no more than a stopgap, it provided the col-lege with grounds to declare his fellowship void the fol-lowing April.

A far better position then materialized—consul at Smyrna for the Turkey Company, 'a good post for honour and revenue' (Sherard to Royal Society, 1703, RS, Sherard MSS, letter 625), which he took in the full expectation that it would be for life. Although lucrative, lack of necessary books and poor communications with Europe impeded work on his *magnum opus*, while local botanizing proved feasible only with many companions for protection. His energies consequently became sidetracked into the col-lecting of coins and medallions and copying of church inscriptions, many of the latter published in Edmund Chisnell's *Antiquitates Asiaticae* (1728). However, fortu-nately for botany, the country house at Sedi-Keui, seven miles outside Smyrna, which he had bought in 1711, was burgled and many of his coins stolen in the mistaken belief that they were silver. Their loss subverted this com-peting interest and took him back to the *Pinax*, but he was increasingly forced to recognize that his return to Eng-land was essential if it was to further progress.

Having reluctantly resigned his position, Sherard left for London in November 1716, but the intentionally leis-urely journey back stretched out to a whole year when plague broke out on his ship and it was held in quarantine at Leghorn. On arriving home, sufficiently well off now to be able to devote all his time to botany, he settled into chambers in Barking Alley, resumed his London friend-ships, and stood for election to the Royal Society, going almost at once on to its council in 1719–20. About the same time his brother James, who had risen to great wealth as an apothecary, acquired an estate at Eltham, on the city's south-east outskirts, and, sharing his enthusiasm for bot-any, invited Sherard to assist him in his soon-realized aim of turning its garden and hothouses into the most richly stocked in Britain. In May 1721 the two travelled to the con-tinent, partly to buy plants and partly to try to entice a ris-ing young Hessian with expertise especially in mosses and fungi, Johann Jakob Dillenius, to move from Giessen to help with their respective projects. Dillenius succumbed and went to live in London with Sherard that autumn, but though both worked hard on the *Pinax*, its completion was held up by a temporary dispute between Sloane and Sher-ard, and the former's consequent denial to them of access to the collections of Petiver and Plukenet. On top of Sher-ard's perfectionism and continuing continental distrac-tions this was eventually to prove the work's death-blow.

In the meantime, though, work on the *Pinax* continued to provide a justification for Sherard's unending botanical acquisitiveness. In 1721 he organized the dispatch of Mark Catesby back to North America to collect natural history specimens for a syndicate, and the next year rounded up another set of subscribers to send the 'pilgrim botanist', Thomas More, to do the same in New England. In 1722, however, the king of France outbid him for the herbarium of Sébastien Vaillant, who had died without completing his life work, the *Botanicon Parisiense*. Before his death Vail-lant had sought to persuade Hermann's successor at Lei-den, Boerhaave, to complete it, and Sherard now pre-vailed upon that long-time friend of his to do so, promis-ing his assistance. This required his making two more visits to the Netherlands preparatory to the book's publi-cation in 1727.

In the autumn of 1724, needing more space for arran-ging his herbarium, Sherard moved with Dillenius to a house on Tower Hill, where the two bachelors were looked after by a housekeeper. But their enjoyment of these improved conditions was brief: by April 1728 Sher-ard was withering away there from what friends described as 'senile marasmus' and his death finally came during the night of 11–12 August. He was buried on 19

August in the churchyard at Eltham, but the precise location of his grave is now unknown. Two years earlier he had donated £500 towards the cost of enlarging the conservatory at the Oxford Physic Garden, along with many duplicate specimens and rare books for its library. In his will he further underlined his debt to his alma mater by bequeathing it his herbarium of some 12,000 sheets, his library of more than 600 volumes, his paintings, drawings, and the manuscript of the *Pinax*. However, a series of conditions was attached: a new chair of botany was to be established at the botanic garden (for which £3000 was offered as its endowment), Dillenius was to be its occupant for life, and the university was to pay £150 annually towards the upkeep of the garden and its library. Seven years of wrangling over the details followed before his intentions were eventually realized and Dillenius took office as the first Sherardian professor. By thus inserting into this key position one of Europe's ablest botanists, Sherard arguably achieved more for the study posthumously than all he accomplished during his lifetime.

Three of his friends named genera in Sherard's honour, but it was the *Sherardia* that Dillenius bestowed on field madder that later secured adoption by Linnaeus and has thereby been perpetuated. Another common British wild flower, *Rosa sherardii*, commemorates him at the species level. D. E. Allen

Sources G. Pasti Jr, 'Consul Sherard: amateur botanist and patron of learning, 1659–1728', PhD diss., University of Illinois, 1950 · H. M. Clokie, *An account of the herbaria of the department of botany in the University of Oxford* (1964), 17–30 · B. D. Jackson, 'A sketch of the life of William Sherard', *Journal of Botany, British and Foreign*, 12 (1874), 129–38 · R. Pulteney, *Historical and biographical sketches of the progress of botany in England*, 2 (1790), 141–50 · W. L. Tjaden, 'William and James Sherard and John James Dillenius: some errors in their biographies', *Journal of the Society of the Bibliography of Natural History*, 8 (1976–8), 143–7 · B. Henrey, *No ordinary gardener: Thomas Knowlton, 1691–1781*, ed. A. O. Chater (1986) · G. A. Lindeboom, *Herman Boerhaave: the man and his work* (1968) · *Boerhaave's correspondence*, ed. G. A. Lindeboom, 1 (1962), 38–162 · *Extracts from the literary and scientific correspondence of Richard Richardson*, ed. D. Turner (1835) · F. Le Sueur, *Flora of Jersey* (1984), xxxiii–xxxv · E. C. Nelson, 'Sir Arthur Rawdon, 1662–1675, of Moira: his life and letters, family and friends, and his Jamaican plants', *Proceedings and Report of Belfast Natural History and Philosophical Society*, 10 (1977–82), 30–52 · Mrs E. P. Hart, ed., *Merchant Taylors' School register, 1561–1934*, 2 vols. (1936) · RS, Sherard MSS, letter 625
Archives BL, journal of Bernard Mould and notes, Add. MS 65142A–B; notes on Asia Minor, Add. MS 10101 · Bodl. Oxf., library and MSS · Musée d'Histoire Naturelle, Paris, specimens · NHM, department of botany, notes and observations on Ray's *Historia plantarum*, Banksian MS 80 · NHM, papers · NHM, specimens · RS, corresp. and papers, MSS 252–256, 88 · U. Oxf., department of plant sciences, herbarium · Zürich Central Library, Switzerland, letters | BL, Sloane MSS, letters to James Petiver · BL, letters to Sir Hans Sloane
Likenesses oils (of Sherard?), Oxford Botanic Garden
Wealth at death £20,000: will, PRO

Sheraton, Thomas (1751–1806), furniture designer and author, was a native of Stockton-on-Tees, co. Durham. His father, also named Thomas Sheraton (*b.* 1725/6, *bur.* 1792), was a schoolmaster from whom he must have received an education, although he later described himself as a 'mechanic, and one who never received the advantages of a *collegial* or *academical* education' (T. Sheraton, *A Scriptural Illustration of the Doctrine of Regeneration*, 1782). Nevertheless, he must have obtained a good training in cabinet-making, perhaps from one of the cabinet-makers in the town, and in draughtsmanship possibly from the local shipbuilding traditions with which his future wife's family were connected.

Sheraton's early years remain obscure. It seems unlikely that he ever set up a cabinet-making business of his own, probably because he lacked capital. He was described as having been 'for many years a journeyman cabinet maker' (*GM*), and he himself wrote in his *Cabinet Dictionary* (1803): 'Having possessed a strong attachment and inclination for carving in my youth, I was necessarily induced to make attempts in this art, and was employed in the country occasionally in it' (Sheraton, *Cabinet Dictionary*, 136). His more profound interests lay elsewhere for by 1782, if not several years earlier, he had become a devout Baptist. In that year he published a tract entitled *A Scriptural Illustration of the Doctrine of Regeneration*, to which was added *A Letter on the Subject of Baptism Written to a Gentlewoman at her Request*, which expressed 'the sentiments of my heart'. On 8 February 1779 he married Margaret Mitchinson of Norton, co. Durham, with whom he is said to have had two children. He may also have found work as a draughtsman and drawing-master: two views of Stockton High Street, engraved 'after T Sheraton', were published by a local bookseller in 1785 and 1795.

About 1790 Sheraton moved to London and was recorded at 4 Hart Street in 1791, 41 Davies Street in 1793, and 106 Wardour Street in 1795. His motives for moving south are unclear, but in 1791 his masterpiece, *The Cabinet Maker and Upholsterer's Drawing-Book*, began to be published by subscription in fortnightly sections (forty-two in all), priced 1s. A slightly larger second edition appeared in 1794 and a third with some small amendments in 1802. A German version was translated by G. T. Wenzel and published in Leipzig. It was intended for practising members of the trade, and addressed 'to Cabinet-Makers and Upholsterers in General'. The 717 subscribers were almost entirely established furniture makers, in contrast to those of Thomas Chippendale's *Gentleman and Cabinet Maker's Director* (1754, 1755, and 1762) which had included members of aristocracy and gentry. Sheraton's intention (inspired perhaps by his nonconformist background) was to improve the work of uneducated artisans by teaching them proportion and perspective drawing, since previous manuals had been deficient in this. He firmly believed in the immutable laws of 'Geometry and real Science' and wished to show how these could be applied to the ephemeral nature of taste particularly in furniture design. In his own words his intention was to make the *Drawing Book* 'as permanently useful as I could and to unite with usefulness the taste of the times' (Sheraton, *Drawing Book*, 1802 edn, 355).

Thus the first two parts were given over to geometry, perspective, and the orders of architecture, all deliberately calculated to the needs of furniture making. Parts three and four, on the other hand, described and illustrated 'a great variety of Original Designs' and ornamental details for fashionable middle-class furniture. The overall style was an elegant neo-classicism with a Francophile bias, in some cases reminiscent of the prince of Wales's architect, Henry Holland. Indeed, the 120 engravings (many of which were accompanied by interesting technical instructions) included views of the prince's Chinese drawing room at Carlton House. How far Sheraton was an innovator or merely following fashionable taste has been debated. He himself described how he had tried to collect ideas from the best sources (Sheraton, *Drawing Book*, 1802 edn, 353), and he was scrupulous in naming those from whom he had taken novel forms, as well as crediting himself where appropriate. In general his designs reflected the fashionable (but not aristocratic) taste of his time and the effect of his publication was to disseminate forms and ornament widely so that they remained in production (albeit often somewhat coarsened) for the next twenty-five years.

About 1799 Sheraton returned to co. Durham, where he became a Baptist minister in the following year. By 1802 he had returned to London and was residing at 8 Broad Street. In 1803 he published his second furniture book, *The Cabinet Dictionary*, containing 134 engraved designs and a lengthy text. By this date avant-garde taste had moved towards the more massive and archaeologically correct vocabulary of classicism advocated by C. H. Tatham, but not yet popularized. Sheraton included ornamental features of this type in the dictionary, but married somewhat awkwardly to more conventional forms. The strength of the dictionary lay more in its detailed descriptions of the production, use, and function of different types of furniture and of the interiors for which they were intended. Its weakness was the author's verbosity and tendency to stray into irrelevant areas.

During his first London period Sheraton's elegant trade card had described him as a teacher of 'Perspective, Architecture and Ornaments' who 'makes Designs for Cabinet-makers and sells all kinds of Drawing Books etc'. Despite this claim, only one manuscript design by Sheraton has survived: a pen and wash drawing for an ornate looking-glass dating from about 1790 (V&A). His only documented and extant commission is the piano ordered by Don Manuel de Godoy in 1796 for presentation to Queen Maria Louisa of Spain and made by Broadwood (now at the Heritage Foundation, Deerfield, Massachusetts).

Sheraton continued to work as a draughtsman after his return to London in 1802, no doubt combining this with his duties as a Baptist minister. But he did not prosper. A glimpse of him is provided by the future publisher Adam Black, then seeking his fortune in London, and who worked for Sheraton briefly in 1804:

> He lived in an obscure street, his house half shop, half dwelling-house, and looked himself like a worn-out Methodist minister, with threadbare black coat … My host seemed a good man, with some talent. He had been a cabinetmaker, was now author and publisher, teacher of drawing, and, I believe, occasional preacher. I was with him for about a week, engaged in most wretched work, writing a few articles, and trying to put his shop in order, working among dirt and bugs, for which I was remunerated with half a guinea. Miserable as the pay was, I was half ashamed to take it from the poor man. (Fastnedge, 22–3)

Adam Black wondered 'how a man with such abilities and resources is in such a state? I believe his abilities and resources are his ruin, in this respect, for by attempting to do everything he does nothing' (ibid.).

The work to which Black was asked to contribute was Sheraton's last and most ambitious project, *The Cabinet-Maker, Upholsterer, and General Artists' Encyclopaedia*. It was to be published in 125 parts by subscription; in the event only thirty sections, from A to C, appeared before the author's death in 1806. The entries were rambling and eccentric, suggesting a loss of mental faculties. The plates, despite being poorly produced, showed stylish furniture in the new early Regency taste. One thousand copies were sold, Sheraton having travelled to Ireland to solicit customers. He died at his home, 8 Broad Street, London, on 22 October 1806 'of a phrenitis', leaving his wife, Margaret, and their two children 'in distressed circumstances' (*GM*), and was buried on 27 October at St James's, Piccadilly, London. In 1812 eighty-four of Sheraton's plates, compiled from all his publications, were reissued by J. Taylor as a single folio volume entitled *Designs for Household Furniture by the Late Thomas Sheraton*.

Sheraton's influence on furniture design was widespread and lasted for at least a generation, not only with successful firms in Britain such as Gillows, but in America and Europe. His plea for an understanding of geometry, proportion, and perspective by aspiring artisans was eventually implemented by the curricula of the government schools of design which became established after the parliamentary enquiry of 1835. During the late Victorian period Sheraton's name became synonymous with the elegant furniture of the 1790s. A facsimile reprint of the *Drawing Book* published in 1895 helped to promote a revival of the beautifully proportioned and finely executed furniture he had advocated.   JAMES LOMAX

Sources C. Gilbert and G. Beard, eds., *Dictionary of English furniture makers* (1986) • R. Fastnedge, *Sheraton furniture* (1962) • T. Sheraton, *The cabinet-maker and upholsterer's drawing book*, 3rd edn (1802); repr. with introduction by L. O. J. Boynton (New York, 1970) • T. Sheraton, *The cabinet dictionary* (1803); repr. with introduction by W. P. Cole and C. F. Montgomery (New York, 1970) • T. Sowler, 'Thomas Sheraton, 1751–1806', *Bulletin* [Cleveland and Teesside Local History Society], 33 (1977), 10–18 • *Memoirs of Adam Black*, ed. A. Nicholson (1885) • S. Jervis, *Penguin dictionary of design and designers* (1984) • *GM*, 1st ser., 76 (1806), 1082 • parish register, London, St James, Piccadilly, 27 Oct 1806

Wealth at death £200: letters of administration granted to his widow, Margaret (Wills Registry, PRO), Nov 1807

Sherborn, Charles Davies (1861–1942), geologist and scientific bibliographer, was born on 30 June 1861 at 5 Gunter Grove, Chelsea, London, the eldest child of Charles William *Sherborn (1831–1912), a metal-engraver and etcher, and his wife, Hannah Simpson Wait (née Davies; d. 1922). He was educated at local schools from the age of three, but left St Mark's College School, Chelsea, at fourteen in order to work in a fashionable stationers.

(Sherborn always maintained that this experience of the book trade was invaluable for his later bibliographical work.) During 1884-5, when on the continent, he availed himself of the opportunity to attend lectures and meet distinguished zoologists and geologists. Over the next decade, employed in various clerical positions throughout London, he pursued his interests in books, antiquities, and natural history. Access to the exhibits and libraries of London's museums enabled Sherborn to further his knowledge of many subjects.

As a young man, Sherborn accompanied many distinguished geologists on their excursions. In the 1880s he was engaged by T. Rupert Jones to assist in the preparation of material for monographs on Tertiary Entomostraca (1889) and Crag Foraminifera (1895-7). This grounding in scientific methods, together with his interest in natural history, persuaded Sherborn to seek a career in science. His association with Rupert Jones had other benefits apart from their joint publications of 1887, 1888, and 1889; it resulted in further introductions to many geologists. He assisted William Topley in editing the Geological Record for 1884-5 and then became editor himself for the 1885-8 volume. In June 1888 Sherborn began his long association with the British Museum (Natural History) when Dr Henry Woodward engaged him to mount and prepare fossils in the collections of Sloane, König, Sowerby, and Phillips. Between 1892 and 1899 he served on the editorial committee of the critical monthly journal Natural Science.

With limited resources for fieldwork, Sherborn devoted his spare time to producing indexes and reference works. A Bibliography of the Foraminifera (1888) was followed by An Index to the Genera and Species of Foraminifera (1890), both published in America. He then collaborated with Arthur Smith Woodward in compiling A Catalogue of British Fossil Vertebrata (1890), and he was asked to catalogue the collections and library of the Geological Society of London. He then became involved in sorting the papers of Sir Richard Owen for the eventual biography by Revd R. Owen (1894). Between 1894 and 1908 he undertook a survey of the zones of the White Chalk of the English coast with Arthur Walton Rowe and was largely responsible for their publication. Inspired by the Index Kewensis Sherborn undertook to provide a complete list of all generic and trivial names given to recent and fossil animals from the time of Linnaeus, together with references to the date and place of their publication. The Index animalium, 1758-1850 became the basis for zoological nomenclature and was compiled single-handed over forty-three years. The first volume (1758-1800) was published in 1902 and the ten volumes 1800-1850, published under the auspices of the British Museum (Natural History), were completed in 1933. During its preparation, Sherborn published numerous bibliographic papers that verified the dates and history of many works and periodicals. This information was incorporated by B. B. Woodward into his Catalogue of Books … in B. M. (N. H.) (1903-15).

Sherborn joined the Geologists' Association in 1883, and became a fellow of the Geological Society (1887) and the Zoological Society (1890), and an associate of the Linnean Society (1912). He was made a life member of both the Zoological Society (1907) and the Geologists' Association (1924) for his services. In 1890 he was awarded the Geological Society's Lyell fund for his bibliographical work and received the Foulerton award from the Geologists' Association in 1922. In 1931 he received an honorary DSc from Oxford University. After helping to found the Society for the Bibliography of Natural History in 1936, he became its first president. Sherborn particularly enjoyed his membership of several select dining clubs of these professional societies for the regular opportunity they gave for scientific discussions.

By living a relatively spartan life, Sherborn was able to collect books, Byzantine bronze coins, and antiquities of all kinds. His deep concern that these objects should rest with 'those who could best appreciate them' (Norman, Nature, 150, 1942, 146) led to numerous donations to institutions. He also ensured that the library of the British Museum (Natural History) acquired many of the works it lacked. His encyclopaedic knowledge, wit, and generosity were widely acknowledged. Like his alleged antipathy to women (especially their attendance at society meetings), his later gruff and brusque manner was essentially a cloak that could be shed when its protection was unnecessary.

After his health declined in 1938, Sherborn's attendance at the British Museum (Natural History) lessened, but even in the 1940s he maintained a weekly visit. He collapsed in his bath following a heart attack on the morning of 22 June 1942 and died that afternoon at his home, 49 Peterborough Road, Fulham, London. His remains were cremated at Golders Green crematorium on 26 June. He was unmarried and was survived by two brothers.

R. J. CLEEVELY

Sources J. R. Norman, Squire: memories of Charles Davies Sherborn (1944) • J. R. Norman, Nature, 150 (1942), 146-7 • A. S. W. [A. S. Woodward], Quarterly Journal of the Geological Society of London, 98 (1943), lxxxi-lxxxii • G. F. Elliott, 'Charles Davies Sherborn, 1861-1942: an appreciation', Foraminifera, 3 (1978), 267-73 • H. B. Thalmann, 'Charles Davies Sherborn, 1861-1942', The Micropaleontologist, 3/3 (July 1949), 19-21 • F. J. Griffin, 'Charles Davies Sherborn, 1861-1942: some personal recollections', Journal of the Society of the Bibliography of Natural History, 3 (1953-60), 1-4 • A. S. Woodward, 'Charles Davies Sherborn', Proceedings of the Linnean Society of London, 154th session (1941-2), 295-6 • J. R. Norman, 'Charles Davies Sherborn, 1861-1942', Proceedings of the Malacological Society, 25 (1943), 126-7 • GS Lond.

Archives BL, autograph collection, Add. MSS 42575-42585 • Geologists' Association • Institute of Geological Sciences, Keyworth, Nottinghamshire, fossils • NHM, corresp. and papers • V&A, prints | BM, scientific and literary corresp. acquired from T. R. Jones, W. Clift, H. Woodward, and H. G. Seeley, donated by Sherborn • NHM, scientific and literary corresp. acquired from T. R. Jones, W. Clift, H. Woodward, and H. G. Seeley, donated by Sherborn • RCS Eng., scientific and literary corresp. acquired from T. R. Jones, W. Clift, H. Woodward, and H. G. Seeley, donated by Sherborn • Royal Society of Medicine, London, scientific and literary corresp. acquired from T. R. Jones, W. Clift, H. Woodward, and H. G. Seeley, donated by Sherborn

Likenesses double portrait, photograph, 1898 (with A. W. Rowe), BM • photograph (at age sixty-one), repro. in Norman, Squire: memories, facing p. 30 • photograph, repro. in Thalmann, 'Charles Davies Sherborn' • photograph, BM, Palaeontology Library • photographs (GA excursion; twenty-five years of age; thirty-two years of age; in museum library at seventy-four years of age), repro. in Norman, *Squire: memories*, facing p. 31

Wealth at death £11,619 1s. 8d.: probate, 5 Sept 1942, *CGPLA Eng. & Wales*

Sherborn, Charles William (1831–1912), etcher and engraver, was born on 14 June 1831 at 43 Leicester Square, London, the eldest son of Charles Sherborn (*b.* 1796), an upholsterer, and his wife, Mary, the daughter of Richard Bance, of Newbury. He was educated first at a local school and then at Cave House, Uxbridge. In 1845 he left school and began attending the government school of drawing and design at Somerset House, while at the same time being apprenticed to Robert Oliver, a silver-plate engraver in Rupert Street, Soho. In October 1852, having served his apprenticeship, he went abroad, staying in Paris from some ten months and afterwards travelling in Italy. In September 1853 he settled in Geneva, where he remained for three years, working as a goldsmith's designer and engraver. He returned to London in September 1856 and began engraving for the London jewellers, first in his father's house, and then in Jermyn Street, in a partnership which proved unsuccessful and was dissolved in 1860; however, the same year he began again in Warwick Street, Regent Street. On 14 August 1860 he married Hannah Simpson (*d.* 1922), the daughter of Thomas Davies, a watchmaker, and the widow of Thomas Wait, a draper, of Liverpool; they had four sons, including the geologist Charles Davies *Sherborn (1861–1942), and a daughter.

In 1872, on account of financial difficulties, Sherborn abandoned business and decided to work independently as an etcher and engraver. His early training had been limited, and it was chiefly with reproduction work after contemporary portrait and subject painters, and later on with bookplates, that he gained a livelihood. He had always undertaken original work for his own pleasure, and his etchings of London architecture and riverside deserve praise for their sincerity. *Chelsea*, *Westminster Abbey*, and *Battersea Bridge* were all published by E. Parsons. His finest achievement is a series of more than 350 bookplates which he designed and engraved chiefly between 1881 and 1912. They are mostly of the armorial type, but some are pictorial and a few are portraits. A contemporary remarked after his death that his mastery of fine engraving technique was unrivalled among the working engravers of his time, and came into its own in reproducing these formal and intricate designs. Between 1874 and 1894 he exhibited plates regularly at the Royal Academy; these were mainly portraits and some allegories and mythological subjects, including *Pope Pius IX* (1876), *Allegory of Life and Death* (1878), *Apollo, God of the Sun* (1881), and *The Earl of Carlisle* (1894), after Henry T. Wells.

Sherborn was elected a member of the Society of Painter–Etchers in 1884. He died at his home, 1 Finborough Road, South Kensington, London, on 10 February 1912, and was buried in Highgate cemetery on 14 February. He and his family presented a complete set of his bookplates, engravings, and etchings to the British Museum, and representative selections of the bookplates to the national collections in France, Germany, and the United States.   H. M. HAKE, rev. JOANNA DESMOND

Sources C. D. Sherborn, *The life and work of Charles William Sherborn* (1912) · R. K. Engen, *Dictionary of Victorian engravers, print publishers and their works* (1979) · Graves, *RA exhibitors* · *CGPLA Eng. & Wales* (1912)

Archives BL, corresp. with Sir F. S. Haden, Add. MS 39581

Likenesses C. W. Sherborn, self-portraits, etchings, 1856–1900, repro. in Sherborn, *Life and work of Charles William Sherborn* · A. Ellis, wash drawing, 1898, BM · C. W. Sherborn, self-portrait, etching, 1900, NPG · W. F. Hopson, wood-engraving, 1903 (after drawing by A. Ellis), UCL · C. W. Sherborn, self-portrait, etching, BM · S. L. Smith, etching, BM · photograph, BM

Wealth at death £5103 13s. 10d.: probate, 25 March 1912, *CGPLA Eng. & Wales*

Sherborn [Sherborne], **Robert** (*c.*1454–1536), bishop of Chichester, was born at Basingstoke, Hampshire, admitted as a scholar of Winchester College in 1465, and went to New College, Oxford, in 1472, where he was a fellow until 1486. He graduated BA in 1477, and subsequently MA and BM. He was the scribe (secretary) to the university, *c.*1480–86. An example of his hand survives in his transcription of 1481 of a Salernitan medical text (Edinburgh University Library, MS 169).

While still at Oxford, in 1482, Sherborn received a prebend of Salisbury Cathedral. When in 1486 he became secretary to Archbishop John Morton of Canterbury (*d.* 1500), further preferment followed rapidly, although, surprisingly, he received no benefices in Canterbury diocese. In 1486 he became treasurer of Hereford, and in successive years from 1488 to 1490 received prebends at Lincoln, St Paul's, and Wells. In 1492 he was admitted as warden of Kingsthorpe Hospital, Northamptonshire, and master of St Cross Hospital, Winchester. As well as various rectories thereafter (the first, Childrey in Berkshire, was granted in March 1491), he secured a prebend at Chichester. In the diocese of Lincoln he was successively archdeacon of Huntingdon (1494–6) and Buckingham (1496–1505); he was also archdeacon of Taunton (1496–1505), and in 1499 (when he was ordained subdeacon) was elected dean of St Paul's. Only on 6 March 1501 was he ordained priest.

Between 1490 and 1492 Sherborn administered for the archbishop during vacancies in the sees of Lichfield, Hereford, Wells, Exeter, and Winchester. In 1494 he first appears in royal service, supervising the building of the new tower at Portsmouth. By 1496 he was secretary and councillor to Henry VII, and in July of that year he conducted his first diplomatic mission to Rome, where he was sent to signify the king's willingness to join the Holy League. He returned there in 1504 to seek from Julius II (*r.* 1503–13) a papal dispensation for the marriage of Prince Henry to the widowed Katherine of Aragon. On his first visit he became warden of the English hospice, which was now transformed by Henry VII into a royal institution. Although Sherborn acted by deputy, he drew up new statutes, remedied the dangerous financial situation, and spent lavishly on the reconstruction of the church, rededicated in 1501.

Back in England, between 1498 and 1500 Sherborn was

engaged in the exaction of heavy fines on the west-country adherents of Perkin Warbeck, and in summer 1503 was one of the commissioners who treated with Scottish envoys about Princess Margaret's dowry. In the new reign, and after his elevation to the episcopate, his diplomatic role was more ceremonial; he received Cardinal Campeggi in Kent in 1518 and again in 1528, while in 1522 he was sent to greet Charles V (*r.* 1519–56) at Calais and escort him to London.

On 5 January 1505 Sherborn was provided by the pope to the see of St David's. Allegations that he forged the bull of provision were undoubtedly a gross exaggeration. The point at issue—an erasure and the inflation of the income of St Cross, Winchester, which he was to retain but which he also restored—was magnified to suit the interests of competing ecclesiastical factions in England and at Rome. Sherborn was vigorously supported by the king, and was consecrated on 11 May 1505. Within three years Henry VII was pressing for his translation to Chichester, to which he was provided by Julius II on 18 September 1508.

Analysis of the records of Sherborn's administration at Chichester has shown that he was an active and effective diocesan bishop. He engaged upon a campaign to increase episcopal authority by a thoroughgoing reform of the church courts, which were amalgamated so as to eliminate competing jurisdictions, and he was prepared to pay Cardinal Wolsey to preserve their independence from legatine intervention. He was active as diocesan in monastic visitation, in which he had been well trained as Morton's commissary, and was also commissioned by Wolsey to conduct the legatine visitation of Premonstratensian Bayham, Sussex. He made a concerted attempt both to improve the condition of the fabric of parish churches, and to maintain and foster the standards of pastoral ministry. He was greatly assisted by administrators recruited from the alumni of New College, and in 1524 he founded in his cathedral church four new 'Wiccamical' prebends, reserved for former scholars of Winchester and New College. To the latter foundation he gave a message at Harrow, Middlesex, to provide for masses for the scholars' souls, and land near High Wycombe, Buckinghamshire, to provide a stipend for a scholar. A visitor in 1526 complimented the furbishment of his episcopal palace and its fine grounds.

By the time of the crisis of the early 1530s Sherborn was a very old man, described in 1532 as 'aged and sickly' (*LP Henry VIII*, 5.506), although in 1535 as 'in good health and merry' (*LP Henry VIII*, 8.402). He was by generation and inclination a member of the 'conservative episcopate', but he bowed to reality by renouncing papal jurisdiction on 26 February 1534, and on 15 June 1535 preached personally in Chichester Cathedral when announcing the king's supreme headship of the Church of England. On 1 June, however, he was examined by Dr Richard Layton (*d.* 1544), and in early June of the next year, at the king's request, he resigned his see. On the following 21 August he died at Chichester, and was buried in an altar tomb, with alabaster effigy, in the south ambulatory of the cathedral choir. His last will, orthodox in tone and sentiment, was made

nineteen days before his death, and proved on 24 November 1536. His career is an excellent example of one who laboured hard in the service both of his king and of the universal church, in the last years when such loyalties were compatible. CHRISTOPHER HARPER-BILL

Sources Emden, *Oxf.*, 3.1685–7 · S. Lander, 'Church courts and the Reformation in the diocese of Chichester', *Continuity and change: personnel and administration of the Church of England, 1500–1642*, ed. R. O'Day and F. Heal (1976), 215–37 · *The Venerabile*, 21 (May 1962) [sexcentenary issue: *The English hospice in Rome*] · W. Campbell, ed., *Materials for a history of the reign of Henry VII*, 2 vols., Rolls Series, 60 (1873–7) · *LP Henry VIII*, vols. 1–5, 8 · J. Gairdner, ed., *Letters and papers illustrative of the reigns of Richard III and Henry VII*, 2 vols., Rolls Series, 24 (1861–3) · *The register of John Morton, archbishop of Canterbury, 1486–1500*, ed. C. Harper-Bill, 1–2, CYS, 75, 78 (1987–91) · will, PRO, PROB 11/25, sig. 4 · records, Winchester College
Archives W. Sussex RO, register, Ep. 1/1/3–4
Wealth at death see will, PRO, PROB 11/25, sig. 4

Sherborne, Robert. *See* Sherborn, Robert (*c.*1454–1536).

Sherbrooke. For this title name *see* Lowe, Robert, Viscount Sherbrooke (1811–1892).

Sherbrooke, Sir John Coape (1764–1830), army officer and governor-in-chief of British North America, was baptized on 29 April 1764 at Arnold, Nottinghamshire, the third son of William Sherbrooke JP, born Coape, of Farnah in Duffield, Derbyshire, and Arnold, Nottinghamshire, who had taken the name of Sherbrooke on his marriage in 1756 to Sarah, one of the three coheirs of Henry Sherbrooke of Oxton, Nottinghamshire. John was commissioned as ensign in the 4th foot in December 1780 and promoted lieutenant in December 1781. He was given a company in the 85th foot in March 1783, and in June 1784 became captain in the 33rd foot, then stationed in Nova Scotia; he returned to Britain in 1786. Having advanced to major in September 1793 and lieutenant-colonel in May 1794, Sherbrooke served with his regiment successively in the Netherlands, the Cape, and finally India. He was promoted colonel in January 1798, and fought in the Anglo-Mysore War of 1799. His health suffered so severely that in January 1800 he had to return to England, where he was placed on half pay in 1802. The following year he took command of the 4th reserve battalion in the eastern counties.

In January 1805 Sherbrooke advanced to major-general and in June was sent to Sicily, where he became commander of the troops at Messina. He went to Egypt in May 1807 on a diplomatic mission. During the first half of 1808 he took temporary command of all British forces in Sicily. Although French activities in southern Italy made his duties arduous, he resolutely confounded the intrigues of the court at Palermo. Henry Edward Bunbury, a fellow officer, described Sherbrooke as

> a short, square, hardy little man, with a countenance that told at once the determined fortitude of his nature. Without genius, without education, hot as pepper, and rough in his language, but with a warm heart and generous feelings; true, strait forward, scorning finesse and craft and meanness. (Bunbury, 329)

Having been relieved by Sir John Stuart, Sherbrooke went home in June 1808. He transferred to the 68th foot in

May 1809, and served in the Peninsular campaign, with the local rank of lieutenant-general, as second in command to Arthur Wellesley. In recognition of his exploits in the battles of Oporto and Talavera, Sherbrooke was made KCB in September 1809. Ill health again forced him to return to England the following May. In June 1811 he became lieutenant-general and on 19 August was appointed lieutenant-governor of Nova Scotia. Five days later he married Katherine (Katherina), the daughter of the Revd Reginald Pyndar, rector of Madresfield, at Areley Kings, Worcestershire.

From his arrival in Halifax on 16 October, Sherbrooke's governorship was dominated by war with the United States, which broke out in June 1812, and measures for the colony's defence. At first the dictates of security and commerce encouraged him to adopt a friendly stance towards the New England states where there existed hostility to the war and a willingness to continue trading with the maritime provinces of Canada by licences as well as clandestinely. This uneasy but highly profitable relationship ended in 1814 when the defeat of Napoleon in Europe induced the British authorities to act more aggressively towards the United States government by occupying part of what was to become Maine. In August Sherbrooke commanded an expeditionary force which landed at Castine and successfully subdued the region between the Penobscot and the St Croix rivers. This remained a British enclave for eight months, though Sherbrooke himself returned to Halifax within four weeks. A grateful house of assembly later voted him £1000 for the purchase of plate, and in January 1815 he received the GCB.

On 10 April 1816 Sherbrooke was commissioned governor-in-chief of British North America, and arrived at Quebec on 12 July. Confronted by bitter strife between English and French parties, which had been aggravated by the conduct of Governor Sir George Prevost during the American war, he resolved to avoid becoming drawn into partisan politics and to pursue instead a neutral, conciliatory course. His broad-church Anglicanism posed no obstacle to cultivating a cordial rapport with the influential leader of the Roman Catholic clergy, Bishop Joseph-Octave Plessis, who was given a seat on the legislative council in 1818. Another valuable political ally was Louis-Joseph Papineau, the youthful, ambitious speaker of the assembly, later the scourge of less accommodating governors. This good understanding facilitated a temporary settlement of the province's chaotic and contentious financial affairs. In 1818 detailed consideration by the lower house of the annual estimates led to the voting of supplies to cover the ordinary expenditures of government, without recognition of the assembly's disputed right to control all forms of local revenue. Unfortunately, resort to the procedure of an address, rather than a regular appropriation bill, meant that no legislative precedent was established which might have moderated future wrangling over this crucial issue. Nevertheless, despite a fierce temper and an instinctive conservatism, Sherbrooke achieved singular success in operating the constitution of Lower Canada harmoniously and gaining the confidence of all parties, to the enhancement of his own reputation.

Still dogged by ill health, and having been afflicted by a paralytic stroke in February 1818, Sherbrooke resigned his commission and returned that August to Britain. He was promoted general in May 1825 and lived quietly at Calverton in Nottinghamshire. He died there on 14 February 1830 and was buried at nearby Oxton, survived by his wife, who died childless on 15 May 1856.

PETER BURROUGHS

Sources *GM*, 1st ser., 100/1 (1830), 558–9 · H. Bunbury, *Narratives of some passages in the great war with France, from 1799 to 1810* (1854) · P. H. Stanhope, *Notes of conversations with the duke of Wellington, 1831–1851*, 3rd edn (1889); repr. (1973) · A. Patchett Martin, *Life and letters of the Right Honourable Robert Lowe, Viscount Sherbrooke*, 2 vols. (1893) · *Army List* (1780–1830) · H. T. Manning, *The revolt of French Canada, 1800–1835* (1962) · D. C. Harvey, 'The Halifax–Castine expedition', *Dalhousie Review*, 18 (1938–9), 207–13 · C. Brown, *Lives of Nottinghamshire worthies* (1882), 326–7 · B. Murdoch, *A history of Nova Scotia or Acadie* (1865) · J. H. Lambert, 'Monseigneur, the catholic bishop, Joseph-Octave Plessis: church, state, and society in Lower Canada', D-ès-L diss., Université Laval, 1981 · J. Fingard, *The Anglican design in loyalist Nova Scotia, 1783–1816* (1972) · W. S. MacNutt, *The Atlantic provinces: the emergence of colonial society, 1712–1857* (1965) · parish register, Arnold, 29 April 1764 [baptism]

Archives NA Canada, an account of an attack on the Belvidera by an American squadron; corresp. and papers | BL, corresp. with Sir James Willoughby Gordon, Add MS 49494 *passim* · BL, letters to Sir Hudson Lowe, Add. MSS 20189–20190 · Herefs. RO, corresp. with Sir George Airey · NL Scot., corresp. with Sir Alexander Cochrane · PRO, Colonial Office records, CO 42/166–79, CO 43/22–5, CO 217/88–98, CO 218/28–9 · PRO NIre., corresp. with Lord Castlereagh

Likenesses miniature, 1796, repro. in Martin, *Life and letters*, frontispiece · R. Field, oils, Halifax Club, Nova Scotia · photogravure photograph, NPG · portrait, Oxton Hall, Nottinghamshire

Sherburne, Sir Edward (*bap.* 1616, *d.* 1702), translator and poet, was baptized with his twin brother John on 27 September 1616 at St Giles Cripplegate, London, the son of Edward Sherburne (1578–1641), government official and secretary of the East India Company, and his wife, Frances (*bap.* 1588, *d.* 1673), the daughter of John Stanley of Roydon Hall, Essex, and his wife, Beatrix. His grandfather Henry Sherburne, a descendant of Sir Richard Sherburne of Stonyhurst, Lancashire, had grown prosperous from modest beginnings as a groom at Corpus Christi College, Oxford. He was the elder of the twins, and there were four other children in the family.

Education and early years The family lived in Goldsmith's Rents, where Sherburne's schoolmaster, as he recalled to Anthony Wood in 1686, was the famous classicist Thomas Farnaby:

> about the yeare 1624; I began as I may truly call it my Ludus literarius, for I began very early, and by Reason of the Neighbourhood of my Fathers House, being joyned to the Backside of M. Farnabyes, us'd to play among the schollars in long Coats. I continued till the Yeare 1634. (Bodl. Oxf., MS Wood F.44, fol. 272r)

At that time Farnaby moved out of London, and his assistant, the poet Charles Aleyn, became Sherburne's private tutor. Other writers of Sherburne's acquaintance included Thomas Carew, Robert Herrick, Thomas May,

Thomas Randolph, and James Shirley. On 5 February 1638 the king granted Sherburne the reversion of his father's clerkship of the office of ordnance.

Sherburne wrote a prefatory poem for Aleyn's verse *Historie* of Henry VII (1638) and another for Ovid's *Heroical Epistles* (1639), translated by his brother John, who died the following year. His father:

> thought fitt for my better Education to send Me abroad to travell. I sett forward just at Xmas 1640 and continued abroad till the End of (41) haveing spent my Time in viewing a considerable Part of France; and was intended for a Journey into Italy, but then unfortunately calld back by Occasion of my Fathers Sicknesse, who not many Weeks after my Returne dyed some few Dayes before Xmas in the End of (41). (MS Wood F.44, fol. 272v)

Civil war Sherburne succeeded his father at a difficult time for the ordnance officers: on 17 August 1642 the House of Lords committed them to custody for refusing to issue munitions without the king's warrant. On 9 September they were ordered to be freed but not restored to their positions. Six days later Sherburne's mother, 'having Two Sons usually living with her, who are now with the King', was ordered to be removed from their house in the Tower (*JHL*, 1642–3, 448). Sherburne served Charles at the battle of Edgehill on 23 October, and on 22 November the king, holding a council of war at Reading, sent him and others with ordnance to Oxford. He was styled commissary, and his brother Henry (killed in 1646) initially worked in the Oxford ordnance office too. On 20 December both were admitted MA by the king's special command.

Eventually, after the battle of Naseby on 14 May 1645, hostilities moved west and the Oxford ordnance office was reduced until its members 'were gathered by Sherburne himself into an ordinary troop, which was allowed to remain as part of the garrison' (Roy, 1.57). After Oxford's surrender in the following June, he moved back to London, where he lived for some time in the Middle Temple chambers of his cousin John Povey. There he became friends with a more distant relative, Thomas Stanley, for whose *Poems and Translations* (1647) he wrote commendatory verses and also (in some copies) 'Epithalamion' on Stanley's marriage. The following year Sherburne published his verse translations of Seneca's *Medea* and *Answer to Lucilius his quaere; why good men suffer misfortunes seeing there is a divine providence?* He dedicated and presented the latter to 'the King of Sorrows', Charles I, who might perceive in it 'a glympse of Your own invincible *Patience* and inimitable *Magna[ni]mity*; in bearing and ever-mastering *Misfortunes*' (sigs. A2v–3r). Sherburne tactfully omitted the concluding lines, 'being a Stoicall Exhortation to the Anticipation of Death' (ibid., 30).

After Charles's execution Sherburne shared Stanley's retirement in the country homes of the latter's family at Cumberlow Green, Hertfordshire, and parents-in-law at Flower, Northamptonshire. Stanley encouraged his studying French and Italian poets, who are well represented in Sherburne's collection, dedicated to Stanley, *Poems and Translations Amorous, Lusory, Morall, Divine* (1651). These are virtually all translations; indeed, 'Sherburne can hardly

be credited with having written original poems at all' (Praz, 290). They have value, however, as evidence of literary fashion. The same year he contributed a commendatory poem to William Cartwright's posthumous *Comedies; Tragi-Comedies, with other Poems*.

Translating Manilius When young Sir George Savile (later marquess of Halifax) returned from his travels, Sherburne later wrote, 'about the years 1651 or 1652 I was invited to tak upon Me the Charge of his Concernes' (MS Wood F.44, fol. 273r). Sherburne has been identified with the Saviles' steward of the same name at Rufford, Northamptonshire, who was involved in an intended insurrection in March 1655. Sir George's mother recommended Sherburne 'to undertake the Tuition of her Nephew Sr: Jo: Coventry in his Travells abroad', setting out at the beginning of that same month and, 'Haveing run through All France, Italy, some Part of Hungary, the Greater Part of Germany, Holland, and the Rest of the low Countries, and Flandres, returning Home about the End of October 1659' (MS Wood F.44, fol. 273r). In Europe, Sherburne conversed with learned men and at Paris in September 1656 began work on Manilius.

Sherburne preserved the ordnance records during his sequestration. On 17 May 1660 he and the storekeeper Richard Marsh petitioned the House of Lords to restore them to their places; but a counter-claim by the incumbents frustrated them until they successfully petitioned the privy council, probably in June. Subsequently Sherburne asked the Council for '943*l*. 9*s*. 8*d*. owing to his late father, as clerk of the Ordnance in 1641, and for much larger arrears due to himself as his successor, to enable him to pay his father's debts' (*CSP dom.*, 1661–2, 229). He was disappointed by a pension of only £100; but he worked hard and conscientiously, remaining at his post throughout the great plague of 1665. He served on the commission for saltpetre in 1666.

Sherburne shared an interest in astronomy with the surveyor-general of the ordnance, Sir Jonas Moore, and the treasurer, George Wharton. Sherburne's *Sphere of Marcus Manilius Made an English Poem* (1675) was long in preparation and printing; it translated the first of the *Astronomica*'s five books, 'with ample notes displaying a wide reading but no great acuteness or alertness of mind' (Housman, 1.xv). Sherburne advertised this attractively illustrated folio as an initiation for young gentlemen 'in the first Rudiments of Sphericall Learning' (MS Wood F.44, fol. 273r). The catalogue of 'the most eminent astronomers, ancient & modern' attracted particular attention. He next published another translation of Seneca: *Troades: or the Royal Captives* (1679). Nahum Tate's collection *Poems, by Several Hands and on Several Occasions* (1685) included 'The Graces, or Hieron', translated by Sherburne from Theocritus 'above forty years ago' (p. 151).

Later life and death On 6 January 1683 Charles II knighted Sherburne:

> in consideration of his great sufferings, and the long and faithful services by him performed ... having also suffered several indignities from the faction at the time of the Popish

Plot, who endeavoured to out him of his Place, for being, as they supposed, a Rom. Cath. (Wood, *Ath. Oxon.: Fasti*, 2.19)

The Sherburne family was known for recusancy—notably the Stonyhurst branch—but Sherburne is said only to have 'turn'd Roman Catholick in King *Charles* II's time' (Boyer, 232). He had taken the oaths required by the Test Act in 1673. (Several Catholic items appear in his library catalogue of 1670—now BL, Sloane MS 857, fols. 182–94.) He remained financially insecure: on 7 December 1686 his petition for 'the arrears of his patent fees, amounting to 720*l*. 2*s*. 6*d*., out of the rebels' estate in the West' was referred to the lord treasurer (*CSP dom.*, 1686–7, 315); and a year later he hoped Anthony Wood might find him a college lease, for which a relative was providing him a lump sum.

On 28 August 1688 Wood dined with Sherburne, who told him 'he had received orders to give out ammunition and armes for the ships and several seaport townes' (*Life and Times*, 3.276). When King James had to replace the Tower's lieutenant, Sherburne wrote on 4 December, 'We are like to fare yet worse, for Orange they say demands the Towre to be deliverd up to him, trusting in that more then a free Parliam'' (MS Wood F.44, fol. 285*r*). A week later he informed Lord Dartmouth, master-general of the ordnance, 'this morning the Lord Lucas, now Lieutenant of the Tower, showed me a warrant from the Lords Spiritual and Temporal for removing me, as a Roman Catholic, out of the Tower' (*Dartmouth MSS*, 3.136). After initially objecting, he complied. On 18 January 1689 he begged Dartmouth to let Thomas Townsend deputize and himself retain the clerkship's profits, but in August, after he refused to take the oath and declaration, his successor was sworn in.

Sherburne planned further translations but completed only one: *The Comparison of Pindar and Horace* (1696) from the French of François Blondel. He lent Richard Bentley, who was editing Manilius, materials collected by Jean-Gaspard Gevaerts, from which Bentley sent a tract by Albert Rubens to Johann Georg Graevius for publication. Bentley's enemies at Christ Church, Oxford, however, published Sherburne's complaint that Graevius had acknowledged Bentley instead of himself; Bentley fully explained the matter in his revised *Dissertation upon the Epistles of Phalaris* (1699). By this time Sherburne was impoverished: on 27 January 1698 he petitioned the crown for some of £1048 10*s*. owing to him 'that he may pay his debts and be relieved from his starving condition' (*CSP dom.*, 1698, 53). On 9 April he was allowed £100 'in consideration of [his] great age and distressed condition' (*CSP dom.*, 187). Similar petitions and grants followed in 1699, 1701, and 1702.

In 1701 Sherburne reflected, 'tis in vaine to strive / To play the Poet well at Eighty five' (BL, Sloane MS 829, fol. 2*v*). He did, however, publish his collected translations of Seneca's *Tragedies* (1702), adding *Phaedra and Hippolytus* and reprinting *The Rape of Helen* from his collection of 1651. In his prefatory 'Brief discourse concerning translation' he strikes an old-fashioned note defending his 'close Adherence' to the words of the original—obviously a response

to Dryden's practice and theory. But Sherburne's verse, accomplished and often elegantly phrased, had rarely shown the independence of mind that distinguishes the best seventeenth-century poetry, even some of his friend Stanley's. He dedicated the *Tragedies* to young Richard Francis Sherburne of Stonyhurst, Sir Nicholas's son, in gratitude for his family's 'many Favours'. On 4 November 1702 he died, probably at Holborn, and was buried four days later in the chapel of St Peter ad Vincula at the Tower of London, towards the east end, on the north side near the wall. Although he composed an inscription for Sir Nicholas to use, a memorial tablet was placed there only in 1912. No will survives, nor record of his having married. Sir Hans Sloane, who had known him, bought some of his manuscripts. HUGH DE QUEHEN

Sources F. J. van Beeck, ed., *The poems and translations of Sir Edward Sherburne* (1961) · Wood, *Ath. Oxon.*, 2nd edn · *The life and times of Anthony Wood*, ed. A. Clark, 5 vols., OHS, 19, 21, 26, 30, 40 (1891–1900) · M. Praz, 'Stanley, Sherburne and Ayres as translators and imitators of Italian, Spanish and French poets', *Modern Language Review*, 20 (1925), 280–94, 419–31 · I. Roy, ed., *The royalist ordnance papers*, 1642–1646, 2 vols., Oxfordshire RS, 43, 49 (1964–75) · H. C. Tomlinson, *Guns and government: the ordnance office under the later Stuarts* (1979) · *A continuation of Mr Collier's supplement to the great historical dictionary* (1705) · R. Steele, ed., *Tudor and Stuart proclamations, 1485–1714*, 2 vols. (1910), 1.417 · R. Bentley, *Works*, ed. A. Dyce, 1 (1836), xxvii–xl · A. Boyer, *The history of the reign of Queen Anne, digested into annals: year the first* (1703) · IGI · *JHL*, 5 (1642–3), 448 · *CSP dom.*, 1661–2; 1686–7; 1698 · *M. Manilii Astronomicon*, ed. A. E. Housman (1903–30) · *The manuscripts of the earl of Dartmouth*, 3 vols., HMC, 20 (1887–96), vol. 3, p. 136

Archives BL, commonplace books, corresp., and literary papers, Sloane MSS 824, 829, 832, 836–837, 857, 1048 | Bodl. Oxf., letters to Anthony Wood, Wood MS F44, fols. 221–300

Likenesses oils, after 1705, repro. in van Beeck, ed., *Poems and translations of Sir Edward Sherburne*; formerly in the collection of David Minlore, London

Sherek, (Jules) Henry

Sherek, (Jules) Henry (1900–1967), theatre manager, was born at 2 Guilford Street, London, on 23 April 1900, the younger son of Bernard Scherek, merchant, and his wife, Margarette Jacoby. His schooling was scrappy and unconventional because his father, who after retiring from business in middle life had become an international theatrical agent, had only one strongly held principle about education: the need for fluency in foreign languages. The boys were therefore sent, when Henry was nine, to the Waren Gymnasium in Germany. He detested this: the discipline was stern and his schoolfellows were young fire-eaters preparing to be officers in the Kaiser's army; but it taught him fluent German. A few years later a less tough school in Switzerland taught him French.

Without a drop of British blood in him, Henry Sherek grew up a passionate patriot for the country of his birth, and when the First World War broke out he took advantage of the fact that he was a big mature-looking boy to enlist in the army at fifteen. He saw service in the Near East and was severely wounded. After the war and a few more desultory attempts at education, he went at the end of 1923 to the United States, where he spent some eighteen months working first for David Belasco, then for a theatrical agency. After returning to London he joined his father's agency and carried it on when his father died. He found the work pleasant and satisfying. The qualities which were later to carry him to a high place among play producers were such as to make very easy the less responsible enterprises of an agent. He was a very big man and this, combined with an extraordinary energy and zest for whatever he happened to be doing, made him a noticeable figure in any company.

Born as he had been into the world of entertainment, Sherek enjoyed it at all its levels; but this catholicity of judgement did not blunt his natural good taste. He was ready to like almost any kind of thing, but it had to be good of its kind. He was in fact in all his dealings with life a rare mixture of gourmand and gourmet. This was true of him literally as well as figuratively. As a boy he had had an enormous appetite and he grew up to be a trencherman of fame. Indeed, in his later years he became a compulsive eater and put on a great deal of weight. This increase of bulk did not seem to affect his energy, although it may well have shortened his life. Yet he never let quantity impair quality. Both in food and wine his choice was excellent.

Likeable, humorous, and kindly, Sherek was a popular figure in all parts of the world to which his talent-spotting journeys took him. He found the life amusing, and its rewards, though uncertain, were enough to keep a pleasure-loving bachelor in comfort—even in luxury, since in 1936 he was engaged by the Dorchester Hotel to supply them with cabaret revues and was given quarters in the hotel. In the same year, however, he realized that a bachelor existence was no longer what he wanted. A friendship of some years with a rising actress, Pamela Carme—in private life Kathleen Pamela Mary Corona Boscawen (1902–1995), daughter of Evelyn Edward Thomas Boscawen, seventh Viscount Falmouth—deepened into love, and on 22 April 1937 they were married. His wife ceased to act, but became his business partner in management.

From the very first, Sherek showed that as a manager he intended to set his standard of quality high. His opening venture, made before his marriage in the hope of providing him with some working capital, was a light comedy which failed; but his chance for a real start came very soon afterwards, when he was offered the British rights in Robert Sherwood's anti-war play *Idiot's Delight*. It took courage to produce such a piece for a public sick of war talk; but he rose to the occasion and took the risk. The play opened at the Apollo on 22 March 1938 and had an excellent run. Another Sherwood play, *The Petrified Forest*, came his way a year or two later, but by the time it was staged at the Globe in 1942 he had rejoined the army and had to present it in partnership.

Sherek served from 1941 until he was invalided out in 1944 with the rank of major; among his appointments was that of chief weapon training officer in the fighting school at Edinburgh. By 1945 he was back in harness as a play producer and adding quickly to his reputation. Over 110 plays were presented or produced by him in London, New York, and Paris. In 1947 and the years following he was sustained by the great success both at home and in America of a fine play, *Edward, my Son*, and this was followed in 1949 by an achievement which must rank as the peak of his career. Reading *The Cocktail Party* by T. S. Eliot, he was struck by both its quality and its stage potential and made up his mind, come what might, to produce it.

This decision called once again for his special gift of courage, for the play, obscure as it was and written in a subtle form of verse peculiar to Eliot, might well have been rejected by the ordinary playgoing public; and indeed Sherek did take the precaution of giving it a trial trip at the Edinburgh Festival of 1949. But such was the energy, the understanding, and the care in casting which he brought to his task that the play had a triumphant progress, first in New York and subsequently in London. The oddly assorted team—the ebullient Sherek, the austere Eliot, and his meticulous-minded director, E. Martin Browne—worked so well together that two more of Eliot's plays (*The Confidential Clerk*, 1953, and *The Elder Statesman*, 1958) were similarly launched by them to success in the West End.

Among the many other plays of merit for which Sherek was responsible were *Boys in Brown* (Duchess, 1947) and *Under Milk Wood* (New Theatre, 1956); but perhaps *The Affair* (Strand, 1961) calls for special mention. This stage version by Ronald Millar of a novel by C. P. Snow hung fire among the London managers because it dealt with the internal affairs of a Cambridge college and was thought therefore to have no popular appeal. Characteristically Sherek took that risk and equally characteristically scored a success. He died on 23 September 1967 in Venice after some years of retirement in Geneva.   W. A. DARLINGTON, *rev.*

Sources H. Sherek, *Not in front of the children* (1959) · personal knowledge (1981) · private information (1981) · Burke, *Peerage* (1999)

Likenesses R. Cass, photographs, 1961, Hult. Arch.

Sherer, Moyle (1789–1869), army officer and writer, youngest son of Joseph Sherer of Southampton, was born in that city on 18 February 1789. He was descended from the Moyles of Bake in Cornwall. From 1801–7 he attended Winchester College, but left on obtaining a commission in the 34th regiment of foot. In 1809 his corps was ordered to Portugal, and took part in the engagements of Albuera, Arroyo dos Molinos, and Vitoria. In the summer of 1813 Sherer was taken prisoner at the pass of Maya, and was moved to France, where he remained for two years, living chiefly at Bayonne.

In 1818 the 34th went out to Madras, from where Sherer sent home the manuscript of *Sketches of India* (1821), which went through four editions. Encouraged by its success, Sherer produced several more books after his return to England in 1823. *Recollections of the Peninsula* (1823) reached five editions and led Sherer into correspondence with Sir William Napier over Sir John Moore's campaign. This was followed by two travel books, *Scenes and Impressions in Egypt and Italy* (1824), and *A Ramble in Germany* (1826). While in India, Sherer had imbibed evangelical religious views, and, anxious to promote them among his comrades in the army, published in 1827 a treatise named *Religio militis*. He also wrote works of fiction and biography. Some, such as his *Life of Wellington* (1830–32), proved popular; others, such as *The Broken Font* (1837), did not. Perhaps because Sherer's works were published without his name, he has been variously (and apparently erroneously) referred to as Joseph Moyle and Joseph Moyle Sherer.

A keen soldier, Sherer was promoted to a brevet majority in 1830 and became captain in the 96th regiment in 1831, before being placed on half pay in 1832. He had little taste for garrison life, and retired from the army about 1836, to Claverton Farm, near Bath. He remained for many years in the same neighbourhood, but he became mentally ill and had to move from his home at Combe Hay, Somerset, to Brislington House, near Bristol. He died there on 15 November 1869, and was buried in Brislington churchyard. J. W. SHERER, rev. ELIZABETH BAIGENT

Sources private information (1897) · *CGPLA Eng. & Wales* (1870) · F. M. Kircheisen, *Memoiren aus dem spanischen Freiheitskämpfe, 1808–1811* (1908) · Allibone, *Dict.* · d. cert.
Wealth at death under £200: resworn administration, Oct 1871, *CGPLA Eng. & Wales* (1870)

Sheres, Sir Henry (*bap.* 1641, *d.* 1710), military engineer and author, was baptized on 17 June 1641 at St Nicholas's, Deptford Green, a son of Henry Sheres (*d.* in or after 1675) of Deptford, a captain in the interregnum navy, and his wife, Susan Pelly (*b.* 1613). His early years are unknown but in 1666 he went to Spain in the service of the ambassador-extraordinary Edward Montagu, earl of Sandwich, and was the 'trusty and ingenious' messenger employed in September 1667 to carry back to England Sandwich's treaty with the Spanish. On his return to England he became acquainted with Pepys, who found him 'a good engenious man, but doth talk a little too much of his travels' (Pepys, *Diary*, 8.444). In the following spring Pepys became jealous of Sheres's attentions to his wife, Elizabeth, despite his realization that his fears were groundless and that Sheres was 'a very civil and worthy man' (ibid., 9.533). Any potential conflict was averted when Sheres left for Tangier in May 1669. He had been employed in the previous autumn on surveying the fortifications and harbour there, and now became partly responsible for building the great breakwater or 'mole' that was intended to turn the English colony into a great entrepôt for Mediterranean trade. Sheres initially held the position of 'clerk examiner' under the chief engineer, Sir Hugh Cholmley, and in 1669 travelled to Genoa to view the mole there, which he favoured as a model for that at Tangier.

Sheres returned briefly to England in 1675, where he became a fellow of the Royal Society. John Evelyn encountered him at a Royal Society dinner on 4 March; Sheres was evidently still fond of regaling others with tales of his travels, on this occasion holding forth on the subjects of scorpions, locusts, elephants, and chameleons. Damage to the mole over the winter of 1674–5 discredited Cholmley, and Sheres's proposal for completing it by a different (and significantly cheaper) method, which relied on sinking large stone-filled chests, won official approval. Consequently he succeeded Cholmley as surveyor-general, and began work in July 1676. Despite shortages of

money and incessant difficulties with the weather, the Moors, the technology, and his enemies in England and Tangier—especially the disgruntled Cholmley and the local naval commander, Arthur Herbert—Sheres gradually extended the mole to its final length of 479 yards. He played a key role during the siege of Tangier in 1680, organizing the artillery defences and subsequently rebuilding the fortifications.

Sheres also played a significant part in the counter-attack from Pole Fort on 27 October, 'a very hott and bloody piece of service' in which Sheres was 'a principal instrument both by his valour and advice of the victory we obtained' (Routh, 194, 197). When the colony was evacuated in 1683 he wrote the report that condemned his own handiwork, the mole, and oversaw its demolition. Sheres was well aware of the charge of hypocrisy that might be levelled at him: when he showed Pepys his report, the latter commented that 'he did show me his foul draft of the ordinary objections made against the Mole improved the most he could to justify the King's destroying of it, though he did tell me privately that he is able to answer them all' (Chappell, 36–7). By this time Sheres had established or restored a close friendship with Pepys, and had also gained the confidence of the navy's commander, Lord Dartmouth. Indeed in 1682 Pepys had recommended Sheres to Dartmouth in the most fulsome terms as a man possessing 'uprightness of mind, universality of knowledge in all useful learning, particularly mathematics, and of them those parts especially which relate to gunnery and fortifications' (*Letters and the Second Diary*, 144–5).

In 1685 Sheres served with the artillery in the Sedgemoor campaign, but disliked the experience: he argued with other officers over the status and deployment of the artillery, and told Dartmouth that 'in plain English I have seen too much violence and wickedness practised to be fond of this trade … for what we every day practise among this poor people cannot be supported by any man of the least morality' (*Dartmouth MSS*, 3.126). Nevertheless he was rewarded in July with a knighthood and the position of surveyor of the ordnance. During the revolution of 1688 he was recovering from a serious illness, but on 1 November he assured James II that he was well enough to campaign and belatedly set off with an artillery train of 250 carriages, reaching Basingstoke by 14 November. He was regarded afterwards as a potential Jacobite, and was arrested twice, in June 1690 and February 1696. He was in Ireland in 1700; on 30 March he was appointed a trustee to regulate the king's Irish grants, and in March 1701 he was summoned to the House of Lords to explain the proceedings of the trustees. He received a ring at Pepys's funeral in 1703.

Sheres wrote extensively. He composed poetry (one of the attributes that had attracted Elizabeth Pepys to him) and translated some of the classics, especially Polybius and Lucian. He also published *A Discourse on the Mediterranean Sea* in 1703, in which he still bemoaned the loss of Tangier, 'a jewel fit only to adorn the crown that wears it, whose value I can better conceive than write' (Sheres, 20). Sheres edited for publication two works by Sir Walter

Ralegh: *A Discourse on Seaports* (1700) and *An Essay on Ways and Means to Maintain the Honour of England* (1701). Several other discourses circulated only in manuscript: these included 'A discourse touching the decay of our naval discipline' (1694), a damning indictment of faction-fighting, and 'Some directions for my Lord Nottingham's building', which included his thoughts on architecture.

By 1706–7 Sheres was increasingly troubled by illness, particularly gout, and he died on 21 April 1710. He seems never to have married, but Pepys recorded that he had kept a mistress in Tangier. By his will, made in September 1709, he left £1000 to his servant Martha Scarlett, and his library to Henry Overton of Trinity College, Oxford, the son of another former servant. His estate might have been greater if his own claims relating to the mole had been satisfied: in 1700 he calculated that he was still owed £14,000 in arrears of salary and disbursements on stores from his time as surveyor-general. Pepys consulted him on many matters, from gunnery to Noah's Ark, and thought that in comparison with all the other engineers and gunners in England, 'Mr Sheres by his experience exceeds them all' (Chappell, 150). J. D. DAVIES

Sources Sheres's letter-book, 1676–9, Bodl. Oxf., MS Rawl. A. 342 · Sheres's correspondence, 1669–1700, BL, Add. MS 19872 · *Report on the manuscripts of the marquis of Downshire*, 6 vols. in 7, HMC, 75 (1924–95), vol. 1 · *The manuscripts of the earl of Dartmouth*, 3 vols., HMC, 20 (1887–96), vols. 1, 3 · E. M. G. Routh, *Tangier, England's lost Atlantic outpost* (1912) · *The Tangier papers of Samuel Pepys*, ed. E. Chappell, Navy RS, 73 (1935) · Pepys, *Diary* · N. Luttrell, *A brief historical relation of state affairs from September 1678 to April 1714*, 6 vols. (1857) · papers relating to Tangier, BL, Sloane MS 3512 · 'A discourse touching the decay of our naval discipline', 1694, BL, Egerton MS 3383 · Evelyn, *Diary* · F. R. Harris, *The life of Edward Montagu ... first earl of Sandwich*, 2 vols. (1912) · *Le Neve's Pedigrees of the knights*, ed. G. W. Marshall, Harleian Society, 8 (1873) · J. Luke, *Tangier at high tide: the journal of John Luke, 1670–3*, ed. H. Kaufman (Paris, 1955) · H. Cholmley, *An account of Tangier* (1787) · *Letters and the second diary of Samuel Pepys*, ed. R. G. Howarth (1932); repr. (1933) · W. A. Shaw, ed., *Calendar of treasury books*, [33 vols. in 64], PRO (1904–69), esp. vol. 8 [1685–9] · will, PRO, PROB 11/515, fol. 57 · registers, St Nicholas, Deptford, LMA · H. Sheres, *A discourse on the Mediterranean Sea and the Streights of Gibraltar* (1703) · W. Musgrave, *Obituary prior to 1800*, ed. G. J. Armytage, 5, Harleian Society, 48 (1901), 257 · IGI · BL, Add. MS 19972

Archives BL, corresp., Add. MS 19872 · Bodl. Oxf., letter-book | BL, corresp. with Sir W. Trumbull · Staffs. RO, letters to Lord Dartmouth

Wealth at death £1000 bequeathed to servant; unspecified residue went to the children of a former servant; son received library: will, PRO, PROB 11/515, fol. 57

Sherey, John (*d.* 1551). *See under* Sherrey, Richard (*b. c.*1505).

Sherfield. For this title name *see* Makins, Roger Mellor, first Baron Sherfield (1904–1996).

Sherfield, Henry (*bap.* 1572, *d.* 1634), lawyer and iconoclast, was baptized on 13 September 1572 at Winterbourne Earls, near Salisbury, the third son and one of five children of Richard Sherfield or Shervill (*c.*1535–*c.*1620), corn dealer and small farmer, and his wife, Matilda Martin, daughter of John Martin. His life before 1607, when his voluminous papers begin, is badly documented. In 1608 he said that he had been educated 'as well in the country

schools as afterwards in the university' (Jervoise MSS, L64/1), but no evidence has been discovered of his presence at either Oxford or Cambridge. He entered Lincoln's Inn in 1598, at the relatively late age of twenty-six, and seems to have spent some time before then in Southampton, possibly working as clerk to a local lawyer. He was called to the bar in 1606.

Sherfield's religious inclinations may have been formed in the puritan environment of his inn. They must also have been shaped by reaction against those of his father. Richard Sherfield described himself late in life as a 'recusant' (Jervoise MSS, L67, testament in box 3), and that slur was also cast against other members of the family. But Richard's recusancy was intriguingly eclectic, combining a Catholic adoration of the five wounds of Christ with a decidedly sectarian interest in Christology. Sherfield's orthodox Calvinism was at odds with both of these. He also distinguished himself from his father and brothers in his capacity to channel his energy and ability into a successful career. He rapidly became a leading counsel in the court of wards and the favourite of its attorney, Sir James Ley. In 1610 he acted as intermediary in passing a bribe of a gilt cup to Ley, not without qualms of conscience recorded in his private fee book; but thereafter he carefully kept his hands clean of overt corruption, using his clients and patrons, like the Cecils and the Sackvilles, in more acceptable ways to reinforce both his London practice and his influence in the country.

Sherfield's local influence was firmly rooted in the triangle bounded by Salisbury, Southampton, and Winchester. It was strengthened by his marriage in 1607 to Mary Hodgson (*d.* 1613), daughter of a Winchester councillor and widow of George Bedford, a rich Salisbury clothier. Sherfield continued some of Bedford's business activities, including woad and madder growing, and retained an eye for opportunities in small-scale farming, while pursuing his legal and political career from a house in Salisbury and rooms in Lincoln's Inn. He was elected MP for Southampton in 1614 and 1621, and served as the town's recorder from 1618. In 1617 he joined the Wiltshire bench as JP, and in the same year he was appointed steward of the earl of Salisbury's west country estates, using his eldest brother, Richard, as his deputy. He had a finger in several pies, and seems deliberately to have been building a power base for his clan.

Though more successful than his brothers, Sherfield shared their prickly temperament. He was quick to take offence and acutely sensitive to threats to his reputation. When William Cecil, second earl of Salisbury, dismissed Richard as deputy steward in 1624, Sherfield wrote to the earl expressing the 'passion which worms discover when they are tread upon' (Jervoise MSS, L2/15). His papers show something of the 'violent' character attributed to him by his enemies (PRO, SP 16/55/64). They also reveal a profound and calculating introspection. He more than once worked out the costs and benefits of his marriage to Mary, who brought him an estate of £3000 but also six stepchildren still unprovided for. (He had only one child of his own, Matilda, born in 1610.) After Mary's death in 1613, he carefully reassessed his chances in the marriage market, hoping for a rich widow or even Ley's daughter, while proclaiming (to a brother) that he counted 'the selling of my body … a most base, vile and abominable thing' (ibid., L67, box 2). In 1616 he married Rebecca, née Bailey (d. c.1655), widow of Henry Long of Whaddon, a minor Wiltshire gentleman and one of his clients. That was a move up the social scale, although it brought the responsibility of a further eight step-children, and produced (he alleged) a profit of only £555. Yet it was a close and companionate marriage. Rebecca's letters, extending over fourteen years until her eyesight failed, are full of love and concern and reflect a shared puritan piety and considerable mutual trust.

Despite his calculation, Sherfield's finances were always precarious. In the 1620s he was earning as much as £400 a year at the bar, but burdened by the need to provide for a large extended family, and by his readiness to stand surety for his kinsfolk and for friends and clients such as Sir George Wrottesley and Sir Thomas Jervoise. His ambitions and his affections led him into obligations he might have been wise to avoid. His political fortunes were given a considerable boost, however, by his election as recorder of Salisbury in 1623. Already a significant figure in the vestry of St Edmund's parish, where he led a godly party including John Ivie and Peter Thatcher, the rector, he was now able to pursue their programme of civic and social reformation. As Sherfield said, they prided themselves on being engaged in 'wars with the drunkard, with the profane swearer, with the maypole-dancer, with every loose man and swaggerer', despite the accusations of 'preciseness' and the label of 'puritan' which they earned from their opponents in and around the cathedral (Jervoise MSS L67, speech in box 3). Their goal was 'a reformation, a true and real reformation' of the city (ibid., L38/54). In 1630 Sherfield sealed their triumph by obtaining a new charter, confirming the town's independence of the bishop and the close.

As MP for Salisbury from 1624 to 1629, Sherfield sought similar success in parliament, where he could count on support from Jervoise and (after 1625) Walter *Long, his stepson. In 1625 he was one of the first to oppose not only Buckingham, 'a cause of all our calamity' (Jervoise MSS, L21/1), but also Richard Montague and the Arminians. Though toning down some of the zealous rhetoric he employed in Salisbury, and billing himself instead as a 'good commonwealthsman' (ibid., L39/8), he was a consistent hammer of papists and introduced a bill for the protestant education of their children. In 1626 he also drafted a bill to encourage municipal brewhouses like that being used in Salisbury for relief of the poor, and he supported William Noy in his attempt to reform the poor laws. He spoke against martial law and the collection of tonnage and poundage, and collected materials on parliamentary privilege. At the same time, he was buying property in order to gain a controlling interest for himself and his kin in the pocket borough of Old Sarum. Sherfield was aspiring to a commanding parliamentary presence he never quite achieved, however; and after the dissolution of 1629

his prospects collapsed. Opposition to the crown had landed Long in the Tower, Sherfield's creditors were pressing, and he was arrested for the debts of his brother Richard.

Against this background, Sherfield's smashing of a stained-glass window in St Edmund's Church, Salisbury, in October 1630—one of the most famous acts of iconoclasm of the century—looks like an attempt to prop up his local position and reassert his authority. Instead it brought his world crashing about his ears. The window, showing God creating 'the sun and moon with a pair of compasses in his hand', had troubled Sherfield's 'conscience by the space of twenty years, for that he could not come into the church, but he must see it, sitting right opposite to it'. The vestry had authorized its taking down, but Bishop John Davenant issued an injunction protecting it. Determined to 'preserve a good conscience' and remove 'an occasion of idolatry', the recorder, 'all in black' and muttering to himself, witnesses alleged, attacked the image with 'a black staff with a pike in the end of it'. He was summoned before Star Chamber in 1633, with the king himself supervising the arrangements and Noy prosecuting. His supporters put up the best defence they could, John Ivie, for example, even testifying that he had seen Sherfield 'divers times' kneel to receive communion. Among his judges, who included a hostile William Laud and Richard Neile, only Edward Sackville, fourth earl of Dorset, gave him any real support, advocating leniency in order to avoid 'the tumults of the rude ignorant people in the countries where this gentleman … hath been a good governor' (State-Trials, 1.400–04, 415). Although he retained his place as recorder, he was fined £500, forced to make public submission to Davenant, and effectively destroyed.

Sherfield continued to believe his 'afflictions and crosses' the work of a benign divine providence: 'Did not God support me, I should have let go my hold long ere this' (Jervoise MSS, L32/39). In 1633, when he had to humiliate himself before Davenant, when fire destroyed his house at Winterbourne, and when even his own city of Salisbury called him to account for civic funds, it must have been difficult to cling on. He died early in the following year, intestate, with his financial affairs hopelessly and deliberately tangled, and with debts put at £6000. He was buried in St Edmund's churchyard on 28 January 1634. His papers, the remarkable archive of a man impelled to justify himself and to square driving ambition with a godly conscience, came into the possession of Sir Thomas Jervoise, once his debtor and now the chief of his creditors.

PAUL SLACK

Sources P. Slack, 'The public conscience of Henry Sherfield', *Public duty and private conscience in seventeenth-century England. Essays presented to G. E. Aylmer*, ed. J. Morrill, P. Slack, and D. Woolf (1993), 151–71 • Hants. RO, Jervoise of Herriard Park papers, 44M69 • W. R. Prest, *The rise of the barristers: a social history of the English bar, 1590–1640* (1986) • S. Emlyn, ed., *A complete collection of state-trials*, 3rd edn, 6 vols. (1742), vol. 1, pp. 399–418 • W. R. Prest, 'Counsellors' fees and earnings in the age of Sir Edward Coke', *Legal records and the historian*, ed. J. H. Baker (1978), 172–3, 184 • R. Priestley, 'Marriage and family life in the seventeenth century: a study of gentry families in

England', PhD diss., University of Sydney, 1988 · P. Slack, 'Religious protest and urban authority: the case of Henry Sherfield, iconoclast, 1633', *Schism, heresy and religious protest*, ed. D. Baker, SCH, 9 (1972), 295–302 · P. Slack, 'Poverty and politics in Salisbury, 1597–1666', *Crisis and order in English towns, 1500–1700*, ed. P. Clark and P. Slack (1972), 164–203 · G. D. Squibb, ed., *Wiltshire visitation pedigrees, 1623*, Harleian Society, 105–6 (1954), 176–7 · parish register, Winterbourne Earls, 13 Sept 1572, Wilts. & Swindon RO [baptism] · St Edmund's parish, Salisbury, parish register, Wilts. & Swindon RO [Jan 1613; burial; M. Sherfield] · St Edmund's parish, Salisbury, parish register, Wilts. & Swindon RO [28 Jan 1634; burial] · C. Russell, *Parliaments and English politics, 1621–1629* (1979), 231, 345 · R. C. Johnson and others, eds., *Proceedings in parliament, 1628*, 2 (1977), 188–9 · K. Sharpe, *The personal rule of Charles I* (1992), 345–8 · marriage agreement, Wilts. & Swindon RO, 947/903/1 · BL, Add. MS 11757, fol. 147 · PRO, SP 16/55/64

Archives Hants. RO, Jervoise MSS of Herriard Park, corresp. and MSS

Wealth at death £6000 in debt: Prest, *Rise of the barristers*, 390

Sheridan, Caroline Elizabeth Sarah. *See* Norton, Caroline Elizabeth Sarah (1808–1877).

Sheridan [*née* Callander], **Caroline Henrietta** (1779–1851), novelist, was the second daughter of Colonel James Callander (afterwards Sir James *Campbell, 1745–1832) and his third wife, Lady Elizabeth Helena (*d.* 1796), youngest daughter of Alexander Macdonnell, fifth earl of Antrim. Caroline Callander, one of the beauties of her day, was married on 21 June 1805 to Thomas (Tom) *Sheridan (1775–1817), the son of Richard Brinsley *Sheridan, and was mother of 'the three graces': Caroline Elizabeth Sarah *Norton; Helen Selina *Hay, countess of Gifford; and Jane Georgiana, duchess of Somerset. They also had four sons, three of whom predeceased their mother.

In 1813 Caroline Sheridan accompanied her husband to the Cape of Good Hope, where, while serving the office of colonial treasurer, he died of consumption on 12 September 1817. She received a small pension, and rooms in Hampton Court Palace were given to her by the prince regent. She published three novels: *Carwell, or, Crime and Sorrow* (1830), which was designed to expose the inequitable sentences pronounced upon those who had been guilty of forgery; *Aims and Ends* (1833); and *Oonagh Lynch* (1833). *Carwell* was also published in a French edition. She died on 9 June 1851, at 39 Grosvenor Place, London, the house of her daughter Lady Dufferin.

W. F. RAE, rev. K. D. REYNOLDS

Sources Burke, *Gen. GB* · Burke, *Peerage* · *GM*, 1st ser., 75 (1805), 1072 · *GM*, 2nd ser., 36 (1851), 207 · Boase, *Mod. Eng. biog.* · Allibone, *Dict.* · *Songs, poems and verses by Helen, Lady Dufferin*, ed. Marquess of Dufferin and Ava (1894) · A. Acland, *Caroline Norton* (1948) · BL, Egerton MS 2137, fol. 162

Sheridan, Charles Francis (1750–1806), author and politician, was born in June 1750 at 12 Dorset Street, Dublin, the second son of Thomas *Sheridan (1719?–1788), actor and lecturer on elocution, of Richmond, Yorkshire, and Frances *Sheridan (1724–1766), novelist and dramatist, daughter of the Revd Philip Chamberlaine. He was a year older and a much paler literary and political shadow of his better-known brother, the playwright and politician Richard Brinsley *Sheridan. Apart from a short period at Mr

Whyte's school in Dublin, he was educated by his father, who was anxious that his son should become an orator.

In 1772 Sheridan was appointed secretary to the British ambassador to Sweden and he made his literary reputation by writing *A History of the Late Revolution in Sweden* (1778). On his return he entered Lincoln's Inn on 11 May 1775 and he was called to the Irish bar in 1780. At the Irish general election of 1776 Sir Robert Tilson Deane, MP for co. Cork, who wished to obtain a peerage, purchased one of the seats for the borough of Belturbet from Lord Lanesborough for Sheridan. Apart from his connections, the Irish administration probably hoped that they had recruited a good parliamentary speaker, for it was said that:

in his manner, ardour and earnestness prevail, which render it strikingly pleasing. In argument he is strong, subtle and acute; investigating with precision, what he has studied with diligence; diving to the bottom of his subject, not merely skimming it's surface; he answers objections with ability, but avoids all asperity of recrimination. (Johnston-Liik, parliamentary lists, 1799(1))

However, despite his gifts he kept a low parliamentary profile for the fourteen years that he was in parliament.

In 1782 Sheridan considered that nothing except 'the most unequivocal assertion of the total independency of the Irish legislature' would satisfy the country (Grattan, 2.215). In 1782 the lord lieutenant, the duke of Portland, dismissed John Lees, formerly private secretary to lords lieutenant Townshend and Harcourt and an efficient Dublin Castle apparatchik, and appointed Sheridan undersecretary in the military department of the chief secretary's office. Sheridan owed his appointment to the influence of his brother Richard with the Rockingham whigs. The office was worth £1000 p.a. and a house. At the general election of 1783 he was returned for the borough of Rathcormack, through government influence with Richard Tonson, who also wished for a peerage and duly became Lord Riversdale. In spring 1783 he married Letitia Christiana, the daughter of Theophilus Bolton, and they had at least five surviving children, including Thomas, Charles, Letitia, and Caroline.

As was expected of an office-holder, Sheridan voted a solid government line. Nevertheless, Sheridan's situation in one of the key positions in the Irish establishment provided the Portland whigs who went into opposition in 1784 with a valuable ally inside Dublin Castle. As early as 1783 Lord Lieutenant Temple remarked to his brother W. W. Grenville on 'the pleasant private intercourse of the two Sheridans, which you may possibly trace in London as I do here' (*Fortescue MSS*, 3.198). Lord Lieutenant Rutland found his literary gifts useful as a pamphleteer in opposition to parliamentary reform and in support of the commercial negotiations and commented that 'he has dealt honourably with the government he serves, and his principles have not been warped by the influence of private connections' (*Rutland MSS*, 1.242). The Regency crisis in 1789 broke this discretion and, in accordance with his English connections, he voted for a regency. Lord Lieutenant Buckingham promptly dismissed him but granted his 'very handsome and amiable wife' a pension of £600 (*Fortescue MSS*, 3.445). Sheridan declared that 'he was promised a pension of £1,200, £600 of this to his wife' (PRO, 30/8/326, fols. 67–8), but when and whether this materialized is uncertain.

Sheridan's political career ended in 1790. He published two pamphlets: *An Essay on the True Principles of Civil Liberty and Free Government* (1793), which upheld the view of Ireland as an independent kingdom, and *Some observations on a late address to the citizens of Dublin with thoughts on the present crisis* (1797), in which he attributes the troubled state of the country to the example of France. On the whole, however, he spent his retirement in various unsuccessful experiments, for instance, in trying to design a perpetual motion machine. He was a member of the Royal Dublin Society and of the Royal Irish Academy. He did not enjoy good health and died, aged fifty-six, at Tunbridge Wells on 24 June 1806. The *Gentleman's Magazine* declared him to be 'a gentleman of most distinguished talents as an author, both in history and political controversy, and no man was more universally beloved and respected in private life' (*GM*, 679).   E. M. JOHNSTON-LIIK

Sources E. M. Johnston-Liik, *History of the Irish parliament, 1692–1800*, 6 vols. (2002) · *The manuscripts of J. B. Fortescue*, 10 vols., HMC, 30 (1892–1927) · *GM*, 1st ser., 76 (1806), 679 · *The manuscripts of his grace the duke of Rutland*, 4 vols., HMC, 24 (1888–1905) · E. M. Johnston, *Great Britain and Ireland* (1963), 66–7 · H. Grattan, *Memoirs of the life and times of the Rt Hon. Henry Grattan*, 5 vols. (1839–46) · PRO, 30/8/326, fols. 67–8

Archives King's AC Cam., diary and letters

Sheridan [*née* Frewen], **Clare Consuelo** (1885–1970), sculptor and journalist, was born in London on 9 September 1885, the only daughter and second of the three children of Moreton Frewen, landowner and sportsman-adventurer, of Brede Place, Sussex, and his wife, Clara, eldest of the three daughters of Leonard Jerome of New York, the grandfather of Sir Winston Churchill. Clare (who was baptized Claire but dropped the 'i') was educated by governesses at home and at Inishannon, her father's property in co. Cork. She also attended, briefly, a Paris convent and a finishing school in Germany. At the age of seventeen Clare 'came out' under the aegis of her aunts Jennie (the wife of Lord Randolph Churchill, who had died in 1895) and Leonie (the wife of Sir John Leslie of Glaslough). A restless, artistic girl, she did not take to the round of balls and country-house parties. She tried to educate herself by serious reading, and in this endeavour she was helped by William (known as Wilfred) Frederick Sheridan (1879–1915), a London stockbroker, the son of Algernon Thomas Brinsley Sheridan, of Frampton Court in Dorset. Wilfred was amused to learn she had never heard of his great-great-grandfather Richard Brinsley Sheridan.

As well as sketching with her friend Princess Margaret of Connaught, the niece of Edward VII and later married to Crown Prince Gustaf of Sweden, Clare Frewen attempted to write novels. Her parents' friends, the writers Robert Hichens, Rudyard Kipling, and above all Henry James, took pains to advise her but she was discouraged by

the opinions of George Moore. In 1910 she married Wilfred Sheridan at St Margaret's, Westminster, and by the outbreak of war she had borne two daughters, Margaret and Elizabeth. When Elizabeth died in February 1914 she modelled a little angel for the child's grave and realized that she wanted to be a sculptor. Wilfred Sheridan was killed in the battle of Loos in September 1915, a few days after the birth of her son Richard at Frampton Court. Clare remained with her parents-in-law until she settled in a small London studio where she could study sculpture under William Reid Dick. Her first exhibition under the auspices of the National Portrait Society aroused great interest, and subsequent commissions included Lord Asquith, the former prime minister (Oxford Union, Oxford), and the politician F. E. Smith (later Lord Birkenhead). She modelled a head of her cousin Winston Churchill while he tried to paint her.

In 1920 the first Soviet trade delegation visited London. It was headed by Lev Kamenev and Leonid Krasin who invited Clare to Moscow. Refused a visa she sailed with the delegation to Stockholm, where Kamenev procured her an Estonian visa. Civil war was raging in the Crimea and Winston Churchill, the secretary of state for war, was pressing for allied intervention. With displeasure he learned that his cousin was living in the Kremlin in Moscow doing busts of Grigory Zinovyev, Feliks Dzerzhinsky, Kamenev, Lenin, and Trotsky, who invited her to accompany him to the front and to set up a permanent studio in Russia. When she returned to England, Clare found that London society ignored her and Churchill preferred not to see her. So she departed for America.

After publishing her Russian diaries in 1921 (entitled *Mayfair to Moscow* in America and *Russian Portraits* in England), Clare travelled in America and Mexico, made friends with Charles Chaplin, and was astounded when newspaper columnists announced their engagement. She was introduced to Herbert Swope, editor of the New York *World*, and in the summer of 1922 she returned to Europe as that paper's roving correspondent. Within a short time she had made her name by obtaining scoop after scoop. In the Irish civil war she was the only reporter to interview both Michael Collins and his republican opponent Rory O'Connor, who was besieged in the Four Courts in Dublin. She then accepted a commission to cover the Greek–Turkish war and her vivid accounts of the terrible evacuation of Smyrna brought her to the top rank of professional war correspondents. She interviewed Atatürk, and, in Bulgaria, Alexander Stamboulisky, the peasant premier, and King Boris. After interviewing the newly crowned Queen Marie of Romania, she covered the Lausanne conference in 1932. Mussolini invited her to view his nascent organization of young fascists in Rome, but forbade her to publish his conversations in the New York *World*.

A second trip to the Soviet Union, in 1923, proved disillusioning, but Clare fulfilled her contract, providing two articles a week for America. Despite being *persona non grata* with the Russians, on her return to London she persuaded Khristian Rakovsky, the first Soviet representative in London (who had been chairman of the Ukrainian council of people's commissars), to authorize a visa for herself and her brother to tour south Russia on a motor cycle, which they called Satanella. In 1924, with Clare in the sidecar with the luggage, they drove across Germany and Poland to the Ukrainian border, and continued onwards to Odessa, where they spent a week. Having arrived safely by ship in Constantinople, Clare took her two children to live on the Bosphorus, where she wrote another book, *Across Europe with Satanella* (1925). She then gave up journalism for her true métier of sculpture, although the Constantinople sojourn resulted in another book, *A Turkish Kaleidoscope* (1926). In 1925 Clare moved to Algeria where she built a house on the edge of the Sahara (Bab el M'Cid at Biskra). Throughout the remainder of the 1920s and 1930s she concentrated on working as a sculptor, though still found time to write *Nuda veritas* (1927) and *Arab Interlude* (1936), among other books. In 1937 her son Dick died of appendicitis, aged twenty-one, at Constantine in the Sahara. As with the death of her daughter in 1914, Clare turned to sculpture as an expression of her grief. Taking a huge Sussex oak tree from her home at Brede Place, she carved it into a memorial for her son. Whereas before she had modelled busts of such men as Gandhi, Serge Lifar, and Keyserling, from now on she found a new artistic direction in carving wood. Seeking solace and to improve her carving technique she spent a summer in an art colony on a Native American reservation in the Rocky Mountains, and on returning to London her exhibition of American Indian heads whittled from forest trees drew much attention. From this experience she wrote *Redskin Interlude* (1938).

During the Second World War, in 1942, Clare made a bust of Churchill in bronze (versions at Chartwell, Kent, and Harrow School). After the war ended she entered the Roman Catholic church, and moved to the Spanish Arch in Galway. There she continued to carve and model. Her final memoirs, *To the Four Winds*, were published in 1957. She died on 31 May 1970, and was buried beside Brede church, where stands the great oak Madonna memorial to her son, probably her best work. The collection of Clare Sheridan's work from Brede Place, which was owned by Jonathan Frewen, was often shown at Rye Art Gallery, Sussex. Her earliest work is in the churchyard at Peper Harow, near Guildford. Her wood carving *Rising Christ* is in the church of St Catherine, Hoogstraeten, Belgium; a fine cherrywood *Crucifixion* hangs in Salthill church, Galway; a dark wood Madonna, silver-crowned, stands at Allington Castle, Maidstone, Kent; her wood carvings were shown at Charleston Manor, Seaford, Sussex. Many of her works in wood, alabaster, and terracotta are in private collections all over the world.   ANITA LESLIE, *rev.*

Sources C. Sheridan, *To the four winds* (1957) · A. Leslie, *Cousin Clare* (1976) · M. Motley, *Morning glory* (1961) · S. Leslie, *Studies in sublime failure* (1932) · diaries of Captain Oswald Frewen RN · personal knowledge (1981) · private information (1981) · *The Times* (2 June 1970) · *CGPLA Eng. & Wales* (1970) · b. cert. [W. Sheridan]
Likenesses J. Epstein, bust, 1919 · B. Park, chlorobromide print, 1919, NPG · O. Birley, oils (in her studio); known to be in possession of Lady Birley in 1981
Wealth at death £263: administration, 19 Oct 1970, *CGPLA Eng. & Wales*

Sheridan, Denis (*c.*1610–1683?), Church of Ireland clergyman, was the son of Owen Sheridan of Togher in the parish of Kilmore, co. Cavan; his mother was the daughter of Thomas Mac Brady of Ballyhaise. He was orphaned as a boy and brought up nearby in the house of the Revd John Hill, a minister of the Church of Ireland and dean of Kilmore. A committed protestant all his life, he came to the notice of William Bedell, bishop of Kilmore, who sought wherever possible to minister to the Irish in their own language. Impressed by Sheridan's skill in Irish, Bedell ordained him in 1634 and installed him in the vicarage of Killesher, co. Fermanagh. He held this benefice until 1683. In 1641, presumably because of the Irish rising, Sheridan was living in Drumcor in the parish of Kilmore. In 1645 he became vicar of the vacant benefice of Drung and Lara in co. Cavan, which he held in addition to Killesher perhaps until 1661. In 1657, during the Commonwealth, he was minister of religion at a stipend of £60 at Carrigallen, co. Leitrim, also in the diocese of Kilmore.

It has been suggested that Sheridan was ordained a Catholic priest and his being orphaned was a fiction intended to obscure his Catholic past. Yet his son Thomas and William Bedell, son of Bishop Bedell, independently relate that he was an orphan. Moreover Bedell would not have ordained Sheridan if he were already a Catholic priest.

About 1633 Sheridan married Jane (*b. c.*1610), daughter of Anthony Atkinson of Geashill, King's county. In the Irish rising of 1641 Sheridan and his wife opened their house as a sanctuary for many distressed planters. Bedell himself was taken from his own house by Edmund O'Reilly, the leader of the rising, and held captive in Clough Oughter. Because Sheridan, though a protestant, was of a 'name and family powerfull in that countrey' (Shuckburgh, 70), he was able to intercede for Bedell and his fellow prisoners. Bedell was released and took refuge in Sheridan's house at Drumcor, where he died of fever in February 1642. Owen Sweeny, the Catholic bishop of Kilmore, had meanwhile taken over Bedell's episcopal residence and refused to allow Bedell to be buried alongside his wife in Kilmore churchyard. Sheridan and Bedell's son-in-law, Alexander Clogie, went to Sweeny and prevailed upon him to revoke his decision. Sheridan also rescued some of Bedell's papers, including the Hebrew manuscript of the scriptures which he had acquired in Venice, and his manuscript translation into Irish of the Old Testament. These he entrusted to Bedell's executor, Henry Jones, dean of Kilmore and later bishop of Meath.

Sheridan's wife, Jane, died about 1643, it seems, and he married again about 1645. By his first marriage he had two sons, William *Sheridan (1635–1711), born in Togher, and Patrick (1638–1682), born near Enniskillen (perhaps at Killesher). William was named after bishop Bedell, his godfather, who left him 40s. in his will, probably to buy a mourning ring. William and Patrick entered Trinity College together in May 1652 and both became bishops of the Church of Ireland. Sheridan's second wife was called Foster. She was the mother of Thomas *Sheridan (1646–1712) and James (*b.* 1649), who were both born at St John's, near

Trim, co. Meath. Since Denis did not hold a benefice in St John's, it is possible that his second wife's family lived there (Fosterstown and Fostersholding are two townlands in the parish of Trim). Thomas became a noted Jacobite but little is known of James.

Attempts have been made to establish a connection between Denis Sheridan and Dr Thomas Sheridan of Quilca, co. Cavan, grandfather of Richard Brinsley Sheridan, the dramatist. Dr Thomas Sheridan is said variously to have been the son of one of three sons of Denis—William, Patrick, or James. Alternatively Sheridan of Quilca is made a descendant of a certain Patrick Sheridan, who was granted land in co. Cavan in 1637 at the same time as Owen Sheridan. Patrick and Owen are assumed by some to have been brothers, and Owen to have been the father of Denis Sheridan. Since, however, our Denis was an orphan in the 1620s, the Owen in question was not his father nor Patrick his uncle. The connection between Denis Sheridan and Richard Brinsley Sheridan remains unproven.

N. J. A. WILLIAMS

Sources J. G. Simms, 'Denis Sheridan and some of his descendants', *Bréifne: Journal of Cumman Seanchais Bhréifne*, 4 (1973–5), 460–70 · J. E. Bruns [J. E. Burns], 'The genealogy of the Sheridans', *Irish Genealogist*, 3 (1960), 162–9, 217–20 · E. S. Shuckburgh, ed., *Two biographies of William Bedell, bishop of Kilmore, with a selection of his letters and an unpublished treatise* (1902) · *A true relation of the life and death of ... William Bedell*, ed. T. W. Jones, CS, new ser., 4 (1872) · Burtchaell & Sadleir, *Alum. Dubl.*, 2nd edn · S. Bannister, ed., *Some revelations in Irish history, or, Old elements of creed and class conciliation in Ireland* (1870); repr. (1970) · J. B. Leslie, 'Biographical succession lists of clergy of the Kilmore diocese', NL Ire., MS 2685 · GEC, *Baronetage*, vol. 5

Sheridan, Elizabeth Ann. *See* Linley, Elizabeth Ann (1754–1792).

Sheridan [*née* Chamberlaine], **Frances** (1724–1766), novelist and playwright, was born in Dublin, the daughter of the Revd Dr Philip Chamberlaine, prebendary of Rathmichael, archdeacon of Glendalough, and rector of St Nicholas Without, and his wife, Anastasia Whyte. Frances was the youngest of five children, three of whom were boys; her mother died shortly after her birth. Her father considering female literacy 'perfectly superfluous', Frances Chamberlaine was secretly taught to write by her clergyman brother Walter. At the age of fifteen, she wrote a romance, *Eugenia and Adelaide*, published posthumously in 1791, and two sermons which her granddaughter recorded 'were reckoned to display considerable ability' (A. Le Fanu, 9).

During the so-called *Cato* affair (a theatrical quarrel sparked off by the misappropriation of a costume) in Dublin in 1743, Frances Chamberlaine espoused the side of Thomas *Sheridan (1719?–1788), of the Smock Alley Theatre, penning in his defence some verses entitled 'The Owls: a Fable'. She subsequently married the actor and theatre manager, probably in 1747. The couple had six children: Thomas (who died aged three), Charles Francis *Sheridan, Richard Brinsley *Sheridan, Alicia, later Alicia *Le Fanu (1753–1817) [*see under* Le Fanu, Philip (1735–1795)], Sackville (who died in infancy), and Anne Elizabeth.

Frances Sheridan (1724–1766), by unknown artist

As a consequence of financial misfortunes, the Sheridans moved to London in 1754. There, Frances Sheridan met Samuel Richardson who read her unpublished romance and encouraged her to write another. The result was her finest work, the sentimental novel *Memoirs of Miss Sidney Bidulph*, published anonymously, but with a dedication to Richardson, in 1761. A study of the effect of extreme distress on apparently irreproachable virtue, the novel embodies a feminist critique of poetical justice so remorseless as to lead Samuel Johnson, one of many influential admirers, to exclaim, 'I know not, Madam, that you have a right, upon moral principles, to make your readers suffer so much' (Boswell, *Life*, 276). As one whose own writing was influenced by contemporary French fiction, Sheridan received the compliment of finding *Sidney Bidulph* translated into French by the Abbé Prévost as *Mémoires pour servir à l'histoire de la vertu* in 1761; a German translation appeared the following year.

Sheridan next turned from fiction to the theatre, writing a comedy, *The Discovery* (1763), which pleased David Garrick, who staged it at Drury Lane on 3 February 1763, playing the role of Sir Anthony Branville himself with Thomas Sheridan taking the part of Lord Medway. The young John O'Keeffe declared that the comedy 'gave great delight, and the success was perfect' (O'Keeffe, 1.86). It played to full houses for seventeen nights; subsequent revivals included an adaptation by Aldous Huxley in 1924. On 10 December of the same year, a second comedy, *The Dupe* (published 1764), was produced at Drury Lane by George Colman before being withdrawn after three nights, allegedly because 'of the theatrical cabals of a popular actress [Kitty Clive]' (A. Le Fanu, 235–6).

In general Frances Sheridan was much admired by male and female friends alike: from Samuel Johnson, Edward Young, and James Boswell—who considered her 'sensible, ingenious, unassuming, yet communicative' (Boswell, *Life*, 275)—to Sarah Fielding, Catherine Macauley, and Sarah Scott. The Sheridans' continuing financial difficulties constrained them in September 1764 to move to France, where they eventually settled at Blois. There Sheridan wrote the *Conclusion of the Memoirs of Miss Sidney Bidulph*, relating the misfortunes of her heroine's daughters (1767). An unfinished comedy, *A Journey to Bath*, was rejected by Garrick, and eventually published only in 1890. A completion by Elizabeth Kuti was successfully staged in Ireland and Edinburgh in 1999. The play is notable for providing in Mrs Tryfort the prototype of Mrs Malaprop in *The Rivals* by Frances's son Richard Brinsley Sheridan.

Frances Sheridan's final (and posthumously published) work, *The History of Nourjahad* (1767), confirmed her talents as a writer of fiction; another account of virtue under stress and long regarded as the finest oriental tale in English after Johnson's *Rasselas*, the work went through many editions and translation into French, Russian, and Polish and was dramatized by Sophia Lee (1788), among others. Frances Sheridan died at Blois after a short illness on 26 September 1766. She was survived by her husband.

IAN CAMPBELL ROSS

Sources A. Le Fanu, *Memoirs of Mrs Frances Sheridan* (1820) · Boswell, *Life* · J. O'Keeffe, *Recollections of the life of John O'Keeffe, written by himself*, 2 vols. (1826) · E. K. Sheldon, *Thomas Sheridan of Smock-Alley: recording his life as actor and theater manager in both Dublin and London* (1967) · J. Watkins, *Memoirs of the public and private life of the Right Honorable R. B. Sheridan* (1817) · T. P. Le Fanu, *Memoir of the Le Fanu family* (1924) · S. Whyte, *Miscellanea nova* (1800)
Likenesses stipple, 1824, BM, NPG; repro. in *La belle assemblée* · drawing, NPG [*see illus.*]

Sheridan, Richard Brinsley (1751–1816), playwright and politician, was born in September or October 1751 at 12 Dorset Street, Dublin, the third child of Thomas *Sheridan (1719?–1788), actor and orthoepist, and his wife, Frances *Sheridan, *née* Chamberlaine (1724–1766), novelist and playwright. He was baptized at St Mary's Church on 4 November, the register listing him as 'Thos. Brinsley', Thomas also being the Christian name of his grandfather Dr Thomas *Sheridan (1687–1738). His parents, however, called him Richard. Their eldest child, Thomas, died in 1750, the year when their second son, Charles Francis (*d.* 1806), was born.

Early years and upbringing When his parents went to London in 1754, after a riot in the Smock Alley Theatre (then managed by Thomas Sheridan), Richard and his elder sister Alicia, later Alicia *Le Fanu (1753–1817) [*see under* Le Fanu, Philip], stayed in Dublin, looked after by a nurse. The parents were back in Dublin from 1756 to 1758 and Thomas then began his son's education, but when they left for London again Richard and his sister lived with Samuel Whyte, attending his famous school in Grafton

Richard Brinsley Sheridan (1751–1816), by John Russell, 1788

Street. Richard had two years with his family when he and Alicia joined them in Windsor in 1759; he never returned to Ireland.

In 1759 Frances Sheridan taught both her sons, concentrating largely on English. In 1762 Richard was sent to Harrow School where he remained until 1767 or 1768, his parents having decided 'to accustom him early to shift for himself'. Though befriended by a member of the staff, Dr Samuel Parr, he was lonely, missing his parents, who had moved to France to escape creditors. His mother died there when he was fourteen; he was not reunited with the family in London until he was seventeen.

In London, Lewis Ker, a former physician, tutored Sheridan in Latin and mathematics, Domenick Angelo teaching him fencing and horsemanship. Angelo's son became his friend: both boys were also educated by Richard's father, who moved the family to Bath in 1770, teaching elocution and giving his Attic entertainments there.

Richard enjoyed the social life of Bath. He corresponded with Nathaniel Brassey Halhed, a friend at Harrow, now at Oxford; they wrote a farce, *Ixion*, later called *Jupiter*, offered in vain to Garrick and Foote. Their verse translation of the *Love Epistles* of Aristaenetus, published in 1771, was reissued in 1773. They planned a literary periodical to be called *Hernan's Miscellany*, of which Sheridan wrote a draft first issue. Two of Sheridan's poems were published in the *Bath Chronicle*, 'The Ridotto of Bath', a skit, and 'Cleo's Protest, or, The Picture Varnished', addressed to a Bath beauty; both poems were reprinted in pamphlet form.

Halhed's letters praised Elizabeth Ann (Eliza)*Linley (1754–1792), who had sung superbly in oratorios at Oxford. Strikingly beautiful, with a magnificent soprano voice, she was painted at least four times by Gainsborough, and Reynolds described one of his two paintings of her as St Cecilia as the best he had ever painted. She was the daughter of Thomas Linley, a musician whom Thomas Sheridan first met in 1764 and had hired to take part in his Attic entertainments. By 1771 Eliza had become engaged to Walter Long, a Wiltshire squire many years her senior who gave her father £3000 for breach of promise when she told him she could never be happy as his wife. Ensuing gossip prompted Samuel Foote's satiric play *The Maid of Bath*. Pursued by a Captain Mathews, a married man, she confided her anxieties about this situation to Sheridan's sisters. Sheridan's brother Charles was in love with her but withdrew from Bath for fear of displeasing his father, then acting in Dublin, who thought the Linleys socially inferior.

Romantic hero Eliza decided to withdraw from public life as a singer and retire to a convent in France. Richard offered to conduct her there, and, borrowing money, organized their journey to Lille, proposing to her *en route*. They were married by a Roman Catholic priest at a village near Calais but did not consummate the marriage, Eliza taking a place in a convent in Lille; her father, having followed them, insisted she should return to Bath and fulfil some singing engagements. Mathews had attacked Sheridan as 'a L[iar] and a treacherous S[coundrel]' in a letter in the *Bath Chronicle* but when Sheridan, who had returned from France with the Linleys, called on him in London he tried to blame Richard's brother Charles. Back in Bath, Sheridan read the letter, dashed to London, defeated Mathews in a duel and compelled him to retract and apologize in the *Bath Chronicle*. A second duel was fought on 2 July, Mathews having lied about the details of his defeat in the first one; this time Sheridan was seriously wounded.

Both fathers strongly objected to Richard and Eliza marrying, Linley not wanting Eliza to give up her very successful musical career and thinking Sheridan's extravagance likely to ruin her, Thomas Sheridan sending Richard to friends, Mr and Mrs Parker, at Waltham Abbey in Essex to study law before entering the Middle Temple, hoping to keep him out of further quarrels with Mathews and from seeing Eliza. At first Richard kept his promise not to communicate with her, and studied a wide range of subjects, aiming to fit himself for public life. She wrote to him, however, and he managed to meet her secretly; the upshot was that they were married on 13 April 1773, Thomas Linley, apparently acquiescent, attending the service. But Thomas Sheridan now considered he had no son but Charles—whom he had always favoured.

After a blissful time at East Burnham, the young couple bought a London house, in Orchard Street, using some of Eliza's £1000 dowry, taken out of the £3000 paid to her father by Walter Long. After fulfilling her two engagements Eliza never sang professionally again: Sheridan thought it unbecoming for a gentleman's wife to sing for money and she disliked performing in public. But what were they to live on?

Author and theatre proprietor Sheridan, who had given up his studies at the Middle Temple, thought writing the answer, informing his father-in-law in November 1774 that there would be a comedy of his in rehearsal at Covent Garden within a few days. *The Rivals* was withdrawn after the first night, 17 January 1775, but Sheridan rewrote it in ten days and its popularity has lasted ever since. Set in Bath, it owes not a little to his mother's novel *Memoirs of Miss Sidney Biddulph* (1761; 1767) and her unfinished play *A Journey to Bath*, in which her Mrs Tryfort anticipated her son's Mrs Malaprop. The play possesses the originality of true comedy, though it contains many deliberate echoes of other plays. There are many references to and caricaturings of events in Sheridan's own life, Sir Anthony Absolute, mirroring Congreve's Sir Sampson Legend in *Love for Love*, being a father as domineering and opinionated as Sheridan's own. Sir Lucius O'Trigger, toned down in the rewritten version of the play, became more than the blustering stage Irishman, originally acted by John Lee, being now better portrayed by Laurence Clinch, for whose benefit performance Sheridan wrote, reputedly in two days, *St Patrick's Day*, an amusing farce reflecting not only his interest in the American War of Independence but pride in his Irish ancestry. He liked to give the impression of dashing off his writing, Thomas Moore alleging in his discussion of *The School for Scandal* that Sheridan's policy was to gain credit for excessive indolence and carelessness, while few people of such brilliant talent 'ever used more art and circumspection' (Moore, 1.241, 192, 209).

The Duenna, a highly successful comic opera, with songs and music provided by the Linley family, which ran for seventy-four nights, opened on 2 November 1774—four days after the birth of a son, Thomas. Two daughters elope, outwitting tyrannical fathers; a duenna outsmarts her master by marrying the rich suitor chosen for his daughter: here is the intricate plotting of classic comedy, with appearances exposed by reality.

Sheridan was already negotiating to buy David Garrick's controlling share of the Drury Lane Theatre for £35,000. His father-in-law and Dr James Ford, a fashionable 'man midwife', joined him in the complicated financing, Sheridan's £10,000 share obtained largely by borrowing £7700 and raising £1000 by mortgages. The other share, owned by Willoughby Lacy, was sold to Sheridan in 1778 for 30,000 guineas and an annuity of £1000 per year. On 21 September 1776 Drury Lane opened under Sheridan's management. He staged three revised versions of Congreve's comedies and rewrote Vanbrugh's *The Relapse* as *A Trip to Scarborough* (staged on 24 February 1777), giving it 'a little wholesome pruning' (R. B. Sheridan, *A Trip to Scarborough*, II.i). Such Restoration comedies might have seemed too coarse for current taste, but Sheridan was preparing for his own highly successful *The School for Scandal*, with its contrast between the Surface brothers, its exposure of the moralizing Joseph's hypocrisy and the generosity of Charles the 'wild spark'. While mocking excessive sensibility, the play, first staged on 8 May 1778, drew genuine feeling in Lady Teazle's transformation, and reflected current political issues in its reference to the Annuity Act, which necessitated Sheridan's persuading the lord chamberlain that the money-lending scene was general satire, not an attack on Benjamin Hopkins, a respectable rival of the raffish politician John Wilkes for a public office.

The Camp, satirizing military manners and current events, staged on 30 October 1779, ran for fifty-seven performances. Sheridan followed it with *The Critic*, exposing dramatic conventions and clichés, in effect teasing the audience into thinking about the issues involved while mocking contemporary journalism and well-known individuals.

The social man and the politician The Sheridans' social life expanded rapidly; they had given private concerts, and, as Fanny Burney's diary records in April 1773, 'the whole town seems distracted about her. Every other diversion is forsaken. Miss Linley alone engrosses all eyes, ears, hearts' (*The Early Diary of Frances Burney*, ed. A. Raine Ellis, 1907, 1.210). The youthful playwright and manager of Drury Lane conversed wittily and had a charm of manner complementing his wife's attractiveness. They were accepted in aristocratic circles, welcome guests at Devonshire House and Chatsworth, at Holland House, Burlington House, and Carlton House.

Sheridan particularly admired Charles James Fox for desiring political reform and opposing the American war. They became friends, Fox thinking Sheridan the wittiest of men. Proposed by Dr Johnson in 1777, Sheridan became a member of the Literary Club, where he met Edmund Burke. The next year he was elected to Brooks's Club.

Sheridan was now living beyond his means, many of his new friends and acquaintances setting him examples of extravagance supported by vast debts. Gaming and drinking were part of their social life, which condoned sexual irregularity. Sheridan, though happy to make wagers, did not gamble. Optimistic about his ability to repay debts, he spent freely, frequently moving residences and entertaining lavishly.

Sheridan had always wanted a public career. He began it by drawing up a manifesto for the Westminster committee's campaign to promote electoral reform. The next step was to obtain a seat in parliament, but depending on a patron or buying a borough were not possible methods for him; besides, he was determined to be independent; he was elected in Stafford in 1780. Though aided by the duchess of Devonshire and her mother, Lady Spencer, his election depended on the votes of the burgesses, an expensive business, costing him over £1000, probably largely borrowed against his share in Drury Lane. Sheridan envisaged achieving distinction and fortune as an MP and prepared his early speeches carefully, gradually consolidating a reputation for eloquence and wit. He supported the whig opposition, concerning himself frequently with the encroachment of the state on public liberties. When the Rockingham administration came to power in March 1782 it had a liberal, reformist policy, Fox becoming secretary

of state for the northern department (foreign affairs) and Sheridan under-secretary.

In May 1782 this Westminster government repealed the Declaratory Act (6 Geo. I c. 5; which asserted the right of the king and Westminster parliament to make laws binding the kingdom of Ireland), Poynings' law, and the Mutiny Act, Henry Grattan having carried a motion for legislative independence in the Dublin parliament in accord with the resolutions of the Irish Volunteers, about which Sheridan had been informed by his brother Charles, now an MP in the Irish parliament. Sheridan, however, thought that Shelburne, secretary of state for the southern department (which included Irish affairs) was conceding Irish legislative independence rather than regarding it as a right. After Rockingham's death in June 1782, Shelburne was asked by the king to replace him, and Fox, at odds with Shelburne, withdrew from the government, Sheridan and Burke following him. When Shelburne lost office in February 1783 Fox, despite Sheridan's powerful pleas against this, allied himself with Lord North. Sheridan was appointed by them as joint secretary to the Treasury with Burke's son Richard.

Burke, influenced against Warren Hastings, then governor general of Bengal, by Sir Philip Francis, persuaded Fox to introduce bills for governmental supervision of the East India Company. Sheridan supported these bills which were passed in the Commons but rejected in the Lords, largely through the influence of the king, who then dismissed the Fox–North administration, requesting Pitt to form a government.

By 1782 Sheridan was concentrating on politics, leaving the management of Drury Lane largely to his father-in-law, ably aided by Eliza, for over six years. His antipathy to excessive monarchical authority, his increasing dislike of Pitt for representing it—and for having taunted him, in February 1783, for being a dramatist and theatre proprietor, something rebutted by Sheridan's dubbing Pitt, in a phrase from Ben Jonson's *The Alchemist*, the 'Angry Boy'—and his own sympathy for an India under the East India Company's autocratic rule led him, despite the break between himself and Nathaniel Halhed, one of Hastings's lieutenants in India, to attack Hastings after he resigned and returned from India in 1784.

Sheridan, having cross-examined the resident of Lucknow skilfully beforehand in the debate on 7 February 1787, supported the impeachment of Hastings for robbing the begums of Oudh of their treasure and allowing the seizure of their lands. In this five-and-a-half-hour speech, Sheridan showed a masterly ability to handle minute legal detail as well as making general statements which appealed to the sensibility of his audience, the motion being passed by 175 votes to 68. His oratorical powers were further demonstrated at Hastings's trial, begun on 3 June 1789, in a carefully prepared speech lasting over several days and ending with the famous phrase, uttered as he swooned dramatically into Burke's arms, 'My Lords, I have done'.

Personal relationships Sheridan became more directly embroiled with Pitt in February 1785 when Pitt's Irish resolutions for a commercial union, put to the Irish parliament, seemed a denial of Irish independence. He opposed Pitt's plans rigorously in a speech of 20 May which marked his increasing political interest in Irish affairs.

Further differences arose through Sheridan's friendship with the prince of Wales who, opposed to his father in most matters, sympathized with the aims of Fox's party, hoping the Foxites would grant him a handsome income if they came to power. Sheridan, now a *habitué* of Carlton House, grew closer to the prince after his secret marriage in December 1785 to Mrs Fitzherbert, a Roman Catholic, an action illegal under the Act of Settlement and the Royal Marriages Act, glossing over the situation skilfully in the house. His influence increased when the king, suffering from porphyria in October 1788, was thought to have become mad. In the ensuing political crisis—the prince would become regent if the king were declared insane, king if his father died—Sheridan acted as a link between the prince and the politicians, Fox being in Italy. He gave the prince subtle independent advice, drafted his diplomatic reply to Pitt's offer of a conditional regency, and manipulated the press in the manner of some contemporary prime minister's spokesman. The whig leaders Fox and Lord Grey, jealous of Sheridan's position, wasted energy intriguing about the potential allocation of ministries. The prince understood Sheridan's proud nature, his concept of honour, his Anglo-Irish insistence on the importance of being a gentleman, accentuated by awareness of his descent from the O'Sioradain chiefs of co. Cavan, his conscientious scruples, his willingness to grant but not receive favours for himself.

Thomas Sheridan, acting Cato in Covent Garden, had deeply upset Richard by refusing to see him, although he did attend a performance of *The Rivals* with his daughters in 1775. They were reconciled later but he was offended by the terms Richard offered him in 1776 to manage Drury Lane. One condition was that he stop acting, Richard not wanting to be known as a player's son. Thomas nevertheless accepted the position in 1778 and resigned in 1780 in the expectation of being reappointed. When he was not he refused to speak to his son until his last illness when Richard sat by his bedside for his last four days at Margate, where he died on 14 August 1788.

Sheridan's relationships with other women drove Eliza to contemplate separating from him. The romantic marriage had become a mere formality. Sheridan, smitten by his 'Amoret', a whig hostess, Frances Anne Crewe, then married for two years to John Crewe, had sent her 'A portrait' as the dedication of *The School for Scandal*, probably the last copy he revised. His wife seems to have tolerated this affair, which lasted until the middle or late seventeen-eighties, she and Mrs Crewe remaining on friendly terms. But Sheridan's passionate relationship with the duchess of Devonshire's sister Lady Harriet Duncannon (Lady Bessborough after 1793 when her husband Viscount Duncannon succeeded to the earldom) deeply wounded Eliza. In 1789 Harriet's husband decided to divorce her and sue Sheridan but was persuaded out of this by the duke of Devonshire. While Fox was urging Eliza to forgive Sheridan, the prince of Wales was attempting to persuade his brother the duke of Clarence, hopelessly in love with her, not to pester Eliza with his attentions. An absurd situation ensued at Crewe House where Sheridan, pleading for his wife's forgiveness, was discovered locked in a bedchamber with the governess. Eliza was furious but finally agreed to take Sheridan back.

In 1791 Eliza and Lord Edward Fitzgerald became lovers. He was the father of her daughter Mary, born in spring 1792. With her pregnancy Eliza's tendency to tuberculosis returned and she died on 28 June, Sheridan, grief-stricken and guilty, attending her to the last. The daughter was treated as a Sheridan, Sheridan and Fitzgerald remaining on friendly terms, both seeing Eliza reborn in Mary, who died in October 1793. The lives of the two men were further entangled when Madame de Genlis and Pamela (reputedly the daughter of the duc d'Orléans, actually Nancy Sims, an English orphan) came to England. They were Sheridan's guests at Isleworth. Both he and Fitzgerald thought Pamela the image of Eliza, and Sheridan seems to have proposed to her but characteristically did not ensure his letters reached her. After Madame de Genlis and Pamela had returned to France, Fitzgerald married Pamela at Tournai and they moved to Ireland where Fitzgerald became active in the United Irishmen.

Sheridan had been involved in the rebuilding of the Drury Lane Theatre from 1791 to 1794; he intended to finance it by £150,000 of debentures but the cost, which overran the estimates, and the need to purchase a third dormant patent meant £90,000 more had to be found. He became involved in a morass of mortgages, the trustees increasingly impatient with his failure to meet financial liabilities. The strains involved made him aware of his loneliness at forty-three. On 27 April 1795 he married again. His second wife was Hester Jane Ogle (whom he called Hecca), the lively nineteen-year-old daughter of the dean of Winchester. Her father insisted on a trust being established for her, made up of her £5000 dowry and Sheridan's £15,000.

They had a son, Charles, born on 14 January 1796, and bought Polesden Lacey, a manor house with 340 acres, in Surrey, Sheridan raising the money by selling 3000 renters' shares in the theatre. He proved a generous landlord to his tenants. Careless rather than grossly extravagant, he would leave letters unopened, plays unread, and bills, often for more than was owed, unpaid—though they *did* get paid, he told Hecca in reply to her complaints of neglect and indifference to her well-being, which he blamed on his sanguine temper, that his confidence could meet any difficulties. There were many: his chaotic financial arrangements led to borrowing from his associates in the theatre, John Grubb and Thomas Shaw in particular, and urgent letters to Richard Peake, the under-treasurer of Drury Lane, frequently requested small advances, sometimes against his subsistence money of 5 guineas a day (his annual salary in 1807 was £2000). Peake also received many letters covering the administrative expenses of the theatre as well as the salaries of actors and actresses, often in arrears. Letters to Hecca, generally energetic accounts of buoyant activity, convey his regard for her—he can assure her he loves her 'more and more dearly if possible every hour' (letter of 6(?) Oct 1796 from the House of Commons, *Letters of Richard Brinsley Sheridan*, 2.53)—as well as expressing concern for his children and telling her of his own occasional fits of low spirits and melancholia.

The complexities of politics Sheridan, like Fox a supporter of the French Revolution after the fall of the Bastille, argued strongly against the execution of Louis XVI. James Gillray's satirical etching 'The hopes of the party prior to July 14th—from such Crown and Anchor-dreams, good Lord deliver us' refers to the radicals' annual celebration of the taking of the Bastille in 1791—which neither Sheridan nor Fox attended. In it Gillray shows Fox about to chop off King George's head, who is uttering 'What! What! What! What's the matter now' while Sheridan holds him down by the ears. Fox deferred to the views of Burke, then writing his *Reflections on the Revolution in France*. Burke attacked the innovations and abuses of the revolution in a speech of February 1790, accusing some of the whigs of forming cabals to alter the British constitution, an allegation Fox denied, while Sheridan, on whom Burke was casting suspicion, taunted Burke in return, comparing the revolution to the English one of 1688, saying what Burke deplored in France was the result of despotism. This provoked Burke's memorable reply that he and Sheridan were now separated in politics.

Sheridan now sought to ally the whigs' desire for political reform with popular radicalism. With several whig leaders he joined the committee of the Society of Friends of the People which opposed Burke's ideas. It made contact with the Society of United Irishmen, founded in 1791 to unite all religions in Ireland, to make it an independent and democratic country, an aim with which Sheridan strongly sympathized.

After Pitt declared war on France, on 12 February 1793, Sheridan's personal position became hazardous when the increasingly reactionary government instituted a series of prosecutions for treason. But he did not cease to be independent, strongly supporting Thomas Walker, president of the Manchester Constitutional Society, when he was tried—and acquitted. After visiting them in prison, he complained strongly about the treatment of the Scottish radicals Thomas Muir and the Revd Thomas Palmer. And he was in contact with the very radical London Corresponding Society.

After the arrests in April 1794 of the Revd William Jackson in Dublin (he had been sent from Paris to test likely support in England for a French invasion) and of William Stone in London (probably also involved in espionage) in May, Sheridan, who had been visited by Stone, was questioned by the secretary of state's office on 8 May and by the privy council the next day. Pitt was obviously hoping to incriminate him, but Sheridan must have regarded Stone as an *agent provocateur* in this period of increasing repression, with the government using informers and spies, and opening letters. Sheridan called it 'a system calculated to engender suspicion and to beget hostility … where it does

not find suspicion it creates it'. Stone was acquitted, but Jackson, found guilty of high treason, committed suicide. Sheridan's self-confidence was not shaken, and in January 1795 he proposed, unsuccessfully, the repeal of the suspension of the Habeas Corpus Act. In the trial of Horne Tooke, he humiliated Pitt by forcing him to admit his earlier evidence was wrong, thus gaining Tooke's acquittal. To associate with and defend the democratic radicals of the London Corresponding Society was brave. Sheridan's courage was acknowledged by the society in a large public meeting of 25 June 1795 which, in a vote of thanks, praised 'Citizen Sheridan', who had made his final brilliant speech against Hastings four months earlier. Hastings, however, was acquitted. The political climate had changed, but Sheridan's fight had not. He was at once encouraging popular radicalism and supporting the prince of Wales, whose massive debts of £630,000 Pitt agreed to pay—a proceeding to which Sheridan agreed, but not, he argued, as something to be met out of public funds, but, rather, by abolishing sinecures and selling royal forests and crown lands.

Tension in Ireland, increased by the sacking in 1795 of Earl Fitzwilliam, the liberal viceroy who had vainly encouraged Grattan to introduce a bill for Catholic emancipation, was added to by General Lake's repressive measures. The United Irishmen began to plan their revolution, seeking French aid, Lord Edward Fitzgerald and Arthur O'Connor acting as emissaries. A large French fleet sailed into Bantry Bay in 1796 with over 14,000 troops aboard, but bad weather meant the postponement of French plans for an invasion. Naval mutinies in England moved Sheridan to propose a committee to look into the sailors' grievances. After the mutiny—apparently defused by some of the sailors' demands being met—had spread he withdrew his proposal, not wanting any French invasion of England. The movement for reform was now in abeyance, Fox and Grey having virtually seceded from parliament after Grey's motion for reform failed to be carried. Sheridan, however, now became more deeply involved in Irish affairs. Arthur O'Connor, back in England in February 1798 *en route* to seek further French aid for an Irish revolution, was arrested with four others at Margate. At their trial in Maidstone, Sheridan, Fox, and Whitbread gave evidence; the trial ended with only one defendant found guilty. Sheridan said he would never permit Ireland to be seized as a post from which England could be attacked, a view he repeated later. In the riot that followed O'Connor's attempt to escape (possibly organized by Sheridan), Sheridan asked the judges why O'Connor, acquitted, was still being held, and was praised by them for his restoration of order in the courtroom. It was an action which made it unlikely he would himself be prosecuted later.

The rising of the United Irishmen virtually coincided with this trial and Sheridan defended the rebels in the House of Commons, arguing that the struggle in Ireland was between people and government and that a fair presumption was that the government was to blame. He called for an end to the repressive methods used to crush the rising, but after it was over his hopes for a non-sectarian independent Ireland were over too. He continued none the less to state his political beliefs openly, and did so most effectively through the symbolism of *Pizarro*, his adaptation of several translations of Frederich von Kotzebue's *Die Spanien in Peru*, staged on 24 May 1799. Kotzebue was regarded as subversive, but Sheridan, while echoing his own speeches in the Hastings trial, managed to make this play patriotic. In effect, it opposed a French invasion yet supported the United Irishmen with a new definition of treason, not warring against one's native land but against 'those who have usurped its power'. The play was immensely successful, running for thirty-one nights. Acting in it were John Philip Kemble and his sister Sarah Siddons, whose acting had so benefited the theatre at a time when all Sheridan's persuasive charm was needed to offset frequent failures to pay the players' salaries. His own high spirits inspired practical joking in which he was joined by his friends Joseph Richardson and Richard Tickell, husband of Eliza's sister Mary.

Sheridan next battled against the Act of Union, speaking against it five times in 1799. He also pressed for peace with France, something achieved in 1802. This year he defeated a bill brought against him in the chancery court by his creditors. Two years later he was appalled by Napoleon's remorseless progress towards creating an empire. Now liberty seemed the concern of the English alone, and Sheridan, by 1803, became a strong supporter of the volunteer corps.

When his son Tom was offered a place in the household of the duke of York in 1803 Sheridan refused this offer which had been prompted by the king, who wanted Sheridan to join Addington's ministry, which had succeeded Pitt's when he failed to carry Catholic emancipation. Both Fox and the prince of Wales urged Sheridan to accept it, but he told them quixotically that he wanted nothing for himself or his family because this would curtail his freedom of speech and action. He feared Fox would join Pitt in a coalition, a fear that led to a decline in his friendship with Fox. His manoeuvring to create a reforming ministry in Ireland under the prince of Wales as lord lieutenant perturbed his whig associates. In 1804, however, the prince appointed him receiver-general of the duchy of Cornwall; and, having shown his independence by opposing the prince's wish for a military command, Sheridan accepted it, regaining his influence as the prince's adviser when the king again became ill.

The money must have been very welcome. The Sheridans, presumably beset by bailiffs, had moved from their George Street house to lodgings in 3 Cork Street in 1803. And Drury Lane, on which Sheridan relied for his personal finance, on which he based his political career, had reached the end of its golden age in 1802 when Kemble, who had raised its receipts by more than a quarter when manager, moved to Covent Garden, taking Mrs Siddons with him. Now only Mrs Jordan, the high-spirited, exuberant mistress of the duke of Clarence, who had joined the company in 1782, remained of the stars, though the

thirteen-year-old William Betty, known as the Young Roscius or the Boy, who first appeared at Drury Lane in 1804, was to prove an asset for a while, despite the high salary he commanded. 'The theatrical bubble' (1805), yet another Gillray cartoon, shows Sheridan dressed as Punch blowing bubbles from which Master Betty emerges. Sheridan was enthusiastic about the boy, betting on his drawing £50 or more in one night, describing him to his wife as 'the most lovely creature' and, so as not 'to destroy him', arranging he should only appear three times a week.

The Gillray caricature preceded the better-known 'Uncorking old-Sherry', a comment on Pitt's sharp reply of 6 March 1805 to Sheridan's long and somewhat rambling speech opposing Pitt's Additional Force Bill. Gillray's depictions of Sheridan are cruel, but his by now mottled complexion, the effect of his drinking to excess ('an abominable habit' according to his first wife in a letter to him of 1790) and his irregular life, made him easy to caricature.

The political and private roller-coaster: final years Sheridan's private life was as turbulent as his political. His obsession with Harriet Bessborough continued to plague him—and her. Replaced as her lover by Granville Leveson Gower, Sheridan continued to attract and repel and he tried to force his attentions on her. His attitudes were contradictory: high ideals, even puritanical (like his father he wanted to improve the moral and social status of the theatre), warred against the laxity of sexual morals he met in aristocratic circles. His second wife had an affair with Lord Grey, and Sheridan was beset by melancholia in 1806. His heavy drinking was beginning to affect his speeches in parliament, but, between January 1806, when Pitt died, and 1807, his political career seemed to be taking off again.

In the 'ministry of all the talents' Sheridan became treasurer of the navy and was made a member of the privy council. When Fox died on 13 September 1806 Sheridan might have expected to succeed him as head of the party but the whig grandees did not trust him; they supported Lord Percy instead for Fox's Westminster seat. Sheridan withdrew; the young man held the seat for the seventeen days the government stayed in office; and then Sheridan won it after a disorderly election. But after the subsequent dissolution of parliament he lost it, largely because of William Cobbett's attacks on him. Cobbett described Sheridan's 'agony of mortification', his 'rage too violent to admit of concealment' (*Weekly Political Register*, 8 Nov 1806, 715), at the result. These emotions were portrayed in Gillray's savage etching 'View of the hustings in Covent Garden', published for the *History of the Westminster and Middlesex Elections in the Month of November 1806* (1807).

This defeat meant, Sheridan said afterwards, his 'total ruin as a public man' (*The Correspondence of George, Prince of Wales, 1770–1812*, ed. A. Aspinall, 8 vols., 1963–71, 6.68). He stood for Wexford as joint candidate with John Colclough, killed in a duel by one of the tory candidates, William Congreve Alcock, subsequently elected with 875 votes to Sheridan's 729 and acquitted at his trial for murder. In 1803 Sheridan had suggested to the prince of Wales that he should become president of a new Irish council of which Sheridan would be a member, a manoeuvre (scotched by Lord Grenville) which would have enabled him to introduce Catholic emancipation. In 1807, having accepted the seat for Ilchester, in the gift of the prince of Wales—not the kind of seat he wanted, but one which meant he could oppose a repressive Irish Insurrection Bill—he continued to put his views about Irish affairs strongly. In advance of his time in sympathizing with Irish farmers and tenants, in realizing the need for reform of land tenure and in wanting to alleviate the condition of the poor, and, as a protestant, consistently seeking Catholic emancipation for all levels of Irish society, he deplored the ignorance of Ireland displayed by government ministers.

The energy required to fight the elections of 1806 and 1807 was followed by a need for stoic resilience, for his son Tom's affair with a Mrs Campbell meant her husband was awarded £1500 as a result of his bringing a case against Tom for criminal conversation, and, somehow, Sheridan had to find the money. There followed the destruction of the new Drury Lane Theatre by fire. Sheridan refused to accede to the suggestion in the house that proceedings should be adjourned. He later watched the blaze from the Piazza Coffee House, reputedly saying, 'A man may surely take a glass of wine by his own fireside' (Moore, 2.368).

This was a devastating blow for Sheridan. He agreed to Samuel Whitbread taking charge of funding the rebuilding and dealing with the theatre's complex debts. Sheridan and his son were excluded from any share in the management of the new theatre which opened in 1811; Sheridan deeply resented the end of the Sheridan family's connection with it. He told the prince of Wales, however, that his debts would be met by the payment of the £40,000 for his half share of the patent (£24,000) and of Tom's quarter share (£12,000) and the fruit shops (£4000). But Whitbread cautiously withheld the money until the claims against Sheridan, some of them patently false, were met, so that the duchy of Cornwall funds became the Sheridans' only income. When an unexpected £1300 turned up in this account, he and Hecca, in a typically feckless way, took a house in Barnes Terrace, where they blew the money in two or three months' lavish living.

Once the prince became regent in 1811—Sheridan having offended Grey and Grenville by redrafting the prince's reply to a deputation from the two houses—he showed himself lukewarm to Catholic emancipation and reluctant to bring in a whig government. Sheridan, still determined to be independent, giving a 'disinterested denial' to Lord Wellesley's offer of a place in a potential administration, decided to abandon his Ilchester seat. Overestimating likely support, he stood for Stafford again but was defeated in October 1812. The prince offered him an apartment in his palace, but his friendship had cooled, though he sent £3000 to Sheridan's solicitor for the purchase of the Wootton Bassett seat. Sheridan failed to go there to arrange matters, and the money disappeared, probably taken by the solicitor to pay Sheridan's debt to him. The prince later told Croker that he had spent over £20,000 on Sheridan. He had financed, to the extent of £8000, Tom's

three failures to be elected an MP, as Sheridan told Hecca in a letter of April 1810, declaring that even in the greatest distress he had refused the offer of even a modest loan for himself from the prince.

As always deeply anxious about Tom's health, Sheridan managed to get him a post at the Cape of Good Hope in 1813. Hecca, too, was ill, in the early stages of cancer. No longer an MP, Sheridan could now be arrested for debt, and spent a week in a sponging house, raging against Whitbread's refusal to give him £12,000 owed him by Drury Lane, some of which was, however, paid on his release. Tempted by the whigs in the summer asking him to stand for Westminster, he withdrew, thinking correctly that Lord Cochrane had been unjustly expelled from his seat—he was returned unopposed. Sheridan's financial position was now dire: Hecca's trust could not be touched; he was selling or pawning treasured possessions—paintings, books, furniture; he was imprisoned again in August 1815. His moods vacillated between despondency and optimism engendered by the hope that an edition of his plays and poems to be published by John Murray would help to pay his debts, which he thought amounted to £3000; he was owed various sums, one as large as £1400.

Though young enough in mind and spirit to attract the youthful Lord Byron's admiration, Sheridan by 1814 was generally regarded as an old man, though he had survived the tough world of politics and juggled with debts longer than many contemporaries. In December 1815 he became ill, largely confined to bed, but he did manage to attend a few dinner parties and was fêted in the green room at Drury Lane. As ever, terrified of being seized by the bailiffs, 'undone and broken-hearted', he wrote to Samuel Rogers that '£150 could remove all difficulties'. Moore brought him the sum in the morning. Sheridan realized that he was dying, but could joke about his rapidly deteriorating health. On 9 May 1816 his sister 'Lissy' (Alicia), who had married Joseph Le Fanu, wrote him a sympathetic and understanding letter to comfort him. She had always been 'fondly attached' to her brother, and now praised his having:

> always shown a noble independence of spirit that the pecuniary difficulties you often had to encounter could not induce you to forgo. As a public man you have been, like the motto of the Le Fanu family, *sine macula* [without stain]; and I am persuaded had you not been too early thrown upon the world, and alienated from your family, you would have been equally good as a private character. (Moore, 2.452–3)

A friend, Dennis O'Brien, wrote to the *Morning Post* calling on Sheridan's former fellow politicians to come to his aid. His friends, however, refused an offer of £200 from the prince regent but as Sheridan said to Chateauneuf, who had translated his plays, 'quel sujet de honte pour notre régent qui m'abandonne! Non, je vais mourir et je lui pardonne' ('Shame on the regent for abandoning me! No, I am dying and I forgive him').

The prince, when king, gave a vivid but third-hand account of Sheridan's last days. Though the house was stripped virtually bare and the bailiffs were installed in it although forbidden by his doctor to seize him, his son

Charles described newspaper accounts as unfounded: his father had every attention and comfort which could make a deathbed easy. Others said he did not want for medical care or friendship (Lady Bessborough visited him) and Hecca, herself ill, was with him when he died at 17 Savile Row on 7 July 1816. His funeral was attended by dukes, earls, lords, viscounts, the lord mayor of London, and other notables. Sheridan would have preferred to be interred near Fox, and recognized as a statesman, but was buried on 13 July in Poets' Corner in Westminster Abbey.

Posthumous reputation Byron's famous praise of Sheridan was a warm tribute from a much younger man; he regarded whatever Sheridan had done as 'always the *best* of its kind'. Certainly Sheridan's two comedies *The Rivals* and *The School for Scandal* have amused audiences from their early, immensely successful performances up to the present day, for Sheridan is one of the great comic writers in English. He could create original characters and infuse stock ones with new vitality. Perhaps the best known of all his creations is Mrs Malaprop, whose unintentional misuse of words coined the term 'malapropism'. Other characters reveal themselves in lively, witty dialogue. Sir Anthony Absolute and Sir Lucius O'Trigger are both foils to the two very different pairs of lovers in *The Rivals*, while Lady Sneerwell and Sir Benjamin Backbite balance the contrasting Surface brothers in *The School for Scandal*. Sheridan's screen scene in this play employs a classic device of comedy to expose most effectively and dramatically the duplicity of Joseph Surface and the silliness of Sir Peter and Lady Teazle.

Sheridan's wit, his sense of fun, and his mockery of sentimental comedy underpin his depiction of the contrast between appearance and reality. His comic invention exposes folly and hypocrisy through dramatic crises in a timeless way, and this has meant the plays remain alive, not only on stage but in radio and television productions as well. The BBC broadcast no fewer than a dozen versions of *The School for Scandal* between 1939 and 1978. A 1942 Home Service production featured Vivien Leigh as Lady Teazle. The play was also filmed as early as 1914 and has since been adapted for television numerous times. Scenes from *The School for Scandal*, featuring Greer Garson and Campbell Gullan, were televised in May 1937. Tony Britton, Joan Plowright, and Felix Aylmer were the main players in a BBC World Theatre broadcast of 1959, while Jeremy Brett, Edward Fox, and Pauline Collins were among the cast of a 1975 version. *The Critic*, starring John Gielgud and Nigel Hawthorne, was televised in 1984. *The Duenna*, *The Rivals*, *St Patrick's Day*, and *A Trip to Scarborough* also formed part of the radio and television repertoire. The unlimited appeal of the plays is demonstrated by their translation into other languages, including a Swedish version of *The School for Scandal*, *Skandalskolan* (1958), and a Russian adaptation of *The Duenna*, *Duenya* (1978).

Sheridan's own character has attracted many biographers since John Watkins and Thomas Moore. Among them are Margaret Oliphant, W. Fraser Rae, Walter Sichel, R. Compton Rhodes, Lewis Gibbs, William A. C. Darlington, Oscar Sherwin, and Madeleine Bingham. Others who

explore and interpret the complexities of Sheridan's artistic, social, sexual, and political life include Linda Kelly and Fintan O'Toole, who cast fresh light on the apparent contradictions which often emerge. O'Toole's sparkling account of the ramifications of Sheridan's political career is particularly searching and subtle.

Studies of Sheridan's contemporaries, such as those dealing with the duchess of Devonshire and Lady Bessborough, have illuminated aspects of his life, while a work by one of his sisters, *Betsy Sheridan's Journal*, suitably edited by William Le Fanu in 1960, gives a lively, frank view of Sheridan's domestic ménage and some divagations from it.

Since Thomas Moore's edition of *The Works of the Late Richard Brinsley Sheridan* (2 vols., 1821) there have been many editions of the plays over the years, and, in particular, Cecil Price's masterly *Dramatic Works of Richard Brinsley Sheridan* (2 vols., 1973). This work of elegant scholarship was preceded by his scrupulously and skilfully edited *Letters of Richard Brinsley Sheridan* (3 vols., 1966). The amount of continuing scholarship and critical activity testifies to the appreciative, investigative interest which has always been taken in Sheridan's life and work.

A. NORMAN JEFFARES

Sources R. B. Sheridan, *The speeches of the Right Honourable Richard Brinsley Sheridan, edited by a constitutional friend*, 3 vols. (1842) · *The letters of Richard Brinsley Sheridan*, ed. C. Price, 3 vols. (1966) · *The dramatic works of Richard Brinsley Sheridan*, ed. C. Price, 2 vols. (1973) · T. Moore, *Memoirs of the life of the Right Honourable Richard Brinsley Sheridan* (1825) · *Sheridaniana, or, Anecdotes of the life of Richard Brinsley Sheridan; his table talk and bons mots* (1826) · B. Sheridan, *Journal 1774, 76 and 1788–90*, ed. W. Le Fanu (1960) · L. Kelly, *Richard Brinsley Sheridan: a life* (1997) · F. O'Toole, *A traitor's kiss: the life of Richard Brinsley Sheridan* (1997) · C. Cruise O'Brien, *The great melody: a thematic biography of Edmund Burke* (1992)
Archives BL, corresp., literary MSS, and papers, Add. MSS 24228, 24246, 25906–26036, 29764, 35118, 39900–39901, 42720–42723, 58274–77, 63641; RP696, 730, 2032, 3437(i); M/442; Egerton MSS 1975–1976 · BL, papers relating to Drury Lane, Add. MSS 25906–26036, 29709–29711 · Bodl. Oxf., letters and papers · Bodl. Oxf., MS of *The school for scandal* [copy] · Dorset RO, family papers · Folger, papers · Harvard U., Houghton L., corresp. and papers relating to Drury Lane · Harvard U., Houghton L., family corresp. and notes for speeches · Hunt. L., papers · King's AC Cam., letters and literary MSS · NL Ire., letters · Princeton University Library, New Jersey, papers · PRO NIre., corresp., papers · TCD, notebooks · Theatre Museum, London, papers relating to Drury Lane · V&A NAL, notes and memoranda · Yale U., Beinecke L., corresp. and papers relating to prince of Wales · Stafford, William Salt Library, corresp. and papers | Bath Central Library, letters to Mrs Mehitabel Stratford Canning · Beds. & Luton ARS, letters and verses to Samuel Whitbread · BL, corresp. with Lord Holland and Lady Holland, Add. MSS 51635, 51641; Add. MS 30348 · BL, corresp. with Samuel Ireland, Add. MS 30348 · BL, corresp. with Georgiana, Lady Spencer, and literary papers · Cumbria AS, Carlisle, letters to J. W. Croker and Lord Lonsdale · Georgetown University, Riggs Memorial Library, letters, mostly to John Gotobed · NL Ire., corresp. with Richard Peake · NL Scot., letters to Blackwoods · Northumbd RO, Newcastle upon Tyne, letters to Thomas Creevey and Mrs Creevey · priv. coll. (NRA), letters to William Adam · PRO, Granville papers, 30/29/6/1; 30/29/6/2 · PRO NIre., papers · Royal Arch., letters to J. McMahon · Royal Arch., letters to J. W. Payne · Royal Arch., letters to prince of Wales · Royal Irish Acad. · Sheff. Arch., corresp. with Edmund Burke · Theatre Museum, London, letters mainly to Richard Wilson

Likenesses line engraving, pubd 1777 (after unknown artist), BM, NPG · T. Cook, line engraving, pubd 1780 (after D. Dodd), NG Ire. · J. Russell, pastel, 1788, NPG [*see illus.*] · J. Reynolds, oils, 1789, priv. coll.; repro. in Kelly, *Richard Brinsley Sheridan*, facing p. 177 · studio of J. Reynolds, oils, *c.*1789, Garr. Club. · F. Serle, stipple, pubd 1789 (after J. Lochée), NPG · attrib. J. Lochée, marble bust, *c.*1790, V&A · J. Heath, stipple, pubd 1793 (after J. C. Lochée), NG Ire. · etching, pubd 1794, NPG · J. Gillray, cartoons, 1794–1803, repro. in *The works of James Gillray* (1847) · J. Gillray, double portrait, etching, pubd 1809 (with the duke of Norfolk), V&A · G. Garrard, plaster cast of bust, 1813, Sir John Soane's Museum, London · T. Kirk, marble bust, 1824, NG Ire. · S. W. Reynolds, mezzotint, pubd 1836 (after J. Reynolds), NPG · J. Gillray, cartoons, Hult. Arch. · J. Gillray, cartoons, repro. in R. Godfrey, *Gillray and the art of caricature* (2001) · K. A. Hickel, group portrait, oils (*The House of Commons, 1793*), NPG; oil study, Royal Collection · J. Hoppner, oils, NPG · J. Hoppner, oils, The Hermitage, Leningrad · J. Sayers, etchings and caricatures, NPG · F. Wheatley, group portrait, watercolour (*Interior of the Shakespeare Gallery, 1790*), V&A · caricatures, BM · print (after Reynolds), BL, Burney Collection

Wealth at death bailiffs virtually stripped house, though ultimately estate perhaps owed little or nothing since many debts owed to subject: biographies

Sheridan, Thomas (1646–1712), government official and Jacobite pamphleteer, was born at St John's, near Trim, co. Meath, the fourth son of Denis *Sheridan, Church of Ireland clergyman, and an Englishwoman named Foster. Denis came of an old Irish family, but had been raised a protestant; of Thomas's brothers, Patrick became bishop of Cloyne and William *Sheridan bishop of Kilmore. Thomas entered Trinity College, Dublin, in January 1661, graduated BA in 1664, and became a fellow in 1667. In June 1670 he entered the Middle Temple, but soon became involved in the Irish revenue administration and then in a variety of potentially lucrative projects. Early in 1678 he published, anonymously, *A Discourse of the Rise and Power of Parliaments*. It 'said little about parliament' (Hiller, 108), but Sheridan argued that England needed to maximize its economic potential to counter the threat from France. He denounced religious persecution as economically damaging; laws were needed against religious dissidents, but they should be lightly and sensitively enforced. He argued that Ireland too needed to modernize economically, which would require both freedom of trade and the replacement of the Gaelic language by English.

In his search for advancement Sheridan had gained the patronage of James, duke of York. This proved embarrassing during the exclusion crisis, and in December 1680 he was imprisoned and interrogated on suspicion of complicity in the Popish Plot. Released early in 1681, he embarked on a plan to farm the Irish revenue. In 1683 or 1684 he married Helen (*c.*1662–1702), daughter of Thomas Appleby of Lynton-on-Ouse, Yorkshire, a Roman Catholic. Described as 'about forty' when she died in 1702, she was already a widow when she married Sheridan; her first husband was called Ravenscroft. A son, Thomas *Sheridan, was born in 1684; two daughters and another son followed. When James II became king, Sheridan announced his conversion to Catholicism, days after the judges' decision in *Godden v. Hales* (June 1686) opened the way for Catholics to hold offices in England. James, however, had work for Sheridan in Ireland. He regarded Henry Hyde, earl of Clarendon, the lord lieutenant, as prejudiced against protestants, but feared that his Catholic rival, Richard Talbot, earl of Tyrconnell, was so anti-protestant as to cause anxiety among his English protestant subjects and harboured thoughts of separating Ireland from England after James's death. When James appointed Tyrconnell lord deputy in January 1687, in Clarendon's place, he appointed Sheridan his secretary and, later, first commissioner of the revenue. Sheridan proved no match for the formidable Tyrconnell; his complaints that Tyrconnell appointed and dismissed officials purely on religious grounds were countered by Tyrconnell with accusations of corruption. A hearing before a group of judges in Ireland upheld Tyrconnell's allegations and Sheridan was removed from his offices on 20 January 1688.

Sheridan followed James into exile in January 1689, determined to clear his name. He published an anti-Williamite pamphlet (widely ascribed to George Savile, marquess of Halifax) entitled *A Letter from a Nobleman in London to his Friend in the Country* (1690) and wrote several tracts which were not published. Whereas he had earlier advocated a measure of toleration and argued that religion should not influence appointments to office, his later tracts show him as both a bigoted Catholic and a forceful proponent of absolute monarchy. He saw James's religion as the sole reason for his expulsion and argued that there could be no compromising the one true faith. Such views were too extreme and intransigent for a king trying to woo his former subjects and the tracts were never published. He no longer claimed that the Gaels were inferior to the English, arguing that the Irish had been uniquely 'faithful' to the Stuarts. He went on a diplomatic mission to the Palatinate in 1695, and in 1699 he was appointed a commissioner of the royal household. His 'Narrative', written in 1702, 'sheds valuable light on James II's Irish policy' (Hiller, 128). Sheridan died on 7/17 March 1712 at St Germain-en-Laye and was buried there.

JOHN MILLER

Sources J. Hiller, 'Thomas Sheridan (1646–1712) and his "Narrative"', *Irish Historical Studies*, 20 (1976–7), 105–28 · V. Geoghegan, 'Thomas Sheridan: toleration and royalism', *Political discourse in early modern Ireland*, ed. D. G. Boyce, R. R. Eccleshall, and V. Geoghegan (1999) · *Calendar of the Stuart papers belonging to his majesty the king, preserved at Windsor Castle*, 7 vols., HMC, 56 (1902–23), vols. 1, 6 · *The correspondence of Henry Hyde, earl of Clarendon, and of his brother Laurence Hyde, earl of Rochester*, ed. S. W. Singer, 2 vols. (1828) · [T. Sheridan], *Discourse on the rise and power of parliaments* (1678); repr. in *Some revelations in Irish history, or, Old elements of creed and class conciliation in Ireland*, ed. S. Bannister (1870) · *The manuscripts of the marquis of Ormonde*, [old ser.], 3 vols., HMC, 36 (1895–1909), vol. 1 · *Calendar of the manuscripts of the marquess of Ormonde*, new ser., 8 vols., HMC, 36 (1902–20), vols. 6–8 · CSP dom. · *A true and impartial account of all the secret consults of the Romish party in Ireland* (1889) · *A true relation of the life and death of … William Bedell*, ed. T. W. Jones, CS, new ser., 4 (1872) · G. Agar-Ellis, ed., *The Ellis correspondence: letters written during the years 1686, 1687, 1688, and addressed to John Ellis*, 2 vols. (1829) · C. E. Lart, ed., *Parochial registers of Saint Germain-en-Laye*, 2 vols. (1910–12) · J. E. Bruns, 'Some details of the Sheridans (1647–1746)', *Irish Sword*, 2 (1954–6), 65–6 · DNB · *Mr Sheridan's speech* (1681)

Archives Royal Arch., MSS

Sheridan, Thomas [Jacobite Sir Thomas Sheridan, baronet] (1684–1746), Jacobite official, was the eldest of the four children of Thomas *Sheridan (1646–1712), government official and Jacobite pamphleteer, and his wife, Helen (*c*.1662–1702), daughter of Thomas Appleby of Lynton-on-Ouse, Yorkshire, and his wife, Helen. (Family legend maintains that Helen Sheridan was actually the illegitimate daughter of the future James II and Anne Hyde, before their marriage.) Some contemporary documents refer to Sheridan as Irish, but evidence to ascertain if there was more to this than paternal descent is lacking. His mother was a Roman Catholic, and his father converted to Catholicism in 1686. The family followed James II into exile in France following the events of 1688, and Sheridan was educated at the Jesuit Collège Louis-le-Grand in Paris. He may also have spent some time in Rome as a youth.

About 1706 Sheridan went to London to study law, and on 18 January of that year was admitted to the Middle Temple. Following the death of Queen Anne in 1714 he returned to France and became a courier in the Jacobite rising of 1715. In 1717 and 1718 he carried messages back and forth in the Jacobite attempt to instigate a Russo-Swedish alliance against the Hanoverians, travelling widely in northern and eastern Europe. Late 1720 saw him at the Jacobite court in Rome, where he was employed in both secretarial and diplomatic capacities. In 1725 he became under-governor to Prince Charles Edward Stuart, and his indulgent and devoted care of the boy, while not an educational success, none the less created a uniquely strong bond of trust between them. The following year (17 March 1726) Sheridan was awarded an Irish baronetcy by James III (James Francis Edward Stuart). In 1734 he accompanied the prince to his first military engagement—the siege of Gaeta in the kingdom of Naples. He played a key role in the elaborate subterfuge designed to conceal Charles's journey to Paris in 1744, when it was believed that the French were about to restore the Stuarts. Once established in the French capital Charles soon sent for Sir Thomas, who, after a brief period of princely disfavour, became actively involved in the young prince's plans to mount a rising in Scotland. He was one of the 'seven men of Moidart' who landed on the Scottish coast with the prince in July 1745 and was present throughout the subsequent campaign. In poor health and in his early sixties (not seventies as some modern accounts maintain), and lacking a military background, his role was secretarial and advisory. A member of the prince's council, he was criticized by a number of the Scottish members for being a key figure in a perceived Irish coterie around the prince. After defeat at the battle of Culloden in 1746 Sheridan managed to escape to France, whence he was summoned to Rome by James III to explain his part in the recent events. It was in Rome that Sheridan died, unmarried, of a stroke on 23 November 1746; he was buried there the following day in the church of the Twelve Apostles.

VINCENT GEOGHEGAN

Sources J. E. Bruns, 'Some details of the Sheridans (1647–1746)', *Irish Sword*, 2 (1954–6), 65–6 · J. E. Bruns, 'The early years and diplomatic missions of Sir Thomas Sheridan (1684–1746)', *Irish Sword*, 3 (1957–8), 256–9 · *Calendar of the Stuart papers belonging to his majesty the king, preserved at Windsor Castle*, 7 vols., HMC, 56 (1902–23) · M. H. Massue de Ruvigny, ed., *The Jacobite peerage* (1904), 165–6 · C. E. Lart, ed., *The parochial registers of Saint Germain-en-Laye: Jacobite extracts of births, marriages, and deaths*, 2 vols. (1910–12), vol. 1, pp. 116, 124; vol. 2, p. 125 · A. Tayler and H. Tayler, eds., *The Stuart papers at Windsor* (1939) · F. J. McLynn, *Charles Edward Stuart: a tragedy in many acts* (1988) · H. A. C. Sturgess, ed., *Register of admissions to the Honourable Society of the Middle Temple, from the fifteenth century to the year 1944*, 1 (1949), 258 · J. E. Bruns, 'Sheridan letters, 1743', *Irish Sword*, 2 (1954–6), 375 · H. Tayler, ed., *A Jacobite miscellany: eight original papers on the rising of 1745–1746* (1948), 12

Archives Royal Arch., Stuart MSS

Sheridan, Thomas (1687–1738), schoolmaster and Church of Ireland clergyman, was born in co. Cavan, Ireland, the son of Patrick Sheridan, a farmer of whom nothing more is certainly known. He attended the school of John Jones, the Dublin schoolmaster who was Jonathan Swift's contemporary at Trinity College, Dublin, and in 1707, at the relatively late age of twenty, entered Trinity himself. He graduated BA in 1711, was ordained priest in 1712, and took his MA in 1714. In 1710 or 1711, still 'in the mad years of life' (Dolan, 5), he married Elizabeth, only child of Charles and Anne McFadden of Quilca, near Virginia, in co. Cavan.

Sheridan apparently began his teaching career before 1714, in Irish classical schools, which emphasized the Latin classics and trained their boys to be young gentlemen. Like other enlightened schoolmasters of the period he decried teaching Latin through 'a Heap of Rules' and by 'frightening … [boys] out of their Wits' (T. Sheridan, *An Easy Introduction of Grammar in English for the Understanding of the Latin Tongue*, 1714, preface), and in 1714 published his own improved version of Lily's *Royal Grammar*, using English verse as a mnemonic aid. It is not certain how he met Swift but their acquaintance probably began in 1717, when Sheridan was a well-established and notably successful Dublin schoolmaster. His remarkable talents as a classical scholar and modern linguist impressed and attracted Swift, as, even more so, did his taste for satire and wordplay in both verse and prose. He was soon tutoring Swift in Greek, while Swift for his part took an active interest in Sheridan's school, finding peculiar delight in his role as examiner. Sheridan's preference in school for the verbal—rather than the actual—lash found favour with Swift, who described his friend as 'doubtless the best instructor of youth in these kingdoms' (Swift, 216).

Though a priest, Sheridan had no benefice until 1725, when he was thirty-eight, and ran his school as a private enterprise. Probably with an eye to preferment and additional income, he took the degrees of BD in 1724 and DD in 1726. In the meantime, in 1725, Swift interceded with the lord lieutenant of Ireland, Lord Carteret, to obtain for Sheridan the living of Rincurran, in co. Cork, and an appointment as one of Carteret's domestic chaplains. Seldom far from the ludicrous, Sheridan—it seems through sheer carelessness—promptly chose the anniversary of the Hanoverian succession to preach a sermon on the text 'Sufficient unto the day is the evil thereof'. If no malice was intended, such a sentiment coming from a high-church tory was bound to cause comment, and when Carteret was informed of what had happened he stripped Sheridan of the chaplaincy and barred him from Dublin Castle. Subsequent attempts to secure patronage and gain preferment failed, and in 1730 Sheridan exchanged the living of Rincurran for that of Dunboyne and Kilbride, in co. Meath, near Dublin and on the way to his estate in Quilca. In 1735, with the income from his school in Dublin declining, he closed the school and exchanged the Dunboyne living for the Royal School in Cavan, a move that helped to stabilize his always rickety finances.

To a mind teeming with learning and humour were added a feckless and vague character and a build more suited to a mouse than a man, with accompanying shrill and squeaky voice. The nicknames Tom Titt and Tom Dingle suited Sheridan well, as did his *nom de guerre*, Tom Punsibi, under which name his *Art of Punning* appeared in 1719 and which more generally expressed the 'pun-ishment' he took and inflicted on Swift and others in his mock-serious 'pun-ic wars'. On the subject of his unhappy marriage, which produced nine children, including the actor-manager Thomas *Sheridan (1719?–1788), his humour turned to acid, and in 1735 he told Swift that he had been 'linked to the Devil for twenty-four years, with a coal in my heart, which was kindled in the first week I married her' (Dolan, 5). The sad union reinforced his own view of his greatest failing: 'I am famous for giving the best advice and following the worst' (ibid., 22). Consolation came from his intimacy with Swift, and though the relationship was at times strained, since neither was afraid to dwell on the other's faults, its closeness may be seen from their long stays with one another, the financial help given by Swift to Sheridan, and the care that Sheridan bestowed on Esther Johnson (Stella) in her last illness.

Sheridan's literary work was, like Swift's, in large part an extension of his character. Doggerel and other nonsense, including farces performed on the Dublin stage, poured from his pen. On his more serious side, he translated Sophocles, Persius, Guarini, and Tasso. In 1728 and 1729 the Dublin periodical *The Intelligencer* appeared, each number comprising a separate contribution from Swift or Sheridan, with Irish economic, social, and political issues as the general theme.

By 1737 Sheridan was in failing health, and he left the school in Cavan to return to Dublin. According to his son Thomas he was at the end insulted and shunned by the increasingly gloomy dean. He retired to a friend's house in Rathfarnham and died there on 10 October 1738, of 'a dropsy and asthma', according to Swift, or of 'a polypus in the heart', according to his son. In his will he left only 5s. to his 'unkind wife'.   W. R. MEYER

Sources J. Woolley, 'Thomas Sheridan and Swift', *Studies in Eighteenth-Century Culture*, 9 (1980), 93–114 · B. Dolan, 'Tom the Punman', *Journal of Irish Literature*, 16/1 (1987), 3–32 · I. Ehrenpreis, *Swift: the man, his works and the age*, 3 vols. (1962–83), esp. vol. 3, pp. 62–8, 358–68 · J. Swift and T. Sheridan, *The Intelligencer*, ed. J. Woolley (1992) · S. Lane-Poole, 'Dr Sheridan', *Fraser's Magazine*, 25 (Feb 1882), 156–72 · J. Swift, 'Character of Doctor Sheridan', in *The prose writings of Jonathan Swift*, ed. H. Davis (1964–9), vol. 5, pp. 216–17 · *DNB*

Archives Bodl. Oxf., corresp. with Thomas Carte · NL Ire., corresp. with Jonathan Swift

Likenesses T. Cook, line engraving, BM, NPG; repro. in T. Sheridan, *The life of the Rev. Dr Jonathan Swift* (1784)

Sheridan, Thomas (1719?–1788), actor and orthoepist, was probably born in early 1719, though no records of birth or baptism have been found. His father, Dr Thomas *Sheridan (1687–1738), was by then running a highly regarded school at his house in Capel Street, Dublin, but there is a possibility that Thomas, his third son, was born in Quilca, co. Cavan, perhaps in the childhood home of his mother, Elizabeth MacFadden. Jonathan Swift, a close friend of Dr Sheridan, was Thomas's godfather and, by Sheridan's own account, a beneficent influence on him from childhood. Towards the end of his life he published a seventeen-volume edition of Swift's *Works* (1784), of which volume 1 was his own *Life of Doctor Swift*. His early education was at his father's school, where the performance of plays was encouraged. The chance to play Antony in *Julius Caesar* in 1732 may have had a profound effect on Sheridan. Ambitious for his favourite son, Dr Sheridan enrolled him at Westminster School in 1733, but was financially unable to sustain him there, and it was with the aid of a scholarship that Sheridan entered Trinity College, Dublin, in 1735. Dr Sheridan died suddenly on 10 October 1738, a year before his son graduated, leaving his large family in straitened circumstances. The need to make money combined with his love of the theatre to draw Sheridan to the Dublin stage, and he made his first appearance at Smock Alley on 29 January 1743 as Richard III, in which part, in the view of the *Dublin Gazette* (25 January–1 February 1743) he 'vastly excelled whatever had at any Time been seen [in] the Kingdom before'.

This was the beginning of the turbulent history of Sheridan's attempts to raise the standard of the Dublin theatre. It is a mixed history of honest endeavour, social and intellectual snobbery, wise economy, extravagance, and paranoia. Sheridan's ambition is clear from the parts he played in his first season. They included Brutus, Othello, and King Lear. His fiery self-regard is clear, too, in his preparedness to cross swords with a visiting celebrity, Theophilus Cibber. Their quarrel in July 1743 threatened to disrupt the season, and for once Cibber was more in the right than his adversary. Coincidentally the dispute brought about the meeting between Sheridan and his future wife, the novelist Frances Chamberlaine (1724–1766) [see Sheridan, Frances], to whom he was married by 1747. Nurturing managerial ambitions, Sheridan travelled to London at the end of the 1743–4 season. He made his début in *Hamlet* at Covent Garden on 31 March 1744 and joined the Drury Lane company for the 1744–5 season, during which he established an edgy friendship with David Garrick.

Two decisions made in Dublin in 1744–5 were to have a long-term effect on Sheridan's life. The first led to the uniting into a single company of Dublin's two theatres, Aungier Street and Smock Alley, the second to Sheridan's appointment as manager of the united company. His first

Thomas Sheridan (1719?–1788), by John Lewis, 1753

period of management (1745–54) began triumphantly, aided by his recruiting of Garrick and George Anne Bellamy. By July 1746 he was prosperous enough to buy Quilca House, Cavan, from his mother, presumably with an eye to his forthcoming marriage, which probably took place in 1747. Sheridan's second season as manager was marred by an incident that gave rise to the notorious Kelly riot. Kelly, a Galway 'gentleman', had made a drunken assault on one of the Smock Alley actresses at a performance of Vanbrugh's *Aesop* on 19 January 1747, and Sheridan had twice forcibly expelled him from the theatre. Kelly's supporters considered this a player's affront to a gentleman, and expressed their outrage two nights later by breaking up a performance, storming the stage, and physically damaging the backstage area. Kelly's trial was perceived in part, not least by Sheridan, as a test of the manager's right to the status of 'gentleman'. There were sections of the Dublin public that never forgave him. Often high-handed, he lacked the diplomatic skills of a manager. Charles Macklin in 1748 and West Digges in 1754 publicly resented his treatment of them, and he offended Dublin society in March 1750 by refusing to release his musicians for a charity concert at the New Garden. But it was politics that precipitated the crisis of 2 March 1754. As one of the founders of the Beefsteak Club in 1752, Sheridan was readily associated with the 'English' party in Dublin, and it was perhaps unfortunate that George II's proroguing of the Irish parliament coincided with a revival of James Miller's *Mahomet* at Smock Alley on 2 February 1754. A speech susceptible to patriotic Irish sentiment was vigorously encored. In what was to prove a critical moment

in his life, Sheridan resolved on a second performance, and the result, on 2 March 1754, was the riot that wrecked the interior of the theatre and brought Sheridan to financial ruin from which he never fully recovered. In a sad footnote to the riot and ensuing debate, the Sheridans' infant son, christened Sackville in honour of the duke of Dorset (vice-regent of Ireland at the time), died of convulsions.

Sheridan sublet the theatre and took refuge in London, where he performed to lukewarm audiences at Covent Garden during the 1754–5 season most of his favourite leading roles. He was not re-engaged. Instead, he spent the winter of 1755 preparing for publication a book entitled *British Education* (1756) and for delivery a series of twelve lectures on spoken English. Financial constraints drove him to return to the management of Smock Alley in May 1756, though with diminished enthusiasm. This second term was scarred by grudges and disputes, above all with John Lee and Spranger Barry. It was Barry's opening of a new theatre in Crow Street, Dublin, in October 1758 that drove Sheridan back to London. He had recently mortgaged Quilca House for the second time, and his Irish debts amounted to over £7000. The Sheridans now had four children to care for. Thomas, their eldest son, had died aged three, but had been followed by Charles Francis *Sheridan (1750–1806), Richard Brinsley *Sheridan (1751–1816), Alicia, later Alicia *Le Fanu (1753–1817) [see under Le Fanu, Philip], the aforementioned Sackville, and (Anne) Elizabeth Craford (*bap.* 1756). Sheridan was hoping for a new career in education, bolstered by Oxford University's incorporation of him as a master of arts in November 1758 (Cambridge would follow suit in 1769). Between 1759 and 1762 he published discourses on the theatre, on education, and on the English language, and began work on a dictionary towards which he was awarded an annual pension of £200 and which was published in two volumes in 1780. Always liable to live beyond his means, he moved his family with three servants to Windsor in September 1759, planning to live by teaching, lecturing, and publishing, but need impelled him to return to Drury Lane for the 1760–61 season.

A little grudgingly, Churchill's *Rosciad* (1761) placed Sheridan second to Garrick on the scale of genius, but this is to overrate his acting. Physically slight and vocally uneven, Sheridan was ill-suited to the heroic parts he favoured, though he was conscientious in delivering the meaning of his lines and disciplined in his preparation. He continued to act, in short bursts dictated by financial need, until 1777, mostly in London and Dublin, but also in Edinburgh, where he was awarded the freedom of the city on 6 July 1761. Plagued from youth by indigestion and in adulthood by creditors, he took his family to France in 1764, with the declared intention of curing the first and the undeclared intention of escaping the second, but the period of voluntary exile was brought to an end by his wife's death on 26 September 1766.

Sheridan had never had a settled home, and he had few enduring friendships. A brief period of residence in Bath in 1770–71 enabled him, in conjunction with the musical

Linley family, to launch a series of *Attic Evening's Entertainments*, with songs by Thomas Linley sung by his daughter Elizabeth, and recitations by Sheridan. The involvement of his brilliant son Richard Brinsley Sheridan with Elizabeth Linley, and their later marriage, caused a serious breach between father and son, in which Sheridan's tendency to a sense of moral and social superiority was characteristically alert. He was hurt by Richard's failure to invite his assistance in the management of Drury Lane in 1776, and when, in September 1778, 'he agreed to put the management into my hands upon condition that I should not appear as a performer' (letter to Charles Sheridan, dated 15 April 1783), the relationship remained tense. Sheridan worked with his son and Thomas Linley at Drury Lane until the end of the season in 1780, all the time waiting for the call to return to Dublin and save the Irish theatre. He was now being cared for by his younger daughter, Elizabeth, with whom he left Dublin *en route* for Portugal, in search of the Lisbon cure, in 1788. They got no further than Margate, where, on 14 August 1788, Sheridan died, with Elizabeth and a penitent Richard in attendance. He was buried, according to his own wish, where he died and 'in as private and cheap a manner as possible'—in fact, in the centre aisle of St Peter's Church on the Isle of Thanet, on 21 August. In 1823 Samuel Parr arranged for a memorial tablet in praise of Sheridan's intellect. Sheridan left the residue of his estate to his two daughters. All four of his surviving children became eminent in their way, among them the politician Charles Francis *Sheridan.

PETER THOMSON

Sources E. K. Sheldon, *Thomas Sheridan of Smock-Alley: recording his life as actor and theater manager in both Dublin and London* (1967) · Highfill, Burnim & Langhans, *BDA* · A. H. Scouten, ed., *The London stage, 1660–1800*, pt 3: *1729–1747* (1961) · G. W. Stone, ed., *The London stage, 1660–1800*, pt 4: *1747–1776* (1962) · J. C. Greene and G. L. H. Clark, *The Dublin stage, 1720–1745: a calendar of plays, entertainments, and afterpieces* (1993) · W. R. Chetwood, *A general history of the stage, from its origin in Greece to the present time* (1749) · R. Hitchcock, *An historical view of the Irish stage from the earliest period down to the close of the season 1788*, 2 vols. (1788–94) · B. Victor, *The history of the theatres of London and Dublin*, 3 vols. (1761–71)
Archives King's AC Cam., corresp., literary MSS, and papers | priv. coll., corresp. with William Creech · Yale U., Beinecke L., corresp. with James Boswell
Likenesses J. Lewis, oils, 1753, NG Ire. [*see illus.*] · J. Lewis, pastel drawing, repro. in W. Sichel, *Sheridan* (1909) · H. Tresham, watercolour, priv. coll. · engraving (after G. Stuart), repro. in Sheldon, *Thomas Sheridan* · Indian ink drawing, BM · oils (after G. Stuart), Garr. Club · oils, priv. coll. · prints, BM
Wealth at death more debts than value

Sheridan, Thomas [Tom] (**1775–1817**), actor and soldier, was born at Orchard Street, London, on 17 November 1775, the only son of Richard Brinsley *Sheridan (1751–1816) and his first wife, Elizabeth Ann (Eliza) *Linley (1754–1792). His father described him at two months old in typically glowing terms to his maternal grandfather Thomas Linley as having 'talents for music and the most perfect integrity of mind' (*Letters*, 1.101). He sent the boy to Dr Samuel Parr (who had taught him and been kind to him when he was a pupil at Harrow) at the school Parr set up at

Hatton in Warwickshire in 1786. Parr, at Richard Sheridan's request, broke the news to Tom that he was to go to Hotwells, Bristol, where his mother was dying.

After her death, while Tom was a great comfort to his father, he was also running wild at Sheridan's mansion in Isleworth, so Sheridan arranged that William Smyth, a recent graduate from Peterhouse and later professor of modern history at Cambridge, should tutor him. Smyth's *Memoir of Mr Sheridan* (1840) described Richard Sheridan as over-fussy about his son, citing his neurotic anxiety when the tutor allowed Tom to skate on ice he thought strong enough to support a wagon. Charles Grey told Sheridan he should have a glass case made for Tom.

Smyth records Tom's reaction to his father's telling him he was going to marry Hecca, as he called Hester Jane Ogle, a frisky girl of nineteen, making out in two hours' talking that it was the most sensible thing he could do: 'Was this not very clever of him? Well, my dear Mr S., you should have been tutor to him. I am incomparably the most rational of the two.' Smyth describes Tom at Cambridge as the idol of the young men who pronounced him the cleverest man in the place. Cambridge was 'a great expense' and the ruin of all Smyth's schemes for Tom's education.

The question of what Tom was to make of his life was bound up with his father's theatrical and political fortunes. The easy-going Tom was charming and intelligent, but lacked his father's driving ambition and hoped his father, with whom he got on well, would buy him a seat in parliament. Richard Sheridan did better: he got the prince of Wales to finance Tom's three electoral failures, at Liskeard and Stafford. The duke of York offered Tom a post as aide-de-camp, at the king's 'express commands', but his father told him to refuse this. Richard Sheridan was himself being courted by the king and his friend Henry Addington, prime minister since 1801, who wanted him in his administration. Fox and the prince both pressed Richard Sheridan to accept office if only to provide for Tom. On his father's advice Tom rejected the surveyorship of the duchy of Cornwall and the registrarship of the vice-admiralty court in Malta before accepting a cornetcy in the prince of Wales's own regiment, the 10th light dragoons, and becoming aide-de-camp to Lord Moira when he became commander-in-chief, Scotland, in 1803.

In Edinburgh, Tom's affair with Mrs Peter Campbell led to his being sued for and pleading guilty to criminal conversation. The case brought him into some ridicule, Mary Brotherton, the housekeeper, testifying that Tom in his uniform had been at the house when Mr Campbell was in London, leaving only at the housekeeper's threat to shoot him if he didn't leave at once. Campbell was awarded £1500, which Sheridan paid, borrowing the large sum from the Drury Lane actors.

Tom then ran away with Caroline Henrietta Callander (1779–1851) [*see* Sheridan, Caroline Henrietta], marrying her on 21 June 1805. Richard Sheridan pronounced his daughter-in-law lovely and engaging. Tom and she had four sons and three daughters. The eldest son, Richard Brinsley Sheridan, followed family tradition and ran away with Marcia Maria, daughter of Lieutenant-General Sir Colquhoun Grant, a considerable heiress; he sat in parliament from 1845 to 1868 (his son Algernon Thomas Brinsley Sheridan merely resided comfortably in his paternal grandfather's place, Frampton Court in Dorset). The three daughters also married well: the eldest became Lady Dufferin and later countess of Gifford; the second Caroline Norton and later Lady Stirling Maxwell; and the third Lady Seymour and later duchess of Somerset.

Richard Sheridan, appointed receiver-general of the duchy of Cornwall by the prince in 1804, tried in vain to get the prince to transfer the position to the newly married Tom. He had provided handsomely for his other son, Charles, but Tom's financial future still remained a problem. Finally Tom became muster-master general in Ireland in 1806, in which year Richard Sheridan gave him a quarter-share in the Drury Lane Theatre. Tom came back from Ireland to canvass Stafford unsuccessfully in 1806 and 1807. Tom, now sole manager of Drury Lane, negotiated skilfully with the lord chancellor to warn off potential rivals, the non-patent holders; at the same time he became joint proprietor and sole manager of the Lyceum Theatre. A good singer and comic actor, he had inherited the Linley family's musical talents and the Sheridans' literary skills. His poem on the loss of the *Saldanha* was praised; he wrote *Descriptions of Characters* (1808), 'a grand ballet of action' staged in Drury Lane, and his melodrama *The Russian* first staged on 13 May 1813 ran for ten further performances.

That production, however, came after the disastrous fire of February 1808 destroyed Drury Lane. The prince provided £1000 and the dukes of Bedford and Devon £500 each to help Tom through the financial crisis. His health was growing worse: he had inherited the tuberculosis that killed his mother. A stay at Puerto de Santa Maria improved his breathing—a debt of £1400 was cancelled by his father's efforts on his return—but the next year Sicily's climate did not ameliorate his condition.

Both Tom and his father had refused to receive any of the funds they were due until the new Drury Lane Theatre was built (both were excluded from any say in it), but in November 1811 Richard Sheridan told Tom that he would get '£12,000 clear', adding that this was 'the last sum of money in the shape of profit any man will ever get out of a THEATRE' (*Letters*, 3.134). In a letter to his uncle Charles Ward, Tom had earlier blamed his father for what was probably his own lack of independence and ambition, by saying that Richard Sheridan constantly pointed at the theatre as Tom's ultimate object; it was to be his, and so, he said, he had been excluded from all other pursuits.

By February 1812 Tom described himself as 'ill in health and spirits and as thin as a Highland crop of oats' (*Letters*, 3.177n.). He tried Madeira again, and then the duke of York obtained for him the post of colonial treasurer at the Cape of Good Hope, supposedly beneficial for lung complaints. (There was no atom of obligation to the prince or his ministers, his father told him cheerfully.) Taking their daughter Helen with them, Tom and his wife left their other children in the care of relatives and sailed for the Cape in 1813. There Tom died of consumption on 12 September 1817.　　　　　　　　　　　　A. NORMAN JEFFARES

Sources *The letters of Richard Brinsley Sheridan*, ed. C. Price, 3 vols. (1966) · T. Moore, *Memoirs of the life of the Right Honourable Richard Brinsley Sheridan* (1825) · L. Kelly, *Richard Brinsley Sheridan: a life* (1997) · F. O'Toole, *A traitor's kiss: the life of Richard Brinsley Sheridan* (1997) · W. Smyth, *Memoirs of Mr Sheridan* (1840) · *Hieroglyphical advertisement* (1807) · *The trial of Thomas Sheridan, esq. for criminal conversation with the lady of Peter Campbell, esquire, in the sheriff's court on July 7th, 1807: damages of fifteen-hundred pounds!!!* (1859) · BL, Egerton MS 2137, fol. 162
Archives BL, corresp. and papers relating to Drury Lane Theatre · Dorset RO, corresp. relating to rebuilding Drury Lane Theatre | PRO NIre., corresp. with Callander family
Likenesses T. Gainsborough, oils

Sheridan, William (1635–1711), nonjuring Church of Ireland bishop of Kilmore and Ardagh, was born in Togher, near Kilmore, co. Cavan, the eldest surviving son of Denis *Sheridan (c.1610–1683?), vicar of Killesher, co. Fermanagh, and his first wife, Jane (c.1610–c.1643), daughter of Anthony Atkinson of Geashill, King's county. A member of a Gaelic Irish family long associated with the district of Kilmore, his father had been brought up a protestant in the house of John Hill, dean of Kilmore. William was named after his godfather, Bishop William Bedell, who had ordained his father and left the youth 40s. in his will to buy a mourning ring. He had a brother, Patrick (1638–1682), and two half-brothers, Thomas *Sheridan (1646–1712) and James (b. 1649). William was privately educated, partly by his father, before he and his brother Patrick entered Trinity College, Dublin, as fellow-commoners in May 1652. Although his first degree is not recorded, he graduated DD in 1682. At an unknown date he married Mary O'Reilly, presumably also from co. Cavan, with whom he had a son, Donald.

After his ordination Sheridan was chaplain to Sir Maurice Eustace, the first lord chancellor of Ireland after the Restoration, and was subsequently chaplain to the duke of Ormond. Rector of Athenry, co. Galway, in 1667, he became dean of Down two years later (25 August 1669), though he was in England that autumn and had permission to remain there until his health recovered. In fact poor health was to be a recurring theme of his correspondence later in his life. During Ormond's last viceroyalty, and thanks to his influence, Sheridan was formally appointed bishop of Kilmore in January 1682 (though at first intended for Raphoe), holding it with the diocese of Ardagh. His brother Patrick had been appointed bishop of Cloyne in 1679.

Sheridan seems to have left Ireland in the latter part of James II's reign. Unlike four other Church of Ireland bishops, he did not sit in James II's Irish parliament of May–June 1689, though unlike them he was deprived under William III for not taking the necessary oaths prescribed by the 1691 act. As the only nonjuring bishop in the Church of Ireland, he moved to London, where he lived close to other nonjurors. Impoverished, in poor health, and continuing to sign himself 'Wm Kilmore' (sometimes adding 'dispossest.'), he was clearly on the conscience of some at least of the conforming clergy. William King of Derry did what he could to help, and was warmly thanked by Sheridan, as was the tory earl of Huntingdon, for whose 'so often repeated charity … I want words to express my gratitude' (*Hastings MSS*, 2.300).

At the beginning of Queen Anne's reign an attempt associated with the lay nonjuror Henry Dodwell to heal the schism in the Church of Ireland, which by this stage effectively centred on Sheridan, petered out. However, for a time thereafter he was apparently paid an allowance out of Kilmore diocesan coffers, a voluntary support which had come to an end before mid-1707, Archbishop King being told in 1708 that Sheridan's successor but one in Kilmore, Edward Wetenhall, 'has not sent him one penny since last midsummer was a year, and then but tenn guineas' (*Second Report*, HMC, 244). It was ironic that it should be Wetenhall who failed to keep up payments on Sheridan's allowance, as he had sat in James II's parliament as bishop of Cork and had required convincing in 1691 that William and Mary were lawful sovereigns. Having endured years of poor health, during which he was cared for by a niece who herself became ill in the process, Sheridan died in London on 3 October 1711 and was buried later that month at Fulham.

RICHARD BAGWELL, rev. JAMES McGUIRE

Sources *Second report*, HMC, 1/2 (1871); repr. (1874), 241–5 · *CSP dom.*, 1680–81; 1691–2 · *CSP Ire.*, 1669–70 · *Report on the manuscripts of the late Reginald Rawdon Hastings*, 4 vols., HMC, 78 (1928–47), vol. 2, p. 300 · *Report on the manuscripts of F. W. Leyborne-Popham*, HMC, 51 (1899), 246 · J. B. Leslie, *Biographical succession lists of the clergy of Down* (1936) · C. S. King, ed., *A great archbishop of Dublin, 1650–1729; his autobiography, family, and a selection from his correspondence* (1906) · 'The history of the bishops', *The whole works of Sir James Ware concerning Ireland*, ed. and trans. W. Harris, rev. edn, 1 (1739) · H. Cotton, *Fasti ecclesiae Hibernicae*, 6 vols. (1845–78) · J. McGuire, 'The Church of Ireland and the "Glorious Revolution" of 1688', *Studies in Irish history presented to R. Dudley Edwards*, ed. A. Cosgrove and D. McCartney (1979), 137–49 · A. Davies, *Dictionary of British portraiture*, 1 (1979) **Archives** TCD, letters, Lyons (King) MSS | BL, letters to H. Sloane, Sloane MS 4041/4046 **Likenesses** W. Sherwin, line engraving, NPG; repro. in *Sermons* (1704) **Wealth at death** very poor: correspondence, *Second report*, HMC

Sheriff, Lawrence (c.1515–1567), benefactor of Rugby School, was probably born in Rugby or nearby, the son of a wealthy yeoman family. After serving his apprenticeship he became a full member of the Grocers' Company about 1541, living in Newgate Street, London. He built up a prosperous trade in spices, supplying Princess Elizabeth's house at Hatfield during the 1550s. His loyalty is demonstrated by an incident which took place in the Rose tavern, Newgate, in 1554. Farrer, a haberdasher, accused the princess of being involved in Wyatt's rebellion: 'Some of them hope that she shall have the crown, but she, and they, I trust, shall hop headless or be fried with faggots, before she come to it' (Foxe, 3.951). Sheriff protested strongly and took the case before Bishop Bonner who, in the political and religious climate of the time, tried to appease both parties.

Sheriff's loyalty ultimately paid off and in 1559 he was granted a coat of arms bearing the griffin, a mythical beast which supposedly guards the treasures of the East. In 1561, he presented the queen with 'a sugar loaf, a box of ginger, a box of nutmeg and a pound of cinnamon' as a new year's gift, and in return he received 'one gilt salt with a cover (weighing) seven ounces'. In 1566 he was elected vice-warden of the Grocers' Company. On 22 July 1567 he made his will in which he describes himself as 'sick of body'. His request was to be buried in St Andrew's Church, Rugby, though in fact it appears that he was buried in Christ Church Greyfriars, the old Greyfriars Church, which was destroyed in the great fire of London in 1666. A surviving parish register records that he was buried on 16 September 1567. In his will, among other bequests, he gave to his wife, Elizabeth (d. 1579), his 'grey ambling nagge', his 'chayne of gold weighing twenty ounces' and his 'gold ring with a picture of death upon it' (PRO, PROB 11/49).

Sheriff's will also set out his intent to endow 'a free grammar schoole … to serve chiefly for the children of Rugby and … of other places thereunto adjoyneing', to be called 'the free schoole of Lawrence Sheriffe'. Bequests of a charitable nature were not uncommon in the sixteenth century, particularly from one of new wealth and with no hereditary estates to maintain. Protestantism emphasized the importance of education as a means to religious enlightenment, although the desire to perpetuate his name may have been no small inducement. There was to be money for 'a fayre and convenyient schoole house', and also for 'meet and distincte lodgeings for four poor men' to be built nearby, the foundation of today's almshouses. A schoolmaster was provided for with a yearly salary of £12. The four poor men were to have 'sevenpence by the week' (PRO, PROB 11/49). These ventures were to be endowed with all Sheriff's lands in Warwickshire, though, as this would not be sufficient, he added a further £100 for more land to be bought locally. On 31 August 1567 Sheriff added a codicil which revoked the grant of £100 and instead bestowed upon the school 24 acres of land in Holborn, only half a mile from the city of London. The rents from this have helped to sustain Rugby School and Lawrence Sheriff School to this day.

SARAH K. FLETCHER

Sources M. H. Bloxam, *Rugby: the school and the neighbourhood*, ed. W. H. Payne Smith (1889) · Lawrence Sheriff's will, PRO, PROB 11/49 · J. Foxe, *Actes and monuments*, 8th edn, 3 (1641), 951

Sheringham, Robert (c.1604–1678), orientalist, was a son of William Sheringham of Guestwick, Norfolk, and his wife, Elizabeth; he had at least one sister. He was educated at Norwich under Mr Briggs, and entered Gonville and Caius College, Cambridge, as a pensioner on 15 March 1619. He proceeded BA in 1623 and MA in 1626, and was incorporated in the same degree at Oxford on 15 July 1628. Ordained deacon at Peterborough on 28 March 1626 and priest on 29 June, he was elected a fellow of his Cambridge college in the same year. In 1634 he was presented to the rectory of Patesley in Norfolk, a living in the gift of Caius, but he was not resident. In the early years of his fellowship he occupied various posts. He acted as Greek lecturer in 1630, Hebrew lecturer in 1633, and dean in 1642, and in 1644 he was elected one of the proctors of Cambridge University. In the following year he issued his first publication, the text of two elegant sermons delivered at St Mary's, Cambridge, on Psalm 41: 4.

In 1648 Sheringham proved himself an accomplished Hebraist with the publication of a Latin translation of the Mishnaic tractate on priests and sacrifices, *Joma*. It coincided with a plan devised in the circle of Samuel Hartlib, John Amos Comenius, and John Dury to make lesser known Hebrew sources more widely available. Sheringham, however, proceeded independently. His work is a landmark in Hebrew studies. In his preface he presents an eloquent defence of the rabbinic writings and their use for Christian biblicists, and stresses the debt of the gospels to a Jewish tradition which can best be discovered by studying the Talmud. His edition was inferior to the Mishnaic tractates about to be produced at Oxford under the supervision of Edward Pococke, but it remains a pioneering work which marks the beginning of an ever more sophisticated English treatment of Jewish writings. It was reprinted in the Netherlands in 1696, edited by Jacob Rhenferd, one of the foremost experts on the ancient languages of the Near East, of which he was professor at the University of Franeker.

Sheringham was deeply committed to the royalist cause. He dedicated his edition of the *Joma* to a prominent royalist, the mathematician Sir John Heydon, also from Norfolk. In 1651, after refusing to submit to parliament, Sheringham forfeited his fellowship at Caius and departed for the Netherlands. He would seem to have made preparations for his arrival in the previous year as the college registers show that he left Cambridge at the end of October 1649. He may have gone first to London, but he matriculated as a student of medicine at the University of Leiden on 4 March 1650. By November he was back at Caius and was still in England in February of the following year.

In the Netherlands, besides other scholarly refugees such as Thomas Marshall, he found a friend in Sir Edward Nicholas, the former secretary of state. By May 1653 he was in The Hague, temporarily acting as chaplain to Charles I's daughter Mary, who was married to the prince of Orange. Subsequently Sheringham moved to Rotterdam, where he gave tuition to fellow emigrants in Hebrew, Arabic, Aramaic, and Syriac. One of his pupils, Thomas Cawton the younger, the son of the minister of the English church, proceeded to the University of Utrecht in 1657 with what was regarded as a remarkable command of the languages which Sheringham had taught him.

In his first years in the Netherlands, Sheringham composed his justification of royal absolutism warranted, he claimed, by the statutes, common law, and ancient customs of England, *The kings supremacy asserted, or, A remonstrance of the kings right against the pretended parliament*. In 1653 Nicholas sent a copy to Edward Hyde, saying it is 'well worth your perusal, notwithstanding you have read and written much on the same subject' (*Nicholas Papers*, 2.14).

Containing an extensive critique of Philip Hunton's *Treatise of Monarchy* the work was intended to serve as a weapon against the parliamentary agents in the Low Countries. Sheringham had originally hoped to publish it in Dutch, but it appeared in English in 1660, dedicated to Charles II. It was reprinted again in 1682.

With the Restoration, Sheringham returned to Cambridge and was re-elected to his fellowship at Caius. In July 1663 he described himself in a letter to Thomas Marshall as 'being at the University, but living for the most part in London' (Bodl. Oxf., MS Marshall 134, fol. 16). He later spent more time in his college, where he was appointed catechist in 1666, 1672, and 1673 and Hebrew lecturer again from 1674 to 1677. His main work, *De Anglorum gentis origine*, appeared in 1670. Based on a vast assortment of Gothic and early English sources, it argues for the descent of the English from the Getae, whom Sheringham, like many of his contemporaries, identified with the Goths. Rejecting the widespread idea that they were descended from Noah's son Japhet, however, he maintained that they were the descendants of Shem, had moved from Scythia to Scandinavia, had then emigrated to the Baltic and Germany, and had gone from there to Asia and back to Germany. Although the work was never reprinted it was quoted with respect by James Tyrrell in 1698, Thomas Herne in 1744, and David Wilkins in 1748. But by 1770 Thomas Percy was critical of Sheringham's inability 'to distinguish what is true and credible from what is improbable and fabulous in the old Northern Chronicles. Because some parts are true, he receives all for authentic' (Mallet, viii).

At Cambridge, Sheringham was greatly admired as a linguist, his knowledge of Gothic and other Germanic languages as well as the Semitic ones drawing high praise from John Gostlin, the future vice-master of Caius. On 17 April 1678 Sheringham drew up his will 'sick in body', bequeathing most of his library to his college (will, 166). He had already presented Caius with a fine fifteenth-century manuscript, probably written by the Chaucerian copyist Shirley and containing works by Richard Rolle (Gonville and Caius College, MS 669/646), and a copy of the liturgical acts and epistles printed in Church Slavonic in Moscow in 1564. At some point during the next two weeks he died in his rooms in college and was buried at the church of St Michael on 2 May 1678.

ALASTAIR HAMILTON

Sources J. Venn and others, eds., *Biographical history of Gonville and Caius College*, 1: *1349–1713* (1897) · D. S. Katz, 'The Abendana brothers and the Christian Hebraists of seventeenth-century England', *Journal of Ecclesiastical History*, 40 (1989), 28–52 · *DNB* · Venn, *Alum. Cant.* · C. N. L. Brooke, *A history of Gonville and Caius College* (1985); repr. with corrections (1996) · *The Nicholas papers*, ed. G. F. Warner, 2, CS, new ser., 50 (1892) · S. Mandelbrote, 'The Bible and national identity in the British Isles, c.1650–c.1750', *Protestantism and national identity*, ed. T. Claydon and I. McBride (1998), 157–81 · S. Kliger, *The Goths in England: a study in eighteenth-century thought* (1952) · *The life and times of Anthony Wood*, ed. A. Clark, 2, OHS, 21 (1892) · T. Cawton, *The life and death of … Thomas Cawton* (1662) · K. L. Sprunger, *Dutch puritanism: a history of English and Scottish churches of the Netherlands in the sixteenth and seventeenth centuries* (1982) · G. du Rieu, ed., *Album studiosorum academiae Lugduno Batavae, MDLXXV–MDCCCLXXV:*

accedunt nomina curatorum et professorum per eadem secula (The Hague, 1875) · P. H. Mallet, *Northern antiquities* (1770) · Bodl. Oxf., MS Marshall 134, fol. 16 · will, 7 May 1678, CUL, department of manuscripts and university archives, vol. 4, pp. 166–8 · Gon. & Caius Cam., TUT/01/04/02 1618–78 · CUL, Add. MS 5932, fols. 265–7 **Wealth at death** furniture, hangings, library; bequests of £8 10s: will, CUL, Add. MS 5932, fols. 265–7; CUL, department of manuscripts and university archives, vol. 4, pp. 166–8, 17 April 1678

Sherland, Christopher (1594–1632), lawyer and politician, was born in Easton Maudit, Northamptonshire, and baptized on 28 April 1594, the first son of Thomas Sherland esquire of Milden, Suffolk, and his wife, Anne, daughter of Sir Christopher *Yelverton of Easton Maudit. He matriculated from Queen's College, Oxford, on 8 May 1607 aged thirteen and he graduated BA on 31 January 1610. He was admitted to Gray's Inn on 1 November 1604, was called to the bar on 26 June 1617, and he became a bencher in 1627. At an unknown date he married Jane, daughter of Edward Oglethorpe of Smithfield, London.

According to Sherland's contemporary biographer, Richard Sibbes, preacher at Gray's Inn, the dominant influence on Sherland's early years was his uncle Sir Henry *Yelverton, who persuaded him to set aside his early inclination to become a divine and to pursue his studies in the law. It was also on his uncle's recommendation that Sherland was appointed recorder of Northampton on 23 June 1623. During the late 1620s he lived in the town, representing the borough in the parliaments of 1624, 1625, 1626, and 1628–9, and acting as legal adviser to the corporation and to local gentry families, such as the Drydens and the Knightleys. He also formed close links with the network of local puritan ministers, including Thomas Ball of Northampton, Robert Bolton of Weekley, John Dod of Fawsley, and Andrew Perne of Wilby, whom he described in his will as 'my reverend and pious friends' (PRO, PROB, 11/10, Audley, 1632). He was among those who defaulted over payment of the forced loan at Northampton in 1627.

At a national level Sherland was closely involved with the leading puritan opponents of crown policies. He was one of the four lawyers among the feoffees for impropriations established in 1625, and by his will he left £400 to the feoffees 'for furtherance of the preaching of the gospel' (PRO, PROB, 11/10, Audley, 1632). He was also a founding member of the Providence Island Company, set up in September 1630, and, in the same month, he joined William Fiennes, first Viscount Saye and Sele, Sir Nathaniel Rich, John Pym, and John Crewe as members of a trust established by Richard Knightley to support John Dod. He made 'my good friend' John Hampden executor of his will.

In the absence of correspondence, the clearest impression of Sherland's attitudes and concerns is provided by his contributions in parliament, where he was a prominent speaker and committee man. His main priority was the defence of Calvinist orthodoxy. Sibbes described him as someone well versed in 'controverted points of divinity' and, with the exception of John Pym, no MP in the late 1620s was more vigorous in his efforts to demonstrate the dangers presented by Arminianism. His first significant speech was in August 1625 when he opposed a grant of subsidies and suggested that proper enforcement of the recusancy laws would provide the king with a more than adequate revenue. In 1626 he reported to the Commons on the outcome of the York House conference, at which George Villiers, first duke of Buckingham, had declared his support for Arminianism, and when he delivered one of the Commons charges against Buckingham in the Lords he added his own gloss that he was 'the principal patron of a semi-pelagian, semi-popish faction, dangerous to church and state, lately set on foot among us'.

In 1628, like other leading lawyers, Sherland was much involved in the debates leading to the petition of right, but again his main concern was religion. In the debate on the remonstrance against Buckingham in June he argued that the Arminians 'run in string with the papists and flatter greatness to oppress the subject', thereby making what has been described as a new and crucial intellectual link between the alteration of religion and the alteration of government. In 1629 he was again at the forefront of discussions on Arminianism, proposing the Thirty-Nine Articles of 1562 as a basic standard of religious orthodoxy and denouncing the evil influence of Arminian advisers close to the king. Sherland died in February 1632. He had no surviving children. He was regarded by Sir John Eliot as one of the ablest and most articulate critics of Charles I's government. RICHARD CUST

Sources R. Sibbes, 'Christ is best', *The saints cordialls* (1637) · M. Jansson and W. B. Bidwell, eds., *Proceedings in parliament, 1625* (1987) · W. B. Bidwell and M. Jansson, eds., *Proceedings in parliament, 1626*, 4 vols. (1991–6) · R. C. Johnson and others, eds., *Proceedings in parliament, 1628*, 1–4 (1977–8) · Northampton borough assembly minutes, Northants. RO, 3, 1; 3, 2 · Isham correspondence, Northants. RO

Sherley [Shirley], **Anthony** [*known as* Sir Anthony Sherley], **Count Sherley in the nobility of the Holy Roman empire** (1565–1636?), adventurer and diplomat in the Persian service, was born at the family estate of Wiston in Sussex, one of nine children of Sir Thomas *Sherley (*c.*1542–1612) and Anne Kempe (*c.*1542–1623), daughter of Sir Thomas Kempe of Ollantighe, Kent, and brother to Sir Thomas *Sherley and Sir Robert *Shirley. Having matriculated from Hart Hall, Oxford, in 1579 and after graduating BA in 1581, in November 1582 he was elected a probationer fellow of All Souls College, a position he held until 1589. In 1583 he was admitted to the Inner Temple.

War in the Low Countries and Brittany Having acquired, as he was later to write, 'those learnings which were fit for a Gentlemans ornament, without directing them to an occupation' (*Sir Anthony Sherley His Relation*, 1) Sherley left England in 1586 to serve as a captain of infantry under Robert Dudley, earl of Leicester, in the wars in the Low Countries. He first saw action at Brielle, commanding an undisciplined garrison company. In 1588, after his brother Thomas's inept performance at Zwolle, he was assigned to the remnants of Thomas's cavalry company; however,

Magni Sophi Persarum Legatus inuictissimo
Cæsari Cæterisque Principibus Christianis:
huiusce Amicitiæ et Auctor et ductor
EX ORE, AD OS.
S. Cæ.Mtis sculptor Ægidius Sadeler. D D.

**Anthony Sherley, Count Sherley in the nobility of the Holy
Roman empire (1565–1636?), by Aegidius Sadeler, pubd 1612**

upon taking charge it was clear that the force was woefully undermanned. The company was disbanded and Sherley was sent home.

After the Spanish capture of the Breton ports in 1591 Sherley returned to the continent to command one of the earl of Essex's three regiments. Though the campaign itself proved indecisive, in June Sherley distinguished himself in battle near Châtelaudren when a sizeable Spanish force of some 500 horse and 6000 foot descended upon the English. Hard pressed, Sherley led the English cavalry against the attackers, personally killing a Spanish captain, and was credited with single-handedly turning the tide of the battle. The next day, with a force of only fifteen horse, Sherley repulsed a Spanish counter-attack, though his own horse was shot from under him; his courageous conduct during these actions earned him a reputation for bravery and noblesse which served him well for much of his life.

Early in 1593 Sherley was dispatched on a mission to the French court where Henri IV awarded him the knighthood of the order of St Michel. Elizabeth I was furious that he had accepted a foreign honour without her permission and recalled him to England. He was questioned extensively by Lord Keeper Sir John Puckering and Lord Buckhurst about the details of the oath he had taken; when his answers were found inadequate he was tossed in the Fleet prison. When he was released shortly afterwards it was on condition that he resign the robes of the order. Though the title no longer had any official sanction he was commonly known as Sir Anthony.

Privateering At some point in 1594 Sherley secretly married Frances (*bap.* 1573), daughter of Sir John Vernon of Hodnet, Shropshire, and first cousin to Robert Devereux, second earl of Essex. Although the union brought him closer to the earl, whom he was later to call the 'patterne of my civill life' and 'a worthy modell of all my actions' (*Sir Anthony Sherley His Relation*, 2), it also incurred the queen's displeasure. As a result he was exiled from court and moved to Inglefield, in Tilehurst, Berkshire, a property sold to him by Essex. Unfortunately the union did not prove happy, and to escape his domestic situation he fitted out an expedition against the Portuguese settlement on the island of São Thomé, in the Gulf of Guinea. Aided by his father Sherley equipped a fleet of eleven ships and an army of 1500 men at the cost of at least £15,000. However, in order to procure a commission legitimizing his attack he was forced to surrender four ships and 500 men to Essex for his raid on Cadiz. With a much reduced fleet Sherley set sail on 20 May 1596.

Ill fortune dogged the venture from the start as contrary winds caused the sacking of São Thomé to be abandoned and disease left Sherley despairing for his life. Instead the fleet sailed for São Tiago, in the Cape Verde Islands. Here they seized and held the town for two days against some 3000 Portuguese; however, there proved little worth taking and so they continued 10 miles down the coast to the fortified town of Ribeira Grande (now Cidade Velha). In the ensuing battle Sherley's force lost eighty men while inflicting 250 casualties on the Portuguese, but the English feared a counter-attack and so fled back to their ships, resolving to sail across the Atlantic.

The crossing proved wretched and disease again took its toll. On 17 October the fleet put in at Dominica in the Leeward Islands for six weeks to let the crew recover. Early in February 1597, after one ship mutinied near the mouth of the River Magdalena in Colombia, the remains of the fleet landed in the Spanish territory of Jamaica. Set on plunder Sherley marched a sizeable force 6 miles inland to the capital, Santiago de la Veda (now Spanish Town), only to find it deserted and the pickings slim. Putting to sea once more all but one of his remaining ships mutinied off Havana and so Sherley was forced to curtail his voyage. He returned to Dover in July, alive but poor.

The Persian mission Searching for some way to abate his family's ailing fortunes, in winter 1598 Sherley accepted Essex's invitation to conduct a small company of English volunteers to Ferrara to assist Don Cesare d'Este, the late duke's illegitimate son, in his claim to the duchy against Pope Clement VIII. With twenty-five English volunteers Sherley left England in spring 1598; but upon reaching Augsburg he received word that Don Cesare had capitulated. Even though the apparent pretence for the mission had evaporated Sherley continued to Venice, where he was joined by his brother Robert. According to his subsequent account, while in Venice Anthony wrote to Essex, who advised him to continue to Persia for the glory of God and to find parts fit for English navigation. Others were more cynical and charged that having wrung £400 from English merchants in Constantinople and a further £500 from those in Aleppo, billing the sums to Essex, he had gone to seek his fortune (*CSP dom.*, *1598–1601*, 130). Either way the enterprise lacked official sanction. According to a letter of April 1601 penned by the English Jesuit Robert Persons, Sherley became a Catholic during his stay in Venice.

By all accounts Sherley's party was well received in Persia with Sherley granted the rank of *mirza*. But after a stay of five months, Shah 'Abbas accepted Sherley's offer to return to Europe as his ambassador to the Christian potentates, charged with engineering an alliance between Persia and Christendom against the Turks; in exchange for Christian support Persia was to be opened up to Christian merchants. Despite the fact that such an alliance would be injurious to English mercantile interests in the region, its terms seem to betray Sherley's influence, for the shah also promised to force the Armenian church to submit to Rome.

Leaving his brother Robert behind as a hostage, Anthony Sherley left Persia in May 1599, accompanied by Hasain Ali Beg Bayat and an Augustinian friar, Nicolò de Mello. Equipped with an array of gifts for the princes of Europe the party travelled north via the Caspian. But by the time they reached Moscow, Sherley and the friar were at odds: de Mello accused Sherley of stealing 1000 crowns and ninety diamonds from him, while Sherley accused the friar of sodomizing two of his attendants. To this end Sherley denounced de Mello to Tsar Boris Godunov, who had the friar stripped of his possessions and put in a monastery. But Sherley's haughty airs irritated the tsar, for when the party was summoned to an audience he refused to enter behind the Persians, arguing that it was the height of indignity for a Christian to walk behind pagans.

Early in 1600 the party left for Archangel. There Sherley persuaded Hasain Ali Beg Bayat that, in the interests of safety, he should send forward one of the cases of presents given to them by the shah to Rome. Continuing to Prague the two ambassadors presented the idea of a Christian alliance with Persia to Emperor Rudolph II on 7 November 1600. Although the emperor was initially enthusiastic, when Sherley refused to return to Persia immediately and suggested instead that he should proceed to England, his credibility was compromised. As his stay lengthened and it became clear that he was living beyond his means, rumours begin to circulate that he was a Spanish spy. The truth was more mundane, for, by the time he left the court in February 1601, Sherley had contracted debts worth in excess of 46,000 thalers.

In April 1601 the two ambassadors arrived at Rome but were now clearly at odds over the issue of precedence. They quarrelled violently over the matter of accommodation, with Sherley insisting on taking the better of the two apartments given them by the pope. Moreover, it was now clear to the Persian that the presents they had loaded for transport in Archangel had disappeared and he accused

Sherley of stealing them; he alleged that Sherley had become so crushed by debt that now his only interest in proceeding with the embassy was to get money from foreign potentates. Indeed, relations between the ambassadors had deteriorated to such a point that they were granted separate audiences with the pope. The situation was further complicated because in their commission from the shah Sherley was not referred to as 'ambassador'. Sherley argued that the translation was poor but the pope clearly favoured Hasain Ali Beg Bayat and Sherley was dismissed on 2 June 1601. At this news the Venetian ambassador in Rome remarked that Sherley 'has done many out of much money, and loud are the lamentations' (*CSP Venice*, *1592–1603*, 462). At this point Sherley seems to have given up any hope of completing his embassy, for he stayed in Rome secretly, twice offering his services to Cardinal d'Ossat and once making overtures to the French king. He left his brother Robert to his fate in Persia.

From late 1601 until the end of 1604 Sherley was resident in Venice, engaged as a spy for both the Spanish and the Scots, in which capacity he was watched continually by two English agents. In late March 1603 his activities began to concern the Venetian senate and he was arrested for 'insult to the Persian merchant's house' (*CSP Venice*, *1603–7*, 1). His position was further complicated because a ship owned by his brother Thomas had just plundered a Venetian galleon returning fully laden from Egypt. In May 1603 he was released from gaol on condition that he leave Venetian territory, but James I intervened, begging the senate to lift the decree. Free, Sherley began to spy again, but this time for the emperor, furnishing him with reports on Turkish strengths. To the Venetians this was intolerable, for it jeopardized their policy of avoiding antagonizing the Ottomans, a cornerstone of their diplomacy. On 1 December 1604 Sherley was summoned to appear before the council of ten and given four days to leave the demesne, never to return under pain of death (*CSP Venice*, *1603–7*, 194).

Mission to Morocco On 2 June 1605 Sherley returned to Prague, where he was received by the emperor, who commissioned him to create a diversion against the Turks in north Africa. In October, Sherley landed in Safi, calling himself 'ambassador' and living, by all accounts, in the manner of a prince, lavishly entertaining any Christian merchant who came to his door. The money advanced to him by the emperor was quickly exhausted and he resorted to living on credit. In February 1606, with a grand escort of 500 men, he travelled to Marrakesh and the court of Abu Faris. Though he was received with great state, when he came to an entertainment organized by the king he refused to dismount from his horse, instead riding through the hall in a manner befitting royalty. When summoned to the same chamber five days later he found a chain across the entrance. But rather than heed the king's wishes, Sherley was indignant and rode away; the chain, he explained, represented a dishonour to the person he represented.

Despite several meetings, Sherley was unable to persuade Abu Faris to strike against the Turks in Algiers and

Tunis; in late June, he was dismissed. However, as was becoming something of a habit, he had incurred such debts that he was obliged to leave behind two of his company as hostages for a debt of 250,000 florins. He extricated himself from a further 60,000 florins of debt to some local Christian merchants by denouncing them to the king for defrauding the treasury of customs.

In the service of Spain When he was finally able to leave north Africa in autumn 1606 Sherley had with him two Portuguese prisoners he had ransomed, hoping to be well compensated for his expenses from their families; but when he reached Lisbon they refused to pay him. Temporarily without means, Sherley made for the Spanish court in Madrid in an attempt to persuade Philip III to finance a scheme to capture two Barbary ports. Instead he was given a formal commission to harass ships supplying the Turks in the Levant and the Low Countries and admitted to the order of San Iago. It was widely rumoured that he owed this new position to the influence of Anthony Creswell, a notorious English Jesuit implicated in the Gunpowder Plot. A brief visit to Prague in 1607 saw Sherley created count palatine by the emperor.

Over the period between 1607 and 1610 Sherley came to treat his commission as a licence for piracy. When he seized a Venetian ship, selling its cargo in Palermo, the Venetians complained vigorously to the Spanish and Sherley was relieved of his position. Completely discredited he made his way back to Madrid where he met and quarrelled with his brother Robert, the new ambassador from the Persian shah, although Robert probably helped him publish his self-aggrandizing *Relation of his Travels into Persia* in London in 1613. In this work, Sherley presents himself as endowed with a natural nobility; his difficulties, he suggests, are a consequence of the fact that such natural virtue is coming to be regarded as less important than a person's financial worth. While he was sympathetic to Persian customs and evaluated them according to their purpose and effect, he had nothing but bile for the Turks.

Now faced with the direst poverty Sherley was granted an allowance of 3000 ducats a year by the Spanish king out of pity; the greater part of this was spent in paying his creditors. His poverty was such that in December 1619 the English ambassador at Madrid reported that Sir Anthony was on the brink of starvation but was 'as full of vanity as ever he was, making himself believe that he shall one day be a great prince, when for the present he wants shoes to wear' (Penrose, 155).

Through the remainder of his life Sherley tried to ingratiate himself with the Jesuits, and sank to concocting plots against his enemies, all of which came to naught. In March 1618 rumours reached the English court that Sherley intended to flee his creditors and live out his days in the Canaries; but again nothing came of this scheme (*CSP col.*, 3.188). Anthony Sherley died in obscurity, probably in 1636.

In 1607 John Day, William Rowley, and John Wilkins wrote a play entitled *The Travailes of the Three English Brothers*. With a striking affinity to the short tract written by Anthony Nixon, *The Three English Brothers*, published at almost the same time, their play presents a heavily sensationalized version of Sherley's dealings with the shah and the subsequent embassy to Europe. Sherley typifies the honour and nobility of Christendom against the machinations of the shah's counsellors at the Persian court and of the scheming Halibeck with whom he must discharge his mission to the princes of Europe. In 1888 Scott Surtees advanced the rather dubious argument that Sherley wrote all Shakespeare's plays.   RICHARD RAISWELL

Sources B. Penrose, *The Sherlian odyssey* (1938) · D. W. Davies, *Elizabethans errant: the strange fortunes of Sir Thomas Sherley and his three sons* (1967) · S. Purchas, *Hakluytus posthumus, or, Purchas his pilgrimes*, bk 20 (1625); repr. Hakluyt Society, extra ser., 33 (1907) · *Sir Antony Sherley his relation of his travels into Persia* (1613) · *A chronicle of the Carmelites in Persia and the papal missions of the XVIIth and XVIIIth centuries*, 2 vols. (1939), vol. 1 · *A true historicall discourse of Muley Hamets … the adventures of Sir Anthony Sherley, and divers other English gentlemen* (1609) · W. Parry, *A new and large discourse of the travels of Sir Anthony Sherley, knight, by sea, and over land, to the Persian empire* (1601) · A. Nixon, *The three English brothers* (1607) · *CSP Venice, 1592–1607* · *CSP col.*, vol. 3 · R. B. Wernham, ed., *List and analysis of state papers, foreign series, Elizabeth I*, 7 vols. (1964–2000) · W. H. Cooke, ed., *Students admitted to the Inner Temple, 1547–1660* [1878] · M. Burrows, *Worthies of All Souls* (1874) · S. Surtees, *William Shakespeare of Stratford-on-Avon, his epitaph unearthed and the author of the plays run to ground* (1888) · E. P. Shirley, ed., *Stemmata Shirleiana* (1841)

Likenesses J. Orlandi, line engraving, 1601, NPG · A. Sadeler, line engraving, c.1601 (after portrait by Sadeler, 1601), repro. in Davies, *Elizabethans errant* · A. Sadeler, line engraving, pubd 1612, NPG [*see illus.*] · J. Cheere, bronzed plaster bust, 1730–70, All Souls Oxf. · D. Custos, line engraving, BM, NPG; repro. in D. Custos, *Atrium heroicum Caesarum*, 4 vols. (1600–02) · G. Sadeler, line engraving, BM, NPG

Sherley [Shirley], **Sir Thomas** (c.1542–1612), politician and courtier, was the eldest of three children born to William Sherley (c.1498–1551), a gentleman of Wiston, Sussex, and his wife, Mary, daughter of Thomas Isley of Sundridge, Kent. Nothing is known of his education; he did not, as sometimes claimed, matriculate as a fellow commoner from Queens' College, Cambridge, in 1561. Sherley married, about 1559, Anne (c.1542–1623), daughter of Sir Thomas Kempe of Wye, Kent. They had twelve children, including three adventurous sons: Sir Thomas *Sherley (1564–1633/4), Sir Anthony *Sherley (1565–1636?), and Robert *Shirley (c.1581–1628). Herbert referred to the Sherleys as 'A family not needing hyperboles' (Shirley, 234). Three other children died in infancy but six daughters survived, Jane (b. 1571) becoming the grandmother of Sir Thomas *Overbury.

Sherley was elected MP for Sussex in 1572, 1584, and 1593; he sat for Steyning, his pocket borough, in 1601 and 1604. He was appointed deputy lieutenant of the county in 1569, and was only removed from the list in 1601. He had a town house in Blackfriars and was patronized by Robert Dudley, earl of Leicester. The Sherleys have had the reputation of being a recusant family, but there is no proof that Sir Thomas had Roman Catholic tendencies. He was related by marriage to several leading local families, some of whom were recusants who leased small parts of his lands. A distant kinsman and namesake, Sir Thomas Shirley of St Botolph's Bridge, Huntingdonshire, attributed the misfortunes which befell Sherley to his having deserted 'the ancient religion', but there is no proof for this assertion. Sherley was a commissioner for recusancy in 1580 and a commissioner for disarming recusants in 1585. After the Throckmorton conspiracy, Ann, wife of Philip Howard, earl of Arundel, gave birth to her daughter at Wiston in April 1564, where she was kept in custody by Sherley for a year.

Knighted by Queen Elizabeth at Rye on 12 August 1573, Sherley's raised social status dictated the need for a larger country residence. The new house at Wiston was built between 1573 and 1575, probably on or near the site of the old part-stone manor house mentioned in 1357. From November 1577 Sherley served as sheriff of Sussex and Surrey for a year. He was also a justice of the peace for many years, together with his near neighbour Sir Thomas Bishop of Parham, referred to in 1587 as 'good justyces—young men'. Sherley's leased farms supplied him with an annual income of about £1000. He also had connections with the Sussex iron industry, and a furnace erected in 1580 was supplied with wood granted to him under a patent of 1578. In 1588 he was one of fifteen Sussex gentry to pay the highest rate to the Armada fund of £100, though in the same year the sheriff seized many of his goods at Wiston (including 71 feather beds and 32 Turkish carpets) for unpaid debts. He had by now begun on the downward spiral that led to his bankruptcy and disgrace in 1597.

Sherley accompanied the earl of Leicester to the Low Countries in 1585 to aid the rebellion against Spain. He acted as Leicester's go-between with Queen Elizabeth early in 1586 when she was angered that her favourite had accepted the governorship of the United Provinces without consulting her. Made joint treasurer-at-war with William Huddleston in the summer of 1586, Sherley was appointed sole treasurer by Queen Elizabeth on 27 February 1587. He had taken his two eldest sons, Thomas and Anthony, with him, and the three of them each retained a company, which enabled Sherley to engage in much false accounting. He used numerous methods to acquire for himself the money sent out by Lord Burghley to pay debts and equip the troops. Burghley noted in June 1587 that £30,000 had been given to Sherley to pay the debts of the expedition, restore the cavalry to good order, and pay all lendings (half pay for the soldiery) until September. At the end of June Sherley had only £3000 left instead of an expected £18,000. He had spent £8000 before he left England. The enormous sum of £1.5 million is said to have passed through his hands during the ten years he was treasurer-at-war, of which large amounts disappeared into his own pockets. One of his captains revealed that Sherley loaned out much of the cash at interest. Sherley also bought up soldiers' claims to back pay and paid himself the full amount due. Peregrine Bertie, Lord Willoughby, commander of the English forces after Leicester's departure for England in December 1587, believed Sherley was making £20,000 per annum.

Suspicious of his treasurer, Burghley constantly checked on Sherley, and finally the queen reduced his salary. By March 1597 he was bankrupt: 'the Queen is greatly incensed and disquieted with Sir Thomas Sherley's doings … he owes the Queen more than he is worth', wrote a contemporary (Davies, 44). In April he was sent to the Fleet prison and probably released in January 1598. He was finally charged with owing the queen £35,175, a mere fraction of what had been embezzled. Of this sum £12,702 was excused and £10,000 recovered by seizing Sherley's goods and putting extents on his lands. He had also obtained questionable patents on the lands of Norwich Cathedral between 1583 and 1586, paying £300 for lands worth £2000 p.a. The dean of Norwich endeavoured to reach an agreement with him, describing Sherley in 1588 as 'promising much but of a contrary mind to perform nothing … he will so plainly deny the receipt of my letters' (Shirley, 254–5). Sherley also acquired a patent to sell black people from England to Spain and Portugal which did not prosper.

On 20 August 1602 the Wiston estate was sequestrated by the crown. The queen finally lost patience when Sherley reneged on the arrangements to repay his debts. He was able to retrieve his lands in July 1604, when three relatives stood surety for him. Shortly before this, on 15 March 1604, he was again in trouble; elected MP for Steyning, he was riding through London with King James prior to the opening of parliament a few days later when he was arrested for debt by a City goldsmith and taken to the Fleet. This raised the whole question of the privilege of freedom from arrest for MPs, and after several weeks of parliamentary activity, a special bill was passed in haste through both Houses. Sherley was released and triumphantly took his seat. The final form of this law was fixed in 1604 and is known as Shirley's case.

In 1610 Sherley was involved in a scheme for creating a new class of knights, which came to nothing. He is also reputed, together with Sir Robert Cotton, to have created the new honour of baronet, sold by the crown for £1096 in 1611. He obtained no financial advantage from this, not surprisingly in view of his unpaid debts. In 1615, three years after his death, his eldest son Sir Thomas wrote to the king:

> My Father (being a man of most excellent and working wit), did find out the device for the making of Baronets, which brought to your Majesty's coffers well nigh a hundred thousand pounds for which he was promised … good recompence which he never had.   (Davies, 240)

Shortly before his father's demise in October 1612, Sherley the younger tried to commit suicide while in a debtors' prison. Six months later the Sherley inheritance—a burden of debt—fell on him like a ton weight. However, his father had done him a posthumous good turn in that he was able to claim immunity from prison by serving as an MP.

Sir Thomas Sherley died in October 1612, aged about seventy. The black marble obituary tablet from what must have been a grand memorial lies broken in the granary above the Wiston House stables. In 1851 it was said to be on the eastern wall of the family burial place, St Mary's Chapel in St Michael's Church at Wiston (now known as St Mary's Church), surmounted by his effigy and that of his wife, with the arms of his six daughters below. The monument itself may have been damaged during the civil war, and again during church restoration in 1862. The kneeling figures of Sherley and his wife, Anne, their noses and hands chopped off, have been placed on a window sill in the southern aisle of the church. Faint traces of colour remain on the stone. The damaged coat of arms from the monument is in the possession of the Wiston estate office.

It has been incorrectly assumed that the Wiston estate was sold by Sherley's eldest son to Sir John Fagge. James I gave the estate to his favourite the earl of Somerset in 1615. In 1622 it was purchased by Lionel Cranfield. He paid off the creditors of the earl of Somerset with £7000, gave £5400 (by instalments) to Sir Thomas Sherley the younger, paid £400 to Sherley the elder's daughter Cecily, and provided an annuity of £400 for Dame Anne, who spent the last year of her life partly at Parham House with her neighbour Lady Bishop, and partly in London. Wiston House has been leased to the Foreign Office as a conference centre, known as Wilton Park, since 1951.

JANET PENNINGTON

Sources E. P. Shirley, *Stemmata Sherleiana, or the annals of the Shirley family*, 2nd edn (1873) · D. W. Davies, *Elizabethans errant: the strange fortunes of Sir Thomas Sherley and his three sons* (1967) · W. Sussex RO, Wiston archives · *The Wiston archives: a catalogue*, 1, ed. J. M. L. Booker (1975) · *The Wiston archives: a catalogue*, 2, ed. S. Freeth (1982) · CKS, Cranfield papers, U269, U269/1 · T. P. Hudson, ed., *A history of Sussex*, vol. 6, pt 1 (1980) · J. Pennington, 'The Wiston estate, Sussex: crown sequestration and its effects, 1596–1634', MA thesis, Brighton Polytechnic, 1989 · G. W. Prothero, ed., *Select statutes and other constitutional documents illustrative of the reigns of Elizabeth and James I*, 3rd edn (1906) · J. R. Tanner, ed., *Constitutional documents of the reign of James I* (1952) · M. Prestwich, *Cranfield: politics and profits under the early Stuarts* (1966) · M. A. Lower, 'Sussex gentry in 1588, with notes', *Sussex Archaeological Collections*, 1 (1848), 32–7 · M. A. Lower, 'The descent of Wiston, with anecdotes of its possessors', *Sussex Archaeological Collections*, 5 (1852), 1–28 · W. D. Cooper, 'Certificate concerning the justices of the peace in Sussex in 1587', *Sussex Archaeological Collections*, 2 (1849), 58–62 · W. T. MacCaffrey, *Queen Elizabeth and the making of policy, 1572–1588* (1981) · F. G. Oosterhoff, *Leicester and the Netherlands, 1586–1587* (1998) · F. C. Dietz, *English public finance, 1485–1641*, 2nd edn, 2 (1964) · A. Somerset, *Unnatural murder: poison at the court of James I* (1997) · W. McElwee, *The murder of Sir Thomas Overbury* (1952) · *Sussex*, Pevsner (1965) · *CSP dom.*, 1602–3 · K. Sharpe, *Sir Robert Cotton, 1586–1631* (1979) · L. Stone, *The crisis of the aristocracy, 1558–1641* (1965)

Archives W. Sussex RO, Wiston archives, papers | BL, Cotton MSS, papers · BL, Harley MSS, papers · BL, Lansdowne MSS, papers · CKS, Cranfield MSS · Hatfield House, Hertfordshire, Hatfield MSS, papers

Wealth at death in debt: Shirley, *Stemmata Sherleiana*, 256

Sherley [Shirley], **Sir Thomas** (1564–1633/4), privateer and travel writer, was the eldest son of Sir Thomas *Sherley (c.1542–1612) of Wiston, Sussex, and his wife, Anne Kempe (c.1542–1623), daughter of Sir Thomas Kempe of Olantigh, Kent. Sir Anthony *Sherley and Robert *Shirley, Count Shirley, were his younger brothers. Together the three brothers through their exploits in Persia and the Mediterranean earned a reputation in their day in pamphlet and play as champions of Christendom against the Turk. To a more jaundiced twentieth-century eye 'The Sherleys all had unlimited bravura and glib sales talk, everything but a capacity to turn an honest penny' (Prestwich, 390).

Thomas Sherley matriculated at Hart Hall, Oxford, in 1579, but left without graduating. In November 1581 he was admitted to the Inner Temple. In 1584 he was returned for the borough of Steyning, Sussex, for which he was to sit in three other parliaments (those of 1593, 1614, and 1621). In 1585 Thomas Sherley accompanied his brother Anthony and his father to the Low Countries, where he commanded a company of cavalry. In January 1588 he saw his only engagement. Encamped outside the walls of the city of Zwolle, Thomas's company was attacked late one evening after a day spent drinking. In the ensuing battle, only twenty horses and thirty men escaped slaughter at the hands of the Spanish. Despite the fact that Sherley's incompetence was largely to blame for this deadly fiasco, the privy council granted him an allowance to rebuild his company. Within two months Thomas had returned to England and his brother Anthony had taken command of the remnants of his company.

Sherley did not stay in England for long, for he entered service in Ireland where he was knighted by Lord Deputy William Fitzwilliam on 26 October 1589. Back in England, Sherley frequented the court, where he succumbed to the charms of a wealthy widow, Frances, Lady Stourton, the sister of Lord Cobham and sister-in-law of Robert Cecil. Although both families favoured the match, Sherley's gaze proved fickle as he met and secretly married Frances Vavasour, the daughter of Sir Thomas Vavasour, in the summer of 1591. But in order to avoid offending his father he still outwardly confessed his intentions towards Lady Stourton. However, in August 1591, while on progress with the court, the queen found out about the match and was furious. Sherley was sent to the Marshalsea prison where he remained until early 1592.

After serving in the parliament of 1593 Sherley later that year returned to the Low Countries as a captain. The increasingly acute financial difficulties of his family forced him to relinquish his command to his brother-in-law Thomas Vavasour. In 1598 he fitted out a fleet to cruise the seas in search of prizes. Spending the summer off the Portuguese coast, he succeeded in capturing four Lübeck ships, and bringing them back to Portsmouth. Although the freight was Spanish the privy council determined that because the ships belonged to a friendly port, they must be returned. Sherley likely received no return on this venture. Undeterred, he set out again late in 1598 but bad weather damaged his ships and he lost one of his prizes. He was forced to borrow money on the security of his ship in order to get home. Nor did his luck improve, for early in 1599 he captured two more ships, the contents of which the privy council deemed the property of foreign merchants resident in London; Sherley was forced to transport them to the capital and restore anything lost.

Sherley's third privateering voyage was probably his most profitable, for in early 1600 he captured two rich prizes, one of which, a merchantman loaded in the West Indies, was deemed to be good. After this he seems to have contented himself in England for a short while. In the elections to the 1601 parliament his father took the seat in Steyning which the family controlled, but Thomas was returned as MP for both Bramber and Hastings, choosing to sit for the latter.

In March 1602 Sherley returned to the seas but decided to avoid the difficulties of privateering (or piracy) on the high seas, concentrating instead on raiding coastal areas. Ten days after leaving Southampton in May, however, he was forced back to port for want of victuals. Selling four of his ships to outfit his remaining two, he proceeded to cruise the Portuguese coast, sacking two small Portuguese hamlets. According to the letter-writer John Chamberlain, when Thomas returned he hurried to court as if he had succeeded in taking Seville.

In the autumn of 1602 Sherley staked the balance of the credit he could raise from his estate on a final voyage, deciding to cruise the Mediterranean. Off Gibraltar, he took a Flemish ship but the prize proved to hold little. Over the following months his crew became mutinous and at least two of his fleet departed in the night. In February 1603 the remains of his force were driven by contrary winds to the island of Kéa, the most north-westerly of the Cyclades Islands and Ottoman territory. Under cover of darkness Sherley and his force marched on the city, where he and two other Englishmen were captured. The rest of his crew fled, setting sail without making any attempt at rescue. Without their captain, they captured a rich Venetian galleon in late February 1603, severely complicating the precarious position of Thomas's brother Anthony in Venice where the senate was unaware that the fleet was acting independently.

A month after his capture Sherley was taken to Negroponte, and late in July he was moved to Constantinople. Initially his imprisonment was wretched, but in April 1604 some money arrived from his father and he was able to purchase a chamber. However, he remained captive until 6 December 1605, when, after a direct appeal from James I, he was released. The observations he made while returning to England in the spring of 1606 form the content of his 'Discours of the Turkes'. Predictably the tone of this work befits that of one whose author had just been thirty-three months in captivity, for the first half is given over to an ethnography of the Turks which lapses into an especially virulent invective against Turkish vice and irreligion. Sherley also goes to some length to stress that a united effort by all the Christian princes of Europe might succeed in dislodging Ottoman power; this, he feels, would particularly benefit the English whose ships could be used to transport the invaders. The remainder of the work is unremarkable and details the author's passage back to England through Italy and Germany. Although not published until 1936 the pronounced similarity in its phrasing, especially in its section devoted to the origin of the Turks, suggests that Sherley's 'Discours' was one of the sources used by Anthony Nixon for his *Three English Brothers* (1607), a work perhaps owing more to the genre of panegyric than to history. In turn Nixon's work formed the basis for a short and unremarkable play, more noted

for its liveliness than its adherence to the dramatic unities, written by John Day and performed in the same year as Nixon's book was published, *The Travailes of the Three English Brothers*.

Back in England, Sherley was in gaol again by September 1607, probably for trying to interfere with the operations of the Levant Company. In August 1611 he was made a prisoner of the king's bench as an insolvent debtor. In the depths of despair he tried to poison himself in the summer of 1612. On his release he was elected to parliament for Steyning in 1614. Following the death of his first wife, Frances, at some point between 1610 and 1615, Sherley married for a second time on 2 December 1617. His new wife was a widow, Judith Taylor, the daughter of William Bennet of London, a woman whose reputation for promiscuity was a subject of gossip. With his first wife Sherley had four daughters and three sons (of whom one was the playwright Henry *Shirley, run through with a sword by Sir Edward Bishop in the course of a quarrel over debts in 1627); with his second he had a further five sons and six daughters.

In 1622, shortly before his mother's death, Sherley sold Wiston to Lionel Cranfield, earl of Middlesex, and retired to the Isle of Wight, where he lived at Cosham House, Newport, holding the position of keeper of the royal park. Still weighed down by debt, Sherley resorted to the charity of Sir John Oglander, a kinsman on his mother's side, who lent him money freely 'as his kinsman and friend', but with experience learnt wariness: 'yet I knew him to be so ill a paymaster that I was forced to make him honest by taking a pawn for my money' (Bamford, 238). According to Oglander's commonplace book Sherley died on the Isle of Wight in 1633 (on old-style dating, so between 25 March 1633 and 25 March 1634).   RICHARD RAISWELL

Sources D. W. Davies, *Elizabethans errant: the strange fortunes of Sir Thomas Sherley and his three sons* (1967) · B. Penrose, *The Sherlian odyssey* (1938) · E. P. Shirley, *Stemmata Shirleiana* (1841) · A. Nixon, *The three English brothers* (1607) · W. H. Cooke, ed., *Students admitted to the Inner Temple, 1547–1660* [1878] · T. Sherley, 'Discours of the Turkes', ed. E. Denison Ross, *Camden miscellany, XVI*, CS, 3rd ser., 52 (1936) · *A royalist's notebook: the commonplace book of Sir John Oglander*, ed. F. Bamford (1936) · *CSP Venice, 1592–1610* · *CSP dom., 1594–1625* · *APC, 1588–1631* · *HoP, Commons, 1558–1603* · M. Prestwich, *Cranfield: politics and profits under the early Stuarts* (1966)

Sherley, Thomas (*bap.* 1638, *d.* 1678), physician and natural philosopher, the son of Sir Thomas Shirley (*bap.* 1597, *d. c.*1656), of Wiston, Sussex, and his wife, Anne, daughter of Sir George Blundell, of Cardington, Bedfordshire, and grandson of Sir Thomas *Sherley (1564–1633/4), was born in the parish of St Margaret, Westminster, London, and baptized on 15 October 1638. He lived with his father in Magdalen College while the king's troops were in Oxford, and was educated at Magdalen School. It is likely that for a time between 1653 and 1656 Sherley was a pupil of Henry Oldenburg, with whom he formed a lasting friendship. While living in Wigan in 1659 he developed an interest in natural philosophy, as attested by his observations of sulphurous exhalations in Lancashire, which he subsequently published in the *Philosophical Transactions* of the Royal Society (3 June 1667). The report was criticized by

Adam Martindale (1623–1686), a preacher at Manchester, who in a letter to Oldenburg dated 4 November 1670 maintained that Sherley's paper was of little or no interest for natural history. Sherley studied medicine in France, where he took the degree of MD. He was twice married: first to Hannah, daughter of John Harfleet, of Fleet, Kent, with whom he had two daughters, Anne and Margaret. On 5 June 1667 he married Elizabeth, daughter of Captain Richard Baskett, of Apps, Isle of Wight, with whom he had two sons, Thomas and Richard, and a daughter, Elizabeth.

Sherley appears to have had a military career which ended in 1667, when he began to practise medicine in London. By 1672 he was claiming to be physician-in-ordinary to Charles II; in the same year he published his *Philosophicall essay declaring the probable causes whence stones are produced in the greater world*, dedicated to George Villiers, second duke of Buckingham. Sherley's *Essay* was not confined to the study of the generation of stones, but dealt also with the principles of natural philosophy. Sherley stated that the reading of Robert Boyle's works had encouraged him to undertake the writing of his *Essay*. Through Oldenburg, Sherley was acquainted with Boyle, whom he referred to as 'my excellent friend' (*Philosophicall Essay*, 84). Sherley's views, as contained in the *Essay*, were a combination of Jean-Baptiste van Helmont's iatrochemistry with Boyle's corpuscular philosophy. Like Helmont and Boyle, Sherley denied that fire analysis could reduce mixed bodies to the first principles, and, like other Helmontians, he searched for the alkahest—that is, the universal solvent. Sherley, who fully embraced a teleological view of nature, reinterpreted the Helmontian seminal principles to claim that they were particles of matter endowed by God with the power of producing natural bodies.

In 1675 Sherley was involved in an unsuccessful dispute with Sir John Fagg over the Wiston estate in Sussex, then worth about £3000 a year. Sherley had inherited the estate from his father, but it was granted to Sir Thomas Fagg during the civil war. When the case was decided against him in chancery, Sherley appealed to the House of Lords. As Sir John was a member of the House of Commons, Sherley was ordered into the custody of the serjeant-at-arms on 12 May 1675 for bringing an appeal in the House of Lords against a member of the lower house. The matter occasioned a dispute between the two houses.

Sherley published the following translations: *Cochlearia curiosa, or, The Curiosities of Scurvy Grass* (1676) from a work by V. A. Moellenbroek; *A Treatise of the Gout* (1676) and *Medicinal Councels* (1677), both after T. Turquet de Mayerne; and *The Curious Distillatory* (1677), after J. S. Elsholtz. Sherley said the work of translation diverted him from melancholy. He died on 5 August 1678 and was buried in the south-west vault of St Bride's Church, off Fleet Street, London.   ANTONIO CLERICUZIO

Sources Wood, *Ath. Oxon.* · E. P. Sherley, 'Sherley family', *N&Q*, 5th ser., 1 (1874), 294, 477 · *The correspondence of Henry Oldenburg*, ed. and trans. A. R. Hall and M. B. Hall, 1 (1965), 96; 3 (1966), 472–8; 7 (1970), 238 · T. Sherley, 'The description of a well, and earth in Lanchashire, taking fire by a candle approached to it', *PTRS*, 2 (1667), 482–4 · A. G. Debus, 'Thomas Sherley's "Philosophical essay" (1672): Helmontian mechanism as the basis of a new philosophy', *Ambix*, 27 (1980), 124–35 · *Eighth report*, 1, HMC, 7 (1907–9), 137, 162 · *Ninth report*, 2, HMC, 8 (1884), 56–7 · J. Ferguson, ed., *Bibliotheca chemica*, 2 (1906), 381–2 · J. L. Chester and J. Foster, eds., *London marriage licences, 1521–1869* (1887) · BL, Add. MS 22263, fols. 24–6
Archives BL, Add. MS 22263

Sherlock, (Alice) Marjorie (1891–1973). *See under* Sickert, Walter, pupils (*act.* 1890–1939).

Sherlock, Martin (*b.* before **1747**, *d.* **1797**), traveller, was a member, it is supposed, of the Kilkenny family of Sherlock. Nothing is known of his family background or of his early years. He was admitted at Trinity College, Dublin, on 1 November 1763, whence he graduated BA in 1768 and MA in 1773. About 1777 Sherlock became chaplain to Frederick Augustus Hervey, fourth earl of Bristol, and bishop of Derry, and under his patronage travelled extensively in Germany, Switzerland, and Italy between 1776 and 1778. The letters he wrote during his travels are dated from The Hague, Berlin, Dresden, Vienna, Rome, Naples, the Alps, and Ferney, where he visited Voltaire in April 1776. Twenty-seven of Sherlock's two hundred letters were published in Geneva and Paris in 1779 and in Neufchâtel in 1781 as *Lettres d'un voyageur anglois*. In the letters from Berlin, Sherlock described the Prussians as the Macedonians of Germany, but Frederick the Great, who read the book, took this in a sense complimentary to himself, and gave Sherlock an interview in Potsdam on 20 July 1779. An English translation by the Revd John Duncombe was published in London in 1780, before Sherlock's return from Europe and before it was known that he was in holy orders. A German version appeared in Leipzig in the same year. A second series of forty-four letters, *Nouvelles lettres*, was published in 1780 in Paris and London, then translated into English by Sherlock (who claimed, in the preface, that he wrote only for fame) and published in London in 1781 as *New Letters from an English Traveller*. This volume was Sherlock's first work in English and he warned the reader to be patient with his style, which, by now, was affected by writing in Italian and French. The letters contain impressions of Italy, Geneva, Lausanne, Strasbourg, Berlin, Germany, Senlis, and Paris, which he asserts that no traveller ever left without regret of some kind or another. Both volumes were well received in France and in Italy, where reviewers pointed out the originality and impartiality of Sherlock's observations, but had much less success in England than abroad. Sherlock noted the scant success the *Letters* received in England, even though, he claimed, he was forced to pay 2s. a book towards a fine binding in order to increase the prospect of their selling. If it had not been for the sale of 600 volumes in France within four weeks, Sherlock claimed, 'these books would have broken my heart' (Nichols, *Lit. anecdotes*, 8.70). Thomas Carlyle, in the last of his ten-volume *History of Friedrich II of Prussia*, quotes largely from Sherlock's *Letters* to describe the encounter between Sherlock and Voltaire. About Sherlock's volume, Carlyle comments: the book 'is now little other than a Dance of Will-o'-wisps to us. A book tawdry, incoherent, indistinct, at once flashy and opaque, full of idle and exuberances—as is the poor man himself' (Carlyle, 10.70). In the same year as the *Lettres*, Sherlock published in Naples, with some assistance from an Italian friend, the *Consiglio ad un giovane poeta*, of which Sherlock gave 400 copies to the bookseller Gregorio Settazi and instructed the marchese di Maccaroni to distribute the money arising from the sale to poor widows. The book was answered by Bassi, professor of Italian and English language in Paris, in *Observations sur les poètes italiens*, Sherlock having compared the tragic poets of Italy with Shakespeare, with little advantage to the former. Bassi defends Dante, Tasso, Ariosto, Petraica, Chiabreta, and Macini against Sherlock's observations. A portion of the *Consiglio* was translated into French by M. D. R. as *Fragment sur Shakspeare, tiré des conseils à un jeune poète*, published in Paris in 1780. An English translation from the French was published in London in 1786. The English translator, the Revd John Duncombe, claimed that Sherlock's digression on Shakespeare in the *Consiglio* is the only interesting part of the work (hence the *Fragment*). Another English version of the *Fragment*, translated by John Nichols, was republished, together with the two series of *Letters*, in London in 1802. In 1781 Sherlock wrote a volume of thirty *Letters on Several Subjects*, on subjects including Shakespeare, Richardson, Frederick the Great, Voltaire, 'Mr. Sherlock', wit, genius, taste, judgement, delicacy, the French, and women. His former works had all been dedicated to the earl of Bristol, and this was dedicated to the countess. This volume was followed in a few months by a second, dedicated to the earl of Bristol and containing thirty-nine letters.

Sherlock hoped, through the influence of the several authorities and courts he had frequented, to obtain a diplomatic post, and he was spoken of in 1781 as secretary to the embassy in Vienna. He was seen during this season in the salons of Mrs Montagu and Lady Lucan; and Horace Walpole, who was acquainted with Sherlock, wrote of him in 1780:

> I am far from guessing why Mr Sherlock does not write in his own language ... I should think everybody in this age could write best in his own ... Mr Sherlock's Italian is ten times worse than his French, and more bald. He by no means wants parts, but a good deal more judgment. (*Letters of Horace Walpole*, 8.158)

Although Sherlock was disappointed in his expectations of a diplomatic career, his merits were, in some degree, rewarded in Ireland, his native country, where he was appointed surrogate to the united dioceses of Killala and Achonry on 9 October 1781, and obtained through his friend Dr Perry, bishop of Killala, the united vicarages of Castlecomer and Kilglass (13 November 1782). In a letter dated 13 June 1781 written in Limerick to a friend in London, Sherlock complained about his living of £200 a year given by the bishop of Killala prior to Sherlock's appointment in 1781. In the letter he asks his friend to put an announcement in four newspapers stating that he was in fact receiving £400 a year. Sherlock believed that making the public know of his income would encourage the sale

of his books in England: 'the world is very apt (God bless it) to value a man's writings according to his rank and fortune' (Nichols, *Lit. anecdotes*, 8.71–2). On 24 March 1788 Sherlock was appointed by John Law (d. 1810), his last patron (bishop of Killala from 10 November 1787, and afterwards bishop of Elphin, 27 March 1795), to the rectory and vicarage of Skreen, and on 28 October in the same year he was collated to the archdeaconry of Killala. In Ireland, Sherlock felt cut off from the world and expressed his frustrations in a letter dated 21 January 1782 from Ballina:

> The Booksellers in London *have given*, and to my knowledge *do give*, very considerable annual sums to men of talents to write for them. I think I could write as well as most men who have written in prose within the century. One great advantage I have over almost all of them, not excepting Dean Swift or Dr. Johnson; I mean a superior education. (ibid., 8.75)

Sherlock died in Ireland in 1797.   SILVIA LAUZZANA

Sources M. Sherlock, *Letters from an English traveller* (1780) · M. Sherlock, *New letters from an English traveller* (1781) · Burtchaell & Sadleir, *Alum. Dubl.* · Allibone, *Dict.* · *The letters of Horace Walpole, earl of Orford*, ed. P. Cunningham, 7–8 (1858) · H. Cotton, *Fasti ecclesiae Hibernicae*, 4 (1850) · Nichols, *Lit. anecdotes*, 8.67–76 · T. Carlyle, *History of Friedrich II of Prussia, called Frederick the Great*, new edn, 13 vols. (1858–65), vol. 10, pp. 70–74 · *GM*, 1st ser., 49 (1779), 601 · *GM*, 1st ser., 50 (1780), 475 · *GM*, 1st ser., 51 (1781), 30, 132, 230. · *GM*, 1st ser., 70 (1800), 812

Sherlock, Paul (1595–1646), Jesuit and theologian, was born at Waterford on 14 August 1595, the son of Walter Sherlock and Beatrice Leonard. At the age of sixteen he followed his elder brother Patrick to Spain, and entered the Society of Jesus at Salamanca on 30 September 1612. Patrick Sherlock, who had entered the society in 1602, died at Santiago de Compostela in 1614. After studying philosophy at the Jesuit colleges of Valladolid and Santiago, Paul Sherlock was ordained priest at Santiago in 1621. He was preparing to return to Ireland when, in 1624, he was appointed to succeed Thomas White as rector of the Irish College at Santiago, a post which he held until 1628. Subsequently he was rector of the Irish College at Salamanca from 1629 until his death. He was a reluctant rector: both colleges were chronically short of funds, and administration was a burden to him.

Sherlock's lifelong passion was for patristic and scriptural scholarship, which bore fruit in an extended devotional commentary on the Song of Solomon in three folio volumes, *Anteloquia in Salomonis Canticum Canticorum*, later volumes *Cogitationes in Salomonis Canticum Canticorum* (Lyons, 1633–40). This magnum opus was reprinted at Venice in 1641, and Sherlock's earnings, together with a generous subsidy from Fernando de Vera, bishop of Cuzco, enabled him to purchase a large library, ownership of which was disputed after his death between the Jesuits of Salamanca and the Irish College. In 1644, under the semi-pseudonym Paulus Leonardus (using his mother's maiden name) and omitting to declare his membership of the Society of Jesus, he published at Lyons *Responsio ad expostulationes recentium theologorum*, a defence of the Molinist doctrine of *scientia media* against its Dominican critics. Discussion of Molina's attempt to reconcile divine foreknowledge with human free will was at the time officially proscribed by Rome. The work was dedicated to Juan de Palafox, bishop of Puebla and virtual viceroy of Mexico, who was a benefactor of the Irish College. Three years later (1647) Palafox was to become embroiled in a bitter dispute with the Society of Jesus.

The strains of office and a lifelong regime of austerity and self-mortification undermined Sherlock's health. He died at the Irish College, Salamanca, on 8 August 1646, and was buried at Salamanca. The first volume of his unfinished treatise on the creation, *Antiquitatum Hebraicarum dioptra*, was published posthumously at Lyons in 1651 on the initiative of Luke Wadding, another Waterford man and former rector of the Irish College, Salamanca, to whom the work was dedicated by the publishers. Sherlock's brief manuscript autobiography, relating the principal events of his life up to 1645, was published for the first time in 1917.　　　　　　　　　G. MARTIN MURPHY

Sources 'El P. Paulo Sherlock: una autobiografía inédita', ed. A. Huarte, *Archivium Hibernicum*, 6 (1917), 156–74 · A. de Backer and others, *Bibliothèque de la Compagnie de Jésus*, new edn, 7, ed. C. Sommervogel (Brussels, 1896) · J. E. de Uriarte, *Catálogo razonado de obras anónimas y seudónimas de autores de la Compañía de Jesús*, 5 vols. (1904–16), 2.89, 3.384
Archives Salamanca University, MSS

Sherlock, Richard (1612–1689), Church of England clergyman, was born at Oxton, a township on the Cheshire Wirral on 11 November 1612, and was baptized at the parish church of Woodchurch four days later. Although his father, William Sherlock, a small yeoman, died while he was young his mother was determined to give him a good education. A stint at Magdalen Hall, Oxford, when he was aged only fourteen, proved both premature and expensive, and he was transferred to Trinity College, Dublin, where he proceeded MA in 1633. He remained in Ireland as minister of several small parishes until the rebellion of 1641. In September 1643, when the royalist leader the marquess of Ormond made a truce with the confederates and sent over some regiments to help Charles I against the parliamentarian forces, Sherlock returned to England as an army chaplain, but was soon captured in the royalist defeat at Nantwich, Cheshire. When released he returned to Oxford, where he became chaplain of the governor of the royal garrison and then a chaplain of New College, and in 1646, for sermons he had preached at court or before the royalist parliament at Oxford, he was awarded the degree of BD.

Ejected from the university by the parliamentary visitors about 1648 Sherlock became chaplain to Jasper Mayne in nearby Cassington, where he lodged with the mother of Anthony Wood, the antiquary. When Mayne in turn was ejected Sherlock returned north, in 1652, and became chaplain to Sir Robert Bindloss, a royalist baronet who lived at Borwick Hall, near Lancaster. There he was active on two fronts: reproving his patron for his 'love of company and many of the evils that attend it' (Wilson, xxiv) and engaging in debates with the local Quakers. In 1654 Sherlock published *The Quakers wilde questions objected against the ministers of the gospel … with brief answers thereunto*

and a discourse on the operation of the Holy Spirit. After a reply by Richard Hubberthorne, Sherlock reprinted this work late in 1655 (though the title page says 1656), with two additional discourses on divine revelation and error, and thus incurred the wrath of George Fox (who attacked him in *The Great Mystery of the Great Whore Unfolded*, 1659, 242–3).

Sherlock was introduced to Charles Stanley, eighth earl of Derby, who made him his chaplain at Latham, and at the Restoration nominated him to Winwick rectory in Lancashire. The earl also placed Sherlock on an eight-man commission to settle all matters ecclesiastical and civil on the Isle of Man. Having done so 'to the entire satisfaction of the lord and people of that island' (Wilson, xxvi), and been awarded a DD by Trinity College, Dublin, Sherlock finally gained full possession of Winwick, one of the richest livings in England, in 1662, and held it to his death there on 20 June 1689.

Sherlock repaid his patron's generosity by a long ministry of exemplary piety, diligence, and charity that is described fully by two who knew him well, Thomas Wilson (his nephew and curate, and future bishop of Sodor and Man) and Thomas Crane (a friend and local minister). Sherlock's dedication is also revealed in the text of his publications and his will. He was personally very abstemious, fasted regularly, prostrated himself in his private chapel, prayed almost constantly, even in the middle of the night and in company, and daily contemplated death and eternity (leading to his *Practical Meditations upon the Four Last Things*, published posthumously in 1692). For nearly thirty years he was almost perpetually in residence, reading morning and evening prayer daily in church, and constantly preaching 'plain and practical sermons'. He kept at least three curates for the service of the church and chapels in his large parish, so that Winwick 'became a very desirable place for young divines to improve themselves in the work of the ministry' (Wilson, xxvi–xxvii). He was a 'pattern of good works' (Crane, 26), daily ministering to the needy, prisoners, and those in distress. He contributed much to the setting up of a stock of bread and cloth for the poor of his parish, the capital for which was topped up to £300 on his death. His will and inventory show that he had regularly lent sums to the 'miserably poor' with little or no prospect of repayment; he also bequeathed over £100 to the poor of various parishes with which he had been associated, and money to finish the setting up of a free school at Warrington. The only personal item of value listed in the inventory was his library, valued at £64 14s. od. He commissioned his own gravestone for Winwick church, describing himself as 'the most unworthy rector of this church', and ordered it to be placed in the chancel where it would be regularly trampled under foot (will and inventory, Lancs. RO, WCW Richard Sherlock 1689). With no wife and children to look to, Sherlock's bequests to individuals were largely spread among his cousins, nephews, brothers-in-law, and steward and their families.

Two other features struck contemporaries. One was Sherlock's very strict observance of the established church's canons and his insistence on full and decent uniformity in public worship, which were reflected in his *The Irregularitie of a Private Prayer in a Publick Congregation* (1674) and *Several Short, but Seasonable Discourses Touching Common and Private Prayer* (1684). The other was his constant campaign to raise the levels of knowledge and commitment of his parishioners through catechizing and handing out free copies of his own publications. *Principles of Holy Christian Religion* had been written for the Bindloss household in the 1650s and consisted of a paraphrase of the prayer book catechism with extra questions and answers, and prayers. But it proved so useful not only in Winwick but elsewhere too that it sold nineteen editions in England between 1656 and 1699, and was also published in Welsh and in America. *Mercurius Christianus* (1673) or as it was thereafter called *The Practical Christian* was designed as its successor for his Winwick parishioners—the practice to go with the doctrine, explained in plain words that all could understand. Much enlarged in later editions, this work consisted of prayers, meditations, psalms, and hymns, and a treatise on how to examine oneself for sin. To the sixth edition, published in 1713, Thomas Wilson added a life of his mentor, and noted that the impact of the works on Winwick had been visible in the great number of 'constant, devout communicants, as at that time were hardly to be seen in any parish in England' (Wilson, xxvi).

A portrait of Sherlock, in cap, bands, and gown, holding a copy of his *Practical Christian* in his right hand, still hangs in Winwick church. An engraving from this was inserted in some copies of this work.   IAN GREEN

Sources T. Wilson, 'Life of Dr Sherlock', in R. Sherlock, *Practical Christian*, ed. H. H. Sherlock (1841) · T. Crane, *Job's assurance of the resurrection* (1690) · Wood, *Ath. Oxon.*, new edn, 1.259–62 · R. Sherlock, correspondence with Anthony Wood, Bodl. Oxf., MS Wood F. 44, fols. 216, 218–19 · J. Keble, *The life of the right reverend father in God, Thomas Wilson*, 2 vols. (1863) · ESTC · will, Lancs. RO, WCW Richard Sherlock 1689 · letter of Thomas Mullory, 1661, BL, Add. MS 4293, fol. 98 · MS dedicated to Richard Sherlock by Robert Maudsley, BL, Sloane MS 1051, sig. 2r · DNB
Likenesses M. Vandergucht, line engraving, BM, NPG; repro. in R. Sherlock, *The practical Christian*, 6th edn (1713) · portrait, Winwick parish church, Lancashire
Wealth at death approx. £1500: will, 1689, Lancs. RO, WCW Richard Sherlock

Sherlock, Thomas

Sherlock, Thomas (1677–1761), bishop of London, was born in London on 20 November 1677, the son of William *Sherlock (1639/40–1707), subsequently master of the Temple and dean of St Paul's, and his wife, Elizabeth Gardner (d. 1715?). He was baptized on 16 December. In 1689, as a King's scholar, Sherlock entered Eton College (where he became known as a strong swimmer). He was admitted pensioner at St Catharine's College, Cambridge, in January 1694 and matriculated in 1695. He took the degrees of BA (1698), MA (1701), and DD (1714), and was elected a fellow of St Catharine's in 1698.

Sherlock was presented to the living of Therfield, Hertfordshire, in 1702. When, in 1705, his father resigned the mastership of the Temple, he succeeded him, following

Thomas Sherlock (1677–1761), by James Macardell, 1757 (after Jean Baptiste van Loo, 1740)

which he became famous as a preacher and only surrendered the position in 1753. His career advanced rapidly thereafter. In 1711 he was appointed chaplain to Queen Anne, and in 1713 a prebendary of St Paul's. From 1714 to 1719 he was master of St Catharine's, Cambridge, and in 1714–15 was vice-chancellor of the university, in which capacity he upheld certain university privileges *vis-à-vis* the claims of the archdeacon of Ely, Richard Bentley. He now displayed his support for the Hanoverian dynasty. In *A Sermon Preach'd at the Temple-Church* he told his audience to show 'a cheerful and steddy Obedience to the Prince whom God has set over us' (p. 23). The following year he was selected to preach before the Commons on the thanksgiving for the Jacobite rising's suppression, and argued '[i]f … we have any Concern for the Peace and Happiness of our Country … we must detest this Rebellion, and with sincere Hearts adore the Goodness of God, who hath wrought this Deliverance for us' (T. Sherlock, *A Sermon Preach'd before the Honourable House of Commons*, 18). In November 1715 Sherlock had been made dean of Chichester but he was ambitious for a bishopric. He became bishop of Bangor in 1728 but observed, in a letter to Thomas Gooch, ''Tis a pity the Bprick shou'd only be a bridge to a better' (Carpenter, 27). He was promoted to Salisbury in 1734 and, in 1748, raised to London, the see which he held until his death in 1761.

By upbringing and conviction Sherlock was a tory. For this reason Edmund Gibson, bishop of London, had no wish to advance him in the church. Sherlock was, however, perfectly willing to work with the royal family.

Under George I he cultivated the favour of the prince of Wales and of Princess Caroline; it was therefore natural for the latter to support Sherlock's elevation to Bangor, after her husband's accession, and his subsequent appointment to Salisbury. None the less relations with Queen Caroline cooled after Sherlock's opposition to the Quakers Tithe Bill and, following her death in 1737, his standing at court waned.

Sherlock took his political duties seriously though, as time went on, his attendance in the Lords declined. In parliament he was occasionally willing to speak on secular as well as religious subjects, and the duke of Newcastle valued his opinions. He supported Sir Robert Walpole's ministry over the pension bill (1731) and the South Sea inquiry (1733). However, he opposed the ecclesiastical courts and mortmain bills, and joined with Gibson in opposing the Quakers Tithe Bill (1736), in respect of which he produced a pamphlet, *The Country Parson's Plea*. He supported Walpole in the difficult early period of the War of the Austrian Succession, in 1745 he preached against the Jacobite rising, and he entered the debate on the treatment of the highlands following the rising's suppression. He could be forceful in debate. In 1743 he described the Spirituous Liquors Bill as 'the most unchristian Bill that was ever thought of by any government' and therefore concluded: 'I think it incumbent upon me as a christian bishop, to give my testimony against it in the most open and express manner I can' (Cobbett, *Parl. Hist.*, 12, 1743, 1236).

It was regrettable that Sherlock's elevation to the episcopate came so late in life since, as his remaining years passed, he became increasingly incapable of discharging his duties effectively. He went to Bangor and, except in 1731 and 1734, held ordinations in the cathedral. He also enforced the duty of residence through the consistory court. While bishop of Salisbury he lived in the city during the summer and annually held an ordination—and in some years two or more ordinations—at his palace. He conducted a visitation in 1736, of which the *Old Whig* reported that he 'obliged the Clergy throughout his Diocese to make a competent Provision for their Curates; and not only so, but had strictly enjoin'd the *Non-Residents*, hence forward to see to it that they do *reside* on their respective Cures' (23 Sept 1736).

In the 1740s Sherlock's health deteriorated. In the 1750s he became increasingly sick, having suffered 'a very dangerous Illness, from which indeed he recovered, but with almost the total Loss of the Use of his Limbs … [with] soon after his Speech failing him' (Nicolls, 25). In 1754 Edmund Pyle was appalled at his condition, and in 1755 he appeared near death. He ordained until June 1753 but thereafter other bishops had to undertake this duty for him. In 1759 he produced a charge to the London clergy, which was printed and which denounced non-residence. If a living were neglected, 'the People of the Parish, who are religiously disposed, will probably go to the Meeting-house, if there be one near; those who are not religiously disposed, will probably go to the Ale-house' (T. Sherlock, *A Charge Delivered to the Clergy, at a Visitation Held for the Diocese of London*, 36). It caused some controversy since Sherlock himself had been so obvious a pluralist.

On his promotion to London in 1748, Sherlock became alarmed about the see's oversight of the American colonies. He was, he observed in 1752, 'bishop of a vast country, without power, or influence, or any means of promoting true religion: sequestered from the people over whom I have the care, and must never hope to see' (Taylor, 'Whigs, bishops and America', 337). He suggested that the work should be split among several English bishops but then concluded that the establishment of a resident American episcopate would serve the church's interests more effectively, maintaining that it would be 'the glory of my life, if I c'd be the instrument … of putting the Ch. abroad upon a true and primitive foot' (ibid., 341). He produced his 'Considerations … relating to ecclesiastical government in America' (LPL, Fulham MSS, 4, fol. 273) but, while the bishops wanted the reform, the government proved unwilling to support it in case it engendered religious strife. To Sherlock's dismay the ministers killed it by prevaricating and then letting the matter drop.

Sherlock was greatly concerned about the social and moral problems of his age. He saw drunkenness as a great social evil, hence his opposition to the Spirituous Liquors Bill, which he believed would facilitate excessive drinking. In his *Letter … on Occasion of the Late Earthquakes* (1750) he denounced idleness and frivolous activities. Wanting moral regeneration, he maintained:

> Blasphemy and horrid Imprecations domineer in our Streets, and poor Wretches are every Hour wantonly and wickedly calling for Damnation on themselves and others, which may be ('tis much to be feared) too near them already. Add to this the Lewdness and Debauchery that prevail amongst the lowest People, which keeps them idle, poor, and miserable. (pp. 7–8)

He also wished to suppress blasphemous or lewd books.

Imbued with traditional views Sherlock was a formidable controversialist. At the time of the Bangorian controversy he was chosen as chairman of the lower house of convocation's committee to report on Bishop Benjamin Hoadly's sermon, and he entered into the pamphlet war on the issues. In 1718 he produced his *Vindication of the Corporation and Test Acts*, which defended the established church's privileges. He was deeply disturbed by the growth of non-traditional and deist ideas; in two of his books, *The Use and Intent of Prophecy* (1725) and *The Tryal of the Witnesses of the Resurrection of Jesus* (1729), he countered such positions, arguing the traditional case with great clarity. The former work discussed the Old Testament prophecies relating to Christ, and adopted a liberal, rather than a literal, interpretation. And in *The Tryal*, by using conventional and accepted methods of cross-examination and historical investigation, Sherlock sought to prove the veracity of the scriptural accounts of Christ's resurrection. 'His Zeal was warm and fervent in explaining the great Doctrines and Duties of Christianity, and in maintaining and establishing it upon the most solid and sure Foundations', Samuel Nicolls stated in his memorial sermon. 'Witness those Discourses written purposely in

Defence of Christianity, in which the Argument for the Truth of the Christian Religion is carried to its utmost Height' (Nicolls, 28–9). Sherlock's *Letter … on Occasion of the Late Earthquakes* sold in prodigious numbers. In addition many of his sermons and the discourses that he preached at the Temple Church were published.

Sherlock married Judith Fountayne, of a Yorkshire family, in 1707; she survived him and died in 1764. They had no children. According to Samuel Nicolls, '[n]o Man was ever more happy in domestic Life, and no one could shew greater Gentleness, Good-nature and Affection to all around him' (Nicolls, 30–31), though it was also noted, in the *Gentleman's Magazine* for 1773, that '[h]e could bear no opposition in his own house' (p. 385). His portrait at St Catharine's College, Cambridge, shows a man of elegant appearance, intelligent and commanding, with astute eyes and delicate fingers. In later prints his appearance is solemn, his face full. The *Gentleman's Magazine* observed: '[h]is aspect was rather austere, heavy, and forbidding; but, when he was pleased and smiled, he shewed the most amiable change of features' (ibid.). As for his voice:

[though it] was not melodious, but accompanied rather with a Thickness of Speech, yet were his Words uttered with so much Propriety, and with such Strength and Vehemence, that he never failed to take Possession of his whole Audience, and secure their Attention.   (Nicolls, 22)

His later life was dogged by gout and mounting ill health; on this account he declined the see of York and that of Canterbury, in 1743 and 1747 respectively. He died on 18 July 1761 and was buried in Fulham churchyard. He left most of his fortune of £140,000 to his wife and to his nephew Sir Thomas Gooch, and his library to St Catharine's, Cambridge.

Sherlock owed his advancement to his personal abilities, his steadfast religious convictions, his connections, and his shrewd and flexible political behaviour. It is revealing that, in the age of the whig supremacy, the Church of England, backed by the political establishment, could accommodate in its highest echelons a man with both a tory political outlook and high clerical views.

COLIN HAYDON

Sources parish register, London, St George, Botolph Lane, GL, microfilm 4793 · Lincs. Arch., PD 1702/42 · will, 1761, PRO, PROB 11/867 · S. Nicolls, *A sermon preached at the Temple Church, on Sunday, November 15, 1761* (1762) · *GM*, 1st ser., 43 (1773), 385–6 · A. Hartshorne, ed., *Memoirs of a royal chaplain, 1729–1763* (1905) · *The Old Whig: or, the Consistent Protestant*, 81 (23 Sept 1736) · Cobbett, *Parl. hist.*, 12.1236 · E. Carpenter, *Thomas Sherlock, 1678–1761* (1936) · S. Taylor, 'Whigs, bishops and America: the politics of church reform in mid eighteenth-century England', *HJ*, 36 (1993), 331–56 · S. Taylor, 'Sir Robert Walpole, the Church of England, and the Quakers Tithe Bill of 1736', *HJ*, 28 (1985), 51–77 · S. Taylor, 'The bishops at Westminster in the mid-eighteenth century', *A pillar of the constitution: the House of Lords in British politics, 1640–1784*, ed. C. Jones (1989), 137–63 · W. Sterry, ed., *The Eton College register, 1441–1698* (1943) · E. B. Fryde and others, eds., *Handbook of British chronology*, 3rd edn, Royal Historical Society Guides and Handbooks, 2 (1986) · G. Hennessy, *Novum repertorium ecclesiasticum parochiale Londinense, or, London diocesan clergy succession from the earliest time to the year 1898* (1898) · Venn, *Alum. Cant.*

Archives CUL, collections relating to University of Cambridge lands, privileges, and property · Wilts. & Swindon RO, corresp.

and MSS relating to Salisbury | BL, corresp. with Lord Hardwicke, Add. MSS 35586–35909, *passim* · BL, corresp. with duke of Newcastle, Add. MSS 32688–32917, *passim* · LPL, Fulham MSS, American corresp., London diocesan administration MSS, and MSS · Yale U., Farmington, Lewis Walpole Library, letters to Edward Weston

Likenesses Lelius, mezzotint, 1737 (after 'Jones'), BM, NPG · S. F. Ravenet, line engraving, 1756 (after J. Vanderbank), BM, NPG · J. Macardell, mezzotint, 1757 (after J. B. van Loo, 1740), BM [*see illus.*] · Jones, oils, St Catharine's College, Cambridge · J. Vanderbank, oils, St Catharine's College, Cambridge · J. Vanderbank, oils, Fulham Palace, London

Wealth at death £140,000: Carpenter, *Thomas Sherlock*

Sherlock, William (1639/40–1707), Church of England clergyman and religious controversialist, was born in Gravel Lane, Southwark, London, the son of a tradesman. He was educated at St Mary Overie, Southwark, and from about 1653 at Eton College, and was admitted to Peterhouse, Cambridge, as a pensioner under William Falkner on 19 May 1657, aged seventeen. He was elected scholar in 1658, graduated BA in 1660, and MA in 1663. Sherlock spent some years without a steady position in the church, and, if later allegations by Robert South were true, may have been a dissenting preacher, but on 3 August 1669 he was collated as rector of St George's, Botolph Lane, London. This position enabled him to marry Elizabeth Gardner (*d.* 1715?) on 8 February 1673, at the Charterhouse Chapel; her father, whose first name may have been William, lived in the parish of St Andrew Undershaft, London.

Rise of a controversial divine Sherlock's first publication, *The Knowledge of Jesus Christ, and Union with Him* (1674) was aimed at the Independent divine John Owen, who asserted that God's mercy could be known only through Christ. Sherlock's ridicule of this position brought a reply from Owen in which he was supported by several other dissenters, including Thomas Danson, Edward Polhil, and Vincent Alsop. Sherlock answered in *A Defence and Continuation of the Discourse* (1675). This controversy, in which Sherlock's position was attacked by some dissenters as moralist, gave expression to the theological differences between dissenters and Anglicans, although many Anglicans held Calvinist opinions and many dissenters were moralist. One counter-attack was Robert Ferguson's *The Interest of Reason in Religion* (1675) to which Sherlock and Joseph Glanvill, another of Ferguson's targets, replied in *An Account of Mr Ferguson his Common-Place-Book* (1675), ignoring Ferguson's arguments but charging him with extensive plagiarism of Glanvill and other authors. Sherlock attacked Owen again in the anonymous *A Discourse about Church Unity* (1681). *The Case of Resistance to the Supreme Powers* (1684) defended the doctrine of passive obedience. In 1684 he also edited and published William Falkner's *Two Treatises* with his own dedication to the archbishop of Canterbury, William Sancroft.

Sherlock's controversial works accompanied his steady rise in London's clerical world. He became the fourth assistant at Sion College in 1673, rising to second assistant the following year. He was senior dean at Sion in 1680 and served a one-year term as president in 1683. Sherlock received his DD in 1680 and the prebend of St Pancras at St

Paul's Cathedral on 3 November 1681. He also received a lecturership at St Dunstan's and in 1685 he became master of the Temple in succession to Richard Ball, with the use of a house and an annual salary of £100 from the Inner Temple, £70 in lieu of chambers from the Middle Temple, and £37 6s. 8d. from the crown.

Sherlock was a leader among the brilliant group of London divines including Thomas Tenison, William Clagett, and Simon Patrick who carried on the literary defence of the Church of England against Catholicism from late in the reign of Charles II into that of James II. Sherlock's *Protestant Resolution of Faith*, first published in 1683, was republished in 1685, 1686, and 1687, at the height of the struggle under James. Sherlock's concern over James's Catholicism was voiced early in the reign, in a sermon preached before the House of Commons on 29 May 1685, the anniversary of the restoration of the monarchy in 1660. Sherlock attacked Catholicism as tending to disloyalty, while asserting his faith in James personally. The Commons voted Sherlock their thanks and ordered the sermon published. It went through two editions in 1685. In 1686 he was appointed a chaplain to James II.

Sherlock was a prolific author of anti-Catholic publications in James's reign. Of these, the two-part *A Preservative Against Popery* (1688) provided simple versions of the main protestant arguments, enabling ordinary protestants without theological training to defend themselves against Catholic claims. It went through several editions and provoked a response from the Jesuit polemicist Lewis Sabran, *An Answer to Dr Sherlock's Preservative against Popery* (1688). Sherlock replied in *A Vindication of the Preservative* (1688). Several of Sherlock's anti-Catholic writings became part of the canon of eighteenth-century anti-Catholicism by their inclusion in Edmund Gibson's collection, *Preservative Against Popery*. Sherlock, like most of his allies, continued to uphold the doctrine of passive obedience, but refused to read the declaration of indulgence in 1687, by which James granted freedom of worship to non-Anglican Christians. Sherlock feared losing his lucrative position at the Temple and asked the nonconformist minister John Howe what Howe would do if he were offered the position. He was reassured to hear that Howe would take it, but resign the emoluments to Sherlock. Sherlock's house was the meeting place for some bishops and London clergy on 11 May 1688, where they considered responses to the declaration.

The oaths Sherlock's conduct following the revolution of 1688 was disastrous to his reputation, if not his career. At first he took a very high-church line, opposing compromises with the dissenters for a more comprehensive church and publishing *A Letter to a Member of the convention* (1689), which called for James's recall upon conditions. A meeting of the clergy at Ely House on 21 January 1689 saw an argument between Sherlock and William of Orange's leading clerical supporter, Gilbert Burnet. (Burnet had earlier included Sherlock in a list of ten Church of England clergy which he recommended to William.) After some hesitation Sherlock refused to take the oaths to William and Mary, and was reckoned a leading nonjuror. He

attempted to persuade others to follow his example, with some success. When the day arrived for the suspension of nonjurors, 1 August 1689, he did not preach.

On 2 February 1690, the day after the day fixed for deprivation, Sherlock stunned ecclesiastical London by preaching at St Dunstan's and praying for William and Mary as *de facto* sovereigns. At this time he was still not intending to take the oaths. Sherlock was deprived of his position at the Temple, and paid for preachers there out of his own pocket. Shortly after his prayer for the king and queen Sherlock's continuing opposition to the oaths led to a break with Robert South, with whom he had gone over the arguments for and against swearing. In a letter addressed to South on 17 February 1690 Sherlock attacked South for circulating a paper which Sherlock had written supporting taking the oaths, and also ridiculed South's own arguments for taking them. South wrote a scorching reply, breaking off friendly relations.

By the spring Sherlock began withdrawing from his opposition to the oaths, and he took them that August. Sherlock claimed that he had been convinced by canon 28 in the convocation book of John Overall, bishop of Coventry and Lichfield and of Norwich in the reign of James I, which had been published the previous month. This canon endorsed praying for *de facto* sovereigns. Sherlock's claim, made in the preface to his defence of his action, *The Case of the Allegiance due to Sovereign Powers* (dated 1691, but actually published late in 1690) convinced few, although the book was extremely popular, going through six editions. Sherlock's yielding was widely credited to his belief that the Stuart cause was irretrievable after the battle of the Boyne in July, or to the influence of his wife. Elizabeth Sherlock was nearly as much reviled as her husband, being compared to Xanthippe, the shrewish wife of Socrates, and Eve who tempted Adam. Whatever Sherlock's motivations, his career did not seem to suffer. He was restored as master of the Temple, where he remained until 1705, and on 15 June 1691 he was installed as dean of St Paul's, in succession to John Tillotson. The Temple reimbursed him for the expense of the preachers he had hired in his period of deprivation. He also became a chaplain to the king and queen in 1691.

Sherlock's argument for *de facto* obedience, made in *The Case of the Allegiance due to Sovereign Powers*, exposed him to attack from both the nonjurors, who regarded him as a traitor and timeserver, and the whigs, who found his acceptance of William and Mary grudging at best. Whigs also believed that Sherlock's identification of the right of William and Mary as exclusively *de facto* meant that the liberties of Englishmen were now without legal foundation. One of the most effective among many nonjuring replies was John Kettlewell's anonymous *The duty of allegiance settled upon its true grounds, in answer to a late book of Dr Will. Sherlock, entitled 'The case of the allegiance due to sovereign powers'* (1691), while the Revd Samuel Johnson, a whig, published *Remarks upon Dr Sherlock's Book, Intituled, 'The Case of the Allegiance due to Sovereign Powers'* (1690). Sherlock responded to his nonjuring opponents in *The Case of Allegiance due to Sovereign Powers, Further Consider'd, and Defended* (1691).

Practical divinity Sherlock's most frequently reprinted books were not his controversial works but works of religious exposition addressed to a broad Christian audience. During his brief nonjuring period Sherlock published what would be the most frequently reprinted of all his books, *A Practical Discourse Concerning Death* (1689), originally intended as a series of sermons to be given at the Temple, but which Sherlock was unable to preach before he was deprived. It became one of the most popular religious books of the seventeenth and eighteenth centuries, and in addition to many subsequent editions, was published in a Welsh translation by Thomas Williams in 1691 and an anonymous French translation in 1693. The *Practical Discourse* argued that, as human beings were naturally motivated towards pleasure, the superiority of the Christian life could be proved in these terms. The spiritual existence of the human soul was infinitely longer than that of the body, and the pains and pleasures of the soul were correspondingly larger than those which could be experienced by the flesh. Consequently the expectation of pleasure could act as an incentive towards a religious existence on earth. *A Practical Discourse Concerning a Future Judgement* received two editions in 1692, and was also reprinted on several occasions. It was followed in 1694 by *A Discourse Concerning the Divine Providence* and in 1704 by *A Discourse Concerning the Happiness of Good Men*.

The trinitarian controversy Sherlock entered another important theological controversy in 1690, that over Socinianism, the denial of the divine nature of Jesus Christ. Sherlock had been working on trinitarian issues for some time, and intended his *Vindication of the Doctrine of the Holy and Ever Blessed Trinity* (1690) to be a major contribution. He put forth a new interpretation of the Trinity as three persons united by a mutual consciousness. Sherlock was one of the first English thinkers to use extensively the concept of consciousness, in which he may have been influenced by John Turner's *A Discourse Concerning the Messias* (1685). But trinitarian issues were always fraught with danger, and some thought that the vigour of Sherlock's attack on Socinianism had brought him to the opposite error of tritheism, the making of the Trinity into three separate gods. Among those was South, who now saw an opportunity to express his scorn of Sherlock. South's anonymous *Animadversions on Dr Sherlock's Book* (1693) was crushing. Sherlock replied with the anonymous *Defence of Dr Sherlock's Notion* (1694), which South answered in *Tritheism Charged upon Dr Sherlock's Notion* (1695). Other leading English theologians and philosophers involved in the controversy were John Wallis, Richard Burthogge, Edward Stillingfleet, and Francis Gastrell. On the continent Gottfried Wilhelm Leibniz spoke of Sherlock with great respect, and deplored the harshness of South's attack, while agreeing that Sherlock had come very close to tritheism.

Whatever the merits of his case Sherlock got the worst of the dispute. Joseph Bingham's Oxford sermon following Sherlock on the Trinity provoked condemnation of its doctrine by the hebdomadal council as 'false, impious and heretical' on 25 November 1695. Sherlock responded with *A Modest Examination of the Authority and Reasons of the Late Decree* (1696), but the controversy ended after William III, prompted by Thomas Tenison, then archbishop of Canterbury, gave directions, addressed to the Church of England hierarchy, forbidding the use of new terms relating to the Trinity on 3 February 1696. Sherlock's sermon *The Danger of Corrupting the Faith by Philosophy*, preached before the lord mayor and aldermen of London on 25 April 1697, and his *The Present State of the Socinian Controversy* (1698) mark his retreat.

Last years In 1698 Sherlock was appointed rector of Therfield, Hertfordshire, in succession to William Holder. The living was in the gift of the dean and chapter of St Paul's. Much of his later career was devoted to advancing his eldest son Thomas *Sherlock (1677–1761), who succeeded his father as rector of Therfield in 1702 and as master of the Temple in 1705. A younger son, John, entered the law, being admitted to the bar at the Inner Temple on 2 July 1704. Mary Sherlock, one of Sherlock's two daughters, married Dr Thomas Gooch [see Gooch, Sir Thomas, second baronet], the future bishop of Ely, in 1717. William Sherlock continued to defend publicly what he regarded as Church of England orthodoxy. *The New Danger of Presbytery* (1703), a reply to Charles Trimnell's *A Vindication of the Proceedings of some Members of the Lower House of the Last Convocation*, attacked high-church zealotry, while *The Scripture Proofs of our Saviour's Divinity* (1706) rebutted Bishop Edward Fowler's *A Discourse of the Descent of the Man-Christ Jesus from Heaven* (1706). Neither had the success of Sherlock's earlier writings or was reprinted. Sherlock's collected sermons, first published in 1700 as *Sermons Preach'd on Several Occasions*, were issued three times in the eighteenth century, and translated into German in 1744. William Sherlock died at Hampstead, Middlesex, on 19 June 1707, and was buried in St Paul's Cathedral. WILLIAM E. BURNS

Sources *DNB* · W. M. T. Dodds, 'Robert South and William Sherlock: some unpublished letters', *Modern Language Review*, 39 (1944), 215–24 · *ESTC* · J. Spurr, *The Restoration Church of England, 1646–1689* (1991) · E. Gee, *The catalogue of all the discourses published against popery, during the reign of King James II* (1689) · F. A. Inderwick and R. A. Roberts, eds., *A calendar of the Inner Temple records*, 3 (1901) · C. F. Mullet, 'A case of allegiance: William Sherlock and the revolution of 1688', *Huntington Library Quarterly*, 10 (1946–7), 83–103 · G. Reedy, *Robert South, 1634–1716: an introduction to his life and sermons* (1992) · M. R. Antognazza, 'Inediti Leibniziani sulle polemiche Trinitarie', *Rivista di Filosofia Neo-scholastica*, 83 (1991), 525–45 · U. Thiel, 'The Trinity and human personal identity', *English philosophy in the age of Locke*, ed. M. A. Stewart (2000), 217–43 · T. E. S. Clarke and H. C. Foxcroft, *A life of Gilbert Burnet, bishop of Salisbury* (1907) · E. Carpenter, *Thomas Sherlock, 1678–1762* (1936) · E. H. Pearce, *Sion College and Library* (1913) · C. J. Sommerville, *Popular religion in Restoration England* (Gainesville, 1977) · Venn, *Alum. Cant.* · W. Sterry, ed., *The Eton College register, 1441–1698* (1943) · T. A. Walker, ed., *Admissions to Peterhouse or St Peter's College in the University of Cambridge* (1912)
Archives LPL, sermon notebooks
Likenesses R. White, line engraving, 1694, BM, NPG; repro. in W. Sherlock, *A discourse on the divine providence* (1694)

Sherlock, William (*c*.1738–1806), portrait painter and engraver, is said to have been born in Dublin, the son of a fencing master and prize-fighter. In 1759 he was a student in the St Martin's Lane Academy in London, also obtaining a premium from the Society of Arts for figure drawing in the same year and a second in 1760 for engraving. He studied engraving with J. P. Le Bas in Paris in 1761. While there he engraved a large plate of *The Grange*, after J. Pillement, published in 1761. He also engraved the portrait heads for T. G. Smollett's *A Complete History of England* (4 vols., 1757–8; 11 vols., 1758–60). From 1764 Sherlock began exhibiting small portraits, in both oil and watercolours, and miniatures. He was elected a fellow of the Society of Antiquaries in 1771, and became their director in 1774, exhibiting with them until 1777. On 5 October 1775 he married Frances Welker at the Old Church, St Pancras, London. Between 1796 and 1806 he exhibited twenty-five paintings at the Royal Academy. A self-portrait in miniature by Sherlock of 180(5) was sold at Christies (12 July 1988, lot 206, repr.). His *Portrait of Sawrey Gilpin* is in the National Portrait Gallery, and three of his miniatures are in the Victoria and Albert Museum, London. Joseph Farington noted in his diary on 21 February 1799 that 'Sherlock quite broke down sold out of funds' (Farington, *Diary*, 4.1162). He also recorded being informed of Sherlock's death in London in an entry on 14 December 1806 (ibid., 8.2926). From 1813 to 1821 Farington administered Royal Academy donations to a 'Mrs Sherlock'.

Sherlock's son **William Pengree Sherlock** (*b.* 1775) was baptized on 20 August 1776 at St Marylebone, Marylebone Road, Middlesex. He also practised as an artist. He entered the Royal Academy Schools on 31 December 1794, aged nineteen, and then exhibited there from 1801 to 1810, sending a few portraits, but principally watercolour landscapes. He drew most of the illustrations to W. Dickinson's *Antiquities historical, architectural, chorographical, and itinerary, in Nottinghamshire and the adjacent counties* (1801–3), and also painted the miniature of the author from which the frontispiece to the work was engraved. In 1811 and following years he published a series of soft ground-etchings after his own watercolour drawings, and those of David Cox, S. Prout, and T. Girtin, among others. A series of drawings in watercolour, representing views in the immediate neighbourhood of London, is in the British Museum. Joseph Farington records Sherlock's unsuccessful application for the post of drawing master at the Royal Military Academy in 1808 (Farington, *Diary*, 9.3302).

L. H. CUST, rev. TINA FISKE

Sources Farington, *Diary*, vols. 4, 8–9, 17 · W. G. Strickland, *A dictionary of Irish artists*, 2 vols. (1913) · D. Foskett, *A dictionary of British miniature painters*, 2 vols. (1972) · S. C. Hutchison, 'The Royal Academy Schools, 1768–1830', *Walpole Society*, 38 (1960–62), 123–91, esp. 155 · B. Stewart and M. Cutten, *The dictionary of portrait painters in Britain up to 1920* (1997) · Waterhouse, *18c painters* · G. Hall and others, *Summary catalogue of miniatures in the Victoria and Albert Museum* (1981) · K. K. Yung, *National Portrait Gallery: complete illustrated catalogue, 1856–1979*, ed. M. Pettman (1981) · Graves, *RA exhibitors* · Graves, *Soc. Artists* · Redgrave, *Artists* · IGI

Likenesses W. Sherlock, self-portrait, miniature, 1805; Christies, 12 July 1998, lot 206

Wealth at death poor; indolent: Farington, *Diary*, 4.1162 (21 Feb 1799)

Sherlock, William Pengree (*b.* **1775**). *See under* Sherlock, William (*c.*1738–1806).

Sherman, Bim [*real name* Lloyd Jarrett Vincent] (**1950–2000**), singer and songwriter, was born on 2 February 1950 in Westmoreland, Jamaica. In addition to his given name and the name that eventually he usually adopted, the singer had many aliases, among them Jarrett Tomlinson, Jarrett Vincent, Lloyd Vincent, Bim Shieman, Lloyd Tomlinson, and J. L. Vincent. The names Vincent and Tomlinson came from Lloyd's mother and father respectively. Jamaican singers of the 1960s and 1970s often found it a commercial necessity to change names as they moved from label to label, just as North America's rural bluesmen of an earlier age changed names as they moved from town to town.

Sherman did not ascribe his love of music to any one person but rather to his family, with whom he attended church services and Sunday school. As he became older, he went to the local dance-hall and once recalled:

> I always knew I could make the music, ever since I was small and it was all I wanted to do. I remember growing up and listening to it, singing along with it and feeling the power of it, which is the other side of roots, and feeling light-headed. (interview with Steve Barker, 1999)

In the early 1970s the young Sherman swapped trades from fisherman to electrician when he moved in with one of his brothers in central Kingston. His closest musical friends were Keith Porter and Ronnie Davis, who would go on to form the premier vocal group the Itals, but his first recording experience was with his early mentor Gladstone (Gladdy) Anderson at the famous Treasure Isle studios. But things did not work out as well as he had hoped— or as he once put it, 'things just go boof!' The first record he released, cut at the Federal studio with Sid Bucknor as engineer, was '100 Years (in Babylon)'. 'Love Forever' followed, a self-financed affair on the Element label, and there came thereafter a string of tunes now recognized as reggae roots classics on Sherman's own Scorpio, Red Sea, and Sun Dew imprints. These singles met with a degree of local success and appreciation that convinced him to continue, but he observed that in Jamaica there was always pressure from big names of the notoriously cut-throat music business:

> Lots of people like Randy's or Joe Gibbs want to record me, and even producers before them like Coxsone. But it's not easy in JA [Jamaica] to get what you want out of recording and those people have a range of tricks they use to oppress you. (interview with Steve Barker, 1999)

Like so many other young Jamaicans in the 1970s Sherman decided to try his luck in the UK, being persuaded to join the 'Roots Encounter' tour of 1979 alongside Prince Far I, Creation Rebel, and Prince Hammer. His first album, *Love Forever*, had been issued a year earlier on the Tribesman label, and included the title tune plus nine other previous Jamaican singles. Sherman settled in the UK, cementing a friendship and business relationship with the young maverick reggae producer Adrian Sherwood, a long-time admirer of the singer who considered him the pre-eminent Jamaican vocalist. The connection with Sherwood's On U Sound record label led to collaborations with a vast range of musicians, artists, and producers including Gary Clail—with whom he appeared on *Top of the Pops* crooning on the hit single 'Human nature' in 1991—Akabu, Tackhead, Japan's Audio Active, the Sabres of Paradise, Groove Corporation, Bomb the Bass, and latterly Sinead O'Connor. But more importantly the relationship with Sherwood and On U Sound also introduced reggae to an audience predominately brought up on rock music. In 1994 Sherman re-recorded six of his old tunes in an acoustic session at Richard Branson's Manor Studios, accompanied by Skip McDonald on guitar and Talvin Singh on tablas. A trip to Bombay followed where India's finest film musicians provided the extra layers of sound that resulted in the 1994 album *Miracle*, which is certainly Sherman's masterpiece and a fitting testament to reggae's sweetest voice.

Bim Sherman died in London on 17 November 2000. He left five children from two common-law marriages. What marked him out from his contemporaries was not just his plaintive and often haunting vocal delivery, or the matching subtlety of his songwriting, but the fact that throughout his career he maintained a fierce defence of his own independence as an artist, keeping control of his output both creatively and commercially. STEVE BARKER

Sources S. Barker, interviews with Bim Sherman, 1999, priv. coll. · *The Times* (19 Dec 2000) · *The Independent* (Dec 2000)

Sherman, Edward (1776–1866), coach proprietor, was the son of Edward Staniford Sherman and his wife, Mary, and was born in Berkshire and baptized at South Moreton, near Wallingford, Berkshire, on 16 January 1777. It was later recorded that he went to London on foot in 1793, being too poor to pay the fare, and obtained employment at 12s. a week. It has been claimed that he owed his advancement either to success as a stockbroker, or to friendship with Lewis Levy, the great toll lessee and stockbroker, but this rests entirely on later evidence, particularly the fact that Sherman later 'dealt largely' in stocks (*City Press*, 29 Sept 1866, 5).

More credibly, it was stated in 1907 that Sherman married three old and wealthy ladies in succession; the widow who owned the Oxford Arms inn, Warwick Lane, London, followed by her sister, and then the sister's niece. It is certainly the case that, at St Martin Ludgate on 6 August 1803, Sherman, then a bachelor of the parish of St Luke Middlesex, married Ann Palmer, a widow, and on 5 October 1803 he became a member of the Innholders' Company in respect of the Oxford Arms inn, Warwick Lane. However, no subsequent marriage can be traced until 1849, and the date of Ann Sherman's death is unknown.

Sherman's move to the Bull and Mouth, Aldersgate Street, about 1823, brought him to the forefront of the coach trade. By the 1830s his coach business was the third largest in London, with 700 horses at its peak. In 1836 he had sixty-one coaches, including ten mail coaches, leaving London every day. Sherman himself was never seen driving a coach, and was later described as 'not a horsey man'

(Harper, 1.37). He originated the long-distance day coaches; in particular, the Wonder to Shrewsbury, performing the 158 mile journey in fifteen and three-quarter hours, set a new standard in 1825. It was followed by the Telegraph to Manchester in 1833 (186 miles in eighteen and a half hours). His coaches had distinctive yellow wheels and bodies, and, unusually, he owned some himself instead of hiring them. He rebuilt the Bull and Mouth (as the Queen's Hotel) in 1830, with extensive underground stabling. He was also a promoter, and then a director, of the *Thames*, the first steam packet plying between London and Margate in 1814.

Harper, writing in 1907, stated that:

> Without doubt a man of strong character, he had many peculiarities, among them a decided taste for extravagance in dress and jewellery, remarkable even at that time … instead of sporting a shirt front, his chest displayed an expanse of black satin, plentifully covered with diamond pins. (Harper, 1.43–4)

Sherman was apparently unpopular with his country partners, who had difficulty obtaining their share of the earnings from him.

Sherman was the slowest of the great coach proprietors to adapt to the railways. When the Grand Junction Railway opened in 1838 he kept some of his coaches working along its route, not only losing heavily on them, but also forfeiting the opportunity to become one of the railway's agents. However, this does not seem to have diminished his prosperity significantly. Certainly by 1839 he was aware that, where railways existed, only the poor or the timid would travel by coach, and the number of people too timid to use railways was rapidly declining. He later worked omnibuses between Paddington and Bank, and he remained the proprietor of the Queen's Hotel. He was said to have been a shareholder in some of the earliest railways.

Sherman's last wife was Isabella, daughter of Thomas Hunt, whom he married at Christ Church, London, on 14 October 1849. She survived him. No children are recorded in Sherman's will, although he was reputed to have illegitimate children. According to Harper, his family took advantage of his eccentricities to commit him, without reasonable cause, to Bethlem Hospital. He died at an asylum in Chiswick known as the Manor House, on 14 September 1866. DORIAN GERHOLD

Sources *City Press* (29 Sept 1866), 5 · S. Harris, *The coaching age* (1885), 126–45 · C. G. Harper, *The Manchester and Glasgow road*, 1 (1907), 34–44 · parish register, St Martin Ludgate, 1803, GL, MS 10,216/2 [marriage] · *IGI* · will, London, 7 Dec 1866 · Innholders' Company, freedom admissions, GL, MS 6651/1 · *Robson's London Directory* (1836) · 'Select committee on the effect of the formation of railroads on turnpike … trusts', *Parl. papers* (1839), 9.384–8, no. 295 · *VCH Middlesex*, 7.74 · d. cert. · H. W. Hart, 'Sherman and the Bull and Mouth', *Journal of Transport History*, 5 (1961–2), 12–21 · m. cert. · *CGPLA Eng. & Wales* (1866)

Wealth at death under £80,000: probate, 7 Dec 1866, *CGPLA Eng. & Wales*

Sherman, James (1796–1862), Congregational minister, son of an employee of the East India Company and his

Yorkshire wife, was born in Banner Street, Finsbury, London, on 21 February 1796. After education by two local dissenting ministers he was apprenticed to an ivory turner for three and a half years. When convinced of a call to the ministry he applied to the Countess of Huntingdon's College at Cheshunt, and was accepted in November 1815. Three years later he was ordained to the Christian ministry in Sion Chapel, Whitechapel, London, before supplying consecutively three chapels of the Countess of Huntingdon's Connexion, in Plymouth, Bath, and Bristol. In 1821 he began a ministry lasting fifteen years at Castle Street Church, Reading, a secession from St Giles's Anglican church, one of whose vicars had supported the countess of Huntingdon. On 10 January 1822 he married a daughter of Dr Grant of Bristol, with whom he had a daughter and a son. She died on 1 January 1834. While at Reading he became friendly with the Revd Rowland Hill, an earlier associate of the countess of Huntingdon, for whom the independent Surrey Chapel had been built in St George's Fields, Blackfriars Road, London, and occasionally preached there. When Hill died in 1833 the congregation sent an invitation to Sherman, knowing this to be Hill's own wish. At first Sherman refused, but finally accepted in 1836. As the Countess of Huntingdon's Connexion was closely linked with the Congregationalists, it was not unexpected for both church and minister now to associate with them.

At the Surrey Chapel Sherman exercised a notable ministry, for many years in partnership with his second wife, **Martha** [Patty] **Sherman** [*née* Tucker] (1806–1848), daughter of Benjamin Tucker and his wife (*née* Grant) of Enfield, whom he married on 3 March 1835 and with whom he had three daughters. A gifted woman of high-spirited and generous personality, she found an outlet acceptable at the time for her energies and abilities in charitable work at her husband's church—fund-raising through sales, pastoral visiting, and the organization of Maternal Associations. The number of church members doubled to 800, the average congregation rose to almost 3000, the largest in London, and the buildings were extended. Sherman's ardent evangelistic preaching achieved many conversions; it was said that eighty-four people joined his church after one sermon in 1837. He was a moderate Calvinist, of eirenic temper and attractive personality; he disliked controversy, and though his nonconformist convictions grew stronger in later life, he was widely respected outside nonconformist circles. He and his wife were known as convinced total abstainers. Both were interested in, supported, and initiated organizations linked to their church for the improvement of the material welfare of the poorer members. This concern led James Sherman to found the Christian Mutual Provident Society in 1847. In 1842 and 1846 they paid visits to Germany, Austria, and Switzerland in search of better health. Martha Sherman died from consumption on 18 May 1848 at the Surrey Chapel parsonage, and was buried on the 25th in Abney Park cemetery, Stoke Newington.

In 1854 James Sherman resigned from the Surrey Chapel and accepted the pastorate of a new Congregational church in Blackheath, London, established by the London Chapel Building Society. His ministry at Blackheath again drew large numbers; 468 new members were admitted, and congregations of 1000 were common. But after much ill health he died on 15 February 1862 at 12 Paragon, Blackheath, and was buried at Abney Park cemetery on 22 February. He had continued to support Cheshunt College throughout his life, and after his death his friends contributed to a Cheshunt bursary in his memory.

Sherman's published works included *A Guide to Acquaintance with God* (1826) and *A Plea for the Lord's Day* (1830), both of which reached many editions, and a volume entitled *Psalms and Hymns for the Use of Surrey Chapel* (1841). He also published several sermons, and memoirs of Rowland Hill and William Allen.   ELAINE KAYE

Sources H. Allon, *Memoir of the Rev James Sherman* (1863) · J. Dix, *Pen and ink sketches of poets, preachers, and politicians* (1846), 228–32 · J. Grant, *The metropolitan pulpit, or, Sketches of the most popular preachers in London*, 2 (1839), 206–20 · *Congregational Year Book* (1863), 263–6 · *Funeral sermons occasioned by the death of James Sherman* (1862) · N. Hall, *Newman Hall: an autobiography* (1898), 41, 45, 122 · J. Sherman, *The pastor's wife: a memoir of Mrs Sherman of Surrey Chapel* (1848) · *CGPLA Eng. & Wales* (1862)
Likenesses W. Say, mezzotint, pubd 1829 (after F. Lake), BM, NPG · C. Baugniet, lithograph, BM · W. H. Mote, portrait, repro. in Allon, *Memoir* · R. Woodman, stipple (after E. B. Morris), NPG · portrait, Westminster College, Cambridge, Cheshunt Foundation
Wealth at death under £2000: probate, 29 March 1862, *CGPLA Eng. & Wales*

Sherman, John (d. **1671**), historian and Church of England clergyman, was the son of Samuel Sherman (d. 1644), clothier, of Dedham, Essex, and his wife, Esther (d. 1646), daughter of Robert Burgess. Sherman's early life is obscure, but in 1645 he was admitted as a pensioner at Queens' College, Cambridge, and he matriculated in 1647. He graduated BA in 1649–50. He subscribed to the engagement, was elected unanimously a fellow of Jesus College, Cambridge, in 1650, and proceeded MA in 1653. He was incorporated at Oxford the same year.

Two years later, in 1655, Sherman was appointed rector of Graveley, Cambridgeshire. He was university proctor in 1660–61, and the following year the university presented him to Wilmsloe in the diocese of Chester, but he was never instituted because the former incumbent retained the living through the Act of Indemnity. In 1662 Sherman became rector of Harlton, Cambridgeshire. He wrote *Historia Collegii Jesu Cantabrigiae*, recording the histories of the nunnery of St Rhadegund and the college which replaced it from their foundations to Edmund Boldero's mastership (1663–79). Sherman's work is considered diligently researched and fairly reliable, although his royalism distorted his analysis of his own times. J. O. Halliwell printed an inaccurate version in 1840.

In 1663 Sherman was one of the syndics for restoring Lambeth's library, and in 1664 he was one of the twelve university preachers. He also contributed to the marble paving in Jesus College chapel. In 1665 he was admitted DD by royal mandate. A John Sherman was married on 2 November 1666 to Elizabeth Clare at Graveley. Sherman was appointed prebend and archdeacon of Sarum in 1670, died in London on 27 March 1671, and was buried in the chancel of Jesus College chapel. His will was proved on 29 March 1671 by his brother Edmund.

Sherman should not be confused with his namesake John Sherman DD, a graduate of Trinity College, Cambridge, and author of several religious tracts, who died, probably in Norwich, in 1663.

J. B. MULLINGER, *rev.* S. L. SADLER

Sources Graveley parish register index, Cambs. AS · CUL, Baker MSS, xxv 323 · J. Sherman, *Historia Collegii Jesu Cantabrigiae*, ed. J. O. Halliwell (1840) · *The diary and correspondence of Dr John Worthington*, ed. J. Crossley, 1, Chetham Society, 13 (1847), 39, 42 · Foster, *Alum. Oxon.*, *1500–1714*, 4.1348 · Wood, *Ath. Oxon.: Fasti* (1815), 178 · Venn, *Alum. Cant.*, 1/4.62 · E. Carter, *The history of the University of Cambridge* (1753), 219 · J. B. Mullinger, *The University of Cambridge*, 3 (1911), 382 · W. Kennett, *A register and chronicle ecclesiastical and civil* (1728), 213 · *VCH Cambridgeshire and the Isle of Ely*, 3.425 · D. Lysons and S. Lysons, *Magna Britannia Cambridgeshire* (1978), 119–20 · Wing, *STC* · A. Gray and F. Britain, *A history of Jesus College* (1960) · IGI · will, PRO, PROB 11/335, sig. 43 · sentence, PRO, PROB 11/338, sig. 39

Sherman, Martha (1806–1848). *See under* Sherman, James (1796–1862).

Sherman, Roger (1721–1793), merchant and revolutionary politician in America, was born on 19 April 1721 at Newton, Massachusetts, the fourth child, and third son, of William Sherman (1692–1741), farmer and cordwainer, and his second wife, Mehetabel Wellington (1688–1776). As a young man Roger worked on the farm, learned how to work leather, and probably attended the local grammar school in the family's home town of Stoughton; he never went to college.

The family was not well-to-do; when William Sherman died in March 1741 his intestate estate was so small that it 'cannot admit of a division among all his [seven] children without great damage thereto' (Sherman, 140). But there were better prospects on the frontier, and so in June 1743 Roger moved the family to New Milford, in the newly settled north-west quadrant of Connecticut, to where his elder half-brother William had emigrated three years earlier. Sherman embarked on a career as a merchant and store owner, in partnerships until April 1759 and thereafter on his own. In his spare time he taught himself to be a surveyor and made enough connections with important people to receive from the colony's assembly in October 1745 an appointment as the public surveyor for that part of the colony. As his retail business grew, his work as a surveyor—a job he would hold until May 1758—provided a steady income, allowed him to evaluate land for possible purchase, and brought him into contact with prominent people beyond New Milford. Increasingly prosperous, he married Elizabeth Hartwell of Stoughton (1726–1760) on 17 November 1749. With a growing family—the couple had seven children over the next eleven years—Sherman could not waste an opportunity. He parlayed his interest in mathematics into a series of almanacs that he published in New York, New Haven, New London, and Boston from 1750 to 1761. With the same curiosity and enlightened self-interest he had used to master surveying, he undertook the study of the law (the younger but better

educated William Samuel Johnson was his mentor), was admitted to the local Litchfield county bar in February 1754, and soon had a thriving law practice.

Sherman's evident abilities brought him increased public responsibilities. Having tested him in various local offices, in May 1755 the voters of New Milford elected him as one of their two deputies to the general assembly, the lower house of the Connecticut legislature; they re-elected him eight more times in the next six years. His peers in the assembly also recognized his abilities and immediately appointed him a justice of the peace; in May 1759 they promoted him to the Litchfield county court bench. He also began to assume leadership roles in the local Congregationalist church, rising to the position of deacon in March 1755. He was not a controversialist in religious matters. Judging by a statement in his New Haven almanac for 1758 defending the inclusion of 'the observable days of the Church of England' and denying that he was therefore an Episcopalian, he was an advocate of toleration: 'as I take liberty in these matters [of religious belief] to judge for myself, so I think it reasonable that others should have the same liberty' (Sherman, 161–2).

By 1760 Sherman was a respected inhabitant of New Milford. He had prospered in business, having received a commission to supply Connecticut troops at Albany, New York, in 1759, and had even opened a branch store at New Haven in July 1760. He was also rising in public esteem; in October 1760 he garnered enough votes to rank eighteenth on the list of men nominated for the governor's council, the upper house of the legislature.

The death of his wife on 19 October, less than a month after the birth of their seventh child, seems to have changed his life. If he had already been thinking about moving to a larger town, the death of his wife hastened his decision. For the second time in his life, now as a forty-year-old widower with five surviving children, he picked up his family and moved, to New Haven on 30 June 1761, where he settled in and prospered with the same skill he had shown at New Milford. On a trip to visit his younger brother, Josiah, then minister at Woburn, Massachusetts, he met Rebecca (or Rebekah) Prescott (1742–1813) of Danvers, the niece of his brother's wife. Sherman appears to have been smitten, and the couple married on 12 May 1763. They had eight children in the next twenty years, the last when Sherman was nearly sixty-two.

Sherman spent the last thirty years of his life in public service. He undertook a profusion of new responsibilities in the mid-1760s. New Haven voters returned him to the assembly in October 1764, and again in May and October 1765 and May 1766. His assembly colleagues appointed him a New Haven county justice of the peace in May 1765, and a member of the county court bench in October 1765. Yale College named him college treasurer that year, a position he held until December 1776, and gave him an honorary MA degree at commencement in 1768. The Anglo-American crisis set off by the Stamp Act (1765), by which parliament attempted to raise revenue in the colonies, gave him the opportunity to begin playing a larger role in

Connecticut politics. Already in October 1764 the chairman of an assembly committee formed to seek alternative and acceptable forms of taxation, he firmly opposed the act as 'inconsistent with the principles and spirit of the British constitution, and an infringement of the essential liberties of the colonists' (Collier, 51). But he disliked the extra-legal violence the radical association, the Sons of Liberty, directed at supporters of the act, and it is this combination of firm adherence to principles with restraint, moderation, and respect for legal procedure that was the bedrock of his political success. When the voters in May 1766 turned out Governor Thomas Fitch and four assistants for being too willing to accommodate British control, the changes included the election of Sherman to the council, a position to which he was re-elected for the next nineteen years. The assembly followed by elevating him to the superior court bench, where he rode circuit amid a heavy slate of other public duties for the next twenty-three years. Sherman completed his transformation into public servant in December 1772, when he turned the running of his store over to his son William and retired from business.

Sherman, like most colonists, spent the early 1770s thinking through how to respond to Britain's attempts to increase imperial regulation. Although it was bound to hurt his business, he supported the non-importation of British goods to drive home the fact of colonial unhappiness, and regretted the failure of the boycott in 1771. John Adams, who met Sherman in New Haven while both men were on their way to Philadelphia as delegates to the first continental congress in 1774, recounted that when Sherman told him 'that the Parliament of G[reat] B[ritain] had authority to make laws for America in no Case whatever', he also said that it was an opinion he, Sherman, had held since 1764 (*Diary and Autobiography*, 2.100).

Between September 1774 and November 1781 Sherman was actively engaged in congressional business for about six months in each year, and played a role in many of congress's most important decisions. He helped write the declaration of rights and supported the non-importation and non-consumption association among the colonies. In the second congress, beginning on 10 May 1775, he worked on issues involving the provisioning of the American army, colonial trade, and foreign aid. An avowed advocate of independence—a position he had favoured as early as perhaps 1772—he was appointed on 11 June 1776 to the committee to prepare a declaration. He played no part in writing the document, but he was fully in accord with its sentiments, and signed it on 2 August 1776. At the same time he was Connecticut's member on the grand committee to draft articles of confederation, and on 1 August asserted that voting in congress ought to be done on the principle of one state, one vote: 'We ought not to vote according to numbers. We are representatives of states, not individuals' (*Diary and Autobiography*, 2.247). This method prevailed in the final articles of confederation, which would govern the former colonies until the ratification of the federal constitution.

This self-educated, plainly dressed, unpolished delegate from Connecticut made an impression on his distinguished colleagues by applying to federal issues the pragmatism honed in the rough-and-tumble of a Connecticut political culture of biennial elections. He had a significant impact because he was present more frequently than all but a handful of other delegates, because his real métier was working on committees such as the board of war and the board of the treasury, where his compromising temperament and taste for expediency had their fullest opportunity for expression, and because he was a ceaseless advocate of issues that were important to the smaller member states of the coalition that eventually became the United States, such as how to vote in congress, how to keep wartime expenses as low as possible, and how to preserve a share in western lands. His willingness to step forward, his firmly pro-patriot principles, his attention to detail, and what Adams called 'a clear head and sound judgment' more than compensated for the fact that in debate he spoke 'very heavily and clumsily' and carried himself with a demeanour that was 'stiffness, and aukwardness itself, rigid as starched linen or buckram' (*Diary and Autobiography*, 2.150, 173).

Sherman's wartime public service also embraced Connecticut as well as congress. From 1777 to 1779, and again in 1782, he was a member of the council of safety, which advised Governor Jonathan Trumbull between sessions of the legislature, and he was a delegate to two important regional conventions on vital economic issues in 1777 and 1778, at which he favoured stabilizing the inflated currency by 'taxing high and often to defray the expenses of the war' (Collier, 164) and imposing wage and price regulations to spread the financial burden equitably across society.

War-weariness in a state reeling under fiscal problems, plus the voters' inherent suspicion of allowing one man to represent them for too long, led to Sherman's eclipse. The bulk of his service in the continental and confederation congresses was over by November 1781; he returned for the first six months of 1784 only because his successors were disqualified by a provision in the articles of confederation that limited delegates to three years of service in every six. He spent his time at home repairing his own finances, helping to revise Connecticut's statute laws, serving as New Haven's first mayor (from 10 February 1784), sitting on the superior court bench, and serving as an assistant until forced to resign in May 1785 by the terms of an act limiting multiple office-holding in Connecticut.

Sherman's most important public service began in May 1787, when he was appointed a delegate to a convention called to see if and how the cumbersome structure of federal government under the articles of confederation might be repaired. Among the men who convened at Philadelphia at the end of May, only Benjamin Franklin had more political experience; only Franklin, too, at the age of eighty-one, was older. William Pierce of Georgia recorded a character sketch which captures Sherman's strengths and weaknesses:

> He is awkward, un-meaning, and unaccountably strange in his manner. But in his train of thinking there is something

regular, deep and comprehensive; yet the oddity of his address ... and that strange New England cant [in his speaking] ... make everything that is connected with him grotesque and laughable; and yet he deserves infinite praise—no Man has a better Heart or a clearer Head. (Farrand, 3.88–9)

Sherman participated extensively in the debates of what came to be called the constitutional convention—only James Madison spoke more—and, sensitive as always to the wishes of his constituents, sought to strengthen the union of the states while doing as little as possible to weaken the power and integrity of the existing state governments. His best-known and most important contribution was as the prime architect of what became known as the Connecticut compromise. With smaller states threatening to abandon the union if voting in congress were made proportional to a state's population or wealth, on 11 June he proposed that the legislature be bicameral, that representation in the lower house be based on relative population, and that in the upper house each state have one vote. His arguments eventually held sway, and the delegates, including Sherman and William Samuel Johnson, signed an engrossed copy of the constitution on 17 September 1787. After six days of consideration, the Connecticut ratifying convention approved the constitution on 9 January 1788, thanks in part to the 'genuine good sense and discernment' of Sherman (Hoadley and Labaree, 6.564). In October 1788 the legislature elected the younger, better-educated, and more polished Johnson and Oliver Ellsworth as senators; Sherman was chosen as one of five representatives, a mixed blessing since it forced him to give up the seat on the superior court on which he had sat since 1766. In congress from March 1789 to March 1791 he spoke in favour of using high import duties to create a national revenue, supported the full funding of the federal debt and assumption of the states' debts, and insisted that, if a bill of rights were thought necessary, it be appended to, not included in, the constitution. When Johnson resigned from congress in May 1791 the Connecticut assembly elected Sherman to the senate, where he served until 9 March 1793; his efforts there are difficult to discern since senate debates were secret. In deteriorating health for several years, he died of typhoid fever at New Haven on 23 July 1793.

Often overlooked today, Sherman had a major role in the transition of the American colonies into a nation of united states. He signed more important documents than any other of the founding fathers.

HAROLD E. SELESKY

Sources J. H. Trumbull and C. J. Hoadly, eds., *The public records of the colony of Connecticut*, 15 vols. (1850–90), vols. 9–15 · C. J. Hoadly and others, eds., *The public records of the state of Connecticut*, 11 vols. (1894–1967), vols. 1–8 · *Diary and autobiography of John Adams*, ed. L. H. Butterfield and others, 1–4 (1961) · P. H. Smith and others, eds., *Letters of delegates to congress, 1774–1789*, 26 vols. (1976–2000), vols. 1–18, 21 · W. C. Ford, ed., *Journals of the continental congress* (1904–36) · M. Farrand, ed., *Records of the federal convention of 1787*, revised edn (1937) · L. G. DePauw and C. B. Bickford, eds., *Documentary history of the first federal congress of the United States of America*, 14 vols. (1972–98) · C. Collier, *Roger Sherman's Connecticut: Yankee politics and the American Revolution* (1971) · J. P. Boyd, 'Sherman, Roger', *DAB* · R. S.

Boardman, *Roger Sherman: signer and statesman* (1938) · T. T. Sherman, *Sherman genealogy* (1920) · J. G. Rommel, *Connecticut's Yankee patriot: Roger Sherman* (1979) · O. Zeichner, *Connecticut's years of controversy, 1750–1776* (1949) · R. L. Bushman, *From puritan to Yankee: character and the social order in Connecticut, 1690–1765* (1967)
Archives American Antiquarian Society, Worcester, Massachusetts, papers · Connecticut State Library, corresp. · Litchfield Historical Society, Connecticut · Yale U., Beinecke L., papers | Connecticut Historical Society, American Revolution · Connecticut Historical Society, Jonathan Trumbull papers · Connecticut Historical Society, William Williams papers · Connecticut Historical Society, William Samuel Johnson papers · Connecticut State Library, Church records · Connecticut State Library, Connecticut archives · Connecticut State Library, Jonathan Trumbull papers · Connecticut State Library, Superior Court records · L. Cong., Peter Force transcripts · L. Cong., Jeremiah Everts papers · New York Historical Society, Horatio Gates papers · NYPL, Bancroft collection · Yale U., Sterling Memorial Library, Baldwin family collection
Likenesses R. Earle, oils, 1775, Yale U. Art Gallery · J. Trumbull, group portrait, oils, *c.*1791, Yale U. Art Gallery · C. B. Ives, statue, *c.*1870, Statuary Hall, US Capitol · C. B. Ives, statue, *c.*1870, State Capitol, Hartford, Connecticut
Wealth at death approx. £4470: probate inventory, quoted in Sherman, *Sherman genealogy*, 196

Sherpa Tenzing. *See* Tenzing Norgay (1914–1986).

Sherratt, John (*bap.* 1718, *d.* 1788), entrepreneur and social reformer, was baptized on 20 June 1718 at St Martin-in-the-Fields, London, the son of William Sherratt and Mary, *née* Trusler. Sherratt (who also spelled his name Sherrott) had a varied and eventful career as a businessman, through which he became involved in politics, foreign affairs, and social reform. He was twice married: first to Catherine (*d.* 1759), and, second, to Sarah, who survived him; further details of his marriages are unknown. He had numerous children, of whom his eldest surviving son, John, acted as an executor for his will.

Sherratt began life as a London hatter, feltmaker, and broker. He continued his work as a broker and auctioneer throughout his career, dealing in a variety of goods and advertising his business in the London newspapers. It was typical of Sherratt's spirit and ingenuity that his bankruptcy (25 January 1746) did not hinder him from exploiting new business opportunities. In partnership with his uncle, John *Trusler, he now became a manager of London's Marylebone Gardens, which he undertook alongside his broker business in Soho. In the long term, however, both ventures failed to bring the rewards which Sherratt sought, and he filed individually as a Soho bankrupt in April 1754, and jointly with Trusler as a result of financial difficulties with the Gardens three months later.

By this date Sherratt had his eyes on another prize, the privateer *Antigallican*. Sherratt was an active member of an antigallican association, and foiled his creditors once more by secretly investing his assets in the ship. As the probable author of the pamphlet *The Antigallican Privateer* (1757) Sherratt described the fate of this first privateer of the Seven Years' War. Having sailed from Deptford on 17 September 1756 the *Antigallican* captured two French ships before seizing the booty-laden French East Indiaman the *Duc de Penthièvre* off the coast of Spain. But disaster then struck, as the Spanish took possession of both the *Antigallican* and its prize at Cadiz in February 1757. Sherratt's account reveals obvious anger and disappointment. Despite a personal visit to Cadiz, as well as further publications and petitions by the association and attempts to involve the prime minister, William Pitt, the goods of the *Antigallican* were never restored.

Yet another of Sherratt's business schemes had ended unsuccessfully. However, his interests in English liberties now took him in a new direction—the reform of private madhouses—which benefited others as well as himself. On 22 May 1766 Sherratt, describing himself as a notary public, gave an affidavit to the court of king's bench about his recent rescue of Hannah MacKenzie from a private madhouse in Paddington where she had been wrongfully imprisoned by her husband. He claimed that his help was sought by MacKenzie's friends because they knew he had

> caused several cases to be delivered at the door of the Honourable House of Commons … complaining of the cruel acts which have been committed in private Mad houses in this Kingdom to the great oppression, injury, and unlawful confinement of many of His Majesty's Subjects. (PRO, KB 1/16/4)

Sherratt was probably alluding to the pamphlet (of which he is the likely author) *A Case Humbly Offered to the Consideration of Parliament* (1763), which contained a letter from MacKenzie thanking Sherratt for his services in the second edition (1766). Sherratt was well aware that many would doubt the honesty of his intentions in such cases. He told the king's bench that he acted 'from principles of humanity and compassion and for the public good', and that 'he hath had no gratuity or reward for such his good offices'. Yet in view of Sherratt's character, it seems unlikely that he let a potentially profitable business opportunity pass him by. Certainly, he had already obtained a reputation as the rescuer of the wrongfully detained, a celebrity recorded by the poet Christopher Smart, whose *An Epistle to John Sherratt, Esquire* (1763?) was published after he had been liberated by Sherratt from Mr Potter's madhouse at Bethnal Green. While it remains unclear how many people Sherratt helped to free, or how much he stood to profit, he should be credited for bringing the abuses of the private asylums to public notice. But his public works were not enough to impress the writer on music Sir John Hawkins, who was appalled when Sherratt sought to become a Middlesex justice of the peace in 1769. Given that he had twice been declared bankrupt, Hawkins believed that Sherratt's name would be a 'disgrace' to the magistracy (Davis, 226). Sherratt was never sworn in as a Middlesex justice, though he remained on the Westminster Commission until 1775.

On 8 November of that year Sherratt was appointed consul for Cartagena, Spain. This was his final change of occupation but, like so many of the other careers, it also ended in disaster. On arriving in Cartagena in May 1776 he quarrelled first with his Spanish vice-consul and then with John Burrows, who had accompanied him to Spain. His disagreement with Burrows resulted in a fight in a public tavern, upon which Sherratt was arrested and

imprisoned. Having brought disgrace upon the consulate Sherratt returned to England in early 1777. In 1780–81 he was advertising his auction business once again. His petitions to the government, stating that in Cartagena he had been used as a political tool and pleading for financial recompense, evidently fell upon deaf ears. His will, in which he described himself as 'his Majesty's late Consul at Cartagena', left just 1*s.* to his wife. None the less he directed his executors to 'countenance and assist all my daughters in their several trades or businesses if they … should be deemed worthy of favour' (PRO, PROB 11/1165/213). His mixed fortunes as an entrepreneur had apparently not diminished Sherratt's desire that his daughters should follow in his footsteps. He died on 5 January 1788 at Hammersmith, Middlesex. ELIZABETH FOYSTER

Sources B. Rizzo, 'John Sherratt, negociator', *Bulletin of Research in the Humanities*, 86 (1983–5), 373–429 · affidavit of John Sherratt, 22 May 1766, PRO, KB1/16/4 · will, 14 April 1788, PRO, PROB 11/1165, sig. 213 · B. H. Davis, *A proof of eminence: the life of Sir John Hawkins* (1973) · A. Sherbo, *Christopher Smart, scholar of the university* (1967)
Wealth at death 1 shilling to wife; clothes to son; debts to be paid to cousin: will, PRO, PROB 11/1165, sig. 213

Sherrey [Sherry], **Richard** (*b. c.*1505), schoolmaster and author, was born in London diocese about 1505 and admitted as a demy (undergraduate scholar) of Magdalen College, Oxford, in 1522. He graduated as a BA in 1528 and as MA in 1531. From Magdalen he went to Cardinal College, Oxford, founded by Magdalen's alumnus Cardinal Wolsey, where in 1530 he occurs as a minor canon and teacher of grammar to the choristers. He returned to Magdalen, between Michaelmas 1531 and January 1532, as master of the college school, where he remained until Michaelmas 1540. In 1532 he also held a fellowship at University College and was ordained as an exorcist, but it is not clear if he proceeded to major holy orders. On leaving Magdalen College School, Sherrey appears to have moved to London, very probably to another teaching post since his four known published works include two contributions to the study of grammar. His *Treatise of Schemes and Tropes Gathered out of the Best Grammarians and Orators* (1550) was a translation of Erasmus's work *De civilitate morum puerilium*, with an introduction dated at London. *A Very Fruitful Exposition upon the Sixth Chapter of St John*, translated from a work by Johann Brentz the elder, appeared in the same year and describes Sherrey as a Londoner. *A Treatise of the Figures of Grammar and Rhetoric* was published in 1555, and he also published a translation, no longer extant or datable, of *S. Basil the Great his Letter to Gregory Nazianzen*, 'shewing that many 100. years ago, certaine godly men began and used the life commonly called monasticall' (Ames, 1.677). *Schemes and Tropes* was addressed to Master Thomas Brooke esquire, probably the protestant activist of that name, and the work by Brentz to Lord Wentworth, a supporter of the earl of Warwick. These might suggest that Sherrey had protestant leanings, but the *Figures of Grammar* was dedicated to Sir William Paget, a supporter of Mary Tudor, and the translation of *Basil* looks like a work aimed at Catholics. It may be that the works were undertaken largely to earn money, or to attract the patronage of influential people of the day. Nothing is known of his death.

Sherrey shared a surname and London affiliation with **John Sherey** (d. 1551), appointed archdeacon of Lewes, Sussex, in 1542, and precentor of St Paul's Cathedral, London, in 1543. John enjoyed the favour of Thomas Howard, duke of Norfolk, who presented him to the precentorship and to the rectory of Thackham, Sussex, which Sherey was holding in 1545. In that year he is also described as the duke's chaplain. Sherey held other benefices in the 1540s, including the rectory of Hayling, Hampshire, and the vicarages of Horsham and Worth, Sussex. His will, made on 1 August 1551, gave bequests to his poor parishioners, divided his books among three Sussex clergy, and left the majority of his lands and chattels to members of his family (among whom Richard Sherrey is not mentioned); he had died, unmarried, by 22 August. NICHOLAS ORME

Sources Emden, *Oxf.*, 4.514, 701 · N. Orme, *Education in early Tudor England: Magdalen College Oxford and its school, 1480–1540* (1998), 69 · *STC, 1475–1640* · J. Ames, *Typographical antiquities, or, An historical account of the origin and progress of printing in Great Britain and Ireland*, ed. W. Herbert, 3 vols. (1785–90), vol. 1, p. 677 · will, PRO, PROB 11/35, fols. 249v–251r [J. Sherey] · *Fasti Angl., 1541–1857*, [St Paul's, London], 17

Sherriff, George (1898–1967), explorer and plant collector, was born at Carronvale, Larbert, Stirlingshire, on 3 May 1898, the fourth son and youngest of the six children of George Sherriff, a businessman and noted amateur photographer, and his wife, Catharine, an ardent horticulturist, daughter of Alexander Nimmo, a businessman of Falkirk. Educated at Sedbergh School, where he excelled at games, Sherriff, like his brothers, was bent on an army career and went to the Royal Military Academy, Woolwich: he was commissioned in the Royal Garrison Artillery early in 1918. He fought in the First World War in France, where two of his brothers were killed, and he was gassed in June 1918, spending the rest of the war in hospital.

In 1919 Sherriff was sent to India and served in a mountain battery at Nowshera, Waziristan, on the north-west frontier, for which he was mentioned in dispatches. On leave he delighted in visiting remote districts and the mountains, and when he was invited in 1927 to be British vice-consul in Kashgar, Chinese Turkestan, he readily accepted. He later became acting consul-general until he resigned in 1931, believing, unlike his superiors, that communist influence in Turkestan would lead, as it did, to the subjection of that territory.

While at Kashgar, Sherriff took every opportunity to travel widely, reaching Tien Shan (Tianshan) in the north and the Khotan in the east. In September 1929 he met Frank Ludlow (1885–1972), who was on his way to the Tien Shan Mountains and had been invited to spend the winter at Kashgar by the consul, Frederick Williamson; their interests in ornithology, travel, and plants started a lifelong friendship. Williamson became political officer in Sikkim and was able at the time of Sherriff's resignation to provide passports for both Sherriff and Ludlow to travel to Tibet, thus enabling them to put into operation the plans they had made in 1929. In spring 1933 Ludlow, Sherriff, and Williamson, with his wife, travelled along the central highway in Bhutan from Ha to Bumthang, where they met the maharaja. Sherriff and Ludlow entered Tibet by the Kang La (La = pass), striking the Lhasa Road to Nangkartse, and turned west to Gyantse and so back to India: they made 500 gatherings of plants.

This journey initiated a plan to work gradually eastwards through Tibet, collecting plants and birds along the main Himalayan range, until they reached the Tsangpo. In 1934 they worked the Tsona and Mago districts: despite the monsoon and malaria, they procured 600 gatherings of plants. In 1936 they returned, with Dr Kenneth Lumsden, to Tsona, crossing the Nyala La (17,150 feet) into the valley of Chayul Chu, which they followed to Lung. They encountered a semi-barbaric tribe of Daphlas and reached the valleys of the Char Chu and Tsari Chu. Tsari was sacred ground where cultivation and even grazing were forbidden, and the botanical spoils were thus remarkably rich: of the sixty-nine species of *Rhododendron* collected, fifteen were new to science, as were fourteen of the fifty-nine *Primula* species. While Ludlow and Lumsden moved on, Sherriff remained in Tsari, making a circuit of the holy mountain, Takpa Shiri, and discovering the pink *Meconopsis sherriffii*, named, as were seventeen other Himalayan plant species, in his honour. They returned with nearly 2000 gatherings of pressed plants, two crates of living plants, and innumerable packets of seed. The following year Sherriff spent the flowering season in central Bhutan collecting near Black Mountain over 600 gatherings. In 1938 Sherriff and Ludlow were joined by George Taylor of the British Museum (Natural History) in their exploration of the drainage of the Tsangpo from near Molo on the Lilung Chu down to Gyala, where they collected herbarium material in vast quantities (almost 5000 gatherings): 'Taylor collects everything from mosses and fungi upwards to lilies' (Ludlow).

During the Second World War, which temporarily put an end to Ludlow's and Sherriff's plans, Sherriff resumed military service, commanding an anti-aircraft battery in the Digboi oilfields of Assam. Later he entered into political activities in Sikkim, when in charge of the Tibet wool trade in Gangtok and Kalimpong. In April 1943 he was sent as Ludlow's successor to take charge of the British mission in Lhasa, shortly after marrying Elizabeth Hannah (Betty), youngest daughter of the Very Revd John Anderson Graham DD CIE, missionary and founder of the Kalimpong Homes for needy Anglo-Indian children. (There were no children of the marriage.) Continuing to collect within a 60 mile radius of Lhasa, Sherriff made an important series of films of now defunct Tibetan ceremonies. After two years in Lhasa he settled at Kalimpong in north-east India and, in 1946, with his wife, Ludlow, and Colonel Henry Elliot of the Indian Medical Service, he set out for southeast Tibet and the great gorge of the Tsangpo. The Sherriffs descended the Po Tsangpo to its junction with the Tsangpo at Gompo Ne, but Sherriff began to suffer from an overstrained heart, due to having helped one of his porters over a high pass in 1938, and he and his wife reluctantly left for lower altitudes in India, while Ludlow remained to explore the gorge. In 1949 Ludlow and Sherriff retired from India but both had been planning a final expedition—Sherriff to the Mishmi hills and Ludlow to the Tsangpo Gorge. Since permits for both were refused, they went to Bhutan with the maharaja's blessing, separating and working the whole of the alpine and temperate flora from west to east. Ludlow took the west, Sherriff the centre, and Dr J. H. Hicks, the medical officer, with Mrs Sherriff, the east: 5000 gatherings were made.

The expeditions were carried out almost entirely at the expense of Sherriff, whose thought so matched Ludlow's that they rarely disagreed: but, surprisingly in retrospect, they never came to be on first-name terms with one another. Sherriff was able to get the best out of his men, who were well fed, warmly clothed, fairly paid, and very loyal. On the expeditions, Sherriff, highly skilled in the use of both still and cine cameras, took thousands of photographs, the later ones of which, like the 21,000 plant gatherings (some damaged by wartime bombing), field notebooks, and maps are preserved at the Natural History Museum. Sherriff was one of the first to use air transport for getting plant material (short-lived seeds as well as mature plants) back to Europe: many crates were sent thus to the Royal Botanic Gardens at Kew and Edinburgh, to the garden of the Royal Horticultural Society at Wisley, and to private gardens. Their best introductions, besides rhododendrons and primulas, included *Paeonia lutea* var. *ludlowii*, which has made possible the breeding of the less heavy-headed cultivars of yellow and yellow-toned tree-peonies, and, unlike most of their introductions, can be readily grown in gardens throughout almost all of Britain, *Euphorbia griffithii*, *Paraquilegia anemonoides* (*P. grandiflora*), and several superior forms of plants already introduced, such as the elusive blue-flowered *Corydalis cashmiriana*. The richness of the areas covered is shown by the fact that of 129 species of primula they gathered, 27 were new, as were 38 out of 140 saxifrages, and 23 out of more than 100 gentians.

Though the Tsangpo Gorge has still to be revisited, the expeditions provided the stimulus for many Natural History Museum expeditions to Nepal when Tibet was closed, so that today the finest collections of Himalayan plants in the world are to be found preserved in the herbarium at the museum. Ludlow and Sherriff, both excellent marksmen, presented nearly 7000 bird skins to the museum, including specimens of two new species and two new subspecies, one of them named Sherriff's long-tailed wren-babbler, *Spelaeornis soulei sherriffii*. Sherriff's manuscript map of his journeys is preserved at the Royal Geographical Society, while the negatives and plates of his Kashgar days and seven diaries of the same period are preserved in the ethnography department of the British Museum. His cine films, dating back to 1928 (black and white), of Kashgar and the early Bhutan and south-east Tibet expeditions are in the National Film Archive, London, while the later colour films are in the family's possession and his later diaries are preserved at the Royal Botanic Garden, Edinburgh.

Sherriff (who was known as Geordie) was tall and well built, smart in his appearance, traditional and yeomanlike in his outlook, a countryman with a wide-ranging circle of friends. Yet he had a deep dislike of matters metropolitan and of superficial social life of the cocktail-party type. In 1950 he bought an estate at Ascreavie, near Kirriemuir, Angus, where he created a fine garden from a 'wilderness overrun by rabbits' (Ludlow). Here he grew many Himalayan plants with great success. From 1952 to 1956 he commanded the Angus battalion of the Home Guard and was a member of the queen's bodyguard for Scotland. From 1952 to 1966 he served on the Angus county council and district board and was made a deputy lieutenant of Angus in 1954. He was session clerk of Kingoldrum church from 1955 to 1965. Sherriff was appointed OBE in 1947 and the following year the Royal Horticultural Society bestowed its highest honour, the Victoria medal of honour, on him for his services to horticulture. He died at Ascreavie on 19 September 1967, and was survived by his wife.   D. J. MABBERLEY

Sources *The Times* (22 Sept 1967) · W. T. Stearn, 'Frank Ludlow (1885–1972) and the Ludlow–Sherriff expeditions to Bhutan and south-eastern Tibet of 1933–1950', *Bulletin of the British Museum* (*Natural History*) [Botany], 5 (1973–7), 241–89 · H. R. Fletcher, *A quest of flowers* (1975) · Desmond, *Botanists*, rev. edn · B. Henrey, *Watsonia*, 12 (1978), 54–5 · private information (1981) · *CGPLA Eng. & Wales* (1967)

Archives NHM, herbarium specimens, field notebooks, maps · RGS, maps · Royal Botanic Garden, Edinburgh, diaries | BM, department of ethnography, diaries, negatives, plates · Royal Botanic Garden, Edinburgh, corresp. with William Wright Smith | FILM BFI NFTVA, ciné films (black and white) · priv. coll., ciné films (colour)

Likenesses photograph, Hunt Botanic Library, Pittsburgh, Pennsylvania

Wealth at death £221,977 7s. 0d.: confirmation, 25 Oct 1967, NA Scot., SC 47/44/94/590–601

Sherriff, Robert Cedric (1896–1975), playwright and scriptwriter, was born on 6 June 1896 at Hampton Wick, Middlesex, the only child of Herbert Hankin Sherriff, insurance clerk, and his wife, Constance, daughter of Charles Winder, of Iver, Buckinghamshire. Educated at the grammar school at Kingston upon Thames, he was on the London staff of the Sun Insurance office from 1914 and served from 1917 as a captain in the 9th (East Surrey) regiment. He served at Vimy and Loos and was severely wounded at Ypres in 1917. After the war, in which he won the MC, he returned to his job as an insurance official and to his favourite sports.

Sherriff started writing plays for the annual fund-raising event at his Kingston Rowing Club. As a result of *Journey's End*, a play based upon his letters home from the trenches, in the new year of 1929 he became one of the most discussed English dramatists of the day. *Journey's End* had been turned down by various managements but, with some assistance from George Bernard Shaw, it received a critically acclaimed production by the Stage Society at the Apollo Theatre in December 1928 and then began a long London run at the Savoy Theatre. The play is set entirely in

Robert Cedric Sherriff (1896–1975), by Bassano, 1938

a claustrophobic dugout before St Quentin on the eve of the March offensive of 1918. Sherriff, who always favoured naturalism in theatre, had sought to give no more than a straight, simple impression of the terrors of the western front in a play written with so much honesty—no heroics, no pretence—that its characters stamped themselves upon the English theatre of their time: Osborne, the gentle schoolmaster; Raleigh, straight from school to the front line; Trotter, the ranker subaltern without imagination, and Stanhope, the captain with too much; Hibbert, his nerve gone. There were 594 performances in London, and the play was translated and performed in every European language. It toured extensively in the United States (where it had 485 performances in New York) and throughout the world; was made into a film; and in the sixty years after its first production in London, was revived twice.

Sherriff's next two plays, *Badger's Green* (1930) and *Windfall* (1933), were not successful, giving rise to suggestions that he was a one-play man, likely to do nothing else. He decided then to fulfil his long desire to study at Oxford and went up to read history as a special student at New College in 1931. (In 1937 he founded a scholarship at the college.) He thoroughly enjoyed his first year but was invited to write the script for *The Invisible Man* in Hollywood and subsequently decided to give up his study for scriptwriting. In 1935 he returned to the theatre with *St Helena*, an affecting and persuasive portrait of Napoleon at his journey's end. It was written in partnership with the actress Jeanne de Casalis, was acted first at the Old Vic, and then ran briefly at Daly's.

Sherriff's name did not appear again on a West End programme until 1948, but in the meantime he worked for Alexander Korda in writing the scripts for his films *Lady Hamilton*, *This Above All*, and, perhaps the best, *The Dambusters*. He returned to the stage with an ironic comedy, *Miss Mabel* (1948), a likeable confidence trick but less good than its successor, *Home at Seven* (1950). With Sir Ralph Richardson as a City bank clerk of regular habits who inexplicably fails to return home for twenty-four hours (during which anything might have happened), the piece was a sustained exercise in suspense, helped by Sherriff's unfailing ear for dialogue. He wrote four more plays: *The White Carnation* (1953); *The Long Sunset* (1955), a play set in the fifth-century Roman occupation of Britain, reflecting his interest in archaeology; *The Telescope* (1957); and *A Shred of Evidence* (1960). Of these, *The Long Sunset*, originally a radio play, was the most durable; it did not reach London, at the Mermaid Theatre, until 1961, six years after its production at the Birmingham Repertory.

Sherriff wrote several screenplays in Britain and Hollywood, of which some of the most familiar, retrospectively, were *Goodbye Mr Chips* (from the book by James Hilton), *The Four Feathers* (from A. E. W. Mason's novel), and *Odd Man Out*. The best of his novels is the first written, *The Fortnight in September* (1931), a sympathetic, detailed picture of a London suburban family's holiday at the seaside. *Greengates* (1936) also received critical acclaim.

Sherriff, who never married, was devoted to his mother. Lacking self-confidence, he preferred the company of people younger than himself. He was an endearingly kind and gentle man, qualities evident in his memoir, *No Leading Lady* (1968). He spent much of his life, after his early success, at his home, Rosebriars, Esher Park Avenue, Esher, Surrey, later adding to this a farm in Dorset. He was elected FSA and FRSL. He died at Kingston Hospital, Kingston upon Thames, on 13 November 1975.

J. C. TREWIN, rev. SAYONI BASU

Sources R. C. Sherriff, *No leading lady* (1968) · *The Times* (18 Nov 1975) · 'R(obert) C(edric) Sherriff, 1896–1975', *The reader's companion to twentieth-century writers*, ed. P. Parker and F. Kermode (1995), 676–7 · *CGPLA Eng. & Wales* (1976)

Archives Surrey HC, corresp., diaries, and papers | BL, corresp. with League of Dramatists, Add. MS 63439 · BL, corresp. with Society of Authors, Add. MS 63326

Likenesses Bassano, photograph, 1938, NPG [*see illus.*]

Wealth at death £182,202: probate, 10 Feb 1976, *CGPLA Eng. & Wales*

Sherring, Matthew Atmore (1826–1880), missionary in India, was born in Halstead, Essex, on 26 September 1826, eldest of the four sons of John Sherring, manufacturer and deacon of the Old Independent Meeting. Initially articled to a surgeon in Colchester, Sherring went on to London University, attending both Coward College (Congregationalist) and University College; he graduated BA in 1848, LLB in 1849, and MA in 1850. A youthful resolve to offer himself to Christ's service was strengthened by the early deaths of two brothers and his father, and he was ordained by the London Missionary Society (LMS) at King's

Weigh House Chapel on 7 December 1852. Afterwards he sailed for India to take charge of the LMS mission at Benares. On 5 March 1856 he married Margaret, daughter of Robert Cotton Mather, his colleague at Mirzapur, and eight months later he took charge at Mirzapur while Mather returned to Britain on furlough. Mirzapur remained relatively quiet during the 1857 rebellion and by the time the fighting was over Sherring had put together an account, entitled *The Indian Church during the Great Rebellion*, which his father-in-law published in London in 1859. On Mather's return in February 1861 Sherring and his wife went back to their duties at Benares.

Sherring had no illusions about the uphill task facing missionaries in Benares, the most sacred of Hindu cities. His reports home pleaded for understanding of the peculiar difficulties of evangelization in Benares and promoted 'indirect' results, meaning his well-publicized debates with Hindu pandits and his work in fostering the popular mission school. He was fascinated by Hindu society and wrote several books which, though denouncing Hinduism, were novel in both insight and detail; they included *The Sacred City of the Hindus* (1868) and his *magnum opus*, the three-volume *Hindu Tribes and Castes* (1872–81). Predictably enough, Sherring viewed India's pre-British past as stagnant non-history—an absence of progress which he blamed on the inhibiting nature of caste—but he was nevertheless a sufficiently dispassionate observer for cautious historians to be able still to make use of his books.

Sherring's more conventional publications included: *The History of Protestant Missions in India* (1875) and *The Life and Labours of the Rev. William Smith* (1879). He had two lengthy trips home in 1866–9 and 1876–8 but was unable to arrest a decline in health. He died of cholera at Benares on 10 August 1880 and was buried there on the same day. He was survived by his widow, who was widely recognized as an equal partner in his evangelical and academic work, and their five children.   KATHERINE PRIOR

Sources DNB · *Chronicle of the London Missionary Society* (March 1880) · *Chronicle of the London Missionary Society* (Oct 1880) · *Chronicle of the London Missionary Society* (Nov 1880) · *Congregational Year Book* (1881) · G. Pandey, *The construction of communalism in colonial north India* (1990) · University of London, *The historical record (1836–1926)*, 2nd edn (1926) · E. M. Bliss, *The encyclopaedia of missions*, 2 vols. (1891) · district court probates and administrations, India, BL OIOC, L/AG/34/31/1 · ecclesiastical records, BL OIOC, N/11/1, fol. 193

Archives SOAS, Council for World Mission Archives, corresp.

Likenesses J. Cochran, stipple (after photograph), NPG

Wealth at death Rs12,000: district court probates and administrations, India, 1865–1910, fol. 247 (L/AG/34/31/1), BL OIOC

Sherrington, Sir Charles Scott (1857–1952), physiologist, was born on 27 November 1857 in Islington, London, the son of James Norton Sherrington, who died while his children were young, and Anne Brookes Sherrington (*d.* 1907), of Great Yarmouth. His mother having married Dr Caleb Rose of Ipswich, Sherrington and his two younger brothers went to Ipswich grammar school where Charles was deeply influenced by one of the masters, Thomas Ashe, a poet of some note. Sherrington was rather small in stature but sturdy and an excellent athlete. Later he played soccer for Ipswich Town, rugby for St Thomas's Hospital, London, and also rowed for his college, Gonville and Caius, Cambridge.

Influenced towards medicine by his stepfather, Sherrington entered St Thomas's Hospital, London, in 1876 and became a scholar of Gonville and Caius College, Cambridge, in 1881. At Cambridge, Michael Foster selected promising students to carry out research in his physiological laboratory and here Sherrington worked in a stimulating atmosphere with G. W. Balfour, W. H. Gaskell, J. N. Langley, and others. His first publication, in 1884, written with Langley, was read to the Royal Society while he was still a student. It was an anatomical study of the brain of a dog presented before the International Medical Congress in 1881 by Professor F. Goltz of Germany, which directed Sherrington's attention towards the nervous system. The dog had moved about in a placid manner for months after surgical excision of the forebrain.

Sherrington obtained first classes in both parts of the natural sciences tripos (1881–3), and completed his studies at St Thomas's Hospital, qualifying MRCS (1884) and LRCP (1886) and obtaining the Cambridge MB (1885), MD (1892), and ScD (1904). In 1885 he travelled to laboratories in Europe, working in Germany and France, and with C. S. Roy and T. G. Brown made a study of cholera in Spain and later Italy, carrying out autopsies when possible. In 1887 he became a lecturer in systematic physiology at St Thomas's and was made a fellow of Caius. In 1891 he was also made professor-superintendent of the Brown Animal Sanatory Institute in south London, where, among other duties, he became, in 1894, one of the first people in Britain to produce diphtheria anti-toxin.

By the end of the nineteenth century, the view of the Spanish anatomist Ramon y Cajal, who stayed for a short period with Sherrington in London, that the individual nerve cell, or neuron, was the anatomical unit of the nervous system, was gaining ascendancy over that of the Italian Camillo Golgi, who maintained that the nervous system was a continuum of connected nerve cells. Sherrington, influenced by the Spaniard and his own electrophysiological work, coined the word 'synapse' for the gap that Cajal postulated between nerve cells. In 1895 Sherrington became Holt professor of physiology at Liverpool, where he remained for sixteen years. During this period in London and Liverpool he began the neurophysiological researches that were to provide important contributions to the study of the function of the nervous system. He also served as secretary of the Physiological Society (1889–96) to which he had been elected in 1885. From 1892 to 1907 he was secretary of the International Physiological Congress.

Making acute decerebrate preparations and using electrophysiological recording methods and sensitive anatomical tracing techniques, Sherrington studied 'decerebrate rigidity' in experimental animals. He worked out the neuron connections in the spinal cord and brain stem, that control the normal maintenance of muscle tone and the postures or reflex-movements in the limbs as in walking. He also explained the reciprocal innervation of muscles, whereby one set of excited muscles is co-ordinated with another set of inhibited muscles: thus groups of muscles will alternately relax and contract in activities such as limb movement. From this work Sherrington proposed the existence of inhibitory mechanisms in the nervous system. He also mapped out the motor areas of the cerebral cortex of mammals, made a particular study of the physiology of sense organs, and provided a description of the physiological unit of the nervous system, the reflex arc, analogous to Cajal's anatomical unit. Much of Sherrington's work can be summarized in the two major concepts he postulated. 'The final common pathway' was his expression for the confluence of reflex arcs from many different sensory inputs onto one output neuron (the final common pathway) which innervated the effector muscle.

The second of Sherrington's concepts was summarized in the Silliman lectures he gave at Yale in 1904, published in 1906 under the title of *The Integrative Action of the Nervous System*. In this he united his experimental results into a view of nervous function, co-ordination, and connectivity, that provided the basis of modern understanding of the nervous system, and the ways in which it receives, controls, utilizes, and responds to information from the external world. In 1947 the Physiological Society reprinted the book without alteration so that it might be read by 'all students of physiology and reread by their teachers'. As Lord Adrian later remarked, Sherrington's researches had 'opened up an entirely new chapter in the physiology of the central nervous system'. In 1939 the *Selected Writings of Sir Charles Sherrington*, edited by his former pupil D. Denny-Brown, brought together some of Sherrington's most important and influential contributions to the study of the nervous system.

In 1913 Sherrington was offered the Waynflete chair of physiology at Oxford, with a fellowship at Magdalen. He was fifty-six: there was no stated age of retirement, or promise of a pension. But Sherrington accepted, and a pleasant house was found at 9 Chadlington Road, near the laboratory and also near the Cherwell where he and his wife spent pleasant hours in punt or canoe. He sometimes wrote his scientific papers on the river. Oxford society he found 'a trifle rigid' but in the home of the regius professor of medicine, Sir William Osler, there was 'refreshing and stimulating refuge from formality'.

Just before the First World War, Sherrington and other British physiologists visited St Petersburg, where the highspot was meeting Ivan Pavlov, with whom he dined, warned by his host to expect the police as receiving three guests at one time was not permitted in a private house. Another engagement was with the tsar, who asked for news of his cousin. Sherrington had to reply that he had not seen much of the king of England lately.

During the war Sherrington wrote to a friend that he had undertaken unskilled work in a Vickers munitions factory in Birmingham. He was in fact studying industrial fatigue for the War Office, and he became chairman of the

Industrial Fatigue Research Board in 1918. He served also on committees on lockjaw and on alcohol and was Fullerian professor of physiology at the Royal Institution from 1914 to 1917. Throughout the war Sherrington also worked on a laboratory manual for physiology students. *Mammalian Physiology: a Course of Practical Exercises* (1919; new edn with E. G. T. Liddell, 1929) was a unique guide that influenced generations of physiologists in Britain and abroad.

From 1920 to 1925 Sherrington was president of the Royal Society, having been elected a fellow in 1893. He gave the Croonian lecture (1897) and received the society's royal (1905) and Copley (1927) medals. In 1922 he was president of the British Association meeting at Hull and in that year he was appointed GBE. In 1924 he was admitted to the Order of Merit. In the next year, to the surprise of even his closest friends, he published a slender book *The Assaying of Brabantius and other Verse*. Sherrington was never a narrow-minded specialist. Before he left Cambridge he had become a book collector, and made valuable gifts to several libraries. These included the British Museum, of which he was a trustee, and whose keeper of printed books described him in 1947 as 'our best benefactor in modern times'. In 1932 he shared with E. D. Adrian the Nobel prize for physiology or medicine. Other honours and awards came to 'the philosopher of the nervous system' from all over the world and were received with modest surprise. Sherrington's contributions to the study of the nervous system have been likened to those of William Harvey on the circulation.

After retiring from his chair at Oxford at the end of 1935 Sherrington, with regret, left his Magdalen friends. It had been 'a busy and fruitful autumn of scientific endeavour in which much of his earlier work came to full harvest'. In 1937 and 1938 he gave the Gifford lectures at Edinburgh and published them in 1940 under the title *Man on his Nature*. The book was widely read and went into several editions, including an exceedingly popular paperback. Described by the *Sunday Times* as 'one of the landmarks in the history of man's speculation about his own place in the universe', it was reprinted by the Physiological Society and given to every delegate attending the 17th International Physiological Congress in Oxford in 1947. It was selected as one of the hundred outstanding modern British books at the Festival of Britain in 1951. It was here that Sherrington explicitly addressed the mind–brain problem: 'But what of mind? Mind knows itself and knows the world: chemistry and physics, explaining so much, cannot undertake to explain mind itself.' Sherrington continued to believe throughout his life that dualism was as reasonable an assumption to make as was monism. In 1946 Sherrington published an excellent biography of an early French physiologist, *The Endeavour of Jean Fernel*.

In 1950 at a special meeting of the Soviet Academy of Science, Sherrington was referred to as the world's leader in regard to the dualist point of view among physiologists. But Sherrington had concluded only this: 'We have to regard the relation of mind to brain as still not merely unsolved but still devoid of a basis for its very beginning'

(*The Brain and its Mechanism*, Rede lecture, Cambridge, 1933).

In 1891 Sherrington married Ethel Mary (d. 1933), daughter of John Ely Wright, of Preston Manor, Suffolk. She was a musician, a good linguist which made her an excellent comrade on their many trips abroad, and one who loved the out of doors. 'Lady Sherrie' made their home in Oxford a centre of hospitality and much kindness to visitors from around the world. They had one son who became a railway economist.

Sherrington enjoyed skiing in Switzerland, was an ardent sailor, an interested traveller, a lover of art, music, and drama. He was a brilliant conversationalist who always seemed more enthusiastic about the work of others than about his own.

Sherrington died at his home, Olinda, 12 Grassington Road, Eastbourne, on 4 March 1952. In 1948 the Sherrington lectures had been founded in his honour in the University of Liverpool.

WILDER PENFIELD, *rev.* E. M. TANSEY

Sources E. G. T. Liddell, *Obits. FRS*, 8 (1952–3), 241–70 · J. P. Swazey, 'Sherrington, Charles Scott', *DSB* · J. C. Eccles and W. C. Gibson, *Sherrington: his life and thought* (1979) · R. Granit, *Charles Scott Sherrington: an appraisal* (1966) · Lord Cohen, *Sherrington: physiologist, philosopher and poet* (1958) · E. M. Tansey, 'Charles Sherrington and the Brown Animal Sanatory Institute', *St Thomas's Hospital Gazette*, 84 (1986), 5–10 · J. P. Swazey, *Reflexes and motor integration: Sherrington's concept of integrative action* (1969) · *Selected writings of Sir Charles Sherrington*, ed. D. Denny-Brown (1939); repr. (1979) · M. Jacobson, *Foundations of neuroscience* (1993) · Venn, *Alum. Cant.* · personal knowledge (1971) · *CGPLA Eng. & Wales* (1952)

Archives Medical Research Council, London, corresp. and papers · RS, corresp. and papers · U. Lpool, Sydney Jones Library, draft MSS; letters · University of British Columbia, Woodward Biomedical Library, corresp. and papers · Wellcome L., reminiscences | Bodl. Oxf., corresp. with Sir Rudolph Peters · CAC Cam., letters to A. V. Hill · NRA, priv. coll., letters to A. Ruffini · RCP Lond., letters to Sir F. M. R. Walshe · RS, letters to R. A. Granit · Wellcome L., corresp. with Sir Edward Sharpey-Schafer · Yale U., Fulton MSS | FILM British Medical Association Film collection, London, Physiological Society collection, footage, *c.*1941

Likenesses W. T. Maud, group portrait, photograph, 1899, Wellcome L. · W. Stoneman, photographs, 1917–43, NPG · R. G. Eves, oils, 1927, RS · R. G. Eves, oils, *c.*1927, NPG; related charcoal drawing, NPG · W. R. Flint, oils, 1929, Magd. Oxf. · R. J. Bracken, pencil drawing, 1944, FM Cam. · A. John, oils, University Club, Liverpool · W. Thomas, photomechanical print, Wellcome L. · double portrait, photograph (with Harvey Williams Cushing), Wellcome L. · group portrait, photograph, Wellcome L. · photograph, Wellcome L. · photographs, RS · portraits, Woodward Library, Vancouver · portraits, U. Oxf., laboratory of physiology

Wealth at death £21,205 19s. 0d.: probate, 13 May 1952, *CGPLA Eng. & Wales*

Sherrington, Helen Lemmens- (1834–1906), singer, born on 4 October 1834 at Preston, Lancashire, was the daughter of John Sherrington (of a Roman Catholic family long settled in the town), who managed a mill owned by his father. Her mother, whose maiden name was Johnson, a beautiful and promising young singer, retired from the profession on her marriage.

At the time of Helen's birth the family was ruined by a

Helen Lemmens-Sherrington (1834–1906), by Pierre Petit

bank failure. In 1838 her father obtained an appointment at Rotterdam, where good music was available both publicly and privately. There Helen was taught music by her mother, and quickly revealed a rich and pure soprano voice. At an early age she sang in the Roman Catholic church at Rotterdam and fascinated the congregation. From 1852 she studied at the Brussels conservatory under Cornelis; in 1855 she was awarded the first prize for singing and elocution. Already in great request as a concert singer, she became engaged to Jacques-Nicolas Lemmens (1823–1881), an organist and the son of deputy burgomaster Jean Baptiste Lemmens, and was induced by her fiancé to return to England. As she was now a stranger in her own country, she at first experienced difficulty in securing engagements, but at a concert of the Amateur Musical Society in the Hanover Square Rooms on 7 April 1856 she 'produced quite an impression', singing a florid bolero by Victor Massé and Schubert's *Ave Maria*. In the same week she sang with John Sims Reeves in a miscellaneous programme at one of Hullah's concerts, again with brilliant success. She appeared at several other concerts, and the critics agreed as to her high promise. After some study of English oratorio, by which her style was greatly improved, she performed in Mendelssohn's *Elijah* and Macfarren's

Mayday at the Bradford festival (1 August), at the inauguration of the Free Trade Hall, Manchester, in October, and at Liverpool in December. On 7 January 1857 she married Lemmens, and they settled permanently at 53 Finchley Road, St John's Wood, London. On 23 January she made her first appearance with the Sacred Harmonic Society, Exeter Hall, in Mendelssohn's *Athalie*.

Madame Lemmens-Sherrington had now taken her place as one of the leading English lyric sopranos; after the retirement of Clara Novello in 1860 she had hardly a rival. From 1860 to 1865 she sang in English opera. E. T. Smith's company at Her Majesty's and Drury Lane, which she joined in 1860–61, was distinguished (Sims Reeves, Charles Santley, Charles Hallé) but 'there was no attempt at stage management'. Her Marguerite in Gounod's *Faust*, in the English-language season of 1864–5, 'united freshness and purity of intonation to a happy technique and a most correct and tuneful delivery' (Arditi). From 1866 to 1868 she sang in Italian opera at Covent Garden, in such parts as Elvira (*Don Giovanni*), Adalgisa (*Norma*), and Marguerite de Valois (*Les Huguenots*). But she was mainly a concert singer, and with Janet Patey, Sims Reeves, and Santley she completed the quartet of great singers which from 1870 stood for all that was best in English performing art. Her husband had less success as an executive musician than as a composer, and the task of providing for their seven children fell mainly on her. She overworked, travelling great distances to keep engagements: two concerts a day, followed by a performance at an evening party, were not uncommon. Oratorio music displayed her powers to greatest advantage, and she was particularly successful in Haydn's *The Creation*, where the elaborate air 'On mighty pens' precisely suited her. In the autumn of 1875 she undertook a provincial tour, at which she sang in scenes from Wagner's *Lohengrin*, at that time new to England and much discussed. In 1876 she took part at St James's Hall in the first performance in England of Bach's mass in B minor.

In 1879 Lemmens opened a school for Catholic church musicians at Malines, and in January 1881 Madame Lemmens-Sherrington accepted a post as teacher of singing at the Brussels conservatory. Lemmens, however, died on 30 January 1881. From then on she was based in Brussels, where she retained her post until 1891, though she occasionally revisited England. When she sang at a performance of Peter Benoît's *Lucifer* in 1889, Shaw wrote that her excellent technique had kept her voice unimpaired after thirty-three years—'and she has the advantage, not common among artists, of being a clever and sensible woman'. She taught for a time in London at the Royal Academy of Music and in Manchester at the Royal College of Music. On 1 November 1894 she appeared for the last time in public, singing at Manchester in Haydn's *The Creation* in honour of her friend Sir Charles Hallé. Her last years were spent in retirement at 7 rue Capouillet, Brussels, where she died on 9 May 1906.

HENRY DAVEY, *rev.* JOHN ROSSELLI

Sources *The Times* (14 May 1906) · MT, 47 (1906), 395 · L. Arditi, *My reminiscences*, ed. Baroness von Zedlitz, 2nd edn (1896) · G. B. Shaw, *London music as heard in 1888–89 by Corno di Bassetto* (1937) · *From Mendelssohn to Wagner: being the memoirs of J. W. Davison, forty years the music critic of The Times*, ed. H. Davison (1912) · H. Rosenthal, *Two centuries of opera at Covent Garden* (1958) · m. cert.
Likenesses E. Matthews & Sons, lithograph, NPG · Moira & Haigh, carte-de-visite, NPG · P. Petit, photograph, NPG [*see illus.*] · H. Watkins, carte-de-visite, NPG · portrait, repro. in *Musical World* (July 1899) · woodburytype carte-de-visite, NPG

Sherry, Richard. *See* Sherrey, Richard (*b. c.*1505).

Sherwen, John (*bap.* 1748, *d.* 1826), surgeon and apothecary, son of John Sherwen, was baptized at St Michael's, Workington, Cumberland, on 23 April 1748. He was apprenticed to Anthony Harrison, surgeon and apothecary of Penrith, for five years, and then admitted a pupil at St Thomas's Hospital, London, on 4 February 1769. The court of examiners of the London Company of Surgeons passed him as a surgeon to an Indiaman on 1 June, four months later, and by the end of the year Sherwen was at Acheen, Sumatra, the voyage from Falmouth having taken five months; he was afterwards at Calcutta and in the Bay of Bengal.

By 1774 Sherwen had returned to England and was practising with Thomas Prichard, at Enfield, Middlesex; ten years later he took over Prichard's practice. He was also friendly there with Richard Gough, and Isaac D'Israeli, the three forming a literary trio. Sherwen founded the short-lived *Medical Spectator* and contributed to medical journals, and a silver medal for his contributions was given him by the Medical Society of London in March 1788.

Sherwen was admitted MD of King's College, Aberdeen, on 14 February 1798, on the recommendation of William Saunders; and on 4 May 1802 he became an extra-licentiate of the College of Physicians in London. In 1802 he paid a visit to Paris. His first wife was Douglass, posthumous daughter of Duncan Campbell of Salt Spring, Jamaica. She visited Bath for her health, and died there on 16 June 1804. A monument to her memory was erected in Bath Abbey. In 1805 Sherwen settled into practice at Bath, living at 18 Great Stanhope Street. He married again at Birkenhead, his second wife being Lydia Ann (1773–1851), the daughter of the late Revd Dannett of Liverpool, on 12 November 1807. There were no children by either of Sherwen's marriages.

Sherwen made a patient study of early English writers, and he owned some rare volumes of Elizabethan literature and early herbals. From 1808 to 1813 he was a frequent contributor to the *Gentleman's Magazine*, mainly on the authenticity of the 'Rowley' poems, which he believed to be genuine. He assisted John Britton in his work on Bath Abbey, and Britton dedicated to him the view of the abbey church from the south side. In 1809 Sherwen published his *Introduction to an examination of some part of the internal evidence respecting the antiquity and authenticity of certain publications* by Rowley or Chatterton. Sherwen was also a versifier of some merit, writing satirically of pompous squires, members of the local vestry, and Calvinist ministers (Gough MSS). He trained a number of apprentices, including William Gaitskel, who later became important in medical politics.

Sherwen made frequent trips to Enfield and died there in his house in Baker Street on 3 October 1826. He was buried on 12 October at St Andrew's Church, Enfield. After taking care of his wife's needs, his estate, including an annuity and the house at Bath, passed in succession to his dead sister's children, and then to establish a dispensary in Workington or Lamplugh.

W. P. COURTNEY, rev. JUANITA BURNBY

Sources *Old age in Bath: recollections of two retired physicians, Dr. John Sherwen and Dr. Thomas Cogan; to which are added … unpublished remains of William Wordsworth … and Joseph Hunter*, ed. H. J. Hunter (1873) · Introduction, *The Medical Spectator*, 1 (1792) · *GM*, 1st ser., 58 (1788), 358 · *GM*, 1st ser., 50 (1780), 127 · *GM*, 1st ser., 68 (1798) · *GM*, 1st ser., 77 (1807), 1074 · *GM*, 1st ser., 74 (1804), 601 · *GM*, 1st ser., 80 (1810) · *GM*, 2nd ser., 35 (1851), 571 · Munk, *Roll* · Watt, *Bibl. Brit.* · 'Literary verses by Dr Sherwen', ed. A. Gapper, *Bath and Bristol Magazine*, 3 (1834), 422–3 · J. Sherwen, 'Observations on the advantages of artificially scorbuticizing the system in some circumstances', *Edinburgh Medical and Surgical Journal*, 10 (1814), 44–50 · D. O. Pam, *A parish near London* (1990) · *N&Q*, 4th ser., 3 (1869), 15 · J. Burnby, 'Early influences in the life of Isaac D'Israeli', *Heritage*, 3 (1988), 41–5 · parish register (baptism), Workington, St Michael's, 23 April 1748 · parish register (burial), Enfield, St Andrew's, 12 Oct 1826

Archives BL OIOC, surgeon and civil servant records · Boston PL, English literary MSS · Guy's and St Thomas's Hospitals, London, united medical and dental schools · Palmers Green Library, London, Gough MSS, vestry minutes and rates for Enfield · PRO, IR/1/56 · RCS Eng., examination records

Wealth at death £50 p.a. to a niece; £555 to relatives and friends; plus house in Bath and house in Enfield: will, 1826, PRO, PROB 11/1718, sig. 556

Sherwill, Sir **Ambrose James** (1890–1968), bailiff of Guernsey, was born on 12 February 1890 in the Castel parish, Guernsey, the son of James Edgar Sherwill (*b.* 1860), butcher, of Les Landes, Castel, Guernsey, and his wife, Elizabeth Annie, *née* Roberts, dressmaker. He came of a poor family and had to work hard. He was educated at Elizabeth College, Guernsey, from 1903 to 1904 and then at the Lycée de Cherbourg from 1904 to 1905. He read law at the Université de Caen and graduated *bachelier-en-droit* in 1913 and *licencié-en-droit* in 1914. The First World War interrupted his studies. He served in the Royal Naval Air Service from 1914 to 1916 and was then commissioned as a lieutenant in the 8th battalion of the Buffs (East Kent regiment). He was wounded three times, mentioned in dispatches, and awarded the MC, the 1914–15 star, and the victory medal. He was called to the bar (Inner Temple) in 1920 and won the Powell prize for evidence and procedure. On 1 May 1920 he was admitted to the Guernsey bar. On 5 October the same year he married May de Beauvoir Tattersall, *née* Clabburn (1890/91–1970), a widow, and daughter of John George Clabburn of Lammas Hall, Norfolk. There were four sons and one daughter of the marriage.

Sherwill proved to be the best advocate of his generation in Guernsey, and was appointed his majesty's comptroller (solicitor-general) on 3 October 1929 and his majesty's procureur (attorney-general) on 6 April 1935. On the premature death of Arthur Bell he might, as procureur, have anticipated succeeding Bell as bailiff. However, he had only just entered office as procureur and so Victor Carey was appointed. Five years later, with German invasion imminent, the island government was radically altered. The states of deliberation set up a controlling committee, a small 'cabinet' designed to replace the states of Guernsey (the island parliament). Because of his relevant legal experience as procureur, Sherwill was appointed president of this committee.

At first Sherwill entertained ideas of a 'model' occupation: 'On the one hand, tolerance on the part of the military authority, and courtesy and correctness on the part of the occupying forces, and on the other, dignity and courtesy and exemplary behaviour on the part of the civilian population' (Bunting, 77). Soon, however, Sherwill encountered the moral dilemmas of occupation. In August 1940 he gave a broadcast talk on German overseas radio and praised the exemplary conduct of the occupying force in Guernsey. Sherwill intended to reassure those islanders who had evacuated to Britain, but German propaganda imparted its own 'spin'. Then, in September 1940, the Germans introduced anti-Jewish measures, including the requirement that Jews must wear the yellow star of David. Sherwill believed (mistakenly, as it later transpired) that the few Jews living in Guernsey had all evacuated, and accordingly felt that there was no point in declining to register the provision. However, Sir Abraham Lainé refused to concur in the registration, an act which elicited admiration from Sherwill: 'this courageous act of his should never be forgotten. As I sat listening to him, I realised how right he was' (ibid., 106).

In September 1940 Sherwill was preoccupied with the case of Nicolle and Symes. These Guernseymen, serving in the British army, had been landed on the island to gather intelligence. When the return vessel failed to make the rendezvous, they were forced to hide. Their lives, and those of friends and relatives giving them shelter, were in great danger. Sherwill worked energetically to secure their potential status as prisoners of war, and then recommended to Nicolle and Symes that they should give themselves up. Some Germans believed that Sherwill had tricked them and sent him, along with twelve others, to prison in Paris. The German commander of Guernsey intervened, and after three months' incarceration Sherwill was allowed to return to the island. The Germans removed him from the presidency of the controlling committee and from the office of procureur. He supported his family as best he could by growing vegetables and keeping goats. In January 1943 he was deported to Germany and spent the rest of the war at Laufen internment camp. There he gave leadership to his fellow deportees and successfully secured the transfer of the Jerseyman Stanley Green from Buchenwald to Laufen.

On 12 December 1945 Sherwill was made a CBE, and then on 1 March 1946 he was made bailiff. In 1949 he was knighted. He retired as bailiff in 1960, in which year he was advanced to KBE. He died at The Glen, rue des Vinaires, St Peter-in-the-Wood, Guernsey, of heart failure on 25 September 1968, and was buried on 28 September at Castel parish church.

Sherwill's record as president of the controlling committee has intermittently been attacked, although seldom by Guernsey islanders. His ambition was to soften the impact of the occupation on the islanders. He used his legal acumen to try to outwit the Germans, to his cost in the Nicolle–Symes affair. Between the autumn of 1940 and May 1945 he was successively in prison in France, in disgrace with the Germans in Guernsey, and in an internment camp in Germany. The islanders regarded him as a brave man.   GREGORY COX

Sources C. Cruickshank, *The German occupation of the Channel Islands* (1975) · W. M. Bell, *I beg to report … policing in Guernsey during the German occupation* (1995) · F. Falla, *The silent war* (1967) · F. E. Cohen, 'The Jews in the islands of Jersey, Guernsey and Sark during the German occupation, 1940–1945', *Journal of Holocaust Education*, 6/1 (1997), 27–81 · memoirs of Sir Ambrose Sherwill, priv. coll. · M. Bunting, *The model occupation* (1995) · private information (2004) · Greffe records, Royal Court, Guernsey · *WWW*, 1961–70 · Burke, *Peerage* · *Guernsey Evening Press* (30 Sept 1968)
Likenesses A. Michael, oils, Royal Court, Guernsey; repro. in L. J. Marr, *Guernsey people* (1984), pl. 34

Sherwin, Charles (*bap.* 1757). *See under* Sherwin, John Keyse (*bap.* 1751, *d.* 1790).

Sherwin, John Keyse (*bap.* 1751, *d.* 1790), designer and engraver, was baptized on 27 May 1751 at East Dean, near Chichester, Sussex, one of nine children born to Francis Sherwin, a shipyard carpenter's labourer, and his wife Martha Nowell. Sherwin anticipated the 'ploughman poet' Robert Burns and the 'Cornish wonder' John Opie in being catapulted into society from humble circumstances and feted as a genius. He was working as a gardener on William Mitford's estate near Petworth in 1769 when Mitford discovered his talent and sent his drawing 'The Head of a Blackmoor' to the Society of Arts, where it was awarded a silver medal. Sherwin was then enabled to go to London, where he studied painting under the affluent showman John Astley, who had married into society and bought Schomberg House, to which fashionable ladies flocked. Sherwin was taught to engrave by the celebrated royal favourite Francis Bartolozzi, whose bohemian lifestyle exerted an equally malign influence on the impressionable prodigy. In 1770 he was admitted to the schools of the Royal Academy, and in 1772 gained the gold medal for a historical picture.

According to the contemporary artist Edward Dayes his training left Sherwin full of 'impudent assurance' (*Works*, 349). On leaving Bartolozzi in 1774 he set up on his own, his first published plate being *The Madonna* (1775), after Sassoferrato. He exhibited ambitious red-and-black chalk drawings of historical subjects over the next ten years and was appointed 'engraver in the red chalk manner' to George III. He engraved some fine portraits and subjects after Sir Joshua Reynolds, Angelica Kauffman, Thomas Gainsborough, and others and he was undoubtedly talented and skilful. He was chiefly celebrated in his own day for such 'history prints' as his fine altar pieces after Guido Reni at Magdalen College, Oxford, and after Anton Raphael Mengs at All Souls; *The Fortune Teller*, after Reynolds; and *The Death of Lord Robert Manners*, after Thomas

John Keyse Sherwin (*bap.* 1751, *d.* 1790), self-portrait, pubd 1794

Stothard (for which last Thomas Macklin paid him £700). His style in line engraving was distinctively metallic and flashy, tending to stylization and full of bravado. In 1785, on Woollett's death, he became historical engraver to the king. He also began to engrave and publish a series of his own designs, but he lacked a talent for composition: *The Happy Village* and *The Deserted Village* (1787) were ill-conceived and their fashionable mixed-method technique was muddy in effect. Another historical print, *The Finding of Moses* (1789), was a transparently commercial device for grouping portraits of the leading society ladies with the princess royal starring as Pharaoh's daughter. Fashionable ladies flocked to his house, vying for inclusion. He charged a bold 3 guineas for the print, with early impressions costing double that. His oil 'The Installation Dinner at the Institution of the Order of St Patrick in 1783'—some 50 or 60 feet long—was left unfinished at his death, as was his engraving of it.

Such projects tended to justify Dayes's caustic observation that Sherwin's 'vanity was so great that he imagined nothing too difficult' (*Works*, 349), and it was probably these ambitious publishing schemes that ultimately broke him. According to Dodd, Sherwin, 'realizing by his labours considerable affluence … launched into an imprudent course of life by which he destroyed his constitution and met with a premature death … at the age of 37' (Dodd, fol. 232). The unsympathetic Dayes did not mince his words:

> by running from one excess to another, he broke a good constitution, impaired his mind, and so embarrassed his affairs, that he was afraid to appear abroad: under these wretched circumstances he sank into eternity, at the house of Wilkinson, the print-seller in Cornhill. (*Works*, 349)

Sherwin died at a small alehouse in Oxford Road, Westminster, on 20 September 1790. A sale of items from his workshop was held on 9–10 November; Robert Wilkinson acquired his plates.

Charles Sherwin (*bap.* 1757) was baptized on 14 February 1757; he was John Sherwin's brother and worked as his assistant. He completed his brother's portrait of Captain Dampier, after Murray, and those of Viscount Folkestone, after Gainsborough, and George Cleghorne MD. His own work had no special merit and consisted of portraits for books. It is not known when or where he died.

TIMOTHY CLAYTON and ANITA MCCONNELL

Sources D. Alexander, 'Sherwin, John Keyse', *The dictionary of art*, ed. J. Turner (1996) · Dodd, manuscript history of English engravers, BL, Add. MS 33404, fols. 232–7 · admon, PRO, PROB 6/166, fol. 219r · *The works of the late Edward Dayes*, ed. E. W. Brayley (privately printed, London, 1805) · parish register, Sussex, East Dean, 27 May 1751 [baptism] · Redgrave, *Artists*
Archives W. Sussex RO, letters and papers
Likenesses self-portrait, stipple, pubd 1794, BM, NPG [*see illus.*]

Sherwin, Ralph [St Ralph Sherwin] (**1549/50–1581**), Roman Catholic priest and martyr, was born at Rodsley, near Ashbourne, Derbyshire. His parents were probably John and Constance Sherwin. In 1568 he became a fellow of Exeter College, Oxford, and 'progressed with great industry the several classes of logic and philosophy' (Wood, *Ath. Oxon.*, 478). He took his BA on 22 November 1571, and, on 2 July 1574, 'being then accounted an acute philosopher and excellent graecian and hebrician', he took his MA as senior of the act, impressing an audience that included the earl of Leicester, the queen's favourite.

In 1575 Sherwin left Oxford University and embraced Catholicism. 'Having received leave from Sir John Petre to study medicine abroad' (Boase, 76) he went to Douai and after two years was ordained priest by the bishop of Cambrai on 23 March 1577. In August he proceeded to Rome. In the disputes that took place concerning the direction of the English College, Sherwin played a leading part and became the spokesman for those who saw the future of the college to be a place for the preparation of missioners to England rather than a refuge for exiles. The college annals (*Liber ruber*) begin on 23 April 1579 when the college oath was initially administered. Sherwin, aged twenty-nine, was first on the roll, expressing his resolution to go to England 'Today rather than tomorrow'.

On 18 April 1580 Sherwin left Rome in company with other priests, including Edmund Campion and Robert Persons. He arrived in England some time in August, but in the following November he was captured while preaching in the London home of Nicholas Roscarrock, another alumnus of Exeter College. He was taken to the Marshalsea 'where he lay night and day in a great pair of shackles for the space of a month'. He was transferred to the Tower, was racked twice and was offered a protestant bishopric if he would renounce his faith. Two of his letters written at this time are printed in William Allen's *Briefe Historie*.

On 14 November 1581 Sherwin was indicted with seven others, accused of having entered England for the purpose of raising a rebellion and overthrowing the queen. The trial took place in Westminster Hall. The chief proof on which the prosecution relied was the deposition of false witnesses. On 20 November Sherwin, Edmund Campion, and Alexander Briant were condemned to death by hanging, drawing, and quartering, the penalty for common traitors. Two days before he died Sherwin remarked to Campion, pointing to the sun, 'Ah Campion I shall shortly be above yonder fellow'. On 1 December 1581 he was dragged on a hurdle from the Tower to Tyburn where, after the short customary address to the crowd, in which he prayed for the queen, he said he was not guilty of any crime except being a Catholic. Before being hanged he kissed the hands of his executioner which were still wet with the blood of Campion who had just met a similar death.

Sherwin was canonized by Pope Paul VI in 1970. He is venerated as the proto-martyr of the English College, Rome.   MICHAEL E. WILLIAMS

Sources G. Anstruther, *The seminary priests 1: Elizabethan, 1558–1603* [1966], 311–13 · Archdiocese of Westminster, *Cause of the canonization of blessed martyrs John Houghton, Robert Lawrence, Augustine Webster, Richard Reynolds, John Stone, Cuthbert Mayne, John Paine, Edmund Campion, Alexander Briant, Ralph Sherwin and Luke Kirby put to death on England in defence of the Catholic faith (1535–1582)*, Sacred Congregation of Rites Historical Society, 148 (1968) · Wood, *Ath. Oxon.*, new edn, 1.478 · C. W. Boase, ed., *Registrum Collegii Exoniensis*, new edn, OHS, 27 (1894), 76 · W. Kelly, ed., *Liber ruber venerabilis collegii Anglorum de urbe*, 1, Catholic RS, 37 (1940) · DNB · E. Lodge, *Illustrations of British history, biography, and manners*, 2nd edn, 2 (1838), 343
Likenesses portrait?, 17th cent., English College, Rome

Sherwin, Ralph (**1799–1830**), actor, was born on 3 April 1799 at Bishop Auckland, co. Durham. He received a basic education in his birthplace, and subsequently went to school in Witton-le-Wear. For five years he studied medicine in London and Edinburgh, but soon became acquainted with Yates of Covent Garden and was inspired to take to the stage. His first appearance was made in York in July 1818, under Mansell, in the role of Dandie Dinmont in *Guy Mannering*. He remained in the York company for two years, acting in Leeds, Hull, and Sheffield. He then went to Birmingham, under Alfred Bunn, and lost his wardrobe when the theatre was burnt down. At Brighton, under Brunton, he played low comedy and old men. He later rejoined Bunn at Leicester, and appeared in the newly erected theatre in Birmingham. On 14 February 1823, as Sherwin from York, he made his début at Drury Lane, playing Dandie Dinmont in *Guy Mannering* once again. He was engaged for three years, and acted the part of Robin in *No Song No Supper*, Paddock in *My Spouse and I*, and Diggory Delph in *Family Jars*, among others. In 1825 he was the original Shock, a very poor shepherd, in Joseph Lunn's adaptation *The Shepherd of Derwent Vale, or, The Innocent Culprit*, Sam Sharpset in *The Slave*, to W. C. Macready's Gambia, and Russet in George Colman's *The Jealous Wife*. Few opportunities were given him, however, and he played mainly in minor roles. At the end of the three years he was not re-engaged, irregular habits being the reputed cause of his dismissal. He then took to driving a stagecoach, which he upset, but did return for a short time to the stage. Sherwin had a fine face and figure, expressive features, and a smooth and powerful voice. He was a good mimic, could sketch likenesses with remarkable fidelity, and was an efficient representative of Yorkshire characters. He died in 1830, in Durham, at his father's house.

JOSEPH KNIGHT, rev. NILANJANA BANERJI

Sources *Oxberry's Dramatic Biography*, 1/11 (1825) · *The biography of the British stage, being correct narratives of the lives of all the principal actors and actresses* (1824) · Hall, *Dramatic ports.* · Genest, *Eng. stage* · *GM*, 1st ser., 100/2 (1830), 376
Likenesses four prints, Harvard TC · plate, repro. in *Oxberry's Dramatic Biography*

Sherwin, William (1607–1690), clergyman and ejected minister, was born in Nottinghamshire. He entered St John's College, Cambridge, in 1624, but in 1625 migrated to Queens' College, Cambridge, where his tutor, Herbert Palmer, later a member of the Westminster assembly of divines, encouraged him to read the millenarian writings of Joseph Mede. Sherwin graduated BA in 1628, was ordained in May 1630, and proceeded MA in 1631. He was married to Dorothea Swan at Ashwell in Hertfordshire on 11 September 1637; there were at least two children from this marriage, a daughter and a son, William *Sherwin (b. c.1645, d. in or after 1709) the engraver.

In 1645 Sherwin was assigned to the lectureship at Baldock, Hertfordshire, and appointed to the sequestered living of Wallington, in the same county, although in October John Bowles, former incumbent of the latter, was called before the committee for plundered ministers for disturbing him. Describing Sherwin's service in Wallington and Baldock, Edmund Calamy remarked that Sherwin cast 'his Net where there was Plenty of Fish. And he did it to good Purpose: For God blessed his Ministry to that great Congregation very much' (Calamy, 361). In 1660, however, Sherwin was ejected from his living when it was restored to Bowles. He then went to live in Fowlmere in Cambridgeshire with his daughter and son-in-law, John Crakinthorpe, who was rector there.

After his ejection, freed, as he explained, from 'Preaching, Expounding, Catechising, public fasts, &c' (Sherwin, *Times of Restitution*, 3–4), Sherwin resumed his study of apocalyptic prophecy, writing a number of works expounding millenarian doctrines. In 1665 he published *Eirēnikon, or, A peaceable Consideration of Christ's Peaceful Kingdom on Earth to Come*, and *Prodromos: the Fore-Runner of Christ's Peaceable Kingdome upon Earth*. These works set out, albeit moderately and undogmatically, Sherwin's belief that there would be a personal manifestation of Christ in the world to inaugurate the thousand-year millennial kingdom. Sherwin's eschatological thought was influenced by his reading of John Archer's *The Personall Raigne of Christ upon Earth* (1642), and especially by Mede's writings. In the 1670s Sherwin published more millenarian tracts, presenting his conviction that the advent of Christ's kingdom on earth was imminent, and that the conversion of the Jews to Christianity would occur with Christ's appearance in the world; in the meantime he encouraged his readers to seek unity and peace (*The Doctrine of Christ's Glorious Kingdom*, 1672, 1). Having published more than ten new works in the previous seven years, Sherwin's writings ceased abruptly in 1676. His only other extant work is a short tract from 1682 entitled *Of the Two Last Things*, in which he criticized prelacy and the human imposition of laws on worship. Sherwin remained at Fowlmere until his death, and was buried there on 12 June 1690.

WARREN JOHNSTON

Sources *Calamy rev.* · Venn, *Alum. Cant.* · E. Calamy, ed., *An abridgement of Mr. Baxter's history of his life and times, with an account of the ministers, &c., who were ejected after the Restauration of King Charles II*, 2nd edn, 2 vols. (1713) · W. Sherwin, *Chronoi apokatastaseōs pantōn, or, The times of restitution of all things with their neer approach upon the ruine of the beast* (1675), 3–5 · *DNB* · W. Sherwin, *The doctrine of Christ's glorious kingdom* (1672)
Likenesses W. Sherwin junior, line engraving, 1672, BM, NPG; repro. in Sherwin, *Doctrine*

Sherwin, William (b. c.1645, d. in or after **1709**), engraver and inventor of a method of mezzotinting, the son of William *Sherwin (1607–1690), a Church of England clergyman, and his wife, Dorothea Swan, was born at Wallington, Hertfordshire, where his father was rector, about 1645. Nothing is known of his training, and his first datable plate is a portrait prefixed to Richard Atkyns's *History of Printing* in 1664. He had established his own shop in London in Little Britain by 1669, when he published John Leeke's translation of Vignola, entitled *The Complete Architect*. From this time he seems hardly ever to have worked for another publisher. He published few books and hardly any plates made by other engravers.

1669 is the date on Sherwin's portrait of Charles II, which is the earliest dated mezzotint by an Englishman. The Latin dedication of this and its pair, a portrait of Queen Catherine, to Prince Rupert states that the process was revealed to the artist through the prince's kindness. James Granger, however, states that Sherwin had in fact discovered the secret for himself, using a loaded file to lay the ground. Since the method of laying the ground is the key to the process and had been Rupert's contribution to the development of the mezzotint, Rupert suspected that the secret had been betrayed by his servant. But Sherwin managed to disprove this, and Rupert instead helped him perfect his technique.

John Chaloner Smith lists twenty mezzotints made by Sherwin between 1669 and 1703, all of which are so rare that it is clear that Sherwin never managed to exploit the process, whose huge development from the end of the 1670s lay in the hands of others. Sherwin also made numerous portrait engravings, which have never been catalogued, as well as a handful of architectural plates and at least one landscape etching.

The number of Sherwin's prints apparently diminishes after 1676, the year in which he was awarded a patent for inventing a new method of printing calicoes. This seems to be the earliest date for calico printing in Europe, for the first Dutch factory at Amersfoort was only established two years later. Sherwin established a factory at West Ham Abbey in the Lea valley, and in 1696, in a petition in defence of the calico industry, he stated that he and his next neighbour employed about 400 men. He had a secondary factory in London, at Well Yard, near St Bartholomew's Hospital.

In 1672 Sherwin married Elizabeth, the daughter of Thomas Pride, one of Cromwell's aides, and his wife, who was a niece of General Monck. This link may have given him access to the capital he needed to establish such a large business. It certainly cannot have come from his print-making, for this never became a large affair. The quality of his work, although always competent, is not high, for he had no real ability in drawing. The Monck relationship led Sherwin and other relatives into a protracted lawsuit after the intestate death of the second duke of Albemarle in 1688, and the last evidence for Sherwin's being alive is a revival of the lawsuit in 1709.

ANTONY GRIFFITHS

Sources J. Granger, *A biographical history of England, from Egbert the Great to the revolution*, 2nd edn, 4 (1775), 138–9 · J. C. Smith, *British mezzotinto portraits*, 3 (1880), 1052–60 · P. Floud, 'The origins of English calico printing', *Journal of the Society of Dyers and Colourists*, 76 (1960), 275–81 · A. Griffiths and R. A. Gerard, *The print in Stuart Britain, 1603–1689* (1998), 212–14, 267–9 [exhibition catalogue, BM, 8 May – 20 Sept 1998]

Sherwood [*née* Butt], **Mary Martha** (1775–1851), children's writer and educationist, was born on 6 May 1775, at Stanford rectory, Worcestershire, the second child and the older daughter of the Revd George Butt (*d.* 1795), appointed a chaplain in ordinary to George III in 1784, and his wife, Martha, *née* Sherwood (*d.* 1817). She was raised and educated in a prosperous but strict home. Tall, well-formed, and auburn-haired, Mary was called Hygeia by her father. Wearing an iron collar to which a backboard was attached, she stood uncomplainingly for daily lessons from her mother; she learned Latin from her father and Greek from her brother, Marten. At fifteen she was sent as a parlour boarder to the Abbey School for Girls at Reading, run by M. and Mme Saint-Quentin. At seventeen she completed her first published story, *Traditions* (1794), which her father discovered and shepherded into print, for the benefit of their ruined friend, M. Saint-Quentin; lamenting the 'ridiculous and serious defect' of having 'the two wives of the hero existing at the same time' (Kelly, 123), Sherwood recalls her juvenilia in her journal (fifteen volumes edited and abridged to one by her daughter Sophia) as exhibiting 'a mind very far from mature' (Darton, 160).

After George Butt's death, on 29 September 1795, his widow and children settled at Bridgnorth, Shropshire, where Mary wrote *Margarita* (1802), sold in 1798 for £40 to Mr Hazard of Bath, and *Susan Grey* (1802), sold for £10. She admits having her head 'full of romantic imagery' and being 'singularly ignorant of life' (Kelly, 163). At the curate's urging, she and her sister Lucy took charge of the Sunday school, where Mary read successive chapters of *Susan Grey* to the older girls as warnings against the promises of military men, 'who were there today and gone tomorrow' (Kelly, 220). In spite of this view, on 30 June 1803, she married her cousin, Captain Henry Sherwood (1776–1849), of the 53rd foot regiment, who was appointed

paymaster the next year. Life in the barracks at Sunderland, co. Durham, was solitary and bleak. Her first child, Mary Henrietta, was born in 1804 at Morpeth, Northumberland, another military base. She accompanied Captain Sherwood when he was ordered to India in 1805, reluctantly leaving the child with her mother and sister 'to save her health from the effects of other climes' (Kelly, 263).

The four-month journey round the Cape to Madras, while Mary Sherwood was pregnant again, was full of perils, including attacks from French warships. In their ten-year stay in India, the growing Sherwood family moved from Calcutta to Dinapore, Berhampore, Cawnpore, and Meerut. 'Never without a baby' (Kelly, 303), Sherwood bore four daughters and two sons in India; her first son, Henry, and second daughter, Lucy, died in infancy. Sherwood was convinced that the Indian nurse of the beatific Henry, 'paler and fairer than polished marble' (Kelly, 318), had poisoned him with opium. With evangelical fervour, she set up schools in each of the postings and wrote about family life in an Indian setting. From Cawnpore her husband sent the amazingly successful *Little Henry and his Bearer* (1815; 37th edn by 1850), the tale of an angelic, dying eight-year-old British orphan who catechizes and directs the conversion of his Hindu bearer Boosy (with the consequent loss of caste), to her sister, who sold it to Mr Hazard of Wellington for £5; in her lifetime it was translated into French, German, Spanish, Hindustani, Chinese, and Sinhalese. The complementary tract, *Little Lucy and her Dhaye* (1825) highlights a similar turn from Sinbad stories to sacred texts, along with the conversion of the Indian nurse. Despite her contention that *Pilgrim's Progress* was 'ill-suited to the genius of the East', Sherwood relied on 'this work of honest old John's' (Kelly, 417) for two Bunyanesque redactions, *The Indian Pilgrim* (1818) and *The Infant's Progress* (1821), the former concentrating on the supposed depravity and pagan idolatry of Brahmans, fakirs, nautch (dance) girls, and soldiers' temporary wives, and the latter, also composed in India, using abstract topography and introducing Sherwood's own malicious sprite, Inbred-Sin. On the family voyage to Meerut she drafted *The Fairchild Family* (1818; 2nd pt, 1842; 3rd pt, 1847), the quintessential reading experience, according to F. J. Harvey Darton (p. ix), for every nineteenth-century middle-class child. India remained a rich resource throughout her long career, as evidenced in tracts and novels such as *George Desmond* (1821), *Henry Milner* (1823) and its sequel *John Marten* (1844), and *The Indian Orphans* (1839).

On Mary Sherwood's return to England in 1816, with her own family, two adopted orphans, and a motherless girl making up a numerous and expensive brood, she devoted the rest of her long life to writing (over 400 titles are assigned to her) and teaching. Abhorring debt and without 'ready money to throw away' (Darton, 440), she made use of her voluntary work in India by establishing a boarding-school 'for the education of a few young ladies' (Darton, 438–9) in English, French, astronomy, history, geography, grammar, writing, and ciphering, at Wick, Worcestershire. With dogmatic fervour, she edited Sarah

Fielding's *The Governess* (1820), a project promised to her mother, who died on 20 March 1817. On half pay in the Brunswick hussars, Captain Sherwood opened a little school in Henwick, Worcestershire. Her eighth child, George, born in 1819, died in infancy. She taught her children Hebrew while working on a dictionary of Old Testament types; Captain Sherwood laboured for ten years on a Hebrew–English concordance.

Whether writing for children or adults, Mary Sherwood was unwilling to temper her conviction of inherent human corruption. Mr Fairchild conducts his quarrelling youngsters to view the rotting corpse of a fratricide on a gibbet to teach them 'that our hearts by nature are full of hatred' (*Fairchild Family*, 59). Sherwood's visit to her brother's parsonage at Oddingley, Worcestershire, resulted in the two-part *The Oddingley Murders* (1830), a grisly true story of the murder of the pastor, the subsequent execution of the assassin hired by local folk who resisted tithes, and the wanting 'spirit of harmony and benevolence' in this 'unhappy parish' (pp. 6–7). Literature for all ranks had a catechetical utility for Sherwood, whether in the four-volume *The lady of the manor, being conversations on confirmation intended for the use of the middle and higher ranks of females* (1825–9), or her short contributions to *The Youth's Magazine*, or her editorship of *The Child's Magazine*. The dynamics of family life, always reflecting the foundational importance of Christian principles, also informed her work, from the piety of the English boarder in *The Flowers of the Forest* (1830), the Christian education of the boy-narrator in *The Babes in the Wood of the New World* (1830), and the fond memories of *The Happy Family* (1838), to the instructive contrasts between siblings in the historical novels she completed with the help of her daughter Sophia, *The Mirror of Maidens in the Days of Queen Bess* (1851) and *The Two Knights, or, Delancey Castle: a Tale of the Civil Wars* (1851). Although her anti-Catholicism was a staple of the times, it became particularly virulent with her characterization of greedy Father Peter in the allegory *The Latter Days* (1833), her lurid descriptions of the 'frightful prison house' (p. 53) and 'various little low cabals' (p. 2) of the convent in the gothic novel *The Nun* (1833; 5 edns to 1860), and the blistering depiction of religious houses in another gothic, *The Monk of Cimiès* (1834). An abolitionist whose attitude toward the indigene was condescending yet occasionally sympathetic, resolutely maintaining that native beliefs ought to be supplanted by Christianity, she succeeded in creating compelling portraits of Dazee in *The Re-Captured Negro* (1821) and Thomas Wilson in *The Poor Man of Colour* (1830).

Mary Sherwood's travels and acquaintances expanded her circle of influence and experience. She was definitely more at ease during a meeting with William Wilberforce, in 1820, at the china manufactory in Worcester, when he wanted to hear about India, and in her coach ride to Worcester gaol with Elizabeth Fry, in 1821, where they talked about 'the dangers of celebrity, for females especially' (Kelly, 537), than she had been, before her marriage, during an audience at Bath with Hannah More, who 'spoke well' but whose sisters 'gathered up her words carefully,

rather Boswellian-like' (Kelly, 217). Throughout the 1830s the Sherwoods travelled extensively on the continent, especially in France and Switzerland; on the return vessel from Holland, in 1832, she met the frail, invalided Sir Walter Scott, to whom she lent pen and ink. Sherwood's work regimen remained prodigious; until her mid-seventies, she read the smallest print, wrote four to five hours each day, and considered herself 'one of the very happiest old women that ever cumbered this earth' (Kelly, 573). In 1849 Captain and Mrs Sherwood left Worcester for Isleworth and then Twickenham, Middlesex, where Captain Sherwood died on 6 December, Mary Sherwood following him on 20 September 1851.   PATRICIA DEMERS

Sources N. Cutt, *Mrs Sherwood and her books for children* (1974) · F. J. H. Darton, ed., *The life and times of Mrs. Sherwood (1775–1851)* (1910) · P. Demers, 'Mrs Sherwood and Hesba Stretton: the letter and spirit of evangelical writing for children', *Romanticism and children's literature in nineteenth-century England*, ed. J. H. McGavran (1991), 129–49 · S. Kelly, ed., *The life of Mrs Sherwood* (1854) · D. Rosman, *Evangelicals and culture* (1984) · N. Royde-Smith, *The state of mind of Mrs Sherwood* (1946)

Likenesses M. Maskall, lithograph, BM · portrait, repro. in Kelly, *Life of Mrs Sherwood* · portrait, repro. in Darton, ed., *Life and times*

Sherwood, Richard (1828–1883), lawyer and politician, was born in Douglas, Isle of Man, and baptized on 9 November 1828 at St Matthew's Church, Douglas, the eldest among the four sons of Richard Sherwood (*d.* 1857), ironmonger, and his wife, Elizabeth Fitzgerald (*d.* 1867). His father came from Whitehaven, Cumberland, as presumably did his mother. Destined for a legal career, he was articled in 1843. On 4 March 1851 he married Ann Graham (*d.* after 1883) of Bibaloe Mooar, Onchan, and farmed there with his wife's family.

Called to the Manx bar in 1857, Sherwood practised first in Ramsey and then in Douglas. In 1863 he went to Australia with the intention of practising the law in Queensland. The difficulties of qualifying there forced him to abandon the idea, and he returned home by way of the United States in 1864. He again took up the law and became involved in Manx politics. In the year of his return he came to immediate prominence by acting for James Brown, proprietor of the *Isle of Man Times*, who had been jailed by the House of Keys for contempt in relation to publishing an article about their rejection of a bill to enlarge the powers of the commissioners for the town of Douglas. Brown served a seven-week term before the English courts ordered that he should be released (he was awarded £250 damages). This was a popular victory and Sherwood's reputation increased immeasurably as a result, although he was now branded as a reformer.

The lieutenant-governor of the day, Henry Brougham Loch, wielded enormous executive power and managed to reform the corrupt and self-elected House of Keys through the House of Keys Election Act of 1866. This gave Sherwood a chance to get into the Keys, and, having failed to find a seat in the first elections to the reformed house, he was elected two years later in a by-election for Glenfaba, a seat he held until 1883. His constituency included the major fishing port of Peel, which at that time supported some 6000 people and produced revenue (mostly from herring) of £80,000 per annum. His interest in improving its harbour led to the first of many clashes in Tynwald with Loch. The autocratic lieutenant-governor usually bested Sherwood when his authority was challenged, describing him as 'revolutionary, if not communistic'. When Loch left the island in April 1882, the *Isle of Man Times* commented, 'Perhaps no two men in the whole legislature have oftener found themselves on opposite sides than the Governor and Mr Sherwood. Times without number has their warfare been carried into the Tynwald Court to almost an extreme' (Harrison, 353).

Sherwood was none the less an effective reforming politician and battled against both Loch and the entrenched remnants of the unreformed House of Keys who had survived the 1866 election. In effect he was the leader of the new house. He was a firm advocate of lowering the age of franchise and the introduction of a secret ballot, which passed into law in 1874 and 1883 respectively; and as early as 1869 was supporting votes for women. When an act of 1881 enfranchised female property owners (although not occupiers) he proposed without success to give parity of voting to both sexes. He was a leader in the successful bid to have mail sent daily to the island. Outside the house he fought successfully between 1870 and 1873 for a scheme to extend the promenade in Douglas and to link the harbour with the back of the town by means of a new street, a battle he won against opposition from both Loch and an influential reactionary, G. W. Dumbell.

To quote A. W. Moore:

> As a lawyer he had few equals, and no superiors, at the Manx Bar. Between 1866 and 1883, he appeared in every important suit, and gained some great successes, notably in three cases against the Crown, all of which he won.

Of these the most important was the Ballaharra clay case, which firmly established the right of Manx customary freeholders to the sand and clay underlying their farms. These rights were claimed by the crown, but Sherwood appealed to the judicial committee of the privy council, which decided for the plaintiffs. On his voyage to Australia he had written an important treatise on Manx law tenures which, published in 1899, became the authoritative statement on the subject. His legal ability was recognized by his appointment as second deemster in 1883.

Sherwood continued farming on his return from Australia at Coloneys, Braddan, but later moved to Glencrutchery House in Douglas. He clearly made much money from the law, but although he was deeply philanthropic, his finances were generally chaotic. Unusually in the island, he was a Unitarian. He was an excessively bearded man. Separated from his wife, he was something of a womanizer. He committed suicide at Glencrutchery House on 8 December 1883 and was buried on 17 December in Onchan parish churchyard.   A. M. HARRISON

Sources A. M. Harrison, 'Richard Sherwood in Manx politics', *Proceedings of the Isle of Man Natural History and Antiquarian Society*, 8/4 (1982), 349–61 · A. W. Moore, *Manx worthies* (1901), 87–8 · J. W. Belchem, ed., *A new history of the Isle of Man*, 5: *The modern period, 1830–1999* (2000)

Likenesses two photographs, *c.*1883, Manx National Heritage Library, Douglas, Isle of Man · J. Swinnerton, marble bust, 1885, Douglas town hall, Isle of Man

Sherwood, Robert (*fl.* 1622–1634), lexicographer, was born in Norfolk. He entered Corpus Christi College, Cambridge, on 7 June 1622, and graduated BA in 1625/6. His tutor was Richard Sterne, who later assisted in Bishop Walton's polyglot Bible (1657), and became archbishop of York. Sherwood moved to London, established a school in St Sepulchre's churchyard, and compiled the English–French dictionary that was appended to the second edition of Randle Cotgrave's *Dictionary of the French and English Tongues* (1632).

Sherwood was the first lexicographer to compile a word-list appearing in a bi-directional bilingual dictionary in which the English is set before the French. The work was entitled 'A dictionarie English and French; compiled for the commoditie of all such as are desirous of both the languages' and was puffed as 'most copious' on the title-page to Cotgrave's French–English dictionary. His two prefaces were written with an eye to the different needs of both groups of target users. Sherwood apologizes to the English user for the space-saving restrictions imposed upon him by the printer, but makes a virtue of necessity:

> It could not be expected in so small a volume, as I was inforced to contract my selfe into, that (in this English Dictionarie) I should show all the French Nounes, and the conjugation of all French Verbes, which are most sufficiently and at large, alreadie done by M. Cotgrave; to whom I referre you.

In his preface 'Aux favorables lecteurs françois, alemans, & autres' he is keen to stress the comprehensive nature of his word-list, which he claims contains all or most of the words in the English language, and the usefulness of the back-matter, which comprises a pronunciation guide and a list of irregular verbs. Sherwood's work was retained, with minor additions to the back-matter, in the editions of Cotgrave's dictionary that were revised and enlarged by James Howell (1650, 1660, 1673).

In 1634 Sherwood published *The French Tutour, … the Second Edition, Carefully Corrected and Enlarged*. It survives only in this text, though it was entered in the Stationers' register on 3 January 1625, and since no copy has been located, the existence of the first edition is open to question. The grammatical element of the work is largely derived from the revised 1625 edition of Charles Maupas's *Grammaire et syntaxe françoise* (Sherwood, iv). Only one additional fact about Sherwood survives: he was ordained deacon in Norwich on 23 December 1632.   JOHN LEIGH

Sources R. Sherwood, *The French tutor*, ed. R. C. Alston (1969), iv · V. E. Smalley, *The sources of a dictionarie of the French and English tongues by Randle Cotgrave* (1948), 33, n. 52 · Norfolk RO, DN/REG 16, bk 23, p. 22 · K. Lambley, *The teaching and cultivation of the French language in England during Tudor and Stuart times* (1920), 192, 281–2 · *DNB* · R. Masters, *The history of the College of Corpus Christi and the B. Virgin Mary … in the University of Cambridge* (1753), 379 · private information (2004) [archivist, Corpus Christi College, Cambridge]
Archives Norfolk RO, DN/REG 16, bk 23, p. 22

Sherwood [Shirwood], **William of** (*d*. in or before 1272), logician and ecclesiastic, was presumably born in Nottinghamshire. The details of his early career are not known, though it is likely that he studied at Oxford, and he most probably wrote his logical treatises in the late 1230s and 1240s. Some authorities claim that he taught at the University of Paris, but there is no positive evidence for this. He was certainly a master by 27 January 1249, when 'magister Willielmus de Shirwood' was one of the witnesses to the foundation deed of the nunnery of Marham in Norfolk; and he was equally certainly at Oxford in 1252, when 'Magister Wilhelmus de Skirwodde' was one of the northerners who swore to the terms of peace agreed by the northern and Irish scholars (who had recently been involved in violent conflict) at Oxford. He became treasurer of Lincoln no earlier than December 1254, after the death of Peter Chaceporc; and the first surviving document mentioning him as treasurer is dated between December 1254 and November 1258. In 1258 he was granted a papal dispensation to hold a benefice with cure of souls in addition to his post as treasurer; and he was still treasurer in 1263, when he played a prominent role in the settlement of a dispute between the cathedral and the city of Lincoln. A document dated October 1266 refers to him as rector of the prebendal church of Aylesbury, Buckinghamshire, but he ceased to be rector before November 1267. His name also appears in the list of rectors of Attleborough in Norfolk under Henry III, and a reference there to the man who became rector at his death suggests that Sherwood must have died by 1272. If it is assumed that he remained treasurer of Lincoln until his death, this conjecture is supported by the fact that Richard of Battle became treasurer some time between 1269 and 1272.

The most important source of Sherwood's works is a Paris manuscript (Bibliothèque Nationale, MS Lat. 16617), whose first part contains several works written in an English hand. The first item is an *Introductiones in logicam* which is explicitly attributed to Sherwood (ibid., fols. 1–23r), one of several general outlines of logic that survive from the thirteenth century. These include the well-known *Tractatus* (or *Summulae logicales*) of Petrus Hispanus, and the slightly later *Summulae dialectices* of Roger Bacon. Like Petrus Hispanus, Sherwood covers both the basic topics of Aristotle's logic with the exception of the *Posterior Analytics*, and the newly developed logic of terms or supposition theory. There is no evidence that either man knew the other's work, and similarities derive from the fact that they drew on the same tradition. A tract on supposition theory is found in whole or in part in two other manuscripts (Venice, Biblioteca Nazionale Marciana, MS Z.L.302, fols. 161r–162v; Worcester Cathedral, MS Q.13, fols. 58rb–59vb), and its use in teaching is attested by the existence of anonymous *Dubitationes* (Worcester Cathedral, MS Q.13, fols. 59vb–63v) dating from the 1290s. The *Introductiones* are followed by a work on *Syncategoremata* (Paris, Bibliothèque Nationale, MS Lat. 16617, fols. 23r–46r)—that is, special logical terms, such as 'whole', 'only', 'necessarily'. This too is explicitly attributed to Sherwood, as it is in the only other manuscript copy (Bodl. Oxf., MS

Digby 55, fols. 205ra–224rb). Next there are two treatises on *insolubilia*, or semantic paradoxes (Paris, Bibliothèque Nationale, MS Lat. 16617, fols. 46v–50v and 50v–54v) of which the first has been tentatively assigned to Sherwood by its editor, though there is no firm evidence. Finally there is a treatise on *obligationes*, or the rules governing what one is obliged to accept or reject in a certain kind of logical disputation (Paris, Bibliothèque Nationale, MS Lat. 16617, fols. 54v–62v), followed by a treatise called *Petitiones contrariorum*, on solutions to sophismata, or logical puzzle-cases (ibid., fols. 62v–64v). There is no particular reason to think that the last work is by Sherwood, but the *De obligationibus*, which exists in three other manuscripts (Erfurt, Wissenschaftliche Allgemeine Bibliothek, Amploniana MS Q 259, fols. 209r–214v; Paris, Bibliothèque Nationale, MS Lat. 16130, fols. 110v–114r; Venice, Biblioteca Nazionale Marciana, MS Z.L.302 (X 204), fols. 151ra–155va), has caused some controversy. The Paris manuscript attributes it to Magister W, but two other manuscripts attribute it to Walter Burley, and the Venice manuscript attributes it to Burley in the heading and to Sherwood in the *explicit*. There seems no way to settle the issue of authorship at this point. Three theological works were attributed to Sherwood by Leland in the sixteenth century, but even if they were by Sherwood, they have not survived.

Evidence of Sherwood's importance is provided by Roger Bacon. In his *Opus tertium* of 1267 Bacon wrote that Sherwood was 'much wiser than Albert [the Great]; for in *philosophia communis* no one is greater than he' (*Rogeri Bacon opera*, 14); and in his *Compendium studii philosophiae* of 1271 Bacon linked Sherwood with Robert Grosseteste (*d*. 1253) and other wise men of the recent past.

E. J. ASHWORTH

Sources *William of Sherwood: Einführung in die Logik* (*Introductiones in logicam*), ed. H. Brands and C. Kann (1995) · *William of Sherwood's 'Introduction to logic'*, trans. N. Kretzmann (1966) · P. O. Lewry, 'Grammar, logic and rhetoric, 1220–1320', *Hist. U. Oxf.* 1: *Early Oxf. schools*, 401–33 · L. M. de Rijk, 'Some thirteenth century tracts on the game of obligation. III. The tract *De petitionibus contrariorum*, usually attributed to William of Sherwood', *Vivarium*, 14 (1976), 26–49 · R. Green, 'The logical treatise *De obligationibus*: an introduction with critical texts of William of Sherwood and Walter Burley', PhD diss., University of Louvain, 1963 · A. de Libera, 'The Oxford and Paris traditions in logic', *The Cambridge history of later medieval philosophy: from the rediscovery of Aristotle to the disintegration of scholasticism, 1100–1600*, ed. N. Kretzmann, A. Kenny, and J. Pinborg (1982), 174–87 · J. Pinborg and S. Ebbesen, 'Thirteenth century notes on William of Sherwood's "Treatise on properties of terms": an edition of *Anonymi dubitationes et notabilia circa Guilelmi de Shyreswode introductionum logicalium Tractatum V* from MS Worcester Cath. Q.13', *Cahiers de l'Institut du Moyen-Âge Grec et Latin*, 47 (1984), 103–41 · 'The *Syncategoremata* of William of Sherwood', ed. J. R. O'Donnell, *Mediaeval Studies*, 3 (1941), 46–93 · *William of Sherwood's 'Treatise on syncategorematic words'*, trans. N. Kretzmann (1968) · M. L. Roure, 'La problématique des propositions insolubles au XIIIe siècle et au début du XIVe siècle', *Archives d'Histoire Doctrinale et Littéraire du Moyen Âge*, 37 (1970), 205–326 · K. Jacobi, *Die Modalbegriffe in den logischen Schriften des Wilhelm von Shyreswood und in anderen Kompendien des 12. et 13. Jahrhunderts* (1980) · Emden, *Oxf.*, 3.1693–4 · P. V. Spade and E. Stump, 'Walter Burley and the *Obligationes* attributed to William of Sherwood', *History and Philosophy of Logic*, 4 (1983), 9–26 · H. A. G. Braakhuis, *De 13de eeuwse tractaten over syncategorematische termen*, 2 vols. (1979) · *Fr. Rogeri Bacon opera* *quaedam hactenus inedita*, ed. J. S. Brewer, Rolls Series, 15 (1859), 14, 428

Archives Biblioteca Nazionale Marciana, Venice, MS Z.L.302, fols. 161r–162v · Bibliotheca Nazionale Marciana, Venice, MS Z.L.302 (x 204), fols. 151ra–155ra · Bibliothèque Nationale, Paris, MS Lat. 16130, fols. 110v–114r · Bibliothèque Nationale, Paris, MS Lat. 16617 · Bodl. Oxf., MS Digby 55, fols. 205ra–224rb · Wissenschaftliche Allgemeine Bibliothek, Erfurt, Amploniana MS Q 259, fols. 209r–214v · Worcester Cathedral, MS Q.13, fols. 58rb–63va

Sherwood, William (*d.* **1482**), bishop of Meath and administrator, was a priest of the archdiocese of York who was provided to the bishopric of Meath in March 1460. There is no evidence that Sherwood participated with Philip Bermingham, the future chief justice, in the Lancastrian insurrection in Meath in 1462, but he was soon leading the Meath gentry in opposition to Geraldine (Fitzgerald) pretensions there. After Thomas Fitzgerald, seventh earl of Desmond (*d.* 1468), had ignored Edward IV's appointment of Sherwood as deputy chancellor in January 1464, a feud ensued and the two were summoned to court. Sherwood's renewed opposition to Desmond's rule apparently helped to secure the earl's supersession and attainder in 1467–8.

In July 1475 the bishop replaced Thomas Fitzgerald, seventh earl of Kildare (*d.* 1478), as deputy lieutenant, and therefore deputy to George, duke of Clarence, the absent lieutenant of Ireland. The reduction of English financial subventions prompted Sherwood to reorganize the parliamentary subsidy and impose heavy taxation on the English pale. He went to court in 1477, where Edward IV tried to compose new disputes with Kildare; but when, in February 1478, Clarence was executed for treason, thus annulling Sherwood's appointment, Kildare was elected governor instead. This time, serious disturbances followed, which were not finally settled until late in 1479 when the king reconciled Sherwood and Chief Justice Bermingham with Gerald Fitzgerald (*d.* 1513), the young eighth earl of Kildare, now appointed deputy lieutenant, and Lord Portlester, the chancellor. Sherwood became chancellor and served without further trouble until his death in Dublin on 3 December 1482. He was buried at Newtown Abbey, near Trim, Meath. STEVEN G. ELLIS

Sources S. G. Ellis, *Ireland in the age of the Tudors* (1998) · A. Cosgrove, 'The execution of the earl of Desmond, 1468', *Journal of the Kerry Archaeological and Historical Society*, 8 (1975), 11–27 · H. F. Berry and J. F. Morrissey, eds., *Statute rolls of the parliament of Ireland*, 4 vols. (1907–39) · F. E. Ball, *The judges in Ireland, 1221–1921*, 2 vols. (1926) · S. G. Ellis, *Reform and revival: English government in Ireland, 1470–1534*, Royal Historical Society Studies in History, 47 (1986) · T. W. Moody and others, eds., *A new history of Ireland*, 2: *Medieval Ireland, 1169–1534* (1987); repr. with corrections (1993) · *DNB* · D. B. Quinn, 'Guide to English financial records for Irish history, 1461–1558', *Analecta Hibernica*, 10 (1941), 1–69

Shevyngton, Alice (*fl.* **late 15th cent.**). *See under* Women traders and artisans in London (*act. c.*1200–*c.*1500).

Shewalton. For this title name *see* Boyle, David, Lord Shewalton (1772–1853).

Shewen, William (*c.***1631–1695**), Quaker preacher, was of unknown parentage, and nothing is known of him before 1654. By this date Shewen had joined the Southwark Quaker Meeting, which was then gathering in private homes, including Shewen's house at the sign of Two Brewers in Bermondsey Street, Bermondsey. Describing himself in his will as a gentleman, Shewen appears to have been involved in business of some description, for an acquaintance of the Welsh Quaker Richard Davies was apprenticed to him. In 1679 he married Ann Raper (*d.* 1706), with whom he had three children.

Shewen was appointed an elder of the meeting in the parish of St Mary Magdalen, Southwark, and from the 1650s onwards was active in the Quaker movement as both preacher and controversialist. In 1659 he was among a number of Quaker preachers subjected to 'manifold Abuses' by hecklers at meetings in Mitcham, Surrey (Besse, 1.680). In April 1674 he engaged in a public dispute with the Baptist leader Jeremiah Ives in Croydon, Surrey. This doctrinal quarrel continued as a pamphlet controversy throughout that year and launched Shewen's career as a printed author. Over the next two decades Shewen published a number of doctrinal and devotional works. His works pleaded constantly for liberty of conscience and for toleration at the most parochial level, his writing arising from ongoing experience of persecution. In 1683 he was among a number of Quakers who, barred from their meeting-house in Horselydown, were arrested for meeting instead in the street. In March 1686 a royal warrant calling for the halt of legal proceedings against Shewen and his wife, among others, identified the former as a 'recusant' of St Mary Magdalen, Southwark (*CSP dom.*, *1686–7*, 72).

Later that year Shewen and his wife moved to Enfield, Middlesex. It is presumably here that he died on 28 May 1695, aged about sixty-four; he was buried at Bunhill Fields. By the time of his death he was of substantial means, leaving a well-appointed property in Enfield and over £2000 in disposable money. The instructions detailed in his will indicate, moreover, that Shewen had considerable financial acumen.

Despite his regular subjection, as an early Quaker, to prejudice and harassment, Shewen's ministry nevertheless seems to have been combined with a successful business career. Author of 'several seasonable experimental treatises' (Whiting, 508), Shewen is most aptly characterized in his own words: applauding William III's declaration for liberty of conscience, the title-page to his last work, *A Brief Testimony for Religion* (1688), announces that it is written by 'a Hater of no man because of his opinion'. BETH LYNCH

Sources J. Whiting, *Persecution exposed: in some memoirs relating to the sufferings of John Whiting and many others of the people called Quakers*, 2nd edn (1791) · W. Beck and T. F. Ball, eds., *The London Friends' meetings: showing the rise of the Society of Friends in London; its progress, and the development of its discipline; with accounts of the various meeting-houses and burial-grounds, their history and general associations* (1869) · J. Besse, *A collection of the sufferings of the people called Quakers*, 1 (1753) · *An account of the convincement, exercises, services, and travels of … Richard Davies*, 2nd edn (1765) · *CSP dom.*, *1686–7*, 72 · Wing, *STC* · J. Smith, ed., *A descriptive catalogue of Friends' books*, 2 (1867) · *The Christian progress of that ancient servant and minister of Jesus Christ, George Whitehead*, ed. [J. Besse?] (1725) · C. R. Hildeburn, *The issues of the press in Pennsylvania, 1685–1784*, 1 (1885) · PRO, PROB 11/426, sig. 105, fols. 168v–169v

Wealth at death over £2000; plus substantial property and plate: will, PRO, PROB 11/426, sig. 105

Shiel, Matthew Phipps (1865–1947), novelist, was born on 20 July 1865 in Plymouth, Montserrat, West Indies, the ninth child and only son of Matthew Dowdy Shiell (1825–1888), a shipowner and Methodist lay preacher of Irish descent, and Priscilla Ann Blake (1830–1910), who was of mixed race. A precocious juvenile, he wrote newspaper columns and an unpublished novel. At fifteen he was ceremoniously crowned by his father as king of Redonda, a rocky islet near Monserrat, and he allowed his fictitious title to be perpetuated. He was educated at Harrison College, a boarding-school in Barbados. In London after 1883, he matriculated at London University, briefly studied medicine, and became a schoolmaster. By the early nineties he was contributing stories to penny weeklies and associating with such writers as W. T. Stead and Arthur Machen.

In 1895 Shiel (as he thereafter spelled his name), published *Prince Zaleski*, describing mysteries solved by an eccentric Russian. *The Rajah's Sapphire* and *Shapes in the Fire* appeared the next year. On 3 November 1898 he married Carolina Garcia Gomez (1879/80–1903), daughter of Miguel Garcia Gomez, a Seville merchant. They had one child, a daughter. That year *The Yellow Danger* introduced the menace of Chinese domination of the world. *Contraband of War* (1899), an adventure of rival naval innovators, was followed by two historical romances, *Cold Steel* (1899) and *The Man Stealers* (1900). Popularity came with two visionary tales in 1901. In *The Lord of the Sea* an English farmer gains control of the world's seaways, discovers he is a Jew, and seeks to solve the 'Jewish problem' in England and Palestine. In *The Purple Cloud* the sole survivor of universal volcanic asphyxiation wanders Europe burning its dead cities until he finds a second survivor, a young woman, and is redeemed by love. What made these novels literary sensations was their grandiose sweep of imagination, the vigour and inventiveness of their prose, and Shiel's surreal images of obsession, hysteria, and horror.

By 1913 Shiel had published eleven more books, including *The Yellow Wave* (1905), inspired by the Russo-Japanese War, a story of interracial romance and intercontinental warfare, and *The Last Miracle* (1906), about a plot to undermine the church by creating and then exposing false miracles. In December 1914 Shiel was briefly imprisoned in Wormwood Scrubs for reasons undetermined. During the war years he wrote plays that were never published. On 31 January 1919 he married Esther Lydia Furley (1872/3–1943). His second creative period began in 1923 with *Children of the Wind*, an African adventure, followed by *How the Old Woman Got Home* (1927), *Here Comes the Lady* (1928), and *Dr Krasinski's Secret* (1929). Republication of four of his novels by Gollancz in 1929 helped revive Shiel's earlier reputation. His wife divorced him in 1929, and after occupying dozens of lodgings in London, Shiel settled in 1930 at L'Abri, a cottage near Horsham, Sussex. His last five books include a murder mystery (*The Black Box*, 1930), short stories (*The Invisible Voices*, 1935), and a science-fiction fantasy (*The Young Men are Coming*, 1937).

Shiel's thirty books varied greatly in theme and quality. The purple prose and frenzied emotion of the 1901 fantasies were never quite equalled, though 'frenetic vigour' remained the hallmark of Shiel's style (Morse, *Works of M. P. Shiel*, 480). His books embodied preoccupations of his time—imperialism, the yellow peril, spiritualism, scientism, evolution—and encompassed many genres—adventure, romance, mystery, horror, fantasy, science fiction. At his best reminiscent of Poe and Wells, he could descend to potboilers and juvenilia. Misanthropy, racism, and anti-semitism pervade his writing, as does fascination with a masterful, aspiring hero.

Shiel's only autobiographical essay, written when he was thirty-five, is brief and unreliable, and many facts about his life remain obscure. A semi-recluse, he wrote his last five books, received a civil-list pension through the efforts of his first bibliographer, John Gawsworth, and worked on a life of Jesus. Shiel died on 17 February 1947 at St Richard's Hospital, Chichester, and was cremated on 24 February at Golders Green, London. After his death he became a cult figure. ALBERT R. VOGELER

Sources A. R. Morse, *The works of M. P. Shiel* (1979) • A. R. Morse, ed., *Shiel in diverse hands: a collection of essays by twenty-nine students of M. P. Shiel* (Cleveland, Ohio, 1983) • C. J. Keep, 'M. P. Shiel', *Late-Victorian and Edwardian British novelists: first series*, ed. G. M. Johnson, DLitB, 153 (1995) • J. Squires, 'Shiel, M[atthew] P[hipps] 1865–1947', *Penguin encyclopedia of horror and the supernatural* (1986), 382–4 • E. F. Bleiler, 'Matthew Phipps Shiel', *The encyclopedia of science fiction*, ed. J. Chute and P. Nichols, 2nd edn (1993) • S. Moskowitz, 'The world, the devil, and M. P. Shiel', *Explorers of the infinite* (1963) • *The Times* (20 Feb 1947) • *New York Times* (18 Feb 1947) • www.creative.net/~alang/lit/horror/impsbooks.htm [annotated bibliography], 2001 • www.creative.net/~alang/lit/horror/jdsbooks.sht [catalogue of books by and about M. P. Shiel], 2001 • www.creative.net/~alang/lit/horror/shiel.sht, 2001 • www.geocities.com/soho/5900/index.html [Redonda], 2001 • m. cert.

Archives Ransom HRC, corresp. and papers • U. Reading L., corresp. with publishers and corresp. relating to his literary estate

Likenesses photograph, repro. in Morse, ed., *Shiel in diverse hands*, 483 • portrait, repro. in M. P. Shiel, *Science, life, and literature* (1950), frontispiece • portraits, repro. in Morse, *Works*, pp. 602, 430

Wealth at death £1487 7s. 3d.: probate, 4 June 1947, CGPLA Eng. & Wales

Shield, William (*bap.* 1748/9, *d.* 1829), composer, was born at Swalwell in the parish of Whickham, co. Durham, the son of William Shield (*d.* 1757), a music teacher. There appears to be no evidence documenting his birth, although there is reference to a baptism of one William Shields on 5 May 1748, and of another William Shields on 5 March 1749. If the latter, his mother's name was Mary. He was educated by his father until the elder Shield's death, when he was apprenticed to a boatbuilder named Edward Davidson (or Davison) of South (or North) Shields; but he continued his musical studies under the composer and concert organizer Charles Avison, for whom he frequently played the violin at concerts. According to his nineteenth-century biographer John Robinson, it was after one of these concerts that he was introduced to Felice Giardini, who ultimately persuaded him to become a professional musician. Fiske places this fortuitous meeting at Scarborough, to which Shield had moved on the

William Shield (*bap.* 1748/9, *d.* 1829), by Robert Dunkarton, pubd 1788 (after John Opie, exh. RA 1787)

completion of his apprenticeship. It was there, through the instrumentality of John Cunningham, the poet and actor, that he was appointed leader of the band at the theatre and conductor of the concerts. Here he encountered his earliest success as a composer by setting poems by Cunningham to music, and, at the request of Richard Trevor, bishop of Durham, he composed his earliest composition, an anthem now lost, for the consecration of St John's Church, Sunderland, on 6 April 1769. On the death of Avison in 1770 his son Edward Avison engaged Shield as leader at the Newcastle concerts and Shield also held a similar position in Durham. At this time Shield played violin extensively in concerts and theatres throughout the north-east, but concert life slackened during the construction of the new assembly rooms in Newcastle, and in 1773 he accepted Giardini's offer of the post among the violins in the orchestra of the King's Theatre in the Haymarket, London. He is not known to have resided in the north-east again, but returned to visit his mother in 1791. Shield progressed quickly to become leader of the viola section and retained this post for eighteen years. His ability to orchestrate and compose for theatre was learned primarily through his experience playing in this and other metropolitan operatic orchestras. In London, Shield met Ann Stokes, of Marylebone, described in his will in 1826 as his 'beloved partner, Ann, Mrs Shield, upwards of forty years' (Robinson, 13–14). The probate record describes her as 'Ann Stokes, alias Shield, spinster' (Robinson, 13); it is not clear whether they married.

Shield is known to have composed, or contributed music towards at least thirty-six operas and seven pantomimes and pantomime ballets. In addition to these he produced three song collections and published several of his most popular theatre songs independently. His work outside theatre music is relatively modest, including a small number of duets, string quartets, and string trios.

Shield's first operatic venture was the music to *Flitch of Bacon*, a comic opera by Henry Bate, afterwards Sir Henry Bate Dudley. It was produced by George Colman at the Haymarket Theatre in 1778 and shows enormous ingenuity in orchestration. Shield subsequently produced two works in rapid succession: *The Cobbler of Casterbury* (1779) and *The Siege of Gibraltar* (1780), both for Covent Garden, but neither an unmitigated success. In 1782, however, Shield produced *Rosina*, and through its success Shield was appointed house composer at Covent Garden. *Rosina* is set in the north of England, inspiring Shield to end its overture with a tune reminiscent of bagpipes. This tune became much better known as the music to 'Auld Lang Syne' by Robert Burns, whose 'Comin' thro' the rye' was also set to Shield's music. The two never met. Although Shield's operas were produced mostly in vocal score and libretto, *Rosina* is the only one to survive in orchestral parts, and for this reason it is especially significant in assessing Shield's ability to orchestrate for theatre. Such was the extent of Shield's success that in 1791 he entertained Haydn, among others, in his home in Taplow. It was presumably then, as a gesture of mutual respect, that Haydn presented him with his trio *Pietà di me*, complete with concertante parts for English horn, bassoon, and horn. In August 1792 he resigned his office at Covent Garden owing to a financial disagreement, and went to France and Italy with Joseph Ritson, the antiquary. On his return a few months later he was immediately reinstated, but resigned in 1797 and dissolved all connection with the theatre ten years later. In 1793 he, Charles Incledon, Bannister the elder, and others formed the once famous Glee Club; he was also an original member of the Philharmonic Society. The time that Shield had gained by reducing his theatre commitments may have been directed towards writing. In 1800 he published *An Introduction to Harmony*, which was followed in 1817 by *The Rudiments of Thorough Bass*, designed as a teaching aid; in it Shield took the opportunity to publish several of the folk songs he had learned as a child.

On the death of Sir William Parsons in 1817 Shield became master of musicians in ordinary to the king. Shield died at his home, 31 Berners Street, London, on 25 January 1829, and was buried on 4 February in the south cloister of Westminster Abbey, in the same grave as Johann Peter Salomon and Muzio Clementi. He left his fine Stainer viola to George IV who, however, insisted on paying Ann Stokes its full value. On 19 October 1891 a memorial cross to Shield was erected by public subscription, supported by the newspaper publisher Joseph Cowen, in Whickham churchyard, and on 25 January 1892 a memorial stone was placed over his grave in Westminster Abbey.

R. H. LEGGE, *rev.* BENNETT MITCHELL ZON

Sources R. Fiske, 'Shield, William', *New Grove* · J. Robinson, *Memorial to William Shield, musician and composer with a sketch of the life*

of Shield (1891) • J. L. Chester, ed., *The marriage, baptismal, and burial registers of the collegiate church or abbey of St Peter, Westminster*, Harleian Society, 10 (1876), 502 • parish register, Whickham, St Mary, March 1696–1751, Durham RO, EP/WHM3 [baptism] • A. P. Stanley, *Historical memorials of Westminster Abbey*, 3rd edn (1869), 339 • *Annual Biography and Obituary*, 14 (1830) • *Quarterly Musical Magazine and Review*, 10 (1828), 273–4 • *MT*, 32 (1891), 654 • W. T. Parke, *Musical memoirs*, 2 vols. (1830) • 'Memoir of William Shield', *The Harmonicon*, 7 (1829), 49–52 • *The Times* (15 Dec 1998)
Likenesses R. Dunkarton, mezzotint, pubd 1788 (after J. Opie, exh. RA 1787), BM, NPG [*see illus.*] • T. Hardy, stipple, pubd 1796, BM, NPG • G. Dance, pencil drawing, 1798, NPG • J. Jackson, watercolour drawing, c.1822, NPG • W. Brockedon, pencil and chalk drawing, 1826, NPG • attrib. T. Hardy, oils, Royal College of Music, London • T. Woolnoth, stipple (after J. Jackson), BM, NPG; repro. in *The British gallery of contemporary portraits* (1822)

Shields, Cuthbert [*formerly* Robert Laing] (1840–1908), university teacher and eccentric, was born on 21 March 1840 in George Street, North Shields, Northumberland, the first child of Robert Laing, master mariner, and his wife, Charlotte Sophia, daughter of Dr Charles Coleman of Maidstone, Kent. His father spent long periods at sea and his mother was responsible for overseeing his education, which he received first at the Moravian schools of Neuwied and Niesky, then at King Edward's School, Birmingham. He matriculated at Wadham College, Oxford, in 1859, gained a first-class degree in jurisprudence and modern history in 1863 (MA 1865), and taught as an assistant master at Radley College. His tutor at Wadham, Walter Waddington Shirley, encouraged him to return to Oxford, where he taught first as a coach, then as a lecturer at Wadham from 1866. He was elected a fellow of Corpus Christi College in 1868. With Edward Stuart Talbot of Christ Church, Charles Lancelot Shadwell of Oriel, and Mandell Creighton of Merton, Laing made a major contribution to the development of the school of modern history, establishing the intercollegiate system of lectures and holding lectureships in nine of the Oxford colleges.

Laing abandoned teaching in 1873 to concentrate on research and university reform, encouraged in the latter by John Matthias Wilson, native of South Shields and newly elected president of Corpus Christi College. In a pamphlet, *Some Dreams of a Constitution-Monger* (1876), he summarized his views on university and college reform. In his evidence to the commission of 1877, Laing advocated a more focused basis for the teaching of history. Lack of organization made it very difficult to establish the new subject of study, and enthusiastic individuals could easily be discouraged and leave the university. He also thought that a properly staffed history school 'might do a great deal in the way of giving lectures throughout the country' and thus increase Oxford's hold on the country (*University of Oxford Commission*, 83).

Laing was an interesting and stimulating, if discursive, lecturer. He took an active part in the movement for the higher education of women and gave courses of lectures in several provincial towns. His autobiographical notebooks (Bodl. Oxf., MSS Don. e. 183–9) reveal that he found lecturing a considerable strain. It was when lecturing on the French Revolution to ladies in Oxford that Laing came into contact with Alice Liddell, later Hargreaves (1852–

1934), daughter of the dean of Christ Church. He immediately became infatuated with her, and her rejection of his advances, combined with the exertions of campaigning for the Liberal candidates in the 1878 parliamentary by-elections at North Shields and Oxford University—during which he shouted to the crowd outside the Radcliffe Camera, 'Remember Eve!'—led to a complete breakdown. One of his notebooks (MS Don. e. 189) recounts in graphic detail the treatment administered to him as a patient of George Fielding Blandford at Munster House private asylum, Fulham, in the summer of 1878.

Laing returned to Oxford for the Michaelmas term in 1878, but left again shortly, took up residence abroad for at least seven years, much of the time at the Moravian community of Herrnhut, and travelled extensively in continental Europe and the Middle East. Between December 1883 and March 1886 he wrote an apologia for his conduct in 1878, in the form of letters to Oxford colleagues (Bodl. Oxf., MSS Don. e. 185–9). So great was the impact on his personality of this experience of prolonged exile that in 1886 Laing changed his name by deed poll to Cuthbert Shields. He returned to Oxford and to his fellowship at Corpus Christi College, where he acquired the reputation of a mystic and a kindly, entertaining, and eccentric don. His breakfast parties for undergraduates were a major feature of college life. He was an excellent raconteur, but one whose conversation had to be steered away from the occult. He claimed to have second sight, believed in the transmigration of souls, and held that in a former incarnation he had been Zoroaster.

Shields published little beyond a few articles in the *Contemporary Review* and the *Quarterly Review*, which included a lengthy review in the latter of George Eliot's *Middlemarch* in April 1873. He devoted most of his later years to the study of India, and examined on this and other subjects for the civil service commissioners. His function, according to Charles Plummer, 'was rather to stimulate productiveness in others than to produce much himself' (Plummer, 137). He served as librarian, garden master, and vice-president of his college, but had to have more periods of overseas travel to cope with recurring ill health.

Writing in the *Pelican Record* in 1917, Charles Oman recalled Shields's 'broad bald forehead, his eager eyes, his big [amethyst] ring' (p. 187). In group photographs of the Owlets' Club (the college reading club he founded in 1889), he appears a benign senior member, with an enormous white beard. He died at Corpus Christi College 'from an internal complaint' (Plummer, 137) on 20 September 1908 and was buried at Holywell cemetery, Oxford, on 24 September. MARY CLAPINSON

Sources C. Shields, autobiographical notebooks, Bodl. Oxf., MSS Don. e.185–189 • [C. Plummer], 'In memoriam', *Pelican Record*, 9 (1907–9), 135–9 • 'Cuthbert Shields', *Pelican Record*, 9 (1907–9), 141–2, 216–17 • [C. Oman], 'An Oxford prophet at Jerusalem', *Pelican Record*, 14 (1917–20), 187–91 • R. Laing, *Some dreams of a constitution-monger* (1876) • *University of Oxford Commission* (1881), 79–83 • CCC Oxf. • M. McFall, 'Cuthbert Shields, Odd Fellow', *Pelican Record*, 39/3 (1994–6), 62–5 • baptismal register, 22 April 1840, Christ Church, Tynemouth • *The Times* (22 Sept 1908), 9 • *Oxford Times* (26 Sept 1908)

Archives Bodl. Oxf., autobiographical notebooks, MSS Don. e.185–189 | Queen's College, Oxford, letters to Edwin Palmer **Likenesses** group portraits, photographs, 1860–99 (the Owlets' Club), CCC Oxf. **Wealth at death** £3267 0s. 7d.: probate, 31 Oct 1908, CGPLA Eng. & Wales

Shields, Frederic James (1833–1911), artist, was born at High Street, Hartlepool, on 14 March 1833, the eldest of the four children of John Shields (c.1808–1849) and his wife, Georgiana Storey (d. 1853). He was baptized Frederick, but later adopted the spelling Frederic. John Shields was a bookbinder, stationer, and printer who ran a circulating library; his wife was a straw hat maker. In 1839 the family moved to London, where Shields attended St Clement Danes parish school until he was fourteen. John Shields was a good draughtsman who recognized his son's talent and gave him his first drawing lessons. Shields also studied engraving at evening classes at the London Mechanics' Institute, winning a prize for figure drawing at the age of thirteen. After leaving school he studied in the sculpture galleries of the British Museum and attended classes at the School of Design at Somerset House. In October 1847 he was apprenticed to a firm of lithographers. A diary (now lost), begun at this time and kept up until he died, detailed his work and daily life and was quoted extensively in his *Life and Letters* (1912).

In 1847, his business having failed, John Shields returned to the north of England. Shields later joined his father at Newton-le-Willows. After doing odd jobs, such as colouring in figures for advertising posters, Shields found employment in Manchester with the printers Bradshaw and Blacklock, and, after they failed, for a lithographic printer designing labels and tickets. He also attended evening classes at the city's School of Design. He became an assistant to the painter C. H. Mitchell and began to make pencil portraits and to paint in watercolours, exhibiting for the first time at the Royal Institution in 1856. Shields was employed to make drawings of works exhibited at the 1857 Manchester Art Treasures Exhibition, and their subsequent publication brought him to the notice of London engravers. His first important commission was a set of wood-engravings illustrating John Bunyan's *The Pilgrim's Progress* (1859) and for which he sought the advice of the author Charles Kingsley and the critic John Ruskin, both of whom admired his work. Both Ruskin and Dante Gabriel Rossetti praised his illustrations for Daniel Defoe's *Plagues of London* (1863), the original designs for which are in Manchester City Galleries.

In May 1864 Shields met Rossetti for the first time and quickly became a close friend of the artist. Ruskin and Rossetti gave him practical help, for although he was a fine draughtsman Shields was not a good colourist. In 1865 he was elected an associate of the Old Watercolour Society, though his watercolours, and later his oils (which became immensely popular and made him a rich man), were bland and sentimental, while his religious works were cold and austere. In November 1870 *The Graphic* printed his large watercolour *Knott Mill Fair*, one of his most successful works; the first of many drawings he made for *Punch* was also published that year.

Between 1865 and 1867 Shields collaborated with the photographer McLachlan on a group portrait of Queen Victoria and her family, containing twenty-two figures; the project kept Shields in what he described as 'hateful slavery' for these years. It was during this time that he suffered a mental and physical breakdown and developed an intense sensitivity to noise that persisted for the rest of his life. To convalesce he went to Porlock, Somerset, where he painted some of his most famous pictures of children. He lodged in Chelsea for a while but soon returned to Manchester.

From December 1872 Shields made frequent references in his diary to his child model of a number of years, Matilda Booth (b. 1855/6), known as Cissy. By the summer of 1874 her family and Shields's friends were concerned about their relationship, and it was made clear to Shields that Cissy was being compromised. They were married on 15 August 1874 at Irwell Street Wesleyan Chapel; the diary entry for the day ends: 'Off to Blackpool alone with Mac [McLachlan]. Did me wonderful good. Thank God'. He was forty-one and Cissy, left alone with the housekeeper, was eighteen. McLachlan returned home after two days but Shields stayed on in Blackpool for a week. Friends thought him uninterested in women and were astonished at his precipitate marriage. In 1875 Shields announced that he was moving to London, and a farewell exhibition of his work was held in Manchester and a dinner given in his honour. His move was delayed until January 1877 and followed a four-month study visit to Paris and Italy, during which time Cissy was abandoned at a boarding-school in Brighton. On his return Shields and his wife set up home in Lodge Place, St John's Wood. She left him in 1891.

A commission to design stained glass for Sir William Houldsworth's chapel at Coodham in Kilmarnock established Shields's reputation as a decorative artist. This, in turn, brought him a more important commission: to design the stained glass and mosaics for the new chapel at Eaton Hall, Cheshire, owned by Hugh Grosvenor, first duke of Westminster. The windows were larger than any he had previously attempted, and making the necessary large-scale drawings revolutionized his style; daily, devout reading of the Bible and belief in its literal truth also had a profound influence. In addition Shields designed a memorial stained-glass window to Rossetti at Birchington church, Kent, and windows for Cheltenham Ladies' College; however, following a disagreement with the headmistress, Dorothea Beale, he refused to finish the latter commission.

In 1892 Shields received his most important commission, from Emelia Gurney, a campaigner for women's higher education and the widow of the recorder of London, to decorate a chapel of rest. The chapel, by the architect Herbert P. Horne, in Hyde Park Place, Bayswater Road, was designed with unbroken wall spaces and windows placed on high in order to accommodate Shields's cycle of large-scale religious paintings expressing the theme of God's redeeming love. The works were painted in oil on canvas and affixed to blocks of slate riveted to the walls, a process that enabled the artist to begin work on the paintings while the chapel of the Ascension, as it was known, was being built (structure completed 1894). Disputes over Gurney's will (she died in 1896) made Shields's work more difficult, and in 1903 a group of the patron's friends raised £3000 to enable him to complete the commission, a process that took seventeen years. Unfortunately, this major cycle of religious paintings does not survive, as the chapel was partially destroyed by a bomb during the Second World War and was demolished some time after 1950.

In spring 1908 an exhibition of Shields's work was held at Manchester City Art Gallery, and he completed two of his most powerful pictures, *Man* and *His Conscience*, much praised by Ruskin. In July 1910 he recorded in his diary: 'Put up the last two pictures in the chapel', and, in September: 'Finished antechapel'. Shields died on 26 February 1911 at Morayfield, Kingston Road, Merton, Surrey, leaving an annuity to Cissy but the bulk of his fortune to missionary societies. He was buried in Merton Old Church.

P. G. KONODY, *rev.* VIVIEN ALLEN

Sources E. Mills, *The life and letters of Frederic Shields* (1912) · V. Allen, *Hall Caine* (1997) · R. Watkinson, 'Shields in Manchester: the making of an artist', *Journal of Pre-Raphaelite and Aesthetic Studies*, 1/1 (1987), 15–37 · N. K. Farmer, 'Dorothea's disagreement', *Country Life* (14 Jan 1988), 58–9 · F. Shields, *The chapel of the Ascension: a descriptive handbook* (1897) · m. cert. · d. cert. · 'The chapel of the Ascension, Bayswater, London', *ArchR*, 9 (1901), 281–4 · H. E. Scudder, *An English interpreter: a sketch of F. J. Shields and his work at Eaton Hall chapel* (1883)
Archives HLRO, letters to E. Thomson · U. Leeds, Brotherton L., letters to C. Rossetti
Likenesses E. Mason, miniature, exh. 1898–1900 · B. E. Fry & Son, photograph, 1903, repro. in Mills, *Life and letters*, frontispiece · M. Beerbohm, caricature, Tate collection · F. M. Brown, oils, fresco (figure of Wicklyffe in *Wicklyffe on his trial*), Manchester town hall · E. M. Mason, watercolour, Man. City Gall. · photograph, repro. in *The Studio* (15 Nov 1911), 144 · portrait (Head of Wycliffe), Manchester town hall
Wealth at death £6509 16*s.* 8*d.*: probate, 15 March 1911, *CGPLA Eng. & Wales*

Shields, Sir (Thomas) Drummond (1881–1953), physician and politician, was born in Edinburgh on 7 August 1881, the second of the eight children of James Drummond Shields, lithographic printer, and his wife, Agnes Campbell. After an elementary education in Glasgow, he left school when he was twelve and found work with a photographer, continuing his studies at night school. He later set up a photographic studio in Edinburgh with his father and a brother. On 11 August 1904 he married Christian Blair Young, schoolteacher and daughter of Alexander Young, joiner, with whom he had a daughter.

Politically, Shiels became involved with the Edinburgh Fabian Society, but when war broke out in August 1914 he enlisted and was given a commission in the 9th (Scottish) division. In the course of the fighting he was severely wounded in battle, and awarded the Military Cross and the Belgian Croix de Guerre as well as being mentioned in dispatches. After the war he entered the medical faculty of the University of Edinburgh, where in 1924 he graduated with the degrees of MB and ChB. He was elected a Labour member of Edinburgh town council, and just before graduation he was invited to stand for parliament as Labour candidate for Edinburgh East. He won the seat in the 1924 general election and held it for Labour until his defeat in 1931 by the Liberal candidate, D. M. Mason.

While in parliament Shiels became active in the Empire Parliamentary Association and, as a result, was appointed a member of the 1927 special commission on the Ceylon constitution. The commission's report recommended democratic self-government in Ceylon, which eventually came about in 1947. His interest in the empire was recognized by Ramsay MacDonald, who appointed him under-secretary of state at the India Office in 1929, but later that year Shiels was moved to the Colonial Office. While in office he proved to be a progressive champion of the rights of native populations in the British colonies, acutely aware that in resisting nationalist demands for political independence a situation was developing in which violence and revolution would be the eventual arbiters of imperial destiny. The Meerut case, in which thirty-two leading members of the Indian Communist Party were tried for conspiracy against the crown in March 1929, deeply influenced his views on emerging nationalism. He attempted to convince aspiring black nationalist forces to work through constitutional channels rather than revolution. As such he was prepared to oppose his own civil servants and colonial officials in championing political representation for native populations and social rights for all.

This was most evident in Shiels's attitude towards the emerging black nationalist movement in Kenya. In spite of protest from leading officials in the Colonial Office, he met with Jomo Kenyatta, leader of the Kikuyu Central Association, in London in January 1930 and was favourably impressed by him. On the basis of this he urged the governor of Kenya, Sir Edward Grigg, not 'to ignore or crush' the association (Gupta, 193). He also continually intervened on the side of local workers in dispute with imperial authorities and private companies. He was successful in convincing the minister, Lord Passfield (Sidney Webb), to issue a circular asking for the annulment of any law in the colonies which made trade unionism an offence and for legislation which allowed unions to legally register. Within the Colonial Office he set up a standing committee on labour legislation which met frequently in 1930 until the fall of the Labour government.

Most of Shiels's interventions were, however, unsuccessful. Faced with a reactionary colonial administration, and hostile white settlers and business interests, two years of office was hardly long enough to reform the traditional practices and policies of the colonial ruling élites. Moreover, within the Labour Party there existed a paternalism towards native populations which inhibited the drive towards indigenous rule. Passfield himself possessed a hierarchical view of humankind; black West Indians were viewed as Europeans and mature enough to establish self-governing independent states, but the black Africans were seen as primitive and as needing guidance towards self-rule, a process which would take at least a hundred years (Gupta, 192).

Following his defeat in the 1931 general election, Shiels found employment in London as a school medical inspector and as secretary to the British Social Hygiene Council. However, he maintained his interest in Commonwealth affairs. In 1940 he was appointed deputy and, later, acting secretary of the Empire Parliamentary Association, and in 1946 he was made a member of the secretary of state's Colonial Economic and Development Council; in addition, he was a member of the Royal Empire Society, serving as vice-president and editing *The British Commonwealth: a Family of Nations* in 1952. Finally, he was a prominent member of various voluntary societies, including the London Group on African Affairs, the Royal African Society, the East India Association, the Anti-Slavery and Aborigines Protection Society, and the Royal Society for the Prevention of Cruelty to Animals.

In 1939 Shiels accepted a knighthood, after turning down a peerage ten years earlier from Ramsay MacDonald. After 1945 he became public relations officer for the General Post Office and held this position until 1949, when he left to become secretary to the British group of the Inter-Parliamentary Union. His first wife died in 1948. He remarried in 1950, his second wife being Gladys L. Buhler MBE, daughter of John James Buhler, and a member of the imperial studies staff of the Royal Empire Society.

For most of his political life Shiels was on the right wing of the Labour Party. Although his interest in socialism had been fired by early sufferings of poverty, he was said to have held an 'equal contempt for the revolutionary folly of the Clyde and the reactionary conservatism of Government officials' (Webb, 232–3). His Fabianism meant that the achievement of socialism would be through a process of gradual evolution. As such he advocated the nationalization of essential national industries, such as the coalmines and the railways, and condemned unfettered capitalism, saying it was productive of a 'social wickedness of a bad type' (*Hansard 5C*, 5 Feb 1926). However, as he made clear in a letter to Arthur Woodburn, secretary of the Labour Party in Scotland, he was equally critical of trade union influence in the Labour Party, and described many parliamentary candidates from the labour movement as second rate, and advocated that Labour should appeal to a wider constituency than the working class (T. D. Shiels to A. Woodburn, 19 Sept 1932, Box 1, Arthur Woodburn MSS).

In appearance Shiels was tall, with expansive features and limbs, and high cheekbones. Beatrice Webb said of him that 'he takes no exercise, eats and smokes heavily and at bedtime takes copiously of whisky' (Webb, 232–3). The hedonism was complemented by an abrasive and tough-minded manner, an urbane sense of humour, and a conceit with which he regarded himself and his opinions. However, those close to him spoke of his friendliness and sincerity. Shiels died in Hammersmith Hospital, London, on 1 January 1953, survived by his wife.

W. W. J. KNOX

Sources *The Scotsman* (3 Jan 1953) · *The Times* (3 Jan 1953) · *DNB* · *The Scottish socialists* (1931) · *The Labour who's who* (1927) · P. S. Gupta, *Imperialism and the British labour movement* (1975) · NL Scot., Woodburn MSS · *Beatrice Webb's diaries, 1924–1932*, ed. M. Cole (1956) · *Hansard 5C* (1925–9) · b. cert. · d. cert. · *CGPLA Eng. & Wales* (1953)
Archives Bodl. RH, corresp. with Lord Lugard
Likenesses W. Stoneman, photographs, 1930–43, NPG
Wealth at death £718 18s. 0d.: administration, 19 March 1953, *CGPLA Eng. & Wales*

Shiels, George (1881–1949), playwright, was born on 24 June 1881, one of seven sons in a family of eight, to Robert Sheills (*fl.* 1880–1920), and Elizabeth, *née* Sweeny (*d.* 1925), in Ballybrake, near Ballymoney, co. Antrim. Shortly after his birth the family moved into the small town of Ballymoney, where his father was a railway worker. George received the basic primary education then available to about the age of twelve. It is not known how he was occupied between about 1893 and 1900, when he emigrated to the United States. There he worked at a variety of casual jobs, mining and farming, in the west, and may have married in Oregon (the matter remains obscure). Having made his way to western Canada, Shiels suffered a serious accident in 1904 while working on the Canadian Pacific railroad. He spent the rest of his life in a wheelchair. He returned to Ballymoney about 1908 and set up a small travel and shipping business in Main Street.

While in hospital in Canada, Shiels began to read serious literature, and he later said that *Pride and Prejudice* fired his imagination. Thereafter he read widely, and like so many Irish writers of the time was largely self-taught. Once home Shiels took a correspondence course with the Pelman School of the Mind, London, and gradually began to write. His first efforts seem to have been westerns, partly based on his experiences in Oregon and Manitoba. In 1916 two stories appeared in the *Irish Weekly*. He then turned to drama and, under the name George Morshiel, wrote three plays between 1918 and 1920 for the Ulster Literary Theatre (founded on the model of the Abbey Theatre). These plays, 'Away from the Moss', 'Felix Reid and Bob', and 'The Tame Drudge', remain unpublished. Shiels's first play under his own name, the one-act *Bedmates*, staged at the Abbey on 6 January 1921, was published in 1922 and launched the career of one of Ireland's most popular playwrights of the first half of the twentieth century.

Shiels went on to write twenty-one plays for the Abbey, roughly the same number as Lennox Robinson, with whom he may be compared. Shiels was not as sophisticated as Robinson but early learned the skills of the Abbey comedy so ably demonstrated in Robinson's prototypal *The Whiteheaded Boy* (1916). Shiels's *Paul Twyning* (1922) and *Professor Tim* (1925) are similarly genial, gently satirical, and well-crafted comedies of rural Irish life. What lent strength to Shiels's comedies was the fine company of players then working at the Abbey. Thus *Bedmates*, though but a trifle, had in the cast Barry Fitzgerald, Michael J. Dolan, and Maureen Delaney, while F. J. McCormick played the lead in the first *Professor Tim*, accompanied by Sara Allgood as Mrs Scally and Eileen Crowe as her daughter Peggy. The enormous popularity of these and other

Shiels plays, revived again and again for decades, is bound up with the strengths of such performers. To a large extent the plays were vehicles for the Abbey style of acting.

Yet Shiels could also be a serious playwright, and *The New Gossoon* (1930) is usually singled out as evidence of this. Even *Bedmates*, short though it is, offers evidence that Shiels always had ambitions above the writing of farce. That play's basis of a dispute in a guest-house over who should rent a bed, is at the same time a political allegory: a northern protestant and a southern Catholic are set at odds by a conniving Englishman. The issue becomes how the Orangeman and the nationalist can co-habit, without sawing the bed in half! *The New Gossoon* explores the new, post-treaty Ireland, by using the character of Luke Carey on a noisy motorbike to shatter the peace and moral ideas of the older generation. Similarly *The Passing Day* (1936) provides, in a form which goes beyond realism, a fairly hard-hitting critique of the materialism of small-town Ireland. And *The Rugged Path* (1940), as a kind of anti-pastoral play, explores violence in the Irish countryside and the politically contentious issue of informing against wrong-doers. Not surprisingly, Shiels struck a nerve with this play. *The Rugged Path* ran for three months at the Abbey, where a rapid change of programme was the norm. Shiels wrote a sequel, *The Summit* (1941), where social conscience leads to solidarity against the vicious family threatening decent people. Shiels was aware that at this time the question of standing up to the violence of the IRA, then waging a campaign in England, was topical. 'The reaction in Ireland to the Coventry martyrs has amazed me. To advocate the exercise of a public conscience after that would probably be regarded as "playing England's game"' (Kennedy, 53). These two plays challenged traditional attitudes towards the nationalist question. A few years later he was less successful in tackling the issue of the great famine of 1845–7. *Tenants-at-will* (1945), written to commemorate the centenary, proved too serious for the Abbey audience and its failure was a bitter blow to Shiels.

In 1932 Shiels moved to New Lodge, Carnlough, in the Glens of co. Antrim and, abandoning his little business in Ballymoney, lived entirely by his writing, in the company of his brother Eddie and sister Mary. He rarely saw one of his plays on stage. Yet he was not reclusive, and loved to hear news and stories of the people of co. Antrim who provided the raw material of his comedies of manners and intrigue. A modest man, he refused an honorary degree from Queen's University, Belfast, and membership of the Irish Academy of Letters. Shiels was a member of PEN (Dublin centre). He died in New Lodge, Carnlough, on 19 September 1949 after a long illness and was buried in Ballymoney on 21 September.

CHRISTOPHER MURRAY

Sources D. J. Casey, *George Shiels: the enigmatic playwright* (1981) • D. Kennedy, 'George Shiels: a playwright at work', *Threshold*, 25 (summer 1974), 50–58 • R. Hogan, *After the Irish renaissance: a critical history of the Irish drama since 'The plough and the stars'* (1968), 33–9 • K. King, 'George Shiels', *Modern British dramatists, 1900–1945*, ed. S. Weintraub, DLitB, 10 (1982), 154–7 • T. C. Murray, 'George Shiels, Brinsley MacNamara, etc.', *The Irish theatre*, ed. L. Robinson (1939), 119–46 • N. Sahal, *George Shiels: sixty years of realistic Irish drama, 1900–1960* (1971), 120–33 • G. Shiels, *Bedmates* (1922) • b. cert. • *Irish Times* (20 Sept 1949)

Archives Ballymoney Library, Ballymoney, copies of short stories, scrapbook, and typescripts of plays • NL Ire., corresp., literary MSS • University of Ulster, Coleraine, clippings, corresp., notebooks, short stories, and transcripts of plays | TCD, letters to Thomas MacGreevy | FILM BFI(?), adaptation of *New Gossoon* as *Sally's Irish rogue*

Likenesses J. Wilkinson, oils, Abbey Theatre, Dublin

Wealth at death £1560 15s. 4d.: probate, 20 June 1950, CGPLA NIre.

Shiels [Shields], **Robert** (*d.* 1753), compiler, was born in Roxburghshire, Scotland, about the end of the seventeenth century, to humble parents, and went to London as a journeyman printer. He had little formal education but was possessed of 'a very acute understanding' (Johnson, *Poets*, 2.329) and a retentive memory.

In 1748 Samuel Johnson, to whom Shiels was further recommended by his devout Jacobitism, employed him as one of six amanuenses on his *Dictionary*, along with the Macbean brothers, Stewart, Maitland, and Peyton. Interestingly, given Johnson's well known views on that nation, all but the last named were Scots. At the conclusion of his work on the *Dictionary* in 1752 Shiels was commissioned by the publisher Ralph Griffiths to compile *Lives of the Poets of Great Britain and Ireland, to the Time of Dean Swift* (5 vols., 1753), the claim to authorship of which was at the time hotly disputed between him and Theophilus Cibber. Although Shiels was certainly the principal compiler of the work, Cibber had been engaged as editor 'with power to alter, expunge, or add, as he liked' (Boswell, *Life*, 3.30). The two men were quite opposite in character as in politics: Cibber was something of a dilettante, Shiels pernickety and pedantic; the former as staunch a whig as the latter was devout a tory. As well as correcting his style and making judicious additions Cibber felt bound to excise Shiels's tory sentiments wherever he found them surfacing in the text. Shiels, outraged at the mutilation of his copy, was only dissuaded from challenging Cibber to a duel by the intervention of Griffiths. Cibber's name alone duly appeared on the title-page of the first volume (the later volumes generously allowed 'and other hands'). Shiels justifiably felt piqued, although Johnson, always well disposed towards his former employee, went too far when he attributed the whole credit of the work to him (Johnson, *Poets*, 2.329). The compilation was in fact largely based on Langbaine and Jacobs, with the aid of Coxeter's notes, and did not contain much original matter.

Apart from his compilations Shiels also wrote poetry, in a style much influenced by that of James Thomson. His verses include *Marriage* (1747), a didactic poem in blank verse, and *Beauty* (printed in 1766 together with James Grainger's *The Sugar Cane* and wrongly ascribed to that author), a piece which contains praise of Johnson's *Irene* (1749). Above even Dr Johnson, Shiels venerated his countryman Thomson, on whose death in 1748 he published an elegy of some merit, *Musidorus*. Shiels was also Thomson's first biographer (in *Lives of the Poets*). However, his admiration seems to have been rather more fatuous than discriminating, if Johnson may be believed: 'I took down Thomson, and read aloud a large portion of him, and then asked,—Is not this fine? Shiels having expressed the highest admiration. Well, Sir, (said I,) I have omitted every other line' (Boswell, *Life*, 3.37).

Shiels died of consumption in May's Buildings, London, on 27 December 1753. Johnson, who had frequently afforded Shiels financial aid during his last illness, provided his epitaph: 'his life was virtuous, and his end was pious' (Johnson, *Poets*, 2.329).   ANTHONY ESPOSITO

Sources Boswell, *Life* • S. Johnson, *Lives of the most eminent English poets*, ed. P. Cunningham, [new edn], 3 vols. (1854) • W. Raleigh, *Six essays on Johnson* (1910) • *Monthly Review*, new ser., 8 (1792) • *GM*, 1st ser., 23 (1753), 590 • L. Morel, *James Thomson: sa vie et ses œuvres* (Paris, 1895), 176 • Nichols, *Lit. anecdotes*, 5.308 • I. D'Israeli, *Curiosities of literature*, 9th edn, 3 (1834), 375 • *DNB*

Shiels, William (1848–1904), politician in Australia, was born at Maghera, co. Londonderry, on 3 December 1848, the son of Robert Shiels, a farmer, and his wife, Patricia Sarah, *née* Kelly. Robert Shiels and the youngest of their four children died within weeks of the family's arrival in Victoria, Australia, early in 1855. Patricia Shiels married William Dickins in 1857.

Shiels was educated at Scotch College, Melbourne (1862–6), and privately. He then had a brilliant career at the University of Melbourne (1867–73), where, despite interrupting his studies because of ill health, he took a double first, won the vice-chancellor's essay prize, and in 1873 graduated LLB. He began to practise, but overwork weakened his already delicate constitution and caused him to go as a private tutor to landed families in western Victoria and in South Australia. At Naracoorte, South Australia, he met Jane (*b.* 1857/8), the daughter of John Robertson, a prominent pastoralist of Struan House; they married on 6 May 1885 and settled in Melbourne, first at suburban Hawthorn, and later at St Kilda.

Shiels had opposed the radical government of Graham Berry in 1877. Elected in 1880 to the legislative assembly for pastoral Normanby (which he held until the 1904 redistribution), from his maiden speech he established a reputation for liberal views, eloquently expressed. He supported breakaway liberal Presbyterians and opposed strict Sabbatarianism, and the Sunday Society published as its manifesto his parliamentary speech of 4 July 1883 supporting the Sunday opening of the Melbourne Library and Museum. In the interests of women, Shiels carried amendments in the 1880s to the divorce and married women's property acts, and to the law of slander as it concerned allegations of adultery and unchastity. Although his reform initiatives fell short of equal access to divorce for women, his 1887 bill became a test of Australian self-government when the imperial government refused assent. South Australia, New South Wales, Queensland, and Tasmania supported his 1890 visit to London, where his advocacy persuaded the Salisbury government to give way.

Fiscal prudence was the keynote of Shiels's assault on the boom-time extravagances of the Gillies–Deakin ministries (1883–9), including vigorous attacks on the 1886 and 1889 budgets. When he became attorney-general and minister of railways in James Munro's government in November 1890, he wrested political control of railway expenditure from the commissioners and forced their resignations. As premier from 16 February 1892, Shiels— the 'young man with a jaunty air' (Hoare)—won a resounding general election victory on 20 April on a platform of retrenchment. Unable, however, to satisfy the electorate's mood for strict economy and the prosecution of fraudulent boomsters, his ministry was defeated on 18 January 1893.

Ill health, diagnosed as angina pectoris, led to Shiels's frequent absence from parliament. In 1899 he re-emerged to overthrow the liberal Turner government. He became treasurer and minister for railways in the conservative McLean ministry (1899–1900) and again in the Irvine ministry (1902–4). His marathon budget speeches, delivered seated and sustained by draughts of whisky and champagne, excited much admiration. Shiels reduced the public service, cut salaries, raised income tax, provoked and crushed a strike of railway workers, and returned Victoria to solvency. His enemies named him 'Slippery' Shiels.

Deteriorating health obliged Shiels to leave the treasury in July 1903 and retire as a minister the following February, and reduced him to invalidism from early 1904. After months of agony, courageously borne, he died at Struan House, his mother-in-law's home in Naracoorte, South Australia, on 17 December 1904, survived by his wife, three sons, and a daughter. He was buried on 19 December with Presbyterian forms and, according to his wishes, with no flowers or special mourning, in a spot he had chosen in the Struan private cemetery.

Shiels the social liberal was a fiscal conservative. His democratic and egalitarian instincts, including support for women's rights, sat easily with his dedication to financial probity. He was a devoted parliamentarian, a gifted speaker, an able administrator, and a treasurer who possessed what William Irvine called 'the very rare fluency of making an array of figures live and move before his audience' (letter to Jane Shiels, Shiels papers, La Trobe L., Vic.).   JOHN LACK

Sources *The Argus* [Melbourne] (28 March 1890) • *The Argus* [Melbourne] (19 Dec 1904) • *The Argus* [Melbourne] (20 Dec 1904) • *The Age* [Melbourne] (19 Dec 1904) • *The Age* [Melbourne] (20 Dec 1904) • State Library of Victoria, Melbourne, La Trobe Library, Shiels MSS, MS 8730 • B. Hoare, *Looking back gaily* (1927) • T. Waters, *Much besides music: memoirs* (1951) • A. Sutherland, *Victoria and its metropolis: past and present* (1888) • 'Lauderdale', *Victoria's representative men at home*, ed. M. Cannon (1977) • Scotch College History Committee, *History of Scotch College Melbourne, 1851–1925* (1925) • J. Tregenza, *Professor of democracy: the life of Charles Henry Pearson* (1968) • G. Serle, *The rush to be rich: a history of the colony of Victoria, 1883–1889* (1971) • S. M. Ingham, 'Some Aspects of Victorian Liberalism', MA diss., University of Melbourne, 1950 • C. D. Gibson, 'Divorce Law Reform in Victoria, 1883–1893', BA Hons diss., University of Melbourne, 1971 • *AusDB* • *Sands and McDougall's commercial and general Melbourne directory* (1870–1904)

Archives State Library of Victoria, Melbourne

Likenesses Johnstone, O'Shannassy & Co., photograph, Parliament of Victoria Library • J. W. Lindt, photograph, Parliament of Victoria Library

Shiffner [Schiffner], **Mathew** [Matthew, Matthias] (*c.*1690–1756), merchant, was born in Russia in or shortly before 1690. Nothing definite is known about his parentage, though unlikely stories have been circulated by amateur genealogists, for example, that his father was archbishop of Riga—a non-existent position. At an unknown date in his youth he was sent or taken to London, where on 8 October 1711 he became a naturalized British subject and on 19 October a freeman of the Russia Company. Shortly afterwards he returned to Russia (most probably as an agent for Samuel Holden of London), and is recorded in 1714 as an English factor in Riga.

In 1720 Shiffner was described as 'Postdirektor' of Riga, presumably an office that could be combined with private trade. In that year he married (Hedwig) Agnata Bruiningk (1704–1793), the daughter of Heinrich Bruiningk (1675–1736), senior pastor of St Peter's Church, Riga, and *Generalsuperintendant* and *Präses* (moderator) of the established Lutheran church in Livonia. The (von) Bruiningks were a Baltic German family, originally from Lübeck, long established at Narva. Father Heinrich had studied theology at the universities of Kiel, Halle, Leipzig, and Wittenberg, and held various church positions at Narva. After the fall of that city to the forces of Peter the Great in 1704 he became chaplain to the Swedish army until nominated by the nobility of Livonia to the major ecclesiastical post of *Generalsuperintendant*. His sons entered the military and judicial service of the tsar and attained high rank. Agnata's eldest brother, Axel Heinrich, was in 1737 ennobled by the holy Roman emperor Charles VI.

Following the tsar's order in 1723 for foreign merchants to move to the capital, Mathew Shiffner and his family settled in St Petersburg, where records show him exporting hemp to England in 1725 in partnership with Jacob Wolff and John Edwards. Hemp was to remain a major trade for Shiffner, but extraordinary opportunities opened for him in 1730, when the widowed Grand Duchess Anna of Courland, a niece of Peter the Great, became tsarina. Baltic German connections now became very valuable at court. Family tradition records that Agnata had been 'gouvernante' to Grand Duchess Anna, while her younger sister, Anna Lucia Bruiningk (later von Hagemeister), became maid of honour to the tsarina at the Winter Palace in St Petersburg, whither she invited her widowed mother to reside. With such influential court connections, the house of Shiffner and Wolff soon became the most prominent British firm at the Russian capital and received many special commissions from the government. These included orders to purchase uniform cloth for the Russian army and commissions to sell abroad on the government's account monopolized commodities (including potash, iron, and rhubarb). Responsibility for the British phase of such arrangements fell to Samuel Holden, who generally held a one-third or one-half interest in the contract. In Russia, Shiffner continued both to act as Holden's factor and to take shares with him in joint ventures.

These years of prosperity ended with the death of the tsarina Anna in 1740, followed by that of Holden the same year. Shiffner returned to London, where he served as Holden's executor and established a similar business of his own in Broad Street Buildings. He was consulted by the Board of Trade on matters concerning trade with Russia and the Baltic, but never held office in the Russia Company. By the late 1740s he had turned over the commodity side of his business to his sons Henry and John, retaining for himself the merchant banking side. He was later remembered in Riga as a London banker.

Shiffner died in London in December 1756, leaving his widow Agnata (who died in 1793), four sons, and two daughters. Henry, the eldest son, inherited his father's real estate and was a member of parliament for Minehead, Somerset (1762–8). In partnership with his younger brother John, Henry continued their father's business for a number of years, but wound it up after meeting reverses in the early 1760s. Henry retired to his country estate in Herefordshire, while John appears to have emigrated to America for a time. Two other sons, Samuel and Matthew, were educated at the lyceum in Riga, with which their grandfather Bruiningk was long associated. In 1752 Matthew earned a doctorate in medicine at Leiden, while Samuel became a merchant in Jamaica, where he died in 1762. His daughter Catherine married Matthew Dorrien, a London merchant, while his daughter Benigna Gotlieb, to whom the tsarina Anna was godmother, married Vincent John Biscoe, a Surrey gentleman from a London mercantile family. Henry's son George was created a baronet in 1818.   JACOB M. PRICE

Sources HoP, *Commons* · H. von Bruiningk, *Das Geschlecht von Bruiningk in Livland* (Riga, 1913), 33–4, 118 · E. Sussex RO, Shiffner MSS · W. Lenz, *Deutschbaltisches biographisches Lexikon, 1710–1960*, 1970 · *Journal of the commissioners for trade and plantations*, [vol. 7]: *From January 1734/5 to December 1741* (1930), 350 · *Journal of the commissioners for trade and plantations*, [vol. 10]: *From January 1754 to December 1758* (1933), 237–8 · will proved, 1756, PRO, PROB 11/826, sig. 352 · 1728, PRO, C.11/2290/57 [bill in Chancery] · 1714, PRO, C.O. 388/18, fol. 234 · 1714, PRO, C.O. 388/35, fols. 25–7 · PRO, PROB 11/1232, sigs. 283–4 [will of widow Agnata Shiffner] · Journal of S. Holden estate, Som. ARS, DD/HY · GL, Russia Company MSS, 11,741, vol. 3 · PRO, SP 91/13, fol. 285 · PRO, SP 91/19, fol. 6 · F. W. Steer, ed., *The Shiffner archives: a catalogue* (1959) · PRO, ADM 106/3600, fol. 111 [Henry Shiffner, 1746] · D. Reading, *The Anglo-Russian commercial treaty of 1734* (1938) · W. A. Shaw, ed., *Letters of denization and acts of naturalization for aliens in England and Ireland, 1701–1800*, 2, Huguenot Society of London, 27 (1923), 111 · J. F. von Recke and K. E. Napiersky, *Allgemeine Schriftsteller - und Gelehrten-Lexikon*, 5 vols. (Mitau, 1827–61), vol. 4, p. 64 · C. A. Berkholz, *Beiträge zur Geschichte der Kirchen und Prediger Riga's* (Riga, 1867) · *London Magazine*, 25 (1756), 613
Archives E. Sussex RO, family MSS | Som. ARS, Hylton MSS

Shilleto, Arthur Richard (1848–1894). *See under* Shilleto, Richard (1809–1876).

Shilleto, Richard (1809–1876), classical scholar, son of John Shilleto of Ulleskelf, Yorkshire, was born there on 25 November 1809. He was educated first at Repton and then under Dr Samuel Butler at Shrewsbury School, where he was head boy. He was admitted to Trinity College, Cambridge, in 1828 and was made a scholar in 1830. W. H. Thompson, later regius professor of Greek and master of Trinity, was among his exact contemporaries. Shilleto was second in the first class of the classical tripos. In his day, however, candidates for honours had to satisfy the examiners in both this and the mathematical tripos in which Shilleto was unfortunately bracketed bottom in 1832. On 7 January 1834 he married Isabella Snelgar; they had one daughter and seven sons, three of whom followed him to Cambridge. Shilleto proceeded MA in 1835 and was ordained in 1838, but owing to his marriage he could not become the fellow of a college, although he examined in the classical tripos in 1839 and 1840 and was for many years a college lecturer at Trinity and at King's.

The introduction of the classical tripos in 1824 had not resulted in much improvement in the preparation provided by college teachers, so virtually every candidate for honours had to go to a private coach whom he paid to correct the translations and more especially the compositions which formed the bulk of the examination. Shilleto quickly became the most celebrated of Cambridge coaches, a reputation he maintained for over thirty years. He taught most of those who were themselves to become leading school and university teachers, and thus his influence was far wider than that of any other Cambridge classical instructor of the time. His reputation was based upon his industry (in 1859 he was reported as coaching three days of eleven hours and three of twelve each week), the success of his pupils, and his eccentricity. He enjoyed controversy whether in scholarship (as in his intemperate attack, published in 1851, on the accuracy of Grote's knowledge of Thucydides in his *History of Greece*) or local affairs, which he often celebrated in classical or English verse.

Shilleto was a heavy drinker, and this hindered his professional advancement. In 1862 he was an unsuccessful candidate for the chair of Greek at Durham, despite having assembled a dozen impressive testimonials from leading scholars. In 1867 he should have been a strong contender for the regius chair at Cambridge vacated by his contemporary W. H. Thompson, but it was annexed to a canonry at Ely for which he was not deemed suitable. In the same year, however, he was elected a fellow of Peterhouse under a statute which permitted the election of eminent married scholars. He gave up coaching and was appointed assistant tutor, dean, praelector, and librarian. He died at 4 Bateman Street, Cambridge, on 24 September 1876. Despite his years of coaching he left under £3000. His widow was granted a civil-list pension of £150 in 1878, and his daughter, Catherine, one of £50 in 1890.

Shilleto was regarded as the greatest Greek scholar in England since Gaisford. His particular expertise was in Greek prose diction, but he left few published proofs of his learning. His only complete editions were of Demosthenes *De falsa legatione* (1844, and three further editions during his lifetime) and Thucydides book 1 (1872). He produced various 'adversaria' to classical authors, including Thucydides, Hyperides, and Aristotle. Many of his books, some of which are in the Cambridge University Library, contain detailed unpublished marginalia. He contributed to early volumes of the *Journal of Philology* and, under the anagram Charles Thiriold, to *Notes and Queries*. His skill as a

translator into Greek and Latin prose and verse is exhibited by the large selection of his compositions published in 1901, as well as by contributions to the anthologies *Sabrinae corolla* and *Arundines Cami*.

Shilleto's son, **Arthur Richard Shilleto** (1848–1894), translator, was born in Cambridge on 18 June 1848, and educated at Harrow, before proceeding in 1867 to Trinity College, Cambridge, where he graduated BA as a scholar in 1871 and MA in 1876. Ordained deacon in 1871 and priest in 1872, he served curacies until 1877 when he was appointed second master at King Edward VI's Grammar School at Stratford upon Avon. From 1879 to 1882 he was master of Ulverston School. He was curate of Satterthwaite, Lancashire, from 1881 to 1883, and of Lower Slaughter, Gloucestershire, from 1883 to 1885. He produced translations of Pausanias (2 vols., 1886), Plutarch's *Morals* (1888), and *Josephus* (5 vols., 1889–90). He also prepared notes for an edition of Robert Burton's *Anatomy of Melancholy* (1893) and was a frequent contributor to *Notes and Queries* under the anagram Erato Hills. After many years' suffering from mental illness, Shilleto died on 19 January 1894.

RICHARD SMAIL

Sources B. H. Kennedy, *Journal of Philology* (1877), 163–8 · M. L. Clarke, *Classical education in Britain, 1500–1900* (1959) · G. M. Trevelyan, *Sir George Otto Trevelyan: a memoir* (1932) · W. E. Heitland, *After many years: a tale of experiences and impressions gathered in the course of an obscure life* (1926) · Venn, *Alum. Cant.* · Boase, *Mod. Eng. biog.* · *CGPLA Eng. & Wales* (1876)
Archives CUL, papers
Wealth at death under £3000: administration, 21 Oct 1876, *CGPLA Eng. & Wales* · under £50—Arthur Richard Shilleto

Shillibeer, George (1797–1866), omnibus promoter, was born in Tottenham Court Road, London, but nothing else is known about his origins. He entered the navy, but did not remain long in the service, quitting it as midshipman. He then went to a firm in Long Acre to be taught coach-building. In 1825 he sought cabriolet licences in London and a year later was in business with John Cavill, coach builder and livery stable keeper, Bury Street, Bloomsbury. He also possessed what he claimed as 'an establishment' in Paris 'for the sale [sic] of carriages'.

In July 1828 Shillibeer petitioned the Treasury to be allowed to run omnibuses of the sort which had started in Paris two months before—which he had visited Paris to see—under the more English name of 'Economist'. His petition was turned down because of the hackney coach monopoly on London's central streets. This, however, did not prevent him from running under stage coach legislation north of the central area along the new road from Paddington Green to the Bank via Islington. He started a three-horse vehicle on the route carrying twenty passengers all inside on 4 July 1829, charging high middle–class fares—a shilling all the way (6*d*. half way)—and wisely called his vehicle, the latest from Paris, an omnibus not an economist.

Shillibeer knew how to copy the carriage-building ideas of others but was unable to exploit his initial advantage. Although he soon put five more of his larger omnibuses on the route, competitors ran many more, wisely preferring more manoeuvrable two-horse vehicles licensed to carry fifteen (twelve inside and three on the roof by the coachman), which paid lower mileage duty, levied on the vehicle irrespective of the number of passengers carried. Shillibeer was unable to meet the higher mileage duty on his vehicles and a commission of bankruptcy was ordered against him on 4 March 1831, though he continued in business after assignees had been appointed. The others could not withstand the competition much longer and the racing to pick up passengers was proving dangerous. Operators met on 10 September 1831 and, paying Shillibeer the compliment of appointing him to the chair, decided to stop thirty-three vehicles and allocate scheduled times at three-minute intervals to the remaining fifty-seven. These times could be bought and sold, thus enabling larger business to be built up.

Omnibuses were admitted to the central area when the hackney coach monopoly was ended on 5 January 1832 but Shillibeer's larger vehicles were unsuitable for the narrow streets. He ran a three-horse 'New Patent Improved Diligence' from London to Brighton during the 1830s and put omnibuses on the route from London to Greenwich and Woolwich from 1833; but steamboat competition and the opening of the first part of the London and Greenwich Railway diverted passengers. Again he was unable to pay his taxes but this time (1836) all his property was seized and he had to flee to Boulogne to escape his creditors. On his return he was sentenced in the insolvent debtors court to several months in the Fleet prison. When released, he took a job on the London and Southampton Railway but soon found himself inside again after 130 gallons of uncustomed brandy, smuggled from Boulogne, were discovered in premises he owned in Camden Town. From prison he sought Treasury recognition of his services in introducing the omnibus to London either by an appointment as inspector of omnibus duties or permission to operate twenty omnibuses tax-free for seven years. These entreaties came to nothing, however, partly, it would seem, because of the change of government in 1841.

Shillibeer's last years were relatively tranquil and more remunerative. He patented a new type of funeral carriage and, again copying Paris, took the Pompes Funèbres as his model which cut funeral costs, and set up as an undertaker in the City Road. He gave evidence before the Board of Health on the question of extramural sepulture in 1850. He died from a carbuncle, on 22 August 1866, at 7 North Street, Quadrant, Brighton, and was buried in the churchyard at Chigwell, Essex, where in 1929, the busmen of London erected a tablet in the church in memory of the 'inventor of the London Omnibus'. THEO BARKER

Sources T. C. Barker and M. Robbins, *A history of London Transport*, 1 (1963) · 'Select committee on … regulating the hackney coaches: evidence', *Parl. papers* (1830), 10.301, no. 515 · Petition of Shillibeer to treasury, July 1828, PRO, T1/2585 · Shillibeer and Noldwrit's case, PRO, T1/4215 · d. cert. · H. Mayhew, *London labour and the London poor: a cyclopaedia of the condition and earnings of those that will work, those that cannot work, and those that will not work*, [new edn], 3 (1861), 339–41; repr. (1967)
Likenesses photograph, London Transport Museum

Wealth at death under £4000: probate, 1 Oct 1866, *CGPLA Eng. & Wales*

Shilling, Andrew (*d.* 1621), naval officer in the East India Company, of unknown parentage, is first recorded on 25 November 1589, when he married Agnes Poape (*d.* 1620) at Plymouth. His eldest daughter, Damaris (who is mentioned in his will), the first of at least ten children, was baptized at St Dunstan and All Saints, Stepney, on 8 October 1592. Shilling served as master's mate of the *Edward Bonaventure* under Captain James Lancaster on a privateering voyage in 1590 and was master of the *Golden Dragon*, a privateer commanded by Captain Christopher Newport, in 1593.

No evidence has been found to support a statement that Shilling began as a petty officer in the navy, but he was appointed one of the six masters attendant of the navy, whose duties were mainly in harbour, on 30 May 1603. The post did not preclude other employment, and he was master of the *Angel* on merchant voyages to the Mediterranean in 1609, 1612, and 1614. He was an elder brother of Trinity House by 1612. Although considered for employment by the East India Company in 1610 and 1615, neither appointment materialized, but he was master of the *Anne Royal* in the East India Company voyage commanded by Martin Pring in 1617. Apart from an unfortunate incident when the failure of his gunner to remove the shot from a gun before firing a salute resulted in a death ashore, Shilling did well. After accomplishing a mission to the Red Sea to secure freedom of trade in 1618 he arrived back in England in September 1619.

The East India Company quickly decided to appoint Shilling as commander of their next voyage. The lord high admiral was reluctant to grant permission, describing Shilling as one of the most able men in the kingdom. The company retorted that the navy had terminated his appointment as master attendant because of his involvement with them, and eventually agreement was secured. There was friction between Shilling and the company because of his alterations to his ship, the *London*, and his complaints about the state of his fleet, but the ships left Tilbury on 26 February 1620. Two days later Shilling's wife was buried. Before leaving England, Shilling made his will.

After reaching Surat, Shilling sent two ships to the Persian Gulf, but hearing of the presence there of a strong Portuguese squadron, he followed with two more ships, capturing a Portuguese ship on the way. He met the first two English ships returning, but Shilling resolved to fight. The first encounter off Jask on 16 December 1620 was indecisive and the Portuguese prize was mistakenly set on fire. Battle resumed on 28 December, but a calm prevented two of the four English ships engaging. The Portuguese fled, but Shilling was mortally wounded, died on 6 January 1621, and was buried ashore three days later.

G. G. HARRIS

Sources *CSP col.*, vol. 2 (nos. 477, 479, 1044); vol. 3 (nos. 743, 765, 776, 799; p. 345; nos. 806, 816, 825) · *The true relation of that worthy sea fight which two of the E. India ships had with 4 Portingals … with the lamentable death of Capt Andrew Shilling* (1622) · F. C. Danvers and

W. Foster, eds., *Letters received by the East India Company from its servants in the east*, 6 vols. (1896–1902), vol. 6, pp. 114, 174, 270 · parish register, St Dunstan and All Saints, Stepney, LMA · C. R. Markham, ed., *The voyages of William Baffin, 1612–1622*, Hakluyt Society, 63 (1881), xxxiv–xxxv, xxxviii–xxxix, xl–xlii · high court of admiralty, examinations, PRO, HCA 13/28, fol. 364; 13/40, fol. 274 · exchequer, king's remembrancer port books, PRO, E 190/16/2, fol. 32; E 190/18/4, fol. 48v · K. R. Andrews, ed., *English privateering voyages to the West Indies, 1588–1595*, Hakluyt Society, 2nd ser., 111 (1959), 226 · S. Purchas, *Hakluytus posthumus, or, Purchas his pilgrimes*, bk 5 (1625); repr. Hakluyt Society, extra ser., 18 (1905), 241 · *CSP dom., 1603–10*, 11 · M. C. S. Cruwys, ed., *The register of baptisms, marriages and burials of the parish of St Andrew's, Plymouth, co. Devon*, Devon and Cornwall RS, 26 (1954), 218 · will, PRO, PROB 11/139, fols. 459–60

Archives BL, East India Company Archives

Wealth at death see will, PRO, PROB 11/139, fols. 459–60

Shillitoe, Thomas (1754–1836), Quaker minister, was born at Gray's Inn, Holborn, London, on 24 February 1754, the fourth of the six children of Richard Shillito (*d.* in or after 1779), librarian, and Frances, *née* Benson (*d.* in or after 1779). Richard Shillito had in 1750 been appointed librarian of Gray's Inn but shortly after Thomas's birth the family moved to Whitechapel, and in 1766 they took the Three Tuns inn at Islington, where Thomas acted as potboy. He was then apprenticed to a grocer and was for a time at Portsmouth, whence he returned to London in the early 1770s. His upbringing was in the established church, and after his return to London he accompanied his master to the Foundling Hospital chapel for about three years until he met, and enjoyed the company of, a distant relative 'descended from Friends'. Thomas now started to go with him to Friends' meetings but, the relative being far from strict, they spent the rest of the day convivially at fashionable places of resort. After about a year Thomas, now more decided in his Quaker convictions, abandoned frivolity for the afternoon meeting for worship. He joined the Friends (despite the 'great displeasure' of his father) about 1775. His sister Margaret (1748–1795) was travelling a similar spiritual path and became a member of the Society of Friends in December 1776.

Shillitoe was helped to a situation with a Quaker banking firm in Lombard Street (not necessarily Barclays, as Hine asserts). Shocked, however, that, contrary to Friends' principles, the firm handled lottery tickets, he left it in 1778 and learned the trade of a shoemaker, the occupation of his future wife's father. London did not suit his health and he moved that year to Tottenham. On 13 July 1779 he married Mary (1746–1838), daughter of John Pace and his wife, Sarah, *née* Jeynes, of Spitalfields; the couple had three sons and four daughters, of whom one son and one daughter died in infancy. Shillitoe's sister Margaret married in 1786 John Sanderson (1749?–1816), a London tallow chandler; their daughters married into established Quaker dynasties—Mary (1788–1846) in 1821 to Sylvanus Fox (1791–1851) of the woollen manufacturing concern at Wellington, Somerset, and Elizabeth (1793–1901) in 1826 to Cornelius Hanbury (1796–1869), partner in the firm of Allen and Hanbury.

Before he left London, Shillitoe had begun to speak in Friends' meetings, and his gift in the vocal ministry was acknowledged by Tottenham monthly meeting in 1790. By 1806, having made sufficient money to ensure an annual income of £100, he retired from business and devoted himself to his Quaker and philanthropic interests. Thereafter he travelled almost continually throughout Britain, in Ireland (three visits, 1808–11), on the continent of Europe (1821–3, 1824–5), and in North America (1826–30). In 1812 he and his wife (with their daughter Hannah) moved to Barnsley, Yorkshire, to be near their recently widowed daughter Mary, and in 1819 they settled in Hitchin, Hertfordshire, where their daughter Margaret (1784–1847) and her husband, John Whiting (1776–1853), lived. In 1826 Shillitoe's wife returned to Tottenham, where he joined her on his return from America.

About the mid-1780s Shillitoe had become a teetotaller and a vegetarian. Though nervously preoccupied about his health he was in fact physically tough, often walking 30 miles a day; even at eighty he would walk from the City back home to Tottenham. James Everett, a Hitchin Methodist, depicted him:

> he was below the middle height, spare, active, buoyant in spirit, and appeared as if made of wire and muscle. He was generally attired in a 'pepper and salt' suit, with a dowlas shirt often open at the neck, and a chip hat, which he usually carried in his hand, or on his umbrella stick in hot weather. He walked vigorously, often with his coat over his arm. (Hine, 187)

Despite nervous fears (he would run across London Bridge in dread lest it collapse beneath him) he had indomitable moral courage once he was convinced he was doing God's requirings. Thus in Ireland, usually with other Friends, he systematically visited drinking houses (eighty in Waterford alone), speaking with the keepers and also frequently 'to the company sitting in them to drink, who mostly heard quietly what we had to offer and at our parting behaved respectfully' (Shillitoe, 1.91). At the other end of the social scale his 1824 continental visit included 'religious opportunities' with the duke of Cumberland at Hanover, the crown prince of Prussia at Berlin, the king of Prussia at Charlottenburg, the king of Denmark at Copenhagen, and the emperor Alexander I at Petersburg. Back at home he had more than one interview with George IV. He passed by sentries into palaces and by warders into prisons and seemed intuitively to respond to the needs of those to whom he felt called.

Shillitoe's religious temperament was mystical but his theology was orthodox. During his American visit, smelling infidelity in the followers of Elias Hicks, he was more preoccupied in preaching against them than in listening to what they actually said. Thus, though sincere in wanting to promote unity among American Quakers, his visits may well have hastened the disastrous separations of 1827–8. During the 1830s, however, he was alarmed at the increasing emphasis that some British Friends were placing on the scriptures rather than the spirit as a primary rule. His quiet humour remained until the end. He said to his medical attendant: 'I will take any thing in moderation, that will not affect my intellect. I want to go out of the world with a clear head and a clean heart' (Shillitoe, 2.425). He died on 12 June 1836 at Tottenham, where five days later his body was interred in the Quaker burial-ground. He was survived by his wife, who died on 23 February 1838.

CHARLOTTE FELL-SMITH, *rev.* EDWARD H. MILLIGAN

Sources T. Shillitoe, *Journal of the life, labours, and travels*, 2 vols. (1839) · R. L. Hine, *Hitchin worthies: four centuries of English life* (1932), 185–9 · T. E. Harvey, 'Thomas Shillitoe (1754–1836), some hitherto unpublished particulars', *Journal of the Friends' Historical Society*, 42 (1950), 3–15 · B. Forbush, *Elias Hicks, Quaker liberal* (1956) · W. Tallack, *Thomas Shillitoe* (1867) · family Bible, RS Friends, Lond., Temp MS 407/20 [nineteenth-century copy]
Archives RS Friends, Lond., corresp. and MS of journal
Likenesses C. E. Giberne, pen, ink, crayon, and chalk, 1830, RS Friends, Lond.; repro. in *So numerous a family: 200 years of Quaker education at Ackworth, 1779–1979* (Ackworth School, 1979) · S. Lucas, sketch, repro. in R. L. Hine, *The history of Hitchin*, 2 vols. (1927–9) · lithograph (posthumous), NPG · silhouette, RS Friends, Lond.

Shils, Edward Albert (1910–1995), sociologist, was born on 1 July 1910 in Philadelphia, Pennsylvania, USA, the younger son of Nathan Shils (*b.* 1881), a worker in a cigar making factory, and his wife, Esther. His parents were immigrant Russian Jews, his mother a housewife with the conventionally fabled educational aspirations for her sons. Shils was educated at the local high school and local university (the State University of Pennsylvania, where he majored in French literature), from which he emerged with a BA in 1931 to face the severe conditions of the labour market of that decade. At first and briefly he worked as a social worker, but then he gradually found his way as Louis Wirth's research assistant into what he saw as the high intellectualism of the University of Chicago. Unsurprisingly in the 1930s he was a Rooseveltian new dealer but, as he matured in the Chicago atmosphere, he became a liberal, distrustful of 'the powers', bellicose against state tyranny of the right and the left, and a devotee of freedom. In the 1970s he also became a neo-conservative in the twentieth-century American sense, trustful of tradition, seeing social order as rooted in face-to-face ties, and finding his utopia in the networks of scientists and scholars intensively looking for truth and protected by the institutions of free science. Co-founder of the *Bulletin of the Atomic Scientists* and actively opposed to the tendency which manifested itself as McCarthyism during the cold war, he defended democratic pluralism in his *Torment of Secrecy* (1956). He was among the last passionate missionaries of academic freedom, enamoured of German universities in their Humboldtean heyday, always seeking to preserve and to reinvent what he increasingly feared to have been lost by Marxist ideological betrayal and state patronage.

At Chicago, Shils taught first in the college where Hutchins had pioneered the 'great books' tradition as a suitable modern but traditional education for undergraduates. He was influenced by Robert Park in the period of Chicago empirical sociology, by Frank Knight in the pursuit of a rigorous logic, and by Leo Szilard in the relentless search for persuasion of the political authorities. He occupied himself energetically with the associated movements towards international control of nuclear weapons. Yet he was faithful to his academic calling, reading the European classics and modern American empirical work, working closely with Talcott Parsons, and publishing widely. Indeed it came to light beyond the circle of his close friends and only on his death that he was engaged on a breathtakingly ambitious, Weber-like project on the movements of knowledge down the ages and across cultures and religions—an unfinished and probably unfinishable programme of scholarly research. Such was the grandeur of his reading and his knowledge of disciplines, languages, and history.

When the USA entered the war Shils seized the opportunity of coming to Europe, not, for obvious reasons, to extend his already formidable knowledge of German sociology, but to visit England where he worked jointly for the British government and for the US office of strategic services, interviewing German prisoners. His conclusion, confirmed by later research, was that the influence of primary group loyalties rather than the Nazi ideology sustained the fighting power of the Wehrmacht. Meanwhile he soon penetrated and enjoyed the London circles of European intellectuals, including Raymond Aron (then a member of the Free French forces). After the war he became one of the first 'transatlantic' academics, with a joint post at the London School of Economics (LSE) and Chicago. He became interested in monarchy, writing perceptively on the coronation of 1953 in the *Sociological Review*. Later, in 1961, he went to King's College, Cambridge, and later still (in 1970) to Peterhouse to escape the influence of Edmund Leach, who was referred to by Lord Dacre as 'the swinging provost' (*Minerva*, 92). He meanwhile retained his connection to Chicago where he had, with John Nef, founded the Committee on Social Thought. He knew an extraordinary number of intellectuals in Europe, North America, and Africa, as well as in India—where he made a special study of their place in society and wrote a much discussed monograph, *The Intellectual between Tradition and Modernity* (1961). He seemed to be in perpetual motion, arriving everywhere to congresses, conferences, and conversations, yet he was an essentially private man.

Shils was also a busy man, with a fresh, freckled face and ginger hair, aggressive, and either scowling in the face of an enemy or smiling at the sight of a friend, 'Not', as Noel Annan has written, 'afraid to bludgeon with his erudition those who did not realise sociology was a subject that rested on a great European intellectual tradition' (Annan, 255). For the students at the LSE after the Second World War there was as magnificent a professorial presentation of the social science scenery as could be found in the Western world. For a small minority of them, mostly grammar school boys returned from the war, the ambition to become professional sociologists formed the first generation of a remarkable group of academics who went on as the vanguard of a rapid expansion of the subject in the British provincial universities. Two men stood out as their guides—David Glass and Edward Shils. Both, oddly enough, were indifferent lecturers, but they were endowed with a compelling charisma (a word which came into lay vogue in the 1940s). Glass was precise in research technique and learned in the LSE tradition of demographic and statistical investigation. Shils provided an alternative spur to their implausible academic aspiration. He not only presented classical European sociology to them but did so in an American voice which simply assumed that undergraduates would become graduate students and subsequently professionals. His blend of tutorial ferocity and Olympian erudition challenged their still half-formed ambition to fearful effort. His *Current State of American Sociology* (1948) conveyed the conviction that a subject of great difficulty and worth was at once both dignified in its European antiquity and accessible in its American modernity. Sociological research beckoned as a living practice as well as a hallowed tradition.

Perhaps Shils's most enduring interest was in the university as an organization for the creation and preservation of important knowledge. To this end he founded *Minerva* in 1962 and was its active, some thought over-active, editor until the end of his life. Many if not most contributors would have their scripts returned and find them cascaded in showers of green ink by the editor's comments and suggestions—in effect rewritten. For Eric Ashby this gave Shils a claim to being the outstanding editor of the century. Certainly no editor put a firmer stamp on his journal. Accordingly he earned many enemies, not only as an overbearing editor but as a rancorous disputant and a ruthless manipulator of colleagues and students. Yet he also had the love of many friends, as the memorial issue of *Minerva* amply showed.

Shils was a complicated man. Sometimes his prose could be turgid, sometimes weighty and incisive. Sometimes his conversation could be portentous and delivered in long, Latinate, and periodic paragraphs. At other times he could relax over a good meal, perhaps one he himself had cooked, to retail academic and literary gossip and anecdotes in short, sharp, racy quips from the New York and Chicago Jewish communities. Community is what he longed for. He could not find it in marriage: he was married twice (first to Ruth Almond, second to Irene Coltman), and was divorced twice. Even survey interviewing was seen by him as a kind of moral conviviality. He was a Jew who neither believed nor practised, but he was nevertheless proud of his ancestry and deeply if sceptically pious, knowing and deploring the secular tendency among his colleagues towards the false belief that reason could put religion to flight. For him the unsolved mystery of life was that the roots of rationality lay in human emotions. A large picture of him is hung in the Shils Seminar Room at the University of Chicago. He was a generous benefactor to Peterhouse, Cambridge, both to the college library and in endowing the Dacre lectures. He died of cancer in Chicago on 23 January 1995, leaving one son from his second marriage. His ashes were scattered over the river in Philadelphia.   A. H. HALSEY

Sources *Minerva*, 34/1 (spring 1996) [Edward Shils memorial issue] · *The Times* (28 Jan 1995) · personal knowledge (2004) · private information (2004) [J. E. Floud, S. Grosby] · N. Annan, *Our age: portrait of a generation* (1990)
Archives University of Chicago, Joseph Regenstein Library, MSS

Likenesses photograph, repro. in *The Times* · portrait, University of Chicago, Shils Seminar Room
Wealth at death £131,935—effects in England: administration with will, 21 Sept 1995, *CGPLA Eng. & Wales*

Shimmin, Hugh (1819–1879), journalist and journal editor, was born on 6 September 1819, in Castletown, Isle of Man. His father was a stonemason but very little is known about his parents.

Shimmin's life might be rendered as a Smilesian story of triumphant self-help and character, pulling the protagonist up from humble origins in defiance of all temptations. Of Manx extraction, he spent his early years in Whitehaven, migrating to Liverpool in his teens with his mother to join his father, a stonemason with a drink problem. The evidence is not entirely conclusive, but he seems to have been brought up in poverty and sent to work at eight years old. His father died in the fifth year of his apprenticeship to a bookbinder. Shimmin then supported his family by collecting rents for his landlord, while impressing his employer sufficiently to take charge of the bookbindery after completing his apprenticeship, incurring the hostility of colleagues who resented his opposition to drinking customs. With this abstemiousness went the pursuit of self-improvement through education, as Shimmin joined the Mental Improvement Society at the Liverpool Institute and then the mechanics' institution in his mid-twenties, coming into contact with Unitarian and Methodist social reformers. He was an active Wesleyan at this stage. At some time, probably in the 1840s, he made a prudent (though childless) marriage: the savings of his wife, Jane (of whose origins nothing has been discovered), were exactly sufficient to buy the bookbinding business.

By his mid-thirties Shimmin was established as a modestly successful businessman. From the mid-1850s his writing gave him a public face and local fame. He began with occasional articles on various subjects in the Liverpool press, but during 1855–6 he wrote a series of exposés of Liverpool's drinking dens, cheap music-halls, dog-fighting taverns, and other haunts of iniquity and vice, which disturbed and titillated readers of the *Liverpool Mercury*. These were later published in book form as *Liverpool Life* (1857) and *Liverpool Sketches* (1863). His brutally frank *Pen-and-Ink Portraits of Liverpool Town Councillors* (1866) had originally appeared in 1857. From this journalistic success Shimmin moved on to be editor and joint proprietor of the new satirical weekly, *The Porcupine*, which appeared in 1860 and which outlived him, surviving until 1913. Its scarifying denunciations of sanitary conditions and moral failings, and deflations of municipal pomposity, found a ready audience. Shimmin's blunt and moralistic rhetoric made him enemies as well as friends. In 1870 he was imprisoned for libel after accusing maritime interests of insurance frauds, despite the sympathetic intervention of many leading citizens, including Charles Booth. In later life he retreated from radical liberalism and became a fervent Anglican. But he remained active in educational and other charities, and his funeral attracted an immense crowd.

Shimmin said little about working conditions and practices, or about ethnic and sectarian divisions. He resisted the contemporary temptation to blame the Irish for social problems. He ascribed social ills to individual failings, although not solely to working-class ones. He disliked misplaced and maladministered charity, blaming drink for many social problems while remaining hostile to the temperance movement. These attitudes, like his emphasis on female virtue and steadiness and on frugal domestic management, flowed from his own experience. His pertinacity and powers of observation gave him enough material to make him an important commentator on Victorian urban provincial life.

Shimmin was a lively and combative journalist under whose editorship *The Porcupine* became famous for campaigns against the evils which were pungently described in its pages, and for unsparing commentaries on local politics and politicians. His writings offer insights into popular enjoyments, working-class domestic life, and the problems of charitable and municipal initiatives for social improvement during the mid-Victorian years in Liverpool, then Britain's second city, which was famous not only as the focal point of the Atlantic economy, but also for appalling living conditions, death-rates, immorality, and vice. He described these conditions, and the problems of policing a great seaport, in graphic detail, but failed to explain their roots or propose ways of ameliorating them. Nevertheless, his work stands comparison with better-known commentators such as Henry Mayhew. Shimmin died of 'apoplexy' at his home, 5 Radstock Road, Liverpool, on 12 January 1879 and was buried on 15 January at Anfield cemetery. His wife survived him.

JOHN K. WALTON and ALASTAIR WILCOX

Emanuel Shinwell, Baron Shinwell (1884–1986), by Walter Bird, 1958

Sources J. K. Walton and A. Wilcox, eds., *Low life and moral improvement in mid-Victorian England* (1991) · A. Wilcox, 'The unknown Shimmin: themes from a mid-Victorian Liverpool observer', MA diss., Lancaster University, 1990 · [H. Shimmin], *Harry Birkett: the story of a man who helped himself* (1860) · H. Hardknot [H. Shimmin], *Rambles in the Lake District* (1857) · *The Porcupine* (18 Jan 1879) · *Liberal Review* (18 Jan 1879) · *Liverpool Daily Post* (13 Jan 1879)
Likenesses O. Silk, engraving, repro. in *Liberal Review*
Wealth at death under £5000: probate, 23 Jan 1879, *CGPLA Eng. & Wales*

Shinwell, Emanuel, Baron Shinwell (1884–1986), politician, was born on 18 October 1884 in Spitalfields, London, the eldest in a family of thirteen children of Samuel Shinwell, a clothing manufacturer of Polish-Jewish origin, and his Dutch wife, Rose Konigswinter. The family moved to Glasgow but Shinwell left school at the age of eleven to be apprenticed to the tailoring trade. He joined his first trade union, the Amalgamated Society of Clothing Operatives, at the age of seventeen and was elected to Glasgow Trades Council in 1906. He was to serve twice as its president. He became an early member of the Independent Labour Party and was an active socialist crusader. In 1911 he was prominent on the Clyde during the national dock strike.

Shinwell continued his militant union activities during the war and was wrongly alleged to have been involved in the disturbances in George Square, Glasgow, between striking workers and the police on Red Friday (31 January 1919). As a result, he spent over five months in Calton gaol, Edinburgh. He was now turning to thoughts of a political career. In the 1918 general election, he stood unsuccessfully as Labour candidate for Linlithgow (West Lothian); in 1922 he was elected to parliament there.

Shinwell served as parliamentary secretary to the mines department in the first Labour government of Ramsay MacDonald in 1924. Defeated in the 1924 general election, he was re-elected in a by-election in 1928 and served in junior offices in the second Labour government, as financial secretary to the War Office in 1929–30, and again in the mines department in 1930–31. He had an immense admiration for MacDonald and tried in vain to persuade him not to head the National Government in August 1931. In the subsequent general election, Shinwell was defeated again.

Shinwell now decided to challenge MacDonald directly and in the 1935 general election handsomely defeated his old leader at Seaham Harbour. After a redistribution of seats, the constituency was later renamed Easington. Shinwell was always a pugnacious member of parliament. In 1938 he caused a sensation by striking a Conservative, Commander Robert Bower (as it happened, a former naval boxing champion), when the latter made a hostile interjection in debate. During the war years Shinwell was a vigorous, though always patriotic, critic of Winston Churchill's coalition government. He and the tory sixth Earl Winterton were popularly christened Arsenic and

Old Lace. Shinwell was also prominent in Labour's policy making committees, notably those dealing with coal and energy.

When Labour won the 1945 general election, Attlee appointed Shinwell to the cabinet as minister of fuel and power. Here he achieved the nationalization of coal in 1946 and also negotiated the so-called miners' charter with the National Union of Mineworkers. He caused much controversy by declaring that the middle class was 'not worth a tinker's cuss'. He served as chairman of the Labour Party in 1947–8. However, his reputation slumped during the acute fuel crisis of January–March 1947, at a time of an exceptionally severe winter. He was accused of complacency and failing to plan to deal with basic problems of coal production. That October, much to his chagrin, Shinwell was demoted by Attlee to the War Office, outside the cabinet. Hugh Gaitskell took his place and thereby earned Shinwell's undying enmity, reinforced by Gaitskell's public-school background. Shinwell was also attacked by younger men such as James Callaghan for being less than ardent over nationalization. However, Shinwell proved to be a vigorous war minister, in tune with army sentiment, and Attlee reappointed him to the cabinet in March 1950 as minister of defence. Here Shinwell dealt energetically with the emergency in Malaya and war in Korea. In the summer of 1951 he urged the cabinet to send British troops to protect the oil refineries at Abadan, which the Persian government had nationalized, but he was successfully resisted by other ministers.

After Labour fell from office in 1951, Shinwell lost ground. He was defeated in elections for the party national executive in 1952 and left the shadow cabinet in 1955. Gaitskell was elected party leader that year; Shinwell had backed his fellow veteran, Herbert Morrison. However, despite being in his seventies, he continued to play a lively role in politics. He changed his stance on nuclear weapons and campaigned against the stationing of American Polaris submarines at Holy Loch. The election of Harold Wilson as party leader after Gaitskell's death gave Shinwell new opportunities. Although now eighty, he was appointed by Wilson as chairman of the Parliamentary Labour Party in October 1964, and worked hard to secure support for a government whose initial majority was only four. However, he came into conflict with ministers from 1966, especially with the equally aggressive foreign secretary, George Brown, since Shinwell was a vehement enemy of British entry into the European Common Market. He resigned as party chairman in 1967; in 1970 he became a life peer.

Shinwell's career was still far from over. He became chairman of the all-party Lords' defence study group. He voted against his own Labour government in 1976 and in March 1982 resigned the party whip in protest against left-wing militancy, though he remained a Labour Party member. He was now a legendary figure, and his hundredth birthday was celebrated in the House of Lords in 1984 (during a national miners' strike) with considerable enthusiasm.

With his stocky figure and Glaswegian accent, Manny Shinwell was pugnacious in parliament and on the platform. Appropriately, his enthusiasms included professional boxing. Though not religious, he was also much involved with the Jewish community. His performance in office was marred by the 1947 fuel crisis, while as a service minister he showed a jingoism some thought inappropriate. However, he had the gift of striking up friendships across the spectrum, including with the first Viscount Montgomery of Alamein and the editor of the *Sunday Express*, Sir John Junor. He was kindly towards the young. He was a major personality over sixty years, and a notable pioneer in Labour's long march to power in 1945. He wrote several autobiographical works, of which *Conflict without Malice* (1955) is the most important. He was married (and widowed) three times. In 1903 he married Fay (Fanny) Freeman (*d.* 1954); they had two sons and a daughter. In 1956 he married Dinah (*d.* 1971), daughter of Carol Ludwig Meyer, of Denmark. In 1972 he married Sarah, former wife of Alfred Hurst and daughter of Solomon Stungo. She died in 1977. Shinwell himself died on 8 May 1986 at the age of 101, at his St John's Wood flat in London, and was cremated at Golders Green crematorium.

KENNETH O. MORGAN, rev.

Sources E. Shinwell, *Conflict without malice* (1955) · E. Shinwell, *I've lived through it all* (1973) · E. Shinwell, *Lead with the left: my first ninety-six years* (1981) · E. Shinwell, *Shinwell talking: a conversational biography to celebrate his hundredth birthday*, ed. J. Doxat (1984) · *The Times* (9 May 1986) · *The Guardian* (9 May 1986) · BLPES, Shinwell MSS · BLPES, Dalton MSS · Nuffield Oxf., Gaitskell MSS · labour party archives, Manchester · private information (1996)

Archives BLPES, corresp. and papers | BLPES, corresp. with Independent Labour Party · King's Lond., Liddell Hart C., corresp. with Sir B. H. Liddell Hart · Labour History Archive and Study Centre, Manchester, corresp. with Morgan Phillips · PRO, corresp. with Ramsay MacDonald, 30/69/1/205

Likenesses W. Stoneman, photographs, 1924–58, NPG · H. Coster, photographs, 1930–39, NPG · W. Bird, photograph, 1958, NPG [*see illus.*] · G. Argent, photograph, 1968, NPG · G. Davien, caricature, plaster head, NPG

Wealth at death £271,509: probate, 28 July 1986, *CGPLA Eng. & Wales*

Shipley, Sir Arthur Everett (1861–1927), zoologist, was born on 10 March 1861 at Walton-on-Thames, the second son of Alexander Shipley, of The Hall, Datchet, Buckinghamshire, and his wife, Amelia, daughter of William Henry Burge, of Windsor. He attended University College School, London (1877–9), whence he entered St Bartholomew's Hospital as a medical student. In 1880 he proceeded with a scholarship in natural sciences to Christ's College, Cambridge. He obtained first classes in both parts of the natural sciences tripos (1882 and 1884); in the second part he took zoology as his subject. At Cambridge, Shipley came under the influence of Francis Maitland Balfour, professor of animal morphology. Balfour had recently published *Comparative Embryology* (1880–81), revealing a new field for zoological research. Moreover, the study of the morphology of the smaller animals and embryos had been greatly facilitated by the invention in

Sir Arthur Everett Shipley (1861–1927), by Philip A. de Laszlo, 1925

1883 of the rocking microtome, which enabled a series of microscopic sections to be cut and mounted. This invention was fully employed by Shipley and his contemporaries.

Shipley's early interest in zoology and his capacity for research were shown by a visit to the Stazione Zoologica at Naples, and by the publication of the results of his work there in a paper on the structure and development of the Brachiopoda, before he had taken the second part of his tripos. His next publication was an account, which appeared in 1887, of the development of the river lamprey. However, Shipley's early publications gave little indication of the lines of work which established his reputation as a zoologist. After the publication of an important memoir on one of the Gephyrean worms (*Quarterly Journal of Microscopical Science*, 31, 1890), he turned his attention to the study of parasitic worms: his published work on this subject, which eventually extended to nearly fifty papers in scientific journals, gradually built up his scientific reputation as a competent and successful researcher, and led in 1904 to his election as a fellow of the Royal Society.

At Cambridge, Shipley successively held the posts of university demonstrator in comparative anatomy (1886), lecturer in the advanced morphology of the Invertebrata (1894), and reader in zoology (1908). This last post he resigned in 1920, after which he held no official teaching post in the university. Shipley's teaching was enlivened by many touches of humour, which were also present in all his writings. In addition to his scientific papers, he produced in 1893 a textbook, *The Zoology of the Invertebrata*, which was much used by students. He collaborated with Professor Ernest MacBride in writing a *Textbook of Zoology*, which was published in 1901 and passed through four editions, the last in 1920. He also collaborated with S. F. Harmer in editing the *Cambridge Natural History*, a work in ten volumes which appeared between 1895 and 1909, and of which Shipley himself wrote several sections. He edited the biological series of the Pitt Press Natural Science Manuals and, for a time, the Fauna of British India series. He was co-editor with Professor G. H. F. Nuttall of the journal *Parasitology* from 1908 to 1914, and also assisted in editing the *Journal of Economic Biology* from 1905 to 1913.

Shipley was perhaps at his best when writing as a popular exponent of zoology. His first book of this nature was a collection of essays entitled *Pearls and Parasites*, published in 1908. It was about this time that he gave up active research in zoology, and turned to literary work. He published '*J*': *a Memoir of John Willis Clark* in 1913. *The Minor Horrors of War* (1915) passed rapidly through three editions and was so successful that a year later he wrote *More Minor Horrors*. These two books introduced parasitology to a public which had at the time practical experience of the parasites described there. *Studies in Insect Life* appeared in 1917, and in 1923 Shipley published a small book entitled *Life*, which had a very wide circulation and encouraged the teaching of elementary biology in schools. In 1924 appeared *Cambridge Cameos* and *Islands: West Indian and Aegean*. Shipley's last book, *Hunting under the Microscope*, was posthumously published in 1928. Shipley was for many years Cambridge University correspondent of *The Times*, and he contributed many articles to that paper, as well as to many other papers, encyclopaedias, and reviews, on a great diversity of subjects.

Shipley was elected a fellow of Christ's College in 1887. At the time of his election the study of natural sciences in Cambridge was beginning to make great strides. Shipley's reputation as a scientist was overshadowed by that of some of his particularly distinguished contemporaries, but his intellect was essentially versatile. As early as 1887 he was sent by the Colonial Office to the Bermudas in order to investigate a plant disease. This was the beginning of a connection with the Colonial Office which lasted until his death. In the administration of his college and of the university Shipley played a leading part. In 1891 he was appointed secretary to the museums and lecture rooms syndicate, a post which constituted him virtually business manager of the university laboratories and museums. In the following year he became tutor in natural sciences at Christ's College. From 1896 to 1908 he was a member of the council of the senate of the university, besides serving on many other boards and syndicates. Shipley made administration easy by an unusual sympathy with all sorts of people, and by a gift for entertaining, which made his hospitality famous in Cambridge. He travelled a great deal, frequently visiting the USA. It was on one of these visits that he received the honorary degree of DSc from Princeton University (1906); on another occasion (1909) he visited Canada in order to preside over the zoological section of the British Association, which was meeting in Winnipeg. He could always entertain a large company with a good story well told.

Outside the university Shipley accomplished a notable amount of public work. He was chairman of the Marine Biological Association, treasurer and vice-president of the Research Defence Society, and a member of the Central Medical War Committee and of the managing committee of the Imperial Bureau of Entomology. He was also a member of the royal commissions on the civil service (1912), on Trinity College, Dublin (1920), and on the importation of store cattle (1921). He was appointed chairman of a tropical agriculture committee in 1919. When the Imperial College of Tropical Agriculture was established in Trinidad in 1921, Shipley was appointed chairman of the governing body.

In 1910 Shipley was elected master of Christ's College. Under his direction the much altered master's lodge was largely restored to its original condition, and became one of the most interesting of the older buildings in Cambridge. He furnished it with great taste. To his frequent lunch and dinner parties there he invited not only people of distinction, but also undergraduates; and it was remarkable how he was able to bring together people of dissimilar ages and vocations. During the First World War he entertained at the lodge a long succession of convalescent officers.

From 1917 to 1919 as vice-chancellor of the university Shipley visited the United States as a member of the British university mission, which was sent out in 1918 by the Foreign Office on the invitation of the council of defence at Washington, to counteract German propaganda in American universities, and to make known the facilities for postgraduate work in British universities. He was in America when the armistice was signed on 11 November. He wrote an amusing account of this visit in *The Voyage of a Vice-Chancellor* (1919).

In 1920 Shipley was created GBE in recognition of his public services. Although he took no part in university administration from this time, he still entertained, wrote, and kept his interest in his college. Moreover, he did not retire from public work outside the university, and in 1924 he visited Trinidad in order to lay the foundation stone of the new buildings of the College of Tropical Agriculture.

In the early part of 1927 Shipley suffered from a serious illness. Although he recovered, a second attack later in the same year proved fatal, and he died at the master's lodge on 22 September. He was not married.

In appearance Shipley was dark and short. Latterly he gave up his earlier regular exercise and became, as he himself expressed it, 'quite rotund'. He was a person of regular habits, who maintained a high standard of private and public duty. He was both punctual and punctilious, and it was an ideal of his to answer all his correspondence by return of post. In spite of his many administrative and social duties, Shipley's literary output was considerable, largely because he could write at odd moments, even when others were talking in the room, as was often the

case during the war, when convalescent officers were staying in his lodge. He had a keen appreciation of painting and architecture. He also collected furniture, and he filled his rooms in college, and later his lodge, with many valuable pieces, which he delighted to show to his visitors.

J. T. SAUNDERS, rev. V. M. QUIRKE

Sources S. F. H., *PRS*, 103B (1928), i–viii • *The Times* (23 Sept 1927) • W. T. Stearn, *The Natural History Museum at South Kensington: a history of the British Museum (Natural History), 1753–1980* (1981) **Archives** U. Cam., department of zoology, corresp. and papers | BL, corresp. with Macmillans, Add. MS 55223 • King's AC Cam., letters to Oscar Browning **Likenesses** P. A. de Laszlo, oils, 1925, Christ's College, Cambridge [*see illus.*] • J. Nicholson, oils, Imperial College of Agriculture, Trinidad • photograph, RS **Wealth at death** £41,999 1s. 8d.: resworn probate, 13 Jan 1928, CGPLA Eng. & Wales

Shipley, Sir Charles (1755–1815), army officer and colonial governor, was born on 18 February 1755 at Copt Hall, Luton, Bedfordshire, the son of Richard Shipley, of Stamford, Lincolnshire, and of Copt Hall, a cavalry captain, and his wife, Jane, the daughter of Robert Rudyerd, of Wormley, Hertfordshire. The latter was great-grandson and representative of Sir Benjamin Rudyerd (1572–1658) of West Woodhay, Berkshire. On the death of Shipley's mother's only brother, Captain Benjamin Rudyerd of the Coldstream Guards (who was aide-de-camp to Lord Stair at the battle of Dettingen, and whose various accomplishments were celebrated by Smollett in the *Memoirs of a Lady of Quality* as those of Mr R—), his mother became sole heir of the families of Maddox and Rudyerd, but, owing to his father's extravagance, Charles Shipley inherited little.

On 1 April 1771, after a period at the Royal Military Academy, Woolwich, Shipley, aged sixteen, was commissioned ensign and practitioner engineer. In 1772 he went to Minorca. On 4 March 1776 he was promoted lieutenant and sub-engineer. He returned to England in 1778, and was stationed at Gravesend as engineer on the staff. In Gravesend, in May 1780, he married Mary (d. 1820), the daughter of James Teale and his wife, Mary, the daughter of Dr Ralph Blomer, prebendary of Canterbury. They had three daughters.

From 1780 to 1783 Shipley reportedly served in the Leeward Islands, and in 1788 he went to the West Indies and was stationed at Antigua. Early in 1792 he returned to England to be court-martialled for disobedience to regulations in employing his own slaves in Antigua on government fortification work. The court sat at the Horse Guards from 23 February to 1 March, found Shipley guilty, and sentenced him to twelve months' suspension from rank and pay, but stated that his conduct did not stem from any corrupt motive.

On 15 August 1793 Shipley was promoted captain. At the request of Sir John Vaughan, commander-in-chief in the West Indies, he again applied to be sent thither, and embarked in November with his family in the government storeship *Woodley*. After leaving Plymouth severe storms compelled them to put into Gibraltar and Cadiz for some weeks, and when at length they arrived within a few miles of Barbados they were captured by the French corvette *Perdrix*. The prisoners were confined in hulks at Guadeloupe, and suffered great hardships; but Shipley's wife was set free, and eventually managed to obtain the liberation of her husband from the notorious French republican commander Victor Hugues.

Shipley was promoted major in the army on 6 May 1795. In May 1796 he sent home reports on the defences of Martinique and of Prince Rupert's Head, Dominica, and on 20 October that year he was appointed commanding royal engineer of the Windward and Leeward Islands. In February 1797 he accompanied Sir Ralph Abercromby as commanding royal engineer of his expedition to Trinidad; the Spaniards surrendered the island on the 17th. He also accompanied Abercromby as commanding royal engineer, and took part in the unsuccessful attack on Puerto Rico in April. The British failed to capture San Juan, and re-embarked. This marked the end of the British offensive expeditions to the Caribbean: 'the heyday of Caribbean warfare was over' (Duffy, 291). On 11 September 1798 Shipley was promoted lieutenant-colonel in the Royal Engineers.

In 1799 Shipley was sent by Lieutenant-General Thomas Trigge in the *Amphitrite* to examine the coasts in the neighbourhood of the Surinam River for a landing-place to attack Surinam. Trigge, in his dispatch (22 August 1799), stated that Shipley acted with great zeal and judgement. Surinam surrendered on 20 August but was soon retaken. Shipley also took part, during March, in the capture of the islands of St Bartholomew, St Martin, and St Thomas, and of Santa Cruz. On 21 and 22 June 1803 he commanded a detachment of infantry at the capture of St Lucia. In April 1804 an expedition was sent under Brigadier-General Charles Green, temporarily commanding in chief in the Leeward Islands, against Dutch Guiana. Shipley accompanied it as commanding royal engineer, and, having landed with Lieutenant Arnold of the Royal Engineers and a small party, reconnoitred the defences of Surinam, which was again captured. Green, in his dispatch to Lord Camden, dated 13 May 1804, admitted obligations to Shipley, as commanding engineer, 'far beyond my power to express'.

On 13 July 1805 Shipley was accordingly promoted colonel in the Royal Engineers, and on 12 June 1806 brigadier-general to the forces serving in the West Indies. In that year, under orders from the Board of Ordnance, he made the circuit of the coast of Jamaica and explored the interior with a view to a survey. In 1807 he accompanied the expedition from Barbados against the Danish West Indian islands under General Bowyer and Rear-Admiral Sir Alexander Cochrane. They arrived before St Thomas on 21 December, when Shipley was sent ashore to demand from the governor, von Scholten, the surrender of St Thomas and St John, which capitulated the next day. On 23 December the expedition sailed for Santa Cruz, and Shipley was again sent on shore to negotiate terms. The governor would capitulate only if some of his officers were allowed to inspect the British ships and troops and satisfy his honour that the British force was so strong that resistance would be hopeless. Shipley agreed, and the island capitulated on 25 December 1807.

On 22 March 1808 Shipley was knighted, and in that same year he sent home proposals for strengthening the defences of the island of St Thomas. In January 1809 he took part in the expedition against Martinique under Lieutenant-General Sir George Beckwith. He landed on 30 January and began operations against Pigeon Island, admirably supported by Captain George Cockburn (1772–1853) of HMS *Pompée* and his sailors. The night after the batteries opened fire the enemy surrendered, and Pigeon Island fell to the British on 4 February, followed by Fort Bourbon and Fort Royal, and on 23 February by the whole island of Martinique. Shipley received the thanks of both houses of parliament.

In February 1810 Shipley commanded the 2nd division of the army in the successful operations against Guadeloupe. Brigadier-General Harcourt, in his dispatch of 7 February, expressed his indebtedness to Shipley during the operations, and especially in the action of 3 February at Ridge Beaupaire, St Louis, in front of Bellair.

Shipley was promoted major-general on 4 June 1811. On 27 February 1813 he was appointed governor of the island of Grenada. His administration was reportedly mild and just, and he dispelled those party feuds to which small colonies were prone.

After Bonaparte's return from Elba, a naval and military expedition, under Admiral Sir Philip Durham and Lieutenant-General Sir James Leith, was sent to secure the French West Indian islands for Louis XVIII, from whom they had revolted, and in June 1815 Martinique and Marie Galante were reoccupied without trouble. Guadeloupe, however, held out for Bonaparte (by then a British prisoner sailing to St Helena), and did not yield without fighting—the last between Bonaparte's troops and the allies. The British attacked on 8 and 9 August 1815, and Shipley commanded the 1st brigade. The enemy were defeated with few British casualties. Following negotiations, on 10 August Guadeloupe surrendered. Both naval and military commanders in their dispatches highly praised the 'distinguished and indefatigable engineer' Sir Charles Shipley. He received, by the command of the prince regent, a medal for Martinique with a clasp for Guadeloupe.

A skilful engineer and soldier, Shipley in July 1815 declined promotion out of the corps of Royal Engineers, of which he was senior regimental colonel, preferring to wait for his battalion. Ever careless of personal exposure, excessive fatigue at the attack on Guadeloupe apparently brought on an illness which ended in his death, at St George, Grenada, on 30 November 1815. He was buried in the church of St George's, Grenada.

His widow died at Boulogne (where she was granted a residence by Louis XVIII for her husband's services in the French West Indies) on 6 August 1820. Their youngest daughter, Elizabeth Cole (d. 1828), married in 1809 Henry David Erskine, twelfth earl of Buchan.

ROGER T. STEARN

Sources PRO, war office records · Royal Engineers Institution, Chatham, royal engineers records · *LondG* (1792–1815) · *Jerdan's*

National Portrait Gallery, 4 (1833) · *GM*, 1st ser., 85/2 (1815), 257 · *GM*, 1st ser., 86/1 (1816), 276–7 · W. Porter, *History of the corps of royal engineers*, 1 (1889) · M. Duffy, *Soldiers, sugar and seapower: the British expeditions to the West Indies and the war against revolutionary France* (1987) · D. Haggard, 'The last fight for Napoleon', *Journal of the Society of Army Historical Research*, 14 (1935), 231–2 · J. Black, *Britain as a military power, 1688–1815* (1999) · A. J. Guy, ed., *The road to Waterloo: the British army and the struggle against revolutionary and Napoleonic France, 1793–1815* (1990) · R. Muir, *Britain and the defeat of Napoleon, 1807–1815* (1996) · C. D. Hall, *British strategy in the Napoleonic War, 1803–15* (1992)

Archives NL Scot., reports and letters to Sir Alexander Cochrane **Likenesses** H. Cook, stipple (after J. Eckstein), BM, NPG; repro. in W. Jerdan, *National portrait gallery of illustrious and eminent personages*, 4 (1833)

Shipley, Conway (1782–1808). *See under* Shipley, William Davies (1745–1826).

Shipley, Georgiana (*c*.1755–1806). *See under* Naylor, Francis Hare- (1753–1815).

Shipley, Jonathan (1713–1788), bishop of St Asaph, was baptized in the united parishes of St Stephen Walbrook and St Benet Sherehog, London, on 2 October 1713. It is likely that his birth (in London) preceded this date by only a few days. He was the second, and eldest surviving, son of Jonathan Shipley (1676–1719), stationer, of London, and of Martha Davies (*d.* 1757) of Twyford House, Hampshire. His younger brother William *Shipley was subsequently the founder of the Royal Society of Arts. Shipley was briefly apprenticed as a stationer (Allen, 137, n. 16) and after attending a school at Reading he won a scholarship to St John's College, Oxford, in 1731. Having migrated to Christ Church he graduated BA in 1735; three years later he graduated MA and took holy orders. In a career move of decisive importance he became tutor to the family of Charles Mordaunt, third earl of Peterborough, and on 1 September 1743 he married the latter's niece, Anna Maria Mordaunt (1716/17–1803). She was celebrated in youth for her beauty and had served as a maid of honour to Queen Caroline (*GM*, 1st ser., 13, 1743, 498; Hare, 1.89). They had one son, William Davies *Shipley, who was later appointed dean of St Asaph, and five daughters.

Shipley proceeded to acquire substantial ecclesiastical preferment. In 1743 Bishop Benjamin Hoadly appointed him a prebend of Winchester and used his influence to secure him the rectorships of Silchester and of Sherborne St John, Hampshire. In 1745 he served as chaplain-general to the army of William, duke of Cumberland, in the continental campaign that included the defeat at Fontenoy. In 1748 he was made DD at Oxford and a canon of Christ Church. In June 1760 he was appointed dean of Winchester and rector of Chilbolton, Hampshire. In retaining his other livings he was not the only Anglican clergyman who found pluralism to be entirely consistent with latitudinarian principles. During the ministry of Augustus Fitzroy, third duke of Grafton (1768–70), Shipley advanced to the bench. He was consecrated bishop of Llandaff in February 1769 and was translated to St Asaph the following September. At this point he relinquished his other livings with the exception of Chilbolton.

In the House of Lords, Shipley gradually associated with

Jonathan Shipley (1713–1788), by John Raphael Smith, pubd 1777 (after Sir Joshua Reynolds, 1776)

the followers of William Pitt, earl of Chatham, in their criticisms of the administration of Lord North. An 'address to the reader' in Shipley's *Works* claims that the parliamentary opposition was 'a set of men to whom he was a perfect stranger, but who appeared to him to understand, and pursue the true interests of their country' (2.61). During the 1770s he became very friendly with Benjamin Franklin, whose opinions on the American question he shared, and with the radical dissenters Joseph Priestley and Richard Price (*Papers*, 29.147–9, 407–9, 635–7). In 1773 he preached before the Society for the Propagation of the Gospel a sermon in which he described North America as 'the only great nursery of freemen left on the face of the earth' (*Works*, 2.191–2). The sermon was praised by Franklin, and Chatham declared himself 'charmed and edified' by it (*Correspondence of William Pitt*, 4.302). In 1774, in a speech prepared for the Lords but not delivered, Shipley was strongly critical of the bill for altering the Massachusetts charter, declaring 'arbitrary taxation is plunder authorized by law' and 'There are methods of making reasonable concessions, and yet without injuring our dignity.' Without condoning the Boston Tea Party he praised the colonists as 'coheirs of liberty with ourselves' (*Works*, 2.161, 179, 181, 187). At the same time he displayed his latitudinarianism by sympathy with the dissenters. Although in 1772 he voted against the dissenters' bill for relief for their ministers and schoolmasters from the rigours of subscription to the Thirty-Nine Articles, and did not support a similar bill the following year, he spoke in favour of a third relief bill, which was passed in 1779 (Ditchfield, 64, 68–9). In a speech that was widely reported he claimed that the bill did not go far enough and that all legislation against the dissenters should be repealed (*Works*, 2.233–5). He was present in the Lords on 7 April 1778 and witnessed the collapse of Chatham. However, the opposition was consistently outvoted in the Lords as well as in the Commons until the disaster of Yorktown led to the fall of North's ministry in March 1782.

Shipley appeared to be in high favour with the new administration of Rockingham and Shelburne. He urged Shelburne to adhere to his 'good principles and your generous views for the public service', adding: 'If you find yourself entangled and embarrassed, like Lord Chatham, in Court artifices, break through the mercenary chains at once, and assert your liberty and honour' (Hare, 1.87). He urged Shelburne to retain his alliance with Rockingham. In July 1782 Charles James Fox told the duke of Grafton that Rockingham had been 'quite decided that Bishops Shipley and Hinchcliffe should have the offer of any opening that presented itself' (A. H. Fitzroy, duke of Grafton, *Autobiography*, ed. W. R. Anson, 1898, 329). Horace Walpole expected Shipley to be offered the see of Salisbury (Brown, 324) but Rockingham died on 1 July 1782 and Shipley seems to have quarrelled with Shelburne. None the less when the death of Frederick Cornwallis created a vacancy at Canterbury early in 1783 it was widely believed that Shipley was a serious candidate and there is evidence that Shelburne solicited George III in his favour (Sykes, 400). The king, however, disapproved of Shipley's political opinions, and the archbishopric was ultimately conferred upon John Moore. Shipley, like Richard Watson of Llandaff, received no further translation.

Thereafter Shipley's attendance in the Lords became more intermittent. He did not vote in the crucial divisions over the India Bill in December 1783 that brought down the Fox–North coalition. In 1787 he was one of only two bishops who, at a private meeting summoned by Pitt to consider an application from the dissenters, favoured the repeal of the Test and Corporation Acts (Sykes, 341). He shared many of the liberal opinions of Sir William Jones, who married Shipley's daughter Anna Maria and on whose behalf Shipley gave a warm recommendation to Pitt. He maintained a general commitment to mild parliamentary and economic reform, published a relatively small number of sermons, was admired in dissenting circles, and enjoyed a convivial social life at his London residence and at the bishop's palace at St Asaph. Despite their differences over America he also enjoyed the friendship of Samuel Johnson, who had visited him at St Asaph in 1774 and described him as 'knowing and conversible'. He belonged to the Literary Club and was on easy social terms with Edmund Burke and Sir Joshua Reynolds. Hannah More recalled a lively evening in his company and that of Horace Walpole (Walpole, *Corr.*, 31.211). He and his daughter Georgiana kept up an affectionate correspondence with Franklin.

Shipley died at Chilbolton on 6 December 1788 after an 'apoplectic seizure' and was buried at Twyford. There is a monument in Twyford church. The *Gentleman's Magazine*, which reported that he died at his London house in Bolton Row, Piccadilly, described him as possessing 'learning without pedantry, patriotism without faction and politeness without affectation' (*GM*, 1179). He was survived by

his wife, who died on 9 March 1803. Shipley was a man of considerable intellectual gifts, although his published works (despite the two-volume edition published in 1792) were not extensive. Within the Church of England he was a conscientious pastor, according to his own lights and those of his age. He conducted his diocesan visitations regularly and dutifully. Although adhering to orthodox Anglican doctrines he was unperturbed by the development of trinitarian heterodoxy and shared the optimistic assumption that truth would prevail in a free intellectual climate. In political terms he represented an Erastian form of whiggery that had passed from fashion during his later years. In declaring (1779) that religious toleration was a matter for the state rather than the church he showed himself to be an apt pupil of Hoadly. Even before the French Revolution his opinions were becoming marginalized among the Anglican hierarchy.

G. M. DITCHFIELD

Sources *The works of the Right Reverend Jonathan Shipley DD, lord bishop of St Asaph*, 2 vols. (1792) · P. Brown, *The Chathamites* (1967), 325–8 · Foster, *Alum. Oxon.* · *GM*, 1st ser., 58 (1788), 1130, 1179 · D. G. C. Allen, *William Shipley, founder of the Royal Society of Arts: a biography with documents* (1968) · A. J. C. Hare, *Memorials of a quiet life*, 18th edn, 2 vols. (1884) · W. B. Bannerman and W. B. Bannerman, jun., eds., *The registers of St Stephen's, Walbrook, and of St Benet Sherehog, London*, 1, Harleian Society, register section, 49 (1919) · *Correspondence of William Pitt, earl of Chatham*, ed. W. S. Taylor and J. H. Pringle, 4 vols. (1838–40), vol. 4, pp. 299–302 · *The correspondence of William Wilberforce*, ed. R. I. Wilberforce and S. Wilberforce, 2 vols. (1840), vol. 1, pp. 47–8 · *The historical and the posthumous memoirs of Sir Nathaniel William Wraxall, 1772–1784*, ed. H. B. Wheatley, 5 vols. (1884) · Boswell, *Life*, vols. 3–5 · G. M. Ditchfield, 'The subscription issue in British parliamentary politics, 1772–1779', *Parliamentary History*, 7 (1988), 45–80 · N. Sykes, *Church and state in England in the XVIII century* (1934) · *The papers of Benjamin Franklin*, 29, ed. B. B. Oberg and others (1992) · E. B. Fryde and others, eds., *Handbook of British chronology*, 3rd edn, Royal Historical Society Guides and Handbooks, 2 (1986)

Archives NL Wales, letters to his son, William Davies Shipley | BL, Add. MSS 33090, 35636, 35639, 42560, 42561 · BL, Newcastle MSS, Add. MSS 32902, 32918, 32920, 32925, 32960 · BL, Stevens transcripts, Add. MS 42309 · priv. coll., corresp. with Lord Shelburne

Likenesses J. R. Smith, mezzotint, pubd 1777 (after J. Reynolds, 1776), BM, NPG [*see illus.*] · B. Reading, line engraving, pubd 1788 (after medallion), BM; repro. in *European Magazine* (1788) · T. Trotter, line engraving, pubd 1792 (after J. Reynolds), BM · attrib. A. Devis, portrait, Bodrhyddan Hall, Denbighshire · studio of J. Reynolds, oils, Bodrhyddan Hall, Denbighshire · engraving (after T. Trotter; after J. Reynolds), repro. in *Works*, vol. 1 · Wedgwood medallion, Wedgwood Museum, Barlaston, Staffordshire

Wealth at death lands and tithes in several parishes, incl. leasehold estate in the parish of St Martin's, near Oswestry; government stock annuities to four unmarried daughters: will, PRO, PROB 11/1183, fols. 60v–62r · left £40,000 (est.) on his death: Brown, *The Chathamites*, 337

Shipley, Joseph (1795–1867), merchant and banker, was born on 12 April 1795 in Shipley House, on the corner of 16th and French streets, Wilmington, Delaware, USA. He was the eleventh of twelve children of a Quaker, Joseph Shipley (1752–1832), whose grandfather William Shipley had left his native Leicestershire to settle at Wilmington, and of Mary Levis (*d.* 1843) of Springfield, Delaware county, Pennsylvania. Although there is no definite information, it is evident from his correspondence that he received a good general and an excellent business education. It is likely he worked as a clerk for Samuel Canby, jun., of Philadelphia, whose letters reveal a fatherly interest in him.

Shipley's first definite employment was with John Welsh, a leading Philadelphia merchant, who sent him to Virginia to buy depreciated southern banknotes during the panic of 1819. Welsh then sent him to Liverpool, first as his agent in Joseph Shipley Jr & Co., Welsh being represented by '& Co.', then from January 1822 as his Liverpool partner, in Shipley, Welsh & Co. By 1825 Shipley had conducted affairs so well that he was invited by William Brown, of William and James Brown & Co. of Liverpool, to become from January 1826 a junior partner in that firm.

Shipley thus joined the leading firm in Atlantic commerce, with branches in Baltimore, Philadelphia, and New York, as well as in Liverpool, and with agents in the southern United States cotton ports. The firm consigned British manufactured goods to the USA, received huge volumes of American staples, especially cotton, ran packet lines, offered advances and credits to smaller merchants, and negotiated foreign exchange. Shipley at first was a partner only in the Liverpool house, but in 1837 he joined all the houses and in June 1839 the Liverpool firm's name was changed to Brown Shipley in recognition of his services during the financial panic of 1837.

This crisis was caused by the collapse of an unsustainable boom in the USA, but Browns and the other large Anglo-American houses bore the main pressure. In late 1836 the Bank of England, afraid of gold outflows, put increasing pressure on the Liverpool houses to restrict American credits. The consequence in America in early 1837 was widespread financial collapse. By May 1837 the Browns were in severe difficulties: remittances due from America for previous credits were unpaid and cotton prices had collapsed. Shipley wrote to his cousin in Philadelphia on 14 May,

> Such a revolution in commerce in the short space of three months surely never was (hitherto) witnessed … the mind can scarcely realise it. It has been only in the last week to ten days that I have begun seriously to apprehend the possible loss of nearly all the earnings of eleven laborious, anxious years. (Shipley to Newlin, 14 May 1837, Hargraves collection)

In these circumstances Shipley, William Brown being ill, visited London several times in late May and early June, and with the help of the Browns' bankers, Joseph Denison & Co., persuaded the Bank of England to offer Browns a loan of £2 million, a quite unprecedented sum. Shipley argued that 'two thirds of all our engagements arise out of the export of British manufacturers', and that 'disastrous consequences would follow our stoppage' which 'would be more felt than that of any other house in England' (Brown, 83–4). He was thus able to exploit fear of a systemic collapse, while the accounts showed that Browns was fundamentally sound.

Shipley gradually became the active partner in Brown Shipley as William Brown developed political interests. However, although in 1846 Brown became the free-trade member of parliament for South Lancashire, he still remained the senior partner, and he and James Brown still owned four-fifths of the capital. Fortunately Shipley agreed with William Brown on most important matters. Under this joint management Browns became the largest negotiator of sterling–dollar exchange and the leading financier of Anglo-American trade. This was inevitably at the expense of its traditional wider interests. Hence when James Brown involved the firm in financing the Collins Line steam-packet ships in the late 1840s, both William Brown and Shipley opposed him. Shipley's importance to the firm is indicated by William Brown's reaction to this deal. He wrote to James Brown:

> Mr Shipley says little, but he seems so vexed at this transaction, I think it not at all improbable he will give us notice of retiring. If so I must do the same, for I cannot at my time of life (even if I resign my seat in Parliament) undertake the management of the business here without the assistance of a partner who I have so long known, and in whom I have every confidence as the first man of business in the Kingdom.

He later revised this letter before transmission, but repeated his comments on Shipley, only replacing the last phrase with: 'as a man of strict integrity and probably the best man of business in the Kingdom' (Brown, letter-book, 23 and 29 Jan 1848).

Despite his doubts about the steamers Shipley remained with the firm until 1850, when he retired because of worsening gout. He returned to his family home in Wilmington, Delaware, and built a house, Rockwood, in Brandywine hundred, in the English style, and lived there with his two maiden sisters. He remained unmarried. His Liverpool house ultimately became part of Liverpool University. However, he retained a strong interest in the firms and regularly wrote them useful letters at critical times, such as in the panic of 1857 and during the civil war. He died on 8 May 1867 at Rockwood, Wilmington, and was buried at the Quaker burial-ground there.

J. R. KILLICK

Sources William Brown, letter-book, Brown Shipley, London · Joseph Shipley MSS, Eleutherian Mills Historical Library, Wilmington, Delaware, Hargraves Collection, accession 1266 · J. C. Brown, *A hundred years of merchant banking: a history of Brown Brothers and Company, Brown Shipley and Company and the allied firms* (privately printed, New York, 1909) · A. Ellis, *Heir of adventure: the story of Brown, Shipley & Co., merchant bankers* (privately printed, London, 1960) · J. A. Kouwenhoven, *Partners in banking: an historical portrait of a great private bank, Brown Brothers, Harriman & Co., 1818–1968* (1968) · E. J. Perkins, *Financing Anglo-American trade: the house of Brown, 1800–1880* (1975) · J. R. Killick, 'Risk, specialization and profit in the mercantile sector of the nineteenth century cotton trade: Alexander Brown & Sons, 1820–80', *Business History*, 16 (1974), 1–16 · M. Collins, 'The Bank of England and the Liverpool money market, 1825–50', PhD diss., U. Lond., 1972 · J. T. Scharf, *History of Delaware, 1609–1888*, 2 vols. (1888)

Archives Eleutherian Mills Historical Library, Wilmington, Delaware, Farnum collection, accession 1267 · Eleutherian Mills Historical Library, Wilmington, Delaware, Hargraves collection, accession 1266 · Hist. Soc. Penn., Cope MSS · Lpool RO, Brown Shipley & Co. MSS · New York Historical Society, Brown Brothers Harriman records

Likenesses portrait, repro. in Kouwenhoven, *Partners in banking*, 56; priv. coll. · portrait, repro. in J. C. Brown, *A hundred years of merchant banking* (1909), 73

Shipley, Orby (1832–1916), liturgical scholar and Roman Catholic convert, was born on 1 July 1832 at Twyford, Hampshire, the fourth son of the Revd Charles Shipley, rector of Mappowder, Dorset, and his wife, Charlotte, daughter of Orby Sloper. His grandfather was William Davies *Shipley, dean of St Asaph, and his great-grandfather was Jonathan *Shipley, bishop of St Asaph. Two brothers were generals, and other relatives had distinguished military careers. Educated at a private school, Shipley entered Jesus College, Cambridge, in 1850, graduating BA in 1854 and MA in 1858. His first publication, *The Purgatory of Prisoners* (1857), proposed half-way houses for newly released convicts, an idealistic scheme based on reforms introduced by his brother-in-law Walter Crofton (1815–1897), prison inspector in Ireland. Ordained deacon in 1855 and priest in 1858, Shipley served as a curate at St Thomas the Martyr, Oxford, whose vicar, Thomas Chamberlain (1810–1892), was a prominent high-churchman. Shipley subsequently joined his ritualist mentor, the Revd Alexander Heriot Mackonochie, in London in 1863 at the new church of St Alban the Martyr, Holborn. There Shipley was married by Mackonochie in 1868 to Zoë Wilson, fourth of the six daughters of James *Wilson; his brothers-in-law included Walter Bagehot and W. R. Greg.

Shipley's contributions to books he edited, *The Church and the World* (1866; 3rd edn, 1867), *Ecclesiastical Reform* (1873), and *Studies in Modern Problems* (1874), proved him to be a most trenchant, if idiosyncratic, proponent of extreme high-church polity. Advocating disestablishment as the only means of preserving the church's spiritual integrity, he none the less avoided identification with the political agenda of the Liberation Society. His self-consciously paradoxical argument in *The Four Cardinal Virtues* (1871) was that disestablishment had to be resolutely pursued even though it was the irresistible will of God, and he counselled Anglicans on the moral temptations they would face in the transition from a captive to a free church. Passage of the Public Worship Regulation Act of 1874 precipitated his call for open defiance of the law in *Ought we to obey the new court created by the W. P. R. Act?* (1875).

Shipley's anguish over the established church was resolved on 24 October 1878, when Cardinal Henry Edward Manning received him into the Roman Catholic communion, three days after his wife's conversion. Many Anglicans ostracized him, and as a married man he had to sacrifice his priestly vocation. But the loss of his clerical living was offset by income from family landholdings, and he was able to publish articles and reviews on religious, literary, and historical subjects for over thirty years.

Both as an Anglican and a Roman Catholic, Shipley was a prodigiously productive scholar, editing tracts, essays, and books that, taken together, constitute a virtual library of Catholic spirituality. These editions include devotional manuals, spiritual exercises, lives of saints, prayers, invocations, meditations, sermons, homilies, and hymns dating from the patristic age to the eighteenth century, most translated from Greek, Latin, Spanish, Italian, or French sources. Shipley's own collected sermons and lectures reveal his special interest in the Virgin Mary (*Carmina Mariana*, 1893; second series, 1902), and in sin, confession, and penance (*Six Short Sermons on Sin*, 1867; *A Theory about Sin*, 1875; *Principles of Faith in Relation to Sin*, 1879). He conveyed a Roman perspective in *The Ritual of the Altar* (1871), a compendium of writings on the Anglican communion service.

Ascetic in appearance and self-effacing in manner, Shipley was self-assured in print. His wide-ranging historical scholarship testified to his personal piety and veneration of tradition and authority. He died at Colway House, Lyme Regis, on 5 July 1916, leaving bequests to Catholic causes. Obituaries failed to do justice to his remarkable religious career. Zoë Shipley died aged eighty-four in 1923.

ALBERT R. VOGELER

Sources *Men and women of the time* (1899) · Venn, *Alum. Cant.* · F. C. Burnand, ed., *The Catholic who's who and yearbook* (1909) · M. Westwater, *The Wilson sisters: a biographical study of upper middle-class Victorian life* (1984) · M. Reynolds, *Martyr of ritualism: Father Mackonochie of St Alban's, Holborn* (1965) · A. R. Vogeler, 'Disestablishmentarianism', PhD diss., 1973 [microfilmed diss.] · d. cert.

Wealth at death £7479 0s. 5d.: probate, 18 Sept 1916, *CGPLA Eng. & Wales*

Shipley, William (bap. 1715, d. 1803), founder of the Society for the Encouragement of Arts, Manufactures, and Commerce, was baptized on 2 June 1715 at St Stephen Walbrook, London. He was the third son of Jonathan Shipley (1676–1719), a native of Leeds and a citizen and stationer of London, and Martha Shipley (d. 1757), daughter of William Davies (1658–1727) of Twyford in Hampshire. His oldest surviving brother was Bishop Jonathan *Shipley. Brought up by his mother and grandfather at Twyford he received nine years of grammatical schooling from about 1725 to about 1734 and was then apprenticed for seven years to the painter Charles Phillips, who lived and worked in Great Queen Street, London. Shipley frequented Old Slaughter's Coffee House in St Martin's Lane, which was a favourite resort of the leading artists of the time. In 1741 he obtained a place as a gentleman pensioner at arms but resigned from it after four years because its rules forbade him to practise as a professional artist. He then travelled the country drawing perspective views of noblemen's and gentlemen's estates before settling as a teacher of drawing and painting in Northampton in 1747.

Shipley was warmly welcomed into the Northampton Philosophical Society, 'the Royal Society in miniature', as he called it (W. Shipley to H. Baker, 18 Oct 1747, English MSS 19, 3, 154), on account of his friendship with Henry Baker FRS FSA, to whom he communicated matters of interest to the Royal Society and the Society of Antiquaries. He also gained support for a philanthropic scheme to buy winter fuel for the poor of Northampton in 1751 and for his *Proposals for raising by subscription a fund to be distributed in premiums for the promoting of improvements in liberal*

William Shipley (*bap.* **1715,** *d.* **1803**), by Richard Cosway, exh. Royal Society of Arts 1760

arts and sciences, manufactures, etc, a broadsheet pamphlet which he eventually published in June 1753. Soon afterwards, on Baker's advice he went to London and published his *Scheme for putting the proposals in execution modelled partly from the plan used by the Dublin Society* (7 December 1753). Two original features of his *Scheme* were that women as well as men could become members of the proposed society, and that medals could be given for especially valuable inventions and improvements, or as honorary awards. Through the clergyman-scientist Stephen Hales DD FRS Shipley met lords Folkestone and Romney, two influential peers who were already considering a scheme to award artists and inventors. After an extensive and largely fruitless canvass, a meeting took place at Rawthmell's Coffee House, Henrietta Street, Covent Garden, on 22 March 1754. Only ten persons besides Shipley, who acted as secretary, were present, but they confidently announced the foundation of the Society for the Encouragement of Arts, Manufactures, and Commerce and offered rewards for the discovery of cobalt, the raising and curing of madder, and for the best drawings by boys and girls. In February 1755 Shipley sub-let two rooms to the society in a house he had rented in Craig's Court, Charing Cross, and in June 1756 he moved with the constantly expanding institution to John Fielding's house in Castle Court, Strand, and was briefly in residence in the magnificent premises designed for the society in 1759 by William Chambers.

Shipley remained secretary of the Society of Arts until 1757 and was its register (or curator) from 1757 to 1760. He had been elected a perpetual member in 1755 and received

the honorary gold medal in 1758. After 1760 he remained active as a member. In 1762 he proposed, without success, the establishment of a 'repository of arts', but his scheme to increase the national supply of fish by stocking (1763) resulted in the society offering premiums for the establishment of scallop-beds. Even after he retired to Maidstone in 1768 he frequently travelled to London to attend meetings of committees of the society. He received the honorary silver medal in 1777 'for his invention of a floating light'. His method of insulating shoes from the damp by the use of tin foil (1781) and his improved gardening tools (1787) received the thanks of the society. An ambitious proposal to reform teaching methods resulted in the society's offer of a premium for teaching languages, and an award to Dr James Egan of Greenwich in 1787. On 1 July 1803, six months before his death, a ceremonial tribute was paid to Shipley at the society's prize-giving ceremony.

From 1754 to 1761 Shipley conducted a drawing school, first sharing premises with the Society of Arts and then at Beaufort Buildings in the Strand, where he rented a magnificent Great Room measuring 65 by 30 feet. Many artists of distinction were trained by him, including Richard Cosway, Ozias Humphry, John Hamilton Mortimer, Joseph Nollekens, and William Pars. The latter, with his brother Henry Pars, continued to manage the school after Shipley's retirement. In November 1767 he married Elizabeth Miller (*c.*1730–1806) at St George's, Hanover Square, and within a year was settled in Maidstone, Kent, where his friend and patron Lord Romney had his country seat. He made friends with his neighbours the Peale family, and his only surviving offspring, Elizabeth (1771–1836), married Richard Peale junior. He was a member of the masonic Lodge of Fortitude and was the treasurer and probably the founder of the Maidstone Society for Promoting Useful Knowledge. Lord Romney was president and Benjamin Franklin, Arthur Young, and Richard Cosway were honorary members. In 1783 Shipley assisted the Maidstone Society's efforts to combat the outbreak of fever in the county goal and in 1786 he published his *Proposal to Establish a Society for Promoting Useful Knowledge in the County of Kent,* which led to the expansion of the Maidstone Society. In spite of his advancing years Shipley was active in the enlarged organization. In 1791 he was elected a fellow of the Linnean Society of London and in 1795 he served on the governing committee of the reformed Kentish Society. In 1796 he resigned from the Linnean Society 'having scarce been in London since that time [his election]' (W. Shipley to T. Marsham, 9 May 1796, Linn. Soc.).

Shipley was known for his taciturnity and absent-mindedness. The miniature by William Hincks (1786), and the earlier portraits by James Barry (*c.*1779) and Richard Cosway (exh. Royal Society of Arts, 1760), confirm Joseph Moser's description of him as having 'something of the heavy appearance of the late Dr Johnson'. Yet, continued Moser, 'under this unpromising aspect he possessed a most benevolent heart, joined to an inquisitive, intelligent and highly cultivated mind' (Moser, 176). His oil painting entitled *A Boy Blowing a Firebrand* after Schalcken (*c.*1751) and his miniature portrait of Henry Baker (before 1766) suggest that he was skilled at copying but hesitant at portraits. His landscape pictures remain untraced. Shipley probably retired from public life during the last eight years of his life. He died at Knightrider House, his home in Maidstone, on 28 December 1803, aged eighty-nine, and was buried at All Saints' Church, Maidstone.

D. G. C. ALLAN

Sources D. G. C. Allan, *William Shipley, founder of the Royal Society of Arts: a biography with documents*, 2nd edn (1979) · D. G. C. Allan and J. H. Appleby, 'James Theobald's "missing" MS history of the Society of Arts and his "chronological register" of the present age', *Antiquaries Journal*, 76 (1996), 201–14 · letters of W. Shipley to H. Baker, JRL, English MS 19 · [T. Mortimer], *A concise account of the rise, progress and present state of the Society for the Encouragement of Arts, Manufactures and Commerce, instituted at London, 1754* (1763) · G. Smith, *Use and abuse of freemasonry* (1783) · letters of W. Shipley to T. Marsham, Linn. Soc. · J. Moser, *European Magazine and London Review*, 44 (1803), 173–80, esp. 176–8 · J. M. Russell, *The history of Maidstone* (1881) · H. T. Wood, *History of the Royal Society of Arts* (1913) · W. T. Whitley, *Artists and their friends in England, 1700–1799*, 2 vols. (1928) · minutes of the society, and of the society's committees, *c.*1754–1803, RSA · W. B. Bannerman and W. B. Bannerman, jun., eds., *The registers of St Stephen's, Walbrook, and of St Benet Sherehog, London*, 1, Harleian Society, register section, 49 (1919), 49–50 · will, Maidstone Museum and Art Gallery · funeral monuments, parish church, Twyford, Hampshire · J. H. Chapman, ed., *The register book of marriages belonging to the parish of St George, Hanover Square*, 1, Harleian Society, 11 (1886), 170

Archives Museum and Art Gallery, Maidstone, MSS · RSA, loose archives, [R]SA minutes, letters, and memoranda addressed to officers and members of the society, RSA MS transactions, guardbooks | American Philosophical Society, Philadelphia, Franklin MSS · BL, letters to Arthur Young and Joseph Banks, Add. MSS · JRL, English MSS, Henry Baker's corresp. · Linn. Soc. · Maidstone Museum and Art Gallery, Maidstone, Hazlitt MSS · Maidstone Museum and Art Gallery, Maidstone, Clement Taylor Smythe MSS · RA, Humphry MSS

Likenesses R. Cosway, oils, exh. Royal Society of Arts 1760, Royal Society of Arts [*see illus.*] · J. Barry, oils, *c.*1779, Royal Society of Arts · W. Hincks, watercolour on ivory miniature, 1786, Royal Society of Arts · W. Hincks, engraving (after miniature by W. Hincks, 1786), repro. in *Transactions of the Society of Arts*, 4 (1786)

Wealth at death approx. £8000: will, Maidstone Museum and Art Gallery, Kent

Shipley, William Davies

Shipley, William Davies (1745–1826), Church of England clergyman, was born on 5 October 1745 at Midgham, Berkshire, the only son among the six children of Dr Jonathan *Shipley (1713–1788), bishop of St Asaph, and his wife, Anna Maria, *née* Mordaunt (1716/17–1803), and nephew of William *Shipley. He was educated at Westminster School under William Markham and then at Winchester College; he matriculated from Christ Church, Oxford, on 21 December 1763, from where he graduated BA on 19 January 1769 and MA in 1771.

Shipley was ordained priest and followed his father's example in rapidly accumulating benefices in plurality. As the new bishop of St Asaph, Jonathan Shipley appointed his son vicar of Ysgeifiog on 19 March 1770. Other livings in that diocese soon followed, including the vicarage of Wrexham, Denbighshire, on 6 February 1771 and the sinecure rectory of Llangwn on 11 April 1772, which Shipley exchanged first for Corwen (1774–82) and subsequently for Llanarmon yn Ial (1782–1816). He was additionally

William Davies Shipley (1745–1826), by Albin Roberts Burt, pubd 1820

appointed chancellor of the St Asaph diocese in 1773 and named dean of the cathedral on 27 May 1774, and held all these posts until his death. They were collectively worth more than £2000 p.a. in the early 1780s. He married, on 28 April 1777, Penelope (*d.* 1789), elder daughter and coheir of Ellis Yonge of Byrn Yorkin, near Wrexham, and next of kin to Sir John Conway, third and last baronet, her maternal great-grandfather. The Conways' holdings included Rhuddlan Castle and a sugar plantation in St Kitt's. The marriage made the Shipleys one of the wealthiest families in north Wales.

Shipley gained national notice from his involvement in a seditious libel case that drew attention to his own whiggish politics as well as his obstinacy. In August 1782 William *Jones (who married Shipley's sister Anna Maria in April 1783) published anonymously, under the auspices of the Society for Constitutional Information, a reformist political tract called *The Principles of Government, in a Dialogue between a Scholar and a Peasant*. As chairman of the Flintshire Association and Correspondence (for parliamentary reform) Shipley publicly read a copy of Jones's pamphlet at the county meeting of 7 January 1783 without previously familiarizing himself with its contents, and carried a resolution that it be translated into Welsh. However, once he had been privately advised that the proposal might be misinterpreted the project was dropped.

The Flintshire committee had already been criticized for its initial approbation of Jones's pamphlet, and Shipley now committed the tactical error of rushing to its defence. On 24 January 1783 he took a copy of the *Dialogue* and with his own hand substituted throughout the words 'gentleman' and 'farmer' for 'scholar' and 'peasant'. He then asked his curate at Wrexham to have a few copies of the amended tract reprinted by a Wrexham bookseller. His precipitate action brought down all the wrath of his political opponents on his head. At a county meeting in March 1783 the high sheriff of Flintshire, Thomas Fitzmaurice (brother of the recent prime minister, William Petty, earl of Shelburne), castigated Shipley as a preacher of sedition, and travelled to London to request his prosecution by the government for seditious libel. The law officers refused to act but Fitzmaurice, undeterred, proceeded privately. Shipley was indicted at the Wrexham great sessions in April 1783 for publishing a seditious libel. The case came for hearing at Denbighshire grand sessions, in Wrexham, in September, with Lloyd Kenyon as presiding judge and Thomas Erskine as Shipley's counsel, retained by the Society for Constitutional Information. Jones had meanwhile made known to Kenyon that he was the author of the tract, a confession that had not prevented his nomination as a judge of the supreme court of Bengal. Shipley had also complained to the Society for Constitutional Information on 16 June 1783 that he had been singled out 'for the object of a Prosecution founded on an anonymous letter, supported by anonymous abuse and lying Reports, and carried out under a false name, with the clandestine Malignity of an Informer that feels ashamed of his own malice' (*Public Advertiser*, 30 July 1783).

The Wrexham hearing having been postponed on legal grounds, the case was removed in March 1784, by a writ of *certiorari*, to the king's bench and then remitted for trial to Shrewsbury assizes, where it was finally heard before Mr Justice (Francis) Buller on 6 August 1784. Buller directed that the jury was merely to find on the fact of publication and the truth of the innuendoes as laid; whether the words constituted a libel or not was for the court. Erskine resisted this view, and the jury's initial verdict was guilty of publishing only. Buller intervened to ask them to reconsider their verdict, and following his directions the jury again decided that Shipley was guilty of publishing but did not find on the question of whether the tract was a libel or not.

On 16 November 1784 Erskine, before the court of king's bench, argued on grounds of misdirection for a new trial, which the lord chief justice, William Murray, Baron Mansfield, refused. However, the defendant was not committed, and Erskine went on to present a motion to the court in arrest of judgment. Mansfield ruled that as the publication was abstract no part of the publication was really criminal, and the dean was discharged as a free man. The news was well received in north Wales, and bonfires were lit and houses illuminated as Shipley proceeded in December first on a visit to his father at Twyford, near Winchester, and subsequently through Shrewsbury, Wrexham, and Ruthin to Llannerch Park (his father's other seat, in Denbighshire), and then to his own residence near St Asaph. The interest that the protracted proceedings evoked—the greatest of all trials for seditious libel, according to Holdsworth—increased pressure from the Portland whigs in parliament to transfer the decision of what is libellous from judge to jury, a change embodied in Fox's Libel Act, 1792 (32 Geo. III, c.60).

Shipley's action ended his prospects of a bishopric, made him suspect to government supporters in Flintshire, and reduced the credibility of the proponents of reform in north Wales. A vague proposal to recommence proceedings against him is mentioned in a letter addressed in the aftermath of the 1796 general election to Lord Chief Justice Kenyon by Thomas Pennant, who passes on some spiteful stories of the dean—'that profligate man'—noting the extent to which Bishop Lewis Bagot was under his thumb and concluding bluntly 'the manner he has past his probation from that time [of his trial] to this, convinces everyone of his incorrigibility' (*Kenyon MSS*, 545). Two months later, on 8 January 1797, Pennant was gleefully telling Kenyon about reports of a trespasser being shot by the dean on his land after a quarrel about a pig. 'Enraged, he ran after the divine with his spade, but could not overtake him. I am told the affair was made up with a sum of money' (ibid., 546). Shipley's character was always considered suspect by Pennant and other north Wales Pittites but against this view should be set his undoubted warm-heartedness (which could so readily turn into impetuousness) and the affection in which he was held by many dissenters. Throughout life he was known for his 'sincere attachment … to those liberal principles which produced the Revolution [of 1688]' (*GM*, 96/2, 641).

Shipley published little apart from a sermon for Chester Infirmary in 1790. He wrote a preface to the edition of his father's works published in 1792, in which he justified the bishop's sympathy for the American revolutionaries, but this does not appear in ordinary copies of the work. He also assisted his widowed sister in collecting the letters and other literary remains of Sir William Jones, published in 1799. Most of his energies went into maintaining St Asaph Cathedral. While he was dean the chapter house was taken down (1779) and the fabric of the cathedral repaired: the choir was rebuilt, a new episcopal throne and pulpit provided, and a reredos erected (1810). The money to pay for many of these improvements was provided by the St Asaph Cathedral Act of 1814. Shipley died at his residence, Bodrhyddan, near St Asaph, on 7 May 1826. He was buried at Rhuddlan, in Denbighshire, where a tablet was raised to his memory. His wife had died in childbirth at Llannerch on 15 November 1789, leaving five sons and three daughters.

The eldest son, William Shipley (1778–1820), was whig MP for Flint boroughs from 1807 to 1812 and for St Mawes from 1812 to 1813. He had been expected by his patrons, the Wynns and the Grenvilles, to become an effective politician but instead proved more interested in grouse, and was killed in a shooting accident; his son William, on the dean's death, assumed the name Conwy. Shipley's eldest daughter, Penelope, married Dr Pelham *Warren, a prominent London physician; the second, Anna Maria, married

Colonel Charles A. Dashwood; and the third, Amelia, married the Revd Reginald *Heber in April 1809. It was while on a visit to his father-in-law that Heber composed, at the old vicarage, Wrexham, his popular hymn 'From Greenland's icy mountain'. Shipley's fourth son, **Conway Shipley** (1782–1808), entered the navy in 1793 as a midshipman under Thomas Pakenham on the *Invincible*, and served on that ship at the battle on the 'glorious' 1 June 1794. After service on the frigate *Phoebe* under Sir Robert Barlow he was commissioned lieutenant in 1800, and in 1804, when in command of the corvette HMS *Hippomenes*, captured a French privateer, *L'Egyptienne*, of much greater tonnage. He was consequently made post captain and commanded the frigate *Nymphe* in the Tagus expedition under Sir Charles Cotton. He was killed in a cutting-out expedition on the Tagus on 23 April 1808. A monument was erected on the river bank by his fellow officers. Shipley's fifth son, the Revd Charles Shipley (1783–1834), was deprived of his fellowship at All Souls, Oxford, in 1810, despite a charge of assault with indecency against an Oxford bookseller's boy failing at the Oxford Lent assizes in 1809; he was rector of Mappowder, Dorset, from 1814. Charles Shipley's fourth son was Orby *Shipley. NIGEL ASTON

Sources *GM*, 1st ser., 59 (1789), 1058 · *GM*, 1st ser., 78 (1808), 467, 555 · *GM*, 1st ser., 96/1 (1826), 645 · *GM*, 1st ser., 96/2 (1826), 641–3 · *Old Westminsters*, 2.844–5 · Foster, *Alum. Oxon.*, *1500–1714* · *Fasti Angl.* (Hardy), 1.83 · Nichols, *Illustrations*, 2.451–2; 3.155 · Nichols, *Lit. anecdotes*, 3.241 · [A. Heber], *The life of Reginald Heber*, 2 vols. (1830), 1.254 · *State trials*, 21.847–1046 · J. Towers, *Observations on the rights and duty of juries, in trials for libel* (1786) · J. Gurney, *The whole proceedings on the trial … against the Rev. William Davies Shipley, dean of St. Asaph, for a libel … at Shrewsbury* (1784) · *The speeches of the Hon. T. E. Erskine*, 4 vols. (1810), 1.137–393 · *The manuscripts of Lord Kenyon*, HMC, 35 (1894) · G. T. Kenyon, *Life of Lloyd, 1st Lord Kenyon* (1873) · Holdsworth, *Eng. law*, 10.675–80, 686 · P. Brown, *The Chathamites* (1967), 373–82 · E. Wyn Jones, 'Diocesan discord: St Asaph, 1779–1786, a family affair', 1982, NL Wales [typescript] · J. A. Lovat-Fraser, *Erskine* (1932), 26–8 · B. Willis, *Survey of St Asaph*, 2nd edn, 2 vols. (1801), 1.182 · D. R. Thomas, *Esgobaeth Llanelwy: the history of the diocese of St Asaph*, new edn (1874), 206–7, 244, 497, 556, 625, 689, 857 · P. B. Ironside Bax, *The cathedral church of St Asaph* (1904), 14, 50 · A. N. Palmer, *The history of the parish church of Wrexham* (1886), 45, 57, 67–70 · A. H. Dodd, *A history of Wrexham, Denbighshire* (1957) · H. Taylor, *Historic notices of the borough and county town of Flint* (1883) · R. G. Thorne, 'Shipley, William', HoP, *Commons, 1790–1820* · W. James, *The naval history of Great Britain, from the declaration of war by France in 1793, to the accession of George IV*, [3rd edn], 6 vols. (1837), 5.38–40 · J. McManners, *All Souls and the Shipley case (1808–1810)* (2002) · Burke, *Gen. GB* (1937) · Burke, *Peerage* (1999) · *DNB*

Archives NL Wales, corresp. and papers, 2788 D.Misc; 2598C Shipley trial · Warks. CRO, corresp. | BL, corresp., Add. MSS 35126, fol. 298; 42058, fol. 208; 52485, fol. 137

Likenesses A. R. Burt, engraving, pubd 1820, NPG [*see illus.*] · J. Ternmouth, statue, 1829, St Asaph Cathedral · attrib. W. Beechey, oils, Bodrhyddan Hall, Denbighshire

Shipman, David Herbert (1932–1996), film historian, was born on 4 November 1932 at Lyndale, Waldemar Avenue, Upper Hellesdon, Norwich, the younger child and only son of Alfred Herbert Shipman (1898–1981), a commercial traveller in electrical appliances, and his wife, Ethel May Deakes (1903–1988), clerical worker and daughter of a piano-tuner. Both parents were Londoners, and the family moved back to the capital, to Eltham, in 1940, only to be evacuated in the following year to Pensilva, Cornwall. David was educated variously at primary schools in London, then, on a junior county scholarship, at Callington county school, Cornwall, where he spent 'some of the happiest years of my life' (Shipman). With the end of the Second World War he went to Shooters Hill grammar school, which he left in 1949, aged sixteen, after taking his school certificate, to become a clerk in the planning office of the London county council.

Snow White and the Seven Dwarfs (1937), seen on holiday in Great Yarmouth when he was five, was the film that ignited Shipman's cine-enthusiasm, but he might have been condemned to the 'sheer boredom' (Shipman) of town-planning paper pushing had it not been for national service. In 1951, against his will, he joined the RAF, on the clerical side, and in its democratic conviviality discovered a self-confidence that he never, despite many buffets and supposed buffets, entirely lost. The following year he spent in Singapore, in Changi, where an RAF chaplain, the Revd James Tinline, introduced him to the films of Greta Garbo and the Marx brothers, and persuaded him to take three A levels and try for Oxford University. Shipman went up to Merton College in 1954 to read English and, although he failed his first-year preliminary examination twice and was sent down after only one year, he enjoyed himself thoroughly. He acted and sat on the Film Society committee, he fell in love with Judy Garland, and he had found a way out.

For the next ten years Shipman worked as a publisher's representative, first on staff, for Victor Gollancz, Methuen, and the Curtis Publishing Company, and after 1963 as a freelance, for Paul Hamlyn, Hale, and Panther. His favourite years were from 1961 to 1963, when he lived in Paris for Curtis, acting as European representative for Bantam Books, and travelled the continent, returning, sometimes just for a night, to London for performances at the National Film Theatre. In 1962 he started contributing to the magazine *Films and Filming*. In December 1964 he met Felix Otto Brenner (b. 1923), the New York-born art director of Hamlyn, who was to be his partner for the rest of his life. He moved into Brenner's London flat, at 2 Callow Street, Chelsea, in March 1965, and in September he gave up travelling. In 1968, with an editor from Hamlyn, he hatched the plot of his first great work, *The Great Movie Stars*, published in two volumes as *The Golden Years* (1970) and *The International Years* (1973); a follow-up volume, *The Independent Years*, appeared in 1991. In 1982–4, again in two volumes, appeared the book of which he was proudest, initially commissioned in 1972 by Phaidon to be a companion to Ernst Gombrich's *The Story of Art* (1950): *The Story of Cinema: an Illustrated History*, a vast compendium, from *Fred Ott's Sneeze* to *Missing*.

Before Shipman there had been *ad hoc* film critics aplenty, but few prepared to take the long view. The history of film was, after all, young; Shipman was to publish his centenary celebration *Cinema: the First Hundred Years* (1993) only three years before his death. Much cinema literature had been ephemeral, much of it hagiographical, much driven by the studios' marketing departments.

Shipman, hailing Paul Rotha as his mentor, combined exceptional diligence and an original amateur's enthusiasm. He kept notes of every film he had ever seen (and refused to write critically of a film he had not). He was as much interested in studio history, budgets, salaries, and box-office returns as in individual actor filmographies. He was passionate about the stars he liked, imperiously acidulous about those he did not. He was a populist who was also devoted to the films of Satyajit Ray and Akira Kurosawa. His tours through star careers could be whirlwinds of excitement or brutal exercises in deprecation. He was for Marilyn Monroe ('she glowed, like a moth in candlelight'; *The International Years*, rev. edn, 1989, 398) and Buster Keaton; he was against Marlene Dietrich ('Age does not wither her, nor custom stale her infinite sameness'; *The Golden Years*, rev. edn, 1989, 166) and Alfred Hitchcock. His vigorous turn of phrase, his large sense of film context, and his independence of judgement marked him out among the swelling ranks of film encyclopaedists.

Shipman's big books never made him rich, and his publishers seemed reluctant, despite their persistent popularity, to keep them in print. This rankled with the author, who felt he had never been adequately recognized. He was a programme consultant to the National Film Theatre, lectured at the University of East Anglia and for the British Council, and served for eight years as film critic of the *Contemporary Review* and for eight as principal film obituarist of *The Independent*, but he necessarily derived his income from more ordinary output such as his books *Movie Talk: Who Said What about Whom in the Movies* (1979), *The Good Film and Video Guide* (1984), *A Pictorial History of Science Fiction Films* (1985), and *Caught in the Act: Sex and Eroticism in the Movies* (1985). He wrote two biographies, *Brando* (1974, enlarged as *Marlon Brando*, 1989) and *Judy Garland* (1992). He was working on a third, of Fred Astaire, when he died in his sleep of a heart attack at home, in the house that had been his mother's, 64 Woodlands, Overton, Hampshire, on 22 April 1996. He was cremated at Aldershot crematorium on 2 May.

David Shipman was outdatedly dapper in appearance, sometimes with a discreet beard, and liked a hat. Outside film his enthusiasms were theatre, opera (Maria Callas), pictures (the early Sienese), and travel. There was something eternally boyish about him. This was usually endearing, occasionally infuriating.   JAMES FERGUSSON

Sources *Daily Telegraph* (26 April 1996) · *The Independent* (24 April 1996) · *The Times* (25 April 1996) · personal knowledge (2004) · private information (2004) [Felix Brenner] · D. Shipman, notebook, priv. coll.
Wealth at death under £180,000: probate, 2 Feb 1998, *CGPLA Eng. & Wales*

Shipman, Thomas (1632–1680), poet, the eldest son of William Shipman (1603–1658) and Sara, daughter of Alderman Parker of Nottingham, was born at Scarrington, near Newark, in November 1632, and baptized there on 8 November. The eldest of eleven or twelve children of his father's second marriage, he received his early education at Sleaford School and was admitted as a pensioner to St John's College, Cambridge, on 1 May 1651. There is no record of his having taken a degree. He married Margaret (d. c.1696), daughter of John Trafford, who brought him a good inheritance; they had several sons, the third of whom, William, became high sheriff of Nottingham in 1730.

In the preface to a collection of some 200 poems which he was compiling at the time of his death, Shipman confessed that he still retained his youthful love of poetry and could see 'no cause but *Dotage* to make it be left off'. The poet Thomas Flatman, who eventually saw the volume through the press as *Carolina, or, Loyal Poems* (1683), informed prospective readers that his friend was 'a Man every way accomplish'd', whose conversation had recommended him to 'the best Wits of the Age'. Shipman's political sympathies are evident in poems on the royal martyr, the passing of Cromwell ('The Arch-Traitor'), the restoration of Charles II, and the virtues of the duke of Monmouth ('The Hero').

Having preserved the family estate by retiring from public life during the protectorate, Shipman entered into his full inheritance as a cultivated country squire after 1660, living on familiar terms with the local aristocracy and assisting Dr Robert Thoroton in his study of Nottinghamshire antiquities. He also became a captain of the trained bands in the county. Shipman's heroic tragedy, *Henry the Third of France*, performed at the Theatre Royal, Drury Lane, in 1678, was designed to support Monmouth at the time of the Popish Plot. In a preface to the published text, he defends the use of rhyming couplets, generously praises *Paradise Lost* as 'noble, strong and fanciful', and imagines 'what a *Poem*' it might have been if Milton had not eschewed rhyme.

Shipman died at Scarrington, where he was buried on 15 October 1680. He was survived by his wife.

ROBERT WILCHER

Sources V. De Sola Pinto, 'Thomas Shipman (1632–1680): a forgotten Nottinghamshire poet', *Transactions of the Thoroton Society*, 53 (1949), 42–61 · R. Thoroton, *The antiquities of Nottinghamshire* (1677), 119–20 · *DNB* · T. Shipman, *Carolina, or, Loyal poems* (1683) · T. Shipman, *Henry the Third of France* (1678) · Venn, *Alum. Cant.*
Wealth at death father had 'a considerable estate' at Scarrington; wife 'brought him a good inheritance at Bulcote': Thoroton, *The antiquities* · was saved 'from a total Ruine' during the 1650s by retiring from public life and not antagonizing the authorities: Shipman, *Carolina*

Shipp, John (1785–1834), army officer and author, younger son of Thomas Shipp, a marine, and his wife, Laetitia, was born at Saxmundham, Suffolk, on 16 March 1785. His mother died in poor circumstances in 1789, his elder brother was lost at sea, and John became an inmate of the parish poorhouse; he was apprenticed by the overseers to a neighbouring farmer, a brutal taskmaster, from whom he escaped by enlisting as a boy in the 22nd (Cheshire) regiment, at Colchester, on 17 January 1797. Through the kindness of his captain he picked up some education, and, after service in the Channel Islands and the Cape, sailed for India, where, having risen to be a sergeant in the grenadier company, he served against the Marathas under Lord Lake. He was one of the stormers at the capture of Dig on 24 December 1804, and three times led the forlorn

John Shipp (1785–1834), by William Thomas Fry, pubd 1832 (after J. Buchanan)

hope of the storming column in the unsuccessful assaults on Bharatpur (January–February 1805). He was severely wounded, but his bravery was rewarded by Lord Lake with an ensigncy in the 65th foot. On 10 March in the same year he was gazetted lieutenant in the 76th foot.

Returning home after two and a half years' further service, Shipp found himself forced to sell out on 19 March 1808 in order to obtain a sum (about £250) to pay his debts. After a short interval he found himself in London without a shilling, and resolved to re-enlist in the ranks. He returned to India as a private in the 24th light dragoons, and rose by 1812 to the position of regimental sergeant-major. In May 1815 the earl of Moira reappointed him to an ensigncy in the 87th (the Prince of Wales's Own) Irish regiment of foot (later Royal Irish Fusiliers), lately arrived in India from Mauritius. Shipp had thus performed the unique feat of twice winning a commission from the ranks before he was thirty-two.

Shipp distinguished himself greatly by his bravery in the second campaign of the Anglo-Nepal War, notably in a single combat with one of the enemy's *sirdars* near Makwanpur. He was on the staff of the left division of the 'grand army' under the marquess of Hastings in the Third Anglo-Maratha War (1817–18), and was promoted lieutenant on 5 July 1821. He seems to have been popular in his regiment for his bravery; but during 1822, while quartered at Calcutta, he was inveigled into a series of turf speculations which proved disastrous. Shipp imprudently commented in writing on the behaviour of a superior officer in regard to these transactions, and was discharged from the

service by a court martial held at Fort William, Calcutta, between 14 and 27 July 1823. He was, however, recommended to mercy, 'in consideration of his past services and wounds, and the high character that he had borne as an officer and a gentleman'. When he sold out, on 3 November 1825, the East India Company granted him a pension of £50, upon which he settled near Ealing, Middlesex.

Shipp then wrote his successful *Memoirs of the Extraordinary Military Career of John Shipp* (1829 and later editions), in which he refrained from recriminations. In 1831 he published *Flogging and its Substitute: a Voice from the Ranks*, in the form of a letter to Sir Francis Burdett, an indictment of the 'cat', which, as he claimed, 'flogged one devil out and fifty devils in'. Burdett sent him £50, and most of his suggestions were later adopted by the military authorities. In 1830 Shipp was offered an inspectorship in the Stepney division of the new Metropolitan Police by Sir Charles Rowan; he was shortly afterwards appointed superintendent of the night watch at Liverpool, and in 1833 was elected master of the workhouse at Liverpool, where he was reportedly highly esteemed. He died at Liverpool, in comfortable circumstances, on 27 April 1834, and was buried in Liverpool.

Shipp was married twice, first, in 1816 in Cawnpore, to Anne. She died in 1823 or 1824, in childbirth, aged twenty-two, and the two sons from the marriage were adopted. Shipp remarried, probably in 1826. There were children from the second marriage. His second wife survived him.

THOMAS SECCOMBE, rev. JAMES LUNT

Sources *Shipp's memoirs*, several edns (1890) [with introduction by H. Manners] · *The path of glory: being the memoirs of the extraordinary military career of John Shipp*, ed. C. J. Stranks (1969) · *GM*, 2nd ser., 2 (1834), 539–42 · [Clarke], *The Georgian era: memoirs of the most eminent persons*, 2 (1833), 143 · J. Gorton, *A general biographical dictionary*, 3 vols. (1841) · J. A. Picton, *Memorials of Liverpool*, rev. edn, 2 vols. (1875) · *London Monthly Review*, 118, 283 · Fortescue, *Brit. army*, vols. 5–8

Likenesses W. T. Fry, stipple and line engraving, pubd 1832 (after J. Buchanan), BM, NPG [*see illus.*] · J. Buchanan, oils (in regimentals), NPG · B. Holl, engraving (*Lieut. J. Shipp, 87th REGT. leading the troops into the Fort of Huttrass*; after portrait by Wageman), BM

Shippard, Alexander (1771–1841), naval officer, was born on 3 March 1771, the youngest son of Alexander Shippard (d. 1803), a purser in the Royal Navy, and his wife, Margaret Walkinshaw. The father was with Horatio Nelson in the *Vanguard* in 1798 and received a medal for the battle of Abu Qir Bay. The younger Shippard entered the navy in 1786 on the *Irresistible*, bearing the broad pennant of Sir Andrew Snape Hamond. From 1788 to 1792 he served in the *Scipio*, *Bellerophon*, and *Vengeance*—all in the English Channel. In 1792 he went out to Newfoundland in the *Assistance*, and on 23 October 1793 he was promoted lieutenant in command of the tender *Placentia*. In 1795 and 1796 he served in the storeship *Camel* in the Mediterranean; in 1797 he took command of the *Monarch* and cut out vessels off Texel, the Netherlands; subsequently, to 1801, he was in the *Montagu*, for the most part in the Mediterranean but afterwards in the West Indies.

In 1801–2 Shippard was in the *Monarch* in the North Sea,

and in 1803 he commanded the cutter *Admiral Mitchell* (12 guns) attached to the fleet under Lord Keith to guard the narrow seas. On 21 August 1803 he landed Georges Cadoudal, the Chouan leader, at Biville, between Dieppe and Tréport, and on 16 January the following year he landed the French general Pichegru at the same place. On 31 October 1803, with the advanced squadron off Boulogne, he ran inshore and engaged a gun-brig in charge of six sloops, some of which were armed. After an action of two and a half hours, during which the squadron was prevented by the contrary wind from giving him assistance, he drove the brig and one of the sloops on shore. Following Keith's report on this, Shippard received a sword of honour from the patriotic fund at Lloyd's and was promoted commander on 3 March 1804. He was later appointed to the *Hornet* in the West Indies.

In 1805 Shippard commanded the *Surinam* in the Mediterranean, and on 22 January 1806 he was advanced to post rank. In May 1807 he was appointed to the *Banterer* (22 guns), which, by the culpable negligence of the lieutenant of the middle watch and of the master who both went to drink grog in the gun room, was lost in the St Lawrence River on the night of 29 October 1808. The court martial found that Shippard had made every possible exertion to save the ship, and afterwards to preserve the stores. He was acquitted of all blame and was shortly afterwards appointed to the *Namur* (74 guns), flagship of Vice-Admiral Thomas Wells at the Nore. In 1812–13 he commanded the *Asia* (74 guns) in the North Sea. He had no further service but became rear-admiral on 28 June 1838, received a pension for meritorious service, and died at Malta on 4 April 1841. Shippard married Jane, daughter of Admiral Sir John *Knight, and they had at least one child.

Shippard's elder brother, **William Shippard** (1764–1856), naval officer, was born on 17 February 1764 near Bo'ness, Linlithgowshire, and entered the navy on the *Medea* in June 1778. He was on the *Nonsuch* in the West Indies in 1782 and served in the battle of 9 April. In August 1797 he was at the blockade of Cadiz, under Lord St Vincent, and in the subsequent battle. In 1801 he served in the battle of Copenhagen. He was advanced to post rank and placed on the retired list in 1846, and died, without children, on 6 July 1856.

J. K. LAUGHTON, rev. ANDREW LAMBERT

Sources D. Syrett and R. L. DiNardo, *The commissioned sea officers of the Royal Navy, 1660–1815*, rev. edn, Occasional Publications of the Navy RS, 1 (1994) · *LondG* (8 Nov 1803) · *Navy List* · O'Byrne, *Naval biog. dict.* · J. Marshall, *Royal naval biography*, suppl. 1 (1827), 106

Shippard, Sir Sidney Godolphin Alexander (1837–1902), colonial official and associate of Cecil Rhodes, was born at Brussels, Belgium, on 29 May 1837. He was the eldest son of Captain William Henry Shippard of the 29th regiment and Elizabeth Lydia, *née* Peters, and the grandson of Rear-Admiral Alexander *Shippard. After education at King's College School, London, he was admitted to Oriel College, Oxford, in 1856 and then to Hertford College, Oxford, as a scholar in 1857. Seven years later he took a BA in law and modern history, graduating a year later with BCL and MA. Also in 1864, at the age of twenty-seven,

he married Maria Susanna (*d.* 1870), daughter of Sir Andries *Stockenstrom of Cape Colony. After pursuing legal studies at the Inner Temple, and being called to the bar in January 1867, Shippard and his wife settled down to life in Cape Town, where in 1868 he was admitted to practise as an advocate of the supreme court. Tragedy, however, struck in 1870 with his wife's death, leaving him with three young children. In January 1873 he took up the post of attorney-general, at first in an acting capacity and then from August 1875 substantively, in the new British colony of Griqualand West which had been set up to enclose the diamondiferous area north of Cape Colony. In the rough frontier town of Kimberley he stood out as a man of cultural refinement, with a particular taste for music, and associated himself with other men of his class such as the Rhodes brothers, with whom he regularly dined.

In Griqualand West, Shippard was notable (or notorious) for his bias in favour of white settlers and for his espousal of Cape colonial expansion. He rode roughshod over African rights in the 1877 land settlement, and came into conflict with imperial officials, notably Charles Warren, Owen Lanyon, and Sir Bartle Frere. He resigned his post, and returned to Oxford to obtain the degree of DCL with a dissertation on Roman-Dutch law entitled 'De vindicatione rei emtae et traditionae' (1878). Shippard's influence on the young Rhodes can be seen in his being named an executor of Rhodes's extraordinary will of 1877, which entrusted Shippard and the colonial secretary in London with a fortune to found a secret society for Anglo-Saxon world domination. In 1878 Rhodes and Shippard were also together at Oxford; Shippard later recalled 'discussing and sketching out the whole plan of British advance in South and Central Africa' as they walked in Christ Church meadow.

Shippard returned to South Africa to re-enter the judicial service of Cape Colony as a judge of the eastern districts court. His published legal judgments included the case of the *Bishop of Grahamstown* v. *Merriman* and other cases carried in Buchanan's Cape law reports for 1880–85. In 1885 he sat on an Anglo-German commission looking into property claims of British citizens in newly proclaimed German territory on the coast of south-west Africa. On 30 September 1885 he was appointed administrator (and chief magistrate) of the new colony of British Bechuanaland, and deputy commissioner for the newly proclaimed Bechuanaland protectorate. Based at Vryburg, Shippard followed the brief given him to administer 'in a manner consistent with the policies of the Cape Colony'. He presided over a land commission which was again noted for blatant bias in favour of white land claimants over black. Meanwhile, in the protectorate he saw his task as playing off the British ally Khama against other chiefs, and containing the 'white tide' of prospectors and speculators seeking their fortunes towards the Zambezi. Shippard cajoled and helped to deceive many African chiefs, including Lobengula of Matabeleland in 1888, into giving mineral and land concessions to Rhodes's British South Africa Company. For this he earned the name Morena Maaka ('lord of lies').

Described as short and balding, 'rotund, squeaky voiced', with mutton chop whiskers and a handlebar moustache, Shippard was created CMG in 1886 and KCMG in 1887. In 1891 he was redesignated as resident commissioner of the Bechuanaland protectorate. On 18 December 1894 he married a second wife, Rosalind, a widow with children, the daughter of W. A. Sanford of Nynehead Court, Somerset. In November 1895 he retired from colonial service.

Informed gossip named Shippard as Rhodes's nominee for administrator of the Transvaal after the overthrow of the Kruger regime. When the Jameson raid failed Shippard earned Rhodes's gratitude by rushing to Johannesburg to persuade the Uitlander rebels to surrender gracefully. In April 1898 he became a director of the British South Africa Company and gave 'wise and loyal service'. He moved to London, where he died in his sixty-fifth year at his home, 15 West Halkin Street, Belgravia, on 29 March 1902. He was buried at Nynehead, Somerset. He was survived by his second wife.   Q. N. PARSONS

Sources S. Shippard, 'Bechuanaland', in [W. Sheowring], *British Africa* (1899), 46–68 • A. Sillery, *Founding a protectorate: history of Bechuanaland, 1885–1895* (1965) • P. Maylam, *Rhodes, the Tswana, and the British: colonialism, collaboration, and conflict in the Bechuanaland protectorate, 1885–1899* (1980) • J. M. Chirenje, *A history of northern Botswana, 1850–1910* (1977) • D. Trevor, 'Public opinion and the acquisition of Bechuanaland and Rhodesia', PhD diss., U. Lond., 1936 • J. A. I. Agar-Hamilton, *The road to the north: South Africa, 1852–1886* (1937) • R. I. Rotberg, *The founder: Cecil Rhodes and the pursuit of power* (1988) • I. Colvin, *The life of Jameson* (1922) • K. Shillington, *The colonisation of the southern Tswana, 1870–1900* (1985) • L. Cohen, *Reminiscences of Kimberley* (1911) • F. J. Ramsay, 'The rise and fall of the Bakwena of south-central Botswana, 1820–1940', PhD diss., Boston University, 1991 • N. Parsons, 'Colonel Rey and the colonial rulers of Bechuanaland: mercenary and missionary traditions in administration, 1884–1955', *People and empires in African history: essays in memory of Michael Crowder*, ed. J. F. A. Ajayi and J. D. Y. Peel (1992), 197–215 • *DNB* • *South Africa*, 25 (19 Jan 1895), 166 • *The Times* (31 March 1902) • *South Africa* (5 April 1902)
Archives Botswana National Archives, Gaborone, high commissioner and resident commissioner records • Cape Archives, Cape Town, British Bechuanaland and Griqualand West records • National Archives of Zimbabwe, Harare, high commissioner records • PRO, Colonial Office records | Bodl. RH, Anthony Sillery MSS • National Archives of Zimbabwe, Harare, corresp. with Francis Newton
Likenesses photograph, c.1890, repro. in H. M. Hole, *The making of Rhodesia* (1926), 72 • photograph, 1895, repro. in *Review of Reviews*, 12 (1895), 311 • photograph, National Archives of Zimbabwe, Harare
Wealth at death £17,254 2s. 9d.: probate, 8 May 1902, CGPLA Eng. & Wales

Shippard, William (1764–1856). *See under* Shippard, Alexander (1771–1841).

Shippen [*married name* Livingston], **Anne** [Nancy] (1763–1841), journal writer, was born on 24 February 1763 at Shippen House in Philadelphia, the elder surviving child and only daughter of William Shippen (1736–1808), physician and professor in anatomy, and his wife, Alice (1736–1817), daughter of Colonel Thomas Lee and sister of Richard Henry Lee and Arthur Lee.

Anne Shippen and her only brother, Thomas (1765–1798), grew up in their father's elegant town house on the corner of Fourth Street, Philadelphia, between Walnut and Spruce streets, opposite the anatomy theatre in which he lectured on anatomy and midwifery. Between her fourteenth and sixteenth years, while Philadelphia was occupied by the British army during the war of independence, Nancy (as she was known) was sent to Mrs Rogers's school in Trenton, New Jersey. Occasionally she and her mother visited her father at army camp, where he was briefly and controversially director-general of the continental army's hospital department.

On her return to Philadelphia in 1779 Anne was heavily courted by Louis Guillaume Otto, youthful delegate to the French legation. Otto wrote her impassioned and teasing love letters, apparently with some success. Her mother offered tentative support for the match but her father, mindful that 'a Bird in hand is worth 2 in a bush' (*Nancy Shippen: her Journal Book*, 101), married her on 11 March 1781 to the wealthy, well-established, but rakish Colonel Henry Beekman Livingston (1750–1831) of New York. On the day after Christmas that year Anne gave birth to a daughter, Margaret (Peggy; 1781–1864). But the marriage was not a success; within two years Anne was living again under her father's roof and, within three, all hope of returning to her husband had faded. Only a brief reconciliation would occur, in February 1785.

Anne Livingston began her journal in the spring of 1783, on her return to the paternal household. It inspired or was inspired by the journal of her friend Bushrod Washington, son of Martha Washington, and by proclaimed impulses of self-improvement and regulation. The journal documents her attendance at the Second Presbyterian Church and her religious and secular readings alone and with friends. In the vellum-covered volumes, prompted by the emerging culture of sensibility, she dwelt on her feelings and sentiments. The journal lays out her hopes for her daughter's education and the companionate ideal of marriage that had eluded her, drawing on the moral and fictional writings of Rousseau and Richardson. 'Why was I form'd with a heart of sensibility!' she asked rhetorically (Library of Congress, journal, 8 April 1784). The journal reveals, too, her informal and formal socializing—sledding, sewing circles and tea-tables, Bartram's Gardens and Peale's Museum, balls and assemblies. But Otto's return to Philadelphia and his short-lived marriage to her sister-in-law Elizabeth Livingston (d. 1787) tried her tranquillity.

The journal was kept carefully for several years but dwindles to a melancholy religiosity and a resigned celebration of duty over happiness. Beyond its pages the historical record tells only of Anne Livingston's failed attempt to divorce her husband—after Elizabeth Livingston's death—in 1789. The difficulty of obtaining a divorce in New York was only sharpened by her parents' resistance and by the troubling implication that she would lose custody of Peggy to her husband, though she was by now supported by her impressive mother-in-law, Margaret Beekman Livingston. Eventually, and after Otto's departure, her husband arranged a divorce in Connecticut; the final diary entry of the journal book (1791) mentions the divorce as a fact. From 1797 to her death in Philadelphia on 23 August 1841 Anne Livingston and her spinster daughter lived, seemingly quietly and permanently together, in Philadelphia.   SARAH KNOTT

Sources *Nancy Shippen: her journal book*, ed. E. Armes (1935) • R. Klein, *Portrait of an American family: the Shippens of Pennsylvania across five generations* (1975) • L. K. Kerber, *Women of the republic: intellect and ideology in revolutionary America* (1980) • C. Kierner, *Traders and gentlefolk: the Livingstons of New York* (1992) • A. Livingston, journal, L. Cong., manuscript division, Shippen MSS
Archives Hist. Soc. Penn., family MSS • L. Cong., corresp. of Anne Home Livingston, family MSS • L. Cong., journal of Anne Home Livingston, family MSS | Hist. Soc. Penn., Charles Swift Riché Hildeburn collection • Hist. Soc. Penn., society collection
Likenesses portrait (after miniature by B. Trott), repro. in Armes, ed., *Nancy Shippen* (1935); priv. coll.

Shippen, Robert (*bap.* **1675**, *d.* **1745**). *See under* Shippen, William (*bap.* 1673, *d.* 1743).

Shippen, William (*bap.* **1673**, *d.* **1743**), politician and Jacobite sympathizer, was baptized at Prestbury, Cheshire, on 30 July 1673, the second son of the parish priest, William Shippen. Educated first under Roger Dale at Stockport grammar school, on 16 July 1687, aged fourteen, he entered Brasenose College, Oxford, as a commoner. Barely a year after his matriculation, however, he moved from the university to be elected a king's scholar at Westminster, where he came under the influence of Richard Busby. He was admitted a pensioner at Trinity College, Cambridge, on 26 June 1691 and became a scholar there in 1692 before going to the Middle Temple in 1693. He graduated BA in 1694 and was called to the bar in 1699.

The early years of Queen Anne's reign witnessed a growing polarization of the English political nation and saw Shippen working hard to establish his reputation as a tory polemicist. His first literary effort, a verse satire published in 1704 with the title *Faction Display'd*, depicted the junto lords as the traitorous Catiline conspirators. This jibe won the accolade of a paragraph-by-paragraph rebuttal from whig hacks, prompting Shippen to follow up his success with a second poem, *Moderation Display'd*. Both pamphlets ran into several editions and marked their author out as a promising candidate for political advancement. His literary output was not sustained, but in 1732 he did publish a defence of Charles I's conduct in which he sought to vindicate Clarendon's *History of the Rebellion*. Shippen first entered parliament as the tory member for Bramber in Sussex, which he represented from 1707 to 1713 on the interest of Lord Plymouth, whose son, Dixie Windsor, later became his brother-in-law. Although he possessed little patrimony of his own, on 17 July 1712 he married Frances Stote (*d.* 1747), the daughter and coheir of Sir Richard Stote of Jesmond Hall, Northumberland, with whom he acquired a fortune of £70,000. In the following year he was returned on the Buller-Carew interest at Saltash in Cornwall, but, being hard pressed by the duke of Wharton's interest there, in 1715 he prevailed upon another brother-in-law, the nonjuring Peter Legh of Lyme, to be returned at his Lancashire pocket borough of Newton,

William Shippen (*bap.* 1673, *d.* 1743), by Thomas Hudson

which he represented at Westminster for the remainder of his life.

In the House of Commons, Shippen became identified as a zealous party man and useful speaker on contentious issues. Following establishment of the tory ministry in 1710 he emerged as a prominent member of the October Club, and a year later he was elected one of the seven commissioners of public accounts set up to discredit the previous whig administration by means of an inquiry into the alleged financial irregularities of the duke of Marlborough. He was a strong proponent of the occasional conformity and schism bills, and in August 1714 stood out brazenly against the offer of a reward for the Pretender's capture. By the time of the queen's death later that month the tory party had become deeply divided; but in the short term, far from resorting to the standard of 'King James', most of its representatives in parliament competed fiercely with their whig enemies to pass 'loyal and lucrative legislation on behalf of her Hanoverian successor' (Colley, 26). Shippen, for example, seconded a motion by Horace Walpole for the payment of arrears to the Hanoverian troops who had fought in the War of the Spanish Succession, offering the ingenuous admission that 'he had opposed that payment in the late reign, but … was for it now' (ibid.).

But such dalliance with the new regime was to be short-lived. As early as April 1715 Shippen was warning his patron Legh that 'all our Letters are opened in defyance of an Act of Parliament' (Shippen to Legh, 13 April 1715, JRL, Legh of Lyme MSS). Following the arrest of Edward Harvey in September on charges of treasonable correspondence, and the latter's attempted suicide while in prison, a report began circulating in London that Shippen himself had 'given Information at the Secret Office ag[ains]t several Persons, s[ai]d to be concerned in a Plot & an intended Invasion from abroad' obliging him to post a personal denial at the Royal Exchange ('Declaration of William Shippen'). Thereafter, a combination of the earl of Oxford's arrest and committal to the Tower, the flights of Bolingbroke and Ormond to St Germain, the sweeping governmental victories at the general election of 1715, and the proscription of rank-and-file tories from both national and local office following the failure of the Jacobite rising did much to harden partisan attitudes and determine future dynastic loyalties.

Shippen's own reaction to these events was to identify himself unequivocally with the small band of those prepared to work actively for a second Stuart restoration. Although he was ready to write whips soliciting the attendance of tory colleagues at Westminster and to raise funds for the Jacobite cause, his main value was as a parliamentary performer. While not a first-rate orator by reason of his low voice and a tendency to cover his mouth with his glove, for more than a quarter of a century 'honest Shippen' raked and harried successive whig ministries with his sometimes intemperately anti-Hanoverian rhetoric, thereby emerging as principal spokesman for the motley crew of parliamentary Jacobites who continued to oppose Hanoverian rule. He was forthright in his opposition to the Septennial Bill and the Mutiny Bill, spoke vehemently against repeal of the Occasional Conformity and Schism Acts, and on 4 December 1717 was committed to the Tower for a provocative speech in a committee on the Army Supply Bill, the house resolving that he had used words which were 'highly dishonourable to, and unjustly reflecting on, his Majesty's Person & Government'. He was charged with having referred to the king's speech as 'rather … calculated for the Meridian of Germany, then for Great Britain', and to King George himself as 'a Stranger to our Language and Constitution' ('Mr Shippen's case'). Despite being implicated also in the ill-starred Gyllenborg plot, he was soon at large once more, subdued but in unrepentant mood. By March 1718 he was assuring the Pretender that all of his commands would be obeyed 'with the utmost pleasure as well as fidelity' (Stuart Papers, 6.260). In fact, throughout the whig schism of 1717 to 1720, and the South Sea fiasco which brought it to an end, he worked diligently to prevent the emergence of a mixed ministry of the type that had been common in the two preceding reigns. Indeed, his services in this regard, so the Pretender was informed, could 'never be sufficiently acknowledged' (ibid., 5.558).

Shippen was also persuaded to act as the main channel of communication between the English and Scottish Jacobites, and in the late summer of 1721 he met with George Lockhart in Newcastle to work out the logistics of their correspondence. The two men further discussed the approaches lately made by Lord Sunderland to the English tories, who, according to Shippen, had resolved 'to enter into no concert with any of the two contending powers at Court, but to stick together and wait till it pleased God

some event might occurr, that would give them occasion to doe [King James] and the country service' (Letters of George Lockhart, 161–6). In the event, Sunderland's premature death and Robert Walpole's emergence as first minister temporarily reunited most of the whigs in parliament, eliminated whatever slim chance there might have been for a parliamentary restoration, and set the scene for another round of plotting and intrigue.

In the longer term, however, scarcely veiled attacks on the king and his ministers combined with a principled hostility to political compromise were bound to prove a self-defeating strategy—one that played increasingly into the hands of Walpole and his associates who used Shippen's all-too-public displays of disaffection to damn all tories as Jacobites and foment mistrust between the whig and tory elements of the patriot opposition beginning to emerge in parliament. Temporary truces between Jacobites and Hanoverian tories were occasionally possible. For example, with a major row brewing at the prospect of a tobacco excise, the 1733 session opened with an attack on the king's address by all members of the opposition as part of a concerted thrust against the ministry. Typically forthright, Shippen's speech of 16 January made ominous references to 'Jealousies and Suspicions without Doors'. There was, he told the house, such a general spirit abroad that it could not:

> be ascribed to any one Set of Men: They cannot be branded with the Name of Jacobites or of Republicans. No; the whole People of *England* seem to be united in this Spirit of Jealousy and Opposition; and it ought not to be entirely neglected. (*GM*, 1st ser., 3, 1733, 393)

In 1734 Shippen again distinguished himself, speaking forcefully in debates on the address, the Seville treaty, the army, and the Septennial Act; but, with the excise crisis and general elections passed, he showed himself determined once more to prize open fissures within the opposition's ranks. In February 1737 he was among forty-five tory MPs who absented themselves from the division on Pulteney's motion to increase Prince Frederick's allowance, as much perhaps from a distrust of the prince and an unwillingness to be seen coercing the Hanoverian monarchy as from any explicit motives of Jacobitism. Yet, despite the libertarian rhetoric which he frequently used in debates, it would be wrong to view Shippen as either a 'pioneer of constitutional opposition' or as a proto-democrat. His purpose throughout was to advance the Stuart cause by any means that seemed likely to prove effective.

As an associate of Francis Atterbury, the Jacobite bishop of Rochester, Shippen was perhaps fortunate not to be taken up in 1722 for complicity in the Atterbury plot. This, together with his sojourn in the Tower in 1717, may well explain his reluctance to commit himself when approached to engage in real business by the Pretender's emissary, who came to England in 1740 to canvass support for a rising of English Jacobites backed by French troops. The agent found King James's friends 'more timorous and backward than heretofore, and yet as full of good inclinations as ever'. It was, he reported, 'impossible to form any plan of business with them; they shudder at the thought of an attempt when they find it can be compass'd, and yet wish it, and even seem to long for it'. While some remained hearty enough, Shippen in particular, he noted, 'trembles, and infuses his fears into the gentlemen to whom the King [that is, James Stuart] wrote' (Sempil to James Stuart, 28 March 1740, Stuart Papers, 221/109). Consequently, he would be left out of future consultations altogether.

In February 1741 Shippen was among the tory members who quit the house rather than vote for Samuel Sandys's motion addressing the king for Walpole's removal, and afterwards could scarcely conceal his contempt for the patriot whigs: 'Robin and I are two honest men, he is for King George and I for King James; but those men with the long cravats [meaning Sandys and his associates] only desire places either under King George or King James' (HoP, *Commons*). He would not, he asserted, 'pull down Robin on republican principles' (ibid.). His last recorded speech in the House of Commons was in February 1742 against the army estimates which were adopted without a division, 'Shippen alone', as Horace Walpole observed, 'unchanged and opposing' (ibid.).

Shippen died, childless, at his Norfolk Street home on 1 May 1743, leaving his small estate to be divided between his brothers Robert and John. He was buried at St Andrew's, Holborn, on 7 May. His misanthropic widow lived separately at Richmond and died on 22 August 1747.

William's eldest surviving brother was **Robert Shippen** (*bap.* 1675, *d.* 1745), college head, who was baptized at Prestbury, Cheshire, on 27 July 1675. He was educated at Stockport grammar school, matriculated from Merton College, Oxford, on 6 April 1693, and graduated BA in 1696. He then became a fellow of Brasenose, from where, having served as a tutor for several years and proceeded MA in 1699, he was elected professor of music at Gresham College in 1705 and fellow of the Royal Society a year later. In 1710 he returned to Brasenose as principal, resigning his professorship in favour of his brother Edward (1671–1724), and was created DD. In the same year he married Frances, Lady Clerke (*d.* 1728), the widowed daughter of Richard Legh of Lyme. He was presented successively to the rectories of Great Billing, Northamptonshire (1710), Whitechapel, London (1716), and Amersham, Buckinghamshire (1744). Allegedly chosen head of house by a body of slothful fellows anxious to avoid disruptive change, he became 'well known as an overbearing tyrant within the walls of his college' (Bennett, 149), and was soon embroiled in university politics, being engaged as an ally by Atterbury, then dean of Christ Church, in his bid to break the dominance of William Lancaster, the provost of Queen's. He was vice-chancellor from 1718 to 1723 and died on 24 November 1745 at Brasenose College, Oxford, where he was buried. STEPHEN W. BASKERVILLE

Sources G. V. Bennett, *The tory crisis in church and state: the career of Francis Atterbury, bishop of Rochester* (1975) · L. Colley, *In defiance of oligarchy: the tory party, 1714–60* (1982) · HoP, *Commons* · Royal Arch., Stuart papers, 221/109 · W. R. Ward, *Georgian Oxford: university politics in the eighteenth century* (1958) · *Calendar of the Stuart papers belonging to his majesty the king, preserved at Windsor Castle*, 7 vols., HMC, 56 (1902–23), vol. 5, p. 558; vol. 6, p. 260 · JRL, Legh of Lyme MSS · 'Declaration of William Shippen', Bodl. Oxf., MS Rawl. D. 842, fol. 382 · 'Mr Shippen's case', Bodl. Oxf., MS Ballard 21, fol. 206 · *Letters of George Lockhart of Carnwath, 1698–1732*, ed. D. Szechi, Scottish History Society, 5th ser., 2 (1989) · *GM*, 1st ser., 3 (1733), 393 · Venn, *Alum. Cant.* · Foster, *Alum. Oxon.* · *DNB*

Archives Bodl. Oxf., Ballard MSS · Bodl. Oxf., MSS Rawl. · JRL, letters to Peter Legh the Elder · Royal Arch., Stuart MSS

Likenesses T. Hudson, oils, Badminton Park, Gloucestershire [*see illus.*] · lithograph (after T. Hudson), repro. in F. G. Waldron, *The biographical mirrour*, 3 [1810], 88

Shipton, Mother (*supp. fl.* **1530**), supposed witch and prophetess, is a mostly legendary figure. The only historical support for her existence as a woman living in Tudor York is found in the slim pamphlet *The Prophesie of Mother Shipton in the Raigne of King Henry the Eighth* (1641), which opens with an account of the prediction which apparently brought her national fame. In 1530, when she heard that the disgraced Cardinal Wolsey was intending to make his very first visit to York, of which he had been made archbishop by proxy in 1514, she declared that though he might see the city he would never reach it. According to the pamphlet Wolsey went to the top of the tower of Cawood Castle, saw York some 8 miles distant, and vowed that when he reached the city he would have Mother Shipton burnt as a witch. He also sent three of his high-placed friends to her house to interrogate her. It is a matter of record that Wolsey, on 4 November 1530, three days before his planned lavish enthronement in York Minster, was arrested at Cawood on a charge of high treason. He became ill on the journey to London and died in Leicester Abbey.

This 1641 pamphlet also contains Mother Shipton's prophecies concerning York, including one which could be said to have anticipated the siege of York at the time of Marston Moor (1644). There are gory descriptions of forthcoming wars, one between England and Scotland, and the concluding lines of this short pamphlet refer to the master of a ship sailing up the Thames and finding that London has been devastated. This was taken to be a prediction of the fire of London, as we know from a reference in the diary of Samuel Pepys (20 October 1666), who stated that when Prince Rupert on board ship heard of the fire he simply said 'now Shipton's prophecy is out' (Pepys, 7.333).

The 1641 pamphlet was reprinted in various forms, some with woodcuts showing Wolsey looking out from the tower, confronted by a hideous witch, some with commentaries on how the prophecies had been fulfilled, notably in William Lilly's *Ancient and Modern Prophesies* (1645). The York provenance is confirmed by accurate local references in the 1641 pamphlet and by the description of Mother Shipton as the 'Sibylla Eboracensis' ('the Sibyl of York') in the early pamphlet *Nuncius propheticus* (1642). Her birthplace, however, is later given as 'Naseborough' (Knaresborough), some 16 miles to the west of York, in a grossly fictitious and salacious version of her life by Richard Head, *The Life and Death of Mother Shipton* (1667).

Head claimed that she was born, a daughter of the Devil, in a house near the Dropping Well in 1486 or 1487. It is significant that John Leland, who, unlike Head, visited

Knaresborough and its petrifying well (about 1538), made no mention of the prophetess. By this time she would have been well known for her prediction concerning Wolsey, and any Knaresborough connection would presumably have been noted by an antiquarian as close to Henry VIII as Leland. Head added to his account of Mother Shipton's phenomenal ugliness and supernatural powers (levitation, poltergeist effects) a number of fabricated prophecies—all relating to events which had taken place by 1667—such as

The Western Monarch's Wooden Horses
Shall be destroyed by the Drake's forces,

purporting to forecast the Spanish Armada.

An anonymous pamphlet based on Head's version, *The Strange and Wonderful History of Mother Shipton* (1686), adds that she was baptized by 'the Abbot of Beverley' as 'Ursula Soothtell' (in later versions 'Southiel' or 'Sonthiel') and that at the age of twenty-four she married a carpenter named Toby Shipton of York. It also states that she died (presumably in York) at the age of seventy-three, having predicted—as Nostradamus is said to have done—the day and hour of her death. Alleged tombs of Mother Shipton, both in York and near Williton, Somerset, have no historical basis.

Interest in Mother Shipton's prophecies was maintained over the next couple of hundred years by the steady appearance of reprints, sometimes in chapbooks of fortune telling. By the end of the eighteenth century she was well-known as a pipe-smoking puppet and a popular pantomime dame, with a song (set to the tune of 'Nancy Dawson') referring to her role in several Covent Garden productions, from about 1770 to *Mother Shipton Triumphant, or, Harlequin's Museum* (1793). In these pantomimes she was a kind of ugly fairy godmother responsible for spectacular transformation scenes. Her face, with the classic hooked nose and upturned chin of a witch, was now sufficiently familiar for a British moth (*Euclidia mi*, later renamed *Callistege mi*), with a similar profile on its wings, to be officially named the Mother Shipton.

A boost to flagging interest in Mother Shipton was provided in Victorian times by Charles Dickens, who printed a story by Dudley Costello in *Household Words* (1856) linking her with the Rollright Stones, and especially by the Brighton bookseller Charles Hindley. In 1862 Hindley printed a set of bogus rhymed prophecies, claiming they had been found in a manuscript in the British Museum. (After they had been reprinted in *Notes and Queries* he wrote to the editor in 1873 confessing he had written them all himself.) In these much-quoted fabrications Mother Shipton is supposed to have predicted railways, iron-hulled ships, wireless telegraphy, and so forth. The last lines of Hindley's doggerel aroused much interest and alarm:

The world then to an end shall come
In Eighteen Hundred and Eighty One.

In a version of the prophecies printed in Knaresborough in 1910 this date was changed to 1991, and there are still local claims that Mother Shipton predicted that the world will end when Knaresborough's High Bridge collapses for a third time. This story can be traced back to the actual collapse of the railway viaduct over the River Nidd in 1848, after which it was alleged that the prophetess had always said it would fall down twice and stand for ever when built a third time.

Although traditions or sayings concerning Mother Shipton have appeared in Somerset, Norfolk, Cambridgeshire, Oxfordshire, London, and elsewhere, she is now especially associated with Knaresborough, where much of the legend and fabrication has for years been presented as fact. Until about 1908 visitors to the town were being shown a house near Low Bridge where Mother Shipton was said to have been born. Now her birthplace is commercially promoted as a cave near the Dropping Well.

Although almost everything written about Mother Shipton and attributed to her has been invented, she was in all probability a veridical woman living in York about 1530. Whether her prediction concerning Wolsey was shrewd guesswork or genuine clairvoyance, it was sufficient to assure her a unique place in English folklore as its best-known witch and prophetess—a convenient peg on which to hang many a fanciful claim.   ARNOLD KELLETT

Sources *The prophesie of Mother Shipton in the raigne of King Henry the Eighth* (1641) · Pepys, *Diary*, 7.333 · W. Lilly, *Ancient and moderne prophesies* (1645) · *Nuncius propheticus* (1642) · R. Head, *The life and death of Mother Shipton* (1667) · *The strange and wonderful history of Mother Shipton* (1686) · *A correct account of Harlequin's museum* (1793) · C. Hindley, *The life, prophecies and death of Mother Shipton* (1862) · *N&Q*, 4th ser., 11 (1873), 355 · W. Camidge, *Mother Shipton, the Yorkshire sybil* (1898) · *Palatine Note-Book*, 1 (1881), 64 · A. Kellett, *Mother Shipton, witch and prophetess* (2002)

Likenesses portrait, BL; repro. in Head, *The life and death of Mother Shipton*, frontispiece · portrait, BL; repro. in *New Wonderful Magazine*, 2 (1793), 225 · portrait, BL; repro. in R. S. Kirby, *Kirby's wonderful and eccentric museum*, 2 (1820), 146 · woodcut, BL; repro. in *Foure severall strange prophesies* (1642), title-page · woodcut, BL; repro. in *Fourteene strange prophesies* (1648)

Shipton, Eric Earle (1907–1977), explorer and mountaineer, was born on 1 August 1907 in Ceylon, the younger child and only son of Cecil Shipton, a tea planter, and his wife, Alice Lilian Earle (*d.* 1943). His father died before he was three and his upbringing, in his mother's hands, was characterized by constant travelling between Ceylon and Europe. Suffering from dyslexia, he failed to pass the common entrance examination for entry to public schools and at eighteen had no enthusiasm for university or for any conventional career.

Following holidays in France and Norway, Shipton's interest in travel had become focused on mountaineering; he did a number of climbs in the Alps. But climbing did not offer a career and in 1928 he went to Kenya to work on a coffee plantation. He expected to spend the rest of his life there but three things conspired to make this otherwise. Shipton's plantation was only 20 miles from the twin peaks of Mount Kenya, of which Batian had been climbed but once while Nelion remained virgin. As climbing companion he found first Percy Wyn-Harris, a notable Cambridge athlete and mountaineer with whom he made the second ascent of Batian and the first of Nelion. Shortly after this he found another companion who was to play an

Eric Earle Shipton (1907–1977), by unknown photographer, 1939 [at Snow Lake, Karakoram]

even bigger part in his life, Harold William Tilman, with whom he made the first complete traverse of the twin peaks.

In 1931 some neighbours found a rich gold deposit close at hand and invited Shipton to join in exploiting it, but this opportunity he declined in order to join the expedition led by Francis Sydney Smythe to Kamet in Garhwal Himalaya. It was to be the first of a whole series of Himalayan ventures that occupied the rest of the 1930s, and shortly after Kamet, with prospects depressed by the world slump, he abandoned his Kenya interests altogether.

After the success of Kamet, Shipton was a natural choice for the Mount Everest expedition of 1933 on which he reached 27,900 feet, but the experience of those two lavishly organized undertakings convinced him that this was the wrong way to travel in the Himalayas and his next venture was in stark contrast. In company with Tilman and three Sherpas he spent three months in Garhwal Himalaya living largely off the country and at a total cost of £286. Instead of travelling as sahibs and retainers they went as companions, sharing the same food and privations. In this remarkable journey they forced an entry, for the first time, up the formidable Rishi gorge and into the Nanda Devi sanctuary which, with its satellite peaks, they surveyed.

In the years that followed there were further expeditions to the north side of Everest (1935, 1936, and 1938), and two journeys of exploration to the remote areas of the Karakoram bordering on Tibet and Sinkiang (Xinjiang) (1937 and 1938).

While preparing to leave the region after the 1936 expedition Shipton met Pamela Freston, with whom he struck up a romance which lasted three years. They subsequently maintained a warm friendship which continued for the rest of Shipton's life. Although she was not a professional writer, Pamela edited Shipton's books and acted as his chief literary guide and mentor. In 1938 Shipton was awarded the Patron's medal of the Royal Geographical Society and his reputation and style were well established. He was not really a professional but had no other career

and made do with modest earnings from books and lectures.

Preparing for the 1940 expedition, Shipton was in Kashmir when he met Diana Kendall Channer (b. 1916/17), whose father, Frederick Francis Ralph Channer, was in the Indian forest service. At the outbreak of the Second World War, Shipton was engaged on the second Karakoram expedition. Diana left for Britain, where she joined the ATS, leaving Shipton to console himself with Beatrice Weir, an old flame. The Indian government offered him the post of consul-general at Kashgar, which he accepted with enthusiasm as an opportunity to see another region of central Asia. It was, however, a difficult assignment, his freedom of action being curbed by Chinese hostility combined with Russian suspicion.

Shipton returned to Britain in 1942 and married Diana Channer at Lyme Regis a few days later, on 16 December. Their honeymoon was brief for Diana went back to her unit and Shipton took up a Foreign Office posting to Persia. From time to time their paths crossed, and their first son, Nicholas, was born in 1945 and the second, John, in 1950. Shipton had a second tour of duty at Kashgar from 1946 to 1948. This, in turn, was followed by two years as consul-general at Kunming in Yunnan (1949–51), an unhappy experience owing to increasing pressure from the communist authorities which concluded with his expulsion from the country and an agonizing journey, with wife and children, to the coast.

Although the reassertion in 1950 of Chinese authority in Tibet had put an end to any early prospect of using the northern approach to Everest, Nepal was gradually becoming accessible and in 1951 a reconnaissance of the south side of the mountain was being planned. On Shipton's return from China he was immediately invited to lead this undertaking. The task was successfully completed, thus demonstrating that despite a dangerous icefall there was indeed a feasible route. By then, however, the British no longer had a monopoly of access to Everest; for 1952 the Swiss had permission from the Nepalese government to attempt to climb the mountain. Britain had to await its turn in 1953.

The Himalayan Committee set up to plan this expedition comprised old hands from the Royal Geographical Society and the Alpine Club. The question of a leader was much debated, but a few of the individual members of the committee, mostly elderly and well connected, approached their own favourites and made offers without general approval. Shipton was an obvious candidate for leader; he was a nationally admired figure, respected by other mountaineers, but known to be averse to elaborate planning and to dislike large expeditions and national rivalries. He was criticized, moreover, for failing to press the assault of Cho Oyu. There was support for a military officer, such men being competent organizers and likely to be given leave. Colonel John Hunt was known to only one of the committee, but gradually his name came to the fore, first as organizing secretary, then as deputy to Shipton, although all the approaches made came from individuals rather than formally from the committee.

On 28 July 1952 Shipton was invited to give the committee an account of the Cho Oyu expedition and discuss plans for the Everest assault. The committee's view was then that he should lead, although no deputy had been chosen. Shipton later wrote that he had been hesitant regarding the leadership. More correspondence ensued. When Hunt and Shipton met on 22 August, Shipton thought that Hunt was to be the organizing secretary, while Hunt supposed that he was to be deputy leader, and declined the other job. More campaigning ensued in support of Hunt as leader, and it was proposed to Shipton that he and Hunt should be co-leaders up to base camp and that Hunt should lead from that point. Finally it was put to Shipton that Hunt should be sole leader—unable to accept this, he stormed out of the meeting, ending his involvement with the expedition.

At a loss for what to do, Shipton took an unsuitable job as warden of the Outward Bound Trust school in Eskdale. But this too was an unhappy episode: Diana fell for David Drummond, one of the instructors, and Shipton ardently pursued Susan Denholm, the bursar's wife. The ensuing storm led to Shipton's being sacked at the end of 1954. He moved with Susan to Shropshire, where he worked as a forester, but their brief affair ended when she returned to a forgiving husband. Diana obtained a divorce and married Drummond, although she and Shipton maintained a friendly correspondence. In 1955 he was appointed CBE. Shipton's next move was to Wiltshire, where he became friendly with Geoffrey and Phyllis Wint. Phyllis was caring for her alcoholic husband, and by the time of his death in 1959 Shipton's moral support had warmed into another love affair. He moved into her house and they lived together as man and wife until his death nearly twenty years later.

By the end of the decade Shipton emerged from the shadows and started with a fresh group of friends on a series of exploratory journeys (1958–64) in Patagonia and Tierra del Fuego, at that time virtually unknown country. This period culminated in his appointment by the Chilean government as their adviser in the boundary dispute with Argentina. He was president of the Alpine Club in 1965–7.

Shipton was a good-looking man with intense blue, deep-set eyes. He was gregarious and interested in people, ready to talk on any subject, with friends of both sexes and various nationalities. His travels are well recorded in his books: *Nanda Devi* (1936), *Blank on the Map* (1938), *Upon that Mountain* (1948), *Mountains of Tartary* (1951), *Mount Everest Reconnaissance Expedition* (1951), *Land of Tempest* (1963), and the autobiography, *That Untravelled World* (1969). He died on 28 March 1977 at The Manor, Anstey, Wiltshire. His body was cremated.

PETER LLOYD, *rev.* ANITA McCONNELL

Sources E. Shipton, *That untravelled world* (1969) · personal knowledge (1986) · private information (1986) · P. Steele, *Eric Shipton: Everest and beyond* (1998) · WWW · m. cert. · d. cert. · *The Times* (30 March 1977) · *The Times* (5 April 1977) · *The Times* (7 April 1977)
Archives GL, corresp. with publishers
Likenesses photograph, 1939, RGS [*see illus.*]
Wealth at death £55,198: probate, 28 June 1977, *CGPLA Eng. & Wales*

Shipton, John (1680–1748), surgeon, son of James Shipton (*b.* 1637?), an apothecary living in Hatton Garden, London, was apprenticed on 2 February 1696 for seven years to William Pleahill, paying £20. He served his time and was duly admitted to the freedom of the Company of Barber-Surgeons on 7 March 1703. He served the office of steward of anatomy in 1704, and on 1 June 1731 he was fined rather than serve as steward of the ladies' feast. He was elected an examiner in the company on 27 August 1734, and on 17 August 1738 he became a member of its court of assistants. He then paid a fine of £30 to avoid serving in the offices of warden and master, to which he would have been elected in due course. He lived for many years in Brooke Street, Holborn, London, where he enjoyed a lucrative practice. He was called into consultation by John Ranby when Caroline, the queen of George II, was mortally ill of a strangulated hernia. Shipton sided in this consultation with Ranby against Paul Buissière, who was in favour of an immediate operation. Lord Hervey says of him that he was 'one of the most eminent and able of the whole profession' (Hervey, 507). He died on 17 September 1748.

D'A. POWER, *rev.* MICHAEL BEVAN

Sources P. J. Wallis and R. V. Wallis, *Eighteenth century medics*, 2nd edn (1988) · *GM*, 1st ser., 18 (1748), 428 · J. Hervey, *Memoirs of the reign of George the Second*, ed. J. W. Croker, 2 vols. (1848), vol. 2, p. 507
Archives Barbers' Hall, London

Shipton, William (*bap.* 1640?, *d.* in or after 1672), poet, was probably the William Shipton, son of Thomas Shipton of Lythe, Yorkshire, baptized on 2 August 1640 at Whitby. A Richard Shipton, son of Thomas, had been baptized there three years before. William Shipton was admitted pensioner at Clare College, Cambridge, on 28 April 1657. He matriculated that year. On 6 April 1659 he migrated to Magdalene College, Cambridge, and graduated BA in 1660 and MA in 1664.

In 1659 Shipton published a collection of poetry and prose under the title of *Dia: a Poem*. The introductory portion extends to thirty pages, comprising a dedication 'to the Truly Noble Edward Trotter Esquire', and commendatory verses by 'Jo. Cooke, Gent., Aulae Clar.', and by Richard Shipton (possibly the poet's brother). Besides a series of poems in praise of his mistress Dia, the volume contains elegies on Thomas Shipton (who was drowned) and on Lord Sheffield; poems on gunpowder treason and on Robert Wilson (a noted musician); and a prose essay entitled 'Cupid made to see and love made lovely'. His poems are full of extravagant and complex metaphors, and his prose is even more fantastic.

Shipton was ordained a priest on 27 May 1661, and was appointed vicar of Escrick, Yorkshire, in 1663 (retaining the appointment until 1672) and vicar of Lythe in 1664. One of his sermons was published in 1668 under the title *The Mystery of Afflictions*.

E. I. CARLYLE, *rev.* JOANNA MOODY

Sources Watt, *Bibl. Brit.* · M. R. Woodhead, 'A mid seventeenth century allusion to "The exstasie"', *N&Q*, 219 (1974), 21, 413 · Venn, *Alum. Cant.* · ESTC · IGI

Shirley. *See also* Sherley.

Shirley, Elizabeth (1564/5–1641), Augustinian nun and author, was the daughter of Sir John Shirley of Shirley in Leicestershire. Sickly in childhood and adolescence she was raised a protestant until at the age of about twenty she went to live as housekeeper to her unmarried Catholic brother, Sir George Shirley of Staunton-Harrold in Leicestershire. Although initially resistant to his efforts to convert her Elizabeth was eventually persuaded by miraculous stories, Catholic literature, and an apparition of the Holy Ghost. Following the marriage of her brother the pressures of recusancy, her ill health, and a reluctance to marry convinced her to enter a convent. After some doubts regarding her vocation she finally joined the Flemish Augustinian cloister of St Ursula's in Louvain, where she made her religious profession on 10 September 1596. In 1608, when the English nuns there decided to establish a separate house, Elizabeth was appointed procuratrice, responsible for its finances, and temporary prioress of the proposed venture. She remained in charge from the nuns' arrival at the new convent on 10 February 1609 until the election of a permanent superior in November, after which she became the sub-prioress, a position she held until infirmity forced her to resign in 1637.

As a capable administrator Elizabeth was principally responsible for establishing the English Augustinian cloister of St Monica's in Louvain. Since the 1569 election of an English prioress, Margaret Clement, in the Flemish convent about twenty-eight women had crossed the channel and entered there. Upon Clement's retirement in 1606 the disputed election of a Flemish superior culminated in the move for a separate convent. The English feared that St Ursula's would no longer receive recusant novices in the face of competition from the recently founded Benedictine monastery in Brussels and a proposed Poor Clare house at St Omer. Elizabeth Shirley was eminently qualified to organize and execute the venture. Her experience in supervising a secular household, coupled with the financial generosity of her family, enabled her to solicit funds, negotiate renting a suitable house, secure as many household and religious furnishings as the Flemish sisters would donate, and facilitate the removal of the six founders and their belongings from St Ursula's to St Monica's. The first few months in the new house were marked by strong religious fervour, tempered by severe financial shortfalls. As procuratrice Elizabeth feared that the cloister would fail, but she managed to secure sufficient alms to avoid dissolution, even putting some money aside to purchase a permanent residence. Although her sisters ultimately elected Jane (Sister Mary) Wiseman as the first prioress, Elizabeth's appointment as sub-prioress affirmed their confidence in her continuing capacity to manage their temporal concerns. She is regarded as instrumental in the foundation of St Monica's in all accounts of the cloister's establishment.

However, Elizabeth Shirley is also known as an author. In 1626 she composed the biography of St Ursula's English prioress whose success in attracting English novices paved the way for St Monica's. Written fourteen years after Margaret Clement's death Elizabeth's hagiographical text offered not only the life of her former prioress and the early history of the English Augustinians in Louvain, but it also aspired to provide spiritual and practical guidance to her sisters and their superiors. Deprecating her skill and worthiness as the recorder of Clement's virtue Elizabeth defended her assumption of the task, declaring:

> I thought it my duty & part to geve her some Littell mytt of my good will … beseeching allmighty god to geve me his grace that I may in som littell thing emmitate her & allso to inspire all those that shall hereafter posses her place & offis of government, that they may sett her as a true pattron & example before them & I assure my self they shall make a happy progres. (Shirley, fols. 62–3)

As a writer, therefore, Elizabeth cemented the economic and administrative foundations she had laid in 1608 by establishing herself as a custodian of the cloister's heritage and adviser to future generations of nuns.

Elizabeth Shirley died, aged seventy-six, on 1 September 1641 at St Monica's, where she was buried. Upon her death her sisters warmly acknowledged her contributions, noting that deafness in old age had deprived them of her much appreciated counsel. Although Elizabeth Shirley was destined to play second fiddle to other superiors in her long religious career of forty-six years, her achievements show how the cloister provided capable and well-connected women considerable scope for institutional governance in early modern society.

CLAIRE WALKER

Sources A. Hamilton, ed., *The chronicle of the English Augustinian canonesses regular of the Lateran at St. Monica's in Louvain*, 1 (1904), 18–20, 33, 59–80, 102–7; 2 (1906), 168–9, 186–8 · E. Shirley, 'The lyfe of our moste reverent mother Margrit Clement', 1626, Priory of Our Lady, Sayers Common, Sussex, MS, fols. i–87 · 'Beginning of St Monica's Louvain to 1622', Little Chronicle, vol. 1, Priory of Our Lady, Sayers Common, Sussex, MS, fols. 47–129 · 'An account of the nunnery of St Monica in Lovain', c.1745, BL, Add. MS 5813, fols. 31–2 · 'A record of all our benefactours', Priory of Our Lady, Sayers Common, Sussex, MS P1, fols. 1, 3–5, 7–8, 12, 25 · P. Guilday, *The English Catholic refugees on the continent, 1558–1795* (1914), 377–82 · C. S. Durrant, *A link between Flemish mystics and English martyrs* (1925) **Archives** Priory of Nazareth, Bruges · Priory of Our Lady of Good Counsel, Hassocks, West Sussex, St Monica's MSS

Shirley, Evelyn Philip (1812–1882), antiquary and genealogist, was born in South Audley Street, London, on 22 January 1812, the eldest son of Evelyn John Shirley (1788–1856) of Ettington Park, Warwickshire (the Shirleys were a branch of the family of the earls Ferrers). His mother was Eliza (d. 1859), only daughter of Arthur Stanhope. He was educated at a preparatory school at Twyford, near Winchester, and afterwards by a private tutor. In 1826 he went to Eton College. He matriculated as a gentleman commoner from Magdalen College, Oxford, on 15 October 1830, graduated BA in 1834, and proceeded MA in 1837.

Shirley owned property at Lough Fea in co. Monaghan, Ettington in Warwickshire, and Houndshill on the borders of Worcestershire. After he succeeded his father, he made considerable alterations to Ettington Park. Here, and at Lough Fea, he built up a large library and picture collection. Benjamin Disraeli portrayed Shirley in *Lothair* as Mr Ardenne, 'a man of ancient pedigree himself, who knew everybody else's'.

Shirley was a Conservative, who opposed the disestablishment of the Church of Ireland, and believed in the union of secular and religious education. However, he, unlike his father, was tolerant towards the Catholic priesthood on his co. Monaghan estate. He was MP for co. Monaghan from 1841 to 1847, and from 1853 to 1865 he represented Warwickshire South. In 1837 Shirley was high sheriff for co. Monaghan, and in 1867 he became high sheriff for Warwickshire.

Shirley's first interest, however, was genealogy and local history, and he rarely took part in parliamentary debates. He wrote a number of books and articles on the history of the Shirley family and their estates, both in England and Ireland. He also wrote on the Church of Ireland and on genealogy. He was a frequent contributor to *Notes and Queries*. Shirley was a fellow of the Society of Antiquaries, and a corresponding member of the New England Historic Genealogical Society. In 1881 he was awarded an honorary LLD at Dublin. He was also a trustee of Rugby School and of the National Portrait Gallery.

On 4 August 1842 Shirley married Mary Clara Elizabeth (1823–1894), eldest daughter of Sir Edmund Hungerford Lechmere. She greatly encouraged the school of Irish lace which was established at Carrickmacross, near Lough Fea. They had a son and three daughters. Shirley died at Ettington Park on 19 September 1882, and was buried there in the family vault on 26 September.

W. P. COURTNEY, *rev.* MARIE-LOUISE LEGG

Sources The Times (21 Sept 1882), 10 · E. C. Waters, *The Academy* (7 Oct 1882), 260–1 · *WWBMP* · K. T. Hoppen, *Elections, politics, and society in Ireland, 1832–1885* (1984), 123 · H. E. C. Stapylton, *The Eton school lists, from 1791 to 1850*, 2nd edn (1864) · Foster, *Alum. Oxon.*
Archives Bodl. Oxf., notes on the Mordaunt family · NRA, priv. coll., corresp., diaries, and estate papers · PRO NIre., political and estate corresp. and papers · Warks. CRO, corresp. and papers | BL, Gilbert collection · BL, letters to J. Hunter, Add. MS 24875 · Bodl. Oxf., corresp. with Sir T. Phillipps · Dublin Public Library, Gilbert collection · Leics. RO, letters to the Shirley family
Likenesses T. C. Thompson, portrait, 1839
Wealth at death £41,044 19s. 3d.: resworn probate, March 1883, *CGPLA Eng. & Wales* · £18,675 7s. 9d.: probate, 6 March 1883, *CGPLA Ire.*

Shirley, Frederick Joseph John (1890–1967), headmaster, was born in Oxford on 24 February 1890, the fourth child of William Shirley, carpenter, and his wife, Louisa Ellen Harris. His childhood was poor, but he was greatly influenced by the Anglo-Catholic parish church of St Barnabas. He was educated at its school, at Oxford high school, and at St Edmund Hall, where he obtained second-class honours in history in 1912. He then taught in private schools, and had the enterprise to read law while commissioned in the Royal Naval Volunteer Reserve in the First World War. He took second-class honours in law in London University (1920) and was called to the bar by Lincoln's Inn.

Shirley found his vocation when, on returning to teaching in 1919, he was given scope for his talents on the staff of Framlingham College in Suffolk and was ordained (deacon 1920, priest 1921). He enjoyed a brief spell as the part-time rector of Sternfield (1923–5). All this prepared him for the challenges he faced on becoming headmaster of St Cuthbert's College, Worksop, in 1925. This was one of the poorest of the schools founded by Nathaniel Woodard, a network of Anglican schools run on more economic lines than most public schools. Shirley set himself to raise its standards and multiply its amenities: new buildings arose, the educational achievements were transformed, and both the grounds and the number of boys were expanded. Everything was stamped with Shirley's personality, which had become powerful and idiosyncratic. If governors of the school were cautious, or pupils non-cooperative, they experienced wrath and a relentless drive; but parents and other visitors were charmed, and increasingly the boys were caught up in the excitement of an ambitious adventure.

This panache was greatly needed at Canterbury, where the King's School, inheriting a tradition of education linked with the cathedral over thirteen centuries, was slow to adapt to modern needs and was burdened by problems of finance and morale. Some boys who moved in 1935 with Shirley from Worksop (to the indignation of his fellow headmasters, whose code was thereby breached) became the nucleus of a renaissance only partly reflected in the school's ever-increasing size and only temporarily halted by the outbreak of the Second World War and the evacuation to Cornwall.

The success made of Worksop was repeated, but with appropriate variations. Shirley was enthusiastic in acquiring or constructing more spacious premises for his boys around the cathedral and in the city. His building programme was initially made possible by the agreement of the dean and chapter to commute for a cash sum their perpetual obligation to provide King's scholarships; and the programme was crowned by the erection of an assembly hall, later the Shirley Hall. He persuaded two authors, Sir Hugh Walpole and W. Somerset Maugham, who both had unhappy memories of their own schooldays at Canterbury, to vie with each other in generosity among the many benefactors now enlisted. This team of supporters included some members of the royal family as well as many grateful parents.

Shirley's delight in the beautiful surroundings of the King's School inspired him to develop its music and drama to exceptionally high levels. He was also determined that more and more of the boys should proceed to the universities, if possible after winning scholarships, and although he did little teaching in class he attracted an able staff. Victories on the river and the playing fields were, however, not despised.

The untiring competitiveness which Shirley encouraged arose from his memories of his own underprivileged boyhood and slow start in life, and often amounted to a frank worldliness. But particularly in his later years, the style was so warmly human, and his devotion to the boys under his care was so evident, that he was loved as well as admired. Signing himself John Shirley, he was Fred to the boys. To the end he was lively and affable in his copious conversation. He was a pioneer among headmasters in encouraging a more relaxed, almost domestic, atmosphere in which each individual could discover and develop his own interests. Many hobbies flourished.

Shirley threw himself with an equal zest into his responsibilities as a canon of the cathedral, and in his latter years also as treasurer and librarian, especially since the dean of Canterbury, Hewlett Johnson, was handicapped by political unpopularity and old age. He became noted for his eloquence in preaching a simple gospel as well as for his administrative and financial exertions, other aspects of a complex character. He published a number of historical studies, among them *Richard Hooker and Contemporary Political Ideas* (1949). He was DD (Oxford, 1949), PhD (London, 1931), an honorary fellow of St Edmund Hall, Oxford, and a fellow of the Royal Historical Society and of the Society of Antiquaries.

In 1926 Shirley married Dorothy, daughter of John Howard, a company director. They had two sons and one daughter. Shirley retired from the King's School in 1962 and died in Canterbury on 19 July 1967. He was buried in Canterbury Cathedral.   DAVID L. EDWARDS, *rev.*

Sources D. L. Edwards, *F. J. Shirley: an extraordinary headmaster* (1969) · *CGPLA Eng. & Wales* (1967) · R. Pittman, ed., *Fred remembered* (1997)
Likenesses A. Devas, oils, King's School, Canterbury · B. Leighton, oils, Worksop College, Nottinghamshire
Wealth at death £43,117: probate, 2 Dec 1967, *CGPLA Eng. & Wales*

Shirley, Sir Henry, second baronet (1589–1633), landowner and local politician, was born on 4 January 1589 at Somerton, Oxfordshire, the eldest of the five children of Sir George Shirley, first baronet (1559–1622), and his first wife, Frances (*c*.1564–1595), daughter of Henry Berkeley, Lord Berkeley, and his wife, Catherine, daughter of Henry *Howard, styled earl of Surrey.

Shirley's childhood was spent largely at Astwell Castle, Northamptonshire, his father's preferred home. He was educated by a private tutor, John Collyns BA. A memoir by his brother Thomas *Shirley records that he attended Oxford University but his name does not appear in the published records of university membership. From Oxford, Shirley travelled abroad before returning to the court of Henry, prince of Wales. On the death of the prince in 1612, Shirley returned to the family seat at Staunton Harold, Leicestershire. On 18 May 1615 he married Lady Dorothy Devereux [see Stafford, Lady Dorothy (1600–1636)], the daughter of Robert *Devereux, second earl of Essex. The marriage produced three children: a daughter, Laeta (Leta, Lettice; *b*. *c*.1619), his heir, Charles (*b*. 1623), and a second son, Robert (*b*. 1629/30) [see Shirley, Sir Robert, fourth baronet]. The barren years between 1623 and 1629 almost certainly represent a period of marital discord, even separation. In 1626 or 1627 Shirley was sued for non-payment of alimony, responding with wounding personal allegations and the argument that Lady Dorothy's prosecution for recusancy nullified her claim for unpaid maintenance. The birth of Robert and a reputed fourth

pregnancy of Lady Dorothy at the time of her husband's death, with the affectionate references to her in his will, suggest some degree of reconciliation in the late 1620s.

The marriage may not have prospered but the Shirley family did. For several generations the Shirleys had contrived to marry widows and heiresses, such that on his father's death in 1622, Shirley found himself the possessor of properties in Leicestershire, Northamptonshire, Huntingdonshire, Warwickshire, Derbyshire, and Staffordshire, and an income from which his father had readily drawn several legacies of £2000 each.

Shirley then entered local politics with two advantages beside his wealth and family connections: the friendship of the duke of Buckingham and the social precedence of an inherited baronetcy which dated from 1611. His weaknesses were a pomposity fuelled by his brother's indefatigable genealogical delvings, which had brought to light an aristocratic lineage stretching back beyond the Norman conquest, and a taste for confrontation and controversy which verged on self-destruction. There was also the taint of Roman Catholicism, a cause which his parents had openly espoused but that Shirley kept at bay by occasional displays of conformity.

At first Shirley prospered. In 1624 he was pricked as high sheriff of Leicestershire, the following year making the most of his office by himself reading the proclamation of Charles I's accession in Leicester's market place. He was paramount too as the most active local opponent of Leicestershire's lord lieutenant, the earl of Huntingdon. But he was not content to keep his attacks on Huntingdon political. In 1627 an absurd squabble with a gentleman of the earl's household highlighted the personal nature of Shirley's campaign. The affair cost him a few days' imprisonment and house arrest before the embarrassment of a public apology set him free. Shirley's hauteur was bolstered by the support of friends at court and he returned to Leicestershire boasting of the offer of a barony as compensation should he fail to be selected as an MP in the coming elections and the promise of the lieutenancy within a year. His shocking declaration despite the lenient treatment he received from the privy council, that he 'cared for never a Lord in England a fart, except the Lord of Hosts', was widely reported (Cogswell, 164). In May 1628 he was summoned before the House of Lords. Huntingdon had had enough and petitioned the committee of privileges, complaining of 'divers scandalous speeches spoken against him' (*JHL*, 1628, 783). On 7 June Shirley was committed to the Fleet Prison, where he remained four days until the house heard his apologies and ordered that they be published at the next assizes in Leicester.

Shirley continued to play a contentious part in local politics but increasingly ill health and other preoccupations, rebuilding his house at Ragdale, Leicestershire, and research into his family's ancient lineage occupied his time. After a 'long lingering disease' (T. Shirley, 'Genealogical history', fol. 109) he died on 8 February 1633 having, according to his brother, Sir Thomas Shirley, openly sought consolation from the Roman Catholic church. He was buried the following day alongside his parents, on whose monument he is commemorated, in the Shirley family chapel at Breedon on the Hill, Leicestershire.

ROBIN P. JENKINS

Sources T. Shirley, 'Genealogical history of the house of Shirley', BL, Harley MS 4928 · E. P. Shirley, *Stemmata Shirleiana* (privately printed, 1841) · Leics. RO, Shirley family papers, 26D53 · T. Cogswell, *Home divisions: aristocracy, the state and provincial conflict* (1998) · R. Cust, 'Catholicism, antiquarianism and gentry honour', *Midland History*, 23 (1998), 40–70 · IGI · submissions concerning a writ for maintenance v. Sir Henry Shirley, BL, Add. MS 46189, fol. 30 · *State trials*, 2.1455-6 · parish register, Breedon on the Hill [burial], 9 Feb 1633
Archives Leics. RO, MS 26D53 · Northants. RO, executorship, accounts, and papers
Likenesses attrib. G. Hollemans, effigy on monument, alabaster, 1598, parish church, Breedon on the Hill, Leicestershire

Shirley, Henry (1591×7–1627), playwright, was the second son of Sir Thomas Shirley the younger (*c*.1564–1633) of Wiston, Sussex, traveller and member of parliament, and his first wife, Frances, daughter of Henry Vavasour of Coppenthorp, Yorkshire. His exact date of birth is unknown, but he must have been born between his parents' secret marriage in late 1591 and the baptism of his younger brother, Thomas, on 30 June 1597. His childhood was no doubt somewhat unsettled, for his father ran up many debts travelling to Portugal and Turkey and was imprisoned several times.

Shirley's one surviving play, *The Martyred Soldier*, is a Christian martyr play set among the medieval Vandals and Goths. It concerns the noble warrior Bellizarius and his wife, Victorina, converts to Christianity who endure much hardship for their beliefs. They are comforted by angels who sing a number of songs, one of which is preserved in a contemporary setting in a manuscript in the Bodleian Library (MS Don. c.57, fol. 24). Eventually the pair are martyred, but their daughter Bellina marries and converts Hubert, who becomes the first Christian king of the Vandals and Goths. The play was licensed in 1622–3 for Lady Elizabeth's Men at the Cockpit and then for Palsgrave's Men at the Fortune, but it was not entered in the Stationers' register until 15 February 1638 and was published that year, with a title-page declaring that it had been 'acted at the Private house in Drury lane, and at other publicke Theaters. By the Queenes Majesties servants'. The dedication to Sir Kenelm Digby was signed by John Kirke, an actor–playwright long associated with the Red Bull theatre.

Shirley's only other surviving work is a set of verses in another manuscript in the Bodleian Library (MS Ashmole 38, fol. 75), entitled 'The Battaile the Combattantes, Sr Ambrose Vaux Knight; and Glascott the Bayley of Southwarke'. John Davies of Hereford's *Scourge of Folly* (1611) has a poem addressed to 'Henry Sherley, Esquire', but this is probably too early to be the dramatist. Four plays were attributed to Shirley in a Stationers' register entry of 1653 but are now lost. These include 'The Duke of Guise' and 'Giraldo, the Constant Lover', about which nothing more is known; 'The Dumb Bawd of Venice', which was performed by the King's Men at court in 1628; and 'The Spanish Duke of Lerma', which was owned by the King's Men in 1641 and adapted by Sir Robert Howard in 1668 as *The Great Favourite, or, The Duke of Lerma*.

In 1622 Shirley's grandmother Lady Anne Shirley left him £40 per annum in her will, to be paid out annually by Sir Thomas Bishop. However, Shirley ran up debts and was chronically short of money. In October 1627 he went to the lodging of Sir Edward Bishop (Sir Thomas's son) in Chancery Lane, London, to demand his annuity, whereupon Sir Edward slew the unarmed Shirley with a sword. Bishop was originally sentenced to be burnt on the hand, but was pardoned on 21 October. The incident was gleefully recounted four years later by William Prynne in *Histriomastix*, and in two newsbooks of 1645. Shirley apparently never married, and died without children.

DAVID KATHMAN

Sources G. E. Bentley, *The Jacobean and Caroline stage*, 7 vols. (1941–68), vol. 6, pp. 1056–64 · E. P. Shirley, ed., *Stemmata Shirleiana, or, The annals of the Shirley family*, 2nd edn (1873) · J. P. Cutts, 'Henry Shirley's *The martyred soldier*', *Renaissance News*, 12 (1959), 251-3 · M. Crum, ed., *First-line index of English poetry, 1500–1800, in manuscripts of the Bodleian Library, Oxford*, 2 vols. (1969) · N. W. Bawcutt, ed., *The control and censorship of Caroline drama: the records of Sir Henry Herbert, master of the revels, 1623–73* (1996), 143-4
Wealth at death debts of at least £47: Bentley, *Jacobean and Caroline stage*, 6.1057

Shirley, Sir Horatio (1805–1879), army officer, born at 13 Gloucester Place, Portman Square, London, on 8 December 1805, was the fifth son of Evelyn Shirley (1756–1810), of Eatington (Ettington) Park, Warwickshire, and his wife, Phyllis Byam (*d*. 1836), the only daughter of Charlton Wollaston of Horton, Dorset. His father's eldest brother, Evelyn John Shirley, was the father of Evelyn Philip *Shirley (1812–1882). Following his education at Rugby School (from May 1820 to 1823) and Trinity College, Oxford (where he matriculated on 10 May 1823), Shirley became second lieutenant in the British army (by purchase) in May 1825, lieutenant (by purchase) in October 1826, captain (by purchase) in July 1833, major (by purchase) in December 1841, lieutenant-colonel in January 1848, and colonel of the 88th foot (Connaught Rangers) in 1854. He served with distinction in the Crimean War, taking part in the battles of Alma and Inkerman with his regiment. At the siege of Sevastopol he was general officer of the trenches in the attacks on the quarries on 7 and 18 June, and was commended by Lord Raglan for his 'arduous services'. In the storming of Sevastopol on 8 September he was wounded and invalided home. He was appointed CB on 5 July 1856 and KCB on 2 June 1869 and promoted major-general on 24 October 1862, lieutenant-general in 1871, and general on 1 October 1877. He was colonel of the 61st foot from February 1870 to September 1874 and of the 88th foot from September 1874 until his death. He died, unmarried, on 7 April 1879, at his house at Puddletown, near Dorchester, Dorset.

E. I. CARLYLE, *rev.* ROGER T. STEARN

Sources Ward, *Men of the reign* · *The Times* (15 April 1879) · *Dorset County Chronicle* (17 April 1879) · A. W. Kinglake, *The invasion of the Crimea*, [new edn], 9 (1888) · Foster, *Alum. Oxon.* · [F. Temple], ed.,

Rugby School register from 1675 to 1867 inclusive (1867) · Boase, *Mod. Eng. biog.* · Burke, *Gen. GB* (1914) · *Hart's Army List* (1854) · A. D. Lambert, *The Crimean War: British grand strategy, 1853–56* (1990)
Archives Warks. CRO, military MSS, 1848–79, CR 229, CR 2131, CR 464, CR 2485
Wealth at death under £6000: probate, 7 May 1879, *CGPLA Eng. & Wales*

Shirley, James (*bap.* 1596, *d.* 1666), playwright and poet, was baptized on 7 September 1596 at St Mary Woolchurch, London, the oldest of five children of James Shirley (1569–1617) and his wife, Catherine. His father and grandfather and their children appear in the same parish records, but there remains little verifiable information about the family; it is likely that they had a small shop. Shirley was enrolled in the Merchant Taylors' School, London, on 4 October 1608. There he gave an average performance until he left, almost certainly on 11 June 1612, though the record is missing. Probably from then until 1614 he worked for the scrivener William Frith.

According to his early biographer, Anthony Wood, Shirley next entered St John's College, Oxford, then presided over by the future archbishop of Canterbury, William Laud. Wood retails the anecdote that Dr Laud:

> had a very great affection for him, especially for the pregnant parts that were visible in him, but then having a broad or large mole upon his left cheek, which some esteemed a deformity, that worthy Doctor would often tell him that he was an unfit Person to take the sacred function upon him. (Wood, *Ath. Oxon.*, 2.260)

But Wood's story has never been substantiated. There is a record of Shirley's matriculation at St Catharine's College, Cambridge, in Easter term 1615 and of his BA on 4 April 1617. Soon afterwards, on 4 January 1618, his first known poem 'Ecco and Narcissus the 2 Unfortunate Lovers' was entered in the Stationers' register. No copy of this remains, although editors agree that it is probably the poem about Narcissus in the 1646 edition of Shirley's poems.

On 2 November 1618 Shirley was guaranteed to succeed as master of the grammar school at St Albans. The following year, on 19 September, he was ordained and, according to Wood, soon afterwards 'became a Minister of God's word in, or near to S. *Albans*' (Wood, *Ath. Oxon.*, 2.260). There is no record as to when Shirley assumed and left the post at the school, but he held it by January 1621 and he was succeeded in January 1625. Meanwhile on 1 June 1618 he had married Elizabeth Gilmet (*d.* c.1645) of St Albans. Since her father, Richard, served as mayor, and since the mayor—along with the governor of the school, the mayor's brother Robert—controlled the appointment of master of the grammar school, it may be assumed that Shirley was promoted by prominent in-laws. One Shirley daughter was baptized at St Albans on 27 December 1619 and another was born and buried there in 1622.

Wood also claims that about the time Shirley became a schoolmaster he 'changed his Religion for that of *Rome*' (Wood, *Ath. Oxon.*, 2.260). Ever since, most scholars of Shirley except Bas have assumed that Shirley became a Roman

James Shirley (*bap.* 1596, *d.* 1666), by unknown artist

Catholic, yet all have confessed that there is little substantive evidence to support this assumption. He could not have converted as early as Wood claimed, since he subscribed to the Thirty-Nine Articles in 1617, was ordained an Anglican priest in 1619, and signed a writ of excommunication as priest on 10 November 1623. Moreover, his children were baptized Anglican in the early 1630s, as was his last son in 1641. Finally, on 18 August 1662, four years before his death, he signed assent to the Bill of Uniformity, which required an oath subscribing to the Book of Common Prayer from all who preached or taught. It is true that Shirley sought and received patronage in the circle of the queen, Henrietta Maria, a Roman Catholic; but he sought and gained patronage elsewhere as well. Probably he looked for patronage where it was available, among aristocrats estimated for their means, not their faith. Relatively few of his acquaintances were known Catholics, and the rare references in his works to Catholicism are ambiguous, so critics insistent on his Catholicism are reduced to supposition and innuendo.

Wood writes that when Shirley found teaching 'uneasie to him, he retired to the *Metropolis*, lived in *Greys* inn, and set up for a play-maker' (Wood, *Ath. Oxon.*, 2.261). The birth of his first son, Mathias, was recorded at St Giles Cripplegate on 26 February 1625 and by 1627 the family had moved to Holborn near Gray's Inn, one of the four inns of court, the personal and professional quarters for the legal establishment and their literary coteries. The parish register for St Andrew's, Holborn, records the births of two more sons, Thomas and James, and one more daughter, Mary, between 1628 and 1633, along with their baptisms and the deaths of Thomas and Mary.

Early London stage career About the time Shirley moved to St Giles, at the age of twenty-eight, his career as a 'professional playwright' began. 'Professional playwright' designates both one who earned his primary livelihood writing plays for stage companies to produce for paying audiences and one whose craft was perfected through intensive study and extensive use of dramatic techniques proven popular by William Shakespeare, Ben Jonson, John Fletcher, and other forebears. In the Caroline era Shirley and his contemporaries Philip Massinger, John Ford, and Richard Brome were thereby distinguished from courtier playwrights against whom they waged poetic arguments. These gentlemen amateurs generally produced only a play or two during their active years rather than the professional average of two plays per year and relied on the expensive spectacle of elaborate stage machinery and props, rich costumes, intricate music, formal dance, and highly wrought language. Shirley and his peer 'professionals' relied more on the craft of traditional dramatic situations, characters, plotting, and language. The professionals occasionally borrowed from each other and honoured each other. Shirley provided commendatory poems for plays by each of the others and received poetic compliments from Massinger and Ford.

Shirley and his professional colleagues wrote for private playhouses. These indoor theatres, which cost about six times more for admission than public theatres, catered to a privileged, typically well-born or wealthy or educated clientele. This audience was generally sophisticated and knowledgeable in its dramatic tastes and it sustained the three playing companies for which Shirley was successively the principal playwright. His dramatic career is thus conveniently divided into the three periods when he wrote for the impresario Christopher Beeston and the company that became Queen Henrietta Maria's Men at the Phoenix or Cockpit in Drury Lane (1625–36), for John Ogilby in Dublin mainly at the St Werburgh Street Theatre, producing plays for the court of Thomas Wentworth, earl of Strafford and lord deputy of Ireland (1636–40), and finally back in London again for the King's Men at Blackfriars (1640–42).

On 11 February 1625 Sir Henry Herbert, the master of the revels, licensed Shirley's first known play, *Love's Tricks, or, The School of Compliment*, to be played at the Cockpit under the management of Christopher Beeston. Both titles characterize a play in which twin sisters love the same gentleman but, with their friend, keep mistaking the identities of different potential partners, changing among them, and among various desires, until three couples finally meander into suitable matches. Along the way they have to evade the restrictions and demands of fathers and the preferences of a mother. A bumpkin country suitor who would be a gallant, and a hopeful poet, Caperwit, supply interlocking minor plots, and a fourth mismatched couple. The play sets a characteristic beginning for Shirley's complicated romance plots, which depend on young lovers managing to come together despite blocking fathers and competing wooers, mistaken identities, manipulations, and confusions among stock characters.

The subtitle takes its name from a scene in the middle, a genial satire on characters presuming to climb the social ladder by imitating the manners and language that mark their betters. As *Love's Tricks* this first play led to others such as *The Wedding* (1626?, published 1629), *The Witty Fair One* (1628, published 1633), *The Changes, or, Love in a Maze* (1632, published 1632), *Hyde Park* (1632, published 1637), *The Bird in a Cage* (1633, published 1633), and *The Opportunity* (1634, published 1640), all plays that emphasize romantic comedy and display wit. As *The School of Compliment* Shirley's first play introduced *The Humorous Courtier* (1631, published 1640), and *The Lady of Pleasure* (1635, published 1637), plays that focus on mild satire of manners and witlessness.

Shirley's second play licensed for performance was *The Maid's Revenge* (9 February 1626) which on publication years later (in 1639) he claimed to be his second tragedy. After this play, which begins like a comedy then abruptly turns deadly, his next tragedy, *Love's Cruelty* (1631, published 1640), is also atypical. Whereas his other tragedies are based more in machiavellian court intrigues over power, *Love's Cruelty* centres on adulterous and fatal sexual compulsions. *The Traitor* (1635, published 1635) is more representative.

The Grateful Servant (1629, published 1630) was Shirley's first tragicomedy, a popular kind of play featuring a mixed tone that complicates a tragic situation rising from significant personal and social issues until it achieves a resolution dependent on miracles and charitable forgiveness. This was followed by *The Young Admiral* (1633, published 1637), *The Coronation* (1635, published 1640), and *The Duke's Mistress* (1636, published 1638). All of the plays in this first period were produced by Christopher Beeston companies except for *The Changes*, which was produced at the Salisbury Court Theatre, the third of the prestigious private indoor theatres after the King's Men's Blackfriars and Beeston's Cockpit.

Hyde Park, first performed in 1632, featured three polite competitions for women in the setting of a foot race, a horse race, and other gaming activities at the annual spring opening of the fashionable London resort. It is an outstanding representative of Shirley's comedies. The characters are subjected to a series of love tests. One lady demonstrates her enduring fidelity to her long-lost husband. Another resists the seductive wiles of an aristocratic lover until this prodigal reforms. A third beats off the advances of unscrupulous adventurers to achieve union with her gentleman lover who has learned to admire his future wife's qualities in the course of their courtship. The most distinctive trait of *Hyde Park* is the mannered language which tests all of the characters for their appropriate status.

Stock characters generally populate Shirley's plays, and are exposed through their language. These include machiavels male and female, misled princes, greedy old men, blunt soldiers, lusty and foolish young suitors, witty gentlemen and even wittier ladies, clever servants, and gullible dupes and clowns. Model characters search for some sort of distinction in manners and language, personal styles that entertainingly adapt but do not violate acceptable social and dramatic roles; occasionally they pledge avowals to virtue. Villains search for inventions to enable them to defraud others; on discovery they confess in long repentances. Satiric characters demonstrate their lack of wit and their failure to advance socially. The traits of all these characters are revealed as much by the style of the language they speak as by their actions. Heroes and heroines are adept at speaking readily, cleverly, and figuratively, what the era called *sprezzatura*. Villains use debased forms that prove self-undermining, fools use language that is trite, over elaborate, strained, obvious, and lacking in any decorum. All of these characters take time to admire their own successes and applaud or make fun of their fellows.

Towards the end of the first phase, Shirley's dramatic career culminated in the wondrously productive season of 1633–4. His *Young Admiral* received Sir Henry Herbert's warmest praise when it was licensed. 'Being free from oaths, prophaneness, or obsceanes', Herbert wrote, '[it] hath given mee much delight and satisfaction in the readinge, and may serve for a patterne to other poetts, not only for the bettring of maners and language, but for the improvement of the quality' (*Dramatic Records*, 19). Herbert arranged for a performance for Charles's birthday and reported that the king and queen liked it. The play appeals through extended set speeches that speak of high ideals and the difficult choices facing the hero, appropriately named Vittori, his father, the lady he serves, and the princess of Sicily destined for the prince of Naples, Cesario.

Like most tragicomedies, *The Young Admiral* focuses on major concerns of aristocratic adolescents making crucial choices about love and marriage and about the honour of inherited martial status. But unlike tragedies, wherein extreme ambitions and commitments result in disaster, tragicomedies are governed by charitable forgiveness and miraculous conversion; they offer hope. Prince Cesario sets *The Young Admiral* in motion through his excessive pride over Naples and his desire for a Neapolitan lady. He has insultingly rejected a Sicilian match, setting off a war. And, risking all, he has pressed his attentions on a lady promised to Admiral Vittori, a man whose naval skills are essential to the survival of Naples. He has wrongfully imprisoned Vittori's father for treason, and locked the gates of Naples against the victorious return of Vittori and the fleet. Through elaborate plot twists, various disguises and missions, and mistaken inferences, Vittori at different times is forced to choose between ideals of loyalty to country, loyalty to family, loyalty to honour, and loyalty to his lady; he faces the prospects of sacrificing his father, his lady, his country, and his own life. Repeatedly choosing self-sacrifice in fidelity to the crown even when wronged and banished, then agreeing in turn to surrender his family and his lady (whom he momentarily mistakes to be unfaithful), he exhibits the honour that makes him a man of true worth. His irascible father, his devoted lady, and the princess of Sicily who loves Cesario also prove their

nobility. So does Cesario in a final reconversion. Similar concerns with honour are reflected in a comic tributary plot.

Later that same season, 1633–4, Herbert reported that Charles thought Shirley's *Gamester* to be 'the best play he had seen for seven years'. This was scarcely a surprise as the play had come from 'a plot of the king's' supplied to Shirley by Herbert himself (*Dramatic Records*, 54–5). The play followed shortly after Shirley's production of *The Bird in a Cage*. On the title-page of that play (published 1633), Shirley is described as 'Servant to Her Majesty'. In it he offered a sarcastic dedication to William Prynne, a counter-attack on Prynne's polemic against the theatre and, perhaps inadvertently, the court, that had cost him his ears.

Masques and moral interludes In January 1634 Shirley was admitted to membership of Gray's Inn as 'one of the Valets of the Chamber of Queen Henrietta Maria' (Shirley, *Poems*, xv). He was commissioned by the inns of court to write the most expensive and elaborate masque of the time as a reconciliatory offering to the king, a presentation on 3 February 1634, that so pleased the royal couple that the king commanded a rare second performance a few days later. *The Triumph of Peace*, staged by Inigo Jones with music by leading composers William Lawes and Simon Ives, proved to be an enormous success in demonstrating the legal establishment's affection and loyalty to the king, despite the attack of Prynne, a barrister. The king was gratified by the action that depicted him bringing together peace and law in a spirit of justice, and pleased at the support of his reforms expressed in the antimasque scenes. Shirley himself, to judge by his description in the preface to the first edition, was pleased with the rank, quality, and sumptuous attire of his audience.

As Shirley's allegiance to royalism is affirmed in his masque, so his adherence to the established social hierarchy is affirmed in his moral interludes—didactic plays which presented social ethics in allegorical form. The short, early interlude *Contention for Honour and Riches* (published in 1633, and later expanded into *Honoria and Mammon*, published in 1659) focuses on relationships between the professions and the estates. The interlude features a scholar, a military officer, a courtier, a lawyer, a citizen merchant, and a bumptious country gentleman, all seeking to marry two desirable ladies, Lady Honoria and Lady Mammon. The scholar Alworth gains honour, and Colonel Conquest wins riches. The citizen and countryman show the deferential cowardice supposedly appropriate to their status, and in the interests of the commonwealth those of lesser station accede to the political visionary and state guardian. Meanwhile, the courtier shows promise in diplomacy and the lawyer reforms to promote justice rather than gain. Phantasms of a sick body politic are also portrayed and then dismissed to make way for the prophecy of a sound one.

Irish and late London stage career A period of severe plague that closed the theatres for seventeen months beginning on 12 May 1636 marks Shirley's second period. At the age of forty he moved with John Ogilby, who became master of the revels in Ireland, in the train of the lord deputy. During his four years in Dublin, Shirley not only wrote as many as eight new plays, but also wrote prefaces to the plays of John Fletcher, Ben Jonson, Thomas Middleton, and others, revised a number of plays for new productions by the St Werburgh Street Theatre, and published sixteen of his earlier plays, or revisions of them, in London. His new plays were mainly comedies, *The Constant Maid* (published 1640), *The Royal Master* (1638, published 1638), and tragicomedies, *The Doubtful Heir* (*Rosania, or, Love's Victory*, 1638?, published 1652) and *The Gentleman of Venice* (1639, published 1655). They include, however, one tragedy, *The Politician* (1639?, published 1655), and the pageant of the early life and miracles of the island's patron saint, *St Patrick for Ireland* (published 1640).

The final three years of Shirley's active playwriting career begin with his return to London in April 1640, to the King's Men and Blackfriars after the death of their principal playwright, Philip Massinger. Shirley had staged one tragicomedy, *The Imposture* (1640), and one tragedy, *The Cardinal* (1641, published 1652), when his last play, the comic *The Sisters* (1642, published 1652), appeared on stage before the civil war closed the theatres in 1642. One new tragicomedy, *The Court Secret*, was printed in 1653 but not played until the Restoration.

The Cardinal is an example of a late revenge tragedy employing a host of elements that characterize a genre popular since Kyd's *The Spanish Tragedy* in the 1580s. According to his dedication and preface, Shirley considered it among the best of his plays. Like *The Young Admiral*, *The Cardinal* focuses on honour and love, but now these are complicated by the passions of revenge. Since the play is founded in a series of vendettas, hell intervenes as well as heaven. Hell comes dressed as heaven in the Cardinal, head of a noble house, favourite of the King of Navarre, and a master machiavel. After the death of the duchess Rosaura's betrothed before consummation of the marriage, the Cardinal persuades the king to arrange her marriage to his nephew, the war hero Columbo, instead of her beloved Count d'Alvarez. When she persuades Columbo, away besieging a city, to release her from the contract, and then weds Alvarez, Columbo returns and—disguised as a player in a wedding masque—assassinates Alvarez. Then the Cardinal protects his nephew while Rosaura seeks revenge. Disguising her intention in cunning madness, she secretly allies herself with Hernando, an insulted colonel, who challenges and kills Columbo in a duel then seeks out the Cardinal, who has been made the protector of the duchess. In the final scene, the Cardinal tries to rape Rosaura, Hernando kills the Cardinal and then himself, and Rosaura is fatally poisoned in a trick devised by the Cardinal.

Shirley employed the tried techniques of revenge tragedy such as a masque murder, a deadly duel, poisoning, multiple intrigues and deceptions, spying, employment of a future lover to avenge a dead one, feigned madness, and multiple killings. He also created a pattern of imagery to complement his themes of arrogant evil and wilful pride among the high born. Both villains and victims are throughout marked by the fire and lightning, storm and fury of their wilful desires, demands, and hatreds. They seek and expect the honour due their station and their political, martial, and amatory skills. Above justice, they relentlessly pursue status and vengeance. The characters' obsession with rank, honour, and revenge is projected in images of purple and red—from the Cardinal's robes to the countess's flushed cheeks. The imagery of violence suffuses this powerful and carefully wrought play.

Quest for patronage and political stance In disillusioned retrospect Shirley believed that the depletion of élite, knowledgeable playgoers was as responsible as the civil war for closing the theatres. In 1640 in his prologue to the production by the King's Men in the Globe, a public theatre, of *Rosania*, written for the Dublin private theatre, he expressed consternation. To open 'A *Prologue at the* Globe *to his Comedy call'd* The Doubtfull Heire, *which should have been presented at the* Black-Friers', he asserts that

> Our Author did not calculate his Play,
> For this Meridian; The Bank-side he knowes
> Is far more skilful at the ebbes and flowes
> Of Water then of Wit

and he admonishes hearers to behave 'As you were now in the *Black-Friers* pit' (Shirley, *Poems*, 32). In Ireland in a prologue to *The Toy* he had lamented that plays 'Ligitimate in Art' were received as stillborn while silly spectacles won applause, even from audiences in private theatres (ibid., 30). By the prologue to *The Sisters*, the last of his plays staged before the closing of the theatres, he was deploring the fact that the King's Men could not draw a crowd for their repertory of Shakespeare, Jonson, and Fletcher, the great names of the English theatre. Thirteen years later, in his dedication (1655) of *The Politician* to the honourable Walter Moyle, esquire, he blamed the despised crowds who demanded worthless entertainment for the ban on plays.

From the late 1630s Shirley needed more patronage than before in order to survive, although he was somewhat diffident in applying for it. Some literary historians applaud the apparent indifference to patronage that Shirley expressed in his dedication of *The Maid's Revenge* to Henry Osborne in 1639: 'I never affected the ways of flattery; some say I have lost my preferment, by not practising that Court sin.' They take as evidence of lost preferment the royal appointment of Sir William Davenant as virtual laureate instead of Shirley, Herbert's censorship of the representations of polite society in the production of *The Ball*, Shirley's amiably satiric observations in *The Humorous Courtier*, *The Lady of Pleasure*, and other works during the early 1630s, and Shirley's move to Ireland. But the record shows that Shirley assiduously sought both ideological and financial support. He had strong social aspirations: the engraving of his bust in the 1659 edition of his *Contention of Ajax and Ulysses* exhibits prominently a coat of arms. The Anglican divine Abraham Wright recorded that 'I beeleeve [*The Grateful Servant* was] purposely so studied by him for to take the court' (Kirsch, 257). He assiduously sought the favour of the nobility in his dedications. *The Grateful Servant* was dedicated in 1630 to the earl of Rutland, the great-grandson of Sir Philip Sidney. In 1637 Shirley dedicated the publication of *The Young Admiral* to the learned and wealthy George, Lord Berkeley, and the same year he dedicated *Hyde Park* to Henry Hyde, earl of Holland, knight of the Garter, and member of Charles's privy council. In Ireland he dedicated *The Royal Master* to the earl of Kildare, the esteemed Irish lord; then he provided for the play a new year epilogue that praised Charles and Charles's lord deputy of Ireland, the earl of Strafford. To Strafford's son Shirley later dedicated *The Court Secret*. Other plays he dedicated to worthies who remain only tentatively identifiable by initials and status such as esquire, knight, or baronet. In 1635 Shirley made his most worthwhile dedication, of *The Traitor*, to William Cavendish, earl of Newcastle. This patron of Jonson, Ford, and Brome was to become Shirley's primary patron.

In various prefaces, most notably in his introduction to the 1647 Beaumont and Fletcher folio, Shirley commends the power of the poet to present pleasurable and profitable models of ideal courtly conduct for young gentlemen and ladies. Often in the plays he promotes the values of the élite, but at the same time he suggests through curative satire the need to correct the failures and abuses of status. That is, he presents both an imitable golden mirror and a critical steel glass. From his first monarch in *The Grateful Servant* to his last in *The Court Secret* he reaffirms a divine right of kings because loyalty to royalty and nobility appears to be the only alternative to chaos. Shirley's weak or vacillating tragicomic monarchs or tragic misled ones are typically rehabilitated and their vain or machiavellian magistrates blamed.

Repeatedly Shirley presented the related theme of the irrepressible nature of noble blood. In *The Coronation*, for example, amid political confusion caused by a machiavellian regent attempting to usurp power, royal scions unaware of their origins demonstrate their true nature by trying to rebel and to take over government, until they are recognized as rightful rulers. Similarly in *The Gentleman of Venice*, the son of a wet-nurse exchanged at birth for the true prince shows his base nature despite regal nurture, while the prince shows his regal nature despite nurture as a groundskeeper. Such exchanges and proofs hold true as well for women. In *The Sisters* the real daughter Angellina proves noble and wins a prince while her changeling 'sister' demonstrates common vanity and social climbing until she is married off to a bandit.

Shirley aims his satire at social and economic climbers. Plays such as *The Opportunity*, *The Humorous Courtier*, and *The Ball* repeatedly demonstrate that while pretenders can ape the manners of their betters, finally their origins and shameful self-seeking will be revealed. The ambitions of all the machiavellian villains of the tragedies, however harmful to others, always destroy their own pretensions to status and honour.

Revolution and Restoration After the closing of the theatres, Shirley, in his mid-forties, joined his patron William Cavendish, earl of Newcastle,

to take his fortune with him in the wars, for that Count had engaged him so much by his generous liberality towards him, that he thought he could not do a worthier act than to serve him, and so consequently his Prince. (Wood, *Ath. Oxon.*, 2.261)

Later Shirley paid a sequestration fine for his military service in the royalist cause from 1642 to 1644. It seems likely that he helped Cavendish write his play *Captain Underwood* during this period. 'After the Kings cause declined', writes Wood, Shirley 'retired obscurely to *London*, where, among other of his noted friends, he found *Tho. Stanley*, Esq' (ibid., 2.261). He seems to have returned to London and to his family about 1645. His feelings about absence from his wife may well be expressed in his poem 'To Odelia'. Shirley now became the poetic centre of a coterie promoted by Thomas Stanley, in which he was able to show his loyalty to the royalist cause during its eclipse. He contributed a poetic commendation to Stanley's *Poems* of 1647, an epithalamion for Stanley's wedding in 1648, and a dedication to Stanley's publication of *The Brothers* in 1652.

In his poem 'On a Black Ribband' Shirley flaunted his fidelity to the royalist cause by speaking of his pride in wearing a black armband as a sign of sympathy with the king's troubles. This poem was published in the 1646 edition of his *Poems*, a volume that was fronted by an engraving of the poet by William Marshall, and included verses of cavalier gallantry, songs, prologues, and epilogues from plays, and a masque. Some scholars are inclined to infer from certain lyrics in the volume that Shirley's wife had recently died. In 1647 Shirley was chosen to address readers of the third great folio of English renaissance plays, that of Beaumont and Fletcher. In the troubled time before the execution of Charles I, this folio served to rally the royalists of England with a nostalgic recollection of the theatrical achievements of the Stuart age.

Some time during the period of Stanley's patronage, Shirley resumed his long-interrupted career as a schoolmaster. One consequence of this move was his publication of two Latin grammars, the *Via ad Latinam* (1649) and the *Rudiments of Grammar* (1656), later expanded. About this time he composed and revised several masques and interludes appropriate for schoolboys. One of these masques was *Cupid and Death*, written originally for private performance some time between 1651 and 1653. This masque in a more elaborate form was presented as an entertainment for the Portuguese ambassador who had come to negotiate a treaty of amity with Cromwell's government. Accompanied by fine new music by Matthew Locke and Christopher Gibbons, enlivened by dances by Luke Channen, and fitted out with splendid scenery, *Cupid and Death* was performed, probably at Whitehall, on 26 March 1653, an unexpected revival of the masque in Commonwealth England. The action, in which Cupid and Death lodge at the same inn for the night, and their arrows become exchanged, so that thereafter Cupid's targets die and Death's victims become rejuvenated, seems to have been a nostalgic allusion to the old Caroline court world disrupted by the ravages of civil war. The masque was revived for a public performance in 1659.

In the mid-1650s, when he was about sixty years old, Shirley married a widow, Frances Blackburne. The retirement of the schoolteacher was not as complete as Wood averred, however, as Shirley actively published his plays as well as the grammars and masques. The publication of eight unpublished plays began with the important *Six New Plays* of 1653 that includes a valuable 'Catalogue' that identifies Shirley's plays. After the Restoration Shirley saw a number of his plays reproduced in print and, more importantly, in the repertories of the re-established theatrical companies.

Shirley's end was hastened, in the autumn of 1666, by the great fire of London. Wood records that Shirley and his wife

> were driven by the dismal conflagration that hapned in *London* an. 1666, from their habitation near to *Fleetstreet*, into the Parish of *St. Giles in the Fields* in *Middlesex*, where being in a manner overcome with affrightments, disconsolations, and other miseries occasion'd by that fire and their losses, they both died within the compass of a natural day: whereupon their bodies were buried in one grave in the yard belonging to the said church of S. *Giles* on the 29 of *Octob*. (Wood, *Ath. Oxon.*, 2.262)

In a will the previous July Shirley testified to considerably more wealth than could have been anticipated for a poet and schoolmaster, leaving belongings to his widow, three sons, two daughters and sons-in-law, one grandchild, and several friends.

Shirley's career flowered in the Indian summer of the Caroline stage. During the civil war years and the Commonwealth he struggled to survive, lacking the theatre or suitable patronage, and ill at ease in a republican setting. 1660 brought only a partial restoration of his fortunes, but his works remain a highly expressive record of the fashionable world of late Caroline England. Although his reputation declined—he was charged with dullness by Dryden in *Mac Flecknoe*—Shirley's plays continued to be plundered for the stage into the eighteenth century, and they have been republished and read ever since. The hybrid tragicomedy was predominant among new plays when Shirley was writing and its vogue continued throughout the century. Tragedies dominated tastes in the era before Shirley wrote and again in the nineteenth and early twentieth centuries. But it was his social and romantic comedies that were most appreciated in the Caroline era, the Restoration, and again in the last half of the twentieth century.   IRA CLARK

Sources G. E. Bentley, *The Jacobean and Caroline stage*, 7 vols. (1941–68), vol. 5, pp. 1064–170 · A. H. Nason, *James Shirley dramatist: a biographical and critical study* (1915) · S. A. Burner, *James Shirley: a study of literary coteries and patronage in seventeenth-century England* (1988) · J. Shirley, *The poems of James Shirley*, ed. R. L. Armstrong (1941) · *The dramatic works and poems of James Shirley*, ed. W. Gifford, 6 vols. (1833); repr. (New York, 1966) · Wood, *Ath. Oxon.*, 1st edn, 2.260–62 · *The dramatic records of Sir Henry Herbert, master of the revels, 1623–1673*, ed. J. Q. Adams (1917) · A. C. Baugh, 'Some new facts about Shirley', *Modern Language Review*, 17 (1922), 228–35 · A. C. Baugh, 'Further facts about James Shirley', *Review of English Studies*, 7 (1931), 62–6 · A. H. Stevenson, 'James Shirley and the actors at the first Irish theater', *Modern Philology*, 40 (1942–3), 147–60 · A. H. Stevenson, 'Shirley's years in Ireland', *Review of English Studies*, new ser., 20 (1944), 19–28 · R. K. Zimmer, *James Shirley: a reference guide* (1980) · B. Lucow, *James Shirley* (1981) · I. Clark, *Professional playwrights: Massinger, Ford, Shirley, and Brome* (1992) · G. Bas, 'The misrepresented biographical documents concerning James Shirley', *Review of English Studies*, new ser., 27 (1976), 303–10 · J. P. Feil, 'James Shirley's years of service', *Review of English Studies*, new ser., 8 (1957), 413–16 · G. E. Bentley, *The profession of dramatist in Shakespeare's time, 1590–1642* (1971) · A. C. Kirsch, 'A Caroline commentary on the drama', *Modern Philology*, 66 (1968–9), 256–61 · R. S. Forsythe, *The relations of Shirley's plays to the Elizabethan drama* (1914) · M. Butler, *Theatre and crisis, 1632–1642* (1984) · D. B. J. Randall, *Winter fruit: English drama, 1642–1660* (1995) · M. Butler, 'Politics and the masque: *The triumph of peace*', *Seventeenth Century*, 2 (1987), 117–41 · L. Venuti, 'The politics of allusion: the gentry and Shirley's *The triumph of peace*', *English Literary Renaissance*, 16 (1986), 182–205

Likenesses W. Marshall, line engraving, 1646, NPG · R. Gaywood, etching, pubd 1653 (after G. Phenik), BM, NPG; repro. in J. Shirley, *Six plays* (1653) · oils, Bodl. Oxf. [*see illus.*]

Wealth at death £950—cornelian seal ring, silver watch, clothing, silver ring with 'Turkey stones', small diamond, plus more estate (at one time a home and property), plate, money, jewels, linens, bedding, brass, pewter, etc.: will dated July 1666 entered with deletions/changes, probate records 3 Nov 1666. The will is quoted and documented in Nason, 158–60, according to Beal, *Index*, a little inaccurately

Shirley, John (*c.*1366–1456), author, translator, and scribe, is recorded in the early years of the fifteenth century in the service of Richard Beauchamp (*d.* 1439), who became earl of Warwick in 1401. In 1403 Shirley was in Warwick's retinue in the campaign against Owain Glyn Dŵr; in 1414 he collected wages from the exchequer for Warwick's retinue in France (the first of a number of such missions) and is specified as the earl's secretary in 1420–21. Warwick returned to England between 1428 and 1430 as tutor to Henry VI, from whom Shirley, as one of two recipients noted as being with the earl, received a new year's gift in 1428. In June 1428 Shirley and other members of the Beauchamp family and household were admitted together to confraternity of St Albans Abbey. On later occasions, often in connection with members of the Beauchamp household, Shirley is described as esquire of London. In 1432–3 he was comptroller of petty customs in the port of London, and in 1436 he was recorded in the London subsidy as having an income of £10 from lands in Hertfordshire. When Warwick and his wife both died in 1439, Shirley was still in their service. Shirley is mentioned in various legal and property transactions, noted as tenant of a house near St Bartholomew's Hospital from about 1438 in a document of 1444. In his will, dated 1 November 1452, Shirley asked to be buried in the lady chapel at St Bartholomew's, near his mother and first wife, Elizabeth. His second wife, Margaret, survived him. The will names executors, including John Wakering, master of St Bartholomew's Hospital (1423–66), John Cok, priest and brother of St Bartholomew's, Richard Caudray, dean of St Martin's-le-Grand, and Edward Norys, citizen and scrivener of London. Shirley died on 21 October 1456 and was buried at St Bartholomew's Hospital. His epitaph was recorded by the Elizabethan antiquary John Stow, who later owned several manuscripts copied by or associated with Shirley.

Between about 1438 and his death Shirley also rented four shops from St Bartholomew's Hospital in Doke Lane and on the basis of manuscripts copied for him, or in his hand or clearly associable with him, some have speculated that Shirley ran a scriptorium, lending library, or some other sort of book business based in these properties. Shirley certainly both translated works from French and Latin and appears to have collected and annotated copies of contemporary vernacular authors, such as Chaucer and Lydgate, providing versified tables of contents and other commentaries to certain compilations. He received at least one set of verses from Richard Sellyng to correct. The surviving manuscripts associated with Shirley can be categorized in three groups: those in Shirley's own hand; those that passed through his hands and were annotated by him; and those apparently derived from manuscripts probably owned or annotated by him. Manuscripts copied by Shirley or containing substantial items in his hand: Cambridge, Trinity College, MS R.3.20; BL, Add. MS 16165, and Harley MS 78, folios 80r–83v; London, Sion College, MS Arc. L.40.2/E.44; Bodl. Oxf., MS Ashmole 59; San Marino, Huntington Library, MS EL 26.A.13. Manuscripts annotated by Shirley or containing his distinctive mark of ownership and motto, a crowned A with the words *ma ioye* or other mottoes: Cambridge, Corpus Christi College, MS 61; Cambridge, Gonville and Caius College, MS 669*/646; CUL, MS Ff.1.33; BL, Royal MS 20 B.xv; LUL, MS 1; New Haven, Yale University Library, Osborn MS a 29; Tokyo, priv. coll. ('Master of game'). Manuscripts apparently or possibly derived in part from exemplars written or annotated by Shirley: Cambridge, Trinity College, MSS R.3.19 and R.3.21; Cambridge, Mass., Harvard University, Houghton Library, MS Eng 530; BL, Add. MSS 5467 and 34360, Cotton MS Titus A.xxvi, Harley MSS 2251 and 7333.

JEREMY GRIFFITHS

Sources A. I. Doyle, 'More light on John Shirley', *Medium Aevum*, 30 (1961), 93–101 · J. Boffey and J. J. Thompson, 'Anthologies and miscellanies: production and choice of texts', *Book production and publishing in Britain, 1375–1475*, ed. J. Griffiths and D. Pearsall (1989), 279–315 · A. Brusendorff, *The Chaucer tradition* (1925), 207ff., 453ff. · M. Connolly, 'The dethe of the kynge of Scotis: a new edition', *SHR*, 71 (1992), 46–69 · J. Griffiths, 'A newly identified manuscript inscribed by John Shirley', *The Library*, 6th ser., 14 (1992), 83–93 · E. P. Hammond, *English verse between Chaucer and Surrey* (1927), 191–7 · N. Moore, *The history of St Bartholomew's Hospital*, 2 (1918), 34ff. · M. A. Manzalaoui, ed., *Secretum secretorum*, EETS, old ser., 276 (1977), xxxvii–xxxix, 227–313 · J. Stow, *A survay of London*, rev. edn (1603); repr. with introduction by C. L. Kingsford as *A survey of London*, 2 vols. (1908); repr. with addns (1971), 2.23–4, 360–61
Archives BL, Add. MS 16165 · BL, Harley MS 78, fols. 80r–83v · BL, Royal MS 20 B.xv · Bodl. Oxf., MS Ashmole 59 · CCC Cam., MS 61 · CUL, MS Ff.1.33 · GL, Sion College MS Arc. L.40.2/E.44 · Gon. & Caius Cam., MS 669*/646 · Hunt. L., MS EL 26.A.13 · LUL, MS 1 · Trinity Cam., MS R.3.20 · Yale U., Osborn MS a 29

Shirley, John (*bap.* 1648, *d.* 1679), author, was baptized at St Botolph, Aldersgate, London, on 18 August 1648, one of the sons of John Shirley, bookseller, and his wife, Anne. He matriculated from Trinity College, Oxford, on 17 March 1665, becoming a scholar in 1667. He graduated BA on 18 February 1668 and proceeded MA on 28 November 1671. His ability was soon recognized and, according to his brother Benjamin, he wrote a life of Sir Walter Ralegh as the preface to an edition of Ralegh's *History of the World*. In 1673 he acted as *terrae filius*, a privileged orator of the university, and was made a fellow of his college. But within the probationary period he was expelled for immoral conduct and returned to London. He married the daughter of an innkeeper of Islington and made his living by writing and by correcting for the press. He died in Islington on 28 December 1679 and was buried there on 30 December.

He was not the only John Shirley writing at that time. **John Shirley** (*fl.* 1678–1682), author, who claimed to be a doctor of medicine, wrote two medical books, *A Short Compendium of Chirurgery* (1678) and *The Art of Rowling and Bolstring* (1682), providing advice on how to deal with wounds, ulcers, and fractures.

John Shirley (*fl.* 1685–1688), writer, was author of *The Famous History of Palmerin of England* (1685), an adventure story with a hero fighting giants and wild bears while crossing Europe, and two lively popular works in praise of women, *The Illustrious History of Women* (1686) and *The Triumph of Wit* (1688), which had reached an eighth edition by 1724. His name occurs with the preface to *A true account of the enterprise of the confederate princes against the Turks and Hungarian rebels* (1685). That work was published by William Thackery, Duck Lane, London, who also published many works by **John Shurley** (*fl.* 1681–1702), writer, who sometimes used the name of J. S. Gent. His range of works included an account of the life of Guy, earl of Warwick (1681), the story of Reynard the fox in heroic verse (1681), *Ecclesiastical History Epitomized* (1682), an account of the life of Jesus, and *Visions of Don Francisco de Quevedo Vellegass* (1682). *The Compleat Courtier, or, Cupid's Academy* (1683) provided a popular lively collection of love songs, poems, epistles, and dialogue, and his *Young Man's Resolution of the Maiden's Request* (1695) followed a similar theme. His final work, an abridgement by J. S. Gent, was the *History of the Renowned and Valiant Prince Amadi of Gaul* (1702).

F. D. A. BURNS

Sources Wood, *Ath. Oxon.*, new edn · Foster, *Alum. Oxon.*, 1500–1714, vol. 4 · *BL cat.* · *IGI* [St Botolph Aldersgate parish register]

Shirley, John (*fl.* **1678–1682**). *See under* Shirley, John (*bap.* 1648, *d.* 1679).

Shirley, Laurence, fourth Earl Ferrers (**1720–1760**), murderer, was born on 18 August 1720, the eldest son of Laurence Shirley (1693–1743) and his wife, Anne (*d.* 1782), fourth daughter of Sir Walter Clarges, first baronet. His father was the fourth son of Robert Shirley, first Earl Ferrers. Laurence matriculated at Christ Church, Oxford, in 1737, but did not take a degree. He succeeded to the peerage and estates on the death in 1745 of his uncle Henry, third Earl Ferrers, who had been confined as a lunatic. He was inactive in the Lords, but did enter a protest against the war in Flanders on 2 May 1746, and another against the bill for the abolition of heritable jurisdictions in Scotland on 21 May 1747. On 16 September 1752 he married Mary (1737/8?–1807), fifth daughter of Amos Meredith, of Henbury, Cheshire, and sister of Sir William *Meredith, third baronet. The marriage was childless. He was an aggressive

Laurence Shirley, fourth Earl Ferrers (1720–1760), by Anthony Walker

husband who imprisoned his wife in his house at Staunton Harold in Leicestershire until the king's bench with difficulty obtained her release. The London consistory court took the severe step of excommunicating him for contempt in 1757 after his wife had initiated a separation suit in that court. She separated from him on the grounds of his cruelty, by act of parliament, in 1758. Thereafter he lived at Staunton Harold with his mistress, 'Mrs' Margaret Clifford, whose father, Richard Clifford, farmed nearby at Breedon. Ferrers and his mistress had four daughters.

Although often lucid and businesslike, Ferrers had phases during which he was distracted or ungovernably excited. In these fits his gesticulation, grimacing, and suspicion of secret plots were wild. He became so overwrought after quarrelling with Sir Thomas Stapleton in 1758 that his family considered taking out a commission of lunacy against him. In addition to his brutal temper, he was prone to other freaks of behaviour. Under the act of separation of 1758 Ferrers's estates were vested in trustees, and John Johnson, who had been in the service of the Shirleys for many years, was appointed receiver of the rents. Ferrers developed an obsessive resentment of his steward, and on 18 January 1760 shot him with a pistol in a locked room at Staunton Harold. Johnson languished for a day before dying. The crime was premeditated, and afterwards Ferrers, both sober and drunk, upbraided Johnson as a villain. On 19 January the earl was spotted crossing his bowling green, armed with a blunderbuss, dagger, and pistols, trying to escape the crowd of colliers that had come to detain him. He was apprehended, and after examination at the bar of the House of Lords (13 February) was committed as a prisoner in the Tower of London.

Ferrers's trial by his peers began on 16 April in Westminster Hall. At his brothers' prompting, he tried to escape a capital sentence by arguing that he was periodically insane, and not responsible for his actions at the time of the murder. He called the Bethlem doctor John Monro as an expert witness, whose testimony raised important issues of criminal responsibility and lunacy. Horace Walpole, who attended the trial, described its 'pomp and awfulness' to George Montagu.

> In general he behaved rationally and coolly; though it was a strange contradiction to see a man trying by his own sense to prove himself out of his senses. It was more shocking to see his two brothers brought to prove the lunacy in their own blood, in order to save their brother's life. Both are almost as ill-looking men as the Earl. (Walpole, *Corr.*, 9.279)

Despite his efforts, on 17 April the Lords unanimously found Ferrers guilty of felony and murder. The next day the lord keeper, Robert Henley, first Baron Henley, acting as lord high steward, sentenced him to death. The grandeur and solemnity of the occasion were impressive despite the 'modish' nature of some spectators. According to Elizabeth Montagu, 'ladies crowded to the House of Lords to see a wretch brought loaded with crime and shame to the bar, to hear sentence of a cruel and ignominious death; which, considering only this world, cast shame back on his ancestors, and all his succeeding family' (*Letters*, 4.261–2). During the trial and after his conviction he was regularly visited by his cousin Selina Hastings, countess of Huntingdon, the prominent Methodist, who concerned herself with his spiritual welfare, and prevented him from seeing his mistress before his execution.

Ferrers was hanged on 5 May at Tyburn gallows. William Hickey attended the execution:

> His lordship was conveyed to Tyburn in his own landau, dressed in a superb suit of white and silver, being the clothes in which he was married, his reason for wearing which was that they had been his first step towards ruin, and should attend his exit. (*Memoirs of William Hickey*, 1.20)

According to Walpole, 'this horrid lunatic ... shamed heroes' in his final comportment. 'He was stopped at the gallows by the vast crowd, but got out of his coach as soon as he could, and was but seven minutes on the scaffold, which was hung with black ... The mob was decent, admired him, and almost pitied him' (Walpole, *Corr.*, 9.283). The tradition that Ferrers was hanged by a silk cord instead of a hemp rope was denied by the *Dictionary of National Biography*, and is not mentioned by any of the eyewitness accounts, but has become part of the mythologized story of the execution. His remains were dissected by anatomists before burial under the belfry at St Pancras, but were reinterred at Staunton Harold on 3 June 1782.

Ferrers was said to have left £4000 in East India Company bonds for the benefit of his mistress, Margaret Clifford, and their children, and to the family of his victim, Johnson. Johnson's family were also made the beneficiaries of £6000 raised from Ferrers's estate and held in trust for their use. Ferrers's wife married, on 28 March 1769, at St Martin-in-the-Fields, Lord Frederick *Campbell (1729–1816), and was killed in a fire, supposedly caused by an accident with a light while she was reading in bed, at Coombe Bank, Kent, on 26 July 1807.

Ferrers's brother **Washington Shirley**, fifth Earl Ferrers (1722–1778), naval officer, was born on 26 May 1722, and entered the navy around 1738. He was made second lieutenant on 6 January 1741, promoted first lieutenant on 9 January 1746, and post captain on 19 April 1746. On 1 December 1747 he married Anne (1722/3–1791), daughter of John Elliot, of Plymouth, Devon, at St George's, East Stonehouse, Devon. He took his seat in the House of Lords a fortnight after his brother's execution (19 May 1760), and by a patent of 6 December 1763 George III granted to him the family estates which had been forfeited by his brother as a felon. This patent was confirmed by act of parliament in 1771. Ferrers was promoted rear-admiral of the white on 31 March, vice-admiral of the blue on 7 December 1775, and vice-admiral of the white on 29 January 1778. Casanova, visiting London, was surprised that he was not 'dishonoured' (Casanova, 5.203), or ostracized, as a result of his brother's crime.

In 1763 Ferrers began to transform his seat at Staunton Harold, which in its location and surroundings is an exceptionally pure example of rural England. The Shirley family had lived there since the fifteenth century. He remodelled the north front, extended the east front, and added a south front. The exterior style of the house is Palladian, with widely spaced windows and Doric columns, but the interior has many neo-classical features. He retained the Gothic chapel, built during the Commonwealth, standing at an angle to the house on the southeast, adding to the air of calm and measured beauty. The overall effect is highly accomplished if, as seems likely, Ferrers was his own architect. At the time of his death these alterations were almost complete. The old formal gardens, with basins and canals, were also replaced by fashionable landscaping with two lakes. These improvements were partly financed by sales during the mid-1760s and in 1775 of ancestral properties in Northamptonshire and Derbyshire.

Ferrers was evidently a virtuoso among admirals, for he was elected FRS in 1761 as recognition of his observations on the transit of Venus and for other mathematical investigations. He was grand master of the freemasons (1762–4). He died on 1 October 1778 at Chartley Manor Place, Staffordshire, the ancient home of the Ferrers family, and was buried on 11 October at Staunton Harold. His wife died at Hampton Court, Middlesex, on 26 March 1791. They had no children, and Ferrers was succeeded in the earldom and estates by his brother Robert (1723–1787). Another brother was the Methodist preacher Walter *Shirley (1725–1786).　　　　　　RICHARD DAVENPORT-HINES

Sources State trials · The trial of Lawrence, Earl Ferrers for the murder of John Johnson (1760) · An account of the late Lawrence, Earl Ferrers (1760) · Earl Ferrers's trial (1760) · A. Knapp and W. Baldwin, The Newgate calendar, comprising interesting memoirs of the most notorious characters, 2 (1825) · J. Coote, Memoirs of Lord Ferrers (1760) · J. Andrews and A. Scull, eds., Undertaker of the mind (2001), 193–225 · 'Unhappy affair of the Earl Ferrers', London Magazine (April 1760), 206–7 · Walpole, Corr., vols. 9, 21 · Memoirs of William Hickey, ed. A. Spencer, 1 (1913) · Letters of Mrs. Elizabeth Montagu, 4 (1813) · J. Casanova, The memoirs of Jacques Casanova de Seingalt, ed. A. Machen, 5 (1960) · Quispian, 'The memoir of a wicked nobleman', Temple Bar, 53 (1878), 316–33 · Country Life (5 April 1913), 490–96 · Country Life (12 April 1913), 526–33 · DNB · Burke, Peerage (1999)

Archives Leics. RO, accounts and papers, incl. orders [Washington Shirley] · Leics. RO, corresp. | PRO, KB 1/12, 1/13 · PRO, KB 33/20/3 · PRO, DL/C/554/073 · Staffs. RO, Chartley and Staunton Harold estate papers

Likenesses engraving, 1760, repro. in Royal Magazine, 2 (1760), 226 · etching, c.1760, Bodl. Oxf., bookstack Vet d 782; repro. in Andrews and Scull, eds., Undertaker, 194 · engraving, 1825, repro. in Knapp and Baldwin, The Newgate calendar, 275 · Audran, line engraving, BM, NPG; repro. in J. Caulfield, Portraits of remarkable persons from … 1688 to the end of the reign of George II, 4 vols. (1819–20) · R. Carriera, pastel drawing; on loan to Leicester Museum · Roberts, line engraving (after Vangro), NPG · Valois, line engraving, BM, NPG · A. Walker, etching (after unknown artist), NPG [see illus.] · A. Walker, line engraving, NPG · etching (in white satin-lined coffin, after being taken down from the scaffold), repro. in Royal Magazine, 2 (1760), 230 · etching, NPG

Shirley, Sir Robert, Count Shirley in the papal nobility (c.1581–1628), diplomat, was born at the family estate of Wiston in Sussex, the youngest son and one of nine children of Sir Thomas *Sherley (c.1542–1612) and Anne (d. 1623), daughter of Sir Thomas Kempe of Ollantighe, Kent. While details of his education are unclear, given the state of the family fortune by the early 1590s it is unlikely that it was as rigorous as that of his elder brothers, Sir Thomas *Sherley (1564–1633/4) and Sir Anthony *Sherley (1565–1636?). He certainly did not attend university, for in 1598 he was resident at the court of Ferdinand, grand duke of Tuscany, where he had been for five years.

When Anthony Sherley's scheme to incite war over Ferrara collapsed in 1598, Robert Shirley travelled to Venice to join him. Seduced by stories of Persia's wealth, about May 1599 the brothers sought passage on an Italian merchantman bound for Aleppo. But, with poor weather impeding their progress and with tempers running high, an altercation broke out after Anthony had one of the Italian crew flogged for insulting the queen. The situation escalated when Shirley gave the ship's captain a 'sound boxe' (Parry, 5–6) after the latter tried to reassert his authority. Bloodshed was averted only when Italian merchants on board suggested that the English be left at Zante. The party finally reached Aleppo in September; from there they travelled overland to Qazvin in Persia, where they arrived in December.

After a series of meetings with Shah ʿAbbas I through the spring of 1600, Anthony was dispatched to negotiate an alliance with the princes of Europe against the Turks; Robert remained behind as a hostage. Initially he was treated well and seems to have helped the shah reorganize his army. Probably about 1603, while in the shah's service, he was converted to Catholicism by the Augustinian friar Antonio de Gouveia. By 1605 though, with no news from Anthony, the shah became markedly cooler towards his guest; in a letter to his brother dated 10 September 1606 Shirley lamented that he was esteemed little more than 'a common liar' (*CSP col.*, 2, no. 353). In February 1608 he married Sampsonia (*c*.1590–1668), the daughter of a Christian Circassian chieftan, Isma'il Khan. She was baptized by the Carmelites and given the name Teresa.

Having heard nothing from Anthony in seven years, 'Abbas selected Shirley to lead a second embassy to Europe. The Shirleys left Persia on 12 February 1608, and in the autumn reached Cracow, where they wintered at the court of Sigismund III. With Teresa housed in a Polish convent, Shirley continued on to Prague, where he was received by Emperor Rudolf II, who knighted him and made him a count palatine in June 1609. After a month in Florence, Shirley entered Rome on 27 September 1609, dressed in his characteristic Persian garb, a gold crucifix affixed to his turban. When he met Pope Paul V two days later he delivered a letter from the shah urging the pope to induce the princes of Christendom to unite and fight the Turks. For his efforts, the pope created Robert a count of the Lateran.

From Rome, Shirley continued to Spain where he met Philip III in January 1610. However, the king regarded the shah's suggestion that the Spanish attack the Turks through Aleppo and Anatolia coolly. With commercial negotiations between the two realms proceeding slowly, in May Shirley sent to Poland for his wife. However, his standing as an emissary was undermined in February 1611 by the arrival of a new Persian ambassador, Dengil Beg Rumlu. Thus in the summer of 1611 Shirley and the pregnant Teresa left Spain, reaching England in August. On 1 October Shirley was received by James I at Hampton Court, where they discussed the shah's offer to give English merchants free use of two Persian ports and a monopoly over the Persian silk trade. While James himself was not uninterested in the idea of an alliance with Persia, given that the scheme was calculated by the shah to redirect the silk trade away from the Turks, it was opposed by the Levant Company. A month later, on 4 November 1611, Shirley announced the birth of his first and only child, a son, who was named Henry.

Although negotiations dragged on into 1612, news of peace between the Turks and Persians rendered Shirley's mission moot. Thus in January 1613, leaving Henry at Wiston, he and his wife boarded *The Expedition* to return to Persia, resolving to sail to Gwatar Bay in Baluchistan and then travel overland back to Esfahan. However, when they landed in August they overheard a plot to kill their party and to loot their baggage. They were forced to sail east down the coast to the mouth of the Indus, where they disembarked in late September 1613. Here they only narrowly escaped a conspiracy orchestrated by the Portuguese in collusion with the local viceroy to blow up their lodgings in Tatta. Determined to seek redress for his injuries from the Mughal emperor, in the spring of 1614 Shirley travelled to Ajmer. There he was well received by Jahangir

and met Thomas Kerridge, factor of the East India Company in Surat, to whom he furnished a description of the Persian ports suitable for English ships along the Arabian Sea. At the end of September he joined a caravan bound for Persia and, about Christmas near Lahore, he met Thomas Coryate. The party finally reached Esfahan in March 1615.

Shirley did not remain in Persia long, for in the summer 'Abbas asked him to return to Europe, this time to reassure the Spanish while the shah sought the support of a maritime power to help against the Portuguese at Hormoz. Reluctantly Shirley agreed to go. However, before he left he helped Richard Steel and John Crouther, the first representatives of the East India Company to reach Persia, to secure a series of trade concessions. After boarding a Portuguese ship in November, Shirley and his wife arrived in Goa in late February 1616 but had missed the annual convoy for Spain. Delayed in Goa for another year, it was not until September 1617 that they finally reached Spain, where they remained engaged in fruitless negotiations until 1622.

Shirley and his wife left Spain in March 1622 and were in Rome by the end of July. Here, in full Persian dress, they both sat for paintings by Sir Anthony Van Dyck. Details of Shirley's activities over the next year are decidedly sketchy; however, he does seem to have had an audience with the emperor in Vienna in late 1622.

Late in 1623 the Shirleys arrived in England and on 28 January 1624 Shirley was granted an audience with the king in which he proposed a scheme which would effectively secure for the English a monopoly over the Persian silk trade. While James liked the idea, the merchants of the East India and Levant companies seriously doubted the capacity of the European market to absorb the volume of silk the shah proposed to export and felt that such a scheme would damage irreparably their Indian and Turkish trade.

Through the rest of 1624 and until James's death in March 1625 tensions between the king and the companies ran high over the scheme, the king going so far as proposing to venture personally into the Persian trade. While Charles I also expressed interest, Shirley's position was seriously compromised by the arrival, in February 1626, of a second emissary from the shah, Naqd Ali Beg. However, when the two ambassadors met in early March Naqd Ali Beg attacked Shirley, beating him severely. As a result, Charles resolved to send Sir Dodmore Cotton to Persia as an envoy; Shirley was to accompany him as a private citizen in order to clear his name. To this end the king demanded that the company transport Shirley's party to the Persian Gulf with its next India fleet. However, when the party arrived in Deal on 20 April 1626, they found the company's ships had already left. After a further year in England, Cotton, Shirley, and his wife boarded *The Star* in March 1627 for the voyage to Persia. Naqd Ali Beg returned home on *The Hart* only to die from an overdose of opium on 30 November, the day before the fleet reached Swally Road.

It was not until May 1628 that Shirley finally reached

Ashraf, where he was favourably received by the shah late in the month. Although he followed when the shah moved his court to Qazvin in June, he had no further audience with the potentate. Suffering from a fever, Robert died on 13 July 1628 at Qazvin, where he was buried by his friends under the threshold of his house. Lady Shirley left Persia shortly afterwards and stayed in Constantinople for three years before retiring to Rome in December 1634. In 1658 she had her husband's remains reburied in the church of Santa Maria in Trastevere, where she herself was buried in 1668.   RICHARD RAISWELL

Sources W. Parry, *A new and large discourse of the travels of Sir Anthony Sherley, knight, by sea, and over land, to the Persian empire* (1601) · T. Herbert, *A relation of some yeares travaile* (1634) · A. Nixon, *The three English brothers* (1607) · *Chronicle of the Carmelites in Persia* (1939) · *CSP col.*, vols. 1–4 · *CSP dom.*, 1547–1631 · *CSP Venice, 1610–29* · T. Middleton, *Sir Robert Sherley, sent ambassador in the name of the king of Persia to Sigismond the third, king of Poland and Swecia* (1609) · B. Penrose, *The Shirleian odyssey being a record of the travels and adventures of three famous brothers during the reigns of Elizabeth, James I, and Charles I* (1938) · D. W. Davies, *Elizabethans errant: the strange fortunes of Sir Thomas Sherley and his three sons* (1967)
Archives Bodl. RH, journal of voyage to Persia as ambassador
Likenesses D. de Astor, engraving, 1609, BM · A. Van Dyck, oils, 1622, Petworth House, Sussex · M. Greuter, line engraving, BM · P. Oliver, miniature, Buccleuch estates, Selkirk · oils, Berkeley Castle, Gloucestershire

Shirley, Sir Robert, fourth baronet (1629–1656), royalist conspirator, was the second son of Sir Henry *Shirley, second baronet (1589–1633), of Eatington, Warwickshire, and Staunton Harold, Leicestershire, and his wife, Dorothy Devereux (1600–1636) [*see* Stafford, Lady Dorothy], second daughter of Robert Devereux, second earl of Essex. A descendant of the ancient family seated at Eatington, his father and grandparents were recusants, but he was brought up within the Church of England by his mother. He was admitted to Corpus Christi College, Cambridge, on 12 August 1645. The following year, on the death of his elder brother, Charles, he inherited the baronetcy and also married, against the wishes of his family, Katharine (d. 1672), daughter of Humphrey Okeover, of Okeover, Staffordshire. They would have five children.

Following the death of his uncle, the earl of Essex, Shirley received a moiety of the large possessions of the Devereux family in England and Ireland. After the execution of Charles I he worked in close contact with those aiming for the restoration of monarch and church. He first clashed with the government in 1648 when he confronted soldiers at the parliamentary garrison at Ashby-de-la-Zouch. His association with Staffordshire opponents of the republican regime led to his first imprisonment in the Tower of London on 4 May 1650 and the sequestration of his estates, though he was soon released and the sequestration lifted. In 1654 he was involved in attending secret meetings to support the exiled king by royalists living in the midland counties, and had become the 'chief man in the Royalist organization' in his area (Underdown, 144), and a recipient of arms. He was again arrested and sent to the Tower. While there he was appointed the royalists' financial agent, having already given substantial sums for the king's service. From there too, in 1656, he

drew up proposals for royalist reorganization on the basis of complete identification of the royal cause with the Church of England, urging that 'whosoever in these times of persecution professes himself a son of the Church will also by the same principles be a loyal subject'. With clergy acting as agents, bishops would be required to resume their episcopal responsibilities, and the laity must refuse any ministry by ministers lacking episcopal ordination. Weekly communions were advocated, as were alms to provide for the support of the clergy, but the proposals failed to bear fruit.

Shirley had sheltered, supported, and employed as his chaplains many of the deprived clergy, among them Robert Mapletoft, Gilbert Sheldon, Henry Hammond, and Peter Gunning. From 1653 he rebuilt the church at Staunton Harold in pure Gothic. The inscription noted 'In the year 1653 when all things Sacred were throughout the nation Either demolisht or profaned Sir Robert Shirley Barronet, Founded this Church; whose singular praise it is to have done the best thing in the worst times and hoped them in the most callamitous' (Lacy, 25). Although he died before the whole church was finished he left explicit instructions in his will as to how the church, the interior especially, should be completed.

A few days before his death in the Tower on 28 November 1656, probably of smallpox, Shirley set apart £600 per annum for the king's cause. The funeral oration by Sheldon, his chaplain, had an apt text, Luke 7: 5, 'He loved our nation and he hath built us a synagogue'. He was buried on 22 December at the church at Breedon on the Hill, Leicestershire, the burial place of his ancestors, and in 1661 his remains were removed to Staunton Harold and buried in the chancel of Holy Trinity Church. In his will he sought to ensure that any profits he had made from church lands or tithes were shared among the distressed orthodox clergy. Writing to Secretary Nicholas on 17 December 1656 Hyde expressed his hopes that 'the news may not be true of the honest gentleman in the Tower, whose loss at this time cannot be repaired' (*Clarendon State Papers*, 3.215).   M. DORMAN

Sources A. C. Lacy, 'Sir Robert Shirley and the English revolution in Leicestershire', *Leicestershire Archaeological and Historical Society Transactions*, 58 (1982–3), 25–35 · E. P. Shirley, ed., *Stemmata Shirleiana* (1841), 48, 109–21 · D. Underdown, *Royalist conspiracy in England, 1649–1660* (1960) · R. S. Bosher, *The making of the Restoration settlement: the influence of the Laudians, 1649–1662* (1951), 30–31 · Venn, *Alum. Cant.* · *Calendar of the Clarendon state papers preserved in the Bodleian Library*, 3: 1655–1657, ed. W. D. Macray (1876), 49, 89, 152–263 *passim*, 385 · Thurloe, *State papers*, 3.89, 95; 4.439, 583; 5.273 · F. L. Colvile, *The worthies of Warwickshire who lived between 1500 and 1800* [1870], 686–9 · J. Nichols, *The history and antiquities of the county of Leicester*, 3 (1800–04), 713–14 · R. Borough, 'The private chapel of the Earl Ferrers at Staunton Harold', *Proceedings of the Society of Antiquaries of London*, 2nd ser., 26 (1913–14), 121–2 · T. Staveley, *The history of churches in England* (1773), 143–5 · *Leicestershire and Rutland*, Pevsner (1984), 390–91 · Wood, *Ath. Oxon.*, new edn, 4.141 · R. Loder, *The history of Framlingham in the county of Suffolk* (1798), 218 · PRO, SP 18/125/2; 18/130/16
Archives Leics. RO, papers about royalist activities
Likenesses Van Dyck, portrait, *c.*1650, Staunton Harold church, Leicestershire · J. Basire, line engraving, BM, NPG; repro. in

Nichols, *History and antiquities* · portrait, vicarage, Pees, Shropshire · portrait, Sudbury Hall, Derbyshire

Wealth at death had been deprived of much of his lands and wealth by Cromwell: will, proved 11 July 1657, Shirley, *Stemmata Shirleiana*, 117-19

Shirley, Sir Thomas. *See* Sherley, Sir Thomas (1564-1633/4).

Shirley, Sir Thomas (*c*.1590-1654), antiquary, was the third son of Sir George Shirley (1559-1622) of Staunton Harold, Leicestershire, and his wife, Francis (1564-1594), daughter of Henry, Lord Berkeley of Berkeley, Gloucestershire. He married Mary (*b. c*.1596, *d*. after 1650), daughter of Thomas Harpur of Rushall, Staffordshire, about 1616; they had seven children. Shirley was knighted on 22 May 1622. His elder brother, Sir Henry Shirley, bt, inherited the family's main estate in Leicestershire, Northamptonshire, and Warwickshire and Sir Thomas was left with the family's manor of Botolph's Bridge in Huntingdonshire as his chief property. He mainly resided there and at the family's principal mansion at Staunton Harold, Leicestershire.

Shirley's main claim to fame was as a member of the circle of midland antiquarians associated with William Burton, William Dugdale, Sir Simon Archer, and Thomas Habington. He exchanged references with Archer and Burton, who visited him at Staunton Harold in the late 1620s; he collaborated with fellow Catholic Habington on his history of Worcestershire during the 1630s; and in May 1638 he joined with Dugdale, Sir Edward Dering, and Sir Christopher Hatton to form a group calling itself the Students of Antiquity who were dedicated to co-operative research in the London archives. Out of the researches of the midlands circle came a scheme for a series of county histories to match Burton's *Description of Leicestershire*, published in 1622. Shirley offered his services as historian of Warwickshire in 1631, but soon after decided to concentrate on the history of his own family and the work was assigned first to Archer, and then, later, to Dugdale. Shirley's 'Genealogicke history', which traced the achievements of his family from the time of their Anglo-Saxon ancestor, Sewale of Ettington, to his brother Sir Henry, was completed in the late 1630s, but never published. It also provided the material for the remarkable Shirley roll, a huge illuminated pedigree commissioned in 1632 which depicted the family's descent along with coloured drawings of deeds, armorial glass, and funeral monuments.

Sir Thomas's other principal work, a massive compendium entitled 'The Catholic armorist', combined his love of heraldry with his devotion to the Catholic religion. His parents were both dedicated Catholics and his wife's father was renowned for suffering for his faith during Elizabeth's reign. Thomas followed their examples. He remained a recusant throughout his life, enduring heavy financial penalties—which led to the seizure and mortgaging of his manor at Botolph's Bridge—and also a spell of imprisonment. This commitment was expressed in 'The Catholic armorist' which took the form of a study of coats of arms into which he worked a defence of the Catholic faith and an account of the families that had remained loyal during the years of persecution. The work was finished about 1650, but was never published. It was apparently intended that it should circulate in manuscript among the families whose achievements Shirley recorded.

Sir Thomas spent part of the 1640s in exile in France, but had returned to Staunton Harold by 1653 and died the following year; he was buried in the church of St Peter Paul's Wharf, London, on 4 February 1654. RICHARD CUST

Sources R. P. Cust, 'Catholicism, antiquarianism and gentry honour: the writings of Sir Thomas Shirley', *Midland History*, 23 (1998) · E. P. Shirley, ed., *Stemmata Shirleiana, or, The annals of the Shirley family*, 2nd edn (1873) · J. Nichols, *The history and antiquities of the county of Leicester*, 4 vols. (1795-1815) · P. Styles, *Studies in seventeenth century west midlands history* (1978) · J. R. Broadway, 'Antiquarianism in the midlands and the development of county history, 1586-1656', PhD diss., U. Birm., 1997 · T. E. Cogswell, *Home divisions: aristocracy, the state and provincial conflict* (1998) · IGI

Archives Leics. RO, family papers, MS 26 D 53 | BL, Harley MSS 4028, 4928, 6680; Lansdowne MS 870 · Northants. RO, Brudenell MSS · PRO, SP 9/9, 19 · Queen's College, Oxford, MSS 89, 104, 141, 142, 143, 144, 148, 153, 160

Shirley, Sir Thomas, first baronet (1727-1800). *See under* Shirley, William (1694-1771).

Shirley, Walter (1725-1786), Methodist preacher and hymn writer, the fourth son of the Hon. Laurence Shirley (1693-1743) and Anne (*d*. 1782), daughter of Sir Walter Clarges, was born on 23 September 1725 and baptized at Doveridge, Derbyshire, on 7 October. His father was the youngest son of Robert, first Earl Ferrers, by his first wife, Elizabeth Washington. Little is known of Shirley's early life, which may possibly have been spent in Ireland, but he entered New College, Oxford, in 1742 and graduated in 1746. Almost immediately he was ordained and became rector of Loughrea, co. Galway. There he settled into the life of an Irish country parson. However, at some date before 1755 he encountered the Methodists, possibly during one of John Wesley's brief visits to Ireland, and was converted. In 1755, when on a visit to England, probably to see his brother Laurence Shirley, fourth Earl Ferrers, at Staunton Harold, he met Francis, tenth earl of Huntingdon, who provided him with an introduction to his mother (Shirley's first cousin), Selina, countess dowager of Huntingdon, whose efforts to aid the Calvinistic Methodists were just beginning. Family quarrels and legal disputes had disrupted the Shirley family and Lady Huntingdon welcomed the first member of her own family to follow her example and join the ranks of the Calvinistic Methodists.

Walter Shirley soon came to divide his time between Ireland, where he employed a series of evangelical curates to serve Loughrea, and England, where, with headquarters at Bath, he served the increasing number of chapels built or supported by Lady Huntingdon. Shirley was the first and probably the best of her agents in this work since his 'conciliatory temper' (E. P. Shirley, 199) enabled him to settle problems in the congregations and to soothe the countess's readiness to complain of their behaviour. She also consulted him about the affairs of the college which she founded in 1768 at Trefeca, near Brecon, to train evangelical ministers. In Ireland, Shirley met with increasing opposition, especially from his diocesan, who cancelled the licence of one of his curates, Richard De Courcy, and preached against Shirley from his own pulpit at Loughrea.

In 1770, after George Whitefield's death, Lady Huntingdon appointed Shirley to succeed him as one of her chaplains. Soon afterwards she entrusted him with the delicate task of trying to reconcile the differences between the Wesleyans and the Calvinists—a duty formerly undertaken by Whitefield and Howell Harris. At his conference in 1770 John Wesley had again raised the question of justification by faith or works and implied that the Calvinists were antinomians. Lady Huntingdon proposed that Shirley should lead a delegation of ministers and laymen to the 1771 conference at Bristol either to meet with the members or to debate the subject afterwards. John Wesley reluctantly allowed the delegation to attend the last day of the conference and a statement was drawn up and signed by those present withdrawing the objectionable parts of the 1770 resolution. However, Wesley almost immediately insisted on publishing, against the author's own wishes, John Fletcher's manuscript 'Checks against antinomianism', which was written before the agreement. This revived the controversy and led to violent attacks by the Calvinists Toplady and Romaine on Wesley, despite all the efforts of Walter Shirley. It marked the end of all co-operation between the two parties.

Shirley's hymn writing and his part in the compilation of Lady Huntingdon's early hymnbooks is somewhat obscure. Julian lists only five hymns written by him, but it is clear from his letters to the countess that he played an important part in revising and improving the hymns and, in conjunction with Benjamin Milgrove of Bath, in providing suitable tunes. Shirley's only other publications were *Gospel Repentance* (1760), *Twelve Sermons*, with a poetical appendix (1761), and an account of the 1771 conference.

Walter Shirley married Henrietta Maria Phillips (*d*. 1792), daughter of John Phillips of Dublin, on 27 August 1766. They had two sons—John and Walter, born at Loughrea on 26 September 1767 and 11 October 1768—and three daughters—Fanny and Henrietta, born at Bath on 6 May 1770 and 11 August 1772, and Ann-Augusta, born on 29 November 1775. Walter Shirley died in Dublin on 7 April 1786 and was buried in the city's St Mary's Church. He was survived by his wife, who died on 15 December 1792. His eldest son, John, predeceased him, leaving Walter Shirley junior as his executor. Unfortunately the family and legal disputes of the Shirleys meant that there was no family fortune, and attempts to improve Walter Shirley's income in his lifetime were unsuccessful. Lady Huntingdon gave him the advowson of Aldwincle All Saints, Northamptonshire, but the incumbent, Thomas Haweis, survived him by more than thirty years. Lord Dartmouth attempted to find an English living which he could exchange for Loughrea, but without success. As a result Walter junior spent much of his life as a penniless curate never far from bankruptcy.　　EDWIN WELCH

Sources W. Shirley, *A narrative of the principal circumstances relative to the Rev. Mr Wesley's late conference held in Bristol, August the 6th* (1771) · E. P. Shirley, ed., *Stemmata Shirleiana* (1841) · E. Welch, *Spiritual pilgrim: a reassessment of the life of the countess of Huntingdon* (1995) · J. Julian, ed., *A dictionary of hymnology*, rev. edn (1907) · Burke, *Peerage* · Foster, *Alum. Oxon.*
Archives Drew University, Madison, New Jersey, United Methodist Archives and History Center · Leics. RO | Westminster College, Cambridge, Cheshunt Foundation, corresp., mostly with countess of Huntingdon
Likenesses J. Dixon, mezzotint, pubd in or before 1773 (after R. E. Pine), BM · line engraving, BM; repro. in *Journal Magazine* (1775)

Shirley, Walter Augustus (1797–1847), bishop of Sodor and Man, was born on 30 May 1797 at Westport, co. Mayo, Ireland, where his father was curate. He was the only son of Walter Shirley (1768–1860) and his wife, Alicia, the daughter of Sir Edward *Newenham. His grandfather, also Walter *Shirley (1725–1786), was a cousin and collaborator of the countess of Huntingdon. At the age of nine Shirley was placed under the care of the Revd Legh Richmond, but as he seemed to be making little progress he was soon sent to a school at Linton in Cambridgeshire, and in 1809 he became a scholar of Winchester College. Six years later he was elected to a fellowship at New College, Oxford, which he held until 1828, and graduated BA (1819) and MA (1823). In 1822 he gained the chancellor's English essay prize for an essay entitled 'On the study of moral evidence'.

Immediately after his ordination in 1820 Shirley took charge of the parish of Woodford, Northamptonshire, one of the livings held by his father. The following year he became curate of Parwich in Derbyshire, and in 1822 he was appointed lecturer at Ashbourne and curate of Atlow. He acted as English chaplain at Rome in the winter of 1826, where he got to know Thomas Erskine, the painter Charles Eastlake, and Baron von Bunsen, the German diplomat, and his wife, Frances. On 4 September 1827 in Paris he married Maria (*d*. 1854), daughter of William Waddington of Impington Hall, Cambridgeshire. They had a daughter and a son, Walter Waddington *Shirley (1828–1866), afterwards regius professor of ecclesiastical history at Oxford. In 1828 he succeeded his father as vicar of Shirley in Derbyshire, the ancient estate of the family, combining it with the adjoining parish of Brailsford from 1839 and with the archdeaconry of Derby from 1840. He was also rector of Whiston, Yorkshire, from 1837 to 1839.

In November 1846 Shirley was appointed bishop of Sodor and Man by Lord John Russell, but because he was seriously ill, the consecration was delayed until 10 January 1847. He had been elected Bampton lecturer at Oxford for that year, but lived only long enough to deliver two of the lectures, which with two others (undelivered) were published posthumously as *The Supremacy of Holy Scripture* (1847).

Shirley received a strict evangelical upbringing, but his kindly disposition prevented him from running to extremes of partisanship. Indeed in 1829 he alienated some of his friends by his outspoken advocacy of Catholic emancipation, as in later years he estranged others by refusing to support extreme measures against the Tractarians. In politics he was a constitutional whig, and both as an incumbent and as an archdeacon he exercised an energetic and effective ministry. He died at Bishop's Court, Isle of Man, on 21 April 1847, and eight days later was buried in the family vault of the church at Shirley.

R. L. DOUGLAS, *rev.* STEPHEN GREGORY

Sources *Letters and memoir of the late Walter Augustus Shirley,* ed. T. Hill (1849) · D. M. Lewis, ed., *The Blackwell dictionary of evangelical biography, 1730–1860,* 2 vols. (1995) · *Annual Register* (1848), 224 · E. P. Shirley, ed., *Stemmata Shirleiana, or, The annals of the Shirley family,* 2nd edn (1873) · J. S. Reynolds, *The evangelicals at Oxford, 1735–1871: a record of an unchronicled movement* (1953) · J. Foster, *The peerage, baronetage, and knightage of the British empire for 1881,* [2 pts] [1881] · Foster, *Alum. Oxon.* · private information (1897)

Archives Leics. RO, family corresp. · Staffs. RO, family corresp. | BL, corresp. with Sir Robert Peel, Add. MSS 40526–40529

Likenesses H. B. Hall, stipple print (after portrait by O. Oakley), NPG

Shirley, Walter Waddington (1828–1866), ecclesiastical historian, the only son of Walter Augustus *Shirley (1797–1847), bishop of Sodor and Man, and his wife, Maria (d. 1854), daughter of William Waddington of Impington Hall, Cambridgeshire, was born at Shirley, Derbyshire, on 24 July 1828. He was educated at Rugby School under Thomas Arnold. His closest friend at school and throughout his life was his cousin, William Henry Waddington, later the French foreign minister. In June 1846 Shirley matriculated at University College, Oxford, but in the following year he migrated to Wadham College, where he had gained a scholarship. He obtained a first class in mathematics in 1851, and in 1852 was elected a fellow of his college. He was compelled to vacate his fellowship three years later, when his mother's death brought him into possession of a small landed property. He married on 4 July 1855 Philippa, daughter of Samuel Knight, of Impington, Cambridgeshire. They had three daughters and three sons, one of whom died young. The eldest surviving son, Walter Knight Shirley, succeeded to the earldom of Ferrers, as the eleventh earl, in 1907.

From 1855 to 1863 Shirley was tutor and mathematical lecturer at Wadham. It was during this period that he began to devote his greatest energy to historical study. A patient and impartial researcher, the master of a clear and dignified style, he came to be regarded by many of his contemporaries, in both England and Germany, as one of the ablest of the new kind of Oxford historian, employing carefully researched evidence and maintaining a detached and objective stance. In 1858 his edition of *Fasciculi Zizaniorum magistri Johannis Wyclif* was published in the Rolls Series. His introduction attracted the admiration of historical students though it was savagely reviewed in *The Athenaeum* by a reviewer who resented what he called Shirley's 'endeavour to exhibit Wycliffe as little of a Reformer as possible'. Thereafter he commenced the preparation of a life of Wyclif which he did not live to complete. In 1865, however, he published a *Catalogue of the Original Works of John Wiclif* and in 1862 he edited for the Rolls Series *Royal and other Historical Letters Illustrative of the Reign of Henry III,*

the master of the rolls, Lord Romilley, thereby demonstrating continued confidence in the scholarship exhibited in Shirley's earlier volume for the series. There has been no edition of *Fasciculi zizaniorum* since Shirley's and it is still very widely used though it suffers somewhat, as one would expect, from the fact that the work was done as long ago as the mid-nineteenth century. His *Catalogue,* on the other hand, has been rendered out of date by more recent research and scholarship.

Shirley's theological views underwent considerable change and began to lean more towards the opinions of the Tractarians. Having been in his early days a disciple of Arnold, he ultimately came to regard 'undogmatic Christianity' as a contradiction in terms. Finally, in May 1863, he preached in the university church a sermon—which created a great impression at the time of its delivery and was subsequently published—in which he sought to demonstrate the unreasonableness of Arnold's teaching. Two or three months after the delivery of this sermon he was made regius professor of ecclesiastical history and canon of Christ Church. His appointment met with general approval among people of very divergent views because he was regarded as scrupulously fair in controversy and free from party spirit and because of the mingled strength and simplicity of his character. He was one of the pioneers of the university extension movement, and played a prominent part in the early history of the founding of Keble College. His promising career was cut short at the age of thirty-eight. He died on 20 November 1866 at the Canon's House, Christ Church, Oxford.

The theological position which Shirley occupied at the time of his death was still regarded by him as a provisional one, as he believed that any moral or intellectual position should always be open to revision. In addition to the works already mentioned, he published a lecture, *Scholasticism,* delivered before the University of Oxford in 1866. After his death a small volume of his writings, edited by William Bright and entitled *Some Account of the Church in the Apostolic Age,* was published by the Clarendon Press.

R. L. DOUGLAS, *rev.* PETER HINCHLIFF

Sources *Letters and memoir of the late Walter Augustus Shirley, bishop of Sodor and Man,* ed. T. Hill (1849) · Burke, *Peerage* · J. W. Burgon, *Lives of twelve good men,* new edn (1891), vii · Foster, *Alum. Oxon.* · R. B. Gardiner, ed., *The registers of Wadham College, Oxford,* 1 (1889) · *The Athenaeum* (2 Oct 1858), 415–16 · *The Athenaeum* (9 Oct 1858), 454 · *Chichele professorship of modern history: testimonials in favour of the Rev. Walter Waddington Shirley* (1862) · CGPLA Eng. & Wales (1866)

Archives Leics. RO, family MSS

Likenesses portrait (after photographs), Keble College, Oxford

Wealth at death under £30,000: probate, 14 Dec 1866, CGPLA Eng. & Wales

Shirley, Washington, fifth Earl Ferrers (1722–1778). *See under* Shirley, Laurence, fourth Earl Ferrers (1720–1760).

Shirley, William (1694–1771), colonial governor and army officer, was born on 2 December 1694 at Preston, Sussex, the son of William Shirley (1667–1701), London merchant, and his wife, Elizabeth, daughter of John Godman of Ote

William Shirley (1694–1771), by Thomas Hudson, 1750

Hall, Wivelsfield, Sussex. He grew up in a family with aristocratic pretensions but without the economic wherewithal to support that style of life. His father died when he was very young, and William was left with relatively little property. He attended the Merchant Taylors' School in London and Pembroke College, Cambridge, as a pensioner, graduating BA in 1715. He entered the Inner Temple in 1714 and was called to the bar on 20 July 1720, practising law for the next eleven years. He was a clerk in the London government from 1717 to 1719. Some time before 1720 he married Frances, daughter and heir of Francis Barker, a London merchant. They had nine children before she died on 31 August 1745. A daughter, Frances, also died in 1745. Although he achieved a good legal reputation and made a number of influential friends, he did not prosper financially. He lost money on the South Sea Bubble and other speculative fiascos, and grew determined to recoup his fortunes in American colonial administration.

In 1731 Shirley emigrated with his family to Boston, Massachusetts, seeking a place in government. Before long he had secured the patronage of his friend Thomas Pelham-Holles, duke of Newcastle, who had connections in the ministry of Sir Robert Walpole. In 1733 Shirley was appointed judge of the vice-admiralty court and shortly thereafter advocate-general of that court. He vigorously attempted to enforce British trade laws while also developing a private law practice and petitioning officials in London for various offices without success. He became associated with a group of colonial businessmen and landowners who were opposed to the governor, Jonathan Belcher, and he began to undermine Belcher's position.

He dispatched his wife to England with instructions to petition the duke of Newcastle, then secretary of state, for various offices and emoluments for him. After she had made several unsuccessful attempts, she began disparaging Belcher and petitioning for her husband's appointment in his stead. With the assistance of powerful allies in both London and Boston, she succeeded on 25 May 1741 in having Belcher dismissed and Shirley commissioned governor of Massachusetts.

Confronted with economic difficulties left to him by his predecessor, Shirley rose to the occasion and quickly established a reputation as an astute servant of the crown. He eliminated various competing banks and restored a sound currency without antagonizing anyone unduly, thereby winning the respect of both the colonists and his superiors in London. Building on this success, he forged a powerful following in Massachusetts by gaining privileges for leading colonists from the British government in exchange for their co-operation. He secured for them war contracts for provisions, military commissions, and civil positions, and prevailed upon Newcastle to relax enforcement of the trade laws. He also built up the colony's defences by persuading the general court to appropriate money for the repair of Castle William and other fortifications in Massachusetts. Hence, when Britain declared war upon France in 1744, he had put the colony on a sound financial footing and in a reasonable state of defence. Seeing the war as an opportunity to improve the colonists' strategic and economic situation, he urged the ministry to seize the weakly held French fortress of Louisbourg on Cape Breton Island. Undeterred by the lack of support or encouragement from Britain, he proposed to the general court of Massachusetts that an expedition be organized by the New England colonies. He ably negotiated with all the parties to cobble together an expedition, to be led by William Pepperrell with the assistance of a British fleet under Commodore Peter Warren. The fortress fell on 17 June 1745, and Shirley was rewarded by being appointed colonel of a British regiment to be recruited from New England provincial troops. In the late 1740s he used hard currency provided by parliament as reimbursement for war expenses to replace some of the paper money of Massachusetts.

The war ended in 1748, and a year later Shirley was appointed to a commission meeting in Paris to determine the boundary between New England and French Canada. Shortly after his arrival in France he married a young Frenchwoman named Julie, the daughter of his landlord; they had no children. The negotiations went on interminably, with Shirley attempting to push the boundaries of British North America into the Ohio valley. Sensing that war between Britain and France would soon break out again, he returned to Massachusetts in 1753. In January 1754 he wrote to the ministry in London, urging the necessity of uniting the colonies and emphasizing the importance of Crown Point (Ticonderoga) to colonial defence. In the summer he led an expedition up the Kennebec River, vainly seeking Frenchmen to fight, and he laid plans to attack the French in eastern Canada. In February 1755 he was promoted major-general, as the British ministry laid plans for all-out war with the French in America. Two months later he attended a council of war with the commander of the British forces in America, General Edward Braddock, and four other governors in Alexandria, Virginia, where a concerted plan of action against the French was agreed upon. Braddock appointed Shirley his second-in-command, then marched against Fort Duquesne while Shirley led an unsuccessful expedition against Niagara. When Braddock was killed in a French ambush in July 1755, Shirley became commander-in-chief, but for the remainder of the year managed only a few military gains in Nova Scotia. His eldest son, William, had been killed while serving as Braddock's secretary, and his second son John had died of fever during the Niagara campaign.

In 1756, with limited support from Britain, Shirley laid plans for another campaign against the French but acted indecisively in carrying them out. Hence he lost Fort Oswego to the enemy. In July 1756 he was replaced as commander-in-chief by John Campbell, fourth earl of Loudoun, and ordered home to answer for his mismanagement of military affairs and for irregularities in his financial accounts. Officials in the war office wanted to court-martial Shirley, but lack of evidence forced the dropping of all charges in the autumn of 1757. Meantime he had been removed as governor of Massachusetts. In late 1758 he was promoted lieutenant-general and given the governorship of the Bahama Islands. Taking up residence in December 1759, he spent the next eight years working to suppress smuggling, improve education, and bolster the islands' defences. In 1767 he relinquished his office to his son, Thomas [see below], and retired on the half pay of a colonel. Two years later he returned to his country estate, Shirley Place, in Roxbury, Massachusetts. There on 24 March 1771 he died. He was buried on 1 April in King's Chapel, Boston, beside the bodies of his first wife and daughter.

The third and only surviving son of William and Frances Shirley, **Sir Thomas Shirley**, first baronet (1727–1800), army officer and colonial governor, was born in London in 1727 and accompanied his parents to Boston. He was enrolled in the Boston Latin school in 1737 but evinced little taste for classical learning. His father appointed him a captain in the British army in 1745. He was promoted major in 1759, and in 1767 succeeded his father as governor of the Bahama Islands. A year later he and his bride, Anna Maria Weston, took up residence there. He was appointed governor of Dominica in 1774. During the American War of Independence he and his family were prisoners of war for a time. In 1781 he was commissioned colonel of the 91st regiment and made governor of the Leeward Islands. He was created a baronet on 27 June 1786, and was promoted lieutenant-general in 1793 and general five years later. He died at Bath on 11 February 1800 and was succeeded in his title by his second son, William Warden Shirley.   PAUL DAVID NELSON

Sources *Correspondence of William Shirley*, ed. C. H. Lincoln, 2 vols. (1912) • G. A. Wood, *William Shirley: governor of Massachusetts, 1741–* 1756 (New York, 1920) • J. A. Schutz, *William Shirley: king's governor of Massachusetts* (1961) • L. H. Gipson, *The British empire before the American revolution*, 15 vols. (1936–70) • T. Thayer, 'The army contractor for the Niagara campaign', *William and Mary Quarterly*, 14 (1957), 31–46 • D. E. Leach, *Arms for empire: a military history of the British colonies in North America, 1607–1763* (1973) • W. R. Nester, *The first global war: Britain, France, and the fate of North America, 1756–1775* (2000) • J. A. Schutz, 'Shirley, William', *ANB* • F. Anderson, *Crucible of war: the Seven Years' War and the fate of empire in British North America, 1754–1766* (2000) • P. D. Nelson, *William Alexander, Lord Stirling* (1987)

Archives BL, corresp., Add. MS 40760 • Mass. Hist. Soc. | American Antiquarian Society, Worcester, Massachusetts, corresp. with J. Bradstreet • BL, letters to duke of Newcastle, etc., Add. MSS 32688–33067, *passim* • Hunt. L., Loudoun MSS • New York Historical Society, W. Alexander MSS • U. Mich., Clinton MSS

Likenesses T. Hudson, oils, 1750, priv. coll. [*see illus.*] • J. Macardell, mezzotint (after T. Hudson), NG Ire.

Wealth at death left house, Shirley Place, Roxbury, Massachusetts; finances improved after 1765; all lost during American Revolution: Schutz, *William Shirley*, 264, 266

Shirley, William (*fl.* **1739–1777**), playwright, was also a merchant who for many years conducted business in Portugal. In 1753 he argued with the English consul at Lisbon, which resulted in an order from the Portuguese government to leave the country within five days. From that time he lived in London, though he occasionally went abroad, and even revisited Portugal, where he narrowly escaped with his life in the earthquake of 1755. He was an authority on affairs of trade and international commerce, and wrote several letters in the *Daily Gazetteer*, signed Lusitanicus, on the relations of Portugal and Britain. He also wrote on currency in Sir William Browne's *Proposal on our Coin* (1771); and produced his *Observations on a Pamphlet Lately Published Concerning a Portuguese Conspiracy* (1759).

Shirley also wrote plays, but his output was far greater than his talent. His earliest play was a tragedy called *The Parricide* which appeared at Covent Garden on 17 January 1739, but was never performed again as there was a riot in the audience. Shirley defends himself in a later published preface to the work, claiming that the riot was planned: 'their expelling the ladies from the pit, and sending for wine to drink, were likewise strong indications of their arbitrary and violent dispositions', and says 'faulty as it is, it deserv'd a better fate than it met with'. Genest, on the other hand, finds 'nothing in it either pleasing or interesting', and this seems to be the view which has lasted.

Shirley's next play, *King Pepin's Campaign*, was performed at Drury Lane in 1745 and published in 1755, but the reviews felt that for a burlesque comedy it was sadly lacking in humour. After this he wrote *Edward the Black Prince*, which appeared at Drury Lane on 6 January 1750, with David Garrick in the part of Edward and Spranger Barry as the French nobleman, Lord Ribemont. Opinions were mixed: the audience mostly applauded, while groaning at the hackneyed love scenes; others found it dull and considered it to be an unsuitable vehicle for an actor such as Garrick. Shirley soon afterwards quarrelled with Garrick and took his revenge in 1758 by printing a pamphlet entitled *Brief Remarks on the Original and Present State of the*

Drama, with a humorous dialogue called 'Hecate's Prophecy', in which Garrick was criticized under the name of Roscius.

The two men seem, however, to have been reconciled, for when new proprietors acquired Drury Lane from Garrick in 1776, one of the terms of sale was that a new piece by William Shirley be performed as soon as possible. *The Roman Sacrifice* opened on 18 December 1777, but closed after four nights of decreasing audiences. According to Horace Walpole it was 'without a tolerable line' (Walpole, *Corr.*, 23 Dec 1777). Shirley wrote several other plays which were not published; nothing further is known about his life.   JO PAYNE

Sources DNB · Genest, *Eng. stage* · W. Shirley, *The parricide* (1739) · W. Van Lennep and others, eds., *The London stage, 1660–1800*, 5 pts in 11 vols. (1960–68) · Nichols, *Lit. anecdotes*, vol. 3 · Walpole, *Corr.*, vol. 32

Shirreff, Emily Anne Eliza (1814–1897), educationist and writer, was born on 3 November 1814, the second of four daughters and two sons born to Rear-Admiral William Henry Shirreff (1785–1847), of Huguenot ancestry, commander of the Portsmouth Dockyard at the time of his death in 1847, and Elizabeth Anne, eldest daughter of the Hon. David Murray and grandniece of the sixth Baron Elibank. During her childhood her father's naval career took the family abroad for substantial periods. In the 1820s the Shirreff family lived in France, first at St Germain-en-Laye, near Paris, and then in Normandy. From 1830 to 1834 they lived in Gibraltar, where William Shirreff was captain of the port. Along with her sisters, Caroline (b. 1812), Maria (b. 1816), and Katherine (b. 1818), she was educated by a Swiss-French governess, Adèle Piquet. Both brothers died young, William in 1829 and Henry in 1833. Emily remained unmarried, the only one of the sisters to do so. An early portrait of Emily and her sisters in adolescence depicts the group as fashionably attractive and appropriately feminine.

The family's circle of friends included prominent intellectuals, women and men, and Emily Shirreff grew up in the company of some of the best-known nineteenth-century scientists—Mary Somerville, Charles Lyell, William Whewell, and John Herschel—as well as among leading literary figures. Never healthy herself, and battling frequent bouts of neuralgia after an early encounter with infantile fever, she none the less spent her younger adult years nursing various family members through sickness. She was close to her younger sister, Maria Georgina *Grey, with whom she collaborated both on numerous writing projects and on the feminist educational campaigns which would secure her name for posterity. When her sister's husband, William Thomas Grey, died in March 1864, the joint career upon which the two sisters had already embarked blossomed into increasing prominence.

As young women, the Shirreff sisters had enjoyed considerable publishing success, first in 1835 with their *Letters from Spain and Barbary*, then in 1841 with a novel, *Passion and Principle* (reissued in 1854 as part of Routledge's Railway Library). In 1850 Maria Grey's husband financed the publication of their first major work, *Thoughts on Self-Culture Addressed to Women*, a work which heralded the interest of the sisters in furthering the educational opportunities available for women of their class. *Thoughts on Self-Culture* espoused an intellectual independence for women firmly based on notions of reason and Christian humanism. Their belief in the perfection of the mind and the importance of developing the intellect clearly foreshadows their active commitment to the principles of women's education. *Intellectual Education and its Influence on the Character and Happiness of Women*, Shirreff's first major single-authored work, appeared in 1858, and further developed the principles of this earlier discussion. It was in the 1870s, after their responsibilities as family nurses declined, that Shirreff and her sister turned their attention more fully to the far-reaching and highly successful campaigns they were to spearhead.

Emily Shirreff was actively involved in fund-raising for the North London Collegiate School and its planned sister school, the Camden School, both founded by Frances Buss. She publicly supported the medical education of women, and played a key role in developing both secondary and tertiary educational openings for women. She was mistress of the newly founded Hitchin (later Girton) College for women during the Lent term of 1870 (writing an account of the college in the *Fortnightly Review*, 1873), and in 1871 launched, with her sister, the National Union for the Improvement of the Education of Women of all Classes. Widely known as the Women's Education Union, and inaugurated in November 1871 at the Royal Society of Arts with Lord Lyttelton presiding, the union's aim was to provide secondary schools for girls and to raise the status of teaching as a profession, especially for women. To these ends, the union helped to found a number of academically rigorous girls' schools and worked to improve and formalize teacher training opportunities for women.

Under the aegis of the union, Shirreff and her sister launched the Girls' Public Day School Company (GPDSC) in June 1872. The company offered £5 shares as a way of raising money to finance the opening of new non-denominational girls' schools. Shareholders received dividends on the profit made from tuition fees, which ranged from 2 to 8 guineas termly; by 1883, with twenty-six schools in operation, shareholders were paid an annual 5 per cent on their investment. The money raised in shares was used for renting, purchasing, or building premises for the schools and for furnishing them. The daughters of shareholders were given priority as entrants, provided they met the entrance requirements. The first of the GPDSC schools opened in London, at Norland Square, Chelsea, in January 1873, with twenty pupils. The school's initial mission was to prepare the girls for the local examinations administered by Oxford and Cambridge as well as those of the College of Preceptors. The schools were deeply influenced by the educational philosophy which Shirreff shared with her sister Maria; both were company vice-presidents. Their view of education stressed both intellectual and physical accomplishment, and saw pleasure as well as discipline as key elements in a successful education. As a result, the schools founded under their influence encouraged girls in physical education, in an appreciation of nature, and in music, as well as in more traditional aspects of the nineteenth-century curriculum. Shirreff, like her sister, was a liberal educationist whose views were grounded in a humanitarian Christianity. Her lecture published in 1875 as *The Enjoyment of Life* outlines these principles. The success of the company schools was such that the Church Schools Company, which was founded in 1883, deliberately emulated the policies pursued by the GPDSC. By 1879 the GPDSC itself boasted seventeen schools enrolling 2804 students.

Shirreff was both the honorary secretary of the Women's Education Union and co-editor of its house journal, the *Journal of the Women's Education Union*. The first of the nine volumes of the journal appeared in January 1873, edited by Shirreff and George C. T. Bartley, author of *Schools for the People*. The journal was a considerable drain on the union's resources, and by 1878 had been reduced to little more than a broadsheet of four pages. Shirreff frequently contributed articles to the journal. Shirreff was also involved in the union's foundation of an evening college for women, which opened at 1 Queen Street, Brompton, in London, in 1878, and in the Governess Registry which it sponsored in 1880. She was also present at the founding meeting (1887) of the Parents' National Union, of which she was a vice-president.

Emily Shirreff was an avid supporter of the education principles of Friedrich Froebel, and one of the founders of the Froebel Society. She was the first secretary of the society from 1874 to 1876, when she was elected its president, a position she held until the end of her life. Many of her later writings reflect her interests in this area. In 1876 she published *The kindergarten: principles of Froebel's system; also remarks on the higher education of women* (2nd edn, 1880). The following year she contributed a sketch of her mentor's life to Berta Maria, Baroness Marenholtz-Bülow's *Reminiscences of Friedrich Froebel*. Many of the talks she gave on Froebel's system at the Royal Society of Arts, the Froebel Society, and the National Association for the Promotion of Social Science over the years were published as pamphlets. She also contributed a monthly column to *The Governess*, 'The kinder-garten at home'. *Moral Training: Froebel and Herbert Spencer* appeared in 1892.

Emily Shirreff's writings were not, however, confined to the topic of education. In 1864 her pamphlet *The Chivalry of the South*, published by the Ladies' London Emancipation Society at the time of the American Civil War, was a fierce denunciation of the continued existence of slavery in the American south. In politics she was a Liberal who strongly supported women's suffrage. But unlike her sister, whose sympathies were increasingly democratic, she was opposed to further extensions of the franchise after the 1867 Reform Act; Shirreff's Liberalism was of an older vintage and she did not seek to extend the franchise vertically to the unpropertied, merely horizontally to suitably qualified women. Her works *Wasted Forces* (1880) and *The Work of the World and Women's Share in It* (1881) both enunciated her feminist principles. She declined an invitation to stand as a Liberal candidate for the new London school board in

1870. In 1874 she joined the Women's Peace and Arbitration Auxiliary, which later changed its name to the London Peace Society.

In 1872 Emily Shirreff contributed a biographical sketch of Henry Thomas Buckle to the posthumous edition of his works which Helen Taylor was overseeing. Shirreff had been close to Buckle as a young woman and profoundly influenced by him intellectually. There is evidence that he had made a proposal of marriage to her, but that she had, on finding that his moral practices did not match her own principles, declined. After the death of her sister's husband in 1864 Shirreff and Maria Grey lived and travelled together, dividing their time between Italy and London. They lived first at Cadogan Place, and later at 41 Stanhope Gardens, Queen's Gate, London. It was here that Emily Shirreff died on 20 March 1897. She was buried in Brompton cemetery four days later.

While politically more conservative than her sister and partner, Emily Shirreff was a formidable force in the cause of women's education, where her campaigning skills and breadth of interest touched upon a wide range of educational issues. She was a principled campaigner, a prolific and impassioned author, and a woman of deep Christian convictions. It was, thus, with women's moral and spiritual contributions and talents that she was most concerned.   PHILIPPA LEVINE

Sources E. W. Ellsworth, *Liberators of the female mind: the Shirreff sisters, educational reform and the women's movement* (1979) · T. Stanton, ed., *The woman question in Europe: a series of original essays* (1884) · *The Times* (24 March 1897) · *Journal of the Women's Education Union* · B. Stephen, *Emily Davies and Girton College* (1927) · S. Fletcher, *Feminists and bureaucrats: a study in the development of girls' education in the nineteenth century* (1980) · C. Dyhouse, *Girls growing up in late Victorian and Edwardian England* (1981) · J. S. Pedersen, *The reform of girls' secondary and higher education in Victorian England: a study of elites and educational change* (1987) · J. Kamm, *Hope deferred: girls' education in English history* (1965) · O. Banks, *The biographical dictionary of British feminists*, 1 (1985) · *Wellesley index* · d. cert.

Archives CUL, letters to Miss Maria Grey

Likenesses photograph, Girton Cam.

Wealth at death £9105 9s. 11d.: probate, 21 April 1897, *CGPLA Eng. & Wales*

Shirreff, John (1759–1818), agricultural writer, was born at Captainhead, Haddington, the son of Matthew Shiraff (d. c.1785), a Haddingtonshire tenant farmer, and Jean Maitland, probably his wife. Very little is known about his early life, wife, or children, though he was said to have received a liberal education. As a young man he was for a number of years a merchant in the West Indies with his brother-in-law, Mr Burton. Following the death of his father he returned home to take on the tenancy of the family farm and to develop a number of agricultural innovations. In 1793, in conjunction with Robert Brown and George Rennie, he was appointed by the board of agriculture to undertake the survey of the West Riding of Yorkshire. Their impressive report, of which Brown was the main author, was widely praised by William Marshall, who had been critical of the accounts of other counties. On his return from Yorkshire, Shirreff attempted to popularize a number of agricultural innovations including a wind driven threshing machine and to encourage the use of bonemeal as an agricultural fertilizer. His success in persuading other farmers to adopt these methods was very limited.

In 1801 Shirreff obtained an award from the board of agriculture for an essay on the most appropriate ways of cropping and reseeding pasture fields. He also compiled an account for the London Society of Arts on the osier plantations on his farm. The death of his eldest two sons in their early twenties devastated him. He sublet the farm, moved initially to Craigside, Abbeyhill, and later to other residences in the Edinburgh region. He made a precarious living from writing articles and reports (on various scientific subjects and the rural economy) which were published primarily in the *Farmers' Magazine* and *Scots Monthly Magazine*. These included 'Discussions on turnips, potatoes and apple trees', 'Curled disease in potatoes', 'Introduction of exotic heaths', and 'Method of stacking turnips to preserve them through the winter'. His main achievement was to undertake, for the board of agriculture, separate surveys of the Orkney and Shetland islands, which included detailed suggestions for improving their subsistence farming methods.

Shirreff was a recognized authority on agriculture and botany, and was widely consulted by agriculturists. His knowledge of Poa, Festuca, and Tritica and the smaller grasses was described in his obituary in the *Farmers' Magazine* as perhaps superior to that of any other man in existence. His countenance and figure were denoted as being exceedingly manly and graceful, with highly prepossessing manners and address. According to his obituary he was rather outspoken, which meant that in spite of all his advantage 'he was ill-calculated to secure the patronage of the great' (*Farmers' Magazine*, 207–9). During the last years of his life he lived in the countryside, taking responsibility for the management of several estates. Following a prolonged illness, during which he was looked after by his wife, his children, and his brother, Alexander Shirreff, he died on 2 November 1818 and was interred at the burial-ground of his ancestors at Prestonkirk, Haddingtonshire.

ERNEST CLARKE, rev. JOHN MARTIN

Sources *Farmers' Magazine* (1821), 207–9 • 'General view of the agriculture of the West Riding of Yorkshire', *Farmers' Magazine*, 6 • Branch 11, 'Review of agricultural publications', *Farmers' Magazine* (Aug 1814), 15 • P. Horn, *William Marshall (1745–1818) and the Georgian countryside* (1982) • J. D. Chambers and G. E. Mingay, *The agricultural revolution, 1750–1880* (1966) • M. Overton, *Agricultural revolution in England: the transformation of the agrarian economy, 1500–1850* (1996) • bap. reg. Scot.
Wealth at death poor: *Farmers' Magazine*

Shirreff, Maria Georgina. *See* Grey, Maria Georgina (1816–1906).

Shirreffs [Shirrefs], **Andrew** (*bap.* 1762, *d.* 1807?), poet, was baptized in Aberdeen on 9 February 1762, the son of David Shirreffs, carpenter, and his wife, Ann Lunan. Two of his brothers attained some distinction in Aberdeen. James was minister of St Nicholas's Church from 1778 to 1814, and Alexander was sheriff-clerk-depute and latterly president of the Society of Advocates. Andrew Shirreffs was

educated at the grammar school, entered Marischal College in 1779, and graduated MA in 1783. He lost both legs and consequently abandoned the intention of following a learned profession, and began business in Aberdeen as a bookseller and bookbinder.

Shirreffs corresponded with John Skinner and James Beattie. Burns in the notes of his northern tour mentions having seen him, and describes him as 'a little decrepid body with some abilities'. He was best-known as the author of *Jamie and Bess*, a pastoral five-act comedy, written avowedly in imitation of Ramsay's *Gentle Shepherd*. It was performed in Aberdeen in 1787, and in Edinburgh, for the author's benefit, in 1796, where he appeared and sang his own song, 'A Cogie o'yill and a pickle Aitmeal'. In May 1787 he joined with others in starting the short-lived *Aberdeen Chronicle* (not to be confused with the paper of the same name started in 1806), and became proprietor and joint editor of the *Caledonian Magazine*. The latter ceased in 1790, and he went to Edinburgh as a bookseller and printer. Inglis mentions a short piece, *The Sons of Britannia*, said to have been acted in Edinburgh in 1796, but it does not seem to have been printed. In 1790 Shirreffs published in Edinburgh *Poems, Chiefly in the Scottish Dialect*.

In 1798 Shirreffs left for London, after which it is impossible to trace him. The date of his death is given as 1807, but this cannot be confirmed; and from his not appearing with his brothers in the will of his first cousin Alexander, a Jamaica planter, who died in 1801, it might be inferred that he was dead before that date. His dramatic and poetic works were reprinted in 1996.

J. C. HADDEN, rev. S. R. J. BAUDRY

Sources R. Inglis, *The dramatic writers of Scotland* (1868) • W. Walker, *The bards of Bon-Accord, 1375–1860* (1887) • R. Burns and others, *The Scots musical museum*, ed. J. Johnson and W. Stenhouse, new edn, 4 (1853), 479, 526 • parish registers, Aberdeen • IGI • bap. reg. Scot.
Likenesses Beugo, oils, repro. in A. Shirreffs, *Poems, chiefly in the Scottish dialect* (1790)

Shirwood, John (*d.* 1493), bishop of Durham, was the son of John Shirwood of York, the city's common clerk, and Agnes, his wife. He was educated at both Cambridge and Oxford, for as MA and BTh of the former he supplicated for DTh at the latter in 1456. By this time he had already been admitted to his first living, that of Terrington in his native Yorkshire. He owed his further advancement to the patronage of George Neville, who at the age of twenty-five was consecrated bishop of Exeter in 1458, and for whom Shirwood acted as Latin secretary. He became chancellor of Exeter Cathedral in 1460 and followed Neville to York in 1465, being collated archdeacon of Richmond on 5 July 1465 and receiving the 'golden prebend' of Masham on 5 August 1471; these two livings alone provided him with an income of some £350 p.a. Pardoned by Edward IV in 1471 for his acquiescence in Henry VI's readeption, he became a king's chaplain and within three years had taken up residence in Rome. In 1476 he became an apostolic protonotary, and in the following year was made the king's proctor at the curia, which he remained until Edward IV's death in 1483.

Shirwood is sometimes said to have returned to England in time to participate in Richard III's coronation, but this seems to be based on a confusion with Bishop William Dudley of Durham whom he was shortly to succeed. The evidence implies that he was continuously in Rome, and he was certainly there as Richard's representative early in 1484. Elected on 30 January and provided by 29 March 1484, he was consecrated at Rome on 26 May as bishop of Durham. Richard III also recommended to Sixtus IV that he be made a cardinal. He was almost certainly engaged, unsuccessfully, in pressing Sixtus's successor Innocent VIII not to sanction Henry Tudor's cause, being advocated early in 1485 by his fellow bishop, John Morton (then in exile). He remained in Rome after Richard III's overthrow, being willing to serve his new king, Henry VII, as proctor from February 1486. He probably returned to England thereafter, but was almost immediately sent back to Rome, as one of the king's envoys to tender his obedience, and arrived there on 8 May 1487. He had not as yet visited his diocese, the temporalities of which had been restored to him only on 16 August 1485, very shortly before Bosworth. A series of undated letters to him from John Auckland, prior of Durham, the last probably written on 1 February 1488, anticipated his arrival in the north-east. But he probably did not set foot in the palatinate until towards the end of 1489, his first recorded action being the appointment of Alexander Lee as his chancellor on 12 January 1490. He stayed in his diocese for little more than two years, before he was once more appointed the king's proctor and orator at the curia. He was in London in February 1492; and arrived in Rome on 14 June. He died, after a short illness, on 14 January 1493 and was buried in the English hospice, of which he had been a member since 1475, chamberlain from 1476 to 1483, and where he had lived in some style from 1480 to 1486.

Shirwood's greatest fame lies in his being one of the earliest English humanists. His library, which he left at Bishop Auckland in 1492, and which was donated by his successor Bishop Richard Fox to Corpus Christi College, Oxford, was collected by him in England and Rome between 1461 and 1487. It contained over three dozen, mainly printed, works, predominantly of classical Roman authors, but also including some moderns. But more significantly he was one of the first Englishmen to learn Greek, possibly being taught first by Manuel of Constantinople, who dedicated a Greek text to George Neville in 1468, then by George Hermonymos in the early 1470s, and perfecting the language later in Rome. He reputedly owned Greek manuscripts which remained in store at Bishop Auckland and disappeared during the Reformation. His support for Greek exiles in England is well documented, extending to exhortation in 1471 to the no doubt bemused inhabitants of Richmondshire to contribute to a collection on behalf of Demetrius Rosato. Shirwood's only surviving writing, which reveals his polished Latin style, is a treatise on the game of *Arithmomachia*, a sophisticated variant of chess, which, so he states in his preface, he taught Archbishop Neville in 1475 during a visit to Calais.

Before his career under Neville took flight Shirwood was attracted to the Carthusian order, which he considered joining in 1458—a leaning which suggests an outlook akin to that of later Christian humanists like John Colet and Sir Thomas More. His attention to his ecclesiastical duties in England was slight. He was for most of his career an absentee from Richmondshire and Durham; his monition to the clergy of Richmondshire in January 1471 against non-residence might perhaps cause modern eyebrows to rise. He left little mark on his diocese. He served three kings loyally as proctor in Rome, which probably says less about the fickleness of his political allegiance, and more about the solidarity and corporate spirit of the episcopate of his day, and an emerging sense of duty to the crown of England as distinct from the individual wearing it. Perhaps his other masters would have concurred with Richard III's recommendation of him to Sixtus IV in 1484 as one 'whose integrity of life, exceptional gentle manners together with the unparalleled virtue with which he is endowed, draw and attract our love to him' (Rymer, *Foedera*, 12.214).

A. J. POLLARD

Sources Emden, *Oxf.* · P. S. Allen, 'Bishop Shirwood of Durham and his library', *EngHR*, 25 (1910), 445–56 · R. Weiss, *Humanism in England during the fifteenth century*, 3rd edn (1967) · Durham Chancery records, PRO, Durh 3 · W. Hutchinson, *The history and antiquities of the county palatine of Durham*, [2nd edn], 1 (1823), 449–56 · A. J. Pollard, *North-eastern England during the Wars of the Roses: lay society, war and politics, 1450–1500* (1990) · C. S. L. Davies, 'Bishop John Morton, the Holy See, and the accession of Henry VII', *EngHR*, 102 (1987), 2–30 · Rymer, *Foedera*, 1st edn, 12.214
Archives CCC Oxf.
Wealth at death approx. £3000: episcopal estate account

Shirwood, Robert (*fl.* 1519–1523), Hebraist, was born in Coventry and educated at Oxford University, where 'he made considerable progress in logicals, but more by far in the Hebrew and Greek languages' (Wood, *Ath. Oxon.*, 1.58). But who could have taught him Hebrew in early sixteenth-century Oxford remains a mystery. To further his knowledge of oriental languages, Shirwood travelled abroad and eventually settled in Louvain, attracted by the presence of the eminent English Hebraist Robert Wakefield at the Collegium Trilingue. By December 1519 he was considered a linguist of sufficient calibre to replace Wakefield as professor of Hebrew. But he resigned after only one month and eventually returned to England. He spent the rest of his life as rector of Dyrham, Gloucestershire.

Shirwood's significance in the history of scholarship rests not only on the fact that he was one of the first Hebrew scholars in Tudor England, but also on his use of rabbinic commentators to elucidate the text of scripture. Though he is credited with making a Latin translation of the Hebrew Bible, his only extant work (apart from a few sermons) is a Latin version of Ecclesiastes, published together with a commentary at Antwerp in 1523. In the preface Shirwood emphasizes that his translation is not a paraphrase but a verbatim rendering of the Hebrew, which students should find helpful because of its literalness and accuracy compared to the Vulgate. Difficult words and phrases are explained by using the Targum and the comments of medieval rabbis. His intention is not to censure the Vulgate, but to rectify errors and omissions and make the meaning of the text that much plainer. He is also anxious to rescue Ecclesiastes from the obscurity into which it had apparently fallen, and to encourage others to study it. A mark of the esteem in which Shirwood's version was held is that the Jesuit scholar Juan de Pineda included it alongside those of Jerome, the Septuagint, and the Targum in his 1620 polyglot edition of Ecclesiastes on the grounds that it was true to the Hebrew original.

The notes provided for the guidance of the reader reveal a competent Hebraist familiar with the rabbis. Almost a decade before Pagninus and Sebastian Muenster demonstrated the value of rabbinic commentaries for a better understanding of the Hebrew Bible, Shirwood had recognized the relevance of the Jewish exegetical tradition for Christians. He was one of the earliest English scholars to appreciate post-biblical Jewish writings.

G. LLOYD JONES

Sources Wood, *Ath. Oxon.*, new edn, 1.58 • V. Andreas, *Fasti academici studii generalis Lovaniensis* (1650), 284 • H. de Vocht, *History of the foundation and rise of the Collegium Trilingue Lovaniense, 1517–1550*, 1 (1951), 500ff. • J. Lelong and C. F. Boerner, *Bibliotheca sacra*, ed. A. G. Masch (1783), vol.1, pt 2, 548 • R. Shirwood, *Ecclesiastes Latine ad veritatem Hebraicam recognitus* (1523) • G. Lloyd Jones, *The discovery of Hebrew in Tudor England: a third language* (1983), 188–9

Shirwood, William. *See* Sherwood, William of (*d.* in or before 1272).

Shoberl [Schoberl], **Frederic** (1775–1853), journalist and writer, was born in London of German descent, and educated at the Moravian school at Fulneck, near Leeds. He settled in London with his family, having married before 1802. He and his wife, Theodosia, had two sons, William and Frederic. Shoberl became, with Henry Colburn, the originator and co-proprietor of the *New Monthly Magazine*, which began in February 1814. For some time he acted as its editor, and contributed original articles and reviews. He was long associated with Rudolph Ackermann, whose *Repository of Arts* he edited from March 1809 to December 1828. He conducted Ackermann's English annual, *The Forget-me-Not*, from 1822 until 1834, and also edited the *Juvenile Forget-me-Not* from 1828 to 1832. In addition to his work for Ackermann, Shoberl was printer and publisher of the *Cornwall Gazette, Falmouth Packet, and Plymouth Journal* (1818–19), a Conservative paper issued at Truro.

As well as his journalistic writing, Shoberl produced numerous other works reflecting his varied interests. In 1814 he published *A History of the University of Oxford*, followed by *A History of the University of Cambridge* in 1815 and *An Historical Account of the House of Saxony* in 1816. He had already published a variety of travel literature: *Travellers in Switzerland* (1803), *Travels in Greece, Palestine, Egypt and Barbary* (translated from a French original, 1812), and *Travels in Caucasus and Georgia* (translated from a German original, 1814). Later he became involved in producing a large number of translations from, among others, Klopstock, Kotzebue, Alfred de Vigny, Thiers, and Chateaubriand. He was also involved in the continuation, with J. Nightingale and others, of Brayley and Britton's *Beauties of England and Wales*, having compiled volume 14 containing Suffolk,

Surrey, and Sussex in 1813. With J. Watkins he compiled *A Biographical Dictionary of Living Authors* (1816).

Shoberl died at Thistle Grove, Brompton, London, on 5 March 1853, and was buried in Kensal Green cemetery on 12 March. His wife had predeceased him on 18 December 1838, as had his younger son, Frederic, who had been printer to Prince Albert at 51 Rupert Street and had died on 22 March 1852, aged forty-eight. Shoberl was survived by his elder son, William, who was first an assistant to the publisher H. Colburn, and then a publisher in his own right at 20 Great Marlborough Street, London.

G. C. BOASE, *rev.* NILANJANA BANERJI

Sources *GM*, 2nd ser., 39 (1853), 446 • *GM*, 2nd ser., 37 (1852), 532 • Allibone, *Dict.* • Boase & Courtney, *Bibl. Corn.* • [J. Watkins and F. Shoberl], *A biographical dictionary of the living authors of Great Britain and Ireland* (1816) • *The Athenaeum* (12 March 1853), 324 • C. H. Timperley, *Encyclopaedia of literary and typographical anecdote*, 2nd edn (1842), 933, 954
Archives Sheff. Arch., letters to James Montgomery • U. Edin. L., letters to James Halliwell-Phillipps

Shoenberg, Sir Isaac (1880–1963), television engineer, was born on 1 March 1880 at Pinsk, in Russia, the eldest son of Yuli Shoenberg, whose profession was forestry. The family were Jewish. He studied at the Kiev Polytechnical Institute, where he read mathematics, mechanical engineering, and electricity. He always retained a keen interest in mathematics, and later received from Kiev a gold medal for his work in this field. After graduation, Shoenberg worked briefly in a sugar-beet factory, and in 1903 he married Esther, daughter of Solomon Aisenstein, hotel owner; they had five children: Mark, a mathematician; Rosalie, a gynaecologist; Alexander, an insurance broker; David, professor of physics at Cambridge University and a fellow of the Royal Society; and Elizabeth, a consultant psychiatrist.

In 1905 Shoenberg joined S. M. Aisenstein at St Petersburg in what, in 1907, became the Russian Wireless Telegraph and Telephone Company, and in 1911 the Russian Marconi Company. He was the chief engineer of this pioneer enterprise, responsible for the research, design, and installation of the earliest wireless stations in Russia. The links between the British and Russian Marconi companies brought him into touch with England, and he became much attracted to its people, and what he saw as its liberal system of government. He wanted to develop his mathematics; accordingly, in 1914, he went to London with his wife and four children. He was admitted to work for a higher degree at the Imperial College of Science and Technology in South Kensington. On the outbreak of war, he volunteered for military service, but was turned down on medical grounds. He then joined the British Marconi Wireless and Telegraph Company. Since he possessed a remarkable aptitude for the complex business of managing patents, he soon became head of the patents department, and then general manager. He became a British subject in 1919.

Shoenberg always had a love of music, and became keenly interested in sound recording, about which he had some original ideas. At that time, gramophone disc recording in Britain was dominated by two firms, the Gramophone Company (His Master's Voice), and the Columbia Graphophone Company, the head of which was Louis Sterling. The two men became friends, and Sterling invited Shoenberg to join Columbia and to introduce his ideas. So successful was this that, in 1928, Sterling appointed Shoenberg general manager.

About this time, the Gramophone Company began to work on the development of television, but when the country was hit by an economic slump, which curtailed the sales of gramophone records, it merged, in 1931, with the Columbia Graphophone Company, assuming the new title of Electric and Musical Industries (EMI). Shoenberg became director of research and head of patents under Sterling as managing director. The important question was whether the company should, at a time of severe recession, continue with television, which was showing little promise, and was viewed with scepticism. Mechanical methods had no future, and no electronic solution was in sight.

Shoenberg now showed himself to be an inspired visionary. He had supreme faith that the problems could eventually be surmounted by his team. He therefore advised his board to pursue an expensive research programme, and his advice was accepted. Work started, and Shoenberg was everywhere, encouraging and drawing out the members of his teams in exhaustive debates, listening carefully to what they said, and often deliberately taking an opposing view in order to stimulate his juniors into argument. He would then meditate on these discussions and make the strategic decisions. In 1932 the team succeeded in making an electronic television picture-generating tube. The pictures were crude, and once again Shoenberg had to decide whether to continue. Courageous as ever, he decided to do so—a decision which was not only fully justified by events, but was also the undoubted origin of the strong position which Great Britain established in the field of television.

In 1935 a government committee under Viscount Ullswater recommended that a public television service should be started by the BBC. Shoenberg had to decide what line standard EMI should offer the government, remembering that it would have to remain in force for a long time, but that the higher it was, the greater both the cost and the technical difficulties. He took a bold scientific risk and recommended 405 lines—a standard far higher than seemed possible with the electronic technology of the time. His decision, which is considered to have been the most difficult that he ever made, was triumphantly vindicated. The 405-line standard was the higher of the two in use (the other being John Logie Baird's 240-line system) when the world's first high-definition public television service was opened by the BBC on 2 November 1936.

Shoenberg was outstandingly brilliant. He was not only a trained scientist of most marked ability, but he had a far-reaching imagination, which was, nevertheless, controlled by the rigour of his logic. He was also an excellent linguist, speaking and reading Russian, German, French, and Hebrew, as well as English. Allied to these numerous attributes was a warm and sensitive nature, and great charm of manner. He was a shy man in his private life, and this became metamorphosed in his professional work into a deep suspicion of publicity, which resulted in much of his unique work receiving inadequate recognition until some years after his death. In 1954 he was awarded the Faraday medal, the highest honour that the Institution of Electrical Engineers can bestow. In 1955 he became a director of EMI, and in June 1962 received a knighthood. In his honour, the Royal Television Society instituted the Shoenberg memorial lecture, sponsored by EMI, and given by some person of distinction in the science of television. Shoenberg died of coronary thrombosis at his London home, 203 Willesden Lane, Willesden, on 25 January 1963. D. C. BIRKINSHAW, *rev.*

Sources personal knowledge (1970) · private information (1970) · *CGPLA Eng. & Wales* (1963) · d. cert. · *The Times* (26 Jan 1963), 10 · *The Times* (28 Jan 1963), 12c
Archives Inst. EE, corresp. and papers
Wealth at death £57,827 18s. 11d.: probate, 26 March 1963, *CGPLA Eng. & Wales*

Shone, Sir Robert Minshull (1906–1992), economist and public servant, was born in Birkenhead, Cheshire, on 27 May 1906, the eldest of the three sons and five daughters of Robert Harold Shone, steel stockholding merchant, and his wife, Hannah, *née* Minshull, a farmer's daughter. Educated at Sedbergh School and at Liverpool University he graduated MEng with a first-class degree in metallurgy in 1929. After two years selling steel for the family business he was awarded a Commonwealth Fund fellowship at the University of Chicago, where he graduated with a master's degree in economics in 1934. After six months of unemployment, when he often watched enviously others better situated consuming large meals in Lyons corner houses while he toyed with a coffee, he joined the British Iron and Steel Federation, of which Sir Andrew Duncan had recently been appointed the first independent chairman. Although briefly enticed away by an appointment as lecturer in industrial economics at the London School of Economics, he was persuaded to return at the end of the academic year as head of the Steel Federation's economic and statistical department. Following the outbreak of war in September 1939 virtually the whole of the federation staff, together with numerous experts in the industry in a range of raw materials and products, were seconded to the Ministry of Supply's iron and steel control. Shone played a key role in the central management as general director of costs, prices, and statistics.

Late in 1945 Shone was appointed economic director and secretary of the British Iron and Steel Federation. Since the election of a Labour government in August 1945, the key issue for the industry had become the government's commitment to nationalize the steel industry. This was Shone's chief staff responsibility, together with prices, development, labour matters, and public relations. Responsibility for raw material and steel supplies lay with the commercial director. In 1950 Shone was appointed director of the federation. The nationalization of steel was a controversial issue because the steel industry had already accepted, in the early 1930s, the principle of steel price supervision by the import duties advisory committee, and the need for central co-ordination to ensure an appropriate degree of development of the industry's resources. Attlee agreed with Duncan that the possibility of attaining the objectives of nationalization by other means should be explored. Following discussions between Herbert Morrison and John Wilmot for the government and Duncan, Sir Ellis Hunter (the federation president), and Shone for the industry, it was jointly recommended that instead of steel nationalization there should be a transfer of key federation staff to an iron and steel board having power to acquire or participate in companies in case this was needed for reasons of defence or default. This proposal was not, however, accepted by the full cabinet, and nationalization of the main steel companies came into effect on 14 February 1951. This was after the Labour government's majority had been reduced from 146 to 8 in the February 1950 election.

In October 1951 the Labour government was replaced by a Conservative government committed to the denationalization of steel, and in May 1953 a new Iron and Steel Act provided denationalization of the nationalized steel companies by an iron and steel holding and realization agency, and public supervision of the industry by a statutory iron and steel board with particular responsibility for prices and development. The board had three full-time members: an independent chairman, Sir Archibald Forbes (from the milling industry); a deputy chairman, Sir Lincoln Evans (former general secretary of the industry's main union); and an executive member. At the suggestion of Sir Ellis Hunter, Shone was appointed to this third post. He strongly influenced all the board's activities, particularly the replacement of basing maximum prices on average costs by that of basing them on new plant costs. John Boys, the senior member of the board's staff, said that when Shone left it felt as if the board had lost its mainspring. Shone's achievements were recognized by his appointment as CBE in 1949 and the award of a knighthood in 1955, and by his appointment to the executive boards of the Royal Statistical Society and the National Institute of Economic and Social Research, and as an honorary fellow of the London School of Economics.

Late in 1961 Shone was appointed by the chancellor of the exchequer, Selwyn Lloyd, as director-general of the newly formed National Economic Development Council (NEDC), comprising representatives of industrial management, trade unions, and government departments, together with some independents, co-operating to improve economic performance and to increase the rate of sound growth. Sir Donald MacDougall, the economic director, recruited university economists, and Tom Fraser, industrial director, recruited managers and trade unionists from industry, generally on the basis of secondment. The government provided the secretary from the Ministry of Labour together with accommodation in Millbank Tower and a grant. Within a year of its first meeting the NEDC published the 'green book' *Growth of the UK Economy*

to 1966, which examined the implications of a 4 per cent overall growth rate for seventeen major industries and services, and for manpower, investment, and the balance of payments; and also the 'orange book' *Conditions Favourable to Faster Growth*. A further reassessment, *The Growth of the Economy*, came one year later. In 1964 came the first of the economic development committees (or 'Little Neddies') for over a dozen industries or services. These had quadripartite membership, like the NEDC, together with a member and a secretary provided by the National Economic Development Office. Some, such as that for mechanical engineering, did constructive work appreciated by the industry or service concerned, and a few, such as that for traffic congestion, were still continuing in 1999 by means of the committee converting itself into a private company when the NEDC was abolished in 1992. Others did not succeed in finding a useful role and were wound up and replaced by economic development committees covering other sectors.

For almost three years Shone and the NEDC had a good press and were well supported. But in October 1964 the balance of the whole concept was undermined by Labour's narrow election victory and the establishment of a new Department of Economic Affairs with George Brown as first secretary of state. This quickly robbed the NEDC of MacDougall and most of his key staff, and it started preparing a very detailed government plan in which industrial management, the trade unions, and the independent element of the NEDC played a very minor part. MacDougall had a particularly close view of Shone's role in the NEDC in 1961–6. In his obituary of Shone he wrote:

> Once the main documents had been agreed, the council did indeed spend many months discussing pay, prices, profits, productivity, and their relation to growth and jobs. The TUC was not prepared to make a deal with a Conservative government, but the mutual understanding resulting from these discussions greatly helped the incoming Labour government to put a prices and incomes policy into place after October 1964. So Neddy achieved quite a lot during its early years and a great deal of credit must go to Robert Shone. Highly intelligent but modest, persistent but a good listener, he had considerable diplomatic talents. He did much to overcome potential discord between the unions, a Conservative government and the employers. He helped indeed to get a consensus between the three parties—and, I believe, the Labour Opposition … He was saddened by Neddy's demise but proud that it had survived for 30 years, albeit in a much less influential form than in its youth. I should not be surprised if it were reinvented in some form or other. (*The Guardian*)

Shone would have retired late in 1965 on completion of his four-year appointment, but was persuaded by George Brown to wait until the election of March 1966 had determined the fate of the Labour government and of the NEDC. Shortly after his retirement Shone was appointed a fellow of Nuffield College, Oxford (1966–7), then visiting professor of the City University (1967–83), and a special professor at Nottingham University (1971–3). He was also a director of APV Holdings, the M and G group, and the Rank Organisation. His research and writings, notably his book *Price and Investment Relationships* (1975), particularly concerned the principle of basing prices on new plant rather than average costs, which he had introduced into the steel industry.

Shone had many friends, women as well as men. He and a Canadian lady had at one stage intended to get married but this proved impossible (she being a Catholic). He enjoyed golf, art, and travelling, particularly cruising. In his last years he suffered from naso-pharyngeal cancer. He died at the Royal Free Hospital, Camden, London, on 13 December 1992, of pneumonia.   BERNARD KEELING

Sources B. Keeling, 'Shone, Sir Robert Minshull', *DBB*, 5.121–5 · B. S. Keeling and A. E. G. Wright, *The development of the modern British steel industry* (1964) · D. Burn, *The steel industry, 1939–1959: a study in competition and planning* (1961) · K. Middlemas, *Industry, unions and government: twenty one years of NEDC* (1983) · *The Guardian* (28 Dec 1992) · *The Independent* (30 Dec 1992) · *Daily Telegraph* (21 Dec 1992) · *The Times* (16 Dec 1992) · *The Times* (30 Dec 1992) · *WWW*, 1991–5 · personal knowledge (2004) · private information (2004) · d. cert.
Archives U. Nott. L., papers | BLPES, corresp. with the editors of the *Economic Journal*
Likenesses photograph, repro. in *Daily Telegraph* · photograph, repro. in *The Times* (16 Dec 1992) · photograph, repro. in Keeling, 'Shone, Sir Robert Minshull', 121
Wealth at death £1,144,083: probate, 27 April 1993, *CGPLA Eng. & Wales*

Shonfield, Sir **Andrew Akiba** (1917–1981), political economist, was born on 10 August 1917 at Tadworth, Surrey, the fourth of six sons and the fifth of the seven children of Rabbi Victor Schonfeld, of north London, and his wife, Rachel Lea, daughter of Josef Sternberg, of Budapest. He was educated at the Jewish secondary school founded by his Hungarian-born father, at St Paul's School (foundation scholar), and at Magdalen College, Oxford (demy; chancellor's English essay prize, 1938). He obtained second-class honours in philosophy, politics, and economics in 1939. He later changed his name to Shonfield. Shonfield served in the army (Royal Artillery) from 1940 to 1946, with the final rank of major, general staff, and was mentioned in dispatches. In 1942 he married Zuzanna Maria, daughter of Alfred Przeworski, a Polish industrialist; they had one son and one daughter. He spent fifteen years in journalism: with the *Financial Times* (1947–57) as a features writer and from 1950 as foreign editor, and with *The Observer* (1958–61) as economic editor.

In the twenty years of his subsequent career Shonfield was director of studies at the Royal Institute of International Affairs (1961–8), chairman of the Social Science Research Council (1969–71), director of the Royal Institute of International Affairs (1972–7), professor of economics at the European University Institute, Florence (from 1978), and consultant to multinational and UK firms. His public activities included lectures and membership of the royal (Donovan) commission on the reform of the trade unions and employers' associations (1965–8), the departmental committee on overseas representation (the Duncan committee, 1968–9), the EEC 'Vedel group' (1972), and of international discussion groups with policy makers and academics.

Shonfield's writings included *British Economic Policy Since the War* (1958) and *The Attack on World Poverty* (1960). *Modern Capitalism* (1965) surveyed post-1945 changes in the Western capitalist system. It examined new approaches to economic management aimed at full employment, improvement for the disadvantaged, and growth, and drew upon comparative European and American evidence. It gave expression to the optimism then so widespread and reinforced perceptions about the directions in which capitalist societies appeared to be moving. His minority report to the Donovan commission stressed that trade unions outside the law could only diminish liberty. *Europe: Journey to an Unknown Destination* (1973) encompassed his 1972 Reith lectures, and won the Cortina-Ulisse literary prize. It was followed by *International Economic Relations of the Western World, 1959–71* (1976). Shonfield died while engaged in reconsideration of the changed conditions of his earlier assumptions and in the study of political, administrative, and social factors affecting how Western democracies and Japan coped with the strain. *The Use of Public Power* (1982) and *In Defence of the Mixed Economy* (1984) posthumously recorded his conclusions. His wide-ranging critique of capitalism in developed democratic societies was influential internationally in the debate about the balance between private and public power.

Shonfield's intellectual leadership derived as much from the qualities of his personality as from those of his mind. His clarity of exposition and ability to remove confusion and reduce something complicated to its simple elements led him sometimes disconcertingly straight to the point. But his was an allusive mind and he would sometimes circle round a subject in order to see it better and reconnoitre before taking a firm position. His charm, generosity of spirit, attractive and distinct voice, and occasional dry comment imparted sheer pleasure to his listeners. He was ready to engage in reasoned discussion with anyone, was tough in debate, and challenged others in order to find out what he really thought himself. At meetings he could change the atmosphere, speaking with energy and emphasis in a constructive tone and in a manner that invited co-operative rather than aggressive responses.

The family influence of Orthodox Judaism and Talmudic study had a powerful effect on Shonfield. He was a rebel against tradition who had escaped after great struggle. The environment of the 1930s made him feel a revulsion against totalitarianism and a sense of the needs of others which went beyond mere justice towards active kindness. He described *Modern Capitalism* as an oblique record of his conversion from one view of the world, with strong elements of the cataclysmic, to a more hopeful standpoint. With no pronounced party political stance in his utterances his influence was the wider. His words 'groping for the shape of contemporary history' defined an approach in which beliefs played little part, but guiding principles did: people were seen as ends not means, and truth was paramount. He had a love of fiction and a covert passion for creative writing; he published one novel.

Shonfield was knighted in 1978, became a fellow of the Imperial College of Science and Technology (1970), and received an honorary DLitt from Loughborough University (1972). He died in St George's Hospital, Tooting, London, on 23 January 1981.   ARTHUR KNIGHT, rev.

Sources *Financial Times* (24 Jan 1981) · *The Times* (24 Jan 1981) · A. Bullock, *International Affairs* (spring 1981) · personal knowledge (1990) · private information (1990) · *CGPLA Eng. & Wales* (1981)
Archives BLPES, MSS | Bodl. Oxf., corresp. with Sidney Dell, MS Eng. c. 5861 | FILM BFI NFTVA, documentary footage | SOUND BL NSA, performance recordings
Likenesses photograph, repro. in *The Times*
Wealth at death £14,954: probate, 18 Feb 1981, *CGPLA Eng. & Wales*

Shoosmith, Arthur Gordon (1888–1974), architect, was born in St Petersburg on 30 June 1888, one of the five sons of Henry Shoosmith (*d.* 1918), entrepreneur, then resident there, and his wife, Alice Southern. Shoosmith was brought up in Russia and Finland before being sent to Latymer School and then to Haileybury College after winning a scholarship. In 1906 he was articled to C. Smith & Son, architects, in Reading, and attended evening classes at University College, Reading. After 1909 he worked as an assistant to M. S. Ward, Ralph Knott and E. Stone Collins, R. Frank Atkinson, and H. S. Goodhart-Rendel in succession while attending evening classes first at the Architectural Association School of Architecture and after 1911 at the Royal Academy Schools. There he became friends with Cyril Farey (1888–1954) and Alick Horsnell (1882/3–1916), both brilliant draughtsmen; he also knew J. W. Whitelaw (1886–1913), about whom he later wrote a memoir for the memorial book published after his accidental death. Shoosmith was unfit for active service in the First World War but his knowledge of Russian and German was used by the intelligence corps in prisoner of war camps in Scotland.

Shoosmith returned to Goodhart-Rendel's office in 1919 and then worked for Sir John Burnet. In 1920 he won the Soane medallion and travelled in Italy. In that same year he was recommended to Sir Edwin Lutyens by the Royal Institute of British Architects to succeed John Greaves as his permanent representative in New Delhi. Shoosmith's task was to supervise the construction of Viceroy's House, and in the opinion of Henry Alexander Nesbitt Medd (1892–1977)—his opposite number in Herbert Baker's office and later the last chief architect to the government of India—'its success was in no small measure due to his meticulous insistence on the highest standards of workmanship in his interpretation of the drawings sent out from London' (note in photo album III, Medd papers, department of south Asian studies, University of Cambridge). Shoosmith greatly admired Lutyens's achievement in New Delhi in which, he argued, 'East and West so blend their music that one is unaware of difference of origin. The effect is of something astonishingly original, and yet nowhere is there a wilful departure from sanctified tradition' ('The design of New Delhi', *Indian State Railways Magazine*, 4/5, Feb 1931, 428).

Shoosmith was responsible for two buildings in Delhi on his own account. The Lady Hardinge Serai (1930–31) was a rest house for travellers and their beasts of burden which owed much to Lutyens's stylistic synthesis. As he came only second in both of the competitions held in 1927 for the Anglican and Roman Catholic churches in New Delhi, both won by Medd, Shoosmith was recommended by Lutyens as architect for the new military church to be built in the cantonments to the west of the city. Built in 1928–30, this was his masterpiece. Lutyens encouraged him in using simple brickwork: 'My dear Shoo, Bricks! … The Romans did it! Why should not Britons? You will get a fine wall, and their mass, proportion, with precious fenestration, will do the rest' (letter of 28 Feb 1928, Hussey, 493). Shoosmith's massive brick walls step back to enclose the interior volumes, creating an austere and sublime mass which echoed both the monuments of the ancient world and modern industrial structures; although exotic, however, the result was recognizably a Christian church. Contemporaries were deeply impressed; 'It is *superb*', wrote Robert Byron (postcard to Shoosmith, 4 May 1931, formerly in possession of Mrs Shoosmith), while Christopher Hussey argued that this 'Elemental' conception

> has very definite style, appropriate both to the climate and the building's purpose. Had this church been the work of a French or German architect, Europe would be flabbergasted by the magnificently simple and direct design. But since it is the work of an Englishman, it will probably never be heard of abroad.   (*Country Life*, 69, 9 May 1931, 582)

The first baby baptized in St Martin's, in 1931, was Shoosmith's daughter and only child. In 1927, in Rangoon, he had married Marjorie Cartwright Reid (1894–1996), the daughter of Herbert Cartwright Reid, military dock engineer; she had been brought up in Edinburgh and studied at the Edinburgh School of Art before travelling with her parents to India. Marjorie Shoosmith advised Lutyens on inscriptions used inside Viceroy's House and executed a portrait group in the style of a Mughal miniature depicting the architects presenting models of the government buildings to the viceroy, Lord Irwin (original now in possession of the earl of Halifax). Both Shoosmith and his wife became deeply interested in the culture of India.

Following the inauguration of New Delhi in 1931, Shoosmith was appointed OBE and returned home. With Britain in depression it was a difficult time to attempt to set up in private practice after so long an absence. Prospective commissions at home and elsewhere in the British empire all evaporated. A design for a viaduct on Western Avenue, London, made during a trial partnership with William Robert Davidge in 1937, remained unexecuted, and all Shoosmith managed to carry out were alterations to a factory in Smithfield. He was also depressed to observe that developments in Europe were undermining New Delhi as an influence in India, so that 'it is in danger of appearing as a splendid culmination to the old epoch instead of inaugurating a new' ('Present-day architecture in India', *The Nineteenth Century and After*, 120, Feb 1938, 209). In 1942 he joined the Ministry of Works, and in the following year he became an inspector in the new Ministry of Town and Country Planning; his widow considered that 'though sadly frustrated in his creative urge to design buildings, he did find some outlet in writing about them, and influencing the decisions to preserve those of value to posterity' (private information). He retired in 1957 and died of bronchopneumonia at his home, Wade's Cottage, Slindon, Sussex, on 14 January 1974.

'Shoosmith I used to meet at lunch at the A. A. (1939–40) … [A] tired, gentle little man, quite nice to talk to but somehow crushed', recalled Sir John Summerson when discussing the several architects who had immersed themselves in India only to return to a Britain which did not care. 'All sad men … It all fits into the picture of latter-day India which Paul Scott's *Raj Quartet* gives us' (private information). Shoosmith nevertheless deserves to be remembered. He was responsible for only two buildings, but one of them is among the most remarkable churches of the twentieth century, for in the Delhi cantonments he displayed genius. Arthur Shoosmith may also be taken as representative of so many talented architects who devoted their careers to service far away in British India.

GAVIN STAMP

Sources private information (2004) [Marjorie Shoosmith, widow; H. Medd; J. Summerson; Genevieve Warwick, granddaughter; Clare Warwick, daughter] · fellowship nomination form, RIBA BAL · G. Stamp, 'Indian summer', *ArchR*, 159 (1976), 365–72 · C. Hussey, *The life of Sir Edwin Lutyens* (1950)
Archives RIBA Drawings Collection, drawings
Likenesses photographs, priv. coll.
Wealth at death £52,605: probate, 6 Feb 1974, *CGPLA Eng. & Wales*

Elizabeth [Jane] **Shore** (*d.* 1526/7?), by unknown artist

Shore [*née* Lambert], **Elizabeth** [Jane] (*d.* 1526/7?), royal mistress, was the daughter of John Lambert (*d.* 1487), citizen and mercer of London, and Amy (*d.* 1488), daughter of Robert Marshall, citizen and grocer of London. She married William Shore (*d.* 1494), a London mercer, but the marriage was annulled in 1476, at her petition, on the grounds of his impotence. The main source for her relationship with *Edward IV is Thomas More, who is responsible (in his *History of Richard III*) for the story that Edward claimed to have three concubines: the merriest, the wiliest, and the holiest harlot in his realm. 'Shore's wife' (the name Jane was attached to her by the dramatist Thomas Heywood in 1599) was the merriest; in More's words: 'a proper wit had she, & could both rede wel & write, mery in company, redy & quick of aunswer, neither mute nor ful of bable, sometime taunting without displesure & not without disport'. More continued with a famous tribute:

> For many he had, but her he loved, whose favour to saithe trouth … she never abused to any mans hurt, but to many a mans comfort. … And finally in many weighty sutes, she stode many men in gret stede, either for none, or very smal rewardes, & those rather gay then rich: either for that she was content with the dede selfe well done, or for that she delited to be suid unto, & to show what she was able to do wyth the king … (More, 56)

Perhaps predictably, no source from Edward's reign names Elizabeth Shore as a royal mistress, but she does enter the historical record in the next reign. The king's death on 9 April 1483 apparently left her in need of a new protector, and a contemporary reference casts Thomas

Grey, marquess of Dorset in that role. In October 1483, when he was in rebellion against Richard III, he was accused of holding 'the unshameful and mischievous woman called Shore's wife in adultery' (*CPR, 1476–85*, 371). The great chronicle of London and Thomas More, by contrast, link her instead with Edward's friend and chamberlain William, Lord Hastings. According to the *Great Chronicle*, she was called to answer for some of Hastings's goods after his death in June 1483 and her own goods were attached by the sheriffs of London. She was also put to public penance 'for the lyfe that she ledd with the said lord hastyngys and othir grete astatys' (Thomas and Thornley, 233). More's account of that penance is another famous set piece: 'In which she went in countenance & pace demure so womanly, & albeit she were out of al array save her kyrtle only: yet went she so fair & lovely … that her great shame wan her much praise' (More, 54–5).

The claimed association of Elizabeth Shore with Hastings led some later historians to argue that she was an intermediary in a Woodville–Hastings plot against Richard, duke of Gloucester, in June 1483. There is no contemporary support for the claim, and More himself, the source for the story, explicitly dismisses it as an implausible fiction put about by Gloucester. Elizabeth was, however, in political trouble of some sort after Edward's death, and was imprisoned in Ludgate at the commandment of Richard III, as Gloucester became. This is made clear by an undated letter from Richard to the bishop of Lincoln, announcing that the king's solicitor, Thomas Lynom, had contracted matrimony with her, being 'merveillously blynded and abused' (Horrox and Hammond, 3.259). The king hoped that the bishop might be able to talk him out of his infatuation but, failing that, Elizabeth was to be released from gaol if she could find sureties for her good behaviour and given into her father's keeping until the king's return to London. Lynom evidently remained unmoved by episcopal argument, for the will of Elizabeth's father, made in September 1487, makes it clear that the two had married. Elizabeth was bequeathed a bed of arras and (rather pointedly, perhaps) a painted cloth of Mary Magdalen and Martha. Lynom managed to transfer his services to the Tudors and was active on the Welsh border under Henry VII and in the early years of Henry VIII. He was a councillor of Prince Arthur and controller of the rolls of his household.

Lynom was dead by 29 July 1518, and this perhaps provides the context for More's description of Elizabeth fallen into penury in her old age. But More's claim that she had to resort to begging seems overdrawn, particularly if the Thomas Lynom who was active in Wales after 1518 was her son. No definite identification of her children can, however, be made. Her father's will mentions a Julian Lynom, bequeathed 40s., who was perhaps the first child of the marriage, but he cannot be traced. It is not known exactly when Elizabeth died. More writes of her as still alive, though very old, when he was composing his *History of Richard III* in the second decade of the sixteenth century; a variant text of the *History* states that she died in the eighteenth year of Henry VIII (1526/1527). Though not implausible, the date cannot be proved. As Jane Shore she enjoyed a considerable literary afterlife, as the subject of poems, ballads, and plays; the most notable of the latter was Nicholas Rowe's *Tragedy of Jane Shore*, first produced in 1714. She also appears in a number of historical novels.

ROSEMARY HORROX

Sources N. Barker, 'The real Jane Shore', *Etoniana*, 125 (1972), 383–91; 126 (1972), 410–14 · R. Birley, 'Jane Shore in literature', *Etoniana*, 125 (1972), 391–7; 126 (1972), 399–407 · St Thomas More, *The history of King Richard III*, ed. R. S. Sylvester (1963), vol. 2 of *The Yale edition of the complete works of St Thomas More* · A. H. Thomas and I. D. Thornley, eds., *The great chronicle of London* (1938) · R. Horrox and P. W. Hammond, eds., *British Library Harleian manuscript 433*, 4 vols. (1979–83) · J. B. Smith, 'Crown and community in the principality of north Wales in the reign of Henry Tudor', *Welsh History Review / Cylchgrawn Hanes Cymru*, 3 (1966–7), 145–71
Likenesses oils, Eton [*see illus.*] · on brass (of her father, John Lambert), Hinxworth, Hertfordshire

Shore, (Margaret) Emily (1819–1839), writer and naturalist, was born on 25 December 1819 at Bury St Edmunds, Suffolk, the eldest of the children of Thomas *Shore (1793–1863) [*see under* Shore, Louisa Catherine] and Margaret Anne Twopeny. A writer and educator who declined preferment in the Church of England on matters of conscience, Thomas Shore received private pupils at his home, where he also educated his daughters. All three of Shore's daughters distinguished themselves as writers and editors. Arabella Shore and Louisa Catherine *Shore (1824–1895), Emily's younger sisters, were poets, critics, and translators, who eventually served as editors of the

(Margaret) Emily Shore (1819–1839), by unknown engraver

remarkable *Journal of Emily Shore*, published in 1891 and reissued with illustrations in 1898.

Emily Shore herself was a prodigious young polymath who, according to her sisters' introduction to the journal, also produced natural histories, histories of the Jews, the Greeks, and the Romans, two novels, three epics, many poems, and a translation of Xenophon's *Anabasis*. Of these works only two short essays survive, 'An account of a cuckoo' and 'The Golden Crested Wren', both published by the *Penny Magazine* in December 1837. Her literary reputation, therefore, rests with her journal, kept from 5 July 1831 until 24 June 1839, a short time before her death at the age of nineteen. It is written in a fine, printed hand and runs to twelve octavo volumes. Only three of these are known to be extant, but portions from all twelve volumes were published in the 1890s editions, more than fifty years after its initial writing.

Emily Shore's exceptional journal is a *tour de force*, the product of a finely tuned intellect and giving evidence of an unslakeable thirst for learning. Shore, who served as a tutor to her younger siblings, read, digested, and wrote about everything from Shakespeare to Charles Babbage's *Economy of Manufactures*, from contemporary newspapers to classical texts, from the working of printing presses to the classification of flowers. Although she was young and removed from mainstream life, she had her fingers on the pulse of her time. In her journal she commented not merely on daily events in her own life but on institutions such as the London Zoo, and on the Reform Bill of 1832 and the new poor law of 1834. Every day she also spent hours recording the habits of birds in the family garden at

Woodbury, Potton, Bedfordshire, observations which were partly detailed in her journal and would lead to her essays in the *Penny Magazine*.

Emily Shore's journal is therefore memorable for a number of reasons. First, it offers the life story of the coming of age both of a young woman and of an early Victorian intellect—one without benefit of formal education. She was initially tutored by her parents but soon became an autodidact. As her sister Arabella said, 'She made her whole existence a happy schoolroom' (Shore, vi). This was particularly true of the natural world. At work on her journal when the 'crazes' for natural history were in full bloom, she was a keen observer and recorder who aimed at working with scientific precision, noting that 'in the study of natural history it is particularly important not to come too hastily to conclusions, but to study facts from observation frequently and most carefully before an inference is drawn' (ibid., 119). The journal also offers one of the finest early examples of a diarist commenting on and experimenting with the diary form. Far from lacking in sophistication, her journal is finely crafted, another example of her care in learning; she found 'the use of the pen … among the most valuable means of improving the mind' (ibid., 138).

As well as an index to Emily Shore's learning, her feelings, and her sense of the journal form, in its last volume the journal becomes a unique, detailed nineteenth-century meditation on death by tuberculosis. When her family moved her to Madeira for her health's sake, she continued to record her impressions of self and surroundings, but as a naturalist had little energy to learn of new species or to enjoy their beauty and peculiarities. Instead, in the end she turned to read her own body and spirit and wrote the story of their struggles and of the body's ultimate decline. Although she ceased writing letters, which became 'an effort of mind and body which I dread to attempt' (Shore, 345–6), she continued to document her illness in her journal: 'I feel weaker every morning, and suppose I am beginning to sink; still I can at times take up my pen' (ibid., 351). Loath to let her journal go, she would hold a pen at least one more time, on 24 June 1839, a fortnight before her death, when she made a last journal entry in a weakened hand. Emily Shore died of consumption on 7 July 1839 at Funchal, Madeira, and was buried there in the Strangers' burial-ground.

BARBARA T. GATES

Sources E. Shore, *Journal*, ed. B. T. Gates (1991) [incl. introduction by B. T. Gates] · 'Shore, Louisa Catherine', *DNB*

Likenesses M. E. Shore, portrait, 1837 · portrait, 1839, repro. in Shore, *Journal*, 351 · engraving, NPG [*see illus.*]

Shore, James (1805–1874), founder of the Free Church of England, was born on 31 July 1805 in Haselbury Plucknett, Somerset, the third son of Thomas Shore (*c*.1776–1833), merchant, of Nottington, Broadway, Dorset, and his wife, Frances (*c*.1776–1828).

Shore was educated at Norton-sub-Hamdon, Somerset, and Dorchester before matriculating on 6 February 1824

at Sidney Sussex College, Cambridge, from where he graduated BA in 1828 and MA in 1831. On 27 June 1827 he married Susannah Gream (1800–1868), originally of Godstone, Surrey, but now resident in the parish of St Andrew's, Plymouth (where the wedding took place), with whom he had three daughters: Julia Berry (*b*. 1828), Emily Frances (*b*. 1830), and Susannah Isabella Pomeroy (1830–1860). Shore was ordained deacon by William Carey, bishop of Exeter, on 19 October 1828 and priest on 25 October 1829, and served as curate at the parish of Berry Pomeroy, Devon. In 1830 he was appointed minister of the chapel of ease at nearby Bridgetown, Totnes.

Shore's adherence to the principles of 'serious religion', as evangelicalism was then known, eventually brought him into sharp conflict with his unsympathetic diocesan, Henry Phillpotts, bishop of Exeter and a strong high-churchman. In 1843 a complicated and acrimonious legal dispute broke out between Shore, Phillpotts, and Edward Adolphus Seymour, eleventh duke of Somerset (patron of Berry Pomeroy). Consequently Shore became, albeit momentarily, one of the most celebrated religious figures in England—a martyr, in the view of his numerous sympathizers, to ecclesiastical despotism and oppression.

The Shore case involved the legal right of a clergyman to secede from the established church, given the alleged indelibility of Anglican orders. Unable to secure a new licence to officiate from Phillpotts, Shore seceded and formed, at Bridgetown Chapel, the first congregation of a new denomination: the Free Church of England. Phillpotts countered by filing charges in the ecclesiastical courts arguing that the seventy-sixth canon prohibited clerical secession from the church; secession, the bishop claimed, would destroy all sense of episcopal discipline over the clergy. The case, known officially as *Barnes v. Shore*, was a protracted and costly affair which provoked a substantial public campaign on behalf of Shore and the cause of religious liberty. It also led to a heated debate over the indelibility of Anglican orders and prompted, in February 1849, the introduction of a Clergy Relief Bill in parliament providing legal protection for seceding clergymen.

Ultimately the case was decided for Phillpotts by the judicial committee of the privy council, and Shore was imprisoned at Exeter gaol (9 March – 30 May 1849) under the pretext of the non-payment of court costs, but effectively for seceding from the Church of England. After paying costs, and in deteriorating health, he was released, returning to his Bridgetown congregation where he remained until 1862, when he moved to Matlock, Derbyshire. Here Shore became associated with John Smedley and his famous hydro. Several years later he moved to Buxton, Derbyshire, where he became the successful proprietor of the Malvern House Hydropathic Hotel (later the Buxton Hydropathic) and minister of the Free Church of England. Shore died at Hartington, Derbyshire, on 12 August 1874 as the result of a riding accident, and was buried, amid much local ceremony, four days later at Bridgetown. He became an important *cause célèbre* in English evangelicalism, his case adding to the crisis of confidence which seized not only evangelicalism, but the Church of England itself, in the mid-nineteenth century.

GRAYSON CARTER

Sources G. Carter, 'The case of the Reverend James Shore', *Journal of Ecclesiastical History*, 47 (1996), 478–504 • J. Shore, *The case of the Revd James Shore, MA, by himself* (1849) • J. Shore, *A statement of the proceedings of the bishop of Exeter in the case of the Revd James Shore, MA* (1848) • H. Phillpotts, *The case of the Revd James Shore* (1849) • W. B. Cosens, *The case of the Revd James Shore, as between the patron and the vicar, in a letter to his parishioners* (1849) • C. Eardley, *An appeal to the country on behalf of the Revd James Shore* (1849) • G. C. B. Davies, *Henry Phillpotts, bishop of Exeter* (1954) • F. Vaughan, *A history of the Free Church of England* (1938) • F. S. Merryweather, *History of the Free Church of England* (1873) • T. E. Thoresby, *The Free Church of England* (1873) • J. E. P. Robertson, *Reports and cases argued and determined in the ecclesiastical courts at Doctors' Commons* (1845), 382–99 • J. L. Adolphus and T. F. Ellis, *Queen's bench reports* (1848), 640–73 • Venn, *Alum. Cant.* • *Buxton Advertiser* (15 Aug 1874) • *Buxton Advertiser* (19 Aug 1874)
Archives Dorset RO | Devon RO, Seymours of Berry Pomeroy MSS • Exeter Cathedral, dean and chapter library, Bishop Phillpotts MSS
Likenesses portrait, repro. in Vaughan, *History of the Free Church*, 2nd edn (1960)
Wealth at death under £9000: administration, 23 March 1875, *CGPLA Eng. & Wales*

Shore, John (*c*.1662–1752), trumpeter, was born in London, the son of Matthias Shore (*d*. 1700), trumpeter, one of a family of three celebrated trumpeters at the court of the late Stuart and early Hanoverian sovereigns. Already one of the trumpeters-in-ordinary from 30 March 1688, he seems to have joined the court band as a musician-in-ordinary in 1695; he became sergeant-trumpeter in 1707 on the death of William Shore, his uncle or, less probably, brother, and he lived to serve George II. He was also appointed lutenist of the Chapel Royal in 1715.

Shore significantly developed a style of playing by which the trumpet escaped from the restrictions of a purely military style and took its place in England as an orchestral instrument, so giving valuable stimulus to Henry Purcell and making it possible for English trumpeters to meet the requirements of the music of G. F. Handel. He is said to have produced 'a tone as sweet as that of a hautboy'. In view of the technical advance implied it is thought that it was probably he who was the 'Mr Showers' who was complimented in the *Gentleman's Journal* of January 1692 for having played in hitherto impossible keys and 'with all the softness imaginable'; but at that date the reference might conceivably be to his father or, less probably, his kinsman William. Be that as it may, his playing attracted the attention of Purcell before 1694. He was a minor composer for the instrument.

It was Sir John Hawkins, writing in 1776, who stated that John Shore devised the tuning-fork, which he used in preference to the pitch-pipe when tuning his lute. The precise form of the appliance is not stated. Shore died in London on 20 November 1752.

WATKINS SHAW, *rev.*

Sources *Gentleman's Journal* (Jan 1692) • Burney, *Hist. mus.*, 3.499 • J. Hawkins, *A general history of the science and practice of music*, new edn, 3 vols. (1853), 752 • E. F. Rimbault, ed., *The old cheque-book, or book of remembrance, of the Chapel Royal, from 1561 to 1744*, CS, new

ser., 3 (1872), 28, 229 • A. Ashbee, ed., *Records of English court music*, 9 vols. (1986–96) • D. Smithers, 'Shore', *New Grove*

Shore, John, first Baron Teignmouth (1751–1834), governor-general of Bengal and founder and first president of the British and Foreign Bible Society, was born on 8 October 1751 at St James Street, Piccadilly, where the family were living temporarily, and was baptized in St James's Church on 23 October. He was the elder of the two children of Thomas Shore (*d. c*.1759), a supercargo in the East India Company trading to China, and his second wife, Dorothy (*d*. 1783), daughter of Captain Shepherd of the company's naval service. The family lived in Melton Place, near Romford in Essex, where John Shore attended school until he was seven, when he was sent to a school in Tottenham. At fifteen he went to Harrow School, where he developed a taste for the Latin and Greek classics which remained with him throughout his life. Nominated for a writership in Bengal by Frederick Pigou, a family friend who was a proprietor of the East India Company, he left Harrow for a commercial school at Hoxton to study bookkeeping and accounts, the formal requirement for appointment as a writer in the company's civil service.

Bengal, 1769–1785 Shore sailed for Bengal late in 1768, arriving in May 1769. Appointed as a writer to the secret political department, in 1770 he was sent as assistant to the controlling council of revenue at Murshidabad, one of the two divisions for the collection of the revenue of the company's Bengal territories. Shore became, *de facto*, the company's chief agent in the vast district because his superiors were busy elsewhere on their own business or, as he reported to his mother, were indolent and indifferent to their responsibilities (Shore, *Memoir of … Teignmouth*, 1.28). During Shore's first year in Murshidabad, as the revenue system was breaking down under years of mismanagement and corruption by the company's and the nawab's local officials, an appalling famine, one of the worst in Indian history, devastated the area. The company's officials in the area were charged, in both India and England, with manipulating the food supply for their own profit, and Shore himself was accused of corruption, but after an investigation his name was cleared.

Shore's opportunity to show his ability came in 1772 with the changes instituted by Warren Hastings, the governor-general of Bengal. The directors in London had decided that the company should no longer try to manage the revenues through Indian intermediaries, but should take direct control, and Shore was posted to Rajshahi, one of the most important districts, as assistant to Samuel Middleton. He also had the temporary post as Persian translator at the nawab's court in Murshidabad. Although at first he had no grammars or dictionaries, he managed through oral instruction from local teachers to study Arabic, Persian, Hindustani, and Bengali, becoming one of the first of the company's servants to achieve reasonable literacy in Indian languages. He maintained his proficiency in Persian throughout his life.

Shore's growing reputation led to his appointment by Hastings in 1775 as one of five members to the provincial

John Shore, first Baron Teignmouth (1751–1834), by George Richmond, 1832

revenue council at Calcutta. This was the period of the great quarrels between Hastings and his leading councillor, Philip Francis, but, although Shore was known to share many of Francis's views, Hastings recognized his ability, and in 1780, when the revenue council was replaced by the committee of revenue, he was appointed to it, serving on it until he left India in 1785, and becoming its acting head. In addition, he was sent by Hastings to make revenue settlements in the districts of Patna and Dacca. In 1785 he summed up the committee's work, and indeed his view of the company's administration in general, when he wrote that the members were vested with vast power, but to pretend that they were able to carry out their duties responsibly would be 'folly and falsehood' (Shore, *Memoir of … Teignmouth*, 1.73).

While an immense official correspondence bears witness to Shore's energy, hard work, and mastery of the intricacies of the Bengal revenue system, surviving letters to his mother and other friends in England give little indication of his private life. The company servants were still making fortunes through private trade, commissions on the revenue collections, and gifts from the nawab and his officials, but, as Shore complained to his mother, 'the road to opulence grows daily narrower, and is more crowded with competitors', restricted by stricter supervision in London. By 1781 he had acquired enough, however, through savings from his salary, trade, and investments, to offer his mother £1000 a year, which she did not accept,

and he spoke of his 'handsome emoluments' from his position in the revenue departments as 'avowed, authorised, and liberal' (Shore, *Memoir of … Teignmouth*, 1.79–84).

Of the friends Shore made in Bengal, two were of particular importance to him. One was Sir William Jones, the great scholar who came out as judge of the supreme court. On Jones's death Shore succeeded him as president of the Asiatic Society of Bengal, and he later edited a collection of Jones's letters (*Memoirs of … William Jones*). The other was Charles Grant, who later became a dominant figure in the East India Company and the leading advocate for the evangelization of India, but at this time he was seeking spiritual advice from Shore, which led to his acceptance of Shore's evangelical Christianity. Shore's own religious attitude is summed up in a comment he made about his mother's religion as being, after the fashion of the time, a 'dwelling principally on the morality of the Gospel, and little on the fundamental doctrine of the Atonement' (Shore, *Memoir of … Teignmouth*, 1.6). His private correspondence throughout his life would be permeated by his anxiety about sin and the need for salvation. He disliked India, partly because he was ill much of the time, perhaps from malaria, and he suffered so much from insomnia that he once said he had never slept more than two hours a night in India (ibid., 1.112). But he also disliked its customs and especially its religion, while being critical of what he regarded as the licentious behaviour of many of the company's servants in his time. Light is perhaps cast on his personal sense of sin, especially sins of the flesh, by the comment that in his early years in Bengal he did not resist bad examples and 'lived as other young men did' (ibid., 1.26). Shore apparently had a mistress, presumably an Indian woman, for the records list the baptism of three illegitimate children of John Shore. John was baptized in October 1777, and Francis and Martha on 2 February 1785, but the mother's name is not given (BL OIOC, N/1/2, fol. 285, and N/1/4, fol. 11). A letter in December 1783 from one of his friends in Bengal, G. G. Ducarel, to another, David Anderson, confirms this, noting that Shore had held positions in Bengal which 'a person with a less delicate Sense of Honour' would have used to make a fortune, but as he thought of returning to England he had less than £7000, and he had to provide for 'two natural Children at present in being and one more in expectation' (BL, Add. MS 45435, fol. 264). That these children are not mentioned by Shore's detractors, especially those who disliked his piety, suggests how commonplace this aspect of his behaviour was among the company's servants. He left Bengal in 1785, on the same ship as Warren Hastings, who impressed him with his friendliness and scholarly interests.

England, 1785–1786 Shore arrived in England in June and spent the first few months visiting friends. In November he met Charlotte Cornish (*d.* 1834) of Teignmouth, described as 'a young lady of great personal attractions', and they were married on 14 February 1786 (Shore, *Memoir of … Teignmouth*, 1.117). The marriage appears to have been happy, despite their long separations when either his wife did not accompany him to India or had to return home because of illness. They eventually had nine children, two of whom died in infancy.

Shore thought in 1786 that he was through with India, but within two weeks he was asked to go back as a member of the supreme council of the new governor-general, Lord Cornwallis. Shore's appointment came from the dominant group within the company, who recognized that his experience and knowledge of the revenue system, and his reputation for integrity, would serve its interests, especially as Cornwallis had no knowledge of the subcontinent. Shore accepted the appointment, despite his dislike of India, as his marriage meant he needed more money. He sailed in April 1786, leaving his new wife behind.

Revenue reform As a member of the supreme council, Shore did not have specific duties, but Cornwallis relied on him in making the administrative and judicial changes that transformed the government of Bengal, especially in relation to the collection of revenue. While it is difficult to summarize Shore's intricate writings, especially as he was always arguing against other interpretations of the available data and changing his views as he gained new information, he asserted that the historical evidence showed that throughout Mughal times the *zamindars* were not just tax collectors, but had been the hereditary proprietors of the soil. Giving the company maximum revenue while providing stability for agriculture could only be done, he insisted, through standardized assessments with the *zamindars* as the acknowledged owners of the land. While he agreed that the fairest system would be to make a settlement directly with the peasants, he felt that the company had neither the knowledge nor the personnel to institute such a drastic change from the system they had found. A ten-year settlement, he was convinced, would give the *zamindars* an assurance of stability, and the government could get a clearer understanding of how the system worked. Against Shore's advocacy of a decennial settlement were those like the influential Thomas Law and James Grant who argued for a permanent settlement, which meant not only recognizing the *zamindars* as landlords, but guaranteeing that the revenue payment fixed at the beginning would be perpetual. Shore argued that not enough was known about the actual state of the economy to justify the British making a permanent revenue commitment that would prevent them from profiting from any increase in agricultural productivity. While acknowledging that Shore's knowledge of the Indian revenue systems was unmatched and that his reasoning on most points was persuasive, Cornwallis decided that a permanent settlement would best serve the needs of the British while making their subjects in Bengal 'the happiest people in India' (*Correspondence of … Cornwallis*, 1.460–74, minute, 19 Feb 1790). Shore always remained doubtful about the wisdom of the decision.

England, 1790–1792 Shore left Bengal at the end of 1789, arriving back in England in April 1790 to be greeted by his wife and their first child, a daughter, Charlotte, whom he had not seen before. He estimated his income at this time at £900 a year, from savings from his salary of £10,000 a year while on the supreme council, and he once more expected to retire to reading the classics in Devonshire. In 1790 he gave evidence in Hastings's favour during his impeachment, insisting, based on his knowledge of the period, that Hastings was never personally corrupt, while, he wrote privately, of the two main accusers, Edmund Burke was mad and Philip Francis, once his friend, was 'malicious and revengeful' (Shore, *Memoir of … Teignmouth*, 1.206). Then, to his surprise, he was asked to go back to India as governor-general, as Henry Dundas, the president of the Board of Control, the government's agency for influencing the East India Company, and Shore's friends among the directors of the company saw him as the best hope for continuing the reforms begun by Cornwallis. Shore, having been created a baronet, sailed for India on 26 October 1792, arriving in Calcutta in March 1793.

Governor-general, 1793–1798 Shore was in a somewhat awkward situation at first, as Cornwallis had stayed on in Bengal, expecting an outbreak of war with France, and Shore did not take office as governor-general until 28 October. Accounts of Shore's administration have compared him unfavourably with his famous predecessors, Clive and Hastings, and his successor, Lord Wellesley, citing his preoccupation with carrying out Cornwallis's planned judicial and revenue reforms, instead of seizing opportunities that might have brought more territory and more influence to the British. He was, however, following the explicit instructions of the company and of the British government not to intervene in the internal wars of India but to follow Cornwallis's administrative policies, which he had helped to shape. Not only the implementation of those policies, but to a considerable extent their codification, including the permanent settlement, which was finally accepted by the directors in 1793, were Shore's contribution to building a state in India with an organized bureaucracy carrying out defined legislative and judicial functions.

Shore's adherence to a policy of non-intervention in the affairs of other Indian states was tested in 1794, when the Marathas, with their headquarters at Poona, attacked the nizam of Hyderabad. The company had made a defensive treaty with both the nizam and the Marathas against Tipu Sultan of Mysore, and the nizam claimed that the British, by the terms of the treaty, were obliged to defend him. Shore refused, explaining in one of his long memoranda that the treaty was only against a common enemy, and that, in any case, the nizam had provoked the Marathas, and that no British interests were at stake (Malcolm, 1.xliv–lxv). An annoying side issue was an attack made by Lord Hobart, the governor of Madras, on Shore in 1796 for not supporting him in his intervention in the affairs of the nawab of Arcot. Denouncing Shore in astonishingly vituperative terms, he demanded his recall, but Henry Dundas at the Board of Control replied that Shore had the confidence of both the company and the government as 'a most able and upright servant of the Public' (Furber, 186).

Serious criticism of Shore's policies surfaced in London, however, in regard to his handling of a threatened mutiny by the officers of the company's army in 1795–6. Rumour that the London authorities intended to reform the company's army by increasing pay but doing away with corrupt and oppressive practices had alarmed the officers, and they talked of seizing the governor-general and his council. Shore urged caution in making changes that might inflame the officers further, and felt that the situation was so dangerous that he made concessions on pay and supplementary expenses to the officers. The directors, annoyed at what seemed to be his weakness, decided to recall him and asked Lord Cornwallis to go out to restore order in the army, but, as dispatches arrived from Calcutta in 1797, it became apparent that Shore's action had in fact succeeded in re-establishing the authority of the Bengal government. Cornwallis declined the appointment, and Shore stayed on (Callahan, 198).

The non-interventionist policies, based on what Lord Hobart sneeringly called Shore's principle that 'What is morally wrong cannot be politically right' (Furber, 195), did not preclude direct action, however, when he thought British interests were threatened by the behaviour of the ruler of Oudh, who paid large subsidies to the company for the support of its troops. The death of the nawab, Asaf ud-Daula, in 1797 led to changed relations, for his adopted son, Wazir Ali, appeared to be making military preparations to assert his independence. In addition, Shore received reports that he was behaving in a licentious and degrading manner, that he was base-born, and that factional strife in the court at Lucknow would lead to anarchy in the state, not only depriving the company of the valuable subsidies but threatening the stability of the whole region. Shore went to Lucknow at the end of 1797, and quickly decided that Wazir Ali must be replaced with Saadat Ali, a half-brother of the former nawab, who was more amenable to British control. While he was still at Lucknow in 1798, Shore received word that Lord Mornington (later Marquess Wellesley) had been appointed to succeed him, and that the king had agreed to create Shore Baron Teignmouth in the Irish peerage.

Critics of Shore's non-interventionist policy in the internal affairs of the Indian states have seen in it proof of his lack of understanding of British destiny in India (Lyall, 235), and this in a sense is true, for Shore had no vision of all the subcontinent permanently united in a British India, but only of the necessity for preserving Bengal for the East India Company and Great Britain. He was convinced, as he wrote in 1794, that the territories in India would not remain 'fifty years longer under our dominion' (Shore, *Memoir of … Teignmouth*, 1.185). At the same time, during his term of office he had come to the conclusion that a great change had taken place in India since he had first arrived thirty years before. British power had become, as he put it, 'a Sovereignty', from having been 'a mere Dependency', but this fact had not been realized in England (ibid., 1.328–9).

President of the British and Foreign Bible Society, 1798–1834
Despite thirty years of intense involvement in India, after his return to England in 1798 Shore seems to have lost interest in the affairs of the East India Company. Instead,

as Lord Teignmouth, he settled in 1802 into the life of a country gentleman at Clapham, then a rural village outside London, acting as a justice of the peace and deputy lieutenant of Surrey. He also began what amounted to a new career as the first president of the British and Foreign Bible Society, a position that he held until his death in 1834, and which he regarded as of more significance to his own life, and to the world at large, than his service in India. The Bible Society is not given much attention in the standard histories of the nineteenth century, but it was an important component of the evangelical movement in the Church of England that was claiming a new role for the Christian laity, especially among the upper classes, that was reshaping British society. From 1802 to 1808 his neighbours and close friends at Clapham were a group of evangelical Christians who became known as the 'Clapham Sect', including William Wilberforce, Charles Grant, Henry Thornton, John Venn, and Zachary Macaulay. The anti-slavery campaign is the best known of their activities, but they regarded the Bible Society as fundamental to their work, along with closely related plans for missionary work throughout the world, but especially in India. Teignmouth wrote much of the annual reports of the Bible Society and he also engaged in long debates, through tracts and pamphlets, with its opponents. Some of these argued that the company had wisely forbidden missionaries to work in its territories, and that it was wrong for a former governor-general to use his prestige to encourage conversion to Christianity in India, where such activity would create hostility that might lead to the overthrow of British rule. Others attacked the society because it included nonconformist clergy in its membership and because it did not publish the Book of Common Prayer along with the Bible. Teignmouth answered these attacks in methodical detail.

In 1807 Teignmouth was appointed a member of the Indian Board of Control, and at the same time he was sworn of the privy council, occasionally hearing appeals relating to India. His authoritative knowledge of British rule in India led to his being called to give evidence, somewhat unwillingly, before committees of the House of Commons on 18 June 1806 and again on 30 March 1813, at a more important session, when the select committee was hearing evidence on the renewing of the company's charter, which he supported as necessary for maintaining British authority. Free trade would not lead, he insisted, to an increase in imports, as the Indian people neither wanted nor could afford British goods; but, reflecting a major concern of his Clapham friends, he saw no reason for continuing to restrict the entry of Christian missionaries to the company's territories, as there was no evidence that their work would antagonize the people of India.

The Teignmouths left Clapham in 1808, and moved to 4 Portman Square in London, to a house where they lived for the rest of their lives. His personal letters to his children and friends, as well as his articles for the *Christian Observer* and other religious publications, are marked by a fervent and a pervasive piety, which was based, he said, on 'the doctrines of the Church of England, as those which were delivered by Christ to the Apostles'. These were 'the inherent depravity of man' and salvation by faith alone, to the exclusion of all merit from good works (Shore, *Memoir of … Teignmouth*, 2.46–7).

Teignmouth died at home in Portman Square on 14 February 1834, and was buried in the parish church of St Marylebone, where his wife, who died on 13 July 1834, was also buried. The monument in the church in their memory states that he was president of the Bible Society before noting that he was governor-general of Bengal. His eldest son, Charles John Shore, succeeded to the title.

Assessment Although Teignmouth's achievements as a revenue official are perhaps remembered only by specialists, all the public and private evidence suggests that he was greatly respected during his Indian career for his hard work, detailed knowledge of revenue systems, financial probity, and sense of justice. Lord Bexley, the son of a former governor of Bengal, Henry Vansittart, and Teignmouth's successor as president of the Bible Society, wrote of 'his dignified courtesy of manners', his 'great sagacity', and his 'utmost candour', and this is affirmed by many others ('Sketch', 274). There is, however, a very different judgement that needs to be noted, considering its source and its appearance in a well-known publication. Lord Wellesley, his successor as governor-general, declared that Teignmouth's 'low birth', added to 'indolence, timidity, and bad health', established 'a systematic degradation of the person, dignity, and authority of the Governor General' (GEC, *Peerage*). This can only be squared with the widespread judgement that he was a man of 'integrity, humanity, and honour' (Stephen, 277) by recognizing that Wellesley was writing from a new day of pomp and power, of which Teignmouth disapproved, but that, ironically, he had helped to make possible.

AINSLIE T. EMBREE

Sources C. J. Shore, second Baron Teignmouth, *Memoir of the life and correspondence of John, Lord Teignmouth*, 2 vols. (1843) • *Correspondence of Charles, first Marquis Cornwallis*, ed. C. Ross, 3 vols. (1859) • H. Furber, *The private record of an Indian governor-generalship* (1933) • W. K. Firminger, ed., *The fifth report from the select committee of the House of Commons on the affairs of the East India Company, dated 28th July 1812*, 2 (1917–18); repr. (1969) • biographical series, 1702–1948, BL OIOC, 1/9/0 • Shore's minutes, BL OIOC, HMS, vols. 159, 207, 381, 384 • personal records, BL OIOC, O/6/1 • writers' petitions, BL OIOC • Bengal baptisms, 1713–1890, BL OIOC • 'Sketch of the life of Lord Teignmouth', *Christian Observer*, 34 (1834), 261–300 • J. Stephen, 'The Clapham sect', *EdinR*, 80 (1844), 251–307 • W. Canton, *A history of the British and Foreign Bible Society*, 1 (1904) • E. M. Howse, *Saints in politics: the 'Clapham sect' and the growth of freedom* (1952) • P. J. Marshall, *East Indian fortunes: the British in Bengal in the eighteenth century* (1976) • A. T. Embree, *Charles Grant and the British rule in India* (1962) • R. Callahan, *The East India Company and army reform, 1783–1798* (1972) • R. Guha, *A rule of property for Bengal: an essay on the idea of permanent settlement* (Paris, 1963) • J. Malcolm, *The political history of India, from 1784 to 1823*, 2 vols. (1826) • 'Select committee on the affairs of the East India Company: minutes of evidence', *Parl. papers* (1812–13), 7.9–20, no. 122 • *JHL*, 45 (1805–6) • B. B. Srivastava, *Sir John Shore's policy towards the Indian states* (1981) • GEC, *Peerage*, new edn • *GM*, 2nd ser., 1 (1834), 552–3 • *GM*, 2nd ser., 20 (1843), 339–56 • A. Lyall, *The rise and expansion of British rule in India* (1907) • *Memoirs of the life, writings and correspondence of Sir William Jones*, ed. Lord Teignmouth [J. Shore, first Baron Teignmouth] (1804)

Archives BL, corresp., Add. MSS 12583, 13522–13523, 13583, 13600 *passim* • BL OIOC, corresp. and papers relating to India • BL OIOC, family corresp., MS Eur. E 307 • CUL, British and Foreign Bible Society archives, letter-book • University of Minnesota, Minneapolis, Ames Library of South Asia, corresp. | Bible Society, Swindon, letter-book • BL, Add. MS 4528, fols. 1–128 • BL, corresp. with David Anderson, Add. MS 45428 • BL, corresp. with Warren Hastings and his wife, Add. MS 29152–29194 *passim* • BL OIOC, corresp. with Lord Hobart, Reel 643 [microfilm] • BL OIOC, BM, NPG • Lord Hobart • Bucks. RLSS, corresp. with Lord Hobart • NA Scot., corresp. with Lord Melville • PRO, corresp. with Lord Cornwallis, PRO 30/11

Likenesses T. R. Poole, wax medallion, 1818, NPG • H. Dawe, mezzotint, pubd 1823 (after H. P. Briggs), BL OIOC, BM, NPG • G. Richmond, watercolour drawing, 1832, NPG [*see illus.*] • T. Phyffers, statue, *c.*1867, BL OIOC • T. Cheesman, stipple (after M. Keeling), BM, NPG

Wealth at death £25,000: 1798, Shore, *Memoir*, vol. 1, 244 • modest: Shore, *Memoir* • will, PRO

Shore, Louisa Catherine (1824–1895), poet and writer, was born at Potton, Bedfordshire, on 20 February 1824. She was the fourth of at least five children and the youngest of the three daughters of **Thomas Shore** (1793–1863), Church of England clergyman and author, son of the Revd Thomas William Shore (1755/6–1822) of Otterton, Devon, and Juliana Mackworth Praed (*b. c.*1758), who were married at West Teignmouth, Devon, on 8 November 1785. Thomas Shore came from a good family; he was the nephew of John Shore, first Lord Teignmouth (1751–1834), and his mother was the aunt of the poet Winthrop Mackworth Praed. Thomas Shore matriculated at Wadham College, Oxford, on 9 June 1810 and graduated BA in 1814 and MA in 1818. He was a scholar at the college from 1812 to 1818. He took orders and married Margaret Anne Twopeny (*d. c.*1859), daughter of the Revd R. Twopeny, at Little Casterton, Rutland, on 19 December 1818. They had at least four other children in addition to Louisa Catherine Shore: (Margaret) Emily *Shore (1819–1839), Richard Noel Shore (*bap.* 1821), Arabella Susanna Shore (*bap.* 1822, *d.* in or after 1897), and Mackworth Charles Shore (*bap.* 1825, *d.* 1860). After a short career as a schoolmaster at Bury St Edmunds, Suffolk, and a period at Potton, Bedfordshire, Thomas Shore settled at Everton, Bedfordshire, where he received private pupils, some of whom later attained distinction—notably Charles John, Earl Canning, George Francis Robert, third Lord Harris, and Granville George Leveson-Gower, second Earl Granville. He also served as curate in the neighbouring parish of Cockayne Hatley. He wrote many classical and theological works but, holding somewhat unorthodox views on religion, declined preferment in the church. In 1863 he published *The Churchman and the Freethinker, or, A Friendly Address to the Orthodox*, a pamphlet which attracted notice. Thomas Shore died on 4 July 1863, at his home at Elmers End, Beckenham, London.

Shore's three daughters were endowed with great literary gifts and enthusiasm for learning. (Margaret) Emily Shore was a gifted poet and writer whose life was cut short by tuberculosis. Louisa Shore spent time in Fulham, Middlesex, as a young woman, where she met Fanny Kemble and Sara Coleridge. She also travelled to France and spent eighteen months in and around Paris between 1851 and 1853. Her first published work was 'War Music', a poem on the Crimean War, which had been sent without her knowledge to *The Spectator* by her sister Arabella. The poem was reprinted in *War Lyrics* (1855), a collaboration between the two sisters, who produced three more volumes of poetry together. Louisa Shore's elegy on the deaths of her sister Emily and brother Mackworth Charles (lost at sea in 1860) was favourably compared to George Eliot's 'Oh! may I join the choir invisible' (Shore, 43). In 1861 she published *Hannibal: a Poem of Two Parts*, which received good reviews in *The Athenaeum* and the *Saturday Review*.

Louisa and Arabella Shore were early and enthusiastic advocates of the cause of women. An article by Louisa Shore in the *Westminster Review* for April 1874, reprinted several times as a pamphlet, contains a prescient discussion of the directions subsequently taken by the women's movement. She lived during the latter part of her life with Arabella at Orchard Poyle, Berkshire, near Taplow, Buckinghamshire. She died, unmarried, at 16 Hillside, Wimbledon, Surrey, on 24 May 1895 and was cremated in Brookwood cemetery, near Woking, Surrey.

L. H. CUST, *rev.* MEGAN A. STEPHAN

Sources L. Shore, *Poems: with a memoir by Arabella Shore and an appreciation by Frederic Harrison* (1897) · Blain, Clements & Grundy, *Feminist comp.*, 979 · S. J. Kunitz and H. Haycraft, eds., *British authors of the nineteenth century* (1936), 559–60 · *CGPLA Eng. & Wales* (1895) · IGI [Thomas Shore] · Foster, *Alum. Oxon., 1715–1886* [Thomas Shore] · personal knowledge (1897) · private information (1897) · *CGPLA Eng. & Wales* (1863)

Likenesses portrait, repro. in Shore, *Poems*, frontispiece

Wealth at death £8227 3s. 9d.: resworn probate, Nov 1895, *CGPLA Eng. & Wales* · under £12,000—Thomas Shore: probate, 11 Nov 1863, *CGPLA Eng. & Wales*

Shore, Thomas (1793–1863). *See under* Shore, Louisa Catherine (1824–1895).

Shore, Thomas William (1840–1905), geologist and antiquary, was born on 5 April 1840 at Wantage, Berkshire, the third of the five children of William Shore (1803?–1845), builder, and his wife, Susannah, *née* Carter (1807–1858). Nothing is known of his early life or education; after obtaining a Department of Science and Art certificate he became a schoolmaster in Gloucester (by 1861). On 24 January 1861 he married Amelia (1832/3–1891), daughter of John Lewis, shop man, at Christ Church, South Hamlet, Gloucester. They had two sons and three daughters.

In 1865 Shore was appointed organizing secretary of the East Lancashire Union of Institutions, a movement for the encouragement of science teaching fostered by Sir James Kay-Shuttleworth. Kay-Shuttleworth spoke highly of Shore's powers of organization, his efficiency as a teacher, and his general experience in educational matters. In 1873 he supported Shore's successful application for the post of secretary, executive officer, curator, and librarian to the Hartley Institution, Southampton. Shore held this post for twenty-three years and it allowed him to get to know every part of Hampshire; he became a renowned authority on the county's geology and antiquities. Shore greatly

expanded and improved the Hartley Library and Museum to represent the geology, archaeology, flora, and fauna of Hampshire and its neighbourhood, as well as illustrating the principal arts and manufactures. He was an enthusiastic walker and became known as the Hampshire Tramp. Shore was elected a fellow of the Geological Society in 1878 and acted as secretary of the geological section of the Southampton meeting of the British Association in 1882. He founded the Hampshire Field Club in 1885. After being forced to retire in 1896 Shore moved to London and founded the Balham Antiquarian Society and in 1900 became joint secretary of the London and Middlesex Archaeological Society.

Shore was a ready and an accomplished author, especially on Hampshire geology and archaeology. In addition to writing popular books on Hampshire and Southampton he was keen to emphasize the economic importance of the county's geology and he published on the local geological conditions affecting forestry; the uses of clays (1890); water supply from springs and streams (1891); river deposits and their uses (1893); and on valleys and waterways (1895). Shore explained the influence of geology upon archaeology and settlement. His antiquarian writings ranged from Anglo-Saxon Hampshire charters, churches, prehistoric earthworks, roads and fords, street and place names, to weapons and implements, and wishing wells. Following his removal to London he also researched Anglo-Saxon London and Middlesex. His major work on the origin of the Anglo-Saxon race—a study of the settlement of England and its tribal origins—appeared posthumously in 1906.

Shore died suddenly at home, 157 Bedford Hill, Balham, London on 15 January 1905 owing to influenza, bronchitis, and heart failure, and he was buried at Woolston cemetery, Southampton, on 20 January. On learning of Shore's death Canon Benham penned the following tribute for the *Church Times* of 20 January 1905:

> I have lost a dear friend and Hampshire one of its most brilliant antiquaries. I knew Shore as a lovable man, a most affectionate son and brother. He … spared no pains to get his facts right, most industrious, most acute, and—a higher gift than these—with a real love and human interest in the places he laboured to throw light upon.

W. H. GEORGE

Sources J. E. Marr, *Quarterly Journal of the Geological Society*, 61 (1905), lviii–lix · *Geological Magazine*, new ser., 5th decade, 2 (1905), 143 · G. W. Minns, *Shore memorial volume* (1908–11), v–viii · A. T. Patterson, *The University of Southampton: a centenary history of the evolution and development of the University of Southampton, 1862–1962* (1962) · *Church Times* (20 Jan 1905) · *Hampshire Advertiser County Newspaper* (21 Jan 1905) · *Hampshire Independent* (21 Jan 1905) · *Southampton Times* (21 Jan 1905) · *The Times* (17 Jan 1905) · *CGPLA Eng. & Wales* (1905) · b. cert. · d. cert. · m. cert. · parish records, Buckland, Berkshire, 15 July 1807 [baptism] · parish records, Buckland, Berkshire, 28 Oct 1858 [burial] · burial register, Wantage, Berkshire, Oct 1845

Archives Hants. RO, notebooks mainly relating to sundry aspects of the history of Hampshire · Hants. RO, texts and papers read by him at the Hants Field Club outings · U. Southampton L., MS notes, offprints, and corresp.

Likenesses photograph, repro. in Minns, ed., *Shore memorial volume* (1908–11), iv

Wealth at death £3279 2s. 8d.: probate, 15 Feb 1905, *CGPLA Eng. & Wales*

Shoreditch, Sir John (d. 1345), administrator and diplomat, was of obscure origins. He was styled *magister* in 1315, presumably of Oxford—two years later an inquiry was ordered into an allegation that he had been abducted and robbed there. By 1321 he occurs as DCL.

Sworn of Edward II's council on 18 October 1321 at the Tower, Shoreditch was appointed keeper of the rolls of king's bench on 11 September 1323, and he also became involved in diplomacy. He departed for France on 28 November 1323 bearing Edward's excuses for his inability to come to Amiens to pay homage to Charles IV (r. 1322–8) for Guyenne. Shoreditch left Paris in January 1324 but in June returned to France with the earl of Pembroke for a further postponement of homage. He was then one of those directed to surrender the castle of Montpezat in Gascony, and on 18 August was appointed a keeper of the castle; but before the letters arrived the French destroyed it. Between 21 August and 29 September he was in the company of Edward's envoy Henri de Sully, but Charles IV, angered by the destruction of the St Sardos bastide in 1323 and by the English king's failure to perform homage, had confiscated Guyenne and refused to give him audience, an intransigence stressed by Edward in a proclamation of 30 September. On 10 September 1325 Shoreditch received protection for accompanying Prince Edward to France for his investment as duke of Guyenne, but he remained consistently loyal to the Despensers, for which he received a pardon in 1327. Nevertheless, in the parliament of November 1330 he sought redress because Queen Isabella had deprived him of Passenham Manor, Northamptonshire, a gift from the king in 1325.

With the new reign Shoreditch acted as an advocate in the court of arches (1328–9), but he soon resumed diplomatic activity, being appointed in September 1329, and again in 1330, to treat with Philippe VI of France (r. 1328–50). In response to Philippe's demand for liege homage he was directed to study the documents concerning Guyenne, and in January 1331 was a member of the embassy that concluded the treaty of Paris (9 March). With Bishop John Stratford he travelled in December 1331 to Bois-de-Vincennes to discuss a wide range of topics, and returned early in the new year.

By 1332 Shoreditch was married to a woman named Helen or Elena, and in February 1333, having renounced his clergy at the king's command, he assumed knighthood with a grant of £40 a year. In 1335 he was granted exemption from serving on juries and assizes for life, on account of loyal service. He was appointed a baron of the exchequer on 10 November 1336 and was deputed to deal with petitions of Gascony, Wales, Ireland, and Scotland in the 1340 parliament. But after Stratford's dismissal in 1341 he was deprived until April 1345 of his keepership of the rolls of king's bench.

From 1332 Shoreditch was frequently abroad. In 1334 he was a member of an embassy to France led by Archbishop Stratford to deal with matters concerning France, Gascony, Ponthieu, and Brittany, and in 1335–6 was engaged in negotiating a prospective marriage between Edward III's infant daughter, Joan of the Tower (d. 1362), and Friedrich, son of the duke of Austria, and in seeking alliances with the archbishop of Cologne, the duke of Brabant, and others. As a diplomat he could be aggressive. Baker records (in a narrative misplaced under 1339) that Philippe idiosyncratically complained, not that Edward had adopted his arms, but that in quartering his own with those of France he had placed the leopards of the little island of England in the first quarter. To this Shoreditch responded that the king had adopted current practice (*usitato more modernorum*) in placing *his* progenitors' arms before those acquired *iure materno* and thus styled himself king of England and France—in that order. Murimuth recounts his belligerence at the papal curia in 1343, when he expressed the opinions of parliament and king on papal provision, and branded the would-be dean of York, Cardinal Talleyrand, 'the enemy of both king and kingdom' (*Adae Murimuth continuatio chronicarum*, 230). In December of that year, and again in 1344 he was appointed envoy to Alfonso XI, king of Castile (r. 1312–50).

In the 1330s Shoreditch assisted the Westminster monks in the appropriation of Longdon church, Worcestershire, and was granted a mortmain licence in 1338 to found a chantry of three chaplains in the abbey; in the event, a chantry for two monk-chaplains was established at St Benedict's altar. Shoreditch was murdered on 10 July 1345 in his house at Ware, Hertfordshire, by four of his servants, who were subsequently hanged.

ROY MARTIN HAINES

Sources Rymer, *Foedera* · *Chancery records* · PRO, Chancery Misc., C 47/28/2 m.9 [re diplomatic processes for Shoreditch 1331–2] · *List of various accounts and documents connected therewith, formerly preserved in the Exchequer*, 35 (1912); repr. (1963) [Nuncii's accounts] · *RotP* · P. Chaplais, ed., *The War of Saint-Sardos (1323–1325): Gascon correspondence and diplomatic documents*, CS, 3rd ser., 87 (1954) · *Chronicon Galfridi le Baker de Swynebroke*, ed. E. M. Thompson (1889) · *Adae Murimuth continuatio chronicarum. Robertus de Avesbury de gestis mirabilibus regis Edwardi tertii*, ed. E. M. Thompson, Rolls Series, 93 (1889) · 'Chronica Guillielmi Thorne', *Historiae Anglicanae scriptores X*, ed. R. Twysden (1652), col. 2052 · E. H. Pearce, *The monks of Westminster* (1916) · Tout, *Admin. hist.*, 3.35n · J. C. Davies, *The baronial opposition to Edward II* (1918), 151 (n. 10), 157, 227, 280 · P. Chaplais, 'Le Duché-Pairie de Guyenne: l'hommage et les services féodaux de 1303–1337', in P. Chaplais, *Essays in medieval diplomacy and administration* (1981), 135–60 · N. P. Zacour, *Talleyrand, the cardinal of Périgord* (1960) · G. P. Cuttino, *English diplomatic administration, 1259–1339* (1940), 40 · R. M. Haines, *Archbishop John Stratford: political revolutionary and champion of the liberties of the English church*, Pontifical Institute of Medieval Studies: Texts and Studies, 76 (1986) · R. M. Haines, *The church and politics in fourteenth-century England: the career of Adam Orleton, c. 1275–1345*, Cambridge Studies in Medieval Life and Thought, 3rd ser., 10 (1978) · R. M. Haines, *Ecclesia Anglicana: studies in the English church of the later middle ages* (1989), 10, 224, 241, nn. 71, 73 · Emden, *Oxf.* · B. Harvey, *Westminster Abbey and its estates in the middle ages* (1977), 395 · *CPR, 1330–34*, 380

Short, Augustus (1802–1883), bishop of Adelaide, third son of Charles Short, barrister, of the Middle Temple, London, was born on 11 June 1802. In 1809 he entered Westminster School, where his early days were the 'most wretched' in his life, though relieved by the kindness of Charles Thomas Longley, afterwards archbishop of Canterbury. He was withdrawn for a time to a school at Langley Broom, near Slough, but returned to Westminster in 1811. He passed to Christ Church, Oxford, in May 1820, where he was placed under his cousin, Thomas Vowler Short, and took a first class in classics in 1823. He graduated BA in 1824 and MA in 1826. Short at first taught as a private tutor, but in 1826 he was ordained deacon at Oxford, and in 1827 priest, and licensed to the curacy of Culham, Oxfordshire. He resigned in 1829, on becoming tutor and lecturer at Christ Church; he was appointed librarian and censor in 1833, and in 1843 was select preacher to the university. In 1835 he accepted the living of Ravensthorpe, Northamptonshire, and in the same year he married Millicent Clara, née Phillips. The parish had been neglected, but Short rapidly organized it on a satisfactory basis. He had many friends among the Tractarians, and wrote (but did not publish) a defence of Tract 90, though he voted for the condemnation of W. G. Ward's *Ideal of a Christian Church* in 1845. In 1846 he delivered at Oxford the Bampton lectures entitled *The Witness of the Spirit with our Spirit.*

On the foundation in 1847 of the colonial sees of Cape Town, Melbourne, Adelaide, and Newcastle, Short was offered the choice of Adelaide or Newcastle. He chose the former, and was consecrated on 29 June 1847 and created DD of Oxford on 16 June. He sailed in September, and reached his diocese in December. There were on his arrival only eight Anglican clergy in his huge diocese (which included South and Western Australia), and the bishop's difficulties were further increased in 1851 by the discontinuance of the vote for maintenance of public worship. The young diocese was thus cast entirely upon its own resources. However, on a visit to England in 1853, Short found that the diocese could be organized with a constitution of its own, and he proceeded to set its affairs in order. In this he was completely successful, and showed himself a very capable administrator, his first synod being assembled in Adelaide in January 1855. He did his best to meet the needs of scattered communities in the bush, was keenly interested in work for the Aborigines (writing *Mission to the Heathen* in 1853), did much for the organization of education in the colony, and secured the building of Adelaide Cathedral in 1849. He was active in founding the University of Adelaide and was its vice-chancellor in 1874 and its chancellor from 1876. Short was, however, quite a controversial bishop, in that his Tractarian sympathies upset his chiefly evangelical flock. He visited England for the Lambeth conference of 1878.

Short was attacked by heart disease in 1881, and resigned the see. He left Australia in 1882, amid general expressions of respect, and took up his residence in London; but his illness returned, and he retired to Eastbourne, Sussex, where he died at his home, Sultan House, on 5 October 1883, his wife surviving him.

His eldest brother, **Charles William Short** (1799–1857), joined the Coldstream Guards as ensign in 1814, was present with his regiment at Quatre Bras and in the defence of Hougoumont at Waterloo, and served in the army of occupation. In 1837 he left the army as captain and lieutenant-colonel, and became a merchant. In 1852 he went to live at Odiham in Hampshire, where, as in London, he was noted for his religious and philanthropic activity. He published treatises on the duties of the soldier, which had a wide circulation. He died at Odiham on 19 January 1857.

A. R. BUCKLAND, rev. H. C. G. MATTHEW

Sources F. T. Whittington, *Augustus Short, first bishop of Adelaide* (1888) · *The Times* (8 Oct 1883) · D. Pike, *Paradise of dissent: South Australia, 1829–1857* (1957) · J. M. Brown, *Augustus Short* (1974) · AusDB · CGPLA Eng. & Wales (1884)
Archives Mitchell L., NSW · National Archives of Australia, Adelaide | LPL, letters to Baroness Burdett-Coutts
Likenesses J. Thomson, stipple, pubd 1849 (after G. Richmond), BM, NPG
Wealth at death £1503 1s. 4d.: probate, 17 Jan 1884, CGPLA Eng. & Wales

Short, Charles William (1799–1857). *See under* Short, Augustus (1802–1883).

Short, Sir Francis Job [Frank] (1857–1945), printmaker and teacher of printmaking, was born at High Park, Wollaston, Worcestershire, on 19 June 1857, the second of the four children of Job Till Short (*b.* 1832), an engineer, and his wife, Emma (*b.* 1832), the daughter of William Millward, also an engineer at Wollaston. He left school at the age of thirteen to train as an engineer, and he was an associate member of the Institution of Civil Engineers from 1883 until his resignation in 1904. For a short time he attended evening classes in the Stourbridge School of Art and then, after a period of engineering work in London, abandoned his original profession and entered the National Art Training School (later the Royal College of Art), South Kensington, though he also attended a life class at the Westminster School of Art, under Frederick Brown. Although he painted in watercolour throughout his life, and was elected a member of the Royal Institute of Painters in Water Colours in 1917, Short's career centred on the practice and teaching of printmaking.

While still a student at South Kensington in 1885, and with the approval and involvement of John Ruskin and other Turner scholars, Short began to produce mezzotints after Turner's *Liber Studiorum*. Encouraged by Ruskin's enthusiasm, he devoted much of his life to the reproduction of Turner's paintings, and he mezzotinted forty-seven plates related to the *Liber*, including thirty based on unpublished plates or unengraved drawings. To many of Short's contemporaries, such plates as the *Via Mala* and *Lucerne* were superior even to those produced by engravers who had worked under Turner's own guidance. Their craft had died with them, but Short revived mezzotint and made it a new and vital art in his translations not only of Turner, but of Reynolds, Constable, DeWint, Watts, and other painters. He investigated new possibilities for the medium, using its qualities of tone and mass for his original landscapes, such as *The Lifting Cloud* (1901) and *When the Weary Moon was in the Wane* (1894). Entirely his own, too, was his work in aquatint, another method which he revived and developed; his *Sunrise o'er Whitby Scaur* (1899) or *A Silver Tide* (1912) are arguably unrivalled in technical accomplishment and atmospheric effect.

When his early etching *Sleeping till the Flood, Bosham* (1887) was exhibited at the Hogarth Club in Albemarle Street it attracted the attention of James Abbott McNeill Whistler, who, from 1888 to 1900, frequently visited Short's Chelsea studios and then the Brook Green studio in Hammersmith for help with technical matters and printing. Short's etched work in bitten line, drypoint, or soft ground was a direct interpretation of nature by means of straightforward, frequently outdoor, work upon the plate. Like Rembrandt and Whistler, he believed firmly in purity of line and clean printing, as may be seen in such plates as *Low Tide and the Evening Star and Rye's Long Pier Deserted* (1888) and *A Wintry Blast on the Stourbridge Canal* (1890). On 17 April 1889, in the Presbyterian meeting-house in Stourbridge, Worcestershire, Short married Esther Rosamond (1866/7–1925), the daughter of Benjamin Barker, an engineer, of London; they had one son, who died on active service in 1916, and one daughter.

Short's outstanding powers led to his appointment in 1891 as teacher of etching and then professor of engraving at the Royal College of Art; he retired in 1924. Many subsequently distinguished artists owed much to his training, his high standards, and his constant advocacy of earnest and serious craftsmanship. Perhaps his own early training in science and engineering engendered in him a confident and positive attitude towards experimentation: he made his own tools and invented new ones, and he probed the traditional printmaking processes and discovered new ways of manipulating their materials and techniques. Influenced by his early contact with the gifted printer Frederick Goulding, he adopted an inquisitive attitude to inks, papers, plates, and presses, affirming the reliance of artistic expression on the printing process itself.

Convinced that the wider public, as well as art students, would benefit from a deeper understanding of printmaking, Short published books on the subject: *On the Making of Etchings* (1888), *Etchings and Engravings: What they Are and Are Not* (1911), and *British Mezzotints* (1925). In addition he served on the committee which arranged the Loan Exhibition of British Engraving and Etching held at the Victoria and Albert Museum in 1903. Having helped select prints from the museum's collections for the exhibition, Short successfully argued for the inclusion of relevant tools and materials which would illustrate the various processes of printmaking. With the help of Constance Mary Pott, one of his assistant teachers, he arranged an exhibit that incorporated etching and engraving tools, explanatory plates in various states of completion, a ruling machine, a steel-facing tank, and a copperplate printing press; he also prepared several pages of technical notes which were published in the exhibition catalogue. When the exhibition closed the collection of tools and materials was retained as a permanent feature of the museum, perhaps the first of its kind in the world. In 1904 Short's technical notes and guide to the exhibit were published as a separate pamphlet by the museum's board of education; they were republished in several later editions.

Short was 'physically strong, with a powerful frame, a massive head, and large and benevolent eyes … a man of quiet manner and kindly impulse, but of firm character and great strength of will' (*DNB*). A remarkable teacher and an influential leader in the art world of his day, he won deserved honour for his personal contribution to the art of engraving. He was elected a fellow of the Society of Painter-Etchers in 1885 and succeeded Sir F. Seymour Haden as second president in 1910; he retired in 1938. He was elected an associate of the Royal Academy in 1906 and Royal Academician in 1911 and was treasurer from 1919 to

Sir Francis Job Short (1857–1945), by Malcolm Osborne, 1931

1932. He was awarded gold medals for engraving at Paris in 1889 and 1900, was master of the Art Workers' Guild in 1901, and was knighted in 1911.

The catalogue raisonné prepared with Short's assistance towards the end of his life (Hardie, 1938–40) is punctuated by evocative and informative anecdotes; these serve to clarify that blend of respect for tradition and commitment to innovation so characteristic of his art and so crucial to the subsequent development of modern British printmaking. Collections of his work are in the British Museum, the Victoria and Albert Museum, and the Royal Academy, London; the last-named also has numerous drawings and sketchbooks. He frequently inscribed his prints 'Frank Short' in pencil below the image; occasionally a monogram, the letter S inside a shield, is etched in the plate. A tablet put up by the London county council in 1951 at 56 Brook Green, Hammersmith, commemorates Short's residence there. He died at Jointure Cottage, Ditchling, Sussex, on 22 April 1945; he was cremated and his ashes buried in Hammersmith cemetery on 1 May. In an appreciation published in *The Times* on 25 April Sir Henry Badeley remarked that Short:

> combined with an outstanding knowledge of technique in every branch of engraving a power of imparting that knowledge, whether by lecture or by criticism, which made him unique as a master. … Those of us who were privileged to know him and his work intimately must ever feel admiration for the artist, respect for the master, but, above all, affection for the friend.

JUDY CROSBY IVY

Sources M. Hardie, *The Liber studiorum mezzotints of Sir Frank Short* (1938) · M. Hardie, *The mezzotints and aquatints of Sir Frank Short* (1939) · M. Hardie, *Etchings, dry-points, lithographs by Sir Frank Short* (1940) · Frank Short nominal file, V&A NAL · exhibition of engraving and etching file, 1903, V&A NAL · M. C. Salaman, 'The mezzotints of Mr Frank Short', *The Studio*, 50 (1910), 2–15 · E. F. Strange, 'The mezzotint and etched work of Frank Short', *The Studio*, 38 (1906), 50–57 · E. F. Strange, *The etched and engraved work of Frank Short* (1908) · R. Garton, ed., *British printmakers, 1855–1955* (1992) · M. C. Salaman, *Sir Frank Short* (1925) · *The Times* (24 April 1945), 6 · *The Times* (25 April 1945), 8 · *The Times* (27 April 1945), 7 · *The Times* (2 May 1945), 7 · *The Times* (20 July 1945), 7 · *CGPLA Eng. & Wales* (1945) · *DNB* · *The Times* (20 June 1911), 10 · IGI · m. cert.

Archives Bankside Gallery, London, papers · Hammersmith and Fulham Archives and Local History Centre, corresp.

Likenesses Bassano, photograph, 1914, NPG · A. W. Peters, chalk drawing, *c*.1914, NPG · A. Hacker, oils, exh. RA 1918, RA · W. Rothenstein, lithographic chalk drawing, 1921, NPG · M. Osborne, drypoint, 1931, Garton & Co., Devizes, Wiltshire [*see illus.*] · W. Strang, etching, Art Workers' Guild, London · three portraits; formerly priv. coll.

Wealth at death £22,027 2s. 4d.: probate, 13 July 1945, *CGPLA Eng. & Wales*

Short, James (1710–1768), maker of optical instruments, was born in Edinburgh on 10 June 1710, the son of William Short, a wright, and his wife, Margaret Grierson; he was supposedly named after James Francis Edward Stuart, the Old Pretender. Following his parents' deaths he was accepted as a pupil in George Heriot's Hospital on 18 April 1720, and then at the age of twelve transferred to the Royal High School, Edinburgh, where he showed considerable ability in the classics. After matriculating in 1726 at Edinburgh University, he followed the arts courses but did not graduate. A pious grandmother had prevailed on him to enter the church, so he studied divinity and is said to have passed his trials for the ministry in 1731. However, he was inspired by the lectures of Colin MacLaurin, professor of mathematics at the university, to abandon divinity for mathematics and astronomy.

Under MacLaurin's guidance and friendship Short developed an interest in astronomical optics, and used his friend's rooms for early attempts at making telescopes in 1732. Soon he improved the metallic specula prescribed by Newton for the reflecting telescope, and, having mastered the art of grinding and polishing parabolic mirrors, he was making sophisticated instruments of several different sizes by 1734. He was far excelling other makers, according to MacLaurin, who drew the Royal Society's attention to his talent in 1735. Tests of his instruments followed in 1736, and that summer in London he instructed William, duke of Cumberland, in mathematics. His skills as a maker were recognized by his election to the Royal Society on 24 March 1737. The annular eclipse of 1737 and a comet that year stimulated astronomical activity in MacLaurin's circle and helped lead to the formation of the Philosophical Society of Edinburgh, of which Short was a founder member and the only one engaged in trade. Through the society's concentration of the professional and landed classes, Short found patronage for his telescopes and participated in astronomical observations. He enjoyed the particular favour of Lord Aberdour, later the earl of Morton, for whom he carried out survey work on his Orkney lands in 1739, and both made and repaired instruments. He also executed a model straw cutting machine in 1742 to satisfy Morton's agricultural interests, and made astronomical observations with him.

Short produced about 180 telescopes in Edinburgh before moving to London in April 1738, no doubt attracted by its wider horizons as a leading centre of European science. His earnings in Scotland had been considerable as early as 1736, when he acquired £3000 Scots of Bank of Scotland stock. The earl of Buchan stated that he banked £500 profit by the time he left Scotland, when he sensibly appointed a factor to look after his Scottish finances. His business acumen was considerable, for he continued to prosper in London as a pre-eminent maker of a range of sizes of reflecting telescopes, charging double his rivals' prices. His output from his workshop in Surrey Street, Strand, was exceptionally specialized but it was steady, and he made about 1370 reflecting telescopes in all.

Short's British reputation was quickly established and spread wider as scientists and academics across Europe sought him out. Among his commissioned instruments was one of an 18 inch aperture for the king of Spain, completed in 1752 and costing £1200. An instrument for Uppsala gained for him the rare distinction of foreign membership of the Royal Swedish Academy of Science in 1758. Such honours mattered to him, for he successfully applied to the University of St Andrews for the degree of MA in 1753. His instrument sales were helped by the vogue for astronomical observations among gentlemen and academic scientists, with whom he frequently made observations, notably during the transit of Venus in 1761, when he was one of the Royal Society's observers and supplied instruments. Interest in this event generated commissions in anticipation of the 1769 transit. As an active member of the society, Short communicated many of his observations from 1736 until 1763, including his calculation of solar parallax from the 1761 transit, which was long accepted. He occasionally assessed others' contributions.

Short numbered London's leading instrument makers among his friends. He made observations with George Graham, and early encouraged John Dollond's improvements to the achromatic refracting telescope which ultimately provided instruments to rival his own. An interest in calculating longitude led to his appointment in 1763 to the parliamentary committee to test a timekeeper devised by John Harrison, with whom he became friends. He may have penned an anonymous account of Harrison's work printed that year. His support for Harrison's claim to the longitude prize seems to have caused his patron Lord Morton, then president of the Royal Society, to oppose his candidature for the post of astronomer royal in 1764, though he reportedly acknowledged Short's superior qualifications. Short's criticisms of observations at Greenwich perhaps contributed to his failure to gain the office.

Before the rift with his patron, Short was a friend to the family and an occasional agent in its affairs. This reflected his links with other Scots in London, and his continuing ties to Scotland, where his brother Thomas traded as an instrument maker in Leith, and from whence he derived income from his stock and personal loans, as well as the occasional commission. In London, as well as his social connections through the Royal Society and the Royal Society of Arts, of which he was a founder in 1754, Short was friendly with migrant Scots. It was to him that James Watt carried an introduction in 1755, and through him found employment. David Hume joked in 1759 that Short was secretly married to a Miss Elliot, who with her sister ran the respectable boarding house where Hume and other Scots stayed, though it is known that he died unmarried.

Short remained active until his death from a disease of the bowel, which occurred on 15 June 1768, at his lodgings at Newington Butts near London. His business was continued by his brother Thomas Short from 1768 until 1776, when he returned to Edinburgh. James Short left most of his considerable fortune derived from his skill at polishing metal mirrors to his nephew, as well as bequests to friends. Among them was Lady Mary Douglas, Lord Morton's eldest surviving daughter, to whom he left £1000 and the reversion of his estate, which may have amounted to as much as £20,000.   TRISTRAM CLARKE

Sources G. L'E. Turner, 'James Short, FRS, and his contribution to the construction of reflecting telescopes', Notes and Records of the Royal Society, 24 (1969–70), 91–108 · D. J. Bryden, 'James Short, MA, FRS, optician solely for reflecting telescopes', University of Edinburgh Journal, 24 (1969–70), 251–61 · T. N. Clarke, A. D. Morrison-Low, and A. D. C. Simpson, Brass and glass: scientific instrument making workshops in Scotland (1989), 1–6 · The collected letters of Colin MacLaurin, ed. S. Mills (1982) · D. S. Erskine, 'Life of Mr James Short, optician', Transactions of the Society of Antiquaries in Scotland, 1 (1792), 251–6 · The letters of David Hume, ed. J. Y. T. Greig, 1 (1932), 168 · Bengt Ferrner, Resai Europa en astronom, industrispion och theaterhabitué … 1758–1762, ed. S. G. Lidberg (1956) · Bank of Scotland Archives, Adventurers' journals and ledgers, 1736–1769, 1/91, 1/92 · BL, letters to Dr Thomas Birch, 1752–1764, Add. MSS 4318, fols. 156–69; 4443, fols. 239–40, 244–5; 4444, fols. 25–6, 176–7; 4475, fols. 179, 201 · George Heriot's Hospital admission register, 1720, NA Scot., GD 421/10/7 · NA Scot., letters to earl of Morton, 1742, GD 150/3485-6

Archives BL, letters to T. Birch, Add. MSS 4318, 4443-4444, 4475 · BL, R. Graham MSS, Add. MSS 4433, 4434 · MHS Oxf., telescopes · NA Scot., Morton MSS, GD 150/3485-6 · Royal Museum, Edinburgh, telescopes · Sci. Mus., telescopes · Whipple Museum, Cambridge, telescopes

Likenesses attrib. B. Wilson, oils, c.1758, MHS Oxf. · eleventh earl of Buchan, pencil and chalk drawing, Scot. NPG · attrib. B. Wilson, oils, Royal Observatory, Edinburgh

Wealth at death over £20,000: Turner, 'James Short, FRS'; Erskine, 'Life of Mr James Short'

Short, (Hugh) Oswald (1883–1969), aeronautical engineer, was born on 16 January 1883 at Stanton by Dale, Derbyshire, the fourth son and fifth child of Samuel Short, engineer, and his second wife, Emma Robinson. His formal education ceased on his father's death but he trained as an engineer by self-help and hands-on instruction from his brothers Horace Leonard (1872–1917) and (Albert) Eustace (1875–1932).

Short first worked as an office boy in Derby in the 1890s and founded a balloon business with Eustace in 1898. The two brothers built their first passenger-carrying balloon at Hove in April 1901 and moved their factory to Maple Mews, Tottenham Court Road, London, about 1902. The partnership's first sales were observation balloons for the government of India (October 1903). In 1905–6 the brothers made contacts in the Aero Club and moved their factory to railway arches at Battersea in June 1906. Balloons were sold to, for example, C. S. Rolls, J. T. C. Moore-Brabazon, and T. O. M. Sopwith, and the brothers established a reputation for quality, becoming the club's official aeronauts (1907) and aeronautical engineers (1908).

Short tried unsuccessfully with Eustace from 1907 to build aeroplanes designed by club members, until Horace left employment with Charles A. Parsons in December 1908 to form the tripartite partnership, Short Brothers, Aeronautical Engineers. In March 1909 Wilbur Wright chose Shorts to build six Model A Flyers (the United Kingdom's first batch contract); these were constructed in the country's first purpose-built aircraft factory, Shellbeach, Isle of Sheppey, as were the Short no. 1 and Short no. 2. In October 1909, in a Short no. 2 powered by an engine designed by Gustavus Green, Moore-Brabazon won the Daily Mail's £1000 prize for the first circular mile by an all-British aircraft. The brothers owed the success which followed to cultivating the civilian market and to their hard-headed practical approach, whose directness sometimes offended. In 1911 Shorts provided the Royal Navy's first two aircraft, becoming principal suppliers to the naval wing, Royal Flying Corps (later the Royal Naval Air Service).

Short established both Shorts' seaplane factory at

(Hugh) Oswald Short (1883–1969), by unknown photographer

Rochester (1913–14) and the airship works at Cardington, Bedfordshire (1916); he became wholly responsible for Shorts' designs in 1917 when Horace died. He experimented with light alloy construction from about 1916, pioneering and patenting the smooth-skinned monocoque light alloy construction ('stressed skin') in the UK with Silver Streak (1920). He applied a non-corrosive form of the technology to flying boats in 1924. Short persevered with stressed-skin construction in the face of official indifference and sustained Shorts in the 1920s by building omnibus bodies until the Royal Air Force and Imperial Airways accepted stressed-skin aircraft. His technology was licensed in the United States, France, and Japan.

The Short partnership was incorporated as Short Brothers (Rochester and Bedford) Limited in 1919 with Short as chairman and joint managing director; he became sole managing director on Eustace's death and retained both posts when Shorts became a public company in 1935. Contracts for Short Empire flying boats for Imperial Airways and Sunderlands and Stirlings for the Royal Air Force in the mid-1930s, and the incorporation of a subsidiary, Short and Harland, in Northern Ireland, marked the peak of his career. Bureaucrats regarded him as a difficult man and his factories were taken over by the government in both world wars.

In 1935 Short married Violet Louise Blackburn, née Lister

(d. 1966); they had no children. An unassuming, courteous man, whose physical courage was proven as an aeronaut, pilot, and observer on test flights, Short was a lover of music and animal life; his labour relations were paternalistic, with a Victorian sense of fair play. His health failed under the stresses of the 1930s and the early war years and, when the government expropriated the shareholders in 1943, he resigned as chairman and director of Shorts, accepting the honorary title of life president. In these later years he was overshadowed by his protégé Arthur Gouge (1890–1962).

From 1943 Short lived quietly in retirement, latterly at Linchmere, near Haslemere, increasingly grieved by the loss of his company and haunted by the fear that history would overlook the Short brothers' achievements. He had none of the nation's honours: he declined appointment as MBE in 1919 as inappropriate to the firm's achievements but his peers in the aircraft industry honoured him as an honorary fellow of the Royal Aeronautical Society and president of the Society of Aviation Artists. He was admitted freeman of the City of London (1933), and honorary freeman of the City of Rochester (1949), and was also a fellow of the Royal Astronomical and Zoological societies. He died at his home, Gillhams Farm, Linchmere, Sussex, on 4 December 1969.

The Short aircraft company was renamed Short Brothers Limited in 1977 in honour of the brothers but the memorial to Short's own genius is the world-wide acceptance of stressed-skin construction.

GORDON BRUCE, rev. ROBIN HIGHAM

Sources DNB · R. Higham and D. J. Jeremy, 'Short, Hugh Oswald', DBB · C. H. Barnes, Shorts aircraft since 1900, rev. D. N. James (1989) · The Times (6 Dec 1969) · JRAeS [centennial issue] (1966) · R. Higham, The British rigid airship, 1908–1931 (1961) · b. cert. · d. cert.
Likenesses F. O. Salisbury, portrait; known to be at Short Brothers Ltd, Belfast, in 1981 · D. Smith, bronze bust; known to be at Royal Aeronautical Society, London, in 1981 · photograph, Royal Aeronautical Society [see illus.] · photographs, Short Brothers & Harland Ltd, Queen's Island, Belfast
Wealth at death £43,247: probate, 22 April 1970, CGPLA Eng. & Wales

Short, Thomas (1635–1685), physician, son of the Revd William Short and his wife, Mary, was born on 25 November 1635 at Euston, Suffolk. He was sent to the grammar school of Bury St Edmunds, and from there to St John's College, Cambridge, where he was admitted a sizar on 25 February 1650, aged fourteen. He graduated BA in 1654 and was created MD by royal mandate on 26 June 1668. Short settled in London and was admitted a candidate at the College of Physicians in December 1668, but was not elected a fellow until 29 July 1675. He had joined the Church of Rome, and, in accordance with an order of the House of Lords for the ejection of Roman Catholics, was summoned to attend a meeting of the Royal College of Physicians on 14 April 1679. He did so, but the feeling of the college was against intolerant proceedings; a quorum was not present, and no steps were taken. He attained considerable practice, and Thomas Sydenham, who had met him in consultation, found his 'genius disposed for the practice of physick' (Whole Works, 339), and praised both his learning and sagacity. Sydenham prefixed to *A Treatise of the Gout and Dropsy* a letter to Short in which occurs a famous passage on posthumous fame which Fielding quoted in *Tom Jones*. Short, who had a son, William (*b.* 1672), died on 28 September 1685, and was buried in St James's Chapel, London. Bishop Burnet, who thought that Charles II died of poison, also believed that Short was poisoned by his co-religionists for asserting that the king was poisoned (*Bishop Burnet's History*, ed. Burnet and Burnet, 1.609). Richard Lower and Walter Needham seem to have been unable to resist an opportunity of imposing upon the whig historian's credulity.

NORMAN MOORE, rev. MICHAEL BEVAN

Sources Munk, *Roll* · Venn, *Alum. Cant.* · *Bishop Burnet's History of his own time*, ed. G. Burnet and T. Burnet, 2 (1734) · Philophilus, *A pindarick elegy … on the universally lamented death of the incomparable Dr Short* (1685) · C. Dodd [H. Tootell], *The church history of England, from the year 1500, to the year 1688*, 3 (1742) · *IGI* · *The whole works of … Thomas Sydenham*, ed. and trans. J. Pechey, 9th edn (1729)

Short, Thomas (*c.*1690–1772), physician, was born in the south of Scotland, and, after graduating in medicine, settled in practice at Sheffield.

In 1713 William Steel told him the secret, which he afterwards published, of making cerated glass of antimony as a cure for dysentery. He made several journeys to visit the mineral springs of Yorkshire and of other parts of England, becoming an expert on the medicinal uses and analysis of water. Following thirty years of research in the chemical analysis of mineral waters, in 1766 he published the first attempt to systematize tests, entitled *Institutes, or, An Introduction to the Examination of Mineral Waters*. Prior to this he had published *A Rational Discourse on the Inward Use of Waters* (1725). In 1750 Short published *New Observations on the Bills of Mortality*, in which he continued the work of John Graunt and Sir William Petty, and treated the subject in relation to observations he had made on the effect of the air on health. He spent eighteen years on this work.

Short wrote several other works on medicine, among them studies on the medical effects of tea, milk, sugar, and spirits. In 1767 he published *A Comparative History of the Increase and Decrease of Mankind*, in which he advocated early marriages, denounced alcohol 'as a Stygian poison', and collected much historical and medical information. He died in 1772.

NORMAN MOORE, rev. PATRICK WALLIS

Sources N. G. Coley, 'Physicians, chemists and the analysis of mineral waters', *The medical history of waters and spas*, ed. R. Porter (1990), 56–66 · Watt, *Bibl. Brit.*
Archives BL, letters to Sir Hans Sloane, etc.

Short, Thomas Vowler (1790–1872), bishop of St Asaph, was the eldest son of William Short (*d.* 1826), archdeacon of Cornwall, and his wife, Elizabeth, daughter of William Hodgkinson, headmaster of the grammar school at Exeter. Augustus *Short was his cousin. He was born on 16 September 1790 at Vicarage House, Dawlish, Devon, where his father was curate. After spending a year at Exeter grammar school Short was sent to Westminster School in 1803, from where he passed with a studentship to Christ Church, Oxford, in 1809. He took a first class in classics

and in mathematics in 1812, and in the following year was ordained deacon by the bishop of Oxford. He graduated BA in 1813, MA in 1815, BD in 1824, and DD in 1837. In 1814 Short became perpetual curate of Drayton, Oxfordshire, but he resigned this cure in 1815 in order to undertake academic offices in Christ Church. He became successively tutor and censor (1816–29), librarian (1822), and catechist and Busby lecturer (1825); in 1823 he was proctor. Having served as an examiner at Oxford between 1820 and 1824 he published influential suggestions (1822) for the improvement of the examination system, but the changes he sought were not effected until 1830. He published *Twenty Sermons on the Fundamental Truths of Christianity* in 1829. Though Short left Christ Church before the Oxford Movement really began, he was well acquainted with most of its leaders. Pusey, a favourite pupil, always acknowledged his influence, and 'Short held a first place in his affection and respect to the last hour of his life' (Liddon, *Life of Pusey*, 1.24). Short examined Newman for his degree, and Keble he numbered among his close friends. W. E. Gladstone was one of his pupils. Short is to be distinguished from Thomas Short (1789–1879), a celebrated contemporary and tutor of Trinity College.

Short's departure from Oxford in 1829 followed the fiasco of Sir Robert Peel's defeat in the university election, Short having been one of Peel's most energetic supporters. He had held the Christ Church living of Cowley from 1816 to 1823, when he was presented to the rectory of Stockleigh Pomeroy, Devon. In 1826 he succeeded his father to the rectory of King's Worthy, Hampshire, which was in the gift of his father's kinsman Sir Thomas Baring. He went to reside there in 1829, forming a household with his mother (the subject of his *Letters to an Aged Mother* published in 1841) and two sisters. A member of the National Society and of the Winchester Bible Society, he was a keen promoter of education, building a school in his parish in 1830. In 1832 he published a two-volume history of the Church of England to 1688, which went through several editions and was widely used by ordinands. He married on 26 February 1833 Mary, daughter of Revd Charles Davies of Pembroke College and widow of John Josias Conybeare.

In 1834 Short was presented by the lord chancellor, Brougham, to the rectory of St George's, Bloomsbury, where he acquired a reputation as a conscientious parish priest. He promoted benefit societies, a Sunday school, a lending library, and a visiting society, which he described in tracts published as *Parochialia* (1842) for the guidance of other clergy. Reckoned a serious-minded practical clergyman, tending to evangelicalism, though regarded by Richard Whately as being intellectually of 'third rate talents' (Brent, 130), he was in 1837 appointed deputy clerk to the closet to the queen. His former pupil Francis Baring advanced his claims as an earnest churchman, and Lord Melbourne appointed him bishop of Sodor and Man, where he was consecrated on 30 May 1841. His first charge (1842) lamented the widespread disaffection from the church and he set about visiting the parishes and improving the education of candidates for ordination. On 27 October 1846 he was translated, on the recommendation of Lord John Russell, to the see of St Asaph. He immediately established a diocesan board of education, building new schools, developing a reading method known as the 'look and say' system, and providing textbooks in which lessons were printed in both English and Welsh. In a public controversy with one of his clergy Short was accused of the inability to read Welsh or conduct services in the language and of harbouring an animosity towards the Welsh people (*Correspondence and statement of facts, connected with the case of the Revd Richard Williams Morgan*, 1856). When he resigned the see on 22 February 1870 it was stated that every parish had a school and a resident incumbent, Short himself having for many years spent half of his episcopal income on diocesan purposes. Short died on 13 April 1872 at Gresford vicarage, Denbighshire, the home of his brother-in-law and former chaplain, Robert Wickham (d. 1880). A. R. BUCKLAND, rev. M. C. CURTHOYS

Sources 'Memoir', T. V. Short, *Sketch of the history of the Church of England*, 9th edn (1875) · Boase, *Mod. Eng. biog.* · Foster, *Alum. Oxon.* · Ward, *Men of the reign* · D. A. Jones, *A history of the church in Wales* (1926) · P. Johnston, 'Thomas Vowler Short, rector of King's Worthy, 1826–34', *Hatcher Review*, 3/25 (1988), 228–37 · R. A. Soloway, *Prelates and people: ecclesiastical social thought in England, 1783–1852* (1969) · R. Brent, *Liberal Anglican politics: whiggery, religion, and reform, 1830–1841* (1987) · *GM*, 1st ser., 103/1 (1833), 264
Archives Christ Church Oxf. · NL Wales, commonplace book; letter-book
Likenesses E. Dent, mezzotint, *c.*1841 (after T. Bridgford), BM · M. A. Shee, oils, exh. RA 1842, Christ Church Oxf. · E. Dent, engraving (after portrait by T. Bridgford), repro. in D. J. Pound, *Drawing room portrait gallery of eminent personages*, 3rd ser. (1860) · D. J. Pound, stipple and line engraving (after photograph by Mayall), NPG · portrait, repro. in *ILN*, 10 (1847), 201
Wealth at death under £14,000: resworn probate, Aug 1872, CGPLA Eng. & Wales

Shortal [Shortall], **Sebastian** (*d.* 1639), Cistercian monk and titular abbot of Bective, Meath, was born in co. Kilkenny. There he received his primary education before travelling to Spain about 1610, where he became a Cistercian monk at Nucale in Galicia. He taught philosophy in the seminary of St Claudius in Nucale and later in the monastery of Mons Ramorum. In 1619 he set out for Ireland accompanied by the Cistercian chronicler Malachy Hartry. *En route* Shortal was taken captive by Moors. On his release he proceeded to Ireland, where he was appointed abbot of St Mary's in Bective some time before 1621. The abbey was long deserted so he settled down nearby and engaged in pastoral activity. In 1626 he was among the signatories of an 'Attestation of Cistercians' in favour of the Franciscan Thomas Fleming, archbishop of Dublin, who was experiencing opposition from his clergy. In 1628 he signed a letter to the abbot of Cîteaux and in 1631 he rallied to the defence of certain Dublin regulars in a bitter dispute with a number of secular priests.

About this time Shortal became involved in a dispute with the bishop of Meath, Thomas Dease, concerning Shortal's title to Bective Abbey. Relations between regular and secular clergy were frequently tense at this time because of competition for scarce resources, jurisdictional problems concerning pre-Reformation privileges, and disagreements over disputed titles. In 1633 Shortal

participated in the regulation of a serious matter of discipline concerning the titular abbot of Abbeyleix, Gerard Purcell. Just before his death on 11 December 1639 he was one of the readers of Hartry's *Triumphalia sanctae crucis*, which he approved for publication.

Shortal was an accomplished composer of Latin verse. He wrote a verse history of the institution of the feast of Corpus Christi called *Historia institutionis festivitatis v. sacramenti B. Julianae Corneliensi ord. Cist. divinitus revelatae, versu hexametro*, a verse life of the Irish Cistercian Candidus Furlong (1576–1616) entitled *Vita Candidi Furlongi, monachi Nucalensis, heroico carmine*, and a collection of pieces in honour of the same person called *De laudibus Candidi Furlongi: hymi, variaque ac erudita epitaphia*. According to Hartry, Shortal was buried in the ruined monastery of St Dominick. THOMAS O'CONNOR

Sources F. Hogan, 'The last monks and abbots of Bective', *Riocht na Midhe*, 6/2 (1976), 3–15 · *DNB*

Shorter, Clement King (1857–1926), journalist and magazine editor, was born on 19 July 1857 in Southwark, London, the youngest of three sons of Richard Shorter (*c.*1827–*c.*1867), a liveryman on the London–Cambridge route, and Elizabeth, *née* Climenson (1824–*c.*1887). His father, whose career was ruined by the completion of the Great Eastern Railway, emigrated to Australia, where he died, leaving Clement, still a child, to be raised by his fundamentalist Christian mother. Between 1863 and 1871 he was educated at a private academy in Downham Market, Norfolk, before leaving to work for four years for a number of London booksellers. In 1875 he returned to Downham Market for a three months' civil service course. From 1877 until 1890 he served as a clerk in the exchequer and audit department at Somerset House, while taking evening classes in languages and literature at the Birkbeck Institution.

Literature and journalism, books and newspapers, became the central passion of Shorter's life. He rapidly built a career as an influential Fleet Street editor whose position and *bonhomie* allowed him to champion particular authors in the columns he regularly wrote for the papers he owned. By 1889 he was writing a twice-weekly book column for *The Star* and a similar weekly piece for *The Queen*, as well as doing editorial work for the *Penny Illustrated Paper*. By 1891, the year after he left his civil service post for full-time work in journalism, he had assumed the editorship of both the *Illustrated London News* and the *English Illustrated Magazine*. As the titles of these papers suggest, he was interested in reaching a wide audience, in popularizing literature, in the business and pleasure of the written word, and in the club life and drawing rooms of more or less established literary London. A solid figure, conventionally attired in stiff collar and pince-nez, he sported a bushy moustache and leonine hair to set off his large features and intense eyes. Not a sophisticated man, his tastes and pronouncements were generally conventional and his style florid and arch, but his good humour and energy made him popular, while his unreflective judgements also made him a frequent subject of satire in the London press.

Shorter's rise was due in part to his early friendship with Sir William James Ingram, who owned a controlling interest in all of the papers which Shorter edited, including *The Sketch*, a popular illustrated paper which he founded in 1892, and *The Album* and *Pick-me-up*, yet two more papers which he was editing by 1897. Seeking more editorial independence, he founded *The Sphere*, another illustrated weekly, in 1900, and *The Tatler* in 1901, both of which later received financial support from his new patron, the shipping magnate Sir John Ellerman. *The Sphere* became his particular favourite, and as editor he contributed a weekly literary column until the year of his death. Here he would write regularly on his personal preferences, contributing frequent articles on the Brontës, George Borrow, Samuel Johnson, and Napoleon. In 1896 he published his first book, *Charlotte Brontë and her Circle* (reissued in 1914 as *The Brontës and their Circle*), followed in 1905 by *Charlotte Brontë and her Sisters*, and in 1908 by a two-volume collection *The Brontës: Life and Letters*. These books, as well as the *Complete Poems of Emily Brontë* (1910), and an edition of *Wuthering Heights* (1911), reveal his enthusiasm and popularizing impulse rather than scholarly competence or academic rigour.

Shorter married the Irish nationalist poet Dora Sigerson on 9 July 1896 [*see* Shorter, Dora Mary (1866–1918)]; it was a childless love match which lasted until her death. In his unfinished autobiography, published posthumously in 1927, he praised her as 'by far the most brilliant, the most gifted, the most richly endowed with genius and intellect of all the women I have ever known' (Shorter, *Autobiography*, 133). This passionate attachment was characteristic in linking him with a literary figure whose deep feeling and slightly bohemian nature kept him in touch with contemporary artistic circles while preserving an essentially conservative life. His good friend J. M. Bulloch, in his introduction to the autobiography, noted that 'For him, journalism was always a personal equation' (Bulloch, xi) and that 'Most of all, he liked to meet literary folk' (ibid., xiii). With Sigerson, Shorter achieved both the 'personal equation' and the literary connection he found so quickening. They divided their time between residence in London at Marlborough Place and in the countryside at Knockmoroon, the house he had built in Buckinghamshire, a county to which he became devoted, as revealed in his *Highways and Byways in Buckinghamshire* (1910).

Shorter was devastated by his wife's death in 1918, but continued a social life, befriending younger and more avant-garde writers such as Richard Aldington and H. D. (Hilda Doolittle), both of whom he met through Ellerman's daughter Winifred (whose pseudonym was Bryher), in whom he was briefly interested romantically. Bryher introduced him to her schoolmate Annie Doris Banfield (*c*.1894–*c*.1980), the manager of a flower farm and the daughter of Ellerman's colleague the Penzance ship-owner John Banfield, whom he married on 23 September 1920. Their only child, Doreen Clement, a name which echoes the forenames of both of his wives as his own

name echoed his mother's, was born in 1922. From 1925 Shorter suffered from a heart condition. He died at Knockmoroon on 19 November 1926; his body was cremated at Golders Green, Middlesex, where his ashes were interred.   CAROLINE ZILBOORG

Sources C. K. Shorter, *C. K. S., an autobiography*, ed. J. M. Bulloch (privately printed, Edinburgh, 1927) · J. M. Bulloch, introduction, in C. K. Shorter, *C. K. S., an autobiography*, ed. J. M. Bulloch (privately printed, Edinburgh, 1927) · C. Zilboorg, 'A new chapter in the lives of H. D. and Richard Aldington: their relationship with Clement Shorter', *Philological Quarterly*, 68 (1989), 241–62 · C. Zilboorg, 'Richard Aldington in transition: his pieces for the *Sphere* in 1919', *Twentieth Century Literature*, 34/4 (1988), 489–506 · *DNB* · *Richard Aldington and H. D.: the early years in letters*, ed. C. Zilboorg (1992) · C. Shorter, *Highways and byways in Buckinghamshire* (1910)

Archives BL, corresp. and papers relating to petition for reprieve of Roger Casement, Add. MS 63596 · Duke U., Perkins L., letters · NRA, corresp. and literary papers · U. Leeds, Brotherton L., corresp. and papers | BL, corresp. with Lord Northcliffe, Add. MS 62174 · Bodl. Oxf., letters to William Montgomery Crook · Bodl. Oxf., Bertram Dobell MSS · LUL, letters to Austin Dobson · NL Ire., letters to T. Dawson · Richmond Local Studies Library, London, corresp. with Douglas Sladen · TCD, letters to Edward Dowden · University of York, archives, letters to Clement William Scott · University of York, archives, letters to Herbert Gladstone Wright

Likenesses O. E. Galsworthy, photograph, 1916, NPG · photograph, Dec 1922 (after H. Winston), repro. in Shorter, *C. K. S.*, frontispiece · Spy [L. Ward], chromolithograph caricature, NPG; repro. in *VF* (20 Dec 1894)

Wealth at death £54,752 15*s*. 2*d*.: probate, 8 March 1927, *CGPLA Eng. & Wales*

Shorter [*née* Sigerson], **Dora Mary** (1866–1918), poet and journalist, was born at 17 Richmond Hill, Dublin, the elder daughter of George Sigerson (1836–1925), Dublin physician and scholar, and his wife, Hester, *née* Varian (1828–1898), poet and novelist. Her sister Hester (later Piatt) also became a writer. Dora and her brother George were educated at a dame-school until the family moved to the more central location of 3 Clare Street, where the children were taught by their mother and aunt until Dora was seventeen; she then had a governess for a few years and thereafter she attended the Dublin School of Art.

Although her parents' marriage was unhappy, the family home became a Dublin salon where Dora met the leaders of Irish literary and political life. This period coincided with the beginning of the Irish literary revival, and she threw herself into the cultural life of Dublin, becoming a member of the Pan Celtic Society in 1888 and of the National Literary Society in 1892; she also contributed poems, reviews, and articles to Irish periodicals, and her first book, *Verses* (1893), was financed by Father Matthew Russell, editor of the *Irish Monthly*, in which most of the poems had first appeared. Soon after this the rising English journalist and journal editor Clement King *Shorter (1857–1926) met and fell in love with the beautiful Dora Sigerson; after a persistent courtship on his part they were engaged in September 1895, and married on 9 July 1896. In London she and Shorter held Wednesday dinner parties for writers, politicians, and journalists at their home in Marlborough Place, St John's Wood. She contributed poems, articles, and reviews to numerous British and Irish

Dora Mary Shorter (1866–1918), by Josephine Webb

journals, and continued to publish volumes of verse and prose sketches at regular intervals, and a *Collected Poems* was issued in 1907. Her verse was generally well received, although some critics complained about the irregularity of her metrics. She took pleasure in frequent trips to the continent with her husband, and in 1904 they bought a country cottage in Great Missenden, Buckinghamshire.

Although Dora Sigerson Shorter played a vigorous role in the intellectual and cultural life of London (she counted George Meredith and Thomas Hardy among her friends and was a founding member of the Lyceum Club), her Irish sympathies strengthened; she joined the Irish Literary Society and later the Irish National Club, and according to the Fenian Mark Ryan wrote a pamphlet to dissuade Irishmen from enlisting in the British army during the Second South African War. She was deeply affected by the Easter rising in 1916, and with her husband organized an unsuccessful campaign to save Roger Casement from hanging. She designed and sculpted a memorial to the events of 1916 now in Glasnevin cemetery. The poems in her *Love of Ireland* (1916) and *The Sad Years* (1918) indicate a growing despair at British conduct in Ireland, and friends, such as Katherine Tynan, believed that her anguish over the political situation there was the major factor in her physical decline and premature death. Chronically ill during the previous year, she died on 6 January 1918 at 16 Marlborough Place, and she was buried in Glasnevin graveyard, Dublin.   JOHN KELLY

Sources C. K. Shorter, *C. K. S., an autobiography*, ed. J. M. Bulloch (privately printed, Edinburgh, 1927) · D. Sigerson Shorter, *The tricolour: poems of the revolution*, rev. D. Barry, new edn (1976) [contains memoir by K. Tynan] · D. J. O'Donoghue, *The poets of Ireland: a biographical and bibliographical dictionary* (1912) · E. Rhys, *Wales England wed* (1940) · K. Tynan, *Twenty-five years: reminiscences* (1913) · K. Tynan, *The middle years* (1916) · M. F. Ryan, *Fenian memories*, ed. T. F. O'Sullivan (1945)

Archives NL Ire., letters | NL Ire., letters to T. Dawson · NL Ire., letters to Mary Thompson

Likenesses J. B. Yeats, oils, 1899, Hugh Lane Gallery of Modern Art, Dublin · J. Lavery, oils, 1919, NG Ire. · J. Webb, pastel drawing, NG Ire. [*see illus.*] · J. B. Yeats, drawing, Colby College, Waterville, Maine, Healy Collection; repro. in W. Murphy, *Prodigal father* (1978) · portrait, repro. in D. Sigerson, *The tricolour* (1922)

Wealth at death £2498 9*s.* 7*d.*: administration, 22 March 1918, CGPLA Eng. & Wales

Shorthouse, Joseph Henry (1834–1903), novelist, was born in Great Charles Street, Birmingham, on 9 September 1834, the eldest of the three sons of Joseph Shorthouse (1797–1880) and his wife, Mary Ann, *née* Hawker. He grew up in Calthorpe Street, Edgbaston. His father had inherited the family chemical works, and manufactured vitriol, and his mother similarly came from a manufacturing family: her father founded the first glasshouse in Birmingham. Both families belonged to the Society of Friends, and the boy (known as Henry) was brought up devoutly by religious parents.

Shorthouse's early education was at home with governesses and tutors, although he spent a brief time at school with a little girl who later became his wife. When he was ten he went to a nearby day school kept by the Quakers. He had by then developed a bad stammer which afflicted him throughout his life, and the year he spent at Tottenham College when he was fifteen increased this difficulty. He came home at sixteen, and tutors were engaged for him, but he soon entered the family business, completing his education himself with wide reading.

Shorthouse married Sarah Scott (1832–1909), eldest daughter of John and Elizabeth Scott, at the Friends' meeting-house at Warwick on 19 August 1857. A short time after this, two events of lifelong importance to him occurred: his conversion to the Church of England in 1861, and his first attack of epilepsy in January 1862. The seizure was severe, and was followed by others. In his weakened condition and with the rest and calm which were prescribed, Shorthouse's active life was much impaired. Although the condition went into remission for long periods, it threatened him for the rest of his life.

Although a Quaker from birth, Shorthouse found himself powerfully attracted to the traditions and liturgy of the Church of England ('His wide reading especially of the older English divines, made the idea of an historic and national church particularly attractive to him'; Shorthouse, 64), and in August 1861 he and his wife were baptized at St John's, Ladywood, by the Revd F. Morse. From then on the church was an increasingly important part of his life. He was particularly attracted by the Anglicanism of the seventeenth century as he saw it, and his inclination was to the school of theology which he later referred to as that of 'the new Oxford school of High Churchmen' (ibid., 309). His interest in mysticism, and in the tensions between Anglicanism and Roman Catholicism, form a

Joseph Henry Shorthouse (1834–1903), by unknown photographer

part of this. He later lived within a stone's throw of Cardinal Newman at the Oratory, and his mysticism had something in common with Newman's. Yet he was resolutely hostile to the Roman church, firmly rejecting the submission of private judgement to the authority of the church for the freedom and reason of the Church of England.

For the next years Shorthouse worked with the family firm, and took on a life of intense study as he prepared the material for the novel he was determined to write. He reflected that the seventeenth century was the nearest to his own in terms of its religious intensity and political struggles, and determinedly immersed himself in the theology and writings of diarists, philosophers, travel writers, and historians. Only a plot was wanting, and by and by he found just what he was after: the story of a knight, who, on returning from a crusade, met and forgave the murderer of his brother. Around this one incident was woven the story of *John Inglesant*. Shorthouse worked sporadically at the novel for ten years, and it was finished at Llandudno in 1876. It was then laid aside. Publishers were not interested, and the Shorthouses were about to move to an expensive new house, which absorbed both energy and capital. In 1880 a hundred copies were published at the author's expense, and one found its way into the hands of Mrs Humphry Ward, who, much struck with it, forwarded it to the publisher Alexander Macmillan. Macmillan had already read a review in *The Guardian*, and now wrote to Shorthouse asking to publish the novel. Thus in the summer of 1881 *John Inglesant* appeared before the public. The novel was an instant success. It captured the mood of the moment, which was marked by religious controversy and a fresh wave of interest in the Catholic question (Mrs Humphry Ward's own best-sellers, *Robert Elsmere*, 1886, and *Helbeck of Bannisdale*, 1898, were further landmarks), and the public responded enthusiastically to the romantic mysticism of the 'philosophic romance' (Shorthouse, 126).

Shorthouse had soaked himself so intensely in the writings of the seventeenth century that it became his own style, and reads almost like pastiche. Interpolated with his own writing is passage after passage of (unacknowledged) quotation from countless sources such as *Leviathan*, *The Anatomy of Melancholy*, and *Brief Lives*, all so skilfully interwoven that the mosaic is complete. The novel was a triumph, and brought Shorthouse attention and admiration from such extremes of opinion as T. H. Huxley, Charlotte Yonge, and Edmund Gosse. He was fêted throughout the literary world, and invited to breakfast with Gladstone at 10 Downing Street.

Shorthouse wrote other books after the success of his first, works such as *The Little Schoolmaster Mark* (1884), *Sir Percival* (1886), *The Countess Eve* (1888), *Blanche, Lady Falaise* (1891), and other stories and essays. None of these, however, attracted the adulation secured by *John Inglesant*. Shorthouse's health began to fail in 1900, and he died at home at Lansdowne, 60 Wellington Road, Edgbaston, on 4 March 1903. He is buried, with his wife, in the old Edgbaston churchyard. They had no children.

BARBARA DENNIS

Sources S. Shorthouse, ed., *Life, letters, and literary remains of J. H. Shorthouse*, 2 vols. (1905) • *The Times* (6 March 1903) • *The Times* (11 March 1903) • *The Guardian* (25 March 1903) • *The Spectator* (14 March 1903) • *The Observer* (7 May 1905) • E. W. Gosse, *Portraits and sketches* (1912) • DNB

Archives Wellcome L., observations relating to extraction of teeth | Birm. CA, Birmingham, letters to M. Evans and her notes relating to letters • BL, letters to William Boyd Carpenter, Add. MS 46723 • BL, corresp. with Macmillans, Add. MSS 54933–54934 • U. Leeds, Brotherton L., letters to Edmund Gosse

Likenesses photograph, NPG [*see illus.*]

Wealth at death £4477 17s. 6d.: probate, 6 May 1903, CGPLA Eng. & Wales

Shortland, Edward (1812–1893), physician and ethnographer in New Zealand, born at Courtlands, near Lympstone, Devon, and baptized at Charles, Devon, on 19 May 1812, was the third son of Captain Thomas George *Shortland, of Courtlands, and his wife, Elizabeth, the daughter of Peter Tonkin of Plymouth. His brothers were Willoughby *Shortland and Peter Frederick *Shortland. He was educated at Exeter grammar school, and Harrow School, and Pembroke College, Cambridge, where he matriculated in 1831 and graduated BA in 1835 and MA in 1839. He then studied medicine, and was admitted an extra-licentiate of the Royal College of Physicians in 1839. In 1841 he travelled, apparently at his brother Willoughby's suggestion, to New Zealand, where on 25 June 1841 he became private secretary to the governor, William Hobson. In 1842 he was appointed police magistrate and sub-protector of aborigines. On 10 August 1843 he landed at Akaroa on Banks peninsula, to act as interpreter to Colonel Godfrey's court of inquiry into the land claims of the French company which was then endeavouring to establish itself in that area. After the court was closed he took a census of South Island Maori settlements, travelling extensively in Otago and coastal Canterbury. His authoritative observations on Maori life, traditions, and language were recorded in his journals. He continued in government employment as sub-protector of aborigines and interpreter until his departure for Europe in 1846.

The Southern Districts of New Zealand (1851) and *Traditions and Superstitions of the New Zealanders* (1854) were published while Shortland was living in Plymouth and practising medicine. In 1860 he served in Garibaldi's Sicilian campaign. In 1862 he returned to New Zealand as civil commissioner appointed to manage Maori affairs in the Hauraki area, and on 14 August 1863 he was appointed native secretary, but he returned to England in 1865. From 1869 to 1873, and from 1880 to 1889, he again resided in New Zealand. During this time he published his major work, *Maori Religion and Mythology* (1882), as well as contributing a seminal article to the first volume of *Transactions of the New Zealand Institute* and publishing a Maori-language textbook (1883).

On his final departure for England in October 1889 Shortland was described as 'the most efficient Maori scholar probably the colony possesses', and he was competent and far-sighted in his administrative positions. He died at Colguill Villa, Compton Gifford, Devon, on 2 July 1893, survived by his wife, Eugenia, *née* Hardie, whom he had married at an unknown date, and with whom he had had four sons and seven daughters. JANE TUCKER

Sources A. Anderson, 'Shortland, Edward', *DNZB*, vol. 1 · A. H. McLintock, ed., *An encyclopaedia of New Zealand*, 3 vols. (1966) · R. S. Hill, *Policing the colonial frontier: the theory and practice of coercive social and racial control in New Zealand, 1767–1867* (1986) · Venn, *Alum. Cant.* · *Auckland Weekly News* (19 Aug 1893)
Archives University of Otago, Dunedin, Hocken Library
Likenesses sketch, repro. in *New Zealand Herald* (16 Aug 1893)
Wealth at death £506 18s. 10d.: probate, 2 Aug 1893, CGPLA Eng. & Wales

Shortland, John (1769–1810), naval officer, born on 5 September 1769, was the elder son of Commander John Shortland (1736–1804), with whom he has sometimes been confused; he was the elder brother of Thomas George *Shortland (1771–1827). He entered the navy in 1781 under his father, then employed in transport service to and from North America. He was afterwards in the *Surprise*, and from 1783 to 1787 in the frigate *Latona* in the West Indies. On his return to England in 1787 he joined the *Sirius* (Captain John Hunter) and in her went out to New South Wales, made the voyage to the Cape of Good Hope, and was wrecked at Norfolk Island, from where he returned to England with Hunter in April 1792. On 10 October 1793 he was promoted lieutenant of the *Arrogant*, and in 1795 he was selected by Hunter as first lieutenant of the discovery

vessel *Reliance*, in which Hunter was going out as governor of New South Wales. As Hunter's duties detained him on shore, Shortland was in acting command of the ship, in which he made several voyages to the Cape of Good Hope, Tahiti, and New Zealand. He was granted land in Australia but returned to England with Hunter in 1801, and, having been promoted commander on 1 January 1801, he was appointed transport agent for the expedition to Egypt. The following year he commanded the cutter *Dolphin*, from which he was moved to the sloop *Trompeuse* (18 guns) going out to the Guinea coast, where, on a death vacancy, he was promoted captain of the *Squirrel* (24 guns). On his return to England his commission as captain was confirmed, to date from 6 August 1805. He was then sent out to the Halifax station, where, in February 1809, he was transferred to the frigate *Junon* (36 guns). In September he sailed for the West Indies, being then a hundred men short of complement, and on 13 December fell in with four large frigates sailing under Spanish colours. They proved able to answer the private signals, and Shortland consequently stood towards them to gain intelligence of the enemy. But, when the *Junon* was well within gunshot, they struck the Spanish colours, hoisted French, and poured in their broadsides. Notwithstanding the odds against him he defended his ship with the utmost gallantry until he was carried below, dangerously wounded. The *Junon*, which had lost ninety men killed and wounded, was then boarded and captured, but she was such a complete wreck that she was cleared out and set on fire. Shortland had both legs and his left arm shattered, and also had a severe wound in his side, and others less serious. His mangled body was taken on one of the French frigates and was afterwards sent, 13 miles in a canoe under a blazing sun, to the hospital at Guadeloupe, where he died, unmarried, on 21 January 1810 and where he was buried at Basse Terre with military honours.

J. K. LAUGHTON, rev. ANDREW LAMBERT

Sources W. P. Gossett, *The lost ships of the Royal Navy* (1986) · M. Gillen, *The founders of Australia* (1989) · W. James, *The naval history of Great Britain, from the declaration of war by France in 1793, to the accession of George IV*, [5th edn], 6 vols. (1859–60), vol. 5, p. 47 · *Naval Chronicle*, 24 (1810), 1–21 · *GM*, 1st ser., 80 (1810), 394 · A. McMartin, 'Shortland, John', *AusDB*, vol. 2 · J. J. Colledge, *Ships of the Royal Navy: an historical index*, 1 (1969)
Likenesses H. R. Cook, stipple (after R. Field), BM, NPG; repro. in *Naval Chronicle*

Shortland, Peter Frederick (1815–1888), naval officer, born on 15 November 1815, was the son of Captain Thomas George *Shortland RN (1771–1827) and his wife, Elizabeth, *née* Tonkin. His brothers were Willoughby *Shortland and Edward *Shortland. He entered the Royal Naval College at Portsmouth in January 1827, and, having passed with distinction, served afloat until 1834, when, on 4 December, he passed the examination for lieutenant. In 1836–8 he was a mate on the *Rattlesnake* in Australian waters, and, on the settlement of Melbourne, made a survey of Port Phillip. After returning to England in 1838 he obtained leave, matriculated at Cambridge as a member of Pembroke College, and in 1842 graduated seventh wrangler. He then applied to join the *Excellent* to compete for the commission at that time offered as a prize to young officers passing a course of gunnery and mathematics; but, as the advent of a seventh wrangler seemed likely to kill all competition, the Admiralty promoted him at once, on 1 April 1842. He was then appointed to the steamer *Columbia* for surveying duties on the coast of North America.

Soon after arriving on station Shortland succeeded to the command. In 1848 he married Emily Marilin, the daughter of Captain Thomas Jones of the 74th regiment; they had children. As lieutenant, as commander (20 January 1848), and as captain (1 January 1859) Shortland continued on the same station until 1865, making a complete survey of the coast of Nova Scotia, including the Bay of Fundy, for which he was specially thanked by the Admiralty. He was then appointed to the *Hydra* for surveying service in the Mediterranean, but in 1867 was sent to the East Indies to take a line of deep-sea soundings from Aden to Bombay. The *Hydra* was paid off in 1868, and Shortland, at the request of the Admiralty, wrote an account of the operation in *A Sounding Voyage of HMS Hydra* (1868). On attaining the age of fifty-five in 1870 he was placed on the retired list. He then qualified as a barrister and on 27 January 1873 was called to the bar; he practised in the Admiralty court. He became rear-admiral on 21 September 1876 and vice-admiral on 3 January 1881. He was the author of *A Short Account of the Laws which Govern HM Navy* (1886) and of *Nautical Surveying* (1890), published posthumously. He died at his home, 6 Hoe Villas, Plymouth, on 18 October 1888, survived by his wife.

J. K. LAUGHTON, rev. R. O. MORRIS

Sources *The Times* (19 Oct 1888) · L. S. Dawson, *Memoirs of hydrography*, 2 vols. (1885) · Venn, *Alum. Cant.*
Wealth at death £1531 19s. 11d.: probate, 10 Nov 1888, *CGPLA Eng. & Wales*

Shortland, Thomas George (1771–1827), naval officer, son of Commander John Shortland (1736–1804) and younger brother of Captain John *Shortland (1769–1810), was born at Portsea, Hampshire, on 10 May 1771. In January 1785 he entered the navy on the *Irresistible*, flying the broad pennant of Sir Andrew Snape Hamond in the English Channel. In March 1787 he was moved to the *Alexander*, one of the little squadron going out to New South Wales with Commodore Arthur Phillip, and served in her until her return to England in May 1789. He was then employed in the channel and the North Sea, and on 19 November 1790 was promoted lieutenant of the sloop *Speedy*. In January 1793 he was appointed to the frigate *Nemesis*, which accompanied the fleet under Lord Hood to the Mediterranean. In September 1794 he was moved into the *Romney*, with Sir Charles Hamilton whom, in April 1795, he followed to the *Melpomene*. On the night of 3–4 August 1798 he commanded the boats of the frigate in cutting out the armed brig *Aventurier* from under the batteries in the Bay of Corréjou, on the north coast of Brittany—a gallant exploit, for which he was promoted commander on 20 April 1799 and appointed to the sloop *Voltigeur* on the Newfoundland station. In summer 1801 he was appointed

temporarily to the 80-gun ship *Donegal*, then in dock at Plymouth, and, as a reward for his extraordinary exertions in fitting her for sea, he was made acting captain of the frigate *Dédaigneuse* (36 guns; rank and command confirmed on 1 March 1802). He took her to the East Indies but was compelled by ill health to return to England in spring 1803. He was afterwards for a short time captain of the *Britannia* (100 guns), and of the *Caesar* (80 guns) bearing the flag of Sir Richard John Strachan.

In summer 1806 Shortland joined the *Canopus* (80 guns), as flag captain to Sir Thomas Louis and commanded her when she led the squadron of Sir John Thomas Duckworth through the Dardanelles in February and March 1807. After the death of Louis, Shortland continued for some months in command of the *Canopus*, but in September 1807 he was moved into the *Queen* (98 guns), still in the Mediterranean, and remained in her until the end of 1808. In 1809 he commanded the *Valiant* (74 guns) in the expedition to the Scheldt; in 1810–11 the frigate *Iris*, off Cadiz and in the West Indies; and in 1812–13 the *Royal Oak* (74 guns) as flag captain to Lord Amelius Beauclerk. In November 1813 he was appointed agent for prisoners of war at Dartmoor; from April 1816 to April 1819 he was captain-superintendent of the ordinary at Plymouth; and for the next three years he was comptroller-general of the preventive boat service. On 14 July 1825 he was appointed resident commissioner at Jamaica, where he died towards the end of 1827. He married Elizabeth, daughter of Peter Tonkin of Plymouth; they had a large family. Three of their sons, Edward *Shortland, Peter Frederick *Shortland, and Willoughby *Shortland, are separately noticed.

J. K. LAUGHTON, rev. ANDREW LAMBERT

Sources D. Syrett and R. L. DiNardo, *The commissioned sea officers of the Royal Navy, 1660–1815*, rev. edn, Occasional Publications of the Navy RS, 1 (1994) · M. Gillen, *The founders of Australia* (1989) · J. Marshall, *Royal naval biography*, 2/1 (1824), 482–8 · P. Mackesy, *The war in the Mediterranean, 1803–1810* (1957) · J. J. Colledge, *Ships of the Royal Navy: an historical index*, 1 (1969)

Shortland, Willoughby (1804–1869), naval officer and colonial administrator, born at Plymouth, Devon, on 30 September 1804, was the son of Captain Thomas George *Shortland, of Courtlands, near Lympstone, Devon, and his wife, Elizabeth, the daughter of Peter Tonkin of Plymouth. His younger brothers were Edward *Shortland and Peter Frederick *Shortland. He was educated at the Royal Naval College, Portsmouth (1818–20), having entered the service on 9 January 1818. He was gazetted a lieutenant on 18 August 1828 and served on the Jamaica station. On 21 March 1831 he took the command of the *Skipjack*, a schooner of five guns, and remained with her in the West Indies until he was invalided home in June 1833. In 1839 he accompanied Captain William Hobson, the first governor-designate of New Zealand, to that colony via New South Wales, where Hobson appointed him chief magistrate and superintendent of police for New Zealand.

In 1841 Shortland married Isabella Kate Johnston, the daughter of Robert A. Fitzgerald, of Geraldine, co. Limerick, Ireland, and in May 1841 he was appointed colonial secretary. He proceeded to Port Nicholson, Wellington, and in dissolving the settlers' council there he aroused resentment among the New Zealand Company settlers. After the death of Captain Hobson on 10 September 1842, Shortland administered the government of New Zealand until his dismissal by the newly arrived Captain Robert FitzRoy on 31 December 1843. During Shortland's temporary government he was widely slated for financial and tactical imprudence. Following the fatal encounter between Maori and settlers at Wairau on 17 June 1843, in his dispatches to the home government he expressed his disapproval of the conduct of the settlers, to which he attributed the massacre. This action made him unpopular, and, when a report of his nomination as governor of New Zealand was circulated, a petition was sent from Auckland praying that he might not be appointed.

Still in favour with the Colonial Office, however, Shortland was in 1845 appointed president of Nevis in the Leeward Islands, and from 10 January 1854 until 1856 served as governor of Tobago. In July 1864 he retired from the navy with the rank of commander. He returned to England and resided on his property, Courtlands, Charleton, Kingsbridge, Devon, until his death there on 7 October 1869.   G. C. BOASE, *rev.* JANE TUCKER

Sources A. H. McLintock, ed., *An encyclopaedia of New Zealand*, 3 vols. (1966) · A. H. McLintock, *Crown colony government in New Zealand* (1958) · P. Mennell, *The dictionary of Australasian biography* (1892) · R. S. Hill, *Policing the colonial frontier: the theory and practice of coercive social and racial control in New Zealand, 1767–1867* (1986) · W. Gisborne, *New Zealand rulers and statesmen, 1840–1885* (1886)
Likenesses lithograph (after drawing by his niece; after portrait), Webster Collection, London
Wealth at death under £800: probate, 14 Nov 1869, *CGPLA Eng. & Wales*

Shorton, Robert (*d.* 1535), college head, is of unknown parentage and place of birth, although a northern origin is likely. He graduated BA from Jesus College, Cambridge, in 1501, is recorded as fellow of Jesus in 1503, and was elected fellow of Pembroke College on 25 November 1505, treasurer in 1509, and lector in divinity some time between 1509 and February 1511. Shorton's treasurership prepared him for his duties at St John's, of which he was officially designated master in its foundation charter (9 April 1511). He owed his preferment to John Fisher as his letter of thanks, dated 6 February 1511, makes clear. He remained master until an uncertain date in 1516. His main task was to supervise the building of the college, and his accounts survive between 31 January 1511 and 21 January 1516. Legal problems, including a boundary dispute with the King's Hall, also had to be resolved. At an unknown date he donated £10 to the college to pave the hall.

On 21 October, most probably in 1516, the fellows of Pembroke College invited Shorton to return as master, stressing his virtue and learning, and the advantage to the college of having as master one who had been nurtured by it. They were correct in anticipating generosity. Shorton added properties near and at Orton Waterville, Huntingdonshire, to the manor and advowson of Orton already

owned by the college. These were the manor of Chesterton Vescie, conveyed in 1518, and Rowse's estate, consisting of a messuage, three tofts and gardens, and 61 acres, conveyed in 1525. He also gave Pembroke chapel sets of white damask vestments for priest, deacon, and subdeacon, for the soul of Master William Thomson.

In the 1520s Shorton rose to eminence. He gained high-church preferments, some via the patronage of Cardinal Wolsey, for whose college at Oxford he selected some scholars. By 1527 he was dean of the cardinal's own chapel, and in that year was appointed canon and prebendary of St George's Chapel, Windsor. From 1529 he was dean of the collegiate college of Stoke by Clare, Suffolk, and archdeacon of Bath. He resigned the mastership of Pembroke in 1534 or early 1535. He was almoner to Queen Katherine of Aragon, and is reported to have spoken in her favour when consulted about her divorce from Henry VIII. Nevertheless, Shorton maintained amicable relations with Cromwell. He wrote on 27 June 1535 approving Cromwell's reformation of Stoke College, and bequeathed him five pieces of arras.

Shorton's will, dated 8 October 1535, requested burial at the college of Stoke by Clare, and left sums for the poor of twenty towns, including Newport, Essex, where he was master of St Leonard's Hospital, and to his tenants at Wells, probably Norfolk, and his parishes of Sedgefield, co. Durham, and Lowther, Westmorland. Noteworthy among the bequests was a gilt salt with a cover 'antyke' to Thomas Legh, and the sum of £40 to maintain highways in Essex. Separately he arranged for obits at Pembroke, St John's, St Catharine's, and Peterhouse, accompanied by distributions to the fellows. That at Peterhouse contains a reference to keeping the obit for twenty years 'or for so long as the king's laws will suffer it'. In 1546 it was reported that he had left the funds to buy the greater part of a farm at Whittlesford to endow his obit at Pembroke. He died on or about 17 October 1535, and his will was proved on 8 November.   MALCOLM G. UNDERWOOD

Sources Emden, *Cam.* · letter, 21 Oct [1516?], Pembroke Cam., Archives, register I alpha, 10.1, fol. 78 · Pembroke Cam., Archives, register C beta, p. 6 · obits., Pembroke Cam., Archives, College Box L26–L28 · Pembroke Cam., Archives, College Box Q3 · PRO, PROB 11/25, sig. 28 (Hogen) · letter, 6 Feb 1511, St John Cam., D105.90 · building accounts, 1511–16, St John Cam., Archives, D6.31 · list of benefactors, St John Cam., Archives, C7.2, fol. 44 · accounts, 1545–6, St John Cam., Archives, D106.17, fol. 305 · *Letters of Richard Fox, 1486–1527*, ed. P. S. Allen and H. M. Allen (1929) · Cooper, *Ath. Cantab.*, 1.55–6
Archives Pembroke Cam. · St John Cam.
Likenesses oils, 17th cent. (after wood panel), St John Cam. · wood panel, Peterhouse, Cambridge
Wealth at death approx. £110: will, PRO, PROB 11/25, sig. 28

Shortt, Doreen Constance. *See* Ingrams, Doreen Constance (1906–1997).

Shortt, Edward (1862–1935), politician, was born at Byker, Newcastle upon Tyne, on 10 March 1862, the second son of Edward Shortt (*b. c.*1828), vicar of St Anthony's Church, Byker, who was descended from an Irish family in co. Tyrone, and his wife, Josepha, daughter of Joseph Rushton of Alderley Edge, Cheshire. Shortt was educated at Durham

School and at Durham University, where he was Lindsay scholar and graduated in classics in 1884. In 1890 he married Isabella Stewart, daughter of A. G. Scott of Valparaiso. They had a son, who was killed in action in 1917, and three daughters.

In 1890 Shortt was called to the bar by the Middle Temple, of which he was elected a bencher in 1919, and joined the north-eastern circuit. He was recorder of Sunderland from 1907 to 1918 and took silk in 1910. Elected to parliament as a Liberal for Newcastle upon Tyne in January 1910 he retained the seat (western division, 1918–22) throughout his parliamentary career.

Shortt made no great success at the bar. He was a clear and lucid debater in parliament but his *Times* obituary noted that 'his political success he practically owed to the War' (*The Times*, 11 Nov 1935, 14). He had spoken frequently on the Home Rule Bill of 1912 but after that he contributed little in the house. However, in June 1917 he was appointed chairman of a select committee set up to review the general administration of the Military Service Acts, which reported in August, recommending that medical examinations should be transferred from the War Office to a civilian authority. Through his intelligent and tactful handling of a subject bristling with difficulties for the government he attracted the attention of Lloyd George, who in April 1918 appointed him to succeed Henry Edward Duke as chief secretary for Ireland. In that post Shortt was quickly confronted by serious trouble linked to 'German intrigue' in Ireland (ibid.). Shortt swiftly organized the arrest of 150 Sinn Féiners but later told American diplomats that the government 'would have to make peace with those people [Sinn Féin]' (Mansergh, 159). In January 1919 Shortt was transferred to the Home Office in the midst of a threatened police strike. There he contributed to a satisfactory settlement, and his popularity with the force was shown by a tribute he received upon his losing office with the fall of the coalition government in October 1922. He did not stand for parliament again and his political career came to an end. As a minister he had on occasion caused difficulties for himself through the laxness of his answers in the House of Commons. *The Times* said that he was 'somewhat indolent in the routine work of the office and in detail' (ibid.). He was also criticized for his apparent bias towards members of the north-eastern circuit in his legal appointments as home secretary.

Shortt was sworn of the privy council and of the Irish privy council in 1918. His old university, Durham, conferred the honorary degree of DCL upon him in 1920. He subsequently held a number of official posts, including the chairmanship of the committees on the rating of machinery, trusts, heavy motor traffic, and the investigation into the Agricultural Marketing Act. In November 1929 Shortt succeeded T. P. O'Connor as second president of the British Board of Film Censors, a salaried appointment but independent of the film industry. He had little interest in the cinema (indeed, he disliked sound films) and proved a restrictive censor; between 1930 and 1935 120 films were banned and in 1932 a record 382 films were cut. Among the films that Shortt rejected, in 1933, was *Red-Headed Woman*, starring Jean Harlow. One of his daughters became a censor in 1934. Shortt died at his home, 140 Oakwood Court, Kensington, London, of septicaemia, following influenza, on 10 November 1935; he was survived by his wife.

E. I. CARLYLE, rev. MARC BRODIE

Sources *The Times* (11–12 Nov 1935) · *The Times* (15 Nov 1935) · N. Mansergh, *The unresolved question: the Anglo-Irish settlement and its undoing, 1912–72* (1991) · F. Stevenson, *Lloyd George: a diary*, ed. A. J. P. Taylor (1971) · T. Wilson, *The downfall of the liberal party, 1914–1935* (1966) · J. Turner, *British politics and the Great War: coalition and conflict, 1915–1918* (1992) · WWBMP · Burtchaell & Sadleir, *Alum. Dubl.*, 2nd edn · J. C. Robertson, *The British Board of Film Censors: film censorship in Britain, 1896–1950* (1985) · J. C. Robertson, *The hidden cinema: British film censorship in action, 1913–1975* (1989) · CGPLA Eng. & Wales (1935)
Archives Nuffield Oxf., corresp. [copies] | HLRO, corresp. with Andrew Bonar Law · HLRO, corresp. with David Lloyd George, etc. · Wilts. & Swindon RO, corresp. with Viscount Long
Likenesses W. Stoneman, photograph, 1920, NPG · R. G. Eves, pencil drawings, 1922, NPG · photograph, repro. in *The Times* (11 Nov 1935), 14
Wealth at death £7056 6s. 9d.: probate, 9 Dec 1935, CGPLA Eng. & Wales

Shortt, William Hamilton (1881–1971), railway engineer and horologist, was born on 28 September 1881 at 22 Courthope Villas, Worple Road, Wimbledon, Surrey, the only son of Charles Henry Shortt (1852–1915), civil engineer, and his wife, Fanny Catherine Lise, *née* Dobson (1855–1950), sister of the poet Austin Dobson. He was educated at Christ's College, Blackheath, and the Goldsmiths' Technical Institute before joining the London and South Western Railway (LSWR) in 1902, as an articled pupil of the chief engineer, J. W. Jacomb-Hood. During his three years under Jacomb-Hood he continued to study at the Goldsmiths' Institute and also at Birkbeck Institute and King's College, London. Jacomb-Hood demonstrated his confidence in his pupil's ability by calling upon him to establish a civil engineering laboratory. In 1907 Shortt was elected to associate membership of the Institution of Civil Engineers, by which time he had already laid the foundations for a successful career as a railway engineer. However, a series of events occurred which added another dimension to his life, and one for which he is principally known.

In 1906 a serious accident occurred on the LSWR when an express train was derailed at Salisbury Station with the loss of twenty-eight lives. The Board of Trade inquiry concluded that the derailment was caused by excessive speed on a curve, and in 1908 a subcommittee of the Railway Engineers Association was formed to report on this issue, under the chairmanship of Jacomb-Hood. Shortt acted as secretary and technical assistant to the subcommittee from 1908 to 1910 and in this capacity he devised an instrument for accurately recording the speed of trains. The speed was determined by measuring the time taken to traverse a known length of track, and this kindled in Shortt an interest in precision time-measurement which was to last all his life. At the same time he described a graphical method for improving existing railway curves, a subject to which he was to return in 1923.

In 1910 a meeting took place between Shortt and Frank

Hope-Jones (1868–1950) which was to have a significant effect in briefly regaining for England the pre-eminence in precision clockmaking that it had once enjoyed. Hope-Jones was the proprietor of the Synchronome Company and had been largely responsible for establishing the electric clock as a reliable timekeeper in the UK. Hope-Jones and Shortt were kindred spirits, professional engineers outside the horological establishment, and receptive to new ideas. Encouraged by Hope-Jones, Shortt began a series of meticulous experiments at his home workshop at Bramcote Road in Putney and also at the Synchronome workshops in Clerkenwell in order to improve the performance of the pendulum clock. This occupied most of his spare time until 1916, when he was released from his railway duties to serve in France as a captain in the Royal Engineers. Following demobilization in 1919 he resumed his position with the LSWR and continued his horological experiments.

It had been recognized for some time that the ideal mechanical timekeeper was a pendulum swinging freely in a vacuum with the least possible interference, but there was no consensus about how this could be realized in practice. Hope-Jones, who was strongly influenced by the work of R. J. Rudd, was convinced that this could be achieved by using a separate slave clock to perform the normal functions of a clock and to provide an impulse to keep the free pendulum swinging. Eventually Shortt also adopted this method and was able to construct an effective free-pendulum clock, which he installed at the Royal Scottish Observatory in Edinburgh during Christmas 1921. Figures published by the astronomer royal for Scotland, Professor Sampson, in 1924 showed that the performance of the Shortt free-pendulum clock exceeded that of other mechanical timekeepers. The Synchronome Company produced a sightly modified version of this clock, which became the standard timekeeper in many observatories and institutions throughout the world.

Early in 1922 Shortt moved to Exeter, and following the regrouping of the railways he became district engineer of the western district of the Southern Railway, a post which he was to occupy until his retirement twenty-four years later. On 1 June 1937 he married Katherine Winifred Messer (1905–1968); they had three daughters. Shortt was a shy and retiring man who was confident in the areas of his expertise. Although he was not directly involved with the development of precision clocks after his move to the west country, he continued to be a director of the Synchronome Company which had the benefit of his advice. His contributions to horology were recognized by the award of a gold medal by the British Horological Institute in 1931, the John Price Wetherill silver medal of the Franklin Institute in 1935, and the Tompion medal of the Worshipful Company of Clockmakers in 1954. He was made a liveryman of the company in 1931 and master in 1950.

In 1946, when Shortt retired from the railway, Dame Georgiana Buller was establishing the firm of Devon Instruments to provide employment for disabled persons. Shortt acted as technical adviser to the firm, which made a range of clocks, and when Dame Georgiana died in 1953 he succeeded her as chairman of the company, a post which he occupied until 1966. He died on 4 February 1971 at the Royal Devon and Exeter Hospital, at Exeter, survived by his three daughters. He was cremated on the 10th in the Exeter and Devon crematorium.

DENYS VAUGHAN

Sources *PICE*, new ser., 50 (1971), 396–7 · 'Railway news section', *Railway Gazette* (25 Oct 1946) · W. H. Shortt, 'Some experimental mechanisms, mechanical and otherwise for the maintenance and vibration of a pendulum', *Horological Journal*, 71 (1928–9), 224–6, 245–7 · F. Hope-Jones, *Electrical timekeeping*, 2nd edn (1949) · W. H. Shortt, 'Precision timekeeping', *Horological Journal*, 54 (1911–12), 86–126 · patents, nos. 12328 of 1911; 9527 of 1915; 187 and 814 of 1921 · R. A. Sampson, 'Studies in clocks and timekeeping, no. 3: comparative rates of certain clocks', *Proceedings of the Royal Society of Edinburgh*, 44 (1923–4), 56–76 · W. H. Shortt, 'A new method for the improvement of existing railway curves', *Selected engineering paper of the Institution of Civil Engineers*, 3 (1923) · F. Hope-Jones, 'The free pendulum', *Journal of the Royal Society of Arts*, 72 (1923–4), 446–60 · private information (2004) · *The Shortt speed recorder for railways* [brochure for James A. Sinclair & Co., Ltd] · b. cert. · d. cert.
Archives Royal Museums of Scotland, Edinburgh, original free-pendulum clock (SHO) · Sci. Mus., prototype of the Shortt-Synchronome free-pendulum clock (GC)
Likenesses photograph, repro. in *PICE*, 50 · photograph, repro. in 'Railway news section'
Wealth at death £26,101: probate, 6 May 1971, *CGPLA Eng. & Wales*

Shotton, Frederick William (1906–1990), geologist, was born on 8 October 1906 in Exhall, near Coventry, the younger child and only son of Frederick John Shotton, an industrialist specializing in drop forged products, who was manager of the Albion Drop Forging Company of Coventry, and his wife, Ada Brooks. He was educated at Bablake School in Coventry and Sidney Sussex College, Cambridge. He obtained first classes in both parts (1926 and 1927) of the natural sciences tripos (geology), and was awarded a Harkness scholarship in 1927. In 1929 he was appointed assistant lecturer at the University of Birmingham, where he remained until returning to Cambridge as a lecturer in 1936. After war service he became Sorby professor of geology at Sheffield University in 1945 and in 1949 he took up the post of Lapworth professor of geology at Birmingham University, from which he retired in 1974. He was vice-principal of Birmingham University in 1965–71.

Shotton made contributions in three main areas: as a military geologist, as a Quaternary stratigrapher and geomorphologist, and as a student of the Mesozoic and Palaeozoic. His career as a military geologist started in 1938 when he joined the Army Officers' Emergency Reserve. He was called up in May 1940 and commissioned into the Royal Engineers. He took responsibility for geological activities in north Africa and the Middle East and was particularly concerned with the provision of water supplies. Indeed, the success of the advance from El Alamein owed much to Shotton's hydrological studies in parched desert terrain. In 1943 Shotton, now a major, was recalled to Britain as geological adviser on the staff of the chief engineer at the headquarters of Twenty-First Army group under the command of Sir Bernard Montgomery. There he worked on the assessment of the character of the invasion beaches prior to Operation Overlord and, *inter alia*, cross-country mobility along the line of advance towards the Rhine. He was three times mentioned in dispatches. After demobilization he retained his links with the army and acted as the geological adviser to the chief scientist (army) until the post was abolished in 1970.

Shotton's career as a Quaternary scientist was an important one and dominated the last three decades of his life. At Birmingham he created one of the outstanding British centres for Quaternary research, establishing a radiocarbon dating laboratory and a renowned centre for the study of Quaternary beetles. He helped to launch the Quaternary Field Study Group (eventually the Quaternary Research Association) in 1964 and presided at the International Quaternary Association in 1977. He made fundamental contributions to the study of Quaternary sediments and land forms in the English midlands and was the editor of (and contributed to) *British Quaternary Studies* (1977). With characteristic vigour and forthrightness he argued and debated the issues until the end; he was one of the physical and intellectual giants of British Quaternary geology.

As a mainstream geologist Shotton wrote extensively on the stratigraphy, structures, and sedimentology of a range of rocks, particularly from the English midlands. Especially important was his work on the Bunter Sandstones, for which he reconstructed palaeo-wind patterns from Aeolian cross stratification. As head of the geology department at Birmingham University he introduced both geophysics and hydrogeology into the curriculum and instituted MSc courses in them.

Shotton was appointed MBE in 1945. He became a fellow of the Royal Society (1956), and president of the Geological Society of London (1964–6), Section C of the British Association for the Advancement of Science (1961–2), and the International Quaternary Association. He was awarded honorary membership of the Royal Irish Academy (1970), the Prestwich medal of the Geological Society of London (1954), and the Stopes medal of the Geologists' Association (1967).

Shotton was large, bespectacled, and a smoker. In 1930 he married Alice Louise, daughter of John Linnett, a draper from Coventry; they had two daughters. She died in 1979 and in September 1983 he married a widow, Lucille Frances Bailey, daughter of David Ray Matteson, chief accountant of the Spokane, Portland, and Seattle Railway in Portland, Oregon, USA. Her career was in psychology and education. Shotton died on 21 July 1990 in the East Birmingham Hospital.   ANDREW S. GOUDIE, rev.

Sources M. S. Rosenbaum, 'Professor F. W. Shotton', *Royal Engineers Journal*, new ser., 104 (1990), 289–90 • P. Worsley, *Proceedings of the Geologists' Association*, 102 (1991), 322–3 • E. P. F. Rose and M. S. Rosenbaum, 'British military geologists: through the Second World War to the end of the cold war', *Proceedings of the Geologists' Association*, 104 (1993), 95–108 • G. R. Coope, *Memoirs FRS*, 39 (1994), 417–32 • *The Times* (2 Aug 1990) • *The Independent* (28 July 1990) • personal knowledge (1996) • private information (1996) • *CGPLA Eng. & Wales* (1991)

Archives Shrops. RRC, corresp. with L. F. Chitty and others
Likenesses photograph, repro. in *Memoirs FRS*, 416
Wealth at death £911,126: probate, 11 Feb 1991, *CGPLA Eng. & Wales*

Shovell, Sir Cloudesley (*bap.* 1650, *d.* 1707), naval officer, baptized on 25 November 1650 at Cockthorpe, on the north Norfolk coast, was the son of John Shovell (1625–1654), from a Norwich family of property and distinction, and Anne (*bap.* 1628, *d.* 1709), daughter of Henry Jenkinson of Cley. His unusual forename derives from the family name of his maternal grandmother, Lucy Cloudesley (1608–1627), and his uncle Cloudesley Jenkinson (1639–1696). Cloudesley Shovell's father died when he was about four and his mother married John Flaxman (*d.* 1687) in 1659.

Early naval career Shovell first went to sea through his father's connections with two naval officers from Cockthorpe, Sir Christopher Mynges and Sir John Narbrough. In 1663 he was with Mynges in the West Indies as a cabin-boy and servant. After Mynges's death in the Four Days' Battle in June 1666 he continued with Narbrough in the same capacity. He was with him in 1667 when Narbrough took Cayenne and perhaps on Narbrough's voyage to the Pacific in 1670–71. The first official record of Shovell's naval service is dated 22 January 1672, when he entered as a midshipman on board the duke of York's flagship *Royal Prince* seventeen days after the duke appointed Captain Narbrough his first lieutenant in that ship.

With Narbrough, Shovell was present at the battle of Solebay on 28 May 1672. On 17 September 1672 he followed him as a master's mate, one of the 210 volunteers from *Royal Prince* who moved into *Fairfax*. When Narbrough shifted command to *St Michael*, Shovell followed in the same capacity. Later in the same year he followed him again to *Henrietta*, where, through Narbrough's influence, Shovell was appointed second lieutenant on 23 September 1673. Shortly afterwards they sailed to the Mediterranean for the naval campaign against Tripoli. In 1675 Narbrough moved to the *Harwich*, and Shovell followed as a lieutenant. On 14 January 1676 Shovell commanded the squadron's boats that burned shipping in Tripoli harbour and earned himself fame through Narbrough's dispatch describing the action, which was subsequently printed (*London Gazette*). Even before its publication Pepys wrote to Narbrough about 'Lieutenant Shovell, with whose management his Majesty and my lords are most particularly satisfied' (Tanner, 3.179; 4.295). Narbrough rewarded the boat crews with 1956 pieces of eight, of which Shovell received 80, the largest amount, and to which Charles II added a further reward, including a medal valued at the exceptional amount of £100. On 3 May 1677 Shovell was appointed first lieutenant in Narbrough's flagship, the *Plymouth*, and joined Narbrough in attesting to a report on the satisfactory state of work being done on the new mole at Tangier.

In September 1677, when Thomas Harman died of his wounds in the action with the *Golden Horse*, Narbrough appointed Shovell to take Harman's place in command of the 28-gun *Sapphire*. In her he made a dramatic chase of a

Sir Cloudesley Shovell (*bap.* 1650, *d.* 1707), by Michael Dahl, *c.*1702–5

44-gun Turkish warship from Tripoli to the Spanish coast, which only narrowly escaped capture in October 1677. As Narbrough prepared for his departure for England in the spring of 1679, Shovell assisted the admiral and the commissioners who concluded a peace treaty with Tripoli, for which Shovell received £100 as a reward. Narbrough and his vice-admiral, Arthur Herbert, shifted Shovell from one command to another as they attempted to deal with the conflicting demands of the Algerine war and the defence of Tangier from Salé. In April–May 1679 Herbert placed Shovell in command of the 36-gun *Phoenix*; then, in May, the Admiralty ordered him back to *Sapphire*. In July 1680 Herbert moved him to the *Nonsuch*, then, in September, at Shovell's request, returned him to the *Sapphire*. Finally, in April 1681, Herbert moved him to the 30-gun *James Galley*, where he remained for the next five years. In her he assisted the *Sapphire* in capturing the 32-gun Algerine cruiser *Half Moon* in September, and in December joined the *Adventure* in driving the 34-gun Algerine corsair *Flower-Pot* ashore near Mazagan. In April 1682 he assisted Herbert in the treaty that ended the four and a half year long war with Algiers. In May and in November he was also at Tripoli for negotiations. When the Admiralty ordered Herbert home, Shovell remained for a year in command of the five-ship Mediterranean squadron.

At Cadiz on 23 June 1683 to convoy English merchantmen, Shovell was pressured by the conde de Aguilar into saluting the Spanish king without receiving a return salute to his own sovereign. He complied with this demand to protect the merchantmen, whose cargoes

would have otherwise been seized or destroyed, but his decision outraged Pepys and Lord Dartmouth, both of whom vowed to court-martial him. However, when the circumstances were reported to the king, Charles II placed no blame on Shovell.

Shovell irritated Pepys again after Dartmouth arrived with the fleet in the Mediterranean to dismantle the garrison at Tangier. This time Shovell, along with Wheeler and Aylmer, produced friction when they were clearly reluctant to sign the report justifying the destruction of the new mole at Tangier. After dismantling the garrison, Dartmouth returned to England, leaving Shovell in charge of a seven-ship squadron. He towed the Tangier pontoon to Cadiz and later cruised off Salé and the Strait of Gibraltar.

Shovell returned to England at the end of 1686 and in April 1687 took command of the 62-gun *Anne*, flagship of the duke of Grafton. In her he escorted the queen of Portugal from Rotterdam to Lisbon and then returned to the Mediterranean to ensure that the treaty with Algiers was not broken, negotiating for the release of some English prisoners. In June 1687 he detained the *James and Mary*, commanded by William Phipps, to secure the silver plate Phipps had recovered from a wrecked galleon in the West Indies.

In April 1688 Shovell took command of the *Dover*. When William III sailed from the Netherlands in November, Shovell was assigned to Dartmouth's fleet, but was cruising independently until 9 November. A few days later Russell named Shovell as one of eight captains 'resolved to salute Dartmouth and come over to us' (BL, Egerton MS 2621). After William III accepted Dartmouth's profession of loyalty and ordered him with the main fleet to the Nore, William ordered the *Dover* to remain with a dozen more vessels at Spithead under Sir John Berry. There, they served to guard against any French attack and to prevent any suspicious movements at Portsmouth. In particular, Shovell was assigned to take precautions against attempts to smuggle the infant prince of Wales to France.

The Nine Years' War In mid-January 1689 the fleet was reorganized and Shovell joined the newly formed squadron under Commodore John Ashby. In April he took command of the 70-gun *Edgar*, assigned to Herbert's fleet, which was one of nineteen ships that engaged the French at Bantry Bay, on 1 May 1689. After the battle the fleet returned to Portsmouth, where the king knighted Shovell and Ashby on board the flagship of the newly created earl of Torrington at Portsmouth on 15 May.

On 24 October Shovell shifted to command the *Monk*. His initial assignment to join the West Indies squadron in her was scrapped and instead he commanded a small squadron cruising between the Isles of Scilly and Ireland. As early as January 1690 Shovell was marked for promotion to rear-admiral of the blue, but this did not take place until June, after it was clear that he had no role in a conspiracy in the fleet. In the spring of 1690 he saw action near Dublin and oversaw the transport of the army and its equipment to Ireland. As part of this movement, on 11

June the king embarked in the yacht *Mary* (Captain Grenville Collins) at Hoylake and sailed to Carrickfergus, with 288 transports carrying 36,000 troops under Shovell's escort. On arrival William shifted to Shovell's barge to land. Occupied on this duty, Shovell was unavailable when the French fleet attacked Torrington off Beachy Head.

On receiving news of the battle, the queen's council sent orders to Shovell and to Vice-Admiral Henry Killigrew, returning with his squadron from the Mediterranean, to join Torrington. Shovell immediately sailed for Plymouth, where he met up with Killigrew. In London, both Shovell and Killigrew were mentioned as possible candidates to be one of the joint admirals to succeed Torrington in command of the main fleet. In the course of this discussion, Queen Mary told the king that her advisers considered Shovell 'the best officer of his age' (Mary to William, 6/16 July 1690, *CSP dom.*, *1690–91*, 53). The presence of the French fleet in the channel, however, prevented the detached squadrons from reinforcing the main fleet. In light of this, Shovell was ordered to cruise in the Soundings and guard against any French attempt to attack Ireland. On reports that French frigates were at Kinsale, he sailed there, where the enemy had just surrendered to English forces under Major-General Kirke. With Duncannon Castle still resisting, Shovell immediately ordered several frigates to bring about its reduction on 28 July. From there, he sailed for Plymouth, but was recalled to form a squadron to intercept a French squadron reportedly covering the evacuation of Galway and Limerick. Interrupted in this by other demands, Shovell was ordered by the Admiralty to sail for the Downs. Arriving on 10 October, he received new orders to take all available ships to Plymouth and to cruise for the protection of trade in the Soundings. He returned to the Downs in mid-January 1691 to join the fleet escorting the king to the Netherlands. At The Hague, on 17 February, the king appointed him major of the 1st marine regiment. Upon his return, he joined the main fleet under Russell. His early naval patron Sir John Narbrough had died in the West Indies in 1688, and on 10 March 1691 Shovell married his widow, Elizabeth, *née* Hill (1659–1732).

In July 1691 Shovell was sent to get intelligence of the French fleet at Brest and proceeded close inshore, imitating a returning French fleet with English prizes. With this ruse, he seized several French merchant vessels loaded with money and ascertained that an unexpectedly powerful force of eighty-four ships of the line lay at Brest. At the end of the campaigning season ashore, he escorted the king from the Netherlands to Margate, where the king landed on 19 October. While still at the camp at Ath, the king additionally commissioned Shovell lieutenant-colonel of the 2nd marine regiment. In January 1692 Shovell was promoted rear-admiral of the red and in March again escorted the king back to the Netherlands. Afterwards he rejoined Herbert's fleet and was among the eighty ships with him on 19 May, when they encountered the French fleet off Barfleur.

Shovell commanded the rear division of Herbert's centre squadron. At 11 a.m. the opposing fleets opened fire in light west-south-westerly winds at such close, musket-shot, range that Shovell later remarked he had never before seen two fleets engage at such short distance. After about two hours the wind shifted, giving Shovell the opportunity to luff up into the new breeze and break through the French line. Seven of his nine ships were able to follow his manoeuvre. The Dutch, in the allied van, made a similar tactical manoeuvre and forced the French to double back on their own line. When the fog cleared momentarily, Shovell engaged Tourville's flagship and six others, but the wind quickly died again and, as the tide turned and began to sweep the opposing fleets to the east, Tourville anchored. Shovell followed suit, but the opposing ships could only exchange fire from their stern and bow guns. Shovell immediately attempted to dislodge the French by sending down fireships on the tide. Shortly thereafter he faced nine French ships coming down the tide. In the face of this new threat, he cut his anchor cables and drifted past Tourville's squadron, which succeeded in heavily damaging Shovell's ships at close range. By ten in the evening the engagement had ended, but the larger English force had not destroyed the smaller French fleet.

Shovell pursued the main body of the French fleet as it moved westward. About midnight the next day, with his flagship nearly disabled by the heavy fire it received, Shovell shifted his flag to the frigate *Kent*. Continuing westward, he soon led the chase with ten ships. He came nearly within gunshot off Cherbourg on 21 May, but withheld fire, awaiting reinforcements. He followed the French to the roadstead of La Hogue and anchored offshore. The following morning Russell ordered him to attack, but he could not, without wind. At this point Shovell reported that he was suffering from a sudden and severe illness, probably blood poisoning from the splinter wound in the thigh received during the fleet action. Rooke took Shovell's place and carried on the attack. Shovell returned to the *Royal William* and proceeded to Portsmouth for repair, later going on the Chatham Dockyard. He came ashore on 28 May to recuperate at Fareham.

In late 1692 the dispute that had arisen between Russell and Nottingham over the conduct of the fleet developed into a party political battle in parliament as well as a conflict between Commons and Lords. As a result it became difficult to choose any one individual to command the fleet for the 1693 season. It was 23 January 1693 before three flag officers were appointed to jointly command the fleet. They were Killigrew and Delaval, two officers with tory political leanings, and Shovell, who was known as a whig. Shovell was the junior of the three and appointed admiral of the blue. On 27 April he joined his father-in-law, John Hill, as an extra commissioner of the Navy Board.

On 15 May 1693 the joint admirals met and considered a plan to convoy a large number of merchantmen to the Mediterranean. Not knowing the exact location of the enemy fleet, the admirals waited until they could obtain more information. A few days later, at the queen's command, the Admiralty overruled this decision, whereupon the joint admirals decided to take the main fleet to accompany Rooke's convoy escort to a position 90 miles west-south-west of Ushant. There they planned to leave Rooke to proceed on his own. On reaching that position the joint admirals still had no information on the whereabouts of the French fleet and decided to stay with Rooke for an additional 60 miles. On 7 June the joint admirals turned to the north, thinking that the longer they stayed with Rooke, the more they were leaving England open to attack from Brest. Not knowing that the French fleet had sailed to the south, they had unwittingly left Rooke and his fleet to fall into the hands of the combined Brest–Toulon squadrons lying in wait at Lagos Bay on the south coast of Portugal.

News of the disastrous attack on the Smyrna merchantmen reached London in mid-July 1693 and the joint admirals' entire conduct of the operation came under tumultuous parliamentary criticism. Although the joint admirals escaped censure, they were dismissed from their joint command and Russell was recalled to replace them and to serve as first lord of a newly reconstituted Admiralty board.

Later, Shovell was named to command the squadron for the West Indies, but Francis Wheeler replaced him before it sailed. In 1694 he purchased an estate, May Place, at Crayford, Kent, and later that year returned to sea as vice-admiral of the red in the main fleet under Lord Berkeley. He participated in the expedition to Camaret Bay which carried the troops under Lieutenant-General Thomas Talmash and also included some of William Meester's 'machine vessels' (vessels of 20–100 tons filled with explosives; towed inshore just before a naval bombardment, they were detonated by a preset firing mechanism, the explosions signalling the main attack). In November Shovell was again the centre of attention. In the Downs, he ordered the *Stirling Castle* to fire on the 56-gun Danish warship *Gyldenløve*, commanded by a future Danish admiral, Captain Niels Lauritzen Barfoed, for failing to strike her pendant in salute to the queen's flag in English home waters.

In May 1695 Shovell was promoted and retroactively paid the allowance of his earlier rank as admiral of the blue from 1 January 1694. In 1695 he was in command of the *Cambridge* as well as acting as Berkeley's second flag officer while in command in the attacks on St Malo and Dunkirk. In August he was spoken of for commanding a small Mediterranean squadron, but eventually Russell was sent with a full fleet of fifty-six ships. In December he took command of the *Duchess*. In April 1696 he commanded the *Victory* as well as being admiral of the blue at the bombardment of Calais. After he had operated in the Bay of Biscay in July and August, the Admiralty sent orders to Shovell to command the fleet in the Mediterranean, but when the French Toulon squadron slipped into Brest that plan was not put into effect. He commanded the Channel Fleet in the remainder of the war in 1697 and in March succeeded Lord Berkeley as colonel of the 2nd marine regiment.

Shovell was appointed commander-in-chief of vessels in the Thames and Medway in August 1698, providing escort for the king on his return from the Netherlands in November. In the parliamentary election of 1698 he was returned as second member for Rochester and retained that seat until 1701. In March 1699 he exchanged his position as an extra commissioner to be one of the principal officers of the Navy Board as controller of victualling accounts.

Shovell returned to command the Channel Fleet again in 1701. It was probably in the early months of Anne's reign that John Macky wrote his posthumously published note on Shovell:

> No man understands the Affairs of the Navy better, or is beloved of the Sailors so well as he. He loves the *Constitution* of his *Country* and serves it without *factious aim*; he … proves a very grateful Husband … hath very good Natural Parts; familiar and plain in his Conversation; dresses without affectation; is a very large, fat, fair Man. (*Memoirs of the Secret Services*, 121)

War of the Spanish Succession Shortly after Anne's accession to the throne, Shovell was promoted admiral of the white (May 1702) and presided over the court martial of Rear-Admiral Sir John Munden. Then he returned to sea as second in command to Rooke. When Rooke sailed to attack Cadiz, he ordered Shovell to cruise in the Atlantic in search of the French naval squadron escorting the returning Spanish bullion fleet. Receiving news that it had arrived at Vigo, Shovell rushed to support Rooke, arriving four days after the initial attack. When Rooke left for home with the main fleet, he remained behind to manage the aftermath of the action, to repair and re-rig the captured vessels, and to supervise the care of disabled ships, destroying those that could not be taken to sea. In particular, he was ordered to prevent any embezzlement of prize goods. He completed this work and departed Vigo on 25 October, but was delayed in his return by bad weather.

In early 1703 Shovell became one of the advisers to the newly formed ordnance establishment and was also present at the opening of the goods from Vigo and to make an account of them. That same year he commanded the squadron in the Mediterranean, where he first attempted to make contact with the Camisard rebels in the Cévennes, then sailed for Leghorn, where he arrived on 19 September. When he found that the Austrians had no plans for the fleet to support their military operations, he departed for England.

A few days after his return, Shovell and several vessels had anchored at the Gunfleet on 27 November 1703 before proceeding up the Thames. Caught there by the great storm, his flagship, *Triumph*, broke her anchor and had her rudder torn off. Dragging her bower anchor and driving toward the Galloper sand, the ship was saved by Shovell when he ordered the main mast to be cut down.

In early 1704, on reports that the Brest fleet had sailed to the Mediterranean, Shovell was ordered to take a large reinforcement of twenty-five ships to Rooke's assistance. Joining with Rooke on 16 June off Lagos Bay, he took part in the capture of Gibraltar, a place that he knew well from his earlier postings in the Mediterranean, and in the fleet battle off Vélez-Malaga on 13 August. In September he returned to England with Rooke's fleet. On 25 December he left office as controller of victualling accounts and on 26 December 1704 became rear-admiral of England and a member of the lord high admiral's council. On 13 January 1705 he succeeded Rooke as admiral of the fleet. Later in the year he was returned as member of parliament in the first seat for Rochester.

On 1 May 1705 the lord high admiral appointed Shovell and the earl of Peterborough joint admirals for an expedition to the Mediterranean to seize Toulon. The fleet of twenty-nine ships of the line sailed from St Helens on 23 May, and reached Lisbon on 11 June. The Toulon operation and other alternatives were set aside when, at the express desire of King Charles, the Austrian candidate for the Spanish throne, the fleet sailed to Barcelona. Peterborough landed with the troops without opposition on 12 August, accompanied by King Charles and the prince of Hesse-Darmstadt. After considerable debate between the Dutch, King Charles's court, Shovell, and Peterborough over the next step, they agreed to besiege Barcelona, which capitulated three weeks later, on 23 September. With no appropriate winter base in the Mediterranean, Shovell left Peterborough at Barcelona and returned to England.

In 1706 Shovell embarked troops to make a false attack on Normandy, but, when bad weather prevented that attack, he proceeded to Portugal with the troops. The original plan was to land the forces in Portugal for an overland attack on Madrid, but an English council of war objected to the Portuguese plan to divide English forces between two armies. Declining this, Shovell landed them in February 1707 at Alicante. Ordering Sir George Byng to support operations, he returned to Lisbon to refit. Two months later he went to Barcelona where Byng, with Vice-Admiral Phillips van der Goes and the Dutch squadron, rejoined him on 20 May. There, Shovell was instrumental in persuading Charles III to implement the long-planned assault on Toulon. In July, near Toulon, Duke Victor Amadeus II of Savoy and Prince Eugene of Savoy consulted with Shovell on board his flagship, *Association*. After Shovell agreed to keep ships available throughout the following winter, the commanders resolved to march the allied armies directly on Toulon. More than 100 cannon were landed from the fleet, and allied forces were in such force that the French sank many of their warships in Toulon harbour. The siege continued until 4 August, when French troops rallied. The allied generals decided they could not prevail. By 23 August the armies had dispersed and Shovell, deeply disappointed, sailed for Gibraltar.

Continuing on with twenty-one ships in the main fleet, he reached the Soundings on the morning of 21 October. On the following day, while trying to confirm its position, the fleet lay to in hazy weather from early in the afternoon until nightfall, and Shovell detached three vessels for Plymouth, apparently thinking the fleet was further to the eastward than it was. Shortly after six, still unable to confirm his position, Shovell ordered the fleet to continue up the channel in fleet formation. At about eight, in dark and rainy weather, lookouts in several ships suddenly saw rocks and the loom of the St Agnes light. Several warning guns were fired, but before the flagship could manoeuvre she struck the Outer Gilstone Rock in the Isles of Scilly and sank quickly. Most of the nineteen vessels in the fleet escaped a similar fate, but the 54-gun *Romney* was wrecked on the same rocks, while the 70-gun *Eagle* sank off the Tearing Ledge, just south-east of the Bishop and Clerks rocks. Of the 1315 men in these three ships, there was only one survivor, a quartermaster from the *Romney*. Shovell's body came ashore from the wreck on the south side of St Mary's Island at Porth Hellick Cove. The fact that he came ashore more than 6 miles from the wreck site, in close proximity to the bodies of his two stepsons—Sir John Narbrough and James Narbrough—a pet dog, and the flagship's captain, suggest that they had been able to leave the wreck together in a boat. Numerous legends and traditional stories surround these events. The most persistent is the alleged confession of a woman in the 1730s, who on her deathbed reported that she had found Shovell alive on the beach and, coveting the emerald ring on his finger, took his life. As her dying wish, the parish priest sent the ring to James, earl of Berkeley. In 1879 a similar ring was in the possession of the Berkeley family, but has not been traced since.

The *Salisbury* carried the body to Plymouth, where Dr James Younge embalmed it at the Naval Hospital, before it was taken by land to London. Shovell's death, with the loss of the *Association* and her consorts, was a great national disaster and accompanied by a great outpouring of grief. The embalmed body lay in state at the queen's expense at Shovell's home in Frith Street, Soho. Two months after the accident, on 22 December 1707, it was borne in an elaborate hearse to Westminster Abbey, where he was buried in the south choir aisle, near the east cloister door. John Molesworth summarized Shovell's reputation when he wrote to his mother, on hearing the news of his death: 'He is universally regretted for his courage, capacity, and honesty, which it will be hard to parallel in another commander' (*Various Collections*, 8.240).

Shovell left his London house, an estate at Crayford, Kent, and a considerable fortune. Survived by his mother, who died in 1709, and his wife, who lived until April 1732, Shovell also left two daughters. The elder, Elizabeth (1692–1750), married Sir Robert Marsham (1685–1724), created Baron Romney in 1716. After his death she married John Carmichael, third earl of Hyndford, the English minister at Berlin (1741–4), St Petersburg (1744–9), and at The Hague, where she died in 1750. Shovell's second daughter, Anne (1696–1741), married, first, the Hon. Robert Mansell (*d.* 1723), and, second, John Blackwood.

JOHN B. HATTENDORF

Sources PRO, ADM 6/3, 6/4, 6/5, 6/6, 6/8 · list of captains, 1688–1715, NMM, Sergison MS SER/136 · Pitcairn-Jones, 'Ship histories', NMM [card file] · *CSP dom.*, 1682; 1687–1704 · *Report on the manuscripts of the marquis of Downshire*, 6 vols. in 7, HMC, 75 (1924–95), vol. 1 · *Report on the manuscripts of Allan George Finch*, 5 vols., HMC, 71 (1913–2003), vols. 2–4 · P. McBride and R. Larn, *Admiral Shovell's treasure* (1999) · E. B. Powley, *The naval side of King William's war*

(1972) • P. Le Fevre, 'Sir Cloudesley Shovell's early career', *Mariner's Mirror*, 70 (1984), 92 • *The Tangier papers of Samuel Pepys*, ed. E. Chappell, Navy RS, 73 (1935) • J. R. Tanner, ed., *A descriptive catalogue of the naval manuscripts in the Pepysian Library at Magdalene College, Cambridge*, 4 vols., Navy RS, 26–7, 36, 57 (1903–23) • J. Ehrman, *The navy in the war of William III, 1689–1697* (1953) • *LondG* (21 July 1676) • BL, Egerton MS 2621 • *Memoirs of the secret services of John Macky*, ed. A. R. (1733) • *Report on manuscripts in various collections*, 8 vols., HMC, 55 (1901–14), vol. 8, p. 240 • R. D. Merriman, 'Gilbert Wardlow's allegations', *Mariner's Mirror*, 38 (1952), 106–31 • R. C. Anderson, 'An Anglo-Dutch incident in 1694', *Mariner's Mirror*, 14 (1928), 175–6 • F. E. Dyer, 'An Anglo-Dutch incident in 1694', *Mariner's Mirror*, 14 (1928), 278–81 • *The manuscripts of the House of Lords*, new ser., 12 vols. (1900–77), vols. 6–7, 9–10 • *The manuscripts of his grace the duke of Portland*, 10 vols., HMC, 29 (1891–1931), vol. 10 • *The manuscripts of the earl of Dartmouth*, 3 vols., HMC, 20 (1887–96), vol. 3 • F. J. C. Krämer, *Archives, ou, Correspondence inédite de la maison d'Orange Nassau*, 3rd ser., 1 (Leyde, 1907) • *The parliamentary diary of Sir Richard Cocks, 1698–1702*, ed. D. W. Hayton (1996) • *The London diaries of William Nicolson, bishop of Carlisle, 1702–1718*, ed. C. Jones and G. Holmes (1985) • J. B. Hattendorf and others, eds., *British naval documents, 1204–1960*, Navy RS, 131 (1993) • J. Burchett, *A complete history of the most remarkable transactions at sea* (1720) • E. B. Powley, *The English navy in the revolution of 1688* (1928) • F. E. Dyer, *The life of Sir John Narbrough* (1931) • *An exact and faithful account of the late bloody fight between Captain Hastings commander of the Saphire, Captain Shovel, commander of the James Galley and Jonas Raile, captain of the Half-Moon of Algier … September 22nd 1681* (1681) • *The new proceedings of the English affairs in Ireland … relating what past with the fleet under that valiant commander Sir Cloudesley Shovell before Dublin, and the great conduct of it against the Irish there* (1690) • *A true and impartial account of a great and bloody fight between part of the English fleet commanded by Sir Clovesly Shovel and the French at sea* (1690) • B. Burke, ed., *The general armory* (1878) • P. Le Fevre, 'The battle of Bantry Bay, 1 May 1689', *Irish Sword*, 18 (1990–91), 1–16 • *Piracy and diplomacy in seventeenth-century North Africa: the journal of Thomas Baker, English consul in Tripoli, 1677–1685*, ed. C. R. Pennell (1989) • S. R. Hornstein, *The Restoration navy and English foreign trade, 1674–1688: a study in the peacetime use of sea power* (1991) • R. Walcott, *English politics in the early eighteenth century* (1956) • J. D. Davies, *Gentlemen and tarpaulins: the officers and men of the Restoration navy* (1991) • will, PRO, PROB 11/499, fols. 166v–169v

Archives CKS, corresp. and papers, U1515/011–18 • E. Sussex RO, family papers • Hunt. L., corresp. and papers • LUL, papers • NMM, letter-book | BL, corresp. with Sir John Norris, Add. MSS 28141, 28153 • BL, corresp. with Lord Nottingham, Add. MS 29591 • CAC Cam., corresp. with Thomas Erle • Leics. RO, corresp. with Lord Nottingham

Likenesses oils, *c.*1692–1694, NMM • M. Dahl, oils, 1702, NMM; version, NPG • M. Dahl, oils, *c.*1702–1705, NMM [*see illus.*] • attrib. G. Gibbons, tomb effigy on monument, Westminster Abbey • J. Smith, mezzotint (after W. de Ryck), BM, NPG

Wealth at death £5000 to wife and £6000 each to two daughters; plate, jewels, and income from lands, including May Place, Crayford, Kent; townhouse, Frith Street, Soho, London; other lands in Norfolk and Kent: will, PRO, PROB 11/499, fols. 166v–169v

Shower, Sir Bartholomew (1658–1701), lawyer, was born on 14 December 1658 in Northgate Street, Exeter, Devon, the fourth of five children of William Shower, merchant, and his wife, Dorcas (*bap.* 1630), daughter of Exeter merchant John Anthony. Shower attended school in Exeter, and moved to London in 1675, where he initially resided at Newington Green. Shower was raised in a dissenting family. His uncle Mark Down (who baptized him on 26 December 1658) was one of the ministers ejected from his living as a result of the Act of Uniformity of 1662 and his brother John *Shower was a prominent Presbyterian preacher.

Shower was admitted to the Middle Temple on 9 September 1676, called to the bar on 21 May 1680, named king's counsel on 14 February 1688, and called to the bench on 25 May 1688. He was a reader at the Middle Temple for the autumn term 1691 and was elected its treasurer on 27 October 1699. Shower later said that he joined the Church of England when he was aged eighteen, but he seemed to retain some dissenting sympathies, advocating greater freedom for dissenting academies and defending the Toleration Act, though he did criticize occasional conformity. In 1699 he prepared a bill against prostitution and adultery, perhaps reflecting his brother John's passionate interest in the reformation of manners.

In some sketchy autobiographical notes published by Butt, Shower indicated that he married on 21 January 1682, but he did not name his wife, nor did he identify her in his will, which left a life estate to 'my dear and loving wife'. The will, written only months before his death, mentioned no children of his own, though it bequeathed some property to his nephew Bartholomew and to his niece Dorcas.

Shower first gained public notice with his tract *An Antidote Against Poison* (1683), which vehemently attacked Lord Russell's purported scaffold speech that protested his innocence. Shower was appointed deputy recorder of London on 14 April 1686 and in that capacity he achieved notoriety by sentencing four soldiers to death for desertion, despite the known doubts of the recorder, Holt, that desertion constituted a capital crime in peacetime. Shower was knighted on 14 May 1687 upon presenting James II with an address from the Middlesex grand jury that thanked him for the declaration of indulgence. Shower was appointed recorder of London on 6 February 1688, but was removed later that year following the restoration of London's charter. He was also one of the prosecutors of the seven bishops, though in a subordinate role.

As a supporter of James II, Shower fell out of political favour with the revolution of 1688, but he remained active in both law and politics. He published no fewer than three tracts in 1689, defending his earlier work against Lord Russell from attacks by Sir Robert Atkyns and others, though Shower now emphasized the integrity of the prosecution and called for a general amnesty. In 1692 he published *A Reason for a New Bill of Rights*, in which he advocated a more specific bill of rights, especially the enactment of the recently unsuccessful Trials for Treason Bill. Shower collaborated with high-church tories, providing the initial idea for Francis Atterbury's *Letter to a Convocation Man* (1697), and he published a bitter attack on Dean William Sherlock regarding the Bingham affair (1696).

Although he was born into a fairly prosperous mercantile family, Shower later remarked that he had been poor as a young lawyer. Be that as it may, his law practice flourished, enabling him to buy a house in Chelsea in 1691 and subsequently to purchase estates in Middlesex at Pinner, Ruislip, and Northolt. Shower represented a number of prominent Jacobite and tory clients throughout the 1690s, such as the Scottish Lord Preston in 1691; several of the conspirators in the assassination plot against William III, among them Sir John Fenwick in 1696; and Charles Duncombe and the old East India Company, both in 1698. He also represented Sir Edward Seymour in his suit against Captain Kirke, and Bishop Watson against efforts to deprive him of the bishopric of St David's.

On 29 August 1698 Shower was sworn in as a freeman of Exeter and as one of its counsels. Later that year he and Seymour were chosen as that city's members for parliament by a larger than expected majority. He was re-elected in 1700 and again in 1701. Shower quickly became one of the leading tory spokesmen in the Commons, supporting the Disbanding Bill (1698), attacking the whig ministry over the grant to Captain Kidd (1699), and speaking at length against the Kentish petition (1701). He also served as one of the Commons' managers of the impeachment against the Junto Lords. On 17 June 1701 he was elected as one of the seven commissioners of accounts, and he was at least mentioned as a candidate for both attorney-general and speaker. His early death cut short a promising political career.

Eleven works of Shower's, on law and politics, were published, some posthumously. He was the first to publish (in 1698) the judicial decisions of the House of Lords, but the printing ceased when the Lords voted the publication a breach of privilege. Two volumes of Shower's law reports were posthumously published from his manuscript notes. These reports have been much criticized, but both Wallace and Holdsworth note that Shower had not prepared them for publication. George Butt brought out a third edition of Shower's *Reports* (1834), correcting numerous transcription errors in the two earlier editions and adding the reports for the Michaelmas term of 1688, but curiously it was the second edition of 1794 that was reprinted in *The English Reports* (vol. 89, 1908) and hence is usually cited. Shower became suddenly ill at Temple Church on Sunday 30 November 1701, and he died four days later, on 4 December, from pleurisy at his home in Temple Lane. He was buried on 12 December 1701 at Pinner, where there is a monument to him in the chapel.

An avid and active partisan, Shower was a controversial figure in his day. The country whig Sir Richard Cocks called him 'the littlest maliciousest man living' (*Diary of Sir Richard Cocks*, 73), but the tory newspaper *Post Boy*, in an unusually long and fulsome obituary, lauded his generosity, 'great veracity', and 'sprightly way of pleading' (*Post Boy*, nos. 1023, 1025). Such differing opinions continued into the nineteenth century: to Macaulay, Shower was a 'base and hard-hearted pettifogger' (Macaulay, 5.360), while Butt claimed Shower was 'the most accomplished lawyer of his time', save Holt (Shower, xi). The more distant twentieth century has tended to regard Shower more dispassionately as an inveterate tory and a skilful lawyer.

ROBERT J. FRANKLE

Sources B. Shower, *Reports of cases adjudged in the court of king's bench in the reigns of Charles II, James II, and William III*, ed. G. Butt, 3rd edn (1834) · *The parliamentary diary of Sir Richard Cocks, 1698–1702*, ed. D. W. Hayton (1996) · N. Luttrell, *A brief historical relation of state affairs from September 1678 to April 1714*, 6 vols. (1857) · D. Lysons, *The environs of London*, 2nd edn, 2 (1811) · J. W. Wallace, *The reporters*, 4th edn (1882) · *State trials*, vols. 9, 12–14 · J. B. Williamson, ed., *The Middle Temple bench book*, 2nd edn, 1 (1937) · Holdsworth, *Eng. law*, vol. 6 · *DNB* · T. B. Macaulay, *The history of England from the accession of James II*, new edn, 5 vols. (1885), vol. 5 · *IGI* · parish register, Exeter, St Petrock's

Archives BL, law reports and autobiographical notes, Lansdowne MS 1105

Likenesses J. Nutting, line engraving, BM, NPG; repro. in *The reports of Sir Bartholomew Shower*, 2 vols. (1708)

Wealth at death estates at Pinner, Ruislip, Northolt, all in Middlesex: will, 2 Sept 1701

Shower, John (*bap.* 1657, *d.* 1715), Presbyterian minister, was born in the parish of St Kerrian, Exeter, and was baptized there on 18 May 1657, the second son of William Shower (*d.* 1661), a wealthy Exeter merchant, and his wife, Dorcas Anthony (*bap.* 1630), daughter of John Anthony. Sir Bartholomew *Shower (1658–1701), recorder of London, was a younger brother. Shower's father died in 1661 but left his wife and children well provided for. Shower was encouraged in his studies by his mother and by his uncle Richard Down, who, following his ejection from the rectory of Winterborne Monkton, Dorset, became pastor to a congregationalist meeting at Bridport. He attended the school run at Exeter by Mr Bradford before entering, in 1671, the academy of Matthew Warren at Otterford, Somerset, with a view to entering the ministry. It was probably here that he acquired his belief in the free and critical study of the scriptures. Shower went on to study at Charles Morton's academy at Newington Green, Middlesex (where his fellow pupils were Daniel Defoe and Timothy Cruso), and completed his course of ministerial training at Edward Veal's academy in Wapping.

At the age of twenty, in 1677, Shower delivered his maiden sermon at Thomas Vincent's meeting-house in Hand Alley, Bishopsgate, London. His reputation as a preacher grew, and in the following year he became one of a group of evening preachers (who also included Theophilus Dorrington) at a merchant's lecture set up in the large room of a coffee house in Exchange Alley. He was ordained on 24 December 1679 by five ejected ministers, headed by Richard Adams. He at once became (while still retaining his lectureship) assistant to Vincent Alsop in Tothill Street, Westminster. In 1681 Shower published his first work, by far his most enduring and popular, *An Exhortation to Youth to Prepare for Judgement* (1681). This had reached its sixth edition by the time of his death thirty-four years later; the twentieth and last edition was published in 1826.

In 1683 Shower relinquished his posts when the whig politician Sir Samuel Barnardiston sent him abroad with two other young ministers as companions to his nephew Samuel Barnardiston. They made the grand tour, visiting France, Switzerland, Italy, and the Rhine. At Amsterdam in July 1684 they parted. Shower remained in the Netherlands until 1686. Having returned to England, he resumed his lecture at Exchange Alley, but the extreme pressure to which nonconformists were then subjected led him to return to the Netherlands in late 1686 or early 1687. He joined his fellow London Presbyterian minister John

Howe at Utrecht. There he met and married, on 24 September 1687, Elizabeth Falkener (d. 1691), niece of the merchant and whig politician Thomas Papillon, and a fellow exile. They had three children but only the eldest, Ann, survived beyond infancy. At the end of 1687 Shower and his wife moved to Rotterdam, where for three years he served as evening lecturer in the Presbyterian Church of England, of which Joseph Hill was a pastor.

Shower returned to London upon receiving a call (19 January 1691) to succeed Daniel Williams as John Howe's assistant at Silver Street. Shower remained there for only a few months; on 8 May 1691 he accepted the call to replace Samuel Borfett as minister of the Presbyterian meeting at Curriers' Hall, Cripplegate. He retained this charge until his death, having been 'married' to his flock by Matthew Mead, as Edmund Calamy put it (DNB). His wife died later the same year, on 24 August. His funeral oration for her was published the following year under the title The Mourning for the Dead. On 29 December 1692 he married Constance White (d. 1701), daughter of an eminent London merchant. They had several children, but only three, Martha, Bartholomew, and John, survived their father.

The congregation at Curriers' Hall grew in numbers and in 1692 was obliged to move to more commodious accommodation in Jewin Street, where, his funeral sermon recorded, he 'continued his work in a very zealous, lively manner, with great diligence and remarkable success' (Tong, 63). When this also proved too small for the growing congregation a new meeting-house was erected in the Old Jewry in 1701, the required funds being raised by the merchants and shopkeepers who made up the congregation. Here Shower had one of the 'most considerable assemblies about the city' (ibid., 68), and Timothy Rogers and Joseph Bennet were successively appointed as his assistants.

Shower was elected a manager of the Common Fund in 1692, and was retained when, following the breakdown of relations with the Independents, it was reconstituted as the Presbyterian Fund in 1695. He was a member of a club of ministers in which Edmund Calamy was the leading spirit; for some years from 1692 it held weekly meetings at the house of Dr Upton in Warwick Lane. In 1697 Shower succeeded Samuel Annesley as one of the Tuesday lecturers at Salters' Hall.

Shower was a prolific writer of religious works, and the author of over twenty publications. Most of these were funeral sermons (he had the reputation of an emotional preacher), such as those for Mrs Mary Doolittle (1693), Nathaniel Oldfield (1697), Jane Papillon (1698), and Nehemiah Grew (1712). In 1693 he published a historical and providentialist account of earthquakes, Practical Reflections on the Late Earthquakes, stimulated by the destruction of Port Royal, Jamaica, the previous year. Among his other works were Some Account of the Holy Life and Death of Mr Henry Gearing (1694), Winter Meditations (1695), and Serious Reflections on Time and Eternity (1696).

Shortly after his move to Old Jewry, Shower's wife died in childbed on 18 July 1701, and on 7 December 1707 Ann, the daughter of his first marriage, suffered the same fate. Shower himself almost died in 1706, when 'seized by a very malignant fever' (Pike, 110). He never fully recovered and became increasingly frail, though John Fox, who visited him in 1712, was impressed by his 'state and pride' (DNB). On 14 September 1713 he suffered a stroke, and though he was able to preach again, he delivered his last sermon at Old Jewry on 27 March 1715. Less than three months later, on 12 June, he was 'seized with a nervous asthma' (Tong, 74). He died at his home in Stoke Newington, Middlesex, on 28 June, and was buried at Highgate on 7 July. His funeral sermon was preached by William Tong at the Old Jewry on 10 July 1715.   M. J. MERCER

Sources W. Tong, Some memoirs of the life and death of the Reverend Mr John Shower (1716) · W. Wilson, The history and antiquities of the dissenting churches and meeting houses in London, Westminster and Southwark, 4 vols. (1808–14), vol. 2, pp. 308–20 · Protestant Dissenter's Magazine, 4 (1797), 41–7 · Protestant Dissenter's Magazine, 6 (1799), 212–17; 254–8 · G. H. Pike, Ancient meeting houses of nonconformity in old London (1870), 102–16 · A. Gordon, ed., Freedom after ejection: a review (1690–1692) of presbyterian and congregational nonconformity in England and Wales (1917), 252 · H. McLachlan, Education under the test acts (1931), 70, 72, 76, 80 · E. Middleton, Evangelical biography, new edn, 4 vols. (1816) · Surman, index of nonconformist ministers, DWL · DNB

Archives BL, letter to J. Boyce, MS 4276, fol. 139 · BL, letter to J. Spademan, MS 4276, fol. 142 · BL, letter to R. Stretton, MS 4276, fol. 141

Likenesses M. Vandergucht, line engraving, BM, NPG; repro. in J. Shower, Practical reflections on the late earthquakes (1693) · R. White, line engraving, BM, NPG; repro. in Tong, Some memoirs · engraving, repro. in Wilson, History, vol. 2 · oils, DWL

Showering, Francis Edwin (1912–1995), drinks manufacturer, was born on 10 July 1912 at The Ship inn, Kilver Street, Shepton Mallet, Somerset, one of the four sons of Albert Edward Showering, an innkeeper and brewer, and his wife, Ethel May née Dyke. He was educated at Shepton Mallet grammar school and then spent two years in Bristol training as a chemist before (like his three brothers, Arthur, Herbert, and Ralph) he joined the family brewing business, Showerings Ltd, which had been brewing beer and making cider in Shepton Mallet since the early nineteenth century. On 25 August 1934 he married Hilda Florence Foote (1911/12–1980), the daughter of James Henry Foote, a cheese factor, of Shepton Mallet. There were no children of the marriage.

Showerings Ltd was a small local business which found it increasingly difficult to compete with the large national manufacturers. After the Second World War, Showering, by then managing director, turned his attention to perry, made from pear juice, which, unlike cider, had never been made on a large scale because of problems with the control of fermentation and the prevention of deposits and cloudiness. He began to research new methods of fermentation, and in 1946 developed a low-alcohol sparkling drink made from pear juice, which was given the name Babycham. This sparkling perry, attractively packaged in small bottles with gold foil round the top, was launched in

Francis Edwin
Showering (1912–
1995), by unknown
photographer

became Allied-Lyons in 1979) from 1975 until his sudden death in 1982, when Showering became vice-chairman. Showering was appointed CBE in 1982. A keen sailor and a first-class shot, he was a generous local benefactor and financed the modern development of the centre of Shepton Mallet. His first wife having died in 1980, he married, on 7 October 1981, his former secretary, Rita Matthewman (*b.* 1928/9), the daughter of Ernest Matthewman, an army officer.

After an unsuccessful attempt to buy back Showerings in 1991, when Allied-Lyons decided to sell it, Showering, together with the four sons of Sir Keith Showering, formed a new drinks company, Brothers Drinks, and invented a new drink, Straight 8. He remained chairman of Brothers Drinks until his death on 5 September 1995, of a heart attack, at his home, Silton Lodge, Silton, Gillingham, Dorset. He was buried on 13 September at the parish church in Shepton Mallet. He was survived by his second wife.   ANNE PIMLOTT BAKER

Sources L. C. Luckwill and A. Pollard, eds., *Perry pears* (1963), 11–12 · *The Times* (8 Sept 1995) · *The Independent* (9 Sept 1995) · b. cert. · m. certs. · d. cert.
Likenesses photograph, News International Syndication, London [*see illus.*] · photograph, repro. in *The Independent*
Wealth at death £2,139,362: probate, 12 Dec 1995, *CGPLA Eng. & Wales*

Showering, Sir Keith Stanley (1930–1982), food and drink company executive, was born on 6 August 1930 at The Cloisters, Draycott, Shepton Mallet, Somerset, the only son and the eldest of five children of Herbert Marquis Valentine Showering (1906–1974), brewer, and his wife, Ada Agnes, *née* Foote. He was educated at Wells Cathedral school, followed by a year at the laboratories of Long Ashton research station, a department of Bristol University, where he studied the chemistry of cider making. He joined the family business of Showerings Ltd, cider makers, in 1947. He began work as a salesman but then worked in all other departments, being particularly interested in financial matters. He became a director of the firm in 1951. On 30 June 1954 he married Marie Sadie (*b.* 1935/6), daughter of Charles Wesley Golden, a company director; they had four sons and two daughters. For his fiftieth birthday his wife commissioned a head to be sculpted by Dame Elisabeth Frink.

When Showering joined the family firm it was undergoing a period of rapid and unparalleled expansion due to the invention of Babycham, a perry which, through strong marketing and advertising, came to appeal to younger women. As sales grew, and Babycham came to be stocked in almost all public houses, the family, led by Showering's father and three uncles—one of whom, Francis, had invented Babycham—looked for diversification. Showering was involved in negotiations which led to the acquisition of Britvic, Vine Products, and Whiteways; he was founder director upon the merger of these companies, becoming deputy chairman in 1964. He was chief executive from 1971 to 1975. In 1965 the family sought to break into the imported wine market. They were initially unsuccessful, but by the end of the year Harveys had been

the west country in the early 1950s and began to be distributed nationally in 1953, accompanied by skilful advertising. Babycham was targeted mainly at young women, as a drink they could order in pubs, served in a saucer-shaped champagne glass; it was marketed as 'the genuine champagne perry sparkling in its own glamorous glass', with the slogan 'I'd love a Babycham' and the brand symbol of a small blue and yellow Chinese water deer. In 1955 it was the first alcoholic drink to be advertised on television. An instant success, Babycham was in short supply to begin with, as production could not keep up with demand. Many of the old perry pear orchards of the west midlands had been neglected or grubbed up, so Showerings bought farms in Somerset, not traditional perry-growing country, and planted new pear orchards on them to supply the Shepton Mallet factory. By 1966 this was producing 108,000 bottles an hour. Factories were built in Ireland and Belgium, as Showerings managed to keep imitators at bay in a series of court cases and resisted the objections of the French champagne houses to the description of Babycham as 'champagne perry'.

Following the success of Babycham, Showerings became a public company in 1959 and went on to acquire other drinks manufacturing firms, including William Gaymer, Vine Products, Whiteways, Britvic fruit juices, and, in 1966, Harveys of Bristol. In 1968 Showerings was sold to Allied Breweries for £108 million, and Showering became a director of the merged company. Showering's nephew Sir Keith Stanley *Showering (1930–1982) was chairman and chief executive of Allied Breweries (which acquired. It held a unique position in the sherry market and also sold port and fine table wines, including Latour. Showering was managing director of the Harveys companies from 1966 to 1971 and chairman in 1971.

In 1968 the family successfully negotiated for Showerings to be merged into Allied Breweries, of which Showering became vice-chairman in 1969 and deputy chairman and chief executive in 1975. Allied soon moved into the Scottish whisky business, acquiring Teachers in 1976, then, on Showering's initiative, into food and catering by acquiring the old-established business of Lyons in 1979. This was a major step away from reliance on alcoholic beverages, taking the company into a new, but closely related, field. Lyons had recently been experiencing a difficult period but as part of Allied-Lyons, as the new group came to be called, it was soon restored to profitability. A small family brewing business had now emerged into the greatest combined force in the United Kingdom in the manufacture and sale of food and drinks. At the time of Showering's death in 1982 Allied-Lyons Ltd was the tenth-largest British company and the most broadly based food and drinks group in Europe. Showering himself spent much time building up the group's interests in Australia and the United States. In 1981 he was knighted for his services to industry. He was master of the Brewers' Company in 1981–2.

Apart from Allied-Lyons, Showering's other business interests included becoming vice-chairman of the Guardian Royal Exchange Assurance Company in 1974 and a director of Midland Bank in 1979. He was also a director from 1976 of Castlemaine Tooheys Ltd of Sydney, Australia, and of the gun making firm of Holland and Holland from 1978.

As a young man Showering had been a good athlete, particularly interested in rugby and boxing. Outside business his greatest interest was in farming, particularly cattle breeding. He had pioneered the importation of Charollais, Simmental, and Canadian Holstein breeds, which changed the face of British dairy- and beef farming. He was also the first British financer and importer of the ovary transplant fertilization technique. Always a first-class shot, a collector of firearms, and a keen fisherman, he also had a true countryman's concern for wildlife conservation. He was a trustee of the World Wildlife fund (UK). He also had a passionate interest in the arts, being a trustee of both the Glyndebourne arts trust and the London Philharmonic Orchestra. In 1982 he was appointed high sheriff of Somerset. Showering was taken ill on 23 March 1982 at the Bank of England in London while attending a meeting of industrial leaders, presided over by the governor. He died the same day, in St Bartholomew's Hospital, London. ROBERT SHARP

Sources personal knowledge (1990) [*DNB*] · private information (1990) · *WWW* · *The Times* (25 March 1982), 14g, 18g · *The Times* (24 April 1982), 14e [memorial service] · *The Times* (6 Oct 1982), 14c [will] · b. cert. · m. cert. · d. cert. · *CGPLA Eng. & Wales* (1982) · *The Times* (8 July 1974), 16g

Likenesses photograph, repro. in *The Times* (1974–82)

Wealth at death £3,618,126: probate, 24 Sept 1982, *CGPLA Eng. & Wales*

Shrapnel, Henry (1761–1842), army officer and inventor of the Shrapnel shell, was born on 3 June 1761, the youngest son of the nine children of Zachariah Shrapnel (1724–1796) from Midnay Manor House, Bradford-on-Avon, Wiltshire, and his wife, Lydia (*née* Needham). The family name appears as Shrapnell in a number of contemporary sources, including Wellington's dispatches and editions of the *Army List*. Shrapnel was commissioned into the Royal Artillery on 9 July 1779; he served in Newfoundland from 1780 to 1784, and advanced to first lieutenant on 3 December 1781. After returning to England in 1785 he began to develop, at his own expense, an explosive shell capable of being fired from existing artillery pieces; the device was in the form of a hollow spherical case, filled with small, round shot and a charge of powder, which was ignited by a fuse of variable length inserted in the base of the shell. The released shot, he hoped, would lethally spray the enemy. Before his experiments had been completed he served in Gibraltar (1787–91), where he was encouraged to find that mortar shells had been fired from 24-pounder guns over Spanish positions in the recent siege with similar intent and some success. Then, for two years, Shrapnel served in the West Indies, successively at Barbados, St Vincent, Grenada, Dominica, Antigua, and St Kitts.

Shrapnel was promoted captain lieutenant on 15 August 1793, and eleven days later he left England with the third Royal Artillery detachment to join the duke of York's expeditionary force in Flanders; he was wounded at the unsuccessful siege of Dunkirk in September. During the British withdrawal from there Shrapnel recommended that the wheels of gun-carriages be locked, so that they skidded over the sand, and that decoy fires be lit at night away from the army's true bivouac position to attract harmless enemy fire. He remained with the British force as it fell back towards Bremen, reaching Woolwich again on 8 May 1795. Shrapnel was promoted captain on 3 October 1795, brevet major on 29 April 1802, regimental major on 1 November 1803, and regimental lieutenant-colonel on 20 July 1804. Meanwhile he had resumed work on his invention, still at his own expense and in his own time. In 1799 he submitted a proposal to the Board of Ordnance that it be adopted for use in the army; this was eventually approved in 1803. Shrapnel became the first assistant inspector of artillery at Woolwich on 10 February 1804, with wide responsibility for ordnance research and development in addition to shells. Thus, in January 1807, he recommended to Lieutenant-General Sir Arthur Wellesley (later Viscount Wellington) new, large-calibre siege-guns from the Carron works in Scotland.

Shrapnel's shell received favourable reports after its use during the capture of Surinam in April–May 1804; and in the light of operational experience further technical improvements were made to enhance its performance. In 1808 Wellesley wrote approvingly of its worth during his first campaign in Portugal; though he argued that for security reasons its novel nature should not be publicly

Henry Shrapnel (1761–1842), attrib. Thomas Arrowsmith, 1817

October 1814, Major A. Macdonald and Lieutenant J. Sinclair described how devastating the shells had proved against exposed French field batteries at Salamanca. Three days after the victory at Waterloo, Colonel George Wood, the artillery commander, underlined his approval of the shell to its inventor. Nor was the Royal Navy unimpressed. In 1813 Vice-Admiral Sidney Smith, following correspondence with Shrapnel, privately ordered 200 shells directly from the Carron works to compensate for a shortfall in official supplies.

Shrapnel married on 5 May 1810 Esther Squires (1780–1852) at St Mary's Church, Lambeth, in the bride's parish; they had two sons and two daughters. Shrapnel was promoted brevet colonel on 4 June 1813, and regimental colonel on 20 December 1814. He complained to the Board of Ordnance on 10 September 1813 that he had spent several thousand pounds of his own money over twenty-eight years to develop his shell, but the board replied that it had 'no funds at their [sic] disposal for the reward of merit'. In 1814, however, a pension of £1200 p.a. for life was granted by the government, in addition to his service pay and allowances. In fact the award was deemed to apply to all his inventive work, not just the spherical case-shot. Furthermore a narrow, bureaucratic interpretation of the terms of the award ensured that, in reality, he enjoyed scant financial gain.

Shrapnel advanced to major-general on 12 August 1819, and retired from active service on 29 July 1825. Nevertheless he did not stop experimenting, and in 1834 patented a percussion lock for small arms. Indeed, in addition to this and his shell, Shrapnel compiled invaluable artillery range tables, invented the brass tangent slide, and improved the efficiency of mortars and howitzers by the introduction of parabolic chambers. He is credited with devising a duplex disappearing mounting for two pieces of ordnance, so that the recoil of one gun lowered it under cover as the second was raised into a firing position. Important advances in small arms, ammunition, and fuses were also ascribed to him during his time at Woolwich. He was appointed a colonel-commandant of the Royal Artillery on 6 March 1827, and became lieutenant-general on 10 January 1837. Shortly afterwards, at Brighton, he was a guest of William IV, who extolled the virtues of his achievements. On 23 April his private secretary wrote to Shrapnel, intimating that the king intended to bestow a baronetcy on him. William IV died in June, and nothing more was heard on the subject.

On 13 March 1842 Shrapnel died at his residence, Peartree House, Southampton; he was buried in the family vault at Bradford-on-Avon church, Wiltshire. Several military figures, including Major-General William Nott and Lieutenant-General Sir Hugh Gough, expressed their high regard for Shrapnel to his eldest son, Henry Needham Scrope (1812–1896), who later submitted unsuccessful claims to the government and to parliament for further recompense for his father's inventions, given that the special pension had terminated with his death. The generic term 'shrapnel', widely used to describe fragments of metal from explosives, has perpetuated Henry Shrapnel's

revealed. This, he acknowledged, would deprive Shrapnel of overt recognition, but the 'ingenuity and the science which he has proved he possesses by the great perfection to which he has brought this invention' (*DNB*) should in itself be sufficient reward. Wellesley confirmed to Shrapnel that his shell had been most effective in the battle of Vimeiro (21 August 1808); and, in another personal letter, Lieutenant-Colonel William Robe, commanding the Royal Artillery in the Peninsula, emphasized that its 'dreadful' impact had been noted 'by the French and all our own general officers, in a way highly flattering to us' (*DNB*). Captain H. B. Lane described to Shrapnel the 'immense slaughter the enemy sustained' (Duncan, 2.277) from his shells at Busaco on 27 September 1810, an outcome confirmed separately by Major J. May. However, after his initial enthusiasm Wellington told the earl of Liverpool on 12 March 1812 that his opinion in favour of the shells had lately been much shaken. He believed that difficulty in judging distance meant that fuse lengths were incorrectly set and seldom readjusted. Furthermore the wounds inflicted were 'of a trifling description; and they kill nobody'; he likened their effect to that of 'duck shot', which accidentally hit 'the face of a person' and could be easily plucked out (*Dispatches*, 8.659). Three weeks later, on 3 April 1812, Wellington revoked his extreme criticism, acknowledging that 'the spherical case shot called Shrapnell's [sic] shells' had been 'very destructive of the enemy' at the siege of Badajoz. Nevertheless he had directed that some shells in future be loaded with 'musket balls' to counteract the fact that the wounds currently inflicted 'do not disable' (*Dispatches*, 9.28). In further letters to Shrapnel from the Peninsula on 9 May 1813 and 22 name and until the end of the First World War shells were still being manufactured according to his original principles. JOHN SWEETMAN

Sources Army List · F. Duncan, ed., History of the royal regiment of artillery, 2 vols. (1872–3) · The dispatches of … the duke of Wellington … from 1799 to 1818, ed. J. Gurwood, 8–9 (1837) · J. Kane, List of officers of the royal regiment of artillery from the year 1716 to the year 1899, rev. W. H. Askwith, 4th edn (1900) · DNB · W. Reid, The lore of arms (1976) · G. A. Shepperd, Arms and armour, 1660–1918 (1971) · E. Longford [E. H. Pakenham, countess of Longford], Wellington, 1: The years of the sword (1969)
Archives Royal Artillery Institution, Woolwich, London, papers | Wilts. & Swindon RO, letters to Revd Thomas Spencer, etc.
Likenesses attrib. T. Arrowsmith, oils, 1817, Royal Artillery Institution, Woolwich, London [see illus.]

Shrewsbury. For this title name see Montgomery, Roger de, first earl of Shrewsbury (d. 1094); Montgomery, Hugh de, second earl of Shrewsbury (d. 1098); Bellême, Robert de, earl of Shrewsbury and count of Ponthieu (bap. c.1057, d. in or after 1130); Talbot, John, first earl of Shrewsbury and first earl of Waterford (c.1387–1453); Talbot, Margaret, countess of Shrewsbury (1404–1467) [see under Talbot, John, first earl of Shrewsbury and first earl of Waterford (c.1387–1453)]; Talbot, John, second earl of Shrewsbury and second earl of Waterford (c.1413–1460); Talbot, George, fourth earl of Shrewsbury and fourth earl of Waterford (1468–1538); Talbot, Francis, fifth earl of Shrewsbury (1500–1560); Talbot, George, sixth earl of Shrewsbury (c.1522–1590); Talbot, Elizabeth, countess of Shrewsbury (1527?–1608); Talbot, Gilbert, seventh earl of Shrewsbury (1552–1616); Talbot, Charles, duke of Shrewsbury (1660–1718); Talbot, John, sixteenth earl of Shrewsbury and sixteenth earl of Waterford (1791–1852).

Shrewsbury, Arthur (1856–1903), cricketer, was the fourth son of seven children of William Shrewsbury and Elizabeth Ann Wragg. He was born in Kyle Street, New Lenton, Nottinghamshire, on 11 April 1856. His father, a designer, draughtsman, and lace manufacturer, was also proprietor of the Queen's Hotel, Nottingham. His elder brother William (1854–1931), who succeeded their father as proprietor of the Queen's Hotel in 1885, had made nine appearances for Nottinghamshire (1875–9) before he emigrated to Canada in 1891. He returned to be a first-class umpire (1896–1904). After being educated at the People's College, Nottingham, Shrewsbury himself became a draughtsman. He showed promise in local cricket, and also in football, and he quickly became a professional cricketer, modelling his style on that of Richard Daft. He first appeared at Lord's for the Colts of England against the MCC in May 1873. Ill health, which dogged him throughout his life, prevented him from playing in 1874, but the following year he began a long association (1875–1902) with Nottinghamshire and in June 1876 he scored his first century (118 against Yorkshire) in first-class cricket.

In 1880 Shrewsbury established an athletic outfitter's business in Queen Street, Nottingham, with Alfred Shaw, and so began a business relationship which led the two men to organize four tours of Australia (1881–2, 1884–5, 1886–7, 1887–8). Shrewsbury and Shaw, together with James Lillywhite, made a profit on the first three ventures but lost £2400 on the final one. This was immediately followed by a rugby football tour to New Zealand, in which Shrewsbury and Shaw lost a further £800. As a player, however, Shrewsbury was consistently successful on all four cricket tours, finishing the last with two double centuries and an average of 58.92.

Shrewsbury's financial losses were to some extent compensated for by benefits from Nottinghamshire in 1893 and 1900, the former—for £600—being at the time the second highest to have been awarded to a Nottinghamshire player. More importantly, his business acumen made him an example of a new type of professional cricketer, as too did the awareness he showed of his rights: with Shaw he participated in 1881 in an unsuccessful strike against the Nottinghamshire authorities for better conditions. Despite a few brief years of prosperity, even cricketers of Shrewsbury's calibre often died in straitened circumstances.

Shrewsbury was successful for the remainder of his career, and headed the English batting averages on six occasions including 1902, his last season. He believed that his 164 for England against Australia at Lord's in July 1886 was his own best innings and contemporaries thought no one—not even W. G. Grace—could have batted better. In 1887 he played eight three-figure innings (including 267 against Middlesex), scored 1653 runs, and had the highest average (78.71) ever recorded in first-class cricket up to that point. In May 1890, with William Gunn, he created another record by putting on 398 for the second wicket for Nottinghamshire against Sussex. In his last season (1902) he scored two separate centuries (101 and 127 not out) in the match against Gloucestershire at Trent Bridge. During his career he scored fifty-nine centuries in first-class cricket, made 26,505 runs, and appeared in twenty-three test matches.

The main features of Shrewsbury's batting were his strong back-foot play and his perfect timing. His strong defence, caution, and unwearying patience also made him one of the greatest players ever on treacherous wickets. His fielding was outstanding, especially close to the wicket.

Towards the end of his life, W. G. Grace was asked who had been the greatest batsman of his day. After agreeing he himself should be considered hors concours, he replied 'Give me Arthur' (H. S. Altham, History of Cricket, 1926, 182). Although he was of a modest and retiring nature, Shrewsbury was a shrewd judge of his own qualities. If not out at lunch, he would instruct the Trent Bridge dressing-room attendant to bring him out a cup of tea at 4.30. When coaching the Warwickshire players in 1892 he put a half-sovereign on the stumps for anyone who could bowl him out. No one did so in a month.

An awareness that he might be no longer able to support himself financially may have contributed to Shrewsbury's death. Believing he had an incurable complaint, he became mentally disordered and shot himself at his sister's residence, The Limes, Gedling, Nottinghamshire, on 19 May 1903. He was buried in the churchyard of Gedling parish church.

W. B. Owen, *rev.* Gerald M. D. Howat

Sources *The Times* (20 May 1903) • *Cricket* (21 May 1903) • *Cricket* (28 July 1892) • *Cricket* (29 Dec 1892) • *Baily's Magazine*, 61 (1894), 413–14 • *Wisden* (1890) • *Wisden* (1904) • R. Daft, *Kings of cricket* (1893) • W. Caffyn, *Seventy one not out* (1889) • E. F. Benson and E. H. Miles, *The cricket of Abel, Hirst and Shrewsbury* (1903) • R. Sissons, *A social history of the professional cricketer* (1988) • P. Bailey, P. Thorn, and P. Wynne-Thomas, *Who's who of cricketers*, rev. edn (1993)
Likenesses sketch, *c*.1885, repro. in Daft, *Kings of cricket* • Hawkins of Brighton, photograph, 1888, repro. in *Wisden* (1890) • Hawkins of Brighton, photograph, 1888, Marylebone Cricket Club, Lord's, London • R. H. Thomas, photograph, *c*.1890, repro. in *Cricket* (3 Aug 1899)
Wealth at death £7149 8*s.* 9*d.*: probate, 14 July 1903, *CGPLA Eng. & Wales*

Shrewsbury [Bolde], **Ralph** (*c*.1286–1363), bishop of Bath and Wells, was of obscure origins, but he may have been connected with the Bold family of the parish of Aston Botterell, Shropshire. Through much of his life he had strong ties with Shrewsbury Abbey, where he probably gained his early education, and his toponym was perhaps as much derived from the abbey as the town. His first certain connection with the abbey was his appointment to the rectory of Edgmond, Shropshire, in its patronage in July 1305. The income from this, his first benefice, helped him to study at Oxford University and by 1308 he had graduated MA. For the next twenty years his life was devoted to study. He gained the unusual distinction of two doctorates, the first by 1317 in canon law, and the second, by 1329, in theology. His standing at Oxford led to his appointment as chancellor of the university in the course of 1328, a post he retained until November 1329.

While he was at Oxford, Shrewsbury's career progressed slowly by the standards of successful clerics of his day and, unlike them, he is not known to have undertaken royal or ecclesiastical service. Edgmond remained his only benefice until 1317, when he became a canon of Wells. Shrewsbury Abbey continued to be his patron thereafter, presenting him to the rectories of Walton-on-Trent, Derbyshire, in 1319 and Hodnet, Shropshire, in 1328. On the death of Bishop Droxford of Wells, Shrewsbury was elected his successor by the chapter of Wells on 2 June 1329. Although the royal assent quickly followed, on 28 June, and although by 3 September he had been consecrated, it soon became clear this would be a contested appointment. An alternative candidate emerged, in the form of Robert Wyville, Queen Isabella's secretary. On 12 June and 2 August royal letters were sent to Pope John XXII unsuccessfully pressing Wyville's claim, probably at the queen's instigation. For nearly a year Shrewsbury's position was insecure, until his rival was papally provided to the see of Salisbury. After a long series of letters by Shrewsbury to the pope and leading cardinals, an appeal for support to Roger Mortimer, a testimonial from the chancellor of Oxford University, and the payment of a substantial sum of money, Pope John confirmed his appointment on 30 May 1330, six weeks after Wyville's provision.

Shrewsbury's lasting importance rests on his pastoral activities during the thirty-four years he was a diocesan bishop. Historians have regarded him as an exemplary medieval bishop and in his lifetime he gained a reputation for sanctity. His register, which survives for the bulk of his episcopate, shows him to have been a conscientious pastor. From July 1331 he spent most of his time in his diocese, rarely leaving for more than a few weeks each year and scarcely at all during the last decade of his life. He regularly travelled round it, diligently carrying out his episcopal functions, until illness and advancing age confined him to a favourite manor. He sought to improve the standards of the clergy, beginning with regular visitations of the diocese in the 1330s which seem to have continued for the rest of his episcopate. To the same end he encouraged clerical education by frequently granting dispensations for absence to study. The same mixture of discipline and encouragement was applied to the major religious houses of the diocese. In 1337 he secured the right to disafforest the manor of Cheddar, ending the use of forest law there and earning popular approval in the diocese. During the black death his pastoral care extended to arranging emergency provision for the sick to make confession to the laity where no clergy were available.

Shrewsbury was a notable benefactor of Wells Cathedral, taking a close interest in it throughout his episcopate and making a visitation of it three times. In 1335–7 he revived the requirement of the chancellor to lecture on theology or canon law, modelling it on the practice at Oxford University. His principal benefactions at Wells were to the minor clergy, enabling the vicars and choristers to live a communal life. The Vicars' Hall, begun in 1348, and probably the Vicars' Close, were built at his expense and at the same time they received a new constitution and endowment. In 1349 the choristers also received an endowment, and in 1354 a house was built for them. Shrewsbury was a keen builder, responsible for the magnificent moat and walls of the bishop's palace in Wells, begun after 1340, and for work at several episcopal manors, some of which the chapter later regarded as unduly extravagant. He increased the revenue of the see by appropriating the rectory of Great Chew to it in 1341.

As bishop, Shrewsbury was able to repay the earlier generosity of Shrewsbury Abbey by establishing a chantry there in 1345, endowed with the manor of Burton near Condover, Shropshire, and cancelling a debt of £20 in his will. His last years, burdened with ill health, were largely spent at Wiveliscombe where he died on 14 August 1363 aged nearly eighty. He was buried in Wells Cathedral in front of the high altar, beneath an alabaster effigy which can now be seen in the north choir aisle. For some thirty years after his death his tomb was a popular place of veneration. In this respect Shrewsbury takes his place within a wider fourteenth-century tradition of unofficial cults around saintly bishops.

D. N. Lepine

Sources T. S. Holmes, ed., *The register of Ralph of Shrewsbury, bishop of Wells, 1329–1363*, 2 vols., Somerset RS, 9–10 (1896) • Emden, *Oxf.* •

Calendar of the manuscripts of the dean and chapter of Wells, 2 vols., HMC, 12 (1907–14) · J. A. Robinson, ed., 'The *Historia minor* and the *Historia major* from the Wells *Liber albus II*', *Collectanea I*, ed. T. F. Palmer, Somerset RS, 39 (1924) · F. W. Weaver, ed., *Somerset medieval wills*, 2, Somerset RS, 19 (1903), 286–7 · L. S. Colchester, ed., *Wells Cathedral fabric accounts* (1983), 5–16 · J. A. Robinson, ed., 'Household roll of Bishop Ralph of Shrewsbury, 1337–8', *Collectanea I*, ed. T. F. Palmer, Somerset RS, 39 (1924), 72–124 · *Chancery records* · LPL, estate document 224A · *CEPR letters*, vol. 2

Archives LPL, household roll, 1337, estate document 224A · Som. ARS, register, SRO D/D/B, Reg 1, fols. 276–89, Reg 2

Likenesses alabaster effigy on monument, *c*.1363, Wells Cathedral

Shrewsbury, Robert of (*d*. 1168), hagiographer and abbot of Shrewsbury, was successively monk, prior (from 1137), and fifth abbot (from *c*.1148) of the Benedictine abbey of Shrewsbury. He is known to have recovered the substantial tithes of Emstrey, which had been alienated by his predecessor. In 1139 he had written a life of St *Gwenfrewi (Winefride) after her supposed relics had been removed from Gwytherin to Shrewsbury the previous year: it was dedicated to Warin, prior of Worcester (*d*. 1140). This life augmented the first life by Pseudo-Elerius (*c*.1100) and survives with it in BL, Cotton MS Claudius A. v. It was translated by William Caxton (1485) and by the Jesuit John Falconer (1635). Reprinted in 1712, it was republished by William Fleetwood in his *Life and Miracles of St Wenefrid* (1713). Several subsequent editions, the most recent in 1976, testify to modern interest in the work. Robert's achievement was to strengthen in England the cult of this obscure Welsh saint of the seventh century and to develop her shrine at Holywell, the goal of pilgrimages from Shrewsbury and elsewhere from the fourteenth century until the present day. This legend of Gwenfrewi made her a girl living at home, whom a Prince Caradoc tried to seduce. After she refused him, he cut off her head. She was miraculously restored to life and then lived as a nun (and abbess) at Holywell. An alternative story made her an anchoress at Gwytherin. In the later middle ages Gwenfrewi was regarded as a patron saint of Wales. The Holywell shrine, rebuilt by Margaret Beaufort in 1485, remained in the seventeenth and eighteenth centuries as a notable centre of Catholic recusancy and is the best-preserved medieval pilgrimage centre in Britain.

Robert died in 1168 and was probably buried at Shrewsbury Abbey. D. H. FARMER

Sources Robert of Shrewsbury and others, 'Vitae S. Wenefredae', *Acta sanctorum: November*, 1 (Paris, 1887), 691–759 · *Bibliotheca hagiographica latina antiquae et mediae aetatis*, 2 vols. (Brussels, 1898–1901) [suppls., 1911 and 1986, 8847–54; 8847–8, 8853, 8854*b*] · C. de Smedt, 'Documenta de S. Wenefreda', *Analecta Bollandiana*, 6 (1887), 305–52 · *VCH Shropshire*, 2.30–37 · U. Rees, ed., *The cartulary of Shrewsbury Abbey*, 2 (1975), esp. 340–41 · R. W. Eyton, *Antiquities of Shropshire*, 12 vols. (1854–60) · D. Knowles, C. N. L. Brooke, and V. C. M. London, eds., *The heads of religious houses, England and Wales*, 1: *940–1216* (1972), 71 · J. Dolan, 'Gwenfrewi', *Bibliotheca Sanctorum*, 7 (1966), 553–5 · *Ann. mon.*, 1.50 · D. H. Farmer, *The Oxford dictionary of saints*, 3rd edn (1992)

Archives BL, Cotton MS Claudius A.v

Shrubb, Alfred (1879–1964), athlete, was born at Battle's, Slinfold, near Horsham, Sussex, on 12 December 1879, the son of William Shrubb, an agricultural labourer, and his wife, Harriett, *née* Dench. He had three elder brothers and three elder sisters. His first indication of athletic talent came in 1898, when he ran 3 miles across country to help fight a fire in a neighbouring village. Shortly afterwards he joined the local athletic club and won the Sussex championships for 1, 3, and 4 miles. By 1900 Shrubb, a bricklayer, was being coached by the professional trainer Harry Andrews, and was competing in his first national Amateur Athletic Association (AAA) championships. He was beaten, but between 1901 and 1904 won ten AAA championships at distances between 1 and 10 miles. As well as southern and national cross-country titles, Shrubb won the first two international cross-country championships in 1903 and 1904. By 1904 it was obvious that he was the outstanding distance runner of his generation; in one race, on 5 November 1904 in Glasgow, he set world records at every distance from 2 to 10 miles. When the International Amateur Athletics Federation (IAAF) produced its first list of official world records in 1921, Shrubb held the records for all distances between 2 and 10 miles; no subsequent British athlete was to break a record for a distance event until Gordon Pirie in 1953.

Shrubb had come to prominence running for the Sussex-based Horsham Blue Star club, but by 1904 he was running for the South London Harriers, and it was clear that his earnings from bricklaying could not be sufficient to fund his expenses as an athlete training and competing across the country. There were rumours that Shrubb would request a piano as a prize at races, which would later be sold by a relation who owned a piano shop. Travelling expenses to athletes were forbidden unless competing in inter-club or AAA championship meetings. In December 1904 the AAA agreed to a request from the New Zealand AAA for Shrubb to make an expenses-paid tour. In the following year the AAA rules on payment of amateur expenses were further tightened and a similar request from the South African AAA was refused. In August 1905 Shrubb was suspended by the AAA for 'irregularities' surrounding the purchase of a ticket to travel to Canada; the AAA southern committee had refused permission for him to make a tour, but he had continued negotiations. Shrubb appealed in January 1906, but his suspension was upheld, and the South London Harriers club were also suspended. The athletic press dubbed the scandal the 'Shrubb sensation', and it coincided with wider debates in the sporting world about who should be considered an 'amateur'. The National Cycling Union was openly challenging the AAA definition of amateurism and promoting athletic meetings under its own code, which allowed amateurs and professionals to compete against each other. Shrubb made his professional début at a Southern Counties Cycling Union meeting on Good Friday 1906, but despite this high-profile support the new style of meetings failed to win popular support.

Shrubb was never as dominant in his professional career as he had been as an amateur, and his best times were set as an amateur. He quickly went to America, where he competed widely, including racing against Johnny Hayes and Dorando Pietri, stars of the 1908 Olympic marathon, who had also turned professional. He wrote *Running and Cross-Country Running* (1908), in which he described himself as the 'world's greatest pedestrian' and urged athletes to 'train consistently and constantly, and always to bear in mind that they could always do better'. Known in his prime as the Little Wonder and the Irrepressible, Shrubb continued to compete into his forties. He returned to Britain and was the professional coach to Oxford University athletics club between 1920 and 1926, before emigrating to Canada in 1928. He visited Britain in 1952, when he met his fellow South London Harrier and successor as a world record holder, Gordon Pirie, and was reinstated as an amateur by the AAA. He died in Bowmanville, Ontario, on 23 April 1964.   M. A. BRYANT

Sources P. Lovesey, *The kings of distance: a study of five great runners* (1968) · P. Lovesey, *The official centenary history of the Amateur Athletic Association* (1979) · b. cert. · census returns, 1881

Shrubsole, William (1729–1797), Independent minister and mastmaker, was born at Sandwich, Kent, on 7 April 1729 and baptized at St Clement's, Sandwich, on 18 April, the son of Edward Shrubsole and Mary Chapman, who had married on 1 July 1726. In February 1743 he was apprenticed to George Cook, a shipwright at Sheerness, whose daughter Margaret (*d.* in or after 1796) he married in 1757. He was converted to a religious and godly life by reading a work of Isaac Ambrose, and in 1752 he was asked to lead the small Independent congregation at Sheerness on Sunday afternoons. In 1763 the congregation erected a meeting-house, and Shrubsole frequently acted as their minister. About 1767 he began regular public preaching in Sheerness and other towns in Kent. In 1773 he was appointed master-mastmaker at Woolwich but later in the year he was promoted at Sheerness. There, in 1784, a new chapel was built for him, which was enlarged in 1787. In 1793 he had a paralytic stroke and a co-pastor was appointed.

Shrubsole's most popular work was *Christian Memoirs* (1776), an allegorical work in the style of Bunyan, featuring representations of John Wesley and George Whitefield; the countess of Huntingdon was among the subscribers. The book was written, as Shrubsole explains, to divert his mind after being bitten by a mad dog in 1773. A second edition (1790) contained an elegy written in 1771 on the death of Whitefield; a third edition (1807) was edited by his son, with a life of the author. Shrubsole also published a pamphlet arguing for increased pay for shipwrights (1770) and wrote on infant baptism (1794). With Samuel Denne he was the author of *The History and Antiquities of Rochester* (1772). He died at Sheerness on 7 February 1797 and was survived by his eldest son, **William Shrubsole** (1759–1829), bank clerk and hymn writer, who was born at Sheerness on 21 November 1759. He became a shipwright in Sheerness Dockyard and later an officer's clerk. In 1785 he went to London as a clerk in the Bank of England, and eventually he was appointed secretary to the committee of Treasury. He was one of the first secretaries of the London Missionary Society and contributed to the Religious Tract Society. He published hymns in various religious publications from 1775 to 1813. His best-known hymn, 'Arm of the Lord! awake, awake' (1795), is attributed in some works to his father. His hymn 'Bright as the sun's meridian blaze' was written in 1795 for the London Missionary Society. Shrubsole, who had a daughter, Mrs Cunliffe, died at Highbury on 23 August 1829 and was buried in Bunhill Fields. He was not connected with William Shrubsole (*bap.* 1760, *d.* 1806), the composer and organist.

J. C. HADDEN, *rev.* EMMA MAJOR

Sources *GM*, 1st ser., 67 (1797), 173, 250 · *ESTC* · W. Shrubsole, 'Life of William Shrubsole', in W. Shrubsole, *Christian memoirs*, 3rd edn (1807) · will, 1797, PRO, PROB 11/1286, sig. 117 · Allibone, *Dict.* · *IGI* · J. Morison, *The fathers and founders of the London Missionary Society*, new edn [1844] · J. Julian, ed., *A dictionary of hymnology* (1892)
Likenesses Ridley, stipple, NPG; repro. in *Evangelical Magazine* (1797) · portrait (William Shrubsole the younger), repro. in Morison, *Fathers and founders*
Wealth at death household possessions; property; stocks: will, PRO, PROB 11/1286, sig. 117

Shrubsole, William (1759–1829). *See under* Shrubsole, William (1729–1797).

Shrubsole, William (*bap.* **1760**, *d.* **1806**), organist, the youngest son of Thomas Shrubsole, a farrier, was born at Canterbury and baptized on 13 January 1760. He was a chorister in the cathedral from 1770 to 1777, and organist at Bangor Cathedral from 1782 to 1784, when he was dismissed for frequenting conventicles. He then became organist of Spa Fields Chapel, Clerkenwell, London, a post he held until his death. He was a successful teacher in London, and among his pupils were William Russell (1777–1813), the organist of the Foundling Chapel, and Benjamin Jacob, of Surrey Chapel. The 1794 musical directory describes him as an alto singer, and in that capacity he is said to have performed at Drury Lane and Westminster Abbey. Shrubsole composed the famous hymn tune known as 'Miles Lane', set to the hymn 'All hail! the power of Jesus' name', by Edward Perronet. 'Miles Lane' was first published anonymously in the *Gospel Magazine* in November 1779, and then under Shrubsole's name in S. Addington's *Collection of Psalm Tunes* (1780). Shrubsole became intimate with Perronet at Canterbury, and Perronet, besides making him one of his executors, left him a substantial share of his property in 1792. Shrubsole died in London on 18 January 1806 and was buried at Bunhill Fields. The first strain of 'Miles Lane' was engraved on his tombstone.   J. C. HADDEN, *rev.* NILANJANA BANERJI

Sources Brown & Stratton, *Brit. mus.* · *New Grove* · J. Love, *Scottish church music* (1891) · Dotted Crotchet, 'Canterbury Cathedral', *MT*, 47 (1906), 373–83, esp. 379 · M. L. Clarke, *Bangor Cathedral* (1969) · J. D. Brown, *Biographical dictionary of musicians: with a bibliography of English writings on music* (1886) · D. Baptie, *A handbook of musical biography* (1883)

Shuckard, William Edward (1802/3–1868), entomologist, was the eldest son of Johann Leonhardt Schuckardt of Frankfurt am Main, Germany, who settled in England in 1787 and married in 1793. Johann Schuckardt Anglicized his name to Leonard Shuckard, and about 1802 leased the Old Ship (then Brighton's principal hotel), in partnership with Alexander Hicks.

William Shuckard was well educated, and then placed in the house of Baldwin, Craddock, and Joy, publishers, of Paternoster Row, London. He lodged first with his maternal uncle, William Bernard *Cooke (1778–1855) [see under Cooke family (per. c.1800–1865)], a line engraver of Soho Square. However, Shuckard's fondness for 'midnight readings' led to friction with his uncle (and the resultant oversleeping led to several threats of dismissal from work). Shuckard moved from his uncle's house and for some time lodged instead at Bateman's Buildings, Holborn, but continued neglect of his duties led to his dismissal. He returned to live with his father at Brighton, where it was hoped he would start up as a bookseller. His father was also keen for him to gain some experience of the German book trade, and sent Shuckard to a firm of booksellers, possibly at Frankfurt or Leipzig.

On 19 November 1829 at St Pancras Old Church, Shuckard married Sarah Ann, daughter of Mr Martin of Horsted Keynes, Sussex. From about 1832 Shuckard attempted to move into writing, and took on occasional sub-editing duties at a local Brighton newspaper. His leisure hours were devoted to entomology, and he soon became an expert in the study. He was a member of the Entomological Society's publications committee, and on 2 April 1835 was appointed librarian to the Royal Society. He held the latter post until 9 November 1843, when he was dismissed for being insolvent, the result of 'the too strenuous pursuit of the science of entomology and the publication upon it' (MC 3.310, Royal Society).

In 1844, through the influence of the entomologist William Wilson Saunders (1809–1879), Shuckard obtained the post of editor of Lloyds List, which he held until his retirement in 1861. In that same year, Shuckard borrowed a large number of insects from the Entomological Society, the East India House, and his fellow entomologists Frederick William Hope and John Obadiah Westwood. However, at some later stage, financial difficulties led to Shuckard's pawning the borrowed specimens, and subsequently being unable to buy them back. As a result, Westwood had to re-purchase both his own insects and those belonging to Hope.

Despite being dogged by financial troubles Shuckard saw a number of works into print, including Essay on the Indigenous Fossorial Hymenoptera (1837); Elements of British Entomology (1839); The British Coleoptera Delineated, with drawings by William Spry (1840); 'On the history and natural arrangement of insects', in Lardner's Cabinet Cyclopaedia, 10 (1840), written in conjunction with William Swainson; Catalogues of the miscellaneous manuscripts and of the manuscript letters in the possession of the Royal Society (1840); and British Bees (1866).

Shuckard also produced a number of works that were translations of German originals. They included A Manual of Entomology, from the German of Dr Hermann Burmeister (1836); Travels in the East (1847), from the work by Tischendorf; and Chamber and Cage Birds (1848), a translation of Johann Bechstein's work, which went through many editions. Some sixteen papers on entomological subjects were also written by him, and appeared in various scientific journals between 1836 and 1842. He died on 10 November 1868 at the Oval Road, Kennington, and was survived by at least one son. YOLANDA FOOTE

Sources The Entomologist, 4 (1869), 180–82 · private information (1897) [from G. C. Shuckard, subject's son, and R. Harrison, assistant secretary, Royal Society] · BL cat. · Catalogue of scientific papers, Royal Society · Boase, Mod. Eng. biog. · A. Z. Smith, A history of the Hope entomological collections in the University Museum, Oxford (1986) · RS, MS MC. 3.310 · R. Flower, The Old Ship—a prospect of Brighton (1986)

Shuckburgh, Sir (Charles Arthur) Evelyn (1909–1994), diplomatist, was born at 33 Iverna Gardens, Kensington, London, on 26 May 1909, the eldest son in the family of three sons and two daughters of Sir John Evelyn *Shuckburgh (1877–1953), a civil servant in the India Office (and later deputy under-secretary in the Colonial Office), and his wife, Lilian Violet, elder daughter of Arthur George Peskett, classicist and fellow of Magdalene College, Cambridge. He was educated at Winchester College, and at King's College, Cambridge.

After joining the Foreign Office in October 1933 Shuckburgh (always known as Evelyn) served for four years in London during which time he married on 25 September 1937 Nancy Mildred Gladys Brett (b. 1918), second daughter of Oliver Sylvain Baliol Brett, third Viscount Esher, and his wife, Antoinette, née Heckscher (from Philadelphia). His first overseas appointment, shortly after his marriage, was to the Cairo embassy as private secretary to the ambassador, Sir Miles Lampson. Although Britain had recently signed a defence treaty with Egypt replacing the existing imperialistic arrangements, Lampson continued to run the mission like a grand outpost of empire (as indeed it effectively was). Shuckburgh's duties were confined largely to the social sphere, making him feel like a 'hired footman' (Shuckburgh, 7). Newly married and starting a family, it was nevertheless a carefree period, despite the looming threat of war. He and Nancy went on to have a daughter, Catherine (b. 1939), and two sons, Julian (b. 1940) and Robin (b. 1948).

Shuckburgh returned to the Foreign Office in October 1939, having been promoted to second secretary a year earlier. In the following June he was seconded to Britain's high commission in Ottawa as administrative assistant to help organize the transport of Canadian troops to Britain. In October 1942 he was transferred to Buenos Aires, where he monitored Argentina's neutrality along with its belated declaration of war on Germany in March 1945. He was promoted to acting first secretary in September 1943 and served as chargé d'affaires in 1944.

Shuckburgh's next posting placed him on the front line of the developing cold war. Arriving at the Prague embassy in September 1945 he reported on the Czechoslovakian elections of March 1946 that saw the communists emerge as the largest party with 36 per cent of the popular vote. He returned to London in April 1947—as head of the Foreign Office's South American department—and so was not present for the communist coup in February 1948, but like many others in the Foreign Office he despaired of the

Sir (Charles Arthur) Evelyn Shuckburgh (1909–1994), by Walter Bird, 1962

Czechoslovakian people for embracing the communists in the first place. He was promoted counsellor in June 1948 and appointed CMG in the following June.

The immediate post-war years were a boom time for the creation of international bodies and the Foreign Office reorganized accordingly. Shuckburgh took charge of the Western department in 1949, which was having to cope with the demands of European reconstruction and the cold war. Within a year he had partitioned off the institutional aspects of this wide remit, helping to establish the Western organizations department, with himself as head, to deal with the politico-military affairs of NATO, the Council of Europe, and the Organization for European Economic Co-operation.

Having thrived on managing busy departments, Shuckburgh moved to the centre of the Foreign Office in August 1951 as principal private secretary to the secretary of state. He initially worked for Herbert Morrison, who had little experience of international affairs or of foreigners. They got on well together and Shuckburgh was sorry to see him leave in October. Morrison's successor was Anthony Eden, who knew the Foreign Office and international affairs inside out, giving Shuckburgh's job a very different aspect. 'Instead of being concerned to explain and justify the Foreign Secretary to the Office', he found himself 'justifying the Office to the Secretary of State and defending startled officials from his all too experienced and well-documented strictures' (Shuckburgh, 12). A crucial part of being private secretary entailed sharing the preoccupations of the minister and, despite the relatively junior status of the job, also having an opinion on all policy issues.

Shuckburgh excelled in the role and became an influential proponent of withdrawal from the Suez base, bolstering the foreign secretary when Winston Churchill went on the warpath against the 'scuttle' in Egypt. Eden had acquired from Churchill the habit of conducting business from bed, making it Shuckburgh's responsibility to guide in hesitant ministers and officials. Relentless proximity, coupled with the intractable problems besetting Britain, resulted in an association that was often fraught. Nevertheless, Shuckburgh had a respect and affection for Eden which was reciprocated. Indeed, Eden may have seen something of his younger self in Shuckburgh—the swept-back black hair and urbane features.

In May 1954 Shuckburgh (who had been made CB in January that year) was promoted under-secretary of state in the Foreign Office, with responsibility for Middle Eastern affairs. The new job testified to his expertise on the Egyptian question, upon which Britain's influence in the region hinged. In July he accompanied Antony Head, the secretary of state for war, on the mission to Cairo which concluded an agreement with Nasser (detailing a phased withdrawal of the Suez garrison by June 1956). A new era of co-operation was meant to ensue, but instead Britain's accession to the Baghdad pact in April 1955 soured relations—Nasser seeing the organization as a threat to Egypt's regional leadership. Meanwhile, Shuckburgh headed the British side in the secret Anglo-American initiative to settle the Arab-Israeli dispute, Project Alpha, which also drowned in regional rivalries. He found the Palestinian issue profoundly depressing, just as his father had in the 1930s: Zionists saw both father and son as hostile. By 1956 the physical and mental demands of trying to balance contradictory policies began to take its toll on Shuckburgh: 'I could not see any sense or prospect of sense in our Middle East policies', he wrote in his diary late in 1955 (Shuckburgh, 293). After asking for new responsibilities in April 1956, he was seconded to the Imperial Defence College as chief civilian instructor in June.

Being away from the Foreign Office was a tremendous relief to Shuckburgh, especially after the Suez crisis erupted on 26 July. He regarded the invasion in November as folly, but he felt that Britain, having gone in, should not have stopped. He diverted himself by learning to play the guitar and translating from sixteenth-century Spanish Juan de Iciar's *Arte subtilissima* (published by Oxford University Press in 1960). After a two-year academic interlude he became assistant secretary-general of NATO in Paris (from September 1958), working as the political adviser to Paul-Henri Spaak, the secretary-general. He was knighted KCMG in January 1959.

Shuckburgh returned to the Foreign Office between 1960 and 1962 as deputy under-secretary, with responsibility for relations with the Soviet Union in Europe. He was deeply involved in Britain's response to the crisis triggered by the construction of the Berlin Wall in August 1961, when a confrontation with the Soviet bloc was a distinct possibility. He then returned to Paris (a city he loved) as Britain's permanent representative on the NATO council, and played an important role in the vigorous British diplomacy which helped prevent the organization from collapsing after France decided to withdraw from its integrated activities in February 1966.

The ambassadorship to Italy (from December 1966 to September 1969) concluded Shuckburgh's diplomatic career, and he was promoted GCMG in 1967. Aside from some turmoil created by De Gaulle's second 'Non' to Britain's proposed entry into the EEC in May 1967, it was a happy posting. He learnt Italian, arranged classical concerts, travelled widely, and restored Keats's grave in Rome's protestant cemetery. A latent Bohemian streak was allowed to flourish with the growth of a bushy, white-speckled beard. But nor did he ignore the disquiet back at the Foreign Office caused by George Brown's rude behaviour towards officials. After leaving the foreign service he publicly rebuked Brown.

Upon retirement Shuckburgh returned to his home, High Wood, in Watlington, Oxfordshire. Already a skilled carpenter of elaborate furniture, he learnt how to make clavichords. He also served assiduously for the British Red Cross Society and the International Red Cross (with spells as chairman of both), and as chairman of the northern home counties regional committee of the National Trust. Anticipating the release of the British documents on Suez, he published his diaries written between 1951 and 1956. Entitled *Descent to Suez* (1986), the book gave a vivid and intimate account of the inner workings of Whitehall under Churchill and Eden. While the big picture that emerged was of a great power struggling with decline, it was the details of Eden's unpredictability, under the pressure of events and ill health, which caught attention. A few critics commented on a public servant breaking confidence in this way, but Eden had been well aware of Shuckburgh's diary-keeping: 'Put that down on your tablets, Evelyn' stands as the preface to the volume. Less contentiously, Shuckburgh translated *The Memoirs of Madame Roland* (1989) which had the backdrop of revolutionary France. He died, of cancer of the prostate at his home in Watlington, on 12 December 1994, survived by his wife and three children. A memorial service was held at St Mary's, Ewelme, Oxfordshire, on 7 January 1995.

MICHAEL T. THORNHILL

Sources E. Shuckburgh, *Descent to Suez: diaries, 1951–56* (1986) · *Daily Telegraph* (15 Dec 1994) · *The Independent* (19 Dec 1994) · *The Times* (15 Dec 1994) · D. Carlton, *Anthony Eden* (1981) · K. Kyle, *Suez* (1991) · P. Gore-Booth, *With great truth and respect* (1974) · *WWW, 1991–5* · Burke, *Peerage* · *FO List* (1969) · will · b. cert. · m. cert. · d. cert. · *CGPLA Eng. & Wales* (1995)
Archives Bodl. Oxf., papers and corresp. relating to Argentina · NRA, priv. coll., papers | U. Birm. L., corresp. with Lord Avon |SOUND BL NSA, current affairs recordings
Likenesses W. Bird, photograph, 1962, NPG [*see illus.*] · photographs, repro. in Shuckburgh, *Descent to Suez*
Wealth at death under £125,000: probate, 30 May 1995, *CGPLA Eng. & Wales*

Shuckburgh, Evelyn Shirley (1843–1906), classical scholar, was born at Aldborough in Norfolk on 12 July 1843, the third and eldest surviving son (in a family of twelve children) of Robert Shuckburgh, rector of Aldborough, and his wife, Elizabeth (*d.* 1876), daughter of Dr Lyford of Winchester. Shuckburgh was educated for some time at a preparatory school kept at Winchester by the Revd E. Huntingford DCL. From there he proceeded to Ipswich grammar school, under Dr Hubert Ashton Holden, the editor of Aristophanes, of whose teaching Shuckburgh always talked with enthusiasm. His father died in 1860, and in 1862 Shuckburgh entered Emmanuel College, Cambridge, as an exhibitioner. He was made a scholar in 1863. He was short-sighted, which probably prevented his taking an active part in athletics, but he took the lead in the intellectual life of the college, and as a speaker at the Union Debating Society became widely known in the university. He was president of the union in 1865, and graduated as thirteenth classic in the classical tripos of 1866.

From 1866 to 1874 Shuckburgh was a fellow and assistant tutor of Emmanuel College. In 1874 he vacated his fellowship on his marriage to Frances Mary, daughter of the Revd Joseph Pullen, formerly fellow and tutor of Corpus Christi College, Cambridge, and Gresham professor of astronomy, and accepted an assistant mastership at Eton. There he remained for ten years, when he returned to Cambridge. He was soon appointed librarian of Emmanuel College, and devoted himself, apart from his comparatively light duties in this capacity, to teaching and writing.

Shuckburgh wrote with great facility, and immediately after his degree had published anonymously various translations of classical works for university examinations. On his return to Cambridge he undertook the editing of many volumes of elementary school classics, chiefly for Macmillan and the Cambridge University Press. For his skill in such work he was selected by Sir Richard Jebb to adapt his edition of Sophocles for use in schools. Shuckburgh, however, lived only to publish the *Oedipus Coloneus, Antigone*, and *Philoctetes*. His translations included Polybius and Cicero's letters and in 1896 he produced an edition of Suetonius's life of Augustus, for which he gained the degree of LittD from Cambridge in 1902. He also wrote various short histories of the classical world, edited some English texts, and produced several works connected with the history of Emmanuel, including a volume in Robinson's series College Histories (1904). He wrote essays and verses for literary journals and prepared some entries for the *Dictionary of National Biography*. Shuckburgh devoted much time to examining in his own and other universities and in the public schools. In 1901 he was appointed by the intermediate education board for Ireland to report on secondary education in Irish schools. He died suddenly on 10 July 1906, in the train between Berwick and Edinburgh, while on his way to examine at St Leonard's School, St Andrews, and was buried at Grantchester, where he had lived for some years. He left a family of two sons and three daughters.

PETER GILES, *rev.* RICHARD SMAIL

Sources J. Adam, *Emmanuel College Magazine*, 17 (1906–7), 1–20 · Venn, *Alum. Cant.* · *CGPLA Eng. & Wales* (1906)
Archives King's AC Cam., letters to Oscar Browning

Likenesses E. Gillick, bronze relief; known to be at Emmanuel College, Cambridge, in 1912 · photograph; known to be at Emmanuel College, Cambridge, in 1912

Wealth at death £2560 14*s.* 7*d.*: probate, 1 Oct 1906, *CGPLA Eng. & Wales*

Shuckburgh, Sir John Evelyn (1877–1953), civil servant, was born on 18 March 1877 at Eton, Buckinghamshire, the eldest son of Evelyn Shirley *Shuckburgh (1843–1906), classical scholar and assistant master at Eton College (1874–83), and his wife, Frances Mary, the daughter of the Revd Joseph Pullen. Shuckburgh was a scholar at Eton (1889–96) and at King's College, Cambridge (matriculated 1896, first-class honours in the classical tripos, BA 1899, MA 1906). In 1900 he passed the civil service first-division examination and entered the India Office, where he was successively junior clerk, store department (1900); private secretary to Sir Arthur Godley (later first Baron Kilbracken), the permanent under-secretary of state (1902); senior clerk, political department (1906); editor, telegraphic code (1907–12); assistant secretary, political department (1912–17); and secretary, political department (1917–21). He had long experience of dealing with Indian princely states. During the First World War, he was private secretary to an important advisory committee on certain post-war issues, and in 1918 was made a CB. On 24 September 1906 he married Lilian Violet, the elder daughter of Arthur George Peskett, a fellow of Magdalene College, Cambridge; they had three sons and two daughters. His eldest son was (Charles Arthur) Evelyn *Shuckburgh (1909–1994), a diplomat; his youngest son was killed in action over France in 1941.

During the First World War Britain's responsibilities in the Middle East were considerably enhanced. Palestine, Transjordan, and Iraq, previously part of the Ottoman empire, were governed by Britain under League of Nations mandates. Their administrative needs were such that a new government department had to be created to deal with them. In February 1921 Churchill became colonial secretary in Lloyd George's coalition government, his responsibilities to include the Near East (then and later also called the Middle East) with, as Churchill had advocated, a new Middle East department. Churchill had already been assembling data on the area and in 1920 had received a report by Shuckburgh on Mesopotamia. Churchill's first choice for his senior civil servant adviser was Sir Arthur Hirtzel, assistant under-secretary of state (1917–21) at the India Office, but he declined and recommended Shuckburgh: 'you would find in him a most valuable head … really first rate—level headed, always cool, very accurate & unsparing of himself: his only fault perhaps a tendency to excessive caution' (Gilbert, *1916–1922*, 524). In 1921 Shuckburgh was transferred to the Colonial Office and appointed assistant under-secretary of state, the permanent head of the new department. Its four senior administrative officials were all old Etonians. Shuckburgh made the new department an efficient administrative organization.

Shuckburgh advised and assisted Churchill on policy for

Sir John Evelyn Shuckburgh (1877–1953), by George Charles Beresford, 1929

the troubled, violent, and controversial area. Most difficult, and arguably insoluble, was the problem of Palestine, wherein, by the Balfour declaration (1917), the British government had promised a 'national home' for Jews. Key members of the coalition government were pro-Zionist—Lloyd George, Balfour, Churchill, and Amery—and British policy favoured the Zionists while hoping Zionist settlement would not harm the interests of the Palestinian Arab majority. In 1920 a British Jewish Zionist, the Liberal politician Herbert Samuel, had been appointed high commissioner of Palestine. Palestinian Arabs resisted Zionist settler encroachment—while Arab absentee landlords, including Palestinian Arab leaders, sold land to Zionists at inflated prices—and violence was endemic.

Shuckburgh accepted the government pro-Zionist policy, writing to Churchill that 'we are committed to this policy and have got to make the best of it' (Gilbert, *1916–1922*, 615), and he was more positive towards Zionism than the average official dealing with Palestine. He realized the difficulties of ruling Palestine, and wrote: 'we are confronted with two distinct obligations … it will be a difficult and dangerous task' (Gilbert, *Winston S. Churchill*, pt 3, p. 1499). He advised against further public definition of the Balfour declaration, and recommended co-operation with Chaim Weizmann, 'the best and most reliable of the Zionists' (ibid., 1672). He also suggested reconciling the Arabs to the Zionist policy by showing them the benefits from Zionist enterprise, and he supported the 1922 hydroelectric scheme concession to Piotr (Pinhas) Rutenberg, a

Russian Jewish engineer. In May 1921 Arabs attacked Jewish immigrants in Jaffa and elsewhere. The British suppressed the disturbances, but Samuel attempted to conciliate the Arabs, including by not enforcing the collective fine of the Jaffa Arabs. Shuckburgh criticized Samuel, alleging he was afraid, and proposed the fine be imposed; Churchill agreed. Shuckburgh and Samuel largely drafted the June 1922 'Churchill' white paper which tried to reassure the Arabs but reaffirmed commitment to the Balfour declaration and continued Jewish immigration. In summer 1921 an Arab delegation arrived in London, refusing to accept the Balfour declaration and demanding immediate self-government. In September Shuckburgh wrote to Churchill that their uncompromising attitude 'makes further negotiation with them useless' (Gilbert, 1916–1922, 633). In November he wrote that they were 'a hopeless body to deal with … being Orientals they will understand an order, and if once they realise that we mean business, may be expected to acquiesce' (Wasserstein, *British in Palestine*, 116). Critics alleged the Middle East department was too pro-Zionist. General Sir Walter Norris Congreve, British commander in the Middle East, asserted it was 'pursuing an unfair policy in favour of the Jews' (Gilbert, 1916–1922, 636).

However, while helping to implement the government's Palestine policy, Shuckburgh privately was dejected and pessimistic. In April 1923 he 'very confidentially' told Sydney Moody, a younger official, of his disappointment and frustration. He saw no purpose to the mandate and no solution. His department had tried but failed to reconcile Arabs and Jews. The former were embittered, the latter were dissatisfied and accused British officials of taking an anti-Jewish line: 'We are unfortunate in our clients' (Friesel, 202). He felt the British were in the dark, without direction, and that the two-faced policy was inappropriate and disgraced him personally. The Balfour declaration had not been worth it, but Britain was bound by the bargain. Yet the logical conclusion was 'our final[ly] disembarrassing ourselves of these promises' (Wasserstein, *Herbert Samuel*, 26). He apparently favoured Jewish autonomy in the framework of an Arab state. In that year Shuckburgh was on a committee with military experts to consider Palestine's strategic value. He argued the 'imperial interest', that 'to lose Palestine is to lose Arabia' (Segev, 198), and that it facilitated the defence of Egypt. The committee failed to agree: the general staff argued Palestine was not necessary for the defence of Egypt and India. Shuckburgh, however, alleged military experts were unreliable: they disagreed and kept changing their positions. In 1922 he was made a KCMG. In March 1925 he accompanied L. S. Amery, colonial secretary (1924–9)—then promoting 'our Zionist policy' (Amery, 306) and resisting British press demands for a 'scuttle' from the Middle East—to Transjordan, Iraq, and Palestine.

Shuckburgh's responsibilities at the Colonial Office were gradually widened and more departments placed under him, and in 1931, as part of an office reorganization, he was appointed to the new post of deputy undersecretary of state. In 1939 he was designated governor of Nigeria, but because of the war continued at the Colonial Office, retiring in 1942. From 1942 to 1948 he was narrator at the historical section of the Cabinet Office, writing a history of the colonial empire in the war. Fond of sport and in his earlier years a competent cricketer, he was cultured, an authority on Dickens, and considered a fine English stylist. He contributed to *The Spectator*, the *National Review*, *Country Life*, *Blue Peter*, the *Tree Lover*, the *Manchester Guardian*, and other publications. In 1946 he published *An Ideal Voyage*, a book of his essays—light, largely retrospective *belles-lettres*—from *The Spectator* and other periodicals. He died on 8 February 1953 at his home, 37a Connaught Street, Bayswater, London, survived by his wife.

ROGER T. STEARN

Sources DNB · *The Times* (10 Feb 1953) · *The Eton register*, 6 (privately printed, Eton, 1910) · Venn, *Alum. Cant.* · Burke, *Peerage* (1939) · *WWW*, 1951–60 · M. Gilbert, *Winston S. Churchill*, 4: 1916–1922 (1975) · M. Gilbert, *Winston S. Churchill*, companion vol. 4 (1975) · B. Wasserstein, *The British in Palestine: the mandatory government and the Arab–Jewish conflict, 1917–1929* (1991) · T. Segev, *One Palestine, complete: Jews and Arabs under the British mandate* (1999) · B. Wasserstein, *Herbert Samuel: a political life* (1992) · B. Morris, *Righteous victims: a history of the Zionist–Arab conflict, 1881–1999* (1999) · E. Friesel, 'British officials and the situation in Palestine, 1923', *Middle Eastern Studies*, 23 (1987), 194–210 · D. Framkin, *A peace to end all peace: creating the modern Middle East, 1914–1922* (1989) · A. W. Kayyali, *Palestine: a modern history* · L. S. Amery, *My political life*, 2: *War and peace, 1914–1929* (1953) · E. Monroe, *Britain's moment in the Middle East, 1914–1956* (1963) · K. Jeffery, *The British army and the crisis of empire, 1918–22* (1984)

Archives BL, corresp. with Sir Arnold Wilson, Add. MS 52456 · Bodl. Oxf., corresp. with Lord Lugard · CUL, corresp. with Lord Hardinge and papers | FILM IWM FVA, recorded talk

Likenesses G. C. Beresford, photograph, 1929, NPG [*see illus.*]

Wealth at death £12,296 6s. 11d.: probate, 21 May 1953, CGPLA Eng. & Wales

Shuckburgh, Sir Richard (1596–1656), royalist army officer and antiquary, was the second son of John Shuckburgh (d. 1631), gentleman, of Shuckburgh, Warwickshire, and his wife, Margery (d. 1629), eldest daughter of Richard Middlemore of Edgbaston, Warwickshire. He was educated at Lincoln College, Oxford, and graduated BA on 3 May 1615. On the death of his childless elder brother, John, in 1625 he became heir to the family estates. On 30 November 1627 he married Mary Crompton, the widowed daughter of Ralph Sneyd of Keele, Staffordshire. Mary died childless on 5 September 1629 and on 10 December 1630 Shuckburgh married Elizabeth, daughter of Sir Robert Lee of Billesley, Warwickshire. Shuckburgh's father died in 1631 and his second wife two years later, leaving him an eligible, childless widower. On 4 February 1634 he married Grace (d. 1677), daughter of Thomas *Holte of Aston, one of the foremost landowners in Warwickshire. In 1635 a son, John, was born.

In 1635 Shuckburgh was appointed to the Warwickshire bench and in 1640 he secured the second Warwickshire seat in the Long Parliament. Despite his kinship with the Middlemores, a prominent Catholic family, he was a convinced Calvinist and co-operated fully with the Long Parliament's anti-papist actions. On the outbreak of civil war he attempted to maintain a neutral stance. He was imprisoned by the House of Commons in September 1642, but bailed the following month and returned to Warwickshire. By tradition he was hunting on his estates when he encountered Charles I on the march to Edgecot and was personally enlisted by the king. In October 1642 he was present at Edgehill, where he was knighted. According to the family tradition he returned to Shuckburgh after the battle and defended the house unsuccessfully but with great bravery against a parliamentarian force. He was sequestered and imprisoned for a time, but benefited from the influence of powerful friends. When his case was discussed by the county committee, the earl of Denbigh was reported to have 'excused his going to the king and said it might be to do good offices' (*CSP dom.*, 1649–50, 444–5). He was acquitted by the sequestration committee at Westminster in March 1647 and survived a further attempt to convict him of royalism in November 1651.

In his retirement Shuckburgh interested himself in history and antiquities, assisting with the research for William Dugdale's *Antiquities of Warwickshire*. Thomas Fuller dedicated to him the third section of the fifth book of the seventeenth century of his *Church History*. Shuckburgh died in London on 13 June 1656 and was buried at the church of St John the Baptist, Upper Shuckburgh. He and Grace had four surviving sons and two daughters. His heir, John, married Catherine, daughter of Sir Hatton Fermor of Easton Neston, Northamptonshire, in December 1656, and was created a baronet in 1660 in recognition of the service of his father and maternal grandfather to Charles I. Shuckburgh's wife survived him and subsequently married John Keating, chief justice of the common pleas in Ireland. She died in Dublin in April 1677.

JAN BROADWAY

Sources A. Hughes, *Politics, society and civil war in Warwickshire, 1620–1660* (1987) • Foster, *Alum. Oxon.* • *The life, diary, and correspondence of Sir William Dugdale*, ed. W. Hamper (1827), 239–40, 244–5, 285 • F. L. Colvile, *The worthies of Warwickshire who lived between 1500 and 1800* [1870], 689 • *Miscellanea genealogica et heraldica*, 2nd ser. (1884–93), 3.353 • *VCH Warwickshire*, 6.217–18
Likenesses P. Bennier, bust on funeral monument, St John the Baptist Church, Upper Shuckburgh, Warwickshire

Shuckford, Samuel (1693/4–1754), Church of England clergyman and author, was born at Norwich, the son of Samuel Shuckford, landowner, of Palgrave in Suffolk. He was educated at the grammar schools of Norwich and of Botesdale in Suffolk. In 1712, aged eighteen, he was admitted as a scholar to Gonville and Caius College, Cambridge, where he graduated BA (1716) and MA (1720); he subsequently obtained the Lambeth degree of DD. He was ordained deacon on 16 June 1717 and priest on 28 October of the following year. In 1722 he was presented to the rectory of Shelton in Norfolk, resigning in 1746. This he held with the living of Hardwick, as well as being vicar of Seething and Mundham, all Norfolk parishes. On 21 March 1738 he was instituted to the tenth prebend in Canterbury Cathedral. Subsequently he obtained the living of All Saints, Lombard Street, London, and it is said that between 1732 and 1754 he served as a chaplain to George II.

Shuckford was the author of *The Sacred and Profane History of the World* (1728), which he intended to serve as an introduction to Henry Prideaux's *Historical Connection of the Old and New Testament*. It was subsequently reprinted on several occasions between 1731 and 1808, and in 1810 there appeared a new edition by Adam Clarke, printed with Shuckford's 1753 treatise, *The Creation and Fall of Man*. Shuckford died in London on 14 July 1754 and was buried in Canterbury Cathedral.

THOMPSON COOPER, *rev.* PHILIP CARTER

Sources Venn, *Alum. Cant.* • *N&Q*, 3rd ser., 3 (1863), 286–7, 335 • *GM*, 1st ser., 24 (1754), 340 • *The works of … George Horne … to which are prefixed memoirs of his life, studies and writings*, ed. W. Jones, 2nd edn, 6 vols. (1818) • Nichols, *Illustrations*
Archives CUL, library catalogue

Shudi [Tschudi], **Burkat** (1702–1773), harpsichord maker, was born at Schwanden in the canton of Glarus, Switzerland, on 13 March 1702, the second son of Joshua (or Josua) Tschudi, wool merchant, surgeon, and councillor of Schwanden. His mother's maiden name was Elmer. The Tschudi family believed it could trace its origins back to a Johann Tschudi who in 870 had supposedly been mayor of Glarus, while another ancestor, Heinrich (1074–1149), had been appointed landholding tenant of the Glarus region in 1128.

Because of the local abundance of wood, the main trade in Glarus was the making of wooden frames for school slates and various articles of furniture. A shortage of wood supplies in the early eighteenth century, however, the result of deforestation, led several woodworkers to become wood merchants. Many families were put out of business when the local parliament decreed that for ten years no wood might be sold outside the country. Despite the flexibility shown by some in becoming cotton weavers, the young Shudi could see little future in remaining at Glarus, and at the age of sixteen, having been taught joinery and cabinet-making by his uncle, he emigrated to London. There at some time in the 1720s he was apprenticed to Hermann Tabel, the Flemish-born harpsichord maker whose apprentices also included Jacob Kirkman.

Shudi's earliest surviving instrument, closely based on Tabel's only extant one of 1721, is a two-manual harpsichord of 1729, which carries on the reverse of the nameboard the inscription: 'QUESTO CIMBALO É DEL^a SIG^{ra} ANNA STRADA 1731, LONDON'. It is believed that the instrument was given to Anna Strada, a celebrated singer, by Handel, with whom Shudi was friendly. Since Tabel had been trained in the workshop of the Couchets in Antwerp, the 1729 Shudi harpsichord is a direct link with those of the Flemish tradition. Shudi must have been free of Tabel by 1729, and it was at about this time that he married Catherine Wild (1704–*c*.1758), daughter of Hans Jakob and Salome Wild (*née* Kubli), natives of Schwanden by then resident in London. Following his first wife's death he married Elizabeth Meier.

Shudi's business was at first conducted from his house at what is now 1 Meards Street, off Dean Street. Later, in 1742, he moved to 33 Great Pulteney Street, where his sign displayed the plume of feathers, a reflection of the patronage of Frederick, prince of Wales, which he enjoyed. The two-manual harpsichord he made in 1740 for the prince has been on view at Kew Palace. It was probably in 1745 that the German painter Marcus Tuscher executed the charming and well-known portrait of the Shudi family. Shudi made a total of five harpsichords for Frederick the Great of Prussia, and it is thought that the first, of about 1745, is the one illustrated in the Tuscher painting. In 1761 a young Scottish cabinet-maker, John Broadwood, was apprenticed to Shudi; he married Shudi's daughter, Barbara, in 1769 and later in the same year was taken into partnership by Shudi. Thereafter the harpsichords made by the firm were signed 'Burkat Shudi et Johannes Broadwood' and continued to be signed thus even after Shudi's retirement in 1771 to a house in Charlotte Street and his death at the same house on 19 August 1773.

Shudi made instruments similar to those of Kirkman, usually in traditional English cases with exteriors of panels of walnut or mahogany, surrounded with ornamental stringing and cross-banding. The majority of the surviving harpsichords have two manuals with the specification of two 8 foot registers and one 4 foot, and a lute register available on the upper manual. Single-manual instruments were also made with two 8 foot and one 4 foot or simply two 8 foot registers. Machine stops and buff (or harp) stops are to be found, and some of the more elaborate harpsichords have the Venetian swell (patented by Shudi on 18 December 1769). It seems that Shudi also collaborated with Samuel Green and John Snetzler in the making of claviorgana. By good fortune a sizeable amount of archival material concerning the production of the Shudi and later the Shudi and Broadwood workshops survives, from which it is clear that instruments were made for a number of famous people in eighteenth-century England and were also exported to many parts of Europe and beyond. CHARLES MOULD

Sources W. Dale, *Tschudi the harpsichord maker* (1913) · D. Wainwright, *Broadwood by appointment: a history* (1982) · D. H. Boalch, *Makers of the harpsichord and clavichord, 1440–1840*, ed. C. Mould, 3rd edn (1995) · D. Wainwright and K. Mobbs, 'Shudi's harpsichords for Frederick the Great', *Galpin Society Journal*, 49 (1996), 77–94 · Broadwood Trust papers, Surrey RO · Bodl. Oxf., MSS Eng. misc. b. 107, c. 529, c. 663
Archives Bodl. Oxf., MS Eng misc. b. 107 · Bodl. Oxf., MS Eng misc. c. 663 · Bodl. Oxf., MS Eng misc. c. 529 | Surrey HC, Broadwood Trust papers
Likenesses M. Tuscher, group portrait, c.1742 (with his family), NPG [*see illus.*]
Wealth at death considerable wealth

Shufflewick, Mrs. *See* Jameson, Rex (1924–1983).

Shuja ud-Daula (d. 1775). *See under* Oudh, nawab wazirs of (*act.* 1754–1814).

Shuldham, Molyneux, Baron Shuldham (1717/18?–1798), naval officer and politician, was the second son of the Revd Samuel Shuldham of Dublin and his wife, Elizabeth, daughter of Daniel Molyneux of Ballymurray, co. Longford. He entered the navy in 1732 as captain's servant in the *Cornwall*, with Captain George Forbes (later the earl of Granard). He afterwards served in the *Solebay* with Captain Charles Fanshawe, and for upwards of four years in the *Falkland* with Fitzroy Henry Lee. He passed his lieutenant's examination on 25 January 1739, being then described on his certificate as 'near twenty-two'.

On 31 August 1739 Shuldham was promoted lieutenant of the *Tilbury*, one of the ships which went to the West Indies with Sir Chaloner Ogle, and in 1741 he took part in the unsuccessful attack on Cartagena. In 1742 he was the *Tilbury*'s first lieutenant when, on 21 September, she was set on fire in a drunken squabble between a marine and the purser's boy and burnt, with a large proportion of the ship's company. Shuldham, with the captain and other officers, was tried by court martial on 15 October, but was acquitted of all blame. As commander of the bomb-vessel *Blast*, Shuldham fought with considerable gallantry to prevent her, ultimately unsuccessfully, from being taken by two Spanish privateers in the West Indies (19 October 1745). In recognition of his efforts he was on 12 May 1746 promoted captain of the frigate *Sheerness*, then employed on the coast of Scotland (BL, Add. MS 15956, fol. 191). In

Burkat Shudi (1702–1773), by Marcus Tuscher, c.1742 [*The Shudi Family Group*: Burkat Shudi (left), with (left to right) Joshua Shudi, Catherine Shudi, and the younger Burkat Shudi]

December 1748 he was appointed to the *Queenborough*, and in March 1749 to the *Unicorn*. In October 1754 he was appointed to the *Seaford*, from which, in March 1755, he was moved to the *Warwick* (60 guns), going to the West Indies, where, near Martinique on 11 March 1756, she fell in with a French 74-gun ship and two frigates, which overpowered and captured her. War had not then been declared, but hostilities had been going on for several months. Shuldham, with the crew of the *Warwick*, was sent to France, kept a prisoner at large at Poitiers for nearly two years, and returned to England in a cartel on 16 March 1758. A second court martial acquitted him of all blame for the loss of the ship.

On 25 July 1758 Shuldham was appointed to the *Panther*, in which he joined Commodore John Moore in the West Indies and took part in the reduction of Guadeloupe and its dependent islands from March to May 1759. In July he was moved by Moore into the *Raisonnable*, which was lost on a reef of rocks at Fort Royal off Martinique as she was standing in to engage a battery on 8 January 1762, when the island was attacked and reduced by Rear-Admiral George Rodney. In April Rodney appointed Shuldham to the *Marlborough*, from which a few days later he was moved by Sir George Pocock to the *Rochester*, and again by Rodney after a few weeks to the *Foudroyant*, in which he returned to England in 1763. In December 1766 he was appointed to the *Cornwall* guardship at Plymouth, and in November 1770 to the *Royal Oak*, then commissioned in readiness for the expected conflict with Spain. On 14 February 1772 he was appointed commodore, governor, and commander-in-chief on the Newfoundland station, which office he held for three years, and on 31 March 1775 he was promoted rear-admiral of the white.

Meanwhile in 1774 Shuldham was elected MP for Fowey, Cornwall, and became a loyal supporter of the North ministry. On 29 September 1775 he was appointed commander-in-chief on the coast of North America from the St Lawrence River to Cape Florida. He went to Boston with his flag in the *Chatham* (50 guns), arriving there on 30 December after a passage of sixty-one days. On 5 February 1776 he was promoted vice-admiral of the blue. His work was limited to covering the operations of the troops, and preventing the colonial trade, a task far beyond his resources. In June 1776 he was superseded by Lord Howe. Both Sandwich and the king sympathized with Shuldham and he was given an Irish peerage as Baron Shuldham (31 July 1776). That he was a brave and capable officer is well attested.

Early in 1777 Shuldham returned to England, and from 1778 to 1783 he was port-admiral at Plymouth. He was promoted admiral of the blue on 24 September 1787 and admiral of the white on 1 February 1793. On 4 October 1790 he married Margaret Irene, daughter of John Sarney of Somerset House, London, and widow of John Harcourt of Ankerwyke, Buckinghamshire; the couple had no children. He died at Lisbon in the autumn of 1798, whereupon the title became extinct. Shuldham's body was brought home from Lisbon in the same ship (the *Colossus*) as Sir William Hamilton's famous collection of Greek vases. The ship was wrecked in the Scillies and, though many of the vases were lost, Shuldham's body was recovered by heroic efforts.

J. K. LAUGHTON, *rev.* RUDDOCK MACKAY

Sources N. A. M. Rodger, *The insatiable earl: a life of John Montagu, fourth earl of Sandwich* (1993) · *The private papers of John, earl of Sandwich*, ed. G. R. Barnes and J. H. Owen, 4 vols., Navy RS, 69, 71, 75, 78 (1932–8) · W. L. Clowes, *The Royal Navy: a history from the earliest times to the present*, 7 vols. (1897–1903); repr. (1996–7), vol. 3 · D. Syrett, ed., *The siege and capture of Havana, 1762*, Navy RS, 114 (1970) · M. M. Drummond, 'Shuldham, Molyneux', HoP, *Commons, 1754–90* · D. Syrett and R. L. DiNardo, *The commissioned sea officers of the Royal Navy, 1660–1815*, rev. edn, Occasional Publications of the Navy RS, 1 (1994)
Archives Mulgrave Castle, Yorkshire, archives · NMM, corresp. with Lord Sandwich · PRO, Admiralty records
Likenesses W. Dickinson, mezzotint, pubd 1780 (after N. Dance), BM

Shurley, John (*fl.* 1681–1702). *See under* Shirley, John (*bap.* 1648, *d.* 1679).

Shute, Christopher (*d.* 1626), Church of England clergyman and religious controversialist, was probably a younger son of Christopher Shute of Oakington, Cambridgeshire, and younger brother of Robert *Shute (*d.* 1590), the future judge, who was born at Gargrave, Yorkshire. He matriculated as a pensioner from Pembroke College, Cambridge, in the Michaelmas term of 1561, graduated BA early in 1565, and proceeded MA in 1568. 'Hand-picked' (Collinson, 208) by Archbishop Edmund Grindal, who had been master of the college when he was first an undergraduate, Shute was ordained at York in August 1572 and licensed to preach throughout the diocese and province. On the presentation of the queen, but probably through the influence of either Grindal or George Clifford, earl of Cumberland, the local magnate, Shute was on 15 July 1576 instituted vicar of Giggleswick, Yorkshire.

The following year Shute published the first edition of his catechism, *The Testimonie of a True Fayth*, and *A verie godlie and necessary sermon preached before the young countess of Cumberland … the 24 of November 1577*. The latter stressed obedience to the word of God and Christian assurance, and called for right administration of the sacraments and for ecclesiastical discipline. Shute proceeded BD in 1580, and in 1581 issued a new version of his catechism as *A Compendius Forme and Summe of Christian Doctrine*. Its dedication to the earl of Cumberland acknowledged his patronage and emphasized the role of the Christian magistrate.

Shute was, or became, one of Cumberland's wealthier tenants in the lordship of Craven. On 17 August 1581 at Giggleswick he married Katherine Newhouse. They had at least five sons—Robert (*bap.* 1584), Nathaniel [*see below*], Josias *Shute (*bap.* 1588, *d.* 1643), Thomas [*see below*], and Timothy [*see below*]—and two daughters, Margaret and Mary.

Shute was almost certainly the author of *A Brief Resolution of a Right Religion, Touching the Controversies that are nowe in England* (1590). He explained to his readers that 'I shall hazard my person in running upon the cragged rockes of the pestilent toonged papistes … howbeit I mean well even to the Romish Catholickes themselves'. In his dedication to Francis Flower, esquire and JP, the publisher John Proctor declared that, of all those tackling the subject, 'none ... so largelie, and in such sweet maner deciphered true religion before, wherein contrarie sects are utterly put down, altogether making manifest what true faith is'. The work contained a further commendation from 'R. Armin'.

Shute was emerging as the pre-eminent leader of a flourishing and sometimes radical puritan tradition in Craven. As early as 1582 a Kirkby Malhamdale man had been presented before the northern court of high commission for misbehaving during one of his sermons, 'sayinge that it was a shame for him to tarry so longe in the pulpytt' (Marchant, 278). Ten years later, in 1592, records of a case of defamation brought before the same court reveal him as a participant in 'exercises' at Gargrave. In 1594 Shute himself became a member of high commission, yet the same year was presented for not using the cross in baptism and then, following his compliance on this point, for other nonconformist practices. However, such trouble as he experienced over the affair seems to have arisen from a quarrel with some parishioners: that he remained a commissioner and that the court's sole requirement was that he should preach a sermon approving the Book of Common Prayer is testimony both to the strength of puritanism and its patrons in the area and to the authorities' perception of the imperative for providing an effective preaching and pastoral ministry. In 1599 Shute was nominated a member of the commission for the investigation of schism in the northern province.

By the end of the century Shute was acting as the chairman of the governors of Giggleswick School, and in that capacity he began in 1599 to keep minutes of their meetings, preserved at the school in the 'Shute book'. At least three of his sons were pupils there, and between 1615 and 1619, probably as a temporary expedient, Shute also served as headmaster. He died at Giggleswick shortly after making his will on 9 October 1626, and was buried there on 14 October. His wife survived him, but was dead by 1 May 1628, when her will was proved.

All five of Shute's sons entered the ministry, a fact noted and celebrated by David Lloyd in his memoir of Josias. Robert, of whom little is known, was vicar of Lyn and predeceased his father. **Nathaniel Shute** (*bap.* 1587, *d.* 1638), who graduated BA from Christ's College, Cambridge, early in 1604 and proceeded MA in 1607, was rector of St Margaret Moyses, London, from 24 February 1614 to 1618, and of St Mildred Poultry from 23 January 1618. Described by Lloyd as 'an excellent scholar and solid preacher' (p. 295), he published only *Corona charitatis: the Crown of Charity* (1626), a funeral sermon for his friend Richard Fishburne, merchant, preached at the Mercers' chapel on 10 May 1625. Shute died in 1638 and was buried on 11 August, his funeral sermon being preached by Richard Holdsworth; admonition of his will was granted on 24 September to his son Christopher.

Thomas Shute (*bap.* 1590, *d.* 1618x26) matriculated from Trinity College, Cambridge, in 1605, graduated BA

from Peterhouse in 1609, was ordained deacon and priest in Chester on 17 February 1611, and proceeded MA in 1612. He became domestic chaplain to Bishop George Lloyd of Chester and preached his funeral sermon in 1615. He was still a preacher in the city in 1618 but dead by the time his father made his will in October 1626. **Timothy Shute** (*bap.* 1592, *d.* in or before 1659) matriculated from Peterhouse, Cambridge, in the Easter term of 1609, graduated BA in 1613, and proceeded MA in 1616. It was almost certainly he who married Precilla Spackman on 21 October 1619 at St Nicholas Cole Abbey, London; their son Christopher was baptized there on 28 November 1623, but was not among the three sons and three daughters of the marriage named in Shute's will, dated 1645. Timothy was rector of Holy Trinity, Exeter, from 1628 and a prebendary of Exeter Cathedral from 1630. On 6 October 1636 he married at St Thomas the Apostle, Exeter, Joane or Jane Moore, a widow with two sons. According to John Walker, on his refusal to take the covenant Timothy Shute was ejected from his Exeter livings in 1645 and disqualified from holding others, but in 1645 and 1647 he appears as rector of Lawhitton, Cornwall, and in 1650 as rector of Farway, where on 8 January 1655 he or his son was admitted by the triers. The date of his death is unknown. In his will he left, among many other bequests, works by George Downame, Richard Holdsworth, and Aquinas; notes he and his brother Josias had compiled went to his sons Thomas and Timothy, who were destined for the ministry. They proved the will on 24 February 1659.　VIVIENNE LARMINIE

Sources Venn, *Alum. Cant.* · T. D. Whitaker, *The history and antiquities of the deanery of Craven, in the county of York*, 3rd edn, ed. A. W. Morant (1878), 166–9 · R. Marchant, *The puritans and the church courts in the diocese of York, 1560–1642* (1960), 22–4, 31, 278 · P. Collinson, *Archbishop Grindal, 1519–1583: the struggle for a reformed church* (1979), 208, 211 · R. T. Spence, *The privateering earl* (1995), 27, 34 · T. Brayshaw and R. M. Robinson, *A history of the ancient parish of Giggleswick* (1932) · *Walker rev.*, 123 · D. Lloyd, *Memoires of the lives ... of those ... personages that suffered ... for the protestant religion* (1668), 293, 295 · G. Hennessy, *Novum repertorium ecclesiasticum parochiale Londinense, or, London diocesan clergy succession from the earliest time to the year 1898* (1898), 285 · copy of Chancery probate file of will of Christopher Shute, Feb 1626 [1627], Borth. Inst. · will, 1 May 1628, Borth. Inst., V 20 [Katherine Shute], fol. 198 · PRO, PROB 6/16, fol. 207r [administration for Nathaniel Shute, son] · PRO, PROB 11/288, fol. 99r–v [will of Timothy Shute, son] · *IGI* · Rymer, *Foedera*, 3rd edn, 7/1.225

Shute, John (*d.* 1563), writer on architecture, was probably born in Cullompton, Devon. A painter–stainer by training, he is presumably the 'John Shute paynter' whose new house in Grantham Lane, London, is referred to in a deed dated 6 December 1550. In 1561 Shute was paid £12 for making the Merchant Taylors' Company's pageant at the lord mayor's show. He may also be identified with the limner, or miniature portrait painter, named as Shoote in Richard Haydocke's *A Tracte Containing the Artes of Curious Painting Carvinge & Buildinge* (1598, 126). But nothing else is known of his professional life, and no paintings have been attributed to him.

By Shute's own account, it was as a servant of John Dudley, first duke of Northumberland, that he was sent to Italy in 1550 'ther to confer with the doinges of the skilful maisters in architectur, & also to view such auncient Monumentes hereof as are yet extant' (Shute, dedication). His itinerary certainly included a stay in Rome, and he returned to England with drawings of buildings, sculptures, and paintings. Northumberland showed these to Edward VI, but it was not until 1563—ten years after Northumberland's death—that Shute published *The first and chief groundes of architecture used in all the auncient and famous monymentes: with a farther & more ample discouse uppon the same, than hitherto hath been set out by any other.* Dedicated to Queen Elizabeth, it was the first architectural treatise published in Britain, and the first in the English language. A licence for printing it in London was granted to Thomas Marshe some time between 20 March and 22 July 1563. The title-page description of Shute as a 'Paynter and Archytecte' need not imply that he ever practised architecture.

The First and Chief Groundes is principally concerned with the origins and proportions of the five classical orders of architecture (Tuscan, Doric, Ionic, Corinthian, and Composite), as established in a similar treatise by the Italian architect Sebastiano Serlio (*Regole generali di architetura*, 1537). Shute relates each of these to the personification of an appropriate Greek deity. He also describes a sixth order, the Attic, citing Vitruvius, Pliny the elder, and the arch of Septimius Severus and the Pantheon in Rome, and throughout the treatise develops fresh interpretations of his subject, based on reading and observation. The text is illustrated with original woodcuts and metalcuts after Shute's own designs; if he executed the latter, which is plausible, he is the first English-born engraver whose name is known.

Scholars are divided as to the influence of Shute's treatise. He himself confessed that his subject was 'knit unto all the Mathematicalles' (Shute, preface): thus he was forced to introduce unfamiliar terminology into the English language, which would have made his text difficult to comprehend. There is hardly any surviving evidence that his designs were imitated: pilasters at Kimbolton Castle and Kirby Hall were copied from the title-page border design, but this woodcut was almost certainly not drawn by Shute. Only the Roman Doric order of the nearly contemporary screen at Middle Temple Hall has been positively linked to Shute's illustrations. On the other hand, his book was directed at a wide range of artisans besides architects, and it was popular enough to be abridged for a new edition dated 1587. There is good evidence to suggest that it was also reprinted or reissued in 1580 and 1584, although no copies of these printings can now be traced. Shute intended to publish more on architecture, but he died in the year *The First and Chief Groundes* was published. He was buried in the church of St Edmund, King and Martyr, Lombard Street, London. A verse epitaph giving his date of death as 25 September 1563 was recorded before its destruction in the great fire. GERALD BEASLEY

Sources J. Shute, *The first and chief groundes of architecture*, ed. L. Weaver (1912) • E. Harris and N. Savage, *British architectural books and writers, 1556–1785* (1990) • A. Wells-Cole, *Art and decoration in Elizabethan and Jacobean England* (1997) • V. Hart, 'From virgin to courtesan in early English Vitruvian books', *Paper palaces: the rise of the Renaissance architectural treatise*, ed. V. Hart and P. Hicks (1998), 297–318 • Bryan, *Painters* (1903–5) • J. Stow, *A survay of London*, ed. A. M. [A. Munday], rev. edn (1618), 382–3 • J. Robertson and D. J. Gordon, eds., 'A calendar of dramatic records in the books of the livery companies of London, 1485–1640', *Malone Society Collections*, 3 (1954), 41–4

Shute, John (*fl.* 1557–1598), translator and soldier, is of unknown origins. His first translation from the Italian, *Two very notable commentaries, the one of the originall of the Turcks and empire of the house of Ottomano, written by Andrew Cambini and the other of the warres of the Turke against George Scanderbeg, prince of Epiro* was published in 1562. It was dedicated to his singular good lord and master Sir Edward Fynes, Lord Clinton, high admiral of England and Ireland. This suggests that he was the Captain John Shute who was included in the list of names of the lords and gentlemen who attended Clinton to France in 1557. Clinton became governor of the Tower of London in 1553 and Shute was made a gunner of the Tower of London and yeoman of the ordnance for life in 1569. In his dedicatory epistle to Clinton, Shute promotes the idea that a trained, skilful, and fit soldier was better than an untrained man. Shute uses examples from classical literature to reinforce this. He apologizes to the reader for the roughness of the translation, as he had not been brought up in schools. He added a table of contents and marginalia to the original.

Shute's *The firste parte of the Christian instruction and generall some of the doctrine, conteyned in holy scriptures*, translated from the French of Peter Viret and published in 1565, was dedicated to the earl of Leicester by 'a simple solider, better practised abroad in martial arts than furnished at home with the cunning of the school'. A continuation of *Christian Instruction* was translated and published in 1573 dedicated to Clinton's wife, Elizabeth, countess of Lincoln. Another translation of a work by Viret, *The principal points which at this day are in controversie concerning the holy supper of Jesus Christ, and the mass of the Roman Church* (1579), was dedicated to Sir Francis Walsingham. Shute had been connected with Walsingham from December 1573 to January 1574 when he travelled to Lowestoft in Suffolk to view soldiers returned from Holland with captains Bingen and Morgan, for which he was paid £10. During the Armada scare of 1587–8 Shute raised 2000 footmen and 200 horse from Surrey and Sussex, receiving £20 for this. He had retired from the post of yeoman of the ordnance by 1600 as a letter from his successor dated in that year says that as a yeoman Shute had refused to conduct the ordnance from place to place on the grounds that he was a leader of men not of carts. Shute had been given a pension by Bishop Horne of Winchester. In 1598 Shute had to write to Sir Robert Cecil to ask for his intercession in getting the pension paid. When Cecil had arranged this Shute wrote him a note of thanks. This is Shute's last appearance in the records. E. LORD

Sources *Two very notable commentaries, … by A. Cambini*, trans. J. Shute (1562) • P. Viret, *The firste parte of the Christian instruction*, trans. J. Shute (1565) • P. Viret, *A Christian instruction*, trans. I. S. [J. Shute] (1573) • [J. Shute], *The principal points* (1579) • APC, 1571–5, 1587–8 • C. T. Martin, ed., 'Journal of Sir Francis Walsingham, from

December 1570 to April 1583', *Camden miscellany, VI*, CS, 104 (1871) · *Calendar of the manuscripts of the most hon. the marquis of Salisbury*, 24 vols., HMC, 9 (1883–1976), vols. 1, 8, 10 · *CPR, 1566–9* · *CSP dom.*, 1547–80

Shute, Josias (*bap.* 1588, *d.* 1643), Church of England clergyman, was baptized on 11 August 1588 in Giggleswick, Yorkshire, the fifth of the nine children of Christopher *Shute (*d.* 1626), vicar of Giggleswick, and his wife, Katherine Newhouse. He was educated at the free school in Giggleswick, and in 1602 matriculated from Trinity College, Cambridge, where he graduated BA in 1605 and proceeded MA in 1609. He was ordained priest on 3 June 1610, and on 30 November the next year was instituted to the rectory of St Mary Woolnoth, London, where he remained until his death. On 25 April 1614 he married Elizabeth Glanvild, one of his parishioners, whom he later described in his will as 'my truly loving and dear wife'; they had no children.

Shute was one of the most widely respected preachers of his day: John Hacket styled him 'Generalis Praedicatorum', the preacher-general of the City of London. According to Ephraim Udall, in the 1645 edition of Shute's *Judgement and Mercy*, he preached 'thrice a weeke ordinarily, and often upon other occasions', and habitually rose from bed at 4 a.m., spending the day 'pinned in his chair to his study and to his bookes, being not willing to be troubled'. None of his sermons was printed during his lifetime, although he bequeathed 'all my paper books and writings' to his brother Timothy *Shute [*see under* Shute, Christopher], perhaps with a view to posthumous publication. Such was his popularity, however, that notes from his sermons were frequently taken down by members of the audience, and some of these later found their way into print. Notes from his sermons on Exodus 4: 21–7, probably preached about 1628–9, are preserved in the British Library (Add. MS 14900), and nine sermons on Exodus 8: 1–10, evidently part of the same series, were published under the title *Judgement and Mercy* (1645). Excerpts from another course of sermons on the book of Ezra were published as *Divine Cordials Delivered in Ten Sermons* (1644) from the shorthand notes of one William Reynolds, but the sole authorized edition of any of Shute's sermons was *Sarah and Hagar* (1649), a series of nineteen sermons on Genesis chapter 16, 'published according to his own original manuscripts, circumspectly examined and faithfully transcribed' by Edward Sparke, rector of St Martin Pomeroy, Ironmonger Lane, London. Shute was also much in demand as a preacher to the East India Company: in September 1633 he preached 'a sermon of thanksgiving to Almighty God for returning their ships and estates in safety' in which he protested against the recent reduction in mariners' wages (*CSP col.*, 8.457, 468).

Shute was later described as one of those divines 'whose standing in the gap, when superstition was rushing in, drew upon them that venerable nickname of Puritans', and this was said to be the reason why he received no preferment until April 1642, not long before his death, when he was appointed archdeacon of Colchester. However, he was equally firm in his opposition to religious radicalism, and the same account describes him as 'so earnest a lover of union and right devotion that the dividing Separatist and superstitious Papist received a wound from him at every Lecture' (*An elegiacall Commemoration*). In November 1642 he was ordered to be imprisoned for refusing to contribute to the support of parliament, but it is not clear whether he was actually sent to prison: according to Robert Chestlin, he was merely 'molested, and vext to death, and denyed a Funerall Sermon to be preached by Dr Holdsworth as he desired', while another account states that he continued preaching until three months before his death, and then retired to the country house of one of his parishioners, a few miles out of London. His last recorded sermon, probably preached in 1642 or 1643, warns that 'Reformation must not bee by Faction and Tumult', and complains: 'The Impudency of some new preachers now, and the Ignorance of others, will foole us out of our Religion' (CUL, MS Dd.5.31, fol. 136). In 1643 he was appointed a member of the Westminster assembly, but did not live to attend it. He died on 13 June 1643, and was buried in the chancel of St Mary Woolnoth on 14 June, when several thousand people attended his funeral. His will bequeathed the sum of £5 per annum to the governors of Giggleswick School to establish a university exhibition there. His wife outlived him by nearly thirty years, dying on 11 June 1670 at the age of over a hundred.

ARNOLD HUNT

Sources J. Shute, *Judgement and mercy, or, The plague of frogges inflicted, removed* (1645) · *An elegiacall commemoration of the pious life … of Mr Josiah Shute* (1643) · [Chestlin], *Persecutio undecima: the churches eleventh persecution* (1648) · J. Hacket, *A century of sermons upon several remarkable subjects* (1675) · parish register, Giggleswick, 11 Aug 1588, N. Yorks. CRO, PR/GGW/1 [baptism] · will, LMA, DL/C/421 (bundle 21/9) · J. M. S. Brooke and A. W. C. Hallen, eds., *The transcript of the registers of … St Mary Woolnoth and St Mary Woolnoth Haw … 1538 to 1760* (1886) · *CSP col.*, vol. 8 · notes on sermons by Shute, BL, Add. MS 14900 · notes on sermons, CUL, MS Dd.5.31 · *Walker rev.*, 57

Archives CUL, sermons, Add. MS 8469

Likenesses W. Marshall, line engraving, BM, NPG; repro. in J. Shute, *Sarah and Hagar* (1649)

Wealth at death land valued at £7 2s. p.a.; cash bequests of £110: will, LMA, DL/C/421

Shute, Nathaniel (*bap.* 1587, *d.* 1638). *See under* Shute, Christopher (*d.* 1626).

Shute, Nevile. *See* Norway, Nevil Shute (1899–1960).

Shute, Richard (*d.* 1660), merchant and local politician, was a resident of St Lawrence Jewry in or before 1629. In that year his infant son was baptized there, the first of three of his children whose baptisms were recorded in the parish register, but nothing is known about the family or geographical origins of Shute or his wife, Mary. In the early 1630s Shute served as a sidesman and collector for the poor in St Lawrence Jewry. A member of the Haberdashers' Company, he was apparently not as prosperous in his early career as he later became. In a London assessment of 1638 he was rated with the middling sort, and a political detractor ridiculed him in 1643 as 'that broken citizen, out at elbowes, called Satten Shute' ('Letter from Mercurius Civicus', 4.596).

Some time before 1640 Shute seems to have become a

factor for Maurice Thompson (or Thomson), an interloping colonial trader and one of the most notable London merchants of the era. Thereafter Shute became highly visible among the new colonial merchants who gained commercial and political ascendancy in London during the civil war years: in 1642 he became a commissioner for the 'additional sea adventure' to Ireland, an enterprise in which numerous investors undertook to raise a military expedition in return for lands confiscated from Irish rebels; and the following year he became collector of tonnage and poundage for the port of London. In 1647 Shute and Thompson were part of a syndicate that sought to replace the existing customs commission, and in 1648 they were involved in a contract for provisioning the army in Ireland. By the late 1640s the geographical scope of Shute's commercial interests had extended to Brazil, to the East Indies (as an interloper), and possibly to the Guinea–West Indies slave trade. In 1648 one of several ships of which he was part owner was lost to the Dutch off the coast of Brazil with a cargo valued at £30,000.

Shute emerged as a militant London puritan spokesman in the early 1640s. In September 1640 he and Thompson presented a petition, which they had promoted in the City, to Charles I at York. Reportedly bearing 10,000 signatures, it demanded a meeting of parliament and an end to the regime's fiscal and religious innovations. When relations between the king and the leadership of the Commons collapsed in January 1642, Shute was named to the London militia committee, and he also served as treasurer of the parliamentary committee of safety. He worked with Lord Mayor Isaac Penington to assist John Pym and the Commons leaders in organizing their war effort.

With Sir David Watkins, Randall Mainwaring, and others, Shute presented petitions to the Commons in November and December 1642 that condemned efforts at reconciliation with the king and deplored the inadequate organization of the parliamentarian army. The petitioners offered to raise a London cavalry troop and Shute became active in raising funds for it. The petitioners also proposed two innovations for financing the war. The first of these was the system of weekly assessments in London that was quickly adopted by parliament and extended throughout the country; Shute served as a treasurer for the weekly assessments in London. The second proposal, which encouraged the imposition of reparations on active royalists, was not fully adopted until 1644. Shute was eventually appointed to the commission for compounding with royalists who were delinquent in paying their fines.

The culmination of Shute's petitioning activities came on 30 March 1643 when he and his associates presented a further 'petition and remonstrance' to common council and to parliament. Their offer to raise and finance volunteer troops was accepted by parliament, and the committee established at Salters' Hall to superintend this endeavour superseded Shute's earlier military fund-raising. The language of the remonstrance reflected the advanced constitutional position occupied by Shute and his friends. Anticipating some of the Leveller programme, it asserted that 'originally the Supreme power' was 'in the whole people' and that annual parliaments should exercise that power in trust, without royal restraint, for the peace and safety of the kingdom (*Remonstrans Redivivus*, 4).

Shute was less active after 1643, having been reprimanded by the Commons in December 1642 for his intemperate denunciation of a London peace petition. He was a member of the vestry for the parish of St Katharine Cree in 1644–6, and in 1645–8 he was a trier in the London classis of the reformed national church. However, Shute's association with London Independent clergy such as Jeremiah Burroughs, John Goodwin, and Hugh Peters during the petitions of 1642–3 suggests that his identification with the national establishment was weakening. He was an author of the 1647 *Declaration by Congregational Societies in, and about the City of London*, which sought to distance religious Independency from the Levellers.

After the New Model Army's intervention in London in 1648 Shute was returned to the common council for the ward of Langbourn in 1649 and 1650. He was a prominent civic friend of the army leadership and served on new commissions for the London militia and assessments and for the navy and customs. He supported the revolution in city politics that transferred power from the lord mayor and aldermen to the common council, and he was a member of a civic delegation to the Rump Parliament that demanded that Charles I be held accountable for warring against the nation. He was twice nominated for the court of aldermen in 1649 and was nominated again in 1651, but he was not elected. He sat on a court that tried prominent royalists in 1649, and was appointed to the high courts of justice of the Commonwealth and protectorate in 1650, 1653, and 1654. He was one of the signatories of another declaration of the London independent churches in 1651. In 1653 Shute and two partners made an unsuccessful proposal to take over the foreign post for England, Scotland, and Ireland.

Shute was apparently still in England in 1658, but he died in 1660, between 2 August, when he made his will, and 25 October, when it was proved, 'in parts beyond the seas'. He had perhaps emigrated or fled after the Restoration (Blagg, 544). GARY S. DE KREY

Sources R. Brenner, *Merchants and revolution: commercial change, political conflict, and London's overseas traders, 1550–1653* (1993) • C. H. Firth and R. S. Rait, eds., *Acts and ordinances of the interregnum, 1642–1660*, 1 (1911), 9–10, 795, 872, 914, 1191, 1259, 1261; 2 (1911), 38, 302, 365, 471, 668, 781, 917, 1015 • K. Lindley, *Popular politics and religion in civil war London* (1997), 10, 32, 293, 306–10, 335, 338 • *CSP dom.*, addenda, 1625–49, 654; 1649–50, 33, 287, 349, 505; 1650, 214, 404, 423; 1651–2, 84, 312, 445; 1652–3, 178, 448–9; 1653–4, 266, 549; 1654, 425; 1655, 133; 1657–8, 515 • Greaves & Zaller, *BDBR*, 167–8 • V. Pearl, *London and the outbreak of the puritan revolution: city government and national politics, 1625–1643* (1961), 174, 252–3, 255, 260–61 • A. W. Hughes Clarke, ed., *The register of St Lawrence Jewry, London*, 1, Harleian Society, registers, 70 (1940), 41–2, 45 • Tai Liu, *Puritan London: a study of religion and society in the City parishes* (1986), 85, 100, 185, 231 • M. Tolmie, *The triumph of the saints: the separate churches of London, 1616–1649* (1977), 140–41, 169–71 • *A true copie of the remonstrance and petition, presented to the honourable the House of Commons … by Sir David Watkins knight, Mr Shuite, and others* (1642) • *Remonstrans redivivus, or, An accompt of the remonstrance and petition* (1643) • 'A letter from Mercurius Civicus to Mercurius Rusticus', *A collection of scarce* *and valuable tracts ... Lord Somers*, ed. W. Scott, 2nd edn, 4 (1810), 596 · T. M. Blagg, ed., *Index of wills proved in the prerogative court of Canterbury*, 8 (1936), 544 · T. C. Dale, ed., *The inhabitants of London in 1638*, 1 (1931), 84 · *A declaration by congregational societies in and about the City of London* (1647) · *A declaration of divers elders and brethren of congregationall societies* (1651) · M. A. E. Green, ed., *Calendar of the proceedings of the committee for advance of money, 1642–1656*, 1, PRO (1888), 3, 6 · M. A. E. Green, ed., *Calendar of the proceedings of the committee for compounding ... 1643–1660*, 1, PRO (1889), 8, 10, 30 · W. A. Shaw, ed., *Calendar of treasury books*, 1, PRO (1904), 47 · *JHC*, 2 (1640–42), 847, 857, 887 · A. B. Beaven, ed., *The aldermen of the City of London, temp. Henry III–[1912]*, 1 (1908), 13, 95, 149 · J. Farnell, 'The politics of the City of London, 1649–1657', PhD diss., University of Chicago, 1963, 240, 257, 365 · B. Manning, *The English people and the English revolution, 1640–1649* (1976), 223 · PRO, PROB 11/300, sig. 172 (fol. 95v)

Shute, Robert (*d.* 1590), judge, was born at Gargrave in Yorkshire but his father, Christopher Shute, resided at Oakington, Cambridgeshire, and it was there that Robert made his home. Cooper said he was probably educated at Christ's College, Cambridge, perhaps because it was his son's college, though he is more likely the Shutte admitted as a scholar of Peterhouse in 1542 or 1544. What is known for certain is that he studied at Barnard's Inn in the late 1540s before being admitted to Gray's Inn in 1550. He was doubtless patronized by his neighbour Sir John Hynde, justice of the common pleas and former bencher of Gray's Inn, whose widow left Shute £4 a year in 1555, 'towards his fyndynge at the innes of court' (PRO, PROB 11/37, fol. 262). By 1557 he was an ancient of Gray's Inn, and the following year the borough of Cambridge elected him as their recorder in succession to George Freville. He made a Latin oration to the queen when she visited Cambridge in 1564, and represented Cambridge in the parliaments of 1571 and 1572–81. In November 1577 he was created serjeant-at-law, his patrons being Lord Burghley and Lord North, and gave a double reading in Gray's Inn as serjeant-elect.

Shute's appointment as second baron of the exchequer on 1 June 1579 made a new departure. Until then the junior barons had never been serjeants and therefore did not go on circuit as assize judges, associate with the judges of the coif in the serjeants' inns (except by invitation), or wear full judicial robes with linings. After Shute the barons were always serjeants and became full members of the higher judiciary. Shute's patent gave him 'the same order, rank, estimation, dignity, and pre-eminence' as the puisne justices of the benches, and an increased stipend of £80, though parity of stipend with the other courts was not reached until 1645. On 8 February 1585 Shute was translated to the queen's bench, with arrears of salary from the death of his predecessor, William Ayloffe, in November 1584. On his deathbed, on 14 April 1590, he said to his wife, Thomasine, 'Thou haste ben a good wife to me and I have ben true to the, and I do give the all my worldlie goodes' (PRO, PROB 11/75, fol. 236). This nuncupative will was proved on 5 May. Thomasine was the daughter of Christopher Burgoyne of Long Stanton, Cambridgeshire. She was the judge's only wife, and they had at least eight children. The eldest son, Francis, settled at Upton, Leicestershire, and was the ancestor of John Shute *Barrington,

first Viscount Barrington (1678–1734). Shute was probably buried at Oakington.

Shute's fourth son, **Robert Shute** (*d.* 1621), matriculated from Christ's College, Cambridge, in 1598, and graduated bachelor of arts in 1601–2. He was admitted to Gray's Inn in 1600 and called to the bar in 1605. He seems to have lived a disreputable life; he became heavily in debt, and was outlawed seventeen times. Attaching himself to George Villiers, the future duke of Buckingham, he secured through his influence the chief clerkship of the king's bench (jointly with Robert Heath) in 1616, under a settlement by John Roper, first Lord Teynham, against the wishes of Sir Edward Coke. On the death of Richard Martin in 1618, Shute became the court candidate for the recordership of London, but was refused on account of his past and Heath was elected instead. In 1620 Shute's reputation underwent a change. During Lent he delivered a reading in Gray's Inn, where he had been a bencher since 1617, and on 29 December he was returned to parliament for St Albans. John Lewis dedicated *Ignis coelestis* to him the same year. The recordership becoming vacant again on Heath's appointment as solicitor-general, Shute was elected on 20 January 1621, the king remarking that, although there was formerly some colour for the objections against him, 'there was none now, besides which he hath since been reader of that society, whereby he hath given public satisfaction of his worth and ability in that profession' (Overall, 294, 303). However, he died within a few days of achieving his ambition, before 10 February.

J. H. BAKER

Sources Foss, *Judges* · HoP, *Commons, 1558–1603*, 3.379–80 · Baker, *Serjeants*, 57, 172, 305, 434, 537 · Sainty, *Judges*, 30, 104, 106, 122 · Cooper, *Ath. Cantab.*, 2.92 · Venn, *Alum. Cant.*, 1/4.71 · *N&Q*, 7th ser., 3 (1887), 203 · R. J. Fletcher, ed., *The pension book of Gray's Inn*, 1 (1901) · PRO, PROB 11/37, sig. 35 [Ursula Hynde's will] · will, PRO, PROB 11/75, sig. 30 · T. A. Walker, *A biographical register of Peterhouse men*, 1 (1927), 137, 144 · W. R. Prest, *The rise of the barristers: a social history of the English bar, 1590–1640* (1986), 391 · *CSP dom., 1603–25* · *Analytical index, to the series of records known as Remembrancia, preserved among the archives of the City of London*, Corporation of London, ed. [W. H. Overall and H. C. Overall] (1878), 294, 303 · *DNB*

Shute, Robert (*d.* 1621). *See under* Shute, Robert (*d.* 1590).

Shute, Samuel (*d.* 1685), local politician, was the son of Francis Shute and his wife, Elizabeth. A linen draper by trade, he lived in the parish of St Peter's Cornhill, London, from 1658, when he married Anne Caryl (*d.* 1711), daughter of the Independent divine Joseph *Caryl. They had at least five children: three sons (two of whom died before Samuel and the third the year after) and two daughters, both of whom were alive when he made his will in April 1684.

Uncertainties in the Shute genealogy make Samuel's relationship to the civil war activist Richard Shute unclear, but they were probably closely related. Samuel and his brother Benjamin, with whom he has been confused, moved in the same London Independent circles that had attracted Richard Shute. They and their wives belonged to Joseph Caryl's gathered church; and, when Caryl's church merged with that of Dr John Owen after

Caryl's death in 1673, they were friends of their new pastor and his assistant, Robert Ferguson. Yet Samuel and Benjamin Shute also held offices that point to the prominence the London Shutes had achieved during the civil war and the interregnum: Samuel was the king's draper in 1681; and the brothers were controllers for the ports of Cardiff and Swansea.

Samuel Shute played a leading role, as a major civic whig, in the London conclusion to the parliamentary crisis of 1678–83. In 1681 he became prime warden of the Dyers' Company. He was nominated for aldermanic vacancies in 1681–2, but he was passed over by the tory aldermanic majority. He served on common council for Cornhill in 1682–3 and, contrary to the wishes of Charles II, he was elected sheriff of London and Middlesex, with Thomas Pilkington, for 1681–2.

As sheriff Samuel Shute was fully involved in whig efforts to prevent Charles from regaining control of the corporation of London. He and Pilkington impanelled the London juries that returned *ignoramus* verdicts to the government's indictments of Stephen College in July 1681 and of the earl of Shaftesbury in November 1681. Indeed Shute reportedly encouraged the whig crowds that celebrated Shaftesbury's acquittal with the words, 'Shout, boys, … shout' (*CSP dom.*, *1680–81*, 583). Shute and Pilkington were similarly instrumental in securing common hall majorities for whig candidates in the London shrieval election of 1682, only to see them overturned by the crown's agents. They clashed repeatedly with the loyalist lord mayor about polling, defied orders of the privy council, and were dispatched to the Tower at one point by an enraged monarch. Shute was one of fourteen leading civic whigs charged with riot in this election, a charge of which they were convicted in 1683. Shute was then fined 1000 marks.

Tory satirists such as John Dryden and Nahum Tate dismissed Shute as 'hot-brain'd', as a lightweight 'shuttlecock', and as being as often 'warm with wine' as he was 'drunk with zeal' (Lord and others, 3.275, 195). Shute was regularly in the company of whig grandees such as Shaftesbury and Monmouth during his shrievalty; and, after the disclosures about whig plotting in 1682–3, Lord Howard of Escrick claimed that he had been told that Shute was 'ready for action' (*CSP dom.*, *July–September 1683*, 92). Shute's son Francis, who died in 1683, apparently acted as an intermediary between Howard and Robert West, one of the masterminds of the Rye House Plot. In the absence of other evidence, the government ignored Howard's information about Samuel Shute.

Shute died in 1685 with personalty worth about £9000, city property, a house in Essex, and lands in Shropshire, Glamorgan, and Montgomeryshire. He was buried on 12 November 1685 in the parish church of St Peter's Cornhill. Two kinsmen preserved the family's prominence into the next generation. Samuel *Shute (1662–1742) was governor of the Massachusetts Bay Colony from 1716 to 1727. John Shute *Barrington (1678–1734) was MP for Berwick upon Tweed from 1715 to 1723.　　　　　GARY S. DE KREY

Sources J. R. Woodhead, *The rulers of London, 1660–1689* (1965), 149 · A. B. Beaven, ed., *The aldermen of the City of London, temp. Henry III–[1912]*, 1 (1908), 42, 61 · CSP dom., 1679–80, 264, 274–5; 1680–81, 328, 330, 332–4, 440, 477, 574, 583, 588; 1682, 11, 53, 147, 264, 270, 272, 316, 412, 415, 417, 548, 561, 584; Jan–June 1683, 41; July–Sept 1683, 92; 1684–5, 258 [with the exception of the 1679–80 vol., Samuel Shute was consistently and incorrectly indexed in *CSP domestic* as Benjamin Shute] · will, PRO, PROB 11/341 [Joseph Caryl, father-in-law], quire 33 · will, PRO, PROB 11/367 [Benjamin Shute, brother], quire 123 · will, PRO, PROB 11/381, sig. 196 · G. de F. Lord and others, eds., *Poems on affairs of state: Augustan satirical verse, 1660–1714*, 7 vols. (1963–75), vol. 3, pp. 195, 275 · N. Luttrell, *A brief historical relation of state affairs from September 1678 to April 1714*, 1 (1857), 102, 119, 124, 129, 156, 194, 199–200, 207, 225, 230, 243, 245, 250, 257, 263 · *State trials*, 9.187–298 · Newdigate newsletter, 25 June 1681, Folger, L.c.1092 · T. G. Crippen, 'Dr Watts's church-book', *Transactions of the Congregationalist Historical Society*, 1 (April 1901), 28 · G. W. G. Leveson Gower, ed., *A register of … the parish of Saint Peeters upon Cornhill*, 2 vols., Harleian Society, register section, 1, 4 (1877–9), vol. 2, pp. 89, 90, 95, 97, 99, 109, 123 · K. H. D. Haley, *The first earl of Shaftesbury* (1968), 657, 669, 681, 693, 699–700, 703, 717, 718 [Samuel Shute misidentified as Benjamin Shute] · T. Harris, *London crowds in the reign of Charles II* (1987), 130, 181, 185 · R. L. Greaves, *Secrets of the kingdom: British radicals from the Popish Plot to the revolution of 1688–89* (1992), 37, 96, 152, 170, 383, 386 [Samuel Shute misidentified as both Benjamin and Richard Shute] · M. S. Zook, *Radical whigs and conspiratorial politics in late Stuart England* (1999), 16, 18

Wealth at death personalty value approx. £9000; plus city property; house in Essex, lands in Shropshire, Montgomeryshire, Glamorgan: will, PRO, PROB 11/381, sig. 196; Woodhead, *Rulers of London*, 149

Shute, Samuel (1662–1742), colonial governor and army officer, was born on 12 January 1662, the son of Benjamin Shute and Patience, the daughter of Joseph *Caryl, clergyman and ejected minister. Shute was educated initially by Charles Morton, Puritan minister, was admitted to the Middle Temple on 23 November 1683, then to Christ's College, Cambridge (leaving without taking a degree), and finally to the University of Leiden. He preferred a military career, however, serving as a captain in Marlborough's European campaigns. He was wounded at the battle of Blenheim (1704) and ultimately rose to the rank of lieutenant-colonel in the 3rd dragoon guards.

As a reward for his service Shute became governor of Massachusetts in 1716. He landed in Boston that October, and found himself embroiled in the factional struggles that remained from the administration of his predecessor, Joseph Dudley. Dudley and his son Paul favoured the issuance of paper currency by the government, whereas the popular party, headed by Elisha Cooke, had proposed a privately run land bank. Dudley had won the Massachusetts assembly's support on this issue, and Shute continued his policies.

Cooke, who speculated heavily in Maine lands, retaliated in 1718 by charging that John Bridger, the surveyor of the king's woods, had been collecting bribes that allowed some people to cut down trees reserved for the Royal Navy while preventing others from engaging in legitimate lumbering. Shute backed Bridger while Cooke persuaded the assembly his cause was just. The governor removed Cooke as clerk of the superior court and refused to allow his election to the provincial council in 1718. In defiance the house elected Cooke speaker in 1719, a choice Shute vetoed.

Shute had little peace for the rest of his administration. The assembly cut his salary by twenty per cent, refused to provide presents for the Abenaki Indians in Maine, and then declined to vote funds to fight them when war subsequently broke out. A drunken Cooke accosted him on the street and called him a blockhead. Instead of dealing with a minor Indian menace his successor easily handled, Shute and the assembly debated that body's power to adjourn without the governor's consent and argued constantly for the last three years of his administration.

Shute suddenly left for England on 1 January 1723, after someone took a pot shot at him in his home, narrowly missing him. He was followed by Cooke, who joined province agent Jeremiah Dummer in debating the same two issues of the house's right to self-adjournment and independently to elect its speaker. Finally, in 1726, the crown forced the Massachusetts legislature to accept an explanatory charter which gave the governor the right to veto the house speaker and only allowed the house to adjourn for two days, or over the weekend, without the governor's permission.

Although Shute was vindicated he was in no hurry to return to Massachusetts. When George I died in 1727, and all royal commissions were thus vacated, the ministry replaced Shute with William Burnet, who would continue to argue with the Massachusetts assembly over the limits of its privileges. Shute tried in vain to recover his unpaid salary from the Massachusetts legislature, but was placated with a royal pension of £400 per year. He retired to private life, and died on 15 April 1742 while living in Westminster. He probably never married, for his will left several hundred pounds to nephews, nieces, a sister, and to several dissenting church charities in equal proportion, without mention of a wife or children.

Shute is a prime exemplar of the many military men sent by Britain to govern the colonies in the hopes that their experience could discipline the unruly provincials. But in time of peace there was little incentive for a colony to co-operate with British desires to curtail the liberties which the local legislatures claimed. Shute had begun as a friend of the colonies, thinking his dissenting connections would make his rule easy. He soon learned that he had no choice but to assert his prerogatives fruitlessly or capitulate to the wishes of his constituents.

WILLIAM PENCAK

Sources M. L. Lustig, 'Shute, Samuel', *ANB* · W. Pencak, *War, politics and revolution in provincial Massachusetts* (1981) · T. H. Breen, *The character of a good ruler: a study of puritan political ideas in New England, 1630–1730* (1970) · P. Miller, *The New England mind*, 2 (1953) · R. Bushman, *King and people in provincial Massachusetts* (Chapel Hill, NC, 1985)
Archives Mass. Hist. Soc., Mather papers
Wealth at death several hundred pounds plus chattels distributed to relatives and charities: PRO, PROB 11/718, sig. 171

Shute, Thomas (*bap.* 1590, *d.* 1618×26). *See under* Shute, Christopher (*d.* 1626).

Shute, Timothy (*bap.* 1592, *d.* in or before 1659). *See under* Shute, Christopher (*d.* 1626).

Shuter, Edward [Ned] (1728?–1776), actor and singer, may have been born in 1728 but, as with so much else regarding the early life of this most colourful of actors, this is conjectural. Contemporary accounts such as the *Theatrical Biography* (1772) say that he was the son of a chair-man and an oyster woman and was born in a cellar in Covent Garden, whereas Shuter said:

> my Mother sold Oysters in the Winter, and Cucumbers in the Summer, yet I do solemnly aver, that I was not born in a Cellar, but in a front room up two pairs of stairs, at one Mr. Merit's, an eminent Chimney-Sweeper, in Vine-street, St. Gile's. (Highfill, Burnim & Langhans, *BDA*)

It is possible that his father was Edward Shuter, the son of Francis and Mary Shuter, born on 18 May 1699 and baptized at St Anne's, Westminster, on 28 May.

The majority of accounts refer to Shuter working as a pot-boy in taverns in and about Covent Garden, where he made acquaintance with actors by delivering beer to the theatres. It is likely that his informal connection with the stage began in 1741, when he was associated with John Frederick Lampe and his wife, Isabella, the actor James Worsdale, and the actor–manager Thomas Chapman, who formed a company to perform Lampe's operas in Preston and Chester. Shuter was seen by the young Charles Burney, who recorded:

> young Shuter, who had attended Mr & Mrs Lampe as a footboy in Preston, and who now served them in that capacity at the Golden Falcon at Chester … was such a pickle, and contrived to mount the stage in the absence of Worsdale, and took him off so exactly that he rec'd even more applause than Worsdale. (C. Burney, 'Fragments of an autobiography', BL, Add. MS 48345)

Shuter's more formal introduction to the stage evidently occurred at this time through Chapman, who managed the summer theatre in Richmond, Surrey, from 1730 through to 1747. Chapman acted in the patent theatres during the winter, ran a billiard room in Bow Street, and taught acting. The Richmond Theatre playbill of 8 September 1744 announces 'Master Shuter' as the Cook in Henry Carey's *Chrononhotonthologos*, but, according to a memorial notice in the *Town and Country Magazine* (November 1776), it is likely that he continued his tavern life by working as a 'billiard marker'.

Shuter first appeared at Covent Garden Theatre for Chapman's benefit on 15 April 1745—billed as one who had 'never appeared on the stage before'—playing the title role in the afterpiece *The Schoolboy*, by Colley Cibber. On 13 June 1746 Chapman played Laertes to David Garrick's Hamlet with Shuter taking the part of Osric. He concluded the season at Covent Garden on 27 June by appearing as one of the witches to Garrick's Macbeth before accompanying Chapman for the summer to Richmond. He played a recruit in George Farquhar's *The Recruiting Officer*, Daniel in Richard Steele's *The Conscious Lovers*, Clencher in Farquhar's *The Constant Couple*, and Gage in John Crowne's *Sir Courtly Nice*, and was given two benefit nights, one in Richmond and one in Twickenham. Shuter spent the 1746–7 season at the illegal Goodman's Fields Theatre, where he began in earnest to compile his portfolio of roles. Among thirty which he played were Sir Jasper in Henry Fielding's *The Mock Doctor*, Taylor in John Vanbrugh's *The Provoked Husband*, Filch in John Gay's *The Beggar's Opera*, Syringe in Vanbrugh's *The Relapse*, Dr Caius in *The Merry Wives of Windsor*, Brazen in *The Recruiting Officer*, Flash and Fribble in Garrick's *Miss in her Teens*, and Polonius in *Hamlet*.

When Goodman's Fields was closed down after the 1746–7 season Shuter joined Samuel Foote in his attempt to evade the 1737 Stage Licensing Act. Foote hired the Haymarket Theatre and offered, for 2 April 1747, 'a Concert of Music. With which will be given Gratis a New Entertainment, call'd "The Diversions of a Morning"'. Foote's ruse failed to deceive, and Shuter returned to Richmond.

Shuter's comic skills must have pleased Garrick, who engaged him when he took over Drury Lane Theatre in 1747. Shuter played there until 1753 (with an unexplained absence during 1748–9) and spent his summers at Richmond and Twickenham. Garrick's prompter, Richard Cross, notes both his rising popularity as a comic actor and also his developing reputation for exchanging comment with his audience. He notes that, when Shuter played Perriwinkle in Susannah Centlivre's *A Bold Stroke for a Wife*:

> At ye end of ye play, a voice call'd out to Shuter; Perriwinkle— which he answer'd—what do you want? This set ye audience in such a roar, that they insisted upon his giving out ye play, wch he did with great Applause, this wch would have been call'd Impudence in another was look'd upon, in him, as Humour; so rising is he in opinion.   (Highfill, Burnim & Langhans, *BDA*)

At Covent Garden the manager, John Rich, had developed a reputation for spectacle, music, and pantomime, and Shuter's popularity in these areas caused his move to the theatre in 1753–4. With the exception of occasional benefit performances at Drury Lane, he remained at Covent Garden for the winter seasons until his last performance during 1775–6. But, like most actors of the eighteenth century, he spent the summer months in the provinces. He was in Dublin and Cork for the summer of 1760 and during 1762 he returned to Richmond. In 1763 he appeared again in Dublin and in Norwich. The Haymarket Theatre now enjoyed a summer licence, and Shuter appeared there during 1765, 1766, and 1767. He was at Bristol in 1768 and again in 1769. By the early 1770s his reputation for farce and audience involvement made him an attractive 'guest' playing his favourite parts on many of the provincial touring circuits. In this way he visited Edinburgh in 1773, then joined Tate Wilkinson's company based at York and Charles Mate's company at Canterbury. He made his last provincial foray in 1775 to Liverpool and York.

Shuter's comic and ribald talents also drew him to the entertainment booths of Southwark and Bartholomew fairs. In September 1757 he advertised: 'This day at noon, Mr Yates of Drury Lane and Mr Shuter of Covent Garden Theatres at the new erected Great Concert Hall, the Greyhound Inn, Smithfield, intend to divert the Town … with a variety of Entertainments'. The *Daily Advertiser* for 3 September 1757 states: 'the bold Shuter' would 'review his Troop … attended by Mammamawks, Papapawks, and Tomahawks … The Lords may laugh, the Ladies may laugh, and the Commoners may laugh … and that will make me laugh'. Shuter continued to present at fairs in 1760 and 1761, offering to give 'a new Exhilaration to Mirth, and dilate the Sides of Laughter, make Vice bleed under corrective Lash, and give a Lecture that shall Stimulate Virtue to pursue the Road to Happiness'.

Shuter played a range of parts, all following distinctive 'lines' of business—farcical servants, country boys, ageing squires, old beaux, comical judges, and assorted eccentrics, including burlesque women's parts. Typical of his range are Old Sly in Cibber's *Love's Last Shift*, Clincher Junior in *The Constant Couple*, Sir Amourous La Foole in Ben Jonson's *Epicoene, or, The Silent Woman*, Sir Callaghan O'Brallaghan in Charles Macklin's *Love à la Mode*, and Lady Pentweazle in Foote's *Taste*. His Shakespearian roles included Dogberry in *Much Ado about Nothing*, Touchstone in *As You Like It*, Feste in *Twelfth Night*, Stephano in *The Tempest*, and, probably his most remembered role, Falstaff in 1 *Henry IV*. Shuter should be remembered for giving the first performances in two of the century's great plays: Hardcastle in Goldsmith's *She Stoops to Conquer*, on 15 March 1773, and Sir Anthony Absolute in Sheridan's *The Rivals*, on 17 January 1775. His final performance, as Falstaff, was for his benefit at Covent Garden on 10 May 1776. He returned for Mrs Gardiner's benefit to perform Scrub and to speak the epilogue from the back of a donkey on 23 September 1776.

Shuter's lack of education, his indolence, and his contractual carelessness, coupled with a predilection for hot gin, reduced his performing capacity and led to dissolution and illness. The actor John Moody wrote to Garrick from Liverpool in the summer of 1775: 'Shuter is a deplorable object! … He is profligate and wicked; he has been but once on the stage these last six weeks' (*Letters*, 1026). But William Parsons was unstinting in his praise: 'to see Corbachio [in Ben Jonson's *Volpone*] acted to perfection, you should have seen Shuter; the public are pleased to think that I act the part well, but his acting was as far superior to mine, as Mount Vesuvius is to a rushlight' (Kelly, 159). His unpredictability was loved, and he clearly represented that vein of comic observation and easy delivery that his theatre admired. Francis Gentleman, in *The Dramatic Censor* (1770), describes his Harry Sycamore in Isaac Bickerstaff's *The Maid of the Mill* (1765) as 'a talkative, vain, ignorant baronet, well calculated for Mr SHUTER, who exhibits him with whimsical pleasantry'; however, 'he seems too sensible of his own humour, and palpably chuckles where he should leave that totally to the audience'. He warns Shuter of a:

> swift-approaching age,
> When lost to action, he must quit the stage … Avert the
>   storm, in time; lay by some pence;
> They'll yield thee comfort, and proclaim thy sense.

Doran's summary is revealing and credible:

his life was one of intense professional labour, with much jollification, thoughtlessness, embarrassment, gay philosophy, hard drinking, and addiction to religion, as it was expounded by Whitfield. ... Of all the frequenters of Whitfield's tabernacle in Tottenham Court road, there was no more liberal giver than the shattered, trembling, laughing, hoping, fearing, despairing—in short, much perplexed actor and man who oscillated between Covent Garden stage and the Tabernacle pulpit, and meditated over his pipe and bottle in Drury Lane upon the infinite varieties of life. (Doran and Lowe, 2.335–6)

He had never married, but from about 1758 he engaged in a widely reported liaison with the dancer Nancy Dawson (1730?–1767). Shuter died at his lodgings in Windmill Street on 1 November 1776 and was buried five days later in St Paul's, Covent Garden, leaving, as far as is known, no will.   Christopher Baugh

Sources Highfill, Burnim & Langhans, *BDA* · G. W. Stone, ed., *The London stage, 1660–1800*, pt 4: 1747–1776 (1962) · C. B. Hogan, ed., *The London stage, 1660–1800*, pt 5: 1776–1800 (1968) · M. Kelly, *Reminiscences*, 2nd edn, 2 vols. (1826); repr., R. Fiske, ed. (1975) · *The letters of David Garrick*, ed. D. M. Little and G. M. Kahrl, 3 vols. (1963) · J. Doran and R. W. Lowe, 'Their majesties' servants': annals of the English stage, rev. edn, 3 vols. (1888) · S. West, *The image of the actor: verbal and visual representation in the age of Garrick and Kemble* (1991) · *Morning Post* (Nov 1776)

Likenesses group portrait, 1756, Folger · J. Zoffany, group portrait, oils, c.1768, Detroit Institute of Fine Arts · P. Dawe, engraving, 1773, BM · T. Parkinson, group portrait, oils, exh. RA 1774, priv. coll. · T. Parkinson, ink and watercolour drawing, 1776, BM · attrib. B. Downes, oils (as Scapin in *The rival queens*), Garr. Club · T. Parkinson, ink and watercolour drawing, BM · J. Roberts, drawing (as Lovegold), BM · I. Taylor, ink and watercolour drawing (as Obadiah Prim), BM · prints, BM, NPG

Wealth at death presumed none: Highfill, Burnim & Langhans, *BDA*

Shuttlewood, John (1632–1689), clergyman, ejected minister, and nonconformist tutor, was born on 3 January 1632 at Wymeswold, Leicestershire, the son of William Shuttlewood of Wymeswold. After attending grammar school in Leicester he was admitted to Trinity College, Cambridge, in 1650, and elected a scholar in 1651. He married Elizabeth (c.1635–1705), daughter of Humphrey Carter of Draycot, Derbyshire, on 26 April 1652. Having been approved by the Wirksworth classis, Shuttlewood was ordained on 26 April 1654 as the minister of Ravenstone, Derbyshire, apparently in the place of Samuel Hacksup. Shuttlewood appears to have held the rectory with the perpetual curacy of Hugglescote in Leicestershire. An English translation of his confession of faith, given originally in Latin, was published in Samuel Palmer's *Nonconformist's Memorial*.

As an intruding minister Shuttlewood was displaced from Ravenstone in 1660 on the return of Hacksup, the sequestrated minister, and presumably ejected from Hugglescote on his refusal to conform in 1662. By 1669 he had retired to Stoke Golding, a parish on the Warwickshire border near Hinckley in Leicestershire. He was an active nonconformist minister and was reported in the 1669 conventicle returns as preaching in eight parishes around Hinckley, Market Harborough, and Lutterworth in south-west Leicestershire, generally with Matthew Clarke, another ejected minister. He was cited in the archdeaconry court for taking part in the burial of Samuel Hall, a nonconformist gentleman, in Sibson church, in defiance of the Act of Uniformity. Shuttlewood was to be considerably troubled by informers, in particular Charles Gibbons, a quarter-master in the trained bands. In December 1668 thirty or forty horsemen with drawn swords surprised Shuttlewood and many others at a meeting, during the singing of a psalm. Taken before William Street, a county magistrate, Shuttlewood was sent to prison on refusing to promise that he would attend his parish church the following Sunday, despite his never having been charged with being absent from church. He remained in prison until 24 February. Soon after the second Conventicle Act came into force Gibbons surprised him and six or seven others at a house in Theddingworth. Although Gibbons would not swear to its being a conventicle, the men were convicted upon notorious evidence, and Shuttlewood was distrained £20 as the preacher. In May 1672 he obtained a licence under Charles II's declaration of indulgence to preach as a presbyterian at his own house in Lubenham, near Market Harborough. Despite the licence Gibbons took him before a justice, who at first refused to act but subsequently issued warrants. In February 1674 Gibbons interrupted another meeting at Shuttlewood's house in Lubenham, and, though appointed to appear before the justices, those present were never summoned but were distrained none the less. Gibbons's death in December 1675, after falling in a ditch and drowning when returning home drunk, removed Shuttlewood's worst tormentor, but he still found it necessary to make frequent moves to avoid arrest and finally moved to Northamptonshire. Edward Pearse, in his *Conformist's Fourth Plea* (1683), included details of Shuttlewood's sufferings. In a letter to Richard Baxter, Pearse also provided an account of Shuttlewood's attempts to gather meetings at Little Creaton, where he lived, and Welford, in Northamptonshire, shortly after James II issued in his indulgence in 1687.

Shuttlewood conducted one of the earliest nonconformist academies, preparing candidates for the ministry at Sulby, near Welford, from the late 1670s. Because of the troubled times he only educated 'a Few, (and it was but a Few)' students, though they 'proved valuable and useful Men' (Calamy, *Funeral Sermon*, 34; Calamy, *Continuation*, 2.587). There are few details about the academy or Shuttlewood's teaching. His students included Thomas Emlyn, who entered in 1678 and stayed four years, though he briefly left after only a year to enter Emmanuel College, Cambridge, in 1679 because of his dissatisfaction with Shuttlewood's library, which consisted of 'very few books, and them chiefly of one sort' (*Works*, 1.vi).

The Shuttlewoods' only son, John Shuttlewood (1667–1737), was minister of Mill Yard Independent meeting, Goodman's Field, London, and his youngest daughter married Thomas Gibbons, tutor at Homerton Academy. Gibbons had a number of Shuttlewood's manuscripts which Palmer used in his *Nonconformist's Memorial*. Shuttlewood died at Little Creaton on 17 March 1689 and was buried in the churchyard. His monument inscription recorded that he was 'Multum dilectus multum deflendus' ('greatly loved, greatly to be mourned').

DAVID L. WYKES

Sources *Calamy rev.*, 441–2 · E. P. [Edward Pearse], *The conformist's fourth plea for the nonconformists. Wherein several considerations are offered for Christian forbearance. With some relations of some of their sufferings, humbly submitted to authority, in order to move compassion. Together with some account of the infamous lives and lamentable deaths of some informers, &c.* (1683), 79–82 · E. P. [Edward Pearse], letter to R. Baxter, 23 Dec 1687, DWL, Baxter letters, VI 210, I 62 [parts 1 and 3 (of 3)] · E. P. [Edward Pearse], letter to R. Baxter, part 2 (of 3), 23 Dec 1687, BL, Egerton MS 2570, fols. 128–9 · *The nonconformist's memorial … originally written by … Edmund Calamy*, ed. S. Palmer, [3rd edn], 2 (1802), 395–400 · E. Calamy, ed., *An abridgement of Mr. Baxter's history of his life and times, with an account of the ministers, &c., who were ejected after the Restauration of King Charles II*, 2nd edn, 2 vols. (1713), vol. 2, pp. 423–4 · correction court act books, 1669, Leics. RO, Archdeaconry court papers, 1 D 41/13/68–70, 76–82 · E. Calamy, *A continuation of the account of the ministers … who were ejected and silenced after the Restoration in 1660*, 2 vols. (1727), vol. 2, p. 587 · *Walker rev.*, 105 · G. L. Turner, ed., *Original records of early nonconformity under persecution and indulgence*, 1 (1911), 70–74, 497 · J. Toulmin, *An historical view of the state of the protestant dissenters in England, and of the progress of free enquiry and religious liberty, from the revolution to the accession of Queen Anne* (1814), 238–9, 586–91 · E. Calamy, *A funeral sermon for the late Reverend Mr John Sheffield* (1726), 34 · *The works of Mr Thomas Emlyn … to the whole are prefixed, memoirs of the life and writings of the author*, 4th edn, 3 vols. (1746), vol. 1, p. vi · H. I. Longden, *Northamptonshire and Rutland clergy from 1500*, ed. P. I. King and others, 16 vols. in 6, Northamptonshire RS (1938–52), vol. 12, p. 167 · will, Northants. RO · parish register, Wymeswold, 6 Jan 1632, Leics. RO [baptism]

Sir James Phillips Kay-Shuttleworth, first baronet (1804–1877), by unknown engraver, pubd 1877 (after C. A. Duval)

Shuttleworth, Sir James Phillips Kay-, first baronet

(1804–1877), civil servant and educationist, was born James Phillips Kay on 20 July 1804 in Rochdale, Lancashire, the eldest of the six children of Robert Kay, cotton merchant, and his wife, Hannah Phillips. The Kays were intensely devout and brought up their children in tight Calvinistically inclined Congregational communities, most of the rearing being done by Hannah as Robert was an inaccessible parent, often afflicted by depression. James Kay emerged from the enclosed, God- and Mammon-haunted cauldron of his family with fervent religious convictions, a consciousness of the temptations and vanities of the world, an obsession with worldly success, and a perilously uncertain belief in his ability and worth.

Education and medicine From 1815 to 1819 Kay was educated in the tradition of the dissenting academies at the privately owned Leaf Square grammar school in Pendleton, Salford. He then worked for about three years in a Rochdale bank but was dissatisfied and asked to study medicine. Instead, his father placed him in the cotton trade. In 1824, still dissatisfied, Kay gained permission to study at the University of Edinburgh.

Between 1824 and 1827 Kay completed his MD with a thesis on asphyxia in warm-blooded animals which challenged the work of the French anatomist and physiologist Marie-François-Xavier Bichat. An impressive student, he joined the Royal Medical Society and became its senior president for the 1825–6 session. He gained the coveted clerical clerkship with the distinguished physician William Pulteney Alison and accompanied him on his hospital rounds, wrote case histories of his patients, and recorded the treatment that Alison prescribed. A fellow student of Kay's remembered that Alison was impressed with his clerk's 'extraordinary mental power and stern unwearied industry' (notes by W. Charles Henry, Kay-Shuttleworth MSS, no. 1109).

Alison boosted Kay's reputation by drawing attention in his own scientific papers to work published by Kay in the *Edinburgh Medical and Surgical Journal*. He also introduced him to the New Town Dispensary which provided medicine and medical assistance on its premises and in the homes of the poor. By working at the dispensary Kay obtained insights, which were sharpened during an outbreak of typhoid fever, into the lives of Edinburgh's poor. Shocked by the physical conditions under which they lived and by the suffering and illness which afflicted them, Kay began to believe that poverty, disease, and misery were not caused by the failings of the poor, as many of his contemporaries insisted, but were social disasters which required explanations beyond the weakness of individuals.

Kay had literary aspirations and produced a quantity of awkward poetry while in Edinburgh. But his medical studies and professional experience diminished his literary ambitions and he began to study political and social issues. He read Adam Smith and Thomas Chalmers, who emphasized the role of education in improving the moral and physical condition of the poor. Under these influences Kay began to ask questions (to which he returned throughout his life) about capital and labour, the distribution of wealth, the causes of destitution, the means to alleviate it, and the relationship between poverty and the physical and moral condition of the people.

Kay's application to work and anxiety about his progress brought him close to a nervous collapse before he successfully completed his final examinations in 1827. The following year, his health restored and his reputation buoyed by his academic achievements, he set out to establish a private practice in Manchester. He had neither adequate family connections nor sufficient capital and the medical world in Manchester was overcrowded. Moreover, doctors were in the process of constructing themselves as a profession: general practitioners were emerging from the ranks of surgeon-apothecaries and trying to distinguish themselves from the fiercely competitive colleges of physicians and surgeons and the lesser denizens of the medical world—midwives, druggists, and what the nascent profession referred to as 'quacks'. Kay plunged enthusiastically into this turbulent world. He was one of the founders of the Ardwick and Ancoats Dispensary (1828) and a founding editor of the *North of England Medical and Surgical Journal* (1830), through which provincial medical practitioners sought to define their profession. When the cholera epidemic reached Manchester in 1832, Kay served on the local board of health and at the Knott Mill Cholera Hospital. He flung himself into his work with typical and frightening intensity and became one of Manchester's most prominent medical identities.

Kay showed wider social interests by joining the Manchester Literary and Philosophical Society which brought him in touch with Manchester's influential middle class, as did his membership, begun in the early 1830s, of the Manchester Mechanics' Institute. He was active politically, publicly supporting the 1832 Reform Bill, and producing an anonymous pamphlet, *A Letter to the People of Lancashire* (1831), which revealed his admiration of Lord John Russell and the whig cause.

Pamphlet on cotton workers' conditions In April 1832 Kay published the first edition of his pamphlet, *The moral and physical condition of the working classes employed in the cotton manufacture in Manchester*. With passion, fascinated disgust, and considerable bravery, he graphically described the conditions in which industrialization and urbanization had left Manchester's poor. The morality of his Congregational childhood, his experiences in Edinburgh, his reading, and knowledge he had gained as a dispensary doctor combined to picture a city of filthy streets, towering mills, and cruelly crowded houses; of drunkenness, improvidence, greed, irreligion, and the exploitation of children. His passionate ambiguities gave the pamphlet its power. Believing that these evils could not be 'the necessary results of the commercial system', Kay found other explanations by blaming the poor (especially the Irish) for bringing about their own demoralization. Yet he also understood that industrialization was changing not merely the working habits but the characters of the poor, and that mill workers were 'drudges who watch the movements, and assist the operations, of a mighty material force, which toils with an energy ever unconscious of fatigue' (*Moral and Physical Condition*, 49, 10).

The growth of social science and the poor law Some of Kay's recommendations made him a pioneer of public health and wrenched him from a free-trade position: restraints should be placed on private speculators who had built unplanned and wretched houses in narrow unpaved streets; the law should protect the rights of communities; the building of streets should be supervised; landlords should provide drainage; and inspectors of housing should be appointed. It is not surprising that Engels spoke favourably of Kay's pamphlet, which ultimately is as fascinating for what it reveals of the ambiguities in the feelings and thoughts of a liberal member of Manchester's middle class, as for its description of working-class living conditions.

Kay became convinced that a social science was possible and in 1833 played a leading part in establishing the Manchester Statistical Society, the first such society in England. Using survey techniques, it gathered statistics on matters such as the education, religion, accommodation, amusements, and literacy of the poor. Kay insisted that objectivity in social matters was possible, and that policy could be based on scientific information which avoided prejudice or partiality. He did not notice that his unprejudiced analysis of social problems focused on the powerless while the powerful were left unstudied.

Kay's time in Manchester ended in disaster. In 1834 he sought to marry Helen Kennedy, the daughter of James (recently deceased) and June Kennedy, from the wealthy Manchester cotton family. His pamphlet had not endeared him to such families, his private practice had not been particularly successful, and his courtship was importunate and clumsy. He was humiliatingly rejected.

Almost immediately Kay suffered an equally decisive professional defeat. He had remained active in medical affairs, helping to establish the Manchester and Salford District Provident Society (1833) and the Manchester Medical Society (1834). Also in 1834 he wrote an analysis of the defects of dispensaries and published *The Physiology, Pathology, and Treatment of Asphyxia* for which the Royal Humane Society later awarded him the Fothergillian medal. In 1835 he stood for election as an honorary physician to the Manchester Infirmary, a major step towards professional acceptance. He had sought election only months after arriving in Manchester and had been rejected. Despite his seven years of professional activity, he was once more defeated. Broken, he fled from Manchester to become an assistant poor law commissioner. He never practised medicine again.

His self-importance gradually restored, Kay saw himself as rescuing the paupers of Suffolk, and later Norfolk as well, from self-destructive dependence. He implemented the new poor law rigorously, and in his own mind fairly, though to the paupers he cross-questioned and forced into the workhouses he appeared an unfeeling zealot. He pressed individual parishes into the unions the poor law required, and when violence erupted he quelled it. The effect of the poor law, he told a friend, was almost magical; he 'lived a new life of high moral and intellectual enjoyment in effecting and witnessing this mighty change' (Kay to Samuel Robinson, 25 June 1836, Kay-Shuttleworth MSS, no. 176).

Believing that the workhouse schools were producing a

new generation of young felons and so perpetuating the evils he saw in their parents, Kay became preoccupied with the education of pauper children, and became convinced that education held the secret to society's regeneration. He travelled to Scotland in 1837 to examine the pioneering work of John Wood and David Stow, he visited Holland and Belgium briefly, and he studied the ideas of continental reformers such as De Fellenberg. His *Report on the Training of Pauper Children* (1838) established his authority in the field of pedagogy. He drew on Stow's innovations, insisting that children ought to be ruled by affection not fear, and that they should not rely on rote learning but should understand what they were taught. He rejected corporal punishment and the monitorial system, favouring the pupil-teacher system which he claimed (erroneously) to have devised. In 1838 he began to use a pauper establishment at Norwood, in south London, as a model school for the training of teachers and as means of demonstrating his ideas.

Educational reforms In 1839 Melbourne's whig administration established the committee of the privy council on education to administer the government grant to education which had existed since 1833. Kay was appointed the committee's assistant secretary, effectively its senior bureaucrat. In the nine years he held this position he laid the foundations of the British public elementary school system. Four of his contributions were crucial. First, he continued to publicize the pedagogical reforms he had advocated as an assistant poor law commissioner. Second, in 1840 he established Battersea College, the most important of the early English teachers' colleges and a model for other colleges, including those established by the churches. He and Edward Carleton Tufnell privately supported Battersea until 1843 when the financial and administrative burden grew too great and the college was transferred to the Church of England which, ironically, had opposed the establishment of the committee of council and Kay's appointment as its assistant secretary. The church's opposition to Kay may have had an additional edge because by this time he had conformed, though it is not clear when or why. Third, through official pamphlets such as *Recent Measures for the Promotion of Education in England* (1839) and *The School, in its Relations to the State, the Church and the Congregation* (1847) he asserted the state's right, as against that of the churches, in the provision of education. His ideas, decisions, and personal character were constantly attacked by the established church and at various times by dissenters. But Kay helped to place government involvement in education beyond effective political challenge.

Fourth, Kay was a brilliant civil servant. Neither a subtle manipulator of politicians nor their self-effacing servant, he was, like Chadwick, whom he knew and disliked, a zealot who pursued his own agenda whichever government he served. He compromised and suffered defeats, but, using the power which government funding gave him, he forced through regulations and a system of inspection which affected how and what children were taught, the design of school buildings, the structure of the teaching profession, and the ways schools were governed. He also created an educational bureaucracy whose influence burgeoned in the following century.

Illness, retirement, family, and estate In 1848 the stress of ideological battles, long working hours, the rapid expansion of his office, his disregard for bureaucratic niceties of funding, and the embarrassment his dedication caused to supporters such as Lansdowne and Russell, placed Kay in a difficult political situation. It became untenable when on 9 December 1848 he collapsed in the council office with an epileptic fit. Until this collapse his condition was unknown outside his family, and perhaps not even there. His desperate efforts to recover his health were unsuccessful; and neither Lansdowne nor Russell gave him strong support, though after petty bickering they offered him a baronetcy. Clutching that consolation, he resigned in December 1849.

On 24 March 1842 Kay had married Janet Shuttleworth, who was born on 9 November 1817, the daughter of Robert Shuttleworth and his wife, Janet Marjoribanks, the daughter of Sir John Marjoribanks, baronet, of Lees. Robert Shuttleworth died four months after the birth of his only child, leaving her the heir to his estate centred on Gawthorpe Hall in Padiham, Lancashire. In 1825 Janet Shuttleworth married again, this time to Frederick North, who later became MP for Hastings. The younger Janet Shuttleworth grew up deeply interested in the affairs of her estate and in 1839 she wrote to Kay asking him to find her a suitable schoolmaster. To the horror of the Shuttleworth and North families, who considered Kay a fortune-hunting interloper, their acquaintance ripened and they married. As part of the marriage agreement Kay added the name Shuttleworth to his. The Kay-Shuttleworths had five children of whom the eldest, Ughtred James (1844–1939), had an honourable parliamentary career and was created Baron Shuttleworth in 1902.

Kay-Shuttleworth had always worked to improve his wife's estate and to renovate Gawthorpe Hall. After his resignation the estate became of even greater significance, despite his unsuccessful travels to continental and English health resorts. It is possible, though not certain, that he may also have suffered from tabes dorsalis, a form of quaternary neurosyphilis. Janet Kay-Shuttleworth's own health deteriorated and the pair were often separated as her husband attended to affairs at Gawthorpe. The marriage degenerated, because of Kay-Shuttleworth's illness and corroding depression at his expulsion from public life, Janet's fear of the effects of epilepsy on any further children they might have, and her increasing dependence on Rosa Poplawska, her maid and the governess to the children. By mid-1855 Janet Kay-Shuttleworth had settled with Rosa Poplawska at Bad Homburg, in Germany, and informed her husband that she intended to live there with their children. Kay-Shuttleworth's efforts to change her mind finished in farce and tragedy when, in mysterious circumstances, he was arrested in Bad Homburg and spent a short time in gaol. Janet Kay-Shuttleworth did not live with her husband again, though she returned intermittently to England. The official explanation for the separation—the requirements of Janet's health—was assiduously maintained, but neither the couple nor their children doubted its permanence.

Throughout the bitter years of the 1850s Kay-Shuttleworth flirted with a return to public life. He considered entering parliament, was active behind the scenes in educational affairs, and produced *Public education as affected by the minutes of the committee of the privy council from 1846 to 1852* (1853), an almost unreadable defence of the committee of council and his work. He supported the careers of his brothers, Edward Ebenezer *Kay (1822–1897), who became a queen's counsel and a lord justice, and Joseph *Kay, queen's counsel and writer on economics. He befriended Charlotte Brontë, unsuccessfully offered her husband a living, introduced her to Elizabeth Gaskell, and, when Brontë died, secured the manuscript of her novel, *The Professor*, and other papers which Gaskell subsequently used in her biography. In 1860 he published, anonymously and to muted critical acclaim, his own novel, *Scarsdale*.

Kay-Shuttleworth returned briefly to the limelight when, in his *Letter to Earl Granville, K.G., on the Revised Code of Regulations* (1861) he powerfully attacked the code of regulations for government grants to elementary schools (embodying payment by results) which Robert Lowe had introduced. During 1862 and 1863 he worked to relieve those affected by the Lancashire cotton famine. He became involved with the National Association for the Promotion of Social Science and developed a new interest in middle-class education when in 1864 he was appointed a governor of the endowed school at Giggleswick in the West Riding of Yorkshire; he also endeavoured to improve the education of middle-class girls. Spurred by the passage of the 1867 Reform Bill, he produced his *Memorandum on Popular Education* (1868), stressing the civilizing power of education and continuing his attack on the revised code. Forster's Education Act of 1870 firmly established public elementary education and Kay-Shuttleworth heard Ughtred, then twenty-five years old, devote his maiden speech in the House of Commons to the bill. In 1870 he was made an honorary DCL at Oxford University and was appointed a member of the royal commission on scientific instruction.

Kay-Shuttleworth made another, unsuccessful effort to enter parliament, standing as a Liberal for North-East Lancashire in 1874. The Gawthorpe estate came to symbolize the extent to which he still remained outside the gentry into which he had married: when Janet Kay-Shuttleworth died on 14 September 1872 (she asked to be buried on the continent), Ughtred, as the heir, moved into Gawthorpe Hall, while his father retired to another part of the estate at Barbon in Westmorland. He continued writing: *Ribblesdale*, a historical novel, was published in 1874 and a third novel remained unpublished at his death, which took place at 68 Cromwell Road, London, on 26 May 1877; he was buried in Brompton cemetery.

A disappointed life In his last years, despite declining health, Kay-Shuttleworth worked at an autobiography which was not published until 1963. The autobiography is a sad testament to a disappointed life. It is concerned entirely with his public career and is flawed by his determination, sharpened by awareness of approaching death and the disappointment of his public life, to claim as much credit for himself as he could. Of the complexities and tragedies of his personal life it says nothing, thus making him seem far less interesting than he was and hiding the extent to which his unsuccessful search for personal acceptance drove his public career.

R. J. W. SELLECK

Sources R. J. W. Selleck, *James Kay-Shuttleworth: journey of an outsider* (1994) · Frank Smith, *The life and work of Sir James Kay-Shuttleworth* (1923) · *Autobiography of Sir James Kay-Shuttleworth*, ed. B. C. Bloomfield (1963) · J. R. B. Johnson, 'The education department, 1839–64', PhD diss., U. Cam., 1968 · D. G. Paz, *The politics of working-class education in Britain, 1830–50* (1980) · *CGPLA Eng. & Wales* (1877) · Kay-Shuttleworth MSS, JRL
Archives CUL, corresp. · JRL, corresp. and papers · Lancs. RO · Lord Shuttleworth's estate office, Cowan Bridge, Lancashire · NRA, priv. coll., papers | Bodl. Oxf., corresp. with Byron and Lovelace families
Likenesses photograph, *c*.1860, JRL, Shuttleworth MSS · photograph, *c*.1860, priv. coll. · wood-engraving (after C. A. Duval), NPG; repro. in *The Graphic* (1877) [*see illus.*]
Wealth at death under £70,000: probate, 29 July 1877, *CGPLA Eng. & Wales*

Shuttleworth, Joseph [*formerly* Joshua] (1819–1883), agricultural engineer, was born at Dog Dyke on the Witham River in Lincolnshire on 12 July 1819, the son of John Allenby Shuttleworth of Coningsby, a boat builder, and his wife, Rebecca Newton. He was baptized Joshua. He left school at the age of fourteen to follow his father's trade, and two years later in 1835 took over the management of a boat-building yard at Lincoln, which his father had acquired. Within a few years the increased prosperity of the yard had so impressed John Shuttleworth that he turned the business over to his son.

Nathaniel Clayton was working in adjoining premises as an iron-founder and steam-packet owner, and in 1842 he and Shuttleworth established the firm of Clayton, Shuttleworth & Co. Iron-founding soon became their main interest, with the railway boom at first providing a rapidly expanding market. This was followed by the start of their rise to prominence as agricultural engineers. With some financial backing from a local firm of corn merchants and millers they began the manufacture of portable steam engines in 1845, and steam threshing machines in 1849. They were one of the first, and certainly one of the most successful, manufacturers of steam-powered farm machinery. They were not outstanding, however, as technical innovators, preferring simply to adopt, or in some cases adapt, the best of the available designs and put their efforts into efficient manufacture, a high standard of materials and workmanship, and competitive marketing. At an early stage in their expansion they came to realize the opportunities presented by overseas markets, and they established an office and works in

Vienna in 1857 to serve the countries of central and eastern Europe. A decade later they developed a substantial export trade to Australia and South America. By the time of Shuttleworth's death the firm had manufactured 19,000 portable steam engines and 17,000 threshing machines, as well as finishing machines, straw and hay elevators, and portable grinding mills.

Shuttleworth's other business interests included, at various times, directorships of the Metropolitan Railway, the Great Northern Railway, the Sutton Bridge Dock Company, and the Agricultural Hall Company, and he was a valued member of the council of the Royal Agricultural Society. He was elected a vice-president of the Agricultural Engineers' Association when it was formed in 1875. He was active also in the volunteer militia (forerunner of the Territorial Army), in which he rose to the rank of captain. For many years he was a member of the town council of Lincoln, and in 1858–9 was chief magistrate. He was a JP and deputy lieutenant of the county of Lincoln, and in 1881 was elected high sheriff of Bedfordshire. The local charities found in him a generous benefactor.

In 1842 Shuttleworth married Sarah Grace, daughter of the elder Nathaniel Clayton and sister of his partner. They had two sons. His first wife died in 1849, and in 1861 he married Caroline Jane, daughter of Lieutenant-Colonel Richard George Ellison of Boultham Hall. They had no children. He died at home at Hartsholme Hall, Skellingthorpe, near Lincoln, on 25 January 1883.

RONALD M. BIRSE, rev.

Sources D. C. Philips, 'Shuttleworth, Joseph', DBB • Journal of the Royal Agricultural Society of England, 2nd ser., 19 (1883), 270–76 • Engineering (2 Feb 1883), 115–6 • CGPLA Eng. & Wales (1883) • d. cert.
Wealth at death £554,612 12s. 8d.: resworn probate, Sept 1883, CGPLA Eng. & Wales

Shuttleworth, Obadiah (c.1675–1734), organist, was born in London, the son of Thomas Shuttleworth of Spitalfields, a teacher of music and transcriber of Corelli's works. He became a skilled violinist, took part in Thomas Britton's concerts, and was leader of the concerts established about 1728 at the Swan tavern, Cornhill. In 1724 he succeeded Philip Hart as organist of St Michael Cornhill, and was one of the organists at the Temple Church. His playing at the Temple attracted large crowds, although some claimed he was a better harpsichordist than organist. He composed much violin music, but only two concertos, adapted from sonatas by Corelli, were published (c.1726). An Obadiah Shuttleworth and his wife, Anne, had five children baptized between 1724 and 1732; when Shuttleworth died on 2 May 1734, he was apparently survived by a widow and two daughters.

L. M. MIDDLETON, rev. K. D. REYNOLDS

Sources J. Hawkins, A general history of the science and practice of music, 5 vols. (1776) • O. Edwards, 'Shuttleworth, Obadiah', New Grove • 'Shuttleworth, Obadiah', Grove, Dict. mus. (1927) • GM, 1st ser., 4 (1734), 274 • IGI

Shuttleworth, Philip Nicholas (1782–1842), bishop of Chichester, was born at Kirkham, Lancashire, on 9 February 1782, the second son of Humphrey Shuttleworth (1734/5–1812), vicar of Kirkham from 1771 to 1812, and of

Preston, Lancashire, from 1784 to 1809, who wrote some tracts against the papal pretensions. His mother was Anne, only child of Philip Hoghton. Philip was educated at Preston grammar school, and in 1796 entered Winchester College, where Dr Goddard nominated him to a scholarship. He was elected a scholar of New College, Oxford, in 1800, and graduated BA in 1806, MA in 1811, and BD and DD in 1822. In 1803 he won the chancellor's Latin verse prize, the subject being Byzantium. Soon after graduating he became tutor to the Hon. Algernon Herbert, and at a subsequent date to Lord Holland's son, Charles Richard Fox, later a general and distinguished numismatist. He was admitted to the Holland circle, and visited the continent with Lord and Lady Holland in 1814 and 1815. Shuttleworth was tutor and fellow of New College until 1822, and proctor of the university in 1820.

In October 1822 Shuttleworth was unanimously chosen warden of New College, an academic position which enabled him to marry on 29 July 1823 Emma Martha, daughter of George Welch of High Leck, Tunstall, Lancashire. The eldest of their children was the translator and poet (Emma) Frances *Bevan. On 19 November 1824 Lord Holland presented him to the rectory of Foxley, Wiltshire. As a strong whig, Shuttleworth's election was welcomed by Samuel Parr as 'a triumph of learning over pedantry and of constitutional principles over sacerdotal intolerance' (Works of Samuel Parr, 8.223). He supported Catholic emancipation and, as a member of the university's hebdomadal board, proposed in 1834 a relaxation of the religious tests which excluded dissenters. In 1836 he defended R. D. Hampden, the heterodox divinity professor. An effective preacher from the university pulpit, he published two volumes entitled Sermons on some of the Leading Principles of Christianity (1827–34). A textbook, A Paraphrastic Translation of the Apostolic Epistles (1829), reached a fifth edition in 1854. His The Consistency of the Whole Scheme of Revelation with itself, and with Human Reason (1832) was recommended to students as a supplement to their reading of Bishop Butler. His churchmanship was orthodox, though his attack on the Tractarians, who regarded him with particular aversion, in a sermon Not Tradition but Scripture (1838), was admired by evangelicals. In his own college he attempted reforms, notably presiding over the surrender of the ancient privilege by which New College men were exempt from university examinations. The deviser of a railway to speed the circulation of port in the senior common room, he was a noted wit, whose ambitions for ecclesiastical promotion were predicted in his schoolboy verse 'Make me, O Sphere-descended Queen, A Bishop, or, at least, a Dean' (Tuckwell, 169).

Shuttleworth's trimming tendencies delayed his advancement. 'His conscientiousness, tho' sincere, has the gait of indecision and his conciliation and ingenuity assume the appearance, and perhaps in some degree the reality, of timidity and compromise', Lord Holland noted (The Holland House Diaries, 1977, 344). He gave offence to his whig patrons by signing an address early in 1835 urging Peel to remain in office, Melbourne subsequently passing him over for vacant mitres (notably Salisbury in 1837) and only with reluctance promoting him to the see of Chichester in September 1840. His most significant act as bishop was ironically to appoint, in disregard of his wife's opposition, the 'Puseyite' Henry Manning to an archdeaconry.

Shuttleworth died at the episcopal palace, Chichester, on 7 January 1842. Pusey saw in the sudden removal of this inveterate opponent of Tractarianism a token of God's presence within the Church of England (H. P. Liddon, *Life of Edward Bouverie Pusey*, 2, 1893, 294). Shuttleworth was survived by his widow, a son (who died in 1848), and three daughters. His occasional verse was published after his death in the *Gentleman's Magazine* (3rd ser., 11, 1861, 245, 542) and in the *Life of William Buckland* (1894). His 'Specimen of a geological lecture' was included in C. G. B. Daubeny's collection of *Fugitive Poems Connected with Natural History and Physical Science* (1869).

C. W. SUTTON, rev. M. C. CURTHOYS

Sources GM, 2nd ser., 17 (1842), 209 · W. Tuckwell, *Reminiscences of Oxford*, 2nd edn (1907) · O. Chadwick, *The Victorian church*, 1 (1966) · W. R. Ward, *Victorian Oxford* (1965) · J. Buxton and P. Williams, eds., *New College, Oxford, 1379–1979* (1979) · GM, 1st ser., 93/2 (1823), 368
Archives Bodl. Oxf. | BL, corresp. with Lord Holland, Add. MS 51597 · Bodl. Oxf., letters to Henry Manning · Bodl. Oxf., corresp. with wife, Emma · LPL, corresp. with Charles Golightly
Likenesses S. W. Reynolds, mezzotint, pubd 1826 (after T. Kirkby), BM, NPG · T. Phillips, oils, 1842, New College, Oxford · T. Kirkby, oils, New College, Oxford · R. Smith, portrait

Shuttleworth, Robert James (1810–1874), botanist and conchologist, was born at Dawlish, Devon, in February 1810, the eldest son of James Shuttleworth (d. 1846) of Barton Lodge, Preston, Lancashire, and his first wife, Anna Maria, daughter of the Hon. and Revd Richard Henry Roper, dean of Clones. His mother died of consumption a few weeks after his birth; his father married again in 1815 and settled in Switzerland. Shuttleworth was chiefly brought up by his mother's relatives. He was sent to school at Geneva, studying under Seringe, keeper of the Candolle Herbarium, and botanizing on the mountains near Geneva. At the age of eighteen he went to Germany, passing a winter at Saxe-Weimar where he enjoyed the court life and came to know Goethe. He also spent some time at Frankfurt and Heidelberg before being recalled to his father's house at Soleure (apparently his father feared his becoming too irresponsible and boisterous if left to his own devices).

Retaining his interest in botany, Shuttleworth made a considerable collection in the Jura during the summer of 1830. From the autumn of that year until the end of 1832 he studied in the medical faculty of the University of Edinburgh. During this period he also made a vacation tour in the highlands, and helped his stepbrother Blake on his estate in the west of Ireland during the famine of 1831 and 1832. On 11 January 1833 Shuttleworth was appointed to a captaincy in the duke of Lancaster's own regiment, but after returning to Soleure in the following winter he married Susette, daughter of Comte de Sury of Soleure, and settled at Bern. The couple later had a son, Henry, and a daughter who died in childhood.

In Switzerland, Shuttleworth resumed his botanizing. He collected on the Grimsel and the Oberland, and worked particularly on red snow (*Chlamydomonas*) and other freshwater algae, until weak eyesight compelled him to abandon the microscope. In 1835 he purchased the extensive herbarium and library of Joseph August Schultes of Zürich. Between 1840 and 1850 he became interested in conchology, an interest sparked by a friendship with Jean de Charpentier of Bex, himself a zealous conchologist.

Shuttleworth spent money freely on his researches. He sent the collector Blauner of Bern to Corsica, the Canaries, and ultimately to Puerto Rico (where he died of consumption). Other collectors in the Americas were also supported through Shuttleworth's purchase of their shells, plants, and seeds. He worked up a large number of the plants, forming a very extensive annotated herbarium.

Shuttleworth suffered from gout, a condition which led him to winter in the south, where he botanized in the Var and Alpes-Maritimes. This resulted in a *Catalogue des plantes de Provence* (1889). Indeed, many of his botanical discoveries were in part due to his constant comparison of French with Italian types. His letters and the notes in his herbarium also evince the critical caution which made him apt to recognize minute differences. However, following the death in 1866 of his son, Henry, then a medical student, Shuttleworth moved to Hyères, and gave up scientific work.

Shuttleworth joined the Botanical Society of Edinburgh as an original member in 1836, became a fellow of the Linnean Society in 1856, and was awarded an honorary doctorate by the University of Basel. Following his death, at Hyères on 19 April 1874, Shuttleworth's collection of shells, considered by Mousson (*Journal de Conchyliologie*, 23.99) one of the most remarkable in Europe, was presented to the state museum at Bern. His herbarium of more than 150,000 specimens of flowering plants and 20,000 cryptogams was added to the British Museum collection. An account of the various collections comprised in this herbarium appears in the official report of the department of botany in the museum for 1877 (*Journal of Botany, British and Foreign*, 2nd ser., 7, 1878, 179–80).

Shuttleworth was the author of some twenty papers, including several on the land and freshwater shells of Corsica. He also published *Nouvelles observations sur la matière coloriante de la neige rouge* (1840), and *Notitiae malacologicae* (1856). *Notitiae* contained nine lithographic plates, of which eight were unsigned, and presumably by Shuttleworth. The second part of *Notitiae* was issued in 1878, edited with synonymy by Dr Paul Fischer and containing a 'Nekrolog von R. J. Shuttleworth', by Guthnick, director of the Bern Botanical Garden.

G. S. BOULGER, rev. PETER OSBORNE

Sources Desmond, *Botanists*, rev. edn, 628 · J. Foster, ed., *Pedigrees of the county families of England*, 1: *Lancashire* (1873) · P. Whittle, *The history of the borough of Preston*, 2 (1837), 235 · R. J. Shuttleworth, *Notitiae malacologicae*, 2 (1878), preface
Archives NHM · RBG Kew · state museum, Bern, Switzerland
Wealth at death under £14,000: probate, 18 May 1874, CGPLA Eng. & Wales

Siaosi Taufa'ahau Tupou I (1797?–1893), king and unifier of modern Tonga, is thought to have been born in 1797 on the island of Lifuka, Ha'apai, Tonga. He was a son of Tupouto'a (d. 1820) (sometime tu'i kanokupolu or ruling chief of Tonga) and Taufahoamofaleono, the daughter of the holder of the Ma'afu title. Taufa'ahau's paternal grandfather was Tuku'aho, the tu'i kanokupolu, whose assassination in 1799 led to a protracted series of civil wars and destroyed the former unitary Tongan polity.

On the death of his father in 1820, Taufa'ahau claimed the rulership of the Ha'apai group of islands. This claim was disputed by the chief Laufilitonga (1797?–1865), heir to the tu'i Tonga title or supreme chieftainship of Tonga. After defeating Laufilitonga at the battle of Verata in 1826 Taufa'ahau's ambition to reunite Tonga under his own leadership was clear but unwelcome to the various territorial chiefs who had become accustomed to independence. Taufa'ahau's claim to inherit his father's title, and its authority to govern, was subverted by the dissident chiefs installing his elderly, mild uncle, 'Aleamotu'a. 'Aleamotu'a's weakness, however, made him a proxy for Taufa'ahau, who fought several short civil wars on his behalf during the 1830s.

Taufa'ahau was attracted to the teachings of the Wesleyan mission which had become established in 1826. He was baptized on 7 August 1831 and became a class leader and lay preacher, encouraged the conversion of his people, and sponsored Tongan missionaries in the neighbouring archipelagos of Samoa and Fiji. On baptism he took the name George (Siaosi in Tongan) and was known thereafter to Europeans as King George. As a Christian he was required to have no more than one wife, and in 1834 married Lupepau'u, baptized as Charlotte or Salote (d. 1889), a woman among the most highly ranked in the Tongan aristocracy. Soon after his baptism he persuaded the ruling chief of the northern group of Tonga, Finau 'Ulukalala Tuapasi, to convert. He subsequently repressed a rebellion for 'Ulukalala, who afterwards named him as his successor. 'Ulukalala died in 1833, and Taufa'ahau duly succeeded as tu'i Vava'u (king of Vava'u).

Taufa'ahau's work of nation building began almost immediately, though he proceeded cautiously. During the 1830s he decreed against various customs that had pagan associations and which also served to enforce the people's servitude to their chiefs. In 1838 he issued the first formal code of laws (the Vava'u code), a set of morality injunctions based on the ten commandments, but providing also for the appointment of judges, fixed fines for offenders, and the universal application of the laws. When 'Aleamotu'a died in 1845 there was no effective resistance to Taufa'ahau becoming Tu'i Kanokupolu, and *de facto* and *de moribus* master of the whole of Tonga, who extended the application of his laws throughout the archipelago. Thereafter he was known by the regnal name Tupou.

The law code was enlarged and extended in 1850, among other things giving formal definition to the relationship between chiefs and people, thus implicitly limiting chiefly authority. This measure sparked the last serious rebellion of Tupou's reign in 1852. Hitherto, his missionary friends had been almost his only source of information about modern government, and of the dangers posed to independence by interaction with foreigners. He sought advice from the chief justice of New Zealand, and in 1853 travelled to Sydney, New South Wales, to observe western society and government at first hand. En route to Sydney, he visited Fiji to arrange restraint for Tongan migrants who were a significant and largely independent political force. He also visited the powerful but beleaguered chief Seru Cakobau (1817?–1883) and advised him to convert to Christianity.

In 1855 Tupou returned to Fiji, where his warriors defeated the last of Cakobau's enemies at the battle of Kaba (17 April 1855), a turning point in Fijian history which strengthened the standing of the Tongans there, but also limited the spread of their power. Over the next few years Tupou faced difficulties with French officials, ostensibly over freedom of religion for Catholics, and was obliged to accept a treaty dictated by the French in 1855. This incident taught Tupou the absolute nexus between modern formal government and the preservation of independence, and he worked steadily to evolve a form of government which would attract formal recognition from other states, especially Britain.

Accordingly, in 1862 Tupou issued a new code of laws. Often called the edict of emancipation because it terminated the serf-like status of the common people, the code was just as important in defining the form of government, the duties of officials, the obligations of citizens, and the manner in which law should be created in future. This important document was Tonga's first constitution, though it still described an essentially tribal society. A radically different constitution followed in 1875, drafted by a missionary, the Revd Shirley Baker. This constitution prescribed the form of government, included a declaration of rights, and enunciated land and other laws. For the first time a law of royal succession was established. The old chieftainship was abolished, and a new, much smaller nobility was created. Treaties recognizing Tongan statehood followed with Germany in 1876, Britain in 1879, and the United States in 1886. The final mark that Tupou left on his kingdom was the creation in 1885 of an independent Christian church, the Free Church of Tonga.

Tupou died at Nuku'alofa on 18 February 1893, aged probably ninety-five, and was buried in the royal cemetery in Nuku'alofa. His longevity was not only remarkable but was a significant factor in his political achievement. The modernization and continued independence of Tonga during the nineteenth century could scarcely have happened but for the authority of a single masterful personality. His personal talents were exceptional: he was a powerful, athletic man and a formidable warrior; he had an acute intelligence; he was a master strategist in both war and politics; and he was faithful to his adopted religion to the end of his life. He was resourceful in opposition and generous in victory, and he accomplished an orderly political and social transformation unique in the history of the Pacific islands.

Tupou had two sons with his wife Lupepau'u, but both died young. Earlier unions gave him two sons and a daughter, all of whom predeceased him. He was succeeded by his great-grandson, Taufa'ahau Tupou II.

I. C. CAMPBELL

Sources S. Latukefu, 'King George Tupou I of Tonga', *Pacific islands portraits*, ed. J. W. Davidson and D. Scarr (1970) · S. Latukefu, *Church and state in Tonga* (1974) · N. Rutherford, *Shirley Baker and the king of Tonga* (1971) · I. C. Campbell, *Island kingdom: Tonga ancient and modern*, 2nd edn (2001) · N. Rutherford, ed., *Friendly islands: a history of Tonga* (1977)

Sibbald, James (*c*.1595–1647), Church of Scotland minister, said to have been of an ancient family in the Mearns, matriculated at Marischal College, Aberdeen, in 1614 and graduated MA in 1618. Two years later he was the first person appointed to act as regent of fourth-year classes in natural philosophy, continuing in that position until 1626. Appointed in 1625 to the first charge of St Nicholas's Church in New Aberdeen, in 1627, following presentation of a thesis later published, he was made a BD by King's College, Aberdeen, and in 1628 a DD, though the non-academic use of that degree was disputed in Scotland at the time. He was noted for his abilities in oriental languages, and in both divine and secular studies.

Sibbald was one of the Aberdonian divines who preached at the funeral of Patrick Forbes of Corse in 1635. His sermon, published as *Holinesse to the Lord* and based on Exodus chapter 28, expressed anti-Catholicism and Calvinist ideas of predestination, both recurrent themes in his writing. In 1637 Sibbald, along with John Forbes of Corse, Alexander Scrogie, William Leslie, Robert Baron, and Alexander Ross, encouraged the unification schemes of John Durie by giving him their opinion that Lutherans agreed with the doctrine of the Church of Scotland in those points which were agreed by the ancient church. In 1638, when the national covenant was being promoted in Aberdeen, those six ministers, together with William Guild, for a time, prepared questions for the covenanting representatives and went on to engage them in a lengthy printed debate on the authority and doctrine of the covenant. In early October of that year, Sibbald signed the king's covenant which was being circulated in opposition to the national covenant. He was elected, along with Robert Baron, to the general assembly of 1638, but neither attended.

In 1639 Sibbald left Aberdeen for England, where he and Baron offered their services to Charles I, but, having met a cooler reception than expected, Sibbald returned to Aberdeen, which had been occupied by covenanters in his absence. In Aberdeen he accepted the political and ecclesiastical situation to the extent of reminding his parishioners not to keep Christmas day, as celebration of it had been banned by the general assembly. Despite some outward appearance of conformity he continued to refuse to subscribe the national covenant, and was at the Aberdeen general assembly of 1640, charged on this count, together with Arminianism and circulating William Forbes's unpublished writings. It was also claimed that he maintained the blessing of private baptism, approved of Lent,

called communion *viaticum* and taught that alms would discharge sin: all these were contrary to the covenanters' interpretation of Calvinist doctrine; all were admitted by Sibbald. He was deposed on 6 August of that year, and was replaced as minister at St Nicholas's by Andrew Cant, one of the region's covenanting ministers. Sibbald's books and papers were seized, but returned to him.

In 1640 Sibbald again sailed for England, and from there went to Ireland, where he received a benefice. He spent the remainder of his career as a protestant episcopalian minister in Dublin, where he was noted for his work with the poor and ill. In 1646 he petitioned Ormond, the lord lieutenant, to preserve episcopalian protestantism in the forms of the Book of Common Prayer, public worship, and episcopacy.

Sibbald died in Dublin in 1647 of plague, contracted while working with the ill of that city. He left a widow, Elizabeth Nicolson, and two children, who were granted £200 Scots (£16 13*s*. 4*d*. sterling) by the Scottish parliament of 1661, after the restoration of both the monarch and episcopacy, and because of his support for both institutions. After his death, fifteen of his sermons were published as *Diverse Select Sermons* (Aberdeen, 1658).

R. P. WELLS

Sources J. Sibbald, *Diverse select sermons upon severall texts of holy scripture* (1658) · P. J. Anderson, ed., *Officers and graduates of University and King's College, Aberdeen, MVD–MDCCCLX*, New Spalding Club, 11 (1893), 9–10, 98, 109, 181 · *Fasti Scot.*, new edn, 6.36–7 · J. Stuart, ed., *Extracts from the council register of the burgh of Aberdeen, 1625–1747*, 1, Scottish Burgh RS, 8 (1871), 114, 138, 235 · J. Spalding, *Memorialls of the trubles in Scotland and in England, AD 1624 – AD 1645*, ed. J. Stuart, 2 vols., Spalding Club, [21, 23] (1850–51) · J. Gordon, *History of Scots affairs from 1637–1641*, ed. J. Robertson and G. Grub, 3 vols., Spalding Club, 1, 3, 5 (1841) · G. Grub, *An ecclesiastical history of Scotland*, 4 vols. (1861), vol. 2, p. 372; vol. 3, pp. 56, 73–7, 78–9 · J. Row, *The history of the Kirk of Scotland, from the year 1558 to August 1637*, ed. D. Laing, Wodrow Society, 4 (1842), 495, 501 · *Fasti academiae Mariscallanae Aberdonensis: selections from the records of the Marischal College and University, MDXCIII–MDCCCLX*, 2, ed. P. J. Anderson, New Spalding Club, 18 (1898) · *The letters and journals of Robert Baillie*, ed. D. Laing, 1 (1841), 136, 248, 365 · J. Stuart, ed., *Selections from the records of the kirk session, presbytery, and synod of Aberdeen*, Spalding Club, 15 (1846), 113 · D. Stevenson, *King's College, Aberdeen, 1560–1641: from protestant Reformation to covenanting revolution* (1990), 75, 110, 112, 117

Sibbald, James (1747–1803), bookseller and journal editor, was born at Whitlaw farm, Roxburghshire, the third of the seven children of John Sibbald (1714–1781), farmer, and Margaret Grieve. After attending the Selkirk grammar school he worked as a farmer, grazing his sheep at the farms of Newtown and Borthwickbrae, while living at Whitlaw and reading in his leisure hours such works as Withering's *Botany* and Mair's *Book-Keeping*, bought from his bookseller cousin Charles Elliot of Edinburgh. At thirty-two he gave up the land for the book trade and journalism, and became a scholar of Scottish literary antiquities.

Sibbald started up in trade by buying the Edinburgh Circulating Library of Mrs Margaret Yair, which formerly belonged to Allan Ramsay. In preparation, he left his brother John and a friend to sell off the sheep, and went to

James Sibbald (1747–1803), by unknown artist

London in February 1779 with money to buy a large stock of books, over the next seven months lodging with a Miss Moore, milliner, at 178 Bishopsgate Street. He inspected circulating libraries, drawing ideas from Thomas Lowndes's and particularly from John Bell's British Library. Sibbald's rapid and intense introduction to bookselling, and to the relationship of the Edinburgh and London trades, can be traced in the letters of Charles Elliot, which contain a torrent of introductions, commissions, and advice. Copyright was one issue. 'Dear Jamie,' Elliot wrote early on, 'take great care when in company of great London booksellers and offer no books from me that have first been printed in London. You may not be properly acquainted with their fine ideas of Literary property' (Elliot to Sibbald, 26 April 1779). Sibbald carried out book exchanges and other business around St Paul's Churchyard with John Rivington, Joseph Johnson, and Carnan and Newbery; in Paternoster Row with Thomas Longman, George Robinson, John Bew, and Richardson and Urquhart; in Fleet Street with George Kearsley and John Murray; and in the Strand with John Nourse, John Knox, Thomas Cadell, James Mathews, and Alexander Donaldson; and he also visited William Fox, Thomas Bell, Charles Dilly, the printer William Strahan, and the stationer William Bloxham. Sibbald acquired from Bloxham a list of English country booksellers, looked after a pamphlet on the American war, *Historical Anecdotes* (1779), that Elliot published as 'London: printed for J. Bew', registered this title for Elliot at Stationers' Hall, and completed the first transaction for himself by exchanging George

Carr's *Sermons* (an Elliot and Cadell publication) for Robinson and Bew books. Asked to send up the best printing ink to Edinburgh, he was warned to go through a friendly bookseller to avoid a curious London practice: 'when they learn it is for Scotland they often send their Trash or spoiled kind' (Elliot to Sibbald, 3 May 1779).

Late in September 1779 Sibbald returned to Scotland on a borrowed horse and worked for some weeks at Elliot's shop in Parliament Square in Edinburgh for a guinea a week, double the wage of Elliot's clerk Thomas Dobson. Meanwhile he wrote his first catalogue for 20,000 titles in English, French, and Italian, as well as music, then reopened the expanded circulating library a few doors away at 28 Parliament Square in November, at the start of university classes. Burns visited in 1786–7, and the shop was frequented by the young Walter Scott. Scott said he fastened 'like a tiger, upon every collection of old songs or romances which chance threw into my way, or which my scrutiny was able to discover on the dusty shelves of James Sibbald's circulating library in the Parliament Square'. He said the library contained

> many rare and curious works, seldom found is such a collection. Mr. Sibbald himself, a man of rough manners but of some taste and judgment, cultivated music and poetry, and in his shop I had a distant view of some literary characters, Burns among others. (Lockhart, 46)

Sibbald contributed to an Edinburgh fad in the early 1780s when he sold the latest coloured mezzotint engravings from London, advertising in the *Caledonian Mercury* favourite titles with the public, such as *Kate of Aberdeen* (7 August 1782; March–July 1783). Elliot described him as a 'perfect judge', who 'from his extensive dealing in prints, has spread such a rage for purchasing, that no gentle house is without its select collection', Elliot's home included (Elliot to David Mitchell, Gothenburg, 15 Sept 1783). Public interest is said to have lessened when Sibbald was discovered colouring the prints himself.

Sibbald multiplied his activities when he established both a magazine and a newspaper and managed a paper mill. In 1785 he began the *Edinburgh Magazine, or, Literary Miscellany*, a journal of literary sophistication which regularly had an engraved view and a page of music; it appeared monthly and sold for 1s. An agreement was made with John Murray the next year to exchange 100 copies of the magazine for the *English Review* and for both booksellers to share the imprints. One of the regular contributors was Lord Hailes, whose attention was first caught by Sibbald's articles, unsigned, on Scottish antiquities. Sibbald was the first reviewer to acclaim the genius of Robert Burns, and his Kilmarnock poems in the October 1786 number: 'The author is indeed a striking example of native genius bursting through the obscurity of poverty and the obstructions of laborious life.' Sibbald continued to promote him with extracts over the next two months. In the December issue he reprinted Henry Mackenzie's review in *The Lounger* and said, 'His fame is now spreading rapidly.' Burns responded with gratitude for the way Sibbald had 'befriended an obscure man and young Author in your last three Magazines—I can only say, Sir, I feel the weight of the obligation' (Burns to Sibbald, Jan 1787). In 1790 Sibbald also started a thrice-weekly newspaper, the *Edinburgh Herald*, in which he proposed to have literary intelligence and essays on life and manners as well as public and political news and advertisements. He published Burns's 'Tam o' Shanter' on 18 March 1791, a month before the poem appeared in Grose's *Antiquities of Scotland*. The *Herald* was characterized by its enemy the *Political Review* on 20 June 1792 as 'a vehicle for ministerial dirt' taken from *The Times* and *The Oracle* of London, and 'dealt out in pailfuls more offensive than before' (Couper, 2.184).

From 1788 to 1798 Sibbald was managing partner of the Auchendinny paper mill on the North Esk, 8 miles south of Edinburgh. Auchendinny served the Scottish and London trade and gave Sibbald the opportunity of a substantial income; in 1798 his joint cash account with the owner, William Cadell, stood at nearly £1500 (Cadell of Grange papers). While there Sibbald experienced the temper of the author James Bruce of Kinnaird. After Bruce signed a contract with Robinson of London to publish *Travels to Discover the Source of the Nile* (in an edition of 2000 copies, for a payment of £6666), Sibbald seized the chance of being associated as the printer. He brought in the printer James Ruthven of Edinburgh as a partner, offered the low price of £495 to print 360 sheets in five volumes quarto, and signed a contract with Bruce between April and May 1789; Auchendinny would also supply the paper. Bruce drew for him a mock title-page whose imprint began 'Edinburgh, printed by J. Sibbald, under the author's immediate inspection' but this was a false promise. Sibbald said that while he was ill with a fever in June and July 1789 and away from the project, Bruce induced Ruthven to increase the production to twelve sheets a week instead of nine by substituting his name for Sibbald's on the imprint; this deletion caused Sibbald to be 'chagrined a little' (Bruce v. Sibbald and Ruthven). The relationship, poor during printing, grew worse when Bruce accused Sibbald of sabotage. He said 'that Arch rascal Sibbald' had deliberately supplied a batch of yellowed and underweight paper for the book and asked Cadell to dismiss him; Cadell found the charge was unjustified (Cadell of Grange papers). Later, when the imperial paper sent to London for the king's presentation copy was found to be badly soiled, Bruce said it was intentional on Sibbald's part, and in November 1790 sued Sibbald and Ruthven at the court of session for failing to deliver the book in a workmanlike manner, claiming £216 in loss and expenses. After much evidence from both sides the case hinged on a letter from Bruce's clerk, which Sibbald produced, acknowledging arrival of the printed sheets in London in good order, and in 1792 Sibbald and Ruthven were cleared of the charge.

Sibbald gave over the running of the *Edinburgh Magazine* to Laurie and Symington in 1791 and ended his editorship in June 1792, passing it on to Dr James Anderson. He stopped editing the *Edinburgh Herald* by 1796. Sibbald also rented his circulating library to Laurie and Symington from 1790 to 1800, for an annual fee of £200, which dropped to 100 guineas. He continued the bookshop for a few more years—publishing Thomson's *The Seasons* (1789),

and *The History of Tom Jones* (1791)—and took to the court of session to recover debts, suing, among many others, the estate of Adam Smith for £1 12s. 6d. He also won a judgment against Thomas Dobson for £42 worth of books sent to Philadelphia. In February 1796 he sold his house in Mausie Smith's Close in the Canongate, and was referred to as 'late bookseller, Edinburgh, now in London' (register of Sasines, Edinburgh, no. 6404). He had visited London frequently, and this sojourn, which was to last several years, appears to have been relaxed: when a relative sought his whereabouts, he replied 'My lodging is in Soho, and my business is so so' (Chambers, *Scots.*, 260). While in London he wrote *The Record of the Public Ministry of Jesus the Christ* (printed at Edinburgh in 1798). He returned to Edinburgh by 1800, when he took back his circulating library. His *Chronicle of Scottish Poetry: from the Thirteenth Century to the Union of the Crowns* (4 vols.), published on 4 December 1802 and priced £1 4s. in boards, offered the public extracts from the Bannatyne manuscript and followed earlier collections by Allan Ramsay and Lord Hailes. Walter Scott, picking up on a footnote, remarked that 'A heavy personage here of the name of Sibbald' had criticized his tardiness in publishing *Sir Tristrem*, but advised that the book be bought as the fourth volume 'contains some curious remarks on the ancient Scottish music & an uncommonly good glossary' (Scott to George Ellis, Dec 1802); he praised the glossary publicly in the *Edinburgh Review* of October 1803.

Sibbald, described as 'a man of eccentric, but benevolent and amiable character' (Chambers, *Scots.*, 261), was a member of many convivial clubs. In a John Kay caricature of 1785, *Connoisseurs*, he is portrayed with a group of friends, looking through a glass at a print of *The Three Graces*. The centrality of his circulating library in Edinburgh life is depicted in the 1856 painting by W. Borthwick Johnstone of Scott seeing Burns there; others in the group include James Bruce, while Sibbald is shown fetching a book from a shelf for Lord Monboddo. Sibbald died, unmarried, at his home in Leith Walk on 9 April 1803, and was buried on 12 April in South Leith churchyard, in William Sibbald's tomb.

WARREN McDOUGALL

Sources Charles Elliot ledgers and letter-books, John Murray, London, archives · J. Sibbald, letter to John Sibbald junior, 9 June 1779, NL Scot., MS 585, no. 1052, fols. 29–30 · J. G. Lockhart, *Memoirs of the life of Sir Walter Scott*, 1 (1837) · *Edinburgh Magazine, or, Literary Miscellany* (1786) · W. J. Couper, *The Edinburgh periodical press*, 2 vols. (1908) · NL Scot., Cadell of Grange MS Acc. 5381, box 36, no. 2 · James Bruce of Kinnaird v. James Sibbald and James Ruthven, NA Scot., CS237/B/6/45 · Chambers, *Scots.* (1864), 4.259–61 · Robert Burns, letter to James Sibbald [Jan 1787], *The letters of Robert Burns*, ed. H. D. Ferguson, rev. G. R. Roy (1985), vol. 1, no. 71 · *The letters of Sir Walter Scott*, ed. H. J. C. Grierson and others, centenary edn, 12 vols. (1932–79) · G. Tancred, *The annals of a Border club*, 2nd edn (1903) · *Edinburgh Evening Courant* (1779) · *Caledonian Mercury* (1782–3) · *Edinburgh Evening Courant* (May 1790) · 'Sibbald v. late Adam Smith', NA Scot., CS238/S/12/39 · 'Sibbald v. Thomas Dobson of Philadelphia', NA Scot., CS226/8695 · bap. reg. Scot., 775/1, Selkirk, Galashiels, births 1714–1819 · bur. reg. Scot., 692/2/16, South Leith, deaths 1791–1810 · *Scots Magazine*, 65 (May 1803), 362 · Register of Sasines, Edinburgh, NA Scot., no. 6404, 5 Feb 1796 · J. Kay, *A series of original portraits and caricature etchings … with biographical sketches* *and illustrative anecdotes*, ed. [H. Paton and others], new edn [3rd edn], 1 (1877), 162, p. 411

Archives NA Scot., MS letter to George Robinson, London; MS contract with James Bruce; Court of Session defender's documents: in James Bruce of Kinnaird *v.* James Sibbald and James Ruthven, CS237/B/6/45 · NA Scot., MS summonses against debtors at Court of Session, CS238/S/12/39; CS238/S/12/44; CS238/S/12/80; CS238/S/12/81; CS29/8; CS226/8695 · U. Edin. L., MS letter to James Cumming, La.II.82 | John Murray archives, London, Charles Elliot letter-books, 1287, 1293, 1306, 1311, 1313, 1315, 1319, 1323, 1328, 1331, 1332, 1333, 1346, 1349, 1357, 1358, 1363, 1375, 1410, 1413, 1439, 1452, 1454, 1760, 1774, 3006, 4111 · John Murray archives, London, Charles Elliot ledgers, L1/67, L1/321, L2/119, L4/100, L4/101 (2 entries) · NA Scot., court of session records · NL Scot., letter to William Cadell, MS Acc. 5381, box 36 (1 and 2) · NL Scot., letter to John Sibbald junior, MS 585, no. 1052, fols. 29–30

Likenesses W. B. Johnstone, group portrait, oils, *c.*1856 (*Meeting of Sir Walter Scott and Robert Burns in 1786: James Sibbald's bookshop*), Writers' Museum, Edinburgh · J. Kay, group portrait, etching (*Connoisseurs*), BM; repro. in *Kay's Edinburgh Portraits: a series of anecdotal biographies chiefly of Scotchmen*, ed. J. Paterson, 2 vols. (1885), vol. 2, facing p. 47 · oils, Scot. NPG [*see illus.*]

Sibbald, Sir Robert (1641–1722), physician and geographer, was born on 15 April 1641 in Blackfriars Wynd off Edinburgh's High Street, the fifth child and third son of David Sibbald (1589–1660), of Rankeillour, Fife, keeper of the great seal of Scotland, and his wife, Margaret Boyd (1606–1672), eldest daughter of Robert Boyd (1575–1645), advocate, of Kippis, near Torphichen, Linlithgowshire. Little is known of Sibbald's early days. His autobiography (which is incomplete and selective) relates how, although 'a tender child', he managed to get 'past all the diseases commonly incident to children without any manifest hazard' (*Memoirs*). In 1645 the family fled Linlithgow because of the plague. In 1650, as the family estate was in Fife, Sibbald was sent to the high school in Cupar. During the following year he witnessed Monck's sacking of Dundee. Sibbald was also educated at the Royal High School in Edinburgh and was a student at the university there from 1653 to 1659, studying under William Tweedy. After receiving his MA on 14 July 1659 Sibbald studied divinity at Edinburgh for about six months, stimulated mainly by Principal Robert Leighton, later archbishop of Glasgow. Sibbald's scholarly habits—'I shunned the playes and divertissements the other students followed' (*Memoirs*)—earned him the nickname 'Diogenes in dolio'.

Leighton's influence turned Sibbald aside from the factionalism of church and state, and in March 1660 he sailed to Leiden to study medicine. He stayed in Leiden for eighteen months, and studied anatomy and surgery under Van Horne and Franciscus Sylvius, botany under Adolphus Vorstius, and chemistry under Christian Marcgraf. Sibbald also met Niels Stenson, who, as Nicolaus Steno, later became professor of anatomy at Padua, and theorist on the earth sciences. Sibbald was also familiar with chemistry and materia medica. Each of these influences helped to shape his later interests. From Leiden he went to Paris, and after a nine-month stay, in which he met Gui Patin, he moved to Angers, where he graduated MD on 17 June 1662. He then briefly resided in London, where he met Sir Robert Moray and other virtuosi introduced to him by his

Sir Robert Sibbald (1641–1722), by John Alexander, 1721

cousins, Andrew *Balfour (1630–1694), a pupil of William Harvey and a later scientific associate of Sibbald, and Patrick Drummond. Sibbald returned to Scotland on 30 October 1662.

Sibbald's intentions on settling in Edinburgh were not ambitious: 'The designe I proposed to myself was to passe quietly through the world, and content myself with a moderate fortune' (*Memoirs*). But from this period he began to develop a deeper interest in natural history, geography, and antiquarianism, which were all to form parts of his vision for the creation of useful natural knowledge. By late 1667 he and Balfour had established a botanical garden in Edinburgh, in grounds belonging to Holyroodhouse. Both there and in the second site in the Trinity Hospital the garden became a major site for plants of use in materia medica. It was run by James Sutherland, later first professor of botany at Edinburgh University and author, with Sibbald's assistance, of the unpublished 'Hortus medicus Edinburgensis'. Between 1679 and 1680, Sibbald, together with Balfour, Thomas Burnet, Alexander Stevenson, and Archibald Pitcairne, founded a medical virtuoso club, which became from 1681 the Royal College of Physicians of Edinburgh (RCPE). Like the botanic garden, the RCPE owed much of its success to political influence, particularly that of James Drummond, fourth earl of Perth and chancellor of Scotland, through whose patronage Sibbald was knighted on 30 September 1682, appointed physician-in-ordinary to the king, and made geographer royal for Scotland.

In 1684 Sibbald produced a *Pharmacopoia Edinburgensis*

and on 4 December of that year was elected president of the RCPE. On 5 March 1685 he was appointed the first professor of medicine at Edinburgh University. Influenced by his patron, Sibbald became a Roman Catholic in 1685, a conversion which shocked his contemporaries, prompted a riotous mob to storm his house in Edinburgh's Carrubers Close, and led him to resign his presidency of the RCPE and flee to London. There he met Sir Robert Boyle, Samuel Collins, Thomas Witherley, Walter Charleton, and other members of the Royal Society, and on 29 March 1686 was elected a fellow of the Royal College of Physicians. Sibbald later renounced Catholicism and re-joined the Protestant church. Boswell claimed later that Sibbald's return to Protestantism was because 'he found the rigid fasting prescribed by the Church very severe upon him' (*TLS*, 8 Dec 1932). However, what was perceived as his lack of principle harmed his reputation; and these events, together with the fact that he had no salary guaranteed, influenced him not to take up the chair at Edinburgh.

Sibbald formally began his geographical work in 1682, although he had already been collecting chorographical and antiquarian material with a view to the description of Scotland. During that year he published an *Advertisement* and a broadside circular requesting geographical information for an intended two-volume description of Scotland. Some of this never-completed work appeared in his 1683 *Nuncius Scoto-Britannus, sive, Admonitio de Atlante Scotio, seu, Descriptione Scotiae antiquae et modernae*. In 1684 he published his most elaborate work, *Scotia illustrata, sive, Prodromus historiae naturalis*, an essay on Scotland's natural history in the widest sense, from natural phenomena, through the plant and animal kingdoms, to human disease. From then until his death Sibbald was active in the fields of natural history, chorographical description, and Roman antiquities, and in promoting useful knowledge as the basis of Scotland's national identity. His cabinet of natural history specimens, gathered together with those of Balfour, was presented to the University of Edinburgh with a catalogue, *Auctarium Musaei Balfouriani e Musaeo Sibbaldino* (published 1697), modelled on Nehemiah Grew's catalogue of the Royal Society's Repository. This collection became an important part of Edinburgh University's Natural History Museum. Between 1698 and 1701 Sibbald twice proposed the founding of a Royal Society of Scotland, an institution to mirror the Royal Society of London and the Dublin Philosophical Society. His 1699 pamphlet on *Provision for the Poor in Time of Dearth and Scarcity* and his unpublished 'A discourse anent the improvements may be made in Scotland for advancing the wealth of the kingdom' (1698) show Sibbald to have been concerned with promoting Scotland's interests through moral enlightenment and economic improvement.

Sibbald's geographical and natural history work reflects but develops the chorographic traditions of Robert Plot, William Petty, William Camden, and others. He extended antiquarian chorographies by practising a Baconian empiricism as a means of consolidating royal authority and as a basis to inductive national and natural knowledge. Sibbald's commission on appointment as geographer royal was to produce a natural history of Scotland, and a geographical description that combined historical data with the results of contemporary survey, which was to be based on returns to his circulated questionnaire. Geography as a whole was for Sibbald not only 'of much use for the life of man' and 'a noble Science' (*Nuncius Scoto-Britannus*), it was also crucial to correct understanding 'in Theology, Natural Philosophy, History, ... Merchandising and the Practice of Medicine' (ibid.). Geography's place within a wider useful natural knowledge embracing natural history and medicine is perhaps unsurprising, given Sibbald's own interests and disciplinary training. But it is of interest to see how he undertook his work.

Sibbald knew and drew from ancient and classical geographers, as well as from contemporary scholars, and drew together existing manuscripts. He also collaborated with the map maker John Adair (although the two had an uneasy relationship). Sibbald worked with John Slezer in the production of his *Theatrum Scotiae* and was a contributor to the 1695 edition of William Camden's *Britannia*; through connections with Edward Lhuyd and the Royal Society he used Martin Martin, author of *A Late Voyage to St Kilda* (1698) and *A Description of the Western Islands of Scotland* (1703), as a source of knowledge on the Hebrides and the highlands. Sibbald also drew together many of the maps of Robert Gordon of Straloch, and some of those from Timothy Pont's geographical survey of Scotland in the late sixteenth century. There is no complete list of respondents to his 1682 enquiries, but surviving manuscript material records about sixty-five local respondents. Many were ministers. For example, James Wallace, who compiled a lengthy report for Sibbald on Orkney, was a Puritan natural historian and physician, and author of *A Description of the Isles of Orkney* (1693), to which Sibbald added an essay on ancient geography.

For various reasons—too little cash, confrontations with Adair and Slezer, too much material, lack of focus—Sibbald's intended 'Scottish Atlas' was never published. The 1683 *Nuncius* and his 1684 *Scotia illustrata* are the only major published expressions of Sibbald's view of geography as a means to national natural knowledge. The material contains Hippocratic discourses on the quality of places, sections on flora and fauna, mountains, forests, arable and other agricultural geographies, and topographical features. The inhabitants of Scotland are viewed as 'products of their country, fitted both for war and the practice of the arts by virtue of the roughness of their native soil and the purity of the air'. Some of the regional material was later expanded and separately published, notably his *History Ancient and Modern of the Sheriffdom of Fife and Kinross* (1710) and *The Description of the Isles of Orkney and Zetland* (1711).

As a physician Sibbald, who was physician to James VII, advocated what has been termed an 'old-new' medicine, a medicine improved by a return to classical principles, but supported by modern observations. He paid close attention to the predisposing causes of disease and to the nature of disease, and explored the efficacy of botanical cures by drawing on Scottish plant life. His lectures on medicine and natural history, advertised in 1706, were never given, as Sibbald considered the students ill prepared and his topics too advanced. His botanical work was admired by Linnaeus, who named the genus *Sibbaldia* in his honour, but Sibbald saw greater value in his natural and medical work, not as classificatory knowledge for its own sake, but as a means to advance both Scotland and the empirical natural sciences.

Sibbald's influence rests, then, in his attention to what he called 'the Knowledge of Natural things that are the products of this Country' as 'usefull to human lyfe' (*Memoirs*). Like his counterparts in Europe, Sibbald was concerned with contemporary survey as current knowledge and as a means to the future condition of the nation. Sibbald's manuscript 'Description of Scotland' pays considerable attention to the economic potential of the nation. His archaeological and antiquarian pursuits and numerous publications on Roman Scotland established the utility of artefacts to national identity. A similar set of interests informed his 1701 'Caetologia', an unpublished marine natural history. Sibbald was much interested in whales, commenting on specimens washed ashore in east Scotland in 1691 and 1701. The blue whale was once known as *Balaenoptera Sibbaldi*. In addition to natural observation, this 1701 work remarks on potential improvements in navigation and the connections between profitable fisheries and national well-being, issues he earlier explored in his 1698 'Discourse anent the improvements'. The focus here was on the state of the nation in the future; as Sibbald put it: 'What is wanting to make the people in all those places Happy'.

Sibbald's personal life was often less than happy. On 26 April 1677 he married Anna Lowes of Merchiston, who miscarried twin boys in a fall that year. A daughter, Katherine, born on 12 October 1678, died soon after, and his wife died on 27 December 1678. He married Anna Orrack in November 1682: a daughter, Elizabeth, born on 9 April 1685, died in 1686. A further daughter was stillborn in 1686. Two daughters survived—Elizabeth, born in November 1687, and Euphame, born 2 September 1688—but a further child, Jean, born on 4 September 1690, died of smallpox in 1692. He lost many personal papers in a house fire on 20 March 1694, was struck in the face by a golf club in October 1690, and had a serious fall in July 1692 after tangling his spurs; and financial difficulties forced him to sell a large proportion of his library in 1707–8.

Sibbald's work and ideas have enduring significance. They are representative of contemporary interest by virtuosi in useful natural knowledge. In his view, geography, medicine, botany, and archaeology were all part of utilitarian and systematic natural philosophy. It was once thought that Sibbald's reputation as a geographer rested on what he took from others. More recent scholarship has pointed to his key role in promoting national knowledge through survey and questionnaire; in being part of European interests in so doing; and, for Scotland, in being central to early Enlightenment debates about the value of

natural knowledge as a means to national improvement. It does not help to describe his interests and work in modern disciplinary terms. For Sibbald, as for so many of his contemporaries, geography was closely allied to natural history, and was both a product, and a means to what we might understand as utilitarian medical-topographical knowledge. It was also a practice that embraced the formal languages of mathematics and geometry and used them to measure and to survey peoples, nations, and nature as a whole. Sibbald died on 9 August 1722, following which the remainder of his library was sold.

CHARLES W. J. WITHERS

Sources The memoirs of Sir Robert Sibbald, 1641–1722, ed. F. P. Hett (1932) • R. Sibbald, 'Memoirs of my lyfe', *c*.1695, NL Scot., Adv. MS. 33.5.1 • J. Maidment, ed., *Remains of Sir Robert Sibbald, KNT, MD, containing his autobiography, memoirs of the Royal College of Physicians, portions of his literary correspondence and an account of his MSS* (1837) • R. L. Emerson, 'Sir Robert Sibbald Kt, the Royal Society of Scotland and the origins of the Scottish Enlightenment', *Annals of Science*, 45 (1988), 41–72 • C. W. J. Withers, 'Geography, science and national identity in early modern Britain: the case of Scotland and the work of Sir Robert Sibbald, 1641–1722', *Annals of Science*, 53 (1996), 29–73 • [H. H. Child], 'Sir Robert Sibbald', *TLS* (8 Dec 1932)
Archives BGS, collections for a natural history of Scotland [copy] • NA Scot. • NL Scot., papers • Royal College of Physicians of Edinburgh • S. Antiquaries, Lond., transcriptions from his collections made for Walter MacFarlan • U. Glas. L. | BL, Sloane MSS, letters mainly to Sir Hans Sloane • RS, letters to Royal Society
Likenesses J. Alexander, oils, 1721, Royal College of Physicians of Edinburgh [*see illus.*] • W. H. Lizars, line engraving (after J. Alexander), BM, NPG, Wellcome L.; repro. in W. Jardine, ed., *The naturalist's library*, 24 (1843), frontispiece
Wealth at death manuscripts and books sold at auction (5 Feb 1723) for £342 17*s*.: *Memoirs*, ed. Hett, 10

Sibbald, William (*d.* 1650), soldier, was 'a Fyfe gentleman borne' (*Diary of Mr John Lamont*, 19), though his parentage is unknown. He recorded that 'I have been from my youth a Souldier' ('Speech', 200), and probably made his career as a mercenary in the Thirty Years' War. He first appears (with the rank of colonel) as the commander of the covenanter garrison placed in the House of Airlie at the end of June 1640 by the earl of Montrose to prevent it falling into the hands of the earl of Argyll, his rival. About a week later Argyll arrived, removed Sibbald, and destroyed the castle.

Sibbald is next mentioned in August 1644, when he was one of Montrose's two companions when, in disguise, he made his way from England to the highlands. In November 1644 he left Montrose and joined the covenanters, and he has been roundly condemned for this. Montrose's 'courtesies and other noble benevolences' had been repaid with ingratitude (Gordon, 71) by a man who 'deserted him in his greatest need' (Wishart, 50). However, it is possible that his 'desertion' was part of some secret plan. Nathaniel Gordon, who also 'deserted' at this point, was believed to have been sent to persuade Lord Gordon to leave the covenanters and join Montrose, and Sibbald may have been acting on secret orders for some other covert mission. Certainly Sibbald, like Nathaniel, later returned to serve Montrose and, as the final episode of his life shows, he was fully trusted by him. He probably went into exile with Montrose in 1646, and about the end of 1649 was dispatched with letters from Montrose to royalist leaders. Major-General James Turner travelled with him from Hamburg to Rotterdam, and since Sibbald was short of money gave him a letter to his wife in Edinburgh, telling her to lend him some. She did so, but 'he had his head chopt of not long after … so I losd both my friend and my money', as Turner briskly relates (Turner, 92). This shows that Sibbald reached Edinburgh, but he was arrested in Musselburgh, where he was a prisoner by 23 April 1650. After Montrose's attempt at a rising had been defeated and he had been executed, the Scottish parliament turned its attention to Sibbald's fate. Montrose's trust in was indicated by the fact that the letters that Sibbald carried but had not delivered told the recipients to give 'absolute crydit' to what he said (*Historical Works of Balfour*, 4.22). Sibbald was an unco-operative prisoner, and on 18 May parliament threatened him with torture unless he satisfied his interrogators. If the report of a French agent is to be trusted, under torture he revealed a royalist plot to seize Edinburgh Castle. After a trial by the committee for processes, parliament gave orders on 4 June that he be beheaded. The sentence was carried out on 7 June at the Mercat Cross, High Street, Edinburgh, Sibbald being beheaded by the Maiden, the Scottish precursor of the guillotine. He had been prevented from reading a speech he had prepared declaring his loyalty to the king and true protestant religion, and by one account he died 'verrie obduredlie' (obdurately) in that he refused to accept his guilt (Nicoll, 15). A royalist account describes, in an idealized vision of a martyr's death, how on the scaffold Sibbald 'smil'd a while, and talk'd to the disorderly rabble that was about him: then with such an heroick gesture march'd to the block, as if he had been to act a gallant in a Play' (Wishart, 270n.). DAVID STEVENSON

Sources DNB · G. Wishart, *The memoirs of James, marquis of Montrose, 1639–1650*, ed. and trans. A. D. Murdoch and H. F. M. Simpson (1893) · 'The speech of Collonel William Sibbald', in G. Wishart, *Montrose redivius* (1652) · APS · S. R. Gardiner, *History of the Commonwealth and protectorate, 1649–1656*, new edn, 4 vols. (1903) · NA Scot., PA12/5 · P. Gordon, *A short abridgement of Britane's distemper*, ed. J. Dunn, Spalding Club, 10 (1844) · J. Turner, *Memoirs of his own life and times, 1632–1670*, ed. T. Thomson, Bannatyne Club, 28 (1829) · *The historical works of Sir James Balfour*, ed. J. Haig, 4 vols. (1824–5) · J. Nicoll, *A diary of public transactions and other occurrences, chiefly in Scotland, from January 1650 to June 1667*, ed. D. Laing, Bannatyne Club, 52 (1836) · *The diary of Mr John Lamont of Newton, 1649–1671*, ed. G. R. Kinloch, Maitland Club, 7 (1830)

Sibbes [Sibs], **Richard** (1577?–1635), Church of England clergyman, was born in 1577 according to his friend Zachary Catlin, although statements of his age at various dates place his birth anywhere between 1576 and 1581; the claim that he was baptized at Tostock, Suffolk, on 6 January 1580 lacks evidence. His parents, Paul Sibbes (*d*. 1610), wheelwright, of Tostock, and his wife, Joane, moved their family 2 miles west to the town of Thurston while he was still young. He was educated locally, attending first the petty school at Pakenham run by Richard Brigs, a graduate of St John's College, Cambridge, and then the well-known King

Richard Sibbes (1577?–1635), by John Payne

Edward VI Free School at nearby Bury St Edmunds. Catlin recorded that Paul Sibbes was persuaded to continue Richard's education only because of 'the Importunity of Friends'. 'His father at length grew weary of his expense for booke-learning' and made an investment in some tools for him, so that he could be set up in his own trade. But the younger Sibbes seemed ill-suited to it. Walking home from school, while his friends played games, Sibbes would 'take out of his Pocket or Sachel, one Book or other, and so to goe reading and meditating, til he came to his Father's house, which was neere a mile of, and so as he went to schole agen' (*Works*, 1.cxxxv).

Cambridge, 1595–1617 In 1595, perhaps due to the influence of John Knewstub, rector of Cockfield, Suffolk, Sibbes matriculated at St John's College, Cambridge. During his years as an undergraduate an allowance of just over £8 per year from his father was supplemented by aid from friends and a sub-sizarship from the college. He graduated BA in 1599. Not quite two years later, on 3 April 1601, he was admitted as a foundress fellow of St John's and in 1602 he proceeded MA. He served in a variety of college posts, including Fell chaplain and sublector (1603), examiner (subject unspecified, 1604–8), Lady Margaret chaplain (1612–18), and Dr Thompson chaplain (1612–18), and he was also taxor for the university in 1608. In 1615 he was elected both senior dean and lector domesticus of St

John's College. In 1619, when he had already left for London, he was elected senior fellow.

At some point, probably soon after he became a fellow of St John's, Sibbes's life changed direction. 'It pleased God to convert him by the Ministry of Master Paul Baines, whilest he was Lecturer at Saint Andrews in Cambridge' (Clarke, 143). On 21 February 1608 he was ordained deacon and priest and on 1 March 1609 he was elected as a college preacher, whose duties included preaching to the townspeople. Despite his stuttering, he evidently succeeded and gained wide repute as a preacher. In 1610 Sibbes was created BD. That same year the minister, churchwardens, and twenty-nine other parishioners of Holy Trinity Church, Cambridge, established a public lecture for the town by popular subscription, to be held in the church at one o'clock on Sunday afternoon; on 22 November they offered the position to Sibbes at a salary of £40 a year. When he preached Holy Trinity was so crowded that a new gallery needed to be built to accommodate his listeners.

It has long been asserted that Sibbes subsequently lost his positions in Cambridge due to his puritan convictions, but, the confusion of later scholars notwithstanding, he was not deprived of his fellowship at St John's in 1615. The college rental books record quarterly payments to him as a fellow continuously through the first quarter of 1626. Nor is there evidence that Sibbes was deprived of the Holy Trinity lectureship. A memorandum from the vice-chancellor's court dated 6 December 1616 relates that when he 'was asked by Mr Vice-Chancellor whether he would subscribe to the 3 articles required to be subscribed unto by the Canons [of 1604] [he] refused'. Answers to diverse accompanying questions supplied in Sibbes's own hand explained, 'I said that the signe of the cross [in baptism] was dangerous', but qualified his reservations to a significant degree. 'My meaning was in regard of those that be not well instructed and not otherwise. I said that there is nihil impie in the booke of ordination. I add it is not contrary to the word of God, but allowable' (Cambridge University Archives, vice-chancellor's court, I.42, fol. 202). The next day, John Hills, master of St Catharine's College and vice-chancellor, wrote to James Montagu, bishop of Winchester, stating that 'Mr. Sibbs at first made Some Quastion and Seemed lesse Setled in Opinion, but upon a Second conference he also Submitted and Subscribed' (Cambridge University Archives, letters 11.A.A.8.d).

London and Cambridge, 1617–1635 Less than two months later, on 5 February 1617, by the influence of Sir Henry Yelverton, Sibbes was chosen preacher (or lecturer, or reader of divinity) of Gray's Inn, London. By 1624 his ministry had been so well-received that, just as at Holy Trinity Church, the auditorium had to be enlarged. His presence at Gray's Inn was crucial to the growth of his network of friendships. Such a prominent platform gave opportunity for both his reputation and his influence to increase beyond what was possible simply as a provincial lecturer.

Sibbes did more than preach in London. In 1625 he was part of a group of twelve Londoners who formed themselves into an unincorporated, self-perpetuating group of trustees in order to 'raise funds with which to acquire ecclesiastical revenue in the hands of laymen to be used for the maintenance and relief of a godly, faithful, and painstaking ministry', particularly in borough towns (Calder, vii). As they gained control of livings, these feoffees did not simply fill vacancies with any duly ordained clergyman; they wanted godly preachers to fill the pulpits. The feoffees worked to that end for eight years, collecting more than £6000 and funding eighteen preachers in eleven counties. In February 1633, after lengthy hearings, the feoffees for impropriations were dissolved in the court of exchequer for having formed a self-perpetuating corporation without having obtained a royal charter. While judiciously observing his obligations to the church, Sibbes was not beyond trying the boundaries of those obligations, or at least working apart from them.

In 1626 Sibbes was appointed to the mastership of St Catharine's College, Cambridge. The college prospered under his leadership. He brought in increased numbers of students, large benefactions, and successfully promoted new construction. Although residing in Cambridge sometimes, Sibbes maintained his post and chambers at Gray's Inn. He also continued to be active in London circles. On 2 March 1627, with William Gouge, William Taylor, and John Davenport, Sibbes circulated a letter appealing for aid especially for the destitute ministers from the upper Palatinate. For their efforts, Sibbes and his co-petitioners were brought before Laud and the high commission and reprimanded. While such aid was not inconsistent with English foreign policy to help the protestants on the continent, publicly circulating a letter could have been seen as an inappropriately direct involvement of private persons in state affairs, and as therefore implicit criticism of government inactivity. Nevertheless, Sibbes continued to prosper. On 9 October 1627 he proceeded DD at Cambridge. On 1 November 1633 he was presented by the crown to the perpetual curacy of Holy Trinity, Cambridge. This was to be his last new appointment.

Death and writings Sibbes preached his final sermon at Gray's Inn, on 28 June 1635. That evening he fell sick. Samuel Hartlib noted that in Sibbes's final days he was unshaken: 'being asked how hee … did in his soule replied I should doe God much wrong if I should not say very well' (Hartlib, 'Ephemerides', 1635). He was obviously in control of his mental faculties. He finished his preface to *The Soul's Conflict, and Victory over itself by Faith*, the following Wednesday, 1 July, at Gray's Inn. Catlin reported that 'his Physitian, that knew his Body best' was 'then out of the Citty'. On Saturday, 4 July, Sibbes clearly knew himself to be dying. That day he revised his will, being 'weake in body, but of perfect memory', leaving his goods to family, friends, and servants at Gray's Inn. In his chamber at Gray's Inn, on 5 July 1635, Sibbes died. He had never married. His body was buried the next day in St Andrew's, Holborn, where the members of Gray's Inn had maintained a chapel from medieval times. His funeral sermon, preached by William Gouge, has not survived.

Sibbes prefaced thirteen volumes of sermons, including those by Paul Baynes, Ezekiel Culverwell, John Preston,

John Smith, Henry Scudder, Thomas Gataker, Robert Jenison, John Ball, and Richard Capel. His own sermons were either published or reprinted almost every year from 1618 to 1664. While over thirty volumes appeared in his lifetime, most were collected and published after his death, many collected and edited, at Sibbes's request, by Thomas Goodwin and Philip Nye. His most celebrated and frequently reprinted work—both during his life and afterwards—is *The Bruised Reed and Smoking Flax*, a series of sermons on the words of Isaiah quoted by Jesus in Matthew 12: 20, 'A bruised reed shall he not break, and smoking flax shall he not quench, till he send forth judgment unto victory.' From the book's first printing (1630) to the most recent reprint (1998), the tender meditations of *The Bruised Reed* have been devotional favourites. The most recent edition of his collected works (1862–4; repr. 1973–83) fills seven volumes.

Reputation Sibbes has been presented as one of a number of early Stuart preachers who neither approved nor practised kneeling in communion, wearing the surplice, or signing the cross in baptism, and yet who remained within the established church. He was, it has been reported, constantly troubled by William Laud, archbishop of Canterbury. Doubly deprived, censured, and silenced, Sibbes was supposed to have been a model for his numerous disciples—such as Thomas Goodwin, John Davenport, and John Cotton—who later found their way into dissent. It has been supposed that only the power of his lawyer friends and noble patrons allowed him to retain his later ministry at Gray's Inn for almost two decades. After his death, his writings became almost entirely the possession of nonconformists, and Sibbes came to be read through separatist spectacles.

Although Sibbes was popular, even celebrated, during his life, his thought could hardly be said to have been seminal, nor his career determinative for the fortunes of the godly in early Stuart England. Contrary to previous presentations of him, it now appears that Sibbes did subscribe to the three articles, conform, and retain his positions in Cambridge. His move to London in 1617 is much more explicable in terms of his talent for fostering friendships, combined with his obvious abilities as a preacher. His sociability certainly helps to account for his successes with the feoffees (before their dissolution) and at St Catharine's College, and perhaps for much more. It does not, however, suggest any religious radicalism which would encourage separation. Radicalism is also ruled out when account is taken of his explicit defences of the Church of England (for example, his *Consolatory Letter to an Afflicted Conscience*), together with the general tone of his writing and indeed the direction of his whole career.

Yet as godly preaching—which Sibbes had taken to be quite literally the salvation of the Church of England—became increasingly hindered by those in authority, his own position in the church certainly appeared more incongruous. His loyalty to the Church of England was consistent with his theology. He understood the church to be a covenant community far more extensive than the elect, intended to be filled with people in various spiritual

states. Therefore imperfection was expected and tolerated, though not excused, and the use of means vigorously encouraged. Indeed, even more than creation, the covenant obliged one to live a life of holiness. Sibbes's interiorization of piety—not unique to Sibbes, but powerfully communicated in his sermons—accounts at the same time for his popularity with disparate groups, his ability to conform to the demands of the church, and yet also for the potential for a Christianity lived in disobedience to ungodly earthly authorities. Ironically, all of the misrepresentations of Sibbes as a doubly deprived puritan legend have led to a very different impression of him from what is gathered by reading his writings and contemporary testimonies about his character and temperament. Yet, with the deprivations removed from the foreground, the conciliating tone of his writings begins to appear more consistent with his own person, and his later preferments become more understandable. The picture of Sibbes which results—of Sibbes as a reformer, but a cautious reformer, as a puritan, but a moderate puritan—is consistent with the rest of Sibbes's life and activities.

MARK E. DEVER

Sources *Works of Richard Sibbes*, ed. A. Grosart, 7 vols. (1862–4) • S. Clarke, 'The life of Doctor Sibs, who dyed Anno Christi 1635', *The lives of thirty two English divines*, in *A general martyrologie*, 3rd edn (1677), 143–45 • M. E. Dever, *Richard Sibbes: puritanism and Calvinism in late Elizabethan and early Stuart England* (2000) • I. M. Calder, *Activities of the puritan faction of the Church of England, 1625–1633* (1957) • C. H. Cooper, *Annals of Cambridge*, 3 (1845) • S. Hartlib, 'Ephemerides' (1635), Sheffield University, Samuel Hartlib MSS • Norfolk RO, ORR/1/2, fols. 80–81 • CUL, department of manuscripts and university archives, vice-chancellor's court, I.42, fol. 202 • CUL, department of manuscripts and university archives, letters 11.A.A.8.d • St John Cam., Archives, SB4.4, fol. 163

Archives CUL, letters, Lett. 11.A.A.8.d | CUL, vice-chancellor's court, I.42 • Norfolk RO, ORR/1/2

Likenesses P. Lachman, portrait, repro. in Dever, *Richard Sibbes* • W. Marshall, line engraving (aged fifty-eight), BM; repro. in R. Sibbes, *A fountain sealed* (1637) • J. Payne, line engraving, BM, NPG [*see illus.*] • engraving, repro. in R. Sibbes, *Bowels opened*, 3rd edn (1648) • oils, Bodl. Oxf.

Wealth at death approx. £940: will, 1635, repr. in *Works*, ed. Grosart, vol. 1, pp. cxxviii–cxxx

Siberch, John [*formerly* Johann Lair von Siegburg] (*c.*1476–1554), printer, was born in Sieglar (Lair), near Siegburg, Germany, the son of Peter von Lair (*d.* 1533), a wool weaver, and his wife, Lena. He took his name from Siegburg, where the family moved in his childhood. On 5 December 1492 he matriculated at the University of Cologne. Probably in 1512, or later, he married a sister of Gertrud van Amersfoort, a member of the bookselling and printing family of Franz and Arnold Birckmann of Cologne, and thus became related to some of the major north European humanist printers and booksellers. They had two daughters: the elder, Katharina, married Georg Kessel of Cologne, and the younger was called Baetzgen.

For a while during the second decade of the sixteenth century Siberch was in the service of another Cologne bookseller, Hans Beck; and it was as a bookseller that he moved to Cambridge, possibly influenced in this by Richard Croke, whom he probably met at Leipzig. The first publication bearing his imprint, a work by Croke (1520), was printed by Eucharius Cervicornus at Cologne.

Siberch established his press in Cambridge in 1520 or 1521 with the help of a loan of £20 from the university. His house was on the site of what is now Tree Court, Gonville and Caius College, and his first book was Henry Bullock's *Oratio*, a tribute on the occasion of a visit to the university by Cardinal Wolsey in autumn 1520. In 1521 Siberch printed at least seven short books, including an unauthorized edition of *De conscribendis epistolis* by his friend Erasmus and Thomas Linacre's translation of Galen's *De temperamentis*. Subsequently his authors included John Fisher and Sir Thomas Elyot; he also sought the assurance of an educational market with an edition of Erasmus and Lily's grammar *De octo partium orationis constructione*. After a period of considerable activity in 1521, the pace of his printing declined sharply, and Siberch's later work includes more ephemera, such as indulgences, rather than books. He ceased to print at Cambridge probably by the end of 1523. He was also associated with a binding shop, possibly as a part of his bookselling business.

Despite the fame of his authors, Siberch was not commercially very successful as a printer in England. By early 1524 he had left Cambridge, possibly going to Antwerp to work with Franz Birckmann and other members of his wife's family. His wife died in England in the mid-1520s, after which time his relations with her family seem to have become strained. By 1538 he had been ordained priest, and for the remainder of his life he served a parish in Siegburg, where he died at some time before 28 September in 1554. He was probably buried at St Servatius's Church, Siegburg.   DAVID McKITTERICK

Sources O. Treptow, *Johann Siberch Lair von Siegburg—John Siberch—der Erstdrucker von Cambridge und seine Welt* (Siegburg, 1964) [trans. and abridged as *John Siberch, Johann Lair von Siegburg* (1970)] · E. P. Goldschmidt, *The first Cambridge press in its European setting* (1955) · STC, 1475–1640

Sibley, George (1824–1891), civil engineer, born on 12 August 1824, was a son of Robert Sibley (1789–1849), then county surveyor of Middlesex and one of the early members of the Institution of Civil Engineers. An older brother, Robert Lacon Sibley (c.1818–1882), continued his father's architectural practice. From 1831 to 1838 Sibley attended University College school, London. After serving an apprenticeship in his father's civil engineering and architectural practice in London, he obtained employment in 1845 as assistant engineer on the Bristol and Exeter Railway under Isambard Kingdom Brunel, and afterwards under Charles Hutton Gregory.

In 1851, through James Meadows Rendel, Sibley was appointed an assistant engineer on the East India Railway, in charge of the Chandernagore district. His promotion was rapid. In August 1853 he was placed in charge of the Birbhum district as resident engineer, and in this position designed the two largest brick arch bridges in India, those over the Adjai and More. In December of the same year he was made a district engineer. About 1857 he was appointed deputy chief engineer under George Turnbull, and in 1859 chief engineer of the North-Western Provinces division. On the death of Samuel Power he became, in April 1868, chief engineer of the East India Railway and a member of the board of agency. During his service in the northwest Sibley was responsible for the completion of the Allahabad Jumna Bridge, then the largest railway bridge in the world, designed by A. M. Rendel and G. W. Rendel. He also constructed the Delhi Jumna Bridge, personally designing the foundations, and designed all the works at Delhi connected with the railway.

In 1869 Sibley was involved in a controversy with the Indian government, which had issued a notification implying that the civil engineers received commissions from others than their employers. The accusation does not appear to have been justifiable and Sibley, with the other engineers, addressed a strong remonstrance to the government, supported by the Institution of Civil Engineers.

In January 1875 Sibley left India on furlough, and retired a year later. In consideration of his services he was made a companion in the Order of the Indian Empire. He lived in England in a house, The Mount, which he built of concrete on the summit of Whitehill, Caterham, devoting himself to literature and science. Sibley was always an individualist, marked by his becoming a vegetarian at the age of nineteen. He died of heart disease at his home on 25 October 1891, leaving funds for engineering scholarships and encouraging native students at Calcutta University.

A brother, **Septimus William Sibley** (1831–1893), surgeon, distinguished himself as a student at the Middlesex and University College hospitals, where he defeated Lord Lister in competition for medals in both medicine and surgery. He was successively house surgeon, medical registrar, and lecturer in pathology at Middlesex Hospital. Becoming FRCS in 1857, he was the first general practitioner elected to the council. An active member of the British Medical Association, he published *A History and Description of the Cholera Epidemic in London in 1854*, besides papers in *Medico-Chirurgical Transactions*.

Sibley married Clara F. Carden, daughter of Sir R. W. Carden, bt, MP; their son Walter Knowsley (1862–1944) followed his father into the medical profession.

E. I. CARLYLE, *rev.* MIKE CHRIMES

Sources PICE, 108 (1891–2), 409–11 · *The Times* (28 Oct 1891) · Colvin, *Archs.* · WWW, 1941–50 [Walter Knowsley]
Archives BL OIOC, minutes of East India Railway Co. · Inst. CE, membership records
Likenesses Maull & Fox, carte-de-visite, Inst. CE, archives
Wealth at death £12,717 9s. 5d.: probate, 12 Nov 1891, CGPLA Eng. & Wales

Sibley, Patricia Jacqueline. *See* Shelton, Anne (1923–1994).

Sibley, Septimus William (1831–1893). *See under* Sibley, George (1824–1891).

Sibly, Ebenezer (1751–c.1799), astrologer and physician, was born in Bristol on 30 January 1751. The names of his parents are not known. The Swedenborgian preacher Manoah *Sibly was his brother, and there was also another brother and a sister of whom nothing is known. Their father was described as a mechanic. His mother died in 1768, whereupon he was removed from school, perhaps to assist in his father's business. None the less, he continued to study on his own, becoming a formidable polymath in medicine, natural philosophy, and occultism, both traditional and contemporary.

By 1784 Sibly was living in Portsmouth, where he was initiated into freemasonry—the beginning of a lifelong involvement, in the course of which he joined several different lodges, and founded one. In this context he was sometimes known as Noah Sibly or Father Noah. He also completed his first book there, from an address somewhere on Portsmouth Common: it was a massive compendium of astrology, occult philosophy, and magic, entitled *A New and Complete Illustration of the Celestial Science of Astrology*, first published in four parts (1784–8). It obviously met a need, for by 1812 there had been twelve editions, some appearing under the title *A New and Complete Illustration of the Occult Sciences*. The last known edition appeared in 1826.

About 1785 Sibly returned to Bristol. He acted briefly as an official agent for the sale of lottery tickets but this aspect of his career was cut short when he was duped into selling false tickets by one John Wilkes of Winchester and the racket was discovered. Sibly swore his innocence in an affidavit before the mayor of Bristol on 31 January 1786, and there the matter ended. By about 1788, Sibly had moved to London, where he remained. In 1795 his address was 1 Upper Titchfield Street, and the following year he was living at 40 New Bridge Street, near St Paul's Cathedral.

In 1789 Sibly founded a new lodge of freemasonry—no. 253, later known as the Lodge of Joppa—which met at The Globe inn, Hatton Garden. He had marked political views, and was a supporter of the American War of Independence. In 1790 he briefly moved to Ipswich in order to campaign vigorously (and successfully) for the whig candidate, Sir John Hadley D'Oyly. On 20 April 1792 he obtained his MD from King's College, Aberdeen (there is no evidence he ever actually lived there).

Meanwhile, Sibly had also become a fellow of the Harmonic Philosophical Society, founded in Paris to promote mesmerism. He quickly incorporated mesmerism, or animal magnetism, into his system, as another example of new discoveries confirming and extending ancient wisdom concerning forces of sympathy and antipathy. More work was also forthcoming. In 1789, a new edition of the extremely popular and durable *Culpeper's English Physician and Complete Herbal* appeared, with fourteen editions under Sibly's name by 1813; in 1794 came Sibly's *A Key to Physic and the Occult Sciences*, which reached five editions by 1814; *The Medical Mirror* reached six editions by 1814; and the first volume of the *Magazine of Natural History* appeared in 1796.

This prodigious output amounted to about 2500 quarto pages, and all the major works were available until well into the first half of the nineteenth century. Their chief interest lies in the way they straddle and unite what are often thought to be the two irreconcilable worlds of ancient magic and modern science: that is, hermetic magic and occultism, with its focus on the sympathetic and antipathetic connections between macrocosm and microcosm, whether human or natural, and contemporary Enlightenment demonstrations of progress, both in human affairs and in knowledge. Sibly thus combined his whig reforming-populist zeal and freemasonic esoteric idealism with the tradition of vulgate self-help manuals of physic and astrology (the poor man's science, so to speak) initiated by Culpeper and other radicals during the revolution in English astrology. He freely mixed the experimental natural philosophy of Newton, Lavoisier, and Priestley with the cosmologies of Hermes Trismegistus, Paracelsus, and the alchemists. Unusually for an eighteenth-century figure, Sibly believed that the experimental and observational discoveries of the modern natural philosophers refined and developed the insights of the alchemical and magical cosmologists, while the vitalism and spirituality of the ancients corrected the tendencies toward atheism and materialism of the moderns.

Sibly's presentation of physic was also suffused with the natural magic of alchemy and astrology, whereby every organ and function has both macrocosmic and microcosmic counterparts within a system of spiritual hierarchies and occult properties. By this reasoning the heart, for example, relates to the sun, to certain herbs such as St John's wort, to gold, and to other items which bear sun-like qualities. When focused on plants and metals, this logic suggests appropriate natural remedies for diseases. Such medicines were often cheaply available, unlike more expensive and invasive procedures. Sibly's *Medical Mirror* was another instance of medical popularization, offering an accessible (if rather florid) account of human anatomy and physiology, including the delicate subject of reproduction.

Within the astrological tradition, Sibly's *Illustration* was the first comprehensive textbook for decades, covering judicial astrology (including both the genethliacal, or natal, and the horary branches) as well as mundane and meteorological applications. Also included were sections on natural and occult philosophy, witchcraft, ceremonial magic, and necromancy—the last presented as a warning, in a satisfyingly sensational manner. Synthetic, eclectic, and populist, it incorporated a largely magical worldview, all things for which it was strongly criticized by the only other nationally known astrologer of the day, and an Aristotelian rationalist, John Worsdale. But it was precisely this approach that guaranteed Sibly the wide readership that Worsdale never attained.

Sibly also continued the provocative tradition of apparently correct astrological predictions (or prophecies) of spectacular public events. In an essay first published in 1787, analysing the sun's ingress into Aries (at the vernal point) on 19 March 1789, Sibly concluded that:

> here is every prospect … that some very important event will happen in the politics of France, such as may dethrone, or very nearly touch the life of, the king, and make victims of many great and illustrious men in church and state,

preparatory to a revolution … which will at once astonish and surprise the surrounding nations.   (Sibly, 1051)

A century earlier, such a forecast and its fulfilment (with the French Revolution of 1789) would have guaranteed its author national fame and/or notoriety, as happened in the case of William Lilly and the great fire of London. But, at the end of the eighteenth century, it drew little or no comment, any more than the rest of Sibly's voluminous published work, despite its popularity, received informed appraisal from his educated and professional contemporaries. This reception points to the way professional and disciplinary boundaries of knowledge had hardened, firmly excluding anything explicitly identifiable as occult, magical, or astrological.

At the same time, however, the middle classes at the end of the eighteenth century were beginning to grow in power and complexity, and, as part of that process, began showing patchy signs of intellectual independence from patrician hegemony. One early sign was the new market Sibly found (and helped create) among semi-erudite middle-class urban readers for a popular magical science. This was a niche that the new almanacs of Zadkiel and Raphael would further exploit and develop from the 1830s onwards. Sibly is thus a key figure in the revival of astrology and natural magic after its apparently terminal decline during the Enlightenment.

Sibly is believed to have died in London about 1799, in an obscurity that says as much about his times as it does about himself.   PATRICK CURRY

Sources E. Sibly, *A new and complete illustration of the celestial science of astrology*, 4 pts in 2 vols. [1790] · A. G. Debus, 'Scientific truth and occult tradition: the medical world of Ebenezer Sibly (1751–1799)', *Medical History*, 26 (1982), 259–78 · D. Timson, 'Ebenezer Sibly: freemason extraordinary', *Transactions Lodge of Research*, 2429 (1964–5), 62–7 · E. Ward, 'Ebenezer Sibly: a man of parts', *Ars Quatuor Coronatorum*, 71 (1958), 48–52 · BM, Add. MS 19166, fol. 396 · *DNB*
Archives Wellcome L., papers
Likenesses portrait, repro. in E. Sibly, *The medical mirror* (1795), frontispiece · portrait, repro. in E. Sibly, *A new and complete illustration of the occult sciences* (1790), following p. 390 · portrait, repro. in E. Sibly, *The medical mirror* (1796), frontispiece

Sibly, Sir (Thomas) Franklin (1883–1948), geologist and university administrator, was born in Bristol on 25 October 1883, the only son (there was also a daughter) of Thomas Dix Sibly, a solicitor, and his wife, Virginia, daughter of the Revd Franklin Tonkin, vicar of Madron, Penzance. He was educated at Wycliffe College, Gloucestershire, which had been founded by his uncle, and at St Dunstan's, Burnham-on-Sea. His career as a student was precocious; in 1903 he obtained first-class honours in experimental physics as an external candidate at London University, studying at University College, Bristol, while still under twenty years old. He was guided into postgraduate research in geology, a subject that had captured his interest. Having been awarded an 1851 Exhibition scholarship, he studied the constitution and structure of carboniferous limestone in the Mendip hills and the Forest of Dean. His series of articles, mainly written between 1905 and 1920, was soon regarded as among the classics of

Sir (Thomas) Franklin Sibly (1883–1948), by William Dring, 1947

carboniferous stratigraphy. He was to serve as chairman of the Geological Survey Board from 1930 to 1943.

Having achieved the degree of DSc in 1908, at the early age of twenty-five, Sibly was appointed lecturer in geology at King's College, London. There he worked under Professor Harry Govier Seeley and he came to know the leading figures in the geological world. Many were subsequently personal friends, thanks to his engaging manner, keen and receptive mind, and willingness to undertake any task to further the science. In 1913 he became professor of geology at University College, Cardiff. He was an inspired teacher, his lectures and talks being clear and stimulating. With too few outstanding students between 1914 and 1918, he took on the part-time war job of a temporary officer in the geological survey, inspecting the iron ore deposits of the Forest of Dean. In 1918, before moving to a chair at Armstrong College, Newcastle upon Tyne, he married Maud Evelyn, second daughter of Charles L. Barfoot of Newport; she had been one of his pupils at Cardiff. They were to have one son.

To widespread surprise and some dismay, in 1920 Sibly became principal of the newly founded University College, Swansea: a change of tack by one who, despite being still under forty years old, was already in the first rank of geologists in England. However, he had already developed an interest in, and liking for, university administration, enjoying a reputation for tackling problems with insight and for a largeness of vision beyond his years. Thanks to his enthusiasm and drive, departments were set up from scratch and made into viable teaching and research centres. In 1925–6 his experience as vice-chancellor of the

University of Wales widened his horizons further. He left Wales in 1926 to become principal officer—later principal—of the University of London.

Sibly's period in London was undoubtedly the most frustrating of his life. The University of London Act of 1926, with its centralizing powers (especially in finance), had to be implemented through statutes that were finally promulgated in 1929, after much resistance in some quarters. He also had to reach agreement with the London county council over the extensive site in Bloomsbury, earmarked as the university's eventual headquarters. His days were therefore spent in a sequence of negotiations at the highest level, and he felt deeply his inevitable remoteness from the teaching staff and students, groups with which he had always sought and enjoyed close relations. When in 1929 he was invited to the University of Reading as vice-chancellor, he accepted gladly. This was a far smaller institution which had received its charter as recently as 1926 and was struggling with inadequate funds; yet its residential system, developed by his predecessor William Macbride Childs, greatly appealed to Sibly.

Sibly husbanded the young university's meagre resources so that they could be laid out to best effect. Although the number of teaching staff did not increase and tutorial students were no more than 600, the number studying for higher degrees more than doubled. By 1939 Reading was one of the main centres in the country for the study of agriculture in its practical aspects. Sibly achieved progress by strength of character rather than by exerting his authority; a kindly man, he could severely reprimand wayward members of staff, but his forceful and ever ruthless manner as a committee chairman immediately relaxed into cheerful informality once he doffed his gown at the conclusion of meetings. He took much trouble to get to know his junior colleagues.

Sibly's readiness to be put upon for the public good was thereafter shamelessly exploited. From 1929 to 1934 he was chairman of the executive committee of the Universities Bureau of the British Empire. In 1938, the year he was knighted, he became chairman of the Committee of Vice-Chancellors and Principals (CVCP). When war came in the following year that post became one of considerable responsibility as the chief intermediary between the universities and government. He was swamped with committees, personal discussions, and correspondence on every aspect of the universities' contributions to the war effort, only occasionally letting his weary but polite impatience show when he was bothered with trivia. Even so, through his aptitude for looking ahead, he set on a steady course plans for the post-war development of the university sector.

In 1943 Sibly was made KBE. That November his always frail health broke down and he had to give up his chairmanship of the CVCP. Although he remained as vice-chancellor of the University of Reading until 1946, he never fully recovered: he 'was one of Reading's war casualties' (Holt, 116). He died at his home, 21 Brooklyn Drive, Reading, on 13 April 1948. His funeral took place on 16 April at St Mary's, Reading. Of medium height and balding early, he had in his younger years played golf and tennis, but later became a very keen gardener. Even to the end his first academic love, geology, remained a recreation and a solace. T. A. B. CORLEY

Sources DNB · J. C. Holt, *The University of Reading: the first fifty years* (1977) · A. E. T. [A. E. Trueman], *Quarterly Journal of the Geological Society of London*, 104 (1948), lxiii–lxv · WWW · U. Reading, archives · *The Times* (16 April 1948) · *The Times* (22 April 1948) · *The Times* (24 April 1948) · *The Times* (30 April 1948) · *Reading Standard* (16 April 1948) · *Reading Standard* (23 April 1948) · *Nature*, 161 (1948), 672
Archives U. Reading L.
Likenesses W. Stoneman, photograph, 1931, NPG · W. Dring, oils, 1947, U. Reading [*see illus.*] · W. Dring, oils, U. Wales, Swansea
Wealth at death £3906 12s. 9d.: probate, 18 Sept 1948, CGPLA Eng. & Wales

Sibly, Manoah (1757–1840), Swedenborgian minister and banker, was born at Bristol on 20 August 1757. He was the brother of Ebenezer *Sibly (1751–c.1799), a notable publisher of esoteric lore, and was himself an autodidact and nonconformist, self-taught in the classical and biblical languages, part of the self-taught artisan culture. He specialized in alchemy and astrology, and became for a period a bookseller in Goswell Street, London, specializing in books on the occult, some of which his brother was then publishing. He himself translated two astrological works by Palcidus de Titis, but his first work, *A critical essay on Jer. xxxiii.16 (latter part) wherein the misinterpretations of the sacred text are confuted* (1777), demonstrated his competence in Hebrew scholarship. He also served as a shorthand writer, and wrote the transcripts of the trials of Thelwall and Hardy. On 7 May 1780, at St Luke, Old Street, Finsbury, he married an orphan named Sarah Lack (d. 1829), and they lived happily until her death, with eleven children, although only two survived him.

It fitted entirely with his idiosyncratic radicalism that in 1787 Sibly adopted Swedenborgian ideas, and, after serving as a lay preacher along with others, was ordained a minister of the New Jerusalem church on 7 April 1790, although serving the London congregation only on a part-time basis. After a schism in 1793 he was appointed minister of a congregationally based group meeting first in Store Street, Tottenham Court Road, then in Red Cross Street, Cripplegate, then the Cross Street Chapel, which Joseph Proud had abandoned, then at Cateaton Street; the meeting erected its own chapel in Friars Street, Blackfriars, in 1803. Although never attracting as many followers as Joseph Proud's London chapel, it was generally reckoned to provide a purer species of Swedenborgian dogma, for Sibly provided a rather meticulous and knowledgeable interpretation of Swedenborgian doctrines, yet to judge from his published sermons (twelve of which were published in 1796 and another seven at other times during his ministry), he remained a rather inward-looking pedant. From 1797 he served in the Bank of England in order to avoid Sunday work, and rose to head their chancery office. He died on 16 December 1840, and was buried in Bunhill Fields. PETER J. LINEHAM

Sources H. B., *Intellectual Repository and New Jerusalem Magazine* (1841), 140–44 · P. J. Lineham, 'The English Swedenborgians, 1770–1840: a study in the social dimensions of religious sectarianism',

DPhil diss., U. Sussex, 1978 • *N&Q*, 3rd ser., 7 (1865), 260 • T. C. Shaw, *A sermon preached … 3 January 1841 on occasion of the removal into the spiritual world of Rev. Manoah Sibly* (1841) • *DNB* • *IGI*
Archives New Church Conference Office, Bedford Road, London, archives
Likenesses W. Wise and W. Hutin, stipple (after J. Clover), BM

Siborne [Siborn], William (1797–1849),

army officer and military historian, was the son of Captain Benjamin Siborn of the 9th (East Norfolk) regiment, who was wounded at the battle of the Nivelle in the Peninsular War, and died while serving with his regiment at St Vincent in the West Indies on 14 July 1819. William Siborne was born on 15 October 1797 and educated at the Royal Military College, Sandhurst. He was commissioned ensign in the 9th regiment on 9 September 1813. He joined the 2nd battalion at Canterbury, and accompanied it to Chatham in February 1815 and to Sheerness in the summer. In August he was one of those drafted to join the army of the duke of Wellington. Siborne was promoted lieutenant in his regiment on 8 November 1815, and at about that date he accompanied it to Boulogne as part of the British army of occupation. In February 1817 the regiment was reduced to one battalion, and Siborne was placed on half pay. He was brought back to full pay as a lieutenant in the 47th (Lancashire) regiment on 11 November 1824.

In March 1826 Siborne was appointed assistant military secretary to Lieutenant-General Sir George Murray (1772–1846), commanding the forces in Ireland, and held the same appointment with Murray's successors, Sir John Byng, Sir R. Hussey, and Sir Edward Blakeney, until 1843. He was promoted captain unattached on 31 January 1840, and on the same date was placed on half pay, although he continued to hold the staff appointment of military secretary in Dublin.

Siborne published in 1822 *Instructions for Civil and Military Surveyors in Topographical Plan-Drawing* and in 1827 *A Practical Treatise on Topographical Surveying and Drawing*. He married, in 1824, Helen, daughter of Colonel Aitken of Todhall, near Cupar, Fife, and they had two sons and two daughters.

In 1830 Siborne was commissioned by the commander-in-chief to construct a model of the field of Waterloo. He lived for eight months at the farm of La Haye-Sainte on the field of battle, and made a survey of the whole ground, upon which he based his model. The execution of this work occupied some years, as Siborne devoted to it only such time as his professional duties permitted. In 1833 the progress of the work was interrupted by the refusal of the new ministry to allot funds for it. Thrown upon his own resources he continued the work until its completion in 1838, at a cost of nearly £3000. The model was publicly exhibited in London and elsewhere, but the receipts barely covered the expenses of exhibition, and Siborne never recovered the cost of its construction. It was later the property of the Royal United Service Institution, then of the National Army Museum, London. Siborne also constructed a smaller model on a larger scale of a portion of the field of battle, and a *Guide to Captain Siborne's New Waterloo Model* was published. Having amassed much information from surviving officers on the battle and the entire campaign, Siborne in 1844 published his two-volume *History of the War in France and Belgium in 1815* (with folio atlas); it long remained a standard work.

On 6 November 1844 Siborne was appointed secretary and adjutant of the Royal Military Asylum at Chelsea, and died there while holding the appointment on 9 January 1849. He was buried at Brompton cemetery. Siborne's second son, Major-General Herbert Taylor Siborne, born on 18 October 1826, edited in 1891, with explanatory notes, *Waterloo letters: a selection from original and hitherto unpublished letters bearing on the operations of the 16th, 17th, and 18th June 1815, by officers who served in the campaign*—a selection from the letters his father received on the battle and campaign of Waterloo. The complete collection of letters became the property of the British Museum. Herbert Siborne died on 16 May 1902.

R. H. Vetch, *rev.* James Falkner

Sources *Army List* • H. T. Siborne, ed., *Waterloo letters* (1891) • *Hart's Army List* • WWW
Archives BL, corresp. and papers relating to battle of Waterloo, Add. MSS 34703–34708 | NAM, corresp. with Sir Henry Murray
Likenesses S. Lover, miniature, oils, *c.*1833; formerly in possession of his daughter Clara in 1897

Sibson, Francis (1814–1876),

physician, was born on 21 May 1814 at Cross Canonby, Cumberland, the third of the five sons of Francis and Jane Sibson. His family moved to Edinburgh in 1819, where he was baptized at St Peter's Episcopal Church. Aged fourteen he was apprenticed to the surgeon John Lizars. He received his diploma from the Royal College of Surgeons of Edinburgh on 21 December 1831. During the cholera epidemics of 1831–2 he worked in cholera wards in Leith, Newhaven, and Edinburgh. Following a brief period in general practice in Cockermouth he continued his medical studies at Guy's Hospital, London, coming under the influence of the physician Thomas Hodgkin.

In 1835 Sibson was appointed resident surgeon and apothecary at Nottingham General Hospital. During his thirteen years at Nottingham he laid the foundations of his subsequent anatomical and clinical research. His 1844 paper, 'On changes induced in the situation and structure of the internal organs under varying circumstances of health and disease', gained him professional repute. His acquaintance with the naturalist Charles Waterton encouraged his interest in the action of narcotics, especially curare, in the treatment of hydrophobia and tetanus. A prolific yet careful writer, he published papers on the mechanics of respiration, the blowhole of the porpoise, the treatment of gout and rheumatism, the use of ether and chloroform in the treatment of neuralgia, and the 1847 typhoid epidemic in Nottingham.

Funded by a testimonial from his supporters in Nottingham, Sibson moved to London in 1848, taking a first in the University of London MB in 1848 and the MD in 1849. He was elected a member of the Royal College of Physicians in 1849 and a fellow in 1853. His election as fellow of the

Royal Society in 1849 recognized his painstakingly accurate work on the anatomy of the healthy and diseased viscera. Establishing his own practice in Brook Street in 1849 he began a well-attended series of demonstrations in visceral anatomy. He also lectured at Samuel Armstrong Lane's school of anatomy in Grosvenor Place. Four lecturers from Lane's school, including Sibson as physician, were elected to the honorary staff when St Mary's Hospital, Paddington, which Lane had promoted, opened in 1851. Planned as a teaching hospital from its foundation, St Mary's opened its medical school in 1854 with Sibson as lecturer on medicine.

In 1858 Sibson married Sarah Mary Ouvry, younger daughter of Peter Aimé Ouvry of East Acton. They hospitably hosted regular breakfast parties for his medical firms at their home, where prayers might punctuate a discussion of a post-mortem. A fair, broad-shouldered athletic man of middle height, he was noted for his obsessive punctuality and intolerance of tardiness. An art connoisseur, he collected Wedgwood china and architectural drawings.

An inspirational clinical teacher and accurate diagnostician, Sibson showed little interest in therapeutics, uniformly prescribing tincture of perchloride of iron regardless of his own precise and painstaking diagnosis. His main interests lay in cardiac, renal, and pulmonary disease. His practice of keeping interesting cases of aortic aneurysm on the wards for months brought conflict with the board of governors keen for earlier discharge of patients blocking beds. His enthusiastic lecturing and bedside teaching on ward rounds were backed by the relish which this morbid anatomist showed in autopsies. His cases at St Mary's Hospital provided the raw materials for his 1869 book *Medical anatomy, or, Illustrations of the relative position and movements of the internal organs*.

Sibson was a member of the council of the Royal Society, 1872–4, and joint treasurer of the Royal Society Club. He was successively Goulstonian, Croonian, and Lumleian lecturer at the Royal College of Physicians. He was curator of the museum of the Royal College of Physicians and censor in 1874. A member of the Provincial Medical and Surgical Association from 1843, he was initially opposed to its transformation to the British Medical Association but became the latter association's president in 1866, and held the post until 1869. He was elected to the senate of the University of London in 1865 and opposed the admission of women to its degrees as fervently as he led the opposition to a suggestion that St Mary's Hospital medical school admit women medical students in 1869. He was, nevertheless, a supporter of the training of nurses. An active member of the Metropolitan Asylums Board from 1875, he was involved in the planning of isolation hospitals.

Sibson, an ardent mountaineer, died suddenly at the Hotel des Bergues, Geneva, during his annual holiday on 7 September 1876 from an aortic aneurysm, ironically the main focus of his research. He was buried in St Mary's churchyard, Acton, Middlesex. KEVIN BROWN

Sources W. M. Ord, 'A short account of the life and writings of Dr Sibson', in *Collected works of Francis Sibson*, ed. W. M. Ord, 1 (1881), ix–xlii • E. Owen, 'Clinical teaching and Francis Sibson', *St Mary's Hospital Gazette*, 9 (1903), 2–3 • E. Owen, 'Reminiscences of Sibson', *St Mary's Hospital Gazette*, 15 (1909), 64–6 • *The Lancet* (20 Sept 1876) • *BMJ* (30 Sept 1876), 446–8 • minute books of board of governors of St Mary's Hospital, St Mary's Hospital archives, SM/AD 1/2–13 • minutes of medical committee of St Mary's Hospital, St Mary's Hospital archives, SM/AD 13/1–2 • J. R. Maltby, 'Francis Sibson, pioneer and prophet in anaesthesia', *Anaesthesia: essays on its history*, ed. J. Rupreht (1985), 28–31 • CGPLA Eng. & Wales (1876)

Archives RCP Lond., anatomical illustrations for his *Medical anatomy*

Likenesses photograph, St Mary's Hospital, London, archives

Wealth at death £6000: probate, 8 Nov 1876, CGPLA Eng. & Wales

Sibson, Thomas (1817–1844), book illustrator, son of Francis Sibson, an unsuccessful farmer, and his wife, Jane, and younger brother of Francis *Sibson MD (1814–1876), was born in the parish of Cross Canonby, Cumberland, in March 1817, and baptized along with his four brothers in 1819 after the family moved to Edinburgh. Sibson initially trained as an accountant and until he was nearly twenty-one he worked in his uncle's mercantile firm at Manchester. Then late in 1837, despite his family's disapproval, he left the firm and moved to London, where he studied with the painter Ralph Nicholson Wornum (1812–1877), later keeper of the National Gallery. Over the next several years Sibson, 'a pictorial Boz' (Grego, 1.456), published extra illustrations to Dickens's *Pickwick Papers* (ten etchings and illustrated wrapper, 1838) and *Master Humphrey's Clock* (seventy-two etchings in eighteen monthly parts, 1840–41; copies were re-etched by J. Yeager for the Philadelphia edition of *Barnaby Rudge*), alongside *Sibson's Sketches of Life and Humour* (1838).

Sibson was a tall, sinewy youth with a winning manner, quaint humour, and earnest determination, who quickly earned the devoted friendship of the poet and painter William Bell Scott (1811–1890) and the wood-engraver William James Linton (1812–1897). He produced many octavo drawings for Linton's projected *History of England*, then tore them up before they were carved into the block and replaced them on a larger scale. His work, exploiting a sprightly brio, clean linearity, and considerable antiquarianism, received high praise from friends and later critics. He was much in demand, designing many of the illustrations to Samuel Carter Hall's *Book of Ballads* and the Abbotsford edition of the Waverley novels. Moved by the plans to decorate the rebuilt houses of parliament with frescoes depicting British history, Sibson decided to become a history painter. In September 1842, after taking a strenuous walking tour through Wales with Linton, Sibson went to Munich to study with Wilhelm von Kaulbach (1804–1874), court painter to Ludwig I. Although Kaulbach had ceased to take pupils, he was so impressed by Sibson that he gave the student free lessons and studio space. But Sibson, suffering from advanced tuberculosis, was compelled by his failing health to return home early in 1844. Too weak to walk, he was cared for by Linton, who brought him wild flowers from Hampstead Heath for him to draw. Richard Twentyman of Bennoch and Twentyman, silk and gimp dealers, provided money for Sibson to winter at Malta. Accompanied by Linton, Sibson set forth from Newcastle; their ship struck a reef on the Yorkshire coast and they barely made it to land. He then stayed with his physician brother in Nottingham for a few weeks to recover his strength before once more setting out for Malta. Shortly after arriving there he died, on 28 November 1844. An album containing 1426 chalk, ink, and water-colour studies that Sibson made before his visit to Munich was bequeathed to Scott, purchased at the sale of Scott's collections in 1890 by Linton, and by him presented to the British Museum. Another sketchbook is in the Victoria and Albert Museum, London.

F. M. O'DONOGHUE, rev. ROBERT L. PATTEN

Sources [W. Bell Scott], *Art Union*, 7 (1845), 37–8 · *Autobiographical notes of the life of William Bell Scott: and notices of his artistic and poetic circle of friends, 1830 to 1882*, ed. W. Minto, 2 vols. (1892) · W. J. Linton, *Threescore and ten years: 1820 to 1890* (1894) · J. Grego, ed., *Pictorial Pickwickiana*, 2 vols. (1899) · J. Turner, ed., *The dictionary of art*, online edn, 4 Nov 2000
Wealth at death presumably under £100; he probably possessed only his clothes, toilet articles, and art supplies

Sibthorp, Charles de Laet Waldo [*known as* Colonel Sibthorp] (**1783–1855**), politician, the second of five sons of Colonel Humphry Waldo Sibthorp (1744–1815) and his wife, Susannah, daughter of Richard Ellison of Thorne in Yorkshire and Sudbrooke Holme in Lincolnshire, was born on 14 February 1783 at North Mimms, Hertfordshire. The Sibthorps were a long-established gentry family which had close connections with Lincoln. The Oxford professor of botany Dr Humphrey Sibthorp (1713?–1797) was Charles's grandfather; John *Sibthorp, the botanist, was his uncle, and the clergyman Richard Waldo *Sibthorp was his youngest brother.

Sibthorp attended a school in Chiswick and matriculated at Brasenose College, Oxford, in 1801, but did not graduate. He was commissioned in the Scots Greys in 1803 and subsequently served in the Peninsular War as a captain in the 4th dragoon guards. In later life he always saw himself as a military man. He married on 21 February 1812 Maria, daughter of Ponsonby Tottenham, from co. Wexford, Ireland. They had four sons, but she was estranged from him in later years, although reconciled before his death.

On the death of his elder brother Coningsby in 1822, Sibthorp succeeded to the family estates. He left the army, and was elected, in 1826, member of parliament for Lincoln, a borough which had previously been represented by his brother, his father, his great-uncle, and his great-grandfather. He also followed in a family succession as colonel of the South Lincoln militia, and was a deputy lieutenant and magistrate for the county. Except for a brief interval in 1833 and 1834, when Sir Edward Bulwer ousted him by a small majority, Colonel Sibthorp continued until his death to be re-elected for Lincoln, on personal rather than on political grounds, and often unopposed.

Sibthorp was an industrious parliamentarian and a very active participant in debate. He tenaciously adhered to ultra-tory and ultra-protestant views and defied fashionable and progressive trends. Partly by his uncompromising opinions, partly by his blunt expressions, and partly

Charles de Laet Waldo Sibthorp (1783–1855), by H. B. (John Doyle), pubd 1840

by an eccentricity that did less than justice to his real abilities, he made himself for many years rather a notorious than a respected figure in political life. His moustachioed and bewhiskered face and colourful style of dress were frequently caricatured. Charles Dickens considered him 'the most amusing person in the House' (*Sketches by Boz*, 1837, 233). His speeches were sometimes witty and polished, but they were too often personal and offensive. He opposed in all their stages the Catholic Emancipation Bill and the Reform Bill, considering the latter worse than the cholera morbus because it undermined the ancient constitution (*Hansard 3*, 14.1285). Sibthorp claimed that the 'Chandos' clause of the Reform Bill, which gave the vote to £50 tenants at will in the counties, had originally been his own idea (ibid., 9.811). The provision in the act to make better provision for the residence of the clergy (1 & 2 Vict. c. 106, section 36), which enabled widows of deceased incumbents to retain possession of the parsonage house for two months after the incumbent's death, also was strongly supported by him.

Sibthorp opposed the ministerial proposal for a grant of £50,000 per annum to Prince Albert on 27 January 1840, largely from suspicion of foreign influences, and it was his amendment for its reduction to £30,000 which, with the support of Peel, was eventually carried. He was a die-hard opponent of free trade, savagely denouncing Peel's 'betrayal' of the country in 1846 and adhering to the tory rump who censured Lord Derby for abandoning protection in 1852. His denunciation of the 1851 Great Exhibition arose in large measure from his associated anxiety to protect British industry from foreign competition. His xenophobia had religious as well as economic roots: he was staunchly protestant (but not evangelical) and was unflagging in his opposition to the expansion of the Roman Catholic church in England. His feelings on this subject were no doubt intensified by the conversion of his brother Richard Waldo to the Church of Rome in 1841. He was also inveterately hostile to railways, particularly because of their encroachments on private property, and was instrumental in preventing Lincoln from being served by a main line.

Sibthorp died at his house in Eaton Square, London, on 14 December 1855, after a long illness, and was buried at Canwick church, near Lincoln. His eldest son, Gervaise Tottenham Waldo Sibthorp (1815–1861), succeeded him as MP for Lincoln. J. A. HAMILTON, rev. JOHN WOLFFE

Sources GM, 2nd ser., 45 (1856), 84–6 · The Times (17 Dec 1855) · A. R. Maddison, An account of the Sibthorp family (privately printed, Lincoln, 1896) · F. Hill, Victorian Lincoln (1974) · 'A group of parliamentary oddities', Fraser's Magazine, 36 (1847), 462–5 · R. J. Olney, Lincolnshire politics, 1832–1885 (1973) · Burke, Gen. GB · Foster, Alum. Oxon. · Army List · Hansard 3 (1831), vol. 9, col. 811; (1832), vol. 14, col. 1285 · Lincs. Arch., Sibthorp papers
Archives Lincs. Arch., Sibthorp family MSS
Likenesses H. B. [J. Doyle], lithograph, pubd 1840, NPG [see illus.] · J. Doyle, caricatures, BM · J. Doyle, drawing, BM · Fernely, portrait (commanding the South Lincolnshire militia) · A. Forrester, lithograph, BM · A. Forrester, satirical statuette, BM · Hayter, crayon (after portrait known to be at Canwick in 1896) · Robertson, miniature (after portrait known to be at Sudbrooke in 1896) · portrait, repro. in Maddison, Account of the Sibthorp family, 83

Sibthorp, Sir Christopher (d. 1632/3), lawyer and pamphleteer, was the third son of John Sibthorp of Much Bardfield, Essex. He matriculated at Queens' College, Cambridge, in 1580 but took no degree and instead went on to the Middle Temple in 1584. In June 1588 he was expelled for nonconformity but readmitted 'on his petition showing his detestation of the popish religion' (Hopwood, 1.300). After being called to the bar in February 1594 Sibthorp next appears as third justice of the king's bench in Ireland on 11 May 1607. Also that year he was sent to Ulster to indict the earls of Tyrone and Tyrconnell. His links with Ulster persisted and he became an undertaker in the Fermanagh plantation and MP for the borough of Limavady from 1613 to 1615.

Sibthorp's professional efforts were rewarded by a knighthood on 3 May 1618 and appointment as treasurer of the King's Inns in 1629. 'Detestation' of Catholicism led him to defend the exclusion of Catholic lawyers from practice and into writing three controversial tracts. Attached to the first of these, A Friendly Advertisement to the Pretended Catholickes of Ireland (1622), was a letter from James Ussher, archbishop of Armagh, on 'The religion anciently professed by the British and Irish'. Sibthorp remained a justice of king's bench in Ireland until his death, which occurred some time between March 1632

and March 1633, but it is on account of his association with Ussher that he has been chiefly remembered. He was married, but nothing is known of his wife or any family.

JOHN McCAFFERTY

Sources CSP Ire., 1606–25; 1633–47 · C. H. Hopwood, ed., Middle Temple records, 4 vols. (1904–5) · J. Morrin, ed., Calendar of the patent and close rolls of chancery in Ireland, of the reign of Charles I (1863) · F. E. Ball, The judges in Ireland, 1221–1921, 2 vols. (1926) · B. T. Duhigg, History of the King's Inns (1806) · R. Lascelles, ed., Liber munerum publicorum Hiberniae … or, The establishments of Ireland, later edn, 2 vols. in 7 pts (1852) · Venn, Alum. Cant. · C. Kenny, King's Inns and the kingdom of Ireland (1992) · D. Gaffney, 'The practice of religious controversy in Dublin, 1600–1641', The churches, Ireland, and the Irish, ed. W. J. Sheils and D. Ward, SCH, 25 (1989), 145–58 · W. C. Metcalfe, A book of knights banneret, knights of the Bath and knights bachelor (1885)

Sibthorp, John (1758–1796), botanist, was born in Oxford on 28 October 1758, the only son of Humphrey Sibthorp (1713?–1797), Sherardian professor of botany at Oxford, and his second wife, Elizabeth, née Gibbes (d. 1780). The elder Sibthorp, a fellow of Magdalen College, Oxford, in 1734–44, took his MB in 1743 and his MD in 1745. Tradition has it that as holder of the Sherardian chair from 1747 to 1783 he presented but one lecture, which was not a notable success. He was said to have done more for botany by raising his son than through any research or writing of his own. Linnaeus, one of the senior Sibthorp's botanical correspondents, named Sibthorpia europaea (Cornish moneywort), a small creeping plant with tiny flowers, after him.

John Sibthorp attended Magdalen College School and Lincoln grammar school, and went on to Lincoln College, Oxford, where he earned his BA in 1777 when he was nineteen. He studied medicine for a year (1778–9) at the University of Edinburgh and took his MA at Oxford in 1780. His mother died in 1780, leaving him a considerable legacy which took the form of a substantial allowance from his father. During the year 1781–2 Sibthorp studied botany with Antoine Laurent de Jussieu at the Jardin des Plantes in Paris. This was followed by ten months of further botanical study with Auguste Brissonet at Montpellier University. On his return to Oxford in October 1783 he received a £300 a year Radcliffe travelling fellowship. Two months later his father, who had earlier inherited property from an older brother in Canwick, Lincolnshire, resigned his chair in his son's favour. Sibthorp took his MD at Oxford in January 1784, and in March, aged twenty-five, was named Sherardian professor. It is not known whether there were other aspirants for this position. In that year he attempted to buy the library and collections of Linnaeus for Oxford, but his friend, the botanist James Edward Smith (1759–1828), outbid him; these materials later went to the Linnean Society of London.

Having no immediate desire to teach, Sibthorp turned his instructional responsibilities over to George Shaw (1751–1813), the very capable departmental lecturer, later keeper of the natural history section at the British Museum. Sibthorp spent the winter of 1784–5 studying at Göttingen, and the summer of 1785 herborizing (Sibthorp's term) in Germany. In the autumn of 1785, while working with Nikolaus Joseph von Jacquin in Vienna, he was shown a fifth-century copy (now in the Botany School

Library at Oxford) of the *Materia medica* of Pedacius Diosco-rides, a first-century Greek army surgeon. Sibthorp decided to study the Greek flora, identify all 700 plants mentioned by Dioscorides, and ascertain their medicinal value. He taught himself modern Greek so that he could converse with local residents concerning plant life. With the Austrian Ferdinand Bauer (1760–1826), who became one of the greatest botanical artists of all time, he visited Cyprus, Crete, Athens, mounts Parnassus and Athos, Salonika, many of the Greek islands, Izmir, and Bithynia between March 1786 and September 1787. Uncertain political conditions, the threat of war in the region, and the onset of plague in Thessaly precluded Sibthorp's travelling through the Greek mainland. He returned to England with some 2000 plants, together with many mammal, bird, and fish specimens. During the period from 1787 to 1794, he lectured according to the advanced taxonomic principles of Linnaeus, added many specimens to the Sherardian herbarium, and completed his father's catalogue of the university's botanical garden. There were insufficient funds to improve the garden, but he did some planting, exchanging some specimens with Kew Gardens. He published *Flora Oxoniensis* (1794), a student's guide describing some 1200 plant species of Oxfordshire, and cared for an estate he had purchased at South Leigh, outside Oxford. One of the founding members of the Linnean Society of London in 1788, he was named a fellow. In that same year, he also was elected a fellow of the Royal Society. Although Sibthorp periodically suffered from malaria, contracted on his first Greek expedition, he was determined to return for additional specimens for a projected *Flora Graeca*. Since Bauer would not accompany him (Sibthorp treated Bauer as a servant, which the younger man bitterly resented) Sibthorp left England in March 1794 with Francis Barone, a congenial young botanical assistant. They took two months to reach Constantinople overland; having arrived there exhausted and ill, Sibthorp was obliged to spend the summer recovering from his journey, after which they moved on to Athens. Barone was killed in an accident there while sleepwalking in their quarters, but Sibthorp was joined by an English friend, John Hawkins (1758–1841). The two men spent the autumn of 1794 visiting Troy and Athens before overwintering on the island of Zakinthos. March and April 1795 were spent botanizing in the south central Peloponnese.

Sibthorp set sail for England at the beginning of May while Hawkins remained in Greece, but his trip was arduous in the extreme. Sibthorp was obliged to spend two miserable weeks in a small Adriatic island hut owing to violent storms. He had begun his trip with a bad cold and fever, which grew worse and was complicated by dysentery. After landing in central Italy he completed his journey home by road, but on arrival in England in July he was suffering from tuberculosis. He survived six months, dying, unmarried, at Bath, Somerset, on 8 February 1796 at the age of thirty-seven. He was buried in Bath Abbey. His plant collections, including the 3000 species upon which the *Flora Graeca* was later based, are still retained at Oxford. Much of his correspondence, which had been kept by his father and then his sister, Lady Sewell, was sold as waste paper following the death of the latter.

In his will Sibthorp left his estate to Oxford University, but directed that his three executors, Hawkins, Thomas Platt, and the Hon. Thomas Wenman, arrange for the completion of the *Flora Graeca*. With the aid of Sir Joseph Banks, Smith was engaged, at a salary of £150 per annum, to draft the text of the *Flora*, and was expected to finish this task within eleven years. Smith began working in 1799 but his assignment was still incomplete when he died in 1828 after twenty-nine years' labour. The entire task ultimately consumed more than forty years. Sibthorp's handwriting was execrable, he had not completed the correlation of his field notes with his specimens, and some of the latter were not labelled. Hawkins would in 1800 commiserate with Smith by writing, 'it is certainly a pity that Dr. Sibthorp did not mark all his specimens, but he trusted to his memory and dreamed not of dying' (Stearn, 'Sibthorp, Smith', 170). Smith completed six lavishly illustrated volumes and part of the seventh (published 1806–32) before his death. The remainder of the seventh and the final three volumes, which appeared between 1832 and 1840, were authored by the botanist John Lindley (1799–1865). All volumes were published in two fascicles. The faithful Hawkins, who with his surviving co-executor Platt had loyally carried out his deceased friend's charge since 1796, died early in 1841. No less faithful was Ferdinand Bauer, who, despite his treatment by the cosmopolitan and erudite Sibthorp, completed all the illustrations for *Flora Graeca*. Only twenty-five sets of *Flora Graeca*, containing 966 plates, were finally published by the Oxford University Press, at a cost of £620 each. These were sold to subscribers for £239 8*s.* Sibthorp's estate made up the deficit of more than £9000. The publisher Henry Bohn later bought the remaining oddments of text and plates from the University Press, reprinted what was missing, and produced another forty sets in 1845 and 1846, which he sold for £63 apiece. No more were printed. The overburdened Smith also produced a four-part *Florae Gracae prodromus*, without illustrations, which appeared in two volumes between 1806 and 1816. Sibthorp willed that on completion of *Flora Graeca* the balance of his estate should endow a Sibthorpian chair of rural economy to be held by the professor of botany. Only the additional stipend (£200) would secure a dedicated botanist for the university. The prospect induced Charles Daubeny to seek the botany chair in 1834, and he became first Sibthorpian professor in 1840.

KEIR B. STERLING

Sources M. R. Bruce, 'John Sibthorpe', *Taxon*, 19 (1970), 353–60 · W. T. Stearn, 'From Theophrastus and Dioscorides to Sibthorpe and Smith: the background and origin of the *Flora Graeca*', *Biological Journal of the Linnean Society*, 8 (1976), 285–298 · W. T. Stearn, 'Sibthorp, Smith, the *Flora Graeca* and the *Florae Graecae prodromus*', *Taxon*, 16 (1967), 168–78 · F. A. Stafleu and R. S. Cowan, *Taxonomic literature: a selective guide*, 2nd edn, 5, Regnum Vegetabile, 112 (1985), 577–80 · A. M. Coats, *The plant hunters* (1969) · A. M. Coats, 'Notes on some portraits of British botanists and gardeners', *Huntia*, 2 (1965), 185–215 · H. M. Clokie, *An account of the herbaria of the department of botany in the University of Oxford* (1964), 38–42 · *Memoir and correspondence of the late Sir James Edward Smith*, ed. Lady Smith, 1 (1832),

131, 460, 463, 465, 467, 471 · R. T. Gunther, *Oxford gardens* (1912), 20–21 · *Hist. U. Oxf.* 5: *18th-cent. Oxf.*, 721–2 · W. Lack, ed., *The 'Flora Graeca' story* (1998) · DNB

Archives BM, duplicate specimens · BM, letters · Bodl. Oxf., lecture course, MS Sherard 219 · Lincs. Arch., family corresp.; MSS · NHM, letters · U. Oxf., department of plant sciences, corresp., diaries, herbarium, and papers · U. Oxf., department of plant sciences, original specimens and manuscripts for the *Flora Graeca* | Linn. Soc., letters to Sir James Smith · NRA, corresp. with Sir Joseph Banks · W. Sussex RO, letters to John Hawkins

Likenesses miniature, NPG · oils, U. Oxf., school of botany · print, Library of the Botanic Garden, Oxford

Wealth at death over £15,572 6s.: Stearn, 'From Theophrastus and Dioscorides to Sibthorpe and Smith', 295

Sibthorp, Margaret Shurmer (*b. c.*1851), journal editor, was born Margaret Shurmer in Scotland, and married Stephen James K. Sibthorp, a chemist (*d.* 1902), when they were both aged twenty-two, about 1873. They had two children, a son, Shurmer Llewellyn W. Sibthorp (*b.* 1873), and a daughter, Shurmer Ada M. M. Sibthorp (*b.* 1875). In the 1891 census return Margaret Sibthorp's occupation was given as 'writer and secretary'. Prior to moving to London, the Sibthorps had resided in Liverpool (their son's place of birth) and Wolverhampton (where their daughter was born). Margaret remarked 'Only those who have lived in small towns in the country, can know how difficult it is to raise any enthusiasm of feeling in regard to any new movement' (*Shafts*, 10 Dec 1892).

Sibthorp was editor of the pioneering women's periodical *Shafts* from 1892 to 1899. *Shafts*, which she described as 'the outgoing of my vital breath; the result of the anxious yearning of my inmost spirit; the manifestation of my deep desire to serve the cause of women' (*Shafts*, Aug 1893), bears the impress of a distinctive personality. Sibthorp's 'earnest desire' to edit such an organ was 'held perforce in check for many years', but following 'the request of many friends of Woman's Freedom' (ibid., 31 Dec 1892) *Shafts* began its career in November 1892 with funding from an anonymous lady friend, and was published from an office in Arundel Street off the Strand. In 1899 Sibthorp paid tribute to four (unnamed) friends who had helped 'faithfully and nobly' to keep it going (ibid., Jan–Feb 1899). The financial basis of the journal was never secure and frequent appeals were made for funds. From 1892 to February 1893 it appeared weekly; then monthly; and by 1898 bi-monthly. From 1895 to 1899 it was published from Westbere Road, West Hampstead, Sibthorp's residence. Undaunted, Sibthorp declared 'for the last ten years it has been my desire to start a woman's daily paper' (ibid., May–June 1898). However, the long hiatus after the January–February 1899 issue (presumably due to Sibthorp's recuperation from a complete health breakdown caused by her struggles) was followed in the July–September number by the news that *Shafts* would become a quarterly. It moved to new premises near the Strand about October 1899, promising a new start from January 1900, but seems to have ended with the century.

Shafts (initial subtitle 'Light comes to those who dare to think', later 'A journal for women and the working classes', and subsequently 'A monthly journal of progressive thought') constitutes an important source for feminist debates and related causes in the 1890s. It gave much attention to general questions of women's emancipation, contemporary debates on social purity, and issues such as rational dress, women's free and responsible choice of motherhood, the need for sex education, opposition to cruelty to animals and children, and vegetarianism—'all reform' (*Shafts*, Jan–Feb 1899).

The considerable space given to occult, psychical, and mystical teachings is not surprising, given that Sibthorp had become a member of the Theosophical Society in 1891, though her membership lapsed in 1894, and was associated with the Blavatsky Lodge. In 1909 she was a founder member of the League of Isis, which promoted the ideas of Mrs Frances Swiney concerning the paramount importance of healthy motherhood and the absolute right of woman to regulate sexual intercourse.

Although Sibthorp believed that 'few evils existing in great strength in the world … are not traceable to the subjection of women' (*Shafts*, 26 Nov 1892), her membership of any suffrage society cannot be traced. She believed an essential new 'aristocracy of character, of will, of mind' would emerge from 'our WOMEN and our WORKMEN' (ibid., 3 Nov 1892), presumably exempting the latter from claims that 'Humanity—which ought to be composed of the united strength of all—is split into two parts: the SUBJECTION of Woman and DOMINATION of Man' (ibid., 3 Dec 1892). Her editorial rules included avoidance of the masculine pronoun when 'expressing general thoughts and facts' (ibid., 3 Nov 1892) and eschewing any titles not 'earned by merit and work' (ibid., 24 Dec 1892). Her ideal was to provide a forum for free and frank discussion, taking 'no side save that of justice and freedom' (ibid., 3 Nov 1892), in 'a wide, honest spirit of love and great intention' (ibid., 24 Dec 1892).

Sibthorp spoke on diverse subjects at a variety of meetings reported or advertised in *Shafts*. Physiology classes for girls and discussion groups on 'all humanitarian and other subjects' (*Shafts*, 25 Feb 1893) were held at the editorial office. Sibthorp thus, by publishing *Shafts* and providing a forum for more intimate debate, fulfilled her desire to give women 'an opportunity of expressing publicly their thoughts' (ibid., March 1894). Her own thoughts remain to us, arising out of obscurity and sinking back into it: no record of her death has been traced.

LESLEY A. HALL

Sources *Shafts* (1892–9) · *The Anglo-Russian* · street directories · census returns, 1891 · 50 Gloucester Place, London, records of the Theosophical Society

Sibthorp, Richard Waldo (1792–1879), Church of England clergyman and Roman Catholic convert, born at Canwick Hall, near Lincoln, on 4 October 1792, was the fifth and youngest son of Colonel Humphry Waldo Sibthorp (1744–1815), MP for Lincoln, and his wife, Susannah, daughter of Richard Ellison of Sudbrooke Holme, Lincolnshire. Colonel Charles de Laet Waldo *Sibthorp was his brother. After an elementary education in a private school at Eltham, Kent, he was sent to Westminster School on 25 rare, and his defection excited considerable alarm. Sibthorp studied divinity at Oscott for a few months, was ordained priest on 21 May 1842, and was then attached to the cathedral church of St Chad, Birmingham, though he subsequently moved into a house which he bought for himself at Edgbaston. Dissatisfied with his position, and mentally disquieted after a serious accident, he left Edgbaston in June 1843 and purchased a cottage near St Helens, Isle of Wight, where he continued to say mass until October. Then he returned to the communion of the established church.

After three years of retirement at Winchester, Sibthorp made a fruitless petition to Bishop Charles Richard Sumner to be reinstated as an Anglican clergyman. After settling at Lincoln in 1847 he established a liberally endowed St Anne's bede-house, and in the same year he was readmitted to discharge the functions of the Anglican ministry. Sibthorp resigned the chaplain-wardenship of St Anne's at the close of 1864, and on 25 January 1865 resumed the privilege of saying mass in the private chapel of Cardinal Wiseman. In December 1865 he was attached to the cathedral of St Barnabas, Nottingham. He frequently preached there, but, 'though now a Roman Catholic priest, his feelings, his language, his general teaching, were, in some very important respects, still evangelical' (Fowler, 177). He was placed on the list of retired priests in December 1874, and died at Nottingham on 10 April 1879. Following a Catholic requiem mass at Nottingham, he was buried in Lincoln cemetery where, in accordance with his express desire, the Anglican service was read over his grave.

Sibthorp was unquestionably devout and sincere (and Gladstone thought him 'a holy man'; *Diaries*, 21 April 1880), but he was never able to satisfy himself that he was in the true church. Certainly he never accepted the full range of Catholic dogma in his Catholic periods. In addition to several sermons and pamphlets, he published *Psalms and Hymns* (1831), *The Family Liturgy, being a Course of Morning and Evening Prayers for a Family* (1836), and *Daily Bread, being a Few Morning Meditations for the Use of Catholic Christians* (1876; rev. and enlarged edn, 1879). His apologetic, *Some Answer to the Inquiry 'Why are you become a Catholic?'* (1842), elicited a series of replies from Oxford friends, including William Dodsworth and William Palmer, and a further reply from Sibthorp.

THOMPSON COOPER, *rev.* MICHAEL CLIFTON

Richard Waldo Sibthorp (1792–1879), by James Scott, pubd 1839 (after Edward Turtle)

March 1807. He matriculated at University College, Oxford, on 12 December 1809, and in 1810 was elected to a demyship at Magdalen College.

Attracted by the Roman Catholic faith, in the Michaelmas term of 1811 Sibthorp went to Wolverhampton, where he spent two days with Bishop John Milner, with the intention of entering the Roman communion. He was brought back, under police surveillance and chancery order, by an elder brother. He graduated BA in 1813, took Anglican orders in 1815, and was appointed curate of Waddington and Harmston, Lincolnshire. There he 'preached with all the enthusiasm of a Whitefield' (Palmer, 22). He graduated MA in 1816, and afterwards became curate to John Scott (1777–1834), incumbent of St Mary's Church, Hull. In July 1819 he was elected a fellow of Magdalen College, Oxford, and in the same year became vicar of Tattersall, Lincolnshire. He proceeded BD in 1823. In 1825 he took the charge of Percy proprietary chapel, St Pancras, London, and was subsequently evening lecturer at St John's Chapel, Bedford Row. At this period he was recognized as one of the leaders of the London evangelicals, and he was one of the founder members of the Islington Clerical Society. In 1829 he gave up his connection with London chapels and went to reside at Magdalen College as a fellow. From 1830 to 1841 he was incumbent of St James's Church, Ryde, Isle of Wight.

On resigning the living Sibthorp was received into the Roman Catholic church at St Mary's College, Oscott, on 27 October 1841 by Bishop (afterwards Cardinal) Wiseman. Clerical conversions to Catholicism were at that period

Sources J. Fowler, *Richard Waldo Sibthorp: a biography* (1880) · C. Sykes, *Two studies in virtue* (1953) · *London and Dublin Orthodox Journal*, 15 (1842), 187, 396 · *The Tablet* (19 April 1879) · *The Times* (2 Feb 1892) · *Nottingham Guardian* (12 April 1879) · Foster, *Alum. Oxon.* · J. R. Bloxam, *A register of the presidents, fellows … of Saint Mary Magdalen College*, 8 vols. (1853–85), vol. 4, pp. 200–46 · R. D. Middleton, *Magdalen studies* (1938), 195–238 · W. Palmer, *A narrative of events connected with the publication of the Tracts for the Times*, [new edn] (1883) · Gladstone, *Diaries*
Archives Magd. Oxf., Bloxham MSS · Magd. Oxf., corresp. with M. J. Routh · Pusey Oxf., letters to J. R. Bloxam
Likenesses J. Scott, engraving, pubd 1839 (after E. Turtle), NPG [*see illus.*] · J. Waldo, mezzotint, pubd 1839 (after E. Turtle), BM,

NPG · photograph, repro. in Fowler, *Richard Waldo Sibthorp*, frontispiece

Wealth at death under £16,000: probate, 7 May 1879, *CGPLA Eng. & Wales*

Sibthorpe [Sibthorp], **Robert** (*d.* 1662), Church of England clergyman, has often been confused with namesakes, including the bishop of Limerick who died in 1649. Nothing is known of his parents or early life, and the attendance at Lincoln College, Oxford, indicated on his funeral monument, lacks clear confirmation. It was as a BA that he was ordained priest at Peterborough on 21 September 1606, and on 13 February 1608 he obtained through royal patronage the vicarage of St Giles, Northampton.

Sibthorpe soon began service in the Peterborough diocesan courts, where John Lambe, whose sister he had married, was an ecclesiastical lawyer. Like Lambe, Sibthorpe had strongly ceremonialist and absolutist convictions: he detested the word-centred piety prevailing in the Jacobean church, which he stigmatized as puritan, and longed to replace it with a piety centred on sacraments and ceremonial conformity. As he attempted to impose this in 1610 the boycotting of his ministry by godly parishioners provoked a flurry of court activity. In 1615 Sibthorpe, Lambe (now chancellor of the diocese), and the controversialist David Owen again tried to impose ceremonial conformity, especially kneeling during receipt of communion, but without support from the establishment success was limited. In *A Counterplea to an Apostataes Pardon* (1618), a Shrove Tuesday Paul's Cross sermon, Sibthorpe, like Owen, called for an abandonment of toleration of nonconformity: by their disobedience to divinely ordained episcopacy puritans were damning their souls and should be punished; they should not be permitted to equivocate over taking oaths of conformity.

From 1616 Sibthorpe had been serving in the cure of St Sepulchre in Northampton; in 1619, having received from Lambe formal appointment there, he resigned his St Giles living. In 1622 he relinquished his cure on receiving from the patron, William Lisle, the rectory of Brackley, and was appointed a collector of aid for the distressed ministers of the Rhine palatinate. Meanwhile he held in plurality, until he resigned it in 1627, the living of Water Stratford, Buckinghamshire, obtained from Sir Arthur Throckmorton.

The accession of Charles I brought Sibthorpe's views into vogue. Around 1625 he was made a JP and gained a doctorate of divinity, but national notoriety was only achieved on 22 February 1627, when he preached in favour of payment of the forced loan at Northampton assizes. Those who were disobedient to divine right monarchy he denounced as puritan rebels and damned souls, proclaiming 'if Princes command anything which is against the lawes of God or Nature or impossible yet Subjects are bound to undergoe the punishment without … resistance', and 'he that resisteth the Prince resisteth the power and ordinance of God, and consequently shall receive damnation' (R. Sibthorpe, *Apostolike Obedience*, 1627, 13, 3). Archbishop Abbot's refusal to license such absolutist ideology for the press was a factor in his downfall, since the king clearly agreed with Sibthorpe's ideas, and in his eclipse by the faction of Bishop Laud, whose colleague Bishop George Montaigne of London licensed the sermon. Sibthorpe's rewards were a royal chaplaincy and the vicarage of Burton Latimer, Northamptonshire (8 April 1629). However, he was condemned in the parliaments of 1628 and 1629, and narrowly escaped impeachment. With Lambe he was questioned over his support for Laud in his feud with Bishop John Williams, which persisted into an abortive 1630s Star Chamber case.

William Piers, bishop of Peterborough from 1630 to 1632, appointed Sibthorpe chief lecturer at Kettering, and by 1633 John Towers was suggesting that Sibthorpe replace him as dean of Peterborough. In 1634 he contributed towards Archbishop Laud's prosecution of Charles Chauncy's opposition to the altar policy. Indeed, Sibthorpe had come to regard Laud and Lambe (now dominant in the central courts) as his only protectors against a ubiquitous puritanism threatening the king, the church, and himself. However, Bishop Francis Dee's drive for conformity in Peterborough in 1637 gave Sibthorpe the chance to realize his vision of the church since, in a new departure, Dee's church survey addressed liturgical practice and the whole groundplan of parochial worship. All parishes were to possess an east end, railed altar, all clergy were to administer communion from within the rails, and all communicants were to receive there kneeling. Together with Samuel Clarke (*d.* 1641), archdeacon of Derby, Sibthorpe executed the commission with customary zeal, making Dee's success possible. He ensured that the minister (Thomas Ball) and churchwardens of All Saints', Northampton, and Miles Burkit, vicar of Pattishall, were harried for their opposition to the altar policy. The prerogative tax of ship money was seen as another test of loyalty so when Thomas Bacon, lord of the manor of Burton, defaulted over payment, Sibthorpe prosecuted him in Star Chamber. He supported the conformist cleric Richard Powell, who preached in favour of paying the tax but was accused of preaching against it by defaulters. Violent arguments broke out with Sir Richard Samwell, a godly JP who was detailed to investigate the case, but the privy council backed Sibthorpe's notion of a puritan conspiracy to undermine the tax and removed Samwell from the commission of the peace. At Brackley, Sibthorpe perceived another puritan conspiracy, led by the godly JP John Crewe, to oust him from the living and control the Wednesday lecture. He despised Crewe's sabbatarianism in attempting to brand as vagrants a group of musicians invited to play at Brackley fair, as part of the latitude permitted by the Book of Sports. Through Lambe and John Towers, bishop of Peterborough from March 1639, Sibthorpe secured the establishment of a heavily regulated combination lecture to be delivered only by himself and preachers approved by the bishop. Its future survival was linked, uniquely, to full performance of Laudian ceremonial by both preacher and congregation. The climax of Sibthorpe's anti-puritan paranoia came with the bishops' wars of 1639, which he regarded as 'Rebellio Puritanica' (Stowe MSS, 3 June 1639). When his ally, George Plowright, was pressed as a soldier by the godly deputy lieutenant Sir

Rowland St John, he reported the matter via Lambe to the privy council. Again the explanation was a puritan conspiracy to ruin him, but this time the case backfired; ironically, in view of the sentiments expressed in *Apostolike Obedience*, he was advocating resistance.

The Long Parliament moved swiftly against such a zealous instrument of Charles I's personal rule; according to Sir Thomas Aston, one of the four 'greatest Enemies to church and state that ever was' (J. Maltby, *Prayer Book and People in Elizabethan and Early Stuart England*, 1998, 163–4). Sibthorpe was sent for as a delinquent by the House of Lords in December 1640 and accused by Bishop John Williams of secular absolutism and religious innovation. On 21 January 1641 the Lords removed him from the commission of the peace, although he was later given leave of absence to go to Northamptonshire. He escaped to the royalist headquarters at Oxford in 1643 and was soon sequestered by the Northamptonshire county committee. His successor at Burton Latimer was admitted on 11 June 1644. In 1646 he was granted a university licence to preach in any part of the kingdom, and he seems to have spent some time in London: his will later mentioned a Mrs Daraston of Long Acre, London, who with her husband had 'done mee many friendly offices in the late tymes of my trouble' (*Walker rev.*, 284). At the Restoration, Sibthorpe was reinstated. He died in April 1662 and was buried in Burton chancel on 25 April. His wife had predeceased him.

J. FIELDING

Sources A. J. Fielding, 'Conformists, puritans and the church courts: the diocese of Peterborough, 1603–1642', PhD diss., U. Birm., 1989 · H. I. Longden, *Northamptonshire and Rutland clergy from 1500*, ed. P. I. King and others, 16 vols. in 6, Northamptonshire RS (1938–52), vol. 12, pp. 169–71 · R. P. Cust, *The forced loan and English politics, 1626–1628* (1987) · Sibthorpe, letters to J. Lambe, 1639, Hunt. L., Stowe papers [unfoliated] · *Walker rev.*, 284 · Wood, *Ath. Oxon.*, new edn, 2.549–52, 99–100 · V. L. Stater, 'The lord lieutenancy on the eve of the civil wars: the impressment of George Plowright', *HJ*, 29 (1986), 279–96 · Northants. RO, Peterborough diocesan records, misc. document 88
Archives Hunt. L., Stowe MSS, letters to Sir John Lambe
Wealth at death £103 9s.: inventory, 26 April 1662, Longden, *Northamptonshire and Rutland clergy*, vol. 12, pp. 169–71

Sichel, Edith Helen (1862–1914), historian and philanthropist, was born on 13 December 1862 at 25 Princes Gardens, London, the daughter of Michael Sichel (*d*. 1884), a cotton merchant, and his wife, Helena Reiss (*d*. 1888); her parents were Christians, but of German Jewish descent. She was well educated, becoming proficient in French, German, and Latin. In 1876 she met and formed a close friendship with Mary Elizabeth Coleridge (1861–1907), with whom she went to read Greek classics with William Johnston Cory (1823–1892), the poet and former master at Eton. She also attended Professor John Wesley Hales's lectures on Elizabethan and Jacobean drama in 1880.

At the age of twenty-three Edith Sichel joined the Whitechapel branch of the Metropolitan Association for Befriending Young Servants. Through her work here she met Canon Samuel Barnett and his wife Henrietta, and also Emily Ritchie, who became her closest friend. Her philanthropy, informed by her deep Christian faith, was essentially conservative and individualistic: accepting as God-given the class system of Victorian society, she held that the core of her mission was the creation and development of personal friendships, and had little interest in administrative and committee work which resulted from the growth of institutional social work.

Sichel's faith in personal initiative in philanthropic work was evidenced by her private projects, pursued after bad health had forced her to abandon her work in the East End in 1891. In 1889 she and Emily Ritchie established a nursery for East End workhouse children in Chiddingfold near Witley, where they were renting a cottage. When they moved to The Hurst, Hambledon, in 1891 they started a home for Whitechapel girls, where they intended to train them for domestic service. In 'The confessions of an amateur philanthropist' (reprinted posthumously in *Old and New*, 1917) Edith Sichel gave an amusing description of her endeavours with her protégées: working with about six girls at a time, she combined domestic training in housework and cookery (a laundry proved unsuccessful) with outdoor rambles, intended to improve their health and—with the aid of poetry and botany—widen their minds. A similar project for older girls proved unsuccessful, but the original home was still thriving when Sichel died. She was also treasurer of a boys' home in Islington for twenty-two years, and from 1893 to 1905 she was manager of the Ashburnham and Park Walk Schools in Chelsea. Subsequently she assisted school-leavers seeking employment.

However, Edith Sichel's leading interest from the 1890s was her literary career. Her first published work, the tale of a Wapping girl entitled 'Jenny', which appeared in the *Cornhill Magazine* in 1887, was inspired by her East End work. She became a steady contributor to journals and magazines, including *The Pilot*, the *Monthly Review*, the *Times Literary Supplement*, and the *Quarterly Review*, revealing herself to be an enthusiastic, perceptive, and generous reviewer of histories, biographies, and memoirs. In 1893 she published *Worthington Junior*, an undistinguished novel, before turning to the more congenial pursuit of French history. *The Story of Two Salons* (1895) described the salons of the Suards and Pauline de Beaumont, while *The Household of the Lafayettes* (1897) dealt with the pre- and post-Revolution history of a prominent French family. In 1903, with G. W. E. Russell, she published *Mr Woodhouse's Correspondence*, a collection of comic correspondence (which had originally appeared in *The Pilot*) between the family and associates of the imaginary Algernon Wentworth-Woodhouse, a rich, miserly, and valetudinarian egotist. This was followed in 1906 by *The Life and Letters of Alfred Ainger*, a tribute to a close friend. Another such tribute appeared in 1910, when she contributed a memoir to *Gathered Leaves*, a posthumous collection of pieces by Mary Coleridge, whose death in 1907 was a considerable blow. *Women and Men of the French Renaissance* (1901) foreshadowed more directly her *magnum opus*, a two-volume account of the life and career of Catherine de' Medici, published as *Catherine de'Medici and the French Reformation* (1905) and *The Later Years of Catherine de'Medici* (1908). The

Renaissance, written for H. A. L. Fisher's Home University Library of Modern Knowledge series, and *Michel de Montaigne*, both published in 1911, were the last of her works to appear in her lifetime. In humorous self-deprecation, Sichel described herself as 'only a gossiping lady's maid who curls the hair of History'. In fact her histories were well researched in primary as well as secondary sources, and she believed that a woman historian could have a distinctive and serious role in exploring the more personal and domestic aspects of history. Vivid, impressionistic portraits of many leading figures in French courts and salons bear witness to her appropriately Renaissance belief that history was 'human life remembered' (Ritchie, 147, 45).

In 1911 Edith Sichel began to hold classes for female prisoners at Holloway Prison, where her sister was already a visitor. She became deeply interested in the 1914 Prison Reform Bill, drawing up a report for the commissioners of prisons and attending police courts to examine sentencing. This additional work may have contributed to her unexpected death, on the night of 13 August 1914, while visiting friends at Borwick Hall, near Carnforth, Lancashire.

Edith Sichel was remembered by her contemporaries as a woman of great charm, witty, cultivated, and cheerful, with a genius for friendship. Both her books and her letters reveal an attractive and vivacious personality. While her poetry is generally third rate and laboured, her prose is elegant, absorbing, and seasoned with epigrams. Her appearance was striking rather than handsome—photographs show a large-featured, dark-haired woman, a sort of beautified George Eliot—but observers commented on her expressive face, 'full of mobility, vigour and refinement' (Cornish, 217). ROSEMARY MITCHELL

Sources E. M. Ritchie, *Edith Sichel: letters, verses and other writings* (1918) · A. C. Bradley, 'Introduction', in E. Sichel, *Old and new* (1917) · F. W. Cornish, 'Edith Sichel: a study in friendship', *Cornhill Magazine*, [3rd] ser., 39 (1915), 217–30 · *WWW*, 1897–1915 · b. cert. · d. cert.

Likenesses photograph, *c.*1887, repro. in Sichel, *Old and new*, facing p. 191 · photograph, 1913, repro. in Sichel, *Old and new*, frontispiece

Wealth at death £6787 19s. 8d.: resworn probate, 11 Sept 1914, CGPLA Eng. & Wales

Sickert, Walter Richard (1860–1942), painter, was born in Munich on 31 May 1860, the first of the six children (five sons and one daughter) of Oswald Adalbert Sickert (1828–1885), a Danish painter and illustrator born in Schleswig-Holstein, and Eleanor Louisa Moravia Henry (1830–1922). Oswald's father, Johann Jörgen Sickert, was also a painter. Eleanor was the natural daughter of the English astronomer Richard Sheepshanks (1794–1855) and Eleanor Henry, a dancer of Irish birth who emigrated to Australia about 1842 leaving her daughter behind. As Eleanor's guardian, Sheepshanks had arranged for her schooling in Dieppe and a subsequent stay in Altona, near Hamburg, to learn German. There she met her future husband. They married in Hendon on 3 August 1859 and went to settle in Munich where Oswald had been appointed as illustrator

on the weekly comic newspaper the *Fliegende Blätter*. However, when the treaty of 1864 between Germany and Denmark decreed that in January 1867 natives of Schleswig-Holstein were to be declared citizens of Prussia, Oswald Sickert decided to leave Germany. The family, now with three more children, settled in Bedford, England, in 1868. They moved to London in 1869 where two more children were born. Oswald Sickert later acquired his wife's nationality.

Life and art to 1905 In the summer of 1878 Sickert matriculated from King's College School, London. Oswald Sickert, having nurtured his son's love of art and above all his abiding admiration for both German and English graphic illustrators, is thought to have discouraged Walter from choosing painting as a career. Sickert's first idea was to join the staff of the British Museum Library, but in 1879 he decided instead to indulge his talent as an actor. Under the pseudonym Mr Nemo he played minor parts in the London and provincial productions of several well-known companies.

When Sickert abandoned the professional stage in 1881 he did not stop acting. He loved dressing up and relished his lifetime roles as playboy, dandy, impresario, guru, and *grand maître*. However he could never have doubted his true vocation. While working as an actor he had spent his holidays sketching. In October 1881 he signed up for a year's 'general course' at the Slade School of Fine Art but this formal training did not meet his needs. In March 1882 he left the Slade to become pupil and assistant to James McNeill Whistler whose 'immense genius' he had recognized in May 1879 (letter to A. Pollard, Baron, *Sickert*, 7). His wit, charm, good looks, and talent combined to ensure that he was soon established as the most trusted pupil of 'The Master'.

When Sickert joined Whistler's studio as an apprentice, the American-born, Paris-trained painter was the undisputed leader of the avant-garde in London. Every facet of Sickert's tough apprenticeship yielded results. He learned to sketch landscapes and portraits from nature, in melting, tonal washes of thin paint; his visual memory was trained during memorizing expeditions preceding a Whistler nocturne; he gained experience in etching techniques when helping to print Whistler's plates. He learned the importance of art politics, the techniques of polemics, and the power of the pen. Even his position as studio errand boy had far-reaching consequences when in April 1883, armed with two letters of introduction, one to Degas and one to Manet, he acted as Whistler's courier and took *Portrait of the Artist's Mother* to Paris for exhibition at the Salon. Manet (who died on 30 April) was too ill to see him personally. Degas liked Sickert enough to take him to his studio and show him his work.

On 10 June 1885 Sickert married Ellen Melicent Cobden (1848–1914), daughter of Richard *Cobden, the radical MP who had died in 1865. After a European tour, the newly married couple spent the rest of the summer in Dieppe. There Sickert cemented his friendship with the painter Jacques-Emile Blanche, whose seafront house was the meeting place for many French writers and painters, including Degas. The debonair figure of Sickert is the focal figure in the pastel drawing by Degas *Six Friends at Dieppe* (1885; Museum of Art, Rhode Island School of Design, Providence). Their friendship deepened in the autumn when Sickert again visited Degas in Paris.

The significance of Degas's example for Sickert was two-fold. Sickert became aware of the limitations of Whistler's method of painting spontaneously from nature, in wet touches upon wet, and learned instead to paint away from nature, using oil sketches and drawings as preparatory documents. Degas's example also encouraged Sickert to extend the range of his subject matter. In 1887 he began to paint the interiors of London music halls, working as Degas advocated in the studio from countless drawings made on the spot. His skill matured fast so that by 1888–9 he was able to achieve the complex construction of *Little Dot Hetherington at the Old Bedford* (priv. coll.) in which audience, orchestra, stage, even artistes waiting in the wings, are all seen as reflections in a great glass mirror.

Meanwhile Sickert outgrew Whistler's patronage. In 1887 he had cast off his nomenclature as 'pupil of Whistler' and exhibited by invitation with Les XX in Brussels. Seurat was a co-exhibitor at this prestigious showplace for progressive art. At the end of the year he joined the New English Art Club (NEAC), created in 1886 as a membership society the exhibitions of which would provide a radical alternative to the Royal Academy. Although 'radical' meant little more than sympathetic to French impressionism, the NEAC immediately became a battleground for different factions. In April 1888 Sickert's 4 foot-high portrayal (destr.) of *Katie Lawrence* behind the footlights at

Gatti's Hungerford Palace of Varieties caused critical furore. He was vilified for finding the bawdy cockney music hall a proper subject for painting. By 1889 he was chief spokesman for the progressive nucleus of the club who, under the title 'London impressionists', staged an independent exhibition at the Goupil Gallery in December. The catalogue preface is Sickert's earliest coherent manifesto. Impressionism, he wrote,

> is not realism. It has no wish to record anything merely because it exists. It is not occupied in a struggle to make intensely real and solid the sordid or superficial details of the subjects it selects. ... It is ... strong in the belief that for those who live in the most wonderful and complex city in the world, the most fruitful course of study lies in a persistent effort to render the magic and the poetry which they daily see around them.

Each summer Sickert painted townscapes abroad, mostly in Dieppe. In 1895 and 1896 he painted in Venice. His unorthodox approach to theatre representation was confirmed in *The Gallery of the Old Bedford* (prime version *c*.1895, Walker Art Gallery, Liverpool) in which he used a mirror image to present a double-angled view of the steeply raked gallery and its motley occupants gawping at the (unseen) stage below. In the interests of earning a living he tried to establish a fashionable portrait practice. He launched this endeavour by drawing portraits for publication in journals, beginning in 1890 with thirteen portraits for *The Whirlwind*. He painted several good working likenesses, usually in head and shoulders format, of distinguished radicals from his wife's circle such as *Charles Bradlaugh* (1890; National Liberal Club, London). However, the range and power of Sickert's talent as a portraitist are best

Walter Richard Sickert (1860–1942), self-portrait, 1907 [*The Painter in his Studio*]

found in the consummate images he created of his friends, such as *George Moore* (exh. 1891) and *Aubrey Beardsley* (1894) (both Tate collection).

As the 1890s progressed Sickert's private life disintegrated. His attempt to establish a commercial portrait practice failed. His marriage, and with it his financial security, broke down. In 1895 Ellen had found a compromising letter to her husband but forgave him and they went together to Venice. However, Sickert's numerous infidelities continued and they finally parted in September 1896. His wife was granted a divorce on 27 July 1899. Despite his flagrant conduct, Ellen continued to help her former husband when he was ill or hard up until her death in 1914. Her private feelings can best be gauged from *Wistons: a Story in Three Parts*, a novel she published in 1902 under the pseudonym Miles Amber, in which the character and failings of her hero, Robin, and the feelings of his wife, Esther, reflect her experience of marriage.

From the winter of 1898 until 1905, interrupted only by three long visits to Venice (1900, 1901, and 1903–4), Sickert lived in Dieppe. There he settled down to earn his appellation by J.-E. Blanche as its 'Canaletto' (Blanche, 45). He rarely exhibited in London. Instead, the Paris dealers Durand-Ruel (who gave him a one-man exhibition in 1900) and Bernheim-Jeune (who mounted one-man shows in 1904, 1907, and 1909) handled his work.

On his last visit to Venice in 1903–4, at the age of forty-three and after five years devoted almost exclusively to landscape, Sickert began to paint the intimate figure subjects for which he is best known. In a sustained sequence of paintings, he presented his Venetian prostitute models within the simple setting of his rooms at 940 calle dei Frati, furnished with a wooden bed, a washstand, and a couch with curved arms. He began to tackle two-figure subjects, sometimes representing his models nude or part-dressed, which anticipate the 'conversation pieces' of his Camden Town period.

Life and art, 1905–1922 Sickert returned to London in 1905 with a repertoire that included subjects suited to the grey light of the dingy lodging houses, many in and around Camden Town, where he habitually rented studios. He taught a group of younger colleagues and pupils to discover magic and poetry in the most unpromising subjects from everyday life: coster girls in dingy bedsitters, dusty bric-à-brac on mantelshelves, the back streets of run-down areas of London, dishevelled and ill-favoured nudes on iron bedsteads. Led by Sickert, this group exhibited, discussed, and sold their work to discerning patrons on Saturday afternoons in a studio they rented in Fitzroy Street, and in 1911 established the *Camden Town Group. Sickert alone developed the two-figure subjects which have come to personify Camden Town painting. Those showing a nude woman together with a clothed man were frequently called *The Camden Town Murder*, a title Sickert borrowed from the sensational press coverage of the murder of a prostitute in September 1907. Other less dramatic clothed figure subjects evoked the boredom and petty conflicts of married life; the most famous example is *Ennui*

(1914; Tate collection). Although Sickert delighted in encouraging, through his titles, dramatic interpretations of his paintings, their implicit tensions arose almost accidentally when he juggled with the formal relationships between his figures. Thus *L'affaire de Camden Town* (1909; priv. coll.), the most brutal painting with the 'murder' title, was based on a tender study of two women entitled *Conversation* (Royal College of Art, London). Sickert christened his paintings when they were finished and his choice was so arbitrary that one work can have separate, anecdotally incompatible, titles. *Summer in Naples* and *Dawn, Camden Town* are authentic titles of a single painting of 1909 (priv. coll.).

Sickert was a prolific, entertaining, and illuminating writer on art. He addressed his readers in discursive, conversational mode, scattering his observations with pertinent phrases in French, German, and Italian, while never losing sight of the plan and purpose of each article. To this day Osbert Sitwell's anthology of his writings is used as a dictionary of quotations on art. During the pre-war years, Sickert's often weekly articles in the *New Age* and *Art News* gave him a platform from which to conduct a passionate polemic against the 'puritan standards of propriety' ('A critical calender', *English Review*, March 1912, 717) that bedevilled British painting. He inveighed against tasteful artificiality. Instead of painting the model ('Tilly Pullen') all dressed up in a glitzy setting, he advised:

> let us strip Tilly Pullen of her lendings and tell her to put her own things on again. Let her leave the studio and climb the first dirty little staircase in the first shabby little house. Tilly Pullen becomes interesting at once. She is in surroundings that mean something. She becomes stuff for a picture. Follow her into her kitchen, or, better still, … into her bedroom; and now Tilly Pullen is become the stuff of which the Parthenon was made. ('The study of drawing', *New Age*, 16 June 1910)

This message underpins Sickert's most quoted dictum:

> The more our art is serious, the more will it tend to avoid the drawing-room and stick to the kitchen. The plastic arts are gross arts, dealing joyously with gross material facts, … and while they will flourish in the scullery, or on the dunghill, they fade at a breath from the drawing-room. ('Idealism', *Art News*, 12 May 1910)

Sickert's innovative approach to subject matter during the Camden Town period—between 1905 and the outbreak of war in 1914—paralleled his experiments with technique and style. Between 1907 and 1910 he used fatter, more oily paint, applied in a dense and bumpy carpet of broken touches and colours. However, he was led to a technical impasse. He disliked thick impasto; he disliked thin paint. He wanted to achieve a paint surface that remained lucid in texture even when built up in multiple coats. In 1913–14 he discovered his ideal technique: he mapped his design on canvas as a tonal, two-coloured underpainting which did not become rough in texture or dirty in colour even when worked over in successive layers. The final coats of local colour could then be brushed on in dry, undiluted paint to produce a surface at once thick, smooth, and clean. His colours became lighter and brighter; his canvases coarser; and he often worked on a larger scale. This method, with minor modifications, remained the basis of his painting for the rest of his life.

Throughout the Camden Town period Sickert devoted much time to printmaking, charting the evolution of his ideas in a sequence of critical essays published between 1908 and 1915. Sickert's prints cannot be assessed in isolation. Whether in his lightly worked vignettes of the early 1880s, his richly varied series published by the Carfax Gallery in 1915, or his austere prints of the 1920s, Sickert tackled on copper the same problems of subject, composition, style, and execution as he did on paper or canvas. Just as he had rejected thick impasto in his paintings, by 1915 he had rejected rich, picturesque, tonal effects in his prints. His ideal in printmaking, as in painting, became to achieve weight and quality without coarsening, dirtying, and compromising his medium.

1910–11 was a busy time in Sickert's personal life. He had enjoyed many amorous friendships since his divorce. His looks and charm were as irresistible in middle age as in his youth. Few women, old, young, grand, or humble, could deny him. However, he found it harder to find a wife than a mistress. He courted three women in one year. The first refused him. The second, a student from his class at Westminster Technical Institute, jilted him on 3 June 1911, it is said on the way to Camden Town register office. Undeterred, by 5 June he had transferred his affections to another student from his private art school at Rowlandson House, Christine Drummond Angus (c.1877–1920), daughter of John Henry Angus, a Scottish leather merchant. They married at Paddington register office on 29 July 1911. Christine was an accomplished embroideress; one of her pieces, a blue damask tunicle in Westminster Abbey, was used for the 1937 coronation. Slim, fine-featured, and delicate, she was likened by Sickert to a pelican. With her quiet humour and intelligence, she was the ideal wife for Sickert.

Sickert was too old to play an active part in the war. Denied his regular summer visits to Dieppe, he escaped to Chagford, Devon, in 1915, visited Bath several times between 1916 and 1918, and devoted much of his energy in London to teaching, writing, and etching. After the war he and Christine decided to make Envermeu, a village outside Dieppe, their home. There, from 1919 to 1920, he painted the lush landscape of the Arques valley and a series of kitchen still lifes. In October 1920 Christine died of tuberculosis. Sickert, who had refused to accept that her health had long been failing, was devastated by her death. His behaviour was bizarre. He had a death mask made. At her funeral, wearing a black velvet coat with his head shaven, he scattered her ashes to the winds; it settled like a fine white dust on the mourners. Some months later he moved to Dieppe where, until his return to London in 1922, he roamed the town at night to paint the harbour cafés and the casino.

Life, art, and character, 1922–1942 In later years, Sickert's behaviour—ever unpredictable—became increasingly eccentric. The one-time dandy took to dressing incongruously, for example, sporting slippers and loud checked suits on formal occasions. In April 1925 he decided to call himself by his full name, Walter Richard Sickert; by the autumn he often dropped the Walter and Richard Sickert was born. This perverse change of name may have been designed to help Sickert retain the uncluttered sense of self essential to his art. As he had confessed to Nina Hamnett in 1918: 'the one thing … I cling to is my coolness and leisurely exhilarated contemplation' (Baron, *Sickert*, 182). To this end his lifelong habits of adopting different roles, changing his appearance by shaving his head bald or growing a huge spade beard, changing his habitat whether by renting countless separate studios (sometimes in different towns and countries) or by changing his circles of friends, colleagues, and lovers, may all be seen as devices to insulate him from emotional engagement. He spent his life shedding the accumulated baggage of former existences. His was a complex, layered personality. The core of his being lay in his art. His steadfast devotion to his muse was unmatched by devotion to anything or anyone else. Generous and selfless in supporting and promoting the work of his professional colleagues, in his personal life he was capable of boundless egoism, not a little cruelty, and on occasion startling hypocrisy. But none of this seems to have tested the loyalty of his friends.

Sickert's third wife was **(Elaine) Thérèse Lessore** (1884–1945), painter. Like his former wives, Ellen and Christine (and unlike his mistresses, many of whom had been physically sumptuous), Thérèse was delicately made; Sickert compared her to a Persian miniature. Her background echoed his, in that she came from a line of continental painters. She was born on 5 July 1884 at Albion Street, Southwick, near Shoreham, Sussex, the youngest daughter of the French painter and etcher Jules Frederick Lessore (1849–1892), who had settled in England in 1871, and his wife, Ada Louisa Cooper. On leaving the Slade School of Fine Art in 1909 she married the painter Bernard Adeney (1878–1966). She was elected to the London Group at a meeting of the Fitzroy Street Group in January 1914 over which Sickert presided. During the war Sickert found her an exhilarating friend, and in January 1918 wrote an enthusiastic article on her painting for *Art and Letters*, reprinted in November as the preface to the catalogue of her exhibition at the Eldar Gallery, London. He admired her sense of design, her spare style, and her technical skill in extracting value from the interplay of coloured underpaintings and final coats of local colour. These qualities were especially close to Sickert's own ideals after 1914 and it is a moot point how far each influenced the other. She and Sylvia Gosse each came to France to help Sickert through the months of black despair following Christine's death. Both remained devoted to him thereafter. Thérèse divorced her husband in 1921. In London, Sickert and Thérèse indulged their shared love of music halls as entertainment and as a subject for painting. They married on 4 June 1926.

The last major development in Sickert's artistic life occurred during the mid-1920s when photographs gradually ousted drawings as the basis for his portrait, landscape, and theatre pictures. When he lost interest in drawing, he abandoned his career as a printmaker. From 1927 onwards he found ready-made subjects for his anecdotal paintings in Victorian illustrations (aptly given the generic description of 'echoes'). The best of the late photo-based paintings, such as the heroic series of self-portraits in which Sickert cast himself in biblical roles, are intensely personal and subjective. Photographs influenced Sickert's art in practical ways. He could paint portraits without sittings or commissions. Thus we have royal portraits painted from newspaper photographs, for example, *Edward VIII* in two versions (priv. coll. and Beaverbrook Art Gallery, Fredericton, Canada) painted during his brief reign in 1936. His flamboyant life-size, full-length portraits became the talking points of Royal Academy summer exhibitions between 1925 and 1935 and a stream of one-man exhibitions, principally at the Leicester Galleries and the Beaux Arts Gallery (run by Frederick Lessore, brother of Thérèse, and his wife, Helen Lessore), kept his recent work on constant view in London throughout the 1930s.

Because Sickert's art was based on photographs his subject matter was no longer conditioned by where he lived. At the end of 1934 he moved from London (Islington) to St Peters in Thanet, Kent. His flow of portraits continued unabated, as did his sequence of theatre pictures. Throughout the 1930s, using press and publicity photographs, he was able to depict his favourite players, for example Peggy Ashcroft and Gwen Ffrangçon Davies, in their classic roles. In 1938 Sickert moved from Thanet to St George's Hill House, Bathampton, Wiltshire. With increasing assistance from his wife and from Sylvia Gosse, he continued to paint local subjects, such as the garden of his house and the townscape of Bath, until 1940. He died at home after a succession of strokes on 22 January 1942 and was buried in Bathampton cemetery. Thérèse Lessore died in St Mary Abbot's Hospital, Kensington, on 10 December 1945, and was also buried in Bathampton cemetery.

There is no firm evidence to support the suggestion that Sickert had children. His three marriages were without issue. It is often claimed (Browse, 36; Sutton, 153) that he fathered Maurice, one of the sons of Madame Augustine Villain, the beautiful red-haired doyenne of the fishmarket in Dieppe, with whom Sickert lived from 1899 until 1902. However, it is doubtful whether Sickert knew Madame Villain when Maurice (*b.* 23 Dec 1895) was conceived. It is more probable that Sickert and his mistress's young son enjoyed an adoptive rather than a blood relationship. He took an interest in Maurice's welfare and painted him in uniform, bearing the Croix de Guerre, during the First World War. A claim to Sickert as father has also been made by Joseph Gorman (*b.* 1926), who first concocted the story, elaborated by the writer Stephen Knight and others, that Sickert was Jack the Ripper. That suggestion is fantasy.

Sickert received little in the way of official honours. In 1932 he received the honorary degree of LLD from the University of Manchester and in 1938 that of DLitt from the University of Reading. Among the many societies to which he was periodically elected and from which he periodically resigned were the New English Art Club; the Royal Society of British Artists (president, winter 1927; resigned 1929); the London Group; the Royal Academy (ARA 1924, RA 1934, resigned 1935); the National Portrait Society; and the International Society of Sculptors, Painters, and Gravers. His work was exhibited widely during his lifetime in all major group shows and with many commercial dealers in London and Paris. In 1930 and 1932 he exhibited in the British section of the biennale in Venice. A big retrospective exhibition organized by Lillian Browse was held at the National Gallery in the autumn of 1941.

Influence For sixty years, in his several roles as painter, teacher, and polemicist, Walter Sickert was a source of inspiration and influence to successive generations of British painters. He taught, on and off, from 1890 to the late 1920s. His longest-lasting official teaching appointment was at the Westminster Technical Institute (1908–18, with a break in 1914), but he also held classes for a brief time in 1926 at the Royal Academy Schools. He opened his first private school (Glebe Place, Chelsea) in 1890, when barely past the apprentice stage himself. Thereafter, when he lived in London, a Sickert atelier could usually be discovered somewhere in inner London. In later life he was in great demand as a lecturer. He successfully toured the country in 1923 and 1924 with 'Straws from Cumberland Market'. In 1938 he addressed the Euston Road School. His last lectures were given at the Bath School of Art in 1939. His output of paintings, drawings, and prints was vast. His subject matter embraced landscape, townscape, portraits, music halls and theatres, intimate interiors with figures, still life, and towards the end of his life the 'echoes', recreations in colour of anecdotal nineteenth-century black and white illustrations. Sickert may be judged equally as the last of the Victorians and as a major precursor, especially in his photo-based paintings, of significant international developments in later twentieth-century art. Sickert would have approved this duality, maintaining: 'There is no such thing as modern art. There is no such thing as ancient art ... History is one unbroken stream. If we know Degas, Degas knew Ingres, and so on, *ad infinitum*' ('A monthly chronicle: o matre pulchrâ', *Burlington Magazine*, 29, 1916, 34–5).

Sickert's art defies categorization. He was neither impressionist nor post-impressionist; neither realist nor intimist. As he wrote: 'Let us leave the labels to those who have little else wherewith to cover their nakedness' ('Mr Ginner's Preface', *New Age*, 30 April 1914). He is often called a painter's painter. He appeals primarily to artists working in the figurative tradition, but not only to artists with a Sickertian vocabulary of subjects. He was a brave painter, unafraid of failing. His subject matter was so various, his investigations of technique so searching, his experiments with style so daring, that each generation of painters since his return to London in 1905 has found abiding inspiration in one or other aspect of his work. There are few British figurative painters whose development can be adequately discussed without reference to Sickert, whether the influence transmitted is obvious or less tangible. The fascination his work holds for painters continues unabated.   WENDY BARON

Sources W. Baron, 'Chronology', *Sickert, paintings*, ed. W. Baron and R. Shone (1992), 33–54 [exhibition catalogue, London and Amsterdam, 20 Nov 1992 – 31 May 1993] • W. Baron, *Sickert* (1973) • R. Shone, *Walter Sickert* (1988) • O. Sitwell, ed., *A free house! or, The artist as craftsman being the writings of Walter Richard Sickert* (1947) • H. M. Swanwick, *I have been young* (1935) [autobiography] • R. Emmons, *The life and opinions of Walter Richard Sickert* (1941) • M. Lilly, *Sickert: the painter and his circle* (1971) • W. Baron and R. Shone, eds., *Sickert, paintings* (1992) [exhibition catalogue, London and Amsterdam, 20 Nov 1992 – 31 May 1993] • L. Browse, *Sickert* (1960) • S. Pakenham, *60 miles from England: the English at Dieppe, 1814–1914* (1967) • D. Sutton, *Walter Sickert* (1976) • J.-E. Blanche, *Portraits of a lifetime: the late Victorian era, the Edwardian pageant, 1870–1914* (1937) • b. cert. [E. T. Lessore] • d. cert. [E. T. Lessore] • M. Sturgis, biography of Sickert [forthcoming] • West Sussex County Library, Cobden papers • letters of Ellen Cobden, W. Sussex RO • Tate collection, corresp. with Ethel Sands and Nan Hudson

Archives Islington Central Library, papers of and relating to him • NL Scot., corresp. and papers | HLRO, corresp. with Lord Beaverbrook • King's AC Cam., letters to J. M. Keynes • RA, letters to Royal Academy • Tate collection, corresp. with the Angus family • Tate collection, corresp. with Gwen Ffrangçon-Davies • U. Birm. L., corresp. with Sir William Eden | FILM BFI NFTVA, footage dating from *c.*1953 • BFI NFTVA, footage by Jake Auerbach, *c.*1993 | SOUND BL NSA, recorded interviews

Likenesses W. R. Sickert, self-portrait, ink, 1882, Islington Public Libraries, London • T. Stirling Lee, bronze roundel, *c.*1882, priv. coll. • E. Degas, group portrait, pastels, 1885 (*Six friends at Dieppe*), Rhode Island School of Design, Providence, Museum of Art • J. McNeill Whistler, oils, *c.*1886, Hugh Lane Municipal Gallery of Modern Art, Dublin • W. R. Sickert, self-portrait, oils, *c.*1890, Art Gallery of New South Wales, Sydney • P. W. Steer, oils, 1890, NPG • P. W. Steer, portrait, 1890–1899?, NPG • W. R. Sickert, self-portrait, oils, *c.*1896, Leeds City Art Gallery • C. Holroyd, metal-point drawing, 1897, BM • J.-E. Blanche, oils, 1898, NPG • W. R. Sickert, self-portrait, charcoal, pen, and ink, *c.*1903–1904, AM Oxf. • W. R. Sickert, self-portrait, oils, 1903–4, AM Oxf. • W. R. Sickert, self-portrait, oils, 1907, Southampton Art Gallery • W. R. Sickert, self-portrait, oils, 1907, Hamilton Art Gallery, Ontario [*see illus.*] • W. Orpen, group portrait, oils, 1909 (*Homage to Manet*), Man. City Gall. • W. Orpen, group portrait, oils, 1909 (*The selecting jury of the New English Art Club*), NPG • H. W. Barnett, three photographs, *c.*1910–1920, V&A • G. C. Beresford, photographs, 1911, NPG • W. R. Sickert, self-portrait, oils, 1913–15, priv. coll. • S. Gosse, oils, *c.*1923–1925, Tate collection • F. D. Wood, bronze bust, 1925, RA • H. Tonks, group portrait, oils, 1926–9 (*Sodales—Mr Sickert and Mr Steer*), Tate collection • W. R. Sickert, self-portrait, oils, 1927, priv. coll. • W. R. Sickert, self-portrait, oils, *c.*1929, Tate collection • W. R. Sickert, self-portrait, 1930–1939?, NPG • H. Rayner, drypoint, 1931, NPG, V&A • J.-E. Blanche, oils, 1935, Man. City Gall. • C. Beaton, photograph, 1940, NPG • E. Kapp, pen-and-ink drawing, 1940, NPG • M. Beerbohm, caricatures, drawings, BM • M. Beerbohm, caricatures, drawings, U. Texas • E. Kapp, pen and Indian ink drawing, FM Cam. • T. Lessore, watercolour, Man. City Gall. • W. R. Sickert, self-portrait, National Gallery of Victoria, Melbourne • P. W. Steer, sketch, V&A • photographs, repro. in Baron and Shone, eds., *Sickert paintings* • photographs, Islington Public Libraries, London

Wealth at death £145 4*s.* 3*d.*: probate, 4 May 1942, *CGPLA Eng. & Wales*

Sickert, Walter, pupils (*act.* 1890–1939), painters, encompass generations of aspiring artists who from 1890 to 1939 attended painting, drawing, and etching classes held by Walter Richard *Sickert (1860–1942) in a succession of private rooms, private studios, and official art schools. Many

students found recipes for successful picture-making in Sickert's precepts: draw by the background spaces; define objects not in terms of outline but as maps of light and shade; plan the execution of pictures through a tonally prepared underpainting. As a result, work by Sickert pupils is ubiquitous.

A distinction must be made between those artists who benefited from Sickert's tuition early in their careers, those who were overwhelmed by him, and those who based their practice on his instruction but retained an independent vision. The first group included Roger *Fry (1866–1934) and William *Rothenstein (1872–1945) who attended Sickert's evening classes at The Vale, Chelsea, in 1893; Ambrose *McEvoy (1878–1927) who in 1909 attended his etching class at 31 Augustus Street; David *Bomberg (1890–1957) who attended his classes at the Westminster Technical Institute; and the talented amateur Winston *Churchill to whom he gave private tuition from 1927 to 1928. Some from the second group enjoyed a brief moment of credibility when in July 1913 the Carfax Gallery put on an exhibition, 'Paintings, drawings, and etchings by past and present pupils of Mr. Sickert'. This umbrella sheltered 101 works by twenty-eight artists of whom some twenty are now forgotten. As Enid *Bagnold (1889–1981), his erstwhile pupil, recalled, Sickert 'was such a teacher as would make a kitchen-maid exhibit once' (*Autobiography*, 1969, 73). The few artists remembered from that exhibition are John Doman Turner (*c.*1872–1938) and Malcolm Drummond (1880–1945), both members of the *Camden Town Group; Mary Godwin (1887–1960); Jean McIntyre (1889–1967); Charles Maresco Pearce (1874–1964); Louise Pickard (1865–1928); and John Wheatley (1892–1955). The third group represents the few men and women who had talent, staying power, and a temperament strong enough to withstand prolonged exposure to Sickert.

Among the best of these was the artist **(Laura) Sylvia Gosse** (1881–1968), born in London on 14 February 1881, the youngest of the three children of Sir Edmund *Gosse (1849–1928) and his wife, Ellen, *née* Epps. Gosse's training began at the St John's Wood School of Art, and continued from 1903 to 1908 at the Royal Academy Schools. In 1908 Sickert—a family friend—took over her education. She learned her formidable skill as an etcher at his classes at the Westminster Technical Institute, at 31 Augustus Street, and perhaps at the school for etching that he ran with the practical and financial help of young Madeleine Knox (1890–1975) first at 209 and then at 140 Hampstead Road. Sickert christened the latter address Rowlandson House in homage to the comic draughtsman and expanded the curriculum to include drawing and painting. When Miss Knox resigned in March 1910, worn out by coping with Sickert, Gosse took over management of the school. A few months later she became a full partner in the enterprise.

Gosse adopted Sickert's subject matter: the townscapes, domestic interiors with figures—clothed and unclothed—iron bedstead scenes, music halls. She adopted his working practices, painting (sometimes after the passage of many years) from squared-up drawings made on the spot and in later life from photographs. She adopted in earlier career his broken touch as both etcher and painter, and in later career his habit of building an abstract jigsaw pattern of colours conceived in terms of their tonal equivalents. She and Thérèse *Lessore [see under Sickert, Walter Richard (1860–1942)] were the painters Sickert most readily entrusted to prepare his later works by transferring his designs to canvas and laying in their tonal underpaintings. However, although Gosse's artistic personality was closely dependent upon Sickert for inspiration, there were qualities innate to her work, in particular her spare touch and bold sense of design, from which he in turn derived nourishment. Her documentary subject painting *Madrid Crowd* (1931; priv. coll., repr. Fisher, between 56-7), clearly based on a newspaper photograph, was painted four to five years before *The Miner* (Birmingham Art Gallery), Sickert's own essay in contemporary reportage.

Gosse, although shy, self-effacing, and reclusive by nature, had confidence in her work. She exhibited with all the major groups including the Allied Artists' Association (from 1909), the London Group (from 1914), the New English Art Club (from 1911), and the Royal Academy (from 1912). Behind the scenes, she devoted much of her energies and her money to helping Sickert at various times of his life. She bought his paintings anonymously when financial support was crucial to his well-being (donating some to the Johannesburg Art Gallery); she tended Christine Sickert during her terminal illness and nursed Sickert back to health and sanity following Christine's death in 1920 at Envermeu, Dieppe; in 1934 she organized the Sickert fund to raise enough money to enable the seventy-four-year-old painter to work free from financial anxiety; she helped Thérèse Lessore look after her husband during the last years of his life.

During Sickert's lifetime, Gosse often lived in his shadow, renting rooms in and around Camden Town and a house in Envermeu, Dieppe. She is sometimes pitied for having twice failed to win Sickert as a husband, first in 1911 and more emphatically after Christine's death when she and Thérèse Lessore were considered by their mutual acquaintance to be joint favourites. Almost certainly this pity is misplaced. There is no evidence to suggest that Sylvia Gosse wished her devotion to Sickert as man and mentor to be rewarded with the doubtful pleasure of marriage to him. It is probable that she preferred to remain single and single-minded in the pursuit of her career as an artist.

Failed eyesight compelled Gosse to give up painting in 1961. She died of heart failure in hospital on 6 June 1968. Her paintings and drawings are in public galleries throughout the United Kingdom while her graphic work is well represented in the British Museum, the Victoria and Albert Museum, and the Ashmolean Museum, Oxford.

(Alice) Marjorie Sherlock (1891–1973), artist, was born at Fir Tree Cottage, George Lane, Wanstead, Essex, on 3 February 1891, daughter of Henry Alexander George Sherlock, a civil engineer, and Alice Mary Sherlock, *née* Platts. She came into Sickert's orbit during the First World War, when she studied at the Westminster Technical Institute as a pupil of Sickert and of Harold Gilman. A woman of distinct and forceful character, she married—and later divorced—her first cousin, Major N. K. Tufnell-Barrett. She lived the last thirty years of her life in an isolated rambling house at Ottery St Mary, near Axminster in Devon. There she carried on working to a rigorous routine and managed to live on a meagre income by making her own clothes and growing her own vegetables.

Sherlock learned her craft from Sickert and Harold Gilman, but retained a distinct vision. As an oil painter she was precocious. Her powerful rendering of Liverpool Street Station (1917; Gov. Art Coll.; another version National Railway Museum, York) was exhibited at the Royal Academy in 1917. In 1926 she resumed her education by going to study etching at the Royal College of Art. She was an accomplished draughtsman on copper, in pencil, and in pen and ink. Her etching of Waterloo Station demonstrates her ability to control the broad structure of a complex composition without losing her delicacy of touch in the detail. Many of her etchings were published: *Egyptian Etchings* (1925), *German Etchings* (1929), and *Indian Etchings* (1932). She visited America during the depression and worked with André Lhote and Dunoyer de Segonzac in Paris in 1938. On moving to Devon she met Orovida, daughter of Lucien Pissarro, who lived near by. Orovida financed their occasional trips abroad in later years. Marjorie Sherlock died at home of heart failure on 2 April 1973.

Sherlock had no solo exhibitions, but her work could be seen in many mixed exhibitions including Royal Academy summer shows, the New English Art Club, the Carnegie Institute, Pittsburgh, the Society of Graphic Art, the International Society of Sculptors, Painters, and Gravers, the Royal Society of British Artists, and the Chicago Society of Etchers.

(Edith) Wendela Boreel (1895–1985), artist, was born on 18 March 1895 at Pau in France and came to England when her father, Jonkheer Boreel, a Dutch diplomat, was posted as minister to London. Her mother, Edith Margaret (*née* Ives), was American. In 1911 she went to the Slade School of Fine Art and to Sickert's evening classes at the Westminster Technical Institute. Her sultry beauty appealed to Sickert as much as her evident talent. Believing that her potential was as a painter in oils, he gave her the use of one of his painting studios in Mornington Crescent. Marjorie Lilly recalls (Lilly, 67-8) that in 1917 Boreel's remarkable aptitude for gouache painting inspired Sickert, and through him his wider circle of colleagues and pupils, to experiment with this difficult medium. Boreel was also a skilful etcher. Her subject matter included portraits, landscapes, townscapes, and figures. She exhibited with the Allied Artists' Association, the London Group, the New English Art Club, the Royal Academy, and the Royal Society of Painter-Etchers and Engravers (of which she became an associate in 1923). After her marriage in

1924 to Leslie George Wylde, a New Zealander, she went to live in Bray, Berkshire. They assembled a fine collection of paintings by Sickert, including his self-portrait, *The Juvenile Lead* of 1907, now in the Southampton Art Gallery. After her husband's death in 1935 she spent much of her time away from England, mostly in France and, during the Second World War, with her son in the United States of America. She died at home in Castelnau-le-Lez, France, on 13 April 1985. Her etchings can be seen in the Victoria and Albert Museum; a polymorphic painting, *Landscape in Nude*, bearing no trace of Sickert's influence, belongs to the Government Art Collection.

Among Boreel's contemporaries at the Slade were Marjorie Lilly (1891–1976) and Christina Cutter (1893–1969), who entered Sickert's Fitzroy Street circle in 1917 and were stimulated as much by his enlightening intelligence in regard to art as by his practical instruction. Lilly, Boreel, and Cutter held several joint exhibitions between 1922 and 1939. Cutter, who was born in Wisbech, Cambridgeshire, and died in Chichester, had married George, brother to Marjorie Lilly, in 1918. Her paintings are characterized by a clear grasp of structure expressed through an emphatic pattern of light and shade and a joyous sense of colour. *A Park in Vienna* (exh. 1921; priv. coll.) is closer to Charles Ginner than to Sickert. Lilly was born, lived, and died in Camden Town. Few of her paintings survived bombing raids during the Second World War. Her inestimable legacy is the lively account she published, *Sickert: the Painter and his Circle* (1971). Lilly quoted the prospectus Sickert published in 1917 in relation to his classes at 8 Fitzroy Street:

> Mr Sickert retains the option of accepting such students only as he believes are likely to profit by his method of training. To avoid correspondence, it may be found convenient to state the principles by which Mr Sickert would be guided in his acceptance of students. Unlikely to benefit would seem to be: (i) painters whose practice is already thoroughly set in methods its continuance in which Mr Sickert would be unable to encourage and indisposed to check; (ii) students who have already studied with him long enough to have absorbed—or failed to absorb—the little he has to teach. An intelligent student who cannot learn whatever is to be learnt from a teacher in three years will learn no more in thirty. Mr Sickert prefers not to be a party to the creation or perpetuation of what may be called the professional or eternal student, with no other aims than to haunt the art schools as an occupation or distraction in itself. (Lilly, 63)

Sickert's last private school, which opened in 1927 at 1 Highbury Place, was restricted to male students. Only a handful applied, of whom several were amateurs. They included Sickert's ophthalmologist Dr Cobbledick; Sickert's biographer Dr Robert Emmons; and Sickert's dealer from 1928, Mark Oliver. Two students were to become serious professional painters: Paul Ayshford *Methuen, fourth Baron Methuen (1886–1974), and Morland Lewis.

(Edward) Morland Lewis (1903–1943) was born on 25 May 1903 in Carmarthen, youngest of the eight sons of B. A. Lewis. He studied (like Gosse some twenty years before) at the St John's Wood School of Art and the Royal Academy Schools before joining Sickert's class in 1927. He painted landscapes and townscapes in England and France, adapting the lessons of Sickert, for instance the use of underpaintings, to produce rich-toned and lively records of the everyday scenes around him. He painted the streets of London and Paris and landscapes in Ireland and around Ferryside, a fishing village near his native Carmarthen. He exhibited with the London Group from 1929 (member 1932) and married the painter Katherine Mary Faussett-Osborne. During the Second World War he served as a camouflage officer in north Africa where he died of malaria on 4 August 1943. Paintings by Lewis are in the Tate collection, London, the Government Art Collection, and the National Museum and Gallery of Wales, Cardiff.

The widespread dissemination of Sickert's precepts had a profound impact on the character of British art throughout the twentieth century. Because Sickert had so many pupils over so long a period, because many went on themselves to become teachers, and because Sickert's maxims were so direct and memorable, art students long after his death were being instructed by Sickert at second—or even third—hand. To paraphrase Sickert, if he taught Bomberg, Bomberg taught Auerbach, 'and so on, *ad infinitum*'.

WENDY BARON

Sources K. Fisher, *Conversations with Sylvia* (1975) · M. Lilly, *Sickert: the painter and his circle* (1971) · W. Baron, C. Haenlein, and M. Parkin, *The Sickert women and the Sickert girls* (1974) [exhibition catalogue, Parkin Gallery, London] · [J. Sansom], *Marjorie Sherlock (1897–1973)* (1973) [exhibition catalogue, Maltzahn Gallery, London, Nov–Dec 1973] · *The Times* (17 Aug 1943) [Edward Morland Lewis] · *Walter Sickert: the artist, his wife, his mistress, his friends and one enemy* (1992) [exhibition catalogue, Michael Parkin Gallery, London, 2 Dec 1992 – 15 Jan 1993] · b. cert. [Marjorie Sherlock] · d. cert. [Marjorie Sherlock]

Likenesses H. Gilman, oils, 1913 (Laura Sylvia Gosse), Southampton Art Gallery

Sicklemore, John. *See* Ratcliffe, John (d. 1610).

Siddal, Elizabeth Eleanor (1829–1862), painter, was born at 7 Charles Street, Hatton Gardens, Holborn, London, on 25 July 1829, the third of eight children of Charles Siddall (d. 1859), ironmonger, and his wife, Elizabeth Eleanor Evans (d. 1892). Of respectable working-class background with some pretensions to gentility, without formal education, she nevertheless possessed an instinctive refinement of manner. Her deportment, said to be 'like a queen', was perhaps formed by her work at the dressmaking and millinery shop in Cranborne Alley, Leicester Square, to which she journeyed from Southwark, where her family was living. In 1850 she was noticed by the artist Walter Deverell, who asked her to act as a model for him and a group of young friends who were beginning to distinguish themselves as the Pre-Raphaelite Brotherhood. She agreed, and sat for Deverell, William Holman Hunt, and for John Everett Millais as the drowned Ophelia. Within a short time she was sitting only for Dante Gabriel *Rossetti (1828–1882).

Siddal's features are apparent in nearly all Rossetti's work until her death, most notably in *Beata Beatrix* (c.1860–64; Tate), *Regina cordium* (1860; Johannesburg Art Gallery), *A Christmas Carol* (1857–8; Fogg Art Museum, Harvard University), and *Writing on the Sand* (1859; British Museum). By

Elizabeth Eleanor Siddal (1829–1862), by Dante Gabriel Rossetti, 1860

4) is in private hands, as too are *Lady Clare* (1857) and *The Quest of the Holy Grail* (1855). Some of her designs were included in the 1857 Pre-Raphaelite exhibition in Russell Square. John Ruskin praised her watercolours and wished to settle money on her in exchange for any work her health permitted.

Siddal also wrote verse of a disillusioned and morbid character, echoing her own sense of neglect, for the passionate love of the early years had turned to disenchantment. With sadly impaired health and frustrated by Rossetti's reluctance to commit himself to marriage, and his too apt inclination to infidelity, she resorted to ever-increasing doses of laudanum. Finally, on 23 May 1860 Rossetti married her at St Clement's Church, Hastings; a year later a child was stillborn. Elizabeth Siddal committed suicide on 11 February 1862 with an overdose of laudanum, in their rooms at 14 Chatham Place, Blackfriars. She was buried on 17 February with other members of the Rossetti family in Highgate cemetery. Rossetti's complex feelings of remorse and guilt for the discords and disillusions of their life together fluctuated with the years though the haunting recollection of his wife was translated into a few lines, scribbled in his notebook:

As much as in a hundred years, she's dead:
Yet is to-day the day on which she died.
(*The Collected Works of Dante Gabriel Rossetti*, ed. W. M. Rossetti, 1886, 1.380)

In October 1869 Siddal's coffin was opened by her husband's wish and a book of his poems, laid beside her at death, was removed. These he published in *Poems* (1870).

VIRGINIA SURTEES

Sources J. Marsh, *The legend of Elizabeth Siddal* (1989) • V. Surtees, *Rossetti's portraits of Elizabeth Siddal* (1989) • A. I. Grieve, *The art of Dante Gabriel Rossetti: watercolours and drawings of 1850–55* (1978) • J. Marsh and P. G. Nunn, *Pre-Raphaelite women artists* (1997) [exhibition catalogue, Manchester, Birmingham, and Southampton, 22 Nov 1997 – 2 Aug 1998] • parish register, Holborn, St Andrew'sk, 23/8/1830 [baptism] • m. cert. • coroner's inquisition, CLRO

Likenesses W. H. Hunt, oils, 1850 (*A converted British family sheltering a Christian priest from the persecution of the Druids*), AM Oxf. • W. H. Hunt, oils, 1851 (*Valentine rescuing Sylvia from Proteus*), Birmingham Museums and Art Gallery • D. G. Rossetti, watercolour, 1851 (*Beatrice*), AM Oxf. • J. E. Millais, oils, 1851–2 (as Ophelia), Tate collection • D. G. Rossetti, watercolour, 1853 (*The first anniversary of the death of Beatrice*), AM Oxf. • D. G. Rossetti, watercolour, 1855 (*Dante's vision of Rachel and Leah*), Tate collection • D. G. Rossetti, oils, 1857 (as St Catherine), Tate collection • D. G. Rossetti, watercolour, 1857 (*The tune of Seven Towers*), Tate collection • D. G. Rossetti, watercolour, 1857 (*The wedding of St. George and the Princess Sabra*), Tate collection • D. G. Rossetti, watercolour, 1857–8 (*A Christmas carol*), Harvard U., Fogg Art Museum • D. G. Rossetti, watercolour, 1858 (*Before the battle*), Museum of Fine Arts, Boston • D. G. Rossetti, watercolour, 1859 (*Writing on the sand*), BM • D. G. Rossetti, drawing, 1860, FM Cam. [see illus.] • D. G. Rossetti, oils, 1860 (*Regina Cordium*), Johannesburg Art Gallery • D. G. Rossetti, oils, c.1860–1864 (*Beata Beatrix*), Tate collection; pencil study, William Morris Gallery, London • D. G. Rossetti, oils, 1874 (model for Beatrice), Birmingham Museums and Art Gallery; pencil and watercolour studies, Birmingham Museum and Art Gallery • J. E. Millais, pencil study, Birmingham Museums and Art Gallery • D. G. Rossetti, drawings and sketches, Birmingham Museums and Art Gallery • D. G. Rossetti, drawings and sketches, Courtauld Inst. • D. G. Rossetti, drawings and sketches, FM Cam. • D. G. Rossetti, drawings and sketches, V&A • D. G. Rossetti, drawings and sketches, Cecil

pen and pencil he conveyed in his innumerable studies of this quite ordinary girl, the fragility of an idealized beauty, and the paths of ill health, for in an enfeebled frame she seemed to carry the seeds of consumption. These studies, rare in quality, present a unique series; Sir John Ward considered that there was nothing comparable in European art. The pathos of her strange beauty is recorded in heavy lids drooping over agate-coloured eyes, wings of copper-red hair framing a face singular in its remoteness. Languor informed every portrayal, whether sleeping, reading, or (rarely) standing. In these representations 'stamped with immortality', she seemed to Ford Madox Brown 'thinner & more deathlike & more beautiful & more ragged than ever' (*The Diary of Ford Madox Brown*, ed. V. Surtees, 1981, 101). Guggum or the Sid were her pet names; the final 'l' in her surname was discarded to please Rossetti.

Rossetti fostered Siddal's slight talent for drawing, largely derivative from his own work, and saw genius in her strangely haunting imagery. She worked hard and for a short time attended an art school at Sheffield. Her early drawings, *Pippa Passes* and *Lovers Listening to Music* (both 1854; Ashmolean Museum, Oxford), show some technical proficiency, while the slightly later watercolours executed as her strength diminished are those of an amateur. The figures are awkwardly flattened, without any semblance of life, and are dependent on the emotional context of the subject. These—taken from medieval lore, border ballads, and from works by Keats, Browning, and Tennyson—are placed within tightly enclosed spaces and illustrated by strangely remote figures largely imbued with her own melancholic nature. Examples include *Sir Patrick Spens* (1856; Tate collection), *St Agnes Eve* (c.1856; Wightwick Manor, Wolverhampton), and *Clerk Saunders* (1857; Fitzwilliam Museum, Cambridge). Her *Self-Portrait* (1853–

Higgins Art Gallery, Bedford · D. G. Rossetti, drawings and sketches, AM Oxf. · D. G. Rossetti, drawings and sketches, Wightwick Manor, Wolverhampton · D. G. Rossetti, drawings and sketches, BM · D. G. Rossetti, drawings and sketches, Tate collection · D. G. Rossetti, drawings and sketches, Leicester Museum and Art Gallery · D. G. Rossetti, drawings and sketches, Man. City Gall. · D. G. Rossetti, drawings and sketches, Norfolk Museum, Virginia · D. G. Rossetti, drawings and sketches, National Gallery of Victoria, Melbourne · D. G. Rossetti, drawings and sketches, Iowa Historical and General Library, Des Moines

Siddall, Henry (*d.* 1572), Church of England clergyman, is first recorded in 1530 as a petty canon of Cardinal College, Oxford, where he was admitted BA on 10 March 1531. He was expelled the following year on royal orders when the college failed after Wolsey's fall, and endured considerable difficulties as a result. In June 1535 he supplicated for the degrees of BCL and BCnL, and was admitted on 12 July, having been excused payment of his fee of 1 gold noble on the grounds of his poverty. In the meantime he had been ordained subdeacon on 24 February 1532 (he is not known to have proceeded to higher orders), and on 24 May 1533 was admitted vicar of Farnborough, Warwickshire, though he had resigned it by the end of 1534. On 1 December 1540 he was collated to a canonry in Lichfield Cathedral with the prebend of Stotfold, exchanging the latter for Tervin on 2 December 1547. He also became master of Yotton's chantry in that cathedral. On 12 May 1546 he was admitted rector of Barrow, Cheshire.

Under Edward VI, Siddall showed strongly protestant sympathies. On 30 April 1547 he was presented by the crown to the fifth prebend at Christ Church, Oxford, and in July he was licensed as a preacher. When Pietro Martire Vermigli (known as Peter Martyr) began to preach in Oxford in the spring of 1548, Siddall was prominent among his supporters. In January 1550 he was appointed to a commission to proceed against Anabaptists, then making headway in Essex and Kent. Recorded as vice-dean of Christ Church in 1552, in the same year he supplicated for the degree of DTh. Following the succession of Mary, however, Siddall was quick to conform to Catholicism, thereby retaining his benefices. Active in trying to persuade Thomas Cranmer to follow his example, he was one of the witnesses to the archbishop's fifth recantation, of 26 February 1556, and gave him assurance that his life would be spared. Yet after the accession of Elizabeth he was among the first to subscribe to the royal supremacy, the Book of Common Prayer, and the royal injunctions of June 1559. He may have become rector of Thames Ditton, Surrey, but clearly remained closely attached to Christ Church. In 1571 Siddall presented books by Erasmus to the college, and it was probably there that he died on 2 May 1572, being buried on the south side of the chancel of Oxford Cathedral. He had never married, and on 8 May letters of administration were granted to his sister Elizabeth Costerdyne. Siddall is recorded by his college as 'a man inconstant in religion but a loyal steward or treasurer of this church' (Emden, *Oxf.*, 4.551).

E. I. CARLYLE, *rev.* ANDREW A. CHIBI

Sources Emden, *Oxf.*, 4.551 · *Fasti Angl.* (Hardy) · administration, PRO, PROB 6/1, fol. 173*v* · D. MacCulloch, *Thomas Cranmer: a life*

(1996) · J. E. Oxley, *The Reformation in Essex to the death of Mary* (1965) · Wood, *Ath. Oxon.: Fasti* (1815), 100, 136 · J. Strype, *Memorials of the most reverend father in God Thomas Cranmer*, 2 vols. (1848) · J. Strype, *Ecclesiastical memorials*, 3 vols. (1822) · Foster, *Alum. Oxon., 1500–1714*, vol. 4 · *Fasti Angl., 1541–1857*, [Bristol] · *Hist. U. Oxf.* 3: *Colleg. univ.*

Siddeley, John Davenport, first Baron Kenilworth (1866–1953), manufacturer of motor vehicles and aero-engines, was born on 5 August 1866 at Cheadle Hulme, the eldest son of William Siddeley and Elizabeth, *née* Davenport. He was no academic, and left school to work in his father's business as an apprentice hosier. The meagre rewards led him to enrol in evening classes, where he developed his mechanical acumen to the extent that in 1885 he began designing bicycles. In 1893 he married Sarah Mabel Goodier of Macclesfield. They had three sons and two daughters.

Siddeley's design work took him to Beeston with the Humber cycle company, whence he became Dunlop's sales manager in Belfast, before returning to the midlands to run Dunlop's subsidiary, the Clipper Tyre Company. For publicity, Siddeley became the first person to ride a bicycle from John o' Groats to Land's End. He then became involved with motor cars, at first through pneumatic tyres, which led him to form the Siddeley Autocar Company in 1902, utilizing Peugeot designs under licence. His success persuaded Wolseley to hire him and there he honed his management skills before resigning as general manager in 1909. He became managing director of the struggling Deasy Motor Car Manufacturing Company in Coventry and so transformed its position that the marque was renamed Siddeley-Deasy.

The war was the making of the company, leading first to government orders for lorries and motor cars and then, most significantly, to aero-engine and airframe production. Siddeley persuaded the directors to sanction a move into the aviation field. Siddeley's engineers resolved the teething problems of the Beardmore-Halford-Pullinger aero-engine and it became the Siddeley Puma; it proved so reliable that it was the principal design in use by British bombers at the war's conclusion. The engineering staff was considerably strengthened when a number of distinguished personnel arrived from the Royal Aircraft Factory at Farnborough in 1917.

To support his ambitious post-war plans, Siddeley arranged a take-over by the armaments and shipbuilding giant Armstrong Whitworth, in April 1919, with Siddeley-Deasy becoming Armstrong Siddeley Motors. Later, in July 1920, Sir W. G. Armstrong, Whitworth Aircraft Ltd was formed. Both companies were under the umbrella of a holding company, the Armstrong Whitworth Development Company. During the 1920s Armstrong Siddeley compensated for depressed home sales through overseas demand, especially from the Australasian dominions. Siddeley was also always willing to explore new fields—Armstrong Siddeley even brought out an electric cinema projector with a patented device to eliminate flicker. Siddeley made successful strides into the armaments field, receiving a knighthood in 1932 for the tank engine supplied to Vickers.

John Davenport Siddeley, first Baron Kenilworth (1866–1953), by unknown photographer

The major success story of the decade was with the Jaguar air-cooled aero-engine, which was developed from a Farnborough design with Siddeley insistently prodding on the project. Its success was such that until the late 1920s Armstrong Siddeley was the major recipient of government orders for military aero-engines. Siddeley utilized this favourable position to full advantage by having airframes designed around the Jaguar. The Siskin 3A single-seater fighter aircraft was a notable outcome. The Jaguar was also a huge success abroad, with orders generated by record-breaking flights orchestrated by Siddeley. In civil aviation, the Armstrong Whitworth Argosy entered service with Imperial Airways in 1926 powered by three Jaguars.

The ailing fortunes of the parent company provided Siddeley with the opportunity to gain control of his companies. This was achieved with a loan of £1.5 million, most of which was arranged by Reginald McKenna, chairman of the Midland Bank. By February 1927 Siddeley was chairman of all three, with the holding company renamed the Armstrong Siddeley Development Company. In his final years, Siddeley expanded his business empire through a number of astute take-overs, which included the aeronautics firm A. V. Roe, the piston supplier Peter Hooker (which became High Duty Alloys), and Improved Gears Ltd (later Self-Changing Gears), whose gearbox was highly successful.

While Siddeley was enjoying his success with the Jaguar engine his rivals, especially Bristol and Rolls-Royce, were busy producing high-power designs which Armstrong Siddeley was unable to match in the 1930s. Siddeley has been accused of complacency, of not devoting sufficient funds to research and development, and of undue interference with engine design, which led two of his major designers to leave. The death of two other critical engine staff was also crucial in diminishing Armstrong Siddeley's design capabilities, while Siddeley's reputation as a domineering employer deterred others of similar calibre from filling the vacancies. A major blow was sustained in 1934 when the Air Ministry preferred the Bristol-powered Gloster Gauntlet to the Armstrong Whitworth Scimitar.

Fortunately for Armstrong Whitworth the Air Ministry, concerned at German re-armament, decided to place orders straight from the drawing board without awaiting the results of prototype trials, and asked the company to supply its Whitley bomber on this basis. It was not a happy choice; the aircraft was late going into production and Lord Weir, industrial adviser to the Air Ministry, wanted outside assistance brought in, but doubted if Siddeley would accept. Although the Whitley was eventually mass-produced, its shortcomings were soon exposed when war came.

By 1935 Siddeley was nearing seventy. He had accumulated a large personal fortune and had no need to continue working. He arranged a merger with Hawker, for which he received £1 million and numerous benefits, officially retiring from his executive positions on 30 September 1936. Siddeley became a tax exile in Jersey, while maintaining several British homes. In 1937 he purchased Kenilworth Castle (later giving it to the nation) and the same year was created Baron Kenilworth.

A rigid disciplinarian at home, as he was at work, Siddeley had a lighter side, indulging in painting and gardening. His gifts to charity were considerable, totalling over £300,000 in his last eighteen years. He died at the Bon Air Nursing Home, St Saviour, Jersey, on 3 November 1953, heartbroken by the death of his wife a fortnight earlier. His estate in England was valued at £354,597 (though his total wealth was probably much greater).

STEVEN MOREWOOD

Sources R. Higham and R. P. T. Davenport-Hines, 'Siddeley, John Davenport', *DBB* · N. Baldwin, 'Siddeley before Armstrong', *Classic and Sportscar* (1983) · M. Redman, *The evening and the morning* (1957) · O. Tapper, *Armstrong-Whitworth aircraft since 1913* (1973) · N. Baldwin, 'Siddeley after Armstrong', *Classic and Sportscar* (1983) · R. Schlaifer and S. D. Heron, *Development of aircraft engines* (1950) · F. R. Banks, *I kept no diary: 60 years with marine diesels, automobile and aero engines* (1978) · A. G. Wilson, *Walter Wilson: portrait of an inventor* (1986) · W. Boddy, 'Talking with Ernest Siddeley', in W. Boddy, *Motor sport* (1980) · K. Richardson, *Twentieth-century Coventry* (1972) · Lord Kenilworth file, *Coventry Evening Telegraph* library, Coventry, Warwickshire

Archives Anstey, near Coventry, Warwickshire, Rolls-Royce Heritage Trust collection · Coventry City RO, Armstrong-Siddeley Motors · Coventry City RO, Deasy Motor Car Manufacturing Co. · priv. coll., Ernest Siddeley MSS · Royal Air Force Museum, Hendon, Bulman MSS | SOUND Coventry University, Richardson Audio Archive

Likenesses group portrait, 1892, Coventry Local Studies Library · photograph, Quadrant Picture Library, London [*see illus.*]

Wealth at death £354,597: Lord Kenilworth file

Siddiqui, Kalim (1933–1996), journalist and Muslim activist, was born on 2 July 1933 near Hyderabad, Deccan, India, one of a family of ten children. While he was still a small child the family moved to Sultanpur, a town between Allahabad and Fyzabad in Uttar Pradesh, where his father worked as a policeman and where Siddiqui was educated. In 1950 he moved to Karachi, in West Pakistan, and four years later he moved to Britain, where he lived in and around London for the rest of his life. He married Suraiya Siddiqui in Lucknow, India, on 11 January 1960; they had two daughters and a son.

Kalim Siddiqui (1933–1996), by Michael Powell

Siddiqui's first interest was in journalism and it was to get training that he moved to London. After working on various local newspapers he held a job as sub-editor on *The Guardian* from 1964 until 1972. During this period he found time to study economics and political science, and gained an MSc and then a PhD degree from University College, London, in 1972. His PhD thesis was published the same year as *Conflict, Crisis and War in Pakistan*. By this time he had developed an increasingly active interest in Islamic issues.

In 1972 Siddiqui left *The Guardian* to found the Muslim Institute, whose director he remained until his death. The main activity of the institute was to sponsor conferences and publications. Its funding sources were never publicized, but observers often assumed that they were primarily in Saudi Arabia. Through the 1970s Islamic political movements were becoming increasingly active, and Siddiqui played a leading part in publicizing the so-called Islamic Movement, a loose alliance of like-minded groupings presenting themselves to the Western public, including the Muslim minorities, under this title. His ideas were put together in two pamphlets published in 1980: *Beyond the Muslim Nation-States* and *The Islamic Movement: a Systems Approach*. In response to the Islamic revolution in Iran in 1979–80 he allied the Muslim Institute publicly with the

revolution and its leader, Ayatollah Khomeini. Through the 1980s it was widely assumed that Iran had become the institute's main source of financial support, although Siddiqui also found considerable encouragement from leading Indian Muslim families in Durban and Transvaal, South Africa. During the period 1980–86 the institute published a series of annual volumes of lectures and papers by its director under the title *Issues in the Islamic Movement*.

In 1989 Siddiqui provoked media controversy by strongly supporting the campaign against Salman Rushdie's *The Satanic Verses*, which first caught wide public attention in January of that year, and then by identifying himself with Ayatollah Khomeini's *fatwa* and death sentence against Rushdie. It was a stand he continued to take repeatedly in public, even when it became an annoyance to the Iranian authorities as they were beginning to distance themselves from the *fatwa* in the mid-1990s. Both on this occasion and later, when he called for armed support for the Muslims in Bosnia against Serb and Croat attacks, the authorities wisely refrained from taking legal action against him.

Siddiqui again attracted headlines when on 14 July 1990 at a public meeting he presented the Muslim Institute's publication of *The Muslim Manifesto*. In the *Manifesto* he proposed the establishment of a Muslim 'parliament' to represent all trends among British Muslims, including a significant representation for young people and women. Its purpose would be to act as a representative body to work with the UK government and other institutions for both Muslim and common interests. In the document the 'parliament' was proposed as an equivalent to the synod of the Church of England or the Board of Deputies of British Jews. While the document itself was worded very carefully and in moderate tones, in his provocative public presentation of it Siddiqui showed his understanding of how to attract the anger of parts of the press and thus the favour of a new generation of young Muslims, frustrated at the discrimination which blocked their full access to employment.

The Muslim parliament, with its membership of 150 selected by Siddiqui and a small circle of associates, first met in 1991. Under his leadership it established a number of subject committees, while the parliament itself met usually twice a year in plenary. The great majority of existing Muslim organizations around the country remained sceptical and were never reconciled to the existence of the parliament. However, there is no doubt that it identified a number of practical issues which affected many Muslims directly. The unreliability of provision of correctly prepared (*halal*) food prompted the parliament to establish a *halal* food authority, but the costs involved prevented it from attracting sufficient support. It was also the Muslim parliament which first took the initiative to encourage the opening of 'tutorial colleges' for Muslim children who were not doing well in school, an idea which was subsequently widely copied by other groups in the form of homework clubs. On several occasions the parliament showed its independence by rejecting or amending proposals put to it by Siddiqui.

Siddiqui died of a heart attack on 18 April 1996 while on a visit to Pretoria, South Africa. He was buried in Slough cemetery, having lived in the town for many years. He was survived by his wife and three children. After his death the Muslim parliament was for a time rent by internal divisions but settled down to a much quieter and more routine existence.   JØRGEN S. NIELSEN

Sources The Independent (20 April 1996) · The Guardian (26 April 1996) · J. S. Nielsen, 'A Muslim agenda for Britain: some reflections', New Community, 17 (1990–91), 467–76 · CGPLA Eng. & Wales (1996) · private information (2004) [family] · U. Lond., Senate House
Likenesses M. Powell, photograph, News International Syndication, London [see illus.] · photograph, repro. in The Guardian
Wealth at death under £180,000: administration, 11 Sept 1996, CGPLA Eng. & Wales

Siddons, Harriet (1783–1844). *See under* Siddons, Henry (1774–1815).

Siddons, Henry (1774–1815), actor and playwright, born in Wolverhampton on 23 October 1774, was the eldest child of the actor William Siddons (d. 11 March 1808) and the renowned actress Sarah *Siddons (1755–1831). His first appearance on stage was in 1783, when his mother brought him to London to play Child to her Isabella in David Garrick's *Isabella, or, The Fatal Marriage* at Drury Lane. He was sent first to Dr Barrow's academy in Soho Square and then for five years to Charterhouse, where he acquired a thorough knowledge of the classics. At the age of fifteen he wrote an interlude called *Modern Breakfast, or, All Asleep at Noon*, which was acted for the benefit of his aunt Elizabeth Kemble at the Haymarket in 1790.

After leaving school Siddons went with his father to France, and on his return joined the company of his uncle Stephen Kemble in Sheffield, appearing as Zanga in Edward Young's *The Revenge* in November 1792. He then performed at Lancaster, Liverpool, Bath, and other provincial theatres and also began to write more dramatic pieces of his own; among those produced were *Sicilian Romance, or, Apparition of the Cliffs* (1794), *Adventures of Tom Trip*, *What we have been and what we may be* (1796), and *Zelida, or, The Pirates* (1799). Siddons accompanied Kemble to Newcastle and Edinburgh, and showed such talent in playing the parts of the Stranger in *Douglas* and Rolla in *Pizarro* that his mother, who had originally intended him for the church, withdrew her earlier objections to his becoming an actor, and was induced to recommend him to Harris, the proprietor of the Covent Garden Theatre in London. She even acted Lady Randolph to his Douglas in Hannah More's *Percy* in May 1802, on the occasion of his benefit.

Siddons was engaged by Harris for three years, and in October 1801 made his first appearance at Covent Garden, as Herman in a play called *Integrity*. His future wife, the actress Harriet Murray [see below], daughter of the actor Charles *Murray, played in the same piece. They were married on 22 June 1802. There were children of the marriage. Siddons remained a member of Covent Garden until the spring of 1805. In September 1805 he made his first appearance at Drury Lane, playing the Prince of Wales to Elliston's Hotspur in *Henry IV*. Next he appeared

Henry Siddons (1774–1815), by Samuel John Stump, 1808

as Romeo and Sir G. Touchwood in *The Belle's Stratagem*. During his stay at Drury Lane he played a variety of leading roles, including Banquo in *Macbeth*, Jaffier in *Venice Preserv'd*, and Claudio in *Much Ado about Nothing*. He terminated his connection with the London stage at the close of the season of 1808–9.

Largely through Sir Walter Scott's influence, Siddons secured the patent of the Edinburgh Theatre Royal. The theatre was then over forty years old and a change of management was definitely required; Henry Siddons, his wife, and his wife's brother William Henry *Murray were thought to be ideal for the job. Siddons left the old building, transferred the royal sanction to the Circus in Leith Walk, and opened the New Theatre Royal, Leith Walk, in November 1809 with John Tobin's *The Honeymoon*, in which he played the Duke and his wife played Juliana. This opening was eminently successful. To maintain the popularity and high standard of the theatre, the Siddonses engaged Sarah Siddons and Stephen Kemble for a season. Siddons and his wife regularly appeared together, as the Count de Valmont and the Unknown Female in *The Foundling of the Forest*, as Leonatus and Paulina in *The Winter's Tale*, and so on. When, around September 1814, Drury Lane asked Harriet Siddons to play Juliet to Edmund Kean's Romeo, she declined without hesitation, preferring to remain with her husband. By then Siddons was fighting a losing battle, however. His play *Friend of the Family* was reproduced in December 1814 under the new name of *Policy, or, Thus Runs the World Away*, but played only twice. In February 1815 *The Comedy of Errors* was performed in Edinburgh for the first time in thirty years, with Murray and Samuel Russell as the two Dromios, but it could not turn the fortunes of the theatre. On 1 March 1815 Siddons appeared on stage for the last time, as Captain Downright in *The Wild Indian Girl* for his wife's benefit. On 12 April 1815 he died in Edinburgh, leaving his wife and the theatre in severe financial difficulties.

Siddons made a great effort to be an efficient and innovative manager and bring success to the theatre, but as an actor he was at the disadvantage of having to suffer constant comparison with his more talented relatives the Kembles, and as a result never received the acclaim that he perhaps deserved. His plays *Time's a Tell-Tale*, *The Russian Imposter*, and *Tale of Terror, or, Castle Without a Spectre*, produced at Covent Garden for Murray's benefit in 1803, as well as his other pieces, were not very successful either. He adapted from a work by Engel *Illustrations of Gesture and Action* (1807), and published three novels, *William Wallace*, *Leon, a Spartan Story*, and *Somerset*.

Siddons's wife, **Harriet Siddons** (1783–1844), actress, appeared as a child at Bath as Prince Arthur in *King John* for her father's benefit on 1 July 1793. Her London début was at Covent Garden, as Perdita in *The Winter's Tale* (May 1798). She remained at that theatre until the summer of 1805, playing with success a large range of parts, from the Shakespearian heroines Rosalind, Viola, Desdemona, Portia, and Beatrice, to Lucy Ashton in Calcraft's Waverley drama *The Bride of Lammermoor*, Lady Teazle in Sheridan's *The School for Scandal*, and Miss Hardcastle in Goldsmith's *She Stoops to Conquer*.

In 1805 Harriet joined the Drury Lane company together with her husband and had an immediate success playing Juliet to Elliston's Romeo. Her first appearance in Edinburgh was in 1808, at the Theatre Royal, where she played Belvidera in *Venice Preserv'd* to the Jaffier of her husband and Ophelia to his Hamlet. She shared managerial duties with her husband from 1809 to 1815; even after his death, when the affairs of the theatre were in a bad state, she was determined to survive with her brother's help in management.

In January 1816 Mrs Siddons made her first appearance since her husband's death, playing Viola in *Twelfth Night*. Murray played Sebastian, and the strong resemblance between brother and sister contributed to the success of the performance. They acted together again in *The Belle's Stratagem* in 1819, Harriet playing Letitia Hardy and Murray playing Flutter. Their wisest decision was to stage the various adaptations of Sir Walter Scott's novels, whose success really helped to raise the fortunes of the house. Daniel Terry's adaptation of *Guy Mannering* was the first of the Waverley dramas performed at the Theatre Royal, in 1817, with Harriet as Meg Merrilees. She also played Jeanie Deans in *The Heart of Midlothian* (1820), Amy in Tom Dibdin's version of *Kenilworth, or, The Merry Days of Old England* (1822), and Diana Vernon in *Rob Roy*, which was produced on the occasion of the visit to Edinburgh by George IV in 1822. In May 1825 the production of a series of Waverley dramas commenced with *The Rose of Ettrick Vale*, Harriet Siddons playing the title role. Murray also took part in all these plays. Harriet took her farewell benefit on 29 March 1829, as Lady Townly in Vanbrugh's *The Provoked Husband*. The address she delivered on this occasion was written by

her great patron, Sir Walter Scott. This was not her last appearance, however, as during her brother's illness she helped out in a number of casts. She died in Edinburgh on 2 November 1844.

J. C. DIBDIN, *rev.* NILANJANA BANERJI

Sources J. C. Dibdin, *The annals of the Edinburgh stage* (1888) · *The thespian dictionary, or, Dramatic biography of the present age*, 2nd edn (1805) · T. Gilliland, *The dramatic mirror, containing the history of the stage from the earliest period, to the present time*, 2 vols. (1808) · D. E. Baker, *Biographia dramatica, or, A companion to the playhouse*, rev. I. Reed, new edn, rev. S. Jones, 3 vols. in 4 (1812) · Hall, *Dramatic ports*.

Archives NL Scot., letters

Likenesses S. J. Stump, miniature, 1808, NPG [*see illus.*] · W. Hamilton, oils, Scot. NPG · W. Ridley, stipple (after H. Edridge), BM; repro. in *Monthly Mirror* (1802) · miniature, wash, Garr. Club · portrait (Harriet Siddons), repro. in *Monthly Mirror* (1802)

Siddons [*née* Kemble], **Sarah** (1755–1831), actress, was born on 5 July 1755 at the Shoulder of Mutton inn in Brecon, the first of the twelve children of Roger *Kemble (1722–1802), an actor and theatre manager, and his wife, Sarah Ward (1735–1807), the daughter of John and Sarah Ward. Like her sisters, she was baptized into her mother's religion as a protestant (her brothers were baptized, after their father, as Catholics), at St Mary's Church, Brecon, on 14 July 1755. Seven of her siblings (four sisters and three brothers), including Charles *Kemble, Ann Julia *Hatton, and Stephen George *Kemble, also entered the acting profession, and her brother John Philip *Kemble became the most important actor and manager of his time; Siddons was to establish herself as the most acclaimed tragic actress of her own age, and she has subsequently been widely regarded as the greatest female performer in English theatrical history. In her own lifetime she achieved the status of a popular icon, playing a key role in the social legitimation of the acting profession, moving from the reputedly disreputable world of provincial touring theatre to the salons of the aristocracy, and amassing substantial personal wealth. Her public success, however, was attended by a great deal of personal sadness: her marriage to the philandering and feckless William Siddons, although nominally enduring, was an unhappy one and ended in informal separation, and she outlived five of her seven children.

Early life and career Although Sarah Kemble's life was spent in the theatre from the very beginning, she entered the profession itself in the face of some parental opposition. To a certain extent this repeated the pattern seen in her own parents' careers, in that her maternal grandfather, John Ward, had initially opposed his daughter's choice of Roger Kemble as a husband. With the Kembles on the road for most of the year, Sarah received her formal education at a succession of day schools in the midlands and the north of England and was trained in elocution and singing by her mother. By the age of twelve she had managed to cultivate such a sufficiently convincing demeanour of gentility that she was invited to attend, free of charge, Mrs Harris's School for Young Ladies at Thornloe House in Worcester. Treated with condescension by her more well-heeled fellow pupils, she discovered that she was here that Siddons's talents first came to the notice of certain well-connected and influential individuals who were to prove instrumental in the advancement of her career. Her portrayal of Belvidera in Thomas Otway's *Venice Preserv'd* (which was to prove one of her most popular roles) attracted the attention of Thomas Brudenell-Bruce, second Baron Bruce of Tottenham, and his much sought-after stepdaughter Henrietta Boyle; Henrietta, who became a lifelong friend, was sufficiently impressed by Siddons to offer to supervise and supplement her wardrobe with her own clothes. Lord Bruce, in addition, recommended Siddons to David Garrick on his return to London.

During the Cheltenham season Siddons was pregnant, and she gave birth to her first son, Henry, in Wolverhampton on 4 October 1774. Garrick, meanwhile, responded to the recommendation he had received by sending one of the leading members of his company, Tom King, to observe Siddons in Cheltenham. Although King reported very favourably back to Garrick, it was not until 1775, when the actor–manager received word from a friend, the Revd Henry Bate, confirming King's account, that he arranged to engage Siddons with his Drury Lane company. By this time Siddons was heavily pregnant with her second child (this did not prevent her from playing Rosalind in *As You Like It*); according to Bate, her face was 'one of the most beautiful that ever I beheld', although he added that her voice struck him as 'at first rather dissonant' and 'somewhat grating', and he speculated that 'her figure must be remarkably fine, when she is delivered of her big belly, which entirely mars for the present her whole shape' (Manvell, 23). An exchange of letters between Bate, Garrick, and William Siddons followed, as they negotiated over the date for Sarah to join the Drury Lane company following the anticipated birth. The issue was resolved when Siddons went into labour during a performance in Gloucester on 4 November; the next day her first daughter, Sarah Martha, was born. Urged by Garrick to make the journey to London at the earliest opportunity, Siddons and her family moved to the capital in the middle of December.

Sarah made her first foray onto the London stage on 29 December 1775, as Portia in *The Merchant of Venice*. This début, which was billed as that of 'a Young Lady (being her first appearance)', was a disaster. Siddons misjudged the scale of the Drury Lane Theatre, which was considerably larger than those in which she was accustomed to performing; she was badly costumed, and, intimidated by the London society audience, she moved awkwardly and hesitantly and lost her voice. It is fair to assume that the effect of an extremely recent birth, the demands of caring for two very young children, the fact that her family was existing on very limited means, and the hostility and suspicion with which she was regarded by the other actresses in Garrick's company also contributed to her failure of nerve. The judgement of the press was almost unanimously negative; most damningly, the *Morning Chronicle* of 30 December recorded that she had 'vulgarity in her tones'. For six months she struggled miserably through a

Sarah Siddons (1755–1831), by Sir Joshua Reynolds, 1783–4 [*Mrs Siddons as the Tragic Muse*]

could find favour by shining in school theatricals. During this period she began to appear with Kemble's company in a variety of parts (her first recorded role being Ariel in *The Tempest* in Coventry at the end of 1766). Also in the company at this time was the actor William Siddons (1744–1808), whom she was later to marry. About 1770, at the age of fourteen or fifteen, Sarah began a romance with William; when her parents, sceptical about William's prospects, opposed it, it merely served to strengthen the relationship. The Kembles had also encouraged the advances of a local Brecon squire, Mr Evans, who was infatuated with Sarah; when William discovered this he accused Roger Kemble of treachery and was as a consequence dismissed from the company. Sarah, however, refused to marry Evans, and in 1770 was sent into service with the Greatheeds of Guy's Cliffe, Warwick, where she remained for two years, first as a maid and then as Lady Mary Greatheed's companion. She continued to correspond with William throughout; in the end the Kembles withdrew their opposition to the match, and on 26 November 1773 William and Sarah were married at Holy Trinity Church, Coventry. The couple rejoined Kemble's company for a year, then left in 1774 to join Chamberlain and Crump's company and set up for the summer in Cheltenham, which was becoming an increasingly fashionable spa town. It succession of parts in comedies for which she was clearly ill-suited (the *Morning Chronicle* concluded that 'she had no comedy in her nature'), while also being (as she later interpreted it) exploited by Garrick as part of his manoeuvring against two of his leading actresses, Mrs Yates and Miss Younge. Siddons left London for the 1776 summer season in Birmingham, hopeful of securing further employment at Drury Lane in the winter. While at Birmingham she was informed by Garrick's prompter that she was not to be re-engaged.

Town and country, 1776–1782 Mortified by her experience at Drury Lane, and in poor health, Siddons resolved to carry on, for the sake, as she repeatedly put it, of her 'poor babies' (Manvell, 38). She spent the next six years in a wide variety of theatres outside London; in 1776–7 this included spells in Liverpool and Manchester and with Tate Wilkinson's company at York. Before long she began to rebuild her confidence and her battered reputation, achieving growing recognition and acclaim as it became increasingly evident that her most powerful talents were for tragedy rather than comedy. Wilkinson, who was working hard to improve the conditions of the acting profession outside London by attempting to extricate it from its disreputable, provincial associations, and who was one of Sarah's most generous supporters, recorded that there was never 'so great a favourite, as a York actress, as Mrs Siddons was in that short period' (Wilkinson, 255). In 1777 her brother John Philip Kemble joined her in Joseph Younger's company in Liverpool, and in January 1778 Siddons played Desdemona opposite Kemble's Othello. This was followed, in March, by a piece of casting which gives a good indication of where her reputation stood in relation to his, by her playing Hamlet to his Laertes.

For the autumn season of 1778 Siddons was engaged by John Palmer the younger at his Theatre Royal in Bath, the city which was now the centre of fashionable society outside London. It was here that she established herself as the most popular, acclaimed, and sought-after actress of her time. In her first season, aged twenty-four and pregnant with her second daughter, Maria (*b.* 1 July 1779), Siddons worked tirelessly, rehearsing and performing nearly thirty roles while also travelling between theatres in Bath and Bristol. In the following season, beginning in September 1779, she took on the roles for which she would become legendary, including Constance in *King John*, Queen Katherine in *Henry VIII*, and Lady Macbeth, and she became an increasing object of interest to fashionable society, being befriended by socialites such as Sophia Weston, Mrs Hester Thrale (Mrs Piozzi), Fanny Burney, and Georgiana, duchess of Devonshire. It was in Bath that she first encountered the child prodigy and painter Thomas Lawrence. Socially and professionally successful, Siddons had every intention of remaining in Bath, but by the end of the 1770s the fear of financial insecurity which she never managed to overcome made it inevitable that she would move to London, where her earnings could be vastly increased. From 1780 onwards, Richard Brinsley Sheridan, who had taken over the management of the Drury Lane Theatre, made repeated attempts to persuade her to return to the London stage, and in 1782 she finally acquiesced. On 21 May she played her last benefit in Bath, and, in a *coup de théâtre* which a number of her fellow performers thought in rather dubious taste, revealed her 'THREE REASONS' for her departure by bringing her children onto the stage. It was not the last time that Siddons's professional and maternal identities would be so publicly linked. She was, moreover, pregnant with her fifth child, Eliza Ann, who was born on 2 June (her fourth, Frances Emilia, who was baptized on 6 April 1781, had died as an infant). Siddons gave final appearances in Bath, Bristol, and Cheltenham and, at the end of September 1782, moved to London.

Triumph and tragedy, 1782–1800 There could hardly have been a greater contrast between Siddons's ignominious departure from Drury Lane in 1776 and her triumphant return there six years later. Sick with apprehension, she made her first appearance on 10 October 1782 in the title role in Garrick's version of Thomas Southerne's *Isabella, or, The Fatal Marriage*. It was an immediate success. Reports rapidly began to circulate of the majestic scale and intensity of her acting, and of the scenes of near-hysteria that it tended to provoke. In his *Memoirs of Mrs Siddons* James Boaden records 'sobs and shrieks among the tenderer part of her audiences', and

> those tears, which manhood at first struggled to suppress, but at length grew proud of indulging ... the nerves of many a gentle being gave way before the intensity of such appeals, and fainting fits long and frequently alarmed the decorum of the house, filled almost to suffocation. (Boaden, 195)

A contemporary commentator tells of how Siddons's Jane Shore made 'two ladies among the spectators fall into hysterics, and one of them had to be carried out, laughing convulsively' (Booth, 19). That such breaches of decorum took place so repeatedly and in so spectacular a fashion may testify to Siddons's power and charisma as a performer, but they also suggest a deeper catharsis, in that the specific kinds of tragic suffering that she conveyed (more often than not, blameless women victimized, exploited, and destroyed by men) had particularly painful resonances for her audiences (and, perhaps, for Siddons herself) in the context of a society wherein the majority of women 'lived in a world of men who defined and circumscribed them, and denied them ... the most basic of civil rights' (ibid., 31). Such emotional reactions were unprecedented, as was the hyperbolic vocabulary of grandeur, majesty, and awesomeness which contemporary commentators on Siddons employed to describe her stage presence, technique, and acting style. Siddons's characteristic performance style is best thought of in terms of the transition from neo-classicism to romanticism—the first aspect becoming visible in a classically inspired, literally statuesque composition of posture, gesture, and costume which rendered her characters as legendary, iconic figures, the second element being found in the focused emotional intensity of her delivery. As audience reactions indicate, it was a mesmerizing combination that seemed to transform the actress into a force both of and beyond nature, and which readily lent itself to romantic notions of the sublime.

Still in her late twenties, Siddons became a cult figure, an object of veneration, even near-worship, and was greatly in demand in fashionable society. She received her first invitation to read before the king and queen early in 1783; at the queen's command, she was appointed reader to the royal princesses. Her earnings rapidly multiplied. In common with all married women of the time, however, she had no control over her income, which legally belonged to and was managed by her husband. This would eventually exacerbate the Siddonses' marital difficulties, as William proved to be quite inept in his handling of the finances. In June 1783 Sarah travelled to Dublin to play Isabella at the Smock Alley Theatre, and in October returned to Drury Lane. The following summer, at the end of the Drury Lane season, she initiated a pattern of work that she maintained for the next decade, by embarking upon a punishing schedule of touring in the north of England and Scotland. Despite the fact that she was now earning quite considerable sums of money, Siddons continued to work compulsively (and to the detriment of her health). This did not always reflect entirely favourably upon her, particularly on the occasions when she became entangled in the inevitable jealousies and ill feeling generated by the benefit system (whereby individual actors could collect the proceeds of a night's performance or offer them for charitable purposes), and she acquired a reputation for meanness and ruthless self-interest. In one particularly damaging instance it was rumoured that, during her 1784 visit to Dublin, she had refused to offer a benefit for the actor West Digges, who had been paralysed some months before (although she eventually did so, rather reluctantly, on 23 August). In October of the same year the story went round that she had similarly refused to offer a benefit for the actor William Brereton (who was in reality fairly well-off and hardly in need of charitable support), which resulted in her being hissed offstage by a hostile Drury Lane audience, although she eventually succeeded in placating her critics. Such gossip was connected to other rivalries: between Brereton and John Philip Kemble, and between Siddons and the actress Anne Crawford, who was in her late forties during the period of Siddons's ascendancy, and whose position as London's pre-eminent tragic actress was rapidly being eclipsed by the rival who was twenty years her junior. Crawford had performed in Dublin during Siddons's first visit there, and in November 1783 she tried to challenge Siddons directly by playing Lady Randolph in John Home's *Douglas* (a part closely associated with Siddons) at Covent Garden; sadly for Crawford, the comparisons that were drawn between the two actresses were unanimously to her detriment.

On 30 September 1783 John Philip Kemble made his own London début, as Hamlet, and made almost as much of an impression as Siddons had the previous year. Brother and sister first appeared together at Drury Lane in Edward Moore's *The Gamester* on 22 November, and they followed this with *King John* on 10 December, in which Kemble played the King and Siddons Constance. Although Constance appears in only three scenes, this was one of her most impressive portrayals (it was assisted by some deft reordering of the text so that Constance became the play's dominant force), and it entailed an identification with the role that was far in advance of its time. As she later recalled, Sarah would leave her dressing-room door open between her scenes; thus, overhearing events on stage, she could work herself into an appropriate frenzy, as they would cause 'bitter tears of rage, disappointment, betrayed confidence, baffled ambition, and, above all, the agonizing feelings of maternal affection to gush into my eyes'. Consciously or not, her account of Constance's 'maternal tenderness desperate and ferocious as a hunted tigress in defence of her young' (Campbell, 1.215) recalls the ever-present rationale for her own reputed ruthlessness. Constance was one of a succession of portrayals of Shakespearian tragic heroines in which Siddons stressed elements of thwarted, distorted, or betrayed conjugal or maternal love, and which included Lady Macbeth, which she first played in London in February 1785 (and which, as her most significant role, is discussed in more detail below), Volumnia in *Coriolanus* in 1787, Katherine in *Henry VIII* in 1788, and, in 1801, her final new role, Hermione in *The Winter's Tale*.

By the mid-1780s Siddons was established as a cultural icon. If her charismatic presence in the theatre produced delirious results, the circulation of her image throughout middle-class English culture in the late eighteenth century in a variety of narrative and visual forms both underpinned and further contributed to her mythical and monumental status. The already considerable impact of her performances was magnified beyond their immediate moment as she, and they, became the subject of discourse and debate within the rapidly expanding and proliferating genres of theatre journalism and commentary, which were in turn addressing themselves to a growing, increasingly critical readership; as it did in person, the figure of Siddons in print provided a focus for the emotional exploration and moral evaluation of a range of contemporary preoccupations and anxieties, particularly in the area of female sexuality. Siddons was also the subject of a wide range of visual representations, as she was commemorated in paintings, sketches, prints, and caricatures in the roles for which she became famous. During the 1783–4 season she sat for Sir Joshua Reynolds as *The Tragic Muse*, which soon became one of the most well-known images of the actress. Seated on a throne, flanked by allegorical personifications of Pity and Terror, Siddons is simultaneously tragedy's source of inspiration and its monumental embodiment. By the mid-1780s Siddons was settling into her niche in London society, mixing with the nobility, writers, and politicians; her acquaintances included Dr Johnson, Edmund Burke, and William Windham. For the next fifteen years she maintained the pattern of alternating between Drury Lane in the winter months and regional tours in the summer.

Although this period of her life saw her at the height of her popularity and critical acclaim, it was also one in which Siddons experienced professional and personal difficulties. On the former count, the continuing saga of her reputed meanness was further complicated by the difficulties that arose from Richard Brinsley Sheridan's haphazard and less than scrupulous management of Drury Lane, which led to her breaking with the theatre for the 1789–90 season. In April 1788 she suffered a miscarriage; two weeks later her youngest daughter, Elizabeth Ann, died, aged six. The 1790s also saw a marked deterioration in her relationship with her husband. Although he had shown early signs of promise, William Siddons's own career as an actor had long since petered out in the shadow of his wife's, and his main role had been to manage the money that she earned but which he legally owned. Rumours of his infidelities began to emerge, which eventually proved to be of substance when (according to her close confidante, Mrs Piozzi) Sarah discovered in August 1792 that the ill health that had afflicted her for a decade was the result of venereal infection from her husband. According to Mrs Piozzi, the façade of loyalty and marital harmony that Siddons continued to maintain masked deep resentment and 'indignant melancholy' (Manvell, 184). Her seventh child, Cecilia, was born on 25 July 1794; she was back acting at the Haymarket a month later. During this period the Drury Lane Theatre was rebuilt on a far larger scale than before, and this was to confront Siddons with the problem that had caused her so much anxiety at her London début. Having thrived upon the relative intimacy of the old theatre, she was now faced with the need to adjust the scale of her performances to the altered size and configuration of the new auditorium. When Drury Lane reopened on 12 March 1794, with Siddons and John Kemble in a lavish new production of *Macbeth*, it quickly became evident that the enlargement of stage and auditorium, and the increased sophistication of the stage machinery, had shifted the emphasis towards elaborate spectacle. Although Siddons was initially enthusiastic about the theatre, it would prove to render her own mode of acting obsolete. Throughout the 1790s financial pressures drove her through a succession of parts in plays of inferior quality; the greatest indignity was her performance as Elgiva in Fanny Burney's disastrous tragedy *Edway and Elgiva* in March 1795. Even 'the solemn accents of Siddons herself' failed to rescue its 'ludicrous circumstance' (Campbell, 2.192); mortifyingly, Siddons's death scene was played to ribald laughter. Siddons continued to act at Drury Lane until the turn of the century, by which time Sheridan owed her more than £2000 in unpaid salary, while William Siddons negotiated to no effect on her behalf.

The final decade of the eighteenth century brought the Siddons family heartache in the form of its entanglements with the portrait painter Thomas Lawrence, whom Siddons had encountered in Bath a decade earlier. From the moment of his arrival in London in 1787 at the age of eighteen, Lawrence was a celebrity: precociously talented, impulsive, narcissistic, charming, and extravagantly irresponsible in his financial and emotional affairs, he was both a charismatic figure and a dangerous one. In 1796 he began an affair with Siddons's daughter Sally, then twenty-one, which led to a marriage proposal the following year. Sarah and William Siddons refused to consent to the match. Siddons's doubts were complicated by her own attachment to Lawrence and the fact that her relationship with William Siddons was becoming increasingly distant. When the relationship between Lawrence and Sally cooled, the latter's eighteen-year-old younger sister Maria stepped in, arranging clandestine meetings with the painter which culminated (again, in the face of stiff parental opposition) in a formal engagement early in 1798. At this point, however, Maria's health began to deteriorate, prompting Lawrence to attempt to renew his attentions to Sally. As Maria's state steadily worsened, Lawrence became increasingly desperate and obsessive in his efforts to gain access to Sally; Sarah Siddons, meanwhile, was torn not only by work commitments, which were enforcing separation from a daughter who was terminally ill with consumption, but also by the conflict between her desire to protect Sally and Maria from Lawrence and her own feelings of sympathy and affection for him. Maria died on 7 October 1798, but not before she had extracted on her deathbed a solemn promise from her sister not to undertake any further liaison with Lawrence. Siddons's opposition to the relationship, which had taken its toll on her own health, confirmed the pact; none the less, she continued to maintain a friendship with Lawrence for the next thirty years until his death. Sally Siddons was rather less fortunate; she died five years after her sister.

Lady Macbeth Although Siddons owed her popular success to her command of a wide range of tragic roles, many of them in plays by her contemporaries which have since vanished from the repertory, her most celebrated part, and the one with which she continues to be associated, is that of Lady Macbeth. Not only her contemporaries but many later commentators have considered her portrayal to be definitive; in 1812 Charles Lamb, who tended to doubt that Shakespeare's tragedies could or should be staged at all, wrote that 'we speak of Lady Macbeth, while we are in reality thinking of Mrs S'. The association was to become firmly fixed in the English cultural imagination by the numerous paintings, sketches, and engravings of her in the role. Siddons first tackled the part in her early twenties during her time in Cheltenham, and she continued to play it throughout her career, up to and after her retirement in 1812. Her prolonged immersion in the part took place in the context of the intense and sustained interest in *Macbeth* within late eighteenth-century English literary and theatrical culture—an interest that was substantially motivated by the play's perceived relevance to events of the French Revolution. As a study in regicide, *Macbeth* afforded English theatre audiences a glimpse of something both fascinating and unspeakable; in the figure of Lady Macbeth, Siddons and her spellbound spectators found a focus for their own darkest fears. Siddons's accounts of her approach to the role are revealing, in that they indicate that her attempts to find her way into the character through imaginative identification and empathy did not just constitute a new and innovative acting method, but also took her into potentially dangerous psychological territory. As she later recalled, she was in the habit of learning her parts at night when she first took on the role, and had planned to rote-learn the part on the eve of the first performance, naively believing that 'little more was necessary than to get the words into my head'. However, as she went on 'in the silence of the night' to the assassination scene:

> the horrors of the scene rose to a degree that made it impossible for me to get further. I snatched up my candle, and hurried out of the room in a paroxysm of terror. My dress was of silk, and the rustling of it, as I ascended the stairs to go to bed, seemed to my panic-struck fancy like the movement of a spectre pursuing me. (Fitzgerald, 1.32–3)

Siddons's record of her appalled reaction to Shakespeare's text, which seems designed to establish her moral distance from her character, actually leads her into an uncanny, and troubling, identification with it, as she echoes Lady Macbeth's ascent to the bedchamber (where, ironically enough, she finds her 'husband fast asleep'). As Siddons depicts herself climbing guiltily towards a bedchamber containing not a soon-to-be-murdered king but the husband who, by the time she narrated this incident, had given her more than enough cause for resentment, the distinctions between the evil character and the good mother, wife, and actress seem less clear-cut than propriety might demand. For Siddons, the moral of this story was that she was sufficiently shamed by the result of (as she saw it) her own immaturity, idleness, and complacency that it 'cured me of procrastinating my business for the remainder of my life'; but it also indicates that the embryonic psychological approach to character could also subtly destabilize the conventional moral categories within which a figure such as Lady Macbeth had previously been assigned.

Siddons's task with Lady Macbeth, as she saw it, was that of finding points of sympathy rather than presenting her (as had previous actresses) as a 'fiend-like Queen' who was, in Dr Johnson's words, 'merely detested'. As Siddons put it in an essay written some time around 1816, Lady Macbeth's propensity for evil had to be seen neither as innate and immutable nor as her sole defining characteristic; she should be regarded rather as a woman riven with conflicts between her feminine nature and ruthless ambition. Adopting what was at the time the new approach of conceiving the role as an organic whole rather than as a series of spectacular but isolated moments, she suggested that Lady Macbeth should be 'most captivating to the other sex,—fair, feminine, nay, perhaps, even fragile' and 'captivating in female loveliness' (Campbell, 2.11); for only this could explain her hold over her husband. Thus Macbeth was driven towards regicide by the goadings of his wife, who, once the murder had been committed, collapsed with remorse as her essential femininity reasserted itself. This was an innovative reading of the part, not just because it contained the suggestion that the Macbeths' criminal acts were the perverse consequence of a profound marital love and loyalty, but also because it

secretly questioned the moral priorities associated with the play. If the wickedness of Macbeth and Lady Macbeth was a matter not of nature but of the circumstances within which they found themselves, might this not put the murder of the king (which had such powerful resonances for late eighteenth-century English audiences) in a different light?

In fact, the effect of Siddons as Lady Macbeth in performance was at first less ambivalent than her considered and sympathetic account of the character suggests. She first played the part in London, on 2 February 1785, opposite William Smith, who was generally agreed to be a weak foil to her; however, when John Kemble took over the part of Macbeth in March, their partnership became legendary. Where Kemble presented Macbeth as an introspective and naturally virtuous man, wracked with guilty imaginings the deeper he progressed in crime, Siddons was mesmerizingly powerful, a terrifying rather than a delicate and pathetic figure. Her most unforgettable moment was the sleepwalking scene, in which Siddons caused some consternation by breaking with the established stage tradition of carrying a candle throughout, choosing instead to set it down to concentrate on the washing of her hands. If this was perceived as faintly disrespectful to her predecessors in the part (notably Hannah Pritchard, who had played opposite Garrick, and whose interpretation had until then been regarded as definitive), Siddons silenced criticism by stamping her unquestionable authority on the role. Although she envisaged Lady Macbeth as a woman deserving of understanding and sympathy, she was apprehended as a vast, malign force beyond nature. William Hazlitt wrote:

> we can conceive of nothing grander … it seemed almost as if a being of a superior order had dropped from a higher sphere to awe the world with the majesty of her appearance. Power was seated on her brow, passion emanated from her breast as from a shrine; she was tragedy personified … she glided on and off the stage like an apparition. To have seen her in that character was an event in every one's life, not to be forgotten. (Hazlitt, *Characters of Shakespeare's Plays*)

History was to prove Hazlitt right: Siddons's Lady Macbeth continues to be regarded as the one against which all later interpretations have been judged.

Final years, 1800–1831 The turn of the nineteenth century marks the beginning of the final phase of Siddons's stage career. In March 1802 she studied her last new role, that of another wronged wife and mother, Hermione in *The Winter's Tale*. Although she was still much acclaimed, it was becoming evident that she was no longer at her best: she was beginning to tire more rapidly, and ticket sales, particularly for her London performances, began to decline. In the summer months she continued her heavy provincial touring schedule. From 1801 onwards she suffered from erysipelas, as well as from rheumatoid arthritis; she was also prone to bouts of depression and sickness. At the end of the 1801–2 season she and John Kemble resigned from Drury Lane; he bought into the Covent Garden Theatre while she went to Ireland with Tate Wilkinson's daughter Martha (known as Patty), who had become her constant companion and would remain so until Siddons's death. Although she continued to impress critics and audiences, it was reported that she was visibly putting on weight and that her voice was sounding strained. None the less, she managed to draw large crowds in Dublin for an interesting experiment in cross-dressing, her portrayal of Hamlet on 27 July 1802. Siddons's swordplay in the final scene attracted praise: she had been tutored by a fencing instructor, Mr P. Galindo, who also played Laertes. Siddons's close friendship with Galindo and his wife, Catherine, an actress who had played alongside Siddons in Ambrose Philips's *The Distrest Mother*, was another unfortunate liaison, which in 1809 led to Mrs Galindo publishing accusations of an illicit affair between the actress and her husband, and of her subsequent betrayal of her family. Siddons had been introduced to the Galindos by Patty Wilkinson; according to Catherine, Galindo had fallen in love with her, abandoned his wife, and spent much of his time driving her about in his carriage.

Whether or not there was a covert relationship between Siddons and Galindo, she was made godmother to the Galindos' daughter in July 1803. In March 1803 Siddons learned that her father, Roger Kemble, had died the previous December. On her return to England in April she stopped in Shrewsbury, where she received a letter from her husband written an hour before the death of her daughter Sally. This was followed by confirmation that Sally had died on 24 March. In London she made overtures to Thomas Harris, the manager of Covent Garden, to employ Galindo. When John Kemble, who had been abroad, got to hear of the plan he was outraged, and ordered Harris to retract the offer. The Galindos followed Siddons to London (where, Mrs Galindo alleged, Galindo was secretly her constant visitor), and the association continued for the next four years. Siddons lent Galindo £1000 to enable him to buy into a partnership with William Macready for a theatre in Manchester. When the venture collapsed, Siddons called in the debt; according to Mrs Galindo, this was a calculated and vindictive attempt to ruin them. Siddons did not get her money back, and the relationship was finished. Meanwhile stories were circulating of an affair between Siddons and Thomas Lawrence, for whom she had sat in March 1804. William Siddons was driven to issue a press advertisement offering a reward of £1000 for information about who was responsible for the rumours, to no effect. In any case, William and Sarah Siddons, who had spent the last few years increasingly apart, were informally separated by October. William moved to Bath, where he died on 11 March 1808. Together with Patty Wilkinson and her sole surviving daughter, Cecilia, Siddons moved to Hanover Square.

Siddons continued to tour during the first two decades of the nineteenth century. She was briefly engaged at the rebuilt Covent Garden Theatre, which opened on 18 September 1809 with *Macbeth*. Once again, the move to a new theatre was an unhappy experience for Siddons, this time because the management's decision to raise admission charges and increase the number of expensive private boxes precipitated the protests from the pit that came to be known as the Old Price (or OP) riots. Kemble's attempt to move the theatre upmarket (and, in the process, subtly to alter the social composition of its audiences) was viewed by the OP protesters as an assault upon the ancient rights and privileges of common theatregoers, as denying them access to the nation's drama (and, in particular, to Shakespeare). After thirty-seven nights of barracking, Kemble acceded to the rioters' demands; ticket prices were brought down and the number of boxes was reduced. Unsurprisingly, Siddons was appalled by what she, along with many other commentators, regarded as an outbreak of radical militancy. She wrote to her daughter-in-law, Harriet Siddons, that the riots were a 'barbarous outrage to decency and reason', adding ominously, 'where it will end heaven knows' (Manvell, 295). If the OP protests represented a temporary victory against theatrical profiteering, they also constituted a challenge to the authority of the patent theatres themselves, with which Siddons's Shakespearian career had been closely associated. She played her final season at Covent Garden in 1811–12, ending with a highly emotional farewell benefit on 29 June 1812, when she played Lady Macbeth. According to Joseph Farington, her rendition so affected the spectators that they again exercised their power to curtail the performance by refusing to let the play continue after the sleepwalking scene. After a considerable time had elapsed, a curtain was drawn back and Siddons was discovered 'sitting at a table in her own character'. Veiled and dressed in white satin, she stood up to face the cheers and applause, finally enforcing silence by a bow and curtsy. She spoke a farewell address which lasted eight minutes: 'having finished, the loudest claps followed, and she withdrew bowing and led off by an attendant … her appearance was that of a person distressed and sunk in spirits' (*Farington Diary*, ed. Greig, 7.89).

Siddons returned to Westbourne Farm, Harrow Road, London, where she had lived since 1805, to spend her time entertaining, sculpting, and travelling with her daughter and Patty Wilkinson. Although she continued to offer private readings and recitals at home, she at first kept away from the theatre as far as was possible, with the exception of rare appearances in benefits for members of her family. Concerted efforts were made to lure her back to the stage; within a year of her official retirement a petition calling for her return was organized. Siddons sensibly resisted the call, perhaps aware that her waning powers risked blighting her glorious reputation. Her occasional appearances in the next decade proved that she could still move and impress; none the less, in 1817 William Hazlitt severely criticized what he regarded as Siddons's prevarication over her retirement, wishing that she 'would either return to the stage, or retire from it altogether', since by her 'uncertain wavering between public and private life, she may diminish her reputation, while she can add nothing to it'. As the embodiment of a sublime conception of tragedy in Hazlitt's account, Siddons's status as a figure of sublimity in memory and imagination was now such that her actual living presence was not only no longer necessary but positively unwelcome:

> if we have seen Mrs Siddons in Lady Macbeth only once, it is enough. The impression is stamped there for ever, and any after-experiments and critical inquiries only serve to fritter away and tamper with the sacredness of the early recollection. (Hazlitt, *Criticism and Dramatic Essays*, 276)

Siddons's earlier performances had acquired an afterlife which would prove to be enduring. Absolutely her final stage appearance was on 9 June 1819, in a benefit for Charles Kemble, although the private recitals continued. Her forty-year-old son, Henry *Siddons, had died of tuberculosis in 1815; Siddons recorded that this loss 'seems to have laid a heavier hand on my mind than any I have sustained' (Campbell, 2.360). Mrs Piozzi died in 1821, John Kemble in 1823; Siddons passed the final decade of her life in a state of deep melancholy. Her niece Fanny *Kemble (who was later to achieve a level of celebrity as an actress that would rival that of her aunt) recorded her 'vapid vacuity' and 'apparent deadness and indifference to everything' (Kemble, 64); invoking the romantic image of Hamlet, she described a weary, solemn figure, dressed in black: 'She has stood on a pinnacle till all things have come to look flat and dreary; mere shapeless, colourless, level monotony to her' (ibid.). The friendship with Thomas Lawrence was maintained, with a final twist in 1828 in that the painter developed an intense but brief romantic interest in Fanny Kemble, who was said to bear an uncanny resemblance to both Sarah and Sally Siddons. He died on 7 January 1830.

On 31 May 1831, aged seventy-six, Siddons fell ill with acute erysipelas. This quickly led to severe sickness and fever, and she fell into a coma on 7 June. She died at her house at 27 Upper Baker Street the next morning, 'peaceably, and without suffering, and in full consciousness', in Fanny Kemble's account. Her funeral, which took place on 15 June, featured eleven coaches of mourners, which included the Drury Lane and Covent Garden companies, and drew crowds of more than 5000. She was buried in St Mary's churchyard in Paddington. Sarah Siddons was already established as a mythical figure well before her death, to the extent that she was discouraged from making live stage appearances in her final years because they tended to corrupt the image of greatness that had been established early in her career. Since she was the subject of countless visual representations as well as reviews, eulogies, panegyrics, letters, and diary accounts, Siddons's likeness and personality were very much in the public domain in her own lifetime; posterity has continued to afford her a hallowed space in theatrical tradition and cultural history. In the final years of her life Siddons collaborated with her biographers: James Boaden's *Memoirs of Mrs Siddons* appeared in 1827, and Thomas Campbell's *Life* in 1836. Campbell sculpted a statue of her for the north transept of Westminster Abbey in 1849; L. Chavalliaud's sculpture (modelled on Reynolds's *Tragic Muse*) was unveiled by Sir Henry Irving on Paddington Green in 1897. A range of popular and scholarly biographies was published in the late nineteenth and twentieth centuries. Siddons continues to exert a fascination in part because her biography (like those of many successful women) appears to conform to a familiar pattern of public success shadowed by personal tragedy, and also because she seems both to belong to natural thespian aristocracy and to embody a vanished golden age of classical acting that could seemingly move spectators almost beyond the bounds of endurance. Ultimately, however, Siddons's enduring significance may lie less in the written records than in the pictorial representations of her, both within and out of roles. Whatever view is taken of her acting or of her personal character, in this respect her status as icon seems assured.   ROBERT SHAUGHNESSY

Sources R. Manvell, *Sarah Siddons: portrait of an actress* (1970) · J. Boaden, *Memoirs of Mrs Siddons*, 2 vols. (1827) · T. Campbell, *Life of Mrs Siddons*, 2 vols. (1834) · Highfill, Burnim & Langhans, *BDA* · C. Parsons, *The incomparable Siddons* (1909) · Y. Ffrench, *Mrs Siddons, tragic actress* (1954) · M. Booth, ed., *Three tragic actresses* (1996) · T. Wilkinson, *The wandering patentee, or, A history of the Yorkshire theatres from 1770 to the present time*, 4 vols. (1795) · P. Fitzgerald, *The Kembles: an account of the Kemble family*, 2 vols. (1871) · *The Farington diary*, ed. J. Greig, 8 vols. (1922–8) · W. Hazlitt, *Characters of Shakespeare's plays* (1817) · W. Hazlitt, *Criticism and dramatic essays* (1851) · F. A. Kemble, *Record of a girlhood*, 3 vols. (1878)

Archives Bath Central Library, notebooks · Folger · Harvard TC · JRL, papers | BL, letters to Lady Barrington, Dep. 9389 · BL, letters to Lord Hardwicke, Add. MS 35350 · Bodl. Oxf., corresp. with Noel and Byron families · JRL, letters to Hester Lynch Piozzi · U. Hull, Brynmor Jones L., letters to Charles Hotham

Likenesses T. Cook, line engraving, pubd 1783, BM, NPG · G. Romney, oils, 1783, priv. coll. · J. Reynolds, oils, 1783–4, Hunt. L. [see illus.] · J. Flaxman, Wedgwood medallion, 1784, Wedgwood Museum, Barlaston, Staffordshire · H. Hone, watercolour miniature, 1784, NG Ire. · F. Bartolozzi, stipple, pubd 1785 (after H. Hone), NG Ire. · T. Gainsborough, oils, c.1785, National Gallery, London · T. Lawrence, portrait, 1786, Tate collection · J. Downman, chalk drawing, 1787, NPG · W. Beechey, oils, 1793, NPG · T. Lawrence, oils, 1796, NPG · T. Lawrence, oils, c.1797, NPG · J. Webb, line engraving, pubd 1798 (after J. Reynolds, 1784), NG Ire. · R. Dighton, etching, 1799, BM, NPG · T. Lawrence, oils, 1804, Tate collection · J. Henning, enamel paste medallion, 1807, NPG · plaster medallion, 1807 (after J. Henning), Scot. NPG · G. H. Harlow, group portrait, oils, 1817 (*Court for the trial of Queen Catherine, Henry VIII*), Royal Shakespeare Memorial Theatre Museum, Stratford upon Avon · G. F. Phillips, stipple, pubd 1825 (after enamel miniature by H. Hone; after his watercolour miniature), NG Ire. · J. Hayter, chalk drawing, 1826, BM · C. Turner, mezzotint, pubd 1826 (after T. Lawrence), BM, NPG · F. Chantry, statue, 1831, Westminster Abbey, London · J. Bromley, mezzotint, 1832 (after J. Reynolds), NPG · T. Campbell, statue, 1849, Westminster Abbey, London · T. Campbell, marble relief, NPG · L. F. Chavalliaud, marble statue, Paddington Green, London · R. Crosse, miniature, V&A · A. Edouart, drawing, silhouette, NPG · G. H. Harlow, oils (as Lady Macbeth), Garr. Club · G. H. Harlow, pencil and wash drawing, Brodie Castle, Grampian · G. H. Harlow, pencil drawing, Bowood, Wiltshire · T. Lawrence, pencil drawing, Garr. Club · J. Reynolds, oils, second version, Dulwich Picture Gallery, London · S. Siddons, clay bust, V&A · attrib. G. Stuart, oils, NPG · R. Westall, oils (as Lady Macbeth), Garr. Club · prints, BM, NPG · watercolour on card (S. Siddons?), Scot. NPG

Sidebotham, Herbert (1872–1940), journalist, was born at Salford, Lancashire, on 21 December 1872, the only son of Edmund Sidebotham, an insurance agent, and his wife, Agnes Greaves Dixon. Educated at Manchester grammar school, he won a scholarship at Balliol College, Oxford, where he gained firsts in classical moderations (1893) and in *literae humaniores* (1895). He won a Craven scholarship (1892), Gaisford prizes for Greek verse (1893) and prose (1894), and was *proxime accessit* for the Ireland scholarship (1894). He was called to the bar by the Inner Temple (1912), but never practised. In 1899 he married Florence, daughter of Thomas Stephens, a Salford alderman, with whom he had three daughters.

In 1895 Sidebotham joined the editorial staff of the *Manchester Guardian* and served that newspaper with distinction for twenty-three years. Though his editor, C. P. Scott, never fully appreciated Sidebotham's extraordinary abilities, the proprietor, Edward Taylor, and the chief leader writer, C. E. Montague, readily acknowledged that their shy, bespectacled, scholarly colleague was 'a real first-rater … [with] the completest knowledge of the whole machinery of journalism' (Ayerst, 313–14). Sider, as he was familiarly known by everyone, possessed 'a genius for fellowship and a broad humanity', that both attracted and influenced his colleagues, 'from leader writers to the junior members of the reporting staff' (Nichols, 119). He wrote upon a wide range of political topics, foreign and domestic, serving in turn as news, then foreign, editor.

A passionate advocate of the cause of peace, paradoxically Sidebotham became well known to his readers as Student of War. Under that pen-name he wrote brilliantly about engagements upon the frontiers of the British empire, of the Second South African War, and of the Russo-Japanese War. In the First World War he wrote a twice-weekly appreciation of events. He also planned, edited and contributed more than half a million words to a fortnightly serial *Manchester Guardian History of the War*. His careful analyses, his thoughtful commentaries, an admirable mixture of idealism and realism, informed and impressed lay and expert readers alike. Foch stated that his writing was 'the only thing of the kind in the press worth reading' (Nichols, 120). Lloyd George instructed the cabinet secretary, Hankey, to keep for reference the articles of 'much the best military critic' (Ayerst, 378). Sidebotham had advertised his good opinion of Lloyd George's outstanding capacities as a military strategist and leader (H. Spender, *The Prime Minister*, 1920, 122; T. Jones, *Lloyd George*, 1951, 53).

Sidebotham's military knowledge inspired his Zionism. He shared that belief with another gentile, his friend and colleague W. P. Crozier. Sidebotham became the ideologue of the British Palestine Committee, a pro-Zionist organization formed in 1916. With a younger colleague, Harry Sacher, he edited the monthly journal *Palestine* (1917–20). In his campaign for the Balfour Declaration, as earlier, in his writing on the triple entente, he enjoyed Scott's unalloyed support. For two decades Zionism remained an absorbing interest. He wrote about it frequently and published two books: *England and Palestine: Essays towards the Restoration of the Jewish State* (1918) and *Great Britain and Palestine* (1937).

Overworked, underpaid, and insufficiently appreciated by his editor, in 1918 Sidebotham reluctantly acceded to the blandishments of *The Times*. Years later Scott admitted

to him that he had made a grave mistake in not holding onto Sidebotham, 'the greatest fault I committed in the conduct of the paper' (Ayerst, 396). In his three years with *The Times* his best work was a series of brilliant political character sketches, reprinted as *Pillars of the State* (1921). They reflected his interest and emphasis upon personality and individuality in politics. He despaired of *The Times* where, despite editorial apologies and assurances, his work was persistently cut. He left Printing House Square with the intention of freelancing. At Lloyd George's insistence, however, for a very large salary he was prevailed upon to join the *Daily Chronicle* as a political adviser. There was insufficient work to occupy him. In 1923 he joined the *Sunday Times* as Scrutator, and wrote in lighter vein as Candidus for the *Daily Sketch*. When the Berry brothers secured the *Daily Telegraph* in 1928, Sidebotham resurrected his old pen-name Student of Politics. Uniquely his writing straddled the quality and popular press, exercising influence and providing entertainment. Arguably he was the best-known columnist of the inter-war years. He collected his Candidus articles in a book, *The Sense of Things* (1938).

Sidebotham's conversation like his writing reflected his complete freedom from snobbery and humbug. He combined scholarship effortlessly with a wide knowledge of the ways of the world. He set little limit to his interests, reading widely and voraciously. At the *Sunday Times* he was 'the revered arbiter of any Latin or Greek which went into the paper' (Hobson, Knightley, and Russell, 135–6). He never forsook his love of the classics, publishing privately in 1937 twenty Shakespeare sonnets done into Latin elegiacs. A talented amateur pianist, he was addicted to Mozart and Beethoven. He died at his home, 7 Heathview Gardens, Roehampton, Surrey, on 19 March 1940.

A. J. A. MORRIS

Sources DNB · *The Times* (20 March 1940) · D. Ayerst, *Guardian: biography of a newspaper* (1971) · H. D. Nichols, 'Scott's lieutenants', *C. P. Scott, 1846–1932: the making of the Manchester Guardian*, ed. [A. P. Wadsworth] (1946), 114–20 · H. Hobson, P. Knightley, and L. Russell, *The pearl of days: an intimate memoir of the Sunday Times, 1822–1972* (1972) · *WW* · *The political diaries of C. P. Scott, 1911–1928*, ed. T. Wilson (1970) · [S. Morison and others], *The history of The Times*, 4/1 (1952) · S. A. Cohen, *English Zionists and British Jews: the communal politics of Anglo-Jewry, 1895–1920* (1982) · F. Hardie and I. Herrman, *Britain and Zion* (1980)
Archives JRL, Manchester Guardian archives
Likenesses photograph, repro. in Nichols, 'Scott's lieutenants', facing p. 144
Wealth at death £5517 16s. 11d.: probate, 3 June 1940, CGPLA Eng. & Wales

Sidesterne, Robert (*d.* in or after **1316**), physician, took his name from the Norfolk village of Sidesterne (modern Syderstone), but his precise origins are unknown. He probably studied at Oxford, but he first occurs, as 'Master Robert de Sidesterne', or 'de Cisterne', subdeacon, on 22 February 1288, when he was collated to the rectory of Newchurch, Kent, and shortly afterwards ordained deacon. He held the rectory of Newchurch only briefly, for on 15 September 1289 a new rector was instituted, and one of the witnesses was 'Master Robert de Cydesterne, physician [*medicus*]' (Davis and others, 87). He soon obtained two other rectories, for on 24 September 1291 the pope granted a faculty to the archbishop of Canterbury to confer the church of Hadleigh, Suffolk, on Master Robert de Sidesterne, who already held the rectory of Bacton (in either Suffolk or Norfolk) in the diocese of Norwich, with dispensation to hold both. On 8 October 1292 Sidesterne was collated to a canonry and prebend in the collegiate church of Wingham, Kent. He continued to hold both rectories, however, for on 28 September 1294 'Master Robert de Cisterne, parson of the churches of Baketon and Hadleghe' (CPR, 1292–1301, 92, 94), was listed among the ecclesiastics who received royal letters of protection for a year, after they had paid Edward I's clerical tax of half their revenues.

In December 1292 Sidesterne was present at the deathbed of John Pecham, archbishop of Canterbury, perhaps as his physician. By May 1301 he was serving as physician to Edward, prince of Wales (later Edward II). The latter's accession to the throne, on 8 July 1307, was probably responsible for Sidesterne's sudden acquisition of additional benefices. By July 1308 he had obtained a canonry and prebend in Exeter Cathedral. On 13 July 1308 he was made vicar of Chesterton, Oxfordshire (presented by Osney Abbey, Oxford; vacated by February 1315), and on 27 July he exchanged his canonry and prebend in Exeter for a canonry and prebend in Crediton, Devon (vacated May 1316). In 1310 Sidesterne used his influence with the king at least twice to aid others: on 23 March, described as 'Master Robert de Cysterne, king's clerk and leech' (CPR, 1307–13, 220), he obtained a royal exemption for Robert Burdeyn from serving as sheriff, coroner, or in other royal offices; and on 16 July Edward II granted a licence to the nuns of Flixton Priory, Suffolk, 'at the instance of Master Robert de Cisterna, our leech' (Catalogue of the Stowe Manuscripts, 1.756–7; CPR, 1307–13, 268), to acquire lands to the value of £10 per annum to increase their endowment.

Sidesterne's flow of benefices resumed a few months later. He was made provost of Holyhead, Anglesey (granted 19 November 1310); canon and prebendary of Wells (admitted 15 October 1311); and rector of Gilling in Rydale, Yorkshire (presented 22 August 1313, but possibly not instituted; a new rector, Walter de Sutton, was presented on 24 March 1314). Sidesterne was still holding the prebend of Wingham on 16 May 1313, when Edward II petitioned the pope to grant 'Master Robert de Cisterne, our clerk and physician', a dispensation for non-residence; the king described Robert as the man 'who knows our constitution and the state of our body better than anyone' (Rymer, Foedera, 2/1.39). However, Sidesterne vacated his vicarage of Chesterton by February 1315, and his canonry and prebend of Crediton in May 1316. He last occurs on 26 June 1316, when Bishop John Droxford of Bath and Wells (d. 1329) granted him an annual pension of 10 marks, to be received until the bishop should grant him a new benefice.

Sidesterne is credited with having written a long treatise in seven books, consisting largely of remedies for ailments. It survives in two copies in the British Library (Sloane MS 75, fols. 4–93, and Sloane MS 418, fols. 189–317) under the title Cure magistri Roberti de Cisterna super Viaticum. It has been inferred from its failure to mention Sidesterne's position as a royal physician that the Cure was written before 1301. It was designed to serve as a companion volume to the Latin translation by Constantine the African (fl. 1065–85) of the Viaticum of Ibn al-Jazzar (d. 1009). Sidesterne followed the topical sequence of the Viaticum and its division into seven books, discussing the various ailments and diseases of the body from head to foot. Thus the first book deals with head ailments (vertigo, lethargy, frenzy, epilepsy, paralysis, spasmus, and tremor); the second book with the face and teeth; and so on. For each ill the remedy is described, but little is said of either the disease itself or its symptoms—these are discussed in the Viaticum. For some ailments, such as spinal injury or hernia, surgery is recommended; a leaden truss is also recommended for the latter. At least two of Sidesterne's remedies (applying the fat of green tree-frogs to decayed teeth to make them fall out, and wrapping a smallpox patient in scarlet cloth) were later used by the more celebrated John Gaddesden, and were included in his Rosa anglica, but C. H. Talbot has dismissed the Cure in general as 'a work without any intrinsic interest or merit' (Talbot, 107–8). MARTHA CARLIN

Sources Emden, Oxf., 3.1700 · C. H. Talbot and E. A. Hammond, The medical practitioners in medieval England: a biographical register (1965), 302–3 · C. H. Talbot, Medicine in medieval England (1967), 107–8, 113 · F. N. Davis, ed., The register of John Pecham, 1, CYS, 64 (1908–10), 44, 72, 87, 252 · D. Douie, ed., The register of John Pecham, 2, CYS, 65 (1969), 3 · CPR, 1292–1301, 92, 94; 1307–13, 220, 268, 289; 1313–17, 13 · F. C. Hingeston-Randolph, ed., The register of Walter de Stapeldon, bishop of Exeter (1892), 15, 103, 205, 212 · E. Hobhouse, ed., Calendar of the register of John de Drokensford, Bishop of Bath and Wells, Somerset RS, 1 (1887), 45, 110 · Registrum Roberti Winchelsey, Cantuariensis archiepiscopi, AD 1294–1313, ed. R. Graham, 2, CYS, 52 (1956), 739 · CEPR letters, 1.544 · The register of William Greenfield, lord archbishop of York, 1306–1315, ed. W. Brown and A. H. Thompson, 3, SurtS, 151 (1936), p. 79, n.4 · L. Thorndike and P. Kibre, A catalogue of incipits of mediaeval scientific writings in Latin, rev. edn (1963), col. 205 · Rymer, Foedera, 3rd edn, 2/1.39 · Catalogue of the Stowe manuscripts in the British Museum, 1 (1895), 756–7 · E. J. L. Scott, Index to the Sloane manuscripts in the British Museum (1904), 111 · M. McVaugh, 'Constantine the African', DSB · BL, Harley MS 4304, fol. 12v · BL, Stowe Charter 319 · Canterbury Cathedral, Register Q, fol. 24 · register of John Dalderby, bishop of Lincoln, 1300–20, vol. 2, fols. 154v, 165v

Archives BL, Sloane MSS 75, fols. 4–93; 418, fols. 189–317

Sidgreaves, Sir Arthur Frederick (1882–1948), businessman, was born on 12 June 1882 probably in the Straits Settlements where his father, Sir Thomas Sidgreaves, was chief justice; his mother was Barbara Catharine, daughter of George Young, of Saverley House, Staffordshire. He was educated at Downside School and in 1902 joined the commercial side of D. Napier & Son Ltd, in which he acquired his first interest in motor-car development. In the First World War he served in the Royal Naval Air Service and the Royal Air Force, and was latterly engaged in the Ministry of Munitions upon the production of aero-engines, some of which were of Rolls-Royce design. He was appointed OBE in 1918.

After returning for a time to D. Napier & Son, in 1920 Sidgreaves joined Rolls-Royce as export manager in the London offices. In 1926 he became general sales manager and in 1929 managing director. At this time the company was developing the R engine and in 1931 the R-engined Supermarine S.6 made aeronautical history by winning the Schneider Trophy for Great Britain. The experience gained in the development of this engine and the intensive teamwork which lay behind its production enabled the company to provide the engines which sustained the Royal Air Force in the battle of Britain ten years later.

When the government introduced its shadow factory programme just before the outbreak of war in 1939, Sidgreaves with Ernest Walter Hives, the general manager, undertook on behalf of Rolls-Royce to build an entirely new factory at Crewe to augment production of the Merlin engine at Derby. Another factory was later built at Hillingdon, Glasgow, and went into production within six months of the commencement of building. In addition to these factories, the Merlin engine was also made by the Ford Motor Company in Manchester and by Packards in America. This enormous production drive was supported by Sidgreaves's calm counsel and acceptance of the drain of effort and resources as a mortgage on the future. Disclaiming any technical ability he was able and quick to detect flaws in technical arguments with a gift of realistic appreciation. A man of kindly heart, simple, almost austere, he was a great reader, of discriminating yet catholic taste, interested in the arts, and, although by nature a recluse, a charming host and witty conversationalist. In 1938 he married Dorothy Jessica, daughter of the late Thomas Henry Bryant. An earlier marriage with Mabel Winifred Winter, with whom he had two sons, had been dissolved.

Sidgreaves was president of the Society of British Aircraft Constructors, 1942–3, and in 1945 he was knighted for his services during the war. He retired in 1946. On 7 June 1948, disturbed by the prospect of an unfavourable medical report which he was anticipating, he threw himself under a train at Green Park underground station.

[ANON.], rev. ANITA MCCONNELL

Sources *The Times* (19 June 1948), 3b [inquest] · *The Times* (8 June 1948), 4f · *CGPLA Eng. & Wales* (1948) · d. cert.
Archives Rolls-Royce Heritage Trust, private papers
Wealth at death £115,887 13s. 10d.: probate, 19 Oct 1948, *CGPLA Eng. & Wales*

Sidgreaves, Walter (1837–1919), Jesuit and astronomer, was born on 4 October 1837 in Grimsargh, near Preston, Lancashire, the second son of Edward Sidgreaves and a member of a remarkable family in the history of English Jesuits. His elder brother, Henry Sidgreaves (1835–1852), a novice who died at the early age of seventeen at Stonyhurst, was allowed to take his vows as a Jesuit priest on his deathbed. His younger brother, Edward Sidgreaves (1840–1930), worked most of his life as a Jesuit priest in West Demerara (now Guyana), and his two sisters were devoted assistants to the Jesuit clergy in their priestly work at Preston. An older cousin, the Revd George Sidgreaves (1829–

1910), became the procurator of the Jesuits for the province.

After his training at Stonyhurst College, Sidgreaves went to St Beuno's College, near St Asaph, for theological studies. He entered the Society of Jesus in 1855 and was ordained a priest in 1871. Among the offices he held were those of minister of Mount St Mary's, Beaumont, and the English College, Malta, and for twenty-five years he taught physics at St Mary's Hall, Stonyhurst.

Sidgreaves's most lasting contribution was to astronomy, for he was responsible for the erection and adjustment of all the instrumental equipment of the Stonyhurst observatory. His first directorship of the observatory was between 1863 and 1868, when Father Stephen Perry, an astronomer of international repute, was engaged in theological studies. A pioneer in the science of terrestrial magnetic observations, he installed in 1866 a suite of the self-recording meteorological instruments in the Stonyhurst observatory; this persuaded the Board of Trade to use the observatory as one of the seven principal meteorological stations in Britain. Sidgreaves accompanied Perry in several of his scientific expeditions. In 1868–9 they went on a magnetic survey of the western and eastern regions of France, and later undertook two government expeditions to observe the transit of Venus across the sun's disc, the first to Kerguelen Island in the Indian Ocean in 1874 and the second to Madagascar in 1882. After Perry died in 1889 on the expedition to observe the total eclipse at Salut Isles, French Guiana, Sidgreaves resumed his duties as director of the observatory, where he devoted his skills to stellar spectroscopy. He devised efficient instruments and took a series of photographs of stellar spectra, in particular of the new stars which appeared in 1892 and 1901. For this photographic work he was awarded a gold medal in the St Louis Exhibition of 1904 and a *grand prix* at the Franco-British Exhibition of 1908; he also received a second blessing from Pope Leo XII. Because of his severe deafness and shyness he was reluctant to accept invitations to lecture outside Stonyhurst, but he did deliver an important lecture before the Royal Astronomical Society in 1904 on the star Beta Lyrae (he had been elected a fellow in 1891 and served on the society's council). Some of his astronomical jottings appeared in the *Memoirs* and in the *Monthly Notices of the Royal Astronomical Society*.

Sidgreaves observed the magnetic elements until the last month of his life. He died at Stonyhurst on 12 June 1919 and was buried there on 14 June. His grave is located between the church and the observatory, the two most significant institutions of his life.

D. BEN REES

Sources WWW · *Letters and Notices* [Society of Jesus], 35 (1919–20), 119–23 · *The Times* (14 June 1919) · private information (2004) · C. Fitzgerald-Lombard, *English and Welsh priests, 1801–1914* (1993) · *The Tablet* (21 June 1919), 768
Archives RAS, letters to Royal Astronomical Society
Likenesses photograph, repro. in *Letters and Notices*

Sidgwick, Arthur (1840–1920), educationist and classical scholar, was born at Skipton in Yorkshire on 9 April 1840, the fifth of six children of the Revd William Sidgwick (*d.* 22 May 1841), headmaster of Skipton grammar school, and his wife, Mary (*née* Crofts). William's early death left his widow to bring up the four surviving children, three boys and a girl. They moved to Clifton in 1844 and in 1853 to the Blue House at Rugby, where the household included a sister of Mary's and two cousins of the Sidgwick family, Ada *Benson and Edward White *Benson. Edward Benson, then a master at Rugby School, married the youngest of the Sidgwick family, Mary ('Minnie'), in 1859 and was a formative influence on the education of the two younger Sidgwick boys. The eldest, William Carr Sidgwick (*b.* 1834), went to a private school and Oxford, but Arthur followed his brother Henry *Sidgwick as a day boy at Rugby, the most liberal and academically successful of the reformed public schools, and to Trinity College, Cambridge. Both had brilliant undergraduate careers, winning many university prizes. Arthur went up to Cambridge in 1859. In 1863 he was second in the first class of the classical tripos and fourteenth senior optime in mathematics, and was also president of the union. He was a scholar of Trinity (1861–4) and later a fellow (1864–9).

More robust than his brother Henry and lacking his early vocation for scholarship, Arthur Sidgwick accepted an invitation from Frederick Temple to return in 1864 as assistant master to Rugby. He remained there for fifteen years, teaching classics, English, history, and divinity, but did not lose touch with the movement for university reform, with which all three brothers identified, meeting regularly at dinners of the Ad Eundem Club, founded in 1864 by his brother William (then a fellow of Merton) to bring Oxford and Cambridge liberals together. Arthur backed Henry's revolt against the Anglican religious tests imposed on fellows (abolished by parliament in 1871): in 1869 both resigned their Trinity fellowships. At Rugby he was a leading opponent of Temple's successor as headmaster, the Conservative Henry Hayman, who dismissed him in September 1873. Sidgwick's future was still in doubt when, on 30 December 1873, he married Charlotte Sophia Wilson (1853–1924), the sister of a Rugby colleague, James Maurice Wilson. A term without teaching duties allowed them a prolonged honeymoon in Europe, and in April 1874 Sidgwick was reappointed at Rugby. Beautiful and intense, Charlotte was a much-loved wife, wholly identifying with her husband's values. Their five children were born between 1877 and 1882: Rose *Sidgwick, Ethel, and Frank at Rugby, and Margaret (Margie) and (Arthur) Hugh at Oxford, where the Sidgwicks moved in August 1879.

Corpus Christi College, a small, intellectually ambitious college, recruited Sidgwick as tutor for classical moderations, a post he held from 1879 to 1902. Between 1882 and his death in 1920 he was a fellow of Corpus (with an interval as honorary fellow, 1902–4) and between 1894 and 1906 university reader in Greek. Returning to academic life at the age of forty he impressed early pupils, several of whom became close friends (including Oliver Elton, L. T. Hobhouse, Gilbert Murray, Henry Newbolt, E. K. Chambers, P. S. Allen), by his excellence as a teacher and his magnetic personality. He looked more like a painter than

a schoolmaster, with his thick silver hair and flowing beard, striking eyes, and 'favourite garb of dusty grey or the like, worn with a certain amused contempt for the tailor' (*Pelican Record*, 16, 1920, 19–20). At Corpus he became the most successful tutor of his time and a central figure in college life; in the university he was an active participant in literary and reforming circles, while always preserving a distance between academic society and a private life that centred on family, friends, and home—first at 77 and then at 64 Woodstock Road in north Oxford.

Arthur Sidgwick's life of his more eminent Cambridge brother, *Henry Sidgwick: a Memoir* (1906), written in collaboration with his sister-in-law, Eleanor Mildred Sidgwick, does full justice to Henry's work for university reform in the reactionary late Victorian era. Arthur's own work for similar ends continued into the twentieth century, when he became the (anonymous) Oxford correspondent of the *Journal of Education* and a supporter of moves for a new royal commission on the ancient universities. His memorandum to the Bryce commission on secondary education shows his particular concern to broaden the university's work so as to meet the needs of secondary schools, poor students, and women ('Memoranda and answers', 47.231–43). Although keen to popularize the cultural heritage of the ancient world he attacked the requirement (abolished only in 1920) that all undergraduates must know the rudiments of Greek. He was a tireless worker for the university delegacies (committees) that ran extension lectures, examined and inspected secondary schools, and launched in 1897 Oxford's programme for secondary teacher training. Sidgwick's own lectures on English as well as classical literature—to undergraduates, women students, and extensionists—helped to make the case for modernizing the curriculum. A few highly regarded lectures on pedagogical subjects reached a wider audience and were published as: *Form Discipline* (1886), *On Stimulus* (1888), and 'The teaching of classics as literature', *Journal of Education*, 235, (1889), 115–18, the last having been delivered to the Oxford branch (which he founded) of the Teachers' Guild.

Sidgwick's most important work in Oxford was in connection with 'the great business of women's education' (Bodleian, MS Murray 168, fol. 61). The Association for Promoting the Higher Education of Women at Oxford (AEW) had been founded in 1878: it shared the cautious philosophy behind the Cambridge lecture scheme initiated by Henry Sidgwick and his hall at Newnham, providing at first separate courses for women students. Arthur Sidgwick taught for the AEW from 1879 and was its secretary (1882–1907, working in tandem with Bertha Johnson and Annie Rogers as lady secretaries), treasurer (1902–6), and president (1907–15). He was also on Somerville's council and the committee responsible for home students. Two of his daughters, Rose and Margie, read modern history as home students and two Benson nieces were early students at Lady Margaret Hall. Sidgwick was in a strong position to mediate in divisions within the Oxford women's movement, and much depended on his firm but tactful handling of issues that divided it, notably relations between the AEW and halls, and the opening of degrees to women. Prominent in the hard-fought battle to open undergraduate examinations in 1884, Arthur welcomed the trend towards assimilation of women's and men's studies, while continuing to take pride in the AEW's pioneering honours courses in English and modern languages. In 1894 (ahead of the Newnham Sidgwicks) he came out for access to the BA degree for women, believing that it would benefit them not only professionally but also educationally by encouraging them to follow a structured course of study. The degree campaign of 1895–6 failed, leaving supporters to fight off counter-proposals for a separate university for women. But the backing of Oxford's Edwardian chancellor, Lord Curzon, brought new hope of success. In 1911 Sidgwick, a suffragist since the 1860s, bet his youngest daughter 'an even half-crown' that women would get degrees at Oxford or Cambridge before they got the vote (Bodl. Oxf., MS Eng. lett. c. 473, fol. 47). He lost the bet, yet no man did as much to pave the way for the admission of women to Oxford degrees in 1920.

As a Liberal Sidgwick drew his ideas chiefly from J. S. Mill, while following the progressive idealist tradition of T. H. Green and Arnold Toynbee that demanded engagement with the local community. Unlike most academic liberals he remained a staunch follower of W. E. Gladstone. Chairman of the Oxford City Liberal Association 1886–1911 and for ten years a director of the *Oxford Chronicle*, he ensured that opponents were given a good run for their money in what became a safe Unionist seat. He supported agricultural trade unionism and tramped miles to speak at evening village meetings. Within the university he presided in 1887 over the formation of the Home Rule League, known for its hilarious annual dinners, regaled on ginger beer and militant but entertaining speeches. In 1888 he moved the memorial of support sent to Gladstone by seventy-four Oxford MAs. Conservative colleagues learned to be wary of his witty, though always courteous, repartee ('Sidgwickedness')—sharpened, no doubt, by dismay at his brothers' conversion to unionism. 'I belonged to a united family, who are now united against me, and nothing can be more painful than that', he noted privately (Sidgwick to Johnson, 10 Feb 1895, Oxford, St Anne's College, Bertha Johnson MSS). Sidgwick's own breach with the local Liberal Party came only in 1913, when he joined twenty-eight university colleagues in withdrawing support from its anti-suffragist candidates in Oxfordshire (*Oxford Chronicle*, 12 December 1913).

When Corpus elected the Conservative Thomas Case as president in 1904 in preference to Sidgwick, he recorded in his journal (kept for over forty years), 'I am content' (Bodleian, MS Eng. misc. e. 658, fol. 156). He would have been a popular choice among past and present students. His qualities were recognized outside Oxford too: Liverpool College had tried to tempt him away as principal; Glasgow had conferred on him in 1898 (as did Leeds University in 1910) an honorary doctorate; and he was on the council of the Classical Association and had accepted in 1903 a commission (resigned when his health began to fail

in 1911) to produce a revised edition of Liddell and Scott's *Greek Lexicon*. But he was associated with unpopular causes, and his published work—school editions of classical texts and entertaining textbooks (one still in print in the 1980s) on Greek prose and verse composition—did not suggest serious scholarship, despite the unrivalled mastery of the language shown in his own Greek verse. Arthur was, perhaps, as Henry once commented, '*too* successful, professionally and socially, in a certain limited way' to feel the spur of ambition (Sidgwick and Sidgwick, 446).

Noted for his humorous touch on serious subjects, Sidgwick took hobbies seriously: walking and climbing in England and Europe, often on family holidays; games of all sorts—golf, billiards, card and word games; amateur entomology, a passion since childhood. His collection of British Lepidoptera was given to the University Museum in 1922. Bug-hunting companions included a scientist nephew, Nevil Sidgwick. Charlotte shared his love of literature, as did their children, whose careers reflected a range of Sidgwick's interests. Rose *Sidgwick became an academic; Ethel (1877–1970) a novelist; Frank (1879–1939) an author and publisher, helped by his father in a somewhat impecunious retirement to found the firm Sidgwick and Jackson; Margie (1881–1948), the 'home daughter', a voluntary worker in Oxford; Hugh (1882–1917) a distinguished Balliol graduate, an essayist, and civil servant at the Board of Education.

Sidgwick died at his home on 25 September 1920 of pneumonia and was buried on 29 September at Wolvercote cemetery, Oxford. The eclipse of his reputation after his death is due in part to a long final illness—its cause unknown—that left him by the time of Hugh's death in Flanders in 1917 'remote from all knowledge' (Bodl. Oxf., MS Eng. lett. c. 473, fol. 88). The characteristically Victorian and English qualities recalled by obituarists implied that he had outlived his time, representing an intuitively literary tradition of scholarship and a high-minded devotion to duty rooted in a religious faith that deserted him by stages, as the unorthodox but devoted Christian who bore witness in his Rugby *School Homilies* (ed. J. M. Wilson; 2 vols., 1915, 1916) turned into a humanist or 'naturalist'. In a longer perspective he stands out as a university liberal of rare consistency and stamina: a progressive bridging Victorian and Edwardian generations, and pre-eminent among the male dons who made a place for women's higher education in Oxford.   JANET HOWARTH

Sources *Hist. U. Oxf. 7: 19th-cent. Oxf. pt 2* · *Oxford Magazine* (1886–1911) · *Oxford Magazine* (29 Oct 1920) · *Oxford Chronicle and Berks and Bucks Gazette* (28 April 1911) · *Oxford Chronicle and Berks and Bucks Gazette* (1 Oct 1920) · *Pelican Record*, 15 (1920–22), 19–28 · A. Sidgwick, 'Teachings of classics as literature', *Journal of Education*, new ser., 11 (1889), 115–18 · *Journal of Education*, new ser., 12 (1890) · *Journal of Education*, new ser., 23–33 (1901–11) · A. Sidgwick, 'Notes on girls' education', *Journal of Education*, new ser., 33 (1911), 218–19 · A. Sidgwick and E. M. Sidgwick, *Henry Sidgwick: a memoir* (1906) · A. C. Benson, *The life of Edward White Benson*, 1 (1899) · A. Baer, 'The Sidgwicks', in *Frank Sidgwick's diary and other material relating to A. H. Bullen and the Shakespeare Head Press at Stratford-upon-Avon* (1975), appx C · W. F. R. Hardie, 'Corpus Christi College, Oxford, 1851–

1905', CCC Oxf. · G. B. Grundy, *Fifty-five years at Oxford: an unconventional autobiography* (1945) · AEW reports and calendars, 1879–1920, Bodl. Oxf. · 'Memoranda and answers to questions', *Parl. papers* (1895), 47.231–43, C. 7862-IV [royal commission on secondary education] · A. Sidgwick, 'Our public schools, 1V – Rugby', *New Quarterly Magazine*, 2nd ser., 2 (1879) · 'Royal commission to inquire into … certain colleges and schools', *Parl. papers* (1864), 21.296–304, no. 3288 [Sidgwick's evidence] · J. M. Wilson, *An autobiography, 1836–1920* (1932) · H. Newbolt, *My world as in my time* (1932) · P. R. L. Horn, 'The farm workers, the dockers and Oxford University', *Oxoniensia*, 32 (1967), 60–70 · d. cert.

Archives Bodl. Oxf., diaries, MS Eng. misc. d. 699, e. 655–659 · Oxf. U. Mus. NH, Hope Library, entomological corresp., diaries, and papers | Bodl. Oxf., Bryce MSS · Bodl. Oxf., letters to Gilbert Murray · Bodl. Oxf., Ethel Sidgwick MSS · Bodl. Oxf., Sidgwick and Jackson MSS · Castle Howard, Yorkshire, letters to earl of Carlisle · King's AC Cam., letters to Oscar Browning · St Anne's College, Oxford, Bertha Johnson MSS · St Anne's College, Oxford, Annie Rogers MSS

Likenesses Beerbohm, caricature, *c.*1890, Bodl. Oxf., MS Top. Oxon. c. 264 · drawing, crayon, *c.*1890, repro. in *Oxford academical portraits and caricatures*, Bodl. Oxf., MS Top. Oxon. b. 92–29 · lithograph, 1896, repro. in W. Rothenstein, *Oxford characters: a series of lithographs*, 2nd edn (1896) · Hall & Saunders, photographs, *c.*1911, repro. in *Oxford Chronicle* (28 April 1911) · Hall & Saunders, photographs, *c.*1911, repro. in *Oxford Chronicle* (1 Oct 1920) · photographs, CCC Oxf. · photographs, Bodl. Oxf., Eng. misc. MS d. 699

Wealth at death £24,350 16s. 8d.: probate, 13 May 1921, *CGPLA Eng. & Wales*

Sidgwick [*née* Balfour], **Eleanor Mildred** (1845–1936), college head, known to family and friends as Nora, was born at Whittingehame, East Lothian, on 11 March 1845, the eldest of a family of five sons and three daughters born to James Maitland Balfour (1820–1856) MP, and his wife, Lady Blanche Mary Harriet Gascoyne Cecil (1825?–1872), daughter of the second marquess of Salisbury. It was a wealthy family and a lively and brilliant one. Closest to Mrs Sidgwick always was her brother Arthur *Balfour, long-serving cabinet minister and prime minister. Among her other four brothers were Gerald William *Balfour and Francis Maitland *Balfour. Lady Frances Balfour was her sister-in-law. She was educated at home and given particular and advanced teaching in mathematics, her natural bent. Lady Blanche saw to it that all the children were properly educated and received independent fortunes from her husband, he having died during their childhood. When her mother withdrew into invalidism, Nora became the chatelaine of the three great Balfour houses.

In 1876 Nora married Henry *Sidgwick (1838–1900), who was then teaching philosophy at Trinity College, Cambridge. He had earlier sought her interest and financial support for the college for women he had helped found, Newnham. It was a marriage which delighted friends and family: an alliance of two people who shared not only a practical devotion to the cause of higher education for women but an intense interest in paranormal phenomena. The marriage may not have been physically consummated, but it was suffused with affection and tender respect and was a model partnership of two working people, remarkable for its time. They were complementary characters: he witty, eloquent, disorganized; she silent, methodical, austere, but given nevertheless to

Eleanor Mildred Sidgwick (1845–1936), by Sir James Jebusa Shannon, 1889

laughter and to exchanging a Balfour wink in a conspiratorial way.

Their home was to be the centre of much social, intellectual, and musical life; their circle included many London and international figures as well as other Balfours working in Cambridge at the time. Lord Rayleigh, her brother-in-law, was professor of experimental physics. Mrs Sidgwick collaborated with him in his work on measurements of electricity; her name appears jointly with his on three papers published by the Royal Society. Later it was said that he used to save up problems for her to solve with him as a particular treat. At the same time she taught mathematics at Newnham and was responsible for college finances. In 1880, when she was appointed vice-principal on the opening of a new hall, the Sidgwicks moved into rooms there in term time, bringing with them into student life not only their close personal involvement but their lively friends and conversation. In 1891, on the death of the first principal, Anne Jemima Clough, Mrs Sidgwick, to her husband's concern, became her successor. He worried that her work for the Society for Psychical Research (SPR), which he had founded, would suffer. Nevertheless, he continued to play his part in college life with grace and charm. They moved into the newly built principal's flat and watched over every detail of administration as well as campaigning for a greater role for women students in the university. Women had been admitted to examinations in 1882 but subsequent efforts for them to be given degrees were thwarted by the old guard for more than the Sidgwicks' lifetimes.

Mrs Sidgwick may have energetically chased twopences in the accounts but she had the far-sighted strategy to organize a new road to ensure a 'campus' site for Newnham and to buy adjoining land, realizing the importance of sound finances. She had a broad vision of the education Newnham should offer; she thought that women should take a share in 'the work of the world' and that they had a right to the kind of happiness which can come only from work. Nevertheless she saw women's lives in the context of the day and accepted conventional wisdom about home ties. She balanced this with a stress on the importance of scholarship and research. Her enlightened outlook encompassed co-educational classes for her students and robust responses to current fears about the effect of higher education on women's health and child-bearing capacities.

It was a golden age for the college, a coming to maturity under the benign Sidgwick regime. Despite her reputed remoteness Mrs Sidgwick became an almost iconical figure, worshipped with reverential affection. Many students realized how readily she would enter into their problems and that, although her regime was one of steely discipline, her laughter echoed down the long college corridors. The college grew in buildings and numbers; benefactors gave generously. Mrs Sidgwick herself contributed £30,000. W. E. Gladstone and his wife visited Newnham on 31 January 1887 to plant a tree; their daughter, Helen Gladstone, assisted Mrs Sidgwick and was later her vice-principal.

Mrs Sidgwick's increasing influence and authority in the wider world of education was marked by her appointment as one of the three women appointed to serve on the royal commission for secondary education in 1894 and by her confident addresses to those universities where she was invited to speak. She always stressed that an educated woman's influence could be felicitous for the whole family. Her concern for women to be regarded as rational creatures naturally led her to support the growing campaign for women's suffrage. However, in a later speech in 1913 on the progress of the women's suffrage movement (delivered as her presidential address to the Cambridge branch of the Conservative and Unionist Women's Franchise Association), she deplored suffragettes' violent tactics as diminishing this image of good sense and judgement. Her own good sense made her resist an angry riposte to a journalist's article which reflected current concerns as to whether too much study might undermine women's physique, thus weakening the nation's breeding stock. Instead she sent out a questionnaire to past students and their sisters and based her refutation of his claims on statistics garnered from their answers (see her *Health Statistics of Women Students of Cambridge and Oxford and of their Sisters*, 1890). Statistics were her passion in the academic and SPR worlds; questions asked may seem amateurish to modern experts but the intention was sound.

Simultaneously with her work for Newnham and for the educational world in general, entirely and deliberately separately, Mrs Sidgwick continued to work on SPR matters, sifting evidence, writing papers, and scrutinizing, not always successfully, the various mediums at seances. Her work on hallucinations appeared in the same year as her appointment to the royal commission. Part of the Sidgwicks' vacations were spent in vain ghost hunts or attending international conferences on the paranormal, always with a distaste for emotional excess and a cool regard for the truth.

Henry Sidgwick's death in August 1900 left her to reign solitarily at Newnham for the next ten years, and to combine this with membership of the council of the SPR and later the honorary secretaryship and presidency. With admirable dedication she started immediately to edit her husband's papers and to write, together with his brother Arthur, a memoir. This biography, published in 1906, is remarkable for its detached appraisal; no personal note intrudes, but devotion of purpose transparently illuminates both the subject and the writer. 'I never *mean* anything' she once said to an importunate questioner.

Mrs Sidgwick's growing reputation as an educationist made her greatly in demand as a public speaker and a consultant; she was given honorary degrees by Manchester, Edinburgh, St Andrews, and Birmingham universities. She remained near the college when she retired in 1910, still running its finances and serving as a member of the college council until her death. In 1916 she moved to live with her brother Gerald's family near Woking, returning to Cambridge for Newnham parties and council meetings. (Her close involvement in college affairs was not always welcome to younger dons.) Family life now claimed her attention; she particularly enjoyed the company of its younger members. Elder sister to the last, she was at her brother Arthur's side when he died in 1930. Although her withering gaze was still directed on some evidence for supernatural claims, as the years passed and she grew closer to 'my Henry' she authorized her brother Gerald, as president of the SPR, to affirm her convinced belief in an afterlife. She died, at his home, Fisher's Hill, near Woking, Surrey, on 10 February 1936 and was buried in Terling, Essex; her last words were, appropriately, 'that is a very bold hypothesis'.

A portrait of Mrs Sidgwick by J. J. Shannon hangs in Clough Hall. It reflects her still containment and withdrawn detachment and the veiled radiance many sensed about her. From her own evidence, in one of the many questionnaires she instituted, she was of slight build with fair curly hair. Judging from photographs and the portrait, either her hair was under strict control or she was, for once, under a misapprehension. Stories about her suggest her independence of spirit and style; in a conventional age she supported its ways but often behaved with donnish or aristocratic disregard for them herself. (The fact that her mother was the duke of Wellington's goddaughter was not for nothing.) Her spirited stance in the struggle for fairness, truth, and informed help for the world is a large part of her legacy to Newnham College and to the University of Cambridge.　　HELEN FOWLER

Sources E. Sidgwick, *Mrs Henry Sidgwick: a memoir* (1938) · A. Sidgwick and E. M. Sidgwick, *Henry Sidgwick: a memoir* (1906) · Newnham College, Cambridge · NA Scot., Balfour MSS · *Proceedings of the SPR* · *Journal of the SPR* · Gladstone, *Diaries*

Archives Air Force Research Laboratories, Cambridge, Massachusetts, laboratory notebooks · Trinity Cam., corresp. and papers | BL, corresp. with Arthur James Balfour, Add. MS 49832 *passim* · BL, corresp. with Macmillans, Add. MS 55159 · Bodl. Oxf., letters to Gilbert Murray · CUL, letters to Lord Acton · King's AC Cam., letters to Oscar Browning · Society for Psychical Research, London, corresp. with Sir Oliver Lodge · Trinity Cam., letters to Mr and Mrs F. W. H. Myers

Likenesses J. J. Shannon, oils, 1889, Newnham College, Cambridge [*see illus.*]

Wealth at death £15,363 0s. 9d.: probate, 2 April 1936, *CGPLA Eng. & Wales*

Sidgwick, Henry (1838–1900), philosopher, was born at Skipton in the West Riding of Yorkshire on 31 May 1838, the elder brother of the classical scholar Arthur *Sidgwick and fourth of the six children of the Revd William Sidgwick, headmaster of Skipton grammar school, and his wife, Mary Crofts, whose family came from the East Riding of Yorkshire. William Sidgwick graduated from Trinity College, Cambridge, in 1829, and was appointed to his headmastership in 1836. He died on 22 May 1841; his wife survived him until 17 January 1879.

Early years After being educated privately, Henry Sidgwick was sent to a school run by the Revd H. Dale at Blackheath in 1850, and then in September 1852 to Rugby, where his mother took a house the following year. Edward White Benson, a cousin of the family, took up a teaching post at the school at the same time, and soon came to exercise a strong intellectual and moral influence over Sidgwick. In 1859 he married Sidgwick's younger sister Mary and he went on to follow a distinguished career in the Church of England, becoming archbishop of Canterbury in 1882. Sidgwick was a precocious and bookish boy, not given to the usual energetic sports and outdoor activities; at the age of seventeen he was urged to apply for a scholarship at Balliol College, Oxford, the great prize for outstanding boys from the school, but, wanting to follow in Benson's footsteps, he chose to go to Trinity College, Cambridge, which he entered in October 1855. From this date until his death forty-five years later Sidgwick was to spend only one term away from Cambridge.

Sidgwick's undergraduate career was one of great distinction: he won the Bell and Craven scholarships in his first two years, was elected a scholar of Trinity, and in 1859 he graduated with a 'double first', top of the list in the classical tripos and thirty-third wrangler in mathematics; he was also awarded the chancellor's medal. In the same year he was elected a fellow of Trinity and appointed assistant tutor in classics. But at least as important as his conventional studies during this period was his membership of 'the Apostles', the highly selective (and secretive) discussion society that had been founded in the 1820s. What Sidgwick so valued about these weekly meetings was the complete frankness and intellectual sincerity with which the society's members were required to express their views, no matter how fundamental or controversial the topic under discussion. It was these gatherings rather

Henry Sidgwick (1838–1900), by Elliott & Fry

than his formal education that revealed to Sidgwick his true vocation, which he later characterized simply as 'thought exercised on the central problems of human life' (Sidgwick and Sidgwick, 35).

Inevitably, the central problem for an intellectually serious young man in the 1860s was the problem of 'belief', the problem of the intellectual status of the 'truths' of Christianity. Sidgwick, a clergyman's son whose attitudes had been deeply shaped by Benson's practical piety, had begun to have serious doubts about his inherited Anglicanism while still an undergraduate, and in the course of the 1860s he moved, unsteadily and with considerable anguish, towards a more sceptical position, while always hoping that historical research or philosophical reasoning might yet ground the central claims of revealed religion on a more credible footing. He was drawn by turns to the relentless empiricism of John Stuart Mill and the sociological positivism of Auguste Comte, but his was too honest and fastidious a mind ever to subscribe without reserve to any of the great intellectual systems of his age. In the early 1860s he began to learn Hebrew and Arabic in the hope that a study of the historical and textual origins of Christianity might make it possible to winnow the grains of spiritual truth from the chaff of superstitious accretion, but in the course of the decade he moved more and more towards purely philosophical investigations.

From this point on, his personal quest and his intellectual career coincided very closely. In 1865 he examined for the moral sciences tripos for the first time, and in 1867 he began lecturing on 'mental and moral philosophy'. During the next three decades Sidgwick's was to be the guiding influence in the teaching and administration of the 'moral sciences' in Cambridge, studies which at the time included a good deal of psychology, politics, and economics as well as all the main branches of philosophy.

His increasing religious scepticism, together with the public campaign against the restriction of college fellowships at Oxford and Cambridge to members of the Church of England, led the always scrupulous Sidgwick to conclude that he could no longer in good conscience hold an appointment that required formal subscription to the Thirty-Nine Articles, and so in 1869 he resigned his fellowship and tutorship. The college indicated its regard for his worth, and for his evident sincerity, by immediately electing him to a lectureship (without a fellowship), which allowed him to carry on his teaching as before. Sidgwick's example greatly boosted the campaign to abolish such religious 'tests', a measure eventually carried in 1871. For him the episode was also a pressing example of the kinds of dilemmas faced in practical moral reasoning, an experience that drove him to deeper enquiries into the nature of ethical first principles.

The Methods of Ethics It was at about this time that Sidgwick began work on what was to be his major intellectual achievement, *The Methods of Ethics*, first published in 1874 and several times revised (the 6th edition was published in 1901). This book has frequently been seen as a defence of utilitarianism, the ethical position associated above all with Jeremy Bentham and John Stuart Mill, which claims that the ultimate criterion for the rightness or wrongness of actions is to be found in their consequences for the greatest happiness of the greatest number. Recent scholarship, however, has convincingly established the work's more systematic and less partisan aspirations. Essentially, Sidgwick was enquiring whether the human mind could establish any principled basis for rationally determining how one ought to act. One of the distinguishing features of the book (in which it is closer to Aristotle than to most modern ethical theory) is the serious attention which it gives to the 'morality of common sense' as a defensible guide to action, a feature that has been taken to give the book an ethically conservative colouring. But after much careful analysis Sidgwick concludes that the rules underlying common sense morality can only be given a coherent form and made to yield consistent practical guidance if they are in turn derived from implicitly utilitarian premises. However, he conceded that the axiom of utilitarianism could not be justified within the terms of utilitarianism itself; it required a rationally groundable intuition of the kind that lay at the heart of the rival nineteenth-century ethical doctrine of intuitionism. Moreover, he concluded that there was no rational way to overcome what he called 'the dualism of practical reason', that is, no demonstrable ground for asserting the superiority of rational altruism over rational egoism. The consistent pursuit of one's own interest provided a no less coherent and justifiable principle of action than did the consistent pursuit of the welfare of others, and the first edition of the *Methods* notoriously ended with the admission that without some notion of a divine system of reward in the hereafter, this conflict is irresolvable; hence, 'the Cosmos of Duty is thus really reduced to a Chaos; and the prolonged effort of the human intellect to frame a perfect ideal of rational conduct is seen to have been foredoomed to inevitable failure' (*The Methods of Ethics*, 1874, 473); the passage was softened and revised in a more optimistic direction in later editions.

The Methods of Ethics has been recognized as one of the few indisputable classics in the history of moral philosophy; it was described by the later Cambridge philosopher C. D. Broad as 'on the whole, the best treatise on moral theory that has ever been written' (Broad, 143). Its stature partly derives from its sustained architectonic conception: partial or intermediate conclusions are allowed no rest until they have been chased down to first principles that form part of rational human understanding as such. But much of the book's force also comes from its painstaking analysis of the unobvious subtlety of 'common-sense morality' and from its patient demonstration of the adaptability and capaciousness of utilitarian moral reasoning. Its density and restraint meant that it was unlikely to attain the cachet among non-philosophers briefly enjoyed by, for example, the *Principia ethica* (1903) of Sidgwick's former pupil G. E. Moore, but it exercised considerable influence over Anglo-American moral philosophy in the twentieth century. The American moral philosopher John Rawls has awarded the book the dubious accolade of being 'the first truly academic work in moral philosophy' (Schultz, 49), while late twentieth-century critical estimation placed it in the company of the ethical treatises of Aristotle, Hume, and Kant.

Reformer and professor On 4 April 1876 Sidgwick married Eleanor Mildred (Nora) Balfour (1845–1936), who, as Eleanor Mildred *Sidgwick, was a significant promoter of university education for women. She was a sister of the Tory politician Arthur Balfour (a former pupil of Sidgwick's). They had no children. For some years after their marriage, the Sidgwicks lived at Hillside, Chesterton Road. From 1893 they lived in Newnham College. Sidgwick had long been sympathetic to the cause of women's education. In 1869 he helped to initiate a scheme of lectures for women at Cambridge and in 1871 set up, at his own expense, a house for these students, inviting Ann Jemima Clough, sister of the poet Arthur Hugh Clough, to become its superintendent. In 1875 the Newnham Hall Company was formed, supported by public subscription, to finance the first building of what became Newnham's established site, leading to the foundation of Newnham College in 1880, with Eleanor Sidgwick as vice-principal. She succeeded Ann Jemima Clough as principal in 1892 and was one of the college's principal benefactors in her own right. Sidgwick later helped the new college acquire the freehold of its site; in his honour, a road built to replace one occupied by college buildings was named Sidgwick

Avenue. He successfully campaigned for the admission of women to university examinations in 1881, and freely gave his time, money, and increasing reputation to further the cause of women's education in other ways.

In 1872 Sidgwick had unsuccessfully applied for the Knightbridge chair of moral philosophy following the death of its holder, F. D. Maurice. At this point he did not have any substantial philosophical publications to his name, and he was passed over in favour of a prominent evangelical clergyman, T. R. Birks. However, when the post next fell vacant following Birks's death, Sidgwick's claims were unrivalled, and he was elected to the chair in 1883. By inclination as well as appointment, his was a thoroughly academic career, and he was one of the earliest figures to have been recognized as a fully professional philosopher. In this spirit, he was a frequent contributor to (and financial supporter of) *Mind*, the first specialist journal of philosophy in Britain, founded in 1876. He constantly referred to the obligations of his academic position, and the title 'professor' became as constitutive a part of his public identity as the name of his diocese is of a bishop's. In 1881 he was awarded an honorary LLD by Glasgow University and made an honorary fellow of Trinity College. He received further honorary degrees from St Andrews and Edinburgh in 1884, from Oxford in 1890, and from Budapest in 1896.

A cause peculiarly dear to Sidgwick's heart was that Cambridge University should deploy its considerable resources and reputation to enrich the national culture and further international scholarship. He involved himself in numerous schemes of reform designed to move the obstructive federation of sinecure-ridden colleges a little further along the path of becoming a university seriously committed to education and research. In 1877 a commission was established by act of parliament to determine new statutes for Cambridge University and its colleges. When these came into effect in 1882, Sidgwick became a member of the newly constituted general board, the body largely responsible for the academic policy of the university; he retained this position until 1899. In addition, he served from 1890 to 1898 as a member of the council of the senate, as well as being on several other special boards and syndicates, where he devoted countless hours to the numbing minutiae of academic administration. On all these bodies he took a leading part, and there is abundant testimony not just to his grasp of detail and his procedural fertility, but also to the persuasiveness exercised by a personality in which the passion to find the least bad outcome carried the force of disinterested reason. Inevitably, he came to be regarded in some of the more conservative quarters of the university as a troublesome meddler, and occasionally his schemes would fail as a result of their excessive ingenuity and complication, as in an abortive scheme to extend the taxation of the colleges for university purposes. He also supported several new academic ventures with his own money, financing professorships and readerships, helping to sustain an arrangement for the education of future members of the Indian Civil Service, making a substantial donation towards the costs of a building for the department of physiology, and so on. As one obituarist observed: 'His truest monument is ... the difference between Cambridge as it is now and the Cambridge of forty years ago' (Schultz, 364).

As a teacher, Sidgwick was too cautious and too thorough (and, as a lecturer, too boring) ever to attract a large undergraduate following, but he won the unstinted devotion of a small number of able pupils. He was wryly self-conscious about the contrast between his own lack of popularity and the crowded lecture-halls that hung upon the not notably clear words of his Oxford counterpart, the neo-Hegelian philosopher T. H. Green. His ingrained scepticism debarred him from imparting a doctrine or message; it was rather the example of his unceasingly probing analytic method that impressed itself on his admirers, most of whom, such as the historian F. W. Maitland, were not destined to be professional philosophers. As his one-time pupil and eventual successor W. R. Sorley put it, 'his teaching was a training in the philosophic temper—in candour, self-criticism, and regard for truth' (Schultz, 2).

Political philosophy This analytical method—'i.e. the method of reflection on the thought we all share, by the aid of the symbolism we all share, language' (H. Sidgwick, *Philosophy: its Scope and Relations*, 1902, 49)—was deployed with particularly telling effect in the two treatises that represented Sidgwick's attempt to bring professorial rigour and detachment to bear upon the major questions of policy and legislation. *The Principles of Political Economy* (1883) was an intellectually conservative work in two ways: first, its analytical or deductive method signalled its adherence to the style of classical political economy, rather than adopting the more historical or more mathematical approaches then in vogue; and second, it included within the scope of the subject not just the 'science' of economic analysis, but also the 'art' of political economy, that is, an examination of the (limited) role of state action in economic life. Implicitly, the work attempted to fend off the twin challenges to the status of traditional political economy posed by the late nineteenth-century enthusiasm for socialism and sociology. Sidgwick accepted the criticism of the historical school to the extent of acknowledging that the premises of political economy were not timeless truths, but he maintained that they did 'correspond broadly to the facts of modern societies' (p. 36). Moreover, his focus was upon matters of policy, on how to decide what to do under present conditions—a task, he argued, for which the fashionable emphasis on historical and cultural diversity was of only limited value. The book was regarded respectfully by the increasingly professionalized economists of the next generation, but Sidgwick was, as John Maynard Keynes later observed, one of the last of those who 'could take [economics] in his stride' as 'one Moral Science out of several' (Collini and others, 309).

The Elements of Politics (1891) was informed by a similarly practical purpose. As Sidgwick explained, in characteristic terms:

> The primary aim of the political theory that is here to be expounded is not to supply an entirely new method of

obtaining reasoned answers to political questions; but rather, by careful reflection, to introduce greater clearness and consistency into the kind of thought and reasoning with which we are all more or less familiar. (p. 1)

In this vein, the book addressed itself to institutional and procedural matters as well as to more purely theoretical issues, attempting to show how analytical reasoning based on 'certain propositions as to human motives and tendencies which are derived primarily from the ordinary experience of civilized life' (ibid., 11) issued in broadly utilitarian conclusions. But as one reviewer noted, 'If this is Benthamism, it is Benthamism grown tame and sleek' (Collini and others, 291), and Sidgwick's practical concentration on the kinds of consideration which were at the heart of policy-making by the late-Victorian governing élite meant that the work displayed none of Bentham's strong critical antagonism to the political institutions of his time. Though *The Elements of Politics*, like Sidgwick's other treatises, never achieved any popular success, for some years it enjoyed considerable academic standing (a 4th edition was published in 1919), but it was thereafter largely neglected by historians of political theory.

In his early years Sidgwick had been a frequent contributor to the periodicals of general culture, writing essays on a range of literary, historical, and cultural subjects (some of which were included in the posthumously published *Miscellaneous Essays and Addresses*, 1904), but from the 1870s onwards he increasingly concentrated upon his work in moral and political philosophy. His later treatises had usually first been sketched in courses of lectures, and his occasional pieces were now predominantly published in the recently established specialist journals. At the time of his death he had been preparing *The Development of European Polity* (1903) for publication, and a further three volumes deriving from his professorial lectures were published posthumously: *Philosophy: its Scope and Relations* (1902), *Lectures on the Ethics of T. H. Green, H. Spencer, and J. Martineau* (1902), and *Lectures on the Philosophy of Kant and other Philosophical Lectures and Essays* (1905). His little handbook *Outlines of the History of Ethics for English Readers*, which had first appeared in 1886, was published in its fifth edition in 1902, and continued to be used for teaching purposes for many years.

Other activities A major expression of Sidgwick's open-minded search for truth about the 'ultimate questions of human life' (especially, in this case, the possibility of an afterlife) was his interest in psychical research. Throughout his adult years, Sidgwick eagerly collected reports and conducted experiments concerning various alleged manifestations of psychic phenomena, from hypnotism and hallucinations through thought transference to 'table-rapping' and other supposed communications from the dead. He was active in the founding of the Society for Psychical Research in 1882, serving as its first president, and he and his wife took leading parts in the society's efforts to secure intellectual respectability for its proceedings. In conducting these investigations Sidgwick was far from credulous, always sought corroborated and verifiable evidence, and participated in the exposure of several

fraudulent mediums or spiritualists. But he continued to devote much time, energy, and money to these enquiries, combining a never entirely stilled scepticism with a never entirely abandoned hope.

Another aspect of Sidgwick's constant efforts to expand the range of shared truths about fundamental questions was his membership of discussion societies made up of distinguished individuals who held very divergent religious and philosophical beliefs. He was a founder member of the Metaphysical Society (1869–80) and later of the Synthetic Society (1896–1900), as well as a member of several groups confined to Cambridge. Characteristically, he observed of the first of these societies that its aim was to attain 'not agreement, which was of course beyond hope, but a diminution of mutual misunderstanding' (Sidgwick and Sidgwick, 221). In such discussions, as in his contribution to more public debates, he steered a middle course between the aggressive positivism of the agnostic scientists and the convinced transcendentalism of the orthodox churchmen. The subsequent reminiscences of participants in these discussions concur in reporting how Sidgwick's dialectical ingenuity and resourcefulness, combined with the evident sincerity of his desire to learn from others, soon earned him a commanding position in their company despite a manner that could appear hesitant and even self-effacing.

Politically one of the young 'lights of Liberalism' in the 1860s, Sidgwick was on the side of 'reform' in both national and academic politics. But his social and economic views reflected the individualism typical of the mid-Victorian intellectual, leaving him increasingly at odds with the more 'collectivist' ideas of the 1880s and 1890s, and his cautious and sceptical temperament meant he was bound to be resistant to the various forms of organized enthusiasm in politics. Intellectually, he was an apprehensive political traveller, nervously rehearsing the potential mishaps of any journey and made edgy by the uncertainty of the destination: the longer he studied the brochures for utopia, the more he warmed to the idea of staying at home. Nor was this simply timidity or unimaginativeness, though Sidgwick had his share of those qualities; it sprang, rather, from a kind of unshowy moral seriousness about the temptations to self-deception offered by political excitement, and an intellectual conviction that only immediate consequences could be calculated with any reasonable reliability. After the home-rule split of 1886, he (like many of the other former 'academic liberals' of the 1860s) became a Liberal Unionist, a political home that at first appeared to suit his combination of intellectual principle and cautious prudence. However, he greatly distrusted Chamberlain's imperialist adventures, and at the end of his life his deep-rooted liberalism manifested itself in his distaste for the militarism and jingoism expressed in Britain's prosecution of the Second South African War.

Last years and reputation In Sidgwick's last years there was no diminution in the range of his activities. He was president of the second international congress of psychologists in 1892, and a member of the Gresham commission on the University of London from 1892 to 1894; he submitted a memorandum to the royal commission on the financial relations between Great Britain and Ireland in 1895 and one to the royal commission on local taxation in 1899; he was prominent in the (unsuccessful) campaign for women to be granted degrees at Cambridge; and he published a collection of his addresses, as *Practical Ethics* (1898). At the close of the century he was also the prime mover in establishing a learned body that might represent scholarship in the humanities as the Royal Society did for the sciences, though he died shortly before its official recognition as the British Academy.

Sidgwick's personality seems to have attracted exceptionally wide respect and affection. As one obituarist recorded: 'It was impossible to know him without feeling that incomparably the most impressive thing about him was his character. ... There was in him an extraordinary simplicity and goodness' (Sidgwick and Sidgwick, 591). His speech was marked by a slight stammer, which added to his air of sincerity without detracting from his gentle wit. Partly because his tastes inclined to the ascetic, his income easily exceeded his needs, enabling him to be a generous supporter of academic, philanthropic, and personal causes. There has been speculation that Sidgwick was impotent (Rothblatt, 135). Several of his closest friends, such as Roden Noel and H. Graham Dakyns, as well as his brother Arthur (a master at Rugby and later fellow of Corpus Christi College, Oxford), were practising homosexuals, but there is no evidence that sexual desire of any kind played a significant part in Sidgwick's life. The surviving likenesses portray the gravity characteristic of widely admired members of the Victorian professional élite, while also catching something of the philosopher's partly abstracted liveliness of mind.

In the decades immediately following his death, Sidgwick's reputation suffered as part of the general reaction against 'Victorianism': on reading the *Memoir*, the young John Maynard Keynes hyperbolized: 'He never did anything but wonder whether Christianity was true and prove that it wasn't and hope that it was' (Harrod, 135). He was also overshadowed philosophically by the great impact of G. E. Moore and Bertrand Russell in the early part of the twentieth century, and subsequently by that of Ludwig Wittgenstein. But the later decades of the twentieth century saw a strong revival of interest in utilitarianism among moral philosophers, and *The Methods of Ethics* was widely regarded as a more careful and philosophically more interesting presentation of the utilitarian position than may be found in the work of the leading representatives of that school, such as Bentham and Mill. In addition, the more nuanced and discriminating understanding of Victorian cultural history that has been achieved by recent scholarship has made clear Sidgwick's central role in many aspects of late nineteenth-century British intellectual life.

Sidgwick died of cancer on 28 August 1900 at Terling Place, Terling, near Witham, Essex, the home of his brother-in-law the distinguished physicist J. W. Strutt, third Baron Rayleigh. He is buried in Terling churchyard.

Had the Anglican service not been used, his preference was to have the following sentences delivered at his graveside: 'Let us commend to the love of God with silent prayer the soul of a sinful man who partly tried to do his duty. It is by his wish that I say over his grave these words and no more' (Sidgwick and Sidgwick, 599).

STEFAN COLLINI

Sources A. Sidgwick and E. M. Sidgwick, *Henry Sidgwick: a memoir* (1906) · B. Schultz, ed., *Essays on Henry Sidgwick* (1992) · J. B. Schneewind, *Sidgwick's ethics and Victorian moral philosophy* (1977) · S. Collini, D. Winch, and J. Burrow, *That noble science of politics: a study in nineteenth-century intellectual history* (1983) · *The Monist*, 58/3 (1974) [special issue devoted to Sidgwick] · C. D. Broad, *Five types of ethical theory* (1930) · S. Rothblatt, *The revolution of the dons: Cambridge and society in Victorian England* (1968), 133–54 · R. McWilliams-Tullberg, *Women at Cambridge: a men's university—though of a mixed type* (1975) · R. F. Harrod, *The life of John Maynard Keynes* (1951)
Archives King's Cam., lecture notes · Trinity Cam., personal and family corresp. and papers | BL, letters to Arthur Balfour, Add. MS 49832 · BL, corresp. with Macmillans, Add. MS 55159 · Bodl. Oxf., corresp. with Mary Benson; letters to Blanche Clough · CUL, Maitland MSS, corresp. with Lord Acton · DWL, letters to Edward Enfield · King's AC Cam., letters to Oscar Browning · Trinity Cam., letters to Mary Benson; letters to F. W. H. Myers; letters to A. J. Patterson · U. St Andr., corresp. with Wilfred Ward
Likenesses J. J. Shannon, oils, 1889, Newnham College, Cambridge · S. A. Walker, photograph, 1894, repro. in Sidgwick and Sidgwick, *Henry Sidgwick* · L. C. Dickinson, oils, 1902, Trinity Cam. · G. W. Bayes, bronze relief, 1905, Newnham College, Cambridge · Elliott & Fry, photograph, NPG [*see illus.*] · S. A. Walker, photograph, NPG · photograph, Girton Cam.
Wealth at death £12,000 13s. 3d.: probate, 28 Nov 1900, *CGPLA Eng. & Wales*

Sidgwick, Nevil Vincent (1873–1952), chemist, was born in Oxford on 8 May 1873, the only child of William Carr Sidgwick (1834–1910) and Sarah Isabella Thompson (d. 1915). There were intellectuals on both sides of the family: his father had been a classical fellow of Merton College and later a university lecturer in politics and political economy, and his uncles included Henry Sidgwick, professor of moral philosophy at Cambridge, Edward White Benson, who later became archbishop of Canterbury, and Sir Benjamin Collins Brodie, second baronet, who was Aldrichian professor of chemistry at Oxford from 1855 to 1872.

Sidgwick was educated at Summer Fields School (near Oxford) and at Rugby School. In 1892 he won a science scholarship to Christ Church, Oxford, where his tutor was A. G. Vernon Harcourt. He gained first-class honours in natural science in 1895, and two years later first-class honours in *literae humaniores* (Greats). After a year's demonstrating at Oxford and a period in Leipzig, in the autumn of 1899 he went to Tübingen University, where in 1901 he was awarded a DSc degree, *summa cum laude*, for work in organic chemistry.

Sidgwick took up a tutorial fellowship at Lincoln College, Oxford, in October 1901; the college was his home for the rest of his life. From 1903 to 1907 he was also lecturer in chemistry at Magdalen College. From 1901 to 1916 he and his students carried out research, mainly on the physical properties of organic compounds, in Magdalen's Daubeny Laboratories. In 1910 he published his first book,

Nevil Vincent Sidgwick (1873–1952), by John Merton, 1954

Organic Chemistry of Nitrogen, which attracted some attention; apart from that he did little work of any distinction until he was in his late forties, although during the First World War he worked on a number of special research problems for the government.

In 1916 Sidgwick moved to the new Dyson Perrins Laboratory, which was devoted to organic chemistry. The laboratory was under the direction of the Waynflete professor, William Henry Perkin junior, and the two men could scarcely tolerate each other. Sidgwick had a deep interest in physical chemistry, which Perkin thought a waste of time; Sidgwick claimed that Perkin on several occasions said to him 'Physical chemistry is all very well, but of course it doesn't apply to organic compounds' (Sutton, 312). In 1919 Sidgwick applied unsuccessfully for the Dr Lee's professorship at Oxford. Nevertheless, in 1922 Sidgwick was elected a fellow of the Royal Society, and two years later was appointed University Reader in Chemistry, a post he held until 1945.

Sidgwick's later success in his researches followed a suggestion in 1914 from Ernest Rutherford that he should attempt to relate chemical properties to the new electronic and quantum theories. His work in this field led to his second book, *The Electronic Theory of Valency* (1927), which was soon recognized to be a scientific classic. In it he skilfully applied electronic theories to a wide range of chemical compounds and lucidly gave a fresh unity to the whole of chemistry. He made a clear distinction between the ionic bonds between atoms, and the covalent bond which involves the sharing of electrons between two atoms. He also emphasized the importance of a third type of bond: the French chemist Alfred Werner (1866–1919)

had postulated that a special secondary bonding occurs in certain complex inorganic molecules; Sidgwick showed that these bonds are simply covalent bonds in which both of the bonding electrons are provided by one of the atoms.

Paradoxically, the quantum theory on which Sidgwick's book was based was already out of date when the work appeared; quantum mechanics had begun to supersede it. Nevertheless, the book had a wide influence, since the presentation was such that readers could easily translate its ideas into the new quantum-mechanical concepts as they developed.

Sidgwick was invited by Cornell University to be the George Fisher Baker lecturer in chemistry for 1931. The required book based on the lectures appeared in 1933 with the title *Some Physical Properties of the Covalent Link in Chemistry*. This was a useful addendum to his *Electronic Theory*, but again little was said about the new quantum-mechanical ideas, which Linus Pauling in particular was applying very skilfully to chemical problems.

From then on Sidgwick's energies were mainly devoted to expanding and applying in much greater detail his previous formulation of the electronic theory. He also wanted to prepare a new edition of his *Organic Chemistry of Nitrogen* but in the end the task was completed by Wilson Baker and T. W. J. Taylor. The book's title, *Sidgwick's Organic Chemistry of Nitrogen*, delighted Sidgwick; 'Like *Plutarch's Lives*' (Sutton, 316), he remarked.

For more than twenty years Sidgwick gave at Oxford a scholarly and comprehensive series of lectures on inorganic chemistry, and at the same time worked on his final book, *The Chemical Elements and their Compounds* (2 vols., 1950). A massive work of 750,000 words, it was written in a lively style, and gave a synoptic view of much of chemistry. It quickly became a classic.

Sidgwick received a number of honours, including a royal medal of the Royal Society, and the Longstaff medal and Liversidge lectureship of the Chemical Society. He served as president of the Chemical and Faraday societies. In 1935 Oxford conferred on him the personal title of professor, and in the same year he was appointed a commander in the Order of the British Empire.

In appearance and personality Sidgwick was unusual. Sir Henry Tizard described him in 1905 as 'An elderly looking man, almost bald, with a fringe of grey hair' (Tizard, 240). He was then thirty-two, and over forty years later he looked much the same. He was always conventional in dress, and invariably carried an umbrella; even in the hot California sun he would wear a felt hat, a thick English suit, and a raincoat. He cared very little about his surroundings, and his rooms in Lincoln College always looked shabby and untidy. During the Second World War the college was taken over as a nurses' hostel, but Sidgwick refused to move.

In his relationships with others Sidgwick was very prejudiced, either completely approving or completely disapproving; he 'made no attempt to conceal his personal prejudices, which were usually irrational and often productive of his wittiest remarks' (Tizard, 254). He would aggressively pounce on any loose or inaccurate statement, and so made a few enemies; others became immune to being bitten. He was, however, quite prepared to adjust his prejudices if confronted with adequate evidence. Before his first visit to the United States in 1931 he announced that he was sure he would not like the place, but soon he had completely reversed his opinion. On his first visit he was fifty-eight, and quite set in his ways. Oxford students had always been in awe of him, but the Cornell students saw him differently and treated him with familiarity, even calling him 'Gran'pa', which delighted him. They paid him the great compliment of inviting him to stay at their fraternity, Telluride House, which he greatly appreciated and enjoyed. From then on he returned whenever he could, and became one of the best known British scientists in the United States; in the end he had visited forty-six of the forty-eight continental states. In 1951 he was in failing health but made what he knew must be his last visit. After undergoing an operation he returned to Telluride House, where the students helped him to go up and down stairs and took him for trips to see the autumn colours. He had a stroke on the boat returning to England, and spent his final months in the Acland Nursing Home, in Oxford, where he died peacefully, on 15 March 1952. He never married. Throughout his adult life he insisted that he had no belief in God or in an afterlife.   KEITH J. LAIDLER

Sources DNB · H. T. Tizard, *Obits. FRS*, 9 (1954), 237–58 · L. E. Sutton, *Proceedings of the Chemical Society* (1958), 310–19 · K. J. Laidler, 'Chemical kinetics and the Oxford college laboratories', *Archive for History of Exact Sciences*, 38 (1988), 197–283 · private information (2004) · *CGPLA Eng. & Wales* (1952)
Archives Lincoln College, Oxford, corresp. and papers · MHS Oxf., notebooks incl. work on history of chemical theory · Oxf. U. Mus. NH, entomological papers | IWM, corresp. with Sir Henry Tizard
Likenesses W. Stoneman, photograph, 1933, NPG · J. Merton, oils, 1954, Lincoln College, Oxford [*see illus.*] · J. Merton, oils, Lincoln College, Oxford
Wealth at death £67,025 9s. 11d.: probate, 18 April 1952, *CGPLA Eng. & Wales*

Sidgwick, Rose (1877–1918), university teacher, was born at 13 Bilton Road, Rugby, Warwickshire, on 9 January 1877, the second daughter of Arthur *Sidgwick (1840–1920) and his wife, Charlotte Sophia Wilson (1853–1924). Her father, an assistant master at Rugby School, became a classical tutor at Oxford, where he was a strong supporter of the movement for women's higher education. Her uncle was the Cambridge philosopher Henry *Sidgwick, and his wife, Eleanor Sidgwick, became principal of Newnham College, Cambridge.

Rose therefore grew up in a circle not only of academic distinction but of involvement in educational, social, and religious issues. On leaving Oxford high school she remained at home in north Oxford, registering with the Society of Oxford Home Students (which in 1952 became St Anne's College), and gaining first-class honours in modern history in 1899. She took as her first post a lectureship at the Oxford Pupil Teacher's Centre, and in 1903 she was awarded the Oxford diploma in education with distinction. She then became for a year a temporary tutor in history at Somerville College, where the impressive library building, designed by Champneys, was nearing completion. Rose helped Margery Fry, the librarian, to arrange the books, and when Margery left to become warden of a small residence for women students at Birmingham, Rose became librarian, receiving among other gifts 2000 volumes from the library of John Stuart Mill.

In 1905 Rose Sidgwick obtained a lectureship in history at Birmingham University. She joined Margery at the Hagley Road Women's Residence, which moved in 1908 to new premises, University House, in Edgbaston. The friendship was deeply emotional on Rose's side, as happened at a time when academic life for women had become almost exclusively celibate. Early in her life at Birmingham, however, she composed for herself 'a New Decalogue'; the first line was 'Thou shalt not cling, thou shalt not clutch'. The friendship was invaluable to both women: Rose found Margery 'a kind of spiritual sea-side' but Margery's mind, sternly nurtured by her father and brother, was widened by Rose's feminine culture. Rose's sister Ethel Sidgwick had published her first novel in 1910: a collection of Rose's verse was published posthumously, *Writings by R. S.* (1920).

Rose Sidgwick was above all a teacher, at a time when universities did not demand research and publication. The records of her twelve-year lectureship are scanty. She was an enthusiastic supporter of the Workers' Educational Association, founded in 1903. She joined Margery Fry on the Staffordshire education committee. In 1914 University House, the fine building which Rose had seen built and helped to plan, was commandeered as a military hospital. The students were temporarily housed, and Margery and Rose rented a house: they bought furnishings from Roger Fry's Omega Workshop in Bloomsbury. For several months the house was lent to Belgian refugees. Margery left to organize relief work with British Quakers in the Marne: Rose joined her in vacations.

In 1918 Rose Sidgwick took Margery Fry's place on the British Universities Mission to the USA. She was a great success, 'the master-bowman of the group' said Sir Henry Jones, professor of philosophy at Glasgow. She died at New York of the influenza that was sweeping through Europe and North America on 28 December 1918, while on the homeward journey. Alumnae of all the American universities she had visited founded the Rose Sidgwick memorial scholarship to enable a British woman graduate to study in an American university (*Times Educational Supplement*, 19 June 1919, 308).

Rose Sidgwick was forty-one when she died, young in appearance and fresh in mind according to Margery Fry, who recalled 'her gentle and dignified manner with its slight but ineradicable touch of the academic' (Fry, 136). People spoke of the sweetness of her nature, as they had of her uncle, Henry Sidgwick. Like him, she had an indestructible faith in some form of personal survival, though she had grown up among people who wanted to apply the tests of reason and science to religion. She sometimes found their iconoclasm hard to bear. Her own religion seems to have been a Wordsworthian natural piety.

ENID HUWS JONES

Sources S. M. F. [S. M. Fry], *Oxford Magazine* (24 Jan 1919), 130 · *Somerville College register, 1879–1971* [1972] · E. H. Jones, *Margery Fry: the essential amateur* (1966) · private information (2004) · b. cert.
Likenesses photograph, BL, writings of Rose Sidgwick, cat. 122/2 cc 21

Sidley, Samuel (1829–1896), portrait painter, was born in York. He studied at the Manchester School of Art and the Royal Academy Schools, and first exhibited at the Royal Academy in 1855. By the end of his life he had exhibited thirty paintings at the Royal Academy and eleven at the Society (from 1887 Royal Society) of British Artists. He was best-known as a portrait painter and was commissioned to paint official and presentation portraits, including those of Professor Henry Fawcett, John Colenso, bishop of Natal (National Portrait Gallery, London), and the duke and duchess of Buckingham. His other paintings included *Alice in Wonderland* and *The Challenge*, which were engraved by C. A. Tomkins. He collaborated with the animal painter Richard Ansdell, and one of their joint paintings was of the children of Angus Holden, with a pony by Ansdell.

Sidley was elected a member of the Royal Society of British Artists in 1890, and he was an associate of the Royal Cambrian Academy. He died on 29 June 1896 at his home, 8 Victoria Road, Kensington, London, leaving a widow, Betty Ferns Sidley.

L. H. CUST, *rev.* ANNE PIMLOTT BAKER

Sources Wood, *Vic. painters*, 3rd edn · J. Johnson, ed., *Works exhibited at the Royal Society of British Artists, 1824–1893, and the New English Art Club, 1888–1917*, 2 vols. (1975) · B. Stewart and M. Cutten, *The dictionary of portrait painters in Britain up to 1920* (1997) · Graves, *RA exhibitors* · Boase, *Mod. Eng. biog.* · *The Times* (10 July 1896) · private information (1897)
Wealth at death £10,314 7s. 10d.: probate, 16 July 1896, *CGPLA Eng. & Wales*

Sidmouth. For this title name *see* Addington, Henry, first Viscount Sidmouth (1757–1844).

Sidney [Sydney], **Algernon** (1623–1683), political writer, was born at Baynard's Castle, London, on 14 or 15 January 1623, the second surviving son of Robert *Sidney, second earl of Leicester (1595–1677), diplomat and politician, and Dorothy Percy (d. 1659), daughter of Henry *Percy, ninth earl of Northumberland. His older brother was Philip *Sidney (1619–1698), Viscount Lisle and later third earl of Leicester, Cromwellian politician; his older sister was Dorothy *Spencer (1617–1684), countess of Sunderland and Waller's Sacharissa; and a younger brother was Henry *Sidney (1641–1704), earl of Romney and later an intimate of William III. From the Sidneys, Algernon inherited a humanist culture and protestant cause, from the Percys an ancient lineage and ungovernable pride. His great-uncle was Sir Philip Sidney, Elizabethan soldier and poet, the fame of whose protestant martyrdom at Zutphen (1576) resonated into Algernon's lifetime. It was because he saw his own struggles against popery and arbitrary power as continuing those of Sir Philip that Algernon's

Algernon Sidney (1623–1683), attrib. Justus van Egmont

1659 entry in the signature book of the University of Copenhagen read: 'PHILIPPUS SIDNEY MANUS HAEC INIMICA TYRANNIS EINSE PETIT PLACIDAM CUM LIBERTATE QUIETEM' ('This hand, enemy to tyrants, by the sword seeks peace with liberty'; 'Lantiniana', 101). His imperiousness was improved by his early (1650s) residence at Petworth, household of his uncle Algernon, tenth earl of Northumberland. His *Court Maxims* described the 'powerful, gallant' nobility of 'the Plantagenet Age', when Percy power was at its zenith (Sidney, *Court Maxims*, 67); his *Discourses* praised the king-making prowess of Henry Percy, first earl of Northumberland, 'and his brave son Hotspur' (Sidney, *Discourses*, in *Works*, 205). Thus Burnet explained that on the one hand Sidney 'had studied the history of government in all its branches beyond any man I ever knew', and that on the other he was 'a man of most extraordinary courage … but of a rough and boisterous temper, that could not bear contradiction' (*Burnet's History*, 2.341). This lineage helped to establish two features of Sidney's perspective. The first concerned the importance of arms, whether against Counter-Reformation popery or over-mighty kings. The second observed the decline in family fortunes under the Stuarts. In both respects, under the militarily invincible republican government of 1649–53, he was to discover a cause for life.

Early life, 1623–1649 Sidney was raised at the family seat of Penshurst Place, Kent, where the family's chaplain from 1633 was the divine and scholar Henry Hammond, echoes of whose work have been detected in Sidney's own writings. Sidney may have attended boarding-school for part of this period. In 1632, with his brother Philip, he accompanied his father on an embassy to Denmark. In 1636 Leicester was appointed ambassador-extraordinary to France; he arrived at Paris in May, again bringing his two eldest sons. Algernon would remain for five years in France, where his education was completed, either in Paris or at the Huguenot academy at Saumur, founded in 1602 by Sir Philip Sidney's friend Philippe Du Plessis Mornay. In Paris the Sidney family attended services at Charenton, where the minister was Jean Daillé, formerly chaplain to Du Plessis Mornay at Saumur, and praised by Algernon in the *Court Maxims*. In November 1636 the countess of Leicester wrote to her husband that she heard Algernon 'much comended by all that comes from you … [for] a huge deall of witt and much sweetness of nature' (*De L'Isle and Dudley MSS*, 6.64). In 1640 his uncle Northumberland tried to procure military employment for him with the prince of Orange. In 1641 the family returned to an England in crisis. On 14 June Leicester was appointed lord lieutenant of Ireland to replace the executed earl of Strafford, but in October Ireland was convulsed by rebellion. Over the winter of 1641–2 forces backed by the English parliament arrived in Dublin to suppress the rebellion containing, by February 1642, Lord Lisle in command of a cavalry regiment and Algernon as captain of a troop of horse.

At a court martial in Dublin on 5 April 1643 the Sidney brothers and four other commanders of cavalry were cleared of the charge of cowardice on 28 March near Old Ross, co. Wexford. A letter to his mother in June explained Sidney's desire both to leave Ireland ('that which is … bad for that which may be better, I think not possibly worse') and to avoid the civil war in England:

> Nothing but extreame necessity shall make me thinke of bearing arms in England, and yet … theare is so few that abstaine from warre for the same reason I doe, that I doe not know wheather in many mens eyes it may not prove dishonourable to me. (J. T. Gilbert, ed., *History of the Irish Confederation*, 7 vols., 1882–91, 1.xlviii–xlx)

Granted leave to return he landed, on 22 June, with Lisle at Chester, where their horses were stolen by royalist marauders. His letter to Orlando Bridgeman threatening to pursue this matter with his father at Oxford was intercepted by the parliamentary committee at Lancaster. The brothers were arrested and taken under guard to London. On 15 April 1644, however, Algernon Sidney was appointed colonel in the earl of Manchester's regiment of horse in the eastern association. His attainment of a parliamentarian command may have been assisted by the king's replacement of Leicester as lord lieutenant (October 1643) with Ormond, while his uncle Northumberland was a leading, if on occasion wavering, parliamentarian peer.

On 2 July, at Marston Moor, Sidney charged

> with much gallantry at the head of my lord's regiment of horse, and came off with much honour, though with many wounds, to the grief of my lord, and many others, who is since gone to London for the cure of his wounds. (*Ash's Intelligence from the Armies in the North*, no. 6)

Forty years later he would be depicted in a ballad declaiming: 'View my Hack'd Limbs, each honourable wound The

Pride and Glory of my numerous Scars in Hell's best Cause the old republic Wars' (*Algernon Sidney's Farewel*, 1683). This action was the baptism by fire of what his *Paper Delivered to the Sheriffs* (1683) would call his adherence to 'that OLD CAUSE in which I was from my youth engaged, and for which thou hast often and wonderfully declared thyself' (Sidney, *Paper Delivered to the Sheriffs*, in *Works*, 39–40). In April 1645 he declined a command in the New Model Army with 'extreame unwillingnesse … by reason of my lamenesse' (BL, Sloane MS 1519, fol. 112). In May he became governor of Chichester, for which Northumberland had served as an MP in the 1620s: the earl's signature headed his letter of appointment. In December 1645 Sidney became MP for Cardiff. Thereafter his votes in the house allied him with Northumberland and others, including Lord Saye and Sele, Sir John Evelyn, and William Pierrepoint. In September 1646 he and his brother Philip carried a banner at the funeral of the earl of Essex. In February 1647 both returned to Ireland, having been appointed respectively governor of Dublin and lord lieutenant of Ireland. After a brief stay in Munster they returned on 21 April, Lisle having been superseded in his command by Lord Inchiquin, lord president of Munster, Algernon Sidney losing his post to Colonel Michael Jones. Instead, in mid-1648 Sidney was appointed to the strategic governorship of Dover Castle.

Republic and protectorate, 1649–1659 In 1659 Sidney was to defend the regicide as 'the justest and bravest act … that ever was done in England, or anywhere' (BL, Add. MS 32680, fols. 9–10). In 1649, however, he disapproved of the army's interference in parliamentary politics as much as he had of that earlier by the king. To the managers of the trial he argued:

> First, the King could be tried by noe court; secondly, that noe man could be tried by that court. This being alleged in vaine, and Cromwell using these formall words (I tell you, wee will cut off his head with the crowne upon it) I … immediately went out of the room, and never returned. (Blencowe, 236–9)

Subsequently in the house he joined Sir Henry Vane jun. and Sir Arthur Hesilrige in speaking against an oath of allegiance which would have approved the judicial proceedings against Charles I. This made 'Cromwell, Bradshawe, Harrison, Lord Grey and others, my enemys, who did from that time continually oppose me' (ibid., 238). It may also have contributed to the rift between Sidney and local army officers which culminated in his replacement as governor of Dover in May 1651. Until late 1651 Sidney's parliamentary attendance was moderate and he served on six or seven committees. The most important was for Irish affairs, in the post conquest settlement of which he played a major role, and upon which by 1653 he was the government's senior authority. For his services in Ireland he was voted £1809 13s. 6d. arrears of pay in October 1649.

From 1652 Sidney's political commitment deepened and he was elected to the council of state in November. His work over the following six months was dominated by foreign affairs (reporting between December and April on meetings with the public ministers of Portugal, Spain,

France, Sweden, Hamburg, Tuscany, Holland, and Austria) and, with Vane, by the First Anglo-Dutch War (1652–4). Vane had worked in naval administration under Northumberland; Sidney was to ascribe to him the invention of 'the Frigat' (Sidney, 'Character'). In this war the two men established a locus of military power alternative to that of the army. Both accordingly featured centrally in the drama of the Rump's ejection by Cromwell on 20 April 1653, of which Sidney left the most important eyewitness account. Thus when he later produced the most striking evocations of the republic's remarkable military achievements he was speaking of a personal experience which furnished the basis of his republican belief.

> [S]uch was the power of wisdom and integrity in those that sat at the helm, and their diligence in choosing men for their merit was blessed with such success, that in two years our fleets grew to be as famous as our land-armies; the reputation and power of our nation rose to a greater height, than when we possessed the better half of France, and the Kings of Scotland and France were our prisoners. All the states, kings and potentates of Europe, most respectfully, not to say submissively, sought our friendship. (Sidney, *Discourses*, in *Works*, 240–41)

Four years of kingless government had turned the Stuart record of military failure on its head.

In 1683 Sidney said of Cromwell: 'you need not wonder I call him a tyrant, I did so every day in his life, and acted against him too'. On 17 June 1656 Lord Lisle complained to his father about 'a play acted' at Penshurst 'of publike affront' to the lord protector during which the audience were so 'exceedingly pleased with the gallant relation of the chief actor in it … that by applauding him they put him severall times upon it' (*De L'Isle and Dudley MSS*, 6.400). Thus grew the legend of Sidney playing Brutus in Shakespeare's *Julius Caesar*. Lisle had been estranged from his father since December 1652 and the principal subject of his letter was the 'extreamest vanity' of 'the younger sonne' who 'now so dominere[s] in your house … [as to] command the whole' (Blencowe, 270–71). Algernon's ascension to the position of *de facto* heir apparent coincided with his rise to republican power. It was no coincidence that his later *Discourses* took as its subject for refutation the primogeniture politics of Sir Robert Filmer's *Patriarcha*. Between 1648 and 1659 he became closely involved with his father's estate and legal affairs. From this developed his entanglement with those of his cousin and (from 1650) brother-in-law Thomas Smith, first Viscount Strangford. By 1655 he had become trustee of Strangford's estate, charged with managing it to clear his debts. In 1657 he became sole resident of Strangford's principal seat of Sterry in Kent. The process of reorganization, mortgage, and sale was still incomplete when, in May 1659, the restored Rump Parliament 'coma[n]ded … [him] into Sweadland in the Quality of a publique minister' (PRO, chancery pleading, C7 327/50).

Baltic ambassador, 1659–1660 In the restored Rump, Sidney's work was again dominated by European (including naval) affairs, alongside Vane, and by the settlement of Ireland. The dominant concern was war between Denmark and Sweden threatening English naval supplies from the Baltic Sound. This was an interest shared with the Dutch, who had lent naval support to Denmark against Charles X of Sweden, a Cromwellian ally. Vane's reorientation of English policy sought Anglo-Dutch co-operation in keeping local control of the sound divided. Sidney left for the sound in June. One of the other plenipotentiaries was Vane's brother-in-law Sir Robert Honeywood. The initial choice as third, Bulstrode Whitelocke, declined partly because 'I knew well the overruling temper and height of Colonel Sydney' (Whitelocke, 4.351). The mission would indeed be dominated by Sidney's unorthodox diplomatic style ('a few shots of our cannon would have made this peace'; Scott, *Republic*, 129). Observers remarked 'We shall soon see the results of such unprecedented methods of negotiation' (*CSP Venice*, 1659–61, 64), and Samuel Puffendorf's *History of the Reign of Charles X* begins a new chapter at this point entitled 'Étrange conduite des ambassadeurs anglois'.

The envoys arrived at Elsinore on 20 July 'avec une magnifique escorte' under the command of the Cromwellian Edward Montague. As the Swedish king was not immediately available to receive them, and although Sidney 'confess[ed]' that this was 'contrary to the ordinary way of ceremony', they began by meeting the Dutch to discuss the creation of a joint fleet capable, if necessary, of imposing peace terms. Relations with Charles X deteriorated rapidly, the king expressing amazement at the English 'wish to command all, as if they were masters' (*CSP Venice*, 1659–61, 66). With the Dutch, Sidney personally handed the king a treaty proposal already accepted by Denmark, and based upon the treaty of Roskilde (1658), threatening military action against the refuser. The king 'in great choler … told us, that we made projects upon our fleets, and he, laying his hand upon his sword, had a project by his side' (Sidney, 'Letters from Thurloe's state papers', in *Works*, 16). 'Everyone is amazed', it was reported, 'how Sidney stood up to him' (F. Guizot, *History of Richard Cromwell*, 2 vols., 1856, 1.160). It was in this context that the new Danish hero signed the visitor's book at the University of Copenhagen, quoted above, furnishing what would become the motto of the state of Massachusetts, USA.

Yet trouble for this strategy was brewing from a crucial direction. When Montague announced his intention of returning with the fleet to England, Sidney gave 'his opinion, [that] for sending away the whole fleet he thought he should deserve to lose his head' (F. R. Harris, *The Life of Edward Montagu*, 2 vols., 1912, 1.149). Although the Venetians reported that the subsequent departure 'does not prevent the English from being held in great respect and practically the arbiters of the whole business' (*CSP Venice*, 1659–61, 90), in practice it severely undermined England's influence. After their capture of the Swedish island of Funen, Sidney's relations with the Dutch cooled. Following the sudden death of Charles X on 12 February 1660 he reported that though 'violently transported by ambition and choller' the Swedish king was in fact 'a man of exceeding good wit, valiant, industrious, vigilant … whoe, by the many and great actions of his short reign deserves to be remembered with honour' (Blencowe, 166, 174–6, 177–8). Despite these and other difficulties a treaty was eventually signed by the Danes, Swedes, and all three mediating powers (including France) on 27 May 1660 which restored something like the *status quo ante* of 1658.

Rome, 1660–1663 Late in 1659 Sidney had begged White-locke for more information concerning the fortunes of 'that cause, which by the help of God I shall never desert' (Blencowe, 170–71). His initial response to the restoration of Charles II was to acknowledge its parliamentary authority.

> Since the Parliament hath acknowledged a king, I knowe … I owe him duty and the service that belongs unto a subject, and will pay it. If things are carried in a legall and moderate way, I had rather be in employment, than without any.
> (ibid., 186)

Yet reports of his opinionated republicanism in Scandinavia had reached the English court. This included not only 'rough' behaviour toward 'the King of Denmark, as also to the King of Sweden', but most damagingly a spirited defence of the regicide. 'If it were true' responded the earl of Leicester, 'he must not thinke of coming into England, when that acsion was so much abhorred by all men, and by me in particular, that am his father' (BL, Add. MS 32680, fols. 9–10). In addition, while prepared to 'submitte', Sidney drew the line at 'acknowledgement of our faults, in having bin against this king, or his father … I shall be better contented with my fortune, when I see theare was noe way of avoiding it, that is not worse than ruine' (Blencowe, 187–8).

> I knowe the titles that are given me of fierce, violent, seditious … turbulent … I know people will say, I straine at knats, and swallow camels; that it is a strange conscience, that lets a man runne violently on, till he is deepe in civill blood, and then stays at a few words and complements … I have enough to answer this in my own minde; I cannot help it if I judge amisse … I walk in the light God hath given me; if it be dimme or uncertaine, I must beare the penalty of my errors: I hope to do it with patience, and that noe burden shall be very grievous to me, except sinne and shame.
> (ibid., 194–8)

On 28 July 1660, after the receipt of letters from England, he resolved against return for the time being. Despite his father's advice that he should live in Hamburg he reported: 'I dislike all the drunken countries of Germany, and the north, and am not much inclined to France. I think I shall choose Italy' (ibid., 195). The earl responded 'what to advise you, truly I knowe not; for you must give me leave to remember, of how little weight my opinions and counsel have been with you … in almost everything' (ibid., 239–40).

In Rome, while Sidney found that the city did not 'beare such signs of Ease, Satisfaction and Plenty' as on his first visit in 1638, 'the Company of Persons excellent in all Sciences, which is the best Thing Strangers can seeke, is never wanting' (Collins, 2.700). An English observer reported: 'Colonel Sidney … has put himself into very great equipage, his coach and three lackeys; he is very gracious with some of the Cardinals, which some impute to his own Parts and wit, others to some recommendation

from [Christina] the [ex] Queen of Sweade', whom Sidney had met in Hamburg (*Egmont MSS*, 1.616). With the cardinals, particularly Christina's friend Azzolini, he became sufficiently familiar to send his father 'Characters' of them in April 1661. 'I have much more Aquaintance amongst the prelates, than the nobility of this place,' he reported, 'the most auncient Familyes [here], have lost all the Vigour and Virtue of their Auncestors' (Collins, 2.705). By mid-1661 he was living at the Villa de Belvedere at Frascati, at the invitation of Prince Pamphili, nephew of the previous pope.

> I … live now as a Hermite in a Palace. Nature, Art and Treasure, can hardly make a place more pleasant than this … In theis last Monethe … I have applied myself to studdy, a littel more thaen I have done formerly; and … I find soe much Satisfaction in it, that for the future I shall very unwillingly … put myself into any [other] Way of living.
> (ibid., 2.718–21)

Yet his contentment did not last. There was his isolation 'when I wander as a Vagabond through the World, forsaken of my Friends, poore, and knowne only to be a broken Limbe of a Ship-wrecked Faction' (ibid., 2.720). There was the 'Ruin of my Fortune' in England, reducing him to financial dependence upon a father 'lesse carefull to give me some reliefe, than I hope[d]' (Blencowe, 190). This was particularly painful 'in a Place farre from Home … wheare I am knowne to be of a Quality, which makes all lowe and meane Wayes of living shamefull and detestable' (Collins, 2.717). Finally Sidney would complain that although he had 'hoped that noe man would … disturbe me in a most innocent exile … I was defended from such as [in Rome] designed to assassinate me, only by the charity of strangers' (Sidney, *Apology*, in *Works*, 3).

The exiles, 1663–1666 In mid-1663, on his way to the Low Countries, Sidney visited Edmund Ludlow and other exiles at Vevey. Although his *Apology in the Day of his Death* later claimed that this trip was for 'the care of my private affaires' (Sidney, *Apology*, in *Works*, 3), Ludlow recorded that Sidney 'Now thinkes it seasonable to draw toward his Native Country, in Expectation of an Opportunity wherein he might be more Active … [in republican] Service' (Ludlow, 977). After presenting his host with a pair of Italian pistols, and thanking the magistrates of Bern for their care of the exiles, he visited the Calvinist academy at the University of Geneva where he inscribed the visitor's book: 'SIT SANGUINIS ULTOR JUSTORUM' ('Let there be revenge for the blood of the just'; C. Borgeaud, *Histoire de l'Université de Genève*, 5 vols., 1900–59, 1.442–3). This was the blood not only of the regicides but in particular of Vane, executed in 1662 ('noble Vane … thy death gave thee a famous victory and a never perishing Crown'; Sidney, *Court Maxims*, 49). In Brussels in December Sidney sat for the portrait by Justus van Egmont which was later hung at Penshurst. From Brussels he informed Leicester of his thoughts of spending 'the next summer as a Volunteere in Hungary' (Collins, 2.725). His hopes of transporting there 'a good strong Boddy of the best Officers and Soldiers of our old Army' may have connected to another plan closer at hand. In early 1664 in the United Provinces, however, he found 'the spirits of those who understood seasons farre better than I … not to be fully prepared' (Blencowe, 259–60). He retreated to Augsburg, where, in April 1665, he was the target of another assassination attempt.

Thereafter Sidney returned to the United Provinces: 'Certaine I can have no peace in my owne spirite, if I doe not endeavour by all meanes possible to advance the interest of God's people'. The context for this renewed hope was the Second Anglo-Dutch War (1665–7). Burnet recorded: 'Algernon Sidney … came to de Wit, and pressed him to think of an invasion of England and Scotland … and they were bringing many officers to Holland to join in the undertaking' (BL, Add. MS 63057, 1.393). Ludlow was reluctant to join the Dutch, whom he blamed for the failure to protect the regicides Okey, Corbet, and Barkstead, kidnapped in Delft in 1662 by the English ambassador, Sir George Downing. In early 1666 Sidney's entreaties to his colleague culminated in a 'Letter stuffed with Invectives from the beginning to the End. Justifying the Dutch in what they did as to the delivery of our three freinds to be butchered', and accusing Ludlow of fixing himself 'unmoveably upon your own Imaginations, grounded upon the vainest, and most frivolous mistaken Informations that can possibly be given in things of such Importance' (Ludlow, 1079–80, 1105). Sidney's other problem was the English republic's own previous military record. As De Witt asked: 'What would the effect be of turning England into a Commonwealth, if it could possibly be brought about, but the ruin of Holland?' (BL, Add. MS 63057, 1.393). By the middle of the year Sidney was in Paris, where the young Louis XIV, a Dutch ally, recorded: 'Sidney, an English gentleman, promised me to produce a great uprising … but the proposition he put to me to advance him 100,000 ecus … was more than I wished to expose on the word of a fugitive [so] I offered him [initially] only 20,000' (Louis XIV, *Mémoires Pour les années 1661 et 1666*, ed. J. Lognon, 1923, 213). As divisions among the exiles continued, and following a failed attempt, with French assistance, to spring John Lambert from prison on Jersey, Sidney received a pass from the French king to retire to Montpellier.

Court Maxims, 1665–1666 The most important literary product of 1665–6 was Sidney's *Court Maxims*, not published until 1996. Emotionally more intense than the later *Discourses*, its objective is the same: to argue for rebellion against the restored monarchy. In the process, particularly by its use of Grotius, it anticipates key features of Locke's as well as Sidney's later classic justifications of resistance. As the most important surviving attack upon the restoration process it seeks to persuade the English people that 'nothing is more reasonable than that they should repent of their choice *and endeavour to unmake what they have made*' (Sidney, *Court Maxims*, 7). In particular it appeals to the godly to resist the restoration of religious persecution.

> Who will endure that bishops, the greatest incendiaries in the whole world, should now preach the highest meekness? They who said it was better that all the streets in England and Scotland should run with blood than that the power of the clergy be diminished, say now, it is better that England should be dispeopled, and the best men in the nation banished and destroyed, than that their lusts should be resisted … At this day we find none to espouse … [non-resistance] but our Quakers, some few Anabaptists in Holland and Germany, and some … Socinians in Poland. … all christian churches have … made use of the sword … against such princes and their ministers as have governed contrary to law.   (ibid., 101–3)

More broadly the *Court Maxims* is a systematic assault upon monarchy: 'as death is *the greatest evil that can befall a person, monarchy is the worst evil that can befall a nation*' (Sidney, *Court Maxims*, 20). This involves deploying an argument in interest language common to English and Dutch antimonarchism. As monarchy is private interest government and republicanism government in the public interest each is 'irreconcileably contrary' to the other. The maxims of monarchy, in both domestic and international affairs, inevitably oppose the public interest of a nation. '[A]ll people grow proud when numerous and rich … The least injury puts them into a fury. But if poor, weak, miserable and few they will be humble and obedient' (ibid., 72). On the basis of this analysis, developed from Machiavelli's *Discourses*, book 2, chapter 1, Sidney asserts an Anglo-Dutch republican 'unity of interest' in 'extirpat[ing]' the two detested families of Stuart and Orange' (ibid., 176). Finally to the 'maxims' of princes the *Court Maxims* opposes the classical republican life of virtuous self-government.

> We need seek no other definition of a happy human life in relation to this world than that set down by Aristotle as the end of civil societies, namely, that men may in them enjoy *vita beata secundum virtutem* (Aristotle, *Politics*, bk III). For as there is no happiness without liberty, and no man more a slave than he that is overmastered by vicious passions, there is neither liberty, nor happiness, where there is not virtue. (ibid., 24)

France, 1666–1677 Sidney spent most of his exile in a country in which he had previously not only lived but been educated. His later return to England he intended to be temporary, before final settlement in Gascony. In 1683 he was to inform his English fellow conspirators of the French saying that 'He who draws his sword against his prince … ought to throw away the scabbard' (Scott, *Crisis*, 289). The *Discourses* praises the readiness of the French nobility to act 'in the defence and vindication of their violated liberties … [if] the king … do [anything] against their laws' (Sidney, *Discourses*, in *Works*, 254–5). Above all those families listed as having rebelled in the past 'fifty years … the houses of Conde, Soissons, Montmorency, Guise, Vendome, Angoulesme, Bouillon, Rohan, Longueville, Rochefoucault, Espernon' include most of Sidney's own French associates. Rohan had been a friend of the earl of Leicester. Most important to Sidney were de Bouillon, Turenne, and De la Rochefoucauld, principal powers of the southwest and survivors of the noble Fronde (1650–52).

From Montpellier in 1666 Sidney sent his Quaker friend Benjamin Furly in Rotterdam his transcription of 'A Prophesy of St Thomas the Martyr' (Bodl. Oxf., MS Eng. lett. C200, fols. 24–5). He argued violently with a local doctor whose services had not pleased him ('A physician does not exercise his art for himself, but for his patients'; Sidney, *Discourses*, in *Works*, 342). He sought the assistance of Sir William Temple, ambassador in Brussels, in the passage of letters to his uncle Northumberland. In 1670 he paid an extended visit to Paris, coinciding with one by the Northumberland family. During the same period he called upon Turenne at Versailles and made, through him, an attempt to 'render his services to … the King of Great Britain', advising his majesty to found his 'security' upon the provision of 'liberty of conscience' to all his subjects (Paris, Archives du Ministère des Affaires Étrangères, du Roy à Colbet, 29 July 1670). While rejecting this overture by 'a man of great courage and spirit, though also the most opinionated republican he had in his realm', Charles nevertheless attempted to implement this advice two years later (PRO, Baschet correspondence 31/3, no. 125, 4 Aug 1670). About the same year Sidney retired to Nérac, in Gascony, within the duchy D'Albret of Turenne's nephew Maurice-Godefroi de la Tour, duc de Bouillon. Bouillon's grandfather was the Huguenot Henri de la Tour, 'ancien compagnon d'Henri IV, marechal de France' and friend of Philippe Du Plessis Mornay. A letter written from Nérac in early 1677 informs us that Sidney occupied himself with riding and hunting, advising the duc de Bouillon about the corruption of his local officials, and visiting De la Rochefoucauld at his seat at Verteuil. It was during another visit to Paris in late 1676 that Sidney met his greatnephew George Savile, and the boy's uncle Henry Savile. From Nérac on 18 December he wrote to the latter that he did 'not value the leave you have obtained for me to return into my country after so long an absence, at a lower rate than the saving of my life' (Sidney, 'Letters to Savile', in *Works*, 56–7). On his way back to England the following year Sidney had the series of conversations with Jean-Baptiste Lantin about his political experiences and opinions which remain recorded in the Bibliothèque Nationale, Fr MS 23254, fols. 99–101.

Family politics and Restoration crisis, 1677–1683 In 1678 Sidney explained: 'my desir of being … somme service unto my old father perswaded me to ask leave to comme over' (Forster, 79–80). He returned in early September 1677 and Leicester died on 2 November. Thereafter, he wrote:

> I have no other businessse heare then to cleare some small contests that are growne between one of my brothers and me concerning that which he hath left me, and [then to] retire from hence … to purchase a convenient habitation in Gascony … where I may in quiet finish thoes days that God hath appointed for me. (ibid.)

In the event, in the words of his *Apology*:

> When I prepared myself to return into Guascony … I was hindered by the earl of Leicester my brother, who questioned all that my father had given me for my subsistence; and by a long and tedious suite in chancery, detained me in England, until I was made a prisoner.

In fact Robert Sidney's provision for his younger sons Algernon and Henry was punitively generous. Algernon collected £5000 immediately, but was forced to seek a remaining £5000, plus various rents and annuities, through proceedings in chancery. Pending settlement,

and as executors of the earl's estate, Henry took up residence at Penshurst, and Algernon at Leicester House in London. It was from there that he became drawn into the gathering political crisis.

Naturally one aspect of this involvement consisted of contacts with the French ambassador, Barillon. On 6 October Barillon reported:

> At the moment my most intimate liaison is with Mr. Algernon Sidney; he is the man in England who seems to me to have the greatest understanding of affairs; he has great relations with the rest of the Republican party; And nobody in my opinion is more capable of rendering service than him. (Paris, Archives du Ministère des Affaires Étrangères, correspondance politique, Angleterre XLI)

After assisting the French-engineered fall of Danby in December 1678 Sidney received a payment of 500 guineas, and another a year later. Over the following three years, through the French ambassadors in England and the United Provinces, he sought to construct an Anglo-Dutch republican alternative to Stuart–Orange foreign policy. Equally he attempted to convince Barillon 'that it is an old error to believe that it is against the interest of France to suffer England to become a republic' (Dalrymple, 2, appx, 313). Meanwhile Barillon reported Sidney's involvement with the politics of London:

> He is in the party of the independents and other sectaries … [who] were masters during the late troubles … they are strong in London … and it is through the intrigues of … Sidney that one of the two sheriffs, named Bethel, has been elected. (PRO, Baschet correspondence, 147, 402–3)

In 1679 the post-Danby court was dominated by two nephews of Sidney's, Halifax and Sunderland, and one cousin, Essex. Over the following five years close relationships with the former two gave way to a treasonable partnership with the latter. Until 1681 the other aspect of Sidney's personal political involvement was parliamentary. Despite his earlier promise to the king to steer clear of politics, he stood as a candidate in all three parliamentary elections of this period. His ally in these campaigns was the Quaker William Penn, to whom he may have been introduced by their mutual friend Benjamin Furly. Despite an apparent victory at Amersham in August 1679 described by William Harrington as 'the most remarkable thing about the[se] elections' (*Fitzherbert MSS*, 19), the result was disputed. A by-election was ordered in December 1680, the result of which was never adjudged by the interrupted Oxford parliament. Accordingly Sidney's influence upon the parliamentary campaign of this period was wielded primarily through his close friendship with the person who emerged as the leader of the House of Commons by late 1680: Sir William Jones. Following the king's dissolution of his last parliament at Oxford in April 1681 *A Just and Modest Vindication of the Proceedings of the Two Last Parliaments* (1681), called by Burnet 'the best writ paper in all that time … was at first penned by Sidney … and corrected by Jones' (*Burnet's History*, 2.276–7).

Discourses, 1681–1683 Many echoes of the *Vindication* appear in Sidney's *Discourses Concerning Government*, written between 1681 and 1683. Although long and sometimes repetitive the *Discourses* places Sidney alongside Milton as the master of republican eloquence. It is the power of its prose, as much as any aspect of its content, which helps to account for the work's exceptional subsequent impact in Britain, continental Europe, and America. Polemically a refutation of Sir Robert Filmer's *Patriarcha* (1680), the practical purpose of the *Discourses* is again to argue for armed resistance to oppression.

> If the laws of God and men are therefore of no effect, when the magistracy is left at liberty to break them, and if the lusts of those, who are too strong for the tribunals of justice, cannot otherwise be restrained, than by seditions, tumults, and war, those seditions, tumults and wars, are justified by the laws of God and man … they who deny this deny all help against an usurping tyrant, or the perfidiousness of a lawfully created magistrate, who adds the crimes of ingratitude and treachery to usurpation. (Sidney, *Discourses*, in *Works*, 188, 193–4)

Beyond this task, which includes the only explicit seventeenth-century defence of 'rebellion', both word and thing, the *Discourses* has three notable features. One is the most sustained English development of Machiavelli's republican militarism: 'when a people multiplies, as they will always do in a good climate under a good government, such an enlargement of their territory, as is necessary for their subsistence, can only be acquired by war' (ibid., 178–9). The second is its related defence of change.

> Changes are … unavoidable … To affirm [otherwise] … is no less than to render the understanding given to men utterly useless … whatever we enjoy, beyond the misery in which our barbarous ancestors lived, is due only to the liberty of correcting what was amiss in their practice, or inventing that which they did not know. (ibid., 304–5, 404)

The third is its defence of the principles (liberty, reason, and virtue) informing that classical moral philosophy which established the necessity of republican political architecture. Finally the *Discourses*, like the *Court Maxims*, was a defence of something going on in Sidney's life in practice. This was that self-defence of protestants, against persecution and popery, in which his ancestors had long been involved, and which had once again become necessary in England following the loyalist reaction.

Imprisonment, trial, and execution From February 1683, following the death of the earl of Shaftesbury, Sidney and his friends, the younger John Hampden, the earl of Essex, and Lord Howard, became involved in treasonable discussions with Shaftesbury's associates Lord Russell and the duke of Monmouth. As in 1665 Sidney's plan was for a 'war in both kingdoms', beginning this time with a rebellion by the persecuted godly people of Scotland, which would, as in 1640, force the summoning of an English parliament upon a militarily ineffective arbitrary monarch. When the legal crackdown began in mid-1683 Sidney's arrest warrant was the first to be issued, on June 25. During the arrest a copy of the *Discourses* was discovered in his house and also taken into custody. Alongside an embellished subsequent 'confession' by Howard, the government lacked a second witness to Sidney's treason. There followed several months in the Tower while it attempted to construct a case.

During this period Sidney wrote a series of letters to his fellow prisoner John Hampden. These stressed the innocence of their actions, involving nothing

> which doth not agree with the Character of gentleman and Christian … Somme say the protestants of Holland, France, or … Piedmont were guilty of treason, in bearing arms against their princes, but [this] is ridiculous … when it is certaine, they sought noe more than the security of their own lives. (E. Sussex RO, Glynde Place MS 794, letter 1, 6 October)

They made detailed preparations for any future trial, 'confident', however, in the absence of a second witness, 'that such rules being observed as the law requires, it is not possible to bring us into danger, though they could bring Jezabel's witnesses from hell to strengthen the Ld Ho[wa]rds testimony' (ibid., letter 7). This confidence disappeared in late October when an application by the prisoners for release under the provisions of the Habeas Corpus Act forced the government to determine its legal strategy. This was, remarkably, to use the manuscript *Discourses* as the second witness against Sidney: in the famous ruling of Lord Chief Justice Jeffreys: 'Scribere est agere' ('to write is to act'). 'I could hardly believe he had said this', recorded Burnet, 'till I read it in the Printed Tryall' (BL, Add. MS 63057, 2.158).

Sidney was arraigned on 7 November and tried, amid great public interest, on 21 November. His defence was legally weak, but politically extremely effective. At the insistence of his counsel his defence depended upon the attempt to deny authorship of words and actions which he would rather have owned. In practice the defence strategy may have been almost powerless to affect the outcome, given the role being played in this crisis by treason trials in general, and by politically selected juries in particular. Of this fact, as Jeffreys pointed out, Sidney was more aware than anyone, having earlier helped his friends Sheriff Bethel and Attorney-General Jones to develop this system. Under these circumstances, given his inability to save his life, his achievement became to expose as much as possible of what was taking place in order to do the government lasting harm. He drew attention to the political selection of the jury, to his own aristocratic ancestry, and to the extraordinary invocation of the death sentence for possession of an unpublished manuscript. While giving a fine display of stoic indifference to his personal fate, he raised a series of procedural objections, drawing attention to the wider fate of later Stuart political legality. Throughout the trial and at the arraignment he confronted the lord chief justice personally, depicting him as a social inferior and an irascible bully ('Lest the means of destroying the best protestants in England should fail, the bench must be filled with such as had been blemishes to the bar' (Sidney, *Paper Delivered to the Sheriffs*, in *Works*). Thus if 'The scandale of this Tryall was so gross that I never met with a man that offered to defend it' (BL, Add. MS 63057, 2.158); if it laid the basis for the subsequent fame both of the *Discourses* and its author; and if the execution which followed was the last in this series for this reason, these were largely Sidney's personal achievements. As his uncle Halifax said two years later: 'Westminster Hall might be said to stand upon its head ... when the reason of him that pleads is visibly too strong for those who are to judge and give sentence' (H. C. Foxcroft, *The Life and Letters of George Savile, Bart., First Marquis of Halifax*, 2 vols., 1898, 2.285–6).

Between sentence, passed on 26 November, and his execution, on 7 December, Sidney extended this public campaign. His *Apology* elaborated the case against the trial and set it in the context of his lifelong struggle

> to uphold the Common rights of mankind, the lawes of this land, and the true Protestant religion, against corrupt principles, arbitrary power and Popery ... I doe now willingly lay down my life for the same; and having a sure witness within me, that God doth ... uphold me ... am very littell sollicitous, though man doth condemne me. (Sidney, *Apology*, in *Works*)

Finally his paper delivered to the sheriffs on the scaffold sensationally owned the principles informing the *Discourses*. Having given the *Apology* to his servant Joseph Ducasse for transmission to posterity, he made sure to consign copies of the paper 'to my friends'. Within a few days 'the Town was full of written copys' (BL, Add. MS 63057, 2.158–9) and the government was forced to accede to a publication which attracted many replies. Sidney was beheaded on Tower Hill on the morning of 7 December 1683. On the scaffold he explained that he had come 'not to talk, but die ... I have nothing to say to men' (*Account ... of what Passed at Algernon Sidney's Execution*, 1683). The following day the king gave permission for his burial in 'the sepulchar of his family' in the parish church at Penshurst (*CSP dom.*, 1683–4, 138).

Biographical fortune and historical significance During his heyday as a whig patriot–hero and martyr Sidney was the subject of many biographies, some appended to editions of the *Discourses* (of which there were at least fourteen between 1698 and 1805). That of G. W. Meadley, *Memoirs of Algernon Sidney* (1813), may be considered the best, and the fullest A. C. Ewald, *The Life and Times of Algernon Sidney* (2 vols., 1873). From 1885 he disappeared from view until in 1945 and 1947 two American scholars, Zera Fink and Caroline Robbins, laid the basis of twentieth-century interest in his political writings. Since 1985 a dramatic resurgence of work on both his life and thought has yielded six books and many articles, among which Blair Worden's 'The Commonwealth Kidney of Algernon Sidney' (published in the *Journal of British Studies*, 24, 1985) was the first, and Jonathan Scott's two-volume study is the most comprehensive. With this have come numerous manuscript discoveries including that of the *Court Maxims*.

It owed much to the high profile given to the *Discourses* by Sidney's martyrdom that for subsequent influence in Enlightenment Britain, America, the United Provinces, Germany, and France he had no seventeenth-century rival except John Locke. For modern scholars his claim to a major place among early modern political writers rests upon two foundations. The first, alongside Locke, is as one of the two pre-eminent seventeenth-century English

resistance theorists, a status underlined by the recovery of the *Court Maxims*. The other is as the most influential of the English republicans. In particular his works exemplify two features of seventeenth-century English republicanism. The first is its debt, within a religious framework, to the moral philosophy of Greek antiquity (its Christian humanism). The second is its Machiavellian and Roman militarism. JONATHAN SCOTT

Sources A. Sidney, *Sydney on government: the works of Algernon Sydney*, ed. J. Robertson (1772) [incl. *Discourses concerning government; The apology of Algernon Sydney in the day of his death; The arraignment, trial and condemnation of Algernon Sydney; The very copy of a paper delivered to the sheriffs*; 'Letters of Algernon Sydney taken from the Sydney Papers'; 'Letters of Algernon Sydney taken from the state papers of John Thurloe'; 'Letters to Henry Savile jnr'] · A. Sidney, *Court maxims*, ed. H. Blom, E. H. Mulier, and R. Janse (1996) · J. Scott, *Algernon Sidney and the English republic, 1623–1677* (1988) · J. Scott, *Algernon Sidney and the Restoration crisis, 1677–1683* (1991) · H. Sydney and others, *Letters and memorials of state*, ed. A. Collins, 2 vols. (1746) · *Report on the manuscripts of Lord De L'Isle and Dudley*, 6 vols., HMC, 77 (1925–66) · R. Blencowe, ed., *Sydney papers* (1825) · A. Sidney, letters, 1683, E. Sussex RO, Glynde Place archives, no. 794 · CKS, De Lisle papers · T. Forster, ed., *Original letters of Locke, Algernon Sidney, and Anthony Lord Shaftesbury* (1830) · 'Lantiniana', Bibliothèque Nationale, Paris, Fr MS 23254 · PRO, Baschet correspondence 31/3, nos.125, 140–56 · *Bishop Burnet's History of his own time: with the suppressed passages of the first volume*, ed. M. J. Routh, 6 vols. (1823) · transcript of Burnet's 'History', BL, Add. MS 63057, 2 vols. · Sidney MSS, BL, Add. MS 32680 · E. Ludlow, 'A voyce from the watch tower', Bodl. Oxf., MS Eng. hist. c. 487 · A. Sidney, 'The character of Henry Vane jnr', in V. A. Rowe, *Sir Henry Vane the younger: a study in political and administrative history* (1970), appx F · J. Dalrymple, *Memoirs of Great Britain and Ireland*, 3 vols. (1771–8), vol. 2, appx · Algernon Sidney chancery pleading, PRO, C7 327/50 · [A. Sidney and W. Jones], 'A just and modest vindication of the proceedings of the two last parliaments' (1681), 4 *State tracts of the reign of Charles II* (1689), 4, appx 15 · correspondance politique, Angleterre, Archives du Ministère des Affaires Étrangères, Paris · Algernon Sidney to Monsieur Bafoy, Archives Nationales, Paris, R2/82 · B. Whitelocke, *Memorials of English affairs*, new edn, 4 vols. (1853) · *The journal of Edward Mountagu, first earl of Sandwich, admiral and general at sea, 1659–1665*, ed. R. C. Anderson, Navy RS, 64 (1929) · earl of Tankerville [F. Grey], *The secret history of the Rye House plot* (1754) · B. Haydon, 'Algernon Sidney, 1623–83', *Archaeologia Cantiana*, 76 (1961), 110–33 · *DNB* · *CSP dom.*, 1683–4, 138 · *Report on the manuscripts of the earl of Egmont*, 2 vols. in 3, HMC, 63 (1905–9) · *The manuscripts of Sir William Fitzherbert ... and others*, HMC, 32 (1893)

Archives S. Antiquaries, Lond., MS notes · Sevenoaks Library, Kent, MSS | Chatsworth House, Derbyshire, Halifax collection, A.1–14 · Chatsworth House, Derbyshire, letters to Henry Savile · CKS, letters to his father · CKS, De Lisle MSS · E. Sussex RO, Glynde Place archives, letters to John Hampden, no. 794 · PRO, chancery court pleadings, C5–C10 · Yale U., Beinecke L., letters to Benjamin Furly

Likenesses I. W., oils, 1647; Sothebys, 14 March 1990 · J. Hoskins, miniature, 1659, FM Cam. · J. Van Egmont, oils, 1663, Penshurst Place, Kent; copy, NPG · G. Bower, silver medal, BM · J. Hoskins, miniatures, Buccleuch estates, Selkirk · attrib. J. Van Egmont, portrait; Christies New York, August 2002 [*see illus.*] · oils, Anglesey Abbey, Cambridgeshire

Wealth at death estate forfeit to crown upon conviction for treason 1683; last known letter, written between 22 and 25 Nov 1683, enclosed gifts totalling £1883 to an unidentified 'dear friend and kinsman': Glynde Place archives no. 794, letter 10, E. Sussex RO

Sidney [*née* Gamage], **Barbara, countess of Leicester** (*c*.1559–1621), noblewoman, was the only child of John

Gamage (d. 1584), lord of the manor of Coety in Glamorgan, and his wife, Gwenllian, daughter of Sir Thomas ap Jenkin Powell of Glynogwr and widow of Watkin Thomas. On her father's death in September 1584 Barbara's marriage became an important bargaining counter in Welsh political infighting. She was courted by her cousins Thomas Jones of Abermarlais, Sir James Whitney of Whitney, and Herbert Croft of Croft Castle; the privy council and Lord Burghley (acting in his capacity as master of the wards) and her influential uncles Sir Walter Ralegh and Lord Howard of Effingham sent contradictory instructions. But her guardian, Sir Edward Stradling, succumbed to even more powerful persuasions and accepted the suit of Robert *Sidney (1563–1626), younger brother of Sir Philip Sidney. Robert's father, Sir Henry *Sidney, was lord president of the council in the marches (and the leading opponent of the Croft faction on the council) and the family was connected by marriage with the earl of Leicester, Sir Francis Walsingham, and the earl of Pembroke. According to one tradition, it was Barbara who was attracted to young Sidney and persuaded her guardian to approve him. More conventional accounts emphasize that Barbara was married within weeks of her father's death to a man she had probably never met before, and one whose family connections were diametrically opposed to her own.

Whichever version of events is nearer the truth, it was apparently a happy and successful marriage. Barbara Sidney's local influence provided Robert with the county seat for Glamorgan in the parliaments of 1584–5 and 1593, and her estates helped to restore the Sidneys' overstretched finances. She may have accompanied him on the campaign of 1585–6 in which his elder brother, Philip, was killed. She certainly went with him to Flushing, where he was governor, in 1590 and 1592 and again in 1597–8. Her early experiences may have left her vulnerable and insecure: on the rare occasions when they were apart, Robert's letters to her are full of anxious reassurance. Unfortunately, none of her letters to him has survived, though there are references to them in letters from others. It is even possible that she was unable to write and dictated her letters to an amanuensis, though the personal tone of Robert's letters to her suggests they were written for her own eyes.

As both her confidence and their family grew (she and Robert had eleven children, including Robert *Sidney and the poet Lady Mary *Wroth), Barbara Sidney spent more time at Penshurst, with occasional and reluctant visits to London. At Penshurst she kept house in the traditional Welsh manner with a household that was unfashionably large by English standards. She seems to have been equally unfashionable in her devotion to her children. She was unwilling to leave them in England when she visited the Netherlands, and she kept her eldest son at home long after her husband considered he should have been sent to a tutor. While Sidney was absent in Flushing she was his representative at court and with the influential members of their family connection, especially with his sister, the gifted and distinguished Mary Herbert,

countess of Pembroke. Barbara appears never to have returned to Wales after her marriage, though she maintained her connections there and Sidney planned to send her there for safety during the Armada crisis. She died in 1621, and was buried at Penshurst on 26 May 1621.

MADELEINE GRAY

Sources *Report on the manuscripts of Lord De L'Isle and Dudley*, 2–5, HMC, 77 (1933–62) • G. Williams, ed., *Glamorgan county history*, 4: *Early modern Glamorgan* (1974) • J. M. Traherne, ed., *Stradling correspondence: a series of letters written in the reign of Queen Elizabeth* (1840) • DWB • HoP, *Commons, 1558–1603* • G. T. Clark, *Limbus patrum Morganiae et Glamorganiae* (1886) • R. Denning, ed., *The story of St. Donat's Castle and Atlantic College* (1983)

Sidney, Sir Henry (1529–1586), lord deputy of Ireland and courtier, was the eldest and only surviving son of Sir William Sidney and Anne (d. 1543), daughter of Sir Hugh Pagenham and widow of Thomas Fitzwilliam, elder brother of William Fitzwilliam, earl of Southampton; he was born, probably at Baynard's Castle, London, on 20 July 1529.

His father, **Sir William Sidney** (c.1482–1554), courtier, was the son of Nicholas Sidney and Anne, sister of Sir William Brandon, father of Charles, duke of Suffolk. The Sidneys were Sussex–Surrey landowners who acquired wealth and local eminence in the mid-fifteenth century. William Sidney entered court through the patronage of his maternal uncle, Sir Thomas Brandon, a prominent courtier under Henry VII and his son. William Sidney lived with his uncle until the latter's death in 1510. In 1511 he attended Lord Darcy on his abortive expedition to aid Spain against the Moors, lingering after Darcy's rapid return to England in a visit to the Spanish court, where he was reputedly offered and declined a knighthood.

Some time before 1512 Sidney became an esquire of the body. For the following decades he pursued a career which combined martial and courtly pursuits. In 1513 he commanded the right wing at Flodden, for which he received a life annuity of 50 marks. In 1512 and 1513 he captained a ship royal and fought in battle against the French off Brest, where he was knighted, on 18 April 1513. During 1514 he was the agent of his cousin, the duke of Suffolk, in the Low Countries, where he had gone to learn the language with a royal letter of recommendation. He was closely involved in Suffolk's affairs when the duke secretly married Princess Mary in Paris. In the following years he served Wolsey as a messenger in French business. He was prominent in the tiltyard in these years, and served as captain in Suffolk's 1523 expedition. In 1517 he married Anne Fitzwilliam. For his career in later years the evidence is scant, but it involved service on investigating commissions and on juries during the Pilgrimage of Grace, and supervision of coastal defences. In 1538 his service was rewarded with office when he was appointed chamberlain of Prince Edward's household; in 1544 he was advanced to be steward to the prince. He was also awarded the Garter in 1542.

Sidney benefited handsomely from the royal bounty; as early as 1514 he had a grant in tail male of two Yorkshire manors, Kingston upon Hull and Myton. In 1521 he

Sir Henry Sidney (1529–1586), attrib. Arnold Bronckorst, 1573

became keeper of the scales in London, a post he held for ten years. In 1539 he exchanged the Yorkshire properties for the lands of Robertsbridge Abbey in Kent and Sussex. (He sold off his inherited lands in Surrey.) To these were added in 1541 the lands of St Swithin's Priory in Hampshire. Finally, in 1552 his royal master gave him Penshurst in Kent. He had the keepership of the honour of Otford and Knole with an annual fee, and he shared in the disposal of the Brandon lands after Duke Charles's death.

Sidney fathered, besides Henry, four daughters: Mary, wife to Sir William Dormer and mother to Jane Dormer [see Suárez de Figueroa, Jane, duchess of Feria]; Lucy, wife to Sir James Harrington of Exton, Rutland; Anne, wife to Sir William *Fitzwilliam; and Frances *Radcliffe, wife to Thomas, third earl of Sussex. His wife predeceased him, dying on 22 October 1543; he died of the stone at Penshurst on 10 February 1554 and was buried in the parish church.

Early career Henry Sidney was eight years senior to the young prince whose constant companion he became from 1538, when his father became chamberlain to the prince of Wales. He shared in the royal education and when Edward became king, the companionship continued, Sidney becoming one of the principal gentlemen of the privy

chamber. In October 1551 he was knighted, significantly at the ceremonies attending John Dudley's creation as duke of Northumberland. Nine months earlier (29 March 1551) Sidney had married Mary (d. 1586), Dudley's only daughter. Northumberland obviously thought his son-in-law's closeness to the new king an asset worth acquiring. From Sidney's point of view his marriage meant access to the innermost political circle. His father-in-law made use of him in confidential state business; in early 1553 he was sent on a mission to France to sound out Henri II on the prospect of English mediation between France and the emperor. (Sidney commanded both French and Italian.) In the parliament of 1547 he sat for Brackley; in that of 1553 for Kent. This hopeful phase of Sidney's career ended with Edward's death, in his arms—yet in spite of his Dudley ties, Sidney speedily disentangled himself from their misfortunes. He had a pardon from Mary before the end of July 1553, followed by a confirmation of most of his father's land grants. (He had to surrender a deathbed grant from Edward.)

In the new reign Sidney accompanied the earl of Bedford's mission to Spain to obtain Philip's signature to the marriage treaty. He probably owed this appointment to his language skills. Purportedly Sidney's private mission was to solicit pardon for his brothers-in-law. Sidney clearly gained Philip's goodwill, and on 30 November 1554 the king stood godfather to his first son, Philip *Sidney. He would have been sent as agent to the emperor to report the birth of a royal child had that occurred. Sidney's acceptance into the Marian court may have owed something to the influence of his niece, Jane Dormer, Mary's lady-in-waiting and prospective wife of the Spanish envoy, the duke of Feria. She and Sidney were to maintain a correspondence in later years.

In 1555 Sidney found a new patron to his career. He accompanied his new brother-in-law, Thomas *Radcliffe, earl of Sussex, to Ireland where in 1556 the latter took up the office of lord deputy. Sidney went as vice-treasurer of Ireland and second in command. Sussex spent long intervals in England when Sidney, as lord justice, was his substitute. In the two years 1557–9 he stood in for the deputy some sixteen to seventeen months.

The Dudley connection In the new reign Sidney realigned his court connection, now that the Dudley star was ascendant, his brother-in-law Robert *Dudley prime favourite in the new court. He resigned his Irish office (to another brother-in-law, Fitzwilliam). Sidney was now enlisted in the Dudley following, a tie which would endure for decades. In 1565 he would write to Leicester (as he now was), 'I care not in regard of any subject your enemy in England but would be accounted a feather in your wing and a principal one too' (CSP dom., addenda, 1547–65, 524). In Ireland, as a token of loyalty, Sidney would display on his personal standard the bear and the ragged staff of the Dudleys. Loyalty to his brother-in-law did not preclude good working relationships with other councillors, most notably Cecil and later Walsingham. Indeed in 1569 there was a negotiation for a match between Philip Sidney and Cecil's daughter, although it did not materialize.

Yet, even if Sidney benefited richly from Leicester's patronage, there was a price to pay. When Sidney went to Ireland he found himself entangled in the strings of his brother-in-law's other patronage dealings. The new deputy was perforce linked to Leicester's Geraldine protégés, the earls of Kildare and Desmond, and correspondingly an enemy of the powerful Butler interest, privileged by the queen's favour to her kinsman Ormond. The hostility of the latter lord in turn frustrated Sidney's own Irish policy. Similarly the Leicester–Sussex feud made attacks on his conduct in Ireland an issue in the partisan slanging match at court, filling the royal ear with allegations Sidney was ill-situated to counter.

In 1559 Sidney was soon pressed into the service of his brother-in-law Robert. He and his wife, one of the queen's ladies, were put to work as go-betweens with the Spanish ambassador, De Quadra. Initially it was Lady Sidney, who spoke Italian, who pressed the ambassador, in her brother's name, to back the Austrian marriage. There was talk of her husband going to Spain to advance the cause, or alternatively to the emperor. Then the death of Amy Robsart opened the way for Dudley's own pursuit of the royal hand in marriage. In January 1561 Sidney approached De Quadra in his brother-in-law's behalf, soliciting Philip's support for the match. He suggested that Dudley would in return back English participation in the Council of Trent, and hinted at the possibility of an entente with Rome. Sidney continued in this role for several months; at one point Dudley boasted that his brother-in-law would become a privy councillor and lord privy seal. Then Cecil, by dissuading the queen from participation in the council, spiked the whole intrigue. In May 1561 Sidney was dispatched to Ludlow, the seat of his new Welsh presidency.

Welsh presidency Early in 1560 Sidney had reaped the first fruits of his attachment to Dudley, appointment as president of the council of Wales and the marches; a post he would hold until his death, in spite of prolonged absences. There he presided over a court with wide judicial powers which brought to bear the crown's delegated authority in an area where the common-law courts were imperfectly effective. The president was as much a political as a judicial figure. He had to deal with a clutch of regional magnates and greater gentry, whose preponderance in the localities echoed something of the traditions of a more unruly age. The greatest of these was in fact Leicester; and at least part of Sidney's function was to secure the earl's interests, and assure him of a leading role in local affairs, which involved a working relationship with the other magnates. Sidney was largely successful in maintaining Leicester's predominance in the region; the marriage of Sidney's daughter Mary [see Herbert, Mary, countess of Pembroke] to Henry *Herbert, second earl of Pembroke, in 1577 secured the co-operation of the weightiest of the south Wales magnates.

The performance of the council in its judicial role under Sidney was mixed. At the end of his first period of extended residence, 1571–5 (after nearly five years in Ireland), there was a burst of criticism from the working members of the council which led to new instructions from the privy council. In 1577 John Whitgift, then bishop of Worcester, was appointed vice-president. He criticized Sidney, who returned from Ireland in 1578, for laxness in enforcing laws against recusancy, quarrelled with Leicester, and formed an alliance with Sir James Croft of Herefordshire, the malcontent magnate on the council. During Whitgift's term as vice-president (1577–80) there was continued friction; the final years of Sidney's tenure were quiet. In general little was done to remedy the complaints levied against the council. Aside from unresolved functional problems, there was a perception that when the interests of the grandees were at stake judgments were political rather than judicial in character and inevitably favourable to members of Leicester's connection.

When Robert Dudley became active in the plan to occupy Newhaven (Le Havre) in 1562, Sidney was employed in the queen's business. During the preliminaries of that enterprise he was sent on an abortive mission to Paris to offer Elizabeth's mediation between the contending religious parties. Later he went north to explain to Mary Stuart that the planned interview between the queens was to be postponed because of the French crisis. In early autumn 1562 he accompanied his brother-in-law Warwick to Newhaven where the latter assumed command of the occupying English force, Sidney then returning home to report. In summer 1563 he was sent to Portsmouth to oversee provisioning for the beleaguered garrison at Newhaven. In the following year he was honoured with the Garter.

The Irish career: first term, 1566–1571 Another major appointment came in 1565—the deputyship of Ireland, again thanks to Leicester's patronage. Ireland had in the last four decades become part of the English political scene, a place where aspiring Englishmen might make a profitable career, enjoying office and acquiring property. Leicester had staked out a considerable sphere of influence in the island and had played a large role in discrediting the previous deputy, the earl of Sussex. Placing an ally in office at Dublin was an obvious move. From the queen's point of view Sidney was recommended by his considerable previous experience in the island during Sussex's tenure of the deputyship in Mary's reign.

Although backed by Sussex's enemy, Sidney went to Ireland armed with a programme of action outlined by the outgoing deputy. In a detailed set of recommendations presented to the queen in 1562 Sussex had proposed the establishment of provincial councils, modelled on the councils of Wales and the north, each headed by an English president with a board of local associates. Each president would have a small armed force at his disposal. He also proposed the councils should use law codes which would blend common law and Brehon (Gaelic) law. This was a strategy which aimed at a bolder and more far-reaching effort than in the past. Sussex had limited himself to defending Leinster, in effect an enlargement of the pale. Sidney proposed to establish an effective royal authority and a meaningful presence in the Gaelic areas. The means were to be persuasive rather than coercive, but the new presidents would have a reserve force at hand to be used if persuasion failed.

Sidney's first tenure of the deputyship was divided into two portions. The first lasted from January 1566 to October 1569. His initial task was one inherited from his immediate predecessor, Sir Nicholas Arnold, who filled the office after Sussex's departure from May 1564 to January 1566. In 1565 the earls of Ormond (Butler) and Desmond (Fitzgerald) had waged private war, the last instance of such conflict. The earls, arrested for their offence, had been released under bond pending royal arbitration. Sidney set out to deal with this situation by creating the proposed Munster presidency with Sir Warham St Leger (the son of an earlier deputy) as acting president.

At this point English politics intruded again on the Irish scene. Leicester had patronized the Geraldine Desmond. Sidney attempted to balance even-handedly their interests with those of the Butlers, but the queen, solicited by Ormond and his allies, intervened in their behalf. (Ormond was a favourite at court, thanks in part to his royal cousinage on the Boleyn side.) Ormond objected to St Leger because of the latter's ancestral claim to some of the Butler lands. Sidney had to dismiss Sir Warham; no one was appointed in his place, while he had to arrest Desmond. Munster fell into disorder. At court Sidney's reputation was assailed by his predecessor as the Leicester–Sussex feud flared up.

Sidney also inherited an urgent problem in Ulster where the O'Neill chief, Shane, was expanding his power. Elizabeth, as always, hoped for a peaceful (and cheap) solution, but she finally agreed to armed measures. There followed a campaign in which the O'Neill lands were ravaged but the chief himself avoided capture. Then an unlucky explosion destroyed the strategic fort erected at Lough Foyle. Ultimately the O'Neill problem was resolved, but not by the deputy. Shane, beaten by the rival Ulster lord, O'Donnell, fled to the Antrim Scots (the MacDonalds), his ancient foes. Seizing the opportunity, they cut off his head and sent it, pickled, to Dublin.

Sidney had been so depressed by the Lough Foyle disaster that he sought recall. He did indeed return to England in October 1567, his reputation at court somewhat repaired by O'Neill's death. Nevertheless, when he arrived at court, where Sussex's influence was at the moment strong, he was coldly received, his recent actions devalued, and his proposals rejected. His stand-in appointee in Munster was sent to the Tower while his schemes for reordering Ulster were dismissed. He had urged the establishment of an Ulster presidency and an earldom for the O'Neill chief, Shane's successor, Turlough Luineach. The queen instead favoured his rival, Hugh O'Neill. Sidney now suffered a severe attack of the stone, which disabled him for some months until he passed a stone the size of a nutmeg. It was presumably at this time that Sussex made his unsuccessful bid to wrest the Welsh presidency from Sidney, a move thwarted by Leicester. In

1568 Sussex went to York as president of the council of the north, necessarily diminishing his influence at court.

During 1568 various proposals were canvassed in the council, including the notion of planting English colonies, initially in Ulster but later in Munster as well. Sidney was accounted a supporter of such schemes but at the time avoided commitment to any one of them. Council discussions led to no agreement as to policy either in Ulster or Munster. By the autumn, grave disorders required immediate attention and Sidney, reluctantly, returned. He went with solid council backing and Cecil's active patronage but without specific instructions other than the observance of strictest economy. Sidney on his part was determined to press ahead with the creation of more provincial councils, for which he had royal consent.

Most immediately, a few months after his arrival, the queen authorized Sidney to summon parliament, the first meeting of the body since 1560. The legislative programme, approved already at Westminster, included some twenty bills, of which the most notable was that for abolishing coign and livery, the ancient right of clan chieftains to levy exactions in money, kind, or service on their dependants. Its elimination would shatter the whole Gaelic social order. It would deprive the chieftains of their power to make war; force would be a governmental monopoly. As compensation the dependants would have fixed financial obligations in place of the old arbitrary assessments, while the greater lords would have a steady, calculable income (while paying an assessed tax to the crown). A second bill attainted the late Shane O'Neill, a measure which placed large parts of Ulster in royal hands. Others dealt with fiscal measures designed to increase the scant royal revenues in the island. All in all, this constituted a coherent legislative programme to extend royal authority in the island and to advance the progress of Anglicization.

Almost every bill met protracted opposition, and what was to have been a brisk six-week session became in fact eight sessions, the last of which sat in 1570. In the end little more than half of the bills laid before the house were passed, including Shane O'Neill's attainder and some of the fiscal legislation, but the attack on coign and livery failed. Throughout, the members showed a growing distrust of the government. The palesmen's distrust of Sidney was heightened by the establishment of English colonies in Munster and even more by Sidney's encouragement of Sir Peter Carew, who successfully laid claim to ancestral rights in lands in the pale and in Munster. Such actions heightened fears of an officially sponsored takeover of Irish lands at the hands of English adventurers.

During the years in which parliament sat, the deputy had to face two revolts in Munster, one led by a brother of Ormond, Sir Edmund Butler; the other by a Desmond kinsman, Fitzmaurice, in which the traditional enemies collaborated. The former was driven to revolt when the earl agreed to surrender coign and livery in June 1569. Ormond, a courtier moving high in governmental circles, saw potential advantage for himself in ending endemic disorder, while for his brethren the measures spelled doom to their way of life. The Desmonds were in a worse state, their earl disgraced, alien colonists in their lands, and the success of Carew threatening their whole position. Desperate, they began seeking foreign aid. For the nonce the two parties acted together until checked by Sidney's belated arrival, followed by Ormond's appearance on the scene to receive the surrender of his kin. This last move was a blow against Sidney by his long-term enemy, since it implied the deputy was incapable of managing the situation. Sidney got his own back by an act of attainder against the Butler brothers, but even here royal intervention pulled the teeth of the condemnation. Sidney did lead the forces which broke the back of the Desmond rebellion, but Fitzmaurice sustained a guerrilla war which ended after Sidney's return home, and martial law prevailed in the province until 1571.

The queen had allowed the establishment of a Connaught presidency under Sir Edward Fitton, a Cecil protégé whose tactless inflexibility provoked an uprising. Ormond, with whom Sidney was newly reconciled, suppressed it. Sidney in the meantime sponsored another colonization project, in Ulster. He proposed that the lands east of the River Bann be occupied by English settlers, some of them discharged soldiers, others husbandmen and artificers, the tenants of gentlemen adventurers who would thus carve out their own estates.

By 1571 the country was relatively quiet and Sidney's recall, decided the previous summer, ensued. He was himself begging release. Fate was unkind to him. Beset by the disorders within the island, he was ill-supported at court. Beside the active enmity of Ormond, he suffered neglect at the hands of the council. Cecil frankly admitted that the affairs of the Scottish queen 'excluded all audience from other causes' (PRO, SP 63/26/57; Brady, 133). Sidney had also incurred royal displeasure by the mounting costs of his government. He had projected a saving of Ir£4600 on his predecessor's budget. Since 1568 the queen had spent Ir£148,000 and had accumulated debts of Ir£73,000. Nor did she favour Sidney's encouragement of colonization schemes, which so agitated both the Old English and Gaelic communities.

Sidney was coldly received at court. Disillusioned, he begged Leicester to free him from further Irish service. Nevertheless, he was soon involved in ruthless attacks on the conduct of his successor (and brother-in-law) Sir William Fitzwilliam and from 1572 began a campaign for reinstatement. In pursuit of this goal he put forward a far-reaching programme of reform, devised originally by Edmund Tremayne, at one time his private secretary. Composition, as it came to be called, attacked head-on the vexed problems of coign and livery and of the cess. In this scheme, the provincial presidents would renounce cess, their rights of billeting, purveyance, and military service, for a fixed annual rent from the chieftains, who would in turn exchange their exactions on their dependants (coign and livery) for fixed payments. The English model of tax-paying subject and rent-paying tenant would come into being. The use of force would be a royal monopoly.

Sidney had a rival in his bid for the deputyship—the earl of Essex, proprietor of a colony in Ulster. Their competition was fiscal in nature. As always the queen had her eye on costs. Essex claimed that the profits of his colony would soon yield an annual rent to the crown of £5000, easily repaying an initial royal outlay. Sidney countered with a proposal by which, implementing his programme of compositions, he would render the Irish government self-sufficient within three years at a cost of £60,000, to be paid by the queen in instalments. Elizabeth accepted and a contract was accordingly signed.

The Irish career: second term, 1575–1578 It was on these challenging terms that in September 1575 Sidney returned to a country which he 'cursed, hated, and detested'. Yet he was hopeful he 'could do that which had not been done before … where others had missed' ('Sidney's memoir', 5.308). Landing at Drogheda, he summoned the palesmen and, in accordance with his plan, offered to replace the variable burden of the cess (money, kind, and service) for a low monetary tax. He was resisted and negotiations dragged on until 1577. The deputy fared no better when he approached the Gaelic chieftains. In both Munster and Connaught his demands were termed extortionate. It was only after repressing revolt in Connaught that he won reluctant consent to composition. In the meantime the angry palesmen sent an unlicensed delegation to London where, after a rebuke for their unauthorized action, they won a hearing. Sidney sent his chancellor, William Gerard, to counter their argument. Gerard, on hearing the palesmen's case, changed his mind and backed their complaints, offering an alternative scheme which would have dismantled Sidney's programme.

Sidney continued to face opposition; public opinion turned against him as the rumour spread that he had taken the whole country in farm, that is, in lease. Worse still, from Elizabeth's standpoint, Sidney was overrunning his cost estimates. Even in the second of the three years she had held back her payment. By Michaelmas 1577 Sidney had exceeded his original costing by more than £14,000. The plaints of both the palesmen and the Gaelic chiefs, added to the deficit, destroyed both royal confidence, always uncertain, and that of leading councillors, even his supporter (his son's father-in-law) Secretary Walsingham. In March 1578 instructions for Sidney's recall ended his Irish career. He departed in September. This was the second time that he had returned under a cloud. But in 1571 he had at least laid the foundations of his proposed provincial councils. In 1578 he left a society in which palesmen and Gael were united in their anger. A keen ear could hear the underground rumblings of a coming volcanic explosion.

From the 1570s on the English government had pursued a course of action in Ireland which aimed at the Anglicization of that island, namely the full acceptance, at least by the Irish élite, of English institutions, social, political, and legal. This was to be accomplished as far as possible by persuasion, backed by force, but force used only when inescapably necessary. Sidney in his two terms of office brought this process to a culmination, acting on the basis of considered, clearly articulated programmes, which laid out the means for its fulfilment. Yet in spite of a consistent and conscientious effort, his record was largely one of failure. Moreover, his departure was not merely a changing of the guard. It proved to be the end of the half-century effort, described above, to bring Ireland peacefully into the English fold.

How far was Sidney to blame? Some would see him as the architect who destroyed his own work by his advocacy of English colonization and even more specifically by his backing for Carew, whose claims seemed to endanger all land titles. Certainly the distrust this aroused engendered deep fears as to the intentions of the English government, and led to the defeat of Sidney's first attempt at a radical reform of Irish society—the bill to abolish coign and livery in the 1569 parliament. His second attempt to achieve the same goal by the different approach of the composition programme of 1575 foundered on Sidney's highhanded impatience, which drove both palesmen and Gael to determined resistance. He had irreparably damaged the trust of the Irish (both Old English and Gael) in English intentions on which a policy of assimilation had to rest.

It should be said in Sidney's defence that he laboured under frustrating difficulties. Given were the homegrown problems of a dysfunctional, violence-ridden society. Added were those created, on the one hand by meddling interference from London, motivated by court intrigue, and on the other by the indifference—or at least inattention—of the council. It is hard to envision a recipe which would have ensured success.

The last years Sidney on his return took the seat in the privy council to which he had been appointed in 1575. In 1579 he attended with modest regularity; thereafter he was not to be seen at court. Whether his absence was voluntary or whether it was at royal command is impossible to say. In any case it meant that Sidney played no role in the centre of power either as councillor or courtier. These years were spent at Ludlow; yet even here he suffered royal rebuke—first for too frequent absence on private visits, then for his leniency to recusants. He enjoyed, however, a personal triumph in these years. His opponent in council, the Herefordshire landowner and privy councillor, Sir James Croft, had his eyes on a local heiress, Barbara Gamage, for his son's hand in marriage. With the aid of Leicester and of his son-in-law Pembroke, Sidney carried off the lady and her fortune, marrying her to Robert *Sidney, his younger son.

There was one more encounter with Irish matters; in 1582 Sidney's return to the island was under consideration. He made it plain he would only go if granted a peerage, the lands to support it, the dignity of lord lieutenant, and the company of his son Philip. The queen refused to accede to these demands and the matter ended. Sidney

died at Ludlow on 5 May 1586. Fortunately he did not live to know of his son's death in the following October. At the queen's command his body was buried in Penshurst church, his heart at Ludlow. Lady Sidney followed him to the grave. She was buried, also at Penshurst, on 11 August 1586.

Sidney died a disappointed man. He had gained neither the grant of lands nor the peerage which were reasonable hopes for a royal servant who had held two great offices. In 1582, after the queen's refusal to grant title and land, he wrote a long letter to Walsingham, whose daughter was about to marry his son Philip. In it he recounted in detail all his years of strenuous service in Ireland and Wales. In each of his three terms in Ireland he had suppressed rebellion; in each he had expended privately Ir£5000. Yet for all this he had nothing to show in material reward. A title was talked of in 1572, but without land. (Mary Sidney had written to oppose the bestowal.) Now, he lamented, he was forced to sell land to settle his debts. He was in fact disposing of considerable parts of his Brandon inheritance in the midlands.

Sidney's disappointment in his career reflects as much unfavourable circumstance as lack of ability. It was not only the intrinsic difficulties of the job—the clash of two divergent cultures—but also the meddling from the court and the low priority given Irish affairs by the council against which the deputy had, often unavailingly, to struggle. There was also the practical disadvantage of having 'his service subject to the ear and not to the eye' of the sovereign (Sydney, *Letters*, 1.93). This disadvantage stemmed in no small part from Sidney's dependence on his brother-in-law Leicester. However generous the queen was to her favourite, she frowned on the formation of factional groups either in court or in council, based in this case on family ties. She preferred that Sidney should serve her in remote Ludlow or transmarine Dublin. He thus remained on the outer edge of the court solar system where the sun's warmth was hardly felt.

WALLACE T. MacCAFFREY

Sources H. Sydney and others, *Letters and memorials of state*, ed. A. Collins, 2 vols. (1746) · *Report on the manuscripts of Lord De L'Isle and Dudley*, 6 vols., HMC, 77 (1925–66) · S. Haynes, *A collection of state papers relating to affairs from the year 1542 to 1570*, 2 vols. (1740) · H. Ellis, ed., *Original letters illustrative of English history*, 1st ser., 3 vols. (1824) · *Second report*, HMC, 1/2 (1871); repr. (1874) [Carew] · J. G. Nichols, ed., *The chronicle of Queen Jane, and of two years of Queen Mary*, CS, old ser., 48 (1850) · 'Sidney's memoir or narrative addressed to Sir Francis Walsingham, 1583', *Ulster Journal of Archaeology*, 1st ser., 3 (1855), 37–44, 91–9, 346–53; 1st ser., 5 (1857), 305–15; 1st ser., 6 (1858), 179–95 · *Calendar of the manuscripts of the most hon. the marquis of Salisbury*, 1, HMC, 9 (1883) · C. Brady, *The chief governors: the rise and fall of reform government in Tudor Ireland, 1536–1588* (1994) · N. Canny, *From Reformation to Restoration: Ireland, 1534–1660* (1987) · S. G. Ellis, *Ireland in the age of the Tudors* (1998) · *CSP dom.*, 1547–53; addenda, 1547–79 · *CSP for.* · *CSP Spain*, 1552–79 · *CPR*, 1549–51, 1553, 1555–7, 1558–60, 1560–63 · *APC*, 1578–80 · HoP, *Commons, 1509–58*, vol. 3 · HoP, *Commons, 1558–1603*, vol. 3 · *LP Henry VIII*, vols. 1–5, 8, 10–14, 16–17, 19, 21, 28

Archives CKS, corresp. and papers · TCD, letters

Likenesses attrib. A. Bronckorst, oils, 1573, Petworth House, West Sussex [*see illus.*] · attrib. A. Bronckorst, oils, versions, NPG;

Penshurst, Kent • Passe, line engraving, BM, NPG; repro. in H. Holland, *Herōologia* (1620)

Sidney, Henry, **first earl of Romney** (1641–1704), politician and army officer, was born in Paris during the spring of 1641. He was the fourth surviving and youngest son of Robert *Sidney, second earl of Leicester (1595–1677), and Dorothy Percy (*bap.* 1598, *d.* 1659), eldest daughter of Henry *Percy, ninth earl of Northumberland.

Early career Sidney grew up at the Sidney family seat, Penshurst Place, Kent, a favourite of his mother and an unusually good-looking child as an early portrait of him by Lely reveals. Much of his youth was spent in the company of Robert *Spencer, second earl of Sunderland, son of his older sister Dorothy *Spencer, countess of Sunderland, but almost an exact contemporary in age. Apparently educated together under the tutelage of Dr Thomas Pierce, the two boys became fast and lifelong friends. Sidney and Sunderland travelled on the continent in Pierce's charge in 1658–9 and made a return visit a few years later with Henry Savile, spending the better part of 1664 in Italy as part of a congenial group of young Englishmen that also included Henry Compton, Sidney Godolphin, and William Trumbull. Sidney then gravitated to the court of Charles II looking for employment, as did many other landless younger sons of good family. It was about this time, according to the *Mémoires de la vie du comte de Gramont*, that he courted Anne Temple (*d.* 1718), who later married Sir Charles Lyttelton. He may also have been involved simultaneously in a relationship with Grace Worthley, a widow of some social standing—she was related to several landed Cheshire families, including the Gerards, Fittons, and Minishulls—with whom he had a son, Henry Worthley. Grace Worthley remained his mistress until about 1682, when Sidney seems to have abandoned her, perhaps to help with protracted marriage negotiations over a Dutch heiress.

Sidney's charm also helped him towards office. In 1665 he secured appointment as groom of the bedchamber to James, duke of York, and subsequently as master of the horse to the latter's wife, Anne. 'The hansomest youth of his time' (*Memoirs of Sir John Reresby*, 55), Sidney allowed himself to get caught up in a serious flirtation with the duchess, which led to his dismissal after their conduct became the subject of widespread gossip. His offence, however, was not serious enough to deny him a commission in 1667 as captain of a new company of foot added to the Holland regiment commanded by his brother Robert. In the following year, while stationed at Carlisle, he declared his candidacy in a by-election at Appleby, but withdrew in the face of powerful local interest exercised on behalf of Thomas Tufton. In 1669 and again in 1672 he visited France on extended leave, the second time carrying a message of condolence from Charles II to Louis XIV upon the death of the latter's daughter.

Charles appointed Sidney master of the robes in July 1675, a post he purchased and which returned a minimum of £500 annually if managed properly. In a real sense it represented Sidney's first step out of relative obscurity.

Henry Sidney, first earl of Romney (1641–1704), by Samuel Cooper, 1669

The Netherlands A more decisive development came on 25 February 1678, when Sidney was commissioned as colonel to raise a new regiment of foot. That May the regiment was sent to join the British expeditionary force in Flanders, and while there he established the beginnings of a friendship with William, prince of Orange, marked by a depth and 'dignified by consistency of which the time affords few examples' (Foxcroft, 1.165). The relationship became a factor in the decision taken in June 1679 to send him as envoy-extraordinary to the states general of the United Provinces, an appointment engineered by Sunderland, then secretary of state for the north, but also supported by Sir William Temple, Sidney's immediate predecessor at The Hague as well as another good friend and something of a mentor. His official brief was to maintain a defensive alliance with the Netherlands, a fixed point of English foreign policy since the Danby ministry. It was a difficult assignment, given doubts about whether Charles II could secure the backing of parliament if a crisis arose. The situation was further complicated that autumn when the French ambassador Count D'Avaux launched a serious effort to win over the Dutch, a move that would have left England diplomatically isolated and the Southern Netherlands vulnerable. During negotiations in late December 1679 Sidney trumped the French with a proposal to the states general actually drafted at a secret meeting with the grand pensionary, Gaspar Fagel, and William himself. News of the Dutch decision to ratify a new treaty redounded to his credit. The countess of Sunderland, as frequent a correspondent as her husband, wrote early in the new year that Sidney's 'praise is up to great height, your health drank with great ceremony in the City, and everybody that's good for any thing talks of you as their guardian angel almost' (countess of Sunderland to Sidney, 13 Jan 1680, *Diary of ... Sidney*, 1.231). In addition to such public business, however, he also had a brief from Sunderland and a group of moderates on the privy council to serve as a private conduit of information to and from the prince. Sunderland, in particular, used him repeatedly to advocate the importance of the prince's coming over to England. There, William could protect the rights of his wife during the exclusion crisis, and counter the activities of Anthony Ashley Cooper, first earl of Shaftesbury, and the pretensions of James Scott, duke of Monmouth, to the succession.

Sidney was not a member of the first Exclusion Parliament, and was abroad when elections were held to the second, later in summer 1679. A promise by William Harbord to secure him or Sir William Temple a seat at Launceston, Cornwall, came to nothing, but Sidney was returned from Bramber, Sussex, after his older brother Algernon *Sidney—with whom he was not on good terms—was forced out of the contest. Judicious expenditure of almost £300 by Gilbert Spence, a trusted family retainer, and the influence of his brother-in-law Sir John Pelham were sufficient to win over a constituency in which he was unknown. There followed a year-long series of prorogations, a conscious policy of delay pursued by Charles II in the hopes that passions would cool. Finally in September 1680 Sidney returned to London in the expectation that parliament would be allowed to meet, and was party to a series of meetings aimed at trying to forge a coalition perhaps willing to accommodate exclusion, but bent on foreclosing the possibility of Monmouth's coming to power. Generally counted a whig at this time by historians of the period, Sidney took his seat in the Commons in late October, but was assigned to no committees and, Rapin and Cobbett to the contrary, left no record of participation in the debates that took place during the first week or so of the session. In fact, by 3 November he was back at The Hague under instruction from Sunderland to make a last-ditch effort to persuade the prince of Orange to declare his interest.

News that the House of Lords had rejected exclusion produced a Dutch crisis of confidence in an alliance with a nation so deeply divided. It was at this point that Sidney finally abandoned the delicate political balance that had allowed him to serve Charles II while discreetly advancing William's cause simultaneously. On 25 November he transmitted to the king a memorial from the states general urging him to come to terms with parliament and suggesting indirectly that acceptance of exclusion was the only way to do so. By a manoeuvre instigated by William with the assistance of both Fagel and Sidney, D'Avaux reported to Louis XIV that the English envoy had even gone so far as to send off manuscript copies to friends in parliament, thereby virtually ensuring the document would appear in print. Sidney's actions at this time were supported and prompted by William and Fagel.

Just his agency in the document's delivery was sufficient to earn Sidney the king's displeasure and a stern reprimand, which was delivered through secretary of state Leoline Jenkins now that Sunderland had fallen from power. While the prince of Orange and others expected the affair would lead to Sidney's immediate recall, it was not until June 1681 that he was summoned back to England and received by Charles more graciously than expected. Contrary to expectations Sidney was allowed to retain his position as master of the robes, and ultimately received reimbursement for all outstanding expenses from his embassy. However, the king did reject a request from William later that summer to appoint Sidney commanding general of the British brigade in the service of the states general, but early in 1682 he was given leave to return to the Netherlands to take up a commission as colonel of one of the six regiments. Thereafter he disappeared from the English political stage for the remainder of the reign, apart from an unsuccessful attempt to intercede on behalf of his brother Algernon after the latter's conviction for treason in late 1683. Sidney was allowed to arrange for Algernon's burial at Penshurst and to claim his estate.

The revolution With the accession of James II, Sidney lost his position at court and was recalled from military service in the Netherlands in the spring of 1685. Unlike the case of a number of other officers removed about the same time, his loyalty was never in question. Rather, it was a case of James's asserting his right to select the commander of the British forces in the Netherlands, a position Sidney had managed to secure *de facto* during the last years of the reign of Charles II, even though lacking appropriate military rank. Given dim prospects of alternative employment in the new regime, he left for the continent in November 1685, and the following year found him variously at The Hague, with William at a meeting of German princes at Cleves, and, both Burnet and Macky suggest, travelling in Italy for more than just pleasure. Sidney's especial value to the prince, however, was as a point of contact with members of his own class in England out of sympathy with James during a period of watchful waiting in 1686 and the earlier part of 1687, and then proving adept at taking on a more proactive role on his behalf after news of the queen's pregnancy radically changed the dynamics of the equation. As William gravitated toward a firm decision to intervene directly, Sidney was 'the man in whose hands the conduct of the whole design was chiefly deposited, by the prince's own order' (*Burnet's History*, 3.264). Only six others—Bishop Compton, Danby, Devonshire, Lumley, Admiral Russell, and Shrewsbury—joined him in adding their ciphers to the cautiously phrased invitation sent off on 30 June 1688. None the less the conspiracy had a considerably broader base of support, or at least promises of neutrality from some of more timorous temperament, with the secret so well kept that Sidney could secure an official pass to take the waters at Aix-la-Chapelle when he left to join the prince in late August.

By mid-September, according to Luttrell, Sidney had been commissioned a major-general in the invasion force. He landed with William at Torbay on 5 November 1688.

His role as a senior commanding officer, member of the general staff, and long-time confidant of William was very important, but in the absence of any serious military engagement that autumn it received little or no attention in contemporary accounts of the drama unfolding. In January 1689 Sidney secured a seat in the convention after a contested election at Tamworth. He is classed by Burnet, in the supplement to his *History*, as one of the moderate Church of England men constant in their support for putting William and Mary on the throne, but in general he does not figure prominently in the proceedings of the lower House. In coronation day honours he was created Baron Milton and Viscount Sydney of Sheppey on 9 April 1689, and took his seat in the House of Lords less than a week later. Other tokens of royal favour and friendship recognized both his vital contribution to the success of the revolution and a continuing record of military and administrative service. In mid-February 1689 William had made him a member of the privy council, and that same year he was also appointed lord lieutenant and vice-admiral of Kent, a justice of the peace, and *custos rotulorum* for the county, and in 1691 lord warden of the Cinque Ports and constable of Dover Castle. He retained most of these positions until his death, though in 1692 and 1693 he shared the lord lieutenancy of Kent with Vere Fane, fourth earl of Westmorland, because of commitments in Ireland. Sydney was also first gentleman of the bedchamber (1689–1700) and groom of the stole (1700–02). Important to him professionally were a commission as colonel of the 1st regiment of foot guards (1689–90 and again 1693–1704) and a special non-regimental commission in May 1691 as commander of all foot in the king's absence while on campaign with William in Flanders. Sydney was also the recipient of a grant of almost 50,000 acres in Ireland in 1690, but title to it and a substantial annual income were lost with the resumption of Irish forfeitures by parliament in 1699.

In the service of William III The final phase of Sydney's career can be said to have begun in the summer of 1690, when he accompanied William III to Ireland, continuing a family tradition of involvement in Irish affairs dating back to the reign of Elizabeth I. Both his father and elder brother Philip *Sidney, third earl of Leicester, had held high office in the Irish administration. He was one of the principal officers at the battle of the Boyne and during the mop-up operation that followed, including the siege at Limerick, where the troops he commanded personally had some success before the king withdrew in the face of bad weather. At the beginning of September, William returned to England after naming Sydney and Thomas Coningsby lords justices to act in his stead, with a third person to be added to the commission at a later date. It was a particularly difficult assignment, with military operations still in progress and widespread economic distress and popular unrest a constant worry. Almost immediately the two men issued a series of proclamations from Dublin aimed at trying to restore some degree of order and stability, but nothing much of substance was accomplished before Sydney was recalled in early December to take on

the post of secretary of state for the north. During his first few months in office he was based in London, while his counterpart, Daniel Finch, second earl of Nottingham, and William went to The Hague. The two secretaries then swapped places after the king briefly returned to England in April 1691, and then set off for a summer campaign in Flanders, for which Sydney's credentials as a seasoned military commander made him doubly useful, as well as a congenial companion.

Shortly after Sydney and the king returned to England in October, rumours about the possibility of his appointment as lord lieutenant of Ireland began to circulate: however, it was not until the beginning of March 1692 that he surrendered his seals of office, and the middle of that month before his new commission officially took effect. In two sets of instructions William gave Sydney extensive powers over both the civil administration and all military forces, as well as a particular mandate to summon parliament to ratify the provisions of the articles of Limerick signed the year before. The king also provided him with an annual salary in excess of £6500, a substantial supply of plate, and an additional allowance of £3000 for equipage. Various factors conspired to delay Sydney's departure, but he finally arrived in Dublin at the end of August, and immediately issued writs summoning parliament to meet on 5 October. It was a session that spun out of control quickly. An exclusively protestant lower house vehemently opposed making a reality out of promises of toleration for Catholics, and a request for new taxes to help cover an anticipated shortfall between revenues and expenditures gave it some leverage in the situation. Even though Sydney seems to have understood that it would be difficult to get the king's business done without organizing a leadership group in the Commons, his lack of success in doing so tempted, if it did not actually provoke, the constitutional challenge to Poynings' law that followed. On 3 November Sydney prorogued parliament after delivering a stiff speech on the rights and prerogatives of the crown, even though it meant losing the tax bills pending. Echoes of the dispute were carried to England that winter by six members of the Irish Commons who met with William, as well as with committees from both houses of parliament, in an attempt to explain their conduct and to further their complaint that Sydney was too tolerant of Catholics, and a corrupt administrator as well. Although the king's support was unwavering, clearly his lord lieutenant had become sufficiently compromised in the eyes of the emerging protestant ascendancy to have lost his effectiveness.

Sydney's recall from Dublin came in late spring 1693, and on 28 July it was followed by appointment to the office of master-general of the ordnance. The post represented neither a sop intended to allow him to save face, nor simply a vehicle for lining his pockets, as some have alleged. Rather, given William's military ambitions and the functions attaching to the job since the department had been reconstituted in 1683, it was a substantial vote of confidence in Sydney's abilities. William's continued respect for Sydney's qualities was confirmed in May 1694, when he was promoted lieutenant-general and created earl of Romney. For the remaining years of the reign Romney was immersed in matters ranging from weapons development and procurement, to construction and maintenance of fortifications and supply depots throughout the British Isles and the colonies. Provision of armaments and munitions for the fleet and efficient dispatch of trains of artillery to the continent were the obvious business with which he dealt, but a host of lesser matters occupied his attention as well—including arrangements for spectacular public firework displays in St James's Square to celebrate the great victory at Namur in 1695, and again on the king's birthday and return to England after the treaty of Ryswick was signed in 1697. In that same year Romney was called upon for the first time to serve as one of the lords justices while William was abroad, and it is also when he purchased the office of ranger of Greenwich Park from Charles Sackville, fourth earl of Dorset, to have use of the Queen's House as his equivalent of a country seat. During Peter the Great's stay in England in the winter of 1698, Romney showed off new naval construction to the tsar, and also helped William entertain his difficult guest privately. He was again appointed a lord justice later that spring, and then in each of the following three years accompanied the king to The Hague, where, in the summer of 1701, Luttrell notes that he was associated with John Churchill, earl of Marlborough, during the negotiations leading to a revival of the grand alliance against France.

The death of William III and the accession of Queen Anne led Romney largely to disappear from the political stage. His employments at court came to an end immediately, though he was continued as lord lieutenant of Kent and granted a handsome pension. A man really outside party in the years after the revolution, Romney continued to attend sessions of the House of Lords on occasion, but was never much interested in the parliamentary arena and not an influential voice there. He died of smallpox on 8 April 1704 at his house, 16 St James's Square, and was buried ten days later in the chancel of St James's, Piccadilly. While the circumstances of his death were noted by a few contemporaries, he had already begun to slip into relative obscurity after the passing of Sunderland and William III had removed the men who defined the parameters of his public life.

Romney has been the subject of widely divergent views about both his capacity and character. Macaulay dismissively described him as 'incapable, ignorant, and dissipated' (Macaulay, 3.1050), and insisted elsewhere that the invitation to William must have been 'drawn up by some person better skilled than Sydney in the art of composition' (ibid., 3.1053), despite the fact that the document is in his hand. In turn, Macaulay seems to have been influenced by Jonathan Swift's disparaging references, one differing only slightly from the other, to the effect that Romney was 'an idel, drunken, ignorant rake, without sense or honour' (Prose Works, 5.288). Thomas Bruce, second earl of Ailesbury, hardly a friendly witness, took a much more charitable view of his character, while John Macky called

him the linchpin of the planning effort for the revolution, a man of honour and honesty who served William to the best of his ability. Both Burnet's History and the supplement to that work provide an even fuller portrait. It is certainly one of an individual with flaws, but also remarkable for his even temper, straight dealing, good judgement, and a knack for gaining the trust of others. Perhaps more dependable than gifted, Romney becomes in this view a person in whom it then becomes possible to understand why William placed such a high degree of confidence over such a long period of time.   DAVID HOSFORD

Sources Diary of the times of Charles the Second by the Honourable Henry Sidney (afterwards earl of Romney), ed. R. W. Blencowe, 2 vols. (1843) • R. W. Blencowe, ed., Sydney papers (1825) • N. Luttrell, A brief historical relation of state affairs from September 1678 to April 1714, 1–4 (1857), vols. 1–4 • CSP dom., 1658–1702 • W. A. Shaw, ed., Calendar of treasury books, [33 vols. in 64], PRO (1904–69), vols. 6–16 • Bishop Burnet's History of his own time: with the suppressed passages of the first volume, ed. M. J. Routh, 6 vols. (1823), vols. 1–4 • Report on the manuscripts of Allan George Finch, 5 vols., HMC, 71 (1913–2003), vols. 2, 4 • A supplement to Burnet's History of my own time, ed. H. C. Foxcroft (1902) • C. Dalton, ed., English army lists and commission registers, 1661–1714, 6 vols. (1892–1904), vols. 1, 3–4 • Memoirs of the secret services of John Macky, ed. A. R. (1733) • J. Dalrymple, Memoirs of Great Britain and Ireland, 3 vols. (1771–8), vol. 2 • Report on the manuscripts of Lord De L'Isle and Dudley, 6, HMC, 77 (1966) • J. P. Kenyon, Sunderland (1958) • H. C. Foxcroft, Halifax (1898), vols. 1–2 • S. Baxter, William III (1966) • T. B. Macaulay, The history of England from the accession of James II, new edn, ed. C. H. Firth, 6 vols. (1913–15), vols. 3–5 • H. Sidney and others, Letters and memorials of state, ed. A. Collins, 2 vols. (1746) • Memoirs of Sir John Reresby, ed. A. Browning (1936) • Pepys, Diary, vols. 6–7 • T. P. Courtenay, Memoirs of the life, works and correspondence of Sir William Temple, 2 vols. (1836) • The prose works of Jonathan Swift, ed. H. Davis, 5: Miscellaneous and autobiographical pieces, fragments, and marginalia (1962) • K. H. D. Haley, Shaftesbury (1968) • T. W. Moody and others, eds., A new history of Ireland, 4: Eighteenth-century Ireland, 1691–1800 (1986) • M. Thompson, The secretaries of state, 1681–1782 (1932) • O. F. C. Hogg, 'Forerunner of the army council', Army Historical Research, 11 (1932), 101–28 • G. H. Chettle, The Queen's House, London Survey Committee, 14 (1937) • JHL • Memoirs of the Comte de Gramont, trans. P. Quenell (1930) • A. M. Mimardière, 'Sidney (Sydney), Hon. Henry', HoP, Commons, 1660–90 • DNB • GEC, Peerage
Archives Althorp, Northamptonshire, corresp. • BL, corresp. and diary, Add. MSS 32680–32682 • CKS, corresp. and papers • PRO, official corresp. and papers relating to various phases of career • TCD, letters | BL, letters to first marquess of Halifax and second marquess of Halifax, C8 • Leics. RO, corresp. with earl of Nottingham • PRO NIre., letters to Thomas Coningsby • U. Nott. L., letters to first earl of Portland
Likenesses P. Lely, oils, c.1650–1654, Penshurst, Kent • S. Cooper, miniature, 1669, priv. coll. [see illus.] • G. Kneller, oils (in later life), Penshurst, Kent • P. Lely, oils (as a child); at Penshurst, Kent, in 1897 • P. Lely, portrait; in possession of Earl Spencer in 1897 • J. B. Medina, oils, Gov. Art Coll. • engraving (after G. Kneller), repro. in J. E. Doyle, The official baronage of England, 3 vols. (1886)
Wealth at death left £450 for relief of poor; bulk of estate to John Sidney, second son of earl of Leicester; papers and other items to Thomas Pelham (both nephews): will, Collins, Letters

Sidney [née Dudley], **Mary**, Lady Sidney (1530×35–1586), courtier, was the eldest daughter of John *Dudley, duke of Northumberland (1504–1553), politician, of Halden, Kent, and his wife, Jane *Dudley (1508/9–1555) [see under Dudley, John], daughter of Sir Edward *Guildford of Halden, Kent, and his first wife, Eleanor. The Dudley genealogies do not supply dates of birth and they separate the five daughters from the eight sons. Mary Dudley may have been born as early as 1530, but equally possibly after Robert *Dudley (1532/3–1588). Her brothers included Ambrose *Dudley, Henry *Dudley [see under Dudley, John], and Guildford *Dudley. No details of her education are known, but she is said to have had an understanding of French, Latin, and Italian. Her intellectual interests included romances (Geoffrey Fenton dedicated his *Certaine Tragicall Discourses* to her in 1567), versifying, and alchemy.

Mary Dudley married Henry *Sidney (1529–1586), courtier, of London, first son of Sir William *Sidney [see under Sidney, Henry], and his wife, Anne. The marriage took place at Esher, Surrey, on 29 March 1551, a ceremony repeated publicly at Ely House, London, on 17 May. Sidney was a gentleman of the privy chamber in Edward VI's household; he was knighted in October that year. It is not impossible that like that of her brother Robert, Mary's marriage was a romantic one, and it was certainly highly compatible. The surviving Sidney papers contain a wealth of personal information about her, including a record of the births of most of her children in the family psalter, but unlike her children neither she nor her husband has yet received a full biographical treatment.

Both were members of the court at Edward's death (Mary Sidney apparently brought the news to Lady Jane Grey that she was to be queen), and the disaster attending her father, now duke of Northumberland, in July 1553 placed them in an extremely difficult position. Like the rest of Northumberland's children she was included in his attainder. Sidney himself had been with Northumberland at Cambridge, but he was able to make his peace with Mary I quickly, thanks in part to three sisters who were members of her household. Nevertheless, he did not sever relations with his wife's family. He served in an embassy to Spain in the spring of 1554 partly to secure the release of his brothers-in-law from the Tower of London. Mary Sidney's brother John *Dudley, Viscount Lisle and earl of Warwick [see under Dudley, John (1504–1553)], died at Penshurst on his release in October 1554. Her first child, Philip *Sidney (1554–1586), born on 30 November, was given a significant combination of godparents: Philip II and the dowager duchess of Northumberland. When the duchess died in January 1555, Sidney was the executor of her will.

Mary Sidney accompanied her husband when he went to Ireland as vice-treasurer in 1556. It was about this time that her second child, Mary Margaret (d. 1558), was born. She returned to England in September 1558, having benefited from the repeal of the Dudley attainder (4 & 5 Philip and Mary c. 12) passed earlier in the year. In January 1559 she was appointed a gentlewoman 'without wages' of Elizabeth I's privy chamber (PRO, LC 2/4/3/104), and thereafter, like her brothers, was at the centre of the new court. In the autumn of 1559 the queen employed her to tell the imperial ambassador that Charles von Habsburg, archduke of Styria, should visit her immediately. When Elizabeth later hedged the proposal with a number of qualifications, Mary Sidney claimed that the queen and her brother had exploited her.

Sidney returned from Ireland at the end of 1559. Mary

Sidney's service at court was thereafter shaped by the demands of her family and her husband's public career (in particular his appointment as lord president of the council of Wales and the marches in 1560 and then his three postings as lord deputy of Ireland). In October 1560 she used Robert Dudley's house at Kew for the birth of her third child, her daughter Elizabeth (who died in Dublin in 1567). In 1561 she accompanied her husband to the marches, and her fourth child, Mary (1561–1621) [see Herbert, Mary], the future countess of Pembroke, was born on 27 October at Tickenhall, Worcestershire. Her most dramatic if unfortunate service in the privy chamber occurred in October 1562 when she nursed Elizabeth through her near-fatal attack of smallpox. Sidney's account of the effect on their lives in his 'Memoir of services' in March 1583 deserves quotation in full. It follows his complaints about the queen's failure to reward his manifold services and her claims that he was living too extravagantly:

> I spend above xxxli a weke, here some will object that I upon the same kepe my wief and her followers. True it is she is now with me and hath ben this half yere and before not in many yeres and if both she and I had our foode and house roome free as we have not in conscience, we have deserved it. For my parte I am not idle but every daye I work in my function and she for her ould service and marks (yet remaining in her face) taken in the same meriteth her meat. When I went to Newhaven [Le Havre] I lefte her a full faire Ladye in myne eye at least the fayerest, and when I retorned I found her as fowle a ladie as the smale pox could make her, which she did take by contynuall attendance of her majesties most precious person (sicke of the same disease) the skarres of which (to her resolute discomforte) ever syns hath don and doth remayne in her face, so as she lyveth solitairilie *sicut Nicticorax in domicilio suo* ['like a night-raven in the house', Psalm 102, verse 6] more to my charge then if we had boorded together as we did before that evill accident happened.   (PRO, SP 12/159, fol. 38r–v)

There is no evidence to support claims that Mary Sidney only appeared in public afterwards in a mask. This seems to have originated in a comment by Sir Fulk Greville that 'she chose rather to hide herself from the curious eyes of a delicate time than to come upon the stage of the world with any manner of disparagement' (Hay, 18). Neither her court service nor their married life came to an end in 1562 as Sidney seems to imply; he often wrote in an exaggerated manner and this is no exception. Robert *Sidney (1563–1626) was born at Penshurst on 19 November 1563 and Ambrosia (d. 1575) was born in 1564 or 1565. Mary Sidney accompanied her husband to Dublin at the end of 1565 when he took up his first lord deputyship, losing her 'whole apparail and all her jewels' when one of their ships was wrecked on the voyage over (PRO, SP 15/12/245). In 1567 she succumbed to the strains of the criticisms of him, 'as she fell greveously sick upon the same and in that sicknes remayned ones in traunce above fifty-two houres, upon whose recoverie I sent her into England' (PRO, SP 12/159, fol. 38r–v).

Mary Sidney did not accompany her husband to Ireland for his second lord deputyship at the end of 1568, thanks probably to her pregnancy with her last child, Thomas

(1569–1595), who was born on 25 March 1569. Sidney expected her and their son Philip to join him in 1570 but he was recalled in March 1571 instead. After his second recall he spent most of his time in Wales and she at court, and this seems to have been the period when they lived apart most extensively. Thanks to her unwaged status in the privy chamber, Mary was dependent on annual stipends from her husband. More of her correspondence survives from this period than for any other and, like her husband's, it has a definitely querulous tone. Both complained increasingly of ill health and of Elizabeth's failure to reward their various services. In May 1572 Mary Sidney interceded with William Cecil, Baron Burghley, lord treasurer, to have the promised offer of a barony to Sidney withdrawn if it was not accompanied by an increase in his estate. Accommodation at court was another issue, over which she appears to have gone on a virtual strike in 1574, by refusing to attend if she did not retain the chambers she had come to regard as hers. There has been a temptation to interpret this incident as a form of political harassment by the new lord chamberlain, her brother-in-law, Thomas Radcliffe, third earl of Sussex. But if Sussex displayed a certain officiousness on taking up a new post, the Sidneys' well-cultivated sense of injustice was undoubtedly a factor.

After the death of Ambrosia at Ludlow, Shropshire, in February 1575, Sidney received one of Elizabeth's famous letters of condolence and an invitation to send young Mary to court as a maid of honour. The family as a group joined the progress to Kenilworth in 1575, where Lady Sidney killed a buck. It was from Kenilworth that Sidney departed on what became his last lord deputyship, but this time there appears to have been no question of his wife's accompanying him. In the spring of 1577 she was superintending the arrangements for Mary's wedding to Henry *Herbert, second earl of Pembroke, probably at Penshurst. Her court career came to an end some eighteen months later. On 6 July 1579 Don Bernardino de Mendoza, the Spanish ambassador, reported that a sister of the earl of Leicester (Robert Dudley), of whom the queen was very fond and to whom she had given rooms at court, had retired to her own house. Ill health was probably the cause, although by 1582 she had joined her husband at Ludlow. In March 1583 Sidney alluded to the possibility that he could remarry and have a second family as his wife was not 'so healthie'. As it transpired, his health gave out first and he died on 5 May 1586; but although she attended his funeral at Penshurst in June Mary did not survive him for very long (Coll. Arms, Dethick's book, fols. 1–2). She died on 9 August, possibly at her son Philip's lodgings in Walsingham House, London, and was then buried with full dignities in her husband's tomb at Penshurst.

The Sidneys were in some respects the golden couple of the court in the early years of Elizabeth's reign. But from the end of the 1560s they became increasingly embittered by what they regarded as shabby treatment at the queen's hands. The extent to which they were justified is still debated. The nature of their relations with Elizabeth in the later years is best expressed in a letter of Mary Sidney's, written during the course of the dispute over accommodation in 1574: 'old Lord Harry and his old Moll [probably Elizabeth's nicknames for them] will do as well as the[y] can in [accepting?] lyck good friends the small portion alotted our long servis in Courght; which as lyttle as hit is, seams somethynge to mooche' (Collins, 1.272).

SIMON ADAMS

Sources A. Stewart, *Philip Sidney: A double life* (1998) · M. A. S. Hume, ed., *Calendar of letters and state papers relating to English affairs, preserved principally in the archives of Simancas*, 4 vols., PRO (1892–9) · K. Duncan-Jones, *Sir Philip Sidney: courtier poet* (1991) · P. J. French, *John Dee: the world of an Elizabethan magus* (1972) · M. P. Hannay, *Philip's phoenix: Mary Sidney, countess of Pembroke* (1990) · S. Adams, *Leicester and the court: essays on Elizabethan politics* (2002) · CKS, Penshurst papers, U1475 · Kenilworth game book, CKS, U1475/E 93 · PRO, LC 2/4/3 [Coronation roll, Elizabeth I] · S. Adams, ed., *Household accounts and disbursement books of Robert Dudley, earl of Leicester, 1558–1561, 1584–1586*, CS, 6 (1995) · PRO, SP 12 [state papers, domestic, Elizabeth I] · PRO, SP 15 [state papers, domestic, addenda] · M. V. Hay, *The life of Robert Sidney, earl of Leicester (1563–1626)* (Washington, DC, 1984) · U. Edin. L., Laing MSS · BL, Cotton MSS · W. Dethick, 'Book of funerals of the nobility', 1586–1603, Coll. Arms · H. Sydney and others, *Letters and memorials of state*, ed. A. Collins, 2 vols. (1746)

Archives BL, dispersals from, Add. MS 15914 · CKS, papers, U 1475 · PRO, letters, SP 12/86 · Trinity Cam., dispersals from, MS M.17.2 · U. Edin. L., Laing MSS, dispersals from | BL, letters, Cotton MSS Titus B.ii, Vespasian F.xii · BL, letters, Lansdowne MS 17

Likenesses attrib. H. Eworth, portrait, c.1550–1555, Petworth House, West Sussex; repro. in R. Strong, 'Hans Eworth', *The Tudor and Stuart monarchy*, 1 (1995), 125, pl. iii

Wealth at death died intestate

Sidney, Mary. *See* Herbert, Mary, countess of Pembroke (1561–1621).

Sidney, Sir Philip (1554–1586), author and courtier, was born on 30 November 1554 at Penshurst, Kent, the first of seven children of Sir Henry *Sidney (1529–1586) and his wife, Mary *Sidney (1530x35–1586), daughter of John *Dudley, duke of Northumberland, and his wife, Jane Guildford. Through his mother's relations in particular, Philip was born into a highly important family. Mary's brothers were Guildford Dudley, who married Lady Jane Grey, Robert Dudley, who was created earl of Leicester in 1564, and Ambrose Dudley, who succeeded his father as earl of Warwick in 1561; in the same year Henry Hastings, husband of Mary Sidney's sister Katherine, succeeded to the earldom of Huntingdon. On his father's side, Sidney's aunt Frances was the wife of Thomas Radcliffe, third earl of Sussex, and Sidney's first cousin Jane Dormer had married the count of Feria, a leading member of the retinue of Philip II of Spain. Queen Mary's husband, after whom Sidney was named, stood as godfather at his baptism, with his grandmother the duchess of Northumberland and John Russell, first earl of Bedford, whose daughter Anne became Ambrose Dudley's third wife, as the other godparents.

Early years and education to 1572 Philip Sidney's early childhood was probably spent at Penshurst. His first sister, Margaret, was born in 1556 (*d.* 1558); she was followed about 1560 by Elizabeth (*d.* 1567), in 1561 by Mary, who as Mary

Sir Philip Sidney (1554–1586), by unknown artist, 1578

*Herbert became countess of Pembroke, and in 1564 by Ambrosia (d. 1575). His two brothers, Robert *Sidney, who became earl of Leicester, and Thomas, were born in 1563 and 1569 respectively. Sidney may have suffered the attack of smallpox that badly scarred his face in 1562, when his mother lost her looks nursing the similarly afflicted Queen Elizabeth.

Sidney's earliest tutor seems to have been Johan or Jean Tassel, probably a Huguenot exile, who may have taught him the French in which he was later so fluent, and accompanied him to Shrewsbury School. The school is close to Ludlow where Sir Henry Sidney had his residence as lord president of the council in the marches. Sidney entered the school on 17 October 1564, on the same day as his future friend and admirer Fulke *Greville. The school's headmaster was Thomas Ashton, a former fellow of Trinity College, Cambridge, and under his direction Sidney studied Latin and some Greek, and may have taken part in Latin plays. He lodged in the town with George Leigh, six times MP for Shrewsbury, and his wife, and was godfather to one of their sons.

Sidney spent part of the new year of 1566 at Eton near Wroxeter with Sir Richard Newport and his wife, returning to them again in May when the school was visited by sickness: he also stayed then with Sir Andrew Corbet of Moreton Corbett, whose eldest son, Robert, later accompanied him on his European travels. In August he travelled to Leicester's magnificent castle at Kenilworth, and then, accompanied by Thomas Wilson, went on to Oxford where Queen Elizabeth was entertained with speeches and plays. There is no certain evidence that he was presented to the queen on this occasion, but his family connections, not least with Leicester who was chancellor of the university, were such as to suggest that he may have been. His subsequent relationship with the queen, however, though not easy to interpret—no letter from her to him survives—seems generally to have been problematic.

On 2 February 1567 Sidney was enrolled as a member of Gray's Inn, and a year later, aged thirteen, he began his career as an undergraduate at Christ Church, Oxford. He lodged with the dean, Thomas Cooper, who also acted as his tutor along with Thomas Thornton and Nathaniel Baxter. Another pupil of theirs at this time was William Camden, and Sidney's other Oxford contemporaries included his schoolfriend Greville, Richard Hakluyt, Richard Carew, Thomas Bodley, Walter Ralegh, Richard Hooker, George Peele, and perhaps John Lyly. His three earliest surviving letters, addressed to Sir William Cecil between 12 March 1569 and 26 February 1570, were all written from Oxford.

Sidney became engaged to Cecil's elder daughter, Anne, and a formal marriage contract was drawn up on 6 August 1569 and signed in September. Within two years the contract seems to have broken down, for in the summer of 1571 Anne was betrothed to the seventeenth earl of Oxford, who became Sidney's enemy. Some time during that year an Oxford mathematician, perhaps Thomas Allen, cast Sidney's horoscope, with sections concerning marriage and journeys. When plague broke out at Oxford in the summer or autumn Sidney moved to Reading with other students. But though he may also have attended Cambridge University for a short time, he did not take a degree at either university.

Sidney's first visit to the continent took place in 1572 when he accompanied Edward Fiennes de Clinton to sign the treaty of Blois, which allied England and France against Spain and seemed to offer some protection to French protestants: Clinton was created earl of Lincoln for the mission. Sidney's passport was signed by the queen on 25 May 1572, and allowed him to travel abroad for two years but not to consort with unlicensed English exiles. His companion for this visit was Lodowick Bryskett, and he took three servants with him. The English mission arrived just outside Paris on 8 June. The treaty was signed a week later, and on 23 June Lincoln's party left Paris, but Sidney stayed on for the next two and a half months, lodging with his future father-in-law, the English ambassador Sir Francis Walsingham. On 9 August he was created a gentleman of Charles IX's bedchamber and a baron.

Sidney was in Paris for the marriage on 18 August of King Henri of Navarre and Marguerite de Valois, and for the elaborate celebrations that followed it. When the massacre of St Bartholomew's day (24 August) broke out, Sidney observed it from the safety of Walsingham's embassy, where he met Timothy Bright and Pietro Bizari. Among those killed in the massacre was the celebrated protestant logician Pierre de la Ramée (Petrus Ramus) with whom Sidney had become friendly. Other friends made on this,

his only visit to Paris, included the protestant theologian and political theorist Philippe Du Plessis Mornay, the lawyer Jean Lobbet, the young count of Hanau, the printer Andreas Wechel, and perhaps also the poets Pierre Ronsard and Guillaume de Saluste Du Bartase, the former chancellor Michel de l'Hôpital, and the diplomat, political thinker, and follower of Melancthon Hubert Languet.

On 9 September the English privy council wrote to Walsingham instructing him to send Sidney home, but by the time the letter reached Paris Sidney and his party had left in the company of John Watson, dean of Winchester. Sidney's constant travelling over the next three years was intended to further his education and also to establish him as an internationally recognized figure who might be called upon to unite and lead the various protestant factions throughout Europe. That he should have been prepared thus for so important a role suggests that the great hopes already invested in Sidney arose as much from his personal qualities as from his birth. His guiding spirit during the tour was Languet, and an important Latin correspondence between the two survives. It is clear that Sidney frequently found the older, unmarried man's constant advice and reproaches trying: he often did not do as he was told and was not entirely open with him about his activities or his intellectual and aesthetic interests.

European tour, 1573–1575 Sidney's initial destination was Frankfurt, where he stayed with the printer Wechel: Languet was a fellow guest. There he also met Théophile de Banos, the Huguenot minister, who dedicated to Sidney his commentaries on the work of their joint friend Ramée. As ambassador to the elector of Saxony, Languet was sent to Vienna, and Sidney followed him there in the early summer of 1573. On the way he met the French printer Henri Estienne (Henricus Stephanus), who gave him a manuscript collection of Greek proverbs and in 1576 dedicated his edition of the Greek New Testament to him. Having reached the imperial court in Vienna, in August 1573 Sidney went to Pressburg (Bratislava) in Hungary near the border with the Ottoman empire, and there he met Georg Purkircher and the botanist Charles de l'Ecluse. Before winter set in he left Vienna with his cousin Thomas Coningsby, Bryskett, and a Welsh servant named Griffin Madox, and set off for Venice, where he joined the count of Hanau, later following him to Padua. Until August 1574 he moved constantly between Venice and Padua, except when in March 1574 he went to Genoa and Florence. In Padua on 20 June 1574 he bought a copy of Guicciardini's history of Italy. In Venice he met two poets—Cesare Pavese, a friend of Torquato Tasso's father, and the French protestant writer François Perrot de Mésières—and also hesitated as to whether to have his portrait painted by Paolo Veronese or by Tintoretto: he chose Veronese, but the portrait, which he sent to Languet, is lost, as are two portraits of him made at Vienna by the imperial artist Antonio Abondio.

Sidney left Venice in the late summer of 1574 and in the autumn went from Vienna, where he had been ill, to Cracow, hoping to see the French crown prince, Henri de Valois, installed as king of Poland: however, following the death of Charles IX, Henri had returned hurriedly to France. This occasion may have been the basis for the myth, promoted by Robert Dow in *Exequiae*, the Oxford volume of elegies for Sidney, and later popularized by Sir Robert Naunton, that Sidney was offered the throne of Poland. He spent the winter of 1574–5 in Vienna where he became friendly with the diplomat Edward Wotton, whom he mentions in the opening sentence of *A Defence of Poetry*. A proposed meeting with Languet in Frankfurt in the spring of 1575 did not take place; in Heidelberg he met the English ambassador Thomas Wilkes. Eventually he was summoned back to England by the queen, but although he travelled in great haste, he was delayed for nearly a month at Antwerp. On this return part of the journey Sidney was joined by Wotton: their relationship endured and Sidney remembered him in his will.

His travels had allowed Sidney to see and admire the splendours of European Renaissance courts, the paintings of Titian, Tintoretto, and Veronese, and the wonders of mannerist art; he learned at first hand about different political systems and paid attention to the arts of war and horsemanship. The friendships he made were extensive and brought him into touch with rulers, scholars, diplomats, and politicians: his new friends tended to be better and more regular correspondents than he was. At the beginning of the tour Leicester had described his nephew to Walsingham as 'young and raw' (Wallace, 115); he returned a grown man, with the manner of a prince.

The reasons for Sidney's rapid return and the nature of his position when he arrived back in England are uncertain. In April 1574 Sir Henry Sidney had reportedly offered his service to King Philip of Spain with 6000 men, pledging his son—then in Italy—'as security for the fulfilment of it' (Duncan-Jones, *Sidney: Courtier Poet*, 88). Leicester, who had had a son from his liaison with Douglass Sheffield in August 1574 and may by the next year have begun an affair with Lettice Devereux, countess of Essex, found himself in a compromised position with Elizabeth: he may have found the return of his promising nephew a convenient way of distracting the queen from his own activities. Furthermore, if Leicester really thought that he might marry the queen, then in her early forties, but might fail to have children with her, then Sidney's position as a possible successor could have appeared strong. Sidney's own thoughts about his new standing are unknown, since no letters from him survive between the time of his return in June 1575 and November 1576.

Return to England, 1575–1577 Sidney reached England on 31 May 1575, and came to court shortly afterwards. After a brief illness he set off on the queen's progress, centred on her visit to Leicester's castle of Kenilworth, beginning on 9 July. Accounts of this visit suggest that the earl's courtship of the queen lay behind some of the entertainments. Early in August, however, Sidney left the progress to accompany his father, who had been reappointed lord deputy in Ireland, to Shrewsbury. He witnessed his father's will on the 20th and rejoined the queen's party early in September, probably at Woodstock, where he may have first met the poet and courtier Edward Dyer: the two became closely associated in their literary careers, and Dyer, by some eleven years the older man, seems to have largely supplanted Languet as Sidney's adviser and close friend, much to Languet's disappointment.

Sidney returned to London for the winter of 1575–6 and became prominent as a courtier. He assisted his aunt the countess of Warwick at the baptism of her niece Elizabeth, daughter of Lord and Lady Russell, in Westminster Abbey on 27 October, and may have begun his career as a tilter at Woodstock or in the Accession day tilt of 17 November. It was probably at this time that he was appointed royal cup-bearer: a post which his father had held, it was perhaps given to him when he came of age on 30 November 1575. Sidney's recurrent attempts to find employment, preferably involving military action, appear to have begun at this time. In the spring of 1576 there was a plan that he should join François Hercules, duc d'Alençon, the French king's brother and as the duc d'Anjou Queen Elizabeth's later suitor, in a revolt near the Loire, but this came to nothing.

Instead, in July 1576 Sidney went to Ireland, probably accompanying Walter Devereux, first earl of Essex, who had recently been appointed earl marshal of Ireland for life. On 10 August he joined his father at Kilcullen outside Dublin, and stayed with him for two weeks in Dublin Castle before setting off for the west of the country to mop up the remaining followers of the sons of the earl of Clanricarde, latterly in revolt. In Galway he met the chieftain Grania, or Grace, O'Malley, described by Sir Henry as 'a most famous feminine sea-captain' (Wallace, 167). Sidney was still in Ireland when Essex died at Dublin Castle on 22 September, and he became friendly with the earl's secretary Edward Waterhouse, but by 4 November he was back in England, and reported on the situation in Ireland to the queen at Greenwich.

Sidney spent the winter of 1576–7 at court, where he was joined by his younger brother Robert: by February 1577 it had been arranged that their sister Mary should marry Henry Herbert, second earl of Pembroke. On 16 January 1577 Sidney joined Leicester and Dyer in a meeting with John Dee, possibly to discuss exploration and imperial aspirations. Sidney, his mother, and Dyer had each invested £25 in Martin Frobisher's first voyage in 1576; for his second voyage of 1577 Sidney and Dyer put in £50 each. At other meetings about this time, before his embassy to Rudolf II, Sidney read the first three books of Livy's *Roman History* with the Cambridge academic Gabriel Harvey. It may have been through Harvey that Edmund Spenser, who had once been his pupil, was brought to Sidney's attention. The exact nature of the relationship between the two poets and its duration are unknown, but neither Spenser nor Harvey accompanied Sidney on his European mission. Those who went included his friends Greville, Dyer, Henry Brouncker, Sir Henry Lee, and Sir Jerome Bowes. Sidney was appointed to convey the queen's condolences to two courts: to Rudolf II on the death of his father, Maximilian II, and to the counts palatine, Ludwig and Johann Casimir, on the death of their father, the elector Friedrich III. The further purpose of Sidney's mission was to investigate the possibility of promoting a protestant league with these leaders, and to gather intelligence about political and religious affairs.

Mission to Rudolf II, 1577 Sidney was now a considerable figure who enjoyed the added status which came from being employed on the queen's business: as an international diplomat he was to meet important and powerful figures. During his journey a tablet describing his relationship to the 'pro-rex' of Ireland, as his father was described, and to the earls of Leicester and Warwick, was hung outside buildings where he stayed. From Brussels he went on to Louvain where on 6 March 1577 he met Don John of Austria, the victor of Lepanto. A meeting with Johann Casimir took place at Heidelberg: Sidney reported on the growing differences between Casimir and his brother in a letter to Walsingham of 22 March. At Nuremberg, where he arrived on 29 March, Sidney was reunited with Languet; they dined with Philip Camerarius, and Sidney explained why there are no wolves in England, and talked about Ireland. Prague was reached on 4 April, which was Maundy Thursday, and Sidney had his first interview with the emperor on Easter Monday, finding him 'sullen of disposition, very secret and resolute' (Wallace, 177).

The Jesuit Edmund Campion was among those Sidney came across in Prague: he had disputed before the queen at Oxford in 1566 and Sidney may have attended his lectures as an undergraduate. Sidney saw Campion in private on several occasions in Prague, and may even have heard him preach. Contemporary Catholic accounts suggest that Sidney was deeply influenced by Campion: 'he professed himself convinced, but said that it was necessary for him to hold on the course which he had hitherto followed; yet he promised never to hurt or injure any Catholic' (Duncan-Jones, *Sidney: Courtier Poet*, 125). Both Sidney and his father appear to have been generally opposed to harsh measures against Roman Catholics. In Venice he had consorted with Catholic friends, including his kinsman Richard Shelley and the devout Edward, third Lord Windsor: Sidney later engaged in court entertainments with Windsor's son Frederick. His interest in New World exploration and settlement may well reflect a desire to provide a tolerant society for recusants. Yet although Sidney appears to have been sympathetic towards and friendly with Catholics, and associated with them throughout his life, he was no closet adherent to their faith. His political affiliations, including his eventual marriage to Sir Francis Walsingham's daughter, and his later literary projects, like his translations of the Psalms and of *De la verité de la religion chrestienne* by his friend Du Plessis Mornay, point rather to an essentially protestant outlook.

After a fortnight in Prague, Sidney and his party retraced their steps, via Nuremberg, Heidelberg, where he met Ludwig, the other palatine count, and Cologne where he said farewell to Languet. The queen had recalled him to England, but she now directed him to visit William of Orange. He missed the Dutch leader at Brussels, went on to Antwerp which he left on 27 May, and met William at the fortress-town of Geertruidenberg. The party moved to Middelburg where Sidney stood deputy to Leicester as godfather to the second daughter of William of Orange and his third wife, Charlotte de Bourbon. Earlier in the mission there had been talk that Sidney might marry a German princess, perhaps either Casimir's sister or Elizabeth von Anhalt. Now it seemed possible that he would marry Marie von Nassau, William's daughter from his first marriage. After a week at William's court, however, Sidney had left by 5 June and by the 10th he was back at court in England. Sidney's friends and supporters promoted the idea that the mission had been a great success, but in truth the arrangements for a protestant league had made scarcely any progress.

First writings, 1577–1582 Sidney's return from the continent was not followed by any progress about his marriage either. Furthermore the queen conspicuously failed to reward him with a knighthood or to give him a suitable post. On his return he had his portrait painted, and also became more involved with Du Plessis Mornay, who was beginning to write *De la verité de la religion chrestienne*, a work concerned with geography and politics as well as religion. In June 1578 he became godfather to Du Plessis Mornay's daughter Elisabeth. During the summer Sidney thought about joining his father in Ireland, visited his newly married sister at Wilton in late August and early September, and finally quarrelled with the eleventh earl of Ormond who was undermining Sir Henry Sidney's position with the queen. This row, which was current during September, led to Sidney's refusing to answer Ormond when he spoke to him, 'but was in dead silence of purpose', as Waterhouse described it (Wallace, 191): Sidney was treating a courtier nobler in birth than himself with open contempt. The dispute prompted Sidney to write a defence of his father's conduct, particularly over his imposition of the cess, a tax on Irish lords living within the pale. The work seems to have had some success, for on 1 November the queen and the privy council allowed that Sir Henry's imposition of the cess was legal. Philip Sidney returned to Wilton with his uncles Leicester and Warwick, and on 16 December wrote from there to the earl of Sussex, who was lord chamberlain, asking to be excused from court over the Christmas season. He did, however, exchange new-year gifts with the queen, giving her a cambric smock.

Although various plans for further overseas travel are mentioned in Sidney's correspondence at this time, nothing came of them. The contacts he had made with Casimir and William of Orange did not result in a role as a European military leader; the protestant league did not materialize. When Frobisher returned from his second voyage in September 1577, Sidney thought of accompanying him to the New World, while in March 1578 he had an 'Indian project' in mind: he invested £67 10s. in Frobisher's third voyage which began in May. But in the end he stayed in England spending his time at court and at Wilton, and launched his career as an imaginative writer by making a start on what became the first version of the *Arcadia*, now known as the *Old Arcadia*: as he put it, 'in these my not old years and idlest times', he 'slipped into the title of a poet' (*Miscellaneous Prose*, 73). It combines poetry and prose, with verse eclogues placed at the end of each of the first four (out of five) books or acts. The poems show Sidney displaying a wide range of poetical forms, including experiments in writing English poetry in classical metres.

In the meantime Sidney was also involved in the political events, the courtly entertainments, and the literary activities associated with the second courtship of the queen by the duc d'Anjou (formerly Alençon) (1578–82). It is almost certain that he took a leading part in the Accession day tilt in November 1577, contributing at least three poems to it. His verses provide further evidence that Sidney had now become an accomplished poet, had devised his pastoral persona of the melancholy shepherd Philisides, and had begun to use *imprese*, emblematic devices accompanied by apt mottoes, to sum up his feelings and ideas about his life. Among the personal *imprese* and mottoes he is known to have used are *Vix ea nostra voco* ('I scarcely call those things my own'), and *Sic nos non nobis* ('Thus we do [or are], not for ourselves'). Then in May 1578, just after he had received the earl and countess of Pembroke at Penshurst, he wrote an entertainment, known as 'The Lady of May', for Queen Elizabeth's visit to Wanstead in Essex where Leicester received her. Among the characters who appear in the show is Rombus, perhaps played by Richard Tarlton: Sidney was his son's godfather.

Court politics, 1578–1579 Sidney was still with the queen at the end of May 1578 when he wrote a short and bitterly aggressive letter to his father's secretary, Edmund Molyneux, accusing him of opening his letters to his father, and making an unambiguous threat that if Molyneux offended again 'I will thruste my Dagger into yow' (*Complete Works*, 3.124): the secretary denied the charge. In April and May Count Johann Casimir sought support from the queen for an invasion of the Low Countries, and wanted Sidney appointed to lead the English forces; but although the queen gave him permission to go in July Leicester was opposed, and by the end of the year nothing had come of it. Abraham Fraunce may have prepared a manuscript summary of Ramist logic accompanied by a collection of *imprese* (Bodl. Oxf., MS Rawl. D.345) as a farewell gift on this occasion.

Gabriel Harvey also refers to Sidney's imminent departure in a volume of Latin poems, usually known as *Gratulationes Valdinenses*, prompted by the queen's visit during her summer progress to Audley End, Essex, where the University of Cambridge joined her for academic disputations. The visit took place between 26 and 30 July, and by September Harvey had written, collected, and printed the Latin verses. The poems in the last of the four books are addressed to Oxford, Hatton, and Sidney. Although the ones to Sidney are extravagant in their claims of affectionate friendship and their praise for him as the perfect courtier, they are not as tactless as two pieces praising Leicester at the expense of Machiavelli (standing probably for Anjou), and urging the queen to marry her English suitor. However, on 20 September Leicester secretly married Lettice Devereux, who may have been pregnant at the time. When Sidney learned of the wedding he must have realized that his position as his uncle's heir was no longer secure. His expansive and undated letter of advice about foreign travel to his brother Robert probably belongs to this period, late in 1578: Robert Sidney set out on a continental tour in February 1579.

For his new-year gift at the beginning of 1579, Sidney gave the queen a white sarcenet waistcoat. Johann Casimir now decided to visit England to make an appeal for aid to Elizabeth in person: among the party was Languet. Sidney and his father went to meet Casimir on the Kent coast and accompanied him to London, where he arrived at the Tower on 22 January. The visit was a social success with extravagant gifts and entertainment, but the queen would not accede to any of the prince's requests, and the party left on 14 February, in such a hurry—'as if they were taking leave of enemies, not of friends' (Duncan-Jones, *Sidney: Courtier Poet*, 158)—that Languet did not have the chance to say farewell properly to Sidney and Dyer. The disappointment of this visit was compounded by the arrival in England on 5 January of Jean de Simier, Anjou's agent, whose task it was to open negotiations for his marriage to the queen. The debates at court and within the privy council over the marriage continued throughout the year: Sidney was bound, not least by family ties, to be part of the anti-marriage faction that gathered around Leicester, Walsingham, Pembroke, and Hatton, and which was opposed by a smaller group, led by Burghley and Sussex, which, if it did not fully support the marriage, did not wish to rule it out immediately. In July Simier revealed Leicester's secret marriage to Elizabeth (who was furious), and the earl's faction received another blow when Anjou himself arrived in England on 17 August.

Those opposed to the marriage responded with the publication in 1579 of John Stubbe's book *The Discoverie of a Gaping Gulfe* in print, and the circulation in manuscript of Sidney's *A Letter to Queen Elizabeth Touching her Marriage with Monsieur*. Sidney's widely circulated tract, arguing against change to the queen's state, since it made her popular and had brought safety to the country, was probably commissioned at a meeting at which Leicester was present, held at Baynard's Castle, the earl of Pembroke's London house, shortly after Anjou's arrival in mid-August. Whereas Stubbe and his publisher William Page were punished with the loss of their right hands on 3 November, it seems that Elizabeth did not respond badly to Sidney's unsolicited advice. She did, however, reprove him for his quarrel on the tennis court with the earl of Oxford which had taken place by 28 August, when Sidney referred to it in a letter to Hatton.

The chief source for this incident is Greville's *A Dedication*, in which—surprisingly—he makes no connection between the quarrel and the Anjou marriage which Oxford, a Catholic sympathizer, seems to have supported. The quarrel probably took place on the tennis court at Greenwich Palace where Sidney was playing. Upon Oxford's demanding the use of the court, Sidney replied

that if he had asked politely he would have given it to him. Oxford responded by calling Sidney 'by the name of puppy'. The row attracted members of the French embassy, and Sidney challenged Oxford to repeat the insult in front of them, which he did, whereupon Sidney 'gave my lord a lie impossible … in respect all the world knows puppies are gotten by dogs and children by men'. He and his companions then left the court, defeated. Oxford sent Sidney a challenge a couple of days later, perhaps through Ralegh, but the queen now reminded Sidney of his inferior position to Oxford and of the monarch's need to maintain differences of rank. According to Greville, Sidney's response was to point out that 'the difference of degrees between free men could not challenge any other homage than precedency' (*Prose Works*, 39).

Family matters, 1579–1581 Although he was not punished either for *A Letter* or for his quarrel with Oxford, Sidney seems now to have chosen to withdraw from public and political life and to pursue his writing career: further plans to join William of Orange and to see Languet again came to nothing. The bulk of the *Old Arcadia*, begun in 1578 after his return from his imperial mission, was probably composed between the autumn of 1579 and the spring of 1581 at the latest: Sidney then revised the work several times during 1581–2. He dedicated it to his sister and said that it was mostly written in her presence, and so presumably at Wilton. A glimpse of Sidney's literary activities at this time is provided by an exchange of letters between Gabriel Harvey and Edmund Spenser which was published in August or September 1580. In them Harvey seeks to associate himself with Sidney and Dyer, stressing their common interest in writing English verse in classical metres: his reference to an academy or learned society (the 'Areopagus') where this practice is discussed is probably a joke. Harvey linked Sidney and Dyer with the diplomat and neo-Latin poet Daniel Rogers, and it was mainly through Rogers and the English ambassador Thomas Randolph that Sidney and his circle became involved with the Scottish poet and historian George Buchanan, whose literary and political interests they shared. Buchanan's enthusiasm for 'divine' poetry, especially the translation of the Psalms into Latin verse, his writings on political theory, and above all his close involvement with James VI and with developments at the Scottish court, all proved deeply sympathetic to Sidney and his friends: their concern with Scottish affairs, especially in regard to the succession to the English throne, continued after Buchanan's death in 1582.

Sidney was at court for the Accession day tilt of 1579, and gave the queen a crystal cup with a cover as his new-year gift in 1580. But by 22 May he was back at Wilton, where he wrote a long letter of advice, in effect a reading list, to Edward Denny, a courtier and soldier who was about to go to Ireland with Lord Grey, the newly appointed lord deputy (a post Sidney himself hankered after), and also with Spenser. On 8 April Sidney's sister gave birth to a son, William Herbert, and Sidney stood deputy to Leicester as godfather at the baptism at Wilton in May. When he wrote again at length to his brother Robert on 18 October about the latter's education, and promising to send him 'My toyfull booke', almost certainly the *Arcadia*, by the following February, he was at Leicester House (*Complete Works*, 3.132).

Sidney probably spent most of the winter and spring of 1580–81 at court, signalling his submission to the queen with a new-year gift to her of a jewel in the form of a diamond-studded gold whip. In April 1581 the countess of Leicester gave birth to a son, Robert, Baron Denbigh (*d.* 19 July 1584), who now displaced Sidney as the earl's heir: Camden reports that Sidney marked the birth by appearing at the next tilt with the crossed-through motto *Speravi* ('I hoped'), and he was largely written out of the new will which Leicester drew up in January 1582. January 1581 saw the arrival at court of Sidney's aunt the countess of Huntingdon, along with Penelope Devereux [*see* Rich, Penelope] (then about eighteen) and her sister Dorothy. The countess had been largely responsible for their upbringing at Ashby-de-la-Zouch after the death of their father, the earl of Essex, in Ireland in 1576. It is just possible that Sidney may have met Penelope when she was a very small child, before her arrival at court: her father had wished just four days before his death that Sidney should marry her. But at the end of February the second Lord Rich died, and his son Robert succeeded to the title and to considerable wealth. In under a fortnight he was spoken of as a suitable match for her, and they were probably married on 1 November.

Back at court, 1581 While this business was going on Sidney was particularly busy with courtly and political events; he was also finishing and revising the *Old Arcadia*. He sat as a member for Shrewsbury in the 1581 session of the parliament of 1572: there is no evidence that he ever spoke in the House of Commons, but on 25 January he sat on a committee for the subsidy and on 1 February on one dealing with slanderous speeches and seditious practices against the queen. On 22 January he took part with Philip Howard, the future earl of Arundel, and Edward, Lord Windsor, in a court entertainment, the 'Callophisus Challenge': its participants sought the queen's favour, and Sidney may have written his own speech as the Blue Knight. A second tournament, known as the 'Four Foster Children of Desire' or the 'Fortress of Perfect Beauty', in which Sidney appeared again with Arundel, Windsor, and Greville, was conceived on a far grander scale. It took place in a specially erected banqueting house in Whitehall over two days, 15–16 May, in front of the French ambassadors. Sidney probably helped devise the entertainment, almost certainly contributing two sonnets, and may have been responsible for some of the speeches in it, but even with the assistance of a contemporary account by one Henry Goldwell, published in 1581 and partly reprinted in Holinshed's *Chronicles*, its narrative is hard to follow. The tilting, tourney, and barriers seem to have been designed to show that the Fortress of Perfect Beauty, presumably representing the queen, could not be taken. Whatever the entertainment signified, negotiations during the summer for the royal marriage gave way to no more than an Anglo-French treaty.

That summer also saw the distribution on 27 June of Campion's *Decem rationes* in the university church at Oxford, timed to coincide with Leicester's visit as chancellor. Sidney may have been with the earl on this occasion, and may have attended his former friend's interrogation at York House on 26 July. He was also involved with Dom Antonio, the Portuguese pretender, who sought the queen's help in winning his kingdom and wanted to enlist Sidney in any expedition. When the pretender left Sidney accompanied him to Dover, where by the end of September he had become weary with waiting for him to go. About then he probably heard of the death of Languet (on 30 September) and of Penelope Devereux's marriage. Once more back in London in October, he wrote earnestly to Sir Christopher Hatton on 14 November in connection with an unnamed office, and three days later may have taken part in the Accession day tilt in front of Anjou, who had returned for a private visit. A month later he was at Wilton with his sister, who had given birth to a girl, Katherine, on 15 October. In December he supported Tobie Matthew who was lobbying to become dean of Durham. At the end of the year he found himself in the awkward position, in view of his tolerant religious principles, of being invited to profit from the confiscated goods of Roman Catholics.

Poetry and money, 1582 Sidney was absent from court at new year 1582 (though he gave the queen a diamond-studded jewel in the form of a castle, intended to hold flowers), and so he missed the elaborate and magnificent tilt that was staged for Anjou. But he accompanied the latter to Dover later in January and was one of the party, including Leicester, that went on to Antwerp. It was against this background of Penelope Devereux's marriage to Lord Rich and Sidney's own involvement at court during 1581 that *Astrophil and Stella* grew. The sequence of 108 sonnets, interspersed with eleven songs, tells of the unhappy and unresolved love of Astrophil, the star-lover, for the married Stella, the star. There can be no doubt that Penelope's marriage to Lord Rich provided the inspirational spur for the poem. The sequence invites the reader to identify Astrophil, whose father is governor of Ireland, with Sidney himself, and Stella, who 'Hath no misfortune, but that Rich she is' (sonnet 37), with Penelope, but it does not form a simple autobiography and carefully evades telling a straightforward personal story or providing a plain historical narrative. It is therefore impossible to tell exactly how important Penelope Devereux was in Sidney's life, as opposed to her part in his poetry.

In the spring of 1582 Sidney retired again from court and spent some time in Hereford and the Welsh marches with his father, probably with a view to eventually succeeding him as lord president. It seems likely that he composed a version of most of his sonnet sequence then, and *A Defence of Poetry* may belong to the same period: however, the composition of both works may well have extended into 1583. Absence from court may not only have assisted literary composition, it also saved money, and the Sidney fortunes were now approaching a crisis. The family were not great landowners and Sir Henry's service in Ireland and

Wales was expensive; the problem was compounded by his and his wife's keeping separate establishments, by his daughter Mary's £3000 dowry, by their eldest son's extravagance, and by the latter's failure to receive a significant official position.

As early as 1564 Philip Sidney received the income of a church benefice in Wales; to this he added a Welsh prebend in the next year, and more may have followed. Later he derived some money from his offices as royal cupbearer and as steward to the bishop of Winchester (a position granted in 1580), and from work in the ordnance office. Additional funds seem to have come from fines raised on recusants. But he continually had to borrow money against his uncle's inheritance, both to finance his life and to invest in speculative expeditions. In keeping with his status he spent lavishly during his continental tour of 1572–5, and in January 1575 Languet agreed to make a gift or loan to him of all his savings. The mission to the emperor in the spring of 1577 cost the Sidneys a further £840. Sidney's patronage, including his literary patronage, was also considerable.

Marriage, 1583–1584 The queen's unwillingness to give Sidney any important office sprang from a variety of reasons: he was irascible, ambitious, proud, and perhaps unreliable; his religious faith may not have been certain; he behaved and was received as a powerful figure abroad; it may therefore have seemed best to keep his power base at home as narrow as possible. When he was finally knighted on 13 January 1583, it was because Johann Casimir had named him as his proxy for his own installation as a knight of the Garter. The rumour in March that Sidney was to be made captain of the Isle of Wight proved false. Later in the spring the Polish prince Olbracht Laski came to England, and with Sidney visited John Dee on 15 June. Another visitor, Henri of Navarre's agent, Jacques Ségur-Pardailhan, went to Wilton in July with Sir Philip who introduced him to Archibald Douglas, a further sign of Sidney's developing concern with Scottish affairs. About this time he also began to lay down plans for investing in North American discoveries. Perhaps the most interesting of Sidney's new friends during this period was the philosopher Giordano Bruno, who stayed in England from the spring of 1583 until nearly the end of 1585: he spent three months at Oxford, but lived most of the time in the London house of the French ambassador, Michel Castelnau de Mauvissière. It is likely that Sidney was present at the Ash Wednesday meal in Greville's house on 15 February 1584 which forms the setting for Bruno's *La cena delle ceneri* (1584).

Deprived of office and advancement, Sidney's best hope lay in making a wealthy marriage. He had been proposed as the husband for several young women: in 1573 while he was on his European tour, it was planned that he should marry one of the daughters of Henry, Lord Berkeley, perhaps to end disputes between Leicester and the Berkeleys; according to Leicester's will of 1582, there was a similar possibility that he might marry Penelope Devereux's sister Dorothy. These and other marital schemes came to nothing, and it may have seemed that like his closest friends, Dyer, Greville, and Languet, he would die unmarried. Nevertheless, by 19 March 1583 a match between Sidney and Frances Walsingham (then fifteen) had been formalized, to the annoyance of the queen, who had not been told about it. The marriage itself took place on 21 September, and as part of its settlement Walsingham agreed to underwrite up to £1500 of Sidney's debts. Marriage brought Sidney new homes at Barn Elms in Surrey and Walsingham House in Seething Lane, London, but the relationship between him and his young wife seems to have been detached: his identification with his father-in-law's political outlook appears, however, to have been quite strong.

The year following Sidney's marriage was perhaps the most intense and complicated of his life: it was also the year in which he probably completed a radical revision of the *Old Arcadia*, transforming it into the work now known as the *New Arcadia*. Conceived as a larger, darker, more complex and epic romance than the *Old Arcadia*, it runs to twice the length of the original version. However, the revision ends in mid-sentence in the third book, and it is possible that Sidney broke off partly because he at last was to be employed by the queen. On 10 June 1584 Anjou died; this was followed on 10 July by the assassination of William of Orange. These deaths destabilized the Low Countries.

Elizabeth now chose Sidney to lead a diplomatic mission to convey her condolences to Anjou's mother, Catherine de' Medici, and to enlist French support against Spain in the Low Countries. The mission set out from London on 10 July but abandoned its journey at Gravesend on receiving news that Henri III had broken up his court, leaving Paris largely deserted. There is some evidence that Sidney may have tried to take out his frustration over the failed mission on the English ambassador to France, Sir Edward Stafford. On 21 July he wrote to Stafford encouraging him 'to begyn betymes to demand something of her Majesti as might be found fitt for yow', implying that Stafford had already incurred the queen's displeasure. In the same letter Sidney mentions that he and others are 'haulf perswaded … very eagerli' to join Sir Humphrey Gilbert's expedition to Newfoundland which established the first English colony on the American mainland (*Complete Works*, 3.145). In the summer of 1582 Sidney had bought the right to some 3 million acres which he hoped Gilbert would discover in America: Sir Thomas Gerrard and Sir George Peckham, who were both Catholics, received similar grants, and it seems that part of the plan was to establish a colony where Catholics could live freely. A year later, in July 1583, Sidney granted part of his own lands to Peckham to equip a ship for the next expedition.

Two days before Sidney wrote to Stafford, Leicester's infant son and heir Robert, Baron Denbigh, died at Wanstead. This gave Sidney hopes of restoring his future fortunes. Almost at once his loyalties towards Leicester were tested by the publication in September of the brilliant attack on his uncle known as *Leicester's Commonwealth*. In keeping with his new position as his heir, Sidney's *Defence of the Earl of Leicester* is much concerned with the question of the gentility of the Dudley family, in this perhaps reflecting his own earlier quarrels with the earl of Oxford, whose friend Charles Arundell was thought to be the leader of the Catholic exiles held responsible for *Leicester's Commonwealth*. It is interesting that on 27 August 1584 the Catholic Henry Howard, later earl of Northampton, wrote to Sidney from prison, rehearsing his troubles and asking Sidney to renew his assured friendship on his behalf. Howard was closely associated with the circle responsible for *Leicester's Commonwealth*, but unfortunately no evidence survives for Sidney's response to his appeal.

Sidney offered to fight his uncle's libeller 'in any place of Europe' (*Miscellaneous Prose*, 140). However, his longing to leave England having been thwarted by the failure of his French mission, as well as by his not joining Gilbert's expedition, Sidney instead found himself increasingly drawn to domestic affairs. In the first part of 1583 he had begun agitating for a post in the ordnance office: in the winter of 1582–3 his uncle the earl of Warwick, who was master of the office, had petitioned the queen that Sidney should join him there. He was not granted the post until July 1585, but during the summer of 1584 he was engaged in its business, in particular in strengthening Dover harbour.

Elected a knight of the shire for Kent in the parliament that assembled in November 1584, during the following winter and spring Sidney sat on several Commons committees, one of them concerned with Ralegh's letters patent for exploration and another with legislation against Jesuits and seminary priests. At court he took part in the Accession day tilt and on 6 December was one of ten married men who fought with swords at Westminster against ten bachelors.

Seeking employment, 1584–1586 It is particularly hard to judge Sidney's state of mind during 1584–5. Early in January 1585 he must have learned that his wife was pregnant. In the following summer he was much occupied as an intermediary between three banished Scottish noblemen, the earls of Mar, Angus, and Glamis, James VI's ambassador the master of Gray, and Queen Elizabeth. This involvement in Scottish affairs led James to develop a great admiration for Sidney, which the latter returned. At some point in 1585 or 1586 Sidney commissioned an opinion from the civilian John Hammond concerning the legitimacy of the imprisonment and execution of Mary, queen of Scots. Largely absent from the court during the later part of the summer, Sidney soon found himself at the centre of affairs again, when Ralph Lane wrote to him in August, inviting him to become governor or general of the English colonists in Virginia: Sidney might have gone on the expedition that had left for America in the previous spring, but now Lane suggested that the way to diminish Spanish power was to attack their mines in the New World.

Sidney did not pursue this offer, but it was rapidly followed by another opportunity. In the first week of September 1585 he and Greville hurriedly went to Plymouth to join Sir Francis Drake's voyage to the West Indies. According to Greville, Sidney's excuse was that he wanted to see Dom Antonio again. Sidney may secretly have hoped to share the leadership with Drake of this expedition, whose purpose seems to have been to intensify the war against Spain: but his plans were thwarted, not least because Drake was unwilling to be involved covertly and against the queen's wishes with Sidney, who was soon summoned back to court. The latter's motives in this episode are not clear, but they may have been connected to the events in the Low Countries. By September 1586 it had been agreed that Leicester would lead English forces there: their costs were to be paid by the Dutch and three ports were to be placed under English rule as security for the payment. The queen was initially unwilling to appoint Sidney to be governor of Flushing, one of these cautionary towns, and Drake's expedition may have looked especially appealing while he waited for the office. On his return to court from Plymouth, however, the queen's anger at his suddenly seeking to leave the country was mitigated by her after all appointing him to the governorship.

Service in the Netherlands, 1586 Sidney's daughter Elizabeth was born in October 1586 and baptized on 20 November at St Olave, Hart Street: the queen herself was present as godmother. Sidney missed the baptism, for he had been granted letters patent for his appointment on 9 November; the next day he was at Gravesend, writing to the queen, sending her 'such a cypher as little leysure coold afoord me' (*Complete Works*, 3.147)—his father had been Edward VI's chief cipherer. Before then Sidney had had to gather men, money, horses, and arms to equip his own entourage, which included his brother Robert; Greville was not allowed to go to the Low Countries and the two schoolfriends never met again. The party arrived at Rammekens, 4 miles from Flushing, on 19 November. Sidney's melancholy mood was immediately apparent, and it became clear, as Greville reported, that almost from the start his friend had few illusions about the chances of an English success in the war against the Spanish. Furthermore, again according to Greville, Leicester had a low opinion of his nephew's capabilities, 'despising his youth for a counsellor, but withal bearing a hand upon him as a forward young man' (*Prose Works*, 18).

Sidney rented a house in Flushing from Jacques Gelée, and found the English troops already in the town to be ill, hungry, and in poor spirits. On 22 November he was sworn as governor, and set out to deal with his men's problems. He hoped that things would be much improved by Leicester's arrival. On 10 December the earl was welcomed there, along with William of Orange's young son Prince Maurice, and Sidney then accompanied his uncle on his progress around the country. At Leiden on 9 January 1586 Sidney was nominated as one of Leicester's deputies in negotiations with the states general, and became involved in the decision taken on the 24th (to the queen's fury) that the earl should take the title of governor-general. Partly as a reward for his support, Sidney was made the colonel of a Zeeland regiment, and it was also suggested that he might replace Prince Maurice as governor of the isles. None of this pleased the queen, who still suspected Sidney of over-weening ambition. In fact Sidney wanted to extend the role of the English forces from a defensive to an offensive one, and at the beginning of February he began a plan to take Steenbergen. The English attempt on the town at the end of the month failed, and Sidney was left in a state of troubled depression: he ruled out the possibility that his wife might come and stay in a house in Bergen op Zoom, and when his father died on 5 May the queen refused to grant him leave to return home.

Instead Frances Sidney came to join her husband late in June, staying with William of Orange's widow, Louise de Coligny, in Flushing. At the same time Sidney was engaged with his brother and Count Hohenlohe in attacking Spanish troops around Breda, and with Prince Maurice in an assault on the town of Axel, which was taken on 7 July. A week later Sidney was nearly captured by the Spanish in a trap set for him at Gravelines, where about forty of his troops were killed. On 9 August his mother died, and his sister was said to be unwell. His troops in Flushing were in a bad way and unpaid; he began to criticize his uncle's policies and behaviour, while quarrels broke out among the English and Dutch allies.

At the beginning of September Sidney was present at the successful siege of the town of Doesburg, and by the middle of the month he was with his uncle and brother at Deventer. From there on 14 September Leicester and Sidney went towards Zutphen, fearing that the duke of Parma and the whole Spanish army were on their way there. The plan was for the English commanders, Sir John Norris and Sir William Stanley, to intercept a supply convoy; Sidney, who had left his regiment in Deventer, was to fight as an independent soldier. On the morning of 22 September in thick mist the English attacked enemy forces which turned out to be greater than expected. Sidney had one horse killed under him, and while rescuing Peregrine Bertie, Lord Willoughby, was hit by a musket shot just above the knee of his left leg: he was not wearing thigh armour. The skirmish failed to stop the Spanish relief of Zutphen.

Death and funeral, 1586–1587 Leicester was moved by the courage with which his nephew endured his wound, and had him taken in his own barge down the River Issel to Arnhem. There he lay for twenty-five days in the house of Mlle Gruithuissens. His shattered leg appeared to be healing, and by 2 October Leicester reported to Walsingham that the worst was over, that Sidney was eating and sleeping well. But soon after a visit by Leicester on the 7th, Sidney's health began to decline dramatically. With his shoulder bones rubbed raw through lying down for so long, enduring more treatment from his doctors, Sidney realized that his leg had developed gangrene: the bullet lay too deep to be extracted and amputation was apparently not considered. He had written his will on 30 September. On 15 October his uncle paid him a final visit. During the evening of 16 October he wrote a desperate letter to Jan Wier, physician to the duke of Cleves, begging him to come. He died between 2 and 3 p.m. on the 17th, having dictated a codicil to his will.

Sidney's body was taken from Arnhem to Flushing on 23 October and on 5 November was brought back to England, where it lay in the Minories while Walsingham tried to sort out his son-in-law's financial problems, a task that is said to have cost him some £6000: at the end of the year his daughter Frances Sidney miscarried. Sidney's funeral did not take place until 16 February 1587. Some 700 mourners processed from the Minories to St Paul's Cathedral where he was buried. His father-in-law was later buried beside him, but no permanent memorial was ever erected to Sidney; Greville's scheme of 1615 for a double tomb for himself and Sidney was not carried out.

Sidney's death was mourned by many of the poets of the time, among them Breton, Constable, Daniel, Drayton, Gorges, Jonson, Ralegh, and Spenser. The memorial volumes published at the time of his death included ones by Churchyard, Day, and Whetstone, and collections of Latin verse from the English universities, as well as one from Leiden by Georgius Benedicti. The first poem in the Cambridge collection of *Lachrymae*, edited by Alexander Neville, was by James VI; the first elegy was by Gabriel Harvey. The Oxford volume, *Exequiae*, was edited by William Gager; a volume from New College was edited by John Lloyd. Drawings of Sidney's funeral procession made by Sidney's servant the musician and herald Thomas Lant, were engraved by Theodore de Bry to form a panorama over 35 feet in length.

In his will Sidney divided most of his estate between his wife and his brother Robert. Among many bequests to his family, relations, friends, and servants, he left his books to Dyer and Greville and his best sword to Robert Devereux, earl of Essex, who later married his widow. The will displays Sidney's characteristic generosity, but his estate was not great enough to fulfil his bequests: legal and financial arguments over his will continued for some time.

Patronage and servants Sidney's extensive literary patronage led him to receive the dedications of many printed books and several manuscripts from English and continental writers. Notable among them were Spenser's *The Shepheardes Calender* (1578); Stephen Gosson's *The Schoole of Abuse* (1579), to which Sidney supposedly replied in *A Defence of Poetry*; Richard Hakluyt's first book, *Divers Voyages* (1582), with a polar map of North America also dedicated to Sidney by Michael Lok; Bruno's two works *De gl'heroici furori* (1584) and *Spaccio de la bestia trionfante* (1585); Alberico Gentili's *De legationibus* (1585); the elder Janus Dousa's *Odarum Britannicarum liber I* (Leiden, 1586); and Justus Lipsius's *De recta pronuntiatione Latinae linguae dialogus* (Antwerp, 1586). He also received manuscript dedications from Abraham Fraunce, Henry Finch, and William Temple. Latin poems were addressed to him by Daniel Rogers and an important English one was intended for him by Geoffrey Whitney, but presented instead to Dyer.

Sidney had a number of other servants and employees. The only secretary he is known certainly to have employed was Stephen Le Sieur, but the scribe of the Clifford manuscript of the *Old Arcadia* (now in the Folger

Shakespeare Library) can be identified as Richard Robinson, who recorded that Sidney and his father were 'many tymes benevolent unto my pore study' (BL, Royal MS 18 A.lxvi, fol. 5v). The printer John Wolfe called himself Sidney's servant on the title-page of Jacobus Acontius's *Una essortatione al timor di Dio* (1579?). In addition to the lost portraits by Veronese and Abondio, likenesses of Sidney were commissioned in the summer of 1577 after his mission to Rudolph II and in 1583 or 1584, perhaps in connection with his marriage. These portrait types have been attributed respectively to Cornelis Ketel and John de Critz. It seems that Nicholas Hilliard too painted a full-length miniature of him; in his *The Arte of Limning* Hilliard reports a conversation with Sidney concerning the problems of proportion in full-length miniatures. That the young composer Daniel Bachelar accompanied him to the Low Countries as a servant suggests the importance of music and song to Sidney.

Works and canon With the possible exception of the two sonnets he may have contributed to Goldwell's account of the 'Fortress of Perfect Beauty' entertainment of 1581, Sidney probably never saw any of his writings in print. During his lifetime they circulated, if at all, in manuscript: only one of his poems survives in his own autograph. His preference for publication in manuscript was common at the time among writers who were not professional authors. When in the dedication to his sister he describes the *Old Arcadia* as 'but a trifle, and that triflingly handled' (Sidney, *Old Arcadia*, 3), or when he makes Astrophil lament that 'My youth doth waste, my knowledge brings forth toyes' (sonnet 18), he is striking a characteristically Renaissance pose of studied negligence. In fact the care with which he revised and rewrote some of his works, most notably the *Arcadia*, shows his deep concern for his art. Sidney does not seem to have written to gain patronage or to win general applause, but rather to entertain his friends, family, and the court; to address and influence specific political issues; and to explore and perhaps relieve his own feelings of frustration in love and worldly affairs.

Sidney's most widely copied work was *A Letter to Queen Elizabeth*, but he allowed multiple copies of the *Old Arcadia* to be made, and some of the poems incorporated in it and others in *Certain Sonnets* were also allowed to circulate: the few surviving manuscripts of *Astrophil and Stella* and *A Defence of Poetry* suggest that he kept those works to a very small circle. Those with access to his manuscript writings tended to be his family (the countess of Pembroke), friends at court (Sir Henry Lee), poets (Abraham Fraunce and Samuel Daniel), and especially school and university friends (Arthur Ottley, Humfrey Coningsby) and East Anglian music lovers: an unusually large number of these appear to have been recusants (Edward Bannister, the Paston and Cornwallis families, Sir Edmund Huddleston). The most enthusiastic of the later admirers of his work in manuscript was Sir John Harington.

The business of transferring Sidney's works to print had begun by November 1586, when Greville reported to Walsingham that an edition of the *Old Arcadia* was threatened.

This was stopped, but the attempt to halt the publication of *A Woorke Concerning the Trewnesse of the Christian Religion*, Arthur Golding's translation of Du Plessis Mornay, failed: it was published in 1587 with the incorrect claim that Sidney was its joint author. Sidney had produced a translation of Mornay, probably late in his life, and Greville wished to include it in a collected volume of his friend's religious writings, along with his version of Du Bartas's *Semaine* and of the forty or so psalms that he translated into various metres, also probably in his last years. The volume never appeared. Instead Greville, with the help of Matthew Gwinne and John Florio, prepared an edition of the *New Arcadia* which was published in the spring of 1590.

This was followed a year later by two editions of *Astrophil and Stella*, both published by Thomas Newman. The first was apparently unauthorized and was suppressed by the Stationers' Company with the assistance of Lord Burghley: in addition to a text of the sequence which differs from most others, it contained a dedication from the publisher to Francis Flower, a brilliant epistle by Thomas Nashe, a series of sonnets by Samuel Daniel, and seven further poems, two of them by Thomas Campion and Greville. All these additional elements were omitted from the second quarto of 1591 which provided a different text of Sidney's sequence up to sonnet 95, but the extra poems were included in a third printing of about 1597–8.

Greville's edition of the incomplete *New Arcadia* was followed in 1593 by one for which the countess of Pembroke was responsible, assisted by her husband's secretary Hugh Sanford and perhaps by Samuel Daniel. This omitted the chapter headings written for 1590, revised its text, and completed it by appending the last three books of the *Old Arcadia*: a complete edition of Sidney's works was promised. In 1595 two editions of *A Defence of Poetry* were published: one, issued by William Ponsonby who had published the *Arcadia* editions of 1590 and 1593, was titled *The Defence of Poesie*; the other, issued by Henry Olney, was called *An Apologie for Poetrie*. It was Ponsonby's version that was reprinted by the countess in her 1598 edition of her brother's works: the latter, also published by Ponsonby, provided a definitive text of his works and established Sidney's reputation as a secular, erotic, and imaginative writer. The volume opened with the hybrid version of the *Arcadia*, followed by the hitherto unprinted collection of *Certain Sonnets*, which Sidney had probably written between 1577 and 1581, *A Defence of Poetry*, and *Astrophil and Stella* (which included sonnet 37, playing on Lord Rich's name, for the first time); the volume closed with the untitled entertainment known as 'The Lady of May'. The 1598 volume, pirated in Edinburgh in 1599, became the standard edition of Sidney's works, and was reprinted in 1605 and 1613 (with a new poem) and frequently thereafter.

Literary qualities and influence Although he valued some earlier vernacular literature, especially Chaucer's *Troilus and Criseyde* and the ballad of 'Percy and Douglas', Sidney's particular preoccupation was to modernize writing in

English, seeking to do this by imitating and adapting classical and contemporary European literature. In his poetry he was especially concerned with experimenting with different metres and verse forms. His interest in developing English took him on a different course from Spenser's exploration of an antique literary language, but he is constantly aware of the limitations of words themselves. Joseph Hall singled Sidney out for praise because of his introduction into English poetic practice of the French fondness for compound adjectives. In both its versions the *Arcadia* represents an extraordinary development of the handling of erotic and epic themes in romance, showing in their accounts of the relations between the sexes a particular engagement with women's experience of love and courtship, and with their potential for individual tragedy. The romances also share a practical and theoretical concern with political thought and the nature of government, and especially with the relationship between liberty and monarchy.

The sonnet craze of the 1590s was largely begun by the appearance in print in 1591 of *Astrophil and Stella*, the first such sequence to tell a story. Sidney's concern in his imaginative writings is centred on the experience of love, on the telling of stories, and on their endings. All his works display a consummate ability to control and organize his material, while maintaining a playful and usually good-tempered authorial voice. That voice, however, is never entirely free of a degree of melancholy and of a strong sense of frustration, which can rapidly change to anger and the threat of violence. The cult of the melancholy poet and lover which is so prominent in late Elizabethan and Jacobean literature owes much to Sidney's influence.

Reputation It was not until 1906–7, when Bertram Dobell obtained three manuscripts of the *Old Arcadia*, that Sidney's original work was discovered: it was printed in full for the first time by Albert Feuillerat in 1926. The hybrid *Arcadia*, in which the ending bore little relation to the beginning, was the one known to generations of readers: the work was published with supplements and passages designed to bridge the gap between the two versions by William Alexander (1613), Richard Beling (1624), James Johnstoun (1638), and Anna Weamys (1651). It was immensely influential: the tragic story of Argalus and Parthenia was widely admired; Shakespeare took the Gloucester sub-plot in *King Lear* from it; the author of *Eikon basilike* (1648) accused Charles I of using Pamela's prayer when he was imprisoned, a charge taken up by Milton in *Eikonoklastes* (1649). The *Arcadia* was one of the first English vernacular works to achieve a European readership, with translations into French (1624–5), German (1629), Dutch (1639), and Italian (1659). The last folio edition of Sidney's works, and the first to be illustrated, was printed in 1724 by Samuel Richardson who took the name of the heroine of his novel *Pamela* from one of the princesses in the romance. Sidney's reputation began to decline later in the eighteenth century, however, and his work was unfavourably criticized by Horace Walpole, William Hazlitt, and

T. S. Eliot, though it was defended by Charles Lamb and Virginia Woolf.

Sidney's translation of the Psalms, which did not reach print until 1828, was admired by John Ruskin, who produced a selected edition with commentary in 1877. Many of Languet's letters to Sidney were published at Frankfurt in 1633, reprinted at Leiden in 1646, and edited by David Dalrymple, Lord Hailes, at Edinburgh in 1776: some of these were printed in translation with Sidney's replies by Steuart A. Pears in 1845. Sidney's letters were collected in Albert Feuillerat's edition of his writings (1912–26), and can be supplemented by continental correspondence published in J. M. Osborn's *Young Philip Sidney* (1972). In addition to the lost translations of Du Bartas and Du Plessis Mornay, Sidney's version of the first two books of Aristotle's *Rhetoric* and his epistle to the unidentified Belerius remain undiscovered.

As well as being extremely clever, with a well-developed sense of humour, Sidney wrote fluently and often with a very light touch. Bookish, arrogant, prickly, and often willing to take offence when none was intended, he struck some of his contemporaries as solemn, aloof, and overserious: his health was not robust. His evident preference for male companions and friendship makes his sexual inclinations as uncertain as his religious views. He acquired his image as the perfect Renaissance courtier, simultaneously a poet, a lover, and a heroic soldier, during his lifetime, and embodied it in his own writings through the use of his personae Philisides and Astrophil. It was enshrined during and after his death in early biographical accounts, such as the one attributed to George Gifford, in which on his deathbed Sidney is reported to have said 'There came to my remembrance a vanity wherein I had taken delight, whereof I had not rid myself. It was my Lady Rich' (*Miscellaneous Prose*, 169). Another early life, *Nobilis*, was written by his sister's physician, Thomas Moffet, as an exemplary model for the young William Herbert. It was Fulke Greville who promoted the myths that his friend had dispensed with thigh armour because the marshal of the camp, Sir William Pelham, had done so, and that as he was being carried from the field at Zutphen he gave the contents of his bottle to a dying soldier with the words 'Thy necessity is yet greater than mine' (*Prose Works*, 77). This was the version of Sidney enshrined in P. B. Shelley's 'Adonais'.

The recovery and re-editing of Sidney's writings during the twentieth century have led him to be seen as among the most influential authors of the Elizabethan age. It can be claimed that he was the most important English writer since Geoffrey Chaucer, whose *Troilus and Criseyde* was one of his favourite works. Not only did he largely initiate the revival of the sonnet, his *Arcadia* popularized and domesticated chivalric romance for aristocratic and low-born audiences to such an extent that some readers found it hard to separate the world of his fiction from real life, and *A Defence of Poetry* supplied readers with one of the first formal pieces of vernacular literary criticism. His interest in political ideas meant that his work continued to be read well into the seventeenth century, and he has been seen as an important influence on radical and republican thought.

H. R. WOUDHUYSEN

Sources M. W. Wallace, *The life of Sir Philip Sidney* (1915) · K. Duncan-Jones, *Sir Philip Sidney: courtier poet* (1991) · *The poems of Sir Philip Sidney*, ed. W. A. Ringler (1962) · *Miscellaneous prose of Sir Philip Sidney*, ed. K. Duncan-Jones and J. van Dorsten (1973) · P. Sidney, *The countess of Pembroke's 'Arcadia' (the 'Old Arcadia')*, ed. J. Robertson (1973) · P. Sidney, *The countess of Pembroke's 'Arcadia' (the 'New Arcadia')*, ed. V. Skretkowicz (1987) · *The complete works of Sir Philip Sidney*, ed. A. Feuillerat, 4 vols. (1912–26) · *The prose works of Fulke Greville, Lord Brooke*, ed. J. Gouws (1986) · *The correspondence of Sir Philip Sidney and Hubert Languet*, ed. S. A. Pears (1845) · J. M. Osborn, *Young Philip Sidney* (1972) [includes continental correspondence] · D. Kay, ed., *Sir Philip Sidney: an anthology of modern criticism* (1987) [includes bibliography of early editions] · M. J. B. Allen, D. Baker-Smith, and A. F. Kinney, *Sir Philip Sidney's achievements* (1990) [includes account of portraits] · T. Moffet, *Nobilis, or, A view of the life and death of a Sidney, and Lessus lugubris*, ed. and trans. V. B. Heltzel and H. H. Hudson (1940) · J. Buxton, *Sir Philip Sidney and the English Renaissance* (1954) · K. Duncan-Jones, *Sir Philip Sidney: life, death and legend* (1986) · HoP, *Commons, 1558–1603*, 3.382–4 · R. M. Sargent, *The life and lyrics of Sir Edward Dyer* (1968) · *The works of Edmund Spenser*, ed. E. Greenlaw and others, 11 vols. (1932–57) · R. Kuin, 'Querre-Muhau: Sir Philip Sidney and the New World', *Renaissance Quarterly*, 51 (1998), 549–85 · V. Stern, *Gabriel Harvey: his life, marginalia and library* (1979) · H. R. Woudhuysen, *Sir Philip Sidney and the circulation of manuscripts, 1558–1640* (1996) · B. Worden, *The sound of virtue: Philip Sidney's 'Arcadia' and Elizabethan politics* (1996) · Bodl. Oxf., MS Bodley 858

Archives BL, corresp., Add. MS 15914 · BL, corresp., RP 125 [copies] · BL, corresp. and papers, Harley MSS · CKS, papers and related material | BL, letters to Walsingham and papers, Cotton MSS

Likenesses oil on panel, c.1576, NPG · C. Ketel?, oils, c.1577, Longleat, Wiltshire; version, Warwick Castle · portrait, 1578, Longleat, Wiltshire [*see illus.*] · J. de Critz?, oils, c.1583–1584 (version), Knebworth, Hertfordshire · J. de Critz?, oils, c.1583–1584 (version), Penshurst, Kent · J. de Critz?, oils, c.1583–1584 (version), Hall i'the Wood Museum, Bolton · attrib. J. de Critz, oils, c.1585, Penshurst, Kent · after J. de Critz, oils, Blickling Hall, Norfolk · Passe, line engraving, BM, NPG; repro. in H. Holland, *Herōologia* (1620) · oils (after Ketel?, c.1577), NPG

Wealth at death will bequeathed more than estate was worth; cost father-in-law, F. Walsingham, £6000: *Miscellaneous prose*, ed. Duncan-Jones and van Dorsten

Sidney, Philip, third earl of Leicester (1619–1698), parliamentarian army officer and politician, was born at Baynard's Castle, London, on 10 January 1619, the eldest son of Robert *Sidney, second earl of Leicester (1595–1677), and his wife, Dorothy (*bap.* 1598, *d.* 1659), eldest daughter of Henry *Percy, ninth earl of Northumberland. Philip's younger brothers included the republican theorist Algernon *Sidney (1623–1683) and the whig politician Henry *Sidney, earl of Romney. His sister Dorothy (1617–1691) became countess of Sunderland [*see* Spencer, Dorothy]. A group portrait by Van Dyck of Philip and his brothers Algernon and Robert is at Penshurst Place, Kent. From 1626, when his father succeeded as earl of Leicester, until his own accession to the title in 1677, Philip bore the courtesy title Viscount Lisle.

Lisle matriculated at Christ Church, Oxford, on 26 July 1634. He accompanied his father on his embassy to Denmark in 1632, and on his embassy to France in 1636. By then the earl's preference for his second son over his heir was already apparent: Algernon was more often in Paris with his father, while Philip was generally left to languish in a French country town. According to Algernon, the earl held 'a sinister opinion' of Philip from when he was a boy, and in later years vainly demanded that his heir 'should leave the lewd, infamous and Atheisticall life that he led' (Scott, *English Republic*, 60).

Lisle returned to England to serve in the second bishops' war, where he commanded the cuirassiers who formed the bodyguard of his uncle Algernon *Percy, tenth earl of Northumberland. In the Short Parliament of April 1640, and in the Long Parliament, Lisle represented the borough of Yarmouth in the Isle of Wight, doubtless owing his election to the patronage of his uncle Northumberland, the lord high admiral.

When the Irish uprising broke out Lisle was sent to Ireland by his father, the lord deputy, in command of a regiment of 600 horse, which landed at Dublin in April 1642. He relieved Geashill Castle in King's county, commanded a plundering expedition into the Irish quarters which advanced as far as Monaghan, and performed other exploits. Lisle held the rank of lieutenant-general of the horse under the earl of Ormond, and the parliamentarian sympathizers in the Irish government would gladly have seen him commander-in-chief in Ormond's place. His support of the parliamentary commissioners Reynolds and Goodwin in their intrigues against Ormond greatly hindered the public service, and Ormond wished to exclude him from the Irish council. Ormond's chaplain, Creichton, charged Lisle with misconduct at the battle of Ross (18 March 1643); while Sir John Temple, a client of the Sidney family, asserted that Lisle did very good service in Ireland, and was systematically discouraged and affronted.

When Ormond's negotiations for the cessation began Lisle resolved to leave Ireland, saying, in an intercepted letter to his father, 'that no good is to be done in this place', and that he feared an oath against the English parliament was about to be imposed on the officers serving in Ireland (Gilbert, 2.60). Though arrested on landing in England, he was speedily released and voted £1000 for his services. Lisle married Lady Catherine Cecil (*b.* c.1628–1652), daughter of William *Cecil, second earl of Salisbury, on 19 May 1645.

In 1646, as soon as parliament was able to think of sending fresh forces to Ireland, Lisle was appointed lord lieutenant (21 January 1646). It has been argued that his appointment was closely connected with factional rivalries at Westminster, marking an attempt by the Independents to undermine their presbyterian opponents, in pursuit of an 'imperial' vision of the three kingdoms united under English rule. Whether or not that is the case, Lisle's lord lieutenancy was a troubled and ineffective attempt to pacify Ireland. Lisle's commission is dated 9 April 1646, but not until 1 February 1647 was he able to start for his charge. He landed in Munster, bringing with him 120 horse and 5000 foot, but was able to accomplish nothing, and became involved in a violent quarrel with Lord Inchiquin. Lisle's commission expired on 15 April 1647; he returned at once to England, and was thanked by parliament on 7 May, though his command was not renewed. At the height of the presbyterian putsch at Westminster that summer Lisle fled to the safety of the army. Like his brother Algernon he was appointed one of the judges for the trial of Charles I, but declined to act. He did not, however, feel any scruples about supporting the republic, and was a member of the first, second, fourth, and fifth councils of state elected during the Commonwealth, the last of which he chaired briefly as lord president in 1653. A few of his letters on public affairs during this period are printed by Collins. On 31 December 1652 Lisle was selected to go as ambassador to Sweden, and accepted, but his instructions were not ready until 22 March 1653, and he had not started when Cromwell turned out the Long Parliament. He then resigned his mission, pleading ill health.

Lisle was high in Cromwell's favour. He was summoned to sit in the 'Little Parliament' (Barebone's Parliament) and was a member of both the councils of state elected by it, but he was 'a lazy councillor and … avoided parliamentary committees like the plague' (Woolrych, 313–14). He was also a member of each of the two councils of state of the protectorate, and was summoned to sit in Cromwell's House of Lords. At the ceremony of Cromwell's second installation as protector (26 June 1656) he took a prominent part, and a letter disapproving of his brother Algernon's ostentatious opposition to the protector has been preserved.

Lisle signed the proclamation declaring Richard Cromwell protector, and was a member of his council. In spite of the important positions he held he seems to have exercised very little political influence, and therefore incurred very little danger when the Restoration took place, but he provided against possible trouble by obtaining a pardon under the great seal (30 October 1660).

Lisle took no further part in public affairs. He succeeded his father as earl of Leicester on 2 November 1677. According to the eighteenth-century account of Arthur Collins, in his later years Leicester was a patron of literature, used to entertain the greatest wits of the age at his house at Sheen, and set apart one day in the week for the entertainment of men of letters. Overshadowing the Restoration years, however, were the family feuds set in train by the second earl's distaste for his eldest son and his willingness to trample over the principles of primogeniture. When Lisle married Catherine Cecil in 1645 the settlement of the Sidney inheritance then made brought out into the open, and in due course irreparably widened, the breach between Lisle and his father. Lisle would inherit the estate as eldest son, but the earl maintained financial control over the future of the estate by reserving to himself the right to charge the estates with bequests up to £29,000 as he chose, which would have to be paid before Lisle could inherit. Father and son quarrelled bitterly. When Lisle's allowance was cut following the death of his wife in childbed on 18 August 1652 he sent his father word by his mother that 'he esteemed himself discharged of all duty and obedience towards him', and in a furious row struck his father in the face (Scott, *English Republic*, 61). Over the years the earl took ample opportunity of the discretion he had allowed himself, adding to and altering his will a

dozen times between 1660 and his death. In return Lisle refused in 1672 to co-operate in his father's schemes to develop Leicester Fields, bitterly reflecting that for the last thirty years he had received from his father but one suit of clothes for his son, and declaring that he would now 'unwillingly lett goe any slender hold I retaine upon my naturall or legall rights' (Scott, *Restoration Crisis*, 91). With his father's death Philip became locked into a bitter struggle through the courts with his surviving brothers, Algernon and Henry, to whom he was expected to pay £20,000 or £29,000 plus extensive rents and annuities, and who as executors of the will held control of the estate. The younger brothers won their case in chancery, but Henry, recognizing the distance between winning and enforcing a judgment, used the verdict as a bargaining tool and came to terms with the earl. These family conflicts received resolution only in late 1683 when the more implacable Algernon lay in prison awaiting execution; Leicester reportedly sent him part of the money still at issue, 'because he could no longer hold up the cudgells' (ibid., 99).

Leicester died at Leicester House, London, on 6 March 1698, and was buried at Penshurst on 17 March. He was succeeded by his son Robert Sidney (apparently his only surviving legitimate child), born in 1648 or 1649, who had been summoned to the House of Lords as Baron Sidney of Penshurst by William III on 11 July 1689. Robert died on 11 November 1702. Leicester had never remarried but in his will made very generous provision for three adult sons and a daughter evidently fathered by himself outside wedlock, the offspring of liaisons with Grace Saunders, *née* Pensar, and Jane Highems, *née* Pensar. The mothers received £600 apiece.   C. H. FIRTH, rev. SEAN KELSEY

Sources DNB · GEC, *Peerage*, 7.556–7 · Keeler, *Long Parliament*, 50 · D. Underdown, *Pride's Purge: politics in the puritan revolution* (1971) · B. Worden, *The Rump Parliament, 1648–1653* (1974) · A. Woolrych, *Commonwealth to protectorate* (1982) · J. Adamson, 'Strafford's ghost: the British context of Viscount Lisle's lieutenancy of Ireland', *Ireland from independence to occupation, 1641–1660*, ed. J. Ohlmeyer (1995), 128–59 · will, PRO, PROB 11/444, fols. 263r–269v (sig. 78) · *History of the Irish confederation and the war in Ireland … by Richard Bellings*, ed. J. T. Gilbert, 7 vols. (1882–91) · H. Sydney and others, *Letters and memorials of state*, ed. A. Collins, 2 vols. (1746) · *Report on the manuscripts of Lord De L'Isle and Dudley*, 6, HMC, 77 (1966) · R. W. Blencowe, ed., *Sydney papers: consisting of a journal of the earl of Leicester, and original letters of Algernon Sidney* (1825) · [T. Carte], *The life of James, duke of Ormond*, new edn, 6 vols. (1851) · J. T. Gilbert, ed., *A contemporary history of affairs in Ireland from 1641 to 1652*, 3 vols. (1879–80) · R. Cox, *Hibernia Anglicana*, 2 vols. (1689–90), vol. 2 · J. Scott, *Algernon Sidney and the English republic* (1988) · J. Scott, *Algernon Sidney and the Restoration crisis* (1991) · Foster, *Alum. Oxon.*

Archives CKS, corresp. and papers | BL, legal papers of the Sidney earls of Leicester, Add. MSS 32683, 43465

Likenesses P. Lely, oils, *c*.1642–1645 (probably Philip Sidney), Althorp, Northamptonshire · G. Kneller, oils, 1685, Penshurst, Kent · A. Van Dyck, group portrait, oils (with his brothers Algernon and Robert), Penshurst, Kent · oils, Penshurst, Kent

Wealth at death He devised real estate, personal estate, and a £6000 debt to his eldest son, and made bequests worth well in excess of £20,000 to (legitimate and illegitimate) children, grandchildren, friends, executors, and servants: PRO, PROB 11/444, fols. 263r–269v

Sidney, Robert, first earl of Leicester (1563–1626), courtier and poet, was born at Penshurst, Kent, on 19 November 1563, and baptized there nine days later, the second son of Sir Henry *Sidney (1529–1586) and his wife, Mary *Sidney (d. 1586), daughter of John *Dudley, duke of Northumberland. Robert *Dudley, earl of Leicester, was his uncle and godfather, and Sir Philip *Sidney (1554–1586) his elder brother.

In the shadow of Philip Sidney Robert Sidney received a first-rate humanist education. He attended Christ Church, Oxford, from 1575 to 1579, without graduating; he then departed on a tour of the continent that lasted—with one interruption—from 1579 to 1582. While he was travelling his brother Philip wrote him two famous letters of advice concerning his studies and activities. His primary base while he was abroad was Strasbourg, where Hubert Languet arranged for him to lodge with the famous pedagogue Johannes Sturm. But he also journeyed to the Low Countries, Germany, Prague, and Paris, making the acquaintance of many political leaders and scholars along the way.

On 23 September 1584 Sidney married Barbara Gamage (c.1559–1621) [see Sidney, Barbara, countess of Leicester], the much-sought-after heir of the recently deceased John Gamage of Coety, Glamorgan. Forewarned by Sir Francis Walsingham that the queen was sending a message forbidding Barbara's marriage without royal approval, Sidney's friends hastily arranged a wedding ceremony that concluded only hours before the command arrived. His marriage to Barbara proved close and supportive, and produced eleven children, five of whom survived him, including the poet Lady Mary *Wroth.

Sidney's father urged him to imitate his elder brother in all things, and Philip became a major influence on Robert Sidney's outlook and aspirations. The Sidneys aligned themselves with those at court, led by Leicester and Walsingham, who favoured an active English role abroad against Spain and Catholicism. In 1585 Elizabeth finally authorized armed intervention on behalf of the Dutch rebels and named Leicester the general of the English forces. Sidney accompanied the army as a captain and served in the Low Countries throughout 1586. He fought at the battle of Zutphen (22 September 1586), where Philip received the wound that eventually led to his death. On 7 October Leicester knighted Sidney for his bravery at Zutphen. Ten days later he was at his brother's bedside during his final hours, where Fulke Greville describes Robert as shedding abundant tears.

Philip's death made Robert the head of the Sidney family, their father having died six months earlier. Sidney inherited extensive properties but also extensive debts, and his need to advance his political career increased accordingly. Following Philip's death Sidney returned to England to settle the complicated family estate. During the Armada crisis in 1588 he attended the queen at Tilbury. As the Armada approached Elizabeth dispatched Sidney on an urgent mission to James VI to ensure Scotland's support against Spain. Although he had to disavow some promises made by the previous envoy, Sidney brought the mission to a successful conclusion. His charm and handsome appearance made a lasting impression on James, who thanked Elizabeth for sending him 'so rare a gentleman' (Letters, ed. Bruce, 54). In 1589 Elizabeth named Sidney the governor of Flushing (Vlissingen), one of the cautionary towns the Dutch had granted England as security for the large loan Elizabeth had provided.

Flushing, the protestant cause, and the court This appointment seemed to launch Sidney on the first steps of a potentially glittering political career. In the event, however, the 1590s turned out to be a difficult and frustrating decade for him. The governorship of Flushing was a responsible position. The port had strategic military importance, and the town provided a useful listening post on the continent. But Sidney's duties in Flushing kept him away from the centre of power at the royal court. He campaigned relentlessly to obtain leaves from his post to return to England, but his political rivals tried just as vigorously to convince the queen that he needed to stay in the Low Countries. Sidney spent about half of the time between 1589 and the end of Elizabeth's reign in honourable isolation in Flushing, which significantly impeded his hopes of political advancement.

In addition the deaths of Leicester in 1588 and Walsingham in 1590 deprived the protestant internationalists of their leading champions. Sidney, along with many others in this camp, gravitated towards Robert Devereux, second earl of Essex, and looked to his leadership; already in April 1588 Sidney had been created MA at Oxford alongside Essex and other members of his circle. Essex's patronage proved a dubious benefit to Sidney, however. Essex rose in Elizabeth's favour, but the rival faction around the Cecils was able to block significant promotions for most of Essex's friends and followers. In 1597 Sidney, who had already served in parliament for Glamorgan in 1584 and 1593, had the satisfaction of being elected senior knight of the shire for Kent over Sir William Brooke, the younger brother of his bitter enemy Henry Brooke, eleventh Baron Cobham. But other political successes were elusive. In 1597–8 Essex tried energetically to gain Sidney a number of posts and promotions, including warden of the cinque ports, vice chamberlain, and promotion to a barony. But Essex's efforts all proved fruitless, and Sidney became increasingly despondent as the 1590s progressed.

During the periods when he was in Flushing Sidney administered the garrison, provided intelligence reports, and maintained relations with Dutch officials. In early 1594 Sidney went on an embassy to Henri IV of France, whose recent conversion to Catholicism had raised concerns in England. Sidney was able to gain reassurances from Henri about his intentions, and won the warm personal regard of the king. Sidney also developed a close friendship with Count Maurice of Nassau and sometimes joined him in the field against the Spanish, playing a significant role in the battle of Turnhout (24 January 1598).

Sidney's correspondence from the 1590s is a rich source for the period. When Sidney was in Flushing he received regular letters from his man-of-business Rowland Whyte, who provided vivid reports on developments at court and his activities on behalf of his master. Factional manoeuvring frequently produced situations rife with tension. As Whyte commented, 'It is a very hard matter to know who are frends now a daies' (Collins, 2.37). Sidney's own letters—and those of his lieutenants, when he had permission to return to England—depict the tedium and alarms of the protracted struggles in the Low Countries and France. Sidney emerges from this correspondence as a man who was well aware of the Machiavellian nature of court politics and was willing to fish in those waters, but who was also a dedicated and effective administrator. In addition he possessed a strong streak of personal honour—for example, he indignantly refused a suggestion from the privy council that he offer a suspected Catholic spy a safe conduct in order to lure him to Flushing and then seize him, saying that such deceit would be unworthy of him.

The Essex rebellion and Jacobean fortunes The same prudence and discretion that made Sidney a successful ambassador helped him survive the treacherous crosscurrents at court towards the end of Elizabeth's reign. By the late 1590s Sidney was growing disillusioned about Essex's ability to help him. His position as Flushing's governor made it his duty to correspond regularly with Lord Burghley and Sir Robert Cecil, and he used this opportunity to stay on reasonably good terms with them. After Essex went to Ireland in 1599 Sidney distanced himself further from the earl and his circle. This proved fortunate, for it kept him from being implicated in Essex's disgrace after he returned without authorization from Ireland in September 1599. Sidney was at court on leave when Essex launched a desperate uprising on 8 February 1601. Sidney joined the hastily mustered forces that surrounded Essex House after the rising collapsed. As one of the few individuals who were trusted and respected by both sides, Sidney played a crucial role in preventing what could have been a bloody finale. He parleyed with Southampton and Essex, who addressed him as 'brother' (Essex had married Philip's widow), and finally the two earls agreed to surrender. Even this service brought Sidney no significant reward, however.

When James VI of Scotland succeeded to the throne of England as James I in 1603 Sidney's fortunes finally began to change. James was sympathetic to former Essexians and still remembered Sidney's visit of fifteen years earlier. By this time, however, Sidney was forty years old, and he had already begun to focus his aspirations on status rather than political power. As early as 1598 Sidney had told Essex that if it came to a choice between the vicechamberlainship and a barony, he would prefer the barony. No evidence exists that he campaigned vigorously for high office after James became king. On 13 May 1603 Sidney received the title of Baron Sidney of Penshurst, and shortly afterwards James named him lord chamberlain of the queen's household and surveyor of the queen's revenues. Because the queen's lord steward, Sir Robert Cecil, normally attended the king, Sidney was usually the presiding official at the queen's court, which limited his opportunities to influence the king. Sidney continued as

governor of Flushing, but since he now rarely left England, his lieutenant executed those duties.

On 4 May 1605 James granted Sidney the title of Viscount Lisle. In 1613 Lisle joined the magnificent entourage that accompanied James's daughter Elizabeth, newly married to the elector palatine, to her new home in Germany. When financial exigencies led James to return Flushing to the Dutch in 1616 Lisle received an annuity of £1200 per annum to compensate him for the loss of his governorship, and James also named him a knight of the Garter (he was installed on 7 July 1616). Lisle maintained his staunchly protestant and anti-Spanish outlook, and with his nephew William Herbert, third earl of Pembroke, and others who shared these views, he supported George Villiers as a counterweight against the Howards and Somerset. In 1618 he finally achieved one of his long-standing ambitions when James created him earl of Leicester, a title Lisle had long claimed as the closest legitimate heir of Robert Dudley. Leicester called his new title '[the queen's] worck' (*De L'Isle and Dudley MSS*, 5.416), and he apparently did not pay for it. The timing—only a few days after the earl of Suffolk's fall—suggests that Villiers may have played a role too.

Poetry and Penshurst Leicester also had literary and scholarly interests. In the second half of the 1590s, when his political frustrations were at their greatest, he worked on a collection of poetry that included sonnets as well as other poems in a variety of metrical forms. The notebook containing them is the longest autograph manuscript by an Elizabethan poet that still survives and allows one to see the revisions and reorderings that he made in the sequence. An edition of these poems appeared in 1984. The collection has some resemblances to *Astrophel and Stella*, though the quality of the verse is uneven: the sonnets tend to be stiff, but some of the songs are lively and engaging. Starting around 1600 Leicester also began compiling several commonplace books on political topics, in which he organized episodes drawn from history into politically meaningful categories. These commonplace books, which give considerable attention to the problems that can afflict monarchies, form a link in the anti-absolutist political tradition of the Sidney family.

Leicester carried out major building projects at Penshurst, including a fashionable long gallery. He also maintained the stately aristocratic lifestyle there that Ben Jonson idealized in 'To Penshurst'. Household accounts and an inventory of 1623 reveal the lavishness of the family's wardrobe and furnishings. As a result, while Leicester's income increased during James's reign, so did his expenditure, leaving him in chronic financial straits. In 1607 Leicester wrote despairingly to his wife, 'If my ill-willers should know in what state I were, it were subject enough for them to laugh at mee for ever' (*De L'Isle and Dudley MSS*, 3.432). In the end, however, he managed to avoid financial disaster, as he had avoided political disaster earlier.

In May 1621 Leicester's wife, Barbara, died. Early in 1626 he married Sarah Smythe, *née* Blount (*d.* 1655), the recently widowed third wife of Sir Thomas Smythe (*d.* 1625). Leicester died barely six months afterwards, at Penshurst Place on 13 July 1626, after falling suddenly ill in London. He was buried at Penshurst three days later. He died intestate, and was succeeded by his only surviving son, Robert *Sidney, who became second earl of Leicester.

ROBERT SHEPHARD

Sources CKS, De L'Isle papers · *Report on the manuscripts of Lord De L'Isle and Dudley*, 6 vols., HMC, 77 (1925–66), vols. 1–5 · H. Sydney and others, *Letters and memorials of state*, ed. A. Collins, 2 vols. (1746) · M. V. Hay, *The life of Robert Sidney, earl of Leicester (1563–1626)* (Cranbury, New Jersey, 1984) · *The poems of Robert Sidney*, ed. P. J. Croft (1984) · PRO, state papers foreign, Holland, SP 84 · PRO, state papers foreign, France, SP 78 · *CSP Scot., 1586–8* · Hatfield House, Hertfordshire, Salisbury MSS · *Calendar of the manuscripts of the marquis of Bath preserved at Longleat, Wiltshire*, 5 vols., HMC, 58 (1904–80), vol. 5, pp. 277–81 · F. Greville, *Life of Sir Philip Sidney* (1652) · *Letters from Sir Robert Cecil to Sir George Carew*, ed. J. Maclean, CS, 88 (1864) · GEC, *Peerage* · [T. Birch and R. F. Williams], eds., *The court and times of Charles the First*, 2 vols. (1848) · *Letters of Queen Elizabeth and King James VI of Scotland*, ed. J. Bruce, CS, 46 (1849)

Archives BL, notebook of sonnets and poems, Add. MS 58435 · BL, corresp., Add. MS 15914 · BL, corresp. · CKS, papers, De L'Isle MSS · LPL, letters | BL, letters to W. Trumbull · Hatfield House, Hatfield, Salisbury MSS, letters and reports · PRO, state papers foreign, Holland, letters and reports, SP 84 · PRO, state papers foreign, France, letters and reports, SP 78

Likenesses oils, c.1585–1588, New College, Oxford · oils, c.1588; on loan to the ministry of public buildings and works at Lancaster House · oils, c.1589, NPG; on display at Montacute House, Somerset · N. Hilliard, oils, c.1590, V&A · attrib. R. Peake senior, oils, c.1605, Penshurst Place, Kent · portrait, c.1610, Penshurst Place, Kent · M. Gheeraerts the younger, portrait, c.1615, Longleat, Wiltshire · S. de Passe, line engraving, 1617, BM, NPG

Wealth at death see administration, 23 June 1627, GEC, *Peerage*

Sidney, Robert, second earl of Leicester (1595–1677), diplomat and landowner, was born on 1 December 1595 at Baynard's Castle, London, the youngest but only surviving son of Robert *Sidney, first earl of Leicester (1563–1626), and his first wife, Barbara *Sidney, *née* Gamage (c.1559–1621), daughter of John Gamage of Coety, Glamorgan. When he was baptized at the end of the month his godparents were Charles Blount, Lord Mountjoy, Lord William Compton (later earl of Northampton), and Penelope, Lady Rich.

Early life, 1595–1632 With his older brother William (*d.* 1612), Sidney matriculated from Christ Church, Oxford, on 27 February 1607; he was still at Oxford in October 1610. William was knighted in January 1610 but Robert received the higher honour of a knighthood of the Bath the following June; the same year his father, who was governor of Flushing, one of the English cautionary towns in the Netherlands, made Robert captain of a foot company there. Robert visited Flushing in 1613 but was back in England the following year when he was MP for Wilton (one of the boroughs of his cousin the earl of Pembroke) in the Addled Parliament; he was appointed to a few committees but appears to have been relatively inactive. Perhaps rebelling against his father's attempts to marry him off (at least two engagements were proposed for him in 1613), in 1615 he secretly married Lady Dorothy Percy (*bap.* 1598, *d.* 1659), daughter of Henry *Percy, ninth earl of Northumberland (1564–1632), and his wife, Lady Dorothy Devereux, daughter of the earl of Essex; the marriage, which was not

Robert Sidney, second earl of Leicester (1595–1677), by unknown artist

discovered until a year later, linked Sidney with two of the most powerful noble families in the realm, and the Percy connection in particular was to be an abiding influence on his career. It was probably the marriage that led to a bitter quarrel between Sidney and James Hay, Viscount Doncaster, who had married Dorothy's sister Lucy Percy, in the course of which the two men came to blows in 1620.

When in the spring of 1616 Flushing and Brill were restored to the United Provinces their English garrisons were reconstituted into a regiment under Sidney's command and retained in Dutch service. He visited the Low Countries later that year and journeyed on to Paris; he was again with his regiment in 1620–21 and retained the command into the 1640s, but latterly it was principally a pecuniary interest. He was admitted to Gray's Inn on 25 February 1618 and when, in the August of that year, his father was made earl of Leicester, he was henceforth styled Viscount L'Isle. In the 1621 parliament he was MP for Kent and in those of 1624 and 1625 sat for Monmouthshire, but he left only a minor mark in the records. On his father's death on 13 July 1626 he succeeded as second earl of Leicester.

Embassy to Denmark, 1632 In April 1632 Charles I announced Leicester's appointment as ambassador-extraordinary to Christian IV of Denmark. The ostensible and public purpose was to offer condolences on the death the previous year of Charles's maternal grandmother, Queen Sophia Frederica; the secret aim of the mission was to stir Christian to action in the Thirty Years' War and to see how Denmark stood in relation to Sweden's proposed anti-

Habsburg league. Leicester left for Denmark on 15 September 1632 with a retinue of fifty-five including, as his secretary, James Howell, and had his first audience with the Danish king on 1 October. Leicester was struck by Danish customs, especially the debauchery of the court, noting in his journal that Christian led 'a strange life … drunk every day, lying with a whore every night', but he showed that he could hold his own in the mammoth drinking binges that passed for royal entertainment in Denmark. At the feast marking the end of Leicester's short embassy on 15 October, which stretched from 11 a.m. until evening, the earl proudly noted that after thirty-five toasts he could still manage stairs unassisted, while the king had to be carried from the table in his chair. Outdrinking the Danes was, perhaps, Leicester's principal achievement on the embassy, for he achieved little else, apart from some minor trading concessions. He returned via Hamburg and reached England on 2 November 1632. Only a few days later all his negotiations were overtaken, and the whole European situation was altered, by the death of Gustavus Adolphus of Sweden at the battle of Lützen.

Embassy to France, 1636–1641 Leicester's family traditions (his uncle had been Sir Philip Sidney) and his Dutch command inclined him to support a policy of vigorously pursuing the protestant interest in the Thirty Years' War, while his Percy connections tied him to the circle of Queen Henrietta Maria in the mid-1630s, a time when her court briefly represented a 'puritan' clique pushing for war with Spain. He professed himself the queen's 'Slave' (Collins, 2.387) and, with her influence over affairs growing, in April 1636 Henrietta Maria procured Leicester's appointment as ambassador-extraordinary to France, seconding the mission of the ambassador-in-ordinary, Viscount Scudamore, whose negotiations with the French had proved unsuccessful. Leicester arrived in Paris on 3 June 1636 (NS) and promptly fell out with Scudamore. The two men could agree on nothing: they employed different solicitors and different agents, they took contrary positions in many diplomatic questions, and they even went to different church services, Scudamore worshipping in his own chapel, Leicester attending the services of the French Reformed church at Charenton in a gesture of solidarity with Huguenots and in defiance of the predilections of Charles and Archbishop William Laud. Leicester successfully ridiculed Scudamore and undermined his credit at the English court, while his own reputation was safeguarded by the strenuous efforts of the earls of Northumberland and Holland, Henry Percy, and the countess of Leicester, who remained in England. Behind these differences lay a deeper division over policy. While Scudamore inclined to a pro-Spanish neutrality, Leicester agitated actively for an Anglo-French alliance against the Habsburgs, telling the secretary of state, Sir John Coke, that 'nothing can be more glorious, nor more religious in the sight of God and man then such a war' against Spain (PRO, SP 78/101, fol. 400). When Charles preferred to pursue a negotiated settlement Leicester reiterated his belief that 'the diseases of Christendome are not to be cured like the King's evil with touching, but with striking' (PRO, SP

78/102, fol. 279). Throughout 1636 Leicester frequently twisted and even ignored his diplomatic instructions in an attempt to persuade Charles and Louis XIII into an alliance. While his words and actions caused some consternation in England, in December 1636 the king showed his support for him against Scudamore by raising his allowance to unprecedented heights.

When the principal negotiations between England and France were remitted to a proposed peace conference at Hamburg in 1637, the nature of Leicester's mission changed, as did the queen's circle, which saw renewed intrigues against Cardinal Richelieu. Leicester negotiated the change successfully. By August 1637 he was drawn into Charles's secret negotiations on behalf of Marie de' Medici's circle in Flanders. He was also implicated in the notorious La Porte affair, a conspiracy involving the exiled Marie de' Medici and her court in Brussels, and the French queen, Anne of Austria, and aiming both to overthrow Richelieu and frustrate the proposed Anglo-French treaty that Leicester had pressed so hard for only recently. Leicester's secretary, Réné Augier, provided the means by which Anne's letters to the Habsburgs could be sent to the Spanish Netherlands. Leicester's negotiations were thwarted by the French, however, whose spies had penetrated the English court, who were intercepting Leicester's post, and who were almost certainly receiving information from Augier himself.

The earl was left with little purpose to his mission. He was temporarily recalled in February 1639, at the same time as Scudamore's mission was ended, but was sent back alone to France in August. The English government was entirely preoccupied by its Scottish and domestic troubles, and Leicester was instructed by Charles in the spring of 1639 to 'mesnage the proceedings by such degrees, that you cum to no conclusion til wee bee freed from our trobles at home' (PRO, SP 78/107, fol. 154v).

From August 1637 Leicester had been scheming to be recalled to England and to be made secretary in place of Coke. Two years later an alternative was suggested by Northumberland, that he should succeed Thomas Wentworth, Viscount Wentworth, as lord deputy of Ireland. He was constantly frustrated. Although he was sworn a privy councillor on 5 May 1639, further preferment was blocked by Laud, who opposed Leicester on account of the earl's treatment of his friend Scudamore. Laud represented Leicester to the king as a puritan, an accusation which Leicester strenuously denied. The earl's preferment of Henry Hammond to the living of Penshurst, the Sidneys' seat, in 1633, after hearing him preach at court, does not suggest any radical religious leanings.

The fall of Strafford created the opportunity, the fall of Laud removed the obstacle; Leicester was again recalled to England in May 1641, and on 14 June 1641 he was appointed lord lieutenant of Ireland. He returned to France in August to conclude his embassy, and arrived back in England at the beginning of October.

Lord lieutenant of Ireland and the English civil war, 1641–1644
Leicester was thus ready to take up his commission just as the Irish rising broke out, preventing his travelling to

Dublin. The next three years were the most testing of his life. The appointment which he had sought, and which Charles had hoped would placate some of his godly opponents in parliament, succeeded in satisfying no one. As Leicester later rued, 'that which should have bin for my good became unto me an occasion of falling' (De L'Isle and Dudley MSS, 6.555). Although he sent his sons Philip *Sidney (1619–1698) and Algernon *Sidney (1623–1683) to Ireland in April 1642 with 600 horse, he never managed to get there himself. Leicester was caught between king and parliament as they argued and divided over who should control the army sent to crush the Irish rebels. The lord lieutenant's position was probably impossible. For Leicester, who according to the earl of Clarendon was 'rather a speculative than a practical man', and who 'expected a greater certitude in the consultation of business than the business of the world is capable of' (Clarendon, Hist. rebellion, 2.531), it proved personally disastrous.

None the less, Leicester retained the confidence of the Lords until the summer of 1642, acting as temporary speaker of the house in May and June, and appointed parliament's lord lieutenant for Kent. As England drifted into civil war, however, he was unable to choose between the two sides and irresolutely sought to satisfy both. He repeatedly refused to grant commissions to his deputy lieutenants under the militia ordinance, stymying efforts to raise Kent for parliament until he was replaced in mid-August 1642. That month he bewailed his plight to the countess of Carlisle, his sister-in-law:

> I am environed by such contradictions, as I can neither get from them, nor reconcile them. The Parliament bids me go presently; the King commands me to stay till he dispatch me. The supplyes of the one, and the authority of the other, are equally necessary. I know not how to obtain them both, and am more likely to have neither; for now they are at such extremes, as to please the one is scarce possible, unless the other be opposed … I am suspected and distrusted of either side. (Blencowe, xxi–xxii)

When parliament insisted on seeing his instructions from the king, Leicester initially refused, increasing the suspicions by then harboured by many in the Commons and the Lords about his intentions, but in October 1642 he yielded, so incurring the king's displeasure. In late November, with Leicester in Chester on the point of embarking for Dublin, Charles, preferring to use Ormond, whose loyalty he did not doubt, forbade him to go and summoned him to Oxford where he arrived shortly after Christmas.

Leicester passed the next year in the royalist headquarters in a tortured state, declining to take any part in the king's affairs. Penshurst was sequestered by the Kent county committee on the grounds that Leicester had flown to an enemy garrison, but the countess, probably with the help of Northumberland, one of the most influential parliamentarian peers, persuaded the parliament to lift the sequestration. In November 1643 the king induced Leicester to resign the lord lieutenancy so that he could appoint Ormond in his place. Leicester remained in Oxford, expecting that he would be appointed governor to Prince Charles. His refusal in January 1644 to sign the letter from the English peers at Oxford to the Scottish privy council urging them not to support the covenanters' invasion of England, however, lost him all hope of preferment, and in June 1644 he left Oxford to make his peace with parliament before retiring to Penshurst, where he attempted to sit out the war quietly, declining to seek readmission to the House of Lords.

Retirement and later life, 1644–1677 Leicester was a broken man and spent almost all of his remaining three decades in retirement at Penshurst, occasionally visiting his London residence, Leicester House, and concerning himself with his estates and scholarly pursuits. Clarendon described him as 'very conversant in books, and much addicted to the mathematics' (Clarendon, Hist. rebellion, 2.531). He possessed a large library, valued at £100 at his death, and his reading concentrated on the politics, religion, customs, and history of ancient and modern nations of the world. Many of his notes and reflections from these survive, and show that he could write interchangeably in five languages (English, Latin, French, Spanish, and Italian). His son Algernon later claimed that Leicester 'writ his own mind to see what he could think of it another time, and blot it out again may be' (Scott, 56). His studies tended towards the relativism and scepticism fashionable in the intellectual circles he had encountered in Paris, where he also met, and clearly admired, Hugo Grotius, the exiled Dutch philosopher who was ambassador of Queen Kristina of Sweden. Leicester was much preoccupied with 'the opinions and fancyes of men' (Scott, 55) and differing political and legal customs. While such relativist thoughts encouraged some, notably his son Algernon, towards radical politics and republicanism, in Leicester they reinforced his tendency towards indecision, what Clarendon called 'the staggering and irresolution in his nature' (Clarendon, Hist. rebellion, 2.531).

Although two of his sons—Philip, Lord Lisle, and Algernon—served the regimes of the interregnum in various capacities, Leicester refused to have much to do with the Commonwealth or protectorate. The countess was, however, through the influence of her brother Northumberland, given the care of two of the late king's children in May 1649. The duke of Gloucester and Princess Elizabeth lived at Penshurst from 14 June 1649 to 9 August 1650, when they were removed from the countess's care and sent to Carisbrooke Castle by the council of state. The earl took the engagement on 18 April 1650, but only because 'if I had not don so I could not have bin plaintiffe nor have sued in any Court of Justice upon what occasion soever' (De L'Isle and Dudley MSS, 6.598). He had, indeed, a stack of suits to prosecute and defend, concerning both his own estate and that of his nephew, Philip Smythe, Viscount Strangford, whose wardship he reluctantly took on in December 1649 after the death of Strangford's former guardian, Sir Thomas Fotherly. He even more reluctantly agreed the following August to the marriage of his daughter Isabella to Strangford, a union pressed on him by the couple and his wife. Strangford, however, was an easily misled drunkard and his affairs were hopelessly chaotic.

Strangford initially accused Fotherly of embezzlement and launched a legal suit against the family which Leicester had to prosecute, before, in 1653, revoking Leicester's title to his guardianship and pursuing the Sidneys through the courts on the same charge of embezzlement. A further case concerned a diamond that Princess Elizabeth, who had died shortly after her removal to Carisbrooke, had bequeathed to the countess of Leicester. Long proceedings ensued, the trustees for the sale of the goods of king and queen claiming that they belonged to the state, the Sidneys basing their title on the princess's personal ownership of the jewel, as originally a gift from her brother-in-law the prince of Orange.

Leicester employed his second son, Algernon, as his principal assistant and agent in the management of his estate and legal affairs from 1648 to 1659. The earl's preference for the able Algernon in preference to his dull and indolent elder brother, Philip, caused a permanent estrangement between the father and his heir. In December 1652 Philip struck his father in the face and proclaimed himself discharged of all duty towards him; three and a half years later Philip complained that the earl allowed Algernon to domineer and command at Penshurst. Two decades later, when the earl's attempts to develop his London property at Leicester Fields had led him into further legal difficulties, it was Algernon's support and advice he sought, procuring a pass for Algernon, in exile on the continent since the Restoration, to return to England. Algernon, however, did not return until after his father's death.

In April 1660 Leicester took up his seat in the House of Lords. Charles II made him a privy councillor on 31 May 1660, but in October 1660, after the adjournment of the parliament, he obtained the king's permission to retire to Penshurst on the grounds of ill health. On the same grounds his attendance at the coronation in April 1661 was also dispensed with. The countess's death on 20 August 1659 had prompted the earl to announce his own imminent end, but he went on to enjoy a further eighteen years of ill health, obsessively writing and rewriting codicils to his will to exclude his son Philip from the estate and control the portions of his other children according to their current standing in his affections. He died at Penshurst on 2 November 1677 and was buried there six days later.   IAN ATHERTON

Sources *Report on the manuscripts of Lord De L'Isle and Dudley*, 6 vols., HMC, 77 (1925–66), vols. 2–6 · H. Sydney and others, *Letters and memorials of state*, ed. A. Collins, 2 vols. (1746) · R. Blencowe, *Sydney papers, consisting of a journal of the earl of Leicester, and original letters of Algernon Sydney* (1825) · state papers foreign, France, PRO, SP 78 · J. Scott, *Algernon Sidney and the English republic, 1623–1677* (1988) · Clarendon, *Hist. rebellion* · I. J. Atherton, *Ambition and failure in Stuart England: the career of John, first Viscount Scudamore* (1999) · R. Cant, 'The embassy of the earl of Leicester to Denmark in 1632', *EngHR*, 54 (1939), 252–62 · GEC, *Peerage*, 7.553–5 · *CSP dom.*, 1610–61 · *JHL* · Foster, *Alum. Oxon.*, 4.1449 · will and codicils, PRO, PROB 11/355, fols. 215, 337r–343r · A. Everitt, *The community of Kent and the great rebellion, 1640–60* (1966) · J. Foster, *The register of admissions to Gray's Inn, 1521–1889, together with the register of marriages in Gray's Inn chapel, 1695–1754* (privately printed, London, 1889), 149 · J. Howell, *Epistolae Ho-elianae*, ed. J. Jacobs, 2 vols. (1890–92) · M. Jansson, ed., *Proceedings in parliament, 1614 (House of Commons)* (1988) · W. Notestein, F. H. Relf, and H. Simpson, eds., *Commons debates, 1621*, 7 vols. (1935) · *Report on the manuscripts of the marquis of Downshire*, 6 vols. in 7, HMC, 75 (1924–95), vols. 3, 5

Archives BL, corresp., Add. MS 15914 · CKS, De L'Isle MSS, corresp. and papers

Likenesses C. Johnson, oils, 1632, Penshurst, Kent · Van Dyck, portrait (as a child) · double portrait, oils (as a boy, with brother William), Penshurst, Kent · oils, Althorp, Northamptonshire [*see illus.*]

Wealth at death his personal possessions at Penshurst were valued at £3415 19s. on his death; his income from his estates in the later 1630s was probably about £4000 a year: *De L'Isle manuscripts*, vol. 6, pp. 554, 634–47; will and codicils, PRO, PROB 11/355, fols. 215, 337r–343r

Sidney [*formerly* Solomon], **Samuel** (1813–1883), writer on agriculture, was born on 6 February 1813 in Paradise Street, Birmingham, where his father, Abraham Solomon MD, practised as a physician. He was educated for the law, and acted for a short time (about 1834) as a solicitor in Liverpool. He soon took, however, to journalistic and literary work, using the *nom de plume* of Sidney, which he afterwards adopted for all purposes. His earlier writings dealt largely with railways and the gauge question and attacked Isambard Kingdom Brunel and the Great Western Company. Most of his works on this subject appeared between 1846 and 1848, notably pamphlets on the gauge controversy and his *Railways and Agriculture in North Lincolnshire* (1848), which suggested the benefits of railways in the era of 'high farming' following the repeal of the corn laws. He followed this with an account of *Rides on Railways* (1851) to the scenic regions of the Lake District, north Wales, and Derbyshire dales. In 1847 the return of his brother John from Australia appears to have aroused Sidney's interest in the colonies, and he wrote much on emigration and colonization between 1848 and 1854. In collaboration with his brother he edited *Sidney's Emigrant's Journal* between 1848 and 1850, when it was discontinued 'as barely paying its necessary expenses'. From 1847 to 1857 he wrote regularly for the *Illustrated London News*, acting as hunting correspondent, and visiting agricultural exhibitions in Britain and abroad. He wrote also for the *Live Stock Journal* a series of articles extending over many years entitled 'Horse chat' and signed Cavalier. He contributed many articles to the earlier volumes of *Household Words*, and wrote a novel dealing with Australian life, entitled *Gallops and Gossips in the Bush of Australia* (1854), which he dedicated to Charles Dickens.

In 1850–51 Sidney became one of the assistant commissioners for the Great Exhibition, and was afterwards for some years assistant secretary to the Crystal Palace Company. In 1859 he was an unsuccessful candidate for the secretaryship of the Royal Agricultural Society, and in the following year he became secretary of the Agricultural Hall Company. In 1864 he organized the first horse show held at that hall, and he later acted as manager of many succeeding horse shows there.

In 1857 Sidney edited and in great part rewrote W. C. L. Martin's book *The Pig*; and in 1860 he re-edited William Youatt's book of the same name. But by far his most important contribution to literature was *The Book of the Horse*, for which he had long collected materials and which was first published in 1873. It is a mine of information on the various breeds of horses, British and foreign, on fox-hunting and deer-hunting, on horsemanship and horsewomanship, on the management of the stable, breeding, breaking, and so on. It is in this work that Sidney's versatile pen appears at its best. The book became popular at once, and was reissued five times up to 1898. In its compilation he had valuable assistance from many leading experts, but he was himself a good judge of a horse, and was a fine rider in his early days. His wife, Marie, was a journalist. He died of heart disease at his home, 10 Bethune Road, Stamford Hill, London, on 8 June 1883, and was buried at Highgate cemetery.

ERNEST CLARKE, rev. JULIAN LOCK

Sources *Agricultural Gazette*, new ser., 17 (1883), 598 · Boase, *Mod. Eng. biog.* · private information (1897) · CGPLA Eng. & Wales (1883) · census returns, 1881
Likenesses portrait, repro. in *ILN*, 82 (1883), 648
Wealth at death £1985 2s. 4d.: probate, 3 Oct 1883, CGPLA Eng. & Wales

Sidney, Sir William (c.1482–1554). *See under* Sidney, Sir Henry (1529–1586).

Sidney, William Philip, first Viscount de L'Isle (1909–1991), army officer and politician, was born on 23 May 1909 in Chelsea, London, the only son of William Sidney, fifth Baron de L'Isle and Dudley (1859–1945), barrister and politician, and his wife, Winifred Agneta Yorke, *née* Bevan (d. 1959), elder daughter of Roland Yorke Bevan. He had an older sister, Mary Olivia (1906–1959). His father, the fourth son of the second Baron de L'Isle, was mayor of Chelsea in 1906–8, and a Conservative member of the London county council from 1922 to 1934; he acceded only briefly to the barony, two months before his death.

Bill Sidney was educated at Eton College and at Magdalene College, Cambridge, where he devoted himself more to sports and the Officers' Training Corps than to academia. In 1929, from Cambridge, he was commissioned as a second lieutenant in the supplementary reserve of the Grenadier Guards. During the next nine years he worked hard in the City of London where, in gaining valuable business experience, he qualified as a chartered accountant. At the same time he helped his father to nurse his extensive estates at Penshurst Place near Tonbridge, Kent, and at Inglesby Manor, Great Ayton, Yorkshire. In the process he became an enthusiastic countryman.

Following the outbreak of the Second World War in September 1939, Sidney, by now a captain, joined his regiment and served with the British expeditionary force in France until, in May 1940, he returned home from the beaches of Dunkirk with his commanding officer, General Sir Harold Alexander; he was among the last to leave under heavy German air attack. Back in London, he married on 8 June 1940 Jacqueline Corinne Yvonne Vereker (1914–1962), the only daughter of John Standish Surtees Prendergast *Vereker, sixth Viscount Gort VC, who had been his commander-in-chief throughout the battle of France. They had four daughters and a son.

After various postings and intensive commando training in England, Sidney was promoted major and served in north Africa. On 22 June 1944, as a company commander with the 5th battalion, Grenadier Guards, he landed on the Anzio beachhead in Italy with the British Sixth Army corps, led again by General Alexander. At first almost unopposed, the British force was rapidly challenged by greatly superior German numbers, strongly supported by the *Luftwaffe*. In fierce fighting at Carrocento throughout the night of 7–8 February 1944, Sidney, in command of a support company of a battalion of the Grenadier Guards, led a counter-attack with hand grenades at the head of the crew of a 3 inch mortar. His citation for the Victoria Cross read:

> Dashing forward with superb courage and utter disregard for danger he was wounded in the face by a German grenade which killed the grenadier at his side. Though further wounded in the thigh, Sidney sent back the remainder of his company to bring up more ammunition and grenades while, virtually single-handed and at point-blank range, he kept the enemy at bay with his tommy gun, driving them back with many casualties until the ammunition-party returned to continue the fierce fighting for another hour. Only then, gravely wounded and weak from loss of blood, did he allow himself to be assisted so that his wounds could be dressed. There is no doubt that, as a result of his action, in the face of great odds, the battalion's position was re-established with far-reaching consequences on the battle as a whole.

Invalided out of the army, and while still suffering from his wounds, Sidney received the Victoria Cross from George V at Buckingham Palace on 12 October 1944; it was accompanied by a piece of VC ribbon cut from Lord Gort's tunic. Two days later, transferred to the regular army reserve for parliamentary duties, Sidney was returned, unopposed, as the Conservative member of parliament for his birthplace, Chelsea, in succession to Sir Samuel Hoare, who had become Lord Templewood in Winston Churchill's administration. Shortly thereafter, as parliamentary secretary to the Ministry of Pensions, and now beginning to climb the political ladder, Sidney was selected to deliver his maiden speech during his first month in the House of Commons, in reply to the king's speech to Parliament. In 'ringing phrases' he gave a much praised, authoritative comment on the state of the war.

Sidney's time in the House of Commons was, however, short. The death of his father on 18 June 1945 took him to the House of Lords. There followed, on 26 July 1945, the general election which brought Clement Attlee's Labour government to power for the next six and a half years. During that time de L'Isle worked in the City of London, was appointed joint treasurer of the Conservative Party, and maintained and improved his historic country seat and gardens, at Penshurst Place, which held a special nostalgia for him as the home of his forebear, Sir Philip Sidney, the gallant Elizabethan poet, diplomat, courtier, and embodiment of chivalry. De L'Isle especially enjoyed showing visitors the remarkable collection of arms and armour in the crypt, the oak-panelled long gallery, the Elizabethan gardens, and the beautiful lake, first mentioned in family records more than 500 years before. At this time also he forged his first contacts with aviation through the Air Ministry's continuously open and lighted Penshurst landing ground at Chiddingstone Causeway on the top of the North Downs; with its telephone link to Croydon airport and an automatic wind indicator, Penshurst began to be used frequently by private flyers, who enjoyed the hospitality extended whenever he was at home by de L'Isle himself.

When on 26 October 1951 a Conservative government under Sir Winston Churchill returned to power with a slim majority, de L'Isle was appointed secretary of state for air, to his special delight and outstanding success. He quickly displayed an enthusiasm for the service which won the unstinted regard of senior officers and all other ranks. He showed his determination for practical involvement by learning to fly at the Royal Air Force Central Flying School, also setting an example by becoming the first air minister to fly by both day and night—and the first to fly a jet aircraft (a Canberra). During his fifty active months as secretary of state for air, the Royal Air Force was more than doubled in strength, from less than 125,000 personnel in 1951 to more than 269,000 in 1955. At a time of rapid technical development, not only did the RAF capture the world's air-speed record at more than 727 m.p.h., but also the first V-bombers were brought into service in the form of the Vickers Valiant in January 1955, followed by the further advanced Avro Vulcan and Handley Page Victor. De L'Isle's term at the Air Ministry also saw a major advance in the equipment of the RAF in helicopters and guided weapons.

De L'Isle worked closely and cordially with Sir William Dickson, chief of the air staff, and then with his successor, Sir John Slesser. Throughout his time at the Air Ministry he was seen by the RAF as one of the most effective and respected of air ministers, devoted to the service in the mould of Lord Trenchard. With his quiet but immensely competent interest in every aspect of the service, he was highly regarded by all ranks wherever his duties took him. His private secretary wrote:

> Numerous visits to Harwell, Windscale, Aldermaston and the major factories of the aircraft industry registered his concern. Yet one's abiding impression, however serious the subject, was that laughter and immense enjoyment of the human comedy were never far away. To be with him, in the office or outside, was much more a pleasure than a duty. (*The Times*, 30 April 1991)

In August 1952 de L'Isle made an 8000 mile tour of inspection of RAF establishments in the Middle East. He had proposed to continue to Singapore, Hong Kong, and on to the United States and Canada. These plans were, however, turned down by the prime minister who, despite his own worldwide overseas visits, wrote to de L'Isle: 'The power of a Secretary of State is best wielded from his desk' (*The Times*, 30 April 1991).

When Anthony Eden succeeded Winston Churchill as prime minister in April 1955, he decided that his secretary of state for air must be responsible to the House of Commons. Loyally, but reluctantly, de L'Isle accepted his replacement by his well-trained parliamentary secretary, Nigel Birch. De L'Isle left the Air Ministry in December

1955. In January 1956 he was made a viscount, dropping from his title the term 'and Dudley', recalling with amusement that at a lunch at the United States headquarters in Ruislip, Middlesex, two places had been laid for him—one on each side of the chairman.

In August 1961 de L'Isle was welcomed by the Australian prime minister, Robert Menzies, to be governor-general of Australia, the last Englishman to hold that post. At once de L'Isle disarmed any incipient criticism by his courtesy and by the informality of his presence, his delightful sense of humour, and by the extent of his local knowledge. He reinforced his regard for Australia by purchasing two properties in New South Wales and by setting up a local company to tend them. He was appointed GCMG in 1961 and GCVO in 1962. In November 1962 his wife died.

After four well-regarded years in Australia, de L'Isle returned to England in September 1965. He married on 24 March 1966 Margaret Eldrydd, Lady Glanusk, daughter of Major-General Thomas Herbert Shoubridge, and widow of Wilfrid Russell Bailey, third Baron Glanusk. With his second wife de L'Isle delighted once more in his historic seat at Penshurst Place, and again extended hospitality and personally conducted inspections to visitors to Penshurst. His cheerful company in the family home, together with his courteous, relaxed, and enthusiastic presence, was much valued, and he was always calm, considerate, and the essence of courtesy. At the same time his business acumen began to be much sought after. He was chairman of Phoenix Assurance and Parmerston Property Development, and a director of the British Match Corporation, Lloyds Bank, the Yorkshire Bank, and Schweppes. He was a trustee of the RAF Museum, the Churchill Memorial Trust (1975–91), the British Museum (1950–64), and the National Portrait Gallery (1965–72), and from 1968 to 1984 he was chancellor of the Order of St Michael and St George. He was appointed KG in 1968. His concern for human rights was displayed by his chairmanship and then presidency of the Freedom Association.

De L'Isle, 'a brave and distinguished nobleman' (*The Independent*, 13 April 1991), died at Penshurst Place on 5 April 1991. He was survived by his second wife and the five children of his first marriage. He was succeeded as second viscount by his son, Major Philip John Algernon Sidney (*b.* 1945). A memorial service was held in the guards' chapel, Wellington barracks, London, on 23 May 1991.

PETER G. MASEFIELD

Sources *The Times* (8 April 1991) · *The Times* (30 April 1991) · *The Times* (24 May 1991) · *The Independent* (8 April 1991) · *The Independent* (10 April 1991) · *The Independent* (13 April 1991) · Burke, *Peerage* · *WWW* · personal knowledge (2004) · private information (2004) **Archives** priv. coll. | Bodl. Oxf., corresp. with Lord Woolton · CAC Cam., corresp. with E. L. Spears · CUL, Templewood papers, corresp. with Samuel Hoare **Likenesses** J. Ward, chalk drawing, 1975, NPG · photograph, repro. in *The Times* (8 April 1991) · photograph, repro. in *The Independent* (8 April 1991) · photograph, repro. in *The Independent* (13 April 1991) **Wealth at death** £4,678,883: probate, 3 Jan 1992, *CGPLA Eng. & Wales*

Siebe, (Christian) Augustus (1788–1872), engineer, was born in Saxony, southern Prussia; the details of his parentage and place of birth are unknown. During the 1790s Augustus, as he was called throughout his life, moved with his family to Berlin, where he showed an aptitude for mechanical and handicraft skills. After leaving school he was apprenticed to a master caster in the capital and soon won medals at fourteen or fifteen for his work in modelling, chasing, and watchmaking.

At twenty-four, according to his own account, Siebe served as an officer of artillery in the Prussian army and was wounded in the battle of the Nations at Leipzig in 1813. After leaving the army at the end of the Napoleonic wars he went first to Denmark and then to England to find employment. He worked for a time with Garrards of London, the royal jewellers, and then as an instrument maker. After a brief period as a manager for an engineering firm he decided to set up for himself as a watchmaker and silversmith at 145 High Holborn.

After some success in mechanical inventions and in business, Siebe moved in 1829 to larger premises nearby—at 5 Denmark Street, Soho. This substantial terraced house gave the Siebe family domestic accommodation as well as workshop space and a shopfront from where he could sell his many mechanical products. Among these were a rotary water pump, which was a great financial success, and the world's first dial weighing machine, which reputedly weighed and measured new recruits for the Crimean War. Siebe later manufactured under licence the Australian James Harrison's ice-making machine, which worked on the ether principle. In 1823 he won the Vulcan medal from the Royal Society of Arts for an improved screw threading tool.

Siebe's major claim to fame, however, was to improve and develop an invention not his own. In 1827 he met Charles Anthony Deane, who in 1823 had invented a smoke helmet for use in fire-fighting. Deane commissioned Siebe to make up a few sets, and the design was very soon adapted for use as a diving helmet, developed in conjunction with Charles Deane's younger brother John. Before this, the centuries-old diving bell, a cumbersome and unwieldy tool, had been used for shipwreck salvage and other underwater work. The naval establishment and the wider maritime economy were ready for something better. The Deanes and Siebe provided the answer. In 1830 they collaborated in producing a complete diving apparatus kit, which consisted of a beaten copper helmet with windows fixed to a corselet. This metalwork was worn over an all-enveloping india-rubber suit, with chest weights and heavy boots. The helmet was supplied with air through a hose connected to a pump operated from above; the exhaled air bubbled out from the rim of the corselet and was known as the 'open helmet'. The 'closed helmet' incorporated a loose flange sealing the dress to the helmet around the edge of the corselet, a modification devised and given freely to Siebe by George Edwards, the engineer in charge of Lowestoft harbour in 1840. These suits gradually proved themselves over the next ten years or so, until in 1840 Siebe supplied a few suits to Colonel Pasley of the Royal Engineers, then engaged in removing the wreck of the *Royal George*, lost some fifty years before in the main anchorage of Portsmouth harbour. This government recognition firmly established 'Siebe's patent diving dress' as the accepted replacement for the outmoded bell system, despite Siebe's having no patent and being essentially a manufacturer and promoter. The apparatus was, however, greatly improved by the provision of a two- or three-cylinder pump of his own manufacture. The use of these instead of a bellows pump enabled air to be forced down to much greater depths.

The invention was much copied in the United Kingdom and in other countries and remained in its use until the SCUBA-type equipment replaced it in the 1950s. Until the 1970s Siebe & Co. and the successor firm of Siebe Gorman & Co. published several manuals and other related books that became standard works in the industry. The company stayed in business until the 1990s, when the expanded nature of its business and a change of name effectively subsumed it.

Augustus Siebe married Susannah Glidden (1796–1856) of Sherwell, Devon, at St Anne's Church, Soho, on 11 July 1819. They had six children of whom his second son, Henry Herepath, together with his son-in-law William Gorman, succeeded him in business on his retirement in 1868.

Siebe died at his home in Denmark Street on 15 April 1872 and was buried in Norwood cemetery, London. The Institution of Civil Engineers described him in their *Proceedings* as 'retiring, kind of heart, and upright and honourable in his dealings' (vol. 36, 1873). Although not the originator of either the closed or open diving helmet dress, Siebe certainly prompted its eventual improvement and development. One of the best and most imaginative machinists of his time, he took the novel but sometimes crude ideas of others and combined them in an improved form to produce what became known throughout the world as 'the standard diving dress'. Old Siebe helmet dresses can still be found in many countries and are a monument to his effort and genius.

WILLIAM RONALD BRAITHWAITE and JOHN BEVAN

Sources *The Engineer* (26 April 1872) · *PICE*, 36 (1873) · J. Bevan, *The infernal diver* (1996) · J. Bevan, biographical notes on C. A. Siebe (1788–1872), *Submex* (29 Jan 1994) · births, marriages, and deaths, General Register Office for England · rate books, City Westm. AC · Siebe Gorman & Co., Submarine Engineers, London, various publications · R. Davis (of Siebe Gorman & Co.), London, various publications · H. Siebe, *Conquest of the sea* (1872) · Sci. Mus., Archive
Archives Inst. CE · Sci. Mus. · Sci. Mus., Siebe Gorman & Co., Submarine Engineers Museum collection | Submex Ltd, London, John Bevan collection
Likenesses E. A. Becker, oils, Sci. Mus.

Sieff, Israel Moses, Baron Sieff (1889–1972), retailer and business innovator, was born at 28 Clarence Street, Cheetham, Manchester, on 4 May 1889, the eldest of three sons and two daughters of Ephraim Sieff and his wife, Sarah Saffer, who had arrived in Britain as penniless immigrants from Lithuania. Beginning with a handcart, his father built up a textile scrap business in Manchester enabling him to purchase the established textile firm of

Israel Moses Sieff, Baron Sieff (1889–1972), by Baron Studios, 1966

Beaumont & Co. This subsequently became Sieff and Beaumont, and made Sieff a wealthy man.

Israel Sieff was brought up in the same street as Simon *Marks (later Lord Marks of Broughton), the son of Michael Marks, founder of Marks and Spencer Ltd. The boys became close friends, passed through Manchester grammar school in the same class, and each married the other's sister. Their friendship was based on common origins as well as personal liking. In 1909 Sieff took a degree in economics at Manchester University, before joining his father's firm. On 15 June 1910 he married Marks's sister Rebecca Dora Marks (1890–1966) [see Sieff, Rebecca Dora]; they had three sons, one of whom died in 1933, and a daughter. In 1915, to help his friend, then about to become chairman of Marks and Spencer, to ward off a take-over bid, Sieff joined Simon Marks on the board, helping him with a substantial loan.

Having joined the Manchester Zionist Organization at seventeen, in 1913 Sieff encountered Chaim Weizmann, then a lecturer at Manchester University, and 'fell under his spell'. With Simon Marks's ardent support, he became Weizmann's unpaid personal assistant. In 1918, as secretary to the Zionist Commission, which was to report on how the Balfour declaration of 1917 was to be implemented, he accompanied Weizmann to the peace conference at Versailles, and in 1920 to the conference of San Remo. His wife, one of the six co-founders of WIZO, the Women's International Zionist Organization, was similarly active and was appointed OBE in 1960. Together they

spent many months in Palestine throughout the 1920s as Weizmann's 'eyes and ears'.

In 1926 Sieff became vice-chairman and joint managing director of Marks and Spencer (posts he held until 1964) at a time when the company was embarking on an ambitious expansion programme based on new methods of retailing. It was Sieff, according to Simon Marks, who spearheaded the new policy, starting with the issue of store organization and the creation of a personnel department to increase efficiency. When Sieff first moved to London he lived with his brother-in-law, Marks, and together they formed a close association often discussing the possibilities for the company long into the night. In effect they became 'the board in permanent session' on the company's affairs. This partnership brought Marks and Spencer great commercial success based on a reputation for high-quality products that represented good value for the customer. Such a policy was based on knowing what the consumer wanted and in turn creating a new kind of relationship with suppliers. It fell to Sieff to rove the country seeking manufacturing firms willing both to bypass the traditional wholesalers and to produce goods at lower costs, while still maintaining quality.

It was Sieff, with Marks's wholehearted approval, who developed a progressive and enlightened attitude to staff relations. Sieff had a keen awareness of how, under modern industrial conditions, the worker might suffer from feelings of alienation. To counteract this he ensured good working conditions for all the company's employees. He brought to the company a broad humanistic view of what the object of business should be. Together he and Simon Marks forged Marks and Spencer into a national institution.

During the depression of the 1930s Sieff made a series of broadcasts for the BBC in which he developed his views on economic planning. This and his writings in the *Morning Post* brought him into the sphere of the Political and Economic Planning (PEP) group. He was invited to become chairman of the influential PEP industry group. With his practical knowledge and personal skills he soon set about steering the group into more practical discussions. He produced the PEP's first report, known as A1, on industrial problems, which became the model for other publications by the organization. He remained chairman until 1939, and thereafter was vice-chairman until 1964.

During the Second World War Sieff made a major contribution to the nation's war effort. In 1940 he made a hazardous Atlantic crossing to America in a bid to try and sell as many goods as possible to earn dollars in order to help finance the war effort. As part of this strategy Marks and Spencer established a smaller subsidiary firm in the United States to conduct the new business and breach the American high tariff barriers.

Sieff had wide interests. For academic studies he particularly favoured the Royal Anthropological Society, of which he was a fellow. He bred prize-winning cattle on his estate in Berkshire, developed strawberry cultivation, and was an expert grower of orchids. His love of music was deep and well informed. He was an elegantly though quietly dressed man, an excellent host, and a master of the anecdote. His mild wise words disarmed critics and quietened troublemakers. Sieff was a natural diplomatist, with skills that were enhanced by his work with Weizmann. He enjoyed the company of men and women, loved good food, and was a connoisseur of claret. At the age of eighty-one he published his memoirs, only, he said, to record his gratitude to the two families and his friends that had enriched his life.

Sieff was created a life peer in 1966. He was FRGS, and was made honorary FRCS (1968) and LLD (Manchester, 1969). Sieff died at his home, Flat 147, Dorset House, Gloucester Place, London, on 14 February 1972. His younger surviving son, Marcus Joseph (b. 1913), was created a life peer, Baron Sieff of Brimpton, in 1980.

KENNETH HARRIS, rev. GARETH SHAW

Sources DNB · P. Bookbinder, *Marks & Spencer: the war years, 1939–1945* (1989) · G. Rees, *St Michael: a history of Marks and Spencer*, rev. edn (1973) · C. Weizmann, *Trial and error* (1949) · *The Times* (15 Feb 1972) · I. Sieff, *Memoirs* (1970) · personal knowledge (1986) · b. cert. · d. cert.
Archives Marks and Spencer plc, London, archive, corresp. and papers · U. Hull, Brynmor Jones L., arbitration papers | University of East Anglia Library, Norwich, corresp. with J. C. Pritchard · Wellcome L., corresp. with Charles Singer
Likenesses Baron Studios, photograph, 1966, NPG [see illus.] · H. Coster, photographs, NPG · photograph, Marks and Spencer, London · photographs, repro. in Rees, *St Michael*, 1st edn (1969)
Wealth at death £164,808: probate, 8 March 1972, CGPLA Eng. & Wales

Sieff, Rebecca Dora (1890–1966), feminist and Zionist, was born on 23 February 1890 at 38 Copenhagen Street, Leeds, the eldest daughter of Michael *Marks (1859–1907), founder of the Marks and Spencer retailing group, and his wife, Hannah Cohen. At the time of Rebecca's birth her mother, being illiterate, inscribed the birth certificate with a tiny cross. There was one son, Simon, born two years before Rebecca, who was always destined to take over the business, and three younger sisters. In 1894 the family settled in Manchester, where Michael Marks rented his first high-street shop. By this time he had joined forces with Tom Spencer, his cashier, and in 1903 the firm of Marks and Spencer Ltd was registered.

As the business prospered Rebecca was able to attend Manchester High School for Girls, a non-denominational school of high academic standing which encouraged women's higher education. In 1908 she enrolled to study English literature at Manchester University and on 15 June 1910, aged twenty, married 21-year-old Israel Moses *Sieff (1889–1972)—an economics graduate from Manchester University and also the son of a Lithuanian refugee pedlar—on the roof of Manchester's Midland Hotel. They had three sons and a daughter.

Manchester's spectacular growth in the nineteenth century as a centre for business, commerce, and the chemical industry attracted enormous Jewish settlement as the great wave of Russian pogroms broke out. In the years before the First World War key friendships were made between Chaim Weizmann, a brilliant young scientist appointed reader in chemistry at Manchester University,

his wife, Vera, and C. P. Scott, editor of the *Manchester Guardian*. At the same time as Weizmann won the sympathetic ear of politicians such as Winston Churchill, David Lloyd George, and Arthur James Balfour, he was forging close friendships with the Sieff and Marks families, who by this time had sufficient financial resources and business skills to help promote his Zionist ideas.

Although there were, from at least 1909, various women's groups and individuals working for the welfare of women and girls in Palestine, Rebecca Sieff took the lead in the struggle to weld them into one force which would ultimately be active in the practical work of building the state of Israel. Her approach to the Zionist movement was much influenced by what she witnessed in the suffragette movement, for she campaigned also for votes for women, equal pay and working conditions, equality of opportunity within trades and professions, and for the economic independence of women. Although the relationship with the English Zionist Federation (EZF) was always slightly uneasy as some felt that the splitting away of the female workers could only weaken the whole, Rebecca was adamant that for women to take part on an equal basis they must organize and work as women and not as an adjunct to the men's movement.

In early 1919 Sieff, together with Vera Weizmann, Olga Alman, and Romana Goodman, finally persuaded the EZF leadership to allow the formation of a separate women's federation. Sieff was elected their first president, and in July 1920, following her first visit to Palestine, the Women's International Zionist Organisation (WIZO) was formed in London 'to promote the welfare of women and children in Palestine and to carry out specific works in the reconstruction of Palestine', according to the words of the official resolution.

In 1926 Israel and Rebecca Sieff and their four children—Michael, Marcus, Daniel, and Judith—moved to London, where Rebecca became well known as an elegant society hostess organizing balls and galas for Jewish and non-Jewish events. In 1933, when Hitler came to power in Germany, she immediately established the women's appeal committee of the central British fund to rescue thousands of women and children from Nazi-dominated Europe. But that year personal tragedy struck too when their son Daniel died. The family founded a scientific research institute in his honour, known today as the Weizmann Institute of Science at Rehovot, Israel. During the 1930s Sieff travelled around the world for Zionist and anti-Nazi causes but she also campaigned vigorously for fuller parliamentary representation of women via the Women for Westminster group, which she founded, as well as demanding equal compensation for civilian women injured in bombing, equal rights in welfare and legal status.

In June 1946 Sieff headed a march to Downing Street of 200 women protesting against the British government's raid on the Jewish Agency's office in Jerusalem. In September she spent time with Holocaust survivors still living in a displaced persons' camp at Bergen-Belsen and two months later, in an impassioned speech to the United

Nations Special Committee on Palestine, demanded both the rescue of Jews stranded in displaced persons' camps and the immediate establishment of the Jewish state.

Following the proclamation of Israeli independence in 1948, Rebecca Sieff made Israel her permanent home. The years after independence demanded great flexibility within WIZO, of which she had been world president since 1920, as waves of immigrants flooded the new country and the organization placed more emphasis on traditionally 'female' issues, especially the care of home and family, while Sieff continued to fight for women's political rights.

In 1956 a bomb at Sieff's home in Tel Mond killed her gardener, but she was unhurt. In 1960 the British government appointed her an OBE and, three years later, when she resigned her executive position in WIZO, she was appointed honorary life president. She died at the Ichilov Hospital, Tel Aviv, Israel, on 8 January 1966, a few days after her husband, Israel, had been created a life peer. She was buried on 10 January at Tel Mond.

Sieff's level of commitment and her concentration on the struggle for women's rights in a male-dominated Zionist movement marked her out from the start among Zionist philanthropists. Yet, in common with many nineteenth-century pioneers of women's rights, while she promoted the centrality of the family in women's lives, her many involvements inevitably took her away from her own family for long periods.

ANNE M. SEBBA

Sources R. Gassman-Sher, *The story of the Federation of Women Zionists of Great Britain and Ireland, 1918–68* (1968) · G. Rees, *St Michael: a history of Marks and Spencer* (1969) · *Speaking for women: Rebecca Sieff and the WIZO movement* (1990) · *CGPLA Eng. & Wales* (1966) · b. cert. · m. cert. · d. cert. · I. Sieff, *Memoirs* (1970) · C. Weizmann, *Trial and error: the autobiography of Chaim Weizmann* (1949)
Archives Central Zionist Archives, Jerusalem · LMA, corresp. [copies] · Manchester Jewish Museum · Marks and Spencer, Wood Green, London, archives · Marks and Spencer plc, corresp. and papers · World WIZO, Tel Aviv, Israel | Women's Library, London, papers on political activity
Likenesses F. Beltran-Masses, oils, 1934, priv. coll. · photographs, Manchester Jewish Museum · photographs, Women's International Zionist Organisation, Tel Aviv, Israel · photographs, Central Zionist Archives, Jerusalem
Wealth at death £207,939: probate, 8 Feb 1966, *CGPLA Eng. & Wales*

Siegburg, Johann Lair von. *See* Siberch, John (*c.*1476–1554).

Sieghart [*formerly* Alexander], (**Henry Laurence**) **Paul** (1927–1988), law reformer, was born on 22 February 1927 in Vienna, Austria, the only child of Ernst Alexander and his wife, Marguerite, daughter of Rudolph Sieghart. Following his parents' divorce about 1930, his mother resumed her maiden name for herself and her son. Sieghart came from a remarkable background. His grandparents were Jewish by birth but had converted to Catholicism. He was brought up as a pious Roman Catholic, unaware of his Jewish ancestry until 1938. His maternal grandfather entered the Austro-Hungarian civil service and became *chef de cabinet* to the emperor Franz Josef.

Sieghart's mother was the first woman to obtain a doctorate of law at Vienna University.

In January 1939 Sieghart (knowing no English) and his mother fled to England from Austria. After one unhappy term at Harrow School in 1940 he moved to Berkhamsted School (1941–4). He went on to read mathematics at University College, London, in 1944 but decided to leave two years later without taking a degree, believing that he had not done enough work to obtain the outstanding result of which he was capable. After a succession of short-term and very varied jobs, Sieghart decided to read for the bar, to which he was called by Gray's Inn in 1953. He was talent-spotted by John Foster, who invited him to join his chambers. Sieghart quickly developed an enormous commercial and tax practice, but—probably because he had made enemies among the judiciary—his first application for silk was rejected in 1966. He promptly quit the bar.

Thereafter Sieghart earned money as a consultant and arbitrator, but devoted most of his time and energy to the advancement of human rights. Foster had introduced Sieghart to the law reform organization Justice. This became his main forum and he chaired its executive committee from 1978 until shortly before his death. Sieghart was almost single-handedly responsible for the enactment of the Rehabilitation of Offenders Act (1974). He wrote and lectured frequently on human rights. His book *The International Law of Human Rights* (1983) was a masterly analysis of the principal international human rights instruments. *The Lawful Rights of Mankind* (1985), aimed at a less expert readership, was also an outstanding book. Sieghart became a governor of the British Institute of Human Rights in 1974 and a trustee of the European Human Rights Foundation in 1980. The quickness of his mind, breadth of his intellectual interests, skill in argument, and enthusiasm for his causes made Sieghart a leading contributor to the development of human rights law both in Britain and beyond.

Sieghart was fascinated by many aspects of science, including computers and nuclear energy, and by medical ethics. He linked these interests with his concern for human rights by founding the Council for Science and Society in 1972 and by his publications *Privacy and Computers* (1986) and *Plutonium and Liberty* (a Justice report, 1978). He pushed the Home Office into setting up the committee (of which he was an influential member) which resulted in the Data Protection Act of 1984.

Although not devout, Sieghart retained close links with the Roman Catholic church and was a member of the hierarchy's Commission on International Justice and Peace (1976–80). One of his last acts was to address a Vatican conference, attended by the pope, on human rights. He was a regular contributor to *The Tablet* and a trustee of the Tablet Trust (from 1976). Sieghart proved to be a superb television performer as the moderator of discussion programmes. One of his programmes won a Royal Television Society award. He was a fellow of the Royal Society of Arts and a freeman of the City of London.

Gaunt, beak-nosed, a chain smoker (he died of lung cancer), Sieghart aroused strong personal reactions. He could be difficult and self-centred, but he could also exercise a compelling fascination. In 1954 he married Rosemary, daughter of Commander Charles E. Aglionby DSO, of the Royal Navy. She died of cancer in 1956, leaving Sieghart with an infant son and daughter. On 18 August 1959 he married Felicity Anne Olga Howard, daughter of Alfred Max Baer, chairman of Rio Tinto Zinc, with whom he had a further son and daughter. Sieghart died in Islington, London, on 12 December 1988, shortly after returning home from a dinner given by Justice in his honour. He was buried in Highgate cemetery.   WILLIAM GOODHART, *rev.*

Sources *The Times* (14 Dec 1988) · *WWW* · personal knowledge (1996) · private information (1996) [family] · *CGPLA Eng. & Wales* (1989)
Archives U. Hull, Brynmor Jones L., arbitration papers
Likenesses P. Benney, portrait, priv. coll.
Wealth at death £559,209: probate, 22 May 1989, *CGPLA Eng. & Wales*

Siemens, Alexander (1847–1928), electrical engineer, was born on 22 January 1847 in Hanover, Germany, the son of Gustav Siemens, a judge, and his wife, Sophie, *née* Heisse. His father was a third cousin of the engineers Charles and William *Siemens, and, after his education at the polytechnic in Hanover, Alexander arrived in England in 1867 to gain practical experience working with William at Siemens Brothers, Woolwich. In the following years he travelled extensively in Europe, the Middle East, and North America. In 1868 he returned to Germany to study at the University of Berlin, although his studies were interrupted when he was sent to Persia to assist with the building of the Indo-European telegraph. In 1869 he was working on cable-laying in the Black Sea.

When Prussia annexed Hanover, Siemens became a Prussian citizen, and he served as a private in the Prussian army in the Franco-Prussian War of 1870–71. He was wounded at the battle of Beaune la Rolande, and was awarded the Iron Cross. After the war he returned to England, and again worked with William Siemens, assisting with the building of regenerative gas furnaces for producing wrought iron and steel direct from the iron ore. He was also involved in the development of the furnace for cremation. In 1875 he joined the cable ship *Faraday* and took part in several cable-laying and cable-repairing expeditions, mainly in the north Atlantic. In 1876 and 1877 he spent some time in Canada and the USA, building furnaces there.

Siemens returned to England in 1877, and became a naturalized British subject in 1878. Most of his work thereafter was electrical, and he became manager of the electric light department of Siemens Brothers in 1879. The company manufactured electric generators, arc lamps, and cables for the lighting industry, but was not initially involved in the manufacture of filament lamps.

In 1881 Alexander Siemens married Louisa Frances Dodwell of Campden, Gloucestershire; they had three daughters. In the autumn of that year the world's first public electricity supply system, supplying electricity to a small number of private houses as well as street lighting, opened in Godalming, Surrey. Siemens Brothers' initial involvement was just to supply the equipment. Later they took over the enterprise, which was never viable, in order to gain practical experience of the emerging electric lighting industry. Alexander Siemens continued to be involved in submarine telegraphy, including laying a telegraph cable in the Amazon River in 1896.

Practical electric motors for railway traction were being developed from about 1890. In 1892 Siemens read a paper to the British Association on 'Electric locomotives on the City and South London Railway', the first deep-level 'tube' underground railway.

When Siemens Brothers became a limited company in 1880, Siemens became a director, and he was made managing director in 1889, a post he held until 1899. In that year the firm was reorganized, with new capital being brought in. George von Chauvin became managing director, although Siemens remained on the board until his retirement in 1918.

In 1871 Siemens was a founder member of the Society of Telegraph Engineers and Electricians, which became the Institution of Electrical Engineers (IEE) in 1888. His contributions to discussions on papers read at the institution showed a grasp both of technical detail and of the wider commercial and legal considerations affecting the electrical industry. He became president of the institution in 1894, and again in 1904, and he was president of the Institution of Civil Engineers in 1910–11. His first presidential address to the IEE included an analysis of the various orders and licences granted under the Electric Lighting Acts, 1882 and 1888. The acts had been much criticized for retarding the development of the electrical industry, but Siemens argued that considerable blame lay with those promoting electrical enterprises, who had had exaggerated expectations and made reckless assertions. In his second presidential address he made a strong plea for the introduction of the metric system, so that everyone would enjoy the benefit, which electrical engineers already had, of standard units of measurement.

As a leading figure in the electrical industry, and with a known interest in standards, Siemens was appointed by the British government as one of the British delegates to the International Electrical Congress at Chicago in 1893. In 1901 he was appointed a delegate to the similar congress in Paris. His interest in standards of measurement also led in 1897 to his appointment to a government committee considering the desirability of setting up a national physical laboratory. When the laboratory was established, in 1901, he served on its executive board. In retirement he lived at Westover, Milford-on-Sea, Hampshire, where he died, from heart failure, on 16 February 1928. He was survived by his wife.   BRIAN BOWERS

Sources J. D. Scott, *Siemens Brothers, 1858–1958* (1958) · *Electrical Trades Directory* (1907) · 'Siemens, Sir William', *DNB* · *Journal of the Institution of Electrical Engineers*, 66 (1928), 1242–3 · 'Reminiscences of Alexander Siemens', Inst. EE, I/6.2 · R. Appleyard, *The history of the Institution of Electrical Engineers, 1871–1931* (1939)
Archives Inst. EE, memoirs, I/6.2
Likenesses photographs, Inst. EE
Wealth at death £7277 13s. 8d.: probate, 3 May 1928, *CGPLA Eng. & Wales*

Siemens, Sir (Charles) William [*formerly* Karl Wilhelm] (1823–1883), electrical engineer and metallurgist, was born at Lenthe, Hanover, the fourth son of Christian Ferdinand Siemens (1787–1840) and his wife, Eleonore, *née* Deichmann. To avoid confusion with his younger brother Karl Heinrich, he was known as Wilhelm in Germany and as William in England. Together with their elder brother Werner, who remained in Germany, William, who spent most of his life in England, and Karl Heinrich, who worked in Russia, were in business as electrical engineers, concentrating first on the electric telegraph and later on electric lighting.

Early life and education in Germany Christian Siemens, a farm manager, had eight sons and a daughter who lived to adulthood. On his death Werner, the eldest surviving son, who was then an officer in the Prussian army, had to care for the younger brothers, a responsibility in which William later shared.

William was educated at a commercial school in Lübeck, then at a technical school in Magdeburg, where Werner was stationed. From there he went to Göttingen University, where he studied under Professor Himly, who had married his elder sister, Mathilde. It having been decided that William was to be an engineer, Werner obtained a place for him in the Stolberg factory at Magdeburg in 1843. Here Werner and William collaborated on their scientific and mechanical ideas, including improvements in the then novel application of electricity to the deposition of metals, for which Werner had already obtained a Prussian patent, specifying a thermo-electric battery to supply the electric current, and improvements in the solutions (alkaline hyposulphites) used for gilding and silvering.

Arrival in England For some reason, probably because it was in England that the greatest progress had been made in electroplating, the brothers determined to try to dispose of the invention there. William was dispatched in 1843 for the purpose. Speaking many years afterwards at a meeting of the Birmingham and Midland Institute (of which he was then president), he gave an account of the difficulties attending this first visit, when he was so ignorant of the language of the country that he was led to visit an undertaker, under the idea that this was the proper person to take up and dispose of his invention. Ultimately, however, perseverance triumphed over difficulties, and he sold his process to Elkington for £1600.

Such a success stimulated the brothers to fresh efforts. William gave up his position at the Stolberg factory in 1844 and started for London with two fresh inventions—a 'chronometric governor' for steam engines, devised by Werner and worked out by William, and the process of 'anastatic printing', invented by Baldamus of Erfurt and developed by the brothers. However, they set too high a value on these two inventions, and no capitalist could be found willing to purchase either, meritorious as they were. The 'governor' was an instrument of extreme ingenuity; it was fully appreciated by leading mechanical engineers, and obtained prizes from the Society of Arts in

Sir (Charles) William Siemens (1823–1883), by Rudolph Lehmann, 1882

1850 and at the Great Exhibition of 1851. It did not, however, come into practical use for its intended purpose—a purpose, indeed, for which it was too delicate—though it was afterwards successfully applied by Sir George Airy for regulating the movement of certain instruments at the Royal Greenwich Observatory.

The anastatic process was employed for the reproduction of printed matter until superseded by modern photographic methods. It was a transfer process. The page to be copied was moistened with acid and laid down on a metal plate. On pressure being applied, the result was a slight etching of the metal by the acid in the parts in contact with the unprinted portions of the paper and a slight setting off of the ink from the printed portions. The plate could then be inked up and printed from by the usual lithographic methods. The process, however, brought no profit to its introducer, and the factory which he started for its application was a source of considerable loss. The first five years of Siemens's stay in England were so discouraging that in 1849 he even discussed the idea of emigrating with Karl and Frederick, another brother, to California, then in the first flush of the gold discoveries.

The next invention about which the brothers busied themselves, though it contained within itself the germs of ultimate success, was no more profitable than its predecessors. The regenerative steam engine and condenser, worked up by William Siemens from earlier ideas, sought to prevent the great waste of energy which occurs in all forms of heat engine in consequence of the high temperature at which the products of combustion are discharged, and also from the steam being condensed to water after a portion only of its heat has been utilized as energy. The most important feature of the invention was that the steam after use in the cylinder passed through a heat-exchanger, and reached the condenser in a partly cooled state. The water from the condenser was afterwards forced back through the exchanger, absorbing its heat and causing its own temperature to rise on its way to the boiler. In spite of all the labour and ingenuity expended between 1847 and 1859, the brothers' hopes were never realized. That the merits of the invention were recognized is shown by the fact that a leading firm of Birmingham engineers, Fox and Henderson, paid Siemens a considerable sum for a share in the patent, and also engaged his services at a salary which provided him with a sufficient means of livelihood. In addition to this he was now earning money in other ways, and in 1851 he produced a water meter, which fulfilled its intended purposes so well, and was so superior to other instruments, that in a year or two it was producing a handsome income from royalties, and the inventor's long struggle against adverse fortune was at an end.

The regenerative furnace The success of the meter, however, was soon eclipsed by that of the great invention with which the names of William and Frederick Siemens must always be connected—the regenerative furnace. The brothers had long endeavoured to apply the principle of their condenser to various manufacturing processes, especially to those in which, as in salt extracting, large quantities of liquid have to be evaporated. Their efforts met with little practical success until they finally hit on the very simple idea of applying the principle of the condenser to furnaces, an idea which was embodied in a patent taken out by Frederick in 1856. The products of combustion from the furnace, instead of passing direct to the chimney, were led through a chamber filled with refractory brickwork, to which they gave up their heat. As soon as the chamber was sufficiently hot the current was shut off, and the air supply of the furnace led through it. The air thus reached the burning fuel hot, instead of cold. By the use of two chambers used alternately to receive and give out the heat, the process was made continuous. By a further improvement gas was used in place of solid fuel, and this was passed through the 'regenerator' so that it arrived at the place of combustion in a highly heated state. Not only was there an enormous economy of heat, but the gas could be made from fuel of a very inferior sort, while processes formerly requiring crucibles were now conducted in the open furnace. The first practical application of the furnace was to the melting and reheating of steel in 1857. It was soon after applied, in a modified form, to heating the air for blast furnaces, then to glass making (the subject of the last lecture ever given by Faraday was the use of the furnace at Chance's glassworks), and eventually to a large number of industrial processes where great heat is required. Its most important application was to the manufacture of steel, either by melting wrought iron and cast iron together on the open hearth of the furnace or direct from iron ore. The former was known as the 'Siemens–Martin' process, and the latter as the 'Siemens'

or 'ore' process. For the manufacture of steel the 'Siemens' process was first used in 1865 or 1866; its employment spread rapidly, so that by 1882 it was estimated that 4 million tons of steel had been produced by it, and in 1896 the output for the whole world was calculated at over 7 million tons as compared with over 11 million tons produced by the Bessemer process. In Great Britain 2,355,000 tons were produced in 1896 by the Siemens process, and 1,845,000 by the Bessemer process.

In order to develop the process, and to test its working on a large scale, Siemens, with some personal friends, formed a company, and works were established at Landore in south Wales in 1869. Though for a time the company promised well and held a leading place among the steelworks of the United Kingdom, it was not commercially successful, and the attempt was abandoned about 1888.

Electrical sciences Siemens became a naturalized British subject in 1859, the year in which he married Anne (d. 12 April 1901), the daughter of Joseph Gordon, an Edinburgh lawyer and the brother of Lewis Gordon, professor of electrical engineering in the University of Glasgow. The couple had no children of their own, but they adopted Alexander *Siemens, the son of a third cousin. Siemens obtained medals at the exhibitions of London in 1862 and of Paris in 1867. In 1860 he became a member of the Institution of Civil Engineers, in special recognition of his merits—since he was a manufacturer rather than an engineer—and in 1862 he was elected a fellow of the Royal Society.

Meantime Siemens had turned his attention to electrical science, and was building up another reputation. On the first introduction of the electric telegraph, Werner Siemens appreciated its possibilities, and determined to devote himself to its development. In 1847 he associated himself with Halske and founded in Berlin the great firm of Siemens and Halske, of which William was appointed the London agent. Werner invented the method of insulating telegraph wires with gutta-percha, and the use of such wires for conveying messages under water led to the invention of submarine cables. The first of these was the Dover to Calais cable, laid, after an unsuccessful attempt in the previous year, in 1851. This was soon followed by others, with many of which the firm of Siemens and Halske was associated. In 1858 this department of their business had developed to such an extent that the brothers determined to establish works in England, and a small factory was started in Millbank, afterwards in 1866 transferred to Charlton in Kent, where the great works of Siemens Brothers (Werner, William, and Karl) were eventually established. These works in course of time occupied an area of over 6 acres, and employed more than 2000 people. Of the undertakings carried out by the brothers, one of the greatest was the telegraph line from Prussia to Tehran, a length of 2750 miles, which formed a principal part of the direct line from England to India. This was carried out by the London and Berlin firms jointly in 1869. A few years later a still more important undertaking was brought to a successful issue by the London firm alone, which in 1874 laid the direct Atlantic cable. For this the cable ship *Faraday* was specially designed by William Siemens, though he had no previous knowledge or experience of marine engineering. The execution of works of such magnitude, indeed, involved the designing and construction of much new machinery and apparatus. In all this detailed work Siemens took his full share, though as time went on, and the concerns with which he was associated increased in importance, he withdrew from detail work and confined himself more to supervision and initiation.

When the Society of Telegraph Engineers (later the Institution of Electrical Engineers) was formed in 1871, Siemens was elected its first president, and he was very influential in the society's early development as a body bringing together both practical engineers and academic researchers.

The electric telegraph was the first widespread industrial application of electricity, but two inventions made electric lighting the focus of attention. The first was the self-excited electric generator, a machine in which the current for energizing the field windings came from the output of the generator itself. The importance of this was that electrical generation was no longer dependent on permanent magnets, and much higher currents could be produced. The self-excited principle was announced at a meeting of the Royal Society on 14 February 1867, when both Siemens and Charles Wheatstone, working quite independently, described the principle. It was then found that Cromwell F. Varley was applying for a patent for the same idea. The second invention was the development about 1879 of a successful incandescent filament lamp by Joseph Swan, the American Thomas Alva Edison, and several other inventors. The Siemens undertakings took up the manufacture of generators and of arc lamps, but not filament lamps, though none of the leading inventions connected with electric lighting can be associated with the name of William Siemens. The firm supplied some of the machines first used for lighthouse illumination, and one of the earliest electric light installations in London—that of the British Museum—was carried out by them in 1879.

The first time that an electricity supply was made available to people in their own homes was in the autumn of 1881, at Godalming, Surrey. The supply was provided by a firm whose main interest was street lighting, and they used a Siemens generator, driven initially from a waterwheel in a local mill. Neither William Siemens nor any other member of the family seems to have been involved in the original undertaking, but before long they had taken over the running of it. In May 1882 Siemens gave evidence to the House of Commons select committee on the Electric Lighting Bill, in which he described the experience gained at Godalming.

William Siemens was also one of the first to suggest the transmission of power by electricity, and to apply electric power to locomotion, in the Portrush Railway, in 1883. When invented in 1879 his electric furnace had no practical application, but it later found a place in industry as a

means of reaching otherwise unattainable temperatures. His 'bathometer' for estimating sea depths without a sounding line, though ingenious, was impractical. His electric thermometer proved useful in cases where it was required to record temperatures at inaccessible or scarcely accessible positions, though not, as he had hoped, in deep-sea investigations, where the cable failed before the apparatus itself. His researches into the effect of electric light on plants were carried far enough only to prove the possibility of aiding the growth of plants and fruit by its means. His patent of 1855 led to a means of achieving extremely low temperatures by the expansion of liquefied gases already cooled down to the lowest attainable point. How prolific was his inventive faculty is shown by the fact that no fewer than 113 British patents were taken out in his name.

Rewards, honours, and death Siemens's inventions and his scientific work brought him many honours. He was president of the mechanical section of the British Association in 1869, and president of the association itself in 1882; he was the first president (1871) of the Society of Telegraph Engineers, and in 1878 he became president of the same society for the second time; he was president of the Institution of Mechanical Engineers (1872) and of the Iron and Steel Institute (1877), and chairman of the council of the Society of Arts (1882); he was an honorary DCL of Oxford and LLD of Dublin and Glasgow. He received the Albert medal of the Society of Arts in 1874, the Howard prize of the Institution of Civil Engineers in 1883, and the Bessemer medal of the Iron and Steel Institute in 1875. He received many foreign orders, including the French Légion d'honneur, and in 1883, only seven months before his death, he was knighted in recognition of his services.

Siemens made few contributions to pure science. In 1882 he sent some ingenious speculations as to the source of solar energy to the Royal Society. Among these was a theory, well received at the time, that gaseous matter might be dissociated by radiant solar energy and driven out by centrifugal action at the sun's equator, to be drawn in towards the poles and subjected to intense combustion. This was his last important piece of work. He died at his home, 3 Palace Houses, Bayswater Road, London, of heart disease and pneumonia, on 19 November 1883, and was buried in Kensal Green cemetery after a funeral service in Westminster Abbey, where a memorial window was set up in his honour.

William Siemens was a born inventor, but he was also, what so few inventors are, a shrewd and capable man of business. He made a large fortune, and used it liberally. He established prize medals at King's College, London, at the Birmingham and Midland Institute, and at the City and Guilds of London Technical Institute. After his death Lady Siemens provided funds for the foundation of a Siemens electrical laboratory, as a memorial, at King's College, London.

Siemens's collected works, including his very numerous addresses, lectures, and papers to scientific societies, were edited by E. F. Bamber, after his death, in three volumes (1889), uniform with the biography by Dr William Pole FRS. H. T. WOOD, *rev.* BRIAN BOWERS

Sources W. Pole, *Life of Sir William Siemens* (1888) · J. D. Scott, *Siemens Brothers, 1858–1958* (1958) · C. W. Siemens, 'Presidential address', *Journal of the Society of Telegraph Engineers*, 7 (1878), 3–19 · C. W. Siemens, 'On measuring temperature by electricity', *Journal of the Society of Telegraph Engineers*, 1 (1872), 123–33 · 'Select committee on the Electric Lighting Bill', *Parl. papers* (1882), 10.198–206, no. 227 [minutes of evidence] · d. cert. · *CGPLA Eng. & Wales* (1883)
Archives Siemens Institute, Munich | CUL, letters to Sir George Stokes
Likenesses M. Thomas, oils, 1876, Inst. CE · R. Lehmann, oils, 1882, NPG [*see illus.*] · R. Lehmann, oils, Inst. EE · Lock & Whitfield, woodburytype, NPG; repro. in T. Cooper, *Men of mark: a gallery of contemporary portraits* (1883) · G. J. Stodart, stipple (after photograph by Van der Weyde), NPG · photograph, repro. in Scott, *Siemens Brothers* · woodcuts, NPG
Wealth at death £393,857 10s. 2d. in UK: resworn probate, Feb 1885, *CGPLA Eng. & Wales* (1883)

Siepmann, Otto (1861–1947), teacher of modern languages, was born on 9 May 1861 at Waldbröl, near Cologne. He was the eldest of the nine surviving children of August Siepmann (1835–1908), insurance broker, and his wife, Wilhelmine Henriette Hasenbach (1836–1891). The Lutheran Siepmann family came from a long line of wealthy landowning Rhineland farmers. Siepmann's education in Colmar, Alsace-Lorraine—which was annexed by Prussia in 1871—influenced his keen linguistic and cultural awareness and engendered his detestation of Bismarck's political ambitions. After study at university, probably Strasbourg, and military service in which he distinguished himself as a marksman, he began teaching as well as dabbling in journalism.

In 1885, finding his liberal outlook unwelcome in Germany, Siepmann moved to Britain, taking a language teaching post at Westgate-on-sea, Kent. Appointed to Inverness College in April 1888, he developed an enthusiasm for the Gaelic language and the Celtic tradition, and he there became engaged to Grace Florence Baker (1858–1937), daughter of John Baker, naturalist, of Cambridge, whom he married in 1889.

He moved in 1890 to Clifton College, Bristol, by then firmly established as one of the most successful English public schools founded in the mid-Victorian period. Siepmann found himself in an especially congenial atmosphere. The college's pioneering work in the teaching of 'modern' subjects provided him for the next thirty-one years with an ideal environment in which to identify the best classroom practice in the art of language teaching and to devote himself to the publishing of textbooks. The latter furthered his pedagogical ideas and, incidentally, financed the education of his three sons and three daughters.

Siepmann's involvement in the founding of the Modern Language Association in London in 1892, and his subsequent engagement in its national and international affairs, influenced his work. Soon after his appointment in 1900 as the founding head of modern languages at Clifton, he reformed the curriculum there radically, securing on the timetable daily an hour of French and an hour of German. This unusual arrangement produced a steady stream of modern languages scholars destined for the universities of Oxford and Cambridge.

Admiration of the British public-school education system led Siepmann to obtain naturalization as a British subject in 1905. Seeing both the strengths and the weaknesses of the direct method of language teaching and its exclusion of the mother tongue, then in vogue in Britain, Siepmann developed what he termed a *via media*, preserving the grammatical training and practice of classical teaching but founding it on the spoken language. This approach was followed in his three major groups of publications: French and German primers; his famous *Word and Phrasebook* series; and annotated editions of French and German classics. All of these enjoyed immense success and made his name well known to generations of schoolchildren in Britain and across the British empire.

With his wife and family, Siepmann spent the academic year 1907–8 on sabbatical leave in Karlsruhe, Baden. During the First World War, while his two elder sons served with distinction in action in the British army, he continued to pursue at Clifton his work on the theory and practice of modern language education. Deeply hurt by wartime anti-German feeling in Britain, he quietly withdrew from the Modern Language Association, but his offer in 1916 to remove his name from his successful series of language textbooks was declined by his publisher, Macmillan. His advocacy of the systematic use of topical newspaper articles to support language teaching, then unheeded, was seventy years ahead of its time. In 1930, the BBC used his *Primary German Course* for pioneering language education broadcasts, and his novel series of twenty-four German language gramophone records, released by His Master's Voice in 1932–3, underscored his belief in the importance of phonetics.

In 1917 Siepmann gave evidence to the national committee of inquiry into the teaching of modern languages, under the chairmanship of Stanley Leathes (1861–1938), and was appointed reviser to the Northern Universities' Joint Matriculation Board language examinations. On his retirement to Godalming, Surrey, in 1921, he became an occasional inspector for modern languages for the Board of Education and an examiner both for the Oxford and Cambridge Schools Examination Board and for the civil service commissioners. In 1932, he gave up all other work to concentrate on writing. He spent the winter of 1937–8 in Germany, after the death of his wife, before settling in Crowthorne, Berkshire.

Siepmann's authority and reputation as an educationist rested on carefully articulated principles. A practical teacher rather than an academic scholar, he was strict but kindly. Tireless and industrious in his work, his character was serious and he did not laugh easily. He was agnostic, though a regular chapel attender at Clifton. When his eldest grandson joined the British army in 1940, Siepmann declared that he intended to remain alive until his return, as he wanted 'to see the end of Hitler'. An inveterate pipe smoker, he doubled his consumption of tobacco as his contribution in tax to the war effort. Retaining a strong

German accent into old age, he continued to be a voracious reader and a player of ferocious croquet and of billiards at home, as well as being a keen golfer. He died of heart failure at his home, Ellesmere, Crowthorne, on 11 January 1947 and was cremated at Woking four days later.

MAURICE WHITEHEAD

Sources *The Times* (13 Jan 1947) · *The Cliftonian* (March 1947) · *The Cliftonian* (July 1947) · *Modern Languages*, 28 (1947), 117 · Otto Siepmann, 1861–1947: correspondence with Macmillan & Co., 1889–1941, BL, Add. MSS 55168–55170 · Otto Siepmann: naturalization papers, 1905, PRO, HO 144/789/129004 · certificate of naturalization, 6 Dec 1905, and oath of allegiance, 30 Dec 1905, PRO, HO 334/41/15640 · private information (2004) · J. Houseman, *Run-through: a memoir* (1972) · J. Houseman, *Unfinished business: a memoir* (1986) · E. O. Siepmann, *Confessions of a nihilist* (1955) · H. A. Siepmann, *Echo of the guns: recollections of an artillery officer, 1914–1918* (1987) · d. cert.

Archives BL, corresp. with Macmillans, Add. MSS 55168–55170 · PRO, naturalization papers, HO 144/789/129004, HO 334/41/15640

Likenesses photograph, *c.*1890 · F. Von Kamptz, oils, *c.*1920, Clifton College, Bristol · photograph, *c.*1920, repro. in Houseman, *Run-through*

Wealth at death £9257 19s. 4d.: probate, 1 May 1947, CGPLA Eng. & Wales

Sieveking, Sir Edward Henry (1816–1904), physician, was born on 24 August 1816 at 1 St Helen's Place, Bishopsgate, London, the eldest son of Edward Henry Sieveking (1790–1868), a Hamburg merchant of Lutheran Westphalian stock, and his wife, Louisa Francesca Margaret, *née* Meyer (1789–1861), also of Hamburg. Both parents came from influential families, a maternal aunt being Amelia Wilhelmina Sieveking (1794–1859), founder in Germany of the first protestant Sisterhood of Mercy at Hamburg. In 1830 Sieveking began his secondary education at Ratzeburg and Berlin. In 1837 he entered the University of Berlin to study anatomy and physiology, the latter under the celebrated neurophysiologist Johannes Muller (1801–1858). After a short spell in Bonn, and two years studying medicine at University College, London, he graduated MD from Edinburgh in 1841 with a thesis on erysipelas. He then returned to Europe, studying in Paris under the neuropathologist Gabriel Andral (1797–1876) and the venereologist Philippe Ricord (1800–1889), and in Vienna some ophthalmology under Frederick Jaeger (1784–1872). For four years Sieveking then practised in Hamburg, lecturing and founding with his aunt Amelia a children's hospital there. Back in England he took the licentiate of the Royal College of Physicians in 1847 (he was elected FRCP in 1852). His marriage on 5 September 1849 to Jane (*b.* 1815/16), daughter of John Ray of Finchley, brought them eight sons, two of whom died in infancy and one as schoolboy at Marlborough College, which all his sons attended. There were also three daughters.

Sieveking set up home and practice in London, in Brook Street and later in Bentinck Street; in 1857 he moved to Manchester Square. Meanwhile in 1851 he had become assistant physician to the recently founded St Mary's Hospital, Paddington, to which he was connected until his death. At an early stage he lectured on materia medica, and in 1860 he became a full physician; he retired from

Sir Edward Henry Sieveking (1816–1904), by William Salter Herrick, *c.*1860

that position in 1888 when he was placed on the consulting staff. He was physician to the London Lock Hospital from 1864 to 1869, and to the National Hospital for the Paralysed and Epileptic from 1864 to 1867. In 1855 with John Propert he founded Epsom College, also known as the Royal Medical Benevolent College, a public school for the sons of medical men. He took a prominent part in matters at the Royal College of Physicians, being censor between 1869 and 1881 and vice-president in 1888. He gave the Croonian lectures (1866), 'On the localisation of disease', and the Harveian oration (1877) on a description of a manuscript of Harvey's lectures.

Several of Sieveking's publications had their origin in his early and postgraduate training. In 1858, in connection with his interest in the nervous system, he invented an aesthesiometer for testing sensation of the skin. He produced manuals on ventilation (1846), on training institutions for nurses and workhouses (1849), on pathological anatomy with C. Handfeld Jones (1854), on epilepsy (1858), on laryngoscopy (1862), and on life assurance (1873 and 1882). His intimate knowledge of German allowed him to translate C. von Rokitansky's *Pathological Anatomy* (1849) and M. H. Romberg's *Nervous Diseases* (1853) for the Sydenham Society. He also edited the *British and Foreign Medico-Chirurgical Review* from 1855 to 1860.

Sieveking was an all-round general physician and diplomatic careerist, advising not only St Mary's Hospital for many years, but also the British Medical Association and the Royal College of Physicians. The college's president, Sir James Clark, recommended him in 1863 as physician-in-ordinary to the prince of Wales, who had recently married the German-speaking Princess Alexandra, daughter of the heir to the throne of Denmark, but he was never called after December 1869. In 1873 he was made physician-in-ordinary to Queen Victoria. He received the honorary degree of LLD (Edinburgh) in 1884 at the tercentenary of the university, was knighted in 1886, and in 1896 was gazetted a knight of grace of the order of St John of Jerusalem for good works for that order. He died at his home, 17 Manchester Square, on 24 February 1904, and was buried on 28 February at Abney Park cemetery, Stoke Newington, London; his wife survived him.

MICHAEL ANTHONY WAUGH

Sources *The Lancet* (5 March 1904), 680–83 · *Medico-Chirurgical Transactions*, 88 (1905), cviii–cix · N. M. Goodman, 'Medical attendance on royalty: the diaries of Dr Edward Sieveking', *Medicine and science in the 1860s*, ed. F. N. L. Poynter (1968), 127–36 · *The Times* (25 Feb 1904), 4a · *The Times* (29 Feb 1904), 10e · *CGPLA Eng. & Wales* (1904)

Archives RCP Lond., diaries, corresp., and papers · U. Edin. L., lecture notes on popular physiology

Likenesses W. S. Herrick, oils, *c*.1860, RCP Lond. [*see illus.*] · R. T., wood-engraving, NPG; repro. in *ILN* (27 March 1886) · R. Tousse, oils, Royal Society of Medicine, London

Wealth at death £23,935 17*s*. 3*d*.: resworn probate, 7 April 1904, *CGPLA Eng. & Wales*

Sieveking, Lancelot de Giberne (1896–1972), writer and radio and television producer, was born in Harrow on 19 March 1896, the third son and third child (there was also a daughter) of Edward Gustavus Sieveking, timber merchant, and his wife, Isabel Giberne, writer and suffragist and cousin of Gerard Manley Hopkins. His godfather was G. K. Chesterton, described by Lancelot as 'the first great friend I ever had', and he was the great-nephew of Sir Edward Sieveking, physician. He was removed from prep school when the family doctor said he had 'outgrown his strength'. He was tutored at home from the age of thirteen to eighteen. Writing later, he much regretted the absence of childhood friends. But this at least enabled him early to indulge his literary bent. His first novel, *Stampede!*, begun at the age of thirteen, was published in 1924. His first book, *Dressing Gowns and Glue*, a slim volume of nonsense verse published in 1920, ran through four editions.

When the First World War was declared in 1914 Sieveking joined the Artists' Rifles but soon transferred to the Royal Naval Air Service. On active service, first in east Africa, later in France, he went on night bombing raids, was promoted captain, and was awarded the DSC. But on 28 October 1917 he was shot down behind the German lines and imprisoned until war's end.

In 1919 Sieveking went to St Catharine's College, Cambridge. There, for the first time (apart from the abnormal war years), he was able to make friends with his contemporaries as well as many of the leading literary figures of the day. A major influence and lifelong friend was the eccentric genius C. K. Ogden, who, Sieveking claimed, 'managed everything I did for the next seven years'. It was Ogden who encouraged him to buy and edit the *New Cambridge*. After failing to qualify for the English tripos, he went down and for a while drifted from job to job, toured

as an actor (1919–22), took the unlikely post of assistant inspector of taxes in Sussex (1922), and then rejoined the Royal Air Force, in which from 1923 to 1924 he was stationed in India.

On 13 September 1924 Sieveking married April Constance Corona (*b*. 1901/2), daughter of Harry *Quilter, artist and writer; they had one son. In April of the following year, his life began to take on greater shape and direction. He applied and was accepted for a job at the BBC, then in existence for only four years. Sieveking was 6 feet 6 inches tall, handsome, and elegant. Anyone less like an assistant to the director of education (for such was his title), whether in appearance or professional experience, would be hard to imagine. But then seldom had the term education been applied to so grotesque a miscellany of duties. Sieveking's main tasks combined public relations (wining and dining distinguished public figures to win their goodwill for a fledgeling and not yet respected institution), editing news bulletins, and organizing topical talks and the first outside broadcasts to be put on the air.

Despite the rampant amateurism of these early days at the BBC, Sieveking soon found his proper niche and, with a small band of fellow workers, lent his imagination to creating a new, distinctive art—radio drama. His output over the next fifteen years was prolific (he produced over 200 plays and wrote several books) and original. In 1926 he produced *The Wheel of Time*, the first feature programme to be broadcast, and this was followed in 1928 by *Kaleidoscope*, the first multi-studio production. This, like everything else he did, provoked both favourable and hostile opinions. His first marriage ended in divorce in 1928, and on 24 August 1929 he married Natalie Alice Denny (*b*. 1908/9), the daughter of Court Denny, a City merchant; they had two daughters.

After 1938 Sieveking ceased to be a dominant influence in broadcasting. Though he produced the first television play (in 1930), he never achieved comparable success in this new medium. 'In three-quarters of a century', he wistfully wrote, 'no one in any field of activity has been anything but friendly and co-operative—except in the field of television. Why?' In 1938–9 he was seconded to the Canadian Broadcasting Corporation, and in 1939 he was transferred to BBC Bristol as a producer in the feature and drama department. From 1942 to 1944 he was the BBC's west regional programme director. But administration bored him and in 1944 he accepted the job of drama script editor, a post he held until he was retired in 1956.

Sieveking's second marriage was dissolved in 1939 and on 12 May 1949 he married Maisie (*b*. 1907/8), the divorced wife of James Leslie Taylor, and the daughter of Max John Christian Meiklejohn, writer and publisher. They had one son. Sieveking lived his last years at the White House, Snape, Suffolk, entertaining and delighting his friends with lively conversation and a fund of anecdotes. He died of heart failure on 6 January 1972 in Ipswich Hospital, Foxhall, Suffolk.

C. A. SIEPMANN, *rev.*

Sources L. Sieveking, unpublished autobiography, BBC WAC · private information (1986) · m. certs. · d. cert. · *The Times* (10 Jan 1972) · *The Times* (20 Jan 1972) · *CGPLA Eng. & Wales* (1972)

Archives BBC WAC, corresp. with BBC staff · BL, letters to D. E. Collins, former secretary of G. K. Chesterton, and related material, Add. MS 73226 B, fols. 146–7, 167, 169; Add. MS 73232 B, fols. 164–6; Add. MS 73240, fol. 16; Add. MS 73455 D, fol. 101; Add. MS 73475 A, fol. 154; Add. MS 73475 B, fols. 26, 30, 35, 38, 83, 86, 93, 96 · Tate collection, letters to Paul Nash · U. Reading, letters to the Bodley Head Ltd
Wealth at death £2067: probate, 7 April 1972, CGPLA Eng. & Wales

Sievier, Robert William (1794–1865), engraver, sculptor, and scientist, was born in London on 24 July 1794. He decided to become an engraver after gaining a silver medal from the Society of Arts in 1812 for a pen-and-ink drawing. He trained under John Young and afterwards with Edward Scriven, and on 8 January 1818 entered the Royal Academy Schools. He produced at this time a large number of stipple engravings after artists such as Hans Holbein, Sir Thomas Lawrence, William Etty, and G. S. Newton.

To improve his knowledge of the figure Sievier learned to model in clay and studied anatomy under Joshua Brookes. Subsequently, around 1823, he gave up engraving in favour of sculpture. 'Rapidly improving', according to Redgrave, 'his great facility of seizing the likeness and characteristic expression of his sitters led many persons of distinction to his studio' (Redgrave, *Artists*, 394). His portrait busts included those of Lord Chancellor Eldon (exh. RA, 1825), Sir Thomas Lawrence (1830; Soane Museum, London), and Prince Albert, the prince consort (1842; Royal Collection). He also executed several memorial statues, including those of the physician Edward Jenner (1825; Gloucester Cathedral) and William Harcourt, third Earl Harcourt (1832; St Michael, Stanton Harcourt, Oxfordshire), and a large number of church monuments. He exhibited at the Royal Academy from 1822 to 1844, at the British Institution from 1825 to 1831, and at the Society of British Artists from 1829 to 1843. Sievier's portraiture was characterized by a bold naturalism which sometimes tended towards exaggeration, especially in the depiction of facial expressions and fleshy form—a manner in which his work is comparable to that of his contemporary Samuel Joseph. He had an eye for detail—for example, in his reliefs for monuments—gained from his training as an engraver. Sievier also designed some 'ideal' works, including figures of a *Bacchante Asleep* (1824) and *Musidora* (1830), which were formerly in the collection of Joseph Neeld at Grittleton House, Wiltshire, *The Three Graces* (1824; Birmingham Museum and Art Gallery), after Canova, and genre subjects such as *Boy and Tortoise* (exh. RA, 1829). His chimney-piece figures of *Bacchus* and *Ariadne* (1833) are at Chatsworth, Derbyshire.

In the latter part of his life Sievier abandoned sculpture and devoted himself to science, being involved in rubber production and in the early development of electric telegraphy. According to Redgrave he was 'of an active inventive mind … and distinguished also by his manners and power of conversation' (Redgrave, *Artists*, 395). He was elected a fellow of the Royal Society in 1841. Sievier died on 28 April 1865 at his home, 35 Rochester Road, Camden Town, London, and was buried in Kensal Green cemetery.

With his wife, Ann Eliza (b. c.1811), Sievier had a son, Robert Moore Sievier (b. c.1827), who was admitted to the Royal Academy Schools on 2 April 1845 to study sculpture.   MARTIN GREENWOOD

Sources R. Gunnis, *Dictionary of British sculptors, 1660–1851* (1953); new edn (1968) · Redgrave, *Artists* · M. Greenwood, 'Sievier, Robert William', *The dictionary of art*, ed. J. Turner (1996) · B. Read, *Victorian sculpture* (1982) · Graves, *RA exhibitors* · Graves, *Brit. Inst.* · J. Johnson, ed., *Works exhibited at the Royal Society of British Artists, 1824–1893, and the New English Art Club, 1888–1917*, 2 vols. (1975), 423 · *Engraved Brit. ports.* · Thieme & Becker, *Allgemeines Lexikon* · CGPLA Eng. & Wales (1866)
Archives Edinburgh Central Reference Library, Kenneth Sanderson collection, corresp. and notes
Wealth at death under £200: probate, 21 Jan 1866, CGPLA Eng. & Wales

Siferwas, John (fl. 1380–1421), manuscript artist, was active in the late fourteenth and early fifteenth centuries. He depicted himself several times in the habit of a Dominican friar, and is probably identifiable as the 'John Cyfrewas' of the Dominican community in Guildford who was ordained acolyte at Farnham on 19 May 1380 by William Wykeham, bishop of Winchester, and as the 'Johannes Sifirwas, brother of the Order of Preachers' to whom the widow Joan Elveden, from Muchelney (Somerset), bequeathed 'one pair of jet praying-beads' in her will dated 4 September 1421. After his ordination Siferwas perhaps moved from Guildford to the Dominican community in Salisbury or Ilchester. All his surviving work was done for religious houses in the south-west.

Siferwas's work survives in three manuscripts: a Pentateuch commentary from Glastonbury Abbey, at Trinity College, Cambridge; the Sherborne missal, in the British Library (Add. MS 74326); and the fragmentary Lovell lectionary, in the British Library (Harley MS 7026). His work on the missal is datable within the period 1396–1407: one of the patrons of the manuscript was Bishop Richard Mitford of Salisbury, whose episcopate spanned those years. Siferwas depicted John Whas, the scribe of the missal, as a Benedictine. Whas probably belonged to the Benedictine abbey of Sherborne, for which the missal was made, and Siferwas may have resided at Sherborne while decorating the manuscript.

Siferwas must have completed the decoration of the lectionary before 1408, the year of the death of John, fifth Baron Lovell of Titchmarsh, who commissioned the manuscript for Salisbury Cathedral. On folio 4 verso, Siferwas depicted himself presenting the manuscript to Lovell. The picture is among the finest examples of early English portraiture.

The sumptuous Sherborne missal represents the high point of Siferwas's art. He decorated most of the first half of the 700-page manuscript himself, leaving much of the rest to assistants of lesser ability. His own contribution comprises a full-page crucifixion, historiated and ornamental initials, and elaborate borders densely populated with biblical scenes, angels, 'portrait' heads, scenes of courtly life, drolleries, and representations of flora and fauna both conventionalized and naturalistic. His sensitive depictions of birds are justly famous for their realism.

Several borders include a pinnacled tabernacle containing figural scenes. These tabernacles are a hallmark of his art, and recur in the Lovell lectionary.

Siferwas painted in the international Gothic style established in England, probably under north-German influence, in the late fourteenth century. Characteristic of the style are the use of rich, warm colours, skilful treatment of architecture, and painterly modelling of the human figure. The Sherborne missal is the masterpiece of the style. Yet because Siferwas worked outside the main centres of manuscript production, his influence was less than his achievement merited.   TIMOTHY GRAHAM, *rev.*

Sources J. A. Herbert, *The Sherborne missal* (1920) · E. G. Millar, *English illuminated manuscripts of the 14th and 15th centuries* (1928) · M. Rickert, *Painting in Britain: the middle ages*, 2nd edn (1965) · R. Marks and N. Morgan, *The golden age of English manuscript painting, 1200–1500* (1981)
Archives BL, Harley MS 7026 · BL, Sherborne missal, Add. MS 74326 · Trinity Cam., Pentateuch commentary from Glastonbury Abbey, B.3.7
Likenesses J. Siferwas, self-portrait, BL, Lovell lectionary, Harley MS 7026, fol. 4v

Sifton, Sir Clifford (1861–1929), politician in Canada, was born on 10 March 1861 in the family farmhouse near Arva, Middlesex county, Upper Canada, the third of three children of John Wright Sifton (1833–1912), entrepreneur and politician, and his wife, Kate Watkins (*c.*1833–1909). His parents were both of Anglo-Irish descent; their Methodist faith, belief in temperance, and commitment to the politics of reform-liberalism were absorbed by their children, Sophia (*c.*1856–1892), Arthur Lewis (1858–1921), and Clifford. The boys were educated in schools at Dundas and London, Ontario; and, after their father secured some contracts for railway construction in the west, at Wesley College in Winnipeg, Manitoba. In 1876 the boys were sent to Victoria College at Cobourg, Ontario, from which Clifford graduated BA in 1880 as the gold medallist of his class. He seems to have tried to compensate for partial deafness contracted during his childhood by cultivating rigorous work habits and physical and mental discipline; the deafness, unhappily, worsened throughout his life. He was said to have been about 6 feet tall, of 'excellent carriage' and 'splendid physique', and was held to have been one of the best lacrosse players in Manitoba. A friend described him as 'burly, ruddy, an outdoorsman, a man of physical activity, a man of large impulses' (*Brandon Sun*, 19 Nov 1896; *Saturday Night* [Toronto], 27 April 1929; *Toronto Star*, 18 April 1929).

After two years of study in law in Winnipeg Sifton was called to the Manitoba bar, and in 1882 established a practice in the western Manitoba town of Brandon, where he became city solicitor, astutely invested in real estate, and aided in his father's political campaigns. He married on 13 August 1884 Elizabeth Armanella Burrows (*c.*1861–1925); they had five sons: John W. (1886–1932), Winfield B. (1890–1928), Henry A. (1891–1934), Clifford (1893–1976), and W. Victor (1897–1961).

Minister of the interior: development of western Canada, 1888–1904 Running as a supporter of the Liberal premier

Thomas Greenway, Sifton was elected to the Manitoba legislature on 11 July 1888; his remarkable abilities as debater, political organizer, and astute tactician soon led to his appointment as attorney-general, 14 May 1891 to 15 November 1896, provincial lands commissioner, 15 May 1891 to 7 October 1896, and minister of education, May 1892 to 15 November 1896. Sifton quickly emerged as the principal tactician in Manitoba's defence of its 1890 Public Schools Act, which sought to establish a 'national' school system at the expense of separate (French and Catholic) schools, against constitutional challenges brought by the dominion government on behalf of the minority. His brilliant and successful performance led to his appointment from 17 November 1896 to 28 February 1905 as minister of the interior and superintendent-general of Indian affairs in the new National Liberal government led by Wilfrid Laurier.

Having moved from Brandon to Ottawa, Sifton quickly abandoned the regional rhetoric favoured by western politicians, and advised Laurier that the problems facing the government were essentially three: adjustment of the tariff to stimulate economic growth; attracting large numbers of immigrants, particularly farmers, for the prairie west; and developing a national transportation infrastructure to allow Canadians to keep trade in 'exclusively Canadian channels'. The successful implementation of these policies, substantially derived from the 'national policy' of Sir John Macdonald, would, he asserted, 'wholly transform the financial difficulties of the country' (Sifton to Charles Fitzpatrick, 18 Dec 1902, Sifton MSS, 249.748–53).

As minister of the interior Sifton had primary responsibility for attracting immigrants and getting them settled on the land. He was blessed by favourable circumstances beyond his control: recovery of the international economy after years of depression; industrialization in Europe which both created demand and higher prices for Canadian foodstuffs and other natural products, and generated the last great wave of emigration from Europe; and the perception of the end of availability of free land in the American west, leaving the lands of western Canada as the last great North American frontier of settlement. Moreover years of failure for many farmers gave way to success with new farming techniques and strains of grain adapted to the prairie region, and with an effective transportation infrastructure and declining costs for getting their products quickly and efficiently to market. None the less, Sifton also played a role in the populating of the prairies with a newly aggressive policy to attract agriculturalists: paying immigration agents by commission; selling the west with millions of advertisements in Britain, Europe, and the United States; and active promotion of group settlement projects for American, British, and various European ethnic groups.

Through settlement of outstanding railway land claims, development of extensive irrigation projects, and formation of land companies, Sifton facilitated agricultural development. He also encouraged exploitation of mineral and timber resources, and expanded the boundaries of the Rocky Mountains National Park. As superintendent-general of Indian affairs, Sifton was mainly preoccupied with minimizing expenses, ensuring that the native Indians would not be a complicating factor in the settlement process, and encouraging the development of boarding-schools for native children rather than the more costly and less effective industrial schools. He also initiated the negotiation of treaty eight (1899) with the native peoples of the drainage basin of the Peace River.

Administration of the Yukon during the gold rush after 1897 also fell primarily to Sifton. He had the difficult task of imposing a system of government on a district remote from Ottawa, and in particular of devising a method to extract some royalties from the gold mined to compensate to some degree for the cost of government, and also to impose a restrictive moral regime on a somewhat unruly and independent-minded mining population. At the same time, Sifton was clearly complicit in a system that permitted patronage, graft, and corruption on a scale exceeding that in the rest of the country. The administration was complicated by the fact that the United States, through the Alaska panhandle, controlled the best routes, and therefore much of the trade, into the Yukon. This intensified the need to reach agreement on precisely where the Alaska–Canada boundary lay. In 1903 Sifton was British agent during hearings before an international tribunal. Ably as he organized the Canadian case, it was the weaker of the two and the Americans won on most points in contention. However, the unnecessary flexing of American diplomatic muscle, and British acquiescence, turned Sifton to a strong Canadian nationalism.

Sifton also played a significant role in the development of the government's railway policy. While in the Manitoba government he had devised an apparently painless system of encouraging railway building through government guarantees of railway bonds; this later was used by the Laurier government. Sifton was instrumental in getting the Crow's Nest pass line built by the Canadian Pacific Railway in 1897–9, with a concomitant agreement to reduce freight rates on goods in and out of the prairie west. In the development of the government's larger transcontinental railway policy, Sifton was the vigorous and successful defender of the interests of the Canadian Northern Railway, popular in western Canada, with the result that both it and the Grand Trunk Railway, favoured by central Canadian politicians, were enabled from 1903 to expand across the continent in an orgy of overbuilding fuelled by excessive optimism about Canada's ability to sustain this development. Sifton originally had favoured requiring the two railroads to co-operate in a single national enterprise, but Laurier was unwilling to force the ambitious promoters to comply.

Resignation and break from Liberals, 1905–1918 Having been instrumental in organizing Liberal electoral victories in 1900 and 1904, Sifton unexpectedly resigned from the government on 27 February 1905. He disagreed with Laurier's policy with respect to education in the constitutions of the two new provinces of Saskatchewan and Alberta, being created in 1905. He believed that the position of the

French Catholic minority should remain unchanged from where it stood under the 1901 ordinances of the North-west Territories, and in his opinion Laurier's draft clause would open the door to increased privileges. His resignation forced Laurier to modify the clause to satisfy Sifton, in order to prevent further resignations from his cabinet. The resulting controversy was, at least in part, a product of Sifton's insensitivity to the aspirations of the French and Catholic minority in Canada, an issue of at least as much importance to the Canadian state as the material issues about which he had been so perceptive.

Sifton remained in parliament as a private member until the general election of 1911. He appeared rarely, mainly to defend his record against charges of corruption and to promote civil service reform. Laurier approached Sifton in 1907, and possibly in 1908, to return to the cabinet, but Sifton declined, partly because Laurier showed no other inclination to reform his ageing and failing ministry, and partly because he would have been expected to resume charge of political organization, which he dreaded.

The final break with Laurier came in 1911 with the government's proposed reciprocity agreement with the United States. Sifton had consistently favoured the government's policy of moderate protection, implemented in the budget of 1897. The reciprocity agreement, Laurier thought, was a return to traditional Liberal free-trade doctrine which should be popular with the country's farmers, reduce the cost of living, and give a fillip to a moribund government. Sifton contended that the proposals reversed historic Canadian national policies of development, opened the door to American domination, and spelt 'retrogression, commercial subordination, the destruction of our national ideals and displacement from our proud position as the rising hope of the British Empire' (Canada, House of Commons, *Debates*, cols. 4385–409, 28 Feb 1911). Sifton lent his formidable powers as an organizer and speaker to the Conservative opposition, led by Robert Borden, who enjoyed a smashing electoral victory in September 1911.

In May 1909 Laurier had appointed Sifton the first chairman of the Canadian commission of conservation. He led the commission in broadly based studies of fisheries, animals, forests, water resources and water power, and public health; and tirelessly promoted the cause of conservation, by which he meant responsible and sustainable exploitation of resources. He resigned from the commission in November 1918.

Later life and business interests During the First World War Sifton had a deep commitment to the allied cause: four of his five sons were in uniform, and two (Clifford and Victor) were wounded in action. He was instrumental in the formation and financing of the automobile machine gun brigade no. 1, later renamed 1st Canadian motor machine-gun brigade. Sifton was knighted on 1 January 1915 for his war contributions as well as his political achievements. He helped to engineer the formation of the pro-conscription union government under Sir Robert Borden in 1917, and its triumphant victory in December 1917, which proved to be his last significant political involvement.

After the war Sifton returned mainly to his business interests. Of these, by far the most important was his ownership of the *Manitoba Free Press*, the newspaper which he had acquired in 1897, and which under the brilliant editorial leadership of John W. Dafoe from 1901 had become the dominant Liberal paper in western Canada. By the end of the 1920s Sifton and his sons had also acquired the Saskatoon *Star-Phoenix* and the Regina *Leader-Post*. Sifton further had a wide range of other financial interests, including land, timber berths, and oil and natural gas, in Canada and Central America. He indulged a lifelong passion for horses, particularly hunters and jumpers, and his horses were frequent prize-winners at national and international competitions.

Sifton also spoke out frequently to urge the Canadian government of William Lyon Mackenzie King to insist upon Canada's equality of status with Great Britain, and the right of the governments of Canada to manage internal and external relations in the same way as the British parliament did for Britain. He strongly approved of the Balfour declaration on equality of status for the self-governing dominions in 1926.

Following the death of Lady Sifton on 19 February 1925 Sir Clifford faced declining health and turned control of Armadale Corporation—the holding company for the Sifton interests—over to his sons. He died while in New York city to consult a heart specialist on 17 April 1929, and was buried two days later in Mount Pleasant cemetery in Toronto, Ontario. His estate was valued at C$3,287,231 but the Ontario government claimed that the Armadale Corporation shares transferred to his sons in 1926 were worth a further C$5,978,425.98 and should be considered part of the estate, and that the proper evaluation of the estate should be nearly C$10 million. Sifton gave his name to a number of places in Canada: Lake Sifton in the province of Quebec; Mount Sifton in the Selkirk mountains, British Columbia; and Sifton mountains and Sifton Pass in the Yukon district.   D. J. HALL

Sources D. J. Hall, *Clifford Sifton*, 2 vols. (1981–5) [incl. comprehensive bibliography] · J. W. Dafoe, *Clifford Sifton in relation to his times* (1931) · *DNB* · [C. Sifton], *The Sifton family record* (privately printed, Toronto, 1956) · NA Canada, Sifton collection
Archives NA Canada · Provincial Archives of Manitoba, Winnipeg | NA Canada, Sir Robert Borden MSS · NA Canada, John Wesley Dafoe MSS · NA Canada, Sir Wilfrid Laurier MSS · Provincial Archives of Manitoba, Winnipeg, Thomas Greenway MSS · University of Manitoba, Winnipeg, Elizabeth Dafoe Library, John Wesley Dafoe MSS
Likenesses K. Forbes, portrait, priv. coll.; [*DNB*] · W. Grier, portrait, priv. coll.; [*DNB*] · photographs, repro. in Hall, *Clifford Sifton*
Wealth at death C$3,287,231—estate and possessions

Sigeberht (*fl.* 630/31–654), king of the East Angles, is known only from Bede's *Historia ecclesiastica gentis Anglorum*, where it is stated that he was the brother of Earpwald, son of *Rædwald. William of Malmesbury and John of Worcester say that he was Earpwald's half-brother by his mother. It is uncertain whether they had additional information or whether they were reading more into

Bede's wording than may have been intended. So it is an open question whether Sigeberht was Rædwald's son or his stepson. During Rædwald's reign he was in exile in Francia, where he was converted to Christianity and baptized. After the death in 627 or 628 of Earpwald, Rædwald's successor, a period of three years' disorder ensued in East Anglia. After Sigeberht became king, in 630 or 631, he obtained the help of Felix, a Burgundian ordained in Francia. Felix had come to Honorius, archbishop of Canterbury, who sent him to East Anglia. He was given an episcopal *sedes* at 'Dommoc', which may have been Dunwich, or Felixstowe, or somewhere else. With Felix's assistance Sigeberht set up a school for children, after the model of those at Canterbury. He patronized an Irish monk, Fursa, and gave him the site for a monastery at Cnobheresburg. The oft-repeated statement that this was at Burgh Castle, Suffolk, is probably erroneous. At some stage (probably somewhat before, possibly long before, 654) Sigeberht resigned the kingdom to his kinsman Ecgric, who had previously been ruling a subordinate part, and entered a monastery. The statement of the twelfth-century *Liber Eliensis* that this was at Betricheswor∂e (later Bury St Edmunds) is untrustworthy. Upon Penda, king of the Mercians, assaulting East Anglia, Sigeberht was urged to leave his monastery and lead the army. He did so, reluctantly; but he would not bear arms, carrying only a rod into the battle in which he was killed. Bede's summary indications are of a career of interest and importance, not least for its place in a context of relations with Frankish Gaul. That Sigeberht's name was one borne by Frankish kings and that he spent his exile in Gaul are, like the Merovingian coins at Sutton Hoo, suggestive of a stronger East Anglian connection with Francia than is directly demonstrable.   J. CAMPBELL

Sources Bede, *Hist. eccl.*, 3.18–19 · F. M. Stenton, *Anglo-Saxon England*, 3rd edn (1971) · F. M. Stenton, 'The East Anglian kings of the seventh century', *Preparatory to 'Anglo-Saxon England': being the collected papers of Frank Merry Stenton*, ed. D. M. Stenton (1970), 394–402 · B. A. E. Yorke, *Kings and kingship in early England* (1990)

Sigeberht (*d.* 757), king of the West Saxons, became king on the death of *Cuthred in 756 and was murdered the following year. He is not named in any of the extant genealogies of the West Saxon kings, and nothing definite is known of his ancestry and connections, except that he had a brother, Cyneheard. According to the Anglo-Saxon Chronicle, Cyneheard was descended in the paternal line from Cerdic, but such claims cannot be taken at face value since genealogies were sometimes manipulated to provide the descent which was considered to confer legal title to rule. Virtually nothing is known of Sigeberht's brief reign, but he is recorded as granting lands in what are now Somerset and Dorset, possibly to the monasteries of Glastonbury and Sherborne respectively.

Sigeberht's rule was successfully challenged in 757 by Cynewulf, who obtained the support of most of the West Saxon councillors. For a while Sigeberht retained a power base in the area of modern Hampshire and the support of Ealdorman Cumbra; but eventually he killed Cumbra and was driven out into the weald, probably in Sussex. On venturing back westwards, he was stabbed to death at Privett (near modern Petersfield) by a swineherd who was avenging the ealdorman.

The fact that Cyneheard attempted to secure the kingship twenty-nine years later, when he fought and killed Cynewulf, suggests that the brothers were very young in 756–7, and the unjust acts which the Anglo-Saxon Chronicle mentions as the cause of Sigeberht's loss of support in Wessex may have been the errors of youth and inexperience. Nothing in his story suggests that he was very capable, and he presumably acquired the kingship for other reasons, possibly as the rightful heir of his predecessor. Cumbra, who stood by him longest, was an ealdorman in the reign of Cuthred and it is possible that Sigeberht and Cyneheard were the sons of Cuthred. Cyneheard was buried at Axminster, but Sigeberht's place of burial is not recorded.   HEATHER EDWARDS

Sources ASC, s.a. 756, 757 [texts A, E] · AS chart., S 1680 · F. M. Stenton, *Anglo-Saxon England*, 3rd edn (1971) · H. Edwards, *The charters of the early West Saxon kingdom* (1988) · D. N. Dumville, 'Kingship, genealogies and regnal lists', *Early medieval kingship*, ed. P. H. Sawyer and I. N. Wood (1977), 72–104

Sigeberht I (*fl.* 626). *See under* East Saxons, kings of the (*act.* late 6th cent.–*c*.820).

Sigeberht II (*fl. c*.653). *See under* East Saxons, kings of the (*act.* late 6th cent.–*c*.820).

Sigebert. *See* Sigeberht I (*fl.* 626) *under* East Saxons, kings of the (*act.* late 6th cent.–*c*.820); Sigeberht (*fl.* 630/31–654); Sigeberht II (*fl. c*.653) *under* East Saxons, kings of the (*act.* late 6th cent.–*c*.820); Sigeberht (*d.* 757).

Sigeheard (*fl.* 693/4). *See under* East Saxons, kings of the (*act.* late 6th cent.–*c*.820).

Sigehere (*fl.* 663–664). *See under* East Saxons, kings of the (*act.* late 6th cent.–*c*.820).

Sigered (*fl.* 762–765). *See under* Æthelberht II (*d.* 762).

Sigered (*fl.* 811). *See under* East Saxons, kings of the (*act.* late 6th cent.–*c*.820).

Sigeric (*d.* in or after 798). *See under* East Saxons, kings of the (*act.* late 6th cent.–*c*.820).

Sigeric (*d.* 994), archbishop of Canterbury, formerly a monk at Glastonbury, was elected abbot of St Augustine's, Canterbury, in 980, and was consecrated by Archbishop Dunstan. He was made bishop of Ramsbury in 985 through the influence of Dunstan, who consecrated him, and perhaps retained his abbacy until he was elected to Canterbury at the beginning of 990. He went to Rome for his pallium, and an account of his travels records twenty-three churches which he visited, his midday meal with Pope John XV, and the seventy-nine stages of his homeward journey from Rome to the place of his embarkation for England, at or near Calais. According to John of Worcester, Sigeric, together with the ealdormen Æthelweard and Ælfric, advised Æthelred II to render tribute to the vikings in 991. Text A of the Anglo-Saxon Chronicle identifies his co-adviser as Bishop Ælfheah of Winchester. In 994 Sigeric rendered a further tribute to stop the Danes from burning down Canterbury Cathedral. He is said to have turned out the secular clerks from Christ Church, Canterbury, and to have put monks in their place. He is also said to have advised King Æthelred to found Cholsey Abbey for the soul of his brother Edward the Martyr and to commemorate Edward at Shaftesbury. Sigeric died in old age on 28 October 994, and was buried in the crypt of Christ Church. Abbot Ælfric (*fl. c*.950–1010), dedicated his first and second series of *Catholic Homilies* to him. Sigeric had a valuable collection of books, which he left to Canterbury. He bequeathed to Glastonbury Abbey seven wall-hangings decorated with white lions, with which the whole of the Old Church was hung on his anniversary.

EMMA MASON

Sources D. Knowles, C. N. L. Brooke, and V. C. M. London, eds., *The heads of religious houses, England and Wales*, 1: *940–1216* (1972), 35 · William of Malmesbury, *Gesta regum Anglorum / The history of the English kings*, ed. and trans. R. A. B. Mynors, R. M. Thomson, and M. Winterbottom, 2 vols., OMT (1998–9), vol. 1 · *Willelmi Malmesbiriensis monachi de gestis pontificum Anglorum libri quinque*, ed. N. E. S. A. Hamilton, Rolls Series, 52 (1870) · *The historical works of Gervase of Canterbury*, ed. W. Stubbs, 2 vols., Rolls Series, 73 (1879–80) · S. Keynes, *The diplomas of King Æthelred 'The Unready' (978–1016): a study in their use as historical evidence*, Cambridge Studies in Medieval Life and Thought, 3rd ser., 13 (1980) · John of Worcester, *Chron.* · P. M. McGurk, D. N. Dumville, M. R. Godden, and A. Knock, eds., *An eleventh-century Anglo-Saxon illustrated miscellany (British Library Cotton Tiberius B.V. part I)*, Early English Manuscripts in Facsimile, 21 (1983) · V. Ortenberg, 'Archbishop Sigeric's journey to Rome in 990', *Anglo-Saxon England*, 19 (1990), 197–246 · M. K. Lawson, *Cnut: the Danes in England in the early eleventh century* (1993) · M. Blows, 'A Glastonbury obit-list', *The archaeology and history of Glastonbury Abbey: essays in honour of the ninetieth birthday of C. A. Ralegh Radford*, ed. L. Abrams and J. P. Carley (1991), 257–69

Sigerson, Dora Mary. *See* Shorter, Dora Mary (1866–1918).

Sigfrid (*d.* 689), co-abbot of St Peter's, Wearmouth, was a monk and deacon of that house and was elected abbot during the absence of Benedict Biscop on his fifth journey to Rome. Bede gives a contemporary account of Sigfrid in his *Historia abbatum* of Wearmouth and Jarrow. On his departure Benedict had left the monastery under the charge of Eosterwine, who, together with a large number of the brethren, died of the plague about 686. Those who were left, on the advice of Ceolfrith, abbot of the daughter monastery at Jarrow, elected Sigfrid in his place. Sigfrid was well versed in the scriptures, but he suffered from an incurable disease of the lungs. On his return Benedict was pleased at his election and confirmed it, assigning to him the active charge of the monastery, and devoting himself to teaching and prayer. Before long Sigfrid's health became much worse, and, Benedict also falling sick, the two lay helpless in their separate cells until one day both desired to be brought together, and Sigfrid was carried into Benedict's cell, where the brethren supported the two abbots so as to enable them to give each other a farewell kiss, and Benedict, with the consent of all, appointed Ceolfrith abbot of Wearmouth as well as of Jarrow. The anonymous historian of Wearmouth and Jarrow, who closely followed Bede's account, states that Sigfrid died on 22 August 689. After the death of Benedict, apparently on 12 January following, the bodies of Sigfrid and Eosterwine were laid with his body in the church of Wearmouth.

WILLIAM HUNT, *rev.* MARIOS COSTAMBEYS

Sources 'Historia abbatum auctore Baeda', *Venerabilis Baedae opera historica*, ed. C. Plummer, 1 (1896), 364–87 · 'Historia abbatum auctore anonymo', *Venerabilis Baedae opera historica*, ed. C. Plummer, 1 (1896), 388–404

Sigfrid [St Sigfrid] (*fl.* mid-10th–early 11th cent.), missionary bishop, eludes biography. No record of his activities survives before the late twelfth century, after which Icelandic saga literature and Swedish hagiography combined to produce conflicting accounts of his career. His place of origin in England is nowhere reliably identified in those sources. 'Sigefridus', a bishop, is remembered in an obit list in a thirteenth-century custumary from Glastonbury Abbey (BL, Add. MS 17450, fol. 5v; under 5 April); in William of Malmesbury's *De antiquitate Glastonie ecclesie* (*c.*1130) 'Sigefridus' is identified as *episcopus Norwegensis* and a monk of Glastonbury, possibly during the time of King Edgar (*r.* 957–75). Some have seen this bishop as the (unnamed) churchman who accompanied King Hákon Adalsteinsfóstri (Hákon Athelstan's Foster-Son) from England to Norway in the mid-tenth century. Others have associated him with the bishop named in the thirteenth-century sagas of Óláf Tryggvason as the English companion of that Christianizing king (*r.* 995–999/1000). A Bishop Siward, who returned to Ramsey Abbey from a period as a missionary in Scandinavia some time after 993 and before 1009, may have been the same man, although the name (probably originally Sigeweard) may invalidate the identification. Óláf Tryggvason's bishop, known in Norwegian and Icelandic saga sources as Jón-Sigurd, is said to have turned his attention to Sweden after the death of his Norwegian patron, and to have converted and baptized King Olof Skötkonung (*r.* 995–1022) and many Swedish heathens. He reputedly returned to Norway to assist King Óláf Haraldsson (*r.* 1014–30) to further the conversion there, after which he resumed his Swedish mission. His place of burial is claimed to be the cathedral of Växjö, in southern Sweden, of which see (along with Skara, in Västergötland) he was purportedly the founder.

No authority is known for the statement of the seventeenth-century Swedish Catholic writer Vastovius (*Vitis aquilonia*, 32) that Sigfrid was canonized by the English pope Adrian IV in 1158, but in the thirteenth century his cult blossomed in Sweden and he was revered as the nation's apostle. Swedish hagiography identified him as an archbishop of York whom the English king, Milred, had sent to King Olof. If there was originally any basis of fact in the Swedish lives, it had clearly been lost or confused before this thirteenth-century flowering, as no contemporary Archbishop Sigfrid or King Milred is known (although a Sigeferth was bishop of Lindsey from *c.*996 to *c.*1004. The conversion histories fostered by the different Swedish dioceses sought not so much to preserve a historical account of Sigfrid's life and work as to claim for their churches Sweden's 'first' saint and missionary, thereby

establishing their primacy. His name stood for missionary endeavour *par excellence*, so much so that the credentials of contemporary churchmen came to be established by relationship with him: he is credited with a suspicious number of nephews. The date of his death is unknown, but he is commemorated on 15 February in medieval Scandinavian calendars. His apparent longevity and ubiquitousness (and, potentially, two obit dates), suggest that several Sigfrids were at work in the Scandinavian mission field, but the evidence does not allow separate identities and achievements to be distinguished.

L. ABRAMS

Sources E. M. Fant and others, eds., *Scriptores rerum Suecicarum medii aevi*, 3 vols. in 6 (Uppsala, 1818–76), vol. 2, pt 1, pp. 344–6 · T. Schmid, ed., 'Trois légendes de Saint Sigfrid', *Analecta Bollandiana*, 60 (1942), 82–90 · B. Sawyer, 'Scandinavian conversion histories', *The Christianization of Scandinavia*, ed. B. Sawyer and others (1987), 88–110 · T. Schmid, *Den helige Sigfrid* (1931) · C. J. A. Oppermann, *The English missionaries in Sweden and Finland* (1937) · J. Vastovius, *Vitis aquilonia, seu, Vitae sanctorum que Scandinauiam*, ed. E. Benzelius (Uppsala, 1708)

Sigillo, Nicholas de (*fl.* 1156–*c.*1187), administrator and priest, was a royal clerk in the exchequer, where he held the office of *clericus de sigillo*, or *magister scriptorii*, in which capacity he ranked next to the chancellor. He derived his name, 'de Sigillo', from his office, as did Robert de Sigillo, the bishop of London, who held the same position in the reign of Henry I. It is possible, although far from certain, that Nicholas served King Stephen. Between 1148 and 1160 the bishop of Lincoln confirmed the church of Warboys to Ramsey Abbey in Huntingdonshire, stating that Nicholas was to hold it for life unless he became a monk. In 1156 he accounted for two hawks in Lincolnshire, and in 1157 was involved in the administration of Henry II's expedition to Wales. Between 1157 and 1159 he was a witness to royal charters, and in September 1173 he tallaged the king's demesnes together with Richard fitz Nigel and Reginald de Warenne. He succeeded Henry of Huntingdon as archdeacon of Huntingdon, probably between 1164 and 1166, and received a letter of congratulations from John of Salisbury, commenting that Nicholas would now have to change his mind about the small hopes of salvation enjoyed by archdeacons. He is last mentioned as archdeacon about 1187. A case of John's reign mentioned that he gave a messuage in Southampton to his niece (or conceivably his granddaughter) Emma.

C. L. KINGSFORD, *rev.* JOHN HUDSON

Sources Pipe rolls · *Fasti Angl., 1066–1300*, [Lincoln] · D. M. Smith, ed., *Lincoln, 1067–1185*, English Episcopal Acta, 1 (1980) · *Curia regis rolls preserved in the Public Record Office* (1922–), vol. 3 · A. Saltman, *Theobald, archbishop of Canterbury* (1956) · R. W. Eyton, *Court, household, and itinerary of King Henry II* (1878) · *The letters of John of Salisbury*, ed. and trans. H. E. Butler and W. J. Millor, rev. C. N. L. Brooke, OMT, 2: *The later letters, 1163–1180* (1979), 24–7 [Lat. orig. with parallel Eng. text]

Sigillo, Robert de (*d.* 1150), administrator and bishop of London, is first found in Henry I's reign, *c.*1121, as master of the royal writing office; his name refers to his duty to keep the king's seal. He was in effect second in command to the head of the Chapel Royal, the chancellor. And, probably when his superior, Geoffrey Rufus, was made bishop of Durham in 1133, and not replaced, Sigillo's emoluments were increased to a daily livery of 2s., 4 gallons of table wine, one loaf of best-quality bread, one large candle, and twenty-four candle-ends, an appreciable increment, but still a saving for the parsimonious king. The Chapel Royal travelled with the king; Sigillo attested ninety-six of Henry I's acts, which show that he accompanied the king on all the latter's visits to Normandy after 1121. When Henry died on 1 December 1135 on the Norman frontier at Lyons-la-Forêt, it fell to Sigillo and the royal constable to conduct the embalmed corpse on its slow voyage to its burial in Henry's great foundation, Reading Abbey, on 4 January 1136.

Meanwhile Stephen's seizure of the throne at the expense of Henry's 'true heir', his daughter, the Empress Matilda, and his appointment of Roger le Poer as chancellor, cost Robert de Sigillo his post; and some time before 1141, probably about 1135, he followed Henry into Reading Abbey, as a monk. However, in 1141, after Stephen's capture at Lincoln, Sigillo was appointed in July by Matilda to the long-vacant see of London, but they were both expelled almost immediately by the Londoners and took refuge at Oxford. Robert's consecrator is unstated; but eventually he made his profession of obedience to Archbishop Theobald. It says much for his talents and reputation that, after Stephen recovered his liberty and much of his power at the end of 1141, Robert was able to make his peace with his king, his metropolitan, and his chapter. Indeed, he steered his way through the ensuing political and ecclesiastical turmoil in the kingdom adroitly, despite some awkward strains in 1147–8, at the time of the Council of Rheims. He died on 28 or 29 September 1150—according to rumour, a victim together with many of his household, learned men of high renown, of poisoned grapes.

Robert de Sigillo seems to have been generally well regarded. Although when a chancery clerk he was probably married (he had a son, named after his royal master, whom later he made a canon of St Paul's Cathedral and who survived into the 1190s), the Westminster monk Osbert of Clare commiserated with him for having to dwell in 'that Babylonish furnace', the royal court. And he is believed to have reduced the power of the dynasties established in his chapter by his two predecessors by introducing more suitable men. John of Hexham considered him a good man, a holy bishop; and John of Salisbury would seem to agree. Henry of Huntingdon called him *vir animo magnus*, a man of spirit. He was clearly a man of many parts.　　　　FRANK BARLOW

Sources Symeon of Durham, *Opera*, vol. 2 · [Nigel, bishop of Ely ?], 'Constitutio domus regis', in R. Fitz Nigel [R. Fitzneale], *Dialogus de scaccario / The course of the exchequer*, ed. and trans. C. Johnson (1950), 128–35 · John of Salisbury, *Historia pontificalis: John of Salisbury's memoirs of the papal court*, ed. and trans. M. Chibnall (1956) · Ordericus Vitalis, *Eccl. hist.* · *The letters of Osbert of Clare, prior of Westminster*, ed. E. W. Williamson (1929) · Henry, archdeacon of Huntingdon, *Historia Anglorum*, ed. D. E. Greenway, OMT (1996) · A. Saltman, *Theobald, archbishop of Canterbury* (1956) · C. N. L. Brooke and G. Keir, *London, 800–1216: the shaping of a city* (1975) · J. A. Green,

The government of England under Henry I (1986) · A. Morey and C. N. L. Brooke, *Gilbert Foliot and his letters* (1965) · *Reg. RAN*, vol. 2

Sigtryggr Cam. *See* Sihtric Cam (*fl.* 962) *under* Óláf Sihtricson (*c*.926–981).

Sigurd (II) Hlödvisson [Sigurðr Hlöðvisson, Sigurd Digri, Sigurðr inn Digri] (*d.* **1014**), earl of Orkney, is called Digri ('the Stout') in *Orkneyinga Saga* (composed *c*.1200). The same epithet is given to King Óláf Haraldsson (St Olaf), and carries the connotation of 'powerful warrior'. The genealogy of the earls of Orkney, compiled *c*.1420, describes him as 'robustus ac corpolentis, magnus et strenuissimus bellifer' (in the Scots translation 'the wicht and corpolent, ane grete and maist stowt battellare'). He was remembered as 'a great chieftain [who] ruled over several dominions' (*Orkneyinga Saga*, chap. 11), although he was not counted among the three most powerful earls (Sigurd (I), Thorfinn (II), and Harald Maddadson).

Son of Earl Hlödver and of Eithne, daughter of King Kjarval (Cerball) of Osraige in Ireland, Sigurd had interests in the west, and is said to have gone on viking expeditions every summer, 'plundering in the Hebrides, Scotland and Ireland'. He eventually met his death striving to win power in the Norse kingdom of Dublin. Initially he was concerned to establish earldom authority over the north mainland of Scotland, which had been hard to maintain since the conquests of Earl Sigurd inn Riki (Sigurd the Mighty) in the late ninth century. He was challenged by a Scottish 'earl' called Finnleik (Finnlaech) to fight at Skitten Mire in Caithness, where his uncle Earl Liot Thorfinsson had fought a battle previously (there is a possibility that this is a mistaken reference to the earlier battle). Already at this date the earl had to persuade the Orkney farmers to support his campaign in Caithness, and did so by 'giving them back their land-rights'. This is a very interesting reference to the evident disagreement between earls and farmers over the status of their lands. It was believed that even in the time of Einarr (Torf-Einarr) in the early tenth century the farmers had lost their udal right over their lands to the earl. Their success in winning it back from Sigurd indicates the power of the farmers to bargain when the earl requested military service outside the island earldom. There is no reason to doubt that the status of their lands was a point of dispute with the earl, although whether the information that it was negotiated over in this way can be relied on, is unprovable.

Sigurd was successful in his campaigns on the north Scottish mainland, remembered as being 'powerful enough to defend Caithness against the Scots', who at this date must have been the mormaers of Moray. Indeed, *Njals saga* claims that he also dominated 'Ross and Moray, Sutherland and the Dales', which suggests much wider-ranging conquests. The memory of his victory at Skitten Mire is bound up with the legends about his raven banner, woven for him by his mother, with magical properties that brought victory to the man before whom it was carried, but death to the man who carried it. At the battle of

Skitten Mire the earl lost three standard-bearers, but none the less won the battle. Sigurd's ambitions clearly extended further south and west than Caithness and evidence for an alliance with Earl Gilli of Coll (recorded only in *Njals saga*), as well as the probable imposition of ounceland units in the Western Isles at this date, suggest that he exercised some control in this locality.

The information devoted to Sigurd in the main Icelandic text of *Orkneyinga Saga* is surprisingly brief for such a famous warrior. There is in additional texts the well-known story of his forced conversion by Óláf Tryggvason, who was returning to his homeland to claim the throne of Norway from his campaigns in England in 995, an incident much recounted in saga history. The two met at Osmundwall, in south Hoy, where Sigurd was taken aboard Óláf's ship and baptized, handing over his son Hundi as a hostage. The saga's statement that 'all Orkney embraced the faith' is probably overstated, although one version adds that priests were left behind in the islands by Óláf. As Sigurd renounced his allegiance to Óláf after his son Hundi died, his Christian allegiance may also have wavered. None the less the fact that he married the daughter of Malcolm, king of Scots (probably Malcolm II, who ruled from 1005 to 1034), means that he must have been considered an acceptable Christian ally by the established dynasty of the southern kingdom. This is the first recorded alliance of an earl with the Scots and it suggests that the earl and the king saw mutual advantages in being united against the dynasty of Moray established between them. *Thorfinn (II) Sigurdson was the famous son of this alliance, younger than his three half-brothers Sumarlidi, Brúsi, and Einarr, who must have resulted from one or more previous liaisons.

These three elder sons were left in charge of the earldom when Sigurd embarked on his last campaign in Ireland in 1014 (the date of 1005 is erroneously given in *Orkneyinga Saga*). This was in support of *Sihtric Silkenbeard, king of Dublin, in his struggle with Brian Bóruma, king of Leinster, for continued control of eastern Ireland. Sigurd's ambitions (as recalled in *Njals saga*) included the hand of Sihtric's mother in matrimony and the kingship of Ireland. The battle of Clontarf is recorded in many different sources to supplement *Orkneyinga Saga*'s meagre information. Passages in *Njals saga* describe scenes at Sigurd's Orkney residence before the earl left for Ireland, as well as fully recounting the drama of the battle action at Clontarf, just outside Dublin, on Good Friday (23 April) 1014, when the earl was forced to carry his bewitched raven banner, at the cost of his own life, and the collapse of his Irish ambitions. On this occasion the banner did not bring victory to the army before whom it was borne, and the result in several respects foretold the end of an era.

BARBARA E. CRAWFORD

Sources H. Pálsson and P. Edwards, eds. and trans., *The Orkneyinga saga: the history of the earls of Orkney* (1978) · 'Genealogy of the earls', *The Bannatyne miscellany*, ed. D. Laing, 3, Bannatyne Club, 19b (1855), 63–85 · H. Magnusson and H. Palsson, trans., *Njal's saga* (1964) · B. E. Crawford, *Scandinavian Scotland* (1987)

Sihtric [Sigtryggr Óláfsson, Sigtryggr Silkiskegg] (*d.* 1042), king of Dublin, was the son of *Óláf Sihtricson (*d.* 981), sometime king of Dublin and Northumbria, and Gormflaith (*d.* 1030), daughter of Murchad mac Finn, king of Leinster; his alternative Old Norse name, Sigtryggr Silkiskegg, may be translated as Sihtric Silkenbeard. Sihtric acceded to the kingship of Dublin after the murder of his paternal half-brother Glúniairn in 989. In 994 a rival viking leader named Ívarr of Waterford forced him from the city, but he was reinstated by the following year. He was allied with his mother's brother Máel Mórda, who was soon to be king of Leinster, when the pair were defeated late in 999 at the battle of Glenn Máma (Wicklow) by the future high-king Brian Bóruma mac Cennétig. Brian captured Dublin on new year's day.

For more than a decade Sihtric was a faithful subordinate, but in 1013 challenges appeared to Brian's lordship, and Sihtric and Máel Mórda rose in revolt. A campaign against Dublin by Brian late in the year achieved nothing, so he made plans to return in the spring. Sihtric sought support from the viking settlements round Britain; an account of his mission to Sigurd, earl of Orkney, is found in *Njals saga*. At the eventual confrontation, the famous battle of Clontarf fought on Good Friday (23 April) 1014, Sihtric and Máel Mórda had in their ranks vikings from Orkney, the Hebrides, the Isle of Man, and northern England, in addition to troops from Leinster and Dublin. On the actual day of battle Sihtric remained aloof and watched the conflict from the walls of Dublin, although his sons and kinsmen fought. Even though Clontarf is considered to have been a victory for Brian, it was a Pyrrhic victory; the high-king was slain, his army sustained heavy losses, and Sihtric remained in control of Dublin.

By this time Dublin was one of the leading ports on the Irish Sea, and Sihtric had to contend with Irish princes who wanted a share of Dublin's riches. A brief glimpse of this wealth can be seen when, in 1029, he had to pay a ransom for his son Óláf, which included 1200 cows, 120 Welsh ponies, 60 ounces of gold, and another 60 ounces of silver. In 1030 Sihtric allied with the king of the English, Cnut, and their fleets raided Wales, after which a Dublin colony was established in Gwynedd. For the following years Sihtric was at the height of his power, defeating neighbouring Irish kingdoms, including an alliance of three at the Boyne in 1032, and executing rivals at Dublin. Sihtric was forced to abdicate, however, in 1036 in favour of Echmarcach Rögnvaldsson, lord of the Isles. He died in exile, at an unknown place, in 1042.

Sihtric was also a patron of the arts, a benefactor of the church, and an economic innovator. Verses survive that were composed in his honour by the Icelandic poet Gunnlaug Serpent-Tongue. He established a bishopric at Dublin in addition to beginning the construction of Christ Church Cathedral, and in 1028 he made a pilgrimage to Rome. In the last decade of the tenth century Sihtric founded a mint at Dublin, the first mint in Ireland. His wife was Sláine, daughter of Brian Bóruma. Their son Óláf was killed in England in 1034, but Óláf's dynasty ruled in Wales after his grandson Gruffudd ap Cynan took lordship of Gwynedd. Other children of Sihtric were Artalach (*d.* 999), Óláf (*d.* 1013), Glúniairn (*d.* 1031), Guthfrith (*d.* 1036), and Cellach (*d.* 1042).   BENJAMIN T. HUDSON

Sources W. Stokes, ed., 'The annals of Tigernach [pt 4]', *Revue Celtique*, 17 (1896), 337–420 · J. H. Todd, ed. and trans., *Cogadh Gaedhel re Gallaibh / The war of the Gaedhil with the Gaill*, Rolls Series, 48 (1867) · B. T. Hudson, 'Knútr and viking Dublin', *Scandinavian Studies*, 65 (1994), 319–35 · E. Ó. Sveinsson, ed., *Brennu-Njáls saga* (1954) · A. Jones, ed. and trans., *History of Gruffydd ap Cynan* (1910) · *Ann. Ulster* · *AFM* · M. C. Dobbs, ed. and trans., 'The Ban-shenchus [3 pts]', *Revue Celtique*, 47 (1930), 283–339; 48 (1931), 163–234; 49 (1932), 437–89

Sihtric Cáech [Sigtryggr Cáech] (*d.* 927), king of York, was a grandson of *Ívarr the Boneless, probably the son of the Sihtric who ruled in Dublin from 888 until his death in 896, and probably also brother of his predecessor as king at York, *Ragnall. The annals of Ulster describe Sihtric Cáech (whose epithet means 'the Squinty') as 'king of the Finngaill and the Dubhgaill' (the 'Fair Foreigners' and the 'Dark Foreigners', that is, the Norwegian and Danish settlers in Ireland and northern England). Most of what is known about Sihtric comes from English and Irish annals, but their ambiguity is such that reconstruction of his career is very difficult and many uncertainties remain.

It seems that, together with other grandsons of Ívarr, Sihtric was expelled from Ireland in 902. He may have been the Sihtric active in the eastern Danelaw, who ruled as an earl in Cambridgeshire, where coins were issued at this time bearing the legend SITRIC COMES and the mint name SCELDFOR (Shelford). The possible identity of the two Sihtrics becomes less implausible when one recalls that Ívarr the Boneless was one of the vikings who slew King Edmund of East Anglia. Coin evidence shows links between York and the eastern Danelaw at this period. The chronology of the two Sihtrics also dovetails. The Danes of Cambridgeshire surrendered to King Edward the Elder in 917, but the fate of their Earl Sihtric is not recorded in English sources. It seems more than a striking coincidence that in the same year Sihtric Cáech arrived with a fleet off Ireland and established himself at 'Cenn Fuait', presumably Glynn in the south of co. Carlow. There he was attacked unsuccessfully by the forces of the high king Niáll Glúndub. Sihtric then occupied and fortified Dublin and when Niáll attacked on 17 December 919 he was killed, together with twelve satellite kings, by Sihtric's forces. A year later Sihtric departed for York, where he succeeded as king his kinsman Ragnall. Sihtric signalled his arrival by a raid on Davonport in Cheshire, but there is no record of further conflict with the southern English. Instead, after King Æthelstan's accession, Sihtric sent an embassy to the new king's court, which led to their meeting at Tamworth in Mercia on 30 January 926, when Sihtric accepted Christian baptism and took Æthelstan's sister as his wife. Very soon afterwards he renounced her and reverted to paganism. Roger of Wendover, who names Sihtric's wife as Eadgyth, records that she retired to a nunnery at Polesworth (about 3 miles from Tamworth), where she was revered as a saint. The choice of Tamworth for the meeting-place between the two kings may indicate that

Sihtric's kingdom then extended much further south than has generally been conceded. Numismatists have suggested that the coins bearing his name, SITRIC REX, were struck at Lincoln, as also were those bearing the 'St Martin' legend; others, with the legend 'St Peter', were struck at York during his reign.

Sihtric had several children, the most famous being *Óláf Sihtricson, king of Northumbria and of Dublin. Another was Gytha, who married *Óláf Tryggvason, king of Norway. Sihtric died at York in 927, some time before the end of June. He was followed there as king by his kinsman **Guthfrith** [Guðrøðr] (*b.* before 920, *d.* 934), another grandson of Ívarr, who had fought with Ragnall at the first battle of Corbridge and replaced Sihtric at Dublin late in 920. Guthfrith was soon driven out of York by King Æthelstan, but he returned to Dublin, where he remained king until his death in 934. Irish sources have a good deal of information concerning Guthfrith's adventures there, but little is known concerning his time at York, and no coins attributable to him have survived.   CYRIL HART

Sources W. M. Hennessy and B. MacCarthy, eds., *Annals of Ulster, otherwise, annals of Senat*, 4 vols. (1887–1901), vols. 1–2 · 'Historia regum', Symeon of Durham, *Opera*, vol. 2 · *AFM* · *ASC*, s. a. 923, 925, 926 [D, E] · [Roger of Wendover], *Rogeri de Wendoveri chronica, sive, Flores historiarum*, ed. H. O. Coxe, EHS, 1 (1841) · A. P. Smyth, *Scandinavian York and Dublin: the history of two related Viking kingdoms*, 2 vols. (1975–9) · C. Hart, *The Danelaw* (1992) · C. E. Blunt, B. H. I. H. Stewart, and C. S. S. Lyon, *Coinage in tenth-century England: from Edward the Elder to Edgar's reform* (1989)

Sihtric Cam (*fl.* 962). *See under* Óláf Sihtricson (*c.*926–981).

Sihtric [Sigtryggr] **inn Gamli** (*d.* 871), viking leader, fought and was slain, along with his namesake, **Sihtric** [Sigtryggr] **inn Ungi** (*d.* 871), at the battle of Ashdown. Both men were earls ('the Old' and 'the Young' respectively) and they were among the five who jointly headed a division of the heathen army during the battle.

MARIOS COSTAMBEYS

Sources *ASC*, s.a. 871

Sihtric inn Ungi (*d.* 871). *See under* Sihtric inn Gamli (*d.* 871).

Sike, Henry (*bap.* 1669, *d.* 1712), orientalist, the son of Heinrich Sieke and his wife, Gerti, was born in Bremen where he was baptized on 3 January 1669 at the church of St Stephen. In April 1687 he entered the local *Gymnasium Illustre*, and attended courses in Latin grammar, Hebrew, Greek, and mathematics. On leaving the *Gymnasium*, about 1690, he seems to have enlisted in the Danish army and to have served as a soldier in the Levant. By 1693 Sike was in Holland. He matriculated as a student of theology at the University of Leiden on 11 September. He probably taught himself Arabic (as well as Syriac, Turkish, and Persian). But although he is unlikely to have learned Arabic in Leiden, where the chair remained vacant throughout the period of his studies, he made good use of the Arabic collection at the university library.

In 1697 Sike was welcomed to Utrecht by the two German classical scholars at the university, Johann Georg Graevius and Ludolf Küster. There he published the text of the apocryphal Arabic 'Infancy gospel', a late work probably dating from about the fifth or sixth century. In the notes Sike examined the use to which the legends in the book had been put by Muslims, quoting extensively from the eleventh-century historian al-Kisa'i. He also drew on the Koran, of which he prepared a Latin translation and commentary which would remain unpublished.

With his publication Sike came to occupy a prominent position in the contemporary movement to accompany the study of the early church by a particular concern with the New Testament apocrypha. This movement would bear fruit in the great collection of biblical pseudepigrapha and apocrypha that Johann Albert Fabricius started to publish in Hamburg in 1703 and in which Sike's 'Infancy gospel' was included. Sike's still remains the edition on which most later versions of the text are based.

Once his name as an orientalist was established, Sike collaborated in 1699 with the short-lived *Bibliotheca librorum novum*, founded in Utrecht by Küster two years earlier. Although he held neither a degree nor a university post, he taught Arabic to Hadrian Reland, appointed professor of oriental languages at Utrecht in 1701, and provided him with material for his *De religione Mohammedica* (1705), one of the first truly informed and enlightened studies of Islam ever to be published. He also became a close friend of Graevius's favourite pupil, Pieter Burman, who occupied the chair of history. But while Sike appears to have been generally liked, he was the subject of damaging gossip. He was rumoured to have sympathies with Spinoza and not to have taken communion for over twenty-four years—allegations that he denied in a letter to his publisher, François Halma (Leiden University Library, MS Pap. 15).

In the spring of 1703 Sike set out as the travelling companion and interpreter of George Hastings, eighth earl of Huntingdon, who had been serving under Marlborough in the Low Countries, and to whom he had been recommended by the professors at Utrecht. Although Huntingdon intended to visit Constantinople, he in fact went no further east than Vienna, and then travelled south to Italy, staying in Venice and Rome.

Graevius and Küster had long been in touch with the classicist Richard Bentley, master of Trinity College, Cambridge, whose attention they had drawn to Sike as early as 1702. On 3 February 1704 Cambridge University agreed to consider appointing Sike regius professor of Hebrew (a chair in the gift of Trinity College). But first Sike needed a degree. He therefore matriculated at Utrecht and, on 7 February 1705, proceeded MA and PhD. On 16 April, thanks to Bentley, he received an honorary doctorate of law at Cambridge. On 24 April he at last took up his appointment as professor at an annual salary of £40 and moved into Trinity College.

While he was at Cambridge Sike was highly esteemed in the world of learning, an intimate friend of Bentley, on good terms with his colleagues (who included Isaac Newton and John Covell), and in close touch with scholars such as David Wilkins and John Chamberlayn. He took part in a number of the learned controversies and enterprises of the time, sharing in Burman's criticisms of Jean Le Clerc's edition of Menander and assisting Peter Needham with his edition of Hierocles. Even the acerbic Thomas Hearne admitted, after initial misgivings, that he was 'an excellent Scholar' (*Remarks*, 3.367). He also had connections with the book trade. Lord Huntingdon's sister, Lady Elizabeth Hastings, called on him to arrange for the sale of her brother's library after the earl's death in February 1705, and in March 1706 he was importing Armenian grammars.

With no academic obligations other than to give occasional tuition, Sike spent much of his time working on early Islamic history. On 24 July 1706 he was admitted to the Bodleian Library in Oxford, in the hope of preparing an edition of Abu'l-Fida and, more important still, of pre-Islamic poets—a plan, wrote Bentley, which will 'bring a great honour to you, as well as benefit to Learning' (*Correspondence*, 244). He made no contribution to Hebrew studies, however.

Sike, who was heavily addicted to smoking and accused by his detractors of a certain slovenliness in his dress, was apparently prone to bouts of depression. On 20 May 1712 he was found dead in his rooms in Nevile's Court at the south end of the library. He had hanged himself with the cord of his dressing gown. His friends, including Burman in Holland and the Danish orientalist Mathias Anchersen, were amazed and horrified at what Bentley described as 'the hardly reparable damage to letters' (*Correspondence*, 433). ALASTAIR HAMILTON

Sources L. Forster, 'Henry Sike of Bremen (1669–1712), regius professor of Hebrew and fellow of Trinity', *Transactions of the Cambridge Bibliographical Society*, 10 (1991–5), 249–77 • *The correspondence of Richard Bentley*, ed. C. Wordsworth, 2 vols. (1842) • H. Sike, ed., *Evangelium infantiae, vel, Liber apocryphus de infantia servatoris* (Utrecht, 1697) • A. Nicoll, *Catalogi codicum manuscriptorum orientalium bibliothecae Bodleianae*, 2 (1835) • G. H. Wheler, *Hastings Wheler family letters, 1693–1704: Lady Betty Hastings and her brother* (1929) • H. Reland, *De religione Mohammedica* (Utrecht, 1705) • *Remarks and collections of Thomas Hearne*, ed. C. E. Doble and others, 1, OHS, 2 (1885) • *Remarks and collections of Thomas Hearne*, ed. C. E. Doble and others, 3, OHS, 13 (1889) • D. A. Winstanley, *Unreformed Cambridge* (1935) • G. Schneider, ed., *Evangelia infantae apocrypha / Apocryphe Kindheitsevangelien* (Freiburg, 1995) • *Album studiosorum academiae Rheno-Traiectinae MDCXXXVI–MDCCCLXXXVI: accedunt nomina curatorum et professorum per eadem secula* (Utrecht, 1886) • G. du Rieu, ed., *Album studiosorum academiae Lugduno Batavae, MDLXXV–MDCCCLXX: accedunt nomina curatorum et professorum per eadem secula* (The Hague, 1875) • W. W. Rouse Ball and J. A. Venn, eds., *Admissions to Trinity College, Cambridge*, 3 (1911) • Leiden University, Leiden, MS Pap. 15

Archives Bodl. Oxf., transcriptions of Arabic and other texts, MSS Bodl. Or. 248, 377, 380, 381, 406, 407, 408, 409 • Trinity Cam., literary corresp. • University of Leiden, commonplace book with transcriptions of Arabic and other texts | University of Leiden, letter to François Halma • University of Leiden, letters to Burman

Sikes, Sir Charles William (1818–1889), banker, was born on 15 February 1818 in Huddersfield, the second son of Shakespear Garrick Sikes, banker, and his wife, Hannah, daughter of John Hurst of Huddersfield. In 1833 he entered the office of the Huddersfield Banking Company, in 1837 became cashier, and in 1881 managing director.

In 1850 Sikes wrote anonymously to the *Leeds Mercury* to propose the establishment of savings banks, and in 1854 developed his proposals in a pamphlet entitled *Good Times, or, The Savings Bank and the Fireside*. A state savings bank had been proposed on a number of occasions in the past, by Jeremy Bentham in one instance, who suggested the creation of 'frugality banks'. Sikes's initial proposal was to reform the existing trustee savings banks, which were run by local trustees on a voluntary basis; all deposits were handed to the national debt commissioners who paid interest at a fixed rate. The problem was that the hours of opening and coverage of the banks were inadequate, and Sikes's solution was to utilize mechanics' institutes as 'feeders' to the nearest trustee savings bank, with a central guarantee fund to provide security. The Yorkshire Union of Mechanics' Institutes adopted his suggestion, but it was clearly only a partial solution. In 1859, in an open letter to the chancellor of the exchequer, William Gladstone, he suggested that the Post Office should take on the role of 'feeder', remitting sums of £1 and above to a central savings bank in London by means of its existing money-order system; in return, depositors would receive 'interest notes' paying 2½ per cent. Sikes assumed that the central bank would be a separate institution, and that the existing transfer services of the Post Office would simply offer a means of providing an adequate coverage of the country.

The plan was drawn to the attention of Rowland Hill by Edward Baines, one of the members for Leeds, and it became the basis of a dispute within the Post Office on the limits of state action. On the one side Rowland and Frederic Hill insisted that the money orders should pay the full rate, and that transfers should be limited to multiples of £1, so as to prevent any competition with commercial banks in transmitting money or with the trustee savings banks, and to remove the danger that it would be a distraction from the main business of the Post Office. On the other side were Frank Ives Scudamore and George Chetwynd, who were eager for the Post Office to expand, particularly where competition between public and private concerns was possible as a guarantee of efficiency. Sikes's scheme was transformed by Chetwynd and Scudamore, in opposition to the Hills, whose caution was overruled by the postmaster general: money orders and interest notes were abandoned, and the Post Office simply entered deposits, of any amount, in a bank book; funds were transferred to a central Post Office Savings Bank which was an integral part of the department.

This expansion of the Post Office was accepted by Gladstone as a solution to the financial problems of the trustee savings banks. The national debt commissioners paid more to the banks than was received from investment in government securities, and Gladstone's attempt to resolve this problem had resulted in deadlock. The Post Office Savings Bank offered a solution, for deposits were transferred to the national debt commissioners which paid only the actual interest earned. The Post Office Savings Bank started operation in 1861, in a form far removed from the suggestion of Sikes, whose proposal had fortuituously coincided with the tussle between minimalists and expansionists within the Post Office, and with Gladstone's desire to prevent the trustee savings banks from imposing a financial drain. Sikes was knighted in 1881 in recognition of his role in the creation of the Post Office Savings Bank. He died unmarried on 15 October 1889 at his home, Birkby Lodge, Huddersfield.

MARTIN DAUNTON

Sources H. O. Horne, *A history of savings banks* (1947) · M. J. Daunton, *Royal Mail: the Post Office since 1840* (1985) · *Huddersfield Chronicle* (16 Oct 1889) · *CGPLA Eng. & Wales* (1889) · Boase, *Mod. Eng. biog.*
Archives W. Yorks. AS, Wakefield, corresp. and papers
Likenesses R. Taylor, wood-engraving, NPG; repro. in *ILN* (2 Nov 1889) · portrait; known to be in possession of Huddersfield council in 1897
Wealth at death £141,414 0s. 9d.: probate, 18 Dec 1889, *CGPLA Eng. & Wales*

Silberrad, Oswald John (1878–1960), chemist and explosives expert, was born at Buckhurst Hill, Essex, on 2 April 1878, the third son of Arthur Pouchin du Toict Silberrad, thirty-eighth baron (Franconian creation, 1002) of the house of Willigis (von der Silber-Rad), prince of the Holy Roman empire (1840–1916), merchant, and his wife, Clarissa Lucy Savill (1852–1921), sister of Thomas Dixon Savill. His aunt Emma married Sir Charles Wyndham. His sister Una Lucy was a novelist. He was educated at Dean Close Memorial School, Cheltenham, the Central Technical College, Finsbury, and the University of Würzburg.

In 1902 Silberrad was appointed head of the experimental establishment at Woolwich of the War Office explosives committee, of which Lord Rayleigh was chairman. Neither Silberrad nor the small staff of six chemists with whom he worked had prior experience with explosives, but under his directorship the fundamental research carried out proved of inestimable value to the military services. Most notable among the explosives that he developed was trinitrophenylmethyl nitroamine, which was introduced into service in 1903 as Silberrad's explosive S. 15 and was later known as tetryl. Through its agency he found a means of causing lyddite to detonate effectively in shell, which it had conspicuously failed to do during the Second South African War. Sir William Crookes, impressed by the work, minuted the War Office emphasizing the need for larger laboratories and additional staff. Of Silberrad he wrote that it was 'wrong to employ a racehorse to cart bricks'. As a result Silberrad was instructed to design new buildings and to begin metallurgical research. He was appointed superintendent of chemical research and a member of the explosives committee.

In 1906 this committee was disbanded and Silberrad resigned to become for the rest of his career a consulting research chemist and director of the Silberrad Research Laboratories, first at Buckhurst Hill, then at Loughton. Although primarily a chemist he had picked up a valuable knowledge of metallurgy and in 1908, at the instigation of the director of naval construction, he investigated the cause of a form of erosion in ships' propellers so severe that it appeared that the application of the steam turbine to shipbuilding was doomed and that a speed exceeding about 20–22 knots was impracticable for surface craft. Silberrad discovered the cause of this erosion and produced a bronze which withstood it and with which propellers were then made throughout the navy. It was also used in other high-speed ships, including destroyers and liners. With the firm of Hotchkiss he worked on erosion-resisting gun steel, which rendered the 75 mm gun a practical proposition during the First World War.

In 1915 the scientific committees advising the Ministry of Munitions had insisted that lyddite could be made only in earthenware, so that its manufacture from dinitrochlorbenzene via dinitrophenol, requiring a high temperature, was impracticable. Silberrad, who was honorary consultant to the ministry during the war, showed how it could be made safely in iron vessels, and many thousands of tons were made by this method in both world wars. He developed a flashless propellent for use in large howitzers, utilizing his earlier discovery (1902) of the cause of the flash from a gun. He discovered how to make dyestuffs from a special type of carbon and also from the residues of TNT manufacture. Among his many other discoveries was a new chlorinating agent, a method for manufacturing isoprene, the artificial retting of flax, a plastic explosive free from nitroglycerine, and a new method of blasting petroleum wells. He was the author of numerous scientific papers and of a treatise on the chemical stability of nitrocellulose. He was a fearless experimenter, on one occasion making a kilogram of nitrogen iodide, an explosive which when dry detonates on the slightest touch. He had great personal charm and was altogether a lovable man.

In 1922 Silberrad married Lilian Glendora, daughter of Edward George, knight of the order of Militia Templi, of Ballinasloe and Oxford; they had one son. Silberrad died at his home, Dryads' Hall, Loughton, Essex, on 17 June 1960 and was buried on 21 June. His wife survived him.

GODFREY ROTTER, rev. K. D. WATSON

Sources *Nature*, 187 (1960), 553–4 · *Proceedings of the Chemical Society* (1961), 29 · *The Times* (18 June 1960), 12 · *The Times* (22 June 1960), 14
Archives Sci. Mus., financial and personal papers, corresp. and patent material, incl. papers relating to Silberrad Research Laboratories; corresp. and papers
Wealth at death £13,957 10s. 6d.: probate, 7 Oct 1960, *CGPLA Eng. & Wales*

Silberrad, Una Lucy (1872–1955), writer, was born on 8 May 1872 at Sunnycroft, High Road, Buckhurst Hill, Essex, the eldest daughter and second of the nine children of Arthur Pouchin du Toict Silberrad (1840–1916), bulb merchant, and Clarissa Lucy, *née* Savill (1852–1921), sister of Thomas Dixon Savill (1856–1910), whose wife was Agnes Forbes, *née* Blackadder, MD (1876–1964). Her favourite brother, Oswald John *Silberrad (1878–1960), provided the scientific detail for her novels. Their father was of the third generation of his father's family to be a freeman of the City of London and also a liveryman of the Fletchers' and Longbowstringmakers' Company, of which he was elected upper warden in October 1864, and master in October 1888 and in October 1903. Admiration for the

integrity and straight dealing of the City is a recurrent theme in Una Silberrad's novels. Not for her any despising of the middle class and their values; that she would have regarded as an absurd affectation.

Una Silberrad was educated privately and at Newnham House School, Loughton, and while still a child she displayed her talent as a story-teller by her ability to compose extempore narratives to amuse her siblings and hold their attention. But she began to write only after leaving school and her first book, *The Enchanter* (1899), 'took two years to write and two years to publish' (*Local Review*, 217). *The Lady of Dreams* (1900), *Princess Puck* (1901), *The Success of Mark Wyngate* (1902), *Petronilla Heroven* (1903), and *The Wedding of the Lady of Lovell* (1905) followed. Their popularity was such that Silberrad was described as 'this favourite novelist of the day' in *Pearson's Magazine* (p. 306), where she contributed an essay entitled, 'Woman as man's equal' to '1896–1906–2006—What will be the future of women?—a collection of eminent opinions'. She followed this concept in *The Affairs of John Bolsover* (1909), where she explored the possibility of a woman prime minister a decade before women had the parliamentary franchise. Silberrad also commented on another controversial topic of the day, cremation, arguing in relation to the victims of an epidemic that it was 'the only sensible thing to do in the circumstances' (U. Silberrad, *Curayl*, 1906, 106). Both these books show that she was her own woman, as does *Success* (1912), a book without love interest that she wrote although convinced, as were her publishers, that it would be a failure. In the event, contrary to this expectation, it lived up to its title. Her *Times* obituarist asserted that it was 'perhaps the best' of her novels (*The Times*, 9 Sept 1955).

Silberrad touched upon the war of 1914–18 in *The Mystery of Barnard Hanson* (1915), *The Lyndwood Affair* (1918), and *Jim Robinson* (1920). Her *Letters of Jean Armiter* (1923) take the form of an exchange of correspondence and her description, the 'flapper-seat of a motor-cycle', gained her an entry in *The Oxford English Dictionary*. She wrote in total forty novels, and with Sophia Lyall described *Dutch Bulbs and Gardens, Painted by Mima Nixon* (1909).

Silberrad, who never married, had only two homes, Sunnycroft for the first sixty years of her life, and Wick House, Burnham-on-Crouch, for the remainder. Both were substantial houses standing in their own grounds where she enjoyed gardening. She also loved to walk in Epping Forest and on the Yorkshire moors. She was an accomplished needlewoman and embroiderer, specializing in the reproduction of flowers from her own drawings. The historical accuracy of her novels attests to the wide range of her reading. Of medium build and about 5 feet 2 inches in height, she had a most attractive smile and a puckish sense of humour, as is shown by the title of her book *Declined with Thanks* (1911) with its subtitle, 'because polite but discriminating editors have declined most of the tales in this collection'. At both Buckhurst Hill and Burnham-on-Crouch she was a member of the Women's Institute; at Burnham she helped with the production of plays, amateur dramatics being one of her hobbies.

Silberrad was not a member of the Society of Friends but had a profound respect for the Quaker way of life. The many quotations from scripture her novels contain show her detailed knowledge of the Bible and on the fly leaves of most of her novels that she kept she wrote a Biblical text. She was a regular worshipper at the parish church of Buckhurst Hill, where she and all her siblings were baptized. She later attended the church at Burnham-on-Crouch. Una Silberrad had just returned from evensong on 28 August 1955 when she had the stroke from which she died at her home on 1 September 1955. Her funeral took place at Burnham-on-Crouch church, where a memorial to her memory was placed. She was buried at Burnham-on-Crouch cemetery on 5 September 1955.

J. H. W. SILBERRAD

Sources *WWW*, 1951–60, 999 · *DNB* · records of the Fletchers' and Longbowstringmakers' Company · *Pearson's Magazine* (1906) · Neanias, 'A noted novelist: a talk with Miss Una L. Silberrad', *Local Review*, 5/58 (June 1912) · *Encyclopaedia Britannica*, 10th edn (1902–3), vol. 27, p. 267 · *The Times* (2 Sept 1955) · *Burnham-on-Crouch and Dengie Hundred Advertiser* (10 Sept 1955)
Wealth at death £10,164 3s. 9d.: probate, 15 Dec 1955, *CGPLA Eng. & Wales*

Silcock [*married name* Fairhurst]**, Helen H.** (*b.* 1866), trade unionist and suffragist, was born in Newcastle upon Tyne, one of ten children of John Silcock, a collier and strong trade unionist, and his wife.

The family moved to Wigan, Lancashire, where at the age of fifteen Helen Silcock began work in the cotton weaving sheds in one of the local mills. She joined the Wigan and District Association of Weavers and Winders in 1890, the year of its founding. As Wigan was a mining as well as a mill town, most men became miners and members of a strong trade union, enjoying high wages. The weavers' union was virtually all female and weak. In 1894 Helen Silcock was unanimously elected president of the Wigan and District Weavers' Association and invited a Women's Trade Union League (WTUL) organizer to visit Wigan to endeavour to strengthen the weak link in Lancashire's organization.

Helen Silcock began speaking in public in 1895 at a large labour day demonstration in Hyde Park. Her leadership qualities were noted and in 1897 the WTUL engaged her as a full-time salaried president-organizer, charged with the task of improving the low rates of pay for women in Lancashire. She and WTUL organizers from London toured the mill towns, holding recruiting meetings—often a thankless task when they had to be cancelled because of a low turn-out. In some cases they shared the platform with such speakers as Harry Quelch, who was editor of the Social Democratic Federation's paper, *Justice*. A determined and dedicated worker in the socialist cause, Helen joined the federation, and also became a member of the Wigan Trades Council. She was one of the few women delegates to the Trades Union Congress (TUC) in her own right—one of three in 1901.

Discouraged by the slow progress in improving wages and conditions for women workers, and the indifference of men trade unionists, Helen Silcock became more interested in the suffrage movement. The vote could give working women the means to bring about legislation to improve their economic situation. A textile workers' campaign to promote the issue had been launched by Esther Roper in 1893 (she became secretary of the Lancashire and Cheshire Women's Suffrage Society) and by 1900, it was supported by influential trade union organizers. Helen Silcock joined this radical group and welcomed visiting suffrage speakers to Wigan.

In 1901 at the TUC congress with her union's support she demanded the parliamentary vote for women. As a member of the TUC's franchise committee, she put forward a resolution asking for the vote for women on the same terms as men. The result was that the committee's position on women's suffrage changed from indifference to outright hostility and an alternative motion demanding full adult suffrage (all men and women) was agreed. Helen Silcock was allowed to present this resolution to congress. Although the adult suffrage notion was held by acclamation by the TUC, she had not changed her mind. She supported suffrage petitions taken to Westminster signed by women workers of Lancashire, Cheshire, and Yorkshire in 1901 and 1902, speaking as representative of the Wigan Weavers at both occasions. She also shared platforms locally with leaders of the northern suffrage movement.

On 31 March 1902, at the age of thirty-six, Helen Silcock married Joseph Fairhurst, ten years her junior, a hairdresser and a prominent Wigan trade unionist. She did not retire from her union post and returned to the TUC that year in another attempt to win delegates over to women's suffrage. She again failed, but narrowly. After her second defeat she began to have doubts as to whether women should get priority in the fight for universal suffrage and cut herself off from the radical suffragist campaign. Her basic aim as a trade unionist was to improve women's industrial conditions. In 1905, when the Adult Suffrage Society was formed, led by Margaret Bondfield, she became a member. However, little local progress was made as Wigan was essentially a coal town and the miners were opposed to women's suffrage. As Helen Silcock was heavily involved in local politics she took no further part in the suffragist campaign until 1913.

Just before the outbreak of war, the National Union of Women's Suffrage Societies canvassed support for the Labour Party, which had adopted women's suffrage as part of its platform. Trade unions, the TUC, trades councils, and Labour Representation Committees were urged to adopt resolutions backing Labour (and hence the vote for women) and Helen Silcock again committed herself, becoming secretary of the Wigan Suffrage Society in 1914. She disappeared from active public life after the war but her career exemplifies the coming together of two strands in the fight for women's rights: trade unionism and the suffrage movement.

JANET E. GRENIER

Sources J. Liddington and J. Norris, *One hand tied behind us: the rise of the women's suffrage movement* (1978) · *Women's Trade Union Review* (Oct 1894) · *Women's Trade Union Review* (Jan 1897) · *Women's Trade Union Review* (Jan 1899) · *Women's Trade Union Review* (April 1900) ·

Women's Trade Union Review (Oct 1901) · *Women's Trade Union Review* (April 1902) · *Women's Trade Union Review* (Jan 1903) · *Women's Trade Union Review* (June 1905) · *Wigan Observer* (5 April 1902) · N. C. Solden, *Women in British trade unions, 1874–1976* (1978), 51–77 · A. L. Morton and G. Tute, *The British labour movement* (1956) · 'The Trades Union Congress and women's suffrage', *Englishwoman's Review*, 32 (1901), 244–5 · 'The Trades Union Congress and women's suffrage', *Englishwoman's Review*, 33 (1902), 248–9 · E. Gore-Booth, 'The women's suffrage movement among trade unionists', *The case for women's suffrage*, ed. B. Villiers (1907) · m. cert.

Lucy Mary Silcox (1862–1947), by Sir Stanley Spencer, 1925

Silcox, Lucy Mary (1862–1947), headmistress and feminist, was born on 11 July 1862 at Warminster, Wiltshire, the eldest of four daughters of the Revd John Wesley Silcox, Methodist minister, and his wife, Betsy, *née* Parkinson. She was educated at Chelsea High School for Girls and at Newnham College, Cambridge, 1881–5. She was awarded a college scholarship in 1883 and passed part two of the classical tripos with first-class honours, later becoming a distinguished associate of Newnham College for thirty years from 1894.

Between 1885 and 1889 Lucy Silcox worked as a teacher of classics at the recently founded Liverpool High School for Girls, where, as her pupil Mary Sheepshanks testified: 'Her flashing eyes and gypsy look gave a hint of a warm and tempestuous nature, and her recherché and at times exotic dress expressed a love of beauty which in her was a dominating passion. ... Lucy Silcox gave and inspired love' (Sheepshanks). In 1890 Lucy Silcox was appointed the (very young) first headmistress of the new Girls' Public Day School Company East Liverpool High School for Girls. Soon after taking up that post she made time after school hours to coach, successfully, an ill-prepared Eleanor Rathbone in Latin and Greek for Oxford. She was succeeded as head of East Liverpool by her younger sister Alice. From 1900 to 1908 Lucy Silcox was headmistress of West Dulwich High School for Girls, and finally, between 1909 and 1926, she was head of the girls' public boarding-school St Felix, Southwold (founded in 1897).

Lucy Silcox, in the judgement of those who encountered her, including Sir Ernest Gowers, was 'one of the greatest headmistresses of all time' (*The Felician*, Sept 1946–7, 8). She was an idealist in her educational philosophy, dedicated to inspiring her pupils with a love of beauty, goodness, and truth; to that end she tried to allow the girls the maximum freedom, both in their choice of studies and in their organization of the school. She believed in treating the girls as reasonable people, capable of self-government and self-imposed discipline—there was extraordinarily little 'policing' by the staff. In her first address at St Felix, Lucy Silcox described the school as a ship in which each member felt her partial responsibility for the well-being of the whole, and where there was 'a real spontaneity and elasticity and freedom [in] the give and take with each other ...—the giving and asking for nothing in return, ... which alone is free from the spirit of barter' (*The Felician*, July 1909, 5–6). In her time at St Felix, Lucy Silcox could not shower enough beauty and intellectual inspiration on 'her' school. There were music recitals by Viennese chamber quartets and Myra Hess—who had to have her Steinway steered delicately up the fire escape

into the Hall—and by Adele Focini who played Brahms on her great-uncle Joachim's violin; talks by the poets De La Mare, Masefield, and Rabindranath Tagore; visits by the painters Cammaerts and Walter Sickert, who, alone, was a disaster. Lucy Silcox collected good paintings and fine pieces of old furniture for the school and she herself directed the girls in Greek plays, sometimes partly in her own translation: *Iphigenia in Tauris*, *Antigone*, *The Trojan Women*. As her way of commemorating the suffering and needed rebirth after the First World War, she managed to acquire a Mestrovic bust of a young girl for the school and she planted a large, sunken water garden in the grounds.

Lucy Silcox's socio-political commitment was feminist and humane. Her life's work as a teacher testified to her belief in the education of girls and, before the First World War, she campaigned actively for the vote. Not only was she president of her local branch of the National Union of Women's Suffrage Societies but she also toured the surrounding Suffolk villages, speaking up for 'the cause' from her pony trap. Sometimes an apple would be shied at her, but much more often she would hold her audience. She also worked, successfully, for the election of women candidates in local government. During the First World War—a very difficult period for the school since it was evacuated three times and one part split off to what the girls called the Funkhole in deepest Wales—Lucy Silcox would testify to unpopular moral restraint in warfare. One pupil never forgot how 'We had been receiving news of some new atrocity perpetrated by the Germans, which had caused much controversy about the rightness or advisability of retaliating in kind. Miss Silcox revealed her thinking on the situation by quoting from a classical author who had said "If we perish we perish but we will not do this thing"' (private letter from Rose Tebbutt, 7 May 1990, St Felix School Archive).

Possessing a passionate temperament, which could occasionally descend into immediately repented temper, Lucy Silcox was an eager, loving friend, the brilliance and colour of her appearance expressing an inner fire. Her friends included Jane Harrison, John Masefield, Gilbert Murray (who wrote a tribute to her in *The Times*, January 1947), Bertrand Russell, Paul Nash, Ray Strachey, and Eleanor Rathbone, but her lifelong companion was the fellow headmistress Olive Dymond, whom she had first met at Newnham. Her limp, the legacy from infantile paralysis, never prevented her from strenuous travels, exploring with gusto Corsica, Spain, Egypt, Palestine, Syria, and of course, Greece. Her remarkable face with its large liquid eyes, wide forehead, strong mouth, and map of lines has been finely drawn by many artists, including Stanley Spencer. Lucy Silcox died on 11 January 1947 at her home, Foxcombe End, Boars Hill, Oxford, listening to a favourite symphony with friends, and was buried in Oxford. She left 2000 books and her collection of paintings by Corot, Derain, Gertler, Christopher Wood, Matthew Smith, Chirico, Epstein, Ivon Hitchens, Frances Hodgkins, and Vanessa Bell to be shared between St Felix and Newnham. The paintings were sold to Leicester Art Gallery. A uniquely vivid, magnetic personality, no one who knew Lucy Silcox ever forgot her.			SYBIL OLDFIELD

Sources *Newnham College Report* (1948) · [A. B. White], ed., *Newnham College register*, 1: *1871–1923* (1964) · G. Murray, *The Times* (30 Jan 1947) · 'St Felix School, Southwold', *The Graphic* (1 April 1922) · F. B. Low, 'A happy school, in bracing surroundings, St Felix, Southwold', *The Queen* (30 June 1926), 18–20 · M. Lilley, *Sickert: the painter and the circle* (1971) · S. Oldfield, *Spinsters of this parish* (1984) · *The Felician* [magazine of St Felix School, Southwold] (July 1909) · *The Felician* [magazine of St Felix School, Southwold] (Sept 1946–1947) · *The Times* (14 Jan 1947) · M. Sheepshanks, 'The long day ended', Women's Library, London · archive, St Felix School, Southwold **Archives** St Felix School, Southwold **Likenesses** group photographs, 1885, Newnham College, Cambridge · pastel drawing, 1914, St Felix School, Southwold · H. Becker, oils, 1921, St Felix School, Southwold · S. Spencer, drawing, 1925, priv. coll. [*see illus.*] · J. K. G., drawing, 1926, St Felix School, Southwold **Wealth at death** £13,056 2s. 11d.: probate, 25 July 1947, *CGPLA Eng. & Wales*

Sìleas nighean Mhic Raghnaill. *See* NicDhòmhnaill, Sìleas (*c*.1660–*c*.1729).

Silkin, John Ernest (1923–1987), lawyer and politician, was born on 18 March 1923 in London, the third and youngest son (there were no daughters) of Lewis *Silkin, later first Baron Silkin (1889–1972), solicitor, who became minister of town and country planning in the Labour government of 1945–51, and his wife, Rosa Neft (1889/90–1947). It was a Jewish, intellectual, Labour family, and his brother Samuel Charles *Silkin (later Baron Silkin of Dulwich), the second son, became a somewhat controversial attorney-general in the Labour governments of 1974–9. John Silkin was educated at Dulwich College and for a short period at the University College of Wales, Cardiff, before going to Trinity Hall, Cambridge, where he obtained a second class (division one) in part two of the law tripos in 1942. He was then called up for the Royal Naval Volunteer Reserve. He became a lieutenant-commander in the intelligence branch and saw service in the Far East. On demobilization he entered the family firm of solicitors. He was admitted a solicitor in 1950. In that

year he married an actress, Rosamund *John (1913–1998), formerly the wife of Lieutenant-Commander (Hugh) Russell Lloyd, of the Royal Naval Volunteer Reserve, and daughter of Frederick Henry Jones. They had one son.

Silkin's first attempt to enter parliament in the Labour interest was in the general election of 1950 for the London constituency of Marylebone. It was a hopeless seat for any Labour candidate. Having unsuccessfully contested West Woolwich in 1951 and South Nottingham in 1959, Silkin finally entered the House of Commons in July 1963 for the south London constituency of Deptford, and very soon began to move upwards within the Parliamentary Labour Party. In 1966 he became chief whip in the government of Harold Wilson, a position which he filled with an agreeable competence until 1969, at a time when Labour had a majority of only three. He was deputy leader of the House of Commons in 1968–9 and minister of public building and works in 1969–70. It was in this period that he became close to Richard Crossman, whose diaries for these years offer a favourable commentary on Silkin's personality and political skills.

In the last Wilson government of 1974–6 Silkin was given the office of minister for planning and local government. It was not a very happy appointment and in 1976 he was moved to the Ministry of Agriculture, where he was much more successful. During the years to 1979 he became well known through extensive press coverage of his disputes with the Brussels officials of the European Community. Silkin's own personal politics were now directly involved. He belonged to the left of the Parliamentary Labour Party, which clustered around the journal *Tribune*. In foreign affairs he was a unilateralist on the issue of the atomic bomb, and a vigorous opponent of Britain's entry into the European Community. His tenure at the Ministry of Agriculture was notable for the tough stance he took on European matters, using a strongly nationalist approach to the much debated issues of fishing rights, and agricultural policies in general. His public quarrels with Brussels greatly extended his political image among the British electorate. His general opposition to the European Economic Community was based upon his acceptance of what was known at the time as 'the alternative economic policy': import controls and the protection of Britain's industrial base, a withdrawal from Europe, and a renegotiation of the terms for a possible future entry.

The Labour Party lost the general election of 1979 and a year later, after James Callaghan had resigned from the leadership of the party, there was an election for his successor. For reasons which are difficult to justify, John Silkin confidently believed that he was a serious candidate as a compromise between Denis Healey on the right of the party and Michael Foot on the left. Barbara Castle wrote in her diary in 1976 that Silkin was 'the kindest chap, but has not yet proved himself a political heavyweight'; it must have been his success against the Brussels officials that warped his judgement. In the first round of the leadership election he received 38 votes against Healey's 112, Foot's 83, and Peter Shore's 32. Nor did Silkin succeed in the election for deputy leader. This serious miscalculation concerning his own position weakened his general standing in the Parliamentary Labour Party.

In the years that followed, although he was on the Labour opposition's front bench, Silkin became involved in various disputes that he was to find very wearing. His own constituency Labour Party was much to the left of his own position and there were serious attempts to replace him as the candidate for the next election. They failed for the general election of 1983, but the continued friction helped to push Silkin into deciding in 1985 that he would not stand again. He was also much involved in a bitter internal quarrel over the control of *Tribune*, the organ of the moderate left.

Silkin had been brought up in an affluent family and he added to his inherited wealth during his own lifetime. His parliamentary salary was augmented by his continued practice as a solicitor. Among his clients was Robert Maxwell, which meant that Silkin had a place on the board of Pergamon Press. Silkin died before Maxwell was exposed as a fraudulent swindler on a very large scale. Silkin also benefited financially from property deals, one of which—a family affair involving his father in earlier years—prompted discussion in the national press in 1974. John Silkin publicly, and vigorously, defended his position.

Slightly taller than average, Silkin was well built. He died suddenly, of a heart attack, at his London home, 4 Dean's Yard, Westminster, on 26 April 1987. A memorial service was held at St Paul's, Deptford, on 23 June 1987.

JOHN SAVILLE, rev.

Sources *Sunday Times* (30 June 1974) · R. H. S. Crossman, *The diaries of a cabinet minister*, 3 vols. (1975–7) · R. H. S. Crossman, *The Crossman diaries: selections*, ed. A. Howard (1979) · *The Castle diaries, 1974–1976* (1980) · N. Wapshott, *The Times* (3 Nov 1980) · *The Times* (27 April 1987) · *The Times* (24 June 1987) · *CGPLA Eng. & Wales* (1988)
Archives CAC Cam., corresp. and papers
Wealth at death £379,521: probate, 20 Jan 1988, *CGPLA Eng. & Wales*

Silkin, Jon (1930–1997), poet and editor, was born on 2 December 1930 in London, the only child of Jewish parents: Joseph Silkin (1904–1990), a lawyer, and his wife, Doris Rubenstein (1905–1996). His maternal grandparents, Harris and Matilda Rubenstein of Llanelli and Swansea, and paternal grandparents, Abraham Silkin (*c.*1865–1948) and Fanny Sopher (*d.* 1924), had left Lithuania to escape the pogroms. Harris Rubenstein, who started a wallpaper and decorating business, had been on his way to the United States of America when the ship stopped for water in Swansea, and he decided to stay there, establishing a connection with Wales that was important for Jon Silkin. Abraham Silkin had settled in the East End of London, where he 'cleaned the toilets of the Synagogue, gave Hebrew lessons, and sold fruit off a barrow' (Silkin, 'The first twenty-four years', 244). Joseph Silkin's elder brother Lewis became a clerk in the Millwall docks and then a lawyer, an MP, and the first Baron Silkin. Lewis's sons, Sam and John Silkin, became Labour cabinet ministers.

Jon Silkin was named after Jon Forsyte in *The Forsyte Saga*. His early childhood was spent in Herne Hill and he attended Dulwich Hamlet School. His was a relatively secure, middle-class upbringing in a home which radiated warmth, intellect, political commitment, and Jewishness (his father organized League of Nations Union meetings on foreign affairs from 1937 to 1939 and specialized in naturalization proceedings for refugees, some of whom stayed in the Silkin household on their arrival in England). Aged seven Jon began his religious education at the synagogue and had Hebrew lessons for two years at home. In 1939 his school was evacuated to Kent, and in the following year he stayed with relations in Swansea, where he attended Parc Wern school before it too was evacuated. At Dolau Cothi in Carmarthenshire he spent a happy year with virtually no formal education. In the winter of 1941 he attended the Methodist public school Wycliffe College in Lampeter, but asked to be excused from Christian worship. He read the Jewish Bible and, even if he understood little, absorbed much of its language and rhythms. In 1945 he returned to London and attended Dulwich College, where he studied little, enjoyed athletics and rugby, became interested in music, and when music failed, turned to poetry. At fifteen he attempted to versify the book of Exodus and read John Milton, T. S. Eliot, and James Joyce; he was expelled for truancy in 1947.

Silkin worked as an insurance clerk and a journalist in south London, before being called up for national service (he became a sergeant instructor in the education corps). He collected his early verse and poems written during army service into a privately printed volume, *The Portrait and other Poems* (1950), published just after he was discharged. Although required to be an army reservist, he refused to serve in the Korean War and was eventually released. He then found work as a grave filler in Fortune Green cemetery. He lived in, and was evicted from, various furnished rooms, and may have spent some time living rough. Sacked from the cemetery for sitting on a grave reading Bernard Shaw's *Saint Joan*, he got a job with the National Cash Register Company, which dismissed him shortly afterwards for trying to form a union.

With £5 back pay in February 1952 Silkin started the literary magazine *Stand*, which he edited until his death. He also worked for a time as an English master in a boys' prep school, and between 1956 and 1958 he taught English to foreign students. He lived with Cynthia Redpath, with whom he had three sons. The death of their eldest son, Adam, informed his most famous poem, 'Death of a Son (who Died in a Mental Hospital Aged One)'. John Berryman thought it did 'not edge into the terror, but starts there and stays there ... and it is as brave, and harrowing, as one might think a piece could be' (Berryman, 317). His collection *The Peaceable Kingdom* (1954) was later judged by the critic Merle Brown as 'the finest first volume of poetry written by a living English poet' (Brown, 363). A further collection, *The Two Freedoms*, appeared in 1958. In the same year he was awarded the Gregory fellowship in poetry at the University of Leeds, where he took a first-class degree in English in 1962 (he wrote on himself in an open finals question), and then embarked on postgraduate work on the First World War poets.

In 1960 Silkin relaunched *Stand*, which had run out of money, with the encouragement of local benefactors in Leeds and the staff of the school of English, including Norman Jeffares and G. Wilson Knight. The magazine quickly established an international readership, publishing Samuel Beckett, Alan Sillitoe, and R. S. Thomas, as well as translations of Jean-Paul Sartre, Aleksandr Blok, Pablo Neruda, Bertolt Brecht, and Luigi Pirandello, and writers he had known in London including Alan Brownjohn, Philip Hobsbaum, and Harold Pinter. Translators and poets such as Edwin Morgan, Michael Hamburger, and Christopher Middleton found *Stand* to be one of the most important outlets for their translations from Russian and German. The magazine took a 'stand' against apathy towards young writers, publishing early work by Ken Smith, who became co-editor in 1963, and Tony Harrison, as well as important poems by Geoffrey Hill. The *Stand* editors, with John Barnard and Andrew Gurr of the Leeds school of English, founded Northern House, a small press which published first collections by Smith and Harrison as well as Silkin's own *Flower Poems* (1964). In 1965, when *Stand* was offered funding by Northern Arts in Newcastle, Jon Silkin settled there. In that year his collection *Nature with Man* won the Geoffrey Faber memorial prize, and he visited America for the first time, teaching at the University of Denison, Granville, Ohio. He also visited Israel in 1966, which led to important relationships with Dennis Silk and Natan Zach, whose work he later translated from Hebrew. A further visit to America in 1967, and a year as visiting lecturer at the University of Iowa (1968–9), informed *Amana Grass* (1971), which also contains significant poems reflecting his visit to Israel. In 1972 Silkin produced *Out of Battle*, an influential study of the poetry of the First World War and one of the first of its kind.

In 1974 Silkin married Lorna Tracy, the American fiction writer whom he had met in 1968. Having met and corresponded with Edmund Blunden, David Jones, and Siegfried Sassoon, he anthologized *The Penguin Book of First World War Poetry* (1979). He visited Israel again in 1980 as visiting writer at Mishkenot Sha'ananim, Jerusalem. He was Bingham visiting professor at the University of Louisville in 1981, and Elliston visiting poet at the University of Cincinnati in 1983. Silkin was also involved in a number of high-profile debates in the early 1980s. He relished controversy, and as part of his personal sense of commitment (best summarized in his introduction to the *Stand* anthology, 1973), he became involved in a prolonged debate with writers such as C. H. Sisson and Donald Davie, stimulated by implications in the post-war attitudes he saw as related to T. S. Eliot's famous claim in 1928 to be 'classicist in literature, royalist in politics, and anglo-catholic in religion'. Passionately argued positions from Raymond Williams, Robert Conquest, Terry Eagleton, Michael Schmidt, and E. P. Thompson also appeared in *Stand* and *PN Review* in the late 1970s. In 1985 Silkin's edition of Wilfred Owen's poetry for Penguin was withdrawn because of Jon Stallworthy's objection that it contravened the copyright of his own edition. A lively discussion between Silkin and Stallworthy on the legalities of copyright was aired in the *Times Literary Supplement*, and Silkin's edition finally appeared in a revised form in 1995.

Silkin was made a fellow of the Royal Society of Literature in 1986, distinguished writer-in-residence, American University, Washington, DC, in 1988, and literary fellow of Dumfries and Galloway Arts Association in 1990. In 1989 he published *The Penguin Book of First World War Prose*, co-edited with Jon Glover. After many years of writing, travelling, and working together as co-editors of *Stand*, Lorna Tracy and Jon Silkin were divorced in 1994. He formed a relationship with the poet Toshiko Fujioka (*b.* 1947) in Japan when he was foreign professor at the University of Tsukuba between 1990 and 1994. They returned to Newcastle, where Silkin edited *Stand*; it continued to attract internationally respected writers. In the early 1990s he was diagnosed with late onset diabetes and a heart condition.

Short and powerfully built, Silkin preferred clothes bought from markets at home or abroad. His black beard and hair (which he cut himself if it seemed necessary) were white in later life. He was a spellbinding speaker and continued to give readings in schools and arts centres until he was taken to hospital in Newcastle, where he died from a heart attack on 25 November 1997. He was buried at Bushey cemetery on 28 November 1997, with the stone setting on 29 November 1998. He was survived by his three children, David Emanuel, Richard Lindsay, and Rachel. Silkin was a prolific poet, still held in high esteem at the time of his death. He had just published the original *The Life of Metrical and Free Verse in Twentieth-Century Poetry* (1997), and had completed a further volume of poetry, *Making a Republic*. Some of his poems on his Jewish inheritance were collected in *Testament without Breath* (1998).

JON GLOVER

Sources J. Silkin, 'The first twenty-four years', *Contemporary authors: autobiography series* (1987), 243–65 • J. Silkin and C. Simpson Stern, 'Jon Silkin', *Contemporary poets*, ed. T. Riggs, 6th edn (1996), 1003–6 • A. C. Jacobs, *Collected poems and selected translations*, ed. J. Retty and A. Rudolf (1996) • M. Duggan, 'From the soul of Silkin', *Northern Echo* (1 Sept 1997), 7 • R. Gardner, 'Silkin purse', *The Guardian* (26 March 1971), 12 • A. Rudolf, 'Tribute to Jon Silkin', *Jerusalem Review*, no. 4 (1999/2000) • J. Silkin and M. Walters, 'Attend to the unnecessary beasts: a conversation with Jon Silkin', *Vanderbilt Poetry Review*, 1/2 (summer 1973) • J. Silkin and another, 'The small magazine since 1960: a recorded conversation with Jon Silkin', *British poetry since 1960*, ed. M. Schmidt and G. Lindop (1972) • J. Silkin, 'Joy lined with metal', 1977, priv. coll. [autobiographical note to poems] • J. Silkin, 'Living through the sixties', *Agenda*, 31/2 (1993), 57–9 • J. Silkin, 'Listening to Smetana's D minor quartet', priv. coll. [autobiographical talk given at the Whitworth art gallery, Manchester, 1997; typescript with annotations] • *The Times* (1 Dec 1997) • *Daily Telegraph* (11 Dec 1997) • *The Guardian* (1 Dec 1997) • *The Guardian* (4 Dec 1997) • *The Independent* (1 Dec 1997) • *Jewish Chronicle* (12 Dec 1997) • *Stand*, 39/2 (spring 1998) • *PN Review*, 24/4 (March–April 1998) • *Poetry Review*, 88/1 (spring 1998) • *Acumen*, 30 (Jan 1998) • *Stand* (1952–97) • J. Silkin, *Selected poems*, 3rd edn (1993) • R. Huk, 'Poetry of the committed individual: Jon Silkin, Tony Harrison, Geoffrey Hill, and the poets of postwar Leeds', *Contemporary British poetry*, ed. J. Acheson and R. Huk (1996) • P. Lawson, 'Rosenberg and Silkin', PhD diss., U. Southampton, [forthcoming] • M. Brown, 'Stress in Silkin's poetry and the healing emptiness of

America', *Contemporary Literature*, 18/3 (summer 1977), 363 · J. Berryman, 'Despondency and madness: on Lowell's "Skunk hour"', *The freedom of the poet* (1976), 317
Archives U. Leeds, MSS and corresp. · University of Florida, Gainsville, corresp., literary MSS, and papers | SOUND State University of New York, Brockport, *Writers Forum* series, recording of interview, 4 Nov 1971 · recordings of poems, BBC · conversations · plays, incl. Jon Silkin's *The people*, 9 July 1973 · poems set to music by John Casken
Likenesses photographs, U. Leeds

Silkin, Lewis, first Baron Silkin (1889–1972), politician, was born in Poplar, London, on 14 November 1889, the seventh child of Abraham Silkin, teacher of Hebrew and wholesale grocer, and his wife, Fanny Sopher. The family had only recently arrived in Britain from Lithuania, settling in the East End of London. At eleven, Lewis won a scholarship to the Central Foundation School, City Road, London; he then attended the East London College, from where in 1909 he won a mathematical exhibition to Worcester College, Oxford. His parents were too poor to send him to university, so he went to work in the East India docks. Determined to triumph over his circumstances, he became a clerk to a solicitor, qualified as a solicitor himself, and then set up his own law firm. On 30 July 1915, while still an articled clerk, he married Rosa (1889/90–1947), daughter of Israel Neft, an accountant, of Neath, Glamorgan. They later bought a house in Balham, south London, where they brought up their three sons, two of whom—John Ernest *Silkin and Samuel Charles *Silkin—became Labour MPs like their father.

Though no orator himself, Lewis absorbed socialism by listening to speeches outside London's dock gates. On regular trips to the countryside, during which he sang as he walked, he acquired a love of rural England. Like many Edwardian radicals, he was influenced by Robert Blatchford, whose *Merrie England* celebrated a pre-industrial nation of co-operative village communities. But Silkin buttressed Blatchford's romanticism with the practical outlook of a good solicitor. In 1925 he was elected to the London county council (LCC) for South-East Southwark, having stood unsuccessfully as Labour parliamentary candidate for Wandsworth Central (1922) and Stoke Newington (1924), and he became leader of the opposition Labour group on the LCC in 1930. He did not oppose Herbert Morrison's bid for the post in 1933, and after Morrison's appointment he loyally served the party as deputy leader instead. When Labour won power in the capital in 1934, Silkin also became chairman of the housing and public health committee. He did much to improve the lives of ordinary Londoners, for example, by championing the 'green belt' scheme which checked the city's chaotic sprawl across south-east England. In May 1936, at a by-election, he was elected to parliament as Labour member for the Peckham division of Camberwell.

Silkin believed that for economic and environmental reasons new industry and housing should be located away from major cities. At the same time enough of the countryside needed to be preserved for farmers to make their living and for holiday-makers to enjoy the beauty of Britain. This could only be done, he argued, if the profit

Lewis Silkin, first Baron Silkin (1889–1972), by Howard Coster, 1945

motive was regulated by effective planning controls and if the fortunes made by individual developers were taxed for the benefit of the whole community. During the war years Silkin's reputation in the party grew with that of the planning movement as a whole. In 1945 Clement Attlee appointed him minister of town and country planning with a brief to reform the way in which the natural environment was utilized in the United Kingdom, though without a seat in the cabinet. Assisted by a brilliant private secretary, Evelyn Sharp, and by a host of experts anxious to realize their vision of the future, Silkin repaid Attlee with three major pieces of legislation. The Town and Country Planning Act (1947) was the centrepiece. It nationalized development rights, giving local authorities sweeping powers compulsorily to purchase land for building in the public interest. They were also empowered to collect development charges on land if its value had been improved by private enterprise. A central land board was set up to assess the charges. Finally, the act enabled local authorities to save buildings of historic interest more effectively by listing and legally protecting those deemed by conservationists to be part of the nation's heritage. As a consequence of these measures the Attlee government was better able to erect badly needed homes, schools, and hospitals in carefully chosen areas. At the same time, by discouraging speculative construction, it reduced the loss of agricultural land to half that of the pre-war period. Thus Silkin also contributed in a small way to the massive growth in British food production which followed the establishment of state farming subsidies in the 1940s.

Silkin's New Towns Act (1946) designated fourteen such towns—eight in the Greater London area, three in the north of England, one in Wales, and two in Scotland. His aim was not just to house people but 'to get different classes … actually mixing together' (Matless, 234). William Beveridge was among the Liberal grandees who chaired the new town corporations. They met with stiff resistance, especially in the home counties, where existing residents were furious at the prospect of working-class Londoners coming to live in their green and pleasant land. Wartime evacuees had been one thing, but Silkin's cockneys were there to stay. Opposition to the act was a clear sign that the class camaraderie fostered by the Second World War had not lasted much beyond VE-day. In Stevenage a 'residents' protection committee' was set up. One of its supporters was E. M. Forster, who had written about the area in his novel *Howards End*. At a public meeting cries of 'dictator' greeted Silkin's rather bombastic announcement that 'People from all over the world will come to Stevenage to see how we here in this country are building for the new way of life' (ibid., 207). Antisemitic claims that the minister planned to erect a synagogue in Stevenage and that locals were being 'crucified on the cross of progress' merely hardened his resolve. Protesters changed platform signs at the town's railway station to read 'Silkingrad' (ibid., 208). But still the working classes alighted to start a new life. Twenty-five new towns were eventually built around the UK, housing over 2 million people.

National parks were an American invention of the 1870s, copied in some British colonies but not brought to the UK until Silkin's National Parks and Access to the Countryside Act (1949). This designated ten areas of England and Wales as national parks, run by local authorities and protected by a commission which drew up the countryside code (1951) to foster urban respect for rural ways. The act also enabled Britons to claim recreational access to private land, and it empowered local authorities to purchase land where no fair agreement could be reached with the owner. In parliament Silkin declared:

> This is not just a Bill. It is a charter—a people's charter for the open air, for the hikers and ramblers, for everyone who loves to get out into the open air and enjoy the countryside. Without it they are fettered, deprived of their powers of access and facilities needed to make holidays enjoyable. With it the countryside is theirs to preserve, to cherish, to enjoy, to make their own. (*Hansard 5C*, 463, 31 March 1949, 1485–6)

'Lewis was an improbable symbol of the hiker's friend', wrote Silkin's colleague Barbara Castle. 'Portly, expensively suited and rather prim, he looked and was the successful city solicitor, but he had not forgotten the rambling days of his youth and the Bill delighted us with its comprehensiveness' (Castle, 169). A total of 130,000 miles of public footpaths, many of them ploughed over or overgrown since the enclosures of the eighteenth century, were restored to life under civic control. But in many respects the act was toothless. The Dower and Hobhouse

reports on the subject (1945, 1947) had recommended blanket public access to uncultivated land. Under Silkin's system the onus remained on the citizen to prove that any right of way was desirable. Furthermore the act did not include Scotland until 1967 or Northern Ireland until 1983. By the end of the twentieth century, less than half of 1 per cent of the UK's countryside was covered by access agreements.

Silkin's attempt to open up rural Britain to holiday-makers was hampered by the Attlee government's fear of upsetting landowners and rural authorities, whose co-operation it needed in order to maximize food production and to implement pressing capital projects like the electrification of the countryside. The minister was no revolutionary himself. Indeed, he saw all his legislation as a way of burying the issue of wholesale land nationalization, which had excited socialists since the 1880s and which still lingered on the left of the Labour Party. 'After all', he told parliamentary comrades when justifying the compromises of his access act, 'in the existing state of society, a person's land is his land'. Silkin's work was also devalued by the architectural developments of the 1950s, 1960s, and 1970s. The many atrocious buildings built during that period turned town planners into public enemies. Silkin personally disliked the modernist style. But what he disliked even more was that so many examples of it were erected by the local authorities to whom he had naively entrusted his legislation. In 1965 he was awarded the gold medal of the Royal Town Planning Institute and appointed Companion of Honour. Though he accepted these honours with grace, they were scant consolation for a man whose career declined so soon after achieving so many of its aims.

While he was serving as minister of town and country planning, Silkin's parliamentary seat was abolished by a redrawing of the electoral map and he was not asked to contest another one. He generously campaigned for other Labour candidates in south London during the general election of 1950 before reluctantly going to the House of Lords, as Baron Silkin, in July 1950. From 1955 to 1964 he was deputy leader of the opposition there. In old age he discovered a new cause: the rights of women. He campaigned vigorously to legalize abortion, and in 1965 he introduced a bill in the House of Lords to that effect. Though unsuccessful it excited some attention and helped to clear the way for David Steel's historic private member's bill of 1967.

Nevertheless, Silkin's reputation as a second-rate busy-body stuck—partly because of his lack of personal charisma, but also because the labour movement did not celebrate his achievements. Environmental planning never had the popular appeal of the National Health Service or the radical cachet of the nationalized industries. And when the party became embarrassed by the mistakes of socialist planners and bureaucrats, it happily marginalized the man who was seen to have sponsored their work. Lewis Silkin's political legacy was undeniably flawed. However, he did leave a positive mark on British society. The bare bones of his legislation remained intact at the beginning of the next century, as did the public culture of responsible building which it eventually fostered. Silkin codified and institutionalized the progressive aims of the British planning movement, and in doing so he improved countless lives. Millions who enjoy the beauty of the UK's national parks have reason to thank him, as do those who exchanged inner-city slums for the relative affluence of new towns, and as does every Briton whose environment has been protected by the state's regulation of unscrupulous property developers. Silkin did not create the arcadia dreamed of by his hero Blatchford. But he did ensure that the relationship between landowner and citizen was a more just one, and that between town and country was a more balanced one.

After the death of his first wife Silkin married second, on 5 October 1948, Frieda (d. 1963), widow of J. F. Fiedler Johnson and daughter of the Revd Canon Pilling of Norwich; and third, on 26 March 1964, Marguerite, daughter of Karl Schlageter, a company director. He died in the National Hospital, St Pancras, London, on 11 May 1972.

RICHARD WEIGHT

Sources DNB · *The Times* (12 May 1972) · *The Times* (16 May 1972) · B. Castle, *Fighting all the way* (1993) · D. Hardy, *From new towns to green politics* (1991) · D. Matless, *Landscape and Englishness* (1998) · H. Newby, *Country life: a social history of rural England* (1987) · m. cert. [Rosa Neft] · m. cert. [Marguerite Schlageter] · d. cert. · *The Labour who's who* (1927) · Burke, *Peerage* (2000), 109 · *The political diary of Hugh Dalton, 1918–1940, 1945–1960*, ed. B. Pimlott (1986) · *The Second World War diary of Hugh Dalton, 1940–1945*, ed. B. Pimlott (1986) · K. O. Morgan, *Labour in power, 1945–1951* (1984) · B. Donoughue and G. W. Jones, *Herbert Morrison* (1973) · *Oxford University Gazette*, 39 (9 March 1909), 504

Archives Wellcome L., papers relating to abortion law reform | University of Strathclyde, Glasgow, corresp. with G. L. Pepler · Welwyn Garden City Central Library, corresp. with Sir Frederic Osborn

Likenesses H. Coster, photograph, 1945, NPG [*see illus.*] · W. Stoneman, photograph, 1945, NPG · W. Bird, photograph, 1962, NPG · H. Coster, photographs, NPG

Wealth at death £157,035: probate, 18 Aug 1972, CGPLA Eng. & Wales

Silkin, Samuel Charles, Baron Silkin of Dulwich (1918–1988), barrister and politician, was born on 6 March 1918 in Neath, Glamorgan, the second in the family of three sons of Lewis *Silkin, later first Baron Silkin (1889–1972), solicitor, who became minister of town and country planning in the Labour government of 1945–51, and his wife, Rosa Neft (1889/90–1947). John Ernest *Silkin was his younger brother. Educated at Dulwich College and Trinity Hall, Cambridge, he obtained first classes in both parts of the law tripos (1938 and 1939), and in his bar finals was awarded a certificate of honour and the Harmsworth law scholarship. He was called to the bar by the Middle Temple in 1941. A formidable cricketer, he played for Glamorgan in 1938. In 1941 he married Elaine Violet (d. 1984), daughter of Arthur Stamp, headmaster, of London; there were two sons and two daughters of the marriage.

In the Second World War Silkin achieved the rank of lieutenant-colonel in the Royal Artillery. He was on the staff of 12th corps during the invasion of France in 1944 and was mentioned in dispatches. He presided at two trials of major Japanese war criminals. After the war he practised from the chambers of Edmund Davies. Careful and methodical in style, he acquired a substantial practice, particularly in the planning field.

Silkin took silk in 1963 and in 1964 he entered parliament as Labour member for Camberwell, Dulwich. He served on the royal commission on the penal system in 1965–6. An enthusiastic European, he led the British delegation to the Council of Europe in 1968–70; there he formed a friendship with Robert Maxwell. Unlike his brother John Silkin, he was never associated with the left of the Labour Party, and he was one of the sixty-nine Labour MPs who in 1971 defied a three-line whip to support British entry to the European Economic Community. During this time he was also recorder of Bedford (1966–71). From 1970 to 1974 he served on the opposition front bench, on law office matters, and it was no surprise when in 1974 Harold Wilson, the incoming prime minister, appointed him attorney-general. He was then sworn of the privy council. He began on a controversial note, by declining to accept the knighthood which, for 400 years, had been bestowed upon law officers on their appointment. From 1974 to 1983 he was MP for Southwark, Dulwich.

Shortly afterwards the government introduced the Housing Finance (special provisions) Bill, granting retrospective immunity to the Clay Cross councillors in Derbyshire, who faced surcharges and disqualification from office for refusing to increase council rents under the Housing Finance Act of 1972. It fell to Silkin to speak in the Commons on the legal aspects of the bill and the opposition was able to produce a leaked letter written by him to a front-bench colleague advising against the principle of the bill. He was the subject of press criticism, which seemed destined to continue throughout his period of office.

In 1974 the literary executors of Richard Crossman proposed publication in the *Sunday Times* of his diaries, including his records of confidential discussions within the Labour government of 1964–70. In accordance with the established convention, they submitted them to the cabinet secretary, who declined to agree to their publication without excising the offending passages. The *Sunday Times* announced that it proposed nevertheless to publish. The affair was presented in sections of the press as a blatant attempt to suppress publication of embarrassing material. Ironically, the government would have preferred to see the material published, in order to establish that there were no secrets. But Silkin was his own man, and insisted that the public interest in the enforcement of constitutional conventions must take precedence over the political interests of the government. The lord chief justice (Lord Widgery) held that the convention existed, and that the courts would enforce it, but that, given the long interval which had elapsed since the events which formed the subject matter of the entries, no damage would be done by publication, and he declined to issue the injunction. The purpose of upholding the convention had been achieved, but the public perception was that Silkin had 'lost'.

In 1977, when Silkin declined to authorize a relator action which would have enabled John Gouriet, of the National Association for Freedom, to proceed against the Union of Post Office Workers, Lord Denning, master of the rolls, used language in the Court of Appeal which was construed by the press as imputing improper motives to Silkin. In the House of Lords he was completely vindicated, but the outcome received less publicity than the earlier judgment. Silkin ceased to be attorney-general in 1979, when the Labour government left office.

In court and in the house Silkin's contributions were quiet, well reasoned, and delivered in a slow, carefully formulated style, which did not appeal to the media. Arising as it did from a preoccupation with the logical form of the argument, it ensured that he was rarely guilty of fallacious reasoning, but tended to conceal his passionate commitment to social justice and human rights. He retired from the Commons in 1983 and entered the House of Lords as a life peer. There he found the style of debating more congenial. He became a director of two of Robert Maxwell's companies, Pergamon Press and the British Printing and Communications Corporation.

Silkin was tall and well made and his face was frequently softened in a smile. In 1984 his first wife died, and in 1985 he married an old friend of the family, Sheila Marian, widow of Walter Swanston and daughter of Arthur Jeal, an executive of a small gas company who owned property and land. Silkin died in the Churchill Hospital, Oxford, on 17 August 1988.

ARCHER OF SANDWELL, *rev.*

Sources H. Young, *The Crossman affair* (1976) · *The Independent* (19 Aug 1988) · *The Times* (19 Aug 1988) · *WWW* · personal knowledge (1996) · *CGPLA Eng. & Wales* (1989)

Archives CAC Cam., political and legal papers

Wealth at death £413,378: probate, 11 April 1989, *CGPLA Eng. & Wales*

Sillán moccu Mind (*d.* 610). *See under* Ulster, saints of (*act. c.*400–*c.*650).

Sillery, Charles Doyne (1807–1837), poet, born at Athlone, Ireland, on 2 March 1807, was the son of an Irish artillery officer, Captain Charles Doyne Sillery, a native of Drogheda, co. Louth, who died of wounds received at the battle of Talavera in 1809, and Catherine, youngest daughter of Barclay Fyfe of Leith, Midlothian. She later married James Watson of Tonthey Hall, Berkshire. The younger Charles entered the navy at an early age, serving as a midshipman on a voyage to China and India. Delicate health prevented him from following a naval career, and in 1828 he settled in Edinburgh in order to study surgery at the university there. The university records make no mention of him after 1829. Besides three small religious works, entitled respectively *A Discourse on the Sufferings of Our Saviour* (1833), *An Essay on the Creation of the Universe* (1833), and *The Man of Sorrows*, published posthumously, he published the following volumes of verse: *Vallery, or, The Citadel of the Lake* (1829), *Eldred of Erin* (1830), *The Royal Mariner and other Poems* (1834), and *The Exiles of Chamouni* (1834). He also

contributed verses to the *Edinburgh Literary Journal*. He died in Edinburgh on 16 May 1837 as a result of pulmonary consumption. Several of his poems have been included in Scottish literary anthologies.

D. J. O'DONOGHUE, *rev.* REBECCA MILLS

Sources C. Rogers, *The modern Scottish minstrel, or, The songs of Scotland of the past half-century*, 4 (1857), 174–8 · D. J. O'Donoghue, *The poets of Ireland: a biographical dictionary with bibliographical particulars*, 1 vol. in 3 pts (1892–3), 230 · Allibone, *Dict.* · private information (1897) [H. A. Webster, University of Edinburgh]

Likenesses A. Edouart, silhouette, 1830, Scot. NPG

Sillett, Emma (*bap.* 1802, *d.* 1880). *See under* Sillett, James (1764–1840).

Sillett, James (1764–1840), painter, son of James Sillett of Eye, Suffolk, was born in Norwich, where he was apprenticed as a heraldic painter. He moved to London, possibly in 1781. Initially employed as a copyist for the Polygraphic Society, he later joined William Capon as a scene-painter at Drury Lane Theatre. Various sources, including Sillett himself (*Norwich Mercury*, 4 July 1812), claim that he studied at the Royal Academy Schools. He is not, however, entered in the register, although his ticket for admission to the winter lectures for 1796 exists in the Reeve collection at the British Museum. In 1801 he married Ann Banyard of East Dereham, through whom he came into property. They had five children, three of whom died in infancy, the two surviving being his daughter Emma [*see below*], baptized at St Stephen, Norwich, on 21 February 1802, and son Edwin James, born on 16 April 1803.

Sillett returned to Norwich in 1801, advertising private tuition, evening classes, and afternoon schools in the local press. He was swiftly established within the local artistic scene, associating with the leaders of the Norwich Society of Artists, founded in 1803. He remained there except for a four-year period between 1804 and 1808 when he relocated to Norfolk Street, King's Lynn, teaching drawing and, in January 1808, exhibiting examples of his own work at Mr Lockett's coffee house in the Market Place. His association with King's Lynn endured, and he produced the illustrations for William Richard's *History of Lynn* of 1812.

Sillett exhibited forty-three works at the Royal Academy between 1796 and 1837, including miniatures, landscapes, and still lifes. It was for his paintings of game, fruit, and flowers that he was chiefly known. These are characterized by immaculate draughtsmanship, precise finishing, and by their debt to Dutch masters. In particular, Sillett's more academic style distinguishes his landscapes from those of Norwich contemporaries who painted local scenery with a more open mind to nature. Examples include *Flowers and Fruit* (1827) and *Thorpe Garden Public House* (1818; Norwich Castle Museum), *Garden Mallows* (BM), and *Hollyhocks* (1807; V&A). Claims in 1812 that his own specialization in still life restricted his teaching practice led Sillett to state publicly 'that his mode of teaching is by no means confined to fruit, flowers &c as has been insinuated, but extends to the practice of Drawing in general' and at the same time to suggest: 'there is more beauty in the delineation of a pig-sty or cart than in the human figure or the beautiful of the flower garden' (*Norwich Mercury*, 4, 11 July 1812).

Between 1806 and 1833 Sillett exhibited 289 works at the Norwich Society of Artists at Sir Benjamin Wrench's Court, and was vice-president, then president in 1814–15. In 1816 he was one of a group of artists who broke away from that organization and in that same year was involved in the formation of the short-lived Norfolk and Norwich Society of Arts. He exhibited with other members of this society, including Robert Ladbrooke and John Thirtle, at the Theatre Plain, Norwich, until the group disbanded in 1818 and Sillett resumed his contributions to the Norwich Society of Artists. From 1823 he exhibited in other provincial centres such as Newcastle. Ackermanns, the artists' colourmen, published his *Grammar of Flower Painting* (1820). In 1828 he published a set of fifty-nine views of public edifices in Norwich, and travelled to Holland, visiting Rotterdam and Leiden, of which he exhibited views at the Norwich Society of Artists. Sillett died at St Peter per Mountergate, Norwich, on 6 May 1840. His wife and children survived him.

Emma Sillett (*bap.* 1802, *d.* 1880) was herself a highly competent flower painter. Taught by her father, she is said to have been his nearest rival and began to assist him with his teaching in 1817. She exhibited forty-eight paintings at the Norwich Society of Artists between 1813 and 1833. There is no record of her having married. She died in 1880. TINA FISKE

Sources *Norwich Mercury* (30 Jan 1808) · *Norwich Mercury* (4 July 1812) · *Norwich Mercury* (11 July 1812) · *Norwich Mercury* (23 Aug 1823) · *Art Union*, 2 (1840), 91 · *N&Q*, 3rd ser., 1 (1862), 39, 135, 194, 358 · A. W. Moore, *The Norwich school of artists* (1985); 2nd impression (1995) · T. Fawcett, *The rise of English provincial art: artist, patron and institution outside London, 1800–1830* (1974) · W. F. Dickes, *The Norwich school of painting: being a full account of the Norwich exhibitions, the lives of the painters, the lists of their respective exhibits, and descriptions of the pictures* [1906] · M. Rajnai, *The Norwich Society of Artists, 1805–1833: a dictionary of contributors and their work* (1976) · J. Walpole, *Art and artists of the Norwich school* (1997) · Graves, *RA exhibitors* · *Catalogue of pictures, drawings, etchings and bronzes in the picture gallery of the Norwich Castle Museum*, Norwich Castle Museum, 3rd edn (1904) · L. Binyon, *Catalogue of drawings by British artists and artists of foreign origin working in Great Britain*, 4 vols. (1898–1907) · L. Lambourne and J. Hamilton, eds., *British watercolours in the Victoria and Albert Museum* (1980) · P. Kennedy Scott, *A romantic look at Norwich school landscapes by a handful of great little masters* (1998) · *IGI* · d. cert.

Likenesses J. Sillett, self-portrait, oils, 1803, Norwich Castle Museum; repro. in Moore, *Norwich school*

Wealth at death £300; £142 9s. 5d. in annuities and bequests; also paintings, drawings, prints, books, and household effects: will, 31 July 1839

Sillitoe, Sir Percy Joseph (1888–1962), police officer and intelligence officer, was born at Tulse Hill, London, on 22 May 1888, the second son and second child of Joseph Henry Sillitoe, average adjuster, and his wife, Bertha Leontine Smith. There was also a younger sister. The family suffered from the improvidence of Sillitoe senior. After leaving St Paul's choir school in 1902, Percy Sillitoe lived at home for three years during which he received some private tuition. From 1905–7 he worked for the Anglo-American Oil Company and in 1908 became a trooper in the British South Africa police, a tough, highly disciplined

Sir Percy Joseph Sillitoe (1888–1962), by Bassano

paramilitary force, in what was then Southern Rhodesia. He transferred to the Northern Rhodesia police in 1911, was commissioned, and in 1913 became engaged to Dorothy Mary, daughter of John Watson, of Elloughton, Yorkshire, surveyor and justice of the peace; he had met her on board ship when returning to Africa from sick leave. He took part in the campaign in German East Africa, and afterwards served as a political officer in Tanganyika from 1916 to 1920, when he resigned from the Northern Rhodesia police, and returned home. In 1920 he married Dorothy, and they had a daughter and two sons.

A further two years as a colonial service district officer in Tanganyika followed, but his wife disliked the life, and after suffering a serious illness himself Sillitoe resigned in 1922. Prompted by his father-in-law he applied for the post of chief constable in Hull, but this application, and another to Nottingham, were unsuccessful. Sillitoe spent the winter of 1922–3 reading for the bar as a student of Gray's Inn, without finding much satisfaction in his studies and becoming increasingly depressed. However, in the spring of 1923 he applied successfully for appointment as chief constable of Chesterfield and began the career in which he was to achieve distinction.

At Chesterfield, where he stayed two years, Sillitoe made a considerable mark and, after a year as chief constable of the East Riding of Yorkshire, he was appointed chief constable of Sheffield on 1 May 1926. Here he commanded a substantial force badly in need of rejuvenation and strong leadership and faced serious problems of law and order, gangs having at this time virtually complete control of the poorer parts of the city. In the course of five successful years Sillitoe revitalized and modernized the force, broke the power of the gangs by the use of plain-clothes police patrols prepared to use 'reasonable force', and acquired a reputation as administrator, disciplinarian, and resolute upholder of the law.

This led to Sillitoe's appointment in 1931 as chief constable of Glasgow to command a force of 2500 men, second in size to the Metropolitan Police, and to face problems similar to those which he had mastered in Sheffield. His tenure of the post, which lasted twelve years, further enhanced his reputation. In the words of one of his subordinates, himself a future chief constable of Glasgow, his arrival was 'like a breath of fresh air' from which the whole of the police service in Scotland ultimately benefited. He was appointed CBE in 1936 and knighted in 1942, and the following year was invited to take command of the new Kent joint force in which the county and nine city and borough forces were combined to facilitate planning and co-operation with the fighting services prior to the invasion of Europe. This was his last police appointment which he held until he became director-general of MI5 on 1 May 1946, in succession to Sir David Petrie.

Sillitoe had a commanding presence. To his men he was the Captain or the Big Fellow, an autocrat and strict disciplinarian leading in a style which was still acceptable between the wars. In the interests of morale and efficiency he was ruthless in requiring senior officers to retire on qualifying for full pension. He chose his subordinates well, left them to do their work without interference, gave them credit for it with outside contacts, and defended them against criticism. He disapproved of the Hendon Police College experiment, believing that officers should rise through the ranks, but was an advocate of women police. Without himself possessing the policeman's professional skills, or being an original thinker, he was alive to the need to bring technical resources to bear on the prevention and detection of crime. He persuaded the police authorities which he served to loosen the purse strings to provide proper accommodation, transport, communications, and support services for fingerprinting, photography, and forensic examination. Resolute, independent, and forthright (as chief constable of Kent he disregarded an instruction to do nothing to prevent the merged forces again becoming independent after the war), his relations with the police authorities were nevertheless generally very good.

Sillitoe wrote in his autobiography that he wished he could persuade himself that his appointment as director-general fulfilled his life's ambition. He had been invited to apply for the post by the Home Office: it was not, he said, one to which the aspirations of a policeman would normally have turned. In fact he was unhappy in it. Times were difficult. His period of office coincided with a high season of Russian espionage and saw the trials of Alan Nunn May and Klaus Fuchs and the defections of Pontecorvo, Guy Burgess, and Donald MacLean. Sillitoe, who had immense concern for his public reputation, had to answer for what with hindsight could sometimes be seen as blameworthy mistakes. The problem of communists in government service required flexibility and political judgement which were not his strong suits. MI5 needed a different style of leadership from a police force. Moreover, Sillitoe had no liking for people whom he called 'book-learned intellectuals'—a category to which (in his view) many MI5 officers could be consigned. For their part the senior staff of MI5, backed by considerable wartime achievements, had had their own favoured candidate for director-general and resented the choice of an outsider whose career had not tended to develop the particular skills which the post required. A rift developed at a high level which was never closed.

Sillitoe's most valuable contribution was made overseas in extending collaboration with, and promoting organization for security in, the old Commonwealth countries and in assisting colonial governments to establish machinery to cope with the security problems which accompanied the evolution of colonial rule into self-government. Here the resolution and forthrightness which had helped to make him a successful chief constable again served him well—although his predilection for publicity shocked traditionalists at home. Sillitoe was made KBE in 1950. Despite setbacks and public criticism he enjoyed Clement Attlee's confidence throughout the latter's premiership.

After retiring from MI5 in 1953 Sillitoe became head of the International Diamond Security Organization established by De Beers to curb the flow of diamonds bypassing the De Beers Central Selling Organization. The main leakage (from Sierra Leone via Liberia) was successfully plugged and the International Diamond Security Organization was wound up in 1957. Sillitoe later became chairman of Security Express Ltd. He died at Eastbourne on 5 April 1962.   ANTHONY SIMKINS, *rev.*

Sources P. Sillitoe, *Cloak without dagger* (1955) · A. E. Cockerill, *Sir Percy Sillitoe* (1975) · personal knowledge (1981) · private information (1981) · *CGPLA Eng. & Wales* (1962) · *WWW* · *The Times* (6 April 1962) · R. Deacon, *The greatest treason: the bizarre story of Hollis, Liddell and Mountbatten*, rev. edn (1990) · P. Murphy, 'Game to Sir Humphrey', *The Guardian* (18 May 2000)
Likenesses W. Stoneman, photograph, 1947, NPG · Bassano, photograph, NPG [*see illus.*] · portrait (after photograph by M. McLellan); known to be in the possession of Strathclyde police force in 1981
Wealth at death £27,004 12*s*. 8*d*.: probate, 5 June 1962, *CGPLA Eng. & Wales*

Silva, Duarte da (1596–1677), merchant, was born in Lisbon and baptized there at St Nicholas's Church in 1596, the son of Diogo da Silva, merchant, and Catarina Henriques, who were both New Christians. He migrated to Brazil, served as a private soldier in the militia, and was promoted captain. When the Dutch captured Bahia in 1624, he was taken to the Netherlands as a prisoner of war, together with the governor of Brazil, but escaped to Flanders. Back in Portugal, he married Branca da Silva, daughter of a female cousin in Viana. He lived there for two years before moving successively to Lisbon, to Brazil, and back to Lisbon, where he became a major sugar importer. In 1639 he and his partners entered into a contract to supply 1 million cruzados for the defence of Brazil. This was cut short by Portuguese independence from Spain, whereupon he became an important tax farmer and financier of João IV's government. In 1641 he, together with Francisco Botelho Chacão, lent João IV 30,000 cruzados. In 1647 he arranged the financing of the Portuguese armadas, which broke the Dutch blockade of Bahia and recaptured Angola from the Dutch. He also arranged remittances to Amsterdam and Hamburg to buy warships and munitions. He was then reputed the richest merchant in Lisbon.

In December 1647 the Inquisition arrested da Silva, together with his two younger sons, daughter, and two brothers-in-law, on charges of Judaism. He had brought up his children as Catholics, and when his eighteen-year-old daughter, Catarina, was tortured, she called for help in the names of Jesus and of the Virgin. Da Silva evinced no obvious enthusiasm for Judaism, but the inquisitors kept the property they confiscated, and his large fortune was tempting. They had collected a denunciation from his eldest son's discarded mistress that he secretly kept Jewish fasts and did not eat pork. The king intervened to debar a death sentence, but da Silva and his children were tortured twice and imprisoned for five years. However, at the suggestion of Father Antonio Vieira SJ the king changed the rules and prohibited property confiscations by the inquisitors. Duarte and his family were paraded and sentenced at an *auto-da-fé* in 1652 and released. His commercial recovery was slow. Queen Luiza de Gusmão, as regent of Portugal, made him a knight of the royal household (*cavalheiro fidalgo da casa real*) and created his sons Francisco [*see below*] and João knights of the order of Christ, Portugal's first order of chivalry, overruling their disqualification because of Jewish ancestry and condemnation by the Inquisition.

The marriage of Catherine of Braganza to King Charles II with a dowry of 2 million cruzados (£350,000) enabled Duarte and his family to leave Portugal with their possessions. He arrived in England with Queen Catherine in May 1662 as the procurator, responsible for paying the first half of her dowry within two months. However, Queen Luiza fell from power in June and the remittances from Portugal ceased, leaving some £40,000 outstanding. Late in 1662 Charles II had Duarte da Silva arrested and imprisoned until April 1663, when the remainder of the first half of the dowry was paid. It seems to have been while he was in the Tower that he drafted a proposal for a drastic reform of the Portuguese Inquisition and a general pardon of its prisoners in return for a tax on the New Christian merchant community. In February 1663 the inquisitors procured a papal brief *ex omne fide* denouncing it. In 1665, jointly with Gomes Rodrigues and Fernão Mendes da Costa, da Silva persuaded the East India Company to carry their diamond trade with Goa. He then received a substantial diamond shipment, and in March 1668 the company sent a consignment of silver to Goa for him. He moved to Antwerp, where he died and was buried in 1677.

Duarte da Silva traded in partnership with his second son, **Francisco Dias da Silva**, marquess of Montfort in the nobility of the Holy Roman empire (1634–1688), who

was appointed Queen Catherine's treasurer-general. Francisco had married a daughter of his Antwerp correspondent Gaspar Rodrigues Passarinho, but she must have died, because about 1670 he married, also in Antwerp, Filippa de Castro. In 1682 the emperor made Francisco a marquess of the Holy Roman empire. The reason for this dramatic promotion is not known, but it suggests that he had given Austria valuable political or financial service. He died and was buried in Antwerp in 1688. Francisco's son, Antonio da Silva y Castro, second marquess of Montfort (*b.* 1671), settled in Amsterdam and joined the synagogue.

EDGAR SAMUEL

Sources A. Baião, *Episódios dramáticos da inquisição Portuguesa*, 3rd edn, 2 (Lisbon, 1973) · *The manuscripts of J. M. Heathcote*, HMC, 50 (1899) · *Photographic facsimile of the original charter granted by Leopold of Austria in 1682 to Francisco de Sylva creating him marquis de Montfort, etc.* (1936) · W. A. Shaw, ed., *Calendar of treasury books*, 1, PRO (1904) · D. G. Smith, *The mercantile class of Portugal and Brazil in the seventeenth century: a socio-economic study of the merchants of Lisbon and Bahia, 1620–1690* (Ann Arbor, MI, 1975) · C. H. Boxer, *Salvador de Sá and the struggle for Brazil and Angola* (1952) · J. C. Boyajian, *Portuguese bankers at the court of Spain, 1626–1650* (1983) · C. Roth, 'An excursus upon the history of the Capadose family', in I. da Costa, B. Brewster, and C. Roth, *Noble families among the Sephardic Jews with some account of the Capadose family and an excursus on their Jewish history* (1936) · *CSP dom.*, 1661–2 · will, PRO, PROB 11/391, sig. 68 [will of Duarte da Silva]

Archives Jewish Museum, London, charter of the emperor Leopold creating Francisco da Silva marquess of Montfort | BL, Add. MS 40699, fols. 49, 64, 65, 66, 100 · Portuguese National Archives, Lisbon, Inquisition trials

Silva, Francisco Dias da, marquess of Montfort in the nobility of the Holy Roman empire (1634–1688). See under Silva, Duarte da (1596–1677).

Silver, George (*fl.* 1580–1599), swordsman and writer on fencing, was the eldest son of Richard Silver of Ropley, Hampshire, and his wife, Agnes, daughter of Thomas West, one of the ramified West family of Sussex and Hampshire, of whom the barons De La Warr were the chief representatives. Nothing is known of his early life, but Silver was probably ordinarily resident in London by early 1580. On 24 March of that year he married in St Clement Danes, Mary Heydon, a spinster of the city of London whose father, George Heydon of Norwich, was the son of Sir John Heydon of Baconsthorpe, Norfolk. It is not known where or how George Silver acquired his mastery of fencing. There was in London a society of swordsmen known as the 'masters of defence', originally chartered as a corporation by Henry VIII, but Silver was not a member; he thought these men were worthy, but lacked the finest skills.

Silver's book *Paradoxes of Defence* was entered in the register of the Stationers' Company on 30 January 1599. In it Silver recalled two Italians, Ieronimo, an apprentice, and Vincentio, a master identifiable as Vincentio Saviolo, who had for seven or eight years earned a living in England teaching the technique of the rapier to gentlemen:

> These two Italian fencers, especially Vincentio, said that Englishmen were strong men, but had no cunning, and they would go back too much in their fight, which was great disgrace unto them. Upon these words, my brother Toby Silver and myself made challenge of them both, to play with

them at single rapier, rapier and dagger, the single dagger, the single sword, the sword and target, the sword and buckler, and two hand sword, the staff, battle axe and morris pike, to be played at the Bel Savage upon the scaffold, where he that went in his fight faster back than he ought, of Englishman or Italian, should be in danger to break his neck off the scaffold. (*Paradoxes*, 66)

Such was their confidence, Silver here suggested, that they had consented to fight at the Bel Savage on Ludgate Hill, an inn which also served as a playhouse, even though its small stage would greatly disadvantage those who fought in rapid retreat, as the English were said to. Fencing contests were familiar sights in London, for they were used by the masters of defence as tests whereby students advanced to full membership of their society, and many were held in playhouses as a kind of theatrical entertainment. George and Toby Silver posted 'five or six score bills of challenge … from the Southwark to the Tower, and from thence through London unto Westminster'. When they arrived at the Bel Savage on the appointed day, there were 'a multitude of people there to behold the fight', but the Italians did not appear (*Paradoxes*, 66–7). The credibility of the account is damaged by the author's apparent belief that the virtue of courage was not to be found among men of Italian nationality. His prefatory admonition to Englishmen urges them to reject the influence of foreign teachers, and, 'casting off these Italianated, weake, fanatical, and most divellish and imperfect fights' return to their natural style (ibid., 1). But what was this? Silver's complaint against the Italian teachers was that they 'did not teach defence but offence' (ibid., 77).

For very nearly 300 years Silver's fame rested upon this single published book, yet he also produced a second work, which is in many respects more interesting but which remained in manuscript until its eventual publication in 1898 by Captain C. G. R. Matthey in *The Works of George Silver*. This was entitled 'Bref instructions upo my paradoxes of defence', clearly intended as a companion to the published work. It sets out a series of tactical precepts and techniques, which rest upon a distinctive strategic approach: 'Silver lays great stress upon defence … and it is only when in safety that he advises counter-attack or riposte' (*Works*, xvi). For Matthey, the manual was of more than academic interest: it could be 'put into practice in sword encounters with highly successful results, especially when they take place against men of savage or barbarian races that Her Majesty's troops are now so frequently sent to face in various quarters of the globe' (ibid., xv). According to a later authority, the work

> describes an advanced technique of short sword fencing which we would recognise as somewhat similar to nineteenth-century sabre fencing. Silver was teaching a new and radical technique of parrying with the edge of the light short sword, and with this considerable improvement in technique had evolved an early and effective sabre style,

suitable not just for duelling but for street fighting and battle (Jackson, viii). Silver's manual reveals him as an expert technician, whose impatience with his rivals was not merely arrogance or chauvinism.

Nothing more is certainly known about George Silver's life, but his wife, Mary, married a second husband, Edward Edwards of Hoddesdon, Hertfordshire, and this may suggest that Silver died young. In 1599 the administration is recorded of the property of a Tobias Silver, who had been killed in Ireland. This was probably the brother, and partner, of whom Silver wrote. *Paradoxes of Defence* contained a preface dedicated to Robert, earl of Essex. It may be that the two brothers enlisted together as swordsmen in the earl's expedition to Ireland in 1599, and that George, like Toby, did not return.   STEPHEN WRIGHT

Sources *The works of George Silver: comprising 'Paradoxes of defence' and 'Bref instructions upo my paradoxes of defence'*, ed. C. G. R. Matthey (1898) [incl. reproductions of BM MSS] · G. Silver, *Paradoxes of defence wherein is proved the true grounds of fight to be in the short ancient weapons, and that the short sword hath advantage of the long sword or long rapier … together with an admonition to … Englishmen, to beware of false teachers of defence* (1599) · W. H. Rylands, ed., *Pedigrees from the visitation of Hampshire … 1530 … 1575 … 1622 … 1634*, Harleian Society, 64 (1913) · J. L. Chester and G. J. Armytage, eds., *Allegations for marriage licences issued by the bishop of London*, 1, Harleian Society, 25 (1887) · J. L. Jackson, ed., *Three Elizabethan fencing manuals* (1972) · E. Castle, *Schools and masters of fence*, 3rd edn (1969) · M. Fitch, ed., *Index to administrations in the prerogative court of Canterbury*, 4: 1596–1608, British RS, 81 (1964) · W. Rye, ed., *The visitacion of Norffolk … 1563 … 1613*, Harleian Society, 32 (1891) · E. K. Chambers, *The Elizabethan stage*, 4 vols. (1923), vol. 2

Silver, Jonathan (1949–1997), businessman and gallery owner, was born on 21 October 1949 at 217 Horton Lane, Bradford, Yorkshire, one of the two sons of Sydney Samuel Silver (*b.* 1917), retail draper, and his wife, Irene Betty, *née* Morris, who ran a boarding-house for Jewish refugees. Educated at Bradford grammar school, he was consistently in the bottom stream; but he spent his lunch breaks in auction rooms buying and selling bric-a-brac, and his spare time buying antiques from large houses that were being demolished, and selling them to antique shops in London. He enlisted in the Israeli army after the Six Day War in 1967, and spent a few weeks in a tank regiment before his age was discovered. After four weeks at Enfield College of Technology he entered the University of Leeds in 1968; he graduated in 1971 with a second-class degree in textile management and art history. On 7 August 1972 he married Margaret (Maggie) Jackson (*b.* 1948/9), secretary, and daughter of Arnold Jackson, an area manager; they had two daughters.

In 1971, with his father and his cousin, Silver opened a shop in Manchester selling cheap but fashionable men's clothing. He went on to build a chain of thirteen Jonathan Silver menswear shops in the north and the midlands, with its headquarters in Bradford: he sold the chain in 1979. From 1977 to 1979 he also had a shop in Manchester with his brother, Art and Furniture, selling antiques, prints, and paintings. Through the clothing business he came into contact with the textile manufacturer Ernest Hall, and they went into partnership to buy and develop redundant mill buildings in Yorkshire, where the textile industry was in rapid decline, buying C. and J. Hirst, an old mill in Huddersfield. In 1983 they bought Dean Clough, the Crossley carpet factory in Halifax which had closed in 1982, and began letting space to small businesses.

Although the partnership was dissolved in 1984, with Silver selling his 50 per cent share in Dean Clough to Hall, they remained friends, and while Hall went on to develop Dean Clough as an arts and business centre, Silver took his wife and children travelling round the world for three years.

In 1987 Silver bought Salts Mill in Saltaire, near Bradford, a large Victorian textile mill built by Sir Titus Salt, who made his fortune from alpaca and created Saltaire, a model industrial town, to house the mill workers. Illingworth Morris, the owners of the mill, had closed it in 1986, and it was under threat of demolition when Silver bought it. He went on to develop Salts Mill on the lines of Dean Clough, as an arts and business centre; the rental income from the small businesses attracted to the site financed the arts ventures.

A long-standing friend and admirer of the painter David Hockney, also born in Bradford, Silver opened the 1853 Gallery in the former spinning mill in November 1987 after Hockney agreed to lend fifty-three paintings. Over the next ten years he built up what became the largest single collection of Hockney's work in the world, buying over 100 pictures himself and borrowing others from Bradford council and the Hockney family. The 1853 Gallery was filled with antiques and plants, and his own collection of Burmanstofts vases (made in Leeds at the end of the nineteenth century by the Leeds Fireclay Co. Ltd), with books lying around for sale, and operas, usually by Wagner, playing in the background. After he learned that Hockney had sent paintings down the telephone line for an exhibition in Brazil, Silver persuaded him to fax a painting from Los Angeles to Salts Mill on 10 November 1989: *Tennis*, made up of 144 sheets, took forty-five minutes to arrive over two machines, and as the faxes came in the guests at the evening event watched the painting being assembled on the wall, amid a blaze of media publicity. Special Hockney exhibitions included his 'Very New Paintings' in 1993, which developed out of the stage designs he did for the Strauss opera *Die Frau ohne Schatten*, and an exhibition of drawings of his family and friends, including several of Silver, in 1993–4. A new Hockney gallery, designed by the painter in the Florentine style, opened in 1994. Hockney painted Silver's portrait in 1996. Although Silver had persuaded Sir Roy Strong, director of the Victoria and Albert Museum, to move part of the museum's collection of south Asian art to Salts Mill, the trustees of the museum later voted against the proposal.

In the former weaving and cloth-finishing sheds Silver drew in opera and theatre productions, beginning with Opera North's performance of *West Side Story* in 1988 and including the Royal National Theatre production of *The Trackers of Oxyrhynchus* (1990) by Tony Harrison. Silver commissioned Harrison's *Poetry or Bust* (1993), the story of the Victorian poet John Nicholson, an employee of Sir Titus Salt. He also opened the Diner, a very successful restaurant. In 1994 Salts Mill won the Arts Council's 'centres for arts' award. Silver's development of Salts Mill generated jobs for over 1000 people, and inspired other companies and organizations to undertake restoration projects: in

1996 Prince Charles launched his 'regeneration through heritage' initiative from Salts Mill. In 1997 Saltaire was awarded the prestigious Europa Norton IBI medal for conservation and restoration, and in 2001 it was designated a UNESCO world heritage site.

With great reserves of energy and a low boredom threshold, Silver nevertheless maintained a very relaxed style, with his ponytail and informal way of dressing. He described himself as a Jewish atheist. He died of cancer on 25 September 1997 at his home, Keldale, Linton Lane, Linton, Wetherby, Yorkshire, and was survived by his wife. ANNE PIMLOTT BAKER

Sources J. Greenhalf, *Salt and Silver: a story of hope* (1997) · *The Guardian* (26 Sept 1997) · *The Independent* (31 Oct 1997) · b. cert. · m. cert. · d. cert.
Likenesses photograph, 1987, repro. in Greenhalf, *Salt and Silver*, 83 · D. Hockney, portrait, 1996, Salts Mill, Bradford, West Yorkshire · Asadour Guzelian, photograph, repro. in *The Guardian* · D. Hockney, drawings, repro. in D. Hockney, *Some drawings of family, friends, and best friends, 1993–4* (1994) · photograph, repro. in Greenhalf, *Salt and Silver*, 71 · photograph, repro. in *The Independent*

Silverman, (Samuel) Sydney (1895–1968), politician and penal reformer, was born at 33 Elizabeth Street, Liverpool, on 8 October 1895. He was the second of four children, only two of whom survived to maturity, of Myer Silverman, general draper, and his wife, Blanche Stern. Little is known about his mother, except that she came from a long-established Jewish family in Manchester.

The Silvermans were poor, but their poverty was not that of nineteenth-century industrial labour, for Myer Silverman was a pedlar or, more properly, a chapman, who lived as a small-time entrepreneur among his labouring fellows. He was never materially successful, probably because his sympathy for his impoverished customers did not allow him to enrich himself at their expense. His children therefore had to make their own way. Sydney obtained a scholarship to the Liverpool Institute, a prestigious grammar school, and, from there, two further scholarships, one to the University of Liverpool and the other to Oxford. With characteristic realism he saw that his family could not afford the expense of an Oxford scholarship; he took up the Liverpool offer and began his studies in English literature.

Conscientious objector and Liverpool solicitor This career was interrupted by the Military Service Act of 1916 which introduced conscription. Silverman, now twenty-one, registered as a conscientious objector. His pacifist beliefs were influenced to some degree by Bertrand Russell but he had his own developing vision of the brotherhood of man, a vision which survived repeated sentences of imprisonment, for his pacifist position was absolute. He rejected completely the arbitrament of war and could not accept any of the alternatives to military service which would rescue him from imprisonment. Serving sentences in gaols as far apart as Preston and Wormwood Scrubs, he learnt at first hand of the need for penal reform.

When the war was over Silverman returned to university and completed his degree. Immediately after the war,

(Samuel) Sydney Silverman (1895–1968), by Bassano, 1947

however, jobs in England were hard to come by, especially for one who had refused military service. He applied successfully for a teaching post at the University of Helsinki, and went there in 1921. It was the typical academic slavery of early twentieth-century Europe: a six-month semester paid at a pittance, followed by six months unpaid leave. Silverman enjoyed the work sufficiently to stay for four years, learning something during this time of the wider world of European politics for which his early training in Liverpool had not prepared him.

Returning to England in 1925, Silverman registered at Liverpool University for a degree in law. This he completed with distinction in two years and found himself, in 1927, a qualified lawyer who could not pay the registration fee (a sizeable amount at that time) that would allow him to practise as a solicitor. He was persuasive enough, however, to obtain a loan of £100 from a hard-headed bank manager. The registration fee was paid and a long and successful career as a solicitor began. His clients were mostly the poor neighbours of his childhood, whom he defended and supported in landlord–tenant disputes, workmen's compensation claims, and criminal cases. In these early years he learnt how much skilled help and support was needed by the labouring poor in their confrontations with the law. His hard work, professional skill, and sympathy for his clients so enlarged his practice that he was joined by like-minded lawyers and his firm became one of the best-known in Liverpool. In later years, when he entered the House of Commons, he opened an office in London and did much of his own work there.

Labour MP for Nelson The imprisoned pacifist and the poor man's lawyer could not, however, remain content with occasionally rectifying individual injustices by legal processes. Political solutions had to be found to the poverty and discrimination which Silverman had suffered and had seen others suffer throughout his early manhood. He threw himself into local politics and became a city councillor in 1932. In 1933 he married Nancy, daughter of L. Rubinstein, whose family had fled to Liverpool from the Russian pogroms in the late nineteenth century. She was an accomplished musician as her father had been before her. They had three sons.

Silverman's skill as a speaker and in political manipulation earned him a considerable reputation throughout the industrial north and the Labour Party nominated him for the constituency of Nelson and Colne. He was elected to parliament in 1935 and retained the seat until his death in 1968.

At the time of Silverman's election, the Labour Party was committed to the principle that elected members were there to further the interests of the party in the House of Commons. That meant that every Labour member must put general issues concerning the whole country and the whole party before constituency matters. This political stance was particularly suited to Silverman. He became a true House of Commons man, throwing himself into its business and procedures with typical enthusiasm. None the less his constituents were not allowed to suffer. Besides dealing conscientiously with their problems, he wrote constantly for the *Gazette*, the Labour Party weekly of the Nelson area. In this he explained what he was trying to do and described the major issues which were taking up parliamentary time. He was well aware, however, that justice and injustice in Britain and Europe, and matters concerning foreign policy and defence expenditure, could not be dealt with in Nelson but had to be determined in parliament. His constituents agreed with him and never withdrew their support.

From Silverman's entry into the House of Commons until the slow abandonment of peace in 1938–9 no issues troubled his conscience. The activities of Mosley and attacks on Jews in London and elsewhere were matters for action and protest rather than for a re-examination of his principles. Nevertheless, the outbreak of war presented him with a difficult choice. As a pacifist earlier imprisoned for rejecting force as an instrument of policy, he was bound to oppose any moves that would make war inevitable. However, it was claimed that destruction of the Jews in Europe could be ended only by armed intervention. Silverman accepted this argument and, with many protests about how the war was being fought, did not insist. At the same time he took strong exception to the Churchillian policy of 'unconditional surrender', arguing that carefully drafted peace aims would end the war more quickly. In this, as in many other matters at this time, he was in a minority.

Palestine and the Soviet Union When the Labour Party came into office in 1945 there were many who expected that Silverman's long service and parliamentary skill would be rewarded by a government post. This never happened, and Silverman's later career of opposition to the party establishment ensured that he would remain a back-bencher. Silverman approved of open access to Palestine for all refugee and stateless Jews who wished to go there. His parliamentary record does not show him to be a passionate Zionist; his aim was simply to secure for each surviving Jew of Europe the settlement and lifestyle which he most desired, whether in Palestine or Colombia. His advocacy derived its urgency not only from the fact that he himself was an Orthodox, though not a practising, Jew, but also because he had been chairman of the British section of the World Jewish Congress and had learnt through this organization of the sufferings of his race in Europe. In addition he visited Buchenwald immediately after it was relieved, as a member of an all-party delegation of members of parliament invited there by Eisenhower. Silverman's memory of what he saw never left him.

Opposition to the government's policy in Palestine and to the treatment of Jewish refugees in general did not endear Silverman to the foreign secretary, Ernest Bevin. Moreover, Silverman fiercely criticized the foreign secretary's handling of relations with the Soviet Union, for he claimed that Bevin negotiated with Russia as if it were the Communist Party which, in Britain, was both feared and despised; instead he thought that the Soviet Union embodied a great people whose rights and dignity should be respected.

Silverman's concern with foreign policy and defence arose from his fundamental objection to the use of force. This belief had yielded second place to the need for Jews to survive during the war. When the war was over he campaigned strongly against the use of any kind of nuclear weapons and became a vigorous member of the Campaign for Nuclear Disarmament. Gaitskell's decision to oppose the rejection by the Labour Party conference of a nuclear defence policy made Silverman angry. Later Silverman was expelled from the parliamentary party (along with Michael Foot and three others) for refusing to accept the convention that the Labour Party in opposition did not vote against the defence estimates.

Campaign against capital punishment All these concerns—defence, Palestine, and the attitude to the Soviet Union—suggest that Silverman's interests were international. Indeed they were, but he will be remembered principally for his long campaign for the abolition of the death penalty. In 1948 the Labour government introduced a criminal justice bill, backed by many reformers, except that it contained no provision about the death penalty. Silverman introduced a clause which provided for a five-year suspension of the penalty but the Lords threw this out. The government tried again and suggested that certain types of murder should be excluded from the mandatory death sentence. The House of Lords rejected this amendment too. To get other parts of the bill enacted, the capital punishment provisions were dropped, but the abolitionists within the house regrouped under Silverman's leadership.

Thereafter Silverman was the acknowledged parliamentary protagonist of abolition, although outside the house and in the newly founded Campaign for the Abolition of the Death Penalty he had neither the reputation nor the force of the other determined reformers, Sir Victor Gollancz and Arthur Koestler. But the battle had to be fought and won in the House of Commons. Silverman, at a second attempt, introduced a private member's bill for abolition in 1956. After obtaining a second reading in the House of Commons, it was defeated in the Lords. Feeling outside the house ran so high that the home secretary, R. A. Butler, introduced and negotiated through both houses a compromise bill which distinguished between capital and non-capital murder. The act's provisions gave rise to many difficulties and anomalies, but there was no opportunity for changing the law until the Labour Party took office in 1964. Silverman had been returned to parliament with an increased majority (in a fierce contest where one of the candidates, although professedly Labour, made his platform the return of capital punishment for all murder). In the light of this resounding success Silverman was given the signal honour of having his proposed private member's bill for abolition of the death penalty referred to in the queen's speech.

In a powerful address, delivered without notes, Silverman moved the second reading of his new bill. There was now no doubt about the result in the House of Commons and, in due course, the bill went to the Lords, which had rejected all previous attempts to abolish capital punishment. But the Campaign for the Abolition of the Death Penalty had done its work well and the bill went through. This was the climax of Silverman's parliamentary career, for he died before the expiry of the five years' suspension period.

Silverman had a passion for justice and equality that kept him well to the left of his party, so that he did not commend himself to the establishment. Besides, he was not good at collective action; most of his battles he fought alone, for he enjoyed twisting the tails of his antagonists and might have been denied this enjoyment if he had worked with others. Crossman commented that Silverman was 'really magnificent—the Lion of Juda' in opposing Bevin on Israel in 1945–8, but that he was 'vain, difficult and uncooperative. No one could get him to work in any kind of a group. All his life he remained an individualist back-bencher' (Crossman, 2.675). Nevertheless his contribution to the thinking of his party, to the progress of penal reform, and to the welfare of his fellow Jews remains unquestioned. To his constituents and to his agent he was unfailing in his service. They responded with a warm personal devotion to him. He wrote, as he spoke, easily and well, contributing articles to many journals. He produced pamphlets to promote the several campaigns in which he was involved and published one book (with Reginald Paget) which described three cases where the death penalty seemed to have been unjustly imposed (*Hanged, and Innocent?*, 1953). Silverman died in hospital in Hampstead on 9 February 1968. A bronze bust by Sam Tonkiss is in Silverman Hall, the Labour Party headquarters in Nelson. A plantation of trees, donated by the World Jewish Congress, grows on a slope outside Jerusalem.

SARAH McCABE, rev.

Sources *The Times* (10 Feb 1968) · E. Hughes, *Sydney Silverman: parliamentary rebel* (1969) · E. O. Tuttle, *The crusade against capital punishment in Great Britain* (1961) · private information (2004) · b. cert. · R. H. S. Crossman, *The diaries of a cabinet minister*, 2 (1976) · CGPLA Eng. & Wales (1968)
Likenesses Bassano, photograph, 1947, NPG [*see illus.*] · Daily Herald, photograph, NPG · S. Tonkiss, bronze bust, Silverman Hall, Nelson, Lancashire
Wealth at death £63,548: administration, 15 March 1968, CGPLA Eng. & Wales

Silvester, Eusebius (*bap.* **1714**, *d.* in or after **1759**), lawyer and projector, was baptized at Tamworth, Staffordshire, on 19 January 1714, the first of the eight children of Nicholas Silvester (1680–1745), gentleman, and his wife, Susanna, daughter of Euseby Dormer and his wife, Mary (*née* Fenwick). Feckless, self-pitying, and importunate, he owes his reputation to his correspondence of the 1750s with the novelist Samuel Richardson, which Richardson closed by threatening to circulate or publish as 'a *Warning Piece* to Posterity' (Forster MSS, XV, 1, fol. 58).

Early in the correspondence Silvester wrote that his life had been 'a confused Scene of Advers Perplexitys almost from my Cradle', owing first to the worldly failure of a father

> defeated by those very Qualitys which ought rather to have merited success; an open frankness and generosity of Heart, which led him, to place too much Confidence in those, who by an abuse of it, were the occasion of a series of Misfortunes which at length … weighed him down & deprived him of his life! (Forster MSS, XIV, 4, fol. 4)

The misfortunes, and the speculative and litigious temperament that drew them on, are copiously documented in chancery records concerning Nicholas Silvester. He shared with his son ambitious theories of land improvement, and ran into financial difficulties following his lease from Lord Weymouth in 1714 of property in Bangley Park, Staffordshire, and his later lease from Ralph Floyer of 'many hundreds of acres of waste and barren land' in Hints, Staffordshire, which he claimed to have 'improved at vast expense' (PRO, C 11/2053/18). He first became mired in chancery proceedings in 1724 over a disputed legacy, and subsequent family wrangles, together with actions for arrears and debts arising from failed agricultural projects, involved him in protracted and ruinous litigation for the next two decades.

In his late teens Eusebius Silvester served for two and a half years as articled clerk to his uncle Thomas Harris of Dorking, but left about 1734, probably in connection with the family quarrels. He later served for two and a half years as clerk to George Garnett of Took's Court, Holborn, the address he gave when swearing an affidavit in May 1738 to secure his recognition as a qualified attorney. He duly appears in the rolls of the common bench attorneys, which give his place of residence as Middlesex until, in Michaelmas 1745, the addition 'now Warwick' (where he remained) appears against his name.

In 1754 Silvester used a letter praising *Sir Charles Grandison* to initiate his correspondence with Richardson, which ended acrimoniously in 1759 after two meetings and at least forty-five letters. At the outset he made much of his refusal to conform to professional type, lamenting that his honesty gave him 'no great reason to believe, that I … ever shall attain to any great Eminence in my Profession', and made fellow attorneys think him 'a Dastardly Unnatural Brother' (Forster MSS, XIV, 4, fol. 5). Though Richardson later rebuked Silvester for his 'parading Epistles' (ibid., XV, 1, fol. 58), he seems to have been favourably impressed, and in November 1755 was still applauding 'that good Heart which so visibly dictates to y^r Pen' (ibid., XIV, 4, fol. 8). At this point he seems to have complied with Silvester's request that he print 'a manuscript containing some Observations on Agriculture' (ibid., fol. 7), now untraced, but outlining ideas which, if ministerially adopted, would make his fortune: a later note by Richardson records that the project 'was to obtain Grants to himself of thousands of Acres … to be cultivated according to a Method invented by himself, and Father, he being a great Schemer in Agriculture' (ibid., fol. 26). At the same time Richardson advanced the first of two loans of £25 in response to Silvester's worry that 'just in the very Crisis & turn of my Fortune, I sho'd, after so many Years Painful Struggles, be dashed down & sunk again … for want of that small Assistance' (ibid., fol. 11). It was only when repayment failed to materialize that Richardson's opinion began to change. Late in 1756 he frostily declined to print a further piece 'on a Popular Subject now under the Consideration of our Legislators' (ibid., XV, 1, fol. 38), and relations subsequently collapsed. Understandably, though perhaps unjustly, Richardson ended by thinking Silvester a cynical confidence-trickster, berating him for 'the Repetition of such gross Pretensions to *Integrity* of *Heart*, as you abounded with in every Letter, and continue thro' *Detection*' (ibid., fol. 58).

Undaunted by Richardson's refusal to touch the second piece, Silvester succeeded in publishing it (with a dedication dated 12 December 1757 to Francis Greville, Earl Brooke, of Warwick Castle) as *The causes of the present high price of corn and grain, and a state of the abuses and impositions practised … by the millers or meal-men*. A year later, in similar fraud-busting vein, he submitted a memorial to the Treasury commissioners, detailing how tanners were evading the duty on hides, and hoping to 'meet with Your Lordships Favour and Encouragement' (BL, Add. MS 32886, fol. 92). Thereafter he fades from the record, and his last surviving correspondence with Richardson is dated August 1759.

THOMAS KEYMER

Sources V&A NAL, Forster Library · T. C. D. Eaves and B. D. Kimpel, *Samuel Richardson: a biography* (1971) · E. W. L. Keymer, 'Chancery tales', *PROPhile*, 10/1 (April 1999), 22–4 · T. Keymer, *Richardson's 'Clarissa' and the eighteenth-century reader* (1992) · E. Silvester, 'Memorial', BM, Newcastle papers, vol. 201, Add. MS 32886, fol. 92 · common bench attorneys roll, Michaelmas 1745, PRO, CP 11/12 · affidavit by Eusebius Silvester, May 1738, PRO, CP 5/5/3 · IGI · ESTC · Floyer v. Silvester, 1732, PRO, C 11/2053/18
Archives BL, Newcastle papers, vol. 201, Add. MS 32886, fol. 92 · V&A, Forster MSS, Richardson corresp.

Silvester, Sir John, first baronet (1745–1822), barrister and judge, was born in London on 7 September 1745, the son of Sir John Baptist Silvester (d. 1789) of St Peter's, Cornhill, London, a doctor of medicine, and Alathea Catherine D'Aulnis, daughter of Colonel D'Aulnis of the Dutch service. Silvester was educated at the Merchant Taylors' School and from 1764 St John's College, Oxford; he took the degree of BCL in 1771 and was created DCL in 1818. Admitted to the Middle Temple on 19 April 1766, he was called to the bar on 8 February 1771. He was elected FRS in 1780 and FSA in 1804.

As a barrister Silvester was unsuccessful in Westminster Hall, but he appeared regularly at the Old Bailey and in the City of London's customary courts where, by virtue of his purchase of a City common pleadership in 1774, he enjoyed with three other pleaders monopoly of practice in the lord mayor's and sheriffs' courts. During the Gordon riots of 1780 Silvester, a 'loyal subject' who would 'support the constitution of the country' (Silvester MS 7067), was made a justice of the peace for Middlesex, and on 23 April 1799 he was appointed deputy lieutenant of that county.

Precisely when Silvester began to practise regularly in London's criminal courts is unclear. A criminal bar was only beginning to emerge in London in the 1780s and he was among its first members. By the early 1780s he had established a lead in business at the Old Bailey, although his career there was eclipsed by the arrival of William Garrow in 1783. Somewhat unusually, Silvester appeared most frequently for the prosecution. His reputation as a barrister was unenviable: one contemporary described him as 'vulgar and ineloquent' and commented 'The Prisoners Calendar he distinguishes by the elegant and humane appellation of a Bill of Fare. He is said to have made much money by his practice; if so, he has derived it from the groans of the gallows' (City Biography, 116–17).

In 1790 Silvester was elected common serjeant of London and he became recorder in 1803 (he was made a bencher of the Middle Temple in the same year). On 27 December 1814 he was created a baronet (described as of Yardley House, Chingford, Essex); the Morning Chronicle noted that his politics had made him a favourite at court and that he 'presented the solitary instance of the Baronetage having been conferred on a possessor of the office of Recorder' (Morning Chronicle, 1 April 1822).

'Black Jack' Silvester quickly earned a reputation for severity as a judge. He clearly favoured law and order over the rights of individuals, and he is on record as opposing any amelioration of England's 'bloody code', a system of criminal justice which relied on the terror of capital punishment to deter criminals. Among the papers he left are notebooks recording details of London's criminal underworld and four weighty volumes of indictment precedents. His obituary in the Gentleman's Magazine praised him for discharging his judicial duties 'in a faithful, zealous, and conscientious manner' (GM, 371), but others held different opinions. Silvester was accused of demanding sexual favours from a woman who approached him to appeal for his assistance in obtaining a pardon for her husband and he was widely condemned for his severe summing up in the trial of Eliza Fenning, a servant-girl hanged for the attempted murder of her master and his family who was popularly believed to be innocent. A restrained assessment of Silvester's career indicated that his 'public character' was not 'peculiarly calculated to inspire respect for the judicial office' (Morning Chronicle, 1 April 1822).

Silvester was married twice: firstly, on 8 October 1772, to Susanne Hoissend (d. 1785), widow of Daniel Hoissend; and secondly, on 11 December 1793, to Harriet Speed (d. 1843), daughter of the Revd Owen Davies and widow of the Revd John Mylles Speed, vicar of Eling in Hampshire. There were no children from either marriage. Silvester died in his sleep at his home in Bloomsbury Square, London, on 30 March and was buried at Chingford church on 6 April 1822. The baronetcy passed to his nephew Sir Philip Carteret *Silvester.   ALLYSON N. MAY

Sources GM, 1st ser., 92/1 (1822), 370–71 • The Times (1 April 1822) • The Times (8 April 1822) • GL, Silvester MSS, MS 7067 • Browne's General Law List (1779–97) • New Law List (1798–1802) • Clarke's New Law List (1803–22) • The whole proceedings on the king's commission of the peace (1783–90) [Old Bailey sessions papers] • City biography: containing anecdotes and memoirs of … the aldermen and other conspicuous personages of the corporation and City of London, 2nd edn (1800), 116–17 • W. Jerdan, The autobiography of William Jerdan: with his literary, political, and social reminiscences and correspondence during the last fifty years, 4 vols. (1852–3), vol. 1, p. 131 • Foster, Alum. Oxon. • J. Silvester, 'Notebooks relating to crime in London, 1800–16', BL, Add. MS 47466, Egerton MS 3710 • V. A. C. Gatrell, The hanging tree: execution and the English people, 1770–1868 (1994)

Archives BL, notebooks relating to crime in London, Add. MS 47466; Egerton MS 3710 • GL, MSS relating to family history

Likenesses T. Blood, engraving (after S. Drummond), repro. in London Review (Nov 1815), 386 • Sievier, plaster bust, City of London Corporation

Silvester, Sir Philip Carteret, second baronet (1777–1828), naval officer, was the son of Rear-Admiral Philip *Carteret (1733–1796), the circumnavigator, and his wife, Marie Rachel (d. in or after 1797), daughter of Sir John Baptist Silvester (d. 1789), born in France but educated in the Netherlands, and physician to the British army in the Low Countries, under the duke of Cumberland, during the War of the Austrian Succession (1740–48). His mother's brother, whose title and name he eventually inherited, was Sir John *Silvester, first baronet (1745–1822).

Philip Carteret entered the navy in 1792 under the care of his father's old lieutenant, Captain Erasmus Gower, on the Lion, in which he went out to China, and returned in 1794. He was then with Gower in the Triumph (74 guns) and was slightly wounded in the partial engagement with the French fleet on 17 June 1795. On 8 October of that year he was promoted lieutenant of the frigate Impérieuse; he afterwards served in the Greyhound, Britannia, and Cambrian in the English Channel and on the coast of France; and on 29 April 1802 he was promoted commander of the sloop Bonne Citoyenne in the Mediterranean. She was paid off in 1803, and the following year he was appointed to the brig Scorpion (18 guns), in which he served in the North Sea, and on 11 April 1805 captured a Dutch vessel bound for the West Indies with a cargo of arms and military stores. In

December 1805 he was sent out to the West Indies, where, during the greater part of 1806, he watched and sent intelligence of the French squadron under Willaumez, so that it was not until his return to England in spring 1807 that he received his commission as post captain, dated 22 January 1806.

In 1809 Carteret served as a volunteer on the *Superb*, flagship of Sir Richard Goodwin Keats, in the expedition to the Scheldt, where his conduct, especially in covering the evacuation of Walcheren, was highly commended by Sir Richard John Strachan, the commander-in-chief, and Commodore Owen, in actual command of the operations. In summer 1811 Carteret was appointed to the frigate *Naiad* (46 guns), in which on 20 September he was off Boulogne when a division of the French flotilla got under way and stood along the coast under the eyes of Napoleon, who on the next day witnessed a detachment of this division cut off, brought to action, and captured by the *Naiad* with three gun-brigs in company. The rest of the division escaped under the guns of the batteries which lined the coast.

Towards the end of 1812 Carteret was moved into the frigate *Pomone* (46 guns), employed on the coast of France and the Lisbon station. On 21 October 1813, in hazy weather in the Bay of Biscay, she fell in with a French frigate under jury masts, much disabled by a recent gale, and at the same time sighted another large ship which was supposed to be also a frigate. Carteret went to engage her, but found she was a Portuguese East Indiaman. Meanwhile the disabled French frigate had escaped, only to be captured, after very feeble resistance, by the *Andromache* two days later. At Lisbon it was reported that the *Pomone* had fled from the frigate, and Carteret applied for a court martial, which was held, on his return to Plymouth, on 31 December. He was acquitted of all blame and continued in command of the *Pomone* until the end of the war. On 4 June 1815 he was made a CB and about the same time was appointed to the *Désirée* (36 guns), from which in October he was moved to the *Active* (38 guns). In her he served two years on the Jamaica station. After returning in autumn 1817 he had no further employment. In January 1822 he took the name of Silvester in addition to Carteret, and on the death of his uncle, Sir John Silvester, without issue, on 30 March 1822, he succeeded to the baronetcy, by a special clause in the patent. He died, unmarried, of 'apoplexy', at Leamington, Warwickshire, on 24 August 1828, when the title became extinct; he was interred at the parish church at Leamington.

J. K. LAUGHTON, *rev.* ANDREW LAMBERT

Sources D. Syrett and R. L. DiNardo, *The commissioned sea officers of the Royal Navy, 1660–1815*, rev. edn, Occasional Publications of the Navy RS, 1 (1994) • *GM*, 1st ser., 98/2 (1828), 273 • J. Marshall, *Royal naval biography*, suppl. 1 (1827), 66 • J. J. Colledge, *Ships of the Royal Navy: an historical index*, 1 (1969)
Archives Boston PL, letter-book while in HMS *Active* • Mitchell L., NSW, corresp. and papers, incl. logbooks • NMM, corresp., logbooks, and papers

Silvester, Tipping (1700–1768), Church of England clergyman and religious writer, was born in the parish of St Mary Woolnoth, London, the son of John Silvester, linen draper of that parish, and Grace (*d.* 1705), daughter of George Tipping, draper, who was descended from the Tipping family of Shabbington in Buckinghamshire. He matriculated from Pembroke College, Oxford, on 13 July 1717, and graduated BA in 1721 and MA in 1724. He was elected a fellow of his college and, having taken holy orders, he was presented by Prudence Tipping, on 21 March 1737, to the vicarage of Shabbington. There he lived until his death.

Having published *Original Poems and Translations* (1733) Silvester confined himself to theological debates. His *Critical Dissertation on Titus iii.10, 11* refuted the heretical arguments of James Foster; this provoked a burlesque reply from Joseph Danvers, entitled *Tipping Tipt Justice* ([1735]), in which Danvers suggested that Silvester's defence of the Church of England was largely self-interest. Silvester replied in *The Evidence of the Resurrection* (1744). Silvester also published several sermons on various subjects and edited Thomas Cockman's *Select Theological Discourses* (1750). He died at Shabbington in 1768.

E. I. CARLYLE, *rev.* EMMA MAJOR

Sources Foster, *Alum. Oxon.* • J. Danvers, *Tipping tipt justice* [1735] • *ESTC* • J. M. S. Brooke and A. W. C. Hallen, eds., *The transcript of the registers of … St Mary Woolnoth and St Mary Woolnoth Haw … 1538 to 1760* (1886) • will, PRO, PROB 11/948, fols. 328–9 • G. Lipscomb, *The history and antiquities of the county of Buckingham*, 4 vols. (1831–47), vol. 1, pp. 450, 453
Wealth at death £1100; plus mortgages, shares, and land of unspecified value: will, PRO, PROB 11/948, sig. 183

Silvester, Victor Marlborough (1900–1978), ballroom dancer and bandleader, was born on 25 February 1900 at the vicarage of St John's Church, Wembley, the second of six children and younger son of the Revd John William Potts Silvester and his wife, Katherine (*née* Hudson). His first name was given to celebrate news of a victory in the Second South African War, his second to honour the bishop of Marlborough. His father, stern in religion, did not indulge his children, but his mother was more approachable. Silvester disliked schooling, running away first from Ardingly College, Sussex, then St John's School, Leatherhead, and, in November 1914, from John Lyon's School, Harrow, to become an under age First World War recruit. His musical education was obtained from a Prussian piano teacher, Fräulein Schmidt, and harmony lessons at Trinity College, London. He spent six months at the front near Arras, France, in 1917 but, his true age discovered, was transferred to the 1st British ambulance unit in Italy. He was wounded and gained the Italian bronze medal for military valour for his part in the evacuation of San Gabriele. He was at Worcester College, Oxford, in 1918/19 but, having acquired a commission just as the war ended, he was offered a place at the Royal Military College, Sandhurst.

At a tea dance in Harrods' Georgian Restaurant the organizer, Belle Harding, offered Silvester work 'partnering unattached ladies' at her headquarters, the Empress Rooms (Royal Palace Hotel, Kensington). After two weeks, during which he received tuition, he joined her team of

Victor Marlborough Silvester (1900–1978), by unknown photographer

instructors. He then left for Sandhurst, in September 1919, but returned to Harding's employment three weeks later. The next February he began studying entomology at Imperial College, London, but again returned to the Empress Rooms, now owned by the caterer J. Lyons. There, in 1922, he met Dorothy Francis Newton (1896/7–1981), then in the chorus of a musical at the London Palladium; they married on 17 December 1922. The same month he and Phyllis Clarke won the world ballroom dancing championship at Queen's Hall, London. Silvester's early style was modelled on contemporary ballroom dancers but he began inventing new figures, such as a clockwise turn in the waltz and double pivot in the one-step. Dorothy became his partner after Phyllis's marriage in 1923, and they opened their first dancing school that year at Rector's Club, near Goodge Street Station. Their only child, Victor Newton Silvester [see below], was born in February 1924.

In 1924 Silvester helped the newly formed ballroom branch of the Imperial Society of Teachers of Dancing to devise a procedural code for ballroom dancing, as ballet-derived technique gave way to movement from the hip, stepping out at the same time. A syllabus was produced for the examination of teachers, standardizing an 'English style'. He later chaired the society (1945) and became its first life president in the 1960s. He overworked himself during the Charleston craze of 1926, and an abscess on the lung put him out of action for most of 1927. However, he conceived the idea of *Modern Ballroom Dancing* (1927), a book offering a complete course of lessons. It sold 100,000 copies within the year, and by 1990 sales had reached 600,000. Later books included *Theory and Technique of Ballroom Dancing* (1932), *Sequence Dancing* (1950), and his autobiography, *Dancing is my Life* (1958).

In the early thirties few records were suitable for dancing: bands chose a tempo they thought appropriate for the tune, not the dance, or treated tempo too flexibly. Silvester persuaded Parlophone to release some piano records in 'strict tempo', a term he made his own. Their success encouraged him to form his Ballroom Orchestra in 1935, a small band comprising saxophone doubling clarinet, bass, drums and, unusually, two pianos, one playing melodically while the other provided what he called 'lemonade'—high trickling notes between chords. The first two records sold 31,000, and the first to be released contained 'You're Dancing on my Heart' (by Al Bryan and George M. Meyer), which became Silvester's theme tune. He later put together a second orchestra called Silver Strings for Latin American dances and Viennese waltzes, and in 1943–4 made records with a jive band, a response to American swing and the presence of GIs in the UK.

Silvester's first radio broadcasts were in 1937. His BBC Dancing Club began in 1941 during the Second World War (and lasted until 1958) to provide dancing lessons over the air to service men and women overseas; it popularized his catch-phrase 'slow, slow, quick quick slow'. 1948 saw the start of Silvester's request programme for the BBC World Service (which ran until 1975) and the Television Dancing Club which survived until 1964. Collaborating with the Rank Organisation in 1957, he opened the first of a chain of twenty-three dance studios. The next year he featured in the royal command performance. As late as 1970 he began a new association with Pye Records, though his son took over his orchestra in 1971. His many awards included appointment as OBE for services to ballroom dancing (1961), Carl-Alan awards for the same reason (1954–6 and, posthumously, 1978), and a BBC golden microphone in recognition of forty years of broadcasting (1977). In 1972 he was made president of the Lord's Taverners. He was tall and slim with auburn hair, keen on physical fitness, a football enthusiast (supporting Chelsea), and good humoured. He died of a heart attack on 14 August 1978 after swimming at Aiguebelle, near Le Lavandon, in the south of France. With record sales of more than 75 million, he outsold every other dance orchestra in the world.

Silvester's son, **Victor Newton Silvester** [*known as* Victor Silvester junior] (1924–1999), bandleader, was born on 17 February 1924 and educated at Orley Farm preparatory school, near Harrow, and Berkhamsted School, Hertfordshire. He learned to play the clarinet at an early age, and was influenced by Artie Shaw and Benny Goodman. After a brief spell as a BBC engineer he was commissioned in 1942 in the Hampshire regiment. He lost the sight of his left eye in a training exercise. When recovered he joined the British forces radio network, and by the end of his army service in 1947 he was second in command of the network's unit in northern Italy. He then joined his father's business, initially as bookings manager, but with an increasing role both administrative and musical. He replaced his father as bandleader occasionally from 1956 and formally from 1971. Under his leadership the Victor Silvester Orchestra broadened its repertory and recorded albums with, among others, Max Bygraves and Edmundo Ros. Silvester was married three times, and had a son and a daughter. His last appearance was at Pontins in Pakefield, Suffolk, in August 1998. He died of lung cancer on 15 October 1999, survived by his son and daughter.

DEREK B. SCOTT

Sources V. Silvester, *Dancing is my life: an autobiography* (1958) · *DNB* · *The Guardian* (15 Aug 1978) · *The Times* (15 Aug 1978) · P. Gammond, *The Oxford companion to popular music* (1991); repr. with corrections (1993), 529–30 · C. Larkin, ed., *The Guinness encyclopedia of popular music*, 4 vols. (1992), 3786–7 · V. Silvester, *Modern ballroom dancing* (1927); rev. edn (1974) · m. cert. · *CGPLA Eng. & Wales* (1978) · *Daily Telegraph* (20 Oct 1999)
Archives FILM BFI NFTVA, documentary footage · BFI NFTVA, performance footage | SOUND BL NSA, oral history interview · BL NSA, performance recordings
Likenesses photograph, NPG [*see illus.*]
Wealth at death £93,957: probate, 18 Dec 1978, *CGPLA Eng. & Wales* · under £200,000—Victor Newton Silvester: probate, 23 Feb 2000, *CGPLA Eng. & Wal.*

Silvester, Victor Newton [Victor Sylvester junior] (1924–1999). *See under* Silvester, Victor Marlborough (1900–1978).

Silvey, Robert John Everett (1905–1981), developer of broadcasting audience research, was born on 19 June 1905 at 38 Hammelton Road, Bromley, Kent, the son of Robert Silvey (1865–1915), Baptist minister, and his wife, Maud Caroline Everett (1874–1924). He completed his education at Taunton School from 1917 to 1921 and then spent six years in the offices of the Booth Steamship Company Ltd in Liverpool. During this period he studied accountancy but he moved on to be a statistician at the London press exchange from 1929 to 1936. It was in this post that he first became involved in research by questioning samples of the general public.

On 6 August 1931 Silvey married Elspeth Mary Grant (1905–1968), daughter of a schoolmaster, Mathew George Grant, at the Friends' meeting-house, Jordans, Buckinghamshire. He and Elspeth were staunch members of the Society of Friends all their lives, becoming well-loved members of the Quaker community in Welwyn Garden City, where they lived for more than thirty years. There were three children from the marriage.

When, after much anguished debate, the BBC decided that it should embark on the systematic study of the listening audience, Silvey was appointed listener research officer, taking up the post on 1 October 1936. He later recorded in his book *Who's Listening?: The Story of BBC Audience Research* (1974) that he was never given any formal terms of reference for the job:

> Curiously, perhaps, this role was never specifically defined by my superiors … As I saw it, it would be for audience research to gather such information about the public as was at once relevant to the needs of the BBC and susceptible of study by the methods of social research … Obviously the responsibility for defining relevance was crucial. This too was never precisely spelled out. (p. 33)

After some preliminary trials, Silvey devised two research instruments that proved practical, robust, and reliable. They were 'the continuous survey of listening' (extended at the end of 1951 to include viewing) to provide estimates of audience size for individual programmes, and 'panels' of listeners and viewers who were sent batches of questionnaires weekly to obtain their opinions of selected programmes. The survey, which involved interviewing a representative sample of people about their listening and viewing 'yesterday' ran, day-in day-out, from December 1939 until long after his retirement, with no more than a short break when the department—as it had then become—was moved from war-torn London to Bristol. The panels came into operation a few years after the daily survey, and proved equally long-lasting.

No less demanding a task than setting up his research tools was gaining acceptance for the results within the corporation, and in this, too, Silvey triumphed. Fears of 'the tyranny of the ratings' were stilled, doubts about their accuracy put to rest, and replaced by a 'how did we ever manage without it?' mentality. By 1948 he began to feel that the time had come for him to move on. However, he had no sooner tendered his resignation from the BBC to take up a directorship of the London press exchange when an eye infection resulted in blindness in one eye and limited vision in the other. The BBC generously offered to reinstate him, and he resumed his duties with the aid of a large magnifying glass and the Braille edition of *Radio Times*. Gradually the sight in his good eye improved and he dispensed with the magnifying glass.

When independent television arrived and adopted a totally different method of measuring television audiences, the two systems inevitably produced what appeared to be divergent results, which led to sporadic bouts of press stories about who was right. In fact, the major reason for the apparent differences was that they were, in effect, measuring different things. This point was made abundantly clear by Silvey in his BBC lunchtime lecture *The Measurement of Audiences* (published in 1966), but regrettably it did not put the argument to rest; the discrepancies made too good a story. Incidentally, though he was always known as Robert, never Bob, formality was utterly foreign to his nature. He was unfailingly understanding and courteous. Only two things really irritated him: he could never abide the pronunciation of 'research' as 're-search', and he heartily disliked the idea of publishing 'top twenty' lists of audiences, which, as he argued in his BBC lecture, encouraged 'an entirely fallacious' impression of the real significance of audience size.

As research into the mass media became more widely practised academically, Silvey recognized that the activities of his department had to be expanded. From the early fifties onwards, special research projects were mounted to explore the needs of the audience and the effectiveness of broadcasting in meeting those needs. This side of the department's work furnished material for an earlier BBC lunchtime lecture, *Reflections on the Impact of Broadcasting* (1963). His unique contribution to British broadcasting was recognized in 1960 by appointment as an OBE.

After retiring from the BBC in 1968, Silvey participated

actively in voluntary work, first by helping in the adult literacy campaign, then at its height, and later by assisting for many years in the work of Amnesty International. He died of a heart attack on 15 April 1981 at the Queen Elizabeth II Hospital, Welwyn Garden City, and was cremated at Garston, Hertfordshire. B. P. EMMETT

Sources R. J. E. Silvey, *Who's listening? the story of BBC audience research* (1974) · staff files, BBC WAC, L 1/1618 · private information (2004) [private memoir written by Robert Silvey] · *The Times* (23 April 1981) · d. cert.
Archives BBC WAC
Likenesses photograph, repro. in *The Times* (18 April 1968)
Wealth at death £85,168: probate, 30 July 1981, *CGPLA Eng. & Wales*

Silvy, Camille-Léon-Louis (1834–1910), photographer, was born on 18 May 1834 at Nogent-le-Rotrou (Eure-et-Loire), France, the son of Onésipe-Tullius-Émile-Léon Silvy (1799–1889), lawyer and banker, and Marie-Louise Pied. Camille Silvy, as he is usually known, came to prominence as a photographer in 1858–9 when his earliest works—exquisite landscape photographs—were exhibited in Edinburgh, London, and Paris. His *River Scene, France* (also known as *Vallée de l'Huisne*) was taken in his native Nogent-le-Rotrou in the summer of 1858. This celebrated work has been widely exhibited in recent years and in 1992 became the subject of the first monograph devoted entirely to a nineteenth-century photograph. Silvy's artistic training included drawing lessons from Hippolyte de Lalaisse, but his true masters were the photographers Gustave Le Gray and Count Olympe Aguado. His large compositions brought him to the attention of the French imperial court in 1859, but he chose to pursue a career in London. He took a studio at 38 Porchester Terrace, Bayswater, in 1859 and established himself as the master of a new form of portraiture which soon swept the world—the carte-de-visite, or album portrait. This new technique was based on the idea of taking six or eight small portraits, in several different poses, on one glass negative. The sitter could then select from the results. Such portraits were sold cheaply but in large quantities—by the dozen, the score, or the hundred. During the carte-de-visite craze of the early 1860s—which made Silvy famous and wealthy—acquaintances exchanged their likenesses. Celebrity portraiture also blossomed, selling by the hundred thousand: collectors assembled albums of portraits of members of royal families, actors and actresses, politicians, and socialites. Silvy photographed 'the upper ten thousand' in his fashionable studio across from Hyde Park.

Silvy's success lay in his skilful posing of his sitters, who included children and those in equestrian portraits. Each sitter was personally posed by the white-gloved master in his luxuriously appointed premises. He used an elaborate system of natural lighting and a variety of elegantly painted backdrops indicating broad landscapes and distinguished interiors, as well as sumptuous accessories such as bronze sculptures executed by his associate, the sculptor Carlo Marochetti. However, the studio was also a factory with a staff of forty:

One room is found to be full of clerks keeping the books, for at the West End credit must be given; in another scores of employees are printing from the same negative. A large building has been erected for the purpose in the back garden. In a third room are all the chemicals for preparing the plates; and again in another we see a heap of crucibles glittering with silver. All the clippings of the photographs are here reduced by fire, and the silver upon them is thus recovered. One large apartment is appropriated to baths in which the cartes de visite are immersed, and a feminine clatter of tongues directs us to the room in which the portraits are finally corded and packed up. Each portrait taken is posted in a book and numbered consecutively. (A. Wynter, 'Cartes de visite', *Once a Week*, 25 Jan 1862, 137)

These books are now in the National Portrait Gallery, London, and provide an unrivalled insight into the workings of a major nineteenth-century photographic studio. However, Silvy's portraits turn up in albums everywhere—easily identifiable by the elegance of lighting and composition, the well-preserved rich purple of the prints, and his trademark facsimile signature—'C. Silvy'—printed in red on the reverse. He also made exquisite exhibition photographs of the effects of twilight and fog outside his London studio.

A pen portrait of Silvy himself has been left by fellow photographer and journalist Thomas Sutton, who remembered his first meeting with 'this photographic genius':

It was late on a fine afternoon in May, and as I was strolling along the hot pavement towards the celebrated suburban studio a cab dashed past me, pulled up at the gate, and out jumped first a Newfoundland dog dripping with water, and then its tall, powerful, energetic young master, who had been having a bathe also after the last guinea portrait had been taken that day. (*British Journal of Photography*, 6 Oct 1871, 476)

Silvy married (Louise-Marie-Elisabeth-Lucie-) Alice Monnier (1839–1913) on 7 June 1863 at Jeurre; they had a daughter, Louise-Marie-Elisabeth-Angèle Silvy (1866–1934) and a son, Jean-Marie-Léon-Lazare-Oenée Silvy (1868–1905). In 1868 he sold his photographic business and studio. He served in the *garde mobile* during the Franco-Prussian War, was wounded, and was mentioned in dispatches. Silvy spent many of his last years in *maisons de santé* and in 1881 was committed to the asylum in St Maurice, near Paris, where he eventually died, on 2 February 1910. He was buried in the Père Lachaise cemetery in Paris. The Victoria and Albert Museum and the National Portrait Gallery in London have collections of his photographs.

MARK HAWORTH-BOOTH

Sources M. Haworth-Booth, *Camille Silvy: 'River scene, France'* (1992) · A. Hales, 'The album of Camille Silvy', *History of Photography*, 19 (1995), 82 · private information (2004)
Likenesses A. S. Adam-Salomon, albumen print, *c*.1859, Bibliothèque Nationale, Paris, Collection Société Française de Photographie · C.-L.-L. Silvy, self-portrait, photograph, *c*.1859–1866, NPG

Sim, Alastair George Bell (1900–1976), actor and director, was born on 9 October 1900 at Lothian Road, Edinburgh, the youngest in the family of two sons and two daughters of Alexander Sim, tailor and clothier, and his wife, Isabella McIntyre. He was educated at the James Gillespie School at

Alastair George Bell Sim (1900–1976), by Arthur Evans, 1946 [in the film *Green for Danger*]

Edinburgh, which he left at the age of fourteen, taking successive jobs as a delivery boy, a clerk with Gieves the outfitters, and, later, a post in the borough assessor's office. He had ideas, at this time, of becoming an analytical chemist and was studying at Edinburgh University, leaving it to join the Officers' Training Corps. The war ended before he had any opportunity of putting his military training to the test.

Sim's first connection with the stage was from 1925 to 1930 when he was Fulton lecturer in elocution at New College, Edinburgh, a post which he obtained as a result of his work in the Edinburgh Provincial Training Centre. While holding this post he established his own school of drama and speech training. It was in Edinburgh that he first met Naomi Merlith Plaskitt [*see below*]. They married on 2 August 1932 and she was able to help him, professionally and enthusiastically, throughout his subsequent career. They had one daughter, Merlith Naomi.

At the comparatively late age of thirty Sim played his first part on the professional stage, doubling the roles of messenger and sentry in the Savoy Theatre production of *Othello* (1930) in which Paul Robeson and Peggy Ashcroft played the principal parts. This was followed by two years at the Old Vic. He was then out of action for a year with a slipped disc which was put right by an osteopath, and in the mid-1930s his face and personality became increasingly familiar to audiences in a series of film comedies and comedy-thrillers: the Inspector Hornleigh series, Edgar Wallace's *The Squeaker* (1937), *Alf's Button Afloat* (1938), and *Wedding Group* (1936), in which Sim played the Scottish minister and his wife the maid-of-all-work.

A return to the stage and to more serious work was signalled by the last of the pre-war Malvern drama festivals where he took one of the leading parts in *What Say They?* (1940) by O. H. Mavor (James Bridie). It was the beginning of a valuable, though not always peaceful, association as Bridie wrote and Sim both acted in and directed plays of the calibre of *Mr Bolfry* (1943), *Dr Angelus* (1947), *The Forrigan Reel* (1945), and *Mr Gillie* (1950).

It was in *Mr Bolfry* that Sim introduced one of his best-remembered directorial touches. The play dealt with a confrontation between a Scots minister and the devil. As written by Bridie (who, said James Agate, could never construct a satisfactory third act) the devil turned out to be an escaped lunatic. Sim reacted strongly against the feebleness of this. He insisted 'the Devil must be the Devil'. The difficulty was how to get him off the stage at the end of the play and back where he belonged. Sim's solution was a *coup de théâtre*. The devil, off stage at that point, had left his umbrella propped in a corner. The door opened. No one appeared. The umbrella picked itself up and walked slowly out by the far door.

The death of Bridie in 1951 put an end to this fruitful association and in some ways Sim never achieved the same magical alchemy which results when the separate talents of author, actor, and director are fused into a single whole. He gave many notable performances on stage and screen. On the screen he played in *Scrooge* (1951) and (fondest memory for many) *The Happiest Days of your Life* (1950) with Margaret Rutherford. He was also memorable in *The Belles of St Trinian's* (1954) and *Blue Murder at St Trinian's* (1957). On the stage there were William Golding's *The Brass Butterfly* (1958), annual appearances as the sardonic old Etonian Captain Hook in Barrie's *Peter Pan*, and towards the end of his career two notable successes at the Chichester Festival, both of which came subsequently to the West End, *The Magistrate* (1969) and *Dandy Dick* (1973) by A. W. Pinero.

In 1948 Sim achieved a remarkable feat, being elected rector of Edinburgh University by a majority greater than that achieved by any of the prime ministers and field marshals who had preceded him. His address ('the only one of eight that I have actually been able to hear', said Bridie) was delivered to that most critical of audiences, with all his professional skill. As one reads it one can hear it being spoken, in the inimitable Sim manner: the clipped words, the sardonic intonation, the crocodile smile. His own character appears in every line:

> I admit that even to this day I enjoy being called an artiste, and if anyone likes to qualify it with some such adjective as 'great', 'incomparable', 'superb', then you can rely on me to finish the ritual by reacting with becoming modesty. But I shall know it is all nonsense.

He was as devastating at the pricking of pomposity in others as in himself.

Sim was made an honorary LLD of Edinburgh University in 1951 on his retirement as rector, appointed CBE in 1953, and refused the knighthood offered to him by Edward Heath on the grounds that it would be ridiculous to be addressed as Sir Alastair. He died in London on 19 August

1976 and was survived by his wife. There is a portrait of him by Edward Seago in the Garrick Club of which he was a long and enthusiastic member and from which he regularly threatened to resign.

Sim's wife, **Naomi Merlith Sim** [*née* Plaskitt] (1913–1999), actress and writer, was born on 30 November 1913 at 30 The Embankment, Bedford, the younger daughter of Hugh Plaskitt (1880–1917), an alcoholic solicitor, and his Scottish wife and cousin, Norah Frances (1880–1963), daughter of Colonel David Cowie, army officer. They separated in 1913 and Norah Plaskitt brought up the daughters; Hugh Plaskitt died on 12 November 1917 of malaria contracted while on active service as a lance-corporal in the Army Service Corps in Africa. Naomi was educated at Bedford high school, a school in Callander, Perthshire, and St George's High School for Girls, Edinburgh. Keen on acting, at twelve she was in the Scottish Community Drama Association production of Yeats's *The Land of Heart's Desire*. There she met and fell in love with Sim. At fourteen she left school and became a pupil at his school of drama and speech training; she later became his secretary. In 1930 she won a scholarship to the Royal Academy of Dramatic Art, but after her two years there gave up any thought of an acting career: 'Alastair was always the most important thing in my life' (*The Independent*, 16 Aug 1999). Following their marriage she devoted herself to his career. They appeared together in one film, *Wedding Group* (1936). Generous and hospitable they quasi-adopted several young people, including George Cole (later in the St Trinian's films and the television series *Minder*). After Sim's death Naomi wrote an autobiographical memoir, *Dance and Skylark: Fifty Years with Alastair Sim* (1987), and contributed to *The Oldie* magazine. She died on 3 August 1999 at Forrigan Bungalow, Newnham Hill, Henley-on-Thames, Oxfordshire, following a stroke. She was survived by her daughter, Merlith. MICHAEL GILBERT, *rev.*

Sources personal knowledge (1986) · private information (1986) · I. Herbert, ed., *Who's who in the theatre*, 16th edn (1977) · *WW* · *CGPLA Eng. & Wales* (1976) · N. Sim, *Dance and skylark: fifty years with Alastair Sim* (1987) · *The Guardian* (7 Aug 1999) · *Daily Telegraph* (9 Aug 1999) · *The Independent* (16 Aug 1999) · b. cert. [Naomi Plaskitt] · m. cert. · d. cert. [Naomi Sim]

Archives NL Scot., MSS | U. St Andr. L., letters to C. Thorpe Davie | FILM BFI NFTVA, *Those British faces*, Channel 4, 20 June 1993 · BFI NFTVA, *Heroes of comedy*, Channel 4, 30 April 1997 · BFI NFTVA, 'Alastair Sim: a qualified fool' · BFI NFTVA, news footage · BFI NFTVA, performance footage

Likenesses A. Evans, photograph, 1946, NPG [*see illus.*] · H. Coster, photographs, NPG · E. Seago, oils, Garr. Club

Wealth at death £11,619: probate, 15 Oct 1976, *CGPLA Eng. & Wales*

Sim, Naomi Merlith (1913–1999). *See under* Sim, Alastair George Bell (1900–1976).

Simcocks [*alias* Manners, Grosvenor], **John** (1609–1695), Jesuit, was born in London on 28 September 1609. Nothing is known of his parents. He was educated at the English College at St Omer in Flanders from 1628 to 1631 and in the latter year entered the Society of Jesus at Watten in Flanders as John Manners, the name which he seems to have used more often than not. He was ordained priest about

1640. At about this time he was transferred from the English province to the Roman province of the Jesuits and for some years his name does not appear in the annual English catalogues. After lecturing in philosophy at Perugia he was appointed in 1649 director of studies at the English College, Rome, and in 1655 was named rector, an office he held until the end of 1658. He was then sent as English penitentiary to Loreto to hear the confessions of English pilgrims to the shrine.

In 1663 Simcocks was spiritual director at the English Jesuit college at Liège and it was probably at this time that he met Lady Trevor Warner who entered among the Poor Clare nuns at Gravelines in 1666. His high opinion of her was quoted by Edward Scarisbrick in his life of her published in 1691. He crossed over to England in 1669 and served as a missionary in the Suffolk district until 1678. A controversial work, *An Invitation of a Seeker*, by J. S. (John Simcocks) was published in 1670.

From 1679 Simcocks was at Ghent or Brussels and from 1682 he was working in London. He retired to France in 1689 and remained at St Germain at the court of James II until his death there in 1695. It was recorded under the name John Grosvenor.

E. I. CARLYLE, *rev.* GEOFFREY HOLT

Sources H. Foley, ed., *Records of the English province of the Society of Jesus*, 7/1 (1882), 485 · H. Foley, ed., *Records of the English province of the Society of Jesus*, 7/2 (1883), 1388 · W. Kelly, ed., *Liber ruber venerabilis collegii Anglorum de urbe*, 2, Catholic RS, 40 (1943), 58–60 · T. M. McCoog, *English and Welsh Jesuits, 1555–1650*, 2, Catholic RS, 75 (1995), 237 · G. Holt, *St Omers and Bruges colleges, 1593–1773: a biographical dictionary*, Catholic RS, 69 (1979), 170 · Gillow, *Lit. biog. hist.*, 4.408 · records and catalogues, British province of the Society of Jesus, 114 Mount Street, London · M. E. Williams, *The Venerable English College, Rome* (1979), 236 · A. de Backer and others, *Bibliothèque de la Compagnie de Jésus*, new edn, 7, ed. C. Sommervogel (Brussels, 1896), 1213 · T. H. Clancy, *English Catholic books, 1641–1700: a bibliography*, rev. edn (1996), 105, 144 · Wing, *STC*, C574, S40 · [E. Scarisbrick], *The life of the Lady Warner* (1691), 77

Simcoe [*née* Gwillim], **Elizabeth Postuma** (1762–1850), diarist and artist, was born in September 1762 and baptized on 22 September at Aldwincle, Northamptonshire, the only child of Lieutenant-Colonel Thomas Gwillim (*bap.* 1726, *d.* 1762?) and Elizabeth Spinckes (*bap.* 1723, *d.* 1762). Her father died before her birth and her mother in childbirth. The orphaned heir to land in Northamptonshire and Herefordshire was given the name of Postuma in recognition of her situation. She was not, however, alone in the world. Her childhood was spent with loving grandparents and aunts on both sides of the family, principally her mother's younger sister, Margaret, who, when she married Admiral Samuel Graves in 1769, took Elizabeth to live with her in Honiton, Devon. The admiral seems to have been responsible for her unusually broad education. It was at his home that she met his godson, Lieutenant-Colonel John Graves *Simcoe (1752–1806), whom she married on 30 December 1782. The couple had eleven children. Although the match between her property and his impecunious ability was logical, it seems also to have been a marriage of genuine affection.

The Simcoes built Wolford Lodge on the Devon estate

Elizabeth Postuma Simcoe (1762–1850), by Mary Anne Burges, 1790

that Elizabeth inherited, and set about improving and extending the estate, all the while seeking a military or colonial appointment for Simcoe, who had field rank but no regiment. Finally, in 1791 he was appointed lieutenant-governor of the new colony of Upper Canada. With the two youngest of their six children, the Simcoes sailed from Weymouth in September 1791.

Elizabeth Simcoe's renown in Canada is based on the diaries she began keeping on that trip. Until she returned to England five years later she kept daily notes, which were later expanded into longer diary entries and incorporated into letters to family and friends. Until early in the twentieth century the diaries remained unpublished and Canadian interest was centred on her husband as the first governor. Her diaries are attractive because of their infectious enthusiasm. Where other women in the colony complained of hardship, Elizabeth saw only adventure. Despite her involvement in her husband's activities she rarely mentioned politics. The people who appear in her diaries tended to be social contacts of her own class: the governor's military colleagues, visiting dignitaries, and women who maintained rounds of visits as if still in England. Her enjoyment of her role as the governor's wife no doubt added to her delight in all that she saw and did. In addition to the diaries Elizabeth, a talented artist, made many sketches, later turned into watercolours, which are frequently reproduced today as the most accurate records of a time and place. On their return to England, a set of

thirty-two watercolours was presented to George III. She was particularly attracted to 'sublime' scenery, but she also made detailed drawings of flora and fauna, of aboriginal peoples, and of local curiosities. A number of maps from this period are also attributed to her drawing ability. The exception to the happy accounts of her life in Canada was the death of a daughter, born at Niagara, who lived only a year. Although she had now borne seven children, this was the first infant death.

Governor Simcoe, who had been seriously wounded during the American War of Independence, found that the climate of Upper Canada adversely affected his health and requested leave to return to England. According to her diary (21 July 1796), Elizabeth Simcoe 'cried all the day' when they left Upper Canada.

As soon as her husband's health was restored, Elizabeth was involved in the process of finding him another appointment. In 1798 he was gazetted lieutenant-general, and given command of the western district, which was vulnerable to the expected attack from France. A surviving diary records a journey of inspection on which she accompanied the general that year. In July 1806 Simcoe was appointed commander-in-chief in India, with a knighthood promised, but while Elizabeth was purchasing her wardrobe Simcoe was sent on a special mission to Portugal. He took ill aboard ship, returned to England, and died at Exeter a few days after his return. Elizabeth, who by now had nine living children, seven of whom were daughters, lost her natural ebullience. She had no financial problems, and she was an educated, intelligent woman with a large circle of friends and relatives, but her life had lost its focus.

Elizabeth's childhood friend, the naturalist Mary Ann Burges, had purchased a home near Wolford and was her principal emotional support in this period. Almost immediately her maternal duty required that she turn her attention to launching her eldest son, Francis, in a career. In the family tradition, he chose the military and, sponsored by Lord Moira, was commissioned in 1807. He was killed at Badajoz in 1812. The next year Mary Ann Burges died.

Elizabeth and her husband had always been devout members of the Church of England. Governor Simcoe had built a chapel at Wolford, and had been assiduous in seeing to the establishment of the Anglican church in Upper Canada. After the loss of husband, friend, and favourite child, Elizabeth turned increasingly to the evangelical wing of the Church of England, which she supported financially and with personal activity, since she considered it the best means of counteracting what she saw as the dangerously democratic tendencies of the period. Determined that her only surviving son, Henry Addington *Simcoe (1800–1868), would not enter the army, she destined him for the church and campaigned for his advancement.

As a widow, Elizabeth Simcoe did not withdraw from society. With her daughters, she wintered at Bath and Cheltenham, where they had many friends. When they were not receiving guests at Wolford, all the female family members seem to have gone on rounds of visits to titled friends. Although she never again travelled outside Britain, diaries survive for visits to Wales in 1814 and 1831. They reveal the same delight in awe-inspiring scenery, and the same determination to sketch what she saw, found in the Canadian diaries. In Wales she also looked for traces of her Gwillim ancestors.

A notable aspect of Elizabeth Simcoe's life, and that of her daughters, is the intensity of female friendships revealed in their journals and correspondence. The women in these networks lived in the country, were all highly intelligent, interested in science, art, and languages, and seem to have been in control of their lives.

Contact with Upper Canada was maintained. The Simcoe family owned property there, managed by an agent, until 1826. Sir Frances Head, a later lieutenant-governor, was a family connection, whose wife kept them abreast of political developments. Elizabeth Simcoe helped pay for the Cambridge education of the Revd Henry Scadding, the son of their agent, and also for at least one of the sons of John Strachan, first bishop of Upper Canada. After her mother's death the eldest daughter, Eliza, was still donating money for missionary activities in Upper Canada and writing to ecclesiastical authorities in England on behalf of the Canadian church.

Elizabeth Simcoe died at Wolford on 17 January 1850, aged eighty-seven, and was buried on 27 January at the chapel there beside the husband she had survived for forty-four years. She had complained of declining health for some time, but was still active well into her eighties. It was Eliza who preserved her mother's diaries, drawings, and correspondence. Had it not been for her, Elizabeth Simcoe would be known only as the shadowy wife of a colonial governor, and a beneficent member of the Devon gentry, instead of her present status as one of the most admired founders of modern Ontario.

MARY LU MACDONALD

Sources Public Archives of Ontario, Toronto, Simcoe MSS, F47/1–17 · maps and drawings, Public Archives of Ontario, Toronto, Special Collections, F47/1–17 · NA Canada, John Graves Simcoe collection, MG23-HI1 · *Mrs Simcoe's diary*, ed. M. Q. Innis (1965) · M. B. Fryer, *Elizabeth Postuma Simcoe, 1762–1850: a biography* (1989) · Metropolitan Toronto Central Reference Library, Elizabeth Russell MSS, L21 · J. Bailey, 'A few remarks on the lives of General and Mrs. Simcoe from 1802 to 1850', *The diary of Mrs John Graves Simcoe, wife of the first Lieutenant-Governor of the province of Upper Canada* (1911)
Archives Devon RO, diaries of travel in Canada · NA Canada · Public Archives of Ontario, Toronto, diaries and sketch books
Likenesses M. A. Burges, drawing, 1790, NA Canada [see illus.] · miniature, NA Canada [photocopy]
Wealth at death £27,000—cash and landholdings in Northamptonshire, Herefordshire, and Devon: will, *Mrs Simcoe's diary*, ed. Innis

Simcoe, Henry Addington (1800–1868), theologian, was born on 28 February 1800 in Plymouth, son of Lieutenant-General John Graves *Simcoe (1752–1806) and his wife, Elizabeth Postuma *Simcoe (1762–1850), the diarist and artist, only daughter of Thomas Gwillim of Old Court, Herefordshire. He was educated at Eton College and at Wadham College, Oxford, where he matriculated on 13 April 1818, obtaining his BA on 17 December 1821, and his MA on 3 November 1825. He married, on 8 February 1822,

Anne (d. 1840), second daughter of the Revd Edward Palmer, vicar of Moseley in Worcestershire and Stogumber in Somerset; they had five sons and four daughters. Following his ordination Simcoe was in 1826 appointed curate at Egloskerry with Tremaine in Cornwall.

After the death of his father in 1806 Simcoe had inherited the estate of Wolford at Dunkeswell in Devon; in 1826 he inherited the estate of William Walcot of Oundle, Northamptonshire, the Simcoes' native county, and through his mother's family he acquired property in Herefordshire. In 1830 he purchased the picturesque Jacobean manor house of Penheale in Egloskerry, with its gardens, fishponds, and avenue of lime trees. Simcoe maintained a private printing press at Penheale, producing over twenty theological works and nine volumes of a periodical, *Light from the West, or, The Cornish Parochial Visitor*. His interests also included agriculture, chemistry, and medicine; he acted as unofficial medical adviser to his parishioners, providing them with free drugs developed in his own laboratory. Anne Simcoe died on 6 December 1840, and two years later, on 21 December 1842, Simcoe married Emily (d. 24 May 1877), second daughter of the Revd Horace Mann, rector of Mawgan with St Martin, Cornwall; they had two daughters.

Simcoe was instituted perpetual curate of Egloskerry and Tremaine on 4 July 1846 (he had recently acquired the advowson) and he also served as rural dean of Trigg Major. During his long incumbency he held four services with sermons every Sunday in each of his two churches, a feat remarked upon in the sermon delivered at his funeral. Simcoe died at Penheale House on 15 November 1868, and was buried in Egloskerry churchyard on 24 November; his obituary in *One and All* described him as 'a much-esteemed clergyman of the Evangelical school', while an illuminated address, presented to his widow by the parishioners, praised his great physical strength, punctuality, benevolence, and 'uncompromising support of Protestant and Evangelical truth': he was known locally as the Apostle of the West.

W. P. COURTNEY, *rev.* CHRISTINE NORTH

Sources Burke, *Gen. GB* (1914) · Boase & Courtney, *Bibl. Corn.*, 2.650–52, 3.1336, 1457 · G. C. Boase, *Collectanea Cornubiensia: a collection of biographical and topographical notes relating to the county of Cornwall* (1890), 529, 899 · Foster, *Alum. Oxon.* · J. Polsue, *A complete parochial history of the county of Cornwall*, 1 (1867), 323–8 · R. B. Gardiner, ed., *The registers of Wadham College, Oxford*, 2 (1895), 279, 280 · *One and All* (Nov 1868) · address presented to Mrs Simcoe, 4 Feb 1869, Cornwall RO · *CGPLA Eng. & Wales* (1869)
Archives Devon RO | Cornwall RO, Parnall MSS
Wealth at death under £8000: probate, 5 Jan 1869, *CGPLA Eng. & Wales*

Simcoe, John Graves (1752–1806), army officer and colonial governor, was born on 25 February 1752 at Cotterstock, Northamptonshire, the third son (and only child to reach adulthood) of Captain John Simcoe (1710–1759), a naval officer of middle-class family who had obtained a grant of arms in 1747, and his wife, Catherine Stamford (d. 1766). After his father died in command of the man-of-war *Pembroke* early in the 1759 Quebec operations, the family moved to his mother's Exeter home, from where Simcoe was well educated for an army officer, at Exeter grammar

John Graves Simcoe (1752–1806), by John Wycliffe Lowes Forster, c.1900 (after unknown artist)

school (1760–65), at Eton College (1765–8), and Merton College, Oxford (1769–70). He was also admitted in February 1769 at Lincoln's Inn, before leaving for the army.

After a year with a military tutor at Exeter, through the influence of his mother's family Simcoe was commissioned ensign on 27 April 1770, by purchase, in the 35th foot, then serving in England; he embarked with his regiment for Ireland in April 1773, and was promoted lieutenant (by purchase) on 12 March 1774, serving as adjutant from 27 March 1772 until leaving the 35th. He sailed from Cork in April 1775, the 35th forming part of the first embarkation of Irish reinforcements for the army at Boston, arriving there from 11 June. In the Boston garrison Simcoe purchased a captaincy in the 40th foot, on 27 December 1775; and with the 40th he served on the 1776 New York and 1777 Philadelphia campaigns, being severely wounded at Brandywine. After being refused permission to raise a corps from the free black inhabitants of Boston, on 15 October 1777 he took command of the Queen's rangers, a loyalist 'legion' of mixed light horse and foot; at first with the provincial rank of major, and later of lieutenant-colonel commandant, Simcoe made his name in the *petite guerre* of raids, reconnaissance, and outpost skirmishing that characterized its service. As contemptuous of the military capacity of his adversaries as he was of their republicanism, his leadership made the Queen's rangers the most successful of the American loyalist corps. He was captured in 1779 and spent six months as a prisoner. He was made brevet lieutenant-

colonel in the army, on 19 December 1781, not long after being invalided home to Exeter, ending his six and a half years' service in the American War of Independence.

On 30 December 1782 Simcoe married Elizabeth Postuma Gwillim (1762–1850) [see Simcoe, Elizabeth Postuma], daughter of Lieutenant-Colonel Thomas Gwillim of Old Court, Ross, Herefordshire, and niece and ward of Simcoe's godfather, Admiral Samuel Graves. A wealthy heiress, she brought him a 5000 acre estate at Dunkeswell, near Honiton, Devon, on which they built Wolford Lodge, where they lived from 1788. Their marriage was happy, and they had three sons and eight daughters. Among their sons was the theologian Henry Addington *Simcoe. After being put on half pay late in 1783 with the disbandment of the Queen's rangers, Simcoe devoted his years at Exeter to convalescence and study, publishing there in 1787 his important military work, the *Journal of the Operations of the Queen's Rangers*, the outstanding tactical study of the *petite guerre* to emerge from the eighteenth-century American wars, an invaluable training and tactical manual for officers soon to be engaged with the light forces of the French revolutionary armies. Prefixed to the copy presented to the king was an essay summarizing Simcoe's views on the organization, training, and tactics of mixed light troops. He also published *Remarks on the Travels of the Marquis de Chastellux* (1787), condemning French intervention in America.

Having turned down Pitt's offer of 1788 that he stand for Honiton as a friend of government, Simcoe entered parliament in 1790 as member for the marquess of Buckingham's freeman pocket borough, St Mawes, Cornwall. A supporter of the administration, he spoke on several occasions and took a particular interest in colonial issues, but his goal was a military or colonial posting, which he secured when appointed lieutenant-governor (his commission dated 12 September 1791) of the new province of Upper Canada, under the Canadian governor-in-chief, Lord Dorchester. Simcoe, his wife, and two youngest children sailed from England on 26 September 1791, arriving on 11 November at Quebec, where they wintered. They reached the temporary capital, Newark (modern Niagara on the Lake), on 26 July 1792. He had in the meantime been made colonel in a general brevet promotion of 18 November 1790, and colonel-commandant of the reconstituted Queen's rangers, his commission dated 1 September 1791. The new Queen's rangers, raised for service in Upper Canada, were intended by Simcoe as military pioneers, to form the nuclei of new, well-ordered settlements, but in fact they were used mainly to open strategic roads to funnel settlement to the west of the province and to facilitate troop movements, then later for garrison duties. He was promoted major-general, in Canada, on 3 October 1794.

Simcoe threw himself into his governorship with the excessive enthusiasm that was characteristic of the man and, as so often in his career, his projections were on a scale beyond the resources provided for the Upper Canadian establishment. His task was to erect a framework of English civil government in the infant loyalist province, a land distribution system that would encourage settlement, and a structure for defence based on a militia and a small marine. His particular interest was in opening the trade and settlement of the south-western part of the province. Though he moved the provincial capital to the fortified harbour at York (Toronto), he envisioned the province as a strategic, offensive–defensive bulwark wedged into the heart of the north-west, with naval bases on the lakes linked by roads radiating from a centrally located, inland 'place of arms' at London (which he founded for that purpose) to forestall future American aggression. He cherished plans to create a flourishing educational system and Church of England in the province—this, like his conception of the reraised Queen's rangers, to create a bastion of social and political conservatism and to prevent the emergence of American-style frontier democracy. However, his plans for municipal corporations, schools, a provincial university, and a full endowment of the Anglican church in Upper Canada were refused by the British government. A warm and sympathetic man, obviously zealous for the good of the province, he was apparently liked by Canadians. A lake, town, and county in Ontario were named after him. His governorship—though the extensive goals that he set for it were mostly checked by the authorities at home, the Quebec governor-general, or his own legislative council, and though it has remained controversial among historians—was generally successful, but the illness that dogged his career forced him to return home in the summer of 1796, resigning his governorship early in 1798.

Simcoe was appointed governor of San Domingo, with local rank as lieutenant-general dated 10 November 1796. In the island, where he arrived early in 1797, he worked to improve the defences against the insurgency of slaves and people of mixed race inspired by the French. His switch to the offensive displeased the British government, which had expected him to oversee a withdrawal to the western tip of the island. In July, his health failing him again, he was obliged to leave for home, though the following January he offered to return to the West Indies. By late 1797 he was at Exeter, in command of the western military district, to which he was sent under the ministry of his friend Henry Addington. He was promoted lieutenant-general on 1 January 1801. Plans to stand in the government interest for Plymouth at the election of 1802 were frustrated. He was given the colonelcy of the 81st foot on 18 January 1798, leaving it on 18 June 1798 for the colonelcy of the 22nd foot, which he retained until his death.

In July 1806 Simcoe was appointed commander-in-chief in India but in the meantime was sent with Lord St Vincent and Lord Rosslyn on a mission to Portugal. Ill health intervened, however, and Simcoe returned to Exeter, where he died on 26 October 1806. Simcoe was an inspiring soldier and a brilliant tactician, an affable and loyal comrade, and a lifelong student of history and writer of verse, but he was too great a projector, and his ambition outran the uncertain health that plagued him from early manhood. He was buried on 4 November 1806 in the chapel at Wolford Lodge. J. A. HOULDING

Sources W. R. Riddell, *The life of John Graves Simcoe, first lieutenant-governor of the province of Upper Canada* (1926) · *The correspondence of Lieutenant Governor John Graves Simcoe*, ed. E. A. Cruikshank, 5 vols. (1923–31) · S. R. Mealing, 'Simcoe, John Graves', *DCB* · M. MacLeod, 'Fortress Ontario or forlorn hope? Simcoe and the defence of Upper Canada', *Canadian Historical Review*, 53 (1972), 149–78 · *Mrs Simcoe's diary*, ed. M. Q. Innis (1965) · J. Hitsman, *Safeguarding Canada, 1763–1871* (1968) · *Army List* (1782–1802) · *GM*, 1st ser., 76 (1806), 1165–6 · N. B. Leslie, *The succession of colonels of the British army from 1660 to the present day* (1974) · 'Succession books', PRO, WO.25/211, 35th foot, 40th foot; WO.25/213, queen's rangers · I. R. Christie, *British 'non-élite' MPs, 1715–1820* (1995) · W. P. Baildon, ed., *The records of the Honorable Society of Lincoln's Inn: admissions*, 1 (1896), 463 · Foster, *Alum. Oxon.* · M. Duffy, *Soldiers, sugar, and sea power: the British expeditions to the West Indies and the war against revolutionary France* (1987) · D. P. Geggus, *Slavery, war and revolution: the British occupation of Saint Domingue, 1793–1798* (1982) · *HoP, Commons, 1790–1820*, vols. 2, 5

Archives Colonial Williamsburg Foundation, Williamsburg, maps and papers · Devon RO, corresp., colonial governors' papers · Devon RO, corresp. · Hunt. L., journal and letterbook · Public Archives of Ontario, Toronto, corresp. and papers relating to North America · U. Mich., Clements L., corresp. and papers | BL, corresp. with Lord Grenville, Add. MS 59005 · Devon RO, corresp. with Lord Sidmouth, etc. · PRO, letters to William Pitt, PRO 30/8

Likenesses J. W. L. Forster, portrait, *c*.1900, NA Canada [*see illus.*] · oils, NA Canada · photographic print (after crayon drawing, 1796), NAM · portrait; in family possession in 1923

Wealth at death 5000 acres of Upper Canadian settlement lots; 5000 acre estate, acquired through marriage, on which he built a large seat in 1788

Simcox, Edith Jemima (1844–1901), anthropologist and political activist, was born on 21 August 1844, the youngest child and only daughter of George Price Simcox, merchant, and his wife, Jemima (1816–1897), daughter of Lancelot Haslope and his wife, Harriet. Edith Simcox grew up in an educated middle-class family. Her two older brothers Augustus and William became fellows of the Queen's College, Oxford. Edith, too, had a strong intellectual bent: she was well grounded in philosophy, learned French and German at school, had a thorough grasp of Latin, some knowledge of Greek, Italian, and Spanish, and acquired a smattering of Dutch and Flemish.

Simcox took an eager interest in radical social reform and the improvement of the status of women. In 1875 she was one of the first female delegates who was admitted to a trade union conference in Glasgow. From 1875 to 1884 she helped her friend Mary Hamilton to conduct a small co-operative shirt and collar manufacturing enterprise in Soho, which employed women under decent conditions in one of the worst of the sweated trades. Her experiences during this period are recorded in an article entitled 'Eight years of co-operative shirtmaking', which was published in the *Nineteenth Century* in June 1884. During these years Simcox also served as a member of the London school board from 1879 to 1882 and promoted compulsory secular elementary education for all children. After 1884 she continued to work for the trade union movement in Britain and on the continent. Her varied language skills were put into practice in letter-writing campaigns with a view to the enhancement of the movement's international influence.

Simcox's wide-ranging interests in politics, the arts, literature, history, and philosophy were reflected in numerous articles, which were published in periodicals such as the *Manchester Guardian*, *The Times*, *The Academy*, the *Fortnightly Review*, *Fraser's Magazine*, the *Nineteenth Century*, the *North British Review*, *Co-operative News*, the *Labour Tribune*, and the *Women's Union Journal*. In addition, she translated political and philosophical writings and was the author of three books. Her first work, *Natural Law: an Essay in Ethics* (1877), was an attempt to define the ethical position of the utilitarian and scientific rationalism with which Simcox associated herself. In this context, she referred to the philosophy of Kant, Hobbes, Bentham, and Schopenhauer. Her second work, the fictional *Episodes in the Lives of Men, Women and Lovers* (1882), is a collection of stories and philosophical musings. They include autobiographical allusions to Simcox's adoration of her idol, George Eliot, and the emotional strains caused by the death of G. H. Lewes, Eliot's grief, her subsequent marriage to J. W. Cross, and eventually Eliot's death in 1880. Simcox started to plan her third work, *Primitive Civilizations: Outlines of the History of Ownership in Archaic Communities* (1894), shortly after the publication of *Natural Law*, and the completion of this two-volume study took the author over fifteen years. Despite this substantial scholarly effort, *Primitive Civilizations* attracted less attention than Simcox's first book. On the one hand, the work can be regarded as a detached academic account of the history of ownership in ancient Egypt, Mesopotamia, and China. Among the topics Simcox explored were the social, economic, legal, agricultural, and domestic arrangements in these civilizations. On the other hand, the treatise was also a radical tract through which the author hoped to improve the social and political conditions of her own lifetime. By alerting her readers to the fact that the prosperity of these three long-lived ancient societies was not built on the idea of economic *laissez-faire* individualism, Simcox indirectly criticized the capitalist traits of her own culture. She considered it to be a particular strength of these civilizations that the organization of the public political sphere was modelled on the domestic arrangements of the family community and its unselfish reciprocity. What is more, an analysis of the material arrangements led Simcox to the conclusion that the women of the three ancient societies she examined in many respects enjoyed a higher status than women in Victorian Britain. In the light of these considerations, Simcox's socialist ideals in politics can be interpreted as a modern version of what she described as the domestic or feminine values which, in her view, were responsible for the success of the ancient communities she analysed. The findings of her research thus challenged the male, and at times racist, anthropological discourse of her own days.

Edith Simcox regarded the ethos of maternal sympathy, which she sought to implement in her own society through her political activism, as one of the crucial elements in the fiction of George Eliot. She first met the novelist in December 1872, shortly before her review of *Middlemarch* was published in *The Academy*. Simcox was then twenty-eight and Eliot fifty-three. She was devoted to Eliot, whom she called 'the one great joy and blessing' of her life (McKenzie, 108). Her passionate desire for the novelist, however, remained unreciprocated. The story of the friendship between the two women is documented meticulously in Simcox's secret diary entitled 'Autobiography of a shirt maker', which is a crucial source for the reconstruction of Edith Simcox's biography. This manuscript journal, held in the Bodleian Library, Oxford, covers the years from 10 May 1876 to 29 January 1900, even though there is a long gap in the record from July 1891 to December 1897. Two-thirds of the entries in Simcox's private journal were written between 1876 and 1881, the last years of George Eliot's life. After Eliot's death in 1880 Simcox published a personal appreciation of the author's life in the *Nineteenth Century* in May 1881. Her article commemorated the woman who was not only the focus of her emotional life but also a significant source of intellectual inspiration for her own literary and political work. Simcox frequently addressed Eliot as 'mother', and to a certain extent her admiration for the novelist echoes her strong feelings of filial affection towards her own mother, with whom she lived for most of her life. Simcox ranked her mother, who died in 1897, above her 'other love in perfection for all human relations' (Simcox, 29 Jan 1900).

Simcox was first troubled by asthma in 1886. An inflammation of the lung was recorded in a diary entry in 1895; subsequently she was sent to Egypt by her family. After an improvement in the state of her health she suffered from another serious fit of asthma in 1899. Edith Simcox died on 15 September 1901 at 10 Lansdowne Road, London, after a long illness; her ashes were placed in her mother's grave at Aspley Guise, near Bedford.   SUSANNE STARK

Sources K. A. McKenzie, *Edith Simcox and George Eliot* (1961) · G. Beer, 'Passion, politics, philosophy: the work of Edith Simcox', *Women: A Cultural Review*, 6/2 (1995), 166–79 · F. Gordon, 'Anthropological analogies: Edith Simcox and Madeleine Pelletier', *Wollstonecraft's daughters: womanhood in England and France, 1780–1920*, ed. C. C. Orr (1996), 168–85 · N Vince, 'The fiddler, the angel and the defiance of Antigone: a reading of Edith Simcox's *Autobiography of a shirtmaker*', *Women: A Cultural Review*, 6/2 (1995), 143–65 · P. Hollis, *Ladies elect: women in English local government, 1865–1914* (1987) · P. Levine, *Feminist lives in Victorian England* (1990) · J. Todd, ed., *Dictionary of British women writers* (1989) · J. Shattock, *The Oxford guide to British women writers* (1993) · E. Simcox, 'Autobiography of a shirt maker', Bodl. Oxf., MS Eng. misc. d.494

Archives Bodl. Oxf.

Wealth at death £1556 6s. 11d.: probate, 19 Oct 1901, *CGPLA Eng. & Wales*

Sime, James (1843–1895), journalist and writer, born on 31 October 1843, was the eldest son of the Revd James Sime of Airdrie, minister of the Independent congregation in Fraserburgh, Aberdeenshire, and afterwards of Wick and Thurso, Caithness (d. 19 September 1865 at Thurso, aged sixty), and his wife, Jane Anderson of Glasgow (d. 28 January 1889 at Edinburgh). He was educated at Anderson's Gymnasium, Aberdeen, which he left in 1859 for Edinburgh University (MA 1867). He married, on 6 October 1865, Jessie Aitken Wilson (youngest sister of Sir Daniel Wilson, president of Toronto University, and of Professor George Wilson of Edinburgh University). In 1866, having given up the idea of entering the ministry, he went to Germany, and studied German literature and philosophy, first at Heidelberg University, and afterwards at Berlin. During his stay in Germany he collected materials for his *Life of Lessing*, and he visited most of the places connected with his hero and with Goethe and Schiller. On his return from Germany he settled at Norland Square, Notting Hill, London, in 1869, and began journalism. In 1871 he joined the staff of the Edinburgh Academy but, finding the work uncongenial, resigned and returned to London in 1873 to writing, which occupied him until his death.

Sime was successively connected with *The Globe*, the *Pall Mall Gazette*, and the *St James's Gazette* (under Frederick Greenwood), writing mainly on social and educational topics, and continental politics. He was a frequent contributor to *The Athenaeum*, the *Saturday Review*, and the *English Illustrated Magazine*, did weekly work for *The Graphic* and the *Daily Graphic* for many years, and for some time was on the staff of *Nature*. He had planned a history of Germany on a fairly large scale, but his everyday work and premature death prevented the achievement of this ambition. From 1880 he lived at 1 Queen Anne's Grove, a house which he had built in Bedford Park (the new 'arty' garden suburb of London at Chiswick, designed by Norman Shaw).

Sime's publications included *History of Germany* (1874), *Life of Lessing* (2 vols., 1877), *Schiller* (1882), *Mendelssohn's Letters* (1887), *Life of Goethe* (1888), and numerous articles on German history, literature, and biography for the ninth edition of *Encyclopaedia Britannica*. Sime died at his home, 1 Queen Anne's Grove, Bedford Park, Middlesex, of influenza, on 20 March 1895, and was buried on 25 March at Hampstead cemetery, London. His wife and their daughter, Georgina Jessie, survived him.

F. Y. POWELL, rev. ROGER T. STEARN

Sources personal knowledge (1897) · private information (1897) · Boase, *Mod. Eng. biog.* · *ILN* (20 March 1895), 374 · *CGPLA Eng. & Wales* (1895) · b. cert.
Archives U. Edin. L., corresp. | NL Scot., letters to Blackwoods
Likenesses engraving (after photograph) · portrait, repro. in *ILN* (20 March 1895), 274
Wealth at death £1133 4s. od.: probate, 19 April 1895, *CGPLA Eng. & Wales*

Sime, Sidney Herbert (1864×7–1941), illustrator and caricaturist, was born between 1864 and 1867 in the Hulme district of Manchester, the second of six children of David and Helen Sime, who were both Scottish. His marriage register entry (1898) gave his age as 31, meaning he would have been born in 1866 or 1867; however, in the letter of administration taken out by his widow in 1941 his age was put at 76, suggesting that he was born in 1864 or 1865. According to his nephew John Sime it was probably the latter. Nothing is known about his parents beyond the fact that when he was an infant they moved to Liverpool, where his father was employed in a furniture warehouse.

Sime probably received little formal education before going to work underground in a Yorkshire colliery. His five years as a pit boy left him with memories of pushing trolleys down tunnels only 2–3 feet high and nearly being buried alive by a roof-fall. He then worked for a linen draper, a shoemaker, and a baker before becoming successful as a signwriter. This enabled him to attend Liverpool School of Art, where he won prizes for drawing in 1885 and 1888 and decided on a career as an illustrator. He moved to London, probably in 1893.

Sime's first illustrations were made for the halfpenny comic papers. His breakthrough came in 1895 when the magazine *Pick-Me-Up*, which employed distinguished artists, started to publish his cartoons about the afterlife. Treating the netherworld with ominous humour (perhaps connected with his experience down the mine), his cartoons upset the devout and created something of a sensation. Soon his sombre fantasies were appearing in many magazines, notably *The Idler*, *The Sketch*, *The Butterfly*, and the *Pall Mall Magazine*. Between autumn 1897 and February 1898 he edited the short-lived magazine *Eureka*, in which post he took a nonchalant view of his duties. At the end of 1897 Sime was being talked of as one of the country's leading artists in black and white, influenced like most of his contemporaries by Beardsley and Japanese prints but a pioneer of the comic-grotesque style (*Windsor Magazine*, December 1897).

Another side of Sime's talent was seen in the theatrical caricatures published in *Pick-Me-Up* in 1896–8 and *The Tatler* in 1902–4. Sir David Low praised Sime for these, describing him as 'the most notable' of the theatrical caricaturists of the nineties, 'a beautifully imaginative artist with a mordant fancy which sometimes overlaid his observation of character but whose studies of people nevertheless are full of fine and well-balanced caricature' (Low, 38). As well as cartooning, Sime also painted allegories, portraits, and landscapes in oil, some of which were exhibited at the Royal Society of British Artists between 1896 and 1903.

Sime's uncle, William Sime, who had been a prosperous solicitor in Edinburgh, died in 1898, leaving him about £14,000 and a house with a small estate at Aberfoyle, Perthshire. In the same year on 14 July he married in Edinburgh Mary Susan Pickett, a miniature painter and illustrator. For the next few years they spent half their time at Aberfoyle, where Sime painted landscapes.

With some of his new wealth, Sime bought *The Idler* and installed himself as co-editor in 1899. Partly through his own neglect it proved a disastrous investment, with Sime selling the goodwill in 1901 for £5. After 1900 he had a diminishing appetite for magazine illustration, but in 1905 he was tempted to visit the United States by William Randolph Hearst. Despite being offered a handsome retainer he stayed only six months.

From the magazines which he called 'those Godforsaken sponge-cakes of the suburban soul' (letter to Josef Holbrooke, 18 Aug 1910, priv. coll.) Sime turned to illustrating books, predominantly the fantasies of Edward Plunkett, eighteenth baron of Dunsany. Starting in 1905 with *The Gods of Pegana*, Dunsany's tales of wonder, set in other worlds and written in prose-poetry, gave Sime, in Rossetti's phrase, a perfect opportunity for 'allegorizing on one's own hook'. While illustrating ten books (some with only a frontispiece) he went to stay with Dunsany at his castle in Ireland, where he proved a highly entertaining guest.

Another noble collaborator and generous friend was Thomas Scott-Ellis, eighth Baron Howard de Walden. Like Dunsany he had a preoccupation with myth and a conviction that Sime was a genius. Sime designed sets and costumes for the trilogy of operas based on the Mabinogion, staged in 1912, 1914, and 1929, for which Holbrooke wrote the music and Howard de Walden the libretto.

In 1903 Sime had bought Crown Cottage, Worplesdon, Surrey, which he converted from a public house. After selling his house in Scotland he lived there for the rest of his life, increasingly withdrawn from the art world. Given a measure of independence by his inheritance and supported by his noble patrons, he painted when he felt inclined. Walter Emanuel wrote, 'one of the most acute individualities in the world of black-and-white is Mr. S. H. Sime—that he produces so little nowadays is a calamity'. He called Sime 'a great master of the grotesque' (*Strand Magazine*, November 1915, 592). In July 1918 Sime was conscripted into the Army Service Corps, and on 11 November, armistice day, he was invalided out. His *Bogey Beasts* with music by Josef Holbrooke was published in 1923, and reasonably successful exhibitions of his work were held at the St George's Gallery, London, in 1924 and 1927; otherwise he spurned dealers, read voraciously (acquiring a deep knowledge of William Blake and other visionary writers), backed horses, and spent every evening at the local public house.

Sime's strong personality and powers of conversation could astonish his audience. During his youth his appearance was as outré as his art: Max Beerbohm's caricature published in *The Idler* of August 1900 made him look like a Buddha in a bearskin. The novelist Desmond Coke called his presence 'overwhelming, as of a chunky Chinese idol' and his conversation 'shattering' (Coke, 225).

Sime's originality in appearance, conversation, and darkly imaginative art, coupled with his rise from pit boy to magazine proprietor, was such as to make him a 'man of the nineties', the friend of Max Beerbohm and Frank Harris, and one of the creators of the *fin de siècle* mood. His decline after the turn of the century was due partly to his contemptuous rejection of the art market and partly to the change in taste whereby the public came to see humour and weird fantasy as incompatible. Apart from a small coterie, the hyperbole evaporated, but Sime continued to have admirers: Dr Gordon N. Ray wrote in 1976, 'of all the English black-and-white artists more or less in the Beardsley tradition he was the most original' (Ray, 201).

Sime died on 21 May 1941 at the Royal Surrey County Hospital, Guildford, Surrey, and was buried nearby in the graveyard of Worplesdon parish church. His widow died in 1949, leaving his remaining pictures, with an endowment, to the trustees of the Worplesdon Memorial Hall to form the Sime Gallery. The couple had no children.

SIMON HENEAGE

Sources S. Heneage and H. Ford, *Sidney Sime* (1980) · G. Locke, *From an ultimate dim Thule* (1973) · J. Lewis, 'The fantasy world of Sidney Sime', *Saturday Book*, 34 (1975) · J. Thorpe, 'Sidney Sime', unpublished typescript, 1948, Worplesdon Memorial Hall, Surrey · D. Low, *British cartoonists, caricaturists and comic artists* (1942) · A. Lawrence, 'The apotheosis of the grotesque', *The Idler* (Jan 1898), 755–66 · E. S. Valentine, 'Mr S. H. Sime and his work', *Strand Magazine*, 36 (1908), 394–401 · F. Harris, *Contemporary portraits: second series* (1919) · E. J. M. D. Plunkett, Lord Dunsany, *Patches of sunlight* (1938) · D. Coke, *Confessions of an incurable collector* (1928) · 'From pit boy to artist', *Liverpool Echo* (24 June 1927) · G. N. Ray, *The illustrator and the book in England from 1790 to 1914* (1976) · private information (2004) · CGPLA Eng. & Wales (1941) · m. cert.

Archives Worplesdon Memorial Hall, Surrey, Sime memorial gallery

Likenesses photograph, 1897, repro. in Lawrence, 'The apotheosis of the grotesque' · E. O. Hoppé, photograph, 1911, Worplesdon Memorial Hall, Surrey; repro. in Heneage and Ford, *Sidney Sime* · M. Beerbohm, caricature, repro. in Heneage and Ford, *Sidney Sime*

Wealth at death £1851 3s. 7d.: administration, 12 Aug 1941, CGPLA Eng. & Wales

Simeon of Durham. *See* Symeon of Durham (*fl. c.*1090–*c.*1128).

Simeon of Warwick. *See* Warwick, Simon of (*c.*1225–1296).

Simeon, Charles (1759–1836), Church of England clergyman, was born on 24 September 1759 at Reading, the fourth son of Richard Simeon (*d.* 1784), attorney and son and grandson of successive vicars of Bucklebury, Berkshire, and his wife, Elizabeth Hutton. His mother came from the same family as two archbishops of York, one in the sixteenth century, the other in the eighteenth. His elder brother was Sir John *Simeon, first baronet (1755/6–1824). Simeon went to Eton College in 1766, where his ugliness gained him the nickname of 'Chin Simeon'. Looking back on his school-days there, he said that he found no inspiration from its low religious standard: the emphasis was placed on the study of the classical authors, and the scriptures were neglected. He was noted for his extravagant dress and able horsemanship, though at the same time his companions thought him unusually religious, particularly when he observed a national day of fasting and prayer, which had been called during the American War of Independence, by shutting himself up in his study and eating only a single hard-boiled egg at dinner.

Conversion Simeon went as a scholar on 29 January 1779 to King's College, Cambridge, where four days after his arrival an incident occurred that changed his whole life. The provost of the college announced that all its members would be required to participate in the mid-term celebration of holy communion in the chapel. Simeon anxiously doubted his spiritual fitness to do this. During some three months of great uneasiness he read the only devotional manual known to him, *The Whole Duty of Man*, which brought him no help. Then he turned, as likely to be more relevant to him in his situation, to *A Short and Plain Instruction for the Better Understanding of the Lord's Supper* (1733) by Bishop Thomas Wilson, who wished the sacrament to have a more important part in Anglican worship; and he

Charles Simeon (1759–1836), by William Say, 1822 (after John Jackson)

found a sentence in this which relieved his sense of guilt: 'The Jews knew what they did when they transferred their sin to the head of their offering' (Carus, 9). These words aroused in him the belief that he could gain salvation by transferring away his sins to 'the sacred head of Jesus' (ibid.). He went to communion on Easter day and recorded, 'At the Lord's table in our chapel I had the sweetest access to God through my blessed Saviour' (ibid.), though he considered the service in the chapel 'very irreverently performed' (ibid., 10).

The result of this conversion was to make Simeon a devoted, practising Christian, which he remained, though this was at first seriously interrupted by a bout of drunkenness, for the rest of his life. He endeavoured to influence his university friends and during the long vacation instructed the servants at home and introduced morning and evening family prayers. He now looked forward to obtaining holy orders. In January 1782 he succeeded as an Etonian to a King's College fellowship and on that title was ordained deacon by the bishop of Ely on 26 May 1782, though he was still under the canonical age and did not graduate BA until January 1783. He was ordained priest by the bishop of Peterborough on 28 September 1783.

Simeon had been brought up as a high-churchman, and at first he felt an affinity with high-churchmen such as Thomas Wilson, but he soon came under the influence of the evangelical movement. Since the evangelicals were still in a minority in the Church of England, they tended to gather in groups in a certain few centres of the kingdom, and one of these was Cambridge. An evangelical clergyman there was Christopher Atkinson, vicar of St

Edward's Church, and Simeon began his ministry by taking duty for him during the long vacation. Atkinson introduced him to others of that persuasion, including John Venn, rector of Clapham, who put him in touch with the outstanding members of that other concentration of evangelicalism there. John Venn also introduced Simeon to his father, Henry Venn, rector of Yelling, some 15 miles from Cambridge, who had a decisive influence upon him. Henceforward he found their outlook congenial, though he called himself 'a moderate Calvinist' (Carus, 418).

Early ministry in Cambridge In 1782 the vicar of Holy Trinity Church, Cambridge, died. The church's size and position made Simeon wish 'I might preach the Gospel there and be a herald for Him in the University' (Elliott-Binns, 285). He persuaded his father to induce the bishop of Ely to appoint him there, but the parishioners wanted to have their afternoon lecturer as their incumbent, and Simeon was not popular as an evangelical. The seat-holders left the church, locking the doors of their pews to prevent anyone else using them. When Simeon placed benches in the aisles, the churchwardens threw them out into the churchyard, and for more than the first ten years of his ministry the congregation had to stand.

In addition, Simeon's reputation for piety made him unpopular with many of the undergraduates. They interrupted his sermons, sought to break up the services, and roughly treated people leaving the church. He restored order in the church by appointing watchers to stand in the aisles, and when the service was ended he went immediately to stand at the north door to confront his opponents. On weekdays he met with shouts of derision in the streets, and so did his curates, even though some of them, such as James Scholefield, were known for their academic distinction in the university (Scholefield, 27). Nevertheless he persevered, steadily gaining support, and had a ministry of fifty-four years there.

Simeon achieved this despite 'an infirmity of temper' described by Charles Jerram, a fellow evangelical divine: 'He was naturally of a haughty, impatient and impetuous temper, and these defects were sometimes exhibited in a way which was painful to the feelings of others' (Memoirs … of the late Rev. Charles Jerram, 124). Simeon was aware of his weaknesses of character and constantly struggled against them, seeking to acquire humility and spiritual discipline. Throughout the year he rose at four o'clock in the morning to give himself to private prayer, self-examination, and devotional Bible reading until he called his servant at eight o'clock to join with him in praying together. As he grew older, it was notable that his character considerably mellowed, and fewer people were offended by his approach to them.

Simeon's access to members of the university was helped by his official position in his college; he was thrice one of its deans, second bursar from 1798 to 1805, and vice-provost from 1790 to 1792, the duties of all of which posts he performed conscientiously. Apart from his benevolent care for the afflicted during the corn famine of 1788, when he organized a subscription to enable bread to be sold at half-price in Cambridge and twenty-four neighbouring villages and rode round on horseback each Monday to make sure that the bakers were doing this, the long period of his incumbency was singularly unmarked by notable incidents, but he was an assiduous, many-sided pastor. George Corrie, later master of Jesus College, was told, when going up to Cambridge, that Simeon was seen 'either in the stable with his horses or by the sick bed of his parishioners' (Moule, 55).

Preacher of the gospel Simeon did his best to make use of the opportunity to preach which he had foreseen Holy Trinity Church would give him. Like other evangelical preachers, he broke away from the ethical sermons of Archbishop John Tillotson, which had dominated eighteenth-century preaching, and proclaimed the symbol of the cross as the supreme expression of the love of God for sinners through which they might enter into the new life of the spirit. While his emphasis was on the salvation of individual souls, he insisted also that those who accepted the faith 'became a member of Christ's mystical body', the church (Simeon, *Horae*, sermon 183).

Like the evangelicals also, Simeon was concerned with the technique of preaching. He particularly set out to achieve a planned framework for his sermons. 'I have been preaching for forty-five years,' he said in 1827, 'but for the first seven of those years I did not know the head from the tail of a sermon.' He preached 'usually to the small door in the west gallery of Trinity Church' (Brown, 178), because, 'When I perceive that the door distinctly hears me, then I know that all the congregation may' (ibid., 186). The effect of his sermons was increased rather than diminished by certain peculiarities of phrase and style. A common gesture in the pulpit looked as if he were catching a fly between his thumb and forefinger. He preached from notes and after each service wrote out more fully the chief headings and subject matter of the sermon. These substantially formed twenty-one volumes of the 2536 sermon outlines of his *Horae homilecticae, or, Discourses digested into one continued series, and forming a commentary upon every book of the Old and New Testament* (1819–28), with his 'Essay on the composition of a sermon', translated from the work by the Huguenot Jean Claude.

Simeon's preaching increasingly attracted more and more of the once generally hostile undergraduates to his church. He wrote on a Sunday in 1818:

> As for the gownsmen, never was anything like what they are at this day. I am forced to let them go up into the galleries which I never suffered before; and notwithstanding that, multitudes of them are forced to stand in the aisles for want of a place to sit down. (Carus, 496)

Simeon regretted the lack of specialized, professional training provided by the Church of England to candidates for the ministry; and he was a pioneer in undertaking this in his rooms in King's College. In 1790 he started fortnightly sermon classes in term-time for ordinands, at first on Sunday evenings and later on Fridays. Each class lasted for an hour. He gave instruction in sermon composition, voice production, reading, and delivery from the pulpit, with such advice as 'A sermon should be like a telescope: each successive division of it should be as an additional

lens to bring the subject of your text nearer and make it more distinct' and 'Form your voice not in your chest, not in your throat, not in the roof of your mouth, but simply with your lips and teeth' (Brown, 183, 187). In addition, the class was given a text upon which each man during the coming fortnight wrote a sermon outline to be read at the next meeting and criticized by Simeon.

Conversation parties In 1812 Simeon started as well his weekly conversation parties, which were also held in his rooms on Friday evenings. After two waiters had handed tea round to those present, he sat on a high mahogany stool with his small old quarto Bible beside him and said, 'Now, if any of you have any question to ask, I shall be happy to hear it and to give what assistance I can.' The questions asked covered a variety of subjects, from meditation and Christian living to slavery and national education. He earnestly explained the religious implications of such matters, but promptly rebuked flippant or foolish questions (Carus, 648–54). There were many ordinands among those who attended these parties, but there were also others who were to attain such positions in society as lawyers, politicians, soldiers, and landed gentlemen. And Henry Kirke White, the poet, was among those he helped.

Lord Macaulay, remembering the time when he was at Cambridge, wrote in 1844:

> As to Simeon, if you knew what his authority and interest were, and how they extended from Cambridge to the most remote corners of England, you would allow that his real sway in the Church was far greater than that of any primate. (Trevelyan, 1.67)

Simeon's ministry, preaching, and particularly his classes and parties did indeed gain him the support of innumerable members of the university who later widely upheld his beliefs and spread his message. Although, like the nonconformists, the evangelicals regarded the church as an invisible communion in which all believers had their proper place and function irrespective of ecclesiastical organization, he always took care to make it clear to them that he was a firm Anglican, saying, 'The Bible first, the prayer book next and all other books and doings in subordination to both' (Carus, 12), so retaining many, both clergymen and laymen, as upholders of the evangelical party within the church at a time when Methodism flourished. Bishop Charles Wordsworth, who knew Oxford during the early days of Tractarianism, made this comparison with the then preacher at its university church, when he said that Simeon 'had a large following of young men—larger and not less devoted than that which followed Newman—and for a much longer time' (Wordsworth, 335).

Simeon further strengthened the position of evangelicalism in the church through the purchase of advowsons. By English law advowsons were regarded as a right of property which could be transferred by gift or (until 1924) by sale. In 1813 John Thornton of Clapham died, leaving the patronage of ten livings, which his wealth had enabled him to acquire, to trustees. Simeon became one of these, and they developed into the Simeon trustees. He used a legacy left to him in 1800, together with substantial gifts from sympathizers, to purchase further advowsons for the trustees. These included fashionable watering-places such as Cheltenham, Bath, and Bridlington, and industrial centres such as Northampton, Birmingham, and Bradford. A great opportunity came to him with the passing of the Municipal Corporations Act of 1835, which compelled the corporations to dispose of livings in their gift. By the time of his death the trust possessed twenty-one livings, a number which increased to 150 during the next century.

Influence on missionary societies Simeon's influence extended not only further than Cambridge but also beyond Britain itself. He was among the founders of the Church Missionary Society in 1797 and actively supported the British and Foreign Bible Society, the Religious Tract Society, the Colonial and Continental Church Society, and the Church Mission to the Jews. His association with these societies showed his willingness to co-operate with both Anglicans of varying churchmanship and nonconformists.

Simeon himself was mainly concerned with missionary work in India, where his interest was aroused by a memorial in 1788 from Charles Grant and other wealthy merchants in the East India Company advocating missionary and educational work there. When Grant became chairman of the court of directors of the company in 1805, he was able, though missionaries were forbidden to go to India, to enable Simeon to secure the appointment of chaplains employed by the company there, who were evangelists among the natives as well. Among these were several of his curates, notably Henry Martyn.

In the last part of his life Simeon, having contributed greatly to the evangelical revival, and despite the widely disseminated effect of his ministry, still valued his fellowship of King's College. He died, unmarried, at King's College, Cambridge, on 13 November 1836 and was buried six days later, at his wish, in its chapel.

LEONARD W. COWIE

Sources H. E. Hopkins, *Charles Simeon of Cambridge* (1973) · *The memoirs and a selection from the letters of the late Rev. C. Jerram*, ed. J. Jerram (1855) · G. O. Trevelyan, *The life and letters of Lord Macaulay*, another edn, 2 vols. (1889) · W. Carus, ed., *Memoirs of the life of the Rev. Charles Simeon* (1847) · A. W. Brown, *Recollections of the conversation parties of the Rev Charles Simeon* (1863) · H. C. G. Moule, *Charles Simeon* (1892); repr. (1948) · C. Smyth, *Simeon and church order* (1940) · A. Pollard and M. Hennell, eds., *Charles Simeon* (1959) · H. Noel, *Charles Simeon of Cambridge* (1890) · F. Close, *The character and last days of Charles Simeon* (1836) · J. Williamson, *Memoir of the Rev. Charles Simeon* (1863) · L. E. Elliott-Binns, *The early evangelicals: a religious and social study* (1953) · M. L. Loane, *Cambridge and the evangelical succession* (1952) · D. A. Winstanley, *Unreformed Cambridge: a study of certain aspects of the university in the eighteenth century* (1935) · H. Gunning, *Reminiscences of the university, town, and county of Cambridge, from the year 1780*, 2nd edn, 2 vols. (1855) · C. Simeon, *Horae homilecticae*, 17 vols. (1819–28) · C. Wordsworth, *Annals of my early life, 1806–1846: with occasional compositions in Latin and English verse*, ed. W. E. Hodgson, 2 vols. (1891–3) · [H. C. Scholefield], *Memoir of the late Rev. James Scholefield … by his widow* (1855)

Archives CUL, corresp., notebook, diaries, and papers · LPL, diary and corresp. · Ridley Hall, Cambridge, papers | U. Birm. L., letters to Henry Venn

Likenesses oils, *c*.1808, King's Cam. · J. Northcote, oils, 1810, King's Cam. · W. Say, mezzotint, 1822 (after J. Jackson), BM, NPG [*see illus.*] · A. Edouart, silhouettes, 1828, King's Cam. · S. Manning junior, marble bust, *c*.1838, CUL · W. Finden, stipple (after W. Beechey, *c*.1800), BM; repro. in Carus, ed., *Memoirs* · C. J. Kay, etching, BM

Wealth at death £5000: Moule, *Charles Simeon*, 265

Simeon, Sir John, first baronet (1755/6–1824), lawyer and politician, was baptized on 18 March 1756 at St Laurence's Church, Reading, the second son of Richard Simeon (*d.* 1784), attorney, of Reading, and his wife, Elizabeth Hutton. His brother Charles *Simeon became one of the most prominent evangelicals in the Church of England. The family were of French extraction. Simeon was educated at Eton College, which he entered in September 1765, becoming a king's scholar in 1771. He matriculated at Merton College, Oxford, on 23 October 1775, aged nineteen.

Having become a student of Lincoln's Inn on 12 November 1773, Simeon was called to the bar in Trinity term 1779. The same year he was elected recorder of his native town of Reading, and held that position until his resignation in 1807. He was also elected to represent the town in parliament in June 1797. On 14 June 1783 he married Rebecca (*d.* 1830), the eldest daughter of John Cornwall of Hendon, Middlesex, a wealthy Russia merchant. The couple had three sons and three daughters. Simeon had estates at Walliscot and Gresley, Oxfordshire.

In the Commons, Simeon was normally a supporter of William Pitt's government, but was not afraid to criticize some of its measures. He lost his seat in 1802, but subsequently re-established his position by means of 'an expensive programme of ostentatious charity and some dubious business transactions' (HoP, *Commons, 1790–1820*, 175). Simeon was elected unopposed in 1806, and continued to represent Reading until 1818, when failing health forced him to retire from politics.

In 1789 Simeon published *A Treatise on the Law of Elections*, which was well received by the profession; a second edition appeared in 1795. Simeon also proposed measures to improve knowledge of electoral law, but his action was frustrated. He was a frequent speaker on the poor laws and sat on the 1817 and 1818 select committees, but was averse to schemes of radical reform. His bill of 1800, to allow transfers of stock in equity suits, passed into law in amended form.

In November 1795 Simeon was appointed a master in chancery in ordinary, and discharged the duties of the office for twenty-eight years; for the last sixteen years of his life he was senior master. On 7 March 1812 he was placed at the head of the commission, composed of himself, Count Münster, and General Herbert Taylor, for placing George III's real and personal estate in trust during his majesty's illness; this delicate business was executed without salary. He acted as a commissioner for the protection of the king's property until his majesty's death in 1820. In consideration of his services a baronetcy was conferred upon Simeon on 22 May 1815, and by royal licence on 26 May 1820 he received a grant of supporters to be borne by him and his successors in the title. On 9 July 1817 he petitioned to be called to the bench of Lincoln's Inn, but his application was not granted.

Sir John was described by Mary Russell Mitford as having been 'stationary as Southampton Buildings, solid as the doorpost, and legible as the letters on a brass plate' (HoP, *Commons, 1790–1820*, 175). He died on 4 February 1824, and was succeeded as second baronet by his eldest son, Sir Richard Simeon. His wife survived him.

W. R. WILLIAMS, *rev.* ROBERT BROWN

Sources Foster, *Alum. Oxon.* · W. P. Baildon, ed., *The records of the Honorable Society of Lincoln's Inn: admissions*, 1 (1896) · Burke, *Peerage* · J. Wilson, ed., *A biographical index to the present House of Commons* (1805) · J. Man, *The history and antiquities … of the borough of Reading* (1816) · J. Haydn, *The book of dignities: containing lists of the official personages of the British empire*, ed. H. Ockerby, [new edn] (1890) · HoP, *Commons, 1790–1820* · R. A. Austen-Leigh, ed., *The Eton College register, 1753–1790* (1921) · GM, 1st ser., 94/1 (1824), 459

Simmonds [Simmons; *née* Calvert], **Martha** (*bap.* 1624, *d.* 1665), Quaker and author, was baptized at Meare, Somerset, on 28 January 1624, the daughter of George Calvert (*d.* 1628), vicar of Meare, and his second wife, Ann Collier; she was the younger sister of the booksellers George and Giles Calvert. Giles's shop at the Black Spread Eagle in St Paul's Churchyard, London, was the leading outlet for the works of early Quakers until 1656. Although perhaps a Seeker from about 1640 Martha was an early convert to Quakerism about 1654–5, writing several pamphlets, three of which were published by her brother Giles: *When the Lord Jesus Came to Jerusalem* (April 1655); *A Lamentation for the Lost Sheep of the House of Israel* (October 1655); and *O England, thy Time is Come* [n.d., c.1656–7]. The first two were printed together in a second edition of *A Lamentation* (1656).

At the time of her conversion Martha had been living in London since probably the 1640s (most likely at her brother's shop) and in *A Lamentation* she describes many years of spiritual seeking. About 1655 she married Thomas Simmons or Simmonds (*b. c.*1618) who had recently returned to London after several years as a bookseller in Birmingham. In March 1655 the Quakers established the Bull and Mouth as their main London meeting place, where Thomas opened his bookshop; he became their principal publisher the following year. During his Birmingham years he had connections with George Calvert, and Giles Calvert may have supported the London venture as an extension of his own Quaker publishing. Martha, however, soon left London for Essex. By December 1655 she had been imprisoned several times in Colchester for interrupting church services and enacting signs, and walking through the town in sackcloth and ashes. She also visited Ware and Hertford and in *O England* writes of almost two years spent in crying repentance 'in thy Cities, Towns, and Market-Streets' (1–2).

Martha's part in the events of summer 1656 has been variously interpreted as female hysteria, witchcraft, or a challenge to male Quaker leadership. A group of women including Martha began in 1656 to interrupt Quaker meetings led by Francis Howgill and Edward Burrough, singing and chanting 'innocency'. The women, condemned by Burrough, William Dewsbury, and Richard Hubberthorn, turned to James Nayler for justice. Martha's powerful appeal triggered a spiritual crisis in Nayler, who stayed at her house for three days, an episode leading to accusations by George Fox of witchcraft. In July, Friends tried to part Nayler and Martha forcibly by taking him to Bristol, though George Bishop later denied her account of being thrown downstairs. Nayler proceeded towards Exeter, where shortly afterwards he was imprisoned, while Martha returned to London and offered herself as nurse to Major-General John Desborough's wife, a sister of Cromwell. As reward for her services she obtained an order for Nayler's release which, with her husband and Hannah and John Stranger, she delivered to Exeter in October.

Now began the series of events which would culminate in Nayler's trial for blasphemy, Martha's ostracism by London Friends, and serious damage to the reputation of the Quaker movement. While Thomas Simmons returned to London, the rest of the Exeter group—Nayler, Martha, Hannah and John Stranger, Dorcas Erbury, Timothy Wedlock, Samuel Carter, and Robert Crab—set off for Bristol, passing in procession through Wells and Glastonbury where they strewed the way with their garments. On 24 October they reached Bristol, entering the city in what many interpreted as a blasphemous re-enactment of Christ's entry into Jerusalem: the men went bareheaded, Nayler riding on horseback while Martha and Hannah walked at either side, singing 'Holy, holy, holy, Lord God of Israel'. Ending their procession at the city's high cross they then met local Friends at the White Hart, whereupon they were immediately arrested, imprisoned, and questioned by Bristol magistrates. Martha's testimony that her actions were inspired by the Lord and that 'James Nayler will be Jesus, when the new life is born in him' confirmed suspicions of Nayler's blasphemy (Deacon, 27). A letter to Martha from her husband laments the rashness of the group's actions at Bristol: 'If there was such a glory amongst you; why were you not silent, and have let the people cry Hosanna'. His suggestion that Martha was 'the chief leader in that action' is suggestive: Martha's preoccupation with the biblical episode of Christ's entry is clear from her first publication. Thomas's postscript offers an analogy with the Levellers: 'part of the Army that fell at Burford, was your figure' (Farmer, 21).

News of the incident quickly spread and a parliamentary committee, set up on 31 October to consider Nayler's misdemeanours and blasphemies, sent for the prisoners; they left Bristol for London on 10 November. Nayler was found guilty of blasphemy and after debate the committee rejected the death penalty. On his first appearance in the pillory, on 18 December, he was whipped 300 times. Protests at this brutality included a petition to parliament that his next punishment be postponed; the only stationer who signed was Giles Calvert, Martha's brother. On 27 December, when Nayler's tongue was bored and his forehead branded, Martha, Hannah Stranger and Dorcas Erbury sat at the foot of the pillory in a tableau recalling the three Marys at the foot of the cross, while Robert Rich put up a sign reading 'This is the King of the Jews' above Nayler's head. The following day a sympathetic and noisy Quaker demonstration gathered at the Rose in the new market place, Westminster, where Martha and the other women were in custody.

A report that Martha, the Strangers, and Dorcas Erbury, still undischarged and under custody, went to Westminster Abbey and listened quietly to sermons seems unreliable. *O England* (with texts by Martha, Nayler, Hannah Stranger, and William Tomlinson) is defiantly celebratory of Nayler's Christ-like suffering, and letters from Friends indicate that, with Nayler imprisoned in Bridewell, the women continued to disrupt Quaker meetings. On one occasion Martha and Mildred Crouch sang a psalm, read from Ezekiel and performed a parodic communion. In April 1657 they attempted reconciliation with the Quaker movement: 'The Agents of J[ames] N[ayler] have come creeping on their Bellies to be owned yea: Martha their Miserable Mother, this day hath been [at?] us, & all her witchery & filthy enchantments is set at Naught' (Swarthmore MS 5.27). The group probably fragmented for, in August, Salisbury Friends 'received some hurt by some of Martha Simmonds company which came there about to dwell' (Swarthmore MS 2.129). By autumn Hubberthorne detected 'something of God stirring' in Martha (Caton MS 3.391). Although Thomas Simmons continued publishing for Quakers until 1661, Giles Calvert thereafter published few Quaker authors other than Nayler. The exact details of Martha's death in 1665 are unclear: a letter of 7 April 1665 reports her death *en route* for Maryland but her death in St Mary Magdalen's parish, Bermondsey, on 27 September 1665 and burial the same day in Southwark are also recorded. MAUREEN BELL

Sources K. L. Carroll, 'Martha Simmonds, a Quaker enigma', *Journal of the Friends' Historical Society*, 53 (1972–5), 31–52 · J. Deacon, *The grand impostor examined* (1656) · R. Farmer, *Sathan inthron'd in his chair of pestilence* (1657) · L. Damrosch, *The sorrows of the Quaker Jesus: James Nayler and the puritan crackdown on the free spirit* (1996) · M. Simmonds, *A lamentation for the lost sheep of the house of Israel* (1655) · M. Simmonds, *O England, thy time is come* [n.d., c.1656–1657] · E. Thomas, 'A purveyor of soul-poysons: an analysis of the career of Giles Calvert, a publisher and bookseller in mid-seventeenth century London', PhD diss., La Trobe University, 1999 · RS Friends, Lond., Swarthmore papers · RS Friends, Lond., Caton papers · G. Bishop, *The throne of truth exalted over the powers of darkness* (1657) · M. R. Brailsford, *A Quaker from Cromwell's army: James Nayler* (1927) · E. Fogelklou, *James Nayler, the rebel saint, 1618–1660*, trans. L. Yapp (1931) · W. Grigge, *The Quaker's Jesus* (1658) · N. Penney, ed., 'The first publishers of truth': being early records, now first printed, of the introduction of Quakerism into the counties of England and Wales (1907) · 'Dictionary of Quaker biography', RS Friends, Lond. [card index] · burial digest, London and Middlesex quarterly meeting, RS Friends, Lond. · B. Smith, '"By word, by writing and by signs": the testimony of Martha Simmons, Quaker', MPhil diss., U. Birm., 2001

Simmonds, Peter Lund (1814–1897), newsagent and journalist, was born on 24 July 1814 in Aarhus, Denmark. He was adopted by Lieutenant George Simmonds RN—but his precise origins and the events leading to his adoption are obscure. The Simmondses were a naval family and their home at Portsea Island, Hampshire, was near the country's chief naval dockyard. From the age of twelve Peter served as a midshipman on the *Cygnet*, under the command of his uncle, James Gooding. In 1831 he was sent to Jamaica as a bookkeeper. The West Indies, in this tumultuous period of slave emancipation, made a deep impression on him; the experience formed the basis for all his later interests. His return to England in 1834 coincided with a remarkable proliferation of periodicals and he first emerged as a journalist editing *The Garland* (1836), a provincial miscellany of news and literature, and as main contributor to *The Alligator* (1841) which was devoted to West Indian matters. On 1 January 1838 he married Ellen Mary Molesworth (it seems that they later separated), and set up in Chichester as a 'newspaper agent', obtaining and circulating newspapers and journals from around the world, until 1841, when he moved to London to become secretary to the dynamic William Shaw, editor of the *Mark Lane Express*. Simmonds's interest in the overlap of science and trade was signalled by his membership of the Statistical Society of London; his essay in this society's *Journal*, 'Statistics of newspapers in various countries' (1841) remains a useful survey of the world's press of that period. From 1842 to 1844 he served as sub-editor of the *Farmer's Encyclopaedia*, and was at some time later engaged as city editor of *The Globe*. In 1844 he began to publish *Simmonds' Colonial Magazine* which promoted the cause of colonial development, and criticized governmental 'apathy and supineness on the one hand and gross ignorance and misrule on the other' (*Simmonds' Colonial Magazine*, 7, 1846, preface). By this time he had established a worldwide communications network of impressive efficiency, and contributed to an enormous range of publications on a wide variety of subjects. In 1848, in keeping with the family tradition, he became a freemason. After the Great Exhibition of 1851 Simmonds was engaged to help with the display in South Kensington of 'trade products and objects of natural history' sponsored by the Royal Society of Arts, of which he became a member in 1853. Subsequently he delivered nineteen major papers and published thirty-three substantial articles in the society's *Journal*, was made an honorary life member in 1862, and three times received the society's silver medal. It was Simmonds who successfully proposed Karl Marx for membership of the society. In 1861 he began a new periodical, *The Technologist: a Monthly Record of Science Applied to Art and Manufacture*. Its main concerns were with informed descriptions of natural resources and their acquisition, processing, and utilization, combined with the promotion of emigration as the solution to social problems. To these interests he added another, in which he was far ahead of his time—the recycling of materials. His book *Waste Products and Undeveloped Substances, or, Hints for Enterprise in Neglected Fields* (1862) is a wide-ranging treatment of the subject. During these years he was closely involved with many international exhibitions, including those in London of 1862, Paris of 1867 and 1878, and Melbourne of 1880, and he was made chevalier of the Légion d'honneur in 1878, and a knight of the Crown of Italy in the same year. He helped establish natural science museums in Australia and Japan. His involvement with *The Technologist* ceased in 1866; in 1870 he started *The Journal of Applied Science* which covered similar topics, and continued for 146 issues until 1882. Thereafter, he was unable to sustain the journalism and lecturing which had been his main sources of income, though he continued to produce works such as *A Dictionary of Useful Animals* (1883). Despite a life of constant labour he was not prosperous and became increasingly impecunious. In 1892, sponsored by the prince of Wales and the archbishop of Canterbury (both freemasons), he was granted a pensioner's place at the Charterhouse in London. In mid-September 1897 he was knocked down by an omnibus in the Gray's Inn Road and died at the Charterhouse two weeks later, on 3 October. He was buried at Charterhouse burial-ground in Bow cemetery. DAVID GREYSMITH

Sources *Journal of the Society of Arts*, 45 (1896–7), 1150 • *Men and women of the time* (1891) • Boase, *Mod. Eng. biog.* • *The Times* (6 Oct 1897) • *The Freemason* (9 Oct 1897) • P. L. Simmonds, *Illustrated history of the St Mark's Mark Lodge* (1895), 83 • *The Garland, or, Chichester, West Sussex and East Hampshire Repository*, 1/1 (1836), 2, 131 • *Journal of the Statistical Society*, 4 (1841), 111–36 • *Simmonds' Colonial Magazine and foreign miscellany of trade, commerce and banking*, 1–15 (1844–8) • *The Technologist: a monthly record of Science Applied to Art and Manufacture* (1861–6) • *The Journal of Applied Science and Record of Progress in the Industrial Arts*, 1–146 (1870–82) • D. G. C. Allen, 'The red doctor among the virtuosi: Karl Marx and the society [pts 1–2]', *Journal of the Royal Society of Arts*, 129 (1980–81), 259–61, 309–11 • Admiralty records, PRO, ADM/6/107, ADM/37/4812–13, ADM/37/7083 • archives, LMA • RGS, Simmonds papers
Archives LMA, archives of the Royal Society of Arts • RGS, corresp. • St Peter the Great, Chichester, Sussex, parish register | PRO, ADM/37/4812–4813, ADM/37/7083, ADM/6/107 • W. Sussex RO, letters to duke of Richmond
Likenesses photograph • portrait, CUL, Royal Commonwealth Society archives • portrait, repro. in Simmonds, *Illustrated history*, facing p. 82
Wealth at death in 'pecuniary difficulties': *Journal of the Society of Arts*, 45, 1150

Simmons, Bartholomew [*pseud.* Harold] (1804–1850), poet, was born at Kilworth, co. Cork, the eldest son of an English exciseman, and a Miss Luddy of Kilworth. He was educated at Birmingham School and Quigley's school, both in Cork. Simmons's first poems were published shortly after his twentieth birthday in *Bolster's Magazine*, to which he was a regular contributor during the next three years, during which time he also contributed, sometimes under the pseudonym Harold, to *Blackwood's Magazine*, which printed his most famous poem 'Napoleon's Last Look'.

Simmons could not, however, live by his poetic gifts alone, and so in 1830 entered the excise branch of the civil service, a sinecure obtained with the help of his father's old landlord Lord Mountcaskell. But Simmons did not cease to write altogether, and was a key member of Lady Blessington's literary circle, whose collected poems were published in London in 1843.

Unmarried to the end of his life, Simmons died of cancer on 21 July 1850 at his lodgings in 29 Acton Street, Gray's Inn Road, London, his death hastened by the shock from an explosion that occurred while he was sailing up the Thames. He was buried in Highgate cemetery. Thanks to the repeated anthologization of his poem on Napoleon,

and to Christopher North's eulogistic reference to his poetic gift in the *Noctes Ambrosianae*, Simmons's name was remembered well into the nineteenth century. JASON EDWARDS

Sources R. R. Madden, *The literary life and correspondence of the countess of Blessington*, 3 vols. (1855) • *GM*, 2nd ser., 34 (1850), 558 • J. Wilson and others, *Noctes ambrosianae*, rev. edn, 5 vols. (New York, 1863–6) • D. J. O'Donoghue, *The poets of Ireland: a biographical dictionary with bibliographical particulars*, 1 vol. in 3 pts (1892–3), 230 • 'Selections from the poems of Bartholomew Simmons', *Journal of the Cork Historical and Archaeological Society*, 3 (1894), 279–90, esp. 279–83 • *DNB*
Archives NL Scot., corresp. with Blackwoods

Simmons, Jack (1915–2000), historian, was born at Manaton, College Road, Isleworth, Middlesex, on 30 August 1915, the only child of Seymour Francis Simmons, a hosiery manufacturer then serving as a private in the Royal Fusiliers, and his wife, Katherine Lillias, daughter of Thomas Finch MD of Babbacombe, Devon. His father was killed on the Somme in France in 1918, and Simmons's mother, restless and unhappy, moved for several years from place to place, often returning to her kin in Devon and the Gower peninsula. After some years she settled in Surrey, and thereafter followed the path of Simmons's career. He lived with her until she died in 1971.

Simmons was educated at Rushmore School, Bedford, and at Westminster School, which he entered in 1928. He became a king's scholar in 1929, and in 1933 matriculated from Christ Church, Oxford, where he held a Hinchliffe scholarship. He had a mild spinal deformity which was severely aggravated by a fall in Oxford, and he had to suspend his studies for a year, taking schools in modern history in 1937. He then spent a year in Paris before returning to Oxford as assistant to Sir Reginald Coupland (1884–1952), Beit professor of colonial history. He was medically unfit for military service in the war, though he served in London as a fire-watcher at St Paul's. In 1943 he was appointed Beit lecturer in the history of the British empire, and pursued his own studies. He collaborated with Margery Perham in *African Discovery: an Anthology of Exploration* (1942), and in 1945 he published *Southey*, a biographical study which led to his election as a fellow of the Royal Society of Literature.

Simmons was joined at Christ Church in 1934 by Michael Robbins, a fellow pupil at Westminster with whom he shared a lifelong interest in railway history. He was also strongly influenced by Alfred Leslie Rowse (1903–97), whose *Tudor Cornwall* (1941) opened new vistas in local and regional studies. Simmons was as well read in English literature and topography as in imperial history, and a purposeful traveller in space as well as in time, as his edition of *Murray's Handbook for Travellers in Switzerland* (1970) testifies. His wide-ranging interests were closely integrated, and he was fascinated by the nexus of imperial and domestic history. He was not, however, familiar with the east midlands, where in the event he spent most of his life, and it was probably Rowse who in 1946 persuaded him to apply for the new chair of history at University College, Leicester, which he held from 1947.

The college, founded in 1921, prepared students for the external degree examinations of the University of London. It had only recently been recognized by the University Grants Committee, and the establishment of ten chairs between 1946 and 1948 was a significant step towards autonomy. With the demand for university places after the war the number of students grew rapidly, and the new professors and their colleagues would have been adequately occupied with present needs if they had not also to plan for the future. Simmons at once found himself in his element. He excelled as a teacher. While managing his own department with tact and good humour he also busied himself with the college library, a cornerstone of any academic development, and with a publications board of senate, which later became Leicester University Press. He also encouraged the appointment of William George Hoskins, newly returned from the wartime civil service, as head of the first department of English local history in the country. Simmons went on to play a leading part in the exacting campaign to obtain a university charter for Leicester, and described the process with engaging lucidity in *New University* (1958). It is a work which surveys everything except his own influential role, and includes a cogent sketch of the expansion of university education in England from the early nineteenth century.

Over the following decades Simmons served the university as public orator, pro-vice-chancellor, and acting vice-chancellor (in 1962), and sat on many boards, always incisively. He was successively honorary editor and president of the Leicestershire Archaeological and Historical Society, and he was a member of advisory committees on archives and museums in and out of the county. He was a well-regarded contributor to the overseas service of the BBC, and in 1967 became the founding chairman of the Leicester local broadcasting council, monitoring the BBC's first such venture.

In 1953, in partnership with Michael Robbins, Simmons established the *Journal of Transport History*, and he maintained it energetically. At the same time he launched A New Survey of England, a topographical series published by Collins. It was intended to match the highly successful series of monographs New Naturalist, from the same house, but foundered on rising costs, despite the distinction of its first volumes: *Middlesex*, by R. M. Robbins (1953), and *Devon* by W. G. Hoskins (1954). Simmons, who was preparing what would have been an exemplary volume on Berkshire, was much disappointed, but after publishing *Livingstone and Africa* (1955) under Rowse's editorship, he turned to edit a pioneering series called A Visual History of Britain, to which he contributed two notable volumes, *Transport* (1962), and *Britain and the World* (1965). His interest now focused on the reign of Victoria, and particularly on the history of the railway as a defining force of the age. He published *The Railways of Britain: an Historical Introduction* in 1961, the first of several studies which culminated in *The Oxford Companion to British Railway History* (1997), which he compiled with Gordon Biddle. The *Companion* is

an impressive work, but Simmons is at his most characteristic in *St Pancras Station* (1968), a biography of a great building which deploys his wide learning, his aesthetic sense, and his sympathetic grasp of practical affairs.

Those qualities also made him influential in establishing the National Railway Museum, which opened in 1975, the year in which he retired from his chair, and the National Museum of Photography, Film, and Television. He long remained as active in retirement as in office. Despite failing sight he continued to the end to write and, by various ingenious contrivances, to read. He was appointed OBE in 1999. He died in the Nightingale Nursing Home, 35 Aylstone Lane, Wigston, on 3 September 2000, of a metastasized cancer, and was cremated on 15 September at Gilroes cemetery. He was unmarried.

Despite his spinal injury Simmons had an imposing and dignified bearing. Although shy and fastidious he could readily command an audience. His conversation in familiar company was lively, and no one could be more rewardingly moved to laughter. His written style was unmistakably and elegantly measured, and inescapably recalls to those who knew him the distinctive cadence and timbre of his voice.   G. H. MARTIN

Sources WW (2000) · M. Robbins, 'Jack Simmons, 1915–2000', *Journal of Transport History*, 3rd ser., 22 (2001), 1–5 · H. J. Dyos, 'Jack Simmons: an appreciation', *Journal of Transport History*, new ser., 3 (1975–6), 133–44 · M. Robbins, 'Jack Simmons: the making of an historian', *The impact of the railway on society in Britain: essays in honour of Jack Simmons*, ed. A. K. B. Evans and J. V. Gough (2003), 1–7 · D. Jeffreys, *The Times* (13 Sept 2000) · C. Ford, 'Jack Simmons', *The Guardian* (13 Sept 2000) · R. B. Peberdy, 'Jack Simmons', *History Today*, 50/12 (2000), 6–7 · b. cert. · R. M. Robbins and N. Scarfe, 'Professor Jack Simmons', *The Independent* (6 Sept 2000) · A. Newman, 'Emeritus professor Jack Simmons, OBE', www.le.ac.uk/ua/rg/dnotices/j_simmons_obit.html, May 2001

Archives National Railway Museum, York, papers | University of Leicester, University Archives | FILM priv. coll., 35mm cinematic film

Likenesses photograph, repro. in Dyos, 'Jack Simmons' · photograph, National Railway Museum, York, Simmons library

Wealth at death under £210,000: probate, 28 Nov 2000, *CGPLA Eng. & Wales*

Simmons, Sir John Lintorn Arabin

Simmons, Sir John Lintorn Arabin (1821–1903), army officer, was born on 12 February 1821 at Langford, Somerset, the fifth son of twelve children of Captain Thomas Simmons (d. 1842), Royal Artillery, of Langford, and his wife, Mary, daughter of John Perry of Montego Bay, for many years judge of the supreme court of Jamaica. Six of his eight brothers were officers in the army.

Educated at Elizabeth College, Guernsey, and at the Royal Military Academy at Woolwich, Simmons was commissioned in the Royal Engineers on 14 December 1837, and embarked for Canada in June 1839. He was promoted first lieutenant on 15 October 1839. While in Canada he was employed for three years in disputed territory on the north-east frontier of the United States of America, constructing defence works and reconnoitring the territory.

Simmons returned to England in March 1845, and married on 16 April 1846 his cousin Ellen Lintorn Simmons at Keynsham, near Bristol. She died on 3 October 1851, leaving a daughter, Eleanor Julia, who died unmarried in 1901.

Simmons was stationed in the London district for a year, and was then an instructor in fortification at the Royal Military Academy, Woolwich. Promoted second captain on 9 November 1846, he was appointed the following month inspector of railways under the railway commissioners. In 1850 he became secretary to the railway commissioners and, when the commission was absorbed by the Board of Trade on 11 October 1851, secretary of the new railway department of the board.

In October 1853 Simmons travelled on leave in eastern Europe, where war had been declared between Turkey and Russia. After his arrival at Constantinople, he was of service to the British ambassador, Lord Stratford de Redcliffe, in reporting on the defences of the Turkish Danube frontier and of the Bosphorus, and he also visited the Black Sea ports.

Promoted first captain on 17 February 1854, Simmons was preparing to leave for England when on 20 March the British ambassador sent him to warn Omar Pasha, the Turkish commander on the Danube, of the Russian intention to cross the lower Danube near Galatz. He reached Omar at Teryukhan, and the hasty retreat of the Turkish army prevented catastrophe. Meanwhile, in reply to a demand from the Board of Trade to return home at once or resign his appointment, Simmons sent in his resignation. When at the end of March the western powers allied themselves with Turkey against Russia, Simmons was formally attached to Omar's army on the Danube as British commissioner. He gave advice and help in the defence of Silistria, which he left during the siege on 18 June to join Omar and the allied generals at Varna. Five days later the siege of Silistria was raised, and the generals at Varna decided that Omar should take advantage of this success to cross the river and attack the Russian army at Giurgevo.

On 7 July Simmons was in command of 20,000 men of all arms at the passage of the Danube and the battle of Giurgevo. He constructed the lines of Slobodzie and Giurgevo in the presence of the enemy, who tried to prevent him, while a Russian army of 70,000 men was within 7 miles. For his services with the Turkish army and his share in the defence of Silistria and the battle of Giurgevo, when the Russians were routed, Simmons was promoted brevet major on 14 July 1854, and given the local rank of lieutenant-colonel (a brevet lieutenant-colonelcy following on 12 December). During the retreat of the Russians and the occupation of Wallachia by the Turks, Simmons was frequently in charge of reconnaissances upon the enemy's rear until they had evacuated the principality.

In the meantime the allies had invaded the Crimea and besieged Sevastopol. Simmons opposed Napoleon III's proposal that the Turks should advance on the Pruth so as to act on the Russian line of communications with the Crimea. Realizing the weakened condition of the allies after Inkerman and that there were no reserves nearer than England and France, he urged that the Turkish army should reinforce the allies in the Crimea. After much discussion the advanced guard of the Turkish army in January 1855 occupied Eupatoria, which Simmons at once

placed in a state of defence, in time to repulse a determined attack by the Russians on 17 February. The Russians were 40,000 strong, while the Turkish garrison was small. After this action the remainder of the Turkish army arrived from Varna, and Simmons constructed an entrenched camp. From April to September 1855 he was with Omar's army before Sevastopol, taking part in the siege until the place fell. He was created CB on 13 October.

When, after the fall of Sevastopol, Omar took his army to Armorica to operate against the Russians south of the Caucasus, Simmons continued with him as the British commissioner. Omar, advancing into Mingrelia with 10,000 men, encountered 12,000 Russians on the River Inguri on 6 November 1855. Simmons commanded a division which, crossing the river by the ford of Ruki and turning the Russian position, captured the enemy's works and guns and compelled them to retreat. The casualties were small, so sudden and unexpected was their turning movement; Omar in his dispatch attributed the success mainly to Simmons. Unfortunately the campaign began too late to enable the relief of Kars to be effected and it capitulated on 26 November.

Early in 1856 Omar sent Simmons to London to explain his views for the next campaign in Asia Minor against Russia, but by the time he arrived in England peace negotiations were in progress, and the treaty of Paris was signed on 30 March. Simmons received the Turkish gold medal for the Danubian campaign, the third class of the Mejidieh (the second class was sent by the sultan, but the British government refused permission for him to accept it because of his rank), and the French Légion d'honneur (fourth class); the sultan of Turkey also presented him with a sword of honour and made him a major-general in the Turkish army. In his service with the Turkish army Simmons had shown a knowledge of strategy and a power of command which should have led to further command in the field, but did not.

On 20 November 1856 Simmons was married, to Blanche, only daughter of Samuel Charles Weston. They had one daughter, also named Blanche. In March 1857 he was nominated British commissioner for the delimitation of the new boundary under the treaty of Paris between Turkey and Russia in Asia; Major-General Charles George Gordon was one of three engineer officers who accompanied him as assistant commissioners. The whole frontier from Ararat to the Black Sea was traversed and questions of principle were settled by the commission; the actual marking of the boundary line was carried out by their expert assistants in the following year. Simmons returned home in December 1857, and was promoted to a brevet colonelcy.

For two years (20 February 1858 – January 1860) Simmons was British consul at Warsaw. Promoted regimental lieutenant-colonel on 31 January 1860, he was for the next five years commanding royal engineer at Aldershot. He sat on several important committees during his command, including one in 1865 on the Royal Engineers establishment at Chatham, presided over by the quartermaster-general, Sir Richard Airey. In September 1865 Simmons became director of the Chatham establishment (later the School of Military Engineering) with a view to carrying out the recommendations of the committee.

In October 1868 Simmons relinquished this appointment after his promotion as major-general (6 March), and in March 1869 he was made lieutenant-governor of the Royal Military Academy at Woolwich, becoming KCB on 2 June. From this time on he was known as Sir Lintorn Simmons. In 1870 he became governor at Woolwich with full responsibility. On 27 August 1872 he was promoted lieutenant-general and made a colonel-commandant of Royal Engineers. The French prince imperial became a cadet at Woolwich in December, and thenceforth the Empress Eugénie regarded Simmons as a personal friend. While governor at Woolwich, Simmons was a member of the royal commission on railway accidents in 1874 and 1875. After six successful years he left the academy on his appointment as inspector-general of fortifications at the War Office (1 August 1875). He was chief technical military delegate with Disraeli and Salisbury at the Berlin Congress of 1878. He had been promoted general on 1 October 1877, and on 29 July 1878 was awarded the GCB. He was also chief technical military delegate with the British plenipotentiary, Lord Odo Russell, at the international conference at Berlin, in June 1880, on the Greek frontier question.

After leaving the War Office in the summer of 1880 Simmons served on Lord Carnarvon's royal commission on the defence of British possessions and commerce abroad. He was also a member of Lord Airey's committee on army reorganization, and had published a pamphlet on the subject, *The Military Forces of Great Britain*, in 1871.

Appointed governor of Malta in April 1884, Simmons did much to improve the island, and especially its drainage, water supply, and coinage. On 24 May 1887 he was awarded the GCMG. He remained at Malta until his retirement on 28 September 1888. In 1889 he took part in a special mission to Pope Leo XIII concerning the religious establishment in Malta.

On 14 March 1890 the sultan of Turkey conferred on Simmons the first class of the Mejidieh, and on 21 May 1890 Queen Victoria made him a field marshal. As a friend of General Gordon, Simmons was chairman of the Gordon Boys' Home. Simmons's second wife died in February 1898, and he spent his last years with his son-in-law and daughter, Major and Mrs Orman, at Hawley House, near Blackwater, Hampshire, where he died on 14 February 1903. He was buried at Churchill, Somerset, beside his wife. R. H. VETCH, *rev.* JAMES LUNT

Sources W. Porter, *History of the corps of royal engineers*, 2 vols. (1889) · *The Times* (10 Feb 1903) · C. M. Watson, 'Field Marshal Sir J. Lintorn A. Simmons', *Royal Engineers Journal*, 33/394 (1 Sept 1903), 202–4 · *Hart's Army List*

Archives BL, letters to Lord Carnarvon, Add. MS 60812 · ING Barings, corresp. with earl of Northbrook · NAM, letters to Lord Raglan · PRO, corresp. and papers, FO 358 · PRO, corresp. with Stratford Canning, FO 352

Likenesses F. Holl, oils, 1883 (as a general), Royal Engineers headquarters mess, Chatham, Kent · H. Hente, oils, c.1890; known to be

in possession of his daughter, Mrs Orman, 1912 · Ape [C. Pellegrini], caricature, NPG; repro. in *VF* (1 Dec 1877) · R. T., woodengraving, NPG; repro. in *ILN* (31 May 1890)

Wealth at death £20,841 0s. 1d.: resworn probate, Sept 1903, CGPLA Eng. & Wales

Simmons, Mary (*d.* 1686×7). *See under* Simmons, Matthew (*b.* in or before 1608, *d.* 1654).

Simmons, Matthew (*b.* in or before **1608**, *d.* **1654**), bookseller and printer, was the son of Thomas Simmons (*d.* in or before 1624), a husbandman from Middleton, Warwickshire. Thomas Simmons, the Quaker bookseller and husband of Martha Calvert, was not the brother of Matthew, as has sometimes been supposed. Matthew Simmons was apprenticed to the London printer John Dawson senior on 20 November 1624 and was freed into the Stationers' Company, when he would have been at least twenty-four, on 14 January 1632. He was active as a bookseller at a shop near Moorgate in London in 1634, when he took the first of six apprentices, and had moved to the sign of the Golden Lion in Duck Lane by the following year. In November 1637 he was in the Netherlands meeting Dutch booksellers; in the same year imprints locate his house in the Barbican near the Red Cross, and in 1640 he was in Goldsmiths' Alley in Red Cross Street. Most of the items he published before that date had been produced with his former fellow apprentice Thomas Paine, and in 1640 he became a partner in Paine's printing shop in the same street.

Simmons was married by 1639 as that year he baptized a son, Lazarus, in St Giles Cripplegate; his wife was **Mary Simmons** (*d.* 1686/7). (An earlier baptism of Mary, the daughter of Matthew and Mary Symons at St Olave, Silver Street, in September 1634 probably does not refer to the same couple.) The parish registers record the burial of another son in 1640 and the baptism of two more children, including **Samuel Simmons** (1640–1687) who, although he was apparently born on 8 April 1640, was not baptized until 15 October 1643. At some point the family moved to Aldersgate Street; a daughter of theirs was baptized in St Botolph, Aldersgate, in February 1646. Simmons was made a liveryman of the Stationers' Company on 12 April 1647.

Simmons was a favoured printer for independents and radicals during the civil war period. Most notably, in 1643 he printed Milton's *Doctrine and Discipline of Divorce*, beginning a professional association between the poet and the Simmons family that would last over thirty years. Simmons himself printed Milton's *The Judgement of Martin Bucer* (1644), *Articles of Peace* (1649), *Eikonklastes* (1649), and *The Tenure of Kings and Magistrates* (1649), and he may also have been involved in the production of *Areopagitica* (1644), *Of Education* (1644), *Tetrachordon* (1645), and *Colasterion* (1645). Curiously, he entered *Eikon basilike* in the Stationers' register in March 1649, although this was crossed out two years later. The registers of St Botolph, Aldersgate, record the death of Simmons on 19 May 1654; the administration of his estate was granted to his wife, Mary, although the date given (6 May) must be erroneous.

Mary Simmons succeeded to Simmons's printing business and proved an active printer, entering titles in the

Stationers' register and binding apprentices. Samuel was sent to the Merchant Taylors' School, London, in 1656 before formally joining his mother's business, with his freedom by patrimony into the Stationers' Company on 3 March 1662. The two seem to have operated in partnership until at least 1673, with Mary being evidently in charge for at least part of that time. The hearth tax of 1666 noted that her establishment had thirteen hearths, making her printing house the largest such recorded on the tax roll, and a census made two years later of London's printing houses listed her as operating two presses with five workmen and one apprentice.

Although Samuel's name appears as a printer on imprints from 1662 onwards, he did not enter a work in his own name into the Stationers' register until 1667. The work in question was *Paradise Lost*, the first Milton work the Simmons family had printed for nearly two decades. The publication was also notable for one of the earliest survivals in England of a detailed contract between author and printer, in which Milton received £5 in advance with a further £5 (and 200 copies) payable at the end of the first three impressions. Samuel also printed Milton's *Accedence Commenc't Grammar* (1669) and the second and third editions of *Paradise Lost* (1674 and 1678). He became a liveryman in July 1669. Jacob Tonson, writing later in the century, described Simmons as someone who 'was lookt upon an able & substantial printer' (Dobranski, 194). Simmons was also responsible for the ambitious attempt to publish by subscription a complete edition of Joseph Caryl's *Exposition with Practical Observations upon the Book of Job*, a work that his parents had published in parts from 1650. Mary assigned all her interests in Caryl's work to her son in 1673 and Samuel announced the proposed publication that same year; however, although the work appeared in two volumes during 1676–7, by 1677 Simmons acknowledged that the project had been 'long a doing … to the great vexation and loss of the Proposer' (Lindenbaum, 184). By 1690 the work was being remaindered.

Mary Simmons died at some point between 24 December 1686 when she collected her annual dividend from her husband's share in the Stationers' Company's joint-stock venture and 11 May 1687 when the share was transferred to a new stationer. In her will, drawn up on 27 May 1684 and proved on 7 July 1687, she described herself as living at a farm in Dagenham, Essex, suggesting that she had retired from the printing business, probably about 1675. She left her estate principally to her son Samuel, who was to act as executor; however, although he was alive on 11 May, he too had died by the time the will was proved.

I. GADD

Sources private information (2004) [M. Treadwell, Trent University] · D. F. McKenzie, ed., *Stationers' Company apprentices*, [2]: *1641–1700* (1974) · *STC, 1475–1640* · Wing, *STC* · H. R. Plomer and others, *A dictionary of the booksellers and printers who were at work in England, Scotland, and Ireland from 1641 to 1667* (1907) · H. R. Plomer and others, *A dictionary of the printers and booksellers who were at work in England, Scotland, and Ireland from 1668 to 1725* (1922) · P. Morgan, *Warwickshire apprentices in the Stationers' Company of London, 1563–1700*, Dugdale Society, 25 (1978) · W. E. Miller, 'Printers and stationers in the parish of St Giles Cripplegate, 1561–1640', *Studies in Bibliography*, 19 (1966), 15–38 · D. F. McKenzie, 'Milton's printers: Matthew, Mary and Samuel Simmons', *Milton Quarterly*, 14 (1980), 87–91 · D. F. McKenzie, 'Bibliography and history: seventeenth-century England', priv. coll. [typescript of Lyell lectures] · D. F. McKenzie, 'The economies of print, 1550–1750: the scales of production and conditions of constraint', *Produzione e commercio della carta e del libro secc. XIII–XVIII: atti della 'Ventitreesima Settimana di Studi'*, ed. S. Cavaciocchi (Florence, 1992), 389–425 [Prato, 1991] · S. B. Dobranski, *Milton, authorship, and the book trade* (1999) · W. R. Parker, 'Milton, Rothwell, and Simmons', *The Library*, 4th ser., 18 (1937), 89–103 · P. Lindenbaum, 'Milton's contract', *The construction of authorship: textual appropriation in law and literature*, ed. M. Woodmansee and P. Jaszi (1994), 175–90 · administration, PRO, PROB 6/28, fol. 108r [Matthew Simmons] · will, GL, MS 9171/40, fols. 449v–450v [S. Simmons] · will, PRO, PROB 11/388, fol. 63r [Mary Simmons] · dividend book, Stationers' Hall, London

Simmons, Samuel (1640–1687). *See under* Simmons, Matthew (*b.* in or before 1608, *d.* 1654).

Simmons, Samuel (*c.*1777–1819), actor, born in London, first appeared at the Haymarket on 21 September 1785, when, as Master Simmons, he played the Duke of York in Cibber's *Richard III* and showed promise. Next he appeared as Tom Thumb, and is said also to have played other juvenile characters at Covent Garden. His first adult role at Covent Garden was on 5 November 1796, when he was the original Momus in John O'Keeffe's *Olympus in an Uproar*. Endless in Prince Hoare's *No Song, No Supper* followed, and in April 1797 he was the original Premiss, a lawyer, in Hoare's *The Italian Villagers*. Simmons remained at Covent Garden until his death, playing such parts as Daniel in Richard Steele's *The Conscious Lovers*, Master Matthew in Ben Jonson's *Every Man in his Humour*, and many roles (chiefly small) in farces which did not survive their own era. He also took many minor parts in Shakespearian plays, such as Feeble in 2 *Henry IV*, Pistol in *Henry V*, Shallow in *The Merry Wives of Windsor*, Lord Sands in *Henry VIII*, Peter in *Romeo and Juliet*, Stephano in *The Tempest*, and Flute in *A Midsummer Night's Dream*. However, he created several original roles in contemporary plays. He was the first Jerry in William Drummond's *Seaside Story* (1801), the original Manikin and Squire Supplejack in Dibdin's *The Cabinet* and *Family Quarrels* respectively, and the original Jonathan Oldskirt and Stubby in Colman's *Who Wants a Guinea?* (1805) and *We Fly by Night* (1806). In the meantime, about 1803, Simmons married. His wife's name was Margaret. In March 1816 he was the first Bailie Macklethrift in Daniel Terry's version of *Guy Mannering*, and in April 1819 the first Saddletree in *The Heart of Midlothian*. On 8 September 1819 Simmons played his old part of Moses in *The School for Scandal*, and died suddenly of apoplexy three days later, on 11 September 1819.

Simmons was a useful, unostentatious actor, to whom very few challenging characters were assigned. His best parts were Mordecai in Charles Macklin's *Love à la Mode*, Master Matthew Fainwou'd in James Kenney's *Raising the Wind*, and Alibi in *The Sleep Walker*. His exclamation 'What do you think of that, eh?' is said to have been a popular catchphrase. He was very natural in his style, which, however, had no great variety. He was a good comic singer, had great freedom of action, and was popular in pantomime. He was very useful in taking at short notice parts for which absent actors had been cast, and in comic waiters and old men showed much genuine and unforced humour with no trace of affectation or extravagance. Though his voice was powerful, Simmons was small in person, and was popularly called 'Little Simmons'.

JOSEPH KNIGHT, rev. NILANJANA BANERJI

Sources Hall, *Dramatic ports.* · *Oxberry's Dramatic Biography*, new ser., 2/1 (1827) · *Era Almanack and Annual* (1892) · *The thespian dictionary, or, Dramatic biography of the eighteenth century* (1802) · *The thespian dictionary, or, Dramatic biography of the present age*, 2nd edn (1805) · T. Gilliland, *The dramatic mirror, containing the history of the stage from the earliest period, to the present time*, 2 vols. (1808) · Genest, *Eng. stage*

Likenesses S De Wilde, pencil drawing (as Simkin in Dibdin's *Deserter*), Royal Collection · S. De Wilde, drawing (as Jonathan Oldshirt in *Who wants a guinea?*), Garr. Club · S. De Wilde, oils (as Master Matthew in *Every man in his humour*), Garr. Club · S. De Wilde, oils (as Baron Mordecai in *Love à la mode*), Garr. Club · J. Turmean, two pencil drawings, Garr. Club · plate, repro. in J. Cawthorne, ed., *Cawthorne's minor British theatre*, 6 vols. (1806) · plate, repro. in *Monthly Mirror* (1808) · plate, repro. in *Theatrical Inquisitor* (1815) · plate, repro. in Terry, *Theatrical gallery* (1822) · prints, BM, NPG · prints, Harvard TC

Simmons, Samuel Foart (1750–1813), physician, the only child of Samuel Simmons (1724–1766), town clerk of Sandwich, Kent, and his first wife, Katherine (1726–1750), daughter of Josiah Foart, was born on 6 March 1750, presumably in Sandwich. After education at a seminary in France, he studied medicine at Edinburgh and graduated MD at Leiden in 1776, with a treatise on measles. He then travelled, visiting continental universities and calling on Petrus Camper, Albrecht von Haller, and Voltaire. In Paris in 1778 he became a member of the Société Royale de Médecine. Established in London, he became a licentiate of the Royal College of Physicians in the same year. Simmons had a paper published in *Philosophical Transactions* in 1773, and on 4 November 1779 he was, on the recommendation of William Cullen, elected a fellow of the Royal Society. In 1780 he was appointed physician to the Westminster General Dispensary; and in 1781, physician to the Bethlem Hospital.

Simmons published a number of papers on a variety of subjects, mainly accounts of work by other people, reviews of current medical practice, or cases confirming earlier observations. He published as *Elements of Anatomy and the Animal Economy* (1775), a translation with a commentary of a work by Claude Person. He also published one volume of a projected *Anatomy of the Human Body* (1780). He provided no new medical insights. His contributions to medicine lay in his publication of the *Medical Register* in 1779, 1780, and 1783. Though unofficial and incomplete, the registers were of use both to the profession and to laymen, as they displayed the extent of medical provision in England, listing practitioners with their qualifications and hospitals, and noting the availability of charitable provision for the sick poor.

More important was Simmons's publication between 1781 and 1790 of eleven volumes of the *London Medical Journal*, and, between 1791 and 1800, eight volumes of *Medical Facts and Observations*. Other medical journals were published by professional societies, but Simmons offered medical men outside societies an opportunity to publish their interesting cases. The journals also contained reviews of new medical works, accounts of papers in other journals, 'medical and philosophical news', and quarterly catalogues of medical books; all of particular interest to provincial practitioners. In 1780 Simmons was president of the Medical Society of London, founded by J. C. Lettsom. When the president of the Society of Collegiate Physicians, William Hunter, died in 1783, Simmons, as a member of the society, though little acquainted with Hunter, offered a eulogy on him, which was subsequently published (1783).

When George III's illness returned in 1804, Simmons, as an expert on insanity, was called to look after him and on 15 May was gazetted physician-extraordinary to the king. His treatment relied on total restraint and the king loathed the 'horrible doctor', his son Richard, and the 'shabby attendants' who assisted them. The king was unco-operative, and on 18 August the doctors were virtually dismissed. In 1810 the king was again taken ill and, in spite of opposition from the royal family, Simmons was sent for. He demanded sole management of the case, and when this was refused, he withdrew. The king remained ill and on 6 August 1811 Simmons with others was consulted, but would not give advice without seeing the patient. The queen objected particularly to Simmons's being allowed near the king, because previously 'his Conduct and Proceedings … had rendered him *justly* obnoxious to the King, to myself, & to the whole Royal Family & to every individual attendant' (Macalpine and Hunter, 161–2). Nevertheless, they were allowed to observe but not to talk to the king. In January 1812 Simmons believed with others that the king would not recover, and the temporary regency was made permanent. Later that same year Simmons refused to give evidence at the trial of John Bellingham, who had assassinated the prime minister, Spencer Perceval, when an attempt was made to prove that Bellingham was insane; he was found guilty and executed.

Simmons had been elected to the Society of Antiquaries in 1791, and was an honorary member of the Manchester Philosophical Society, a member of the medical societies of Nancy, Montpellier, and Madrid, a foreign associate of the École de Médecine, and a correspondent, première classe, of the Institut impérial. By contributing 100 guineas, he became a hereditary governor of the British Institution for the Promotion of the Fine Arts and a proprietor of the Royal Institution.

In 1780 Simmons was living in Bentinck Street, Cavendish Square; later he lived in Poland Street, Westminster. His wife's name was Susanna; the date of their marriage and the names of her parents are unknown. Richard was their only son. On 10 April 1813 Simmons was taken ill with violent vomiting and died on 23 April. He was buried in St Clement's churchyard, Sandwich, on 2 May. He made an ample fortune from his private madhouse, but its location is not known. By his will he left to his wife the house in Poland Street and its furnishings, and £23,900 in trust, provided that she did not remarry. Near relatives, six charities, and servants were all remembered. Land, houses, and premises in Sandwich went to his son, his residuary legatee, who became so wealthy that he had no further need to practise medicine.   HELEN BROCK

Sources GM, 1st ser., 83/1 (1813), 587–8 · W. Boys, *Collections for an history of Sandwich in Kent*, 1/2 (1892, [1792]), 489 · I. Macalpine and R. Hunter, *George III and the mad-business* (1969), 132–4, 137, 145, 161 · *The correspondence of George, prince of Wales, 1770–1812*, ed. A. Aspinall, 5: *1804–1806* (1968), 63 [re Simmons' dismissal, 18 Aug 1804] · G. Clark and A. M. Cooke, *A history of the Royal College of Physicians of London*, 2 (1966), 601–2 · will, PRO, film 1544, May 268
Archives BL, Add. MSS 26, 35057 · BL, Egerton MS 2351 · RS
Wealth at death £23,900—in trust; property: will, PRO PROB 11/1544, sig. 268

Simms, William Henry

Simms, William Henry (1811–1882), engraver, was born on 11 June 1811 in St Pancras, London. Of his parents nothing is known. He was a pupil of William Finden (1787–1852), from whom he learned the craft of line engraving in copper, a method of pictorial reproduction widely used until about the fourth decade of the nineteenth century, by which time Simmons and many of his colleagues had turned to working in the much more durable medium of steel. Though beautiful when employed by a skilled craftsman the method was laborious and slow, and in response to the burgeoning demand for reproductions of popular pictures Simmons turned to the speedier technique of mixed mezzotint (in which tones and textures are achieved by a rich combination of etching, mezzotint, and engraved line). It is in this style that most of his mature work is executed. His prolific output includes many engravings after such celebrated paintings as *The Last of the Clan* and *Highland Mary* by Thomas Faed; *The Marriage of Their Royal Highnesses the Prince and Princess of Wales* by William Powell Frith; *Christ Weeping over Jerusalem* by Sir Charles Eastlake; and *The Sanctuary* by Sir Edwin Landseer.

Examples of Simmons's work were exhibited at the Royal Academy on twenty-one occasions between 1857 and 1882, years during which his skills were in constant demand by such leading print-publishers as Thomas Agnew, Henry Graves, and Ernest Gambart. When Agnew commissioned him to engrave Landseer's *Well-Bred Sitters* (eventually published in 1879), Simmons worked directly from the original canvas, which he promised to lock in his bedroom every night during progress on the large plate. It is a reflection of the arduousness of an engraver's life that Simmons undertook to complete the large image (*c*.22×29 in.) in fourteen months for a fee of £500, and of the publisher's typical anxiety for speedy results that he was offered a bonus of £25 for completion in twelve months (undated letter, Agnew's agreements book, Agnew's, London).

Perhaps Simmons's finest work is his engraving after William Holman Hunt's *The Light of the World*, the publication of which was announced by Gambart in August 1858 (that is, the intention to publish was notified to the Printsellers' Association, formed in 1847 to prevent the production of proofs beyond an openly declared number).

Gambart had been on the lookout for an appropriately skilled interpreter and his eventual choice of Simmons was applauded by the painter John Everett Millais, to whose *Proscribed Royalist* (of which a print was declared for publication, also by Gambart, in January 1858) the engraver must have been turning his attention at about the same time. On 17 November 1858 the *Illustrated London News* announced the completion of the plate of *The Light of the World*, declaring that 'considered both as the translation of a picture and simply as a work of the burin, it is one of the most perfect things modern art has produced … a great triumph'.

Though the sale of prints of *The Light of the World* alone established Hunt's international fame and brought Gambart huge financial rewards, there is no evidence that the engraver—one of the most eminent of his profession—was ever compensated by more than a modest living for his years of expert accomplishment. According to the 1881 census Simmons, by then a widower, lived at 247 Hampstead Road, St Pancras, London. The house was shared by his unmarried sister, Maria; his widowed daughter, Ann Hollyer; Ann's son, Christopher; an apprentice engraver named Herbert Wilde; and a housemaid and a cook. Simmons died there on 10 June 1882, leaving unfinished an engraving of Rosa Bonheur's *The Lion at Home* (which was later finished by a colleague, T. L. Atkinson). He was buried in Highgate cemetery. Examples of Simmons's prints are in the British Museum.   ANTHONY DYSON

Sources G. W. Friend, ed., *An alphabetical list of engravings declared at the office of the Printsellers' Association, London*, 2 vols. (1892) · R. K. Engen, *Dictionary of Victorian engravers, print publishers and their works* (1979) · J. H. Slater, *Engravings and their value*, rev. F. W. Maxwell-Barbour, 6th edn (1929); repr. (1978) · Graves, *Artists*, new edn · undated letter concerning Agnew's/Simmons contract, agreements book, Agnew's, London · J. Maas, *Gambart, prince of the Victorian art world* (1975) · census returns, 1881 · A. Dyson, *Pictures to print: the nineteenth-century engraving trade* (1984) · *DNB* · H. Beck, *Victorian engravings* (1973) [exhibition catalogue, V&A] · CGPLA Eng. & Wales (1882) · M. B. Huish, ed., *The year's art* (1883) · *Art Journal*, new ser., 2 (1882), 224
Wealth at death £700: administration, 12 July 1882, CGPLA Eng. & Wales

Simms, Frederick Richard

Simms, Frederick Richard (1863–1944), mechanical engineer and businessman, was born on 12 August 1863 in Hamburg (where his grandfather had established a business), the son of Frederick Louis Simms and his wife, Antonia, *née* Herman. Simms was educated in Germany and London and also attended the Polytechnisches Verein in Berlin after serving his apprenticeship with the AG für Automatischen Verkauf in Hamburg and Berlin. Simms was twice married. His first wife was Austrian, but nothing else is known about her; there were two daughters of his second marriage, in 1910, to Mabel Louise, daughter of Joseph Worsley, a cotton merchant.

Simms's European background and contacts contributed to his role as mediator of developments in his chosen fields of activity, the internal combustion engine and its components, and the motor vehicle. A key event was his meeting with Gottlieb Daimler when Simms was superintending the erection of an aerial cableway of his own design at the Bremen Exhibition in 1889. Simms negotiated British patent rights for Daimler engines and in 1890 founded Simms & Co., consulting engineers, which introduced Daimler engines into the United Kingdom, applying them to launches, rather than road vehicles. This work was carried out by the Daimler Motor Syndicate, which Simms founded in 1893 and sold to the financier H. J. Lawson in 1895. This proved to be Lawson's most significant acquisition and led to the foundation of the British motor industry, in the shape of the Daimler works at Coventry Motor Mills. Simms was, however, sufficiently foresighted to keep his own business affairs distinct from those of Lawson. Between 1898 and 1900 Simms operated the Motor Carriage Supply Company Ltd and was in contact with such well-known motoring contemporaries as Emil Jellinek, who stimulated the development of the Mercedes car, and Count Zborowski.

In 1900 Simms became a vehicle manufacturer, with the establishment of the Simms Manufacturing Company Ltd. This produced cars and commercial vehicles in small quantities at the Welbeck Works, Kilburn, from 1904 to 1907–8, as well as engines for other manufacturers. Simms was interested in the military application of the motor vehicle, mounting a Maxim machine gun and an armoured shield on a De Dion quadricycle as the Simms Motor Scout and designing a heavier Motor War Car. They foreshadowed later armoured vehicles, but given the stage reached by automotive technology at the turn of the century, did not directly lead to a line of military vehicles.

Simms's principal legacy to the automotive world was in the field of components, especially magnetos. The Simms Magneto Company Ltd was established in 1907, after he had obtained UK manufacturing rights from Robert Bosch, the German electrical engineer, but small production runs could not compete with the foreign product and the company closed early in 1913. It had been preceded by the joint Compagnie des Magnetos Simms-Bosch (c.1899–1906), which foundered on the personal differences of the principals. Yet Simms may be considered to have played a significant role in magneto development, by his stimulus to Bosch and his colleagues to develop their product, and by opening up the important French market for Bosch.

In 1913 Simms started another business, Simms Motor Units Ltd, initially as a sales and repair organization for motor components, especially dynamos and magnetos. Manufacture was initially undertaken by others on behalf of the firm, an important source in the First World War being the Simms Magneto Company Ltd, of New Jersey, established by Simms in 1910. The English workforce, however, grew from twelve in 1913 to more than 300 by early 1919 and a subsidiary, the Standard Insulator Company Ltd, was established in 1915.

To build on his wartime success, Simms established Simms Motor Units (1920) Ltd in extensive premises in East Finchley. The virtual destruction by fire of the Kilburn works in 1920 and the slump of 1920–21 in the engineering industry brought about the cessation of manufacture until 1926. The Finchley factory was retained, however, trading profits improved, and a separate concern was established in Lyons to produce the Simms–Vernier coupling. In 1930, five years before Simms's retirement, the company moved in new directions to match changing automotive technology, moves culminating in the joint development, with Leyland Motors, of the Uniflow injection pump (1937). In his later years Simms's interests widened to include a tour of inspection of southern Africa in 1928 on behalf of the British motor trade and experimentation in compound metals for electrical contacts, with the establishment of Compound Electro Metals Ltd.

As well as being a businessman, Simms was also a man of affairs in the motor world. Concerned at the close involvement of H. J. Lawson's business interests with his Motor Car Club, Simms launched the Automobile Club of Great Britain and Ireland in 1897. This was joined by Sir David Salomons's Self-Propelled Traffic Association in 1898 and became the Royal Automobile Club in 1907. The problem of trade shows, exacerbated by cycle manufacturers' attempts to include cars in their shows, was met by Simms's foundation in 1902 of the Society of Motor Manufacturers and Traders, which elected him as its first president. With an interest in aviation, Simms also contributed to what was to become the Royal Aero Club.

In a long, active life Simms touched many aspects of the evolving motor industry, perhaps spreading his talents too thinly for a single, wholly outstanding, achievement. However, the importance of his contribution to the establishment of the motor and component industry and to motoring in the UK should not be under-rated. It is in his role as a catalyst and intermediary between the UK and Europe and, to a lesser extent, the United States that his lasting significance lies.

Simms's wife predeceased him, and his own death occurred on 22 April 1944 at Dunbarty, Stoke Poges, Buckinghamshire. He was cremated at Streatham Vale, London, and his ashes were placed in the Annunciation churchyard beside those of his wife.

RICHARD A. STOREY

Sources F. R. Simms, *How I formed the SMMT*, privately printed (1936) · F. R. Simms, *The history of the magneto*, privately printed (1940) · St J. C. Nixon, *The story of the SMMT, 1902–1952* (1952) · St J. C. Nixon, *The Simms story* (1955) · H. O. Duncan and E. Vavin, *The world on wheels* (privately printed, Paris, [1926]) · K. Richardson and R. Storey, 'Simms, Frederick Richard', *DBB* · T. Heuss, *Robert Bosch: Leben und Leistung* (1946) · *Bromley and West Kent Mercury* (28 April 1944) · d. cert. · Lord Montagu and D. Burgess-Wise, *Daimler century* (1995) · P. Brendon, *The motoring century: the story of the Royal Automobile Club* (1997) · private information (2004)

Archives LUL · NRA, papers | British Motor Industry Heritage Trust, corresp. and papers · Royal Automobile Club, London, corresp. · Veteran Car Club of Great Britain, corresp. and papers

Likenesses M. Milbanke, portrait, Royal Automobile Club, London

Wealth at death £90,221 15s. 9d.: probate, 2 Sept 1944, *CGPLA Eng. & Wales*

Simms, Frederick Walter (1803–1865), engineer and technical writer, was the seventh of nine children of William Simms (1763–1828), manufacturer of scientific instruments, and his wife Sarah, *née* Thompson (1767–1834). He was born on 24 December 1803 in the parish of St Ann Blackfriars, London. Apprenticed about 1818 to Robert Wilmott, cabinet-maker, he was turned over to his father and completed his training in 1825. He then obtained a place on the Irish Ordnance Survey, and was soon promoted to be head of the computing department. After some years in Ireland, in 1829 he was appointed assistant astronomer at the Royal Observatory, Greenwich. While there he married, in the summer of 1832, Caroline Nutting (1804–1846), whose elder sister was married to his elder brother William *Simms (1793–1860). Of their five children, only Frederick Walter (1835–1891) survived into adulthood.

Simms was poorly paid at the observatory and took on other work, teaching, and adjusting ironships' compasses. He began technical writing and left the observatory to become assistant to Henry Robinson Palmer on the South Eastern Railway and other works in 1834. In 1837–8 he visited Paris as an engineer of the Asphalte Company, to study the French method of working the preparation. His next employment was under Sir William Cubitt, then engaged in laying the South Eastern railway line. In 1842 he received the Telford medal from the Institution of Civil Engineers, which he had joined in 1838, for two papers on tunnelling which were based on his work for the South Eastern line. After working on railways in England and France, including the Bordeaux–Cette line, he was appointed in 1845 consulting engineer to report to the East India Company on the advisability of constructing railways in India. The Indian climate proved too much for his health, and his wife died there. Furthermore, he was overruled as to the course of the East Indian line. At the end of his five years' engagement he declined reappointment and on his return to England was appointed consulting engineer to the London, Chatham, and Dover Railway. He was unable to deal with the stress of the post, and retired from professional employment.

In addition to his membership of the Institution of Civil Engineers, Simms was a fellow of the Royal Astronomical and Geological societies. His most significant achievement was as the author of several important engineering textbooks, which went into many editions These included *A Treatise on the Principal Mathematical Instruments Employed in Surveying, Levelling, and Astronomy* (1834; 8th edn, 1860) and *A Treatise on the Principles and Practice of Levelling* (1837; 6th edn, 1875), which helped to promote his brothers' instruments. He edited part of *Public Works of Great Britain* (1838) for the publisher John Weale, and became involved in a subsequent copyright dispute. His *Practical Tunnelling* was the leading authority on tunnelling techniques of the time. For the last three and a half years of his life Simms suffered from heart disease. He died at his home, 50 Torrington Square, London, on 27 February 1865.   E. I. CARLYLE, *rev.* MIKE CHRIMES

Sources E. Mcnnim, *Reid's heirs* (1989) • A. McConnell, *Instrument makers to the world: a history of Cooke, Troughton & Simms* (1992) • *PICE*, 25 (1865–6), 519–22 • *CGPLA Eng. & Wales* (1865)
Archives BL OIOC • Inst. CE, archives | PRO, London, Chatham & Dover, SE Railways
Likenesses Maull & Polyblank, photograph, 1855, NPG • photograph, 1855, Vickers Archives, York
Wealth at death under £40,000: probate, 3 April 1865, *CGPLA Eng. & Wales*

Simms, George Otto (1910–1991), Church of Ireland archbishop of Armagh, was born in Dublin on 4 July 1910, the third of the four children of John Francis Arthur Simms, of Combermore, Lifford, co. Donegal, crown solicitor for co. Tyrone, and his wife, Ottilie Sophie, *née* Strange (1879–1960). His mother had been born in Australia, the daughter of Otto Georg Christian Strange, a professor of music. The family returned to Germany on the death of her mother, and she was educated in Germany and England; she married Simms's father in 1903. The Simms family had been resident in co. Donegal since the seventeenth century. J. F. A. Simms was scholarly, gracious, kind, and deeply involved in the life of the Church of Ireland, a member of the general synod and legal assessor to the bishop of Derry and Raphoe.

Simms attended the Prior endowed school in Lifford, beside the family home (1915–20). In May 1920 he went to St Edmund's School, Hindhead, Surrey, where W. H. Auden was head boy, and where Simms himself was also later head boy. There he showed a strong propensity for classics. In 1924 he entered Cheltenham College on winning a scholarship. He took an enthusiastic part in all aspects of college life, including sport, scholarship, and social and cultural activities. He considered ordination seriously at this time. In January 1929 he entered Trinity College, Dublin, to read classics, ancient history, and political science. He was elected a foundation scholar in classics in 1930 and was awarded the Berkeley gold medal for Greek, the vice-chancellor's Latin medal, and the Booke prize for classics. He won a double moderatorship in 1932, then won a theological exhibition and graduated BD in 1935. He was ordained deacon in the Church of Ireland on 25 March 1935 for the assistant curacy of St Bartholomew's parish, Dublin, where Walter Cadden Simpson, a strong Oxford Movement Christian socialist, was vicar. In 1938, at the invitation of Eric Abbott, supported by William Temple, he became chaplain of Lincoln Theological College. There he developed his interest in modern European theology, assisted by his fluency in German and French, and made many long-lasting friendships in the Church of England.

In 1940 Simms returned to Ireland as dean of residence (chaplain) at Trinity College, Dublin. He transformed this office into a vital part of university life, having an effective ministry to the whole university by force of his personality and commitment. He augmented his salary of £212 p.a. by lecturing in theology and examining in classics. In 1943 he was appointed chaplain-secretary of the Church of Ireland Training College (for primary teachers). His fluency in the Irish language was vital for this post. He carried a very heavy burden of work which was necessary in later years to support a growing family, having married, in September 1941, Mercy Felicia Gwynn (1915–1998), a lecturer in Italian at Trinity College and daughter of Brian James Gwynn, of Temple Hill, Terenure, Dublin. The Gwynns were a family of distinguished scholars who, like the Simms, had settled in co. Donegal in the seventeenth century. Simms and his wife—who were to have three sons and two daughters—shared a strong commitment to the social expression of Christianity. During the difficult war years Simms kept alive a strong Christian witness in Trinity College, organizing reading parties, conferences, and missions, and promoting ecumenism through the Mercier Society, a group of Anglican and Roman Catholic scholars which flourished in Dublin in the 1940s. Tall, handsome, with elegant classical features, Simms grew skeletally thin, kinder if possible and holier, as he flew from one commitment to another on a ramshackle bicycle in the midst of Dublin traffic, a well-known and greatly loved figure in university, church, and the city. While chaplain at Trinity College he commenced his life's scholarly work. He collated the manuscript of the Book of Kells and wrote the introduction for a facsimile edition (3 vols., 1950–51) as joint editor with Ernest Henry Alton (provost of Trinity College) and Peter Meyer. Simms was awarded the degree of PhD by Trinity College for his work on the Book of Kells in 1950 and an honorary DD degree in 1952. More than a dozen of his later published works were on the Book of Kells and other early Irish manuscripts (including the Book of Durrow), and on figures from the early Irish church, such as St Patrick, St Brendan, and St Columba.

In 1951 Simms was appointed dean of Cork; he was installed on 16 April 1952. He immediately opened up St Fin Barre's Cathedral to the public, and published a monograph and guide to it. In October 1952 he was elected bishop of Cork, Cloyne, and Ross. His energy was prodigious. He organized a diocesan conference in Cork city hall which attracted in excess of 2000 people per night for five nights. Henry Robert McAdoo, who succeeded him as dean, described Simms's episcopate as 'a sort of springtime in the diocese' (The Independent, 23 Nov 1991). In 1953 he commenced writing a weekly article on spiritual matters for the Irish Times, 'Thinking aloud', which he continued to write for thirty-eight years.

In December 1956 Simms was elected archbishop of Dublin and primate of Ireland. He was enthroned in Christ Church, Dublin, on 25 January 1957. His election was widely welcomed by all denominations and by all sections of the state and the community in Ireland, he being perceived as representing a new generation of the Church of Ireland. He played a major part in each of the Lambeth conferences which he attended, in 1958, 1968, and 1978. In 1958 he was chairman of the liturgy committee, the report of which was very well received. His wisdom and dexterity in ecumenical matters won the admiration of Archbishop Michael Ramsey, who appointed him co-chairman of the Anglican–Roman Catholic international commission on the theology of marriage and its application to mixed marriage. In 1975 this committee

produced a report indicating constructive ways ahead, some of which were adopted and implemented. In 1963 he attended the Toronto Anglican Congress, and in July 1963 he represented the Church of Ireland at the fourth assembly of the World Council of Churches in Uppsala. His contribution at both conferences was widely reported and appreciated. His activity in the Church of Ireland was also noteworthy. He was instrumental in establishing ecumenical conferences and he revived unity talks with the Methodists and Presbyterians. Together with his wife, he helped establish the Church of Ireland marriage counselling service, which soon became non-denominational and state funded. He also helped to establish a central advisory council of training for the ministry and a new election process for bishops. He chaired the liturgical advisory committee for eighteen years. He also chaired the advisory committee on administration which produced a radical and far-reaching report in 1967, which, however, did not find the support of the general synod.

In July 1969 Simms was elected archbishop of Armagh and primate of all Ireland. He was enthroned in St Patrick's Cathedral, Armagh, on 25 September 1969. Northern Ireland was by then in the grip of political turmoil and violence. Simms spent himself in every endeavour to restore peace in the province, to the point of exhaustion: visiting riot areas in Belfast, making a television appeal, preaching in churches throughout Northern Ireland, and writing pastoral letters. On the most dangerous missions and in the most dangerous areas he always refused police protection, as he felt that it could interfere with his pastoral freedom and credibility. It was said that 'in all his years in Armagh the hostility he encountered was rarely from Roman Catholics, but rather from extreme Protestants' (The Times). During this troubled and dangerous period he never neglected the burden of the administration of the whole of the Church of Ireland, and his wider remit on international and inter-church bodies. He kept a peaceful mind in the midst of turmoil through prayer and meditation. He retired in February 1980. Basil Blackshaw's portrait of him (1979), which was later hung in the Alexander Synod Hall in Armagh, shows him careworn and tired, in comparison with other portraits from his early days as archbishop of Dublin.

Simms retired to live in a semi-detached house in Terenure, Dublin. There he enjoyed good health and an extensive programme of ministry, conducting quiet days, taking services to assist clergy, and, at the request of his successors, remaining president of the Sunday School Society; president of the Association for Promoting Christian Knowledge; chairman of the board of Search (a theological journal); a member of the religious education curriculum committee of the general synod Board of Education; and president of the Leprosy Mission. He enjoyed occasional commissions as lecturer on a Swan Hellenic tour, and lectured extensively in Germany in 1983 while representing the Church of Ireland at the Lutheran quincentennial celebrations. In retirement he was also able to return to his first love—the early history and great religious manuscripts of the Irish church. Among his many books were *Irish Illuminated Manuscripts* (1980), *In my Understanding* (an exploration of the spiritual wisdom of the Celtic church, 1982), and biographies of Brendan the Navigator (1989) and St Patrick (1991). He wrote or co-operated in writing several parish histories. He also wrote innumerable articles in theological journals, mainly on subjects related to Celtic spirituality. He kept up a correspondence by letter with friends, fellow scholars, pupils, and people he met incidentally, in several languages. Communicating by letter was a great part of his faithful ministry. He continued to give his greatly appreciated illustrated lectures on the Book of Kells to the end of his life, by which time he had given more than 450 lectures all over the world. He brought a freshness and enthusiasm to each one. He died after a brief illness at the Meath Hospital, Dublin, on 15 November 1991, and was survived by his wife and five children. His ashes were interred in the churchyard of St Maelruan's parish, Tallaght, co. Dublin, after cremation on 23 November.   DONALD A. R. CAIRD

Sources L. Whiteside, *George Otto Simms: a biography* (1990) · The Representative Church Body Library and Archive Collection, Dublin, Simms papers · *The Church of Ireland Directory* (1936–90) · *The Times* (18 Nov 1991) · *The Independent* (21 Nov 1991) · *The Independent* (23 Nov 1991) · *WWW*, 1991–5 · personal knowledge (2004) · private information (2004)
Archives Representative Church Body Library, Dublin, papers · TCD | SOUND Radio Telifis Éireann Archives, Dublin
Likenesses J. B. Schwatschte, oils, *c.*1968, Representative Church Body Library, Dublin · B. Blackshaw, oils, 1979, Alexander Synod Hall, Armagh, Northern Ireland · P. Fitzgerald, oils, 1993, Church of Ireland College of Education, Dublin · photograph, repro. in *The Times* · photograph, repro. in *The Independent* (21 Nov 1991)
Wealth at death £229,855 Éire: probate, 23 March 1992, *CGPLA Éire*

Simms, Robert (*bap.* 1761, *d.* 1843), businessman and Irish nationalist, was baptized in Belfast on 20 March 1761, the fifth child in the family of five sons and two daughters of Robert Simms, merchant and tanner, and his wife, Elizabeth Stevenson of Belfast. With his brother William *Simms he owned a tan yard in North Street, Belfast (until 1794), a flour mill in Crumlin (until 1798), and a paper mill in Ballyclare (from 1798). He subscribed to Belfast's New White Linen Hall in 1782—a gesture marking him out as one of that group of successful and civic-minded merchants for which Belfast was then noted. On 8 August 1786 he married Mary Gilliland (*d.* 1832) of Colin, near Belfast. They had four daughters and a son.

The Simms family were members of the Third Presbyterian Congregation in Rosemary Street, and as such not opposed to subscription to the Westminster confession of faith. Already a supporter of political reform in the 1780s, in October 1791 Simms was one of the thirteen founders of the Society of United Irishmen and a proprietor of its newspaper, the *Northern Star*. From the outset he was the society's key leader in the north. In May 1794 he and his brother were tried for, and acquitted of, publishing a seditious address in the *Northern Star*. By May 1797, when the paper was finally suppressed, they were its sole remaining proprietors.

After 1795—when the United Irish Society went underground as an armed, revolutionary movement—Simms remained prominent. He was one of fewer than a dozen leaders conversant with the society's policy of seeking French military help, and in 1796 he was appointed to the movement's first national executive committee. He was arrested and detained in Newgate prison in Dublin from February to June 1797. In late 1797 he was elected adjutant-general for co. Antrim, and preparations began for a rising. When it erupted prematurely in Leinster the following May he refused to lead another in Ulster before the expected French help arrived, and resigned his command. Five days later the Ulster rising went ahead under new leaders and was savagely suppressed. Simms maintained his silence on the reason for his withdrawal, and in 1842 he refused to give an interview to R. R. Madden, then writing his history of the United Irishmen. This is why we know so little about Robert Simms, though most contemporaries thought him too moral a man to have acted dishonourably. He was nevertheless arrested in 1798 and transferred in 1799 to Fort George in Scotland. He was released back to Belfast in December 1801. Although the government continued to suspect him he seems not to have taken any further part in rebellious activities and tried to dissuade his old friend Thomas Russell from organizing another rising in 1803.

Simms was on the committee for the Belfast Harpers' Festival of 1792 and maintained an interest in Irish traditional music throughout his life. He was secretary to the Belfast Society for Promoting Knowledge (the future Linen Hall Library) from 1794 to 1796 and assistant secretary to the Royal Belfast Academical Institution from 1812 to 1843. His personal character is difficult to fathom but he had a capacity for deep and long-lasting friendships. Affectionately nicknamed 'the Tanner' in the journals of Theobald Wolfe Tone, he appears as a person of wisdom and integrity. He died in Belfast, at Franklin Place, on 23 June 1843.   MARIANNE ELLIOTT, *rev.*

Sources M. Elliott, *Partners in revolution: the United Irishmen and France* (1982) · M. Elliott, *Wolfe Tone: prophet of Irish independence* (1989) · C. Dickson, *Revolt in the north: Antrim and Down in 1798* (1960) · G. Chambers, *Faces of change: the Belfast and Northern Ireland Chambers of Commerce and Industry, 1783–1983* (*c.*1984) · N. E. Gamble, 'The business community and trade of Belfast, 1767–1800', PhD diss., University of Dublin, 1978 · private information (1993) [C. J. Woods, Robert Bonner]

Simms, William (*bap.* 1763, *d.* 1843), businessman and Irish nationalist, was baptized in Belfast on 6 June 1763, the sixth child in the family of five sons and two daughters of Robert Simms, merchant and tanner, and his wife Elizabeth Stevenson of Belfast. With his elder brother Robert *Simms he owned a tan yard in Belfast, a paper mill in Ballyclare, and a flour mill in Crumlin. He was a member of the Third Presbyterian Congregation in Rosemary Street, a noted reformer in the 1780s, one of the founders of the Society of United Irishmen and its secretary in 1791, and a proprietor of its newspaper, the *Northern Star*. His house, The Grove, on the Shore Road in Belfast, became one of the meeting-places of the society, and with his brother he subscribed heavily to its finances. In May 1794 he was tried for, and acquitted of, publishing a seditious address in the *Northern Star*, of which he remained a proprietor until its suppression in May 1797.

William Simms is overshadowed by his brother Robert but he too was a dedicated revolutionary. Indeed some thought him more active than Robert but that he escaped notice, being 'more artful and cunning'. He was detained in Newgate prison in Dublin in 1797 but he appears to have taken little part in the 1798 rising and was not among the state prisoners incarcerated after its suppression. He does not figure in R. R. Madden's history *The United Irishmen, their Lives and Times* (7 vols., 1842–6) and has been neglected in consequence. Although the government continued to think him dangerous—and there are signs that he may have remained in the revamped United Irish movement during his brother's imprisonment—in 1803 he advised Thomas Russell against rebellion and there is no evidence of treasonable activity thereafter.

Simms was married with a son and four daughters, all of whom died before the age of ten. He was named one of the managers of the Belfast Academical Institution in 1810. He died at his Belfast home on 2 August 1843 and was buried in Knockbreda.   Marianne Elliott, *rev.*

Sources M. Elliott, *Partners in revolution: the United Irishmen and France* (1982) · W. T. W. Tone, *Life of Theobald Wolfe Tone*, 2 vols. (1826) · H. Joy, *Historical collections relative to the town of Belfast, from the earliest period to the union with Great Britain* (1817) · baptismal and marriage records of the Third Presbyterian Congregation, Presbyterian Historical Society of Ireland, Belfast · G. Benn, *A history of the town of Belfast from the earliest times to the close of the eighteenth century*, 2 vols. (1877–80)

Simms, William (1793–1860), maker of scientific instruments, was born on 7 December 1793 in Birmingham, the second of nine children of William Simms (1763–1828), toy maker, and his wife, Sarah, *née* Thompson (1767–1834). In 1794 the family moved to London where the father turned to the manufacture of marine compasses. William was apprenticed to Thomas Penstone, a working goldsmith, in 1808, and turned over to his father the following year to complete his apprenticeship, taking his freedom in the Goldsmiths' Company in 1815. He married Ann Nutting in 1819 and set up house in Islington where several children were born. He worked alongside his father and brothers at Bowman's Buildings, off Aldersgate Street, London, until 1826, when he entered into partnership with Edward Troughton (1753–1835), the most respected astronomical instrument maker of his day. It seems that James South introduced the two men; certainly Troughton employed William Simms as an outworker from at least 1823, and by June 1824, writing to the astronomer royal, Joshua Pond, could refer to him as 'the best [workman] I know' (Royal Society, MS Gh. 1. 30). Simms was certainly keen to improve his skill at hand-dividing large instruments, as his notebook shows, and to educate himself generally. He and his brothers were among the members of the London Mechanics' Institution, founded in 1824. He became a member of the Institution of Civil Engineers in 1828.

When Troughton and Simms joined forces, Simms moved to Troughton's house at 136 Fleet Street where his wife cared for the elderly bachelor. The partnership prospered, supplying superb major instruments for observatories at Greenwich, Cambridge, Edinburgh, Lucknow, Madras, and Cracow, for many private observatories, and for the survey of India under Captain George Everest, besides selling numerous lesser surveying, navigational, and mathematical instruments. When Troughton died in 1835 Simms wisely continued to trade as Troughton and Simms, and he inherited from Troughton the onerous duty of supplying and maintaining the apparatus at the Royal Greenwich Observatory. In 1838 the firm displaced W. D. and T. Gilbert as suppliers to the East India Company, and thus gained access to a vast market for mathematical and surveying instruments for the company's engineers, revenue officers, and schools. Another line of business which Simms dominated was that of producing standards of length. Building on Troughton's reputation, he benefited from the rising demand for accurate standards for trigonometrical surveys in Ireland, India, the United States of America, and elsewhere. When the national standards were lost in the fire which destroyed the houses of parliament in 1834, the authorities turned immediately to Simms as the most reliable contractor to construct replacements—a lengthy business which involved countless hours of tests and experiments to determine the best metal, the best shape of bar, and the corrections for temperature.

Several of the Simms family found employment with Troughton and Simms. William's sons William Henry (*b.* 1820) and James (1828–1919) were bound apprentice to him in 1834 and 1843 respectively, while his nephew William (1817–1907) joined him in 1836. His brother-in-law John Nutting kept the books until his early death around 1837, when brother Henry Simms (*b.* 1800) succeeded to the post. William's brother Frederick Walter Simms (1803–1865), who had been employed on the Irish survey and then as an assistant at the Greenwich observatory before taking up the profession of railway engineer, wrote several books on surveying and the use of instruments in which he publicized Troughton and Simms instruments, thus carrying their fame still further afield. In 1846 Simms took as apprentice Joseph Beck, the fee of 200 guineas for this binding reflecting his high status in the trade.

Simms's residence in Fleet Street brought him obligations: he served as constable of St Bride's parish in 1836 and as a trustee from 1836 to 1839. After the death of his first wife, about 1840, William married Emma Hennell, and raised several more children. In 1841 the collapse, following a fire, of two houses adjacent to his own brought an opportunity for limited expansion. Simms leased no. 138 and erected a new house on Fleet Street with workshops behind, and moved into his new premises by 1844. He moved his own family to Carshalton around this time. The new workshops, like the old ones, were reached through the narrow entrance to Peterborough Court and this restriction obliged him to continue the practice of putting out all the casting and turning of large items, usually to the engineering firms of Maudslay and Field or Donkin, both of which were situated on the south bank of the Thames. The smaller instruments were graduated in house; Simms constructed the first self-acting dividing engine, driven, like clockwork, by a falling weight which moved down the exterior wall of the workshop. It was completed by 1843, to much acclaim in the engineering world. Troughton had built an observatory on the roof of no. 136 for testing his astronomical instruments before they were sent out, and Simms replicated this when he moved to no. 138. He was a keen astronomer, building an observatory at his Carshalton home. He had been a member of the Astronomical Society since 1831, serving from time to time on its council and joining the Astronomical Dining Club, so that he was on familiar terms with his more important customers.

In 1852 twenty leading astronomers and engineers proposed Simms for election to the Royal Society, testifying that he was:

> the author of several papers … the inventor of a self-acting machine for dividing circles … distinguished for his acquaintance with the science of practical optics and astronomical mechanics … eminent as an astronomical observer and as an artist in the construction of philosophical apparatus, telescopes, instruments etc.

Despite this tribute to a man who was universally admired for his skill and respected for his kind, modest, and gentle nature, there were by then ominous signs that Troughton and Simms was neither maintaining its high standard nor keeping up with technical developments. There were justified complaints about defects in several costly astronomical instruments, notably those consigned to Harvard, and rumbles of dissatisfaction from India, where the levels fitted to Simms's theodolites had to be replaced by German ones. In England, too, Airy was recognizing the superiority of German instruments.

Simms died at Carshalton on 21 June 1860 and was buried at Norwood cemetery. His estate, which included the goodwill and assets of the firm, was valued at just under £80,000. Simms's son James (1828–1915) entered into a partnership with his cousin William (1817–1907), which lasted until the latter retired in 1871. In 1864 the partners built new workshops at Charlton, Kent, where they remained until 1922 when failing business led to an amalgamation with one of their main competitors, Thomas Cooke & Sons of York, owned by Vickers. The company was re-formed as Cooke, Troughton, and Simms, and the Charlton business relocated in York, where it continued until 1988 (by then known as Vickers Instruments) when Vickers, having no further use for it, sold off the business assets and closed it down.   ANITA McCONNELL

Sources A. McConnell, *Instrument makers to the world: a history of Cooke, Troughton and Simms* (1992) • E. Mennim, *Reid's heirs* (1989) • *Monthly Notices of the Royal Astronomical Society*, 21 (1860–61), 105–6 • *PICE*, 20 (1860–61), 167–8 • J. Weale, *London and its vicinity* (1851), 683 • E. Mennim, *Transit circle: the story of William Simms, 1793–1860* (1992)

Archives BL OIOC, invoices and letters • priv. coll. • RAS, letters and observations | Borth. Inst., Vickers Instruments archive • CUL, Greenwich Observatory archives
Likenesses photograph, Borth. Inst., Vickers Instruments archive
Wealth at death under £80,000—incl. assets and goodwill of business: probate, 17 July 1860, *CGPLA Eng. & Wales*

Simnel, Lambert (*b.* 1476/7, *d.* after 1534), impostor and claimant to the English throne, was born probably in Oxford, the son of Thomas Simnel, a carpenter, organ maker, or cobbler. His origins are obscure, even in official accounts; his mother is unknown and he may have been illegitimate. Nothing is known of his upbringing.

Simnel's identity cannot be established with any certainty. Over the winter of 1486–7 a pretender claiming to be Edward, earl of Warwick, son and heir of George, duke of Clarence, the last surviving male of the house of York, was being acknowledged in Dublin. The Tudor regime rapidly set out to unmask the impostor. He was stated to be the son of an organ builder at the University of Oxford and the earliest documentation about him that names him says he was the son of Thomas Simnel, lately of Oxford, a joiner. These accounts do have a certain consistency. A Thomas Simnel worked in Oxford in the late 1470s and held a tenement on the conduit towards St Thomas's Chapel from Osney Abbey in 1479. The organ builder William Wooton was a neighbour, suggesting Thomas Simnel was a carpenter by trade who built organs. He was probably Flemish. His son was described by the historian Polydore Vergil in his account of the plot as 'a comely youth, and well favoured, not without some extraordinary dignity and grace of aspect' (*DNB*). With his father probably dead by 1496, Lambert Simnel was an ideal candidate to play the impostor.

Simnel was put forward by former Yorkists, disgruntled with the new king, Henry VII. The mystery surrounding the fate of Edward IV's sons provided fertile ground for pretence. There may have been similar uncertainty as to the fate of Warwick. In 1485 Henry transferred him from Sheriff Hutton Castle in Yorkshire to the Tower of London, but in 1486 there were reports of his escape. To add to the confusion, stories may have continued to circulate that Clarence had plotted in 1478 to have his son sent for safety to Ireland, and to have his place in the nursery taken by a local child. William or Richard Simonds, a priest, was brought before John Morton, archbishop of Canterbury, at convocation on 17 February 1487 and confessed to having organized the imposture late the previous year and then taken Simnel to Ireland. On 2 February the king's council had decided to parade the real Warwick through the city from the Tower to St Paul's Cathedral. If Henry hoped that he would settle minds by presenting Warwick in this way, he was to be disappointed. John de la Pole, earl of Lincoln, another nephew of Edward IV and possible claimant to the throne, supported Simnel, declaring him to be the real Warwick. Simnel's plot was now escalating as other people offered support because it suited their own agenda.

Almost all that is known about Simnel derives from

sources close to the Tudor regime. It had some incentive to appear to know more than it really did about the plot, and even to resort to disinformation. With its comical and exotic sound, Lambert Simnel's name appears custom-made to provoke derision and the herald who witnessed his capture said that his 'name was indeed John'. There is some confusion about whether Simnel affected to be War-wick or Richard, duke of York, the younger of Edward IV's sons. Bernard André, Henry's panegyrist, who said that Simnel claimed to be York, was certainly muddled. Per-haps, as Vergil states, the conspiracy shifted its focus early on from York to Warwick. In Vergil's account, however, the priestly mentor is named Richard Simonds, not Wil-liam Simonds. Vergil's insistence that the plot was hatched by a single priest likewise sits uneasily with his statement that the king regretted Lincoln's death in battle because it prevented his plumbing the depths of the con-spiracy. None the less, the official line on Simnel has a cer-tain economy and is not wholly lacking in corroboration.

The plot was set in train in 1486, if not earlier. With a floating population of clerks and scholars, Oxford was a natural location for a conspiracy based on impersonation. While it may have originated in the mind of a single priest, who is said to have refined Simnel's manners at Oxford, it is perhaps no coincidence that two of the lead-ers of the subsequent revolt had their principal seats near the town: Lincoln at Ewelme and Francis Lovell, Viscount Lovell at Minster Lovell. Then there was Robert Stilling-ton, bishop of Bath, who had retired to his old college at Oxford after the battle of Bosworth, whom Henry had good reason to suspect of involvement in a plot on behalf of Clarence's son. The king summoned him in February 1487 to answer charges regarding certain conspiracies.

During autumn 1486 there were reports of a Yorkist pre-tender overseas, though Simnel need not have been the only horse in the race. By the end of 1486 he was estab-lished in Ireland, with the backing first of Thomas Fitzger-ald, chancellor of Ireland, and later of his brother Gerald Fitzgerald, eighth earl of Kildare, the king's deputy, and Walter Fitzsimons, the archbishop of Dublin. According to André, Henry sent a herald to question him on his back-ground, and indeed in March a payment was made to Fal-con pursuivant for a mission to Ireland in the king's ser-vice. Simnel must have had some former courtiers in his entourage. Lovell, who had been at large since Bosworth, may already have been active in the conspiracy. Simonds confessed that after he took the boy to Ireland he had been with Lovell in the Furness Fells in Cumbria, to reconnoitre a suitable landing place. Early in 1487, too, Margaret of York, dowager duchess of Burgundy and Clarence's sister, began to lend support to the enterprise, providing a base for defectors and financial assistance. Shortly after the February council, Lincoln slipped out of England and joined his aunt at Malines or Mechlin in the province of Antwerp. By the end of April, Lincoln, Lovell, and other Yorkist exiles, and a company of German mercenaries under the Swiss captain Martin Schwartz, sailed to Ire-land. With the arrival in Dublin of Lincoln, the stage was set for a most remarkable piece of theatre, the coronation

of the young boy in Holy Trinity on 24 May. The fact of the coronation, and the reference to the king as Edward VI, attests that the focus of the impersonation was now War-wick. A parliament was held in Dublin in the new king's name, and coins struck. Proclamations were issued. Henry was later to make fun of the gullibility of the Irish, claim-ing that they would crown apes at last. The men of the city of Waterford, which remained loyal during the revolt, likewise mocked the Dubliners for taking an organ mak-er's son as their king.

The invasion of England was a serious affair. Simnel, Lincoln, and a mixed force of Yorkist diehards, 1500 Ger-man mercenaries, and about 4000 poorly armed Irish kernes (light infantry), landed in Furness on 4 June. From its secure beachhead, the army moved rapidly eastwards, crossing the Pennines into Wensleydale, where it found recruits among the local gentry. On 8 June a letter in the name of 'Edward VI' was dispatched from Masham to York, advertising his cause and seeking 'relief and ease of lodgings and victuals' (York City archives, House Book 6, fol. 97). Two local magnates—John Scrope, fifth Baron Scrope of Bolton, and Thomas Scrope, sixth Baron Scrope of Masham—led a company of horsemen to York and pro-claimed the new king at Bootham bar; but the city held firm for Henry. Meanwhile the main rebel host had pressed south, desperately hoping to skittle the Tudor regime by the speed of their advance.

Henry was well-prepared, having positioned himself strategically to raise support, and advanced purposefully northwards from Leicester. There were some moments of unease, and not all the forces summoned arrived on time. Rumours of a rebel victory prompted some Londoners to take to the streets on Simnel's behalf. None the less, by the time the king left Nottingham on 15 June he had at his command twice as many men as his opponents. On the morning of 16 June the rebels crossed the Trent upstream from Newark and positioned themselves on the hillside overlooking the road from Nottingham. The battle of Stoke was a sharp and brutal encounter. Lincoln, who was regarded as the real leader of the rebellion, was slain, but Lovell escaped and fled to Scotland. A herald, who was at the battle and wrote an early account of it, records that 'the lad' whom the 'rebels called King Edward' was cap-tured by Robert Bellingham (BL, Cotton MS Julius B XII, fol. 29r).

According to Vergil, Henry spared Simnel, and put him to service, first in the scullery, and later as a falconer. The Book of Howth, a later compilation drawing on family tradition, repeats this story, adding the detail that Henry had his new scullion formally presented to a group of Irish lords to underline the folly of their actions in 1487. Vergil reports that Simnel was still alive at the time of writing, 1534. For a royal servant, Lambert remains oddly elusive. The only known documentation of his later life is the issue of robes to him at the funeral of Sir Thomas Lovell, courtier and counsellor of Henry VII, in 1525. Given the rarity of the surname in England, Richard Simnel, canon of St Osith's in Essex at the time of the dissolution in 1539, may have been his son.   MICHAEL J. BENNETT

Sources M. Bennett, *Lambert Simnel and the battle of Stoke*, pbk edn (1993) · *The Anglica historia of Polydore Vergil, AD 1485–1537*, ed. and trans. D. Hay, CS, 3rd ser., 74 (1950) · BL, Cotton MS Julius B XII, fols. 27v–29v · M. T. Hayden, 'Lambert Simnel in Ireland', *Studies: an Irish Quarterly Review*, 4 (1915), 622–38 · G. Smith, 'Lambert Simnel and the king from Dublin', *The Ricardian*, 10 (1994–6), 498–536 · RotP, 6.397–8 · D. Wilkins, ed., *Concilia Magnae Britanniae et Hiberniae* (1737), 3.618 · Bodl. Oxf., MS Wood F. 10, fol. 197r · BL, Add. MS 12462, fol. 10r · W. Campbell, ed., *Materials for a history of the reign of Henry VII*, 2 vols., Rolls Series, 60 (1873–7) · York City archives, house book 6, fol. 97 · J. S. Brewer and W. Bullen, eds., *Calendar of the Carew manuscripts*, 5: *1603–1623*, PRO (1871) · DNB

Simon (*d. c.*1162). *See under* Kyme family (*per. c.*1080–*c.*1380).

Simon de Wells. *See* Wells, Simon of (*d.* 1207).

Simon of Faversham. *See* Faversham, Simon of (*d.* 1306).

Simon [Simeon] **Stock** [St Simon Stock] (*supp.* **1165–1265**), hermit and monk, is said to have been born in Kent in 1165. Although he is celebrated as the sixth prior-general of the Carmelite order, there are no contemporary references to him, unless the mention by the mid-thirteenth-century Dominican Gerard de Frachet of a Simon who is described as prior of the Carmelite order refers to Simon Stock. The earliest surviving list of priors-general of the order to list Simon dates from 1396. From the early fifteenth century a fuller tradition of his career emerged. A legendary preserved in three fifteenth-century manuscripts celebrates Simon as the eleventh out of sixteen notable saints of the order. According to his legend, Simon lived as a solitary hermit in the trunk of a tree, the practice to which he owed his cognomen. In 1201, aged thirty-six, he joined the Carmelite order, and later entered the convent at Hulme in Northumberland. Elected prior-general of the order in 1245, Simon oversaw the modification to the order's rule by Innocent IV (*r.* 1243–54) in 1247 that brought it closer into line with other mendicant orders. In some versions of his legend he performed a miracle of turning water into wine in a consecrated chalice. He is also, in one version, credited with being the first Carmelite to receive a bachelor's degree at Oxford University. The most celebrated incident of his career was the vision granted to him in 1251, in which the Blessed Virgin instructed Simon to introduce into the order the wearing of the scapular, a garment consisting of two bands worn over each shoulder. Any friar wearing the scapular would be guaranteed his salvation. Later Carmelite historians, such as Bradley, Paleonydorus, Bostius, and Bale, embellished the outlines of this tradition. Most versions of the legend supply a note of those Englishmen of noble birth, including Edward II (*d.* 1327) and Henry, duke of Lancaster (*d.* 1361), said to have adopted the scapular on their deathbeds.

The 'scapular promise' appears independently of Simon Stock in the literature of the order—initially in the 1360s in an acrostic by Johann von Hildesheim (*d.* 1375). The tradition of the scapular promise, with its special grant of protection from the Blessed Virgin, developed from the papal protection granted to the Carmelites in the mid-

thirteenth century to aid them in their expansion in western Europe. The legend of the scapular has obvious parallels with similar traditions developed by the Dominicans in the thirteenth century of divine approbation granted to the garments worn by the order, and is part of a wider concern among all mendicants to endow their habits with a distinctive spiritual identity.

By the fifteenth century the chronology of the Carmelites' migration to the West from the crusader states had been distorted. The Simon Stock legend thus has him joining the order in 1201, although the hermits of Mount Carmel were only recognized as an order by the papacy in 1226, and did not reach England until 1242. A hermit accustomed to the solitary life would have been an appropriate recruit for the order in its early days, but if an Englishman called Simon was among those hermits of Mount Carmel who formed a distinct community around 1200 and adopted a rule *c.*1205–14, and was in 1245 elected prior-general of the order, he must have been born rather later than 1165. Simon is not mentioned in the *De adventu Carmelitarum in Angliam* of William of Coventry (*c.*1365) although an English Carmelite senior enough to be elected prior-general ought to have been at the forefront of the settlement in England. The legend of Simon Stock was ascribed by Launoy (1653) to Paleonydorus, who was writing in the 1480s, but it is evidently earlier than this, and possibly dates from the later fourteenth century. John Bale listed as Stock's works collections of homilies, pastoral letters, and hymns, but there is no other testimony for these. Simon supposedly died in 1265 in Bordeaux and was buried there.　　　ANDREW JOTISCHKY

Sources B. Xiberta, *De visione sancti Simonis Stock* (1950) · Bodl. Oxf., MS Laud misc. 722 · BL, Harley MS 3838 · Bale, *Cat.* · S. C. Ceroke, 'The credibility of the scapular promise', *Carmelus*, 11 (1964), 81–123

Likenesses Lombard school, fresco medallion, 1472, Santuario del Carmine, S. Felice del Benaco, Brescia, Italy

Simon the Norman. *See* Ételan, Simon d' (*d.* 1249).

Simon, Abraham (*bap.* **1617**, *d. c.***1692**), medallist, was baptized on 27 April 1617 at the French protestant church in Threadneedle Street, London. He was the third son of Peter (or Pierre) Simon, a merchant, and his wife, Anne (*b. c.*1588), the daughter and heir of Gilles Germain, a merchant of St Peter Port, Guernsey, and the brother of the medallist and seal engraver Thomas *Simon (*bap.* 1618, *d.* 1665); his other siblings were Peter (*b. c.*1612x14), Hannah, William (*bap.* 1616), Samuel (*bap.* 1619), Nathaniel, and Laurence. Abraham matriculated at Queen's College, Oxford, on 8 May 1635, and was created MA in 1646. He studied law for seven years, being admitted a student of Gray's Inn in 1640 and again in 1642.

By 1645 Simon was making medals and wax models of leading parliamentarians and others, working both independently and in collaboration with his brother Thomas. Abraham's medals, a number of which bear his signature, 'AS', were cast and chased. Signed examples include those of John Campbell, first earl of Loudoun (1645), William Pope (1645), the ambassador Albert Joachim (1646), Sir Sydenham Poyntz (1646), John Maitland, second earl of

Lauderdale (1646), and Charles Seton, second earl of Dunfermline (1646).

Simon's movements after the late 1640s are unclear. He may possibly have visited the Netherlands, before or after travelling to Sweden. John Evelyn met him in London in June 1653, and in 1654 Simon was also in England as he produced a medal of Henry Cromwell. However, that same year he was in Sweden, where he made the coronation medal for Queen Hedvig (unsigned), for which he was paid the sum of 800 dalar in October 1654. Unusually for Simon, the medal die was engraved rather than cast using a wax model. Vertue claimed that Simon travelled with Queen Kristina on a visit to Louis XIII of France, and that the queen was in love with him. In fact Kristina visited the court of Louis XIV in 1656 (following her abdication in 1654), and as the Swedish royal household did not pay Simon that year it is probable that he accompanied Kristina. Vertue records that during this visit Simon was nearly arrested when taking a wax portrait of the king from the gallery of the royal chapel on account of his peculiar appearance. He was 'a man of small stature; of a primitive philosophic aspect, always wearing his hair and beard, according to the mode of his ancestors' (Vertue, *Medals, Coins, Great Seals*, 58). Court accounts record that Simon was in the service of Karl X Gustav and Hedvig between 1655 and 1660, although no medals from this period are known. He probably left Sweden for good in 1658, and possibly settled in the Netherlands for a few years. It is unclear whether it was during this or an earlier visit that he was in the company of the diplomat Sir William Temple.

After the Restoration, Simon returned to England, where he found favour at court. He modelled the portrait of Charles II at the price of 100 broad-pieces. The duke of York afterwards had his portrait done, but proposed to pay him only 50 broad-pieces: Simon then took up the wax model, and in the duke's presence deliberately defaced it. This act lost him favour at court, and other sitters often complained of his impatience when they offered any criticism of his work. Vertue records that his unconventional appearance, 'constantly wearing boots and spurs, with his long sword *en cavalier*, made him everywhere remarkable' (Vertue, *Medals, Coins, Great Seals*, 58). He was also in considerable demand as a model because 'His hirsute picturesque was of a kind, exploited by Van Dyck in his studies of apostles's heads, that remained very popular throughout the seventeenth century' (Vertue, *Note books*, 1.124). Indeed, he was painted three times by Sir Godfrey Kneller, once as a hermit. Sir Peter Lely also painted Simon's portrait.

In later life Simon seems to have encountered difficulty attracting patronage, and he died in obscurity about 1692. He left two daughters, Anne and Judith.

W. W. WROTH, *rev.* DEBORAH GRAHAM-VERNON

Sources G. Vertue, *Medals, coins, great seals, and other works of Thomas Simon* (1780) · H. E. Pagan, 'Presidential address, 1988', *British Numismatic Journal*, 58 (1988), 179–89 · Vertue, *Note books* · N&Q, 2nd ser., 12 (1861), 2, 357, 403, 510 · S. Stenström, 'Abraham Simon i Sverige', *Nordisk Numismatisk Årsskrift*, 7 (1942), 204–11 · E. J. Pyke, *A biographical dictionary of wax modellers* (1973) · H. Farquhar, 'Thomas Simon, "one of our chief gravers"', *Numismatic Chronicle*, 12 (1932), 274–310 · E. Hawkins, H. Grueber, and A. W. Franks, *Medallic illustrations of the history of Great Britain and Ireland* (1885) · H. Groeber, *Handbook of the coins of Great Britain and Ireland in the British Museum* (1970) · J. D. Stewart, *Sir Godfrey Kneller* (1983)

Likenesses attrib. A. Simon, oils, c.1670–1680, NPG · A. Blooteling, mezzotint (after P. Lely), BM, NPG · A. Simon, sculpture, wax model, BM · A. Simon, three self-portraits, etchings, BM · G. Vertue, line engraving, BM, NPG; repro. in Vertue, *Medals, coins…* (1753) · G. Vertue, red chalk and Indian ink drawing (after G. Kneller), BM

Simon, André Louis (1877–1970), writer on wine and food, was born on 28 February 1877 in rue Taranne, in the sixth *arrondissement* of Paris, the second son and second child in the family of six sons and one daughter of Ernest Constant Simon (c.1848–1895), artist and former *zouave pontifical*, and his wife, Jeanne, daughter of Emile Dardoize, artist. He was educated at Le Petit Séminaire, Notre Dame des Champs, in Paris, and after failing his *baccalauréat* he worked for a few months in 1894 for *L'Avant Garde, gazette bi-mensuelle des Zouaves Pontificaux*, a royalist journal. He then worked in England, improving his English, before three years' military service at the École Militaire in Paris, on the staff of the *Revue d'Artillerie*. On 17 October 1900 he married Edith Winifred (1879–1963), daughter of Henry Bond Symons, a former railway engineer, of Southampton, whom he had met in England. They had two sons and three daughters; one son became a Jesuit priest, and two of their daughters became nuns.

In 1899 Simon began an apprenticeship with the champagne house Pommery and Greno, in Rheims, and was sent to London in 1902 to Pommery's London agent, to work as a champagne shipper. At the outbreak of the First World War, Simon reported to his regiment, the 13th artillery regiment, at Vincennes, Paris, and spent most of the war as an interpreter, including two years with the 50th (Northumbrian) division. He was awarded the British Military Medal in 1916.

In 1905 Simon published the first of more than 100 books and pamphlets, *The History of the Champagne Trade in England*, a scholarly work based on records in the Guildhall Library, followed by his *History of the Wine Trade in England* (1906–9) in three volumes. He was one of the founders of the Wine Trade Club in 1908, and as chairman of the education committee he gave regular lectures about wine, many of which were later published, and built up a wine library, while at the same time forming his own private collection. *The Art of Good Living* (1929), a guide to the wines appropriate to different dishes, his first book about food, was followed by an exhibition at the First Edition Club of early printed books and manuscripts from his collection, including a leaf from the Gutenberg Bible with Isaiah's prophecy of the vine. He travelled to South Africa, and was active in La Ligue Internationale des Adversaires des Prohibitions, which was wound up in 1933 after the American Congress repealed the Prohibition Act. In 1931 Simon was one of the founders of the Saintsbury Club, a dining club formed in honour of George Saintsbury (1845–1933), the literary critic and author of *Notes on a Cellar Book* (1920).

André Louis Simon (1877–1970), by Howard Coster, 1933

In 1932 Simon found himself without a job when Pommery appointed a new agent for the sale of the firm's champagne. He became managing director of the Madeira Wine Association Ltd, formed to popularize madeira in England after he had visited Madeira in 1933, but this was short-lived. He was also asked by Constable to edit *Constable's Wine Library*, a new series of popular books on wine. He wrote *Madeira: Wine, Cakes, and Sauce* (1933), *Port* (1934), and *Champagne* (1934) himself, and commissioned friends to write the others.

It was through Ye Sette of Odd Volumes, a literary dining club, that he met A. J. A. Symons (1900–1941), founder of the First Edition Club, and in October 1933 they started the Wine and Food Society, a private venture. Symons became secretary, and Simon organized the lunches, dinners, and wine tastings, and edited the quarterly journal *Wine and Food*. 212 attended the first meal, an Alsatian luncheon at the Café Royal, and by the end of the first year there were more than 1000 members. The society's first birthday was celebrated with a banquet at the Royal Pavilion, Brighton, marking the centenary of the death of Antonin Carême, chef to the prince regent. Simon visited the United States for the first time in 1934, founding several branches of the society.

The Second World War put an end to the society's dinners, and after the death of A. J. A. Symons in 1941 Simon carried on alone, continuing to bring out *Wine and Food*, with editorials dismissing the idea that wartime food had to be dull. The whole of the winter 1941 issue was devoted to the sausage, and Ernest Oldmeadow, an expert on frugal cookery, contributed a series of recipes. Simon published cookery pamphlets, including *Soups, Salads, Souses: Wartime Fare for the Fastidious* (1944), and also completed his *Concise Encyclopedia of Gastronomy* (1939–46). After the war the dinners and wine tastings resumed. Simon travelled all over the world, visiting the many branches of the society: in 1954, its twenty-first birthday, there were twenty branches in England, twenty in the United States, and twelve elsewhere. In his late eighties Simon toured Australia and published *The Wines, Vineyards, and Vignerons of Australia* (1967). He withdrew from the management of the Wine and Food Society in 1967, when he was ninety.

André Simon was regarded as the leading authority in the world on wine and gastronomy, although he himself never learned to cook. His philosophy of life is best expressed in *Tables of Content* (1933), a record of special occasions over the previous five years: here he says that the greatest joy is good wine in good company, and refers to a birthday dinner in 1914, 'What a dinner it was! What anecdotes, reminiscences, jokes and arguments flowed good-humouredly with every one of those perfect wines!' (xviii). He remained a French citizen, and retained a strong French accent. From 1919 he was president of the French Benevolent Society, founded in 1842 to care for destitute French immigrants in London. He published *Les pauvres de France en Angleterre* in 1924, with illustrations by well-known artists. But he also loved England: he had his own cricket field in the grounds of his Sussex house, and he believed that English food was as good as the best anywhere, especially when partnered with French wines. Jovial, enthusiastic, and good-natured, Simon had thick snowy white hair and a portly figure. In 1968 he claimed never to have had a day's illness, and he continued his life-long habit of opening a bottle of champagne at eleven every morning. He published two volumes of memoirs, *By Request* (1957) and *In the Twilight* (1969).

Simon was made an honorary CBE in 1964 and an honorary freeman of the Vintners' Company in 1968. He died on 5 September 1970 in the Middlesex Hospital, London. A memorial requiem mass was held in Westminster Cathedral on 19 October 1970.   ANNE PIMLOTT BAKER

Sources P. Morrah, *André Simon: gourmet and wine lover* (1987) • A. L. Simon, *By request: an autobiography* (1957) • A. Simon, *In the twilight* (1969) • J. Symons, *A. J. A. Symons: his life and speculations* (1950); pbk edn (1986), 139–160 • *The Times* (7 Sept 1970) • *Wine and Food* (Sept 1970) • *WWW* • m. cert. • d. cert.

Likenesses H. Coster, photograph, 1933, NPG [*see illus.*] • Y. Carter, drawing, repro. in Simon, *By request*, frontispiece • J. Gunn, portrait, repro. in Morrah, *André Simon*, 96 • photograph, repro. in Simon, *In the twilight*, frontispiece

Wealth at death £8778: probate, 31 Aug 1971, *CGPLA Eng. & Wales*

Simon, Ernest Emil Darwin, **first Baron Simon of Wythenshawe** (1879–1960), industrialist, politician, and public servant, was born in Didsbury, Manchester, on 9 October 1879, the eldest son of Henry Gustav Simon (1835–1899), industrialist, and his second wife, Emily Stoehr (1858–1920). Henry Simon had been born in Silesia, but as a liberal had moved to Switzerland owing to the autocratic political climate prevalent in Prussia. In 1860 he

Ernest Emil Darwin Simon, first Baron Simon of
Wythenshawe (1879–1960), by Lafayette, 1926

emigrated from Zürich to Manchester, where he established two engineering firms: Henry Simon Ltd, which produced flour milling machinery, and Simon–Carves Ltd, which became one of two leading British manufacturers of coke ovens. These were both very successful, and became in due course the Simon Engineering Group with a worldwide market.

Ernest Simon was educated at Rugby School and in 1898 entered Pembroke College, Cambridge, where he read for the mechanical sciences tripos and gained a first in part one in 1901. His father's death brought him heavy family responsibilities at a young age, and he immediately joined the Simon Engineering Group on leaving Cambridge. He planned the expansion of the company into building grain silos, and travelled widely on company business. Subsequently, the company's success gave him the financial resources to pursue his wide-ranging interests outside industry, and enabled him to take an independent line in politics.

Although he was a member of the Liberal Party and subsequently the Labour Party, Simon was not a rigid party politician; for him political parties were the means to achieve progressive reform. He established a close interest in social reform during the first decade of the twentieth century, which was in part fostered by his close friendship with Sidney and Beatrice Webb. This relationship with the Webbs ensured that he played an instrumental role in founding the *New Statesman* (1913), of which he became a director and subsidizer. On 22 November 1912 he married Shena Dorothy Potter (1883–1972) [*see* Simon, Shena Dorothy]. The marriage was an effective, happy

partnership similar to that of the Webbs; both were insatiable social reformers with a capacity to focus on particular problems. They had two sons and a daughter (who died at the age of twelve).

Manchester politics and housing reform   Simon was elected to Manchester city council in 1912 as Liberal member for Didsbury. The city council provided Simon with a platform to press for the implementation of progressive reform, notably smoke abatement and the improvement of housing conditions. He was appointed a member of the housing committee, becoming chairman in 1919, a role in which he played a principal part in tackling the post-war housing shortage in Manchester. He was lord mayor of Manchester in 1921–2, the youngest person at the time to hold the office. In 1926 he published *A City Council from Within*, based upon his years on the Manchester corporation. The work is, by the standards of such local government studies, lucid and readable, embodying Simon's belief that the largest urban authorities could combine administrative efficiency with a concern for the well-being of the local community.

Simon's growing involvement in national politics after the First World War was fostered by his relationship with Manchester Liberalism and with the editor of the *Manchester Guardian*, C. P. Scott. It was stimulated by his recognition that national legislation, particularly in the area of housing reform, was essential if real change was to be effected. However, the Liberal Party was divided between the rival factions of Asquith and Lloyd George, and more importantly for Simon it lacked a concrete policy with which to appeal to the new post-war electorate. The greatest weakness Simon perceived was the party's lack of an industrial policy. He began, with a group of younger Manchester Liberals, to press the party nationally to adopt an industrial policy that addressed the problems facing British industry in the aftermath of the First World War. This agitation produced a meeting at Simon's Herefordshire farm, Leadon Court, in May 1921 which provided the impetus for the creation of the Liberal summer school movement, which recruited intellectuals to the Liberal Party and provided a forum at which experts could float their ideas about contemporary economic, social, and industrial questions.

In December 1923 Simon was elected Liberal MP for Manchester Withington. He did not enjoy parliamentary life. He found the procedures of the House of Commons frustrating, which combined with its partisan atmosphere militated against the achievement of real progressive change. However, it provided him with the opportunity to establish his reputation as an expert on the question of housing reform within the national arena. He delivered his maiden speech on the topic, and in 1924 successfully piloted a private member's bill through parliament, the Prevention of Evictions Act. He lost his seat to a Conservative opponent at the 1924 general election and decided not to seek re-election to Manchester city council in 1925. In his period out of the Commons, during the 1924–9 parliament, he bought Wythenshawe Park and Wythenshawe Hall, and presented them to the city of Manchester to allow the development of a model satellite town for the relief of Manchester's overcrowded centre.

Simon took part in the Liberal summer school gatherings which produced the 'yellow book', *Britain's Industrial Future* (1928). This set out a comprehensive, well defined industrial policy, which formed the basis of the Liberal Party's national campaign in the May 1929 general election. Simon himself regained his Manchester Withington seat at the election. After the formation of the National Government in August 1931 Ramsay MacDonald appointed him parliamentary secretary at the Ministry of Health. Simon had already resolved not to contest the Withington constituency again, and stood for Penryn and Falmouth at the October 1931 general election in order to remain in office. But he was defeated, and consequently only held the ministerial post for a fortnight. He received a knighthood in 1932.

After his defeat in 1931 Simon adopted an increasingly independent stance, gradually withdrawing from Liberal party politics. He was particularly disturbed by the decision of the National Government in the 1930s effectively to abandon the previous decade's efforts to solve Britain's housing shortage through local authority building. His 1933 book *The Anti-Slum Campaign* showed him to be a convinced municipalist in housing matters. He maintained that 'the municipalities tend to build better, that they always build cheaper for letting', that too many private builders were interested only in profit ('we know only too well the kind of house they built in pre-war days'), and that the private sector should concentrate on providing for the owner-occupier (E. E. D. Simon, *The Anti-Slum Campaign*, 1933, 80, 145). The book criticized the redirection of national housing policy towards piecemeal slum clearance. Simon anticipated the planning movement of the post-1945 era in his call for 'a carefully thought-out plan … so as to avoid the errors of our ancestors and to try to produce a city that shall be beautiful, healthy and convenient' (ibid., 95). His growing interest in holistic planning, however, coupled with a disenchantment with the slow progress of the Wythenshawe scheme, led Simon to see the enlightened state rather than the municipality as the agent of urban renewal, particularly after the election of the Attlee government in 1945. Like most of his generation of British town planners, though, Simon was anxious to detach planning doctrines from an association with authoritarianism evident on the continent in the 1930s. He sought to do this less by restraining the state than by educating the citizenry.

Simon turned his attention to the future of democracy, and along with Eva Hubback founded the Council for Education for Citizenship. This initiated and financed a campaign to promote the teaching of civic and social philosophy in secondary schools. Simon believed that the survival of democracy depended on the education of the citizen as much as on the machinery of democratic government, a theme which he pursued in *Training for Citizenship*, which he co-wrote with Hubback in 1935.

At the outbreak of the Second World War, Simon resolved to devote his energies to ensuring that the Simon engineering firms adapted their techniques to the needs of the war, while also contributing to civil administration. After spells of involvement with the Ministry of Information and the Ministry of Aircraft Production he became deputy chairman of the Building Trade Council in the newly formed Ministry of Works. This position provided him with the opportunity to look beyond the immediate concerns of the war towards post-war reconstruction. It gave him valuable information on the structure and potential of the British building industry, which served as the basis for his book *Rebuilding Britain: a Twenty Year Plan*, published in the spring of 1945.

Labour peer In 1946 Simon contested a by-election for the Combined English Universities seat as an independent. He was defeated after the intervention of a second independent candidate. However, he was now considering his future political affiliation, and resolved to join the Labour Party, a move which he had contemplated twenty years earlier but rejected because of the party's rigid commitment to nationalization. His position was eased by the party's decision to concentrate on specific nationalization projects. He also recognized that as the Labour Party was in power with a large majority, by working from within the party he could press the causes he considered important: education, housing, and town planning. His influence was strengthened when he was raised to the peerage as Baron Simon of Wythenshawe on 17 January 1947.

Simon's membership of the Labour Party led to his appointment as chairman of the British Broadcasting Corporation in 1947, for a five-year term. He invested his immense energies in the position, viewing the BBC as the ideal instrument for the education of democratic citizens. He strongly supported the preservation of the BBC as a public service monopoly during the controversy surrounding the question of the renewal of its charter. A visit to the United States persuaded Simon of the need to oppose commercial television; he fought a tenacious, but ultimately unsuccessful, rearguard action against the campaign waged to secure commercial television, which was supported by the Conservative Party. His period as chairman prompted him to publish *The BBC from within* (1953).

In the immediate post-war years Simon believed that the future of humanity was under threat from two developments: overpopulation and the growth of nuclear weapons. The first concern prompted him to undertake a visit to Barbados to study the relationship between population and economic resources on the ground; he concluded that more effective birth control was required. He gave active support to the International Planned Parenthood Federation, and contributed to the propaganda activities of the British Family Planning Association. After his death the work continued through the endowment of the Simon Population Trust for research and education on population issues. He also became involved with the Campaign for Nuclear Disarmament. Although he was concerned at the tactics of some of his fellow campaigners, who advocated civil disobedience, he was active in pursuing the issues raised by the question of nuclear disarmament, not least in challenging government nuclear policy through debates in the House of Lords, and financing a book on the subject by Wayland Young.

Simon's longest association was with the University of Manchester; he was elected a member of the court and council in 1915, remaining a member, except for a brief interlude, until his death. He was treasurer from 1932 to 1941, and chairman of council from 1941 to 1957; in the latter role he helped pilot the university through the spectacular years of university expansion covered by the first post-war quinquennium of the University Grants Committee. He received an honorary degree from the university in 1944, and in the same year endowed the Simon Fund to provide research fellowships. In 1959 he was granted the freedom of the city of Manchester.

Throughout the post-war years Simon pursued the problems which were faced by the universities; his election literature during the Combined English Universities by-election in 1946 was dominated by these issues. He initiated a number of debates in the House of Lords that focused attention on the failings of government provision for university and technological education. Simon's final contribution to public life was to introduce a motion in the House of Lords on 11 May 1960 calling on the government to establish a committee to inquire and report on tertiary education. The government's initial response was one of indecision, which disappointed him, but in December 1960 it announced the appointment of a committee under the chairmanship of Lord Robbins. The announcement came too late for Simon, who after suffering a stroke while on holiday in the Lake District died in a Manchester nursing home, Nathan House, Christie Hospital, in Withington, on 3 October 1960. His wife survived him.

BRENDON JONES

Sources M. Stocks, *Ernest Simon of Manchester* (1963) · B. Simon, *In search of a grandfather: Henry Simon of Manchester, 1835–1899* (1997) · 'A long career of public service', *Manchester Guardian* (4 Oct 1960) · *The Times* (4 Oct 1960) · Man. CL, Manchester Archives and Local Studies, E. D. Simon MSS · M. Freeden, *Liberalism divided: a study of British political thought, 1914–1939* (1986) · J. Campbell, *Lloyd George: the goat in the wilderness* (1977) · M. Tylecote, *The work of Lady Simon of Wythenshawe for education in Manchester* (1974) · *The Guardian* (18 July 1972) [obit. of Lady Simon of Wythenshawe] · Man. CL, Manchester Archives and Local Studies, S. D. Simon MSS · *CGPLA Eng. & Wales* (1961)
Archives Man. CL, Manchester Archives and Local Studies, corresp. and papers | BLPES, corresp. with Lord Beveridge · CAC Cam., letters to A. V. Hill · JRL, letters to the *Manchester Guardian* · King's Lond., Liddell Hart C., corresp. with Sir B. H. Liddell Hart · Man. CL, Manchester Archives and Local Studies, S. D. Simon MSS · McMaster University, Hamilton, Ontario, corresp. with Bertrand Russell · Welwyn Garden City Central Library, corresp. with Frederic Osborn | FILM BFI NFTVA, documentary footage
Likenesses Lafayette, photograph, 1926, NPG [*see illus.*] · T. C. Dugdale, oils, 1944, Simon Engineering Ltd, Stockport, Cheshire · J. Epstein, bronze bust, Simon Engineering Ltd, Stockport, Cheshire · photographs, Simon Engineering Ltd, Stockport, Cheshire
Wealth at death £397,564 0s. 5d.: probate, 6 Jan 1961, *CGPLA Eng. & Wales*

Simon, Sir Francis Eugen [Franz] (1893–1956), physicist, was born on 2 July 1893 in Berlin, the only son and second of the three children of Ernst Simon, a well-to-do real estate developer, and his wife, Anna (d. 1946), daughter of Philibert Mendelssohn, a surveyor and an able mathematician. An ancestor was the brother of Moses Mendelssohn, the eighteenth-century Jewish philosopher; two of Simon's cousins became scientists: K. Mendelssohn FRS, reader in physics in the University of Oxford, and H. Mendelssohn, professor of zoology at the University of Tel Aviv. At the Kaiser Friedrich Reform Gymnasium in Berlin, which Simon attended from 1903, his talent for mathematics and physics soon showed itself. After overcoming strong family opposition—his father thought physics an insecure profession—he matriculated in 1912 at the University of Munich where he spent two semesters followed by one at Göttingen. His studies were interrupted first in 1913 by compulsory military service, then by the First World War, in which he served in the field artillery, mainly on the western front. He became an officer, was twice wounded, and was one of the earliest poison gas casualties. In the spring of 1919 Simon resumed his studies of physics and chemistry at the University of Berlin, where he came under the influence of Planck, von Laue, Haber, and in particular of Nernst, then director of the Physikalisch–Chemisches Institut of the university, under whom he did his thesis work on specific heats at low temperatures. He became DPhil in December 1921 and spent the next ten years in the same laboratory, becoming in 1924 a *Privatdozent* and in 1927 an *Extraordinarius* (associate professor). In 1922 he married Charlotte, daughter of a successful Berlin businessman, Sigismund Münchhausen; they had two daughters.

The Berlin period was a most fruitful one and established Simon's reputation as a great thermodynamicist and the outstanding low temperature physicist of his generation. Much of his work in Berlin was directly connected with the Nernst heat theorem, which in its fifteen years of existence had already proved its worth by enabling the prediction of chemical equilibrium with the help of the postulate of vanishing entropy differences between condensed phases at the absolute zero of temperature. There were, however, a number of cases which seemed to contradict the Nernst heat theorem, and in the ensuing controversy Simon took the line that these were only apparent violations and were due either to incorrect extrapolation of specific heats to absolute zero or to the fact that the system was not in internal equilibrium and hence thermodynamic arguments were not applicable. Many specific heat measurements were carried out in his laboratory to prove this view and it is largely thanks to Simon's work that the Nernst heat theorem has come to be regarded as the third law of thermodynamics, equal in fundamental importance to the first and second laws.

It was in Berlin that Simon began his extensive researches on fluids at high pressures and low temperatures in what he called model experiments. The basic idea was that by studying the melting pressures of substances with low boiling-points, that is, weak intermolecular attractive forces, one could predict how other substances would behave under conditions difficult to realize in practice. Thus, his success in solidifying helium at 50 °K, that is, ten times the critical temperature, enabled him to make hypotheses about the earth's core. These and other experiments required liquid hydrogen and liquid helium, and the Berlin phase was notable for the development of many new low temperature techniques. For the liquefaction of helium on a small but useful scale Simon developed the desorption method and in 1927 his laboratory became the fourth institution in the world where experiments down to the temperature of liquid helium could be carried out.

Early in 1931 Simon succeeded A. Eucken as professor of physical chemistry at the Technische Hochschule of Breslau: an appointment of some piquancy in view of Simon's recent heated controversies with Eucken about the third law. The spring semester of 1932 was spent as visiting professor at the University of California at Berkeley, where Simon conceived and developed his idea of the so-called expansion method for helium liquefaction and he was thus the first person to liquefy helium in the United States. The simplicity and cheapness of the method made it the mainstay of many low temperature laboratories for the next twenty years; it was with one of the earliest Simon expansion liquefiers installed at the Clarendon Laboratory in Oxford in 1933 that helium was first liquefied in Britain.

When Hitler came to power Simon decided to leave Germany although, as a war veteran and holder of the Iron Cross first class, he was exempt from the decree dismissing Jews from university posts. He correctly foresaw the trend of events and in August 1933, at the invitation of F. A. Lindemann (later Viscount Cherwell), he moved to the Clarendon Laboratory in Oxford on one of the research grants provided by Imperial Chemical Industries for refugee scientists from Germany. He became reader in thermodynamics in 1936 and was accorded the title of professor and became a student of Christ Church in 1945; in 1949 a chair of thermodynamics was specially created for him. In Britain he was to be known as Francis, though Franz remained his formal name.

The Clarendon Laboratory when Simon came to it was small and not too well equipped, but the period of 1933–9 was nevertheless rich in achievements. The magnetic cooling method to reach temperatures down to 0.001 °K, proposed in 1926 by Debye and by Giauque, fascinated Simon, who had earlier carried out experiments to estimate the scope of the method and now devoted much of his energy to developing it as a practical technique for experimenting in an entirely new temperature range. This work, carried out with a small group of collaborators, led to the discovery of new superconductors and new magnetic phenomena in paramagnetic substances and included experiments on thermal conductivity and thermal relaxation. It was during the same period that experiments with helium II (the 'superfluid' low temperature modification of liquid helium) led Simon to postulate the existence of a mobile helium II film on all surfaces in contact with the liquid.

The outbreak of war in 1939 brought this research work to an end. Simon, a naturalized British subject since 1938, tried hard to contribute to the war effort but there was reluctance to entrust secret work to ex-enemy aliens. With other refugee scientists, notably R. E. Peierls and O. R. Frisch, he became interested in the possibility of an atomic bomb and began to work on the problem before it had become an official project: hence the paradoxical fact that in its early days the 'Tube Alloys' project (as the British atom bomb project was code-named) was run mainly by foreign-born scientists. Simon was mainly concerned with the separation of the uranium isotopes by the gaseous diffusion method and his report in late 1940 contained the first realistic proposal for a sizeable separation plant. He was also involved in many other aspects of atomic energy and his stimulating views played a part in Britain's atomic energy developments both during and after the war.

With the resumption of peacetime research at the Clarendon Laboratory, Simon, while continuing some of the earlier work, turned his attention to some new fields. With H. Halban he initiated work on nuclear orientation: the study of the anisotropy in the intensity of radiation emitted by preferentially oriented radioactive nuclei, a technique fruitful for both nuclear and solid state physics. Even more spectacular were the experiments on nuclear cooling, an extension of the magnetic cooling method to nuclear magnetic moments, which resulted in temperatures of about a millionth of a degree absolute.

During the last ten years of his life Simon devoted much of his time to the wider social and political aspects of science and technology. His varied activities had one basic idea: an uncompromising dislike of waste in any form. He castigated the government for its lack of an integrated power and fuel policy; he deplored the waste of fuel in open grates and the waste of scientific manpower through the lack of good technological education or through the ineffective use of the intellectual potential of the country. Many of his ideas found expression in his articles in the *Financial Times*, of which he was scientific correspondent between 1948 and 1951. His immediate impact on public affairs was only slight, partly because the uncompromising crusading fervour with which he propounded his many ideas tended to put people off. But through public discussions, stimulated by his views, he did ultimately influence Britain's thinking.

Underlying Simon's whole work was a vivid appreciation of thermodynamics, which to him was a living subject, drawing strength continuously from the interpretation of new phenomena. His career roughly coincided with the period during which low temperature physics grew into a varied yet unified discipline and he was the outstanding figure of that era. It was largely thanks to him that the Clarendon Laboratory came to possess one of the world's largest and most renowned low temperature schools. As chairman of the commission of very low temperatures of the International Union of Pure and Applied

Physics, and as president of the first commission of the International Institute of Refrigeration, he played an important part in fostering international collaboration and the exchange of ideas in these fields. He was elected FRS in 1941 and received the society's Rumford medal in 1948. He became an honorary foreign member of the American Academy of Arts and Sciences in 1952 and was awarded the Kamerlingh Onnes gold medal of the Dutch Institute of Refrigeration (1950) and the Linde medal of the German Refrigerating Association in 1952. He was appointed CBE in 1946 and knighted in 1954.

On Cherwell's retirement in 1956 Simon succeeded him as Dr Lee's professor of experimental philosophy and head of the Clarendon Laboratory, but within a month of taking up his new position he died of coronary heart disease at the Radcliffe Infirmary, Oxford, on 31 October 1956. He was survived by his wife.

Simon's most notable quality was a profound and warm-hearted interest in people for their own sake. He was kindly and generous, devoid of all pomposity; he made friends easily and was particularly successful in gaining the confidence and devotion of young people. He was proud of his pupils—many of whom reached prominence in academic and industrial life—and tended to regard them as members of a large family. His influence as a teacher and as the founder and head of a great low temperature school was mainly through personal contact; lecturing was not his strength. Although tolerant by nature he was uncompromising on matters of principle. To the end of his life he could neither forget nor forgive the record of Nazi Germany and remained convinced that the spirit which made Nazism possible was still alive in Germany. He was a scientist to the core. His scientific outlook permeated his whole life and coloured his judgements on public affairs and his relations with others. It was the blend of lovable subjective qualities with the disciplined objectivity of the physicist which gave Simon's personality its cachet.   NICHOLAS KURTI, *rev.*

Sources N. Kurti, *Memoirs FRS*, 4 (1958), 225–56 · N. Arms, *A prophet in two countries* (1966) · personal knowledge (1971)
Archives RS, corresp. and papers | Nuffield Oxf., corresp. with Lord Cherwell · Oxf. U. Mus. NH, letters to Octavius Pickard-Cambridge · RS, corresp. with Lord Blackett · University of Bristol Library, corresp. with Charles Frank
Likenesses photograph, repro. in *Memoirs FRS*, facing p. 225
Wealth at death £8303 17s.: probate, 24 May 1957, CGPLA Eng. & Wales

Simon, (William) Glyn Hughes (1903–1972), archbishop of Wales, was born on 14 April 1903 at Swansea, the son of the Revd John Simon and his wife, Caroline Margaret Hughes. He came from a family whose roots were in Carmarthenshire. His father was one of the first students to attend the new theological college of St Michael and All Angels established at Aberdâr in 1892. Glyn Simon was throughout his life to remain loyal to the Tractarian principles the college was founded to promote, and his own period as warden of the college was a significant time in the institution's life. His mother was born and brought up in Cardiganshire. Simon was at first educated privately in

Swansea, where his father was then a curate, and proceeded to Christ College, Brecon, in 1913. His time there was not happy, and, although he went on to Jesus College, Oxford, in 1922, his school days had done nothing to nurture his social and personal confidence. To the end of his life, his manner was often diffident in conversation; as though to compensate, it could also be sharp to the point of waspishness in content.

Simon obtained second-class honours in Greats in 1926, and a first in theology the following year, after twelve months' residence at St Stephen's House, Oxford. In that year he was ordained to a curacy at St Paul's, Crewe, in the diocese of Chester, where he exercised a devoted ministry in the classic Anglo-Catholic style, spending many hours in visiting, and living simply in the middle of a fairly deprived and difficult area. He returned to Wales in 1930 as warden of the Church Hostel in Bangor, at that time an uneasy mixture of a university hall of residence and a hostel for ordinands. The warden's duties involved not only the pastoral and administrative oversight of the hostel, but also responsibilities in the teaching of theology. His regime was severe, and not all the students found the Catholic, indeed semi-monastic, atmosphere congenial: the poet R. S. Thomas, who took up residence in the hostel in 1932, left a none-too-sympathetic portrait of Simon in his autobiography, though he speaks with appreciation of the warden's unfailingly challenging sermons. Simon evidently polarized opinion not a little in the Church in Wales: his reputation among Anglo-Catholics was deservedly high as a teacher, preacher, and confessor, but his cutting tongue and his tendency to look down somewhat on both less well-educated Welsh Anglicans and the Welsh free churches intimidated and alienated a good many.

In 1938 Simon was an unsuccessful applicant for the principalship of Lampeter; had he been successful, he might well have found it a hard furrow to plough, as it represented so much of the Welsh Anglican ethos he disliked and even despised; certainly in later life he showed little sympathy for Lampeter. In 1939 he became warden of St Michael's College, now removed from Aberdâr to Llandaff, on the outskirts of Cardiff. In this role, he exercised a vast influence upon generations of Welsh clergy, and under his government St Michael's took on a good many of the features of Simon's own theological college, St Stephen's House. Here as in Bangor, he insisted on rigorous discipline; and here too his acerbic style was much in evidence. The austerity of college life was intensified when the community was forced to move to St David's after the Llandaff site suffered bomb damage in 1941.

Simon had regularly encouraged his students to celibacy, and was generally regarded himself as a confirmed celibate; his marriage on 7 September 1941 to Sheila Roberts came as a great surprise, even to quite close friends. He had prepared her for confirmation at Bangor, and she had begun to study theology under his guidance. Of strong nonconformist background, she represented a politically alert and radical strain in Welsh culture which Simon had not until this period taken too seriously. Her influence on his development was marked; and her personal charm made her widely loved in Llandaff after the marriage. A first child died in infancy, but three children were born of the marriage (Nicholas in 1946, Robin in 1947, and Perpetua in 1948). Sheila Simon continued to be a powerful support to her husband's ministry until her death from cancer in 1963.

In 1948 Simon was appointed dean of Llandaff and embarked immediately upon the enormous task of supervising the restoration of Llandaff Cathedral, badly damaged during the war. The rededication of the restored cathedral in 1960, with the celebrated Jacob Epstein figure *Christ in Majesty* as its centrepiece and the new chapels and furnishings, represented the culmination of work begun by Simon, whose artistic flair and boldness undoubtedly set the tone for all that was to follow. The restored cathedral seemed to many to stand for a fresh vision for the Welsh church: confident, articulate, and culturally sophisticated. The poet and critic Moelwyn Merchant has written of the strong sense of a Welsh Anglican renaissance in the late forties and fifties; Glyn Simon was a central figure in this.

His election as bishop of Swansea and Brecon in 1953 (he was consecrated in January 1954) provided Simon with a wider stage to implement his vision. He encouraged a number of missions, making use of the village evangelists in the sparsely populated northern regions of the diocese, but was also remembered as active in improving the living conditions of the clergy. He emerged more and more in the public eye as a commentator on national and international affairs, and began also to develop a concern with Welsh identity and the Welsh language (not a native speaker, he worked hard to attain a reasonable fluency in his years as a bishop)—though he had attracted criticism in 1950 for some characteristically barbed remarks about the pseudo-antique rituals of the national eisteddfod. This new-found enthusiasm for things Welsh found rather unhappy expression in 1957. He had been translated to the diocese of Llandaff in October of 1957, and an archiepiscopal election followed in November, at which the bishop of Monmouth, Edwin Morris, was elected. Morris was an Englishman, though one who had spent his entire ministry in Wales; Simon expressed some unease, early in 1958, in his diocesan newsletter, about the principle of electing non-Welsh speakers to Welsh dioceses, and to the archbishop's office. Morris took great offence (though Simon made it clear that he intended no personal criticism of Morris) and relations were strained for some time.

The period as bishop of Llandaff unquestionably saw Simon at his very considerable best. He engaged, as practically no previous Welsh bishop had done, with the world of industry, appointing an industrial chaplain for the great steelworks at Port Talbot, commenting and intervening in industrial disputes and winning much trust and affection from the unions in the steel and coal industries. For many, his most powerful public intervention was his broadcast reflection on the appalling tragedy at Aberfan in October 1966, when 116 children and 28 adults were killed in a landslip of colliery waste. His own experience of bereavement was movingly evoked as he spoke of the 'commonwealth of suffering' which alone makes such pain bearable. His personal involvement, including his forthright denunciation of negligence on the part of the National Coal Board, gave him a massive moral authority in much of Wales. He had also won a reputation elsewhere in the Anglican communion, preaching and teaching widely, leading a significant university mission in Durham in 1963, and emerging as a vocal critic of apartheid and nuclear weaponry. His theology remained resolutely traditional, but his public face was clearly identified with the political left (he remarked to an ordinand in 1971 that he believed in being 'bright blue in theology and bright pink in politics'). And while these public stands attracted predictable criticism, his rapport with the young became constantly easier; to his ordinands and younger clergy, he was the object of a certain amount of hero-worship, and he found student audiences enthusiastically receptive.

In 1968 he succeeded Edwin Morris as archbishop of Wales. The transition was not unlike that between Fisher and Ramsey at Canterbury: Morris, like Fisher, had been a man of great ability and natural authority, but generally unfriendly to innovation; Simon, like Ramsey, brought to the office not so much a programmatic radicalism as a certain freedom of spirit, informed by Catholic theology and spiritual discipline, that allowed more scope for engagement with contemporary issues. As archbishop he continued his support for Welsh-language concerns, expressing some sympathy with campaigns of 'direct action'. But his health was already failing: by 1969 Parkinson's disease had been diagnosed, and this took an increasing toll. In April 1971 he retired. He had remarried on 2 February 1970 and, with his new wife, Camellia (widow of Trevor Pritchard Rees), he moved to Goathurst in Somerset. On 14 June 1972 he suffered a fatal heart attack and died at the Dower House, Goathurst. His body was returned to Llandaff for burial. He was survived by his second wife.

Simon's published remains—a commentary on 1 Corinthians, a collection of visitation charges, and a little book on pastoralia (*Feeding the Flock*, 1964)—do less than justice to his influence and ability. Arguably the greatest ornament of the Welsh bench since disestablishment, he gave the Welsh church a new degree of confidence and public credibility that lasted long after his death.

ROWAN WILLIAMS

Sources O. W. Jones, *Glyn Simon: his life and opinions* (1981) · O. W. Jones, *St Michael's College, Llandaff* (1992) · D. Walker, M. Walker, and others, *Swansea & Brecon, 1923–1973* (1973) · R. S. Thomas, *Neb* (1985) · M. Merchant, *Fragments of a life* (1990) · personal knowledge (2004)
Archives NL Wales, papers, incl. MS autobiography | NL Wales, letters to Thomas Iorwerth Ellis · NL Wales, Llandaff diocesan archives
Likenesses S. M. Brown, portrait, priv. coll.
Wealth at death £7651: probate, 10 Aug 1972, *CGPLA Eng. & Wales*

Simon, John (1675–1751), mezzotint engraver, was born into a Huguenot family in Normandy and is said to have belonged to an artist family connected with the protestant church at Charenton, near Paris. After training in Paris as a line engraver he moved to England and rapidly adapted to the medium of mezzotint. His earliest prints were published from Cross Lane, Long Acre, during the middle years of Queen Anne's reign. Their spare and powerful style soon attracted the notice of Sir Godfrey Kneller, who about 1708–9 had quarrelled with his principal engraver, John Smith, and in the period before the dispute was settled Simon obtained several of Kneller's commissions. This assured his reputation, and Simon became a founding subscriber to the Academy for Artists in Great Queen Street, set up under Kneller's patronage in 1711.

Simon was a prolific engraver, particularly noted for his portraits, of which Chaloner Smith (in *British Mezzotinto Portraits*) details 170 examples, above all after Kneller and Dahl, but also after Gibson, Murray, Mercier, and Seeman. His subjects represented all points of the political spectrum. Thus, while engraving three separate portraits each of the duke of Marlborough (nos. 93, 94, 96) and of Sir Robert Walpole (nos. 158–60), he also engraved Jacobites, including Francis Atterbury, bishop of Rochester (no. 19), George Keith, the Earl Marischal (no. 92), Lord North and Grey (no. 112), and the duke of Ormond (no. 115). Simon's numerous portraits of members of the Hanoverian royal family were similarly balanced by portraits dating from *c.*1730 of the exiled Stuart king James III (no. 143), with Queen Clementina (no. 144) and the young princes Charles Edward (no. 145) and Henry Benedict (no. 146). Hardly surprisingly, these last were untitled and unsigned, but Chaloner Smith considered the attribution as 'certain' (p. 1118) on stylistic grounds. Simon also engraved a notable sequence of twenty-four *Poets and Philosophers of England*, published on six plates (*c.*1727), and many religious and decorative subjects, such as *Christ Restoring the Blind Man's Sight*, after Laguerre, *Four Elements*, after Amiconi, and *Four Seasons*, after Rosalba. Particularly notable was a version of the *Raphael Cartoons* at Hampton Court (no. 173), engraved in the early years of his career and published by Edward Cooper, for whom Simon worked extensively until *c.*1720. Thereafter he mostly published his own prints from a series of addresses in the vicinity of Covent Garden, including King Street (the Seven Stars), Villiers Street (the Golden Eagle), and New Street, before retiring from active engraving about 1742. He died in London on 22 September 1751, and his remaining stock of plates was sold in November 1761.

RICHARD SHARP

Sources J. C. Smith, *British mezzotinto portraits*, 3 (1880), 1060–130 · Vertue, *Note books* · T. Clayton, *The English print, 1688–1802* (1997) · Thieme & Becker, *Allgemeines Lexikon* · Bryan, *Painters* (1849) · *DNB*

Simon, Sir John (1816–1904), surgeon and public health officer, was born in the City of London on 10 October 1816, the sixth child of Louis Michael Simon (1782–1879) and his second wife, Mathilde Nonnet (1787–1882). Both parents were second-generation French immigrants; his father, initially a shipbroker, later became a stockbroker and a prominent member of the London stock exchange, serving on its governing committee from 1837 to 1867. John Simon was educated first in Pentonville, and then, when the family moved out of the City to Blackheath, at the

Sir John Simon (1816–1904), by Charles Baugniet, 1848

Greenwich preparatory school of the Revd Dr Charles Parr Burney, which he disliked. In 1831 he was sent to lodge with the Revd Leonard Molly of Hohensolms near Wetzler, in what was then Rhenish Prussia, to learn German.

Medical training and academic career In 1833 Simon was apprenticed to Joseph Henry Green, surgeon to St Thomas's Hospital, London, and professor of surgery at King's College, for a premium of 500 guineas. In the first three decades of the nineteenth century surgery had become a prestigious and lucrative profession for a well-connected gentleman. Consultant surgeons such as Astley Cooper and Benjamin Brodie had incomes in the range of £10,000 per year. Simon and Green had much more than surgery in common: they shared interests in German Romantic literature and philosophy, as well as in biology, and their relationship was longlasting; in 1865 Simon prepared a memoir of Green for inclusion in Green's *Spiritual Philosophy*, a digest of Coleridge's philosophy.

In 1838, a year before the expiration of Simon's apprenticeship, Green presented him for the examination to become MRCS, in order that Simon might be eligible for appointment as demonstrator in anatomy at King's College. Simon passed the examination and took up the position in conjunction with Francis MacDougall in 1839. On the opening of King's College Hospital in 1840, Simon also became senior assistant surgeon. He held both of his honorary posts until 1847, when he was appointed lecturer in anatomical pathology at St Thomas's at £200 per annum. He retained the surgical post at King's until 1853, and became full surgeon at St Thomas's in 1863; he held that post until 1876. He had resigned the pathology lectureship in 1871. In 1844 he was elected an honorary fellow of the Royal College of Surgeons. He served on its council from 1868 to 1880 and was vice-president in 1876–7 and president in 1878. He was also president of the Pathological Society in 1867.

In 1845 Simon published *A Physiological Essay on the Thymus Gland*, which had won the first Astley Cooper prize of the Royal College of Surgeons (worth £300) and led to Simon's election to the Royal Society in the same year. His lectures on pathology were published in 1850 as *General pathology as conducive to the establishment of rational principles for the diagnosis and treatment of disease*. He also published articles on clinical surgery and on inflammation in T. Holmes's *System of Surgery* (1860).

Medical officer of health   In 1848 Simon was elected the first medical officer of health to the sewers commission of the City of London over a number of better-known and more senior candidates. Simon's appointment made him the second medical officer of health in the country (Liverpool had introduced the position in 1847). The post was established as the City sought to retain its independence from the public health legislation that parliament was enacting for the country as a whole and for the metropolis in particular. Although a member of the Health of Towns Association, Simon was not known for his expertise or interest in sanitary matters, nor was he closely associated with the sanitary movement led by Edwin Chadwick and Thomas Southwood Smith. These facts, along with his father's longstanding influence in the City, contributed significantly to his election. In taking up the position at a salary of £500 (later £800) a year, Simon kept his positions at King's and St Thomas's, and his private practice as a surgeon.

Far from keeping a low profile Simon quickly began a series of passionate, eloquent, and sometimes sarcastic *exposés* of health conditions in the City, chiefly in his annual reports, which were well publicized by *The Times*. He urged reform in many areas: water supply, sewerage and drainage, burial practices, butchering and other noxious trades, food adulteration, and overcrowded and substandard housing. While reform was not forthcoming in many of these areas during Simon's tenure, he did much to persuade the public that it was ultimately necessary. Although initially his blunt criticism of the City and its institutions made him unpopular, by the mid-1850s Simon's perseverance and tact had won over many of his early enemies. He shrewdly distanced himself from the increasingly unpopular Edwin Chadwick, whose insistence on regional and national co-ordination of public health threatened the City's autonomy, all the while supporting many of Chadwick's programmes. Simon's breadth of concern, powerful reports, and careful use of morbidity and mortality data to identify areas where public intervention was needed did much to set the model of the medical officer of health. On the formation of the Association of Metropolitan Medical Officers in 1855 Simon was elected its first president. In 1854 the series of annual reports was unofficially published as *Reports Relating to the Sanitary Condition of the City of London*.

In 1854 Chadwick and his associates were purged from the General Board of Health, and in 1855 Simon accepted the invitation of Sir Benjamin Hall, MP for Tower Hamlets and president of the reorganized Board of Health, to become the board's chief medical officer at a salary of £1500 a year. At this point he gave up private surgical practice while maintaining his appointments at St Thomas's. Simon's metropolitan popularity and defence of local self-government made him an enormously attractive candidate to Hall, who had been one of the stoutest critics of the Chadwickian centralists. When the board was dissolved in 1858, Simon's work of investigating outbreaks of disease and co-ordinating the nation's response to them was transferred to the privy council, and his salary was raised to £2000.

This arrangement, at first temporary, lasted until 1871, when many of Simon's duties were transferred into the new Local Government Board (the rest were transferred in 1874). Simon and other members of the medical profession were able to influence the royal sanitary commission of 1869–71, which recommended the reorganizations of public health institutions that were carried out in a series of acts between 1871 and 1875. However, matters of disease prevention and the investigation and control of epidemics were a low priority for the board, which was concerned with administering the poor law and with overseeing all manner of local-government activities. Accustomed to direct ministerial access at the privy council and to the freedom to organize his own work and that of his staff as he thought fit, Simon found himself frustrated with mundane administration and rigid routine. In 1876 he resigned, having demanded a series of procedural changes which had been refused. He received a pension of £1333 per annum and was created CB.

During the late 1870s and early 1880s, Simon, now retired from his administrative and teaching posts, continued to be active—as a reforming president of the Royal College of Surgeons, as a founder and administrator of the Grocers' Company scholarships in sanitary science, and as an influential member of the General Medical Council. He was created KCB in 1887 and awarded honorary degrees by Oxford (DCL, 1868), Munich (MChD, 1872), Cambridge (LLD, 1880), Edinburgh (LLD, 1882), and Dublin (MD, 1887). He was also awarded the Harben medal of the Royal Institute of Public Health (1896) and the Royal Society's Buchanan medal (1897). For much of the last decade of his life, however, he was incapacitated and nearly blind.

Surgeon and pathologist   While Simon's most visible contributions were in public health, he was influential also as a surgeon and pathologist. As a surgeon he was associated not with major innovations, but with significant improvements in ophthalmic, urological, and orthopaedic surgery. He was conservative and painstaking, preparing for every novelty of procedure by long practice on cadavers. He was similarly well-respected as a lecturer in the relatively new science of pathology, and known for the thoroughness with which he kept abreast of continental work.

Simon's most important research in public health was done as the chief member of the committee for scientific inquiries on the cholera epidemics, established by Sir Benjamin Hall's General Board of Health in 1854. Following the initial work of John Snow, Simon established, with much greater confidence, the link between cholera incidence and faecally contaminated water. He was reluctant, however, to conclude that contaminated water was the common means of transmission of a specific cholera agent. Thereafter his main works during his years as the nation's chief health officer were the annual reports of the medical officer of the privy council, begun in 1858–9.

In these reports, Simon introduced the conclusions of a growing number of scientists and inspectors, most of them ostensibly temporary staff but in practice relatively permanent. Their inquiries were of three sorts. Beginning with his *Papers Relating to the Sanitary State of the People of England* (1858), based mainly on the work of Simon's assistant E. H. Greenhow, Simon undertook to identify the independent sources of excess mortality by re-analysing the data on the registration of deaths, to discover which diseases accounted for deaths in particular sectors of the population and in particular localities. These led to a number of studies by staff members on occupational disease (by Greenhow and J. S. Bristowe) and on the nutritional status of the population (by Edward Smith). Other studies, such as that by Greenhow on infant diarrhoea, identified the pathogenicity of social institutions—for instance, where mothers of small children were employed in factories, or where people worked in agricultural groups. Karl Marx drew on several of these reports to illustrate the concept of surplus value in the first volume of *Capital*.

Simon's staff also undertook epidemiological investigations of the causes of severe local outbreaks of infectious diseases, particularly of typhoid fever and of an apparently new disease, diphtheria. The studies were of dubious value since it was not yet clear that such diseases had specific causes and means of transmission, and because Simon's inspectors were in no position to compel local authorities to take remedial measures. Finally, beginning in 1867 and using as a precedent the substantial expenditure on the cattle plague of 1865–6, Simon persuaded the Treasury to allot up to £2000 per year for basic scientific research on the 'intimate pathology' of several diseases. Recipients of these commissions included John Burdon Sanderson and J. L. W. Thudichum. Here too, despite some suggestive findings, the research projects were usually too tentative, and too isolated from the (mostly German) mainstream of biomedical science, to produce much that was directly useful in the control of disease. In 1887 Edward Seaton, Simon's long-time assistant and successor at the Local Government Board, published in conjunction with the Sanitary Institute of Great Britain two volumes of Simon's *Public Health Reports*; these consisted mainly of the annual reports to the City of London and of extracts from his annual reports to the privy council.

Simon's achievements In 1890 Simon published his *English sanitary institutions reviewed in their course of development and in some of their social and political relations*, a historical polemic dealing at length with the marginalizing of state medicine by the Local Government Board, but placing public health within a long series of social and political reforms that included the abolition of slavery and the reform bills. Simon's efforts established the potential of state medicine as a central part of Fabian socialism and were ultimately more influential on such figures as Beatrice and Sidney Webb than the virulent anti-medical perspective of their fellow Fabian, George Bernard Shaw. Yet Simon himself was for much of his career a reluctant socialist, treating much sanitary improvement as a branch of philanthropy, or a division of 'practical Christianity'.

Simon is often commended for having replaced Chadwick's exclusive focus on sanitary engineering with a more empirical and a more medical approach to public health administration. The comparison is misleading inasmuch as Simon's privy council medical office was only in part a replacement of Chadwick's Board of Health, whose functions in overseeing sanitary public works were continued by the local government act office of the Home department, between 1858 and 1871, the period of Simon's near-autonomy in the council.

Simon's strengths as a health officer were in the disclosure and effective publicizing of underestimated public health problems. During his years as an anxious young surgeon Simon had extensively studied the classics, as well as English literature, and German and oriental art and philosophy. Like his close friend John Ruskin he sometimes became persuaded that the astonishing power of his prose could effect great change. Among his close friends were several journalists, and he had uncommon access to the editorial pages of *The Times* and other newspapers. Simon's pen was most clearly effective in 1862–3 when he blocked an effort, supported by William Farr, Florence Nightingale, and Edwin Chadwick, to relocate St Thomas's Hospital to a presumably more salubrious countryside site. He was not skilled as a legislative draftsman and was almost wholly uninterested in the minutiae of administering public health law. He was an opportunistic administrator with powerful friends, particularly during Liberal administrations, and he was able to persuade the reluctant Treasury to sponsor a remarkable range of activities, with the result that the post of medical officer of health became a much larger part of government than had been originally intended.

Nevertheless, two factors ultimately undermined the credibility of the claim that the activities Simon had initiated were vital to the well-being of the state. These were the anomalous status of the privy council itself as a department able to issue extra-parliamentary 'orders', together with the fact that Simon, with the possible exception of the control of vaccination, carefully kept the medical officership free from entanglement in any of the growing administrative domains of the state. Finally, as an administrator of scientific investigations of disease, both in the field and in the laboratory, Simon the pathologist was in conflict with Simon the epidemiologist. He was reluctant to acknowledge what was becoming increasingly plain to continental researchers in the 1860s and 1870s: that for many diseases it was enough to know that microbes of a particular kind, transmitted by a particular means, had invaded a body. Simon, however, like other philosophical pathologists, believed that the answers to deeper questions of the biochemistry of pathological processes would provide practical knowledge for control and prevention. Unfortunately, the biochemistry and cellular biology of the day were incapable of shedding much light on those questions, and the agenda itself diverted attention from the more pragmatic matter of epidemiological generalization. This tension is reflected in his last significant medical publication, an article entitled 'Contagion' in Richard Quain's *Dictionary of Medicine* (1878).

On 22 July 1848 Simon had married Jane O'Meara (1816–1901), daughter of Matthew Delaval O'Meara, who had been deputy commissary-general in the Peninsular War. The couple had no children of their own, but adopted Simon's two-year-old niece and godchild, Jane Faulkner, in 1853, after the death of her mother. Legend has it that she, or her elder sister, was Algernon Swinburne's 'Boo'. Socially the Simons moved more in artistic and literary circles than in scientific and medical ones. Their home at 40 Kensington Square, London, became something of a salon. Their closest friends included Ruskin, whom Simon met in the Italian Alps in 1856, and the American philologist Charles Eliot Norton and his wife; they were also friendly with the Burne-Joneses and many of the other Pre-Raphaelites. In 1894 Simon prepared a short volume, *Personal Recollections*, which was privately printed, and revised and reprinted in 1903.

Simon died at his home in Kensington Square on 23 July 1904 and was buried at Ladywell cemetery, Lewisham. He bequeathed the ultimate residue of his estate to St Thomas's Hospital, London.   CHRISTOPHER HAMLIN

Sources R. Lambert, *Sir John Simon, 1816–1904, and English social administration* (1963) · J. Simon, *Personal recollections of Sir John Simon* (privately printed, London, 1894) · E. Seaton, ed., *John Simon, public health reports*, 2 vols. (1887) · J. B. Sanderson, *PRS*, 75 (1905), 336–46 · V. G. Plarr, *Plarr's Lives of the fellows of the Royal College of Surgeons of England*, rev. D'A. Power, 2 (1930), 296–8 · *St Thomas's Hospital Reports*, new ser., 33 (1905) · C. Bellamy, *Administering central–local relations: the local government board, 1871–1919, in its fiscal and cultural context* (1988) · A. MacNalty, *The history of state medicine in England* (1948) · C. E. A. Winslow, *The conquest of epidemic disease: a chapter in the history of ideas* (1943)
Archives RCS Eng., corresp. and papers | Bodl. Oxf. · Bodl. Oxf., letters to Sir Henry Wentworth Acland · GL, City of London commissioners of sewers · Harvard U., Charles Eliot Norton MSS, letters · JRL, corresp. with A. Severn and J. Severn · PRO, Ministry of Health MSS · PRO, Privy Council Office MSS · PRO, Treasury MSS · UCL, Chadwick MSS, letters · University of Lancaster, Ruskin Galleries, letters · University of Lancaster, Ruskin Library, corresp. with John Ruskin
Likenesses C. Baugniet, lithograph, 1848, Wellcome L. [*see illus.*] · G. Jerrard, photograph, 1881, Wellcome L. · C. Baugniet, lithograph, BM · T. Woolner, marble bust, RCS Eng. · photographs, repro. in *BMJ* (1904), 2.265
Wealth at death £26,635 8s. 8d.: probate, 17 Aug 1904, *CGPLA Eng. & Wales*

Simon, Sir John (1818–1897),

serjeant-at-law, was born at Montego Bay, Jamaica, on 9 December 1818, the only son of Isaac Simon, a Jewish merchant, and his wife, Rebecca, only daughter of Jacob Orobio Furtado. Rebecca Simon was descended from Balthasar Orobio, who, on account of his adherence to the Jewish faith, spent three years (1655 to 1658) in the prison of the Spanish Inquisition, and whose father, Caesar Orobio, was burnt at the stake. Simon was educated at a public school in Jamaica, and a private school in Liverpool. He went on to study at University College, London, and graduated LLB in 1841 at London University. He entered the Middle Temple on 29 October 1839 and on 4 November 1842 he was called to the bar, the second Jew to be admitted. In 1843 he married Rachel, fifth daughter of Simeon Kensington Salaman of Portman Square, London, and sister of Charles Kensington Salaman, the composer. Rachel Simon was a writer. Together they had five surviving children—two sons, Charles Moncrieffe Simon and Oswald John Simon, and three daughters.

After practising for two years in Jamaica, Simon returned to England in 1845, and became a leader on the common-law side on the northern circuit. In April 1858 he successfully defended Simon Bernard from the accusation of complicity with Orsini in the attempt to assassinate Napoleon III. On 15 April 1864 he was appointed a serjeant-at-law, and in February 1868 he received a patent of precedence, which gave him the privileges of queen's counsel, with the right of holding briefs against the crown. On 27 November 1868 he was returned to parliament as a Liberal for the borough of Dewsbury in Yorkshire. In the House of Commons it was said that he swiftly commanded attention as an authority on legal questions. He made significant speeches on the Oaths Bill (1880–83), which he had introduced, allowing for an affirmation to be given by those who objected to taking an oath. He also spoke extensively on the government of Jamaica in 1884 and played an important part in the restoration of representative government.

In parliament and outside Simon was an untiring advocate of Jewish interests. Besides organizing the Mansion House meeting in 1870 to protest against the persecution of the Jews in Romania and Serbia, he entered a vigorous protest in parliament against the pogroms in Russia in 1882. He was one of the founders of the Anglo-Jewish Association in 1871. On 24 August 1886 he was knighted and in 1888 he retired from parliament. He was a member of the Reform Club. He died at his London residence, 36 Tavistock Square, on 24 June 1897, and was buried that month at Golders Green cemetery.

    E. I. CARLYLE, *rev.* ERIC METCALFE

Sources *WWW* · *WWBMP* · J. Foster, *Men-at-the-bar: a biographical hand-list of the members of the various inns of court*, 2nd edn (1885) · *Jewish Chronicle* (2 July 1897) · *Dewsbury Reporter* (3 July 1897) · *Annual Register* (1858) · Walford, *County families* · Burke, *Peerage*
Likenesses W. Goodman, painting (Bernard/Orsini trial); known to be at 63 Tavistock Square, London, in 1897 · S. J. Solomon, portrait; known to be at 63 Tavistock Square, London, in 1897 · Spy [L. Ward], chromolithograph caricature, NPG; repro. in *VF* (25 Sept 1886)
Wealth at death £1075 5s. 11d.: probate, 22 Oct 1897, *CGPLA Eng. & Wales*

Simon, John Allsebrook, first Viscount Simon (1873–1954),

politician and lawyer, was born on 28 February 1873

John Allsebrook Simon, first Viscount Simon (1873–1954), by Bassano, 1931

at 16 Yarburgh Street, a terraced house in Moss Side, Manchester, the only son and elder child of the Revd Edwin Simon (1843–1920) and his wife, Fanny Allsebrook (1846–1936). Edwin Simon, like three of his five brothers, was a Congregational minister, pastor of Zion Chapel in the Hulme district of Manchester. Fanny was the daughter of William Pole Allsebrook, a Worcestershire farmer, although she claimed descent from Margaret, countess of Salisbury, niece of Edward IV.

Education, the bar, and marriage Simon was educated at kindergarten in Manchester until he moved to King Edward's School, Bath, where his father had become president of the Somerset Congregational Union. From there he won a scholarship to Fettes College in Edinburgh. At Fettes his outstanding intellectual ability first became apparent and in 1891 he secured an open scholarship to Wadham College, Oxford, where his contemporaries included F. E. Smith and C. B. Fry.

After a distinguished undergraduate career, crowned by a first in Greats and the presidency of the union, Simon was elected a fellow of All Souls in 1897. Thus began a connection which he would maintain to the end of his life and which became increasingly important to him in his later years. After coming down from Oxford at the end of 1898 he was called to the bar at the Inner Temple, where he was a pupil of A. J. Ram and then of Sir Reginald Acland. In court his strength lay in his ability to analyse and clarify issues of great complexity. His preferred style was to persuade a jury through logic and reason rather than oratory

or histrionics. But, notwithstanding his undoubted legal talents, he never looked upon the law as more than a stepping-stone towards a career in politics.

On 24 May 1899 Simon married Ethel Mary Venables, daughter of Gilbert Venables, and the niece of the historian J. R. Green. She was a student when they met at Oxford, and became vice-principal of St Hugh's Hall. Two daughters were born in 1900 and 1901, but Mrs Simon died shortly after the birth of a son, Gilbert, in September 1902. It is difficult to exaggerate the impact this tragedy had upon the young lawyer. Even three years later he spent Christmas day walking aimlessly in France to try to escape from his sorrow. In time he recovered, to the extent that on 18 December 1917 he remarried. His second wife was Kathleen Manning (1863/4–1955) [see Simon, Dame Kathleen Rochard, Viscountess Simon], the widow of Thomas Manning, a Dublin doctor, and daughter of Francis Eugene Harvey. But in other respects the impact of this early bereavement was never erased. His natural shyness intensified, and he devoted himself with reinforced and sometimes obsessive commitment to his work.

Liberal lawyer At least Simon's legal career prospered. In 1903 he acted for the British government in a complicated dispute concerning a boundary between Canada and Alaska, and he was made a KC in 1908. More importantly, he secured election to the House of Commons as member for Walthamstow in the Liberal landslide of January 1906. In parliament he rose rapidly, despite the amount of competition on the packed Liberal benches, and was appointed solicitor-general on 7 October 1910, with the customary knighthood. At thirty-seven he was the youngest holder of this office since the 1830s. In February 1911 he successfully conducted the prosecution of Edward Mylius for criminal libel, the defendant having published allegations that George V was a bigamist. Promoted to attorney-general with, unusually, a seat in the cabinet on 19 October 1913, he was widely seen as one of the rising stars of the Liberal government and was even spoken of as a possible successor to Herbert Asquith for the premiership.

The First World War, however, saw a distinct downturn in Simon's political prospects. Though he became home secretary at the formation of the first coalition on 25 May 1915, turning down an offer of the lord chancellorship since the resulting peerage would have curtailed any prospect of future political advance, he had accepted British involvement in the conflict with marked reluctance. For the first time both colleagues and opponents sensed the equivocation which became his trademark. His position within the government became increasingly uneasy, and he resigned in January 1916 over the introduction of conscription.

Simon, however, was no pacifist. His opposition to conscription was on the narrow but important principle of a man's right to decide for himself whether or not he fought for his country. Accordingly, in 1917 he served with distinction in the Royal Flying Corps, attached to General Trenchard's staff. He remained loyal to Asquith and opposed the Lloyd George coalition. Not surprisingly, he lost his parliamentary seat in the 1918 'coupon' election, sharing the fate of the vast majority of independent Liberals, and Lloyd George successfully thwarted his attempt to return to the Commons at the Spen Valley by-election in 1919.

Post-war politics Simon did manage to secure the Spen Valley seat at the general election of 1922 and soon became deputy leader of the Liberal Party. But that party was no longer the vehicle for political advancement which it had been before the First World War. Simon now seemed destined to play out the remainder of his political career confined to the ranks of permanent opposition. At the beginning of the 1920s he stood as the champion of independent Liberalism. But as the decade progressed he became increasingly disillusioned with the party's prospects. Simon's relations with Lloyd George remained poor, notwithstanding the apparent reunion of the warring Liberal factions for the general election of 1923. He found himself repeatedly at odds with Lloyd George over party tactics, particularly over the question of how Liberals should respond to the advent of Labour as a governing party. But it was Lloyd George rather than Simon who emerged as Liberal leader after Asquith's retirement in October 1926.

Increasingly, Simon was coming to see socialism as the ultimate political evil. Such thinking no doubt helped to prompt his famous declaration in the House of Commons on 6 May 1926 that the general strike was illegal. At the same time he recognized in the Conservative Party of Stanley Baldwin a reflection of some of the Liberal values which he continued to espouse. Yet while Lloyd George remained Liberal leader it seemed possible that Simon might withdraw from politics altogether. His legal career was at its peak and he was now the highest-paid barrister of his generation. In 1927 he accepted the government's invitation to chair a statutory commission on Indian constitutional development following the Montagu–Chelmsford reforms of 1919, and in 1930 he headed an inquiry into the R101 airship disaster. His Indian report was a classic of its kind, a lucid exposition of the problems of the subcontinent in all their complexity. But it was hamstrung by the government's terms of reference and was largely pre-empted by the declaration on dominion status made by the viceroy, Lord Irwin, in October 1929.

Foreign secretary in the National Government The political and economic crises of the Labour government of 1929–31 opened up the possibility of a revival in Simon's career. The mounting problem of unemployment even compelled him to question his adherence to the traditional Liberal doctrine of free trade, thus facilitating a *rapprochement* with the Conservative Party. Frustrated by Lloyd George's refusal to put the minority Labour government out of office, Simon and about thirty Liberal supporters broke away to form the Liberal National group in June 1931. Simon received his reward when appointed foreign secretary on 5 November in Ramsay MacDonald's National Government. When members of the mainstream Liberal Party, now led by Herbert Samuel, withdrew their support from the government over the introduction of tariffs in 1932, going into formal opposition in November 1933, the breach in the historic Liberal Party became permanent. Critics have argued that Simon and his band of supporters now became prisoners of a government dominated by the Conservative Party, and that Liberal Nationals and Conservatives rapidly became indistinguishable. More charitably it may be suggested that the Liberal National grouping enabled Simon to sustain his political philosophy while accepting the electoral reality that the Liberal Party itself was no longer a serious aspirant for power.

Simon entered office in an atmosphere of considerable goodwill. When he moved to the Home Office in June 1935 his period as foreign secretary was almost universally condemned, even by his governmental colleagues, as a disaster. One wit judged him the worst foreign minister since Ethelred the Unready. But these were years in which it would have been difficult for any incumbent to have made a success of the Foreign Office. It was Simon's misfortune that his tenure witnessed the first major challenge to the authority of the League of Nations with the Japanese attack on Manchuria, the rise of Hitler to power in Germany, the collapse of the World Disarmament Conference of 1932–4, and the first stirrings of Italian aggression in Africa. All this was at a time when Britain's defence capability was at its lowest level in the whole inter-war period.

With hindsight the Manchurian episode took on a symbolic importance as a decisive first step in the process of appeasement which culminated at Munich seven years later. But this was not how it was seen at the time. None the less, the speech which Simon made to the league assembly on 7 December 1932, in which he declined to deliver an unqualified denunciation of Japan's conduct, was to haunt him for the rest of his days. He was always sceptical about the prospects for disarmament, but did put forward one of the conference's more constructive proposals, that for qualitative rather than quantitative disarmament. He showed no particular insight into the unique threat posed by Hitler, but the external menace inherent in the Nazi regime only became fully apparent after Simon had left the Foreign Office. That said, his ministry was characterized by indecision and hesitation. His complex mind could always see too many dimensions in any given problem to render decisions and action easy. Throughout his life he was always more confident in analysing situations than in drawing conclusions from his analysis.

Home secretary and chancellor of the exchequer Simon's temperament was more suited to the Home Office, where he served between 7 June 1935 and 28 May 1937. There his legal skills enabled him to play an important behind-the-scenes role in handling the constitutional aspects of the abdication crisis of 1936. Within the ranks of the National Government his standing recovered considerably with the result that, when Neville Chamberlain became prime minister, Simon was promoted to be chancellor of the exchequer in Chamberlain's place. As chancellor he continued the management of the economy along the orthodox lines already laid down by his predecessor. Believing that a strong economy would represent the nation's 'fourth arm of defence' in any future war, he was careful to limit expenditure on rearmament. This policy now seems less culpable than it once did, but it meant that Simon would inevitably occupy a high place among those 'guilty men' who were held to have brought Britain to the brink of military disaster in May and June 1940. To his credit he led a group of cabinet ministers on the evening of 2 September 1939 in insisting to Chamberlain that there could be no further delay in Britain's declaration of war following the German invasion of Poland.

Lord chancellor As a close colleague of Chamberlain and a leading advocate of the policy of appeasement, it was not surprising that Simon was excluded from the higher direction of the war effort when Churchill formed his government in May 1940. But his talents were too great to be dispensed with altogether. He now served with distinction for five years as lord chancellor, elevated to the woolsack (13 May 1940) as Viscount Simon of Stackpole Elidor, the small Pembrokeshire village from which his father's family hailed. In this position he was responsible for interrogating Hitler's deputy, Rudolf Hess, after the latter's bizarre flight to England in May 1941. In his judicial capacity Simon was outstanding. Some of his judgments relating, *inter alia*, to the principles upon which damages as regards expectation of life should be calculated in cases of death by negligence and the principles upon which a jury should be directed in a murder case where there is a possible alternative defence of manslaughter, became landmarks in English law. Despite his own preferences it is difficult to escape the conclusion that the lord chancellorship was his rightful destiny, and that he was more successful as a lawyer than as a politician.

Assessment of career Simon's ministerial career came to an end in July 1945 after the defeat of the Conservative Party in the general election. He remained, however, active in politics and the law in the House of Lords and the judicial committee of the privy council, and entertained hopes of being reappointed lord chancellor when Churchill formed his peacetime government in October 1951. The position went, however, to Lord Simonds. By this time Simon was seventy-eight years old, but still mentally and physically vigorous. He now regarded himself as for all practical purposes a Conservative, although Churchill firmly resisted his attempts formally to join the party. In his final years Simon completed a disappointingly uninformative volume of memoirs, *Retrospect* (1952). Of more lasting value was *Simon's Income Tax*, whose publication he supervised in 1948 and which became a standard text. But his most revealing piece was probably the short memoir of his mother, to whom he was devoted, which he had published in 1936, *Portrait of my Mother*, in which Simon revealed flashes of a softer, warmer personality than he usually displayed in public.

Simon's array of high offices in a career at or near the top of British public life of more than thirty years marks him out as a figure of distinction. He was appointed KCVO in 1911 (for his defence of George V in the libel case), GCSI

in 1930, and GCVO in 1937. In 1948 he succeeded Lord Sankey in the honorific post of high steward of the University of Oxford. His great intellect was matched by a distinguished appearance. Tall, slim, athletically built, with graceful limbs and sensitive hands, he had, judged one contemporary, 'the most remarkable head in London' (Leslie Hore-Belisha in the *Evening Standard*, 27 Nov 1924). A fine portrait by Sir Gerald Kelly of Simon in the robes of the chancellor of the exchequer hangs at the National Liberal Club in Whitehall Place. Yet it remains difficult to assess his career, at least as a politician, without a strong feeling of failure and disappointment. His career peaked in the 1930s, a decade which damaged, often beyond repair, the historical reputation of many British ministers. But the failure surrounding Simon reflects also his inability to secure the affection or even respect of most of his contemporaries. Many indeed made a point of recording their dislike of him. 'I am always trying to like him', stressed Neville Chamberlain, 'and believing I shall succeed when something crops up to put me off' (Chamberlain to Lord Irwin, 12 Aug 1928, Irwin MSS, MS Eur. C/152/18). Throughout his career he had difficulty in convincing others of his sincerity, the consequence perhaps of the facility with which the lawyer–politician became the advocate of the cause which it fell to him to champion at any given moment. For this reason he was always a more effective speaker in the courts of law than in parliament.

Simon knew that his manner tended to alienate others, but seemed incapable of doing anything about it. His outstanding intellect was in one sense his most notable attribute. But it could also be a considerable handicap, since he found it difficult to strike up an easy relationship with those possessed of more commonplace minds. Some sign of human frailty might have made him a more congenial colleague. As it was, Simon remained, as Asquith styled him, 'the Impeccable'. His ability to see all sides of a complicated question easily degenerated into an irritating inability to make up his mind. As the cartoonist David Low explained: 'I sometimes draw him with a sinuous writhing body because that conveys more or less his disposition to subtle compromise' (D. Low, *Ye Madde Designer*, 1935, 55). Yet Simon's unctuous attempts to ingratiate himself probably reflected the efforts of a lonely and insecure man to compensate for his innate shyness.

Simon suffered a stroke during the Christmas recess of 1953, and died in the Westminster Hospital, London, on 11 January 1954. Despite his upbringing as a son of the manse he lacked religious faith and, following his own instructions, was cremated in his Oxford robes without religious ceremony. His second wife survived him.

D. J. DUTTON

Sources D. Dutton, *Simon: a political biography of Sir John Simon* (1992) · Bodl. Oxf., MSS Simon · R. F. V. Heuston, *Lives of the lord chancellors, 1940–1970* (1987) · C. E. B. Roberts, *Sir John Simon* (1938) · E. B. Segal, 'Sir John Simon and British foreign policy: the diplomacy of disarmament in the early 1930s', PhD diss., U. Cal., Berkeley, 1969 · [J. Allsebrook, first Viscount Simon], *Retrospect: the memoirs of the Rt. Hon. Viscount Simon* (1952) · R. Bassett, *Democracy and foreign policy* (1968) · *The Times* (12 Jan 1954) · N. Rostow, *Anglo-French* *relations, 1934–36* (1984) · D. J. Dutton, 'John Simon and the post-war national liberal party: an historical postscript', *HJ*, 32 (1989), 357–67 · R. Jenkins, 'Sir John Simon', *The chancellors* (1998), 365–92 · G. D. Goodlad, 'The liberal nationals, 1931–1940: the problems of a party in "partnership government"', *HJ*, 38 (1995), 133–43 · private information (2004) · corresp. with Lord Halifax, BL OIOC, MS Eur. C 152/18

Archives BL OIOC, corresp., evidence, and papers as chairman of Indian statutory commission, MS Eur. F 77 · Bodl. Oxf., corresp., diaries, and papers · NRA, priv. coll., MSS including scrapbooks, visitors' books, photographs · PRO, foreign office corresp, FO 800/285–291 | All Souls Oxf., letters to Sir William Anson · BL, corresp. with Lord Cecil, Add. MS 51082 · BL, letters to Lord Gladstone, Add. MSS 46062–46085 · BL OIOC, corresp. with Lord Halifax, MS Eur. C 152 · BL OIOC, Reading MSS · Bodl. Oxf., corresp. with Asquith · Bodl. Oxf., letters to A. L. Goodhart · Bodl. Oxf., corresp. with Lord Monckton · Bodl. Oxf., corresp. with Gilbert Murray · Bodl. RH, corresp. with Lord Lugard · Borth. Inst., corresp. with Lord Halifax · CAC Cam., corresp. with Sir Eric Phipps · CUL, corresp. with Sir Samuel Hoare · HLRO, corresp. with Bonar Law · HLRO, letters to David Lloyd George · HLRO, corresp. with H. Samuel · JRL, letters to the *Manchester Guardian* · Lpool RO, corresp. with seventeenth earl of Derby · NA Scot., corresp. with Lord Lothian · Nuffield Oxf., corresp. with Lord Cherwell · PRO NIre., corresp. with Edward Carson · U. Birm., Avon MSS · U. Birm., Neville Chamberlain MSS · U. Newcastle, Robinson L., corresp. with Walter Runciman | FILM BFI NFTVA, documentary footage · BFI NFTVA, recorded talk [Britain under National Government] · BFI NFTVA, news footage · BFI NFTVA, propaganda film footage | SOUND BFI NFTVA, news footage

Likenesses F. Dicksee, line print, 1922, NPG · G. Kelly, oils, c.1924, Wadham College, Oxford · Bassano, photograph, 1931, NPG [*see illus.*] · M. Beerbohm, caricature drawing, 1932, All Souls Oxf. · O. Birley, oils, 1933, lord chancellor's office, London · O. Birley, oils, 1933, Inner Temple, London · D. Low, pencil drawing, before 1933, NPG · H. Coster, photograph, c.1935, NPG · W. Stoneman, photograph, 1937, NPG · G. Kelly, oils, 1938, National Liberal Club, London · F. O. Salisbury, portrait, c.1945–1946, judicial committee of the privy council, Downing Street, London · C. Beaton, photograph, NPG · E. I. Halliday, pencil drawing, priv. coll. · K. Kennet, bust, All Souls Oxf. · K. Kennet, bust, Fettes College, Edinburgh · P. A. de Laszlo, portrait, All Souls Oxf. · WH [W. Hester], caricature, NPG; repro. in *VF* (18 Oct 1911)

Wealth at death £93,006 12s. 0d.: probate, 12 Feb 1954, *CGPLA Eng. & Wales*

Simon, John Peter (1764?–c.1810). *See under* Boydell, John, engravers (*act.* 1760–1804).

Simon [*née* Harvey], **Dame Kathleen Rochard**, Viscountess Simon (1863/4–1955), slavery abolitionist, was born in Kyle, co. Wexford, Ireland, the elder of the two daughters of Francis Eugene Harvey of Kyle and his wife, Frances Elizabeth, daughter of John Pollock. In later years she ascribed her love of liberty and hatred of servitude to her parents' influence. She was educated privately and at various schools in Dublin. She trained as a nurse and worked in some of the poorest districts of London where she learned the conditions under which women had to bear and try to rear their babies. On 21 February 1885 she married Dr Thomas Manning MD of co. Kerry, and she then accompanied him to Tennessee. It was there that she first encountered white racism when she saw a young girl excluded from a gathering because of her colour. 'My name is Kathleen, what is yours?' she asked as she held out her hand (Harris). That girl was the 'Amanda of Tennessee' to whom, together with 'all those who have suffered and still suffer in slavery', Kathleen Simon later dedicated her book on twentieth-century slavery. It was the revelation of continuing racial discrimination in the United States, in the aftermath of slavery, that led her to join the Anti-Slavery Society on her return to Britain.

After her husband's death Kathleen Manning moved to England, where on 18 December 1917 she married, as his second wife, the widower Sir John Allsebrook *Simon, later first Viscount Simon (1873–1954). She had been a governess to his children after the death of his wife and had renewed acquaintance with him in 1917 when she sought his assistance when her son by her first marriage, serving in the Irish Guards, became a prisoner of war. During the period of the Black and Tans in Ireland, Kathleen Simon worked on behalf of the nationalist Irish and urged her husband to speak against the actions of the Black and Tans. Then, throughout the 1920s, she researched for her important work on the survival of chattel slavery throughout the world, including the British empire and British protectorates. Her resulting study was greeted as a 'startling indictment of modern civilisation' (*Sunday Times*, 1929) and it was acknowledged that: 'This country cannot wash its hands of responsibility' (*Daily News*, 1929).

Kathleen Simon revealed that slavery was still socially accepted in Abyssinia, Sudan, Arabia, the British protectorate of Sierra Leone, Liberia, China, Hong Kong, Burma, and Nepal. But she also looked at less blatant forms of servitude including peonage, indentured labour, and debt bondage in South America and Asia, and she even confronted—and excoriated—the current British colonial policy of exacting forced labour by Africans in east Africa. She estimated that the number of slaves, worldwide, might exceed 6 million, and that there was one feature common to all shades of slavery: 'the individual ceases to possess the rights of a human being and becomes a property' (K. Simon, *Slavery*, 1929, 2). She did not blench from spelling out that slavery all too often involved flogging, sexual abuse, and even torture and killing of the victims, many of them children.

Kathleen Simon's uncovering of the slave-owning wealth of the rulers of Abyssinia embarrassed the supporters of Haile Selassie against the aggression of Italy. Her championing of the domestic girl slaves, officially—and very euphemistically—called *mui tsai* or 'adopted daughters', in Hong Kong, Malaya, and Ceylon, was part of a campaign over several decades for their emancipation by Lieutenant-Commander and Mrs Haslewood, Edith Picton-Turbervill MP, and Eleanor Rathbone MP, together with Chinese and Ceylonese activists on the ground. She attacked forced labour in British Africa as incompatible with the principles of trusteeship under the League of Nations, and was supported in this by the International Labour Organization's body of experts, including Lord Lugard and Sir Selwyn Fremantle who reported that 'the only way to prevent forced labour from developing into "conditions analogous to slavery" *was to abolish it altogether*' (K. Simon, *Slavery* 1929, 190).

Kathleen Simon did not only use her pen in monographs, articles (for example, in the *Empire Review*, 1930), and book reviews for the *Anti-Slavery Reporter and Aborigines' Friend*, she also travelled the country indefatigably, speaking at innumerable meetings to rouse public opinion and raise funds for emancipatory campaigning, in tandem with John Hobbis Harris and his wife, Alice. For example, in October and November 1933 she spoke in Sale, Letchworth, Hull, Oxford, and London. In February 1934 she spoke in Fulham; and in November she spoke in Belgravia; at Wisbech, the birthplace of Thomas Clarkson; and in Sutton. That year alone she addressed about 10,000 people.

Once the racist persecution of Jews under German Nazism was under way, Lady Simon, created DBE in 1933, took up the Jewish cause and was sympathetic to Zionism. She also raised a great deal of money for the work of the Anti-Slavery Society of which she was joint president and to which she gave her library of books on slavery. In April 1940 she organized an African Conference at 11 Downing Street on native races and peace terms, emphasizing the obligation to train for self-government and oppose racial discrimination and the colour bar. Crippled by painful osteoarthritis and having to walk with a stick, she was unquenchable and inspirational to the end. 'For Lady Simon slavery was a flaming injustice. She could not live in peace in the same world with a single man who claimed another as his property' (*Annual Report of the Anti-Slavery Society*, 31 March 1955). 'It is hardly an exaggeration to say that she filled the place in Britain that Harriet Beecher Stowe had earlier filled in the United States' (*The Times*, 21 April 1955). Small, cheerful, and outgoing, Lady Simon died at her home, 10 Linnell Drive, Golders Green, Middlesex, on 27 March 1955 and was cremated at Golders Green. Her age was variously given as eighty-two or eighty-three; in fact she was ninety-one.   SYBIL OLDFIELD

Sources *Anti-Slavery Reporter and Aborigines' Friend* (1930–55) • *The Times* (21 April 1955) • *Annual Report of the Anti-Slavery Society* (31 March 1955) • A. Harris, Tribute in, *Anti-Slavery Reporter* (May 1955) • *Manchester Guardian* (28 March 1955) • S. Miers, 'Britain and the suppression of slavery in Ethiopia', *Slavery and Abolition: Journal of Slave and Post-Slave Studies*, 18/3 (Dec 1997) • Burke, *Gen. Ire.* (1958) [Harvey, formerly of Bargy Castle] • D. Dutton, *Simon: a political biography of Sir John Simon* (1992) • *CGPLA Eng. & Wales* (1955) • *WWW*, 1951–60 • d. cert.
Archives Anti-Slavery International, London, speeches, reviews, and reports for the Anti-Slavery Society • Bodl. Oxf., corresp. • Bodl. RH, corresp., notebooks and papers relating to Anti-Slavery Society | PRO, corresp. with colonial secretary, CO 967131
Likenesses photograph, c.1935, Anti-Slavery International, London • Stobl, marble bust, Anti-Slavery International, London
Wealth at death £3751 16s. od.: probate, 3 May 1955, *CGPLA Eng. & Wales*

Simon, Oliver Joseph (1895–1956), printer, was born on 29 April 1895 at Sale, Cheshire, the eldest son of Louis Simon (1861–1937), cotton merchant, and his wife, Louisa (1870–1918), sister of Sir William *Rothenstein and Albert *Rutherston. He was educated at Charterhouse and at a boarding-school in Jena, Germany. In the First World War he served in Gallipoli, Egypt, and Palestine, places which made a profound impression on him. Later he revisited Palestine and his intense interest in the country led to the founding of the Paladin Club. The membership included Sir Ronald Storrs, Chaim Weizmann, Lord Samuel, Malcolm MacDonald, and Norman Bentwich.

With no certain idea of what his future should be, Simon went to London in 1919. Seeing a bookseller's window display of finely printed books, he realized immediately that his life's work must be with printing. Albert Rutherston, an artist and illustrator, helped him with introductions and, after a short time as a pupil with Charles T. Jacobi at the Chiswick Press, he met, through Joseph Thorp, Harold Curwen, who agreed to take him for a year's training at the Curwen Press at Plaistow, east London. In July 1921 he persuaded Curwen to let him stay on and examine the prospects of adding book printing to the Curwen activities, with the result that he remained with the press for the rest of his life; in 1949 he became its chairman. (In 1933 he was joined at the press by his brother Herbert, whose *Song and Words: a History of the Curwen Press* was published in 1973.)

In 1923 Simon published the first volume of *The Fleuron*, a journal of typography of which seven substantial and finely produced numbers were published. The first four issues were edited by Simon and printed at Curwen; the last three were edited by Stanley Morison and printed at Cambridge University Press. It was characteristic that the first number contained no introduction with elaborate statement of aims and objects, and no promises for the future.

Simon and Hubert Foss, helped by two or three others, founded in 1924 the Double Crown Club, a dining club for typographers, designers, artists, authors, and publishers. Its influence on the design and production of British books cannot be exactly measured, but it has certainly been highly influential in fostering and encouraging a sound contemporary style of printing in all its forms.

He married on 27 February 1926 (Winifred) Ruth (1905–1967), daughter of Christopher Henry Ware, of Herefordshire; they had one daughter and one son.

In November 1935 Simon brought out the first number of a periodical, *Signature*, which was to appear two or three times a year until 1954 with the exception of the war years, 1941–5. It contained articles on the arts of design, illustration, printing, and calligraphy, and provided a fitting monument to his own ideals of beautiful production. In 1945 he published *Introduction to Typography* which was quickly accepted as a standard work.

Although Simon was recognized internationally as a typographical authority with an intimate knowledge of the importance and influence of English fine printing, his aim was to do first-rate contemporary and commercial work. Under his guidance and that of Harold Curwen, the Curwen Press played a major part in the improvement of printing in all its aspects after 1918, not least in the illustration of books. His uncle William Rothenstein, principal of the Royal College of Art, encouraged his staff and students to use their talents in the direction of illustration and book design at Curwen, among them Eric Ravilious, Paul Nash, Barnett Freedman, Edward Ardizzone, Edward

Bawden, Reynolds Stone, Rex Whistler, John Piper, and Graham Sutherland.

Printer and Playground (1956), Simon's autobiography, is the story of an idealist, a man dedicated to his calling, a typographical craftsman of uncompromising standards, but no pedant. He appears sociable but not gregarious, ever modest of his own accomplishments, affectionate, humorous, with an invincible courage and unflinching tenacity of purpose.

Simon was appointed OBE in 1953 and died in London, where his address was 40 Downshire Hill, Hampstead, on 18 March 1956. His son, in turn, became a director of the Curwen Press.   G. W. HOWARD, rev. JOHN TREVITT

Sources O. Simon, *Printer and playground: an autobiography* (1956) · H. Simon, *Song and words: a history of the Curwen Press* (1973) · private information (2004) · *The Times* (20 March 1956) · personal knowledge (1971) · private information (1971)
Likenesses B. Robb, oils, c.1950, Curwen Press, Chilford Hall, Linton, Cambridge · B. Robb, drawing, repro. in Simon, *Printer and playground*, frontispiece · photograph, repro. in Simon, *Song and words*
Wealth at death £20,818 15s. 8d.: probate, 4 July 1956, *CGPLA Eng. & Wales*

Simon [*née* Potter], **Shena Dorothy**, Lady Simon of Wythenshawe (1883–1972), politician and educational reformer, was born in Croydon, Surrey, on 21 October 1883, the second of nine children of John Wilson Potter (1856–1933), a shipowner of Scottish descent, and his wife, Janet Boyd, *née* Thompson (d. 1946). Educated at home, she passed the higher local education examination and went on to read economics at Newnham College, Cambridge, from 1904 to 1907. She narrowly missed a first in the new economics tripos and in 1907 began postgraduate study at the London School of Economics, where she developed a close friendship with Beatrice Webb, and came into close contact with the new Liberal theorists Graham Wallas and Leonard Hobhouse. She failed to complete her thesis, which focused on the emergence of the Labour Party, largely because she undertook the role of honorary secretary to the legislative committee of the National Union of Women Workers. This prompted an interest in wage boards, which she investigated in Australia and New Zealand. This in turn led to her involvement in a special committee formed to ensure that the rights of married women were safeguarded in Lloyd George's 1911 National Insurance Bill.

Shena Potter was also closely involved in the female suffrage campaign. Despite opposition from her family she spoke at suffrage meetings and joined marches. She admired the militant leaders and recognized the value of militant tactics for the vote to be gained, but she herself refused to participate in any militant actions. Her Newnham contemporary Eva Hubback introduced her to the Mancunian social reformer Ernest Emil Darwin *Simon (1879–1960), who 'wanted a wife who could play Beatrice to his Sidney Webb' (Harrison, 285). They married on 22 November 1912 in a register office, since both were agnostics, and formed a happy and effective partnership, moving in progressive intellectual circles between the wars. Settling in Manchester, they started a family: a first son

was born in 1913, a second son in 1915, and a third and last child, a girl, was born in 1917, but died aged twelve after a long illness.

After her marriage Shena Simon became increasingly involved in Liberal politics in Manchester, and was elected in 1924 as a Liberal city councillor representing Chorlton ward. She quickly established a reputation as a leading radical on the city council, pursuing educational reform. She became chairman of the education committee in 1932, the first woman to hold that office. She was also closely involved with the development of the Wythenshawe estate, developed after Ernest bought Wythenshawe Park and Wythenshawe Hall and presented it to the city of Manchester to allow the development of a model satellite town for the relief of Manchester's overcrowded centre. Shena Simon sat on the city council's Wythenshawe estate special committee from 1928, becoming its chairman in 1931. In 1933 she was defeated in Chorlton as a result of a Conservative backlash. In 1935, after a period out of party politics, she joined the Labour Party a decade before her husband. Although she failed to be elected when she contested the Moston ward in 1936, she returned to the education committee as a co-opted member and continued to hold this position until she retired in 1970.

Shena Simon's work was not confined to Manchester city council. Between 1929 and 1931 she served on the royal commission on licensing and in 1931 she was appointed to the consultative committee of the Board of Education, contributing especially to its work on secondary education. She served on the University of Manchester council from 1921 until 1966. In 1938 she served on a departmental committee on rating and valuation, her appointment reflecting her reputation as a notable authority on a highly technical subject. In 1942 she was involved in forming the Council for Educational Advance. In the years following the Second World War she was a strong advocate of comprehensive education in Manchester. Her *Three Schools in One* (1948) was an influential contribution to the debate on the tripartite system of secondary education in England. Her other publications addressed topics of local government finance and administration.

Shena Simon also continued to pursue feminist issues. In 1922, as lady mayoress, she refused to attend a function at a hospital with no women on the medical staff or the board of management. This action forced a change in policy. Her membership of the city council enabled her to champion feminist causes, the most notable being a campaign against the marriage bar on women teachers in Manchester, which was lifted in 1928 as a result of her efforts. Like others who had campaigned for women's suffrage, she became involved in the inter-war movements for equal citizenship, and was a founder of the Manchester and Salford Women Citizens Association. With her husband she also helped to found in 1934 the Association for Education in Citizenship to promote the study of democratic politics in schools and universities. Her civic consciousness underlay her reforms in the field of public housing, and her advocacy for raising the school-leaving age and for the introduction of comprehensive schools.

Shena became Lady Simon in 1932 when her husband was knighted. In 1947 her husband was raised to the peerage as the first Baron Simon of Wythenshawe. After his death in 1960 she considered moving to London, but resolved to stay in Manchester. She wanted to continue to serve the university and the education committee. A number of personal honours followed in later life: in 1964 she was made a freeman of the city of Manchester; in 1965 she became an honorary fellow of the London School of Economics; in 1966 she was awarded an honorary degree by the University of Manchester. In her later years she allowed more time for the leisure pursuits that she had enjoyed throughout her life, especially detective novels, cinema, and the music of Gracie Fields. She continued to lead a full and active life until her death, in Manchester, owing to failing health through old age, on 17 July 1972. Her contribution to education in Manchester was recognized in 1982 with the opening of Shena Simon College.

BRENDON JONES

Sources *The Guardian* (18 July 1972) · Man. CL, Manchester Archives and Local Studies, S. D. Simon MSS · M. Tylecote, *The work of Lady Simon of Wythenshawe for education in Manchester* (1974) · J. Simon, *Shena Simon: feminist and educationalist* (privately printed, 1986) · O. Banks, *The biographical dictionary of British feminists*, 2 (1990) · M. Stocks, *Ernest Simon of Manchester* (1963) · Man. CL, Manchester Archives and Local Studies, E. D. Simon MSS · B. Harrison, *Prudent revolutionaries: portraits of British feminists between the wars* (1987)
Archives BLPES, corresp. and papers relating to population of England · Man. CL, Manchester Archives and Local Studies, corresp. and papers · Women's Library, London, corresp. and papers including unpublished biography | Man. CL, Manchester Archives and Local Studies, letters to Sir Maurice Pariser and Lady Pariser · Man. CL, Manchester Archives and Local Studies, E. D. Simon MSS · U. Sussex, corresp. with Leonard Woolf · U. Sussex, corresp. with Virginia Woolf
Likenesses pencil drawing, Newnham College, Cambridge
Wealth at death £305,710: probate, 20 Sept 1972, *CGPLA Eng. & Wales*

Simon, Thomas (*bap.* 1618, *d.* 1665), medallist and seal-engraver, was baptized on 26 April 1618 at the French protestant church in Threadneedle Street, London. He was the fourth son of Peter (or Pierre) Simon, a merchant, a native of London but of French descent, and his wife, Anne (*b.* c.1588), the daughter and heir of Gilles Germain, a merchant of St Peter Port, Guernsey, and the brother of the wax modeller and engraver Abraham *Simon (*bap.* 1617, *d.* c.1692). His other siblings were Peter (*b.* c.1612x14), Hannah, William (*bap.* 1616), Samuel (*bap.* 1619), Nathaniel, and Laurence. On 30 August 1633 Thomas was apprenticed for eight years to a London goldsmith, George Crompton. However, in 1635, probably through the commendation of Sir Edward Harley, he began a seven-year apprenticeship to Edward Greene, also a goldsmith, and chief engraver at the mint. Greene was himself subject to the direction of Nicholas Briot, whose artistry undoubtedly influenced Simon. Simon's first attributed work was the Scottish rebellion medal of 1639 commemorating the treaty of Berwick.

The apprenticeship ended during the civil war, when Simon's French protestantism ensured his loyalty to parliament. Although he was not yet a member of the mint establishment he continued to work there, making, on the order of parliament, a new great seal, for £100 (which had been taken to the king at York in 1642). After the death of Edward Greene in 1644, Thomas Simon and Edward Wade were appointed joint chief engravers on 4 April 1645. The quality of the coinage during the latter half of the 1640s is not impressive: it is assumed that Wade did this work and Simon the medals. On 15 February 1649 Simon married Elizabeth, the daughter of Cardin Fautrart. They were married at All Saints', Maidstone, Kent, though his wife's family originated from Guernsey. They had three sons and two daughters, of whom Samuel (*b.* 1 April 1653), Elizabeth, and Ann survived into adulthood.

Simon became a freeman of the Goldsmiths' Company on 12 June 1646: his first apprentice was his brother Laurence. From that time he produced portrait medals of eminent contemporaries, often working in collaboration with his brother Abraham, who produced many of the wax models from which they were cast. Examples include *Sir James Harrington* (1653), *John Thurloe* (1653; British Museum), and *Edward Hyde, First Earl of Clarendon* (1662).

Wade died in 1648 and, in the appointments that followed the execution of Charles I, Simon was appointed chief engraver. He engraved a great seal bearing the arms of the Commonwealth, but the haste in which it was required is evident in the artistry. His second great seal of the Commonwealth produced in 1651 was of much greater complexity and of magnificent craftsmanship. In 1650 the committee of the army sent Simon to Edinburgh to sketch Oliver Cromwell for the medal to commemorate the battle of Dunbar. The lord-general in his reply declared that his own portrait should not appear: gratitude to the army might better be expressed by having 'Parliament on one side, and on the other an Army.' In the same letter Cromwell asked the committee to confer upon Simon 'the imployment in your service which Nicholas Briott had before him, indeed the man is ingenious and worthie of encouragement' (Farquhar, 'Thomas Simon', 274). On 27 November 1656 Simon was ordered by the council at Whitehall to produce portrait coinage of Oliver Cromwell, for 5s. in silver and 20s. in gold—the obverse showing the protector in profile and of bust length, and the reverse showing the heraldic arms of the Cromwell family. These were struck on the newly designed mill and screw press of Pierre Blondeau.

Simon made many seals for the public service, including, in 1655–6, the great seals for Scotland and for Ireland, and seals for the English, Scottish, and Irish councils, the English law courts, and the admiralty. On 14 January 1657 he laid before the council his account for making medals, badges, silver boxes for treaties, and presses for seals amounting to £1728 5s. 8d. In the following year he was still asking that the debt be honoured. 'I beg you', he writes, 'to consider that I and my servants have wrought five years without recompense, and that the interest I have to pay for gold and silver eats up my profit.' In 1658 he was employed to model the face of the effigy of Cromwell, carried in the protector's funeral procession on 23 November 1658.

At the Restoration Simon petitioned Charles II 'for the employment as Chief Engraver to His Majesty and the Mint … and for Pardon because by order of Parliament he made their Seal in 1643.' He was refused, as the title was restored to Thomas Rawlins, who had held it under Charles I. None the less, it was Simon who was instructed to prepare the patterns for the new coinage of 1660. On 31 May 1661 he obtained the grant of the office of one of the gravers of the king's arms, shields, and stamps; and on 2 June 1661 he was made by patent one of the king's chief gravers of the mint and seals, with the salary of £50. At this time he prepared the great privy seal, the great seal of Ireland, the great seal of Jamaica, and seals for the Order of the Garter, the lord high admiral, the council of Wales, and the Royal Society. In 1661 he visited Paris on official business of the mint.

In January 1662 Simon and John Roettiers were ordered to engrave dies for the new 'milled' coinage. However, they could not agree 'by reason of a contest in art between them' (Farquhar, 'Thomas Simon', 297), and so on 7 February they were each instructed to submit to the king a trial piece for a silver crown. Charles decided in favour of Roettiers. The following year Simon engraved the Petition Crown, so called because of its two-line edge inscription: 'Thomas Simon most humbly prays your Majesty to compare that his tryll piece with the Dutch and if more truly drawn and embossed more gracefully ordered and more accurately engraven to relieve him' (ibid., 298). This was a magnificent example of Simon's abilities, but his petition went unheeded. A specimen is in the Ashmolean Museum, Oxford.

Nevertheless, the king continued during 1662 to employ Simon as 'one of Our Cheife Gravers'. He was granted warrants to make the great seal of Charles II and the seal of the court of exchequer; on 25 August the king's silver and gold coinage; on 18 September an angel golde showing St George slaying the dragon and, on the reverse, a man-of-war; and the Scottish coinage, of which only two silver coins were completed. His last known work is the dominion of the seas medal commemorating the English naval victory over the Dutch in June 1665. He died, possibly of the plague, that same year and was buried on 26 July at the parish church of All Saints, Maidstone, Kent. His body was probably later reinterred at St Clement Danes, in accordance with his will, proved on 23 August 1665. He left his son, Samuel, a farm at Shorne, Kent, together with paintings, drawings, and medals. To his nephew William, the son of his brother Nathaniel (deceased), he left his punches and graving tools. Simon's widow petitioned the king about 1669 for the sum of £2164, claimed by her as arrears of payment due to her husband.

Simon's outstanding achievement was to bring together exquisite artistry and technology at the mint:

this received national recognition in 1753, when the publisher Vertue was instructed by act of parliament to produce a major account of his work. Simon's sketchbooks containing figure, portrait, and animal studies, and the designs for his seals and coinage, which passed into the possession of his daughter Mrs Hibberd, were sold at Christies, London, on 14 July 1987.

W. W. Wroth, *rev.* Matthew Craske and Lesley Craske

Sources G. Vertue, *Medals, coins, great seals, and other works of Thomas Simon* (1780) · H. E. Pagan, 'Presidential address, 1988', *British Numismatic Journal*, 58 (1988), 179–89 · H. Farquhar, 'Thomas Simon, "one of our chief gravers"', *Numismatic Chronicle*, 12 (1932), 274–310 · H. Farquhar, 'New light on Thomas Simon', *Numismatic Chronicle*, 14 (1936), 210–34 · D. Allen, 'Thomas Simon's sketchbook', *Walpole Society*, 27 (1938–9), 13–54 · *N&Q*, 2nd ser., 12 (1861), 2, 357, 403, 510 · E. Hawkins, H. Grueber, and A. W. Franks, *Medallic illustrations of the history of Great Britain and Ireland* (1885) · H. W. Henfrey, *Numismata Cromwelliana* (1877) · *CSP dom.*, 1649–65 · will, CKS, PRC 32/53/301

Archives BL, account books, Add. MSS 45190, 59792 · BL, royal warrant for him to engrave the great seal of England, with his drawing thereof, Add. MS 71450

Likenesses G. Vertue, line engraving, BM, NPG; repro. in G. Vertue, *Medals, coins … from the elaborate works of Thomas Simon* (1753)

Wealth at death see will, CKS, PRC 32/53/301

Simon, Ulrich Ernst (1913–1997), theologian, was born in Berlin on 21 September 1913, the younger son of James Martin Simon (1880–c.1944), concert pianist and composer, and his wife, Anna, *née* Levi (1885–1969), a freelance broadcaster on literary matters. This cultured environment was to bear fruit in the breadth of his learning and culture. He met among others Thomas Mann and Dietrich Bonhoeffer, being a near contemporary of the latter at Grunewald Gymnasium, which he attended from about 1923 to 1931. (The school was later renamed the Walther Rathenau Schule, and Simon retained vivid memories both of the man and of the assassination which took place nearby in 1922.) After escaping from Germany in 1933—his father was later to perish in Auschwitz, his brother, Jörn Martin (1910–1937?), almost certainly under Stalin—he moved to London and, after a brief employment in a small firm in the City, trained for the Anglican priesthood, first at King's College, London (1935–8), and then at Lincoln Theological College (1938), having been baptized in July 1934. He was ordained deacon in 1938 and priest in 1939. In 1949 he married Joan Edith Raynor Westlake (*b.* 1920), daughter of Canon Herbert Francis Westlake (1879–1925), custodian and historian of Westminster Abbey. His wife was herself a teacher of classics and divinity. They had three children: Sophia Anne (*b.* 1950), Martin Francis Andrew (*b.* 1952), and Peter Paul (*b.* 1954).

After serving in two curacies—St Helier, Southwark (1938–42), and Upton with Chalvey, Slough (1942–5)—Simon returned to King's College in 1945 and devoted to it his whole career until retirement in 1980. He taught both Old Testament and Christian theology, and, beginning as lecturer in Hebrew and Old Testament, achieved in 1959 both a DD of London University and a readership in theology. He became in 1971 professor of Christian literature, devoting his inaugural lecture to Mann's *Der Zauberberg* ('The Magic Mountain'). He was elected a fellow of King's College in 1957.

Simon's outlook matched his experience, and he commented pungently and often pessimistically on his times, being particularly caustic about sloppy thinking which ignored the signs of the times. Indeed, it was his unerring sense of evil which drove his impatience with what he saw as effete and blind liberalism—he described John Robinson's best-selling *Honest to God* (1963) as a 'mean little book'. His final years at King's were as dean of the college, in which post he succeeded Sydney Evans in 1978, adapting the office to the reduced circumstances forced on it by changes in the college's constitution. There he both revealed his priorities and strained the patience of his secretary by insisting on reading for a period—a passage from Proust for instance—before he faced the morning's correspondence.

Simon's intellectual achievement was various and reflected the range of his teaching responsibilities and the breadth of his interests. Noteworthy among his ten books was *A Theology of Auschwitz* (1967), which was unique among the vast literature generated by that evil. More than anything, it was a meditation on the suffering of Simon's own people in the light of the passion of Christ. Other books included *Theology of Crisis* (1948), *Heaven in the Christian Tradition* (1958), *A Theology of Salvation* (1961), a theological commentary on Isaiah 40–55, *The Trial of Man* (1973), and *Story and Faith* (1975). He was firmly of the opinion, if that is not too weak a word, that those who have no music in their soul should leave theology alone; indeed, what he took to be a slighting reference to Bach once induced anger. Mozart was another love, one shared with Karl Barth, the theologian who influenced him most, sustaining him during the war and giving him breathing space on a visit to Basel after it, and whose later neglect he deplored. And into all his thinking was fed his reading of literature—Dante, Shakespeare, and Dostoyevsky perhaps most prominent, but also Goethe, Mann, Milton, and Kierkegaard.

In 1978 Simon published the characteristically titled *Sitting in Judgement, 1913–63: an Interpretation of History*. A kind of autobiography, as the first date in the title implied, it was, like many of Simon's writings, idiosyncratic and unusual, far exceeding the expectations aroused by the genre. It both told the story of his first fifty years—ending in time, though not in the organization of the narrative, with the assassination of Kennedy, which shocked him deeply—and was the vehicle for characteristic judgements on his times. One chapter, 'This precious isle', took over from the allusion to Shakespeare's words both love for his adopted land and church and sharp observations on those whose apostasy threatened the nation's integrity and liberty. The chapters on the Second World War provided a unique perspective on British society and its leaders, cameos of figures as different as Bishop George Kennedy Allen Bell of Chichester and Victor Gollancz helping to illuminate the atmosphere of the times. One review described the book as 'dazzling in its virtuosity, devastating in its accusation, yet offering hope and not despair' (*Expository Times*, 1978, 288). Similarly, his public speaking was eloquent, pungent, and beautifully organized, often with the help of a few scribbled notes.

Simon's writing virtually ceased after his retirement, reflecting, it would seem, a measure of disillusionment with developments in the Church of England. His musical activities became his main interest; the day before his death (of an aneurism, at his home, 22 Collingwood Avenue, London) on 31 July 1997 he had bought a new set of strings for his violin, of which he was an accomplished player. His ashes were buried in Coton churchyard, Cambridgeshire, on 5 July 1999; he was survived by his wife.

COLIN GUNTON

Sources U. E. Simon, *Sitting in judgement, 1913–63: an interpretation of history* (1978) · private information (2004) [Mrs J. Simon] · *The Times* (5 Aug 1997) · *Daily Telegraph* (6 Aug 1997) · *The Independent* (16 Aug 1997) · *The Guardian* (7 Oct 1997) · staff records, King's Lond., archives · WWW · Crockford (1980)
Likenesses photograph, repro. in *Daily Telegraph* · photograph, repro. in *The Independent* · photograph, repro. in *The Times*
Wealth at death £120,697: probate, 12 Nov 1997, *CGPLA Eng. & Wales*

Simonds, Gavin Turnbull, Viscount Simonds (1881–1971), lord chancellor, was born at The Point, Bath Road, Reading, on 28 November 1881 and came from a family of brewers. His father, Louis de Luze Simonds (1852–1916), was born in New York after Gavin's grandfather had emigrated from England, and had married Sophie de Luze, the daughter of a French *émigré* family. Louis himself went to England and in 1880 married Mary Elizabeth (1857–1930), daughter of Gavin Ainslie Turnbull, surgeon-general. Of their five children Gavin was the second eldest.

Early years Enjoying a comfortable childhood Simonds went to Winchester College in 1894 and attended New College, Oxford (1900–04), where he gained firsts in classical moderations (1902) and *literae humaniores* (1904), and excelled in soccer and tennis. Called to the bar (Lincoln's Inn) in November 1906, he joined the chambers of James Austen-Cartmell, the Treasury devil in Chancery cases, in 1908 and remained there until taking silk in 1924.

On 28 March 1912 Simonds married Mary Hope (d. 1973), daughter of the county court judge Francis Hamilton Mellor KC (whose alleged laziness was blamed in 1914 for the build-up of arrears of cases in Manchester). They had three sons who all tragically predeceased the couple. The eldest, Robert Francis, died in infancy while the twins, Gavin Alexander and John Mellor, who were born in 1915, both died on active service. Gavin, who never married, succumbed to a rare disease contracted in east Africa in 1951 while his younger brother, John, a major in the army, and who had become a communist in 1936 after meeting D. N. Pritt, was killed at Arnhem in September 1944.

Simonds himself had been invalided out of a territorial battalion of the Royal Berkshire regiment in 1916 after falling seriously ill with diphtheria just before being posted to France. He returned to Austen-Cartmell's chambers and began to acquire a sizeable war-related practice, including prize court cases. A Chancery silk from 1924, his practice expanded greatly, especially in the appellate courts and privy council, where intellectual argument could flourish.

Outside the courts Simonds filled a number of public appointments. He was an active member and part-draftsman of the famous Donoughmore committee report on ministers' powers (1929–32) and in 1936 he was a member of the tribunal of inquiry (with Mr Justice Porter and Roland Oliver KC) investigating the leak of budget secrets, which led to the resignation of J. H. (Jimmy) Thomas from the post of secretary of state for the colonies.

On the bench In March 1937 Simonds replaced the long-serving Sir Harry Eve as Chancery judge and received the customary knighthood. His thorough knowledge of equity principles and the clarity and speed of his decisions were soon recognized. He determined not to reserve judgments in his first term. The future Lord Pearce, who as a barrister appeared before him in the Chancery Division, observed that he was 'courteous, attentive, human, quick, with no time to waste on what was *clearly* rubbish—but *never, never* domineering or overbearing, and *never* discourteous' (Heuston, 144). Another distinguished equity judge, Sir Robert Megarry, memorably recalled that, 'In some ways he [Simonds] was an equitable counterpart of Goddard, though a much more profound lawyer. For him, argument was a forthright process' (ibid., 145). Given the fierce controversy over Goddard's reputation, one wonders what Simonds would have made of even the limited comparison.

Further committee work included chairing a committee on law reporting set up by Lord Chancellor Maugham in 1939. Then in 1940 Simonds was appointed by Ernest Bevin, minister of labour, to a rather different and demanding job which occupied much of his time until 1944, that of chairing successfully the National Arbitration Tribunal, which sought to settle wartime wage disputes without resort to industrial action.

In April 1944, without having sat in the Court of Appeal, Simonds replaced Lord Romer as the Chancery law lord, with a life peerage, and embarked upon an appellate career which established him as the most significant exponent of English judicial conservatism of the twentieth century. Indeed, it has been stated that during the period from 1952 to 1972 he was one of the 'triumvirate of legal giants [the others were lords Reid and Radcliffe] whose shadow has loomed so large as to dominate the course of judicial business in the House of Lords' (Blom-Cooper and Drewry, 156). But the unexpected interlude of his time as lord chancellor in Churchill's government, between 1951 and 1954, must first be addressed.

Lord chancellor Simonds received the great seal on 30 October 1951. He had had little active involvement in politics and was mystified by his appointment. He had never met Churchill (who probably had never heard of him) and reached the woolsack (probably on Lord Woolton's advice to the prime minister) only after Cyril Asquith had turned

it down because of poor health. Maxwell Fyfe famously noted that Simonds was 'as innocent of politics as a newly baptized babe, and obviously enjoyed his immersion immensely' (Kilmuir, 194). Yet it may perhaps be more accurate to say that the administrative and political aspects of his appointment proved tiresome, frustrating, and uncongenial to his more intellectual cast of mind. He endured rather than enjoyed the non-judicial functions of his office, and regularly had to wrestle with politically sensitive issues which he probably saw as an unavoidable, and in some cases distasteful, diversion from his true mission, his judicial work.

As lord chancellor Simonds continued to consult over new judicial appointments and pressed for improved judicial salaries. When the press took an interest, the flak began to fly. 'Poor Simonds could not understand what had hit him' (Stevens, *Independence*, 129). None the less the first reform of judicial salaries for 120 years was successfully achieved during his tenure. As head of the judiciary he was prepared to discipline judges who meddled in political issues, such as Mr Justice Lloyd-Jacob who had written to *The Times* in 1954 to condemn nations which used the hydrogen bomb. Judge Gaman was forced to apologize in open court in 1952 for apparently implying in an adultery case that the 'morals of West Hartlepool seem to be lower than any other place in the country' (ibid., 91). When the Foreign Office sought a judicial contribution to the *United Nations Yearbook on Human Rights* in 1953, Simonds vetoed Denning, whose name had been suggested by his officials but whom he did not trust to write with tact. Birkett was chosen instead (Denning was none the less acceptable to Simonds in a less sensitive role as chairman of a Church of England committee). Indeed, despite his own previous experience, Simonds was uncomfortable with appointing judges for non-judicial activities such as remuneration committees or for the Monopolies and Restrictive Practices Commission. The attempts to resolve the Rinfret controversy, which concerned the Canadian chief justice's efforts to remain on the judicial committee of the privy council after Canada had created its own final appeal court, sorely tried Simonds's patience.

Simonds's involvement in politically sensitive matters revealed his own inexperience in such areas. 'He was too apt to interpret opposition as an insult to himself or [to] the office which he held' (Heuston, 150). Lord Reith's attack on the government's plans in 1952 for commercial television was perceived as questioning his integrity. Unlike seasoned politicians he got angry (when he should have got even) at an injudicious and possibly insulting remark by Lord Simon regarding Simonds's adhesion to the Donoughmore report. Mutterings from the woolsack when socialist peers such as Lord Chorley made their points were not uncommon.

In 1954, following the troubles in Kenya, Simonds gave questionable advice to the cabinet in a paper, 'The attorney-general and public prosecutions', which (notwithstanding the Campbell case in 1924 and the careful guidance in 1951 of Hartley Shawcross) appeared to blur the line between considerations of public policy whenever the attorney-general considered a prosecution in which a minister would be interested and, on the other hand, the political considerations of government. As one authority later noted, the 'intervention of the Lord Chancellor, with respect to an office he had never occupied, was extraordinary' (Edwards, 322n.). In parliamentary debates he supported Lord Goddard's proposal in 1952 that the court of criminal appeal be empowered to order a retrial (the power was granted only in 1964) but he opposed Goddard's motion to restore, indeed to extend, corporal punishment, which had been abolished in 1948. Yet, although he was an unenthusiastic law reformer, he somewhat surprisingly revived in 1954, albeit in a modest fashion, the Law Reform Committee created by Sankey twenty years earlier. Its first report, recommending the repeal of certain obsolete provisions of the Statute of Frauds of 1677 requiring written evidence of sales over £10, led to the enactment of the Law Reform (Enforcement of Contracts) Act of 1954.

Simonds's visit to North America in August and September 1953 as lord chancellor to address the annual conventions of the American and Canadian bar associations gave him immense pleasure. Professor A. L. Goodhart of University College, Oxford (and himself an American) acted as an informal intermediary, informing the lord chancellor that the supreme court judge, Felix Frankfurter, had suggested that Simonds could perform a great service if he indicated in his address to the American Bar Association how the basic aspects of Anglo-American convictions about human dignity had remained the same despite the political shifts through National, Labour, and Conservative governments. Simonds's speech, which was later published under the title, 'Liberty within the law' in the *American Bar Association Journal*, would have disappointed Frankfurter. It was bland, predictable, and uninformative.

Unceremoniously and unexpectedly shunted aside to make room for Maxwell Fyfe on the woolsack in October 1954, Simonds did not hide his disappointment and displeasure at being replaced by a much younger and considerably less talented lawyer. In his unpublished 'Recollections' he constantly referred to the new lord chancellor Kilmuir as Fyffe [sic]. Partly mollified by the grant of a viscountcy (he had been granted a hereditary peerage in June 1952), he resumed as a lord of appeal in ordinary following Lord Porter's retirement, though not without a further departmental failure to follow the correct statutory sequence in making the offer. 'Once again', noted an official, 'things have gone far ahead of protocol' (PRO, LCO 6/2718). Simonds himself wrote:

Thus after three years my 'political adventure' [which, enigmatically, was the title of Maxwell Fyfe's autobiography] ended and once more I was back in the familiar world of law and lawyers. And now as I write it nearly ten years later, it sometimes seems like a strange dream. (Heuston, 157)

The fact is that Simonds was 'more judge than politician' (Stevens, *Independence*, 143).

House of Lords judge Simonds's reputation is founded on his being the foremost twentieth-century exponent of judicial conservatism (or of what specialists call legal formalism). This doctrine holds that the judicial role is to ensure certainty and predictability in the law rather than to shape it to the needs of society or of 'justice'. The task of the courts is 'to consider what the law is, not what it ought to be' (*Jacobs* v. *London County Council*, 1950). The latter was the responsibility of the legislator, not the judge. His exchanges with Lord Denning, with whose vision of the judicial task he fundamentally differed, were legendary (the evidence for personal animosity is inconclusive). Yet Simonds was usually supported by a majority of his fellow law lords when issuing his decisions, which were marked by their scholarship and logical coherence rather than by dramatic literary flourishes. It is difficult to imagine that he would have welcomed the House of Lords practice statement of 1966 permitting the highest judicial forum to depart from its own previous decisions (he had opposed the idea in 1962).

Between 1954 and 1966 (he sat on a handful of cases after his retirement) Simonds attended 174 House of Lords appeals, delivering judgments in 149 cases, including eight full dissents, and concurring in twenty-five cases. Out of thirty-five House of Lords judges during this period, only Lord Reid could boast a more productive record. In an examination of Simonds's contribution to legal doctrine, attention is invariably drawn to a number of classic utterances, many of which constitute robust rejections of Denning's pioneering efforts to reform the law without the assistance of parliament. Thus in *Scruttons Ltd* v. *Midland Silicones Ltd* (1962) he firmly rejected the efforts of his fellow law lord, Denning (which the latter had previously attempted in a number of Court of Appeal judgments) to alter an aspect of the law of contract by establishing third-party rights (which would be enforceable by one who was not a party to the contract). This provoked Simonds to endorse counsel's (Ashton Roskill QC's) view that 'it is more important that the law should be clear than that it should be clever' and to pronounce memorably:

to me heterodoxy, or, as some might say, heresy, is not the more attractive because it is dignified by the name of reform. Nor will I easily be led by an undiscerning zeal for some abstract kind of justice to ignore our first duty, which is to administer justice according to law, the law which is established for us by Act of Parliament or the binding authority of precedent. The law is developed by the application of old principles to new circumstances. Therein lies its genius. Its reform by the abrogation of those principles is the task not of the courts of law but of Parliament. (*Scruttons Ltd*, 467–8)

Like a previous master of the rolls, Thomas Cromwell, Denning later admitted that he had been 'verbally beheaded' (Denning, *Family Story*, 202). On questions of statutory interpretation Simonds rejected the Denning approach which was that 'we sit here to find out the intention of Parliament and of Ministers and carry it out, and we do this better by filling in the gaps and making sense of the enactment than by opening it up to destructive analysis' (Lord Denning, *The Discipline of Law*, 1979, 13). By contrast Simonds insisted that the courts were simply to apply the ordinary meaning (the literal interpretation) of words to the particular statutory provision and not to seek the policy behind the parliamentary enactment. To explore policy rather than merely to interpret the words would be a 'naked usurpation of the legislative process'. Moreover even if the statutory words were ambiguous, a voyage of discovery must be strictly limited (*Magor and St Mellons R.D.C.* v. *Newport Corporation*, 1952). Only if a literal interpretation would lead to 'absurd' results, he declared elsewhere, would a 'contextual' approach be permissible. Moreover the pursuit of 'justice' could only be undertaken where no precedent bound the house. Notwithstanding those exceptional situations, it was a case of Lord Halsbury revisited, with a clear and unbridgeable division between law and policy and a generally passive role for the courts.

Simonds also insisted that judgments should be based on the arguments of counsel presented in court and not on researches which had not been aired before judges and counsel. In what was perceived as a rebuke to Denning he repudiated the latter's action in *Rahimtoola* v. *Nizam of Hyderabad* (1958) in choosing to examine some authorities not cited by counsel because, as Denning had explained, the issue at stake was important, the legal position unclear, and the Lords should take the opportunity to tidy up the law. Simonds would have none of this and added a note at the end of his speech, to which the other judges in the hearing assented, dissociating himself from Denning's view (there was more tolerance for the latter's approach in later years). Yet Simonds himself had been guilty of the same 'offence' ten years previously, in *National Anti-Vivisection Society* v. *Inland Revenue Commissioners* (1948), when he based an important section of his decision on a statement in a relatively unknown book not referred to by counsel.

Dissenting in very few cases, Simonds hated being in the minority and took it personally. He would therefore assume 'task leadership' as the senior judge to try to persuade those whom he respected to change their opinions. How successful he was is difficult to say (it is evident in the speeches of other judges in *National Anti-Vivisection Society*). He certainly did not attempt 'social leadership', that is, to identify agreed ground if that did not correspond to his own view.

Simonds's influence in the House of Lords did, however, steadily decline in his last few years there. Lord Reid, for example, questioned effectively whether certainty of legal doctrine did in fact lead to predictable future decisions and, expressing a view with which Devlin and Evershed were sympathetic, considered that legal formalism had a habit of leading to unreasonable results. Yet two major judgments by Simonds stand out during this closing period. First was the important restatement of the principles governing remoteness of damage in tort which he delivered in the privy council decision in *The Wagon Mound* (No. 1) (1961), following an oil spillage in Sydney harbour. The second was his highly controversial judgment in *Shaw* v. *Director of Public Prosecutions* (1962), the 'Ladies' [i.e. prostitutes] Directory' case, in which he upheld the existence of the criminal offence of conspiracy to corrupt public morals. The severe criticism levelled against him was that his decision created a new offence. Not only was this inconsistent with the approach of a judicial conservative but it was especially regrettable in the criminal law where it was widely considered that judicial activism should be kept on a short leash. His speech did not mince words:

> In the sphere of criminal law I entertain no doubt that there remains in the courts of law a residual power to enforce the supreme and fundamental purpose of the law, to conserve not only the safety and order but the moral welfare of the State, and that it is their duty to guard it against attacks which may be the more insidious because they are novel and unprepared for. That is the broad head (call it public policy if you wish) within which the present indictment falls. It matters little what label is given to the offending act.

Here was the genuine voice of the social authoritarian (rather than of the social libertarian). But how it squares with legal formalism presents formidable difficulties of analysis. Despite the widespread academic criticism of the decision, A. L. Goodhart, editor of the *Law Quarterly Review*, viewed Simonds's reasoning as an important contribution to the common law.

Other activities Simonds's contribution to Lords debates after 1954 was modest, although it included a speech in his eighty-seventh year opposing the introduction of 'breakdown of marriage' as a ground for divorce in the Divorce Reform Bill (1969). In 1958 he opposed the introduction of an assizes system for the judicial committee of the privy council (only Denning and Reid favoured such a scheme). Then in 1959–60 he chaired a committee which recommended that disciplinary tribunals be granted legal powers to subpoena witnesses and secure the production of police evidence unless disclosure was against the public interest.

Simonds's interests outside the law lay in the countryside. He was a bird-watcher and fished and was apparently a good shot. He wrote little. His writings included a chapter in *The Character of England* edited by Sir Ernest Barker (1947). As a former lord chancellor, he was editor-in-chief of the third edition of *Halsbury's Laws of England*. He also received many honours. He was elected a fellow of Winchester in 1933 and warden in 1946 (where he opposed expanding the school's shares portfolio beyond investments in land and government stocks) and was elected an honorary fellow of New College, Oxford, in 1944. He was Oxford's high steward from 1954 to 1967, a bencher of Lincoln's Inn from 1929 and treasurer in 1951. He received honorary degrees from Reading University (1947), Laval University (1953), and Oxford (1954); was made an honorary FRCOG (1954) and professor of law at the Royal College of Arts (1951). In physical appearance he projected an image of a 'bluff, big, highly educated and very able squire', according to Lord Pearce (Heuston, 141). He was bespectacled, though was not always seen wearing his glasses, and was slightly balding with prominent and bushy eyebrows.

Conclusion Simonds has been correctly described by Stevens as the 'High Priest of the new orthodoxy' of substantive formalism (Stevens, *Law and Politics*, 342). The essence of legal formalism was its purported non-political flavour. Yet this is to assume that legal doctrine whose 'certainty' is to be judicially nourished has no pedigree and no history, being forged by judges who themselves had no pedigree, no history, and who occupied a space cocooned from their society. This is a questionable argument. For Simonds's judicial conservatism could be as 'political' as Denning's pervasive radicalism and Reid's reform of public law. Thus Simonds's contentment with the then underdeveloped state of judicial review, effectively offering wide ministerial immunities until the transformations which commenced in the 1960s, together with the lipservice he paid to civil liberties issues, were not value-free. In private law 'his penchant for the established order was clear from the first' (ibid., 346). Thus whether in respect to the terms of a will, or to a taxation statute, or to workers' protection under the factories legislation, whenever he insisted that the literal meaning of words should prevail, and that intent and statutory purpose be disregarded, his judicial conservatism disguised his social conservatism.

None the less there remains more than a hint of intellectual fudging. Apart from the apparent inconsistencies of his 'egregious performance' in *Shaw*, as one critic put it (Stevens, *Law and Politics*, 353n.), and his own invocation of authority in *National Anti-Vivisection Society* which had not been cited before the court, he sought to explain in a tax case burdened with an 'inconvenient' late nineteenth-century precedent where 'certain observations … [had been] made without full consideration of their consequences', that while he yielded to no one in the importance of precedent, none the less 'this case stands alone in my experience' (*Public Trustee* v. *Inland Revenue Commissioners*, [1960] A.C.398, 415–16). It was at best a limp rationale, but perhaps it reminds us that for every general proposition there will always be exceptions.

Government and politics, it is clear, were merely an interlude for Simonds and, on balance, an uncomfortable one. Indeed his happiest time as lord chancellor was probably when the great seal was temporarily 'in commission' during his visit to North America in 1953. It is scarcely surprising, therefore, that as lord chancellor his reputation and achievements were limited but that as a House of Lords judge his reputation and achievements were surpassed by few. Whether one condemns or applauds his judicial philosophy, he was undoubtedly one of the greatest judges of the modern age. Though he suffered a stroke one month after delivering his judgment in *Shaw*, prompting his resignation as a lord of appeal in ordinary on 31 March 1962, he remained active from time to time for the next few years. He died at 54 Rutland Gardens, London, on 28 June 1971, and was cremated at Golders Green, London, on 2 July.　　　　　G. R. RUBIN

Sources R. F. V. Heuston, *Lives of the lord chancellors, 1940–1970* (1987) · L. Blom-Cooper and G. Drewry, *Final appeal: a study of the House of Lords in its judicial capacity* (1972) · A. Paterson, *The law lords* (1982) · R. Stevens, *The independence of the judiciary: the view from the lord chancellor's office* (1993) · R. Stevens, *Law and politics: the House of Lords as a judicial body, 1800–1976* (1979) · B. Abel-Smith and R. Stevens, *Lawyers and the courts* (1965) · J. L. J. Edwards, *The attorney-general, politics and the public interest* (1984) · PRO, LCO 6/2718; LCO 6/2210; LCO 2/5650; LCO 2/5684; HO 287/1417 · G. T. Simonds, '"Liberty within the law": the lord chancellor's address', *American Bar Association Journal*, 38 (1953), 1059–62, 1114–17 · A. Flanders and H. A. Clegg, *The system of industrial relations in Great Britain* (1963) · earl of Kilmuir, *Political adventure* (1964) · D. N. Pritt, *The autobiography of D. N. Pritt*, 1–2 (1965–6) · F. Bresler, *Lord Goddard* (1977) · Lord Denning, *The family story* (1981) · Lord Denning, *The closing chapter* (1983) · DNB

Archives Winchester College, Winchester, memoirs · 'Recollections' (unpublished TS) [cited in Heuston Lives] | Bodl. Oxf., letters to A. L. Goodhart | FILM BFI NFTVA, news footage

Likenesses W. Stoneman, photograph, 1946, NPG · C. Beaton, photograph, 1953, NPG · G. Kelly, oils, c.1953, Lincoln's Inn, London · Lord Methuen, portrait, 1953, repro. in Heuston, *Lives* · Lord Methuen, group portrait, oils, c.1954 (*The lord chancellor on the woolsack*), Palace of Westminster, London · photograph, repro. in *The Times* (29 June 1971) · photograph, Hult. Arch.; repro. in Heuston, *Lives* · photograph, repro. in *ABA Journal*, 38 (1953), 1061

Wealth at death £312,537: probate, 25 Aug 1971, *CGPLA Eng. & Wales*

Simonds, James Beart (1810–1904), veterinary surgeon, was born at Lowestoft, Suffolk, on 18 February 1810, the first child of James Simonds (1786–1810), and his wife, Mary, daughter of Robert Beart of Rickenhall, Suffolk, an agriculturist and horse breeder. His paternal uncle, Samuel Simonds, had married Mary's sister. Samuel Simonds was in practice with his father, Samuel Simonds (b. 1754), in Bungay, Suffolk, when he died suddenly, in February 1810, leaving a widow and an infant; his brother James returned from Lowestoft to help, but himself died in October, leaving Mary pregnant. James Beart Simonds was then brought up in Bungay, Suffolk, by his grandfather Samuel.

Simonds was educated at Bungay grammar school. He entered the Veterinary College in Camden Town, London, in January 1828, but found the course limited to the diseases of horses. He sought and attended external lectures, including in chemistry and anatomy. He received his diploma to practise in March 1829, and joined his uncle Robert Beart's veterinary surgery at Bungay. In 1833 he married his 'beloved cousin' Martha, daughter of Robert Beart (Simonds, 320). They had two daughters and a son, James Sexton Simonds, for some time chief of the Metropolitan Fire Brigade. Martha died in August 1851. Simonds later married Harriet Driffill, who survived him.

In 1836 Simonds's career was transformed by the sudden death of a cousin from whom he inherited a veterinary practice in Twickenham. Simonds moved there and renewed his connections with his tutors and friends in London. In the same year he became a founder member of the Veterinary Medical Association which subsequently played a significant part in the creation of the British veterinary profession. Two months after its founding in 1838, Simonds became a member of the English (later Royal)

Agricultural Society. He was made an honorary member in April 1849, and a foundation life governor in March 1890. He promptly took part in organizing the scientific work connected with the animals of its farm. He was invited by the society to serve on a subcommittee to consider ways of co-operating with the governors of the Veterinary Association to include farm animals in the curriculum. In 1839 his diagnostic tests for 'cattle epidemic' (foot-and-mouth disease) and sheep rabies led to Simonds's being appointed to the first professorship of cattle pathology at the Veterinary College in London, and consulting veterinary surgeon to the Royal Agricultural Society (a position he held for sixty-two years until his death). He disposed of his Twickenham practice, settled in London, and thereafter played a crucial role in expanding the scope of the profession to encompass the food-animal industry.

Simonds was active in the movement for obtaining the charter which was granted on 8 March 1844 to the Royal College of Veterinary Surgeons, of which he was president from 1862 to 1863. He took a prominent part in the efforts of the Royal Agricultural Society to popularize among farmers information on diseases of animals, and he investigated the causes and means of prevention. He diagnosed sheep pox in 1847, showed it was contagious, and pressed for measures to control it, and he was involved in the campaign to free the British Isles of the disease; in 1852–3 he helped to rid the royal herd at Windsor of pleuropneumonia. He carried out an inquiry on the continent into the cattle-plague epidemic in 1857, and made a detailed report, and he also diagnosed swine fever in 1862.

Simonds's information on cattle-plague was useful during an outbreak of that disease in London in June 1865; the privy council office delayed orders for slaughtering and burying affected animals in quicklime, and the infection spread over a great part of England. A veterinary department was set up at the privy council. Simonds was appointed chief inspector and professional adviser; among his assistants was Professor George Thomas Brown. The outbreak cost at least £5 million. The veterinary department was continued as a permanent department, with Simonds at its head until November 1871, when he resigned in order to become principal of the Royal Veterinary College, in succession to Professor Charles Spooner. He conducted a detailed inquiry into the educational system there, and completed the incorporation of the college in 1875 by royal charter.

Early in 1881 Simonds's health failed, and in June he retired to the Isle of Wight, though he remained senior consulting veterinary surgeon to the Royal Agricultural Society. His health recovered, but he never returned to full-time work. Instead he farmed and served as a JP. Simonds was a tall, dignified, and handsome man, grave and serious by nature. He died at his home, St John's Villa, St John's Park, St Helens, in Ryde, Isle of Wight, on 5 July 1904, of pneumonia. He left a large and unique collection of books, pamphlets, nine massive scrapbooks, and notebooks, which are important to historians of his profession. Many letters show that he was respected and liked by his peers.   ERNEST CLARKE, rev. LINDA WARDEN

Sources J. B. Simonds, 'James Beart Simonds, late principal of the Royal Veterinary College, professor of cattle pathology etc.', *The Veterinarian*, 67 (1894), 315–24, 401–12, 487–500, 573–85, 651–62, 736–49, 811–23, 889–99 · J. Kingsley, 'The scrapbooks of the Simonds Collection at the Royal Veterinary College', *Veterinarian History*, new ser. 7/2 (1992), 39–45 · 'Professor J. B. Simonds, J. P.', *Veterinary Record* (9 July 1904), 917 · I. Pattinson, *A great British veterinarian forgotten: James Beart Simonds, 1810–1904* (1990) · d. cert. · personal knowledge (1912) · IGI

Archives Royal Veterinary College, London, corresp. and papers relating to the profession and cattle diseases

Likenesses photograph, repro. in Kingsley, 'The scrapbooks of the Simonds Collection', 45 · photograph, repro. in *Veterinary Record*, 916

Wealth at death £4093 2s. 3d.: probate, 29 Aug 1904, CGPLA Eng. & Wales

Simons, Joseph. *See* Lobb, Emmanuel (1594–1671).

Simonsen, Sir John Lionel (1884–1957), organic chemist, was born in Levenshulme, Manchester, on 22 January 1884, the only son of Lionel Michael Simonsen, a velveteen merchant, and his wife, Anna Sophie Bing. His parents were naturalized British citizens of Danish origin; his father was of Jewish descent, and they had relatives in academic circles in Denmark and Sweden. He was educated at Manchester grammar school, where he was stimulated by Francis Jones, a distinguished pioneer in the teaching of chemistry. His summer holidays were spent in the Copenhagen laboratory of an uncle by marriage, Professor V. Henriques, a physiologist. This experience and other contacts with his Danish scientific relatives probably helped to determine the direction of his interests. Forfeiting a scholarship in modern languages, he became in 1901 a student in the school of chemistry of Manchester University, a leading centre of research. He graduated with first-class honours in 1904, obtained his DSc in 1909, and from 1907 was assistant lecturer and demonstrator.

The professor of organic chemistry at Manchester, W. H. Perkin, was an authority on the chemistry of natural products, and Simonsen began his research in this field. Even in those early days he was recognized as a talented experimentalist. His main task was to find a synthesis of norpinic acid, the end-product of a degradation of α-pinene carried out by Adolph von Baeyer in Munich. A successful synthesis proved elusive, but syntheses arrived at during the study gave fresh starting points in other directions. Simonsen recorded new syntheses of terebic acid and two homologues and in collaboration with Robert Robinson reinvestigated rhein and aloe-emodin, which were shown to be 1, 8-dihydroxyanthraquinone-3-carboxylic acid and the related 3-hydroxymethyl compound respectively.

In 1910 Simonsen went to Madras as professor of chemistry at the Presidency College. There he devoted himself to the improvement of Indian scientific work and education beyond the limits of his post. He took the initiative in 1914 in helping to found the Indian Science Congress Association, of which he was general secretary until 1926 and which owed its success largely to his efforts. Simonsen also assisted the government in various ways: during the First World War he was controller of oils and chemical adviser to the Indian munitions board. In 1919–25 he was chief chemist of the Forest Research Institute and College at Dehra Dun and in 1925–8 professor of organic chemistry at the Indian Institute of Science at Bangalore. In 1913 he married Jannet (Nettie) Dick Hendrie (d. 1960), the eldest daughter of Robert Hendrie of Nairn, Scotland. At the time of her marriage she was a skilled surgeon and in charge of the Caste and Gosha Hospital, Madras. They had one child, an adopted daughter.

In 1928 Simonsen returned to the UK and worked for a time at the chemical laboratory of Guy's Hospital, but in 1930 he was appointed professor of chemistry at the University College of North Wales, Bangor, where he remained until 1942. The main area of his mature scientific work was the chemistry of terpenes and sesquiterpenes. His name will always be associated with the interesting discovery of carene in Indian turpentine. This compound proved very useful in determining the structure of sylvestrene, a hydrocarbon obtained from Swedish pine oil. Some of his studies of sesquiterpenes were started in India, but the greater part of this important work was carried out in Bangor, partly in collaboration with A. E. Bradfield and often with A. R. Penfold, director of the Museum of Applied Arts and Sciences in Sydney, Australia. This long-distance arrangement was very effective; Penfold isolated new natural products and Simonsen developed their chemistry. Their labours led to the establishment of the structure of the sesquiterpenoid ketone, eremophilone, although not without difficulties on the way. In the course of this work an intramolecular migration of a methyl group was recognized, and this type of rearrangement was later found to play a part in the biogenesis of the sterols. Simonsen and his colleagues determined the structures of α- and β-cyperones, discovered the cyclobutane element of the caryophyllene molecule, and laid the foundations for the determination of the structure of longifolene. He made numerous further significant contributions to knowledge which are described in about 180 papers. He also published a comprehensive account of the terpenes in five volumes (1947–57, with L. N. Owen, D. H. R. Barton, and W. C. J. Ross), which was for a time the standard work of reference in the field.

In 1943–52 Simonsen was director of research of the Colonial Products Research Council. He also worked on the insecticide panel and stored foods committee. He was appointed a member of the Agricultural Research Council in 1945 and was British delegate to the Food and Agriculture Organization specialists committee in London in 1947. In all this work he displayed impressive energy and administrative ability. In 1944 with Sir Robert Robinson he visited the USA and the Caribbean. Results of this visit were the founding of the Microbiological Institute in Trinidad and the clearance of mosquitoes from the coastal strip of British Guiana. This work helped contribute to the dramatic reduction of the infant mortality rate. In 1946 with Sir Ian Heilbron he visited eastern and southern

Africa. The necessity for a wider front than that implied by 'colonial products research' became apparent and eventually the term 'tropical products research' was adopted.

Simonsen was an experimentalist of a high standard, and he had little interest in theory. He had many students and junior collaborators whose subsequent achievements bear testimony to his ability as a teacher. At the same time exacting and generous, he could be formal when the occasion demanded it, but was always warm-hearted. He was elected a fellow of the Royal Society in 1932 and was awarded the Davy medal in 1950. He was the first recipient of the American Chemical Society's Fritzsche award (1949) and received honorary degrees from the universities of Birmingham, Malaya, and St Andrews. He served periods as a vice-president of the Chemical Society and on the council, and was honorary secretary (1945–49). He was knighted in 1949. He died at his home, 3 Wildcroft Manor, Putney Heath, London, on 20 February 1957.

ROBERT ROBINSON, rev. JOHN SHORTER

Sources R. Robinson, *Memoirs FRS*, 5 (1959), 237–52 · personal knowledge (1971) · *CGPLA Eng. & Wales* (1957)
Archives RS, corresp. with Sir Robert Robinson on alkaloids
Likenesses W. Stoneman, photograph, 1945, NPG · W. Stoneman, photograph, 1946, RS · photograph, Royal Society of Chemistry, London
Wealth at death £19,596 3s.: probate, 1 May 1957, *CGPLA Eng. & Wales*

Simpson. *See also* Simson.

Simpson family (*per.* 1894–1990), clothing manufacturers, came to prominence with **Simeon Simpson** (1878–1932). Born in London and apprenticed as a tailor, he is said to have opened a workshop in the East End of London in 1894. A highly skilled cutter and designer, a good organizer with the ability to retain a loyal workforce, he enjoyed increasing success and after expanding out of several East End workshops, opened his first purpose-built factory at 109 Middlesex Street, London E1, in 1917, largely in response to the demand for uniforms in the First World War. He married Sarah (1880–1959); they had at least two sons and a daughter.

In the difficult post-war years Simpson concentrated on good quality ready-to-wear suits as well as providing provincial tailors and outfitters with a swift, reliable, mail-order wholesale bespoke service, with the suits fitted by the retailer but made in the factory. With prices about two-thirds lower than those of completely custom-made garments, demand outgrew supply and in 1929 he built a new factory at 92–100 Stoke Newington Road, London, promoted as the largest and most modern clothing factory in the world. Despite active participation in the management of the factory and travels to Europe and the USA for style ideas and manufacturing techniques, Simeon Simpson was active in Jewish communal and local municipal affairs. He was elected as Municipal Reform candidate for Hackney borough council in 1925, and in 1931, after the family had moved to 88 Fitzjohn's Avenue, Hampstead, to Hampstead borough council.

Simpson died on 12 July 1932, from a perforated ulcer, at Hallam House, Hallam Street, London. He was mourned, with a sincerity which appears to be justified, as 'a good man, a good son, a good husband, a good father, a good friend and a model employer' (*Hackney Gazette and North London Advertiser*, 22 July 1932). After a legacy to his married daughter Rebecca Woolf, whose City solicitor husband Arthur was later to become a director of the firm, his estate was left equally between his wife, remembered as a warm-hearted and positive partner in the family and the business, and his sons, Alexander and Samuel Leonard.

It was his younger son, **Alexander Simpson** (1902/3–1937), who took over the running of the firm. Known as Mr Alex to his employees, he was an enthusiast for style and quality who had saved pocket money for good, smart clothes while a child. Alexander entered the trade at fifteen, straight from Westminster City School, learned the business thoroughly at home and abroad, and at the age of twenty-one became his father's right hand in the planning of the new factory and partner in charge of sales. He shared with his father the credit for introducing the adjustable self-supporting trouser, obviating the need for belts or braces, patented in 1932. As Daks slacks they were the first fashion sports trouser and so convinced were Simeon and Alex Simpson of the quality of the design that they made 10,000 pairs in advance of the first sale. The trade mark Daks, registered in 1934, is, according to family legend, a combination of Dad and slacks, a late night inspiration of Alex and his brother Samuel Leonard, approved by William Crawford, their advertising agent and friend. Demand was great and by 1936 when S. Simpson Ltd changed from being a private to a public company, it had an issued capital of £350,000, all held by the family, and employed 2500 people. In April 1936 Simpson married Ceridwen Catherine Rees Roberts, the daughter of a neighbour.

Alexander Simpson had a particular flair for promotion. In 1934 he and William Crawford organized a very successful Simpson stand at the British Industries Fair. This was the first to use live male models and sports demonstrations. In the same year he began to plan a permanent showplace for Simpson clothes, a prestige London shop. After acquiring the Piccadilly site, he commissioned a design team for what he intended as the most modern shop in London, with a unique feature, the largest curving plate glass windows in the world. Correspondence shows him to have worked closely and amiably with the architect Joseph Emberton. Interiors were designed by László Moholy-Nagy, design and lettering concept by Ashley Havinden. The shop became a listed building, acknowledged as a modernist classic. It had been financed by the parent company, with a supplementary loan arranged by the Yorkshire wool magnate Lord Barnby, later a director. In just over two years the shop was complete, opening on 24 April 1936, and by 1939 edging into profit. Only thirteen months after the store opened, Alexander Simpson's life was cut short by leukaemia; he died at Rookery Wood, Highwood Hill, Mill Hill, Hendon, on 15 May 1937.

The shock to the trade was great, for Mr Alex was popular and admired. Dark haired like his father, he was similarly active in Jewish and local affairs, especially those relating to young people. Of large build, he was lively, a good communicator, and 'never made a boring speech in his life' according to *Mens Wear* (1937). Fond of amateur football, boxing, and fast cars, he had the family ability to get on with staff of any age and level. Knowledgeable about all aspects of the men's wear, he was a perfectionist with a sense of style and quality which included but went far beyond clothes.

The direction of the family business then passed to Alexander's brother **Samuel Leonard Simpson** (1900–1983), known in the firm as the Doctor. Although he was educated like his brother at Westminster City School, his career had taken a different path. A Cambridge scholar and prizeman with a double first in the natural science tripos, he was also a boxing blue and in 1922 captain of the university boxing team. However, he refused the invitation to become a professional boxer. After qualifying as a doctor at the London Hospital in 1926, he worked at the Mayo Clinic in New York, as well as in Berlin and at the Lister Institute in London. He became a specialist in endocrinology and his book, *Major Endocrine Disorders* (1938; 3rd edn, 1959), became a standard work. He was already a distinguished and established physician so the decision to run the clothing business could not have been an easy one. On the advice of his Cambridge professor, he decided to divide his time between his practice and the family firm. He was fortunate in that, as part of a close family, not only had he already absorbed many of the essentials of the family business, he also had the help of long-standing employees of the firm. Solomon Klein (Mr Solly), for instance, had been apprentice and assistant to his grandfather, a director of the parent company from 1935, of Simpson Piccadilly from 1936, and was to become managing director in 1940 and joint managing director in 1949. In 1940 Simpson married Heddy Monique, Baroness de Podmansky (1908–1994); they had one daughter.

Urbane, considerate, and very organized, as adept in staff management as his father and brother, Samuel Leonard Simpson spent Tuesdays and Thursdays at Simpsons, the last week of every month at meetings, and combined research, business, and lecture trips overseas. His medical interests also extended to metabolic research. A generous donation in 1964 to the medical school at St Mary's Hospital, London, where he was to become honorary consultant endocrinologist, was instrumental in founding the Alexander and Leonard Simpson Laboratory for Metabolic Research, a memorial to his brother. His industrial psychological work was relevant when he became director of personnel and chairman of the appointments board of Simpsons. His joint consultation committee on staff matters (1947) was as effective in staff management in the difficult post-war period as his brother's earlier concept, 'Partners in Progress', had been with staff and retailers in the economically fraught years of the 1920s and 1930s.

Initially vice-chairman, Samuel Leonard Simpson was precluded by his profession from taking up the chairmanship of S. Simpson Ltd, Simpsons (Piccadilly) Ltd, and Daks Simpson Ltd, until 1957. He then held these positions until retirement in 1983, his international as well as his sporting interests suggesting useful new directions for the firm. He is credited with the 1940 formation of the Simpson Service Club which performed an important public service role for the allied forces as well as providing a venue for prestige patriotic entertaining and exhibitions, events which were to continue as features of Simpson publicity. Simpson also developed a concerted export plan: Simpson Imports Incorporated was established in New York in 1941 and Daks Canada in 1950. From 1948 to 1952 he was a member of the grand council of the Federation of British Industries. He was also a member of the Carlton Club. By 1966 Daks Simpson were the biggest exporters of British menswear. The manufacturing side was similarly well served. The Stoke Newington factory, damaged by bombing in 1940, was finally replaced with a purpose-built factory at Larkhall, near Glasgow, in 1949, and was extended in 1963.

Golf, another of Samuel Leonard Simpson's pursuits, also became a Simpson speciality. Tournaments were regularly sponsored, most notably from 1961 the Walter Hagen annual award, which he was himself to receive in 1977. His interest in horses, which he bred on his estate at Grouselands, Sussex, and which he shared with his family, led the firm to sponsor many equestrian events. The Doctor was also an amateur painter of some skill but though he exhibited, this was in the main a private pleasure. His interest in the arts led to an important gift of current fashions to the Victoria and Albert Museum in 1979.

Heddy Simpson, who became a director in 1947, was vivacious and elegant. She was notable hostess at their London home (formerly that of Winston Churchill), 28 Hyde Park Gate, and was influential in the fashion focus of the Jermyn Street extension of the Piccadilly store opened in 1957. It was a role her daughter Georgina, who became a director in 1976, was to perform with great flair in 1977 for the opening of 'SJS' and 'Young and Gay', new Simpson departments aimed at the youth market.

Sports sponsorship, export achievement, and a traditional English quality image became the Daks Simpson hallmark. As their prestige grew, they were awarded a royal warrant by the duke of Edinburgh in 1954, by the queen in 1962, and the prince of Wales in 1982. Samuel Leonard Simpson died peacefully at Crawley Hospital, Sussex, on 3 August 1983. On the sale of the firm to Sankyo Seiko Osaka in 1990, for £65 million, the formal family association with the firm ceased. The Simpson Family Charity Trust, founded in the same year, nevertheless perpetuated the family's philanthropic commitment.

M. GINSBURG

Sources D. Wainwright, *The British tradition: Simpson—a world of style* (1996) · *60 celebrating a diamond jubilee, style for men*, 1954, Simpson (Piccadilly Ltd), London, Simpson archives · *To record twenty-one years … Doctor S. Leonard Simpson, MA, MD, FRCP*, 1959, Simpson (Piccadilly) Ltd, London, Simpson archives · *Hackney Gazette and North London Advertiser* (22 July 1932) · *Mens Wear* (1937), *passim* · Simpson (Piccadilly Ltd), London, Simpson archives, *passim* · WWW · DBB · private information (2004) · d. certs. · *CGPLA Eng. & Wales* (1932) · *CGPLA Eng. & Wales* (1937) · *CGPLA Eng. & Wales* (1984)

Archives Simpson (Piccadilly) Ltd, London, Simpson archives

Likenesses portraits, Simpson (Piccadilly) Ltd, London, Simpson archives

Wealth at death £80,224 8s. 6d.—Simeon Simpson: resworn probate, 13 Oct 1932, *CGPLA Eng. & Wales* · £53,473 11s. 4d.—Alexander Simpson: probate, 9 Aug 1937, *CGPLA Eng. & Wales* · £1,647,153—Samuel Leonard Simpson: probate, 9 March 1984, *CGPLA Eng. & Wales*

Simpson, Mrs. *See* Simpson, (Bessie) Wallis, duchess of Windsor (1896–1986).

Simpson, Alexander (1902/3–1937). *See under* Simpson family (*per.* 1894–1990).

Simpson, Archibald (1790–1847), architect, was born on 4 May 1790 at 15 The Guestrow, Aberdeen, the fifth of five sons and the youngest of nine children of William Simpson (1740–1804), clothier in Aberdeen, and his wife, Barbara (*c*.1750–1801), eldest daughter of the Revd Francis Dauney, minister of Banchory Ternan. He was educated at Aberdeen grammar school and then briefly at Marischal College in 1803–4. His maternal uncle William Dauney had been an architect in Aberdeen. He received his initial training in architecture from James Massie (*d.* 1816), an Aberdeen builder. In 1810 he moved to London and found employment with Robert Lugar and David Laing, for whom he prepared plans of a house in Aberdeen. His struggles in London, in spite of letters of introduction, are recorded in two letters to his family. In 1813 he returned to Aberdeen after a tour of Italy.

It was an opportune moment to return, because the citizens of Aberdeen had embarked on a series of ambitious street improvements at the same time as the technology had developed to enable the exploitation of the plentiful local granite for building purposes. Simpson was to emerge as the leading architect of the city, which he stocked with a fine series of public buildings, distinguished not only by his skill in seizing town-planning initiatives but also by the splendour imparted by their finely jointed and polished granite masonry. In these works he had to endure the rivalry of the city architect, John Smith (1781–1852), who had the advantage of being longer established in their profession.

Simpson's first public building was the Gothic St Andrew's Chapel of 1816. His skill as a classical designer in the Greek revival style found expression in the Medico-Chirurgical Hall of 1818 and the porticoed county assembly rooms of 1820. These were followed by a wide range of commissions which display his inventive powers, including the Gothic Marischal College of 1837, the New Market of 1840, and in the same year his headquarters of the North of Scotland Bank, with its quadrant corner screen and richly decorated interior incorporating the Parthenon frieze. In 1843 he designed his celebrated 'triple kirks' for three Free Church congregations whose financial constraint is reflected in their brick spires. Simpson also dominated architecture in the north-east of Scotland. He added to many existing houses and castles, but his finest design is probably Stracathro House, Forfarshire, of 1828 with its noble Corinthian portico. He also designed elegant classical villas such as Park House, Aberdeenshire, of 1822. St Giles's Church, with its portico and tower, is a powerful essay in the Greek revival style and provides the focal point at the heart of Elgin.

Simpson was of slight build and 'shy and retiring' in character. He was remembered as 'a little, active man, always to be seen carrying plans under his arm'. He loved music and played the violin. He died intestate on 23 March 1847 at his home, 1 East Craibstone Street, Aberdeen. He was unmarried. He was buried in the East Church of St Nicholas, Aberdeen.   IAN GOW, *rev.*

Sources G. M. Fraser, *Aberdeen Weekly Journal* (5 April 1918) · G. M. Fraser, *Aberdeen Weekly Journal* (11 Oct 1918) · Colvin, *Archs.* · *The Archibald Simpson centenary celebrations* (1947) [reproduced from the *Quarterly Journal of the Royal Incorporation of Architects in Scotland*] · *Archibald Simpson*, Aberdeen Civic Society (1978)
Likenesses J. Giles, portrait, after 1843, U. Aberdeen, Marischal College; repro. in *Archibald Simpson*, Aberdeen Civic Society · J. Giles, portrait (when young), U. Aberdeen, Marischal College · J. Giles, portrait, Aberdeen Art Gallery

Simpson, Cedric Keith (1907–1985), forensic pathologist, was born on 20 July 1907 at 138 Beaconsfield Villas, Preston, Brighton, Sussex, the second son and second of three children of George Herbert Simpson, a general medical practitioner, and his wife, Maud Annie May, a nurse, daughter of Joseph James Bussell. Simpson left Brighton and Hove grammar school in 1924 to study medicine. He completed his studies for the degree of MD at Guy's Hospital in 1932, with a speciality in pathology, and won prizes in pathology, clinical surgery, physiology, dissection, and bacteriology. That year, promoted to senior demonstrator in the pathology department, he married, on 4 June, a Guy's nurse, Mary McCartney Buchanan (*d.* 1955), with whom he raised three children. As a young member of the staff at Guy's in the early 1930s he undertook post-mortems at the nearby Southwark mortuary. From this work he grew interested in assisting the police with murder investigations.

Simpson began practising forensic medicine at a time when any duly qualified medical practitioner might be asked to carry out medico-legal post-mortem examinations. Sir Bernard Spilsbury, who like Simpson lived and worked in London, was at the height of his fame when Simpson entered the field. Spilsbury, although renowned among the public and the police for his expertise, stood aloof from his professional colleagues and was loath to train students or serve as a mentor. It was Spilsbury's reluctance to assist the authorities with cases which were not sufficiently complex to hold his attention which gave Simpson the opportunity to make a name for himself.

Aside from Spilsbury and a few other pathologists at regional hospitals, in the early twentieth century almost no other physicians had the training, technique, experience, or equipment to carry out complex medical enquiries into criminal cases. Simpson and his contemporaries, among them Sir Sydney Smith at Edinburgh, and fellow Londoners Donald Teare and Francis Camps, through their advocacy of forensic investigation as a medical speciality greatly enhanced the stature of the field of forensic

pathology. In time Simpson joined the few pathologists whom the Home Office designated as official investigators. As his reputation grew he served as an expert in investigations all over Britain and abroad. With the death of Spilsbury in 1947 Simpson became the leading forensic pathologist in Britain.

Simpson held faculty positions in forensic medicine at the University of London, where he was named reader in 1946 and professor in 1962, and at Oxford, where he was named lecturer in 1961. He retired from the faculty at Guy's Hospital medical school in 1972. He helped to solve several sensational murder cases, including the Haigh case (1949), in which John George Haigh had attempted to dispose of his victims' bodies in an acid bath. In 1943 he performed autopsies on the bodies of several dozen victims of an accident in which 173 persons had been crushed when they were entering an underground station during an air raid. This helped Simpson to refine his detection of death by asphyxiation—a subject upon which he became an authority. In 1948 Simpson's knowledge of forensic odontology proved relevant in the notorious Gorringe case, where for the first time a British court accepted evidence that bite marks on a body could have been made by only one set of teeth—in this case that of Mrs Gorringe's husband, who was duly convicted of her murder.

Simpson was meticulous in work habits, collegial with peers, and on good terms with the police. He was known as an extremely effective expert witness. He appeared non-partisan in the witness box and was invariably well prepared. His crime scene notes were models of detail and keen observation. He was unruffled by vigorous cross-examination, and could make technical points comprehensible to a lay jury. Not all Simpson's careful fieldwork and persuasive courtroom testimony, however, resulted in convictions. During the Second World War he noted that juries were reluctant to convict servicemen of violent crimes, while on other occasions no charges were even brought.

Simpson travelled widely and participated actively in several organizations. He was a founding member of the British Association in Forensic Medicine, and served as its president in 1966–7; he was president of the Medico-Legal Society in 1961–3. He was a member of the councils of the Royal College of Pathologists and the Medical Protection Society. He was awarded honorary degrees from Ghent and Edinburgh, and was a member of the Société de Médecine Légale and the American Academy of Forensic Sciences. In 1975 he was appointed CBE.

His editorship of the eleventh and twelfth editions of Taylor's *Principles and Practice of Medical Jurisprudence* marked Simpson as an authority in the field. His own *Forensic Medicine* (1947) was published in multiple editions and earned the Swiney prize of the Royal Society of Arts. His *A Doctor's Guide to Court* (1962) went to a second edition in 1967. Simpson wrote more than 200 articles in learned publications about topics in pathology (including cardiomyopathy and pulmonary embolism), as well as subjects more medico-legal in nature, such as the identification of the physical marks of child abuse. In 1983 he drew both professional support and public criticism by refusing to perform a post-mortem examination on the body of a victim of AIDS.

Simpson helped to make forensic medicine accessible to the general public not only through his many courtroom appearances but in radio and television interviews and with his writings for lay people. His autobiography, *Forty Years of Murder* (1978), was an international best seller. Simpson's wife died of multiple sclerosis in 1955; on 15 March 1956 he married Jean Anderson Scott Dunn, his secretary for the previous ten years. She died of cancer in 1976 and on 2 July 1982 he married Janet Thurston, *née* Hazell, widow of the coroner Gavin Thurston, who survived him. He died on 21 July 1985 at St Bartholomew's Hospital, London. ELISABETH A. CAWTHON

Sources K. Simpson, *Forty years of murder* (1978) · 'Professor Keith Simpson', *The Times* (23 July 1985) · B. H. Knight, 'Professor Keith Simpson', *Journal of the Forensic Science Society*, 5 (1985), 403–4 · 'Professor Cedric Keith Simpson', *Guy's Hospital Gazette* (Aug 1985), 282–4 · CGPLA Eng. & Wales (1986) · b. cert. · m. certs. · d. cert.
Likenesses G. Argent, photograph, repro. in Simpson, *Forty years*, 200 · photograph, repro. in *The Times*
Wealth at death £182,072: probate, 19 March 1986, CGPLA Eng. & Wales

Simpson, Christopher (*c*.1602–1669), composer and musician, was the eldest son of Dorothy Pearson (*d*. 1628) and Christopher Sympson (*b*. *c*.1580, *d*. in or after 1616). Originally from Nottinghamshire, the family had settled in Yorkshire by the mid-sixteenth century. Simpson was probably born at Egton in the North Riding, where his parents moved after their marriage. In official documents his father is described as a 'cordwainer' (shoemaker), but he was also actor–manager of a theatre company patronized by wealthy Catholic families in the area. This duality may be explained by the need for Catholic recusants, such as the Simpsons were, to maintain a discreet profile during a period of religious and political turbulence.

That nothing is known of Simpson's education, formidable as it was, or his early career, probably reflects such considerations. Indeed, a tantalizing theory has been propounded (Urquart, 'Was Christopher Simpson a Jesuit?') that Simpson may have led a double life and is to be identified with a contemporary named Simpson (or Sampson) who received a Jesuit education on the continent, leading to ordination in 1629. Many features of the career of this Yorkshire-born priest, who finally returned to the Jesuit college of St John at Durham in 1649, are not entirely incompatible with the composer's known activities. The evidence for the musician's death in 1669, however, is at odds, at least on the face of it, with the notification from London to the Jesuit authorities in Rome of the priest's death on 3 March 1674.

Simpson first emerges from obscurity about 1642 during the civil war, when he enlisted in the royalist army under William Cavendish, duke of Newcastle, at York, where Charles I had established a base in response to the threat from Scotland. In the summer of 1643 Newcastle's forces

Christopher Simpson (*c*.1602–1669), by William Faithorne the elder, pubd 1659 (after John Carwarden)

were in Lincolnshire, and it was probably there that Simpson came into contact with Sir Robert Bolles, a noted patron of music, of Scampton manor, just north of Lincoln. Some time between 1645 and 1649 Simpson became resident musician and tutor to Sir Robert's son John. Simpson had earlier inherited from his father Hunt House, a smallholding at Pickering, but he settled this property on his nephew Christopher, and continued to reside with the Bolles family, either at Scampton or in London, until the end of his life.

As a theorist, Simpson first contributed to Playford's *A Brief Introduction to the Skill of Musick* (2nd edn, 1655), providing annotations to a chapter based on a short treatise by Thomas Campion (1613). He established a national reputation with *The Division-Violist* (1659), a viol tutor culminating in a comprehensive elucidation of the art of spontaneous extemporization over a repeated bass theme, then a widely practised and highly esteemed art. He dedicated the first edition to Sir Robert Bolles, under whose roof 'the work had both its conception and production' (dedication), and the second (1665) to his highly talented son, for whose use the treatise was written. With a view to exploiting the continental market, the latter edition incorporated a translation into Latin. Roger L'Estrange, himself an accomplished amateur violist, wrote in his foreword: 'Whoever has this book by him, has one of the best tutors in the world'.

In 1665 Simpson published a modest primer on the rudiments of music, *The Principles of Practical Musick*, dedicated to another young pupil, Sir John St Barbe, whom he had begun to teach in 1663. A much enlarged treatise, *A Compendium of Practical Musick*, followed in 1667, dedicated to the duke of Newcastle. The first part is based on *The Principles* and is followed by four additional sections devoted to composition, discords, figurate descant, and canon respectively. By 1775 the *Compendium* had reached its ninth edition and even Burney, who was sceptical of the efficacy of such publications, acknowledged 'the considerable merit of its clearness and simplicity' (Burney, *Hist. mus.*, 3.473).

Simpson's compositions were written almost exclusively for consorts of viols, or mixed consorts, in various combinations with continuo, or for solo viol. They were widely disseminated in manuscript copies, but none was printed in his lifetime, apart from those included in his treatises for illustrative purposes. Reflecting the growing ascendancy of the violin family during the seventeenth century, it is evident that the treble parts in consort pieces, including those ostensibly for viols, were increasingly played by, and sometimes even conceived for, the violin. Furthermore, two divisions on a ground specifically for violin were attributed to Simpson and published posthumously by John Playford in *The Division-Violin* (1684).

In his treatise on the making of divisions Simpson affirmed that it was essentially an improvisatory art; at the same time, in the sets of divisions he wrote down, a remarkable inventiveness, melodic gift, structural grasp, and delight in instrumental display are evident. His *Twenty 4-Part Ayres* are grouped by key into suite-like sets, each one containing one or two airs interspersed within a succession of dances—pavans, galliards, courantes, and sarabands—and written for the relatively uncommon combination of two trebles and two basses. These pieces, with their subtle varieties of texture, may well have been inspired by the similarly scored works of Simpson's distinguished colleague and friend John Jenkins.

Many important sources for Simpson's music are now preserved at the British Library, the Bodleian Library, Oxford, and the Henry Watson Library, Manchester. Modern editions of his works include four fantasia-suites in *The Seasons*, twelve virtuoso fantasias in *The Months*, *A Little Consort* for lyra viol, treble viol, and bass viol, *Six Sets of Divisions* for treble and bass viol, and *Twenty-Two 3-Part Airs*, in which a tendency towards a polarity between the two upper parts and the bass suggests the pervasive influence of the Italian trio sonata.

Simpson made his will at Lincoln on 5 May 1669, and it was proved in London on 29 July. He died at a house of Sir John Bolles, probably that in Holborn, but possibly Scampton Hall in Lincolnshire; exactly when is not known. Simpson was widely recognized as one of the most accomplished musicians of his generation. Thomas Mace placed him alongside Jenkins and William Lawes at the pinnacle of their profession:

> These three famous men … by their most singular and rare works *they live*; and may so easily be distinguished, the one from the other, and as exactly known, which is which, as if they were present in person, and should speak words. (Mace, 151)

Matthew Locke, the most prominent English composer immediately after the Restoration, praised Simpson as 'a person whose memory is precious among good, and knowing men, for his exemplary life and excellent skill' (Locke, 32). IAN BARTLETT

Sources Simpson family genealogical table, BL, Harley MS 5800 · P. J. Lord, introduction, in C. Simpson, *A compendium of practical musick*, 2nd edn, repr. (1970) · *The life and times of Anthony Wood*, ed. A. Clark, 2, OHS, 21 (1892) · M. Urquart, 'Was Christopher Simpson a Jesuit?', *Chelys*, 21 (1992), 3–26 · M. Urquart, *Sir John St. Barbe, bt of Broadlands* (1983) · L. Hulse, 'Apollo's Whirligig: William Cavendish, duke of Newcastle and his music collection', *Seventeenth Century*, 9 (1994), 213–46 · *New Grove*, 2nd edn · M. Locke, *Observations upon a late book, entituled, 'An essay to the advancement of musick, etc.'* written by Thomas Salmon, M.A. of Trinity College in Oxford (1672) · T. Mace, *Musick's monument, or, A remembrance of the best practical musick, both divine, and civil, that has ever been known, to have been in the world* (1676) · Burney, *Hist. mus.*, vol. 3 · J. Playford, *A brief introduction to the skill of musick*, 2nd edn (1655) · J. Hawkins, *A general history of the science and practice of music*, 5 vols. (1776); new edn, 3 vols. (1875), vol. 2 · T. Campion, *A new way of making foure parts in counterpoint* (1613) · P. Holman, *Four and twenty fiddlers: the violin at the English court* (1993)
Archives BL · Bodl. Oxf. · Henry Watson Library, Manchester · Royal College of Music, London | NL Scot., Panmure MSS
Likenesses attrib. J. Carwarden, oils, *c.*1650, U. Oxf., faculty of music · W. Faithorne, line engraving, BM, NPG; repro. in Simpson, *Compendium* · W. Faithorne the elder, line engraving (after J. Carwarden), BM, NPG; repro. in C. Simpson, *The division-violist* (1659); 2nd edn (1665) [*see illus.*] · C. Grignion, print (after J. Carwarden), repro. in Hawkins, *General history* · line engraving, NPG; repro. in C. Simpson, *The division-violist* (1659)
Wealth at death over £71; two rings; Hunt House at Pickering, Yorkshire; smallholding with cottage: will, PRO, PROB 11/330, sig. 90

Simpson, David (1745–1799), Church of England clergyman and author, was born on 12 October 1745 at Ingleby Arncliffe, near Northallerton, Yorkshire, the son of Ralph Simpson, a farmer. His father expected his son to follow the same occupation, but, according to Simpson's own account, while he was still a boy he heard one evening during family prayers a voice within him calling him to go to be instructed for the ministry. His father, though initially sceptical, eventually gave way and Simpson received a classical education, first from the Revd Mr Dawson of Northallerton and then at Scorton grammar school. He was admitted to St John's College, Cambridge, on 19 June 1765 and graduated BA in 1769 and MA in 1772. Simpson's sense of calling led him to take seriously his preparation for ministry, and early in his university career he visited Theophilus Lindsey, then vicar of Catterick (but later a Unitarian minister), who directed him to a close study of the scriptures. This, together with a terrifying encounter with a highwayman, led him to serious religion, and although at first afraid of being identified as a 'Methodist' he began to associate with a group of evangelical undergraduates, particularly Rowland Hill, who was a member of his own college.

Simpson was ordained deacon in September 1769 and served an initial curacy at Ramsden Bellhouse, Essex. Thereafter, his early career was characterized by a turbulence not untypical of clergymen associated with Methodism. In 1771 he was ordained priest and became curate of Buckingham, but was forced to leave within twelve months because of opposition to his evangelical preaching. In 1772 he moved to Macclesfield at the invitation of Charles Roe, a leading evangelical manufacturer, and became assistant curate at St Michael's Church. In the following year, on 27 May 1773 he married Ann Yaldy, who died after only fifteen months, leaving one daughter, also named Ann. He remarried in October 1776; his new wife was Mrs Elizabeth Davy, with whom he had three children. Simpson's activity at Macclesfield, especially his close friendship with John Wesley, did nothing to decrease his reputation for Methodism and a group of parishioners induced Dr Markham, the bishop of Chester, to deprive him of his curacy. Shortly afterwards he was offered the prime curacy at St Michael's by a friend, who had the right of presentation. However, his opponents continued their protests and at this juncture Roe again intervened, offering to build a new church for Simpson. Christ Church, Macclesfield, was consecrated and Simpson licensed by the new bishop of Chester, Beilby Porteus, in December 1779; he continued as minister there until his death.

Although Simpson was an evangelical Arminian in his theology and associated most naturally with clergy of similar views, he maintained a wide acquaintance among evangelicals and was a regular correspondent of Rowland Hill, Thomas Robinson, and several others with whom he engaged in a concert of prayer. At Macclesfield he combined a regular ministry to a settled congregation with itinerant preaching in the surrounding area. He was a popular preacher and an energetic pastor, who visited regularly throughout his parish, ministered to the legal and medical needs of the poor, and founded friendly societies, charity schools, and Sunday schools. As a consequence, he attracted large congregations and often had six or seven hundred communicants. He was an early pioneer of congregational hymn singing, and a collection of hymns formed one of his earliest publications in 1776. Simpson was a prolific author and published more than thirty works including sermons, tracts, essays, and more substantial volumes of apologetic. Particularly interesting is *A Plea for Religion and the Sacred Writings etc* (1799), which included an appendix announcing his intention to secede from the church, partly because of conscientious objections to the damnatory clauses in the Athanasian creed (although Simpson himself was an orthodox Trinitarian) and partly because of corrupt practices within the church—an issue rendered more urgent by a lively sense of impending divine judgment. Only twelve days before the planned formal announcement of this decision Simpson died at Macclesfield after a brief illness on Easter Sunday, 24 March 1799; his second wife had died eleven days earlier. He was buried on 26 March at Christ Church, Macclesfield. MARK SMITH

Sources J. B. Williams, 'A life of the author', in D. Simpson, *A plea for religion and the sacred writings etc* (1837) · Venn, *Alum. Cant.* · IGI
Archives St John's College, Cambridge, papers
Likenesses J. Collyer, stipple (after J. Russell), NPG · engraving, repro. in D. Simpson, *A key to the prophecies etc* (1801), frontispiece

Simpson, Edward (1578–1651), Church of England clergyman and author, was born at High Cross, Tottenham, Middlesex, on 9 May 1578, the son of Edward Simpson, rector of the parish. He was educated first at Westminster School and then at Trinity College, Cambridge. Admitted in 1596, he was a scholar of the college in 1597 and elected a fellow in 1601, graduating BA the same year and proceeding MA in 1604, BD in 1611, and DD in 1624. Between 1611 and 1614 he acted as chaplain to Sir Moyle Finch of Eastwell, Kent, known for his puritanism and militant antipopery, and on 2 January 1617 was presented by Finch's widow, Lady Elizabeth Finch, to the rectory of Eastling, valued at £129 per annum; he did not resign his fellowship until 1628. On 4 August that year Simpson was collated to the prebend of Corringham in the diocese of Lincoln, and installed by proxy on 13 August. He was married twice, first to a daughter of Sir Richard Barham; of his second wife, nothing at all is known.

In 1636 Simpson issued a chronology of the Christian religion, *Chronicon historiam catholicam complectens*, which appeared in expanded form in 1652. The Leiden edition of 1729 contains a miniature portrait of Simpson, with a white beard and skull-cap, the miniature being born aloft by cherubim and seraphim in a larger scene depicting the banishment of superstition, and the progress of light and learning, during the days of the Christian emperors of Rome. Simpson's biographer Thomas Jones, whose account of his life prefaced the 1652 edition, credited him with other publications, but there is no evidence for this.

Simpson remained at Eastling through the 1640s but at some point after September 1643 replaced the intruded minister, one S. Jemmatt, at Pluckley in the same county. He had resigned by 1649, when he was succeeded by Israel Tonge. Simpson died in 1651 and was buried on 9 June at Eastling. Administration of his estate was granted on 27 June to the guardian of his only child, Jane, who subsequently married Tonge. STEPHEN WRIGHT

Sources T. Jones, preface, in *Chronicon historiam catholicam complectens / Edwardus Simson* (1652); [another edn] (1729) · *Old Westminsters* · *Fasti Angl., 1541–1857*, [Lincoln] · *Walker rev.*, 214, 225 · E. Hasted, *The history and topographical survey of the county of Kent*, 2nd edn, 12 vols. (1797–1801); facs. edn (1972) · Venn, *Alum. Cant.* · Wood, *Ath. Oxon.*, new edn · P. Clark, *English provincial society from the Reformation to the revolution: religion, politics and society in Kent, 1500–1640* (1977), 137, 262, 306 · DNB · STC, 1475–1640 · Wing, STC
Likenesses line engraving (aged seventy-three), BM, NPG; repro. in Simpson, *Chronicon* (1652) · line engraving, NPG · miniature, repro. in Simpson, *Chronicon* (Leiden, 1729), frontispiece

Simpson, Edward [nicknamed Flint Jack] (c.1815–c.1880), archaeological forger and craftsman, was possibly born in the Whitby region of Yorkshire, but nothing is known for certain about his parentage or early life. He went by a variety of aliases, the best known of which was 'Flint Jack'. He also used the name John Wilson. Other nicknames included 'Bones', 'the Old Antiquarian', 'Fossil Willy', 'Cockney Bill', and 'Shirtless'.

Simpson's activities began to be noticed in 1853, when Charles Roach Smith wrote to warn Thomas Bateman of forgers at Whitby. In 1855 and 1857 Bateman received further letters complaining about forgers in the town called John Wilson, alias 'Bones', and Jerry Taylor. These two, particularly 'Bones', sold forgeries of prehistoric flint tools, pottery vessels, and jet seals. During this period Edward Tindall, an antiquary and collector of Bridlington, Yorkshire, formed an archaeological collection which attracted some interest. But when Tindall exhibited this in York at the Yorkshire Museum in 1857 many items were condemned as the product of the forger known as 'Bones', 'Flint Jack', or 'Shirtless'.

Awareness of his activities caused Simpson to leave Yorkshire and roam Britain selling forgeries (his identification with John Wilson, alias 'Bones', is confirmed by works which mention his early association with Jerry Taylor). In 1857 a collector at Blackheath, Surrey, purchased forged archaeological items; twelve years later he saw a photograph of Simpson, whom he identified as the vendor.

Simpson became well known to archaeologists, who called him 'Flint Jack', seldom using any proper name. In 1862 he demonstrated flint-knapping techniques for the Geologists' Association. The following year he visited Salisbury, where he manufactured flint tools for the museum and was photographed at work. He returned to Yorkshire in August 1863 and received a month's imprisonment for petty theft at Bridlington.

In 1866 Simpson was the subject of a long article in the *Malton Messenger*, the newspaper of Malton in Yorkshire, which claimed to use information supplied by the forger himself. Afterwards published in pamphlet form, this has served as the basis of later biographies, but there are difficulties with its chronology. The article claimed that Simpson began making flint tools in 1843 and first left Yorkshire in 1846. This is at variance with his documented activities by ten years. His visit to Salisbury Museum is dated to 1854, but the museum was not founded until 1860.

James Wyatt, a Bedford journalist, described a visit from 'Flint Jack' in his diary in 1867. Shortly afterwards Simpson was arrested for theft and sentenced to a year's imprisonment in Bedford gaol. While he was in prison a financial appeal on his behalf appeared in *The Reliquary*. In 1872 Simpson formed a surprising partnership with Alfred Elliot, a retired policeman, at Stamford. Elliot took Simpson's photograph, which allegedly sold many copies.

Simpson's fame rests on his career as a manufacturer of flint tools. Sometimes he passed these illicitly, at other times he openly made them as replicas. His itinerant life presumably prevented marriage or acquisition of wealth. Those who met Simpson, alias 'Flint Jack', commented on his untidy appearance, and photographs show him badly shaven and wearing torn clothes. Sometimes appearing unintelligent, and clearly lacking formal education, he displayed knowledge of and enthusiasm for prehistoric

archaeology. During his wanderings he looked for genuine flint tools, which he sold or even gave to those who appreciated them.

There is no record of his activities after 1878. It is believed that he died in poverty in a Yorkshire workhouse at about this time. Items made by 'Flint Jack' remain in the museums at Whitby, Hull, Salisbury, and Bedford. The Royal Scottish Museum in Edinburgh possesses tools used by him.   ROBERT HALLIDAY

Sources 'Flint Jack, or, A notice of the life of Edward Simpson', *Malton Messenger* (29 Dec 1866) • Sheffield City Museum, Bateman MSS • E. T. Stevens, *First descriptive catalogue of the Salisbury and South Wiltshire Museum* (1864) • J. Blacking, 'Edward Simpson, alias "Flint Jack"', *Antiquity*, 27 (1953), 207–11 • L. Jewitt, 'Flint Jack: a memoir and an appeal', *The Reliquary*, 8 (1867), 65–76 • H. Cuming, 'A few words on forgeries', *Journal of the British Archaeological Association*, 25 (1869), 389–92 • T. Sheppard, 'Forgeries and counterfeit antiquities', *The Antiquary*, 44 (1908), 209–15, 301–4 • 'An antiquarian at fault, or, The biter bit', *Bridlington Free Press* (29 Aug 1863) • 'Flint Jack again', *Whitby Gazette* (29 June 1872) • 'Flint Jack', *People's Magazine* (6 July 1867) • 'British antiquities', *GM*, 4th ser., 4 (1867), 446–7 • R. Corlass, 'Flint Jack: an east Yorkshire character', *Driffield Observer* (18 May 1878) • J. Wyatt, diary, Beds. & Luton ARS, X567/99

Archives Bedford Museum, items made by Simpson • Hull Museum, items made by Simpson • Royal Scottish Museum, Edinburgh, flint knapping tools used by Simpson • Salisbury Museum, items made by Simpson • Whitby Museum, items made by Simpson

Likenesses F. Treble, photograph, 1863, repro. in Blacking, 'Edward Simpson, alias "Flint Jack"'; copy, Hull Museums • A. Elliot, photograph, 1872, repro. in T. Sheppard, 'Forgeries and counterfeit antiquities'; copy, Hull Museums • engraving (after photograph), repro. in 'Flint Jack', *People's Magazine*, 425; copy Hull Museums

Simpson [*formerly* Sinovitch]**, Esther** [Tess] (1903–1996), worker for refugee scholars, was born Esther Sinovitch on 31 July 1903 at 33 Lower Brunswick Street, Leeds, the youngest child and only daughter of Ilya (later Ellis) Sinovitch (later Simpson), textile worker, and his wife, Sara Liba (later Sarah), née Peravosnick. Esther's parents were late nineteenth-century Jewish immigrants from Shtayochisik, in eastern Lithuania. After attending Leeds Girls' Modern School (1914–20), she won one of the twenty city scholarships to Leeds University in 1921, and graduated with a first-class degree in French and subsidiary German in 1924. She then taught herself the Gregg system of trilingual shorthand for English, French, and German, and became a sought-after secretary-cum-translator-cum-interpreter, working first in Germany and France and then for the International Fellowship of Reconciliation in Vienna and, briefly, for the World Alliance of the YMCA in Geneva. It was her brother, a conscientious objector during the First World War, who first introduced her to the Society of Friends, and she related to all she met, believing and responding in the Quakerly way to that which is of God in every one, ever after.

Appalled by Hitler's wholesale dismissal of Jewish lecturers and professors from German universities Tess Simpson asked Leo Szilard if she could be of use to the Academic Assistance Council recently founded in London by William Beveridge, Maynard Keynes, Gilbert Murray,

Esther Simpson (1903–1996), by unknown photographer

Ernest Rutherford, and others, to help these persecuted scholars. In July 1933 she was appointed assistant secretary—on a third of her previous salary—of the emergency funding centre and international academic labour exchange that the council set up in two small offices of the Royal Society's rooms in Burlington House. This Academic Assistance Council, renamed the Society for the Protection of Science and Learning in 1936, was an organization run by British scholars to rescue other scholars regardless of their race, nationality, political beliefs, or religion. Tess Simpson was to persevere in that endeavour for the next sixty years. When challenged, late in life, about the council's exclusive focus on intellectuals, she replied: 'What was happening [in Germany] … was anti-human and I wanted to do something to mitigate against that … Each [refugee organization] could only do so much but of course I felt terrible about the plight of others' (The Times, 1 July 1992).

At first almost all the refugees were Jews. But after the Nuremberg laws of 1935 German academics could be expelled if they had just one Jewish grandparent or a Jewish wife. Between 1933 and 1940 Tess Simpson became a one-woman reception centre for nearly 2600 refugee intellectuals. They arrived in Britain rejected, nearly destitute, and traumatized by the humiliation and hatred meted out to them by Nazis, and found themselves in a country still suffering massive unemployment, whose popular newspapers were as hostile to Britain's being 'flooded' by foreign asylum seekers as at any other time, before or since. Tess Simpson was almost always the first person to meet each new arrival and she greeted him or her with warm sympathy, high intelligence, and immense practicality, setting them 'on the stairway to survival and success' (Hampstead and Highgate Express, November 1996). Many of these desperate people were eventually to become among the most eminent thinkers in their fields

in the world, but they all started in Britain as Tess Simpson's 'children' for whom she found a new life, often locating work for them in small colleges in the United States or in university colleges in the British Commonwealth, if not at first in Britain.

After the fall of Norway in 1940, the British government, headed by Churchill, panicked about these and other 'enemy aliens' in Britain and decided to intern them all. To her horror Tess Simpson learned that over 500 of 'her' refugee scholars, many of them now doing work of national importance and of course anti-Nazis to a man, were about to be arrested, sent to camps surrounded by barbed wire, and possibly even deported. She made vain protests to the Home Office and had to spend the next year accumulating the most meticulous documentation attesting to the integrity of every single individual case in order to give Professor Archibald Vivian Hill, MP for Cambridge University and vice-president of the executive committee of the society, and Eleanor Rathbone, MP for the Northern Universities, the evidence they required before they could succeed in their joint effort, helped by Bishop George Bell of Chichester, to have all these interned intellectuals released. 'Do you know the story of Bruce and the spider? I am that spider', she later remarked (Cooper, Refugee Scholars, 134).

Tess Simpson continued to work for the Society for the Protection of Science and Learning, often in a voluntary capacity, from the end of the Second World War until her official—but not actual—retirement at the age of seventy-five. She gave help to refugee scholars fleeing Czechoslovakia in 1948, Hungary in 1956, apartheid South Africa after 1960, Czechoslovakia again in 1968, and Poland, Chile, Greece, Brazil, Argentina, Bangladesh, Zambia, Rhodesia, Iraq, Persia, and China—in fact wherever and whenever a brutal regime targeted independent-minded, critical intellectuals. It was said of her phenomenal 'computer' brain that all her refugees and their families lived inside her head and that she was forever working out the right contacts—and possible sources of funding—for each of them that would enable them to survive and fulfil their potential. The list of her refugees from Nazism alone included at least sixteen future Nobel laureates and many other outstanding thinkers and artists (including Karl Popper, Claus Moser, Hans Kornberg, Ernst Gombrich, Nikolaus Pevsner, Marie Jahoda, Geoffrey Elton, Ludwig Guttmann, Otto Deutsch, Max Rostal, Peter Schidlof, and Rudolf Peierls—among many, many others). 'Yours was a truly personal success, the giving of yourself and your friendship unstintingly in a way that literally changed the cultural history of the world' was the tribute to her from Sir Walter Adams, former director of the London School of Economics and general secretary of the Society for the Protection of Science and Learning, in 1966 (Cooper, Refugee Scholars, 235). In addition, between 1944 and 1966, Tess Simpson worked as secretary of the Society for Visiting Scientists, which was in fact a one-woman band, sponsored by the British Council and supported by fellows of the Royal Society.

Small, dynamic, austere in her personal spending, Tess

Simpson lived mostly on bread and cheese, fruit, and vegetables; the luxuries she indulged in were good talk and the playing of music. She was a dedicated and immensely talented violinist and viola player until deafness struck her in her seventies. In 1949 she was given the ordre des Palmes Académiques of the French government; in 1956 she was made an OBE; she received honorary doctorates from the universities of London and Leeds, in 1984 and 1989 respectively; in 1991 she was elected an honorary member of the Royal College of Physicians; and in 1995 Austria gave her the Oesterreichische Ehrenkreuz für Wissenschaft und Kunst. Four years before her death from a heart attack in Hampstead, London, on 19 November 1996 (she said she had too much work to do to go into hospital), the Nobel laureate Max Perutz said of her: 'I cannot think of anyone else with the same combination of warm affection for the individual scholars and iron toughness in the face of officialdom' (report of reception at the Ciba Foundation, 2 July 1992). At her request, her body was donated for medical science.   SYBIL OLDFIELD

Sources R. Cooper, *Refugee scholars: conversations with Tess Simpson* (1992) · *The Times* (1 July 1992) · report of reception at the Ciba Foundation, 2 July 1992 · *The Times* (30 Nov 1996) · *The Independent* (24 Dec 1996) · *Hampstead and Highgate Express* (Nov 1996) · *Jewish Chronicle* (13 Dec 1996) · *Yorkshire Post* (25 Nov 1996) · *Daily Telegraph* (3 Dec 1996) · *The Guardian* (21 Dec 1996) · R. Cooper, *Retrospective sympathetic affection* (1996) · b. cert. · private information (2004) [Dr Vivian Simpson] · *CGPLA Eng. & Wales* (1997)
Archives Bodl. Oxf., MSS · U. Leeds, corresp. and papers | Bodl. Oxf., Society for the Protection of Science and Learning archive | SOUND IWM · U. Leeds, Brotherton L.
Likenesses J. Kramer, portrait, 1929, U. Leeds; repro. in Cooper, *Refugee scholars* · H. Schiff, portrait, 1933, Vienna; repro. in Cooper, *Refugee scholars* · photograph, repro. in *The Times* (1 July 1992) · photograph, News International Syndication, London [see illus.] · photograph, repro. in *Yorkshire Evening Post* (1989)
Wealth at death £587,639: probate, 1997, *CGPLA Eng. & Wales*

Simpson [née Spearing], **Evelyn Mary** (1885–1963), literary scholar, was born on 2 September 1885 at 2 Park Terrace, Cambridge, the daughter of James Spearing, solicitor, and his wife, Fanny Elizabeth, née Clayton. She was educated at the Perse School, Cambridge, where she was remembered as one 'whose learning already created awe in those around her' (*Newnham College Roll Letter*, 1964), and at Newnham College, Cambridge (1905–9), gaining a first in medieval and modern languages in 1908. After teaching at Bedford College, London University (1909–11), in 1911 she became a fellow of Newnham, the title 'fellow' being associated at Newnham at that time specifically with research.

In 1912 Spearing published *The Elizabethan Translations of Seneca's Tragedies* and her work on *Studley's Translations of Seneca's Agamemnon and Medea* appeared in Louvain in 1913. She interrupted her research on Elizabethan drama—the second volume of her endeavours was lost when the Louvain University Press was destroyed—to work as a nurse, first during 1914–15 at a Red Cross hospital in Cambridge for wounded Belgian soldiers and subsequently, from the autumn of 1915, at military hospitals in France. In 1917–18 she worked as a general service superintendent at Eaton Hall Military Hospital, Chester.

It was an act of considerable courage for a pioneering woman university teacher and scholar to interrupt an academic career in Cambridge to work as a voluntary aid detachment (VAD) nurse in the difficult conditions prevailing in France in 1915. In her account of her experiences, *From Cambridge to Camiers under the Red Cross*, published in 1917, Evelyn Spearing shows a profound and tender compassion for the ordinary wounded combatants in her care. In 1918 she was mentioned in dispatches.

Spearing was appointed tutor in English literature at St Hugh's College, Oxford, in 1919. On 16 August 1921 she married the English scholar Percy *Simpson (1865–1962), fellow of Oriel College from 1921 to 1936 and latterly Goldsmiths' reader in English at Oxford University. The following year she became the first woman to be awarded the DPhil degree at Oxford and in 1924 she published a study of the prose works of John Donne based on her doctoral thesis. Her marriage, however, marked the end of her tutorship at St Hugh's but the beginning of a long-standing editorial collaboration, described as 'one of the most remarkable partnerships in the history of scholarship' (*The Times*, 12 Sept 1963). Percy Simpson was some twenty years older than his wife and for many years had been engaged, with C. H. Herford (1853–1931), on the Oxford edition of Jonson's works, the first two volumes of which were to appear in 1925. Following Herford's death Evelyn Simpson worked with her husband on the remaining volumes of text and accompanying commentary, the whole edition of eleven volumes being completed in 1952. The Jonson edition stands as a lasting monument to the Simpsons' meticulous research and editorial skills; it 'remains one of the great editions of its age. Its commentary is a masterpiece of wide, profound, and exact scholarship' (*DNB*).

While the great work on Jonson was nearing completion, Evelyn Simpson's work on Donne's sermons, commissioned by the University of California at Berkeley, though it had been interrupted by research for the Jonson edition, was also taking shape, the first volume appearing in 1953. She too suffered the loss of a co-editor with the death of George Reuben Potter (1895–1954) and continued as sole editor, completing the ten-volume work in some nine years.

Evelyn and Percy Simpson had two children: a son, Edward Spearing Simpson (b. 1923), who died in an accident on Mont Blanc in 1953, and a daughter, Mary, born in 1924. Percy Simpson died at the age of ninety-seven in 1962, and Evelyn's death followed less than a year later; she died, of heart failure following pneumonia, at Sun Court Nursing Home, Sheringham, Norfolk, on 7 September 1963, aged seventy-eight, and was buried at Old Headington cemetery, Oxford.   D. PHILLIPS

Sources *Newnham College Roll Letter* (1964) · *The Times* (12 Sept 1963) · E. Spearing, *From Cambridge to Camiers under the Red Cross* (1917) · *DNB* · *CGPLA Eng. & Wales* (1964)
Wealth at death see probate, 13 Jan 1964, *CGPLA Eng. & Wales* (no value given)

Simpson [née Way; other married name Leach], **Dame Florence Edith Victoria** (1874–1956), controller of Queen

Mary's Army Auxiliary Corps, was born on 9 October 1874, possibly in London, the daughter of Colonel Wilfred Fitzalan Way. Virtually nothing is known about her early years except that her first husband was Captain Henry Edmond Burleigh Leach; they were later divorced. In her role as a military wife she felt compelled to assist the war effort and in 1915 became a prominent member of the Women's Legion. At this time senior military personnel were experiencing a severe shortage of cooks. The inability to ensure that British troops were adequately nourished presented a potential problem for Britain's fighting performance in battle. Lady Londonderry, as president of the Women's Legion, stepped into the breach and offered to provide additional cooks for military service. The first party of Women's Legion military cooks arrived at a convalescent base on 3 August 1915. As a member of this initial party Florence Leach readily accepted responsibility for the staffing of army cookhouses. Such was her organizational ability that she became commandant of the cookery section of the Women's Legion between 1915 and 1917. Furthermore, on the formation of the Women's Army Auxiliary Corps in 1917 she became controller of inspection for this organization and in 1918 was promoted to controller-in-chief. By this time the corps had received royal patronage and was given the new title of Queen Mary's Army Auxiliary Corps. The corps contained approximately 57,000 women.

In recognition of her services Florence was appointed CBE in 1918 and DBE in the new year honours list of 1919. In the aftermath of the First World War senior members of Queen Mary's Army Auxiliary Corps lobbied War Office officials in an attempt to establish a permanent women's service within the British armed forces in peacetime. However, the war cabinet adhered to the 'ten year rule'. This maintained that a future conflict was unlikely to occur for at least a decade, the women's services (with the exception of the military nursing services) consequently being disbanded.

On her retirement from military service in 1920 Florence assisted in the formation of the Queen Mary's Army Auxiliary Corps Old Comrades Association. On 12 January 1922 she married a widower, Edward Percy Simpson (1865–1925), company director, the son of James Simpson, a civil engineer. Florence, as president of the Old Comrades Association, continued her work with the Queen Mary's Army Auxiliary Corps. Following the Second World War this organization of old comrades was renamed the Women's Royal Army Corps Association.

By this stage the War Office had decided to retain a permanent women's service, primarily because of a severe shortage of manpower within the armed forces overall. Florence continued to demonstrate an interest in the lives and welfare of servicewomen, particularly those with whom she had served during the First World War. Described by her good friend Dame Helen Gwynne-Vaughan (the first director of the WRAF) as beautiful, elegant, and charming, Florence was also renowned for her organizational qualities and independence of spirit. In later life she lived with her stepdaughters on Moyeni

Farm, Orange Free State, South Africa. On becoming ill, however, Florence decided to spend her final months at Arlesheim, Switzerland, in a private clinic, the Klinisch-Therapeutisches Institut. She died there on 5 September 1956.

As one of the first military dame commanders Florence Simpson nurtured the spirit of comradeship among those women who had served their country. More significantly, her involvement with the Queen Mary's Army Auxiliary Corps provided a concrete foundation for the countless future generations of women who chose to follow her path.   PENNY STARNS

Sources H. Gwynne-Vaughan, *The Times* (10 Sept 1956) · S. Bidwell, *The Women's Royal Army Corps* (1977) · PRO, WO/222 · PRO, WO/32/12330 · WWW · m. cert. [Edward Percy Simpson] · d. cert. **Archives** NAM, papers

Simpson, Frederick Arthur (1883–1974), historian and eccentric, was born at Caldbeck in Cumberland on 22 November 1883, the second son in the family of two sons and one daughter of William Frederick Simpson, rector of the parish, and his wife, Frances, daughter of Edward Fidler JP, of Standing Stone, Wigton, Cumberland. He was educated at Rossall and at Queen's College, Oxford, where he obtained a third class in classical honour moderations in 1904 and a first in modern history in 1906. He was awarded a research studentship, something which was then a rarity.

When he followed in his father's clerical footsteps in Cumberland, becoming curate of Ambleside from 1909 to 1911, Simpson busied himself writing up his research. It was to yield a four-volume work on Louis Napoleon, sometime emperor of the French. The first volume came out in 1909 as *The Rise of Louis Napoleon* and was extremely well received, for its judicious judgements, fresh information, extracted with extraordinary ingenuity and persistence from the archives, and what was frequently referred to as its lapidary style. The book attracted the attention of a scholar on the way to becoming the best-known historian in the country, G. M. Trevelyan of Trinity College, Cambridge. Simpson himself became a fellow of Trinity in 1911, and remained so until his death sixty-three years later at the age of ninety. From 1915 to 1918 he was a chaplain in the forces.

One further volume of his promised series appeared after a dozen years, *Louis Napoleon and the Recovery of France* (1923). This is, however, the only title Simpson had to show for half a century and more of a scholar's life. The reason was believed to have been a hostile review of his second book, in fact two reviews, the one in the *Times Literary Supplement* being anonymous, both of them by the historian and journalist Philip Guedalla. Work was certainly done towards the later volumes, for a chapter was published in 1962 (*Historical Journal*, 5/2). To all intents and purposes, nevertheless, Simpson's career as a historical writer was over in his fortieth year.

There was an exception, if a five-page article could be said to qualify, in a commentary which he published as a

Frederick Arthur Simpson (1883–1974), by Adrian Savage, 1929

note to the 1943 Rede lecture on G. Lytton Strachey by Sir Max Beerbohm. Simpson caught Strachey cheating in his account of Cardinal H. E. Manning in *Eminent Victorians* (1918). Apart from this, the intellectual activity of this quintessentially donnish, unmarried college figure, who scarcely stirred out of Cambridge, seems to have consisted in the chiselling out of a few sermons. Each of those he did compose he delivered, with electric effect, on many occasions. He was twice select preacher at Oxford, and three times at Cambridge. There were also his required university lectures, and his college supervision attended by generation upon generation of Trinity undergraduates.

Nearly all the rest of his time, for the remainder of his life, was given over to his eccentricities. These developed themselves as he inhabited his college: at the common table in hall, in his rooms in the Great Court, and above all as a walker through Trinity and its neighbours, snipping, clipping, pruning, lopping the leaves, the twigs, and the branches of the trees and bushes. He seemed omnipresent and could be pointed out with satisfaction to the wondering visitor as Snipper Simpson, the college eccentric. His rooms finally contained a glittering array of pruning instruments, from scissors to pole secateurs. His track round the courts and walks could often be traced by the litter of vegetation which he left behind him.

In his earlier years Simpson had made rather bolder excursions into oddity: he owned and had flown for him his own aeroplane of what he would have called a Heath Robinsonian kind. This was piloted by a series of persons who became distinguished aviators, and stories of his flying adventures proliferated. For all the narrowness of his ambit, he was well informed, if sometimes inaccurate in his statements, and could argue with considerable skill even with the most distinguished college guest. He made important and often surprising friends among the hierarchy of the Church of England in spite of the fact that in his later years his belief in the divinity of Jesus seems to have become uncertain. He was undoubtedly popular with undergraduates, to whom he made a number of little benefactions, and showed considerable skill in reconciling the society of fellows to his vagaries, though the long-suffering college servants were naturally the least amenable.

Simpson had the capacity to sustain an attitude and a way of living which were almost entirely anachronistic in his own time, and to attain a degree of eminence in spite of that fact, or even because of it. By the end of his long life—and his reputation was due in no small degree to his longevity—he acted as if he were the last representative of an otherwise extinct race of bachelor don, of Christian priest whose vocation was pulpit eloquence, and of conscious, deliberate eccentric, able to behave in ways which successive cohorts of colleagues and students delighted to make good stories out of.

Nevertheless, Simpson was a man of real gifts as a writer, and as a historian of the early twentieth-century type. If ever a tradition of the haunting of the Great Court at Trinity College, Cambridge, should arise, it must inevitably be the shade of F. A. Simpson which walks in it: a tall, dark, stooped, craggy-faced man in a cloth cap and a dangling grey scarf, in his hand the ghostly glitter of a pair of pruning shears. Simpson died on 6 February 1974 at Cambridge. PETER LASLETT, *rev.*

Sources E. James, 'A last eccentric', *The Listener* (30 Oct 1980) • *Mr. Simpson portrayed*, undated pamphlet repr. from a Trinity College publication • F. A. Simpson, 'A fragment of autobiography', *Trinity Review* (1964) [repr. separately, 1972] • personal knowledge (1986) • private information (1986)
Likenesses J. K. Green, drawing, 1924, Trinity Cam. • A. Savage, pencil drawing, 1929, Trinity Cam. [*see illus.*] • G. Leet, pencil drawing, 1947, Trinity Cam.
Wealth at death £118,006: probate, 8 April 1974, *CGPLA Eng. & Wales*

Simpson, Sir George (1786/7?–1860), governor of the Hudson's Bay Company, was born in the parish of Lochbroom in the Scottish highlands, son of George Simpson. An illegitimate child, he was brought up by his father's family, particularly by his aunt Mary Simpson. After attending the parish school he seems to have gone to London about 1800 where he was found employment by his uncle Geddes Mackenzie Simpson, partner in the London sugar brokers Graham and Simpson. This partnership merged with Wedderburn & Co. in 1812 and, through Andrew Wedderburn, Simpson was brought into contact with the Hudson's Bay Company.

In the first twenty years of the nineteenth century, the Hudson's Bay Company fought a bitter battle with the rival Canadian-based North West Company, a battle which was increasingly inimical to the successful prosecution of trade. Wedderburn—who by now had changed his name to Colville and was on the governing body of the

Hudson's Bay Company—successfully urged the appointment of Simpson as locum governor-in-chief in 1820, hoping that his unemotive business sense and bargaining ability would put the area's trade on a steadier and more rational footing. Surprised by the appointment to a part of the world of which he knew little, Simpson immediately sailed for North America, arriving in Montreal in 1820. He at once began negotiations for an end to hostilities with the North West Company, ever ready to use the expertise and experience of Hudson's Bay officers, and quick to perceive that what was needed was a business accommodation, not a battle treaty in the style of the earlier, rather theatrical, dealings between the two companies. In March 1821 the companies amalgamated: Simpson was appointed one of two governors and, unexpectedly, found himself in charge of the northern department, the more promising of the two areas into which the companies' territories had been divided.

Simpson proved an able if autocratic governor, adept at reconciling officers who had a little earlier been bitter rivals, and shrewd at spotting and rewarding talented fur traders. He was helped by the fact that the fur trade prospered and the men were well rewarded. In 1824 he began the most remarkable of his transcontinental journeys during which he acquired the reputation for keen observation, determination, and great speed of travel. He reached the Pacific Ocean from Hudson Bay in eighty-four days (twenty fewer than the previous record), and, once there, set about plans to expand trade in the face of competition from the Russians and the Americans. His vigour and vision were rewarded in 1839 when he was made governor of both departments of the company. He moved his headquarters from York Factory to Lachine, which was close to Montreal, more accessible from England, and the base for company canoes bound for the west. He continued the rapid journeys across the company's territories, cultivating his reputation for action and enabling him to prepare detailed firsthand reports for the company's London committee on new trading areas and routes.

In 1829 he visited to England to seek a wife, finding one in his cousin Frances Ramsay Simpson (1812/13–1853), daughter of his uncle Geddes; they married on 24 February 1830. Simpson's earlier relationships with several women of mixed European/Amerindian blood had been formalized as marriages, according to local custom, but, unlike other officers in the same position, he treated the liaisons simply as arrangements for his sexual gratification. He cut all contact with his former partners after his marriage, and, although he continued to provide for his several illegitimate children in Britain and Canada, he kept them at a distance from his wife and their five surviving children. The marriage was not very happy: Simpson was far older than his wife and rather autocratic; she found life in Canada isolated and her health suffered, particularly after the death in infancy of one of their children.

Simpson became one of the leading figures of the Montreal business community, using his political and business contacts in the company's interests and to promote his own banking, rail, and mining ventures. His position in the company earned him the nickname the Emperor of the Plains. He was knighted in 1841 in recognition of his services to Arctic exploration after having encouraged the journeys of Thomas Simpson, his nephew, and Peter Warren Dease.

Simpson's position brought him into the world of politics as well as trade. In 1838 he visited St Petersburg and negotiated a treaty by which the Russians leased the Alaskan peninsula to the Hudson's Bay Company. He tried to resist American penetration of the Columbia River territories and helped shape British government policy in the area, although American interests ultimately prevailed. Hoping to observe the situation in the Pacific west and in Alaska, at the same time as realizing a personal ambition, he decided in 1841 to travel round the world, accompanied (because of failing eyesight) by a secretary, Edward Martin Hopkins. Setting out from London in 1841, he reached North America, and then crossed it, riding eleven hours a day to gratify his passion for speed. Travelling up the west coast he decided to rationalize the company's organization by closing all but one of the permanent trading posts. He then pressed on to the Sandwich (later, Hawaiian) Islands, forming the opinion that the company's interests would be best served if they remained independent; an opinion which in 1842 and 1843 he succeeded in persuading the British, French, and Belgian governments to adopt. After a further quick visit to Alaska, he headed for Russia and thence London, where he arrived in October 1842 after a journey remarkable for its speed despite his business engagements *en route*. He continued his voyages almost to the end of his life, finding canoe travel particularly invigorating, but he became increasingly firmly based in Montreal and in 1849, at his request, relinquished the supervision of the Red River territory.

In 1857 Simpson successfully resisted plans that control of Rupert's Land pass from the company to Canada, although this was to happen after his death. By 1859 he was physically weakened and announced his intention to retire. In 1860 he suffered attacks of apoplexy, from which he recovered enough to entertain the prince of Wales, who visited Montreal that summer, before a renewed attack rendered him unconscious and led to his death on 7 September 1860 at Lachine, Montreal. He was buried at Mount Royal cemetery, Montreal, next to his wife. He left over £100,000, principally to his surviving son John Henry Pelly Simpson, with substantial grants to his four legitimate daughters and a tiny annuity to one of his illegitimate children. Ruthless and autocratic at times, he served the interests of the Hudson's Bay Company with great devotion and very considerable business acumen.

ELIZABETH BAIGENT

Sources J. S. Galbraith, 'Simpson, Sir George', *DCB*, vol. 8 • J. S. Galbraith, *The Hudson's Bay Company as an imperial factor, 1821–1869* (1957) • A. S. Morton, *Sir George Simpson* (1944) • *Letters of Sir George Simpson, 1841–1843*, ed. J. Shafer (1908) • *Peace River: a canoe voyage from Hudson's Bay to Pacific, by Sir George Simpson … in 1828; journal of the late chief factor, Archibald McDonald … who accompanied him*, ed. M. McLeod (Rutland, VT, 1971) • G. L. Nute, 'Simpson as banker', *The*

Beaver [Hudson's Bay Company], outfit 286 (1956), 51–2 · A. Simpson, *The life and travels of Thomas Simpson, the Arctic discoverer* (1845) · Hudson's Bay Record Society, vols. 10, 29 [correspondence] · Hudson's Bay Record Society, vol. 30 ['Character Book']
Archives Provincial Archives of Manitoba, Winnipeg, corresp., letter-books, journals, and papers · Provincial Archives of Manitoba, Winnipeg, Hudson's Bay Company archives | Bodl. Oxf., letters to Sir John Crampton
Likenesses Scott, mezzotint (after S. Pearce), NPG · stipple, BM; repro. in G. Simpson, *Narrative of a journey round the world* (1847)
Wealth at death under £20,000: probate, 4 Feb 1864, *CGPLA Eng. & Wales* · over £100,000: total probate value (including Canadian): *DCB*, vol. 8

Simpson, Sir George Clarke (1878–1965), meteorologist, was born in Derby on 2 September 1878, the second son and third of the seven children of Arthur Simpson (1851–1917), a small businessman who became mayor of Derby, and his wife, Alice Lambton (1853–1937), daughter of Thomas William Clarke, a wharfinger of Sutton Bridge, Lincolnshire. He was educated at the diocesan school, Derby, left school at sixteen and entered his father's business, but, inspired by reading popular science in his spare time, joined evening classes to improve his mathematics. He persuaded his father to let him sit the entrance examination for Manchester University, which he passed at the first attempt. In 1897 he entered Dalton Hall and, though he was less well educated than most students, was allowed (with Professor Arthur Schuster's help) to register for the honours physics degree which he passed with first-class honours in 1900. An appointment as tutor in physics without salary but with free board and lodging, and a university scholarship of £50, then gave him financial independence and time for research on the resistance of bismuth to an alternating current in a strong magnetic field on which he published two papers in the *Philosophical Magazine*. Meanwhile he had been accepted by Captain R. F. Scott to join his first Antarctic expedition as a physicist but failed the medical examination for a slight defect which was later corrected by a minor operation.

In 1902 Simpson was awarded an 1851 Exhibition scholarship to study at the Geophysikalisches Institut, Göttingen, where he investigated the problem of the earth's permanent negative charge. He showed that this could not be maintained by absorption of negative ions from the atmosphere as suggested by Julius Elster and H. F. Geitel. Believing that such problems of atmospheric electricity could best be studied in high latitudes, where the large seasonal variations in solar radiation might have greater effect on the ionization of the atmosphere, he spent a year in Lapland where he obtained continuous records of the atmospheric potential gradient and thrice daily measurements of air conductivity and ionization. He thus established the diurnal and seasonal variations.

In 1905 Simpson was appointed lecturer in meteorology in Manchester, the first in any British university, but soon afterwards accepted an appointment in the Indian meteorological office under Gilbert T. Walker and began, in Simla, his lifelong studies of thunderstorm electricity, starting with the electrical charges on raindrops. He found that the charge carried by thunderstorm rain was predominantly positive. He also made the important discovery that large water drops breaking up in a strong vertical air current became positively charged. This, together with P. Lenard's discovery that freely falling water drops broke up if they were more than 6 mm in diameter, led Simpson to the view that large raindrops falling from thunderstorms could disintegrate and generate electric charges and fields strong enough to produce lightning. This theory had to be abandoned when it became clear that it was incompatible with the distribution of electric charge within thunderstorms as deduced from measurements of the electric field by C. T. R. Wilson, and later by Simpson himself using an ingenious, simple, balloon-borne instrument which produced the first measurements within actual thunderclouds. The Simpson drop breaking mechanism may, however, be partly responsible for the subsidiary centre of positive charge present in the base of thunderstorms which appears to trigger (rather than generate) lightning flashes.

In 1909 Captain Scott again invited Simpson to join him on an Antarctic expedition. C. S. Wright and he made a most valuable series of meteorological and electrical measurements, which Simpson published and discussed in three volumes appearing between 1919 and 1923. However, he had to cut short his stay in Antarctica because of Walker's illness in India. He returned to India in 1912 and spent the First World War there, part of the time on secondment to the Indian munitions board.

In 1914 Simpson married Dorothy Jane (*d.* 1978), daughter of Cecil Stephen, a barrister in New South Wales, who was the son of Sir Alfred Stephen and first cousin of Sir Leslie Stephen. They had four children, all of whom achieved distinction in different fields. Simpson was elected to fellowship of the Royal Society in 1915 and appointed CBE in 1919. In 1920 he was invited to succeed Sir William Napier Shaw as director of the British Meteorological Office, and devoted most of his energies during the following eighteen years to building up an efficient unified organization serving the armed forces, civil aviation, and the general public. He now had little time for research but managed to publish three papers on the radiation balance of the earth and atmosphere in 1928–9. Although always interested and active himself, he did not encourage his staff to do original research, and under his leadership the Meteorological Office budget for research remained absurdly low. His contributions to meteorology and the public service were recognized by his appointment as CB in 1926 and KCB in 1935.

After retirement, and on the outbreak of war, Simpson took charge of Kew observatory where he continued his research on the electrical structure of thunderstorms and electrification of precipitation until November 1947. His outstanding work in this and related fields was summarized in two very lucid and stimulating presidential addresses in 1940 and 1941 to the Royal Meteorological Society which had awarded him the Symons gold medal in 1930. Among his other honours were DSc (Manchester, 1906, and Sydney, 1914), honorary LLD (Aberdeen, 1925), and honorary FRSE (1947). He served on the council of the

British Association from 1927 to 1935 and was a corresponding member of many foreign societies.

Although physically fit and agile for his years, Simpson suffered from deafness which made him appear rather remote and forbidding to his subordinates. He did not suffer fools gladly and could be brusque but, during his latter years at Kew observatory, he was kind and considerate to all members of his small staff and much concerned to set them a good example in adapting to wartime living. The last years of his retirement were spent at Westbury-on-Trym. He died at Clifton Court, Clifton, Bristol, after a short illness on 1 January 1965.   B. J. MASON, *rev.*

Sources E. Gold, *Memoirs FRS*, 11 (1965), 157–75 [incl. photograph and bibliography] · private information (1981) · personal knowledge (1981) · *CGPLA Eng. & Wales* (1965)
Archives Scott Polar RI, journal | Nuffield Oxf., corresp. with Lord Cherwell · Scott Polar RI, letters mainly to Arthur Schuster | FILM BFI NFTVA, 'British Antarctic expedition, 1910–1913', 1924
Likenesses H. G. Ponting, photographs, *c.*1911–1912, Scott Polar RI · W. Stoneman, two photographs, 1943–54, NPG · D. G. Lillie, caricature, watercolour, Scott Polar RI · photograph, repro. in Gold, *Memoirs FRS*, facing p. 157 · photographs, RS
Wealth at death £35,399: probate, 4 June 1965, *CGPLA Eng. & Wales*

Simpson, George Walter Gillow (1901–1972), naval officer and sheep farmer, was born on 6 June 1901, the second son of the Revd Robert Henry Bridges Simpson (1862–1935), vicar of Oakwood, Surrey, and his wife, Sophie, née Thomson. He became widely known by his sobriquet, Shrimp, throughout a naval career spanning nearly forty years from cadet to rear-admiral. The nickname was justified by his bare 5 feet and 2 inches; but it did not prepare unknowing challengers for the crackling blue eyes set in craggy features surmounting a sturdy figure—a figure that was liable to sway back on its heels before delivering a pungent comment beginning, good-naturedly enough, 'I say, old chap …'. Simpson attended the Royal Naval College at Osborne and Dartmouth from 1915 for two and a half years before he was promoted midshipman early, with his term-mates, and sent to sea at the age of sixteen in accordance with Admiralty directives for young gentlemen in the First World War.

Simpson was thrilled at the thought of active service, but became disillusioned after arriving in one of the sadistically administered gunrooms of the period to be bullied and beaten as a junior wart. The experience scarred; but it forced Simpson to reflect on the cause of stultifying conditions, unrelieved boredom, and poor morale in generally idle capital ships. It was a situation engendered, in his opinion, by tradition—a word he described as the harlot of vocabulary, and which he resisted thereafter when proposing policies that did not always suit the Whitehall hierarchy. However, while railing against the worst aspects of tradition Simpson ignored the best, which he himself so well exemplified. And, as he proved in his professional autobiography *Periscope View* (1972), the Royal Navy demonstrated superb fighting qualities in the Second World War.

The Submarine Service, more vigorous and less traditional than the surface fleet, was a natural choice for

George Walter Gillow Simpson (1901–1972), by unknown photographer, 1943

Simpson's career: he joined it in 1921, but an anticipated early command was delayed by his studying to become a Russian interpreter and a spell as first lieutenant of the big submarine *Thames* (which required a qualified commanding officer as second in command) followed by a staff course. He commanded *L27* briefly in 1935 and, for some fifteen months from August 1938, the large minelaying and general purpose submarine *Porpoise* where he made a somewhat contentious mark by stressing the effectiveness of torpedo attacks compared (by implication) with big-ship gunnery. However, Simpson's greatest service to the navy was compressed into two strenuous years from January 1941 to January 1943 while he commanded the flotilla of submarines (to become famous as the Fighting Tenth) based on the beleaguered island of Malta.

Malta, in the centre of the Mediterranean and the only British harbour between Gibraltar and Alexandria, had long been crucial to the Royal Navy's strategy; but now the small island, wholly reliant on seaborne supplies for its military and civilian needs, was susceptible to siege by air forces and very difficult to defend. Grand harbour could not safely be used by surface ships, but submarines were able to lie in Marsamxett where the solid old Lazaretto isolation hospital offered protection for personnel and some shelter for submarines alongside. None the less, several submarines were destroyed or damaged by bombing in Maltese harbours; and Simpson sometimes had to order boats to dive by day, albeit jeopardizing maintenance and relaxation between patrols. He noted that pre-war excavation of cave-like pens had been halted for the sake of economy: the entire project would have cost the same as one medium-sized submarine.

Admiral A. B. Cunningham, commander-in-chief, Mediterranean, assigned Simpson the prime task of preventing supplies and reinforcements from Italy reaching axis armies in north Africa. The enemy supply lines could be reached in a day or so by the slow, small U-class submarines which constituted the flotilla proper: temporary visitors of other classes were generally employed further afield. Proximity permitted three or four regulars to be on patrol at any one time; but wartime dangers were exacerbated by confined and revealingly clear waters, a shortage of torpedoes, and increasingly expert enemy countermeasures. Submarine casualties were heavy throughout the Mediterranean. Twenty-three boats were sunk during his time at Malta: twelve had sailed from his flotilla and two were bombed in harbour. But Simpson, with a cheerfully unpretentious brand of leadership and an absurdly small staff, consistently ran the show at peak efficiency despite daunting discouragements. More to the point his tenth flotilla did all that was required of it, and more.

Simpson was relieved by George Phillips in January 1943 and was taking passage in HMS *Welshman* when she was sunk by *U-617*; but he was able to take up an appointment at Londonderry in the battle against U-boats, and he went on to command the cruiser *Birmingham*. He became first naval member and chief of New Zealand navy staff in 1948, flag officer, Germany, in 1951, and he was flag officer, submarines, from 1952 until he retired in 1954. He had married, in 1945, Alison, daughter of Captain L. J. Hall. They had two sons and a daughter. In retirement, with his wife and young family, he took up a new and physically demanding sheep-farming life in New Zealand. He died there on 2 March 1972, at 70 Kiripaka Road, Whangarei, Northland, New Zealand.

Simpson was utterly dependable. In a memorial address Admiral Sammy Woods recalled his strength: 'Looking back ... I am chiefly struck by the man's rock-like stability' (Woods).   RICHARD COMPTON-HALL

Sources Royal Naval Submarine Museum, Gosport, personnel (officers) archival files · W. J. W. Woods, 'memorial service address', general archival files, 1972, Royal Naval Submarine Museum, Gosport · F. W. Lipscomb, *British submarines* (1954) · Royal Naval Submarine Museum, Gosport, submarine (individual) archival files · personal knowledge (2004) · private information (2004) · R. Compton-Hall, *The underwater war, 1939–1945* (1982) · G. W. G. Simpson, *Periscope view: a professional autobiography* (1972) · S. W. Roskill, *The war at sea, 1939–1945*, 3 vols. in 4 (1954–61) · J. Allaway, *Hero of the upholder: the story of Lieutenant Commander M.D. Wanklyn VC DSO* (1991) · A. Marr, *British submarines at war, 1939–1945* (1971) · *WWW* · Venn, *Alum. Cant.*
Archives Royal Naval Submarine Museum, Gosport
Likenesses photograph, 1943, IWM [*see illus.*] · portrait, repro. in Simpson, *Periscope view*

Simpson, James (1781–1853), advocate and author, was born in Edinburgh, the son of William Simpson, minister of the Tron Church, Edinburgh, and his wife, Jean Douglas Balderston. His grandfather James, and great-grandfather John Simpson were also ministers of the Church of Scotland. James was called to the bar in 1801. In early life he was acquainted with Sir Walter Scott, and was among those to whom *Waverley* was submitted for criticism before publication.

In 1815 Simpson visited Waterloo immediately after the defeat of the French, and then proceeded to Paris, at that time in the hands of the allies. In the same year he published a vivid description of the scenes in the neighbourhood of the battlefield, entitled *A Visit to Flanders and the Field of Waterloo* (1815), which rapidly went through nine editions. In 1853 he published an account of his experiences in Paris, under the title *Paris after Waterloo*, which included a tenth edition of his earlier work. His impressions of Paris are interesting, and include some recollections of Sir Walter Scott. In 1823 Simpson was associated with George Combe and his brother in establishing the *Phrenological Journal*, to which he was a constant contributor until it ceased to appear in 1847.

Simpson took a deep interest in the movement for better elementary education. He was one of the founders of the Edinburgh modern infant school, in which he attempted to solve the problem of religious education by allowing parents to select religious instructors themselves. Failing to receive adequate support, however, the school was ultimately sold to the kirk session of New Greyfriars. Simpson continued devoted to the cause of non-sectarian education, and lectured on the subject throughout Britain. In 1837 he appeared as a witness before the House of Commons select committee on education, and his examination lasted seven days. He expressed his views on the need for educational reform in several publications including *The Necessity of Popular Education as a National Object* (1834), and *The Philosophy of Education* (1836). He also wrote *Hints on the Principles of a Constitutional Police* (1822), and *The State of the Representation of Edinburgh in Parliament* (1824). Simpson died on 2 September 1853, at his house, 33 Northumberland Avenue, Edinburgh.

E. I. CARLYLE, *rev.* DOUGLAS BROWN

Sources *The Scotsman* (15 Sept 1853) · *Fasti Scot.*
Archives Bodl. Oxf., letters · Wellcome L., lecture notes | NL Scot., corresp. with George Combe · U. Newcastle, Robinson L., letters to Sir Walter Trevelyan · W. Sussex RO, corresp. with Richard Cobden
Wealth at death £874 4s. 5¾d.: registration, NA Scot., SC 70/1/82/387–93

Simpson, Sir James (1792–1868), army officer, born in Edinburgh, was the son of David Simpson of Teviotbank, Roxburghshire, and his wife, Mary, daughter of John Eliott of Borthwickbrae and grandson of the Revd James Simpson, minister of Wilton, Scotland. Educated at the University of Edinburgh (c.1808–1810), he was commissioned as ensign and lieutenant in the 1st (Grenadier) guards on 3 April 1811. Throughout his career he was the tallest officer in the British army. In 1812 he was sent to Spain, and served there in the 3rd battalion from May 1812 to May 1813. He took part in the defence of Cadiz and relief of Seville, and, joining Wellington's army in the autumn at Salamanca, shared in the retreat from Burgos. He subsequently served with the 2nd battalion in the campaign of 1815, and was severely wounded at Quatre Bras.

Simpson became lieutenant and captain on 25 December 1813, and was made adjutant on 8 February 1821. He was promoted captain and lieutenant-colonel on 28 April 1825, went on half pay soon afterwards, and was made lieutenant-colonel of the 29th regiment on 10 June 1826. He took his regiment to Mauritius, and remained there with it until 1837, when it returned to England. On 28 June

Sir James Simpson (1792–1868), by Roger Fenton, 1855

1838 he became colonel in the army. In 1839 he married Elizabeth, second daughter of Sir Robert Dundas, bt, of Beechwood, Midlothian. She died in 1840.

Simpson exchanged to half pay in 1839, but returned to the command of the 29th in 1842, and took the regiment to Bengal. He was soon appointed to take charge of the Benares division, and in 1845 was sent to Sind to act as second in command to Sir Charles Napier in his operations against the hillmen of Kachhi. He led the column which advanced up the Teyaga to Dera, and, when the whole force had united there, took part in the movements which led to the final submission of the tribes. He was 'an officer peculiarly exact in following his instructions' (Napier, 202).

Simpson returned to England in 1846, went on half pay from the 29th on 8 December, and was made commandant at Chatham. He was promoted major-general on 11 November 1851 and to the command of the south-west district. In February 1855 he was sent out to the Crimea, with the local rank of lieutenant-general, as chief of the staff. The new war minister, Lord Panmure, especially ordered him to report on the standard of the officers in the Eastern Army. He landed at Balaklava on 15 March, and on 26 April he reported that, though he had come out with some degree of prejudice, he found that there was none he would want removed, and did not think a better selection of staff officers could be made.

On Lord Raglan's death on 28 June 1855, Simpson succeeded to the command of the British troops as senior officer, and was confirmed in that post. He was given the rank of lieutenant-general, and of local general, from that date. The feeling in the army was that he was 'a good man,

a long-headed Scotchman', but hardly equal to so great a responsibility. On 8 September the final assault on Sevastopol was delivered by the French on the Malakhov, and by the British on the Redan. The arrangements for the latter were unsatisfactory. Simpson had chosen the second and light divisions, but these contained many raw recruits. The assaulting column of 1000 men, preceded by a covering party of 200 and a ladder party of 320, and followed by an armed working party of 200, reached the Redan, but the men lost all cohesion in their advance, and many in their confusion would not follow their officers inside the work. The first supports, amounting to 1500, joined them, but did not press the attack. Further supports from the remainder of the two divisions and other troops did not come forward. Simpson afterwards wrote that, because the trenches were so crowded after this attack, he was unable to organize a second assault using the highlanders. The French capture of the Malakhov secured the fall of Sevastopol. Pélissier, in his joy, embraced Simpson and kissed him. 'It was a great occasion,' Simpson said, 'and I couldna' resist him.' Simpson was promoted general from 8 September 1855, received the GCB on 16 October, and was given the colonelcy of the 87th regiment.

In October further successes were obtained at Kinburn and Eupatoria, but the main Russian army remained strongly posted to the north of the Chernaya and the harbour. The British government was impatient to see it driven out of the Crimea, but the allied commanders were finding it difficult to agree on concerted action. Simpson determined to resign a command which he had accepted with hesitation and for which he felt ill-equipped. On 10 November 1855 he handed it over to Sir William Codrington. He received the grand cross of the Légion d'honneur and of the military order of Savoy, and the Mejidiye (first class).

Simpson was made colonel of his former regiment, the 29th, instead of the 87th, on 27 July 1863. He passed the rest of his life in retirement, and died at his home at Horringer, near Bury St Edmunds, on 18 April 1868.

E. M. LLOYD, rev. JAMES FALKNER

Sources Army List · The Times (21 April 1868) · Hart's Army List · F. W. Hamilton, The origin and history of the first or grenadier guards, 3 vols. (1874) · S. J. G. Calthorpe, Letters from head-quarters … by a staff officer, 2 vols. (1856) [with illustrations by G. Cadogan]; abridged edn as Cadogan's Crimea (1979) · A. W. Kinglake, The invasion of the Crimea, 8 vols. (1863–87) · H. Tyrrell, The history of the war with Russia, 2 vols. (1855–8) · W. F. P. Napier, History of … Sir Charles Napier's administration of Scinde, and campaign in the Cutchee Hills (1851) · Boase, Mod. Eng. biog.

Archives NA Scot., corresp. with Lord Panmure · NL Scot., corresp. with Sir George Brown

Likenesses R. Fenton, photograph, 1855, NPG [see illus.] · G. Cadogan, pencil sketch, repro. in Cadogan's Crimea (1979), 197 · G. Cadogan, watercolour, repro. in Cadogan's Crimea (1979), 224 · J. W. Hunt, stipple and line engraving (after photograph by R. Fenton), NPG · engraving, repro. in Nolan, Russian war, 2 (1857), 610 · engraving, repro. in ILN, 27 (1845), 426

Wealth at death under £8000 in UK: probate, 6 July 1868, CGPLA Eng. & Wales

Simpson, Sir **James Young,** first baronet (1811–1870), physician and obstetrician, born on 7 June 1811 at Bathgate, Linlithgowshire, was the seventh son and youngest of eight children of the village bakers, David Simpson (1760–1830) and his wife, Mary (d. 1820), daughter of John Jarvey. Both his mother, who was of Huguenot descent, and his father came from families long established as small farmers in east central Scotland.

Simpson's mother died when he was nine and his sister, Mary, played a substantial role in his upbringing. He attended the local parish school, where he was taught by a Mr Taylor, who had a reputation as an exceptional teacher. Simpson was soon identified as a promising scholar and his father and brothers committed themselves to providing him with the financial support necessary for a college education. Simpson enrolled as an arts student at Edinburgh University in 1825, aged fourteen, and began his medical studies two years later. He supplemented the official medical course by attending extramural classes, notably those in surgery offered by Robert Liston. Simpson became a licentiate of the Royal College of Surgeons of Edinburgh in 1830 and graduated MD in 1832. The quality of his MD thesis (on inflammation) attracted the attention of John Thomson, professor of pathology, who appointed Simpson as his assistant. Simpson was elected senior president of the Royal Medical Society of Edinburgh in 1835, in which year he also embarked upon a European tour, visiting the Paris hospitals. In 1836, while teaching pathology, Simpson secured an appointment to the City Lying-in Hospital in Edinburgh and began to practise midwifery on his own behalf. He undertook research into the diseases of the placenta, and in 1839 began to give extramural lectures on obstetrics. Later that same year he was appointed to Edinburgh University's chair of midwifery. From then on his practice grew rapidly, both in obstetrics and in general medicine.

Since his days as a medical student Simpson had been greatly concerned with the problem of surgical pain. Following earlier experiments in the United States, the first trial of ether as a surgical anaesthetic in a major British centre was undertaken by Robert Liston in University College Hospital, London, on 21 December 1846. Simpson was fired with enthusiasm by Liston's success. On 19 January 1847 he tried ether in a labour complicated by a deformation of the pelvis. Immediately convinced of the utility of anaesthesia he enthusiastically advocated its general adoption. He was using ether routinely within his obstetric practice by the end of 1847, employing an inhaler of his own design. Ether, however, had several disadvantages as an anaesthetic, particularly in domiciliary practice, and Simpson sought to find a substitute. David Waldie, chemist to the Liverpool Apothecaries' Company, suggested that the properties of chloroform might be worth investigating. On 4 November 1847 Simpson and his assistants, George Keith and James Matthews Duncan, tried inhaling a sample, probably supplied by the Edinburgh pharmaceutical company Duncan and Flockhart. In a very short time they collapsed, unconscious, dramatically displaying the substance's efficacy as an anaesthetic. Chloroform

was first employed on an obstetric case on 8 November and its first public trial in surgery was successfully undertaken, by Professor James Miller, on 10 November in the Edinburgh Royal Infirmary. On 20 November 1847, a preliminary report was published in *The Lancet.*

As the leading advocate of obstetric anaesthesia Simpson met with much opposition and prejudice. Whereas the incorporation of anaesthesia within operative obstetrical procedures was relatively uncontroversial, Simpson's extension of its use to alleviate the pains of normal labour excited considerable criticism. A number of medical, clerical, and lay commentators took the view that parturition pains were either salutary or divinely sanctioned or both. But Simpson's advocacy prevailed and anaesthesia, generally with chloroform, quickly became standard obstetric practice. However, though in many ways more convenient than ether, chloroform had its own dangers, and there were deaths from overdosage or adverse reactions before safer anaesthetic agents were found. Nevertheless, credit must go to Simpson for establishing that the relief of pain should be central to an obstetrician's professional concerns.

The introduction of chloroform anaesthesia made Simpson internationally famous. He also made a considerable number of other major contributions, including several technical advances in the practice of obstetrics. He improved the technique of version—manual turning of the foetus—in cases of deformed pelvis; he refined the design of the obstetric forceps; and he pioneered the development of the vacuum extractor. Despite his interest in technological aids Simpson's obstetric practice was significantly, and influentially, more patient and less interventionist than that of many of his colleagues. He was a vigorous champion of breastfeeding and understood the importance of what was later termed as 'bonding' between mother and baby.

Simpson's introduction of a better uterine sound and his invention of the sponge tent technique to produce dilation of the cervix greatly improved the scope of gynaecological diagnosis, even if it required the introduction of aseptic methods for the full potential of these innovations to be realized. Simpson encouraged the development of the operation of ovariotomy and of the surgical repair of vaginal fistula. A study on hermaphroditism was a detailed and influential exposition of a complex subject. Simpson believed that the hermaphrodite was the only true representative of a species:

> the natural characters of any species of animal are certainly not to be sought for solely either in the system of the male or in that of the female; but … they are to be found in those properties which are common to both sexes, and which we have seen combined together by nature upon the bodies of an unnatural hermaphrodite, or evolved from the interference of art upon the castrated male or spayed female. (Moscucci, 21)

Simpson's innovation of acupressure, a technique for controlling arterial haemorrhage after surgery by pinning the ends of the damaged vessels against the underlying tissue, failed to attain the success he predicted. Nevertheless, his book on the subject, *Acupressure* (1864), constituted a major study of wound healing and of the effects of the occlusion of blood vessels. Throughout his career, Simpson was a prolific author of clinical and scientific papers, and for a time he was the proprietor and principal editor of the *Monthly Journal of Medical Sciences*.

Some of the most important work of the later part of Simpson's career concerned the complex problems of hospital infection and surgical sepsis. In 1850 Simpson argued that puerperal fever and surgical fever were identical and that both were contagious. He believed that victims of puerperal fever had been 'inoculated with a materia morbi … and this materia morbi is liable to be inoculated by the fingers of the attendant' (J. Y. Simpson, 414), in a manner analogous to smallpox inoculation. This was still an unpopular idea as late as the 1860s. Simpson advocated that the preventive methods which obstetricians had developed against puerperal fever, which principally entailed careful cleansing of hands and instruments, should be adopted by surgeons against wound sepsis.

Simpson also held post-operative surgical infection to be closely related to defects in the design, ventilation, and management of large hospitals, coining the term 'hospitalism' to describe the morbid conditions so caused. He collected a mass of statistical data to substantiate this relationship, noting in particular that the frequency of death after amputation was highest in large hospitals and lowest where the operation had taken place at home or in a cottage hospital. He also remarked upon a similar pattern in puerperal fever, the incidence of which was much higher in large lying-in hospitals. Simpson put forward a number of innovative ideas on hospital design, maintaining that alterations in layout and management, in particular the housing of patients in small isolated units, could improve the hospital environment to such an extent that the incidence of septic disorders would be greatly diminished. He first articulated this position in 1849 and his views were influential upon many later commentators on hospital conditions, including Florence Nightingale.

Despite his support for a theory of contagion, Simpson, like many of his contemporaries, opposed the Listerian reforms and the Pasteurian germ theory of disease. He held that the answer to surgical sepsis lay not in carbolic wound dressings (which in any case were not, as he pointedly noted, original to Lister) but in the improved design and management of hospitals. He also felt that Lister's sterile catgut ligature was an unnecessary innovation since his own invention of acupressure provided, in his opinion, a better and safer means of controlling post-operative bleeding.

Simpson was formidable in debate and controversy. His sustained opposition to homoeopathy, which he regarded as mere quackery and self-delusion, is noteworthy. He was a major advocate of the importance of science for medical education and practice and was closely involved in the mid-century campaign for medical reform legislation. He was also engaged in the medical planning for the Crimean War and was particularly interested in Isambard Kingdom Brunel's prefabricated pavilion hospital, aspects of which coincided with some of his own principles of hospital design. Less creditably perhaps, Simpson played a full and active role in the internecine quarrelling between the professors which was so characteristic of the Edinburgh medical faculty at this time. The mutual antipathy between Simpson and James Syme, professor of clinical surgery, was particularly bitter and long-lasting. Professional rivalry between the two professors occasioned many disputes, springing largely from what Syme perceived as Simpson's encroachments into what should be considered the rightful sphere of the surgeon. Simpson's proposed innovation of acupressure, for example, received withering criticism from Syme.

An inspiring and vigorous personality Simpson was a most successful lecturer and practitioner. He was always ready to attend the poor, often neglecting to collect a fee. Liberal in his social attitudes he advanced the cause of foreign students in Edinburgh and supported the medical education of women. Emily Blackwell, younger sister of Elizabeth, worked for a time as one of his assistants. He was also a supporter of the anti-slavery movement. His Edinburgh house was a meeting place for people from many walks of life, and a hospitable lodging for many medical visitors to the city. He enjoyed conviviality and believed in the health-giving virtues of red wine. He was a devout adherent of the Free Church of Scotland, but would not sign the Westminster confession of faith, because of its literal interpretation of the book of Genesis.

In 1847 Simpson was appointed one of the queen's physicians for Scotland; and he became a foreign associate of the Academy of Medicine, Paris, the members insisting on his election against the appointing commission which had omitted his name. In 1850, at the remarkably young age of thirty-nine, he was elected president of the Royal College of Physicians of Edinburgh. In 1856 he was awarded the Monthyon prize by the French Academy of Sciences, for 'most important benefits done to humanity'. He received the order of St Olaf from the king of Sweden, and was made an honorary member of nearly every major medical society in Europe and America. In 1866 he was awarded an honorary DCL degree by Oxford University, and in the same year he received a baronetcy, the first given to a doctor practising in Scotland. In 1868 he was awarded the freedom of the city of Edinburgh. A man of wide interests Simpson also devoted much time and energy to archaeological and literary studies. He published work on antiquarian subjects, including leprosy and syphilis in fifteenth- and sixteenth-century Scotland. In 1861 he was elected professor of antiquities by the Royal Scottish Academy.

Simpson married, on 26 December 1839, his cousin Jessie (d. 1870), daughter of Walter Grindlay of Liverpool. Five of their nine children died before him. Having suffered from angina pectoris for a few months, Simpson himself died on 6 May 1870 at his house, Strathavan, 52 Queen Street, Edinburgh. He was succeeded in the baronetcy by his son Walter Grindlay (1843–1898). Simpson's family declined the offer of a grave in Westminster Abbey, and he was buried on 13 May in Warriston cemetery, Edinburgh; the city accorded him a public funeral, which was a major civic occasion. His wife survived him by only a few weeks. A statue was erected to him in Princes Street, but the Simpson Memorial Maternity Hospital, built at the expense of his friends, was his principal monument in Edinburgh. He was also honoured by the placing of a bust in Westminster Abbey, on which it is recorded that to Simpson's 'genius and benevolence the world owes the blessings derived from the use of chloroform for the relief of suffering' (*DNB*). MALCOLM NICOLSON

Sources M. Simpson, *Simpson the obstetrician* (1972) · J. A. Shepherd, *Simpson and Syme of Edinburgh* (1969) · J. Duns, *Memoir of Sir James Y. Simpson, bart.* (1875) · E. B. Simpson, *Sir James Young Simpson* (1896) · J. Y. Simpson, 'On the analogy between puerperal fever and surgical fever', *Monthly Journal of Medical Science*, 10 (1850), 414 · *DNB* · O. Moscucci, *The science of woman: gynaecology and gender in England, 1800–1929* (1990) · Burke, *Peerage* (1879) · Burke, *Peerage* (1907)

Archives Duke U., papers · National Library of Medicine, Bethesda, Maryland · NL Scot., corresp.; lecture notes · NRA, priv. coll., casebooks · Royal College of Physicians of Edinburgh, letterbooks, casebooks, and lecture notes · Royal College of Surgeons, Edinburgh, corresp. and papers · Royal Medical Society, Edinburgh, dissertation · U. Edin. L., lecture notes

Likenesses J. Archer, lithograph, 1848, Wellcome L. · J. Watson-Gordon, oils, *c.*1860, U. Edin. · W. Brodie, bronze statue, 1877, West Princes Street Gardens, Edinburgh · W. Brodie, bust, 1879, Westminster Abbey · Bingham, carte-de-visite, NPG · Bingham, photograph, Wellcome L. · Dalziel, woodcut, BM · W. Hole, etching, NPG; repro. in W. Hole, *Quasi Cursores* (1884) · J. Moffat, photograph, Wellcome L. · J. Moffat, photograph, NPG · J. Stevenson Rhind, marble bust (after P. Park), Scot. NPG · J. G. Tunny, photograph, Wellcome L. · photographs, NPG · wood-engraving (after photograph by Bingham), NPG; repro. in *ILN* (24 Feb 1886)

Simpson [*née* Bell], **Jane Cross** (1811–1886), hymn writer, daughter of James Bell, advocate (*d.* 1826), and his wife, Janet (1780–1855), daughter of the Revd James Hamilton of Cathcart parish church, Glasgow, was born in Glasgow on 12 November 1811. Educated by her father, she studied the classics as well as those subjects which were conventionally considered appropriate for middle-class girls of the time. In her youth she travelled extensively in Europe. From 1822 onwards, Bell was assessor and town clerk of Greenock; his daughter contributed frequently to the *Greenock Advertiser* under the pseudonym Gertrude. In 1831 her hymn on prayer, 'Go where the morning shineth', appeared in the *Edinburgh Literary Journal*, then edited by her brother, Henry Glassford *Bell (1803–1874). On 2 July 1837 she married her half-cousin, James Bell Simpson (*d.* 1874), an artist and bibliographer, who was librarian of the Stirling Library, Glasgow, from 1851 to 1860; he published *Literary and Dramatic Sketches* (1872).

Throughout her adult life Jane Simpson's work, in both prose and verse, appeared in various literary and religious journals, including the *Scottish Christian Herald* and *Good Words*. She published several collections of poems, including *Linda, and other Poems* (1879), which ran to three editions. Her most popular hymns appeared in a number of widely used Victorian collections, including Charles Roger's *Lyra Britannica* (1867), James Martineau's *Hymns of Praise and Prayer* (1874), Ebenezer Prout's *Psalmist* (1878), and the *Scottish Evangelical Hymnal* (1878). These hymns, and indeed her writing in general, addressed some characteristic concerns of nineteenth-century protestant evangelical piety: in particular the death of children, but also the bonds of human affection and domesticity, and the beneficence of God as demonstrated in the beauty of creation. Her rather sentimental style and 'improving' tone is typically Victorian; thus Jane Cross Simpson's work is significant as representative of its time and *œuvre*, rather than for any enduring literary or religious value.

After her husband's death Jane Simpson lived with her daughter, successively in Portobello, Midlothian; Newport, Fife; and Aberdeen. She died in Aberdeen on 17 June 1886. She had eight children, but was survived only by two daughters. T. W. BAYNE, *rev.* LESLEY ORR MACDONALD

Sources *Christian Leader* (24 June 1896) · J. Julian, ed., *A dictionary of hymnology*, rev. edn (1907); repr. in 2 vols. (1915), 1058 · D. H. Edwards, *Modern Scottish poets, with biographical and critical notices*, 9 (1886) · *Fasti Scot.*, new edn · Faculty of Advocates list, NA Scot. · private information (1897) · m. cert.

Simpson, John (1614/15–1662), Fifth Monarchist preacher, was baptized on 25 April 1615 at St Dunstan-in-the-East, London, the son of Fabian Sympson, gentleman, of St Dunstan-in-the-East, London. He matriculated at Exeter College, Oxford, on 2 December 1631, graduating BA on 30 April 1635 and proceeding MA on 18 January 1638. From 22 March 1642 he held lectureships at St Dunstan's, and from 29 April at St Botolph, Aldgate, London, and soon became notorious as one of the leading antinomian preachers in the city.

On 9 October 1643 the Commons took away Simpson's lectureship at Aldgate and banned him from preaching. The ban was not lifted until October 1646, but Simpson ignored it. Parliament ordered his arrest in February 1644 after he clashed at Paul's Cross with the presbyterian Cornelius Burges, and he was soon in trouble again for preaching, allegedly, that Christ was to be found even 'in Hogs and Dogs, or Sheep' (Greaves, 101). In 1647 Simpson became pastor of the gathered congregation at All Hallows-the-Great, London, founded by the antinomian Walter Cradock. Invited to preach to the Commons on 13 March 1651, at the suggestion of Major-General Thomas Harrison, he used the occasion to champion lay preaching by soldiers, when inspired by the spirit, and to damn the professional clergy and human learning. His sermon produced uproar in the house, and he was denied the customary vote of thanks. In 1653 he visited some thirty gathered churches on a preaching tour of Essex and East Anglia, in the company of his friend Henry Jessey. He did not, however, withdraw from the public ministry. He remained a frequent lecturer in the parish church of All Hallows, and in March 1652 he was appointed to the sequestered rectory of St Botolph without Bishopsgate.

When Charles II and the Scots invaded England in 1651

the gathered churches raised forces to fight under Harrison against them. Simpson served as a major in this campaign, which culminated in the victory at Worcester. But by then he had already come to doubt whether parliament shared the commitment he felt, with Harrison, to the kingdom of Christ on earth. In December 1651 he joined Christopher Feake in calling a meeting at All Hallows to rally support for the millenarian cause. It was here that the Fifth Monarchist movement was born, with All Hallows its centre and Feake and Simpson its first leaders. Unlike many radicals, Simpson placed no trust in Oliver Cromwell as the instrument of God. He reported visions in which God had revealed to him Cromwell's lust for power and his impending ruin. When Cromwell became protector in December 1653 Simpson and Feake attacked him ferociously at All Hallows. They were arrested in January 1654 and held in Windsor Castle. At first they continued to rail against the regime, but Simpson's ardour had cooled enough by July for the council to order his release, on condition that he did not come within 10 miles of London. In December, flouting the order, he reappeared at All Hallows and denounced Cromwell's church settlement. Summoned before the protector, Simpson boldly accused him to his face of treason, for taking the government upon himself. Cromwell, remarkably, dismissed him with merely a caution, though the appointment at St Botolph without Bishopsgate was formally revoked a few months later.

Simpson's militancy reached a new peak in December 1655, when he denounced the protector at All Hallows as a tyrannical usurper, and allowed the subversive tract *A Word for God* by Vavasor Powell to be read out to the congregation. He promptly went into hiding but was eventually captured. He was soon released, however, and the news spread that he had abruptly reversed his political stance and was now willing to accept the regime; whether prison or Jessey's advice lay behind the change is unclear. This conversion, welcomed by the government, provoked anger among some of his former supporters. When he preached restraint at All Hallows in February 1656 the meeting broke up in confusion. A considerable part of his gathered congregation, already suspicious after his release in 1654, accused him of apostasy, and in 1656, following an acrimonious dispute, seceded to form a new church. In January 1657 he clashed with Feake at All Hallows over his old ally's continued intransigence. He was also involved in a long-running dispute at St Botolph, Aldgate, with Zachary Crofton, its presbyterian minister. In 1657 Crofton tried to bar him from the pulpit as a heretic and troublemaker. Simpson had the backing of an unlikely alliance of radicals and moderates, driven together by Crofton's rigid principles and choleric nature, and Cromwell and the council upheld his claims. The council even suggested resolving the dispute by building a meeting-house next to St Paul's for him and his followers to use.

Simpson's rehabilitation soon went further. In 1658 he was allowed to preach at Bishopsgate once more, as a Sunday lecturer, and in August 1659 the restored Rump, after much dispute and delay, voted to re-install him as rector. But his triumph proved short-lived. He was forced out of the Aldgate lectureship soon after General George Monck arrived in London, and a new rector was appointed at Bishopsgate on 10 August 1660, shortly after the Restoration. The return of monarchy rekindled Simpson's old militancy. In October 1660, at Bishopgate, he boldly defended the regicides, and at All Hallows he repeatedly urged the godly to stand firm. He was arrested in November 1661 but released after taking the oaths of allegiance and supremacy, which aroused further suspicions of apostasy. He died a few months later, and was buried on 27 June 1662. He seems to have had a wife and at least one child, but nothing is known about them.

Simpson's collected sermons set out the antinomian creed he never retracted. In 1660 he defended free grace in two public disputations at All Hallows against John Goodwin, the champion of free will. He later attacked the Quakers. He was generally known as an Anabaptist, but though he ridiculed infant baptism he insisted that adult or believer's baptism was also unnecessary. His gathered church, like Jessey's, allowed members to decide the issue for themselves. He attached no importance to outward forms, condemning the linking of salvation to ordinances or church membership. Many contemporaries were bewildered by Simpson's volatile and passionate nature and thought him mad. Even a funeral sermon, *The Failing and Perishing of Good Men* (1663), which described Simpson as 'a Moses', was apologetic about the controversies which had dogged his erratic career (sig. B2v). But his power as a preacher was widely recognized, and he remained true to his faith in the Holy Spirit as the sole guide for believers.

BERNARD CAPP, *rev.*

Sources Thurloe, *State papers* · H. Hathorn, *The old leaven purged out* (1658) · Z. Crofton, *The vertue and value of baptism* (1663) · J. A. Dodd, 'Troubles in a city parish under the protectorate', *EngHR*, 10 (1895), 41–54 · B. S. Capp, *The Fifth Monarchy Men: a study in seventeenth-century English millenarianism* (1972) · R. L. Greaves, *Saints and rebels: seven nonconformists in Stuart England* (1985), 99–132 · IGI · *The failing and perishing of good men* (1663)

Simpson, John (*b.* 1709/10, *d.* in or after 1766), evangelist and preacher, was the son of Thomas Sympson, and was brought up in Gainsborough, Lincolnshire. Possibly because of the influence of John Wesley, then living in nearby Epworth, he entered Lincoln College, Oxford, aged eighteen, as a servitor in 1728. There he became Wesley's pupil and a member of the Holy Club (the Oxford Methodists). He graduated in 1731, and after ordination obtained a valuable Leicestershire living.

During the 1730s Simpson kept in touch with Wesley, and when the evangelical revival began, he was drawn into it. By November 1739 he was in London, the centre of the revival. He preached in Benjamin Ingham's Yorkshire societies, and in January 1740 visited Ingham's followers in Nottingham. Wesley seems to have left Simpson in charge of his fledgeling Foundery Society, established for his London followers because he disapproved of the doctrine of 'stillness' which was taking hold of the revival's 'headquarters', the Fetter Lane Society. But by April Simpson had himself espoused 'stillness', rejecting the sacraments, and led opposition to Charles Wesley in both societies. The dispute resulted in the Wesleys' withdrawal from the Fetter Lane Society that July.

In November 1740 Simpson, who had by now resigned his living, moved to Ockbrook, Derbyshire, and became leader of the societies established by Ingham's followers there and in Nottingham. In 1741 Simpson's teaching of 'stillness' annoyed the countess of Huntingdon—although she believed he was 'a good man and means well' (undated letter to James Hutton, Moravian Church House, London, AB88.A3.12.1)—and she asked the Fetter Lane Society to recall him. They replied that they had not sent him, but none the less asked him to return, which he declined to do.

By now the Moravians had taken over the Fetter Lane Society. When Simpson visited them in August 1741, they judged him to be 'ehrlich; aber doch eigen' ('honest but peculiar'; London Moravian diary, 12 Aug 1741). They remonstrated with him for going to Ockbrook, acting unilaterally, and fostering error. In April 1742 Moravian opposition to Simpson's planned marriage to an unconverted woman prompted him to repudiate them. Meetings with Lady Huntingdon and the Wesleys ensued, but he stood by his teachings and, though initially thought to have made common cause with the Wesleys, remained independent.

Simpson's support in Ockbrook grew (two houses were built for him), and he visited Nottingham quarterly, but in 1743 several members of his society withdrew after the Moravians, who thought he acted 'like a madman' (Moravian English Conference minutes, 15 Sept 1742, Moravian Church House, London), publicly disowned him for refusing to obey directions. By May only ten remained; thirty of Simpson's former followers requested Moravian supervision in January 1744.

John Wesley's journal entries recording meetings with Simpson display continued affection: 'Whatever he does is in the uprightness of his heart. But he is led into a thousand mistakes by one wrong principle … the making inward impressions his rule of action, and not the written word' (22 June 1742, J. Wesley, 3.26); he was 'the oddest, honestest enthusiast, surely, that ever was upon earth' (28 Nov 1743, ibid., 3.113); this 'original enthusiast … spoke many good things, in a manner peculiar to himself … what pity it is this well-meaning man should ever speak without an interpreter!' (17 Aug 1745, ibid., 3.202). In November 1747 Simpson aroused Wesley's sympathy when he was drawn to London by the offer of a living, but was then asked to stop preaching outside church—a condition to which he could not agree.

Still living and preaching in Ockbrook, in 1748–9 Simpson's repeated drunkenness and the content of his conversations to and about women gave offence. He railed against the Moravians, seeming 'crazy if not fuddled' (Bedford Moravian Labourers' Conference minutes, 1 Jan 1750, Bedfordshire RO, MO.2) when doing so in a Bedford inn. He was in Derby gaol by January 1751, and still there in October 1753. By 1757 he was out of prison, still living in Ockbrook and preaching to five or six people every Sunday. He is last recorded living in Ockbrook in 1766; details of his date and place of death are unknown.

C. J. PODMORE

Sources *The journal of the Rev. John Wesley*, ed. N. Curnock and others, 8 vols. (1909–16) · *The journal of the Rev. Charles Wesley*, ed. T. Jackson, 2 vols. [1849] · J. Simpson, MS letters, Moravian Church House, London, AB102.A3.1–5 · Fetter Lane Daily Helpers' Conference MS minutes, Moravian Church House, London, 15, 25 May, 19 July, 23 Sept 1742; 17 May, 9 Aug 1743 · Ockbrook Congregation MS diary, Ockbrook Moravian Church, Derbyshire, 16 Jan 1751, 24 Oct 1753, 30 June 1757, 6 Nov 1756 · J. Watson, MS letters, Fulneck Moravian Church, Yorkshire, 83a.8,15, 5 Feb, 14 Sept 1748 · London Moravian MS diary, Unitätsarchiv, Herrnhut, Germany, R13.C1.1, 1/12, 2/13 Aug 1741 · MS extract of London and Yorkshire diaries, Unitätsarchiv, Herrnhut, Germany, R13.C1.6, 24 May/14 June 1742 · Fetter Lane Congregation MS diary, Moravian Church House, London, 8/19 Dec 1742 · J. Bennet, MS diary, JRL, Methodist Archives and Research Centre, PLP Diaries, 71, 27 July 1743 · Foster, *Alum. Oxon.*

Archives Moravian Church House, London, MS letters | Moravian Church House, London, Fetter Lane Daily Helpers' Conference minutes; countess of Huntingdon MS letters; Moravian English Conference MS minutes; Fetter Lane Congregation MS minutes

Simpson, John (1746–1812), Presbyterian minister and religious writer, the youngest son of Nathaniel Simpson, dissenting minister, and his wife, Elizabeth, was born at Leicester on 19 March 1746. After attending school at Kibworth, Leicestershire, under John Aikin and at Market Harborough, he entered Warrington Academy in 1760. He was a student there while Joseph Priestley was a tutor, and during this time developed Arian views. In 1765, after finishing his studies at Warrington, he migrated to Glasgow University, where he was a pupil of William Leechman. After leaving Glasgow in 1767 he spent the next five years in private study at his parents' home in Leicester.

In April 1772 Simpson succeeded Thomas Bruckshaw as junior minister of High Pavement Presbyterian Chapel, Nottingham, and became sole minister on the death of John Milne in the following September. In 1774 George Walker (1735–1807) became his colleague, and together they won back a section of the congregation which had seceded in 1760. In August 1777 Simpson moved to Walthamstow, Essex, to assist Hugh Farmer as afternoon preacher, but resigned this office in 1779 and retired from active duty. He moved to Cottingham, near Hull, where he married in 1780 Frances Watson, daughter of Thomas Woodhouse of Gainsborough and widow of a Mr Watson of Cottingham. From there he moved to Little Woodham, near Leeds, and then to Leeds itself. In 1791 he settled at Bath for the remainder of his days.

Simpson lived much among his books and made few friends. One of the few was Joseph Stock, bishop of Waterford, the translator of Job and Isaiah. Simpson published a few sermons and a number of essays. Those on topics of biblical criticism were collected as *Essays on the Language of Scripture* (1806). Of these the most important was 'An essay of the duration of a future state of punishments and rewards' (1803). This argument for universal restoration was commended by Priestley in his last days. Among other publications were *Thoughts on the Novelty, Excellence and Evidence of the Christian Religion* (1798) and *Thoughts on the New Testament Doctrine of Atonement* (1802). A collection of his sermons was published posthumously in 1816.

Simpson died in Bath on 18 August 1812 and was buried on 31 August at Lyncombe Vale, near Bath, in the cemetery belonging to the Bath Unitarian chapel. He was survived by one son, John Woodhouse Simpson of Rearsby, Leicestershire.

ALEXANDER GORDON, rev. M. J. MERCER

Sources C. Surman, index, DWL · J. Murch, *A history of the Presbyterian and General Baptist churches in the west of England* (1835) · G. E. Evans, *Vestiges of protestant dissent* (1897) · Allibone, *Dict.* · [J. Watkins and F. Shoberl], *A biographical dictionary of the living authors of Great Britain and Ireland* (1816) · PRO, PROB 11/1549, fols. 50v–51r

Simpson, John (*bap.* 1782, *d.* 1847), portrait painter, was baptized in Enfield, Middlesex, on 1 September 1782, the son of John and Martha Simpson. In 1800 he enrolled at the Royal Academy Schools, and he was for many years one of Sir Thomas Lawrence's most active assistants, completing several of his unfinished portraits after his death in 1830. Simpson lived and worked in London, where he obtained some success as a portrait painter, and eventually a very large and flourishing practice. From 1807 to his death he was a frequent exhibitor at the London exhibitions, showing 126 works, the vast majority portraits, at the Royal Academy, as well as portraits at the Society of British Artists and figurative subjects including *Rural Amusement* and *Itinerant Musician* at the British Institution. Many notable people of his day sat to him, including William IV (NG Ire.; Brighton Art Gallery; United Service Club, London), Admiral Sir Charles Napier MP (Scot. NPG; Oporto Museum, Portugal; priv. coll.), Captain Frederick Marryat (*c*.1826; NPG), and Sir Herbert Taylor (1833, exh. RA, 1833; NPG); however, a portrait in the National Portrait Gallery of the engraver John Burnet previously attributed to Simpson is now credited to William Simson. His *Head of a Negro* is also in a public collection (Tate Collection).

In 1834 Simpson received a commission to go to Portugal, where he was appointed portrait painter-in-ordinary to Maria II, queen of Portugal, and spent a brief period painting members of the court circle in Lisbon. Simpson was rather a skilful portraitist than an artist. His portraits are not without power, but lack instinct and penetration. Simpson died in London in Carlisle Street, Soho, in 1847. His estate was administered by his son, George. He left two sons, who practised as artists and continued to exhibit from 10 Carlisle Street, Soho, the usual address of their father. Charles Simpson died young in 1848, having contributed several landscapes, coastal, and genre scenes to London exhibitions (1833–47). The other son, Philip Simpson, was a student at the Royal Academy Schools from 1822 and exhibited regularly from 1824 to 1837. He obtained some success for portraits and small domestic subjects, often of children, such as *I Will Fight* (exh. Society of British Artists, 1824, British Institution, 1827; V&A).

L. H. CUST, rev. ERIKA INGHAM

Sources Graves, *RA exhibitors* · Graves, *Brit. Inst.* · J. Johnson, ed., *Works exhibited at the Royal Society of British Artists, 1824–1893, and the New English Art Club, 1888–1917*, 2 vols. (1975) · R. Ormond, *Early Victorian portraits*, 2 vols. (1973) · R. Walker, *National Portrait Gallery: Regency portraits*, 2 vols. (1985) · K. Garlick, ed., *Sir Thomas Lawrence: a complete catalogue of the oil paintings* (1989) · Redgrave, *Artists* · B. Stewart and M. Cutten, *The dictionary of portrait painters in Britain up to 1920* (1997) · Thieme & Becker, *Allgemeines Lexikon* · Bénézit, *Dict.*, 4th edn, vol. 12 · R. Parkinson, ed., *Catalogue of British oil paintings, 1820–1860* (1990) [catalogue of V&A] · S. C. Hutchison, 'The Royal Academy Schools, 1768–1830', *Walpole Society*, 38 (1960–62), 123–91, esp. 160 · administration, PRO, PROB 6/223, fol. 430r

Wealth at death under £300: administration, PRO, PROB 6/223, fol. 430r

Simpson, John Frederick Norman Hampson [*known as* John Hampson] (1901–1955), novelist, was born on 26 March 1901 at 148 Victoria Road, Handsworth, Birmingham, the fifth of eight children born to Mercer Hampson Simpson (1867–1930) and his wife, Kathleen, formerly Leary. The Simpsons were a prosperous and distinguished family, whose wealth was derived from the family brewing business of Moore and Simpson. John's great grandfather and grandfather, both eldest sons who were given the names Mercer Hampson Simpson, were managers of the Theatre Royal in Birmingham; one of his uncles was Jordan Lloyd, professor of surgery at Birmingham University; his brother Jimmy Simpson was a world famous motor cyclist; his brother-in-law was the racing driver Michael McEvoy.

When in 1907 the family brewery business collapsed, they moved to a terraced house in Leicester, where John Simpson's father found work as manager of the Rudge motor cycle depot. John attended a village school in Broughton Astley, but does not appear to have attended secondary school because of recurring ill health. In 1915 he started work in a munitions factory, followed by several years working in hotels and public houses in Nottingham, Liverpool, London, and Derby. A brief career as a book thief ended in Wormwood Scrubs prison. In 1925 he found employment as a nurse and companion to a Birmingham boy with Down's syndrome; he began to use the surname Hampson, moved to the village of Dorridge, near Birmingham, and began writing novels.

No one would publish Hampson's first novel because of the explicit treatment of its author's homosexuality. His second novel, a study in sister-fixation, was an immediate critical and commercial success. Published by the Hogarth Press, *Saturday at The Greyhound* (1931) went through three impressions in five weeks, rapidly selling 3000 copies and winning Hampson wide critical praise. The novel was translated into French and reprinted by Penguin in 1937, when it sold a further 80,000 copies; it was republished in 1950, and again in 1986. Success brought this striking, tiny man friendships with other homosexual writers such as J. R. Ackerley, William Plomer, John Lehmann, and E. M. Forster. He visited Berlin in 1931. Throughout the 1930s Hampson's stories appeared in the most prestigious literary magazines, such as *Life and Letters, New Writing*, and *New Stories*. Several of his stories were also published in limited editions—*The Sight of Blood* (1931), *Two Stories* (1931), and

Man about the House (1935). But success for Hampson was always ice-thin. His second published novel, *O Providence* (1932), was condemned by critics who mistook its experimental narrative for shapelessness, and his dislike of fine writing for a lack of style. After rejecting a novel about a sexual triangle, based on his visit to Berlin, the Hogarth Press dropped him.

In 1933 Hampson met the critic and novelist Walter Allen, who introduced him to other young writers living in Birmingham, such as Louis Macneice, W. H. Auden, and the short-story writers Peter Chamberlain and Leslie Halward. Hampson helped Walter Brierley write the novel which became the best-selling *Means-Test Man* (1935). The critic Edward J. O'Brien called them the 'Birmingham group'.

In October 1933 Hampson returned to Berlin to report the Reichstag fire trial for *New English Weekly*, an experience which made him a convinced anti-Nazi. While he was in Berlin he had an affair with Martha Dodd, daughter of the American ambassador to Germany. In 1936, however, Hampson entered into a marriage of convenience with the Austrian actress Therese Gift (1897–1975). As Therese Giehse she had played Mrs Peachum in *The Threepenny Opera* (Brecht wrote the 'Plum Song' for her). Because of her activities in an anti-Nazi cabaret in Zürich, the German authorities threatened to withdraw her passport. Auden suggested Hampson should marry her and provide her with a British passport, as Auden himself had recently done for Erika Mann. The marriage took place at Solihull register office on 20 May 1936.

Hampson published four more novels in the 1930s, emotionally violent Freudian dramas of suppressed hatreds, repressed desires, emotional and physical abuse. *Strip Jack Naked* (1934) depicted the consequences of a brother-fixation; *Family Curse* (1936) was a portrait of the barely disguised hatreds which hold an English middle-class family together; *The Larches* (1938) was a ruthless analysis of an unhappy father–son relationship. These novels reveal Hampson's interest in narrative technique; *Family Curse* is written from thirteen separate points of view; *The Larches* (written with the novelist L. A. Pavey) uses an intricate chronology; while *Care of the Grand* (1939) employs seven different narrators.

During the Second World War Hampson tried to enlist in the Royal Air Force, but was rejected on medical grounds. He broadcast for the BBC and put his experience of hotel kitchens to good use in *The English at Table* (1944). His remaining years were marked by deteriorating health and critical neglect. In 1948 he visited India, where he met the educational psychologist Ford Thompson. Hampson wrote a documentary study of his work with maladjusted children, but could not find a publisher for it. His last novel, *A Bag of Stones*, was published in 1952, and formed another terrifying study of an addictive, abusive, father–son hatred.

At the age of fifty-four Hampson suffered a heart attack, and was taken into Solihull General Hospital, where he died on 26 December 1955. John Hampson published only seven novels, and his critical reputation had declined long before his early death. But in the 1930s he briefly pioneered a form of intense autobiographical fiction, combining a 'hard-boiled' prose style with experiments in narrative technique. He found in provincial English middle-class family life the materials of Greek tragedy, and confronted his own sexual history in fiction at a time when honesty in such matters was difficult, championing the emotionally disinherited and the weak in a decade dominated by the institutionalized bullying he so hated.

Andy Croft

Sources M. Simpson, 'The novels of John Hampson', MA diss., U. Wales, 1975 · M. Simpson, 'John Hampson: the novelist as prisoner of the self', unpubd essay, [n.d.], priv. coll. · W. Allen, *As I walked down New Grub Street* (1981) · W. Allen, *Tradition and dream* (1964) · W. Plomer, 'Introduction', in J. Hampson, *Saturday night at the Greyhound* (1950) · A. Croft, *Red letter days* (1990) · b. cert. · *CGPLA Eng. & Wales* (1956)
Likenesses photograph, 1933, priv. coll. · G. Herickx, bust
Wealth at death £549 9s. 2d.: probate, 20 Feb 1956, *CGPLA Eng. & Wales*

Simpson, Sir John Hope (1868–1961), civil servant and colonial administrator, was born on 23 July 1868 at 26 Newbie Terrace, Everton, Liverpool, of Scottish descent, the fourth of eleven children and third of seven sons of John Hope Simpson (1830–1909), general manager of the Bank of Liverpool, and his wife, Margaret, daughter of Thomas Swan, a factor to the earl of Crawford and Balcarres. All their children were christened Hope, and Hope Simpson came to be treated as a double-barrelled name. The parents were pious and puritanical Congregationalists who rejected alcohol, dancing, theatre, and gambling.

Indian Civil Service Simpson was educated at Liverpool College—where, he later said, he 'first learnt to work, and also the value of work' (I. H. Simpson, 224)—until sixteen, then at Bonn Gymnasium and in Switzerland and France. In 1887 he passed into the Indian Civil Service (ICS) fourth on the list. Under Benjamin Jowett, Balliol College, Oxford, especially welcomed ICS probationers and many more studied there than at any other college. Simpson attended Balliol (1887–9), where he played in the rugby and association football teams. ICS probationers then had only two years at university, so in 1889 he left without a degree. Later, on long furlough (June 1907 to October 1908), he returned to Balliol, completed his third year, and gained his degree (BA, 1908; MA, 1937).

Simpson joined the ICS in August 1889 and arrived in India in October 1889. Starting as assistant magistrate and collector, he rose through the ICS hierarchy to magistrate and collector, first grade, in 1911. He served in the North-West Provinces and Oudh. On leave he married at the Presbyterian church, Singleton Road, Salford, on 29 September 1900, Mary Jane (known as Quita) Barclay (1870–1939), youngest daughter of Robert Barclay, South America merchant, of Sedgley New Hall, Prestwich, Lancashire, head of the firm of Noton Barclay of Oldham. Educated at Laleham School and Girton College, Cambridge (1895–8), she was the sister of Sir (Robert) Noton Barclay (1872–1957), banker, Liberal MP for the Exchange division of Manchester (1923–4), and lord mayor of Manchester (1929–30). Simpson and his wife had two sons and three daughters. Physically he was a big man, about 6 feet tall and in his prime about 13 stone, 'not one pound of which was surplus fat' (I. H. Simpson, 240). He retained his religious faith learned in childhood, 'a strong anchor throughout his life' (ibid.). Brought up a Congregationalist, he and his wife became low-church, evangelical Anglicans and were subsequently influenced by the Oxford Group (later Moral Rearmament). He was energetic, and his recreations included fishing.

In 1902 Simpson and his family survived a cholera outbreak at Lucknow. He was registrar of rural co-operative credit societies (1904–7), intended by the government of India to protect peasants from rapacious moneylenders, for Simpson a welcome duty. He served in the Central Provinces (1908–13) and was president of the committee on municipal taxation (1908) and district magistrate, Gorakhpur (1909–13). He served in the United Provinces volunteer horse and led their contingent at the 1911 Delhi Durbar. In 1912 he was visited, on their world tour, by Sidney and Beatrice Webb, who were favourably impressed. Beatrice described him as an 'ideal' official, a 'big burly Englishman with his paternal kindly authoritative manner', 'a tall good-looking middle-aged man … a good sportsman, and a Patriarchal Head of his district, speaking various vernaculars with perfect fluency and associating almost exclusively with the natives' (Letters of Sidney and Beatrice Webb, 2.385, 2.383). In 1913 he was made CIE. He was acting chief commissioner of the Andaman and Nicobar islands (1914, 1916), which were then used for penal settlement, and retired from the ICS in 1916, leaving India in December. His ICS paternalism, and especially his concern to protect indigenous cultivators, apparently underlay his later policies for Palestine and Newfoundland.

Liberal MP, Indian immigration, and Greek refugees On retirement Simpson hoped to serve in the armed forces but failed, and became private secretary to the parliamentary secretary of the new Ministry of Labour (1917). Soon after the war ended (November 1918) he resigned. He considered farming in Canada and in 1919 made an extensive tour there, but he eventually chose Somerset instead. In 1920 he bought Blagroves, a mixed farm (about 250 acres) near the village of Oake, which he worked in partnership with his brother Tom. Taunton constituency had long been a safe Conservative seat and early in 1922 had no Liberal organization or candidate. In 1922 he stood as an independent Liberal, improvising his organization, and in the November general election—to his surprise—was elected MP. In the House of Commons he spoke on agricultural and imperial, especially Indian, issues. He held the seat in 1923 but lost it in 1924.

In 1924 Simpson was appointed by the viceroy, Rufus Isaacs, Lord Reading, to chair the Indian colonies committee on Indian immigrants in the empire, especially in Kenya. The government of India favoured the immigrants' interests over those of the indigenous peoples,

and under Simpson the committee functioned as a pro-immigrant pressure group. Although it failed to enable Indians to buy land in the Kenyan 'white highlands', it contributed to defeating the proposed restriction on Indian immigration into east Africa, and Isaacs was pleased. Apparently because of his work on the committee Simpson was knighted in 1925.

In 1925, after his brother Tom died, Simpson sold Blagroves. Through the influence of a retired ICS colleague, Sir John Campbell, from 1926 to 1930 he was vice-president of the Refugee Settlement Commission in Athens, established by the League of Nations to settle Greek refugees after the Graeco-Turkish War (1920–22). He was awarded the grand cordon of the order of the phoenix, and left Greece in December 1930.

Palestine and China In 1929, in Ramsay MacDonald's second Labour government, Sidney Webb, Lord Passfield, was the dominion and colonial secretary and so responsible for Palestine, which was administered by British authorities under a League of Nations mandate. In 1930 he appointed Simpson, whom he had recently visited in Greece, commissioner to report on land settlement in Palestine; he wrote of Simpson, 'we are lucky to get him' (Letters of Sidney and Beatrice Webb, 3.325). On leave from Greece, he visited Palestine in May and June 1930 and gathered information. He wrote, 'there are a larger number of liars per square yard in Palestine than there are even in Greece' (I. H. Simpson, 82) and that Jewish immigration must be restricted 'otherwise the Arabs will either become a landless and discontented proletariat, or they will be forced to emigrate' (ibid., 96). His 'Palestine: report on immigration, land settlement and development' (Parl. papers, 1930–31, 16, Cmd 3686), which appeared in October 1930 and was known as the Hope Simpson report, was the first detailed attempt to assess Palestine's population capacity, and its estimate of the total cultivable land was almost 40 per cent lower than previous estimates. It claimed that under existing conditions there was 'no margin of land available for agricultural settlement by new immigrants' (Palestine, 141) except land held in reserve by Jewish agencies, and that the 'apparently conflicting duties' (ibid., 142) to Arabs and Jews under the League of Nations mandate could be reconciled only by 'an active policy of agricultural development' (ibid., 142) including large-scale irrigation and intensive cultivation. It advocated limiting the area of Jewish settlement and ending the eviction of Arabs.

Simpson expected 'storms of criticism' (I. H. Simpson, 88) and both his report and the accompanying Passfield white paper, incorporating his main proposals, were attacked by Zionists—who alleged his estimate of cultivable land was wrong—but he did not reply publicly. However, under Zionist pressure and persuasion, in 1931 MacDonald—to whom leading Jewish Zionists had an access denied to Palestinians—reverted to a policy more favourable to Zionist settlement. For financial reasons the development scheme was indefinitely postponed, but the report partly caused the 1933 protection of cultivators ordinance to protect tenants from eviction. From 1944

Simpson was involved in controversy over Palestine in *The Times* and elsewhere, favouring the Arabs and criticizing the Zionists. According to his son, 'Palestine he always regarded as his greatest failure' (I. H. Simpson, 116).

Simpson was reportedly considered for the governorship of Kenya, but was not offered it. In June 1931, seeking an appointment, he wrote, 'I need a salary … all our investments are dreadfully deteriorated' (I. H. Simpson, 118). In August 1931 China suffered catastrophic floods in the Yangtse valley, and its government requested an expert from the League of Nations. In 1931 Simpson was appointed director-general of the national flood relief commission. For three years he was the chief planner of measures for relief and prevention, including a series of dykes, partially implemented despite the Kuomintang government—which he described as 'execrable' (I. H. Simpson, 164)—and hostile action by communists, bandits, and Japanese. He was awarded the order of the brilliant jade. He hoped for the commissionership of the free city of Danzig, a League of Nations appointment, but was not offered it, allegedly because of Zionist pressure.

Newfoundland In the post-1929 depression Newfoundland suffered much and faced bankruptcy. So in 1934, with Newfoundland agreement, the United Kingdom took responsibility and installed a commission of government. Simpson offered his services to J. H. Thomas, the dominions secretary, who in 1934 appointed him commissioner for natural resources, comprising fisheries, forests, agriculture, and mines, the country's basic resources. He and his wife went to Newfoundland in February 1934. Based at the government-owned Newfoundland Hotel, St John's, they travelled much. They were shocked at the poverty, deprivation, and previous misgovernment. Simpson wrote that 'the poverty of the island is appalling' (Neary, *White Tie and Decorations*, 36) and that 'the morale of the whole people is dreadful' (I. H. Simpson, 187). He disliked the local commercial élite: 'a reactionary crowd' with 'no interest outside their own profit' (Neary, *Newfoundland*, 60). He wrote that the country's natural resources had 'been given away with both hands and are now largely held by speculators' (I. H. Simpson, 183), and that the woodsmen and fishermen were 'serfs' (Neary, *Newfoundland*, 60). He alleged hyperbolically, 'It is the Congo over again' (ibid., 61).

Apparently imbued with the ideals of ICS paternalism and of pre-war constructive 'new Liberalism' and its land campaign, Simpson claimed 'our main interest is prosperity for the common folk' (I. H. Simpson, 189), and he wanted to provide opportunities for people to help themselves. He was determined on reform: 'Boy, can he hustle!' said one of his secretaries (I. H. Simpson, 183). He and his British fellow commissioner Thomas Lodge dominated the government from 1934 to 1936 and 'tested the limits of the new system' (Neary, *Newfoundland*, 105) but, against the opposition of powerful local vested interests and with inadequate support locally and from the imperial government, their achievements were limited. With a strong regulatory approach, Simpson attempted to rationalize the fishing industry, reducing the personnel involved, and

established the successful Newfoundland fisheries board (1936). He also established the Newfoundland rangers police, encouraged land settlement schemes and tourist facilities, and secured moderate, compromise improvements in education and forestry workers' conditions. In 1934 the logging town Port Hope Simpson, on the Alexis River in Labrador, was named after him. According to his son, this fulfilled his secret ambition to have a place named after him, and of all his honours gave him the greatest pleasure. He resigned, and left in September 1936. In 1937 he was made a KBE.

Back in England, Simpson was active in the Royal Institute of International Affairs and was director of its refugee survey (1937–9), resigning because of ill health. He published *The Refugee Problem* (1939). His wife died of inoperable cancer on 6 November 1939. On 12 February 1941 he married an old friend from his Andaman Island days, Evelyn (Eve) Brookes, widow of his ICS colleague W. H. Brookes and younger twin daughter of J. Forster Hamilton of London. They set up home in her house, 24 Rosebery Avenue, Worthing, Sussex, where he died in his bath from a massive heart attack on 10 April 1961. His son Ian Hope Simpson, a schoolmaster, wrote an unpublished partial biography of his father and in 1989 deposited it with a collection of his parents' papers in the library of Balliol College, Oxford.

ROGER T. STEARN

Sources I. H. Simpson, 'Jack of all trades, an Indian civil servant in retirement: Sir John Hope Simpson', typescript, [n.d.], Balliol Oxf., box. no. JHS 11 · P. Neary, *White tie and decorations: Sir John and Lady Hope Simpson in Newfoundland, 1934–1936* (1996) · *The Times* (12 April 1961) · *WWW*, 1951–60, 1961–70 · Burke, *Peerage* (1939), (1959) · b. cert. · m. cert. · I. Elliott, ed., *The Balliol College register, 1900–1950*, 3rd edn (privately printed, Oxford, 1953) · K. T. Butler and H. I. McMorran, eds., *Girton College register, 1869–1946* (1948) · *WWBMP*, vol. 3 · F. W. S. Craig, *British parliamentary election results, 1918–1949*, rev. edn (1977) · P. Neary, *Newfoundland in the north Atlantic world, 1929–1949* (1988) · *The letters of Sidney and Beatrice Webb*, ed. N. Mackenzie, 2–3 (1978) · *The diary of Beatrice Webb*, ed. N. MacKenzie and J. MacKenzie, 4 vols. (1982–5), vol. 4 · 'Report on immigration, land settlement and development: Palestine', *Parl. papers* (1930–31), 16.459, Cmd 3686 · *Great Britain and Palestine, 1915–1936*, Royal Institute of International Affairs, Information Department Papers, 20 (1937) · T. Segev, *One Palestine, complete: Jews and Arabs under the British mandate* (2000) · R. Symonds, *Oxford and empire: the last lost cause?* (1991) · M. P. Bunton, 'The role of private property in the British administration of Palestine, 1917–1936', DPhil diss., U. Oxf., 1997

Archives NRA, papers

Likenesses W. Stoneman, photograph, 1922, NPG

Wealth at death £29,764 18s.: probate, 28 June 1961, *CGPLA Eng. & Wales*

Simpson, John Palgrave (1807–1887), playwright and novelist, was born in Norwich on 13 June 1807, the second of the four sons of William Simpson, town clerk of the city of Norwich and treasurer of Norfolk, and his wife, Katherine, daughter of William Palgrave of Coltishall. Both parents descended from old families long resident in the county. His younger brother Palgrave (1815?–1891), a mercantile lawyer of Liverpool, was also a skilled musician and author of *The Bandmaster's Guide* and *A Treatise on Harmony*.

John Palgrave Simpson was educated first at home

John Palgrave Simpson (1807–1887), by Henry Wyndham Phillips, *c*.1849

under private tutors, and afterwards at Corpus Christi College, Cambridge, where he was admitted on 22 November 1824. He graduated BA in 1829 and five years later proceeded MA. On leaving the university he declined to take holy orders in the Church of England, despite his parents' wishes, but travelled at leisure about central Europe, residing principally, during the early part of his tour, in Germany. While at Munich, in 1842, Simpson became a Roman Catholic. Pope Gregory XVI, to mark his approval of the step, enrolled him as a knight of St Gregory. Two years later, while Simpson was still abroad, a bank failure involved his father, and he turned to literature for a livelihood. In 1846 he published a novel, *Second Love*, to which were added two minor tales, 'Pauvrette' and 'The Maiden's Chamber'. In 1847 he published *Gisella*, a romantic, melodramatic novel set in Hungary and dedicated to Hermine, Countess Rasoumoffsky, one of his friends. This was followed immediately by *Letters from the Danube*, a detailed and informative account of Hungarian life, based on his experiences in 1846, when he crossed Hungary 'from its western to its eastern boundaries' (vol. 1, p. 5).

In the 1840s Simpson was a contributor to *The Times*, *Blackwood's Magazine*, *Bentley's Miscellany*, and possibly to *Fraser's Magazine*. For the first three of these publications, he wrote, among other things, eye-witness accounts of the 1848 revolution in France, which were later collected in two volumes, *Pictures from Revolutionary Paris* (1849). In the same year he brought out his third novel, *The Lily of Paris, or, The King's Nurse*, a romance set in 1848, relating to Charles VI of France. In his 'presentation' to Charles Langton Massingberd at the beginning of the book, he wrote

that he had followed 'the picturesque and flowery paths of an historical tale' (vol. 1, p. v).

In 1850 Simpson settled permanently in London. He had already distinguished himself as an amateur actor, and had made himself familiar with English dramatic literature. While living in Europe, he had 'articled himself for a term as a pupil of Eugène Scribe, the popular French dramatist' (Coleman, *Players and Playwrights*, 2.167). He now devoted himself to writing plays, and supplied, within five years, four of the London theatres with eight one-act pieces, principally comediettas. He wrote, singly or in collaboration, some sixty plays between 1850 and 1885, including comedies, melodramas, farces, operettas, and extravaganzas. *A Scrap of Paper*, adapted from Victorien Sardou's *Pattes de mouche* (first produced at the St James' Theatre on 22 April 1861), and *Lady Dedlock's Secret*, adapted from Dickens's *Bleak House* (Her Majesty's Opera House, Aberdeen, 3 April 1874), both became stock theatrical pieces. Also held in high regard was *All for her*, written with Herman Merivale and loosely based on the plots of Dickens's *A Tale of Two Cities* and Thackeray's *Henry Esmond* (Mirror Theatre, Holborn, 18 October 1875). But at least one critic held that Simpson had 'a facile pen, more remarkable for neatness and elegance than strength' (Coleman, *Players and Playwrights*, 169). Charles Reade, however, declared that 'dear old Pal's lines are written in water, but his plots are engraved in steel' (Coleman, *Charles Reade*, 271). In 1865 Simpson produced a *Life of Weber*, an abbreviated translation of the German memoir written by the son of the composer. The *Edinburgh Review* considered this version as 'in more respects than one an improvement of the original' (*EdinR*, 421). The last book published by Simpson was his fourth novel, *For Ever and Never* (1884).

Simpson was a popular and striking figure in society. He was bearded and had a swarthy complexion, and habitually wore a cloak and felt hat. He was a long-standing member of the Garrick and Athenaeum clubs, an assiduous attender of first nights, and the secretary of the Dramatic Authors' Society from 1868 to 1887. He was unmarried, but proud of his adopted son, John Clayton, who held him in deep affection. Simpson died at the age of eighty, on 19 August 1887 at his London residence, 9 Alfred Place West, Thurloe Square, South Kensington, London, and was buried on 23 August in St Thomas's cemetery, Fulham.   CHARLES KENT, *rev.* DONALD HAWES

Sources J. Coleman, *Players and playwrights I have known*, 2 vols. (1888) · *The Times* (22 Aug 1887) · *The Times* (24 Aug 1887) · *Annual Register* (1887) · Venn, *Alum. Cant.*, 2/5 · A. Nicoll, *Late nineteenth century drama, 1850–1900*, 2nd edn (1959), vol. 5 of *A history of English drama, 1660–1900* (1952–9) · *Wellesley index*, vols. 1–2, 4 · J. Coleman, *Charles Reade as I knew him* (1903) · *EdinR*, 122 (1865), 396–421 · Boase, *Mod. Eng. biog.* · *CGPLA Eng. & Wales* (1887)

Archives BL, agreements and account with Richard Bentley, Add. MSS 46614–46615, 46651–46652 · BL, letters to Royal Literary Fund, loan 96 · Herts. ALS, letters to Lord Lytton · NL Scot., letters to William Blackwood & Sons

Likenesses H. W. Phillips, oils, *c*.1849, Royal Collection [*see illus.*] · Bean, photograph, repro. in Coleman, *Charles Reade*

Wealth at death £282 13s. 9d.: administration with will, 3 Oct 1887, CGPLA Eng. & Wales

Simpson, Sir John William (1858–1933), architect, was born on 9 August 1858 at Brighton, the eldest son of Thomas Simpson, architect, of Brighton, and his wife, Clara (née Hart). He was the brother of Gilbert Murray Simpson, architect, and the great-grandson of Robert Simpson. He was educated at private schools and was articled to his father in 1875; he subsequently attended the Royal Academy Schools in 1879.

After travelling in France and Belgium, Simpson became an associate of the Royal Institute of British Architects in 1882 and a fellow in 1900. He was elected vice-president twice and was president from 1919 to 1921. He was nominated to represent the institute on the council of the British School at Rome, and held this appointment for sixteen years, being one of the original members under the royal charter. He was associated with a number of overseas schools of architecture: he was president of the Union Franco-Britannique des Architectes (1922–3), and a corresponding member of the Institut de France, the Sociedad Central de Arquitectos, Buenos Aires, and the Centralvereinigung der Architekten, Vienna.

In Britain, Simpson was in partnership with M. P. Manning from 1881 to 1884 and later with E. J. M. Manning and O. M. Ayrton. He held many public appointments, including that of secretary-general of the town planning conference which was held in London in 1910. He specialized in the design of public buildings, and planned (in collaboration): the Grafton Street Hospital, Liverpool; the National Hospital for the Paralysed and Epileptic, Queen Square, London; the Glasgow Art Galleries for the corporation of Glasgow; and the Victoria Institute, Worcester (1896). He was solely responsible for the offices of the crown agents for the colonies at Millbank and for schools as diverse in character as Roedean, (1898–9, 1906, 1908, 1911), Gresham's School, Holt, and West Downs School, Winchester, and for new buildings at Lancing College and Haileybury College. He also undertook the design of several memorials, including: the Queen Victoria memorial at Bradford; the Royal Sussex regiment memorial at Brighton; the Onslow Ford memorial in St John's Wood; and the Cartwright Memorial Hall at Bradford. He is best known for his work at the British Empire Exhibition which was held at Wembley in 1924, where, in collaboration with his partner, Maxwell Ayrton, he was responsible for the general layout, the stadium, and the palaces of industry and engineering.

As architect to the Honourable Society of Lincoln's Inn, Simpson restored the old hall of the inn and in 1928 published *Some Account of the Old Hall of Lincoln's Inn*. His other works include *Essays and Memorials* (1923) and *Paris Rosemary* (1927), and he revised W. H. Ward's *The Architecture of the Renaissance in France* for a second edition (2 vols., 1926), and wrote an introduction to Sir Lawrence Weaver's *Architectural Copyright* (1911). He also published many professional papers on such subjects as the planning of cities and open spaces, and was editor of the periodical the *Book of Book-Plates* (April 1900 – July 1903), which later continued under the title the *Book-Lover's Magazine*. He was appointed KBE in 1924, was a chevalier of the Légion d'honneur, and was awarded the gold medal of the Société des Artistes Français in 1922.

Simpson died, unmarried, at his home at 39 Brookfield, West Hill, Highgate, Middlesex, on 30 March 1933. His body was cremated at Golders Green on 4 April.

W. G. Allen, rev. John Elliott

Sources *The Builder*, 144 (1933), 568, 573 · *The Builder*, 144 (1933), 614 · R. Unwin et al., 'Sir John William Simpson', *RIBA Journal*, 40 (1932–3), 514–15, 517 · *The Times* (1 April 1933) · *Building News* (1906), 46 · biographical file, RIBA BAL · CGPLA Eng. & Wales (1933)
Archives RIBA, drawings collection · RIBA, photographic collection | RIBA, nomination papers
Likenesses portrait, in or before 1906, repro. in *Building News* (1906), 573 · A. S. Cope, oils, 1922, RIBA · W. Stoneman, photograph, 1930, NPG · portrait, in or before 1933, repro. in *The Times* · portrait, in or before 1933, repro. in *The Builder* (7 April 1933), 573 · photograph, RIBA, photographic collection · photograph, NPG
Wealth at death £9564 8s. 8d.: probate, 26 May 1933, CGPLA Eng. & Wales

Simpson, Maxwell (1815–1902), organic chemist, was born on 15 March 1815, the youngest son of Thomas Simpson of Beach Hill near Newry, co. Armagh. His mother's maiden surname was Browne. He attended Dr Henderson's school at Newry, where fellow pupils included the later 'Young Irelanders' John Martin and John Mitchel. Although never drawn to political action himself, Simpson remained on intimate terms with them. In 1832 Simpson entered Trinity College, Dublin, where Charles Lever, the novelist and doctor, advised him to enter the medical profession. He graduated BA in 1837, but left Dublin without a medical degree. On a visit to Paris he heard a lecture by the chemist Jean Baptiste André Dumas, which inspired him to begin the study of chemistry. For two years he worked under Thomas Graham at University College, London. In 1845 he married Mary Martin (d. 1900), the daughter of Samuel Martin of Longhorne, co. Down, and sister of John Martin, who was enthusiastically interested in her husband's work; they had six children.

On his marriage Simpson returned to Dublin where, in 1847, he took the MB in order to qualify as a lecturer in chemistry in the Park Street medical school. Following the closure of the school in 1849 he became lecturer in chemistry in the Peter Street, or 'Original', school of medicine. By then Simpson had come to realize that chemistry ought to be taught in the practical way that was being made famous by Justus Liebig in Germany. In 1851 he was granted three years leave of absence and took his family to Germany to gain further experience of continental teaching methods. He studied initially under Hermann Kolbe in Marburg (where he began a lifelong friendship with the mathematician Thomas Archer Hirst, who became his brother-in-law) and then with Robert Bunsen in Heidelberg, and accomplished his first original chemical work. In 1854 he returned to his duties in Dublin, but in 1856 he resigned his lectureship and again went to the continent, working chiefly with Adolph Wurtz in Paris until 1859.

In 1860 the family took a house in Dublin, where Simpson fitted up a small laboratory in the back kitchen. There he pursued the chemical investigations that gave him an international reputation as an organic chemist. One of his most important achievements was the development of a method of determining the amount of nitrogen in organic compounds that were difficult to burn (*Journal of the Chemical Society*, 6, 1854, 289). He also pioneered methods of synthesis, his major triumph being the synthesis of succinic and other di- and tri-basic acids (*PRS*, 12 1862–3, 236). Much of this work was inspired by Wurtz, whom he revisited in 1867 before resettling in London. He continued with his private researches, living on a private income and fees from examinerships at Woolwich, at Cooper's Hill Engineering College for the Indian Civil Service, and at the Queen's University in Ireland. In 1872, however, he was appointed professor of chemistry at Queen's College, Cork, and held the post until his retirement in 1891. In the absence of any culture of research among colleagues or any stimulus from local chemical industries, he devoted himself entirely to teaching. After his retirement, the Simpsons returned to London where they regularly entertained members of the scientific and artistic communities at 7 Darnley Road, Holland Park Avenue. Simpson died on 26 February 1902 and was buried in Fulham cemetery.

Simpson was elected FRS in 1862 and was a fellow of the Royal University of Ireland from 1882 to 1891. From Trinity College, Dublin, he received the honorary degrees of MD in 1864 and LLD in 1878, and from the Queen's University of Ireland the honorary degree of DSc in 1882. In 1868 he was elected an honorary fellow of the King and Queen's College of Physicians. He became a fellow of the Chemical Society in 1857, and was vice-president from 1872 to 1874. He was president of the chemical section of the British Association when it met in Dublin in 1878. He was a person of wide culture and lively humour, with a kindly and generous personality. He ranks as Ireland's most distinguished organic chemist. **W. H. BROCK**

Sources D. Reilly, 'Contributions of Simpson to aliphatic chemical synthesis', *Chymia*, 4 (1953), 159–70 · H. D., *PRS*, 75 (1905), 175–81 · *JCS*, 81 (1902), 631–5 · *Nature*, 65 (1901–2), 515–16 · C. Mollan, W. Davis, and B. Finucane, eds., *More people and places in Irish science and technology* (1990), 30–31 · T. A. Hirst, journals, Royal Institution of Great Britain, London · *DNB*

Likenesses carte-de-visite, repro. in Reilly, 'Contributions of Simpson to aliphatic chemical synthesis'

Wealth at death £2686 3s. 9d.: probate, 11 April 1902, *CGPLA Eng. & Wales*

Simpson, Nathaniel (1599–1642), writer on arithmetic, born at Skipton in Yorkshire, was probably a member of the Simpson family of Havery Park. He entered Trinity College, Oxford, matriculating on 10 May 1616, and graduating BA on 25 November 1619 and MA on 26 May 1623. In 1630 Simpson became a fellow of the college, and in the following year took the degree of BD. He died, unmarried, probably at Oxford, on 23 October 1642 and was buried in Trinity College chapel. In 1623 he published *Arithmeticae*

compendium, a very brief arithmetic primer, for the students of the college. The only known copy is in the British Library. **E. I. CARLYLE, rev. H. K. HIGTON**

Sources Wood, *Ath. Oxon.* · Foster, *Alum. Oxon.* · *STC, 1475–1640*

Simpson, Percy (1865–1962), literary scholar, was born at Lichfield, Staffordshire, on 1 November 1865, the son of John Simpson, Post Office clerk, and his wife, Emma Gilbert. Bishop Abraham found him as a small boy reading in the cathedral library, lent him books, and coached him, and Simpson won a scholarship at Denstone College. In 1884 he went as a scholar to Selwyn College, Cambridge, where after taking a second in the classical tripos, he received his BA in 1887 and MA in 1891. He returned to teach at his old school until 1895. At Cambridge, and as a classics master, Simpson read widely in Elizabethan literature, particularly in the drama; and as early as 1888 he embarked on what was to become his life's work by beginning to annotate the plays of Ben Jonson. He moved to Wimbledon in 1896 and from 1899 until 1913 taught at St Olave's Grammar School, Southwark, no doubt lured by the library of the British Museum and the chance of contact with other scholars. At this period of his life he was carrying very heavy family responsibilities, and it was not until 1913, when he was forty-eight, that relief from these enabled him to give up schoolmastering and devote himself to scholarship. In that year he accepted an invitation from Charles Canon of the *Oxford Magazine* to go to Oxford to work for the Clarendon Press. As soon as he arrived Sir Walter Raleigh secured his help as a lecturer in the English faculty and in 1914 appointed him as the first librarian of the new English faculty library, a post he held until 1934. On 16 August 1921 Simpson married Evelyn Mary Spearing [see Simpson, Evelyn Mary (1885–1963)], daughter of James Spearing, of Great Shelford, near Cambridge, and Fanny Elizabeth, *née* Clayton. She was a tutor in English literature at St Hugh's College, and a well-known Donne scholar. They had one daughter, named Mary Fleay, and one son, Edward Spearing, who died on a skiing holiday at Mont Blanc in 1953.

Simpson was a fellow of Oriel College from 1921 until 1936; university reader in English textual criticism from 1927 to 1930; and Goldsmiths' reader in English literature from 1930 until his retirement in 1935. He was also a Leverhulme research fellow from 1935 to 1937. He continued to supervise and examine research students for many years, and in 1946, in his eighties, he even returned for a short time to Oriel, of which he had become an honorary fellow in 1943, as a tutor to help with the flood of returned servicemen.

The Clarendon Press invited C. H. Herford (whose notice Simpson contributed to the *Dictionary of National Biography*) to edit Jonson in 1902. In the following year Herford suggested Simpson should be brought in to assist with the text and commentary. At the initial conference at Oxford the junior editor arrived late, having walked from Reading. (To the end of his life Simpson remained addicted to walking, only in his seventies reducing his daily stint from 15 to 10 miles.) The first two volumes, biographical and

Percy Simpson (1865–1962), by unknown photographer

critical, mainly the work of Herford, appeared in 1925, followed by the first two volumes of the text in 1927 and 1932. Before the appearance of the last of these Herford died. From this time what he had affectionately described as Simpson's 'impossible standard of perfection', and increasing years, made progress almost imperceptible, and in 1937 Evelyn Simpson was brought in as third editor. She laid aside her own work on Donne to help her husband marshal into order the vast amount of material he had amassed over a lifetime, and between them they brought the eleven volumes to a conclusion. Although an editor today would handle the presentation of the text differently, it remains one of the great editions of its age.

In two other works Simpson played a notable part in the history of textual scholarship in English. Like all pioneers he lived to see his conclusions questioned; but he was the first to challenge some long-held assumptions. His first and most original work, *Shakespearian Punctuation* (1911), marked a new era in editorial practice. Before its appearance it had been assumed that an editor could disregard the original punctuation of early printed texts as wholly misleading. Simpson set himself to examine Elizabethan punctuation to discover its principles. His first convert was Herbert Grierson, who in 1912 produced his edition of Donne's poems, the first edition in old spelling and with old punctuation. The book is now outmoded, since Simpson assumed that what is now seen as largely compositorial pointing was authorial; but progress has been from the position he established. His other major contribution was his study of *Proof-Reading in the Sixteenth, Seventeenth and Eighteenth Centuries* (1935). Here again, although in details he has been proved wrong, he successfully challenged the assumption that authors in those periods never read proofs.

Percy Simpson was a dedicated scholar, prepared to take endless pains to settle a textual point or elucidate a reference. He weighed lightly the risk of never finishing against the compulsion to aim at perfection. Short, rosy faced, with his blue eyes twinkling behind his spectacles, he loved to give an impression of extreme scholarly ferocity, and recounted with gusto stories of how he had 'floored' some ignoramus. Although severe to the idle and thoughtless, he was endlessly kind and patient with the serious, and delighted in his pupils' later successes. Simpson received honorary degrees from Cambridge and Glasgow and in 1951 became an honorary fellow of his old college, Selwyn.

Except for his epoch-making book *Shakespearian Punctuation*, all Simpson's important work dates from after 1921, when he was fifty-six; and the edition of Jonson was only completed in 1952, when he was eighty-seven, fifty years from its inception. It was only in his last few years that his mental and physical powers failed and he was moved to his daughter's home at 10 Town Close Road, Norwich. He died on 14 November 1962, at 61 Mount Pleasant, Norwich. His widow died the following year.

HELEN GARDNER, *rev.* REBECCA MILLS

Sources life of Percy Simpson, *A list of the published writings of Percy Simpson* (1950), 5–11 · F. C. Roberts, ed., *Obituaries from 'The Times', 1961–1970* (1975), 730–31 · Venn, *Alum. Cant.*, 2/5.518 · *WWW*, 1961–70, 1961–1970 · *The Times* (16 Nov 1962) · H. G., 'Percy Simpson', *Oxford Magazine* (7 Feb 1963), 164–5 · personal knowledge (1981)
Archives U. Oxf., faculty of English language and literature, corresp. and papers | Bodl. Oxf., letters to Bertram Dobell · NL Scot., corresp. with John Dover Wilson
Likenesses P. Horton, drawing, 1952, U. Oxf., English faculty library · photograph, NPG [*see illus.*]
Wealth at death £9184 14s. 5d.: probate, 15 March 1963, *CGPLA Eng. & Wales*

Simpson, Richard (1820–1876), Roman Catholic writer and literary scholar, was born at Beddington, Surrey, on 16 September 1820, the second son of the four children of William Simpson and his wife, Emily Cranmer, through whom the manor of Mitcham, Surrey, came into the Simpson family. He was educated at Merchant Taylors' School and at Oriel College, Oxford, where he graduated BA on 9 February 1843. In 1844 he became vicar of Mitcham, a family living, which he resigned shortly before his conversion to Roman Catholicism on 1 August 1846. Having married his cousin Elizabeth Mary Cranmer on 29 October 1844, he was unable to pursue his clerical vocation in his new communion. He travelled for more than a year on the continent, learning several languages. After settling at Clapham,

Surrey, in 1847, with an inherited income of several hundred pounds, he devoted himself to literary pursuits, particularly archival research in sixteenth-century history. He was also a prolific musical composer.

In 1850 Simpson began to write for *The Rambler*, a Roman Catholic monthly founded by liberal converts, and in 1856 became its assistant editor; in 1858 he was made editor and a proprietor, Sir John Acton being the principal proprietor. From early on in his participation in *The Rambler*, Simpson came into conflict with members of the Roman Catholic hierarchy, who disapproved of a layman's writing on theology, of his fierce insistence on freedom of scholarship and of philosophic speculation, and of his frequent puckish irreverence towards authority. Simpson's deep faith centred on the dogmatic core of Roman Catholicism, leaving him free to apply his mind (and his sense of humour) to all other subjects. With these views, he joined Acton in making *The Rambler* the organ of the liberal Catholic movement in England, opposing the trend towards ultramontanism. The bishops forced his resignation as editor in 1859, replacing him briefly with John Henry Newman and then with Acton; but Simpson remained a proprietor of and major contributor to the magazine. He was an admirer of Newman, who sympathized with his views but disapproved of his tactics. In 1862 the magazine was transformed into the quarterly *Home and Foreign Review*, one of the most distinguished periodicals of its day, praised by Matthew Arnold ('The function of criticism at the present time') for 'so much knowledge, so much play of mind'. The review was denounced by Cardinal Wiseman and Bishop Ullathorne; Simpson replied with a spirited pamphlet, *Bishop Ullathorne and The Rambler* (1862). But the conflict between liberal Catholic principles and the positions taken by church authorities, and eventually by Pope Pius IX himself, forced its conductors to discontinue the review in 1864.

Simpson participated in other ventures of the Acton circle, *The Chronicle* newspaper in 1867–8 and the *North British Review* in 1869–71, both more Gladstonian Liberal than religious. The definition of papal infallibility in 1870 served as the final blow to liberal Catholicism, and Simpson had already diverted his energies elsewhere. He had published numerous studies of recusant history in *The Rambler*, leading to his principal work, *Edmund Campion: a Biography* (1867), long the standard work on the subject. His studies of the Elizabethan period led him to an interest in Shakespearian studies; he was one of the first to advance the theory that Shakespeare was a Roman Catholic. He was elected a member of the committee of the New Shakspere Society in 1874. His most original work in this field was *An Introduction to the Philosophy of Shakespeare's Sonnets* (1868). In 1872 he published the first of a series of editions of Elizabethan dramas with which it was believed that Shakespeare had been connected. After his death the whole appeared as *The School of Shakespeare* (2 vols., 1878).

Simpson was consulted on some minor points when W. E. Gladstone was preparing his tract *Vaticanism* late in 1874, but the statement in the *Dictionary of National Biography* that Simpson 'was constantly at his side' is wrong.

Simpson had already made his own adjustment to a minimalist acceptance of the dogma of papal infallibility. Simpson died of cancer on 5 April 1876 at Villa Sciarra, Rome; he was buried in Rome. JOSEF L. ALTHOLZ

Sources D. McElrath, *Richard Simpson, 1820–1876* (1972) · J. L. Altholz, *The liberal Catholic movement in England: the 'Rambler' and its contributors, 1848–1864* [1962] · *The correspondence of Lord Acton and Richard Simpson*, ed. J. L. Altholz, D. McElrath, and J. C. Holland, 3 vols. (1971–5) · M. Arnold, *Essays in criticism* (1865) · Gladstone, *Diaries*
Archives Downside Abbey, near Bath, corresp. and papers · Mitcham Public Library | Birmingham Oratory, Newman MSS · CUL, letters to Lord Acton · Jesuit Archives, Brussels, Belgium, letters to Victor de Buck · Shrops. RRC, letters to Lord Acton
Wealth at death £8000: probate, 9 June 1876, *CGPLA Eng. & Wales*

Simpson, Robert (1792/1795–1867), minister of the United Presbyterian church and writer, was born in Edinburgh. Authorities differ on the year of his birth but give it as either 1792 or 1795. Details of his parentage remain obscure, and he apparently never spoke about it. At an early age he went to live with his grandparents in the parish of Stobo, Peeblesshire, where he attended the parish school. He went on to study at Edinburgh University with the intention of entering the ministry of the Church of Scotland, but while there his views changed, and he determined to become a Secession minister. To that end he entered the Divinity Hall at Selkirk under Dr George Lawson in 1814. He was ordained as the first minister of a newly established congregation at Sanquhar, Dumfriesshire, in May 1820. At the time of his call to Sanquhar he was also sought by a congregation in Duns, Berwickshire, and Simpson would have preferred the latter charge. However, the synod directed him to Sanquhar, and he remained there for the next forty-seven years.

Sanquhar had occupied a special position in what had been the heartland of the seventeenth-century covenanting movement. The region, and its turbulent history, became an all-absorbing interest for Simpson. Of his books, *Traditions of the Covenanters* (1843), *History of Sanquhar* (1853), and *Martyrland* (1861) all went to further editions, and the popularity of his work outlived him. During an active ministry he also wrote for religious periodicals and took a keen interest in temperance work. He enjoyed a reputation as a good preacher and a popular minister, and was known widely as simply 'the doctor'.

Simpson married Jean (d. 1879), daughter of Robert Faulds, a banker and manufacturer in Beith. They had two daughters and four sons who predeceased them. Another daughter, Jane, outlived them. In 1853 Simpson was awarded the degree of DD by Princeton University. He died suddenly at Sanquhar on 8 July 1867 and was buried there; a granite obelisk to his memory was erected in front of the North United Presbyterian church at Sanquhar. LIONEL ALEXANDER RITCHIE

Sources M. N. Goold, *United Presbyterian Magazine*, new ser., 11 (1867), 425–7 · R. Small, *History of the congregations of the United Presbyterian church from 1733 to 1900*, 1 (1904), 246–7 · W. Mackelvie, *Annals and statistics of the United Presbyterian church*, ed. W. Blair and D. Young (1873), 149 · T. Wilson, *Memorials of Sanquhar kirkyard*

(1912), 146–50 • J. Brown, *The history of Sanquhar* (1891) • J. M. Porteous, *God's treasure-house in Scotland* (1876), 208
Likenesses photograph, repro. in Wilson, *Memorials*, facing p. 146
Wealth at death £1288 15s. 9d.: inventory, 27 Aug 1867, NA Scot., SC 15/41/13/965

Simpson, Robert Wilfred Levick (1921–1997), composer and radio producer, was born on 2 March 1921 in Leamington Spa, Warwickshire, the son of Robert Warren Simpson, of Scottish descent, and his wife, Helena Hendrika, *née* Govaars, of Dutch descent. Both parents worked for the Salvation Army. His parents intended him for a medical career (Sir James Simpson, the pioneer in the use of anaesthetics, was a forebear), for which he studied in London for two years, but a chance hearing of Beethoven's 'Pastoral' symphony at a BBC Promenade Concert made him wish to become a composer. Owing to the strong Salvation Army influence, he became a cornet and trumpet player, and performed in brass bands. He was educated at Westminster City School, London, then studied composition privately with Herbert Howells in London (1941–4). Although pugnacious in manner, he was a confirmed pacifist, and when the Second World War started he became a conscientious objector, and served in an ARP mobile surgical unit. On 26 April 1946 he married Bessie Fraser (1910/11–1981), daughter of Seymour Fraser, builder. There were no children of the marriage.

After the war, with Donald Mitchell and fellow composer Harold Truscott, Simpson founded the Exploratory Concert Society in London to perform music they believed was undeservedly neglected. He shared with Truscott an enthusiasm for the music of Carl Nielsen, Havergal Brian, and Anton Bruckner, and this led to a gradual revival of their music worldwide. As a brass player Simpson knew nothing of the difficult art of writing for piano, and it was Truscott who assisted him with this for his early piano work *Variations and Finale on a Theme of Haydn* (1948), dedicated to Truscott. It was a seminal work of great distinction; its theme must have haunted Simpson, as it became the basis for the thirty-two palindromic variations and fugue which formed his hour-long string quartet no. 9 (1982). Simpson destroyed four of his early symphonies; the fifth became his symphony no. 1, which he presented for his successful DMus degree at Durham University in 1951. It was later recorded under the auspices of the British Council.

Two other landmarks in 1951 were Simpson's first string quartet and his joining the BBC as a music producer. Within two years he had become second in command of the Third Programme's music section. This was a golden opportunity to make Nielsen and Bruckner better known and more frequently performed. It was largely due to Simpson that both composers were accepted into the standard repertory. Simpson also made important contributions as a writer with his *Carl Nielsen, Symphonist* (1952, revised 1979), *Bruckner and the Symphony* (1960), and *Sibelius and Nielsen* (1965). *The Essence of Bruckner* (1966) was a work of great insight, as was the shorter BBC music guide *The Beethoven Symphonies* (1970). During the musicians' strike of

Robert Wilfred Levick Simpson (1921–1997), by Suzie E. Maeder

1980, when the Proms were cancelled, he resigned from the BBC, publishing a polemic, *The Proms and Natural Justice* (1981), in which he deplored the fact that one director's individual preferences should influence the Proms programme year after year.

The nucleus of Simpson's *œuvre* consists of eleven symphonies, fifteen string quartets, concertos for piano, violin, cello, and flute, some highly effective brass band works (often played in competitions), two choral works (both of great beauty), as well as piano and organ works. Beethoven's influence is felt in a number of chamber works written for imaginative, classical combinations, such as the quintet for clarinet and string quartet (1968), the quartet for horn, violin, cello, and piano (1981), and the quartet for clarinet, bass clarinet, and string trio (also 1981).

Simpson's first wife died in 1981 and on 2 August 1982 he married Angela Mary Musgrave (*b.* 1933), BBC assistant producer, and daughter of Percy Eric Musgrave, army paymaster and subsequently company director. In 1986 the couple moved to Tralee Bay, co. Kerry, Ireland. In 1991 Simpson suffered a severe stroke on a flight home from a lecture tour in England. He remained mentally alert, but new compositions proved impossible, although he managed to complete his second string quintet through dictation (1994); a double concerto for violin, piano, and orchestra was among the manuscripts found after his death, which took place on 21 November 1997 at his home, Síocháin, Killelton, near Camp, Tralee, co. Kerry. There was no funeral: typically for a man of his integrity and humanity, Simpson donated his body to the medical science unit at the University of Cork. He was survived by his second wife. A memorial concert was held on 19 September 1998 at St John's, Smith Square, London.

RICHARD STOKER

Sources L. Pike, *Contemporary composers* (1990) · *Professional Composer* [Association of Professional Composers newsletter] (winter 1997–8) · *New Grove* · *The Times* (22 Nov 1997) · M. Anderson, *The Independent* (24 Nov 1997) · C. MacDonald, *The Guardian* (24 Nov 1997) · *Composer*, 52 (1974), 35 · R. Stoker, *Open window—open door* (1985) · *WW* · L. Ronald, ed., *Who's who in music* (1935) · *Who's who in music*, 3rd edn (1950) · Grove, *Dict. mus.* · J. O. Ward, ed., *The concise Oxford dictionary of music*, 2nd edn (1964) · *Cambridge biographical dictionary* (1998) · *Chambers biographical dictionary* (1998) · A. Jacob, ed., *The Music Yearbook, 1972–3* (1972) · *Handbook and register of members, 1974–5*, Incorporated Society of Musicians, London (1974) · D. Mitchell, *Donald Mitchell on Benjamin Britten* (1978) · personal knowledge (2004) · private information (2004) [A. Jackson, A. Musgrave] · m. certs.

Archives Royal Holloway College, Egham, Surrey, Robert Simpson Society archive | British Music Information Centre, London | FILM 'Carl Nielsen: A Life in Six Symphonies', with Simon Rattle and the CBSO, BBC video cassette | SOUND BBC Gram Library, Broadcasting House, London W1 · BL NSA · British Music Information Centre, London W1, recordings of Simpson's music

Likenesses T. Dorrell, portrait, Liverpool Philharmonic Hall · K. Jones, portrait, priv. coll. · S. E. Maeder, photograph, News International Syndication, London [*see illus.*] · photograph, repro. in *The Times* · photograph, repro. in *The Independent* · photograph, repro. in *The Guardian* · photographs, A. Lengnick & Co., music publishers, London

Simpson, Samuel Leonard (1900–1983). *See under* Simpson family (*per.* 1894–1990).

Simpson, Sidrach (*c.*1600–1655), Independent minister, was born in Lincolnshire, perhaps at Boston; his parents' names are unknown, but he had at least two brothers—Joshua (later of Boston) and Robert (later of Bristol). He was admitted sizar at Emmanuel College, Cambridge, in 1616, but migrated the following year to Queens' College, where he graduated BA in 1622 and proceeded MA in 1625. Ordained in 1623, he seems to have first served as preacher at Black Notley in Essex. He became curate and lecturer at St Margaret's, New Fish Street Hill, London, in 1629. In 1635, he was convened, along with John Stoughton and John Goodwin, before the bishop of London for breach of the canons of the church, but upon 'their promised amendment and submission to the Church in all things' (*Works of … William Laud*, 5.333) Bishop Juxon took no further action against them. However, Simpson decided to leave his living in London and went into exile in the Netherlands either in late 1637 or early 1638. There he renounced his English ordination and joined at Rotterdam an independent English church with John Ward as pastor and William Bridge as teacher. Discord soon arose between him and Bridge over the issue of prophesying; consequently Simpson withdrew and erected a new church with himself as pastor. In his later answers to the charge of schism Simpson maintained that he had not gathered a church against a church and that the place where his church met was 'in an open street, a noted place, neer the Exchange' (S. Simpson, *Anatomist Anatomis'd*, 1644, 11). With Simpson's church at Rotterdam was also associated Joseph Symonds, another London minister in exile.

Simpson returned to London in 1641 and lectured at Blackfriars as well as St Margaret's, New Fish Street Hill.

Mr. Sydrach Simpson late Master of Pembroke-Hall in Cambridge And Preacher of the Gospell in London.

Printed by Peter Cole Printer & bookseller of London at the signe of the printing-press by the Royall Exchange.

Sidrach Simpson (*c.*1600–1655), by unknown engraver

According to Thomas Edwards, Simpson used these lectures frequently to propagate the Independent church way, 'pleading strongly for it, and for pretended liberty of conscience and toleration' (Edwards, 215). In the meantime he had gathered an Independent church in the City, which was, again in the words of Edwards, 'a rich and numerous Church, consisting of so many Gentlemen and Gentlewomen, rich Citizens, rich virgins, &c.' (ibid., 222). No record of Simpson's gathered church in London has survived, but it is known that among its members were some prominent civic leaders in the revolutionary era such as Alderman Thomas Andrewes, Alderman Samuel Warner, and Captain John Stone. Henry Dawson, alderman of Newcastle upon Tyne, was also a member. In a sermon Simpson preached in 1642 before a group of MPs at Westminster he spoke candidly against a national church and religious uniformity. 'God gives gifts and graces diversly', he said, and then added 'Christ hath Sonnes of divers sizes' (Simpson, 31). On 26 July 1643 he was invited by the House of Commons to preach a fast sermon, which he published under the title of *Reformation's Preservation* (1643). In his epistle of dedication he called upon the Commons to save the nation by 'the speedy execution of justice' and 'the vigorous prosecution of the warre'.

Nominated to the Westminster assembly of divines in

June 1643, he appears to have attended its meetings regularly, and he frequently registered his dissent. More important, he joined with Thomas Goodwin, Philip Nye, William Bridge, and Jeremiah Burroughes, all of whom had been in exile in the Netherlands, to form a nucleus of dissent in the assembly. Early in 1644 they published their famous *Apologeticall Narration*, which, though written with studied restraint and moderation, was none the less an open appeal over the assembly to parliament and to the nation for their congregational church way. And in the ensuing two years Simpson took part in all the concerted actions of the dissenting brethren of the assembly in opposition to the establishment of a rigid presbyterianism. In 1647 he became lecturer at St Mary Abchurch, where Joseph Symonds had been chosen minister by the parish, and he succeeded Symonds as minister in 1649. During these years he was apparently associated with more radical men like John Goodwin, John Canne, and Vavasor Powell. In early 1648 he was said to be one of twelve ministers sent for by Cromwell to preach in the army, and on 20 September 1650, not long after Cromwell's victory at Dunbar, he wrote to the lord general and urged him: 'Goe on therefore, my Lord, you are throwing downe what God is throwing downe' (Nickolls, 22–4). Later in the year the parliamentary visitors of Cambridge University appointed him master of Pembroke College.

It was at this juncture that Simpson became more conservative in his religious views. In April–May 1651 he took action against Captain Robert Norwood, a member of his gathered church, who had apparently harboured pantheistic beliefs, and eventually excommunicated him for blasphemy. On 10 February 1652 he appeared with John Owen and other Independent divines before the House of Commons and presented a petition against the anti-Trinitarian Racovian catechism, and a week later they submitted to a parliamentary committee their proposals for the propagation of the gospel. In 1653, at the commencement of Cambridge University, Simpson preached in defence of learning and university education for the ministry, which provoked William Dell, a former army chaplain and now master of Gonville and Caius College, to publish *A Plain and Necessary Confutation*. It has been said that Simpson was imprisoned in 1654 for preaching against Cromwell, but this must have been mistaken. All known facts indicate that he supported the Cromwellian protectorate: on 9 January he signed a circular letter denouncing the Fifth Monarchy Men; on 28 February he was one of the Independent divines consulted by Cromwell for a religious settlement; and on 20 March he was appointed a trier. In the meantime he was proffered by the great seal the rectory of St Bartholomew by the Exchange in spite of the fact that the parish had chosen for the place George Hall, the future bishop of Chester.

Simpson made his will on 2 April 1655, and died shortly afterwards at St Bartholomew by the Exchange, his will being proved on 15 April. He was buried on 18 April at St Bartholomew. He was survived by his wife, Isabella, of whom nothing else is known, and by his children, Sydrach, Katherine (wife of Joseph Denham), and Priscilla; a third daughter (almost certainly deceased) had married James Lane. It appears that Simpson possessed considerable assets at the time of his death, including land and tenements in the parish of Bocking in Essex. Two volumes of Simpson's sermons were published posthumously in 1658 from notes taken in shorthand by Captain Mark Coe, another member of Simpson's gathered church and one of the overseers of his will.   TAI LIU

Sources S. Simpson, *A sermon preached at Westminster before sundry of the House of Commons* (1643) · T. Edwards, *Antapologia* (1644) · [A. Forbes], *An anatomy of Independency* (1644) · *The works of the most reverend father in God, William Laud*, ed. J. Bliss and W. Scott, 7 vols. (1847–60) · *Original letters and papers of state addressed to Oliver Cromwell ... found among the political collections of Mr John Milton*, ed. J. Nickolls (1743) · A. F. Mitchell and J. Struthers, eds., *Minutes of the sessions of the Westminster assembly of divines* (1874) · W. A. Shaw, *A history of the English church during the civil wars and under the Commonwealth, 1640–1660*, 2 vols. (1900) · K. L. Sprunger, *Dutch puritanism: a history of English and Scottish churches of the Netherlands in the sixteenth and seventeenth centuries* (1982) · parish records, St Mary Abchurch, GL, MS 3891/1 · will of Sidrach Simpson, PRO, PROB 11/249, fol. 217v · DNB
Likenesses line engraving, NPG [*see illus.*]
Wealth at death considerable; land and tenements in Bocking, Essex: will, PRO, PROB 11/249, fol. 217v

Simpson, Simeon (1878–1932). *See under* Simpson family (*per.* 1894–1990).

Simpson, Thomas (d. 1584), Church of England clergyman, is first recorded by John Foxe as one of the lay deacons of the secret protestant congregation of London during the reign of Mary I. On one occasion spies were waiting for the congregation near Aldgate, 'and had not Thomas Simpson the deacon espied them, and bid themselves disperse themselves away, they had been taken' (*Acts and Monuments*, 8.558). Foxe also states that Augustine Bernher and Simpson visited the deacon Cuthbert Symson on the night before his martyrdom in March 1558. That Thomas and Cuthbert were brothers, or at least closely related, thus seems highly probable.

What Foxe does not disclose is that, probably in November 1557, Thomas Simpson had been ordained priest in the redundant church of St Mary Axe by the congregation's 'superintendent and *presbyterium*'. The four 'witnesses' were three ordained clergy—William Lyving, Augustine Bernher, and Robert Cole—and Avery Brierton, a merchant tailor of the parish of St Martin Vintry. When Simpson subscribed the oath of supremacy in August 1559 he did so as 'minister in Honey Lane' (Carte antique et miscellanee, XIII/2/57, fol. 2). He was presumably serving as curate in the parish of All Hallows.

Simpson's clandestine ordination was accepted as valid by Edmund Grindal who, in one of his earliest acts as bishop of London, collated him to the vicarage of Brightlingsea, near Colchester, on the Essex coast, on 4 January 1560. Avery Brierton stood surety at the exchequer for Simpson's first fruits along with another member of the former London congregation, Thomas Gee, whose widow later married John Sterne, suffragan bishop of Colchester.

On 12 November 1562 Grindal issued Simpson with letters testimonial rehearsing the circumstances of his ordination 'five years since', and retrospectively ratifying and confirming it. It is implied, though not definitely stated, that it was justified by 'a time of persecution'. It is the only known example of English orders at this time which did not involve the laying on of consecrated hands.

On 2 July 1569 Grindal further collated Simpson to the city rectory of St Botolph without Bishopsgate. He held both his livings until his death, without ever apparently becoming involved in nonconformist activities in the city or in Colchester. The preamble to his will nevertheless trusts that he will 'inherit the kingdom of Glory among the Saints' (will, fol. 324v).

Simpson made his will as a widower, probably in January 1584. Nothing is known of his wife. After monetary bequests to the poor of both his parishes, he left a private house to his son, William, a minor, and his sixth share in a boat. The rest of his goods and possessions were divided between his other sons, Thomas, John, and Josias, who were all apparently of age. His daughters, Martha, Hester, Anne, and Mary, were left monetary bequests totalling £120 and were to inherit at nineteen or marriage. He probably died in May 1584. Thomas and John, named joint executors, were granted probate on 3 June, the day on which Thomas was collated to Brightlingsea as his father's successor in the vicarage.　　　　　　　BRETT USHER

Sources *The acts and monuments of John Foxe*, ed. S. R. Cattley, 8 vols. (1837–41) · B. Usher, '"In a time of persecution": new light on the secret protestant congregation in Marian London', *John Foxe and the English Reformation*, ed. D. Loades (1997), 233–51 · Carte antique et miscellanee, LPL, XIII/2/57 · LMA, DL/C/332, fol. 69v [Grindal's letters testimonial] · registered will, LMA, DL/C/358, fols. 324v–325v · D. MacCulloch, *Tudor church militant: Edward VI and the protestant Reformation* (1999)
Wealth at death probably reasonably well off: property to sons; total of £120 in money to be shared between four daughters: will, 3 June 1584, LMA, DL/C/358, fols. 324v–325v

Simpson, Thomas (*bap.* 1582, *d.* 1628?), violist and composer, was baptized at Milton-next-Sittingbourne, Kent, on 1 April 1582, son of John Simpson. An autograph manuscript volume comprising the bass part of nineteen instrumental 'songes' (Centre for Kentish Studies, Maidstone, U951.z.23)—'the first frute of my unskillfull Laboures'—is dedicated to Sir Norton Knatchbull (1569–1636) of Mersham, Kent, suggesting that Simpson served him before emigrating to Germany. By 1608 he had become a musician at the court of Frederick, elector palatine, at Heidelberg and on 25 June 1609 he married Anna Colin from Jamets, Lorraine, at the Barfüsserkirche there. In 1610 at Frankfurt am Main appeared the first of his published collections, *Opusculum newer Pavanen*, comprising mostly pavan-galliard pairs in five parts. Here Simpson describes himself as 'violist'. No doubt he was present in Heidelberg when the elector brought home his bride, Elizabeth, daughter of James I, in 1613, but between about 1615 and 1622 he served in Bückeburg (near Hanover) at the Holstein-Schaumburg court of Count Ernst III. He published another anthology, *Opus newer Paduanen* (Hamburg, 1617) and single compositions by him are included in collective volumes edited by Hagius (1616) and Oberndörffer

(1620). His last publication, *Taffel-Consort* (1621), contains many works by his Bückeburg colleagues.

Simpson is among the most important English composers working on the continent. His collections mix English and German works, many newly arranged by himself, and also include his own versions of Italianate forms such as the ricercare and canzona, including a beautiful setting of the English folk-song 'Bonny Sweet Robin'. The 1617 collection is much more varied than that of 1610, extending the paired-dance groupings into longer series or suites. Here and in the *Taffel-Consort* Simpson employs two equal (and often florid) treble parts which criss-cross and answer each other in dialogue. *Taffel-Consort* reduces the string texture to four parts (omitting one viola) but includes a continuo—perhaps the first use of a 'string quartet' layout in Western music.

The onset of the Thirty Years' War in 1619 and the death of Count Ernst in 1622 caused Simpson to move to Copenhagen, where he served at court between 7 May 1622 and 4 March 1625. The city bailiff of Copenhagen was asked to collect a debt from his heirs on 20 June 1628, so it seems he had recently died there, perhaps earlier in the year.

ANDREW ASHBEE

Sources P. E. Mueller, 'The influence and activities of English musicians on the continent during the late sixteenth and early seventeenth centuries', PhD diss., Indiana University, 1954 · C. Coxon, 'Simpson, Thomas', *Die Musik in Geschichte und Gegenwart*, ed. F. Blume (Kassel and Basel, 1949–86) · A. Ashbee, 'Simpson, Thomas', *New Grove* · G. Dodd, *Thematic index of music for viols* (1980–) · P. Holman, *Four and twenty fiddlers: the violin at the English court, 1540–1690*, new edn (1993) · J. Bergsagel, ed., *Instrumental ensemblemusik / Music for instrumental ensemble* (Copenhagen, 1988), vol. 2 of *Musik i Danmark pa Christian IV's tid / Music in Denmark at the time of Christian IV* (1988–92) · parish register, Milton-next-Sittingbourne, 1 April 1582 [baptism] · Evgl. Kirchenbuchamp, Heidelberg, KB. IV, 39 [marriage] · CKS, MS U951.z.23

Simpson, Thomas (1710–1761), mathematician, was born on 20 August 1710 at Market Bosworth, Leicestershire, the son of a weaver. It seems that the only formal education he received was from a Richard Smith in a school at Market Bosworth. He moved to Nuneaton, Warwickshire, where he took up the profession of a schoolmaster. He taught himself mathematics, which might seem exceptional but was, however, quite the rule in eighteenth-century Britain: many mathematicians were self-trained. They called themselves 'philomaths' and were often of a provincial background. It is not known exactly which books Simpson read. He was known, because of his reputation as a fortune-teller, as the 'oracle of Nuneaton, Bosworth and the environs'.

About 1730 Simpson married his landlady at Nuneaton, a widow named Swinfield. They had two children, Elizabeth, born in 1736, and Thomas, born in 1738. From 1725 to 1733 he taught mathematics at Nuneaton. He reportedly had to flee to Derby in 1733 after he or his assistant had frightened a girl by dressing up as a devil during an astrology session. In 1736 he was in London, where he continued to work, as a weaver and as a teacher of mathematics. He resided at Spitalfields where he was a tutor at the famous

Mathematical Society. Francis Holliday, and perhaps Francis Blake, were among his pupils. With Blake he corresponded on the foundations of the fluxional method in connection with George Berkeley's *Analyst* (1734), a pamphlet consisting of logical criticisms of Newton's and Leibniz's calculi. He was a friend of John Landen, with whom he frequently corresponded. In 1737 he published *A New Treatise of Fluxions*. This was a high-quality textbook devoted to the calculus of fluxions, the Newtonian version of the infinitesimal calculus. The topic was advanced—it was no trivial exercise to write such a book in the 1730s, when the calculus was mastered by only a few mathematicians in Europe.

Simpson also gained a broader reputation as a mathematician by answering some questions in the *Ladies' Diary*, a mathematical periodical where the British philomaths proposed and answered problems. His answers were published from 1736 under pseudonyms such as Marmaduke Hodgson, Hurlothrumbo, Kubernetes, Patrick O'Cavannah, and Anthony Shallow. He also contributed to the *Gentleman's Magazine* in 1736–8, to *Miscellanea Curiosa Mathematica* in 1745–6, and to the *Gentleman's Diary* in 1746. From about 1753 to 1760 he was editor of the *Ladies' Diary*, succeeding Robert Heath, with whom he had a squabble after Heath accused him of plagiarism. The control over this periodical was much valued and there were factions that fought against each other. Heath was a friend of another writer of mathematical textbooks, William Emerson, and their respective conduct as editor and main contributor to the *Ladies' Diary* has been described as contentious.

In 1743 Simpson was appointed assistant to the chief master of mathematics at the newly formed Royal Military Academy at Woolwich, thanks to the recommendation of Martin Folkes, president of the Royal Society, and perhaps also of William Jones (1675–1749). This remained his position until his death. He was elected FRS in 1745 and in 1758 fellow of the Academy of Sciences in Stockholm. His post in Woolwich led him to consider several problems in engineering, concerning in particular fortifications and the building of bridges. About 1760 he had a controversy with John Muller, chief master of mathematics in Woolwich, on the design for a bridge across the Thames at Blackfriars: Muller defended a project with elliptical arches, while Simpson would have preferred semicircular ones.

Simpson was a prolific writer. His most important works are the *Doctrine and Application of Fluxions* (1750), *Mathematical Dissertations* (1743), and *Miscellaneous Tracts* (1757), the first of which is one of the best treatises on fluxions written in the eighteenth century. The second contains a remarkable treatment of the attraction of spheroids, the solids obtained by rotating an ellipse around one of its axes, which improves on results earlier obtained by Colin MacLaurin. The third is mainly concerned with physical astronomy—the precession of the equinoxes, the orbit of the comets, and the motion of the moon. Simpson also contributed several papers to the *Philosophical Transactions of the Royal Society*.

Simpson's style is quite an exception in the panorama of British eighteenth-century mathematics. Unlike many of his countrymen, he leaned towards symbolical and abstract methods based on algebraical manipulations, and he looked with admiration to the analytical results achieved by continental mathematicians. His model was the French savant Alexis-Claude Clairaut. Simpson's most valuable mathematical achievements include his analytical expression of the so-called Newton–Raphson method of approximation of the root of an equation, his study of the methods for solving 'isoperimetrical problems' (methods in what is now called the calculus of variations), and several works on probability and annuities. This last topic occasioned a polemic over priority with Abraham De Moivre. It is an irony that Simpson is nowadays remembered for 'Simpson's rule' for obtaining the area under a curve, a result which he did not claim as his, and which was well known to Isaac Newton. He was also an accomplished writer of introductory textbooks on algebra, geometry, and trigonometry. His slim volume of *Select Exercises for Young Proficients in the Mathematicks* (1752) was widely used; it ran to further editions in 1792 and 1810, and was partly translated into French in 1771.

Simpson died at Market Bosworth, Leicestershire, on 14 May 1761 and was buried at Sutton Cheynell in Leicestershire. After his relatively early death his widow, who died in 1782, was reportedly granted a pension by the crown in recognition of his merit, a rare distinction for a commoner. A tablet was erected on Simpson's grave in 1790 by John Throsby. His papers were given to Henry Watson of the East India Company, who did not publish them. They are now in the library of Columbia University.

NICCOLÒ GUICCIARDINI

Sources R. V. Wallis and P. J. Wallis, eds., *Biobibliography of British mathematics and its applications*, 2 (1986) • P. J. Wallis, 'Simpson, Thomas', *DSB* • F. M. Clarke, *Thomas Simpson and his times* (1929) • *DNB* • C. Hutton, 'Memoirs of the life and writings of the author', in T. Simpson, *Select exercises for young proficients in the mathematicks*, 2nd edn (1792) • N. Guicciardini, *The development of Newtonian calculus in Britain, 1700–1800* (1989) • I. Todhunter, *A history of the mathematical theories of attraction and the figure of the earth*, 2 vols. (1873) • N. Kollerstrom, 'Thomas Simpson and "Newton's method of approximation": an enduring myth', *British Journal for the History of Science*, 25 (1992), 347–54
Archives Col. U.

Simpson, Thomas (1808–1840), Arctic explorer, the elder son of Alexander Simpson (d. 1821), schoolmaster of Dingwall in Ross-shire, and his second wife, Mary, was born at Dingwall on 2 July 1808. As a boy he was delicate, with a tendency to consumption. He was destined for the ministry, and at the age of seventeen entered King's College, Aberdeen, whence he graduated MA in 1829. He had developed into a strong, active man, so that, instead of proceeding to the ministry, he took a post with the Hudson's Bay Company. This followed the visit in 1825 of his cousin George Simpson, administrator in the company, whose descriptions of Canadian life inspired Thomas, his brother Alexander, and his half-brother Aemilius all to enter the company's service.

Simpson arrived in Canada in 1829, but caused trouble among the métis (of mixed French and Indian blood) at

Fort Garry (Winnipeg). In July 1836 he was appointed second in command, with particular responsibility for surveying and scientific investigations, of an expedition, sent under chief factor Peter Warren Dease, 'to complete the discovery and survey of the northern shores of America'. While Dease, with the party of twelve men, started for Great Slave Lake, Simpson went to Red River settlement, where he spent some months refreshing and extending his knowledge of astronomy and practice in observations. On 1 December he started out to join Dease, whom, after an interesting and adventurous winter journey, he found at Fort Chipewyan, on the shore of Lake Athabasca. In June 1837 they continued their journey, and leaving a few men at Fort Norman, to prepare winter quarters by Great Bear Lake, reached the sea on 9 July. They then turned west, along the coast until, in longitude 154°23' W, the boats were stopped by the ice. It was determined that Simpson should try to reach Barrow Point on foot, which he succeeded in doing on 4 August and there took possession of his discoveries for Britain. On the 6th he rejoined Dease, and on the same day they started for the Mackenzie River, which they reached without accident on the 17th. Their progress up the river was slow and laborious, and they did not reach Fort Norman until 4 September. On the 25th they arrived at the station on Great Bear Lake, which they named Fort Confidence, and there they wintered.

On 7 June 1838 the party started up Dease River, but its ascent proved very difficult because of rapids. Then, carrying their baggage and boats over the watershed, they descended the Coppermine River, and endeavoured to examine the coast to the eastward. The season, however, was so bad that they made but little way, and from Point Turnagain returned to their winter quarters at Fort Confidence, which they reached on 14 September. On 15 June 1839 they again started for the Coppermine, where they had left their boats, and with a more favourable season went eastward as far as the Boothia peninsula. They were, however, unable to determine whether there was any passage to the Gulf of Boothia, or to connect their coast navigation with the known King William Sea to the north. They had almost, but not quite, discovered the north-west passage. The advanced season compelled them to return, and by 24 September they were again at Fort Confidence, whence, after a very severe journey, they reached Fort Simpson on the Mackenzie on 14 October. Leaving Dease there, Simpson set out on 2 December, and reached Red River settlement on 2 February 1840. He remained there until the summer, and on 6 June started for the United States and England hoping to ensure that he, not Dease (whom he considered a ditherer), took the credit for their discoveries, and hoping to secure approval for a further expedition. On 14 June he was killed by a gunshot wound in the head. The men of mixed race who were with him deposed that he went mad, killed two of the party, and then committed suicide; others suggested that he was attacked by his own men, two of whom he shot before he was killed. It is clear that he had made himself unpopular because of his petulance and readiness to criticize, although the latter trait makes his writings a rich source of quotations for later historians. In particular, his aversion to those of mixed race, whose 'extravagant and profligate habits' (Simpson, cited in Sampson, *DCB*) he censured, made him a difficult member of an exploring party and would have made him an impossible leader.

Simpson's *Narrative of Discoveries on the North Coast of America* was edited by his brother Alexander and published in 1843. Alexander corresponded for two years with the London committee of the Hudson's Bay Company to try to clear Thomas's name and to get a pension paid to his mother as a reward for his brother's services. In 1845 he published *The Life and Travels of Thomas Simpson* to try to gain public sympathy for his brother. He was largely unsuccessful, partly because the Royal Geographical Society and the establishment in general tended to underestimate the contribution to Arctic exploration of fur traders, preferring to attribute achievements to the Royal Navy, and partly because of Simpson's pushy character and unpleasant death. ELIZABETH BAIGENT

Sources A. Simpson, *The life and travels of Thomas Simpson, the Arctic discoverer* (1845); repr. (1963) · J. Gellner, introduction, in A. Simpson, *The life and travels of Thomas Simpson* (1963) · C. Holland, *Arctic exploration and development, c. 500 BC to 1915: an encyclopedia* (1994) · K. Abel, 'Simpson, Alexander', *DCB*, vol. 7 · T. H. Levere, *Science and the Canadian Arctic: a century of exploration, 1818–1918* (1993) · W. R. Sampson, 'Dease, Peter Warren', *DCB*, vol. 9
Likenesses J. Cook, stipple and line engraving, pubd 1845 (after G. P. Green), BM, NPG · portrait, repro. in Simpson, *Life and travels*

Simpson, Thomas [Tommy] (1937–1967), racing cyclist, was born on 30 November 1937 at Station Street, Haswell, co. Durham, the youngest of the six children of Thomas Simpson, a conveyor worker in a coal mine who became a glassworker and later a storekeeper, and his wife, Alice Cheetham. He was brought up in Harworth, Nottinghamshire, and as a boy he joined Harworth district cycling club where he was nicknamed Four-Stone Coppi after the Italian champion. While working as a draughtsman in a Retford glassworks he won a bronze medal in the team pursuit at the Melbourne Olympics (1956) and a silver in the individual pursuit at the Cardiff British Commonwealth and empire games (1958). With stamina belied by his fragile appearance, he won his first professional world road championship in 1959 at the Zandewoort circuit in the Netherlands. On 3 January 1961 he married Helen Margaret Sherburn (b. 1939/40), whom he met when she was working as an au pair in France, the daughter of Frank Sherburn, produce merchant. They had two daughters. In 1961 he won the tour of Flanders, the first classic win by a Briton for sixty-five years. Other classic victories followed including Bordeaux–Paris, Paris–Nice, Ghent–Wevelgem, Milan–San Remo, and, in 1965, the tour of Lombardy.

Tommy Simpson was world professional road race champion in 1965 and was voted BBC sports personality of the year. But an injured leg, broken on a family skiing holiday, meant that he missed most of the following season and was unable to exploit his title commercially. Aged twenty-nine, he saw the 1967 tour de France, the world's greatest cycle race, as his last remaining chance to make big money out of the sport. On 13 July 1967, during the thirteenth stage, 133 miles from Marseilles to Carpentras, after remounting twice Simpson finally collapsed in high temperatures half a mile from the summit of the virtually shadeless Mont Ventoux. Attempts at resuscitation failed. His was the first known drugs-related death of a British sportsperson. Although the official cause of his demise was given as dehydration and exhaustion, it was later acknowledged that Simpson, like many other cyclists, had been using amphetamines. Taking such drugs was well established among long-distance racing cyclists in the days when there were no dope controls. Indeed attempts to introduce drug tests in 1966 had been fiercely opposed by leading cyclists, including five times tour winner Jacques Anquetil, who argued that professionals could not cope with their long season without resort to stimulants.

As a mark of respect, the fourteenth stage from Carpentras to Sète was a slow procession with Barry Hoban, a member of Simpson's team, the predetermined winner. A memorial stone was erected near the Ventoux summit, where each year cycling fans still leave mementoes in tribute to a fallen champion. Hoban later married Simpson's widow.   WRAY VAMPLEW

Sources T. Simpson, *Cycling is my life* (1966) · J. Rendall, 'Death of a cyclist', *Sunday Telegraph Magazine* (13 July 1997) · *The Times* (14 July 1967) · R. Hughes, 'Family sustains Simpson's indomitable spirit', *The Times* (14 July 1997) · b. cert. · m. cert. · *CGPLA Eng. & Wales* (1968)
Likenesses photograph, 1967, repro. in J. Huntington-Whiteley, *The book of British sporting heroes* (1998) · photograph, repro. in *Daily Telegraph* (25 July 1998)
Wealth at death £3390: administration, 16 Jan 1968, *CGPLA Eng. & Wales*

Simpson, (Bessie) Wallis. *See* Windsor, (Bessie) Wallis (1896–1986).

Simpson, William (1627?–1671), Quaker preacher, was from Sunbricke or Sunbreak in Lancashire, where he 'also received the truth', being convinced of the Quaker message there (Tomkins, 185). Little is known of his early years and background, except that he came of humble origins and was a husbandman. He may have been the William Simpson baptized on 13 June 1627 in the priory church, Cartmel, Lancashire, the son of Thomas Simpson and Ann Ellithorne. He was married to Ann Symson, who died on 6 December 1669 and was buried at Sunbreak. It is likely that Christopher Simpson of Sunbreak, who married Isabel Birkett in 1675, was their son as his father was William.

Simpson preached in the north at Pardshaw in Cumberland, and along with Thomas Laiton was the first to spread Quakerism in Mitton under Wychwood. He travelled widely and in 1655 is listed as receiving money from the Kendal fund to travel to Scotland and spread the Quaker message.

Simpson is particularly noted for testifying by signs, a practice which was adopted by some followers of the early Quaker movement but gradually died out in the seventeenth century. George Fox, in a testimony to Simpson, noted how Simpson

went three years naked and in sackcloth, in the days of Oliver and his parliament, as a sign to them, and to the priests, showing how God would strip them of their power, and that they should be as naked as he was.

Fox also added how Simpson 'was made oftentimes to colour his face black' as a sign of the spiritual darkness of ministers (Fortescue, 13). Simpson went naked in a number of towns and cities, including Colchester, Cambridge, London, and Oxford. In the latter, accompanied by two other Friends who carried his clothes, he passed from the east gate to the middle of the city, where he was whipped, and then continued through to the north gate, where he met with some scholars. Of interest is Simpson's broadside entitled *Going Naked a Sign* (1660), in which he describes the practice and how he felt moved to testify in this manner. In it he recounts how

> a necessity was laid upon me from the Lord God … to be a sign: but before I was given up to the thing, it was as death unto me, and I had rather, if it had been the Lord's will, have died than gone on in this service.

He was imprisoned with others at Oxford in 1654 for bearing a public testimony against vice and superstition, and in 1655 suffered further incarceration for preaching at Banbury.

Simpson also encountered opposition elsewhere. He was sent out of Evesham in 1657 for telling the inhabitants 'to repent and fear the Lord' (Besse, 2.60). In April of the same year he was arrested at Chipping Camden in Gloucestershire and sent to Lancaster, charged with being a wandering person. Later, in 1659 he was whipped upon his back and breast for going naked through Evesham 'in a prophetic manner' (ibid., 61), and in the same year went naked at Halsted in Essex, where he was badly beaten by a man named John Folks who, according to Besse, died shortly afterwards. In an entry for 1661, but no doubt referring to an earlier date, George Fox noted in his *Journal* how Simpson went naked in Cambridge but was protected by the mayor, who 'did nobly to him; he put his gown about him and took him into his house' (*Journal of George Fox*, ed. Nickalls, 408).

Following the Restoration, Simpson suffered considerably in the Quaker cause but appears to have stopped prophesying by signs around this time. In 1663 he was sent to prison with others for refusing the oath of allegiance after his removal from a meeting at Bugbrook, in Northamptonshire. The next year, according to Fox's *Journal*, he was fined for not attending church. In 1670 he was removed for preaching from Westminster and Devonshire House meetings, and suffered a fine of 20s. for preaching in the street at Ratcliffe after the meeting-house had been barricaded.

On 8 July 1670 Simpson travelled to Barbados to spread the Quaker message with John Burnyeat, who described his close friend as 'a very innocent man, and full of fear and reverence … very sweet and pleasant', and went on to say how they 'walked in great love and unity together; for he was a humble man, and had very low thoughts of himself' (Burnyeat, 39).

Simpson's literary output was very small, but of importance for shedding light on early Quaker practices. In *From one who was Moved of the Lord to Go a Sign* (1659) Simpson wrote with apocalyptic urgency,

> so signs in your streets also must you have, that you may be left without excuse in the day when the Lord will come to reckon with you, that you shall not say you have not been warned, so your blood shall be upon your head if you repent not. (p. 6)

His other writings were generally warnings and reproofs such as *A Discovery of the Priest and Professors* (1660). In *A Declaration unto All, both Priests and People* (1655) Simpson criticized ministers for taking tithes from their congregations and for denying 'immediate revelation' which he said he 'and all the saints have', and for denying 'perfection to be obtained while … in this body of clay' (pp. 3–4).

Not long in Barbados, Simpson was taken ill with 'a violent fever', from which he died on 8 February 1671 (Burnyeat, 39). He is said to have 'departed this life like a lamb', a leaving which it was hoped would 'give content' to his son (Fortescue, 7). He was buried in the garden of Richard Forstal of Bridge-Town, Barbados.

CAROLINE L. LEACHMAN

Sources W. Fortescue, *A short relation concerning the life and death of William Simpson* (1671) · J. Besse, *A collection of the sufferings of the people called Quakers*, 2 vols. (1753) · J. Burnyeat, *Truth exalted in the writings of that eminent and faithful servant of Christ, John Burnyeat* (1691) · J. Tomkins, *Piety promoted … the second part* (1702) · W. Simpson, *Going naked a sign* (1660) · *The journal of George Fox*, ed. J. L. Nickalls, rev. edn (Philadelphia, 1985) · *The journal of George Fox*, ed. N. Penney, 2 (1911) · J. Smith, ed., *A descriptive catalogue of Friends' books*, 2 (1867), vol. 2 · RS Friends, Lond., Swarthmore MS vol. 1, fol. 233 (MS vol. 352) · digest registers of births, marriages, and burials, RS Friends, Lond. · E. E. Taylor, *The valiant sixty* (1951) · N. Penney, ed., 'The first publishers of truth': being early records, now first printed, of the introduction of Quakerism into the counties of England and Wales* (1907) · 'Dictionary of Quaker biography', RS Friends, Lond. [card index] · W. C. Braithwaite, *The beginnings of Quakerism*, ed. H. J. Cadbury, 2nd edn (1955); repr. (1981) · IGI

Archives RS Friends, Lond., letters, portfolio MSS 5/51; 17/2, 96, 98 | RS Friends, Lond., MS 294

Simpson, William (1823–1899), watercolour painter and journalist, was born on 28 October 1823 in a tenement in Carrick Street, Glasgow, the son of James Simpson (1791–1879), a marine engineer and mechanic, and his wife, Ann Johnstone (1786–1854). He spent fifteen months at a writing-school in Perth but thereafter received no regular education. From January 1837 he trained as a lithographer under David Macfarlane in an architect's office in Glasgow. In August or September 1839 he left Macfarlane and from 1840 was apprenticed to the lithographers Allan and Ferguson. Commissioned by David Allan, Simpson sketched the city's old buildings for Robert Stuart's *Views and Notices of Glasgow in Former Times* (Stuart's Glasgow) (1848). He attended the Glasgow School of Design from 1845 and sold his first watercolour in 1850. In 1851 he moved to London and worked for the lithographers Day & Son.

During the Crimean War Simpson became a pioneer

William Simpson (1823–1899), by unknown photographer, 1891

war artist: dispatched by the printsellers Colnaghi & Son (on Day's recommendation), he recorded the naval battles in the Baltic Sea and then went on to Balaklava in November 1854 to make accurate sketches on the spot. The drawings which he made during that terrible winter were submitted to Lord Raglan, sent home to England, and shown to Queen Victoria by the minister of war, the duke of Newcastle. After the fall of Sevastopol he was attached to the duke's party of exploration in Circassia. Eighty of his Crimean drawings were lithographed in *The Seat of War in the East* (2 vols., 1855–6), which was dedicated with permission to Queen Victoria. When the original watercolours were exhibited at Colnaghi's gallery, Lord Elcho and other MPs called for them to be bought by the nation as a historic record of the war. On the advice of Sir Charles Eastlake, this proposal was rejected and the watercolours were sold off separately. Simpson returned to England with a brown beard long enough to button into his waistcoat, and he had an audience with the queen: he showed her his sketches and was much impressed by her grasp of every detail of the war. She commissioned *The Queen Reviewing the Royal Artillery at Woolwich on their Return from the Crimea, 1856*, and over the next thirty years was a steady patron for the painter.

After the Indian mutiny Day & Son sent Simpson to India on a roving commission, to make studies for a large-scale illustrated book. He arrived in October 1859 and joined the party of the governor-general, Lord Canning, on a tour of the area where the mutiny had taken place; he also sketched with Lady Canning. Over three years he visited much of the subcontinent, including Tibet and its Buddhist temples, the Himalayas, Kashmir, and Ceylon. When he returned to England in 1862, he had travelled 22,570 miles. He settled in chambers in London at 64 Lincoln's Inn Fields, worked for four years on Day's project, and completed 250 drawings. However, when the firm of Day & Son went into liquidation, his Indian watercolours were taken over and sold off as bankrupt stock: Simpson received no recompense for seven years of hard work. Finally, fifty paintings were indifferently reproduced in a book with text by Sir John Kaye.

In 1866, through William Ingram, editor and proprietor of the *Illustrated London News*, Simpson became a special artist for the paper, a role for which he was specially suited. After twenty-five years' service for the *Illustrated London News* he wrote:

> I have at all times felt that I was not seeing for myself alone, but that others would see through my eyes, and that eyes yet unborn would, in the pages of the *Illustrated London News*, do the same. This feeling has at all times urged on my mind the necessity for accuracy. (*ILN*, 14 May 1892, 604)

He covered many royal events for the paper. In the autumn of 1866 he went to Dunrobin in Scotland to record the prince of Wales's visit to the duke of Sutherland. At St Petersburg in November 1866 he illustrated the marriage of the tsarevich (later Alexander III) to Princess Dagmar, sister of the princess of Wales, and he accompanied the prince and princess of Wales to Egypt in 1868. In 1875–6 he covered the visit of the prince of Wales to India for the *Illustrated London News* and made over 200 sketches, mostly in sepia with some watercolour. The queen and prince acquired a number of these and a collection, *Shikāre and Tamāsha: a Souvenir of the Visit of the Prince of Wales to India*, was published in 1876; forty-four of Simpson's Indian watercolours are in the Victoria and Albert Museum, London. His last commission from Queen Victoria was in 1889, but for the prince of Wales he drew scenes relating to the death of the duke of Clarence in 1892. He visited Balmoral and Abergeldie castles and Sandringham and was on friendly terms with both the queen and the prince of Wales; fifty of his works are in the Royal Collection.

Simpson travelled round the world for the *Illustrated London News*, and his *Autobiography* (1903) describes his surroundings with clarity and passionate interest. Sketches sent home from abroad were worked up into watercolours on his return. On location he wisely disguised himself by wearing local native costume, a masquerade he obviously enjoyed. As an observer and reporter for over forty years, he had contacts and friends all over the world; he mixed with people of every rank and learned many European and oriental languages and dialects needed on his innumerable travels. In 1868 he accompanied Lord Napier on the Abyssinian expedition: he made archaeological sketches to illustrate the Palestine exploration fund's excavations in the Holy Land, was granted permission to sketch inside the Dome of the Rock, and in 1869 attended the Vatican Council in Rome. He returned to Constantinople to revisit the Crimea, and was present at the opening of the Suez Canal in November 1869. In 1870,

at the outbreak of the Franco-Prussian War, Simpson travelled to Metz and was briefly imprisoned. (Fortunately he had made his drawings on cigarette paper so that, when he was arrested as a spy, he could smoke them in front of his captors.) During the Paris commune he was under fire, and he witnessed harrowing scenes there before returning to London in June 1871. In 1872–3 he went round the world; he visited China to illustrate the marriage of the emperor Tongzhi and saw the Great Wall and the Ming tombs before travelling on via Japan to San Francisco. He was the only eyewitness reporter on the spot able to cover the rebellion of the Modoc Indians, and he visited Salt Lake City, Kentucky, New York, and Niagara, before returning to Liverpool in June 1873. He describes his travels in *Meeting the Sun: a Journey All Round the World* (1874). In 1877 he made sketches of the Schliemann excavations at Troy and Ephesus. He also covered the Second Anglo-Afghan War of 1878–80 and was with the Afghan boundary commission in 1884–5.

Simpson became a good amateur archaeologist, had a profound interest in religions, and was a prolific writer. His published works include *Picturesque People* (1876), *The Buddhist Prayer Wheel* (1896), *The Jonah Legend* (1899), *Glasgow in the Forties* (1899), and many articles, including papers on freemasonry in the *Transactions* of that society, into which he was initiated in 1871. Probably because of the peripatetic life he led it was not until 5 January 1881 that he married the miniature painter Maria Eliza Burt, daughter of Thomas Burt, a contractor's agent; about 1884 the couple had one beloved daughter, Ann Penelope. Simpson became an associate of the Institute of Painters in Water Colours in 1874 and a full member in 1879; he exhibited fifty-nine watercolours between 1874 and 1899. An original member of the Institute of Painters in Oil Colours in 1883, he resigned in 1886. He was also an FRGS, an honorary associate of the Royal Institute of British Architects, and a founder member of the Society of Biblical Archaeology. Simpson spent his last years writing his *Autobiography*, which he stipulated should not be published until after his death, which took place on 17 August 1899 at his home, 19 Church Road, Willesden, London. He was buried in Highgate cemetery, Middlesex. DELIA MILLAR

Sources W. Simpson, *The autobiography of William Simpson*, ed. G. Eyre-Todd (1903) · P. Theroux and S. Peers, *Mr William Simpson of the Illustrated London News: pioneer war artist, 1823–1899* (1987) [exhibition catalogue, the Fine Art Society, London, Edinburgh, and Glasgow] · M. Archer and P. Theroux, *Visions of India: the sketchbooks of William Simpson, 1859–62* (1986) · W. Simpson, *Glasgow in the forties* (1899) [biographical sketch by A. H. Millar] · S. Peers, 'William Simpson's Indian travels', *Antique Collector*, 57 (1986), 70–77 · P. Hogarth, *Artists on horseback: the old West in illustrated journalism, 1857–1900* (1972), 88–108 · E. Clodd, *Memories*, new edn (1926), 86–91 · D. Millar, *The Victorian watercolours and drawings in the collection of her majesty the queen*, 2 (1995), 802–13 · W. Simpson, 'Experiences', Mitchell L., Glas. [description of Simpson's experiences in the Second Afghan War] · m. cert. · d. cert.

Archives CUL, corresp. and papers; corresp. · Mitchell L., Glas., drawings, papers, and scrapbooks · NL Scot., autobiographical notes and reflections, watercolour and photographic album | Keele University Library, letters to W. H. Rylands · NL NZ, Turnbull L., diaries · Royal Arch., corresp.

Likenesses photograph, 1874, repro. in Archer and Theroux, *Visions of India*, frontispiece · photograph, 1891; Christies, 29 April 1999, lot 87 [*see illus.*] · R. Fenton, photograph (in the Crimea), repro. in Theroux and Peers, *Mr William Simpson* (1987), frontispiece · group portrait, wood-engraving, NPG; repro. in *Our artists—past and present*, *ILN* (14 May 1892) · photograph (in old age), repro. in Simpson, *Glasgow in the forties*, 2

Wealth at death £964 12s.: probate, 27 Sept 1899, CGPLA Eng. & Wales

Simpson, William Douglas (1896–1968), archaeologist and historian, was born at 80 Hamilton Place, Aberdeen, on 2 August 1896, the younger son of Henry Fyfe Morland Simpson (1859?–1920), rector of Aberdeen grammar school, and his wife, Jenny Fridericke Simpson, *née* Dohm (1866?–1949). He was educated at the grammar school and at Aberdeen University, where his studies were interrupted by the First World War. Having been discharged from the army for medical reasons, he spent his war service on coast-watching duties and in work for the Ministry of National Service. He then completed his degree with first-class honours in history, being awarded the Caithness prize and Forbes gold medal.

For a year after graduation in 1919 Simpson was assistant to Charles Sanford Terry, professor of history, and then became lecturer in history at Aberdeen University. In 1926 he was appointed university librarian, a post he held until 1966. His interest in the archaeology of castles was already well developed, and over the next thirty years he directed excavations at Kildrummy, Coull, Kindrochit, Esslemont, Dundarg, and Finavon castles, and at the Doune of Invernochty. He published a succession of books, papers, and guides, including many for the office of works and its successors, on these sites and many others in Scotland, England, and Wales. For his book *The Castle of Kildrummy* (1923) the university awarded him the degree of DLitt.

Other books dealt with wider questions of archaeology and history. *The Province of Mar* (1943) and *The Earldom of Mar* (1949) pursued Simpson's studies of north-east Scotland. *The Castle of Bergen and the Bishop's Palace at Kirkwall* (1961), together with his edition of the proceedings of the Viking Congress held at Lerwick in 1950 (1954) and a series of papers on castles of the Teutonic knights in East Prussia, extended his interests further afield. He edited *The Fusion of 1860* (1963)—the volume which commemorated the centenary of the union of King's and Marischal colleges, Aberdeen—and as secretary of the Third Spalding Club supervised the publication of its numerous volumes. The Lincoln Record Society's *Building Accounts of Tattershall Castle* (1960) was published under remarkable difficulties, the manuscript being badly damaged by a monkey which made its way into the editor's house after escaping from a travelling circus. Of his numerous books intended for the general reader, the most widely known was *The Ancient Stones of Scotland* (1965).

The Origins of Christianity in Aberdeenshire (1925), *The Historical St Columba* (1927), *The Celtic Church in Scotland* (1935), and *St Ninian and the Origins of the Christian Church in Scotland* (1940) were regarded by Simpson as an important part of his work. His methodology, however, and the conclusions which he drew from the archaeological evidence, were criticized from the start, and later opinion appears to have agreed that the criticisms were well founded.

Many developments took place in Aberdeen University Library during the forty years in which Simpson was its librarian. Some of his far-sighted proposals were not accepted; even so strong a personality as Simpson had less influence in the university than certain members of his library committee, and he was never a member of senate. In his later years, as his health deteriorated, much of the library's administration and development was handled by others.

When Simpson began his work on Scottish history, the subject tended to be professionally neglected; he was therefore a pioneer. Much of the practical excavation of his sites was done by his faithful boy scouts; he himself was not a trained archaeologist. Some of his conclusions have not stood the test of time, for example those concerning 'bastard feudalism' and the design of later medieval castles. His lasting achievement is to be found in his detailed studies of individual buildings, and the widespread interest in the archaeology and history of Scotland which he generated through his books and lectures. His enthusiasm, fluent delivery, and ebullient personality made him an immensely successful lecturer both in the lecture room and in the field. For many years his extramural classes were crowded with students of all ages and from all walks of life; his successors in the university library long continued to receive enquiries from Scottish exiles on topics of local history and archaeology.

Simpson married on 12 August 1935 Ellen Dorothy Mason (1901–1984), a bank clerk of Dundee, daughter of Joseph Reed Mason, a house furnishing buyer, and Emily Annie Mason of Dundee. They had one daughter. Simpson was appointed OBE in 1954, and CBE in 1962. He was chairman of the Ancient Monuments Board for Scotland, a member of the Royal Commission on the Ancient and Historical Monuments of Scotland, and president of the Scottish History Society. For most of his life he was an enthusiastic scout and he was a lay reader of the Episcopal Church of Scotland. He died of a coronary thrombosis in King's College Library, Aberdeen, on 9 October 1968, and was buried in Springbank cemetery, Aberdeen, on 12 October.   A. T. HALL

Sources personal knowledge (2004) · A. T. Hall, 'A bibliography of W. Douglas Simpson, 1896–1968', in W. D. Simpson, *Dunollie Castle and the Brooch of Lorne* (1991), 1–32 · W. Witte, *Aberdeen University Review*, 43 (1969–70), 24–7 · C. McLaren, *Aberdeen University Review*, 58 (1999–2000), 189–202 · R. B. Strathdee, 'Presentation to W. Douglas Simpson', *Aberdeen University Review*, 42 (1967–8), 247–54 · private information (2004) [G. G. Simpson; C. F. M. O'Boyle] · b. cert. · m. cert. · d. cert. · *Press and Journal* [Aberdeen] (11 Oct 1968) · WWW

Archives U. Aberdeen, collection of MS and typescript notes and papers relating to various historical and archaeological articles, lectures, pamphlets, etc. | Bodl. Oxf., letters to O. G. S. Crawford

Likenesses A. Morrocco, oils, 1967, U. Aberdeen · A. G. Hutchison, drawing, repro. in *Aberdeen University Review*, 42 (1967–8) · H. Lubbock, bust, U. Aberdeen · photograph, repro. in *Aberdeen*

University Review, 42 (1967–8) • photograph, repro. in *Aberdeen University Review*, 58 (1999–2000) • photograph, repro. in Simpson, *Dunollie Castle*

Wealth at death £9170 13*s*. 5*d*.: Scottish confirmation sealed in London, 8 Jan 1970, *CGPLA Eng. & Wales*

Simpson, Sir William John Ritchie (1855–1931), physician and specialist in tropical medicine, was born on 27 April 1855 in Glasgow, the son of John Simpson and his wife, whose maiden name was Arthur. He attended school in Jersey, graduated MB CM at Aberdeen University in 1876, and in 1880 proceeded MD (Aberdeen) and took the diploma of public health at Cambridge. In 1881 he became medical officer of health at Aberdeen, the first full-time officer appointed. While he was medical officer, Simpson argued that research in laboratory medicine would provide public health officers with new means to prevent, control, or cure epidemic diseases. In 1888 Simpson married Isabella Mary Jane, fourth daughter of George Jamieson DD, minister of St Machar's Cathedral, Old Aberdeen; the couple had a son who was killed in the First World War and a daughter.

After studying at King's College, London, Simpson became, in 1886, the first full-time medical officer of health for Calcutta. As medical officer he promoted research in laboratory medicine and he contended that the Indian government must support it. He engaged in research on epidemic diseases including cholera, smallpox, and bubonic plague. With this wide experience gained he was well qualified for the chair of hygiene at King's College, London, to which he was appointed in 1898 and which he occupied until his retirement in 1923. He co-operated with Patrick Manson and James Cantlie in founding the London School of Tropical Medicine, which was opened in October 1899; there he lectured on tropical hygiene from 1898 until 1923. Simpson also taught hygiene at the London School of Medicine for Women from 1900 until 1914. In 1926 he was one of the founders of the Ross Institute and Hospital for Tropical Diseases at Putney, where he became the first director of tropical hygiene, and physician to the attached hospital.

Besides his regular work at London University, Simpson undertook many other important tasks. In 1900 he was a member of a commission to inquire into dysentery and enteric fever among the troops in South Africa. He had hardly completed this task when, in the following year, bubonic plague broke out among the dense mass of refugees from the war area living in overcrowded and insanitary huts in the suburbs of Cape Town. Simpson travelled to Cape Town, where he advised local government officials on how to keep the disease in check. Patrick Manson, the London adviser on tropical medicine at the Colonial Office, considered Simpson to be in the front rank of sanitarians. He suggested that Simpson be appointed commissioner to investigate plague in Hong Kong in 1902; Simpson also investigated sanitation in Singapore in 1906; plague on the Gold Coast, and public health in Sierra Leone, the Gold Coast, and Southern Nigeria in 1908. He reported on plague and public health in east Africa, Uganda, and Zanzibar in 1913, as well as being a member

of a yellow fever commission in west Africa. In 1924 he studied sanitation and plague in the mines and mining villages in the Gold Coast and the Asante kingdom. His last visit to the tropics was in 1929 to the Chester-Beatty group of copper mines in Northern Rhodesia. From 1903 onwards he advocated the policy of Ronald Ross for the control of malaria by reducing the mosquito.

Simpson was a prolific writer, not only of official reports. He was editor of the *Indian Medical Gazette* (1889–96) and joint editor of the *Journal of Tropical Medicine* (London) from its inception. He was author of *A Treatise on Plague* (1905), *The Principles of Hygiene in Relation to Tropical and Sub-Tropical Climates* (1908), and *Maintenance of Health in the Tropics* (1916). He also wrote several papers on vaccination.

For his public services Simpson was appointed CMG in 1909 and knighted in 1923. He was received into the order of St Sava in 1918 for work in Serbia during the First World War. He gave the Croonian lectures in 1907 at the Royal College of Physicians, of which he was elected a fellow in 1899, and he was president of the Royal Society of Tropical Medicine and Hygiene in London from 1919 to 1921.

Simpson died at the Ross Institute, Putney, on 20 September 1931, and was buried four days later at Holy Trinity Church, West Hill, Putney. Simpson's contemporaries described him as light in build, with delicately chiselled features, quiet and charming, though he might be stubborn. He held firm opinions and he was not easily swayed, even under pressure from hostile municipal councils. During the bitter priority disputes of Manson and Ross, Simpson remained a friend to both, a mark of his loyalty and courtesy. It was characteristic of him that his last efforts were directed towards retaining open spaces in London for recreation, particularly the site of the Foundling Hospital.

MALCOLM WATSON, *rev.* MARY P. SUTPHEN

Sources R. A. Baker and R. A. Bayliss, 'William John Ritchie Simpson (1855–1931): public health and tropical medicine', *Medical History*, 31 (1987), 450–65 • *The Lancet* (26 Sept 1931), 712 • *BMJ* (3 Oct 1931), 633 • *Journal of Tropical Medicine and Hygiene*, 34 (1931), 333–4 • Lady Simpson [I. M. J. Simpson], 'Memoir of Sir William Simpson, M.B., C.M., M.D., D.P.H., M.R.C.P., F.R.C.P., C.M.G., K.C.B.', Wellcome L., Simpson collection • M. P. Sutphen, 'Imperial hygiene in Calcutta, Cape Town, and Hong Kong: the early career of Sir William John Ritchie Simpson', PhD diss., Yale U., 1995 • personal knowledge (1949) • Munk, *Roll* • *CGPLA Eng. & Wales* (1931)
Archives Wellcome L. | London School of Hygiene and Tropical Medicine, Ronald Ross MSS • PRO, Colonial Office archives
Likenesses F. Boucher, bust, London School of Hygiene and Tropical Medicine • Elliott & Fry, photograph, Wellcome L. • C. Harris, photograph, Wellcome L. • D. Scott, photograph, Wellcome L.
Wealth at death £586 11*s*. 8*d*.: probate, 22 Oct 1931, *CGPLA Eng. & Wales*

Sims, Sir Alfred John (1907–1977), naval architect, was born on 11 October 1907 in Revelstoke, near Plymouth, the fourth son and youngest of five children of John Thomas Sims, maintenance engineer on the estate of Lord Revelstoke, and his wife, Jessie Finch. He attended Regent Street higher elementary school in Plymouth, from which he entered HM Dockyard Devonport, as an apprentice in 1923. The royal dockyards in those days had excellent schools for the brighter apprentices, from which it was possible to win cadetships to study naval architecture at the Royal Naval College at Greenwich as probationary members of the Royal Corps of Naval Constructors (RCNC), a civilian body whose students by tradition train in naval uniform. Sims, from his early days in Devonport Dockyard school, demonstrated high academic ability combined with great capacity for hard work, and duly won a cadetship and in 1928 entered the Royal Naval College. In 1931 he graduated with an outstanding first-class professional certificate, and embarked on a career in the RCNC that was to bring him eminence in the corps, in the naval architecture profession, and in society at large. He married in 1933 Barbara Mary Hunking, daughter of John Lewis Paul, cabinet-maker of Plymouth, and they had a son and a daughter.

In the eight years between leaving college and the outbreak of the Second World War, Sims gained wide experience of different types of warship in service with the Mediterranean Fleet; at Chatham Dockyard, where he did pioneering work on the application of welding to warship construction; at the Admiralty, where he worked on submarine design; and then on the staff of rear-admiral submarines at HMS *Dolphin*. In the first four war years he worked on submarine design and operation as a constructor commander closely alongside Admiral Sir Max Horton, and won respect for his dedication to duty in those difficult days. In 1943 he was appointed OBE and was sent to the Admiralty at Bath to become, in 1944, a very young chief constructor in charge of submarine design and building—a post he retained for the rest of the war.

In 1947 his career took a new turn as Sims was appointed professor of naval architecture at the Royal Naval College at Greenwich, a position he occupied for five years. This appointment restored an RCNC tradition, which had been interrupted by the war, of having serving officers of high potential with up-to-date design experience to teach RCNC probationers. To this academic role Sims brought not only experience of the lessons learned in the recent war but also a determination to restore the Greenwich course to its pre-war pre-eminence among schools of naval architecture in Britain.

Two years after his return to the Admiralty at Bath in 1952, Sims was promoted to the post of assistant director of naval construction in charge of both aircraft-carrier and submarine design and in-service support, which he occupied until 1958 when, in a drastic reorganization of the Admiralty, he was selected at the relatively early age of fifty to be the first director-general ships, the most senior technical officer responsible to the Admiralty board for all vessels of the Royal Navy. At the same time he became head of the RCNC. In both roles he was the leader of an élite group of professional engineers at the start of a decade in which there were to be profound changes in the surface ships and submarines of the Royal Navy. He was appointed KCB in 1960.

The navy's first nuclear submarine, *Dreadnought*, entered service in 1962, having been designed in the ship department at Bath under Sims's overall direction. This development led to the even more momentous introduction of the Royal Navy's ballistic missile (Polaris) submarines. At the end of the decade, following the cancellation of the navy's last traditional aircraft-carrier design, CVA01, in 1966, a very ambitious design and construction programme was embarked on with a large helicopter-carrying cruiser, a compact guided missile destroyer, a new anti-submarine frigate, and a new mine-countermeasure vessel. The ships were highly innovative with extensive use of electronics, with gas turbine propulsion, and with new weapon systems. It was probably the most intensive period of change the navy had known and Sims presided over the upheaval with calm good humour and considerable industry, harnessing the efforts of a unique group of highly original but sometimes unruly naval constructors. He retired in 1968.

From 1971 to 1975 Sims was the first professional president of the Royal Institution of Naval Architects. In 1975–6 he was prime warden of the Worshipful Company of Shipwrights. He was a member of council of Bath University, which in 1974 conferred on him an honorary DSc. His other interests were wide: from 1969 to 1977 he was president of the Bath Choral and Orchestral Society; he was a Savoyard; a churchwarden of Bath Abbey parochial church council; president of the Bath branch of the YMCA; and from 1967 to 1971 the first chairman of the western branch of the Royal Society of Arts.

Sims's work and social activities were characterized by great energy and drive, boundless enthusiasm, much ambition, and an enormous and rather ruthless capacity for hard work, all coupled with a benign personality, which matched well his rather Pickwickian proportions. He died in the Forbes Frazer Hospital, Bath, on 27 August 1977. L. J. RYDILL, *rev.*

Sources *The Times* (2 Sept 1977) · *Naval Architect*, 5 (Sept 1977), 153 · private information (1986) · personal knowledge (1986) · *WWW* · *CGPLA Eng. & Wales* (1978)

Wealth at death £14,775: probate, 7 March 1978, *CGPLA Eng. & Wales*

Sims, Charles Henry (1873–1928), painter, was born on 28 January 1873 at 133 Balls Pond Road, Islington, London, the eldest son of Adenijah Stephen Sims, costume maker, and his wife, Alice, *née* Metcalf. Lame in the right leg from infancy, he attended Mrs Maw's school in Cliftonville, Margate, Kent, and then in London. Being destined to become a draper in 1887, aged fourteen, he was sent to Paris as an apprentice to a commission agent. There he learned French but little about commerce. He returned to the drapery business in London, but exhibited more interest in music and drawing; transferring to an apprenticeship in engraving did little to increase his business application. Finally, in 1890, he enrolled at the South Kensington College of Art. Thereafter he transferred to the Académie Julian in Paris, where for two years he studied under Jules Lefebvre and Benjamin-Constant. With other cosmopolitan students he learned the rudiments of *plein-air* and decorative painting, and he admired the palette of Jules Bastien-Lepage, the Impressionists' mastery of light, and the monumental symbolism of Puvis de Chavannes.

He was beset by poverty both in Paris and after he returned to England in 1892, when he vainly attempted to establish himself as a landscape painter. By 1893 the need for prizes and scholarships compelled him to enrol at the Royal Academy Schools. He was successful with such honours but his Parisian insolence and cavalier ways alienated the authorities of the schools, and in 1895 he was unceremoniously expelled. All bursaries ceased, but he had gained the confidence to start painting bacchanalian scenes of revelry, executed with astonishing flair. In January 1897 he married Agnes, the elder daughter of the landscape painter John MacWhirter, with whom he had three sons.

The first picture Sims showed at the Royal Academy, in 1896, was *The Vine*, which depicted an orgiastic party and was painted with great facility. The following year he exhibited *Childhood*, which, although establishing his mastery of the effects of sunlight, showed a whimsicality fashionable in Edwardian London but ultimately detrimental to a late-twentieth-century revival of interest in his work. *Childhood* won him a gold medal at the Paris salon and was sold to the Musée du Luxembourg. In 1898 he exhibited *A Fairy Wooing*, a sun-drenched capriccio in the manner of Victorian fairy painters. It is as a painter of an imaginary Garden of Eden, bathed in sunlight, that he emulates the work of John Singer Sargent. Two fantasies, *An Island Festival* (1907, National Gallery of New South Wales, Sydney), possibly his masterpiece, and *The Fountain* (1908, Tate collection), also drew on his formative study of the paintings of Antoine Watteau in the Louvre. With *The Shower* (1912), Sims, as did various continental artists who were trained at the Académie Julian, continued to depict a Theocritean-inspired Arcadian idyll which was shattered by the outbreak of the First World War. This redundant paradise was described by the artist as 'Earth in Heaven': 'I should say that that was my perpetual subject, a formula always in my mind'. Referring to this statement of his father's, Alan Sims continued:

> he could only conceive Heaven as a state of ideal physical existence. When he painted the spirit, he recorded his own figment of a young, flawless body … His quarrel with the apparent world was not for what it did to immortal souls, but for what it did to mortal bodies. (Sims and Sims, 93)

Besides the occasional landscape, Sims utilized his mastery of light in the open air to paint images of women and children, subject matter fashionable at that time. Beginning in 1902 with *Top o' the Hill*, he gained notoriety with such works as *Butterflies* (1904) and *The Kite* (1905, National Museum and Gallery of Wales, Cardiff), and conversation pieces such as *Spreading the Wings* (1901) and *The Little Fawn* (1908, Royal Cornwall Museum, Truro), which depict the joy of family life, springtime, a private Elysium. Idiosyncratic portraits followed, such as *Mrs Harold Phillips* (1907) and *The Countess of Rocksavage* (1921, priv. coll.). His one-man show at the Leicester Galleries in London in 1906 brought him fame and financial rewards sufficient to enable him to relocate his home and studio to Fittleworth in Sussex. In 1908 he was elected ARA; in 1910, when he held another one-man show, he was elected a member of the Royal Society of Painters in Water Colours; in 1912 he won two international gold medals; and in 1915 he was elected RA.

The end of his 'Terrestrial Paradise' came in 1914: his eldest son was killed on active service and, brokenhearted, he moved to London to try to earn a living as a society portraitist and decorative mural painter. For a while he worked as a war artist, and painted a memorial mural in the parliament buildings in Ottawa, Canada. In 1924 he was commissioned to paint the fresco *King John Sealing the Magna Carta* in St Stephen's Hall in the Houses of Parliament, London. Although he had become keeper of the Royal Academy in 1920, neither this fresco nor his portrait of George V (destroyed by the artist) were considered successes. Notwithstanding being honoured with a trusteeship of the Tate Gallery in 1924, in the same year he left England to paint portraits in the United States. This led him, in 1926, to resign the keepership of the Royal Academy. Despite achieving some successful likenesses, his disgust with society both in America and London drove him, by 1926, to abandon portrait painting altogether.

Sims's *Seven Sacraments of the Holy Church* (1917–18, priv. coll.), executed in a modernist yet naïvely archaic style, confused and displeased both the established church and the Royal Academy. A new-found but unconventional religious fervour led him into reclusiveness. His six *Spirituals* (1927–8; one in the Tate collection) depict, in agonized intensity, God's mystic relationship to man. Their modernist style and baffling content resulted in outright rejection by the artistic establishment. (They were only exhibited posthumously at the Royal Academy.) Insomnia, disillusionment, and a paranoid fear of old age weakened his resolve to live, and on 13 April 1928, aged fifty-five, while visiting the Younger family, he drowned himself in the River Tweed, near Ravenswood, St Boswells, Roxburghshire. He left a suicide note to the effect that he could not continue.   SIMON REYNOLDS

Sources A. L. Baldry, 'The paintings of Mr Charles Sims', *The Studio*, 41 (1907), 89–98 · H. Speed, 'Charles Sims RA', *Old Water-Colour Society's Club*, 6 (1928–9), 45–64 · *WWW*, 1929–40 · *The Times* (17 April 1928) · C. Sims and A. Sims, *Picture making, technique and inspiration* (1934) · *DNB* · *CGPLA Eng. & Wales* (1928) · b. cert.
Likenesses W. Stoneman, photograph, 1924, NPG · Elliott & Fry, photograph, NPG · C. H. Sims, self-portrait, repro. in Speed, *Annual Volume*, facing p. 46
Wealth at death £29,037 17s. 8d.: probate, 11 June 1928, *CGPLA Eng. & Wales*

Sims, George Robert (1847–1922), journalist and writer, was born on 2 September 1847 at 8 Newton Terrace, Kennington, London, the eldest among the six children of George Sims and his wife, Louisa Amelia Ann Stevenson (*bap.* 1823). Sims's paternal grandfather was a friend of the scientist Michael Faraday (they were fellow Sandemanians), and his maternal grandfather was a Chartist. In different facets of his life Sims reflected both traditions, though an indulgent sense of fun and panache often made him appear trivial. His father, a wine merchant, became 'a wholesale and export cabinet manufacturer and plate-glass factor' (Sims, *Life*, 31–2) in Aldersgate Street in the

City. His mother was president of the Women's Provident League. Sims grew up in comfortable circumstances in Hamilton Terrace, Islington. His parents entertained a cosmopolitan circle, including the political refugee Karl Blind, the art historian George Zerffi, the theosophist Anna Kingsford, the poet Augusta Webster, Samuel Butler, and the suffragists Frances Power Cobbe and Lydia Becker. This earnestness did not outlaw amusement: from six, Sims accompanied his mother to theatres.

Journalism and social concern After preparatory schooling in Eastbourne, followed by Hanwell College, a crammer for army cadets, Sims was dispatched to France and Germany to complete his education. He was recalled after developing a 'pronounced partiality for the roulette-tables of Ems and Wiesbaden' (Sims, *Limelight*, 157). He acquired some linguistic fluency, however. At Bonn he dabbled in play writing, adapting Benedix's comedy *Dr Wespe*; and in 1874 Chatto and Windus published his translation of Balzac's *Contes drôlatiques*. This offended the strait-laced and was withdrawn, until reissued in 1903. Back home, he entered his father's office, but was not cut out for ordinary business. In the firm's time he scribbled stories and verse. *Fun* began accepting his copy in 1874; among fellow contributors were W. S. Gilbert and Ambrose Bierce, with whom Sims became friendly (Nash, 112–14). On 3 October 1876 while living in London at 24 Addington Square, Camberwell, Sims married Sarah Elizabeth Collis (*b*. 1850/51).

Sims's satire strayed into the libellous in 1876. His open letter 'To a Fashionable Tragedian', while comically charging Henry Irving with inciting mass murder by overdoing the gore in his stage Shakespeare, unwisely accused the actor–manager of bribing hacks to flatter his performances. This landed Sims and his editor Harry Sampson in court. They apologized and Irving withdrew the suit. In 1877 Sampson started a Sunday sports and entertainments paper, *Referee*. Sims wrote its 'Mustard and Cress' columns under the pen-name Dagonet. So successful was Sims's miscellany—particularly the verses which, collated as *The Dagonet Ballads* (1879) and *Ballads of Babylon* (1880), sold in hundreds of thousands and were reprinted over the next thirty years—that *Punch* sought to poach him. Dagonet's droll travelogues were also popular, but the literati thought Sims facile. In 1892 the *National Observer*, mouthpiece of the manly imperialist coterie led by W. E. Henley, sardonically nominated Sims to succeed Tennyson as laureate. More obvious in its attack was Charles Whibley's profile of Sims in the paper's 'Modern man' series in 1889, which even Henley—who normally did not flinch when applying the lash—thought 'a trifle acid' (Connell, 167, 258). Sims fared no better in the estimation of Wildean aesthetes, whose patronizing contempt was echoed in Robert Hichens's spoof *The Green Carnation* (1894).

A solitary line from *The Dagonet Ballads* nevertheless ensured Sims entry into practically every dictionary of quotations: 'It is Christmas Day in the workhouse'. Its sentimentality and social concern struck a chord and betokened Sims's crusading zeal. The characteristics that coloured his literary confections now enlisted public support for his campaigning, especially an eye for that graphic and pathetic detail which dramatized the plight of the suffering victim. Not just evident sympathy but omnipresent wit and reasonableness spared Sims's ethical scorn and solemn warnings from seeming humbug. His articles in the *Sunday Dispatch*, *Pictorial World*, and *Daily News* in 1879–83—'The social kaleidoscope', 'The three brass balls', 'The theatre of life', 'How the poor live', and 'Horrible London' (all later published in book form)—derived from observation of London's slums. The burgeoning debate about landlord–tenant relations and the role of public authorities further involved Sims as a member of an inquiry into social conditions in Southwark in 1882 and as a witness before the royal commission on working-class housing in 1884. He also campaigned against the white slave traffic in articles in the *Daily Telegraph* (published as *London by Night*, 1906, and *Watches of the Night*, 1907); and he was active in the National Sunday League, seeking to dispel sabbatarian gloom by opening museums and galleries and providing concerts. He also wrote tracts against the maltreatment of children, such as *The Black Stain* (1907); he abetted the boys' clubs movement and, with Mrs E. W. Burgwin, headmistress of a Southwark board school, he founded the *Referee* Children's Free Breakfast and Dinner Fund (1880), which by 1900 was generating £4000 a year. It was the capital's largest such charity, whose work anticipated the public provision of free school meals for necessitous children in 1906.

Sims's fascination with London's variety merits for him a place alongside Henry Mayhew, Walter Besant, and Charles Booth. His *Living London*, published by Cassell in thirty-six parts, and as a three-decker book in 1901–3, has been too little regarded. Probably it was his 'Bitter cry of the middle classes' campaign in *The Tribune* in 1906 that forfeited him the goodwill of progressives, for he argued that the clerk, the small independent tradesman, and others of the straitened lower-middle classes were the over-taxed casualties of a new social order which enthroned organized labour, big business, and statism.

Popular dramatist That Sims's campaigning involved sensationalism is unsurprising, because this quality made him a star writer of melodrama, burlesque, pantomime, and comic opera. For *Who's Who* he recited some twenty-eight titles of which he was author or part-author. Mostly adapted from continental stock or following formulas, they were of doubtful originality. Sims did not even bother to list his first hit, *Crutch and Toothpick*, modelled on a French farce, which opened at the Royalty on Easter Monday 1879 and ran for 240 nights. Rightly he began his credits with *The Lights o' London*, which Wilson Barrett produced at the Princess's on 10 September 1881. It stayed for 286 nights, then took hold in the provinces and earned record receipts in America. By 1916, when it was being staged in Copenhagen, it had been playing somewhere in the world non-stop for thirty-five years. *Romany Rye*, which opened at the Princess's on 10 June 1882, was a similar box-office smash. J. M. Barrie and Somerset Maugham are usually credited with the feat of having four plays running concurrently in West End theatres; but it was Sims who first achieved that in the early 1880s—with, additionally, a dozen touring companies performing his work. His play-writing collaborators were numerous (Wilson Barrett, Sydney Grundy, Clement Scott, and Arthur Shirley), and his union with Henry Pettitt was particularly profitable, starting with *In the Ranks*, which opened on 6 October 1883 and ran for 457 nights at the Adelphi; it was followed by *The Harbour Lights*, which played there for eighteen months from 23 December 1885. Their *Faust Up-To-Date*, scored by the Gaiety's musical director Meyer Lütz, was the rage for several years after opening on 30 October 1888; and it inaugurated a new meaning of 'up-to-date' in the language, that of being 'abreast of the time in respect of qualities of style, knowledge, presentation of facts' (*Oxford English Dictionary*).

Sims's craftsmanship should not be disparaged. Writing in the *Contemporary Review* in November 1891 D. Christie Murray expected great things of Sims in what he considered to be a new epoch in the theatre, alongside Arthur Pinero and Robert Buchanan. The latter collaborated with Sims to write five Adelphi melodramas. Typical was *The Trumpet Call*; its plot, mused *The Globe*'s reviewer, advanced from improbability to impossibility. Mrs Patrick Campbell (1865–1940) [*see* Campbell, Beatrice Stella] played the tempestuous Gypsy villainness. This was before she established her credentials with intellectuals by her title role in *The Second Mrs Tanqueray*. The Trumpet Call gave her a different sort of fame when one night her costume collapsed and she was exposed in her drawers. This perhaps extended the play's run. Moreover, Sims and Mrs Campbell became lovers, but Sims's ardour persisted after hers cooled. She accused him of parading her as a trophy 'fruit of his labour for his fellow men to envy' (Peters, 92).

Legal reform and later life On 17 March 1888, as a widower, Sims had married Annie Maria Harriss (b. 1859/60). On 15 August 1901, again a widower, he married Elizabeth Florence Wykes (b. 1873/4). There were no children from any marriage, and all three ceremonies were held in register offices. Sims's parents were Anglicans, but his religious life appears to have been void. From the early 1890s his home was 12 Clarence Terrace, Regent's Park, London, the address of a man who had made it; and he cut a figure in the royal parks driving his trotting ponies. Attending sporting events was a passion, horse-racing and boxing matches especially. Sims exercised at badminton and by strenuous walks; as a patriot he bred prize-winning bull-dogs. The Devonshire ranked foremost among his clubs, though he incurred members' jibes when his marketing of a hair-restorer, Tatcho, supposedly a miracle cure of his own invention, failed to defeat his advancing baldness. What profit he gained from this unorthodox enterprise, wedded to his vast literary earnings, is not known, but his income approached £150,000 in 1898. That he left only £7111 at his death was probably due to his admitted gambling, a recklessness he shared with Buchanan who, despite their money-spinning play writing partnership, died

bankrupt. Sims died at 12 Clarence Terrace on 4 September 1922 from cancer of the liver; his third wife outlived him.

Sims's ideal was to win 'the admiration of the literary school of critics without sacrificing the commercial approval of the general public' (Sims, *Limelight*, 57–9); but, forced to choose, he preferred instant cash and popularity to critical reputation or literary immortality. That Sims's sketches and verses, plays and pantomimes added to the sum of human happiness in his day is plain. Unexpectedly, it is in the history of legal reform that Sims found an enduring place. Intrigued by the psychology of crime for the social pathologies it revealed, as well as for its fictional possibilities—he wrote ingenious detective stories, one, *Dorcas Dene* (1897), involving a pioneering woman detective—Sims enjoyed discussing cases with Conan Doyle, Max Pemberton, and Churton Collins at Arthur Lambton's Crimes Club. He became so wrapped up in the Whitechapel murders that some suspected him of being Jack the Ripper. More pleasingly, it was his campaign, fought through the *Daily Mail*, to release, pardon, and compensate a Norwegian, Adolf Beck, twice imprisoned owing to mistaken identity, that helped to get the court of criminal appeal established in 1907. His dedication was recognized in a knighthood of the order of St Olaf, first class, awarded by the king of Sweden and Norway in 1905.

Sims never received a native honour. His literary output was too prolific and ephemeral, and his social crusading, while spirited and arresting, was spread across too many causes. Yet he possessed uncommon flair and imagination, together with curiosity and concern about people. Sims prompted some indecision when selections were being made in 1934 for inclusion in the *Dictionary of National Biography* supplement. 'G. R. Sims I find we rejected, reconsidered, and again rejected', the secretary to the press R. W. Chapman told the essayist E. V. Lucas on 1 August:

> Do you say that this was wrong, and if so do you want to write a short life of him, (in which I am afraid you must not identify him with Jack the Ripper), or will you very kindly suggest a writer? I have always been very vague about the importance of G.R.S. (Oxford University Press archives, PB/ED/12916/OP1722)

Presumably Lucas was vague too because it was not until *Missing Persons* (1993) that Sims became securely lodged in the public memory.   PHILIP WALLER

Sources G. R. Sims, *My life: sixty years recollections of bohemian London* (1917) · G. R. Sims, *Without the limelight: theatrical life as it is* (1900) · *WWW*, 1916–28 · S. Kemp, C. Mitchell, and D. Trotter, *Edwardian fiction: an Oxford companion* (1997) · M. Peters, *Mrs Pat: the life of Mrs Patrick Campbell* (1984) · L. Irving, *Henry Irving: the actor and his world* (1951); repr. (1989) · K. Powell, *Oscar Wilde and the theatre of the 1890s* (1990) · A. S. Wohl, *The eternal slum: housing and social policy in Victorian London* (1977) · P. J. Keating, *The working classes in Victorian fiction* (1971) · T. H. Darlow, *William Robertson Nicoll: life and letters* (1925) · L. Radzinowicz and R. Hood, *The emergence of penal policy in Victorian and Edwardian England* (1990) · J. S. Hurt, *Elementary schooling and the working classes, 1860–1918* (1979) · J. Connell, *W. E. Henley* (1949); repr. (1972) · E. Nash, *I liked the life I lived* (1941) · S. P. Evans and P. Gairey, *Jack the Ripper: first American serial killer* (1995) [repr.

(1996)] • R. S. W. Bell, 'The houses of celebrated people', *Windsor Magazine*, 2 (July 1895), 3–11 • *Journals*, ed. N. Flower, 1 (1932) • b. cert. • *IGI* • m. certs. • Oxford University Press, archives
Archives U. Leeds, Brotherton L., letters to Clement Shorter
Likenesses sketches, repro. in *M. A. P.* (22 April 1905), p. 396 [advertisement for Tatcho]
Wealth at death £7111 17s. 6d.: probate, 24 Oct 1922, *CGPLA Eng. & Wales*

Sims, James (1741–1820), physician, possibly the son of the Revd Samuel Sims, a dissenting minister, was born in co. Down, Ireland, and after a preliminary education went to study at Leiden, where he proceeded MD in 1764, presenting as his inaugural thesis '*De temperie foeminea et morbis inde oriundis*'. He then returned to Ireland, and after practising for nine to ten years in co. Tyrone, moved about 1773 to London, where he was admitted a licentiate of the Royal College of Physicians on 30 September 1778.

Sims was greatly assisted by John Coakley Lettsom, and soon acquired a lucrative practice. In 1774 Sims was appointed physician to the General Dispensary in Aldersgate Street (established by Lettsom) and also served as physician to the Surrey Dispensary. He was the first chairman and vice-president of the Philanthropic Society. The Humane Society, too, owed much of its early success to his energy. Sims also became an honorary fellow of the New York and Massachusetts medical societies. He joined the Medical Society of London in 1783 and from 1786 he served for twenty-two years as its president. As his presidency progressed he became less popular, but was dislodged only by the strenuous exertions of the younger fellows, such as Astley Cooper and William Babington, some of whom had already left to form the Medical and Chirurgical Society. Sims had a valuable collection of books, which by an unusual arrangement he made over to the Medical Society in 1802, provided that an annuity of £30 be paid to himself and his wife, and £45 annually to the survivor. He made a sufficient fortune to allow himself to retire in 1810 to Bath, where he died in 1820.

William Wadd described him as 'a good-humoured pleasant man, full of anecdote, an ample reservoir of good things, and for figures and facts a perfect chronicle of other times. He had a most retentive memory; but when that failed, he referred to a book of knowledge, from which he quoted with oracular authority'.

There is a good portrait of Sims painted by Samuel Medley (1769–1857). It was engraved by Nathan Branwhite, and issued as a folding plate in the third volume of J. C. Lettsom's *Hints Designed to Promote Beneficence, Temperance, and Medical Science* (1801).

Sims's works are: *Observations on Epidemic Disorders, with Remarks on Nervous and Malignant Fevers* (1773), which went into a second edition in 1776 and was translated into both German and French; *A Discourse on the Best Methods of Prosecuting Medical Enquiries* (1774), a critique of current methods in anatomy, which was translated into French and Italian; and *Observations on the Scarlatina anginosa, Commonly called the Ulcerated Sore Throat*, which appeared in several editions between 1796 and 1803. Sims also completed and corrected Edward Foster's *Principles and Practice of Midwifery* (1781). D'A. POWER, *rev.* KAYE BAGSHAW

Sources C. E. Dukes, 'Dr James Sims (1741–1820): a new appraisal', *Medical History*, 5 (1961), 375–83 • S. Thomson, 'The strenuous life of a physician in the 18th century', *Annals of Medical History*, new ser., 1 (1929), 1–13 • Munk, *Roll* • *GM*, 1st ser., 90/1 (1820), 567 • J. J. Abraham, *Lettsom, his life, times, friends and descendants* (1933) • [W. Wadd], *Nugae canorae, or, Epitaphian mementos of the Medici family of modern times by Unus Quorum* (1899) • S. C. Lawrence, *Charitable knowledge: hospital pupils and practitioners in eighteenth-century London* (1996)
Likenesses attrib. G. Dance, pencil drawing, 1796, RCP Lond. • N. C. Branwhite, stipple, pubd 1799 (after S. Medley), BM, NPG • N. Branwhite, group portrait, stipple, pubd 1801 (*Institutors of the Medical Society of London*; after S. Medley), BM • R. Page, stipple, pubd 1823, NPG • N. Branwhite, engraving (after portrait by S. Medley), repro. in J. C. Lettsom, *Hints designed to promote beneficence, temperance, and medical science* (1801) • S. Medley, group portrait, probably Medical Society of London • S. Medley, portrait

Sims, John (1749–1831), physician and botanist, was the son of R. C. Sims, a member of the Society of Friends, who for sixty years practised as a physician at Dunmow, Essex, and was the author of *An Essay on the Nature and Constitution of Man* (1793), and of *The Constitution and Economy of Man's Nature* (1807). John Sims was born in Canterbury on 13 October 1749, and was educated partly at the Quaker academy in Burford, Oxfordshire, and partly by his father, who was a good classical scholar. In 1770 he proceeded to the University of Edinburgh, and, after passing the session of 1773–4 at Leiden, graduated MD at Edinburgh in 1774, his inaugural dissertation being '*De usu aquae frigidae interno*'.

Sims settled in London and bought the practice of Thomas Cogan in Paternoster Row; in 1779 he was admitted a licentiate of the Royal College of Physicians. He had a large practice, with many of his patients coming from the Quaker community. In 1790 he married Ann (d. 1835) and with her had six children. Sims was obliged to resign from the Society of Friends in 1790 as his wife was not a Quaker. He became physician to the Surrey Dispensary and to the Charity for Delivering Poor Married Women in their own houses. A renowned accoucheur, in 1814 he examined Joanna Southcott, the religious mystic, who had announced that she was pregnant with the Shiloh. Sims wrote an article in the *Morning Chronicle* claiming that Southcott was not pregnant but was suffering from mental delusion and diseased internal organs. After her death in 1818 Sims was present at the examination of her body, but no cause of death was ascertained. Sims also acted as physician to Princess Charlotte and attended her labour in 1817, when complications arose.

Sims edited William Curtis's *Botanical Magazine* from 1801 to 1826, and the *Annals of Botany* from 1805 to 1806, in conjunction with Charles Konig. He was elected a fellow of the Royal Society in 1814 and was a member of the society's midwifery committee. He was also one of the original fellows of the Linnean Society.

Some time after 1826 Sims retired to Dorking, Surrey, where he died on 26 February 1831. He was buried on 5 March 1831 in Fittleworth, Sussex, where his son Courthope was a curate.

Sims was commemorated by Robert Brown in the Mexican genus of Compositae, *Simsia*. His herbarium was purchased by George Bentham, and was located at Kew. Sims contributed an account of the expansion of Mesembryanthemum under the influence of moisture to the *Medical and Physical Journal* (vol. 2, 1799), and a 'Description of *Amomum exscapum*' to the *Annals of Botany* (vol. 1).

G. S. BOULGER, *rev.* KAYE BAGSHAW

Sources L. Dobson, 'The bicentenary of John Sims, MD, FRS', *The Practitioner*, 164 (1950), 156–70 · Munk, *Roll* · *Authentic memoirs, biographical, critical, and literary, of the most eminent physicians and surgeons of Great Britain*, 2nd edn (1818) · J. Britten and G. S. Boulger, eds., *A biographical index of British and Irish botanists* (1893)
Archives RBG Kew, corresp. relating to the *Botanical Magazine* | NHM, letters to members of the Sowerby family
Likenesses D. Lucas, mezzotint, 1839 (after C. R. Leslie, 1824), Wellcome L. · D. Turner, etching (after medallion by B. Pistrucci, 1817), BM, Wellcome L. · engraving, repro. in *Annals of Botany*, 1 (1805)

Simson. For this title name *see* Ashwell, Lena [Lena Margaret Simson, Lady Simson] (1872–1957).

Simson, Alexander (1570–1639), Church of Scotland minister, was a younger son of Andrew *Simson (*c.*1526–1591?), minister of Dalkeith, and Violet, sister of Patrick Adamson, archbishop of St Andrews; among his six brothers and three sisters were Patrick *Simson (1556–1618), William *Simson (*b.* 1562, *d.* in or after 1623), and Archibald *Simson (1564–1628). He was educated at the University of Glasgow, graduating MA in 1590. Alexander was appointed to 'teach' at Muckhart in November 1591, and was on the exercise at Stirling in the same month. He became minister of Alva and Tillicoultry, Clackmannanshire, in the following year. On 9 June 1596 Alexander (along with his brother Patrick and the 'haill ministars and Reidars' of the presbytery of Stirling) 'maid a new covenant with god' by restating his adherence to the solemn oath contained in the confession of faith of 1581 (Stirling presbytery registers, CH2/722/3). He was admitted to the parish of Mertoun, in the presbytery of Earlston, Berwickshire, in 1597. Nothing is known of his life over the next two decades, except that at some date he married and had a son, Andrew. Following the imposition of episcopacy in 1610 he was probably advised by his brother Patrick not to court a high public profile.

A convinced presbyterian, Simson was one of a large number of ministers who gathered at Edinburgh in 1621 to organize opposition within parliament to the intended ratification of the five articles of Perth. In a sermon preached at the 'Grayfrier Kirk' on 22 July, he found fault with the bishops and certain 'ministeris [of both England and Scotland], as not being cairfull watchemen and warneris of his majestie of his synis' (*Reg. PCS*, 12.545), and for 'omitting to putt [the king] in mind of the breache of the covenant' which the Perth articles represented (Calderwood, 7.470). Such was the sensitivity of the issue that the minister was hauled before the privy council the next day. Simson promptly made matters worse by refusing to recognize the jurisdiction of the council over ecclesiastical affairs, and by denouncing John Spottiswoode, archbishop of St Andrews, and three other 'bishops that were present, [as] belligods, and enemies to the Kirk of Christ in this land' (ibid.). As a consequence of Simson's

'undeutifull speecheis' all ministers except those of the burgh and 'such others as may have special warrant' were ordered to quit Edinburgh, 'and not return while parliament is sitting' (*Reg. PCS*, 12.546). Simson was imprisoned at the castle of Dumbarton, at his own expense, to await sentence. On 10 October he was released, and confined to his home parish of Mertoun.

According to the minister and contemporary church historian John Livingstone, Simson 'knew and cared little for earthly things, was unwearied in prayer, and constantly occupied with the Bible' (*Fasti Scot.*, 2.158). Certainly his piety impressed John Stewart, 'Captaine of Dumbartane', who 'beyond all expectation … wold take nothing for [the minister's] interteanement' at the castle (Calderwood, 7.511). Age and infirmity caused Simson to demit his ministry before May 1632, but he remained opposed to the bishops, and was the author of *The Destruction of Inbred Corruption, or, The Christians Warfare Against the Bosome Enemy* (London, 1644). He died on 17 July 1639 and was buried at Dryburgh, Berwickshire.

VAUGHAN T. WELLS

Sources D. Calderwood, *The history of the Kirk of Scotland*, ed. T. Thomson and D. Laing, 8 vols., Wodrow Society, 7 (1842–9) · *Reg. PCS*, 1st ser., vol. 12 · Stirling presbytery registers, Central Region Archives, Stirling, CH2/722/3 [unfoliated] · *Fasti Scot.*, new edn, vols. 1, 2 · J. Livingstone, *Memorable characters … of the most eminent divines* (1759) · Wing, *STC*

Simson, Andrew (*c.*1526–1591?), grammarian and Church of Scotland minister, studied at King's College, Aberdeen, probably under the humanist John Vaus and certainly under his assistant and successor Theophilus Stewart. By late May 1550 he was master of the grammar school at Perth, where he was admitted as a burgess and brother of the guild. It is unclear whether he was the man of that name who studied at St Salvator's College, St Andrews, in 1554, and at St Leonard's College, St Andrews, in 1559. By the mid-1550s Simson had married Violet Adamson (also known as Constyne or Constant), daughter of a Perth baker and sister of Patrick Adamson, the future archbishop of St Andrews (1575–92). They had seven sons (Patrick *Simson, William *Simson, Archibald *Simson, Alexander *Simson, Richard, Abraham, and Matthew) and three daughters (Katherine, Violet, and a third, whose name is unknown). A very popular master, Simson taught as many as 300 students at a time, including sons of prominent nobles and gentry. Although normally a stern teacher who was willing to use a leather strap on the students, he sometimes permitted his charges to play games.

Before his conversion Simson is said by John Row to have been 'a zealous papist' (Row, 1.4), but he became a protestant after reading a book by Sir David Lindsay, probably *Ane Dialog Betuix Experience and ane Courteour* (1553), at the request of one of his students. Simson continued to teach at Perth until 1560, and about 1562 became minister of Dunning, Perth, with responsibility as well for Cargill. On 28 June 1564 the general assembly approved his transfer to Dunbar, where he was also responsible for some of the surrounding districts and taught in the town's grammar school. On 31 August 1568 the government formally presented Simson with the parsonage at Dunbar, where his stipend was £126 13s. 4d. in 1574. In the meantime, on 4 September 1566 he was a signatory of a letter to Theodore Beza approving the second Helvetic confession, with the exception of the provisions recognizing the holy days associated with Christ's life. In 1570 he persuaded a fellow minister, John Kello of Spott, Haddingtonshire, to confess that he had murdered his wife, and seven years later he reportedly prophesied disaster when he saw a thousand fishing boats casting nets on the sabbath: that night 170 boats were said to have capsized in a storm.

In August 1572 the general assembly appointed Simson to the committee responsible for reviewing the visitation records of the archbishop of St Andrews, the superintendents, and the commissioners. Two months later he subscribed the articles of the synod of Lothian, which dealt with administrative matters, the importance of the nobility's participation in general assemblies, and the provision of books to clergy with low stipends. In March 1574 the assembly appointed him to a committee that handled requests and complaints which synods could not settle.

In December 1575 Regent Morton and the privy council named Simson to a committee of grammarians, chaired by George Buchanan and Peter Young, the royal preceptors, whose primary goal was to fashion a national grammar; Simson's task was the preparation of the first and second rudiments. By 1580 he had completed the *Rudimenta grammatices in gratiam juventutis Scoticae conscripta*, which Christophe Plantin published in Antwerp; no copy of this edition is known to have survived. An edition was published at Edinburgh in 1587. Meanwhile Simson resigned as minister at Dunbar before 11 September 1580, perhaps to devote more time to his writing. About October 1582, however, he accepted a position as minister at Dalkeith, with responsibility for the parishes of Lasswade and Glencorse as well. During these years he undoubtedly continued to work on the 'Second rudiments', though this was never published during his lifetime. Indeed, the first recorded licence to print Simson's *Rudimenta* dates only from 1599, but the work was being used as a textbook in Edinburgh two years earlier. One early edition (published in 1597) combined Simson's 'First rudiments' with the 'Second rudiments' from Andrew Duncan's *Studiorum puerilium clavis* (*Key to the Studies of Boys*).

Simson successfully opposed the attempt of the Stirling minister Robert Montgomery, a favourite of the duke of Lennox, to become bishop of Glasgow, attacking him from the pulpit as unfit for the post. In the autumn of 1584 he refused to sign a bond recognizing the crown's spiritual jurisdiction, and he was consequently summoned to appear before James VI and the privy council on 7 December. Rather than subscribe to the official formula Simson was permitted to devise his own words, swearing not to preach heresy or sedition, nor to incite subjects to rebel, and to obey all laws as long as they agreed with the word of

God. For unknown reasons his stipend was given to the abbey of Newbattle in 1587, but it was apparently restored to him in 1589. Simson probably died in early 1591. His son Archibald *Simson (1564–1628), who had been his assistant at Dalkeith since 1586, was ordained as its minister on 3 June 1591. Altogether six of Simson's sons became ministers, including Patrick *Simson, William *Simson, and Alexander *Simson; the seventh, Matthew, was a professor of humanity at Glasgow University. In February 1586 his daughter Katherine married Alexander Home, minister of Dunbar (where he succeeded Simson), and his daughter Violet married James Carmichael, minister of Haddington and rector of its grammar school from 1572 to 1576.

RICHARD L. GREAVES

Sources *Fasti Scot.*, new edn, 1.107, 314, 406; 4.268 · T. Thomson, ed., *Acts and proceedings of the general assemblies of the Kirk of Scotland*, 3 pts, Bannatyne Club, 81 (1839–45) · J. Durkan, 'Education: the laying of fresh foundations', *Humanism in Renaissance Scotland*, ed. J. MacQueen (1990), 123–60 · *Reg. PCS*, 1st ser., 2.478; 3.476, 703, 713 · J. Row, *The historie of the Kirk of Scotland*, ed. B. Botfield, 1, Maitland Club, 55 (1842), 4, 223–4 · H. Robinson, ed. and trans., *The Zurich letters, comprising the correspondence of several English bishops and others with some of the Helvetian reformers, during the early part of the reign of Queen Elizabeth*, 2, Parker Society, 8 (1845), 362–5 · D. Calderwood, *The true history of the Church of Scotland, from the beginning of the Reformation, unto the end of the reigne of King James VI* (1678), 167, 171 · T. McCrie, *Life of John Knox*, [another edn] (1898), 19, 393 · DNB

Simson, Andrew. See Symson, Andrew (c.1638–1712).

Simson, Archibald (1564–1628), Church of Scotland minister, was a younger son of Andrew *Simson (c.1526–1591?), minister of Dalkeith, Edinburghshire, and Violet Adamson, sister of Patrick Adamson (1537–1592), archbishop of St Andrews. Of his six brothers, five became ministers, including Patrick *Simson (1556–1618), William *Simson (b. 1562, d. in or after 1623), and Alexander *Simson (1570–1639); he also had three sisters. He was educated at the University of St Andrews, graduating MA in 1585. In the following year he was appointed assistant to his father and was clerk to the presbytery of Dalkeith in 1588. He succeeded to the latter charge in 1590. On 1 February 1604 Archibald married Katherine Crichton; the couple had three daughters, Christian, Elizabeth, and Jean. Following Katherine's death (before 10 February 1607), Archibald married, on 26 September 1607, Elizabeth Stewart.

A convinced presbyterian, Simson was a constant opponent of James VI's attempts to impose royal authority over the general assembly of the kirk. In 1605 he supported the actions of those ministers who convened at Aberdeen, in defiance of the king's express command. Although their arrival was delayed by inclement weather, he and several other ministers 'finding the Assemblie dissolved … went to the place where the Assemblie was holdin, and … tooke instruments … that were come to have keeped the said Assemblie; and … they did ratifie all the proceedings therof' (Calderwood, *History*, 6.444). Having thus incurred the king's wrath Simson was summoned before the privy council, but was dismissed after promising to moderate his future behaviour. This undertaking, however, was short lived. Simson appeared before the privy council on similar charges in December 1606 after having protested that a convention of ministers at Linlithgow—'convocated at his majestie's desire'—should not be regarded as a lawful substitute for a 'free Generall Assemblie' (ibid., 606–7).

The issue continued to occupy Simson, and—in June 1617—he objected to the proposal that 'whatever his majestie should determine in the external government of the church, with the advice of the archbishops [and] bishops … should have the force of law' (*Reg. PCS*, 11.166). The intended legislation raised presbyterian hackles, since it threatened the institution of a system 'resembl[ing] the convocatioun hous in England' and would inevitably 'prejudice the libertie of our generall assemblies' (Calderwood, 'Trew relatioun', fol. 8*v*). Consequently fifty-five ministers submitted a 'protestatioun' against the scheme, and the proposal was rejected by parliament. The weight of James's resentment fell on the document's principal author, David Calderwood, minister of Crailing, and on Simson, who had acted as 'scribe'. On 12 July, Simson was summoned before the court of high commission, deprived of his charge, and banished to Aberdeen. As before, Simson (probably on the advice of his brother) admitted his offence, and was restored to his parish in December.

Thus Simson emerged relatively unscathed from his encounters with royal authority. Undoubtedly this was due to the influence of his brother Patrick, who was himself a conspicuous opponent of episcopacy. Nevertheless, it was the latter who prevailed upon his brother to 'tolerate' the bishops (Calderwood, *History*, 7.129) and—no doubt—also instilled in him the commonly held belief that an unjust sentence might be admitted, 'howbeit ye do not acknowledge it' (Calderwood, 'Trew relatioun', fol. 4*v*). Archibald's fervent prayer that God might reinforce 'that gift [of toleration] in thir dayes of defection' reflected not only his respect for his brother's advice, but also his determination not to join those of his fellow ministers who 'for fear or gain fall into earthly dispositione' (Wodrow, 125). His own faith can only have been strengthened by the fact that in April 1618 he had to preach Patrick's funeral sermon after dark, 'being silenced and stay[ed] to preach publickly by the persecution of the Prelats' (ibid., 115). But Archibald Simson's principled presbyterianism, tempered by tolerance and common sense, earned him friends in high places. His continued nonconformity attracted the attention of the high commission at Edinburgh in June 1620, but, on the intercession of William, earl of Morton, he was excused. Even after Patrick's death, therefore, he was able to retain both his religious principles and his charge.

Simson dedicated the last years of his life to writing, and published several sermons, including *Christes Testament Unfolded, or, Seaven Sermons, on Our Lords Seaven Last Words* (1620), *Heptameron, the Seven Dayes* (1621), *Samson's Seaven Lockes of Haire: Allegorically Expounded* (St Andrews, 1621), and *A Godly and Fruitfull Exposition on the Twenty Five Psalmes* (1622). In the course of his writings Simson remembered those whose help had sustained him through difficult times. His *Hieroglyphica animalium terrestrium* (1622), for example, contained three Latin poems written by his friend and colleague Patrick Turner, minister of Borthwick and son-in-law of James Law, archbishop of Glasgow, and *A Sacred Septenarie, or, A Godly and Fruitfill Exposition on the Seven Psalmes of Repentance* (1623), was dedicated to William, earl of Morton. Simson's more tendentious works, 'Historia ecclesiastica Scotorum' and 'Annales ecclesiae Scoticanae' (NL Scot., Adv. MSS), were probably written during this period of Simson's life, but, due to the difficulty of the times, were never published. Simson died, probably at Dalkeith, in December 1628. His wife survived him.

VAUGHAN T. WELLS

Sources D. Calderwood, *The history of the Kirk of Scotland*, ed. T. Thomson and D. Laing, 8 vols., Wodrow Society, 7 (1842–9), vol. 6 · *Reg. PCS*, 1st ser., vols. 11–12 · W. K. Tweedie, ed., *Select biographies*, 1, Wodrow Society, 7/1 (1845) · D. Calderwood, 'A trew relatioun of my trall before the high commissioun and my troubles following thereupon', 1617, NL Scot., Wodrow MS Qto 76.1 · *Fasti Scot.*, new edn · *STC, 1475–1640*

Simson, Frances Helen (1854–1938), promoter of women's higher education and suffragist, was born at 13 Bruntsfield Place, Edinburgh, on 2 April 1854, the daughter of William Simson (1811–1858), secretary of the Bank of Scotland, and his wife, Jane Christiana Aberdein (*b*. 1820). She was the seventh of nine children, seven girls and two boys. While she was an infant, the family moved to 9 Eton Terrace, a smart address in an area then being developed to the south-west of the New Town, where she would spend much of her life.

Frances Simson was one of the first eight women to graduate from the University of Edinburgh in 1893 (all MA), following the Universities (Scotland) Act, 1889, which made that possible. At thirty-eight she was the oldest of the group and had studied for her degree at the classes run by the Edinburgh Association for the University Education of Women (EAUEW; formerly the Edinburgh Ladies' Educational Association, ELEA, founded in 1867), in which she enrolled in 1877. Women were first admitted to lectures, examination, and graduation at Edinburgh in 1892, when seventy matriculated, but from 1868 the ELEA held lectures, conducted and examined by university staff, leading to certificates in literature, philosophy, and science; it was the first to do so in Scotland. A year before graduating she began a collaboration with Elizabeth Sanderson Haldane, translating and editing Hegel's *Lectures on the History of Philosophy* (1892–6), first published in German in 1833–6. It remains the standard English translation.

Simson belonged to the management committee of St George's Teacher Training College in Edinburgh and was later a member of the council of St George's School for Girls, both set up by the EAUEW. Once it had succeeded in its aim of entry for women to the Scottish universities, the EAUEW turned its attentions to the women students' well-being, seeing a need for a library, a place of meeting for rest or study, and residential accommodation. She was a member of the sub-committee, set up by Margaret Houldsworth and Louisa Stevenson, to raise subscriptions for the university's first hall of residence for women. When Masson Hall opened in autumn 1897, Frances Simson was deemed to be 'a superintendent of the right sort' (Mrs J. Balfour to Louisa Stevenson, EAUW MSS) and became its first warden, a salaried post which she held for twenty-one years. Working at a large desk in a corner of the library, she gained the respect and affection of many students. She later said that when she was offered the post she 'had never even managed a private house'. Nevertheless she modelled the hall on the home in which she had been brought up, giving the hall 'a peculiar and individual charm' (H. S. Taylor, *Masson Association News Letter*, 1938, 27). The association donated valuable furniture and books to the hall.

Masson Hall remained the centre of the EAUEW's continuing activities and became a focus of women's suffrage activity. It offered a communal life to all women students, many of whom lived at home or more cheaply in lodgings. Isolation, shyness, and inarticulacy were seen as particular problems for Scottish women students. In a climate that was not uniformly welcoming to women—they met with amused toleration and scepticism as to their ability—a supportive centre for women students was needed. It was intended that the hall would develop as a women's college on the model of Girton College, Cambridge. Although its collegiate ambitions were not realized, the hall had a strong collective culture and old girls—Massonians—kept in touch through the Masson Association, of which Frances Simson was president after her retirement as warden in 1918.

Simson played a leading role in the attempt by five women graduates to vote for the university MP at the general election of 1906; the others were Margaret Nairn (also one of the first eight graduates), Dr Elsie Inglis, Chrystal Macmillan, and Frances Melville. The universities of Edinburgh and St Andrews together elected an MP and Glasgow and Aberdeen universities a second MP; the 1906 election was the first time that the joint Edinburgh and St Andrews seat had been contested since women had been permitted to graduate. The women argued that their membership of the general council of each university entitled them to vote, and that the university franchise was unique in both qualification and constituency since it was 'a franchise of education, of intellect' (*Glasgow Herald*, 11 Nov 1908). When the registrar refused to issue them with voting papers, they took the case to the Court of Session in June 1906. Their action failed when 'person' in the relevant legislation was interpreted to mean 'male person' rather than 'human' as the women argued; the denial of the vote to women, Lord Salveson declared, was on the ground of decorum and did not underrate their worth or intellect. The appeal in November 1907 was also lost but the women graduates then took their case to the House of Lords, in November 1908, raising £1000 to do so. Simson, Melville, and Macmillan attended, with Macmillan opening and acting as senior counsel. Simson spoke on the second day of the hearing, 12 November, making a more general argument and closing the case. The *Glasgow Herald* next day described hers as 'a well ordered argument upon the broad grounds'; her main points were that women graduates exercised all privileges as members of the general council except the parliamentary franchise; that women's exclusion from the suffrage generally was by custom rather than a constitutional principle and that society and elections had changed considerably from when that custom had been established; and that male graduates were qualified to vote not as men but as graduates and that women now had identical qualifications. The appeal was dismissed, with costs against the appellants, but generated useful press coverage and sympathetic support.

That women could argue their case so well at the highest court of the land, in the Palace of Westminster where they were otherwise not admitted other than as visitors behind the grille, was in itself a powerful statement. Against expectations there was no accompanying demonstration and the serious and constitutional manner in which they sought the suffrage was emphasized. Although the imposing 'modern Portia', Macmillan, gained more media attention and Simson, dressed plainly in black, was somewhat in her shadow, she was judged 'sufficiently clear and impressive in her manner' (*Glasgow Herald*, 13 Nov 1908). Elizabeth Haldane wrote to her on 16 November 1908: 'Whatever the result this will do great things for the cause and makes me proud of my sex' (NL Scot., Haldane MSS). The case led to the formation of women's suffrage societies in the four Scottish universities and Simson became president of the Scottish University Women's Suffrage Union. She was also vice-president of the Edinburgh National Society for Women's Suffrage (NSWS) and active in the Scottish federation of the National Union of Women's Suffrage Societies; after 1918 she was president of the Edinburgh Equal Citizenship Society, the successor to the Edinburgh NSWS.

When Edinburgh University marked its 350th anniversary, in October 1933, Simson received the honorary degree of LLD, as the only woman graduand, for her role in the cause of the university education of women. The citation described her as 'a survivor of the plucky band of eight ladies' who were first to graduate and referred to the 'useful and decorous' part she played in 'the general struggle for the rights of her sex' (*University of Edinburgh Journal*, 6/2, Jan 1934, 163–4). She saw herself as honoured on behalf of the many women who had worked for women's education—'they knew what they wanted and were determined to get it, and not to accept anything inferior'—and one of those who had been first to reap the fruits of those efforts (*The Scotsman*, 2 Nov 1933). In retirement she spent her summers in highland Perthshire, usually with her sisters and members of their families, and was often visited by former Masson Hall residents. Contemporaries described her as avoiding the limelight but as working quietly and steadily for her ideals (*Masson Association News Letter*, 1938, 27). She died at her home, 9 Eton Terrace, Edinburgh, on 4 September 1938. SUE INNES

Sources W. N. Boog Watson, 'The first eight ladies', *University of Edinburgh Journal*, 23 (1967–8), 227–34 • *Glasgow Herald* (11 Nov 1908), 11 • *Glasgow Herald* (13 Nov 1908), 9 • *Edinburgh Evening News* (5 Sept

1938) • 'Woman pioneer honoured', *The Scotsman* (2 Nov 1933) • S. Hamilton, 'Women and the Scottish universities, *circa* 1869–1939: a social history', PhD diss., U. Edin., 1987 • L. Leneman, *A guid cause: the women's suffrage movement in Scotland* (1995) • *The Scotsman* (24 Nov 1897) • *The Scotsman* (5 Sept 1938) • *University of Edinburgh Journal*, 6 (1933–4), 163–4 • R. Saville, *Bank of Scotland: a history, 1695–1995* (1996) • B. W. Welsh, *After the dawn: a record of the pioneer work in Edinburgh for the higher education of women* (1939) • censuses, 1851–91 • *The Post Office Edinburgh directory* [annuals] • bap. reg. Scot. • d. cert.

Archives NL Scot., Elizabeth Sanderson Haldane corresp. and papers • U. Edin., Edinburgh Ladies' Educational Association and Edinburgh Association for the University Education of Women MSS • U. Edin., Masson Hall MSS

Likenesses group photograph, 1893, repro. in *The Queen* (May 1893) • photograph, 1897, repro. in *The Student* (16 Dec 1897) • photograph, 1934, repro. in *University of Edinburgh Journal*, 6/2 (Jan 1934)

Wealth at death £13,575 8s. 4d.: confirmation, 3 Dec 1938, CCI

Simson, Harold Fraser- (1872–1944), composer, was born at 3 Dawson Place, Kensington, London, on 15 August 1872, the son of a flourishing merchant, Arthur Theodore Simson, and of his Scottish wife, Jane Anne Catherine Fraser, of Reelig. Educated mostly in France, but also at Charterhouse School and King's College, London, he operated as a commercial shipowner from an office in Mincing Lane, while at the same time turning his hand to composing light music in a dilettante way. In 1911 he wrote the musical score, to a colourful if conventional text by the striving stage writer Walter Wadham Peacock, for a comic opera called *Bonita*, and organized a syndicate to produce it in the West End. Several well-known artists were hired to take part, but Simson's coup was the securing of the avant-garde director H. Granville Barker to stage the piece. *Bonita* was not a success, but its music was well received, and thus, five years later, when Howard Talbot and Paul Rubens proved unavailable to set the new libretto by an unknown author being prepared by Bobbie Evett for Daly's Theatre, Simson (some said, at the price of an investment) was offered the job. His score to Freddie Lonsdale's text for *The Maid of the Mountains* (1916, including 'Farewell', 'Love will Find a Way', and 'Husbands and Wives') made him famous.

His reputation secure, as the composer of one of the biggest musical-theatre successes of the era, Simson subsequently supplied Evett with the scores for two other vehicles for the star of *The Maid of the Mountains*, José Collins—the splendidly successful *A Southern Maid* (1917) and a Peg Woffington musical, *Our Peg* (1919). The latter was initially frozen out of the West End because of the success of its long-running predecessors, but it later played at the Gaiety in a revised form as *Our Nell* (1924) with the star as Nell Gwynne.

The composer had less joy with a touring musical called *Missy Jo* (1921) and a vehicle for the comedian W. H. Berry, *Head over Heels* (1923), but he scored another fine success when he returned once again to themes costume and romantic and teamed once more with Lonsdale on a musical about artists in Montmartre, *The Street Singer* (1924). Phyllis Dare purchased the show and had it mounted as a vehicle for her talents, and it ran for nearly a

year at London's Lyric Theatre before going round the country. Thereafter Simson wrote only one further musical play for the West End stage, a charming light romantic piece based on Hastings Turner's *The Lilies of the Field*, which was produced in 1925 under the title *Betty in Mayfair*, with Evelyn Laye featured. However, four years later he supplied the music to A. A. Milne's adaptation of Kenneth Grahame's classic *The Wind in the Willows*, which was produced at Liverpool as *Toad of Toad Hall*. The little show established itself as a perennial favourite, and more than half a century later it was still regularly produced in Britain as a children's Christmas entertainment. The composer achieved one more, posthumous, stage credit when, in 1970, Julian Slade adapted Milne's *Winnie the Pooh* to the stage with his song cycle *The Hums of Pooh* as its musical part.

Simson, who was married to Cicely Devenish, latterly lived his life between London and the family seat at Dalcross Castle, Croy, Inverness-shire, where he died on 19 January 1944. KURT GÄNZL

Sources K. Gänzl, *The encyclopedia of the musical theatre*, 2 vols. (1994) • K. Gänzl, *The British musical theatre*, 2 vols. (1986) • J. Parker, ed., *Who's who in the theatre*, 6th edn (1930) • P. Gammond, *The Oxford companion to popular music* (1991) • A. Lamb, 'Fraser-Simson, Harold', *New Grove* • WWW • b. cert. • d. cert.

Wealth at death £4204 3s. 2d.: confirmation, Scotland, 1944

Simson, John (1667–1740), theologian and university teacher, was born at Cambaston, Scotland, on 13 July 1667, the eldest son of Patrick *Simson (1628–1715), minister of Renfrew, and his second wife, Janet Cullen (*née* Peadie) (*bap.* 1635, *d.* 1714). After receiving his MA from Edinburgh University in 1692 he studied divinity at Glasgow University, where he was bibliothecary and quaestor by December 1693, and appeared on the divinity rolls of 5 February 1694. In 1695 the burgh of Glasgow reappointed him bibliothecary, but he left for the Netherlands in August 1696 to pursue his theological studies. Since Simson later claimed to have studied under Jan Marck (1656–1731), his destination was presumably Leiden. After returning to Scotland in 1697 he passed his trials, signed the Westminster confession of faith, and received his licence to preach from the presbytery of Paisley on 13 July 1698. Although Simson admitted to scruples about the way the confession dealt with the covenant of works and about some of its wording, he stressed that one must 'be satisfied with the Truth of every Proposition and Consequence contained in it' in order to subscribe (*Letters*, 7).

In September 1698 Simson re-embarked for the Netherlands as tutor to John, son of Francis Montgomery of Giffin. They spent two years in Utrecht, then travelled home slowly via Flanders, France, and England. Back in Scotland, Simson acted as assistant to his father in Renfrew until he received a call to the parish of Troqueer (presbytery of Dumfries) in July 1705. He was ordained at Troqueer on 20 September 1705, and served there for the next three years. On 10 April 1708 the University of Glasgow elected him professor of divinity. The commission of the general assembly of the Church of Scotland agreed to his transportation from Troqueer to Glasgow on 7 July, and his formal admission to the chair took place on 10 November of that year. On 31 October 1710 he married Jean Stirling (c.1691–1782), daughter of James Stirling, minister, and niece of Glasgow University's principal, John Stirling, by whom they were married; they had fourteen children born between 1712 and 1735 of whom all but three died in childhood.

Enlightened in outlook and familiar with reformed theology on the continent, Simson introduced into the Glasgow divinity school the work of Marck, along with that of the contemporary Genevan theologian Benedict Pictet. He expounded the Westminster confession, noting its differences from other reformed systems and its superiority to them. His students were allowed considerable latitude of argument in making presentations, refuting Christian writers from various denominations, and having group discussions on difficult scriptural passages. His teaching was based on a belief in the benevolence of God and an assurance that a loving creator would never deny his creatures the means of salvation, which could be discovered through the exercise of reason. Simson's efforts to make such a God conform to late seventeenth-century Scottish Presbyterian orthodoxy led to confrontation with devout zealots shortly after his arrival in Glasgow. The ensuing debates produced a wealth of polemic writing and became entangled with political rivalries.

The first suggestions of unsound teaching were made in 1710 by the orthodox Edinburgh minister James Webster. Apparently satisfied by Simson's explanation of his teaching on the imputation of original sin, political differences over the Act of Abjuration (1712) led Webster to a more extreme position. When he charged Simson with unsound doctrine, the 1714 general assembly of the Church of Scotland sent the case to a committee chaired by William Carstares. Webster's publication (1716?) of Simson's correspondence with Robert Rowan, minister of Penningham, added fuel to the flames. There Simson justified his teaching on federal theology as well as his political views on the Act of Abjuration. Simson's opponents were further alarmed by his refutation of Webster's libel, published in 1716, which reflected his sympathy with the possibility of salvation. Simson's views included an insistence on the likelihood of more souls being elect than reprobate and the probable election of deceased infants, an aversion to the contractual nature of federal theology, and a belief that in hell sinning would cease, as well as an interest in current astronomical discussion leading him to suggest that the moon might be inhabited. The presbytery of Glasgow and Simson's academic colleagues stood firm behind him, united in their political allegiance to the squadrone, whereas Webster was an Argathelian, supporting the Campbells of Argyll. The general assembly of 1717 determined that Simson had merely been guilty of imprudent expressions, which he should avoid in future: a mild reprimand and a victory for the squadrone managers. In Glasgow, however, the Argathelians succeeded in securing the transportation of John Anderson to a city church against the wishes of the squadrone's presbytery members, causing Simson, in a sermon in May, to speak of

'breaking the hearts of five honest men to please one man' (Correspondence of … Wodrow, 2.272).

In matters of ecclesiastic or academic discipline Simson was authoritarian. His study of Samuel Clarke's work on the Trinity and of patristic writers caused new controversy in the mid-1720s. This enthusiasm for research led to rumours that he had adopted Clarke's semi-Arianism, and that within his strict rules of classroom propriety his divinity students had too much freedom of debate. At about the same time Simson was afflicted with an intestinal disorder which sapped his strength. Ill health limited his ability to teach and to defend himself when in 1726 he was accused by the presbytery of Glasgow of making statements in his lectures which seemed to have an Arian tendency. Simson responded that he had come to believe that the Church of Scotland verged on the modalistic heresy of Sabellianism. He said that he now emphasized in his teaching the personal properties of each person in the Trinity to maintain their individual qualities. He assured his colleagues that he adhered to the Bible and the Westminster confession, using their terminology in his lectures. The matter was taken to the general assembly, which appointed a committee to investigate Simson's teaching in co-operation with the presbytery of Glasgow, full details of which were published by the Church of Scotland. Simson reiterated his orthodoxy, and the depositions of his students were inconclusive.

A new pamphlet war between ultra-orthodox and liberal presbyterians resulted in deep divisions in the church. Political realities again affected the outcome. The Argathelians, under the earl of Ilay, were now the dominant faction; Simson returned to his family's traditional support of the Campbells. Appreciating that fanatics made ineffective political allies Ilay opposed any increase in power for the ultra-conservative group. Fear of English interference in Scottish ecclesiastical affairs also played a part in the eventual compromise decision (1729) supported by Ilay to suspend, but not depose, Simson. After Simson's supporters failed in 1730 to have his suspension reversed he continued to live in his university house and act as a member of the Glasgow faculty, although not teaching publicly, until his death on 2 February 1740.

Simson's cases formed a watershed in the development of the Church of Scotland in the eighteenth century. Their significance lies less in the fate of Simson than in the effect they had on the church. The secession of 1733 was partly brought about by the dismay at what the extreme group considered Simson's lenient punishment. Freed from the restrictions imposed by the ultra-orthodox, the church embraced Enlightenment ideals while upholding Calvinist Christianity. ANNE SKOCZYLAS

Sources G. Heath, ed., *Records of the Carrick Moore family* (1912) • J. Simson, *Libel Mr James Webster, against Mr John Simson professor of divinity in the University of Glasgow* (1716?) • *A true and authentick copy of Mr. John Simsons letters to Mr. Robert Rowan, late minister at Penningham, taken out of the originals*, ed. J. Webster (1716) • J. Dundas, *State of the processes depending against Mr. John Simson Professor of Divinity in the University of Glasgow* (1728) • *The correspondence of the Rev. Robert Wodrow*, ed. T. M'Crie, 3 vols., Wodrow Society, [3] (1842–3) • R. Wodrow, *Analecta, or, Materials for a history of remarkable* providences, mostly relating to Scotch ministers and Christians, ed. [M. Leishman], 4 vols., Maitland Club, 60 (1842–3) • C. Innes, ed., *Munimenta alme Universitatis Glasguensis / Records of the University of Glasgow from its foundation till 1727*, 4 vols., Maitland Club, 72 (1854) • testimonial for John Simson, Alexander Wodrow, and John Hamilton, U. Glas., Archives and Business Records Centre, MS 30329 • accounts for quaestor, 1682–1726, U. Glas., Archives and Business Records Centre, MS 58201 • minutes, faculty and university meetings, U. Glas., Archives and Business Records Centre, MSS 26632–5, 26639 • general assembly papers, 1714–18, 1726–31, NA Scot., CH1/1/24, CH1/2/34–38, 52–64, CH1/5/11 • records of the presbytery of Glasgow, Mitchell L., Glas., Strathclyde regional archives, CH2/171/8–10 • J. D. Marwick and R. Renwick, eds., *Extracts from the records of the burgh of Glasgow, AD 1691–1717*, 4, Scottish Burgh RS, 19 (1908) • R. Renwick, ed., *Extracts from the records of the burgh of Glasgow, AD 1718–1738*, 5, Scottish Burgh RS, 23 (1909) • W. J. Couper, 'The Levitical family of Simson', *Records of the Scottish Church History Society*, 4 (1930–32), 119–37, 208–66, esp. 209–40 • A. Skoczylas, 'Professor John Simson and the growth of enlightenment in the Church of Scotland', PhD diss., University of Western Ontario, 1996

Archives Mitchell L., Glas. • NA Scot. • U. Glas. L.

Simson, Patrick (1556–1618), Church of Scotland minister, was born at Perth, the eldest of the seven sons of Andrew *Simson (c.1526–1591?) and his wife, Violet Adamson, sister of Patrick *Adamson, archbishop of St Andrews. His brothers, all but one of whom also became ministers, included William *Simson (b. 1562, d. in or after 1623), Archibald *Simson (1564–1628), and Alexander *Simson (1570–1639). He also had three sisters. His father was schoolmaster at Perth and became minister of Dunning and Cargill shortly after the Reformation, before being translated to Dunbar in 1564. Having been educated in the classics by his father, Patrick entered the University of St Andrews in 1571 and graduated MA in 1575. It was intended that he proceed to Cambridge, but on his way there he met an English gentleman who put the library in his house at Brigstock, Northamptonshire, at Simson's disposal, enabling him to acquire an extensive knowledge of the literary and historical remains of antiquity, both lay and ecclesiastical. His father then fell sick and recalled Simson to Scotland, where he assisted in the school at Dunbar by teaching Greek. In 1577 he was admitted minister of the adjoining parish of Spott, which with Aldhame and the Bass constituted both a prebend in the collegiate church of Dunbar and a free parsonage, and he continued to teach weekly at Dunbar.

In 1582 Simson became minister of Cramond in the presbytery of Edinburgh; he was provided to the vicarage on 30 August 1586. In 1584 the ministers of the presbytery were ordered to subscribe the so-called 'black acts' in favour of episcopacy, and to promise obedience to their bishop on pain of forfeiting their stipends. Although his diocesan was his maternal uncle, Patrick Adamson, Simson refused, showing himself then as always implacably opposed to the reintroduction of bishops. During his time at Cramond he was himself offered a see, but unsurprisingly declined it. He later also refused a pension.

In 1590 the general assembly translated Simson to Stirling, a royal residence. He was admitted on 7 August and received the crown's presentation in May 1591. He held the benefice for the rest of his life. He had considerable influence with the king, to whom he was constantly loyal and respectful, and also with John Erskine, second earl of Mar, a leading courtier and Prince Henry's keeper. When James renewed his efforts to reintroduce episcopacy, however, Simson was once more a leading opponent of royal policy. Early in 1606 he attended the trial for treason at Linlithgow of six ministers who had attended an assembly which the king had banned, and was their main supporter; in July that year he drew up and signed the protest against episcopacy presented to the Scottish parliament; and when Andrew Melville was imprisoned in the Tower of London in March 1607 he organized a subscription for him. In the latter year the general assembly nominated him permanent moderator of the presbytery of Stirling, but he refused the appointment, probably because it appeared dangerously similar to episcopal office. However, on 15 June 1608 Simson was elected moderator of the conference at Falkland between bishops and representatives of the kirk, at which the latter called for the maintenance of presbyterianism. He also opposed the liturgical changes which followed the restoration of bishops, regarding them as the deplorable product of English influence and reportedly declaring: 'Alace! I see all the midden (or dunghill) of the muck of the corruption of the Kirk of Ingland comeing on upon us, and it will wrack us, if God send not help in time' (Mullan, *Scottish Puritanism*, 268).

In spite of his anti-episcopal fervour Simson was by nature moderate, peaceable, and charitable, so much so that he was sometimes blamed for his conciliatory spirit by extremists on his own side. He took a leading part in preventing schism in the church, and urged his brethren to continue to attend synods after the bishops began to preside over them. He attended at least ten general assemblies before 1610 (only one more was held in his lifetime). He continued his studies into his fifties, when he learned Hebrew, and was often consulted by his clerical brethren for his wisdom and learning. A notable preacher and pastor, he was held in considerable affection by his flock, many of whom venerated him as their spiritual father. On his coming to Stirling he found the townspeople disorderly and violent, with merchants and craftsmen apt to engage in bloody combat in the streets, and he restored order to the community. In times of plague he remained in his parish and performed his ministerial duties at the risk of his own life. When he lay dying people of all ranks crowded to his bedside to receive his blessing and brought their children with them. Nearly fifty years afterwards John Livingstone, writing in exile in the Netherlands, looked back to his childhood in Stirling and remembered Simson as 'a man learned, godly, and very faithfull in the cause of God' (Mullan, *Scottish Puritanism*, 35).

Simson married twice. His first wife was Martha Baron, the daughter of an Edinburgh burgess; they had three sons, all of whom became ministers, and a daughter, Lilias, who married John Gillespie, minister of Alva, and was the mother of George *Gillespie and Patrick *Gillespie. Following Martha's death Simson married a daughter of Leslie of Kinnaird. He died after many years of ill health on 31 March 1618 at Stirling and was buried in the choir of

Stirling parish church. It was claimed that owing to 'the persecution of the Prelats' his funeral sermon had to be delivered at night (Mullan, *Episcopacy*, 130). Between 1609 and 1616 he published four works of church history which were subsequently brought together into a single volume by his brother Archibald as *The Historie of the Church since the Dayes of our Saviour Jesus Christ untill this Present Age* (1624). It was dedicated by Archibald to the duke of Richmond, but Patrick Simson's own epistle dedicatory was addressed to Mary, countess of Mar, one of several noblewomen who had held him in high regard.

G. W. SPROTT, *rev.* DUNCAN SHAW

Sources Fasti Scot., new edn, 4.318 • D. Calderwood, *The history of the Kirk of Scotland*, ed. T. Thomson and D. Laing, 8 vols., Wodrow Society, 7 (1842–9), vols. 2–4 • T. Thomson, ed., *Acts and proceedings of the general assemblies of the Kirk of Scotland*, 3 pts, Bannatyne Club, 81 (1839–45) • W. K. Tweedie, ed., *Select biographies*, 2 vols., Wodrow Society, 7 (1845–7), 63–112 • D. Mullan, *Episcopacy in Scotland* (1986) • D. Mullan, *Scottish puritanism, 1590–1638* (2000) • A. R. Macdonald, *The Jacobean kirk, 1567–1625* (1998)

Simson, Patrick (1628–1715), Church of Scotland minister, was born in New Abbey manse, Kirkcudbrightshire, on 2 October 1628, the second son and sixth child of Adam Simson (1594–1642), the minister there, and his wife, Margaret Spens. His early years are obscure. He may not have accompanied his parents when they went about 1632 to Ireland, where his father died ten years later, leaving his wife in penury; he may instead have been brought up by his cousin George Gillespie. He matriculated in arts at Edinburgh in 1643 and was a member of the class of James Wiseman (*d.* 1655), professor of philosophy, but did not graduate. Once licensed (date unknown), he served between 1649 and 1653 as chaplain and tutor to the marquess of Argyll at Inveraray.

Having already been an observer at six general assemblies of the kirk on 11 November 1653 Simson was ordained and inducted to Renfrew. On 30 August 1654 he married Elizabeth Hay, daughter of his predecessor (and successor); they had five children. Little is seen of Simson's Renfrew ministry before his ejection on 1 October 1662. Following the death of his wife on 31 March 1662, on 30 June 1664 he married Janet Peadie (*bap.* 1635, *d.* 1714), widow of Robert Cullen, a Glasgow merchant. Of their seven children, John *Simson became a Glasgow professor of dubious orthodoxy.

After accepting the second Act of Indulgence, Simson was appointed to Kilmacolm in 1672, but the family's unsettled life was not at an end. In 1674 he was charged with ministering outside his parish. He supported the covenanter preacher Alexander Peden during the latter's imprisonment on the Bass Rock in 1677, and, having refused the privy council's summons in 1678–9 to answer for 'keeping of conventicles', was deposed, but the sentence was not enforced for some years. The 1687 declaration of indulgence allowed his reappointment to Renfrew, but this was not implemented until 1690.

In his later years Simson proved a valued counsellor in ecclesiastical business, for example, during the restoration of presbyterianism in 1690 and the union debates of

1707. He served in 1695–6 as moderator at a general assembly which moved towards realizing the Scottish reformation's aim of a school in every parish, was involved in witch trials in 1697, and was dean of the faculties in Glasgow University from 1690 to 1701. The communion cups presented on his ministerial jubilee in 1703 were still in use at the end of the twentieth century, but although plans to authorize for congregational use his *Spiritual Songs, or, Holy Poems* (1685–6), drawn from the Bible, came close to fruition in 1708, they lapsed thereafter. Simson retained a sharp mind and memory, being father of the kirk at the end of his life. His wife having died on 19 September 1714, Simson himself died on 24 October 1715. Robert Wodrow, who knew him well, paid him a glowing tribute. Three of his writings on church controversies survive in manuscript (NL Scot., Wodrow MSS).

D. F. WRIGHT

Sources Fasti Scot. • W. J. Couper, 'The Levitical family of Simson', *Records of the Scottish Church History Society*, 4 (1930–32), 119–37, 208–66, esp. 211–27 • J. Warrick, *The moderators of the Church of Scotland from 1690 to 1740* (1913), 71–91 • A. Morgan, alphabetical listing of the matriculation roll of the University of Edinburgh, arts, 1623–1774, U. Edin. L., special collections division, university archives [typescript], 24 • matriculation rolls, U. Edin. L., special collections division, university archives • A. Dalzel, *History of the University of Edinburgh*, 2 (1862)

Archives NL Scot., Wodrow MSS

Simson, Robert (1687–1768), mathematician, was born on 18 October 1687, probably the eldest of the seventeen children, all male, of John Simson (*d.* 1731), a Glasgow merchant, of Kirktonhall, West Kilbride, Ayrshire, and his wife, Agnes, daughter of Patrick Simson, minister of Renfrew. Thomas *Simson was a younger brother. Robert Simson's name appears in the list of students matriculating in the fourth class at Glasgow University on 3 March 1701. Originally intended for the ministry, he studied under his maternal uncle, John Simson, professor of divinity, and first distinguished himself as a classical scholar. His interests then turned to mathematics, a subject which was in decline at Glasgow. Following the enforced resignation of the professor of mathematics, Robert Sinclair, Simson was nominated to this post on 8 March 1711. At that time he was spending a year in London pursuing his mathematical studies but after his return he was examined on 9 November 1711 and admitted to the professorship ten days later, having just graduated MA, on the 16th. About 1728 he became clerk to the university meeting and fulfilled both functions until he retired in 1761. In 1746 the University of St Andrews conferred on him the honorary degree of MD.

While in London, Simson made the acquaintance of several eminent mathematicians, among them Edmond Halley, whose influence perhaps reinforced his obsession with the works of the Greek geometers. He first directed his attention to Euclid's porisms, which are only known from the short account in the *Collectiones mathematicae* of Pappus of Alexandria. Although Pierre de Fermat claimed to have restored Euclid's work and Halley had edited the Greek text of the preface to the seventh book of Pappus, Simson was the first to throw real light on the matter. In a paper communicated in 1723 to the Royal Society by James Jurin, Simson restored two general propositions in which Pappus summed up several of the porisms (*PTRS*, 32, 1723, 330–40); his further work on the porisms was not published until after his death. In 1735 Simson published *Sectionum conicarum libri V*, which he partly intended as an introduction to the treatise by Apollonius of Perga on the subject; here Simson employed methods of pure geometry rather than algebra. In 1738 he completed the restoration of the 'Loci plani' of Apollonius, a task already attempted by Fermat before 1629 and by Francis Schooten in 1657; his conclusions were published in 1749 in a work entitled *Apollonii Pergaei locorum planorum libri II, restituti a R. Simson*. He next occupied himself with the restoration of the 'Sectio determinata' of Apollonius, which had already been the subject of some investigations by Alexander Anderson in 1612 and by Willebrord Snel in 1634; Simson's version was published posthumously. His most influential work was probably his definitive edition of Euclid's *Elements*, which he published in 1756. Both his Euclid and his *Conic Sections* ran through many editions and were translated into several languages.

In spite of his obsession with Greek geometry Simson was familiar with contemporary mathematics and included the elements of fluxionary calculus in his courses. There is an early manuscript of his dealing with inverse tangent series and their use in calculating π (U. Glas. L., MS. Gen. 1096), and in his paper 'An explication of an obscure passage in Albert Girard's commentary upon Simon Stevin's works' (*PTRS*, 48, 1754, 368–77) he used algebraic methods to discuss a limit involving Fibonacci numbers and an iterative process for finding square roots. Among his manuscripts now in Glasgow University Library are sixteen volumes of 'Adversaria on mathematical subjects, 1716–1767' (U. Glas. L., MS Gen. 256–71).

Simson appears to have been tall and of good stature. In spite of his great scholarship he was a modest, unassuming man who was very cautious in promoting his own work. He enjoyed good company and presided over the weekly meetings of a dining club that he had instituted. In his later years he complained of failing memory which inhibited his work. He had a special interest in botany, in which he was an acknowledged expert.

Simson never married. He died at the University of Glasgow on 1 October 1768 and was buried in the graveyard of Blackfriars Church. He bequeathed his extensive library to the University of Glasgow where it is still preserved as the Simson Collection. His manuscripts were left to his friend and colleague James Clow, professor of philosophy, with the request that he should put them in order and have them published. With financial support from Philip Stanhope, second Earl Stanhope, Clow published some of them in 1776 as Simson's *Opera quaedam reliqua*.

E. I. Carlyle, *rev.* Ian Tweddle

Sources W. Trail, *Account of the life and writings of Robert Simson* (1812) • *Encyclopaedia Britannica*, 3rd edn (1797), vol. 17, pp. 504–9 • C. Innes, ed., *Munimenta alme Universitatis Glasguensis / Records of the University of Glasgow from its foundation till 1727*, 4 vols., Maitland Club, 72 (1854) • J. Coutts, *A history of the University of Glasgow* (1909) • D. Murray, *Memories of the old college of Glasgow: some chapters in the history of the university* (1927) • R. V. Wallis and P. J. Wallis, eds., *Biobibliography of British mathematics and its applications*, 2 (1986), 131–5 • R. Alison, *The anecdotage of Glasgow* (1892), 116–17 • J. M'Ure, *Glasghu facies: a view of the city of Glasgow*, ed. J. F. S. Gordon (1872), 330–31, 650–51 • J. Strang, *Glasgow and its clubs* (1856), 2–24 • J. Paterson, *History of the counties of Ayr and Wigton*, 3 (1866), 61–2, 365–8 • I. Tweddle, 'John Machin and Robert Simson on inverse-tangent series for π', *Archive for History of Exact Sciences*, 42 (1991), 1–14 • I. Tweddle, *Simson on porisms*, Sources in the History of Mathematics and Physical Sciences (2000)

Archives CKS, corresp. with Lord Stanhope • RS • U. Glas., Archives and Business Records Centre • U. Glas. L.

Likenesses P. de Nune, oils, 1746, University of Strathclyde, Glasgow, Collins Art Gallery • W. Cochrane, oils, 1769–70 (after P. de Nune, 1746), Hunterian Museum and Art Gallery, Glasgow • P. de Nune, oils, Royal Technical College, Glasgow • line engraving (after de Nune), NPG; repro. in Trail, *Account*

Wealth at death £519 15*s.* excl. library bequeathed to University of Glasgow; also lands in Ayrshire, chiefly Kirktonhall and Knock Ewart: NA Scot., commissary of Glasgow testaments, vol. 64 (CC 9/7/67)

Simson, Thomas (1696–1764), physician, was born at Kirktonhall in the parish of West Kilbride, Ayrshire, the third son of John Simson (*d.* 1731), a merchant, of Kirktonhall, and his wife, Agnes, daughter of Patrick Simson, minister of Renfrew. The mathematician Robert *Simson was his brother, and the theologian John Simson was his uncle.

In 1721 James Brydges, duke of Chandos, established a medical professorship at the University of St Andrews, and on 10 January 1722 Simson, who had been awarded an MD by Glasgow University in 1720, was admitted as its first incumbent. He was an able and efficient professor who, unusually for the time, taught in the vernacular.

About 1724 Simson married a daughter of Sir John Preston of Prestonhall, Fife, who was deprived of his estates in 1715. They had four sons and two daughters; their son James was professor of medicine at St Andrews in succession to his father from 1764 to 1770.

In 1744 Simson was elected an honorary fellow of the Royal College of Physicians of Edinburgh, and in 1756 he produced *Regulations for the Degree in Medicine* at St Andrews, but his recommendations were not acted upon. He held the chair of medicine until his death in St Andrews on 30 April 1764. Simson was the author of: *De re medica* (1726); *De erroribus circa materiam medicam* (1726); *System of the Womb* (1729); and *Enquiry on the Vital and Animal Actions* (1752).   E. I. Carlyle, *rev.* Kaye Bagshaw

Sources R. G. Cant, *The University of St Andrews: a short history* (1946) • J. D. Comrie, *History of Scottish medicine to 1860* (1927) • J. D. Comrie, *History of Scottish medicine*, 2nd edn, 2 vols. (1932) • *Scots Magazine*, 26 (1764), 167 • J. S. G. Blair, *History of medicine in the University of St Andrews* (1987)

Simson, William (*b.* 1562, *d.* in or after 1623), Church of Scotland minister and Hebraist, was born on 13 August 1562 in Perth, probably the third son of Andrew *Simson (*c.*1526–1591?), rector of Perth grammar school, and Violet, daughter of Patrick Adamson, a Perth baker, and sister of Patrick Adamson (1537–1592). Among his six brothers were Patrick *Simson (1556–1618), Archibald *Simson (1564–1628), and Alexander *Simson (1570–1639). He matriculated at St Andrews in 1577 and graduated MA in

1581. Thereafter his movements are elusive. He probably fled to England with other presbyterians after the pro-episcopal black acts of May 1584, perhaps with James Carmichael (c.1543–1628), who married his sister Violet. Simson contributed a Latin and Greek verse eulogy to Carmichael's *Grammaticae Latinae*, published at Cambridge in 1587.

In 1593 Simson attended the general assembly at Dundee, probably as an elder, since he was named among those about to enter the ministry. By 1597 he was serving as minister of Burntisland, Fife. Its historic church had been built by the town in 1592, but no provision made for stipend. The assembly of March 1600 therefore agreed that Simson should get a share of stipend for assisting at Ceres in Fife, but also gave him liberty to seek a fresh charge. His attendance at the assembly which convened in Burntisland on 12 May 1601 is not recorded. On 23 June that year he was presented by James VI to Dumbarton. He remained opposed to episcopacy and in July 1607 withdrew from the synod of Clydesdale when it accepted a bishop—John Spottiswoode—as moderator. The same year he was chosen master of Dumbarton's grammar school, and in August 1608 was admitted a burgess by the town council. John Skene's *Regiam majestatem Scotiae* (Edinburgh, 1609) contained a Latin verse tribute by Simson (not in the English version of the same year).

By October 1614 the Dumbarton council was seeking a replacement minister because of Simson's absence in England, and by the autumn of 1616 William Blair had succeeded him. Meanwhile, on 22 December 1615 Glasgow commissary court issued letters of 'horneing and poynding' against Simson for non-payment of £66 9s. 6d. to a Glasgow tailor. His presence in England is confirmed by his book *De accentibus Hebraicis*, published in London in 1617, the earliest treatise on Hebrew by a Scot. Its preface, dated 1 September 1617, has a dedication to Sir Christopher Hatton (c.1581–1619), known for other literary and musical patronage, and was written 'ex Musaeo nostro Vanstedano', which must refer to Wanstead, perhaps to Wanstead House, near Barking, but may possibly indicate Hatton's residence at Clay Hall. It also mentions other Hebrew writings—an etymological table and a grammatical analysis of Genesis 1—which scarcity of Hebrew type left unpublished.

Further details of Simson's English sojourns remain to be uncovered. He may have married Alice Wakeman, whose name appears English. He is last sighted writing a preface, 'To the Christian Reader', in the second edition of *The Christian Synagogue* by John Wemyss (d. 1636), another Scottish ministerial Hebraist, published at London in 1623. An alleged sighting of him in Edinburgh in November 1624 (Couper, 128) is a case of mistaken identity. It is not known when Simson died.   D. F. WRIGHT

Sources W. J. Couper, 'The Levitical family of Simsons: final records', *Records of the Scottish Church History Society*, 5 (1933–5), 117–39 · *Fasti Scot.*, new edn, 3.341; 5.81 · F. Roberts and I. M. M. MacPhail, *Dumbarton common good accounts, 1614–1660* (1972) · 'Records of the University of St Andrews', 1579–1747, U. St Andr. · b. cert. · Glasgow commissary of deeds, 22 Dec 1615, NA Scot., CC 9/14/4, fol. 194v · 'A Simson family', *Northern British-Israel Review*, 3/3 (Jan 1913), 167–87 · NL Scot., Denniston MSS, Adv. MSS 19.2.8; 19.2.16 · F. Roberts, *Roll of Dumbarton burgesses* (1937), 54 · J. Kirk, 'The development of the Melvillian movement in late sixteenth century Scotland', PhD diss., U. Edin., 1972 · A. Symson, *The destruction of inbred-corruption* (1644) · HoP, *Commons, 1558–1603*, 2.279 · J. P. Wainwright, *Musical patronage in seventeenth-century England: Christopher, first Baron Hatton (1605–1670)* (1997) · D. Pinto, 'The music of the Hattons', *Royal Musical Association Research Chronicle*, 23 (1990), 79–108 · *VCH Essex*, vols. 5–6

Simson, William (1798/9–1847), painter, second son of Alexander Simson, merchant, was born in Dundee. His father was admitted a burgess of Dundee in 1792, and, though engaged in commerce, was deeply interested in art. Three of his sons became artists: George (1791–1862), a portrait and landscape painter, who became a member of the Royal Scottish Academy; William, the subject of this entry; and David (1803–1874), a successful landscape painter and lithographer. William Simson began his art education in 1818 under the landscape painter Andrew Wilson (1780–1848), master of the Trustees' Academy at Edinburgh. Among his fellow students were Robert Scott Lauder and David Octavius Hill. Simson began exhibiting at the Institution for the Encouragement of the Fine Arts in Scotland in 1821; in 1825 he signed a proposal for the establishment of the Scottish Academy, becoming one of its first academicians. Simson, however, withdrew his membership of the newly established body before the Scottish Academy's first exhibition. It was not until after the union between the institution and the Scottish Academy in 1829 that Simson first exhibited at the Royal Scottish Academy in 1831. He presented the haunting *Solway Moss—Evening* (1830) as his diploma piece.

Simson's early works were local landscapes and seapieces. However, Simson also painted a number of works in response to a visit to the Low Countries in 1827: *A Scene in Holland* (1828; NG Scot.) and *Passage Boats Becalmed on the Maas at Dort* (NG Scot.) are full of serene light and capture the still, flat countryside and waterways, and reflect the influence of the seventeenth-century Dutch masters Albert Cuyp and William van de Velde II. The success of his elder brother George as a portrait painter encouraged Simson to follow temporarily that branch of art. The Royal Scottish Academy owns two of his cabinet portraits: one of Edmund Thornton Crawford (1806–1885), a contemporary marine painter also influenced by the Dutch school, and the other a portrait of the artist's brother David Simson. These portraits are very finely painted with small, tight brushstrokes and great attention to detail. In 1830 he exhibited his *Shooting Party Regaling*—chiefly comprising portraits—at the Royal Academy in London, and from that time until the year of his death (with the exception of 1833, 1835, and 1836) he was a regular exhibitor there. He also sent seventy-two pictures to the exhibitions of the Royal Scottish Academy.

Throughout the 1830s Simson closely followed in David Wilkie's footsteps, imitating his Italian journey in 1834. His work there led to his composition *Cimabue and Giotto*, which was exhibited at the Royal Academy in 1838 and purchased by Sir Robert Peel for 150 guineas. Simson moved to London in 1838, and settled at 97 Dean Street,

Soho, afterwards moving to 12 Sloane Street, Chelsea. Wilkie did much to encourage Scottish artists to move south but this was to prove Simson's undoing as he forsook landscape painting for history paintings, for example *Columbus at the Door of the Convent of La Rabida* (exh. RA, 1839). Simson's genre pieces, for example *A Goatherd's Cottage* (1832; NG Scot.) and *Interior of a Cottage, Killin* (1833; NG Scot.), are also indebted to Wilkie in composition, colouring, and chiaroscuro. Simson even copied Wilkie's paintings, including *The Chelsea Pensioners Reading the Gazette of the Battle of Waterloo*. Such paintings did not meet with critical approval, as Simson did not have the ability to paint interesting and lively historical scenes.

After 1830 Simson's best work is to be found in his drawings and depictions of hunting scenes. The sportsman William Scrope (1772–1852) employed Simson to record events in the field, including *The End of the Day: William Scrope on a White Pony with his Keepers and the Day's Bag* (1840s; priv. coll.). Scrope and Simson may have met at the British Institution, where Scrope was the director and Simson exhibited regularly. Simson died at his home, 12 Sloane Street, Chelsea, London, on 29 August 1847, aged forty-eight, having never enjoyed good health. Posthumously his brother David reproduced some of his drawings as lithographs. An album of 205 drawings dating from 1828 to 1847 in the Royal Scottish Academy comprises portrait and animal studies as well as landscapes and seascapes of such diverse locations as Antwerp, Amsterdam, Bridlington, and Dumfries. Collections of Simson's drawings are also in the City of Edinburgh Library Fine Art Department and the National Gallery of Scotland.

A. H. MILLAR, *rev.* LUCY DIXON

Sources *Art Union*, 9 (1847), 353 · R. Nicholson, *William Simson RSA, 1800-1847: paintings and sketches* (1989) [exhibition catalogue, Fine Art Society, London and Edinburgh, Oct–Nov 1989] · R. Parkinson, ed., *Catalogue of British oil paintings, 1820–1860* (1990) [catalogue of V&A] · W. D. McKay and F. Rinder, *The Royal Scottish Academy, 1826–1916* (1917) · *Early Victorian draughtsmen and the rise of the Scottish Academy*, National Gallery of Scotland (1980) · M. Campbell, *The line of tradition: watercolours, drawings and prints by Scottish artists* (1993) [exhibition catalogue, Royal Scot. Acad., 4 Aug – 12 Sept 1993] · J. Egerton, ed., *British sporting and animal paintings, 1655–1867* (1978) · M. H. Grant, *A chronological history of the old English landscape painters*, rev. edn, 8 (1961) · K. Andrews and J. R. Brotchie, *Catalogue of Scottish drawings* (1960) · H. Smailes, *The concise catalogue of the Scottish National Portrait Gallery* (1990) · A. Graves, *A century of loan exhibitions, 1813–1912*, 3 (1908) · d. cert.

Archives NL Scot., family letters · Royal Scot. Acad., letters, sketchbook

Likenesses D. Simson, plaster bust, Scot. NPG · W. Simson, self-portrait, pen, ink, and brown wash, City of Edinburgh Fine Art Department, sketchbook, WNC 115 567 · W. Simson, self-portrait, scribble in ink, NL Scot., letter, 19 July 1846, MSS 9994.181

Sinclair family (*per.* 1280–*c.*1500), nobility, has a particular importance because of its acquisition of the ancient Norwegian earldom of Orkney in 1379. By the time that the family lost the earldom 100 years later, many individual Sinclair branches had established themselves throughout the Orkney and Shetland islands. The ancient earldom of Caithness (conjoint with the earldom of Orkney from saga times) was not, however, given to the Sinclairs in 1379, but was none the less acquired by the last Sinclair earl in 1455; thereafter many branches of the family similarly sprang up on earldom lands throughout the north mainland of Scotland. This has resulted in the name of Sinclair being one of the most common surnames in northern Scotland and the northern isles today.

Southern origins The first Sinclairs to be recorded in Scotland were based south of Forth in Midlothian, where the lands and barony of Roslin were granted to Sir William *Sinclair on 14 September 1280. Cousland, Roslin, and Pentland were named together as the baronies of the Sinclair family in 1325 but Roslin became the most important seat, and Earl Henry called himself lord of Roslin when granted his Orkney earldom title in the late fourteenth century. It was there that the family's main fortified residence was constructed above the gorge of the River North Esk. Sir William was active in political life under Alexander III and King John, and he and his sons Sir Henry *Sinclair [*see under* Sinclair, Sir William (d. 1299x1303)] and Bishop William *Sinclair all supported Robert I in the wars of Scottish independence. In 1321 Sir Henry appears as royal bailiff in Caithness, a rather surprising move north which anticipates the future role which the Sinclairs were to play in the Scandinavian parts of Scotland. It may have had something to do with his marriage to Alice Fenton, a northern heiress with lands in Ross. He was predeceased by his heir, **Sir William Sinclair** (d. 1330), who was slain, possibly with his brother John alongside him, in battle at Tebas de Ardales in Granada on 25 March 1330, as they were accompanying Sir James Douglas to Palestine with the heart of Robert I. William's heir, another William Sinclair (d. after 1358), was a minor at his father's death. He married Isabella Strathearn, eldest daughter of the second marriage of Malise, earl of Strathearn, Caithness, and Orkney (d. *c.*1350), whose heir she had been designated in 1344. By 1364 Thomas Sinclair, probably another son of Sir William's, was called 'baillie of the king of Norway' in Kirkwall, when he witnessed a charter of resignation of land to Hugh Ross, with whose family he had come to be closely associated. The Ross family dominated events in the whole north of Scotland, including Orkney, in the 1350s and 1360s, by reason of the vacuum left by the death of Earl Malise *c.*1350 without a male heir, and it was evidently through Ross patronage, as well as by marriage and inheritance, that the Sinclairs were raised to a position of power in the north.

Settling in the north Establishing their position in the far north was not a simple matter for the Sinclairs. Earl Malise had had five daughters altogether, from two marriages. The process of dividing his lands among them was a lengthy one, complicated by the differences in inheritance customs in force in Caithness and Orkney. In the former Scottish law prevailed, and though the lands were divided, the title went to the son of Malise's eldest daughter (from his first marriage), Alexander de Ard. In Orkney the earldom rights, though not the title of earl, were also granted to Alexander de Ard, though **Henry Sinclair** (*d*. 1400), as the eldest of Malise's grandsons from his second marriage, did obtain a share of the lands. However, Alexander's government was apparently unsatisfactory, and in 1379, following a meeting with Haakon VI (*r*. 1363–80) at Marstrand in Norway, Sinclair was granted the title of earl of Orkney, as well, probably, as royal lands and rights. A letter survives, issued by the new earl in September 1379, in which he announces that he has promised the Norwegian king not to alienate or pledge any lands or islands of his earldom of Orkney.

The Sinclairs were entering an unfamiliar, essentially Scandinavian, world, but they took on the challenges of their new position with energy and determination. A struggle for power with Malise Sperra, another of Henry Sinclair's cousins, who had probably been given authority in Shetland by Haakon VI, lasted until 1391, when Malise was killed. Sinclair may have had more widespread ambitions in the north Atlantic. The interpretation of the so-called Zeno narrative, relating the voyages in Atlantic waters of two Venetian sailors in association with a local magnate called Zichmni, who is usually identified with Henry Sinclair, is fraught with difficulties. Yet none of the adventures described is impossible, and it is not unlikely that this ambitious and successful overlord of an island dominion might wish to retrace the steps of his Norse ancestors across the northern seas, even though there is no supporting evidence to confirm either the apparent attempt to dominate the Faeroe Islands, or the supposed discovery of North America.

Although the Zeno narrative gives the clear impression that Zichmni was at enmity with the king of Norway, it is known that Earl Henry was in Norway or Denmark in 1389 to acknowledge Erik of Pomerania's claim to the Norwegian throne, and there survives a letter of Richard II of England to Queen Margret of Norway (written between February 1389 and April 1391) showing that Henry enjoyed cordial relations with her. This letter refers in particular to Earl Henry's complaints to Queen Margret of 'the intolerable and extreme hurt committed against him' by Richard's subjects (Perroy, no. 130). The king comments that the same earl and his subjects, together with French and Scots, have notoriously made war against him, and that he does not therefore feel inclined to give the safe conduct to him which Queen Margret is requesting. However, by 1392 Richard had granted a safe conduct to the earl and twenty-four companions to pass through his dominions—presumably to go to Denmark on some royal business. Where exactly the earl had been making war against King Richard is not clear, whether within his own territories or elsewhere, but his reference to attacks against him by English subjects is likely to be connected with fishing disputes in water round the northern isles.

It is this situation of violence in northern waters which was probably responsible for the death of Earl Henry, which is reported in the fifteenth-century 'Genealogy' of the earls as having taken place in Orkney, when 'for the defence of the cuntrie [he] was sclane thair crowellie be

his innimiis' ('Genealogy', 81). This may have been the occasion in 1400 when an English fleet landed in the Orkneys, as recorded by Walsingham. The first earl had at least ten children with his wife, Jean, daughter of Walter Haliburton of Dirleton. However, according to the 'Genealogy', at his death Henry's mother, Isabella, ensconced herself in Orkney, outliving all her sisters and their children, and (perhaps in accordance with Norwegian legal custom) succeeding to nearly all their lands. She held these until her grandson succeeded her, about 1416, which might help to explain why the second earl appears to have had very little to do with his northern earldom. It is doubtful whether this **Henry Sinclair** (*c*.1375–1420) ever visited his Norwegian overlord to receive a grant of the earldom title, although he used it from the date of his succession to his father.

National politics Another reason for the second earl's distancing himself from his Orcadian inheritance must have been his involvement in the affairs of central and southern Scotland, presumably from Roslin, where he probably resided during the 1390s. He fought at Homildon Hill on 14 September 1402, and was one of the numerous prisoners taken by the victorious English, but must have been quickly ransomed. The battle created a power vacuum in Lothian, which Sinclair, thanks both to his landed interests in the region and to his marriage to Egidia Douglas, a granddaughter of *Robert II, aspired to fill. He became very close to the court, witnessing important royal charters from August 1404, and in 1405 leading Scottish troops to Berwick in support of the earl of Northumberland, in revolt against Henry IV. He became one of the guardians of Robert III's young son, Prince James, and was on his way to France with the prince when both were captured by English pirates on 22 March 1406.

Thereafter Sinclair was in and out of custody for some years. But his recorded movements during the decade after 1406 were all southwards; in 1416, for instance, he had a safe conduct with twenty persons to come from and return to Scotland. However, from this same year there is also evidence that he as well as his brother John were becoming more active in the administration of the northern isles, suggesting that their grandmother Isabella died about this time. In a letter of 11 December 1416, Henry Sinclair, styling himself earl of Orkney, appointed his brother-in-law, David Menzies of Weem, to be tutor testamentary of his son and heir, William, and other children, and governor of all the earl's men, lands, rents, possessions, and goods in Orkney until his heirs attained their majority. Then eighteen months later, on 21 September 1418, John Sinclair received the very important grant of Shetland as a life fief with all royal rights, which made him the *foud* (royal official, from Danish *foged*) and provides the first clear evidence that the Sinclair family had acquired control of Shetland. Earl Henry was one of the magnates who died of 'le qwhew', possibly whooping cough, recorded by Bower in 1420.

Although the second Earl Henry's son and heir, **William**

Sinclair, third earl of Orkney and first earl of Caithness (*b.* after 1407, *d.* 1480), appears to have been under age for a few years after his father's death, he was none the less proposed as a hostage for James I in 1421, and received safe conducts in 1423 and 1424. He met James I at Berwick on his return to Scotland in spring 1424, and was one of the assize which condemned the duke of Albany and his sons to death in 1425. By then he had put forward his claim to the earldom of Orkney which had been controlled by the bishop, Thomas Tulloch, for a period since his father's death, followed by David Menzies. The remarkable 'Complaint of the people of Orkney' sent to the queen of Norway in 1425, along with a letter asking that the young earl be appointed their governor, shows clearly that there had been much disturbance in the islands between the followers of David Menzies and of Thomas Sinclair, a member of the earl's family established in Orkney. William was not, however, formally invested as earl by King Erik until 1434.

By this date Earl William had married Elizabeth Douglas, sister of Archibald *Douglas, fifth earl of Douglas (*d.* 1439), and the widow successively of Sir Thomas Stewart (a son of the earl of Mar) and John *Stewart, earl of Buchan. A papal dispensation was granted in 1432 licensing them to remain in matrimony. William was involved in protracted legal battles to assure her legal rights in her second husband's property, and in 1437, just after the murder of James I, she was given a grant of the fruits of the lordship of Garioch, as countess of Buchan and of Orkney. At the time her brother was lieutenant-general of the kingdom; this marriage had brought Earl William into close contact with the royal court, and in 1436 he had been chosen, as admiral of the fleet, to accompany the king's daughter on her journey to France for her wedding to the dauphin.

Sinclair's grip on power strengthened during the minority of James II when his relatives the Douglases were in control, nor did it diminish when the king came of age: he acted as steward at the young king's marriage with Mary of Gueldres in 1449, and in 1454 was appointed chancellor. By this date his wife had died and he had broken with the Douglases. Sinclair was active in the campaign against the Douglas castle of Threave in 1455, and it was to his custody at Roslin that Sir James Hamilton of Cadzow, previously a leading supporter of the Douglases, was entrusted after his submission to James II in the same year. Also in 1455 he was granted the earldom of Caithness, thus succeeding in reuniting the two ancient northern earldoms which had been separated since the death of Earl Malise *c.*1350: it was made in compensation for the lordship of Nithsdale, to which he had a claim through his mother, Egidia Douglas. His southern seat at Roslin was also being developed in a manner commensurate with the standing of a magnate of Earl William's importance. The remarkable church of St Matthew, probably begun in 1446, and given a collegiate constitution in the early 1450s, though never completed beyond the chancel, bears witness through its exotic and elaborate carved stonework to the wealth and taste of its founder. Roslin itself was erected into a burgh of barony in 1456.

The loss of Orkney From this position of power in the kingdom of Scotland, Earl William's star waned rapidly. He ceased to be chancellor in the later months of 1456, and along with Bishop James Kennedy moved to the sidelines as the young James II took a more aggressive line in both internal and external politics. In foreign matters the question of the 'annual' of Norway (the tribute payable by the Scots since 1266 in return for the cession by Norway of the Scottish Western Isles) loomed large, and inevitably meant strained relations with the king of Denmark–Norway (who should have been Earl William's acknowledged overlord for his earldom of Orkney, but there is no evidence that he had gone to do homage since 1434, although he had been summoned in 1446). Negotiations over the 'annual' took place in the late 1450s, and at a meeting of Danish and Scottish envoys in Paris in 1460 it became clear that James aspired to take control of Orkney and Shetland. Earl William, who must have been aware of royal ambitions regarding his earldom, may have attempted to implement delaying tactics. He certainly embarked on an expensive policy of purchasing 'odal' lands (that is, lands not held of any superior lord) in Orkney at this time, apparently with the intention of acquiring an estate which could not be encroached upon by the king. The death of James II in 1460 allowed the earl a breathing space to prepare himself better for the time when royal ambitions would once again focus on his rich northern possessions. Once more he was called upon to guide the kingdom in a period of difficulty, and he acted as one of the seven regents for the minority of James III, which provided him with an excuse for not answering a summons from King Christian (*r.* 1448–81) to attend the Danish court.

With the rise of the Boyds to power in 1466, Earl William faced once more the prospect of aggressive policies directed by the crown towards the northern isles. The situation of tension over the 'annual' was used as a means to achieve royal ambitions, in the marriage negotiations which were conducted at Copenhagen in the summer of 1468. The earl refused all attempts by King Christian to summon him, undoubtedly realizing that his position as vassal of both kings made it exceedingly difficult for him to be involved in the negotiations. These resulted in the extraordinary acquiescence by King Christian in the demands of the Scottish envoys that Orkney be handed over as part of the dowry of the young Princess Margaret. Desperately short of cash, and desperate for a good marriage for his daughter, he agreed to pledge the islands as part payment for the dowry; in the following year he agreed to pledge Shetland for most of the rest. There is little doubt that his transfer included all of the islands, and not just the royal estates. It remained for the ambitious councillors of James III to prevail upon the earl to give up all his rights in his earldom, which he did in 1470, thus ensuring permanent possessions for the Scottish crown in the islands, even if the Danish monarchy should ever succeed in redeeming them. The impression that the earl came out very badly from the 'excambion' of 1470 is probably unjustified, since in exchange for his right in the earldom he received the very fine royal castle of Ravenscraig in Fife, a number of valuable privileges and confirmations which he must himself have stipulated, and a handsome annual pension of 400 merks.

Family settlements From 1470 Earl William was known as earl of Caithness until 1476, when he resigned his earldom in favour of William, the eldest son of his second marriage; thereafter he was only Lord Sinclair. His latter years were occupied with family affairs, although he was named as an envoy to England once or twice. Family matters were problematical, although his second marriage, to Marjory Sutherland, the (possibly illegitimate) daughter of Alexander Sutherland of Dunbeath, was apparently very successful—at least there were fourteen children of it. Alexander Sutherland's will, dated 1456, may indicate that Earl William's liaison with Marjory had not at that time been regularized, although it later was. Such a marriage, to a daughter of a member of the Sutherland family with no standing in the north, is very surprising. However, Alexander's will indicates that he had been a source of credit for the earl, perhaps to help with the land-purchasing policy in Orkney. The children of this marriage clearly took precedence over Earl William's son of his first marriage, William the Waster, who was not considered suitable to be his father's main heir, although he did succeed in getting possession of the Fife estates after his father's death.

In 1476 the old earl did his best to ensure that his main estates went to the elder sons of his second marriage, the earldom of Caithness to William, Roslin and Ravenscraig to Oliver. None the less, shortly after his death, in the early months of 1480, there was serious conflict between the half-brothers, attested by several bonds and agreements. A verdict of idiocy was procured against the elder William in 1482, but the latter's interests were well represented by his own eldest son, Henry, who eventually restored the fortunes of the family in the northern isles, based on the 'conquest' estates which were acquired by the last earl of Orkney, and which did not escheat to the crown along with the earldom lands. He achieved this in conjunction with his uncle, Sir David Sinclair of Sumburgh, an illegitimate son of the old earl who pursued a successful career in the service of both the kings of Scots and of Norway, and who built up a personal estate based on the conquest lands in Shetland, which he prevailed upon all his half-brothers and -sisters to resign to him in 1498. The old earl's foresight had ensured the survival of a large and powerful Sinclair presence in Orkney and Shetland, as well as in Caithness.   BARBARA E. CRAWFORD

Sources B. E. Crawford, 'The earls of Orkney–Caithness and their relations with Norway and Scotland, 1158–1470', PhD diss., U. St Andr., 1971 · *Scots peerage*, vols. 6–7 · GEC, *Peerage*, new edn, vol. 10 · R. St Clair, *The Saint-Clairs of the Isles* (Auckland, 1898) · 'Genealogy of the earls', *The Bannatyne miscellany*, ed. D. Laing, 3, Bannatyne Club, 19b (1855), 63–85 · B. E. Crawford, 'William Sinclair, earl of Orkney, and his family: a study in the politics of survival', *Essays on the nobility of medieval Scotland*, ed. K. J. Stringer (1985), 232–51 · J. S.

Clouston, ed., *Records of the earldom of Orkney*, Scottish History Society, 2nd ser., 7 (1914) · R. H. Major, ed., 'The voyages of the Venetian brothers Nicolo and Antonio Zeno', Hakluyt Society, 1st ser., 1 (1873) · University of Guelph, Ontario, Library Archival Collections, Campbell of Menzie papers · *Norges Gamle Love*, anden raekke, 1: 1388–1447 (1912) [Denrets Historiske Kommissjon, Christiania] · B. E. Crawford, 'The pawning of Orkney and Shetland: a reconsideration of the events of 1460–69', *SHR*, 48 (1969), 35–53 · *The diplomatic correspondence of Richard II*, ed. E. Perroy, CS, 3rd ser., 48 (1933) · R. A. Hay, *Genealogie of the Sainteclaires of Rosslyn* (1835) · W. Bower, *Scotichronicon*, ed. D. E. R. Watt and others, new edn, 9 vols. (1987–98), vol. 8 · G. Burnett and others, eds., *The exchequer rolls of Scotland*, 9 (1886) · C. Innes, ed., *Registrum S. Marie de Neubotle*, Bannatyne Club, 89 (1849) · S. I. Boardman, *The early Stewart kings: Robert II and Robert III, 1371–1406* (1996)
Archives NA Scot., Cookston writs · NA Scot., GD 164 · Wemyss Castle, Fife, Wemyss family papers

Sinclair, Andrew [Anders Sinklar] (1555–1625), army officer and diplomat in the Danish service, was born in Ravenscraig, Scotland, the third son of Henry Sinclair, fifth Lord St Clair (1527–1601), and his first consort, Janet (d. 15 April 1569), daughter of Patrick Lindsay, Lord Lindsay of the Byres. A Scottish nobleman, he was educated in the household of the duc de Guise. In 1591 he became a gentleman of the Danish court under King Christian IV and eventually settled in Denmark, where he was known as Anders Sinklar. He accompanied Christian to Germany in 1597, and acted as a gentleman of the bedchamber to Queen Anna Katrine until he retired from court service in 1600. In that year he married Kirsten (d. 1632/3), daughter of Erik Kaas (d. 1578) and Kirsten Pederrsdatter Galt (1536–1616). They had several children: Henrik, who died as a child, Jacob, Christian, Johanne, Erik, and Christine (mentioned in 1623). Christian IV became godfather to one of their sons in 1607.

Through marriage, Sinclair became *lensman* ('regional governor') of Gladsax, in which capacity he worked until 1620. During his subsequent career, he also acted as *lensman* of Landskrone (1619–21), and of Hammershus with Bornholm (1621–5). During the Danish–Swedish Kalmar War of 1611–13 Sinclair served the Danish-Norwegian army as a captain. After participating in the conquest of Öland in 1611, he became the commandant of Kalmar on its capture from Sweden. By 1615 he had been appointed colonel of the Skåne regiment, and by 1622 was commander of the entire Danish-Norwegian army east of the Baltic Sound. He was ennobled in Denmark in 1616, and was further rewarded in 1617 when he was appointed a member of the Danish *rigsråd* (the state council) at the age of sixty-two. Throughout his career he maintained his links with Scotland, travelling with Princess Anna's ambassador to Scotland in October 1589 to participate in her marriage negotiations with James VI. He joined the Danish embassy to Scotland in summer 1594. He proved to be a useful negotiator, uniquely equipped with a familiar knowledge of both Scottish and Danish language and society. After 1603 he acted on seven occasions as the Danish-Norwegian envoy to the Stuart court (1604, 1606, 1612, 1614, 1618, 1619, and 1621).

Early in 1614 James VI and I was asked by Christian IV to arbitrate in his dispute with Lübeck. Sinclair achieved a short-term settlement in the dispute, which was followed up by Sir Robert Anstruther's embassy in 1615. James's diplomatic intervention on behalf of Denmark–Norway once more proved influential with Christian in resolving the issues peacefully. When negotiations between Denmark and Sweden were held at Ulvsbäck in 1619 Sinclair was present and met the Swedish king, Gustavus Adolphus. With the outbreak of the Bohemian war in 1618, the peaceful policies of James VI and I finally faltered. He relied heavily on Sir Robert Anstruther in Denmark to gain Christian IV's support for his schemes to end the war. Christian in turn sent Sinclair, with Frederick Günther, to the Stuart court in 1621. Christian sought to build up an evangelical military alliance in northern Europe, comprising Denmark–Norway, the German protestant princes of the lower Saxon circle, the British kingdoms under James VI and I, and any of the free German cities that could be persuaded to join in. Sinclair received instructions to persuade King James to take part in order to resist perceived Habsburg aggression in northern Europe. For his part, James believed that he could find a more appropriate diplomatic solution. Sinclair conducted no further missions to Britain for Christian IV, but continued in his other military and diplomatic capacities until his death at Sinklarsholm, Skåne, Denmark, in 1625.

STEVE MURDOCH

Sources C. F. Bricka and others, eds., *Dansk biografisk lexicon*, 27 vols. (1933–44), vol. 13, pp. 399–400 · Danish Rigsarkiv, Copenhagen, TKUA Skotland A II, 4 · James VI to Christian IV, 20 Oct 1604, Danish Rigsarkiv, Copenhagen, TKUA England A 1, 2 · C. F. Bricka and J. A. Fridericia, eds., *Kong Christian den fjerdes egenhaendige breve*, 1: *1589–1625* (Copenhagen, 1887–9), 12–13, 29–30, 63–5, 131, 180–81 · Anglica 3, Spens to Duke Johan of Ostergotland, 10 Jan 1614; Anglica 5, Spens to Axel Oxenstierna, 9 May 1614; Anglica 3, Spens to Axel Oxenstierna, 4 June 1614; Anglica 5, Spens to Axel Oxenstierna, 1 March 1615, 26 May 1615, Riksarkivet, Stockholm · Anstruther to secretary of state, 10 March 1621, PRO, SP 75/5, fols. 235–238 · *CSP Venice, 1613–15*, 88–9, 369–70 · A. Thiset and P. L. Wittrup, *Nyt Dansk adelslexicon* (1904), 261–2 · G. Lind, *Danish officers, 1614–1662* [Copenhagen, 1995 version, lodged in Danish data archive in Odense; computer database, Danish data archives 1573] · J. C. W. Hirsch and K. Hirsch, eds., 'Fortegnelse over Dansu ou Norske officerer med flere fra 1648 til 1814', 12 vols., unpublished MS, 1888–1907, Rigsarkivet, Copenhagen, vol. 10 · T. Riis, *Should auld acquaintance be forgot … Scottish–Danish relations, c.1450–1707*, 2 (1988), 74 · *Scots peerage*, 7.575 · S. Murdoch, 'Scotland, Denmark–Norway and the house of Stuart, 1603–1660: a diplomatic and military analysis', PhD diss., U. Aberdeen, 1998

Sinclair, Andrew (1794–1861), surgeon and naturalist, was born in Paisley, Renfrewshire, on 13 April 1794, the son of John Sinclair and Agnes Renfrew. Between 1814 and 1818 he studied medicine and surgery at the University of Glasgow, at L'hôpital de la Charité in Paris, and finally at the University of Edinburgh, from where he graduated MD in 1818. In 1822 he entered the navy as an assistant surgeon, and from 1823 to 1833 he served on the *Owen Glendower* off the Cape of Good Hope and in the Mediterranean. He also began to collect botanical and zoological specimens which he sent to the British Museum. Sinclair became a surgeon in 1829, and in 1834 was attached to HMS *Sulphur* on a surveying expedition to the South American coast,

under the command of Captain Frederick William Beechey and afterwards of Sir Edward Belcher. Sinclair continued his interest in natural history, collecting plants in 1837 and 1838 in Mexico and Central America.

After a brief period in Britain to recover his health in 1839, Sinclair was appointed surgeon to a convict ship, and he had opportunities of collecting natural history specimens at several Australian ports. He spent some weeks in New Zealand in 1841 with Joseph Dalton Hooker, then naturalist to James Clark Ross's Antarctic expedition, and in 1843 he accompanied Captain Robert FitzRoy as private secretary, when FitzRoy became governor of New Zealand. On 6 January 1844 a somewhat reluctant Sinclair was made colonial secretary in New Zealand, and he served as such under a succession of governors and acting governors until the establishment of parliamentary government in May 1856. He was efficient rather than inspired in office.

In 1856 Sinclair retired to Britain on a pension, and he soon met some of the leading scientific figures of the day, having been elected fellow of the Linnean Society in 1857. He returned to New Zealand in 1858 to collect in the middle and south islands material for a supplement to J. D. Hooker's *Flora*. He made arrangements with Sir John Francis Julius von Haast to explore Mount Cook, but was drowned on 26 March 1861 in endeavouring to cross on foot the River Rangitata, near Canterbury, New Zealand, when it was swollen by flood. He was buried in the nearby Mesopotamia station. Sinclair was unmarried. His zoological specimens, chiefly sponges and zoophytes, were mostly presented to the British Museum, and his plants went to Sir W. J. Hooker and were mainly described in Hooker and Arnott's *Botany of Beechey's Voyage* (1841), and in George Bentham's *Botany of the Voyage of HMS Sulphur* (1844). Sinclair himself published only two papers. He is commemorated in the names of sixteen New Zealand plants, as well as Mount Sinclair and Sinclair River.

G. S. BOULGER, rev. ELIZABETH BAIGENT

Sources *DNZB*, vol. 1 · M. M. Johnson, *The botanical explorers of New Zealand* (1950) · A. Sharp, *The New Zealand colonial secretary's office and department of internal affairs* (1966) · *Proceedings of the Linnean Society of London* (1861–2), xcv–xcvi
Archives NL NZ, Turnbull L.

Sinclair, Archibald Henry Macdonald, first Viscount Thurso (1890–1970), politician, was born on 22 October 1890, the only son of Clarence Granville Sinclair (1858–1895) and his wife, Mabel Sands (d. 1890). His father, a lieutenant in the Scots Guards, was the eldest son of Sir (John George) Tollemache Sinclair, third baronet, of Ulbster, Caithness. His mother, a noted beauty of her day, was the daughter of a wealthy New York businessman, Mahlon Sands. Sinclair's mother died a few days after his birth, and five years later his father also died, leaving the young Sinclair to experience a rather itinerant childhood as he moved about between the houses of various relatives who tried to provide a home for him. Much of his time was spent with his grandfather Sir Tollemache, with his uncle, Archdeacon William Macdonald Sinclair, canon of St Paul's, or at Temple House, Marlow, Buckinghamshire,

Archibald Henry Macdonald Sinclair, first Viscount Thurso (1890–1970), by Augustus John, c.1920–24

the home of his uncle and aunt—Lieutenant-General and Mrs Owen Williams—where he found himself at the heart of fashionable society, for Williams was on excellent terms with Edward VII.

Churchill's aide Educated at Eton College and at Sandhurst, Sinclair entered the army in 1910 in the 2nd Life Guards, and on the death of his grandfather in 1912 he succeeded to the baronetcy and with it the ownership of some 100,000 acres at the northernmost tip of Scotland. In the days before the First World War there were few more glamorous young men in society than Archie. His good looks, charm, and romantic highland aura were spiced with a touch of daredevilry that led him to experiment with a primitive aircraft which he flew before breakfast. Asquith was captivated, and so was his daughter, Violet; but much the deepest friendship which Sinclair made at this time was with Winston Churchill. At heart Sinclair grew up a somewhat shy and reserved young man with no great liking for the crowded events of the social calendar. Churchill in a different way was also a solitary figure. But he and Sinclair at once discovered that they had a vast amount in common. Both felt that circumstances had deprived them of full parental affection, though both had been sustained by a devoted governess. Both had American mothers and swashbuckling Yankee grandfathers. Both were by training cavalry officers with a shared enthusiasm for polo and flying. It was even the case that both had a slight speech impediment. Sinclair in his early twenties was turning towards politics and ready to

trust in an older man as his guiding star; Churchill in his late thirties was already a curiously paternal figure delighted to discover a young disciple. The letters which he and Sinclair exchanged during the First World War are remarkable on both sides for their expression of private feeling, and read like those of a mutually devoted father and son. Sinclair could write to Churchill in April 1916 of 'my keen longing to serve you in politics—more humbly but more energetically than I have been able to in war' (Gilbert, 1494).

Sinclair served on the western front throughout the war. In February 1915 he was appointed aide-de-camp to the Liberal MP and former secretary for war J. E. B. Seely, commander of the Canadian cavalry brigade. In January 1916 Churchill, whose career had been ruined for the time being by Gallipoli, took charge on the western front of the 6th Royal Scots Fusiliers, and for four months Sinclair served as his second in command. 'He is most courageous conscientious and hard-working', wrote Churchill to his wife, 'but he hates every hour of it [the war] with a profound loathing' (Gilbert, 1490). Sinclair ended the war as a major in the Guards Machine-Gun regiment. In 1918, while still on service in France, Sinclair met and after a whirlwind courtship married, on 18 May, Marigold (1897–1975), the daughter of Angela Forbes (who had obtained a divorce from her husband, Marigold's father, Lieutenant-Colonel James Stewart Forbes), who was running a military canteen in Le Touquet. They were married at the office of the British vice-consul in Boulogne. It was the beginning of a long and happy marriage which produced four children: Catherine (b. 1919), Elizabeth (1921–1994), Robin [see below], and Angus (b. 1925).

After the war Sinclair remained for a time in the role of aide to Churchill, serving as his personal military secretary at the War Office (1919–21), and as his private secretary at the Colonial Office (1921–2). But in 1922 he entered parliament as MP for Caithness and Sutherland, taking his stand as a Liberal supporting the Lloyd George (and thus Churchill) wing of the party. In the House of Commons he built up a reputation as a skilful opposition speaker, while playing a part in the comprehensive overhaul of Liberal policy which Lloyd George had initiated. A convinced Scottish home-ruler, he was chiefly responsible for the Liberal 'tartan book', the Scottish version of the party's 'green book' on agricultural reform.

Liberal politician in the 1930s During the second Labour government of 1929–31 the Liberal Party began to disintegrate, a process accelerated by the formation of Ramsay MacDonald's National Government in August 1931. One section of the party, led by Sir John Simon, favoured outright opposition to the Labour government in alliance with the Conservatives. In the economic crisis they were prepared to jettison the historic Liberal creed of free trade, and welcome the National Government as the basis of a permanent association with the tory party. The Liberal Nationals or Simonites were gradually to lose their separate identity and become Conservatives in all but name. Sinclair, who had accepted the thankless task of Liberal chief whip in November 1930, took the same line as the Samuelites, led by Sir Herbert Samuel, who were prepared to support the National Government as a temporary expedient while seeking to maintain the long-term independence of the Liberal Party. They accepted office in August 1931, Sinclair becoming secretary of state for Scotland (he did not have cabinet rank until November). In October they agreed to fight a general election in alliance with the Conservatives, and when the cabinet decided in January 1932 to introduce protection it was announced that the Samuelite ministers would remain in the government under an agreement to differ. No doubt the satisfactions of office were great, but Samuel and Sinclair, who together comprised the Liberal high command, were committed first and foremost to the independence of the party and the ultimate restoration of free trade. In the summer of 1932 a series of discussions took place at Sinclair's home in Caithness which led to the resignation of the Samuelite ministers in September, in protest against the conclusion of the Ottawa agreements.

The post of secretary of state for Scotland had offered Sinclair little scope, coming as it did at a moment of financial stringency. A greater opportunity, at first very effectively disguised, presented itself in November 1935. Samuel, who had led the party since 1931, lost his seat in the general election, and Sinclair was prevailed upon to serve in his place as chairman of the parliamentary party. Sinclair was reluctant to accept the job, and the correspondence preserved among his papers helps to explain why. The Liberals were a deeply demoralized party. Their by-election performance since 1931 had been disastrous, and in 1935 their strength in the Commons was further reduced to twenty-one MPs. There was no easy solution at hand, but enthusiasts were very ready to blame the quality of the party leadership, and there were many prima donnas at hand with schemes to revive the party's fortunes. With all such prickly individuals Sinclair dealt patiently but firmly, anxious not to discourage the efforts of anyone with something to contribute to the cause. In this he relied heavily on the advice and support of his old friend Harcourt Johnstone, generally known as Crinks, who maintained liaison between the whips' office and the constituencies. Although Sinclair could do little to revive the Liberal vote, he succeeded in turning the parliamentary party into a force more powerful than its numbers indicated. From 1935 onwards the crisis in Europe overshadowed all other political issues. The Baldwin and Chamberlain governments pursued a pragmatic policy of piecemeal concessions to Mussolini and Hitler. The Labour Party, while adopting a high moral stance of opposition to fascism and aggression, refused until late in the day to accept the need for rearmament. Under Sinclair the Liberals (though never wholly united on such questions) sought to combine support for collective security through the League of Nations with pressure for a strong air force and secure defences. They were therefore the advocates of a genuine middle way which became increasingly influential, and was indeed adopted by Churchill in his campaign for 'arms and the covenant'. In the House of Commons Sinclair and Churchill worked closely together: in condemning the Munich agreement or urging an understanding with Russia they were of one mind. They also combined to seek the establishment of a Ministry of Supply.

Secretary of state for air At the outbreak of war in September 1939 Chamberlain invited Sinclair to accept office on behalf of the Liberals, an invitation which Sinclair declined. In the critical Commons debate of 7–8 May 1940, which led to Chamberlain's resignation, Sinclair joined in the attack, and on 10 May his old friend and ally Churchill became prime minister. Sinclair was appointed secretary of state for air, a post he retained until the dissolution of the coalition in May 1945.

Sinclair was never one of the major figures in the coalition government. With the prime minister himself directing the chiefs of staff, and the conduct of the war from day to day, the service ministers took little part in military decisions. On a more personal level Churchill continued to treat Archie as a subaltern and social companion, asserting a dominance that Sinclair never seriously contested. Nor did Sinclair possess a strong power base. The Liberal Party was small and faction-ridden. Furthermore Churchill on coming to power had stripped the Air Ministry of its most important function, the production of aircraft, and handed it over to a separate Ministry of Aircraft Production under Beaverbrook. Sinclair was compelled to spend much of his first year in office defending his own department from repeated attempts by Beaverbrook to seize more of its powers.

Sinclair also incurred the enmity of the commander-in-chief of Fighter Command, Sir Hugh Dowding, who blamed him for failing in May 1940 to resist Churchill's demands for the dispatch of fighter squadrons to France, and later never forgave him for the manner in which he was retired from his command in November 1940. It was fortunate for Sinclair that he found a strong ally in the new chief of air staff, Sir Charles Portal. The two men quickly struck up a relationship of trust and friendship. Under Portal's tuition Sinclair was also persuaded to abandon his initial preference for precision bombing in favour of area bombing, with the aim of destroying the morale of the civilian population. In March 1942 he took a prominent part in the struggle to prevent the Admiralty diverting bombers from strategic bombing to long-range reconnaissance duties in the battle of the Atlantic, and obtained Churchill's consent for a resumption of the full bombing offensive. When Lord Cherwell circulated his famous memorandum of March 1942 advocating the 'dehousing' of the German population through the bombing of residential areas, Sinclair commented that he found the argument 'simple, clear and convincing'. In recent years the weight of opinion has been strongly critical of the strategic bombing offensive on the grounds that it was ineffectual and wasteful of resources which could have been better employed. The use of bombing to terrorize and kill civilians has also frequently been condemned on ethical grounds. Sinclair relied on the common-sense judgement that a weapon so destructive as bombing must also be decisive; any secretary for air who thought differently would not have survived the wrath of the air marshals for long. Nor did the moral issue cause him any difficulty: he believed that any measure necessary for the defeat of Germany was justifiable, a severe view which most people accepted in the heat of the conflict. None the less Sinclair thought it prudent not to admit the true nature of the bombing offensive in public, in case opposition was stirred up on grounds of conscience and the morale of bomber crews affected. In a number of speeches Sinclair asserted that strategic bombing was directed primarily against industrial targets, not against residential areas, and that civilian deaths were the by-product and not the objective of the campaign. The most controversial episode of all, the Anglo-American destruction of Dresden in February 1945, was the outcome of direct instructions from Churchill. Churchill soon began to regret this episode and issued a minute (later withdrawn) describing the attack as 'a serious query against the conduct of Allied bombing' (Webster and Frankland, 2.112).

Retirement and peerage Between the wars Sinclair had been able to pay regular attention to his constituency of Caithness and Sutherland, the largest geographically in the United Kingdom. He took care to visit his constituents on annual summer tours, and otherwise kept in touch through his party agent Captain Barrogill Keith, who was also the factor of his estate. The war years cut Sinclair off, and he paid for this in the general election of 1945, coming bottom of the poll in a remarkable result in which only sixty-one votes separated the three candidates. This was in effect the end of Sinclair's career. After failing to be re-elected in 1950 he accepted a peerage in the first honours list of the post-war Churchill government, and was created Viscount Thurso of Ulbster on 10 April 1952. Plans for him to re-enter politics as Liberal leader in the House of Lords were thwarted by illness and he did not take his seat until 1954. For three years he was able to play a prominent part in the debates of the upper house, but it was his fate to spend the remainder of his life as an invalid.

Sinclair enjoyed the world of politics and worked hard at it, but he did not live for his career as Churchill did. He built around himself a secure and happy private life in the company of his wife and children. Except in the war years he guarded his leisure hours, and most of all the weeks devoted every summer to house parties of family and friends at Dalnawillan Lodge, deep in the wilds of Caithness. He enjoyed grouse shooting, won recognition as a very fine salmon fisherman, and played polo and rode regularly until he was about forty. He carefully supervised the accounts of his estate, and kept in touch with his tenant farmers, but was not by inclination an agriculturist. If his heart was in the highlands (he was lord lieutenant of Caithness from 1919 to 1964), his home and his vocation for most of the year were in the south-east. To the life of politics he brought both a clear view of his function and certain definite gifts. He maintained that it was not the job of a politician to take on the role of expert in any particular branch of knowledge, but to make use of the knowledge which experts possessed. The task of the politician

was to organize, to persuade, and to co-ordinate. John Colville wrote:

> Sinclair had an air of distinction. With his fine features, black hair, and swarthy complexion he resembled a Spanish grandee rather than the Highland chieftain that he was. His delivery as a speaker was slow. He had a stammer which attracted attention and lent emphasis … During the Norway debate leading to Neville Chamberlain's fall, his attack was notable for both its venom and its originality. (Colville, 172)

In the Commons Sinclair was an effective speaker, alert to the atmosphere of the house, and skilfully casting his arguments in terms which were likely to exercise the maximum appeal. At the Air Ministry Sinclair was to prove less effective: a conscientious administrator dominated by Churchill and Portal, 'Sinclair did what was required of him', his biographer writes, 'and did it well' (De Groot, 205). Sometimes persuasive, but seldom powerful, Sinclair was a gentlemanly figure with two consistent loyalties which shaped his contribution to public life. He was faithful to Liberalism and helped to ensure the survival of the party during a period in which it was threatened with extinction; and although he did not always agree with Churchill, he was a friend and admirer through all the ups and downs of Churchill's career.

Sinclair was appointed CMG in 1922 and KT in 1941, and was sworn of the privy council in 1931. He died at his London home, Fotheringay House, Montpelier Row, Twickenham, on 15 June 1970, leaving his wife, two daughters, and two sons.

Sinclair's elder son, **Robin Macdonald Sinclair**, second Viscount Thurso (1922–1995), landowner and businessman, was born on 24 December 1922 in London and educated at Eton College and at New College, Oxford. During the Second World War he served as a flight lieutenant in the RAF, undertaking photographic reconnaissance missions in the Far East. After the war he read agriculture at Edinburgh University. He married, on 14 February 1952, Margaret Beaumont Brokensha, widow of Lieutenant Guy Warwick Brokensha, Fleet Air Arm officer, and elder daughter of Colonel Josiah James Robertson, of Caithness; they had two sons, John (b. 1953) and Patrick (b. 1954), and a daughter, Camilla (b. 1957). A Liberal, he was a Caithness county councillor, a Thurso town councillor, and in 1966 an unsuccessful parliamentary candidate for East Aberdeenshire. After inheriting the viscountcy and estates in 1970 he became one of Scotland's leading landowners. He promoted new industries and other ventures in Caithness. Most failed, but Caithness Glass succeeded. He was criticized for supporting the Dounreay nuclear reactor and Nirex, the nuclear waste organization. He was fairly active in the House of Lords, for some years living on a houseboat near Richmond during its sittings. He was lord lieutenant of Caithness (1973–95), president of the Boys' Brigade (1985–93), and a close friend of the queen mother. He died of leukaemia and emphysema on 29 April 1995 at his home, Thurso East Mains, Thurso, Caithness. He was survived by his wife and their three children, and was succeeded as third viscount by his son John, who in 2001 was elected Liberal Democrat MP for Caithness, Sutherland,

and Easter Ross, thus becoming the first hereditary peer to be elected to the Commons following the House of Lords Act of 1999.   PAUL ADDISON

Sources G. J. De Groot, *Liberal crusader: the life of Sir Archibald Sinclair* (1993) · R. Douglas, *The history of the liberal party, 1895–1970* (1971) · C. Webster and N. Frankland, *The strategic air offensive against Germany, 1939–1945*, 4 vols. (1961) · CAC Cam., Thurso MSS · P. Harris, *Forty years in and out of parliament* (1947) · M. Gilbert, ed., *Winston S. Churchill*, companion vol., 3/2 (1972) · J. Colville, *The Churchillians* (1981) · private information (1981) · CGPLA Eng. & Wales (1970) · WW · WWW · Burke, *Peerage* · *Daily Telegraph* (1 May 1995) · *The Times* (2 May 1995) · *The Independent* (2 May 1995) · d. cert. · CCI (1996) [Robin Macdonald Sinclair] · d. cert. [Robin Macdonald Sinclair]

Archives CAC Cam., personal and political corresp. and MSS · priv. coll., papers · PRO, MSS as secretary of state for air, AIR 19/73-557 | Bodl. Oxf., corresp. with Gilbert Murray · CAC Cam., Churchill MSS · CAC Cam., corresp. with Sir E. L. Spears · CUL, corresp. with Sir Samuel Hoare · HLRO, corresp. with Lord Beaverbrook; letters to David Lloyd George; corresp. with Herbert Samuel · IWM, corresp. with Sir Henry Tizard · JRL, letters to *Manchester Guardian* · King's Lond., Liddell Hart C., corresp. with Sir B. H. Liddell Hart · NL Wales, corresp. with Clement Davies · Nuffield Oxf., corresp. with Lord Cherwell

Likenesses photographs, 1904–c.1914, Hult. Arch. · J. Lavery, oils, before 1914, priv. coll. · A. John, oils, c.1920–1924, Scot. NPG [*see illus.*] · O. Birley, oils, 1930–1939?, priv. coll. · S. Sutherland, sculpted head, 1936, Thurso · W. Stoneman, three photographs, 1936–43, NPG · W. Dring, pastel drawing, 1939, IWM · D. Foggie, chalk drawing, 1939, Scot. NPG · N. Parkinson, photograph, c.1955, NPG · W. Dring, oils, IWM

Wealth at death £39,745: probate, 27 Nov 1970, CGPLA Eng. & Wales · £830,026.55—Robin Macdonald Sinclair: confirmation, 6 March 1996, CCI

Sinclair, Catherine (1800–1864), novelist and children's writer, was born in Edinburgh on 17 April 1800. She was the fourth daughter and seventh of the thirteen children of Sir John *Sinclair, first baronet (1754–1835), of Ulbster, first president of the board of agriculture, and his second wife, Lady Diana MacDonald (1769–1845), daughter of Alexander, first Lord MacDonald of Sleat. Sir George *Sinclair, second baronet (1790–1868), Archdeacon John *Sinclair (1797–1875), and the Revd William *Sinclair (1804–1878) were her brothers. She also had two half-sisters from her father's first marriage. She and her sisters were all very tall, and jokes circulated about Sir John Sinclair's 6-and-30 feet of daughters: the pavement outside their house was known as the 'Giants' Causeway'. S. C. Hall states that she was badly scarred with smallpox. She was educated at home, and, from the age of fourteen, acted as secretary to her father, who maintained an extensive correspondence with agriculturists and politicians in Europe and America. It is said that she wrote from his dictation for five or six hours daily for many years. The family were members of the Scottish Episcopal church, and an evangelical protestantism is promoted throughout Sinclair's fiction. Her sister Julia (d. 1868), with whom Sinclair lived in the later part of her life, married in 1824, as his second wife, the fourth earl of Glasgow (1765–1843), and had a son and a daughter, for whom Sinclair's first book, *Charlie Seymour, or, The Good Aunt and the Bad Aunt* (1832), was written. She had earlier published in *Blackwood's Edinburgh Magazine* (25, February 1829, 189–92), one of the horror stories

in which the magazine specialized: 'The Murder Hole: an ancient Legend', which is about a murderous innkeeper, based on a rural legend. After her father's death Sinclair's rate of production increased. She began with a novel of fashionable life, of the then popular 'silver fork' school, *Modern Accomplishments* (1836), which was followed by a sequel, *Modern Society* (1837). *Hill and Valley, or, Hours in England and Wales* (1838) was the first of a series of travel books. But her best book and most enduring success was *Holiday House: a Series of Tales* (1839). Harry and Laura, perhaps based on her nephew and niece, live with their kind grandmother and uncle, and a severe nurse. They are always getting into trouble, unlike their saintly brother Frank, who goes away to sea, returning to die nobly in the last chapter, effecting the conversion of his unregenerate brother and sister. In a preface Sinclair states that Frank's death was based on that of her brother James (d. 1826), and that she wanted to describe 'noisy, frolicsome, mischievous children' rather than the paragons of contemporary children's fiction. The book combines an improving religious message with the entertaining account of Harry and Laura's misdeeds, and was both innovative and popular. *Sir Edward Graham, or, The Railway Speculators* (1849) is a novel for adults, with many of the same characters, in which Harry and Laura both find romance and marriage. Sinclair's other adult fiction, also of markedly evangelical tone, includes the perhaps semi-autobiographical *Jane Bouverie* (1846), and *Beatrice* (1852), which came out in the aftermath of the 'papal aggression' crisis, and has a fiercely anti-Catholic message. She also published tracts and devotional works. A late success was the series of picture letters for children published between 1861 and 1864, in which words and hieroglyphic pictures are appealingly mingled. Sinclair devoted herself to charitable works of a practical as well as religious kind. She founded a mission school at Water of Leith, a volunteer corps, and a Sinclair Cooking Depot in Edinburgh, to provide good cheap food for the poor. She also set up public benches and drinking-fountains in that city. She died at Kensington vicarage, London, the home of her brother John, on 6 August 1864, and was buried in the graveyard of St John's Episcopal Church, Edinburgh, ten days later. After her death a meeting was held in Edinburgh to erect a memorial by public subscription, which still stands on the corner of Albyn Place and North Charlotte Street.

CHARLOTTE MITCHELL

Sources *The Times* (15 Aug 1864), 10 · *The Times* (6 Oct 1864), 7 · J. G. John, 'Catherine Sinclair', *British children's writers, 1800–1880*, ed. M. Khorana, DLitB, 163 (1996), 282–6 · IGI · S. C. Hall, *A book of memories of great men and women of the age*, 2nd edn (1877) · R. Mitchison, *Agricultural Sir John: the life of Sir John Sinclair of Ulbster* (1962) · BL cat. · GM, 1st ser., 70 (1800), 384 · GM, 3rd ser., 17 (1864), 654–6 · W. Anderson, *The Scottish nation*, 3 (1880), 471 · C. Sinclair, introduction, *Holiday house: a book for the young* [1896]

Archives NL Scot., letters | BL, accounts and corresp. with Richard Bentley, Add. MSS 46651–46652

Likenesses J. Archer, crayon

Wealth at death under £25,000: resworn administration, 6 Sept 1864, CGPLA Eng. & Wales

Sinclair, David (d. 1656), army officer in the Swedish service, was born in Scotland. The Swedish peerage notes him as the son of William Sinclair of Seba and his wife, Barbara Halcro, the daughter of Baron Hugo Halcro, although this could not be supported in the Scottish peerage (Scottish lairds were commonly called barons in seventeenth-century Sweden). David went to Sweden in 1630 or 1631 with his elder brother John and his father, and they all entered military service. John became a lieutenant-colonel in 1632 but died soon after at Thorn in Prussia.

David Sinclair appears to have begun his military career as an ensign in Colonel Robert Cunningham's regiment in 1633, but he also served in Andreas Dynn's recruited squadron that year. He may have been in William Gunn's recruited infantry squadron in 1636 but the following year he had returned to Cunningham's regiment, serving alongside his father. In 1638 Sinclair was a lieutenant in his father's regiment. There is no further reference to Sinclair in the Swedish military records for the next eleven years. From 1640 he was involved in the Scottish and later English civil wars. He was known as a staunch royalist in Swedish circles and used to bear the Stuart symbol of a white cockade. However, after the execution of Charles I Sinclair reappeared in Swedish service in Johan Wittkopf's cavalry regiment as an unspecified officer in 1649. He also served in Joakim Ernst Goertzke's cavalry regiment that year. David was soon promoted to lieutenant-colonel and then became the colonel of a foreign recruited cavalry regiment after 1650. Realizing the futility of the royalist cause, David used his father's money, which had been set aside for the family's return to Scotland, to buy property at Finnekumla in Älvsborg in Sweden. In 1651 he married Catherine Makeléer (b. 1637), the daughter of the Scottish merchant John *Maclean (d. 1666), who was based at Göteborg and had become a staunch royalist. They had three children, and one of them, William, later became Baron Sinclair. David Sinclair served as an interpreter for the Cromwellian ambassador Bulstrode Whitelocke on his 1654–5 embassy to Sweden, and the political tendencies of his and his wife's families must have made for interesting conversations. According to the ambassador's diary, Sinclair went to great lengths to inform Whitelocke of the size and strength of Göteborg's fortifications, perhaps in an effort to reveal the power available to the Scottish royalists in Sweden. Sinclair's integration into Swedish society continued as he was ennobled and introduced to the Swedish house of nobility in 1655. He remained in military service on the Polish campaigns of Karl X and was fatally wounded by a cannon-ball while leading a charge at Warsaw in 1656. Although he died shortly afterwards his name was still listed as the colonel of a regiment in the Swedish military muster rolls until 1661. A. N. L. GROSJEAN

Sources military muster rolls, Krigsarkivet, Stockholm, MR 1633/16–22, 25, 1634/12–23, 1635/20–26, 1636/17, 20–22, 1637/13–16, 1638/21, 1649/19, 1655/1, 1656/3, 9, 10, 1657/1, 1661/2 · G. Elgenstierna, *Den introducerade svenska adelns ättartavlor med tillägg och rättelser*, 9 vols. (1925–36), vol. 7 · *The diary of Bulstrode Whitelocke, 1605–1675*, ed. R. Spalding, British Academy, Records of Social and Economic History, new ser., 13 (1990) · H. Marryat, *One year in Sweden including a visit to the isle of Gotland* (1862) · E. M. Furgol, *A regimental history of the covenanting armies, 1639–1651* (1990)
Wealth at death held an estate in Sweden: Elgenstierna, *Den introducerade svenska adelns ättartavlor*

Sinclair, Sir Edwyn Sinclair Alexander-, of Freswick (1865–1945), naval officer, was born in Malta on 12 December 1865, the second son of Captain John Hobhouse Inglis Alexander RN (1832–1875) of Southbar and Boghall, Renfrew, and his wife, Isabella Barbara (d. 1883), daughter of Thomas Cochrane Hume, of Halifax, Nova Scotia, and Isabella, daughter and heir of William Sinclair, of Freswick and Dunbeath in Caithness. He succeeded his elder brother to the Southbar property in 1892, and in 1894, on succeeding his second cousin as laird to the estate of Freswick, adopted the additional surname of Sinclair.

After entering the Royal Navy as a cadet in 1879 Alexander served on the China station from early 1881 in the armour-plated iron ship *Iron Duke*, flagship of George Willes. He was promoted midshipman in August 1881 and sub-lieutenant in January 1886. After serving in the *Active* and taking a staff course he joined the *Fearless* in the Mediterranean in March 1888, but left her on promotion to lieutenant in January 1890 to become flag lieutenant to Richard Tracey in the channel squadron. When Tracey became admiral superintendent, Malta, in 1892, Alexander accompanied him and gained experience in dockyard and administrative work. On 26 January 1892 Alexander married Julia Margaret (d. 1930), daughter of Colonel Charles Vereker Hamilton-Campbell, of Netherplace, Ayrshire. They had two sons and one daughter. On 7 November 1933 he married Maud Kathleen, who survived him, widow of Major William Robinson Campbell, of the 14th hussars, and younger daughter of Captain Samuel Yates Holt Davenport, of the Royal Sussex regiment, Territorial Army.

From 1893 to 1896 he served in the battleship *Ramillies*, flagship of Sir Michael Culme-Seymour, commander-in-chief, Mediterranean, and from 1897 to 1900 was his flag lieutenant when he was commander-in-chief at Portsmouth. After his promotion to commander in 1901, Alexander-Sinclair commanded the destroyer *Albatross* from June 1902 and the dispatch vessel *Surprise* from January 1904. He was promoted captain in June 1905 at the Royal Naval College, Osborne, where he remained until 1908. From 1909 to 1910 he commanded the second destroyer flotilla in home waters and in 1911 became flag captain to Sir Arthur Moore, the commander-in-chief at Portsmouth. He returned to sea in September 1913, as captain of the battleship *Temeraire* in the Home Fleet, and was still in command of her at the outbreak of war in 1914.

As a part of the extensive reorganization of the Grand Fleet which followed the battle of the Dogger Bank in January 1915, Alexander-Sinclair became commodore commanding the 1st light-cruiser squadron with his broad pennant in the *Galatea*. On 31 May 1916 the *Galatea* was part of the screen of the Battle-Cruiser Fleet under Sir David

Sir Edwyn Sinclair Alexander-Sinclair of Freswick (1865–1945), by Francis Dodd, 1917

Beatty when she altered course to examine a neutral merchant vessel. As Alexander-Sinclair closed this ship he sighted two enemy destroyers approaching from the opposite direction. His 'enemy in sight' signal brought the Battle-Cruiser Fleet, and subsequently the whole Grand Fleet, into the action known as the battle of Jutland.

Alexander-Sinclair was appointed CB in 1916. In 1917 he was appointed rear-admiral commanding the 6th light-cruiser squadron with his flag in the *Cardiff*. In November 1917 he played a prominent part in the action with the German second scouting group in the Heligoland bight, after which he was praised by Admiral Beatty, and others, including the Germans, for his 'skill and determination … and resolute manner' in difficult circumstances (Marder, 4.305). Twelve months later he had the role of leading the surrendered German high sea fleet into Rosyth with the British Grand Fleet. For his war services he was appointed KCB. In the spring of 1919 the 6th light-cruiser squadron was transferred to the Mediterranean under his command and renamed the 3rd light-cruiser squadron.

In 1920 Alexander-Sinclair was appointed admiral superintendent, Portsmouth Dockyard. In 1922 he became vice-admiral commanding 1st battle squadron with his flag in the *Barham* and for a while, during the illness of the commander-in-chief, Sir John De Robeck, was senior admiral in the Atlantic Fleet. Arthur Marder has described Alexander-Sinclair as a 'first-class sea officer who rose to command a Grand Fleet cruiser squadron. He

was, however, not gifted with much brain' (Marder, 2.16). However, in June 1925, he became commander-in-chief, China station, with his flag in the *Hawkins*, and showed a great deal of skill and judgement in handling difficult situations during the advance of the Chinese nationalist armies. At an incident in Wanhsien (Wanxian) in September 1926, the 'admirable restraint imposed upon the British seamen' by Alexander-Sinclair was said to be 'appreciated by impartial observers' (*The Times*, 14 Nov 1945, 7). In October 1926 he was promoted to the full rank of admiral and returned to the United Kingdom in 1927 to become commander-in-chief at the Nore. He relinquished his command in May 1930 and became first and principal aide-de-camp to George V. At the end of the year he was placed on the retired list on attaining the age of sixty-five. On his retirement he was promoted GCB.

A 'dour red-haired Scot from the wilds of Caithness, with a scrub-hammock face' (Marder, 2.40), Alexander-Sinclair, during his naval career of more than fifty years, received several foreign decorations, including the American DSM, the French Croix de Guerre, and was appointed a commander in the Légion d'honneur. He died at his home, Dunbeath Castle, Caithness, on 13 November 1945. J. H. LHOYD-OWEN, *rev.* MARC BRODIE

Sources *The Times* (14 Nov 1945) · Burke, *Peerage* · Burke, *Gen. GB* · A. J. Marder, *From the Dreadnought to Scapa Flow: the Royal Navy in the Fisher era, 1904–1919*, 5 vols. (1961–70) · *WWW* · private information (1959) · personal knowledge (1959)
Archives Maritime Museum of British Columbia Society, Victoria, papers relating to surrender of German high seas fleet in 1918
Likenesses F. Dodd, charcoal and watercolour drawing, 1917, IWM [*see illus.*] · A. S. Cope, group portrait, oils, 1921 (*Naval officers of World War I, 1914–1918*), NPG · print, 1939, NPG

Sinclair, George, **fourth earl of Caithness** (*b.* in or before 1527, *d.* 1582), magnate, was the second born but eldest surviving son of John Sinclair, third earl of Caithness (*d.* 1529), and his wife, Elizabeth, daughter of William Sutherland of Duffus. Born before 14 July 1527, his wardship was entrusted at first to Alexander Stewart, bishop of Moray, who died in 1537, and then to James Kirkcaldy of Grange and the courtier Oliver Sinclair. He first sat as a peer in parliament in 1542. In 1544, while the bishop of Caithness was in exile in England, the earl attempted to expand his influence by allying with Donald Mackay, a local chieftain, in order to appropriate some of the landed wealth of the diocese. Caithness took the bishop's castle of Strabister and Mackay took Skibo. When the bishop returned, Caithness and his confederates refused to restore his lands and rents. The earls of Huntly and Sutherland summoned them to appear at Helmsdale where both submitted, but Mackay was imprisoned for a time. On 2 October 1545 Caithness resigned his earldom into the hands of Queen Mary, who granted a charter to his son and heir, John Sinclair, under the usual reservation of a liferent of the earldom to himself. In September 1553 an act was passed resolving a dispute between Caithness and Mackay. Caithness continued to be a volatile influence in the north-east. In July 1555 he refused to convoke his men to appear at the justice ayres summoned by Mary of Guise, the queen regent, during her progress through the north. As a result he was imprisoned, first in Inverness and then in Edinburgh, being released only on payment of a large fine. On 18 December 1556 he was granted a remission for this and many other disorders.

It was later claimed that Caithness, along with other Catholic nobles, sponsored a mission by John Leslie, official of Aberdeen diocese and later bishop of Ross, to the newly widowed Mary, queen of Scots, in 1561 in the hope of persuading her to ally with the conservative faction among the lords, rather than with the earl of Moray and his protestant confederates. The mission was unsuccessful, but Caithness consistently supported the conservative and Catholic cause in the years following the establishment of the Reformation in 1560. His name is not recorded on the sederunt of the Reformation Parliament of August 1560, but Thomas Randolph, the English ambassador, wrote that only the earls of Caithness and Cassillis opposed the abolition of the mass and papal authority and the adoption of a reformed confession of faith at this parliament. Knox claimed that Caithness was present and dissented along with other lords, while Archbishop Hamilton stated that he was absent in order to avoid voting on the issue. Probably he was present but sometimes left the room. In 1563 Caithness was ordered into custody at Edinburgh for the murder of some servants of the Earl Marischal. In the dispute between the earl of Moray and Queen Mary in 1565 Caithness took the queen's side. In February 1566 he willingly accepted Mary's encouragement to attend mass, and he was present in Edinburgh on the night of the murder of her secretary, David Riccio (9 March), although he left the town along with the earl of Atholl and other conservative lords three days after the event. On 17 April he was created hereditary justiciar in Caithness; the appointment was confirmed on 14 February 1567.

Caithness hoped to use this position as a platform to carve out a greater area of secure and independent personal rule for himself in the far north which would render him less vulnerable to his Gordon rivals, the earls of Sutherland and Huntly. In the crises of the last years of Queen Mary's personal rule he remained an ally of the queen. After the murder of Darnley, Caithness acted as foreman of the jury at the sham trial which acquitted the earl of Bothwell of the crime. Caithness protested at the time that no crime should be imputed to the jurors since nobody had appeared to accuse Bothwell of the murder or brought any proof in support of the indictment. However, the members of the Lennox family, who would have pressed the charge, were all intimidated from attending by Bothwell's supporters. Although Caithness supported Bothwell's marriage to Queen Mary, after his 'abduction' of the queen, he reluctantly joined the confederate lords in a rebellion intended to free her from Bothwell's control. After the confrontation at Carberry on 15 June 1567, which ended with Bothwell's flight and Mary's imprisonment in Lochleven, Caithness considered his position. Essentially an opportunist, described by a contemporary as 'making always fair weather with those in authority'

(Hewitt, 24), he remained aloof from subsequent operations, failing to sign the bonds in support of the queen. He rejoined her before the battle of Langside on 13 May 1568 and after her flight to England remained a staunch member of her party in Scotland, even writing to Queen Elizabeth on Mary's behalf in July 1568. But as the tide turned against the Marian party the earl began to detach himself from his former loyalties, and in September 1571 he consented to the election of the earl of Mar as regent of the kingdom. After Mar's death he attached himself to the earl of Morton until the regent's fortunes began to wane in 1578.

In 1575 Caithness was granted a yearly pension by the bishop of Caithness for help given in the gathering and protection of episcopal revenues. In 1568 he secured the wardship of Alexander Gordon, twelfth earl of Sutherland, a rival to the Sinclairs in the region. Caithness forcibly married Alexander, aged fifteen, to his 32-year-old daughter Barbara, in order, it was alleged, to secure control over the Sutherland territories. His plan was thwarted by Alexander's escape from his father-in-law's custody and his subsequent divorce after a long struggle to regain his patrimony. Caithness was also accused of involvement in the poisoning in July 1567 of Alexander's father, Earl John, and his wife and of thereafter attempting to destroy the charters and deeds of the house of Sutherland during Alexander's wardship. His plans were frustrated since Earl John had transferred the charters and deeds to the custody of the laird of Carnegie. Caithness traced a violent course in his dealings with his own neighbours. In 1570 he launched an attack on the Murrays during which the cathedral at Dornoch was burnt. He imprisoned John, his own eldest son and heir, in the castle of Girnigoe for plotting against him. John remained in captivity for about seven years before dying, it was said, of starvation and neglect in 1575.

Caithness died at Edinburgh on 9 September 1582 and was buried in the Sinclair foundation at Roslin, outside the town. His heart was cased in lead and buried in the Sinclair aisle in the church at Wick. It is related that during a raid on the town by the earl of Sutherland in 1588, one of the earl's troops entered the church and found the casket. He opened it in the hope of finding valuables, but simply scattered the contents to the winds. The earl's impressive monument survives, however. Caithness was married to Elizabeth Graham, daughter of the second earl of Montrose. She was dead by 4 April 1576. They had four sons and five daughters: John, master of Caithness, who died in prison; William of Mey, who died without legitimate heirs; George of Mey; David; Barbara, or Beatrix, who married and was divorced from Alexander, earl of Sutherland; Elizabeth, who married first Alexander Sutherland of Duffus, and second Hugh Mackay of Farr; Margaret, married to William Sutherland of Duffus; Barbara, said to have been married to Alexander Innes of Innes; and Agnes who married, as his second wife, Andrew Hay, eighth earl of Erroll. ALLAN WHITE

Sources Scots peerage, 2.338–42 · GEC, Peerage, new edn, 2.479, 14.133 · R. Gordon and G. Gordon, A genealogical history of the earldom *of Sutherland … with a continuation to the year 1651* (1813), 111–12 • J. Lesley, *The history of Scotland*, ed. T. Thomson, Bannatyne Club, 38 (1830), 256 • *John Knox's History of the Reformation in Scotland*, ed. W. C. Dickinson, 2 vols. (1949) • *CSP Scot.*, 1547–83 • G. Donaldson, *All the queen's men* (1983), 44, 72–4, 80–84, 94, 122 • D. Calderwood, *The history of the Kirk of Scotland*, ed. T. Thomson and D. Laing, 8 vols., Wodrow Society, 7 (1842–9), vol. 2, pp. 347–50 • G. R. Hewitt, *Scotland under Morton, 1572–80* (1982)

Sinclair, George, fifth earl of Caithness (1566/7–1643), nobleman, was the son of John Sinclair, master of Caithness (*d*. 1575), and Lady Jean or Janet Hepburn, only daughter of Patrick *Hepburn, third earl of Bothwell (*c*.1512–1556), and widow of John *Stewart (*c*.1531–1563), and was half-brother of Francis *Stewart, first earl of Bothwell (*d*. 1612). His father, imprisoned at Castle Girnigoe on the advice of his grandfather George *Sinclair, fourth earl of Caithness, died there in 1575, after seven years of 'famine and vermine' (Gordon, 164; Calder, 105). After succeeding to his grandfather's title in 1582, Caithness was, according to one source, known as Wicked Earl George, and he lived up to this by murdering his father's gaolers, Ingram and David Sinclair, shooting the former in the head and killing the latter with his sword.

Caithness suffered a diminution of his influence in 1584 when, through George Gordon, sixth earl of Huntly, his office of justiciary of Caithness was reduced. He had his grandfather's 'hatred towards the house of Sutherland' (Gordon, 179); and the earls of Sutherland and Caithness were often called to Elgin where, in the presence of Huntly, 'hereditary judge and arbitrator of all debates and controversies' (ibid., 200), they would make bonds and be reconciled, but never for very long. On 29 July 1585 Caithness married Lady Jean, only sister of Huntly and daughter of George Gordon, fifth earl of Huntly (*d*. 1576), and his wife, Lady Anne Hamilton. Caithness received a remission under the great seal for the murders of a David Hume and of the Sinclairs, but in 1594 or 1595 he was revealed to be one of those nobles of Roman Catholic sympathies who had entered a bond with his rebellious stepbrother Bothwell.

In 1606 Caithness and Sutherland were among a number of nobles suspected of popery, and ordered to confine themselves within the bounds of certain towns and to sign an assurance to keep the peace under pain of rebellion. Caithness then, having mistreated the earl of Orkney's servants, fell into a dispute with him, which came to the attention of the king and the privy council. Under caution of 10,000 marks he was compelled to sign another assurance of peaceable behaviour in 1608 to last until 1610. The two earls were reconciled, and Caithness finally bound himself in future to allow a free and safe passage to all the king's subjects through Caithness to and from Orkney.

On 12 November 1612 Caithness was appointed to the commission of the peace and in the following year recommended himself to the privy council by delivering up his kinsman Lord Maxwell, who had taken refuge at Castle Sinclair. On 26 May 1614 he received a commission for the pursuit, capture, and punishment of pirates infesting the north-east coast between Peterhead and Shetland, and on 12 July was named one of a commission for the apprehension of 'jesuits, seminary priests' and 'verie dangerous pestis in this commonvele' who frequently visited Caithness (*Reg. PCS*, 10.241). On 6 August he was commissioned as king's lieutenant for the suppression of the rebellion of the earl of Orkney, detained in Dumbarton Castle, and his illegitimate son Robert Stewart, who had fortified himself in Kirkwall and openly defied the king's authority. With 100 men he compelled the Kirkwall garrison to surrender, and received a warrant to destroy the castle.

Later in 1614 Caithness visited the king in London and received remission of his past crimes and a yearly pension of 1000 crowns. He was also made a privy councillor in Scotland. However, all these signs of favour were lost within a short time. In 1615 the corn of Lord Forbes's tenants in Sansett was burnt, and, to remove any suspicion from himself, Caithness spread the rumour that the Mackays had committed the offence. After complaints were made to the privy council Caithness was said to have caused the witnesses to be drowned so that no actual proof could be found against him. Lord Forbes demanded a reset of the incendiaries, and on 11 June Caithness was denounced for not exhibiting them, while later in the year he was denounced a rebel for his 'papistical' opinions. He obtained a remission by resigning the sheriffdom of Caithness and by forfeiting his yearly pension.

Eventually Caithness got hopelessly into debt and on 1 June 1619 was denounced for trying to defy outlawry. On 25 October 1620 his eldest son, William Sinclair, Lord Berriedale, who had been imprisoned for some of his father's debts, complained to the privy council, and Caithness was obliged to mortgage several portions of his estate to satisfy creditors. After various ineffectual moves against him in 1621, on 19 December 1622 a commission was issued to Sir Robert Gordon to reduce him to obedience. When negotiation failed, Gordon was given on 10 June 1623 sanction to use 'fire and sword' and 'all the lieges of the north' were commanded to assist (*Reg. PCS*, 13.281, 283). Caithness fled, first to Orkney and then to Shetland. On 30 March 1624 a proclamation warned all mariners against helping him back to Orkney or Caithness, but on 10 June the proclamation against intercommuning with him was cancelled, and a new protection was granted to him to go to Edinburgh and deal with his creditors. Reaching agreement with them, he obtained an extension of his protection and an allowance from his estates for the remaining years of his life.

It is accepted that with his wife, Countess Jean, Caithness had three sons and one daughter: his son William was living in 1623, but died before his father; Francis married Elizabeth, daughter of Andrew Fraser, Lord Fraser; John, a lieutenant-colonel in Swedish service, was killed in the Palatinate in 1632; Elizabeth, his daughter, in 1621 married George Lindsay, fourteenth earl of Crawford. He also had two illegitimate sons: Francis, ancestor of the Sinclairs of Sterkoke, and John. He may also have had an illegitimate daughter who married the laird of Dunn. When Caithness died in February 1643 he was succeeded by his great-grandson George Sinclair (*d*. 1676), William's grandson, who, childless and deep in debt, in 1672 made over the lands and titles to Sir John Campbell of Glenorchy.   ALISON CATHCART

Sources Reg. PCS, 1st ser., vols. 5, 7–11 · R. Gordon and G. Gordon, *A genealogical history of the earldom of Sutherland … with a continuation to the year 1651* (1813) · W. Fraser, ed., *The Sutherland book*, 3 vols. (1892), vol. 1 · *Scots peerage* · GEC, *Peerage*, new edn, 14.133 · J. M. Thomson and others, eds., *Registrum magni sigilli regum Scotorum / The register of the great seal of Scotland*, 11 vols. (1882–1914), vol. 5, 1580–1593 · APS, 1567–1625 · T. Sinclair, *Caithness events* (1899) · J. T. Calder, *Sketch of the civil and traditional history of Caithness* (1861) · D. Calderwood, *The history of the Kirk of Scotland*, ed. T. Thomson and D. Laing, 8 vols., Wodrow Society, 7 (1842–9), vol. 5

Sinclair, George (d. 1696?), natural philosopher and university professor, of unknown birth and parentage, described himself as from the Lothians and possessed property in Haddington, Haddingtonshire. He and his brother John were probably educated at the University of St Andrews. John was for a time regent at St Leonard's College, St Andrews, then from 1647 minister of Ormiston in Haddingtonshire; he left in 1683 for Delft, in the Low Countries, where he died in 1687.

George Sinclair taught at St Andrews before moving to Glasgow in 1655, where he was admitted master and appointed professor of philosophy. In 1656 he gave 100 marks towards the building of Glasgow College, and lent a larger sum which was repaid with interest in 1659. During this time the marquess of Argyll obtained rights to the wreck of the Spanish vessel *Florida*, which had foundered in Tobermory Bay after the defeat of the Armada. Sinclair, 'almost the only cultivator of physics during this age' as Stevenson generously described him (Stevenson, xi), assisted when a diving bell was brought to the site, possibly by Archibald Millar of Greenock. Several pieces of ordnance were recovered before stormy weather ended the exercise. Sinclair subsequently devised his own diving bell and described its use in a stylized classical debate in his *Ars nova et magna gravitatis et levitatis* (1669, pp. 220–44).

Sinclair's four-volume *Tyrocinia mathematica* (1661) was prepared for his students; it was reissued in London as *Principia mathematica* in 1672. When the professors were required to submit to the episcopal form of government, Sinclair, who had been allocated a university house in 1665, declined to do so and resigned his post in 1667. He then found employment in the mines of southern Scotland as a mineral surveyor and engineer, and was the first to suggest a practical method of draining coalmines. He was also among the first in Britain to measure heights and mine depths with a barometer: using a sealed tube and a bottle of mercury he assembled the barometer to take readings at the base and summit of a hill, first on Hartfell, near Moffat, and later on Arthur's Seat, in Edinburgh, and at Leadhills and Tinto. His *Hydrostaticks* (1672) was a gallimaufry of practical and theoretical physics, drawing on his experiences with the diving bell and barometer. His claims to innovation were immediately attacked in a series of anonymous letters ridiculing the novelty of his ideas, which had long been taught at St Andrews. A long satirical attack, under a pseudonym but known to be from James Gregory, professor of mathematics at St Andrews,

was published in 1672. Sinclair penned a riposte, the manuscript of which he presented to the University of Glasgow in 1692.

In 1673–4 Sinclair, then a schoolmaster at Leith, was employed by the Edinburgh magistrates to superintend the bringing of the city's first supply of drinking-water from Comiston, for which he was paid £66 13s. 4d. His *Hydrostaticks* was reissued as *Natural Philosophy … in 1683*, now dedicated to the provost and council of Edinburgh. His *Principles of Astronomy and Navigation* followed in 1688. Besides his practical science, Sinclair was interested in aspects of religion, which led him to issue under his own name *Truth's Victory over Error*, a translation of the Latin lectures on the confession of faith delivered by David Dickson, professor of divinity at Glasgow. The book for which Sinclair was best-known was *Satan's Invisible World Discovered* (1685), a compilation of numerous 'authentic' manifestations of witches, devils, spirits, and other apparitions, in which he defended the popular belief in witchcraft as essential to orthodoxy.

Following the revolution of 1688 Sinclair declared himself willing to swear the oath of allegiance. He was recalled to the University of Glasgow as a regent, and in 1692 became professor of mathematics and experimental philosophy. He is last heard of in April 1696 and probably died later that year.

JOHN ANDERSON, rev. ANITA McCONNELL

Sources C. Innes, ed., *Munimenta alme Universitatis Glasguensis / Records of the University of Glasgow from its foundation till 1727*, 1–3, Maitland Club, 72 (1854) · T. Stevenson, biographical notice, in G. Sinclair, *Satan's invisible world discovered* (1871), ix–liii · R. Wodrow, *Life of David Dickson* (1764) · J. Ray, *Three physico-theological discourses* (1713), 263 · *Chambers, Scots.* (1835) · G. Sinclair, dedication, *Natural philosophy improven by new experiments* (1683) · D. W. Thomson, '2000 years under the sea: the story of the diving bell', *American Neptune*, 7 (1947), 269–70

Sinclair, George (1786–1834), gardener and writer on horticulture, was born at Mellerstain in Berwickshire into a Scottish family which had long been devoted to gardening. His father, George Sinclair (1750–1833), gardener to the Hon. G. Baillie of Jerviswood, was in his earlier years considered to be one of the best horticulturists in the south of Scotland, and his uncle was superintendent of the grounds, gardens, and farms at Bonnington, near Lanark. Sinclair was himself originally in the service of the Gordon family, and became, on the duke's marriage with Lady Georgiana Gordon in 1803, gardener to John Russell, sixth duke of Bedford, at Woburn Abbey.

On instructions from the duke, and under the direction of Sir Humphry Davy, Sinclair conducted an extensive series of experiments on the nutritive qualities of various types of animal fodder. The results were published in 1816 in *Hortus gramineus Woburnensis*, an expensive folio volume containing dried specimens of the grasses. These were replaced by plates in cheaper editions published in 1825, 1826, and 1829, and in a German translation of 1826. The nutritional value of the grasses described in *Hortus* was assessed through comparison of their water-soluble constituents, the theory being that these formed the bulk of the feeding material. As a comparative guide the technique did have some value.

After having superintended the gardens at Woburn Abbey for seventeen years, Sinclair left the service of the duke and entered into partnership about 1824 with Cormack & Son, nurserymen and seedsmen of New Cross. On 26 March 1824 he became a fellow of the Linnean Society, and he was also a fellow of the Horticultural Society and of other botanical organizations. He remained a partner of the firm of seedsmen for some nine or ten years, until his death at New Cross Nursery, Deptford, on 13 March 1834. In addition to producing the *Hortus gramineus* and a subsequent *Hortus ericaeus Woburnensis* (1825), Sinclair edited the *Hortus Cantabrigiensis* of James Donn, the *Essay on Weeds* of Benjamin Holdich (1825), and a *Treatise on Useful and Ornamental Planting*, published by the Society for the Diffusion of Useful Knowledge.

ERNEST CLARKE, rev. ALEXANDER GOLDBLOOM

Sources *Gardener's Magazine*, 10 (1834), 192 · *Quarterly Journal of Agriculture*, 13 (1843), 442 · J. Britten and G. S. Boulger, eds., *A biographical index of British and Irish botanists* (1893) · G. Sinclair, *Hortus gramineus Woburnensis* (1816) · G. Sinclair, *Hortus ericaeus Woburnensis* (1825)
Archives NRA, priv. coll., letters on botanical subjects | Linn. Soc., Smith corresp. · UCL, letters to Society for the Diffusion of Useful Knowledge

Sinclair, Sir George, second baronet (1790–1868), politician, was the eldest son of Sir John *Sinclair, first baronet (1754–1835), of Ulbster, Caithness, and his second wife, Diana (1769–1845), daughter of Alexander MacDonald, first Baron MacDonald of Sleat. He was born in Edinburgh on 28 August 1790; he was the brother of John *Sinclair (1797–1875), William *Sinclair (1804–1878), and Catherine *Sinclair. He was sent to Harrow School, aged ten; Byron and Robert Peel were among his contemporaries. Byron described Sinclair as 'the prodigy of our schooldays. He made exercises for half the school (literally), verses at will, and themes without it. He was a friend of mine, and in the same remove.' He had, his father's biographer notes, 'a touch of the prig' (Mitchison, 99). Sinclair left Harrow at sixteen, and went to Göttingen University. He was arrested as a spy near Jena, and was brought before Napoleon, who examined him and ordered his release; Sinclair issued a privately printed *Narrative* of the interview in 1826. He returned to Britain, and in 1811 succeeded his father as MP for Caithness, which he represented at intervals for many years, sitting as an independent whig. In 1812 he presented a Caithness petition for parliamentary reform, and supported Catholic relief; he was out of the Commons from 1812 to 1818. In 1816 he married, on 1 May, Lady Catherine Camilla, daughter of John Manners of Grantham Grange, and his wife, Louisa, daughter of Sir William Manners, first baronet. They had three sons, and three daughters. Sinclair and his family made their home in Thurso Castle, which he modernized.

Sinclair was re-elected to parliament in 1818. In the Commons he formed a close friendship with Joseph Hume and Sir Francis Burdett. He strenuously advocated Catholic emancipation and the emancipation of the West

Indian slaves, and he severely criticized the pension list. While a member of parliament Sinclair found time to attend lectures at Edinburgh University on chemistry, anatomy, and botany. He took a great interest in the misfortunes of Charles X, and had numerous interviews with the royal exile when he was resident in Holyrood. One of these he described in a racy pamphlet, *Comme Charles X* (1848). In 1831 he was again elected for Caithness and sat continuously until 1841, being re-elected in 1833, 1835, and 1837. He became known for his religion. He supported the Reform Bill of 1832, and in the same year he attracted public attention by refusing William IV's invitation to dine with him on a Sunday. In 1835 he joined the new 'constitutional' party of Lord Stanley and Sir James Graham, who had seceded in 1834 from the government of Earl Grey. On 21 December 1835 he succeeded his father as second baronet. He took an active part, as chairman of Burdett's committee, in the famous Westminster election of 1837; a writer in *Blackwood's Edinburgh Magazine* characterized him as 'one of the manliest and most uncompromising of the constitutional members of the House of Commons; a friend to the church, the king, and the people'. He retired from parliament in 1841.

Sinclair was a faithful supporter of the anti-patronage society with reference to the Church of Scotland; he afterwards joined the Free Church. His last years were passed in seclusion at Thurso Castle and Torquay. His wife died on 17 March 1863. He spent the winter of 1867 at Cannes, and died in Edinburgh on 23 October 1868; he was buried at Harold's Tower, Thurso. He was succeeded in the baronetcy by his eldest son, John George Tollemache Sinclair, who also held the Caithness seat.

Sinclair, as heir to the family estates, was placed in difficulty by his father's bankruptcy, but even so £2000 p.a. was settled on him. He was a voluminous writer for the press and author of many pamphlets. His earliest work, *Travels in Germany* in two volumes, describing his visits to the continent, was printed for private circulation; only one copy is known to exist. He published a number of pamphlets on popery and on the Disruption, and also *Observations on the New Scottish Poor Law* (1849).

GEORGE STRONACH, rev. H. C. G. MATTHEW

Sources *Memoirs of Sir George Sinclair*, ed. J. Grant (1870) · *The Times* (31 Oct 1868) · HoP, *Commons* · R. Mitchison, *Agricultural Sir John: the life of Sir John Sinclair of Ulbster* (1962)
Archives NRA, priv. coll., corresp. and papers | BL, corresp. with Lord Aberdeen, Add. MSS 43239–43243 · BL, corresp. with Sir Robert Peel, Add. MSS 40354–40578 · Bodl. Oxf., letters to Benjamin Disraeli · Lpool RO, letters to fourteenth earl of Derby · NA Scot., corresp. with Thomas, Lord Cochrane · NL Scot., corresp. with Blackwoods · NL Scot., letters to J. W. Croker · U. Edin., New Coll. L., letters to Thomas Chalmers · U. Edin., New Coll. L., letters to A. L. Simpson
Likenesses C. H. Jeens, engraving, 1870, repro. in J. Grant, ed., *Memoirs of Sir George Sinclair*

Sinclair, Sir Henry (d. c.1330). *See under* Sinclair, Sir William (d. 1299×1303).

Sinclair, Henry (d. 1400). *See under* Sinclair family (*per.* 1280–c.1500).

Sinclair, Henry (*c*.1375–1420). *See under* Sinclair family (*per.* 1280–*c*.1500).

Sinclair, Henry (1507/8–1565), judge and bishop of Ross, was the son of Sir Oliver Sinclair of Roslin, Edinburghshire (*d.* 1513), and his second wife, Isabella Livingstone, and grandson of William *Sinclair, third earl of Orkney and first earl of Caithness (*b.* after 1407, *d.* 1480) [*see under* Sinclair family (*per.* 1280–*c*.1500)]. Nothing is known of his early life except for his studies at St Andrews, where he matriculated at St Leonard's College in 1524 and determined in 1524–5. As his areas of study were theology, philosophy, and letters, he very probably went on to take a law degree elsewhere and practised law in some way. On 13 November 1537, on the king's instructions, he was sworn in as an ordinary lord of session. In February 1539 he acted as a commissioner of parliament.

Sinclair sat as a spiritual lord and for the next ten years appears in public records merely as holding various benefices. He is possibly the Henry Sinclair found briefly about this time as official of Moray diocese or the treasurer of Brechin diocese of that name. More probably he is the Master Henry Sinclair presented to the parsonage of Polwarth in 1538. In December 1538, when presented by the archbishop to be parson of Glasgow (Glasgow *primo*, which constituted a cathedral prebend), he was styled cleric of St Andrews diocese. He had been allowed by Rome to remain without taking holy orders for some years, and in April 1539 the king supported his petition for a further respite of seven years and permission to hold three incompatible benefices. There was a legal difficulty over the Glasgow prebend, as a previous incumbent had resigned it in favour of an Italian cardinal who refused to give up his right. The king, for two years and more, insisted to Rome on Sinclair's appointment being accepted. Sinclair resigned the prebend in 1550 but held the liferent until his death.

In February 1541 the king nominated Sinclair to Rome as perpetual commendator of Kilwinning Abbey (the nomination was repeated in December) and on 1 May 1542 bulls for this were issued, but with the incumbent abbot retaining his position and the abbatial revenues. Sinclair was in practical terms his successor. He received a five-year tack (lease) of Kilwinning in 1545 and became commendator in reality on the abbot's death in 1547 or 1548. He was also in 1548 tacksman of Currie church, near Edinburgh. Then, in April 1550, on resigning Kilwinning in exchange for the office of dean in Glasgow diocese, he received a pension for life from Kilwinning revenues.

In August 1550 Sinclair was an envoy to England and Flanders to deal with terms of peace, and in 1554 he is recorded as returning from France, though it is not known how long he had been abroad. Then, perhaps in 1555 and certainly in May 1559, he was one of those empowered to treat with English commissioners over terms of peace.

Having been for some years vice-president of the college of justice, in 1558 Sinclair succeeded Bishop Robert Reid as its president. Then in November that year, following the death of Bishop Panter of Ross, the crown granted to Sinclair the temporalities of the diocese and nominated him to Rome as bishop, but his provision was delayed as Rome at this juncture wanted a guarantee of orthodoxy. Eventually, by bulls of 2 June 1561, he was provided to Ross, with the stipulation that he should resign as dean of Glasgow. After Queen Mary's return to Scotland he sat on the privy council, and he remained in Edinburgh, where the college of justice sat. In 1563 and early 1564 he was involved in arrangements for administering justice throughout the land. Already in September 1562, however, his health was poor, and in July 1563 he went to France for treatment. He travelled through England to France at some point in 1564, was operated on for a kidney stone in September, and died in Paris on 1 or 2 January 1565, in his fifty-eighth year.

A man of distinguished ancestry, Sinclair was related to royal Stewarts and noble Hamiltons, with whom he had property dealings. He also purchased the lands of Stevinstoun, Haddingtonshire, which he granted shortly after, in 1537, to his brother James. To all appearances he made very competent use of church revenues to support himself. As late as 1563, being a lord of session, he remained exempt from the one-third tax on his income from Ross diocese, the Glasgow deanship, and his Kilwinning pension. His career was in the law, with church benefices providing the necessary financial support. In 1549, although a commendator-abbot, he did not attend the provincial church council.

In addition to his many years on the bench, Sinclair made permanent contributions to Scots law. In 1554 he was responsible for introducing improvements in the course of justice, while 'Sinclair's practicks', a compilation of judgments and precedents, proved invaluable (though the credit for this, formerly given to him, is probably due rather to his brother John *Sinclair (*c*.1510–1566), whose career closely paralleled his own). Henry Sinclair was also known for his erudition beyond the law, and indeed the remains of his quite outstanding library show the width of his scholarly interests, embracing Renaissance humanism as well as scholastic theology. Alongside printed texts by classical authors including Plutarch, Cicero, and Horace, the collection contained the writings of such contemporary luminaries as Erasmus, Paolo Giovio, and Juan Luis Vives.

There can be little doubt that Sinclair remained a Catholic after the Reformation Parliament of 1560, though he has been described as indifferent in matters of church allegiance. All indications point to this: his support of Catholics, his relations with France, the hostility of Thomas Randolph (English agent in Scotland), the outright condemnations by John Knox. This commitment to Catholicism, however, was combined with his upholding of the law and his outstanding integrity as a senior judge, exemplified in his personal conduct. This explains his advice that laws against Catholic practice had to be observed, his declaring Knox to be innocent of a treasonable act, his refusal in 1562 to meet the Jesuit Nicholas Goudanus on a clandestine mission to Scotland, his supplying bread and wine (in his capacity of life-renter of

Glasgow parsonage) for protestant communion. Even Randolph praised his public-spiritedness. A contemporary writer declared that never before had two such honest and erudite men as Henry and John Sinclair come from the same family.   MARK DILWORTH

Sources G. Brunton and D. Haig, *An historical account of the senators of the college of justice, from its institution in MDXXXII* (1832) • *CSP Scot., 1547–1569* • *CSP for., 1558–65* • *APS, 1424–1567* • *The letters of James V*, ed. R. K. Hannay and D. Hay (1954) • J. M. Thomson and others, eds., *Registrum magni sigilli regum Scotorum / The register of the great seal of Scotland*, 11 vols. (1882–1914), vols. 2–5 • R. K. Hannay, ed., *Acts of the lords of council in public affairs, 1501–1554* (1932) • *John Knox's History of the Reformation in Scotland*, ed. W. C. Dickinson, 2 vols. (1949) • J. Lesley, *The history of Scotland*, ed. T. Thomson, Bannatyne Club, 38 (1830) • T. Thomson, ed., *A diurnal of remarkable occurrents that have passed within the country of Scotland*, Bannatyne Club, 43 (1833) • J. H. Pollen, ed., *Papal negotiations with Mary queen of Scots during her reign in Scotland, 1561–1567*, Scottish History Society, 37 (1901) • J. M. Anderson, ed., *Early records of the University of St Andrews*, Scottish History Society, 3rd ser., 8 (1926) • G. Donaldson, ed., *Accounts of the collectors of thirds of benefices, 1561–1572*, Scottish History Society, 3rd ser., 42 (1949) • D. E. R. Watt, ed., *Fasti ecclesiae Scoticanae medii aevi ad annum 1638*, [2nd edn], Scottish RS, new ser., 1 (1969) • D. McRoberts, ed., *Essays on the Scottish Reformation, 1513–1625* (1962) • *An introductory survey of the sources and literature of Scots law*, Stair Society, 1 (1936) • T. A. F. Cherry, 'The library of Henry Sinclair, bishop of Ross, 1560–1565', *The Bibliotheck*, 4 (1963), 13–24 • R. A. Hay, *Genealogie of the Sainteclaires of Rosslyn* (1835) • *Thomae Dempsteri Historia ecclesiastica gentis Scotorum, sive, De scriptoribus Scotis*, ed. D. Irving, rev. edn, 2 vols., Bannatyne Club, 21 (1829)

Sinclair, Sir Hugh Francis Paget (1873–1939), intelligence officer, was born on 18 August 1873 in Southampton, the son of Frederick Sinclair, gentleman, and his wife, Agnes May. Sinclair began his career in the Royal Navy at the age of thirteen. His service record before the First World War, a period during which he specialized in torpedo work, repeatedly commended him as a 'most zealous officer' with 'excellent tact and judgment' (Andrew, *Secret Service*, 421). In 1907 he married Gertrude, daughter of William Sydney Attenborough, of independent means. During the First World War Sinclair served successively as assistant director of the mobilization division on the Admiralty war staff (1914–16), commander of HMS *Renown* (1916–17), and chief of staff of the battle-cruiser force (1917–19).

Sinclair's first major involvement in intelligence came as director of naval intelligence from 1919 to 1921. In 1919 he was also given responsibility for founding the new signals intelligence (sigint) agency, the Government Code and Cypher School (GC and CS). Sinclair was promoted rear-admiral in 1920, and after a tour of duty as chief of the Submarine Service from 1921 to 1923, he was appointed chief of the secret service (in which he was known as CSS or C) in succession to Sir Mansfield Cumming. In addition to becoming operational head of the Secret Intelligence Service (SIS), Sinclair also became non-operational director of GC and CS; he was promoted vice-admiral in 1926.

SIS between the wars was a small, under-funded, foreign intelligence agency, staffed mainly by men with a service background. During Sinclair's first decade as CSS, its main priority was intelligence gathering from Soviet Russia.

Sinclair himself had a deserved reputation as 'a terrific anti-Bolshevik' (Andrew, *Secret Service*, 422). His priorities were changed by the rise of Adolf Hitler. By the mid-1930s the Soviet menace had slipped into fourth place in the SIS 'order of priorities' behind Germany, Italy, and Japan.

As the Nazi menace grew, Sinclair's influence in Whitehall increased. He was promoted admiral (retired) in 1930 and dined regularly with Sir Robert Vansittart, permanent under-secretary at the Foreign Office from 1930 to 1937; Vansittart described the political intelligence from SIS in 1936 as 'invaluable' (then probably a somewhat exaggerated estimate of its real significance). Helped by his immense clubbability, Sinclair's influence in the higher reaches of Whitehall by the mid-1930s extended well beyond the Foreign Office. He won the support and friendship of the two most powerful civil servants of the time: Sir Maurice Hankey, cabinet secretary from 1916 to 1938, and Sir N. F. Warren Fisher, permanent secretary at the Treasury and head of the civil service from 1919 to 1939. Sinclair was appointed KCB in 1935.

By the time of the Munich agreement in September 1938, Sinclair also had the ear of the prime minister, Neville Chamberlain. He was a convinced appeaser, pressing strongly that the Czechs accept 'the inevitable' and surrender the Sudetenland to Germany. Sinclair also urged Chamberlain to beware of a pact with Russia, insisting that the Red Army 'could do nothing of real value' (Andrew, *Secret Service*, 593). As war approached, SIS reports on German intentions, like those from other sources, became increasingly confused. Vansittart's successor as permanent under-secretary at the Foreign Office, Sir Alexander Cadogan, complained that 'we had no means of evaluating their reliability' (ibid., 591). Soon after the outbreak of the Second World War, Sinclair was taken in by a deception operation mounted by the German *Sicherheitsdienst* (the SS security service) which led to the capture of two of his officers in the Dutch border town of Venlo.

Sinclair had a reputation as a *bon viveur* as well as a fine sailor. A large crocodile-skin cigar case was usually close at hand, and he had a justly celebrated wine cellar. Even during the First World War, Sinclair prided himself on offering his guests delicacies such as Californian peach-fed ham. He derived his nickname, Quex, from the play *The Gay Lord Quex*, by Sir Arthur Pinero. Like his namesake, playfully described as 'the wickedest man in London' (Andrew, *Secret Service*, 422), Quex had, until his middle years, a stormy private life. In 1920, embarrassingly soon after becoming naval aide-de-camp to George V, Sinclair was divorced. He had two sons and did not remarry; his sister Evelyn subsequently kept house for him. He died at 8 Beaumont Street, Portland Place, London, on 4 November 1939, five days before the Venlo incident.

CHRISTOPHER ANDREW, *rev.*

Sources C. Andrew, *Secret service: the making of the British intelligence community* (1985) • C. Andrew and J. Noakes, eds., *Intelligence and international relations, 1900–1945* (1987) • private information (1993) • *WWW* • *CGPLA Eng. & Wales* (1939) • *The Times* (21 July 1972) [Derek Hugh Sinclair] • *The Times* (23 Nov 1985) [Maurice Hugh Sinclair]

Archives NMM, journals, etc.
Wealth at death £21,391 8s. 8d.: probate, 18 Dec 1939, *CGPLA Eng. & Wales*

Sinclair, Hugh Macdonald (1910–1990), nutritionist, was born on 4 February 1910 at Duddingston House, Edinburgh, the second son and youngest of four children of Colonel Hugh Montgomerie Sinclair, of the Royal Engineers, and his wife, Rosalie Sybil, daughter of Sir John Jackson, civil engineer and MP. He was educated at Winchester College and at Oriel College, Oxford, where he obtained a first class in physiology in 1932. He then went to University College Hospital, London, and qualified as LMSSA (he was master of the Society of Apothecaries in 1967–8) and BM, BCh in 1936. Elected a university demonstrator and lecturer in biochemistry at Oxford, and a fellow of Magdalen College, in 1937, he chose to work on thiamine. He obtained his Oxford DM in 1939. In May 1941 he created the Oxford Nutrition Survey (ONS), of which he was director from 1942 to 1947. Scarcely out of his twenties, he had acquired a mastery of survey technique, and by 1944 was directing twenty-five trained and experienced staff. His work was a springboard for the post-war surveys in the Netherlands and Germany, which he was invited to undertake with the rank of brigadier after his success in assuring the British government that its food policy was working.

Sinclair's reports to the Ministry of Health were brief, but he kept his records well, and his 1940s data were still being written up in the 1990s. Some of the German data were lost as a result of administrative tangles, partly due to Sinclair's delight in twisting the tails of supposed superiors. He was a difficult man to work under, with, or over. He was appointed an officer of the order of Orange Nassau in 1951 and was awarded the US medal of freedom with silver palm in 1946 for his post-war work. He became FRCP in 1964.

By 1947 the ONS had given place to the University Laboratory of Human Nutrition, of which Sinclair was director until 1955. He was reader in human nutrition from 1951 to 1958, but, in a titanic quest for better premises, he fell foul of authority, losing both the directorship (to Sir Hans Krebs) and the readership in the struggle, a calamity that might have been prevented by a better record of publication. His fellowship at Magdalen lapsed with the readership, and he became a research fellow there, with some tutoring, at which he was excellent, at a much reduced stipend. Meanwhile, he was developing his fatty acid hypothesis: having undertaken a compendious review, he concluded in the 'longest and rudest letter' in *The Lancet* (6 April 1956, 381) that a relative deficiency of essential polyunsaturated fatty acids was the main cause of various diseases of civilization. This was thought too speculative by his seniors, and weakened Sinclair's chances of re-election to the readership, for which he did not reapply. Encouraged by the first earl of Woolton, he decided to set up an independent nutrition institute, to which he dedicated his property. He sold his medical library in 1965 for

£90,000 to escape insolvency. The rump of his library, including much erotica (the basis of his wide knowledge of sado-masochism), sold for £70,000 in 1992.

In 1972 Sinclair registered a nutrition 'association' as a charity, which was renamed the International Nutrition Foundation (INF) in 1982. He was its unpaid director and main sponsor, housing it rent-free at his estate, Lady Place, Sutton Courtenay, 10 miles south of Oxford, where he planned to build a research centre. The INF failed to raise the £12 million needed, and after his death its trustees, as the sole heirs of his estate, decided to develop it to raise capital for a university chair of nutrition.

From 1970 to 1980 Sinclair was much appreciated as a visiting professor at Reading, and was still doing scientific work. In his seventieth year he followed an Inuit diet, composed of water, seal, and fish, for three months. His bleeding time rose from three to fifty-seven minutes, thus supporting his view that the unsaturated fatty acids of fish decrease the aggregation of platelets and are effective in diminishing the incidence of coronary thrombosis in persons on a high fat diet. Sinclair continued work on fatty acids to the end of his life, writing or editing ten books, giving lectures, composing critical chapters and reviews, and appearing on television. In all he published about 400 separate pieces, and much enjoyed his final years as the doyen of an international branch of research. He was devoted to scientific truth, but slow to establish it by experiment. Claiming an allergy to publication he produced some important speculation, which he thought more significant than reputation, and throughout his life scrupulously maintained his own education, relentlessly sacrificing home and wardrobe to the work of his beloved foundation, to the acquisition of new texts, and to the cultivation of friendships.

Sinclair's tall mesomorphic physique tempted him to work excessively far into the small and not necessarily productive hours, but, relishing deadlines and crises, he was never late for work in the morning. He had a broad and high forehead, fair colouring, and strongly slanting eyebrows, supercilious at the extremities and contracted downwards at the centre, above stone-blue eyes. He was engaged to be married twice, but one of his fiancées died in 1939 from cancer, and the other died from taking cyanide when captured behind German lines in 1940. He remained unmarried. He died on 22 June 1990 in the John Radcliffe Hospital, Oxford, from a gastric carcinoma, leaving his estate to the INF, which in turn funded the establishment of the Hugh Sinclair Unit of Human Nutrition at the University of Reading. BRIAN B. LLOYD, *rev.*

Sources M. Gale and B. Lloyd, eds., *Sinclair*, Founders of Modern Nutrition no. 3, McCarrison Society (1990) · J. Ewin, *Fine wines and fish oil: the life of Hugh Macdonald Sinclair* (2001) · *The Times* (28 June 1990) · *The Independent* (27 June 1990) · private information (1996) · personal knowledge (1996) · *CGPLA Eng. & Wales* (1990)
Archives U. Reading | SOUND U. Oxf., laboratory of physiology, tape recording
Likenesses photograph, repro. in *The Times*
Wealth at death £1,388,172: probate, 1 Nov 1990, *CGPLA Eng. & Wales*

Sinclair [St Clair], **James** (1687/8–1762), army officer, was the second son of Henry Sinclair or St Clair, tenth Lord Sinclair (*bap.* 1660, *d.* 1723), and Barbara (*b.* 1660), daughter of Sir James Cockburn, first baronet. James Sinclair's father was the only Scottish peer to object to the act settling the crown on William and Mary, and his elder brother, John *Sinclair, master of Sinclair, styled eleventh Lord Sinclair (*bap.* 1683, *d.* 1750), remained true to the Jacobite cause.

James (then a child of about six) was entered in the army in 1694 with an ensign's commission, dated 22 May 1694, in the Royal Scots regiment (1st foot). His active service began during Marlborough's campaigns in Flanders. He was promoted captain in the Royal Scots on 2 November 1708. At the peace of Utrecht in 1713 he was placed on half pay. However, on 19 May 1714 he joined the 3rd regiment of guards (the Scots guards) with the rank of captain and lieutenant-colonel. In 1722 he was made a brevet colonel (a non-regimental rank) and second major in the Scots guards; he became first major in 1723. He was colonel of the 22nd foot (later the Cheshire regiment) between 1722 and 1734, and was made lieutenant-governor of Berwick and Holy Island in 1733.

Sinclair married Janet (1698–1766), youngest daughter of Sir David Dalrymple of Hailes, first baronet, and widow of Sir John Baird of Newbyth, second baronet. In 1735 he purchased the estates of Roslin Castle, Ravenscraig, and Dysart, which he entailed on the male heirs of his sisters, he and his wife having had no children. In 1723 he had inherited the family estates on the death of his father; however, when his brother obtained an act allowing him to inherit property, Sinclair conveyed the estate to him. On 26 June 1737 Sinclair transferred to the colonelcy of his old regiment, the Royal Scots, which he held until his death. On 2 July 1739 he was promoted brigadier-general; he was named major-general on 15 August 1741 and lieutenant-general and quartermaster-general of the British forces in Flanders on 4 June 1745.

In 1746 he was appointed to command an expedition against Quebec, but the fleet's having been delayed in the channel too long to permit its sailing that season it was decided to mount a diversionary attack on the coast of Brittany. Port Lorient, where the French East India Company had its depot of stores and ships, was chosen as the target. With reinforcements bringing the number of troops to 8000 men (many were, however, suffering from sickness due to the crowded conditions on the transports) and a detachment of artillery the expedition sailed from Portsmouth on 15 September 1746. A successful landing was made at Quimperle. Upon reaching Lorient, Sinclair rejected an offer of surrender on good terms from the French governor and a siege was begun. The French had been able to bring reinforcements into the town and the attempt to bring about a surrender by force of arms was soon abandoned. The expeditionary force was re-embarked for England on 17 October, having destroyed the forts in Quiberon Bay.

The comparative failure of the Lorient expedition has not been treated lightly by later historians. Fortescue wrote:

Anything more pointless than the design or more contemptible than the execution of this project can hardly be conceived, for it simply employed regiments which were badly needed in Flanders and America in useless operations, which did not amount to a diversion   (Fortescue, *Brit. army*, 2.156)

Among his contemporaries Sinclair's conduct was defended by a kinsman, the historian David Hume, who was employed as his secretary and held a commission as judge-advocate to the forces on the expedition. Regarding the expedition Hume stated that Sinclair, 'neither proposed it, nor planned it, nor approved it, nor answered for its success' (Hill Burton, 1.455). When Sinclair informed the authorities at Whitehall of his complete lack of knowledge of the French coast or the disposition of French forces he was answered that 'nothing was expected of him but to land where he pleased in France, to produce an alarm and to return safe' (ibid., 440). According to Hume, Sinclair's rejection of the French governor's terms for surrender was based upon the need to make a show of force together with poor advice from his artillery officers regarding the likelihood of a short and successful siege. In fact it soon proved the case that the town could not be invested from all sides, the French were able to bring in reinforcements of militia, and the French batteries proved too strong. Hume thus concluded: 'By his prudence in timely desisting from a fruitless enterprise the misfortune was confined merely to a disappointment without loss or dishonour to British arms' (ibid., 455).

Sinclair endured criticism, but his career did not suffer greatly from the Lorient expedition. In 1748 he was sent on a military mission to the courts of Vienna and Turin. His official purpose was to continue the work of his predecessor, Lieutenant-General Thomas Wentworth, in restoring Austro-Sardinian relations. His secret purpose was to discover whether the smaller allies in receipt of British subsidies were maintaining their quota of troops in the field. Once again David Hume was employed as his secretary and aide-de-camp and left a series of letters to his brother describing the lands through which they travelled.

In 1750 Sinclair's elder brother John died without leaving issue and the family estates once more passed into his possession; and but for the attainder of 1715 he would have become the twelfth Lord Sinclair. By now he was reputed to be a man of considerable wealth, garnered in the main from his collieries. Between 1756 and 1758 the Scottish architect George Paterson (*d.* 1789) designed a new building for Sinclair at Dysart House in Fife. Sinclair sat for many years in the House of Commons and, though the brother of a Jacobite, supported successive whig administrations as an ally of Archibald Campbell, earl of Ilay and later third duke of Argyll. From 1722 to 1734 he sat for the Dysart burghs and from 1736 to 1747 he represented Sutherland. He was defeated at Sutherland in 1747 following criticism of the Lorient expedition, but thereafter sat once again for Dysart burghs until 1754. From then until 1762 he represented Fife. He was the political patron of his nephew Sir Henry *Erskine, whom he made heir to his unentailed estates.

William Pitt the elder pressed Sinclair's claims to succeed as commander-in-chief of the armed forces in 1760, which the duke of Newcastle rejected on grounds of age and deafness, as well as Sinclair's friendship with John Stuart, third earl of Bute, then in opposition. However, following the accession of Bute's pupil, George III, on 10 March 1761, he was promoted general. He died at Dysart House on 30 November 1762, aged seventy-four, being then governor of Cork and a major-general on the staff in Ireland. He was survived by his wife, Janet, who died at Greek Street, in Soho, on 8 January 1766. As the Sinclairs had no children, and the family's entailed estates passed to his nephew Colonel James Paterson Sinclair, the claim to the title of Lord Sinclair passed to a kinsman, Charles St Clair. JONATHAN SPAIN

Sources E. Haden-Guest, 'St Clair, Hon. James', HoP, *Commons, 1715–54* · J. Foster, *Members of parliament, Scotland … 1357–1882*, 2nd edn (privately printed, London, 1882) · C. Dalton, *George the First's army, 1714–1727*, 2 vols. (1910–12) · *Scots peerage* · Burke, *Peerage* (1999) · GEC, *Peerage* · Colvin, *Archs.*, 738 · Fortescue, *Brit. army*, 2nd edn, 2.156 · *The letters of David Hume*, ed. J. Y. T. Greig, 1 (1932) · J. H. Burton, *Life and correspondence of David Hume*, 2 vols. (1846), vol. 1, p. 440
Archives NL Scot., corresp. and papers, MSS Div. Acc 7228–8987 · NL Scot., legal corresp. and papers, MSS Dept. MS 1461–2
Likenesses F. Cotes, oils, 1762, Dunrobin Castle, Highland

Sinclair, James, fourteenth earl of Caithness (1821–1881), scientific dilettante, son of Alexander Sinclair, thirteenth earl (1790–1855), and Frances Harriet (*d.* 1854), daughter and coheir of William Leigh of Rushall Hall, Staffordshire, dean of Hereford, was born on 16 December 1821 at Edinburgh. In 1856–8 and 1859–66 he was a lord-in-waiting, and he sat as a Scottish representative peer from 1858 to 1866 when he was raised to the peerage of the United Kingdom as Baron Barrogill of Barrogill Castle, Caithness. His first wife, whom he married on 17 July 1847, was Louisa Georgina, youngest daughter and coheir of Sir George Richard Phillips, bt, of Weston, Warwickshire. She died on 31 July 1870, having had a son and a daughter. He married, secondly, on 6 March 1872, Marie [*see below*], widow of General the count of Medina Pomar, and daughter of Don José de Mariategui, from which marriage there were no children.

Caithness devoted much time to scientific pursuits, was a fellow of the Royal Society of London, and the inventor of a steam carriage for travelling on macadamized roads, a gravitating compass which came into general use, and a tape-loom which enabled a weaver to stop one shuttle without interrupting the action of the others. In 1877 he published *Lectures on Popular and Scientific Subjects*, which achieved some modest success. He died suddenly, from a heart attack in the Fifth Avenue Hotel, New York, on 28 March 1881, and was buried in the Chapel Royal, Holyroodhouse, Edinburgh.

Marie Sinclair [*née* de Mariategui; *other married name* de Medina Pomar], countess of Caithness (1830–1895), who was created *suo jure* duchess of Pomar in the papal nobility in 1879 by Pope Leo XIII, was prominent in spiritualist

circles, being vice-president of the British National Association of Spiritualists; she also founded the first Theosophical Society in France in 1884. Notable for her attempts to reconcile theosophy, spiritualism, and Catholicism, on which she published a book in 1876, she died at her house, 124 avenue Wagram, Paris, on 3 November 1895. She was buried on 26 November in the Chapel Royal, Holyroodhouse, Edinburgh.

T. F. HENDERSON, rev. K. D. REYNOLDS

Sources GEC, *Peerage* · Burke, *Peerage* · J. Oppenheim, *The other world: spiritualism and psychical research in England, 1850–1914* (1985), 170–72 · *The Times* (30 March 1881) · *The Times* (31 March 1881)
Likenesses U. Heath, carte-de-visite, NPG · F. Sargent, pencil drawing, NPG
Wealth at death £36,842 10s. 5d.: 1881

Sinclair, Janet. *See* Colquhoun, Janet, Lady Colquhoun (1781–1846).

Sinclair, John (*c.*1510–1566), lawyer and jurist, was the fourth son of Sir Oliver Sinclair of Roslin (*d.* 1513) and Isabella Livingstone, his wife. He was a younger brother of Henry *Sinclair (1507/8–1565), bishop of Ross: 'Sik tua honest and cunning letterit men as thir wes will be seindill or rather never seen to come of ane hous and familie of this realme' (Thomson, 98). He is probably identifiable with the person of the same name who graduated at St Andrews in 1527, and was certainly at the University of Paris, where he graduated in arts in 1531 and was proctor of the German nation the following year. He returned to Scotland, and was incorporated at St Andrews as licentiate in civil law in 1537. He lectured in canon law at King's College, Aberdeen, holding the parsonage of Snow (St Mary *ad nives*), the prebend of the canonist, as well as the vicarage of Alford.

Sinclair was admitted as a senator of the college of justice and ordinary lord of session on 23 April 1540, but retained his Aberdeen prebend until 1542, when he was presented by James V to the deanery of the collegiate church of Restalrig. Despite resigning the benefice in the curia in favour of James Lauder in April 1547, he retained possession of it for the rest of his life. He began to preach at Restalrig in 1558 when, according to John Knox, many thought him 'not far from the Kingdom of God', but, as the friars and other Catholics began to whisper against him, not only 'gainsaid he the doctrine of justification and of prayer which before he had taught, but also he set up and maintained the Papistry to the utmost prick' (*Knox's History*, 1.131). Knox includes him among those instigating the French to send an army against the Scottish protestants, who in December 1560 ordered the kirk of Restalrig to be cast down as a monument of idolatry.

Depositions sent to Rome in 1565 in support of his becoming a bishop declared that Sinclair had suffered for his defence of the Catholic church, had been impoverished by the heretics, and obliged to flee to France. There he resumed his connection with the University of Paris, acquiring a doctorate in civil and canon law. Although granted a safe conduct to pass through England in September 1564, he remained in France until after his brother's death on 1 or 2 January 1565, when he took back to Scotland the materials which Henry had gathered for a continuation of Boece's history. He officiated at the marriage of Mary and Darnley at Holyrood on 29 July 1565 and was nominated by the queen to the bishopric of Brechin. Although he received papal provision on 7 September 1565, it is doubtful whether he was ever consecrated. Having resumed his judicial duties on 10 April 1565, he sat as president of the college of justice in succession to his brother from November onwards. He died at the house of James Mosman in Forrester's Wynd, Edinburgh, on 9 April 1566, following an attack of fever. Knox, who dismissed him as 'blind of one eye in the body but of both in his soul', nevertheless acknowledged that he and Henry were 'learned in the laws' (*Knox's History*, 1.112–13, 2.185).

Another contemporary noted Sinclair's 'singulare intelligence had in theologie, and in lykwis the laws' (Thomson, 98). Authorship of 'Sinclair's Practicks' is attributed by some manuscripts to Henry Sinclair but internal evidence points strongly towards John. The earliest collection of decisions of the court of session (1540–49), it is written in an idiosyncratic mixture of Scots and Latin, with some personal comments by the author. His main concern is the relationship between Scots law and the *jus commune*, for which he draws upon a wide range of civilian and canonist authorities. The work is said to resemble similar contemporary European collections. The text survives in a number of defective late sixteenth- and seventeenth-century copies but remains unpublished.

ATHOL MURRAY

Sources A. L. Murray, 'Sinclair's Practicks', *Law-making and law-makers in British history*, ed. A. Harding, Royal Historical Society Studies in History, 22 (1980), 90–104 · *John Knox's History of the Reformation in Scotland*, ed. W. C. Dickinson, 2 vols. (1949) · T. Thomson, ed., *A diurnal of remarkable occurrents that have passed within the country of Scotland*, Bannatyne Club, 43 (1833) · L. A. de Saint Clair, *Histoire généalogique de la famille de Saint Clair* (Paris, 1905) · D. E. R. Watt, ed., *Fasti ecclesiae Scoticanae medii aevi ad annum 1638*, [2nd edn], Scottish RS, new ser., 1 (1969) · J. H. Pollen, ed., *Papal negotiations with Mary queen of Scots during her reign in Scotland, 1561–1567*, Scottish History Society, 37 (1901) · A. I. Dunlop, ed., *Acta facultatis artium universitatis Sanctiandree, 1413–1588*, 1, Scottish History Society, 3rd ser., 54 (1964) · J. M. Anderson, ed., *Early records of the University of St Andrews*, Scottish History Society, 3rd ser., 8 (1926) · J. Durkan and A. Ross, *Early Scottish libraries* (1961) · G. R. Dolezalek, 'Provisional text of "Sinclair's Practicks"', 1996 [unpubd]
Archives NL Scot., 'Sinclair's Practicks', Advocates' MSS 22.3.4, 24.1.11, 25.4.11 [copies] · U. Edin., 'Sinclair's Practicks', Laing MSS III, 429, 488a [copies]

Sinclair, John, ninth Lord Sinclair (*bap.* 1610, *d.* 1674), nobleman and army officer, was baptized at Edinburgh on 29 October 1610, the son of Patrick, eighth Lord Sinclair (*d. c.*1615), and his wife, Margaret, a daughter of Sir John Cockburn of Ormiston. Sinclair had a charter for the baronies of Ravenscraig and Newburgh and, with his wife, for other lands in Fife granted to him on his marriage to Mary Wemyss (*d.* 1657), daughter of John, first earl of Wemyss, in July 1631. They had one daughter, Catherine. During Charles I's 1633 visit to Scotland for his coronation Sinclair attended the first of the fifteen parliaments he would attend. A supporter of the emerging covenanter movement, he attended the general assembly of 1638 and was

on the committee there which judged on the legitimacy of the general assemblies held from 1606 to 1618. In 1639 he accompanied Balmerino's horse and the earls of Home, Lothian, and Rothes, and Lord Yester in the forced removal of the regalia from the king's house at Dalkeith to Edinburgh. His association with the earl of Rothes continued in their shared command of a regiment, with Lord Lindsay, in the first bishops' war.

In the second bishops' war Sinclair had sole command of a regiment of foot raised from Caithness and Orkney in September 1640 which occupied Aberdeen from the end of October until February 1642. Sinclair himself did not remain with his troops throughout, but made repeated trips to Edinburgh because of his duties in parliament, and on the committee of estates and the privy council, to both of which he had been appointed in 1641. His troops' behaviour while occupying Aberdeen was considered unreasonable by the inhabitants, but that does not necessarily reflect directly on Sinclair, who castigated his lieutenant-colonel for executing a deserter, and discharged the lieutenant-colonel for cruelty in 1641.

In early 1642 Sinclair's regiment was one of those sent to Ulster as part of the Scottish government's response to the 1641 rising. It crossed to Ireland from April 1642 and garrisoned Newry. Sinclair served in Ireland from August 1642 until 1643, when he fell ill. Suffering hardships his regiment abandoned Ireland in February 1644, creating disturbances on its arrival in Scotland. It was attached to the army sent to England that year to fulfil Scotland's military obligations to the English parliament. Again Sinclair was not with his regiment for the whole of their service. He was absent at the beginning of their participation in England, acting as colonel of the College of Justice regiment of foot. In 1645 Sinclair was again on the committee of estates. In England he appears to have made contact with agents of Charles I and, in 1646, was called before the estates to answer charges that he had been communicating with royalists, but was acquitted of the accusations. His regiment returned to Scotland in 1647 and, though there was talk of returning it to Ireland, it was disbanded after further disturbances.

Sinclair was a supporter of the engagement agreed between Charles I and some of the more accommodating of the covenanters in December 1647. He raised a horse troop for the engager army which entered England in the king's cause in 1648 and served with it himself. With the collapse of the engager cause and the execution of Charles I, Sinclair, at some point, joined the exiled Charles II at The Hague. He advised Charles to launch his cause in Ireland rather than treat with the kirk party in power in Edinburgh by 1650. When Charles in fact accepted Scottish offers of support, Sinclair was among those barred from returning to Scotland or having access to the king until he reconciled himself to the Scottish parliament. In defiance of this Sinclair accompanied Charles II's invasion of England in 1651, and was taken prisoner at the battle of Worcester. He was imprisoned, first in the Tower, and later in Windsor Castle, until the Restoration, though account was taken of his ill health, and he was granted liberty at various times. He was also granted a pension in 1656 because of poverty demonstrated by the fact that his forfeited estates had been valued at £906 17s. 4d., and his debts at £1660 10s. 6d. In 1654, while imprisoned, he was excluded from pardon under the Act of Grace and Pardon. In 1659 he was again granted liberty for illness.

After the Restoration, Sinclair was released from his imprisonment, and he was made a privy councillor again in 1661. In that same year parliament made him a commissioner for excise for Fife and Kinross. The last fifteen years of his life were uneventful in comparison to the two preceding decades, and there is little note of him after 1661. In 1666 his daughter, Catherine, who had married John St Clair the younger of Herdmanston, Haddingtonshire, died giving birth to the third of their sons. Their elder son, Henry, succeeded his grandfather as the tenth Lord Sinclair after the ninth lord's death on 10 November 1674 at Edinburgh. He was buried at Greyfriars, Edinburgh, later that month. R. P. WELLS

Sources E. M. Furgol, *A regimental history of the covenanting armies, 1639–1651* (1990) · *APS*, 1625–86 · *Scots peerage*, 7.576–7, 586–7 · Anderson, *Scot. nat.*, 458–9 · A. Keith, *A thousand years of Aberdeen* (1972) · J. Gordon, *History of Scots affairs from 1637–1641*, ed. J. Robertson and G. Grub, 2, Spalding Club, 3 (1841), 39, 147 · J. Spalding, *Memorialls of the trubles in Scotland and in England, AD 1624 – AD 1645*, ed. J. Stuart, 2 vols., Spalding Club, [21, 23] (1850–51) · *CSP dom.*, 1651–3; 1655–7; 1659–60 · J. Nicoll, *A diary of public transactions and other occurrences, chiefly in Scotland, from January 1650 to June 1667*, ed. D. Laing, Bannatyne Club, 52 (1836) · *The historical works of Sir James Balfour*, ed. J. Haig, 3–4 (1824–5) · *The letters and journals of Robert Baillie*, ed. D. Laing, 1 (1841) · J. M. Thomson and others, eds., *Registrum magni sigilli regum Scotorum / The register of the great seal of Scotland*, 11 vols. (1882–1914), vol. 9 · D. Stevenson, *Revolution and counter-revolution in Scotland, 1644–1651*, Royal Historical Society Studies in History, 4 (1977) · D. Stevenson, *Scottish covenanters and Irish confederates* (1981) · GEC, *Peerage*

Archives BL, letters to Lauderdale and Charles II, Add. MSS 23114–23133

Sinclair, John, styled eleventh Lord Sinclair [*known as master of Sinclair*] (*bap.* **1683**, *d.* **1750**), Jacobite army officer and writer, the eldest son of Henry, tenth Lord Sinclair (*bap.* 1660, *d.* 1723)—a new creation under the great seal, in June 1677, with the former precedency—and Barbara Cockburn, daughter of Sir James Cockburn of Cockburn, was baptized on 5 December 1683. Entering the army at an early age, John held a captain-lieutenant's rank in Preston's regiment, under the duke of Marlborough. Having been accused by Ensign Hugh Schaw of cowardice during the battle of Wynendaal, Sinclair and Schaw fought with swords in 1708. Schaw was mortally wounded during the encounter. His brother, Captain Alexander Schaw of the Royals, thereupon asserted that Sinclair had previously protected his breast with paper. Resenting this reflection on his courage and honour, Sinclair encountered Schaw at the head of his regiment and, failing to obtain a denial or apology, shot him dead. It was found that Schaw's hand had been laid on his pistol while Sinclair shot him, and it may have been that Sinclair fired either in self-defence or after due warning, but with 'no seconds at either encounter' (GEC, *Peerage*, 11.744) his

fights with the Schaws could hardly be called duels. On his being tried by court martial in the camp on 17 October 1708, his acts were declared to be a breach of the tenth article of war, and he was sentenced to death. Through the duke of Marlborough the case was recommended to the consideration of the queen's privy council, who pronounced the act to be wilful murder; but before the sentence could be carried out Sinclair escaped, probably with Marlborough's connivance, from the camp to the Prussian dominions, and he remained abroad until he received a pardon in 1712.

In 1708 Sinclair was chosen member of parliament for the county of Fife, but, even if the election had not been declared void by reason of his being the eldest son of a peer, it would have been rendered void by the sentence of death. On his return to Scotland, after receiving pardon, he continued to reside at Dysart, Fife, until he was summoned to join the standard under the earl of Mar in 1715. He obeyed the summons with reluctance, not because of lukewarmness as a Jacobite, for indeed he was a passionate patriot and opponent of union, but because he had little or no faith in Mar's ability. Still, to him belongs the credit of one of the brilliant Jacobite achievements of the campaign. Sinclair learned that a vessel with arms and stores from the castle of Edinburgh, intended for the retainers of the earl of Sutherland in the north of Scotland, had been brought to anchor near Burntisland. He set out from Perth with 400 horse and reached Burntisland at midnight. Without losing a moment, a detachment of his soldiers seized some boats in the harbour, boarded the vessel without resistance, and thus obtained 420 complete stand of arms. However, at the battle of Sheriffmuir his action was not at all in keeping with this daring exploit. In command of the Fife and Aberdeenshire horse, he was attached to the division which advanced towards Dunblane. This division met the left wing of Argyll's army and was victorious; but Sinclair, though he writes in high praise of the incredible vigour and rapidity of the Jacobite attack, himself did nothing to turn it to account.

On the return of Mar's forces to Perth, Sinclair left the camp and went north to Strathbogie, and thence to Orkney, where he at last found a vessel to take him to the continent. He was associated with the marquess of Huntly's party, which sought to make peace with the government, an action which led to Jacobite scorn for Sinclair:

The Master with the bully-face,
And with the coward's heart, man,
Who never missed, to his disgrace,
To act the traitor's part, man.
(Sinclair, xix)

Being attainted for his share in the rising, Sinclair remained abroad until 1726, when he received a pardon as regards his life, but without remission of the other consequences of the attainder. On his return to Scotland he received back the estates at the hands of his younger brother, General James *Sinclair, in accordance with the legal formula drawn up to evade the 'consequences of the attainder' (Sinclair, xiii). In 1736 he gained an act of parliament enabling him to inherit property but not the title. He married first, on 16 August 1733, Lady Margaret Stewart, eldest daughter of James, fifth earl of Galloway, and Catherine Montgomerie, dowager of James, fifth earl of Southesk. Lady Margaret died at Edinburgh on 22 July 1747 and was buried at Dysart. On 24 April 1750 he married Amelia (1732–1777), eldest daughter of Lord George Murray and sister of John, third duke of Atholl. Neither marriage produced children. Sinclair died at Dysart on 2 November 1750.

Sinclair's *Memoirs of the Rebellion*, published by the Roxburghe Club in 1858, are curiously cynical and sarcastic, highly critical of the earl of Mar, graphic and clever, and of great value for the light they throw on the inner history of the Jacobite rising. Sinclair has also been credited with the authorship of *A True Account of the Proceedings at Perth* (1716), which provided an account of the debates over and decision to end the Jacobite rising; however, Sinclair's authorship is doubtful as he had left the camp before these debates commenced.

T. F. HENDERSON, *rev.* MURRAY G. H. PITTOCK

Sources J. Sinclair, *Memoirs of the insurrection in Scotland in 1715*, ed. W. Scott (1858) · GEC, *Peerage* · R. Douglas, *The peerage of Scotland*, 2nd edn, ed. J. P. Wood, 2 vols. (1813) · *Scots peerage*

Sinclair, Sir John, first baronet (1754–1835), agricultural improver, politician, and codifier of 'useful knowledge', was born at Thurso Castle, Caithness, on 10 May 1754, the third but only surviving son of George Sinclair (*d.* 1770) of Ulbster and his wife, Lady Janet Sutherland (1720–1795), sister of the seventeenth earl of Sutherland. Three sisters also survived to adult life. This branch of the Caithness Sinclairs was not in line for the earldom of Caithness, but owned about a quarter of the county, including much of the land that had belonged to the earldom and also much of its feudal superiorities on which voting in county parliamentary elections was based.

Sinclair was educated at the Edinburgh high school, the universities of Edinburgh (1765–7 and 1768–9) and Glasgow (1767–8), and also as a gentleman-commoner at Trinity College, Oxford (1775–6). He became a member of Lincoln's Inn in 1774, a member of the Faculty of Advocates in 1775, and was called to the English bar in 1782, but he never practised either Scots or English law.

On 31 August 1770, aged sixteen, he had inherited on his father's death estates in Caithness yielding approximately £3000 a year, and the superiority of Wick and of much of the county. On 26 March 1776 he married Sarah Maitland (*d.* 1785), the daughter of a London merchant, Alexander Maitland, who brought him a dowry of £9000. The marriage produced two daughters.

Politics, 1780–1786 Sinclair entered parliament for Caithness at the general election of 1780. Caithness had a parliamentary seat only in alternate elections, a handicap to the prospect of a political career. Sinclair's politics alternated between supporting and advising governments and, when his advice was consistently ignored, moving to independency and trying to organize other independents into

Sir John Sinclair, first baronet (1754–1835), by Sir Henry Raeburn, *c.*1794–9

a party. He had an exaggerated sense of his own political importance, but since no government could survive without the support of a considerable number of independents, an organizer of such members could affect the outcome of important divisions.

Sinclair started his political career as a supporter of Lord North's ministry, and brashly offered to second the address at the opening of parliament, an offer tactfully declined. In 1782 he began what was to become a vast list of publications with a book, *Thoughts on the Naval Strength of the British Empire*, and also *Lucubrations during a Short Recess*, the latter a theoretical support of the idea of parliamentary reform which did not confront the electoral system by which he had entered parliament. He followed these with a disorganized collection of Scottish verbal usages, *Observations on the Scottish Dialect* (1783), the result of studying to speak the English of the English. Altogether Sinclair was to publish massive volumes on agriculture, political economy, and health, as well as over 350 pamphlets and reprints from newspaper articles: the quality of these productions is very varied.

By the winter of 1782–3 Sinclair was moving to independence and trying to organize other independent MPs in a loose association nicknamed the St Alban's Club because they frequented the St Alban's tavern. In the various divisions which eventually brought down the ministry these men voted in every possible different way, so to call these twenty-three members a club is to overstate their degree of agreement. Under the coalition of Charles Fox and Lord North, which replaced the North ministry, he was able to persuade the government to intervene and dispatch resources valued at £15,000 to the north of Scotland to prevent famine following the failed harvest of 1782. Although he voted for the ministry's East India Bill, he became an enthusiastic supporter of the younger Pitt when he became chief minister in 1784, and was involved in Pitt's approaches to past members of the St Alban's Club. He sent a list of forty names to Pitt with advice about negotiating for their support.

When Pitt dissolved parliament in 1784 Sinclair had to find a seat, since Caithness did not have one. His attempt to use his dominance of Wick to gain the Tain burghs was defeated by Fox. He was allowed by the ministry to purchase a seat in Lostwithiel, one of Lord Edgecumbe's Cornish pocket boroughs, for £3000. Once in parliament he sent the government various letters of unasked-for advice, and on 14 February 1786 was rewarded with a baronetcy with special remainder to his daughters.

Though he was useful to Pitt at various times, and a nuisance at others, Sinclair never became an intimate. Pitt's style of life was aristocratic and expensive, while Sinclair lived as a family man of middling-rank expenditure, using much of his own resources for public ends. Because of his political career he had to have a house in London, but he soon established a family home in Edinburgh and spent half the year there. His mother lived in his home until her death in 1795.

Sinclair became increasingly interested in political economy and the financing of government. In 1784 he produced his *History of the Public Revenue of Great Britain* (2 vols; a further part was added in 1789). This is a useful analysis, once it abandons the medieval period, not only showing financial development but indicating Sinclair's appreciation of the possibilities of government promotion of economic growth. It was unfortunate for Sinclair's political career that he and Pitt had very different ideas of the proper role of government.

Foreign tour, second marriage, and politics Sinclair's wife died on 15 May 1785, leaving him devastated. He withdrew from politics and considered leaving parliament: he offered to vacate his seat if Pitt needed its vote. To distract himself from loneliness he went abroad, first on a short visit to France, later on a carefully worked out assiduous tour of seven months over northern Europe, timed to fit mostly within the parliamentary recess. Given by Pitt the inexplicit title of commercial negotiator to the northern courts, he went through Denmark, Sweden, Russia, Poland, Prussia, Austria, Hanover, the Netherlands, Flanders, and France, meeting the leading political figures and making links that he was to use later with the network of scientific contacts built up by Sir Joseph Banks.

The tour developed Sinclair's enthusiasm for 'useful knowledge' in a wide range of topics. He published papers on the political systems of Denmark, Sweden, and Russia. He was interested in the financial organization of the governments of Russia and Prussia. His permanent interest in the development of agriculture and fisheries dates from this journey, and the journey provided him with a network of correspondents with similar interests. In the long run his new concern for economic development was to widen the gulf between his conception of the function of government and that of Pitt.

Sinclair distanced himself from Pitt over the latter's support for the impeachment of Warren Hastings, with whom he subsequently became friendly, but this was not regarded as a serious deviation by the minister. It was the regency crisis of 1788 that produced the breach. Sinclair again attempted to organize a group of independents, which called itself 'armed neutrality'. It included Lord Moira, Bishop Watson of Llandaff, and Henry Adam.

On 6 March 1788 Sinclair married Lady Diana MacDonald (1769–1845), daughter of Lord MacDonald of Sleat and possessor of a dowry of £4000. Her family were government supporters, but the restitution of family life for Sinclair weakened his political significance, since it removed him to Edinburgh for half the year. Lady Diana provided him with seven sons and a further six daughters, almost all of whom survived him. Their third son was John *Sinclair (1797–1875), author, among other works, of a biography of his father.

The response of the ministry to Sinclair's desertion over the regency issue was an attempt by Henry Dundas to unseat him for Caithness in the general election of 1789 and add that county to the long list of seats controlled by Dundas. For once Dundas failed, and Sinclair continued certain of a seat at every other election. His good relations with Dundas were quickly re-established, and in 1792 Sinclair promised Dundas the vote of Wick in the Tain burghs election. The men were natural allies: both saw ways in which government action could benefit Scotland, and were ready to end the legislative inertia which had hung over the country since the Union.

The *Statistical Account of Scotland* The 1790s were Sinclair's happiest and most creative years. In 1790, as an elder in the general assembly of the Church of Scotland, he launched the idea of a survey of the state of the country, which was to become the twenty-one volumes of the *Statistical Account of Scotland*. It is a detailed account of the geography, history, economy, and society of every parish. He had gathered the word 'statistical' from Germany on his northern tour. He used it to mean information which was desirable for legislative purposes, though not necessarily numerical in form. 'Statistics', he said, 'should reveal the quantum of happiness in a population', as well as 'the means of further improvement'. He saw the proper function of government as intervention or legislative action to promote welfare and economic growth, and recognized that detailed information was necessary for such intervention to be effective. He was not the first to move towards the collecting of detailed local information. In particular, for Scotland Sir Robert Sibbald had made various county reports; Sir James Steuart had recommended such action. Alexander Webster's Scottish census of 1755 was an interpretation of the same idea, as were Macfarlane's Geographical Collections of the early eighteenth century. There were the various parish studies made by the Society of Antiquaries of Scotland and published in 1782. The survey idea was taken further in the census of 1801. The important features of Sinclair's survey were its comprehensive range of topics and the fact that it was fully carried through. All 936 parishes were reported on in the following nine years, and the book as a whole is the most frequently quoted of all Scottish historical sources. There have been two subsequent 'statistical accounts' of Scotland, compiled in the nineteenth and twentieth centuries; they follow the original one and are useful bodies of local information, but they lack the variety and buoyancy of tone of Sinclair's.

Sinclair sent out a basic questionnaire of 160 items in May 1790: he followed this up with a further six queries almost at once, and another five in June 1791, these last covering education which he had, surprisingly, ignored in 1790. Altogether the questions covered geography, history, wages, prices, population, industry, agriculture, fisheries, farm size, the progress of enclosure, poor relief, and the general topic of the manners of the people. Some replies came in very promptly and Sinclair sent copies of the four of these he judged best as samples to the ministers who had not yet responded. Initially he had intended to summarize all the reports, but appreciating their variety and individual flavour he instead put in some minor editorial work, including Webster's figures for the population of the parishes in 1755, tidied up the format, and published the whole.

By June 1792, 525 parish reports had come in and were being edited in Sinclair's London house by a team of young men for publication by William Creech in Edinburgh. It was the extraction of the remaining 400-odd that was the great achievement. In all Sinclair sent out over twenty circulars to goad the clergy into action. Some delayed for laziness, some out of a desire for a full report, some out of general disapproval; Sinclair wrote the report for Thurso himself, his publisher, Creech, covered Edinburgh, and the final twelve recalcitrant parishes were covered by the editorial staff. As an incentive for the clergy he had obtained through Dundas in 1792 a gift from the crown of £2000 for the Society for the Benefit of the Sons of the Clergy, and the profits from the sales of the *Statistical Account* and the copyright were also given to the society. The whole project had depended for its feasibility on the privilege of franking mail enjoyed by Sinclair as a member of parliament.

The practical effects of the whole venture cannot be decisively identified but it seems likely that it influenced legislation. Dundas at the heart of government was prepared to note needs, and some complaints made by many reports were met. These were the burden of the tax on coals carried coastwise, the high level of some multures, and the need for increases in the stipends of schoolmasters and ministers. On all these there was legislative change between 1793 and 1810.

The *Statistical Account* might have been expected to use all Sinclair's energies, but at the same time he was involved in meetings of the Edinburgh Highland Society, from which in 1791 he launched the British Wool Society. This was aimed at developing a better breed of sheep than was usually to be found in the highlands, but Sinclair also wanted to encourage the creation of small sheep farms which would prevent the displacement of the existing tenantry. His new society did not succeed in influencing farming in England, where the breeds and problems were completely different from those in Scotland, and in Scotland the society fell into inanition because Sinclair's agricultural interest had a new focus.

The board of agriculture Sinclair wanted an institution such as the board of agriculture as a means of publicizing agricultural developments, advising the government, spreading information, conducting experiments, and promoting legislation. In the minor liquidity crisis of 1793, caused by the start of the war with France, he used his links with bankers to expedite the transfer of £70,000 of small exchequer bills to firms in the north to stave off bankruptcies. In return Pitt agreed to the setting up of the board on an annual grant of £3000, with Sinclair as its unpaid president and Arthur Young as salaried secretary.

The board was nearer to a voluntary society than to a branch of government. Its main element was a core of thirty-one 'ordinary' members chosen from both houses of parliament, who included the leading agricultural publicists. These formed a closed corporation electing their own successors. To these were added 'official' members, nineteen in all, including the great officers of state, the leading bishops, the mayor of London, and the president of the Royal Society. The board met once a week during the parliamentary session and Sinclair conducted business in its name for the rest of the year. The meetings were like those of a debating society; practical decisions were made by the president. To make the grant go as far as possible Sinclair kept the board in his own London house.

Sinclair had hoped that the board would conduct a survey of England similar to the *Statistical Account*, but this was frustrated by the archbishop of Canterbury, who would not allow an investigation which would lay emphasis on the topic of tithe. Instead Sinclair set on foot a series of county reports for the whole of Britain, the General Views series. These surveys were conducted and published in two groups, between 1794 and 1798, and between 1805 and 1814. The first series was hurriedly drawn up and received much criticism, but the second set is a valuable source.

The board also promoted experimental work on field drainage, advertised the merits of the plans of Macadam for road making, gave advice—largely ignored—on the management of the food shortage of 1795, conducted experiments on farm equipment, and in 1796 unsuccessfully tried to get a bill through parliament for the general enclosure of English agriculture, instead of the dilatory and expensive system of single acts for each parish. On this last topic the board found itself in opposition to powerful interests, particularly those of lawyers and the

Church of England, and achieved only a simplification in the procedure for enclosure acts in the Enclosure Consolidation Act of 1801.

Sinclair found time in 1794 to raise a regiment of fencibles from Caithness with himself as colonel; this was a voluntary militia for home defence, called the Rothesay and Caithness fencibles—Rothesay being a tribute to the prince of Wales's Scottish title. He spent six months in camp with the men, a period which gave him a long-term interest in public health.

Politics, 1795–1804 In 1795 Sinclair was close enough to the ministers to suggest the loyalty loan, a relatively unremunerative patriotic investment. It did not bring him close enough to government to help with his election problem in 1796, when Caithness did not send. He stood unsuccessfully for Orkney, and in January 1797 had to buy himself in for Petersfield. By this time the military, naval, and financial situation of the country appeared disastrous, and in February the government's heavy borrowing led the Bank of England to suspend cash payments. Both as a political economist and as a politician Sinclair was appalled and moved into opposition, where he attempted to organize a peace party. In 1798 he publicized his views in two pamphlets, *Letters on the State of the Nation* and *Hints on the Present Alarming Crisis*. He also opposed Pitt's new scheme of taxation, the increase of the assessed taxes, the conversion of the land tax, and, later, the creation of income tax, and issued a pamphlet calling for a 'broad-bottomed' ministry. *The Times* called him 'the Great Scotch Rat', and Pitt called up the official members to get him deposed from the presidency of the board in 1798. Under its new president the board acquired its own house, but had, as a result, less money for projects, and in any case took some time to recover from Sinclair's inroads on its future grant. It became largely inactive.

For a time Sinclair continued to oppose the government, but he came to support the ministry of Addington over the making of the short-lived peace of Amiens. He also supported the union with Ireland. He had strengthened his electoral position by buying up some more superiorities.

Sinclair was also carrying through reorganization on his Caithness estate, and his dismissal from the presidency of the board led to closer attention to Scottish affairs, including the business of the Highland Society. He carried through the division of joint farms, the enclosure of fields, the creation of new small farms, and the setting up of model villages. He bought the estate of Langwell and attempted on part of it to turn moorland into good pasture. The experiment was a failure, but his general management of the estate sent up its value. He was an enthusiast for the spread of the Cheviot sheep, which became the common flock in the highlands. He held to most of the standard views of improving landowners—their enthusiasm for enclosure, for instance, hostility to commons, and readiness to experiment with new crops. He planned the new town of Thurso, an attractive Georgian suburb. He also persuaded the British Fisheries Society to make Wick into one of its stations, with special arrangements for the

availability of customs-free salt. Wick was enlarged by the building of a suburb and proved the only lasting success of the society. As with most improvers many of his experiments were expensive failures, but he was unworried by his considerable level of debt because he had been promised a legacy of £61,000 by an investor in the racket of the debts of the nawab of Arcot.

Later writings Sinclair proposed a scheme to codify existing useful knowledge under five heads: agriculture, health, political economy, finance, and religion. In 1807 he produced a massive four-volume *Code of Health*, and in 1817 a *Code of Agriculture*. The former book cannot be considered a success, since he failed to take advantage of statistical methods in analysing the impact of disease, but the latter was used as a convenient textbook. He never completed the other planned codes. An effective publication of this period was his *Account of the Systems of Husbandry Adopted in the More Improved Districts of Scotland* of 1812.

The relative inactivity of the board of agriculture when Sinclair was not directing it drove him to reconsider his political position. In 1804, when the war with France restarted, he used his influence with other independents to support Pitt's bid for a return to power. He also voted against the impeachment of Dundas. In 1806 he was allowed re-election as president of the board. At once he set to work to spend the money it had accumulated by inactivity, producing the second set of county reports in the series of General Views, and a further *General Report on the Agricultural State and Political Circumstances of Scotland* (5 vols., 1804), a very miscellaneous collection of information which he put together himself. He made several unsuccessful attempts at a general enclosure act. When in 1813 he finally retired from the presidency the board had used up all available money and had to suspend publications for a while, but he had not run it into debt or confused its finances with his own. In the post-war years the board became a mouthpiece for the agricultural and protectionist lobby until the government stopped its grant in 1821, thereby killing it.

In the unexpected general election of 1806 Sinclair found himself without a seat. His attempt to get that of the Tain burghs would have succeeded only if the Kirkwall representative had failed to get to the meeting. The unexpected dissolution of the next year restored him to the Caithness seat. In this parliament he supported the Portland ministry, except for its ban on distilling. When Spencer Perceval took over he gave him steady support, and in return was made a member of the privy council in 1810.

The bullion debate, bankruptcy, and end of political career In that same year Sinclair gave useful support to the government over the bullion issue, the debate which arose from the publication of the report on the currency position by a committee dominated by monetarist economists. This report pointed out that since the suspension of cash payments by the Bank of England the pound had depreciated by some 15 per cent against gold. The committee held that it should be brought back to its former position in two years, ignoring the discomfort and distress that drastic deflation would bring. Perceval declared that this was impossible if the war was to continue. Sinclair wrote a hurried and bulky pamphlet, *Observations on the Report of the Bullion Committee* (1810), and followed this up with another, *Cursory Hints Regarding Paper Currency*. Having in 1797 opposed the use of paper money he had now come to appreciate its flexibility and convenience, and was groping his way towards the concept of the need for an expanded circulation in an expanded economy. The resulting controversy with the authors of the bullion report, who were backed by Ricardo, was inconclusive, since neither side could appreciate the point of view of the other: in this the *Quarterly Review* (1810 and 1811) contributed an entirely personal attack on Sinclair, ranging up and down his writings for unguarded remarks. The post-war deflation showed that Sinclair's recognition of the discomfort it caused was sound.

Sinclair's political life ended abruptly in 1811 because he faced bankruptcy. The legacy on the debts of the nawab was disallowed by the Carnatic commissioners. Sinclair had been spending beyond his income for many years to support his various enterprises. He claimed that he had spent over £1000 a year on the affairs of the board; like many agricultural improvers he had been over-optimistic on the returns from development, and keeping up houses in both Edinburgh and London had been costly. He sold off the lands and superiorities that he had bought and put the core of his inherited estate into the hands of trustees. Perceval granted him a government sinecure, the cashiership of excise for Scotland, recently reduced in value to £2000 a year, and incompatible with a seat in parliament. So he stood down from Caithness and secured the seat instead for his eldest son, George. In 1815, in an effort to raise further funds, he opened a public subscription to himself: it brought in very little, and led to much mockery and a breach with his old friend and ally Sir Joseph Banks.

By then Sinclair had given up living in two houses. At first he brought the family to London but in 1819 he returned it to Edinburgh. He continued to write on various topics. In 1807 he had brought out the Highland Society's edition of the poems attributed to Ossian, with a dissertation on their authenticity, an unfortunate excursion into unfamiliar territory which reveals that he did not fully understand the reasons for the scepticism held by many about the authorship. His last important work was the *Analysis of the 'Statistical Account'*, long promised but produced only in 1825. In 1831 he published his *Correspondence*, two volumes of letters sent to him by various people of note in Britain and abroad. He was still working on his proposed codes of religion and of political economy, but now in old age he could not keep to his earlier schedule of twelve hours' work a day and had to settle for six. Many of his friends had advised him against writing the 'Code of religion'.

Sinclair was a tall but spare man: he stood 6 feet 2 inches and weighed 11½ stone. His physique is clearly shown in the full-length portrait by Raeburn in the National Gallery of Scotland. He was a man of iron constitution and enormous energy, public spirit, and optimism; abstemious and conscientious, with wide interests in practical matters, he had a very limited sense of humour and a total lack of self-criticism. All through his life he had shown a remarkable talent for hard and sustained work. He had strong family affection and trained his children to act as his secretaries. He engaged in many philanthropic activities and promoted the careers of numerous young men. He was religious in a conventional sense, but immune to the trend towards evangelicalism, except that under its influence he held daily family prayers. His genuine philanthropy is shown in his concern that improvement should not mean the displacement of the small tenantry, and a long letter that he wrote to Dundas in 1804, urging him to do something to reduce highland emigration, may have contributed to the government's programme of highland roads. The village of Hallkirk which he planned was an attempt to create smallholdings. His public spirit is shown in his willingness to serve on tiring committees which might promote development, and in his readiness to use his own money for public ends.

Sinclair died peacefully at his home, 133 George Street, Edinburgh, on 21 December 1835 after a short illness. He was buried on 30 December in Holyroodhouse; Lady Diana, who survived him until 22 April 1845, lies beside him.   ROSALIND MITCHISON

Sources R. Mitchison, *Agricultural Sir John: the life of Sir John Sinclair of Ulbster* (1962) • *Memoirs of the life and works of the late Rt Hon. Sir John Sinclair*, ed. J. Sinclair, 2 vols. (1837) • HoP, *Commons* • D. Withrington, introduction, in J. Sinclair, *Statistical account of Scotland, 1791–1799*, [new edn], ed. D. Withrington and I. R. Grant, 1 (1977) • R. Mitchison, 'The old board of agriculture (1793–1822)', *EngHR*, 74 (1959), 41–69 • J. Henderson, *General view of the agriculture of the county of Caithness* (1812) • *The autobiography of Arthur Young*, ed. M. Beetham-Edwards (1898) • J. Kay, *A series of original portraits and caricature etchings … with biographical sketches and illustrative anecdotes*, ed. [H. Paton and others], 2 (1838), 60–71

Archives Bodl. Oxf., papers relating to West Indies • NA Scot., corresp. • NL Scot., corresp. • NRA, priv. coll., corresp. and papers • Thurso East Mains, Caithness • U. Reading L., corresp. | Birm. CA, letters to Boulton family • BL, letters to Sir Joseph Banks, Add. MSS 33978–33982 • BL, letters to Lord Grenville, Add. MS 58996 • BL, letters to Lord Hardwicke, Add. MSS 35642–35735 • BL, corresp. with Warren Hastings, Add. MSS 29172–29185, 29237 • BL, corresp. with Sir Robert Peel, Add. MSS 40224–40407 • BL, letters to Arthur Young • BL, corresp. with earls of Liverpool, Add. MSS 38219–38311, 38410, 38421, 38572 • California State Library, letters to Sir Joseph Banks • CKS, letters to Lord Stanhope • Col. U., Rare Book and Manuscript Library, corresp. with John Jay • Falkirk Museums History Research Centre, Falkirk Archives, letters to William Forbes • LUL, letters to Lord Sheffield • NA Scot., letters to Sir Archibald Grant • NA Scot., letters to Gilbert Innes • NA Scot., letters to Lord Melville • NL Scot., letters to Robert Douglas • NL Scot., corresp. with Robert Liston • NL Scot., letters to Sir Walter Scott • Northumb RO, Newcastle upon Tyne, corresp. with George Culley • NRA, priv. coll., letters to William Adam • NRA, priv. coll., corresp. with Robert Brown • NRA, priv. coll., corresp. with William Creech • PRO, letters to William Pitt, PRO 30/8 • PRO NIre., corresp. with John Foster • Rothamsted Experimental Station Library, letters to Sir Joseph Banks • Royal Highland and Agricultural Society of Scotland, letters relating to Gaelic dictionary • RSA, letters to Royal Society of Arts • St Deiniol's Library, Hawarden, corresp. with Sir John Gladstone • TCD, corresp. with William Shaw Mason • U. Edin. L., letters to Grimr Thorkelin • U. Edin., New Coll. L., letters to Thomas Chalmers • U. Reading, Rural History

Centre, old board of agriculture MSS · UCL, letters to Lord Brougham · W. Sussex RO, letters to duke of Richmond **Likenesses** W. Skelton, line engraving, pubd 1790 (after T. Lawrence), BM, NPG · J. Kay, etching, 1791, NPG · H. Raeburn, oils, c.1794–1799, NG Scot. [see illus.] · plaster medallion, 1797 (after J. Tassie), Scot. NPG · H. Raeburn, oils, c.1810, NPG · W. Bond, stipple, pubd 1817 (after A. Robertson), BM, NPG · W. Bromley, line engraving (after S. Drummond), BM, NPG; repro. in European Magazine (1791) · attrib. F. Chantrey, statue, Thurso · T. Lawrence, portrait, Thurso East Mains, Caithness · political cartoons · sketch, repro. in Kay, Series of original portraits **Wealth at death** probably £4000–£6000 p.a. from estate, but heavily encumbered

---

Sinclair, John (1791–1857), singer, was born on 9 December 1791 near Edinburgh, the son of David Sinclair, a cotton spinner. He joined the band of Campbell of Shawfield's regiment as a clarinettist, and went to Aberdeen. There he taught singing until he was able to buy his discharge. As he liked the stage and had a fine tenor voice, he went to London to look for work, and on 7 September 1810 appeared at the Haymarket Theatre as Captain Cheerly in William Shield's Lock and Key. After this he became a pupil of Thomas Welsh and was engaged for seven years at Covent Garden, where he created the tenor roles in Henry Bishop's Guy Mannering (1816) and The Slave (1816), John Davy's Rob Roy (1818), and other works. He was the first to sing Bishop's song 'The Pilgrim of Love', and he was very popular as Apollo in Midas. In 1816 Sinclair married a daughter of Captain Norton. One of his daughters, Caroline, was married to the American tragedian Edwin Forrest.

Sinclair went to Paris in 1819 and had lessons from Giulio Pellegrini, then travelled to Milan, where he studied with Davidde Banderali at the conservatory. In May 1821 he sang to Rossini at Naples, and had some lessons from him, and in 1822–3 appeared in opera at Pisa, Bologna, Genoa, Modena, Florence, and elsewhere. At Venice in 1823 Rossini wrote for him the part of Idreno in Semiramide.

By the time Sinclair returned from Italy to England, his voice had greatly improved, and he appeared at Covent Garden on 19 November 1823 as Prince Orlando in T. J. Dibdin's comic opera The Cabinet. From 1828 to 1829 he was engaged at the Adelphi, and from 1829 to 1830 at Drury Lane, and after a short visit to America in 1830–1, where he sang in New York and Philadelphia, he retired to Margate. He was director of the Tivoli Gardens there until his death, in Margate, on 23 September 1857.

Sinclair's voice was a pure tenor, with an unusually fine falsetto, but his style was a little effeminate, and he was known as 'the leddies' bonnie Sinclair'. He was one of the earliest performers of Scottish song. He composed a number of songs, including 'Come, sit ye doon', 'The Bonnie Breast Knots', 'The Mountain Maid', 'Johnny Sands', and others in the Scottish style, all of which were very popular. J. C. HADDEN, rev. ANNE PIMLOTT BAKER

Sources New Grove · Grove, Dict. mus. · Boase, Mod. Eng. biog. · D. Baptie, ed., Musical Scotland, past and present: being a dictionary of Scottish musicians from about 1400 till the present time (1894)

Likenesses S. De Wilde, two drawings, 1812, Garr. Club · G. H. Harlow, oils, Royal Society of Musicians, London · H. Hoppner Meyer, mezzotint (after G. H. Harlow), BM

Sinclair, John (1797–1875), Church of England clergyman, third son of Sir John *Sinclair, first baronet (1754–1835), and his second wife, Diana (1769–1845), daughter of the first Baron MacDonald of Sleat, was born on 20 August 1797, and educated at Edinburgh University. In 1815 he entered Pembroke College, Oxford, where he graduated BA in 1819 and MA in 1822. At Edinburgh he was a founder member of the Rhetorical Society, and at Oxford he helped to lay the foundations of the Union Society. Ordained deacon in 1819 and priest in 1820, he worked at Sutterby, Lincolnshire, at Hackney, and at Edinburgh, before being appointed in 1839 to the secretaryship of the National Society for Promoting the Education of the Poor. As secretary, and subsequently treasurer, of the society he exercised a powerful influence on its activities for more than thirty years, waging a vigorous campaign against government attempts to encroach on the church's monopoly of education. In 1839 he organized the society's successful resistance to the proposal by Sir James Kay-Shuttleworth to give the privy council the right to appoint school inspectors. His policy of non-co-operation forced the government's hand, and produced the concordat of 1840 whereby such appointments were made subject to approval by the provincial archbishops. Bishop Blomfield unreservedly supported Sinclair, whom he made in 1839 one of his examining chaplains, in 1843 vicar of Kensington, and in 1844 archdeacon of Middlesex. He held the last two offices until the end of his life. At Kensington he subdivided the huge parish, and built the new parish church of St Mary Abbots. He acted also as secretary of the Diocesan Church Building Society, which became, under Bishop Tait, the Bishop of London's Fund. Sinclair died, unmarried, at the vicarage in Kensington, after a short illness, on 22 May 1875. He was the author of a biography of his father (1837), and of many minor religious works.

G. MARTIN MURPHY

Sources H. J. Burgess, Enterprise in education (1958) · The Churchman, new ser., 6 (1891), 294, 352 · The Guardian (26 May 1875) · Crockford (1874) · Foster, Alum. Oxon. · Burke, Peerage · Boase, Mod. Eng. biog.
Archives BL, corresp. with Sir Robert Peel, Add. MSS 40413–40557 · LPL, corresp. with Baroness Burdett-Coutts · LPL, corresp. with A. C. Tait and related papers
Wealth at death under £25,000: probate, 21 June 1875, CGPLA Eng. & Wales

Sinclair, John, first Baron Pentland (1860–1925), politician and administrator in India, was born at 6 Moray Place, Edinburgh, on 7 July 1860, the eldest of the three sons of Captain George Sinclair (1826–1871), an officer of the Bengal army, and his wife and cousin, Agnes (d. 1876), daughter of John Learmonth of Dean, coach-builder and lord provost of Edinburgh, who built and presented to the city of Edinburgh the Dean Bridge. His grandfather was Sir John Sinclair of Dunbeath in Caithness, sixth baronet; this branch of the family had been settled at Dunbeath since about 1680.

Sinclair was educated first at Edinburgh Academy (1870–73), then at Wellington College (1873–8), and entered Sandhurst in 1878. He passed out fifth, joined the 5th Royal Irish Lancers in 1879, and served in Ireland from 1881. He acted on occasion as an escort officer for the viceroy, Earl Spencer, and said that it was to him that he 'owed the beginnings of his Liberal faith' (Pentland, 22). His experiences in Ireland also strongly developed his later belief in home rule. He served with the Sudan expedition of 1885 and earned the medal and clasp. In 1886 he unsuccessfully contested the Ayr burghs in Scotland as a Liberal.

Early in 1887 Sinclair left the army; he began to read law and study economics, and was a resident at the recently founded Toynbee Hall. In 1889 he was elected a member of the first London county council, as a Progressive, for East Finsbury but stood aside in 1892 to allow for the candidature of Lord Rosebery, who described Sinclair as 'arduously interested in the work of the Council' (Pentland, 26). Sinclair then obtained Liberal endorsement for the Dunbartonshire constituency, which he won at the general election of 1892. He was appointed assistant private secretary to the secretary of state for war, Henry Campbell-Bannerman, but at the general election of 1895 he lost his seat. He then served for a year (1896–7) as private secretary to Lord Aberdeen, who was at that time governor-general of Canada. Recognized within the party as an excellent and popular campaigner Sinclair re-entered parliament in 1897 at a by-election for Forfarshire; this seat he retained until he was made a peer in 1909. From 1900 to 1905 he was Scottish Liberal whip. On 12 July 1904 he married Lady Marjorie Adeline (1880–1970), only daughter of John Campbell *Gordon, seventh earl and first marquess of Aberdeen; they had one son and one daughter.

In late 1905 Sinclair was being considered for the post of chief whip but commented that he 'does not want to be a whip, dislikes the work, thinks it too hard, and takes him altogether from his wife' (Wilson, 439). He was instead appointed secretary for Scotland, a position he took to with great enthusiasm, as he 'had very definite ideas about Scottish administration. He wanted Scotland to be governed according to Scottish ideas' (Pentland, 106). Sinclair was personally very close to Campbell-Bannerman (who made him his executor and left him his papers) and this enabled him to exercise considerable influence upon the general policy of the Liberal Party, although the relationship was sometimes ridiculed, and Asquith said Sinclair was 'regarded as C. B.'s natural son' (*Liberal Chronicle*, 95). Sinclair's secretaryship was marked by several measures of importance to Scotland, including the National Galleries (Scotland) Act of 1906 and the Scottish Education Act of 1908, which provided for better physical care of children, improved the training of teachers and the secondary school system, and gave greater facilities for continued instruction after school age. His Small Landholders (Scotland) Bill, the object of which was to extend to smallholders in the rest of Scotland the security of tenure already granted to the crofter counties, was severely criticized both outside and within the Liberal Party, and it was only Campbell-Bannerman's strong support that allowed it to be approved by cabinet. It was rejected by the House of Lords in 1907 and 1908, but became law in 1911.

Sinclair was raised to the peerage (as Baron Pentland of Lyth, Caithness) in February 1909, and in 1912 he was appointed governor of Madras. There he was remembered for his efforts to improve the health and social welfare and the economic development of the presidency; he remained until 1919. He was sworn of the privy council in 1905, and created GCIE in 1912 and GCSI in 1918. He died of pneumonia at his home at Frognal End, Hampstead, London, on 11 January 1925, and was buried at Dean cemetery, Edinburgh, on 15 January.

MAURICE HEADLAM, rev. MARC BRODIE

Sources M. Pentland, *The Right Honourable John Sinclair, Lord Pentland, G.C.S.I.: a memoir* (1928) · *The Times* (12 Jan 1925) · *The Times* (13 Jan 1925) · *The Times* (16 Jan 1925) · J. Wilson, *CB: a life of Sir Henry Campbell-Bannerman* (1973) · Burke, *Peerage* · P. Rowland, *The last liberal governments*, 1 (1968) · *A liberal chronicle: journals and papers of J. A. Pease*, ed. C. Hazlehurst and C. Woodland (1994) · *CGPLA Eng. & Wales* (1925)
Archives NA Scot., corresp. and papers [microfilm] | BL, corresp. with Sir Henry Campbell-Bannerman and biographical papers, Add. MSS 41230, 41252, 52520 · BL, corresp. with Lord Craigmyle, MS 41230 · BL, corresp. with Lord Gladstone, Add. MS 45995 · BL OIOC, corresp. with E. S. Montagu, MS Eur. D 523 · CAC Cam., corresp. with David Saunders · CUL, corresp. with Lord Hardinge · NL Scot., corresp. mainly with Sir Patrick Geddes · U. Birm. L., letters to Austen Chamberlain
Likenesses H. Furniss, pen-and-ink caricature, *c*.1905, NPG · W. Stoneman, photograph, 1921, NPG · photograph, repro. in *The Times* (13 Jan 1925), 16 · photographs, repro. in Pentland, *The Right Honourable John Sinclair*

Sinclair, Sir John Alexander (1897–1977), army and intelligence officer, was born on 29 May 1897 in Fulham, the younger son and second of the four children of John Stewart Sinclair, later archdeacon of Cirencester (who was the grandson of Sir John Sinclair, first baronet), and his wife, Clara Sophia, daughter of John Dearman Birchall JP, of Bowden Hall, Gloucestershire. He was educated at West Downs School, Winchester, and the Royal Naval College at Osborne and Dartmouth, finishing his education just in time to serve as a Royal Navy midshipman for the first two years of the First World War. During that time he was almost continuously at sea, mainly in submarines, but scarcely ever free from seasickness. Soon after he had taken part in the landing of the Lancashire Fusiliers on the west beach at Gallipoli his health broke down completely and he had to be invalided out of the navy after only six years' service.

During his long convalescence Sinclair was able to return to West Downs School to do some teaching until well enough to apply for a new career in the army. In 1918 he entered the Royal Military Academy, Woolwich, where he proved himself an outstanding cadet, winning the sword of honour and other academy prizes. Commissioned in the Royal Field Artillery in 1919, he served first with the Murmansk force in northern Russia and then in India. He returned to duty at Aldershot, and married in 1927 Esme Beatrice (*d.* 1983), daughter of Thomas Kark general staff South-Eastern command, and in 1942 deputy chief of the general staff, home forces.

Promoted major-general, Sinclair concentrated on training and planning for the Normandy invasion, though his own hopes of joining the invasion forces were later dashed by the split-up of home forces command and the formation of the Twenty-First Army group of Sir B. L. Montgomery. Instead he was appointed director of military intelligence (DMI) at the War Office in 1944 and thus found himself entering at the highest level a field that was new to him. Intelligence played a great part in the war and was at that time needed more than ever. He quickly showed that he had the qualities for the job; a capacity for detail, good judgement, and a ready acceptance of responsibility. Sinbad Sinclair, as he was called by his colleagues, became a much-respected DMI and held the post until the end of the war.

Near the expected end of his military career a new prospect opened for Sinclair. It was to become in 1951, after first serving as deputy director until 1950, the director of MI6, the civilian intelligence service responsible to the foreign secretary and the prime minister. The choice of a successful DMI, admired for his strong character and organizational skills, was particularly appropriate for the transitional period that lay ahead of the service. A large wartime organization had to be scaled down, new methods and standards of recruitment for permanent staff agreed, and old international alliances renegotiated for new peacetime tasks. He achieved these things in ways that lasted well, while at the same time directing current operations in his usual practical and responsible way. It was therefore unfair to his reputation that the only time he came to public notice was in connection with the intelligence operation of 19 April 1956 in which the diver Commander Lionel Crabb was lost when making an underwater inspection of a Russian ship awaiting in Portsmouth harbour the return of Khrushchov and Bulganin, who were on a goodwill visit to Britain. The intelligence urgencies of those times had led to a hastily planned operation for which he had to accept responsibility without having been able to supervise its details.

Sinclair, who was appointed OBE in 1940, CB in 1945, and KCMG in 1953, was also a commander of the American Legion of Merit (1945). He retired in 1956 leaving behind him the reputation of a notable reformer and much-trusted chief. He was now free to enjoy twenty-one years of a happy and united family life at his home, East Ashling Grange, East Ashling, near Chichester, Sussex, where he died on 22 March 1977. DICK WHITE, *rev.*

Sources personal knowledge (1986) · private information (1986) · *The Times* (24 March 1978) · *WWW* · *CGPLA Eng. & Wales* (1977)
Likenesses W. Stoneman, photograph, 1944, NPG [*see illus.*]
Wealth at death £132,000: probate, 20 June 1977, *CGPLA Eng. & Wales*

Sir John Alexander Sinclair (1897–1977), by Walter Stoneman, 1944

Sopwith, of Maidstone, who was later archdeacon of Canterbury. They had two sons and two daughters.

After serving as adjutant in the Honourable Artillery Company (1929–31) Sinclair went on to the Staff College, Camberley (1932–3), and from 1938 to 1939 he was an instructor at the Senior Staff College at Minley. By the opening of the Second World War his reputation in the army was that of a studious and thoughtful soldier and a fine all-round sportsman. He began the war as an operational planner with the British expeditionary force (BEF). Although the British were always sceptical of one of its basic concepts, namely the impassability of the Ardennes to German armour, the British plans had to be fitted into the overall Gamelin plan. Alec Sinclair drafted the operational order for the advance of the BEF to the River Kyle but having done so was almost immediately recalled to London to become GSO1 in military operations 4 close to the highest levels of command, and at a time when the planners had to take simultaneous account of the calls for reinforcement and the possibility of evacuation. When this phase was over he had become brigadier and deputy director of operations. In 1941 he was appointed brigadier,

Sinclair, Marie, countess of Caithness and *suo jure* duchess of Pomar in the papal nobility (1830–1895). *See under* Sinclair, James, fourteenth earl of Caithness (1821–1881).

Sinclair, Mary Amelia St Clair [May] (1863–1946), novelist and philosopher, was born on 24 August 1863 in Thorncote, Rock Park, Rock Ferry, near Birkenhead, Cheshire, the youngest of six surviving children of William Sinclair (1829–1881), part owner of a Liverpool shipping business, and Amelia (1821/2–1901), daughter of a Belfast merchant, John Hind. In the late 1860s William Sinclair's business began to fail, and about 1870 he became bankrupt, and the family was dispersed. May lived with her mother in Ilford, Cheltenham, and Fairford, Wrexham, Salcombe Regis, and London. She had tuition at home, piano lessons, and access to her father's library, where she read widely in classical and English literature, history, and philosophy. She learned German, Greek, and French before being sent for a year to Cheltenham Ladies' College in 1881, where the influential Dorothea Beale took an interest in her. In that year her father, who had become an alcoholic, died. The family tragedy continued relentlessly with the early deaths of her four brothers from heart failure between 1887 and 1896.

Sinclair's original ambition was to be a poet and philosopher. Her first book, *Nakiketas and other Poems* (1886), was published under the pseudonym Julian Sinclair. *Essays in Verse* (1892) was her first publication as May Sinclair. Her first essay on idealism came out in the *New World* in 1893 (she became the first woman member of the Aristotelian Society after publishing *A Defence of Idealism*, 1917). In 1893 Sinclair met and fell in love with Anthony Charles Deane. However, he was ordained in that year and then married someone else in 1898. When her first novel, *Audrey Craven*, was published in 1897, Sinclair was poor and trapped, looking after her mother in London lodgings at Christchurch Road, Hampstead. The novel's psychological complexity and frankness became her hallmark, as did the relative sexual explicitness of her second, *Mr. and Mrs. Nevill Tyson* (1898). *The Divine Fire* (1904), ironically a critique of the bookselling industry, was her first major success, establishing her reputation not only in Britain, but in America, where it was a best-seller. Like much of her fiction it deals with the emotional and psychological lives of artists.

When Joseph Walter, her last surviving brother, died in 1905, Sinclair assumed responsibility for his children, and then for those of her brother William when his widow died in 1906. In August 1907 she took a flat at 4 The Studios, Edwardes Square, Kensington, London. Her friends included H. G. Wells, Ford Madox Ford (then Hueffer), Wyndham Lewis, W. B. Yeats, and Thomas Hardy. Sinclair concentrated on novels exploring the difficulties women faced in sexual, domestic, and intellectual arenas in *The Helpmate* and *The Judgement of Eve* (1907), *Kitty Tailleur* (1908), and *The Creators* (1910). From 1907 to 1914 she published a series of fine introductions to the Everyman Library editions of the Brontë novels (she wrote a full-length study in 1912, and her novel *The Three Sisters* draws on the Brontë story). In 1912 she wrote *Feminism* for the Women Writers' Suffrage League, of which she was a member. She was also a member of the militant Women's Freedom League. She

Mary Amelia St Clair Sinclair (1863–1946), by Walter Tittle, 1923

supported new literary, social, and intellectual movements such as Tagore enthusiasts, imagists, and vorticists. She championed Ezra Pound, and also wrote essays on her friends T. S. Eliot (who published her in *The Criterion*), Violet Hunt, H. D., and Richard Aldington (whom she may have loved platonically). She had a particularly intense friendship with Charlotte Mew, who was in love with her.

In October 1913 Sinclair attended the inaugural meeting of the Medico-Psychological Clinic of London, 'the first clinic in England to include psychoanalysis in an eclectic array of therapeutic methods' (Boll, 104). Sinclair wrote the prospectus, and was elected as one of the twelve founder members, and as a member of the board of management. *The Three Sisters* (1914) is the first of her novels to explore psychoanalytic concepts such as unconscious motivation. In May 1914 she was also elected to membership of the Society for Psychical Research, which combined interests in scientific psychology and mystical or paranormal phenomena; her *Uncanny Stories* (1923) and *The Intercessor, and other Stories* explore mystical or psychic themes.

Sinclair moved to 1 Blenheim Road, St John's Wood, London, in March 1914. At the outbreak of the First World War she joined Dr Hector Munro's volunteer ambulance corps as secretary, treasurer, banker, financial supporter, and publicist. They left London on 25 September 1914 for Ostend, Bruges, and Ghent. After two and half weeks Sinclair was sent back to England for more funds, and was shocked to discover Munro had replaced her. The proximity of mortal danger had an intense effect on her, which can be gauged in her war fiction, especially *The Tree of Heaven* (1917) and *The Romantic* (1920).

In 1916 Sinclair was elected a fellow of the Royal Society of Literature. In the same year William Lyon Phelps hailed her as 'the foremost living writer among English-speaking women' (*The Times*, 15 Nov 1946), and she published 'Clinical lectures on symbolism and sublimation', one of the few accounts to appear in an English journal of a schism between Jung and Freud. She was among the earliest novelists to explore psychoanalytic ideas in fiction and criticism, and in 1918 was the first to apply William James's term 'stream of consciousness' to literature in an essay on Dorothy Richardson's *Pilgrimage*. In 1919 she published *Mary Olivier: a Life*, a work of experimental modernism, and one of her best novels. Much of her family life formed the basis of this novel: the heroine's love for her brother Mark (Frank); her struggle against the tyranny and religious orthodoxy of the mother, who rejects her daughter's love in favour of her sons; her fear of hereditary madness, alcoholism, and physical weakness; her intense, unconsummated, renounced love for several different men; and the drive to individuation and creativity seeking to escape the trammels of heredity, family, environment, society, and religion. All can be read as fictionalized spiritual biography. By 1920 Sinclair was at the pinnacle of her achievement, and was described by Thomas Moult as 'the most widely known woman artist in the country and America'. *The Life and Death of Harriett Frean* (1922), the only novel to continue the modernist experiments of *Mary Olivier*, was considered by Sinclair to be 'one of the best books I have done' (Boll, 143). It is certainly her most spare and poignant novel, a powerful though understated portrait of female disappointment and repression.

Though her fiction was controversial, Sinclair was personally modest, anxious, fastidious, considerate, fair, and a teetotaller with a passion for being driven in motor cars. Her self-effacing nature—Mark Twain, who sat next to her during a dinner in 1905 in New York in his honour, thanked her for her 'remarkably interesting silence'—gave her a particularly sharp eye for arrogance and egotism, especially in the male, which perhaps accounts for some of the controversy.

From 1919 Sinclair began to use Stow on the Wold in the Cotswolds as a writing retreat. Florence Bartrop joined her then as companion, nurse, and housekeeper, replacing her twin sister Nellie, who had been with Sinclair since 1914, and staying with her for the rest of her life. By 1920 Sinclair began to show signs of Parkinson's disease. She disappeared from literary London, and was forgotten. Her last novels are slight and repetitive, and received poor reviews. She wrote nothing after 1927, and lived as a recluse in childlike dependence on Bartrop. She gave up the rented cottage at Stow for another in the Cornish village of Constantine, next to Dorothy Richardson; then she took a permanent room in the White Hart Hotel in Stow. After living in Little Tingewick, Buckinghamshire, from 1932 to 1936, she finally settled with Bartrop at The Gables, 96 Burcott Lane, Bierton, near Aylesbury, where she died on 14 November 1946. She was cremated at Golders Green, London, on 18 November.

Feminist scholarship recovered Sinclair's importance as a transitional figure in the 1970s. There have been two biographies, by Theophilus Boll (1973) and Suzanne Raitt (2000), who acclaimed Sinclair as 'one of the few brilliant women philosophers of her time' (Raitt, 42).

MAX SAUNDERS

Sources S. Raitt, *May Sinclair* (2000) · T. Boll, *Miss May Sinclair, novelist* (1973) · *DNB* · *The Times* (15 Nov 1946) · M. Sinclair, 'Clinical lectures on symbolism and sublimation', *Medical Press* (9–16 Aug 1916) · M. Sinclair, 'The novels of Dorothy Richardson', *The Egoist*, 5 (April 1918), 57–9
Archives Ransom HRC · University of Pennsylvania, Philadelphia, Annenberg Rare Book and Manuscript Library, papers | NYPL, Berg collection
Likenesses W. Tittle, engraving, 1923, NPG [*see illus.*] · photographs, repro. in Raitt, *May Sinclair*
Wealth at death £10,310 3s. 9d.: probate, 10 Feb 1947, CGPLA Eng. & Wales

Sinclair, Oliver (*d.* in or before **1576**), courtier, was a younger son of Sir Oliver Sinclair (*fl.* 1476–1523) of Roslin and one of his three wives. He had at least seven brothers, of whom William succeeded to the family estates, while Henry *Sinclair (1507/8–1565) became a judge and bishop of Ross and John *Sinclair a judge, and also one sister. The younger Oliver made a career as a 'familiar servant' of James V, being first recorded as receiving his livery in 1536, when he accompanied the king to France, apparently keeping the accounts of expenditure from the royal purse. In June 1537 his services were rewarded with the barony of Pitcairn in Perthshire; contemporary documents often refer to him under this territorial designation, although in January 1545 he sold Pitcairn to Henry Drummond of Riccarton. In 1538 he became a royal cupbearer, and with the treasurer, James Kirkcaldy of Grange, was jointly granted the ward of the earldom of Caithness, the third earl, Oliver's first cousin, having been killed at the battle of Summerdale in 1529. He acquired the barony of Whitekirk in Haddingtonshire from Holyrood Abbey in 1539; the old barn adjacent to the parish church may incorporate the remains of Sinclair's tower house. In 1540 he was granted Tantallon Castle in feu-ferme. Tantallon, an important castle on the coast of Haddingtonshire, was a seat of the earl of Angus, who was then in exile in England. Sinclair was required to supervise building works there. In 1541 he was given a three-year tack of Orkney and Shetland, extended to 1547, along with the keeping of Kirkwall Castle and justiciary powers.

Sinclair is represented in contemporary accounts as a great favourite of James V, one of a small group (which included some senior churchmen) responsible for persuading the king not to meet Henry VIII at York in the summer of 1541, but rather to pursue war against England. Scottish historians writing from a protestant viewpoint see him as an unworthy councillor, pursuing policies in support of the old church. When war with England came late in 1542, Sinclair was apparently appointed to lead the army which came to grief at Solway Moss. Sinclair's role as army commander has given rise to some controversy, and it has been argued that he was not leader at all, but that the story of his appointment was developed after the battle to blacken James's character and discredit ecclesiastical influence on royal policies. There are only one or two indications that Sinclair had previously acted in a military capacity on the king's behalf, taking the English prisoners captured at the battle of Hadden Rigg near Kelso (24 August 1542) back to Edinburgh, and going to Hume Castle in Berwickshire in November 1542, apparently to discuss military tactics with the gentlemen of the region. It was certainly unusual for anyone but a magnate, or the king himself, to lead an army, but Sinclair is described as chief captain of the army, and as having lost the king's banner at Solway Moss, in a letter which was written only a few days after the battle by Sir George Douglas, the earl of Angus's younger brother. Early Scottish historians are consistent in their agreement. Contemporary English sources, notably the full report given by Sir William Musgrave, who was one of the English leaders, do not comment on the Scottish command structure. It is true that the imperial and Venetian ambassadors in London believed that Lord Maxwell was commander, but the latter, at least, were keen to present Maxwell as a heretic deliberately engineering the defeat out of spite against the policies of a government led by Cardinal Beaton.

It is clear that James V did not intend to lead his forces into England, and therefore command must have been delegated to others. If Sir George Douglas is to be believed about Sinclair having the king's banner at Solway Moss, this must be seen as a sign that he was in overall charge of the men there, even if Maxwell was more experienced and on home territory as warden of the Scottish west march. The Scottish forces called out in late November for a raid against the English, perhaps 14,000 men in all, were not marshalled as a single army. On the evidence of the reports of English spies, the Scots had two armies in the field, and it was probably only one of these—the smaller of the two—which advanced into England on 24 November. They were caught at Solway Moss, just inside Cumberland, by an English force about 2000–3000 strong, and were soundly beaten. Sinclair himself was taken prisoner, as were his brothers Alexander and James and a number of Scottish nobles, including the earls of Glencairn and Cassillis and lords Maxwell, Somerville, and Oliphant. As with many battles, accounts of what happened are rather confused, but perhaps the most plausible explanation is that the Scots allowed themselves to be manoeuvred by the English light horse into a tight space flanked by marshy ground and with the River Esk behind them.

Contemporary English accounts, though jubilant about the outcome of the engagement, do not make much of the disparity in size between the opposing armies, as they surely would have done had it been notable. From their point of view it was fitting revenge for the earlier Scottish victory at Hadden Rigg, not a turning point or major achievement. Scottish historians have accused the Scottish nobles at Solway Moss of giving up without a fight, since they were so disgusted at Sinclair's appointment over them, but the report by Sir William Musgrave

specifically states that Lord Maxwell with many other noblemen and courtiers fought valiantly. Once captured, Maxwell requested permission to speak with Sinclair—was this a subordinate looking for a lead from his superior? James V is said to have been devastated by Sinclair's capture but did not live to receive a firsthand report from him on the débâcle, dying before Sinclair was released from captivity early in 1543.

Sinclair seems to have played little part in national affairs for the rest of his life, though he is referred to as involved in border skirmishing in 1543, and seems to have remained on good terms with Cardinal Beaton, receiving a charter from him in 1546. Sinclair married twice. His first wife, apparently married by 1542, was Katherine Bellenden, sister of Sir Thomas Bellenden of Auchnoull and previously the wife of Adam Hopper, provost of Edinburgh, and of Francis Bothwell, provost of Edinburgh and lord of session. They had three children, Henry, who succeeded to Whitekirk, Oliver, and Isabella. Katherine had died by January 1568, and Sinclair later married Beatrice Rollo or Rollock, probably a daughter of Robert Rollo of Duncrub. He also had a natural son named James, who was legitimated in January 1539. Sinclair was presumably dead by 20 April 1576, when Beatrice was granted the life rent of the mains of Whitekirk with the advice of the curators of her stepson Henry.　　　DAVID H. CALDWELL

Sources M. Livingstone, D. Hay Fleming, and others, eds., *Registrum secreti sigilli regum Scotorum / The register of the privy seal of Scotland*, 2 (1921) · J. M. Thomson and others, eds., *Registrum magni sigilli regum Scotorum / The register of the great seal of Scotland*, 11 vols. (1882–1914), vols. 3–5 · J. B. Paul, ed., *Compota thesaurariorum regum Scotorum / Accounts of the lord high treasurer of Scotland*, 6–8 (1905–8) · *Scots peerage* · *LP Henry VIII*, vols. 17–18 · J. Bain, ed., *The Hamilton papers: letters and papers illustrating the political relations of England and Scotland in the XVIth century*, 1, Scottish RO, 12 (1890) · *CSP Spain*, 1541–3 · *John Knox's History of the Reformation in Scotland*, ed. W. C. Dickinson, 2 vols. (1949) · [G. Buchanan], *The history of Scotland translated from the Latin of George Buchanan*, ed. and trans. J. Aikman, 6 vols. (1827–9) · J. Leslie, *The historie of Scotland*, ed. E. G. Cody and W. Murison, trans. J. Dalrymple, 2 vols. in 4 pts, STS, 5, 14, 19, 34 (1888–95) [1596 trans. of *De origine moribus, et rebus gestis Scotorum libri decem* (Rome, 1578)] · *The historie and cronicles of Scotland … by Robert Lindesay of Pitscottie*, ed. A. J. G. Mackay, 3 vols., STS, 42–3, 60 (1899–1911) · J. Cameron, *James V: the personal rule, 1528–1542*, ed. N. Macdougall (1998) · M. H. B. Sanderson, *Cardinal of Scotland: David Beaton, c.1494–1546* (1986) · *CSP Venice, 1534–54*

Sinclair, Sir Robert, of Stevenson, third baronet, Lord Stevenson (1643–1713), politician, was born on 15 October 1643, the younger son of Mr John Sinclair, fiar of Stevenson, Haddingtonshire, and Isabel, daughter of Robert Boyd, sixth Lord Boyd. He succeeded his grandfather and his elder brother John as third baronet on 5 July 1652. His lands of Stevenson were ratified to him by parliament on 4 June 1663, and he obtained a further charter of the lands of Carfrae, Haddingtonshire, on 28 June 1670.

Sinclair was one of the counsel for the defence at the trial of the marquess of Argyll in 1661. He was appointed a commissioner of excise and a justice of the peace for Haddingtonshire on 1 March 1670. In the same year he seems to have aspired to the office of lord advocate, but in this hope he was disappointed. On 29 July 1680 Sinclair was 'pannelled' and rebuked before the privy council 'for seditiously and factiously opposing, at least obstructing his Majesty's service in putting the act of Privy Council to execution for levying 5,500 men out of the militia' (Lauder, 1.111). He was a commissioner of supply for Haddingtonshire in 1678, 1685, 1689, 1690, and 1704.

At the revolution Sinclair represented Haddington constabulary in the convention of estates and subsequent parliament, serving in this capacity from 1689 to 1702. In March 1689 he subscribed both the act declaring the convention to be a free and lawful meeting of the estates, and the letter of congratulation to King William. He was appointed to a number of parliamentary committees, and appears to have regularly attended, apparently supporting Melville's party in its struggle with the 'Club' (Melville, 194, 202). On 7 December 1689 he was appointed sheriff of Haddingtonshire, a privy councillor in May following, and one of the lords of exchequer. He was also named a lord of session as Lord Stevenson, but through his 'uncommon modesty' (Brunton and Haig, 441), he never took his seat, although he remained some years in the nomination, and at his final resignation of this office was succeeded by Sir William Hamilton of Whitelaw, on 29 December 1693. On 17 July 1695 he was granted the right to hold two yearly fairs and a weekly market at Pencaitland Wester. Following the accession of Queen Anne, in 1703 he was again nominated a privy councillor.

Stevenson was twice married: first, at the palace of Holyroodhouse, on 10 September 1663, to Lady Helen, daughter of John Lindsay, seventeenth earl of Crawford, with whom he had six sons and three daughters, and second, to Anne, daughter of Sir William Scott of Ardross, widow of Sir Daniel Carmichael of Mauldslie; they had no children. His daughter Margaret married Robert Dundas, second Lord Arniston, and was mother and grandmother to two successive lord presidents of the court of session who bore that title. Stevenson died in July 1713, and was succeeded by his son Sir John, as fourth baronet, his testament being confirmed at Edinburgh in December.

A. H. MILLAR, *rev.* DEREK JOHN PATRICK

Sources M. D. Young, ed., *The parliaments of Scotland: burgh and shire commissioners*, 2 vols. (1992–3) • G. Brunton and D. Haig, *An historical account of the senators of the college of justice, from its institution in MDXXXII* (1832) • J. Lauder, ed., *The decisions of the lords of council and session*, 2 vols. (1759–61) • Anderson, *Scot. nat.* • APS, 1689–1701 • *Reg. PCS*, 2nd ser. • *Reg. PCS*, 3rd ser. • W. H. L. Melville, ed., *Leven and Melville papers: letters and state papers chiefly addressed to George, earl of Melville … 1689–1691*, Bannatyne Club, 77 (1843)

Sinclair, Robin Macdonald, second Viscount Thurso (1922–1995). *See under* Sinclair, Archibald Henry Macdonald, first Viscount Thurso (1890–1970).

Sinclair, Ronald. *See* Jones, Reginald Teague- (1889–1988).

Sinclair, Sir William (*d.* 1299x1303), baron, was descended from the Anglo-Norman William de Sancto Claro, who received the barony of Roslin from David I. His father, another William, died about 1270 and either he or his son was sheriff of Haddington in 1264 and of Linlithgow and Edinburgh in 1266. In 1279 and 1281 the younger Sinclair

was described as guardian of Alexander, prince of Scotland (*d.* 1284), and in 1284 he attended the meeting which accepted Margaret, the Maid of Norway, as heir presumptive should Alexander die without male heirs. Shortly afterwards he was sent to France with two other ambassadors to find a new wife for the king, choosing Yolande of Dreux. Sir William was also given custody of the royal castles of Dumfries and Edinburgh; these many positions of responsibility suggest that he was indeed 'closer to Alexander III than any other Scot' (Duncan, 588).

After King Alexander's death Sir William served the guardians as sheriff of Dumfries and justiciar of Galloway and attended the parliament at Birgham in 1290 which arranged for the marriage of the Maid of Norway with Edward I's eldest son. After Margaret's death, Sir William supported John de Balliol's claim to the throne of Scotland, acting as one of his auditors; he was present at all the main events of the Great Cause, attesting King John's fealty to Edward I on 20 November 1292. But despite receiving a grant of lands worth 100 merks per annum, Sir William took part in depriving King John of power at a parliament held at Stirling in 1295; he was probably one of the governing council of twelve then appointed.

On the outbreak of war in 1296, Sir William was captured with other members of the Scottish nobility at Dunbar, and was imprisoned in Gloucester Castle. Although his son Henry was released in a prisoner exchange in 1299, Sir William was not set free; however, he escaped some time before 1302, since Walter Beauchamp, who died in that year, was posthumously pardoned for failing to stop him. This suggests that Sinclair had refused to perform homage to Edward I, which would undoubtedly have been a condition for release. There is no mention of him thereafter and he probably died between 1300 and 1303. He is said to have married Agnes, daughter of Patrick, earl of Dunbar, but this is unlikely. One Amicia was described as his widow as early as 1299; the couple had three sons: Henry, William *Sinclair (*d.* 1337), bishop of Dunkeld, and Gregory; and a daughter, Annabel.

Sir Henry Sinclair (*d. c.*1330) swore fealty to Edward I in 1292, but, like his father, joined the patriotic side in 1296 and was duly captured at Dunbar. In 1299 he was released from St Briavels Castle, as part of a prisoner exchange, in return for Sir William Fitzwarin. In September 1305 he was appointed sheriff of Lanark, an office which had until then been held by the earl of Carrick. On 22 June 1306, together with Sir Robert Keith and Sir Adam Gordon, both prominent members of the patriotic government before 1304, he acted as surety for the good behaviour of William Lamberton, bishop of St Andrews. Between 1308 and 1309 Sinclair was paid by the English government for keeping the truce with the king of Scots and 'for going to Robert Bruce on behalf of the King's council in those parts' (PRO, E101/373/24, f. 41). But he had joined Bruce's side by October 1313 and perhaps fought at Bannockburn in 1314. He sealed the declaration of Arbroath in 1320 with the designation of 'panetarius'. In 1328 he was granted a pension of 40 merks to himself and his heirs, until lands of that value could be granted; this was perhaps the repayment of a loan made to the king. He died about 1330. Sir Henry married Alicia Fenton and they had a son, another Sir William *Sinclair [see under Sinclair family], who was killed in 1330 in Spain with Sir James Douglas who carried King Robert's heart.   FIONA WATSON

Sources CDS, vols. 1–5 · J. Stevenson, ed., *Documents illustrative of the history of Scotland*, 2 vols. (1870) · G. Burnett and others, eds., *The exchequer rolls of Scotland*, 1 (1878) · APS, 1124–1423 · *Johannis de Fordun Chronica gentis Scotorum*, ed. W. F. Skene (1871) · RotS, vol. 1 · *Scots peerage*, vol. 6 · A. A. M. Duncan, *Scotland: the making of the kingdom* (1975), vol. 1 of *The Edinburgh history of Scotland*, ed. G. Donaldson (1965–75)

Sinclair, Sir William (d. 1330). *See under* Sinclair family (*per.* 1280–c.1500).

Sinclair, William (d. 1337), bishop of Dunkeld, was the second son of Sir William *Sinclair (d. 1299x1303), lord of Roslin. Sir Henry *Sinclair (d. c.1330) [see under Sinclair, Sir William] was his brother. He was an early opponent of the English domination of Scotland, being captured with other members of his family in Dunbar Castle in 1296 and imprisoned for a while thereafter. In 1309, when he was already a canon of Dunkeld, a university graduate, and in possession of the church of Kinross, Sinclair was elected bishop of Dunkeld by the cathedral chapter on the death of Matthew Crambeth and travelled to the curia to seek consecration. The election was disputed by John Leek, a nominee of Edward II, but following unfinished litigation at the curia Leek's promotion to the archbishopric of Dublin left the path open for papal confirmation of Sinclair's election in May 1312. Although he had made his peace with the English king, he seems to have been treated with some suspicion by Edward II, who, in giving him a safe conduct to Berwick in 1313 (presumably on his return from the curia), made it conditional upon his not proceeding further into Scotland, nor communicating with 'the enemy'.

Sinclair certainly supported Robert I after Bannockburn. He attended several parliaments from 1314 onwards, and the frequency of his appearances in the witness lists of King Robert's *acta* suggests that he was regarded as a favourite of the king. Bower recounts how Sinclair endeared himself to Robert I by personally leading a small force to defeat an attempted English invasion of Fife. He none the less joined the political majority in 1332, adhering to the pro-Balliol faction. On 24 September 1332 he crowned Edward Balliol at Scone, and he was present at Balliol's parliament of February 1334. Later, however, the English appear again to have mistrusted him, for in 1335–6 he was reported as acting contrary to his allegiance, and therefore, although he witnessed none of David II's royal acts, his loyalties may have reverted to the Bruce kingship before his death on 27 June 1337. Apparently active in his diocese as well as at court, Sinclair is credited with achieving significant building work on his cathedral church, where he was buried.

NORMAN H. REID

Sources A. Myln, *Vitae Dunkeldensis ecclesiae episcoporum*, ed. T. Thomson, rev. edn, 1, rev. C. Innes, Bannatyne Club (1831), 12–15 · CDS, vol. 2, no. 177; vol. 3, nos. 301, 655, p. 335 · APS, 1124–1423, 464–5, 289–90, 477–8, 542 · W. Bower, *Scotichronicon*, ed. D. E. R. Watt and others, new edn, 9 vols. (1987–98), vol. 6, pp. 383–5 · G. W. S. Barrow and others, eds., *Regesta regum Scottorum*, 5, ed. A. A. M. Duncan (1988) · CPR, 1307–13, 527 · A. Theiner, *Vetera monumenta Hibernica et Scotorum historian illustrantia* (Rome, 1864), no. 398 · Rymer, *Foedera*, 2.155 · *The chronicle of Walter of Guisborough*, ed. H. Rothwell, CS, 3rd ser., 89 (1957), 279 · D. E. R. Watt, *A biographical dictionary of Scottish graduates to AD 1410* (1977), 496–7 · J. Dowden, *The bishops of Scotland … prior to the Reformation*, ed. J. M. Thomson (1912), 61–3

Sinclair, William, third earl of Orkney and first earl of Caithness (b. after 1407, d. 1480). *See under* Sinclair family (*per.* 1280–c.1500).

Sinclair, William (1804–1878), Church of England clergyman, the fifth son of Sir John *Sinclair, first baronet of Ulbster, Caithness, and his second wife, Diana MacDonald (1769–1845), daughter of Alexander, first Baron MacDonald of Sleat, was born in Edinburgh on 4 September 1804. He was a brother of Catherine *Sinclair (1800–1864), author, of Sir George *Sinclair (1790–1868), and of Archdeacon John *Sinclair (1797–1875). On leaving Winchester College he obtained, at the age of sixteen, a commission as captain in the Madras cavalry, and distinguished himself by leading a forlorn hope at the siege of Kittur. After returning to England he matriculated from St Mary's Hall, Oxford, in 1832 and graduated BA with fourth-class honours in classics in 1835 and MA in 1837. At Oxford he became president of the union when its members included Archibald Tait, Roundell Palmer, Edward Cardwell, and Robert Lowe. Thomas Jackson, in his preface to the Oxford squib *Uniomachia: a Greek-Latin Macaronic Poem* (5th edn, 1877), states that while engaged on it he had a visit from Sinclair, his college friend, who, he says, 'entered heartily into the scheme, and composed many of the best lines and notes'.

Sinclair married in 1837 Helen (d. October 1842), daughter of William Ellice and niece of Edward Ellice the elder. In the same year he was ordained, and he became vicar of St George's, Leeds, in 1839, where his liberal evangelical views are said to have brought him into conflict with W. F. Hook, vicar of Leeds. In 1846, following the death of his first wife, he married Sophia Mary Georgiana, daughter of the Revd James Tripp. Parochial work, such as serving on a committee to consider proposals for tackling the unchurched masses, undermined Sinclair's health, and in 1857 he accepted the rectory of Pulborough, Sussex, where he rebuilt the church and rectory, and started schools and chapels in different parts of the parish. In 1874 he was appointed by Dr Durnford to a prebendal stall in Chichester Cathedral. Sinclair published a manual of prayers and edited his brother's archidiaconal charges as well as books on a military theme. He died at Pulborough on 8 July 1878. There were two sons from his first marriage; the two daughters and three sons from his second marriage included William Macdonald Sinclair (1850–1917), archdeacon of London from 1889 to 1911, and John Stewart Sinclair (1853–1919), archdeacon of Cirencester from 1908 to 1919.   [ANON.], rev. ELLIE CLEWLOW

Sources Boase, *Mod. Eng. biog.* · Foster, *Alum. Oxon.* · Ward, *Men of the reign* · W. R. W. Stephens, *The life and letters of Walter Farquhar Hook*, 2 vols. (1878)
Wealth at death under £10,000: probate, 30 July 1878, *CGPLA Eng. & Wales*

Sinclair, Sir William Japp (1846–1912), obstetrician and gynaecologist, was born on 6 March 1846 at Back-wynd, Forfar, Forfarshire, the fourth of six children of Alexander Sinclair (*b.* 1809x11), railway gate keeper and afterwards linen weaver, and his wife, Margaret MacLacy (*b.* 1811/12). He was reared in humble circumstances in Laurencekirk, Kincardineshire, and retained throughout his life a sympathy for the poor. He attended Laurencekirk public school, Aberdeen grammar school (briefly), and Aberdeen University, with a bursary, graduating MA in natural science in 1869, MB CM with highest honours in 1873, and MD in 1875. After a period as resident physician at Aberdeen Royal Infirmary, Sinclair moved to Manchester in 1873 as house surgeon to St Mary's Hospital for Women and Children, and subsequently the Northern Hospital for Women and Children. In 1875 he spent several months studying obstetrics and gynaecology in Vienna. On his return to Manchester he commenced in general practice, and was appointed honorary physician to the Southern Hospital for Women and Children, under the leadership of the gynaecologist John Thorburn. This was the base from which Sinclair developed his own career as a specialist obstetrician and gynaecologist, a proponent of midwifery, and a key clinician in the medical school developed by Owens College (later the Victoria University of Manchester) on its new site to the south of the city.

From 1878 Sinclair was in charge of the Southern Hospital's women's department, where he was assisted by John Thorburn, then Owens College's first professor of obstetrics and gynaecology. Sinclair was also in charge of the midwifery department, and from 1877 to 1880 he was examiner in midwifery and the diseases of women and children in the University of Aberdeen. A keen champion of the training of midwives, he started courses for them at the Southern Hospital in 1881; it was following his suggestion that the hospital added lying-in beds in 1887. In 1883 Sinclair married Margaret (*d.* 1935), daughter of Andrew Haddon of Denholm, Roxburghshire; they had two daughters.

Proficient in several European languages, Sinclair regularly visited continental clinics. He was deeply interested in cancer of the uterus, and was a pioneer of vaginal hysterectomy and caesarean section. He opposed abdominal operations for cancer, describing them as 'bloody vivisections'. He wrote many papers for medical journals and contributed the article on malignant disease of the uterus in Allbutt and Playfair's *System of Gynaecology*. In 1884, with James Niven, Manchester's medical officer of health, he had founded and co-edited (to 1887) the *Medical Chronicle*, which had a worldwide circulation. In 1887 he contributed to it a series of papers entitled *Gonorrhoea in Women*, which, published with additions in book form the following year, gained him international prominence.

After John Thorburn's death in 1885 Sinclair applied for the chair of obstetrics and gynaecology at Owens College but it went to Charles Cullingworth, the rising star at St Mary's. Three years later, however, when Cullingworth moved to London, Sinclair succeeded him at the university, and as the leading local specialist in obstetrics and gynaecology. It was through Sinclair's influence that the Southern Hospital in 1893 obtained land from Owens College to build a new hospital near the medical school. This project became part of a complex series of negotiations over the re-siting of Manchester's two largest city-centre hospitals—the Royal Infirmary and St Mary's. The outcome was a new maternity hospital in the city centre, together with a new infirmary and a new hospital for women and children—both situated near the medical school. The Southern Hospital merged with St Mary's Hospital in 1904 when Sinclair was appointed honorary physician to the conjoint hospitals.

From about 1890 Sinclair had been prominent in the national campaign for the registration of midwives, in the face of bitter hostility, not least from Manchester general practitioners active in the British Medical Association. When registration became state regulated in 1902 he was appointed to the Central Midwives' Board, serving to 1912. One of his major concerns was puerperal fever, which he believed could be prevented by antisepsis. His attempts to reduce mortality from the disease culminated in his biography, *Semmelweiss: his Life and Times* (1909), which established the legend of the disregarded pioneer of obstetric hygiene. In 1907 Sinclair published a plea for the establishment of a municipal maternity hospital for cases of abnormal labour and puerperal fever.

Sinclair made important contributions to the national organization of his specialty. He was a founder, in 1890, and first secretary of the North of England Obstetrics and Gynaecological Society, and president in 1893 and 1904. He was the chief founder, in 1902, of the prestigious *Journal of Obstetrics and Gynaecology of the British Empire*, which he initially helped edit. He is also credited with the original conception of what eventually became the Royal College of Obstetrics and Gynaecology (1929). He was a fellow of the Obstetrical Society and the British Gynaecological Society, an honorary fellow of the American Association of Obstetricians and Gynaecologists, and corresponding member of the Deutsches Gesellschaft für Gynäkologie and the Budapest Royal Medical Society. He became a member of the Royal College of Physicians in 1892 and was president of the Manchester Medical Society in 1899.

Sinclair was active in party politics. Originally a Liberal, he seceded to the Unionists over home rule. He joined the Manchester branch of the Liberal Unionist Committee and was founder and first chairman of the South Manchester Liberal Unionist Association. He was a JP and represented St Luke's ward on the city council from 1893 to 1897. He was knighted in 1904. One of his later interests was promoting laminaria tent making as an occupation for Scottish crofters.

Sinclair was known for his commanding abilities, ruthless clarity of perception, shrewd wit, and profound sympathy with suffering. He was a 'bonny fighter' whose 'whole life was a struggle with adverse circumstances' (*The Lancet*, 7 Sept 1912). He died at his home, Garvock House, Dudley Road, Whalley Range, Manchester, on 21 August 1912 after a prolonged illness and was buried at Manchester southern cemetery. JOAN MOTTRAM

Sources *Journal of Obstetrics and Gynaecology of the British Empire*, 22 (1912), 171–4 · *Medical Chronicle* (Nov 1912), 63–76 · *Manchester Guardian* (22 Aug 1912) · *Manchester City News* (24 Aug 1912) · *BMJ* (14 Sept 1912), 665–6 · *The Lancet* (7 Sept 1912), 733 · *Manchester Medical Students Gazette*, new ser., 12 (1912), 110 · J. H. Young, *St Mary's hospitals, Manchester, 1790–1963* (1964) · J. V. Pickstone, *Medicine and industrial society: a history of hospital development in Manchester and its region, 1752–1946* (1985) · J. Mottram, 'State control in local context: public health and midwife regulation in Manchester, 1900–14', *Midwives, society and childbirth*, ed. H. Marland and A. M. Rafferty (1997) · JRL, Manchester medical collection · bap. reg. Scot. · census returns, 1851, 1861
Archives JRL, Manchester medical collection, biographical material
Likenesses photograph, repro. in *Manchester Faces and Places*, 359 · two photographs, JRL, Manchester medical collection, Sinclair file
Wealth at death £856 16s. 10d.: probate, 19 Oct 1912, *CGPLA Eng. & Wales*

Sindercombe, Miles (*d.* 1657), parliamentarian soldier and conspirator, was originally from Kent. He was later reported to have been apprenticed to a surgeon near St Catherine's in the Tower, London, before the civil war, but much of his early life is very obscure. At the time of his death his widowed mother, Elizabeth, and his sister Elizabeth Herring were living in London and had visited him in the Tower. Nothing is known of a wife, although an unnamed 'sweetheart' also visited him in the Tower.

Sindercombe first comes to notice in 1649, when quartermaster in the New Model Army regiment of John Reynolds the agitator. In May he was involved when the regiment mutinied, and he may have been a ringleader for he had already apparently developed pronounced Leveller convictions. When the mutiny was suppressed Sindercombe escaped, perhaps around this time (or later) lodging with a hat seller on London Bridge. He re-emerged as an enlisted soldier in Colonel Matthew Tomlinson's regiment of horse in Scotland. Here he continued his scheming, and took part in the so-called Overton plot in late 1654 to seize control of the army in Scotland from General George Monck. The intrigue fell through, and Monck dismissed Sindercombe in January 1655 as 'a busy and suspicious person, and one who was forward to promote such ill designs' (*DNB*). By the time Monck discovered that Sindercombe had actually been one of the chief organizers of the plot, he had fled to Flanders.

In exile Sindercombe fell in with his fellow Leveller Edward Sexby, who encouraged his hostility to the protectorate and eventually engaged him to engineer Cromwell's assassination. Using his Spanish and royalist connections, Sexby was able to provide Sindercombe with £500, weapons, and ammunition. Sindercombe's hope was that with Cromwell's removal the nation could return to the pre-1653 government of the Rump Parliament. However, should the assassination lead to the restoration of the monarchy, he hoped that so much disorder would follow that the people, in whom he placed a great deal of faith, would return Charles II once more into exile or deliver him to a well-deserved death on the scaffold.

On his secret return to England in 1656 Sindercombe first rented a shop in King Street, Westminster, later abandoned as impractical for an assassination attempt. He recruited others into the plot, notably John Cecil, a former trooper, and William Boyes, about whom the plotters knew very little. It was Boyes who assured his companions of royal assistance if and when Cromwell was assassinated, and he may well have been an *agent provocateur*. The group also managed to recruit one of Cromwell's life guards, John Toope, to provide information on the lord protector's movements, for by this stage Cromwell, as befitted his dignity, rarely went anywhere in public without a guard. Toope was to prove the weak link in the conspiracy; although lavished with money and tales of the honours and wealth he would obtain under the new regime after the murder, he soon had misgivings and went on to betray the plotters. Numerous warnings also came to the government through the intelligence agents of John Thurloe, the secretary of state, but this did not hamper the group's schemes to assassinate Cromwell. That they did not succeed was not out of any lack of enterprise, but rather because of a failure of nerve at the final hurdle.

After various attempts to catch the lord protector as he rode in his coach to Hampton Court Palace, the assassins finally thought to kill him as he was taking the air in Hyde Park. They had broken the hinges on the gates of the park in order to make a quick escape after the murder, and while Cecil lurked on the fringes of the protector's retinue, Sindercombe waited for the call outside the gates. Unfortunately for them Oliver, with his eye for good horseflesh, noticed Cecil's horse and called him over to enquire about the animal. Faced with the great man himself Cecil lost his nerve and later claimed that he would have shot Cromwell there and then, but that the horse Oliver was admiring so much was in fact ill with a cold.

The next scheme involved Sindercombe, under the alias John Fish, hiring a house next to Westminster Abbey. From its backyard, the assassins could shoot Cromwell as he proceeded from the abbey to parliament. They began to erect scaffolding under the pretence of building work to cover their real business. On the day parliament was due to meet, Cecil, Sindercombe, and Boyes armed themselves with pistols and waited in the yard. Unfortunately for the murderers some people came into the yard at this point. Boyes immediately decamped into the crowded street and the scheme was abandoned. In order to prove to Sexby that they were not wasting his time, the next scheme followed quickly. This was a design to fire Whitehall Palace by using a special incendiary device planted in the chapel. The plotters managed to break into the chapel and lay the device, but Toope's nerve finally broke and he betrayed the scheme to the regime, subsequently becoming an agent of Thurloe. Cecil and Sindercombe were captured and Boyes escaped. Sindercombe initially fought off the guard sent to seize him, submitting only when one of the guards cut off part of his nose in the struggle. Both he and Cecil were imprisoned in the Tower of London, where Cecil immediately confessed all he knew to Thurloe. As he had with Toope, Thurloe decided to use him as a double agent. The confessions of Cecil and Toope allowed Thurloe to reveal to parliament and the nation Edward Sexby's part in the plot. Sindercombe, however, refused to confess anything and, when tried for treason on 9 February 1657, was found guilty and sentenced to be hanged, drawn, and quartered. Rather than submit to the indignity of the punishment from a state he hated, Sindercombe decided, according to Sexby, to take the Roman way out. Despite being heavily guarded Sindercombe was able to procure some form of poison after a series of visits to his cell by members of his family, and the night before his execution, 13 February 1657, he used it to commit suicide. He died, having first lapsed into a coma some two hours after he had apparently taken the poison. The subsequent inquest could find little evidence of the type of toxin he had actually used, or his means of procuring it. However, Sindercombe had left a suicide note, in which he claimed that 'I do take this course, because I would not have all the open shame of the world executed upon my Body' (*Mercurius Politicus*, 349, 12–19 Feb 1657, 7606). As a consequence the body was drawn to Tower Hill on a hurdle four days later and buried in the manner of a suicide: without ceremony, naked, and with an iron stake through its heart.

Sindercombe's fate made him a martyr to the Good Old Cause, an idea still followed by many in the army and men such as Edward Sexby. Consequently he was given a prominent part in Sexby's pamphlet *Killing Noe Murder, Briefly Discourst in Three Quaestions* (1657). This justified the slaying of Cromwell on the grounds of the lord protector's tyranny. Sindercombe himself seems to have been motivated less by a clearly expressed ideology than by personal bitterness over the way in which the English republic had been distorted by Cromwell's actions in April 1653 when he expelled the Rump Parliament. Nor as a seasoned mutineer, Leveller, and plotter was Sindercombe reluctant to use violent action to remedy the situation. As it was the Sindercombe plot had one significant outcome: it revived discussions as to whether the lord protector should become king, to protect both himself and the nation from any other attempts on his life.

ALAN MARSHALL

Sources *Mercurius Politicus* (29 Jan–19 Feb 1657) · *The whole business of Sindercombe, from first to last: it being a perfect narrative of his carriage, during the time of his imprisonment in the Tower of London* (1657) · *Diary of Thomas Burton*, ed. J. T. Rutt, 4 vols. (1828), 353–65 · *State trials*, 5.841–72 · O. Lutaud, *Dès révolutions d'Angleterre à la révolution Française: le tyrannicide et 'Killing no murder' (Cromwell, Athalie, Bonaparte)* (1973) · R. Overton, *An arrow against all tyrants and tyrany shot from the prison of Newgate into the prerogative bowels of the arbitrary House of Lords* (1646) · C. H. Firth, 'Killing no murder', *EngHR*, 17 (1902), 308–11 · C. H. Firth, *The last years of the protectorate, 1656–1658*, 2 vols. (1909) · D. Wootton, ed., *Divine right and democracy: an anthology of political writing in Stuart England* (1986) · Thurloe, *State papers* · *A true narrative of the late trayterous plot (by Miles Sindercomb and others) against the person of his highness, the lord protector, with the votes of parliament, etc.* (1657) · *A briefe relation of the late dangerous plot, and traiterous design for the destruction of his highness person* (1657) · D. Underdown, *Royalist conspiracy in England, 1649–1660* (1960)

Singer, Burns. *See* Singer, James Hyman (1928–1964).

Singer, Charles Joseph (1876–1960), historian of medicine and science, was born on 2 November 1876 at 22 Brunswick Square, Camberwell, London, the fifth child and fourth son of Simeon *Singer (1848–1906), headmaster of Jews' College School and minister of Borough New Synagogue, and his wife, Charlotte, *née* Pyke. Singer acquired a grounding in Greek, Hebrew, and Bible studies from his father, an erudite scholar who was appointed rabbi of the New West End Synagogue, London, in 1878. He attended the City of London School from the age of twelve, where he became interested in the natural sciences and was persuaded to study medicine. He began the medical course at University College, London, in 1893, but discovered a preference for zoology and won a scholarship at Magdalen College, Oxford, to pursue that subject, which remained a lifelong interest. He graduated BA in 1898 and then returned to the study of medicine, at St Mary's Hospital, Paddington, London, where he graduated BM in 1903. He qualified MRCS and LRCP and was immediately appointed medical officer to a small geographical expedition to Abyssinia, where he spent nearly a year.

On his return Singer completed his residence at St Mary's and graduated BM BCh at Oxford (DM in 1911). He then filled various posts in London, Brighton, and, in 1908, Singapore. Back in London he was admitted MRCP in 1909 and was appointed registrar to the Cancer Hospital, where he undertook pathological research, and physician to the Dreadnought Hospital, where he extended his interest in tropical diseases. He retained these posts until he went to Oxford in 1914 and for a time he was concurrently in consulting practice in Westminster.

On 20 July 1910 Singer married Dorothea Waley Cohen (1882–1964) [*see* Singer, Dorothea Waley], second daughter of Nathaniel Louis Cohen, a City businessman, and sister of Sir Robert Waley *Cohen (1877–1952), oil industrialist. They had a son and a daughter. The Cohens were one of the leading Anglo-Jewish families; Dorothea was a wealthy woman, and her money was vital to Singer's later work. She was already a respected student of alchemical and medieval manuscripts, and she devoted herself to many social and humanitarian activities. Singer's own interest in the history of medicine dated from this time. In 1911 he wrote two papers on Benjamin Marten, seen as a neglected early germ theorist; other historical papers followed over the next three years. In 1912 Singer was a founder member of the History of Medicine section of the

Royal Society of Medicine, and in 1920–22 he was its president. Although he became an enthusiast for the history of medicine, Singer regarded it as an improving study for medical practitioners, rather than as a taught discipline.

When Sir William Osler offered Singer a studentship in pathology at Oxford in 1914—the duties of which were to be mainly historical—the Singers threw themselves into the task of improving the facilities for the study of history of science, spending generously from their own resources and occupying a room in the Radcliffe Camera. During most of the First World War, Singer served as a pathologist, with the rank of captain, in the Royal Army Medical Corps, and was active in Malta and Salonika. While on military service he published fifteen notable papers on medieval and renaissance medicine, and also his first major work, the first volume of *Studies in the History and Method of Science* (1917).

After the war Singer returned to Oxford as lecturer in the history of biological sciences, but he found the atmosphere much changed, and in 1920 he accepted a lectureship in the history of medicine at University College, London. Singer was not a willing teacher, though he was always prepared to lecture on topics of his choice. At University College his lecturing duties were light, but he benefited from the stimulating company and from the copious research help that was available to him, and the next twelve years were richly productive. In 1921 the second volume of his *Studies* appeared. He contributed to *The Legacy of Greece* and to other volumes in the Legacy series, and with E. R. Bevan edited *The Legacy of Israel*, to which both Singers contributed. In the first volume of *Studies* Singer had included his important discussion of the visions of St Hildegard of Bingen, and in 1922 he was awarded a DLitt (Oxon.) for that and other historical essays. He had been elected FRCP in 1917 and in 1923–4 he

gave the Fitzpatrick lectures of that college; they were published in extended form in 1925 as *The Evolution of Anatomy*, the first serious study of that subject in English, and were followed by Singer's translations of significant medieval anatomical works. Dorothea Singer's own monumental catalogue of Greek, Latin, and vernacular alchemical manuscripts in the British Isles was published between 1924 and 1931.

In 1930 Singer gave the first Noguchi lectures at Johns Hopkins University, Baltimore, in the USA, and after a period at the Huntington Library at Pasadena spent three months as a visiting professor at the University of California at Berkeley. In 1931 he declined the invitation to take up a chair at Johns Hopkins as it involved a heavy teaching load and he had just accepted the title of professor of history of medicine in the University of London, which he held until 1942. He returned to teach at Berkeley in 1932, his lectures there being published as his *Short History of Biology* (1931) and *Short History of Science* (1941).

In 1934 the Singers moved to Kilmarth, near Par, Cornwall, where their library could be adequately and more economically housed, and where they could receive more comfortably the stream of scholars from many countries. During the Second World War, Singer taught biology to the boys of King's School, Canterbury, evacuated to Cornwall. In the pre-war years Singer and his wife were very active in assisting Jewish and non-Jewish refugees from Germany, finding them homes and employment, and they were involved with the Society for the Protection of Science and Learning, which helped scholars suffering from Nazi oppression.

Singer's output in the post-war years was prolific and diverse: in 1946 he published with Chaim Rabin a study of the Arabic sources in the *Tabulae anatomicae sex* of Vesalius; in 1948 a sumptuous book on the early history of the alum

Charles Joseph Singer (1876–1960), by unknown photographer

industry; in 1952 a translation and study of the writings of Vesalius on the human brain, and, with J. H. G. Grattan, an important work on Anglo-Saxon magic and medicine; and in 1956 an annotated translation of Galen's *On Anatomical Procedures*. Dorothea's studies on Giordano Bruno were published in 1950. There then emerged under Singer's chief editorship, and generously funded by ICI, the *History of Technology* (5 vols., 1954–8), the first major work in English to embrace the whole subject from the earliest times to the end of the nineteenth century. It attracted mixed reviews but undoubtedly contributed to the growing interest in the subject.

Singer was always very active in the international field, and he was president (1928–31) of the Académie Internationale d'Histoire des Sciences, and of the international congresses held in London in 1922 and 1931. With the award of an honorary DSc degree in 1936, Singer became the holder of the three Oxford doctorates in medicine, science, and letters. He was an honorary fellow of Magdalen College, Oxford, and of the Royal Society of Medicine, and a fellow of University College, London. He was a founder and from 1946 to 1948 the first president of the British Society for the History of Science. He was awarded the Osler medal by the University of Oxford and, jointly with his wife, received the Sarton medal of the American History of Science Society. In 1953 colleagues presented him with a Festschrift, *Science, Medicine and History*, with a bibliography of his published writings.

Singer was sturdily built and enjoyed walking and swimming, though he took little interest in sport. His chief recreations were travel, talking, reading, and, in later life, the cultivation of succulent plants. He was a witty conversationalist, and to the end kept up an immense correspondence. His influence was felt even in fields remote from his main subjects. He died at his home in Cornwall on 10 June 1960.

E. A. UNDERWOOD, *rev.* ANITA MCCONNELL

Sources C. Jilla, 'Charles Singer: his life, aims and achievements in the history of medicine', BSc diss., Wellcome Institute for the History of Medicine, 1991 · *The Times* (13 June 1960) · A. S. MacNalty, 'Charles Singer, the man and the historian', *Proceedings of the Royal Society of Medicine*, 55 (1962), 859–60 · G. Miller, 'Charles and Dorothea Singer's aid to Nazi victims', *Koroth*, 8 (11–12) (1985), 207–17 · personal knowledge (1971) · private information (1971) · M. Kranzberg, 'Charles Singer and *A history of technology*', *Technology and Culture*, 1/4 (1960), 299–302 · V. D. L., 'Simeon Singer', *Encyclopedia Judaica* · b. cert. · d. cert. · m. cert. · *CGPLA Eng. & Wales* (1961)
Archives MHS Oxf., corresp. · U. Southampton L., papers relating to German anti-Semitism · Wellcome L., corresp. and papers | BL, corresp. with Society of Authors, Add. MS 56809 · Bodl. Oxf., letters to O. G. S. Crawford · Bodl. Oxf., corresp. with C. D. Darlington · Rice University, Houston, Texas, Woodson Research Center, corresp. with Sir Julian Huxley · U. Southampton L., corresp. with James Parkes · U. Southampton L., corresp. with Cecil Roth · U. Sussex, letters to J. G. Crowther · Wellcome L., corresp. with E. A. Underwood
Likenesses photograph, *c.*1914–1918, Wellcome L. · double portrait, photograph (with Dorothy Singer), repro. in *Encyclopedia Judaica*, vol. 14, p. 1608 · photograph, Wellcome L. [*see illus.*]
Wealth at death £3352 14s. 11d.: probate, 23 Aug 1961, *CGPLA Eng. & Wales*

Singer [*née* Cohen], **Dorothea Waley** (1882–1964), historian of medicine and philanthropist, was born on 17 December 1882, the second daughter of Nathaniel Louis Cohen (*d.* 1913), stockbroker, and his wife, Julia M. Waley. She took a general arts course at Queen's College, London, and on 20 July 1910 married Charles Joseph *Singer (1876–1960), then employed as a hospital pathologist. They adopted a son, Andrew Waley Singer, and a daughter, Nancy Waley Singer, who in 1949 became the second wife of Edgar Ashworth Underwood (1899–1980). Underwood was at the time director of the Wellcome Institute for the History of Medicine, and later the memorialist of Charles and Dorothea Singer.

The Singers lived in London until 1914, moving to Oxford when Charles Singer embarked on a career in the history of medicine; in 1934 they moved to Cornwall, their principal home thereafter. Dorothea collaborated with her husband on a series of papers dealing with the plague, but soon embarked on her own study of pre-Renaissance scientific manuscripts, publishing a study of over 100 plague tractates dating from about 1348 to 1485. This work led to her endeavour to catalogue and codify those manuscripts in Great Britain and Ireland which related to science and medicine; by 1919 she knew of some 30,000, many of which were copies or variants.

In 1924 the Union Académique Internationale published the first volume of Dorothea's monumental catalogue of alchemical manuscripts, dealing with the Greek texts. Three succeeding volumes (1928–31) dealt with the Latin and vernacular manuscripts. This experience enabled her to lecture on palaeography when she accompanied her husband to the University of California in 1930 and 1932. Her vast calendar of manuscripts with a scientific content is stored on cards at the British Library as the Singer Collection. Alongside these major projects and numerous shorter articles she served on the councils of various learned societies in Britain and abroad; in 1956 Dorothea and Charles Singer were joint recipients of the Sarton medal of the History of Science Society of America.

Prior to the Second World War, Dorothea was among those who pioneered the placing of refugee girls as student nurses, and she continued to be involved with the welfare of refugees from Nazi Germany. Her interest in social welfare led to her biography of the British social worker Margrieta Beer, and she took an active part in the local Women's Institutes and Red Cross. When she became afflicted with increasing deafness, Dorothea entered into an intensive correspondence with otologists and Ministry of Health officials regarding the provision of hearing aids.

Dorothea Singer published in 1950 a catalogue of early manuscripts on the plague, and in the same year her biography of the Copernican Giordano Bruno (1548–1600), with a translation of Bruno's 'On the infinite universe and worlds', and in 1959 a translation from the German of Friedrich Klemm's work, entitled *History of Technology*. The Singers were always immensely hospitable, welcoming visiting historians to Kilmarth, Par, their remote Cornish home. In the years after Charles Singer's death in 1960 the deterioration of her sight and hearing made life very difficult for Dorothea and those who cared for her. She died at Kilmarth on 24 June 1964.   ANITA MCCONNELL

Sources E. A. Underwood, 'Dorothea Waley Singer', *British Journal for the History of Science*, 2 (1964–5), 260–62 • E. A. Underwood, 'Dorothea Waley Singer', *Nature*, 205 (1965), 1262–3 • *WWW* • *Jewish Chronicle* (10 July 1964), 28a • *CGPLA Eng. & Wales* (1964) • m. cert.
Archives U. Birm., catalogue of pre-sixteenth-century British and Irish Latin and vernacular plague texts • Wellcome L., corresp. and papers | U. Sussex, letters to J. G. Crowther
Wealth at death £4460: probate, 14 Dec 1964, *CGPLA Eng. & Wales*

Singer, George John (1786–1817), electrical researcher, was the son of Thomas Singer (*d.* 1793/4), feather and artificial flower maker of 3 Princes Street, Cavendish Square, London, and his wife, Elizabeth Weller. After his father's death Singer helped his mother with the family business, and continued to live at her home, 3 Princes Street. Every spare moment, however, he devoted to scientific study, more particularly to the investigation of electricity and electro-chemistry. He made almost the whole of his apparatus himself, and introduced several improvements, inventing, among other things, the gold leaf electrometer and an electric column comprising 20,000 zinc and silver plates. He also purchased apparatus including a 50 inch diameter electrostatic plate machine that had once belonged to Napoleon, for which he paid £100.

Singer built, almost unassisted, a large room at the back of his mother's house where from at least 1808 he delivered courses of demonstration lectures on electricity and related subjects. From 1810 he also lectured at the Russell Institution and from 1811 he described himself in his papers as 'Lecturer on Chemistry and Natural Philosophy'. Among his auditors were Michael Faraday and Francis Ronalds. Singer referred to Ronalds as his pupil and communicated to the *Philosophical Magazine* Ronalds's first paper. He also made the acquaintance of the electrician Andrew Crosse with whom he collaborated, staying frequently at Crosse's seat, Fyne Court, Somerset, and walking with him on the Quantocks. In 1814 Singer published *Elements of Electricity and Electro-Chemistry*, a work of considerable importance, which was translated into French (Paris, 1817), Italian (Milan, 1819), and German (Breslau, 1819). He died, unmarried, of pulmonary consumption on 28 June 1817 at his mother's house. His collection of apparatus was sold at Stewart's auction room in 1818.

E. I. CARLYLE, *rev.* FRANK A. J. L. JAMES

Sources *Philosophical Magazine*, 50 (1817), 75 • private information (1897) • I. Inkster, 'Science and society in the metropolis: a preliminary examination of the social and institutional context of the Askesian Society of London, 1796–1807', *Annals of Science*, 34 (1977), 1–32 • *Memorials, scientific and literary, of Andrew Crosse, the electrician*, ed. [C. Crosse] (1857) • *The correspondence of Michael Faraday*, ed. F. A. J. L. James, 2 (1993)

Singer, James Hyman [*pseud.* Burns Singer] (1928–1964), writer and biologist, was born on 29 August 1928 in New York, the son of Michael Myer Singer (1900–1959), a second-generation Polish Jewish immigrant born in Manchester, and his second wife, Bertha Burns (*d.* 1951) from Greenock, daughter of an Irish father and a Scottish mother of Norwegian extraction. Singer's father was an unsuccessful salesman hoping to better his career and the poet later recalled 'I spent my infancy in the back of a car or on a ship'. His mature life was to prove equally displacing. A younger brother Michael Myer Singer was born in Greenock in 1930 and eventually the family moved to Glasgow in 1932. With the outbreak of the Second World War, Singer and his brother were evacuated to the village of Maud in Aberdeenshire, but returned to Glasgow in 1940. James, always known as Jimmy to family and friends, entered Glasgow University in 1945, studying English, history, and Italian, but left for London after only two terms. Determined to make his way as a writer—he got to know C. M. Grieve (Hugh MacDiarmid) and other literary figures in Glasgow—he moved to Cornwall in 1946 to be near W. S. Graham, pitching a tent next to the poet's caravan. The following two years were unsettled, with travel and nearly a year spent in Paris (1947–8), before Singer registered once more at Glasgow University (1949–51) as a student of zoology.

Pressed for funds and deeply shaken by his mother's suicide in 1951, Singer left university again, and worked as a scientific assistant in Aberdeen at the marine laboratory, Torry (1951–5). Here he produced most of the poems in *Still and All* with the wartime experiences of a former soldier friend providing inspiration for 'The Transparent Prisoner', the finest long poem in the collection. Singer's scientific studies and trips on fishery research vessels also gave him material for *Living Silver*, a popular study of the fishing industry. Appreciated for his scientific work, but erratic in his habits, Singer was dismissed from Torry in 1955 and made his way to London. Always an intense and depressive personality, frail, blond-haired, and frequently seeking oblivion in drink, the poet attempted suicide at this time, but a meeting with Marie Battle (1919–1986), an African American child psychologist, gave him much needed stability, and the couple were married on 6 June 1956.

Singer's poems were beginning to be published under his pseudonym Burns Singer, and he found employment as a writer for periodicals and radio. In 1957 his work was well received, and *Still and All* (1957) was a Poetry Book Society recommendation, but the poet was suffering from physical and nervous exhaustion and spent 1958 in retreat in Cornwall and Spain. His return to Britain saw the publication of *Five Centuries of Polish Poetry* (1960), a collaboration with Jerzy Peterkiewicz whom he had first met in 1946. The Singers moved to Cambridge in 1962 where Professor Carl Pantin offered James scientific research work in 1963 at the marine laboratory in Plymouth (a Leverhulme fellowship was awarded the following year). Singer continued to write creatively, but died of a heart attack in Plymouth on 8 September 1964. His ashes were scattered from the research trawler *Sarsia*.

Reminiscent of W. S. Graham in his concern with the difficulties of any expressive act, Singer's work is marked by pared-down and epigrammatic phrases, lyrical repetition, and a cerebral but highly personal intensity. *The Collected Poems of Burns Singer* (1970), edited and introduced by W. A. S. Keir, with a preface by Hugh MacDiarmid, is the best edition to date, with a fine memoir by Keir, but a revised and expanded edition with further biographical material has been researched by James Keery.

RODERICK WATSON

Sources H. MacDiarmid, preface, in *The collected poems of Burns Singer*, ed. W. A. S. Keir (1970) · NL Scot., Singer MSS 5083, 5145, 5510 · priv. coll. [to be deposited in NL Scot.] · J. H. Singer, *New collected poems*, ed. J. Keery [forthcoming] · J. Vinson, ed., *Contemporary poets*, 3rd edn (1980) · A. Kamm, ed., *Collins biographical dictionary of English literature* (1993)
Archives NL Scot., corresp. and papers · NRA, priv. coll. | Indiana University, Bloomington
Likenesses photographs, priv. coll.

Singer, John (*fl.* 1583–1603), actor, may have owed money to a Canterbury man in 1571; otherwise his origins are unknown. He was a clown and one of eight experienced actors first chosen in March 1583 to form Queen Elizabeth's Men. At a play of theirs in Norwich on 15 June he was involved in a quarrel that resulted in a murder, for which he apparently escaped punishment. He was with the company in 1588 and probably until 1594, when he joined the Lord Admiral's Men. He was a senior member of the latter and, like others, figures often in the diary of the theatre financier Philip Henslowe. They used the Rose playhouse until summer 1600, the Fortune thereafter.

Singer lived in Shoreditch from 1593 to 1596, then on Bankside, near the Swan playhouse. There in 1600 he and his wife, Alice, took as tenants John and Frances Downell, who soon accused them of misappropriating money and not repaying it. Five children of John Singer, player, were baptized at St Saviour's, Southwark: Thomas (1 August 1597), William (17 June 1599), John (21 September 1600), Elizabeth (30 August 1601), Jane (1 May 1603). On 13 January 1603 Henslowe paid Singer £5 'at the Apoyntment of the companie … for his playe called Syngers vallentarey' (*Henslowe's Diary*, 208), after which Singer disappears from the stage. At the queen's funeral in April he was one of sixteen grooms of the chamber. He probably died before 1608, since Thomas Heywood included him among actors whose 'deserts yet live in the remembrance of many' in his *Apology for Actors* (p. 43), published in 1612 but written about 1608. In 1609 Thomas Dekker mentioned Singer, Richard Tarlton, and Will Kempe as great clowns of the past.

HERBERT BERRY

Sources E. K. Chambers, *The Elizabethan stage*, 4 vols. (1923) · *Henslowe's diary*, ed. R. A. Foakes and R. T. Rickert (1961) · D. Galloway, ed., *Norwich, 1540–1642*, Records of Early English Drama (1984) · W. Ingram, *The business of playing: the beginnings of the adult professional theater in Elizabethan England* (1992) · T. Heywood, *An apology for actors* (1612) · T. Dekker, 'Proemium', *The guls hornbook* (1609) · M. Eccles, 'Elizabethan actors, IV: S to end', *N&Q*, 238 (1993), 165–76, esp. 169 · parish register, Southwark, St Saviour, LMA, P.92/SAV/3001 [baptism]

Singer, Joseph Henderson (1786–1866), Church of Ireland bishop of Meath, was born at Annadale, co. Dublin, in October 1786, the youngest son of James Singer, deputy commissary-general in Ireland, and his wife, Elizabeth, daughter of James Henderson. In 1802 Singer entered Trinity College, Dublin, where he obtained the mathematical and Hebrew prizes. He graduated BA as gold medallist in 1806, became a fellow in 1810, and proceeded MA in 1811, and BD and DD in 1825. In 1822 Singer married Mary, eldest daughter of the Revd Henry Crofton, senior chaplain of Kilmainham, and niece of Sir Hugh Crofton of Mohill in co. Leitrim. They had five sons and four daughters.

Singer was fellow and tutor at Trinity College for many years before succeeding Charles Richard Elrington as regius professor of divinity after the latter's death in 1850. During his time at the university Singer distinguished himself as a leading member of the evangelical party in the Church of Ireland, his views strongly influencing a number of the students in his charge. He was also actively involved in attempts to revive the church through evangelism among Roman Catholics in Ireland. He became rector of Raymochy in the diocese of Raphoe in 1850 and archdeacon in 1851. He was an able preacher, being for many years chaplain of the Magdalen Asylum, and was a regular contributor to the *Christian Examiner*. On the death of Thomas Stewart Townsend in September 1852 Singer was appointed by Lord Derby to the premier bishopric of Meath, and was sworn of the Irish privy council. Much to the disappointment of the evangelical party, however, he was an inactive member and exerted little influence. Singer occupied the see until his death on 16 July 1866 at Dundrum House, co. Dublin. He was buried on 21 July at Mount Jerome cemetery, Dublin.

E. I. CARLYLE, *rev.* DAVID HUDDLESTON

Sources *GM*, 4th ser., 2 (1866), 405 · *Dublin University Magazine*, 42 (1853), 562–9 · D. Bowen, *The protestant crusade in Ireland, 1800–70* (1978) · J. B. Leslie, *Raphoe clergy and parishes* (1940) · *The Times* (19 July 1866) · *The Times* (23 July 1866) · H. Cotton, *Fasti ecclesiae Hibernicae*, 6 (1878), 94 · [J. H. Todd], ed., *A catalogue of graduates who have proceeded to degrees in the University of Dublin, from the earliest recorded commencements to … December 16, 1868* (1869), 517 · Burtchaell & Sadleir, *Alum. Dubl.*, 2nd edn · *CGPLA Ire.* (1866)
Archives TCD
Likenesses J. McGlashan, engraving, 1853, repro. in *Dublin University Magazine*
Wealth at death under £25,000: probate, 30 Aug 1866, *CGPLA Ire.*

Singer, Samuel Weller (1783–1858), literary scholar, born in London, was the son of Thomas Singer (*d.* 1793/4), a maker of artificial flowers and feathers, and Elizabeth Weller. George John *Singer (1786–1817), natural philosopher and inventor, was his younger brother. His father died when Samuel was ten years old, and his mother continued the feather and flower business in Princes Street, Cavendish Square.

Samuel received a limited education at a day school kept by a Frenchwoman. There he learned French, but was mainly self-taught, reading widely and acquiring Italian through frequent visits to the opera. At an early age he was apprenticed to a hatter near Cavendish Square, but he soon returned to work for his mother; and about 1808 he set up for himself in the same trade in Duke Street, St

James's. In the same year he married Harriet Robinson; they had a son, Alfred (1816–1898), and three daughters.

Singer's growing absorption in literature soon prompted him to change his profession and open a bookseller's shop in St James's Street. Book collectors such as Richard Heber, Richard Grenville, and Francis Douce were among his customers, and Douce became a lifelong friend. A tenacious autodidact, Singer quickly began to develop the skills of a literary editor, and in 1811 he prepared for private circulation a limited-edition reprint of Fénelon's *Deux dialogues sur la peinture*, with a preface in French. There followed similar editions of works in both French and Italian.

In 1812 Singer entered into literary controversy for the first time by printing for private distribution fifty copies of *Some account of the book printed at Oxford in* MCCCCLXVIII *under the title 'Exposicio sancti Jeronimi in simbolo apostolorum'*. Singer's argument in this work, that Rufinus's Latin treatise on the apostles' creed was published in 1468 rather than 1478, promised to have important implications for the history of printing in England. It was, however, wholly mistaken, and the author subsequently attempted to recall as many copies as he could (Madan, 22–3). He later made a frank admission of his error in a letter published in Sotheby's *Principia typographica* (3.19).

In 1815 Singer abandoned his bookseller's shop and embarked on a fully-fledged literary career. Retiring from London, he settled first at Bushey, Hertfordshire, and afterwards at Box Hall, Hertfordshire (BM Add. MS 28654, fols. 135–7). In 1816 he produced his best-known original composition, *Some researches into the history of playing cards: with illustrations of the origin of printing and engraving on wood* (250 copies). This lavishly illustrated work won high praise from Thomas Dibdin, the bibliographer and antiquary (Allibone, *Dict.*, 2.2113). About this time Singer first gained employment as a literary editor from Robert Triphook, an antiquarian publisher whose shop was close to Singer's old establishment in St James's Street. Triphook introduced him to Charles Whittingham, proprietor of the Chiswick Press, in 1814, with the result that Singer secured from Whittingham the editorship of a series entitled Early English Poets: it included Marlowe and Chapman's *Hero and Leander* (1821), and Lodge's *Glaucus and Silla* (1819), as well as works by Chalkhill, Marmion, and Lovelace. Among other editorial projects Singer prepared the first complete edition of Cavendish's *Life of Wolsey* (2 vols., 1825–7); the first edition of Philip Sidney's paraphrase of the Psalms (1828); the first full transcript of the *Anecdotes* of Joseph Spence (1820, 1859); and the correspondence and diaries of Henry Hyde, earl of Clarendon, and Lawrence Hyde, earl of Rochester (1828), collated from the manuscripts of his friend William Upcott.

Singer's burgeoning reputation as an Elizabethan scholar was consolidated in 1826, when he prepared a ten-volume edition of Shakespeare's *Dramatic Works* for the Chiswick Press. Singer was responsible for the collation and annotation of the text, while Charles Symmons provided a biographical introduction. The work was illustrated with wood-engravings after the designs of Stothard

and others, and went through a further two English editions (1856, 1875), as well as an American edition (1834), which proved particularly successful.

Meanwhile Singer had extended his linguistic studies to Old English and Norman-French, and began the compilation of an Old English dictionary. He abandoned the project on learning that Joseph Bosworth was engaged on a similar undertaking, but turned his researches to some use in his critical *Remarks on the Glossary* (by Sir Frederic Madden) *of Havelock the Dane* (1829), to which Madden replied. He also printed, with an English translation, *The Departing Soul's Address to the Body*, a semi-Saxon poetic fragment (1845, 100 copies).

Singer was elected FSA in 1825, but in 1827 his literary activities were checked by his acceptance of the office of librarian to the Royal Institution in Albemarle Street, which he retained until 1835. In 1834 his friend Francis Douce died and, to Singer's surprise, left him a competency. Relieved of the necessity of earning a livelihood, Singer finally retired in 1835 to Mickleham, near Dorking, Surrey, and devoted the rest of his life to leisurely study. He edited Herrick's *Poetical Works* (1846), Bacon's *Essays* (1856), and Selden's *Table Talk* (1847); and translated Luther's *Einfältige Weise zu beten* (as *Way to Prayer*, 1846), and in 1847 (with original additions) Depping and Michel's *Veland le Forgeron: dissertation sur une tradition du moyen âge* (as *Wayland Smith*).

While Singer was remembered by contemporaries as both amiable and modest, his rivalry with the well-known Shakespeare scholar John Payne Collier led him late in his life into bitter controversy over the notorious 'Perkins folio', on which Collier based his *Notes and Emendations to the Text of Shakespeare's Plays from Early Manuscript Corrections* (1853). A courteous exchange between the two in *Notes and Queries* was followed by Singer's vituperative *Text of Shakespeare Vindicated* (1853), a work which stopped just short of accusing Collier of forgery and which shocked reviewers (Ganzel, 163–4; *The Athenaeum*, 28 May 1853). He nevertheless retained his reputation as an unassuming, yet shrewd and incisive student of Elizabethan literature.

Singer died suddenly at his residence, Manor Place, Wandsworth Road, Mickleham, on 20 December 1858, and was buried at Mickleham. His library, which included many valuable Italian books, was sold by auction in 1860, along with his small collection of manuscripts, consisting chiefly of the papers of Joseph Spence (*N&Q*, 2nd ser., 4.120).   SIDNEY LEE, rev. P. J. CONNELL

Sources D. Ganzel, *Fortune and men's eyes: the career of John Payne Collier* (1982) • A. Warren, *The Charles Whittinghams: printers* (1896) • *The Athenaeum* (1 Jan 1859), 19 • *The Athenaeum* (3 March 1860), 306 • *The Athenaeum* (2 June 1860), 759 • *N&Q*, 2nd ser., 7 (1859), 19–20 • S. L. Sothcby, *Principia typographica*, 3 vols. (1858) • F. Madan, *A brief account of the university press at Oxford* (1908) • W. R. Arrowsmith, *The editor of 'Notes and Queries' and his friend, Mr. Singer* (1858) • Allibone, *Dict.* • W. D. Adams, *Dictionary of English literature*, 2nd edn [1878]

Archives BL, letters to R. Triphook, Add. MS 28654 • U. Edin. L., letters to James Halliwell-Phillipps

Wealth at death under £9000: probate, 12 Feb 1859, *CGPLA Eng. & Wales*

Singer, Simeon (1848–1906), rabbi, was born in London on 5 November 1848, the youngest son of Julius Singer, a clothier from Raab in Hungary, and his wife, Frederica Wolff of Hamburg. Singer went to the Jews' College School, London, where he subsequently became a teacher. In 1867 he became minister to the Borough New Synagogue, south London, a post which he combined with a variety of Jewish and non-Jewish charitable and philanthropic endeavours, while busying himself also as a prison visitor. On 21 April 1868 he married Charlotte, the youngest daughter of Samuel Pyke; they had five sons, including the medical historian Charles Joseph *Singer, and one daughter. In 1878 Singer was appointed minister of the New West End Synagogue, then in the course of erection in St Petersburgh Place, west London; he served as its minister for the remainder of his life.

Singer thus moved from one of the poorest to one of the wealthiest of the Jewish congregations in London; the transition coincided with a turning point in the development of the Anglo-Jewish ministry. In 1870 the lay leaders of the Ashkenazi congregations in London had established the United Synagogue, over which 'the cousin-hood'—and pre-eminently the Rothschilds—presided. Nathan Marcus Adler, the chief rabbi, became the supreme ecclesiastical authority of this body; ministers of its constituent synagogues were not intended to be rabbinical authorities, but merely preachers and pastors. Singer was an enthusiastic supporter of the concept of the United Synagogue; he moved easily within the world of wealth with which the New West End was associated, enjoyed the friendship of the Rothschild family, and acquired an unrivalled reputation as a preacher of great power and eloquence. At the same time he immersed himself in public service beyond as well as within the Jewish and Anglo-Jewish worlds.

Singer edited, in conjunction with Solomon Schechter, *Talmudical Fragments in the Bodleian Library* (1896). In 1890 he had published, with Nathan Adler's authority, the *Authorised Daily Prayer Book*, which combined accuracy of Hebrew with a vibrant and intelligible English translation. That same year the rabbinical diploma was conferred on him by Rabbi Weiss, lector in Vienna. Singer undertook this study partly as a protest against the lowly status of the Anglo-Jewish preacher, and partly to demonstrate that Anglo-Jewish scholars were capable of securing the rabbinical qualification.

As a Jewish theologian, however, Singer stamped himself as a radical and, in some respects, as a rebel. Though a supporter of Jewish settlement in Palestine, and one of Theodor Herzl's earliest Anglo-Jewish patrons, he opposed Herzl's scheme for a Jewish state as impractical, contrary to the divine will, and subversive of the attachment of the Jew to the state of which he was a citizen. Though Orthodox in his religious beliefs, Singer deplored the division between the Orthodox and Reform camps, preached in the Reform synagogue in Manchester, and was a supporter of the Jewish Religious Union, forerunner of the Union of Liberal and Progressive Synagogues; it was only under intense pressure from within the United Synagogue that he broke off this association.

Singer died at his London residence, 52 Leinster Square, on 20 August 1906, and was buried in the United Synagogue cemetery, Willesden. He was survived by his wife.

GEOFFREY ALDERMAN, rev.

Sources *Jewish Chronicle* (24 Aug 1906), 11–15, 27 · I. Abrahams, ed., *The literary remains of the Rev. Simeon Singer*, 3 vols. (1908) · *CGPLA Eng. & Wales* (1906) · *WWW*
Wealth at death £4913 16s. 10d.: probate, 21 Sept 1906, *CGPLA Eng. & Wales*

Singh, Baldev [known as Baldev Singh Chokar] (1902–1961), industrialist and politician, was born on 11 July 1902 in the village of Dummna, Punjab, India, the son of Inder Singh Chokar, government official and businessman. After his early education in Ambala, Baldev Singh joined the Khalsa College in Amritsar, the foremost Sikh educational institution in pre-independence India. After leaving the college he became a director of his father's steel company in Jamshedpur, Bihar (now in Jharkhand).

Baldev Singh returned to Punjab in the 1930s to begin his political career. His first success was as a Panthic (Akali) Party candidate in the elections of 1937 to the Punjab provincial assembly, the first held under new constitutional arrangements promulgated in 1935. He served as development minister in the short-lived coalition government of Sir Sikandar Hayat Khan between June and December 1942.

Baldev Singh soon rose to prominence as a key representative of the Sikh community in delegations and missions that were important in defining the structure of independent India. Along with three other prominent Sikhs, he was chosen to represent the community before the Cripps mission of 1942, charged with charting India's route to self-determination. He was similarly appointed to represent Sikh interests to the British cabinet mission of 1946 that negotiated the constitutional make-up of post-independence India. During this period he not only met repeatedly with the mission to put forth proposals regarding the Sikh community, but was also consulted by nationalist leaders such as Jawaharlal Nehru, the future prime minister of India, and Mohammad Ali Jinnah, the future governor-general of Pakistan. When the cabinet mission put forth a scheme to safeguard the Muslim minority but not the Sikhs, Baldev Singh joined the Panthic Pratinidhi board set up in Amritsar in June 1946 to oppose it.

The remainder of Baldev Singh's political career took place on the national level, beginning with his nomination in September 1946 as the representative of the provincial Shiromani Akali Dal political party in Jawaharlal Nehru's interim national government. He was appointed defence minister, a post he held through the independence of India in 1947. He led the Indian armed forces through the partition of the subcontinent in 1947, the Pakistani invasion of Kashmir, and the Indian military interventions in Junagarh and Hyderabad in 1948. He was elected to the Lok Sabha, the lower house of the Indian parliament, in the first general election of 1952 and re-elected in 1957, although he did not hold a cabinet post during either period.

After a lengthy illness Baldev Singh died in New Delhi on 29 June 1961 and was cremated with full military honours in his native village of Dummna.

JEEVAN SINGH DEOL

Sources K. Singh, *A history of the Sikhs*, 2 (1966) · G. Singh, *A history of the Sikh people* (1979) · H. Singh, ed., *The encyclopaedia of Sikhism*, 2nd edn, 1 (Patiala, 1995)
Archives U. Southampton L., Mountbatten papers

Singh, Bhagat [*known as* Bhagat Singh Sandhu] (1907–1931), revolutionary and writer, was born in the village of Banga, Punjab, India (now in Pakistan) on 27 September 1907, the second of the four sons and three daughters of Kishan Singh Sandhu, a farmer and political activist, and his wife, Vidyavati. Kishan Singh and his brother Ajit Singh were involved in radical politics, including the Canal Colonization Bill agitations of 1907 and the Ghadr movement of 1914–15.

After his early education to the fifth grade in the village school in Banga, Bhagat Singh enrolled at the Dayanand Anglo-Vedic school at Lahore. He soon left the school for the National College at Lahore in response to Mahatma Gandhi's call for students to boycott government-aided educational institutions. An attempt by his parents to arrange his marriage caused him to leave home for Cawnpore, United Provinces (now Kanpur, Uttar Pradesh) while still studying for his examinations. He returned to Lahore in 1925 only after assurances that he would not be compelled to marry, and remained unmarried for the rest of his life.

Bhagat Singh showed an early interest in revolutionary, socialist, and anti-British literature. While in Kanpur he worked on the nationalist newspaper *Pratap* under the assumed name Balwant Singh and joined the radical Hindustan Republican Association (later known as the Hindustan Socialist Republican Association) in 1924. On his return to Punjab in 1925, a warrant was issued for his arrest on the charge of association with a group of agitators on its way to protest against the British deposition of the maharaja of the state of Nabha. He left Punjab and spent five months living in Delhi, where he worked for the daily paper *Vir Arjun*.

On his return to Lahore, Bhagat Singh established contact with the socialist Kirti Kisan Party and began writing for its magazine *Kirti* ('The Worker') under the pseudonym 'Vidrohi' ('Revolutionary'). In 1926 he was one of the founders of the Naujawan Bharat Sabha, of which he became secretary. An article published in *Kirti* in 1927 on the looting of a train carrying the government treasury near Kakori, United Provinces, in August 1925 by Hindustan Republican Association activists led to his arrest on charges of association with the looters. Some time after his release, he renounced his Sikh religion and cut off the long hair and beard worn by Sikh males. Bhagat Singh wrote numerous articles for the periodicals *Pratap*, *Kirti*,

and *Chand* as well as a number of tracts and revolutionary handbills.

The events that led to Bhagat Singh's execution occurred in 1928. On 30 October 1928 the Lahore police charged a protest procession led by the revolutionary Lala Lajpat Rai, who died on 17 November of the wounds sustained on the occasion. The Hindustan Socialist Republican Association vowed to take revenge: Bhagat Singh, Shiv Ram Hari 'Rajguru', Chandra Shekhar Sharma 'Azad', and Jaigopal were deputed the task of assassinating the superintendent of police, J. A. Scott. On 17 December the men instead shot dead the assistant superintendent, J. P. Saunders, and a head constable, Channan Singh. The association put up leaflets claiming responsibility for the crime, and the four men fled Lahore. Bhagat Singh ended his journey in Calcutta, where he hid for several months.

In early 1929 the Public Safety Bill and Trade Disputes Bill were put before the Indian parliament in New Delhi. The Naujawan Bharat Sabha opposed both pieces of legislation and decided to register their dissent by exploding bombs in parliament's debating chamber. On 8 April 1929 Bhagat Singh and B. K. Dutt exploded two bombs in the chamber and showered it with revolutionary pamphlets. They were arrested, and Bhagat Singh was sentenced to transportation in connection with the bomb case. The trial of Bhagat Singh and a number of his associates from the Hindustan Socialist Republican Association for the killing of Saunders and Channan Singh followed. On 7 October 1929 Bhagat Singh, Rajguru, and Sukhdev Thapar were sentenced to death.

Some controversy surrounds the issue of Bhagat Singh's confessional identity at the time of his death. He wrote a tract, 'Why I am an atheist'—his most famous work—in prison in 1930, but a Sikh religious leader, Bhai Randhir Singh, claims in his autobiography to have reconverted him to Sikhism in gaol, convincing him to keep his long hair and beard once again. There do not, however, appear to be contemporary photographs that would resolve this issue.

Bhagat Singh, Sukhdev Thapar, and Shiv Ram Hari Rajguru were executed by hanging at the central gaol, Lahore, on 23 March 1931. Their bodies were taken by the police to a spot near the village of Husainiwala for a secret cremation, but the ceremony was interrupted by local residents. The remains of the trio were taken on a massive procession through Lahore the next day. Bhagat Singh is remembered by the popular appellation 'Shahid-i Azam' ('the great martyr'). The hanging of Bhagat Singh, Rajguru, and Sukhdev was a central event in the Indian freedom struggle, and Bhagat Singh in particular quickly became an icon for the nationalist movement.

JEEVAN SINGH DEOL

Sources G. S. Deol, *Shaheed Bhagat Singh: a biography* (1969) · F. Singh, ed., *Who's who: Punjab freedom fighters*, 1 (1972) · K. Nayar, *The martyr Bhagat Singh* (2000) · R. Singh, *Jelh Chitthian* (1981) · H. Singh, ed., *The encyclopaedia of Sikhism*, 2nd edn, 1 (Patiala, 1995)

Singh, Sir Bhupinder (1891–1938), maharaja of Patiala, was born on 12 October 1891 in the city of Patiala, Punjab,

Sir Bhupinder Singh (1891–1938), by Vandyk, 1911

India, the eldest son of Maharaja Rajinder Singh (1872–1900), and his first wife, who died in 1897. Upon the death of his father in November 1900 he succeeded to the throne of the largest Sikh-ruled state in India. While a council of regency managed state affairs, the maharaja attended Aitchison Chiefs' College in Lahore from 1904 to 1908 and was subsequently invested with full administrative powers in 1910. In 1908 he married the daughter of Sardar Gurnam Singh, whom he appointed as his confidential secretary, and she became his senior maharani. Tall, well-built, with an imposing face and beard, Bhupinder Singh epitomized the British idea of an Indian prince. Bridging East and West, he enhanced imperial ceremonies with his brocaded silk clothes embellished with opulent pearl or emerald necklaces, but also participated in manly, British sports, first by playing and then by patronizing cricket and polo, as well as the Indian sport of wrestling. He fulfilled the Indian ideal of a beneficent, ecumenical ruler by liberally endowing religious and educational institutions ranging from the Sikh Khalsa College in Amritsar to the Islamic Anglo-Oriental College at Aligarh to Benares Hindu University.

Throughout his lifetime, which coincided with significant political change and upheaval in India, Bhupinder Singh was a generous, conspicuous, but wily military and political ally of the British empire, and a shrewd participant in Sikh political activity in the Punjab. During the First World War he and his state provided troop contingents, equipment, and monetary support. He was an enthusiastic recruiter for the British Indian army, once exhorting his subjects that it was far better to meet the angel of death through a manly demise on the battlefield than through the unmanly diseases of cholera and plague. His state furnished more than 28,000 troops, second in number only to Jammu and Kashmir. In 1918 his contributions were recognized when he represented the Indian states at the Imperial War Conference in London. Bhupinder Singh simultaneously sought to contain political hostility against the British government in connection with the forced return of Sikh immigrants from Canada on the *Komataga Maru*, and the German-financed Ghadr conspiracy in North America. During the 1920s and 1930s he astutely acted as a mediator between the government of India and Sikh political activists supporting the gurdwara reform movement launched by the Shiromani Gurdwara Parbandhak committee. The British crown and government of India recognized his military and political support with the GCIE in 1911, the GBE in 1918, the GCSI in 1921, and the GCVO in 1922. He also served as a representative of India at the League of Nations assembly in 1925.

Possessed of a strong and shrewd personality, Bhupinder Singh could be both charming and autocratic, winning friends and enemies among British officials, his subjects, his princely peers, and British Indian politicians. Among Indian rulers Bhupinder Singh was a formidable figure. Active in the initial organization of the chamber of princes, an advisory body of princes inaugurated in 1921, he was a perpetual member of its standing committee. Oscillating between collaborative junior colleague and ambitious rival of Maharaja Ganga Singh of Bikaner, the first chancellor of the chamber, Bhupinder Singh was elected chancellor in 1926 and served until 1930, again from 1933 to 1935, and from 1937 to 1938. Because of that office he was the official leader of the delegation of Indian princes to the first round-table conference in 1930 at London. However, Ganga Singh of Bikaner emerged more prominently because of his speech offering tentative princely support for a federation with British Indian provinces.

After initially endorsing federation, by mid-1931 Bhupinder Singh promoted confederation as an alternative scheme, partly out of personal pique at his eclipse in princely politics and partly from concern about the consequences of a federation for the future existence of princely states. His action was one factor dividing an already fractious princely order, and federation proposals lost political momentum. By March 1932 he became reconciled with Ganga Singh as an advocate for a reconfigured federation. Subsequently, die-hard Conservative politicians and journalists, particularly those associated with the *Morning Post*, who opposed significant constitutional reforms in India during the 1930s, sought to gain his renewed opposition to federation. While Bhupinder Singh wavered, he ultimately remained committed. However, federation was never achieved.

Among his subjects Bhupinder Singh was noted for his quixotic generosity, his extravagant lifestyle, and his intolerance of political opposition. Popular politicians found him authoritarian, unwilling to accommodate but likely to imprison or co-opt any challengers. In 1930 a scathing attack by the States People's Conference on his dictatorial political practices and financial mismanagement, resulting from his personal indulgences and extensive travels, led to a British investigation of Bhupinder Singh's administration of his state. The Fitzpatrick inquiry cleared him of political wrongdoing, but the government of India imposed constraints on his control of his state's financial affairs. By 1935 challenges from his peers in the chamber of princes, intensified popular, political opposition within his state, and declining health led Bhupinder Singh to be less active in the all-Indian and imperial political spheres. He died on 23 March 1938 in Patiala and was succeeded by Yadavindra Singh, the eldest son of his senior wife. His remains were cremated in Patiala. BARBARA N. RAMUSACK

Sources *The Times* (24 March 1938) · *New York Times* (24 March 1938) · *Manchester Guardian Weekly* (25 March 1938) · M. F. O'Dwyer, 'The maharaja of Patiala: war service to the empire', *The Times* (25 March 1938) · K. M. Panikkar, *The Indian princes in council: a record of the chancellorship of his highness the maharaja of Patiala, 1926–1931 and 1933–1936* (1936) · *Patiala and the Great War … compiled from secretariat and other records* (1923) · B. N. Ramusack, 'Punjab states, maharajas and gurdwaras: Patiala and the Sikh community', *People, princes and paramount power: society and politics in the Indian princely states*, ed. R. Jeffrey (1978), 170–204 · B. N. Ramusack, *The princes of India in the twilight of empire: dissolution of a patron–client system, 1914–1939* (1978) · I. Copland, *The princes of India in the endgame of empire, 1917–1947* (1997) · R. Walia, *Praja Mandal movement in East Punjab states* (1972) · Indian States People's Conference, Patiala Enquiry Committee, *Indictment of Patiala* (1930) · *DNB* · M. Mukherjee, 'Peasant movement in Patiala state, 1937–48', *Studies in History*, 1 (1979), 215–83 · B. Singh, *Public pronouncements in connection with the Indian states committee* (1928)

Archives BL OIOC · National Archives of India, New Delhi · Punjab State Archives, Patiala City, Punjab, Patiala State Records and Records of the Chamber of Princes | CUL, corresp. with Lord Hardinge

Likenesses Vandyk, photograph, 1911, NPG [see illus.] · photographs, BL OIOC

Singh, Duleep (1838–1893), maharaja of Lahore, was born in Lahore on 6 September 1838, the youngest son of Maharaja Ranjit Singh (1780–1839) and Rani Jindan Kaur (1817–1863). With the death of Ranjit Singh came chaos and mayhem as his prized Khalsa army, the lynchpin of his control of the Punjab, became a law unto itself and gave its support to a chain of successors. Each in turn was murdered until, on 16 September 1843, Duleep Singh was declared maharaja. Duleep Singh's early years as ruler of the Punjab were filled with all that the court could provide. He was tutored in Persian and Gurmukhi—the language of the Sikh holy scriptures. He loved falconry and learned to hunt and shoot—a pastime that he continued to enjoy throughout his life.

By 1845 the Khalsa army clamoured for long overdue payment from the child-maharaja. They themselves were in total disarray, with the British provocatively camped on the Punjab's southern border. The scene was set for the First Anglo-Sikh War (1845–6). Following the defeat of the Khalsa army in 1846 Duleep Singh's kingdom was reduced to half its former size, and a British resident installed in

Duleep Singh (1838–1893), by Franz Xaver Winterhalter, 1854

Lahore. Within two years a Sikh revolt led to the Second Anglo-Sikh War (1848–9). By the time of the Sikh surrender in March 1849 the British had entered Lahore and removed Duleep Singh from the Punjab to the town of Fatehgarh in the North-West Provinces of India. The conditions of surrender required Duleep Singh to resign his title to the sovereignty of the Punjab, the confiscation of state property, and the surrender of the famous Koh-i-noor diamond to Queen Victoria. In return Duleep Singh was granted a pension provided he 'remain obedient to the British Government'.

Fatehgarh, famed for its Christian missionary activity, was where Duleep Singh was converted to Christianity in 1853. This act, although facilitated by his guardians, was none the less more rapidly accomplished than even they had expected. A year later, in May 1854, he arrived in England and quickly gained a royal audience, becoming an immediate success with Queen Victoria.

Between 1854 and 1861 the maharaja lived variously in London, in Mulgrave Castle, Yorkshire, and in Castle Menzies, Perthshire, becoming famous for his love of the country and game-shooting. He joined the Carlton Club and became a freemason.

In January 1861 Duleep Singh returned to India to rescue his mother from political exile. For the next two years they were inseparable, but in 1863 she suddenly died. Again the maharaja returned to India, this time to cremate the maharani. He did not return home alone. In Cairo, on 7 June 1864, he married Bamba Müller (1849–1887), a part-Ethiopian, part-German girl from a local mission school. He took her home to his newly acquired home at Elveden, Suffolk. Between 1866 and 1879 they had six children, who were brought up as royalty in the sprawling estate. Duleep Singh loved Elveden and rebuilt the church, cottages, and the school. His fame as a shooter of game was revived in the grounds of the great estate.

Amid European glamour, the spirit that had tasted sovereignty was hibernating somewhere in the mind of Duleep Singh. Prompted initially by his mother, then by his cousin Thakur Singh Sandhanwalia, and finally by the supposed prophecies of the tenth Sikh guru, Duleep Singh began a battle with the British government asserting the illegality of the annexation of the Punjab, and he demanded to be reinstated as maharaja. In 1886 he tried to return to India to place himself as the prophesied head of the Sikh people, but was arrested at Aden. Here he was received back into the Sikh faith.

Duleep Singh was to spend his last six years in Paris leading a crusade to return himself to the throne of Lahore. In his proclamations he signed himself 'the lawful sovereign of the Sikh nation' and the 'implacable foe of the British government'. He conspired with Russian and Irish revolutionaries to take the Punjab through the Khyber pass, the scheme relying on the British being weakened by a mass revolt of Punjabi and Irish soldiers. The grand plan was never to materialize. He was dogged by conspiracy, then in 1887 his most powerful Russian ally, Mikhail Katkov, died, and with him went any chance of Russian support.

In Paris, on 20 May 1889, Singh was married for a second time, to Ada Douglas Wetherill (1869–1930), a young Englishwoman, and they had two daughters. With his health deteriorating, he initiated a reconciliation with Queen Victoria, who responded with a full pardon through the secretary of state on 1 August 1890. Within years his health broke down completely, and on 22 October 1893 he suffered a fatal 'apoplectic fit' in the modest Hôtel de la Tremoille, Paris. His body was taken back to his beloved stately home, Elveden, to be buried next to his wife and youngest son in the graveyard of St Andrew's and St Patrick's Church, on 28 October.

Of Duleep Singh's nine children, Princess Bamba Sofia Jindan Duleep Singh (1879–1957) settled in Lahore, where she died. Victor Albert Jay Duleep Singh (1866–1918) held a commission in the 1st (Royal) Dragoons and married a daughter of the earl of Coventry. Frederick Victor Duleep Singh (1868–1926), who like his brother was educated at Eton and at Cambridge, also held an army commission and saw service in France during the First World War. The princesses Sophia Alexandra Duleep Singh (1876–1948)

and Catherine Hilda Duleep Singh (1871–1942) were both educated at Magdalene College, Cambridge, and Sophia later ruffled feathers at the India Office by defiantly selling *The Suffragette* newspaper outside Hampton Court. All Duleep Singh's children died without issue.

AMANDEEP SINGH MADRA

Sources H. Singh, ed., *The encyclopaedia of Sikhism*, 2nd edn, 1 (Patiala, 1995) · C. Campbell, *The maharajah's box* (2000) · M. Alexander and S. Anand, *Queen Victoria's maharajah* (1980)
Archives BL OIOC, personal and family corresp. and papers, MS Eur. E 377 · Royal Arch., letters | BL, letters to W. E. Gladstone and related papers, Add. MSS 44468–44508, *passim* · Bodl. Oxf., corresp. with Lord Kimberley, MSS Eng. a 2013–2014; b 2047–2049; c 3933–4514; d 2439–2492; e 2790–2797
Likenesses G. Beechy, oils, 1852, priv. coll. · E. Becker, photograph, 1854, Royal Collection · F. X. Winterhalter, oils, 1854, Royal Collection [*see illus.*] · carte-de-visite, *c*.1877, Maharajah Duleep Singh Centenary Trust · Spy [L. Ward], lithograph, NPG; repro. in *VF* (18 Nov 1882) · photograph, Sothebys
Wealth at death £7219 13*s*.: 1894, *CGPLA Eng. & Wales*

Singh, Ganga (1880–1943), maharaja of Bikaner, was born on 13 October 1880 in Bikaner, Rajputana, the younger son of Maharaja Lall Singh (*d.* 1887) and his second wife, and seven years later (August 1887) became the twenty-first ruler of Bikaner, in succession to his half-brother, Maharaja Dungar Singh. The young prince was initially tutored in English, Indian languages, and history by Pandit Ram Chandra Dube, then attended Mayo College in Ajmer from 1890 to 1895, and was trained in administrative practices and the sports of riding and shooting by Brian Egerton from 1895 to 1898. Although the maharaja was an ardent polo player as a young man, he became particularly known as an excellent shot. In 1897 he married Vallabh Kanwar, Maharani Ranwatji (*d.* 1906), the daughter of the ruler of Partabgarh, and they had three children, the third of whom was Sadul Singh, who would succeed his father. His second wife was Krishnakumari, Maharani Chandrawatiniji (*d.* 1922). His third wife, whom he married on 3 May 1908, was Ajab Kanwar, Sri Maharani Bhatiyaniji Sahib (*d.* 1945), with whom he had a further three children. His second wife was childless and this may well be why he married again. He probably never divorced her, but maintained her in a separate establishment.

Upon his investiture with ruling powers in 1898, the maharaja had no easy task in front of him. His state, though it extended over an area of 23,000 square miles, was almost entirely desert. The annual rainfall was 11 inches and precarious. Famine, or at least severe scarcity, was of frequent occurrence. Soon after the maharaja's minority ended, Bikaner and the surrounding states suffered the worst famine of modern times. Ganga Singh undertook relief works with great energy, but realized the need for more permanent measures. After persistent efforts, he succeeded in securing a share in the waters of the Sutlej River and constructed the Gang Canal (opened in 1927), which ran in a cement-lined channel through 90 miles of Punjab territory. The Gang Canal, a revised land revenue settlement, and the absence of large *jagirdars* (landholders) in the state fostered a relatively contented

Ganga Singh (1880–1943), by Sir William Orpen, 1919

peasantry and forestalled extensive peasant political activity in Bikaner.

Another problem which confronted the maharaja was presented by the virtual independence of his *thakurs*. These semi-feudal barons had reasserted their autonomy during the nineteenth century, and there were wide areas in which the authority of the durbar (ruling court) was only grudgingly acknowledged. The maharaja successfully extended state control over these recalcitrant collaborators. He sought to conciliate dominant groups with the establishment in 1913 of a representative assembly whose powers were subject to veto by the maharaja. At first only landholders and larger municipalities elected members, but smaller municipalities and agriculturists were eventually granted limited suffrage.

Ganga Singh firmly believed that the princes should combine together in promoting the common interests of their order. It was mainly at his instigation that during the war of 1914–18 the viceroy initiated an annual conference of rulers which developed into the chamber of princes, officially inaugurated in 1921. The maharaja of Bikaner was elected the first chancellor and held that office continuously for the next five years. At the same time he maintained contacts with Indian nationalist leaders, including Mahatma Gandhi, and publicly spoke in support of Indian nationalism.

In the wider field of Indian constitutional development the maharaja was again in the forefront. In 1930, the year in which he led the Indian delegation to the League of Nations assembly at Geneva, he attended the first round-table conference in London, where he and Nawab Hamidullah of Bhopal were the first two princes to support the scheme propounded by Sir Tej Bahadur Sapru for an all-India federation incorporating the princely states. Extensive negotiations followed, in which Ganga Singh faced an anti-federation campaign led by his successor as chancellor of the chamber of princes, Maharaja Bhupinder Singh of Patiala. This opposition from other princes may be attributed to several factors. First, as the details of what federation would entail in financial commitments and possible limits on internal autonomy were defined, many princes, both smaller ones who might lose their identity and larger ones who would suffer attrition in income, demanded extensive legal guarantees. Second, the government of India at New Delhi, especially the political department, was less supportive of federation than British officials at the India Office in London and did not lobby persuasively for federation. Third, the diehard faction within the Conservative Party in Britain tried to use the princes as one hammer to destroy federation since the diehards opposed the delegation of power to elected Indian politicians, which was a key element in a federated government of India.

As the reforms were incorporated in the Government of India Act in 1935 and in the autonomous provincial governments inaugurated in 1937, the negotiations over federation continued and Bikaner and Patiala were reconciled. In 1938 the Congress Party gave formal sanction to the burgeoning efforts of its members to launch popular political demonstrations in the princely states. These campaigns sought internal state reforms such as guaranteed civil rights, more equitable land taxes, the introduction of the franchise, and representative government, as well as the popular election, rather than princely appointment, of representatives from the princely states to the federation government. These agitations exacerbated already existing princely apprehensions and by 1939 Ganga Singh himself had retreated into hesitant opposition to federation. The outbreak of war in Europe in September 1939 aborted negotiations over federation.

If the maharaja wavered in his support of the federal programme, he never faltered in his devotion to the crown. Always a keen soldier, his first military campaign was during the Boxer uprising of 1900 in China, where he commanded his well-known camel corps, the Ganga Risala. At the outbreak of the war of 1914–18 he placed the resources of his state at the disposal of the crown, and he served personally in France and Egypt. He was a member of the Imperial War Conference of 1917 and a signatory to the treaty of Versailles. He was appointed honorary major-general in 1917, lieutenant-general in 1930, and general in 1937, the first Indian to be given the rank of general in the British army. He was for many years an honorary aide-de-camp to successive British kings. During the war of 1939–45 he substantially increased his state forces, supplied many contingents to the Indian army, and in 1941 visited the Middle Eastern front.

Tall, a formidable public speaker, always elegantly attired whether in Indian or Western clothes, Ganga Singh was prominent in the coterie of Indian princes who

were politically astute, hardworking, benevolent auto-
crats. He assumed that he would be dominant and carefully consulted in any organization or process in which he
participated. Although he could be a charming, considerate host at world famous sand-grouse shoots at his country
palace at Gajner, he was known to terrify officials in his
state. Fellow princes and British officials could find him
brusque and abrasive, but all acknowledged his dedicated
service to the princely order and the British empire. He
was appointed KCIE (1901), KCSI (1904), GCIE (1907), GCSI
(1911), KCB (1918), GCVO (1919), and GBE (1921). He served
as chancellor of Benares Hindu University from 1929 to
1943, and the universities of Cambridge, Edinburgh,
Oxford, Benares, and Osmania (Hyderabad) conferred
honorary degrees on him. Maharaja Ganga Singh died on 2
February 1943 in Bombay and was cremated at Devikund
Sagar, near Bikaner city. He was succeeded by his only surviving son, Maharaja Kanwar Sadul Singh (1902–1950). His
death marked the passing of an era when a few select
Indian princes played significant roles as imperial
politicians.   BARBARA N. RAMUSACK

Sir Hari Singh (1895–1961), by Bassano, 1944

Sources DNB · *The Times* (3 Feb 1943) · *New York Times* (2 Feb 1943),
19 · K. M. Panikkar, *His highness the maharaja of Bikaner: a biography*
(1937) · I. Copland, *The princes of India in the endgame of empire, 1917–
1947* (1997) · B. N. Ramusack, *The princes of India in the twilight of
empire: dissolution of a patron–client system, 1914–1939* (1978) ·
K. Singh, *The relations of the house of Bikaner with the central powers,
1465–1949* (1974) · N. Patnaik, *A desert kingdom: the Rajputs of Bikaner*
(1990) · S. P. Sen, ed., *Dictionary of national biography*, 4 vols. (1972–4),
vol. 4, pp. 213–15 [India] · R. Sisson, *The congress party in Rajasthan:
political integration and institution building in an Indian state* (1972) ·
S. Das, *Bikaner* (1940) · Unpublished genealogy of John McLeod
Archives Rajasthan State Archives, Bikaner, Rajasthan, India,
Bikaner State Records | BL OIOC, crown representative records ·
National Archives of India, New Delhi, India, foreign and political
department files · Punjab State Archives, Patiala, Punjab, India,
Chamber of Princes Records
Likenesses W. Orpen, oils, 1919, NPG [*see illus.*] · W. Stoneman,
photograph, 1930, NPG · J. Guthrie, portrait, NPG · W. Orpen,
group portrait (*The signing of the peace in the hall of mirrors, Versailles*),
IWM · photographs, BL OIOC · photographs, repro. in Patnaik,
Desert kingdom

Singh, Sir Hari (1895–1961), maharaja of Jammu and Kash-
mir, was born at Jammu on 30 September 1895, the son of
General Sir Amar Singh (d. 1909), the brother of Sir Partab
Singh, then the maharaja of Jammu and Kashmir.
Although Partab Singh had adopted a son (Jagatdeo Singh
of Poonch) for religious reasons, the government of India
indicated that they preferred his nephew as his heir. Thus
Hari Singh had been educated to be a 'progressive prince'
at Mayo College in Ajmer and with the Imperial Cadet
Corps in Dehra Dun. When Partab Singh died on 23 Sep-
tember 1925, Hari Singh succeeded.

Although his religiously conservative uncle never left
his state, the future ruler made several visits to Europe.
During one in 1924 he became involved in Paris with a Mrs
Robinson, who had been hired by a blackmailing clique
headed by his aide-de-camp, a Captain Arthur, who had
been recommended by Sir John Wood, then the British
resident at Jammu and Kashmir. Hari Singh initially

agreed to pay £125,000 but then stopped payment on the
cheque. Robinson sued. In a subsequent trial the young
prince was permitted to provide evidence under the
pseudonym of Mr A. His identity soon became known and
the episode became a staple of scandal magazines and
polemical pamphlets. Meanwhile Hari Singh married four
times, his first wife, Baijilal, dying while pregnant and the
next two being childless. His fourth wife, Maharani Tara
Devi, from Kangra, had one son, Karan Singh, on 9 March
1931 in Cannes.

After his succession Hari Singh established a reputation
as a liberal prince at a time when the future of the princes
and their states was increasingly controversial, in the context of Indian nationalism. He was quickly elected to the
standing committee of the chamber of princes and
attended the first round-table conference in London in
1930. There he made a speech supportive of British Indian
aspirations for India's equal status in the British Commonwealth. During the Second World War he was a firm ally.
He had been created a KCIE in 1918, a GCIE in 1929, a GCSI
in 1933, was a representative of India at the war cabinet in
1944, and received the GCVO in 1946.

From 1931 onwards he confronted growing domestic
demands from the Muslim majority community under
the leadership of Sheikh Abdullah for greater representation of Muslims in government service, and from Kashmiri Brahmans for constitutional reforms. Any movement for greater popular political participation in Jammu
and Kashmir would have a tortuous path. The state had a

Hindu ruler who identified with a strong Hindu Dogra Rajput community in Jammu, the winter capital of the state; an overall but sectarianly diverse Muslim majority population; a summer capital at Srinagar in Kashmir which had a Muslim majority of over 90 per cent and an articulate Kashmiri Brahman pandit élite; and a Buddhist minority concentrated in Ladakh.

When the British announced their withdrawal from India in August 1947, Hari Singh initially sought to remain independent. His action has been attributed variously to his indecisive character, to his abhorrence of Pakistan, to his fear of a popular government headed by Sheikh Abdullah, and to his conviction that independence was the best means of ensuring communal harmony in this religiously complex state. Commentators have claimed that either the British tried to promote the accession of the state to Pakistan since it was a Muslim majority area; or Lord Mountbatten, influenced by Jawaharlal Nehru, who sought to include the state in India for sentimental reasons since he was a Kashmiri Brahman or for political reasons to demonstrate that a Muslim majority state could exist in a secular India, manoeuvred to secure Kashmir for India. Pakistani leaders argued that Jammu and Kashmir belonged to Pakistan demographically and geographically.

Once Pakistan was independent and there were indications that Hari Singh might accede to India, elements within the Pakistani military logistically supported an invasion of Muslim tribesmen from Pakistan into border areas of Kashmir and Jammu in October 1947. Hari Singh appealed to India for military aid and signed an accession agreement probably on 25 October. The government of India, with Lord Mountbatten as governor-general, accepted it on 26 October, and Indian troops landed on the following day at the Srinagar airport, just as the tribesmen reached its outskirts. Fighting continued until a United Nations ceasefire came into effect on 1 January 1949. At that point Pakistani forces held approximately two-fifths of the territory of Jammu and Kashmir, an area known as Azad (Free) Kashmir. Subsequently Sheikh Abdullah, as head of the interim government of the Indian state of Jammu and Kashmir, urged Nehru and Sardar Patel that Hari Singh had to abdicate. In response to their pressure Hari Singh agreed to leave his state temporarily and to recognize the appointment of his eighteen-year-old son, Karan Singh, as regent. Hari Singh lived thereafter in Bombay, where he died of a heart attack on 26 April 1961. The problems of Kashmir remained unresolved at the century's end.   BARBARA N. RAMUSACK

Sources *The Times* (27 April 1961) · *New York Times* (27 April 1961) · K. Singh, *Heir apparent: an autobiography*, 1 (1982) · P. S. Jha, *Kashmir 1947: rival versions of history* (1996) · H. V. Hodson, *The great divide: Britain–India–Pakistan* (1969) · I. Copland, *The princes of India in the endgame of empire, 1917–1947* (1997) · U. K. Zutshi, *Emergence of political awakening in Kashmir* (1986) · I. Copland, 'Islam and political mobilization in Kashmir, 1931–34', *Pacific Affairs*, 54 (1981), 228–59 · A. Lamb, *Kashmir: a disputed legacy* (1991) · K. Singh, *Sadar-i-Riyasat: an autobiography*, 2 (1985)
Archives BL OIOC · Jammu and Kashmir State Archives, Jammu · National Archives of India, New Delhi

Likenesses Bassano, photograph, 1944, NPG [*see illus.*] · photographs, BL OIOC

Singh, Kishen (1849/50–1921). *See under* Montgomerie, Thomas George (1830–1878).

Singh, Mani (*b.* in or before **1829**, *d.* after **1868**). *See under* Montgomerie, Thomas George (1830–1878).

Singh, Nain (**1829/30–1882**). *See under* Montgomerie, Thomas George (1830–1878).

Singh, Tara [*known as* Master Tara Singh Malhotra; *formerly* Nanak Chand Malhotra] (**1885–1967**), headmaster and politician, was born on 24 June 1885 in the village of Haryal, Punjab, India (now in Pakistan), the son of Bakhshi Gopi Chand Malhotra, a revenue official and moneylender. Tara Singh was born as a Hindu named Nanak Chand, converting to the Sikh faith in 1902. At his initiation into Sikhism by Sant Attar Singh, he took on the new name Tara Singh.

Tara Singh's early education in the village school in Haryal was followed by a period at the Mission High School, Rawalpindi. He was well known at both schools for tenacity on the playing fields, a quality he later displayed in his political career. Although Tara Singh was unsuccessful in his attempt to go to medical school, in 1903 he received a scholarship to Khalsa College in Amritsar, the leading Sikh educational institution of the time. There he first took an active part in politics, becoming the president of a student agitation committee protesting against government attempts to assert greater control of the college.

After his graduation from the college in 1907, Tara Singh attended a teacher training college in Lahore. On his graduation in the following year he offered to take up a post at a minimal salary if the Sikh community established a Khalsa high school in the market town of Lyallpur (now Faisalabad in Pakistan). He joined the new school as headmaster, gaining the sobriquet 'Master' that he retained for the rest of his life. He remained in the post for six years, his planned departure to England to serve as *granthi* (scripture reader) being cancelled by the outbreak of the First World War. He was headmaster of the Khalsa high school, Kallar, from 1914 to 1916 and at other schools before returning to Lyallpur in 1920.

Tara Singh's career in religious politics began in March 1921, when he was made secretary of the Shiromani Gurdwara Parbandhak committee, newly established to wrest control of Sikh shrines from their hereditary custodians. In this role he was involved in several agitations against the government and was imprisoned on charges of sedition and conspiracy in 1923. On his release in 1926 he became vice-president of the committee. He was first elected president of the committee in 1930 and remained in that office with only short periods of intermission until 1962.

During the late 1920s and 1930s Tara Singh's deft political manoeuvrings made him the most important of Sikh nationalist leaders. During a controversy over the Nehru committee report of 1928, which put forth Indian National Congress proposals for an Indian constitution, he expressed his opposition to the conclusions of the report while maintaining his support for the Congress movement. In 1930 he was gaoled for his participation in the Congress-led civil disobedience movement against British rule.

As leader of the provincial Shiromani Akali Dal political party, Tara Singh led agitations against both the British Indian government and the provincial Unionist government after its election in 1937. His campaigns against the British Indian government concerned both religious issues such as the control of Sikh shrines and political issues such as the representation of Sikhs in the provincial legislature. His agitations against the Unionists were focused on what he saw as their support for Muslim domination of Punjab through the reservation of seats in the legislative assembly on a communal basis.

Tara Singh's reputation as the foremost Sikh political leader was confirmed in the eyes of many due to his campaigns and actions in the run-up to the partition of the subcontinent into India and Pakistan in 1947. In 1943 he put forth the Azad Punjab ('Free Punjab') scheme suggesting the reorganization of Punjab to exclude Muslim-majority districts and began to condemn Congress policies. At the time of the Simla conference in 1945 and the British cabinet mission in 1946, Tara Singh demanded an independent Sikh state in the event of a partition of the subcontinent.

As the communal climate in Punjab deteriorated, Tara Singh was often seen at the head of public rallies that opposed the partition of Punjab and inflamed communal tensions. A particularly fierce protest in Lahore on 3 March 1947 sparked violent rioting in the city that led to open conflict between Sikhs and Muslims. At partition Tara Singh migrated to east Punjab.

After the independence of India in 1947, the Shiromani Akali Dal under the leadership of Tara Singh began to demand the reorganization of the state of Punjab on linguistic grounds into a Punjabi-speaking state, known as the Punjabi Suba. Tara Singh led two major agitations on the issue in 1955 and 1960, both of which led to the arrest of thousands of activists. He undertook a fast to the death in 1961 over the issue, ending it unsuccessfully after forty-eight days. With this, his influence in the Sikh political arena began to wane and his power in both the Shiromani Akali Dal and the Shiromani Gurdwara Parbandhak committee were challenged successfully by a faction led by the rival leader Sant Fateh Singh. The demand for a Punjabi Suba was finally conceded in 1966, during the period of Fateh Singh's leadership of the Dal. In addition to his political activities, Master Tara Singh wrote numerous tracts and newspaper articles. He died on 22 November 1967. The Master Tara Singh Memorial College for Women, Ludhiana, was named after him.   JEEVAN SINGH DEOL

Sources Khushwant Singh, *History of the Sikhs*, 2 (1966) · Gopal Singh, *A history of the Sikh people* (1979) · Harbans Singh, *The heritage of the Sikhs* (1983) · K. C. Gulati, *Akalis past and present* (1974) · Ajit Singh Sarhadi, *Punjabi Suba* (1970) · Baldev Rat Nayar, *Minority politics in the Punjab* (1966) · H. Singh, ed., *The encyclopaedia of Sikhism*, 2nd edn, 4 (Patiala, 1998)
Archives U. Southampton L., Mountbatten papers

Singh, Udham (1899–1940), assassin, was born Sher Singh on 26 December 1899 in the village of Sunam, Patiala, Punjab, India, the second son of Tehal Singh, a smallholder and railway crossing guard, and his wife, Harnam Kaur. Orphaned at the age of eight, he was sent to the Central Sikh Orphanage, Amritsar. Turn-of-the-century Punjab was a hotbed of political unrest and spearhead of direct action against British rule. The state's governor, Sir Michael O'Dwyer, ruled with an iron fist. By 1919 the excesses reached an apex with the infamous Jallianwalla Bagh incident. According to British estimates 379 Indians were killed when Brigadier-General Reginald Dyer marched an armed unit into a public area and fired upon a crowd of protesters. Dyer defended his actions all the way to a court martial; O'Dwyer slipped from public office and retired. The massacre left a profound impact on the Indian people and on Sher Singh, although at the time he was in Africa building British railways.

After returning to the Punjab in June 1919, Singh rallied around communists and liberation parties and, despite a modest education, contributed to a revolutionary newsletter. Stimulated by his politics, he made his way to the United States, where he worked for a time in Detroit and Chicago. He then travelled west to California, home of the Gadhr Party, a militant communist freedom party. A directory of its prominent members lists Singh: in activist terms he had arrived. By 1927 he was back in the Punjab, where his local infamy caught the watchful eye of the authorities. He paid the price for his notoriety by receiving a five-year prison term for illegal possession of firearms.

After being released from prison in 1932, Singh managed to acquire a passport, using the name Udham Singh for the first time, and made his way to Britain. His appearance in London was typical of a 1930s Sikh immigrant moving to the East End to find work around the docks. His revolutionary ideals and boasts of direct action brought suspicion from the Sikh community, but he remained wedded to his politics. For six years he did little other than eke out a living in depression-hit London.

Singh's frustration was real; he desperately needed to prove himself. His chance came on 13 March 1940, when the East India Association hosted a lecture on the Afghan crisis, at Caxton Hall, Westminster. Those attending included Lord Zetland, secretary of state for India, and Sir Michael O'Dwyer—a name that would have been immediately reviled by Udham Singh. The meeting was concluding when Singh pushed his way to the front of the public area. As the audience stood up to leave, he stepped forward and drew his pistol. Just inches from his back, Singh shot O'Dwyer twice. Further shots hit Zetland and two others. Singh was tackled before he could escape. O'Dwyer was killed immediately.

The press photographed Singh as he was led handcuffed from the hall, and his notoriety was sealed the next morning as the story was splashed across the world's front pages. In custody he gave the name of Mohammed Singh Azad—an eclectic mixture of a Sikh, a Hindu, and a Muslim name. His statement ultimately sealed his fate: 'I just shot to make protest. I have seen people starving in India under British Imperialism. I done it … I am not sorry … it was my duty.' The prosecution case was simple, the defence chaotic. Revenge came at a heavy price. On 5 June 1940 Singh was sentenced to death. There was no appeal hearing. On 31 July 1940 he was hanged and his body buried in the unconsecrated grounds of Pentonville prison.

For the ordinary Punjabi, Singh was a great freedom fighter, while the ruling élite held him to be a revengeful killer. The Indian political parties at first distanced themselves from his crime, though not for long. After independence politicians clamoured for the reflected glory of Udham Singh and demanded that his body be returned. In 1974 permission was finally given for his body to be returned to India. He was cremated on 31 July 1974 at his birthplace of Sunam. AMANDEEP SINGH MADRA

Sources N. Singh, *Challenge to imperial hegemony: the life story of a great Indian patriot, Udham Singh* (Patiala, 1998) · R. Perkins, *The Amritsar legacy: Golden Temple to Caxton Hall, the story of a killing* (1989) · H. Singh, ed., *The encyclopaedia of Sikhism*, 2nd edn, 4 (Patiala, 1998)
Archives PRO, 25908, file no. MEPO 3/1743 · PRO, 37513, file no. PCOM 9/872 · PRO, file no. P&J (s) 466/36
Likenesses photograph, repro. in Perkins, *Amritsar legacy*

Singleton, Henry (1682–1759), judge, was the fourth son of Edward Singleton, alderman of Drogheda, co. Louth, and member of parliament for that town. He went to school in Drogheda, matriculated from Dublin University in 1698, entered the Inner Temple in 1702, and graduated as bachelor of arts in 1703. He was called to the Irish bar in 1707. In the same year his sister married Robert Lindsay, later judge of the Irish common pleas. Singleton is mentioned as recorder of Drogheda in 1708, and was returned as its MP in 1713 and in 1715.

In politics Singleton was a tory, a friend of the Foster family of Drogheda, and also of Dean Swift and of Bishop Berkeley. He became prime serjeant, the chief law officer in Ireland, in 1726 and acted continuously as a justice of assize. Returned as MP for Drogheda and Dunleer, in 1727 he elected to sit for Drogheda. He was strongly supported for the position of speaker of the Irish Commons in 1733. In the following year he received an honorary LLD from Trinity College, Dublin. He was appointed chief justice of the Irish court of common pleas in 1740; this was seen as a victory for the Irish bar at the time, since it was then common to appoint Englishmen to the Irish bench. There was no question of his qualification for the post; he had been a barrister for over thirty years, a member of the Irish House of Commons for over twenty-five years, and the chief law officer for fourteen years. He was also sworn of the privy council. In 1753 he surrendered his seat as chief

Henry Singleton (1682–1759), by John Brooks, in or after 1740

justice, and in 1754 he became master of the rolls (not a judicial office in Ireland at this time).

According to a report in the *Dublin Evening Post* of 14 June 1740:

> although to those who did not enjoy a close acquaintance he appeared proud and haughty … [Singleton] was far from deserving that character, and such was his benevolence that within a few weeks of his elevation to the bench, he is mentioned as having expended over four hundred pounds in purchasing oatmeal for the inhabitants of Drogheda, who were suffering, in common with the whole of Ireland, from the terrible famine by which the country was then devastated. (Ball, 2.131)

He was fortunate to survive the subsequent fever, which in 1741 carried off two of his contemporaries on the bench, John Rogerson, chief justice of the king's bench, and John Wainwright, baron of the exchequer.

Singleton died, unmarried, in 1759; he was buried on 12 November in Drogheda in St Peter's Church, where there is a memorial to him, erected by his nephew Sydenham Singleton. The memorial, which includes a bust, was made in 1787 in London by John Hickey, an Irishman and sculptor to the prince of Wales. He lived in Dublin in Jervis Street, in Drogheda in Lawrence Street, and near Dublin at Drumcondra in Belvedere House, which he leased from Sir Marmaduke Coghill, judge of the prerogative court and later chancellor of the exchequer. His house in Lawrence Street, Drogheda, became Drogheda grammar school; in 1989, despite its being a listed building, it was demolished by an impatient and unscrupulous developer.

The development company was later prosecuted and subsequently the judge ordered that the parts of the demolished building be preserved so that the house might be reconstructed at some time in the future (*Irish Times*, 24 Aug 1989). His law library, mostly manuscript works, was acquired by Columbia University, New York, in 1937. It includes a notebook of cases (MS 71) in the Irish courts of chancery and exchequer heard in the years 1716 to 1734, in which Singleton appeared as prime serjeant.

ANDREW LYALL

Sources F. E. Ball, *The judges in Ireland, 1221–1921*, 2 vols. (1926); repr. (1993) · C. J. Smyth, *Chronicle of the law officers of Ireland* (1839) · *Dublin Evening Post* (14 June 1740) · *County Dublin*, 4.171 · G. H. Bassett, *Louth county guide and directory* (1886); repr. (1998) · W. Garner, *Drogheda architectural heritage* (1986) · memorial, St Peter's Church, Drogheda, co. Louth, Ireland · A. P. W. Malcomson, *John Foster: the politics of the Anglo-Irish ascendancy* (1978) · *The correspondence of Jonathan Swift*, ed. H. Williams, 5 (1965), 140 · J. Coghill to Southwell, 13 March 1733, BL, Add. MS 21123, fol. 26 · Jocelyn to Hardwicke, 29 March 1741, BL, Add. MS 35586, fol. 335 · W. N. Osborough, 'Puzzles from Irish law reporting history', *The life of the law* [Oxford 1991], ed. P. Birks (1993), 89–112 · parish register, St Peter's Church, Drogheda [burial] · H. Potterton, *Irish church monuments, 1570–1880* (1975) · *Public Register, or, Freeman's Journal* (2 Aug 1787) · J. P. Campbell, 'Two memorable Dublin houses', *Dublin Historical Record*, 2/4 (1939–40), 141–55

Archives Col. U., Diamond Law Library

Likenesses J. Brooks, engraving, in or after 1740, NG Ire. [*see illus.*] · J. Hickey, bust on memorial, 1787, St Peter's Church, Drogheda, co. Louth

Singleton, Henry (1766–1839), painter, was born in London into an artistic family on 19 October 1766. He lost his father before the age of two, and was brought up by his uncle, William Singleton (d. 1793), a pupil of Ozias Humphry (whom Henry painted: exh. Society of Artists, 1797), and painter of portraits, fancy heads, and miniatures. Another uncle, Joseph Singleton, exhibited miniatures at the Royal Academy between 1777 and 1783.

Henry Singleton was precocious: he worked as a professional portraitist from the age of sixteen, and exhibited at the Society of Artists in Spring Gardens in 1780 *A Soldier Returned to his Family*, a pen drawing, by 'Master H. Singleton, aged ten years'. He attended the Royal Academy Schools from 1783, winning the silver medal in 1784 and the gold medal in 1788 for a painting from Dryden's ode *Alexander's Feast*. He exhibited at the Royal Academy from 1784 until his death, at the British Institution between 1806 and 1839, and at the Society of British Artists from its foundation in 1824.

A measure of Singleton's early promise was the commission he received from the Royal Academy in 1793 to paint a large portrait group of the academicians under their president, Benjamin West, *The royal academicians assembled in their council chamber to adjudge the medals to the successful students in painting, sculpture, architecture, and drawing* (RA). This complex and impressive composition contains forty portraits, with some evidently being added as late as 1798, and was engraved in 1802 by C. Bestland. However, Singleton never became an academician himself, and was unsuccessful in gaining an associateship, first in 1807 and again in 1811.

Singleton was first noted for large historical compositions from the Bible, Shakespeare, or contemporary historical events. Many were engraved in mezzotint on a suitably large scale by Gillbank and Charles Turner and published by James Daniell. Two of the best, *Paul I Granting Liberty to Kosciuszko* (1797) and *The Death of Captain Alexander Hood after Capturing the French 74 'L'Hercule', 21 April 1798*, were engraved, the latter in colours, by Daniell himself (BM). Although Singleton remained a popular artist, whose works were always in demand, he never fulfilled his original promise as a history painter. His figures, compositions, and colour became relatively weak, and most of his sentimental and genre scenes, painted in a manner that blended the styles of George Morland and Francis Wheatley, were designed for stipple engravers such as W. Bond, Thomas Burke, James Godby, and Anthony Cardon. Singleton also provided book illustrations, and those done for Sharpe's classics and other serials have charm. He completed a series of cabinet pictures to illustrate Shakespeare shortly before his death.

Singleton remained an effective portrait painter, in a style somewhat influenced by Romney, and those of, for example, Lord Nelson and Admiral Vernon were engraved. A small but vigorous portrait by him of Lord Howe is in the National Portrait Gallery, London; a portrait group of James Boswell with his wife and family was lent by Ralph Dundas to the Edinburgh loan exhibition of Scottish national portraits in 1884.

In 1807 Singleton married William Singleton's only daughter (d. 1811). His sisters Maria and Sarah Macklarinan Singleton were also artists: the former exhibited at the Royal Academy between 1808 and 1820; the latter was a miniaturist who exhibited portraits at the Royal Academy between 1788 and 1813 and lived with Henry for twenty or thirty years, latterly at 4 Haymarket, London. He lived during the latter part of his life in Charles Street, St James's, London, in comfortable circumstances, and for some years was the oldest living exhibitor at the Royal Academy. He was in Paris briefly in 1813, but otherwise appears not to have travelled save for visits to the country. He died at the house of a friend at 7 Kensington Gore, London, on 15 September 1839, and was buried in the church of St Martin-in-the-Fields. A large collection of sketches is in the British Museum, and other works are in the Victoria and Albert Museum, London, the Scottish National Portrait Gallery, Edinburgh, the Tate collection, the Ulster Museum, and Brighton Art Gallery.

L. H. CUST, *rev.* ROBIN SIMON

Sources B. Stewart and M. Cutten, *The dictionary of portrait painters in Britain up to 1920* (1997) · W. T. Whitley, *Art in England, 1800–1837*, 2 vols. (1928); repr. (1973) · *GM*, 2nd ser., 12 (1839), 430 · d. cert.

Archives East Riding of Yorkshire Archives Service, Beverley, letters to Thomas Grimston

Singleton [Lee], **Hugh** (d. in or before 1593), bookseller and printer, was the son of John Singleton or Lee, citizen and currier of London. His date of birth is unknown but a chancery case of 1589 suggests it may have been before 1518 as Singleton testified that he had been abroad for thirty years, including at the time of his grandfather's death (1541). He was, however, continuously resident in London from 1547, apart from 1553–6 when he lived in Wesel, Germany, so his thirty-year absence must have taken place primarily before 1548, setting his birth before 1518. His family may have come from Enfield, Middlesex; their alternative name Lee was passed down through at least three generations.

Singleton began his career as a bookseller, commissioning other printers to publish works by leading protestants including John Foxe and John Knox. In 1553 he employed Richard Jugge to print *The Copie of a Pistle or Letter Sent to Gilbard Potter* which was highly critical of Northumberland's regime. Later that year, and using a false imprint, Singleton reissued Gardiner's defence of the royal supremacy, *De vera obedientia*, to embarrass Gardiner and the Marian regime. This work was probably printed by Joos Lambrecht in Wesel where typographical evidence suggests Singleton was between 1553 and 1556. This same evidence undermines arguments both that Singleton was arrested with John Day in October 1554 for printing 'noythy books' and that (according to Plomer) he was based in Dublin during 1553–6. Singleton may have begun to print himself from 1555 but no works are known to have been printed by him between 1557 and 1560, and 1562 and 1565. In 1566 and in 1569–70 he was appointed searcher for unlawful books by the Stationers' Company, of which he was a member.

In 1579 Singleton printed John Stubbe's *A Discoverie of a Gaping Gulf* and Edmund Spenser's *The Shepheardes Calendar*. Both works were critical of Elizabeth I's proposed marriage to the duke of Anjou, the French king's brother. The more controversial and outspoken of the two works, *A Gaping Gulf* was condemned by Elizabeth, and Singleton, Stubbe, and William Page (who had tried to distribute fifty copies of the book in the west country) were arrested in October 1579. They were originally tried for felony but, the jury refusing to convict, they were charged with conspiracy to incite sedition. They were tried at queen's bench were they were convicted and sentenced to have their right hands cut off and to imprisonment. The *coram rege* and controlment rolls indicate that Singleton suffered this penalty but the French ambassador, Mauvissière, reported that he was pardoned on account of his age. Camden's eyewitness account of Stubbe's and Page's amputations, given in his *Annales*, fails to record Singleton's presence on the scaffold. Research by H. J. Byrom further suggests that Singleton quickly resumed the printing of *The Shepheardes Calendar* already begun some time in August. No record of a pardon survives although this is not significant as pardons were only enrolled when people paid to do so.

Singleton's involvement in the printing of these two books, and his apparent subsequent pardon, has usually been attributed to his being a client of the earl of Leicester who used the books as part of a propaganda campaign against Elizabeth's marriage. However, there are no discernible connections between the two men and Leicester was out of Elizabeth's favour and absent from court during the trial. Singleton's involvement can more reasonably be attributed to his reputation as seller and printer of protestant or controversial material, such as *The Copie of a Pistle or Letter Sent to Gilbard Potter* and *De vera obedientia*.

Singleton was made printer to the City of London in August 1584, in which capacity he printed official city orders. This appears not to have been lucrative and he received loans from the Stationers' Company; Byrom claims that 'to the end of his days he remained one of the poorest of London stationers' (Byrom, 121). He continued to print and to employ other printers until his death, which occurred before 25 April 1593. He left a wife, Margaret, but it is not known if they had any children.

NATALIE MEARS

Sources H. J. Byrom, 'Edmund Spenser's first printer: Hugh Singleton', *The Library*, 4th ser., 14 (1933–4), 121–56 · H. R. Plomer, 'The protestant press in the reign of Queen Mary', *The Library*, 3rd ser., 1 (1910), 54–72 · STC, 1475–1640 · PRO, C2/Elizabeth I S3/5; C2/Elizabeth I S3/48: 1–3 · *John Stubbs's 'gaping gulf' with letters and other relevant documents*, ed. L. E. Berry (1968) · K. Barnes, 'John Stubbe, 1579: the French ambassador's account', *Historical Research*, 64 (1991), 421–6 · Arber, *Regs. Stationers* · F. Isaac, ed., *Facsimiles and illustrations III: English and Scottish printing types, 1535–38 and 1552–58* (1932) · C. L. Oastler, *John Day, the Elizabethan printer* (1975) · R. B. McKerrow, ed., *Printers' and publishers' devices in England and Scotland, 1485–1640* (1949) · C. Garrett, '"The resurreccion of the masse" by Hugh Hilarie—or John Bale (?)', *The Library*, 4th ser., 21 (1940–41), 143–59 · *The diary of Henry Machyn, citizen and merchant-taylor of London, from AD 1550 to AD 1563*, ed. J. G. Nichols, CS, 42 (1848) · Mauvissière to Henri III, 9 Nov 1579, Bibliothèque Nationale, Paris, MS Fonds français 15973, fols. 201v–202 [19th-century copy in PRO, 31/3/27, fol. 410v]

Archives PRO, C2/Elizabeth I S3/5; C2/Elizabeth I S3/48: 1–3 · PRO, KB 29/215, membranes 6, 17, 20, 25, 30 · PRO, KB 27/1271, membrane 3 (Crown side)

Singleton, John (1715–1795), jockey and racehorse trainer, was born at Melbourne, near Pocklington in Yorkshire. Details of his parents are unknown. His early working life was spent in Ross Moor (Yorkshire), first as a cattleherd and then tending horses in Mr Read's stables. Although barely in adolescence he was so skilled that a particularly fine piece of work prompted his employer to reward him with a ewe. Showing great business acumen Singleton sold the ewe's offspring, using the money to pay for a racehorse, Smiling Tom, to cover a mare belonging to Mr Read. The resulting foal proved to be an excellent horse which Singleton rode to victory in numerous races throughout the north. By then Mr Read was employing him to ride his best mounts, and in 1732 Singleton won His Majesty's Hundred Guineas race at Hambleton. This proved to be the first of many triumphs for Singleton, who established himself as one of the best jockeys of his day.

Typically for his time, Singleton was not sparing in his use of the whip, and Mr Read's horse Jack-come-tickle-me was so named because Singleton had informed him that the animal 'ran better for being tickled (whipped)' (Cook, 1.207). Singleton's expertise attracted the attention of the second marquess of Rockingham, who made him both his rider and trainer, and was rewarded by victories in a string of major races. Throughout his career, which spanned over fifty years, Singleton rode for only two owners, Mr Read and Rockingham. An indication of his status can be gleaned from the remarks of the Jockey Club's historian, Robert Black, who declared that although Mr Read was one of the founder members of the club 'his chief title to commemoration is that he introduced to the turf the celebrated jockey John Singleton' (Black, 130).

In 1769 Singleton married the widow of the jockey Peter Jackson; they had one son, John. Singleton took immense trouble to preserve his health, and remained very fit. At the age of fifty-seven he had a riding weight of just 8 stone 7 lb. Towards the end of his life contemporaries recorded that 'old John could lift a full glass of port without a tremor, for his head and nerves remained as cool as his chest and arms strong and solid' (Cook, 2.353). He made a significant amount of money from horseracing and 'founded the fortunes of his family at Great Givendale, where he was universally loved' (ibid.). He died at Ross Moor in 1795 and was buried in the same church there as his deceased employer, Mr Read. This was in accordance with both their wishes.

John Singleton (1775/6–1802), jockey, was the son of a nephew of the first John Singleton, also named John, and who had also ridden successfully for Lord Rockingham. Although the life and career of the third John Singleton were much briefer than his great-uncle's he rivalled him in fame. His greatest successes came in 1797 when he won both the Derby, riding the duke of Bedford's mount, and the St Leger, on a horse belonging to Lord Fitzwilliam. He was very well regarded by both the nobles and gentlemen who employed him, and his death in an accident at Newmarket at the age of twenty-six was 'sincerely lamented by those who had the pleasure of his acquaintance' (*Sporting Magazine*, 255). While the first and the third John Singletons were the most successful jockeys of the dynasty, they were followed by three other Singleton brothers, Thomas Jackson, Kirton, and Leonard Jewison. Although all three were successful, Leonard Singleton, despite having only one eye, won more Gold Cup races than the others. Also, 'in spite of heavy "wasting", not only in the saddle but in a chancery suit as well, he lived till he was 93' (The Druid, 200).   ADRIAN N. HARVEY

Sources T. A. Cook, *A history of the English turf*, 6 vols. (1901–5) • The Druid [H. H. Dixon], *The post and the paddock: with recollections of George IV, Sam Chiffney, and other turf celebrities* (1856) • R. Black, *The Jockey Club and its founders* (1891) • *Sporting Magazine*, 21 (1803), 255
Likenesses engraving, repro. in Cook, *History of the English turf*, vol. 2, p. 352
Wealth at death founded fortunes of family at Great Givendale, Yorkshire: Cook, *History of the English turf*, vol. 2, division 2, p. 353

Singleton, John (1775/6–1802). *See under* Singleton, John (1715–1795).

Singleton, Sir John Edward (1885–1957), judge, was born on 18 January 1885 at St Michael-on-Wyre, Lancashire, the third son of George Singleton, farmer, of Howick House, Preston, and his wife, Eleanor Parkinson. He was educated at the Royal Grammar School, Lancaster, and Pembroke College, Cambridge, where he obtained third classes in both parts of the law tripos (1904–5) and became an honorary fellow in 1938. He read for the bar first in Lincoln's Inn, afterwards in Liverpool, and was called at the Inner Temple in 1906, when he joined the northern circuit. He quickly built up a reputation as a junior before his career was interrupted by the war, in which he served in France and Belgium in the Royal Field Artillery, was mentioned in dispatches, and rose to the rank of captain. On his return to his practice he soon acquired a large common-law business based on Liverpool and was principally engaged on the northern circuit until in 1922 he took silk and accordingly moved to London, although he never lost contact with, or wavered in his devotion to, his native county. In the same year (1922) he fought the Lancaster division as a Conservative and defeated his Labour opponent, Fenner Brockway, by a large majority; but in 1923 he lost his seat to the Liberal candidate and never afterwards returned to politics. His success in his profession continued and he became a prominent leader of the common-law bar. He was a judge of appeal, Isle of Man (1928–33), and recorder of Preston (1928–34).

A keen, straightforward advocate, devoted to his art and thoroughly competent, Singleton had the highest of standards. In two lectures to students at the instance of the Council of Legal Education and published in book form as *Conduct at the Bar* (1933) he set forth his views on the true professional spirit and the conduct required of a barrister. For many years each student called by the Inner Temple was handed a copy of this book which was consequently in the possession of many hundreds of barristers throughout the Commonwealth; it was not only a valuable work of instruction but a memorial of the esteem in which Singleton was held as an exemplar of the art of advocacy in the courts. The profits went to the Barristers' Benevolent Association.

Singleton was appointed a judge of the King's Bench Division (with a knighthood) in 1934 and a lord justice of appeal (and sworn of the privy council) in 1948, in which office he served until his death, becoming at the end of his career the senior lord justice in the Court of Appeal. In 1949 he received an honorary LLD from the University of Liverpool. Soon after he was appointed judge he was called on to try Dr Buck Ruxton on a charge of the murder of his wife, Isabella, at Manchester assizes. This sensational trial in which eminent counsel were engaged lasted no less than eleven days, at the end of which the accused was convicted.

As a judge Singleton will be remembered as a man of stout Lancastrian common sense, ready to apply the law as he understood it, if possible in the simplest manner, without recourse to subtlety, and anxious at all times to do justice. He may not have had a profound interest in the law as a science, but he was none the less well equipped for his work, for his mind never deviated from the purpose of doing justice in the particular case with which he had to deal. He was not concerned to extend the law or to be remembered for the grace of his judgments but rather to perform what he had to do, not so much as a jurist or a craftsman, but as a just and workmanlike professional. He carried out the judicial task as best he could and continued to find satisfaction in it until the end of his life. He would no doubt like to be remembered as a no-nonsense judge, ready to listen patiently to evidence and to argument, yet intolerant of waste of time or any lapse from the standard of conduct which he expected from the bar.

Singleton became a bencher of his inn in 1929 and in due course treasurer in the year (1952) in which the queen laid the foundation stone for the new buildings to replace those destroyed in the war. He was always devoted in serving the inn for which he had an enduring affection and in which he made his home during the last years of his life.

In the Second World War, Singleton gave valuable service in connection with government inquiries into submarine services, the production of stabilized bomb-sites, and the comparative strength of British and German air forces. In December 1945 he was appointed British chairman of the Anglo-American Palestine commission; this was perhaps the most important of his public services outside his judicial work.

Singleton never married. He was a sturdy and affectionate friend, full of fun, and popular within and without his profession. He enjoyed life in all its aspects, was a keen though indifferent golfer and a good shot, and during the shooting season spent as much time as he could on the Yorkshire moors. It was shortly after returning from a day's shooting on the moors near Pateley Bridge which he loved so well that he died, at the hospital, Lytham, Lancashire, on 6 January 1957.　　HODSON, *rev.* ALEC SAMUELS

Sources personal knowledge (1971) · private information (1971) · *Law Journal* (25 Jan 1957), 62 · *The Times* (7 Jan 1957)
Likenesses W. Stoneman, photograph, 1935, NPG
Wealth at death £83,721 4s. 2d.: probate, 4 April 1957, CGPLA Eng. & Wales

Singleton, Robert (d. **1544**), clergyman, probably belonged to the Singletons of Single Hall, Lancashire. From 1516 he was vicar of Preston and in 1517 he went up to Oxford, moving thence to Cambridge where he was admitted bachelor of canon law in 1521/2. By 1533 he was in the service of Thomas Cromwell, who was to use him as a preacher against purgatory and monasticism; by 1535 he was a chaplain to Anne Boleyn, and that year he became arch-priest of St Martin's-le-Grand, Dover. A sermon he preached at Paul's Cross in 1536 was subsequently published. Singleton pursued advancement through informing Cromwell of the activities of traditionalist clergy and through ostentatious displays of his learning; he wrote several religious and philosophical treatises, most of which are lost, though a treatise 'De septem ecclesiis' ascribed to him by Bale probably survives in BL, Royal MS 18 A.xl. On 8 July 1543 he abjectly recanted unspecified heresies, calling himself 'an unlearned fantastycall foole' (Guildhall MS 9531/12, fol. 45r); this was partly due to his writings, which may also have brought about his execution for treason at Tyburn on 7 March 1544. Bale believed he was condemned for a treatise, since lost, containing an inflammatory exposition of certain prophecies. However, Singleton was involved in murkier matters: about April 1543 he was apparently plotting with Cranmer's agent John Twyne to conceal evidence of heresy in Kent. Bishop Gardiner later reminded Protector Somerset of the threat which 'Singletons conspiracye' had posed (*Letters*, ed. Muller, 422). Foxe called him a martyr, but his fellow penitent Robert Wisdom dismissed him as 'more to be pitied, then regarded' (Cambridge, Emmanuel College, MS 261, fol. 93v).　　ALEC RYRIE

Sources C. Haigh, 'The Reformation in Lancashire to 1558', PhD diss., University of Manchester, 1969 · S. Brigden, *London and the Reformation* (1989) · LP Henry VIII, 6, no. 422; 8, no. 600; 10, nos. 612, 640 · CCC Cam., MS 128, pp. 329, 359 · R. Singleton, 'A lityll tytilling by yor orator Robert syngleton', 1538, BL, Cotton MS Cleopatra E.v, fols. 407–8 · Emden, *Oxf.*, 4.517 · Wood, *Ath. Oxon.*, new edn, 1.144 · GL, MS 9531/12, fol. 45r · *The letters of Stephen Gardiner*, ed. J. A. Muller (1933) · *The acts and monuments of John Foxe*, ed. S. R. Cattley, 8 vols. (1837–41) · R. Wisdom, 'A revocatyon of that shamfull byll that Winchester devised and wisdome reedde', 1543–4, Emmanuel College, Cambridge, MS 261, fols. 88–130 · C. Wriothesley, *A chronicle of England during the reigns of the Tudors from AD 1485 to 1559*, ed. W. D. Hamilton, 1, CS, new ser., 11 (1875) · Bale, *Cat.*, 2.105

Singleton, Robert Corbet (1810–1881), hymn writer, was born on 9 October 1810, the second son of Francis Corbet of Aclare, co. Meath. His father added Singleton to his name in 1820. After attending a series of schools in Dublin, Robert entered Trinity College, where he graduated BA in 1830 and MA in 1833. After his ordination he was appointed first warden of St Columba's College, Rathfarnham, near Dublin, which was opened in 1843. He then proceeded to St Peter's College, Radley, of which he was the first warden (1847–51), and there inaugurated for the boys a rigorous system of religious discipline. While at Radley he published *The Psalter Arranged for Chanting* (1846) and discourses entitled *Uncleanness, the Ruin of Body and Soul* (1850). In 1847 he was admitted *ad eundem* to Trinity College, Oxford. In 1868 he edited, in conjunction with Dr E. G. Monk, *The Anglican Hymn-Book*, which contained nearly thirty original hymns by him, most notably 'With gladsome feet we press', as well as numerous translations from the German and Latin. He died at Petergate, York, on 7 February 1881, and was buried on the 12th in the Corbet vault, St Patrick's Cathedral, Dublin.

D. J. O'DONOGHUE, *rev.* LEON LITVACK

Sources J. Julian, ed., *A dictionary of hymnology*, rev. edn (1907); repr. in 2 vols. (1915) · M. Frost, ed., *Historical companion to 'Hymns ancient and modern'* (1962) · Burial records, St Patrick's Cathedral, Dublin, 12 Feb 1881 · CGPLA Ire. (1881)
Archives NL Ire., priv. coll., corresp. as warden of St Columba's · Radley College, archives, corresp. and papers
Wealth at death under £450: probate, 2 March 1881, CGPLA Eng. & Wales

Singleton, Thomas (1783–1842), Church of England clergyman, born on 25 July 1783, was the only son of Thomas Anketell Singleton, of the family of Fort Singleton in Monaghan, and lieutenant-governor of Fort Landguard in Suffolk, and his wife, a daughter of Francis *Grose the antiquary. He was educated at Eton College from about 1797 and matriculated from Corpus Christi College, Cambridge, in 1800, graduating BA in 1804 and MA in 1826. Singleton was ordained deacon in February 1807 and priest in September 1807. At Eton he acquired the friend-ship of Hugh, Earl Percy (afterwards third duke of North-umberland). Singleton acted as the earl's tutor at Cambridge, and was his private secretary from 1813 onwards. In 1812 the earl presented Singleton to the rectory of Elsdon, and in 1826 he was appointed archdeacon of Northumberland and rector of Howick. In 1829 he became a prebendary of Worcester, and in 1830 received the honorary degree of LLD from Dublin University.

In 1837 Singleton requested Sydney Smith to give his opinion on the recently appointed ecclesiastical commission, and became the archdeacon to whom Smith addressed his published letters on ecclesiastical reform, denouncing the commission and its works. Singleton was also a friend of Robert Peel, usually spending a week with Peel at Tamworth during his residence as canon of Worcester. Singleton died, unmarried, at Alnwick Castle on 13 March 1842.　　　　E. I. CARLYLE, *rev.* ELLIE CLEWLOW

Sources Venn, *Alum. Cant.* · *GM*, 2nd ser., 17 (1842), 560

Archives BL, corresp. with Lord Francis Leveson-Gower, Add. MSS 40366, 40338

Sinha, Satyendra Prasanno, first Baron Sinha (1863–1928), politician, was born on 24 March 1863 at the village of Raipur in the Birbhum district of Bengal, the youngest son of Sitikantha Sinha, a Kayastha *zamindar* and middle-ranking bureaucrat. He passed the entrance examination from Birbhum Zilla school, entering Presidency College with a scholarship in 1878. In 1880 he married Gobinda Mohini (*d.* 1938), daughter of Kristo Chunder Mitter, a landowner; they had four sons and three daughters. He left for England in 1881 without taking a degree. Owing to the prejudice which still prevailed against travel overseas his preparations for departure had to be made in secret, and he arrived in England with insufficient means; but the scholarships and prizes he won relieved him from financial difficulty. In 1886 he was called to the bar by Lincoln's Inn, and returned to Calcutta where he joined the City College as lecturer in law and also began to practise as a barrister.

Sinha soon built up a large practice, and in 1903 was appointed standing counsel to the government of India. In 1905 he was appointed to officiate as advocate-general of Bengal, and was confirmed in the post in 1908, the first Indian to fill the position. He was thus the constitutional legal adviser of the governments of both India and Bengal during the agitation against the partition of Bengal in which many of his friends and associates were taking part. It is a tribute to his personality and reputation for integrity that he retained the respect of his countrymen as well as the British authorities.

In 1909 Lord Morley appointed Sinha to be legal member of the governor-general's executive council. No Indian had previously been a member of the government of India, sharing collective responsibility for the policy of the government. The appointment of an Indian to this post was not universally welcomed, but the manner in which Sinha discharged his duties produced general satisfaction. He resigned over differences with his colleagues regarding a bill to control the press, but later withdrew the resignation. He was, however, suffering huge losses financially, and so he returned to the bar in 1910, experiencing little difficulty in resuming his practice. He was knighted in 1914.

The Indian National Congress elected Sinha its president in 1915. Sir Lawrence Hugh Jenkins persuaded its leaders that the cause of Indian self-government would be advanced by the election of an Indian universally trusted by the English. Sinha, reluctant at first, eventually accepted the office at the request of his friend B. N. Basu. A member of the Indian National Congress from 1896, Sinha was a moderate nationalist with a firm faith in constitutional methods. He believed that India should achieve autonomy within the British empire through 'gradual evolution and cautious progress'. For him, a time when Britain would not be the paramount power in India was unthinkable. His faith in British rule was matched by his belief in India's right to govern herself. In his presidential address to the Congress he put forward a reasoned plea for an authoritative definition of the ultimate goal of British policy for India. Montagu's famous declaration of 1917 was partly in response to that plea. The demands set forth by Sinha also emphasized the need for military training and the admission of Indians to the commissioned ranks of the army. He left the Congress with other moderates when Gandhi initiated the non-co-operation movement in 1920.

Sinha became a member of the Bengal executive council in 1917, but was summoned to Britain almost at once and worked with the secretary of state, E. S. Montagu, first as an assistant, and then as a member of the imperial war cabinet and conference, sharing the deliberations for the settlement of the peace terms. In 1919 he was sworn of the privy council, made parliamentary under-secretary of state for India, and raised to the peerage as Baron Sinha of Raipur. He piloted the Government of India Act (1919) through the House of Lords.

Lord Sinha returned to India in 1920 in order to take the post of governor of Bihar and Orissa under the new constitution. He held this post for eleven months (1920–21). He was not very happy in his new job because he felt acutely his lack of training for the detailed administration required of a governor. The strain on his health compelled him to take a prolonged rest. Towards the close of 1925 he again began to interest himself in public life, contributing a series of articles to *The Bengalee* (he was a member of its editorial board) pleading the cause of political moderation. In the same spirit he welcomed the Indian statutory commission which was boycotted by virtually all sections of political opinion in India. In 1926 he was appointed to the judicial committee of the privy council in London; but he was twice forced by his health to winter in India, and during the second of these trips he died, on 4 March 1928, at Berhampore in Bengal. His wife survived him.

Lord Sinha's interests lay in his own profession of law. His work for the government was undertaken as public duty furthering the political cause he believed in. Socially he appeared to all who knew him a perfect combination of the culture of East and West; and this favourable opinion was heightened by a modesty which no success could spoil. He would have preferred to refuse many of the honours showered on him, but his sense of duty to his compatriots obliged their acceptance. He received the freedom of the City of London in 1917, took silk in 1918 (the first Indian to do so), was created KCSI in 1921, and in 1926 was made a bencher of Lincoln's Inn.

S. V. FitzGerald, rev. Tapan Raychaudhuri

Sources *Speeches and writings of Lord Sinha* (1919) · *The Times* (6 March 1928) · *Calcutta Weekly Notes* (12 March 1928) · S. P. Sen, ed., *Dictionary of national biography*, 4 vols. (1972–4) [India] · S. Sengupta and A. Basu, eds., *Samsada Banali caritabhidhana* (Calcutta, 1976) · GEC, *Peerage* · *CGPLA Eng. & Wales* (1928)
Archives BL OIOC, official papers relating to the Paris peace conference, MS Eur. F 281 [copies] | CUL, Hardinge MSS, letters to Lord Carmichael and W. R. Gourlay |SOUND BL OIOC · National Archives of India, New Delhi · Nehru Museum, New Delhi
Likenesses photograph, National Library of India, Calcutta · portrait, Legislative Assembly, Calcutta
Wealth at death £538 2s.—effects in England: probate, 17 July 1928, *CGPLA Eng. & Wales*

Sinker, Sir (Algernon) Paul (1905–1977), university teacher and civil servant, was born on 13 April 1905 in Slough, Buckinghamshire, the only child of Robert Sinker (1868–1941), a Church of England clergyman, and his second wife, Jessie Mildred, *née* Barrett (1873–1908). Baptized Algernon after a benefactor in his father's parish, he was always known by his second name, Paul. As his mother died just before his third birthday, he was cared for by two aunts until his father remarried in 1914. He had three halfbrothers from his father's first marriage and a half-sister from the third.

Sinker's family was closely connected with the Church of England, Cambridge University, and India. His grandfather Robert Sinker (1838–1913), the librarian and chaplain of Trinity College, Cambridge, was ordained, as were four of his uncles. Of his three half-brothers, George (1900–1986) was a missionary with the Church Missionary Society in both Ceylon and India, the headmaster of Bishop Cotton School in Simla, the bishop of Nagpur, and then on return to England, assistant bishop of Derby and provost of Birmingham Cathedral. The other two halfbrothers joined the Indian army, one being ordained later in life after an injury suffered while playing polo.

Sinker went to Haileybury College, a school associated with the Indian Civil Service, and then in 1924 to Jesus College, Cambridge, with a Rustat scholarship awarded to sons of the clergy. He was confident both physically and intellectually; although punished initially for 'general uppishness', he became head of school. As an undergraduate he took up mountaineering. Having a good eye for ball games he was competitive; even in later life he did not believe in letting children win and enjoyed beating his younger son at tennis. Having an aversion to seaside holidays, partly as a result of his father's parish being in Southport, Lancashire, from 1908 to 1930, he preferred sailing, climbing, and walking. He was awarded a first in both parts of the classical tripos at Cambridge in 1926 and 1927. Jesus College, thinking his all-round qualities would make him an excellent tutor, sent him for a year (1927–8)

to the University of Vienna and elected him a fellow. Settling into the life of a Cambridge don, in 1929 he married a clergyman's daughter, Ruth Nesta (1903–1998), the elder sister of a mountaineering friend, Jack Longland, later director of education for Derbyshire from 1949 to 1970. The couple had two sons and two daughters. Sinker won the prince consort prize in 1930 and published *An Introduction to Lucretius* in 1937. But for the outbreak of war in 1939 he would probably have remained in Cambridge all his life.

Sinker volunteered in 1940 to be a temporary civil servant and was posted to the Admiralty where after a year in Washington, DC, in 1941–2, he achieved distinction as head of its war registry which operated a worldwide communication system around the clock. His competence attracted the attention of Sir Edward Bridges who, as secretary to the Treasury, was looking for an appropriate person to be the first director of training and education in the Treasury, a post created in 1945 to implement the recommendations of the Assheton committee. He was persuaded not to return to Cambridge and began a second career as a public servant. C. P. Snow wrote that 'as soon as he had a taste of administration. … he enjoyed it … [having] never wholeheartedly enjoyed academic life. He was made for authority' (*The Times*, 21 March 1977).

After serving in the Treasury, Sinker was invited by Bridges to become the chairman of the civil service selection board in January 1950 on the understanding that he would succeed Sir Percival Waterfield as the first civil service commissioner when Waterfield retired in 1951. His principal remit was to manage a reduction in civil service commission staff and expenditure after post-war reconstruction work had been completed. The numbers of staff employed fell from 815 in 1949 to 456 in 1954. As first commissioner he presided over the revision of the Method I syllabus and gave evidence to the royal commission on the civil service. But finding himself somewhat underemployed, especially during the months October to March, he volunteered to serve on working parties. Having been adviser to the Egyptian government in 1950, he went to Sierra Leone in 1952 to investigate the salary structure of its civil service. He was knighted in 1954.

Sinker found fulfilment in June 1954 on becoming director-general of the British Council. His name had been kept in reserve by Bridges while the council's executive committee tried to secure first Sir Robert Fraser, who became director-general of the Independent Television Authority, and then Sir Alexander Clutterbuck, whose health had suffered while in the Commonwealth service in tropical climates. His remit on this occasion was to manage an expansion, not a contraction, because the government was expected to implement the recommendations of the Drogheda committee's investigation into overseas information services. He had to wait until 1957 for what he called 'the Hill expansion', the increased allotment to the British Council supervised by Charles Hill as chairman of the cabinet committee on overseas information services. He succeeded in bringing Bridges into the council as its chairman in 1959.

Working in close harmony with Bridges for nine years

Sinker restored the council's morale which had been sapped partly by attacks in the Beaverbrook press. Ministers had not recognized the council as a permanent part of government until 1955 when plans were laid to extend its work in the Middle East. He knew civil service regulations and had a flair for establishment problems, although the pension scheme he negotiated was not as generous as had been hoped. Having been appointed on secondment from the civil service, he identified with the council by becoming a member of its staff in 1959. On his retirement in 1968 the deputy director-general said that 'he had brought many Roman gifts … law, straight roads and a great Empire' (Donaldson, 197).

Sinker moved to Shrewsbury in order to be near two of his children and the Welsh hills, but he continued to travel to London regularly, particularly while he was chairman of the Council for Small Industries in Rural Areas, from 1968 to 1976. He died on 26 February 1977 at Stone House, Kingsland, near Leominster, Herefordshire. He was buried in Kingsland.   J. M. LEE

Sources Burke, *Peerage* (1959) • *The Haileybury register*, 9th edn (1862–1973), 189 • *The Times* (1 March 1977), 16g • *The Times* (3 March 1977), 16h • *The Times* (21 March 1977), 21f • *Annual Report* [Jesus College, Cambridge] (1977) • *Civil Service Commission Reports* (1953–6) • PRO, T 273/26, 76; FO 371/80365; CO 554/406–408; CSC 11/245 • A. J. S. White, *The British Council: the first twenty-five years* (1965) • F. Donaldson, *The British Council: the first 50 years* (1984) • *CGPLA Eng. & Wales* (1977) • private information (2004) [daughter, Dr. P. A. Ovenden]
Likenesses photograph, repro. in Donaldson, *British Council* • photographs, priv. coll.
Wealth at death £18,318: probate, 31 Aug 1977, *CGPLA Eng. & Wales*

Sinklar, Anders. *See* Sinclair, Andrew (1555–1625).

Sinnett, Alfred Percy (1840–1921), journalist and theosophist, was born on 18 January 1840, the son of Edward W. Percy Sinnett (*d.* 1845), journalist, and his wife, Jane, a historian and translator. Educated at London University School, Sinnett joined his father's profession in 1859 by becoming assistant sub-editor of the *Globe*. After holding positions on other London papers, he was named editor of the *Hong Kong Daily Press* in 1865. Back in London three years later, he became leader writer on the *Standard*. In 1870 he married Patience, daughter of Richard Edensor of Shaw Wood, Derbyshire; she became his partner in occult inquiries.

The Sinnetts left England in 1872, when he was appointed editor of the *Pioneer of India*, an Anglo-Indian daily. In India, they fell under the influence of Helena Petrovna Blavatsky who, having arrived there in 1879, recognized the Sinnetts as promising potential converts to her new religion of theosophy (the couple had previous experience of spiritualist séances and practices). Blavatsky favoured Sinnett with letters allegedly dispatched to him by her own superhuman Mahatmas. Drawing on these 'Mahatma letters', he published *The Occult World* (1881) and *Esoteric Buddhism* (1883) to disseminate Blavatsky's divine wisdom; both works attracted considerable attention in the English-speaking world and went through numerous editions.

In 1883 the Sinnetts returned permanently to London, where they rose so rapidly in theosophical circles that, the following year, the *Pall Mall Gazette* described Sinnett as 'the chief theosophist of the London branch of true believers' (26 April 1884). When Blavatsky moved to London in 1887, she inevitably eclipsed his leadership, and, until her death in 1891, the two led rival theosophical lodges, with competing claims to monopolize theosophical truth. Sinnett challenged, for example, Blavatsky's condemnation of the spiritualist belief in communications from the deceased; he was particularly anxious to embrace that possibility after his wife's death in 1908. By then Sinnett had become vice-president of the international Theosophical Society, and until his death he tirelessly promoted his version of occult knowledge, publishing some twenty books and articles on various aspects of spirit development. Condemning western science for its materialism, he sought to revitalize it with the esoteric knowledge of the East. If Sinnett finally recognized that his 'Mahatma letters' were Blavatsky's handiwork, he still believed in cosmic forces that scientists could never quantify. From 1904 to 1907 he published a monthly periodical—*Broad Views*—to challenge 'conventional habits of thought', as the title-page proclaimed. He died on 26 June 1921 at his home, 47 Ladbroke Grove, London.

JANET OPPENHEIM

Sources WWW • *The Times* (27 June 1921), 7 • A. P. Sinnett, *The early days of theosophy in Europe* (1922) • A. P. Sinnett, ed., *Incidents in the life of Madame Blavatsky* (1886) • 'More about the theosophists', *Pall Mall Gazette* (26 April 1884), 3–4 • A. T. Barker, ed., *The Mahatma letters to A. P. Sinnett from the Mahatmas M. and K. H.* (1923) • H. E. Hare and W. L. Hare, *Who wrote the Mahatma letters?* (1936) • A. L. Cleather, *H. P. Blavatsky as I knew her* (1923) • A. H. Nethercot, *The first five lives of Annie Besant* (1960) • A. H. Nethercot, *The last four lives of Annie Besant* (1963) • J. Oppenheim, *The other world: spiritualism and psychical research in England, 1850–1914* (1985) • A. Taylor, *Annie Besant: a biography* (1992)
Archives BL, corresp. and papers, Add. MSS 45284–45289 | Theosophical Society archives, Adyar, Madras, India
Wealth at death £3216 11s. 7d.: probate, 12 Aug 1921, *CGPLA Eng. & Wales*

Sinnich, John (1603–1666), theologian, was born in Cork of Roman Catholic parents, Maurice Sinnich and Eleanor Hogan. He was educated at the University of Louvain, where he matriculated as a 'pauper' on 20 January 1624. The following year he obtained the highest marks in the examinations in the arts, and he proceeded to the study of theology, obtaining his doctorate on 27 September 1639. In 1637 he had been appointed to the secondary chair in theology, attached to a prebend in the collegiate church of St Peter, Louvain. After obtaining his doctorate he was presented to a second prebend, at the collegiate church of Turnhout, which he relinquished in 1640 for a canonry of the cathedral of Bruges. In 1641 he became president of the greater theological college at Louvain, and in 1642 regent of the faculty of theology. Following the death of Cornelius Jansen (Jansenius) he helped edit the *Augustinus* for publication (1640) and followed it with his own *Homologia Augustini Hipponensis* (1641), which argued the conformity of Jansen's teaching to that of St Augustine.

After the publication of the papal condemnation of *Augustinus* in the bull *In eminenti* he was one of two emissaries sent to Rome by the Flemish Jansenists to plead, unsuccessfully, the orthodoxy of the work. He returned to Louvain in 1645 and devoted himself to his academic work.

Eleven works, several published pseudonymously, are attributed to Sinnich, a number of which were placed on the Roman index. His best-known work, *Sanctorum patrum … trias* (1648), was used extensively by Pascal, and the French theologian and Jansenist leader Antoine Arnould considered Sinnich the soundest guide on questions of grace after Jansen's death. Sinnich died at Louvain on 8 May 1666, leaving his personal property to the college to found bursaries to maintain students from Ireland at Louvain, Bruges, or Turnhout. He was buried at the collegiate church of St Peter, Louvain.　　　　PAUL ARBLASTER

Sources L. Ceyssens, 'Sinnich (Jean)', *Biographie nationale*, 33, suppl. 15 (1966) · F. Deiniger, *Johannes Sinnich* (1928) · R. Clark, *Strangers and sojourners at Port Royal* (1932) · T. W. Moody and others, eds., *A new history of Ireland*, 3: *Early modern Ireland, 1534–1691* (1976)

Sinnott, William Veitch [*pseud.* Will Sinn] (1960–1991), popular musician, was born on 23 December 1960 at Calderbank House, Baillieston, Lanarkshire, son of William Veitch Sinnott, a foreman joiner, and his wife, Mary Helen (*née* McLeod). By the mid-1980s he was working as a psychiatric nurse in Aberdeen. In this period he developed a fascination with psychosis and altered states of consciousness which he carried through the rest of his life. Through this he met Colin Angus, also a psychiatric nurse, and member of a rock band called the Shamen. Sinnott had previously been bass guitarist with Edith and the Ladies. Success eluded this band, which Angus described as a 'wild, rockist' group. Late in 1987 Sinnott was planning to leave nursing to teach English in Spain. However, the day before his planned departure Angus invited him to take up the recently vacated position of bass player with the Shamen. Sinnott accepted immediately and joined the band in time for its support slot on a tour with the whimsical, lightly Gothic band All About Eve.

The Shamen at this point were a psychedelic rock band with a growing interest in the synthesizer and sequencing technology being used in the burgeoning acid house dance music scene. They married this to polemical lyrics (one track, 'Shitting on Britain', accused Margaret Thatcher, then prime minister, of this act, to the sampled sound of a toilet flushing) and were developing a fine nose for controversy and its attendant publicity. The brewers Scottish and Newcastle, who were major Conservative Party supporters, were planning to use the band's 'Happy Days' to advertise their McEwan's lager, unaware that the song was an anti-Falklands war polemic. The brewery found out at the last minute and pulled the campaign, and the Shamen resisted their attempts to recoup the substantial amount of money already paid out. *Knature of a Girl*, Sinnott's first recorded outing with the band, also proved controversial: the cover, featuring a thermographic image of a semi-naked woman and a sea slug which many interpreted as sexual, was branded pornographic, and the band

anti-feminist. Angus and Sinnott defended their use of the image on libertarian grounds.

Sinnott and Angus quickly found that they shared many interests and beliefs: both held libertarian attitudes to personal morality, particularly on sexual freedom and the use of psychedelic drugs; both had leftist political convictions, and both thought that rock music had much to gain from absorbing the influences of the dance music styles of acid house and hip hop. Their views on drugs, derived on Sinnott's part from his time as a psychiatric nurse, attracted the censorious attention of the British press. Sinnott explained in an interview with *Melody Maker* in February 1989 that he and Angus believed drugs should be classified as addictive or non-addictive rather than legal or illegal, and that the use of psychedelic drugs (LSD, MDMA known as ecstasy, mescaline, and psyilocybin) 'in the right circumstances by the right people, can be life-enhancing'. He also thought that psychiatric nurses ought to have had at least one experience of LSD to gain insights into psychosis and paranoia.

In the summer of 1988 Sinnott and Angus shed the other two members of the Shamen and moved to London to immerse themselves in acid house culture. The result was their album *In Gorbachev We Trust* (1989). Lyrically the polemical tone remained, with the religious right in the USA as a particular target. However, in their paeans to drug experimentation and sexual freedom there was a definite shift towards the personal, and a psychedelically informed positive attitude. Musically the influence of acid house and hip hop was evident in the rhythms and textures of the sounds. The album was a critical success, but a mainstream chart hit was elusive.

Phorward, a mini-album, followed and helped to fund the band's next venture: an attempt to bring the atmosphere of the acid house rave to the rock concert. The show, called Synergy, fused the band's live performance with DJs, strobe and psychedelic lights, smoke machines, and projectors. This clearly owed a debt to Andy Warhol's Exploding Plastic Inevitables of the 1960s, but where these attacked the audience's senses, Synergy aimed to provide an environment of sound, light, and technology conducive to achieving blissful highs.

This achieved further critical acclaim, but the Shamen thirsted after commercial success. To this end they adopted the radio-friendly 7 inch format, rather than the DJ-friendly 12 inch format they had previously favoured. Paradoxically, they were also appropriating the kind of electronically generated and digitally manipulated sounds associated with the avant-garde end of the popular music spectrum. They finally had a top 40 hit-single with 'Hyperreal', which featured Plavka, a highly photogenic female soul singer. It was from their third full-length album, *En-Tact* (1990). Disillusion with post-Soviet politics and with the continuing dominance of the Conservatives in Britain, together with an increasing interest in the self and in altered states of consciousness, removed the political content from the lyrics on this album. Simon Reynolds in the *Melody Maker* criticized the 'sickly humanism' of *En-Tact*'s lyrics, arguing that, since the music was so expressive of the bliss of ecstasy highs, the words were an unnecessary intrusion. Sinnott himself took forward the view that 'the political content of dance music is intrinsic … offering the experience of unity and affinity with others. This experience invalidates liberal, individualistic ideology and creates true political opposition' (Marshall).

By May 1991 the Shamen had remixed the track 'Pro-Gen' from *En-Tact*, which they were planning to release as 'Move any Mountain—Progen 91', and went to the Canary Islands to shoot the promotional video. On 23 May Sinnott went swimming off the coast of Gomera, near Tenerife. He had apparently been warned of the hazardous currents, but he decided to swim there none the less. The currents proved too strong and Sinnott drowned. His body was taken back to Britain.

Angus, in consultation with Sinnott's family and the band's record label, decided to go ahead with the release of 'Move any Mountain' in July 1991. It entered the charts at number 4. The Shamen went on to further commercial success with the album *Boss Drum*, which included 'Ebenezer Goode', a number 1 single. However, the period between 1988 and early 1991 remains the most interesting in the Shamen's career. It was then that they epitomized (and to an extent pioneered) the shift in British popular culture away from rock music towards dance, and away from traditional political protest to an implied personalized politics of drugs, hedonism, and anarchism.

JOHN MCMANUS

Sources P. Lester, cathedral.then.net/shamen [suppl., *Melody Maker*], 15 March 2000 · www.universalshamen.co.uk, 8 Aug 2000 · J. Marshall, 'The Zippies', www.bis.uni-oldenburg.de/~kropp/wiredzip.htm, Sept 2001 · b. cert.

Sinton, John Alexander (1884–1956), soldier and malariologist, was born on 2 December 1884 at Victoria, British Columbia, Canada, the third of the seven children of Walter Lyon Sinton (1860–1930?) and his wife, Isabella Mary, *née* Pringle (1860–1924). His parents were both from the north of Ireland, of Scottish lowland origins, Quakers on his father's side, Presbyterian on his mother's. The family returned to Ulster in 1890 and that remained Sinton's base throughout his much travelled life. Academically gifted from an early age, Sinton attended the Nicholson Memorial School, Lisburn, and the Royal Belfast Academical Institution before graduating MB BCh BAO (Belfast) in 1908, first of his year, adding DPH (Belfast and Cambridge) in 1910 and DTM (Liverpool) in 1911. He was first in the entrance examination for the Indian Medical Service (IMS) and was gazetted lieutenant IMS in July 1911. However, before being posted to India he was seconded for a year as Queen's University research scholar to the Liverpool School of Tropical Medicine where his contact with Sir Ronald Ross may have influenced his later career as a malariologist.

Sinton served with great distinction in the military branch of the IMS from 1912 to 1921, when he transferred to the civil branch in which he served until his retirement in 1936. In the former he saw action in the turbulent

John Alexander Sinton (1884–1956), by Charles H. Halliday, 1947

North-West Frontier Province, in Mesopotamia, Afghanistan, Waziristan, and Turkestan, and was decorated many times, receiving the Victoria Cross in 1916, the OBE, and the Russian order of St George, and was mentioned in dispatches six times. The citation to his VC, awarded during the Mesopotamian campaign, runs:

> For most conspicuous bravery and devotion to duty. Although shot through both arms and through the side, he refused to go to hospital, and remained as long as daylight lasted, attending to his duties under very heavy fire. In three previous actions Captain Sinton displayed the utmost bravery.

During the transcaspian campaign of 1918–19 Sinton commanded an Indian field ambulance which marched through Persia to Turkestan where he became senior medical officer of the Turkestan military mission. Heavy fighting along the Trans-Siberian Railway resulted in casualties among troops already weakened by cholera, typhus, and malaria. The situation was exacerbated by the 1918 influenza pandemic which left Sinton's unit with no fit men to collect rations. The military hospitals were overwhelmed and sick and wounded overflowed into Russian hospitals. Without Sinton's energy and expert medical knowledge the death rate in this campaign would have been substantially higher.

Although military matters dominated these years,

Sinton found time for research, publishing papers on cholera, leishmaniasis, mosquitoes, and sandflies. Following transfer to the civil branch he was posted to the government of India's principal centre for medical research and vaccine production at Kasauli, in the Punjab, where his academic potential blossomed. Initially Sinton divided his time between the Pasteur Institute and the Central Research Institute, but in July 1921 he was put in charge of the quinine and malaria inquiry under the newly formed central malaria bureau. At Kasauli, Sinton met Eadith Seymour Steuart-Martin (1894–1977), daughter of Edwin Steuart-Martin and Ada May Martin (née Martin), whom he married on 19 September 1923. Their daughter, Eleanor Isabel Mary Sinton, was born at Kasauli on 9 December 1924.

In 1925 Sinton became the first director of the malaria survey of India at Kasauli, a position he held until he retired from the IMS. He was a dynamic leader and established an international reputation for himself and for his unit. He likened India to 'Prometheus bound by chains of apathy to the rock of expediency and financial stringency while the vulture of malaria devours the vitals of her people' (Kitzmiller, 497–9). In his Royal Society obituary Sir Rickard Christophers listed Sinton's contributions to malaria research under three headings: parasites, treatment, and monkey malaria. Sinton made important contributions to the enumeration, identification, pigmentation, and nomenclature of parasites. In the field of treatment he discovered the metabolic effects of quinine, notably hypoglycaemia. By controlled research he distinguished between parasite suppression, which could be followed by recrudescence, and cure which involved parasite elimination, and he defined the principles for the assessment of the efficacy of the antimalarial drugs then being introduced. Drug resistance rendered many of the early synthetic antimalarials useless, and quinine returned to favour. The principles defined by Sinton remain highly relevant in the continuing search for effective antimalarial therapy. The *in vivo* tests for resistance defined by the World Health Organization are based on his ideas. On monkey malaria, Sinton showed that multiple infections and super-infections occurred and that longitudinal studies could detect the presence of more than one plasmodial species in the same host. These observations contributed significantly to an understanding of the mechanisms of immunity in malaria and were still cited in research papers published sixty years later.

After his first retirement Sinton continued malaria research as Manson fellow at the London School of Hygiene and Tropical Medicine and at the malaria laboratory of the Ministry of Health at Horton Hospital, near Epsom. He also became adviser on malaria to the Ministry of Health. With the outbreak of the Second World War, Sinton was recalled as an IMS reservist and commanded a hospital in India. At the age of fifty-five he was again retired, but was appointed consultant malariologist to the east African force and later to Middle East command, retiring with the honorary rank of brigadier in August 1943. Two weeks later he was yet again recalled and appointed consultant malariologist to the War Office, travelling widely to Assam, Australia, Burma, Ceylon, India, New Guinea, and the Solomon Islands, where his expertise in malaria was invaluable. Further military decorations resulted from this period, after which Sinton returned to Northern Ireland and retired to Cookstown. He was elected FRS in 1946.

In his final retirement Sinton's compelling sense of duty was manifested in service to his university and to the local community. At Queen's University, Belfast, he sat on the senate, was pro-chancellor and president of the University Association. He became a JP, high sheriff and deputy lieutenant of co. Tyrone, and held a number of other offices.

Sinton published over 200 scientific papers, many on malaria including a monumental bibliography of 2200 malaria research papers in India from Ross's discovery of the parasite in 1898 up to 1928. Another forty of Sinton's papers were on sandflies and included descriptions of twenty-seven *Phlebotomus* species, sixteen of which were new to science; Sinton named one *Phlebotomus eleanorae* after his daughter, and another *Phlebotomus eadithai* after his wife. Others honoured Sinton by naming three mosquito species, *Aedes sintoni*, *Anopheles sintoni*, and *Anopheles sintonoides*, one sandfly species, *Sergentomyia sintoni*, and one subgenus *Sintonius* of the genus *Phlebotomus*, after him.

Sinton received many awards and was Arnot memorial medallist of the Irish Medical Schools' and Graduates Association (1917); MD (*honoris causa*) of Belfast (1919); honorary fellow of the Ulster Medical Society (1920); DSc of Belfast (1927); Chalmers memorial medallist of the Royal Society of Tropical Medicine and Hygiene (1928); Bisset-Hawkins medallist of the Royal College of Physicians, London (1944); Robert Campbell memorial orator and medallist of the Ulster Medical Society (1946); Mary Kingsley medallist of Liverpool School of Tropical Medicine (1949); and Manson medallist of the Royal Society of Tropical Medicine and Hygiene (1956). He died at his home at Slaghtfreedan Lodge, Cookstown, co. Tyrone, on 25 March 1956 and was buried with full military honours on 28 March at Claggan Presbyterian cemetery in Cookstown. His name is commemorated in a University hall of residence, Sinton Hall, and in Sinton Court, a British Legion home.

Sinton is unique as the only man ever to have been both a holder of the Victoria Cross and a fellow of the Royal Society. In the words of Colonel H. W. Mulligan in an obituary in the *British Medical Journal*: 'Sinton had an exceptionally quick, receptive, and retentive brain, but his greatness sprang not so much from his unusual intellectual gifts as from the simple qualities of absolute integrity and tremendous industry'.   JAMES S. PORTERFIELD

Sources J. A. Sinton, diaries, PRO NIre. · R. Christopher, *Memoirs FRS*, 2 (1956), 269–90 · A. Sachs, 'John Alexander Sinton, V.C., F.R.S. soldier, doctor and scientist', *Ulster Medical Journal*, 41 (1971), 17–32 · *BMJ* (7 April 1956), 806–7 · *The Lancet* (7 April 1956) · *Nature*, 177 (1956), 826 · 'Fourth supplement dated 21st June 1916 to *London Gazette* of 20th June 1916 pp 6191', *Gazette of India*, no. 849 (27 July 1916) [extract from *Gazette of India*] · private information (2004)

[M. W. Service, Liverpool School of Tropical Medicine; V. P. Sharma, Malaria Research Centre, Delhi] · J. B. Kitzmiller, *Anopheline names: their derivations and histories* (1982)
Archives priv. coll. · PRO NIre. | priv. coll.
Likenesses C. H. Halliday, photograph, 1947, RS [*see illus.*] · J. Fairfax Whiteside, oils (on battlefield at Sheikh Sa'ad, Mesopotamia), Royal Army Medical College, Millbank, London · photomechanical print, Wellcome L.
Wealth at death £17,180 16s. 10d.: administration, 28 Oct 1957, *CGPLA NIre.*

Siôn, Syr, ap Rhys. *See* Prise, Sir John (1501/2–1555).

Siôn Cain (d. c.1649). *See under* Rhys Cain (c.1540–1614).

Siôn Cent [John Kent] (*fl.* **1400–1430**), Welsh-language poet, wrote a eulogy to the people and land of Brycheiniog (Brecon) which suggests a link with that area, and, although it was not necessarily his native region, the border area of south Wales was certainly his sphere of activity. Kent was a common enough surname in that area, and is not in itself proof of any link with the parish of Kentchurch in Herefordshire. The portrait at Kentchurch Court once thought to be of Siôn Cent is now known not to be so. Siôn Cent was not a professional bard, but clearly had some bardic training and made effective if unsophisticated use of the *cywydd* metre [*see* Cywyddwyr (act. c.1330–c.1650)]. It has been suggested that he was educated at Oxford University, where he would have been influenced by the empirical philosophy of *scientia experimentalis*, which may have provided a basis for his attack on the Platonic ideals of the Welsh bards. One of his most famous statements is 'Ystad bardd astudio byd' ('The estate of a poet is to study the world'). Learned elements in his poems include references to ecclesiastical authorities such as Peter Lombard and detailed knowledge of the Bible. The only firm basis for dating Siôn Cent's career is his debate with Rhys Goch Eryri, which was a consequence of Rhys's elegy on the death of Gruffudd Llwyd and subsequent debate with Llywelyn ab y Moel in the 1420s. Siôn was not a young man at that time, and it seems therefore that the Glyn Dŵr rebellion and its aftermath was his period of activity, a period which is reflected by the grim spirit of his poetry.

Siôn Cent's critique of Rhys Goch Eryri's work focuses on the claim that the bardic muse was of divine origin, and he argues instead that the falsehoods of praise poetry prove it to be inspired by the devil. In keeping with this rejection of bardic ideals, Siôn Cent's poems ruthlessly demonstrate the worthlessness of all the worldly values celebrated by the bards. Their emphasis is on the transience of life and the horrors of death, with the aim of turning people's attention away from this world to the next. The influence of the preaching friars is clear, and there are many parallels with the religious verse of medieval Europe. Siôn Cent was the first Welsh poet to use the technique of the repeated refrain, which was certainly due to English influence. Although the bards took no account of his moral criticisms of their work, Siôn Cent's influence on Welsh literature of the fifteenth and sixteenth centuries was considerable. There were clearly a number of other poets writing similar verse, whose work is falsely attributed to Siôn Cent in the manuscripts on account of his fame as a religious poet. The attributions total close to one hundred poems, but of these only eighteen are now accepted as genuine.

Siôn Cent the poet was later confused with several other figures of similar name and became a popular character in the folklore of the Welsh marches, famed as a trickster and wizard. Two of these misidentifications, in particular, seem to have contributed to his reputation for learning, namely those with **John Gwent** (d. 1348), Franciscan monk, who died at Hereford, and **John Caerleon** (d. c.1482), also apparently known as John Kent, who is said by Leland to have had a distinguished academic career at Cambridge in the fifteenth century.

DAFYDD JOHNSTON

Sources *Cywyddau Iolo Goch ac eraill*, ed. H. Lewis, T. Roberts, and I. Williams, new edn (1937) · S. Lewis, *Braslun o hanes llenyddiaeth Gymraeg* (1932) · S. Lewis, *Meistri'r canrifoedd: ysgrifau ar hanes llenyddiaeth Gymraeg*, ed. R. G. Gruffydd (1973) · G. Williams, *The Welsh church from conquest to Reformation*, rev. edn (1976) · *Commentarii de scriptoribus Britannicis, auctore Joanne Lelando*, ed. A. Hall, 2 vols. (1709) · J. Pits, *Relationum historicarum de rebus Anglicis*, ed. [W. Bishop] (Paris, 1619)
Archives NL Wales, Peniarth MSS, 53, 54, 55

Siôn Trefor. *See* John Trevor (d. 1410/1412).

Siôn Treredyn. *See* Edwards, John (1605/6–1656).

Siôn Tudur [John Tydder] (c.1522–1602), courtier and Welsh-language poet, was born at the family home, Wigfair, St Asaph, Denbighshire, the son of Tudur ap Dafydd Llwyd and his wife, Margaret, daughter of Ieuan ap Hywel of Mostyn, Flintshire; both parents came of local gentry families and he himself was termed *generosus* (*Wigfair*, 497). As a young man he entered the royal household, served the young Prince Edward, and was retained as yeoman extraordinary when Edward became king in 1547 (BL, Royal MS 7 C XVI, fol. 193). He was probably at the court, at least periodically, during Mary's reign, 1553–8, while references in his poems prove he was in London during the early years of Elizabeth's reign.

As yeoman of the guard, and later yeoman of the crown within the royal palace, Siôn Tudur may have witnessed Elizabeth's coronation and accompanied her on some of her progresses. Yeomen of the crown were not obliged to remain at court; they were allowed to retire to their homes provided they were ready at their sovereign's command should their services be needed. They held the fee of the crown for life (Hennell, 303). It is clear from Siôn Tudur's own words and those of his contemporaries (Bodl. Oxf., MS Jesus College 15, fols. 273–300; NL Wales, Llanstephan MS 36, fols. 127–31) that in his prime, before he became old and lame, he was broad, tall, and handsome, as befitted a guardsman. He was obviously familiar with the cultural life of the court and the city, which may account for the high quality of his own writings.

From the mid-1560s Siôn Tudur seems to have spent more time at home. He was a member of the official order of Welsh poets referred to as Beirdd yr Uchelwyr ('poets of the gentry') so named from their custom of visiting the homes of the gentry, composing greetings, eulogies, and elegies for a fee. He was taught by the great master poet Gruffudd Hiraethog (*d.* 1564) (Bowen, *Gruffudd Hiraethog*, xxxv–xxxix), and at the Caerwys eisteddfod in 1567 graduated as *disgybl pencerddaidd* ('apprentice of the master craft'; Bowen, 'Graddedigion', 131). Contemporary poets in their elegies termed him *pencerdd* ('master craftsman'); if he did acquire this distinction it must have been at a marriage feast as no further eisteddfod was held. He was both poet and patron, visiting the homes of gentry families and welcoming other poets to his home at Wigfair.

A large corpus of Siôn Tudur's poems, from before 1560 to 1601, has survived, scattered, mostly singly, over hundreds of manuscripts in various libraries, mainly the National Library of Wales at Aberystwyth, the British Library, Bangor, Cardiff, and the Bodleian Library, Oxford, with probably no more than three in his own handwriting. Most of his work, in the traditional strict metres, consists of eulogies, elegies, requests, and thanks to some sixty gentry families, together with several love poems. His metrical version of fifteen psalms, composed possibly at the request of Bishop Robinson of Bangor before 1580, was the first attempt in Welsh to versify the psalms. The rest, together with several long poems in free metre, deal with the evils of society, such as usury, avarice, and miserliness, and often bear similarity to the works of London writers such as Robert Greene, Thomas Nash, Thomas Lodge, and Thomas Deloney. However, the fact that some of his poems were written down at an earlier date than the extant published works of the above writers suggests either that all were relying on tracts now lost, or that Siôn Tudur was dealing with topics he had heard discussed in London literary circles. His scathing comments on the contemporary Welsh poets, together with his lament over the death of so many poets, harpists, and crowthers, reveal his concern about the deterioration of the traditional poetic and musical arts. His early works give the impression that he adhered to the Roman faith; by the late 1580s he was a zealous protestant. The claim often made that he held an important clerical office at St Asaph Cathedral derived from a misreading of a manuscript by an eighteenth-century scribe.

Siôn Tudur married Mallt (Matilda), daughter of Pyrs Gruffudd of Llwynyglyniau, Caerwys, Flintshire; they had three children: Thomas, Elizabeth, and Margaret. He died at Wigfair on 3 April 1602 and was buried on 5 April, in the south aisle of the parish church of St Asaph (Thomas, 239). Letters of administration were granted to his widow and son on 20 April 1602 ('St Asaph probate act book', 1593–1602).   ENID ROBERTS

Sources E. Roberts, ed., *Gwaith Siôn Tudur*, 2 vols. (1980) · E. Roberts, 'Siôn Tudur yn Llundain', *Transactions of the Denbighshire Historical Society*, 18 (1969), 50–82 · E. Roberts, 'Rhagor am Siôn Tudur yn Llundain', *Transactions of the Denbighshire Historical Society*, 19 (1970), 103–7 · 'A schedule of the Wigfair deeds and documents', 1973, NL Wales, vols. 2–3 · *Catalogue of Western manuscripts in the old royal and king's collection*, 1, 1921, BL, MS Royal 7 C XVI, fol. 93 · R. Hennell, *The history of the king's body guard of the yeomen of the guard* (1904) · *Report on manuscripts in the Welsh language*, 2 vols. in 7, HMC, 48 (1898–1910), 2/1.1–90 [Jesus College]; 2/2.419–782 [Plas Llanstephen] · D. J. Bowen, ed., *Gwaith Gruffudd Hiraethog* (1990) · D. J. Bowen, 'Graddedigion eisteddfodau Caerwys, 1523 a 1567/8', *Llên Cymru*, 2 (1952–3), 129–34 · *Mynegai i farddoniaeth gaeth y Llawysgrifau*, University of Wales, Board of Celtic Studies, 11 (1978), 3741–94 · D. R. Thomas, ed., *Y cwtta cyfarwydd* (1883) · 'St Asaph probate act book', 1593–1602, NL Wales

Wealth at death value unknown; Wigfair estate

Siôn y Potiau. *See* Edwards, John (*bap.* 1699?, *d.* 1776).

Siraj ud-Daula (*d.* 1757). *See under* Bengal, nawabs of (*act.* 1756–1793).

Sirr, Henry Charles (1764?–1841), police officer, born in Dublin Castle probably on 25 November 1764, was fifth, but eldest surviving, son of Major Joseph Sirr (1715–1799), who, on retiring from the army after twenty years' service, was appointed to the post of chief of the Dublin police or town-major in 1761, and served as high sheriff of the county in 1771. His mother was Elizabeth, daughter of William Hall of Skelton Castle, Yorkshire. Sirr entered the army on 6 June 1778 as an ensign in the 68th regiment of foot; subsequently he was lieutenant in the same regiment, which he accompanied in 1782 to Gibraltar. In 1791 he quitted the service, and was engaged as a wine merchant in Dublin, where he lived successively in French Street and at 77 Dame Street. In the same year he married Elizabeth, daughter of James D'Arcy of Hyde Park, co. Westmeath. They had two sons and two daughters.

In 1796, upon the formation of yeomanry in Dublin, Sirr volunteered and was appointed acting town-major or head of the police, and thenceforward was the chief agent of the castle authorities. In 1798 he was promoted to the position of town-major, and received a residence in Dublin Castle. He proved very active in political repression, and organized an extensive system of spies and informers. He successfully arrested Peter Finnerty, the editor of *The Press*, on 31 October 1797, and was concerned in almost every important capture during the troubled years from 1798 to Emmet's insurrection in 1803. During this period his life was often in serious peril; on no fewer than three occasions in 1798 he barely escaped the attacks of the United Irishmen. The part Sirr played in the capture of Lord Edward Fitzgerald on 19 May 1798 brought him most prominently before the public. In the affray on that occasion Sirr, in coming to the aid of Daniel Frederick Ryan, inflicted on Lord Edward the wound from which he died. In 1802, in the case of *Hevey* v. *Sirr*, he was sued for £5000 damages for false imprisonment, and was held up to execration by Curran, the counsel for the plaintiff. The jury found a verdict against him for £150 and 6*d.* costs, but the government paid Sirr's legal expenses. On 25 August 1803 he was instrumental in the arrest of Robert Emmet and the other insurrectionary leaders. In 1808 Sirr was appointed a police magistrate for the city of Dublin. He continued to discharge his duties as town-major until 1826, when he retired upon full pay, and in consideration of his services was allowed to retain his official residence in Dublin Castle.

Sirr devoted his leisure to collecting curiosities and antiquities. His collection, which included some five hundred paintings, was of considerable value, and was acquired after his death by the Royal Irish Academy. In 1818 he helped to found the Irish Society for Promoting Scriptural Education in the Irish Language. He was an evangelical and an active freemason, and in 1797 joined the Orange order. He died at Dublin Castle on 7 January 1841, and was buried in the graveyard of St Werburgh's, Dublin, in close proximity to Lord Edward Fitzgerald. Sirr transformed the office of town-major from a sinecure into a vital and efficient cog in the Dublin Castle machinery. The authorities came to rely upon him to an extraordinary degree, and he was highly esteemed by them. Robert Peel testified in the House of Commons that Sirr was unswervingly loyal, religious, and humane. Castlereagh also praised 'the unceasing activity of Major Sirr'.

Sirr intended to destroy all his correspondence; but a number of documents, many of them of considerable historical interest, were found after his death, and presented by his elder son to the library of Trinity College, Dublin, where they remain.

Sirr's elder son, **Joseph D'Arcy Sirr** (1794–1868), a graduate of Trinity College, Dublin, rector of Ringwood, and afterwards (1859) of Morstead in Hampshire, was the author of a *Memoir of Power le Poer Trench, Last Archbishop of Tuam* (1845), of *Sacrifices, Past, Present, and Future* (1862), and of a *Life of Archbishop Usher*, prefixed to *The Religion of the Ancient Irish* (1835), in addition to some minor religious works. He died at Winchester on 5 April 1868. The younger son, **Henry Charles Sirr** (1807–1872), of Lincoln's Inn, barrister, was successively British vice-consul at Hong Kong (1843) and queen's advocate for the southern circuit of Ceylon; he was the author of two works of interest, *China and the Chinese: their Religion, Character, Customs, and Manufactures* (1849), which dealt with the evils of the opium trade, and *Ceylon and the Cingalese: their History, Government, Religion, Antiquities, etc.* (1850).

C. L. FALKINER, *rev.* PETER GRAY

Sources R. R. Madden, *The United Irishmen: their lives and times*, 3rd ser., 7 vols. (1842–6) · J. Smyth, *The men of no property* (1992) · T. Pakenham, *The year of liberty: the story of the great Irish rebellion of 1798* (1969) · *GM*, 2nd ser., 15 (1841), 222 · *The Times* (11 Jan 1841) · *Freeman's Journal* [Dublin] (8 Jan 1841)
Archives TCD, papers relating to United Irishmen | BL, corresp. with Sir Robert Peel, Add. MSS 40222–40408, *passim*
Likenesses J. Martyn, engraving, NL Ire. · engraving, repro. in *Irish Magazine* (Dec 1810), 550 · print, BM · print (after ivory relief by W. Ewing), BM
Wealth at death under £2000—Joseph D'Arcy Sirr: probate, 1868

Sirr, Henry Charles (1807–1872). *See under* Sirr, Henry Charles (1764?–1841).

Sirr, Joseph D'Arcy (1794–1868). *See under* Sirr, Henry Charles (1764?–1841).

Sisley, Alfred (1839–1899), landscape painter, was born at 19 rue des Trois Bornes in the 11th *arrondissement* of Paris on 30 October 1839, into a family of Anglo-French descent, the younger son and second of four children of William Sisley (1799–1879), a dealer in imported luxury goods, and his wife and cousin, Felicia Sell (1808–1866), daughter of a saddler from Lydd, Kent. He was educated in Paris. Sisley retained the British nationality inherited from his parents, although he made two unsuccessful attempts in 1889 and 1898 to become a naturalized French citizen. He lived in France all his life and, apart from three years spent in London (1857–60) studying commerce, when he may have become aware of the work of Constable, only visited Britain for short painting expeditions on three other occasions in 1874 (July–October), 1881 (June) and 1897 (July–September). On the first of these brief visits Sisley explored the River Thames, painting for example *Bridge at Hampton Court* (Wallraf Richartz Museum, Cologne) and *Molesey Weir—Morning* (NG Scot.).

From *c.*1860 to 1863 he attended the atelier of the Swiss painter Charles Gleyre in Paris. He then moved out of Paris and lived in villages near the River Seine to the west of the capital—Louveciennes, Marly-le-Roi, and Sèvres—but in 1880 he returned to the area south-east of the forest of Fontainebleau, where he had first painted during the 1860s, and subsequently lived in a series of villages near the confluence of the rivers Loing and Seine—Veneux-Nadon, Les Sablons, and Moret-sur-Loing. These movements are significant for an understanding of Sisley's work.

Sisley was an impressionist painter and exhibited in five of the eight impressionist exhibitions held at irregular intervals between 1874 and 1886. During the 1890s he occasionally exhibited with Les Vingt in Brussels and more regularly with the Société Nationale des Beaux-Arts in Paris. Neither during his lifetime nor since have Sisley's paintings achieved the popularity of those by Monet, Renoir, or even Camille Pissarro, with all of whom he helped to develop the impressionist style. Consequently, he experienced considerable financial hardship which was exacerbated towards the end of his life by illness. For sales he relied upon dealers in Paris such as Paul Durand-Ruel, Georges Petit, and Goupil Boussod-Valadon, as well as upon a small group of patrons such as François Depeaux of Rouen, Henri Vever, and Edmond Decap, but financial success eluded him. On the other hand, certain young critics, especially Adolphe Tavernier (1853–1945), did extol the virtues of Sisley's work. Tavernier remains one of the principal sources for our appreciation of Sisley's style and technique.

Sisley was principally a landscape painter and there are very few still lifes or portraits in an *œuvre* that amounts to some 900 pictures. Drawings and prints by his hand are limited in number, although he was an able practitioner in pastel, which he began to use during the 1880s. Several of Sisley's early paintings dating from the second half of the 1860s were accepted for display in the official Salon, but during the 1870s he began to paint in a fully fledged impressionist style characterized by pure colours applied with broken brush strokes and intense light. Several of his finest works date from these years. Like many of the impressionists, Sisley experienced stylistic difficulties towards the end of the 1870s, but he remained faithful to the technique of impressionism. His mature landscapes are notable for the broad, low horizons, expansive skies, fugitive effects of light, vibrant colours (blue, violet, yellow, red), and rhythmical brushwork. Sisley often painted motifs in series, notably the church at Moret-sur-Loing in 1893 and 1894, inspired by Monet's views of the façade of Rouen Cathedral. During the last two decades of his life Sisley remained independent, although not unaware, of developments in Paris. His work retained a pronounced individuality and originality that has perhaps yet to be properly acknowledged.

During the early 1860s Sisley met (Marie Louise Adélaide) Eugénie Lescouezec (1834–1898), with whom he had one son, Pierre (*b*. 1867), and one daughter, Jeanne (*b*. 1869). The couple were not formally married, however, until 5 August 1897 in Cardiff. Sisley died of cancer of the throat at his home, 19 rue Montmartre, Moret-sur-Loing, on 29 January 1899, his wife having predeceased him in October 1898. He was buried in Moret-sur-Loing cemetery on 1 February 1899.   CHRISTOPHER LLOYD

Sources R. Shone, *Sisley* (1992) · I. Cahn and M. A. Stevens, *Alfred Sisley* (RA, 1992) [exh. cat.] · F. Daulte, *Alfred Sisley: catalogue raisonné de l'oeuvre peint* (1959) · C. Sisley, 'The ancestry of Alfred Sisley', *Burlington Magazine*, 91 (1947), 248–52 · J. Rewald, *The history of impressionism*, 4th revised edn (1973) · J. Turner, ed., *The dictionary of art*, 34 vols. (1996)
Likenesses A. Renoir, oils, 1868, Zürich Bührle Foundation · A. Renoir, oils, 1874, Art Institute of Chicago

Sismondi, Jean-Charles Léonard de (1773–1842), economist and historian, was born on 9 May 1773 in Geneva, the son of Gédéon Simonde, a protestant pastor and grandson of a first syndic of Geneva, and his wife, Henriette, *née* Girod, a lady of means. His father's family had migrated from Dauphiné to Switzerland after the revocation of the edict of Nantes and were citizens of Geneva, where the young Jean-Charles was well educated. Being intended for commerce he was apprenticed as a banker's clerk in Lyons, but the 1792 revolution in Switzerland led him to accompany his family in their flight to London, where he spent eighteen months in exile. This period enabled him to learn English, to study British constitutional politics, and to become acquainted with new historical and economic writing. On returning to Geneva both father and son were the subject of heavy fines and shortly afterwards emigrated to a small farm at Pescia, near Lucca, in Tuscany. Jean-Charles had noted the similarity of his father's (Simonde) family arms with those of the sometime flourishing old Pisan house of Sismondi, and subsequently added that name to his, calling himself Simonde de Sismondi, the latter name alone eventually establishing itself as that by which he is generally known. In Tuscany, Sismondi engaged actively in farming work, but, as a French-speaking person, he encountered hostility locally and returned to Geneva before 1800, where he settled for the rest of his life.

Sismondi's career as a writer started with his *Tableau de l'agriculture toscane* (1801), based on his recent experiences. It was quickly followed by his first book on political economy, *Traité de la richesse commerciale* (1803). After a period as secretary of the département du Léman, during which he assembled useful statistics, he was offered academic chairs in other countries but remained in Geneva, first as professor of philosophy and then of history. Early a follower of Adam Smith and one of his first publicists on the continent, Sismondi's thought evolved, partly through his interest in the role and nature of liberty in society, partly through his comparative studies of societies and literatures. In 1804 he met Madame de Staël and, closely associated with her and her circle at Coppet (even if some, like Schlegel, were not to his liking), he accompanied the writer on her tours of Italy and Germany. Sismondi also made the acquaintance of the elderly countess of Albany, the widow of the Young Pretender, and engaged in an extensive correspondence with her. His sixteen-volume *Histoire des républiques italiennes du moyen âge* (1807–17) established his international reputation as a descriptive historian who, while concentrating on the institutions which (rather than climate) he saw as forming the character of a people, was vague in explanations and essentially interested in the general idea of liberty. The book, a favourite work with Macaulay, did much to create the modern interest in the Renaissance and thus promoted a sense of national unity in Italy, becoming thereby a work of inspiration for the Risorgimento. It was translated into English in 1832. An indefatigable writer, he followed this up with a four-volume study *De la littérature du midi de l'Europe* in 1813. This book, inspired by the ideas of Madame de Staël and the works of Bouterweck, Schlegel, and Andrès, was a founding book of romantic literary criticism, and covered Arabic influence on southern Europe, Provençal, and medieval French literature, Dante and the early Italian Renaissance writers, as well as early Spanish and Portuguese literature. Translated into English by Thomas Roscoe in 1823, it opened the way for Henry Hallam's *An introduction to the literature of Europe during the fifteenth, sixteenth and seventeenth centuries* (1837–9).

In 1813 Sismondi also visited Paris, surprisingly for the first time. Despite his earlier English leanings and liberal views he now endorsed Napoleon's constitutional ideas and indeed met him, although refusing the Légion d'honneur. In 1814 he published his *Considérations sur Genève dans ses rapports avec l'Angleterre et les états protestants*, a work uniting some of his lifelong interests. Two years after the death of Madame de Staël in 1817, on 15 April 1819, at Hanley, Staffordshire, and after a courtship of several years, he married an Englishwoman, Jessica Allen, the eighth child of John Bartlett Allen of Cresselly, Pembrokeshire, and his wife, Elizabeth, *née* Hensleigh. Two of Jessica's sisters married Josiah Wedgwood and John Wedgwood, and another was the wife of Sir James *Mackintosh. Madame Sismondi's English family was therefore much in the centre of the social and literary life with which her husband had close contact during his various visits to England in 1819, 1820, 1826, 1828, and 1832. There were no children of the marriage. He spent his latter years happily in Geneva and wrote one rather unsuccessful novel, *Julia Sévéra, ou, L'an 442* (1822), together with numerous further historical works, including a Gibbonesque *Histoire de la chute de l'empire romain et du déclin de la civilisation de l'an 250 à l'an 1000* (1835) and a thirty-one volume *Histoire des Français*

(1821–44) which, like most of his works, was translated into English. Sismondi's was a social view of history permeated by a belief in the progressive betterment of humanity. His *Histoire des Français* aimed to be 'un tableau moral, où la nation française pourra toujours reconnaître quels fruits amers a apportés le vice, quels fruits excellents a apportés la vertu' ('A moral painting, in which the French nation will be able to discern which bitter fruits have brought vices and which excellent fruits have led to virtue'). More important was his role both as an economic historian and as a political economist. His earlier works, together with the *Nouveaux principes d'économie politique* (1819), *Études sur la constitution des peuples libres* (1836), and his later *Études sur l'économie politique* (1838), place him among the early writers on the nature and function of economic crises, in particular on overproduction, underconsumption, and the proper use of wealth to increase the general happiness of society, views which won the approbation of both Marx and Keynes. A critic of the way in which capitalism had developed during his lifetime (the introduction of machinery, women and children as a major part of the workforce, longer hours, lower wages, unhygienic new accommodation, unemployment), particularly in England, Sismondi was, however, no socialist. Although he foresaw a split between the bourgeoisie and the workers, he believed in private property and supported small-scale industrial and agricultural developments, always stressing the humanitarian aims of social and economic policy.

Sismondi died in Geneva on 25 June 1842. Seen as an early socialist economist, an influential historical writer, and a liberal who always took the side of the oppressed, be they in France, Italy, or Greece, or Irish Catholics, black slaves, or Hindu farmers, he has attracted increasing academic attention, particularly since the publication of J. R. de Salis, *Sismondi* (1932), and outstandingly in Italy. A Société des Amis de Sismondi was established to publish work by or about him. GILES BARBER

Sources J. R. de Salis, *Sismondi, 1773–1842* (1932) · J. R. de Salis, A. Babel, and W. E. Rappard, *Sismondi: discours* (1943) · G. C. L. Sismondi: epistolario, ed. C. Pellegrini, 4 vols. (Florence, [1933–54]) · C. Pellegrini, *Il Sismondi e la storia delle letterature dell'Europa meridionale* (1926) · W. Maturi, 'Sismondi, Jean-Charles Léonard Simonde de', *Enciclopedia italiana*, 31 (1936) · *The new encyclopaedia Britannica: micropaedia*, 15th edn, 10 (1985) · H. Deonna, 'Sismondi, Jean-Charles Léonard', *Dictionnaire historique et biographique de la Suisse*, 6 (1932)

Sisson, Jeremiah (*bap.* 1720, *d.* 1783/4), maker of mathematical instruments, was born in London and baptized at the Presbyterian chapel in Carter Lane, Blackfriars, on 14 December 1720, the son of Jonathan *Sisson, also a maker of mathematical instruments. By 1740 he was one of his father's workmen. According to the French astronomer Joseph de Lalande, writing in 1763, the elder Sisson was so infirm in his last years that it was Jeremiah who actually made the large mural quadrants for the observatories of Bologna, Paris, and Pisa, and for George Parker, second earl of Macclesfield.

When his father died in June 1747, Jeremiah took over a thriving business and the premises at the corner of Beaufort Buildings, Strand. Though his reputation as a craftsman equalled, if not exceeded, his father's, as a businessman he was a failure, being declared bankrupt in 1751. Lalande wrote of him in 1763:

> Sisson has been several times in prison for failing to pay his workmen; he starts many things and finishes nothing: he takes his instruments to the pawnbroker, where they have been seen selling for a tenth of their value. He is obliged to work in great haste, and so achieves nothing worthwhile, but nevertheless there is no one who has as much ability as he.

Though Sisson's main stock-in-trade was probably small surveying and drawing instruments, it was his large astronomical instruments that made his reputation. He made the zenith sector that Nevil Maskelyne took to St Helena in 1761; all the larger instruments for the king's private observatory at Kew; and instruments for St John's College in Cambridge, Naples, Geneva, Milan, and Mitau in Latvia. In 1759 he prepared drawings and a model of a waterpump to be sent to Italy. In 1772 he was appointed mathematical instrument maker to the Board of Ordnance. His duties included the servicing of the instruments at the Royal Greenwich Observatory and making two new equatorial sectors.

In 1775 Sisson was again declared bankrupt and lost the ordnance appointment. However, Maskelyne, who had a high opinion of his abilities, lent him considerable sums and secured for him commissions for instruments, not only for his own observatory at Greenwich, but also for new instruments for Eger in Hungary, Mannheim, and Florence. Then, in 1780, Sisson was forced to vacate his premises in Beaufort Buildings and to make over the lease and mortgage of his house in Southwark to Maskelyne.

Of Sisson's first marriage nothing is known, but he was described as a widower when he married Ann Sidebotham at St Clement Danes on 1 January 1761, and again when he married Grace Plampin at St Anne's, Soho, on 14 February 1774. Of his death, the only reference found is the entry in Maskelyne's account book for 13 March 1784: 'Recd of Mrs Grace Sisson, thro' the hands of Mr Henry Robin Auctioneer my dividend for £88.14.11 due to me from the Estate of the late Jerh Sisson—£15.0.0—and gave it to the Widow.'

DEREK HOWSE, *rev.*

Sources *Jerome Lalande. Journal d'un voyage en Angleterre, 1763*, ed. H. Monod-Cassidy (1980) · Jean Bernouilli, *Lettres astronomiques* (1771) · N. Maskelyne, account book, 1773–85, Wilts. & Swindon RO · *Journal for the History of Astronomy*, 17/4 (1986) [*The Greenwich list of observatories*, ed. D. Howse] · private information (2004) [J. R. Millburn]

Sisson, Jonathan (1690?–1747), maker of mathematical instruments, was born in Lincolnshire, perhaps in 1690. He went from there to London and was established in a workshop on the corner of Beaufort Buildings in the Strand by 1722, probably having worked for George Graham, with whom he remained on very close terms. In 1725 he was employed by Graham to construct the framework of the 8 foot mural quadrant for Edmond Halley at the Royal Observatory, Greenwich. He was appointed mathematical instrument maker to Frederick, prince of Wales, in April 1729, by which time he had a high reputation, particularly as a maker of surveying instruments, being known especially for his accurate division of scales. He manufactured the wooden quadrants invented by John Elton in 1730 and had a considerable number of these in stock at his death. Edward Saul, in *An Historical and Philosophical Account of the Barometer or Weather-Glass* (1735) wrote:

> it may perhaps be an Inducement to some of the Gentlemen of Lincolnshire, to deal with Mr Jonathan Sisson …; that he is their Country Man, and eminent for his great Skill, Accuracy and Fidelity, both in the Construction of his Barometers, and in whatever Work, he undertakes, or delivers out of his Hands.

It was to Sisson that John Hadley turned when he required a copy of his newly invented reflecting octant to be made in brass for the 1731 Admiralty trial in the Thames estuary in the yacht *Chatham*. In 1736 Sisson was commissioned by Graham to construct a 9 foot zenith sector (the arc of which Graham divided himself) for the French Académie des Sciences expedition to northern Sweden under Pierre de Maupertuis to measure the length of a degree of the meridian. Also in 1736 Graham commissioned him to prepare brass rods and scales for the Royal Society and the Académie to show the relation between the English yard and the French half-toise. After each rod had been engraved with both yard and half-toise, and comparisons had been made in London and Paris, in 1742 Sisson divided each measure into three equal parts. The same year, a paper giving an account of a new spirit level invented and made by him was read at the Royal Society.

By this time Sisson's reputation was such that he had begun to receive orders for large astronomical instruments, such as mural quadrants, zenith sectors, and transit instruments for observatories all over Europe: for Utrecht, Bologna, Leiden, Paris, and Pisa, as well as for the private observatory of George Parker, second earl of Macclesfield at Shirburn. Jonathan's son Jeremiah *Sisson was working for his father at this time and about 1740 John Bird also worked for Sisson before setting up his own workshop near by in 1745. Jonathan Sisson was one of the most celebrated instrument makers of his time, fostering the high reputation which the London instrument-making trade acquired in Europe during the eighteenth century, ably followed by John Bird, Jeremiah Sisson, John and Peter Dollond, Jesse Ramsden, and Edward Troughton. Sisson died in London on 13 June 1747.

DEREK HOWSE, rev.

Sources 'Graduation', A. Rees and others, *The cyclopedia, or, Universal dictionary of arts, sciences, and literature*, 16 (1819) • E. G. R. Taylor, *The mathematical practitioners of Hanoverian England, 1714–1840* (1966) • M. Daumas, *Scientific instruments of the seventeenth and eighteenth centuries and their makers* (1972) • *Journal for the History of Astronomy*, 17/4 (1986) [*The Greenwich list of observatories*, ed. D. Howse] • E. Saul, *An historical and philosophical account of the barometer or weather-glass* (1735) • inventory, PRO, PROB 3 46/47

Wealth at death £394; £106 owed by customers; contents of house and workshop, incl. tools, brass, and finished and unfinished instruments: inventory, PRO, PROB 3 46/47

Sitaram Pande (*supp.* **1795?–1873×80?**), supposed army officer in India and autobiographer, may not have existed. The authenticity of what purport to be his memoirs has been disputed, and if they are a work of fiction then so too is this article, which is largely based on them, and statements here about his life should be read in this light. Sitaram (also written Sita Ram) Pande was supposedly born, probably in 1795, in the village of Tilowee, in the Rae Bareli district of Oudh, the son of Gangadin Pande, a prosperous Brahman yeoman farmer who owned over 150 acres and was a man of importance in his village. Sitaram was educated by the family priest and became literate. Before 1857 the East India Company's Bengal army recruited its sepoys largely from Oudh Brahmans. In 1814 Sitaram's maternal uncle Hanuman, an infantry jemadar, visited Sitaram's parents and inspired him to become a soldier. He and Hanuman travelled together, having a narrow escape from thugs who joined their party, and reached Agra. There, in November, Sitaram enlisted in his uncle's unit, the 2nd battalion, 26th Bengal native infantry, and served in his uncle's company, the light company.

Sitaram served in the Anglo-Nepal War (1814–16) and in the Pindari war (1817) against Pindari mounted bandits—'demons from the lowest hell' (Lunt, 36)—and was wounded. His first promotion was to lance-naik. In 1818 he served with the 1st battalion, 25th regiment, at the siege of Asirgarh, and in the assault was wounded when a magazine exploded, killing his uncle and most of his company. His mother arranged his marriage, about 1818, to the daughter of a local landowner, but after the wedding he discovered that she was disfigured by smallpox. He served in the fighting against Maratha chiefs' Arab mercenaries, and in the attack on a fort, Ahunpoora, he rescued a beautiful girl from an Arab. She was the daughter of Makum Singh, a Rajput *thakur* (petty chief) in Bundelkhand, and about 1820 Sitaram made her his second wife.

In 1820 Sitaram joined a new unit, the Fategarh levy (later the 63rd and 64th Bengal Native Infantry). He served with the 63rd, part of Lord Combermere's army, at the siege and capture of Bharatpur (1825–6) and later was promoted havildar. In 1838, as part of Lord Auckland's plan to restore Shah Shuja to power in Afghanistan, a British-subsidized, British-officered force was raised in India, known as Shah Shuja's levy, and Sitaram became a havildar in it. He served in the First Anglo-Afghan War, and in January 1842, on the disastrous retreat from Kabul, was wounded, captured, and then sold as a slave in Kabul. He later escaped to India, reaching Ferozepur in October 1843, and returned to the 63rd. He served in the first and second Anglo-Sikh wars (1845–6, 1848–9) and in 1847 was promoted jemadar. In 1855 he served against the Santal uprising in Bengal.

In 1857 Sitaram warned his commanding officer of sepoy discontent, then went on leave and was in his village when the mutiny began. He remained loyal and was abducted by mutineers, then rescued by European irregular cavalry. He joined a new Punjab regiment, probably the 12th Punjab infantry, whose second-in-command, later commanding officer, was Captain (later Major-General) James Thomas Norgate (1824–1894), and served with them against the mutineers in India and Nepal. His son was captured and executed as a mutineer: 'not for one moment did I consider requesting that his life should be spared—that he did not deserve' (Lunt, 168). After the campaign in Nepal, Sitaram was promoted subedar, but he was then too old. He disliked the post-mutiny army, the Punjabis, and the changed attitudes of British officers. After criticism by officers he retired on a pension in 1860 and returned to his village. During his career he had been awarded six medals. Old and apparently disillusioned, he wrote his memoirs, probably in Adwadhi (western Hindi), comparing unfavourably the army that he had joined with that which he had recently left, criticizing Muslims, and asserting his own loyalty. In 1861 he sent the memoirs to Norgate. He died, presumably at Tilowee, probably between 1873 and 1880.

Norgate translated Sitaram's memoirs and published them in book form at Lahore in 1873; an Urdu translation was published in the same year. In 1911 an Urdu translation from Norgate's version was published as a language text for British officers, and used until 1947. A summary of the memoirs, with comment, was published in 1959 by Sir Patrick Cadell in the *Journal of the Society for Army Historical Research*; and an edition by James Lunt was published in 1970 and has been used as a source by military historians. The memoirs contain many inaccuracies of names and dates, and are vague on the units in which Sitaram served, omitting regimental numbers. They were widely known and long accepted as genuine. After 1947, however, some questioned their authenticity, emphasizing their errors, the fact that Sitaram had too many changes of regiment, and that his adventures were 'too good to be true' (Mason, 208). It was alleged that the memoirs were a deliberate fraud by Norgate; J. A. B. Palmer wrote that they were 'of doubtful authenticity' (Palmer, 1). Others, however, including Cadell and Lunt, maintained that they were genuine. There is no conclusive evidence either for or against their authenticity but they may well be genuine, if sometimes inaccurate and possibly embroidered. If authentic then they are the only account published of an Indian sepoy's experiences during the first half of the nineteenth century, and as such they constitute an important historical source. ROGER T. STEARN

Sources S. R. Pandey, *From sepoy to subedar*, trans. J. T. Norgate, new edn, ed. J. Lunt (1970) · P. Cadell, ed., 'The autobiography of an Indian soldier', *Journal of the Society for Army Historical Research*, 37 (1959), 149, pp. 3–11; 150, pp. 49–56 · T. A. Heathcote, *The military in British India: the development of British land forces in south Asia, 1600–1947* (1995) · P. Mason, *A matter of honour: an account of the Indian army, its officers and men* (1976) · P. Macrory, *Kabul catastrophe: the story of the disastrous retreat from Kabul 1842* (1986) · C. Hibbert, *The great mutiny, India, 1857* (1978); repr. (1980) · J. A. B. Palmer, *The mutiny outbreak at Meerut in 1857* (1966) · D. Omissi, *The sepoy and the raj: the Indian army, 1860–1940* (1994) · P. Spear, *The Oxford history of modern India, 1740–1947* (1965) · P. Moon, *The British conquest and dominion of India* (1989)

Sitch, Charles Henry (1887–1960), trade unionist and politician, was born at Saltney, Chester, on 4 May 1887, the third son of **Thomas Sitch** (1852–1923), chain maker and trade unionist, and his wife, Elizabeth (*née* Young). Thomas Sitch was born at Cradley Heath, Staffordshire, on 23 July 1852, the son of a chain maker. He started work in Cradley Heath at the age of eight and subsequently moved first to Newcastle upon Tyne, where he met and married his wife, and then to Saltney, Chester.

While working in Saltney in 1889 Thomas Sitch formed the Chainmakers' and Strikers' Association of Saltney, Pontypridd and Staffordshire. This was a union for men who worked in factories making big chain, such as ships' cable. The innumerable varieties of small chain were made by outworkers, many of whom were women, so the trade was effectively divided into two branches. In the outwork section unremitting downward pressure on wages arising from intense competition for employment was not conducive to unionization. However, this was not the case in the factory section, and this allowed Sitch to build the Chainmakers' and Strikers' Association into an effective organization and in 1894 he was appointed its full-time general secretary. He then returned to Cradley Heath, the main centre of the chain trade, and became a widely respected public figure. He served with distinction on both Rowley Regis urban district council and Staffordshire county council, being chairman of the former in 1911, and in 1913 he was made a JP. Thomas Sitch died on 23 April 1923 at his home, Unity Villa, Sydney Road, Cradley Heath, which also served as the union office. He was survived by his wife. He was buried in St Luke's churchyard, Cradley Heath.

Charles Henry Sitch moved to Cradley Heath with his parents when he was seven. He went to the local elementary school, leaving at the age of thirteen to work in a grocer's shop. With financial support from the Chainmakers' and Strikers' Association, however, he went to Ruskin College, Oxford, where he studied economics and related subjects for two years. This experience and his family background led naturally to a strong interest in trade unionism and Sitch subsequently played a leading part in union activity in and around Cradley Heath, particularly among the female outworkers in the chain trade. However, it was not until the National Federation of Women Workers (NFWW) began recruiting in Cradley Heath, soon after its formation in 1906, that real progress was made in the unionization of these casual workers. Sitch became secretary of the hand-hammered chain branch of the NFWW and, together with Mary Macarthur, mounted a vigorous campaign to secure statutory protection for the outworkers. The agitation ensured that small chainmaking was included in the 1909 Trade Boards Act, which provided for the establishment of minimum wages in four sweated industries. Sitch was among the first members of the Chain Trade Board which within four years, in addition to setting a minimum wage, raised piece-work rates by up to two-thirds.

The success of the Chain Trade Board led to other Black Country sweated industries being organized on similar lines and Sitch was a central figure in this process becoming, *inter alia*, vice-chairman of the Stourbridge and district firebrick wages and conciliation board and the women workers' representative on the Hollow-Ware Trade Board. In 1913 he was appointed assistant secretary of the Chainmakers' and Strikers' Association and from 1914 to 1918 he was president of the South Staffordshire and Worcestershire Federation of Trades Councils (he was exempted from military service on medical grounds). Away from work his main interest was amateur operatics. He acted as honorary secretary of the Cradley Heath, Old Hill and District Amateur Operatic Society for many years and was also a leading performer in its productions, often appearing with his wife, Mabel Jackson, who came from Goole.

Sitch's work as a union organizer was the springboard for his political career. He was elected to the Rowley Regis urban district council as a Liberal in 1913 but switched to Labour in 1916 and at the 1918 general election he won the formerly safe Conservative seat of Kingswinford with a majority of 2888. He remained in parliament until 1931 but made little impression mainly because from the end of 1922 he had to devote most of his time to the affairs of the Chainmakers' and Strikers' Association following his appointment as general secretary in succession to his father.

Sitch took over the union just as its membership and finances were beginning to decline. One consequence of this was that his wages were progressively reduced to only £2 per week and when he lost his parliamentary salary he could no longer afford the expensive tastes which both he and his wife had acquired. His solution was to use the union's funds, which he controlled virtually unsupervised, for his private purposes. His deception was eventually discovered and in 1933 he was found guilty of fraudulently converting the Chainmakers' and Strikers' Association's funds and sent to prison for nine months.

The disgrace inevitably ended Sitch's public career and on his release from prison he moved away from Cradley Heath. He eventually settled in Leeds where, from 1937, he was employed by *Reynolds News* (later the *Sunday Citizen*) as a collector and organizer for a scheme through which co-operative societies supported the newspaper. He continued to live in Leeds after his retirement in 1952 and died at his home there, 116 Harrogate Road, Chapeltown, on 13 June 1960 from pulmonary tuberculosis. His wife survived him.   ERIC TAYLOR

Sources *County Express* [Stourbridge] (4 March 1933) [issue of warrant] · *County Express* [Stourbridge] (25 March 1933) [committal proceedings and trial] · *County Express* [Stourbridge] (1 July 1933) [trial] · E. Taylor, 'Sitch, Charles Henry', *DLB*, vol. 2 · R. H. Tawney, *The establishment of minimum rates in the chain making industry* (1914) · E. Taylor, 'Sitch, Thomas', *DLB*, vol. 1 · *Souvenir of the Chainmakers' and Strikers' Association semi-jubilee* (1914) · E. Taylor, 'The working class movement in the Black Country, 1863–1914', PhD diss., Keele University, 1974 · E. Taylor, 'A craft society in the age of general unions: the Chainmakers' and Strikers' Association of Saltney, Pontypridd and Staffordshire, 1889–1914', *West Midland Studies*, 5 (1972), 28–32 · private information (2004) · *The Times* (27 April 1923) [Thomas Sitch] · *Dudley Herald* (28 April 1923) [Thomas Sitch] · *County Express* [Stourbridge] (28 April 1923) [Thomas Sitch] · G. C. Allen, *The industrial development of Birmingham and the Black Country, 1860–1927* (1929); repr. (1966) · *Souvenir of the Chainmakers' and Strikers' Association jubilee* (1939) · d. cert. · b. cert.

Wealth at death £1104 4*s*. 6*d*.—Thomas Sitch: probate, 19 June 1923, *CGPLA Eng. & Wales*

Sitch, Thomas (1852–1923). *See under* Sitch, Charles Henry (1887–1960).

Sitwell, Dame Edith Louisa (1887–1964), poet and biographer, was born at Scarborough on 7 September 1887. She was the eldest of three children born to Sir George Reresby *Sitwell, fourth baronet (1860–1943), genealogist and antiquary, and his wife, Lady Ida Emily Augusta Denison (*d.* 1937), fourth child and third daughter of the first earl of Londesborough. Sir (Francis) Osbert Sacheverell *Sitwell (1892–1969) and Sir Sacheverell *Sitwell (1897–1988) were her younger brothers. The Sitwell family traced itself back to the fourteenth century and numbered kings of France, the English Plantagenets, Robert Bruce, and the Macbeths among its forebears. As Sir George put it, the Sitwells 'had been working up to something'; but never did he dream that Edith and his two sons, Osbert and Sacheverell, would make a significant mark on modern literature. When he first learned of Edith's early success with poetry, he lamented that she had made 'a great mistake by not going in for lawn tennis' (Pearson, 107).

Early in the 1920s, Edith, Osbert, and Sacheverell emerged as a literary cult of three. For good and for ill, they struck critics as an amalgam of dadaism, cubism, and futurism. They drew inspiration from the *commedia dell'arte* and the Ballets Russes, from Pope and Swift, from Dickens and D'Annunzio, from Claude and Marinetti, from the baroque and chinoiserie. Frequently attacked as *enfants terribles*, they were none the less widely admired, especially by Evelyn Waugh, who paid them a supreme compliment when he proclaimed: 'They took the dullness out of literature' (E. Waugh, *Sunday Times*, 1 Dec 1952, 7).

That his only daughter should dwell upon poetry, Edith claimed in her posthumously published autobiography, *Taken Care Of* (1965), was a disappointment to Sir George; but she felt that she was a disappointment to him and her mother from the day she was born. She also claimed that her early years were so wretched that she bore psychic scars. Edith, it would seem, was not unwanted and an unloved child, but more of an exasperating one who could not easily be moulded to her parents' wishes. Whenever she became morose and contrary, she would play the brat and assume the pose of an artist. One day she pertly announced that she would grow up and become a genius.

In her early teens Edith developed an insatiable love for poetry. When she was sixteen, a new governess, Helen Roothman, introduced her to the works of Verlaine, Rimbaud, and Mallarmé. More important, her enlightening teacher encouraged her to compose her own poems. In March 1913 one of her earliest works, 'Drowned Suns', was published in the *Daily Mirror*. Thrilled with her first

Dame Edith Louisa Sitwell (1887–1964), by Sir Cecil Beaton, 1926

appearance in print and fearful that it would be impossible for her to be truly creative if she remained in her parents' home, in April 1913 she and her governess, who was by now mentor and friend, went off to London. Three years later, Edith began editing *Wheels*, a modernistic venture that aroused the ire of conservative critics. Her own poems published in *Wheels* occasioned even more negative responses, especially 'The Mother', which served as the lead poem in her first published collection, *The Mother and other Poems* (1915). In quick succession followed *Clown's Houses* (1918), *The Wooden Pegasus* (1920), *Façade* (1922), and *Bucolic Comedies* (1923).

On 12 June 1923 Edith gave a reading of *Façade* in London's Aeolian Hall; overnight she became the most talked-about poet in England. Everything about her public performance provoked controversy. To begin with, she sat with her back to the audience, barely visible behind a transparent curtain adorned with a crudely fashioned moon-face. In order to project her voice, she spoke through a Sengerphone, an instrument made of compressed grasses meant to retain the purity of magnified tonal quality. Disgruntled members of the audience

thought they were victims of a hoax. What they heard sounded like gibberish, but had they listened more closely they might have discovered—in addition to a great deal of humour and gaiety—subtle criticisms of modern life, innuendoes of despair, decay, and death.

Façade had come into being chiefly because of prosodic experiments that Edith was engaged in at the time. She wanted to explore the effect that various impressions have upon the senses and to what extent she could capture notational images. Osbert and Sacheverell suggested that William Walton—at that time a little known young composer who had been living with the Sitwells since 1919—should write the music for Edith's lyrics and give them assorted rhythms of the waltz, the foxtrot, the polka, the mazurka, the tango, the paso doble, and country and sailor dances. To rebut adverse judgements about her efforts, Edith later gave profuse and erudite explanations of the aural techniques and phonological technicalities she employed. But lurking in the minds of many was the overriding question: was she an innovative poet or merely a talented charlatan capable of verbal legerdemain? Over the next years of her life—in volume after volume—she sought to answer the question in her favour.

With *Sleeping Beauty* (1924), *Troy Park* (1925), *Elegy on Dead Fashion* (1926), and *Rustic Elegies* (1927) Edith abandoned some of the eccentricities of her earlier verse. That she was still a master technician and an adroit inventor of rhythms and rhymes remained obvious to her growing number of devotees. Though she had achieved an enviable reputation, now that she was in her forties she began to reflect upon the sterility of her existence. To find some metaphysical resolutions to the enigma of life, she wrote *Gold Coast Customs* (1929), from which she wanted readers, 'to cogitate the rich man's gold and … wheat … blood and fire' and 'the fires of God … marching on' (E. Sitwell, 'Some notes on my own poetry', *Collected Poems*, 1930, xxxvi–xxxvii).

In 1930 Edith published her first important prose work, a biography of Alexander Pope, that 'small, unhappy, tortured creature … who is perhaps the most flawless artist our race ever produced' (E. Sitwell, *Alexander Pope*, 1). The same year saw the publication of her *Collected Poems*. Like another Pope, she had suffered for her art and had tolerated years of prejudice, but with the favourable reception of her *Collected Poems* it was obvious that she was as worthy of her laurels as Pope had been some 200 years before. The Royal Society of Literature certainly thought so when in 1933 it awarded her its coveted medal. In the following year she wrote *Aspects of Modern Poetry*, in which, after she assailed all those who questioned her art, she focused on the achievements of Hopkins, Yeats, Eliot, and Pound. Her second biographical study, *Victoria of England*, appeared in 1936. In the same year she completed her first novel, *I Live under a Black Sun*. Into its narrative, which is based upon the life and loves of Jonathan Swift, she wove many of her own private experiences, especially her failed relationship with the Russian artist Pavel Tchelitchew. She often thought of herself as his muse, and was flattered to sit for six portraits and a sculpture of her head in wax and wire.

She also produced three anthologies, *Edith Sitwell's Anthology* (1940), *Poems Old and New* (1940), and *Look! The Sun* (1941). Shortly thereafter, she published *'Green Song' and other Poems* (1944) and *Song of the Cold* (1945). Then she tried her hand at another biography, *Fanfare for Elizabeth* (1946), in which she drew an excellent picture of sixteenth-century England and a flattering portrait of the monarch, with whom she was prone to identify.

In 1947, Edith Sitwell was selected by Leeds University for an honorary degree. Two years later, Durham bestowed a second honorary degree upon her, and she was named an honorary associate of the American Academy of Arts and Letters. Then, in 1951, Oxford conferred on her the honorary degree of doctor of letters. A fourth honorary degree from Sheffield University followed in 1955. During this same period when so many honours flowed her way, Edith and Osbert Sitwell made a tour of the United States, lecturing and reading from their poetry. They were lionized everywhere they went, and the high point of their visit was a performance of *Façade* at New York's Museum of Modern Art.

Edith and Osbert Sitwell undertook a second visit to the United States in 1950. In Hollywood, she was enthusiastically greeted by such famous personalities as Charlie Chaplin, Greta Garbo, Merle Oberon, and Marilyn Monroe. To them, she was not only a poet *par excellence* but a remarkable character. Tall and august, her pale oval face with its extended aquiline nose and tight lips added to her formidable appearance. Then, too, she always wore a long, loose, flowing robe and a turban-like headdress, and she adorned her slender fingers with huge rings. In short, she was as colourful and flamboyant as the motion picture stars who fawned over her. Further tributes and honours now came her way, the most important of which was her being named dame of the British empire in 1954. None the less, she still experienced a spiritual void in her life, one which she filled in 1955 with her conversion to Roman Catholicism. And never one to let her pen remain idle for long, she published another anthology, *The Atlantic Book of British and American Poetry* (1958); *The Outcasts* (1962), her last volume of poetry; and *The Queen and the Hive* (1962), her last biography, a study of Elizabeth of England and Mary of Scotland.

Now in her seventy-fifth year, Edith was honoured with a celebration in London's Royal Festival Hall. A recitation of *Façade* accompanied by Walton's music produced a tremendous ovation of almost five minutes' duration; after which Edith, overcome, waved to her enthusiastic admirers—and wept. Two years later, on 9 December 1964, she died, unmarried, at St Thomas's Hospital, London. An ecumenical service was conducted by a Roman Catholic priest and an Anglican vicar. Burial followed in the graveyard at Weedon Lois, near Weston, Northamptonshire. A sculpture by Henry Moore depicting the hand of a young child clasping the hand of an old man—an obvious symbol of the continuity of life through the generations—marks her grave.   G. A. CEVASCO

Sources *DNB* · G. A. Cevaso, *The Sitwells: Edith, Osbert, and Sacheverell* (1987) · J. Pearson, *Façades: Edith, Osbert and Sacheverell Sitwell*

(1978) · R. L. Mégroz, *The three Sitwells* (1927) · G. Elborn, *Edith Sitwell* (1981) · J. Lehmann, *A nest of tigers: the Sitwells in their time* (1968) · R. Fifoot, *A bibliography of Edith, Osbert and Sacheverell Sitwell* (1963) · *Selected letters of Edith Sitwell*, ed. R. Greene (1997) · *The Times* (10 Dec 1964) · *CGPLA Eng. & Wales* (1965)

Archives Harvard U., Houghton L., corresp. · London Library, letters · NRA, corresp. and literary papers · Ransom HRC, corresp., notebooks and papers · University of Iowa Libraries, Iowa City, letters and literary MSS · University of York, corresp., literary MSS, and papers · Washington State University Libraries | American Academy of Arts and Sciences, letters to American Academy of Arts and Letters · BL, letters to Lady Aberconway, Add. MS 52556 · BL, letters to John Lehmann, Add. MSS 52609–52611 · BL, letters to Sydney Schiff and Violet Schiff, Add. MS 52922 · Bodl. Oxf., corresp. with Sibyl Colefax · Bodl. Oxf., letters to Jack Lambert · Georgetown University, Washington, DC, letters to Graham Greene · JRL, letters to L. P. Hartley · King's AC Cam., letters to E. J. Dent · King's AC Cam., letters to John Hayward · King's AC Cam., letters to J. M. Keynes · LUL, corresp. with Duckworth & Co. · Royal Society of Literature, London, letters to Royal Society of Literature · Rutgers University, New Jersey, letters to Arthur Waley · U. Durham, letters to William Plomer · U. Sussex, corresp. with Choura Tchelitchew

Likenesses R. Fry, oils, 1918, Sheffield Art Gallery · N. Hamnett, pencil drawing, 1918, U. Texas · A. Guevara, oils, *c*.1919, Tate collection · W. Lewis, pencil drawing, 1921, National Gallery of South Australia, Adelaide · W. Lewis, pencil drawing, 1922, NPG · W. Lewis, pencil and watercolour drawing, *c*.1922–1928, Cecil Higgins Art Gallery, Bedford · W. Lewis, oils, 1923–35, Tate collection · C. Beaton, photograph, 1926, NPG [*see illus.*] · A. Rutherston, charcoal drawing, 1928, U. Texas · P. Tchelitchew, oils, 1937, Tate collection · B. Anrep, sculpture, 1952, National Gallery, London · M. Levy, pencil drawing, 1959, U. Texas · C. Beaton, ink caricature, triptych, U. Texas · B. Brandt, photograph, NPG · H. Coster, photograph, NPG · Z. Czermanski, group portrait, gouache caricature, U. Texas · P. Evans, pencil drawing, U. Texas · M. Gerson, photograph, U. Texas · H. P. Horst, photograph, NPG · B. Patridge, pencil, ink, and watercolour caricature, V&A; repro. in *Punch* (21 May 1928) · A. Rutherston, group portrait, lithograph, Scarborough borough council · R. S. Sherriffs, double portraits, ink caricatures (with George Bernard Shaw), NPG · P. Tchelitchew, oils, U. Texas

Wealth at death £28,836: probate, 5 Feb 1965, *CGPLA Eng. & Wales*

Sitwell, George (*bap.* 1601, *d.* 1667), landowner and ironmaster, was born at Eckington, Derbyshire, where he was baptized on 15 March 1601, the eldest son of George Sitwell (1569–1607) and Mary, daughter of Thomas Walker of Derby, who later married Henry Wigfall, also of Eckington. The Sitwells rose steadily during the sixteenth century from freeholders to gentry through the acquisition of land in Eckington and neighbouring parishes, a transition completed by George Sitwell, who was a JP, served as high sheriff of Derbyshire in 1653, and received a grant of arms in 1660, which he produced, together with a pedigree, at Dugdale's visitation of the county two years later. The family's rise was confirmed by the building of Renishaw Hall at Eckington, probably in the 1620s, which became the centre of their estate and remains their home today.

Sitwell, in common with many landowners of his day, supplemented his income from land through the exploitation of minerals beneath his estate, in his case chiefly iron. His involvement in the industry probably began with the building of a blast furnace at Plumbley, near Eckington, in the 1630s, jointly with his stepfather, Henry Wigfall. This partnership came to an end in 1649 and three years later Sitwell alone built a new furnace at Foxbrooke, close to Renishaw, which by the 1660s was the nucleus of the most extensive group of ironworks anywhere in Derbyshire or Nottinghamshire, including two other furnaces (at Staveley and North Wingfield) and forges at Staveley, Pleasley, Clipstone, and Cuckney. Sitwell also made saws at Pleasley and in 1656 installed near Renishaw the first rolling and slitting mill in the east midlands, the rod iron from which supplied a large number of local nailmakers.

Sitwell remained in personal control of his works until his death and a letter-book covering the last few years of his career shows that he was in business on a large scale, producing pig and bar iron, castings, saws, nails, and other finished goods for sale both locally and in London, where a cousin acted as his factor. Some products, including rolling mills for the West Indies sugar plantations, went abroad. Sitwell sent iron to London both by water (via the River Idle at Bawtry) and by road, employing his own private carrier as well as using public stage wagons. His correspondence also shows how closely a country landowner could keep in touch with public affairs in the capital through his commercial contacts; in addition, although by this date in his sixties, Sitwell visited London regularly. At home, he made extensive purchases of wood from both the crown and private owners in Sherwood and elsewhere, and was an important figure in an extensive regional credit network. He was also much involved in administrative business as a JP at parish and hundred level and to a lesser extent in the county as a whole.

Sitwell, who married Margaret, the daughter of Hugh Childers of Carr House, near Doncaster, was buried at Eckington on 2 August 1667; his wife died in 1658 and was also buried at Eckington. Of their five sons and two daughters who survived into adult life the eldest son continued his father's iron-making activities from his seat at Renishaw and two others became London iron merchants. In the 1690s, however, the works were leased and, although they retained direct management of their collieries until the mid-eighteenth century, the family were henceforth principally landowners, merely drawing rent from industrial enterprises on their estate. Wealth accumulated from both land and industry would later enable Sir G. R. Sitwell (1860–1943) and his children, Osbert, Sacheverell, and Edith to pursue their various literary careers.

PHILIP RIDEN

Sources *George Sitwell's letterbook, 1662–66*, ed. P. Riden, Derbyshire RS, 10 (1985) · P. Riden, 'The charcoal iron industry in the east midlands, 1580–1780', *Derbyshire Archaeological Journal*, 111 (1991), 64–84 · G. R. Sitwell, 'A picture of the iron trade in the seventeenth century', *Journal of the Derbyshire Archaeological and Natural History Society*, 10 (1888), 28–46 · parish register (burial), Eckington parish church, 2 Aug 1667 · J. Hunter, *Hallamshire: the history and topography of the parish of Sheffield in the county of York* (1819), 217
Archives Derbys. RO · Renishaw Hall, Eckington, Derbyshire
Likenesses monument, Eckington parish church, Derbyshire
Wealth at death see will, proved 28 July 1668, Lichfield RO

Sitwell, Sir George Reresby, fourth baronet (1860–1943), antiquary, was born in Green Street, Mayfair, London, on

Sir George Reresby Sitwell, fourth baronet (1860–1943), by Vincent Brooks, Day & Son, c.1900

27 January 1860, the only son of Sir Sitwell Reresby Sitwell, third baronet (1820–1862), and his wife, Louisa Lucy (d. 1911), daughter of Colonel the Hon. Henry Hely-Hutchinson. He succeeded his father in 1862, thereby enjoying a long minority. He went to Eton College, and entered Christ Church, Oxford, in 1879, but left without taking a degree. While at university he gained notoriety by his 'physical capture of a "spirit" at a spiritualist headquarters in London' (*The Times*). In 1886 he married Ida Emily Augusta (d. 1937), daughter of William Henry Forester Denison, Baron (later first earl of) Londesborough, with whom he had three remarkable children: Edith Louisa *Sitwell, (Francis) Osbert Sacheverell *Sitwell, and Sacheverell *Sitwell.

An ardent Unionist, Sitwell contested Scarborough seven times and was successful twice, representing the seat in parliament from 1885 to 1886 and from 1892 to 1895. Later (1908) he became a Liberal, but by then he had abandoned politics, despite a talent for addressing large audiences.

While at his preparatory school Sitwell had taught himself to read black-letter English from family documents, and in 1889, having bought the *Scarborough Post* and a private printing press, he produced his first book, *The Barons of Pulford in the Eleventh and Twelfth Centuries and their Descendants*. The Sacheverell papers which he inherited led to the writing in 1894 of *The First Whig*, an account of the parliamentary career of William Sacheverell, to whom he was related collaterally. He also published *The Letters of the Sitwells and Sacheverells* (1900). His researches among family papers clarified many disputed points in the pedigrees of the older English families and he frequently worked in close co-operation with J. H. Round, never relying on popularly accepted pedigrees but tracing them to their documented origins. He allowed himself the relaxation of writing a book in the form of fiction when he published in 1933 *Tales of my Native Village*, studies of medieval life, manners, art, minstrelsy, and religion. In addition to his studies of genealogical details he paid considerable attention to heraldry, on which he contributed articles to *The Ancestor*.

Sitwell spent much of his time at Renishaw Hall, the family seat in Derbyshire, where he filled seven sitting-rooms with memoranda on a multiplicity of subjects over which his active, inventive, but erratic mind continually ranged and upon which he expected to be consulted as an infallible authority: 'I must ask anyone entering the house never to contradict me or differ from me in any way, as it interferes with the functioning of the gastric juices and prevents my sleeping at night.' To his researches in genealogy and heraldry he added in particular the study of the construction and planning of formal gardens which was of genuine value and led to the publication *On the Making of Gardens* (1909, republished 1949). He redesigned the gardens at Renishaw on a formal plan, at the same time ornamenting the park with a large expanse of landscaped water, and to gain further information on the subject of garden planning he travelled extensively in Italy, a country to which he became progressively devoted. During his travels in the remoter parts of southern Italy between 1890 and 1910 he persisted in changing into full evening dress for dinner however small and primitive the inn.

In 1909 Sitwell purchased the Castello di Montegufoni, formerly the property of the Florentine family of Acciaiuoli and at that time the dwelling place of nearly 300 peasants. 'The roof is in splendid order, and the drains can't be wrong, as there aren't any', he wrote to his elder son, ending with a characteristic warning against extravagance (O. Sitwell, *Great Morning*, 76). The castle had undergone many alterations and Sitwell with the aid of the family documents set about restoring the building to its original design. In 1925 he left England to make Montegufoni his residence, persuaded thereto by his three children, who needed freedom to follow their own brilliant careers:

> The general atmosphere, which was always menacing, the interruptions, the scenes, the surprises, and the ambushes laid, the fussing, the necessity my father felt both for consulting and contradicting me, the economies, the extravagances, all put it beyond possibility to write a line when he was in the house. (O. Sitwell, *Laughter in the Next Room*, 260–61)

Sitwell himself wrote to the archbishop of Canterbury and the chancellor of the exchequer to explain that the newly imposed taxes obliged him to settle in Italy. He had never enjoyed the more obvious pleasures of social life, and in Italy he retreated more and more into the seclusion of his scholarly investigations of Gothic life.

Edith Sitwell wrote that in later life her father 'became very handsome and noble-looking; with his strange, pale, wild, lonely-looking eyes, and his red beard, he resembled a portrait of one of the Borgias, or some other early Italian tyrant' (E. Sitwell, 22). His eccentricities supplied his famous children with 'good material for their prose to embellish', but where 'they were self-consciously original, he was naturally so' (Bridgeman and Drury, 51). When Sitwell died at Villa Fontanelle, Porto Ronco, Locarno, Switzerland, on 9 July 1943, he was proud of the fact that he had been lord of the manor of Eckington for eighty-one years—a longer period than any of his predecessors since the Norman conquest. He was succeeded by his elder son, Osbert, whose autobiography (5 vols., 1945–50) affectionately described his difficult parent as 'one of the most singular characters of his epoch'.

DAVID HORNER, rev. MARK POTTLE

Sources personal knowledge (1959) · O. Sitwell, *Great morning: being the third volume of left hand, right hand!* (1948) · O. Sitwell, *Tales my father taught me* (1962) · O. Sitwell, *Laughter in the next room* (1949) · E. Sitwell, *Taken care of: an autobiography* (1965) · H. Bridgeman and E. Drury, *The British eccentric* (1975) · *The Times* (10 July 1943), 6e · Burke, *Peerage* (1939)

Archives BL, letters to Lady Aberconway, Add. MS 52556

Likenesses H. Tonks, oils, 1898; formerly in possession of Sir Osbert Sitwell, 1959 · V. Brooks, Day & Son, lithograph, *c*.1900, unknown collection; copyprint, Hult. Arch. [*see illus.*] · J. S. Sargent, group portrait, oils, 1900, priv. coll.

Wealth at death £12,271 9*s.* 11*d.*—in England: probate, 26 June 1944, *CGPLA Eng. & Wales*

Sitwell, Sir (Francis) Osbert Sacheverell, fifth baronet

Sitwell, Sir (Francis) Osbert Sacheverell, fifth baronet (1892–1969), writer, was born at 3 Arlington Street, London, on 6 December 1892, the elder son of Sir George Reresby *Sitwell, fourth baronet (1860–1943), genealogist and antiquary, and his wife, Lady Ida Emily Augusta Denison (*d.* 1937), fourth child and third daughter of the first earl of Londesborough. Osbert Sitwell, like his elder sister Dame Edith Louisa *Sitwell (1887–1964) and his younger brother Sir Sacheverell *Sitwell (1897–1988), devoted his life to the arts and literature. Collectively, the trio produced almost 200 volumes of poetry, fiction, biography, music, art, and literary criticism, giving expression to their own kind of modernism, an amalgam of cubism, futurism, and dadaism best described as 'Sitwellism'.

Most of Osbert Sitwell's boyhood was spent at Renishaw Hall, Derbyshire, the Sitwell family seat, and Scarborough, another ancestral home. Early schooling prepared him for Eton College (1906–9), and he planned to attend Oxford. Directed by his father, however, in 1911 he obtained a commission in the Sherwood rangers. Months of boredom and discomfiture convinced him that he was not cut out to be a cavalry officer. After falling off several mounts, he came to detest horses and quipped that he preferred giraffes. He managed a transfer to the Grenadier Guards and was placed on duty at the Tower of London. Not only did he not have to contend with saddling up every day, but the grenadiers seemed a more civilized body of men. During his off-duty hours, Sitwell frequented theatres, art galleries, and concert-halls. At social gatherings he mingled with the most prominent artists, writers, and musicologists of the time. He struck all who

Sir (Francis) Osbert Sacheverell Sitwell, fifth baronet (1892–1969), by Frank Dobson, 1923

met him as suave and sophisticated, handsome, and rather proud of his Hanoverian profile.

Osbert Sitwell lacked the usual martial attributes, but he did not mind being a peacetime gentleman soldier. In November 1914, shortly before his twenty-second birthday, things changed radically when his regiment was activated. Shortly thereafter, he found himself in France where he fought in the trenches. One day while bivouacked near Ypres, he grieved over the barbarity of armed conflict in a short metrical diatribe he entitled 'Babel'. Somehow, although surrounded by death and filled with despair, he found his vocation: he would become a poet. 'Some instinct, and a combination of feelings not hitherto experienced', he later wrote, 'united to drive me to paper' (O. Sitwell, *Laughter in the Next Room*, 1949, 115).

The devastation of war gave meaning to the sacredness of art; the artist, Sitwell intuited, could be a priest, a prophet, an apostle, one who could make others more fully appreciative of life. Having been rather poorly educated in the humanities, he had doubts about playing the role of a poet in earnest. He affirmed, none the less, that as long as he lived he would dedicate himself to the arts. Publication of 'Babel' in the 11 May 1916 issue of *The Times* marked his début as a man of letters. Two years later, a short time after he left the army with the rank of captain, he began to devote himself to poetry, art criticism, and controversial journalism. To fill the vacuum the war had

left in the artistic life of London, along with Sacheverell he sponsored a controversial exhibition of such artists as Matisse, Utrillo, Picasso, and Modigliani. The Sitwell brothers were acknowledged as impresarios and proponents of the modern movement. Of greater importance for Osbert was the publication of his *Argonaut and Juggernaut* (1919), a slender book of fifty poems filled with the indignation and bile that had built up in him during his war years. Two years later, he published another book of bitter poems, *At the House of Mrs Kinfoot*, which satirized common dullness and complacency.

Early in 1924 Sitwell completed his first work of fiction, *Triple Fugue*, a collection of six studies of weird behaviour and egoistic eccentricity. The following year he published *Discursions on Travel, Art and Life*, reflections on visits he had made to Italy, Sicily, and southern Germany. His first novel, *Before the Bombardment* (1926), was his first work to achieve a critical acclaim, but his next three novels, *The Man who Lost himself* (1929), *Miracle on Sinai* (1934), and *Those were the Days* (1937), were not as well received. *Open the Door* (1940), a collection of seventeen short stories, and his fifth novel, *A Place of One's Own* (1940), were moderately successful, as were his *Selected Poems* (1943), and a book of essays, *Sing High, Sing Low* (1944).

On the death of his father in 1943, Sitwell succeeded to the baronetcy. Filled with thoughts of his own mortality, he began to concentrate on what was to become his *magnum opus*, his autobiography, a labour that over the following years would run to five volumes. Having a mild interest in chiromancy, he entitled his initial volume *Left Hand, Right Hand* (1945), from the belief of palmists that the left hand reveals characteristics determined at birth, while the right reflects those determined by an individual's own will. In this volume he scrutinized the two streams in his own life. *Left Hand, Right Hand* proved to be the best of twenty or so works Osbert had written over some twenty-nine years.

In his second autobiographical volume, *The Scarlet Tree* (1946), Sitwell focused on his days at Eton and his first sojourn in Italy under the tutelage of his father. In the third, *Great Morning* (1948), he wrote of his boyhood at Renishaw and his stressful military career. In the fourth, *Laughter in the Next Room* (1949), he covered the period of the First World War and the 1920s. The final volume, *Noble Essences: a Book of Characters* (1950), was devoted to the importance of art and to reminiscences of such talented friends as Sir Edmund Gosse, Ronald Firbank, and Arnold Bennett.

In 1950 Sitwell and his sister Edith visited the United States, where they were lionized by literary critics and Hollywood personalities. The American Academy of Arts and Letters declared Osbert Sitwell an honorary associate. Many other tributes and awards began to come his way, chief among them an honorary DLitt from Sheffield University (1951), appointment as a trustee of the Tate Gallery (1951–8), a CBE (1916), and a CH (1958). In 1962 Sitwell completed *Tales my Father Taught Me*, to serve as a postscript to his autobiographical sequence. The following year he completed his last book, *Pound Wise*, a collection of assorted essays. Now in his seventieth year, the Parkinson's disease from which he had suffered for several years incapacitated him and eventually brought on his death, unmarried, on 4 May 1969, at Montegufoni, a remodelled medieval castle near Florence left to him by his father, at which Sitwell had spent the last years of his life. His body was cremated, and his ashes were interred in a protestant cemetery outside the Italian estate.　　　G. A. CEVASCO

Sources G. A. Cevasco, *The Sitwells: Edith, Osbert, and Sacheverell* (1987) · J. Pearson, *Façades: Edith, Osbert and Sacheverell Sitwell* (1978) · R. Fulford, *Osbert Sitwell* (1951) · R. L. Mégroz, *The three Sitwells* (1927) · J. Lehmann, *A nest of tigers: the Sitwells in their time* (1968) · M. Wykes-Joyce, *Triad of genius* (1953) · R. Fifoot, *A bibliography of Edith, Osbert and Sacheverell Sitwell* (1963) · *The Times* (6 May 1969) · *Sunday Times* (11 May 1969) · *Sunday Telegraph* (24 Aug 1975)
Archives Eton, corresp. and papers · Harvard U., Houghton L., corresp. and papers · NRA, corresp. and literary papers · Ransom HRC, corresp. and papers · University of Iowa Libraries, Iowa City, letters | BL, letters to Sidney Schiff and Violet Schiff, Add. MS 52922 · Bodl. Oxf., letters to members of the Lewis family · CAC Cam., corresp. with Sir E. L. Spears · Herts. ALS, letters mainly to Lady Desborough · JRL, letters to L. P. Hartley · King's AC Cam., letters to E. J. Dent · King's AC Cam., letters to J. M. Keynes · King's AC Cam., letters to J. E. H. Steegman · King's Lond., Liddell Hart C., corresp. with Sir B. H. Liddell Hart · LUL, corresp. with Duckworth & Co. · PRO NIre., letters to Lady Londonderry, D 3099/3/16 · Tate collection, corresp. with Kenneth Clark · U. Durham L., letters to William Plomer · U. Reading L., letters to R. L. Mégroz · University of Iowa, Iowa City, corresp. · Washington State University, letters to Thomas Balston
Likenesses N. Hamnett, oils, *c.*1918, NPG · F. Dobson, painted plaster cast of head, 1922, NPG · F. Dobson, polished brass head, 1923, Tate collection [*see illus.*] · A. Rutherston, charcoal drawing, 1927, AM Oxf. · A. Rutherston, group portrait, lithograph, 1928, Scarborough county council · B. Anrep, mosaic, 1933, National Gallery, London · H. Coster, photographs, 1934, NPG · R. Whistler, pencil and watercolour drawing, 1935, NPG · D. Harmsworth, oils, 1938, U. Texas · photograph, 1951, NPG · F. Dobson, modern cast of bronze head, 1994, NPG · C. Beaton, ink caricature, U. Texas · C. Beaton, photograph, NPG · M. Beck and H. MacGregor, photograph, NPG · Denys, photograph, NPG · P. Evans, pencil drawing, NPG · A. Rutherston, pencil and ink drawing, U. Texas · R. S. Sherriffs, ink caricatures, NPG
Wealth at death £30,057—in England: probate, 8 Sept 1969, *CGPLA Eng. & Wales*

Sitwell, Sir Sacheverell, sixth baronet (1897–1988), writer, was born on 15 November 1897 in his parents' house, Belvoir Terrace, in The Crescent, Scarborough, the third child of Sir George Reresby *Sitwell, fourth baronet (1860–1943), genealogist and antiquary, and his wife, Lady Ida Emily Augusta Denison (*d.* 1937), fourth child and third daughter of the first earl of Londesborough.

Sacheverell Sitwell, like his elder sister, Dame Edith *Sitwell, and his elder brother, Sir (Francis) Osbert Sacheverell *Sitwell, lived for the arts. One of the most prolific of literary families, their reputations varied from decade to decade. Always the centre of spirited controversy, during the period of the Second World War, Edith found her widest audience, Osbert achieved wide acclaim for his autobiographical volumes, and Sacheverell's cultural studies became standard fare for devotees of art, architecture, and music.

Sacheverell's childhood, more indulged than Osbert's and more at a remove from Edith's, was idyllic, according

Sir Sacheverell Sitwell, sixth baronet (1897–1988), by Sir Cecil Beaton

to what he wrote years later in *Splendours and Miseries* (1943). While still in his teens, he carried on extensive correspondence with some of the foremost artists, musicians, and avant-garde figures of the day. When he left Eton College in 1916, he declared himself a bibliophile and dedicated intellectual. 'He set himself', Osbert wrote, 'with an energy and intensity that were remarkable to amass knowledge *he* wanted to amass' (O. Sitwell, *The Scarlet Tree*, 1946, 273). For dubious reasons he found formal education at Balliol College, Oxford, disappointing and did not pursue a degree. Instead, he joined Osbert in London to mount exhibitions of contemporary French art and hold salons to which they invited luminaries from the literary world.

Sacheverell Sitwell's first publication, *The People's Palace* (1918)—a slight work of fourteen poems—received a cool reception; nor did his second collection of verse, *The Hundred and One Harlequins* (1922), impress the critics. Two years later he published *Southern Baroque Art*, his first work of prose; and this study of the painting, architecture, and music of Italy and Spain during the seventeenth and eighteenth centuries drew laudations. *German Baroque Art* (1927), *The Gothick North* (1929), and *British Architecture and Craftsmen* (1945) followed in profusion. Other books, such as *Roumanian Journey* (1938), *The Netherlands* (1948), and *Bridge of the Brocard Sash* (1959), took their origins from his travels.

On 12 October 1925 Sitwell took time from his research and writing to marry Georgia Doble (*d.* 1980), an attractive Canadian from a prominent banking family, in Paris at the Anglican church of St George. They made a handsome pair: he, tall and slim (6 feet 4 inches), with a distinguished look and distinguished carriage; she, stately, slender, dark-haired with light olive skin and widely spaced hazel-green eyes. All things considered, their marriage was a good one, and her death in 1980 was a trying occasion for

Sitwell and their two sons, Francis and Reresby. The award in 1981 of the Royal Society of Literature's Benson medal alleviated some of his pain, as did his being made a Companion of Honour in 1984. Succession to the baronetcy in 1969 upon Osbert's death had followed as a matter of course.

Sitwell's sixteenth volume of poetry, *An Indian Summer* (1982), was his last book. Although this collection of 100 poems is an interesting brew of wisdom and melancholy, beauty and rapture, it is as a prose writer that he will be remembered. His *Collected Poems* (1936) and *Selected Poems* (1948) are worthy of attention, but his strength is to be found in his studies of art and literature. Among his books on music and composers, *Mozart* (1932), *Liszt* (1934), and *Scarlatti* (1935) have the most staying power.

Prominent among Sacheverell Sitwell's more than sixty books are his autobiographical volumes, *All Summer in a Day* (1926), *Dance of the Quick and the Dead* (1936), and *For Want of a Golden City* (1973), in which he wrote of his family and friends, his responses to what he found most appealing. With something of an existential touch, he dilated upon oral and visual memories, focused upon all he preferred to recollect, and glossed over most troublesome aspects of his days and years. He lived latterly at Weston Hall, Towcester, Northamptonshire. Sacheverell Sitwell died on 1 October 1988.   G. A. CEVASCO

Sources G. A. Cevasco, *The Sitwells: Edith, Osbert, and Sacheverell* (1987) · J. Pearson, *Façades: Edith, Osbert and Sacheverell Sitwell* (1978) · R. L. Mégroz, *The three Sitwells* (1927) · J. Lehmann, *A nest of tigers: the Sitwells in their time* (1968) · M. Wykes-Joyce, *Triad of genius* (1953) · S. Bradford, H. Clerk, J. Fryer, R. Gibson, and J. Pearson, *The Sitwells and the arts of the 1920s and 1930s: a pictorial biography* (1996) · N. Ritchie, *Sacheverell Sitwell: an annotated and descriptive bibliography, 1916–1986* (1987) · S. Bradford, *Splendours and miseries: a life of Sacheverell Sitwell* (1993) · G. Sitwell, *Never a dull moment* (1975) · DNB
Archives NRA, corresp. and literary papers · Ransom HRC, notebooks · University of Iowa Libraries, Iowa City, letters and literary MSS · York University, Toronto, Scott Library, literary notebooks | BL, letters to Sydney Schiff and Violet Schiff, Add. MS 52922 · King's Cam., letters to E. J. Dent · LUL, corresp. with Duckworth & Co. · Ransom HRC, letters to E. R. S. Fifoot · Tate collection, letters to Thomas Lowinsky · Washington State University, letters to Thomas Balston
Likenesses A. Rutherston, lithograph, 1928, Scarborough county council · three photographs, c.1940–1984, Hult. Arch. · M. Black, bronze bust, 1985, NPG · C. Beaton, caricature, triptych, U. Texas · C. Beaton, photographs, NPG [see illus.] · M. Beck and H. MacGregor, photograph, NPG · Denys, photograph, NPG · R. S. Sherriffs, ink caricature (with George Bernard Shaw), NPG
Wealth at death £161,284: probate, 11 Aug 1989, CGPLA Eng. & Wales

Siward (*d.* 1048), bishop and coadjutor-archbishop, was a monk of Glastonbury, and succeeded Æthelwine as abbot of Abingdon, probably in 1030. An extant grant by Cnut may have been solicited by Siward to finance his plan to rebuild St Æthelwold's church at Abingdon. But he abandoned the plan and gave the money to the poor instead, after St Æthelwold had appeared to him in a dream and forbidden the destruction of the church.

Eadsige, the archbishop of Canterbury, finding in 1042 that ill health prevented him from discharging the duties

of his office, with the consent of the king and Earl Godwine, consecrated Siward as his suffragan, so that he might act as his coadjutor. Eadsige probably intended that Siward should succeed to the archiepiscopal see: he is described as archbishop of Canterbury in the history of the abbots of Abingdon, and as archbishop in the attestations of three charters, where his name has precedence over that of the archbishop of York. However, in another charter he appears simply as bishop, his name coming after that of the archbishop of York. For six years Siward acted in all things in Eadsige's place. The story that he ill-treated the archbishop and was consequently deprived of the succession may be rejected. He retired on account of ill health in 1048, and was carried back sick to Abingdon. He probably died two months after his return to Abingdon, on 23 October, and was honourably buried there, for he was a munificent benefactor to the monastery, to which he gave Wittenham, near Wallingford, and all the furniture of his chapel. There has been continual confusion between him and the *Siward who held the bishopric of Rochester from 1058 to 1075.

WILLIAM HUNT, rev. MARIOS COSTAMBEYS

Sources F. Barlow, *The English church, 1000–1066: a history of the later Anglo-Saxon church*, 2nd edn (1979) · ASC, s.a. 1046, 1048 [texts C, E] · AS chart., S 1007, 1008, 1010, 1012 · J. Stevenson, ed., *Chronicon monasterii de Abingdon*, 2 vols., Rolls Series, 2 (1858), vol. 1 · E. B. Fryde and others, eds., *Handbook of British chronology*, 3rd edn, Royal Historical Society Guides and Handbooks, 2 (1986)

Siward, earl of Northumbria (*d.* 1055), magnate, first appears witnessing as *dux* in a charter by King Cnut for Archbishop Ælfric of York in 1033. Siward's name (Sigvarthr) suggests that he was of Danish stock, although the names of his parents are unknown. The life of King Edward recorded his nickname as 'Digri', or 'Digara', from the Danish *Diger* meaning 'the Stout', or 'the Strong'. A legend preserved in the twelfth century noted that Siward was descended from the union of a white bear and a noblewoman.

Siward succeeded Earl *Erik of Hlathir in southern Northumbria between 1023 and 1033, the dates of Erik's last appearance in a charter and Siward's first. Siward was one of those to whom Cnut delegated significant authority in England while he was occupied in his Scandinavian lands. The northern part of Northumbria remained in the hands of the earls of Bamburgh. Eadulf Cudel had succeeded his brother Earl Uhtred c.1016 and was, in turn, succeeded by Uhtred's son Ealdred. Earl Ealdred was himself followed by another Eadulf, who was Uhtred's son by another wife. In 1041, however, Siward killed this Earl Eadulf and assumed control of all Northumbria. Siward played a significant role in the politics of the kingdom of the English during the reigns of Cnut, Harthacnut, and Edward the Confessor, often acting in concert with Earl Leofric of Mercia in opposition to the Godwine family. A measure of his activity may be obtained by examining his attestation of royal charters in this period. For example, he witnessed a lease of land by Ælfwine, bishop of Winchester, to Osgod in 1043 or 1044, possibly around the time of the attack on Queen Emma described below. He was also a witness to the endowment of Stow St Mary by Earl Leofric and his wife, Godgifu, between 1053 and 1055. This may reflect his close relationship with the comital house of Mercia. For a time Siward seems to have held the earldom of Huntingdon and there is a semi-legendary account of his slaying of a certain Tostig, earl of Huntingdon.

In 1041 Siward took part in an attack on the monastery and town of Worcester following the murder there of two of King Harthacnut's tax gatherers, Feader and Thurstan. After Edward the Confessor's coronation, Siward, together with earls Leofric and Godwine, advised the king to ride from Gloucester to Winchester. The earls accompanied him and, on 16 November 1043, they arrested Emma, the queen mother. Emma's wealth was confiscated on the grounds that she had not aided Edward as much as she might have done and that she had been harsh towards him. An account of the translation of St Mildrith added that Emma was accused of inciting King Magnus of Norway to attack Edward's realm. During the crisis of 1051–2, when Earl Godwine and his sons collected their forces and threatened the king near Gloucester, Siward acted together with Earl Leofric of Mercia and Earl Ralph in first opposing Godwine and his family on the king's behalf and then allowing them to regain their positions in 1052. The C and D texts of the Anglo-Saxon Chronicle suggest that the earls' hesitancy in attacking Godwine and then allowing his return was born of a fear that civil war would leave the kingdom open to foreign invasion.

Siward is named by the Norman chronicler William of Poitiers as being one of those magnates of England who swore an oath to secure Duke William of Normandy's succession to the English throne. Siward's rule in Northumbria was seen as particularly harsh but effective by contemporary sources. The life of King Edward describes how before the earl's time parties of even twenty or thirty men were not safe from robbers, but that Siward's policy of killing or mutilating the miscreants, however noble, brought security to the region. Siward may also have expanded his control into Cumbria, as a writ issued in the name of a certain Gospatric, ruler of that area, seems to suggest that he was under Siward's overlordship. Siward reinstated Æthelric, bishop of Durham, who had offered him money after being driven out of his bishopric by the community of St Cuthbert in 1045. In 1054 Siward invaded Scotland on behalf of his nephew, *Malcolm Canmore (d. 1093), who claimed the throne of his father, Duncan, in opposition to Macbeth. Soon after Duncan's overthrow in 1040 Malcolm had fled Scotland and found a refuge at his uncle's court in York. According to some sources it was on the order of Edward the Confessor that Siward prepared a land and sea assault against Macbeth. Having routed the Scots and their Norman allies, the earl ravaged the kingdom, so the twelfth-century chronicler Henry of Huntingdon reported. During the decisive battle on the Day of the Seven Sleepers (27 July 1054), fought in Perthshire, north of the River Tay, Siward's son, Osbeorn, was killed together with the earl's nephew, another Siward.

Earl Siward married first Ælfflæd, a daughter of Earl Ealdred of Bamburgh, and they had at least two sons, Osbeorn and *Waltheof; it is not known whether the couple had any daughters. A second wife, Godgifu, is recorded as promising to give the two estates of Belmesthorpe and Ryhall near Stamford to Peterborough Abbey on her death. She predeceased Siward and he made an agreement with the abbey whereby he held both estates until his death. According to Domesday Book the manors were held by Waltheof at the time of King Edward's death and by Waltheof's widow, Judith, in 1086.

Henry of Huntingdon described Earl Siward as a giant of a man 'whose vigour of mind was equal to his bodily strength' (Huntingdon, *Historia Anglorum* (OMT), 376). During an attack on Scotland, when one of his sons was killed, Siward enquired whether he had received his wound in front or behind. When informed that the wound had been received in front, the earl rejoiced that his son had died a fitting death. This may refer to the death of Osbeorn at the hands of the Scots in 1054. Also according to Henry of Huntingdon, Earl Siward himself died of dysentery. He felt ashamed that he was not going to die in one of his many battles and asked to be dressed in his armour, so that, with shield and battleaxe in his hands, he might die a soldier's death. This was at York, before mid-Lent 1055, when he was buried in the monastery which he had founded at 'Galmanho', dedicated to St Olaf, king and martyr—which indicates Siward's continued Danish sympathies. Bootham Bar in York was formerly Galmanhithe and the site of the monastery there was given to St Mary's Abbey, York. The earldom was given to Tostig, son of Earl Godwine of Wessex, possibly because Siward's surviving son, Waltheof, was still young in 1055 and the influence of the Godwine faction at court was overwhelming. According to Domesday Book, Earl Siward and his son held lands worth around £350. This cannot, however, represent the total value of his estates while in office, as Domesday Book did not survey the lands to the north of the River Tees or the larger part of Cumbria. Siward's recorded lands lay in Derbyshire and in Yorkshire, most notably at Whitby.

WILLIAM M. AIRD

Sources ASC, s.a. 1043, 1044, 1048, 1051, 1052, 1053, 1055 [texts C, D, and E] · John of Worcester, *Chron.* · A. J. Robertson, ed. and trans., *Anglo-Saxon charters* (1939) · F. Barlow, ed. and trans., *The life of King Edward who rests at Westminster*, 2nd edn, OMT (1992) · F. E. Harmer, ed., *Anglo-Saxon writs* (1952) · P. A. Clarke, *The English nobility under Edward the Confessor* (1994) · M. K. Lawson, *Cnut: the Danes in England in the early eleventh century* (1993) · F. Barlow, *Edward the Confessor* (1970) · W. E. Kapelle, *The Norman conquest of the north: the region and its transformation, 1000–1135* (1979) · Guillaume de Poitiers [Gulielmus Pictaviensis], *Histoire de Guillaume le Conquérant / Gesta Gulielmus ducis Normannorum et regis Anglorum*, ed. R. Foreville (Paris, 1952) · Henry, archdeacon of Huntingdon, *Historia Anglorum*, ed. D. E. Greenway, OMT (1996) · A. O. Anderson, ed., *Scottish annals from English chroniclers, AD 500 to 1286* (1908)
Wealth at death over £350: *Domesday book*

Siward (*d.* 1075), abbot of Chertsey and bishop of Rochester, was consecrated bishop by Archbishop Stigand in 1058, after he had received his pallium from Pope Benedict X. He assisted at the consecration of Archbishop Lanfranc in August 1070, was allowed to retain his see, and died in possession of it in 1075. At his death his church was in a very impoverished state. This bishop has been confused with Siward (d. 1048), coadjutor of Archbishop Eadsige. WILLIAM HUNT, rev. MARIOS COSTAMBEYS

Sources ASC, s.a. 1058 [texts D, E] • [H. Wharton], ed., *Anglia sacra*, 2 vols. (1691) • E. B. Fryde and others, eds., *Handbook of British chronology*, 3rd edn, Royal Historical Society Guides and Handbooks, 2 (1986)

Siward, Sir Richard (d. 1248), mercenary and courtier, has obscure origins. In his earliest appearances he is Richard son of Siward, indicating English ancestry and the name of a father or earlier progenitor. It is probable that he was the young man of that name from Farnham in Lower Nithsdale, Yorkshire, who was accused of homicide late in John's reign, arrested, but later released into the military household of an unnamed Yorkshire magnate. Coincidentally, the first certain appearance of Sir Richard is about 1215 in the retinue of William de Forz, count of Aumale, lord of Holderness in Yorkshire's East Riding. Along with other former Aumale followers Richard Siward was retained in the household of William (II) Marshal, earl of Pembroke, and appeared with him in London in 1216, by which time he had achieved the status of knight. He was later reputed to have played a role in the sea battle off Sandwich in 1217. He again fought for the count of Aumale in his rebellion at the end of 1220. Siward escaped the siege of Bytham, and for a period of a week or two in February 1221 in the Forest of Cliff, Northamptonshire, he held off a royal army. He surrendered and left the kingdom, but was pardoned in September of that year.

In 1223 Siward was once again in the retinue of Earl William Marshal and followed him over the next few years into Wales, Ireland, and Brittany. He received manors and rents from his patron. The Marshal connection also brought him into friendship with the Basset family of Headington and High Wycombe, for Gilbert Basset was a prominent Marshal banneret. In October 1229 Siward married Philippa *Basset (d. 1265), Gilbert's cousin and daughter of Thomas Basset of Headington, only a few weeks after the death of her first husband, Henry (II) de Newburgh, earl of Warwick. This was the turning point of Siward's career, for Philippa brought him control of her share of the lands of Basset of Headington and her handsome dower settlement from the Warwick estates.

The Basset connection brought Siward less profitable consequences in 1233, when Gilbert Basset fell into royal disfavour. Siward shared in his disgrace, being accused (wrongly) of marrying Philippa without royal licence. Siward and Basset found shelter in Gwent with Earl Richard Marshal, who then rebelled against Henry III. On the earl's behalf Richard Siward led several daring forays out of Netherwent and deep into England. One of these was in late September 1233, when Siward and several score of raiders rode across England into Berkshire and pillaged a manor of Bishop Peter des Roches. On 29 October Siward liberated the fugitive Hubert de Burgh from his sanctuary in Devizes church, leading his force of knights and Welsh mercenaries into the town in a fog, causing the Welsh to give their war-cry and the townspeople and besiegers to flee in the belief that Prince Llewelyn's men had come.

The force and de Burgh returned, meeting boats at Aust, Gloucestershire, on the Bristol Channel, which ferried his party back safely to Chepstow and Earl Richard Marshal, despite encountering a hostile royalist fleet and military force from Bristol. This and like episodes made Siward's name synonymous with opposition to the obnoxious 'Poitevin' regime in 1233–4, and accounts for his subsequent fame.

At the conclusion of the Marshal–Basset rebellion in May 1234 Richard Siward was pardoned, appointed to the king's council, and given temporary keeping of Glamorgan and the castle of Bolsover, Derbyshire. He had fees in Glamorgan from the king or the earl marshal, and in England from de Burgh. Alexander II of Scotland gave him the castle and lordship of Kellie, with other lands in Aberdour, Fife. However, Siward's career was uneven. In 1236 he had both the honour of carrying the sceptre at the queen's coronation, and the disgrace of imprisonment through the machinations of a court cabal. He survived this plot, and was retained in the royal household (for an annual fee of 100 marks), in 1242 serving as a banneret with the king's army in Poitou. It may be that at this time he was retained also by Simon de Montfort, earl of Leicester, who had awarded him a money fee before 1245.

But difficulties began to close in around Siward. His friend Gilbert Basset died in 1241, and Philippa Basset, his wife, somehow managed to obtain a swift divorce from Siward by the autumn of 1242. After this he seems to have retired for a time to his Scottish estates. Siward received another blow when Richard de Clare, earl of Gloucester and Hertford, and lord of Glamorgan, had him arrested on 5 July 1245 while going, unsuspecting, to a meeting of the Glamorgan county court. The earl's avowed justification was that Siward had sided with a Welsh magnate of the area against him, but it is evident that the earl's chief purpose was to reclaim areas of his lordship abstracted from the St Quintin family by Siward while the earl was a minor. Siward's castle of Tal-y-fan and extensive lordship of Llanblethian were confiscated. He disputed the disseisin before the king in 1247 and was still in pursuit of justice in July 1248. He died soon after a crippling stroke, by the end of the same year. He left to the wardship of King Alexander an under-age son, also Richard Siward, whom he had with Philippa, and an adult bastard called Daniel, to whom he had given lands at Merthyr Mawr in Glamorgan before 1245.

Siward's career is a remarkable story of social advancement based solely on military prowess. Like the career of the elder William Marshal, it shows the importance of finding the right patron. It is doubtful whether Siward would have risen far in a hostile and increasingly class-conscious world without such support. A marcher writer calls him Richard Severus, which would seem to be an ironic contemporary nickname for him among the literate clergy and laity, alluding to the great philosopher–emperor, whose urbanity, education, and piety Richard Siward must too obviously have lacked.

DAVID CROUCH, rev.

Sources D. Crouch, 'The last adventure of Richard Siward', *Morgannwg*, 35 (1991), 7–30 · M. L. Colker, 'The *Margam chronicle* in a Dublin manuscript', *Haskins Society Journal*, 4 (1992), 123–48 · D. M. Stenton, ed., *Rolls of the justices in eyre … Yorkshire in 3 Henry III, 1218–1219*, SeldS, 56 (1937) · *Ann. mon.* · Paris, *Chron.* · *Rogeri de Wendover liber qui dicitur flores historiarum*, ed. H. G. Hewlett, 3 vols., Rolls Series, [84] (1886–9) · GEC, *Peerage* · G. T. Clark, ed., *Cartae et alia munimenta quae ad dominium de Glamorgancia pertinent*, ed. G. L. Clark, 6 vols. (1910)

Six, James (1730–1793), silk weaver and natural philosopher, was born in Canterbury, Kent, on 30 January 1730, and baptized there in the Walloon church on 26 February. He was the son of James Six (1695–1743) and his wife, Ester, daughter of Louis Ducaufour, and descended from the Huguenot refugee families who came to Britain in the sixteenth century and settled in Canterbury, where they engaged in the silk weaving trade. Six was brought up in the family business but declining trade prompted him to retire early and devote himself to the wide range of interests typical of an eighteenth-century intellectual, though there is no evidence that he ever received any formal training. He was a good artist, and he was certainly a competent amateur astronomer: he sent several observations of comets and of the planet Uranus to William Herschel, to the *Gentleman's Magazine*, and to the American Philosophical Society, which enrolled him as a foreign member in 1787.

Six is best remembered for the self-registering thermometer which he invented, the first to record maximum and minimum temperatures on a single instrument. He was elected a fellow of the Royal Society in 1792 for this invention and his own temperature observations. His book on these subjects was published posthumously as *The Construction and Use of a Thermometer* (1794); twenty-five experimental forms of air and marine thermometer made by him have been preserved. Six never patented his designs. He sent examples of the air thermometer to friends at home and abroad, and soon after his death it was adopted by the Royal Society and Kew observatory. Versions of his marine thermometer served for deep-sea measurements throughout the nineteenth century. Two centuries after its invention, 'Six's' remained a popular house and garden thermometer.

All accounts of Six describe him as a competent yet modest and unassuming man of great integrity, and a devout Christian. With Robert Deane he founded and supported a Sunday school in the parish of Holy Cross in Kent, which offered religious instruction and taught reading and singing to poor children, and much of his time was devoted to this cause. On 21 May 1754 Six married Mary Riquebourg (1733–1801) of Canterbury; they had four sons, three of whom died in infancy and one in 1786, and a daughter. Six died on 25 August 1793 and was buried at Holy Cross, Westgate, Canterbury. He and his wife, who was also buried at Holy Cross, were commemorated in a tablet within the chancel.   ANITA McCONNELL

Sources J. F. Austin and A. McConnell, 'James Six, FRS: two hundred years of the Six's self-registering thermometer', *Notes and Records of the Royal Society*, 35 (1980), 49–65 · *GM*, 1st ser., 63 (1793), 864 · election certificate, RS · parish register, St Mildred, Canterbury · J. M. Cowper, ed., *The memorial inscriptions in the church and churchyard of Holy Cross, Westgate, Canterbury* (1888) · marriage licence, 1754, diocese of Canterbury

Skae, David (1814–1873), physician and asylum superintendent, was born in Edinburgh on 5 July 1814, one of the two sons of David Skae, builder and architect, and his wife, Helen Lothian. As both Skae's parents died while he was a child, he moved to St Andrews to live with his maternal uncle, the Reverend William *Lothian, who was responsible for his education. At the age of fourteen Skae enrolled as a student in the arts faculty of St Andrews University, leaving at the age of sixteen to work as a clerk in an Edinburgh lawyer's office. He then entered the Edinburgh extra-mural medical school, becoming a licentiate of the College of Surgeons, Edinburgh, in 1835, and a fellow in 1836. After this he became a partner of Dr Davidson, a general practitioner in Edinburgh. In 1836, Skae became lecturer in medical jurisprudence in the extra-mural school, and his lectures proved to be popular. At the same time he became surgeon to the Lock Hospital and held this appointment for ten years. On Christmas day, 1837, he married Sarah, daughter of Major Alexander Macpherson, late of the 2nd West India regiment; they had five sons. Skae was described as a stout figure, with a massive head of brown curly hair, who was jovial and charming in company.

Skae wrote several original articles on syphilis, and was also appointed as an examiner in medicine at St Andrews University, which led to an honorary degree of MD being conferred on him in 1842. In the same year he succeeded Robert Knox as one of the lecturers on anatomy in the extra-mural school in Edinburgh. In 1846 he was appointed physician superintendent at the Morningside Asylum (later the Royal Edinburgh Asylum), and held this post until his death. In 1863 he was president of the Association of Medical Officers of Asylums, and in 1873 was nominated Morison lecturer in insanity at the Royal College of Physicians in Edinburgh.

Skae's most significant contribution was in the field of mental disease. He was judged an able and humane superintendent of the asylum, and in his annual reports he emphasized the need for the careful organization of the institution, and for a healthy and active regime for the inmates. During his period of office the asylum doubled in size, and Skae brought about improvements in the accommodation by providing cottages for small groups of patients. The reputation of Morningside was also enhanced, and several assistant physicians, such as John Batty Tuke, David Yellowlees, and Thomas Clouston, who went on to achieve eminence in the field of lunacy, trained under him. Skae was also an enthusiastic teacher, who set up a regular course of lectures and demonstrations for students.

In his published work Skae was interested in the classification of mental disease, general paralysis, alcoholism, and the legal aspects of lunacy. He was a somaticist in his approach to insanity, defining it as a disease of the brain affecting the mind. Skae made an ambitious attempt at the classification of insanity based on aetiology, which he outlined in his 1863 paper in the *Journal of Mental Science*, and, further, in his series of 1873 Morison lectures, which were completed after his death by his pupil, Thomas Clouston. Skae's classification was not adopted outside Edinburgh and was heavily criticized by his contemporaries. Other important publications by Skae include his 1857 article on 'Mental diseases' in the eighth edition of the *Encyclopaedia Britannica*, his discussions of 'Dipsomania' (1858) and 'General paralysis' (1860), and his two papers on 'The legal relations of insanity' (1861, 1867).

Skae's last years were overshadowed by illness, and he died at his home, Tipperlinn House, Morningside Place, Edinburgh, on 18 April 1873 from cancer of the oesophagus. He was survived by his wife and children.

ALLAN BEVERIDGE

Sources F. Fish, 'David Skae, founder of the Edinburgh School of Psychiatry', *Medical History*, 9 (1965), 36–53 · T. S. C. [T. S. Clouston], *Journal of Mental Science*, 19 (1873), 323–4 · *Edinburgh Medical Journal*, 18 (1872–3), 1055–6 · *BMJ* (10 May 1873), 549 · *The Lancet* (21 June 1873), 897 · H. Freeman and G. E. Berrios, eds., *150 years of British psychiatry*, 1: *1841–1991* (1991) · parish register (marriage), 25 Dec 1837, Edinburgh, St Cuthbert's · d. cert. · *London and Provincial Medical Directory* (1867)

Archives U. Edin. L., Lothian Health Services collection

Likenesses photograph, 1861, NPG · photograph, repro. in Freeman and Berrios, eds., *150 years of British psychiatry*

Skating Minister, the. *See* Walker, Robert (1755–1808).

Skeaping, John Rattenbury (1901–1980), sculptor and teacher of sculpture, was born on 9 June 1901 at South Woodford, Essex, the second son of Kenneth Skeaping (1856–1946), a painter, and his wife, Mary Mathieson, a professional piano teacher. When he was thirteen he studied sculpture for a year at Blackheath School of Art, London, then from 1915 to 1917 attended the school of art at Goldsmiths' College; thereafter he attended the Central School of Arts and Crafts (1917–19) and the Royal Academy Schools (1919–20). 'In the two years I was there I won every prize that was open to sculpture students' (J. Skeaping, 46). In 1920 he won the Royal Academy gold medal and travelling scholarship, which enabled him to visit Rome, Siena, and Florence. Four years later he won the *prix de Rome* for sculpture and returned to Rome, where he learned marble carving from Giovanni Ardini, a professional mason. In Italy, Skeaping met Barbara *Hepworth (1903–1975), who had been runner-up for the *prix de Rome*, and they were married at the Palazzo Vecchio, Florence, on 13 May 1925. In his autobiography he recalled: 'Barbara had a strong influence on me. She was a great admirer of Henry Moore and all things modern. I started to change the style of my own work' (ibid., 71).

The couple returned to England at the end of 1926 and took rented accommodation in St Anne's Terrace, St John's Wood, London. Skeaping and Hepworth held a joint exhibition of their recent carvings and drawings in their St John's Wood studio in December 1927, and then at Tooth's Gallery, Bond Street, London, and the Alex Reid and Lefevre Gallery, Glasgow, in spring 1928. Both shows sold out and improved their financial situations. Skeaping

John Rattenbury Skeaping (1901–1980), by Howard Coster, 1943

and Hepworth were early exponents of direct carving, and Skeaping was probably the first sculptor in Britain to pierce a hole through a stone carving (*c*.1930). His sculpture at this time included animal and figure subjects influenced by non-European traditions. Wedgwood commissioned Skeaping in 1927 to produce a series of ten small animal groups for a fee of £10 per animal, to be cast in glazed coloured ceramics; he produced *Deer*, *Kangaroo*, *Buffalo*, *Sea Lion*, *Monkeys*, *Antelope*, *Bison*, *Duiker*, *Polar Bear*, and *Tiger and Buck*, which were commercially very successful and popular.

Early in 1928 Skeaping and Hepworth moved to 7 The Mall Studios, Parkhill Road, Hampstead, close to Henry Moore, where they became part of a group of avant-garde British artists. Their son, Paul, was born in August 1929. Skeaping was a member of the London Group from 1928 to 1934 and of the Seven and Five Society in 1932, and he taught at the Central School of Arts from 1930 to 1939. He separated from Hepworth in 1931 and they were divorced in 1933. In the early 1930s Skeaping befriended Julian Huxley, secretary to the London Zoological Society, who asked the artist to paint a fresco of animals on the walls of the new restaurant there. Huxley was also responsible for placing a large carved wooden horse by Skeaping at Whipsnade Zoo (now in the Tate collection). In 1933 Skeaping provided the illustrations for *The Whipsnade Animal Book*, and this reinforced his reputation as an animalier.

Skeaping married Morwenna Ward on 7 April 1934, and they had three sons—twins Colin and Christopher (*b.*

1944) and Nicholas (*b.* 1947). Skeaping and his wife left London and went to live on Dartmoor; this allowed him to combine his love of animals with carving the local stone, granite. From 1940 to 1945 Skeaping served in the intelligence corps as an official war artist and spent a short spell with the SAS:

> Even in the army, the style with which he wore his beret was distinctive and at first sight made him look more like a handsome Basque gypsy than a soldier. His irreverence was profound, and of course a great tonic to his colleagues. (Sir John Astor, memorial service address, 24 April 1980)

He taught sculpture at the Royal College of Art from 1948 and was professor of sculpture at the college from 1953 to 1959. During 1949–50 he worked in Mexico, where he studied the pottery techniques of the ancient Mexicans. He was made an associate of the Royal Academy in 1950 and Royal Academician in 1960. In 1959 he left Britain to live in the Camargue, where he was surrounded by horses. His marriage to Morwenna was dissolved in 1969, and on 6 June that year he married Margery Scott in Marseilles.

Skeaping wrote several instructional books, beginning with *Animal Drawing* in 1936; this was followed by *How to Draw Horses* in 1941 and *How to Draw Dogs* in 1961. His more personal writings were *The Big Tree of Mexico* (1952) and his autobiography, *Drawn from Life* (1977). In the 1930s and 1940s he concentrated on animal and figure sculpture, and only later focused on equine subject matter. During the 1960s and 1970s Skeaping was much in demand making bronze portraits of champion racehorses—for example, *Hyperion* for Lord Derby in 1961 and *Brigadier Gerard* for John Hislop in 1972. His sculpture may also be found in a variety of architectural settings; examples include stone corbels (1933) for Ashmore church, Dorset; wooden relief panels (1953) for the United Nations building, New York; and a black limestone relief (1958) over the main entrance of the New College of Science, Kensington, London.

Skeaping was given a retrospective exhibition of bronzes at Arthur Ackermann's Gallery, London, in 1979, and this show travelled to the National Museum of Racing, Saratoga, New York. Skeaping died in London on 5 March 1980, and the Ackermann Gallery mounted a scholarly retrospective exhibition in 1991 which helped to restore his reputation as a pioneer of direct carving. His work may be found in many public collections, among them the Ashmolean Museum, Oxford, the British Museum, the Fitzwilliam Museum, Cambridge, the Victoria and Albert Museum, and the Tate collection. The Hon. J. J. Astor, a long-standing friend of the artist, described Skeaping as

> unconventional … ubiquitous … and basically elusive. He was the best of companions: enthusiastic, sensitive, observant, sharp without being malicious, and his judgments were always worth hearing. Convention meant little to him, and never dictated his way of life. He seemed to be sustained and motivated by some inner vitality and gaiety, which both protected him and adapted him for many backgrounds. He was equally at home with primitive Mexican Indians, working with trainers at Newmarket or

with herdsmen in France. (Skeaping and Hely-Hutchinson, 70)

JUDITH COLLINS

Sources J. Skeaping, *Drawn from life: an autobiography* (1977) · N. Skeaping and N. Hely-Hutchinson, *John Skeaping, 1901–1980: a retrospective* (1991) [exhibition catalogue, Arthur Ackermann & Son Ltd, London, June 1991]
Archives Rice University, Woodson Research Center, corresp. with J. Huxley · V&A, questionnaire completed for Kineton Parkes
Likenesses B. Hepworth, drawing, 1925, Tate collection · H. Coster, photograph, 1943, NPG [*see illus.*]

Skeat, Bertha Marian (1861–1948). *See under* Skeat, Walter William (1835–1912).

Skeat, Walter William (1835–1912), philologist, was born at Mount Street, Park Lane, London, on 21 November 1835, the second son of William Skeat and his wife, Sarah Bluck. He attended King's College School, Strand, where Thomas Oswald Cockayne, one of the best Anglo-Saxon scholars of the time, was his form-master. From there he went to Sir Roger Cholmeley's School, Highgate, and in 1854 entered Christ's College, Cambridge. There C. S. Calverley, J. R. Seeley, and Walter Besant were among his friends. He studied theology and mathematics, took the mathematical tripos (fourteenth wrangler) in 1858, and was elected a fellow of his college in 1860. In the latter year he took orders, and entered on his first curacy at East Dereham, Norfolk. On 15 November 1860 he married Bertha Clara Jones (*b.* 1839/40, *d.* in or after 1912), eldest daughter of Francis Jones, of Lewisham. They had two sons and four daughters, including Bertha Marian Skeat [*see below*]. Two years later Skeat became curate of Godalming, but a serious illness affecting his throat closed his career in the church.

Skeat returned to Cambridge, and was appointed to a mathematical lectureship at Christ's College in 1864. The duties left him ample leisure, and he now began the serious study of Early English, which had first been roused by the extracts in the history book which he used at school; he had worked back to them through the *Faerie Queene*. But it was Frederick James Furnivall who first set him to work as an editor. The discussion of plans for the *New English Dictionary* (later the *Oxford English Dictionary*) had revealed a dearth of trustworthy early texts, and to supply the want Furnivall and Richard Morris formed the Early English Text Society in 1864. Skeat was pressed into service, and punctually edited *Lancelot of the Laik* (1865). In 1866 he began his great edition of *Piers Plowman*, which was finished twenty years later. This remained the standard edition for over a hundred years, and crucially influenced twentieth-century textual scholarship on the poem; his interpretative and historical notes are still referred to by modern critics and editors. The first part of his edition of John Barbour's *The Bruce* appeared in 1870, and by 1872 he had published the *Treatise on the Astrolabe*. This was one of many studies preliminary to his seven-volume edition of Chaucer (1894–7), another standard work which was not superseded until the edition of Robinson in 1933, and

Walter William Skeat (1835–1912), by James Russell & Sons, 1899

whose interpretative and historical notes were regularly consulted by editors working on the Riverside edition of Chaucer, published in 1987. This might seem a life's work, but it is only a part of Skeat's contribution to the study of one century—the fourteenth. He produced two standard works in Anglo-Saxon, the *Anglo-Saxon Gospels* (1871–87) and Ælfric's *Lives of Saints* (1881–1900), and in 1873 he founded the English Dialect Society, which prepared the way for the *English Dialect Dictionary* (edited by Joseph Wright, 1896–1905). Another important book, his *Etymological Dictionary* (1879–82; revised and enlarged, 1910), was begun with the purpose of collecting and sifting material for the use of the *Oxford English Dictionary*. This project was one to which he made an enormous contribution, ranging from editorial work (including supplying numerous quotations) to supporting the dictionary's editor, J. A. H. Murray, with a mortgage to purchase his house.

Besides these larger works, Skeat found time to edit Chatterton (1871), to write many textbooks for schools and universities, to popularize philology and modernize old authors, and to contribute freely to the learned societies and journals concerned with English studies. Furthermore, in his latter years he led the way in the systematic study of place names, county by county. In 1878 he was elected to the new Elrington and Bosworth professorship of Anglo-Saxon at Cambridge.

All Skeat's vast output is distinguished by accuracy in matter of fact, wide learning, and humanity, and most of it he produced without prospect of reward, out of devotion to his subject. His own prescription for such monuments of scholarship was enthusiasm, with unremitting application, and he wasted no time. He could also set practical limits to his curiosity: in the preface to the first edition of the *Etymological Dictionary* he explains that he usually gave three hours to a difficult word—'During that time I made the best I could of it and then let it go.' This requires self-sacrifice in a scholar, but it is the secret of Skeat's great service. According to his obituary in *The Times*, Skeat was the first Cambridge professor to ride a

bicycle, and was in general better known to the general public of Cambridge than were his professorial colleagues. This was partly because of the fame of his etymological dictionary, on which he conducted a vast correspondence with word enthusiasts both professional and amateur, and partly because

> in fine weather he almost invariably walked the mile and a half from his house [2 Salisbury Villas] to the Divinity Schools, where he lectured, in a peculiar ambling trot, with his silk gown caught up behind him on one arm. His white beard at once attracted attention, and it never seemed rude to watch him because he always appeared oblivious of passers-by.   (*The Times*, 8 Oct 1912)

Walter William Skeat died at 2 Salisbury Villas, Cambridge, on 6 October 1912, survived by his wife, two sons, and three daughters. He was buried in the grounds of the parish church of the Ascension, Huntingdon Road, Cambridge. In 1935 a commemorative stained-glass window, designed and executed by one of his grandsons, F. W. Skeat, was placed in the library of his old college. It depicts Geoffrey Chaucer on horseback, with Canterbury Cathedral in the background.

The new school of philology that arose towards 1880, when the lines of Skeat's work were laid down and much of it done, produced men like Zupitza and Sievers in Germany, or Henry Sweet, A. S. Napier, and Henry Bradley in England, who went beyond Skeat in linguistic theory and in exact methods. But Skeat's pioneer work made such advances possible. At a critical moment in English studies he saw the wisdom of Furnivall's doctrine, that the essential thing was to attract workers, and to make available for them quickly a great quantity of materials, edited as well as possible, but always with a time limit in view rather than perfection in minutiae. And perhaps he gained as much ground for his subject by quiet sapping as Furnivall took by storm.

Bertha Marian Skeat (1861–1948), schoolmistress, was born on 30 December 1861 at Quebec Road, East Dereham, Norfolk, the eldest child of Walter William Skeat and his wife, Bertha Clara, *née* Jones. She read medieval and modern languages at Newnham College, Cambridge (1882–6), and gained a first-class examination result in 1886. After obtaining a Cambridge teacher's certificate she took a PhD degree at the University of Zürich, and returned as a lecturer at the Cambridge Teaching College for Women (1890–93). Thereafter she occupied a number of teaching positions before becoming co-founder and principal of Baliol School, Sedbergh, from 1899 to 1932, when the school closed. She published a *Word-List* illustrating the correspondence of modern English with Anglo-French vowel sounds for the English Dialect Society (1884), a primer of historical English grammar, and two anthologies of English literature for use in schools. She also wrote some pleasant but undistinguished verse in late-Victorian sentimental style, including school plays, principally concerning the relations between mothers and daughters; such publications include: *The Lamentations of Mary Magdalene* (1897), *Atalanta's Race* (1907), and *The Crucifixion of Mary,* *and other Poems* [1924]. Bertha Marian Skeat died, unmarried, at Baliol Cottage, Sedbergh, Yorkshire, on 2 December 1948.   KENNETH SISAM, *rev.* CHARLOTTE BREWER

Sources W. W. Skeat, *A student's pastime* (1896) • C. Brewer, *Editing Piers Plowman* (1996), esp. 91–105 • A. Sherbo, 'Walter William Skeat (1835–1912) in the *Cambridge Review*', *Yearbook of Langland Studies*, 3 (1989), 109–30 • private information (1927, 2004) • [A. B. White], ed., *Newnham College register*, 1: *1871–1923* (1964), 73 • m. cert. • b. cert. [B. M. Skeat] • d. cert. [B. M. Skeat] • *CGPLA Eng. & Wales* (1912)
Archives King's Lond., corresp. and papers relating to English Dialect Society • MHS Oxf., corresp. relating to *English dialect dictionary* • U. Oxf., Institute of Social and Cultural Anthropology, notes, papers, and pamphlet collection | BL, corresp. with Macmillans, Add. MS 55016 • Bodl. Oxf., corresp. with Thomas Hallam • Bodl. Oxf., letters to A. S. Napier • JRL, letters to J. H. Nodal • Lincs. Arch., letters to R. W. Goulding • UCL, letters to Karl Pearson
Likenesses C. E. Brock, oils, 1899, Christ's College, Cambridge • J. Russell & Sons, photograph, 1899, NPG [*see illus.*] • C. W. Walton, lithograph, King's Lond.
Wealth at death £38,905 0*s.* 6*d.*: probate, 5 Dec 1912, *CGPLA Eng. & Wales* • £7735 8*s.* 10*d.*—Bertha Marian Skeat: probate, 16 May 1949, *CGPLA Eng. & Wales*

Skeel, Caroline Anne James (1872–1951), historian, was born at Hampstead, London, on 9 February 1872, the sixth in the family of one son and six daughters (two died in infancy) of William Skeel (1822–1899), export merchant, and his wife, Anne, *née* James (1831–1895); they were first cousins and of Welsh descent. Educated initially at home, from the age of eight she attended South Hampstead high school, transferring in 1887 to its sister school at Notting Hill; there she was twice (at junior and then senior level) the top girl in the Cambridge local examinations. Awarded a St Dunstan's scholarship, in 1891 she entered Girton College, Cambridge. Having in 1894 taken a first in part one of the classical tripos, she then took a first in the historical tripos, a feat hailed by some in Cambridge as '*the honour of the year*' (1895). Girton, which rewarded her then and later with its most prestigious prizes, remained a constant source of encouragement. But it was at another women's college, Westfield in Hampstead, soon to be part of London University and closer to home, that she made her career.

Skeel joined Westfield in 1896 as a visiting lecturer in classics, but was soon also placed in sole charge of the embryonic history department and drew on both disciplines in her first original work, *Travel in the First Century after Christ*, which won Girton's Gibson prize in 1898. But it was history that prevailed, as shown by her enrolment in 1901 as a postgraduate student at the London School of Economics to work on the dissertation on the Council of the Marches during the Tudor and Stuart periods, which in 1904 earned her the Hutchinson medal and the London DLitt. Well received on its appearance under Girton auspices as a book in the same year, it long remained a standard work. At Westfield meanwhile she combined a heavy teaching programme with responsibility from 1902 for the college library, attracting gifts in kind from learned societies and others which substantially improved its

stock; in her role as a recognized teacher of London University, she served from 1902 to 1906 as secretary to the board of studies in history.

The onset in 1907 of severe and lasting depression removed Skeel, though only temporarily, from the academic scene, to which she eventually returned on her reappointment to Westfield in 1911; as the college magazine, *Hermes*, put it: 'Present students will be the gainers … past students know best what will be gained' (April 1911). For Skeel herself there was the added bonus of support henceforward from a succession of able young lecturers, to whom she represented, as one said, 'the ideal of university teaching'. Among the first to introduce undergraduates to original sources, she organized visits to historic sites and as the leading collaborator in a series of Texts for Students edited selections from two medieval Latin authors, Matthew Paris and Geraldus Cambrensis (1918). Her own appetite for scholarly research had been revived by the award in 1914 of Girton's Gamble prize for her essay 'The influence of the writings of John Fortescue' (published in *Transactions of the Royal Historical Society*, 1916) and the offer, not taken up, of an honorary research fellowship. Thereafter she maintained a steady flow of contributions to historical and archaeological journals, extensions in some cases of earlier work but also breaking new ground. Many relate to Wales, where her credentials as historian were backed up by family connections, a reading knowledge of Welsh, and cordial relationships with archivists throughout the principality.

Promoted in 1919 to a university readership, Skeel was able to contribute in various ways to the success of a new venture close to her heart, the Institute of Historical Research. Characteristically, she viewed her election in 1921 to the overwhelmingly masculine council of the Royal Historical Society as a tribute not to herself but to women scholars in general. Amid these and other preoccupations, she remained at the disposal of her students, past and present, dispensing sympathetic advice on problems ranging from a difficult essay to 'the deepest and most baffling issues of life'. In 1925, amid great rejoicing, she was advanced to a professorship, the first to be held at Westfield. But within a year symptoms of depression reappeared and in 1929 she took early retirement. Long remembered in Hendon, where she lived quietly until her death at 24 Hayes Crescent, Golders Green, following a stroke on 25 February 1951, as 'a charming gentlewoman who had seen better times', she was in fact the residuary heir to a family fortune amounting at her death to some £270,000 (gross), the bulk of which she bequeathed to Westfield, already the beneficiary of gifts made anonymously during her lifetime.   JANET SONDHEIMER

Sources Queen Mary College, London, Westfield College Archives • J. Sondheimer, *Castle Adamant in Hampstead: a history of Westfield College* (1983) • K. T. Butler and H. I. McMorran, eds., *Girton College register, 1869–1946* (1948) • J. E. Sayers, *The fountain unsealed: a history of the Notting Hill and Ealing high school* (privately printed, Broadwater Press, 1973) • *The Times* (3 March 1951) • d. cert.
Archives Queen Mary College, London, papers

Likenesses A. de Biden Footner, tinted drawing, Queen Mary and Westfield College, Caroline Skeel room · P. Bigland, oils, Queen Mary and Westfield College, Caroline Skeel room

Wealth at death £269,386 2s. 1d.: probate, 18 May 1951, *CGPLA Eng. & Wales*

Skeffington, Clotworthy, second earl of Massereene (1742–1805), landowner and debtor, was the son of Clotworthy Skeffington, sixth viscount and first earl of Massereene (d. 1757), and his second wife, Anne, daughter of Henry Eyre of Rowter, Derbyshire. He was born on 28 January 1742 in Antrim and was educated at Corpus Christi College, Cambridge. From 1756 he was known as Lord Loughneagh, until 1757, when he succeeded to his father's title. The Skeffingtons were a notable Irish political family, of old protestant lineage, with major landholdings in Antrim, which included the manor of Moylinny. They had a group allegiance in parliament, based on the Antrim town borough seats, although Massereene's financial difficulties meant that control of the borough was temporarily devolved upon Lord Antrim. As a group they were generally unsympathetic towards patriotism, particularly after the viceroy, Lord Harcourt, rewarded them in 1775.

It appears that Massereene's mental capacity had been damaged by a fall from a horse. This may have contributed to his willingness to become involved in disastrous financial speculations, which resulted in his imprisonment in France in 1770. His mother refused to send money to pay for his release, in the mistaken belief that this would force Massereene, who had a reputation as an extravagant man of fashion, to manage his financial affairs more carefully. While in the debtors' prison of Fort-l'Evêque he continued to spend lavishly, and after an early attempt to escape—foiled by the bad faith of a turnkey—he settled down to live his prison life in luxury. However, his own depiction of life in La Force, to which he had been transferred in 1780, was much more melancholy. He complained that he was shut up in solitude 'save for the vermin and a mouse which I taught to come for food'. He described himself as 'imprisoned abroad, robbed at home, misrepresented everywhere' (*Leeds MSS*, 22.56). On 13 July 1789, the eve of the fall of the Bastille, he was liberated by the Paris crowd, and he left the prison accompanied by Marie Anne Barcier, the daughter of the prison governor, whom he subsequently married. After presenting himself at the British embassy, Massereene took refuge in the precincts of the Temple, a privileged spot for debtors. But on finding himself in no danger of rearrest, he proceeded to Calais. After narrowly escaping detention he made his way back to England, and then travelled onwards to Ireland. Ironically Lord Massereene's motto on his coat of arms was 'through difficulties to honour'.

At St Peter Cornhill, London, Massereene formally married Marie Anne Barcier, on 19 August 1789, although he was said to have already married her twice while in France. She died in 1800 and he subsequently married Elizabeth Lane (d. 1838). He also formed a relationship with a servant in London, whose discretion was purchased

at great cost after his death. None of these unions produced children. He died on 28 February 1805 at Antrim Castle.

Massereene's descendants included **John Skeffington Foster Skeffington**, tenth Viscount Massereene and third Viscount Ferrard (1812–1863), poet, the son of Thomas Foster, second Viscount Ferrard, and Harriet, daughter of Chichester Skeffington, ninth Viscount Massereene. He was born in Dublin on 30 November 1812 and was educated at Eton College and Christ Church, Oxford. He succeeded his mother as Viscount Massereene, and his father as Viscount Ferrard in 1834, at the same time assuming Skeffington as an additional surname. He was created knight of St Patrick on 3 July 1851. He married on 1 August 1835 Olivia, fourth daughter of Henry Deane Grady of Stillorgan Castle, co. Dublin; they had four sons and four daughters. He was the author of *O'Sullivan, the Bandit Chief: a Romantic Poem* (4 vols., 1844), *Church Melodies* (8 vols., 1847), *A Metrical Version of the Psalms* (8 vols., 1865), and *The Love of God: a Poem* (8 vols., 1868). He died at Antrim Castle on 28 April 1863.

J. G. ALGER, *rev.* MARTYN J. POWELL

Sources S. J. Connolly, ed., *The Oxford companion to Irish history* (1998) · Venn, *Alum. Cant.* · E. M. Johnston, *Great Britain and Ireland, 1760–1800* (1963) · F. G. James, *Lords of the ascendancy: the Irish House of Lords and its members, 1600–1800* (1995) · GEC, *Peerage* · Burke, *Peerage* · *The manuscripts of the duke of Leeds*, HMC, 22 (1888), 56 · M. Bodkin, ed., 'Notes on the Irish parliament in 1773', *Proceedings of the Royal Irish Academy*, 48C (1942–3), 145–232

Archives PRO NIre., papers | BL, corresp. with Lord Hardwicke, Add. MSS 35730–35766, *passim* · CKS, letters to duke of Dorset

Skeffington, Francis Sheehy- (1878–1916), women's rights activist and pacifist, was born on 23 December 1878 in Bailieborough, co. Cavan, and christened Francis Joseph Christopher Skeffington, the only child of Joseph Bartholomew (J. B.) Skeffington (1847–1919), scholar and teacher, and his wife, Rose Magorian (1829–1909), daughter of a farmer in the co. Down village of Ballykinlar. His parents were married in the Roman Catholic chapel in Ballykinlar on 30 September 1869 when his father was twenty-two and his mother forty. Francis Skeffington grew up in Downpatrick, co. Down, where his father, as an official in the national education system, was a district supervisor of education. J. B. Skeffington was opinionated, arrogant, tyrannical, and punctilious. He was also extremely honest, had a great respect for ideas, and a strong sense of order, virtue, morality, and kindliness toward others: these latter qualities his son inherited.

The dominant culture in Downpatrick was protestant, pro-British, anti-Catholic. The Skeffingtons—being devout Catholics—lived in an all-Catholic ghetto. Francis learned early to reject the bigotry of the protestants while, at the same time, viewing with some clarity and scepticism the errors of his own group. Until he entered university, Francis's only teacher was his father. He was well taught and when he entered University College, Dublin, in 1896, his major lifelong goals were fixed. He wanted to improve the world, crusade for political and economic freedom for women, and free Ireland from British rule. In 1909 he joined the Socialist Party, convinced that socialism was the only remedy for the evils of society. Also fixed was his attire: rough, grey tweed suit and knickerbockers, with long stockings—in imitation of George Bernard Shaw. Known to his fellow students as Frank, Skeff, or Skeffy, he was slightly over 5 feet 5 inches, deceptively frail appearing, with a soft, fair, badly trimmed beard. His voice was somewhat high-pitched, his accent that of an Ulsterman. He had a brisk handshake and the humourless habit of concentrating on points made casually. At the university, his closest companions were the writer James Joyce and Thomas Kettle, who would become known as politician, essayist, and poet. Francis is portrayed as McCann in Joyce's *Stephen Hero*, and Joyce draws him as well in *A Portrait of the Artist as a Young Man*. In 1917 a pamphlet, *Two Essays*, by Sheehy-Skeffington and Joyce appeared.

On 27 June 1903 Francis Skeffington and Hanna Sheehy [*see* Skeffington, Johanna Mary Sheehy-], scholar and teacher and the daughter of David Sheehy, a mill owner and nationalist MP, were married. In order to demonstrate their belief in equality for women, he and Hanna took each other's surname. He thus became Francis Sheehy-Skeffington. Their only child was the politician and university teacher Owen Lancelot Sheehy-*Skeffington. That year also he was appointed the first lay registrar at University College, Dublin. The Women Graduates Association was fighting then for admission of women to the university on an equal basis with men and Francis helped to write and circulate their petitions. Since as an officer of the college he had no right to advocate opposition policy, he was asked to resign.

In 1908 the Irish Women's Franchise League (IWFL), militant wing of the Irish suffrage movement, was formed in the Sheehy-Skeffingtons' home. Men were accepted as associate members and Francis promptly joined. The IWFL was attacked by the Irish press for its insistence that any home rule bill must include a plank for women's suffrage, and Francis felt that only a rival paper would serve to counteract the attacks. The first edition of his new paper, the *Irish Citizen*, appeared on 25 May 1912. It proved to be his most ambitious venture and also the longest lasting, most time-consuming, and most rewarding. Its lead editorial stated its aim: 'to win for men and women equally the rights of citizenship and to claim from men and women equally the duties of citizenship'.

When the United Kingdom declared war in August 1914, Francis Sheehy-Skeffington defined war in the *Irish Citizen* of 22 August 1914 as 'one of the social evils, like drink and prostitution that arise from neglect of the feminine point of view and based on a theory of society one-sidedly and arrogantly male', and on 15 August an *Irish Citizen* poster read 'Votes for Women Now! Damn Your War!'

Every Sunday at Beresford Place in Dublin, Sheehy-Skeffington spoke out against the war and urged Irishmen not to enlist to 'fight England's battles for naval supremacy', nor to become part of the English garrison in Ireland. After forty such speeches, he was arrested on 29 May 1915, sent to Mountjoy prison, and sentenced to six months' hard labour and an additional six months in default of bail. When, on 9 June, sentence was imposed, Francis stood and said: 'I will eat no food from this moment, and long before the expiration of the sentence I shall be out of prison alive or dead' (Sheehy-Skeffington, *Speech from the Dock*, 11). For seven days he was on hunger strike, and then released because of his health, under the 'Cat and Mouse Act'. He was using a strategy common to women suffragists in both Britain and Ireland: in 1912 two British women, Mary Leigh and Gladys Evans, who had been demonstrating in Ireland, had received a sentence of five years' penal servitude. They had gone on hunger strike and had been forcibly fed. Four Irish women, among them Hanna Sheehy-Skeffington, who were then serving a month's sentence for vandalizing government property, went on hunger strike for one week to protest against the severity of the British women's sentence. And in 1913 in Dublin, Hanna Sheehy-Skeffington, who had been sentenced to seven days in the Mountjoy prison for assaulting a police officer, went on hunger strike and was released after five days because of her physical condition.

The nationalist James Connolly and Sheehy-Skeffington had become fast friends: their goals for socialism, feminism, and against the war were identical. But Sheehy-Skeffington was absolutely opposed to an armed uprising and never varied in his opinion. 'I would rather be shot than shoot anyone' (Byrne, 122) he told his friend Byrne, and he spoke out at every opportunity for peace and pacifism.

On Tuesday 25 April 1916, the second day of the Easter rising led by Connolly, Sheehy-Skeffington, after witnessing considerable looting on the previous day, tried to recruit volunteers to stop the looting. That evening, walking home over the Portobello Bridge and with bystanders calling out to him by name, he was placed under arrest and taken to nearby Portobello barracks. Reason given: it seemed advisable to arrest pedestrians who were attracting attention in order to avoid altercations. He was detained that night and the next morning, shortly before ten, was taken from his cell by Captain J. C. Bowen-Colthurst of the Royal Irish Rifles. With two other prisoners, Sheehy-Skeffington was taken into the barracks yard and summarily executed. It was Wednesday morning, 26 April 1916.

Every attempt was made to cover up the executions and the events surrounding them. Hanna Sheehy-Skeffington received no notification of her husband's death and was refused any information by the military. Not until Friday, two days later, did she learn the facts. After repeated requests on her part for a public inquiry, a court martial—with attendance by invitation only—was held in Richmond barracks, Dublin, on 6 and 7 June 1916. The court found Captain Bowen-Colthurst guilty but insane at the time of the murders. He was sentenced to detention in an asylum for the criminally insane at Broadmoor in England, the length of time to be at his majesty's discretion. After twenty months he was released and emigrated to Vancouver, British Columbia. Still dissatisfied, Hanna Sheehy-Skeffington pressed for an open inquiry, and on 17 August 1916 a royal commission was convened and a report covering every aspect of the case issued on 29 September. Late in 1916 Hanna Sheehy-Skeffington published her husband's novel, *In Dark and Evil Days*, with a biographical memoir.

On 8 May 1916 Francis Sheehy-Skeffington's body, which had been buried in the mortuary at Portobello barracks, was exhumed and reburied in Glasnevin cemetery in Dublin. This man who had implored Irishmen not to fight England's battles had met his death at the hands of an Irish recruit to the British army, and this man who believed that all problems could be settled without violence had met his death as the victim of violence.

LEAH LEVENSON

Sources L. Levenson, *With wooden sword: portrait of Francis Sheehy-Skeffington, militant pacifist* (1983) · L. Levenson and J. H. Natterstad, *Hanna Sheehy-Skeffington: Irish feminist* (1986) · F. Sheehy-Skeffington, *In dark and evil days* (1916) [with biog. memoir by his widow] · F. Sheehy-Skeffington, *Speech from the dock* (1915) · O. S. Skeffington, 'Francis Sheehy-Skeffington', in O. D. Edwards and F. Pyle, *The Easter rising* (1968), 135–48 · private information (2004) · J. F. Byrne, *Silent years: an autobiography with memoirs of James Joyce and our Ireland* (1953)
Archives NL Ire., papers · TCD | SOUND BBC WAC
Wealth at death £550: administration, 3 Aug 1916, CGPLA Ire.

Skeffington, Johanna Mary [Hanna] **Sheehy-** [*née* Johanna Mary Sheehy] (1877–1946), suffragist and Irish nationalist, was born on 24 May 1877 in the Millhouse, Kanturk, co. Cork, the eldest of four daughters and two sons of David Sheehy (1844–1932), mill owner, and his wife, Bessie McCoy (1851–1918), daughter of Richard McCoy of Curraghmore, co. Limerick. In 1887 the family moved to Dublin where Hanna (as she was always known) attended the Dominican nuns' convent school in Eccles Street. From 1896 to 1899 she studied modern languages in Dublin at the Catholic St Mary's University College for women, receiving a BA with second-class honours. In 1902, after further study in Paris and Bonn, she returned to Dublin and was awarded an MA in modern languages with first-class honours. She then became a part-time teacher of literature and languages, always handicapped by the fact that in Ireland all positions of educational authority in relation to Catholic girls were open only to nuns.

The Sheehy family had a long tradition of nationalist politics. Hanna Sheehy's father had originally been a Fenian but then became a constitutional nationalist and MP for South Galway and later for County Meath. He was imprisoned six times for his opposition to British rule and landlordism. Hanna Sheehy's beloved uncle Eugene, known as 'the Land League priest', was a lifelong Fenian and member of the secret Irish Republican Brotherhood. The Sheehys appear as the Daniel family in James Joyce's *Stephen Hero*. In Hanna's case her Irish nationalism soon became complicated by a feminism influenced not only by the injustice of her own precarious professional position, but also by her friendship with the ardent radical Francis Skeffington (1878–1916) [*see* Skeffington, Francis Sheehy-], Joyce's 'hairy jaysus'. Skeffington was a socialist, pacifist, feminist, anti-vivisectionist, vegetarian teetotaller whose many principles did not prevent him from also being an

Johanna Mary Sheehy-Skeffington (1877–1946), by Poole Studio

endearing companion, warm-hearted, and capable of fun.

The Sheehy-Skeffingtons, as they were known ever after, were married on 27 June 1903; their union was to be a passionately political as well as emotional partnership for thirteen years. In 1909 Hanna definitively broke with her religious background, refusing to have her newborn son, Owen Lancelot Sheehy-*Skeffington, baptized; thereafter she could not teach in convent schools and was to be an outsider in Catholic Ireland. Having founded the militant Irish Women's Franchise League together with Margaret Cousins in 1908, Hanna suffered her first prison sentence as a suffragist in June 1912 for 'wilful damage' to nineteen panes of glass, property of the War Office. She was sentenced to two months' imprisonment—a heavier sentence than that imposed on a wife-beater that same day. Meanwhile in London, her father, the Irish MP, voted in favour of forcible feeding of suffragettes on hunger strike. Hanna herself later embarked on a hunger strike in sympathy with English women prisoners but was released after five days without having been subjected to forcible feeding. It was also in 1912 that Francis Sheehy-Skeffington co-founded the radical paper the *Irish Citizen* for which Hanna wrote numerous articles in support of Irish women's right to vote. In November 1913 Hanna was arrested while attempting to leaflet the Conservative leader Bonar Law in Dublin. She was charged with assaulting the police officer who had in fact seized and shaken her. Refusing bail, she went to prison and, in protest against the magistrate's refusal to hear her counter-charge, went on hunger strike until freed after five days.

The watershed of Hanna Sheehy-Skeffington's life was the Easter rising of 1916. Francis Sheehy-Skeffington was an Irish nationalist but also a pacifist who had written many passionate advocacies of passive resistance as the way to win Irish independence. He was opposed not only to the First World War but also to the attempt by the Irish Volunteers and the Irish Citizen Army to overthrow British rule by force. Nevertheless he was arrested, unarmed and unresisting, while trying to prevent mob looting, and was shot without trial on Wednesday of Easter week by a firing party under a British officer. Thereafter Hanna, always more of an Irish nationalist and less of a pacifist than her husband, became deeply involved with Sinn Féin. In July 1917 she returned secretly to Ireland after a lecture tour of the United States that had raised significant funds for Michael Collins. She was arrested by the British government and imprisoned first in the notorious Dublin Bridewell and then moved to Holloway, London, only to be released after hunger striking. In 1920 she was elected Sinn Féin councillor on Dublin corporation and later, in 1925, on Dublin city council. After the establishment of the Irish Free State, Hanna continued to be a republican gadfly, supporting Maud Gonne and Charlotte Despard in the Women's Prisoners Defence League. Hanna was also a feminist gadfly among the nationalists, whether in Sinn Féin or in de Valera's Fianna Fáil—which she decided to join in 1926, only to resign in 1927 in protest against de Valera's agreement to take the oath of loyalty to the Irish Free State. However her feminism could hardly flourish in a Catholic Ireland that forbade women the basic freedoms of access to sex education, contraception, and divorce. She died in Dublin on 20 April 1946 and was buried in Glasnevin cemetery. Many tributes were paid to her warm, even gentle, private personality. She was judged 'the ablest of the women' in Irish public life by the *Irish Times* of 23 April 1946. She had been a militant nationalist among the pacifist internationalist feminists, a republican among the free staters, a feminist among the nationalists, and an atheist in holy Ireland.

SYBIL OLDFIELD

Sources L. Levenson and J. H. Natterstad, *Hanna Sheehy-Skeffington: Irish feminist* (1986) · L. Levenson, *With wooden sword: portrait of Francis Sheehy-Skeffington, militant pacifist* (1983) · M. Ward, *Hanna Sheehy Skeffington: a life* (1997) · L. Ryan, '*Irish feminism and the vote*, 1912–1920', *Irish Citizen* (1996) · R. C. Owens, *Smashing times: a history of the Irish women's suffrage movement, 1889–1922* (1984) · H. S. Skeffington, 'Irish militants and the war', *Ius Suffragii* (1 April 1915) · *CGPLA Ire.* (1946)
Archives NL Ire., corresp. and papers
Likenesses photograph, *c.*1920, repro. in Owens, *Smashing times*, 41 · Poole Studio, photograph, NL Ire. [*see illus.*]
Wealth at death £369 14s. 3d.: administration, 9 Aug 1946, *CGPLA Éire*

Skeffington, John, second Viscount Massereene (*bap.* 1632, *d.* 1695), nobleman, was baptized on 27 December 1632, the eldest son of Sir Richard Skeffington (*d.* 1647) of Fisherwick, near Lichfield, and Anne Newdigate (1607–1637). His father died in 1647 and in 1652 he succeeded his cousin as fourth baronet at the age of nineteen. As a substantial landowner in both Staffordshire and Warwickshire it was not long before Skeffington arranged a lucrative marriage, on 20 July 1654, to Mary, the only daughter of Sir John *Clotworthy of co. Antrim, who later became first Viscount Massereene. It was his father-in-law's influence which secured him a seat in Richard Cromwell's 1659 parliament as MP for Antrim, Down, and Armagh. He was also elected MP for co. Antrim in the Irish parliament of 1661.

By the death of his father-in-law in 1665, Skeffington became Viscount Massereene and baron of Loughneagh by special remainder and succeeded to a great Irish estate in his wife's right. Thereafter he extended his political influence, as *custos rotulorum* of co. Londonderry (from 1666) and an Irish privy councillor (from 1667). He was also able to secure compensation for lands lost by the Clotworthys at the Restoration. His support for presbyterianism, however, brought him into conflict with the duke of Ormond by the 1670s, and his involvement in the exclusion crisis caused Ormond to target his local power base. The tightening of restrictions against nonconformist JPs and militia officers after the exclusion crisis was partly aimed at Massereene, and in 1682 the earl of Arran announced his intention 'to turn out of all employments the peer himself' (*Ormonde MSS*, new ser., 6.375). In 1683 Ormond threatened to remove Massereene from the privy council, and presented him for nonconformity.

Despite fears of James II's intentions after 1685, Massereene was nevertheless reappointed to his governorship and sworn of the privy council. But it was not long before he was actively supporting a Williamite invasion. When the citizens of Londonderry determined to stand on their defence Massereene helped them with a large sum of money. He was one of those to whom the Enniskilleners specially appealed for help; it was at Antrim Castle that the protestants of the county met under Massereene's presidency, and his only surviving son, Clotworthy, was chosen to command them in the field. Massereene himself withdrew to England soon afterwards. In Tyrconnel's proclamation of 7 March 1689 both father and son were among the ten persons excepted by name from mercy as 'principal actors in the rebellion' (*Ormonde MSS*, old ser., 2.396).

Massereene was in London in November 1689, being one of the Irish committee chosen to confer with William III. He returned to Ireland after the battle of the Boyne, and resumed his seat on the privy council, sat in the parliament which met on 5 October 1692, and was active in the business of the House of Lords. He died on 21 June 1695 and was buried at Antrim. Clotworthy succeeded him as third viscount, and was ancestor of Clotworthy *Skeffington, second earl of Massereene. Of Massereene's three daughters, the youngest, Mary, married Edward Smyth, bishop of Down and Connor.

RICHARD BAGWELL, *rev.* PATRICK LITTLE

Sources HoP, *Commons* [draft] · GEC, *Baronetage* · GEC, *Peerage* · J. Lodge, *The peerage of Ireland*, 4 vols. (1754) · *The manuscripts of the* *marquis of Ormonde*, [old ser.], 3 vols., HMC, 36 (1895–1909) • *Calendar of the Clarendon state papers preserved in the Bodleian Library*, ed. O. Ogle and others, 5 vols. (1869–1970) • *CSP Ire.*, 1647–70 • E. Berwick, ed., *The Rawdon papers* (1813) • PRO NIre., D 207/16 • Venn, *Alum. Cant.*

Archives PRO NIre., Foster/Massereene MSS, D 207/16 | BL, letters to Sir Edward Dering, Stowe MSS 744–746, *passim* • BL, letters to Lord Essex, Stowe MSS 200–212, *passim*

Likenesses P. Lely, portrait, Arbury Hall, Warwickshire

Wealth at death £4340 p.a. in 1689: Lodge, *Peerage of Ireland*, vol. 3, p. 65

Skeffington, John Skeffington Foster, tenth Viscount Massereene and third Viscount Ferrard (1812–1863). *See under* Skeffington, Clotworthy, second earl of Massereene (1742–1805).

Skeffington, Sir Lumley St George, second baronet (1771–1850), fop and playwright, younger but only surviving son of Sir William Charles Farrell Skeffington, first baronet (1742–1815), and Catherine Josepha (*c*.1743–1811), daughter of Michael Hubbert of Tenerife, merchant, was born in the parish of St Pancras, London, on 23 March 1771. He was educated at Newcome's school at Hackney, and, by taking part in the plays for which the institution was famous, acquired a taste for drama. On leaving school he was admitted into the select circle at Carlton House and soon set the fashions for the youth of the day: he was consulted on the subject of attire by the prince regent, and invented a new colour, known as 'Skeffington brown'. His features were large, and he had a sharp, sallow face, with dark curly hair and whiskers. For many years his dress was 'a dark blue coat with gilt buttons, a yellow waistcoat, white cord inexpressibles, with large bunches of white ribbons at the knees, and short top boots'. Among his friends were the actors John Kemble, Mrs Siddons, and 'Romeo' Coates; he never missed a first night or a début, and often visited four theatres on the same evening. Between 1802 and 1813 Skeffington himself wrote a number of dramatic works, trying his hand at comedy, melodrama, and opera, and produced some of them in the theatre; none met with lasting success. Widely ridiculed, he was a natural target for the satirical cartoonist Gillray, who depicted him a number of times.

Skeffington succeeded to the baronetcy and family property on his father's death in January 1815; but he had permitted his father to cut off the entail of their large estates, and his reckless extravagance had wasted the rest of his resources. His debts caused him to spend several years within the rules of the king's bench prison, living near the Surrey Theatre in Southwark. Some time before his death he recovered a hereditary estate producing about £800 per annum; but he failed in his action in 1838 to obtain possession of the Hubbert property at Rotherhithe. He still continued to live in the southern suburbs, and it was at that time that Henry Vizetelly made his acquaintance. He was 'a quiet, courteous, aristocratic-looking old gentleman, an ancient fop ... wore false hair, and rouged his cheeks' (*Glances Back*, 111). He entertained, and had a great store of anecdotes. It was his boast that the secret of life lay in 'never stirring out of doors during the cold damp winter months, and in living in a suite of

Sir Lumley St George Skeffington, second baronet (1771–1850), by Ridley & Holl, pubd 1806 (after John Thomas Barber)

rooms', so that he could constantly shift from one to another (Vizetelly, *Glances Back*, 112). He died, unmarried, on 10 November 1850 in lodgings near the Indigent Blind School, St George's Fields, Southwark, close to the king's bench prison, of which he had again lately been an inmate; he was buried at Norwood cemetery on 15 November. The title became extinct.

W. P. COURTNEY, rev. K. D. REYNOLDS

Sources GEC, *Baronetage* • H. Vizetelly, *Glances back through seventy years: autobiographical and other reminiscences*, 2 vols. (1893) • R. H. Gronow, *The reminiscences of Captain Gronow* (1861) • *The works of James Gillray, the caricaturist, with the history of his life and times*, ed. T. Wright (1873) • *GM*, 1st ser., 75 (1805), 1120–21 • *GM*, 2nd ser., 35 (1851), 198–200, 289

Likenesses J. Gillray, caricatures, repro. in Wright, ed., *Works of James Gillray* • Ridley & Holl, stipple (after miniature by J. T. Barber), NPG, BM; repro. in *Monthly Mirror*, 21 (Jan 1806), frontispiece [*see illus.*]

Skeffington, Owen Lancelot Sheehy- (1909–1970), politician and university teacher, was born on 19 May 1909 in hospital at 122 Lower Baggot Street, Dublin, the only child of Francis Sheehy-*Skeffington (1878–1916), journalist, and Johanna Mary, known as Hanna Sheehy-*Skeffington (1877–1946), lecturer and journalist, eldest daughter of David Sheehy MP. His parents combined Irish nationalism, atheism, feminism, pacifism, and socialism. Sheehy-Skeffington learned to think for himself, coming to share their politics, minus his mother's later abstentionist republicanism.

Sheehy-Skeffington was educated at Rathgar Kindergarten and Training College, Rathmines, from 1913 to 1919, with a brief sojourn in America, where he attended schools in Connecticut and California, St Brendan's School, Sallynoggin, co. Dublin (1919–20), then at Earlsfort House School, Dublin (1920–22), and finally at Sandford Park School, Rathmines, Dublin. In 1927 he entered Trinity College, Dublin, taking first-class honours in 1931. He studied at the École Normale Supérieure in Paris from 1931 to 1933, when he returned to Trinity College to become a lecturer in French. In 1934 he presented a doctoral thesis on Jules Romans, becoming doctor in 1935, permanent lecturer in 1936, and reader in 1954. He was a dedicated and popular teacher but not a published academic. On 23 March 1935 he married Andrée Germaine Denis (1910–1998) of Amiens, with whom he had three children.

In 1934 Sheehy-Skeffington joined the Irish Labour Party. In spite of its increasing conservatism he joined its administrative council in 1941. In 1942 the party's Dublin selection conference was rigged; he publicized this and was expelled for 'bringing the party into disrepute'. Although he kept many friends (to whom he was 'at home' every Friday), he found himself somewhat politically isolated; Catholic faculties barred him from speaking, while Moscow's followers denounced his independence. His wife, Andrée, ran unsuccessfully for the Dublin corporation in 1950. At the general election of the following year Sheehy-Skeffington himself ran (as an independent liberal socialist) for a Seanad university seat. Defeated, he ran again, and was victorious in 1954. He was defeated after an overconfident campaign in 1961, but was returned in 1965 and remained a senator until his death.

As a senator Sheehy-Skeffington spoke mainly on education: he urged lay participation in school management, and was opposed to corporal punishment—three of his speeches on this subject were published in 1956. He was an opponent of capital punishment; a supporter of anti-colonial struggles, and upheld the state's right to suppress militant republicanism under law. He lived to see his initiatives begin to be realized.

Outside the Seanad, Sheehy-Skeffington helped to found the Irish Pacifist Movement, the Irish Association of Civil Liberties, and the Irish Humanist Association. He was deputy correspondent for the International Universities Association and became president of the Dublin University International Affairs Association in 1953. From 1962 he was the student and lecturers' representative on the Trinity College board. He served on the Dublin University Social Service (Tenements) Company, and was governor of St Patrick Dun's Hospital and (until 1962) of his old school Sandford Park.

In May 1956 Sheehy-Skeffington suffered a coronary, and had further heart attacks in November 1964 and May 1970. He suffered a fourth—and fatal—attack at his home, Hazelbrook Cottage, 69 Terenure Road West, Dublin, on 7 June 1970. He was buried two days later at Glasnevin cemetery, Dublin. Until then his healthy lifestyle had preserved him; he had captained the Sandford Park cricket team and boxed for Trinity, was a regular swimmer, and walked or cycled whenever it was practical. Small and

wiry in build, his only apparent disability was inherited short sight.

Skeff, as he was known, was a devoted husband and loving father to his three children, Francis (b. 1945), Alan (b. 1947), and Michelline (b. 1953). Standing alone, he was the most influential Irish university senator before the future president Mary Robinson, many of whose achievements were founded on his work.   D. R. O'CONNOR LYSAGHT

Sources A. Sheehy-Skeffington, *Skeff* (1991) · *Irish Times* (8 June 1970) · *Irish Press* (8 June 1970) · *Irish Independent* (8 June 1970) · *Seanad Éireann: parliamentary debates* (1954–61) [8th Seanad]; (1965–70) [11th–12th Seanad] · *Annual Report*, Irish labour party (1941–2) · Burke, *Gen. Ire.* (1976) · private information (2004) · *Thom's directory* (1910) · b. cert. · d. cert.
Archives SOUND BL NSA, documentary recording
Likenesses photographs, repro. in Sheehy-Skeffington, *Skeff*, following p. 180
Wealth at death £6692.10: probate, 1970, *CGPLA Éire*

Skeffington, Sir Richard (*c.*1590–1647), politician, was the younger son of William Skeffington (*d.* 1635) of Fisherwick, Staffordshire, and his wife, Elizabeth (*née* Dering) (*b.* 1567?), who came from Kent. His father, who gained a baronetcy on 8 May 1627, came from a family prominent in 'the great web of intermarried gentry of Warwickshire and Staffordshire' (Larminie, 74) and with branches in Leicestershire. Richard Skeffington matriculated from Magdalene College, Cambridge, in 1615, but did not take a degree. He acquired estates at Hawkesyard, Staffordshire, and at Arley near Coventry, and a house in the city itself. Knighted in 1624, he was returned as MP for the joint Warwickshire/Staffordshire seat of Tamworth the following year, apparently making no recorded mark whatever in that parliament. In 1626 he married Anne (1607–1637), youngest daughter of Sir John Newdigate (1571–1610) and his wife, Anne *Newdigate (1574–1618), a liaison which confirmed and strengthened the respective positions of both families within midlands society.

There is evidence linking Skeffington with the circles around Robert Greville, Lord Brooke, and he has been described as a puritan. He sided with the parliamentarian cause with the outbreak of civil war, while his brother, Sir John Skeffington (*c.*1589–1651), who had inherited the main family estates at Fisherwick, went the other way, suffering sequestration for his allegiance. Having played little part in local government before 1642, Skeffington now emerged as a vigorous participant in the parliamentary administration of the county. One of the clique opposed to the predominance of the earl of Denbigh within the midlands association, some years later, Richard Baxter praised Skeffington as one of the 'many very godly and judicious gentlemen' in charge of the Warwickshire committee during the war (*Reliquiae Baxterianae*, 43–4, cited in Hughes). He was a commissioner for Staffordshire and Warwickshire in respect of reform of the ministry, collection of taxes and sequestration of royalists, and was added to the Staffordshire bench after Naseby. He and Colonel John Needham, governor of Leicester, played a crucial role in securing the capitulation of Lord

Loughborough's garrison at Ashby-de-la-Zouch in February 1646, mediating with parliament to secure preferential rates of composition for his lordship's party, they having been effectively driven out of Lichfield in the aftermath of a contest for command among the royalists there.

Later that year, after a hotly contested election in August, Skeffington was recruited as MP for Staffordshire with the support of Sir William Brereton, whose second wife was Skeffington's sister, Cicely. Brereton, who thought his brother-in-law 'a most precious excellent man' (Letter Books, 2.216), had previously failed to secure him a seat at Stafford town, where he had been defeated by a single vote. The margin at the county election was not very much wider. Once at Westminster he was appointed to a committee of the House of Commons to discuss officers' indemnity, as well as the publication of the Septuagint Greek translation of the Old Testament in October 1646, briefly excusing himself from the service of the house shortly thereafter. He took the solemn league and covenant on 9 December, and was added to the committee of privileges a week later. He was appointed to a committee to confer with the Lords about the attempt to convey the duke of York away from the earl of Northumberland in the same month. He was added to the committee of accounts in January 1647.

Skeffington was denied the time or the opportunity to establish his political career on the national stage. He died on 2 June 1647 at Broxbourne, Hertfordshire, where he was buried. A memorial inscription commended in him 'that piety which is also peaceable' (Shaw, 1.366). His will was proved by Richard Newdigate, his brother-in-law, and Richard Pyott, two of his executors. Its overseers were Sir William Brereton, Michael Biddulph of Elmhirst, and his cousin, John Swynfen MP. The Skeffingtons had three daughters and three sons. The eldest son, John *Skeffington (bap. 1632, d. 1695), succeeded his cousin Sir William Skeffington as fourth baronet, and then succeeded his father-in-law as second Viscount Massarene.

SEAN KELSEY

Sources V. Larminie, *Wealth, kinship and culture: the seventeenth-century Newdigates of Arbury and their world* (1995), 73–7, 211 · A. Hughes, *Politics, society and civil war in Warwickshire, 1620–1660* (1987), 122, 131, 173, 179, 360–63 · *Reliquiae Baxterianae, or, Mr Richard Baxter's narrative of the most memorable passages of his life and times*, ed. M. Sylvester, 1 vol. in 3 pts (1696), 43–4 · S. Shaw, *The history and antiquities of Staffordshire* (1898), vol. 1, pp. 366, 373 · J. C. Wedgwood, *Staffordshire parliamentary history*, 48–9, 68 · *The letter books of Sir William Brereton*, 2 vols. (1984–90), vol. 1, p. 26; item nos. 206, 222n., 227, 465, 528; vol. 2, item nos. 796, 825, 826, 876, 887, 941, 946, 1001, 1002, 1030, 1037, 1192, 1220; p. 558 · *CSP dom.*, 1645–7, 300, 305, 318, 352, 353, 357, 430 · *JHC*, 4 (1644–6), 453, 694, 695; 5 (1646–8), 7, 14, 27, 62, 84 · GEC, *Baronetage* · will, PRO, PROB 11/214, fol. 160

Wealth at death 'His will gave two younger sons annuities of £40 each and both surviving daughters £1,000 portions': will, PRO, PROB 11/214, fol. 160, cited in Larminie, *Wealth, kinship and culture*, 76

Skeffington, Sir William [called the Gunner] (d. 1535), lord deputy of Ireland, was the eldest son of Thomas and Mary Skeffington of Skeffington in Leicestershire. Having been knighted by Henry VII, he served as sheriff of the counties of Warwick and Leicester and as a justice of the peace for Leicestershire in 1509. In 1510 he was issued with a royal pardon and was subsequently reappointed to the commission of the peace for Leicestershire, a post that he intermittently held throughout his career, even during his service in Ireland. By 1512 he was a captain with responsibility for receipt of ordnance, and in the mid-1510s he again held the position of sheriff of the counties of Warwick and Leicester. In May 1515 Skeffington was appointed master of the ordnance for which he was paid 2s. a day. He continued to hold that position until 1529. In 1520 he was listed among those chosen to attend on Henry VIII at the Field of Cloth of Gold. Throughout the 1520s, in his capacity as master of the ordnance, Skeffington was actively involved in strengthening the fortifications of the English pale in Calais and Guînes. In 1525 he was granted a commission for conducting searches in specific quarters of London. He was knight of the shire for Leicestershire in 1529. By then he had been married twice. By his first marriage, to Margaret, daughter of Sir Everard Digby of Tilton, he had a son and heir, Thomas. He and his second wife, Anne, daughter of Sir John Digby of Kettleby in Leicestershire, had among other children, one son, Leonard, who served as a lieutenant of the Tower of London, as a soldier in Ireland, and as a messenger who regularly represented his father at court.

In a new departure in the governance of Ireland a secret council of three officials acted as deputy to the nominal lieutenant, Henry Fitzroy, duke of Richmond, in June 1529. Skeffington arrived in Ireland the following August, having been dispatched as the king's counsellor and commissioner, charged with the task of compiling a report on the military situation in the lordship. He was involved in negotiating a settlement between Piers, earl of Ossory, and the earl of Desmond and in making arrangements for the governance of the midlands. Early in 1530 Skeffington submitted a detailed report in which he asserted that the secret council lacked the money and men to govern effectively. He returned to England, but following the fall of Cardinal Wolsey, the architect of the conciliar scheme, in the summer of 1529, he was appointed lord deputy of Ireland in June 1530. Skeffington duly arrived in Dublin in August along with Gerald Fitzgerald, earl of Kildare, and was received in a solemn procession at St Mary's Abbey with great applause from the citizens. He was instructed to promote good relations between the earls of Kildare, Ormond, and Desmond, and to secure their co-operation against Gaelic resistance. He was to enjoy the active assistance of the earl of Kildare, convene a parliament, and act only with the approval of the council. He unsuccessfully endeavoured to negotiate for a retroactive extra-parliamentary grant of taxation for the period 1529–30.

Late in 1530 Skeffington led a campaign into the territory of Leix (Laois) against O'More and O'Connor, whom he subdued. Following an inactive winter he and the earl of Kildare made inroads into Ulster early in 1531, capturing and demolishing O'Neill's castle at Kinard and destroying neighbouring territories and villages. In May he was granted a commission to convene a parliament. Later that month he received an indenture of submission to Henry VIII on behalf of Odo O'Donnell at Drogheda. While initially Skeffington and the earl of Kildare maintained amicable relations, by July both men were sending messengers to the court with reports of the other's malpractice, and Kildare was apparently treating the deputy less as the king's representative than as a mere commoner. In an effort to secure greater freedom of action from Kildare's influence Skeffington encouraged the feud between Ossory and Kildare. His critics accused him of supporting Kildare's kinsmen against the earl and of having built up alliances with Gaelic lords bordering on the pale in opposition to Kildare. Skeffington's problems were further compounded by parliament's refusal to grant a subsidy when it met in September and October 1531, thereby forcing him to resort to levying scutage on the king's tenants by knight service.

In May 1532 John Rawson and Chief Justice Patrick Bermingham, both former members of the secret council, presented the English council at Greenwich with a list of accusations of maladministration directed against Skeffington, notably that he had deliberately rekindled the Ossory–Kildare feud and had exhibited partiality towards Ossory. Early in July the earl of Kildare visited the court and was reappointed deputy lieutenant. Soon after he assumed office in mid-August, Kildare set about settling the score with Skeffington by humiliating the former deputy publicly during a muster of his troops. Skeffington was then obliged to wait on Kildare until he received instructions regarding the storage of a sizeable consignment of ordnance and military stores which had been in his custody. In mid-October 1532 he finally entrusted the armaments to the charge of the Irish council. Kildare was summoned to court in September 1533, and by October Skeffington had retired to England to lend weight to the mounting campaign instigated by the Butlers with a view to securing Kildare's recall to court. To that end, in December 1533 he submitted his own indictment of Kildare. While Skeffington was 'scantily beloved' in English government circles, Maguire, lord of Fermanagh, bemoaned his absence from Ireland early in 1534, alleging that he had 'gained the esteem of all' and had 'showed himself most just and indifferent' (*LP Henry VIII*, 7, 1883, no. 1014; Brewer and Bullen, 1.53).

Before May 1534 the decision had been taken to reappoint Skeffington as lord deputy. His instructions, the 'Ordinances for the government of Ireland', served as a manifesto for administrative reform of the lordship. These also stipulated that he was to lead a campaign against the pope, to resist the pope's provisions and jurisdiction, and to enact both measures at the next parliament. Late in May Ossory formally undertook to assist the new deputy. Skeffington appears to have been virtually the only candidate for the post: the imperial ambassador, Eustace Chapuys, expressed surprise at Henry's choice of incumbent since he regarded Skeffington as the most unfit candidate for governing Ireland that could be chosen. In June 1534 Kildare's son and deputy, Thomas,

Lord Offaly, repudiated his allegiance to Henry VIII. In late July preparations were still in progress for Skeffington's dispatch with a modest company of just 150 men, but the situation in Ireland deteriorated when Offaly besieged Dublin Castle in August. The lord deputy dallied in Wales for the months of August and September, blaming desertions, a lack of reinforcements, and poor weather conditions for his failure to sail for Ireland. He sent his son, Leonard, to court to impress upon Henry VIII the dangers of undertaking the crossing without a good company.

By late September 1534 Henry had grown impatient with Skeffington and ordered his immediate departure. On 14 October the deputy and his company finally set sail from Graycott. Skeffington brought heavy artillery with him to Ireland which his forces used to good effect during the siege of Kildare's fortress at Maynooth. Wary of reports that Dublin city and castle had been taken by Offaly, Skeffington opted to land at Waterford. He subsequently changed his itinerary and on 24 October he and his force of approximately 2300 men arrived in Dublin. He was immediately sworn into office. Three days later a friar from Drogheda informed the deputy that Offaly intended laying siege to that town. The following day he set out for Drogheda where he remained stationed for a week. He had Thomas Fitzgerald proclaimed a traitor at the high cross in the town. Having summoned the gentlemen of Louth and Meath to affirm their allegiance Skeffington returned to Dublin via Trim where his son, Leonard, served in skirmishes against Fitzgerald. Immediately upon his return to Dublin Skeffington, along with many of his troops, fell ill. Advanced in age, with a choleric temperament and prone to occasional dysentery, he was prostrated with sickness for much of the winter; he garrisoned the chief pale towns while he lapsed into lethargy, proving both unable and unwilling to control the army. Skeffington used orthodox military tactics in his handling of Lord Offaly, seeing no need to bring the rebel's forces to an engagement, a strategy that frustrated many members of the Dublin government. In December John Alen remarked that 'the deputy is old, and cannot take pains by reason of sickness' (*LP Henry VIII*, 7, no. 1573).

Early in 1535 Skeffington allowed William Brereton and other captains to divide their companies and to burn many Geraldine villages, including Maynooth, Lord Offaly's base. By mid-March the deputy had recovered, and besieged Maynooth Castle which surrendered to him on the 23rd of that month. He authorized the immediate execution of the garrison in what was known as 'the pardon of Maynooth'. Skeffington subsequently made Maynooth his base and campaigned throughout Kildare to suppress Geraldine insurgence. In mid-June Skeffington was informed that O'Neill and O'Donnell were conspiring against him, but while the deputy contemplated an expedition into Ulster, O'Neill pre-emptively sought a parley and in July 1535 signed an agreement with Skeffington at Drogheda, following the example of O'More and MacMurrough. In late July Skeffington was replaced as military commander by Lord Leonard Grey. On 24 August Skeffington notified Henry VIII that Thomas Fitzgerald had surrendered to him and that O'Connor had similarly submitted at Castlejordan following his campaign into the Gaelic lord's territory. Skeffington insisted that no 'condition either of pardon, life, lands or goods' was made with Fitzgerald; yet members of the Irish council admitted that comfortable words were spoken to Thomas 'to allure him to yield' and they interceded with Henry VIII to spare Fitzgerald's life on account of those undertakings (Brewer and Bullen, 1.73, 74).

The deputy, now known as the Gunner by his Gaelic contemporaries, became ill once again in late summer: John Alen and Gerald Aylmer remarked that Skeffington was 'almost dead' on occasions when he had to be out of his bed before ten or eleven o'clock in the day. A planned expedition against Conor O'Brien into Munster had to be postponed. In September William Brabazon, undertreasurer, recommended the recall of Skeffington who had by then sufficiently recovered to attend the takeover of Dungarvan Castle. The deputy himself requested permission to retire from Ireland on grounds of poor health, but in response Henry issued a qualified thanks to him for securing Fitzgerald's submission and insisted that he remain in office, declaring his unabated confidence in Skeffington's capacity for the post. On 31 December 1535 Skeffington died at Kilmainham in Dublin. He was buried before the steps ascending to the altar in the north wing of St Patrick's Cathedral, Dublin, and a monument to his memory was erected at Skeffington.

William Brabazon said of Skeffington: 'He was a very good man of war, but not quick enough for Ireland, and somewhat covetous' (*State Papers, Henry VIII*, 2, pt 3, 279). Several other contemporaries also made the latter observation, and it appears somewhat justified since the deputy died in severe financial difficulties, leaving his widow, Anne, and their children in very precarious circumstances. On 1 January 1536 Lord Leonard Grey was elected justiciar in succession to Skeffington, and in June of that year Thomas Skeffington was granted livery of his late father's property. Skeffington was the first in a long line of exclusively English-born incumbents of the deputyship of Ireland under the Tudor monarchs, and he was also the first military leader to introduce sophisticated weaponry to Ireland.   MARY ANN LYONS

Sources J. S. Brewer and W. Bullen, eds., *Calendar of the Carew manuscripts*, 1: 1515–1574, PRO (1867) · *LP Henry VIII*, vols. 1, 2/1, 3–4/1, 4/3–11 · *State papers published under … Henry VIII*, 11 vols. (1830–52), vol. 2, pt 3 · *Holinshed's chronicles of England, Scotland and Ireland*, ed. H. Ellis, 6 (1808) · R. Chapman, 'The Skeffingtons of Tunbridge', *Archaeologia Cantiana*, 10 (1876), 39–45 · *CSP Ire.*, 1509–73 · J. Lodge, *The peerage of Ireland*, rev. M. Archdall, rev. edn, 7 vols. (1789), vols. 1, 2 · S. G. Ellis, 'Thomas Cromwell and Ireland, 1532–1540', *HJ*, 23 (1980), 497–519 · S. G. Ellis, 'The Kildare rebellion and the early Henrician Reformation', *HJ*, 19 (1976), 807–30 · L. McCorristine, *The revolt of Silken Thomas: a challenge to Henry VIII* (1987) · B. Bradshaw, 'Cromwellian reform and the origins of the Kildare rebellion, 1533–34', *TRHS*, 5th ser., 27 (1977), 69–93 · C. W. Fitzgerald, duke of Leinster, *The earls of Kildare and their ancestors from 1057 to 1773*, 3rd edn, 2 vols. (1858–62) · W. M. Mason, *The history and antiquities of the collegiate and cathedral church of St Patrick, near Dublin* (privately printed, Dublin, 1820) · T. W. Moody and others, eds., *A new history of Ireland*, 10 vols. (1976–96), vols. 2–3, 8–9 · S. G. Ellis, *Reform and revival: English government in Ireland, 1470–1534*, Royal Historical Society Studies in History, 47 (1986) · R. Bagwell, *Ireland under the Tudors*, 1 (1885) · J. Lydon, *The making of Ireland from ancient times to the present* (1998) · R. Cox, *Hibernia Anglicana, or, The history of Ireland from the conquest thereof by the English to the present time*, 1 (1689) · C. Brady, *The chief governors: the rise and fall of reform government in Tudor Ireland, 1536–1588* (1994) · B. Bradshaw, *The Irish constitutional revolution of the sixteenth century* (1979) · C. Lennon, *Sixteenth-century Ireland: the incomplete conquest* (1994) · S. G. Ellis, *Ireland in the age of the Tudors* (1998) · R. Lascelles, ed., *Liber munerum publicorum Hiberniae … or, The establishments of Ireland*, 2 vols. [1824–30], pt 3 · R. Fabyan, *The new chronicles of England and France*, ed. H. Ellis, new edn (1811) · J. L. J. Hughes, ed., *Patentee officers in Ireland, 1173–1826, including high sheriffs, 1661–1684 and 1761–1816*, IMC (1960) · J. Morrin, ed., *Calendar of the patent and close rolls of chancery in Ireland, of the reigns of Henry VIII, Edward VI, Mary, and Elizabeth*, 1 (1861)

Wealth at death in serious debt: *LP Henry VIII*; State papers published under … Henry VIII

Skelhorn, Sir Norman John (1909–1988), lawyer and public servant, was born on 10 September 1909 at Claremont Villa, Spire Hollin, Glossop, Derbyshire, the only child of Samuel Skelhorn (1869–1947), a Congregationalist minister who subsequently took Anglican orders, and his first wife, Bertha Heymann (1871/2–1931). During his early years his father's ministry took the family to a number of different parishes in the south and west of England, and in consequence he received a varied education, eventually completing his schooling at Shrewsbury School.

Although there was no legal tradition in the family, by the age of ten Skelhorn had decided to become a lawyer, and he began his legal training while still in his teens, joining chambers in Bristol. He entered the Middle Temple, was called to the bar in January 1931, at the early age of twenty-one, and rapidly built up a successful practice on the western circuit. On 17 April 1937 he married Rosamund Selina Swain (1904–2001?), the daughter of James Swain, an eminent west country surgeon and professor of surgery at the University of Bristol. They had no children. It was with her encouragement that he decided to move to London, and in January 1938 he joined J. D. Caswell's chambers, at 2 Mitre Court. During the war years he worked from 1940 to 1942 for the trading with the enemy department set up by the Treasury and Board of Trade, and then transferred to the Admiralty, ending the war as head of the naval law branch.

In 1945 Skelhorn resumed his legal practice and in the same year was appointed recorder of Bridgwater, a post he held until 1954. In April 1954 he had become a QC, having set up his own chambers, at 2 King's Bench Walk, two years previously, in order to avoid having too many silks in one set. He served as recorder of Plymouth from 1954 to 1962 and recorder of Portsmouth from 1962 to 1964. He was also chairman of the Isle of Wight quarter sessions from 1951 until 1964, and in 1959 and 1960 was a commissioner of assize, trying cases in Sheffield, Leeds, and Birmingham. He became a bencher of his inn in 1962.

From the late 1950s onwards Skelhorn served on a number of public committees. He was a member of the departmental committee on the Probation Service from 1959 to 1961 and in 1962 was appointed a member of the home secretary's advisory panel on the treatment of offenders.

Sir Norman John Skelhorn (1909–1988), by Walter Bird, 1964

He also served on the home secretary's Probation Advisory and Training Board from 1962 to 1973. He conducted a number of inquiries on behalf of the Board of Trade. In February 1964 he reported on the death of Herman Woolf, who had died of brain injuries following a road accident and a subsequent period of detention by the police. Skelhorn found that the police were not responsible for Woolf's injuries, but that there had been several shortcomings in the way that they had handled the case.

In April 1964 Skelhorn was unexpectedly offered the post of director of public prosecutions. Although acceptance meant a reduction in income and would prevent his becoming a judge, he decided to undertake the position because he felt that 'here was a job in which I could make a real impact' (Skelhorn, 64). In June 1966 he received the knighthood customarily conferred on the holder of the post. After thirteen years in office, he resigned because he wished to serve as recorder of the crown court, a position he occupied until 1981. His successor as director of public prosecutions was Sir Thomas Hetherington, during whose tenure of office the crown prosecution service was created.

Skelhorn was the eighth holder of the office of director of public prosecutions, a non-political post within the civil service with responsibility for prosecuting some categories of offences, deciding on the prosecution of certain others, and advising on criminal matters. Changes made by him in the running of the department included the setting up of two new divisions to deal with police matters and company frauds, and he was successful in obtaining much needed additional office accommodation in order to deal with the additional work arising from criminal bankruptcy legislation.

Although Skelhorn's service as director of public prosecutions was not exceptionally controversial, there were inevitably several cases which attracted public comment. The prosecution of the publishers of the underground magazine *Oz*, in 1971, exemplified the difficulties of obscenity cases, especially in a climate of rapidly changing public taste. Skelhorn subsequently expressed the view that prosecutions for obscenity were seldom in the public interest, as an unsuccessful case only served to advertise the publication. Also controversial was the decision in 1973 to grant immunity from prosecution to the 'supergrass' Derek Smalls, which was severely criticized by Lord Justice Lawton. Skelhorn's department received further criticism in relation to the Confait case, when three youths convicted in 1972 in connection with the murder of a homosexual prostitute, Maxwell Confait, were released following an appeal in 1975. An inquiry in 1977 by Sir Henry Fisher found that, although the director's staff had acted conscientiously, the practices they followed were not wholly satisfactory.

Another case attracting great public interest was the prosecution in 1975 of Peter Hain, then leader of the Young Liberals and a well-known anti-apartheid activist, on a charge of alleged bank robbery. Following Hain's acquittal, in April 1976, the decision to bring the case was widely criticized, and David Steel, leader of the Liberal Party, and five other MPs put forward a motion in parliament calling for Skelhorn's resignation. Skelhorn was strongly supported, however, by Sir Eric Sachs, who argued, in a letter to *The Times* (13 April 1976), that it had been right to put the identification evidence, on which the case turned, before a jury. The attorney-general (S. C. Silkin) refused to agree to a public inquiry, and expressed himself satisfied with the handling of the case.

Skelhorn considered that a degree of reticence was necessary to ensure respect for his office, and his autobiography, *Public Prosecutor* (1981), reveals little of his personality or of the inner workings of his department. He did, however, on several occasions, publicly comment that the right to silence, as it then stood, did little to help the innocent and hampered the police. He supported capital punishment, which he believed discouraged recklessness on the part of criminals, and favoured prison conditions sufficiently severe to deter those criminals who were not capable of reformation.

Skelhorn died at his home, Wyndham, 10 Chiltley Way, Liphook, Hampshire, from heart disease, on 28 May 1988. A journalist who met him in 1986 described him as 'a small, twinkling eyed, rosy cheeked man' (Rozenberg, 32). A keen traveller, both for official and recreational purposes, he visited many countries, including Australia, Russia, and India, and enjoyed country pursuits.

SHEILA DOYLE

Sources N. Skelhorn, *Public prosecutor* (1981) • J. Rozenberg, *The case for the crown: the inside story of the director of public prosecutions*

(1987) • *The Times* (1951–88) • D. Taylor, 'Between the devil and the DPP', *Punch* (24 Nov 1976), 958–9 • *WWW*, 1981–90 • *The Times* (31 May 1988)
Likenesses W. Bird, photograph, 1964, NPG [*see illus.*] • Ffolkes, drawing, repro. in Taylor, 'Between the devil and the DPP', 958 • photograph, repro. in Rozenberg, *Case for the crown* • photograph, repro. in *The Times* (22 April 1964), 14 • photograph, repro. in *The Times* (28 June 1972), 4 • photograph, repro. in *Sunday Times* (30 June 1974), 12 • photographs, repro. in Skelhorn, *Public prosecutor*
Wealth at death £53,090: probate, 12 Aug 1988, *CGPLA Eng. & Wales*

Skellern, (Flora) Eileen (1923–1980), nurse, was born on 14 June 1923 at 54 Old Road, Stone, Staffordshire, the eldest of the three children of Willis Arthur Skellern (1896–1982), commercial traveller, and his wife, Flora, formerly Poole (1900–1986). She was educated at Retford Girls' High School, Nottinghamshire. When she was eighteen Eileen Skellern undertook general nurse training at Leeds General Infirmary, Yorkshire, qualifying as a nurse in 1944. After some placements as a staff nurse, in 1946 she was promoted to ward sister on a medical ward, where there were some psychiatric beds. This led to an interest in modern methods of treating the mentally disordered, and to further this in 1948 Skellern moved to the Cassel Hospital, Richmond, Surrey, where she joined the ward sisters' certificate course in nursing the neuroses and psychological methods of treatment. The Cassel Hospital was known for its progressive open door policy and its emphasis on a therapeutic environment. As a place for further education the Cassel seemed more attractive to Skellern than the traditional psychiatric nurse training in large mental hospitals, which were still teaching custodial methods on closed wards. In 1949 Skellern joined the permanent staff of the Cassel Social Therapy Unit and in 1953 became sister in charge of the Social Rehabilitation Unit at the Belmont Hospital, Sutton, Surrey, where, in addition to administration, she was active in teaching, group work with patients and staff, and social research.

At the age of thirty-four Eileen Skellern began studying for a tutor's diploma at the Royal College of Nursing (1957–9), and then held the post of sister tutor at St Bartholomew's Hospital, London (1959–61). She was appointed superintendent of nursing at the Bethlem Royal and Maudsley hospitals in 1961, but before taking up her post studied to obtain the qualification of registered mental nurse at Cheadle Royal Hospital, Cheshire. From this time she was based in Greater London.

From the beginning, in 1963, of her busy management career Skellern's activities within the Maudsley were supplemented by external committee work, such as advising the Home Office on nursing in the prison service over a period of five years, working with the World Federation of Mental Health in 1966, and also working with the National Association of Mental Health over several years in the late 1960s. Most memorable was the work with the secretary of state, Richard Crossman, reviewing government policy on mental subnormality, following revelations of malpractice at Ely Hospital, Cardiff. The results of this work

were eventually seen in a white paper, *Better Services for the Mentally Handicapped*, in 1972, the year in which she was appointed OBE. Eileen Skellern's remaining years at the Maudsley were marked by a long struggle against cancer, which forced her into early retirement in 1980. Although not without close men friends, she remained unmarried.

The achievements of Eileen Skellern's early career grew out of her clinical work at the Cassel Hospital with Dr Tom Main, with whom she pioneered psychotherapeutic and psychosocial treatments of patients with neurotic illnesses. The therapeutic community initiatives which Dr Maxwell Jones and Skellern developed at the Belmont Hospital heralded important moves forward in the development of psychiatric nursing. The medium of therapy being the whole community, an opportunity was offered for nurses to escape from their former subservient positions. Skellern showed that new roles for nurses in the staff team were becoming available in family work, socialization, and group work. Her vision was that in a variety of settings psychiatric nurses would use their relationships with patients to promote independence and facilitate the transition back to the community. She also showed, with Maxwell Jones, that a psychiatric nurse and a doctor could collaborate on equal terms in the tasks of publishing papers and drawing conclusions from their work, for instance on the topics of social rehabilitation and work therapy. Skellern's publications gave a definitive picture of the new developments in psychiatric nursing in the 1950s. This was a significant contribution to thinking about nursing at a time when psychiatric nurses were emerging from the old custodial roles, and actively developing therapeutic initiatives with patients.

Skellern supplemented this in 1952–3 by writing a historic report for the Royal College of Nursing. This study, 'The role of the ward sister', was the first serious piece of nursing research done in England by a psychiatric nurse, and covered the practical application to ward administration of modern methods in the instruction and handling of staff and student nurses.

In nurse education Skellern's work was always innovative. She had a natural bent for teaching and much of her career was occupied with developing the education and training of psychiatric nurses. She promoted the use of group methods in teaching by the experiential approach, which linked the student's clinical experiences to the classroom. This concern for linking theory to practice was shared by Elliott Jacques, professor of social sciences at Brunel University, who was experimenting with undergraduate courses interspersed with industrial placements. In collaboration with Jacques, Skellern instituted a combined nursing certificate and degree course in 1968, half at the Maudsley and half at Brunel University, which was the first to link nursing and social sciences. In the field of post-basic training Skellern, with Dr Isaac Marks of the Institute of Psychiatry, London University, initiated a course in behavioural psychotherapy for nurses in 1973 which was a notable step in the establishment of nurses as therapists in their own right.

Much of this was done in an era which saw the introduction of the Salmon nursing management structure, giving Skellern, retitled chief nursing officer in 1972 at the Maudsley, much managerial power and responsibility. Her colleagues benefited from her valuable insights into hospital management and her knowledge of health care worldwide. In committees she was firm in her views, which were informed by a strong personal sense of morality. Her religious faith was that of a practising member of the Church of England, and she maintained a warm, concerned, and good-humoured approach to individuals, whatever their status in the organization. She was conscientious and equitable in her dealings with staff. Her fair haired, well built, neatly dressed figure was familiar to hundreds in hospital wards and board-rooms. The stresses of hospital life and of her own chronic illness led her to adopt stress as a topic, on which she spoke publicly in a charismatic way which enlightened and strengthened her hearers.

Eileen Skellern was one of the first British psychiatric nurses of national reputation, making distinguished contributions in the clinical, research, education, and policy making fields. This was recognized when she was made a fellow of the Royal College of Nursing in 1980. On 29 July 1980 she died of carcinoma at her home, 129 Alresford Road, Winchester, and was buried at Winchester cemetery on 4 August. DAVID H. RUSSELL

Sources Bethlem Royal Hospital, Beckenham, Kent, Archives and Museum, Skellern papers · D. Russell, *Scenes from Bedlam* (1996) · M. Skellern and D. Russell, 'Eileen Skellern House', *Royal College of Nursing History of Nursing Journal*, 4/2 (1992–3), 82–4 · personal knowledge (2004) · b. cert. · d. cert. · private information (2004) [Margaret Skellern, sister]
Archives Bethlem Royal Hospital, Beckenham, Kent, Archives and Museum
Likenesses M. Cossey, oils, 1985, Bethlem Royal Hospital, Beckenham, Kent · R. Beattie, oils, 1992, Maudsley Hospital, London
Wealth at death £16,623: probate, 17 Sept 1980, *CGPLA Eng. & Wales*

Skelton, Barbara Olive (1916–1996), writer and literary *femme fatale*, was born on 26 June 1916 at The Croft, Ellington Road, Taplow, Buckinghamshire. Her father, Eric George Skelton, a descendant of the playwright Sheridan, was a major in the West India regiment, but was invalided out of the army at an early age; her mother, Eveline Ada Williams, of partly Danish origin, was a former Gaiety girl. A temperamental child, 'bun-faced, with slanting sludge-coloured eyes' (Skelton, *Tears before Bedtime*, 4), Barbara lost her virginity to a margarine millionaire while still in her teens.

Barbara worked as a model, but after the Second World War began she became a denizen of bohemian London, dividing her amorous favours between Peter Quennell and Feliks Topolski, who came to blows over her one night in the Gargoyle Club. Barbara and Quennell shared an attic in Bedford Square, rented from Cyril Connolly, but in 1942 she went to Egypt, at Donald Maclean's suggestion, to work as a Foreign Office 'cipherine' in Cairo. There she

Barbara Olive Skelton (1916–1996), by unknown photographer

added King Farouk to her list of lovers. Barbara always disdained conventional good looks, once citing Erich von Stroheim as her *beau idéal*: she retained a soft spot for the king, despite his lashing her with his dressing-gown cord.

Back in London, she was re-introduced to Cyril *Connolly (1903–1974), writer and editor; he fell in love with her, and they were married on 5 October 1950. Marooned in Barbara's tiny cottage, high up in the Kentish Downs, with only a ferocious South American coatimundi, some guinea fowl, and a goose to keep them company, the Connollys fought—as he put it—like a couple of kangaroos. Paralysed by writer's block and the melancholy of middle age, Connolly—known to his spouse as Pungle or Pop—lay in bed for hours on end, sucking the sheets and muttering 'Poor Cyril' like a mantra.

On one of the Connollys' trips to London, Barbara began a passionate affair with her husband's new publisher, (Arthur) George Weidenfeld (b. 1919); to complicate matters further, Weidenfeld published her first novel, *A Young Girl's Touch* (1955), which was dedicated to Connolly and was, like all her fiction, thinly disguised autobiography. Connolly was devastated by her intense if transient physical infatuation with Weidenfeld; the affair became the talk of literary London, and after a series of near-farcical comings and goings they reluctantly divorced in the spring of 1956, with Weidenfeld cited as co-respondent.

Shortly afterwards, on 26 August 1956, Barbara Skelton

married Weidenfeld; the newly-weds spent their honeymoon in Italy, on Ischia, where Connolly happened to be staying with W. H. Auden. Life as a publisher's wife proved entirely uncongenial, and passion turned to positive dislike: she had affairs with Alan Ross and the painter Michael Wishart—for whom she was 'as feline in appearance as she later proved to be in character' (Wishart, 149)—but when, in due course, Weidenfeld divorced her, Connolly was cited as co-respondent.

Connolly remained the one great love of Barbara Skelton's life, and after her divorce in 1959 she moved to New York, where she worked in a bookshop and as a dentist's receptionist, and added the critic Kenneth Tynan, the editor Bob Silvers, and the cartoonist Charles Addams to the cast of admirers. In 1966 she was briefly married to Derek Ainslie *Jackson (1906–1982), a war hero living in Paris who combined the Oxford professorship of spectroscopy with success as an amateur jockey; his fortune was founded on the *News of the World* and from then on Barbara was never short of a penny, even though they were divorced after a year. She settled in the south of France, where she enjoyed a tumultuous relationship with the French writer Bernard Frank; while staying with her there in the summer of 1974, Connolly suffered a heart attack, and died in London two months later.

Barbara published a collection of stories, *Born Losers* (1965), and a second novel, *A Love Match* (1969), which had to be withdrawn after John Sutro threatened a libel action. But she is best remembered for her two volumes of autobiography, *Tears before Bedtime* (1987) and *Weep No More* (1989), which combine waspishness and wit in equal measure. She had a keen eye for the absurd, and a ruthless ability to skewer friends and foes alike with an exact and colourful turn of phrase, comparing Farouk in exile to 'a huge sawdust teddy bear badly sewn at the joints', and noting Connolly's 'Chinese coolie's legs protruding from below his knee-length shorts' (Skelton, *Tears before Bedtime*, 91, 110).

To the end of her life Barbara Skelton retained her pantherine good looks, and her hour-glass figure remained as supple as that of a thirty-year-old; she had fair hair, and her high cheek-bones and glittering eyes reminded Quennell of 'the youthful concubine of a legendary Mongol chieftain' (Quennell, 21). Quick-witted, funny, and well-read, she could be alarmingly sullen, moody, and farouche: the important thing was to make her laugh, after which one's sins of neglect were briefly forgiven.

Much to her regret, Barbara was unable to have children. Lonely, restless, and easily bored, she returned to England with her cats in 1993. Towards the end of 1995 she was diagnosed as having a brain tumour. She spent her last weeks with Connolly's daughter Cressida and her family in Worcestershire, and died there, at Wick Manor, Wick, near Pershore, on 27 January 1996. She was buried at Wick. JEREMY LEWIS

Sources B. Skelton, *Tears before bedtime* (1987) · B. Skelton, *Weep no more* (1989) · P. Quennell, *The wanton chase* (1980) · *The Guardian* (31 Jan 1996) · G. Weidenfeld, *Remembering my good friends* (1995) ·

M. Wishart, *High diver* (1977) · E. Wilson, *The fifties* (1986) · F. Topolski, *Fourteen letters* (1988) · letters from Cyril Connolly to Lys Lubbock, University of Indiana, Lilly Library · letters from Cyril Connolly to Barbara Skelton, priv. coll. · diaries and letters of Barbara Skelton, priv. coll. · personal knowledge (2004) · b. cert.

Archives priv. coll.

Likenesses photograph, repro. in B. Skelton, *Tears before bedtime*, facing p. 115 [*see illus.*]

Wealth at death £256,076: probate, 3 April 1996, *CGPLA Eng. & Wales*

Skelton, Bevil (*c.*1641–1696), diplomat and soldier, was the eldest son of the Yorkshire soldier Sir John Skelton (*d.* 1673), lieutenant-governor of Plymouth from 1660, and his wife, Bridget (*d.* 1681), daughter of Sir Peter Prideaux. He later hinted that he served with the tiny royalist army in the 1657 campaign that culminated in the battle of the Dunes. By December 1657 he was a page of honour to the exiled Charles II, and continued in this position briefly after the Restoration, receiving a pension of £120 a year in 1662, the year in which he sold the office. On 11 June 1662 he married Simona Cary (*d.* 1692), the daughter and stepdaughter of prominent soldiers (respectively, Sir Ferdinando Cary and Sir Thomas Blackwell); they had at least three sons, Bevil, Cary, and Charles (1672–1736). The marriage seems to have been happy: in January 1673, while serving in France, Skelton wrote to Simona to assure her 'that I most passionately love thee, being unwilling to express any further discontent and trouble for my being from thee, not questioning you are sufficiently assured of my being, my only joy, thy faithful loving husband' (*Various Collections*, 8.67).

On 27 July 1666 Skelton was commissioned a cornet in the earl of Rochester's horse, and became a captain in Sir Arthur Basset's foot regiment on 13 June 1667. From August the same year he served as quartermaster to Sir George Hamilton's troop in the French army. On 20 November 1668 he was commissioned a captain in the 1st foot guards, and in October 1669 became registrar of the Charterhouse. In 1671 he was with his regiment at York, and received some of the proceeds from the fines on conventicles in Yorkshire. From 1672 to 1674 he served as lieutenant-colonel of the Royal English regiment in France.

Following his return from military service Skelton embarked upon a long and controversial diplomatic career. From August to November 1674 he undertook a secret mission to France for the king. On 29 December 1675 he was accredited as envoy-extraordinary to the imperial court, with an allowance of £4 a day (soon increased to £5), and remained at Vienna until 1681, despite the fact that his overtly francophile stance (epitomized by a close friendship with the French ambassador) made him unpopular with the emperor's ministers. In 1679 Charles II proposed to transfer him to The Hague, but his sympathies for France made him unacceptable to William of Orange and the states general. From 1681 Skelton was accredited to most of the lesser German courts in a peripatetic role, based usually at Hamburg. He had audiences at Brunswick and Saxony in 1682, and also visited the Netherlands on a number of occasions. In the spring of

Bevil Skelton (*c*.1641–1696), by Matthias van Someren, 1678

1684 he made a diplomatic mission to Denmark, and had an audience in May.

Skelton's roving commission ended in March 1685, when he journeyed to The Hague to take up the post of ambassador. This was a posthumous insult to his nephew by Charles II, who had been offended by William's support for the duke of Monmouth and knew that the appointment of Skelton would be seen as a personal affront. Indeed the French ambassador in London even thought that this was deliberately intended to provoke William into a rash gesture, and at first Skelton had orders not to speak to the prince. Not surprisingly Skelton's relations with William of Orange and the Dutch authorities were poor almost from the very beginning, with Skelton again making no attempt to conceal his francophile stance. The Dutch authorities ignored his requests to prevent the sailing of the marquess of Argyll's and Monmouth's expeditions, and resented his subsequent attempts to get opponents of James II expelled from the Netherlands. To compound matters Skelton found out that William was having an affair with Elizabeth Villiers; a letter to him from Princess Mary's chaplain, John Covel, was intercepted, and William attempted to use it to get the despised ambassador recalled. Skelton's one success was to secure the return from the Netherlands of the English and Scottish regiments in the Anglo-Dutch brigade, but even this was very much a qualified success, as the political sympathies of the returning troops lay firmly with the opponents of the king.

Eventually admitting the inevitable James II accredited Skelton as envoy-extraordinary to France on 17 October 1686. In a parting gesture that hardly endeared him to the Dutch, Skelton authorized an attempt to kidnap Sir Robert Peyton, who had been indicted for sedition in the previous year, and to transport him back to England in his diplomatic yacht. However, Peyton had become a citizen of Amsterdam and was rescued by the mob. During his leave in England, Skelton regaled James with exaggerated tales of William's sympathies with the rebels, thereby helping to harden the king's attitude to his nephew. At Versailles, however, Skelton was effectively sidelined, with all serious negotiations being conducted directly through the French ambassador in London, Barillon. His one real initiative, in August 1688, was to advise the presentation of a memorial to the states general threatening French action against the Netherlands if William's preparations against England continued. James took a public position of resenting Skelton's unauthorized initiative and recalled him, committing him to the Tower on his return. This was effectively an attempt by James to convince William and European opinion that he was not in Louis XIV's pocket, but his treatment of Skelton suggests that it was little more than window dressing. The erstwhile ambassador's confinement was brief: on 9 October he was commissioned to command a new foot regiment, and on 6 November succeeded Sir Edward Hales as lieutenant of his so recent prison. He lost this position on 11 December and followed James into exile with two of his sons. Their escape was hair-raising:

> we were pursued by a vessel full of the Dover rabble who had an intent to plunder us, if not to murder us, but after two hours dispute side by side, with matches lighted and pistols cocked expecting who should fire first, they finding nothing was to be had without blows left us, and we sailed on our way. (*Various Collections*, 8.68)

In March 1689 Skelton undertook a mission for James to the imperial diet at Regensburg, and subsequently sought an audience of the emperor. The mission also took in Venice and Turin, where he attempted to win over James's kinsman, Duke Victor Amadeus of Savoy. The duke, who was reluctant to offend William III, managed to avoid Skelton, whose known predilection for France again conditioned the response of a government to him. In February 1690 Skelton returned to Versailles as James II's envoy. He was appointed comptroller of the household at St Germain-en-Laye in June 1690 on a salary of 4200 livres a year, and additionally became a commissioner of the household on 24 December 1694. Skelton converted to Catholicism in 1691.

Following Simona's death on 17 January 1692 Skelton married, on 14 March, Marie (1660/61–1747), daughter of Daniel *O'Brien, third Viscount Clare (*c*.1630–1690). Several children were born in quick succession: James in 1692, Mary (who later married Lord Molyneux) in 1693, and Frances early in 1695. By February 1696 Skelton was dangerously ill, and he died and was buried at St Germain-en-Laye on 28 April, when he was said to be fifty-five. A posthumous son, Daniel Ignatius, was baptized on 31 July (he died in November 1697). In 1701 Skelton's widow petitioned parliament for the recovery of her jointure: disingenuously, she claimed to have married Skelton 'some time before the revolution' (Bodl. Oxf., MS Rawl. A.253, fol. 131), and made no mention at all of their time at St Germain-en-Laye. She eventually returned there and died on 8 November 1747, aged eighty-six.

Skelton was a significant hate figure for supporters of the Williamite revolution, especially the whigs, and their demonization of him has shaped the way in which history has treated him. Skelton, a man who always seems to have found it easier to make enemies than friends, made no secret of his contempt for their opinions: in 1684 he wrote to Sir Richard Bulstrode that 'I wish I could convert my relations that are with you from their damn'd Whiggish principles' (BL, Egerton MS 3681, fol. 132). Gilbert Burnet repaid the compliment in no uncertain terms, condemning Skelton to posterity as

a very weak and passionate man, who neither understands the conduct of affairs, nor can govern his tongue with any sort of temper; for as his passion carries him to fly out on all occasions, so his vanity is so little governed that he discovers all sorts of secrets, even when he can have no other design in it but to let it appear that he knows them. (*Supplement to Burnet's History*, 256)

Skelton was undoubtedly incompetent in his dealings over Argyll's and Monmouth's expeditions, reacting too slowly and approaching the wrong authorities. His love of the French was matched only by his rather less enthusiastic attitude to other Europeans: in 1676 he described his time among the high-ranking German and Austrian dignitaries at Regensburg as being 'confined amongst proud jealous brutes, with whom I have no conversation' (BL, Egerton MS 3681, fol. 2). Skelton sought solace with fellow Britons: '[I] was yesterday (being St Benedict's day) entertained by the abbot of the Scotch Benedictines, a very honest gentleman and a good fellow, for which my head now aches' (ibid., fol. 1). Ultimately, the question of whether Colonel Bevil Skelton was or was not a competent diplomat is perhaps less important than the question of why Charles II and James II consistently employed in such high profile positions an ambassador whose sympathy for only one state and one policy was so transparent. In that respect, Skelton's career perhaps reveals more about their competence in foreign affairs than about his own.

J. D. DAVIES

Sources correspondence with Lord Middleton, BL, Add. MSS 41823–41824, 41842 · PRO, SP 78/136–7, 150–51; 82/16; 84 · *Report on the manuscripts of the marquis of Downshire*, 6 vols. in 7, HMC, 75 (1924–95), vol. 1 · letters to Sir Richard Bulstrode, BL, Egerton MS 3681 · *A supplement to Burnet's History of my own time*, ed. H. C. Foxcroft (1902) · C. E. Lart, ed., *The parochial registers of Saint Germain-en-Laye: Jacobite extracts of births, marriages, and deaths*, 2 vols. (1910–12) · private information (2004) [E. Corp] · *CSP dom.*, esp. 1657–8 · W. A. Shaw, ed., *Calendar of treasury books*, [33 vols. in 64], PRO (1904–69), esp. vols. 1 and 8 · will of Sir John Skelton, PRO, PROB 11/341, fol. 309v · will of Dame Bridget Skelton, PRO, PROB 11/367, fols. 315v–316 · petition of Mary Skelton, Bodl. Oxf., MS Rawl. A. 253, fols. 131–3 · J. C. R. Childs, *Nobles, gentlemen and the profession of arms in Restoration Britain, 1660–1688: a biographical dictionary of British army officers on foreign service* (1987) · G. Hilton Jones, *Charles Middleton: the*

life and times of a Restoration politician (1967) · P. S. Lachs, *The diplomatic corps under Charles II and James II* (1965) · R. Oresko, 'The glorious revolution of 1688–9 and the house of Savoy', *The Anglo-Dutch moment, essays on the glorious revolution and its world impact*, ed. J. Israel (1991), 392–4 · *The manuscripts of the earl of Dartmouth*, 3 vols., HMC, 20 (1887–96), vols. 1, 3 · *Report on manuscripts in various collections*, 8 vols., HMC, 55 (1901–14), vol. 8 · *Report on the manuscripts of Lord Polwarth*, 5, HMC, 67 (1961) · G. M. Bell, *A handlist of British diplomatic representatives, 1509–1688*, Royal Historical Society Guides and Handbooks, 16 (1990) · *Letters of Sir George Etherege*, ed. F. Bracher (1974) · BL, Add. MS 25119, fols. 146–65 · BL, Add. MS 35104, fols. 37–80 · N. Luttrell, *A brief historical relation of state affairs from September 1678 to April 1714*, 6 vols. (1857) · S. B. Baxter, *William III* (1966) · J. Miller, *James II: a study in kingship* (1978)

Archives BL, letters to R. Bulstrode, Egerton MS 3681 · BL, corresp. with Lord Middleton, Add. MSS 41812–41824, 41842 · PRO, SP 78/136–7, 150–51, 80/239, 82/16 · Yale U., Beinecke L., letters to E. Poley

Likenesses M. van Someren, line engraving, 1678, NPG [*see illus.*]

Skelton, John (*c*.1460–1529), poet, may have been born about 1460 in the north of England, possibly Yorkshire. His family name may derive from one of the six places called Skelton in Yorkshire (though the name is found elsewhere also) and a number of his early poems are connected with that county. But about his family and early life no records have survived and his poems are silent on these matters. In fact only about two dozen records relating to his life are extant. These are mainly of a technical nature, and while they are useful, it is to his poems that one must turn for details of what mainly concerned him.

University career In a poem written in 1527 or 1528 against two Cambridge heretics Skelton refers to the university as 'kind parent' (*alma parens*) and says he was once an '*alumnus*' there (*Complete English Poems*, 373), and a sidenote to this passage (which was probably written by Skelton) says that he 'first sucked the breast of learning at Cambridge'. There are several references to students called Skelton at this time but none is indisputably to be identified with the poet. The most likely is that which refers to a 'Dominus Skelton questionist' which might indicate that he was about to supplicate for his BA. But there is no record that Skelton did actually take this degree. He may have been at Peterhouse. In a Latin quatrain added to a poem written in 1489 Skelton refers in affectionate terms to Dr William Ruckshaw, 'most excellent of men' (ibid., 35), fellow of Peterhouse until 1474. Among his other contemporaries at Cambridge were John Blythe, who eventually became chancellor of the university, master of the rolls, and bishop of Salisbury, and John Syclyng, who later became master of Godshouse (now Christ's College). In 1495 all three dined together in London while Syclyng was there representing the University of Cambridge against the town in a legal dispute; and in 1501 Skelton and Syclyng ate together on several occasions.

But it was from the University of Oxford, which Skelton may have attended in some capacity, that his first degree comes: about 1490, in his preface to *Eneydos*, William Caxton refers to him as 'late created poete laureate in the university of Oxford' (A. S. G. Edwards, 43) and Skelton himself refers, in one of his flytings against Sir Christopher Garnesche, to this honour which was conferred 'by hole consent of theyr senate' (*Complete English Poems*, 131). About 1492, according to a laudatory Latin poem in his honour by the grammarian Robert Whittinton, Skelton, 'the glory of English poets', was laureated by the University of Louvain (A. S. G. Edwards, 49–53). No record of this has survived. But it does acquire some confirmation from the terms of the laureateship he received from Cambridge in 1493, which refers to his Oxford degree and to another obtained 'in places across the sea' (*in partibus transmarinis*; H. L. R. Edwards, 287). This record also mentions the fact that Skelton could 'use dress given to him by a prince', which evidently meant that he could wear some distinctive apparel, evidently of white and green with the word 'Calliope' embroidered on it.

These academic distinctions, which others also had, appear to have been given in recognition of Skelton's achievement as a writer, and other evidence confirms his early fame. Caxton, in the preface already quoted, praises him for his classical learning, his skill in translation, and his 'polysshed and ornate termes': 'I suppose he hath dronken of Elycons well'. In 1499 Erasmus, in a letter to the future Henry VIII, mentions that the prince has in his household Skelton, 'a light and glory of English letters' (A. S. G. Edwards, 44). Yet it is impossible to know exactly on what his fame rested, because it is difficult to date his early works and because some of them have undoubtedly been lost. It is fairly certain, though, that, by the time Caxton praised him, he had written the elegy for Henry Percy, fourth earl of Northumberland, killed by a mob of tax rebels on 28 April 1489 at Topcliff, Yorkshire. He had also finished his translation of Diodorus Siculus's 'Bibliotheca historica', the sole surviving manuscript of which (Cambridge, Corpus Christi College, MS 357) was owned by Robert Pen, gentleman of the Chapel Royal. Caxton also mentions that he 'hath late translated' Cicero's letters 'and diverse other werkes out of Latyn in to Englysshe' but none of these have survived in an identifiable form.

Royal tutor and church career What Skelton did after his years at university is not clear. He was evidently associated at some stage with the Percy household. There is a text of the elegy for the fourth earl in London (BL, Royal MS 18.D.ii) that at some stage belonged to Henry Percy, the fifth earl, and which contains a Percy family chronicle, in verse, written by William Peeris, 'clerke and preiste', which views the death of the fourth earl in very much the same light as Skelton had. And though they are lost, Skelton also claims to have composed 'pajauntis [pageants] that were played at the Joyows Garde' (*Complete English Poems*, 351). 'Joyous Garde', Lancelot's castle in *Morte Darthur*, was sometimes considered to be Alnwick and sometimes Bamborough, both of which were Percy castles in Northumberland; and it may well be that Skelton wrote plays which were performed at one or other of them. It seems he was also at Sheriff Hutton Castle as a guest of the Howard family in 1495, when he began to write 'The Garlande of Laurell' in which he describes an embroidery group of Elizabeth Tylney Howard, countess of Surrey, and some of her relatives and friends who embroider a laurel crown in his honour (ibid., 334–43).

Skelton appears to have entered the Tudor royal service in late October or early November 1488. It is not known what his early duties were, but about 1496 he became tutor to Prince Henry, a post he held until about 1502 or 1503. Skelton entered holy orders in 1498: he was ordained subdeacon on 31 March, deacon on 14 April, and priest on 9 June. He was attached to the abbey of St Mary of Graces, a 'free chapel royal' near the Tower of London. He is recorded as having celebrated mass there on 11 November 1498 before Henry VII, who made him an offering of 20s. It appears that Skelton involved himself in the ecclesiastical politics of London: Peter Ottey, a royal chaplain, made a complaint against him at the court of requests on 14 May 1501; and on 10 June 1502 he was imprisoned as surety for William Guy, prior of St Bartholomew's, who was delinquent in a debt. But much of Skelton's time must have been spent on his pedagogical duties, which he recalled with pride years later: 'The honor of England I lernyd to spelle' (*Complete English Poems*, 132).

Skelton's writings in this period reflect the multifaceted nature of his situation. Some are panegyrics, such as the 'Epigramma ad sancti principis maiestatem', written to celebrate Prince Henry's being created duke of York on 1 November 1494. Probably similar was the now lost 'Prince Arturis Creacyon' (*Complete English Poems*, 345) which may have celebrated Arthur's assumption of the title of prince of Wales in 1489. It is likely too that Skelton wrote or translated a number of pedagogical works, such as the 'New Gramer' (ibid., 346), or moral works such as 'the Boke how Men Shulde Fle Synne' or 'the Boke to Speke Well or Be Styll' (ibid., 345), the second of which may well have been a version of Albertanus de Brescia's *Tractatus de doctrina dicendi et tacendi*. Both of these are now lost, as are the texts on government Skelton claims to have written such as 'The Boke of Honorous Estate', 'Royall Demenaunce', and 'Soveraynte a noble pamphelet' (ibid., 345–6). One such book of advice, however, has survived—the brief 'Speculum principis', written in ornate Latin prose for Prince Henry and finished on 28 August 1501. It looks as though Skelton took his duties as royal tutor very seriously.

But some of Skelton's English poems written in this period give a very different impression of his life. 'Manerly Margery Mylk and Ale', which survives with music for three voices by William Cornish in London, British Library, Add. MS 5465 (Fayrfax MS), is a cynical seduction poem. And a lot of the lyrics in the collections entitled *Agaynste a Comely Coystrowne* and *Dyvers Balettys and Dyties Solacyous*, both printed by John Rastell about 1527, but written probably in the 1490s, deal with social and sexual competitiveness in London and at court: two are satires on would-be teachers of music at court; another is about a man deceived by a tavern prostitute; and another is about disquiet in a well-to-do knightly household because the wife of a 'ryght jentyll knyght' is having an affair with the servant in charge of the horses: 'He rydyth wel the horse, but he rydyth better the mare' (*Complete English Poems*, 43). A number of these themes reappear in *The Bowge of Courte*, probably written in the autumn of 1498 and printed by de Worde in 1499. This is a sombre anti-court satire cast as a traditional medieval dream-vision allegory. Skelton, in the thinly disguised character of Drede, a man of 'vertu' and 'lytterkture', finds himself on a ship, 'The Bowge of Courte', steered by Fortune and resorted to by those hoping to make their way at court. He is told by Desyre:

> Bone aventure may brynge you in suche case
> That ye shall stonde in favoure and in grace.
> (ibid., 49)

The ship is peopled by a sinister assortment of thieves, gamblers, pimps, potential murderers—a kind of courtly underclass—who all both flatter and scheme against each other, and try to involve Drede in their plots. The language they use is colloquial and demotic, full of innuendo and threat. It is a poem full of conspiratorial whispering—'I have an errande to rounde in your ere' (ibid., 60)—but the message is never told. It is a depressed analysis, born out of anxiety and insecurity, out of frustration and disappointment, of the milieu in which Skelton had decided to make his career.

Rector of St Mary's, Diss On 29 April 1502 'the duc of Yorks scolemaster' received a gift of 40s. from Henry VII (H. L. R. Edwards, 288–9). If this person is to be identified with Skelton it was probably the last gift of this sort that he received. Perhaps by 1503, but certainly by 10 April 1504, when he witnessed the will of Margery Cowper, one of his parishioners, Skelton was in Diss, Norfolk, where he was rector of the parish church of St Mary's—a post he held until his death. Though the rectorship of Diss was quite a lucrative post, Skelton evidently did not enjoy the experience of being a country clergyman very much. He probably lived mainly in Diss until 1512 or 1513. He does not appear, from the official records, to have been anything other than a dutiful clergyman. In, perhaps, 1506 he wrote a Latin couplet rejoicing in the receipt of tithes from his parishioners. Some time after 25 April 1507 he wrote 'Lamentacio urbis Norwicen', on the second disastrous fire in the city. Between 3 December 1509 and 4 February 1510 he was in attendance at the Norwich consistorial court for the interrogation of Thomas Pykerell of Diss 'for the welfare of his soul'—a heresy trial. On 6 December 1511 he was one of the arbitrators in a dispute between William Dale, rector of Redgrave, Suffolk, and Thomas Revet before Bishop Richard Nykke in Norwich.

But some poems written in Skelton's period at Diss suggest that he did not get on well with some of his parishioners or some of his fellow clergymen. A pair of macaronic satiric epitaphs, perhaps written in 1506, and copied out by the parish priest of Trumpington, Cambridgeshire, take as their subject 'two knaves sometyme of Dis' (Complete English Poems, 106): John Clarke, whose will was proved on 14 April 1506, and Adam Uddersall, two of his parishioners. The epitaph's normal laudation of a life well spent is here replaced by vicious personalized invective. Clarke had, it seems, either calumniated or criticized Skelton, his own rector. There is no doubt, however, about what provoked 'Ware the Hawke', which dates from about the same period: a neighbouring cleric, perhaps John Smith, rector of East Wretham (about 15 miles from Diss),

had allowed his hawk to chase an injured pigeon into Skelton's church. Skelton remonstrated with him:

> But he sayde that he wolde
> Agaynst my mynde and wyll
> In my church hauke styll.
> (ibid., 64)

Skelton implies that he made a formal complaint about the incident which is recorded in 'the offycallys bokys' (ibid.) but that a bribe caused the matter to be dropped, so that the church is 'abusyd / Reproched and pollutyd' (ibid., 66). A better-tempered poem, probably dating originally from before 1505, is 'Phyllyp Sparowe', a mock elegy on the death of a pet sparrow belonging to Jane Scrope, daughter of the twice widowed Lady Eleanor Wyndham, who, with her unmarried daughters, had gone in 1502 to live in Carrow Abbey, a Benedictine house near Norwich, where the unfortunate bird was killed by the nunnery cat. The poem owes something to Catullus's 'Lugete, O veneres cupidinesque', his lament for Lesbia's dead sparrow, and to other classical poems on the deaths of pets, but it is structured around various offices for the dead from the service books of the medieval church, and Latin phrases from these services intersperse Jane's lament.

Something about Skelton's poem offended Alexander Barclay—possibly the parody of the offices for the dead or, more likely, the questionable prurience of some of Skelton's 'commendacions' of Jane—and he referred to it slightingly in a 'brefe addicion to the syngularyte of some newe folys' which he appended to his translation of Sebastian Brant's *Shyp of Folys* (1509):

> Wyse men love vertue, wylde people wantones;
> It longeth not to my scyence nor cunnynge
> For Phylyp the Sparowe the *Dirige* to synge.

This is the first known occasion on which Skelton's writings attract unfavourable notice. Subsequently it becomes more frequent and Skelton becomes more of a controversialist. He responded, characteristically, to Barclay with an 'addicyon' of his own (which made its first appearance in print in 'The Garlande of Laurell', 1523, lines 1261–375, and which was included in all subsequent editions of 'Phyllyp Sparowe') defending his poem and accusing his detractors of envy. However, about 1510, Skelton is mentioned in *The Great Chronicle of London*, along with William Cornish and Thomas More, as contemporary satiric 'poettes ... of fame' (A. S. G. Edwards, 46–7).

Henry VIII's 'orator regius' On the accession of Henry VIII in 1509 Skelton made a determined effort to return to court, hoping that his former pupil might favour him. He wrote 'A Lawde and Prayse made for our Sovereigne Lord the Kyng', perhaps for 24 June when the new king was crowned, praising him for uniting the Lancastrian and Yorkist lines, and confidently expecting him to be 'sage' and 'just', and a protector of the commons. He also sent to Henry VIII a copy of the 'Speculum principis', perhaps for his birthday on 28 June, with the addition of a twelve-line 'palinodium' making many of the same points as the English eulogy. He adds, 'May Jupiter Feretrius grant that I do not pass my time on the banks of the Eurotas'—alluding, in the last phrase, to the Latin proverb connoting enforced idleness and under-employment (*Latin Writings*, no. X). Whether Skelton's bid had any immediate effect is difficult to say. The general pardon roll of 21 November 1509 says that he was 'late of Diss, Norfolk', so perhaps he was living, for at least part of his time, in London or Westminster. He was in Westminster on 15 July 1511 when he dined with Prior Richard Mane, but he was in Norwich in the autumn of that year.

By 1512, however, Skelton was beginning to write poems very different from the outraged invectives and satires on local issues which characterized his period in Diss. In 1512 and afterwards he frequently used the title 'orator regius'—which means probably that he saw himself as a spokesman for the king with a range of duties, sometimes diplomatic, sometimes secretarial, and sometimes poetical. It was a title used also by Bernard Andre, Giovanni Gigli, ambassador to the papal curia, and Jean Maillard, French secretary to Henry VIII. Skelton celebrated his new status, characteristically, with two poems of self-praise— one in Latin, one in English—dedicating himself to Calliope 'for as long as my life lasts' (*Latin Writings*, no. XV, l. 4). And the focus of his poems becomes more national. In this year, at the suggestion of Abbot John Islip, he wrote a Latin epitaph to be displayed on the tomb of Henry VII in Westminster Abbey, celebrating him, among other things, for the fear he instilled in the French and the Scots (ibid., no. XVI, ll. 12–14). He also sent to Henry VIII a copy of the Chronique de Rains, a history of the third crusade, written in French prose, which recounts, among other things, the exploits of Richard I. Skelton attached to it a brief dedicatory Latin poem pointing out that the exploits of the English are usually belittled by French writers (ibid., no. XIV, ll. 10–11). The nationalism and latent aggression of these two texts may suggest that Skelton knew that war was coming and that he was in favour of it.

In May and June 1513 Henry VIII crossed the channel to France with a large and well-equipped army and besieged Therouanne. An attempt by the French to relieve the town on 16 August led to a disastrous defeat at Guinegate, usually called 'the battle of the spurs' because the French ran away so fast. In support of his French ally, with whom he had signed a treaty of mutual aid on 16 March 1512, James IV of Scotland crossed the English border on 22 August. A number of castles fell to the Scots initially, but they were confronted and disastrously defeated at Flodden by an English army under Thomas Howard, earl of Surrey, on 9 September, and James IV was killed. These events provided the material for a number of poems, glorifying the achievements of Henry VIII and belittling his enemies. Where Skelton was during these momentous events—in France with Henry VIII's army, in Diss, or in Westminster—is much argued about, but he got speedy information (not always accurate) about what was happening.

Skelton's 'Chorus de Dys contra Gallos', written on 28 August 1513, celebrates the capitulation of Therouanne, denigrates the French, and praises Henry VIII as Mary's knight who will rule the French nation under her might (*sub ope*; *Latin Writings*, no. XVII). Four poems, however,

deal with the battle of Flodden and its aftermath, and Skelton was clearly principally concerned with the Scottish war. The earliest is 'A Ballade of the Scotyshe Kynge', printed as a single leaf by Richard Fakes, evidently hurriedly because it is full of mistakes. Skelton knows that there has been a battle, but, reflecting earlier reports of it, does not know exactly where it took place and is not sure whether James IV is dead or has been taken prisoner. Most of the poem deals with an interview between the Lyon king of arms, James IV's herald, and Henry VIII in France, of which Skelton obviously had a detailed account. In the style of a flyting Skelton denigrates James IV for his treachery and maintains that through his actions he has forfeited the right to be called noble. At some time probably shortly after 22 September, Skelton revised this poem and reissued it as *Agaynste the Scottes* with a variety of changes: he knew by then that the battle had taken place at Branxton Moor and Flodden Edge, and what had happened to James IV's body. Some of the additions add extra insults to the Scots and their dead. He is also concerned to set the record straight, dismissing derisively the early claims that the Scots had won the battle. He is also clearer about the double intention of the poem: it is to 'angre the Scottes and Irish keterynges' by rejoicing over the death of their king, and to 'comfort with gladnes' the hearts of England (*Complete English Poems*, 117).

To praise the king, celebrate victories in battle, and to denigrate the enemies of England may have represented some of the literary functions of the 'orator regius', but it seems clear that Skelton also had a responsibility to entertain and amuse the court. A number of satires in the form of flytings were written in the years between 1514 and 1518 apparently for this purpose. The most interesting and extensive poems of this sort—four lengthy English offerings and a Latin couplet—disparage the ancestry, personal appearance, moral make-up, and career of Sir Christopher Garnesche, a prosperous East Anglian knight, who had seen service in France and had become gentleman usher to Henry VIII in 1509. There were two sides to this poetical contest, but the poems written on behalf of Garnesche have not survived. In the heading to his second poem Skelton refers to Garnesche's helper as 'Gresy, Gorbelyd Godfrey'—which may refer to Stephen Hawes or to Alexander Barclay (*Complete English Poems*, 122). The latter had attacked Skelton in the same year as 'voyde of wisedom'. From 1515–16 come two other flytings: one against George Dundas, in which all Skelton's anti-Scottish feelings are rehearsed; and 'Against Venemous Tongues', an attack on backbiters at court. In 1517 or thereabouts Skelton wrote 'Elynour Rummynge', an antifeminist diatribe in the guise of describing a tavern, its owner, and its clientele. It was evidently based on a real person: an 'Alianora Romyng' of Leatherhead, Surrey, was described as being a 'common tippellar of ale' and was fined 2*d.* for selling ale 'at excessive price by small measures'.

The only eulogistic poem to date from these years is the Latin elegy for Lady Margaret Beaufort, mother of Henry VII, which is dated 15 August 1516. Lady Margaret had died in 1509 and the occasion for Skelton's poem was probably the completion of Pietro Torregiano's tomb for her in the south aisle of Henry VII's chapel in Westminster Abbey, where the poem was displayed. But in July 1518, or a little later, he wrote another epitaph—satiric and vituperative this time—on William Bedell, Lady Margaret's former treasurer and receiver-general, with whom Skelton would have come into contact when he was in Diss and subsequently in Westminster. Bedell is twice referred to as a hater of priests (*Latin Writings*, no. XXI, ll. 6–8), and since Lady Margaret had significant holdings in the parish of Diss, which she discharged through Bedell, the quarrel may have originated there.

Skelton's most ambitious work from this period is 'Magnyfycence', an elaborate morality play, first performed perhaps in the London Merchant Taylors' Hall (*Complete English Poems*, 179). It is set in London and deals with a struggle for power in the household of a 'prynce', and, though it is peopled by allegorical abstractions, it appears to refer to the 'expulsion of the minions' of May 1519, a move by Henry VIII's council to expel from their places in the privy chamber a group of young men, including Sir Nicholas Carew and Sir Francis Bryan, who were thought to be having a deleterious influence on the king. In Skelton's play, irresponsible and scheming vice figures persuade Magnyfycence to dismiss his steward, Measure, and misappropriate and spend the prince's money, leaving him impoverished and degraded until Good Hope, Redresse, Sad Cyrcumspeccyon, and Perseveraunce bring him back to good order—these last probably a reflection of the 'foure sad and auncient knights, put into the kynges privie chamber' by the council. Skelton, through this play, seeks to persuade Henry VIII to be careful whom he chooses to have as his most intimate advisers, to curb his financial excesses, and to run his household according to the Aristotelian 'golden mean'.

In 1519 Skelton became involved in the 'grammarians' war', which turned on how it was best to teach Latin—by rule and precept, or by means of seeking to imitate the best classical authors and giving less attention to formal grammar. Skelton, predictably, took the part of the more formal traditionalists. He was praised in this year by Robert Whittinton, whose traditionally based *Vulgaria* (1520) was one of the texts at the centre of the quarrel. Skelton, in his turn, attacked William Lyly, headmaster of St Paul's School, London, one of the reformers, in a Latin invective of 64 lines, which has been lost. Lyly wrote a brief but brilliant epigram on Skelton which concludes by describing him as 'neither learned nor a poet' ('doctrinam nec habes, nec es poeta'; A. S. G. Edwards, 48). Skelton returns to this issue in 'Speke Parott' (1521) where he jibes that the modernistic teachers set their minds 'so moche of eloquens' that the complete meaning of things ('hole sentens') is lost (*Complete English Poems*, 235). And he widens his attack to include the way Greek, which had recently become available at both Oxford and Cambridge, was taught. Again it is the non-utilitarian focus which offends him.

Skelton and Wolsey 'Speke Parott', however, is about rather more than grammar, being for the most part a thinly disguised attack on Cardinal Thomas Wolsey for his high-handedness and his manoeuvrings at the Paris peace conference between 2 August and 24 November 1521, which Skelton took to be to serve his own ambitions for the papacy rather than the interests of Henry VIII and England. Skelton uses the Parott of the title as a mouthpiece and pretends to be repeating what he has heard, 'shredis of sentence', around the court, so distancing himself somewhat from what he writes. The learning and allusiveness of the earlier part of the poem evidently made it difficult to understand: according to 'lenvoy primere' some 'folys' who had read it said that it hung together 'as fethyrs in the wynde' (*Complete English Poems*, 239). Skelton rejects this criticism by saying that these cavillers are 'lewdlye … lettyrd' (ibid.). But he responds to the suggestion that he should 'sette asyde all sophysms, and speke now trew and playne' (ibid., 244), and closes off the poem with a set of generalized 'abuses of the age'. And his other poems against Wolsey are simpler and more direct in style. In 'Collyn Clout' (1521–2) Skelton assumes the persona of a poor countryman and abandons the rhyme royal of the previous poem for the simpler short-lined rhyming to which he gave his name—'Skeltonics'. But even though his poem is simple, 'ragged / Tattered and jagged', he asserts that it 'hath in it some pyth' (ibid., 248). It is an attack on various aspects of the contemporary church, particularly on the bishops for dereliction of their duties, greediness, worldliness. In 'Why come ye not to courte?' (November 1522) the approach is a lot plainer. This is a question-and-answer poem which deals with contemporary events in an up-to-date manner. 'What news? What news?' and similar questions produce a review of the political issues of the day. But the latter part of the poem is an attack on Wolsey—direct, trenchant, often highly personal, as in lines 1166–201, where Skelton mentions his eye trouble and suggests he is also syphilitic. But what concerns Skelton principally is the way in which Wolsey, in the council and in Star Chamber, overbears the aristocracy and, he suggests, sets himself up as an equal to Henry VIII:

> Set up a wretche on hye,
> In a trone triumphantlye,
> Make him of great astate
> And he wyll play checke mate
> With ryall majeste.
> (ibid., 293)

It is impossible to tell whether Wolsey was aware of these poems or not: they do not appear to have been printed until after his death, but they may well have circulated in manuscript.

However, when Skelton's 'Garlande of Laurell' was published by Richard Fakes on 23 October 1523 it contained a double dedication—to Henry VIII and, surprisingly, to Wolsey. The latter is reminded that he had promised Skelton a prebend (*Complete English Poems*, 356). Whether Skelton was bought off by patronage (which is what this suggests) or whether he thought England had worse enemies than Wolsey, is impossible to say. But after 1523 most of his poems appear to have been commissioned by Wolsey.

That he could dedicate his poem to the two most powerful men in the kingdom adds something to Skelton's poem, though, because it is very much a summation and justification of his poetic career. Much of the narrative, which relates in a dream-vision how Skelton was accepted into the company of other eminent poets by the Queen of Fame, was probably written in 1495 or a little later. All that he appears to have done in 1522 and 1523, besides write the dedicatory lines, is to update his autobiography (ibid., 346–50). But it is clear that by 1523 Skelton believed that he had achieved distinction in his chosen career and that his position of eminence was assured. The Queen of Fame tells him that 'your place is here reservyd' (ibid., 344).

After this Skelton wrote only two substantial poems, both commissioned by Wolsey, and both dealing with threats to state and church. In early November 1523 John Stewart, duke of Albany and regent of Scotland, crossed the English border with a large force of Scots and Frenchmen and besieged the castle of Wark, but, after a fierce engagement, failed to take it. Skelton celebrates the failed siege in 'The Douty Duke of Albany', written between 6 and 12 November, using material from Surrey's dispatches and ideas from his earlier anti-Scottish poems. The purpose of the poem appears to have been to counter Albany's propaganda as much as to celebrate his discomfiture, and Skelton, in a predictable and personalized way, stresses his unknightly behaviour:

> This Duke so fell
> Of Albany,
> So cowardly,
> With all his hoost
> Of the Scottyshe coost,
> For all theyr boost,
> Fledde lyke a beest.
> (*Complete English Poems*, 359)

Several years later, in late 1527 or 1528, Skelton wrote against two heretics who had appeared before Wolsey in November 1527. Thomas Arthur and Thomas Bilney, both Cambridge scholars, made abjurations (though Bilney's was very oddly framed), and both were imprisoned for about a year. On their release Arthur disappeared from heretical circles, but Bilney, after a while, resumed his heterodox preaching and was burnt as a relapsed heretic on 19 August 1531. Skelton was much involved in countering heresy in 1528: he appeared as a witness in the trial of Thomas Bowgas, a fuller from St Leonard's, Colchester, who was cited before Cuthbert Tunstall, bishop of London, on 4 May. Skelton's poem, *A Replycacion agaynst Certayne Yong Scolers Abjured of Late*, published by Pynson probably in 1528, seems to have been part of an orchestrated strategy: it was commissioned by Wolsey, and bears a marked resemblance to Thomas More's *Dialogue Concerning Heresies* (published in 1529) which was written at Tunstall's request. Skelton accuses the 'recheless yonge heretykes' of overreaching intellectual pride which has taken them 'farther than their wytte wyll reche' (ibid., 374), and advises them to submit to the authority of the 'doctours' of the church (ibid., 381). But though the poem may be unfair in presenting them as bar-room intellectuals, it is also astute in not giving credence to Bilney's abjuration. Skelton asserts that he is 'now as yll … As ye were before' (ibid., 379), and events proved him to be correct.

Death and reputation On 8 August 1518 Skelton is recorded as living within the sanctuary at Westminster in an apartment 'south of the great Belfrey' and it may be assumed that he lived there for the latter part of his life. He died on 21 June 1529 and was buried before the high altar in St Margaret's, Westminster, to all intents and purposes an honoured churchman.

But stories which circulated after his death, especially the *Merie Tales* of 1567, presented him very differently as a scandalous libertine (who kept a concubine with whom he had a child), and an eccentric wit and jester (*Poetical Works*, 1.lxxi–xci). Many of the stories turn on clever retorts or pithy sayings, which are not inconsistent with the reputation he had for learning and for being, as Henry Bradshaw termed him, 'inventive' (A. S. G. Edwards, 47). It is worth noting that both More and Erasmus were renowned as wits and jesters, and John Grange, in *Golden Aphroditis* (1577), links Erasmus and Skelton in this regard: 'by what means could Skelton the Laureat poet, or Erasmus that great and learned clarke have uttered their mindes so well at large, as thorowe clokes of mery conceytes in wryting of toyes and foolish theames?' (ibid., 59). Implicit in such a question is the view that witty jests had serious intentions.

Skelton was the last great poet of Catholic England, and was a determined and thoroughgoing conservative on religious and political issues. He was also the first notable poet whose career coincided with printing. A number of his texts were circulated in the traditional way in manuscript form, but a good many were printed in his lifetime, and this brought him to the notice of a readership from a wide social spectrum. Since he was essentially a public and occasional poet the availability of print was important: his poems had a propagandist value, which was exploited by him and by his patrons. After his death there appeared numerous editions of his works, both single poems and small collections, culminating in Marsh's extensive collection of 1568, *Pithy, Pleasaunt and Profitable Works of Maister Skelton, Poete Laureate*. This was prefaced by an adulatory poem by Thomas Churchyard, comparing Skelton to a list of poets both classical and modern, both European and English. He stresses Skelton's talent for satire: 'His terms to taunts did lean' (A. S. G. Edwards, 56–9). And this was very much the way he was seen in the sixteenth century: according to John Bale, he told the truth 'under a mask of laughter' ('sub persona ridentis'; H. L. R. Edwards, 306). His early followers tended to imitate his controversial and polemical works, especially those in 'Skeltonics'—long leashes of monorhymed short, mainly two-stressed, lines: the earliest is probably William Roy's and Jerome Barlowe's *Rede me and be nat Wrothe* (1528), a vituperative attack on Wolsey, but several controversial works in this form survive from the 1540s and 1550s. Skelton, however, did not see himself exclusively as a satirist.

He had a high view of the worth of poetry and of the dignity of the poet, which is probably why he insists so much on his titles to fame, 'poete laureate', 'orator regius'. In some of the last lines he wrote he asserts that 'God maketh his habytacion' in poets and that it is through 'divyne inspyracion' that poets write. And this, he argues, applies to poetry of all sorts, which are all equally valid, for poets write in all sorts of circumstances:

Somtyme for affection,
Sometyme for sadde dyrection,
Somtyme for correction.
(*Complete English Poems*, 384–5)

Praise, advice, blame—in small compass this is not a bad summary of the nature of his poetry.

JOHN SCATTERGOOD

Sources A. S. G. Edwards, *Skelton: the critical heritage* (1981) · *The poetical works of John Skelton*, ed. A. Dyce (1864) · H. L. R. Edwards, *Skelton: the life and times of an early Tudor poet* (1949) · *John Skelton: the complete English poems*, ed. J. Scattergood (1983) · *The Latin writings of John Skelton*, ed. D. R. Carlson, Texts and Studies (1991)
Likenesses line engraving, pubd 1821 (after unknown artist), BM, NPG

Skelton, Sir John [*pseud.* Shirley] (1831–1897), writer, was born in Edinburgh on 18 July 1831, the only son of James Skelton of Sandford Newton, writer to the signet and sheriff-substitute at Peterhead, Aberdeenshire, and his wife, Margaret, *née* Kinnear. He was educated at the universities of St Andrews and Edinburgh, and in 1854 he was admitted a member of the Faculty of Advocates. However, his interests lay in literature more than in law and he started contributing essays and reviews to *Fraser's Magazine* under the pseudonym of Shirley, from Charlotte Brontë's novel of that name. He had previously received a letter from her for his critical notice of *Jane Eyre*. In 1857 he contributed an essay on 'Early English life in drama' to a volume of *Edinburgh Essays* and was a regular contributor to *The Guardian*, a short-lived Edinburgh periodical, and formed an acquaintance with the editor of *Fraser's*, James Anthony Froude. In 1862 his first independent publication, *Nugae criticae*, was published, a collection of essays which had appeared in various magazines, and in the same year he attempted a political romance, *Thalatta, or, The Great Commoner*, a sketch of a character combining resemblances to both Canning and Disraeli. With his friend William Ellis Gloag, a Scottish judge, he also edited the second edition of Dickson's *Treatise on the Law of Evidence* (1864). In 1865 he edited and published, anonymously, a collection of verse entitled *Spring Songs*. On 30 July 1867 he married Anne Adair Lawrie (*b.* 1846/7), daughter of James Adair Lawrie, professor of surgery at Glasgow. Among their children was the politician Noel *Skelton.

When the Scottish Board of Supervision, which administered the laws respecting the poor and public health, was reconstituted in 1868, Skelton was appointed secretary by Disraeli. It was said that the choice was due to Disraeli's admiration of his literary work. Within a year Skelton published anonymously a sympathetic sketch of his patron, entitled *Benjamin Disraeli: the Past and the Future … by a Democratic Tory* (1868). His earliest official work had

been to administer the Public Health Act of 1867, and to aid its operations he published an edition of the act with notes. In 1876 he published another official work of authority, *The Boarding-out of Pauper Children in Scotland*. The *Handbook of Public Health* (1890–91) and *The Local Government (Scotland) Act in Relation to Public Health* (1890) were valuable contributions to official literature.

Meanwhile Skelton was confirming his literary reputation. His connection with *Blackwood's Magazine* started in 1869 and lasted throughout his life. In 1876 he published his first contribution to the controversy concerning Mary Stuart, entitled *The Impeachment of Mary Stuart*, in which he espoused the cause of the unfortunate queen. This was followed by *Essays in Romance and Studies from Life* (1883), *Maitland of Lethington and the Scotland of Mary Stuart* (1887–8), his most elaborate historical work, and *Mary Stuart* (1893), in all of which he defended Mary against her accusers with ability and careful restraint. In his historical work he characteristically displayed something of the spirit of the advocate. His descriptive powers are seen in his graphic rendering of life at Peterhead in *The Crookit Meg: a Story of One Year* (1880), originally serialized in *Fraser's Magazine*. Of Skelton's more purely literary works the best-known are the *Essays of Shirley* (1882) and *The Table Talk of Shirley* (1895), of which a second series was issued in 1896 under the title *Summers and Winters at Balmawhapple*. The table talk consisted chiefly of reminiscences of Froude, Dante Rossetti, and other personal friends or literary contemporaries. Quaint, almost eccentric, in treatment, Skelton's essays were popular with authors as different as Carlyle, Thackeray, Huxley, and Rossetti.

In 1878 Skelton received the honorary degree of LLD from Edinburgh University; he was created CB in 1887, and KCB in 1897. He retained the post of secretary to the Board of Supervision until 1892, when he was elected chairman. In 1894, when the board was replaced by the Scottish Local Government Board, Skelton became vice-president of the new body. He finally retired on 31 March 1897, when the board recorded in a minute its sense of Skelton's services in diminishing pauperism throughout Scotland. Skelton died on 19 July 1897 at his home, Hermitage of Braid, Edinburgh, survived by his wife and several children.

[ANON.], rev. SAYONI BASU

Sources *The Times* (21 July 1897) · *The Times* (1 April 1897) · *WWW* · T. Royle, *The Macmillan companion to Scottish literature* (1983) · *Men and women of the time* (1895) · *Daily Chronicle* [London] (22 July 1897) · *The Scotsman* (21 July 1897) · m. cert.
Archives NL Scot., corresp. with Blackwoods
Likenesses C. Matthew, wax medallion, 1890, Scot. NPG · portrait, repro. in *Sketch* (28 July 1897), 4
Wealth at death £32,548 13s. 3d.: confirmation, 1 Sept 1897, CCI

Skelton, Joseph (1781/2–1850). *See under* Skelton, William (1763–1848).

Skelton, (Archibald) Noel (1880–1935), politician, was born on 1 July 1880 in Edinburgh, the son of Sir John *Skelton (1831–1897), advocate, author, and civil servant, and his wife, Anne Adair Lawrie (*b.* 1846/7, *d.* in or after 1897). He was educated at Trinity College, Glenalmond, the University of Edinburgh, and Christ Church, Oxford, where he took a second in history in 1903. From 1906 he was an advocate in the Scottish bar. He became a rising figure in Unionist Party politics, one friend recalling (*The Times*, 25 Nov 1935) that he did much 'to make Toryism a live creed in Scotland and to shake the rooted Scottish political traditions'. He stood unsuccessfully as parliamentary candidate for East Perthshire at the December 1910 general election. During the First World War he served with the Scottish Horse, a yeomanry regiment, reaching the rank of captain. Elected as MP for Perth at the 1922 election, he was defeated in 1923 but re-elected at the 1924 and 1929 elections. In the 1931 general election he was returned unopposed for the Combined Scottish Universities. He never married.

During the early 1920s Skelton's pre-war Unionist activism against Liberal predominance in Scotland turned into belief that a progressive Conservatism was needed to defeat the new 'socialist' challenge throughout Britain. Here, for a back-bench MP, he had an unusual and enduring influence. In four articles in *The Spectator* in April and May 1923, republished during the first Labour government in 1924 as a pamphlet entitled *Constructive Conservatism*, he coined the pregnant phrase 'a property-owning democracy'. In truth, encouraging possession of private property among the working population was an obvious strategy against socialist collectivism and was already entering the rhetoric of Conservative leaders, although Baldwin used the precise phrase only in 1931. Nevertheless, in Skelton's presentation the concept was a fresh and radical restatement of Conservative 'philosophy' appropriate for a 'new era': it would stabilize democracy, give wage-earners an economic status commensurate with their political enfranchisement, 'bridge the economic gulf … between Labour and Capital', and be the 'vehicle for the moral and economic progress of the individual' (*Constructive Conservatism*, 7, 24). His ideas appealed strongly to a loose group of younger, idealistic Conservatives in the 1924 parliament, known as the 'YMCA', who supported the progressive elements in Baldwin's Conservative government against what they regarded as the party's reactionary business members. Skelton took a leading part in the lobbying and journalistic activities of the group, his contributions including an article entitled 'Labour in the new era' (*QR*, 244, 1925). Several of the group's members—Oliver Stanley, Walter Elliott, Robert Boothby, and Harold Macmillan—and another friend, Anthony Eden, later became important figures, and through them Skelton unwittingly helped inspire interventionist Conservative 'middle way' thinking from the 1930s. By a 'property-owning democracy' he himself had meant a reinforcement of individualism through industrial profit sharing, agricultural small-holdings, and co-operative schemes. But after Eden revived the phrase at the 1946 Conservative conference and made it a leading party slogan, it became chiefly associated, particularly by Macmillan during the early 1950s, with state promotion of house ownership.

In their memoirs, Skelton's friends recalled him as 'thought-provoking', a 'great political teacher', and a

'superlative talker, with a tremendous vitality and zest for life' (Eden, 12; Macmillan, 177–8; Boothby, 138). But these qualities were imperfectly communicated to wider audiences. While younger associates received early and rapid ministerial promotion, only under the National Government in September 1931 did he become parliamentary under-secretary for Scotland. Here he supervised health, housing, and educational policies, but without striking departures. He served also on the Empire Marketing Board and on the government delegation to the League of Nations. He had one last, curious effect on public life. He stood again for the Combined Scottish Universities at the next general election, but died at 25 Belgrave Crescent, Edinburgh, on 22 November 1935, after the poll but before the declaration of the result—creating the first modern case of a parliamentary candidate elected posthumously. The consequent by-election in January 1936 was notable for being used to secure a parliamentary seat for the former prime minister, Ramsay MacDonald, embarrassingly defeated in Seaham at the general election.

PHILIP WILLIAMSON

Sources *The Times* (23 Nov 1935) · *The Times* (25 Nov 1935) · *The Times* (26 Nov 1935) · *The Times* (6 March 1936) · *WWBMP*, vol. 3 · A. Eden, earl of Avon, *The Eden memoirs*, 1: *Facing the dictators* (1962) · Lord Boothby [R. J. G. Boothby], *My yesterday, your tomorrow* (1962) · H. Macmillan, *Winds of change, 1914–1939* (1966) [vol. 1 of autobiography] · P. Gatland, 'The "YMCA" and the search for a constructive conservatism in Britain, 1924–1929', PhD diss., U. Lond., 1989 · b. cert. · d. cert. · *WWW*

Archives Bodl. Oxf., Harold Macmillan MSS · HLRO, St Loe Strachey MSS

Wealth at death £14,687 17s.: confirmation, 14 Feb 1936, *CCI*

Skelton, Peter Raleigh Ashlin (1906–1970), cartographical historian, born at the family house at 16 Leigham Street, Plymouth, on 15 November 1906, was the second son of John Cecil Skelton, from Long Sutton, Lincolnshire, a marine engineer with the Eastern Telegraph Company, in whose service he moved from port to port. His mother was Agnes Gertrude Gilbert, who claimed descent from the family of Sir Humphrey Gilbert, for whom Raleigh was a family Christian name. He was always known as Peter to his friends, but his marriage and death certificates show him as Raleigh Ashlin Skelton, under which name he also published. Skelton obtained scholarships at Aldenham School and at Pembroke College, Cambridge, where he took a first in part one of the modern languages tripos (1927) and a lower second in part two (1929). He was for two years an assistant master at Berkhamsted School and then in 1931 entered the British Museum as an assistant keeper in the department of printed books. Trained to catalogue accessions and to arrange the entries in the museum's general catalogue, he became a highly efficient library technician, who was also turning himself into a scholar by wide and carefully selected reading. His cataloguing brought him into contact with many of the early voyage collections and atlases and he mastered the bibliography and content of those of the early modern period, which provided him with a starting point for his later studies.

On 24 September 1936, at Earls Court, London, Skelton

married (Mary) Katherine, the daughter of the late Canon William Arthur Macleod, sometime provost of Wakefield. He served in the Royal Artillery from 1939 to 1945, first in the Middle East (1941–4), and later with the monuments, arts, and archives branch of the allied high commission in Austria; he was demobilized with the rank of major.

After returning to the British Museum in 1945 Skelton was seconded to the map room to work with the superintendent, E. W. Lynam, whom he succeeded in 1950 (he was promoted deputy keeper in 1953). The map room was an autonomous unit in the department of printed books, and Skelton used his considerable powers of organization and command to make it unique. He issued clear, precise instructions on what he wished to have done and drove himself and his helpers hard, but he was always ready to explain his reasons and to listen to suggestions. He was continuously concerned with the housing of the rapidly growing collections in a confined space, the conservation of those collections, the radical improvement of the map catalogue (which, in a great burst of energy, he and his staff prepared for publication shortly before he retired), good and well-informed service to a growing body of users of the map room for whom he found space, and good relations with other departments in the museum and with cartographical institutions outside it. The result of his labours was the creation of a cartographical laboratory–library which was in the end without equal.

Elected FSA in 1951, Skelton was involved in the congresses of the International Geographical Union (IGU) from 1949 onwards, especially that of 1964, for which he mounted and catalogued an exhibition, 'The growth of London', at the Victoria and Albert Museum. He became a member of the IGU commission on early maps in 1952 (and its chairman from 1961), and was particularly involved in the organization of *Monumenta cartographica vetustioris aevi A.D. 1200–1500*; his introduction to volume 1 (*Mappemondes*) in 1964 gave an account of the project. He became a member of the Royal Society's committee on cartography and served on the governing bodies of the Royal Geographical Society (he received the Gill memorial in 1956 and the Victoria medal in 1970), the Society for Nautical Research, the Royal Historical Society, the Institute of Historical Research, the British Records Association, and the National Central Library. He was awarded the research medal of the Royal Scottish Geographical Society in 1965.

Skelton's work for the Hakluyt Society, as secretary from 1946 to 1966 and a member of council until his death, was outstanding. He built up its worldwide membership, tightened its editorial standards, got Cambridge University Press to become its publisher (which brought better distribution), and immersed himself in the work of making available early accounts of exploration. He had an exceptional capacity for throwing himself into the problems of each individual editor, acquiring rapidly an expert grasp of his problems and providing assistance, especially contributions on cartographical problems, often unattributed, for successive volumes. His special contribution was in enabling J. C. Beaglehole to complete his classic edition

of James Cook's journals, mobilizing subsidies and helpers, selecting a portfolio of charts (1955), and adding sections of his own on each of the three voyages. More than forty volumes were published by the society under his auspices.

Skelton had also much to do with *Imago Mundi*. As a corresponding editor (from 1950), secretary of its management committee (1959–66), when it was put on a sound footing, and general editor (1966–70), he considerably enhanced its standing as the leading international cartographical journal. He revised and translated the *History of Cartography* (1964) by Leo Bagrow, *Imago Mundi*'s founder. His friendship with Armando Cortesão led him to take an active part in the preparations for the 500th anniversary of the death of Henry the Navigator. He contributed substantially to Cortesão's edition (with A. Teixeira da Mota) of *Portugaliae monumenta cartographica* (6 vols., 1960), revising and adapting the long English introduction and delivering several papers to the celebratory congress in Lisbon.

In 1962–3 Skelton spent a sabbatical leave at Harvard University, setting in order the map collections of the Widener Library and lecturing on cartography. Later, at the Newberry Library, Chicago, he was a consultant on the cartographical collection and gave the Nebenzahl lectures for 1966, published as *Maps: a Historical Survey of their Study and Collecting* (1975).

Skelton's work on Cook's surveys had given him an interest in the early cartography of Newfoundland, which he visited in 1968 to help plan a cartographic bibliography of the island and to receive an honorary DLitt from Memorial University.

From 1960 to 1965 Skelton was involved in the study of the newly discovered Vinland map for the then anonymous American owner (Paul Mellon). This research, carried out under conditions of some secrecy, led him to make a masterly survey of the cartography of the northern regions in the later Middle Ages and to present an effective case for the authenticity of the map, although until his death he was anxious to have it submitted to scientific tests which might establish its authenticity unequivocally. He believed in its authenticity, although he considered it might, conceivably, be a fabrication. The furore which the publication of *The Vinland Map and the Tartar Relation*, by Skelton, T. E. Marston, and G. D. Painter, created in 1965 plunged him for many months into a whirl of international controversy, from which he emerged with the enhanced respect of both his supporters and those who differed from him.

Throughout this period Skelton steadily made contributions to the study of English map making and distribution. His 'Tudor town plans in John Speed's "Theatre"' (*Archaeological Journal*, 108, 1951) and his stress on English examples in *Decorative Printed Maps of the 15th to 18th Centuries* (1952) were the first of many detailed studies. His *County Atlases of the British Isles, 1579–1703*, which had appeared over several years in parts, was published within a few weeks of his death.

Skelton published a series of popular articles in the *Geographical Magazine* from 1953 onwards, using map evidence to bring out precisely what the great explorers had discovered and how the maps that recorded their discoveries often became the fallible guides of the next generation. Collected in *Explorers' Maps* (1958), they had an immediate success. It was, however, to an increasing range of specialists that Skelton became an indispensable guide. He acquired an astonishing familiarity with maps of many periods, but on European maps between the fifteenth and eighteenth centuries he became an internationally recognized authority. Always willing to put his knowledge at the service of enquirers, he found himself exploring cartographical problems of all sorts and often ended by contributing sections to their books.

In the early sixties Skelton became involved in Nico Israel's project to publish facsimile atlases under the imprint Theatrum Orbis Terrarum. For many of them he wrote introductions, and after his retirement he acted as a consultant to the firm. He was opposed to reprints which represented old books without apparatus, but believed in equipping facsimiles with adequate introductions and, where necessary, indexes. He collaborated effectively with D. B. Quinn and Alison Quinn on this basis in the production of Hakluyt's *Principall Navigations* (1589) (Hakluyt Society, 1965).

In 1967 Skelton retired from the British Museum but worked harder than ever. He completed his fine edition and translation of the Yale Pigafetta MS, which was also reproduced in colour-facsimile (Antonio Pigafetta, *Magellan's Voyage*, 1969), and was handling a few hours before he died the final proofs of *A description of maps and architectural drawings in the collection made by William Cecil, first Baron Burghley, now at Hatfield House* (1971), which Lord Salisbury presented to the Roxburghe Club and which Skelton had compiled with Sir John Summerson. Three other volumes in which he had a major part were with the printers at the time of his death.

Skelton had a tall, slim figure, and did not in his latter years look his age. He walked with a military stride and never developed more than a slight suspicion of a scholar's stoop. He had considerable physical energy which he employed in walking and gardening, and also exceptional powers of concentration and endurance, so that he could work long and intensively when writing. His clear, logical mind enabled him to seize on essentials in describing or analysing a map or book, and he showed the same qualities in argument, even if he sometimes developed a case from too narrow premises. He had strong opinions and his judgements tended to be conservative, but in argument he never defended the claims of established authority when new information was presented to him or when an effective case was made out for a novel interpretation. He made an excellent collaborator, conscientious, sympathetic of approaches other than his own, but always strong-minded in defence of his personal views. His originality lay in his determination to use maps as historical documents in every possible way. He was also determined to mobilize the scattered and largely unco-

ordinated corpus of information on maps of the early modern period so that the maps should become intelligible and accessible to students and researchers. His development of precise methods and formulae for cataloguing maps, his enthusiasm for the presentation of effective bibliographies of maps and map literature, and his historical understanding combined to make him the leading cartographical historian in his time and an outstanding exponent of what came to be called cartobibliography.

From shortly after the war until his death Skelton lived with his wife and their two daughters at Street Farm, Tilford, near Farnham. He was closely concerned in the life of the locality, served three terms on the parish council, was chairman of Tilford cricket club (his most cherished distinction), and took an active part in the Surrey Archaeological Society, of which he became president in 1968. Skelton died at Farnham Hospital on 7 December 1970 from injuries received in a road accident.

DAVID B. QUINN, *rev.*

Sources *Imago Mundi*, 25 (1971) [R. A. Skelton memorial volume] · private information (1981) · personal knowledge (1981) · b. cert. · m. cert. · d. cert. · *The Times* (11 Dec 1970) · G. R. Crone, 'Raleigh Ashlin Skelton', *GJ*, 137 (1971), 273–4 · *CGPLA Eng. & Wales* (1971)
Archives Memorial University, Newfoundland, Canada | NHM, corresp. with Warren Royal Dawson
Wealth at death £8770: probate, 11 Feb 1971, *CGPLA Eng. & Wales*

Skelton, Philip (1707–1787), Church of Ireland clergyman and religious controversialist, was born in February 1707 in Derriaghy, co. Antrim, the son of Richard Skelton (*d.* 1718), a farmer who had served an apprenticeship as a gunsmith, and also traded as a tanner. His mother, Arabella Cathcart, was the daughter of a farmer, and the tenancy of the farm at Derriaghy, held under Lord Conway, was her dowry. His paternal grandfather had settled in Ireland during the reign of Charles I. Philip had five brothers, two of whom also became clergymen, and four sisters. He was sent at the age of ten to a Latin school at Lisburn, conducted by a Revd Mr Clarke. He was prompted to be studious there by the suggestion of his father that his alternative to going to university was to be employed as a labourer. His father's death in 1718 curtailed the family's relatively comfortable lifestyle, but Philip continued at Clarke's school. In June 1724 he entered Trinity College, Dublin, as a sizar. Dr Patrick Delany was his tutor, and the two men struck up a lasting friendship. He was elected a scholar in 1726, and graduated BA in July 1728, despite allegations that he was a Jacobite.

After teaching in the endowed school at Dundalk, Skelton was nominated curate to the physician Samuel Madden at Drummully, co. Fermanagh, and ordained deacon by Bishop Sterne of Clogher in 1729. He lived with Madden for two years as private tutor to his sons, as well as attending to his curacy. It was here that Skelton produced the first in a long line of published pamphlets, a short work in support of Madden's scheme for premiums in Trinity College. He also began a lifelong habit of donating part of his salary to the poor. In 1732 he became a curate at Monaghan, where the rector paid him £40 a year, most of which was spent for the benefit of his family or poor parishioners, and in clearing his still outstanding college debts. He attended assiduously to his clerical duties, paying particular attention to the children of the parish. He also performed many specific acts of kindness and Christian endeavour, including securing a pardon for a condemned felon, and using his substantial physique to impress his values on errant spirits. Additionally he studied medicine, and dispensed medical help within the parish.

Skelton found time to publish anonymously a series of short discourses against Socinianism, and in 1736 two ironical pamphlets in support of the established church that purported to be a defence of deism and dissent but were couched in such terms as to appear ridiculous. The following year, again anonymously, he addressed the inadequacies of the Irish legal system in a *Dissertation on the Constitution and Effects of a Petty Jury*, while in 1741, inspired by what he witnessed during a period of famine, he produced *The Necessity of Tillage and Granaries in a Letter to a Member of Parliament*. The latter called for the extension of tillage farming and the erection of public granaries to alleviate future distress. Both works were well received in Ireland.

In 1742 Skelton became for a short time tutor to the politician James Caulfeild, first earl of Charlemont. A quarrel with Lord Charlemont's stepfather led to his returning to his curacy in Monaghan, though Skelton dedicated *Truth in a Mask* (1744), a series of parables, to Charlemont. In 1744 he published *The Candid Reader*, a satirical treatment of a number of well-known contemporary figures, including Samuel Johnson. In the same year he issued *A Letter to the Authors of the 'Divine Analogy' and the 'Minute Philosopher'*, another paper in support of the doctrines of the established church. In 1745 he produced *The Chevalier's Hopes*, a hastily written pamphlet condemning the Pretender, James Stuart.

Skelton travelled to London in 1748 to publish *Ophimaches, or, Deism Revealed*, which he considered too important a text to publish in Dublin. It consisted of eight conversations designed to repudiate the teachings of deists such as John Toland, and bolster again the conventions of reformed Christianity. He received £200 for the manuscript, and was treated in the city as a minor celebrity. He also took the opportunity to preach in several London churches. A second edition appeared in 1751. Though generously commended by Bishop Thomas Sherlock, like most of Skelton's work it lacked a coherent structure, and was largely impenetrable to the ill-informed. His prose was, and remained, excessively rhetorical and unnecessarily elaborate.

In 1750 Skelton was given the living of Templecarn, a large parish in the counties of Donegal and Fermanagh. It included St Patrick's Purgatory, then the primary centre of Catholic pilgrimage in Ireland, of which he later wrote a detailed account. The parish was in a somewhat neglected condition. The state of religious knowledge and observance was poor among the protestant community; there was no rectory, and the parish yielded less than £200

a year. Despite this situation, and Skelton's personal dislike for the area, he continued his ministry and good works, as he had in Monaghan. He preached specifically against whiskey drinking, and also continued writing. In 1751 he published *The Dignity of the Christian Ministry: a Sermon*, which addressed the differences between dignity conferred by worldly wealth, and that inherent in the Christian ministry. This was followed in 1753 by *Consultation, or, A Dialogue of the Gods*, an attack on the Arians. He again visited London in 1754, and published *Discourses Controversial and Practical on Various Subjects*, a collection of his sermons and other works. It was not well received, and he returned to Templecarn frustrated and disappointed. During a famine in 1757 he sold all his books to buy oatmeal for distribution to his parishioners, irrespective of their religion, and to supply the women with flax to spin.

In 1759 Skelton published, as a reply to an Arian pamphlet, *An Answer to 'An Appeal to the Common Sense of All Christian People'*. He was also given the living of Devenish, co. Fermanagh, worth around £300 a year, which allowed him to move to the nearby town of Enniskillen. In Devenish, with a larger congregation, he continued as before. In 1766 he was presented to the more profitable living of Fintona, or Donacavey, co. Tyrone, which proved to be his last. Reputedly he enjoyed some success here in convincing a large number of Presbyterians to conform to the Church of Ireland. In 1770 he published his collected works by subscription, in five volumes; the £500 profit was donated to the Magdalen charity in Dublin. The advent of famine once more in 1778 again saw Skelton sell his library, which he had renewed, in order to provide for the poor. From 1771 he had become non-resident in his parish during the winter months, staying first with a nephew in Drogheda, then in lodgings in Dublin. From 1780 he moved permanently to the capital, while a curate remained at Fintona. In Dublin he continued writing, producing two more volumes to complement his earlier collected works, and a number of hymns and pamphlets.

Skelton died on 4 May 1787 in Dublin, and was buried there on 8 May near the west door of St Peter's Church. His charitable deeds and constant attendance to his clerical duties, lovingly recorded in a hagiographic biography written by his friend and fellow cleric Samuel Burdy, have led to Skelton's being frequently cited by historians of eighteenth-century Ireland as a model clergyman of the Church of Ireland. His published works provide an insight into the mind of a committed reformer, and a devout Anglican. They also reveal a complete aversion to protestant dissent in any form. Despite his professional and personal attributes, and his abilities as a self-publicist, his ambitions within the church were ultimately frustrated. He was apparently denied sustained preferment both by his lack of a powerful patron, and by his own less redeeming qualities of a short temper and a brusque manner.

NEAL GARNHAM

Sources S. Burdy, *The life of Philip Skelton* (1792) · *Report on manuscripts in various collections*, 8 vols., HMC, 55 (1901–14), vol. 6, pp. 440–49 · E. J. Quigley, 'A clerical economist', *Irish Ecclesiastical Record*, 5th

ser., 19 (1922), 15–28 · 'A description of St Patrick's Purgatory', c.1766, BL, Add. MS 35607, fol. 210 · *DNB*
Wealth at death approx. £150: Burdy, *Life of Philip Skelton*, 226–7

Skelton, Robin (1925–1997), poet and literary scholar, was born on 12 October 1925 in the schoolhouse at Easington in the East Riding of Yorkshire, the only child of Cyril Frederick William Skelton (1879–1964) and his wife, Lili (1888–1982), daughter of William Robins and his wife, Eliza, *née* Young. He was educated until the age of almost eleven at Easington village school, where his father was headmaster. He then went as a boarding pupil to Pocklington grammar school. On leaving school in 1943 he was placed on a six-month course, sponsored by the Royal Air Force for potential officers, at Christ's College, Cambridge. His war service in the Royal Air Force was spent mainly in India as a codes and cipher clerk with the rank of sergeant. After demobilization he studied English literature at Leeds University from 1947 to 1950, and obtained a first-class honours BA degree, which was followed by the degree of MA in 1951.

From 1951 to 1963 Skelton was on the staff of the English department of the University of Manchester, initially as an assistant lecturer but from 1954 as a full lecturer. On 27 August 1953 he married Margaret Mary Lambert (b. 1928/9), a schoolteacher; after their divorce he married Sylvia Mary Snow, *née* Jarrett (1927/8–1998), also a schoolteacher, on 4 February 1957. A son, Nicholas, and two daughters, Alison and Brigid, were born from the second marriage.

During his period in Manchester, Skelton became involved in a wide range of literary and artistic activities. As a student he had acquired an interest in a small publishing house, the Lotus Press, and this he continued to manage until 1952. In 1955 he published his first major collection of verse, *Patmos and Other Poems*. This was followed by further collections, including *Third Day Lucky* (1958), *Begging the Dialect* (1960), and *The Dark Window* (1962). To supplement his university salary, Skelton worked part-time for the *Manchester Guardian*, first as a poetry reviewer and later as a theatre critic. He was also an examiner for the Northern Universities Matriculation Board and subsequently became chairman of examiners for its English O level examination. While preparing his work on versification, *The Poetic Pattern* (1956), he made the acquaintance of many of the leading British poets of the time, including William Empson, Louis MacNeice, David Gascoyne, and Kathleen Raine. Always gregarious, Skelton had a wide acquaintance among the local artists and writers active in Manchester, and founded the Peterloo Group in conjunction with Michael Seward Snow and Tony Connor. Later he helped to found the Manchester Institute of Contemporary Arts, drafting its constitution and acting as its first secretary. In 1960 he travelled to Dublin to research into the papers of the Irish playwright J. M. Synge. The visit fostered a lifelong affection and empathy in Skelton for Ireland and its writers, and resulted in a number of publications relating to Irish literature, including an anthology of modern Irish poets, *Six Irish Poets* (1962), and collected editions of Synge, Jack B. Yeats, and David Gascoyne.

The turning point in Skelton's career came in 1963, when he and his young family emigrated to Canada so that he could take up a post of associate professor in the newly created University of Victoria, British Columbia. In this new and growing university he had a fruitful environment in which to develop his considerable and many-sided talents as poet, writer, anthologist, editor, literary and drama critic, collage artist, publisher, administrator, and dedicated teacher. With characteristic energy and industry he soon became immersed in all these activities. After three years as associate professor, in 1966 he became a full professor of English, and was from 1967 to 1973 director of the newly formed creative writing programme which he had inaugurated. This became the department of creative writing in 1973 with Skelton as its chairman until 1976. In 1967 he founded and jointly edited the prestigious *Malahat Review*; he was joint editor until 1971 and sole editor from 1972 to 1983. He received recognition as a Canadian writer, when in 1981 he became vice-chairman and in 1982–3 chairman of the Writers' Union of Canada. Continuing his part-time career as a publisher, Skelton acted as editor-in-chief of two small presses in Victoria, the Sono Nis Press from 1967 to 1982 and the Pharos Press from 1972. His artistic activities included a number of one-man exhibitions of collages, with shows in Victoria in 1966, 1968, and 1980.

Throughout his years in Canada, Skelton continued to produce scholarly critical and literary works. His output was prodigious, with over 100 separate titles to his credit during his long and fruitful career. Apart from the works on the writers of the Irish Renaissance, he wrote a number of books on versification and the craft of poetry, including *The Practice of Poetry* (1971), *The Poet's Calling* (1975), and the posthumously published *The Shapes of our Singing* (2002), as well as editing several anthologies including the Penguin editions *Poetry of the Thirties* (1964) and *Poetry of the Forties* (1968). It is, however, for his own poetry that he is best-known and that he would have liked best to be remembered. Robin Skelton's belief in the importance of poetry as central to his life was held from a very young age. First published in a student magazine at Christ's College, Cambridge, he continued to write and publish poems for the rest of his life, producing an astonishing body of work, which continued to change and develop throughout his career. The earlier poetry published in England in the 1950s and early 1960s was, in the 'new movement' style of the time, relatively low-key and unemotional, but he went on to develop his own distinctive style with the reflective quasi-autobiographical and longer narrative poems of *Timelight* (1974) and *Callsigns* (1976) giving way to the shorter, brighter, almost incantatory poems of *Popping Fuchsias* (1992) and especially *One Leaf Shaking* (1996). Many of Skelton's poems show the strong influence of his boyhood experiences in his natal village located between the North Sea and the wide Humber estuary, and use the imagery of the sea, its tides and pebbled beaches, and the distant horizons across the estuary mudflats. Throughout his life Skelton was fascinated by the varieties of poetic form and his later poems in particular demonstrate an impressive range of forms taken from cultures as diverse as those of Wales and Japan, as well as forms invented by himself.

Robin Skelton was an impressive, even eccentric figure whom many of his students found daunting until they discovered his essential kindness and humility. He has been described as looking like an ancient druid with, in later life, his flowing beard, long white hair, talismanic pentagram, tattooed wrist, and chunky rings on his fingers. Skelton was scornful of convention and social conformism. He became interested in the occult, and while in Canada was initiated as a practising witch in the Wiccan tradition and wrote several works on witchcraft including *Spellcraft* (1978), *Talismanic Magic* (1985), and *The Practice of Witchcraft Today* (1988).

While Skelton was well known and honoured in Canada, in his lifetime he was relatively little known and rarely anthologized in Britain, as he himself complained in his autobiography, *The Memoirs of a Literary Blockhead* (1988). It is perhaps ironic that his decision to move to Canada which so stimulated his development as a poet should have also isolated him from literary attention in his native country. This is much to be regretted, as his poetry is powerful, haunting, and insightful, and he deserves to be more widely known and read.

Robin Skelton died after a short illness, brought on by complications resulting from diabetes and congestive heart failure, at his home in Victoria, British Columbia, on 27 August 1997; he was survived by his wife.

PETER A. CROWTHER

Sources R. Skelton, *The memoirs of a literary blockhead* (1988) • R. Skelton, *Portrait of my father* (1989) • *The Times* (15 Sept 1997) • *The Guardian* (29 Aug 1997) • G. Woodcock, 'Robin Skelton', *Contemporary poets*, ed. T. Chevalier, 5th edn (1991), 909-12 • D. Brown, 'In memoriam Robin Skelton', *Critical Survey*, 10 (1998), 109-10 • L. Sandler, 'An interview with Robin Skelton', *Tamarack Review*, 68 (1976), 71-85 • H. Rheinisch, 'The uncommon poetry of common words', in R. Skelton, *One leaf shaking: collected later poems, 1977-1990* (Vancouver, 2000), xvii-xxiii • '100 Canadian poets—Robin Skelton—profile', www.ucalgary.ca/UofC/faculties/HUM/ENGL/canada/poet/r_skelton.htm [accessed Aug 2002] • private information (2004) • m. certs.

Archives University of Victoria, British Columbia, McPherson Library, corresp. and literary MSS

Likenesses J. Kramer, sketch

Skelton, William (1763–1848), engraver, was born in London on 14 June 1763. He entered the Royal Academy Schools in 1781 and was a pupil first of James Basire and later of William Sharp. Sir Richard Worsley, bt, and Charles Towneley were among his earliest patrons. He was employed on the illustrations of many of the most sumptuous literary and learned publications of the day, notably John and Josiah Boydell's *Shakspeare* (2 vols., 1803); Thomas Macklin's Bible (7 vols., 1800–16); Bowyer's edition of David Hume's *The History of England*; Sir George Staunton's *An Authentic Account of an Embassy from the King of Great Britain to the Emperor of China, Taken Chiefly from the Papers of the Earl of Macartney* (1797); *Plates*, a large folio volume of maps and illustrations for which Skelton engraved

S. Edwards's *The Fire-Backed Pheasant of Java* and *The Pelicanus Sinesis, or, Fishing Cormorant of China*; *A Description of the Collection of Ancient Marbles in the British Museum* (1812–61); and *Specimens of Ancient Sculpture* (2 vols., 1809–35), published by the Society of Dilettanti. Skelton is best known, however, for his many fine portraits of famous contemporaries, chiefly from pictures by Sir William Beechey, the majority of which he published himself between 1790 and 1820; these include a series of George III and his sons, which became extremely popular; Robert Markham DD (1790); Thomas Denman MD (1792); Henry, Lord Mulgrave (1808); Spencer Perceval (1813); and Warren Hastings (1817). His *Wenceslaus Hollar*, engraved on steel, was published in Horace Walpole's *Anecdotes of Painting*, ed. J. Dallaway (5 vols., 1826–8). One of his latest plates was a portrait of Charlotte Augusta, the daughter of George IV, then the dowager queen of Württemberg, after P. Fischer (1827), which he issued in 1828. He also produced portraits of himself and Beechey in lithography.

Skelton resided for many years at Stafford Place, Pimlico, London, and afterwards in Upper Ebury Street, where he died on 13 August 1848, having long previously retired from the profession. He was buried in Brompton cemetery. He was a man of great benevolence, and for over fifty years served on the committee of the Asylum for Female Orphans at Lambeth. He was married with one daughter.

Joseph Skelton (1781/2–1850), brother of the above, was born in 1781 or 1782, and became an engraver in the mixed style of topographical and antiquarian subjects. Before 1819 he went to live in Oxford, where he published *Oxonia antiqua restaurata* (1823), *Antiquities of Oxfordshire*, from drawings by Frederick Mackenzie (1823), *Pietas Oxoniensis, or, Records of Oxford Founders* (1828), and S. R. Meyrick's *Engraved Illustrations of Antient Arms and Armour, from the Collection of Llewelyn Meyrick at Goodrich Court, Herefordshire, after the Drawings and with the Descriptions of Dr Meyrick* (2 vols., 1830). He also engraved the heading to the *Oxford Almanack* for the years 1815 to 1831, from drawings by Mackenzie and Charles Wild, and executed a set of fifty-six etchings for *The Antiquities of Bristol* from original sketches by Hugh O'Neill (1825–[30]). Later Skelton settled in France, where he engraved many of the plates to C. Gavard's *Galeries historiques de Versailles* (7 vols., 44, 1839), J. Vatout's *Le château d'Eu* (1844), and P. A. E. Girault's *Les beautés de la France* (1850). He was elected a fellow of the Society of Antiquaries of London in 1825, but his name disappeared from the lists in 1844. He died in 1850.

F. M. O'DONOGHUE, rev. GREG SMITH

Sources R. K. Engen, *Dictionary of Victorian engravers, print publishers and their works* (1979) • *GM*, 2nd ser., 31 (1849), 324 • S. C. Hutchison, 'The Royal Academy Schools, 1768-1830', *Walpole Society*, 38 (1960-62), 123-91

Archives BM, department of prints and drawings • V&A, department of prints and drawings

Likenesses W. Skelton, lithograph (after W. Beechey), BM, NPG

Skene, Alexander, of Newtyle (1621?–1694), local politician and author, was born or baptized in Aberdeen on 27 October 1621, the eldest son and second of five children born to Marjorie Forbes (d. 1650) and Robert Skene (d.

1643). His father was elected treasurer of the town council, a post reserved for the wealthy, in 1629 and 1633. Robert Skene also served on the town council of 1638–9, a body dominated by covenanters, of which he was almost certainly one. In accordance with the family's wealth and status, Alexander Skene joined the Aberdeen merchant guild before the age of four in 1625. He enrolled at Marischal College, Aberdeen, in 1637. Since his father is known to have taken the sons of other prominent Aberdeen merchants with him on expeditions to the cloth-producing regions of Yorkshire and to London, it is likely that Alexander received similar instruction.

Few details concerning Alexander Skene's business affairs survive, but his career in public office and his writings attest to his involvement in commercial matters. His actions and whereabouts through the civil wars of the 1640s are unknown, but he was married at Kirkcaldy to Lilias Gillespie [see Skene, Lilias (1626/7–1697)], daughter of John Gillespie, the minister there, on 26 August 1646. They had ten children. Their eldest surviving son, John Skene (c.1649–1690), was active in Quaker circles in Aberdeen, emigrated to America in 1682 after his business failed, and was deputy governor of West Jersey (1685–8).

Alexander Skene was first elected to the town council in 1648 (as treasurer, an unusually senior first appointment) in an election from which royalists and moderate covenanters were excluded. He was dean of guild in 1650. In 1651 the Aberdeen kirk session, also dominated by hardline covenanters, elected him ruling elder. At the fractious general assembly of July 1651 he and Aberdeen's other lay and clerical representatives sided with the radical protester minority. After Aberdeen surrendered to the English army in September 1651 the local covenanting élite splintered when Provost Alexander Jaffray of Kingswells and two of the town's three ministers formed a short-lived Independent congregation (Scotland's only such) on the English model. Skene was close to all those involved, but any defection on his part must have been fleeting, as he remained an elder of the kirk. In 1656 he was elected a magistrate (baillie) of the town. His energy and organizational skills were instrumental in the successful introduction of the justice of the peace court, Aberdeen's only major institutional innovation of the seventeenth century.

Skene's connections to the radical cause in church and state worked against him when moderates returned to public life after 1657. He purchased the estate of Newtyle (near Foveran, about 12 miles north of Aberdeen) that year, and was usually referred to thereafter as 'Newtyle'. Though not yet forty he virtually retired from public life. In March 1670 he paid to rebuild Aberdeen's medicinal Well of Spa for the public good, and republished Dr William Barclay's 1615 treatise on the well, to which he appended (under the pseudonym Philopolis) some celebratory verse and an 'Epistle Dedicatory' addressed to the town council. This public-spiritedness may have expedited his political comeback (and counteracted the effects of his wife's avowal of Quakerism the year before), because six months later he was again elected baillie and

elder. His term ended in September 1671 and with it his career in public office, because shortly after he converted to Quakerism himself—not long, he tells us, after suffering painful spasms upon saying of a prominent Quaker, 'It wer well to tak that Villain Georg Keith and hang him up at the [Market] Cross of Aberdeen' ('Brieff historicall account', 31).

In 1672 Alexander Skene joined a tiny Quaker community around Aberdeen that already included such luminaries as Alexander Jaffray of Kingswells (whose son Andrew *Jaffray [see under Jaffray, Alexander] Skene's daughter Christian married), George Keith, and Robert Barclay of Urie. Despite the outburst against Keith, Barclay described the converted Skene as 'a Man very modest, and very averse from giving offence to others' (R. Barclay, 401). Quaker meetings were held in the Skenes' townhouse on the Guestrow. When Quakers were persecuted in Aberdeen between 1676 and 1679 Skene, like every adult male Quaker in the region, spent long stretches in the Tolbooth prison. In 1676 the Scottish privy council assessed fines totalling half his valued rents; when he refused to pay his livestock were seized and auctioned at the Aberdeen market, though the citizenry registered its distaste for this action by refusing to bid. Nevertheless, financial pressures stemming from the years of persecution may account for the sale of Newtyle in 1680.

As soon as he joined the Aberdeen Quakers, Skene set about compiling their history. He was chiefly responsible for two lengthy and wonderfully detailed manuscripts on the subject completed in the early 1680s ('A brieff historicall account' and 'A brieff account of the most material passages'). He is also said to have compiled a manuscript of the coats of arms of all the principal Scottish families. Alexander Skene published on behalf of Quakers on four occasions, beginning in 1675 and 1676 with two accounts, co-authored with his son John Skene and three others, of a celebrated public debate in Aberdeen in April 1675 (moderated on the Quaker side by Alexander Skene) between Barclay and Keith on the one hand, and four over-matched Marischal College divinity students on the other. These were followed by his preface to George Keith's *The Way Cast Up*, dated February 1677 'from the Tolbooth of Aberdeen, where I am prisoner', in which he offers a comparatively measured response to Robert McWard's anti-Quaker tirade appended to the third edition of the letters of Samuel Rutherford. In 1681 he published a solo tract, *A Plain and Peaceable Advice to those called Presbyterians in Scotland*.

Alexander Skene's most important publications dealt not with Quakers but with civic government and urban history. In 1685 he published a remarkable handbook for prospective civic magistrates, *Memorialls for the Government of the Royall-Burghs in Scotland*, under the pseudonym 'Philopoliteius, or a lover of the Publick welfare'. It was dedicated to the Edinburgh town council and bound with a shorter work, *A Succinct Survey of the Famous City of Aberdeen*, dedicated to the Aberdeen council. Attribution is confirmed by an Aberdeen council minute of 18 November

1685 referring to 'the little book latlie emitted be Mr. Alex^r Skene late baillie, dedicated to the Mag^rats and Counsell … to get tuentie thereof for the touns use' (Aberdeen town council register, vol. 57). The *Succinct Survey* is derivative of James Gordon's *A Description of both Touns of Aberdeen*, dating from the mid-seventeenth century, but is none the less a vital source for local historians. The *Memorialls* is a much more original work. It offers a systematic description of the workings of Scottish burghs from the unique perspective of a magistrate of deep experience and frustrated ambitions; it is open to question whether the book would have been written had Skene been able to continue his career in public office. Though laced with classical and biblical citations that establish the author's learning and piety, it is at heart a straightforwardly practical work that sets forth key legislation pertaining to Scottish burghs, explains the duties of each class of civic office-holder, and offers a wide range of advice on such matters as the planting of orchards in towns; the establishment of public libraries stocked with works on government, law, navigation, and commerce; the furthering of trade; the avoidance of faction; and the instilling of youth with virtue and civic-mindedness.

Alexander Skene died in Aberdeen in January 1694 and was buried, as was his wife three years later, in an unmarked grave in the Quaker burial-ground at Kingswells. GORDON DESBRISAY

Sources W. F. Skene, ed., *Memorials of the family of Skene of Skene*, New Spalding Club, 1 (1887), 1–3, 77–81 · J. Robertson, 'Alexander Skene of Newtyle', *Scottish Notes and Queries*, 9 (March 1896), 158–60 · W. F. Miller, 'Gleanings from the records of the yearly meeting of Aberdeen, 1672 to 1786', *Journal of the Friends' Historical Society*, 8 (1911), 40–46, 53–80, 113–22 · 'A brieff historicall account and record of the first rise and progress of the blessed truth, called in derision Quakerism, in and about Aberdeen', NA Scot., CH10/3/36 · 'A brieff account of the most material passages and occurrences that happened to friends of truth during that great and long tryall of sufferings and persecution at Aberdene', NA Scot., CH10/13/35 · *Diary of Alexander Jaffray*, ed. J. Barclay, 3rd edn (1856) · R. Barclay, *An apology for the true Christian divinity*, 4th edn (1701) · W. Barclay, *Callirhoe, commonly called the Well of Spa, or the Nymph of Aberdene, resuscitat by William Barclay* (1670) · G. DesBrisay, '"Menacing their persons and exacting on their purses": the Aberdeen justice court, 1657–1700', *From lairds to louns: country and burgh life in Aberdeen, 1600–1800*, ed. D. Stevenson (1986), 70–90 · G. DesBrisay, 'Quakers and the university: the Aberdeen debate of 1675', *History of Universities*, 13 (1994), 87–98 · G. DesBrisay, 'Catholics, Quakers, and religious persecution in Restoration Aberdeen', *Innes Review*, 47 (1996), 136–68 · Aberdeen town council register, Aberdeen City Archives, vols. 52.1, 53.1, 57 · Aberdeen St Nicholas Kirk session minutes, NA Scot., CH2/448/6 · W. Walker, *The bards of Bon-Accord, 1375–1860* (1887) · A. Tayler and H. Tayler, eds., *The valuation of the county of Aberdeen for the year 1667*, Third Spalding Club (1933) · P. J. Anderson and J. F. K. Johnstone, eds., *Fasti academiae Mariscallanae Aberdonensis: selections from the records of the Marischal College and University, MDXCIII–MDCCCLX*, 3 vols., New Spalding Club, 4, 18–19 (1889–98) · A. M. Munro, ed., 'Register of burgesses of guild and trade of the burgh of Aberdeen, 1399–1631', *The miscellany of the New Spalding Club*, 1, New Spalding Club, 6 (1890), 1–162 · *The papers of William Penn*, ed. M. M. Dunn, R. S. Dunn, and others, 2 (1982) · Aberdeen monthly meeting and quarterly meeting minutes, 1672–92, NA Scot., CH10/3/1 · Aberdeen monthly meeting and quarterly meeting minutes, 1692–1706, NA Scot., CH10/3/2 · book containing much old and miscellaneous writing on many and various subjects, NA Scot., CH10/3/34 · U. Aberdeen L., special libraries and archives, Historic collections, William Walker MS 2774

Archives NA Scot., 'A brieff historicall account and record of the first rise and progress of the blessed truth, called in derision Quakerism, in and about Aberdeen', CH10/3/36 · NA Scot., 'A brieff account of the most material passages and occurrences that happened to friends of truth during that great and long tryall of sufferings and persecution at Aberdene', CH10/3/35

Skene, David (*bap.* **1731**, *d.* **1770**), physician and naturalist, was baptized on 13 August 1731 at the kirk of St Nicholas, Aberdeen. His father was Andrew Skene the younger (1702/3–1767), a physician and surgeon in Aberdeen; his mother was Margaret (1708/9–1755), daughter of David Lumsden of Cushnie. The family owned the mansion house of Pitmuxton in the west end of Aberdeen and Skene was the third of a family of eight—four sisters and four brothers. He was educated at Aberdeen grammar school and from 1744 to 1748 in the arts class at Marischal College, Aberdeen. There he emerged as a polymath whose interests ranged from medicine to geology and botany. His medical training included midwifery and he was one of the first man-midwives in the north of Scotland. Skene completed his training in Edinburgh, London, and Paris with such eminent physicians as Alexander Munro, Sir John Rutherford, William Hunter, and William Smellie. He was so impressed by Smellie's own forceps—'the neatest and smallest, the blades are wrapp'd round with leather'—that he introduced them to Aberdeen to be used in midwifery cases (letter, 5 Dec 1752, U. Aberdeen L., MS 38).

In 1753 Skene joined his father in his Aberdeen medical practice, where he stayed for the rest of his life. One of his first projects was to establish midwifery training in Aberdeen and he ran several courses in the late 1750s and early 1760s 'particularly intended for the instruction of country midwives' (*Aberdeen Journal*, 17 Oct 1758), a subject he also discussed in his paper 'Proposals for supplying country parishes with skillful midwives'. In addition, Skene offered poor women in childbirth the chance to be looked after 'gratis in their own Houses' and 'maintained in Bed and Board at his Expence till their Recovery' ('Proposals', U. Aberdeen L., MS 37, fol. 88). He vaccinated children in his private practice against smallpox and there is some indication from his correspondence that he attempted experiments to vaccinate against measles.

A man of many interests and projects Skene was a manager of Aberdeen Infirmary and also acted on behalf of the commissioners for the sick and wounded seamen. A member of the Gordon's Mill Farming Club that existed from 1758, he probably was the 'inventor' of the moss dunghill usually ascribed to Lord Kames. He was a member of the Edinburgh Philosophical Society from 1765 and a founder member of the Aberdeen Philosophical Society, established in 1758. Members of this latter society included the philosopher Thomas Reid, who wrote a eulogy for Skene. Skene attended over half the meetings and was elected president of the society in 1766. He proposed more than a dozen questions covering many topics and a similar number of discourses falling into four categories: the philosophy of the mind, the nature of happiness, natural history, and plant classification. Thomas Reid proposed that Skene should take up the chair in the theory and practice of medicine at Glasgow University vacated by the move of Joseph Black to Edinburgh in 1763, but Skene refused. In 1764–5 there was a further proposal to make Skene an assistant professor of medicine in Aberdeen, but this fell through. In 1767 the chair of materia medica in Edinburgh was offered to him but the terms proved unacceptable and again he declined. Although he never held a university chair he was annually elected dean of faculty at Marischal College from 1767 until his death.

Skene's interest in natural history and philosophy led him to communicate widely with leading scholars of the day, including the Swedish botanist Carl Linnaeus, Lord Kames, Lord Monboddo, and London amateur botanist John Ellis. His correspondence stretched as far as Philadelphia and St Petersburg. Skene was primarily a classifier and arranger of scientific material whom Linnaeus thought the 'brightest star of enquiry in North Britain'. In the 1750s he visited the Fife coalfields and wrote his 'Notes upon coal'. He helped to classify many of the commercially significant ores and was sent samples from all over the country by Thomas Pennant and John Hope. Sir William Hamilton, editor of Thomas Reid's *Works*, wrote that he was 'one of the most zealous cultivators of the natural sciences in Scotland' (*The Works of Thomas Reid*, 1846, 39). Much of his correspondence survives and is located in the special collections section of Aberdeen University Library. Never appearing to be in good health and often a victim of gout, he died on 27 December 1770 in Aberdeen.

H. LESLEY DIACK

Sources A. Thomson, *Biographical sketch of David Skene MD of Aberdeen* (1859) · B. Lenman and J. Kenworthy, 'Dr David Skene, Linnaeus and the applied geology of the Scottish enlightenment', *Aberdeen University Review*, 47 (1977–8), 32–44, 231–7 · W. R. Humphries, 'The letters of David Skene', *Aberdeen University Postgraduate Medical Bulletin* (April 1970); (Oct 1971); (Feb 1972); (June 1972); (Oct 1972); (May 1973); (Sept 1973) · L. Diack, 'Dr David Skene and his contribution to women's health', *'To the greit support and advancement of helth': papers on the history of medicine in Aberdeen*, ed. A. Adam, D. Smith, and F. Watson (1996), 12–19 · *Aberdeen Journal* (1747–70) · B. Fabian, 'David Skene and the Aberdeen Philosophical Society', *Bibliothek*, 5 (1967–70), 81–99 · H. L. Ulman, ed., *The minutes of the Aberdeen Philosophical Society, 1758–1773* (1990) · U. Aberdeen L., special libraries and archives, MSS 37–40, 471–83, 501, 540 · parish register and kirk session records, St Nicholas, Aberdeen · University lists, U. Aberdeen

Archives U. Aberdeen L., corresp. and papers | U. Aberdeen, Reid MSS

Skene, Felicia Mary Frances [*pseud.* Erskine Moir] (1821–1899), writer and philanthropist, born on 23 May 1821 at Aix-en-Provence, France, was the youngest child of James *Skene (1775–1864), lawyer, of Rubislaw, and his wife, Jane Forbes (1787–1862), daughter of Sir William *Forbes of Pitsligo, sixth baronet. As a child in Paris she was given piano lessons by Franz Liszt. When the family moved to Edinburgh, she played with the children of the exiled Charles X of France at Holyroodhouse and was, on occasion, the preferred companion of her father's friend, the ailing Sir Walter Scott ('he felt unequal to any society but that of his friend's youngest child, who would amuse him with her merry *bavardage*'; 'Glimpses of some vanished celebrities', *Blackwood's Edinburgh Magazine*, 158, 1895, 2). The family lived at Athens between 1838 and 1845, where she became acquainted with Maximilian of Bavaria (and was amused by his use of 'broad Scotticisms'). From Athens the family visited Lord Stratford de Redcliffe, British ambassador at Constantinople. Skene's years spent on the continent rendered her an accomplished linguist. After 1845 the Skenes lived at Leamington Spa, Warwickshire (where Felicia attended school for two years, in 1850–52) before the family took up residence at Frewin Hall, Oxford, in 1850.

It was with Oxford that Skene's subsequent career was most intimately associated. Here she became acquainted with E. B. Pusey and his biographer, Henry Liddon, and became a sympathetic proponent of the Oxford Movement. She also won the active support and admiration of Sir Henry Acland and Benjamin Jowett, as, during the cholera epidemic in the city in 1854, she organized a band of nurses, some of whom were later sent to the Crimea to work with Florence Nightingale. She maintained a correspondence with Nightingale throughout the Crimean War, admiring 'beyond measure her admirable care and accuracy' ('Some episodes in a long life', *Blackwood's Edinburgh Magazine*, 159, 1896, 543). She also supported the antivivisection work of her friend Frances Power Cobbe. Skene took much interest in rescuing girls from prostitution, and from 1878, with Home Office sanction, she dedicated herself to prison-visiting at Oxford gaol. Some of her experiences were described in a series of five unsigned articles published in *Blackwood's Edinburgh Magazine* from November 1888 to August 1889 (reprinted in 1889 as *Scenes from a Silent World, or, Prisons and their Inmates* under the pseudonym Francis Scougal), in her study *Penitentiaries and Reformatories* (1865), and in her article 'Prison visiting' (*Fraser's Magazine*, Dec 1880). Her interest in the 'eminently unsatisfactory existence' of vagrants is evident in her 'Ethics of the tramp' (*Cornhill Magazine*, May 1898, 688).

Skene's earliest published volumes, *Isles of Greece and other Poems* (1843) and *Wayfaring Sketches among the Greeks and Turks on the Shores of the Danube* (1849), drew on her seven years' residence in south-east Europe. Her popular devotional work, *The Divine Master* (1852), which went to several editions, was followed in 1854 by *The Ministry of Consolation*, in 1883 by *The Shadow of the Holy Week*, and by memoirs of her cousin Alexander Penrose Forbes, bishop of Brechin (1876), and of Alexander Lycurgus, archbishop of the Cyclades (1877). She was also the editor of the *Churchman's Companion* (1862–80). Her first novel, *Use and Abuse* (1849), follows the careers of two rivals, Raymond and Arabyn. It was succeeded by *The Tutor's Ward* (1851) and *Hidden Depths* (1866; repr. 1886), the latter a fictional exposure of prostitution in Oxford ('Greyburgh') which, the author claimed, drew on scenes that she had personally witnessed. Her later fiction includes *A Strange Inheritance* (1886), the story of a gentlemanly emigrant's return to Scotland, and *The Lesters: a Family Record* (1887). In the mid-1870s she also serialized novels, in *The Quiver: Still and Deep* in 1875, *Raymond* in 1876, and *More than Conqueror* in 1878. Under the pseudonym Erskine Moir she published *Through the Shadows: a Test of the Truth* (1888) and felt this to be her most important religious work. Apart from her contributions to *Blackwood's Edinburgh Magazine* and *Cornhill Magazine*, she also published articles in the *Dublin University Magazine*, *Macmillan's Magazine*, and *Temple Bar*. Skene died, unmarried, of bronchitis at her home, 34 St Michael Street, Oxford, on 6 October 1899.

ANDREW SANDERS

Sources *The Times* (10 Oct 1899), 4 · E. C. Rickards, *Felicia Skene at Oxford: a memoir* (1902) · *ILN* (14 Oct 1899) · *ILN* (21 Oct 1899) · Mrs W. O'Brien, *Unseen friends* (1912), 168–82 · Boase, *Mod. Eng. biog.* · Allibone, *Dict.*, suppl. · *Wellesley index* · J. Sutherland, *The Longman companion to Victorian fiction* (1988), 583–4 · R. L. Wolff, *Nineteenth-century fiction: a bibliographical catalogue based on the collection formed by Robert Lee Wolff*, 4 (1985) · d. cert.
Archives Bodl. Oxf., letters to Sir H. W. Acland and Sarah Acland · NL Scot., letters to Blackwoods
Likenesses photograph, repro. in *ILN* (21 Oct 1899)
Wealth at death £2449 14s. 1d. (in UK): resworn probate, April 1900, *CGPLA Eng. & Wales* (1899)

Skene, Sir James, of Curriehill, first baronet (1578/9–1633). *See under* Skene, Sir John, of Curriehill (*c.*1540–1617).

Skene, James (1775–1864), friend of Sir Walter Scott, was born at Rubislaw, near Aberdeen, on 7 March 1775, the second son of George Skene, advocate, and his wife, Jean Moir. The family was descended from Thomas, brother of Sir George Skene (*d.* 1707), a Danzig merchant and provost of Aberdeen who left his estate at Rubislaw to James's father. George Skene died in the year after James's birth. In 1783 his widow settled in Edinburgh, for the education of her seven children, and James attended the Edinburgh high school. When his elder brother died in 1791, he became heir of Rubislaw, and was sent to Europe to further his education, becoming an accomplished linguist in due course. Upon returning to Edinburgh, he studied law, and was admitted to the Scottish bar in 1797.

A mutual friend introduced Skene to Sir Walter Scott, who was eager to learn about German literature from him. In spite of their age difference, they found that they had much in common, and remained firm friends until Scott's death. Scott wrote of Skene that he was 'the only one among my numerous friends who can properly be termed *amicus omnium horarum*' ('friend of all hours'; *Journal of Sir Walter Scott*, 66–7). That year they founded the Edinburgh light horse infantry, of which Skene became cornet. The dedication to Skene of the introduction to *Marmion*, canto 4, is charged with reminiscences of their common interests, and J. G. Lockhart's *Memoirs of the Life of Sir Walter Scott* (1837–8) draws heavily on Skene's manuscript memoranda of the friendship.

In 1802 Skene revisited Europe and stayed there for several years. George Bellas Greenough, president of the Geological Society of London, was his travelling companion for a time, and Skene became a member of the society. On his return to Scotland, on 11 September 1806, Skene married Jane (1787–1862), youngest child of Sir William *Forbes of Pitsligo, sixth baronet (1739–1806). She was the sister of Sir William, seventh baronet, who in 1797 married Scott's first love, Williamina Stuart. Jane Skene, like her husband, was highly respected by Scott, who wrote of her that she was 'a most excellent person, tenderly fond of Sophia' (*Journal of Sir Walter Scott*, 54). Three sons and four daughters of the marriage survived; the second son, William Forbes *Skene (1809–1892), was to become a noted antiquary and historian. The youngest daughter, Felicia *Skene, became a popular religious writer. They lived in Kincardineshire for ten years, making frequent visits to Scott's home, and to Edinburgh.

In 1816 the family moved to Edinburgh, and Skene became an active member of various literary and scientific societies including the Society of Antiquaries of Scotland and the Royal Society of Edinburgh, acting for a long time as the curator of its library and museum. He was an original member of the Bannatyne Club, for whom he edited Spalding's *History of the Troubles in Scotland* (1828). In addition, he was for many years secretary to the board of trustees for manufactures. In 1820 he undertook the design of the new Princes Street Gardens.

The Skenes visited France in 1820 and the detailed journal he kept was used by Scott for *Quentin Durward* (1823). The Jewish element in *Ivanhoe* (1819) also drew on Skene's continental experiences (Lockhart, 4.323; cf. ibid., 7.325). In 1829 he produced a series of sketches to accompany the Waverley novels. Scott had a high opinion of Skene's artistic skill, writing that he was 'for a gentleman the best draughtsman I ever saw' (*Letters of Sir Walter Scott*, 1.301). Skene wrote the article on painting which appeared in Sir David Brewster's *Edinburgh Encyclopaedia*.

For health reasons the family went to Greece in 1838, staying for several years near Athens, in a villa built to Skene's own design. He busied himself with art, and is said to have left over 500 watercolours of Greek scenery and antiquities. Returning to Britain in 1845, he settled first at Leamington Spa and then at Frewin Hall, Oxford, where he died on 27 November 1864. He was buried at St John's Episcopal Church, Edinburgh.

T. W. BAYNE, *rev.* SARAH COUPER

Sources W. F. Skene, ed., *Memorials of the family of Skene of Skene*, New Spalding Club, 1 (1887) · *The journal of Sir Walter Scott*, 2 vols. (1890–91) · *The letters of Sir Walter Scott*, ed. H. J. C. Grierson and others, centenary edn, 12 vols. (1932–79) · A. Scott, *The story of Sir Walter Scott's first love* (1896) · B. Thomson, ed., *The Skene papers* (1909) · J. G. Lockhart, *Memoirs of the life of Sir Walter Scott*, 7 vols. (1837–8) · *Familiar letters of Sir Walter Scott*, ed. D. Douglas, 2 vols. (1894) · Burke, *Peerage*
Archives Edinburgh Central Reference Library, albums of architectural drawings and portion of MS of *The Ottoman Empire*; notes relating to his drawings for Chambers's *Reekiana* · NL Scot., artistic corresp. and papers; corresp. and papers · NRA Scotland, priv. coll., papers · priv. coll., papers · U. Aberdeen L., estate corresp. and papers | NL Scot., corresp. with Sir Walter Scott · UCL, letters to G. B. Greenough
Likenesses wash drawing, Scot. NPG
Wealth at death under £200: probate, 13 Dec 1864, *CGPLA Eng. & Wales*

Skene, Sir John, of Curriehill (*c.*1540–1617), jurist, was the sixth son of James Skene in Bandodle (killed at Pinkie, 10 September 1547) and his wife, Janet, daughter of Robert Lumsden of Cushnie. His father was the second son of Alexander, ninth laird of Skene (1485–1507), and progenitor of the Skenes of Westercorse and Ramore. Gilbert *Skeyne (*c.*1522–1599), physician, was his brother. He may have been at Aberdeen grammar school in 1549, and was thereafter at King's College, Aberdeen. In 1556 he incorporated at St Mary's College, St Andrews, where he was a regent in 1565. He spent seven years in Europe (*c.*1567–1574), studying law in Paris and visiting Switzerland, Poland, and Scandinavia before settling in Germany, at the University of Wittenberg. It was probably through his travels that he became, according to James VI, fluent in 'the Dutch and Latin tongues, with great acquaintance with sundry princes in Germany, and the chief learned men about the princes there' (*CSP Scot.*, 1589–93, 305).

After returning to Scotland, Skene was admitted as an advocate on 19 March 1575. He was then recruited by Regent Morton to assist with a project for reviewing the laws of Scotland. In 1577 Morton granted him a pension from the revenues of Arbroath Abbey, to compensate for loss of his legal practice, confirmed by James VI in 1578 and 1579. As a 'disciple' of Sir James Balfour, Skene probably assisted in the compilation of the latter's *Practicks*. When Balfour went into exile in 1579, Skene seems to have expanded his own legal practice, appearing in cases before the privy council. In 1581 the general assembly of the kirk suggested his appointment as procurator for certain ministers and in 1589 he was included in a commission to consult as to measures for 'the weal of the kirk in so dangerous a time' (Calderwood, 5.4).

James VI initially objected to Skene's inclusion in the embassy to Denmark in 1589 for negotiating his marriage, because 'ther were many better lawers', but was assured by Sir James Melville that Skene 'was best acquanted with the conditions of the Germanes, and culd mak them lang harrangues in Latin, and was a gud trew stout man lyk a Dutche man' (Melville, 366). In 1590 James sent him on an extended diplomatic mission to the Netherlands, Denmark, and Germany, where he tried to interest the rulers in supporting plans for a league against Spain. On his return to Scotland, he resumed his duties as joint lord advocate, to which he had been appointed on 20 August 1590.

According to Scot of Scotstarvet, Skene owed his appointment as clerk register on 19 September 1594 to his brother-in-law Walter Stewart, Lord Blantyre. Shortly afterwards, on 30 November 1594, he was appointed a lord of session. As clerk register he inventoried the exchequer records and used them to compile a list of crown property rights that had been lost during royal minorities. From January 1596 he was one of the 'Octavians', the eight commissioners of exchequer, given sweeping powers to overhaul the royal finances. When James VI's impatience with financial restraints and their own growing unpopularity forced the Octavians to resign in January 1597, all were reappointed, but the enlarged commission had more limited powers and was effectively controlled by Blantyre as treasurer. An act of parliament of June 1598 prohibiting permanent commissions of exchequer brought an end to this attempt at financial reform. About ten years later Skene set out a similar programme in his 'Proposals anent the order of the Checker', produced for the then lord treasurer, George Home, earl of Dunbar.

Skene's membership of a commission appointed in 1592 to review and print acts of parliament and other laws resulted in the publication in 1597 of *The Lawes and Actes of Parliament*, containing post-1424 statutes. His *De verborum significatione* (1597), the first published dictionary of Scots law, drew extensively on earlier and non-statutory sources. A second edition of this rather idiosyncratic compilation appeared in 1599, the only new entry being a dissertation on the names of days of the week. According to his assistant Habakkuk Bisset, Skene also prepared a third, unpublished, edition.

De verborum's full title, 'The exposition of the termes and difficill wordes conteined in the four buikes of *Regiam majestatem*', indicates that Skene was already engrossed in the task that was to occupy him for the next ten years. However, the citations in *De verborum* indicate that the text of *Regiam* he was using differed from the one eventually published. A revised text of 1601–2 bears extensive annotations, some showing his awareness of the relationship between *Regiam* and *Glanvill*, which also excited interest among English lawyers in the context of proposals for a legal union of England and Scotland after 1603. In later revisions Skene brought in a fuller range of references to *Glanvill*. By 1607 he was able to lay a finished text before the privy council, which recommended to the king that, as Skene's estate was not equal to his wit, genius, and literature, the work should be printed at public expense, a tax being levied on judges and members of the estates to defray the cost. The volume finally appeared in 1609 in two versions: 'the one in Latyne for the benefyte of strangearis, the uther in Scottishe language for the use of subjectis of the countrey' (*Reg. PCS*, 1st ser., 8.358). Both included legal texts or statutes attributed to monarchs from Malcolm II to Robert III. An edition of the Latin version was published in London in 1613, differing only in its title-page.

Skene's editorial methods have been criticized severely by later writers, notably his uncritical acceptance of the authenticity of *Regiam*, in which he followed legal tradition going back at least two centuries. Its relationship to *Glanvill* seems to have reinforced his conviction that it was authentic legislation of David I, of which *Glanvill* was merely a later English adaptation, whereas Sir Thomas Craig dismissed it as the work of a plagiarist. Skene was, however, fully aware of the many serious discrepancies among the manuscript sources available to him, as shown by his comment 'I fell into an Augean stable, that not even the labour of Hercules can cleanse or purge' (*Regiam majestatem*, Latin preface). Drastic editing produced texts that were logical by his own standards, while his notes showed awareness of parallels in English and civil law. He deserves credit, at least, for providing lawyers with a printed text that answered contemporary needs. Moreover the English version of *Regiam* contained two treatises that were genuinely innovative. The first, 'Ane short form of proces presentlie used and observed before the Lords of Counsell and session', was the first published guide to Scottish court procedure, drawing upon Roman law, as well as native sources. Habakkuk Bisset's *Rolment of Courtis* is a revised and expanded version, using Skene's own emendations of the original. The second, 'Of crimes and judges, in criminall causes, conforme to the lawes of the realme', is a brief, well-planned exposition of different types of crime and the various judges entitled to try them.

Skene, who had been knighted in 1604, had combined his editorial work with involvement in public business. His appointment as a commissioner for negotiating the proposed union with England in 1604 may be the context for his call to the English bar (Middle Temple) in the following year. He served on several other commissions, including one for visiting the University of St Andrews in 1609.

According to Scot of Scotstarvet, Skene's editions of the acts of parliament and *Regiam* brought him 'a great deal of money from the country; for all heritors of land were obliged to buy them, but it did little good; for albeit he lived many years in the place, yet did he purchase but few lands' (Scot, 99). He did not acquire Curriehill, Edinburghshire, until 1604, the year in which he made a first move to ensure his eldest son's succession to the office of clerk register. Although James Skene's [*see below*] commission was not recorded, it evidently involved some form of joint tenure with his father, who also made over to him the minor office of clerk of the bills in 1608. Finally in April 1612 Skene 'being grown in age and infirmity' dispatched James to court 'with a demission of the place but with a charge not to use it unless he found the king willing to admit him'. James, however, 'abused by some politick wits' accepted the lesser position of an ordinary lord of session (*History of the Church*, 3.517). This was attributed to the machinations of Sir Thomas Hamilton, the lord advocate, who became clerk register but quickly exchanged the post for that of secretary of state, his real objective. The incident caused an estrangement between father and son, said to have been healed only by the king's personal intervention. Skene's withdrawal from public life ended with his reappointment to the council in February 1614, from which he retired finally in June 1616.

Skene died on 16 March 1617 and was buried in the Greyfriars' Kirk, Edinburgh. He was survived by his wife, Helen Somerville (*d*. in or after 1625), eldest daughter of Sir John Somerville of Camnethan, whom he had married in 1577. They had four sons and four daughters. He bequeathed her the unsold stocks of *Regiam* and the rest of his books. His library, including a number of incunabula, survived at Mar Lodge, Braemar, into the 1920s but was subsequently dispersed.

Sir James Skene of Curriehill, first baronet (1578/9–1633), judge, the eldest son of Sir John Skene, was admitted advocate in 1603 and was joint clerk register with his

father from 1604 to 1612 and clerk of the bills between 1608 and 1614. Appointed a lord of session in 1612, he was promoted to lord president in 1626. He was a privy councillor from 1616 to 1626, and was created a baronet of Nova Scotia in 1628. On 7 December 1603 he married Janet, daughter of Sir John Johnston of Hilton and Sheen, who survived him. They had eight sons, six of whom died young, and three daughters. Sir James Skene died on 15 October 1633, aged fifty-four, and was buried beside his father.

John Skene of Hallyards (*d*. 1644), the second son of Sir John, was appointed by him keeper of the registers of hornings and inhibitions for life, but in August 1612 the privy council found his gift to be invalid. He succeeded his brother as clerk of the bills in 1614 and by 1618 was a principal clerk of session. On 29 June 1603 he married Alison, sister of William Rigg of Aithernie, who predeceased him; they had three sons and six daughters. The Skene manuscript of 1615–35, containing tunes, chiefly Scottish, arranged for the lute, is partly attributed to him. He died in December 1644.   ATHOL MURRAY

Sources W. F. Skene, ed., *Memorials of the family of Skene of Skene*, New Spalding Club, 1 (1887) · D. Walker, *The Scottish jurists* (1985) · A. L. Murray, 'Sir John Skene and the exchequer', *Miscellany One*, Stair Society (1971), 125–55 · *Reg. PCS*, 1st ser., vols. 2–14 · *Reg. PCS*, 2nd ser., vols. 1–6 · *CSP Scot.*, *1588–1603* · *APS*, 1124–1423; 1593–1625 · J. Hamilton-Grierson, *Habakkuk Bisset's Rolment of courtis*, 3 vols., STS, new ser., 10, 13, 18 (1920–26) · J. Skene, *Regiam majestatem*, ed. T. M. Cooper, Latin edn (1609), Stair Society, 11 (1947) · *Memoirs of his own life by Sir James Melville of Halhill*, ed. T. Thomson, Bannatyne Club, 18 (1827) · J. Scot, *The staggering state of Scottish statesmen from 1550 to 1650*, ed. C. Rogers (1872) · J. Spottiswood, *The history of the Church of Scotland*, ed. M. Napier and M. Russell, 3 vols., Bannatyne Club, 93 (1850) · W. Dauney, *Ancient Scottish melodies, from a manuscript of the reign of James VI*, Bannatyne Club, 59 (1838) · GEC, *Baronetage* · W. Temple, *The thanage of Fermartyn* (1894) · J. M. Thomson and others, eds., *Registrum magni sigilli regum Scotorum / The register of the great seal of Scotland*, 11 vols. (1882–1914), vols. 5–7 · H. Paton, ed., *The register of marriages for the parish of Edinburgh, 1595–1700*, Scottish RS, old ser., 27 (1905) · Edinburgh testaments, NA Scot., CC 8/8/49, fol. 309v · H. J. MacQueen, 'Glanvill resarcopate: Sir John Skene and *Regiam majestatem*', *The Renaissance in Scotland: studies in literature, religion, history, and culture offered to John Durkan*, ed. A. A. MacDonald and others (1994), 385–403 · *An inventory of the ancient and historical monuments of the city of Edinburgh, with the thirteenth report of the commission*, Royal Commission on the Ancient and Historical Monuments in Scotland (1951) · D. Calderwood, *The history of the Kirk of Scotland*, ed. T. Thomson and D. Laing, 8 vols., Wodrow Society, 7 (1842–9)

Archives NL Scot., diary of embassy to protestant princes [copy] | NG Scot., Skene of Hallyards papers, Adv. MS 29.2.10

Wealth at death £4636 13s. 4d. Scots—(£386 sterling): NA Scot. Edinburgh testaments, 8 July 1617, CC88/8/49, fol. 309v

Skene, John, of Hallyards (*d*. 1644). *See under* Skene, Sir John, of Curriehill (*c*.1540–1617).

Skene [*née* Gillespie], **Lilias** [Lillias Skein] (1626/7–1697), Quaker preacher and poet, was the daughter of John Gillespie (*d*. 1627 or *c*.1647), minister of Kirkcaldy; according to conflicting accounts, her father died either around the time of her birth or shortly after her marriage. Her mother was Lilias Simson (*d*. 1627), the daughter of Patrick

*Simson, minister of Stirling. One of at least eight children, her brothers included the Church of Scotland ministers Patrick *Gillespie, principal of Glasgow University, and George *Gillespie, minister of St Giles, Edinburgh.

Lilias Gillespie married at Kirkcaldy on 26 August 1646 an Aberdeen merchant, Alexander *Skene (1621?–1694), magistrate and author of *Memorialls for the Government of the Royall-Burghs in Scotland*. She moved with him to Aberdeen, and between 1647 and 1669 bore ten children. Her eldest surviving son was John Skene (*c.*1649–1690), deputy governor of West Jersey (1685–8) (*Papers of William Penn*, 96n., 105n.). She and her husband were fervent covenanters, respected for the strength of their faith even when their strict presbyterianism became impolitic at the Restoration. It caused a local sensation when, about the time when her last child was born in 1669, she suddenly converted to Quakerism. Her husband followed suit in 1672. Of her own conversion she wrote: 'It is very well known to all that lived in the place where I sojourned, I was none who conversed with them, I was never at one of their meetings, I never read one of their books', yet she experienced 'that thing the school-men call Immediat Objective Revelation' (Skein, 203). She continued to be known locally as Lilias Gillespie, but within Quaker circles she was called, English-style, by her husband's surname.

Lilias Skene was the leading woman in Aberdeen's tiny but influential Quaker community, which included such figures as Robert Barclay, George Keith, and Alexander Jaffray of Kingswells. Quaker meetings were often held in the Skenes' house. She appears to have been the only woman to join the men in adjudicating disciplinary matters. About 1678 she helped establish the first Quaker school in Scotland. Lilias Skene's leadership and activism came to the fore between 1676 and 1679, years of persecution in Aberdeen when every adult male Quaker in the region (about thirty in all) spent months or years in prison—including her husband, eldest son, and son-in-law Andrew *Jaffray [see under Jaffray, Alexander] of Kingswells, who had married her daughter Christian. Quaker women remained at liberty and continued to meet and lobby for the men's freedom. Lilias Skene was very active through this period. In a ferocious letter of 31 March 1677 to the Aberdeen magistrates, she refers to her own preaching ('at severall seasons and in diverse maners I have witnessed') and goes on to condemn their imprisoning 'honest men that have families wives and children … in those cold nasty stinking holes where ye have shutt them up, who have been as neatly handled and tenderly educated and as usefull in their generation as any amongst you' ('Brieff account of the most material passages', 37–9). It has been plausibly claimed, but cannot be confirmed, that she assisted her husband in compiling the two manuscript accounts of the history of Quakerism in Aberdeen which he produced in the early 1680s.

Lilias Skene also turned her pen to epistolary evangelizing. In 1676 Robert Barclay encouraged her to write to Elisabeth, princess palatine of the Rhine (1618–1680), cousin of the Stuart kings, who Quakers hoped would intervene on their behalf even if (as happened) she could not be converted. Barclay introduced Skene to her as 'a woman of great experience and tenderness of heart who through great tribulations both of body and mind hath attained the earnest of the Kingdom [but whose] husband and son-in-law are now in Prison' (Hull, 27). Skene corresponded with the princess and her companion, Countess Anna Maria van Hoorn (or de Hornes), and was invited to visit them at Herford, Westphalia. George Keith's biographer claims she accompanied Keith, Barclay, George Fox, and William Penn on their tour of the Netherlands and Germany in the summer of 1677, and Barclay tells us she intended to go. But neither Penn nor Fox mentions her in their journals of the trip, and in a letter written to her in 1678 the princess seemed to imply that they had not met: 'I love your upright intention to travail (i.e. toil) in spirit for your friends, though unknown to you' (ibid., 33). Skene was in London in the summer of 1677, and also visited the bedridden philosopher and recent Quaker convert Anne, Viscountess Conway, at Ragley in Worcestershire. She befriended and corresponded with Anne Conway, and was entrusted with hiring new household staff for Ragley, all Quakers—a task she could arrange from Aberdeen, thanks to her extensive contacts in the English Quaker community.

Lilias Skene's letters and poems are among the few surviving literary works of non-aristocratic seventeenth-century Scottish women. Her only known publication in her lifetime (the author spelling her name Lillias Skein) was 'An Expostulatory Epistle, Directed to Robert Macquare', dated June 1678 and appended to one of Robert Barclay's polemics in 1679. Macquare (better known as Robert McWard) was a presbyterian dissenter whose vitriolic rants against Quakers had earlier drawn Alexander Skene into print. Lilias Skene's effort was gracious and restrained, but firm: 'O Robert! thy hard speeches have manifested thy own sad acknowledgement to be very true, the Holy fire is gone out with thee indeed' (Skein, 201). In the nineteenth century William Walker published (from his own transcription of a manuscript since lost) selections from thirty lyric poems and three anagrams composed between 1665 and 1697 (Walker, 85–102). Lilias Skene's poetry, like her prose, was filled with mystical allusions and scriptural images of suffering and salvation. The Aberdeenshire poll-tax book of 1696 finds her widowed and living modestly in Aberdeen with her daughter Anna and two servants. She died there on 21 June 1697, three years after her husband, and was buried beside him in an unmarked grave in the Quaker burial-ground at Kingswells.

GORDON DESBRISAY

Sources W. Walker, *The bards of Bon-Accord, 1375–1860* (1887) • W. F. Skene, ed., *Memorials of the family of Skene of Skene*, New Spalding Club, 1 (1887), 1–3, 77–81 • L. Skein, 'An expostulatory epistle', in R. Barclay, *Robert Barclay's apology for the true Christian divinity vindicated from John Brown's examination and pretended confutation thereof* (1679), 196–205 • *The Conway letters: the correspondence of Anne, Viscountess Conway, Henry More, and their friends, 1642–1684*, ed. M. H. Nicolson, rev. edn, ed. S. Hutton (1992) • W. Hull, *William Penn and the Dutch migration to Pennsylvania* (1935) • W. F. Miller, 'Gleanings from the records of the yearly meeting of Aberdeen, 1672 to 1786', *Journal of the Friends' Historical Society*, 8 (1911), 40–46, 53–80, 113–22 •

G. DesBrisay, 'Catholics, Quakers, and religious persecution in Restoration Aberdeen', *Innes Review*, 47 (1996), 136–68 · 'A brieff historicall account and record of the first rise and progress of the blessed truth, called in derision Quakerism, in and about Aberdeen', NA Scot., CH10/3/36 · 'A brieff account of the most material passages and occurrences that happened to friends of truth during that great and long tryall of sufferings and persecution at Aberdene', NA Scot., CH/10/3/35 · W. F. Miller, 'Notes on early Friends' schools in Scotland', *Journal of the Friends' Historical Society*, 7 (1910), 105–13 · *Relique Barclaiana: correspondence of Col. David Barclay and Robert Barclay of Urie and his son Robert* (1870) · J. Besse, *A collection of the sufferings of the people called Quakers*, 2 vols. (1753) · J. Robertson, 'Alexander Skene of Newtyle', *Scottish Notes and Queries*, 9 (1895–6), 158–60 · *The papers of William Penn*, ed. M. M. Dunn, R. S. Dunn, and others, 2 (1982) · L. B. Taylor, ed., *Aberdeen council letters*, 6 vols. (1942–61), vol. 6 · J. Stuart, ed., *List of pollable persons within the shire of Aberdeen, 1696*, 2 (1844) · Aberdeen monthly meeting and quarterly meeting minutes, 1672–92, NA Scot., CH10/3/1 · Aberdeen monthly meeting and quarterly meeting minutes, 1692–1706, NA Scot., CH10/3/2 · book containing much old and miscellaneous writing on many and various subjects, NA Scot., CH10/3/34 · *Fasti Scot.*, new edn, 5.102 · U. Aberdeen L., special libraries and archives, Historic collections, William Walker MS 2774

Archives NA Scot. | U. Aberdeen L., special libraries and archives, Historic collections, William Walker MS 2774

Wealth at death estate valued at 5000–10,000 merks [£3333–6666 Scots] for poll tax in 1696: Stuart, ed., *List of pollable persons*, 614

Skene, William Forbes

Skene, William Forbes (1809–1892), historian and Celtic scholar, the second of seven children of James *Skene (1775–1864) of Rubislaw, near Aberdeen, and Jane (1787–1862), daughter of Sir William Forbes, sixth baronet, of Pitsligo, Aberdeenshire, was born on 7 June 1809 at Inverie, Kincardineshire. He was educated at the high school of Edinburgh, and there began on his own account to study Gaelic, of which he had some opportunity of learning the rudiments through his maternal relationship with MacDonell of Glengarry, but still more through his being boarded for a time at Laggan, Inverness-shire, with the parish minister, Mackintosh Mackay, on the recommendation of Sir Walter Scott, a close friend of his father.

After a session at the University of Edinburgh, Skene went in 1824 with his elder brother, George, to Hanau, near Frankfurt, where he acquired German and a taste for philology, which he afterwards turned to account in Celtic studies. On his return to Scotland he spent a session at St Andrews University (1825–6), then served a legal apprenticeship under his uncle-in-law, Sir Henry Jardine, passing writer to the signet in 1831. He held a post as a clerk in the court of session, becoming depute clerk of session from 1853 to 1867. He also engaged in private practice, and became senior partner of Skene, Edward, and Bilton, writers to the signet, a position which he retained until his death. It was to Skene's firm that Robert Louis Stevenson was attached in 1872 during his brief flirtation with the law.

While never neglecting his professional duties, Skene had his eye from earliest manhood on highland history and Celtic scholarship. In 1833, with Donald Gregory and others, he founded the Iona Club to promote Celtic history and literature. The club's only publication, *Collectanea*

William Forbes Skene (1809–1892), by Sir George Reid, 1888

de rebus Albanicis (1834; repr. 1847), included Skene's earliest transcription and translation of the famous highland genealogical manuscript now known as MS 1467, but there called MS 1450. In 1837 he published, in two volumes, *The Highlanders of Scotland, their Origin, History, and Antiquities*, a landmark in its day, although later research, not least Skene's own, altered many of the views there expressed. In 1862 he contributed an introduction to Thomas M'Lauchlan's pioneering edition of the precious sixteenth-century Gaelic literary manuscript known as the Book of the Dean of Lismore. Skene's rejection there of the chronological scheme of the older school of Irish antiquaries would now be universally accepted; although his defence of James Macpherson's *Ossian* would not.

In 1868 Skene published the manuscripts known as *The Four Ancient Books of Wales* (the Black Book of Carmarthen, the Book of Aneurin, the Book of Taliesin, and the Red Book of Hergest) in two volumes, with a commentary on fifth- and sixth-century British history with particular reference to the *Gwŷr y Gogledd*, the 'men of the north', and to King Arthur, whom Skene took to be a historical character. This ground was not to be traversed again in such scholarly fashion until the publication in 1949 of H. M. Chadwick's *Early Scotland*. In 1869 Skene published an *Essay on the Coronation Stone of Scone*, in which he overthrew the Scottish legend that this stone was the *Lia Fail* on which Irish kings were crowned at Tara.

In 1867 Skene edited *The Chronicles of the Picts and the Scots*, and in 1871–2 he published for the Historians of Scotland series a critical edition in two volumes of the *Chronica gentis Scotorum* of the fourteenth-century Scottish historiographer John of Fordun, with a translation by his nephew Felix Skene. In the former work he collected for the first time the earliest fragments of Scottish history from Irish and Welsh sources, as well as the older medieval legends and annals which had not been absorbed into the chronicles of Wyntoun and Fordun. In the latter he put into the crucible the *Scotichronicon* as published by Walter Goodall in 1759, and by a thorough inspection of the manuscripts distinguished the portion written by Fordun himself from the additions of Walter Bower, and other continuators. He also added several notes, including one on the origins of Scottish thanages. Skene's Fordun has not yet been superseded; and a modern scholarly edition of Bower did not appear until the 1990s.

With his cousin, Bishop Alexander Penrose Forbes of Brechin, Skene reprinted in 1874, in the Historians of Scotland series, Bishop Reeves's edition of Adomnán's *Life of St Columba*, with translation and rearranged introduction and notes. Felix Skene's edition of the *Liber pluscardensis* in the same series (2 vols., 1877, 1880) incorporated his uncle's argument that the author was Maurice Buchanan, treasurer of Princess Margaret, daughter of James I of Scotland, who was married to Louis XI when dauphin. Skene also edited for the New Spalding Club in 1887 *Memorials of the Family of Skene of Skene*.

However, Skene's *magnum opus*, for which he had prepared all his life, was *Celtic Scotland: a History of Ancient Alban*, which appeared in three volumes from 1876 to 1880, taking the story of Scottish history up to 1286. Following in the path indicated by Father Thomas Innes, and with the aid of better and fuller texts, as well as more advanced methods of criticism, both philological and historical, Skene accomplished more for the annals of his native country than any other contemporary writer. He effectively opened out to view a period of more than five centuries, from the reign of Malcolm Canmore back to the time of St Columba. A second edition appeared in 1886–90.

Shortly after Skene's death Alexander Macbain published a paper severely critical of Skene's methods, 'Mr Skene *versus* Dr Skene'. Macbain's main purpose in appealing, as he put it, 'from "Skene Young" to "Skene Old"' was due to the fact that Skene's *Highlanders of Scotland* of 1837 was all too often preferred by 'the popular historian and clan controversialist' to his later, more fully considered *Celtic Scotland*. As Macbain demonstrated, Skene's *Highlanders* was deeply flawed, and much had been corrected, albeit often silently, in *Celtic Scotland*. Even in *Celtic Scotland*, Macbain believed that Skene had erred grievously in suggesting that the northern Picts had spoken Gaelic and were the true ancestors of the highland Scots, and in suppressing a century of Dalriadic history before the reign of Kenneth mac Alpin.

Macbain's *cri-de-cœur* regarding the reliance of clan historians on Skene's *Highlanders* has been echoed by many later scholars. Some writers still do not realize that the MS 1450 of *The Highlanders* and the MS 1467 of *Celtic Scotland* are one and the same, and that the version in the later book is infinitely preferable to that in the former, despite the fact that Macbain produced a second edition of Skene's *Highlanders* with valuable corrective notes in 1902. Macbain included in this volume a short memoir of Skene and there made some amends for his earlier harsh criticism:

> The Celts of Scotland owe Dr. Skene a deep debt of gratitude, for he was the first to draw their early history out of the slough into which it had got, and to make it respectable. For this end he lent the weight of his learning and position to the cause of the Scottish Celt at a time when it was sorely needed; and he made writers of Scottish history devote fuller attention to the Celtic side of Scottish affairs. (Macbain, 'Life of Dr Skene', xiii–xiv)

Macbain's later, more generous opinion has been echoed by later historians. A. O. Anderson shrewdly commented of Skene's critics that 'All those that condemn him use his books' (A. O. Anderson, *Early Sources of Scottish History: AD 500 to 1286*, 1922, 1.lxxxiii). In 1981 Gordon Donaldson, like Skene historiographer royal for Scotland, noted that *Celtic Scotland*, for all its flaws, had not been superseded. Only in the 1990s, one hundred years after his death, is Skene's account of Celtic Scotland gradually being replaced.

Skene was a keen supporter of St Vincent's Episcopal Church in Edinburgh and was instrumental in the union of that congregation with the Scottish Episcopal church. He wrote a *Gospel History for the Young* in three volumes (1883–4). He acted as secretary to the relief committee in the highlands, set up because of the potato famine from 1846 to 1850. He was also for many years a director of the Commercial Bank of Scotland. Skene received the honorary degrees of LLD and DCL from the universities of Edinburgh and Oxford respectively. He was appointed historiographer royal for Scotland in 1881 on the death of John Hill Burton. Skene died at his home, 27 Inverleith Row, Edinburgh, on 29 August 1892. He never married, but brought up as a father several members of the family of one of his nieces.

As Aeneas Mackay rightly concluded, in his *Dictionary of National Biography* article:

> Skene had many advantages for the task of a Scottish historian: a talented father, an intellectual home, a boyhood spent in the atmosphere of Walter Scott, a thorough knowledge of the Highlands and its inhabitants, a taste for languages and philology, especially Celtic, with opportunities for cultivating it both at home and abroad, ample preparation by the study of Celtic sources at first hand, and a long life. Yet all these would not have sufficed had he not possessed an historic instinct and a patriotic desire to enlarge the boundaries of the history of Scotland and throw new light on its darkest age.

A. J. G. MACKAY, *rev.* W. D. H. SELLAR

Sources D. Mackinnon, *Proceedings of the Royal Society of Edinburgh*, 20 (1892–5), viii–xx • W. F. Skene, *Memorials of the family of Skene of Skene*, New Spalding Club, 1 (1887) • A. Macbain, 'Life of Dr Skene', in W. F. Skene, *The highlanders of Scotland*, ed. A. Macbain, 2nd edn (1902), xiii–xiv • *DNB* • A. Macbain, 'Mr. Skene *versus* Dr. Skene', *Transactions of the Gaelic Society of Inverness*, 21 (1896–7), 191–214 • G. Donaldson, 'Historiography', *A companion to Scottish culture*, ed. D. Daiches (1981) • *CGPLA Eng. & Wales* (1892)

Archives NA Scot. • NL Scot., corresp. and papers • NRA Scotland, priv. coll., papers | Bodl. Oxf., corresp. with Sir Thomas Phillipps • NA Scot., Board of Manufacturers MSS, NG series
Likenesses G. Reid, oils, 1888, Scot. NPG [*see illus.*] • A. Edouart, cut paper silhouette, Scot. NPG • Hill & Adamson, two calotypes, Scot. NPG
Wealth at death £27,092 3s. 8d.: confirmation, 26 Oct 1892, *CCI*

Skerning, Roger de. *See* Scarning, Roger of (*d.* 1278).

Sketchley, Arthur. *See* Rose, George (1817–1882).

Skevington [Skeffington; *formerly* Pace], **Thomas** (*d.* 1533), abbot of Beaulieu and bishop of Bangor, was the son of John Pace of Leicestershire and Margaret, daughter and heir of William Cobley; he is reputed to have been born at Skeffington, Leicestershire, the seat of the family of that name, and to have been related to Richard Pace, dean of St Paul's and Henry VIII's secretary. He entered the Cistercian abbey of Merevale, Warwickshire, and was educated there and at the Cistercian college of St Bernard, Oxford, to which he bequeathed £20 in his will. He took a new name when entering religion—Skevington, or Skeffington, from his supposed birthplace, where the church window bore the blazon of his arms. He became abbot of Waverley, Surrey, possibly in 1478, and was still there in 1500, when he was dispensed to hold a benefice *in commendam*. By 1508 he had become abbot of Beaulieu, Hampshire. The last of the pre-Reformation bishops of Bangor, he was papally provided to the see on 23 February 1509 and, like all his predecessors since 1436, he was in religious orders. He was given licence to retain his abbey of Beaulieu *in commendam*. He was consecrated at Lambeth on 17 June 1509 and had his spiritualities restored to him on the 20th.

Skevington seems to have spent more of his time in the congenial surroundings of his Hampshire abbey than in his remote north Wales diocese. One of his enemies reported to Thomas Cromwell, with no little exaggeration, that he was the 'richest monk in England' and that he had not set foot for fourteen years in his diocese, which he had set to farm to his vicar-general, William Glyn (*LP Henry VIII*, 4/3, no. 5533). Some of his Bangor registers survive, giving details of fifty-eight appointments, about one-third of them to clerics outside the diocese. Among them were John Baddesley, abbot of Merevale, and Richard Pace. During his episcopate Bangor was much troubled by disagreements between Sir Richard Bulkeley and Skevington's confidant, William Glyn, chancellor of Bangor and archdeacon of Anglesey. They came to a head in 1524, when Glyn was appointed archdeacon in preference to Wolsey's nominee, Thomas Runcorn, and again in 1529, when there was conflict between Edward Johns (Wolsey's representative) and Glyn.

In spite of prolonged absence from Bangor, Skevington was responsible for extensive building work there—a mark of contrition for past neglect of his church and see, one hostile commentator suggested. In 1529 he rebuilt the previously grass-grown nave, so the priest–poet, Dafydd Trefor, averred; and, according to an inscription over the tower doorway, built the tower and the church ('hoc campanile et ecclesia fieri fecit') in 1533. Trefor maintained that the work cost this 'willing-hearted bishop' a 'goodly chestful of gold' and expressed the wish that he should live as long as St Deiniol and crown his efforts by placing bells high in the steeple (Williams, *Welsh Church*, 310). He is also credited with an inscription over the entrance to the episcopal palace to the effect that 'Thomas Skevington ep'us Bangor fecit', suggesting that he completed the rebuilding begun by Bishop Henry Deane (1496–1500). When Skevington died, on 16 or 17 August 1533, at Beaulieu, he left a will directing that the steeple and loft of the cathedral at Bangor be completed and four bells hung there. He was buried later that month at Beaulieu, but his heart was placed before the picture of St Deiniol on the north wall of his cathedral. GLANMOR WILLIAMS

Sources Emden, *Oxf.*, 3.1707–8 • *Fasti Angl., 1300–1541*, [Welsh dioceses] • *LP Henry VIII*, vols. 1–6 • B. Willis, *A survey of the cathedral church of Bangor* (1721) • A. I. Pryce, *The diocese of Bangor in the sixteenth century* (1923) • M. L. Clarke, *Bangor Cathedral* (1969) • G. Williams, *Welsh Reformation essays* (1967) • G. Williams, *The Welsh church from conquest to Reformation*, rev. edn (1976) • I. George, 'Syr Dafydd Trefor', *Transactions of the Anglesey Antiquarian Society and Field Club* (1934), 69–74; (1935), 90–104; (1936), 33–43 • will, PRO, PROB 11/25, sig. 5
Archives NL Wales, records of Welsh church
Wealth at death see will, PRO, PROB 11/25, sig. 5

Skewys [Skuish], **John** (*d.* 1544), lawyer and chronicler, was the son of John Skewys of Skewys, St Wenn, Cornwall, and his wife, Joan, daughter of Richard Torunpioe. His paternal family had been seated at Skewys as early as the reign of Edward III. According to Wood, Skewys 'was conversant for a time among the Oxford muses, either in Exeter College or in Hart Hall, but whether he took a degree, it appears not' (Wood, *Ath. Oxon.*, 1.58). In fact Hart Hall belonged to Exeter, which often used it to provide accommodation, and it may be that Skewys sometimes resided there as a guest of the college when he was acting as Cardinal Wolsey's agent in Oxford in the late 1520s—Exeter gave him wine in 1525 and gloves on at least three subsequent occasions. But there is no evidence for his having studied at Oxford.

By 1506 Skewys had married Katherine, widow of John Reskymer and daughter of John Trethurffe of Trethurffe, Cornwall. Through his marriage, which produced no children, he became connected with the Courtenay family, his wife's mother being Elizabeth, sister of Edward Courtenay, earl of Devon. The earl appointed Skewys one of the supervisors of his will, and he was later also employed by his wife's cousin the marquess of Exeter and other nobles including the earl of Northumberland. Wood claims further that he 'was held in great esteem by several of the nobility for his proficiency in various sorts of learning' (Wood, *Ath. Oxon.*, 1.58).

Skewys was prominent in Cornish affairs, owning several properties by inheritance and purchase; in a deed of 1539 he disposed of eight manors in the county. In 1509 he was granted the lease of tolls on tin in Tewington, Tywarnhaile, and Helston, Cornwall, for twenty years. He was a JP in the county between 1510 and 1515, an assessor for the duchy of Cornwall in 1514, 1518, and 1521, and high sheriff of the county in 1520.

Skewys's main residence and work, however, were in London, for he took up the law as his profession. He was resident at Lincoln's Inn by 1514, when he was granted the privilege of wearing his hat in the king's presence. Skewys entered Wolsey's service, and remained in the employment of the cardinal until the latter's fall in 1529, when he was appointed to adjudicate all cases committed to chancery by the king or his chief minister. It was probably Wolsey's patronage that brought him the rights, with Sir John Lysle and Robert Cosen, of next presentation to a canonry of St George's, Windsor, in 1516 and 1521. In 1525 he was one of the commissioners for the suppression of St Frideswide's, Oxford, in preparation for the foundation of Cardinal College. He was regularly appointed a JP for Middlesex between 1528 and 1544.

John Bale records two works by Skewys in his *Index*. It would appear that both survive in BL, Harley MS 2258. A note on the verso of the flysheet records the provenance of this volume: 'Raynold Mohun Owner here of by the gyfte of John Skewys lawyar; & borne in the contye of Cornewall Whoo drewe & wrote thys worke wythe hys owne honde & brevyated owte of dyvers antyke auctors'. A substantial index is followed by a brief account of the Trojan war (fols. 34–44), corresponding to one of the writings recorded by Bale. This is succeeded by the other, 'A brevyat of the cronacles of the Ile or realme of gret Bretayn nowe callyd yngland translatyd out of latyn ynto Inglysshe out of the historyens boks', which occupies the rest of the book. After a brief account of Britain in terms of position, climate, and natural products, Skewys begins his narrative with Brutus and the Trojans and ends at the death of Edward III. There is no attempt at originality; up to 1066 he is heavily dependent on John Hardyng, and then abruptly switches his allegiance to Matthew Paris. Thomas Fuller claims to have some 'presumptions to conclude him inclined to the Protestant Reformation', but does not elaborate (Fuller, *Worthies*, 1.317). There are numerous marginal notes drawing attention to the corruption and avarice of the papacy—'at Rome mony makyth all' (fol. 171)—but none that suggest doctrinal protestantism; a story derived from Bede draws the comment 'nota the vertue of the masse' (fol. 86), while Thomas Becket is 'Sent Thomas' throughout, becoming 'This holy martir' at his death (fols. 157*v*–158). The malice and untrustworthiness of the French are attacked at least as often as the Roman church. His 'brevyat' suggests that Skewys was a religious conservative who had accepted the royal supremacy.

Skewys's wife was dead by 3 August 1537, and he died on 16 May 1544, his will having been drawn up in St Sepulchre's parish, London. He was probably in London to prosecute an action for debt against his fellow Cornishman William Trewynnard; the latter was an MP, and the case had significant implications for parliamentary privilege. His male heir was his cousin Lawrence Courtenay, although some property including the Cornish manor of Polrode passed to Anne Hollys and Alice Reskymer, daughters of his nephew John Denysell, sergeant-at-law. Deeds relating to a dispute between the Skewys and Reskymer families in 1543 are preserved in BL, Additional Charters 64516–64527.

PETER SHERLOCK

Sources J. Maclean, *The parochial and family history of the deanery of Trigg Minor in the county of Cornwall*, 3 (1879), 333–4, 385–7 · Wood, *Ath. Oxon.*, new edn, 1.58–9 · *LP Henry VIII*, vols. 1–20 · Bale, *Index*, 255–6 · BL, Harley MS 2258 · BL, Lansdowne MS 207(F) · Emden, *Oxf.*, 4.517 · Fuller, *Worthies* (1840) · N. H. Nicolas, ed., *Testamenta vetusta: being illustrations from wills*, 2 vols. (1826) · HoP, *Commons, 1509–58*, 3.485–6

Skey, Frederic Carpenter (1798–1872), surgeon, second of six children of George Skey, a Russia merchant in London, and his wife, was born at Upton-on-Severn, Worcestershire, on 1 December 1798. He was educated chiefly at the private school at Normanston in Suffolk of Michael Maurice, father of Frederick Denison Maurice, whose friendship he retained until his death. After a short stay at Plymouth with his cousin, Dr Joseph Skey, then inspectorgeneral of army hospitals, Skey commenced his medical education at Edinburgh University, where he spent two years, followed by a few months in Paris. On 15 April 1816 he was apprenticed to John Abernethy, surgeon at St Bartholomew's Hospital in London, paying the usual premium of 500 guineas. After studying at the hospital he was admitted as a member of the Royal College of Surgeons, London, on 5 April 1822. Abernethy had so high an opinion of his pupil's capacities, that even while he was still an apprentice, Skey was entrusted with the care of some of his master's private patients.

Thanks to Abernethy's help Skey was appointed demonstrator of anatomy at St Bartholomew's about 1826. He resigned the office after Abernethy's death in 1831, following a dispute with William Lawrence, but retained the post of assistant surgeon, to which he was appointed on 29 August 1827, the same year that he became consulting surgeon at Charterhouse. The direct outcome of Skey's resignation of his teaching post was the revival of the Aldersgate Street school of medicine, which in the hands of James Hope, Robert Todd, Marshall Hall, Jonathan Pereira, and Francis(?) Kiernan, soon became famous as a private teaching establishment. For ten years Skey taught surgery at the Aldersgate Street school, which for some time competed with the neighbouring medical school of St Bartholomew's Hospital. Skey also maintained a growing private practice at 13 Grosvenor Street in central London, attracting an influential clientele.

Skey was elected a fellow of the Royal Society in 1837, the same year in which the society published his paper on muscular fibre. He was appointed anatomy lecturer at St Bartholomew's Hospital medical school in 1843, and held this post until 1865. He became full surgeon at the hospital in May 1854 and relinquished the position on 18 January 1864 having reached the official retirement age of sixty-five. He was then elected consulting surgeon, and was presented with a handsome testimonial.

Skey filled many important positions at the Royal College of Surgeons. Elected an honorary fellow in 1843 and a member of the council in 1848, he was appointed Hunterian orator in 1850, and in 1852 was made professor of human anatomy and surgery. He was elected a member of the court of examiners in 1855, and in 1863 became president. In 1859 Skey served as president of the Royal Medical and Chirurgical Society, and in 1864, at the instigation of his friend and patient Benjamin Disraeli, was appointed chairman of the first parliamentary committee at the Admiralty to inquire into the best way of treating venereal disease in the army and navy. He was created CB in 1868 for his services in this capacity, and the direct outcome of the committee's report was the framing of the Contagious Diseases Act of 1866.

Skey was a man of genial disposition and great intelligence, and he was known to be fond of animals. He was a good writer, a clear lecturer, and an excellent teacher who concerned himself with the broad principles of his subject rather than with details. An able surgeon, especially when treating exceptional cases, he was extremely skilful in diagnosis and most resourceful when unusual difficulties arose.

Skey published a number of books, wrote several pamphlets, was a frequent contributor to the periodical press, and wrote letters to *The Times* on alcoholic diseases and on the harmful physical effects of rowing, especially those caused by the pace of the university boat race. His works include: *On a New Mode of Treatment in the Cure of Various Forms of Ulcer and Granulating Wounds* (1837), which was followed by *A Practical Treatise on the Venereal Disease* (1840), based on six lectures given at the Aldersgate Street school of medicine. Willing to use innovative methods in surgery, Skey wrote *On a New Operation for the Cure of Lateral Curvature of the Spine* (1841); and his *Operative Surgery* (1850), which was of considerable merit and became a standard student text, explained his opposition to the use of the knife except as a last resort. *Hysteria* (1867) consisted of a series of lectures in which the advantages of the 'tonic' plan of treatment were extolled; it reached three editions.

Skey was married and had four sons and two daughters. His wife, Sarah Sophia (b. 1809/10), pre-deceased him, as did one son. Skey's own health failed during the last two or three years of his life, and after suffering great pain from intestinal ulceration he died at his home at 24 Mount Street, Grosvenor Square, London, on 15 August 1872. He was buried at Kensal Green cemetery on 19 August.

D'A. POWER, *rev.* CHRISTOPHER F. LINDSEY

Sources BMJ (7 Sept 1872), 282–3 · *The Lancet* (24 Aug 1872) · *Medical Times and Gazette* (24 Aug 1872), 211–13 · *The Times* (16 Aug 1872) · *St Bartholomew's Hospital Reports*, 9 (1873), xxi–xxxix · F. C. Skey, 'Athletics', *The Times* (10 Oct 1867) · F. C. Skey, 'Athletics', *The Times* (26 Oct 1867) · V. G. Plarr, *Plarr's Lives of the fellows of the Royal College of Surgeons of England*, rev. D'A. Power, 2 vols. (1930) · *Medical Directory* · 'Select committee on the Contagious Diseases Act', *Parl. papers* (1868–9), 7.1, no. 306; 7.143, no. 306-I · census returns for London, 1861, 1871 · *London Gazette index*, 2 (1868) · DNB
Likenesses T. H. Maguire, lithograph, 1850, RCS Eng., Wellcome L. · Barraud & Jerrard, photograph, Wellcome L.
Wealth at death under £2000: probate, 19 Sept 1872, CGPLA Eng. & Wales

Skeyne [Skene], **Gilbert** (c.1522–1599), physician, born at Bandodle, Aberdeenshire, was the fifth son of James Skeyne or Skene (d. 1547), and his wife, Janet Lumsden. The father practised as a notary public at the farm of Bandodle on the Skene estate, near Aberdeen. Sir John *Skene of Curriehill (c.1540–1617), jurist, was his younger brother Gilbert was educated at Aberdeen grammar school and at King's College, Aberdeen, where he graduated MA. He then studied medicine, graduated MD, and was appointed mediciner or professor of medicine in King's College in 1556. In 1568 he became one of the ordinary regents of the college. Skeyne married Agnes Lawson, widow of John Uddart, in 1569. It was not a happy marriage. Skeyne was collated to the burse of medicine in King's College in 1571. He moved to Edinburgh in 1575 and bought a house in Niddrie Wynd, where he developed a successful practice. On 16 June 1581 he was appointed doctor of medicine to James VI, with a salary of £200.

Skeyne wrote *Ane breve descriptioun of the pest quhair in the causis, signis, and sum speciall preseruatioun and cure thairof ar contenit* (1568). While not dismissing the power of prayer and the need for the repentance of sins, Skeyne considered that the disease arose from 'stench and corruption and filth' (Hamilton, 14). This was the earliest medical work to appear in the vernacular in Scotland. It was reprinted, under the editorship of William Forbes Skene, for the Bannatyne Club (1860). The reprint includes *Ane breif descriptioun of the qualiteis and effectis of the well of the Woman Hill besyde Abirdene* (1580), published anonymously, but now thought to be the work of Skeyne. In it he discusses the healing powers of the well's waters.

Skeyne retired from practice in 1593, and died in 1599, leaving neither children nor a will. His widow engaged in a long legal battle with his family over the estate, which was eventually divided among several nephews and nieces.   THOMPSON COOPER, *rev.* SARAH BAKEWELL

Sources W. F. Skene, 'Notice of Dr Gilbert Skeyne', in *Tracts by Doctor Gilbert Skeyne, medicinar to his majesty*, ed. W. F. Skene (1860), i–xi · H. D. Traill and J. S. Mann, eds., *Social England*, 6 vols. (1901–4), 3.150 · W. F. Skene, ed., *Memorials of the family of Skene of Skene*, New Spalding Club, 1 (1887) · R. Dickson and J. P. Edmond, *Annals of Scottish printing from the introduction of the art in 1507 to the beginning of the seventeenth century* (1890) · J. D. Courie, *History of Scottish medicine*, 2 vols. (1932) · D. Hamilton, *The healers: a history of medicine in Scotland* (1981)
Wealth at death estate was source of long legal dispute between Skeyne's widow and other members of family

Skimmington. *See* Williams, John (fl. 1631–1637).

Skinner, Cortlandt (1727–1799), politician and army officer in America, was born on 16 December 1727 at Perth Amboy, Middlesex county, New Jersey; he was the eldest son of the Revd William Skinner (1687–1758), Scottish-born clergyman in the Church of England, and Elizabeth Van Cortlandt (1694–1763), heir to 8900 acres in New York. On 30 November 1751 he married Elizabeth Kearny (1731–1810), daughter of a New Jersey assemblyman who was acclaimed that colony's foremost lawyer; they raised twelve children to adulthood, one of whom, Maria, was a noted diarist [*see* Nugent, Maria].

Skinner received a classical education from his father, a renowned tutor; by 1776 his library held 482 volumes. He mastered the law at Newark while clerking for David Ogden, a member of the governor's council, and then began practising at Perth Amboy. He became attorney-general aged just twenty-seven, presumably through Ogden's patronage.

Perth Amboy elected Skinner to the New Jersey assembly in 1763. Possessing gifted oratorical talent he gained such respect that he was unanimously chosen speaker two years later. He was the second youngest man to have assumed that position, which he would keep until 1776. The assembly tapped Skinner to replace a speaker who had wavered in his opposition to parliament's first inland revenue upon the American colonies, the Stamp Act. Skinner detested the Stamp Act and presided over the session that condemned it as having 'Endanger'd both their Liberty and Property' (Purvis, 244) but his perspective was essentially pragmatic. He dismissed the idea that George Grenville's ministry threatened American self-government but he firmly believed that parliamentary taxation and Whitehall's efforts to extend royal prerogatives were ill-conceived and counter-productive. He believed that these measures could only engender political discontent among the colonists and carried enormous risk of Britain's 'alienating a people which she might make her greatest prop and security' (Whitehead, 103) by sowing fear that their rights as Englishmen were menaced. He asserted that Britain's greatest advantage lay in encouraging growth and prosperity for the colonies, the largest market for British manufactured goods, because 'the wealth flowing from trade will be more for the Interest of Britain than all the taxes that can be imposed on the colonies' (ibid.).

A strong sense of British patriotism also gripped Skinner, who took pride in his family's military services against the French. His aunt married Admiral Sir Peter Warren, who commanded Britain's naval forces at Louisbourg's capture in 1745. One of his three brothers died a lieutenant-colonel in the royal army and another retired a major.

The governor of New Jersey, William Franklin, strengthened Skinner's sense of obligation to Britain by defending his brother, provincial treasurer Stephen Skinner, when the Skinners' political rivals demanded Stephen's resignation in 1768 after burglars stole £6000 in public funds from his home. The governor appointed Stephen a councillor in 1769 and helped to stave off his resignation until 1774. Franklin left the Skinners profoundly indebted to royal officialdom.

Skinner was offered any civil or military post at the disposal of New Jersey's patriots in August 1775, and they considered his refusal a major setback. Although he still publicly opposed parliamentary taxation he privately believed that the North ministry's ineptitude had allowed incipient discontent to ripen into widespread, armed resistance. After the interception of a letter revealing his contempt for the continental congress he fled to avoid arrest in January 1776.

Skinner was one of just three speakers of colonial assemblies, sitting or former, who actively opposed American independence. Appointed brigadier-general in the British army on 4 September 1776 he recruited the largest of the loyalist units. His 2000 New Jersey volunteers mercilessly harassed their American patriot enemies from New York's defensive outposts on Staten Island throughout 1783. Only three other Americans attained a rank equivalent to Skinner's in the loyalist American corps.

The American patriots confiscated Skinner's estates, worth £10,382, for which parliament authorized compensation of £5169 plus a £500 pension. After the war he brought his family to England and retired in Bristol on his annuity. There he died on 15 March 1799 and was buried at St Augustine's Church.　　　　　　THOMAS L. PURVIS

Sources W. A. Whitehead, *Contributions to the early history of Perth Amboy and adjoining country* (1856) • E. A. Jones, *The loyalists of New Jersey: their memorials, petitions, claims, etc.* (1927) • T. L. Purvis, *Proprietors, patronage, and paper money: legislative politics in New Jersey, 1703–1776* (1986) • W. N. Jones, *The history of St Peter's Church in Perth Amboy, New Jersey* (1924)
Archives New Jersey Archives, Trenton, New Jersey, journals of the New Jersey assembly • PRO, Audit Office papers, claims to be compensated for property seized by revolutionaries, AO 12/109 • PRO, Audit Office papers, pension papers, AO 13/79; 13/111 • Rutgers University, New Brunswick, New Jersey, Gage family papers, corresp. [microfilm]
Likenesses oils, New Jersey Historical Society, Newark
Wealth at death approx. £5169 (compensation from parliament for losses incurred during revolution): will, PRO, PROB 11/1323

Skinner, James (1778–1841), army officer, born in Bengal, was the son of Hercules Skinner (*b. c.*1735), son of David Skinner, provost of Montrose from 1733 to 1743. Hercules Skinner was a Scot in the East India Company's military service, who became a lieutenant-colonel in 1800 and died at Buragaon, Bengal, on 12 July 1803. When an ensign, he had taken Jeany, the daughter of a Rajput *zamindar*, as a mistress, and they had six children, one of whom was James. She committed suicide in 1790 when her daughters were taken from her, out of purdah, and sent to a school for children of Indian and European parentage.

James and his younger brother Robert (*d.* 1821) were sent first to a charity school, then in 1794 to a Calcutta boarding-school; and in 1796 James was apprenticed to a printer there, but at once ran away. His godfather, Captain W. Burn, introduced him to De Boigne, the French general who was in the service of Sindhia, the Maratha chieftain, and Sindhia gave him a commission in his army. Skinner did not join the British forces because of a rule barring anyone whose mother was Indian from holding commissioned rank. During the next ten years he took part in various expeditions and forays, in which M. Perron, De Boigne's successor, was perpetually engaged, including the capture of Delhi in May 1798, and the storming of Hansi, the stronghold of George Thomas the Irish adventurer, in 1799. When the Marathas were defeated by General Gerard (afterwards Viscount) Lake in 1803, some of the sons of British officers and Indian mothers who had served the Marathas were imprisoned by the British, but

James Skinner (1778–1841), by unknown artist

British officials, he was a great patron of artists, employing them to paint portraits of his family and friends. At his parties he often gave pictures to his guests of the dancing girls that had entertained them. He also had pictures painted of the Yellow Boys, and of the many groups connected to Indian armies at the time; these valuable historical records are now in the oriental and India Office collection of the British Library.

The headquarters of Skinner's corps were at Hansi, and there, following attacks of fever, he died on 4 December 1841, and was buried with military honours, his remains being taken to Delhi two months afterwards and deposited in his own church. He is said to have had sixteen wives and mistresses, and left five sons: Joseph (1796?–1855?); James (1805–1862), a colonel in the Indian army; Hercules (1813–1852), major in the Indian army; Thomas (d. 1864); and Alexander (1825–1885). On the death of his youngest son, Alexander Skinner, who had managed the estate for some years, it was divided among Skinner's surviving descendants.

STEPHEN WHEELER, rev. AINSLIE T. EMBREE

Sources J. B. Fraser, *Military memoir of Lieut. Col. James Skinner*, 2 vols. (1851) · D. Holman, *Sikander Sahib* (1961) · *District Gazetteers: Kurnaul and Hissar* · P. Mason, 'A meditation on the life of Colonel James Skinner', *Delhi through the ages*, ed. R. E. Frykenberg (1986) · M. Archer, 'Artist and patrons in "residency" Delhi', *Delhi through the ages*, ed. R. E. Frykenberg (1986)

Archives NAM, memoirs · NRA Scotland, priv. coll., autobiography

Likenesses G. Ali Khan, drawing, c.1827–1828 (*Returning from the review*), NAM · G. Ali Khan, group portrait, watercolour, c.1827–1828, NAM · attrib. W. Melville, oils, St James's Church, Delhi · drawing; Christies, 5 June 1996, lot 25 [*see illus.*] · portrait, BL OIOC

Skinner was offered the command, without a commission, of a body of horsemen who had deserted the Marathas. He accepted with the understanding, it is said, that he would not have to fight his old employer, Sindhia. At the head of his irregular cavalry—known as the Yellow Boys from their uniforms and soon to be famous as Skinner's Horse, a designation inherited by the 1st Bengal cavalry—he distinguished himself in the campaign against Holkar (1805) and in the Pindari war (1817–19). In 1825 he was present with his cavalry at the storming of Bharatpur. The Indian government rewarded him by grants of land at Hansi in the newly acquired territory, and, having purchased other properties, including a large house in Delhi, he became master of a large estate. He spent much on irrigation works, was well spoken of by government officials as a good landlord, and was respected by his tenants. Successive governors-general, from the Marquess Wellesley to the earl of Auckland, spoke of him in the highest terms; in recognition of his military services he was given the rank of lieutenant-colonel in the army, and created a CB (1828). In one of his early campaigns with the Marathas, when wounded and hard pressed by the enemy, he had vowed, if his life were spared, to build a Christian church. So he built, at a cost of £20,000, the church of St James at Delhi. The building was consecrated by Bishop Daniel Wilson of Calcutta on 22 November 1836, and Skinner and his three sons were confirmed there on the same day.

Skinner lived in princely style, and his entertainments were lavish. Like Indian rulers, and some of the early

Skinner, James (1818–1881), Church of England clergyman and religious writer, was born at Forfar, Scotland, on 23 June 1818, the youngest son of John *Skinner (1769–1841) [*see under* Skinner, John (1744–1816)], dean of Dunkeld and Dunblane in the Scottish Episcopal church, and his wife, Elizabeth, daughter of Provost Ure of Forfar. His grandfather was John *Skinner (1744–1816), bishop of Aberdeen. In 1832 Skinner entered Marischal College, Aberdeen, and in the following year, when Durham University was first opened, he was admitted as a foundation scholar. He graduated BA in 1836 and MA in 1840, and was a fellow from 1844 to 1849. From 1839 to 1841 he was a master at King William's College, Isle of Man, where he soon gained a reputation as 'a violent Oxford Tract party man'.

Ordained deacon on 27 June 1841 and priest in the year following, Skinner was successively curate of Burton Agnes in Yorkshire and of Holy Trinity, Windsor (during 1844); chaplain of the district military prison at Southsea Castle (from July 1845); and curate of St Mary's, Reading, from 1846. On 18 July 1848 he married Agnes, daughter of Oliver Raymond, vicar of Middleton, Essex. They had a daughter, Agnes Raymond, who died in 1868.

As his health was deteriorating, Skinner accepted the post of chaplain to the forces in Corfu, but in 1850 he returned to England. In 1851 he was appointed senior curate of St Barnabas, Pimlico, London, by its vicar, Robert Liddell. Since November 1850 this new church with its then advanced ceremonial practices had been notorious as the target of persistent riots, occasioned by the popular outcry against Tractarians as a result of the 'papal aggression' crisis. As a consequence the church's founding vicar, W. J. E. Bennett, had been forced to resign. Skinner, with the help of Liddell and support from his junior curate, Charles Lowder, persisted with these controversial practices, defending them at length in his sermon *Why do we Prize Externals in the Service of God?* (1856) and in the law courts. However, in 1856 failing health forced him to resign.

After an interval in which he was engaged with the organization of the English Church Union, in 1861 Skinner accepted the living of the tiny parish of Newland, near Great Malvern, Worcestershire, and the wardenship of the almshouses for retired agricultural labourers situated there. He quickly increased the frequency with which holy communion was celebrated, built a new parish church in 1864, and steadily developed Newland as a spiritual centre attracting clergy and laity from all over the country for retreats or spiritual and pastoral advice. At this time he also published a number of important works, including *The Daily Service Hymnal* (1864) and *A Plea for the Threatened Ritual of the Church of England* (1865) in support of the new generation of ritualists. In 1877 poor health once again obliged him to move, this time to Ascot, where his final years were spent assisting Pusey. He died at Bath on 29 December 1881, and was buried in the churchyard at Newland; his wife survived him.   GEORGE HERRING

Sources M. Trench, *James Skinner: a memoir* (1883) · L. E. Ellsworth, *Charles Lowder and the ritualist movement* (1982) · *The Guardian* (11 Jan 1882) · *CGPLA Eng. & Wales* (1882)
Wealth at death £7431 7s. 5d.: probate, 9 March 1882, *CGPLA Eng. & Wales*

Skinner, James Scott (1843–1927), violinist and composer, was born in Banchory-Ternan, Aberdeenshire, on 5 August 1843, the younger son of William (Dancie) Skinner (d. 1845), a violinist and dancing teacher, and his wife, Mary, *née* Agnew. He was taught the violin and cello by his brother Alexander and by his godfather, 'Professor' William Scott, whose name he took when he was nineteen, and he learned strathspey playing from Peter Milne (1824–1908). For six years from 1855 he was a member of a touring band of boy players, Dr Mark's Little Men, based in Manchester, during which time he was taught by the French violinist Charles Rougier of the Hallé Orchestra. He won first prize for the sword dance in Ireland in 1862 and for the strathspey and reel in Inverness in 1863. He quickly became known as a dancing-master and solo violinist, especially in north-east Scotland, where he lived with his first wife, Jane, *née* Stuart (d. 1883). In 1893 and 1903 he toured North America with success. He settled in the Dundee area with his second wife, Dr Gertrude Park. Though a highly paid performer, he did not save, and was

granted a civil-list pension. In 1922 he moved to 25 Victoria Street, Aberdeen, where, after an exhausting American visit in 1926, he died on 17 March 1927; he was buried in Allenvale cemetery, Aberdeen.

Skinner composed more than 700 tunes, mostly for the violin, and especially slow strathspeys (he became known as the Strathspey King); his most famous were the march 'The Bonnie Lass o' Bon Accord' (written to pay a bill and inspired by a girl named Wilhelmina Bell) and the slow air 'The Cradle Song', and his best the strathspeys 'Tulchan Lodge', 'The Laird o' Drumblair', and 'The Miller o' Hirn'. His excellent technique led to more complex tunes, and higher performing standards, as did his *A Guide to Bowing* (1900, new edn 1984). He specialized in what he called 'the straight slur', highly influential in Scottish fiddle playing. His many self-financed editions—particularly *The Miller o' Hirn* (1881), *The Elgin Collection* (1884), *The Logie Collection* (1888), *The Scottish Violinist* (1900), and *The Harp and Claymore* (1904)—ensured that many of his tunes became standard, and his prolific recordings captured his assured and florid style. The continental influences evident in his playing contributed to the corruption of authentic Scottish fiddle playing.   H. C. G. MATTHEW

Sources *Aberdeen Press and Journal* (18 March 1927) · *Aberdeen Press and Journal* (21 March 1927) · J. M. Henderson, 'The Strathspey King', *Scots Magazine*, 40 (1943–4), 23, 28 · A. T. McRobert, 'James Scott Skinner', *Scottish Notes and Queries*, 3rd ser., 13 (1935), 83 · M. A. Alburger, *Scottish fiddlers and their music* (1983) · A. J. Hardie, disc notes, *J. Scott Skinner: the Strathspey King* (Topic records, 12T280, 1975) · *New Grove*
Archives Angus Local Studies Centre, Montrose, music MSS
Likenesses D. Waterson, oils, 1912, Scot. NPG · J. Y. Hunter, oils, 1917, Dundee Art Gallery · photographs, repro. in Hardie, *J. Scott Skinner* · photographs, repro. in Henderson, 'The Strathspey King', *Scots Magazine*, 22
Wealth at death £373 19s. 11d.: confirmation, 1928, Scotland

Skinner, John (1721–1807), songwriter and ecclesiastical historian, was born on 3 October 1721 at Balfour in Birse, Aberdeenshire, the only child of John Skinner (c.1696–1776), parochial schoolmaster of Birse, and his wife, Jean Gillanders (d. c.1723), widow of Donald Farquharson of Balfour. He received his early education at the parish school of Echt, to which his father had transferred c.1724, and from 1734 at Marischal College, Aberdeen, graduating AM in 1737. From c.1735 or 1736 to 1740 he worked as assistant teacher at Monymusk, Aberdeenshire, where some of his early poetry was written. About this time he left the Presbyterian for the Scottish Episcopal church. Through the influence of Bishop Robert Forbes (c.1708–1775) he became in 1740 tutor in the family of Robert Sinclair of Scalloway in Shetland. It was here that he met and on 12 November 1741 married Grissel Hunter (c.1719–1799), eldest daughter of the Revd John Hunter, the Scottish Episcopal minister of Shetland. They had three sons and three daughters. Skinner was ordained on 15 August 1742 and appointed to the important charge of Longside, near Peterhead, where he was to minister for the following sixty-four years.

Skinner was not a Jacobite (unlike most of his colleagues), but he incurred the enmity of the fiercely Presbyterian Elizabeth Fergusson, Lady Kinmundy, whose house had been plundered during the rising of 1745, and who returned the compliment by having the Episcopalian chapel burned by government forces in July 1746, Skinner having to take to the heather while she rode round his blazing chapel yelling: 'Haud in the prayer books!' To the scandal of his brethren Skinner tried to avail himself of the Toleration Act of 1746 which meant praying for King George by name and taking the oaths of allegiance and abjuration. He was forced to recant and seek absolution. This, in turn, made him liable to the Penal Act of 1748, which invalidated his orders, and disbarred him from conducting anything but family worship under pain of imprisonment and transportation. In 1753 he was sentenced to six months in gaol at Old Aberdeen for defying its provisions, on information lodged by Lady Kinmundy whom he had in the meantime lampooned as a shrine-destroying Jezebel. As he had also satirized the procurator-fiscal he could expect little mercy from the court.

During the 1750s and 1760s Skinner's influence steadily grew, thanks to his learning and ability and a number of published works, chiefly of ecclesiastical controversy, but including a Hutchinsonian essay on Messianic prophecy. In 1765 he was instrumental in overturning the election of the Jacobite bishop Robert Forbes to the diocese of Aberdeen and having a politically safer candidate installed in his place. Resisting pressure to accept the office himself, he saw his son John become coadjutor bishop in 1782. One of their first acts was to arrange for the consecration of Samuel Seabury as bishop of Connecticut in 1784, a necessary step since Seabury could not take the oaths of allegiance to the British crown. This ensured that the Scottish liturgy was used in America, and that episcopal succession came down through the Scottish rather than the English line. The younger John *Skinner became bishop of Aberdeen in his own right in 1786 and in 1788 primus. Skinner himself was made dean of Aberdeen probably in 1789. Since the main strength of Scottish Episcopalianism lay in the north-east, this left the Skinners effectively masters of the church, and the long struggle between those who continued to owe allegiance to the exiled Stuarts, and those who felt that some accommodation with the Hanoverian state must be reached, was at last resolved. There followed a declaration of severance from the Stuart cause in 1788 upon the death of Charles Edward Stuart and a bill granting relief from the penal statutes in 1792.

Skinner's main fame is as a writer. His polemical and theological works are now forgotten, but he acted as adviser to Dr George Gleig when the latter was editing the *Encyclopaedia Britannica*, and his two-volume *Ecclesiastical History of Scotland* (1788) remains one of the most vigorous and trenchant accounts of its subject, although from a strongly Episcopalian point of view. He was a fluent and nimble verse-maker in Latin, English, and Scots, pioneering the literary use of north-east Scots in poems such as 'The Monymusk Christmas Ba'ing'. Robert Burns greatly admired his work and the two corresponded, Skinner supplying material for *The Scots Musical Museum*. Burns praised 'The Ewie wi' the Crookit Horn' (a comically ambiguous piece which may be understood either in a purely pastoral sense, or as a panegyric to an illicit still) and 'Tullochgorum' which he declared 'the best Scotch song ever Scotland saw' (Walker, 149):

> Come, gie's a sang, Montgomery cried,
> And lay your disputes all aside,
> What signifies't for folks to chide
> For what was done before them:
> Let Whig and Tory all agree,
> Whig and Tory, Whig and Tory,
> Whig and Tory all agree,
> To drop their whig-mig-morum:
> Let Whig and Tory all agree,
> To spend the night wi' mirth and glee,
> And cheerfu' sing alang wi' me
> The Reel o' Tullochgorum.
> (*Amusements*, pp. 55–6)

Skinner was a genial, gregarious, and witty man and greatly loved. He died in Aberdeen at the house of his son, the bishop, on 16 June 1807 and was buried in the churchyard of Longside, where a monument was erected to his memory. WILLIAM DONALDSON

Sources W. Walker, *The life and times of the Rev. John Skinner* (1883) • J. Skinner, *Amusements of leisure hours, or, Poetical pieces, chiefly in the Scottish dialect* (1809) • *Theological works of the late Rev. John Skinner*, 2 vols. (1809) • Chambers, *Scots.* (1835) • W. Stephen, *History of the Scottish church*, 2 vols. (1894–6) • *Journals of the episcopal visitations of the Right Rev. Robert Forbes*, ed. J. B. Craven (1923) • A. Jervise, *Epitaphs and inscriptions from burial grounds and old buildings in the north-east of Scotland*, 2 vols. (1875–9) • J. B. Pratt, *Buchan*, rev. R. Anderson, 4th edn (1901) • R. Burns and others, *The Scots musical museum*, ed. J. Johnson, 6 vols. (1787–1803)

Archives NL Scot., MS 1022 • U. Aberdeen | NL Scot., Abbotsford collection, MS 877

Likenesses T. Woolnoth, stipple, BM, NPG; repro. in Chambers, *Scots.* • oils, repro. in Walker, *Life and times*

Skinner, John (1744–1816), Scottish Episcopal bishop of Aberdeen, was born at Longside, Aberdeenshire, on 17 May 1744, the son of Dean John *Skinner (1721–1807) of Lishart, Scottish Episcopal clergyman and poet, and his wife, Grissel Hunter (c.1719–1799). The elder Skinner was a victim of the harsh anti-Episcopalian laws introduced after the Jacobite rising of 1745 and young John shared his father's imprisonment in Old Aberdeen in 1753. After an early education at the parish schools of Longside and Echt (under his grandfather), he entered Marischal College, Aberdeen, in 1757, leaving in 1761 to become private tutor to the grandson of Sir Hugh Paterson, bt, of Bannockburn, Stirlingshire, a Jacobite family. Skinner followed his father into the Scottish Episcopal church. Ordained deacon in 1763 and priest in 1764 by Andrew Gerard, bishop of Aberdeen, he was appointed at once to the two charges of Bairnie and Chapelhall in the respective parishes of Ellon and Udny, Aberdeenshire. It was a successful ministry. In summer Skinner held a minimum of two services and a new chapel was constructed for the Udny congregation in

John Skinner (1744–1816), by Charles Turner, pubd 1810 (after Andrew Robertson)

1768. Even so, Episcopalians could not take toleration for granted in George III's reign, and in 1775 the Ellon worshippers were driven from their new chapel by persecution. That same year Skinner was chosen to succeed William Smith in charge of the Episcopal congregation in Aberdeen, the focal point for nonjuring Anglicanism in north-east Scotland. Increased accommodation was soon required for his people; the upper floor of his new dwelling house in Longacre was converted into a chapel, holding over 500 people. On 25 September 1782 Skinner was consecrated in the chapel of Luthermuir, Kincardineshire, as coadjutor to Robert Kilgour, bishop of Aberdeen.

The young prelate quickly established himself as a force in the Scottish nonjuring church. Skinner's consecration coincided with the end of the American War of Independence, and the revival of plans for the appointment of a bishop to minister to Anglicans in the new United States. The plan of George Berkeley for the dispatch of a Scottish missionary bishop was dropped in favour of an American candidate, Samuel Seabury from Connecticut. Seabury's inconclusive negotiations with the English hierarchy persuaded him to approach Bishop Kilgour in August 1784. Assured by Berkeley that the archbishop of Canterbury privately had no objection to the proposed consecration, Skinner encouraged Kilgour to make a positive response in order to place the Church of England under an obligation to the Scots and give Episcopalians a renewed national prominence. Seabury was duly consecrated in the upper room of the house at Longacre on 14 November, with Skinner among the participating bishops and causing some consternation with a sermon which contrasted

the 'acts of the apostles' with 'acts of the British parliament'. On 15 November the Scottish bishops, with Seabury, met in synod, and drew up eight articles of a 'concordate' or bond of union between 'the catholic remainder of the ancient church of Scotland and the now rising church in Connecticut'. The fifth article recommended to America the use of the Scottish communion office in preference to the service in the Book of Common Prayer.

On Kilgour's resignation of the see (October 1786), Skinner was appointed bishop of Aberdeen; he was subsequently elected primus in December 1788, on Kilgour's resignation of that office. Not a Jacobite himself, Skinner was anxious to show his church's loyalty to the Hanoverian dynasty at the first opportunity and to achieve its political rehabilitation. He presided at a convocation of bishops, senior clergy, and laity at Aberdeen on 26 April 1788, when it was unanimously resolved that, in consequence of the death of Prince Charles Edward (31 January), the Scottish Episcopal clergy should, from 25 May, pray for George III as king, using the terms of the Anglican prayer book.

Skinner now bent his efforts to the removal of the penal laws still weighing heavily on his church. In early April 1789 he went to London with two other newly consecrated prelates, William Abernethy Drummond, bishop of Edinburgh, and John Strachan, bishop of Brechin, where they were cordially received by Archbishop Moore. Leading Scottish presbyterian divines, headed by William Robertson, favoured their claims, but Anglican clergy officiating in Scotland resisted the concession. A bill passed the Commons, but was lost in the Lords owing to Lord Chancellor Thurlow's intransigence. After returning to Scotland in July 1789, Skinner tried again. A committee was appointed in London to work for repeal of the penal laws, lobbying was undertaken by high-church sympathizers such as William Stevens, and parliament was petitioned by the royal burghs of Scotland in favour of a second Relief Bill, introduced in early 1792. Its success was ensured by Bishop Samuel Horsley's intervention, who had made the bill more acceptable to the Church of England by inserting a requirement of subscription to the Thirty-Nine Articles from Episcopalian clergy. The bill received the royal assent on 15 June 1792. Under its terms, the laity were left free from all penalties and civil disabilities unless they attended a chapel in which the reigning house was not prayed for; the clergy were bound to take an oath abjuring their past loyalty to the Jacobite cause, but unless ordained by a Church of England bishop they could not officiate south of the border. An Episcopalian meeting at Laurencekirk (22 August) approved Skinner's action and agreed on voluntary adoption of the Thirty-Nine Articles.

Skinner wanted to unite all the Anglican congregations in Scotland into one body. He hoped to effect this by the appointment of Jonathan Boucher, vicar of Epsom and high-church American exile, as bishop of Edinburgh, but the scheme was abandoned, owing to the disquiet of the kirk Episcopal clergy in the city ordained by English bishops, and the denial of open support from within the

English hierarchy. Helped by Skinner's impeccable loyalism during the 1790s, relations between Scottish Anglicans continued to improve and terms of union in six articles were finally proposed on 24 October 1804 at a convocation of the clergy in Laurencekirk. These were gradually accepted (including subscription to the Thirty-Nine Articles), with Skinner relieved that the Scottish communion office of 1764 had been retained.

In his own diocese Skinner was a hard-working prelate. At Aberdeen he built a new chapel in 1795, and laid the foundations of St Andrew's Church in 1816. Diocesan meetings of his clergy were revived from 1784; at first biannual, they were held yearly from 1792. Skinner delivered no fewer than thirty-six Episcopal charges. They *inter alia* gave expression to the Hutchinsonian views he inherited from his father, and which he shared with such friends as Boucher. He was the commanding presence in his church, and he dominated the college of bishops. Excessively so for some, one church member describing him as a 'dictator' (M. Irvine to G. Ogilvie of Auchiries, 23 Oct 1794, Aberdeen University Library, Ogilvie-Forbes of Boyndlie MSS, 2740). But he revised the code of canons of the church at the 1811 general synod and also secured primary authority for the Scottish communion office, fearing that it would fall into disuse if attempts continued 'to assimilate our divine Service in every the minutest article to that of the Church of England' (Aberdeen University Library, MS 3320/6/87, 'Thoughts on the English liturgy', 40). Yet careful Anglicizer that he was, Bishop Skinner also made sure that congregations preferring the English prayer book office could freely use it.

Skinner's leadership of the Scottish Episcopal church did not preclude extensive theological activity. Many of his sermons were published in his lifetime including that preached at Bishop Seabury's consecration, which emphasized that the church drew its authority from Christ through the apostolic succession of its ministry. In 1786 he produced *A Course of Lectures* intended to instruct lay members; the lectures convey Skinner's moderate high-churchmanship and his strong sacramentalism: 'the bread and the cup are made unto us, and do become in power and efficacy, the body and blood of Christ' (p. 133). The primus's concern 'to exact a conformity with the ancient standards of Eucharistic service' (Dowden, *Scottish Communion Office*, 98) endeared him to high Anglicans such as Berkeley, Horsley, and George Horne in England who were warm admirers of the anti-Erastian character of Skinner's church. Skinner defended his church's high regard for apostolicity against his fellow Aberdonian, George Campbell, in *Primitive Truth and Order Vindicated* (1803). He also contributed to the *Anti-Jacobin Review*, but on theological rather than overtly political matters.

Skinner married (between 27 August 1764 and 12 September 1765) Mary (d. 1807), a daughter of the Revd William Robertson. Two of their sons, the eldest, John [*see below*], and William *Skinner (1778–1857), his father's successor in the Aberdeen diocese, survived infancy, along with two daughters. The parents felt the loss of their other children in infancy acutely, and Skinner wrote a touching poetic elegy for his daughter Betty, dated 25 February 1795, speaking of her as:

> Beyond the reach of medicinal cure,
> Beyond the strength of childhood to endure.
> (Aberdeen University Library, MS 3320/6/108)

Mary Skinner died on 4 March 1807. John died of a hernia on 13 July 1816, and was buried on 19 July in the Spital churchyard, Aberdeen. His record of achievement still makes it hard to quarrel with William Walker's claim that Skinner was 'the greatest Bishop of the Scottish post-revolution episcopal church' (Walker, 253).

John Skinner (1769–1841), Scottish Episcopal clergyman, was born on 20 August 1769, educated at Marischal College, Aberdeen, and ordained in 1790. After serving as Episcopal clergyman at Banff he was rector of Forfar for forty-five years and became dean of Dunkeld and Dunblane. Skinner contributed to the *Anti-Jacobin* in the 1790s. He was a supporter of allowing laymen to assume greater importance in running the church. His *Annals of Scottish Episcopacy, from the Year 1788 to the Year 1816* (1818) includes a memoir of his father. He married Elizabeth, daughter of Provost Ure of Forfar, with whom he had a son, James *Skinner (1818–1881). Skinner died at Forfar on 2 September 1841.   NIGEL ASTON

Sources W. Walker, *The life and times of John Skinner, bishop of Aberdeen* (1887) · J. Skinner, *Annals of Scottish episcopacy* (1818) [incl. 'Memoir of Bishop John Skinner'] · A. E. Nimmo, 'Bishop John Skinner and the resurgence of Scottish episcopacy', PhD diss., U. Aberdeen, 1996 · *DSCHT* · J. P. Lawson, *History of the Scottish Episcopal church* (1843) · G. Grub, *An ecclesiastical history of Scotland*, 4 vols. (1861), vol. 4, pp. 99, 124–35, 174–89 · M. Lochhead, *Episcopal Scotland in the nineteenth century* (1966) · F. Goldie, *A short history of the Episcopal church in Scotland*, 2nd edn (1976), 66–81 · J. Dowden, *The bishops of Scotland … prior to the Reformation*, ed. J. M. Thomson (1912) · *Fasti academiae Mariscallanae Aberdonensis: selections from the records of the Marischal College and University, MDXCIII–MDCCCLX*, 2, ed. P. J. Anderson, New Spalding Club, 18 (1898), 329 · GEC, *Baronetage*, 4.342 · G. White, 'The consecration of Bishop Seabury', *SHR*, 63 (1984), 37–49 · B. E. Steiner, *Samuel Seabury, 1729–1796: a study in the high church tradition* (1971), 196–217 · F. C. Mather, *High church prophet: Bishop Samuel Horsley (1733–1806) and the Caroline tradition in the later Georgian church* (1992) · F. C. Mather, 'Church, parliament and penal laws: some Anglo-Scottish interactions in the eighteenth century', *EngHR*, 92 (1977), 540–72 · A. Y. Zimmer, *Jonathan Boucher: loyalist in exile* (1978), 256ff. · E. L. de Montluzin, *The anti-Jacobins, 1798–1800: the early contributors to the 'Anti-Jacobin Review'* (1988), 144–6 · J. Dowden, *The annotated Scottish communion office* (1884) · register of baptisms, St John's Church, Longside · *Theological works of the late Rev. John Skinner*, 2 vols. (1809), vol. 1

Archives LPL, corresp. relating to union of English and Scottish Episcopalians [copies] · NA Scot., corresp. and papers; Episcopal church records, CH 12/30/21–117; 12/12 · NRA Scotland, priv. coll. · U. Aberdeen, documents relating to chapel in Long Acre, 1775–1806, MS 3499/14/2 · U. Aberdeen, minute-book containing transactions of committee of an Episcopal congregation in Aberdeen, 1777, MS 3499/14/1 | LPL, Moore MSS, vol. 6 · U. Aberdeen, Episcopal clergy of Ellen & Udney, MS 3220/6/129 [typescript] · U. Aberdeen, Episcopal church records, section 6, vols. 95, 105, 106 · U. Aberdeen, Ogilvie-Forbes of Boyndlie MSS, box 1, bundle 1, MS 2740

Likenesses C. Turner, mezzotint, pubd 1810 (after A. Robertson), BM, Scot. NPG [*see illus.*] · T. Hodgetts, engraving, 1825, vestry of St John the Evangelist's Episcopal church, Aberdeen · Flaxman, memorial, Aberdeen Episcopal cathedral · engraving, repro. in Walker, *Life and times of John Skinner*, 126

Skinner, John (1769–1841). *See under* Skinner, John (1744–1816).

Skinner, John (1772–1839), diarist and antiquary, was born at the Old Hall, Claverton, near Bath, the son of Russell Skinner of Newtown House, Lymington, and Claverton House, near Bath, and his wife, Mary Page. He was educated at Cheam School and at Trinity College, Oxford, which he entered on 16 November 1790, by which time he was already keeping journals of his travels. Skinner graduated BA in 1794 and proceeded MA in 1797; in 1794 he entered Lincoln's Inn, but soon decided to take holy orders. He was ordained deacon in 1797 and served as curate to Richard Graves, rector of Claverton, who interested him in the study of antiquities. In the same year, he made one of his many tours of southern England, exploring Somerset, Devon, and Cornwall; extracts from his journal were published in 1985. In 1799 Skinner was ordained priest, and took up a new curacy at Brent Knoll, Somerset, but in 1800 his uncle purchased for him the living of Camerton, also in Somerset, which he held until his death. On 17 June 1805 he married Anna (*d.* 1812), eldest daughter of Joseph Holmes of Edmonton. They had three daughters and two sons between 1806 and 1811.

Skinner's life at Camerton was soon blighted by a succession of deaths in his family. His eldest brother died in 1810 and his two sisters soon after, followed by his youngest daughter in 1811. In 1812 his beloved wife, Anna, died, the greatest blow of all, and Skinner's anguish was renewed in 1820 by the death of Laura, his eldest daughter.

Skinner found himself increasingly isolated in the midst of his thankless clerical labours. Camerton, a rural parish augmented by a mining community, did not conform to the ideal of an English village, and it provided no intellectual companionship for a man of his scholarly tastes. With the local lady of the manor Skinner was on terms of guarded hostility: he regarded her activities in the parish as meddlesome and was sensitive about her desire to secure the succession of his living for her son-in-law. With local farmers he had periodic feuds over the payment of tithes, one of which culminated in an action for assault being brought against him. Skinner was driven alternately to rage or despair by the church choir, the overseers of the workhouse, teachers at the village school, his own servants, and local miners and publicans. Intolerant of Catholics (except when they were peers), he regarded the local Methodists as canting, illiterate, and hypocritical and was furious when they snatched dying parishioners from the jaws of Anglicanism. As he remarked in July 1821, 'Truly may it be said that Society is out of joint; what with Methodists, Catholics, Colliers, Servants and Attornies, all domestic comfort is estranged' (Skinner, 167).

Nevertheless, Skinner struggled to perform his duties, showing genuine concern for the spiritual condition of his flock. A conventional clergyman of his day, he was overtly paternalistic and often insensitive to his social inferiors. But he was conscientious in his pastoral duties: he visited the sick and dying regularly, organized a village school, and urged his parishioners to attend communion and to bring their children for baptism. Hard-working but humourless, he was, however, as generous with sententious advice as with port wine and money: it is easy to understand why he found many of his humbler parishioners hardened or insolent.

Increasingly, Skinner took refuge in his diaries and his antiquarian researches: 'to me indeed study has been a shield and safeguard against the evils of life' (Skinner, 271). Some of his happiest days were spent in the company of fellow antiquaries such as Sir Richard Colt Hoare of Stourhead and William Lisle Bowles. Although Skinner's archaeological explorations of the Camerton area were significant for later local historians, his deductions were highly speculative. He argued stubbornly that Camerton was the Camulodunum of Tacitus, investing the ugly realities of Camerton life with a touch of historical romance. His obituary in the *Gentleman's Magazine* described his etymological work on Celtic names as 'very wild' (*GM*, 662). Skinner's publications amounted to no more than a few articles on antiquarian subjects, which appeared in *Archaeologia* and the *Gentleman's Magazine*.

Skinner's surviving children afforded him little satisfaction: he frequently quarrelled with his sons, Joseph and Fitz-Owen, who were slow to find themselves careers, and his daughter Anna. After one argument, during which Fitz-Owen resorted to breaking the parlour furniture, Skinner recounted the scene in his journal with 'feelings wounded almost to a pitch of madness' (Skinner, 417). The death of Joseph in 1833 was a further blow to the anxious, affectionate, but demanding father. A decline in Skinner's mental health became increasingly apparent (in 1839 his diary recorded with restrained malice the providential bad ends of his Camerton enemies), and on 12 October 1839 he committed suicide, shooting himself through the head in a wood behind his rectory.

Skinner's will left some 146 volumes of manuscripts, comprising his diaries, tours, and antiquarian notes and essays, to the British Library, with £1000 to fund the publication of his manuscript (never published) 'An analysis of language and symbols of the worship of the sun'. Although his *Dictionary of National Biography* entry presented him solely as an antiquary, Skinner has proved more significant as diarist than as scholar. In 1930 part of his diary dealing with the years 1822–32 was published, and an evocative and sympathetic essay by Virginia Woolf, comparing Skinner and James Woodforde, appeared in *The Common Reader* (1932). A further twenty-five volumes of Skinner's papers were discovered in a London bookseller's in 1933, and in 1971 *The Journal of a Somerset Rector* was republished in an enlarged edition covering the years 1803 to 1834.

Skinner's diaries present a bleak picture of the early nineteenth-century rural English parish, plagued by apathy, immorality, poverty, alcoholism, and dissent. But it is a portrait exaggerated by his own pessimism and inability to empathize with his parishioners, which render his reflections both unintentionally amusing and profoundly moving. Despite his own prickly and suspicious temperament, Skinner emerges as an oddly heroic figure.   ROSEMARY MITCHELL

Sources [J. Skinner], *Journal of a Somerset rector, 1803–1834*, ed. H. Coombs and P. Coombs, rev. edn (1971) · *GM*, 2nd ser., 14 (1840), 661–2 · *DNB*
Archives Bath Central Library, corresp. and papers · BL, corresp., journals, and papers, Add. MSS 28793–28795, 33633–33730, 52417, 52490–52493; Egerton MSS 3099–3123 · Bodl. Oxf., corresp., essays, illustrations, sermons, and verses · Cardiff Central Library, Welsh travel journal · FM Cam., travel diaries relating to Wales, the west country, and Hadrian's Wall · Som. ARS, diaries, travel journals; travel journal of tour mainly of north of England, watercolour drawings of Camerton · Wellcome L., analysis of language | Som. ARS, corresp. with William Stradling and Samuel Hasell
Likenesses J. Skinner, pencil drawing, c.1833, repro. in [J. Skinner], *Journal of a Somerset rector*, ed. H. Coombs and A. N. Bax (1930) · G. Patten, oils · S. C. Smith, oils; known to be at Stourbridge, Worcestershire, in 1897

Skinner, John Edwin Hilary (1839–1894), author and journalist, the elder son of Allen Maclean Skinner QC, and a descendant of Matthew Skinner, was born in London in January 1839, and educated at London University, where he graduated LLD in 1861. In the same year he was called to the bar from Lincoln's Inn, and went on the northern circuit. A first-rate linguist, he obtained a commission from the *Daily News* as special correspondent with the Danish army in the war of 1864. He was present during the campaign until the fall of Alsen at the end of June, whereupon Christian IX awarded him the Dannebrog order. A partial success only can be ascribed to his attempt to unravel the Schleswig-Holstein complication in *The Tale of Danish Heroism* (1865); his opinion as to the superiority of the Prussian breech-loaders, however, was amply vindicated in the following year, when he reported the Austro-Prussian campaign. In the meantime Skinner had visited North America, and on his return wrote two sketchy volumes entitled *After the Storm* (1866). In 1867 he ran the blockade into Crete, and in *Roughing it in Crete* (1867) advocated the cession of Crete to Greece. This, he contended, would not only conciliate liberal opinion, but would concentrate the Turkish power. Nine years later, on this same subject he contributed *Turkish Rule in Crete*, denouncing the 'blighting effect' of Turkish misgovernment, to the Papers on the Eastern Question (9, 1877). During the Franco-Prussian War of 1870, Skinner was attached to the crown prince of Prussia's staff, and described the battles from Wörth to Sedan. He carried his account of the decisive battle from Donchéry, near Sedan, to London, riding neck and neck with W. H. Russell of *The Times*, and crossing from Ostend in the same boat; their narratives appeared simultaneously on 6 September, having been anticipated only in the *Pall Mall Gazette*.

For a short time, in the spring of 1881, Skinner was assistant judicial commissioner in Cyprus. In 1885 he unsuccessfully contested the constituency of South Paddington, standing as a Liberal against Lord Randolph Churchill, and in 1886 he contested the Strand division of London against W. H. Smith, equally unsuccessfully. He died at the Hôtel de France, rue de Constantine, Setif, Algeria, where he had gone for his health, on 20 November 1894; his wife, Louisa Sarah Skinner, survived him. A 'dapper little man', overflowing with vivacity, he was referred to by Archibald Forbes in 1870 as one of the élite of the profession.

                        THOMAS SECCOMBE, *rev.* H. C. G. MATTHEW

Sources *Daily News* (27 Nov 1894) · *The Times* (27 Nov 1894) · Boase, *Mod. Eng. biog.* · *CGPLA Eng. & Wales* (1895)
Wealth at death £4052 1s. 7d.: resworn probate, May 1895, *CGPLA Eng. & Wales*

Skinner, Sir Matthew (1689–1749), serjeant-at-law, was born on 22 October 1689, son of Robert Skinner (1655–1698) of Welton, Northamptonshire, judge of the Marshalsea court, and his wife, Anne, eldest daughter of William Buckby, serjeant-at-law and recorder of Daventry, Northamptonshire. He was the great-grandson of Robert Skinner, bishop of Oxford, sent to the Tower during the civil war. Skinner was educated at Westminster School, where he was a queen's scholar, and matriculated at Christ Church, Oxford, on 18 June 1709. He entered Lincoln's Inn on 20 June 1709, and became a barrister on 21 April 1716, joining the Oxford circuit. In 1719 he married Elizabeth, daughter of Thomas Whitfield of Watford Place, Hertfordshire. They had four sons, only one of whom survived him.

In 1719 Skinner bought the position of one of the four common pleaders of the city of London, thus gaining the right to practise in the lord mayor's court, but he gave this up in 1722 and moved to Oxford, where he had been elected recorder on 30 May 1721, a position he kept until his death. His practice grew rapidly, and he was created serjeant-at-law on 1 February 1724, king's serjeant in 1735, and was first serjeant from 1738. He was knighted in 1735. He served as treasurer of Serjeants' Inn in Chancery Lane, London, from 1737.

Skinner contested Andover unsuccessfully in the parliamentary election in 1727, but was elected MP for Oxford in 1734, with the support of the earl of Abingdon. He sat until 26 November 1738, when he was appointed chief justice of Chester and of the great sessions for the counties of Flint, Denbigh, and Montgomery. He was a counsel for the crown in the trials of the Jacobite rebels on the northern circuit in July 1746, and led for the crown in the trial of the Jacobite Arthur Elphinstone, sixth Baron Balmerino, captured at Culloden, for high treason in the House of Lords later that month.

In 1728 Skinner published his father's *Reports of cases … from the thirty-third year of … Charles the Second, to the ninth year of … William the Third, in the king's bench*. He died in Oxford on 21 October 1749 and was buried in Oxford Cathedral.

                        W. R. WILLIAMS, *rev.* ANNE PIMLOTT BAKER

Sources Baker, *Serjeants*, 537 · W. R. Williams, *The history of the great sessions in Wales, 1542–1830* (privately printed, Brecon, 1899), 46–7 · H. W. Woolrych, *Lives of eminent serjeants-at-law of the English bar*, 2 vols. (1869), 2.520–30 · HoP, *Commons* · Foster, *Alum. Oxon.* · *GM*, 1st ser., 19 (1749), 476

Skinner, Robert (1591–1670), bishop of Worcester, was born on 10 February 1591 and baptized two days later at St Sepulchre, Northampton, the second son of the vicar, Edmund Skinner (c.1554–1628), and his wife, Bridget (d. 1630), daughter of Humphrey Radcliffe of Warwickshire. On 6 August 1594 Edmund was instituted rector of Pitsford, also in Northamptonshire, where he spent the remainder of his ministry and where the younger of his seven sons and four daughters were baptized. Robert attended Brixworth grammar school before matriculating on 11 July 1606 as a scholar from Trinity College, Oxford. He graduated BA in June 1610, became a fellow in 1613, proceeded MA on 25 June 1614, and subsequently acted as vice-president of the college under its energetic president, Ralph Kettell. A younger near contemporary was Gilbert Sheldon, the future archbishop; among his own students were the future traveller Henry Blount, the Commonwealth judge Richard Newdigate, and William Laud's godson William Chillingworth.

Having proceeded BD on 19 April 1621 and been licensed to preach on 14 January 1622, probably about this time, and certainly by 1624, Skinner became lecturer at St Gregory by St Paul's, London. During this period he resigned his fellowship and married Elizabeth (1603–1644), eldest daughter of Bernard Banger (d. 1615), late esquire bedell of divinity at Oxford; their eldest son, Matthew, was baptized at St Benet Paul's Wharf on 11 April 1624. Following the death of his father on 21 May 1628 Skinner was the next day instituted as rector of Pitsford, but this did not signal a move into provincial obscurity. Probably on the recommendation of Laud, recently translated to the see of London, on 8 January 1629 Skinner became a royal chaplain-extraordinary, and on 31 October a chaplain-in-ordinary. On 16 July he wrote to the bishop reporting on a visit to Oxford to attend the annual act in terms revealing of their intimacy and their shared perspective on university and ecclesiastical affairs. Dismissing the degree disputations as 'many Arguments about unnecessary Quaestiones, but not a peece of an Answere to any Argument', his scorn was directed especially at notable Calvinist participants and preachers. While he considered that Mr Williamson allowed an excessive freedom to claim the inspiration of the Holy Spirit in the interpretation of prophecy so dangerously attractive to sectaries that 'I doubt not but weavers & shoemakers will challenge the Spirit as much as any', it was regius professor John Prideaux who drew his heaviest fire. Prideaux 'read of the use which Reason hath in points of Divinity ... very slackly and very tediously, to litle purpose', inventing an enemy in the papists when they were well able to out-argue the Church of England on the point. Later in the proceedings, in criticizing the performance of the up-and-coming young Laudian Thomas Lawrence, Prideaux 'publiquely [professed] himself an Adversary at once of the authority of the Church and of the Demeans thereof'. To Skinner's evident satisfaction Lawrence's performance earned resounding applause; to Skinner's evident delight his glancing tilt at Bishop John Jewel's reputation provoked Prideaux into 'a rage (for I must tell you, it was a meer rage)' and a betrayal of Calvinist feelings of helplessness at the triumph of Laudianism at court (LPL, MS 943, fol. 133).

From 24 January 1631 Skinner was also rector of Launton, Oxfordshire, and thus well placed to continue in the role of informant to Laud on university affairs. His own position is clear from his preaching at Whitehall. Too many 'early green heads ingage themselves in preremptorie opinions, in the parlour, in the pulpitt, in the presse, without preparation or provision beside their own thoughts', he observed in his earliest recorded sermon on 6 December 1631 (BL, Add. MS 20065, fol. 22). His was not just a negative distaste for unregulated controversy, however, but a positive preference for Arminianism. As he put it three weeks later, condemning the 'impious and prodigious errors [that] are crept into the church' in the form of absolute predestination as 'a dangerous position; which at once abolisheth the free grace of God to man, and our due thankfulness to God' while 'we rightly conclude we are elected by grace because we are freely elected' (ibid., fol. 4). 'Seditious opinions, and turbulent positions have beene ever first invented and vented in private', he proclaimed in *A Sermon Preached before the King* (1634). The remedy was public worship undertaken with proper demeanour in a sacred and beautiful place. 'It is not complete worship, without a clear Demonstration of our subjection, without genuflection, or prostration, or some other inclination of the body' (p. 6). The sacraments were to be approached with due reverence, and the very meanings which puritans feared might be read into the prayer book communion service were affirmed as orthodox: 'is it not deepe infidelitie and heresie, to thinke Christ to bee absent from his Body and Blood? Most certainly present he is, though not by his glorious, yet in a singular way, by his gracious presence' (pp. 22–3). The many benefactors who had contributed to the rebuilding fund for St Paul's Cathedral and thus to the removal of 'the abhomination of desolation' (p. 36) from the temple in Israel, earned his approbation; the largest clerical donation to the project came appropriately from Skinner himself.

Promotion was not long in coming. Early in 1636 Skinner resigned Pitsford. In July he was elected bishop of Bristol, on 13 August he was created DD, and on 17 November the king presented him to the rectory of Greens Norton, Northamptonshire. Consecrated bishop on 15 January 1637 he was enthroned by proxy on 13 February. By the previous October he had already made a careful assessment of episcopal revenues, and both his immediate predecessors, George Coke (translated to Hereford) and Robert Wright (now at Coventry and Lichfield), were called to account for missing income and alienated rights. In his letters to Archbishop Laud explaining this and his dealings with Dean Edward Chetwynd and the chapter of Bristol, he was characteristically confident and robust in promoting the endowment of cathedral and diocese. His visitation articles and his speech accompanying the visitation at Dorchester, Dorset, on 18 September 1637, published the same year as *The Speech of Dr Robert Skinner*, echoed his court sermons in their concern not just for peace and conformity but also for fitting ceremonial and consolatory sacrament. Baptism and the eucharist were not 'mere signs' (p. 20); the clergy were to bring their parishioners to confession and 'fit them for Absolution; for Absolution, I say, wherein is the Life and Soul of all the comforts of the Soul' (p. 22); scripture, oath of allegiance, reason, custom, and charity bound observance of kneeling, of the cross in baptism, and of church vestments.

With the calling of convocation in 1640 Skinner emerged as a prominent member of its upper house. He was delegated with Matthew Wren to consult with the lord chief justice over the legal implications of the proposed ecclesiastical canons, and with Wren, Walter Curle, and Joseph Hall to consult with the representatives of the House of Commons over the 'etcetera oath'; before the end of September he had introduced it in his own diocese. In April 1641 he was among members of the Lords who met at the bishop of Lincoln's lodging and condemned the doctrinal content of recent publications. Preaching at court on 1 August a sermon much corrected in the surviving copy, his attention turned to the sight of 'greevous wolves [who had] entered in not sparing the flock, when they cannot but behold ungratious children devouring their owne mother that bear them' (BL, Add. MS 20065, fol. 122). Following a *congé d'élire* of 11 November that year and royal assent on 29 November he was translated to the bishopric of Oxford, also adding nearby Cuddesdon to his livings. Less than three weeks later, on 17 December, he subscribed to the protest of bishops prevented from attendance at the House of Lords and as a result was committed to the Tower, where he spent eighteen weeks before being released on bail.

The nature and extent of Skinner's episcopal ministry over the next two decades is not entirely clear. On 10 June 1642 his daughter Bridget was baptized at Cuddesdon, and it is possible that he spent time in Oxford once the king made the city his headquarters that autumn; his wife died there on 25 June 1644, according to Anthony Wood within a fortnight of her eighteenth confinement. Skinner was sequestered from Greens Norton on 22 July 1643 for his malignancy, and by 13 June 1646 had suffered the same fate at Cuddesdon, although that summer he and his son Thomas put up a fight, allegedly molesting and obstructing his successor. He kept Launton, despite the Lords' attempt to admit T. South on 17 July 1646, and that December he petitioned to compound. A fire at his house had by this time destroyed the parish register there, and with it any record of his previous residence, but Launton seems to have been his base thereafter. With Ralph Brownrigg alone among the bishops to have been granted a licence, he later claimed to Sheldon that 'for preaching I never failed one Sunday for 15 years together' (Skinner, 10). His ordinations of Ralph *Bathurst on 2 March 1644 and of John Martin and others at Trinity College chapel on 21 December 1645 were among the first of many secret ordinations in Oxford and Launton. On his own perhaps

inflated reckoning over the 1640s and 1650s these totalled between four and five hundred 'and not one of them all but subscribed to the Articles, and took the oath of allegiance in those days when, upon discovery, I should have had my books, and my bed taken from me, having little else left me'. He recalled that Thomas Lamplugh, vicar of Charlton-on-Otmoor, 'in those dismall dayes rid not fewer than 300 journeys betwixt Oxford and Launton' to help him with confirmation and ordination (Skinner, 9–10); Bathurst assisted under cover of his medical practice. Skinner also later told Sheldon that where he could he had attempted to control what was heard by congregations:

> I took such care for all Scrip[tures] that were commanded to be read in churches, that constantly every clause that tended to the dishonour of the king or church, was branded aforehand with black lead, and this, by my direction, many did, whom I durst to trust.   (Skinner, 9–10)

Assessment of Skinner's contribution to the survival of prayer book Anglicanism still depends largely on his own claims, but there is some independent evidence that his judgement and authority were recognized at the time. On 4 August 1647 Sheldon, at that point a royal chaplain and perhaps writing at the king's behest, sought Skinner's opinion on 'whether, upon extreme necessity or any exigence of state' a Christian monarch might lawfully tolerate the exercise of more than one religion within his kingdom. Three days later, his experiences doubtless having taught him to temper with pragmatism his previous conformist idealism, Skinner replied that since Charles was indeed standing under 'extreme necessity', such a course was 'not only lawful, but expedient' (Skinner, 7). Characteristically, he added a reminder of a previous request to put before the king his claim to the reversion of the headship of Gloucester Hall, part of the original endowment of the bishopric, but now all the more necessary after his financial misfortunes. However, over the years such apparent acquisitiveness, together with his inexplicable liberty of preaching, convinced Secretary of State Edward Hyde and others that Skinner had not been as energetic in the underground church as he might have been and that his main goal was his future translation to a richer see. Hyde said as much in a letter to John Barwick of 26 September 1659, and his disapprobation was subsequently considered to be the chief obstacle to Skinner's gaining any swift reward for his labours.

Following the Restoration, Skinner regained his livings, and according to White Kennett immediately ordained over a hundred clergy at Westminster Abbey. On 31 July 1660 he was named to a commission of visitors of the University of Oxford, and in concert with others locally began a brisk purge of both university and diocese. Alert as ever to the augmentation of church revenues, this time in relation to Shotover Forest, he also had the foresight to arrange in the summer of 1662 ordinations in anticipation of the vacancies likely to result once the Act of Uniformity came into force on 24 August. Yet he still felt the need to defend his interregnum record in the letter to Sheldon of 17 August, pleading that poverty in the form of debt incurred even before he went to Bristol had tied his hands from doing more. Eventually his deserts or his hints were accepted: on 12 October 1663 he was elected bishop of Worcester, being enthroned by proxy on 20 November.

From Worcester, Skinner retained his close links with Trinity College, of which Bathurst was now president, taking a critical and influential interest in building work and giving generous donations to the library and a new quadrangle. In the mid-1660s he was also in confident form dealing with routine diocesan business and reporting to Sheldon on a dispute over the cathedral organ, but thirty years after he had first become a bishop his age may have been telling. Little evidence survives of his episcopate, and on 28 October 1669 a letter to Secretary of State Joseph Williamson gave erroneous news of his death. Yet when he drew up his will on 2 April 1670 his opinions were as vigorous as ever: he expressed himself 'a true sone of the Church of England' which 'is a true member of the holy Catholique Church'; he had 'ever embraced the liturgie and service of the Church now in use as one of the greatest blessings the heir of Grace ever bestowed upon us of this nation' and implored 'our Lord Jesus Christ lover and author of peace to move all animosities and wilfull opposicons against that most excellent peece of divine service' (PRO, PROB 11/333, sig. 94). On 7 June, Thomas Lamplugh, having commented favourably to Williamson on the loyalty of Worcester itself, where the mayor was 'active and courageous in suppressing conventicles and seditious meetings', wrote that the bishop was 'ill with an issue, but may linger some time, as nature is strong' (CSP dom., 1670, 259). Seven days later Skinner died, and was buried in his cathedral. He left four sons and four married daughters.   VIVIENNE LARMINIE

Sources A. M. Skinner, *A few memorials of the Right Reverend Skinner DD, bishop of Worcester* (1886) · Foster, *Alum. Oxon.* · *CSP dom.*, 1636–43; 1660–70 · H. I. Longden, *Northamptonshire and Rutland clergy from 1500*, ed. P. I. King and others, 16 vols. in 6, Northamptonshire RS (1938–52), vol. 12, pp. 187–91 · *The life and times of Anthony Wood*, ed. A. Clark, 1, OHS, 19 (1891), 202, 323–4, 365 · Wood, *Ath. Oxon.*, new edn, 4.842 · *Fasti Angl., 1541–1857*, [Ely], 107 · *Fasti Angl., 1541–1857*, [Bristol], 10, 76 · *Walker rev.*, 12–13 · LPL, MS 943, fol. 133 · BL, Add. MS 20065 · will, PRO, PROB 11/333, sig. 94 · *Hist. U. Oxf. 4: 17th-cent. Oxf.*, 380, 512 · P. Barwick, *The life of Dr. John Barwick, dean of St. Paul's*, ed. G. F. Barwick, trans. H. Bedford (1903) · J. Davies, *The Caroline captivity of the church: Charles I and the remoulding of Anglicanism, 1625–1641* (1992) · P. Lake, 'Joseph Hall, Robert Skinner and the rhetoric of moderation at the early Stuart court', *The English sermon revised: religion, literature and history 1600–1750*, ed. L. Ferrell and P. McCullough (2000), 167 · J. W. Packer, *The transformation of Anglicanism, 1643–1660* (1969), 46–7 · R. S. Bosher, *The making of the Restoration settlement: the influence of the Laudians, 1649–1662*, rev. edn (1957)
Archives Bodl. Oxf., letters to Gilbert Sheldon, MS Tanner 48 · LPL, letter to William Laud, MS 943, fol. 133 · Warks. CRO, letter to John Newdigate, CR 136, B419

Skinner, Stephen (*bap.* 1623, *d.* 1667), physician and philologist, baptized on 23 November 1623 at St Martin Pomeroy, London, was the son of John Skinner. He matriculated from Christ Church, Oxford, on 6 December 1639, but, the civil war breaking out, he left England and 'served in wars beyond seas'. He was probably the Skinner who was stated by the parliamentary visitors of Oxford to be 'in the service of Ireland'. In 1646 he was again at Oxford,

and in consideration of his foreign service was allowed to accumulate both his arts degrees in that same year, BA on 21 October and MA on 10 November. On 22 April 1649 he entered as a medical student at Leiden, on 6 May 1653 at Heidelberg, and on 4 November 1653 again at Leiden. At the beginning of 1654 he graduated MD of Heidelberg, and on 26 May following was incorporated in that degree at Oxford. Wood says that during his absence from England he 'visited France, Italy, Germany, the Netherlands, visited the courts of divers princes, frequented several universities, and obtained the company and friendship of the most learned men of them'. He was made honorary fellow of the College of Physicians in December 1664. Skinner practised in Lincoln, where he died of malignant fever on 5 September 1667 and was buried in the city's cathedral. Administration of his estate was granted to his sister, Elizabeth Bowyer, and his daughter Stephanie Skinner on 7 September 1667.

Skinner left behind him several philological treatises in manuscript which were enumerated by Wood. These were edited by Thomas Henshaw and published in London in 1671 under the title of *Etymologicon Linguæ Anglicanae*. Samuel Johnson gratefully acknowledged his indebtedness to Skinner in the preface to his *Dictionary* (1755).

BERTHA PORTER, *rev.* MICHAEL BEVAN

Sources Wood, *Ath. Oxon.*, new edn, 3.793–4 · Wood, *Ath. Oxon.: Fasti* (1815), 90–91, 148 · Foster, *Alum. Oxon.* · Munk, *Roll* · IGI · N&Q, 11 (1855), 122, 168 · G. Toepke, ed., *Die Matrikel der Universität Heidelberg*, 7 vols. (Heidelberg, 1884–1916) · G. du Rieu, ed., *Album studiosorum academiae Lugduno Batavae, MDLXXV–MDCCCLXXV: accedunt nomina curatorum et professorum per eadem secula* (The Hague, 1875) · M. Burrows, ed., *The register of the visitors of the University of Oxford, from AD 1647 to AD 1658*, CS, new ser., 29 (1881)

Skinner, Thomas (*c.*1616–1695), merchant, came from a family that originated in Essex, but his father, Daniel, was a merchant in Dover. It seems likely that Thomas Skinner was married to Magdalen, and that some of his eight children, who included Mary, Thomas, and Benjamin, were born in Dover in the early 1650s; all except Benjamin were dead by 1710. However the only certain references describe him as being 'of London'. He and his six brothers—Albertus, Daniel, Frederick, Lyonel, Maurice, and Robert—were involved in an intricate network of international trade and mutual indebtedness; a man of the same name was also secretary of the Merchant Adventurers (*CSP dom.*, 1654, 345–6). Litigation records show that Skinner had trading interests in Ireland, France, and Flanders as well as Indonesia.

During the interregnum the East India trade, previously controlled by the chartered East India Company, became increasingly open, but in spring 1657 the promise of a new charter signalled the closure of the trade. In December Skinner set out on an independent trading voyage to Bantam, where his brother Frederick was the East India Company's factor. He anticipated Frederick's imminent dismissal for trading in defiance of company rules and probably intended to assist him in removing illicit goods (Sainsbury, 22, 25, 295, 320; BL OIOC, G 21/3-3, pt 1). Skinner was, by his own account, well on the way to making a fortune when the East India Company's new agents arrived. They believed (correctly) that many of the goods in Skinner's custody actually belonged to Frederick, and regarded him as an unauthorized trader—an 'interloper'. His property (including a small island, Barella in Sumatra) was seized, and he was forced to return to England overland.

Skinner petitioned the crown for compensation, asking for £40,000 to cover both actual losses and notional profits. His claim ultimately took the form of 39 articles (BL OIOC, H 42, 10-28). Between 1661 and 1666 the crown promoted several attempts to mediate between Skinner and the East India Company. All the hearings were inconclusive: the parties were unwilling to compromise; the distances involved made it difficult to secure accurate testimony; the case also raised difficult legal issues. In December 1666 Charles II referred the case to the House of Lords, and unwittingly precipitated a major constitutional crisis.

When the House of Lords was restored along with the monarchy in 1660, the precise limits of its powers (especially its legal powers) were unclear. Unlike other contemporary courts it had no distinctive body of law to administer, no clear jurisdictional limits, and no established procedures to assist the quest for truth. The peers either did not realize the full difficulties of this case or deliberately chose to ignore them. The case came before them as an original cause. The judges had also advised that all but one of Skinner's grievances were remediable in the lower courts and that the remaining issue, that of the confiscation of his island, was outside the jurisdiction of any English court. Following an initial recommendation of over £28,000, the house awarded Skinner £5000 damages (*Eighth Report*, HMC).

The East India Company petitioned the House of Commons for relief, obtaining a declaration that anyone assisting the Lords in the execution of their judgment 'shall be deemed a betrayer of the commons of England' (*CSP dom.*, 1667-8, 382). Commons hostility initially related to parliamentary privilege, since several members of the East India Company were also MPs, but other issues soon emerged. Whether the Lords had jurisdiction over original causes between subjects was in itself questionable. Its assumption of jurisdiction over issues that were not remediable in an ordinary court of law was interpreted as an attempt to legislate without the concurrence or participation of the House of Commons. Even if the Lords did have jurisdiction it was not clear whether the East India Company were responsible for the actions complained of, or whether their agents had exceeded their authority. Not surprisingly the Commons regarded the proceedings in the Lords as unconstitutional and arbitrary. The Lords, ever sensitive to threats to their privileges and status, interpreted Commons opposition as an attempt to encroach upon the rights of the upper house. The wrangling was so intense that parliament had to be prorogued for nearly two years. It has been suggested that 'the dispute was spun out to frustrate the passage of controversial legislation' and 'was also a reflection of a rift at court and

in the privy council' (Swatland, 132-3), but this kind of political exploitation was only possible because the case did raise genuine constitutional issues. Reconciliation became possible only when both houses agreed to erase all record of the case. This expedient, however weak, brought gains to both sides. The Lords avoided open defeat, but never again heard a case in original jurisdiction; a bill designed to define (and curb) the Lords' judicial powers was dropped (HLRO, LP 181/29).

However the case was not over for Skinner, who continued to petition for compensation, at one stage even offering to help the French capture St Helena, then in the company's possession, as he had suffered 'great wrong and injury, and he might in this or any other way seek his satisfaction' (*CSP dom.*, 1671, 316). In 1691 he commenced an action in exchequer, producing in evidence documentation that he had hoarded for some thirty years (PRO, E 112/682, 258). When he lost in 1693, he appealed the decision to the House of Lords (*JHL*, 15.316b). It was still unheard when he died in December 1695, in his eightieth year. His youngest son, Benjamin, threatened to revive the case in 1710 but does not appear to have made any real effort to do so.

RUTH PALEY

Sources *Eighth report*, 1, HMC, 7 (1907-9), 165-74 · [Denzil, Lord Holles], *The grand question concerning the judicature of the house of peers stated* (1669) · BL OIOC, G 21/3-3, pt 1 · BL OIOC, H42, 10-28 · HLRO, parchment collection, box 182/43 · HLRO, LP 181/29 · BL, Stowe MS 304, fol. 89 · PRO, E 133/112/49 · PRO, E 112/464 · PRO, E 163/19/24 · PRO, E 112/682, 258 [bill of Thomas Skinner] · *CSP dom.*, 1654; 1667-8; 1671 · *JHL*, 15 (1691-6), 316b · J. B. Whitmore and A. W. Hughes Clarke, eds., *London visitation pedigrees, 1664*, Harleian Society, 92 (1940), 126 · *The case of Benjamin Skinner son of Thomas Skinner merchant* (1710) [microfilm copy, Goldsmiths Kress Library of Economic Literature, reel 281, no. 4607, 0-21] · W. R. Scott, *The constitution and finance of English, Scottish and Irish joint stock companies to 1720* (1910) · E. B. Sainsbury, ed., *A calendar of the court minutes ... of the East India Company*, [4]: 1650-54 (1913) · A. Swatland, *The House of Lords in the reign of Charles II* (1996)

Archives BL OIOC, East India Company MSS · PRO, legal actions, Court of Exchequer, E 112/682, 258; E 112/464; E 133/112/49; E 163/19/24

Skinner, Thomas (1629/30-1679), physician and biographer, probably the son of Nicholas Skinner, of Brentwood, Essex, was born there, and educated at Bishop's Stortford, Hertfordshire, before being admitted sizar of St John's College, Cambridge, on 29 May 1646, at the age of sixteen. He graduated BA in 1649 at Cambridge, and DM at St John's College, Oxford, on 17 July 1672, and is described by Foster as sometime of Cambridge University.

Skinner is thought to have been 'physician to the Duke of Albemarle, when residing at New Hall in Essex' (Skinner, 92). He practised in Colchester, Essex, where he lived in All Saints' parish, and later moved to Lincoln, where he died, in 1679. He was buried at St Mary's, Colchester, on 8 August 1679.

Skinner is best-known as the author of *The Life of General Monk, Duke of Albemarle*, published in 1723 by William Webster, curate of St Dunstan-in-the-West, Fleet Street, London, with a preface defending Monck's character, and attributing the manuscript to Skinner. A letter from Skinner to the secretary of state in January 1677 states that he was solicited by the second duke of Albemarle to write a life of his father in Latin, but only this English version of the life has survived. Skinner applied to Samuel Barrow and others for assistance in his task, and claims to have had access to a collection of Monck's papers.

C. H. FIRTH, rev. PATRICK WALLIS

Sources Venn, *Alum. Cant.* · Foster, *Alum. Oxon.* · T. Skinner, *The life of General Monk, late duke of Albemarle* (1723) · F. P. Guizot, *Memoirs of George Monck, duke of Albermarle*, trans. J. S. Wortley (1838) · P. Morant, *The history and antiquities of the most ancient town and borough of Colchester in the county of Essex* (1748) · *N&Q*, 1 (1849–50), 377–8 · *N&Q*, 8th ser., 4 (1893), 421 · Wood, *Ath. Oxon.: Fasti* (1820), 333
Archives BL, Egerton MSS

Skinner, Thomas (*c*.1800–1843), army officer and author, was the son of Lieutenant-General John Skinner. He entered the army on 25 January 1816 as an ensign in the 16th foot; he became lieutenant on 6 August 1819, captain on 9 October 1823, and exchanged into the 31st foot on 25 March 1824. He went with his regiment to India shortly before 1826, and was stationed at Hardwar, in the North-Western Provinces, near the foot of the Himalayas. He made expeditions into the little-known mountainous districts of the area, and described the results of his exploration in *Excursions in India* (1832). After returning home on leave he went back to India in 1833 by the overland route through Egypt, Syria, and Palestine, down the Euphrates, and across the Persian Gulf. He described his journey in *Adventures during a Journey Overland to India* (1836). On 24 November 1835 he was promoted major, and in 1842 he joined the force assembled at Jalalabad under Sir George Pollock for the relief of Kabul. He commanded the 31st foot in the campaign, and on 26 July 1842 was present at the conflict of Mazina, near Jalalabad. He accompanied Pollock's advance, and was entrusted with the task of clearing the hills on the left of the valley of Tezin in the engagement there on 13 September. He received for his services the CB and was gazetted on 23 December brevet lieutenant-colonel. He died at Landour on 6 May 1843 from the results of privations endured during the campaign.

E. I. CARLYLE, rev. M. G. M. JONES

Sources GM, 2nd ser., 20 (1843), 333 · *Army List* · *Hart's Army List* (1843), 342 · J. W. Kaye, *History of the war in Afghanistan*, 3rd edn, 3 (1874), 293, 309

Skinner, Thomas Bridges Boucher (1804–1877), army officer and engineer, born at St John's, Newfoundland, on 22 May 1804, was the son of Lieutenant-Colonel William Thomas Skinner (*d.* 1829), of the Royal Artillery, and his second wife, Mary, daughter of Dr Monier of the Royal Artillery. From 1811 Thomas was at school in England, until in 1818 he went to Ceylon, and obtained a second lieutenancy in the Ceylon Rifles. In 1820 he was employed in road construction. In 1825 he was appointed staff officer of the garrison of Colombo, and on 27 November 1829 deputy assistant quartermaster-general of the forces in Ceylon. In 1832 he opened a road from Arippu, on the western coast of Ceylon, to Anuradhapura. In the following year the public works were transferred to the civil authorities, and Skinner accompanied the surveyor-

general over the country to initiate him in his duties. Subsequently Skinner undertook a survey of the mountain zone, the result of which was embodied in a one-inch sketch map of the Kandian provinces and in a general map of Ceylon. In 1836 he was promoted captain, and in the following year was employed to regulate the surveyor-general and civil engineer's department, which had fallen into great confusion. This occupied him until 1840; but as the department became again disorganized when he ceased directing it, he was appointed permanent commissioner for the roads in Ceylon in 1841. He married Georgina, daughter of Lieutenant-General George Burrell CB, on 19 December 1838. One of their children was Monier Williams Skinner, lieutenant-colonel, Royal Engineers. In 1847 he retired from his regiment with the rank of major, and in 1850 the civil engineer's department was amalgamated with his own. In 1859 he was appointed auditor-general, but because of a disagreement with the governor, Sir Henry Ward, on the coast of a railway from Colombo to Kandy, he was superseded in 1861, and returned to his former post of commissioner of public works, which he continued to hold until, in 1865, he resumed the duties of auditor-general.

Skinner retired to England in 1867, and was made a CMG on 15 February 1869. He resided at Bath. Skinner wrote an autobiography, *Fifty Years in Ceylon*, edited by his daughter Annie Skinner (1891); it contains a history of his branch of the Skinner family. He died at his home, 7 Grosvenor Place, Bath, on 24 July 1877. His services to Ceylon were very great in opening up the country and rendering overland transport possible.

E. I. CARLYLE, rev. M. G. M. JONES

Sources T. Skinner, *Fifty years in Ceylon: an autobiography*, ed. A. Skinner (1891) · *Colburn's United Service Magazine*, 3 (1877), 110
Likenesses portrait, repro. in Skinner, *Fifty years in Ceylon*
Wealth at death under £4000: probate, 15 Aug 1877, *CGPLA Eng. & Wales*

Skinner, William (1699/1700–1780), military engineer and army officer, was born at St Christopher (St Kitts), West Indies, the son of Thomas Skinner, a merchant and younger son of William Skynner, mayor of Hull in 1665. Skinner's parents both died while he was a child, and he was adopted by Elizabeth, his father's sister, who married Talbot Edwards, the military engineer, as her second husband. Edwards, related by marriage to Sir Martin Beckman, chief engineer and master gunner of England, bequeathed his large collection of maps and plans, many of which had been Beckman's, to Skinner. Skinner was from a young age exposed to a culture of military engineering to which he willingly inclined himself.

On 11 May 1719 Skinner was given a warrant as practitioner engineer and the following year was employed at the gun wharf, Devonport. In 1722 he was sent out to Minorca, where the works at St Philip's Castle under William Horneck provided him with practical experience of fortification on a large scale. In the summer of 1724 Skinner was moved to Gibraltar under Jonas Moore. There he participated in the first general survey of the rock and served in its defence during the siege of 1727. He was promoted to sub-engineer on 20 February 1727 and the following year was made barrack-master at Gibraltar in addition to his engineer duties. On 10 March 1730 he was made engineer-extraordinary and acted as chief in Moore's temporary absences in 1736 and 1738. He was promoted engineer-in-ordinary in 1739, and on 1 July 1741, after Moore was killed at Cartagena, Skinner was appointed chief engineer at Gibraltar.

His promotion was then very rapid, for Skinner was named sub-director on 1 January 1744 and director on 30 September 1746. He was given a new challenge when in 1746 he was recalled to London. The board appointed him chief engineer in Scotland on 31 December 1746, with orders to survey the works at Edinburgh, Stirling, Dumbarton, and Blackness, as well as Fort William and Fort Augustus, following the great damage to the fortifications inflicted by the Jacobite rising. This work he began on arrival in Scotland in January 1747. The captain-general, William Augustus, duke of Cumberland, persuaded his father, George II, that a new fortress was required at Inverness, and had already settled on a plan which he ordered to be followed. Skinner postulated many sound reasons for it not to be pursued, and drew up a project of his own, which Cumberland quickly saw was better.

The new fort near Inverness was to extend over 42 acres on a specially purchased site. Begun in 1748 Fort George was many years in the building and cost in excess of £200,000. Lieutenant-Colonel James Wolfe, visiting the site in 1751, forecast that when finished it would be 'the most considerable fortress, and the best situated, in Great Britain' (Wright, 178). Skinner had the undiluted responsibility for directing the works and would not allow the smallest deviation from his plan. The principal contractor, with whom Skinner came to be on familiar terms, was John Adam, older brother of the architects Robert and James Adam.

The summer season of each year found Skinner at the isolated Ardersier Point on the Moray Firth guiding the engineers, overseers, contractors, and soldiery. When absent he insisted on almost daily letters to keep him informed of progress in every detail, firing back trenchant criticisms and detailed instructions, always urging the work forward. Fort George was the culmination of Skinner's ambition, the fulfilment of the professional tradition to which he had been brought up; he called it his 'monument'.

In 1750 Thomas Lascelles retired and, though an appointment was made for a new surveyor-general, the post of chief engineer was left vacant. This deprived the corps of the most senior post they could aim for. Skinner considered himself in line for the promotion and confided, 'it's all I have been aspiring to this thirty-two years, having been so long constantly employed, which is ten years longer than most of the engineers on the establishment have been in the service' (BL, Add. MS 17500, fol. 35). Some weeks later he wrote:

It is very hard that after thirty-two years in the Ordnance service with a good character with great trust and a constant attendance I should be put in competition with my junior

[Thomas Armstrong, chief engineer at Minorca, had applied] who the whole world knows has never made a design in his life, but has always been employed in the executing of the designs of others. (ibid., fols. 48–9)

Nor was Skinner satisfied with his remuneration, pointing out that while he laboured in Scotland for 20s. a day, his counterparts in Minorca and North America had 50s. and 40s. respectively. Skinner was perhaps too useful in Scotland, and particularly at Fort George, for his appointment as chief engineer to be attractive to the board. With no other plausible candidate, the easiest option was to allow the post of chief engineer of Great Britain to lapse. Skinner was chief engineer in all but name, Cumberland referring to him as 'the King's first engineer' (Cumberland MSS, 48/82–3). Skinner waited seven years until the board eventually appointed him to that post, on 14 May 1757, at which time he was also made colonel, the first military rank he had held.

While the works at Fort George proceeded Skinner was often employed in other directions by order of the board. He presided over a committee that in 1754 recommended the erection of magazines at Purfleet as a depot for military ammunition and combustibles. In November 1755 Skinner received orders to proceed to Ireland, where, in conjunction with Thomas Eyre, surveyor-general there, he was to survey the fortifications. Their extensive and handsomely illustrated report in the following year gave account of Duncannon Fort, Kinsale, Limerick, Galway, and Athlone, and recommended the building of a new fort at Cork.

In 1758 Colonel Skinner was called before the bar of the House of Commons in connection with a report he had made on the works carried out at Gibraltar by the governor, James O'Hara, second Baron Tyrawley. Tyrawley had meddled in the fortifications 'with no more economy than governors are apt to do, who think themselves above being responsible', as Horace Walpole put it (Walpole, 3.15). Skinner's report had revealed Tyrawley's defensive innovations as inefficient and lacking in science. Tyrawley, enraged by these insinuations, attended the house and 'leaning on the bar, he browbeat Skinner, his censor, who stood on his left hand, with such arrogant humour, that the very lawyers thought themselves outdone in their own style of worrying a culprit' (ibid.). Skinner presumably allowed such rodomontade to pass over him, while the Commons soon forgot the affair.

During 1758 Skinner was in Scotland and at Milford Haven, Pembrokeshire, supervising the works. In December, on intelligence of a French-inspired plot to take Gibraltar by surprise, he was abruptly dispatched under direct orders from the secretary of state, William Pitt, to take necessary measures for the defence of the rock. The supposed plot was shown to be of no substance even before Skinner's arrival at Gibraltar. Despite his presence there being quite unnecessary, permission for him to return was long sought by Skinner and by the Board of Ordnance before his eventual arrival home in September 1759. Soon thereafter he was ordered to Plymouth to report on the fortifications. He appears to have suffered intermittent poor health at this time, perhaps due to his heavy workload and frequent travelling.

On 18 February 1761 Skinner was promoted to major-general and in May he made a flying visit to Portsmouth and the Isle of Wight, before making his habitual summer journey to Scotland. After arriving in early June he was recalled urgently to London by the king's particular command. His orders were to go to Belle Île, just captured by a British expedition, to report on the defences and draw up plans for accommodating the troops which would garrison the island. Almost certainly he would have been at Belle Île when news reached him of the death on 27 August of his only son, Captain William Skinner, at Coule-hault on the coast of Dominica, while on service with his regiment.

In the winter of 1761–2 Skinner was again ill with what he referred to as 'my old disorder'. The following winter he wrote to his friend John Adam:

> I begin to think a little rest will be necessary; I grow old and think and hope near fifty years servitude intitles me to a little indulgence; my only view is to see my monument on the Point [Fort George] finished with credit, as it has been so long my nursery, a short time more puts it out of our hands. (BL, Add. MS 17501, fol. 148)

But his illness continued to plague him into the summer, when in June he found it necessary to inform the board that he was for the moment incapable of attending to any business. However, despite his ill health at this time, Skinner was to serve many more years as chief engineer. In 1769 he adjudicated on several projects for improving the defences of Gibraltar submitted by colleagues. On 30 April 1770 he was promoted lieutenant-general in the army, and later the same year, after a long period of neglect by the board, his pay as chief engineer was increased to the same as that of colonels-commandant of the Royal Artillery. Among Skinner's later projects were those for enlarging the gun wharf and erecting new magazines at Plymouth; also for remodelling and augmenting the lines at Chatham. The freedom of several Scottish and Irish cities was conferred upon him.

Skinner's great talent lay in his thorough understanding of the principles of fortification and his mastery of the technical repertoire of the engineer. He was thus enabled to fulfil to perfection the duties of chief engineer of Great Britain owing to the superiority of his professional knowledge. Virtually every project or estimate from home and abroad was sent to him by the Board of Ordnance for consideration and report, the principal officers of the ordnance depending on his advice. Sometimes at the Office of Ordnance, but more often at home at Croom's Hill, Greenwich, Skinner examined the proposals of his junior colleagues and dispensed his wisdom.

After sixty-one years' service as an engineer, twenty-three of them as chief engineer of Great Britain, Skinner died at Greenwich on 25 December 1780 in his eighty-first year. He was buried in the churchyard of St Alfege, Greenwich. Margaret Skinner (*née* Caldwell), his widow, applied for and was granted £100 per annum extra to her widow's pension, on the grounds that her husband had saved little

during his working life to provide for her, partly owing to his remuneration not being increased when he could have expected it.

PAUL LATCHAM

Sources J. W. S. Conolly, 'Notitia historica of the corps of royal engineers', MS, *c.*1860, Royal Engineers Corps Library, Chatham · *GM*, 1st ser., 50 (1780), 591 · J. M. Lambert, *The portraits and silver of the RE headquarters mess, Chatham* (1963), 12 [Skinner's portrait] · I. MacIvor, *Fort George*, Historic Scotland guide (1996) · W. Porter, *History of the corps of royal engineers*, 2 vols. (1889) · H. Walpole, *Memoirs of King George II*, ed. J. Brooke, 3 vols. (1985) · R. Wright, *The life of Major-General James Wolfe* (1864) · board of ordnance, minutes, PRO, WO47 · reports on Gibraltar, BL, Add. MS 10034 · corresp. while chief engineer in Scotland, BL, Add. MSS 17499–17501 · MSS relating to Gibraltar, BL, Add. MS 57640 · corresp., Royal Engineers Museum, Chatham, MSS 2001-64/2-64/20; 4501.21; 4601.79, 1–5; 4601.71 · Royal Arch., Cumberland papers, box 22/167–8, 170–71; box 45/82–4; box 48/82–3; box 61/B5A-B; box 66/VII.27.14
Archives BL, Gibraltar map, Add. MS 56092 · BL, maps, plans, and surveys, Add. MS 22875 · BL, maps, plans, and surveys, Maps K.Top.50.7.2, 50.23, 50.27, 50.30, 50.31, 50.33, 50.9 a–i · BL, reports on Gibraltar, Add. MS 10034 · BL, MSS, Add. MSS 33231 A-PP, 33232–33233 · NL Scot., surveys · Royal Engineers Museum, Chatham, corresp., 2001–64/2–64/20, CHARE: 4501.21, 4601.79.1–5 (Belle-Isle), 4601.71 | BL, corresp. with Board of Ordnance while chief engineer in Scotland, Add. MSS 17499–17501 · BL, MSS relating to Gibraltar, Add. MS 57640 · BL, Townshend papers, plans of Fort Monckton, Gosport, Add. MS 50008B, fols. 2, 3 · NL Scot., plans and drawings of Fort George and other Scottish fortifications in the Board of Ordnance series, MSS 1646–1648 · PRO, Board of Ordnance minutes, WO 47 · Royal Arch., William Augustus, duke of Cumberland MSS, box 22/167, 168, 170, 171; box 45/82–84; box 48/82–3; box 61/B5A, B5B; box 66/VII.27.14
Likenesses double portrait, oils (with his daughter), priv. coll. · oils (after portrait), Royal Engineers' mess, Chatham; repro. in Lambert, *Portraits and silver*, 12

Skinner, William (1778–1857), Scottish Episcopal bishop of Aberdeen, the second son of John *Skinner (1744–1816), bishop of Aberdeen, and his wife, Mary Robertson (*d.* 1807), was born at Aberdeen on 24 October 1778, and educated at Marischal College, Aberdeen, and at Oxford University, where he matriculated from Wadham College on 3 March 1798, graduating BA in 1801, and MA, BD, and DD in 1819. Skinner was ordained by Bishop Samuel Horsley of St Asaph in March 1802. After returning to Scotland, he officiated as assistant, and then as colleague, to his father in the incumbency of the Scottish Episcopal church of St Andrew's, Aberdeen. In 1804 he married the youngest daughter of James Brand, cashier of the Aberdeen Banking Company.

On 11 September 1816 Skinner was elected by the clergy of the diocese as successor to his father in the see of Aberdeen, and was consecrated at Stirling on 27 October. George Gleig, primus of the church, sent a severe but fruitless reproof to the dean and clergy of Aberdeen for electing the son of their late bishop. Skinner was one of the bishops who attended the synod held at Laurencekirk on 18 June 1828 to revise the canons of 1811; thirty canons were adopted and duly signed on 20 June. In 1832 Skinner confirmed as many as 462 persons, and a first effort was made in the same year to circulate Episcopalian religious works in the Gaelic language. On 29 August 1838 he attended another synod held in St Paul's Church, Edinburgh, when the canons were again revised. Upon the

William Skinner (1778–1857), by Henry Adlard, pubd 1845

death of Bishop James Walker, Skinner was unanimously elected primus by an episcopal synod held in St Andrew's Church, Aberdeen, on 2 June 1841. During his primacy Trinity College, Glenalmond, near Perth, was founded in 1844, and developed by the Episcopalians in Scotland as a place of education for young men studying for the church. In the previous year a serious controversy had sprung out of the refusal of Sir William Dunbar, minister of St Paul's Chapel, Aberdeen, to receive or to administer the sacrament in accordance with the Scottish ritual. Acting with the concurrence of his synod, Skinner excommunicated Dunbar on 13 August 1843. Among the many pamphlets written on this issue were *A letter to the managers of St Paul's Chapel by Sir W. Dunbar, to which is added Bishop Skinner's declaration* (1843) and *The Rev. Sir W. Dunbar versus the Right Rev. W. Skinner* (1849). Skinner did much during his primacy to consolidate the Episcopal party in Scotland. He died at 1 Golden Square, Aberdeen, on 15 April 1857, and was buried in the Spital cemetery on 22 April.

G. C. BOASE, rev. H. C. G. MATTHEW

Sources *Aberdeen Journal* (22 April 1857) · *GM*, 3rd ser., 2 (1857), 729–30 · M. Lochhead, *Episcopal Scotland in the nineteenth century* (1966) · J. P. Lawson, *History of the Scottish Episcopal church* (1843)
Archives LPL, corresp. [copies] · NA Scot., corresp. and papers · NRA Scotland, priv. coll., corresp. and papers relating to Scottish Episcopal Friendly Society | BL, corresp. with W. E. Gladstone, Add. MS 44300
Likenesses H. Adlard, stipple, repro. in T. Stephens, *History of the Church of Scotland*, 4 vols. (1845), frontispiece [*see illus.*]
Wealth at death £1325 12s. 3d.: confirmation, 19 May 1857, NA Scot., SC 1/36/40, p. 526

Skip, John (d. 1552), bishop of Hereford, is of unknown origins. The suggestion that he was born in Norfolk and the brother of Richard Skip, in 1516 rector of St John's, Ber Street, Norwich, is based on very thin evidence. By 1515,

however, he was certainly studying at Gonville Hall, Cambridge, where he graduated BA in 1515 and proceeded successively MA in 1518, BTh in 1533, and DTh in 1535. Between 1519 and 1521 he was president of Physwick Hostel, a dependency of Gonville's. Traditionally linked with the early development of reformed opinions in religion in Cambridge, he has been named in that context as a member of the group that met at the White Horse tavern there. Although the role of these meetings in the dissemination of protestantism is now perceived as largely imaginary, Skip's credentials as an early supporter of reform are none the less well established. In 1530 Stephen Gardiner listed him as one of the supporters at Cambridge of the king's case for a divorce, along with Simon Heynes, Hugh Latimer, Nicholas Shaxton, Nicholas Heath, and Thomas Goodrich.

In 1534 Skip and Heynes were sent from the court to Cambridge 'for the vindication of the king's supreme authority in his own dominions against the Pope's pretended power' (Strype, 1/1.260). His career prospered, for he was made vicar of Thaxted, Essex, in 1534 and also received an important appointment at court. In 1535, after the elevation of Nicholas Shaxton to be bishop of Salisbury, Skip was made chaplain and almoner to Queen Anne Boleyn; he also succeeded Shaxton as canon of Westminster and prebendary of St Stephen's. (The Dr Skip named as Katherine of Aragon's almoner in 1518 was certainly a different person.) In a position close to a queen with strong evangelical sympathies, he was able to exercise some influence and his well-known friendship with Matthew Parker dated from this time. He served the queen until her death in 1536, and at the time of her fall did what he could in her defence, visiting her frequently in prison and attending her during her final hours: Sir William Kingston, constable of the Tower, wrote to Cromwell in the early hours of 19 May, the day of her execution, 'her Almoner is continewaly with hyr, and has bene syns ii of the clock after midnight' (*LP Henry VIII*, vol. 10, no. 910).

Skip's connection with the executed queen did not hinder his subsequent career. He was named master of Gonville Hall in 1536 and retained that position until 1540. He was also archdeacon of Suffolk from 1536 to 1539, rector of Newington, Surrey, in 1538, and archdeacon of Dorset from 1538 to 1539. It is also to this period that one of the more curious of Skip's contributions to posterity can be dated—a recipe for apple tarts.

On 7 November 1539 Skip was named bishop of Hereford following the translation of Edmund Bonner to London. Little can be said about his administration of his diocese. He presided over the transfer of the Forest deanery to the newly formed diocese of Gloucester in 1541 and over the dissolution of some seventy-seven chantries and chapels. He also made a 200-year lease of his episcopal residence in London to Lord Clinton—a lease that was revoked after Queen Mary succeeded to the throne. Perhaps it was to compensate for this loss that in 1551 he obtained a grant of the advowson of St Katherine's Hospital, Ledbury. After he arrived in his see, Skip appears to have taken the opportunity to have released a large number of clergy from his prison at Hereford, where they had been confined for breaches of ecclesiastical discipline. Whether this was a manifestation of reforming tendencies or simply a general amnesty is unknown.

In fact, although Skip acted in his diocese as the government directed, there is no evidence that he did anything further there to advance the cause of the Reformation. Indeed, his essentially moderate, even conservative, position towards religious change, especially during the reign of Edward VI, seems to indicate a reluctance to advance too far down the protestant road. As early as 1536 Skip was arguing that reform ought not to mean throwing the theological baby out with the bathwater:

> The kynges office is to se thabuses taken awey and not the good thinges themselffes except hit so be that thabuses can nott be taken awey, as Ezechias toke awey the brason serpent when he cowed nott take awey thabuse of hitt.   (PRO, SP 6/1, fol. 10)

For Skip, then and later, reform ought to be cautious and thoughtful or, as he said in a letter to Matthew Parker, 'cold and tardy' (Bruce and Perowne, 9).

Despite his association with Anne Boleyn and leading reformers, Skip's religious opinions never appear to have been radical and he is probably more correctly seen as a Henrician Catholic than as a protestant. Just before the execution of Anne Boleyn, on Passion Sunday (2 April) 1536, he preached a sermon in the king's chapel that caused considerable disquiet. Basing himself on the text 'Quis ex vobis arguet me de peccato?' ('Which of you convinceth me of sin?'—John 8: 46), he launched an attack on the wholesale changes that were then occurring in the church. Aware of the tension that existed between the queen and Thomas Cromwell, especially over the impending dissolution of the lesser monasteries and the use to which the proceeds were to be put, the tone and content of Skip's sermon were extremely critical of Cromwell's intentions to reclaim church lands for the crown, and may also have been implicitly critical of the king. Like the queen, Skip would have preferred the money to be devoted to furthering the cause of reform rather than to filling the king's coffers. The sermon was blunt and he went so far as to modify the biblical story of Haman and Asasuerus to make the point that councillors ought not to deceive the king.

Although his outburst led to Skip's being interrogated, the case went no further. Subsequently he appears to have maintained a cautiously conservative theological position. In 1536 he was consulted over the issues of justification, purgatory, and the numbering of the ten commandments for the forthcoming Bishops' Book. In 1538 he was named to a commission against Anabaptists. In 1543 he was involved in the heresy trial of John Marbeck and is said by Foxe to have been sympathetic to the musician, of whom he was supportive during his fourth examination, and whom he reassured afterwards that there was no substance to the charges against him (unlike his associates, Marbeck escaped the stake). In the same year, however, he is said to have argued with Cranmer over the doctrine contained in the King's Book, and under Edward VI, along with Day and Heath, he was identified by Cranmer as one of the bishops with awkward opinions on the new prayer book of 1549, particularly over the sacraments. The suggestion that he was one of the group of theologians at Windsor that compiled the 1552 prayer book has no foundation.

Skip's apparently ambiguous religious conservatism was put to no further test. He died in London on 28 March 1552, some fifteen months before the accession of Mary, and was buried at St Mary Mounthaw, London.

D. G. NEWCOMBE

Sources *Correspondence of Matthew Parker*, ed. J. Bruce and T. T. Perowne, Parker Society, 42 (1853) · J. Foxe, *Actes and monuments*, 4th edn, 2 vols. (1583) · *LP Henry VIII*, vols. 4–21, *addenda* · A. Gasquet and E. Bishop, *Edward VI and the Book of Common Prayer* (1928) · E. Ives, *Anne Boleyn* (1988) · J. G. Nichols, ed., *Narratives of the days of the Reformation*, CS, old ser., 77 (1859) · J. Strype, *Ecclesiastical memorials*, 3 vols. (1822) · R. M. Warnicke, *The rise and fall of Anne Boleyn* (1989) · Venn, *Alum. Cant.*, 1/4.86 · state papers, theological tracts, PRO, SP6/1 · D. MacCulloch, *Thomas Cranmer: a life* (1996) · L. B. Smith, *Tudor prelates and politics* (1953) · H. W. Phillott, *Diocesan histories: Hereford* (1888) · E. W. Ives, 'Anne Boleyn and the early Reformation in England: the contemporary evidence', *HJ*, 37 (1994), 389–400 · G. Aylmer and J. Tiller, eds., *Hereford Cathedral: a history* (2000)

Skippe [Skipp], **John** (1741–1812), wood-engraver, born on 7 July 1741, was the son of John Skipp of Upper Hall, Ledbury, Herefordshire, where the family had long been settled, J. Skipp of that place having supported Sir Henry Lingen in 1646. His mother, Penelope, was the daughter of Thomas Symonds of Pengethley. He matriculated at Merton College, Oxford, in 1760. After leaving the university he travelled in north Italy, and made many drawings, not without merit, from the old masters. A series of careful studies, done in 1773 from the frescoes by Andrea Mantegna in the church of the Eremitani at Padua, is in the print room of the British Museum. He was the pupil of J. B. Malchair and possibly also of John Baptist Jackson. Skippe is chiefly noted for his series of wood-engravings in chiaroscuro, done in imitation of those works of Ugo da Carpi and other early Italian artists. Skippe's engravings are more artistic than Jackson's, and more nearly approach the work of the older masters, including Parmigianino, Correggio, and Raphael. He is also known to have engraved a plate, dated 1809, after Salvator Rosa. A large collection of colour engravings by Skippe after Michelangelo, Rubens, and others dated between 1770 and 1773 is in the British Museum. Drawings by Skippe of landscape, sacred, and other subjects, executed in bistre with some vigour, are occasionally met with in collections and have sometimes been attributed to the old masters. Skippe died unmarried on 14 October 1812 in Overbury. Further examples of his work are in the Victoria and Albert Museum and the Tate collection, London.

L. H. CUST, rev. CHLOE JOHNSON

Sources J. Chambers, *Biographical illustrations of Worcestershire* (1820), 464 · Redgrave, *Artists* · W. Chatto and J. Jackson, *A treatise on wood engraving* (1839), 711 · Bryan, *Painters* · Foster, *Alum. Oxon.* ·

R. K. Engen, *Dictionary of Victorian wood engravers* (1985) · Bénézit, *Dict.*, 4th edn

Skippon, Philip, appointed Lord Skippon under the protectorate (*d.* 1660), parliamentarian army officer and politician, was the son of Luke Skippon (*d.* 1638), a minor gentleman of West Lexham, Norfolk, and his wife, Anne. The Skippons had been in Norfolk since the thirteenth century, but Philip at a young age took military service on the continent. He married Maria Comes (*d.* 1656) of Frankenthal, Lower Palatinate, on 14 May 1622, and they had eight children, three of whom died in infancy. Since he was married at Frankenthal he was evidently serving in the Palatinate before that date, under Sir Horace Vere. Skippon was wounded during the siege of Breda in 1625, and again at its recapture by the prince of Orange in October 1637. It was at Breda that he first gained his reputation for courage on the battlefield, reportedly with thirty English soldiers driving off 200 Spaniards 'at push of pike' (Walker, 52). He served also under Lord Vere at the sieges of Bois le Duc and Maastricht in 1629.

Having attained the rank of captain in the Dutch service, Skippon returned to England, and went to live at Foulsham, where he had inherited a house and property from an uncle, William Skippon, who died in 1634. In 1639, however, the king recommended him to the Honourable Artillery Company of London for election as their captain. According to Clarendon his experience in the Netherlands had made him disaffected to the Church of England and the Book of Common Prayer, and for this reason he was 'much caressed and trusted' by the king's enemies in England (Clarendon, *Hist. rebellion*, 1.509). After Charles's attempted arrest of the five members in January 1642 the House of Commons requested a guard from the City, and the common council appointed Skippon to take command of the City-trained bands, and raise a guard for parliament's defence. He was appointed at the rank of sergeant-major-general, and voted a salary of £300 p.a., having been made a freeman of the City only four days prior to his appointment. By 20 January the Commons had also given him responsibility for the trained bands of Westminster, Southwark, and the suburbs. During the tense month that followed the House of Commons ordered him to send out mounted scouts and patrol-boats to gather intelligence, to blockade the Tower, and to attempt to seize it by surprise. In the latter case the removal of Sir John Byron put an end to the supposed danger. On 4 February 1642 parliament praised Skippon for his 'diligence, faithfulness, and sufficiency' (*JHC*, 2.412). In a letter of 13 May the king commanded Skippon to attend him at York. But the two houses denounced the order as 'against the law of the land, the liberty of the subject', and 'the privilege of parliament,' and ordered him to continue serving them (*JHC*, 2.575).

The first civil war When the king's forces threatened London after the battle of Edgehill, Skippon was at the head of the trained bands that marched to Turnham Green to defend the metropolis. As he passed before the ranks of

Philip Skippon, appointed Lord Skippon under the protectorate (*d.* 1660), by R. S., pubd 1647

his soldiers he spoke words that echoed his own military motto (*ora et pugna*): 'Come my boys, my brave boys, let us pray heartily and fight heartily; I will run the same fortunes and hazards with you; remember the cause is for God, and for the defence of yourselves, your wives and children: come, my honest brave boys, pray heartily and fight heartily, and God will bless us' (B. Whitelocke, *Memorials of the English Affairs*, 4 vols., 1853, 190–1).

The commander-in-chief of the parliamentarian forces, the earl of Essex, quickly discerned Skippon's worth, and on 17 November 1642 snatched him away from the London common council to make him sergeant-major-general of the infantry in his army. In April 1643 Skippon took part in the siege of Reading, in August and September he accompanied Essex on his march to relieve Gloucester, and in September he performed notable service at the first battle of Newbury. The following month he occupied Newport Pagnell for parliament, and in December he took Grafton House in Northamptonshire. In the late summer of 1644 Essex allowed himself and his army to be drawn into a trap in Cornwall. While the earl escaped by sea from Lostwithiel, it was left to Skippon to arrange the best terms he could. He convoked a council of war, and urged his field officers to imitate the horse by endeavouring to cut their way through the enemy's ranks. This time, however, Skippon's persuasive oratory failed him and he was obliged to surrender.

At the second battle of Newbury (27 October 1644) Skippon had his revenge. According to his own account he, Colonel Barclay, and Lord Roberts saw the hottest action, repulsing three violent charges of Prince Rupert's horse. Had night not fallen, opined Skippon, the parliamentarian army would probably have 'utterly defeated their whole army' (Rushworth, 5.723). Yet two weeks later the king returned to relieve Donnington Castle under the noses of the combined armies of Essex, Manchester, and Waller. Obloquy was poured upon the parliamentarian commanders for this episode, and Skippon received his share. In his defence he noted that Essex's whole army had shrivelled to fewer than 2000 men, and that they had had no assistance from Manchester's horse under the command of Oliver Cromwell.

Skippon's disgrace was only temporary, for with the foundation of the New Model Army in early 1645 he was named sergeant-major-general of the infantry under Sir Thomas Fairfax. The delicate task of condensing the remaining foot from Essex's army into three regiments was entrusted to him. In an 'excellent, pious, and pithy hortatory speech to all his souldiers', he pledged, 'as I have been with you hitherto, so upon all occasion of service to my God and country, I shall by the help of God, be willing to live and die with you' (J. Vicars, *Magnalia Dei Anglicana, or, England's Parliamentary-Chronicle*, 1646, 132; Rushworth, 6.17). His success at this assignment set an example to the others, so that in a short time the balance of Essex's army was merged into the New Model. Skippon took the field with Fairfax in May 1645, and was sent to overrun Borstall House in Buckinghamshire, but he was repulsed with loss.

It was at Naseby that Skippon's work in training the New Model infantry was triumphantly vindicated. Marshalling the parliamentarian foot, he positioned himself on the left centre. In the wake of Prince Rupert's successful charge against the cavalry on the left wing the parliamentarian soldiers of the foot found themselves sorely pressed. The royalist foot under Lord Astley rolled them back until they fell behind the reserves. The reserves, however, remained steady against the onslaught, not only repelling the king's forces but putting them to flight. In the midst of this intense struggle Skippon was dangerously wounded by a shot in the side. Fairfax asked him to leave the field, 'but the old man answered, he would not stir so long as a man would stand', and stayed until the fighting was over (Rushworth, 6.43). He was lucky to escape with his life. Parliament rushed surgeons and apothecaries to treat him, and then brought him to London for many months of convalescent care, at a cost of several hundred pounds.

Skippon saw no further action during the first civil war, but was rewarded for his contribution at Naseby with the governorship of Bristol. He rejoined Fairfax at the siege of Oxford where, in May 1646 he undertook the construction and management of the forts and entrenchments for the parliamentarian besiegers. Although he had transferred to the New Model Army, Skippon remained on good terms with the earl of Essex and preserved his reputation as a political moderate. When Essex died in September 1646 Skippon had the high honour of acting as an armour bearer at his funeral.

In December 1646 the Scots army was preparing to vacate Newcastle and return to its own country. Fairfax recommended, and parliament agreed, that Skippon should be the new governor of Newcastle. He was given command of the convoy of thirty-six carts that hauled the first instalment £200,000 to pay off the Scots and receive the king from them. For his skill in handling this sensitive transaction Skippon won kudos from the parliamentarian commissioners who were with him.

Politics and the army On 29 March 1647 the House of Commons summoned him to resume his duties with the field army, and a week later the presbyterian majority led by Holles and Stapleton pressed him to accept the command of the projected expedition to Ireland. He wrote back, 'I am so sensible of my own exceeding indisposedness of mind, inability of body, and distractedness of estate and family, that I ingenuously confess myself most unfit, and unable to undertake or undergo such an employment' (*JHL*, 9.139). But the presbyterians pressed it on him as his patriotic duty, and in the end he yielded to them.

On the same day Skippon took his seat in the House of Commons as member for Barnstaple. Three troopers representing eight New Model cavalry regiments who had petitioned against disbandment and the Irish expedition at once approached him to support their cause. On 30 April 1647 he laid a copy of the soldiers' *Apologie* before the house. The party of Holles and Stapleton now gave him his most difficult assignment to date: to travel to army headquarters at Saffron Walden with Cromwell, Ireton, and Fleetwood, damp down the flames of discontent, and restore peace within the ranks. Skippon did his best to please his parliamentarian masters. For all his powers of diplomacy, however, he could wring no more from his fellow officers than a commitment to consult their regiments. On 16 May Skippon and the other parliamentarian commissioners gathered at Saffron Walden to hear the results of this consultation. There was sharp conflict between the minority who favoured obedience to parliament, and the majority who advocated defiance. In vain Skippon tried to mediate the 'clashings and jarrings', which he found 'a very great pressure to my spiritt', and to encourage enlistment for Ireland (C. H. Firth, ed., *The Clarke Papers*, CS, 1, 1891, 1.58). Warned by the commissioners that the army was near mutiny, the parliamentarian presbyterians tried to sweeten their offer by repealing the declaration of dislike of 30 March, passing an act indemnifying the soldiers against civil prosecution for crimes committed while in arms, and promising to pay more of their arrears. But these appeasing measures came too late. The army drove out its presbyterian officers, banded together in a solemn engagement not to disband until its grievances were met, and erected a general council to oversee its political affairs. When Skippon and the other commissioners met the army at Thriplow Heath on 10 June to announce parliament's latest concessions they were greeted with cries of 'justice, justice' (Rushworth, 6.556). The response in London to army militancy was an attempted counter-revolution. To further their project of overthrowing the New Model Army the allies of Holles and Stapleton in the City offered Skippon the command of the trained bands. He opted, however, to remain with his comrades in the revolutionary army. This marked the beginning of the politically radical phase of his career. His new alignment was signified by his marching with Sir Thomas Fairfax and the other higher officers at the head of the New Model when they entered London on 6 August.

Controlling London Political duelling between the army and the City dragged on inconclusively until the outbreak of the second civil war, when both City fathers and citizens made their sympathy for a royalist peace settlement increasingly clear. Although they had previously requested that Skippon be placed in charge of all the forces in London and the environs, by the end of May 1648 they were petitioning for his ouster in favour of the covertly royalist sheriff Richard Browne. Parliament, however, resisted these importunities, and Skippon remained the linchpin of their control over the metropolis. The centrality of his role was underlined by his appointment, in the same month, to the Derby House committee. This committee, now purged of Scots and presbyterians, devised and executed parliament's military strategy in the second civil war. Skippon's seat on the committee furnished him with the power he needed to take charge of the metropolis during the eight months that culminated in the king's trial and execution. Most of the policies affecting London seem to have emanated from him, and he always appears to have got his own way. Free from the supervision of the City militia committee, he was accountable to parliament and the Derby House committee alone. During the summer he searched out and impounded the horses, arms, and men being recruited by royalist agents. He also directed an intelligence effort to uncover the places where men and *matériel* were being hidden. Even more important was his recruitment of a thousand horse to keep the City secure, and a further 1500 Londoners, chiefly from the suburbs, to assist Fairfax at the siege of Colchester. His military and political effectiveness was such that the common council of London was moved to petition parliament against him. The core of their complaint was that he was raising servants and apprentices 'in a clandestine way at unseasonable times in the night … tending to the raising of tumults, dividing and breaking of the trained bands and auxiliary forces of this City' (*The Humble Petition of the Lord Major, Aldermen, and Commons of the City of London … to the Right Honorable the Lords and Commons in Parliament Assembled*, 24 July 1648, 1–2).

While the Lords backed the City, the Commons refused to revoke Skippon's authority. In the midst of this political struggle Skippon discovered a hitherto unsuspected talent and relish for political manoeuvre. Besides mobilizing the Derby House committee, he delivered major speeches in the House of Commons and the London common council. He now discarded the mantle of moderation to reveal an unswerving adherent of the revolution. At the end of June, for example, he addressed the corporation of London, deploring the royalism of the citizenry and calling for recruits to the parliamentarian cause. A few days later in the House of Commons he denounced the City's 'malignant' petition for a personal treaty with the king (*Mercurius Pragmaticus*, 4–11 July 1648, sig. P2a.). In November he again addressed the Commons, this speech being on the theme of the soldiers' unpopularity in the streets of London, and the continuing danger from malignants. The following month he promoted the ordinance barring all signers of the petition for a personal treaty with the king from voting in the common council elections. At that same time the men of his own foot regiment in the New Model were billeted in St Paul's Cathedral. They kept themselves warm by tearing down 'the carved timber, scaffolds and other materialls' and making great fires on the cathedral floor (CLRO, repertories of the court of Aldermen, vol. 59, fols. 322–323). More than anyone else it was Skippon who kept a deeply unhappy City in parliament's grip from the outbreak of the second civil war to the time of the king's trial.

Religion and wealth Skippon's radicalism, however, had its limits. Appointed to the high court of justice to try the king, he declined to attend any of its meetings; nor did he put his name to the warrant for Charles's execution. During the Commonwealth and protectorate he continued to hold high office despite his initial refusal to swear the engagement. When Cromwell led the invasion of Scotland in the summer of 1650 Skippon was appointed commander-in-chief of all the forces in and about London. He was also elected to the first, second, third, and fifth councils of state under the Commonwealth. He was not appointed to the council created by the army officers after the expulsion of the Rump; nor was he chosen for Barebone's Parliament in 1653, though a group of gathered churches in Norfolk had nominated him. Yet he was a member of each of the two councils appointed by Cromwell. The protector also commissioned him to command the forces in London in February 1655 to suppress the apprehended rising of the royalists. During the reign of the major-generals (1655–6) Skippon was major-general for the London area. In the parliaments of 1654 and 1656 he represented Lyme, but said little in debate. His one significant intervention came in December 1656 when he repeatedly expressed indignation at the blasphemies of James Naylor. 'The growth of these things', he declared, 'is more dangerous than the most intestine or foreign enemies. I have often been troubled in my thoughts to think of this toleration'. Again, 'if this be liberty, God deliver me from such liberty'; and finally, 'I was always of opinion in the Long Parliament, the more liberty the greater mischief' (*Diary of Thomas Burton*, 1.24–5, 50, 218).

Religion was indeed a matter close to Skippon's heart at all times. Judging by his published writings, his regimental flag, his will, and his recorded utterances, he adhered to an uncomplicated, non-sectarian brand of puritanism.

He sank substantial sums of his own money into the publication of three books, each several hundred pages long, of pious reflection and devotion. They largely consisted of long strings of biblical quotations linked by commentary. Among his favoured themes were the importance of prayer and sabbath observance, and his conviction that 'the scriptures are the infallible truth of God' (*Christian Centurian's Observations*, 1643, 223). He counselled his fellow soldiers not to be intimidated by, but to wear proudly, the labels puritan and roundhead. The emotional power of puritanism for Skippon is reflected in the words he addressed to his troops in early 1644: 'I am almost strucken into a sownd [swoon] for joy, and indeed you have so won my heart … that I … am willing to spend my dearest blood, in this just cause, and amongst you all'. In response, 'the souldiers with loud acclamations cried out that they would lose their lives with him' (*A most Joyfull Declaration*). Bearing witness to his confident providentialism was the flag he designed for his regiment. Beneath the image of a cloud from which an arm extends brandishing an unsheathed sword, it proclaims, 'Pray and fight. Jehovah helps us and help us we will' (*Ora et pugna. Iuvat et iuvabit Iehovah*; BL, Sloane MS 5247, fol. 31v). No sectarian, Skippon supported the Cromwellian church settlement of the 1650s. He was a good friend of the Independent divine Philip Nye, who preached at the wedding of his youngest daughter Susanna in 1655. In the will that he dictated at the end of his life he affirmed his belief in the 'unconceivable essence of the trin-une deitie', original sin, the resurrection of his own body after death, and eternal happiness (PRO, wills, PROB 11/300, fol. 257).

Yet piety for Skippon was no bar to self-enrichment. Parliament at various times awarded him £500, £1000, and £200 towards his arrears and expenses. In addition he acquired confiscated land in every category: crown, church, and royalist. In Norfolk he bought bishops' lands, including the bishop of Norwich's palace, valued at over £2500; in Norfolk and Kent he obtained dean and chapter land for £356; while in Cornwall he purchased the crown manor of Bonalva for £719. When the so-called delinquent or royalist estates came onto the market in 1651 Skippon purchased the manors of Bletchley, Whaddon, Eaton, and Winslow in Buckinghamshire, but then sold them off in small parcels to the tenants.

Last years Lord protector Cromwell showed his high respect for Skippon by naming him to the reinstituted House of Lords in 1657. When the protector died Skippon was one of the signatories to the proclamation of Richard as his successor. The following year the restored Rump Parliament reappointed Skippon major-general of the London militia (27 July 1659), and commander-in-chief of all the forces within the weekly bills of mortality (2 August 1659). As the end of his life approached, however, he played no part in the events leading up to the Restoration. His death occurred some time after 26 June 1660, and his will was proved on 25 October of that year. He left his properties in Acton and other parts of Middlesex and Buckinghamshire to Dame Katherine, whom he commended as 'a most Christian like, tender and carefull wife

and nurse unto mee …' (PRO, PROB 11/300, fol. 259). This was Katherine Philips, whom he had married after the death of his first wife on 24 January 1656: their marriage settlement was dated 22 August 1657. His Norfolk properties he bequeathed to his son and heir, Philip, and an unspecified sum in cash was granted as a marriage portion to his daughter Mary. He also left generous annuities and cash bequests with a capital value in excess of £156 to the poor in various parishes in Buckinghamshire, Middlesex, and Norfolk. For a largely self-educated man his library was impressive: it included the Bible and a Bible concordance, Josephus's *History of the Jews*, the works of Joseph Hall (2 vols.), Samuel Purchas's *Purchas his Pilgrimes* (5 vols.), Speed's and Holinshed's chronicles, Plutarch's lives, 'the Turkish historie', and Henry Hexham's 'two greate vollumes of the mapps of the whole world' (ibid., fols. 261v, 262v).   IAN J. GENTLES

Sources I. Gentles, 'The struggle for London in the second civil war', *HJ*, 26 (1983), 277–305 · I. Gentles, *The New Model Army in England, Ireland, and Scotland, 1645–1653* (1992) · *DNB* · P. Skippon, *A salve for every sore, or, A collection of promises out of the whole book of God, and is the Christian centurion's infallible ground of confidence* (1643) · P. Skippon, *A pearl of price, in a collection of promises* (1649) [enl. edn of *A salve for every sore*] · P. Skippon, *The Christian centurion's observations, advices, and resolutions, containing matters divine and moral, collected according to his own experience, by Philip Skippon* (1645) · P. Skippon, *True treasure, or thirty holy vows, containing a brief sum of all that concerns the Christian centurion's conscionable walking with God* (1644) · *A most joyfull declaration made by Colonell Skipon … at Maiden-head Ian 12* (1644) · PRO, wills, PROB 11/300, fols. 257–263v · exchequer, certificates of the sale of crown land, PRO, E121/1/6/9 · chancery close rolls, PRO, C 54/3465/3; 54/3518/32; 54/3888/37 · BL, Sloane MS 5247, fol. 31v · sales of bishops' lands, Bodl. Oxf., MS Rawl. B. 239, fol. 26 (349) · *JHC*, 2–5 (1640–48) · *JHL*, 7–9 (1644–7) · *CSP dom.*, 1641–9; 1659–60 · J. Rushworth, *Historical collections*, new edn, 5–6 (1721–2) · G. G. Walker, *The Honourable Artillery Company, 1537–1947* (1954) · R. W. Ketton-Cremer, *Norfolk in the civil war: a portrait of a society in conflict* (1969) · *Diary of Thomas Burton*, ed. J. T. Rutt, 4 vols. (1828), vol. 1 · C. B. Jewson, 'Norfolk and the Little Parliament of 1653', *Norfolk Archaeology*, 32 (1958–61), 129–41 · 'Skippon family', *Miscellanea Genealogica et Heraldica*, new ser., 1 (1874), 37–40 · parish register, St Mary's, Acton, Middlesex, 1539–1690, LMA
Archives Bodl. Oxf., corresp.
Likenesses J. Ricraft, line engraving, 1646, BL · R. S., line engraving, pubd 1647, NPG [*see illus.*] · line engraving, 1647, BM; repro. in Vicars, *England's worthies* · engraving, Honourable Artillery Company, London; repro. in Walker, *Honourable Artillery Company*, facing p. 51 · engraving, Bodl. Oxf.; repro. in Gentles, *The new model army*, 251 · print, repro. in J. Ricraft, *A survey of England's champions and truth's faithfull patriots* (1647); copy, line engraving, BM, NPG · stipple, NPG
Wealth at death wealthy; several thousand pounds; £23 in two annuities to poor; £3 6s. 8d. in bequests to poor; £100 in gold pieces; coaches, horses, books, silver plates; several hundred pounds owing to him; extensive landed estates in Middlesex, Norfolk and Buckinghamshire: will, PRO, PROB 11/300, fols. 257–260

Skipsey, Joseph (1832–1903), poet, was born on 17 March 1832 at Percy Main near North Shields, the eighth child of Cuthbert Skipsey (*d.* 1832) and his wife, Isabella (*née* Bell). Cuthbert, overman at Percy Main colliery, was shot dead by the special constable against whom he was defending a pitman in the bitter strike into which Joseph was born. The killer served a six-month sentence, but Isabella

Joseph Skipsey (1832–1903), by unknown photographer

received no pension or relief, and was soon forced to send her children down the pits, where Joseph went at the age of seven. As a trapper, opening and closing ventilation doors for sixteen hours a day, he taught himself to read and write from discarded playbills and advertisements. His first books were the Bible, Pope's *Iliad*, and *Paradise Lost*, gifts from an uncle when he was fifteen. Soon afterwards Skipsey became a putter, with higher pay, and studied Shakespeare, Burns, Blake, and some translations from Latin, Greek, and German, particularly Heine's poems and Goethe's *Faust*.

At twenty Skipsey walked most of the way to London, where in 1854 he married Sarah Ann Hendley (*d.* 1902), his landlady, with whom he soon returned north, first to work in Coatbridge, Scotland, for six months, then at the Pembroke collieries in Sunderland, and subsequently at Choppington. The couple had eight children. Skipsey was a strong and skilful hewer; intelligent and reliable, he was quickly promoted to pit deputy, but disliked the responsibilities and returned to hewing, where he stayed until retirement except for short spells at jobs obtained for him by admirers.

Skipsey's first volume of poems, published at Morpeth, Northumberland, in 1859, went largely unnoticed, and no copy is extant, but it attracted the attention of James Clephan, editor of the *Gateshead Observer*, who got Skipsey the post of an under-storekeeper at Gateshead. In the year of his next publication, *Poems, Songs and Ballads* (1862), 200 men and boys were killed by choke damp in Hartley colliery. In their memory Skipsey wrote 'The Hartley Calamity', a beautiful and dignified ballad which he read at many meetings to raise funds for Hartley widows and orphans. Greatly moved at one of these readings, Robert Spence Watson became a lifelong supporter of Skipsey, obtaining for him the job of assistant librarian to the Newcastle Literary and Philosophical Society in 1863. Meagre pay induced Skipsey to return to the pits—where he would remain for twenty years—the following year, when

The Collier Lad and other Lyrics (1864) was published, followed by *Poems* (1871), and *A Book of Miscellaneous Lyrics* (1878, re-issued with additions as *A Book of Lyrics* in 1881).

By this time Skipsey was enjoying some celebrity as 'the Collier Poet', and in 1880 Thomas Dixon, a Sunderland cork-cutter whose writings had brought him into contact with John Ruskin, took him to London, where he met the leading intellectuals of the day. Largely because of Edward Burne-Jones' influence, Skipsey was granted a civil-list pension of £10, raised in 1886 to £25, with a donation of £50 from the Royal Bounty Fund. Skipsey left the pits again in 1882, when he and his wife became caretakers of the Bentinck board schools in Mill Lane, Newcastle, for three years. Spence Watson's patronage again got Skipsey employment as a porter at the newly opened Armstrong College in 1888, but it lasted only a few months: 'it was quite impossible to have a college where the scientific men came to see the Principal and the artistic and literary men came to see the porter' (Bunting, 10). In 1889 a glittering company, including Burne-Jones, Browning, Tennyson, Dante Gabriel Rossetti, William Morris, and Lord Leighton, sponsored the 'tall, portly, well-proportioned man with a fine grave face' (ibid.) to become custodian of Shakespeare's house at Stratford upon Avon. Skipsey, deeply knowledgeable about Shakespeare's works, could not endure being 'a common showman' of counterfeit relics to troupes of tourists (Bradley) and he returned to the Northumberland pits in 1891. Skipsey's psychological experiences at Stratford suggested the theme of Henry James's story 'The Birthplace', in *The Better Sort* (1903).

Although Skipsey published *Carols from the Coalfields* (1886) during his unsatisfying period away from mining, most of his literary work in the 1880s was as general editor of the Canterbury Poets series, published by Walter Scott at Felling. His lecture 'The poet as seer and singer', was published in 1890. His last volume of poetry was *Songs and Lyrics* (1892). Skipsey later travelled with the Spence Watsons to the Lake District and the Norwegian fjords; he became a spiritualist for a time, believing himself to be clairvoyant. His last year was spent in the care of his twelve-year-old granddaughter, Jane Skipsey, and he died, a year after his wife, in his son's house at Harraton, near Newcastle, on 3 September 1903. He was buried in Gateshead cemetery, and was survived by the eldest of three daughters and two of his five sons: William was inspector of schools for Durham, James a master shifter at Montagu colliery in Scotswood, where the elderly Joseph had sometimes visited the colliery doctor whose son, Basil Bunting, edited a collection of Skipsey's poems in 1976.

Contemporary responses to Skipsey's poetry were mixed. Spence Watson was dismissive; but Oscar Wilde found his work reminiscent of Blake's, and Dante Gabriel Rossetti considered him 'a man of real genius … a poet of the people who describes what he knows and mixes in' (Bunting). *A Book of Miscellaneous Lyrics* was well reviewed by Theodore Watts-Dunton in *The Athenaeum* (16 November 1878), and translations of 'Fairies' Parting Song' and other poems appeared in Ernest de Chatelain's *Beautés de la poésie anglaise*, volume 3. Even Rossetti, however, found some crudeness of diction, rhyme, and rhythm in Skipsey's poems, as did Bunting, his most ardent proselytizer. His best lyrics, about mining life, bring written poetry close to nineteenth-century traditional oral dialect ballads. Although he read his poems in a strong accent and expected others to do so, unlike most dialect poets Skipsey did not attempt to transliterate dialect pronunciation, fully aware that however broadly ordinary working people spoke, they could read only standard English.

JOHN LANGTON

Sources R. S. Watson, *Joseph Skipsey: his life and work* (1909) • J. Skipsey, 'Autobiographical preface', *A book of miscellaneous lyrics* (1878) • B. Bunting, preface, in *Selected poems: Joseph Skipsey*, ed. B. Bunting (1976) • J. L. Bradley, 'Joseph Skipsey', *N&Q*, 223 (1978), 320–21 • G. Clucas, 'Joseph Skipsey', *Agenda*, 16/1 (1978), 106–12 [review] • A. H. Miles, 'Poets and poetry of the century', *The Athenaeum*, 5 (16 Nov 1878) • A. H. Miles, 'Poets and poetry of the century', *The Athenaeum* (12 Sept 1903) • review of *A book of miscellaneous lyrics*, *The Athenaeum* (16 Nov 1878), 618–19 • *Newcastle Daily Leader* (5 Sept 1903)

Archives Newcastle Central Library, MS notes | U. Newcastle, Robinson L., letters to R. S. Watson and E. S. Watson

Likenesses J. Koster, oils, 1894, priv. coll. • R. T. & Co., wood-engraving, NPG; repro. in *ILN* (16 April 1892) • engraving, repro. in Bunting, ed., *John Skipsey: selected poems* • oils (after J. Koster, 1894), Laing Museum and Art Gallery, Newcastle upon Tyne • photographs, repro. in Watson, *Joseph Skipsey* [*see illus.*]

Skipwith, Sir William (*b. c.*1320, *d.* in or before 1398), justice, was probably born about 1320, into an old Yorkshire family that took its name from the village of Skipwith. The second son of William Skipwith and his wife, Margaret, daughter and heir of Ralph Fitzsimon of South Ormsby, Lincolnshire, the younger William entered the legal profession, and became one of the longest-serving justices of the fourteenth century. His career as a lawyer may have begun in York. In 1341 the vicars-choral of St Peter's, York, appointed him their attorney, and in 1348 he represented the city in parliament. By 1345 he had married a Lincolnshire heiress, Alice Hiltoft, who was to inherit the manors of North and South Hiltoft and Ingoldmells from her father Sir William, and the manors of Cawthorpe, Covenham, and Uphall from her mother, Alice Muer, by 1361. At his own father's death (probably before 1361) Skipwith inherited parts of the manors of Skipwith and Menthorpe in Yorkshire, and the Lincolnshire manors of Bigby and Thorpe, his elder brother John having died prematurely. From his mother, he was to acquire by 1369 the manors of South Ormsby and Ketsby in Lincolnshire.

In Michaelmas term 1344 Skipwith was created a serjeant-at-law, and his arguments in court begin to be reported frequently in the year-books. He was retained as a king's serjeant in 1354, and in 1359 was appointed a justice of the common pleas. Within a few months he was knighted, and in June 1361 became chief baron of the exchequer. In 1344 he had received the first of many appointments to oyer and terminer commissions in the midlands and Yorkshire. He rode the midland circuit on assize from 1347 to 1359, and the northern circuit from 1360 to 1365. Throughout his career he saw continuous service on commissions of the peace and gaol delivery in the midlands and Yorkshire, and was also often appointed to survey dikes and ditches there. For six years after its promulgation in 1350 he heard cases under the Statute of Labourers in several counties. Service on judicial commissions had its perils. At an oyer and terminer session in Louth a defendant drew his sword and seized Skipwith by the throat, causing him to adjourn proceedings.

A number of wealthy magnates also sought Skipwith's services, including Ralph Stafford, earl of Stafford (*d.* 1372), and John, Lord Willoughby, to whose son and heir, Robert, Skipwith had married his eldest daughter, Alice, by 1370. But his most important private employer was Edward, prince of Wales, who in September 1355 retained him at 50*s.* per annum to provide counsel and plead; in 1362 this fee was doubled. At the height of his influence, however, in October 1365 Sir William suddenly fell from grace. The chronicler Knighton reports that he and Henry Green (*d.* 1369), the chief justice of the king's bench, were dismissed from office for 'enormous infidelities', and imprisoned until they had paid large fines to the king. No record of proceedings against them survives, but Sir William and several associates, mostly of Lincolnshire, gave two recognizances to the crown for the sum of 4000 marks in April and May 1366. On 10 February 1370, after half the money had been paid, Sir William was pardoned, and five days later he was appointed chief justice for pleas in Ireland. In 1373 he returned to England and began to serve again on judicial commissions. In 1374 he was appointed justice of north and south Wales by the Black Prince, and by October 1376 his rehabilitation was complete, with his reappointment as justice of the common pleas. In the following year he was back on the midland assize circuit, switching in 1385 to the northern circuit. His rapid restoration to office led earlier historians to invent a second Sir William Skipwith, whose first judicial appointment was to the Irish bench in 1370.

By April 1377 Skipwith had entered the service of John of Gaunt, duke of Lancaster, who appointed him his chief justice. Presiding over proceedings brought against William Wykeham (*d.* 1404) at Gaunt's instigation in November 1376, Sir William refused to grant the defendant an adjournment to seek counsel, expressly in retribution for Wykeham's similar treatment of Gaunt's ally, William, Lord Latimer (*d.* 1381), in the Good Parliament earlier that year. The Anonimalle chronicle also reports that Sir William sternly rebutted Wykeham's claim that as chancellor he was not accountable for his office, and Wykeham was fined £64,000.

His memory of his own dismissal probably loomed large in the only crisis Skipwith faced during Richard II's reign. When summoned to the council at Nottingham in 1387 to give an opinion on the king's assertion of his royal prerogative, he pleaded illness, thereby avoiding the fate that subsequently befell his fellow judges. However, he and his two eldest sons were among the Lincolnshire gentry who swore an oath to uphold the lords appellant in 1388. That year he retired from the bench, although appointed a trier of petitions in parliament, as he had been in every parliament from 1362 to 1365, and from 1376 to 1386. In 1390 his service on judicial commissions also ceased, and he was dead by 15 November 1398.

Skipwith was survived by five sons and one daughter. He left an estate further enlarged by marriage and purchase. By 1370 his eldest son, William, had married Catherine d'Avranches, heir to the larger parts of the Yorkshire manors of Skipwith and Menthorpe. His second son, John, married Alice, daughter of Sir Frederick Tilney of Boston, represented Lincolnshire in three parliaments, and eventually inherited the bulk of the family estate from his brother's daughter. A third son, Stephen (d. 1398), was rector of the church of Ingoldmells, and the youngest sons, Patrick and Thomas, were still alive in 1415, when they and their mother received bequests in the will of the judge's second daughter, Margaret, wife of Sir Henry Vavasour of Yorkshire. MAUREEN JURKOWSKI

Sources W. O. Massingberd, *History of the parish of Ormsby-cum-Ketsby* (1893) · C. Rawcliffe, 'Skipwith, John', HoP, *Commons* · *Chancery records* · BL, Harley charters, 49.G.11, 52.A.37, 55.B.24, 56.E.29, 57.G.11, 57.G.16, 58.A.48, 84.A.35 · BL, Add. ch. 19922 · BL, Harley MS 5019, fols. 207v–212 · Lincs. Arch., Massingberd papers, MM1, MM2 · Baker, *Serjeants*, 157, 537 · *List of assize rolls, 1206–1481*, PRO (1986) · M. C. B. Dawes, ed., *Register of Edward, the Black Prince*, PRO, 2–4 (1931–3) · King's remembrancer's miscellanea, PRO, E163/24/1, rot. 7d · R. Somerville, *History of the duchy of Lancaster, 1265–1603* (1953), 467–8 · G. H. Moberly, *Life of William of Wykeham* (1887) · *VCH Yorkshire East Riding*, 2.63, 93 · *RotP*, vols. 2–3 · P. H. W. Booth, *The financial administration of the lordship and county of Chester, 1272–1377* (1981), App. III · J. R. Maddicott, 'Law and lordship: royal justices as retainers in thirteenth- and fourteenth-century England', *Past and Present*, suppl. 4 (1978), esp. 1–88 · *Inquisitions and assessments relating to feudal aids*, 6 vols., PRO (1899–1921) · PRO, C138/25/12 · PRO, C137/72/33

Archives BL, Harley charters, deeds, 49.G.11, 52.A.37, 55.B.24, 56.E.29, 57.G.11, 57.G.16, 58.A.48, 84.A.35 · Lincs. Arch., Massingberd MSS

Wealth at death £300 p.a.: PRO, C 138/25/12; C 137/72/33

Skipwith, Sir William (c.1564–1610), politician and poet, was born at Tugby, Leicestershire, the eldest surviving son of Henry Skipwith (d. 1588) of Cotes and Keythorpe, Leicestershire, and his wife, Jane (d. 1598), daughter of Francis Hall of Grantham, Lincolnshire, and widow of Francis Nele of Prestwold and Cotes, Leicestershire. He was educated at Jesus College, Cambridge, in 1580, and was knighted on 30 April 1603.

Sir William was descended from a long line of Lincolnshire gentry. His family became established in Leicestershire when his father, a younger son and equerry to Queen Elizabeth, married the widow of Francis Nele of Prestwold and Tugby and also purchased the manor of Cotes. William served as a volunteer with the earl of Leicester in the Netherlands in 1586, but after his father's death in 1588 settled down to life in the shire, becoming an influential figure in local politics. He was appointed to the county bench in 1592, served as sheriff (1597–8), was one of the commissioners to deal with the midland revolt and problems of depopulation in 1607, and served as knight of the shire in 1601 and MP for Leicester in the parliament of 1604–10. He also played host to Queen Anne and Prince Henry when they stayed in Leicester on their progress south in June 1603.

Skipwith's role in Leicestershire politics was largely determined by his ambiguous relationship with the Hastings family which dominated the local scene. During the late 1590s he was said to be 'out of frendship' with the fourth earl of Huntingdon, the head of the family (Bodl. Oxf., MS Carte 78, fol. 319) and this probably cost him a seat for the county in the parliament of 1597. By 1601 he had to some extent been reconciled with the family and his election for the county that year was probably with Huntingdon's blessing; however, at hearings during the parliament Skipwith sided with George Belgrave who had snubbed the earl during the election for Leicester. Skipwith was on much friendlier terms with George's grandson Henry, who succeeded to the earldom in 1605; however, in local politics he continued to take an independent line. He voiced loud criticisms of abuses by the local purveyor which reflected badly on the earl's management of the service; he also sided with the Greys and the Beaumonts in quarrels with the earl's great-uncle, Walter Hastings. Perhaps as a result of this Huntingdon never promoted him to the prestigious local office of deputy lieutenant. As an MP Skipwith was not a prominent speaker, confining himself mainly to interventions on local issues. None the less he established a reputation, both in Leicestershire and at Westminster, as an exemplary 'parliament man'.

Skipwith's standing was also enhanced by his religious and literary activities. There is little evidence for his personal piety, but he showed his support for local puritans when the opportunity arose and was regarded as one of their chief allies. In May 1603 he arrested trouble-makers in Leicester who had set up a maypole in defiance of the town's godly ministers; then in January 1605 he joined other leading justices to sign a petition to Viscount Cranborne on behalf of puritan clergy who had been deprived of their livings. He was also a prominent member of a literary circle gathered under the patronage of Sir Henry Goodyer and the fifth earl of Huntingdon. Copies of his poems survive in a commonplace book which belonged to his family and also included works by other members of the network, notably Francis and John Beaumont, John Donne, and Thomas Pestell. Skipwith's verses dwelt on the themes of beauty, romantic love, and the author's obligations to his patron. The lines he composed for the earl's entertainment at Ashby, on the occasion of a visit from his mother-in-law, Alice, countess of Derby, in 1607, included a mock 'chancery bill' indicting the countess and other gentlewomen present for 'stealing the hearts of his Majesty's loving subjects' (BL, Add. MS 25707, fol. 134). In his *Worthies of England*, Thomas Fuller described Skipwith as

a person of much valour, judgement, learning and wisdom, dexterous at the making fit and acute epigrams, poesies, mottoes and devices, but chiefly at impresses neither so apparent that every rustic might understand them, nor so obscure that they needed an Oedipus to interpret them. (Fuller, *Worthies*, 2.258)

Sir William was married twice, first, to Margaret (d.

1594), daughter of Roger Cave of Stanford, Northamptonshire, with whom he had four sons and four daughters, and second, to Jane (d. 1630), daughter of John Roberts and widow of John Markham of Sidebrook. He died in London on 3 May 1610 and was buried at Prestwold church where his second wife erected a large monument to him. The verses inscribed on this, written by his friend John Beaumont, present him as the ideal of the contemporary gentleman: nobly born, hospitable, learned, and the true servant of his country (Nichols, 3.359).

RICHARD CUST

Sources HoP, *Commons, 1558–1603* · P. Watson, 'Skipwith, Sir William', HoP, *Commons* [draft] · J. Knowles, 'WS MS', *TLS* (29 April–5 May 1988), 472, 485 · R. P. Cust, 'Purveyance and politics in Jacobean Leicestershire', *Regionalism and revision*, ed. P. Fleming, A. Gross, and J. R. Lander (1999), 145–62 · R. P. Cust, 'Honour, rhetoric and political culture: the earl of Huntingdon and his enemies', *Political culture and cultural politics in early modern England*, ed. S. D. Amussen and M. Kishlansky (1995), 84–111 · J. Nichols, *The history and antiquities of the county of Leicester*, 3/1 (1800), 357–66 · Fuller, *Worthies* (1840), 2.258 · G. F. Farnham, 'Prestwold and its hamlets in medieval times', *Transactions of the Leicestershire Archaeological Society*, 17 (1932–3), 7–8 · Bodl. Oxf., MSS Carte 77, 78 · BL, Add. MS 25707 · *Records of the borough of Leicester*, 4: *1603–1688*, ed. H. Stocks (1923), 137 · W. Kelly, *Notices illustrative of the drama etc. … extracted from the manuscripts of the borough of Leicester* (1865), 100–09 · PRO, PROB 11/117/42, Wood

Archives BL, family commonplace book, Add. MS 25707

Likenesses funeral monument, Prestwold church, Leicestershire

Skirlawe [Skirlaw], **Walter** (c.1330–1406), diplomat and bishop of Durham, was born in or shortly after 1330 at Skirlaugh in the parish of Swine, near Hull. His family was probably prosperous, since his sister Joan became prioress of Swine. Other recorded relatives are John Skirlawe and John Danby, who received crown benefices, a married brother William, and Robert Custeby, whose education is provided for in his will.

Skirlawe is first recorded as a notary, attesting in the consistory court of York in 1353. He was registrar to Archbishop John Thoresby (d. 1373) by July 1356, and early in 1358 received his first benefice, the rectory of Preston Bisset in Buckinghamshire. In February 1359 he went on a mission to the curia at Avignon, staying for about a year on the archbishop's business. While there, on 30 November 1359, he was provided by the pope to the archdeaconry of the East Riding at Thoresby's request. The archbishop described Skirlawe as his secretary and as a student of canon and civil law for six years, an earlier petition having named him BCL. Other visits to the curia followed between 1360 and 1363, but Skirlawe was perhaps also attending the schools at Oxford: in 1362 he is again described as a student of law, and a royal writ was served on him 'in his hospice in Oxford', apparently in 1364.

A crisis arose in Skirlawe's life when in March 1364 the crown, pretending a spurious vacancy, presented the queen's secretary to his archdeaconry, and then proceeded by *quare impedit* against Skirlawe and his archbishop. The court record demonstrates Archbishop Thoresby's unwillingness to defend the suit, while Skirlawe failed to appear. According to the king's attorney in a

resulting action, disregarding a royal writ of prohibition Skirlawe left the country disguised as a servant in striped clothing, sued in the papal courts at Avignon, and obtained an inhibition forbidding the archbishop to admit the crown presentee, which he caused to be posted on the doors of York Minster. The crown's reaction was to proceed by *praemunire* against Skirlawe and his abettors, notably Peter Stapleton, who had smuggled him abroad, and the prior of Drax, accused of receiving the revenues of the archdeaconry and dispatching them to Avignon. In June 1366 Skirlawe was outlawed.

Skirlawe remained in exile until 1370, described in one instance as continually dwelling at the curia, where he presumably found occupation. Meanwhile his attempted supplanter was not admitted to his archdeaconry, and eventually a settlement was reached: in the course of 1370 Skirlawe was first given safe conduct to return for a year, then pardoned his outlawry, and finally confirmed in his archdeaconry.

After his rehabilitation Skirlawe perhaps returned for a time to Oxford, and certainly to Avignon, for in 1374, by now DCnL, he brought letters from the pope to the king and bishops during preparations for a meeting of papal and royal ambassadors at Bruges, and similarly to London from the nuncios after their arrival. One recipient, the recently consecrated archbishop of York, Alexander Neville (d. 1392), on 19 July appointed him official of the court of York and sent him north to explain to a newly summoned convocation matters raised at Bruges. Skirlawe, described as LLD in October 1374, was official at York for only two years. In 1376 he entered the royal service: a king's clerk by 5 October, he witnessed Edward III's will on 7 October, on 27 November received the deanery of St Martin's-le-Grand, and on 6 March 1377 was granted a salary as a chancery clerk.

Skirlawe's appointment was evidently due to his international experience. He at once began to serve on diplomatic missions, mostly negotiations in Calais for peace with France, but including a journey to Rome. He also went to Brittany, and in 1380 attended the meeting of John of Gaunt, duke of Lancaster, with the Scots. Early in 1381 he helped negotiate the treaty of marriage between Richard II and Anne of Bohemia, and in May was among those dispatched to Prague to obtain its ratification and contract the marriage on Richard's behalf. From there Sir Nicholas Dagworth and Skirlawe travelled on to Rome for prolonged negotiations with the pope and Italian princes, returning to London on 5 August 1382.

Three days later Skirlawe was appointed keeper of the privy seal, an office he held until 23 October 1386. His new responsibilities did not prevent his crossing the channel four times in as many years for negotiations with the French, while in 1385 he accompanied Richard II on his Scottish expedition. Made bishop of Coventry and Lichfield on 28 June 1385, he was consecrated at Westminster on 14 January 1386 in the presence of the king and a notable assembly. On 18 August 1386, again by papal provision, he was translated to Bath and Wells in preference to the king's secretary, Richard Medford, who had been elected by the chapter; the wishes of the king in this matter are obscure. Unusually he retained the privy seal on becoming bishop, but when in October 1386 the earl of Suffolk was dismissed as chancellor and Bishop John Fordham (d. 1425) as treasurer, Skirlawe too left office, although his resignation was not called for in parliament. In spring 1387 he treated for peace with the Scots.

Skirlawe was one of the bishops promoted when the king's personal rule was overturned by the lords appellant, being translated to Durham by papal bull dated 3 April 1388, although not effective until September. In this crisis he does not appear as an active partisan, rather an acceptable and respected administrator, although his credit with Richard II may well have diminished. With William Wykeham (d. 1404) he was enrolled to provide an episcopal element in the committee appointed in January to control the king, but was not reappointed when it was renewed in May. In December he headed an embassy that concluded a truce with France in June 1389. He then presided over five successive conferences to treat for peace. After 1393 he ceased to be employed in the French negotiations, but in August 1394 treated with the Scots, being now more regularly in the north. When, following the parliament of September 1397 at which the king turned the tables on the lords appellant, he obtained exemption from attending parliaments after the session pending at Shrewsbury, he pleaded ill health; whether this was genuine or simply politic, he is not among those mentioned as attending the Shrewsbury session at which the king's personal rule was firmly re-established. In 1398 he was apparently elected archbishop by the chapter of York, but was passed over in favour of Richard Scrope (d. 1405).

In 1399 Skirlawe attended the assembly that received Richard II's abdication, and assented to his imprisonment; he was at Henry IV's coronation feast and attended council meetings during November and early December. He was made chief ambassador for negotiations with the French for continuing the truce and returning Isabella, Richard's queen, and, to this end he crossed the channel four times in the next two years. The treaty of 17 May 1401 was his final success as a diplomat. Thereafter he retired permanently to the north, excusing himself from parliaments on grounds of infirmity.

Skirlawe paid proper attention to the administration of the diocese and the county palatine of Durham, although not always able to prevent royal infringements of his palatine liberty. He was particularly concerned for good order in hospitals and collegiate churches. In 1402–3 he dealt with an outbreak of Lollardy in Newcastle, and Richard Wyche's own account of his examination by Skirlawe provides a glimpse of his personal character. Although described by one of his own household as 'somewhat headstrong and impatient' (Matthew, 534), the elderly bishop appears more concerned to persuade than condemn, giving the accused every opportunity to recant.

A considerable builder and benefactor, Skirlawe rebuilt the parochial chapel at his birthplace, and contributed to other surviving buildings at Durham, Howden, and York. At all four places he founded a chantry, and at Howden a common dwelling for the clergy. At University College, Oxford, he endowed three fellowships in theology open to non-graduates; but there is no known evidence for Anthony Wood's statement that Skirlawe himself once had a fellowship there. He gave books to University College and New College, and made many legacies to churches, friends, and servants. Skirlawe made his will on 7 March 1404, adding numerous codicils during the next fourteen months; they reveal a prodigious personal wealth. On 11 May he attended the translation of the remains of St John of Bridlington (d. 1379), but thereafter is found only at the bishop of Durham's Yorkshire manors of Wheel Hall and Howden, not far from his birthplace. He died at Howden on 24 March 1406 and was buried in Durham Cathedral, in a chantry tomb at the altar of St Blaise and St John of Beverley.

Throughout his life Skirlawe's legal, administrative, and diplomatic expertise brought him numerous rewards in the form of benefices and dignities. He was always useful and evidently highly respected, and it is perhaps a further tribute to his diplomatic skill that any personal antipathies or political antagonisms attending his later career can only be guessed at.   M. G. SNAPE

Sources PRO · Durham dean and chapter muniments, U. Durham L., archives and special collections · York archbishops' registers, Borth. Inst. · *Chancery records* · *CEPR letters* · [J. Raine], ed., *Testamenta Eboracensia*, 1, SurtS, 4 (1836), 306–25 · York *sede vacante* register, BL, MS Cotton Galba E.x · letter of Queen Philippa, BL, Add. ch. 15422 · R. G. Davies, 'The episcopate and the political crisis in England of 1386–1388', *Speculum*, 51 (1976), 659–93 · M. G. Snape, 'Some evidence of Lollard activity in the diocese of Durham', *Archaeologia Aeliana*, 4th ser., 39 (1961), 355–61 · *RotP*, vol. 3 · *Polychronicon Ranulphi Higden monachi Cestrensis*, ed. C. Babington and J. R. Lumby, 9 vols., Rolls Series, 41 (1865–86), vols. 8–9 · *Thomae Walsingham, quondam monachi S. Albani, historia Anglicana*, ed. H. T. Riley, 2 vols., pt 1 of *Chronica monasterii S. Albani*, Rolls Series, 28 (1863–4) · Emden, *Oxf.* · F. D. Matthew, 'The trial of Richard Wyche', *EngHR*, 5 (1890), 530–44

Archives BL, York *sede vacante* register, Cotton MS Galba E.x · Borth. Inst., registers

Wealth at death est. to be over £4000, incl. approx. £2600 in cash and at least £1000 in plate, vestments, hangings, and books: will

Skirving, Adam (*bap.* 1719, *d.* 1803), songwriter, was a son of Archibald Skirvine and Grizell Howdan, and was baptized at Athelstaneford in Haddingtonshire on 27 October 1719. He was educated at Prestonkirk and became a substantial farmer, tenant of Garleton Farm near Haddington. He is credited with two of the most popular songs from the Jacobite rising of 1745: 'Tranent Muir', beginning 'The Chevalier being void of fear did march up Birstle Brae, man', and 'Johnny Cope', one of the most brilliant of Scottish comic songs, celebrating the plight of General Sir John Cope, the government commander at the disastrously lost battle of Prestonpans which took place on 21 September 1745:

> Coup sent a challenge frae Dunbar,
> Chairlie, meet me an ye dare,

And I'll learn you the art of war
If you'll meet me in the morning.
(Ritson, 2.84–6n.)

The song was published in Burns and Johnson's *Scots Musical Museum* (vol. 3, 1790) and in two versions in Joseph Ritson's *Scotish Songs* (1794). However, there are striking differences between these texts in terms of artistic quality, and it seems clear that they were not the product of a single mind. It is not obvious which—if any—of these may have been Skirving's. The richness of Scotland's popular song culture depended on mechanisms that ensured a degree of collective composition, with material in circulation receiving attention from every creative personality through which it passed until eventually a stable form was reached. In the case of 'Johnny Cope' this proved to be the second of Ritson's versions, printed in *Scotish Songs* as an extended footnote.

Skirving married Jean Ainslie (*bap.* 1722) on 25 November 1747. They had at least two sons, Archibald *Skirving, the portraitist, and Robert. It is highly likely that he is also the Adam Skirving of Athelstaneford who married Christian Carnagie on 18 March 1786. He died in April 1803, and was buried in the church of Athelstaneford; his epitaph described him as:

In feature, in figure, agility, mind,
And happy wit rarely surpass'd.
(Wilson, 1.187)

WILLIAM DONALDSON

Sources J. G. Wilson, ed., *The poets and poetry of Scotland*, 2 vols. in 4 (1876–7) · R. Burns and others, *The Scots musical museum*, ed. J. Johnson, 6 vols. (1787–1803) · J. Ritson, ed., *Scotish song*, 2 vols. (1794) · R. Chambers, ed., *Scottish song prior to Burns* (1862) · *The correspondence of Thomas Percy and George Paton*, ed. A. F. Falconer (1961), vol. 6 of *The Percy letters*, ed. C. Brooks, D. N. Smith, and A. F. Falconer (1944–88) · W. Donaldson, *The Jacobite song: political myth and national identity* (1988) · parish register, Athelstaneford, East Lothian, 27 Oct 1719 [baptism] · *IGI*

Likenesses A. Skirving, oils, Scot. NPG · A. Skirving, portrait, Art Gallery of New South Wales, Sydney · portrait, priv. coll.

Skirving, Archibald (1749–1819), portrait artist, the eldest son of the farmer and Jacobite balladeer Adam *Skirving (*bap.* 1719, *d.* 1803) and his first wife, Jean Ainslie (*bap.* 1722), was born at East Garleton Farm, Athelstaneford, near Haddington, in October 1749. Adam Skirving was a tenant farmer on the Charteris-Wemyss estate, then based at Amisfield House, near Haddington, and later at Gosford House, near Longniddry. Archibald Skirving was educated at the local school in Athelstaneford and, according to the writer Henry Mackenzie and the art critic George Cleghorn, at the age of eighteen he was found a job by his father as a junior clerk in the Edinburgh customs office. He began to paint miniatures and oil portraits at this time. Key early works, datable to *c.*1770, are the masterly miniature of his father (Lloyd, 13, fig. 1) as well as the pair of oils of his parents and the youthful *Self-Portrait* (Art Gallery of New South Wales, Sydney; Lloyd, 13 and 15, figs. 2–3 and 5). An autograph variant of the portrait of his father also survives (Scot. NPG). The miniature is notable for its virtuoso technique and penetrating characterization, both aspects of Skirving's later pastels and drawings. The oils are

Archibald Skirving (1749–1819), self-portrait, 1790

painted in a more conventional manner, strongly influenced by the style of Allan Ramsay. At this time it is likely that Skirving studied at the Trustees' Academy in Edinburgh, where Charles Pavillon was master from 1768 to 1772. During this first Edinburgh period he would have been in direct competition as a miniaturist with Henry Raeburn, seven years his junior.

In 1777 Skirving, like many other Scottish artists, moved to London. He had various letters of introduction, including one to John Hamilton Mortimer, the noted painter of conversation pieces. Skirving exhibited his work only once at the Royal Academy during this period. In 1778, described as a miniature painter, he displayed 'a frame with three miniatures'. The exhibition catalogue listed his address or lodgings as 'at Mrs Milward's, Little Brook Street, Hanover Square'. His delicately painted *Unknown Lady* (V&A; Lloyd, 16, fig. 9) is signed and dated 1780.

Skirving must have found it difficult to establish himself in London, as he was back in Edinburgh during the mid-1780s, when he was working on *John Hume* and *Mrs Lockhart*. He was also beginning to create portraits in pastels or crayons, including his first known rendition in this medium: *Catherine Hume of Ninewells, Later Mrs Robert Johnston of Hutton Hall* (NG Scot.). Made *c.*1784–6, this portrait of David Hume's niece is an exuberant study of a fashionable woman, and is notable for its high-keyed colouring and lively characterization. Finding it difficult also to make a successful career in Edinburgh, Skirving decided to study in Rome, like many other Scottish artists before him. He left Leith by boat on 30 November 1786, and did not return until 1795. Primarily based in Rome, Skirving seems to have been supported by his father's landlord, the Hon. Francis Charteris of Amisfield, styled seventh earl of Wemyss from 1787, or by his only son, styled Viscount Elcho. The latter visited Rome with his family in late 1789, where he and his eldest son, later restored as sixth earl of Wemyss, both sat to Skirving in January 1790 for their portraits in pastel (priv. coll.). Skirving also demonstrated his prowess both as a pastellist and as a portrait miniaturist by producing outstanding self-portraits in both media (Scot. NPG), in which he explored subtle changes of mood in the use of the shadow cast on his brow by a wide-brimmed black beaver-fur hat.

While in Rome, Skirving also portrayed in a notably lucid pastel his fellow Scottish artist Gavin Hamilton (1788–9; Scot. NPG), as well as making crayon and black chalk portraits in 1791 of the sculptor John Flaxman (both York City Art Gallery). He also studied and copied classical sculpture, and made a series of delicate landscape drawings of scenes around Rome (NG Scot.). One of his best-known drawings is from this date, the dispassionate yet witty triple portrait *Unknown Family* (1792; priv. coll.; Lloyd frontispiece), a rare image of a British family on the grand tour. Like other artists in Rome, Skirving supplemented his income by acting as an art dealer and agent, in this case for the wealthy retired Scottish judge Francis Garden, Lord Gardenstone.

Skirving departed from Rome on 22 May 1794, but on 4 August he was taken prisoner by the French at sea off Gibraltar, and was imprisoned in Brest as a spy. After months of brutal incarceration, during which he suffered serious eye problems, Skirving was released thanks to the efforts of two fellow artists still in Italy, James Smith and Jean-Bernard Duvivier. They wrote to François Cacault, the French republican chargé d'affaires in Florence: 'c'est artiste nous a toujours manifesté à Rome l'amour la plus grande pour la Révolution française' (Ingamells, 863).

Having landed at Berwick upon Tweed on 12 August 1795, Skirving re-established himself in Edinburgh, purchasing a flat at 3 St James's Square. He also rented an unpretentious two-room studio nearby, at 12 Leith Street (or Terrace)—unusually without a showroom or gallery. He concentrated on producing a small number of very high-quality pastels, portraying only a limited clientele. Up to fifty sittings were sometimes required, and in some instances his fee rose to 100 guineas. To this unusual business practice Skirving added increasingly eccentric habits and frequently impolite behaviour, for which he became well known in Edinburgh society. His strange habits were noted by, among others, Thomas Carlyle, who described him as living 'in complete Hermitage, an indignant but uncomplaining King, supreme sovereign there if nowhere else' (*Reminiscences*, 133–4). Carlyle, who as a young man had met Skirving as an old man, was also aware, however, of the artist's unforgettable appearance, describing him 'with brow, cheek, jaws, chin all betokening impetuosity, rapidity, delicacy and the stormy fire of genius not yet hidden under the ashes of old age' (ibid., 136).

During the eight years from 1795, when Skirving returned to Edinburgh, until 1803, when he retired as a professional portraitist, he produced a small number of outstanding works in pastel. These include portraits of the judges Alexander Fraser Tytler, Lord Woodhouselee (1798; priv. coll.), and William Craig, Lord Craig (Scot. NPG), as well as the mother of the writer John Wilson (Christopher North), Margaret Sym, Mrs John Wilson (Scot. NPG). Equally severe yet sympathetic are the portraits of James Boswell's cousin, the lawyer Robert Boswell of St Boswells (priv. coll.), and his half-sister Janet Skirving, Mrs James Carnegie of Edrom Newton (NG Scot.). Skirving's sensitivity as a portraitist of children is evident in the pastels of the teenager Henry Home Drummond, sixth laird of Blair Drummond and the unique full length of the young boy Robert Dundas of Arniston holding an owl (both priv. coll.). His portrait of the geologist, etcher, and naval theorist John Clerk of Eldin, signed and dated 1800 (but exhibited at the Royal Academy in 1799) and the profoundly moving half length *Unknown Lady*, signed and dated 1803 (both priv. coll.) are equally sensitive portraits of elderly sitters.

Skirving's skill as a portrait draughtsman is also evident in his direct but subtle profile heads, drawn in red or black chalk. Very rarely he drew similar but unusual portraits in white chalk on mahogany panel, such as *The Hon. Charles Napier of Merchiston*, signed and dated 1800 (Glasgow Museums: Art Gallery and Museum, Kelvingrove). During his own lifetime, and ever since, Skirving's most famous portrait has remained his luminous copy drawn in red chalk ('keel'), after Alexander Nasmyth's small oil on panel of Robert Burns (both Scot. NPG). Sir Walter Scott admired this work, and described it in a letter of 30 May 1816 to the poet and collector Samuel Rogers—before Skirving took it to London in that year—as 'the only good portrait of Burns' (*Letters*, 4.243).

Skirving also occasionally painted oil portraits such as that of the pamphleteer the Revd Alexander Carlyle (Scot. NPG). As an old man he was clearly admired by some of the younger generation of Scottish artists. Raeburn portrayed him in oils (priv. coll., USA) for his gallery of eminent contemporaries in his studio at York Place, Edinburgh. Andrew Geddes also portrayed him in oils (NG Scot.) and in an etching, to which Skirving himself added drypoint. In addition George Watson painted two oil portraits of Skirving (Scot. NPG and East Lothian council museums service).

A small number of Skirving's portraits were reproduced as prints, including Robert Scott's stipple engraving *Gavin Hamilton* (1793), William Ward's pair of mezzotints *Mr and Mrs Mark Sprot*, John Beugo's line-engraving after the copy of *Robert Burns*, S. W. Reynolds's mezzotint *John Clerk of Eldin* (1800), and George Dawe's mezzotint *The Hon. William Craig* (1801), as well as the posthumous mezzotint by Charles Turner *Francis Walker* (1821) and a line and stipple engraving by Edward Scriven, *John Rennie*.

Skirving, who never married, spent the last part of his life with his sister Grace, living on her farm at Inveresk, just outside Musselburgh near Edinburgh. He died suddenly on 19 May 1819 leaving a substantial estate of just over £4000, partly indicating the extreme frugality with which he led his life. Skirving was buried in Athelstaneford churchyard in the same plot as his father and grandfather. His tombstone was inscribed with words composed by his brother Robert:

> By peculiar excellence attained eminence
> as a portrait painter;
> and might have lived in affluence,
> had he not aimed at private independence
> by simplifying the comforts of common life.

Skirving's pastel portraits made during the period 1784–1803 in some respects constituted a challenge to Henry Raeburn, who at that time dominated the Scottish market for portraiture in oils. Skirving was the only major pastellist, apart from Catherine Read, to have worked in Scotland. After a first-ever exhibition of his work, held at the Scottish National Portrait Gallery in 1999, Skirving can now be seen as one of the finest European pastellists of the eighteenth century, worthy of comparison with Maurice-Quentin de La Tour, Jean-Étienne Liotard, and Hugh Douglas Hamilton.   STEPHEN LLOYD

Sources S. Lloyd, *Raeburn's rival: Archibald Skirving, 1749–1819* (1999) [exhibition catalogue, Scot. NPG, 22 Jan – 5 Apr 1999] · T. Sundström, 'Aspects of the life and work of Archibald Skirving (1749–1819)', MPhil diss., U. St Andr., 1994 · B. C. Skinner, 'Archibald Skirving and his work', *Transactions of the East Lothian Antiquarian and Field Naturalists' Society*, 12 (1970), 46–56 · J. Ingamells, ed., *A dictionary of British and Irish travellers in Italy, 1701–1800* (1997) · *The reminiscences of Thomas Carlyle: now first published*, ed. J. Clubbe (Durham, North Carolina, 1974) · K. Andrews and J. R. Brotchie, *Catalogue of Scottish drawings* (1960) · Lord Gardenstone [F. Garden], *Travelling memorandums, made in a tour upon the continent of Europe, in the years 1786, 87 & 88* (1791–5); 2nd edn, 3 vols. (1802) · H. Smailes, *The concise catalogue of the Scottish National Portrait Gallery* (1990) · *The letters of Sir Walter Scott*, ed. H. J. C. Grierson and others, centenary edn, 12 vols. (1932–79) · *Portrait drawings by Scottish artists, 1750–1850* (1955) [exhibition catalogue, Scot. NPG] · G. Cleghorn, *Ancient and modern art* (1837), 2nd edn, 2 vols. (1848) · *The anecdotes and egotisms of Henry Mackenzie, 1745–1831: now first published*, ed. H. W. Thompson (1927) · tombstone, Athelstaneford churchyard, near Haddington · IGI

Archives NA Scot., estate papers, SC 70/1/19, fols. 540–44 · NL Scot., NLS Acc. 10102

Likenesses A. Skirving, self-portrait, chalk drawing, 1790, Scot. NPG [*see illus.*] · A. Skirving, self-portrait, miniature, 1790, Scot. NPG · G. Watson, oils, *c*.1800–1810, Scot. NPG · H. Raeburn, oils, *c*.1810, priv. coll. · A. Geddes, oils, *c*.1815–1819, NG Scot.; on loan to Scot. NPG · A. Geddes and A. Skirving, drypoint etching, *c*.1815–1819, Scot. NPG

Wealth at death over £4000: estate papers in Skirving MSS, NL Scot., NLS Acc. 10102

Skirving, William (d. 1796), political reformer, was the son of William Skirving, 'a respectable farmer' (Mackenzie, 3) interested in agricultural improvements, who lived at Liberton, near Edinburgh. After a period of study at the University of Edinburgh, Skirving began to train for the ministry at the Burgher Divinity Academy under John Brown of Haddington. During this time he lived with and acted as private tutor to the family of the physician Sir Alexander Dick of Prestonfield. He later abandoned his theological

studies and returned to the practice and science of agriculture. His first venture, a farm leased at Damhead in Haddingtonshire, was unsuccessful. Meanwhile, he had married Rachel (d. 1801), daughter of Andrew Abercrombie, a Kirkcaldy merchant. She had inherited her father's property, including a farm at Strathruddie, near Lochgelly, which Skirving now took over. He applied unsuccessfully for the new chair of agriculture at the University of Edinburgh in 1790, but he did produce the first volume of his *Husbandman's Assistant* in 1792 (the second volume never appeared).

The final stages of work on this publication had brought the Skirvings to Edinburgh amid mounting enthusiasm for political reform inspired by the French Revolution. In accordance with his seceding background, Skirving became involved with the Association for the Abolition of Patronage and a Repeal of the Test and Corporation Statutes. In July 1792 he joined John Clark, a mason, and John Buchanan, a baker, in forming the (Scottish) Society of the Friends of the People to campaign for parliamentary reform. Skirving acted as secretary to the whole movement, including the period when its three national conventions were held (in December 1792, May 1793, and October–December 1793). He was also sent as a delegate to the conventions by the branches in Portsburgh, Edinburgh, and Leslie, Fife (the latter for the first convention only). During the first convention it was Skirving who proposed that the Scottish radicals should act in concert with their English counterparts, and from May 1793 he began to correspond with prominent English and Irish radicals. This eventually led to the attendance by several of them at the third or 'British' convention, though not until all the Scottish delegates had had to be recalled to Edinburgh. Skirving had carelessly invited the Englishmen and Irishmen to the convention so late that it was impossible for their societies to send delegates in time to arrive for the original dates of 29 October – 1 November 1793. The convention reconvened on 19 November and sat until it was broken up on 5 December.

It was not long before Skirving suffered for his political activities in the alarmist conservative climate of Edinburgh during the French Revolution. He was first arrested in August 1793 for distributing copies of a radical pamphlet written by George Mealmaker of Dundee and printed by Thomas Fysshe Palmer, who was transported for his action. Skirving published a *Complaint of Wrongous Imprisonment*, but he was shortly afterwards released on bail and, though cited as a witness at Palmer's trial, he was not examined. He was arrested a second time, on 5 December 1793, when his papers were seized, and again on 12 December. He was then indicted for sedition together with Maurice Margarot, Alexander Scott, Joseph Gerrald, and Charles Sinclair. Skirving was tried before the high court in Edinburgh on 6 and 7 January 1794, and bravely or unwisely insisted on conducting his own defence. He was sentenced to fourteen years' transportation. After a short period of imprisonment in the Edinburgh tollbooth he was transferred to Newgate, London. The transport, the *Surprise*, left St Helen's on 1 May 1794, carrying Skirving,

Palmer, Margarot, and Thomas Muir, and it arrived at Port Jackson, New South Wales, on 25 October. Skirving bought a small farm shortly after his arrival and named it New Strathruddie in memory of his wife. He died from dysentery in Port Jackson on 16 March 1796.

EMMA VINCENT MACLEOD

Sources P. Mackenzie, *The trial of William Skirving, secretary to the British convention, before the high court of justiciary, at Edinburgh, on the 6th and 7th January, 1794, for sedition; with an original memoir, and notes* (1836) • J. D. Brims, 'The Scottish democratic movement in the age of the French Revolution', PhD diss., U. Edin., 1983 • H. W. Meikle, *Scotland and the French Revolution* (1912) • justiciary records, small papers, main series, NA Scot., JC 26/280 • W. Skirving, *The husbandman's assistant* (1792) • W. Skirving, letter to John Patison, 25 April 1794, U. Edin. L., MS La. II. 509/1238–9 • T. F. Palmer, *A narrative of the sufferings of T. F. Palmer and W. Skirving, during a voyage to New South Wales, 1794, on board the Surprise transport* (1797)
Archives NA Scot., justiciary records, small papers, main series, JC26/280
Likenesses J. Kay, etching, 1794, repro. in J. Kay, *A series of original portraits and caricature etchings … with biographical sketches and illustrative anecdotes*, ed. [H. Paton and others], new edn, 2 (1877), pl. 359
Wealth at death farms at Strathruddie, Fife, and 'New Strathruddie', New South Wales: Mackenzie, *The trial of William Skirving*, 3, 24

Skittles. *See* Walters, Catherine (1839–1920).

Skot [Scott], **John** (*fl.* 1521–1537), printer, not to be confused with the Edinburgh printer John *Scott, was active in London for at least seventeen years, during which time he produced forty or more books; the majority of those known are either undated or fragmentary, making a detailed reconstruction of his activity impossible. His earliest surviving dated book is an edition of the *Body of Policy* of Christine de Pisan, dated 17 May 1521 from St Sepulchre's parish without Newgate. He remained at this address for some time, printing both on his own account and for Wynkyn de Worde; by 1528 he had moved his press to St Paul's Churchyard, where he printed several more books, two of them dated 1528 and 1529. An edition of John Stanbridge's *Accidence* (1530?) describes Skot as 'dwellynge at the George alleygate' in the parish of St Botolph without Bishopsgate. Finally, six books are known giving the printer's address as Foster Lane, in St Leonard's parish, and one of these, an edition of the *Rosary of Our Lady*, is dated 1537.

Skot's output was principally popular in character, including editions of verse narratives such as *Jacob and his Twelve Sons*, the *Book of Maid Emlyn*, the *Jest of Sir Gawaine*, and the *History of Sir Isembras*. In addition to printing books under his own name or device, he produced works for other publishers, including John Butler, Robert Redman, and John Toye. In 1533 Skot apparently confessed to having printed a book written by Elizabeth Barton, the so-called Nun or Maid of Kent. According to a memorandum made by Thomas Cromwell, Skot had been given the manuscript of the book by Edward Bocking, who took 500 copies for himself and left the printer with 200 more. All were seized, and neither the manuscript nor any of the printed books survives; Barton, Bocking, and four others were hanged on 20 April 1534, but Skot himself seems to have escaped punishment. His disappearance in 1537 and the appearance of another printer of the same name at Edinburgh in 1539 have led to their being sometimes mistaken for the same man, but the characteristics of their work show that the two printers are distinct.

JANET ING FREEMAN

Sources *STC, 1475–1640* • E. G. Duff, *A century of the English book trade* (1905); repr. (1948) • E. G. Duff, *The printers, stationers, and bookbinders of Westminster and London from 1476 to 1535* (1906) • E. J. Devereux, 'Elizabeth Barton and Tudor censorship', *Bulletin of the John Rylands University Library*, 49 (1966–7), 91–106 • *LP Henry VIII*, 6, no. 1194

Skrimshire. For this title name *see* Anderson, (Margaret) Betty Harvie, Baroness Skrimshire of Quarter (1913–1979).

Skrine, Henry (1755–1803), traveller, was the eldest of the three children of Richard Dickson Skrine (1719–1791), landowner and JP, of Warleigh Manor, Bathford, Somerset, and his wife, Elizabeth (1726–1800), daughter and heir of John Tryon of Collyweston, Northamptonshire. Henry was educated first at a preparatory school at Claverton, near Warleigh, and then at Winchester College. He entered Christ Church, Oxford, on 24 January 1774 and graduated BCL in 1781. He became a barrister of Stone Buildings, Lincoln's Inn, and was called to the bar in 1782, but whether he ever actually practised law is uncertain.

Skrine's inherited wealth enabled him to spend his time chiefly in travelling as a 'rational' entertainment, and recording his descriptions of both urban and rural Britain. His first published work, *Three Successive Tours in the North of England, and Great Part of Scotland* (1795; 2nd edn, 1813), included his journal of a tour through Derbyshire, Nottinghamshire, and Yorkshire undertaken during the 1780s, together with journals of his two tours to Scotland, in 1787 and 1793. In the first of these Scottish tours he described his journey from the Vale of Trent through the Lake District and the south-western highlands of Scotland to Loch Tay, Perth, Edinburgh, and then south through Durham to Manchester, terminating in south Wales. In the second tour, he travelled from Edinburgh to Aberdeen, Inverness, Fort William, and Blair Atholl, returning south through Glasgow, Edinburgh, and the borders. In his later *Two Successive Tours throughout Wales, with Several of the Adjacent English Counties* (1798; 2nd edn, 1812) he compiled the journals of several tours pursued over successive summers during the 1790s, and described the landscape, inhabitants, and condition of most of Wales. His final publication was another topographical work, *A General Account of All the Rivers of Note in Great Britain* (1801).

Writing for a general audience rather than the specialist topographer or antiquarian, Skrine proved a shrewd observer, providing a well written commentary on the state of the country through which he journeyed. He was particularly concerned with 'improvement', concluding, for example, that by this measurement the Scottish were more than a century behind the English. In particular, in the journal of his 1787 tour, he complained of the 'filth and habitual dirtiness' of the lowlanders of Scotland, contrasting them with the highlanders, 'a manly, bold, and hardy race … often as clean as their poverty will allow' (*Three Successive Tours in the North of England, and Great Part of Scotland*, 2nd edn, 71). On his return to Scotland in 1793 he was disappointed to see no major improvement in the condition of the country, a fact which he attributed to the 'chilling torpor' caused by the effects on commerce of the events of 1793, the beginning of the French Revolutionary Wars (p. 160). Although now little consulted, his works, especially those about Scotland, provide valuable first-hand descriptions of the country and its people. A journal of his two journeys to France in 1788–9 exists in manuscript in the Skrine family papers at Warleigh Manor, and contains an interesting account of revolutionary Versailles.

On 14 March 1787 Skrine married Marianne Chalié (1767–1788), eldest daughter of John Chalié, a wealthy wine merchant of Wimbledon, Surrey. She died in April 1788 after the birth of a son and heir, Henry, whom his father appears to have neglected somewhat. Skrine married second on 26 April 1790 Letitia Sarah Maria Harcourt (1762–1813), daughter and heir of John Harcourt of Dan-y-parc, Crickhowell, Brecknockshire. They had two sons and five daughters.

In 1795 Skrine was high sheriff for Brecknockshire, and at this time he apparently lived at Dan-y-parc, which his wife had inherited. He subsequently moved to the family home of Pyports House, Cobham, Surrey, where he was remembered as 'Mr Skrine, "the tourist"' (Walker, 37), but he moved, finally, to Walton-on-Thames about 1796 or 1797. By this time he was suffering from a painful illness and he died on 27 February 1803 at Walton-on-Thames, where he was buried near the south porch of the parish church.   ANDREW GROUT

Sources E. W. Ainley Walker, *Skrine of Warleigh in the county of Somerset with pedigrees* (1936) · Burke, *Gen. GB* (1972) · Foster, *Alum. Oxon.*

Archives priv. coll.

Likenesses portraits, priv. coll.

Wealth at death substantial, incl. freehold property and farms: will, PRO, PROB 11/1393, sig. 484; Ainley Walker, *Skrine of Warleigh*

Skrine, (Agnes) Nesta Shakespear (1865–1955). *See under* Keane, Mary Nesta (1904–1996).

Skues, George Edward Mackenzie (1858–1949), angler and writer on fly-fishing, was born on 13 August 1858 at St John's, Newfoundland, the eldest of eight children of William Mackenzie Skues (1828–1892), surgeon-general of Aberdeen, and his wife, Margaret Ayre (1836–1890), daughter of Christopher Ayre, clerk of the parliament and acting colonial secretary of Newfoundland.

At the age of three Skues was brought to his grandparents' house in Aberdeen from Newfoundland in a sailing vessel. In July 1872 he won a scholarship to Winchester College, which he left in 1877. After a year in the Channel Islands with his parents, he entered the offices of the family's solicitor, James Powell, and by 1895 had become a partner, remaining active until 1940, when he retired at the age of eighty-one.

Skues learned to fly-fish for trout on the River Itchen while at Winchester, and his fascination with the sport

George Edward Mackenzie Skues (1858–1949), by Howard Coster, 1927

culminated in his becoming probably the finest all-round fly-fisherman and writer on fly-fishing of the twentieth century. The year 1883 was a turning point in Skues's fishing career. He was invited to fish the Abbots Barton stretch of the River Itchen, and fished there until 1938. In 1887 he took up trout-fly dressing after being presented with a copy of *Floating Flies and How to Dress Them* (1886) by the great Frederic Halford, who pioneered the practice of fishing artificial flies upstream on the surface for rising fish. This was adopted by fly-fishermen world wide.

In 1891 Skues met Halford during a week's fishing on the River Itchen. By then he was exploring the theory that when trout were not taking the floating natural fly or dun, it was more profitable to use an upstream sunk wet fly. This led to his use of artificial nymphs, being imitations of the larval stage of the natural fly, fished below the surface. His views, expounded in articles in the *Fishing Gazette* and the *Flyfishers' Journal*, culminated in the publication of his first book, *Minor Tactics of the Chalk Stream*, in 1910. His further researches were embodied, together with an investigation into trout behaviour, in his 1921 book *The Way of a Trout with a Fly*. A further book, *Side-Lines, Side-Lights and Reflections*, published in 1932, was a collection of articles written for fishing magazines including the *Bulletin of the Anglers' Club of New York*. This was the most endearing of his books, with glimpses of the man himself and his sense of humour. Among Skues's attributes were a fluent and lively prose style together with great skill and dedication as a practical angler, despite the handicap of poor sight in one eye.

In 1938 a debate was held at the Flyfishers' Club of London which questioned Skues's theories that the nymph was an effective and ethical way of fishing for chalk-stream trout, and found against him. The disillusioned Skues, at the age of eighty, published a final defence with his 1939 book *Nymph Fishing for Chalk Stream Trout*.

Skues's place as one of the greats in fly-fishing history centres on his discovery that trout in chalk streams feed largely on nymphs, even during hatches, and not on the adult, emerged flies. His dressings of artificial nymphs specifically to represent larvae were new and radical. This was extremely controversial and challenged the rigid dry-fly theories of Halford and his disciples. Halford's greatness lay in his exposition of a method which became universal. Skues's forward-looking theories challenged what had become a rigid aridity with methods that were flexible and thoughtful, and were to become a predominant approach on both sides of the Atlantic.

In 1938, partly because his use of the nymph was not popular with fellow members of his syndicate on the Itchen, Skues left and took a rod on the River Nadder, near Salisbury. He went to live at the Nadder Vale Hotel in 1940 until it closed in 1948, when he moved to be near his brother in Beckenham, Kent. He finally finished fishing at the age of eighty-seven, but continued to maintain an immense correspondence with anglers from all over the world.

Skues died, unmarried, four days short of his ninety-first birthday, on 9 August 1949, at 23 Kelsey Park Road, Beckenham, succumbing to myocardial degeneration. His ashes were scattered on the banks of his beloved Itchen by his old friend William Mullins, the long-serving head keeper of the syndicate that fished the river.

Two more of Skues's books were published after his death. *Silk, Fur and Feather* appeared in 1950, and was a collection of articles on fly tying which had appeared in the *Fishing Gazette* under one of his many pen names, Val Conson. Skues had directed that the second, *Itchen Memories* (1951), should be published only after his death. It is a charming recollection of his days on the river he loved so well.   KENNETH ROBSON

Sources private information (2004) [family] · G. E. M. Skues, 'Trivialities of a long life', Flyfishers' Club Library, 69 Brook Street, London [unpublished MS] · G. E. M. Skues, *Itchen memories* (1951) · C. F. Walker, ed., *The angling letters of G. E. M. Skues* (1956) · T. D. Overfield, *The way of a man with a trout* (1977) · K. Robson, *The essential G. E. M. Skues* (1998) · E. A. Barton, diaries, 1920–30, Flyfishers' Club Library, 69 Brook Street, London · d. cert.
Archives Flyfishers' Club, London, books, documents, flies, rods
Likenesses photographs, 1863–1946, repro. in Robson, *Essential G. E. M. Skues* · H. Coster, photograph, 1927, NPG [*see illus.*]
Wealth at death £13,848 8s. 1d.: probate, 12 Oct 1949, CGPLA Eng. & Wales

Skuish, John. *See* Skewys, John (d. 1544).

Skynner, Sir John (*bap.* 1723, *d.* 1805), judge, was baptized on 15 November 1723 at St Lawrence Jewry and St Mary Magdalen, Milk Street, London, the son of John and Elizabeth Skynner. His mother was heir to the Smyth family, and inherited the estate of Great Milton, Oxfordshire, which later became Skynner's country residence. He entered Westminster School on 10 January 1735 and was elected a king's scholar in 1738. He matriculated from Christ Church, Oxford, on 19 June 1742 and graduated BCL on 27 January 1751. He was admitted to Lincoln's Inn on 21 November 1739 and was called to the bar on 17 November 1748, joining the Oxford circuit. By 1770 he was a leading counsel in the equity side of the exchequer and in chancery.

In January 1771 Skynner was returned to parliament as MP for Woodstock, in the interest of George Spencer,

Sir John Skynner (*bap.* 1723, *d.* 1805), by Thomas Gainsborough, 1785 [replica]

fourth duke of Marlborough. On 28 January 1771 he was made a king's counsel. He also became attorney-general of the duchy of Lancaster, and on 19 June 1771 a bencher of Lincoln's Inn. On 3 April 1772 he was appointed second judge on the Chester circuit. In parliament he usually supported the North ministry but was particularly interested in church questions; he spoke against the Church Nullum Tempus Bill on 17 February 1772, and on 23 February 1773 opposed Sir William Meredith's motion against university subscription to the Thirty-Nine Articles. On 4 May 1774 he took part in the debate on the bill for the impartial administration of justice in Massachusetts Bay, when he argued against the introduction of the appeal for murder into America, on the grounds that it was not practicable. He also took the opportunity to defend William Blackstone's *Commentaries*, which had been attacked in debate, as one of the best books ever written on English law. The clause was dropped, but he still voted against the third reading, on 6 May, being the only member among the noes who was not a committed adherent of the opposition. Despite this stand he was still listed as a supporter by the government in September 1774. On 12 April 1776 he was elected recorder of Oxford and presented with the freedom of the city; in 1789 he presented the corporation with a piece of plate.

Skynner was knighted on 23 November 1777 in anticipation of his appointment as lord chief baron of the exchequer on 27 November, in succession to Sir Sidney Stafford Smythe. On 6 March 1778 he married Martha (*d.*

1797), daughter of Edward Burn and Martha Davie; they had one child, Martha Frederica (*d.* 1821), who on 1 August 1799 married the politician Richard *Ryder (1766–1832). Skynner delivered the ruling of all the judges in the case of *Rann* v. *Hughes* (1778), whereupon the House of Lords overturned Lord Mansfield's contention, in *Pillans* v. *Van Mierop* (1765), that in commercial cases the want of consideration in contracts was not an objection to their validity. For Skynner and his colleagues this was a striking innovation in the law of contract, and it was overturned.

Skynner resigned on 20 January 1787, citing ill health, and was compensated by being sworn of the privy council on 23 March 1787. He retired to Great Milton, where the house was transformed by James Wyatt into 'a convenient and elegant residence' (*GM*). He had retained his connections with his former school and university; he was elected a Busby trustee of Westminster School on 17 April 1780 and was a contributor to the funds of the Bodleian Library in Oxford. He died at Bath on 26 November 1805, and was buried in the south aisle of Great Milton church. Great Milton was inherited by his daughter and son-in-law.

DAVID LEMMINGS

Sources *DNB* · E. Foss, *Biographia juridica: a biographical dictionary of the judges of England … 1066–1870* (1870) · J. Brooke, 'Skynner, John', HoP, *Commons, 1754–90* · Cobbett, *Parl. hist.*, 17.303, 1294–6 · *GM*, 1st ser., 90/1 (1820), 107 · D. Lemmings, *Professors of the law* (2000) · Sainty, *Judges* · Sainty, *King's counsel* · Holdsworth, *Eng. law*, 12.565 · IGI
Likenesses T. Gainsborough, oils, 1785; Phillips, 16 Dec 1997, lot 26 · T. Gainsborough, oils, 1785 (replica), Christ Church Oxf. [*see illus.*]

Skynner, Lancelot (*c.*1766–1799), naval officer, was the eldest son of the Revd John Skynner (1725–1805) of Easton, Northamptonshire. It is possible that he was the nephew of another naval officer, Captain Lancelot Skynner, who had been killed in action against the French on 4 April 1760. He entered the Royal Navy in October 1779, and served in the *Brilliant* and other vessels in the East Indies and home waters. In October 1787 he was promoted lieutenant, but in July 1791 he was discharged to the half pay list. He returned to active service on the outbreak of war with France in February 1793. In July 1794 he joined the *Boyne*, flagship of Admiral Sir John Jervis, and sailed for service in the West Indies. His first independent command was the sloop *Zebra* in November 1794, but he only stayed with her briefly before being made captain of the frigate *Beaulieu*. He commanded this vessel during the campaigns in the West Indies and the capture of St Lucia in April and May 1796. The *Beaulieu* returned to home waters in the autumn and then proceeded to the Downs. Skynner's ship's crew was not immune from the mutinous feelings that developed in 1797, and in the summer of 1798 he was forced to leave the vessel. Apparently, though, he was not held responsible for this event by the Admiralty, since in the summer of 1799 he was appointed to command the frigate *Lutine*.

Skynner's career came to an unfortunate end. In autumn 1799 the *Lutine* was ordered to sail for the Texel.

She carried $600,000 worth (estimated at £140,000 sterling) of specie, to pay Hamburg merchants for their supplies to Britain. Skynner sailed from Yarmouth Roads on 9 October, the weather deteriorated, and some twelve hours after her departure the *Lutine* was wrecked off Vlieland. The whole crew, including Skynner, was lost, the only survivor being a Dutch lawyer, one of several passengers on board. In 1858 £50,000 worth of the ship's cargo was salvaged, along with her bell and rudder. The *Lutine* bell was hung at Lloyd's underwriters and is rung once on news of a total wreck.

MICHAEL PARTRIDGE

Sources *DNB* · *GM*, 1st ser., 70 (1800), 278–80 · *GM*, 1st ser., 69 (1799), 988, 994 · treasury pay books, series 2, 1788, PRO, ADM 34/537, 788 · treasury pay books, series 3, PRO, ADM 35/436, 83, 853, 269, 2079, 221–2 · ships' musters, series 1, PRO, ADM 36/9993; 14633 · W. James, *The naval history of Great Britain, from the declaration of war by France in 1793, to the accession of George IV*, [5th edn], 6 vols. (1859–60), vol. 1, pp. 410–11; vol. 2, p. 474 · T. Grocott, *Shipwrecks of the revolutionary and Napoleonic era* (1997), 79 · G. Chowdharay-Best, 'Ships' bells', *Mariner's Mirror*, 62 (1976), 96

Skyrme, Tony Hilton Royle (1922–1987), theoretical physicist, was born on 5 December 1922 at 7 Blessington Road, Lewisham, London, the only child of John Hilton Royle Skyrme, bank clerk, and his wife, Muriel May Roberts. After attending a boarding-school in Lewisham he won a scholarship to Eton College, where he distinguished himself by outstanding work in mathematics, gaining a number of prizes. In 1940 he became a scholar of Trinity College, Cambridge, reading mathematics, and there he maintained the high standard shown at Eton. He passed part one of the mathematics tripos as a wrangler in 1942, and part three in 1943.

On graduating he was directed by the wartime central register of scientists to Birmingham, where a group under Rudolf Peierls was working on the theoretical aspects of atomic energy, particularly atomic weapons. Here his great ability soon attracted attention. While capable of using abstract reasoning on difficult problems, he was prepared to look at experimental situations and at measurements which needed theoretical analysis. He wrote a number of useful reports, one of which, concerned with neutron scattering, remained in demand for many years. At the end of 1943 several scientists working on atomic energy, including Peierls, were transferred to the United States to assist in the 'Manhattan project'. Skyrme followed a little later, and worked first in New York, on problems concerning the diffusion plant for isotope separation, and then at Los Alamos.

After the end of the Second World War Skyrme spent two years (1946–7) as a research fellow at Birmingham University, where he acquired a command of modern theoretical physics. One of the results he obtained provided a rigorous mathematical proof of an important theorem in nuclear physics. He submitted this for publication, but the referee wanted one section expanded; Skyrme never complied with this request, and the paper remained unpublished. The academic years 1948–9 and 1949–50 were spent at the Massachusetts Institute of Technology and at the Institute for Advanced Study in Princeton, respectively. In 1949 he married Dorothy Mildred, daughter of Francis Charles Millest, commercial traveller; they had no children.

From 1950 to 1962 Skyrme worked at the Atomic Energy Research Establishment at Harwell, and these were his most productive years. Apart from papers relating to the design or interpretation of experiments in nuclear physics, and much work on specific problems of nuclear structure, he made two pioneering contributions to nuclear physics. One was to show how to handle short-range forces in a three-body problem; the other, not unrelated, was a powerful approximation to nuclear forces, later widely used as the 'Skyrme model'. An even more original contribution was a treatment of fundamental particles, in which particles such as neutrons and protons, which obey the Pauli exclusion principle, appear as manifestations of fields such as that of mesons. These ideas were so revolutionary that it was some years before they received adequate attention. Later the study of these 'Skyrmions' became a flourishing branch of theoretical physics. For this work Skyrme was awarded the Hughes medal of the Royal Society in 1985.

During a year's leave from Harwell he and his wife spent a semester in the University of Pennsylvania and then returned via the United States, Australia, and the Far and Middle East, making all the land journeys by Land Rover. They had enjoyed Malaysia, and when changes at Harwell made his condition there less congenial, he accepted a post in the University of Malaysia in Kuala Lumpur, where they arrived, again by Land Rover, in the autumn of 1962. Since the staff of the department was much smaller than he had been led to believe, there were heavy teaching duties and few people interested in research. In 1964 Skyrme accepted an invitation to a professorship in Birmingham, initially as head of the department, but later he was relieved of the administrative duties. He remained in Birmingham until his death.

Skyrme was distinguished by a deep understanding of physics, by a great command of mathematics, and, above all, by an original and fertile imagination. He was of medium height, with light brown hair and brown eyes. As a young man he had a slim, athletic figure; in later life he put on much weight. He tended to be rather quiet, being a solitary person who did not like joint work, but preferred to think about problems on his own. Skyrme died on 25 June 1987 in Selly Oak Hospital, Birmingham, of an embolism after an operation, his wife surviving him.

RUDOLF PEIERLS, rev.

Sources R. H. Dalitz, 'An outline of the life and work of Tony Skyrme', *International Journal of Modern Physics*, A, 3 (1988), 2719–44 · *The Times* (3 July 1987) · *CGPLA Eng. & Wales* (1987)
Archives U. Birm. L., corresp. and papers
Wealth at death £28,783: administration, 21 Aug 1987, *CGPLA Eng. & Wales*

Slack, Anne. *See* Fisher, Anne (1719–1778).

Slack, Henry James [*pseud.* Little John] (1818–1896), writer, was born in London on 23 October 1818, the son of Joseph Slack, a prosperous cloth merchant, and his wife, Grace Elizabeth Christmas. He was educated at North End, Hampstead, and then entered a career in business. In 1840 he married Charlotte Mary Walters. From 1846, Slack became involved in the newspaper industry, working on the *North Devon Journal* and several other provincial papers. In 1852 he became proprietor and editor of the *Atlas*. He also wrote much for the *Weekly Times*, under the signature Little John. From 1862 he edited the *Intellectual Observer* (developed from an earlier journal—*Recreative Science*—and issued as *The Student* from 1868 to 1871). He also published several books. *The Ministry of the Beautiful* (1850) was a dialogue upon aesthetic subjects, while in 1860 he produced an optimistic treatise, *The Philosophy of Progress in Human Affairs*.

The ideas which Slack advocated throughout his life were those of advanced Liberalism, and he was active in causes such as the abolition of slavery, the ending of the paper duties, and the higher education of women. He was a Cobdenite, a forward member of the National Education League, and a warm friend of Kossuth and Mazzini. When specially moved he was an eloquent speaker. But the causes with which he identified most were those espoused by the Sunday League. He was president of the league in 1879, and inaugurated the popular lectures for Sunday evenings. He was no less zealous in the cause of the Sunday opening of museums and picture galleries (the promotion of which was taken up by the Sunday Society, formed in 1875).

In his leisure hours Slack was an ardent microscopist, and he was successively secretary and president (1878) of the Royal Microscopical Society. He published *The Marvels of Pond Life* (1861), an attractive and essentially popular introduction to microscopical study (although most of the ponds to which he referred did not survive into the twentieth century). Slack was a regular contributor to *Knowledge*, *Popular Science Monthly*, the *Meteorological Journal*, and other similar periodicals. His chief theological influence was the unitarian William Johnson Fox, whose works he edited in a *Memorial Edition* (12 vols., 1865–8), in collaboration with William Ballantyne Hodgson. Slack died at his house in Forest Row, Sussex, on 16 June 1896. His wife survived him.

THOMAS SECCOMBE, rev. PETER OSBORNE

Sources *Nature*, 54 (1896), 351 · *Daily News* (27 June 1896) · private information (1897) · *IGI* · *CGPLA Eng. & Wales* (1896)
Wealth at death £9620 8s. 1d.: resworn probate, Nov 1896, *CGPLA Eng. & Wales*

Slack, John (*c*.1721–1768), pugilist, was born in Norfolk of unknown parents. His trade was that of a butcher and he probably served the usual apprenticeship under one John Browne at Norwich, where he first came to prize-fighting prominence, forging a formidable provincial reputation there.

Prior to the pinnacle of his boxing career, his unexpected win over the seemingly invincible John Broughton, Slack was advertised in journals of the day as meeting such first-rate fistic exponents as George Taylor, Thomas Smallwood, James Field, Benjamin Boswell, and John

John Slack (*c*.1721–1768), by George Townshend, first Marquess Townshend, 1751–8

James. It appears he made his London début when he defeated James on 12 October 1743 at the Great Booth, Tottenham Court. Slack at this stage claimed to be unbeaten (*Daily Advertiser*, 12 and 14 Oct 1743). Shortly afterwards he again overcame James but was twice vanquished by Smallwood; in line with the general trend of the era, he certainly fought several of his opponents on more than one occasion. However, it was Taylor the Barber, then considered second only to Broughton, who proved to be Slack's most difficult adversary. On 4 November 1747, at Broughton's Amphitheatre, Oxford Road, Taylor survived a burst blood vessel before recording a thirty-six minute victory and on the 16th of the following month he won again at the same venue, this time in thirty-two minutes. Any lost reputation, though, was completely redeemed by Slack in his confrontation with Field the Sailor on 9 February 1749. The battle lasted about ninety-two minutes and was the 'severest and longest ever seen upon the Stage' (*London Evening-Post*, 9–11 Feb 1749). Before again losing to Taylor, in a desperately hard encounter on 31 January 1750, Slack had also beaten Boswell and the massive Thomas Hawksley (Hawksly). It is clear, therefore, that he was far more experienced and highly regarded prior to meeting Broughton than has been generally accepted.

The Broughton match occurred on 11 April 1750 (*GM*, 1st ser., 20, 1750, 184). It developed after both claimed to have been physically abused by the other, the previous month, at the election at Brentford of a knight of the shire for the county of Middlesex. Broughton, fighting at his amphitheatre, was the early favourite but Slack surprisingly gained a victory in just over fourteen minutes by temporarily blinding his antagonist. It was thought at the time that as a result of his success Slack became richer by at least £600. Historians since the nineteenth century have credited him with championship (of England) status between this success and his defeat ten years afterwards by William Stevens (Stephens) the Nailer, but there is no evidence of this in contemporary journals. Moreover, in February of the year following the Broughton contest Slack suffered yet another loss at the hands of George Taylor. On that occasion a leg injury sustained in the last fall forced a dominant Slack to concede after approximately sixteen minutes (*Read's Weekly Journal*, 9 Feb 1751). Although he easily subdued George Lea (Lee) on 10 February 1752, he had great difficulty beating the cricketer Thomas Faulkner (Falkner) some three months later and, on 15 November of that year, sustained a further defeat when bested by Elias Goddard.

Apart from the Broughton conquest, Slack's other most notable performance was probably against the remarkably strong Pettit on 29 July 1754 at Harlston, Norfolk. Despite throwing Slack off the stage three times, Pettit became so cowed by his indomitable opponent that he walked away after twenty-five minutes, leaving Slack to be awarded the victory the next morning. Also fought out of London were Slack's triumphs over John and Cornelius Harris on 6 February and 6 March 1755 respectively. Both took place in Bristol; the former lasted about six minutes (*Felix Farley's Bristol Journal*, 25 Jan – 8 Feb 1755) and the latter upwards of twenty (*Felix Farley's Bristol Journal*, 1–8 March 1755). Slack's last win appears to have been over one Morton (Moreton) before his final contest in which he lost to Stevens in less than four minutes on 2 June 1760 at the Tennis Court, James Street, Haymarket, London (*Public Advertiser*, 3 June 1760).

Slack was a powerfully built man, standing about 5 ft 8½ in. tall and weighing, in his prime, somewhere between 13 and 14 stone. His physique and fistic attributes were ideally suited to the prevailing style of fighting of the period. He possessed considerable strength and, despite lacking science, when resolved on victory his courage and determination made him a redoubtable adversary. He so abhorred 'shifting' that it is said he 'optionally received a knock-down blow sooner than relinquish his original situation' (Fewtrell, 52). Although later generations of bareknuckle pugilists generally scorned its use, Slack was noted for his success with the 'chopper', a back-handed blow to the face.

It is probable that the John Slack, butcher, sworn in as a freeman of the city of Norwich (1744) and the butcher John Slack who later became a burgess of the city of Bristol (1759) were both the celebrated prize-fighter. At some time between these dates he certainly plied his trade in London, first at Chandos Street, Covent Garden, and then at the now defunct Brooks Market, Holborn. He died at Bristol on 17 July 1768 (*Felix Farley's Bristol Journal*, 23 July 1768).

Slack was the grandfather of the renowned Belcher brothers, James (1781–1811) and Thomas (1783–1854), the former a champion of England and the latter one of the most scientific boxers of his day. TONY GEE

Sources fight reports, etc., *Daily Advertiser* [London]; *London Evening-Post*; *Whitehall-Evening Post, or, London Intelligencer*; *Read's Weekly Journal, or, British-Gazetteer*; *Felix Farley's Bristol Journal*; *GM*; *Public Advertiser*; *London Daily Advertiser*; *Penny London Post, or, The Morning Advertiser*; *Old England*; *General Advertiser* [London]; *Norwich Mercury*; *Public Ledger, or, Daily Register of Commerce and Intelligence*; *Westminster Journal, or, New Weekly Miscellany* • *Felix Farley's Bristol Journal* (23 July 1768) • T. Fewtrell, *Boxing reviewed, or, The science of manual defence* (1790), 51–3 • *Gazetteer and New Daily Advertiser* (26 July 1768) • J. Latimer, *The annals of Bristol in the eighteenth century* (1893); repr. (1970), 313–14, 341 • P. Egan, *Boxiana, or, Sketches of ancient and modern pugilism*, 1 (1812), 60–61 • Norwich freeman's register, 1744, Norfolk RO, fol. 83 • Burgess book, 1755–9, Bristol RO, FC/BB/1 (q) 4, frame 9 • *Sporting Magazine*, 38 (Aug 1811) [obit. of James Belcher] • *Bell's Life in London* (4 Feb 1855) [obit. of Thomas Belcher]

Likenesses G. Townshend, first Marquess Townshend, pen-and-ink caricature, 1751–8, NPG [*see illus.*] • W. Thomas, engraving (after bust by Sivier), repro. in H. D. Miles, *Pugilistica: the history of British boxing*, 1 (1880)

Slack, Kenneth (1917–1987), minister of the Presbyterian Church of England, was born on 20 July 1917 in Wallasey, Cheshire, the second son in the family of two sons and one daughter of Reginald Slack, manager of a small grocery store, and his wife, Nellie Bennett. They lived on a grocer's wage, and providing for Kenneth's education was a struggle. He was educated at Wallasey grammar school and at Liverpool University, from which he graduated with a BA honours degree in 1937. He then studied theology at Westminster College, Cambridge, on a Lewis Gibson scholarship. He was ordained into the Presbyterian Church of England in 1941. In the same year he married (Barbara) Millicent, daughter of William Spong Blake, a traveller for the family printing firm. They had two sons and one daughter.

Throughout the years of Slack's ministry there was a continual and creative movement between service in local churches and leadership within the ecumenical agencies. In both he revealed talents for organization, and preaching and writing skills. His first pastorate was at St Nicholas's Church, Shrewsbury. In 1942 he entered the Royal Air Force Volunteer Reserve as a chaplain. From 1943 to 1946 he served in the Far East, from which he returned with an MBE (1946) and an international dimension to his thinking. He became minister of St James's, Edgware, where his abilities were soon recognized throughout the Presbyterian Church of England, as a vigorous pastor, forthright editor of the church journal, and supporter of ecumenical development.

In 1955 Slack was appointed general secretary of the British Council of Churches (BCC), the first free church minister to hold this position, and as such became the senior civil servant of the ecumenical movement in Britain. It was an ideal appointment, for he was quick to establish excellent personal relations with senior officers of the churches, becoming a trusted colleague at Lambeth Palace and at Archbishop's House, Westminster. The BCC had

been a tender plant in its early years, but Slack was able to give it a higher public profile and a greater priority in the life of the churches. He was also concerned with the local expression of ecumenism, travelling constantly to encourage local councils of churches.

In 1965 Slack returned to local ministry, first at St Andrew's Church in Cheam (1965–7), and then in central London at the City Temple (1967–75). During this time he became well known as a broadcaster, being frequently heard on the BBC's *Thought for the Day*. So skilled was he at the brief, pertinent message that a member of his congregation was moved to ask whether he could not preach as briefly on Sundays. The cause of Christian unity remained a priority to him, and during the 1960s he took a leading part in the discussions between Presbyterians and Congregationalists, which led to the formation of the United Reformed church in 1972. It was no surprise that he was elected its moderator for 1973–4 and stimulated consultation about further unions. He had become a leading public exponent in Britain of the call to remove the ancient barriers between Christian churches.

The broader scene claimed Slack again from 1975 to 1982, when he was director of Christian Aid, the agency through which the churches provided help to the most needy people of the world. This task called for much travel and constant advocacy so that resources could be provided, not only for disaster relief, but to lift the chronic burdens of poverty. Another period of local church ministry followed for him, at Kensington, from 1982 until his death in 1987.

A steady and prolific writer, Slack produced a series of books on World Council of Churches assemblies, biographies of Martin Luther King (1970) and Bishop George Bell (1971), and biblical studies on the Lord's prayer (1973) and the Psalms (*New Light on Old Songs*, 1975). But he was never a cloistered writer. Excelling in conversation and friendship, vigorous and challenging, he was good company, helping many to share his own confidence in the radical power of Christian faith. Tall, upright, and burly, he was a commanding figure, particularly when robed in the pulpit. His air of confidence, good humour, and frequent laughter gave him a welcoming appearance. Southampton University gave him an honorary degree in 1971. Slack died on 4 October 1987 in East Finchley, London, where his home was 184 East End Road. A memorial service was held in Westminster Abbey on 25 November, led by the archbishop of Canterbury.

BERNARD THOROGOOD, *rev.*

Sources *The Independent* (7 Oct 1987) • *The Times* (6 Oct 1987) • *The Times* (26 Nov 1987) • personal knowledge (1996) • private information (1996) [Millicent Slack, widow] • United Reformed Church, 86 Tavistock Place, London, Presbyterian Church of England archive

Wealth at death £38,216: probate, 23 Feb 1988, *CGPLA Eng. & Wales*

Slack, Thomas [*pseud.* S. Thomas] (*bap.* 1723, *d.* 1784), printer and newspaper proprietor, was the eldest son of Joseph Slack (1701–1752?), of Wreay, near Carlisle, and his wife Mary (*née* Stephenson); he was baptized on 18 December 1723 at Hesket in the Forest, Cumberland. Nothing is known of Slack's education and early years. On 15 December 1751 he married Ann (or Anne) *Fisher (1719–1778), daughter of Henry Fisher, a yeoman of Oldscale, in the parish of Lorton, Cumberland. On 18 October 1752 Thomas Slack, as the heir of his father, was admitted tenant of lands at Wreay which, on 16 September 1784, his eldest daughter and heir-at-law, Mrs Mary Blaylock, inherited.

By 1751 Slack was working for the Quaker printer Isaac Thompson, of Newcastle, to whom William Bulmer was later apprenticed. Thompson was proprietor of the *Newcastle Journal*, and Slack was said to have been his manager. Their working relationship is unclear, however, for in 1755 was issued *Lucius and Celadon, or, A Dialogue of the Existence and Immortality of the Soul*, with the imprint 'Printed by I. Thompson and C°, for Tho. Slack'; in the following year *The Newcastle Memorandum-Book* was published with the imprint 'Printed for Tho. Slack, and sold by all Persons who distribute the *Newcastle Journal*'. The *Memorandum Book* survived as an annual publication until 1893, and was widely sold by booksellers in England and Scotland; Charles Elliot, the Edinburgh publisher and bookseller, for example, took 100 copies in 1774. In association with the London publishers, George Robinson & Co., he also published *The Ladies' Own Memorandum-Book*, prepared by his wife; Slack printed the letterpress matter, and the Robinsons dealt with the calendar and ruled matter. This publication continued under his successors until 1805, when the Robinsons failed.

In 1763 Slack started his own printing business, following a disagreement with Isaac Thompson, reflected in correspondence in the local news-sheets. His shop which he named the Printing Press, was at the head of Middle Street, Newcastle upon Tyne. Slack, ably assisted by his wife, sold prints, lottery tickets, and spectacles, in addition to books and stationery. The printing of books formed a large part of their flourishing business. Between 1755 and 1784 his name appeared, as printer, publisher, or bookseller in the imprints of some 150 books, including two editions of *The Pleasing Instructor* (1756) by his wife, writing under her maiden name. Among other books by his wife, of which Thomas Slack printed and published several editions, were *A Practical New Grammar* (1762), *A New English Exercise Book* (1770), *An Accurate New Spelling Dictionary* (3rd edn, 1777), and *The New English Tutor* (1778). An advertisement in the *Newcastle Chronicle* for 16 March 1782 shows that he also published the pastoral poems of John Cunningham, poet and player.

In competition with Thompson's *Newcastle Journal* he established the weekly *Newcastle Chronicle*, the first issue appearing on 24 March 1764. The newspaper remained in the control of his daughter and son-in-law and their sons until 1850. When Joseph Cowen, industrialist and MP, took it over from Mark William Lambert in 1859 it became a radical campaigning journal; it ceased publication in 1953.

Thomas Slack was also an author, writing under the pseudonym S. Thomas, complementing his wife's work with a series of books on business practice: *The British*

Negociator (1759), *The Banker's Sure Guide* (1762), *Britannicus estimator* (1764), which became *The Ready Calculator* (1771), and *The Commercial Palladium* (1775). He also edited W. Webster's *Essays on Book-Keeping* (1779).

Among Slack's competitors in the Newcastle book trade were John White (*fl.* 1711–1769), William Charnley (*fl.* 1755–1803), and Thomas Saint (*fl.* 1761–1788), who worked with and succeeded White. White was the first 'permanent' printer in Newcastle and, in 1711, established the *Newcastle Courant*, which Saint continued. Saint pursued White's policy of concentrating on popular literature, including children's books, often illustrated by Thomas Bewick. Charnley was a considerable bookseller and publisher, helping to establish Fourstones papermill in 1763. Each of these four had, therefore, his own field of specialization, Slack concentrating on more substantial, frequently didactic, works, and all had connections with the London and provincial book trade. Ann Fisher's schoolbooks were frequently reprinted in association with Slack and 'pirated' by Hoey of Dublin, Henry Mozley of Gainsborough, Christopher Etherington of York, and John Soulby of Penrith, among others.

Slack was unusual in the eighteenth-century English provincial book trade in combining authorship (his and his wife's), printing and publishing a wide range of books, newspaper proprietorship, and jobbing printing. In this he was most successful, his will showing that in addition to the property at Wreay and his house and printing workshop in Middle Street, he had other houses and a shop in Newcastle and a one-sixteenth share in the ship *Mary*.

Slack and Fisher had nine children, all girls, three of whom died in infancy; one other, Jane, predeceased her father, dying in 1776, aged twenty-one. Thomas Slack died at Newcastle on 13 January 1784, and was buried at St John's Church there. The printing business was left to his fourth daughter, Sarah, then aged just under twenty-four. Solomon Hodgson (1760–1800), who had probably been working for Slack, married Sarah on 15 February 1785. On 21 February the executors of Thomas Slack's estate transferred to Hodgson the *Newcastle Chronicle*, together with the printing, bookselling, and stationery business.

PETER ISAAC

Sources R. Welford, 'Early Newcastle typography', *Archaeologia Aeliana*, 3rd ser., 3 (1907), 1–134, esp. 33–7 • J. Hodgson the younger, 'Thomas Slack of Newcastle, printer, 1723–1784, founder of the *Newcastle Chronicle*', *Archaeologia Aeliana*, 3rd ser., 17 (1920), 145–51 • R. V. Wallis and P. J. Wallis, eds., *Biobibliography of British mathematics and its applications*, 2 (1986) • 'The *Newcastle Chronicle*', *Monthly Chronicle of North Country Lore and Legend*, 4 (1890), 223–6 [no author] • P. J. W. [P. J. Wallis], 'Piracies: true and dirty', *Durham Philobiblon*, 2 (1955–69), 74–6 • C. J. Hunt, *The book trade in Northumberland and Durham to 1860: a biographical dictionary* (1975) • U. Newcastle, Robinson L., Bell MSS, fol. RB 942.82 – BEL

Archives U. Newcastle, Robinson L., Bell collection

Likenesses oils, repro. in Hodgson the younger, 'Thomas Slack of Newcastle', facing p. 145; priv. coll. • pen-and-ink drawing, repro. in 'The *Newcastle Chronicle*'

Wealth at death died well off: Hodgson the younger, 'Thomas Slack'

Slade, Sir Adolphus [called Mushaver Pasha] (1804–1877), naval officer in the Turkish service and author, was the fifth son of General Sir John *Slade, first baronet (1762–1859), of Maunsel Grange, Somerset, and his wife, Anna Eliza, *née* Dawson (*d.* 1819). In August 1815 he entered the Royal Naval College, Portsmouth, and was to pass with distinction, winning the gold medal. He was on the South American station for three years, and in 1824, as mate of the *Revenge*, flagship of Sir Harry Burrard Neale, was at the demonstration against Algiers. On 20 October 1827 he was in the cutter *Hind*, the tender to the *Asia*, at the battle of Navarino, and on 27 November he was promoted lieutenant. In 1828–9, on half pay, he travelled through France, Italy, and the Greek islands, and reached Constantinople in May 1829. He then went for a cruise in the Black sea with the Turkish fleet, and after the peace of Adrianople, as the guest of Captain Edmund Lyons in the frigate *Blonde*, he visited Russian ports. From Varna he went by land to Adrianople, and for the next two years travelled in the Turkish empire. In 1833 he published *Records of travel in Turkey, Greece, … and of a cruise in the Black Sea with the Capitan Pasha in the years 1829-30-31* (2 vols.).

In January 1834 Slade was appointed additional lieutenant of the *Caledonia*, flagship of Sir Josias Rowley. During the next three years he was employed on several missions to Greece and Constantinople, and once to Sevastopol, on the defences of which and the improved state of the Russian navy he wrote a valuable report. In 1837 he published *Turkey, Greece, and Malta* (2 vols.). Again on half pay he travelled on the continent, and in 1840 published *Travels in Germany and Russia, including a steam voyage by the Danube and Euxine from Vienna to Constantinople in 1838-9*. On 23 November 1841 he was promoted commander. He then studied again at the Royal Naval College, and in 1846–7 commanded the brig *Recruit* off the coast of Spain and at the Azores.

On 10 January 1849 Slade was promoted to post rank. Shortly afterwards, when war appeared imminent between Austria and Turkey, he was lent to the Porte for service with the Turkish fleet. Retaining his rank in the Royal Navy, he entered the Turkish service as Mushaver Pasha, and for the next seventeen years was the administrative head of the Turkish navy, which with much difficulty he brought to relative efficiency. His period of service included the Crimean War.

In June 1853 Slade, supported by Lord Stratford de Redcliffe, persuaded the Turkish government to overhaul the defences of the Bosphorus, to Slade's design. This work played a significant part in averting a Russian *coup de main*. Impatient with the slow advance of the allied fleets, especially after the disaster of Sinope, Slade and Stratford fell out with Admiral J. W. D. Dundas and his French colleague Admiral Hamelin. Slade commanded the Turkish fleet on the Caucasian coast in early 1854, but a very public argument with Dundas in April 1854 over the need to give an active role to the Turkish fleet, which Dundas despised, led to his removal from active operations. His influence with the Turks was based on his connection with the British; once they saw that he had no support from Dundas he was of no further use. His sense of injustice was reflected in *Turkey and the Crimean War* (1867), which adopted a pro-Turkish approach and deprecated the value of the Royal Navy in the strategy of the Crimean campaign.

The Turkish government awarded Slade the Mejidiye and the Osmaniye (both second class), and the British government the KCB on 10 August 1858. On 2 April 1866 he attained, in course of seniority, the rank of rear-admiral in the Royal Navy. He then retired from the Turkish service and lived principally in England. He became a vice-admiral on 6 April 1873, and died, unmarried, at his residence, 3 Hyde Park Gardens, London, on 13 November 1877. His publications include *A Few Words on Naval Construction and Promotion* (1846) and *Maritime States and Military Navies* (1859), both of which reveal a profound grasp of the issues. He was a highly intelligent officer with great linguistic skills and a rare ability to work alone and under difficult circumstances; but his strength of character was also seen in his insubordination and his difficulties with the allied commanders in 1854.

J. K. LAUGHTON, *rev.* ANDREW LAMBERT

Sources A. D. Lambert, *The Crimean War: British grand strategy, 1853–56* (1990) · A. D. Lambert, *The last sailing battlefleet: maintaining naval mastery, 1815-1850* (1991) · A. Slade, *Turkey and the Crimean War: a narrative of historical events* (1867) · A. Slade, *Records of travel in Turkey, Greece, … and of a cruise in the Black sea with the Capitan Pasha in the years 1829-30-31*, 2 vols. (1833) · A. P. Saab, *The origins of the Crimean alliance* (1977) · U. Southampton L., Palmerston MSS · PRO, Stratford de Redcliffe MSS · NMM, Dundas MSS · Burke, *Peerage* · *CGPLA Eng. & Wales* (1878) · *The Times* (15 Nov 1877)

Archives Som. ARS | Bedford estate office, London, letters to Lord George William Russell · Norfolk RO, letters to Sir Henry Bulwer, and other corresp. and reports relating to differences with the British Consulate in Constantinople · PRO, Stratford de Redcliffe MSS · U. Durham L., letters to Viscount Ponsonby

Likenesses wood-engraving (after photograph), NPG; repro. in *ILN* (Dec 1877)

Wealth at death under £80,000: probate, 7 May 1878, *CGPLA Eng. & Wales*

Slade, Felix (1790–1868), art collector and benefactor, was born in August 1790 at Lambeth, the second son of Robert Slade (*d.* 1835), proctor in Doctors' Commons and deputy lieutenant for Surrey, and his wife, Eliza, daughter and heir of Edward Foxcroft of Halstead, Thornton in Lonsdale, Yorkshire. After the death of his elder brother in 1858 Felix (himself a successful lawyer) inherited the whole of his father's considerable estate. He never married and devoted himself to the law and to collecting. A private man, he took no part in public life, but had a wide circle of friends, particularly among collectors. They included Augustus Wollaston Franks of the British Museum, whom he probably first met in 1850, when Franks was secretary to the medieval exhibition at the Society of Arts. Slade was a member of the Athenaeum (he admired its library and bequeathed money to it for the purchase of art books) and of the (Burlington) Fine Arts Club. He was elected a fellow of the Society of Antiquaries in 1866, although—through Franks—some objects from his collection had been exhibited there prior to his election. He lent generously, if with some trepidation, to many of the exhibitions of the mid-nineteenth century, including the great Manchester Art Treasures Exhibition of 1857, but fell out with the South Kensington (later the Victoria and Albert) Museum to the extent that he specifically excluded it from his will.

Slade collected antiquities, books (particularly those with fine bindings), and Japanese ivories, but specialized in glass (on which he spent some £8000) and prints. From time to time he gave to the British Museum specific antiquities, of which the most important is perhaps the 'sword of Tiberius', dated to 15 BC, found in Mainz, and purchased for the museum by Slade in 1866. Slade died at his home in Walcot Place, Lambeth, on 29 March 1868, and left an estate valued at £160,000. Among many charitable bequests he left £45,000 to his executors, £35,000 of which was to be found professorships of fine art at the universities of Oxford and Cambridge, and at University College, London. The rest was to endow six scholarships in fine art at University College for students of 'proficiency in drawing, painting or sculpture'. Oxford and Cambridge each conventionally established a chair, which is now normally held for one year by a distinguished art historian; the first professors were, respectively, John Ruskin and the architect Matthew Digby Wyatt. At University College the £23,000 received from Slade's estate, augmented by gifts from Samuel Sharpe and J. P. Heywood, was used to found and house the Slade School of Fine Art. Its first professor, Edward Poynter, set the long-standing tone of the school by insisting on the importance of life drawing.

Slade devised to the British Museum 944 pieces of glass 'and such other works … as my friend … Franks, out of my executors may select for the British Museum'. This included his Japanese ivories, forty-three finely bound books, 8853 prints, and a number of other items. Franks also oversaw the luxurious completion of the catalogue of Slade's magnificent glass collection, which led to the British Museum's pre-eminence in this field. The print collection is among the ten most important donations of this material ever made to the museum. Although particularly rich in the British school, it also contains a catholic choice from other countries, chosen with extreme care and attention to quality.   DAVID M. WILSON

Sources A. Griffiths, 'Felix Slade (1790–1868)', *Landmarks in print collecting: connoisseurs and donors at the British Museum since 1753*, ed. A. Griffiths (British Museum Press, 1996), 113–33 [exhibition catalogue, Museum of Fine Arts, Houston, TX, 1996, and elsewhere] · *GM*, 5th ser., 1 (1868), 688 · *The Times* (31 March 1868) · *DNB* · H. H. Bellot, *University College, London, 1826–1926* (1929) · *Catalogue of the collection of glass formed by Felix Slade, Esq. FSA, with notes on the history of glass contributed by Alexander Nesbitt FSA* (1871) · *CGPLA Eng. & Wales* (1868)
Archives BL, Add. MS 34580 · BM, department of medieval and modern Europe
Likenesses M. Carpenter, chalk and watercolour drawing, 1851, BM
Wealth at death under £160,000: probate, 21 April 1868, *CGPLA Eng. & Wales*

Slade, James (1783–1860), Church of England clergyman, born at Daventry, Northamptonshire, on 2 May 1783, was eldest of the four children of the Revd James Slade, fellow of Emmanuel College, Cambridge, and his wife, Elizabeth Waterfield of Daventry. He was educated by his father

until 1800, when he went to Emmanuel College, Cambridge, where he graduated in 1804 as ninth wrangler. He became a fellow and tutor of his college, and was ordained at Peterborough Cathedral deacon in 1806 and priest in 1807. He was curate of Willingham from 1806 to 1811, and on 28 May 1812 married Augusta, daughter of the rector there, George Henry *Law. They had three children, only one of whom, Mary Elizabeth Christian (*b.* 1820), survived. She married the Revd Thomas ffoster Chamberlain, vicar of Limber Magna, Lincolnshire, and honorary canon of Manchester.

In 1812 Slade became vicar of Milton, near Cambridge, and in 1813 rector of Teversham. He was appointed examining chaplain by his father-in-law, Bishop Law, and prebendary of Chester in 1816. In 1817 he exchanged the rectory of Teversham for the vicarage of Bolton-le-Moors, Lancashire. During the nearly forty years that Slade was vicar of Bolton he was seldom absent from his church and parish, except for residence as prebendary at Chester. In the same year as he was inducted into Bolton he obtained a king's preachership for the county of Lancaster. In 1818 he was presented to the living of Tattenhall by Bishop Law. Slade married again in 1824; his second wife was Mary, daughter of Edward Bolling. From 1826 to 1829 he held the rectorship of Northenden, and from 1829 until his death that of West Kirby, both in the gift of the dean and chapter of Chester.

As vicar of Bolton Slade attained a wide reputation as a stirring preacher and an able expositor of scripture. He was select preacher at the primary visitation of John Bird Sumner, bishop of Chester, in 1829, and at that of James Prince Lee, first bishop of Manchester, in 1851. During his vicariate fourteen churches were built and consecrated. He was also rural dean of Bolton.

A conservative on constitutional matters, such as Catholic emancipation, Slade nevertheless urged the church to reform itself. In a striking letter to Charles Blomfield, bishop of London, in 1830 he advocated church reform of ecclesiastical laws, liturgy, revenues, and discipline, and remarked on the need for church extension.

Slade believed the education of the working classes to be the key to their mental and spiritual improvement. The Bolton parish church Sunday schools became famous under his care. More than 1300 scholars aged from six to forty years attended those schools, and there were 100 teachers. In 1846 he founded the Church of England Educational Institution for boys and girls of the middle class and for evening students, and this became an important factor in the education of the town, having in 1892 more than a thousand day and evening pupils. He was also the founder of the Poor Protection Society and the first president of the Bolton Savings Bank in 1818 and of the Bolton Temperance Society in 1831. He strongly advocated missionary effort overseas and became the first president of the Bolton Missionary Society in 1824. In 1825 he founded a clerical society.

Slade was elected proctor for the chapter of Chester in York convocation in 1852, and was re-elected in 1857 and 1859. He retired from the vicarage of Bolton at the close of

1856, and spent the remainder of his days between his living of West Kirby and Chester. He died at Crompton Fold while on a visit to Bolton on 15 May 1860, and was buried in the churchyard of St John's, Breightmet, Lancashire, on 19 May.

Slade's most learned work was *Annotations on the Epistles* (1816), which was a continuation of Elsley's *Annotations on the Gospels and Acts of the Apostles*. It met a great want, and went through several editions. He also published several collections of sermons and prayers. His most popular publications were *Lessons for Sunday Schools, Selected from the Scriptures* (1823) and *An Explanation of the Psalms as Read in the Liturgy of the Church* (1832). He was a good musician, and composed several chants and hymn tunes.

J. A. ATKINSON, rev. ELLIE CLEWLOW

Sources J. A. Atkinson, *Memoir of the Rev. Canon Slade MA* (1892) · Venn, *Alum. Cant.* · Boase, *Mod. Eng. biog.* · *GM*, 3rd ser., 9 (1860), 674 · *GM*, 1st ser., 94/1 (1824), 560
Likenesses T. Lupton, engraving (after G. Palten) · G. Palten, oils; known to be at Church of England Institution, Bolton, in 1897
Wealth at death under £4000: probate, 9 Oct 1860, *CGPLA Eng. & Wales*

Slade, Sir John, first baronet (1762–1859), army officer, born on 31 December 1762, was the son of John Slade (d. 1801) of Maunsel Grange, Somerset, a commissioner of the victualling board, and his wife, Charlotte, youngest daughter of Henri Portal of Freefolk, Hampshire. He obtained a commission as cornet in the 10th dragoons on 11 May 1780, and became lieutenant on 28 April 1783, captain on 24 October 1787, major on 1 March 1794, and lieutenant-colonel on 29 April 1795. On 18 October 1798 he exchanged to the 1st dragoons (the Royals). He was appointed equerry to the duke of Cumberland in 1800, and became colonel in the army on 29 April 1802. In June 1804 he was made brigadier, and gave up command of the Royals.

Slade saw no active service until, in October 1808, he was sent to Corunna in command of a hussar brigade. Of limited ability, lacking initiative, and apparently capable only of going forward to carry out a definite order, he was 'nearly useless' (Anglesey, 77). Lord Paget (later first marquess of Anglesey) despised him, 'that damned stupid fellow' (ibid., 350), and transferred his own regiment, the 7th hussars, from Slade's brigade to Charles Stewart's. Slade led the 10th in the cavalry action at Sahagun on 20 December, shared in the arduous work of the cavalry during Moore's retreat, and served as a volunteer at the battle of Corunna, when the cavalry had embarked. He was employed on the staff in England for six months, but returned to the Peninsula in August 1809 with a brigade of dragoons, and served there continuously for four years. He was at Busaco and at Fuentes d'Oñoro. He commanded the cavalry division, in Cotton's absence, during Masséna's retreat from Portugal in the spring of 1811. He was said to have missed opportunities, but Wellington mentioned him favourably in his dispatch of 14 March.

On 11 June 1812, when he was under Hill in Estremadura, Black Jack Slade was beaten by General Lallemand in a cavalry action at Llera. Each had two regiments. The British had the advantage in the first encounter, and followed headlong in pursuit through a defile, beyond which they found the French reserve drawn up. Their own reserve had joined in the pursuit and lost its formation; the brigade panicked, was pursued by the French for several miles, and lost more than 100 prisoners. Slade rode with the leading squadrons, instead of attending to the supports, and Wellington and others blamed him. Wellington was furious: he wrote, 'It is occasioned entirely by a trick our officers of cavalry have acquired of galloping at every thing … They never … think of manoeuvring' (Longford, 275).

In May 1813 Slade's brigade was transferred to General Fane, and he went home, and was employed for a year in Ireland. He received a gold medal and one clasp for Corunna and Fuentes d'Oñoro. He had been promoted major-general on 25 October 1809, became lieutenant-general on 4 June 1814, and general on 10 January 1837. In 1831 he was given the colonelcy of the 5th dragoon guards, on 30 September 1831 he was made a baronet, and in 1835 he received the GCH. He married, first, on 20 September 1792, Anna Eliza Dawson (d. 24 Dec 1819), and second, on 17 June 1822, Matilda Ellen (d. 12 Sept 1868), second daughter of James Dawson of Fork Hill, co. Armagh. He had eleven sons and four daughters. He died on 13 August 1859 at his home, Monty's Court, Norton Fitzwarren, near Taunton, Somerset, 'the oldest living member of the army save one' (*GM*, 307). He was succeeded in the baronetcy by his third son, Frederic William Slade (1801–1863), queen's counsel and bencher of the Middle Temple. Admiral Sir Adolphus *Slade (1804–1877) was his fifth son.

E. M. LLOYD, rev. ROGER T. STEARN

Sources *GM*, 3rd ser., 7 (1859), 307 · C. P. De Ainslie, *Historical record of the 1st dragoons* (1887) · *Supplementary despatches (correspondence) and memoranda of Field Marshal Arthur, duke of Wellington*, ed. A. R. Wellesley, second duke of Wellington, 15 vols. (1858–72), vols. 7, 9, 11 · J. Philippart, ed., *The royal military calendar*, 3rd edn, 2 (1820) · W. Tomkinson, *The diary of a cavalry officer in the Peninsular and Waterloo campaigns, 1809–1815*, ed. J. Tomkinson (1894) · Marquess of Anglesey [G. C. H. V. Paget], *One-leg: the life and letters of Henry William Paget, first marquess of Anglesey* (1961); repr. (1996) · E. Longford [E. H. Pakenham, countess of Longford], *Wellington*, 1: *The years of the sword* (1969) · R. Muir, *Britain and the defeat of Napoleon, 1807–1815* (1996) · A. J. Guy, ed., *The road to Waterloo: the British army and the struggle against revolutionary and Napoleonic France, 1793–1815* (1990) · Boase, *Mod. Eng. biog.* · Burke, *Peerage* (1959) · *CGPLA Eng. & Wales* (1859)
Likenesses W. Theed, terracotta bust, Royal Military Academy, Sandhurst
Wealth at death under £160,000: probate, 26 Sept 1859, *CGPLA Eng. & Wales*

Slade, Matthew (1569–1628), religious controversialist and college head, was born at South Perrot, Dorset, on 9 September 1569, the second son of the rector, John Slade, and his wife, Joan, daughter of John Owsley of Misterton, Somerset. Following his elder brother, Samuel, to Oxford, he matriculated at St Alban Hall on 29 October 1585 and graduated BA on 13 January 1589. Soon afterwards he went to London, where for a period he was a member of the separatist congregation led by Henry Barrow and John Greenwood, but he then returned to the west country, and is believed to have taught at a school in Devon. He married about this time, probably on 20 September 1593, Alethea (*d.* 1608), daughter of Richard Kirford, a man of some means from the Honiton area. Slade may have been among the members of the separatist church who moved to the Low Countries after the execution of Barrow and Greenwood; by about 1595 he had become an elder of their Ancient Church in Amsterdam.

Slade was a noted scholar and linguist and in 1598 he was offered the vice-rectorship of the Latin school in Amsterdam, possibly after having taught there already, possibly (as an eighteenth-century source has it) after having worked as a mason. Some months before he took up his duties on 1 July, a controversy arose in the Ancient Church over his practice of attending Dutch Reformed services. Its course was complicated by existing dissension within the congregation centring on the fraternal rivalry of its recently arrived pastor, Francis Johnson, and his brother George Johnson, of whom Slade was a loyal supporter. Formally censured by the eldership on 30 July, after much delay he was expelled, above all, according to John Paget, because of his defence of the admission to baptism of children of non-members. Slade and his wife, known as Allis, baptized two children at the Nieuwe Kerk in Amsterdam, Cornelius on 24 September 1599 and Marcia on 23 September 1604.

Early in 1602 Slade succeeded Cornelis de Reeckenaar as rector of the Latin school, where he soon became embroiled in disputes with his deputy, Gorisz. In 1607 he quarrelled with Gorisz's successor, Arnold Gregory, this time apparently acting in an insulting and unreasonable manner; the consistory intervened. Slade was appointed municipal librarian of Amsterdam in 1603 and his catalogues, compiled in 1612 and 1622, were enlivened by occasional remarks on volumes such as 'horribly mutilated by a detestable sacrilegist' and 'give back the book, thief, and mend your ways' (Nijenhuis, 11).

When pressures from England and scandals at the Ancient Church encouraged a campaign for a new, respectable, and orthodox church to cater for English immigrants, Slade played a pivotal role. On 5 May 1605 he submitted to the Dutch Reformed consistory a written complaint against the separatists, who 'oppose the authority of the magistrates of this town and … act to the great detriment of the Reformed church of God' (Nijenhuis, 5). He helped block the appointment of the dissident separatist Thomas White as pastor of the new church, founded in 1607 and soon to eclipse the Ancient Church. His wife Allis was a founding member, but he did not join; a request of 1611, renewed in 1615, that he take up an eldership, was rejected by the Dutch, but Slade remained on friendly terms with the pastor, John Paget, and his followers.

Early in 1608 Allis Slade died, and was buried on 12 February. On 6 September Slade married Suzanna de Kampenaer; they baptized four children, Johannes, Janegjen, Mattheus (*d.* 1628), and Suzanna before his wife died in May 1614, or shortly after. She was a step-daughter of the famous high Calvinist Peter Plancius, whose theological views Slade shared, and he plunged into the controversy over the views of Jacob Arminius (*d.* 1609) and his successor as theology professor at Leiden, Conrad Vorstius. In March 1612, on the prompting of the English ambassador, Sir Ralph Winwood, Slade issued the first volume of a Latin refutation of Vorstius's most recent work, opposing as heretical his key doctrine of God's free will and labelling him as a Socinian. To the fury of Hugo Grotius, Slade also volunteered gratuitous remarks against Erasmus, who was in high standing among Vorstius's followers. He corresponded with Sibrand Lubbertus, professor at Franeker, and offered criticism of a manuscript copy of his book on Vorstius. Slade acted as an intermediary between the forces of Dutch and English orthodoxy, translating English into Latin for Lubertus and Dutch into English for his English correspondents, who included George Abbot and Thomas Morton, dean of Gloucester; and he was assiduous in defence of his theology against both Dutch and English enemies. In 1609 and in 1614 he disputed with Thomas Leamer, an exiled English former separatist, now an Arian, and a long-time target of the consistory. On 29 October 1615 he debated at Plancius's house against the remonstrant merchant Rem Egbertsz Bisschop, the brother of Episcopius, and two supporters.

Slade was acquainted with many leading scholars, including Isaac Casaubon, Gerard Vossius, Joseph Scaliger, Hugh Broughton, and Jan Theunitsz. He helped Sir Henry Savile in his (unavailing) attempts to market his edition of Chrysostom in the Netherlands. He was mentioned as a possible candidate for a professorship at Leiden; he himself canvassed Lubbertus for two professorships, of Gröningen (1613), and of the Latin school at Dordrecht (1615). In the latter case, it seems, Plancius refused to recommend his son-in-law, because the magistrates of Amsterdam were unwilling to lose him. His political importance in the years after 1612 is attested by visits from Winwood, Horace Vere, the English military commander in the Netherlands, and Hendrik Alting, tutor of Frederik V of the Palatinate, future husband of Princess Elizabeth. On 6 September 1618 Slade thanked Sir Dudley Carleton, Winwood's successor as ambassador at The Hague, for having recommended him as tutor to the young prince Frederick William of Orange. His thirty-nine letters to Carleton, written chiefly between 1616 and 1620, contain insights into the tumults in Amsterdam in those years. They also leave no doubt that Slade was very useful to the government at Westminster. He served chiefly as a translator and purveyor of detailed news of the theological and political disputes which led to the execution of Oldenbarnevelt and the expulsion of the remonstrants. But at key points he also acted as an agent, supplying, on 12 July 1617, intelligence of Jacques le Maire's discovery of a new route into the Pacific. The following year he reported the support of Amsterdam for the merger of the Dutch and English East India companies, and passed on news of Anglo–Dutch clashes in the East Indies. Slade requested recompense for services rendered, asking Carleton to recommend him as 'one of the basest varlets of his majesty's household' (Nijenhuis, 85), though in this he was disappointed, and his political usefulness declined after the Synod of Dort.

Slade was married twice more, on 2 April 1616, to Catharina van der Veeken, a native of Antwerp, then aged thirty-nine, and on 16 October 1627 to Sara Clercq from Middelburg, but no children are known to have been born of his last two marriages. He died on 10 February 1628 in Amsterdam and was buried there on 14 February in the Zuiderkerk. His eldest son, Cornelius, was appointed professor of Hebrew and other languages and became rector of the Latin school at Amsterdam on 9 May that year, probably in succession to his father. He had married Gertrude, daughter of Luke Ambrose, an English preacher there, and was father of **Matthew Slade** (1628–1689), physician, born on 9 June 1628 in England. He was registered on 8 April 1644 as a student of medicine at the University of Leiden and proceeded MD on 15 October 1649. Two theses, including one on asthma, dedicated to his father, survive in the faculty library of Glasgow University. He wrote several medical treatises, including the pseudonymous *Dissertatio epistolica de generatione animalium contra Harveium* (Amsterdam, 1666), against William Harvey's theory of the circulation of the blood. On 2 December 1684, he sent to Johannes Graevius, professor of history and humane learning at Utrecht, a letter of recommendation for his friend John Locke, a man 'of an inquiring nature, well informed and fond of books' (*Correspondence of John Locke*, 2.656). In autumn 1689, Slade came to England, hoping to further his career as a physician. He stayed chiefly in London, but late in November left for Windsor, where he hoped to view the library of the late Isaac Vossius, canon of Windsor. Arriving in Oxford with Thomas Hyde, Bodley's librarian (1636–1703) on 1 December, he wrote from there to Locke requesting money for his accommodation, bidding 'Goodbye, best of friends, and keep me in your affections' (ibid., 3.731). Philip van Limborch provided a letter of introduction for him to the bishop of Salisbury. Slade also had assistance from another friend of Locke, the writer James Tyrell (1642–1719), who enjoyed his company. He died suddenly on 20 December 1689 between Oxford and nearby Wheatley as he was returning by coach to London after a visit to Tyrell. The latter arranged an autopsy in Oxford, conducted by Dr William Gibbons and other physicians, who agreed that he had 'dyed of an apoplexy; the vessels in the brain being more than ordinaryly distended with blood; and the glandules in the small plexus Choroides being sweld' (ibid.). Tyrell also arranged the funeral at St Peter's-in-the-East, Oxford, on 22 December. Limborch reported the following month that Slade's relations had sent £300 for the funeral and for the repayment of his debts in England.   STEPHEN WRIGHT

Sources W. Nijenhuis, *Matthew Slade, 1569–1628* (Leiden, 1986) • K. Sprunger, *Dutch puritanism* (1982) • B. White, *The English separatist tradition* (1971) • G. Johnson, *A discourse of some troubles* (1603) • Wood, *Ath. Oxon.* • A. C. Carter, *The English reformed church at Amsterdam in the seventeenth century* (1964) • J. de Hoop Scheffer, *History of the free churchmen in Holland* (1922) • J. Paget, *An answer … best* (1635) • G. C. Brodrick, *Memorials of Merton College*, OHS, 4 (1885) • J. Hutchins, *The history and antiquities of … Dorset*, ed. W. Ship and J. Hodson (1861–3) • *The correspondence of John Locke*, ed. E. de Beer, 8 vols. (1976–89), vol. 2, p. 656; vol. 3, letters 1207, 1210, 1215, 1217, 1225, 1227–8 • R. W. Innes Smith, *English-speaking students of medicine at the University of Leyden* (1932) • *The life and times of Anthony Wood*, ed. A. Clark, 3, OHS, 26 (1894) • M. Cranston, *John Locke, a biography* (1985)

Archives BL, letters to Sibrand Lubbert, Add. MSS 22961–22962

Slade, Matthew (1628–1689). *See under* Slade, Matthew (1569–1628).

Slade, Sir Thomas (1703/4–1771), shipbuilder, was born into a well-established shipbuilding family based in Ipswich and Harwich. Benjamin Slade, probably his uncle, who had become the foreman of Deptford yard by 1718 and was promoted to master mastmaker in 1733, became master shipwright at Plymouth in 1746. Thomas Slade probably began his apprenticeship at Deptford yard in 1718. He was sent to Harwich to act as naval overseer in the building of the *Harwich* (fourth rate) in 1742. Two years later he surveyed the harbour at Sandwich and helped draw up plans for improvements at Sheerness; he then became assistant master shipwright at Woolwich. Benjamin Slade was brought to the notice of George Anson in 1747, when the latter was a lord of the Admiralty. He made a very fine model of Anson's flagship, the *Centurion*, which is now in the collections of the National Maritime Museum. When he was ordered to examine the lines of several French prizes, he commissioned his kinsman Thomas to take plans of them to Anson.

When Benjamin died in 1750 Thomas Slade replaced him at Plymouth. He became an Anson protégé, moving to Woolwich in 1752, to Chatham less than three weeks later, and finally to Deptford in 1753, where he was close enough to London to act as an unofficial adviser to Anson. In 1747 Thomas had married Hannah Moore (d. 1763), the daughter of Captain Moore; they had one son, Thomas Moore Slade.

Slade's great opportunity came in August 1755 when the incumbent surveyor of the navy, Sir Thomas Allin, was taken ill and became 'disordered in his senses'. The Admiralty, led by Anson, was clearly determined to get Slade and his colleague William Bately (formerly assistant surveyor of the navy) appointed joint surveyors as quickly as possible. On 7 August they arrived at the Navy Board with warrants to 'inspect the books and papers as joint surveyors of the navy until the patent shall pass for their appointments' (Lavery, 1.96). Allin was pensioned off, though his illness prevented him from taking the necessary oaths; the Admiralty simply ordered that the pension be given to him anyway.

Before becoming joint surveyor Slade had begun his career as a ship designer. Within three weeks of his appointment he produced a draught for two new ships, the first of the Dublin class. Though they were initially described as 70-gun ships, they were in fact the first British-designed 74s, representing a new type of large two-decker that was to dominate the line of battle until after 1815. Anson and Slade cast aside the system of 'establishments' (fixed dimensions and scantlings prescribed for each class of warship), which had handicapped British ship design for half a century. Slade and Bately were the first surveyors to design virtually all the navy's ships themselves. In a previous generation, Jacob Acworth had merely supervised the design, and the process had been taken out of the surveyors' hands while the 1745 establishment was in force. Slade is known to have designed only one ship before his appointment as surveyor, the yacht *Dorset* in 1753. It is remarkable that he produced the plans for the *Dublin* class so quickly, and it would seem that he had been preparing them for some time in advance. The size of Slade's 74-gun ships increased slightly over the next few years, ending with the Bellona and Arrogant classes of 1757–8, at 168 ft on the gundeck. With this the 74s reached a plateau and most ships over the next twenty years were of similar dimensions.

In 1756 Slade turned his attention to smaller ships. Until this time the navy had used single-deckers of 20–24 guns which were too small, and two-deckers of 44 guns which were poor sailers. Following French practice, Slade developed the 'true' frigate, with an unarmed lower deck and a single deck of guns well above the waterline. Previous British ships of this type had carried only 9-pounder guns, but the ships of Slade's Southampton class carried 12-pounders and were powerful enough to fight, but had excellent sailing qualities. As with the 74s, Slade continued to develop the type over the years. The first 36-gun frigates were launched in 1757–8, but this type was not pursued in Slade's lifetime. Meanwhile he altered the layout, especially in the bows where space was limited, and improved the lines and sailing qualities. In 1758 Slade began the design of his only first rate, the *Victory* (100 guns). She was eventually launched in 1765, but saw no service during his life. Her surprisingly good sailing qualities made her a favourite with many of the admirals who used her as a flagship and this resulted in her being rebuilt twice at considerable expense before Nelson died on board her at Trafalgar in 1805.

Slade was aware that different ships needed to be designed for different purposes and he probably inspired a letter from the Navy Board to the Admiralty in 1760, after the board were ordered to design ships of 74, 64, 32 and 28 guns to the lines of the French prize *Aurora*: 'Ships of 74 and 64 guns built strictly similar to her … would require to have their tonnage increased to between 600 and 700 tons more than those of the 74s lately launched … and in respect of the 32 gun ships and under, … she conforming to the *Aurora* in depth in hold will raise the weight of metal too high, and consequently occasion their being tender' (Lavery, 1.206).

Slade, who was knighted on 27 January 1768, died at Bath on 22 February 1771 and was buried in St Clement's churchyard, Ipswich. Though the *Victory*, now preserved at Portsmouth, is his most obvious memorial, he designed many other ships for the navy. It is a measure of his success that his draughts continued to be used after his death. Ten ships of his Arrogant class, for example, were built between 1774 and 1789 while the lines of the *Victory* were copied for the Princess Charlotte class as late as 1813. In Nelson's great victory at the Nile in 1798 eight out of thirteen British ships of the line had been built to Slade

designs. His other achievement was in training new shipwrights and he deserved the eulogy from a later surveyor, Sir John Henslow: 'He was truly a great man in the line he trod, such a one I believe never went before him, and … I may venture to say will hardly follow him' (Lavery, 1.109). Slade introduced no new principles of ship design, though he may have used a slightly more efficient system for drawing the lines, producing a fairer hull. He was aware of the advantages of French design and to a certain extent he was influenced by it, especially in the building of frigates and smaller craft, but he clearly did not want to follow it too slavishly, for fear that British naval architecture would be permanently behind. He was fortunate in the support of Anson in his ventures, and in reaching maturity at a time when the navy was expanding under stress of war, when there was great dissatisfaction with the elder ships and their designers. He was as taciturn as his patron and left very little correspondence beyond what his duty required.

BRIAN LAVERY

Sources A. G. E. Jones, 'Sir Thomas Slade', *Mariner's Mirror*, 64 (1978), 224–6 · D. A. Baugh, *British naval administration in the age of Walpole* (1965) · B. Lavery, *The ships of the line*, 2 vols. (1983–4) · R. Gardiner, *The first frigates* (1992) · J. M. Collinge, *Navy Board officials, 1660–1832* (1978)

Slade, William (d. *c.*1415), abbot of Buckfast and writer on philosophy, evidently read theology at Oxford, but nothing is known of his life until he became abbot of the Cistercian house of Buckfast in Devon soon after 1398. Leland saw his expositions of Aristotle's *Physics*, *De anima*, and *Ethics*, a treatise on universals, some questions on the *Sentences* of Peter Lombard, and *Moralium flosculi*, presumably a collection of materials for preachers, at Buckfast Abbey, and the last also at Fountains. All these were probably his academic notes from Oxford lectures, now put to use, in accord with monastic practice, to instruct the monks of Buckfast. Bale also noted his *Conclusiones ethicorum*, beginning *Memoratio et reminiscibilis*, perhaps the same as his commentary on the *Ethics*, in the library of Magdalen College, Oxford. Neither this manuscript nor any of those at Buckfast and Fountains appears to survive, so none of Slade's works is extant. He died about 1415, the year when a new abbot took office at Buckfast, and was probably buried at the abbey.

JEREMY CATTO

Sources *Commentarii de scriptoribus Britannicis, auctore Joanne Lelando*, ed. A. Hall, 2 vols. (1709) · *Joannis Lelandi antiquarii de rebus Britannicis collectanea*, ed. T. Hearne, 6 vols. (1715), vol. 4, p. 152 · Bale, *Index*, 149 · Bale, *Cat.*, 1.492–3 · G. Oliver, *Monasticon dioecesis Exoniensis* (1846), 371 · F. C. Hingeston-Randolph, ed., *The register of Edmund Stafford, 1395–1419* (1886), 42, 151 · Emden, *Oxf.*, 3.1711–12

Slade, William James (1892–1982), shipowner and master mariner, was born on 28 April 1892, at 18 Irsha Street, Appledore, Devon, the eldest son of William Kingdon Slade (1865–1943), master mariner, and his wife, Rosina Annie Abigail (1865–1964), daughter of Captain Richard Harding of Appledore. Slade attended the Wesleyan elementary school in Appledore from 1895 until 1904, when he was allowed to leave at the age of twelve after passing an examination.

The male members of the Slade family had traditionally

been employed as seamen but, partly as a result of the part-time work of the women of the family in the garments industry, they were just beginning to acquire small vessels of their own. These were employed in the home trade, that is, the coasting trade, and the trade with European ports between Brest and the Elbe. Slade had, since infancy, spent a month or more at sea with his father and his mother (who was an experienced sailor in her own right) in the family's vessels during the summer. Now he went to sea with his father in the ketch *Ulelia* as boy at 1s. (5p) a passage. His duties were to cook, clean, help to work cargo, and assist with the working of the vessel.

Slade's father was barely literate, but he was a hard-driving man with an excellent business sense, and all the secretarial and business work in connection with the operation of the vessel was given to the boy, at his father's dictation, at the end of each working day, which lasted from 6 a.m. to 9 p.m. Increasingly as he grew into his teens Slade was also given responsibility for navigation and pilotage. As a result he was sometimes hardly ashore for months on end, even though the vessels were employed in the home trade. When the *Ulelia* was partly rebuilt at Appledore he spent five weeks working with the shipbuilders.

Although an unbelievably hard life, it was superb training, of which he took full advantage, and as a result at the age of nineteen was given command of, and managing responsibility for, the schooner *Elizabeth Jane*. After a difficult start with a drunken crew Slade prospered with this vessel, and later with the schooners *Millom Castle* and *W. D. Potts*, which was sunk by a German submarine in 1917 when Slade was in command, the ketch *Trio*, and the three-masted motor schooner *Haldon*. In 1930 he lost an eye in an accident ashore but continued in command of the *Haldon* until 1943. In 1944 he sold her. He had by then acquired sufficient capital to maintain himself to his own satisfaction for the rest of his life and settled, after civil defence work during the remainder of the war, at 29 Bridgeland Street, Bideford, where his wife ran a draper's shop.

Although physically small Slade was immensely strong, a very able shipmaster, and an even more able businessman of great personal charm. To the end of his life he spoke with a strong north Devon accent. Slade also had the twin gifts of total recall and an ability to write in a pleasant, easy style. In 1959 his autobiography, *Out of Appledore*, was published. In it he was able to record not merely a form of seafaring life by then completely lost, but the social and economic background to it. The book went into four editions and became a minor classic of its kind. In 1971 he published a collaboration, *Westcountry Coasting Ketches*, of which he wrote much the greater part. Slade married in 1915 May Whitton (1892–1971), daughter of a Baptist minister. He had known her since childhood. They had five sons, all of whom became professional men. He died on 31 August 1982 in Barnstaple Hospital, from the long-term consequences of diabetes, and was buried on 3 September in Bowden Green cemetery, Bideford.

BASIL GREENHILL

Sources personal knowledge (2004) · W. J. Slade, *Out of Appledore*, 4th edn (1980) · W. J. Slade, *Westcountry coasting ketches* (1974) · B. Greenhill and A. Giffard, *Women under sail* (1971) · d. cert. · *CGPLA Eng. & Wales* (1982)
Likenesses photographs, priv. coll.
Wealth at death £42,648: probate, 28 Oct 1982, *CGPLA Eng. & Wales*

Sladen, Sir Charles (1816–1884), pastoralist and politician in Australia, born at Ripple Court, near Walmer, Kent, on 28 August 1816, was the second son of John Baker Sladen of Ripple Court, Kent, a deputy lieutenant for the Cinque Ports, and his wife, Ethelred, the eldest daughter of Kingsman Baskett St Barbe of London. He was educated at Shrewsbury School (1831–4) and Trinity Hall, Cambridge, where he entered as a scholar in 1834 and graduated BA in 1837. He served his articles with a proctor in Doctors' Commons, and proceeded LLB in 1840 and LLD in December 1867. He married, on 11 August 1840, Harriet Amelia (d. 1887), the daughter of William Orton of Stockton-on-Tees.

Thinking, correctly, that his prospects were better in Australia, Sladen emigrated to Port Phillip, where he landed on 14 February 1842. He started practice forthwith as a solicitor at Geelong, and became the head of the firm of Sladen, Martyr, and Taylor. His rapid success enabled him to retire from practice in 1854, when he bought part of the former Wesleyan mission station, Buntingdale, near the modern township of Birregurra. This he called Ripple Vale, and he set about establishing there Victoria's leading Leicester sheep stud.

On 28 November 1855 Sladen was appointed treasurer in Victoria's first ministry under responsible government and nominated as a member of the legislative council. In September 1856 he was elected to represent Geelong in the new legislative assembly, but continued as treasurer until 1857.

After seven years out of parliament, in July 1864 Sladen was elected to the legislative council for the Western Province, and very soon became the acknowledged leader of the conservatives in that house. He led the council's resistance to the attempt by the ministry of Sir James McCulloch to 'tack' controversial measures—in 1865 the tariff and gold duties repeal bills, and in 1867 the 'Darling Grant'—to the annual appropriation bills. When McCulloch resigned in 1868, Sladen formed, as a last resort, a ministry which was in a hopeless minority in the assembly. He was premier and chief secretary from 6 May to 11 July, and resigned one day after Sir Charles Darling's reinstatement in the colonial service removed the *casus belli* between the houses. In August 1868 his seat became vacant by lapse of time, and he did not seek re-election, though he served for six years on the local Winchelsea shire council.

In 1876 Sladen regained his old seat in the council. Here he led the opposition to Graham Berry's proposals for payment of members, levying of a land tax, and reform of the Victorian constitution. At the same time he accepted the need for changes in the council's membership and electorate, but not in its powers. His own proposals proved unacceptable, but, with his support, a Reform Bill was eventually passed in 1881. He had moved to live in Geelong in 1876, but finally retired from politics on 13 December 1882, for reasons of health. Sladen's conservatism was based on principle rather than the more general self-interest. Hence, while he never enjoyed widespread electoral popularity, his sincerity was never questioned nor his integrity compromised. He was gazetted CMG in 1870 and KCMG in 1875.

Outside politics and sheep farming Sladen's main interests were the Church of England and his home town, Geelong. To both his local parish, Christ Church, and the new diocese of Melbourne he gave strong and sustained support. In the Geelong community he associated himself with a wide range of public, philanthropic, and social activities, including the Anglican Geelong grammar school, and from 1878 was the first chairman of the important Trustees, Executors, and Agency Company. Tall, handsome, and of great personal charm, he undertook over three decades the unenviable task of commending conservative principles and policies to a radical colony. He died childless at his home in Barwon Crescent, Chilwell, Geelong, on 22 February 1884, and was buried on 24 February in the eastern cemetery, Geelong.

JAMES GRANT

Sources J. Grant, 'Sladen, Sir Charles', *AusDB*, vol. 6 · *Geelong Advertiser* (4 July 1879) · *Geelong Advertiser* (9 Oct 1883) · *Geelong Advertiser* (23 Feb 1884) · *The Argus* [Melbourne] (23 Feb 1884) · W. R. Brownhill, *The history of Geelong and Corio bay* (1955) · D. Sladen, *My long life* (1939) · G. Goodman, *The church in Victoria* (1892) · A. Sutherland, *Victoria and its metropolis* (1888) · *DNB* · Burial register, Christ Church, Geelong, Victoria, Australia
Likenesses C. Summers, marble bust, 1870, State Library of Victoria, Melbourne, La Trobe Collection · G. F. Folingsby, oils, 1884, State Library of Victoria, Melbourne, La Trobe picture collection · Miss Bell, oils, City Hall, Geelong · print, National Gallery of Victoria, Melbourne
Wealth at death £37,441: probate, Victoria, Australia

Sladen, Sir Edward Bosc (1827–1890), army and political officer in India, born at Madras on 20 November 1827, was the son of Dr Ramsey Sladen (1782–1861), physician-general of the East India Company's service, and his second wife, Emma (*d*. 1850), daughter of Colonel Paul Bosc, commissioner in Mysore. Educated at Oswestry School, Shropshire, he was nominated to an East India cadetship on 14 April 1849, and, going back to India in that year, was posted on 3 September 1850 as second lieutenant to the 1st Madras fusiliers, one of the company's European regiments. He served in the Second Anglo-Burmese War, being present at the relief of Pegu in December 1852, and at the second investment of Pegu in January 1853. Gazetted a lieutenant on 1 February 1853, he was appointed an assistant commissioner in Tenasserim, and in 1856–7 took part in operations against insurgent Shans and Karens in the Yun-za-lin district, when he was severely wounded.

In February 1858 Sladen rejoined his regiment, then serving against the mutineers in upper India, and was present at the capture of Lucknow in March 1858. In the subsequent campaign in Oudh he accompanied Hope Grant's column and acted as brigade quartermaster under Sir Alfred Hastings Horsford. On the return of his regiment to Madras he reverted to district work in Burma, joining the Indian staff corps when the Madras fusiliers became a Queen's regiment. He was gazetted captain on 21 June 1860, major on 14 April 1869, and lieutenant-colonel on 14 April 1875. He married, in 1861, Sophia Catherine, eldest daughter of Richard Pryce Harrison of the Bengal civil service. She died in 1865.

In 1866 Sladen went to Mandalay as agent of the chief commissioner, and in August of that year had a narrow escape from a group of insurgents who had murdered three of the royal princes. During the ensuing disturbances he embarked nearly all the Europeans and other Christians at the Burmese capital on board a river steamer and brought them safely to Rangoon, for which he received the thanks of the governor-general. The insurrection having been put down, he returned to Mandalay, and in May 1867 exerted his influence with the king to prevent the execution of three young princes, two of whom owed their lives to his intercession, the other having been beheaded before the reprieve arrived. Shortly afterwards he obtained the king's assent to a new treaty of commerce and extradition which was ratified by the governor-general on 26 November 1867. In 1868 he was placed in charge of a political mission sent to the Chinese frontier to inquire into the causes of the cessation of overland trade between Burma and China, and to obtain information respecting the Shans, Kakyens, and Panthays. Leaving Mandalay on 13 January, he proceeded via Bhamo to Momein (Tengyue), the frontier town of the Chinese province of Yunnan, where he stayed six weeks, but was prevented from proceeding further by the disturbed state of the country. The mission reached Bhamo, on its return journey, on 3 September, having acquired much valuable information about an almost unknown country. From 1876 to 1885 Sladen was commissioner of the Arakan division; and in the latter year he accompanied the force sent against King Thibaw, as chief political officer. In this capacity, on the arrival of the British troops at Mandalay, on 28 December 1885, he entered the royal palace, and received the king's submission. In a speech on 17 February 1886 the governor-general, Lord Dufferin, made special mention of 'Colonel Sladen, to whose courage and knowledge of the people we are so much indebted for the surrender of the king'. In 1880 he married Katharine (Kate) Jane (*d*. 1890), the daughter of Robert Russell Carew of Carpenden Park, Hertfordshire, who survived him.

On 26 November 1886 Sladen was knighted, and on 14 April 1887 he retired from the service. Besides his *Official Narrative of the Expedition to China via Bhamo* (1869), he published an article on the geographical results of the mission, in the *Proceedings of the Royal Geographical Society* (vol. 15). He died at his London residence, 30 Lowndes Square, Chelsea, on 4 January 1890.

STEPHEN WHEELER, *rev.* M. G. M. JONES

Sources Burke, *Gen. GB* · *Madras Army List* · J. Anderson, *Mandalay to Momein* (1876) · *Parliamentary papers, Burma* (1886) · *British Burma Administration Reports* · *Proceedings* [Royal Geographical Society], new ser., 12 (1890), 113 · Boase, *Mod. Eng. biog.*

Archives BL OIOC, corresp. and papers mostly relating to Burma, MSS Eur. E 290 · RGS, papers relating to Burma

Likenesses wood-engraving, NPG; repro. in *ILN* (12 Dec 1885), 606

Wealth at death £18,019 19s. 2d.: administration, 13 Feb 1890, *CGPLA Eng. & Wales*

Slane. For this title name *see* Fleming, Alice, Lady Slane (*b. c.*1508, *d.* in or after 1540).

Slane, Philip (*d.* 1327), bishop of Cork, was a royal clerk and a member of the Dominican community of St Mary of the Island, Cork. In March 1321, following the translation of John McCarroll to Meath, Slane became the first papal appointee to the bishopric of Cork. The temporalities were restored to the new bishop in July 1321 and shortly afterwards he departed on one of his many visits to England.

From at least 1318 Slane had been a member of the Irish council and he continued to serve on it after his promotion to Cork, receiving a yearly fee of 5 marks. A large part of his career as bishop of Cork was spent on royal business, particularly as an emissary to the papal court then at Avignon. In 1324 he undertook the first of two journeys there to promote a scheme for the reformation of the Irish church. Among the proposals were requests that ecclesiastical censures be implemented against Irish clerics who did not preach loyalty to the king, and a number of suggestions that poor bishoprics (worth under £60 per annum) which were ruled over by the Irish be united to larger ones. Slane's mission, with its decidedly political overtones, was carefully supervised by Edward II, who wrote to prominent continental ecclesiastics enlisting their support.

Pope John XXII received the emissary sympathetically but requested more clarification and more discussion with the Irish clergy. This necessitated Slane's return visit to Avignon in 1325, taking with him a second draft of the reform plan which, according to Edward II, was aimed at curbing the obstinate malice of the Irish. The plan was the result of thorough discussions by the archbishops of Dublin and Cashel, Philip Slane, the Irish council, and the king's council in England. However, apart from promulgating the unification of the diocese of Cloyne with Cork, the pope had taken no immediate steps towards implementing the scheme when Slane died in March 1327.

That the bishop of Cork was a scholar as well as a politician is evidenced by the survival of an abridgement of the *Topographia Hibernica* of Gerald of Wales, entitled *Libellus de descriptione Hibernie*, which was presented to Pope John XXII by 'Philip of the Dominican house of Cork' (BL, Add. MS 19513, fols. 164–188b). This abridgement also formed the basis of a fourteenth-century Provençal version of the *Topographia* (BL, Add. MS 17920, fols. 20–29).

MARGARET MURPHY

Sources E. Bolster, *A history of the diocese of Cork*, 1: *From the earliest times to the Reformation* (1972) · J. A. Watt, 'Negotiations between Edward II and John XXII concerning Ireland', *Irish Historical Studies*, 10 (1956–7), 1–20 · H. G. Richardson and G. O. Sayles, *The Irish parliament in the middle ages* (1952) · *CEPR letters*, vol. 2 · R. Flower, 'Manuscripts of Irish interest in the British Museum', *Analecta Hibernica*, 2 (1931), 292–340, esp. 316–17

Archives BL, Add. MS 17920, fols. 20–29 · BL, Add. MS 19513, fols. 164–188b

Slaney, Robert Aglionby (1792–1862), politician, was born on 9 June 1792, the eldest son of Robert Slaney (1764–1834) of Hatton Grange, Shropshire, and his wife, Mary, daughter of Thomas Mason of Shrewsbury. The family came originally from Slany (Schlan), a small town in Bohemia, near Prague, but had been settled in Shropshire since the end of the sixteenth century (*Visitation of Shropshire*, 1623, Harleian Society, 29, 1889). After a few terms at Trinity College, Cambridge, he married, in 1812, Elizabeth, daughter of William Hawkins Muccleston, physician; she was the heir of Joseph Muccleston of Walford, Shropshire. Slaney was called to the bar at Lincoln's Inn in 1817. He joined the Oxford circuit, and practised until 1826, when he was elected for Shrewsbury, a two-member constituency, one of whose seats the Liberals won in good years.

Slaney soon became known for his 'benevolent exertions to ameliorate the condition of the poor' (speech of the duke of Richmond, *Hansard 3*, 1830, 481), though he was a supporter of the new poor law of 1834. In 1834 he succeeded, on the death of his father, to the property at Hatton Grange. He was defeated in 1835, but was re-elected in 1837, and then held his seat until 1841, when he did not stand against Disraeli. During this period he spoke frequently on subjects dealing with agricultural improvement and economic reform generally, serving also on committees appointed to investigate these and similar subjects. He moved for the appointment of a committee to inquire into the condition of the labouring classes, spoke on national education, the Irish poor laws (1838), enclosure bills, factory regulation, highways, public walks, rating of tenements (1839), duties on timber, the inquiry into charities, emigration, the poor-law commission (1840), the health of the metropolis, and school rates (1841). A member of the Society for the Diffusion of Useful Knowledge, the London Statistical Society, and the Central Society of Education, Slaney was chairman of the select committees on education (in 1838) and the health of the poorer classes in large towns (in 1840); he edited and wrote prefaces for the reports of both committees. From 1843 to 1846 he was an active commissioner on the health of towns, in which capacity he investigated and reported on the sanitary condition of Birmingham and fourteen other towns. In the autumn of 1847 he was again elected for Shrewsbury, holding his seat until 1852. In that year he had secured the legal position of co-operative societies by his Industrial and Provident Societies Act. He was re-elected in 1857, and again in 1859, remaining in parliament until his death in 1862. He was also a JP and deputy lieutenant for Shropshire, and was its high sheriff in 1854.

After the death of his first wife, Slaney married, in 1854, Catherine, daughter of the Revd George Buckston of Bradborn Hall, Derbyshire, and widow of Graves Archer of Mount John, co. Wicklow. In August 1860 he set out on a journey to the United States and Canada, where he visited Boston, Quebec, Montreal, Chicago, St Louis, and Washington, returning in November of the same year. In 1861 he published an account of his tour in *Short Journal of a Visit to Canada and the States of America in 1860*.

Slaney was a bold rider to hounds, a fine shot, a good ornithologist, one of the many minor poets of Shropshire, and a staunch moderate Liberal. He died on 19 May 1862 at his residence, 5 Bolton Row, Piccadilly, London, from the effects of falling through a gap in the floor at the opening of the International Exhibition. His third daughter from his first marriage, Frances Catherine, married Captain William Kenyon MP, and inherited the family estate of Hatton Grange; her husband took the name Kenyon-Slaney [*see* Slaney, William Slaney Kenyon- (1847–1908)].

ERNEST CLARKE, *rev.* H. C. G. MATTHEW

Sources *The Times* (21 May 1862) • Boase, *Mod. Eng. biog.* • *GM*, 3rd ser., 12 (1862), 794 • *Men of the time* (1862) • P. Richards, 'R. A. Slancy, the industrial town, and early Victorian social policy', *Social History*, 4 (1979) • D. G. Paz, *The politics of working-class education in Britain, 1830–50* (1980) • B. Hilton, *The age of atonement: the influence of evangelicalism on social and economic thought, 1795–1865* (1988)
Archives Shrops. RRC, diaries, essays, accounts, travel journals, and election papers; foreign travel journal • U. Birm. L., corresp. and papers; diaries and travel journals | BL, corresp. with Sir Robert Peel, Add. MSS 40310–40580, *passim* • UCL, letters to Society for the Diffusion of Useful Knowledge
Likenesses engraving, 1851 (after photograph by Kilburn), repro. in *ILN*, 28/291 (1851)
Wealth at death under £100,000: probate, 5 Sept 1862, *CGPLA Eng. & Wales*

Slaney, William Slaney Kenyon- (1847–1908), soldier and politician, was born on 24 August 1847 at Rajkot in India. He was the eldest son of William Kenyon, then a captain in the 2nd Bombay cavalry, and Frances Catherine, the daughter and heir of Robert A. Slaney of Hatton Grange, near Shifnal, in Shropshire. On the death of the latter in 1862 the Kenyon family assumed the additional surname of Slaney and William Kenyon-Slaney became the owner of 4000 acres.

While at Eton College between September 1860 and December 1865 Kenyon-Slaney emerged as a talented sportsman. A first-class batsman he played cricket for the MCC and occasionally for Shropshire. In association football his 'skill and dexterity in the dribbling game' was noted. He played for England against Scotland in 1873 and for the Old Etonians in the final tie for the English cup in 1876, and he helped to popularize the association code.

After Eton Kenyon-Slaney spent a brief spell at Christ Church, Oxford (1866–7); but his ambitions were military not academic, and he left Oxford in November 1867 on receiving his commission in the 3rd battalion of the Grenadier Guards. In 1882 he fought in the Egyptian campaign under Sir Garnet Wolseley, being decorated for his part in the battle of Tell al-Kebir (13 September). He became a colonel in July 1887, was placed on half pay in November of that year, and finally retired from the army in 1892. On 22 February 1887, at the age of thirty-nine, he married Lady Mabel Selina Bridgeman, daughter of the third earl of Bradford; they had a son and a daughter.

At Oxford Kenyon-Slaney's political zeal had led to his being summoned before the senior proctor for 'helping to break up a Radical meeting in the Town Hall'. In 1885 he stood unsuccessfully as Conservative candidate for Wellington, but was elected in the following year for the Newport division of Shropshire which he represented until 1908. His advocacy of a tariff in 1885 was a sign that the protectionist tradition in rural toryism was reviving in a period of agricultural depression. By the 1906 general election, when the party as a whole was moving back to protectionism, he insisted that any Unionist programme that excluded tariff reform was 'worthless and hopeless'. As an MP he took an interest in agriculture, the army, Ireland, death duties, and the Pure Beer Bill. He campaigned for the provision of a recreation ground in London for the men of the guards, and organized help for ex-servicemen who had fought in the Second South African War and for their families.

His most noted parliamentary achievement took the form of the 'Kenyon-Slaney clause', an amendment to A. J. Balfour's 1902 Education Bill. This was designed to placate nonconformist criticism of the bill by placing control of religious instruction in denominational schools under the managers as opposed to the trustees or individual clergymen. By employing a popular back-bencher to promote this amendment the government successfully overcame the protests from within the Conservative Party. In November 1902 Kenyon-Slaney declined the offer of a baronetcy, but he was sworn of the privy council in 1904.

A popular figure in Shropshire, where he was known as 'the Colonel', Kenyon-Slaney retained a countryman's love of nature, hunting, and shooting. His role as a squire brought out the paternalistic side to his toryism; he insured his estate workers against accident and equipped his cottages with gardens, drainage, a water supply, and three bedrooms. In parliament he backed legislation designed to promote the purchase of small-holdings by tenants and to provide workers' compensation for injury. On the other hand, he found it hard to tolerate the expression of independent political views on the part of his tenants; and in 1904–5 this led to a controversy with a Mr Frederic Horne who was both a tenant of Kenyon-Slaney and an active Shropshire Liberal; eventually Horne left his farm. In this period the radicals' campaigns against Shropshire landlords had put Kenyon-Slaney onto the defensive and he only narrowly retained his seat in the 1906 election.

In 1908 some 4000 people subscribed towards portraits of Kenyon-Slaney and Lady Mabel, painted by Mark Milbanke, in recognition of his twenty-one years as an MP. However, shortly before the presentation could be made he suffered a severe attack of suppressed gout followed by pneumonia. He died at his home, Hatton Grange, on 24 April 1908, and was buried at Ryton near there.

MARTIN PUGH

Sources W. Durnford, ed., *Memoir of Colonel William Kenyon-Slaney M.P.* (1909) • *The Times* (25 April 1908) • *Newport Advertiser* (25 April 1908) • *Shrewsbury Chronicle* (1 May 1908) • *Hansard 4* (1902), 113.1311–16
Archives Shrops. RRC, papers, scrapbooks, and autobiography
Likenesses M. Milbanke, oils, 1908, Hatton Grange, Shropshire • wood-engraving (after photograph by Russell & Sons), NPG; repro. in *ILN* (29 Nov 1890), 676

Wealth at death £135,502 3s. 9d.: probate, 10 July 1908, *CGPLA Eng. & Wales*

Slanning, Sir Nicholas (1606–1643), royalist army officer, was born on 1 September 1606, the younger of two children of Gamaliel Slanning (1589–1612) of Hele, Devon, and his wife, Margaret, daughter of Edward Marler of Kent, whose wife—Margaret's mother—was Agnes, daughter and heir of Nicholas Slanning (d. 1583) of Maristow, also in Devon. Slanning's parents were thus first cousins, a marriage which was to lead to his inheriting the estates of both branches of his family. He married Gertrude, daughter of Sir James Bagge of Saltram, Devon, on 23 September 1625; they had two sons and two daughters. He had attended Exeter College, Oxford, and entered the Inner Temple in November 1628. He then served in the Low Countries, becoming proficient in the art of war.

On his return to England Slanning was knighted on 24 August 1632 and appointed vice-admiral of both Devon and Cornwall, and on 17 April 1635 he became governor of Pendennis Castle. He was particularly concerned with the danger from Barbary corsairs and rejoiced at the arrival in September 1637 of two ships bringing captives released from Salé after Rainsborough's expedition. Slanning served on both the Devon and Cornish commissions of the peace. The first bishops' war led to his being ordered to take thirteen pieces of ordnance from Pendennis Castle and 100 soldiers by sea to Workington in Cumberland. He had arrived by 13 April 1639 when he was ordered to defend Carlisle with these forces.

Slanning was member of parliament for Plympton Earle in the Short Parliament and for Penryn in the Long Parliament when he showed his support for the king by opposing the attainder of the earl of Strafford. In January 1642 he was accused of ordering Cornish ports to apprehend the five members should they try to escape the king by flight abroad, but he denied this charge. As preparations began for war he was included on the commissions of array for both Devon and Cornwall and so in August was excluded from parliament. Slanning's prime responsibility during the first months of the war was securing the import of supplies. He provided many of the ships needed for this trade and also organized a fleet of royalist privateers to prey on merchant ships and seize goods for the king's service.

During October 1642 Slanning was engaged in recruiting his own regiment. He was replaced as governor of Pendennis so that he could serve in Sir Ralph Hopton's army which entered Devon in early December and took Tavistock and Plympton. On 6 December he accompanied Hopton to Modbury where a posse comitatus had been raised which was numerous but largely unarmed and inexperienced. Colonel Ruthven made a surprise attack on the town, dispersed the raw recruits, and captured the sheriff and some officers though Hopton and Slanning narrowly escaped. In January Slanning's regiment was part of Hopton's force which defeated Ruthven at Braddock Down and in February he was involved in a second action at Modbury.

The inconclusive fighting in the west country led to a truce and Slanning was among the Cornish representatives who negotiated it. Both sides had prepared for action by the time it ended on 22 April 1643. Hopton undertook a night march from Launceston to surprise the parliamentarians at Okehampton, but James Chudleigh ambushed the royalists and their flight was checked only by the force at the rear under Slanning's command. The parliamentarians then advanced into Cornwall and engaged Hopton's army at Stratton on 16 May where Slanning's regiment was among Hopton's victorious troops. Hopton's army now left the west country and Slanning fought at the battle of Lansdowne on 5 July where his horse was killed under him. Finally he took part in Prince Rupert's attack on Bristol on 26 July 1643; he was mortally wounded and died a few days later. Slanning and Colonel John Trevanion, who also died at Bristol, were described by Clarendon as 'the life and soul of the Cornish regiments, whose memories can never be enough celebrated' (Clarendon, *Hist. rebellion*, 4.113). Their deaths, following that of Sir Bevil Grenville at Lansdowne, destroyed the Cornish army as a fighting force.   MARY WOLFFE

Sources W. Jones, 'The Slannings of Leye, Bickleigh and Maristow', *Report and Transactions of the Devonshire Association*, 19 (1887), 451–66 · M. Coate, *Cornwall in the great civil war and interregnum, 1642–1660*, 2nd edn (1963) · Clarendon, *Hist. rebellion* · *Bellum civile: Hopton's narrative of his campaign in the West, 1642–1644*, ed. C. E. H. Chadwyck Healey, Somerset RS, 18 (1902) · *CSP dom., 1635–43* · J. Stucley, *Sir Bevill Grenville and his times, 1596–1643* (1983) · J. Prince, *Danmonii orientales illustres, or, The worthies of Devon* (1701) · E. A. Andriette, *Devon and Exeter in the civil war* (1971) · J. L. Vivian, ed., *The visitations of the county of Devon, comprising the herald's visitations of 1531, 1564, and 1620* (privately printed, Exeter, [1895]) · A. Duffin, *Faction and faith: politics and religion of the Cornish gentry before the civil war* (1996) · J. Rushworth, *Historical collections*, new edn, 8 vols. (1721–2), vol. 4, pp. 688–9; vol. 5, pp. 67, 70, 267 · W. H. Coates, A. Steele Young, and V. F. Snow, eds., *The private journals of the Long Parliament, 1: 3 January to 5 March 1642* (1982) · M. A. E. Green, ed., *Calendar of the proceedings of the committee for compounding … 1643–1660*, 5 vols., PRO (1889–92), 2210 · Commission of the peace for Devon, PRO, C231/5, fol. 171 · Commission of the peace for Cornwall, PRO, C193/13/2; SP16/405 · *A true and perfect relation of the passages in Devonshire this weeke* (1642–3) [Thomason tract E 91(4)] · *Kingdomes Weekly Intelligencer*, 9 (21–8 Feb 1643) [Thomason tract E 91(8)] · *The protestation taken by the commissioners of Cornwall and Devon at Stone-House neare Plymouth* (1642) [Thomason tract E 94(21)] · *Remarable [sic] passages newly received of the great overthrow of Sir Ralph Hopton and his eorces [sic] at Madburie, 12 miles from Plimouth … which particulars were sent in two letters* (1642) [Thomason tract E 130(16)] · *Speciall Passages and Certain Informations* (29 Nov–6 Dec 1642) [Thomason tract E 129(5)] · *A Continuation of Certaine Speciall and Remarkable Passages* (1–8 Dec 1642) [Thomason tract E 244(5)] · *A Perfect Diurnall of the Passages in Parliament*, 38 (27 Feb–6 March 1642) [Thomason tract E 246(37)] · *Mercurius Aulicus* (29 Jan 1642/3–3 Feb 1642/3) [Thomason tract E 246(16)]

Likenesses R. Cooper, stipple, NPG · attrib. Van Dyck, portrait; formerly in the possession of Mr John Chaworth Musters of Colwick and Annesley Park, Nottinghamshire, 1887 · line engraving, NPG · photograph (after Van Dyck?); formerly at Bickleigh Church, near Plymouth, 1887

Wealth at death family compounded for £999 13s. 11d., 16 Sept 1651: *Calendar of the proceedings of the committee for compounding*

Slare, Frederick (1646/7–1727), chemist and physician, was born between 16 December 1646 and 15 December 1647 in Old, Northamptonshire, the son of Frederick

Schloer (*b. c.*1601), rector of Old and an immigrant from Germany, and Anna, daughter of Ralph Malory of Shelton, Bedfordshire. He was baptized in the parish of Old in early 1648. Slare matriculated at the University of Heidelberg in 1666, and after his studies returned to England, where he lived, at least for a time, with his father's cousin Theodore Haak in London. In the early 1670s he began working for Robert Boyle as an amanuensis and laboratory operator, an association to which Slare would later attribute his subsequent scientific success. Indeed, several of Slare's studies continued Boyle's own interests. Many papers in the Boyle archive bear Slare's hand, and Boyle bequeathed him a ring worth £8. Among Slare's work for Boyle was the preparation of various phosphorescent substances, including the newly discovered white phosphorus on which Boyle published in 1680 deploying samples and data prepared by Slare and Ambrose Godfrey. Slare performed a demonstration using white phosphorus before the Royal Society in 1683; he later repeated it before Samuel Pepys and John Evelyn, the latter giving an enthusiastic description of it in his *Diary* (13 November 1685).

Slare obtained an MD from Utrecht in May 1679, and had it incorporated at Oxford on 9 September 1680 and at Cambridge in 1681. On 16 December 1680 he was made FRS; he became extremely active in the Royal Society, acting as chemistry curator for a year beginning on 28 February 1683 and serving on the council for six terms between 1682 and 1699. He published ten papers in the *Philosophical Transactions* and two in R. Hooke's *Collections*, and read thirteen others before the society. He was made a candidate to the Royal Society of Physicians on 25 June 1681, and created a fellow on 21 May 1685. He proved to be an equally active member of that society; he served as censor in 1692, 1693, and 1708, was made elect on 21 September 1708, and was a member of the council from 1716 until his death in 1727. He was also a member of the Society for the Propagation of the Gospel in Foreign Parts. In late 1711 or early 1712 Slare moved to Bath, but eventually returned to the London area. He died on 12 September 1727, and was buried at Greenwich. His sister Jane (1653/4–1734) was buried next to him. There is no record of his having married.

Slare's major interests lay in the application of chemical principles to physiology and medicine, and he deployed chemical observations to explain common phenomena. For example, he related the 'corruscations' observed in white phosphorus to lightning, and the heating and cooling produced when various chemicals were mixed to fevers and chills. Slare's early work, besides that on phosphoruses, included an analysis of mineral and bodily substances. He wrote a treatise on bladder and kidney stones, and published part of it in the *Philosophical Transactions* (1684) to answer queries raised by Sir John Hoskins. Slare's first book, *Experiments and Observations upon Oriental and other bezoar Stones* (1715), is related to these early studies. The book also contains an appendix entitled 'A vindication of sugars', debunking the claim (made by Thomas Willis and others) that sugar contained a corrosive acid salt damaging to teeth. Slare there tells of his maternal grandfather who ate sugar daily and grew a new set of teeth at the age of eighty, which remained sound until his death twenty years later. Slare also had a long interest in the therapeutics of mineral waters. It has been suggested that he is the 'Dr. S. L.' to whom Boyle addressed his 1685 *Short Memoirs for the Natural Experimental History of Mineral Waters*, 'the ingenious Doctor who set me on this task' (Hall, 35). While in Bath Slare studied the local water as well as those of Spa, Tonbridge, and Pyrmont (near Göttingen). He particularly praised the effervescent water of Pyrmont (especially against the more popular Spa water), and demonstrated experiments on it before the Royal Society on 28 February 1717. These studies, first published in the *Philosophical Transactions*, were expanded into his second book, *An Account of … the Pyrmont Waters* (1717). A German translation by Georg Ludwig Piderit was published at Hanover in the following year, with critical annotations by Johann Philipp Seip, who had published his own *Neue Beschreibung der Pyrmontische Gesund-Brunnen* in 1717. The second edition of Seip's book (Hanover, 1719) contains a eulogy of Slare on page 49. Slare's last appearance in print was to defend the newly introduced practice of inoculation against smallpox. His defence was published as an appendix to Perrott Williams's 1725 tract *Some Remarks upon Dr. Wagstaffe's Letter*.

LAWRENCE M. PRINCIPE

Sources M. B. Hall, 'Frederick Slare, FRS, 1648–1727', *Notes and Records of the Royal Society*, 46 (1992), 23–41 • M. Hunter, *The Royal Society and its fellows, 1660–1700: the morphology of an early scientific institution*, 2nd edn (1994) • Munk, *Roll* • RS, classified papers, XI (1) • M. Hunter, *Letters and papers of Robert Boyle: a guide to the manuscripts and microfilm* (1992), xxxv • *Diary and correspondence of John Evelyn*, ed. W. Bray, rev. edn, ed. [J. Forster], 2 (1860), 245
Archives RS, classified MSS and register books

Slate, Richard (1787–1867), Congregational minister, was the son of Thomas Slate, straw-hat maker, and was born at 36 Noble Street, London, on 10 July 1787. In 1803 he became a member of Founders' Hall, Lothbury, and was a Sunday school teacher in connection with the London Itinerant Society. In 1805 he entered Hoxton Academy and was called to Stand Chapel, near Manchester. He began his ministry there on 1 July 1809 and was ordained on 19 April 1810. This was a very successful ministry and a new Sunday school building had to be erected in the first year of his pastorate. He married Ann Watkins on 14 May 1810; she died in 1851. In September 1826 he received a call to the pulpit of Grimshaw Street Chapel, Preston, Lancashire. This was the second Congregational church in the town, opened in 1808. Slate took over at the end of a very troubled period in the church's history, but he rapidly became first the spokesman and then the elder statesman of nonconformity in the town. At Grimshaw Street, where he was pastor for thirty-five years, a new Sunday school building was put up and a new church built in 1859—this was to him the crowning glory of his ministry. In Preston he was active in a variety of temperance, educational, and reform movements: he was also a respected figure in Lancashire Congregational Union affairs. Slate was a keen student of Lancashire nonconformist history: he compiled *Select Nonconformists' Remains* (1814), original sermons of the leading Lancashire ejected clergy of 1662; *Memoirs of the Rev. Oliver Heywood* (1825); and *A Brief History of the Lancashire Congregational Union and the Blackburn Independent Academy* (1840). He contributed to Robert Halley's *Lancashire Nonconformity* and to J. Horsfall Turner's edition of Oliver Heywood's *Diaries*. Benjamin Nightingale used, and thought highly of, his historical writings. Slate died at Preston on 10 December 1867 and was buried at Stand.

C. W. SUTTON, rev. IAN SELLERS

Sources *Congregational Year Book* (1869) · B. Nightingale, *Lancashire nonconformity*, 6 vols. [1890–93], vols. 1, 3 · *Preston Guardian* (14 Dec 1867) · *Preston Chronicle* (14 Dec 1867)
Wealth at death under £1500: probate, 31 Dec 1867, *CGPLA Eng. & Wales*

Slater, Eliot Trevor Oakeshott (1904–1983), psychiatrist, second son of Gilbert *Slater (1864–1938), economic historian and principal of Ruskin College, Oxford, and Violet Oakeshott, was born on 28 August 1904 at 84 Eglinton Road, Plumstead, London. His mother being a Quaker he went to Leighton Park School, Reading, from where he won an exhibition to St John's College, Cambridge, to study natural sciences. From 1925 he continued his medical education at St George's Hospital, London, qualifying as a doctor in 1928. He then spent two years in medical posts in general practice, at St George's, and at the West End Hospital for Nervous Diseases, passing the membership examination of the Royal College of Physicians in 1930. In his 'Autobiographical sketch' (1971) he described his next post, assistant medical officer at Derby County Mental Hospital, as stultifying and was therefore overjoyed to be appointed medical officer at the Maudsley Hospital, London (1931), where, with the encouragement of Aubrey Lewis and Edward Mapother, and the assistance of R. A. Fisher, he developed his interest in the application of statistical methods to the empirical study of mental illness.

In 1934 Slater went to the Research Institute for Psychiatry in Munich, studying psychiatric genetics under Bruno Schulz. He met and, on 24 December 1935, married his first wife, Lydia Pasternak [see Slater, Lydia Elisabeth Leonidovna Pasternak (1902–1989)], a research chemist in the institute in Munich. She was daughter of Leonid Pasternak, and sister of the poet and novelist Boris Pasternak. Their four children (two daughters and two sons) became respectively an English don, a psychiatrist, a mathematician, and a haematologist.

Slater returned to the Maudsley in 1935, continuing his research on the inheritance of mental disorders, but when war broke out in 1939 psychiatric services at the Maudsley were dispersed and he became clinical director of the Sutton Emergency Hospital, where he was responsible for the treatment of some twenty thousand psychiatric casualties. This experience led to the influential book *Physical Methods of Treatment in Psychiatry* (with William Sargant, 1944). From 1946 he was physician in psychological medicine at the National Hospital for Nervous Diseases, Queen Square, London, but he resigned in 1964 in protest

at the hospital's rejection of the offer of a benefaction to establish a chair in psychiatry there. After the dissolution of his marriage he married, in 1946, Jean Fyfe Foster.

As senior lecturer at the Institute of Psychiatry (1950–59) Slater continued to work, notably on the prevalence of psychiatric disorders in twins, assisted by James Shields. In 1959 Slater formed the Medical Research Council Psychiatric Genetics Unit at the Maudsley, which he directed until 1969. This work culminated in *The Genetics of Mental Disorders* (with Valerie Cowie, 1971).

Slater published about 150 books and papers, of which *Clinical Psychiatry* (with Willi Mayer-Gross and Martin Roth, 1954) was long the leading textbook of psychiatry in English. He gave the Litchfield (1959), Galton (1960), and Mapother (1960) lectures, and in the Maudsley lecture (1961) and elsewhere attacked the concept of hysteria as a valid syndrome: in an influential follow-up study of patients diagnosed as suffering from hysteria he showed that serious underlying physical illness emerged later in many of them and that this could in itself account for their allegedly psychological symptoms. As editor of the *British Journal of Psychiatry* from 1961 to 1972 Slater transformed it into a leading European journal. Colleagues noted the hard work and willingness to assist the efforts of others which characterized his editorship. In 1966 he was appointed CBE. He held honorary fellowships of several British and American medical and psychiatric societies, and was fellow and vice-president (1963–6) of the Eugenics Society.

Slater's interests were wide: in 1964 he was a member of the royal commission on capital punishment, and after retirement he joined the Euthanasia Society. He was agnostic, and found himself at times more at home with ideas than with people. He published a statistical investigation of chess openings, pathographic studies of composers, and a book of poetry. An exhibition of his paintings was held in 1977. He remained active long after retirement, being awarded the degree of PhD (London) at the age of seventy-seven for a statistical word study of *Edward III* which provided evidence that the play was written by Shakespeare.

Slater died at his home, the Coach House, 128A Castelnau, Barnes, London on 15 May 1983 of a heart attack. He was survived by his wife and the four children of his first marriage. Although his advocacy of the theory that schizophrenia is inherited by a single partially dominant gene was, and remains, controversial, he had achieved international recognition for his work on psychiatric genetics and the nature of neurosis. By his concern for the systematic collection and critical analysis of data he helped to establish psychiatry as a scientific discipline capable of rigorous empirical study.

HUGH SERIES

Sources *BMJ* (11 June 1983), 1906 · *The Times* (21 May 1983) · *The Lancet* (28 May 1983) · *Bethlem and Maudsley Gazette*, 31/3 (summer 1983), 16–19 · E. T. O. Slater, 'Autobiographical sketch', *Man, mind, and heredity: selected papers of Eliot Slater on psychiatry and genetics*, ed. J. Shields and I. I. Gottesman (1971), 1–23 [incl. bibliography] · private information (2004) · *WWW* · *CGPLA Eng. & Wales* (1983) · b. cert. · d. cert.

Likenesses photograph, repro. in Slater, 'Autobiographical sketch' · studio photograph, priv. coll.
Wealth at death £128,456: probate, 30 Aug 1983, *CGPLA Eng. & Wales*

Slater, Gilbert (1864–1938), economist and social reformer, was born at 1 Braidwood Terrace, Plymouth, on 27 August 1864, the son of Daniel Slater MA, a schoolmaster, and his wife, Ellen Augusta, *née* Trevor. He was admitted at St John's College, Cambridge, in 1882 and graduated BA in 1885 as twentieth senior optime in the mathematical tripos. For much of the next twenty years he was engaged in political and social activity. He was an early member of the Fabian Society, joining it at Plymouth in 1888, and after the dock strike in the following year helped to organize unskilled workers in Plymouth. He became a committee member of the Gasworkers' Union and stood as an independent labour candidate for the school board. After a spell of schoolteaching in Plymouth he moved in 1893 to London, where he was associated with both Balliol House and Toynbee Hall. He began a long association with adult education by lecturing to university extension students. When he married, on 15 April 1897, Violet Oakeshott of Croydon, the third daughter of the late Joseph Oakeshott, a postmaster of Sunderland, his occupation was given as 'General Teacher'. They had three children, including Eliot Trevor Oakeshott *Slater.

A year before his marriage Woolwich in south London had become the centre of Slater's activities. He had joined the settlement work of Charles H. Grinling. But he soon branched out into a range of political and social activities in the newly formed borough. From 1899 to 1902 he edited *Comradeship*, the journal of the Royal Arsenal Co-operative Society, became a borough councillor (1903–6), and was Woolwich's first Labour mayor in 1906–7. He was chairman, vice-chairman, or secretary of many local committees connected with unemployment, the anti-sweating campaign, and the Labour Representation League. In the mean time he was also a research student at the London School of Economics, obtaining the Hutchison Silver medal in 1901, and was awarded a DSc (Econ) in 1905 for his dissertation, published as *The English Peasantry and the Common Fields* (1907).

Slater's social and political activism and his academic background were significant factors in his becoming principal of Ruskin College in 1909. The college had been in turmoil following the dismissal in 1909 of the previous principal, a student strike, and the creation of a separate Central Labour College in intentional opposition to Ruskin College. On his appointment, initially to teach sociology, Ruskin's publicity material gave an outline of his career, emphasizing his work in both the labour movement and education. No member of the small teaching staff up to then had anything like that experience. He was endorsed by the leading lights of the labour movement—George Lansbury, Keir Hardie, Sidney Webb, Will Crooks, Pete Curran, and J. A. Hobson. In 1912 he became a member of Lloyd George's land enquiry committee, and in 1913 he published *The Making of Modern England*.

A major feature of the conflict at Ruskin in 1909 was its constitution. The striking students and their allies demanded that working-class education should be under the control of working-class organizations. Ruskin's governing council included Oxford University dons as well as others from outside the labour movement. Slater made his mark rapidly by recommending a change in the college's structure: in future only representatives of working-class organizations could be represented on the governing council. In February 1910 the provisional committee of the Central Labour College immediately seized upon the significance of the change. It noted that the new Ruskin constitution was precisely the answer to the demands of the striking students and the new college. The committee therefore invited Ruskin and the Central Labour College to meet to consider uniting. Other differences between them proved impossible to resolve, and the two colleges went their own, mutually hostile ways.

Under Slater's principalship Ruskin College settled down and flourished. Student numbers expanded and there were more international contacts. But the First World War intervened. The college closed and there was no salary for him. He taught at Toynbee Hall, on one occasion so absorbed that he failed to notice a Zeppelin air raid, nor the departure during it of some members of his class. In 1915 he accepted the newly created chair of Indian economics at Madras University, and held that post until 1921. He participated in the proceedings of the imperial board of agriculture, notably on the sub-committee on the Indian famine of 1918. As professor, he inspired his students 'to go beyond their classes and text-books and study the human material ready to their hands' (*The Times*, 10 March 1938, 16). His questionnaire was used for these surveys, the results of which were published under his editorship as *Some South Indian Villages* (1917). He stayed one more year in Madras as the publicity officer for the state and as a member of the Madras legislative council. He produced leaflets explaining government policy to counter the opinions of the Congress Party.

Although he left India in 1923, Slater maintained his interest in the subcontinent, and later published *Southern India: its Political and Economic Problems* (1936). In later life he spent his time lecturing and writing on a variety of subjects, including *Seven Shakespeares* (1931). His book *Poverty and the State* (1930) was based on lectures for a course arranged by the Church of England Temperance Society in association with the University of London and for Police Court Missionaries. He lectured at the London School of Economics and to Indian Civil Service students at Oxford, where he died at his home, 4 Park Crescent, on 8 March 1938. He was survived by his wife.

G. D. H. Cole described Slater as 'a keen internationalist, and a firm believer in human brotherhood and equality. A man of very simple, even ascetic tastes, and great moral courage' (*The Times*, 11 March 1938, 16). In the Preface to the posthumously published second edition of his *The Growth of Modern England* (1939; first published 1932), Vera Anstey, 'a friend and pupil', quoted his description of himself as an 'unrepentant Liberal' and an 'active pacifist' (Anstey, vi–vii). She noted that as well as his activity in numerous social movements in England and India 'his writings were characterised by wide social sympathies and interests, which forbade the treatment of economic, or political, or ethical developments as independent specialisms, and necessitated the study of mankind "in the round"' (ibid., x).   HAROLD POLLINS

Sources G. Slater, *Poverty and the state* (1930), preface [autobiography] · *The Times* (10–11 March 1938) · J. Attfield, *With light of knowledge: a hundred years of education in the Royal Arsenal Co-operative Society* (1981) · V. Anstey, 'Preface', in G. Slater, *The growth of modern England*, 2nd edn (1939) · Ruskin College Library, strike records [leaflets on his appointment to Ruskin College] · H. Pollins, *The history of Ruskin College* (1984); repr. (1993) · J. Atkins, *Neither crumbs nor condescension: the Central Labour College, 1909–1915* (1981) · b. cert. · m. cert. · d. cert. · Venn, *Alum. Cant.* · *CGPLA Eng. & Wales* (1938) · R. Rhodes, *An Arsenal for labour: the Royal Arsenal Co-operative Society and politics, 1896–1996* (1998)
Archives Keele University Library, LePlay Collection, corresp. and minute book entries as member of Sociological Society committees · NL Scot., corresp. mainly with Sir Patrick Geddes
Likenesses photographs, 1909, Ruskin College, Oxford, Strike Records, 2, fol. 124
Wealth at death £2221 12s. 5d.: probate, 7 May 1938, *CGPLA Eng. & Wales*

Slater [*née* Evans], **Harriet** (1903–1976), co-operative movement activist and politician, was born on 3 July 1903 at 90 Bond Street, Tunstall, Staffordshire, the daughter of John Edward Evans, a potter's placer, and his wife, Margaret Ball.

Harriet Evans was educated at Chell and Park Road elementary schools, and Hanley high school, Stoke-on-Trent. She trained as a teacher at Dudley Teachers' Training College and taught at Moreland Road Girls' School, moving later to Middleport Senior Girls' School, Stoke-on-Trent. She continued to work as a teacher until she married Frederick Slater, an organizer for the Co-operative Party, in 1931.

Both Harriet and her husband were long-standing members of the co-operative movement and members of their local Burslem society. Both were also members of the Labour Party and Harriet Slater entered local government in 1933 when she was elected to the Stoke-on-Trent city council, on which her husband also served. She remained a councillor until 1949 when she was made an alderman, becoming an honorary alderman in 1966. Her chief interests were education, health, and housing and from 1953 to 1966 she chaired the Stoke education committee.

Harriet Slater was also active in the co-operative movement. For many years she was a director of the Co-operative Society and from 1932 she was president of the Milton guild at Burslem. From 1933 to 1946 she was a member of the Burslem co-operative management committee. She gave up her job as a teacher when she was appointed a national organizer for the Co-operative Party in February 1943 with responsibility for the north-west of England. Her work took her throughout the region lecturing on the work of the Co-operative Party and its place within the wider labour movement. She also taught history for a brief time for the Co-operative Union. Harriet Slater held the post of regional organizer until 1953 when she was selected as Co-operative and Labour Party candidate for the constituency of Stoke-on-Trent North.

Harriet Slater was elected MP in 1953, the sole woman MP representing the Co-operative Party, and easily held on to this seat in the 1955, 1959, and 1964 general elections. Education, particularly the improvement of overall educational opportunities for working-class children, health, and housing were the issues on which she concentrated at Westminster, as she had as a local councillor, although the subject of her maiden speech was the need for the abolition of the colour bar. She was involved in issues such as the standards of teacher training, classroom sizes, and the need for compulsory registration of child-minders. She was an ardent opponent of the means test by local education authorities in the provision of student grants and urged the removal of all impediments to the fullest expansion of sixth-form education. She fought for better standards of health care, housing, and consumer protection. These were all issues which she felt, from her experience in local government, most affected working-class wives and mothers.

After the Labour Party's election victory in 1964 Harriet Slater became the first woman to be appointed a government whip. From October 1964 until March 1966 she was a lord commissioner of the Treasury. In 1965 she was appointed CBE. In 1966 Harriet Slater retired as an MP in order to spend more time looking after her husband who was suffering from ill health. They moved to live at Bull Bay in Anglesey. In the same year she joined the Anglesey health committee and the Anglesey employment committee.

In 1976, only a few months before her death, Harriet Slater and her husband returned to Stoke-on-Trent and it was at her home, Heber, 70 Sytch Road, Brown Edge, Staffordshire, that she died on 12 October 1976. She was cremated at Carmountside crematorium on 18 October after a service at Hamil Road Methodist Church in Burslem. She had no children and was survived for a brief time by her husband.   SERENA KELLY

Sources DLB · WWW · *The Times* (14 Oct 1976) · *CGPLA Eng. & Wales* (1977)
Wealth at death £13,851: administration with will, 21 March 1977, *CGPLA Eng. & Wales*

Slater, James Henry [Jim] (1923–1993), trade unionist, was born at 36 Francis Street, South Shields, on 4 October 1923. One of the thirteen children of Septimus Slater, stevedore, and his wife, Jane Clements, Jim left school after an elementary education and soon went to sea. At first he was a deckhand aboard colliers, carrying coal from northeastern ports to power stations. As a member of the merchant navy he took part in the Second World War, travelling across the Atlantic and to the Soviet Union. On one voyage he was rescued from a lifeboat after a torpedo had sunk his ship—the point at which, he maintained, his wages were stopped. Such experiences fuelled his efforts to improve seamen's conditions. On 19 November 1949 he married Ivy Greenwell (*b.* 1924/5, *d.* in or before 1985); they had a son and daughter. He joined the National Union of

James Henry Slater (1923–1993), by unknown photographer, *c.*1986

Seamen at seventeen, but first became notorious in 1960 as a leader in the north-east of the National Seamen's Reform Movement, a rank-and-file body that opposed the conciliatory policies of the national officials. After helping to organize an unofficial strike, he was among those struck off the register of the merchant navy establishment. This action, taken with the connivance of the official leadership, barred him for a lengthy period from working at sea. To get back a berth, he gave assurances that he would keep to the agreements made by the union. The ban did not, however, prevent him from standing for the post of general secretary in 1962, when he obtained 9855 votes to the 30,879 polled by the successful candidate, Bill Hogarth. In October 1964 Slater was appointed district secretary for the north-east coast, which gave him a seat on the union's national executive.

In 1966 Slater gained wider notoriety during a lengthy seamen's strike. In the House of Commons on 28 June 1966 Harold Wilson asserted that 'a small group of articulate, intelligent and well-briefed members' of the seamen's executive council were exercising 'influence far beyond their number'. He named Slater and Joe Kenny (another militant member of the executive) and continued: 'I can testify to their ability and to their mastery of the details of the seamen's complaints, to their ability to absorb skilled briefings and to their dominance amongst their colleagues' (*Hansard 5C*, vol. 730, col. 1617). He

believed they had been briefed by Communist Party activists and maintained that when in London they stayed in the flat of Jack Coward (whom Wilson had already named as a communist) where they were visited by Bert Ramelson, the party's industrial organizer. Slater always resented Wilson's allegation that he was under the influence of communists who were using the strike for political ends; rather, he simply harboured an uncompromising determination to improve the pay and conditions of seamen. When fighting campaigns his bluff manner, fondness for a drink, and boisterous sense of humour concealed his skills as a negotiator, but few of his members feared he would sell them short. Addressing the men he was in his element. The craggy, ginger-haired Slater would throw off his jacket and roll up his sleeves—thus exposing a tattoo of a serpent entwined around a palm tree, which stretched for the length of his forearm—and talk the language of the seaman.

In 1970 Slater became assistant secretary of the union. On the death of Hogarth in 1973 Slater was elected general secretary, taking up office in the following year after the six-month election campaign provided for by the union's rules. He again challenged the income policies of a Wilson government in 1976 when he pushed through a pay settlement above the level of the existing norms. In 1979 he became a CBE. With the advent of a Conservative government in 1979 Slater saw no reason to temper his left-wing position. Though opposed to the Falklands War in 1982, he secured bonus payments for those merchant seamen who were prepared to enter the war zone. Within a few months of the war ending he bitterly reproached the government, which had praised the seamen's role in the campaign, for using foreign ships to supply the Falkland Islands. He scored a success in 1983 when, in concert with Greenpeace and other unions, he instructed his men not to dump nuclear waste at sea, a policy he persuaded the Trades Union Congress to support (he was on the council of the TUC from 1974 to 1983). Then, unabashed by legislation that made such payments illegal, he ensured that union funds were donated to the miners during their strike of 1984–5. He could do nothing, however, to affect government policy towards the decline of the merchant fleet, and calls for action against flags of convenience met a reply from Margaret Thatcher that she did not believe 'the time has come for us to abandon free trade principles' (Marsh and Ryan, 219). Another Conservative policy led to the end of his general secretaryship. Under the Trade Union Act (1984), voting members of union executives could be elected for not more than five years, while the rulebook of Slater's own union made ineligible candidates over the age of sixty. He might have continued as a non-voting member of the executive, but officials felt that a better option was to support Slater's deputy, Sam McCluskie. The latter, who was a member of the national executive committee of the Labour Party and regarded as a shrewder tactician, was elected general secretary in 1986. Slater accepted the revived post of president of the union. He continued to speak out, supporting the anti-apartheid movement in South Africa, warning of the danger of nuclear power, and generally taking any opportunity to criticize the government. Slater's wife, Ivy, having died, on 30 March 1985 he married Moira Wyn, née Shiels, a former colleague at the National Union of Seamen; they had two daughters.

By this time 'flagging out' had reduced the size of both the British merchant marine and the union's membership. A dispute with P and O European Ferries in 1988 led to the sequestration of union assets and hastened the merger with the National Union of Railwaymen, which in 1990 created the National Union of Rail, Maritime, and Transport Workers. In a sense, therefore, Slater had been in office during a period of near terminal decline, though it is unlikely that a different leader would have avoided this outcome. Indeed, perhaps his skill at managing the National Union of Seamen and his colourful personality helped to sustain an embattled membership. Several anecdotes, some perhaps apocryphal, testify to his never-say-die character. As a young man he was said to have jumped ship in Canada, only to spend some time in gaol as a suspected illegal immigrant—his Geordie accent having been taken for Serbo-Croat. He explained, as the general secretary, that he always emphasized the basic pay of his members, who did not want their wives to find out what they earned with overtime and bonuses. Another story placed him in a seaside hotel, negotiating into the small hours with a group of employers, when a gale blew open a window and scattered their papers. 'Imagine', he urged, 'what it is like for my members out there at sea in that awful weather.' By breakfast the owners had conceded, though to help them save face Slater admitted, with a wink, that he had 'climbed down' (The Independent, 31 May 1993). Slater was in Liverpool for a celebration of the battle of the Atlantic when he suffered a fatal heart attack, and died in Broadgreen Hospital on 30 May 1993.

D. E. MARTIN

Sources A. Marsh and V. Ryan, The seamen (1989) · Hansard 5C (1966), 730.1617 [Harold Wilson's statement 28/06/1966] · Daily Telegraph (31 May 1993) · The Independent (31 May 1993) · The Times (31 May 1993) · TUC Report (1993) · b. cert. · m. certs. · d. cert.
Likenesses photograph, c.1986, Hult. Arch. [see illus.] · photograph, repro. in The Times · photograph, repro. in The Independent
Wealth at death under £125,000: probate, 23 March 1994, CGPLA Eng. & Wales

Slater, Lydia Elisabeth Leonidovna Pasternak (1902–1989), biochemist, poet, and translator, was born on 21 March 1902 in Moscow, the last of four children of Leonid Osipovich Pasternak (1862–1945), painter, and his wife, Rosalia Isidorovna Kaufmann (1867–1939), concert pianist. Despite the artistic milieu surrounding her childhood—Tolstoy, Skryabin, Repin, Rubinstein—she was drawn initially to medicine and studied at the Second Moscow University. She was, however, persuaded to delay by her mother and father, who were afraid that she would be drafted to relieve a typhoid epidemic. That she acceded to their wishes reflects the perceived danger not to herself but to her beloved parents. In 1921 she entered Moscow Lomonosov University to study a broad range of sciences.

In December she emigrated with her sister Josephine and her parents to Germany—a move made possible by the Soviets' new economic policy. In Berlin entry to medical school for Russian citizens was virtually impossible, and she therefore graduated from the Institute of Pharmacology in biochemistry. In 1926 she submitted her dissertation, 'A study of halogenated tyrosine derivatives'. In 1929 she followed her sister Josephine to Munich, where she worked in the chemistry department at the Kaiser Wilhelm Institute for Psychiatry, under Irvine H. Page. Together they worked on new laboratory methods of investigating the metabolism of cerebral lipids and their significance for the development of arteriosclerosis. Between 1931 and 1935 Page and she regularly published articles in the Biochemical Journal, a forum of international repute.

In 1934, with the rise of Nazism, some colleagues demanded that Leonid Pasternak's 'Jewish daubs', hanging in the institute, should be replaced by a portrait of Hitler. Lydia Pasternak wrote mordant satirical verses on Nazi ideology. In 1935 Page's department was closed down. She left the institute. While there she had met Eliot Trevor Oakeshott *Slater (1904–1983), an English psychiatrist on a Rockefeller scholarship from 1934 to 1935, and son of Gilbert Slater, a university professor. They married in Oxford on 24 December 1935—a marriage dissolved in 1945, after producing two sons and two daughters. Lydia was followed to England by her sister's family and her parents. A new life began—a life of real poverty, lodgers, Jewish refugees, child care, and cramped gentility in 20 Park Town, her parents-in-law's house in a beautiful neo-Georgian terrace, which became progressively dilapidated in the following decades. Her father's pictures were hung everywhere—the only painted surfaces that were not peeling.

After his death her father's reputation, necessarily fragmented by his double migration, was the prime concern of Pasternak Slater and her sister. This concern became acute when her brother, Boris, was awarded the Nobel prize for literature in 1958—making the family name world famous, but eclipsing her father's already dissipated artistic standing in the subsequent event-trauma. The two sisters redoubled their efforts to arrange exhibitions, assisted, ironically enough, by Boris's fame. Of course, this pietas for her parent co-existed with a properly intense pride in her sibling. She began to translate his poetry into English. Fifty Poems appeared in 1963. It was twice reprinted. Her translations—which meticulously attempted to reproduce her brother's complex and ravishing word music, his intricate assonances, his bold metres, and satisfying, full rhymes—were misguidedly undervalued by some contemporaries. It is true that her English could seem awkward and even quaint, the aural demands of Pasternak making her over-hospitable to inversion, but the aura of foreignness paradoxically worked in favour of her translations. Where her original English poetry (Before Sunrise, 1971) could be stilted, they felt Russian. The present writer was unsurprised, therefore, when Seamus Heaney told him that he thought her translations the most authentic versions of Pasternak. In this he was probably influenced by another Nobel laureate, Joseph Brodsky, who, like many other important cultural figures, visited her in Oxford for an audience in her cluttered kitchen, where they could experience her weak Nescafé, her tepid macaroni with tinned Italian tomatoes, her Cinemascope grin, and her famous yawn.

Several portraits of Pasternak Slater by her father survive, from swift baby sketches to oils of the young woman—a kind of *ad hoc* Muybridge sequence—but there are no paintings of her weatherbeaten prime, glistening with Nivea, a silk handkerchief doing duty as a bikini top, her muscular toes capable of inflicting a powerful 'horse-bite' on unsuspecting fellow sunbathers. She died of heart failure on 4 May 1989 at Apsley House, 367 Banbury Road, Oxford. Her ashes were buried in Wolvercote cemetery in 1990. She was survived by her four children.

CRAIG RAINE

Sources A. Vogt, *Vom Hintereingang zum Hauptportal—Wissenschaftlerinnen in der Kaiser-Wilhelm-Gesellschaft* (1997), 32–43 · *The Guardian* (8 May 1989) · *Jewish Chronicle* (12 May 1989) · *The Times* (6 May 1989) · private information (2004) · personal knowledge (2004) · m. cert. · d. cert.
Archives Pasternak Trust, Oxford, letters, diaries, MSS, tapes, recordings, publications, a film, and photographs · Stanford University, California, Hoover Institution
Likenesses E. Gabritchevsky, portrait, Pasternak Trust, 20 Park Town, Oxford · L. Pasternak, portraits, Pasternak Trust, 20 Park Town, Oxford · photograph, repro. in *The Guardian*
Wealth at death £15,950: probate, 24 Oct 1991, *CGPLA Eng. & Wales*

Slater, (Charles) Montagu (1902–1956), writer and librettist, was born on 23 September 1902 in St George's Road, Millom, Cumberland, the elder son in a family of two sons and three daughters of Seth Slater, a sub-postmaster and master clothier, and his wife, Rosa Annie Thora Lugsdin. His parents were strict Wesleyan Methodists, and his father a lay preacher.

Educated at Millom secondary school, Slater went up to Oxford as a non-collegiate student in October 1920 and graduated with a second in philosophy, politics, and economics in 1924. He had started writing poetry at Millom, and writing became both his passion and his profession. After leaving Oxford Slater became a journalist on the *Liverpool Post*, and while in Liverpool worked with the unemployed and became active in local left-wing politics. In 1927 he joined the Communist Party, to which he remained committed for the rest of his life. After moving to London in the following year to work on the *Morning Post*, he married Enid Helena (*b.* 1902/3), daughter of Frederick William Mace, a marine surveyor, on 1 May 1929; they had three daughters and lived in north London. In the later 1930s Slater worked as a sub-editor for *Reynolds News*, the Sunday newspaper owned by the co-operative movement, and wrote drama criticism for the *New Statesman*. During the Second World War he served as head of scripts in the film division of the Ministry of Information.

A first novel, *Second City* (1931), drew on Slater's experience of the seamier side of Liverpool life. A second, *Haunting Europe* (1934), was set among young communists in Berlin grappling with the rise of the Nazi regime. Both works reflected his growing political and literary engagements, which bore fruit in October 1934 with the publication of the first issue of the influential *Left Review*. Slater, a founder of the magazine, also served as its first editor.

Slater's subsequent creative works sprang from his involvement with 'left theatre', and mixed ordinary speech with verse and song. The first was a historical play, *Easter 1916*, which depicted the events in Dublin leading up to the Easter rising. This was put on by a trade-union group in London on 5 and 8 December 1935. Another play, *Stay Down Miner*, first performed at the Westminster Theatre on 8 May 1936 by the Left Theatre company, was based on actual events in the Welsh coal industry the year before, upon which Slater had reported. A pithead with its ropes and wheels dominated the set, and the play revolved around a firm stand by the miners: 'We decided to stay down till the blacklegs were dismissed and our men given their rightful jobs again' (Slater, *New Way Wins*, 60).

At the end of the play Slater has the miners—as they ascend to the surface—sing a chorus about the hardness of the miner's lot. The music was by Benjamin Britten, with whom Slater collaborated on a number of dramatic works in the later 1930s. The first of these was a documentary film for the General Post Office film unit, *Coal Face* (1935), directed by Alberto Cavalcanti; Slater wrote the narration, Britten the music for the soundtrack. In addition, Slater wrote verse for a number of quite different dramatic occasions. These included historical pageants: one was a colourful—and broad-brush—depiction of the history of the co-operative movement, with a large cast and music by Alan Bush; another was a pageant of empire, for which Britten again provided music. Slater and Britten subsequently collaborated on two pieces for puppet theatre, *The Seven Ages of Man* and *Old Spain*. These were rehearsed in the Slaters' north London flat and performed at the Mercury Theatre, London, in 1938.

Slater's health was not good—he developed stomach cancer, and had a major operation in the later 1930s—and Enid later recalled how Britten kept her company while the operation was taking place. In 1939 the composer dedicated his *Ballad of Heroes* to the Slaters. The friendship resumed after Britten and Peter Pears returned from the USA in 1942; at a conscription tribunal, Britten's case was supported by both Montagu Slater and William Walton.

Early in 1942 Britten asked Slater to draft a libretto based on the tragic events in the life of Aldeburgh, a small East Anglian fishing village, as depicted in George Crabbe's poem *The Borough*. The collaboration initially went very well. Britten wrote to a friend that Slater had 'splendid ideas', and that the work on *Peter Grimes* was leaping ahead. 'It is getting more and more an opera about the community, whose life is "illuminated" for this moment by the tragedy of the murders' thought to have been committed by fisherman Peter Grimes (Banks, 24–5). To another correspondent Britten wrote, 'I am writing an opera, all about a fishing village, full of storms, and sailing boats, and murders—very exciting' (ibid., 26).

The libretto, according to Slater, was 'written in four-beat half-rhymed verse, as conversational as possible and not too regular' (Crozier, 19). Crabbe's poem was only 'a starting point':

I have taken these character sketches as clues and woven them into a story against the background of the Borough: but it is my story and the composer's (the idea was originally not mine but Britten's) and I have to take the responsibility for its shape as well as its words. (ibid., 26)

The character of Grimes retained the 'hints of loose-living and sadism' developed by Britten and Pears; but the 'crucial expansion of the role of the community and its interaction with Grimes' (Banks, 65), as well as the development of Ellen and the other minor characters, were entirely Slater's contribution. Britten conceded that Slater deftly transformed what might have been 'no more than a rather bloodthirsty melodrama' into a taut drama 'about the precarious balance of responsibility between society and the individual' (ibid., 62). The whole tragedy was set against the struggle with the sea, the angry and lyrical mood of which Britten's music evoked so powerfully.

Following receipt of the libretto there began what Britten described as a period of 'discussions, revision and corrections' (Banks, 2). In January 1944 he began composing the music, and the score was completed in February 1945. Yet as Britten composed he began to realize there were aspects of the libretto that needed recasting; and to do this he turned first to Eric Crozier—who directed the first performance of *Peter Grimes* at Sadler's Wells on 7 June 1945—and then to the writer Ronald Duncan. Slater apparently agreed to the changes, which did not threaten his authorship of the text, but Crozier recalls the writer being 'a silent, rather recalcitrant figure' during a series of tense meetings; not exactly unco-operative, but showing little 'active collaboration' (Mitchell, 37). In the circumstances, Slater's decision to let the Bodley Head publish his original libretto separately—it appeared in 1946 as *Peter Grimes and other Poems*—is understandable. When Britten expressed his dismay, Slater's reaction was, according to Donald Mitchell, uncharacteristically explosive: '"But this is *my* work, this is *my* work", he repeated, and banged the table to emphasise the point' (ibid., 39).

The first performances of *Peter Grimes* were a great success, and reviewers praised the libretto as well as the music: a reviewer in *Modern Music* aptly noted that 'the piece has the quality of a Greek tragedy' (Biswell, 40). Although the opera did not significantly advance Slater's career or reputation—and he did not work with Britten again—his creative output continued undiminished. He wrote at least two other opera librettos in the early 1950s for left-wing composers: *Mimosa* (1951) by Bernard Stevens; and *Yerma* (1956) for Denis ApIvor (adapted from Garcia Lorca's play).

Despite his precarious health Slater published further novels in the 1940s and early 1950s. The most noteworthy was *Once a Jolly Swagman* (1944), depicting the life of a speedway rider, 'the daringest devil on the wall of death' (p. 149); this became a film starring the young Dirk Bogarde. *Englishmen with Swords* (1949) was a lightly fictionalized account of the crushing of the Levellers and other radical groups in the aftermath of the English civil war. In his last book, an influential study of the trial of Jomo Kenyatta—accused of 'managing Mau Mau' in Kenya—Slater drew attention in 1955 to the 'political' nature of the trial. A selection of his verse, put together by Edgell Rickword (fellow poet and editor of *Left Review*), was published posthumously in *The New Reasoner* (vol. 1/4, spring 1958).

Much of Slater's best work was done in the film industry, and one of his film scripts in particular stands out. This was *The Brave Don't Cry* (1952), about a Scottish coalmining disaster. Commissioned by John Grierson, the doyen of documentary films and then head of Group Three films, and directed by Slater's son-in-law Philip Leacock, the film received excellent reviews. 'The varying moods of the trapped miners', wrote Bosley Crowther in the *New York Times*, 'the stoicism of their loved ones above ground, the creeping surrender to frustration and the final lift of heroism in their rescue—these things are beautifully articulated' (Hardy, 184).

Slater died from cancer in the Whittington Hospital in Islington, London, on 19 December 1956. A contemporary recalled that he was 'a dear, small, delicate man' (Rattenbury, *Englishmen*, vi). Modest to the end, he did his best writing in the genre of community drama—whether depicting fishing or pit villages—and in the poetic drama of *Peter Grimes* he undoubtedly helped create one of the great operatic masterpieces of the twentieth century.

ROBERT BROWN

Sources D. Mitchell, 'Montagu Slater (1902–1956): who was he?', *Benjamin Britten, Peter Grimes*, ed. P. Brett (1983) · A. Rattenbury, ed., 'Poems by Montagu Slater', *Renaissance and modern studies* (1976), vol. 20, pp. 120–31 · P. Banks, ed., *The making of 'Peter Grimes': essays and studies* (1996) · A. Rattenbury, 'introduction', in M. Slater, *Englishmen with swords* (1949); (1991) · J. Clark and others, *Culture and crisis in Britain in the thirties* (1979) · H. Carpenter, *Benjamin Britten: a biography* (1992) · A. Biswell, 'Montagu Slater, 1902–1956', *Peter Grimes* [programme of Welsh National Opera production, Oxford, Apollo Theatre, 2 March 1999] · E. Crozier, ed., *Benjamin Britten: 'Peter Grimes'* (1945) · F. Hardy, *John Grierson: a documentary biography* (1979) · V. Cunningham, *British writers of the thirties* (1988); paperback edn (1993) · M. Slater, *New way wins* (1937) · M. Slater, *Once a jolly swagman* (1944) · b. cert. · m. cert. · d. cert.

Archives U. Nott. L., literary MSS and papers | BL, corresp. with League of Dramatists, Add. MS 63443 · BL, corresp. with Society of Authors, Add. MS 63329 · BL, letters to Bernard Stevens with copies of poems, Add. MS 69025

Slater [*formerly* Leschziner], **Oscar Joseph** (1872–1948), victim of miscarriage of justice, was born in Oppeln, Upper Silesia, Germany, on 8 January 1872, the son of Adolph Leschziner (d. 1916), a baker, and his wife, Paula Zweig (d. 1917). The family, which was Jewish, consisted of at least four (and probably six) children. Oscar Leschziner attended the *Gymnasium* in Beuthen, the town where his father had his bakery. At fifteen he was apprenticed to Schuttenberg, a timber merchant in Beuthen. He parted from Schuttenberg on good terms and left Beuthen to work in Hamburg. His attraction to gambling and prostitutes, and to the buying and selling of jewellery, may have started in Hamburg. In 1893 or 1894 he travelled to London, to evade military service, and later worked as a bookmaker. Once in England, and later in Scotland, Leschziner used various names, such as George, Anderson, Sando, Schmidt, and Slater; and it was the latter he now used for official purposes. In 1896 he was prosecuted at north London sessions for malicious wounding. He was acquitted. In 1897 he was prosecuted for assault. He was discharged by the magistrate at Clerkenwell police court.

By 1899 Slater had moved to Edinburgh. He variously claimed to be a gymnastics instructor, a dentist, and (more realistically) a dealer in precious stones. He was known to the Edinburgh police as a notorious gambler and a 'low class foreign bully', although, in fact, he was always dapper in his attire. In November 1899 he was fined by Edinburgh police court for disorderly conduct. By 1901 he was living in Glasgow, but was constantly changing his address. He walked around with a large dog (which he claimed to be a performing circus dog) and he was known to the police as the associate of prostitutes, thieves, burglars, and 'resetters' (the receivers of stolen goods). On 12 July 1901 Slater married in Glasgow Mary Curtis Pryor (*b.* 1878/9) of Norfolk, the daughter of James Pryor, a farmer. After resettling in London and occasionally visiting the USA (where he had an interest in gaming clubs), Slater returned to Glasgow in 1908.

On 21 December 1908 Marion Gilchrist, a rich but reclusive spinster aged eighty-three, was beaten to death at 15 Queen's Terrace, West Princes Street, Glasgow. Her flat had previously been watched by loiterers, including one man who used the pretext of asking for 'Anderson'. This was the name being used by Slater for the purpose of renting premises (a suspected brothel) near by. The motive for the crime, resembling, as it seemed to do, the murder in Dostoyevsky's *Crime and Punishment*, was assumed to be robbery. Slater was suspected because he had been trying to sell a pawn ticket to a brooch. A brooch was the only item that appeared to have been stolen from the victim's flat. He had also left Liverpool for New York on 26 December 1908. The police subsequently admitted that the pawn ticket had been a false lead. They nevertheless persisted in identifying Slater as the prime suspect, interpreting Slater's journey as a 'flight from justice'. The police travelled to New York to apply for Slater's extradition. Slater's lawyer advised him that this application would probably fail. In the event, Slater decided to return to Scotland voluntarily.

Slater was tried for murder at the High Court in Edinburgh on 3–6 May 1909. He did not give evidence in his own defence. The prosecution made much of the 'flight from justice'. They also relied on identification evidence, all of it of a fleeting glimpse nature. Much of it was unreliable, prejudiced, tainted, or coached. Slater's identification parade had consisted of placing Slater (a man of obviously foreign appearance) in a line of nine off-duty policemen and two Scottish railway workers. Many criticisms of the trial were subsequently made by William Roughead in

his introduction to *The Trial of Oscar Slater* in the Notable British Trials series (1910): the prison authorities removed these pages from the book before they allowed Slater to borrow it from the prison library. But the transcript alone showed that the trial had transgressed the rule that a defendant should not be brought to a criminal court to answer for his entire past life. The jury's verdict was a majority of nine votes to six (five being in favour of the Scottish verdict of 'not proven' and one in favour of 'not guilty').

There was no court of criminal appeal in Scotland in 1909. The secretary for Scotland, Lord Pentland, disregarded the advice of his under-secretary, J. M. Dodds, who advised that the death penalty should be carried out. By means of a conditional pardon Slater's sentence was commuted to one of penal servitude for life. Lord Pentland's recorded reasons included the advice of the trial judge (Lord Guthrie), the prejudice caused by publicity in the press, and the jury's knowledge of Slater's 'very abandoned' character. During his imprisonment Slater was recorded to have committed some sixty offences against prison discipline, including idleness, insolence, and destroying library books. Yet during this time Roughead's book continued to impress all who read it. Among those who agitated for Slater's release were his solicitor (Ewing Speirs), Sir Arthur Conan Doyle, Sir Edward Marshall Hall, James Ramsay MacDonald, and (in 1927) Viscount Buckmaster.

In 1914 the secretary of state for Scotland, Thomas MacKinnon Wood, encouraged one of the detectives in the case, John Thompson Trench, to transmit information which had allegedly been concealed by the Glasgow police and which implicated one of Miss Gilchrist's relatives as a suspect. Wood then set up an inquiry but failed to protect Trench from the consequences of his actions. He was dismissed from the police and prosecuted on a trumped-up charge, but was acquitted. If Slater's trial exemplified all the criticisms which can be made of the adversarial system, the inquiry which was set up by Wood exemplified all the disadvantages of the inquisitorial system. The inquiry led to the publication of expurgated witness statements in June 1914, but Wood decided that there was no reason to interfere with Slater's sentence. This only inspired Roughead to bring out a second edition of his book (1915), including his criticisms of 'the secret inquiry'.

In 1927 William Park published his book *The Truth about Oscar Slater*. This proved decisive. The solicitor-general for Scotland, A. M. MacRobert, reported to the secretary of state for Scotland, Sir John Gilmour, that it was no longer proven that Slater had committed the murder. In November 1927 the government secured the passing of a bill to enable the recently established Scottish court of criminal appeal to hear appeals relating to convictions before the original shut-off date of 1 November 1926. Slater was then released from Peterhead prison, on licence, and into the care of Rabbi E. P. Phillips of Glasgow. In July 1928 the Scottish court of criminal appeal quashed Slater's conviction, on the ground that the trial judge had failed to direct the jury, in sufficiently unambiguous terms, about the irrelevance of Slater's supposed character as a pimp. Slater accepted £6000 compensation from the government in August 1928. He lived the remainder of his life in Scotland quietly and respectably, no longer characterized as a 'low-class foreign bully', but resembling a retired army officer.

Slater was 5 feet 7½ inches tall, strongly built, with an apparently distorted nose, memorable to all who saw it. He was briefly interned at the beginning of the Second World War. He had separated from his first wife long before his arrest, and in 1936 he married Lina Wilhelmina Schad (b. c.1902), who was also interned as an enemy alien. There were no children of either marriage. Slater died at 25 St Phillan's Avenue, Ayr, on 31 January 1948, after three years' invalidity from phlebitis, and was cremated. On his death certificate he was described as a retired baker. His second wife survived him.

Slater's wrongful conviction rankled with the Scottish legal system for nearly twenty years and eventually led to a reform of the appellate courts. Slater liked to call himself 'the Scottish Dreyfus'. It is more accurate to evaluate Detective-Lieutenant Trench as the Scottish Colonel Picquart. But Trench, who died in 1919, aged fifty, never lived to see the success of his efforts.

LESLIE WILLIAM BLAKE

Sources W. Roughead, ed., *The trial of Oscar Slater*, 4th edn, Notable British Trials (1950) · T. Toughill, *Oscar Slater: the mystery solved* (1993) · J. House, *Square mile of murder* (1984) · P. Hunt, *Oscar Slater: the great suspect* (1951) · private information (2004) [University of Glasgow, Scottish Jewish Archives Centre, Glasgow] · *Glasgow Herald* · W. Park, *The truth about Oscar Slater* (1927) · lord advocate's department MSS, NA Scot., AD21/5, AD21/6 · home and health department MSS, NA Scot., HH15/20, HH16/109, HH16/110–112, HH60/461 and 480 · m. cert. · d. cert. · d. cert. [J. T. Trench] · b. cert. [M. Gilchrist]
Archives NA Scot., home and health department MSS, HH15/20, HH16/109, HH16/110, HH16/111, HH16/112, HH60/461, HH60/480 · NA Scot., lord advocate's department papers, AD21/5, AD21/6
Likenesses photograph, 1908, repro. in Toughill, *Oscar Slater* · photographs, 1909–27, NA Scot., home and health department MSS, HH15/20 · photograph, 1928, repro. in Roughead, ed., *Trial of Oscar Slater*, frontispiece

Slater, Samuel (1629?–1704), clergyman and ejected minister, was born in London, the son of Samuel Slater (d. c.1670), puritan lecturer at St Katharine by the Tower; he is probably the Samuel Sclater baptized in the parish in November 1629. In January 1645 he entered Emmanuel College, Cambridge, graduating BA in 1648 and proceeding MA in 1658. After serving as vicar of Stoke by Nayland, Suffolk, from 1651, he was appointed lecturer at Bury St Edmunds in July 1654. A zealous proponent of godly rule, he denounced a 'cursed and abominable toleration', and called upon Richard Cromwell to go on 'purging out superstition, extirpating errors … beating down prophaneness … [and] setting up the pure worship of God' (Slater, *Protector's Protection*, 1659, 29, 26). At the Restoration the Bury corporation ejected Slater for nonconformity, along with his colleague Nicholas Clagett. In April 1672 he obtained a licence as a presbyterian teacher

in his house at Walthamstow, Essex, though the authorities rejected his application to preach in Bury. He had ministered to a church in Ropemakers' Alley, London, for a number of years when in July 1680 he succeeded Stephen Charnock as co-pastor, alongside Thomas Watson, of the presbyterian congregation at Crosby Square, Bishopsgate. About this time Slater married Hannah (d. in or after 1704), daughter of the godly London merchant Harman Sheafe and widow of Robert Hood; Slater may have been previously married.

Among the first victims of the tory reaction, Slater was prosecuted in November 1681 for violating the Five Mile Act. In April 1687 he joined such dissenting divines as Vincent Alsop and Stephen Lobb in presenting an address of thanks to James II for his declaration of indulgence. Later that year, preaching before the nonconformist lord mayor, Sir John Shorter, he scolded Anglicans for being so 'wickedly angry' at dissenters for accepting the relief James offered (Slater, *A Sermon Preached*, foreword). Not surprisingly, the king expected Slater and at least a handful of other ministers, including Richard Mayo, Nathaniel Vincent, and Lobb, to express their gratitude again in May 1688 when he reissued his declaration. But, after discussions with John Howe and Daniel Williams, Slater and the others closed ranks and agreed not to address the king; in doing so they revealed the bankruptcy of James's policy. After the revolution Slater encouraged co-operation among London's dissenters and contributed £100 to their Common Fund, which supported deserving candidates for the nonconformist ministry. Although the dissolution of the 'Happy Union' between city Independents and presbyterians in 1694 deeply discouraged Slater, he took comfort in the Williamite regime's commitment to the reformation of manners.

Most of Slater's works 'sold extraordinarily well' (Dunton, 1.171). A noted preacher of funeral sermons, many of which were printed, he also wrote three more substantial volumes: *The Young-Man's Kindness to his God* (1689), *A Discourse of Closet, or Secret Prayer* (1691), and *An Earnest Call to Family-Religion* (1694). Underlying all his works was the conviction that 'hot contentions for lifeless forms and ceremonies not worth a button' had obscured, if not destroyed, old-fashioned godliness (Slater, *Closet Prayer*, foreword). A German translation of the second of his two *Poems* (1679), 'A Dialogue between Faith and a Doubting Soul', enjoyed several editions in the early eighteenth century. Slater died in London on 24 May 1704 and was survived by his wife, Hannah. His assistant, Daniel Alexander, and William Tong of Salters' Hall each published funeral sermons for him. Harman Hood, assistant minister at Little St Helen's, was probably his stepson.

JIM BENEDICT

Sources *Calamy rev.*, 444–5, see also 116, 190 · R. L. Greaves, 'Slater, Samuel', Greaves & Zaller, *BDBR*, 3.182 · E. Calamy, ed., *An abridgement of Mr. Baxter's history of his life and times, with an account of the ministers, &c., who were ejected after the Restauration of King Charles II*, 2nd edn, 2 vols. (1713), vol. 2, p. 646 · E. Calamy, *A continuation of the account of the ministers … who were ejected and silenced after the Restoration in 1660*, 2 vols. (1727), vol. 2, pp. 787–8, 40 · D. Alexander, *A* *funeral sermon preached at Crosby-Square* (1704) • W. Tong, *A funeral sermon occasioned by the death of … Mr. Samuel Slater* (1704) • A. Gordon, ed., *Freedom after ejection: a review* (1690–1692) *of presbyterian and congregational nonconformity in England and Wales* (1917), 164, 353 • J. Browne, *A history of Congregationalism and memorials of the churches in Norfolk and Suffolk* (1877), 151, 403, 419, 590, 596 • R. Thomas, 'The seven bishops and their petition, 18 May 1688', *Journal of Ecclesiastical History*, 12 (1961), 56–70 • *Report on the manuscripts of the marquis of Downshire*, 6 vols. in 7, HMC, 75 (1924–95), vol. 1, p. 279 • *CSP dom.*, 1671–2, 308, 337, 410, 433, 606; 1680–81, 592, 613 • W. Wilson, *The history and antiquities of the dissenting churches and meeting houses in London, Westminster and Southwark*, 4 vols. (1808–14), vol. 1, pp. 338–43, 150–53 • *The life and errors of John Dunton*, [rev. edn], 1, ed. J. B. Nichols (1818), 171 • Bodl. Oxf., MS Walker C.8, fol. 137 • D. R. Lacey, *Dissent and parliamentary politics in England, 1661–1689* (1969), 175–208 • R. L. Greaves, *Secrets of the kingdom: British radicals from the Popish Plot to the revolution of 1688–89* (1992), 93 • *IGI* • S. Slater, *An earnest call to family-religion* (1694) • S. Slater, *A discourse of closet, or secret prayer* (1691) • S. Slater, *The young man's kindness to his God* (1689) • S. Slater, *The protectors protection* (1659) • S. Slater, *A sermon preached before the lord mayor* (1688)

Archives DWL, Morrice MSS, Q, 112, 263, 269

Likenesses R. White, line engraving, 1692, BM, NPG

Slater, William (1796–1889), solicitor, was born at Somerville, Pendlebury, on 18 December 1796, the son of a cotton manufacturer. Slater was educated at the private school of the Revd J. Bell in Alderley, Cheshire, and later at another private school near Halifax. In 1815 he was articled to the firm of Sharpe, Eccles and Cririe, of King Street, Manchester, and was admitted as an attorney in the Hilary term of 1820. He became a partner in the firm in 1823 (a firm whose founder, William Fox, also a partner in the banking firm of Jones Loyd & Co., left £150,000 on his death).

During his long and successful legal career, Slater dealt with private clients, public bodies, and corporations. According to one of his clients, Sir Charles Shaw, a former police commissioner for Manchester, Slater's talents in conveyancing were generally considered to be without equal in Lancashire. He was solicitor to the Liverpool and Manchester Railway, and from 1839 to the Manchester and Birmingham Railway. When the two companies became part of the North Western Company in 1847, Slater was one of the few people to be issued with a life pass to travel anywhere on the railway system. In his capacity as solicitor to the Liverpool and Manchester Railway, he was present at the opening ceremony of the company on 15 September 1830 and witnessed the first railway accident, which resulted in the death of William Huskisson the tory politician.

As a parliamentary lawyer Slater's formidable legal skills ensured that he was much in demand, and to him was entrusted the legal work connected with the promotion of the Manchester Rectory Division Act of 1850, which he piloted through parliament on behalf of the churchwardens of Manchester. He included the Byrom family of merchants and bankers among his clients, and he also acted as solicitor for the Bridgewater and Clowes estates. He was solicitor to the Wilton family and was a personal friend of Thomas, earl of Wilton. Slater also acted as legal adviser to the Mersey and Irwell Navigation Company, the Old Quay Company, Manchester grammar

school, Henshaw's Blind Asylum at Old Trafford, Henshaw's Blue Coat School at Oldham, and a variety of other charities and turnpike trusts. Renowned for his phenomenal memory, in 1885 Slater was called to give evidence before the vice-chancellor of the palatine court of Lancaster regarding certain deeds. This he did *viva voce* and included all the details as to time, place, and even the room in which certain interviews occurred—events which had happened some forty-five years before.

Slater was a founder member of the Manchester Law Association and was elected its president in 1868. He was also a member of the Solicitors' Benevolent Society and for some years was a director of the London and Provincial Law Insurance Society. He was a member of the Union Club, a devout Anglican, and a liberal supporter of the church and its schools. He married Fridiswid Charlotte Worthington, the daughter of W. H. Worthington of Sandiway Bank, Chester; she died in 1849, leaving him with three sons and one daughter. In 1856 the eldest son, William Slater, became a partner in his father's firm. The other sons became farmers, and his daughter, reflecting the circles in which the family moved, married the Revd Thomas Daniels, rector of St Paul's, Stretford Road, Manchester.

In appearance, Slater was a tall, upright figure, even in his later years. An unostentatious and private man, he was noted by family and colleagues for his temperance and his methodical habits. He lived at Park Lane, Higher Broughton, at a distance of about 3 miles from his office and club in Manchester. An early riser, he regularly walked the distance from his home to his work, where he appeared for the last time on the Friday before his death on 12 November 1889. He was ninety-two years of age. His longevity and vast knowledge of the law won him the unofficial title of 'father of the legal profession in Manchester'.

V. R. Parrott

Sources *Manchester Faces and Places*, 1 (1889–90), 44, 52–4 • J. T. Slugg, *Reminiscences of Manchester 50 years ago* (1881) • M. C. H. Hibbert Ware, *The life and correspondence of the late Samuel Hibbert Ware* (1882) • *Manchester Guardian* (13 Nov 1889)

Archives Man. CL • Slater, Heelis & Co. Solicitors, Manchester

Likenesses portrait, Slater Heelis & Co. Solicitors, Princess Street, Manchester; photograph, priv. coll. • portrait (after photograph by M. Savvy, 1886), repro. in *Manchester Faces and Places*, 40–41

Wealth at death £53,083 6s. 6d.: probate, 13 Jan 1890, CGPLA Eng. & Wales

Slater, Sir William Kershaw (1893–1970), chemist and agricultural administrator, was born in Oldham on 19 October 1893, the only child of James Slater (d. 1922), cotton mill manager, and his wife, Mary Ann Kershaw, who came from a Yorkshire farming family. As a child, he suffered severely from asthma, and on his doctor's recommendation was sent to live with the proprietor of a small private school in Bournemouth. Returning to Oldham at the age of fourteen, he attended Hulme Grammar School and was much influenced by F. Potter, the science master.

Slater graduated BSc from the University of Manchester in 1914, with first-class honours in chemistry and the Leblanc medal. He was rejected for military service

Sir William Kershaw Slater (1893–1970), by Walter Stoneman, 1951

because of defective eyesight and began research, but this was soon curtailed for service with the explosives inspectorate. After the war he became assistant lecturer in chemistry at Manchester University. In 1922, after a year in industry, he entered biochemical research, taking up a position under A. V. Hill at Manchester University. Slater obtained, for the first time, a reliable value for the heat of combustion of glycogen, essential for the interpretation of Hill's experiments on muscle. This success won him a Beit memorial medical research fellowship in 1923, with which he followed Hill to University College, London. Here, under J. C. Drummond, he continued work on heats of combustion and clarified some aspects of anaerobic metabolism in lower animals. In 1921 he married Hilda (d. 1966), daughter of Augustus Whittenbury, a merchant of Moss Side, Manchester. They had two sons and a daughter.

Slater's career then took an abrupt turn. Leonard and Dorothy Elmhirst, who had started the Dartington educational experiment in 1925, wanted the help of a scientist and in 1929, on Hill's recommendation, Slater was invited to join them. He set up a laboratory which was soon useful in nearly every part of the enterprise, and especially in soil surveying and soil improvement. Slater's business abilities early led to his acting as managing director of the two limited companies which were formed to take over the activities of the trading and constructional departments of the estate. When Dartington Hall was registered as a charitable trust he became one of the trustees, with a

still greater administrative load, but he did not abandon science. His unassuming enthusiasm imbued everyone at Dartington with the notion that some understanding of science was both practically useful and intellectually rewarding.

In 1941 the minister of agriculture, Robert S. Hudson, set up the Agricultural Improvement Council (AIC) as part of his drive to increase the productivity of British agriculture, and in 1942 Slater joined its staff. There he became associated with James A. Scott Watson in the creation of the National Agricultural Advisory Service (NAAS) and the establishment of a national chain of experimental husbandry farms and horticultural stations. To Slater must go much of the credit for the sound foundations on which the NAAS was built. He became secretary of the AIC in 1944 when John C. F. Fryer moved to the Agricultural Research Council (ARC).

Fryer died suddenly in 1949 and Slater succeeded him as secretary of the ARC, a post in which he continued until his retirement in 1960. Pre-war surveys by the ARC, wartime experience, and a resolve to maintain post-war productivity had led the cabinet in 1946 to approve a greatly expanded programme of agricultural research. In 1956 to make this research effective Slater sought to make the ARC more autonomous and this was achieved with the passing of the Agricultural Research Act, which greatly increased its responsibilities and put a much greater burden on the secretary and his staff, but resulted in more effective research and lower administrative costs. To ensure the high quality of research Slater appointed only first-class scientists, and supported ARC units in universities and the pursuit of basic research.

Slater was appointed KBE in 1951 and elected to the Royal Society in 1957. He was a DSc of Manchester and an honorary DSc of Queen's University, Belfast. He was president of the Royal Institute of Chemistry in 1961–3, a general secretary of the British Association for the Advancement of Science (1962–5), and chairman of a government committee which proposed the creation of a Natural Resources (later Natural Environment) Research Council. Through Elmhirst, and through his membership of the Colonial Research Council, he had long been interested in the problems of food production in less economically developed countries, and after 1960 he gave much time to them. He served as British co-ordinator of several UN conferences and was the British representative on the Cento Council for Scientific Education and Research. He did an immense amount of work for the Freedom from Hunger Campaign, and started the idea of the Food and Agriculture Organization's 1969 *Indicative World Plan for Agricultural Development*. Some of his views are expressed in his book *Man must Eat* (1964).

Slater had an equable temperament, was extremely tenacious in matters that he considered important and yet was an able negotiator. He was friendly and approachable. Slater's last years were clouded by the death of his elder son in 1968. He died at Midhurst, Sussex, near his home at Fittleworth, on 19 April 1970.   E. G. Cox, *rev.*

Sources H. D. Kay, *Memoirs FRS*, 17 (1971), 663–80 · *The Times* (21 April 1970) · personal knowledge (1981) · private information (1981)
Archives CAC Cam., corresp. and papers
Likenesses W. Stoneman, photograph, 1951, NPG [*see illus.*] · Bassano & Vandyk, photograph, RS
Wealth at death £37,323: probate, 22 July 1970, *CGPLA Eng. & Wales*

Slatin, Sir Rudolf Carl von (1857–1932), colonial governor and author, was born on 27 June 1857 at Ober Sankt Veit, near Vienna, the fourth of six children born to Michael Slatin, a silk dyer, and his wife, Maria Anna Feuerstein, who was born in Lwów (Lemberg). Slatin's grandfather was a Jew who had been converted to Catholicism. The family lived at 1 Wolfrathplatz, where their six children were born between 1852 and 1864. Rudolf was baptized Rudolf Anton in the Catholic church at Ober Sankt Veit, but was later known as Rudolf Carl. He entered Oberrealschule am Schottenfelde in September 1866, but his academic record was poor and he left school after three years. In 1870 he entered a commercial school in Vienna, the Wiener Handelsakademie, and graduated three years later.

Aged sixteen, Slatin was eager to begin a life of adventure. Chance decided that it was to be in Egypt, where a bookseller was in need of a clerk and a tutor for his sons. Slatin spent a few months as tutor and left for a trip up the Nile. Once the boat reached Korosko in Turco-Egyptian Sudan, he continued by camel to Berber and then to Khartoum, where he spent two months. He left Khartoum for the Nuba Mountains in southern Kordofan, but for reasons of security was ordered back. Chance intervened when he met Edward Schnitzer—better known by his Muslim name, Emin Pasha—who was about to join the Egyptian service in Equatoria under the governorship of General Charles Gordon. Slatin asked Emin to recommend him to Gordon's attention for future employment. In December 1875 Slatin returned to Vienna and joined the Austrian army, serving with the 18th Bohemian infantry regiment. In December 1877 he was posted to the 19th Hungarian regiment as a sub-lieutenant for service in the lines. In July 1878 Gordon Pasha, now governor-general of Turco-Egyptian Sudan, invited Slatin to join his staff in Khartoum and he accepted eagerly.

Slatin's career in the Sudan covered thirty-six eventful years. He started in January 1879 in the finance department as an inspector with the rank of a *bimbashi* (the Turkish equivalent of a major). Later that year he was appointed governor of Dara, in south-western Darfur, and after less than a year became governor-general of the whole province. In his major publication *Fire and Sword in the Sudan* (1896) Slatin was vague about his duties in Darfur. However, his life as governor-general was soon disrupted by Muhammad Ahmad ibn ʿAbdullahi, who in June 1881 declared himself the *Mahdi* of the Sudan. Soon the Mahdi and his followers (*ansar*) escaped from Aba Island, on the White Nile, to the Nuba Mountains and Slatin became actively involved in the uprising. Many of the tribal and religious leaders in Darfur joined the Mahdi. Slatin led his troops in numerous battles against the Mahdist forces and

lost many soldiers. In January 1883 al-ʿUbayd, capital of Kordofan, fell into Mahdist hands and Darfur was cut off from Khartoum. Slatin decided 'nominally to adopt the Mohammedan religion' since he was told by his Egyptian and Sudanese followers that they had lost confidence in his ability, as a Christian, to win the war against the Mahdi. 'I am not a foreigner, I am not an unbeliever', he responded, 'I am as much a believer as you … I bear witness that there is no God but God and Mohammed is his Prophet' (Slatin, 216–17). However, disastrous defeats at the battle of Shaykan in November 1883 and the fall of al-Fasher, capital of Darfur, convinced Slatin to surrender. He sent a letter to the Mahdi in al-ʿUbayd declaring his submission and in December 1883 he and his troops surrendered at Dara. Slatin was renamed ʿAbd al-Qadir Salatin, a name he carried thereafter.

From 1884 to 1895 Slatin was a prisoner, first of the Mahdi and, following his death in 1885, of Caliph ʿAbdullahi al-Ta ʿaishi. After a brief period in Dara, where he was allowed to live in his old house and keep his servants, Slatin was ordered to join the Mahdi's camp at al-ʿUbayd and to take part in the march to Khartoum. During the siege of Khartoum, Slatin was asked by the Mahdi to write on his behalf to General Gordon and seek his surrender. Slatin, according to his account, attempted to explain to Gordon the circumstances of his conversion to Islam and to justify his surrender. Gordon was willing to forgive Slatin's surrender but not his conversion to Islam. After the Mahdi's death Slatin became the caliph's orderly, and was entrusted with confidential administrative and financial duties. He described the caliph as a 'cruel beast' and accused him of brutalities, but failed to mention how kindly he and some of the other European prisoners were treated. During this period Slatin apparently had two wives, Hassaniyyah, a Fur girl he brought with him when he surrendered to the Mahdi in December 1883, and an Abyssinian, Desta, who bore him a child shortly after his escape from Omdurman in 1895; the child died after a few weeks (Neufeld, 206–7). He left both women behind when he escaped in 1895.

Slatin's problematic relations with the caliph may also be observed in a letter he wrote to the caliph from Cairo on 6 April 1895, some six weeks after his escape from the Sudan. In this letter Slatin asked his former patron to continue to rely on his love and loyalty and to disregard any rumours to the contrary emanating from Cairo. He ended his letter by asking the caliph to forgive him for having left Omdurman without notifying him and offered to return to his service once he received his letter of pardon (Slatin to Caliph ʿAbdullahi, 6 April 1895, Durham University Library, Sudan archive, SAD/100/20).

Of Slatin's value as an intelligence agent there are conflicting views. Few of the communications he smuggled to Cairo contained valuable information. Colonel Reginald Wingate, who since 1887 had served in the military intelligence department of the Egyptian army, ignored most of them as probably written under duress. For intelligence purposes he needed Slatin in Cairo, where he could interrogate him freely. On 20 February 1895 Slatin escaped from Omdurman, led by two guides hired by the intelligence department. He arrived in Cairo on 19 March and was met by Wingate at the railway station. Two days later the Egyptian khedive, Abbas II, received him and raised him to the grade of pasha. His detailed intelligence report to Wingate was entitled 'General report on the Egyptian Sudan, March 1895, compiled from statements made by Slatin Pasha'. Wingate, who helped Slatin to write his memoirs, worked to convince the British government and public opinion that the Sudan had to be reconquered because of the caliph's cruel autocracy, and Slatin's literary contributions were both timely and essential. *Fire and Sword in the Sudan* was published in English in 1896 and was dedicated to Queen Victoria. Its impact on public opinion in Europe was greater than Wingate had expected. It appeared in numerous editions until 1935, and was translated into German, Italian, French, and Arabic. Slatin spent several months of leave, partly with his family in Austria and partly in travelling throughout Europe, receiving decorations from heads of state and lecturing at geographical societies. He had become a celebrity and seemed to enjoy it.

From 1896 to 1898 Slatin was Wingate's assistant director of military intelligence in the Egyptian army. Both were practical and down-to-earth, methodological of mind, and scornful of the abstract. Articulate, uninhibited, and simple, they trusted each other absolutely and became close friends. Although Slatin was a full colonel and a pasha, while Wingate, his superior, was a mere bey and a lieutenant-colonel, this did not affect their close relationship. Their aim was the reconquest of the Sudan and the total destruction of the Mahdist state; nothing else mattered. They therefore cultivated the press, an art at which both men excelled. Eager to return to active service in the Sudan, Slatin was allowed to take part in the final battle, which took place at Karrari, near Omdurman, on 2 September 1898. His knowledge of Omdurman and its people, as well as his fluent command of Arabic, proved to be invaluable.

During the conquest Slatin's views condoning slavery were brought to the attention of Queen Victoria and he was warned to be more careful in future. However, he continued to express his view that black people were inferior and 'do not deserve to be treated like free and independent men', and suggested that black people 'should be made to remain under the protection of their former masters' (Hill, 55–6). The queen forgave Slatin and also overlooked his years as apostate. He became a favourite correspondent and a frequent visitor at Windsor and Balmoral. In 1898 Queen Victoria awarded him a knighthood, and upon his retirement in February 1899 the khedive, Abbas, promoted him to general and granted him a yearly pension. In 1906 he was created a baron of the Austrian–Hungarian empire.

Slatin's retirement did not last long. In the summer of 1900 Wingate, now governor-general, arranged for Slatin's appointment in the Sudan government as inspector-general and director of intelligence. It was, according to Wingate, a personal post which would cease

when Slatin left the service. Given his experience and command of Arabic, his position as Wingate's right-hand man was unchallengeable. His duties and authority were never clearly defined but his role was paramount in shaping the government's Islamic and tribal policy. He knew most of the leaders personally and advised on the establishment of a 'Board of Ulemas', arguing that a government consisting of Christians should not interfere in daily decisions regarding Muslims. Slatin decided who would serve on this board and he acted as the liaison officer between the board and the government. He personally kept in touch with former Mahdist leaders, including members of the families of the Mahdi and the caliph, both for intelligence purposes and because of his loyalty to old friends. His idea was to propagate 'orthodox' Islam as a barrier against Sufi and Mahdist fanaticism. In April 1913 he wrote to Wingate: 'I am expelling 3 fikhis from the Yemen and Hejaz, who were preaching Rott and Nonsense' (Hill, 93). Slatin was more apprehensive regarding Sufism than he was with regard to a possible Mahdist revival. He knew that most of the condominium's Sudanese employees had previously served in the Mahdist state but did not question their loyalty. Slatin himself lacked religious zeal of any kind. Christian missionaries were forbidden to proselytize in the Muslim provinces and were ordered to limit their activities, including education, to the non-Muslim regions. In tribal affairs he sought to strengthen family bonds, tribal leadership, and the administration of justice according to tribal law. He believed that by lowering taxes and encouraging tribes to revert to their traditional economies, the government would be relieved of many of its administrative burdens. He relied on his acquaintances, many former Mahdists, in deciding whom to appoint as tribal sheikhs or in other senior positions. Slatin's British colleagues resented his constant interference in their provinces and one of them claimed that 'he was not popular among the Sudanese as he was supposed to show favoritism to his pals among the tribes' (Butler, journal, 1911, Durham University Library, Sudan archive, 422/12). However, with Wingate's unrelenting support Slatin's position was maintained. On Slatin's departure in 1914 following the outbreak of the First World War the position of inspector-general ceased to exist.

For Slatin it was a difficult decision: he was fifty-seven years old and had served under the British crown for most of his life. Due to his superior knowledge of Turkey and the Middle East he was asked occasionally by the Austrian authorities to give advice. In December 1914 the khedive, Abbas, met Slatin in Vienna and offered to appoint him as his general aide-de-camp, for the duration of the war. Slatin turned the offer down since he did not want to commit himself to active participation in the war against England. His sole active service was in the Austrian Red Cross, in which he served as unpaid head of the division for prisoners of war. In this capacity he also did his best for British prisoners of war in Austrian captivity. However, with the patriotic feelings prevailing in Europe, the British press frequently slandered Slatin as a double-crosser. Wingate came to his defence whenever he could, but the misrepresentations prevailed.

When the war ended Slatin was included in the Austrian delegation to the peace conference and in October 1919 he was offered the post of Austrian minister in London. He declined because of ill health and lack of financial means. During his years of retirement he often travelled to England where he saw Wingate and other old friends who had served with him in the Sudan. He also met George V. On 21 July 1914 he had married Baroness Alice von Ramberg (1873–1921). The couple had a daughter, but Alice died from cancer on 26 June 1921. In the winter of 1927 he made his last visit to the Sudan, as the guest of Sir John Maffey, the new governor-general. He wrote to Wingate following the visit and commented favourably on the vast Gezira irrigation scheme, which Wingate and he had initiated in 1913, but criticized the glorification of Sayyid ʿAbd al-Rahman al-Mahdi, the Mahdi's posthumous son. In his last diary, covering 1932, he noted on 16 March: 'Today it is 37 years that I reached Assouan on my escape from Omdurman' (Sudan archive, 441). He died on 4 October 1932 at the Cottage Nursing Home, Vienna, Austria, and was buried at Ober Sankt Viet.   GABRIEL WARBURG

Sources R. Hill, *Slatin Pasha* (1965) · B. Farwell, *Prisoners of the Mahdi* (1967) · R. C. Slatin Pasha, *Fire and sword in the Sudan: a personal narrative of fighting and serving the dervishes, 1879–1895* (1896) · A. B. Theobald, *The Mahddiya: a history of the Anglo-Egyptian Sudan, 1881–1899* (1951) · C. Neufeld, *A prisoner of the khaleefa: twelve years' captivity at Omdurman* (1899) · G. Warburg, *The Sudan under Wingate: administration in the Anglo-Egyptian Sudan, 1899–1916* (1970) · U. Durham L., department of palaeography and diplomatic, Sudan archive, Wingate MSS
Archives U. Durham L., archive, corresp., diaries, and papers | U. Durham L., letters to Sir Harold Macmichael · U. Durham L., corresp. with Sir Reginald Wingate
Likenesses H. von Angeli, oils, Royal Collection; [commissioned by Queen Victoria] · Spy [L. Ward], watercolour caricature, NPG; repro. in *VF* (5 Feb 1887) · oils, U. Durham, Sudan archive · oils; Governor General's palace, Khartoum, in 1938 · portraits, U. Durham, Sudan archive, boxes 12, 13 · portraits, Nationalbibliothek, Vienna, Py. 3434/0; Py. 3434/1

Slattery, Michael (1783–1857), Roman Catholic archbishop of Cashel, was born in Tipperary town on 1 October 1783, the son of Michael Slattery, a businessman from Tipperary. After completing his secondary education at the Abbey School, Tipperary, Slattery entered Trinity College, Dublin, on 4 November 1799, thus taking advantage of recent legislation in the Irish parliament which allowed Catholics to take degrees in Dublin University. He studied law and obtained his BA in 1804, but did not take his MA until 1832. In 1805 he decided to abandon a promising legal career and offered himself as a candidate for the priesthood in the Roman Catholic diocese of Cashel. He spent the next four years (1805–9) studying philosophy and theology at Carlow College, and was ordained priest in 1809. That same year he was appointed professor of philosophy at Carlow College, a post he held until 1815. During these years he formed a close friendship with James Doyle (J. K. L.), who was on the staff of Carlow College until appointed bishop of Kildare and Leighlin in

1819. Both men took a keen interest in education, especially relating to improved facilities for Irish Catholics.

In 1815 Slattery was appointed parish priest of Oola, co. Limerick. In 1817 he was translated to the parish of Borrisoleigh, co. Tipperary, where he helped to stamp out factional fighting in the district. In June 1833 he was elected president of St Patrick's College, Maynooth, a post he held for only nine months. A vacancy occurred in the see of Cashel in July 1833, when Michael Laffan, the archbishop of Cashel, died. Slattery was appointed his successor on 22 December 1833 and was consecrated on 24 February 1834. He remained in office until his death in 1857.

As archbishop, Slattery showed considerable organizing ability. He never enjoyed good health, and was often confined to his house in Thurles for long periods. He held the important office of metropolitan of Munster at a time when the Irish church was going through a process of transition following the granting of Catholic emancipation by the Westminster parliament in 1829. The population of the country was growing rapidly, and this called for an upsurge in church building to replace the small penal chapels still in use. Slattery held a series of provincial synods to discuss and legislate on a number of issues such as liturgical reform, priestly life, and education. The great famine (1845–9) presented the archbishop with his greatest social challenge. He did not spare himself, collecting large sums of money from at home and abroad for the famine victims. He also had to deal with the question of the English protestant Bible societies, who stepped up their activities in Ireland during the years 1845–55. These societies, centred on Exeter Hall, London, were especially active in co. Limerick and directed their efforts for the most part to the poorer people, offering them money and other material benefits if they changed their religion. Slattery counteracted this proselytizing threat by organizing the first parish 'mission' in the diocese of Cashel in 1853.

When, in 1845, the British government proposed the establishment of three Queen's colleges, in Cork, Galway, and Belfast, Slattery opposed the idea on religious and moral grounds. The Queen's colleges question became a major divisive issue among the four Irish Catholic archbishops during the years 1845–50. Dr Crolly of Armagh and Dr Murray of Dublin were in favour of the colleges, whereas Dr MacHale of Tuam and Dr Slattery of Cashel were utterly opposed to them. In an earlier controversy, during the 1830s, over the issue of non-denominational national schools, Slattery had sided with Crolly and Murray in supporting them, whereas MacHale had been a bitter opponent of the national schools system. In 1850 the first national synod of the Irish Catholic hierarchy since 1642 was held at Thurles in deference to Slattery, who resided in that town. The synod condemned the Queen's colleges, and proposed the setting up of a Catholic university.

Slattery was a distinguished scholar and theologian, though he never published anything apart from his pastoral letters. He left behind him a vast correspondence, witnessing how much he was caught up in the social, ecclesiastical, and political events of his day. He died in Thurles on 4 February 1857 and was buried on the 9th in Thurles chapel. His remains were later re-interred in the sanctuary of Thurles Cathedral. There are portraits of him in the archbishop's house, Thurles, and in St Patrick's College, Maynooth.   D. MARK TIERNEY

Sources Cashel Diocesan Archives, Thurles, co. Tipperary · Paul Cullen MSS, Irish College, Rome · Daniel Murray MSS, Dublin Diocesan Archives · Acta, 1833–4, Propaganda Fide Archives, Rome · 'Scritture riferite nei congressi: Irlanda', Propaganda Fide Archives, Rome, vols. 20, 21 · James Doyle MSS, Kildare and Leighlin Diocesan Archives · *Tipperary Free Press* (1833) · *Limerick Reporter* (1839–49) · *Limerick Reporter* (6 Feb 1857) · *Limerick Reporter* (10 Feb 1857) · *Tipperary Vindicator* (1844–9)
Archives archbishop's house, Thurles, co. Tipperary, MSS · NL Ire., MSS
Likenesses oils, archbishop's house, Thurles, co. Tipperary · oils, St Patrick's College, Maynooth, co. Kildare

Slatyer, William (*c*.1587–1647), Church of England clergyman and author, son of a Somerset gentleman, was born at Tykeham, near Bristol. Having matriculated at Oxford from St Mary's Hall in February 1601, more than two years' absence from the university occasioned by his father's death intervened before he moved to Brasenose in 1607 and then graduated BA in 1609. Although Anthony Wood claimed (Wood, *Ath. Oxon.*, 3.227) that he was made a fellow of Brasenose in 1611, the year he gained his MA, college records cast doubt on this, but he did later return to Brasenose to gain his BD and DD in 1623.

In 1616 Slatyer was appointed treasurer of the cathedral church of St David's, and in 1617 rector of Newchurch, Romney, Kent. A period as chaplain to Anne of Denmark gave rise to his first publication, *Pandionium melos, in perpetuam serinissimae simul ac beatissimae Principis Annae reginae memoriam* (1619), a set of elegies and epitaphs on the queen in Hebrew, Greek, Latin, and English, addressed to Prince Charles. Two years later this was complemented by poems to King James prefacing a 300-page Latin and English poem, *The history of Great Britain from the first peopling of this iland to this present raigne of our happy and peacefull monarke K. James*, supplemented in turn in 1630 by *Genethliacon, sive, Stemma Jacobi*, which, describing itself 'as an appendix' to the earlier work, deduced the descent of James I from Adam.

Meanwhile, in 1625, Slatyer had added to Newchurch the rectory of Otterden, Kent, but any hopes of further preferment he may have entertained as a result of his literary efforts received a setback in 1631 when his next publication got him into trouble. *Psalmes, or, Songs of Zion* (1630) 'intended for Christmas carols' and dedicated to 'his approved worthy friend, Sir Thomas Finch, knight, Lord Maidstone, a true Mecaenas and Patron of the Muses', was on 9 July 1631 ordered to be burned. Summoned before the court of high commission on 20 October, Slatyer confessed that he had 'added thereunto a scandalous table to the disgrace of religion, and to the encouragement of the contemners thereof'; judging from an annotated copy of the work dated 1642, this probably consisted of a list of popular tunes to which the psalms might be sung. After submission and 'a very sharp reproof' from Archbishop

Abbot, Slatyer was dismissed, but recalled by Bishop Laud and censured for wearing riding clothes instead of attire 'fit for a minister' (Gardiner, 186).

Slatyer continued to publish, however, following *A Type of Trew Nobilitye* (*c*.1635) with, in 1643, a catechism entitled *The Compleat Christian*, and *The Psalmes of David in Four Languages*, a high quality edition containing both words and music, the latter principally by Thomas Ravenscroft. Deprived of his Newchurch living in 1645, on the grounds that 'being long absent' he 'had employed a drunken curate ... who had since left' (*Walker rev.*, 225), Slatyer continued at Otterden until his death there on 14 February 1647. He was survived by his wife, Sarah, and succeeded as rector by his son William.

E. I. CARLYLE, *rev.* VIVIENNE LARMINIE

Sources Wood, *Ath. Oxon.*, new edn, 3.227 · *N&Q*, 2nd ser., 11 (1861), 386–7 · *N&Q*, 3rd ser., 3 (1863), 255–6 · S. R. Gardiner, *Reports of cases in the courts of star chamber and high commission*, CS, 39 (1886), 186 · [C. B. Heberden], ed., *Brasenose College register, 1509–1909*, 1, OHS, 55 (1909), 93 · Rymer, *Foedera*, 3rd edn, 8/2.31 · *Walker rev.*, 225 · *BL cat.* · *STC, 1475–1640* · W. Slatyer, *Genethliacon. sive, Stemma Jacobi: genealogia scilicet regia, Catholica, Anglo-Scoto-Cambro-Britannica* (1630) · W. Slater, *The psalmes of David in four languages* (1643)
Likenesses engraving (after oil painting), BM, NPG; repro. in *The psalmes of David in four languages*, rev. edn (1652)

Slaughter, Edward (1655–1729), Jesuit and Hebraist, was born in Herefordshire on 5 January 1655 into a family many of whose members became Catholic priests. He commenced his noviciate with the English Jesuits at Watten in September 1673. After two years at Watten he proceeded to the Jesuit college for higher studies at Liège where he studied philosophy from 1676 to 1678 and theology from 1678 to 1682. During his studies he apparently acquired enough knowledge of Hebrew and mathematics to become a teacher of those subjects in his own college. On 28 March 1682 he was ordained priest. Subsequently he was sent on the mission and worked for one and a half years at Swaffham in Norfolk, in the Jesuit district of 'The college of the holy apostles'. In 1683 he was back at Liège in order to travel on to Ghent where he made his tertianship (1683–4), the final stage of Jesuit higher studies, although it would take until 2 February 1696 before he was professed of the four vows. In the meantime he had taken up residence at Liège and became professor there. Apart from Hebrew he taught mathematics and theology.

During these years Slaughter also published some handbooks directed to his teaching duties. In 1696 a theological treatise entitled *Conclusiones ex universa theologica* appeared at Liège and three years later his most successful work, *Grammatica Hebraica brevi & nova methodo concinnata*, was published at Amsterdam by Allard Aaltsz. Amsterdam was one of the centres for Hebrew publications and Aaltsz was one of the few Catholic publishers there. The book is a well-organized practical guide to the basic principles of Hebrew and testimony to its didactic qualities are the many reprints until well into the second half of the nineteenth century. In 1702 he also published a handbook of arithmetic, *Arithmetica methodice et succincte tradita* (1702).

Slaughter was rector of the college at Liège from 1701 to 1704 and witnessed the siege and occupation of the town in October 1702 by the forces of John Churchill (later duke of Marlborough) whom he apparently met on this occasion. After this period he moved to the English College at St Omer and became its rector. One of his innovations was the introduction of Hebrew for half an hour a day in the school of rhetoric (the sixth form). It was an innovation that was quietly dropped again after his departure in 1709 when he returned to Liège. For the next ten years he taught again at Liège where he became involved in the conflict between the episcopal seminary and the English Jesuits. In order to combat Jansenist tendencies in the episcopal college the prince bishop of Liège, Joseph Clement of Bavaria, appointed English Jesuits as professors of theology, which caused fierce opposition from a large section of the native secular clergy. Slaughter's last official position was rector of the Jesuit house of higher studies at Ghent from 1719 to 1722. In 1722 he returned to Liège where he died seven years later on 20 January 1729.

J. BLOM and F. BLOM

Sources DNB · H. Foley, ed., *Records of the English province of the Society of Jesus*, 5 (1879), 595; 7 (1882–3), 715 · G. Holt, *The English Jesuits, 1650–1829: a biographical dictionary*, Catholic RS, 70 (1984) · *The letter book of Lewis Sabran*, ed. G. Holt, Catholic RS, 62 (1971), 82, 143 · G. Holt, 'The letter book of Fr John Warner, 1678–1686', *Archivum Historicum Societatis Jesu*, 53 (1984), 443–68 · G. Oliver, *Collections towards illustrating the biography of the Scotch, English and Irish members, SJ* (1838) · H. Chadwick, *St Omers to Stonyhurst* (1962), 245 · D. A. Bellenger, ed., *English and Welsh priests, 1558–1800* (1984) · J. P. Delville, *Le grand séminaire de Liège, 1592–1992* (1992)

Slaughter, Stephen (*bap.* 1697, *d.* 1765), portrait painter, was baptized on 13 January 1697 at St Paul's, Covent Garden, London, one of the five children of Stephen and Judith Slaughter. He is first recorded in autumn 1712 studying at Sir Godfrey Kneller's academy in Great Queen Street, London. Soon afterwards he departed for the continent, where he lived for seventeen years, first in Paris and then in Flanders. By 1733 he was back in London but promptly left for Dublin, where he painted Nathaniel Kane, lord mayor of Dublin, a portrait known from an engraving by John Brooks of 1734. Having returned to London he lived in Bloomsbury Square and set up a successful portrait practice, which attracted many notable patrons, such as Sir Hans Sloane (portrait, 1736, NPG). Slaughter's style is meticulous and exacting, with a particular attention to the detail of dress; Vertue praised him for painting this himself rather than using a costume painter (Vertue, *Note books*, 3. 111). He painted and copied a number of oils and pastels in the late 1730s for the Spencer family at Althorp, Northamptonshire, including *The Hon. John Spencer* (1736; priv. coll.) and two of his most ambitious works, *The Hon. John Spencer* and *Lady Georgiana Spencer* (1737; priv. coll.). In 1742 he painted *Sir Robert Walpole* (priv. coll.) and in 1747 the latter's son, Edward, and grandchildren (Minneapolis Institute of Arts). He is known to have bought a number of old masters at the sale of Walpole's collection in 1751.

In 1742 a malicious spoof appeared in the *London Evening-Post* (21–3 October), possibly by an envious Hogarth, stating that Slaughter, then living in Rathbone Place, had received a knighthood from the king for a painting of his son Frederick, prince of Wales. Slaughter did, however, go on to achieve high office in 1745, when he succeeded Parry Walton as surveyor and keeper of the king's pictures, a post that he held until his death, with a salary of £300 per annum. In the 1740s he returned to Dublin, where he had 'great business' (Vertue, *Note books*, 3.123), examples of which survive in many Irish country houses. *John Hoadley, Bishop of Armagh* (1744; NG Ire.) is a fine example of his work in Ireland at this period. By the 1750s Slaughter was again in London, but there are few recorded works during this period, *Sir George Lee* (1753; Tate collection) being an exception. He retired to Kensington and lived with his brother, Edward, and three sisters, Catherine, Judith [*see below*], and Mary, at Church Court. He died there, apparently unmarried, on 15 May 1765 and was buried on 22 May at the church of St Mary Abbots, Kensington.

Judith Lewis (*d.* 1781), artist, was Slaughter's sister. Walpole wrote that she 'excelled in imitating bronzes and bas reliefs to the highest degree of deception' (Walpole, 2.705). She was an honorary exhibitor of crayons, miniatures, and needlework pictures at the Society of Artists. Two of her signed and dated equestrian conversation pieces in the style of John Wootton, of 1755 and 1766, were sold at Christies on 24 June 1960. She died on 6 April 1781 and was buried at St Mary Abbots, Kensington.

EMMA LAUZE

Sources A. C. Sewter, 'Stephen Slaughter: a minor British painter of the 18th century', *Connoisseur*, 122 (1948), 10–15 · E. Einberg, 'The Betts family: a lost Hogarth that never was, and a candidate for Slaughter', *Burlington Magazine*, 125 (1983), 415–16 · Vertue, *Note books*, 3.77, 111, 123, 133 · A. Crookshank and the Knight of Glin [D. Fitzgerald], eds., *Irish portraits, 1660–1860* (1969) [exhibition catalogue, Dublin, London, and Belfast, 14 Aug 1969 – 9 March 1970] · A. Crookshank and the Knight of Glin [D. Fitzgerald], *The painters of Ireland, c.1660–1920* (1978) · R. Paulson, *Hogarth: his life, art and times* (1971) · H. Walpole, *Anecdotes of painting in England: with some account of the principal artists*, ed. R. N. Wornum, new edn, 3 vols. (1849); repr. (1862) · S. West, 'Slaughter, Stephen', *The dictionary of art*, ed. J. Turner (1996) · Waterhouse, *18c painters* · K. J. Garlick, 'A catalogue of paintings at Althorp', *Walpole Society*, 45 (1974–6) [whole issue] · A. Moore, ed., *Houghton Hall: the prime minister, the empress and the Hermitage* (1996) [exhibition catalogue, Norwich Castle Museum and The Iveagh Bequest, Kenwood, 12 Oct 1996 – 20 April 1997] · W. G. Strickland, *A dictionary of Irish artists*, 2 vols. (1913); facs. edn with introduction by T. J. Snoddy (1969) · artist's file, NPG, Heinz Archive and Library · artist's file, Paul Mellon Center for Studies in British Art, London · will, PRO, PROB 11/909, sig. 198
Wealth at death see will, PRO, PROB 11/909, sig. 198

Slaughter, Sir William Capel (1857–1917), lawyer, was born at 9 Langton Place, Vassall Road, Kennington, London, on 11 May 1857 and was the sixth and youngest child, and second son, of Mihill Slaughter (*d.* 1880), the secretary of the railways' department of the stock exchange, and his wife, Ann Erskine, *née* Capel. Little is known about the kind of education the Slaughter children received; the biographical notes that survive suggest that he was educated privately, a euphemism of the period suggesting education at home by a governess or tutor. He did not attend university and his legal training, common at the time, was a five-year period as an articled clerk to a solicitor. Slaughter was articled to the firm of Benjamin Gay

Wilkinson and George Bernard Harvey Drew in Bermondsey Street. Although he learned the fundamentals of law with this firm, it did no commercial work, and Slaughter's first professional exposure to the field of work in which he would make his name occurred in 1879 when he joined the leading firm of solicitors Ashurst Morris Crisp & Co. Here John Morris, a highly respected commercial lawyer, became his mentor.

In 1880 Slaughter's father died and he left £40,000 to be divided among his children, his wife having predeceased him. This gave him a degree of financial security, and together with his legal work enabled him to marry, on 22 September 1881, Ida Mabel (1855/6–1889), daughter of Loraine Wearer, a surgeon. The couple produced four children between 1882 and 1887, two sons and two daughters, although one daughter died of meningitis aged eighteen months. Shortly after his marriage Slaughter was made a freeman of the Clothworkers' Company.

In 1887 Slaughter left Ashurst Morris Crisp to set up his own practice. By an agreement with Morris, Slaughter continued to handle the affairs of some of his clients as agent of Ashurst Morris Crisp but the rest Slaughter was able to keep as his own. It appears that in addition Slaughter had clients who were unrelated to his work for the firm, but acquired mainly through family connections. It was also at this time that Slaughter began his connection with William May, who had also undertaken his articles at Ashurst Morris Crisp. By the end of 1888 they had decided to go into partnership together. On 1 January 1889 they opened a joint bank account and the legal firm of Slaughter and May was established. Shortly afterwards Slaughter's wife Ida died, leaving him with three small children, but his sister Mary stepped in to look after the children and the household, allowing Slaughter to concentrate on his legal practice. On 9 December 1899 he married his second wife, Hester Mary (b. 1867/8), daughter of William Duff Bruce, a civil engineer and vice-chairman of the port of Calcutta; they had one son.

Slaughter's pre-eminence in the legal world arose through his legal knowledge and practical experience of finance and commerce. It was said that there was no man in the City whose advice was valued more on any complicated question of law and finance: 'Ten minutes' consultation with him was worth more than an hour with most men. His brain worked with extraordinary rapidity, and with a fine sense of proportion' (The Times, 13 March 1917). His experience of business was vast, typified by his long connection with the Home and Colonial Stores (a highly successful chain of low-cost but good-quality food retailers), whose founding partner, Julius Charles Drew (formerly Drewe) was his sister's brother-in-law. Slaughter became chairman of Home and Colonial Stores in 1888 and remained so until his death in 1917. He reconstructed the company in 1893 so as to facilitate its expansion, and in 1895 the company was reconstituted again, this time with a capital of £100,000. Although a managing director was appointed in 1899, Slaughter continued his detailed involvement with the company, remaining its primary negotiator with suppliers.

Slaughter's high profile and reputation as a businessman prompted his appointment to the royal commission on sugar supplies, established in August 1914 under the chairmanship of Reginald McKenna. The commission had a mandate to 'purchase, sell, and control the delivery of sugar on behalf of the government', and it was one of the first examples of central control over food resources, a matter which became more prevalent as the war progressed. Slaughter gave 'arduous assistance' to the commission and other government departments, especially the Board of Trade, and was rewarded by the king with a knighthood in the birthday honours list of 1915.

Slaughter appears to have had few interests outside law and business. He founded Kingsgate Golf Club on the Kent coast in the first decade of the twentieth century but it is not known whether he played, although the Sir William Capel Slaughter cup was played for at the club for many years after his death.

Slaughter had always made great demands upon himself and by the middle of the war these were beginning to take their toll. He had suffered bouts of illness since the 1890s, not surprisingly, given that a contemporary described him as working 'unremittingly, allowing no rest by night or day' (Dennett, 145). The end, however, was brought about by cancer: in 1916 he was diagnosed as suffering from cancer of the prostate, and was very ill by Christmas. He died on 10 March 1917 at his London home, 3 Berkeley House, Hay Hill, Mayfair, after a stroke had sent him into a coma, and was buried at Kensal Green cemetery. His wife survived him.

Slaughter was typical of the breed of Victorian solicitors familiar with business yet determined to create and maintain professional respect for the solicitors' profession. Many such solicitors fell victim to the recession of the late 1890s, but those that survived did so with an enhanced professional reputation. At the time of his death, Slaughter and May was established as one of the leading commercial firms, a position that it has retained up to the present day and for which it owes much to its original founder.

MARK LUNNEY

Sources L. Dennett, *Slaughter and May: a century in the city* (1989) · *The Times* (11 March 1917) · *The Times* (13 March 1917) · *Solicitors' Journal*, 61 (17 March 1917), 342–3 · *DBB* · b. cert. · m. certs. · d. cert. · *CGPLA Eng. & Wales* (1917)
Archives Bodl. Oxf., corresp. with Sir Henry Burdett
Likenesses portraits, c.1911, repro. in Dennett, *Slaughter and May*, 114, 144
Wealth at death £99,443 1s. 8d.: administration (will limited), 23 March 1917, *CGPLA Eng. & Wales*

Slazenger, Ralph [*formerly* Ralph Slazenger Moss] (1845–1910), manufacturer of sporting goods, was born Ralph Slazenger Moss at Lymm, Cheshire, the oldest of the twelve children of Joseph Slazenger Moss (1810–1872), a tailor with shops in Warrington and Lancashire, and his wife, Eliza Lazarus. Both were prominent members of the Jewish community in the Manchester area.

Moss was educated at Manchester grammar school until 1859, when he entered his father's business as an apprentice. By the time of his father's death in 1872 the business

Ralph Slazenger (1845–1910), by John Henry Frederick Bacon, 1910

had expanded considerably, with four shops of general outfitters. Together with his brothers Isaac (1857–1940) and Albert (b. 1856), he fostered further expansion, importing goods from abroad and establishing factories in both Manchester and Paris. During this period he claimed to have spent thirty years as a volunteer in the Lancashire light horse, as a keen proponent of national defence.

With an eye on wider markets, Moss left the northern business in the hands of his brothers and moved to London in 1885, starting a new business at 56 Cannon Street, manufacturing indiarubber goods for the growing enthusiasm for middle-class sports. This was more than just a commercial move to exploit new markets; it represented a significant break with his regional and religious roots as he renounced Judaism and shortened his surname officially to Slazenger. One great boost to his personal life, and his business, came with his marriage in 1890 to a wealthy widow, Jane Stokes (d. 1912?), of Hawkes Bay, New Zealand. There were no children but the marriage had other fruits.

Slazenger's business grew rapidly from this time onwards, not least because he became a leading manufacturer of balls and other equipment for the booming late-Victorian middle-class games of golf and lawn tennis. The latter was the focus of a sharp commercial struggle for the publicity which came from providing balls for the All England Lawn Tennis Club's annual Wimbledon tournaments and its ancillary events, such as the tournament at Eastbourne. Slazenger's involvement in this was in large part due to the acumen and rather sharp practices of his manager, Archdale Palmer, who dragged the firm into a scandal amid allegations of attempted bribery at Wimbledon in 1905. This did not, however, harm the firm's reputation or growth and Palmer continued to work for Slazengers. Having moved largely from manual to machine production, Slazenger floated his business on the stock exchange in 1910, increasing profits by fifty per cent, to almost £50,000 per annum, by 1913. Other brothers became involved in the firm, Horatio (1859–1946) as a director and Frank (b. 1860) as the manager of their New York agency.

As his prosperity grew Ralph Slazenger became heavily involved in the corporate life of the City of London, becoming a member of the Spectacle-makers', Shipwrights', Gardeners', Fruiterers', Loriners', and Makers of Playing Cards' livery companies, as well as master of the Needlemakers'. This brought social recognition, the freedom of the City of London, and election to the common council of the City for Dowgate ward in May 1903. In 1909 he was appointed sheriff of London but he was defeated in an election for alderman. Because of his public role in entertaining foreign dignitaries he was honoured by the king of Portugal and by the king of the Belgians, who made him an officer of the order of the Crown in August 1910. His public life extended to visible philanthropy, as a governor of Christ's Hospital and of the Royal School for Deaf Children at Margate; he was also a keen supporter of the Royal Orthopaedic Hospital, where he endowed a children's bed in his own name, a common seeking after immortality for people of similar status. Like many of the affluent middle classes whose leisure he serviced, he was an avid sportsman, a cricketer, golfer, and shot; he also became a member of the Royal Automobile Club.

Slazenger died at his Kensington home, 9 Kensington Court, on 24 October 1910 from bronchitis and influenza; his wish for a non-religious cremation was ignored by his wife who arranged an Anglican service. He was cremated at Putney Vale crematorium on 27 October. At the time of his death the firm that he had founded was one of the most significant sporting goods businesses in Britain.

J. R. LOWERSON

Sources C. Dean, 'Slazenger, Moss and Dean', typescript, Dunlop Slazenger International Ltd, Leatherhead, Surrey · *The Times* (25 Oct 1910) · *Truth* (30 Nov 1905) · *Truth* (14 Dec 1905) · *Truth* (21 Dec 1905) · *Truth* (15 Feb 1906) · *Truth* (22 Feb 1906) · J. Lowerson, *Sport and the English middle classes, 1870–1914* (1993) · private information (2004)

Likenesses J. H. F. Bacon, oils, 1910, unknown collection; copyprint, NPG [*see illus.*]

Wealth at death £56,137 15s. 8d.: probate, 1 Feb 1911, *CGPLA Eng. & Wales*

Sleath, John (1767?–1847), headmaster, son of William and Millicent Sleath, was born probably at Osgathorpe, Leicestershire, where he was baptized on 19 June 1767. He entered Rugby School in 1776, his parents being then described as of Leighton, near Kimbolton, Bedfordshire. In 1784 he went up as a Rugby exhibitioner to Lincoln College, Oxford, but in 1785 was elected to a scholarship at Wadham. He was Hody exhibitioner in 1786–7, and in 1787, before taking his degree, was appointed to an assistant mastership at Rugby. Among his pupils there was Walter Savage Landor, who writes with affectionate remembrance of 'the elegant and generous Doctor John Sleath at Rugby' (*Works and Life of Walter Savage Landor*, ed. J. Forster, 1876, 4.400n.). He was known as a kindly master of the lowest form, comprising boys aged between six and nine. He graduated BA in 1789, MA in 1793, and BD and DD in 1814. He was elected FSA on 9 March 1815, and FRS on 23 March 1820. Having been ordained some time after 1790, he served curacies in West Hadden and other villages around Rugby. From 1799 he had sole charge of the parish of Rugby, the incumbent being non-resident.

On 16 June 1814 Sleath was appointed high master of St Paul's School, and held the office until 10 October 1837. The honours gained at the universities by his pupils from the school were remarkable. Benjamin Jowett, master of Balliol College, Oxford, was one of his scholars, and he could claim nine fellows of Trinity College, Cambridge. In June 1816 he gave evidence on the state of the school to Brougham's select committee on education. Sleath was an imposing figure and carried a natural authority, but his attempts to broaden the curriculum were obstructed by the Mercers' Company, the governing body of the school, who also enforced the rule (to which Sleath objected), that the high master should submit to annual re-election.

Sleath's position at St Paul's brought him to the notice of successive bishops of London. He was made prebendary of Rugmere in St Paul's Cathedral, on 5 July 1822; chaplain-in-ordinary to the king in 1825; subdean of the Chapel Royal, St James's, on 28 June 1833. He became rector of Thornby, Northamptonshire, in 1841, after his retirement from St Paul's. He was married, and his wife predeceased him. Sleath died at his London home in Hertford Street, Hyde Park, on 30 April 1847, and was buried in the crypt of St Paul's Cathedral. He left no family. His elder brother, William Boultbee Sleath (*c*.1762–1843), educated at Rugby and Emmanuel College, Cambridge, was headmaster of Repton School from 1800 to 1832, and like John Sleath produced a number of distinguished pupils.

J. H. LUPTON, *rev.* M. C. CURTHOYS

Sources GM, 2nd ser., 28 (1847), 212–13 · GM, 2nd ser., 19 (1843), 92–3 · E. Abbott and L. Campbell, *The life and letters of Benjamin Jowett*, 2 vols. (1897) · [F. Temple], ed., *Rugby School register from 1675 to 1867 inclusive* (1867) · R. B. Gardiner, ed., *The registers of Wadham College, Oxford*, 2 vols. (1889–95) · M. F. J. McDonnell, *A history of St Paul's School* (1909) · A. H. Mead, *A miraculous draught of fishes: a history of St Paul's School* (1990)

Likenesses I. W. Salter, lithograph, pubd 1834 (after J. Slater), BM, NPG · W. Behnes, marble bust, 1841 · portrait (discovered in 1893)

Wealth at death £12,000: GM (1847), 213

Sleeman, Sir William Henry (1788–1856), army officer in the East India Company and administrator in India, born at Stratton, Cornwall, on 18 August 1788, was the son of Captain Philip Sleeman (*d*. 1798) of Pool Park, St Tudy, Cornwall, yeoman and supervisor of excise, and his wife, Mary Spry (*d*. 1818). In 1809 he was nominated to an infantry cadetship in the Bengal army, and went to India in the same year; he was gazetted ensign on 24 September 1810, and lieutenant on 16 December 1814. He served in the Anglo-Nepal War (1814–16), when his regiment, the 12th Bengal infantry, lost five British officers by jungle fever, and he himself suffered severely from it. In 1820 he was appointed junior assistant to the governor-general's agent in the Saugor and Nerbudda territories. He did not return to military duties, being thenceforth employed in civil and political posts, retaining, however, in accordance with the regulations, his right to military promotion. He was gazetted captain on 23 September 1825, major on 1 February 1837, lieutenant-colonel on 26 May 1843, colonel on 5 December 1853, and major-general on 28 November 1854.

Between 1825 and 1835 he served as magistrate and district officer in various parts of what became the Central Provinces (later Madhya Pradesh). On being posted to the Jubbulpore district in 1828, he issued a proclamation forbidding aiding or abetting suttee, but hardly twelve months later a Brahman widow was burnt alive in his presence, and with his reluctant assent, given when it became evident that the woman would otherwise starve herself to death. In 1831 he was transferred to Saugor where, two years later, he showed his firmness during a time of scarcity, refusing, though urged to do so by the military authorities, to limit the market price of grain. In 1827 he had introduced the cultivation of the Otaheite sugar cane in India.

Sleeman married, on 21 June 1829, Amélie Josephine (*d*. 1883), daughter of Count Blondin de Fontenne, a French nobleman who owned estates in Mauritius; and they had a son, Henry Arthur, born on 6 January 1833 (cornet 16th light dragoons, January 1851), and three daughters. She used to accompany her husband on his journeys in pursuit of thugs.

Sleeman's most memorable achievement was the extirpation of thuggee. The thugs were professional hereditary murderers who worshipped the Hindu goddess Kali and preyed in organized bands on innocent travellers. Thug can be translated as 'deceiver', and the bands' operations were shrouded in secrecy. Thugs were also known as phransigars (stranglers) from their practice of strangling their victims with a noose of twisted yellow or white silk knotted in one corner with a silver coin dedicated to Kali. After death the body was hastily buried after being cut and disfigured to expedite its decomposition. A sacred pickaxe dedicated to Kali was used to dig the grave (in shape it resembled the entrenching tool used by the British army in the First World War).

At first Sleeman received little support in his anti-thuggee campaign, but this changed in 1835 when Lord William Bentinck became governor-general. He made

Sir William Henry Sleeman (1788–1856), by George Duncan Beechey

Sleeman head of a commission for the suppression of thuggee and dacoity (1839–42). During the next two years Sleeman investigated and repressed criminal organizations in upper India. Between 1826 and 1840 more than 14,000 thugs were hanged, transported, or imprisoned for life. Much depended on Sleeman's painstaking collection of evidence regarding thuggee, which included both Hindus and Muslims. Those who were taken and who agreed to talk were known as 'approvers'. They were segregated in confinement in Jubbulpore, where they and their families were taught trades. Sleeman published *Ramaseeana* (1836) on the thugs, their language, and the measures against them.

By 1848 thuggee had virtually ceased. J. W. Kaye stated the contemporary British view: 'The extirpation of Thuggee is an exploit worthy to be celebrated by every writer who seeks to chronicle the achievements of the English in the East' (*History of the Administration of the East India Company*, 1853). One man confessed to having committed more than 700 murders, and his revelations were the basis of Meadows Taylor's *Confessions of a Thug* (1839).

In 1841 Sleeman was offered the post of resident at Lucknow, but he refused to accept this lucrative appointment so that it might be retained by an officer who, as he heard, had been impoverished through the failure of a bank. In 1842 he was sent into Bundelkhand to inquire into the disturbances there, and from 1843 to 1849 he was political resident in Gwalior. Three years after the defeat of the Gwalior troops by a British force at Maharajpur he was able to report that the measures initiated by Lord Ellenborough for the maintenance of British influence in

Sindhia's territory had proved successful. The turbulent aristocracy had been brought under subjection, and the people, delivered from lawless violence, were able to live without fear of robbery or murder. On the residency at Lucknow again becoming vacant, Lord Dalhousie offered it to Sleeman (16 September 1848), who now accepted it. The reports he submitted during a three-month tour in 1849–50 largely influenced Dalhousie in his resolve to annex the kingdom, though this was contrary to the advice of the resident, who believed that reforms were possible under indigenous rule. In December 1851 an attempt was made to assassinate Sleeman. In 1854 he was compelled by ill health to leave for the hills, but the change failed to restore him, and he was ordered home. He died on 10 February 1856 on board the *Monarch*, off Ceylon, on his way to England. He was buried at sea the same day. On Dalhousie's recommendation Sleeman was made a KCB (civil), four days before his death. His wife survived him.   STEPHEN WHEELER, *rev.* JAMES LUNT

Sources W. Sleeman, *Ramaseeana* (1836) · W. Sleeman, *Report on the thug gangs* (1840) · W. Sleeman, *A journey through the kingdom of Oude* (1858) · F. Tuker, *The yellow scarf* (1961) · G. Bruce, *The stranglers* (1968) · E. Eden, *Up the country*, ed. E. Thompson, [new edn] (1937) · J. L. Sleeman, *Thug: a million murders* (1933) · M. Taylor, *Confessions of a thug*, 3 vols. (1839) · Boase, *Mod. Eng. biog.* · S. Wolpert, *A new history of India* (1993) · J. M. Brown, *Modern India: the origins of an Asian democracy*, 2nd edn (1994)

Archives University of Minnesota, Minneapolis, Ames Library of South Asia, papers relating to suppression of thuggee | PRO, letters to Lord Ellenborough, PRO 30/12

Likenesses G. D. Beechey, oils, priv. coll. [*see illus.*]

Sléibíne mac Congaile (d. 767). *See under* Iona, abbots of (*act.* 563–927).

Sleigh, William Campbell (1818–1887), serjeant-at-law, was born in Dublin, the eldest son of William Willcocks Sleigh MD of Bull House, Buckinghamshire, and subsequently of Dublin. He matriculated from St Mary Hall, Oxford, on 9 February 1843, but took no degree. This is perhaps unsurprising as he had already become a student of the Middle Temple on 18 January 1843. On 30 January 1846 he was called to the bar. He practised in London, attending the central criminal court and the London, Middlesex, and Kent sessions. Between 1850 and 1860 he published several legal texts. On 2 November 1868 he was created a serjeant-at-law, being the last person not a judge to be received into Serjeants' Inn. He enjoyed a lucrative practice at the Old Bailey, and took part in many leading criminal trials, being an effective cross-examiner. In 1871 he accepted the first brief for the claimant Arthur Orton, alias Roger Tichborne, in his civil action. He was long retained as leading counsel to the Bank of England, with Hardinge Giffard as his junior. He stood unsuccessfully as a Conservative candidate for parliament in Lambeth on 5 May 1862, Huddersfield on 20 March 1868, Frome on 17 November 1868, and Newark on 1 April 1870. In 1877 he emigrated to Australia, and on 21 March of that year was called to bar of Victoria; but his claim to precedence as a serjeant-at-law was not allowed. He continued to practise in Melbourne until 1886, when he returned to England. He died at Ventnor, Isle of Wight, on 23 January 1887.

G. C. Boase, rev. Eric Metcalfe

Sources Venn, *Alum. Cant.* · *Law Times* (12 Feb 1887), 274 · Serjeant Robinson [B. C. Robinson], *Bench and bar: reminiscences of one of the last of an ancient race*, 2nd edn (1889), 112, 298 · private information (1897)
Likenesses R. T., wood-engraving, NPG; repro. in *ILN* (5 Feb 1887)

Slesser [*formerly* Schloesser], **Sir Henry Herman** (1883–1979), judge and politician, was born on 12 July 1883 at 29 Hamilton Terrace, St John's Wood, London, the second son of Ernest Theodore Schloesser (1837?–1929), leather merchant, and his wife, Anna Gella Schloesser (*née* Seligmann), concert pianist. His parents evidently intended him to receive the education then conventional for children of the prosperous middle class and Schloesser (as he was until he changed his name by deed poll on the outbreak of the 1914–18 war) entered Oundle School in April 1896. But after only two terms he transferred to St Paul's School; and some two years later, aged sixteen, entered the City and Guilds Central Technical College, South Kensington. At eighteen he became a pupil of the chief mechanical engineer of the London and North Western Railway at Crewe. This experience gave him some understanding of the realities of life for industrial workers, but brought about a complete breakdown in his health, always delicate. He wrote that for the next three years he had no occupation except to visit doctors in Harley Street; but in 1903 he took the decisive step of entering the Inner Temple, and was called to the bar in 1906. The solitary, nervous, and mildly obsessive young man lacked any of the obvious characteristics of the successful advocate but undertook the customary pupillage with Robert Colam. It was Slesser's decision (taken on the advice of the journalist and historian R. C. K. Ensor) to join the Fabian Society which proved decisive in setting the direction of his future career.

Slesser's enthusiastic involvement in Fabian activities brought him into contact with many significant figures in the left-wing politics of the day. His legal skills were publicly demonstrated by his work in drafting a fifty-page Prevention of Destitution Bill—the subject of an important parliamentary debate in 1910—intended to give effect to the minority report of the 1906 royal commission on the Poor Law. In 1912 he was appointed standing counsel to the Labour Party. Although he believed that many solicitors refused to instruct him because of his known political sympathies, he nevertheless built up a significant practice (especially in cases involving trade unions and their members) from chambers at 11 King's Bench Walk.

On 24 December 1910 Slesser married Margaret Grant (1887/8–1979) whom he had met at Fabian Society events; she was the daughter of Corrie Grant KC, a Liberal MP. Slesser had been brought up in a cosmopolitan musical and literary environment, and the Slessers' home at Bourne End, Berkshire, became the scene of convivial hospitality for the liberal intelligentsia of the day. For a

period in 1920 and 1921 it was the base for the artist Stanley Spencer (who made Slesser a figure in several of his paintings).

Slesser volunteered for military service in 1914, but his cardiac condition inevitably led to his being rejected. Throughout the war he was active in advising the War Emergency Workers' National Committee on the effects on the working class of legislation—often hurriedly enacted—dealing with housing, pensions, and conscription; and he frequently appeared for the defence of munitions workers prosecuted under the Munitions of War Acts (1915–17). But he had become increasingly sceptical about aspects of the socialist policies then advocated by the Labour Party, preferring to draw on his Anglo-Catholic faith as the main inspiration of social policy.

Slesser stood for parliament as Labour candidate for Central Leeds at the general election of November 1922 and put what he described as the principles of medieval economics, distributive and social justice, guilds, the condemnation of usury and avarice, and the just price in the forefront of his campaign. He attributed his defeat in part to the uneasiness caused to the 'secularist and Hebrew' elements in the constituency by the presence among his supporters of monks from the Community of the Resurrection at Mirfield (Slesser, 88). He was equally unsuccessful in a by-election in summer 1923, and at the general election of 1923.

Had Slesser been elected, his standing in a Parliamentary Labour Party not over-supplied with prominent lawyers would have made him an obvious choice as attorney-general in the first Labour government (1924), notwithstanding the fact that his application for silk had been rejected in 1922. As it was, Patrick Hastings KC not only had a more plausible claim to be treated as the leader of the bar but held a Commons seat, which was at the time regarded as a prerequisite for the office. Slesser was sworn in as solicitor-general on 24 January 1924, having been appointed king's counsel some days previously. He received a knighthood. Throughout the MacDonald administration's short period in office he was active behind the scenes. He served as a member of the home affairs committee and chaired the cabinet committee which successfully formulated an acceptable compromise (in the event brought forward by the Conservative administration in 1925) of the demands of women's groups for equal rights in relation to the upbringing of children and other similar matters.

Slesser was not directly involved in the controversial decisions taken about the prosecution of J. R. Campbell under the Incitement to Mutiny Act of 1797 in respect of articles published in the communist *Workers' Weekly* but he strongly and in public defended what had been done; and Hastings was to record in his autobiography the outstanding debt of gratitude he owed to Slesser for his help. On 8 October 1924 the government was defeated on a vote censuring its conduct of the case.

In the ensuing general election Slesser was returned for the safe Labour seat of Leeds South East and for several years was a prominent critic of the incoming Conservative administration. Slesser (who had, jointly with C. Baker, written the authoritative text *Trade Union Law*) deplored the unions' decision to call a general strike in 1926 but he vigorously and skilfully attacked the view that such a strike was illegal. His encyclopaedic knowledge and experience in this field enabled him to score many points in debate and secure some concessions from the Baldwin government over the provisions of its Trade Disputes and Trade Unions Act of 1927. The reputation of this quick-speaking, 'pallid, dark, bespectacled figure' for 'industrious, pertinacious disputation' (*Morning Post*; Slesser, 230) rose considerably among informed MPs and commentators; but Slesser remained something of a lone and unhappy figure in the Parliamentary Labour Party. His forceful expression of strongly conservative views on social issues such as birth control and the law governing marriage and divorce did not make for popularity with the rank and file, while his frequent references to his Anglo-Catholic beliefs seem to have irritated Ramsay MacDonald, among others.

In June 1929 Lord Justice Sankey was made lord chancellor in MacDonald's second administration; and MacDonald immediately offered Slesser the vacant place in the Court of Appeal. Slesser's appointment as a lord justice (which could certainly have been justified on the basis of his demonstrated ability and learning and reinforced by precedents apparently entitling former law officers to special consideration as candidates for high judicial office) was widely criticized in the profession.

Slesser became intensely sensitive to the suggestion that he owed his office to political considerations; and in 1934 he took strong offence at an apparently innocent provision in a Law Reform (Miscellaneous Provisions) Bill which would have allowed the appointment of a vice-president of the Court of Appeal. Slesser believed this to be an attempt by Lord Hanworth, then master of the rolls, to deprive him of the seniority which was his due. Lord Chief Justice Hewart used the episode as the occasion for an outspoken and bitter public attack not only on bureaucrats in general but on the lord chancellor's permanent secretary, Sir Claud Schuster, in particular. The episode did not enhance the standing of any of those involved.

More than a hundred of Slesser's judgments are to be found in the law reports. The most erudite of these, *Re Carroll (No. 2)*, holding that the Guardianship of Infants Act of 1925 did not affect the rights of a parent to determine his child's upbringing, was overruled forty years later by a House of Lords apparently unimpressed by Slesser's invocation of the views of St Thomas Aquinas and unaware of Slesser's involvement in settling the policy of the 1925 act. The record shows him to have been conscientious and never less than competent as both a first instance and an appeal judge.

In 1940 Slesser retired from judicial office on the ground of ill health, but he continued to write prolifically on legal, political, and religious topics. He was also active in public life, serving for more than twenty years as a county councillor, as chairman of the Dartmoor National Park Committee, and as an active member of the council of the University College of the South-West at Exeter. The man whose frail health had been a concern since infancy died aged ninety-six at his home, Holcombe House, Moretonhampstead, Devon, on 3 December 1979. He had been received into the Roman Catholic church in 1946.

S. M. CRETNEY

Sources H. Slesser, *Judgment reserved* (1941) · J. S. Peart-Binns and J. Saville, 'Slesser, Sir Henry Herman', *DLB*, vol. 9 · R. F. V. Heuston, *Lives of the lord chancellors, 1885–1940* (1964) · *The Times* (5 Dec 1979) · *WWW, 1971–80* · *Hansard 5C* (1925–30) · A. W. B. Simpson, ed., *Biographical dictionary of the common law* (1984) · *The autobiography of Sir Patrick Hastings* (1948) · J. L. J. Edwards, *The attorney-general, politics and the public interest* (1984) · J. Johnston, *A hundred commoners* (1931) · R. Lyman, *The first labour government, 1924* (1957) · S. M. Cretney, *Law, law reform and the family* (1998) · law reports, 1929–40 · H. Slesser and C. Baker, *Trade union law*, 1st edn (1921); 2nd edn (1926); 3rd edn (1927) · b. cert. · d. cert. · P. White, 'Purposeful art in a climate of cultural reaction: Stanley Spencer in the 1920s', *Stanley Spencer*, ed. T. Hyman and P. White (2001)
Archives Labour History Archive and Study Centre, corresp. and papers relating to Labour Party | PRO, corresp. with Ramsay MacDonald, PRO 30/69/1/206 · U. Sussex, letters to Maurice Reckitt
Likenesses S. Spencer, portrait, 1920–21 · W. Dring, portrait, repro. in Slesser, *Judgment reserved* · portraits, repro. in Slesser, *Judgment reserved*
Wealth at death £62,569: probate, 22 Feb 1980, *CGPLA Eng. & Wales*

Slessor, Sir John Cotesworth (1897–1979), air force officer, was born at Ranikhet in India on 3 June 1897, the eldest in the family of three sons and one daughter of Major Arthur Kerr Slessor (1863–1931), of the Sherwood Foresters and later steward of Christ Church, Oxford, and his wife, Adelaide Cotesworth. He was educated at Haileybury College, where he later claimed to have been 'rather an idle boy with a capacity for making friends and getting a good deal of fun out of life, but with a marked distaste for hard work' (*Central Blue*, 2). An attack of poliomyelitis as a child left him lame in both legs, and an army medical board in 1914 rejected him as 'totally unfit for any form of military service'. But a family friend responsible for selecting officers for the Royal Flying Corps enabled him to circumvent regulations. He was commissioned on his eighteenth birthday, and four months later was seeking vainly to engage a Zeppelin night raider over central London.

Posted to 17 squadron in the Middle East, Slessor spent some months bombing and strafing Turks in the Sinai and rebels in the Sudan until in the spring of 1916 he was sent home to England with a wound in the thigh and the MC. After a tour as an instructor at Northolt, he went to France in May 1917 as a flight commander in 5 squadron, with which he served until June 1918. He returned to England to lead a squadron at the Central Flying School, Upavon, of which he briefly took command in September. The armistice reduced him to his substantive rank of flight lieutenant in the new Royal Air Force. Following a bitter quarrel with a senior officer, Slessor became sufficiently disenchanted with service life to request demobilization. But, after just two months as a civilian, early in 1920 he accepted a short-service commission and in the spring of 1921 went to India as a flight commander in 20

Sir John Cotesworth Slessor (1897–1979), by Yousuf Karsh, pubd 1956

squadron, flying Bristol fighters. He then served briefly on the air headquarters staff before attending the third course at the new RAF Staff College at Andover. In 1923 he married Hermione Grace (d. 1970), the daughter of Gerald Seymour Guinness, a merchant banker, and the widow of Lieutenant-Colonel Herbert Francis George Carter; they had one son and one daughter. From 1925 to 1928 Slessor commanded 4 (army co-operation) squadron at Farnborough, and in 1928 he was posted to the plans branch of the Air Ministry's directorate of operations and intelligence, where he remained until 1931.

This was the decisive period in Slessor's formative years. He was already marked as an officer of exceptional ability, charm, and force of personality. But his thinking and most of his experience had centred upon the role of aircraft in direct support of ground forces. In his years at the Air Ministry he now became one of the most passionate disciples of Lord Trenchard and his theories of strategic air power as a war-winning weapon. Slessor was one of that select group of officers which included C. F. A. Portal (later Viscount Portal of Hungerford) and Ralph Cochrane, who were clearly destined for the highest ranks of the air force. In the years that followed he served a second tour of duty in India, where he almost died in the Quetta earthquake and won a DSO commanding a wing in the Waziristan operations. But he achieved greater distinction for his lecturing as an instructor at the Army Staff College, Camberley, for his authorship of the RAF manual on army co-operation, and for his book *Air Power and Armies*, published in 1936. The book reflected the belief not only of

Slessor, but of his generation of senior airmen, in the moral impact of air attack upon civilian populations. He wrote:

> In air operations against production, the weight of attack will inevitably fall upon a vitally important, and not by nature very amenable, section of the community—the industrial workers, whose morale and sticking power cannot be expected to equal that of the disciplined soldier. And we should remember that if the moral effect of air bombardment was serious seventeen years ago, it will be immensely more so under modern conditions. (*Air Power and Armies*, 65)

Here was the core of the strategic theory which would lie at the heart of the British bomber offensive against Germany, and of which Slessor was among the most articulate proponents.

From 1937 to 1940 Slessor held the critical post of director of plans at the Air Ministry. It must be said that in this role he shared his colleagues' delusions about the power of bombers to influence the course of the war even when these were few in number, and were wholly inadequately trained and equipped to carry out the tasks to which the RAF war plans committed them. In a memorandum to the chief of air staff four days after the outbreak of war, Slessor urged an all-out bomber attack on the Germans:

> Although our numerical inferiority in the air is a most important factor, it should not be allowed to obscure other potent considerations. We are now at war with a nation which possesses an impressive façade of armed might, but which, behind that façade, is politically rotten, weak in financial and economic resources, and already heavily engaged on another front [Poland]. The lessons of history prove that victory does not always go to the big battalions. At present we have the initiative. If we seize it now we may gain important results; if we lose it by waiting we shall probably lose more than we gain.

In the two years that followed, the RAF painfully discovered that the difficulties of implementing Trenchard's doctrine were caused not merely by the limits on resources imposed by pre-war politicians, but also by the failure of the service to match its skills and training to the ends it sought to achieve. Slessor must share responsibility with his generation of airmen for the lamentable shortcomings of the RAF in close support of ground and naval forces and low-level bombing techniques. It is impossible to escape the conclusion that their failure to address themselves to these problems in the same fashion as the pre-war Luftwaffe was influenced by the RAF's determination to find a role in war both more decisive than that of mere flying eyes and artillery for the two older services, and independent of them.

At the end of 1940 Slessor went to the United States to take part in the 'ABC' staff conversations. In April 1941 he returned to take command of 5 group of Bomber Command at perhaps the most frustrating period of the air offensive, when this was the sole means of carrying the war directly to Germany, and yet it had become evident that its impact upon the enemy was very small. In April 1942 he became assistant chief of air staff (policy), and played an important role in the development, alongside the American airmen, of the plans for Operation Point-blank (a combined air offensive against Germany, designed specifically to pave the way for the invasion of north-west Europe, which was approved at the Casablanca conference).

In February 1943 Slessor took on the role for which he is best remembered in the Second World War, as commander-in-chief of Coastal Command. He arrived at Northwood at an exceptionally difficult period in the battle of the Atlantic, when sinkings were running at an alarming level. He controlled some sixty squadrons, of which thirty-four (430 aircraft) were committed to the anti-submarine war. Even with the vital assistance of Ultra decrypts of U-boat wireless traffic, which contributed decisively to the Atlantic victory, Slessor faced immense problems in extending air cover into the mid-ocean gap where convoy losses had been so heavy. He possessed only two squadrons of very long-range Liberators with the ability to operate at these distances, and the business of co-ordinating operations not only with the Admiralty but with the American and Canadian navies and air forces taxed Slessor to the utmost. He proved himself both an able administrator of large forces and a sensitive leader and motivator of his command.

In January 1944, a little to his own disappointment, Slessor was taken from Coastal Command to succeed Sir Arthur Tedder, commanding the RAF in the Mediterranean and Middle East and acting as deputy to General Ira Eaker of the United States Army Air Force, who was commander-in-chief of the allied air forces in that theatre. Slessor shared with Eaker the disappointments and frustrations of the Italian campaign, the complexities of support for Yugoslavia, the vain efforts to supply the Warsaw insurgents. In March 1945 he was brought back to London to serve as air member for personnel, a job in which over the next three years he bore responsibility for the demobilization of the huge wartime air force. He served as commandant of the Imperial Defence College until in January 1950 he succeeded Tedder as chief of air staff. The coming of the atomic bomb had provided an entirely new dimension to air power. Both in office and after his retirement in 1953 Slessor was an impassioned advocate of the need for powerful air forces as a deterrent against war. In his retirement, from his home in Somerset, he continued to produce a succession of essays, lectures, broadcast talks, and articles, and he also wrote a lively autobiography. He served as a director of Blackburn Aircraft and of the English and Scottish Investment Trust, and also as a governor of Haileybury, Sherborne, and Wellington schools.

Slessor stood foremost among the second rank of airmen of the Second World War, behind Portal, Tedder, and Sir Arthur Harris. Sir Maurice Dean, among the most prominent civil servants of Slessor's generation at the Air Ministry, wrote of his 'warmth, knowledge, experience and adaptability'. A devoted countryman, he maintained a lifelong devotion to fishing and shooting. His charm and force of personality won him great affection and respect among his contemporaries, although he never achieved the wider celebrity of the top airmen of the war. He shared with his generation the passionate determination to win a place for the air force alongside the two older services in the councils of national defence. His strategic vision, like theirs, was perhaps narrowed by the years of struggle to bring this about. He was appointed air commodore in 1939, air vice-marshal in 1941, air marshal in 1943, air chief marshal in 1946, and marshal of the Royal Air Force in 1950.

For his services during the war of 1914–18 Slessor was awarded the MC (1916), the Belgian order of Leopold (chevalier), and the Belgian Croix de Guerre. He was appointed to the DSO in 1937, and was created CB (1942), KCB (1943), and GCB (1948). He was a member of the French Légion d'honneur, the Greek order of Phoenix, the Norwegian order of St Olaf, and the Swedish order of the Sword; he also held the American Legion of Merit and the Yugoslav Partisan Star. He received the gold medal of the Royal United Services Institute in 1936 and the Chesney memorial award in 1965. Following the death of his first wife, he married in 1971 Marcella Florence, the widow of Brigadier Robert Thomas Priest of the Royal Artillery, and the daughter of Christopher Edward Spurgeon, an engineer. Slessor died on 12 July 1979 at the Princess Alexandra Hospital, Wroughton, Wiltshire.

MAX HASTINGS, rev.

Sources J. C. Slessor, *The central blue: recollections and reflections* (1956) · J. Slessor, *Air power and armies* (1936) · J. Slessor, *Strategy for the west* (1954) · J. Slessor, *The great deterrent* (1957) · air files, PRO · private information (1986) · *Daily Telegraph* (14 July 1979) · *The Times* (19 Nov 1979) · *CGPLA Eng. & Wales* (1979)
Archives King's Lond., Liddell Hart C., corresp. with Sir B. H. Liddell Hart · PRO, papers, AIR 75 · Royal Air Force Museum, Hendon | FILM BFI NFTVA, record footage · IWM FVA, actuality footage | SOUND BL NSA, oral history interview · IWM SA, 'British air marshal served as pilot with royal flying corps', IWM Air Operations, 8 March 1978, 3176 · IWM SA, oral history interview · IWM SA, recorded talk
Likenesses group portrait, photograph, 1946, Hult. Arch. · Y. Karsh, photograph, repro. in Slessor, *The central blue*, frontispiece [*see illus.*] · C. Orde, oils, Haileybury School, Hertfordshire · C. Orde, portrait, IWM; on loan to Royal College of Defence Studies
Wealth at death £112,379: probate, 2 Aug 1979, *CGPLA Eng. & Wales*

Slessor, Mary Mitchell (1848–1915), missionary, was born on 2 December 1848 in Gilcomston, a suburb of Aberdeen, the second of seven children (four of whom reached adulthood) of Robert Slessor, shoemaker, of Buchan, and his wife, Mary Mitchell (1821–1885), weaver, of Old Meldrum. Robert Slessor's alcoholism lost him his job, and in 1859 the family moved to live at 17 Harriet Street, Dundee, to look for work. Mary, aged eleven, became a weaver in the textile mills and was soon the family's principal breadwinner. She received some education at night school, but was largely self-taught.

Active in the local United Presbyterian church, Mary Slessor became a voluntary teacher at Queen Street mission and followed the activities of the church abroad. Her younger brother John's early death and the missionary fervour aroused by the death of David Livingstone in 1873 spurred her into applying for work further afield. Accepted by the foreign mission board as a teacher in Duke Town, Calabar, Nigeria, in August 1876 she sailed for west Africa after three months' missionary training at Moray House, Edinburgh.

Quickly picking up the local Efik language and immersing herself in work among the women, Mary applied for a remote station where she could live frugally and send more of her annual £60 salary to her family in Scotland. Her move 3 miles up river to Old Town was the first step in a gradual journey into the district of Okoyong and away from the European settlement on the coast. When her mother died on 31 December 1885 and her sister Janie died the following year, Mary's last links with home were broken: 'Heaven is now nearer to me than Britain,' she wrote. Moving still further inland, she dispensed with the trappings of the colonial lifestyle—she drank unboiled water, used no mosquito net, walked barefoot, and even went without the indispensable hat. Visitors commented upon the tiny Scotswoman's sunburnt face and unkempt appearance. When the traveller Mary Kingsley visited her at Ekenge in 1895, she found that: 'Miss Slessor ... has lost most of her missionary ideas and bullies the native chiefs in their own tongue ... and is regarded by the other missionaries as mad and dangerous.' Her insistence on setting up lone stations cut off from the central missionary settlement led her into conflict with the authorities, who often thwarted her persistent applications to go further up-country.

In 1891 Mary Slessor was briefly engaged to Charles Morrison, a Scottish missionary teacher at Duke Town and eighteen years her junior. However, when the mission board refused to allow him to join her in Okoyong, the relationship was broken off. Her family became the twins she adopted, whose lives were in danger through local belief that twin births were the result of a coupling with evil spirits. Anxious about leaving her charges when she visited Britain, she began to take them with her, in 1883 first bringing Atim Eso to Dundee, where the six-month-old baby was christened Janie Slessor.

In 1892 Mary was appointed vice-consul in Okoyong, presiding over the native court; later, in 1905, she became vice-president of the Ikot Obong native court. A natural meddler with an iron will, the role of magistrate suited her well. Even after her resignation she continued to petition the district officer concerning injustices and disputes, particularly on behalf of the women for whose rights she continually campaigned. It is said that no woman lost a case while Mary Slessor was presiding.

A heroine of popular culture in Britain and heralded as 'the White Queen of Okoyong', she was shy of the publicity greeting her infrequent visits to her homeland and only reluctantly agreed to lecture to raise money for and to increase consciousness of pioneer missionary work. Back in Africa, by 1907 rheumatoid arthritis had almost crippled her and she suffered long periods of inactivity. However, she refused either to move to the comfort of Duke Town or to return to Britain. In 1913 she received the order of St John of Jerusalem. She died of fever and dysentery on 13 January 1915 in Calabar, and was buried in the cemetery there.   D. J. BIRKETT, *rev.*

Sources C. Christian and G. Plummer, *God and one redhead: Mary Slessor of Calabar* (1970) · W. P. Livingstone, *Mary Slessor of Calabar: pioneer missionary* (1915)
Archives Dundee Central Library, corresp. · Dundee Museums and Art Galleries, corresp., diaries, and papers · National Archives of Nigeria, Ibadan, papers | Dundee City Archives, letters to Charlotte Crawford
Likenesses photographs, repro. in Christian and Plummer, *God and one redhead*

Slezer, John (*d.* 1717), army officer and topographical draughtsman, came from a German-speaking area of Europe, perhaps the upper Rhineland, but his parentage is unknown. In his early years he may have been attached in a military capacity to the house of Orange. He first visited Scotland in 1669. Through his proficiency as a draughtsman he became acquainted with several of the nobility such as the earls of Kincardine and Argyll, who secured him the office of chief engineer in Scotland, at a salary of £10 per annum, on 8 September 1671, whereupon he returned and settled in Scotland for life. He was appointed lieutenant of the artillery, with responsibility for the practical supervision of the Ordnance, on 4 March 1677. In the same year he married Jean Straiton, who came from a military family. They had at least four children, including three sons. Slezer later described himself as 'a foreigner who had been honoured by the patronage of Charles II and the Duke of York'.

One of Slezer's duties was to survey the defences of Scotland and about 1678 he developed a plan 'to make a book of the figures, and draughts, and frontispiece in Talyduce [*taille-douce*, the French term for copper-plate etching] of all the King's Castles, Pallaces, towns, and other notable places in the kingdom belonging to private subjects'. Slezer's ambition was impressive, similar views had been published previously but none had aimed to depict an entire country. This work was also of interest to Scottish antiquaries as it was to contain 'the History of the king's ... from Fergus the first and also particular accounts of the judicatories and universities of the kingdom' (NL Scot., Adv. MS 29.2.11, fol. 198). Slezer travelled through Scotland making drawings of the houses and monuments of the nobility, which ultimately resulted in the publication of his *Theatrum Scotiae*. On 19 April 1678 he was admitted as a burgess by the corporation of Dundee and prepared two views of the town. About the same time Slezer introduced himself to Patrick Lyon, third earl of Strathmore and Kinghorne, whose seat at Glamis Castle he proposed to sketch. Lord Strathmore received the suggestion with enthusiasm, giving Slezer 'liberall money, because I was loath that he should doe it at his owne charge, and that I knew the cuts and ingravings would stand him money' (*Book of Record*, 42, 150). Slezer served with the army at the battle of Bothwell Bridge on 22 June 1679 and his name appeared on a list of those to whom shares were granted out of forfeited estates. Work on the *Theatrum Scotiae* was interrupted in 1681 when Slezer was sent to the Netherlands on Charles II's orders for the purpose of having new guns cast for Scotland. He was also supposed to bring back with him experienced gunners or 'fireworkers', though no record of the entry of any such people into Scotland survives. Slezer's correspondence with the master of the ordnance, John Drummond of Lundin, brother to the earl of Perth, between March and December 1681, is preserved at Blair Drummond Castle. In one of his letters Slezer expressed the hope that his claim on the Treasury for his expenses during the journey had been paid; 'for I suspect,' he adds, 'my wife will be as scairce of siller as myself'. He was admitted a burgess for Linlithgow in 1682 and Edinburgh in 1684.

Slezer was already captain of the Scottish artillery train by May 1687, when the governor deputy of Glasgow was instructed to obey his orders regarding the placement of his guns. At the time of the revolution of 1688 he was, as commander of the artillery train, ordered to proceed against the supporters of the prince of Orange. He went into England with the rest of the Scottish forces in October 1688, detailing his return march to Edinburgh, via Carlisle, to Lieutenant-General James Douglas on 20 November 1688. In March 1689 he was appointed by the Scottish parliament to 'draw together the canoniers and artillery' (*APS*, 1689–95, 492) but he was forbidden to return to Edinburgh Castle until he had taken the oath of fidelity to the committee of estates. He only took the oath after the Williamite victory at Killicrankie on 27 July 1689. After declaring for William he was able to procure a commission, dated 11 January 1690, from the new regime as 'captain of the Artillery Company and surveyor of Magazines' (Dalton, *Scots Army*, 166 n. 6). Slezer visited the court and received an audience with the king in 1690. His commission was later renewed by Queen Anne in 1702.

Following the conclusion of hostilities Slezer devoted himself to the completion of the *Theatrum Scotiae* for which William III, like Charles II and James VII and II, had expressed admiration. The first volume was published by royal authority in 1693, and contained fifty-seven views of palaces, abbeys, and castles of the Scottish nobility. The accompanying text for this edition, the work of the geographer royal Sir Robert Sibbald, was originally written in Latin but Slezer had it translated into English without Sibbald's agreement and published it without acknowledging him, resulting in a breach between them. Slezer did all in his power to induce the book's purchase by the Scottish nobility by including 'the most remarkable houses belonging to Noblemen and Gentlemen and other notable Buildings with the Coats of Arms Crests and Supporters & Mottos of the Noble and Ancient Families of the Kingdom never heretofor published' (NL Scot., Adv. MS 29.2.11, fol. 198). Though the national importance of the book was recognized, its sale failed to cover the amount expended on production.

In 1694 Slezer was recorded as living in Old Kirk parish, Edinburgh, with his wife and four children. In 1695 he exhibited a specimen of his work to the Scottish parliament, petitioning them to grant him £1000 to aid him in issuing two further volumes, titled *The Ancient and Present State of Scotland*, the sketches for which were then ready. Parliament resorted to a curious expedient in order to find the money required by Slezer. Under the Tonnage Act a special tax of 16*s*. Scots was imposed on Slezer's behalf, conjointly with John Adair, the hydrographer, upon every ton of goods exported in foreign ships from Scotland, and of 4*s*. Scots per ton upon every Scottish ship above 12 tons burden exporting merchandise. This tax was to continue for five years. While the act was in force Slezer received, by his own account, £530 sterling; but when it lapsed in 1698 it was only renewed after serious limitations had been adopted, and under the new arrangements Slezer received little or no money. His military pay had also fallen into arrears, and his pecuniary embarrassments rapidly increased. By 1705 he had taken sanctuary from his creditors in Holyrood, the law allowing him to live there during the week and visit his family on Sundays. He was also able to keep his office of captain of the artillery until 1716 when the army was reorganized. In 1705 he petitioned parliament from Holyrood, stating that he was then £650 sterling out of pocket. In 1708 he declared that he ought to have obtained £1130 from the Tonnage Act, but he 'had never received the value of a single sixpence'. His whole claim then amounted to £2347 sterling, part of this sum being for clothing which he had ordered for his artillerymen, as he could not 'suffer them to go naked'. Slezer died in Holyrood in November 1717. His eldest son, who was a master gunner, had died in 1699, but Slezer's widow and his second son, Charles, pursued the government with their claims, obtaining a final settlement in 1723.

Slezer's lasting achievement was the design and publication of his *Theatrum Scotiae*, which went through seven editions (1693; two in 1718; 1719; 1728–9; 1797; 1814). Many of his unpublished drawings were, after his death, frequently reproduced by others. 'As an artist his talents may have been modest' (Cavers, 103), but his work has proved an invaluable visual record of seventeenth-century Scotland.   A. H. MILLAR, *rev.* M. R. GLOZIER

Sources C. Dalton, 'A list of the artillery company in Scotland at the time of the union and their pay', *Minutes of Proceedings of the Royal Artillery Institution*, 22 (1895), 579–89 • C. Dalton, *The Scots army, 1661–1688*, 2 pts (1909), 43, 44, 166 • *Delices de la Grande Bretagne* (1791) • *The book of record: a diary written by Patrick first earl of Strathmore and other documents relating to Glamis Castle, 1684–9*, ed. A. H. Millar, Scottish History Society, 9 (1890) • *Reports on the manuscripts of the earl of Eglinton*, HMC, 10 (1885), 132–5 • *The manuscripts of the duke of Leeds*, HMC, 22 (1888), 25, 42 • *Report on the manuscripts of the earl of Mar and Kellie*, HMC, 60 (1904), 220 • A. H. Millar, *Roll of eminent burgesses of Dundee* [n.d.], 203 • NL Scot., Adv. MS 29.2.11, fol. 198 • W. Nicolson, *The Scottish historical library* (1702), 27 • J. Slezer, *Theatrum Scotiae*, ed. J. Jamieson (1874) • D. Laing, ed., 'Collection of papers relating to the *Theatrum Scotiae* and *History and present state of Scotland* by Captain John Slezer, 1693–1707', *Bannantyne Miscellany*, 2 (1836), 305–44 • K. Cavers, *A vision of Scotland: the nation observed by John Slezer, 1671–1717* (1993)

Sligger. *See* Urquhart, Francis Fortescue, of Urquhart (1868–1934).

Slim, William Joseph, first Viscount Slim (1891–1970), army officer, was born in Bishopston, near Bristol, on 6 August 1891, the son of John Slim, a hardware merchant, and his wife, Charlotte Tucker. Slim's family moved to Birmingham in 1903, where his father rebuilt a small business after a failure in Bristol. Although Slim had a reasonably comfortable upbringing, during which his ambition for a military career took shape, his family circumstances put a commission out of reach. Slim's education began about 1903, at St Philip's Catholic School, Edgbaston, and continued in 1908 at King Edward's School, Birmingham, where he joined the Officers' Training Corps. He also qualified as a teacher. After leaving school he worked first as an elementary teacher, and then with an engineering firm. He had also managed an attachment to Birmingham University's Officers' Training Corps in 1912. Slim was about to start an overseas job with Shell when the First World War began, opening for him a door that would otherwise have remained closed. In September 1914 he was commissioned in the Royal Warwickshire regiment.

The First World War The next four years were crucial to Slim's professional development. The senior officers of the British army in the Second World War were, as a body, strongly conditioned by their experience of combat on the western front in 1914–18. Slim's experience—like that of Field Marshal Sir Claude Auchinleck—was very different. His battalion of the Royal Warwicks went to Gallipoli, where, in the savage battle for Sari Bair Ridge in August 1915, he fought alongside the 1st battalion, 6th Gurkha rifles, the battalion that would eventually become his army home. He was also wounded so badly that he was fortunate to survive. After convalescence in England (where he arranged a regular commission in the West India regiment) he took a draft of replacements to Mesopotamia. There, technically still unfit for active service, he fought for the next six months, winning a Military Cross and observing an early exercise in the transformation of defeat into victory as Lieutenant-General Sir Stanley Maude rebuilt the battered Mesopotamian expeditionary force and led it to the capture of Baghdad. 'To watch an army recovering its morale is enthralling: to feel the process working within oneself is an unforgettable experience', he wrote later (Slim, *Unofficial History*, 42).

Wounded a second time during the advance north after the fall of Baghdad, Slim was evacuated to India. After recovering, he spent two years on the staff of army headquarters, India, where the armistice found him a temporary major. He transferred again, this time to the Indian army, as a captain, in May 1919. Now a regular officer in a service many of whose officers were from backgrounds similar to his own—and quite different from those of the regular British army—Slim finished his time at army headquarters and was posted to the 1st battalion, 6th Gurkha rifles, in March 1920.

India between the wars Gurkha units were an élite within the Indian army, and the network of Gurkha officers within that service would play an important part in Slim's future. His career during the inter-war years included the

William Joseph Slim, first Viscount Slim (1891–1970), by Elliott & Fry, 1950

standard exposure to frontier warfare, an intense tactical education. This was matched by a thorough professional grounding for higher command, first as a student at the Indian Staff College, Quetta, in 1926, where one of the instructors was Percy Hobart, one of the British army's 'apostles of mobility'. After a posting to army headquarters (where he showed a precocious interest in the possibilities of air supply for ground forces in difficult situations) he became the Indian army member of the directing staff at the British army's Staff College at Camberley (1934–6). Only after a further year at the Imperial Defence College (IDC) in London did Slim return again to regimental soldiering.

Mesopotamia and the north-west frontier had initiated Slim into warfare that was more fluid and mobile than the western front experience. He was also familiar with the arguments over mobility that divided British military opinion during the twenties and thirties, as well as mainstream army doctrine derived from the western front. When he took command of the 2nd battalion, 7th Gurkha rifles, at Shillong in Assam early in 1938, however, it may have seemed unlikely that he would ever have the opportunity to utilize his professional qualities in the sort of senior command that many had confidently predicted for him. He was by then a rather elderly lieutenant-colonel. To support his family—he had married Aileen Robertson on 1 January 1926, and they had had two children—he supplemented his salary by writing fiction and essays under the pen-name Anthony Mills (developing the prose style that would make his memoir, *Defeat into Victory*, a classic of its kind). Battalion command, it seemed, might well be the summit of his career. In 1914 Sarajevo had opened a door for him; Hitler was about to open another. Slim had passed through the senior officers' school at Belgaum prior to taking command at Shillong. In April 1939 he returned as commandant. September 1939 found him there, an acting brigadier. Within a fortnight he was a brigade commander.

The war in the Middle East Slim's career over the next two years reflects the enormous importance of the Indian army to the British war effort in the Middle East. As a brigade commander in 10th Indian division he had his initiation into higher command in a confused engagement at Gallabat on the Sudan–Abyssinian frontier in November 1940. With the humility and candour that characterized him, he wrote of it: 'When two courses of action were open to me, I had not chosen, as a good commander should, the bolder' (Slim, *Unofficial History*, 149). Boldness would never thereafter be lacking. It characterized his handling of 10th Indian division in Iraq and Syria the following year. The occupation of Persia in August 1941, in which Slim commanded an improvised combined arms force and had to deal with both the occupied Persians and Britain's Russian allies, was a useful rehearsal for the responsibilities about to fall upon him. In early March 1942 he was summoned back to India.

Retreat from Burma As the Japanese advance into Burma gathered momentum in February 1942 a new commander was sent out from England to try to hold Rangoon (the entry port for China-bound supplies on the Burma Road). Lieutenant-General Sir Harold Alexander was given a corps commander to handle the two weak divisions that were his field force. Since Alexander himself was a British service officer while his troops were largely Indian and Burmese, an Indian army officer was the obvious choice for 1st Burma corps or 'Burcorps'. Both divisional commanders were from the 6th Gurkhas and urged Slim's selection. In London, Lieutenant-General Sir Archibald Nye, the vice-chief of the Imperial General Staff, who had known Slim at Camberley, supported the suggestion. Events were moving so swiftly that Rangoon had been lost by the time Slim reached Burma. He was in time, however, to conduct the longest withdrawal in British military history, which ended with a skeletal but still functioning Burcorps reaching the safety of the Imphal plain in eastern Assam as the monsoon broke.

Alexander had been in overall command, but the unrelenting burden of extricating Burcorps had fallen largely on Slim. His conduct of the retreat demonstrated the truth of the dictum attributed to the elder Moltke: no one should be considered a great general who has not conducted a difficult withdrawal. Slim also drew conclusions about what the army needed to change, in training and tactics—conclusions that he began to put into practice when he took up his next command, 15th corps, in the summer of 1942. The raw Indian units that made up most of Burcorps had shown more cohesion than anyone had a

right to expect. If the deficiencies caused by over-expansion in 1940–41 could be remedied, there was every prospect of a very different result. The 1942 campaign also indicated that there were weaknesses in the apparently invincible imperial Japanese army that better trained and supported opponents might take advantage of—a carelessness about logistics, a rigidity in executing orders, and, above all, an inflexible commitment to the offensive. Standard Japanese tactics—to infiltrate and outflank opponents, cutting their supply lines and tumbling them into disorganized retreat—had served them well in Malaya and Burma. Against better trained opponents, however, who went into an all-round defence—a defended 'box'—and simply switched their supply line from road to air, this tactical ploy would not only lose its efficacy but could even be turned back against the Japanese. It would take time, however, before these ideas would become a reshaped army, ready to assume the offensive. Slim's role in that great transformation almost ended prematurely.

The first Arakan campaign Perhaps the worst-managed British offensive operation of the war, the first Arakan campaign (in the nearly impenetrable coastal belt of Burma bordering the Bay of Bengal), was born, in the autumn of 1942, more of political necessity and unwarranted optimism than operational possibility. Lieutenant-General N. M. S. Irwin, commanding eastern army, exercised direct command of the single attacking division, feeding it reinforcements until the divisional commander was trying to manage nearly a corps. Irwin ignored Slim and his corps headquarters, which was readily available. When the Japanese counter-attacked in April 1943, precipitating a collapse every bit as bad as anything that happened in Malaya or Burma, Slim was brought in, far too late. He succeeded in stabilizing the front but only by pulling it back further than the army commander wished. Sharply critical of Slim's dispositions, Irwin indicated he would be relieved. However, it was Irwin who was replaced, by General Sir George Giffard, who would strongly support Slim over the next critical fifteen months.

Giffard's arrival was part of an extensive reorganization that was a turning point in both the theatre and Slim's career. Field Marshal Sir Archibald Wavell was replaced as commander-in-chief, India, by General Sir Claude Auchinleck. A new Anglo-American theatre command, southeast Asia command (SEAC), headed by Vice-Admiral Lord Louis Mountbatten, came into being. Giffard took over the newly created Eleventh Army group, while Slim became commander of the principal operational formation, christened Fourteenth Army. He would be insulated by Mountbatten and Giffard from the sort of political pressure that had pushed Wavell into the Arakan campaign. An Indian army officer, he would have as well the good fortune to serve in a theatre where the majority of the formations were Indian and where he knew many of his key subordinates well. He benefited also from the renaissance in the Indian army's fortunes after mid-1943. Auchinleck, and his new director of infantry, Major-General Reginald

Savory, began to address the shortcomings in training and support that Slim had identified a year earlier. The way was at last clear for Slim to put into practice his own approach to battle.

Americans and Chindits Nothing, however, was ever straightforward in Slim's theatre. Britain was fighting a coalition war, and Slim had, almost immediately, to deal with two manifestations of this: the American Lieutenant-General Joseph W. Stilwell and Major-General Orde Wingate. Stilwell represented the American determination to sustain China by reopening overland communications through Burma. Slim had met him during the 1942 retreat and realized that personal contact was the key to working successfully with him (Slim's accent and manner, unlike those of Wavell or Alexander, did not arouse Stilwell's simmering Anglophobia.) It was fortunate that this was so, since Stilwell refused to accept orders from Giffard (whom he also disdained) but would from Slim, who was considerably his junior in rank. This makeshift, typical of the theatre, fortunately worked well enough.

Wingate, an eccentric military visionary, who inspired some while infuriating others, was a more intractable problem. His first long range penetration ('Chindit') operation in Burma (February–April 1943) had done the Japanese only slight damage but had provided a flash of offensive success in a theatre hitherto totally devoid of it. Churchill, under intense American pressure over Burma, seized on Wingate and his ideas, presenting both to Roosevelt and the American chiefs of staff at Quebec in August 1943. The consequence was that, when Slim took over the Fourteenth Army, Wingate was back in India with both a direct line to Churchill and authority to raise a corps size 'special force' (at the cost of considerable disruption to formations in India). Supported by an American-supplied dedicated air component, special force was to operate deep in the Japanese rear. The intent was to assist the forward movement of not only Slim but, above all, Stilwell. The Japanese, however, had other plans.

Victory at Arakan and Imphal Shortly after Slim took command it became clear (largely through signals intelligence, which played almost as significant a role in Burma as in Europe) that the Japanese were about to launch an offensive against the British base at Imphal, the staging area for any British offensive into Burma. The Japanese planned to strike first in the Arakan, to draw in British reserves. Slim, fighting his first battle as an army commander (and with a force painfully nursed back to health after the disasters of 1942–3), elected to stand on the defensive, absorbing the Japanese assault, breaking it, and then going over to the attack. He was counting on the fighting qualities of his retrained units and air supply, allied to the tactical rigidity of the Japanese and their habitual logistic optimism, to give him the morale-building victory he needed. The Japanese attack in the Arakan, despite the indications from signals intelligence, achieved considerable tactical surprise, but, after some tense moments, Slim's troops accomplished all that was expected of them. Air supply, especially the 'Dakota'—the

military version of the DC3—proved to be the crucial weapon (paradoxically making the Americans even more important to Fourteenth Army since they controlled most of the air transport assets). Victory in the Arakan was the battlefield turning point in Burma. Another general who had turned defeat into victory, Ulysses S. Grant, had commented:

> troops who have fought a few battles and won, and followed up their victories, improve on what they were before to an extent that can hardly be counted by percentage. The difference in result is often decisive victory instead of inglorious defeat. (*Personal Memoirs*, 355)

Like Grant's, Slim's army would henceforth fight with the knowledge that it had the formula for victory.

As the Japanese thrust in the Arakan faltered, Lieutenant-General Mutaguchi Renya's Fifteenth Army launched its main thrust at Imphal. Once again, despite signals intelligence indications, the Japanese managed tactical surprise. Slim later admitted, characteristically, that he had underestimated the speed at which the Japanese would move and waited too long before ordering the divisions of 4th corps, deployed forward of Imphal, to begin their controlled withdrawal to the edge of the Imphal plain, where the Japanese were to be held and beaten. None the less there was no repetition of 1942–3. The forward units fought their way back, supported by tactical airpower and sustained by smoothly functioning air supply. Conducting the widely separated Arakan and Imphal battles, as well as a separate contest at Kohima, where the Japanese had cut the road that linked Imphal to the railhead at Dimapur, presented Slim with the most complex, geographically sprawling battle managed by any British army commander in either world war. Much of the fighting, like that on the north-west frontier, was intense battalion and company action. Slim was fortunate in having at Imphal a corps commander and two division commanders who were all from the tightly knit world of Gurkha units (the 3rd division was commanded by one of his former staff officers from the 10th Indian division). In three months of tense, complex fighting Slim turned the Japanese obsession with the offensive, and their logistic carelessness, against them. Imphal–Kohima became a killing ground on which the Japanese Fifteenth Army died. When Mutaguchi at last retreated 55,000 of his 80,000 men had become casualties.

To the pressures of his vast, complicated battle, Slim had to add concern for both the Chindits and Stilwell. Wingate's second operation had been mounted just as the Japanese opened their Imphal offensive. Slim's decision to stand initially on the defensive removed much of the operational context for Operation Thursday and the Japanese had no western-style supply lines to disrupt in any case. However, the operation was politically imperative. Deprived by Wingate's death in an air crash on 25 March of his drive and high-level support, his Chindit brigades, while writing an epic of courage and endurance, had little direct impact on Slim's battle. Special force, transferred to Stilwell's command, was kept in the field far too long and badly misused by the American commander. As its battered remnants were withdrawn during the monsoon Slim was moving Fourteenth Army into the pursuit phase of the Imphal battle, determined to campaign through the monsoon, giving the defeated Japanese no respite. 'Some of what we owed we had paid back', Slim wrote. 'Now we were going on to pay back the rest with interest' (Slim, *Defeat into Victory*, 369).

The reconquest of Burma: Operation Capital Slim was knighted at Imphal by the viceroy on 15 December. By that time the unprecedented monsoon pursuit had positioned Fourteenth Army on the edge of the open plains of north central Burma, where British superiority in armour and tactical air support would have maximum impact. The nature of the Burma campaign was changing as well. Stilwell had been recalled, the reopening of an overland link with China (assured by the 1944 campaign) having made his acerbic presence unnecessary to Washington's aims. Special force, decimated by that campaign, was about to be disbanded. If, however, the management of the campaign had become easier, the imperial Japanese army remained. A new Japanese commander, Lieutenant-General Kimura Heitara, appreciated the advantage open terrain and the impending dry season gave Fourteenth Army and pulled his battered forces back behind the mile-wide Irrawaddy, the most formidable defended river barrier faced by any British army commander in the twentieth century. Moreover, the prolongation of the European war precluded an amphibious operation in the Bay of Bengal. If Burma was to be reconquered in the 1944–5 dry season it would be overland, from the north. To this Slim now applied his mind.

The resulting plan, 'Capital', was as bold an operational gamble as the 1940 German offensive in the west. One corps would drive for the Irrawaddy, north and south of Mandalay, where the Japanese expected the main British effort to be made. Another corps in secrecy and radio silence (and aided by imaginative deception) would then strike for the great river well below Mandalay, make an assault crossing and drive for Meiktila, the nodal point of Japanese communications. By late January 1945 Slim's 33rd corps had closed up to the river and had two bridgeheads across it, threatening Mandalay and concentrating Japanese attention on what they believed to be all of Fourteenth Army. Lieutenant-General Sir Frank Messervy's 4th corps then sprang Slim's great surprise, crossing well to the south on 13 and 14 February. By 27 February 1945, 17th Indian division was in Meiktila. Unhinged as thoroughly as the French command had been in 1940, the Japanese reaction was characteristically intense but disjointed. In a month of confused fighting about Meiktila, Kimura's Burma area army was thoroughly beaten. The redoubtable Japanese infantryman still died where he stood, but increasingly to little avail.

The stage was now set for the final phase, the pursuit that would turn tactical success into operational victory. Officially known as 'Extended Capital', it was christened SOB—'Sea or Bust'—in Fourteenth Army. With a creaking, over-extended supply-line looping from central Burma back to Calcutta and employing everything from elephants to Dakotas, Slim needed to take the port of Rangoon before the monsoon broke in May. Moreover his vital air supply was increasingly precarious as the Americans (who controlled most of the theatre's transport squadrons) lost interest in the campaign. In the face of these challenges Slim's plan was as bold as the seizure of Meiktila. When his final drive jumped off on 11 April, he simply dropped his overland supply-line and relied entirely on air supply, leaving Mountbatten to win the battle for enough transport aircraft. Only a mentally tough, and utterly determined, army commander would have taken the risk. Ultimately a furious message from Winston Churchill to the American army chief of staff George Marshall carried the day. Even so, Fourteenth Army had over 300 miles to go, racing the monsoon while overcoming determined, but badly co-ordinated, Japanese resistance. Engineers, moving with the spearhead units, opened a new airheads every 60 miles or so, into which the tireless Dakotas brought the supplies that sustained offensive momentum. It was a display of mobility in exploitation which demonstrated that Slim, the one-time pupil of Hobart, was a master of more than frontier and jungle warfare.

It was also the Indian army's last great campaign. By 1945 manpower shortage had eroded the British component of Fourteenth Army to some 13 per cent. Over 60 per cent of Slim's troops were Indian (the balance being mostly African units). Fittingly, when the monsoon broke and stalled the advance just north of Rangoon, the leading unit was a Gurkha battalion of the 17th Indian division, which had campaigned under Slim since 1942. By that time, Fourteenth Army's advance had levered the Japanese out of Rangoon. One of the most brilliant campaigns conducted by a British general in the modern era came, however, to a victorious conclusion counterpointed by a strange episode in which Slim was almost removed from command.

A reorganization of SEAC in the autumn of 1944 replaced Giffard and Eleventh Army group with allied land forces, south-east Asia (ALFSEA) commanded by Lieutenant-General Sir Oliver Leese, a protégé of Montgomery, who came from Eighth Army in Italy, bringing his key staff officers with him. From the beginning there was some tension between ALFSEA and Fourteenth Army, a product of the differing temperaments of Leese and Slim, the different wartime experiences of the two headquarters, and the fact that while ALFSEA was mostly British army, Fourteenth Army was largely drawn from the Indian service. This came to a head in May 1945, the day after Rangoon fell, when Leese told Slim that he would be replaced at Fourteenth Army, now destined to invade Malaya, and would remain in Burma with an essentially static occupation force. Slim, stunned, requested retirement instead. Leese seems to have believed he had Mountbatten's approval. If so, he was speedily proven wrong. Nor did he find backing in London, while the reaction in Fourteenth Army and at Indian army headquarters in New Delhi was hostile to Slim's removal. Slim did indeed leave

Fourteenth Army, but as a full general, taking Leese's position as commander-in-chief, ALFSEA, on 10 August 1945.

At the Imperial Defence College Slim's new post was, in a sense, anticlimactic. After much needed home leave, he took up the job in the much changed conditions produced by Japan's surrender. Then early in 1946 he returned to London to become commandant of the IDC, responsible for restarting it after its wartime hiatus. During his two years there, the Indian army in which he had made his career, and which he had led to a sunset moment of victory, passed into history. Nehru had indicated in the summer of 1947 that Slim would be welcome as the first commander-in-chief of the new Indian army (Jinnah, the father of Pakistan, thought of him as a potential governor for what became East Pakistan). Slim, however, doubtless wisely, decided on retirement. On 1 April 1948 he left the Indian army to become deputy chairman of the railway executive.

Chief of the Imperial General Staff and governor-general of Australia Slim was, however, not destined to remain out of uniform. Prime Minister Clement Attlee, who along with much of Whitehall had wearied of Montgomery as chief of the Imperial General Staff, chose him to succeed Monty in November 1948. Montgomery, who had in mind a successor from among his own wartime subordinates, argued that, as an Indian army officer, Slim would neither know nor be known by the British army. Slim none the less got the job and with it the complex task of managing the army in the new era of peacetime conscription, nuclear weapons, and declining British power. He also had to deal with Churchill's return to office. Slim was a virtual stranger to Churchill (always a handicap), but the prime minister came to admire him—as did Slim's staff at the War Office. When he finished his tour as chief of the Imperial General Staff in November 1952 he was offered the governor-generalship of Australia.

During Slim's eight years in Australia, where he displayed, in a very different setting, the personal qualities that had drawn people to him throughout his career, he wrote what will be his most enduring monument, *Defeat into Victory* (1956), which stands as the best English-language army commander's memoir of the twentieth century. Written with grace and marked by self-deprecating humour, it describes exactly how he exercised high command, including candid avowals of error. Together with *Unofficial History* (1959), a collection of essays, some dating from his days writing as Anthony Mills, Slim put on paper one of the best and most readable accounts of how a thoughtful and dedicated professional soldier masters his craft.

Slim became a knight of the Garter in 1959 and was raised to the peerage in 1960. After his return from Australia, his final appointment, in 1963, was as deputy constable and lieutenant-governor of Windsor Castle. The following year he became constable and governor, remaining in office until shortly before his death, which occurred on 14 December 1970 in London. After his funeral, at St George's Chapel, Windsor, he was cremated privately. He was survived by his wife, his son John (who succeeded him in the peerage), and his daughter, Una.

Of all the memorials to Slim the one that he would perhaps have cherished most was the impact he made on those he commanded. A half-century later, one of them recalled:

> the burly man who came to talk to the assembled battalion … it was unforgettable. Slim was like that: the only man I've ever seen who had a force that came out of him. British soldiers don't love their commanders … Fourteenth Army trusted Slim and thought of him as one of themselves, and perhaps his real secret was that the feeling was mutual. (MacDonald Fraser, 35–6, 37)

RAYMOND CALLAHAN

Sources Viscount Slim [W. J. Slim], *Defeat into victory*, 2nd edn (1956); unabridged edn (1972) [later edn, 1972] • W. J. Slim, *Unofficial history* (1959) • S. W. Kirby and others, *The war against Japan*, 2–4 (1958–65) • R. Lewin, *Slim: the standard bearer* (1976) [official biography] • L. Allen, *Burma: the longest war, 1941–45* (1984) • R. Callahan, *Burma, 1942–1945* (1977) • G. Evans, *Slim as military commander* (1969) • G. Evans, *The desert and the jungle* (1959) • S. Bidwell, *The Chindit War: the campaign in Burma, 1944* (1979) • P. Mason, *A matter of honour: an account of the Indian army, its officers and men* (1974) • J. Masters, *The road past Mandalay* (1961) • P. Ziegler, *Mountbatten: the official biography* (1985) • G. Macdonald Fraser, *Quartered safe out here* (1992) • G. Smurthwaite, ed., *The forgotten war: the British army in the Far East, 1941–1945* (1992) • *Personal memoirs of U. S. Grant*, ed. E. B. Long (Cleveland, OH, 1952) • private information (2004) • *CGPLA Eng. & Wales* (1971) • *DNB*

Archives CAC Cam., corresp. and papers • priv. coll., papers | IWM, letters to Lt-Colonel H. R. K. Gibbs • IWM, Irwin MSS • King's Lond., Liddell Hart C., corresp. with Sir B. H. Liddell Hart • NAM, corresp. with Sir Roy Bucher • PRO, WO files | FILM BFI NFTVA, news footage • IWM FVA, *The commanders*, BBC, 1973, MBY 123 • IWM FVA, actuality footage • IWM FVA, documentary footage • IWM FVA, news footage | SOUND BL NSA, news recordings • IWM SA, oral history interview • IWM SA, recorded talk

Likenesses W. Stoneman, photograph, 1945, NPG • T. C. Dougdale, oils, *c*.1947, Staff College, Camberley, Surrey • Elliott & Fry, photograph, 1950, NPG [*see illus.*] • J. Pannett, chalk drawing, 1960, NPG • W. Bird, photograph, 1964, NPG • L. Boden, portrait, NAM • T. C. Douglas, portrait • statue, Whitehall, London

Wealth at death £12,249: probate, 14 May 1971, *CGPLA Eng. & Wales*

Slingsby. For this title name *see* Lee, Mary [Mary Slingsby, Lady Slingsby] (*fl.* 1670–1685).

Slingsby, Guilford (1610–1643). *See under* Slingsby, Sir Robert, baronet (1611–1661).

Slingsby, Sir Henry, first baronet (1602–1658), royalist army officer and conspirator, was born on 14 January 1602, second son of Sir Henry Slingsby (*d.* 1634) of Scriven, Yorkshire, and his wife, Frances (*d.* 1611), daughter of William Vavasour of Weston. Although the Slingsbys had settled in the Knaresborough area in the fourteenth century it was not until 1572 that a member of the family represented the borough at Westminster. Slingsby's father was returned for the town in every parliament between 1601 and 1624, served as sheriff of Yorkshire in 1611–12, and for the last five years of his life was vice-president of the council in the north under Thomas Wentworth, first Viscount Wentworth (the future earl of Strafford).

Sir Henry Slingsby, first baronet (1602–1658), attrib. Thomas Rawlins, 1658

Slingsby entered Queens' College, Cambridge, in January 1619, and having become heir to the family estate upon the death of his elder brother in 1617, was accepted as a pupil by the discriminating godly divine John Preston. He took over his father's seat at Knaresborough in the first Caroline parliament (1625), but either did not stand or was defeated in the 1626 elections, and in March of that year obtained a licence to travel abroad. He was back in Yorkshire by 1628, when he stood again for Knaresborough, losing in a contest to the town's deputy steward, Henry Benson. On 7 July 1631 Slingsby married Barbara (*bap.* 1609, *d.* 1641), daughter of the prominent church-papist Thomas Belasyse, first Viscount Fauconberg, of Newburgh Priory, Yorkshire, with whom he had two sons and a daughter.

Following the death of his father in 1634 Slingsby devoted much of his time to improving his inheritance, which was worth about £1800 a year in 1640, and included lands in Knaresborough, several manors in the West Riding, and properties in London, Middlesex, and Essex. On 2 March 1638 he was created a baronet of Nova Scotia. He showed little interest in local politics, avoiding involvement in the quarrel between his father-in-law and Viscount Wentworth. Nevertheless by 1638 he was performing the duties of a deputy lieutenant for the West Riding, though without a formal commission. He regarded the Scottish covenanters' grievances as 'a pretence & cloake for wick'dness' (*Diary*, 12), and in the first bishops' war served in the earl of Holland's troop, taking part in the abortive march to Kelso.

In the elections to the Short Parliament, Slingsby was returned for Knaresborough after a three-way contest with Benson and Sir Richard Hutton of Goldsborough. He received no committee appointments, and apparently spoke only once in debate—on 4 May, when he supported the crown's offer of twelve subsidies in return for the abandonment of ship money. He argued that so long as the king had a legal judgment in support of ship money it was 'Rebellion' not to pay it (J. D. Maltby, ed., *The Short Parliament (1640) Diary of Sir Thomas Aston*, CS, 4th ser. xxxv, 1988, 140). These words were 'vehemently excepted against' (ibid., 141), and Slingsby was fortunate not to have been called to the bar of the house. The determination he showed in beating Benson and Hutton to the senior place at Knaresborough in the elections to the Long Parliament was not matched by his record at Westminster, where he was 'reserved and inactive' (*CSP dom.*, 1658–9, 21). Although he professed to have no obligation to the court he was one of only six Yorkshire MPs who voted against Strafford's attainder. In addition he opposed the bill for abolishing episcopacy, which he saw as a threat to the peace of the church and to the social order in general. On the other hand he supported moves for the exclusion of the bishops from the Lords, having no truck with Laudian clericalism. His approach to religion appears to have combined something of the 'painful' earnestness of the godly with the reverence for order and decency of the Arminians. He greatly admired the Arminian clergyman Timothy Thurcross, though he apparently disapproved of 'new ceremonies' such as 'bowing & adoring towards the altar' (*Diary*, 8).

That Slingsby's sympathies lay with the king by late 1641 is perhaps evidenced in the subtle but deliberate way he frustrated the return of Sir William Constable (a leading Yorkshire puritan) in the Knaresborough by-election in November. Moreover only two of Slingsby's tenants voted for Constable; far short of the 'thirty voices of his dependants' (*Memoirs of the Reign of Charles the First: the Fairfax Correspondence*, ed. G. W. Johnson, 2 vols., 1848, 2.263) that Slingsby could usually command. On 20 May 1642 he left London to join the king at York, having been commissioned on 11 May to command the City regiment of the Yorkshire trained bands. On 13 December he was commissioned by the earl of Newcastle to raise a regiment of foot, which he commanded in the northern campaigns of 1643 and 1644. He was a combatant at Marston Moor, attended the king and the Oxford parliament in December 1644, and was present at the capture of Leicester and the battle of Naseby. In November 1645 he joined the garrison at Newark, and he was there when it surrendered the following May.

In July 1646 Slingsby petitioned to compound for his delinquency on the Newark articles, but this offer was apparently rejected. He refused to compound thereafter, claiming that he had 'nether personal mony to answer the summe, nor credite' (*Diary*, 345), though the main obstacle was his unwillingness to take the negative oath and covenant: 'the one makes me renounce my alegiance; the other my religion' (ibid., 119). He spent the next five years or so at his seat of Redhouse, Moor Monkton, Yorkshire, where he lived in great confinement, fearing arrest. In 1651 he was named in the act for the sale of delinquents' estates, despite the efforts of his friends at Westminster, in particular his nephew Slingsby Bethell and the regicide Sir John Bourchier, to have him exempted. His estate, which was valued at £11,220, was purchased by Slingsby Bethell and another of his kinsmen, Robert Stapleton, who held it in trust for Slingsby's children.

By 1654 Slingsby was in contact with the royalist underground, lending £100 to one of the king's agents, and reportedly delivering a letter from Charles Stuart to Lady Fairfax, aimed at winning over her husband. Implicated in the northern royalist rising of 1655, he was imprisoned at Hull, where he set about trying to subvert several of the garrison officers as part of a plot to betray the town to the king's forces. With the approval of their superiors, the officers played along with his design, and so convincing was their deception that he eventually gave one of them a commission signed by the king. The trap had been sprung, and on 25 March 1658 Slingsby found himself on trial for treason before a newly commissioned high court of justice at Westminster Hall. In his defence Slingsby argued that he had been 'trepanned' by the officers, who had taken seriously what he had spoken only in jest (*Diary*, 427, 431), but the court was not convinced, and on 2 June sentenced him to death. His nephew Lord Fauconberg, who had recently married Cromwell's daughter, interceded on his behalf, but to no avail. He was executed at Tower Hill on 8 June—his final speech reportedly showing 'little sense of sorrow, or fear of Death' (*The Severall Tryals*, 28; *Mercurius Politicus*, no. 419, 3–10 June 1658, 583). His body was given to his family, and he was buried in Knaresborough church. After the Restoration it was alleged that he had died a Catholic, though as late as 1651 he professed allegiance to the Church of England. Slingsby's estate passed to his eldest son, Sir Thomas Slingsby, who was a staunch supporter of the duke of York during the exclusion crisis. Like his father he was suspected of being a Catholic.

Sir Henry Slingsby's 'Diary', covering the years 1638 to 1648, is a valuable source for the civil war in northern England, and provides a revealing insight into the mind of an interesting, if not exactly typical, seventeenth-century country gentleman. The work was strongly informed by Slingsby's reading of Montaigne. The diary was edited from the manuscript in 1836 by the Revd Daniel Parsons, with notes and additions, including *A father's legacy. Sir Henry Slingbey's instructions to his sonnes. Written a little before his death* (1658). DAVID SCOTT

Sources HoP, *Commons, 1640–60* [draft] · *The diary of Sir Henry Slingsby*, ed. D. Parsons (1836) · J. T. Cliffe, *The Yorkshire gentry from the Reformation to the civil war* (1969) · *The severall tryals of Sir Henry Slingsby knt, John Hewet DD, and John Mordant Esq. for high treason* (1658), BL, E753/5 · W. Yorks. AS, Leeds, Yorkshire Archaeological Society, Slingsby MSS, DD 56 · draft constituency article, Knaresborough HoP Trust · R. Carroll, 'Parliamentary representation of Yorkshire', Vanderbilt University, PhD diss., 1964 · R. Marchant, *The puritans and the church courts in the diocese of York, 1560–1642* (1960) · D. Underdown, *Royalist conspiracy in England, 1649–1660* (1960) ·

Thurloe, *State papers*, vol. 4 · P. R. Newman, *Royalist officers in England and Wales, 1642–1660: a biographical dictionary* (1981) · Clarendon, *Hist. rebellion* · IGI

Archives W. Yorks. AS, Leeds, Yorkshire Archaeological Society, family papers, DD 56, 188 | Hunt. L., *An introduction to the Christian faith* · U. Nott. L., Department of Manuscripts and Special Collections, book of memoirs · W. Yorks. AS, Leeds, Yorkshire Archaeological Society, letters to his son · W. Yorks. AS, Leeds, Yorkshire Archaeological Society, diary · Yale U., Beinecke L., diary

Likenesses attrib. T. Rawlins, silver medal, 1658, BM [*see illus.*] · G. Vertue, line engraving (after unknown artist), BM, NPG; repro. in *Loyalists* · portrait; formerly in family possession, 1897 · portrait; formerly in the possession of Mr Talbot of Lacock Abbey Fox Talbot Museum, Wiltshire

Wealth at death estate worth approx. £1800 p.a. in 1640: HoP, *Commons, 1640–60*

Slingsby, Henry (1619/20–1690), master of the mint, was the second son of Sir William Slingsby (*d.* 1634), of Kippax, Yorkshire, and Elizabeth, daughter of Sir Stephen Board of Board Hill, Sussex. Since he was said to be forty-eight in 1668 he must have been born in 1619 or 1620. After matriculating at Oxford in 1635 he went on to build for himself a life of some importance and style. His principal achievement was at the mint, where seemingly he made his first appearance in 1657, authorizing payments for equipment to be installed in the newly mechanized coining process. Subsequently, at the instigation of lords Ashley and Lauderdale, he was successively deputy to master worker Sir Ralph Freeman, joint patentee as master worker with Sir Ralph, and then, upon the latter's death in 1667, master worker alone for almost twenty years at a salary of £500. It was during this long period of control that Blondeau's machinery triumphed over and finally replaced the old hammered process of production. In 1661 Slingsby became a member of the Philosophical Society, being a member of its council at the time it became the Royal Society. On 12 January 1663 he received Charles II at the mint; on 27 August 1666 he went with Evelyn, Wren, and others to examine proposals for repairing St Paul's Cathedral; and between 24 June 1670 and 29 September 1672 was secretary for the council for trade and plantations. In this capacity he fitted out an office in Queen Street and took responsibility for running it. Pepys and he were well acquainted, meeting at court or at the Tower, and it is because of this acquaintance that Pepys has so much to say about the newly mechanized mint. In 1665 he described Slingsby as 'a very ingenious person' with whom he had had many 'fine discourses' on issues such as the size of the circulating medium and the law prohibiting the export of bullion (Pepys, 6.22–3).

Whether Pepys truly befriended Slingsby is hard to say but Evelyn did. It was he who suggested to Slingsby the words 'decus et tutamen' (an ornament and a safeguard) with which to edge mark the new milled coins, who went with him to Borough Green, Cambridgeshire, which Slingsby had acquired through his wife, Ann, daughter of Sir Anthony Cage, to advise where a new house should be built, and who, in 1674, epitomized him as 'my worthy friend and great lover of music' (Evelyn, 4.49). To Evelyn's credit this friendship held good despite Slingsby's expulsion in 1675 from the Royal Society for non-payment of his dues, despite Slingsby's suspension from office at the mint in 1680, and despite Slingsby's ultimate dismissal in 1686. From time to time the two men continued to dine together; in 1684 Evelyn took Slingsby to see 'Mr Sheldon's collection of medals'; and in 1688, when the former master worker was in 'deplorable circumstances', Evelyn betook himself to the lords of the Treasury to ask them 'to be favourable to him' (Evelyn, 4.396, 587).

Man of parts and ability though Slingsby undoubtedly was, his expensive lifestyle, new building, and £4500 of debt inherited from his father-in-law left him living beyond his means and unable to keep straight his accounts for the management of the mint. Not until 1675 did either he or Warden St Leger make any account for the offices they had held since the Restoration and only then for the period 1666 to 1670. The commission of inquiry which was set up on 23 September 1677 to look into these irregularities could make no real headway because both Slingsby and Comptroller Hoare simply refused to co-operate. Slingsby would produce nothing, 'saying it was contrary to law for an accountant to charge himself, and for the books of accounts, he said they were his private books and therefore would not produce them' (Challis, *New History*, 354). When pressed further both Slingsby and Hoare let it be known that they would answer further only through their lawyers. Despite this obstruction the commission of inquiry was left with the clear impression that all was far from well. Quite apart from the missing accounts for the mint's normal activities, no account had been made for the Dunkirk money and there were serious allegations that neither the pyx nor the ledgers were properly kept, that the crown had paid more than was necessary for copper used to make farthings and halfpence, and that the gold and silver coin was worse than standard. Moreover, it had been revealed that for some years the mint officers had bought up old gold to melt it down at a profit.

On 30 January 1678 Lord Treasurer Danby instructed the auditors to require Slingsby and St Leger to make their accounts without delay and as the wheels turned slowly throughout that year and the next Slingsby's fitness to stay in office fell openly in question. By early 1680 his credit had sunk so low that when a warrant was issued to him to receive £600 out of the coinage money in the exchequer it was specifically stated that unless payment was actually made in the presence of the moneyers to whom the money was then to be paid as part of the total sum which Slingsby owed them nothing was to be done. In 1680 he was suspended on full pay and a triumvirate consisting of John Buckworth, Charles Duncombe, and James Hoare was appointed to exercise his office. Slingsby resisted by refusing to give up his keys of office, but with some of his property confiscated and the auditors relentlessly demanding their pound of flesh capitulation was inevitable. Slingsby was a ruined man. For a decade he fought his private creditors, including the moneyers who in 1685 claimed that they had received only £8542 out of £16,109 which was due to them in respect of the gold and silver coinage between 1673 and the date of Slingsby's suspension, 22 July 1680. As far as the crown was concerned it was not until May 1690, after he was dead, that a settlement was finally agreed. Even then, it was only possible because Slingsby's executor, Ann, 'the best of women' as he described her in his will, was allowed to claim for the period of his suspension, first, the fees for himself, his assayer, and his purveyor, secondly, part of the engineer's salary and allowance, and, thirdly, some of the master worker's fee for coining gold and silver. These amounts totalled £13,451, the greater part of the £22,621 in which he finally stood indebted to the crown for the mint and other government services.

By his will, proved on 15 April 1690, in which he requested that he be buried 'without invitation of friends', Slingsby bequeathed to his son Harry (Henry) all his lands in Kippax, together with all his mines and quarries of coal and stone, as well as his possessions in Barwick in Elmet and his windmills in Garforth and Stainforth, Yorkshire. Coal was of the essence because in this, Slingsby had once claimed, lay his chief subsistence. His debts being settled (if his lands allowed), his manors of Borough Green and Croydon were to go to his widow, £2000 to his daughter Elizabeth, £500 to his younger son, Anthony, and £100 p.a. to his sister Elizabeth, whose second husband was John Villiers, Viscount Purbeck, brother to the duke of Buckingham. The manor of Kippax passed on the death in 1695 without issue of Henry Slingsby junior to Henry's brother Anthony and upon his death in 1697, unmarried, to his sister Elizabeth, who married Adlard Cage, of Thavies Inn, London, gentleman.   C. E. CHALLIS

Sources C. E. Challis, 'Presidential address', *British Numismatic Journal*, 61 (1991), 167–76 • W. M. Palmer, *A history of … Borough Green, Cambridgeshire*, Cambridge Antiquarian Society (1939) • *CSP dom.*, 1657–80 • C. E. Challis, ed., *A new history of the royal mint* (1992) • W. A. Shaw, ed., *Calendar of treasury books*, 9, PRO (1931) • *CSP col.*, vol. 7 • *The diary of Sir Henry Slingsby of Scriven, bart.*, ed. D. Parsons (1836), 404 • Evelyn, *Diary* • Pepys, *Diary* • PRO, PROB 11/399, 437 • BL, Add. MS 34358 • priv. coll., Slingsby MSS

Archives Norton Conyers, Yorkshire, mint MSS • Norton Conyers, Yorkshire, MSS, files 1, 2 • Norton Conyers, Yorkshire, family MSS • Norton Conyers, Yorkshire, letters

Wealth at death bequeathed property in Yorkshire (including coal mines) and in Cambridgeshire; also various sums of money; but owed substantial sums to crown, and most likely had other debts

Slingsby, Jonathan Freke. *See* Waller, John Francis (*c.*1809–1894).

Slingsby, Mary. *See* Lee, Mary (*fl.* 1670–1685).

Slingsby, Sir Robert, baronet (1611–1661), naval officer and administrator, was the second of five sons (there were also four daughters) of Sir Guylford Slingisbie or Slingsby (1565–1631) of Bifrons, Canterbury, comptroller of the navy, and his wife, Margaret (*d.* in or after 1661), daughter of William Walter of York. The Slingsby family, staunch royalists, originated from Scriven, near Knaresborough, Yorkshire. In 1630 Sir Guylford sent his son to Bristol to supervise the sale of a royal prize lying there, and in February 1633, his father having recently died, the navy officers urged the admiralty to appoint Robert to command a small vessel, the eighth or tenth *Lion's Whelp* (12 guns), preparing to serve in the channel, from which ship he moved in 1636–7 to the third *Whelp* and then the first *Whelp*. He was soon venturing out of home waters: in 1638 he commanded the *Expedition* as the second vessel escorting the Moroccan ambassador home from Portsmouth, and in January 1640 the *Expedition* convoyed troops and munitions from the Tower of London to Edinburgh for the second bishops' war. In June that year he was back in the channel in the *Happy Entrance*, commanding a small defence squadron—a command he held until June 1642 when he transferred to the *Garland* to convey the Portuguese ambassador to Lisbon.

During the winter of 1641–2 Slingsby had taken lodgings in Russell Street, Covent Garden, where he appears to have been an uneasy link between Admiral Sir John Penington and the king. Unhappy about developments in parliament, he passed 'not a merry Christmas, but the maddest one I ever saw' (*CSP dom.*, 1641–3, 217). On the outbreak of the civil war Penington declared for the king, who appointed him to command the fleet. Slingsby was one of the few captains to support him, refusing to obey parliament's order appointing Warwick to command. Next day Warwick sent an ultimatum and threatened to attack Slingsby in the *Garland* and Baldwin Wake, who was holding out in the *Expedition*. Slingsby and Wake abused the boat crews who brought the message, whereupon the crews seized the two ships and their captains. The pair were held prisoner by Warwick; on 21 July they petitioned the House of Lords to be freed or charged, and they appealed again after seven weeks in gaol in London.

In December, Warwick urged the Lords to release the prisoners; they were called to the bar and freed on condition that they did not accept any employment or command against the interests of parliament, to which they agreed. In December 1643, however, Slingsby received £100 from the king at Oxford and early in 1644 he sailed from Weymouth for France, where he was to gather intelligence and raise funds in Paris and Amsterdam. From April he was awarded 40 shillings a day indefinitely for services abroad, and June that year found him in Paris. He seems to have travelled back and forth, however, for in 1643–5 he set out ships at Bristol for the king at his own expense, and he was probably the Colonel Robert Slingsby who was at Bristol with Prince Rupert in 1645 when the town fell to parliament. With his younger brother Colonel Walter Slingsby, deputy governor of Bristol, he attended a council of war on 5 September 1645, shortly before the surrender. During the years 1643–6 he was also sending arms to the king from abroad, for which in 1660 he petitioned for the sum of £5800 still owed to him.

While Charles was held captive after the war, Slingsby visited him as a confidential messenger, perhaps incognito, on several occasions, and was himself thrown into a 'loathsome dungeon', receiving a royal message of sympathy and reassurance.

In January 1649 Slingsby petitioned parliament from Hemlington, Yorkshire, for permission to compound; he asked again in June, noting that he had never been judicially impeached or sequestered. In March 1650 he was permitted to compound for £200; in February 1652 he asked for the sum to be reduced, and on 3 June the fine was settled at £140. In September he petitioned over his manor at Barkway, Hertfordshire, detained from him by the earl of Arundel. This manor had come to him through his marriage with Elizabeth, daughter of Robert Brooke of Newcells, Hertfordshire, having been sold to the couple by her parents' heir.

Nothing is heard of Slingsby during the remainder of the 1650s, when presumably he was living quietly in Yorkshire. In April 1660 he stood for election as a knight of the shire—perhaps Yorkshire. In May he was in competition with Sir George Carteret for the post of navy treasurer; in August he secured the appointment of comptroller of the navy. Samuel Pepys recorded his first meeting with Colonel Slingsby on 5 September, referring to him by this title until Slingsby was created a baronet on 18 March 1661. He also met and approved of Slingsby's second wife, Elizabeth (daughter of Sir Edward Radcliffe or Radclyffe of Dilston and widow of Sir William Fenwick, baronet), and her daughter. In January 1661 Pepys read Slingsby's 'Discourse upon the past and present state of his majesty's navy' in which he advocated regular payment, prohibition of trading by officers, and the encouragement of merchant shipping. It was presented to the duke of York, then lord high admiral, and remained unpublished until 1801. The original is probably that now in the Pepys Library, Magdalene College, Cambridge, with later copies in the British Library and elsewhere.

Slingsby barely had time to reap the reward of his loyalty for in the autumn he fell sick of the intermittent typhus then circulating in London. Pepys went to visit him on 22 October, and reported on his decline. He died on 26 October 1661 at his house in Lime Street, much regretted by Pepys, who considered him to be a staunch friend and jovial companion, 'he being a man that loved me, and had many Qualitys that made me to love him above all the officers and Commissioners in the Navy' (Pepys, 2.202). Pepys was invited to view the body four days later, but confided to his diary that there had been much disorder in the house, and 'pretending that the corps stinks, they will bury it tonight privately, and so will unbespeak all their Guests, and there shall be no funerall' (ibid., 2.204). Slingsby was buried at St Andrew Undershaft on 30 October; his second wife apparently survived him. There were no children of either of his marriages and the baronetcy became extinct.

Sir Robert's elder brother, **Guilford Slingsby** (1610–1643), graduated MA of St Andrews University in 1628 and was incorporated at Oxford the following year. He was elected to represent Carysfort in the Irish parliament in 1634 and became secretary to the earl of Strafford, who appointed him lieutenant of the ordnance office and vice-admiral of Munster. On Strafford's fall from favour he took refuge in the Low Countries but returned to his estate at Cleveland about December 1642 and levied a regiment there for the king's service. Leading it into battle at

Guisborough on 16 January 1643 he was defeated by Sir Hugh Cholmeley, and taken prisoner. He died shortly afterwards from his wounds, and was buried in York Minster on 26 January.

Arthur Slingsby, one of Sir Robert's younger brothers, who inherited Bifrons, was knighted by the king at Brussels in 1657 and in October 1658 made a baronet by a patent dated from Bruges. He married a Flemish lady, and was the only one of the brothers to leave descendants.

BERNARD CAPP and ANITA MCCONNELL

Sources CSP dom., 1631–61 · Pepys, Diary, vols. 1–2 · Fifth report, HMC, 4 (1876) · The manuscripts of the duke of Leeds, HMC, 22 (1888), 40 · JHL, 5 (1642–3) · B. E. Warburton, Memoirs of Prince Rupert and the cavaliers, 3 vols. (1849), 3.175 · J. R. Powell and E. K. Timings, eds., Documents relating to the civil war, 1642–1648, Navy RS, 105 (1963) · M. A. E. Green, ed., Calendar of the proceedings of the committee for compounding … 1643–1660, 4, PRO (1892) · J. Foster, Pedigrees of the county families of Yorkshire, 2 vols. (1874) · H. Chauncy, The historical antiquities of Hertfordshire, 1 (1826); repr. (1975), 102 · VCH Hertfordshire, 4.29 · J. Burke and J. B. Burke, A genealogical and heraldic history of the extinct and dormant baronetcies of England, Ireland and Scotland, 2nd edn (1841); repr. (1844), 490 · parish register, St Martin-in-the-Fields, City Westm. AC · parish register, London, St Andrew Undershaft, GL [burial]

Slingsby, William Cecil (1849–1929), mountaineer, was

born on 25 May 1849 in Bell Busk, near Gargrave, Yorkshire, the eldest in the family of three sons and two daughters of William Slingsby, mill owner of Carleton in Craven, and his wife, Mary Ann, daughter of Isaac Dewhurst of Skipton. He was educated at Cheltenham College. On leaving school in 1866 he entered his father's cotton mill at Carleton in Craven, where he later became a partner; he retired in 1906. He married on 21 June 1882 Alizon (b. 1859), daughter of William Farrer *Ecroyd, a worsted manufacturer and Conservative MP for Preston, 1881–5. They had two sons and three daughters, of whom the youngest daughter, Eleanor, married the mountaineer Geoffrey Winthrop Young.

Slingsby first visited Norway in 1872 and soon discovered that he was in a country whose temperament and customs were akin to his own. In their turn the Norwegians accepted him as one of themselves. Crossing the Jotunheim in 1872 he had seen Störe Skagastölstind, the Matterhorn of the northern Alps, and resolved to make its first ascent. On 21 July 1876, accompanied by his friends Emmanuel Mohn and Knut Lykken, he attacked the mountain up the steep glacier later known as the Slingsbybrae, reaching the col under the final rock pillar; there the Norwegians refused to go on, considering the peak inaccessible. Slingsby climbed on and reached the summit alone. He made over fifty first ascents of peaks between the Jotunheim and the North Cape. In the early twentieth century he was sometimes known as the 'father of Norwegian mountaineering'. He promoted skiing as a sport and was among the first to introduce Norwegian skis to the Alps.

Slingsby's book Norway, the Northern Playground (1903) gives an account of his adventures and explorations, and also information about the folklore and way of life of the Norwegians. The composer Edvard Grieg was numbered among his many friends. In 1878 he first visited the Alps, where he took part in several first ascents, chiefly with A. F. Mummery. In 1885 he started climbing in the Lake District, where his name is perpetuated in Slingsby's pinnacle and Slingsby's chimney on Scafell. Slingsby died at his home, St Georges, Hurstpierpoint, Sussex, on 23 August 1929 and was buried at St Mary's Church, Carleton in Craven. His wife survived him.

J. S. WINTHROP-YOUNG, rev.

Sources Schule Schloss, Salem, Germany, Slingsby MSS · W. C. Slingsby, Norway, the northern playground, ed. G. W. Young (1941) · E. S. Skirving, ed., Cheltenham College register, 1841–1927 (1928) · CGPLA Eng. & Wales (1929) · gravestone, St Mary's Church, Carleton in Craven
Archives Schule Schloss, Salem, Germany
Wealth at death £2072 4s. 2d.: probate, 9 Nov 1929, CGPLA Eng. & Wales

Sloane, Sir Hans, baronet (1660–1753), physician and col-

lector, was born at Killyleagh, co. Down, on 16 April 1660, the seventh son of Alexander Sloane (d. 1666). His father, a protestant, was by profession agent for James Hamilton, second Viscount Claneboye and later earl of Clanbrassill; he was subsequently receiver-general of taxes for co. Down. Hans's mother, Sarah Hicks, came to Ireland in the company of Anne Carey, daughter of the earl of Monmouth, who later married James Hamilton. Much of what is known of Sloane's childhood and parentage derives from a brief pedigree in the College of Arms and from a memoir by Thomas Birch, now in the British Library (Add. MS 4241). From these we learn that Hans 'was descended of a Family originally of Scotland, but settled in the North of Ireland upon the new Plantation of that Part of the Kingdom in the Reign of King James I'.

Early years and medical training So far as is known Sloane's schooling took place in Killyleagh, where he developed a 'strong Inclination to the study of the Works of Nature'. At the age of sixteen he developed a pulmonary affliction that took three years to subdue and which, despite a prudent regime, was to leave him periodically spitting blood for the remainder of his life.

By the age of nineteen he had recovered sufficiently to further his education in London. There he lodged in a house in Water Lane, adjacent to the Apothecaries' Hall where he studied chemistry. His lodgings were shared by Nicholas Staphorst, the Apothecaries' 'chemical operator', with whom Sloane acquired 'a perfect Knowledge of the Preparations and Uses of most chemical Medicines'. Lectures in anatomy and physic complemented this training, along with botanical studies at the physic garden in Chelsea.

During this time he also came under the influence of two older contemporaries who were to remain his firm friends for the remainder of their lives, John Ray and Robert Boyle. There seems little doubt that the acquaintance of these two scholarly figures and their circle produced a powerful formative influence on the development of Sloane's interests.

After four years of formal education in medicine Sloane

Sir Hans Sloane, baronet (1660–1753), by Stephen Slaughter, 1736

journeyed to Paris, where for some three months he followed an intensive regime 'which afforded him full Employment for the Day', sharing his time between the Jardin Royal des Plantes and the Hôpital de la Charité: Birch records that Sloane was 'assiduous in his Attendance' upon all the Professors, 'by whom he was treated with great Respect as likewise by those of the Royal College & others eminent for their Skill in Physic, Natural History, or Philosophy'. Of his tutors, Joseph Pitton de Tournefort was perhaps to have the most lasting influence.

When the time came for Sloane to take his doctorate, his protestant faith dictated that he should do so at the University of Orange. There, on 27 July 1683, the oral examination was begun and on the following morning was completed; forthwith the university conferred on him the degree of doctor of physic.

Sloane now attended the University of Montpellier. He went there with a recommendation from Tournefort to Pierre Chirac, 'the chief Professor, to whose lectures & those of the other Professors there, he was admitted without any Fee or Reward, & became particularly acquainted with Monsr Magnol the Botanist, whom he accompanied in his herborisations round that City'. There he further studied anatomy, medicine, and botany. Both Tournefort and Pierre Magnol were avid searchers for new species and both were to devise new classificatory schemes; close acquaintance with them undoubtedly had a lasting effect on Sloane's own development. Sloane extended his stay in Montpellier until the following summer when, on 23 May 1684, he set out again for London 'with a Resolution to fix himself there for the Exercise of his Profession'.

On returning to England, Sloane entered into 'the greatest Intimacy of Friendship' with Thomas Sydenham and was

> desir'd by him to settle in his Neighbourhood, that he might introduce him into practice … recommending him in the strongest terms to his Patients, when he was disabled by the Gout from attending them himself, & carrying him to them, when he was able.

Sydenham's skills were quickly communicated to the receptive Sloane, who was soon established to the point where, on 12 April 1687, he was admitted a fellow of the Royal College of Physicians.

Travels with the duke of Albemarle At the same time Sloane received a tempting proposition to join the household of Christopher Monck, second duke of Albemarle, newly appointed governor of Jamaica, as the duke's personal physician. Sloane saw here an opportunity not only to serve his prestigious master and his family but also 'to see what I can meet withal that is extraordinary in nature in those places', acknowledging too that the voyage 'seem'd likewise to promise to be useful to me, as a Physician; many of the Antient and best Physicians having travell'd to the Places whence their Drugs were brought, to inform themselves concerning them' (Sloane, *Voyage*, preface). Ray and another friend, Martin Lister, were particularly encouraging, setting out a number of questions which Sloane might answer on the spot and further desiring him to 'collect & transmitte hither' specimens of all kinds (MacGregor, 'Natural history correspondence', 80). On 12 September 1687 the ducal party set sail from Spithead, proceeding via Madeira and the Canaries; by 25 November they had made land at Bridgetown, Barbados, eventually reaching Jamaica on 19 December 1687.

During the following fifteen months Sloane reports that he took pains 'to search the several Places I could think afforded Natural Productions, and immediately described them in a Journal'. He made notes on the weather, the topography, natural phenomena such as earthquakes, but above all on the flora, penetrating to the north of the island collecting, noting, and recording. Within a year, however, this absorbing activity was interrupted by the death on 6 October 1688 of the duke of Albemarle. Sloane's last duty to his patron was to embalm his body for shipment to England; the upheavals then surrounding the English throne delayed the departure of the dead duke and his household for a further five months, but on 16 March 1689 they sailed for home. Sloane's baggage was swelled by many scientific trophies: his plant collection alone amounted to 800 specimens, 'most whereof were New' (Sloane, *Voyage*, preface).

Marriage and publication of his West Indian research After returning to London on 29 May 1689 Sloane remained for nearly four years in the service of the duchess of Albemarle before setting up in practice in Bloomsbury. There, on 11 May 1695, he married Elizabeth (*d.* 1724), daughter and coheir of John Langley, a London alderman, and widow of Fulk Rose, formerly of Jamaica. The marriage was an advantageous one for Sloane, since his wife inherited not only her father's estate but also one third of the income from her former husband's properties in Jamaica. The newly married couple set up house in what later became 3 Bloomsbury Place, then at the centre of a fashionable residential area. There Sloane established his immensely successful practice, his patients including many of the most prestigious figures of the day.

In the years that followed Sloane began to publish his observations from the West Indies. At first they were submitted to the *Philosophical Transactions of the Royal Society*. There papers by him appeared on species such as coffee and the Jamaican pepper tree, and on the earthquakes that devastated Lima and struck Jamaica in 1687–8 and were felt in Jamaica again in 1692. Six years after his return, in 1696, his *Catalogus plantarum quae in insula Jamaica sponte proveniunt* came to fruition, an octavo volume of 232 pages with a 43 page index, dedicated jointly to the Royal Society and the Royal College of Physicians. Its appearance had been long delayed while Sloane sought opinions and criticism among his friends, notably Ray, and consulted numerous printed authorities. Sloane placed great emphasis on these cross-references, stating that he had endeavoured

> to find if any thing I had observ'd was taken Notice of by other Persons … I therefore looked into most Books of this Nature, and the greatest part of what I found is publish'd [in the *Catalogus plantarum*], which I think, for Synonymous Names of the Plants therein mentioned, is somewhat more Copious and exact than any other before it.   (Sloane, *Voyage*, preface)

The process of collation and rationalization alluded to here represents one of Sloane's most valuable contributions to the advancement of science. His readiness to subordinate his own independent discoveries to the prior claims of others was characteristic of him in a way that was unmatched among his contemporaries. The new volume rendered obsolete many of the clumsy synonyms that littered earlier literature and brought about an improvement in nomenclature that was to be superseded only by the system of Linnaeus. But its value was greater than this: in a letter to Edward Lhwyd, Ray described Sloane's work as 'a great treasure, he having very exactly described every species' (J. Ray to Edward Lhwyd, 15 May 1697, Gunther, 271).

A successful physician On 2 November 1694 Sloane had been appointed physician in charge of Christ's Hospital, London, a post he held until 1730. With a generosity that was also characteristic of him, he returned his salary of £30 a year to the hospital on a regular basis for the relief of needy inmates. He was a supporter of the Royal College of Physicians' dispensary, where medicines could be obtained at cost price. He was always generous with his own money and liberal with medical advice to his friends and to those who were unable to pay, running a free surgery for the poor every morning. He later became a governor of, and financial donor to, most of London's hospitals, giving £100 to each of those with which he was associated.

In 1701 Sloane was awarded the degree of doctor of medicine by the University of Oxford and in 1705 was elected to the College of Physicians of Edinburgh. In 1719, at the age of fifty-nine, he was elected president of the Royal College of Physicians in London, which office he held for sixteen years.

Further recognition of his medical prowess came in 1712 with an appointment as physician-extraordinary to Queen Anne. In 1714 he attended the queen in her final illness. De Beer draws attention to the crucial significance of Sloane's role in prolonging the queen's life to the point where the succession of the protestant George I could be ensured, so thwarting Jacobite aspirations to regain the throne. Under George I, Sloane continued to serve as a physician-extraordinary and on 3 April 1716, shortly after the king's accession, he was created a baronet—one of the first physicians to be so honoured. A court appointment followed in the succeeding reign when, in 1727, Sloane became physician-in-ordinary to George II, 'having been before constantly employ'd about the whole Royal Family, & always honour'd with the Esteem & favour of the Queen Consort'.

Estimates of Sloane's contributions to medicine are generally in line with those of his standing in the broader world of science. He was not a great innovator, but he was cautiously progressive and contributed to the establishment of scientific diagnosis and prescription, based on accurate observation rather than hypothesis. He was a keen promoter (against entrenched medical opinion) of the introduction and practice of inoculation in England, not fearing to apply it to his own family nor to advocate its administration to the children of the princess of Wales. He was never a slavish follower of established practice, and declared himself 'always very attentive to Matters of Fact' concerning the efficacy of cures (Oshlag, 1947). Sloane's name is further linked with the popularization of quinine, distilled from 'Peruvian bark': on returning from Jamaica he is said to have invested most of the fortune he acquired there in the bark, so securing a valuable stock of medicine which he actively promoted by prescription (for a range of complaints beyond those hitherto treated in this way) and by writing about it in the *Philosophical Transactions*. Further, he made a considerable amount of money from the promotion of milk chocolate—a commodity singularly in harmony with the regime of temperance that governed his life.

Publication of his *Voyage to the Islands*; links with the apothecaries In parallel with these highly successful efforts to develop his medical practice Sloane worked towards the completion of the first volume of his major work, the *Voyage to the islands Madera, Barbados, Nieves, S. Christophers, and Jamaica, with the natural history … of the last of those islands*. The first volume (dedicated to Queen Anne) was in due course brought out in 1707, though the scholarly world had to wait until 1725 for the appearance of the second volume (dedicated to George I). It is noteworthy like the earlier *Catalogus* for the pains that Sloane took to acknowledge the opinions of earlier scholars than himself. Furthermore, it is, as Birch acknowledges, 'written with an unaffected plainness and simplicity of Style most suited to the capacity of common Readers, & therefore likely to engage their Attention, & gratify their curiosity'. Critical acclaim was duly forthcoming, and not only in England: the *Journal des Sçavans* reviewed it warmly on 21 May 1708, despite the fact that Britain and France were then engaged in war. The first volume alone, concerned principally with plants, established Sloane's status unequivocally in the academic world. Many illustrations were engraved for it from drawings by Everhardus Kickius and Garrett Moore. The second volume included much more than plants— beasts, birds, fish, insects, reptiles, climate, disease, and trade are all considered. Sloane was able to use his own collection to draw comparisons with species of plants common to Jamaica and England, Spain, Portugal, Barbary, Guinea, and the East Indies.

Sloane's extensive pharmaceutical knowledge is alluded to in an account of a debate at the House of Lords of the Physicians' Bill on 14 April 1720, which he attended with other members of the Royal College of Physicians: when the apothecaries, who were also represented, attempted to insinuate that the physicians 'did not understand drugs', Sloane 'offered to contend with them, & sayd he would bring 500 drugs that all the Apothecarys in town should not know one of' (*Family Memoirs*, 1.74). None the less, the apothecaries remained indebted to him, for since his acquisition of the manor of Chelsea some years earlier, Sloane had become landlord of the physic garden there and in 1722 he entered into an agreement with the society by which, for an annual payment of £5, he conveyed the garden and all its appurtenances to them. The grateful society erected a full-length statue of their benefactor in the garden: the statue and its maquette, both by Rysbrack, were later placed in the British Museum.

Administration of the Royal Society Scholarship was only one of several gifts with which Sloane was endowed and in any assessment of his worth his association with the administration of the Royal Society must merit primary importance. He was elected to the society as a young man of twenty-four on 21 January 1685 (proposed by Lister) and remained an active participant in its affairs for sixty-eight years. He seems to have been encouraged and positively moved by his admission to the Royal Society, as also by his election two years later to the Royal College of Physicians—'unmerited Favours', as he called them, which 'incited me to do what I could to be no useless Member, but to cast in my Mite towards the Advancement of Natural Knowledge … and by that means endeavour to deserve a Place amongst so many Great and Worthy Persons' (Sloane, *Voyage*, preface). In 1693 he was elected second secretary of the society and in 1695 was made first secretary. The appointment carried with it, in addition to a considerable burden of administrative duties, responsibility for publication of the *Philosophical Transactions*. Production of the *Transactions* had lapsed for a number of years before Sloane became involved and the society as a whole was at the time in a state of decline; he played a key role in revitalizing both, and there can be little doubt that the shouldering of these considerable responsibilities

inhibited Sloane's own opportunities for further scientific work.

The appointment placed Sloane at the hub of the learned world. It is hard to conceive that a more appropriate person could have been found to occupy this position, for Sloane's wide circle of acquaintances, his assiduousness as a correspondent, and his easy relations with foreign scholars at a period when the continent was repeatedly riven by warfare helped maintain the Royal Society in a key strategic position within the European scholarly community. His extensive correspondence with the Abbé Bignon, master of the king's library in Paris and editor of the *Journal des Sçavans*, may be singled out as a particularly fruitful conduit through which the latest scientific ideas (and gossip) were transmitted across the channel. The fact that so many of the communications printed in the *Philosophical Transactions* at this time were in the nature of extended letters to the editor underlines the important role played by the editor as correspondent.

Sloane was not without his critics, however. One of the most vociferous was Dr John Woodward, who bore an undoubted enmity for Sloane, fuelled by more than a hint of jealousy, but his antipathy also had a genuine scholarly dimension to it. With some justification Woodward felt that the experimental and philosophical objectives of the Royal Society (as reflected in the papers published in the *Transactions*) were neglected or even undermined during Sloane's secretaryship; not only did Sloane lack the intellectual capacity to forward these pursuits but, in Woodward's opinion, he subverted the course of progress by forwarding the theories of his cronies at the expense of others (notably Woodward himself). Even more devastating in effect was an attack which came in the form of a parody on Sloane and the journal he edited, published anonymously in 1700 by William King, under the title of *The Transactioneer*. Although an official inquiry into its authorship was mounted by the council, King remained undiscovered.

Of as much importance from the society's point of view was Sloane's businesslike outlook, which resulted in many arrears of subscriptions being successfully claimed and in a striking improvement in the society's finances. He also encouraged donations to the 'repository' (the society's museum), which had enjoyed an enhanced degree of direction and purpose since responsibility for it had passed in 1677 to Nehemiah Grew. Sloane himself contributed enormously to the society's collections of plant specimens by including in his agreement with the apothecaries a proviso that the Chelsea Physic Garden should annually supply the Royal Society with fifty specimens of plants of different species, by which means more than 2000 specimens were received.

The president of the society from 1703 was Sir Isaac Newton. Although Sloane lacked the academic stature of Newton, he took on as secretary much of the responsibility for running the society, and when Newton died in 1727 Sloane seems to have been widely perceived as his natural successor in the office. On 29 March of that year the council unanimously voted him president. The membership at large was split in its loyalties (both personal and political), however, and at the annual general meeting on 30 November there was a lengthy debate before Sloane's election was confirmed by a three-to-one majority. He was to remain in office for fourteen years until, at the age of eighty-one, indifferent health caused him to stand down. An impression of the high esteem in which he was held can be gained from the reluctance of the membership to let him go. A medal struck in 1744 commemorates his distinguished presidency, as does the society's portrait by Kneller.

In the course of his term of office honours had come from other bodies. The French Académie Royale des Sciences appointed him correspondent in 1699 and foreign associate in 1709. He was elected to the foreign membership of the Royal Prussian Academy of Sciences in 1712, to the academies of sciences of St Petersburg and Madrid in 1735, and to membership of the Academy of Sciences in Göttingen in 1752, at the age of ninety-two.

Later years and death Sloane's wife Elizabeth had died in 1724. Together they had four children, a son, Hans, who had died in infancy, and three daughters, of whom one, Mary, had also died an infant. Of the surviving daughters, Sarah married George Stanley of Paultons in Hampshire, while Elizabeth married Colonel Charles (later second Baron) Cadogan. Some memory of these dynastic links is preserved in many of the street names in the Sloane Square area of the Cadogan estate in Chelsea.

In 1739, aged seventy-nine, Sloane was smitten by a paralytic disorder from which he never fully recovered. Three years later, in 1742, he retired to Chelsea after a further serious illness. In 1752 Birch found him 'cheerfull and healthfull but … almost incapable of conversation from his Defects of hearing and speech'. He died on the afternoon of 11 January 1753 at the Manor House, Chelsea, and was buried on 18 January next to his wife in the south-east corner of the churchyard at Chelsea old church. Sloane was well loved by his friends such as Ray, Locke, and Pepys and certainly never went out of his way to make enemies, for he had none of the contentiousness characteristic of many of his contemporaries. Self-effacement seems to have been a prominent character trait: in the opening pages of his *Voyage* he had stated: 'I am sensible there are herein a great many faults, not only in Hypotheses or Opinions, which I propose only as Conjectures, and shall easily part with … [knowing] too well how unduly qualified I am for such an Undertaking'. These twin virtues of industry and modesty were further alluded to by William Stukeley in an assessment of Sloane that is otherwise critical enough as to be clearly unbiased:

> Sʳ Hans Sloan is an instance of the great power of industry which can advance a man to a considerable height in the worlds esteem with moderate parts & learning … He has no faculty of speaking, either fluently or eloquently, especially before any number of people, & he do's it with great timidity. His most commendabl quality is his love for natural learning, & the pains he takes to promote it. (Bodl. Oxf., MS Eng. misc. e 260, fol. 101v)

Collections A further dimension to the esteem with which Sloane is remembered is provided by his collecting activities. The first elements of his collection were formed in the course of his youthful botanizing expeditions, while the Jamaican voyage resulted in a very substantial increase both in the size of the collection and in perceptions of its value. As early as 1691 John Evelyn gave a description of the collection that revealed its already considerable size as well as its diversity, describing it as 'an universal Collection of the natural productions of Jamaica consisting of Plants, [fruits,] Corralls, Minerals, [stones,] Earth, shells, animals, Insects, &c: collected by him with greate Judgement' (Evelyn, *Diary*, 5.48). Subsequent development of the collection depended largely on other ready-made museums which Sloane was able to incorporate into his own: of these the most important were those of William Courten, which he acquired on the latter's death; Leonard Plukenet, from whose herbarium Sloane acquired some 8000 specimens; and James Petiver, whose collection Sloane acquired in 1718.

In addition to these major acquisitions a number of smaller but historically important groups were added over the years. In the field of botany, for example, he bought Nehemiah Grew's collection of seeds and fruits; he also acquired collections of plants built up by Christopher Merret, Jakob Breyne of Danzig, James Cunninghame's Chinese plants, and others from the Philippines collected by Georg Joseph Kamel. Smaller numbers of specimens (including shells as well as plants) were contributed directly or indirectly by an array of famous personalities such as William Dampier.

Plants, shells, and other specimens again came to Sloane from the collection of Engelbert Kaempfer (1651–1716), who had spent two years in Japan as physician to the Dutch East India Company between 1690 and 1692. At no small cost Sloane acquired not only the specimens but also many of Kaempfer's papers, including the unpublished manuscript text for Kaempfer's 'History of Japan', the translation and subsequent publication of which were undertaken at Sloane's expense.

Sloane himself was a subscriber to certain plant hunting expeditions. In 1723 Mark Catesby sent plants, birds, and shells from Carolina to Sloane; eight years later, the first volume of Catesby's *Natural History of Carolina* was published with an acknowledgement to his 'curious Friends' to whom he had sent seeds, plants, corals, and so on, 'more particularly (as I had the greatest Obligations) to that great Naturallist and promoter of Science Sir *Hans Sloane*, Bart to whose goodness I attribute much of the Success I had in this Undertaking'.

Sloane's friends and acquaintances contributed smaller amounts of material. Ralph Thoresby and Richard Richardson both sent geological specimens from the coalpits in their native Yorkshire. Others came from the Revd John Morton and from Peter Collinson. Sir Charles Wager, first lord of the Admiralty, collected a variety of curiosities on his voyages (seemingly at the instigation of Collinson), some of which went to swell the Sloane collection. As it grew in size the collection began to present problems of accommodation, which Sloane solved by acquiring 4 Bloomsbury Place, the property adjacent to his own house, for the ever-expanding museum.

A particular virtue of Sloane's was his punctiliousness in compiling catalogues of every aspect of his collection and library. He has indeed been described as 'a pioneer cataloguer who perceived the need to document his collections in a systematic way' (Jones). In a striking self-analysis, Sloane wrote to the Abbé Bignon that 'the collection and accurate arrangement of these curiosities constituted my major contribution to the advancement of science' (Clarke).

Sloane was notably free with access to his specimens and was 'always ready, on proper Notice to admit the Curious to the sight of his Museum' (BL, Add. MS 4241). Neither was he reluctant, on the whole, to share the benefits of his collection with the learned community. He seems to have been motivated by a strong sense of public utility in forming and expanding the collection. Birch, whose notes are thought to have been compiled from direct conversations with Sloane, expressed it as follows:

> It was not ... a trifling or vain Inclination of merely getting together a great Number of uncommon things, that induc'd him to spend 50,000£ in purchasing the Rarities which every country produced. His constant Endeavour was to employ them to the best purposes, by making himself acquainted, as far as possible, with the Properties, Qualities, & Uses, either in Food, medicine, or manufacture of every Plant, Mineral, or Animal, that came into his possession. By which means he became one of the ablest Physicians of his Age and Country; & in this last Character he was so distinguish'd that for many years he had a Flow of Business which inabled him not only to lay out such vast Sums on his Collection, & to portion out his two Daughters to leave besides a Fortune behind him of [£]100,000. (BL, Add. MS 4241)

Meanwhile, the museum became one of the sights of London for visiting connoisseurs and scientists, most notably Linnaeus, who came in August 1736 bearing a letter of introduction from Hermann Boerhaave. There seems to have been little meeting of minds between the two of them, communication being hindered by difficulties of language and a great difference in age (Linnaeus was twenty-nine at the time while Sloane was seventy-six, tending to deafness, and partly paralysed). The old man failed to respond to the innovative theories of the young Swede, published the previous year in his *Systema naturae*, while Linnaeus was evidently disappointed with Sloane's renowned plant collection, finding it 'in complete disorder' (Linnaeus to Olaus Celsius, Dandy, 11).

Sloane was by now in poor health and his medical practice much curtailed. In 1742, with his retirement from practice, the time had come for Sloane to transfer his household, including the collections, to the manor house at Chelsea. Stukeley paid Sloane a visit on 13 April 1743 and found that 'His great house at Chelsea is full throughout; every closet & chimney with books, raritys, &c' (*Family Memoirs*, 1.358). An account of the museum in its new setting was left by Linnaeus's pupil Per Kalm, who called on Sloane on his way to America in 1748, and in the same year the museum received the accolade of a visit from the

prince and princess of Wales, duly recorded in the press. These descriptions provide some character to the lists of exhibits contained in his catalogues (MacGregor, *Sir Hans Sloane*).

Prudence and application, combined with a sober temperament, a philanthropic nature, and a sense of Christian virtue, marked every aspect of Sloane's career from beginning to end. The rather long and grave face alluded to in the earliest description of him, at the age of twenty-one, marks every known portrait of him in later life. There was to be no sequel in maturity corresponding to the youthful promise of his scientific fieldwork in Jamaica, but he earned in his own day almost universal respect for his able administration of the nation's foremost scientific and medical institutions. The richness of the collections he built up has also been acknowledged since that time, as witnessed by Stukeley:

> Industry may be said to have raisd S^r. Hans, as Art did Radcliff, fortune Mead. S^r. Hans has had this piece of luck too, that being a vertuoso has made his fortune, which generally ruins others ... The same industry has made him perfect master of the knowledg of his immense collection, begun by Mr. Charltons gift, carryd on by his own riches & pains & interest, & may be said to be the greatest that ever was a private mans possession. (*Family Memoirs*, 1.125–6)

The Sloane bequest In an effort to secure the continuing integrity of his collection Sloane drafted a carefully worded will, the first version of which, dated 9 October 1739, was reinforced by half a dozen codicils drawn up between 1746 and 1752 and published as *The Will of Sir Hans Sloane* in 1753. Originally three executors were charged to offer the collection for sale, first to the king, then the Royal Society, and then in turn to a number of bodies at home and abroad. Under a codicil of 10 July 1749 these administrative arrangements were transformed, with the appointment of forty-eight trustees acting under a supervisory body of visitors numbering a further thirty-seven persons of influence, acting privately or *ex officio*. In formulating these complex arrangements Sloane was motivated, in Birch's words, by 'the Desire next his Heart ... that his collection might be kept together for the instruction and Benefit of others engaged in the same pursuits'. When George II proved indifferent to the offer the trustees decided instead to petition parliament with a view to securing the collection for the nation. A stipulation of the will was that a legacy of £20,000 for Sloane's two daughters had to be provided by whoever acquired it. With this in mind Sloane's former curator, James Empson, was summoned before parliament to give an estimate of its value which was, in his opinion, some £80,000 if not £100,000; whereupon the members were persuaded that 'it will be for the Honor and Advantage of this Country to accept of Sir Hans Sloane's Legacy' (MacGregor, *Sir Hans Sloane*, 49). As well as the museum collection, the legacy included Sloane's library of manuscripts and printed books; the manuscripts alone, rich in medieval and later tracts on natural science and medicine, collected letters and papers including Sloane's own voluminous correspondence, remain one of the great resources for scholarly research into eighteenth-century intellectual history, though as yet they lack both a definitive catalogue and all but the most partial of topical surveys.

Parliament further decided to purchase the manuscripts from the collection of the Harleys, first and second earls of Oxford, which were then on the market. With the Sloane and Harleian collections were to be combined the manuscripts left to the nation in 1700 by Sir Robert Cotton, all three to form the founding collection of the British Museum, established by act of parliament on 7 June 1753.

ARTHUR MACGREGOR

Sources BL, Add. MS 4241 [memoir by Thomas Birch] · Coll. Arms, MS 3.D.14, pp. 85–6 · G. R. de Beer, *Sir Hans Sloane and the British Museum* (1953) · *DSB* · E. St. J. Brooks, *Sir Hans Sloane: the great collector and his circle* (1954) · A. MacGregor, ed., *Sir Hans Sloane: collector, scientist, antiquary, founding father of the British Museum* (1994) · J. Britten and J. E. Dandy, eds., *The Sloane herbarium* (1958) · P. M. Jones, 'A preliminary check-list of Sir Hans Sloane's catalogues', *British Library Journal*, 14 (1988), 38–40 · A. MacGregor, 'The natural history correspondence of Sir Hans Sloane', *Archives of Natural History*, 22 (1995), 79–90 · J. Jacquot, 'Sir Hans Sloane and French men of science', *Notes and Records of the Royal Society*, 10 (1952–3), 85–98 · J. A. Clarke, 'Sir Hans Sloane and the Abbé Bignon: notes on collection building in the eighteenth century', *Library Quarterly*, 50 (1980) · R. D. Lund, '"More strange than true": Sir Hans Sloane, King's *Transactioneer* and the deformation of English prose', *Studies in Eighteenth-Century Culture*, 14 (1985), 213–30 · I. B. Cohen, 'Isaac Newton, Hans Sloane and the Académie Royale des Sciences', *L'aventure de la science*, ed. A. Koyré (1964), 81–102 · G. R. de Beer, 'Relations between fellows of the Royal Society and the French men of science when France and Britain were at war', *Notes and Records of the Royal Society*, 9 (1951–2), 244–99 · C. G. Thomas, 'Sir Hans Sloane and the Russian Academy of Sciences', *British Library Journal*, 14 (1988), 21–4 · J. A. Oshlag, 'The ethical practices of Sir Hans Sloane', *Bulletin of the History of Medicine*, 21 (1947), 918–21 · M. Ultee, 'Sir Hans Sloane, scientist', *British Library Journal*, 14 (1988), 1–20 · K. Dewhurst, 'The correspondence between John Locke and Sir Hans Sloane', *British Journal of Medical Science*, 6th ser., 143 (1960), 201–12 · W. R. Sloan, 'Sir Hans Sloane, FRS, legend and lineage', *Notes and Records of the Royal Society*, 35 (1980), 125–9 · R. W. T. Gunther, *Further correspondence of John Ray* (1928) · *The family memoirs of the Rev. William Stukeley*, ed. W. C. Lukis, 3 vols., SurtS, 73, 76, 80 (1882–7) · H. Sloane, *A voyage to the islands Madera, Nieves, S. Christophers, and Jamaica, with the natural history … of the last of those islands*, 2 vols. (1707–25) · H. Sloane, *Catalogus plantarum quae in insula Jamaica sponte proveniunt* (1696) · M. J. Crossley Evans, 'The maternal ancestry of Sir Hans Sloane (1660–1753), and the household of Ann Hamilton (c.1612–89), Countess of Clanbrassil', *Antiquaries Journal*, 80 (2000), 302–8 · *The will of Sir Hans Sloane* (1753)

Archives BL, corresp. and papers, Add. MS 29470 · Lincs. Arch., papers relating to Jamaica plantations and regarding marriage settlement · NHM, catalogues of natural history collections · RS, letters and papers | Bodl. Oxf., letters to Richard Richardson · NHM, letters [copies; originals at RS, Linn. Soc., Wellcome L., and a library in Göttingen] · NHM, letters to Johann Jacob Scheuchzer [copies]

Likenesses G. Kneller, oils, 1716, RS · T. Murray, oils, c.1725, RCP Lond. · J. Faber junior, mezzotint, 1728 (after T. Murray), BM, NPG · J. Faber junior, mezzotint, 1729 (after G. Kneller), Wellcome L. · J. Richardson, oils, 1730, Examination Schools, Oxford · S. Slaughter, oils, 1736, NPG [see illus.] · J. M. Rysbrack, statue, 1737, Chelsea Physic Garden, London · Wray, line engraving, 1795 (after T. Murray), Wellcome L. · J. B. Bird, stipple (after S. Slaughter) · J. A. Dassier, medal, BM · attrib. G. Kneller, portrait, TCD · W. H. Lizars, line engraving (after T. Murray, 1722), Wellcome L. · J. M. Rysbrack, terracotta bust, BM · attrib. J. Vanderbank, oils, BM · line engraving (after G. Kneller, 1716), Wellcome L.

Wealth at death £100,000; plus value of collection (perhaps another £100,000): BL, Add. MS 4241 [memoir by Thomas Birch]

Sloggett, Sir Arthur Thomas (1857–1929), army medical officer, was born on 24 November 1857 at 4 Napier Street, Stoke Damerel, Devonport, Devon, the son of William Henry Sloggett, surgeon on HMS *Calypso* (later inspector-general of the Royal Navy), of Tremabyn, Paignton, Devon, and his wife, Elizabeth, daughter of Thomas Cornish-Crossing JP of Stoke Damerel.

Sloggett was educated at King's College, London, and after qualifying MRCS and LRCP (Edinburgh) in 1880 he entered the army as a surgeon the following year. His early service, mainly in the East, included service on the Indian frontier in 1884; he made his name as senior medical officer with the Dongola expeditionary force in 1896, in the Sudan in 1897–8, and in the Second South African War. He was wounded at Omdurman during the charge of the 21st lancers. A young medical officer in India in 1909 later reported that:

> Sloggett was one of the best known, and a long way the most decorated, of the officers of the Medical Service at that time … He had been specially promoted twice and was then far and away the youngest Surgeon-General in the Army. (Blackham, 124)

His marriage in 1881 to Helen Sophia, daughter of John Robert Boyson, resulted in a son and two daughters, but did not impede growth of a reputation for success in the boudoir and in following the hounds.

Sloggett's career advanced in the new RAMC in which he showed great pride in its standing and rights to use full military titles. After service as director of medical services in India between 1911 and 1914 he had returned to the UK as director of the corps. In October he went to France as director of medical services on the western front, while Sir Arthur Keogh returned to the War Office as director, his health precluding service in France. As director-general of medical services on the western front (1914–18), Sloggett provided the leadership and drive to meet the new challenges of trench warfare. By 1916 he was able to contrast the western front with conditions 'in parts of the Mediterranean where nobody seemed to know who was at the head of anything!' (Butler, 869).

Sloggett also supported a new role for leading civilian specialists, such as Almroth Wright, the surgeon Sir Anthony Bowlby, and the American neurosurgeon Harvey Cushing as consultants on the western front. In his journal for 5 May 1915 Cushing records how he first mounted 'the narrow dark stairs to the busy crowded offices of that important person the overseas D.G. General Sir Arthur Sloggett' (Cushing, 65). Many contacts followed. Sloggett formed an effective team with his deputy Macpherson and successor Burtchaell, in managing the services. He also held posts as chief officer of the Red Cross and St John Ambulance, and was thus able to encourage growth of a

Sir Arthur Thomas Sloggett (1857–1929), by Bassano, 1917

voluntary contribution. Sloggett was open to new ideas: for example, after a tour of inspection of the French services in 1915 he secured the introduction of the steel helmet in the British forces. Sloggett was successful in gaining a high priority in resources for the RAMC and in winning the respect of Field Marshal Haig and his staff. He was active in social events at general headquarters, becoming 'the life and soul' of the dinner party celebrating new year 1916 with 'his yarns, some of which were libellous and few of which would have passed muster in a drawing-room' while Haig 'kept silence merrily' (Charteris, 129).

After some delays Sloggett supported an expansion of the role of the casualty clearing stations after 1916 so as to avoid unnecessary transport and movement of wounded men. He stressed the personal responsibility of officers for health and sanitation of their troops, a direct criticism of the Australian approach. There was some friction with the Australian services as Sloggett resisted dilution of his authority. In contrast the Canadian *Official History*, a notably critical source on most issues, paid a warm tribute to Sloggett's team: 'these three bore that heavy burden of war until the end. Few Canadians came in actual contact with them, but all felt their strong sure hand; and to the sick and wounded it was a kindly hand' (Macphail, 338). Sloggett was made CMG (1901), CB (1910), KCB (1915), and KCMG, KCVO (1917).

Sloggett had his critics, such as Viscountess D'Abernon, a luminary of the Red Cross, who described him as 'not unlike Mr Punch' with a 'breezy manner and a crimson nose'. She would have preferred to see 'a younger and

more serious minded man' take his place (*Red Cross and Berlin Embassy*, 4). However, Sloggett's style concealed many achievements of substance. The RAMC accomplished remarkable results in prevention, sanitation, and effective care of the wounded. Sloggett's personal contribution was recognized when he retired on 1 June 1918. Cushing recorded, 'A send-off to General Sloggett—the most elaborate any retiring general has seen. Even French, when recalled, had nothing like it. It betrayed a very genuine affection for Sir Arthur' (Cushing, 367).

From 1921 to 1928 Sloggett was colonel of the RAMC and was active as a company director. He died suddenly as a result of heart disease while walking in Upper Baker Street, London, with his son on 27 November 1929. Sloggett's reputation has today been eclipsed by that of Keogh, but this should not allow the crucial contribution he made in a time of great crisis to go overlooked.

NICK BOSANQUET

Sources W. G. Macpherson, *Medical services: general history*, History of the Great War, 1–3 (1921–4) · A. Macphail, *Official history of the Canadian forces in the Great War, 1914–19: the medical services* (1925), 338 · A. G. Butler, *The western front* (1940), vol. 2 of *Official history of the Australian medical services, 1914–18*, 869 · H. Cushing, *From a surgeon's journal* (1936), 65, 367 · R. J. Blackham, *Scalpel, sword and stretcher* (1932), 124 · J. Charteris, *At G.H.Q.* (1931), 129 · Viscountess D' Abernon, *Red Cross and Berlin embassy, 1915–1926* (1946), 4 · N. Bosanquet, 'Health systems in khaki: the British and American medical experience', *Facing Armageddon: the First World War experienced*, ed. H. Cecil and P. H. Liddle (1996), 451–65 · W. Herringham, *A physician in France* (1919) · B. Oliver, *The British Red Cross in action* (1966) · A. Sloggett, 'The international congress at Lisbon 1906', *Journal of the Royal Army Medical Corps*, 7 (1906), 618–24 · Army medical services, 1898–1968, 7th anniversary edition (1968) · *RAMC News and Gazette* (Jan 1930), 218 · m. cert. · d. cert.
Archives Bodl. Oxf., corresp. with Sir Henry Burdett
Likenesses Bassano, photograph, 1917, NPG [*see illus.*] · photograph, repro. in *ILN* (8 Oct 1898)
Wealth at death £19,476 0s. 11d.: probate, 21 Jan 1930, CGPLA Eng. & Wales

Sloper, Edward Hugh Lindsay (1826–1887), pianist and music teacher, was born in London on 14 June 1826. He studied the piano in London under Ignaz Moscheles until he was fourteen, and then went first to Aloys Schmitt in Frankfurt, later to Vollweiler in Heidelberg to study harmony and counterpoint, and finally to Boisselot in Paris (1841–6). After returning to London in 1846 he appeared occasionally as a pianist at the concerts of the Musical Union (1846) and at the Philharmonic Society (6 May 1850), of which he subsequently became a member. As his teaching commitments grew his public appearances waned, and ultimately he devoted himself entirely to teaching, for which his services were apparently in constant demand. He is reported to have lectured on music in England at Alexandra Palace in May 1876.

Sloper was a prolific composer, chiefly for the piano, and his works include a sonata for violin and piano, studies for piano (opp. 3 and 13), *Pianoforte Instructions, Exercises, and Lessons* (1854), a *Technical Guide to Touch, Fingering, and Execution on the Pianoforte* (1877), transcriptions and arrangements for piano, and songs. He also edited piano pieces and other works by more prominent composers. Sloper died at his London home, 63 York Terrace, Regent's Park, on 3 July 1887.   R. H. LEGGE, *rev.* DAVID J. GOLBY

Sources Brown & Stratton, *Brit. mus.* [incl. work list] • private information (1897) • *CGPLA Eng. & Wales* (1887) • Grove, *Dict. mus.* **Wealth at death** £80 4s. 3d.: probate, 22 July 1887, *CGPLA Eng. & Wales*

Smalbroke, Richard (1672–1749), bishop of Coventry and Lichfield, was born at 19 High Street, Birmingham, and baptized on 3 November 1672 at St Martin's, Birmingham, the son of Samuel Smalbroke (*d.* 1701) of Rowington, Warwickshire, and his wife, Elizabeth Knight (*d.* 1722). He probably attended King Edward's School in Birmingham before admission to Trinity College, Oxford, in 1688 at the age of fifteen. Smalbroke was elected demy of Magdalen in 1689, along with Joseph Addison, and fellow in 1698; he graduated BA in 1692 and proceeded MA in 1695, BD in 1707, and DD in 1708. In 1709 Thomas Tenison, archbishop of Canterbury, appointed him his chaplain and gave him the rectory of Hadleigh, Suffolk. He became a canon of Hereford (1710), vicar of Lugwardine, Herefordshire (1711), the last treasurer of Llandaff to hold the office (1712), and rector of Withington, Gloucestershire (1716). Having been elected bishop of St David's in 1723 he was translated to the see of Coventry and Lichfield in 1731.

Smalbroke entered into the theological controversies of his day as a stalwart champion of orthodoxy. In 1706 he published a university sermon refuting the opinion of the nonjuror Henry Dodwell the elder, that baptism confers immortality. He issued three pamphlets against William Whiston, in which he attacked Whiston's Arianism and his claims for the authenticity of the apocryphal Clementine constitutions. In his *Enquiry into the … Complutensian Edition of the New Testament* (1722) Smalbroke urged the classical scholar Richard Bentley to seek confirmation of 1 John 5: 7, a verse that affirms the Trinity, in an ancient Greek manuscript that was thought to be in the Vatican. He systematically refuted the arguments of the free-thinker Thomas Woolston in *A Vindication of the Miracles of our Blessed Saviour* (2 vols., 1729; 1731), his most significant work, in which he demonstrated both his ability as a patristic scholar and his faith in the literal truth of the Bible. In this and other writings he insisted that the clergy, and even laymen, should report crimes against orthodox religion to the civil magistrate and assist in prosecuting the heterodox, such as Whiston. In his sermons and charges, Smalbroke emphasized the dangers of Quakerism, Methodism, and Roman Catholicism as well as enthusiasm, deism, and Arianism. Against these evils he recommended study of the Bible and reinforcement of discipline.

Smalbroke's polemics provoked many replies, which questioned his judgement and sometimes his motivation. Woolston and others accused Smalbroke of encouraging the civil magistrate to punish him for blasphemy; Woolston insinuated, in the ironical dedication of his *Third Discourse on the Miracles of our Saviour* (1728), that desire for translation to a wealthier see had motivated Smalbroke in

his zeal for upholding orthodoxy. Smalbroke replied angrily to the criticism of Browne Willis, who noted, in his *Survey of the Church of Landaff* [*sic*] (1719), that the roof of the cathedral needed repairs, thereby criticising Smalbroke's diligence in his post of treasurer of Llandaff. Smalbroke was married to Catherine Brookes, with whom he had three sons and four daughters. He was assiduous in reserving clerical preferments for members of his family: he bestowed an archdeaconry on his brother-in-law, Richard Brookes, and distributed two more archdeaconries, a chancellorship, a precentorship, three canonries, a living, the mastership of a hospital, and the registrarship of the diocese among his three sons and three sons-in-law. When he died on 22 December 1749, at Lichfield Cathedral, he owned substantial property in Warwickshire and Worcestershire which he bequeathed to his eldest son, Richard (*d.* 1805), who held the post of chancellor of the Coventry and Lichfield diocese for sixty-four years. Smalbroke provided generously for his widow, but less well for their unmarried son and daughter. In his will he prescribed the place of his tomb in Lichfield Cathedral and the inscription for his memorial on the wall. He also stipulated that Richard Allestree's *The Whole Duty of Man* and William Sherlock's *A Practical Discourse Concerning Death* should be distributed to the poor of Birmingham and that his collection of books should always remain in his family.

WILLIAM H. TRAPNELL

Sources F. L. Colvile, *The worthies of Warwickshire who lived between 1500 and 1800* [1870] • Foster, *Alum. Oxon.* • will, PRO, PROB 11/775, sig. 378 • W. Beresford, *Lichfield* [1883] • J. Hunt, *Religious thought in England from the Reformation to the end of the last century*, 2 (1871), 417–24 • W. Whiston, *Memoirs of the life and writings of Mr William Whiston: containing memoirs of several of his friends also*, 2nd edn, 2 vols. (1753) • *DNB* • *IGI* **Archives** LPL, court of arches, Acts 27 • LPL, archbishop's acts book, 1701–10 **Likenesses** G. Vertue, line engraving, 1733 (after T. Murray), BM, NPG • oils, Magd. Oxf. **Wealth at death** lands in Warwickshire and Worcestershire: will, PRO, PROB 11/775, sig. 378

Small, Ann Hunter [Annie] (1857–1945), missionary and educationist, was born on 26 December 1857 at Polmont, Redding, Stirlingshire, the eldest of the three daughters, all subsequently missionaries, of the Revd John Small (1833–1899), trained teacher and missionary of the Free Church of Scotland in India, and his wife, Nathina Hunter (1824/5 – 14 April 1913). At six she went to India, where she was educated by her mother and learned the local language; from thirteen to seventeen she attended the School for the Daughters of Missionaries at Walthamstow, Essex, where her talents blossomed in a community which fostered individual development.

From 1876 to 1892 Annie Small worked in India, mainly as an agent of the Free Church of Scotland Ladies' Society for Female Education in India and South Africa, specializing in the expanding work among women. Her book, *Light and Shade in Zenana Missionary Life* (1890), graphically described the skills needed—but seldom found—in the new recruits sent out. Based mainly in Poona and influenced by her father's enlightened attitude, she gained deep insight into Indian culture and religion.

Small was invalided back to Britain in 1892, at a time when training for the increasing numbers of women missionaries had become urgent; this was pioneering work as there was then no special training for either male or female missionaries. Appointed in 1894 as the first principal of the Free Church Women's Missionary Training Institute in Edinburgh (later St Colm's Women's Missionary College of the United Free Church of Scotland), she aimed to make the institute a place of training for life, not 'a sort of hothouse for "forcing" a certain type of missionary character' (house guild letter, May 1909, St Colm's College). Treating her students as responsible individuals she sought personal development founded on the strong spiritual life of the college community, while not neglecting modern educational methods. The college attracted students from all denominations throughout Britain and beyond, especially from Switzerland, Germany, and Scandinavia.

Small exemplified her own ideal of the true missionary as 'a throughly furnished man or woman' (Small, *Letters*, 154). She was a slight person, of simple tastes, sane, far-sighted, joyous, and deeply spiritual, an accomplished musician, and a graphic writer—her works ranged from early books on India to biblical and devotional studies, notably *The Psalter and the Life of Prayer* (1912). Her interests ranged from the arts and crafts movement to the late nineteenth-century liturgical revival, from politics to the Celtic church. She is credited with drawing the attention of the Revd George MacLeod to Iona as a centre for his community. A proud presbyterian she nevertheless rejoiced in being part of the worldwide church in all its diversity, and her studies on Islam and Buddhism written for the Student Christian Movement show her enlightened attitude towards dialogue with other faiths—a contrast to the empire-building view of missions of many of her contemporaries.

Annie Small's portrait in the college reveals a serene gentleness, though not the impressive presence radiating goodness remembered by those who knew her. Her ability to get on well with people extended from her students to many of the great figures of the time. Though never associated with the women's movement she was regarded with suspicion in some church circles for her advocacy of women's training. At the Edinburgh World Missionary Conference in 1910 she was secretary of Commission V whose remit was to study the preparation of missionaries; the commission's influential report recognized the excellence of St Colm's College. Honoured in missionary circles she became a sought-after leader of training courses for both sexes. The college became a model for new training institutions in England and abroad.

Small retired in 1913, exhausted—her health was never strong. She continued to live in Edinburgh, a valued speaker at conferences and a profound influence on her many visitors. She died of a heart attack, in an Edinburgh nursing home, on 7 February 1945. In accordance with her will she was cremated, at Warriston crematorium, Edinburgh, on 10 February; she had directed that her ashes should be buried in the family grave at Arbroath Abbey. She never married.   ISABEL LUSK

Sources O. Wyon, *The three windows: the story of Ann Hunter Small* (1953) · A. H. Small, *Memories of fifty years, 1894–1944: the Church of Scotland* (1944) · 'Preparation of missionaries', report of Commission V, World Missionary Conference, Edinburgh, 1910 · private information (2004) · Women's Foreign Missionary Society Training Institute minute book, 1894–1923 (Church of Scotland) · house guild letters and handbooks, Women's Missionary Training Institute and College, St Colm's College, Edinburgh · A. H. Small, *Letters to missionary friends* (1908) · Scottish Foreign Mission records, 1827–1929, NL Scot. · I. Lusk, 'A throughly furnished woman—Annie Small and the training of women missionaries', lecture, 1994, St Colm's College, Edinburgh

Likenesses D. Hole, pencil drawing, 1913, St Colm's International House, Edinburgh · photographs, repro. in Wyon, *Three windows*

Wealth at death £428 3s. 9d.: confirmation, 30 April 1945, CCI

Small, Edward Francis (1890–1958), journalist, trade unionist, and nationalist politician in the Gambia, was born on 29 January 1890, in Bathurst (later Banjul), capital of the British colony of the Gambia. His father was John W. Small, a well-regarded Aku (Sierra Leonian) Methodist tailor and outfitter. He was one of four children—two boys and two step-sisters. An unusually able pupil, he won a government scholarship to Methodist Boys' High School, Freetown, Sierra Leone. He returned home in 1912 and worked as a public works department clerk. Resigning when refused promotion, he taught at the Methodist Boys' High School, Bathurst, and envisaged training as a Methodist minister. He was sent upriver to Ballanghar as a probationary mission agent in 1917, where he clashed with a European trader. The incident, trivial in itself, escalated when the local British administrator, and then the Methodist church, sided with the trader and recalled Small. He was dismissed for insubordination and these events appear to have radicalized him politically.

In 1919, while working upriver at Kaur for a European trading company, Small founded the Gambia Native Defence Union, formed among like-minded Bathurst Akus. In 1919–20 he converted it into the local branch of the inter-territorial National Congress of British West Africa, giving up his job to represent the Gambia at the founding of the Congress in Accra, Gold Coast, in March 1920. As secretary of the Gambia National Congress, essentially a moderate nationalist organization, Small adopted a more radical political position, championing African rights and frequently attacking government in his newspaper, *The Gambia Outlook and Senegambia Reporter*, which first appeared on 27 May 1922, the first newspaper since the demise of *The Intelligencer* in the 1890s.

Undeterred by the collapse of the National Congress of British West Africa and the intermittent appearance of his newspaper, Small went on in 1929 to found both the Gambia Planters' Syndicate (later renamed the Gambia Farmers' Co-operative Association) to fight for improved groundnut prices, and the first trade union in Gambia, the Bathurst Trade Union. In November 1929 he organized one of the most successful strikes in colonial Africa before the Second World War. He also helped bring into existence the important Gambia trade union ordinance of 1932. Ousted from control of the Bathurst Trade Union in a leadership quarrel, he set up in 1935 a rival trade union, the Gambia Labour Union, which still exists today. His trade-union and anti-colonial (but never anti-British) activities led him to establish links with socialist and communist organizations in Britain and Europe; he even attended a communist-backed anti-colonial conference in Hamburg, Germany, in July 1930, organized by the International Trade Union Committee of Negro Workers, an affiliate of the Red International of Labour Unions (Profintern). Small was elected to its presidium and was sufficiently enthused to deliver a paper denouncing British imperialism in the Gambia. Yet it is unlikely that his links with international communism were other than tactical, given his Methodist upbringing and essentially constitutionalist political outlook and the failure of such connections to provide him with expected financial support. Even so, his brief dalliance with European left-wing political organizations, together with his constant attacks on the local administration and European business community, convinced the British and Gambian governments that he was a communist agitator. Official correspondence at this time describe him as a 'link subversive'.

The peripatetic Small continued his political career in Bathurst in the mid-1930s through the Rate Payers' Association, of which he was chairman; but by the late 1930s he gradually mellowed in his attitude towards the government and his strong pro-British stance at the start of the Second World War persuaded the colonial administration to permit his appointment to the legislative council in 1942, as the nominee of the Bathurst municipal authority. Following post-war constitutional reforms, Small won the first direct election to the legislative council in 1947, representing Bathurst. In 1951 he was defeated for re-election to the legislative council by two former acolytes, I. M. Garba-Jahumpa and the Revd J. C. Faye, a painful experience partly ameliorated by Governor Wyn-Harris's reappointment of him to the legislative council in 1954 as a nominated member and his successful recommendation of Small for the OBE. The pre-war radical had now evolved into a far more conservative elder statesman, who was even critical of too rapid an extension of the franchise in the post-war period. During this time he was also active in the anti-communist world trade union movement, obtaining a seat on the general executive council of the International Confederation of Free Trade Unions (which broke away from the communist-dominated World Federation of Trade Unions in 1948), a position he held from 1945 until his death. He died in Bathurst on 3 January 1958 and was buried there in the Christian cemetery. Though regarded during his lifetime as somewhat of a recluse and eccentric in his private life—he never married and seldom socialized, preferring instead to play the piano at his home, 4 Allen Street, Bathurst—'Pa' Small was to be warmly remembered as the 'Watchdog of the Gambia', for his fearless journalism and role as unofficial ombudsman;

and as his country's first modern political leader and founder both of trade unionism and the agricultural co-operative movement in the Gambia.

ARNOLD HUGHES

Sources A. Hughes and H. A. Gailey, *Historical dictionary of the Gambia* (1999) • A. Hughes and D. Perfect, 'Trade unionism in the Gambia', *African Affairs*, 88/349 (Dec 1989), 549–72 • J. Ayodele Langley, 'The Gambia section of the national congress of British West Africa', *Africa*, 34/4 (Oct 1969), 382–95 • D. Perfect, 'The political career of Edward Francis Small', *The Gambia: studies in society and politics*, ed. A. Hughes (1991), 64–79 • D. Perfect, 'Organised labour and politics in the Gambia, 1920–1984', PhD diss., U. Birm., 1994, chaps. 2–5

Archives Gambia National Archives, Banjul, copies of his newspaper • PRO, official corresp. relating to him | Gambia National Archives, Banjul, official corresp. relating to him • Senegal National Archives, Dakar, official corresp. relating to him

Likenesses photographs, Gambia National Archives, Banjul

Small, James (*bap.* **1740**, *d.* **1793**), agriculturist and plough maker, was born at Upsettlington in the parish of Ladykirk, Berwickshire, and baptized in Ladykirk on 28 March 1740; he was the son of John Small, a farmer, and Elspeth Robeson. He served an apprenticeship with a carpenter and plough maker at Hutton, Berwickshire. About 1758 he went to Yorkshire to work for a Mr Robertson, maker of wagons and carriages at Doncaster. He returned to Scotland in 1763 and settled on a farm at Blackadder Mount, Berwickshire, where he also had a blacksmith's shop. Here he started to experiment with ploughs to establish which worked with the least draught. On 30 December 1766 he married Janet Smith at Chirnside, Berwickshire.

There is much speculation about how much Small based his work on his knowledge of developments in England, especially the design of the Rotherham plough introduced during the 1730s. This plough, with a breast covered with iron plate and iron coulter and share, introduced some elements of standardized design and construction. By the time Small was working in Yorkshire, ploughs of the Rotherham type were becoming well known and examples were to be found in the Scottish lowlands. However, he conducted his experiments using the local ploughs of Berwickshire, known as the 'old Scotch' type. They were heavy, needing, it was said, at least a pair of horses and a pair of oxen to draw them with several labourers to control plough and animals. The Berwickshire landowner James Renton of Lammermuir became his patron, financing the establishment of Small's smithy and carpenter's shop, and also advancing the working capital. After years of trials he constructed his first improved plough in 1779–80. It had a mouldboard of iron, cast at the Carron foundry. The reduced friction through the soil of this mouldboard meant that Small's ploughs normally required only a pair of horses and one ploughman. Trials by the Dalkeith Farming Society showed Small's plough requiring only 9–10 cwt of force in ploughing up old pasture compared with 16 cwt needed by the old Scotch type. Small subsequently extended the use of cast iron to other parts hitherto made of wood, including the sheath and head. Small's plough was not suitable for all types of soil and so was not universally popular (the ploughmen in, for example, Lanarkshire being quite against it). There remained room for debate as to the precise design of mouldboards and the mathematics involved. However, Small had established the principles which all subsequent designers followed. In introducing more cast-iron parts he was also opening up a path leading to the establishment of large plough works and agricultural engineering firms.

Small enjoyed patronage from several leaders of Scottish society. Henry Home, Lord Kames, encouraged him in the publication of his treatise. Sir John Sinclair, a leader of progressive agricultural opinion in Scotland, was another champion of Small and his work. Small did not forget his first investor, Renton, who in 1784 became the dedicatee of his *Treatise of Ploughs and Wheel-Carriages*. This book made Small the first to set out the scientific principles of plough design in print, building upon and clarifying the work of previous thinkers on the subject as well as expressing his own theories. The treatise was the standard text on plough design for fifty years.

Small's works employed a number of hands in the manufacture of ploughs, wagons, and carts. He moved in the early 1780s to Rosebank, Ford, Edinburghshire. Here he enjoyed the patronage of Henry Scott, third duke of Buccleuch. His sons, John and Alexander, began to take a more active role in the implement-making business, which continued after his death as Alexander Small & Co. James Small died in 1793. JONATHAN BROWN

Sources H. Cheape, 'James Small and plough innovation', *Acta Museorum Agriculturae*, 19 (1986–7), 93–106 · J. Sinclair, 'Account of James Small and his improvements of agricultural implements', *An account of the systems of husbandry adopted in the more improved districts of Scotland* (1812), appx [separate edn 1811] · A. Bruce, *General view of the agriculture of the county of Berwick* (1794) · J. A. Ransome, *The implements of agriculture* (1843) · G. E. Fussell, *More old English farming books, … 1731–1793* (1950), vol. 2 of *The old English farming books* (1947–91) · J. Small, *A treatise on ploughs and wheel-carriages* (1784) · G. E. Fussell, *The farmer's tools, 1500–1900* (1952) · parish register, Ladykirk, Berwickshire, 28 March 1740 [baptism] · parish register, Chirnside, Berwickshire, 30 Dec 1766 [marriage]

Small, John (1726–1796), army officer, was born at Strathardle, Atholl, Perthshire, the son of Patrick Small, a minister. After serving in the Scottish brigade in the Dutch service, he obtained a commission as ensign in the 42nd highlanders (the Black Watch) on 29 August 1747, and was promoted lieutenant in 1756, on the eve of the 42nd's departure to America to serve under John Campbell, fourth earl of Loudoun (1705–1782). He took part in the unsuccessful attack in July 1758 on Ticonderoga, under Major-General James Abercrombie, when the 42nd and other British units, attacking without artillery, suffered heavy casualties. Small accompanied Sir Jeffrey Amherst in his expedition the following year against French Canada, and in 1760 he went to Montreal. In 1762 he sailed with his regiment against Martinique and was made captain. On 14 June 1775 he received a commission as major to raise a force of highlanders in Nova Scotia to act against the rebel American colonists. He took part in the battle of Bunker Hill (17 June 1775), and shortly afterwards was appointed to command the 2nd battalion, 84th Royal

Engineers, with part of which he joined Sir Henry Clinton at New York in 1779. He was promoted lieutenant-colonel in 1780 and colonel on 18 November 1790. In 1793 he was appointed lieutenant-governor of Guernsey, and on 3 October 1794 he became major-general. He never married, prevented, according to his will, by 'the exigencies of military duty which may affect my life and liberty'. He died at Guernsey on 17 March 1796. His will named his brother Alexander Small, of Ware, Hertfordshire, his sister Margaret Small, and a niece, Susan Robertson, among his heirs, and referred to his friendships with the duke of Clarence (afterwards William IV) and Sir Robert Murray Keith. He left an estate of 1000 acres in Nova Scotia to his cousin Patrick Small, of Wood Street, London, on the condition that he built a mansion house there.

E. I. CARLYLE, *rev.* ROGER T. STEARN

Sources R. Cannon, ed., *Historical record of the forty-second, or the royal highland regiment of foot* (1845) · D. Appleton, *Appleton's cyclopaedia of American biography*, 7 vols. (1886), vol. 5 · N&Q, 8th ser., 4 (1893), 98 · J. Holland Rose and others, eds., *Canada and Newfoundland* (1930), vol. 6 of *The Cambridge history of the British empire* (1929–59) · J. Black, *Britain as a military power, 1688–1815* (1999) · P. Mackesy, *The war for America, 1775–1783* (1993) · S. Conway, *The War of American Independence, 1775–1783* (1995) · E. Linklater and A. Linklater, *The black watch: the history of the royal highland regiment* (1977) · will, PRO, PROB 11/1275, sig. 279

Likenesses P. Jean, miniature, *c.*1783–1787, R. W. Norton Art Gallery, Shreveport, Louisiana · J. Trumbull, group portrait (*The death of General Warren at Bunker's Hill*), Yale U. Art Gallery · chalk drawing, Scot. NPG

Wealth at death see will, PRO, PROB 11/1275, sig. 279

Small, John (1737–1826). *See under* Hambledon cricket club (*act. c.*1750–*c.*1796).

Small, John (1828–1886), librarian, the son of John Small (*d.* 1847) and his wife, Margaret Brown, was born in Edinburgh. He was educated at the Edinburgh Academy and the University of Edinburgh, where he graduated MA in 1847. In the same year, on the death of his father, who was sub-librarian of Edinburgh University Library, he succeeded to the post. In 1854, in succession to Professor Alexander Brunton (1772–1854), he was appointed librarian, with an official residence. He was the first non-professional librarian since the seventeenth century, and in his thirty-two years of service secured extra space, extra assistants, and the receipt of several important collections—notably the manuscripts accumulated by David Laing. Also in succession to his father, he held the office of acting librarian to the College of Physicians (Edinburgh), for which he prepared a catalogue in 1863. He was president of the Library Association in 1880, and in 1886 the University of Edinburgh awarded him the degree of LLD. He was also for some time treasurer of the university musical society.

Small devoted his leisure to a range of literary work. His first large publication was *English Metrical Homilies … Edited, with an Introduction and Notes* (1862), and in 1864 he published biographical sketches of Adam Fergusson and Patrick Fraser Tytler. He was the chief associate of Cosmo Innes in editing the *Journal of Andrew Halyburton*, published in 1867. Subsequently, he spent much of his time editing, with glossaries and indices, the works of early Scottish poets, producing *The Poetical Works of Gavin Douglas* (1874), as well as Sir David Lyndesay's *Monarchie* (1865–6) for the Early English Text Society and *The Poems of William Dunbar* (1884–92) for the Scottish Text Society. In 1885 he re-edited David Laing's *Select Remains of the Ancient Popular Poetry of Scotland* (1822), adding a bibliographical notice of the original editor. He contributed numerous papers to the *Transactions of the Royal Society of Edinburgh* and the *Proceedings of the Society of Antiquaries of Scotland*, and compiled two volumes on *The Castles and Mansions of the Lothians* (1878), still valuable for their contemporary photographs. Among other editorial texts, he gave much assistance to Sir Alexander Grant in writing *The History of the University of Edinburgh* (1884).

After a long illness Small died in Edinburgh on 20 August 1886, and was buried three days later, in the family burial-place in the Grange cemetery. His daughter Jessie (*d.* 1924) bequeathed £5000 to the university for the benefit of its library, especially in early Scottish literature.

GEORGE STRONACH, *rev.* NILANJANA BANERJI

Sources *Library Chronicle* (Dec 1887) · *The Scotsman* (23 Aug 1886) · T. R. Guild and A. Law, eds., *Edinburgh University Library, 1580–1980: a collection of historical essays* (1982)
Archives U. Edin. L., corresp. with James Halliwell-Phillipps
Wealth at death £2476 11*s.* 5*d.*: confirmation, 26 Oct 1886, *CCI*

Small, (Robert) Leonard (1905–1994), Church of Scotland minister, was born on 12 May 1905 in North Berwick, Scotland, son of the Revd Robert Small (1866–1959), minister of the United Free church, and his wife, Marion Cavet McEwen (*b.* 1875). He was educated at North Berwick high school (1910–23), Edinburgh University (1924–8), where he graduated MA with first-class honours in classics, and New College, Edinburgh (1928–30). During his time at the latter, a theological college of the United Free church, it was merged with the faculty of divinity of Edinburgh University when the United Free church was reunited with the Church of Scotland in 1929. Small also undertook further theological study at the universities of Rome, Berlin, and Zürich (1930–31). He was tall and fit and athletic: a keen football player, he was known as the Holy Goalie in his student days.

Small's forty-five-year ministry was marked by pastoral dedication, a growing and established reputation as one of the most effective preachers of his generation in Scotland, active and imaginative community leadership, and increasing recognition as a national church leader. On 22 June 1931 Small married Jane Hay McGregor (*b.* 1908). In the same year he was ordained and inducted to St John's Bathgate on 10 September, and was translated to Kilmarnock, West High parish, in 1935. At the start of the Second World War he served with the Church of Scotland huts and canteens organization as a chaplain in France. He was translated to Cramond in 1944 and to St Cuthbert's, Edinburgh, in 1956, retiring from the latter in 1975.

Cramond suited Small well—and he suited Cramond—an attractive historic village fast becoming a fashionable suburb of Edinburgh, retaining a strong sense of community, with the parish church at the centre. With the

people seated close to the pulpit in pews and galleries, the church matched Small's clear captivating style of preaching. He broadcast frequently from Cramond, where his lively mind and devoted pastoral involvement amply served the flowering of church activity in the years following the Second World War. St Cuthbert's was different, one of central Edinburgh's great churches, the large congregation drawn from every part of the city, the building a large, grand, late nineteenth-century edifice. There his preaching and pastoral care maintained a large and devoted congregation, though his own liturgical preferences contrasted with St Cuthbert's more ornate chancel and its tradition in the high-church legacy of the Scoto-Catholics. His ability to remember people's names and the details of their lives served his deep interest in people and commitment to them. He was chaplain to several schools, and made a deep and lasting impression on young people who heard him and met him.

Small's sermons were marked by vivid anecdotes, such as noting, in a warehouse, boxes with the words stamped on each, 'Soiled goods. Return to maker'; and, commenting on the price paid for a new standard for the Royal Company of Archers, compared to the price of the previous standard, 'Friends, it costs more to bear standards nowadays' (private information). He preached without notes, with great fluency and clarity, without hesitation, and with authority. His theological perspective might be termed liberal evangelical, broadly humane, and pastoral; his ethical approach one of high principles and duty. Though possessed of a sharp intelligence and acquainted with biblical scholarship, he was not inclined to intellectual re-examination of ideas, claims, and beliefs, and urged younger ministers to do nothing which might shake people's faith or increase their doubts. His contribution as a preacher lay in the combination of an attractively strong personality with skilfully articulated communication of protestant Christianity.

Small was prominent in the administration of the Church of Scotland. He was convener of several important committees, and served as moderator of the general assembly (1966–7), and chaplain to the queen (from 1967). He was a DD of Edinburgh University (1957) and appointed OBE (1957) and CBE (1975). He was the first chairman of the Parole Board for Scotland (1967–73). He published a volume of reminiscences entitled *The Holy Goalie* (1993). His other books included *The Problem of Suffering* (1954), *With Ardour and Accuracy* (1959), *No Uncertain Sound* (1963), and *No other Name* (1966).

Leonard Small was a minister of the old school, one of those able and characterful Scots serving as ministers of the church. He died on 8 April 1994 in Murrayfield Independent Hospital, Edinburgh. His wife had predeceased him.

GILLEASBUIG MACMILLAN

Sources personal knowledge (2004) · private information (2004) · R. L. Small, *The Holy Goalie* (1993) · d. cert. · *The Scotsman* (9 April 1994) · *The Independent* (16 April 1994) · *The Times* (29 April 1994)
Wealth at death £179,038.73: confirmation, 9 June 1994, *CCI*

Small, William (1734–1775), physician and natural philosopher, was the third son of the Revd James Small (*d.* 1771), and Lilias, *née* Scott (*d.* 1775), of Carmyllie, Forfarshire, Scotland. He was born there on 13 October 1734 and was educated at Marischal College, Aberdeen, where he received his MA in 1755 and his MD in 1765. In 1758 Small was in America to take up the post of professor of natural philosophy at the College of William and Mary in Williamsburg, Virginia, where he revolutionized the teaching of the subject, introducing a lecture system, newly fashionable in Europe. Among his students were John Page, later thrice governor of Virginia, and Thomas Jefferson, whom he taught ethics, rhetoric, and belles lettres, and with whom he remained in contact. He seems to have met Benjamin Franklin in Williamsburg in the spring of 1763. However, Small was unhappy in Virginia, in poor health (apparently with malaria), and bitterly at odds with other faculty members. When he travelled to London in the autumn of 1764 to buy scientific apparatus, he chose not to return to America.

In London, Small was a guest of the surgeon John Belchier at the Royal Society on 24 January 1765. Following Benjamin Franklin's letter of recommendation on his behalf to Matthew Boulton, Small moved to Birmingham in May, where he quickly became established in the town's medical and scientific network. He shared rooms at 9 Temple Row with John Ash, and became a subscriber to the proposed general hospital; they both served on its founding committee from 1765. In the same year Small joined the embryonic Lunar Society of Birmingham; he was one of its first four members, and increasingly acted as its honorary secretary. Meanwhile, his medical practice was thriving. While holding a daily hour-long free clinic for the poor, he had a prosperous clientele, which included Matthew Boulton and William Russell, a wealthy Birmingham merchant, as well as their families. In his *Medical Miscellany* (1769) Thomas Tomlinson thanked both Ash and Small for their guidance. Small's fees were substantial and from town practice alone he earned an average of £500 a year, rising to £600 in the 1770s. His scientific investments, which were a considerable further source of income, included a share in Boulton's Soho development, where he acted as a technical consultant. Small's friendships and acquaintances were extensive, all based on his wide scientific interests. He was an early supporter and correspondent of James Watt, whom he had known in Glasgow, and seems to have introduced him to Matthew Boulton. Through his connections with Boulton and the Lunar Society, Small was also linked to John Baskerville, Joseph Black, Erasmus Darwin, Thomas Day, Richard Lovell Edgeworth, James Keir, and Josiah Wedgwood. He carried on an extensive correspondence with most of these men and his advice was often sought, for example in the difficulties of extending Watt's patent. Small became involved in town affairs: from 1769 he served on the committee for lighting and improving Birmingham, and became a subscriber to the new theatre in King Street in 1774.

Small's own scientific work was many-sided. He was interested in improving clock mechanisms, in optics (telescopes and microscopes), in geology, metallurgy, ceramics, gunnery, chemistry (especially alkali)—even in making a new kind of lead pencil. He corresponded with Joseph Priestley when the latter was writing his major work on air, and he urged James Watt to publish his research. Small himself took out a patent in 1773 (no. 1048) for a simplified clock design.

Small seems to have had a withdrawn, shy personality; he never married and Erasmus Darwin noted that he lived 'quite a recluse studious life'. Unlike other 'Lunatics', Small did not write for publication, although his correspondence was considerable. He appears never to have enjoyed robust good health and to have always greatly preferred scientific work to medical practice. Even towards the end of his life in 1773 he was considering leaving Birmingham and taking up an academic post in Scotland. However, he died in Birmingham, apparently of 'ague', aged only forty, on 25 February 1775: Boulton had noted how ill Small had been earlier in the month. Small was buried in St Philip's churchyard, Birmingham, on 15 March. Erasmus Darwin wrote an obituary poem to him, and there were many expressions of loss at his death. His portrait sketch shows a simply dressed, plainly wigged man, arms folded defensively, sitting near his quill pen, inkpot, and books—clearly his world. William Withering took over much of Small's medical work when he moved to Birmingham in May 1775.　　　　JOAN LANE

Sources R. E. Schofield, *The Lunar Society of Birmingham* (1963) · J. K. Aronson, *An account of the foxglove and its medical uses, 1785–1985* (1985) · T. W. Peck and K. D. Wilkinson, *William Withering of Birmingham* (1950) · *The letters of Erasmus Darwin*, ed. D. King-Hele (1981) · J. A. Langford, ed., *A century of Birmingham life … 1741–1841*, 2 vols. (1870–71) · J. Dos Passos, *The head and heart of Thomas Jefferson* (1955) · H. W. Dickinson, *Matthew Boulton* (1936) · H. W. Dickinson, *James Watt: craftsman and engineer* (1935); repr. (1936) · A. K. Bruce, *The Engineer* (8 March 1957), 362–6 · H. L. Ganter, 'William Small, Jefferson's beloved teacher', *William and Mary Quarterly*, 4 (1947), 505–11 · *Aris's Birmingham Gazette* (27 Feb 1775) · H. L. Ganter, 'Jefferson's "pursuit of happiness" and some forgotten men', *William and Mary College Quarterly*, 2nd ser., 16 (1936), 558–85
Archives Birm. CA, Boulton and Watt MSS · Birm. CA, St Philip's burial register · Birm. CA, General Hospital, Birmingham, governors' minutes and annual reports · BL, Russell family MSS, Add. MS 44997 · NA Scot., registers · RS, records
Likenesses pencil sketch, Birmingham assay office; repro. in Peck and Wilkinson, *William Withering*, facing p. 1

Smalle, Peter (*b.* 1577/8), poet, was a native of Berkshire. He matriculated from St John's College, Oxford, on 5 November 1596 aged eighteen and graduated BCL on 17 December 1602. In 1604 he became rector of Pinnock in Gloucestershire.

In 1615 Smalle published a poem entitled, *Mans May, or, A moneths minde: wherein the libertie of mans minde is compared to the moneth of May.* It is prefaced by the verses 'To All Gentlemen Students and Schollers', 'To the Reader the Authors Resolution', 'To the right worshipfull, my most loving good friend, Sir Henry Blomar of Hatherup, in the county of Glocester, knight', and finally by a single stanza 'Ad eundem'. The poem, written in rhyming couplets of iambic pentameter, is Smalle's only known work.

E. I. CARLYLE, rev. ELIZABETH GOLDRING

Sources Foster, *Alum. Oxon.*, *1500–1714* [Peter Smale]

Smalley, Beryl (1905–1984), historian, was born at Highfield House, Stockport Etchells, Cheshire, on 3 June 1905, the eldest of the six children of Edgar Smalley, a Manchester businessman, and his wife, Constance Lilian, *née* Bowman. Edgar's family firm dealt in woollen cloths and paper, and as he prospered he moved out of Manchester, first to a country house near Cheadle in Staffordshire, and then, as his family grew, to Taddington Hall, outside Buxton. Beryl had no taste for the outdoor life, and although she nursed and fielded her siblings with good will she greatly preferred the world of books to anything else that the Peak had to offer. She was educated from 1919 to 1923 at Cheltenham Ladies' College, and in 1924 was elected to a Beale history scholarship at St Hilda's College, Oxford.

St Hilda's was a small college, but a home of serious endeavour. Beryl Smalley was greatly influenced by her tutor, Agnes Moncreiff Sandys (*d.* 1952), whom she succeeded in 1943, but by her own account she was a wayward student, inclined only to such subjects as ecclesiastical and diplomatic history, which she found congenial. She probably exaggerated her detachment, but in 1927 she attained only second-class honours in modern history. On the other hand in the previous winter Agnes Sandys had introduced her to the Ford's lecturer for the Hilary term, Professor F. M. Powicke of the University of Manchester. Powicke's lectures, published by the Clarendon Press in 1928 as *Stephen Langton*, were an important contribution to constitutional and political history. He was chiefly interested in the interaction between Langton's studies in Paris and English politics under John and Henry III, but his comments on Langton's academic career also opened other lines of enquiry. None of his distinguished audience carried those themes further than the quiet undergraduate from St Hilda's. In the summer of 1927 Powicke readily accepted Smalley as a graduate student at Manchester. Her subject was Langton's *quaestiones*, a study which he was gratified to see developed. She worked with exemplary speed and thoroughness, and after a year she moved to Paris to study with Georges Lacombe.

Smalley's dissertation was published in 1930, in collaboration with Lacombe, in *Archives d'Histoire Doctrinale et Littéraire du Moyen Âge*. It was a well-executed and auspicious extension of Powicke's approach to Langton and he thought and hoped that she would go on to examine the effect of Langton's scholarship on his political activities. Smalley however, not uncharacteristically, had other ideas. During her work in Paris she had become deeply interested in the great commentary on the Bible which by Langton's day was coming to be known as the *glossa ordinaria*, a summary of patristic commentaries which provided a common work of reference for all biblical students. It was traditionally attributed to a German monk,

Walafrid Strabo, who had begun such a compilation in the ninth century. Modern scholars had doubts that the elaborately refined text in common use in the twelfth century could be closely identified with Strabo's work, but it fell to Smalley to develop a remark by Peter Chanter that the true begetter of the great gloss was Anselm of Laon, director of the school of Laon between 1180 and 1240, whose work was continued by his brother Ralph and by a succession of Parisian masters down to Peter Abelard. She painstakingly pursued that investigation to 1935. It was in some ways a perilous venture. Her father's support had enabled her to complete her dissertation, and from 1931 to 1935 she had a lectureship at Royal Holloway College which supported her adequately though not royally, but Powicke had wished to see her apply her talents to themes more evidently allied to the concerns of the history schools of British universities in the twentieth century than to the syllabuses of the medieval University of Paris.

In 1935 a fortunate vacancy brought Smalley election to a Jex–Blake research fellowship at Girton College, Cambridge. It assured several years' work, and its requirements went some way to meeting Powicke's and indeed in a measure her own concerns, as she was expected to produce a publishable book on a theme of some wider and—in an already circumscribed market—more general interest than a study of a paralysingly technical undertaking by a cleric whose personality at best rested upon a scatter of references to his existence and to the trials and occasional rewards of the conventual life. Her solution was to turn to yet another biographical study of a master with whom she could herself identify, and whom she could justifiably distinguish as a luminary of his time.

The new hero was Master Andrew, an Englishman who joined the Victorine congregation in Paris in 1125, and who returned to England to a small priory at Shobden, Herefordshire, which subsequently moved to Wigmore. In Paris he had studied with Hugh de St Victoire, the most influential of his small but powerful order. Hugh had defined two approaches to biblical exegesis, the allegorical and the literal. The allegorical enjoyed overwhelming success with commentators, and the alternative, the literal, which Andrew explored, was largely ignored and forgotten, though in the long run it emerged in the centre of such studies. In the mean time Andrew, undeterred by obscurity, doggedly pursued his principles, and in particular turned to Jewish scholars to help him understand the origin and evolution of the scriptures. It was a bold resolution in its turn, and may have inspired as well as mirrored Beryl Smalley's own approach to the subject. At all events she now had a congenial course to follow, an exemplar, and at the end a topic.

In a curious way the Second World War came to Smalley's rescue. There were few posts to be filled, but she had a breathing space and some expedients. She traced the development of exegetical studies through the gloss, dilated upon Master Andrew's distinctive contribution, and published *The Study of the Bible in the Middle Ages* in 1941. It did not cause a great stir and the title was not unnaturally misunderstood by some, for such a subject required a library rather than a monograph, but she had staked out a distinctive claim, and found temporary employment in the Bodleian Library. Then in 1943 Agnes Sandys, by then Mrs Kenneth Leys, retired and Beryl Smalley was appointed to succeed her. The price of security was the ramifying demands of a tutorship and the business of a college.

There was no suggestion that the price was too high, even given the pressure on resources in post-war Oxford. A second edition of *The Study of the Bible* appeared in 1952. It was better found than the first, and was enhanced by Smalley's interest in a new character, Herbert of Bosham, a hero and casualty of Becket's costly triumph, and in the role of the friars, first in exegetical studies and then in the elucidation of biblical and ancient history. Work on Bosham issued in the Ford lectures for 1969: 'The Becket controversy and the schools'. The second theme, touching first the Franciscans and then a group of English Dominicans, particularly Robert Holcroft, determined Smalley's studies for the rest of her life. All the characters involved, including herself, had particular qualities in common. They were learned, sometimes stiff-necked, absorbed in the life of the church, but never wholly assimilated by it.

Beryl Smalley's position in Oxford, in and out of college, was distinctive. She discharged her duties as a tutor, a fellow, and as vice-principal of St Hilda's from 1957 to her retirement in 1969, but concerned herself no further with the wider business of the university than she had to. In her scholarship as in some other respects she was an isolated figure. She had an enduring influence on her pupils, but she was in no sense the leader of a group. Her work advanced medieval studies at large, the growing interest in the history of the medieval university, especially in prosopographical studies, and in what came to be called the history of the book. There her closest associates were such scholars as Richard Hunt and Dom Daniel Callus. In 1963 she was elected a fellow of the British Academy. She had twice sought the support of formal organizations, having been received into the Roman Catholic church in 1930 and the Communist Party of Great Britain in the early years of the war, but had distanced herself from both without any formal declaration. Her relations with them would almost certainly have involved others, but she effaced all trace of those and other influences in the systematic destruction of her effects in the last months of her life. She died at her home, 5C Rawlinson Road in north Oxford, on 6 April 1984, and her ashes were scattered at Oxford crematorium.

Smalley was an intensely private person, and yet not wholly self-contained. She maintained an understated elegance in her dress and style. Her pupils were apt to find her formidable. They observed her learning and self-control with awe, and yet were reassured by the enduring warmth of her interest in them. Her capacity for domesticity came as a surprise, and echoes through every account of her life and work. It was one of the few keys to her character that she was willing to display, though that, like everything else, was on her own terms.

G. H. MARTIN

Sources R. W. Southern, *PBA*, 72 (1986), 455–71 · M. E. Rayner, *The centenary history of St Hilda's College, Oxford* (1993) · C. V. B. Brown and M. E. Rayner, eds., *St Hilda's College centenary register, 1893–1993* (1993) · personal knowledge (2004) · b. cert. · d. cert.
Likenesses group photograph (with W. M. Pantin and others), repro. in Southern, *PBA*
Wealth at death £134,144: probate, 22 June 1984, *CGPLA Eng. & Wales*

Smallpeice, Sir Basil (1906–1992), accountant and businessman, was born in Rio de Janeiro, Brazil, on 18 September 1906, the son of Herbert Charles Smallpeice, a senior clerk in the London and River Plate Bank, and his wife, Georgina Ruth, *née* Rust. He suffered a serious bout of malaria at an early age and was brought back to England to be educated, seeing very little of his parents over the next eleven years. He went to Hurstpierpoint preparatory school and then to Mydnehe House, near Eastbourne, before attending Shrewsbury School, from 1920 to 1925. He was then articled to the Norwich and London accountants, Bullimore & Co., qualifying as a chartered accountant in 1930. He also took the external London University BCom degree while working as an articled clerk.

On qualification, Smallpeice moved out of public practice to become assistant secretary at £300 per annum to Hoover Ltd, the vacuum cleaner company, where he learned American cost accounting principles and procedures. On 29 July 1931 he married Kathleen Ivey Singleton (Kay), the daughter of Edwin Singleton Brame, of Surbiton, Surrey; there were no children. Smallpeice remained with Hoover until 1937, when he joined Doulton & Co. Ltd, the china and porcelain company, as secretary and chief accountant responsible for costing and accountancy at the factories, and for financial administration and the company's secretarial work at headquarters. During the war he remained with Doulton, but also performed various minor war-related administrative tasks. It was at this time that he joined the Christian frontier council of the Church of England. In 1948, he moved as director of costs and statistics to the newly formed British Transport Commission, which was then responsible for the nationalized inland transport system. In 1950 he was recruited by Sir Miles Thomas, chairman of the British Overseas Airways Corporation (BOAC), to deal with, as Thomas put it, 'too much delay in presentation of figures and too much confusion in the way they were put forward' (*The Independent*, 17 July 1992). Quickly, he introduced up-to-date management accounting techniques including budgetary control, thereby imposing order on the accounts of this nationalized and troubled concern. These changes helped revive BOAC, and in 1953—the year the company first reported a profit—he joined the board.

Smallpeice was appointed managing director of BOAC in 1956 and succeeded in assembling an extremely strong new top management team to tackle the company's difficulties. BOAC was during this period immersed in a series of catastrophic disasters affecting its Comet aircraft—at one point a Comet broke up in mid-air—but his loyalty to the de Havilland concept and design was rewarded with the successful re-introduction of the Comet (IV) in 1958. Smallpeice's other notable triumph was the introduction of transatlantic jet travel, BOAC's Comets beating Pan American's Boeing 707s to it by three weeks with a same-day return trip to New York. Financial success remained elusive in the fast-developing civil airline business, and differences arose between the board of BOAC and the Ministry of Aviation, then under Julian Amery. The minister called in John Corbett, the senior partner in the leading firm of chartered accountants, Peat, Marwick, Mitchell & Co., to prepare a secret but presumably highly critical report, since Smallpeice and a number of other board members were forced to resign, in November 1963. Ironically, the new management was to benefit from the return to profitability which the work of Smallpeice and his colleagues had ensured.

Smallpeice joined the board of the Cunard Steamship Company the following year, and served as chairman from 1965 to 1971. The company was in dire straits at the time of his appointment because of a fondness for tradition and a neglect of modern management methods. Smallpeice possessed precisely the right management experience and skills to deal with this situation, not shirking the radical decisions required to bring back the company into profit by mid-1968. While there, Smallpeice saw the *QE2* into operation and played a key role in the introduction of cargo containerization. Cunard was taken over by Trafalgar House in 1971 and Smallpeice went on to the main board, before taking over shortly afterwards as non-executive deputy chairman of Lonrho. There, he was increasingly at odds with the major shareholder and chief executive, Tiny Rowland. The outcome of a power struggle was that Smallpeice and seven of his fellow directors resigned in 1973. He continued as non-executive chairman of Associated Container Transportation (Australia) and of its partnership with the Australian National Line until 1979, when he completely retired from business. Meanwhile, Smallpeice's first wife, Kay, died in February 1973, and in November that year he married Rita Burns, who had been his secretary since 1967. Again there were no children.

Smallpeice was appointed KCVO in the 1961 queen's birthday honours list in recognition of his work in connection with her majesty's flights. He was therefore well-known to the queen when he received the prestigious appointment as part-time administrative adviser to her majesty's household in 1964, introducing modern budgetary control methods during an appointment which lasted until 1980.

Despite leaving public practice in 1930, Smallpeice maintained a keen interest in the affairs of the Institute of Chartered Accountants in England and Wales, working hard to raise awareness of responsibilities towards its industrial members. He assembled a ginger group which published critical comment in *The Accountant*, the profession's journal, which did not go unnoticed at the institute's head office in Moorgate Place. The appointment of an industrial member to the council of the institute remained unthinkable at that time, but in 1942 the taxation and financial relations committee was established, and this played an important part in raising the standard of financial reporting in the years that followed. Smallpeice was appointed to the committee but this did not deflect him from continuing to press for industrial representation on the institute's council. When this step was finally taken in 1948, Smallpeice filled one of the industrial appointments until 1957. He also played a prominent role in the affairs of the British Institute of Management, serving as a council member from 1959 to 1964 and again from 1965 to 1975, and as chairman from 1970 to 1972.

Some of Smallpeice's contemporaries believed that his upbringing away from his family accounted for a degree of sensitive diffidence and intellectual arrogance. He was at the same time earnest, sincere, anxious to achieve good personal relations, and always, often justly, suspicious of political motivation. Although not the most robust of individuals, he showed considerable fortitude and possessed undoubted integrity. This latter quality, and his lack of political acumen, sometimes put him at a disadvantage in the boardroom, particularly in a highly visible nationalized industry in the early 1960s and when confronted by the likes of Tiny Rowland. Quiet, unassuming, always impeccably dressed, his manner in business was cautious and precise. His relaxation included chairing the Leatherhead New Theatre Trust and the Air League, while he also enjoyed membership of his London clubs. In retirement he lived at Bridge House, 45 Leigh Hill Road, Cobham. He died in Epsom, Surrey, on 12 July 1992.

JOHN RICHARD EDWARDS

Sources *The Times* (13 July 1992) · *The Independent* (17 July 1992) · R. Higham, 'Smallpeice, Sir Basil', *DBB* · D. J. Jeremy and I. G. Tweedale, *Dictionary of twentieth century business leaders* (1994) · B. Smallpeice, *Of comets and queens* (1981) · *CGPLA Eng. & Wales* (1992)
Archives NL Scot., letters and memoranda to Lady Tweedsmuir
Likenesses photograph, 1973, Hult. Arch. · photograph, repro. in *The Times* · photograph, repro. in *The Independent*
Wealth at death £20,854: probate, 29 Oct 1992, *CGPLA Eng. & Wales*

Smallwood, Charles (1812–1873), physician and meteorologist, was baptized on 10 November 1812 at St Philip's, Birmingham, the son of Edward Smallwood and his wife, Elizabeth. After medical training in London he moved to Lower Canada in 1833, living successively in Huntingdon, St Martin, and Montreal, and was licensed in 1834 to practise medicine in the province. His medical practice was highly successful and led to an appointment as professor of midwifery and diseases of women and children in 1871 at Bishop's College in Montreal. He was appointed dean of the faculty, but declined in order to continue supervision of the meteorological observatory at McGill College.

Smallwood had established an observatory in 1841 at his home, where he kept a daily record of the usual meteorological variables, but also of ozone, atmospheric electricity, and snow crystals. He co-operated with both the Smithsonian Institution and the Toronto Magnetic Observatory. Smallwood's observatory was moved to McGill in 1863, where he had been awarded an honorary LLD and had been appointed professor of meteorology, both in 1856. The observatory obtained a government grant for magnetic research in 1860. In 1871 this support was greatly expanded when Smallwood became the official Montreal observer of the joint meteorological network of the Canadian ministry of marine and fisheries and the United States army signal office. By the 1850s Smallwood was a prominent member of the provincial scientific community. When the American Association for the Advancement of Science met in Montreal in 1857 Smallwood gave the welcoming remarks. He published numerous articles on meteorology and ozone. He was a governor of the College of Physicians and Surgeons of Lower Canada from 1851 and president of the Montreal Natural History Society in 1865. He died at 32 Beaver Hall Terrace, Montreal, after a short illness, on 22 December 1873, and was buried two days later.   E. I. CARLYLE, rev. GREGORY A. GOOD

Sources J. S. Marshall, 'Smallwood, Charles', *DCB*, vol. 10 · *The Gazette* [Montreal] (22 Dec 1873) · *Daily Witness* [Montreal] (26 Dec 1873) · H. J. Morgan, *Sketches of celebrated Canadians, and persons connected with Canada* (1862)

Smallwood, Sir Denis Graham (1918–1997), air force officer, was born on 13 August 1918 at 7 St Alban's Road, Moseley, Birmingham, the son of Frederick William Smallwood, rule manufacturer, and his wife, Irene May, *née* Kentish. Smallwood was educated at King Edward VI School, Birmingham, and joined the RAF in 1938, becoming assistant adjutant and flying instructor in 605 (County of Warwick) squadron, an auxiliary unit flying Gladiator biplane fighters. For most of the Second World War, Splinters Smallwood was attached to Fighter Command, serving as a fighter pilot with 605, 87 and 247 Hurricane squadrons between 1939 and 1942, and leading a Spitfire wing from 1943 to 1944.

On 14 October 1940, at the church of St Agnes, Moseley, he had married Frances Jeanne (1919/20–1992), daughter of Walter Needham, jeweller of Birmingham. They had a son and daughter.

At 87 United Services squadron Smallwood commanded the ground attacks which backed up the abortive Dieppe raid on 19 August 1942 in which 4000 of the 6000 British and Canadian troops were killed, wounded, or captured. Instead of drawing the entire Luftwaffe forces in northern France into an attritional battle over Dieppe, it was the RAF that suffered a defeat with the loss of 109 aircraft. For his bravery that day in leading his squadron into action against German gun emplacements, Smallwood was awarded the DFC (1942). Following a brief spell with 247 squadron, he was placed in charge of a Spitfire wing operating from bases in Cornwall from where he roved over occupied France, attacking targets of opportunity such as trains, vehicle convoys, and gun positions. After the allied landings in Normandy, he led 131 and 165 squadrons carrying out ground attacks in support of the allied advance inland, for which he was awarded the DSO (1944).

Between 1945 and 1946 Smallwood was directing staff at the RAF Staff College, Haifa. From there he went to headquarters British air forces of occupation Germany and in 1948 he received command of 33 squadron, a Tempest fighter squadron in Germany. Between 1948 and 1952 he

was an Air Ministry planner and a member of the Joint Services Staff College. Placed in command of RAF Biggin Hill, he led a large force of jet aircraft on 2 June 1953 for the RAF salute at the queen's coronation.

During the Suez crisis in 1956 Smallwood planned the action of the air task force which neutralized the Egyptian air force. Although the operation was successful, Smallwood, with characteristic forthrightness, called the basis on which he and his fellow planners were expected to work, 'a monumental political cock-up' (*The Guardian*, 19 Aug 1987).

After Suez he commanded the Bloodhound surface to air missile wing at North Cotes in Lincolnshire and in 1961 became commandant of the college of air warfare at Manby. Two years later he was appointed assistant chief of staff (operations). Although a renowned fighter pilot, Smallwood built a new reputation as a bomber leader when appointed to 3 group, Bomber Command, in 1965, senior air staff officer at Bomber Command in 1967, and deputy commander-in-chief, strike command, the following year. From 1969 to 1970 he was air officer commanding the Near East air force and, at the same time, administrator of the sovereign base area in Cyprus. Smallwood returned to Britain where he became vice-chief of the air staff, and from 1974 to 1976, commander-in-chief strike command. From 1975 he commanded Nato's UK air forces.

Smallwood had the distinction of being knighted twice. Having been appointed MBE in 1951, CBE in 1961, and CB in 1966, he received a KCB in 1969 and GBE in 1975.

Following retirement from the RAF in 1976, Smallwood spent six years as a military adviser to British Aerospace, and in his later years indulged his interest in horses, becoming organizer of the Tythrop horse trials near Thame, Oxfordshire, and chairman of the RAF Equitation Society. Other interests included shooting and gundog training, and he played a major part in charitable fields, notably at Pace, a locally based charity to assist children with cerebral palsy. He was chairman of the Air League as well as being co-founder and president of the Friends of St Clement Dane, the RAF central church in the Strand, London.

Splinters Smallwood died from heart disease at his home, 27 Swinnerton House, Phyllis Court Drive, Henley-on-Thames, on 26 July 1997, survived by his son and daughter, his wife having died in 1992.

BRIAN WIMBORNE

Sources *WW* (1990–94) · *Debrett's People of today* · *Daily Telegraph* (28 July 1997) · *The Times* (30 July 1997) · *The Independent* (8 Aug 1997) · b. cert. · m. cert. · d. cert. · *CGPLA Eng. & Wales* (1997)

Wealth at death under £180,000: probate, 11 Sept 1997, *CGPLA Eng. & Wales*

Smallwood [*née* Walford], **Norah Evelyn** (1909–1984), publisher, was born on 30 December 1909 at Glenbervie, Little Kingshill, Buckinghamshire, the third of the four daughters and the fifth of the eight children of Howard Neville Walford, artist, and his wife, Marion, *née* Griffiths. She went to school in Eastbourne and began her publishing career as a secretary in 1936, when she joined Chatto and Windus, the firm to which she devoted the rest of her working life. On 21 December 1938 she married Peter Warren Sykes Smallwood (1909/10–1943), a chartered accountant and the son of John Russell Smallwood, from a long line of Birmingham wine merchants.

Norah Smallwood found in Ian Parsons at Chattos an exceptionally gifted publisher, who soon involved her in the brilliantly original though short-lived weekly magazine *Night and Day*. In the war years that followed she proved to the full both her capabilities and her courage: she not only shared the strain of wartime publishing with her very able but hard-pressed senior partner, Harold Raymond, but also had to bear the loss of her husband, who was serving as a navigator with the RAF when he was killed over Holland in 1943, as well as the death of a much-loved brother, who was also killed on active service.

Widowed and without children, Smallwood poured her energies into Chattos, and in 1945 was made a partner. Two years later she was appointed to the board of the Hogarth Press, the firm which Leonard and Virginia Woolf had founded in 1917 and which had come under Chatto's management in 1946. From then on she worked closely with Leonard Woolf until his death in 1969, doing as much as anyone to foster the separate identity of his list and to care for its authors—Henry Green, William Sansom, Laurens van der Post, A. L. Barker, Laurie Lee, and George Mackay Brown, among many others.

Smallwood was appointed to the board of Chattos in 1953 when it became a limited company and, with Ian Parsons, effectively ran the firm for the next twenty years before succeeding him as managing director and chairman in 1975 until her own retirement in 1982. She also served for fourteen years on the board of the holding company which was formed when Chattos merged with Jonathan Cape in 1969, later to be joined by the Bodley Head (1973) and Virago Press (1982).

By now Smallwood's reputation, both as a dynamic woman publisher in a world still dominated by men, and as a vivid, stylish, generous-spirited if sometimes sharp-tongued personality, was widely known. Professionally, she had acquired expertise in many aspects of book production and liked nothing better than turning her hand to typographical design or commissioning work from such gifted artists as Enid Marx, A. Reynolds Stone, and John Ward. She also excelled in that essential function of any literary publisher—working creatively with her authors, encouraging and helping them with her quick and incisive reading of their manuscripts. She was especially good with fiction, winning the respect, gratitude, and friendship of distinguished writers such as Aldous Huxley, Compton Mackenzie, Sylvia Townsend Warner, Victor Pritchett, Elizabeth Taylor, Elspeth Huxley, Iris Murdoch, A. S. Byatt, Amos Oz, and Toni Morrison. She also contributed imaginatively to Chatto's poetry publishing (with Ian Parsons, Cecil Day-Lewis, and D. J. Enright), to their children's books, and to their educational and academic list, notably with her early recognition of Moses Finley's stimulating influence in the field of ancient history.

It was Smallwood's instinct for quality that brought Dirk Bogarde to Chattos. Her perception of his lively intelligence and sensitive, alert talent soon drew out the writer in him, and led to one of the most rewarding friendships of her latter years. His debt to her is vividly and movingly described in the third and fourth volumes of his autobiography.

Iris Murdoch, eminent among the many authors to whom Norah Smallwood dedicated so much of her life and who in turn dedicated so many of their books to her, remembered her as:

> the most rational person I had ever met … To us writers she was a combination of comrade, leader, mother, business partner and muse … She was always cheerful, always seemed happy, was always joking, was at the same time strong, clever, wise, practical, loyal and absolutely reliable. (Murdoch)

That same virtue, the unqualified trust that she inspired in her authors and friends, was given full public expression by Laurens van der Post in the memorial service held in her honour at St Martin-in-the-Fields, London.

Norah Smallwood was appointed OBE in 1973 and she received an honorary degree of LittD at Leeds University in 1981. She died in Westminster Hospital, London, on 11 October 1984, having for years fought the ill health and crippling arthritic pain with which she was afflicted.

JOHN CHARLTON, *rev.*

Sources *The Times* (12 Oct 1984) · D. Holloway, *Daily Telegraph* (13 Oct 1984) · J. Goldsmith, 'Norah Smallwood, publisher', *The Bookseller* (20 Oct 1984) · I. Murdoch, 'Norah Smallwood', *The Bookseller* (27 Oct 1984) · J. Parfitt, 'Norah Smallwood', *The Sphere* (21 May 1960) · D. Bogarde, *An orderly man* (1983) · D. Bogarde, *Backcloth* (1986) · O. Warner, *Chatto & Windus: a brief account of the firm's origin, history and development* (1973) · personal knowledge (1990) · private information (1990) · b. cert. · m. cert. · d. cert.
Archives U. Leeds, Brotherton L., corresp. and papers | U. Sussex, corresp., notes, and memos with Leonard Woolf and others
Wealth at death £332,349: probate, 18 Dec 1984, *CGPLA Eng. & Wales*

Smallwood, William (1732–1792), revolutionary army officer and politician in America, was born probably at Smallwood's Retreat in Charles county, Maryland, the son of Bayne Smallwood (*c*.1711–1768), wealthy planter, merchant, and politician, and his wife, Priscilla Heabard (*d.* 1784). He had one brother and five sisters. Smallwood was educated in England, first at Kendal and then at Eton College. He was a communicant of the Church of England and served at least one term as a vestryman of Durham parish in Charles county, Maryland. Other local service included terms as a justice of the peace in 1762 and from 1770 to 1773. Smallwood represented his county as a delegate to the lower house of the Maryland legislature from 1761 to 1774. He then served in several of the extra-legal American patriot assemblies that governed the colony between 1774 and 1776.

Having already fought in the French and Indian War, Smallwood returned to military service on 14 January 1776 when commissioned as a colonel in the 1st Maryland regiment. In April he led a contingent of 1400 men from Annapolis to join the continental army, where it participated in the battle of Long Island, protecting the retreat of

George Washington's main forces. Smallwood, however, was away attending a court martial. Though wounded in October of that year at the battle of White Plains, he continued to serve, now as a brigadier-general, in subsequent engagements in New York and New Jersey. Between 1779 and 1780 Smallwood was headquartered in Wilmington, Delaware, charged with surveillance of the Chesapeake Bay and protection of the continental army's stores. In 1780 Smallwood's troops moved south as part of General Gates's army fighting in South Carolina, where in September Smallwood was appointed a major-general and division commander. When he refused to serve under a foreigner, Friedrich Wilheim von Steuben, Smallwood was sent back to Maryland to raise supplies and enlist troops. Smallwood left the army on 15 November 1783. He was elected to the continental congress in 1784 but declined to serve.

Chosen as governor by the legislature in November 1785, Smallwood served three one-year terms (the statutory limit). As governor, he called the Maryland constitutional convention which, despite strong anti-federalist sentiment in the state, ratified the federal constitution in April 1788. Historians have credited Smallwood with encouraging the movement to improve Potomac River navigation, but the negotiations between Maryland and Virginia delegates largely took place before Smallwood became governor, although he was chief executive when the legislature ratified the accord in December 1785.

When his third gubernatorial term ended in 1788 Smallwood retired for a time to the life of a gentleman planter. He was active in the local masonic chapter and helped to organize the Maryland chapter of the Society of the Cincinnati, for which he served as the first president. Smallwood returned to public office in 1791 when elected to the Maryland state senate, where he served as president.

Smallwood never married and left no known children. He died on 14 February 1792, at 'his woodyard' in Prince George's county, according to Annapolis diarist William Faris, and was buried at his plantation, Smallwood's Retreat, in Charles county. During his lifetime Smallwood amassed landholdings of about 9500 acres in Maryland and 2000 acres in Virginia. His estate was heavily indebted, however, and his administrators were forced to sell his land to help settle the claims.

Smallwood is most noted as 'an outstanding military leader' (White, 21) but N. D. Mereness held a more critical view of his performance, noting Smallwood's complaints that he should have been promoted more rapidly and that Maryland deserved more recognition for her contributions to the war effort, as well as 'his offensive attitude toward foreigners. His greatest service in the war was as a drill master, in raising men and supplies, and in administering the other military affairs of his state' (Mereness, 226). In a more recent evaluation, R. J. Brugger records that '[b]y all reports Maryland troops received superior training from Smallwood, a rigorous disciplinarian' (Brugger, 228) and that the Maryland line fought bravely and well in a number of critical engagements. JEAN B. RUSSO

Sources E. C. Papenfuse and others, eds., *A biographical dictionary of the Maryland legislature, 1635–1789*, 2 (1985) [pt of the Maryland State Archives biography project] · F. F. White, *The governors of Maryland, 1777–1970* (Annapolis, Maryland, 1970) · R. J. Brugger and others, *Maryland: a middle temperament, 1634–1980* (1988), 128–9 · N. D. Mereness, 'Smallwood, William', *DAB* · M. B. Klapthor and P. D. Brown, *The history of Charles county, Maryland* (La Plata, Maryland, 1958) · diary of William Faris, entry for 16 Feb 1792, Maryland Historical Society, Baltimore, MS 2160
Archives Maryland Historical Society, Baltimore, MS 1875
Likenesses C. W. Peale, oils, 1781–1782?, Independence National Historical Park, Philadelphia · J. Trumbull, miniature, oils, 1792?, Yale U. Art Gallery · R. Peale, oils, c.1812, Baltimore Museum of Art, Maryland · C. W. Peale, oils, 1823, Maryland Commission on Artistic Property of the Maryland State Archives, Annapolis · R. E. Pine, oils, National Gallery of Art, Washington, DC, Mellon collection
Wealth at death personal property valued at £4761 6s. 7d. (incl. twenty-six slaves and 53 oz of plate); approx. 9500 acres in Maryland and 2000 acres in Virginia; estate heavily indebted, requiring the sale of real estate to cover the debts, est. in 1798 to total £17,500: Papenfuse and others, eds., *A biographical dictionary*, 2.742

Smalridge, George (1662–1719), bishop of Bristol, was born in Sandford Street, Lichfield, Staffordshire, on 18 May 1662 and baptized on the same day at St Mary, Lichfield, a son of Thomas Smalridge, citizen and dyer of Lichfield. His father, who served as sheriff of Lichfield in 1674, was later said to have been 'but very poor' (*Remarks*, 1.236). George had at least two brothers, one of whom, William, later kept the Queen's Arms alehouse in Birmingham, while another was a clothier of Coventry. He was educated first at Lichfield grammar school, where one of his contemporaries was Joseph Addison, and from 1678 at Westminster School. There in 1680, in tribute to his sponsor, the antiquary Elias Ashmole, he composed elegies in Latin and English on the astrologer William Lilly. He also met Francis Atterbury at Westminster, whose career was to follow almost exactly the same path as his own. Proceeding to Christ Church, Oxford, he matriculated on 18 December 1682 and became a college tutor after taking his BA in 1686. His growing reputation for Latin verse composition was confirmed by the publication in 1689 of *Auctio Davisiana*, a description of the sale of the stock of Richard Davis, an Oxford bookseller, reprinted in the celebrated collection *Musae Anglicanae*. After taking his MA degree in 1689, Smalridge was ordained, and in June 1693 he became prebendary of Flixton, in Lichfield Cathedral, a post that he retained until 1714.

Throughout this period Smalridge continued to enhance his reputation in Oxford. In 1694 he was chosen to give the oration in praise of Sir Thomas Bodley, and in 1698, with Atterbury, he took a leading part in the production of *Dr Bentley's Dissertations on the Epistles of Phalaris Examined*, a doomed achievement whose skill nevertheless earned Jonathan Swift's applause in *The Battle of the Books*. Some indeed, including Henry Sacheverell, later assumed that Smalridge had been the author of the *Tale of a Tub*, a supposition that was bitterly refuted. Also in 1698 Smalridge took his BD and was appointed minister of the new Broadway Chapel in Westminster. On 18 July 1700 he married Mary (d. 1729), daughter of Dr Samuel de l'Angle, at Steventon, Berkshire; they had two daughters and two

George Smalridge (1662–1719), by Sir Godfrey Kneller, 1717

sons. On 28 May 1701 he proceeded DD, and on 14 February 1702 he was appointed a Busby trustee of Westminster School. By this time his reputation as an orthodox high-churchman was well established. As early as 1687, in conjunction with Henry Aldrich and Francis Atterbury, he had published *Animadversions on the Eight Theses Laid Down in a Discourse … Lately Printed at Oxford*, a 'clinically exact answer to a wild piece' (Bennett, 28–9) by the Roman Catholic propagandists Obadiah Walker and Abraham Woodhead. In 1690, when the rector of Exeter College, Dr Arthur Bury, published *The Naked Gospel*, repudiating the Athanasian formula of the Trinity, and defied the visitatorial power of the bishop of Exeter, Smalridge took an active part in moves to anathematize Bury's doctrine and to reassert Bishop Jonathan Trelawney's rights. In 1701, writing as 'A Gentleman in the Country', he published *Some Remarks upon the Temper of the Late Writers about Convocations*, a lengthy but restrained vindication of Atterbury's recent book *The Rights, Powers and Privileges of an English Convocation* (1700) against the arguments of seemingly Erastian apologists such as William Wake. From 1700 to 1707 Smalridge acted as deputy to Dr William Jane, regius professor of divinity, and in that capacity he presented John Ernest Grabe, the Prussian patristic scholar then resident in Oxford, for an honorary Oxford DD in 1706. In his Latin address, delivered on that occasion and reprinted in an English translation in 1714, Smalridge ventured to hope that Grabe might in due course receive a Prussian mitre and thereby serve as the instrument of a closer union between the Church of England and the Lutheran churches. Together with Archbishop John Sharp and Bishop

John Robinson he devoted much energy to this cause, corresponding with Daniel Jablonski in Berlin as well as with Grabe, from whom he inherited eighteen substantial volumes of papers after the latter's death, in 1711, which then passed to the Bodleian Library.

To many it was a matter of surprise when Smalridge did not succeed Jane in the regius chair of divinity in 1707. Some specifically attributed his failure to the hostility of John Churchill, duke of Marlborough; others, like Thomas Hearne, saw him as a victim of his qualities: 'an eloquent ingenious Gentleman, an excellent Divine and of a deep, rational Understanding; a true Friend to the Church, resolute and brave, of steady Principles and [therefore] not likely to be turned as the [whig] Party would have' (*Remarks*, 2.88). However, other appointments offered compensation: the lecturership of St Dunstan-in-the-West, London, in succession to Dr Offspring Blackall, in January 1708, and a post as chaplain-in-ordinary to Queen Anne in 1710. Smalridge was also gaining in reputation as a notable tory preacher, and some of his best-known sermons were delivered at the annual commemoration of the martyrdom of Charles I on 30 January. One of these, given in 1702 on Genesis 49: 6 and speaking vehemently against the regicides, who had caused 'the Desolation of a flourishing Kingdom, and the overthrow of a Primitive and Apostolical Church … [and] … the total loss of all … civil Rights' (G. Smalridge, *Sermon 1702*, 20), generated much controversy and was reprinted in 1707 and 1709. When the decision was taken in November 1709 to impeach Henry Sacheverell for his sermon *The Perils of False Brethren, both in Church, and State* Smalridge rallied immediately behind Sacheverell, withdrawing his own acceptance of an invitation to preach before the lord mayor and aldermen at St Paul's at a thanksgiving service less than a month afterwards. Together with other Oxford high-churchmen he supported Sacheverell at his trial, standing behind him at the bar, assisting with the composition of the immensely effective speech that Sacheverell gave in his own defence, helping to marshal the programme of loyal addresses that underpinned the tory election landslide in autumn 1710, and contributing his own *Thoughts of a Country Gentleman upon Reading Dr Sacheverell's Tryal* (1710).

In December 1710 Smalridge presented Atterbury to Archbishop William Wake for confirmation as prolocutor of the lower house of convocation. However, by this time the friendship with Atterbury had begun to cool. In his diary for 6 December 1706 Wake commented that the oration, particularly in its original Latin version, left it far from clear whether Smalridge had 'really intended to praise [Atterbury] or abuse him' (Bennett, 129). Relations between the two men deteriorated further during the following year as a result of a struggle at court over the deanery of Christ Church, vacant following the death of Henry Aldrich, in December 1710. Although both the queen and Archbishop Sharp pressed the claims of Smalridge, a high-churchman of a less inflammatory kind, pressure from Henry St John and Sir Simon Harcourt eventually secured Atterbury's appointment, on 30 August 1711. Smalridge instead, in September 1711, obtained the Christ Church canonry left vacant by the death of Dr Benjamin Woodroffe, and on 3 November he was appointed to succeed Atterbury as dean of Carlisle, a post that he resigned when he finally secured the deanery of Christ Church, on Atterbury's appointment as bishop of Rochester and dean of Westminster. Appointed on 11 July 1713, Smalridge was installed seven days later without any public ceremony. Ill health was the stated reason but the tacit repudiation of the opulent demonstrations that had accompanied Atterbury's installation two years earlier was probably deliberate, Smalridge being 'so noted for his good temper, that succeeding Dr Atterbury in the Deaneries of Carlisle and Christ Church, he was said to carry the bucket to extinguish the fires' (Nichols, *Illustrations*, 3.231). Following the translation of John Robinson to the see of London, on 9 March 1714, Smalridge was appointed bishop of Bristol. At his consecration, on 4 April 1714, the sermon was preached by a colleague, Thomas Terry, regius professor of Greek at Oxford. Bristol being a poor see, Smalridge held it with the deanery of Christ Church *in commendam*. He was appointed lord almoner at the same time but lost this post on the arrival of the Hanoverian dynasty.

For Smalridge, as for many tories, the accession of George I was a difficult time. In his *Poem on the Death of Queen Anne; and the Accession of … King George* (1715), a cautious exhortation of loyalty to George I was accompanied by unconcealed mourning for Queen Anne—'The Public Loss, and Oxford's too' (p. 13). Yet Smalridge, unlike Atterbury, was no Jacobite, and for a few months in autumn 1714 seems even to have been in favour at court, until he was discredited by his tory connections. Although he hardly deserved Thomas Hearne's contemptuous description as 'one of the Sneakers & terribly afraid of disobliging the debauched Court of K. George' (*Remarks*, 5.66) he took care to ensure that the noblemen and gentlemen commoners of Christ Church were prevented from celebrating the birthday of the Stuart pretender, James III, on 10 June 1715. Nevertheless Smalridge remained a tory, even after the defeat of the Jacobite rising in 1715. He voted in support of Robert Harley, earl of Oxford, during impeachment proceedings in late summer 1715; refused, with Atterbury and Francis Gastrell, to sign the declaration against the pretender in the following November, and published his reasons for doing so; and resisted an attempt to procure a loyal address from Oxford for George I on his return from Hanover in 1717. He remained close to some nonjurors and composed an epitaph for Robert Nelson (d. 1715), from whose estate he inherited a *Madonna* by Correggio.

Smalridge's ecclesiastical principles, which remained those of a decided high-churchman, were summarized admirably in the charge delivered at his primary visitation of the diocese of Bristol in 1716. Here 'allegiance to his present Majesty' was justified on the conservative ground of 'those Principles of Loyalty, by which our Church hath been long distinguished' (Smalridge, *Charge*, 22–3), and a caution against 'fiery and hot-headed Zeal' (ibid., 18) was qualified by a reminder that there are 'things, in which it is laudable to excell' and a warning against excessive 'moderation' (ibid., 19). In 1718 he opposed repeal of the Occasional Conformity and Schism Acts and made a 'very animated speech' (Nichols, *Illustrations*, 3.227; Cobbett, *Parl. hist.*, 7.573) in defence of the Test and Corporation Acts. Together with other high-churchmen he was appalled by the promotion of Benjamin Hoadly to the bishopric of Bangor and offered an ingenious proposal (not adopted by the government) for the effective, but indirect, condemnation of the notorious court sermon *On the Nature of the Kingdom, or, The Church of Christ* (1717). However, Smalridge was reluctant to persecute merely speculative opinions; he was reported in 1714 as having said 'that every private Christian was not obliged to believe every Part of the Athanasian Creed' (*Diary of Mary, Countess Cowper*, 17). He remained on cordial terms with the Arian William Whiston, even though his own views were entirely orthodox, and shortly before his death declared to Bishop Trelawney that 'even if it were as … [Whiston] had said, he had no wish to examine it and to find that the Church had been in error for so many hundred years' (*DNB*). Despite his often iterated orthodoxy he was believed to have some respect for the views of the theologian Samuel Clarke, and was later recalled by John Perceval, first earl of Egmont, as having said that 'he could pardon everything in Dr. Clark but his calling the three persons in the Trinity three Beings, which made too great a distinction in the unity of the Godhead' (*Egmont Diary*, 1.233).

Smalridge died suddenly, at Christ Church on 27 September 1719, aged fifty-seven, of 'an apoplexy, having had two Fits before' (*Remarks*, 7.51). He was buried two days later in the north choir aisle of Christ Church Cathedral, an oration being pronounced by John White, censor of Christ Church. A monument, with an inscription by Smalridge's brother-in-law Dr Robert Freind, survived until 1870. His will, proved at Oxford on 10 October 1719, showed that he did not die rich; indeed his wife, Mary, later needed the support of a pension of £300 p.a. from Princess (later Queen) Caroline until her death, on 6 June 1729. Smalridge's surviving son, Philip, followed his father to Westminster and Christ Church (MA, 1723; DD, 1742); he became rector of Christleton, Cheshire, in 1727, and was chancellor of the diocese of Worcester from 1742 until his death, on 23 October 1751.

As a clergyman 'the famous Dr Smalridge' (as Swift called him) stood high in reputation and authority. Long after his death Bishop Thomas Newton remembered him as a prominent figure at Westminster School elections, and Steele characterized him strikingly, as Favonius, in *The Tatler*:

in the midst of a Thousand impertinent Assailants of the Divine Truths, [he] is an undisturbed Defender of 'em. He protects all under his Care, by the Clearness of his Understanding, and the Example of his Life. He visits dying Men with the Air of a Man who hop'd for his own Dissolution, and enforces in others a Contempt of this Life, by his own Expectation of the next. His Voice and Behaviour are the lively Images of a compos'd and well-govern'd Zeal. (*The Tatler*, 24 Sept 1709)

'He abounds with that Sort of Virtue and Knowledge which makes Religion beautiful, and never leads the Conversation into the Violence and Rage of Party-Disputes' (ibid., 31 Dec 1709). A folio collection, *Sixty Sermons … Publish'd from the Originals*, for the benefit of Smalridge's widow in 1724, was a major publishing success. It attracted some 2000 subscribers, most but not all of them high tories, and appeared in a second edition in 1727, followed by reprintings in Oxford and London in the nineteenth century. The sermons were commended by Dr Samuel Johnson for elegance and good style. A portrait of Smalridge by Sir Godfrey Kneller hangs in Christ Church hall and was engraved by George Vertue in 1724.

RICHARD SHARP

Sources DNB · *Remarks and collections of Thomas Hearne*, ed. C. E. Doble and others, 11 vols., OHS, 2, 7, 13, 34, 42–3, 48, 50, 65, 67, 72 (1885–1921) · Nichols, *Illustrations* · G. V. Bennett, *The tory crisis in church and state, 1688–1730* (1975) · N. Sykes, *William Wake, archbishop of Canterbury, 1657–1737*, 2 vols. (1957) · G. Holmes, *The trial of Dr Sacheverell* (1973) · D. F. Bond, ed., *The Tatler*, 3 vols. (1987) · *Hist. U. Oxf. 5: 18th-cent. Oxf.* · Foster, *Alum. Oxon.* · *Old Westminsters* · G. Smalridge, *Sixty sermons preach'd on several occasions … publish'd from the originals* (1724) · G. Smalridge, *The charge of George lord bishop of Bristol, at his primary visitation of his diocese, anno 1716* (1716) · *Diary of Mary, Countess Cowper*, ed. [S. Cowper] (1865) · *Manuscripts of the earl of Egmont: diary of Viscount Percival, afterwards first earl of Egmont*, 3 vols., HMC, 63 (1920–23), vol. 1, p. 233
Archives Bodl. Oxf., letters to Arthur Charlett, MS Ballard 7
Likenesses J. Richardson, oils, 1714; photograph, NPG archive · H. Rodd, oils, *c.*1715–1719, Bristol City Museum and Art Gallery · G. Kneller, oils, 1717, Christ Church Oxf. [*see illus.*] · G. Vertue, line engraving, 1724 (after G. Kneller), BM, NPG; repro. in Smalridge, *Sixty sermons* (1724) · oils, Christ Church Oxf.
Wealth at death presumably not great

Smart, Benjamin Humphrey [*pseud.* Francis Drake] (*bap.* **1787**, *d.* **1872**), elocutionist and grammarian, was born at Princes Street, Leicester Square, London, and was baptized on 1 March 1787 at St Anne's, Soho, London, the eldest son of Benjamin Smart (1757–1833), citizen and goldsmith of London, and his wife, Lucy. He came from a family long associated with the City of London and which included a past sheriff of London, Sir Joseph Smart (1641–1702). Smart's father, who worked as a gold refiner at Princes Street, wrote two tracts in 1811 and 1818 criticizing the government's handling of the currency.

Smart became one of half a dozen elocution teachers in London, and supplemented his income by writing. He inherited his father's literary abilities and commenced a long publishing career with his *Grammar of English Pronunciation* (1810). At this time he owned a house in Plough Court, off Fetter Lane, which conferred a vote in the county of Middlesex. In 1813 he lived at Lamb's Conduit Street, St Andrew's, Holborn, and on 15 April 1813 he married Caroline West of St Luke's, Chelsea. They had five children: Leopold (1816–1867); Caroline Charlotte (*b.* 1818), who was later to marry successively Thomas David Easton and the Revd Simon Sturges; Ellen Julia (*b.* 1820), who was to marry Thomas Hand; Emily Emma (*b.* 1822); and Frances Harriet (*b.* 1824, *d.* before 1867), who became the wife of Francis Lewis Dowling. From 1832 to 1850 the Smart family lived at 55 Connaught Terrace, Edgware Road, Paddington.

Smart had continued to teach and write to support his growing family. He published a Shakespeare anthology and a 'revival and correction and exclusive establishment' of Locke's philosophy and metaphysics, but although he was clearly fascinated by these topics, the bulk of his writing was aimed at the acquisition of both new pupils and royalties. His *Grammar on its true basis: a manual of grammar, containing examination questions, exercises, etc, ancillary to the accidence and principles of English grammar* (1847) and *Manual of rhetoric, with exercises for the improvement of style or diction, subjects for narratives, familiar letters, school orations, etc* (1848) are fine examples of these aims. However, two of his works—*Memoir of a Metaphysician* (1853) and *The metaphysicians: being a memoir of Franz Carvel, brushmaker, written by himself, and of Harold Fremdling, esquire, written and now republished by Francis Drake, esq.* (1857)—were written purely for love of the subject, and were published under the ambitious pseudonym Francis Drake.

On 4 February 1850 Smart was elected to the Athenaeum as 'the author of several works on metaphysics and grammar', his membership having been proposed by the Revd Richard Jones and seconded by the distinguished physicist Michael Faraday. In 1854 Smart's son, Leopold, married Ellen, daughter of Hyam Phillips of Pimlico, an Ashkenazi Jew. Leopold was also an elocution teacher, probably working as his father's assistant. By this year Benjamin Smart had moved to 37 Wyndham Street, Bryanston Square, Marylebone, Middlesex.

After 1857 Smart's prolific pen fell silent. He withdrew from the Athenaeum on 1 January 1869. He died of old age, on 24 February 1872, at 76 Charlwood Street, which he had shared with his son Leopold (until his death in 1867) and daughter-in-law. He left what he described in his will as a 'narrow estate' of under £800. In the year after his death a guide to English pronunciation, 'after Smart', *Deutsch-englisches Vocabular und methodische Anleitung zum Erlernen der englischen Aussprache*, was published in Germany. Smart's emphasis on precision both in grammar and diction was transmitted both to pupils and to his descendants: Leopold's grandson Julius Rietchel was remembered quoting Shakespeare by heart—and with perfect clarity of speech—to his own grandchildren on the beach at Bexhill, Sussex, as late as the 1960s.

ANTHONY R. J. S. ADOLPH

Sources [J. Watkins and F. Shoberl], *A biographical dictionary of the living authors of Great Britain and Ireland* (1816) · Allibone, *Dict.* · private information (2004) [archivist, Athenaeum] · *The Times* (28 Feb 1872) · parish register, Soho, St Anne [baptism] · parish register, Chelsea, St Luke [marriage], 15 April 1813 · *London Directory* · will, proved, 1872, Principal Registry of the Family Division, London · family papers, priv. coll. · d. cert. · BL cat.
Wealth at death under £800: probate, 20 April 1872, CGPLA Eng. & Wales

Smart, Charles Frederick (*b. c.*1780). *See under* Smart, George (1750/51?–1818?).

Smart, Christopher (1722–1771), poet, was born on 11 April 1722 in Shipbourne, near Maidstone, Kent, the

Christopher Smart (1722–1771), by unknown artist, in or after 1765

youngest of three children of Peter Smart (1687–1733), steward to Christopher Vane, first Baron Barnard, and of Winifred Griffiths (d. 1765x7). His mother was a Welshwoman from Radnorshire. His father came of a prominent Durham family, with strong church connections, including the puritan cleric Peter Smart, prebendary of Durham under Charles I, and the sixteenth-century evangelist Bernard Gilpin, equally renowned for his resistance to puritan iconoclasm.

1722–1749: Kent, Durham, Cambridge In 1726 Peter Smart bought Hall Place, an estate in East Barming worth £300 a year. Recollections of a childhood spent among 'the meadows the brooks and the hills' of the Medway valley (Smart, Jubilate, B119) figure in Smart's georgic poem, 'The Hop-Garden', and poignantly in later works, as a period of untroubled happiness and Blake-like infant joy. In Fairlawn, Lord Barnard's estate at Shipbourne, Smart found his Eden:

> Let Mary rejoice with the Carp—the ponds of Fairlawn and
>   the garden …
> For due East is the way to Paradise.
> (Smart, Jubilate, B168)

Smart attended Maidstone grammar school until he was eleven. This phase ended abruptly when his father died in 1733, 'in embarrassed circumstances' (Hunter, 1.ix), compelling his mother to sell most of the Hall Place estate at a loss. Christopher, accompanied by his sister Margaret, was sent north to live with an uncle, John Smart of Snotterton in Staindrop, co. Durham. He also came under the protection of Henry Vane, third Baron Barnard, whose

seat at Raby Castle replaced Fairlawn as a haven for the Smart children. At eleven Christopher fell in love with Vane's daughter, seven-year-old Anne, to whom his poem 'To Ethelinda', is addressed, according to his daughter Elizabeth. This precocious piece of erotic verse, written when Smart was thirteen, took 'such effect that these young lovers had actually set off on a runaway match together', before being 'timely prevented' (Le Noir to E. H. Barker, fol. 245).

Smart was educated at Durham School under the mastership of a classical scholar, Richard Dongworth, and showed early accomplishment as a writer of Latin verse. In 1739 he left school to enter Pembroke College, Cambridge, as a sizar, with a supplementary allowance of £40 granted by the duchess of Cleveland, Henry Vane's sister-in-law. He was described by a Cambridge contemporary as 'a little, smart, black-eyed man' (L. Whibley, 'The jubilee at Pembroke Hall in 1743', Blackwood's Magazine, 221, 1927, 106). His abilities as a classical student were quickly recognized. He won a Watts scholarship in 1740, was chosen for three years running to write the Latin verses published with the tripos results, and won the coveted Craven university scholarship in 1742. Smart's Latin rendering of Alexander Pope's 'Ode to St Cecilia' was printed at the university press in 1743; a copy sent to Pope himself was graciously received. After receiving his BA in January 1744, Smart was elected fellow of Pembroke in July 1745, with praelectorships in rhetoric and philosophy. He seemed to be on course for a steady university career.

Smart's progress at Cambridge, however, was anything but steady. Despite his academic success, 'the favourite studies of this Seat of Learning were not congenial with his mind' (Hunter, 1.viii). He found the emphasis on mathematics cramping, as 'On an Eagle Confined in a College-Court' shows in its Dunciad-like conclusion, when classical learning, 'wit and sense', are engulfed in 'mathematic gloom' (Poetical Works, 4.91). Smart was altogether too high-spirited, convivial, and ambitious to settle to the tranquil existence of a college don. Between 1743 and 1747 he divided his time between Cambridge and London, where he frequented the company of actors, artists, and musicians. Some of these, including Charles Burney, became lifelong friends. Smart's 'Idleness', set to music by William Boyce in 1744, was the first of several of his songs performed in London pleasure gardens, and his poems were frequently printed in London magazines in the 1740s. In Cambridge in 1747 he wrote and produced a comedy, The Grateful Fair, or, A Trip to Cambridge, which was performed in college by students and Smart himself. The play does not survive, but it apparently turned on the visit of a Norfolk country squire and his daughter to a nephew at the university, and thus is probably connected with Smart's 'long but unsuccessful passion' in this period for Harriote Pratt of Downham, Norfolk, the sister of a college friend and the subject of several of his early poems (Hunter, 1.xxxiii).

Smart was by nature 'liberal to excess' and incapable of economy (Hunter, 1.xxvii–xxviii). His extravagance led to a crisis in 1747. That spring the poet Thomas Gray, observing Smart's spiralling debts and unruly behaviour, predicted that 'all this … must come to a Jayl, or Bedlam' (*Correspondence*, 1.275). In October he lost his praelectorships, and in November Gray's prophecy was almost fulfilled when Smart was arrested for debt to a London tailor, and forced to go into hiding while the college fellows paid off the tailor and settled with Smart's numerous creditors in Cambridge. Gray blamed Smart's troubles on drunkenness, a judgement confirmed by Burney and other friends, and by Smart's nephew Christopher Hunter. The continuance of his fellowship after this episode was probably made conditional on living in college, 'soberly, & within Bounds', as Gray recommended (ibid., 1.292). By October 1748 he was restored to grace, reappointed to his praelectorships, and made college catechist, with responsibility for giving religious instruction to undergraduates. Since he was chosen in 1747 to be preacher before the mayor of Cambridge, an office reserved for an 'orthodox divine' (Sherbo, 45), he may also have taken minor orders. 1748–9 was Smart's last year in residence. In July 1749 he stayed at Market Downham and visited Ryston, the Pratt family seat, where, he told Burney, he preferred 'hearing my Harriote on her spinnet & organ at her ancient mansion' to the musical celebrations at Cambridge for the installation of the Chancellor (*Annotated Letters*, 42–3). He did not return to college next term, and effectively left Cambridge for good.

London, 1749–1756 The next seven years were hectic, as Smart tried to juggle practical exigencies and his appetite for popular success against his loftier poetic aspirations. He was introduced by Burney to the bookseller John *Newbery, and enlisted into Newbery's stable of hack writers. In June 1750 Newbery published Smart's satire *The Horatian Canons of Friendship*, printed under the signature Ebenezer Pentweazle, one of numerous pseudonyms Smart adopted for his lighter productions. In the same month he joined Bonnell Thornton as co-editor of *The Student, or, The Oxford and Cambridge Monthly Miscellany* (1750–51), the first of many Newbery enterprises in which Smart was involved. He was editor and principal writer of *The Midwife, or, The Old Woman's Magazine* (October 1750 – June 1753), and a major contributor to the *Lilliputian Magazine*, the first English magazine for children (March 1751 – June 1752).

At the same time Smart was bidding for recognition as a serious poet. In March 1750 he won the Seatonian prize, awarded annually to a Cambridge master of arts for a poem on the perfections or attributes of the supreme being, with his 'poetical essay' in blank verse *On the Eternity of the Supreme Being*. Smart competed and won four more times between 1750 and 1755. The rhetoric of eighteenth-century didactic poems on theological and philosophical subjects now appears somewhat jaded, but Smart's boldness of thought and expression raises his contributions to the genre above the usual standard. Meanwhile his *Poems on Several Occasions* was published by subscription, through Newbery, in 1752. The book was clearly designed as a showcase for Smart's versatile talents.

Together with the tripos verses and many previously printed odes, fables, and miscellaneous pieces, it contained some hitherto unpublished writings, including 'The Hop-Garden' and Latin versions of Pope's *Essay on Criticism* and Milton's *L'allegro*, but not the first two Seatonian poems. In spite of a glowing pre-publication notice by Smart's friend Richard Rolt and an impressive list of over 800 subscribers, critical reception of the book was lukewarm. The translation of Pope's *Essay*, Smart's most ambitious work so far, was received 'with much praise from the learned, but without either profit or popularity' (Hunter, 1.xi), and Smart's very versatility told against him. Admirers of the Seatonian poems lamented the inclusion of so much ephemeral verse, while more light-minded readers were put off by his Latin works and the Miltonic style of 'The Hop-Garden'.

1752 was almost certainly the year of Smart's marriage to Newbery's stepdaughter Anna Maria Carnan (1731–1809), then twenty-one, although the exact date and place is unknown. The romantic story told by Le Noir of a runaway wedding at St Bride's, Fleet Street, without Newbery's consent, before the Marriage Act of 1753 outlawed such ceremonies (Le Noir to C. Sharp, fol. 217), is undocumented and improbable. Smart probably first met Anna Maria in 1750; by June 1751, as he proclaimed in a poem in the *Midwife*, his 'lass with the golden locks' had supplanted his Harriote (*Poetical Works*, 4.192–3). Afterwards the couple lived in apartments in Canonbury House, a large property of Newbery's, where their two daughters were born: Marianne, on 3 May 1753, and Elizabeth Anne [see Le Noir, Elizabeth Anne], god-daughter of Anne Vane, on 27 October 1754. It was not a good match, however. Although Smart was an affectionate father, family responsibilities did not sober him down or curb his feckless generosity. Anna Maria was a very capable businesswoman, but though 'married to an author (or perhaps from that very circumstance) [she] had a great dislike to everything relating to literature' (Le Noir to C. Sharp, fol. 219). Temperamental incompatibility and Smart's drunkenness and irresponsibility were major reasons for marital discord, but overwork, ill health, and Newbery's interference must also have had a corrosive effect.

Newbery had a reputation for benevolence, but he was a businessman first and last, and a relentless taskmaster. Arthur Murphy wrote of Smart in 1753 that, lacking a wealthy patron, 'A bookseller is his only friend, and for that bookseller, however liberal, he must toil and drudge' (Brittain, 33n.). In addition to producing a copious supply of prose and verse for Newbery's magazines, and composing his annual Seatonian prize poems, Smart engaged during these years with Murphy, Henry Fielding, and others in the paper war against the author Dr John Hill. His vivacious satire *The Hilliad* (1753) was an important contribution to the campaign. A more burdensome task was a prose translation for schools of the entire works of Horace. It was so successful that it remained a standard schoolbook for nearly two centuries, but Smart himself received only £13 out of £100 due to him, the rest being retained by Newbery for Smart's wife. On top of all this,

Smart was producer, performer (as 'Mrs. Midnight'), and main supplier of songs and recitations for a variety show, billed as 'Mrs. Midnight's Oratory' or 'The Old Woman's Oratory'. An offshoot of the *Midwife*, and vigorously promoted by Newbery, it was first performed at the Castle tavern in Paternoster Row on 27 December 1751, moved then to the Haymarket Theatre, and was repeated frequently during the next few years. Hester Piozzi described it as 'low buffoonery', but added that 'it pretended to nothing better, and was wondrous droll' (Sherbo, 80).

Meanwhile, Smart and Rolt had signed a contract in November 1755 with another publisher, Thomas Gardner, to provide materials for a monthly magazine, the *Universal Visiter* (January–December 1756). Although contributions by Smart appeared until October 1756, he took no part in its production after the first few numbers, presumably because of ill health. 'Of a very delicate constitution' since childhood (Hunter, 1.vi), Smart suffered periodical attacks of feverish illness from 1750 onwards, culminating in a serious breakdown recounted in a *Hymn to the Supreme being on Recovery from a Dangerous Fit of Illness*, published in June 1756. The *Hymn* marks a turning point in Smart's career. It describes a transformative experience, a reawakening to religious faith and spiritual values, the impact of which is apparent in almost everything he wrote afterwards.

The madhouse years, 1757–1763 In March 1757 a petition was made for Smart's admission to St Luke's Hospital, and he was admitted to the 'curable' ward in May on the recommendation of Newbery and another bookseller. He was discharged uncured in May 1758, but put on the waiting list for readmission. Application for his re-entry was withdrawn in 1760, presumably because by then he was in the private madhouse in Bethnal Green kept by a Mr Potter to which Newbery committed him. Smart's alleged 'madness' has always been debatable. The judgement of William Battie, physician at St Luke's, and the family story of 'paroxysms so violent and continued as to render confinement necessary' (Hunter, 1.xx), have to be weighed against the testimony of friends. It is indisputable that Smart held highly unconventional beliefs, was subject to emotional extremes ('For I have a greater compass both of mirth and melancholy than another'; Smart, *Jubilate*, B132), and had an irrepressible urge to pray loudly in public ('For I blessed God in St James's Park till I routed all the company'; ibid., B89). Whether he was ever clinically insane, however, remains questionable. Samuel Johnson, who visited Smart in the madhouse, said, 'I did not think he ought to be shut up. His infirmities were not noxious to society' (Boswell, *Life*, 1.397), and Hester Piozzi argued that he was only committed to St Luke's because he displayed his eccentricities in public. There is a strong suspicion that Newbery contrived to keep Smart locked up to prevent him from being a nuisance and financial burden to his wife and to Newbery himself. Allegations of wrongful detention of people in madhouses were rife, and a petition to parliament by John Sherratt, a businessman who campaigned for several years for reform of private madhouses, stated that Potter's house was notorious for such abuses.

Smart was not held under close constraint. He was allowed to keep a cat, work in the garden, and have access to books, newspapers, and writing materials; but his sense of humiliation and the anguish of separation from his wife and daughters are movingly expressed in *Jubilate agno*. Anna Maria Smart moved to Dublin in 1758 as Newbery's agent, remaining there for three years. She became a Roman Catholic and sent the children to a convent school in France in 1761. She never returned to her husband but survived him until 1809. Former friends remained loyal, however; David Garrick gave a benefit performance of *Merope* for Smart in 1759, prompting the publication of several verse tributes to Smart. Smart's final escape in January 1763 was engineered by John Sherratt, with the aid of other friends. In Smart's nautical metaphor, Sherratt snatched the ship

> from the pirate's port,
> Beneath the cannon of the fort.
> ('An epistle to John Sherrett, Esq', *Poetical Works*, 4.347)

Sherratt's trick was to get permission to take Smart out to dinner, whereupon 'he returned to confinement no more' (Le Noir to C. Sharp, fols. 217–18).

During these years Smart wrote what are now recognized as his most brilliant and original works: *A Song to David*, the *Hymns and Spiritual Songs for the Fasts and Festivals of the Church of England*, and *Jubilate agno*. The surviving fragments of the last remained unknown until the manuscript was discovered by W. F. Stead and published under the title *Rejoice in the Lamb* in 1939. A new text, retitled and substantially reorganized in conformity with Smart's apparent intentions by W. H. Bond, was published in 1954. *Jubilate agno* is unlike anything written in the eighteenth century prior to Blake's prophetic books. Smart must have been aware that its radical attack on philosophical and scientific orthodoxies, its daring innovations in language, verse, and structure, and its visionary and confessional style would be unacceptable to the public for he made no effort to print it. *A Song to David* however was published at his own expense in 1763. It was praised for its rhapsodic quality and felicities of expression, but the regularity of its formal design was unperceived and it was judged 'a fine piece of ruins' (*Critical Review*, 15, 1763, 324) reflecting the author's disordered mind. The *Hymns*, published with Smart's *Translation of the Psalms of David* in 1765, went entirely unnoticed.

The final phase, 1763–1771 After his release Smart moved into lodgings in Westminster. He was visited in 1764 by John Hawkesworth who found him living 'with very decent people' in rooms overlooking St James's Park, and reported that 'his company as a gentleman, a scholar, and a genius' was sought after as much as before his confinement (Hunter, 1.xxv). Smart charmed the young Fanny Burney, when he visited her father in 1768–9, but she saw 'still great wildness in his manner, looks & voice', and was shocked by his savage references to his wife (*Early Journals*, 1.36, 91).

Smart's creativity in this period was prodigious. He published three small collections of poetry (1763–4); finished the rendering of the Psalms which he had begun in the madhouse; wrote two oratorio librettos, *Hannah* (1764) and *Abimelech* (1768); and produced *A Poetical Translation of the Fables of Phaedrus* (1765), *The Works of Horace, Translated into Verse* (4 vols., 1767), and a versified edition of *The Parables of our Lord and Saviour Jesus Christ* (1768). But nothing Smart published after 1756 prospered. None of these productions earned him either critical acclaim or significant financial reward, and he was soon in financial trouble again. Subscriptions for the Psalms were slow to come in, and despite efforts by Burney and others to help him he was, as ever, incapable of living within his means. He claimed he was 'eight times arrested in six years'; the last time, after 'a fortnight at a spunging-house, one week at the Marshalsea in the want of all things' he 'safely arrived at the King's Bench' on 26 April 1770 (*Annotated Letters*, 132). He was comfortable enough in prison, especially after his brother-in-law Thomas Carnan secured him the 'Rules' (freedom to walk in St George's Fields). While there, he wrote *Hymns for the Amusement of Children*. Dated 1771, it was in fact published by Carnan in December 1770, and reprinted in England, Ireland, and America. Smart however had returned to drinking and he died in the king's bench prison of liver failure on 20 May 1771. He was buried in the church of St Gregory by Paul on 26 May.

In the eighteenth century Smart was admired for the elegance, vivacity, and wit of his minor verse, and above all for his mastery of the religious sublime in the Seatonian poems. Among his lighter poems, the songs and fables were especially popular; Burney rated Smart second only to John Gay as 'the most agreeable metrical Fabulist in our language' (*Early Journals*, 1.40). Smart's later writings, including *A Song to David* were largely misunderstood, derided, or ignored: the posthumous edition of *The Poems of the Late Christopher Smart* (2 vols., 1791), collected by Francis Newbery, omitted almost everything published after 1756 as showing marks of 'the recent estrangement of his mind' (Hunter, 1.xliii). A suggestion made to Newbery by Charles Burney jun. that a third volume containing Smart's translations of Phaedrus and Horace might be added to the 1791 *Poems* was not taken up. The resurrection of *A Song to David* in the nineteenth century, however, led to an even more unbalanced view of Smart. While the energy and originality of its language, its lyrical virtuosity, and breadth of imaginative compass were fully acknowledged, the *Song* was seen as a solitary work of supreme value amid a heap of dross. The myth created by Robert Browning in 'Parleying with Christopher Smart' (1887), of a literary drudge momentarily transformed into a poet of genius, held sway until the early twentieth century, when interest in Smart's other poems began to revive.

It was the discovery of *Jubilate agno* in 1939, however, and the impact on a wider public of Benjamin Britten's setting of Smart's words in his cantata *Rejoice in the Lamb* (1943), that triggered a thorough reappraisal of his standing.

Smart was seen at last as a poet of substantial achievement as well as revolutionary vision. *Jubilate agno* itself now rivals *A Song to David* as a work of intrinsic and historical importance which anticipated by half a century the oracular poetry of the Romantics, and directly influenced many twentieth-century poets in England and North America. A new subgenre of celebratory verse has emerged, based on the 'Cat Jeoffry' section of *Jubilate agno*. The recovery of Smart's hymns and psalms further consolidated his reputation. Recognition for the first time of the superb lyrical technique and sacramental quality of his *Hymns and Spiritual Songs* has earned him a significant place in the long tradition of Anglican devotional poetry. Similarly, *Hymns for the Amusement of Children* have been appreciated for their joyful spirit, their command of a diction ranging from child-like simplicity to a powerfully compressed, allusive syntax, and for the power, conspicuous in Smart's later poetry, to unite the sensuous and the spiritual 'as though the transition was not hard' (Blunden, xi). Study and evaluation of Smart's other neglected writings, notably his fine verse translations of Phaedrus and Horace (the latter unreprinted for two centuries until 1996), has only just begun, but his status as a major poet now seems assured. KARINA WILLIAMSON

Sources C. Hunter, 'The life of Christopher Smart', *The poems of the late Christopher Smart* (1791), vol. 1 • A. Sherbo, *Christopher Smart, scholar of the university* (1967) • C. Mounsey, *Christopher Smart: clown of God* (2001) • C. Smart, *Poems*, ed. R. Brittain (1950), 5–56 • E. Le Noir, letter to E. H. Barker, *c*.1825, Bodl. Oxf., MS 1006, fols. 245–6 • E. Le Noir, letters to Sir C. Sharp, 1831, Durham Cath. CL, MS Sharp 28, fols. 217–45 • *Correspondence of Thomas Gray*, ed. P. Toynbee and L. Whibley, 3 vols. (1935) • Boswell, *Life*, vols. 1–2 • H. L. Piozzi, 'Madness', *British Synonymy 1794* [facsimile reprints 113], 2 (1968) • *The early journals and letters of Fanny Burney*, ed. L. E. Troide, 1: 1768–1773 (1988) • C. Burney, *Monthly Review*, new ser., 7 (1792), 36–43 • R. Lonsdale, *Dr Charles Burney: a literary biography* (1965), 25–8, 66–70, 363, 485–70 • C. Smart, *Jubilate agno* (1980), vol. 1 of *The poetical works of Christopher Smart*, ed. K. Williamson • *Miscellaneous poems, English and Latin*, ed. K. Williamson (1987), vol. 4 of *The poetical works of Christopher Smart* • *The annotated letters of Christopher Smart*, ed. B. Rizzo and R. Mahoney (1991) • B. Rizzo, 'John Sherratt, negociator', *Bulletin of Research in the Humanities*, 86 (1983–5), 373–429 • R. Mahony and B. Rizzo, eds., *Christopher Smart: an annotated bibliography, 1743–1983* (1984) • E. Le Noir, *Miscellaneous poems*, 2 vols. (1825–6) • R. Browning, 'With Christopher Smart', *Parleyings with certain people of importance in their day* (1887) • *Hymns for the amusement of children by Christopher Smart*, ed. E. Blunden (1947)
Archives NRA, letters and poem
Likenesses oils, *c*.1745, NPG • oils, in or after 1765, Pembroke Cam. [*see illus.*] • H. Meyer, stipple, BM; repro. in *The poems of the late Christopher Smart*, 2 vols. (1791) • photograph (after unknown artist), repro. in C. Smart, *Rejoice in the lamb*, ed. W. F. Stead (1939) • portrait, repro. in Smart, *Poems*, ed. Brittain
Wealth at death nil: Brittain, ed., *Poems*; Sherbo, *Christopher Smart*

Smart, Elizabeth (1913–1986), writer, was born on 27 December 1913 in Ottawa, Canada, the third child and third daughter in the family of four daughters (one of whom died in infancy) and one son of Russel Sutherland Smart, a prominent Ottawa lawyer specializing in patents, and his wife, Emma Louise (Louie), daughter of James Alexander Parr, executive in the Montreal Telegraph Company. She grew up in affluent circumstances in

Elizabeth Smart (1913–1986), by Christopher Barker

Ottawa and Kingsmere, where the family had a second house on a lake. She was educated at Ottawa normal school, Elmwood School, and Hatfield Hall in Cobourg, with the exception of one year during which she was obliged to lie in bed with a heart condition, and there began to write. She vacillated between becoming a musician or a writer, and did not go to university. She travelled around the world under the eye of a family friend. In London she studied to become a professional pianist with Katharine Goodson, but with the confidence born of what she called the 'huge luckiness' of her childhood she reacted against the hollowness of her social life and broke away to travel around the world, always gravitating towards artistic rebels. Although she had studied music for thirteen years and played the piano very well she never played again. She lived on an allowance from her father.

Smart expressed her adventurous, romantic nature to the full when, after reading the poems of George Granville *Barker in a Charing Cross bookshop, she promptly fell in love with the poet, who was then working unhappily in Japan. He was the son of George Barker, formerly of the Coldstream Guards, a butler at Gray's Inn. In 1940 she invited Barker and his wife to Canada, raising the cash herself for both their fares, and they then moved to Monterey, California, where she was living. This was the pivotal act of her life: it resulted in a passion-wracked affair, which began in July 1940 and produced four children and her extraordinary novel *By Grand Central Station I Sat Down and Wept*, which she completed in 1941. First published in

August 1945 by Tambimuttu just before the end of the Second World War her novel (or narrative prose poem) remained largely unnoticed in the fray, although Cyril Connolly gave it a certain grudging admiration in *Horizon*.

After the birth of her first love child, a girl, in 1941, Smart went to England in 1943 on a convoy which was torpedoed. Shortly afterwards she produced a son with Barker, whose wife had twins five weeks later. The rigours of bringing up a family with very little money (she was still reliant on an allowance from her father), and without a permanent father figure, gagged her muse, but she became more settled when she moved to a mill house in Essex. She wrote intermittently about the aftermath of her grand passion, but, understandably under the circumstances, her productivity was low. She had another of Barker's sons in 1945 and a daughter in 1947.

From 1949 to 1951 Smart was a sub-editor on *House and Garden*. Separated from Barker, who eventually had fifteen children with different women, she had occasional affairs. By the mid-1950s she supported her family by writing advertising copy. Her large flat at 9 Westbourne Terrace was a centre for London bohemians, many of them distinguished remnants from the old Soho 'Fitzrovia' days (the painters Robert Colquhoun, Robert MacBryde, Patrick Swift, and Craigie Aitchison; the poets Patrick Kavanagh and W. S. Graham; and the inspired drifter Jeffrey Bernard). In 1957, with Agnes Ryan, she published *Cooking the French Way*. Her life began to pick up considerably in 1964 as the children grew up and she began writing for the sparkling new magazine *Queen*, a job she held until 1966.

In 1966 Smart's novel was republished by Panther Books in a silver paperback, with an introduction by Brigid Brophy, who described it as one of the half-dozen masterpieces in the world:

> The entire book is a wound. Even when its rhythm expresses the throb of pleasure, the pleasure is so ardent it lays waste the personality which experiences it … it is one of the most shelled, skinned, nerve-exposed books ever written.

But some critics continued to be affronted by such a metaphor-laden, raw, female emotion, the eternal wail of a woman for her demon lover, and took their refuge in accusations of purple prose, discounting the passages of searing humour.

After her younger daughter became involved with drugs Smart often had full responsibility for the daughter's two children, and she soon moved to a cottage near Bungay, Suffolk, where she became absorbed in creating a garden and writing poetry. She aimed for Blakean simplicity, which did not appeal to the poetry mafia of the period. However, her first collection, *A Bonus*, was published in 1977 and she began to give poetry readings. The publication of *The Assumption of the Rogues and Rascals* in 1978, her long-brewing aftermath novel, and the Canadian publication of her dazzling memoirs, *In the Meantime* (1984), reinforced her growing reputation. Meanwhile the now famous early book was translated into many languages and became something of a cult novel. In 1982 she spent a year as writer in residence at the University of Alberta.

Elizabeth Smart had occasional affairs with both men and women. She was a great beauty, not only in the classical blonde, blue-eyed, well-featured sense, but because of a radiance which, even later, ravaged by age and empathy, could draw so many people to her. She was a bohemian in the best sense of the word, and died on 4 March 1986, of a heart attack, in her son Christopher's flat in the Soho where she had spent so many hours in conviviality, good talk, and freedom from hypocritical moral restraints. Her younger daughter had died from drug taking in 1982. Her journals were posthumously published as *Necessary Secrets* in 1986.   JILL NEVILLE, *rev.*

Sources E. Smart, *In the meantime* (1984) · R. Sullivan, *By heart: Elizabeth Smart, a life* (1991) · E. Smart, *Necessary secrets* (1986) · CGPLA *Eng. & Wales* (1986)
Likenesses C. Barker, photograph, priv. coll. [*see illus.*]
Wealth at death £43,425: resworn probate, 18 Sept 1987, CGPLA *Eng. & Wales* (1986)

Smart, George (1750/51?–1818?), musical instrument maker and music publisher, was possibly born in London. He attained proficiency on the violin, double bass, and clarinet. Evidently a gifted musician, he was possibly the Smart who appears on the records of Covent Garden as early as 22 September 1760 as a band member earning 3s. 4d. daily, although confusion regarding specific details has arisen and persisted owing to the number of musicians simply named Smart who appear in records from the second half of the eighteenth century. The subject of this article was employed from the early 1770s at James Bremner's music shop in New Bond Street before assisting William Napier, a viola player whose music shop was at 474 Strand. He set up his own business as a musical instrument maker and music seller and publisher at the corner of Conduit Street, near Savile Row, in 1773 or 1774. In December 1774 he relocated to the corner of Argyll Street, at 331 Oxford Street, where he remained 'until sometime during the early nineteenth century' (Highfill, Burnim & Langhans, *BDA*). Smart published and edited collections of popular music, mainly songs and dances, and he is the only known maker of the 'sticcado-pastorale', a 'percussion idiophone made of glass' or 'crystallophone' (King): there is an example signed by Smart and dated about 1775.

Meanwhile Smart continued to perform, appearing at Drury Lane as a clarinettist and violinist and on the double bass at the Handel memorial concerts in June 1784. Having been rejected by the Royal Society of Musicians in 1785, possibly because he practised a second profession or because 'he had reported four children when his wife was pregnant with a fifth' (Ehrlich, 29), Smart founded, along with Edward Miller, a rival friendly society which accepted provincial members. The New Musical Fund was set up on 16 April 1786. He served as a member of its court of assistants and as treasurer from 1794 to 1815. There were also performances in Johann Peter Salomon's concert series, the band of the King's Theatre, and the Concerts of Ancient Music.

According to the *Dictionary of National Biography*, Smart also entered the brewery business with his son Henry, but without great success. His children with his wife Ann Embrey (*d.* 1818) included at least three prominent musicians: George Thomas *Smart (1776–1867), Henry *Smart (1778–1823) [*see under* Smart, Sir George Thomas], and **Charles Frederick Smart** (*b. c.*1780). At least two of them appeared with their father, as 'Smart and Sons', in the band that played for Handel's *Messiah* under Samuel Arnold and François Hippolyte Barthélémon at the Haymarket on 15 January 1798. Charles Frederick was a singer and a well-known double bass player in London orchestras and was living in his father's house at 331 Oxford Street in 1794. Some doubt surrounds the date and place of George Smart's death. Nicholas Temperley has suggested that Smart died about 1805, but another authority cites F. Cansick's *A Collection of Curious and Interesting Epitaphs* (1869–72), which quoted Smart's memorial inscription at St James's Chapel, Hampstead Row, London, stating that he died, aged sixty-seven, in Edinburgh on 4 September 1818 (Highfill, Burnim & Langhans, *BDA*). Smart's wife died on 19 October 1818 and was buried beside him at St James's Chapel. The subscribers to the New Musical Fund paid for his memorial tablet there.   DAVID J. GOLBY

Sources Highfill, Burnim & Langhans, *BDA* · W. H. Husk and N. Temperley, 'Smart', *New Grove*, 2nd edn · A. H. King, 'Sticcado-pastorale', *The new Grove dictionary of musical instruments*, ed. S. Sadie, 3 (1984), 454 · C. Ehrlich, *The music profession in Britain since the eighteenth century: a social history* (1985)

Smart, Sir George Thomas (1776–1867), conductor and organist, was born in London on 10 May 1776, the eldest of the six children of George *Smart (1750/51?–1818?), a music publisher and dealer and an amateur bass player, and his wife, Ann, *née* Embrey (*d.* 1818). After schooling in London and Ashford, he began his musical career in 1783 as a chorister at the Chapel Royal, St James's, under Edmund Ayrton, and studied the organ with Thomas Dupuis, the piano with J. B. Cramer, and composition with Samuel Arnold. He sang at the first Handel commemoration festival in Westminster Abbey in 1784, and conducted the last there in 1834. He made his début as a pianist in a concerto by Dussek on 6 March 1790 at a New Musical Fund concert. Having left the chapel in 1793, he occasionally deputized for Arnold as organist, both at the chapel and at Westminster Abbey. He also became organist at St James's Chapel, Hampstead Road, taught singing, and played the violin or viola (which he had learnt from the bass player Garabaldi) in Salomon's orchestra. During Haydn's visit in 1794 he was required to deputize for an absent timpanist, which he did, not very successfully until the composer himself left the keyboard to instruct him. He sang as a bass at the Italian Opera House in 1795 or 1796, and took conducting lessons with Joah Bates.

On 1 January 1811, on a visit to Dublin to conduct a series of concerts, he was knighted by the duke of Richmond, lord lieutenant of Ireland. Two years later he became one of the original members of the Philharmonic Society, for which he often conducted. From 1813 to 1825 he was conductor of the Lenten oratorio concerts, at which in 1814 (following correspondence with Beethoven) he gave the English première of Beethoven's *Christ on the Mount of*

Sir George Thomas Smart (1776–1867), by William Bradley, 1829

Olives in his own arrangement, and the 'Battle' symphony. He also conducted the City Amateur Concerts, where he introduced symphonies by Beethoven and piano concertos by Mozart as well as much new music. He was appointed organist of the Chapel Royal on 25 January 1822.

In 1825 Smart made an extended tour of Europe, partly with Charles Kemble, in the course of which he made thorough notes about musical conditions and practices and met a large number of musicians, including Mendelssohn (whom he encouraged to visit England), Meyerbeer, Spohr, and, especially, Beethoven, whom he visited in Vienna to discover the correct tempos for the symphonies. As he was leaving, Beethoven detained him for two minutes while he composed a canon, 'Ars longa, vita brevis', 'written on the 16th September 1825 in Baden when my dear talented music artist and friend Smart (from England) visited me here'. Smart also visited Weber, then on a cure at Ems and 'lame and out of breath', to discuss details of the planned production of *Oberon* at Covent Garden, and invited him to stay at his house, 91 Great Portland Street; despite all his solicitude, Weber died there early on the morning of 5 June 1826. Smart then attended to the funeral arrangements, organized subscriptions for the erection of the Weber statue in Dresden, and put himself to much trouble in tidying up Weber's affairs.

Smart conducted the first English performance of Beethoven's ninth symphony at the Philharmonic Society in 1826, and that of Mendelssohn's *St Paul* at the Liverpool festival in 1836. Having conducted the music at the funeral of George IV and the coronation and funeral of William IV, he became composer to the Chapel Royal on 1 April 1838; he subsequently conducted and played the organ at the coronation of Queen Victoria and played the organ at her wedding to Prince Albert. In 1845 he travelled to Bonn for the celebrations attending the unveiling of the Beethoven statue. He was greatly in demand as conductor at nearly all the principal music festivals, including Dublin and Norwich (of which cities he was made a freeman), as well as Liverpool, Bath, Newcastle, Edinburgh, Bury St Edmunds, Derby, Cambridge, and Manchester. He conducted with great authority and skill, not using a baton but from the keyboard or organ. He was a life governor of Norwich Great Hospital, and grand organist of the Grand Lodge of Free and Accepted Masons. Much sought after as a teacher of singing until he was past eighty, he was particularly valued for his knowledge, acquired from his father's observation, of how Handel wished his arias to be sung: his students in this included Jenny Lind and Henriette Sontag, and among other pupils were Emma Romer and Louisa Pyne. The copious notes he wrote for the Norwich festival show his meticulous attention to detail. His compositions included glees, anthems, and other church music, and he edited Gibbons's first set of madrigals for the Antiquarian Society (1841) and Handel's Dettingen Te Deum for the Handel Society (1846–7). His journals give graphic accounts of personalities and events of his time, in particular of his travels. On 28 February 1832 he married Frances Margaret, daughter of the Revd C. S. Hope of Derby; they had one daughter. By all accounts, and by his actions on behalf of music and musicians, Smart was a kindly and generous man, and a much loved one. John Sainsbury wrote that

> He has risen into estimation … by a combination of qualities not often to be found in the same individual, namely by extreme correctness and skill in his instrumental performance, by a general acquaintance with the details of musical business, by unassuming and gentlemanly manners, and by integrity and liberality of conduct. (*Dictionary of Musicians*)

He died at 12 Bedford Square, London, on 23 February 1867, and was buried at Kensal Green cemetery.

George Smart's brother **Henry Smart** (1778–1823), violinist, the third child of George Smart senior, studied the violin with William Cramer. At the age of fourteen he was engaged by the orchestras at Covent Garden, the Haymarket, and the Concerts of Ancient Music (where he was principal viola). In 1803 he retired from the music profession to join a brewery with his father, but on its failure he resumed his original vocation and, besides teaching, led the orchestra at the Lyceum Theatre when it opened as the English Opera House in 1809. He was also leader at Drury Lane, from its reopening in 1812 until 1821, at the oratorio concerts under his brother, and, occasionally, for the Philharmonic Society. In 1821 he opened a piano factory in Berners Street, and on 22 July 1823 took out a patent for an improved mechanism for touch; in addition he invented a metronome which was said to give 'simultaneously a visible and an audible beating of every possible division of time'. His ballet *Laurette* was successfully produced at the King's Theatre in 1803. About 1810 he married Ann Stanton Bagnold. He died in Dublin on 27 November 1823.

Henry Smart's son **Henry Thomas Smart** (1813–1879),

organist and composer, was born in London on 26 October 1813. He was educated at Highgate School, and while a boy frequently visited Robson's organ factory, where he learned the elements of his ultimately profound knowledge of organ construction and practical mechanics. After turning down a commission in the Indian army he was articled to a solicitor, but soon abandoned law for music, and built himself a set of organ pedals for his piano. In 1831 he became organist of the parish church at Blackburn, Lancashire, and wrote his first important composition, an anthem for the 300th anniversary of the Reformation, which was performed there on 4 October 1835. In 1836 he was appointed organist of St Philip's, Regent Street, London, and became a teacher and a critic for the *Atlas*. In March 1844 he was appointed organist of St Luke's, Old Street, and remained there until 1864, when he moved to St Pancras Church, Euston Road. All his life Smart suffered from a weakness of the eyes, and by 1864 this became total blindness, when his numerous compositions had to be dictated. These were very popular in his day, and included much church music (especially a widely admired service in F), cantatas, partsongs, and organ works. He designed, among many organs, those in the City and St Andrew's halls in Glasgow and the town hall in Leeds. He also went to Dublin in 1878 to examine and report on the organ in Christ Church. In June 1879 he was awarded a civil-list pension of £100 a year, but he died in London on 6 July, and was buried in Hampstead cemetery.   JOHN WARRACK

Sources *Leaves from the journals of Sir George Smart*, ed. H. B. Cox and C. L. E. Cox (1907) · A. H. King, 'The importance of Sir George Smart', *MT*, 91 (1950), 461–2 · [J. S. Sainsbury], ed., *A dictionary of musicians*, 2nd edn, 2 vols. (1827) · J. E. Cox, *Musical recollections of the last half-century*, 2 vols. (1872) · C. von Weber, ed., *Reise-Briefe von Carl Maria von Weber an seine Gattin Carolina* (1886) · D. Reynolds, ed., *Weber in London, 1826* (1976) · *New Grove* · J. Broadhouse, *Henry Smart's compositions for the organ* (1880) · W. D. Seymour, *Henry Smart* (1880) · W. Spark, *Henry Smart* (1881) · *DNB*

Archives BL, corresp. and papers, Add. MSS 41771, 41778 · BL, corresp. and papers incl. memoranda book, Add. MSS 27741–27744, 41771–41779, 42225, 61933, 69856–69858 · BL, list of festivals conducted, Add. MS 34728 | BL, letters to William Hawes and others, Add. MS 63589

Likenesses J. Green, miniature, exh. RA 1815 · W. Bradley, oils, 1829, NPG [*see illus.*] · F. S. Archer, marble bust, exh. RA 1839 · C. Hodgson, oils, *c.*1856, Royal Society of Musicians, London · C. Baugniet, lithograph on India paper · J. Cawse, oils, Foundling Museum, London · E. Edwards, photograph, repro. in L. Reeve, ed., *Portraits of men of eminence*, 2 (1864) · E. Stalker, engraving (after oil portrait by J. Cawse), Foundling Museum, London

Wealth at death under £30,000: probate, 21 March 1867, *CGPLA Eng. & Wales* · under £300—Henry Thomas Smart: administration, 9 Aug 1879, *CGPLA Eng. & Wales*

Smart, Henry (1778–1823). *See under* Smart, Sir George Thomas (1776–1867).

Smart, Henry Hawley (1833–1893), army officer and novelist, was born at Dover on 3 June 1833, the son of Major George Smart, of an old Kentish family, and Katherine, daughter of Sir Joseph Henry *Hawley. His grandfather, Colonel Henry Smart, had been governor of Dover Castle early in the century. After education by a private tutor, he

received a commission by the influence of Lord Fitzroy Somerset (later Lord Raglan), and was gazetted ensign in the 1st foot (Royal Scots) on 20 October 1849, being promoted lieutenant on 6 July 1852 and captain on 15 May 1855. He served through the Crimean War, returned to England in 1856, and sailed next year for India, where he served during the mutiny. In 1858 he exchanged into the 17th (Leicestershire) regiment, and went to Canada.

Smart left Quebec in 1864, sold out of the army, and, after losses on the turf, became a professional novelist. His models were Lever and Whyte-Melville, and his first novel was *Breezie Langton: a Story of Fifty-Two to Fifty-Five* (1869). He subsequently produced two or more novels a year, amounting to some thirty-eight in total, of which the last, *A Racing Rubber*, was published posthumously in 1895. They were novels of 'society', military life, racing, and hunting, based in part on his own experiences. Entertainment rather than literature, they none the less, especially the army and racing stories, have some force and character.

Smart married, in 1883, Alice Ellen, daughter of John Smart of Budleigh Salterton, who survived him. He died at his residence, Laburnum Cottage, West Hill, Budleigh Salterton, on 8 January 1893, and was buried in Budleigh churchyard.   THOMAS SECCOMBE, *rev.* JAMES LUNT

Sources *The Times* (10 Jan 1893) · *ILN* (14 Jan 1893) · *The Athenaeum* (14 Jan 1893), 56 · *Saturday Review*, 27 (1869), 256–7 · *Our Celebrities*, 38 (Aug 1891) · *Hart's Army List* (1850–64)

Archives BL, corresp. and agreements with Richard Bentley & Son, Add. MSS 46618, 46622

Likenesses Barraud, photograph, NPG; repro. in *Men and Women of the Day*, 2 (1889) · portrait, repro. in *ILN*

Wealth at death £1476 13s.: probate, 16 March 1893, *CGPLA Eng. & Wales*

Smart, Henry Thomas (1813–1879). *See under* Smart, Sir George Thomas (1776–1867).

Smart, John (1741/2–1811), miniature painter, may have come from Norfolk but there is nothing to support that traditional contention, nor are any details of his birth or parentage known. On 5 August 1809 Joseph Farington recorded a conversation he had had that day with Smart, when 'he mentioned Cosway as being a year older than Himself. Cosway, said He, is 67,—but He would have it believed He is younger than that age' (Farington, *Diary*, 10.3523). This information accords with the earliest recorded reference to Smart as an entrant in the competition for children under fourteen run by the Society of Arts in 1755 and, together with his being described in his obituary in the *Gentleman's Magazine* as having died 'in his 70th year' (*GM*, 81/1, 599), indicates that he was born in 1741 or 1742.

Smart's early prowess as an artist is evident from his success in the Society of Arts competitions to which he submitted pencil and chalk drawings. He came second to Richard Cosway in 1755 and won the competition in the next three years (drawings for 1755–6, 1758; RSA). His entry for 1757 was a chalk drawing of William Shipley, founder of the Royal Society of Arts, at whose drawing academy in St Martin's Lane he gained his only formal

John Smart (1741/2–1811), self-portrait, 1797

training as an artist, having enrolled as a student there on 23 September 1755. It is not known who taught Smart the art of miniature painting, and suggestions that he was the pupil of his contemporary Richard Cosway are unsubstantiated. By 1760, however, Smart had become established as a miniaturist in London; his earliest miniature was dated 1760 but, according to Foskett, may have been painted earlier (Foskett, *Miniatures*, 648). He practised from premises in Dean Street, Soho, and from 1765 at 68 Berners Street, working in watercolour on ivory and card. He often worked up his miniatures from pencil sketches but he also produced exquisite finished drawings in pencil and wash on paper, such as that of his grandson, *Robert Woolf Junior* (1796; Huntington Library and Art Gallery, San Marino, California). His work in miniature was distinguished by his excellent draughtsmanship and brilliant colouring, with a tendency towards a reddish-pink flesh tone that became markedly ruddy in some of his male sitters. His superb naturalistic observation of his subjects was recorded in a finish characterized by meticulous brushwork and minutely rendered detail. His fellow miniaturist and competitor Ozias Humphry remarked with some surprise on the 'exactness' of the likeness in Smart's miniature of Mary Boydell and commented that it was painted 'without any flattery' (Humphry MSS, HU 3/49). In this respect Smart's work differed from that of the other leading miniaturist of the period, Richard Cosway, and his followers. Smart usually dated his miniatures and signed them with cursive initials J. S. on the front; those of his miniatures dating from his Indian period are identifiable by the addition of an I after the date.

Smart's clientele was broadly drawn from the wealthy middle class and his business proved lucrative. He not only exhibited at the Society of Artists from 1762 to 1783 but he also became its director in 1771 and made several loans to the society in periods of financial difficulties. His involvement in its affairs was recognized by his appointment as vice-president in 1777 and as president in 1778; a medal modelled by Joachim Smith was cast, bearing Smart's portrait on the reverse, to commemorate the former event. In 1798 Farington recorded: 'Smart says he has realized between 5&£600. He paints miniatures now at 25 guineas a head' (Farington, *Diary*, 3.1040) and eventually he died a wealthy man, having left almost £9000 in his estate. But Smart's financial acumen did not endear him to all; the artist Thomas Jones recorded in his *Memoirs*:

> Everybody who knew Smart must know, however eminent he was in his profession, that he was a man of the most vulgar manners, grossly sensual, and greedy of Money to an extreme—(I have often heard him say 'D— me Sir I can sit on my A— for 18 hours together without stirring & put four & twenty guineas in my pocket at a Sitting') … He was a muckworm. (Oppé)

Notwithstanding his commercial and professional success in London, Smart decided to exploit the market for portraiture in India and obtained permission from the East India Company to travel to Madras in 1784. He set sail on the *Dutton* and on 6 September 1785 arrived in Madras, where he settled in North Street, Fort St George. With the exception of short visits to Bombay and Bengal, Smart remained in Madras for the duration of his stay in India, painting many of the English residents as well as the nawab of Arcot (version in the Nelson–Atkins Museum, Kansas City; another repr. in Foskett, *John Smart*, fig. 62; sketch in the V&A), the nawab's retinue, and the sons of Tippoo Sultan. The preliminary drawings for the lost miniatures of Abdul Khalick and Mooiz ud Din (1794) are in the British Museum. Smart never fulfilled the threat to Ozias Humphry of his working in Calcutta, which Humphry had nervously anticipated on his arrival but, like Humphry, Smart experienced difficulties in obtaining his fees and was still owed a considerable amount by the nawab of Arcot when he decided to return to England in 1795.

Smart quickly re-established his practice as a miniaturist on his arrival back in London. The Society of Artists was no longer in existence when he returned and he exhibited instead at the Royal Academy during the period 1797–1811, at first from a studio at 20 Grafton Street and, from 1799 onwards, from 2 Russell Place, Fitzroy Square. It is thought that at about this time he made a second marriage, to Edith Vere, his first wife (who died in 1778) having eloped to Rome with the artist William Pars, leaving Smart with the upbringing of three children: John (b. 1762), who died young; Anna Maria (1766–1813), later Mrs Robert Woolf; and Sophia (1770–1793), later Mrs John Dighton. From his third marriage, to Mary Morton (1783–1851) on 14 February 1805, Smart had a son, John James (1805–1870), and, from a relationship with Sarah Midgeley before his departure for India, another son, **John Smart**

junior (1776–1809), and a daughter, Sarah (1781–1833). The younger John Smart became a miniature painter, working in a style very close to that of his father. As a child provision was made for him and his sister during his father's stay in India under the guardianship proceedings of the court of chancery (1790), and the miniaturist Robert Bowyer was appointed to supervise his education. It appears that it was his father who taught John Smart jun. to paint in miniature. In a letter to the East India Company of 28 May 1808 John Smart requested permission for his son to travel to India as a miniaturist, stating: 'I respectfully solicit the same indulgence for my son John Smart who had been taught by me and has obtained a proficiency in the same line that will do honor to me and credit to himself' (BL OIOC, East India Company, general correspondence, 1602–1859, MS E/1/118, fol. 112). Father and son shared the same address at this point and it was from 2 Russell Place that John Smart jun. exhibited his miniatures at the Royal Academy from 1800 to 1808. He travelled to India on the *Asia*, possibly in the role of a cadet, as suggested by the *Calcutta Monthly Journal* (12 February 1809) and by the existence of a self-portrait in cadet uniform, dated 1808 (priv. coll.). He arrived in Madras on 11 February 1809 but, despite his stated intention to practise as a miniaturist, one surviving miniature represents the extent of his artistic activity before his death in Madras from unknown causes four months later. The burial register for St Mary's Church, Fort St George, records his date of death as 1 June 1809, although both the *Madras Courier* (7 June 1809) and the *Government Gazette, Madras* (8 June 1809) state that his death occurred on 2 June 1809. The sale of his effects, including his miniaturist's equipment, took place on 17 July 1809 in Madras (BL OIOC, Madras wills and administrations, MS L/AG/34/29/210, fols. 127–135). Although his work has an obvious affinity with that of his father his is clearly weaker. He preferred working on paper or card to ivory and his manner of signing, with the initials J.S.J. and the date, makes any confusion between the work of father and son unlikely. A large group of miniatures by John Smart jun. was sold at Christies on 10 December 1928 (lots 11–16); four of his miniatures are in the Victoria and Albert Museum, London. His self-portrait (1800) was formerly in the collection of Edward Grosvenor Paine, New York, and another pencil drawing of him, by John Smart (1808), was formerly in the Wellesley Collection. The elder John Smart outlived his son by only two years and died after a short illness on 1 May 1811 at his home, 2 Russell Place, Fitzroy Square, London; he was buried in St James's burial-ground, St Pancras. His influence was most evident in the work of his follower Samuel Andrews (1767?–1807), who succeeded Smart in practice in Madras, but also in the prolific copies in the manner of Smart that came into circulation in the nineteenth and early twentieth centuries. The most significant collection of his work is the Starr collection of consecutive dated examples from 1760–1810 in the Nelson–Atkins Museum, Kansas City. Other locations of his work include the Hugh John Burton collection in the Victoria and Albert Museum,

London, the Fitzwilliam Museum, Cambridge, the Metropolitan Museum of Art, New York, the Cleveland Museum of Art, Ohio, and the Yale Center for British Art, New Haven. Smart painted a number of self-portraits, of which the most well known is the ivory miniature (1797) in the Victoria and Albert Museum. John Smart, professionally and financially rewarded in his own lifetime, appears only to have grown in critical and popular estimation in recent times. His miniatures, which 'are of the utmost prettiness' (Reynolds, *English Portrait Miniatures*, 132), are widely collected and merit the accolade of his being 'by general consent one of the greatest English miniaturists' (Long, *British Miniaturists*, 406).   V. REMINGTON

Sources *GM*, 1st ser., 80 (1810), 593 · *GM*, 1st ser., 81/1 (1811), 599 · D. Foskett, *John Smart: the man and his miniatures* (1964) · Ozias Humphry MSS, 8 vols., 1774–1810, RA · G. Reynolds, *The Starr collection of miniatures in the William Rockhill Nelson Gallery* (1971) · *John Smart, miniaturist, 1741/42–1811: Starr collection of consecutively dated miniatures and special loan exhibition* (1965) [exhibition catalogue, Nelson–Atkins Museum of Art, Kansas City, MO, 6 Dec 1965 – 2 Jan 1966] · B. Long, 'John Smart: miniature painter', *The Connoisseur*, 74 (1926), 196–200 · B. S. Long, *British miniaturists* (1929), 405–9 · G. Reynolds, *English portrait miniatures* (1952); rev. edn (1988), 130–34 · M. Archer, *India and British portraiture, 1770–1825* (1979), 390–93 · W. Foster, 'British artists in India, 1760–1820', *Walpole Society*, 19 (1930–31), 1–88, esp. 71 · Farington, *Diary* · A. P. Oppé, ed., 'Memoirs of Thomas Jones, Penkerrig, Radnorshire', *Walpole Society*, 32 (1946–8) [whole issue], esp. 73–4 · Graves, *Soc. Artists* · Graves, *RA exhibitors*, vol. 8 · D. Foskett, *Miniatures: dictionary and guide* (1987) · burial register, St Mary's Church, Fort Museum, Fort St George, Madras · F. T. Cansick, *A collection of curious and interesting epitaphs*, 1 (1869)
Likenesses J. Kirk, medal, *c.*1777, repro. in Reynolds, *Starr collection*, 33 · R. Brompton, oils, *c.*1780, Nelson–Atkins Museum, Kansas City, Starr collection · attrib. G. Stuart, oils, *c.*1783, Joslyn Art Museum, Omaha · J. Smart, self-portrait, miniature, 1786, Museum of Fine Arts, Boston · J. Smart, self-portrait, watercolour on ivory, 1797, V&A [*see illus.*] · attrib. L. F. Abbott, oils, *c.*1800, NPG · J. Smart junior, self-portrait, pencil, 1800 (John Smart junior), repro. in Foskett, *John Smart*, fig. 104 · J. Smart junior, self-portrait, pencil and wash on paper, 1800 (John Smart junior), repro. in Foskett, *John Smart*, fig. 103 · J. Smart, self-portrait, watercolour on ivory, 1802, Cleveland Museum of Art, Ohio · attrib. M. Brown, chalk drawing, Scot. NPG
Wealth at death £8942 18s. 3d.: Foskett, *John Smart*, 26

Smart, John, junior (1776–1809). *See under* Smart, John (1741/2–1811).

Smart, Sir Morton Warrack (1877–1956), manipulative surgeon, was born in Edinburgh on 1 December 1877, the third son of John Smart (1838–1899), a landscape painter, and his wife, Agnes Purdie Main, daughter of Robert Main of Doune, Perthshire. He was educated in Edinburgh, at George Watson's College, the university, and the Royal College of Surgeons, and he graduated MB ChB in 1902 and MD in 1914. He served with the Black Watch in the Second South African War, interrupting his medical studies. In the First World War, though by then a doctor for ten years, he served as a combatant with the Royal Naval Volunteer Reserve in many parts of the world. He reached the rank of commander, was mentioned in dispatches, and was awarded the DSO in 1917. In 1923 he married Lilian Gladys, daughter of William S. Gibson JP, of London, and widow of Major P. V. Lavarack MC. They had no children.

After qualifying as a doctor Smart moved to London, where he joined the medical staff of the Great Ormond Street Hospital for Sick Children, taking charge of the electrical therapy department. In his professional career, he became one of the leading exponents of manipulative surgery and an authority on physical medicine and rehabilitation. He worked with the orthopaedic surgeon Walter Rowley Bristow, developing the Smart–Bristow faradic coil, which became a fashionable form of electrotherapy treatment. He began consulting with Bristow from Harley Street before the First World War and continued on his return from active service. He founded and was for many years in charge of the London Clinic for Injuries at Grosvenor Square. He was manipulative surgeon to kings George V, Edward VIII, and George VI, and to Queen Elizabeth II. He was appointed CVO (1932), KCVO (1933), and GCVO (1949), and received a number of foreign decorations. He was a member of the central medical war committee and of the Empire Rheumatism Council, and a fellow of the Royal Society of Medicine. During the Second World War he acted as consultant in physical medicine to the Royal Air Force at its rehabilitation clinic in Regent's Park. He contributed many articles on muscle and joint injuries to medical journals and encyclopaedias and in 1933 he published *The Principles of Treatment of Muscles and Joints by Graduated Muscular Contractions*. Although he did not regard himself as an orthopaedic surgeon, he made many contributions to the development of that speciality, emphasizing the value of non-surgical techniques and the need to treat patients holistically. He practised essentially as an orthopaedic physician.

Smart was a man of many facets. As well as a pioneer of physical medicine and manipulative techniques, he was a fearless sailor and an early exponent of motor-boat racing. He was a skilled horticulturist, specializing in growing gladioli. He won many prizes for his blooms and served as president of the British Gladiolus Society. He was also a superb raconteur of his experiences in the many spheres of his busy life. He died at his home at Cooden Beach, Bexhill, on 16 March 1956; his wife survived him. W. E. TUCKER, rev. STELLA BUTLER

Sources BMJ (31 March 1956), 750–51 · The Lancet (24 March 1956), 339 · personal knowledge (1971) · W. Waugh, A history of the British Orthopaedic Association (1993) · CGPLA Eng. & Wales (1956)
Likenesses W. Stoneman, photograph, 1933, NPG
Wealth at death £60,545 19s. 9d.: probate, 14 Aug 1956, CGPLA Eng. & Wales

Smart, Peter (1568/9–c.1652), Church of England clergyman and religious controversialist, was one of five surviving sons of William Smart, vicar of Stratford upon Avon, Warwickshire; his mother was probably Katherine Leuce of Stratford, who had married his father in 1559. He was a queen's scholar at Westminster School before matriculating on 25 October 1588, aged nineteen, as a batteler of Broadgates Hall, Oxford. By April 1589 he had been elected to a studentship at Christ Church, where the dean was William James. He graduated BA in 1592 and proceeded MA in 1595.

Following James's translation to the deanery of Durham, in 1597 the new dean appointed Smart to the mastership of Durham School, where he probably remained until 1609. During this period Smart married Susanna, with whom he had several children; their son William was born between December 1602 and December 1603. After James became bishop in 1606 he ordained Smart and made him his chaplain, presenting him to the rectory of Boldon, co. Durham, and to the sixth prebend of the cathedral. Before 1610 Smart also became master of the nearby St Edmund's Hospital, Gateshead, and in 1614 he was advanced to the fourth prebend.

At this time Smart's life was prosperous and untroubled, since he was at one with the Calvinist Bishop James's emphasis on preaching ministries and encouragement of lectures and ministerial exercises. However, on 12 May 1617 the bishop died and the same month newly installed canon Francis Burgoyne had the communion table moved to an altar position at the east end of the cathedral. Smart immediately attacked this policy, calling Burgoyne the first corrupter of religion there, but he held the new bishop, Richard Neile, responsible for the change, even though he was not enthroned until October. Smart, who had known Neile at Westminster, accused him later in *A Short Treatise of Altars* (1629) of seeking preferment, in the light of his deficiencies as a preacher, by advancing 'Catholic pomp and glorious Ceremonies', and compared him with the scarlet woman in Revelation chapter 17 (and thereby with the Roman church). Following the appointment of the Arminian Richard Hunt as dean in 1620 the communion table was replaced with a stone altar adorned with cherubim. Another prebendary, Robert Hutton, attacked Neile for this, but by 1624 numerous deaths among the prebendaries had allowed the bishop to replace them with more Arminians, including John Cosin. By about this time Smart, his disquiet with Arminian changes to the cathedral mounting, had reportedly withdrawn himself from communion there. As a senior prebendary he repeatedly but vainly advised the innovators that their actions were unlawful. In 1625 and again in 1627, like some of his colleagues, he qualified himself as a member of the York province high commission court, but he seldom attended.

Probably stimulated by the fear of a Popish conspiracy against England which affected the country in the spring and summer of 1628, on 27 July that year Smart launched a vehement attack on liturgical changes in a sermon at the cathedral morning service. In *A Sermon Preach'd at Durham* (1628) he claimed they negated the very nature of the Reformation by replacing ministers, communion tables, and sacraments with priests, altars, and sacrifices, and by denying that Christ's was the last sacrifice for sin. With the introduction of anthems which were as incomprehensible as Hebrew or Irish,

the sacrament itselfe is turned neare into a theatricall stage play, that when mens minds should be occupied about heavenly meditations, of Christs bitter death and passion, of their owne sinnes and of faith and repentance, of the joyes of heaven, and the torments of hell, their eares are possest with pleasant tunes, and their eyes fed with pompous spectacles.   (P. Smart, *A Sermon Preach'd in the Cathedral Church of Durham*, 1628, 25)

He attacked as almost blasphemous those who preferred such services to sermons. Comparing these practices to those of the Delos temple of Apollo, he went on to attack their young Apollo, Cosin, for his ornamentation of the choir. He fulminated against such men, and those of higher rank, as blind guides, hypocrites, holders of many rich preferments, non-resident, and limitlessly ambitious. He condemned Neile's acquiescence in the moving of the communion table as presumptuous, and the changes made as illegal and uncanonical. He continued by urging the congregation, 'Stay at home in the name of God, until such things be mended' (ibid., 26), finally admonishing them that the light of God's truth would be removed if they did not repent of such superstitious vanities.

By this time Neile himself had been translated to Winchester, but such a powerful attack, both on Arminianism and upon colleagues in the cathedral chapter and their former bishop and present patron, brought a very swift response. That afternoon Dean Hunt, and the prebendaries Marmaduke Blakeston, John Cosin, and William James met in the dean's great chamber, constituted themselves as members of the York high commission, accused Smart of preaching a seditious sermon against permissible ceremonies, and summoned him to appear immediately. He obeyed, delivered a copy of the sermon, and affirmed he would justify every word. He was bound to appear later on £1000 of his own recognizances. The dean and chapter wrote to Bishop William Laud of London, alleging that Smart had attacked people and places more eminent, including the king's chapel, and appealing for his help, and their preservation from contempt. The affair was taking on a strong personal dimension, as well as wider political and religious ones. The case remained without articles for over two months, but Smart preferred four indictments against the dean and chapter at the August assizes on the grounds that the ceremonies were superstitious and contrary to the Act of Uniformity, causing a local sensation. The grand jury found no case, and the judge, Sir James Whitelocke, rejected the indictment, adding that Smart deserved substantial punishment for acting to disgrace the church and dishonour God's service. Nevertheless Cosin told Laud, 'the fury of so hot a spirit will [not] be stayed till he has set all on fire, unless he be cooled by authority' (*CSP dom.*, 1628–9, 260). The fruits of his prebend were sequestrated on 21 August, according to Smart without a chapter meeting.

This rather heated Smart than chilled him, and he began preferring a bill against the chapter in parliament, against which Cosin sought the help of Neile, Laud, and John Howson, the new bishop of Durham. When articles were finally produced against Smart and given a preliminary hearing in October he retaliated by accusing Cosin of denying that the king was supreme head of the Church of England, and by implying popery as the reason. He used delaying tactics until the commissioners' jurisdiction was superseded by Canterbury's in January 1629. In London he was imprisoned for his defiance, but refused to submit, and remained a captive. He was then returned at his own request to York, where the high commission censured him. By this time his sermon had been printed in Edinburgh to avoid censorship. Archbishop Samuel Harsnett of York had it burnt, at which Smart was furious, describing him as decreasing in grace as he increased in rank. Arguing that the dean and chapter had proceeded illegally against him in July he brought another case at the assizes, this time before Sir Henry Yelverton. Some of the Arminian prebendaries tried to get the case dropped, but Yelverton, who agreed with Smart's sermon, was resolved to act legally. He judged that, as some were punished for refusing ceremonies demanded by law, so others should be for including those not so sanctioned, and the jury preferred the indictment. But he regarded the suit as unchristian and endeavoured in vain privately to reconcile the parties, to the fury of Smart's son-in-law Ogle, who cried out, 'Did we rely upon the Judge for this? hath my father spent £300 for this?' (*CSP dom.*, 1629–31, 19). Yelverton nevertheless stayed the indictment until he had consulted Laud, Howson, and Neile.

Smart remained obdurate in his views, convinced in conscience that he had not offended against the doctrine and discipline of the Church of England. Late in 1630 he resigned Boldon, was prepared to resign his prebend to a sound preacher, and was degraded. His supporters regarded him as a martyr and raised £400 a year to support him and his family. Refusing to pay a fine of £500 he was imprisoned in the King's Bench. Here he was encouraged by his wife, who wrote: 'We cannot but brust fourth into the prasing of such a bountefull God who maide you worthy to suffer for his name', and prayed, 'Let not the Arminions say where is now his God', assuring him of her daily prayers (Hunter, 62–3). In August 1632 he contested deprivation from his prebend at the assizes, arguing either that he could hold it as a layman, or that the procedures for his degradation were illegal, desperately quoting the stipulations of the Council of Trent.

In prison Smart's bitterness remained undimmed, and in April 1640 he petitioned the House of Commons through Sir Robert Harley, and John Pym and John Hampden took up the case next day, seeing his imprisonment as linked with a scheme to crush Calvinists and return the Church of England to Rome. A week after the Long Parliament met in November, with Edward Bagshaw's help, Smart's petition was renewed, and the Commons ordered his immediate release with a keeper until Mr Leighton's committee on prisoners could examine the case. This led to his release in January 1641 and to his being called as a witness in the trial of Cosin. Many accusations came from Smart's sermon and formed part of the impeachment articles.

Smart's celebrity at this time led to engravings of him being printed, one by Wenceslaus Hollar with an approving verse beneath, supposedly written by Archbishop George Abbot. Later, in Archbishop Laud's trial, Smart deposed that Augustine Lindsell had stated that only ignorant Calvinist bishops had put down altars at the Reformation. In 1643 he published *Anti-Christi et hierarchiae connubium*, a Latin verse attack on the Roman church, Arminians, and Arminianism, which he depicted as having led to the oppression of the true bride of Christ until 1642. Doubtless this was intended as part of the campaign for Laud's impeachment.

In 1643 Smart took the covenant. Parliament ordered that he should be reinstated in his prebend and benefices, but he battled for years to try to get arrears. On 22 December 1645 he was admitted to the sequestrated rectory of Bishopstoke, Hampshire, and in 1646 claimed also to have Great Aycliffe, co. Durham. In 1648 he spent some time in London, urging great want of money. He was reported to have died at Baxter-Wood, a hamlet of St Oswald's, Durham, about 1652.   ELIZABETH ALLEN

Sources C. Hunter, *An illustration … of the history of the puritans in the article of Peter Smart A. M.* (1736) · *DNB* · *CSP dom.*, 1628–9, 243, 259, 266; 1629–31, 15, 19–20, 343, 354; 1640, 518 · C. Russell, *The fall of the British monarchies, 1637–1642* (1991), 37, 105–7, 109, 222 · N. Tyacke, *Anti-Calvinists: the rise of English Arminianism, c.1590–1640* (1987), 115–19 · R. Rushworth, *Historical collections*, 3/1 (1691), 208–10 · *JHC*, 2 (1640–42), 25 · R. Lockyer, *Buckingham: the life and political career of George Villiers, first duke of Buckingham, 1592–1628* (1981), 437–44 · R. Savage, ed., *The registers of Stratford-on-Avon*, 3 vols. (1897–1905), vol. 1, pp. 3–4, 6, 11; vol. 2, p. 1; vol. 3, p. 95 [baptisms, marriages, burials] · Venn, *Alum. Cant.* · J. Peile, *Biographical register of Christ's College, 1505–1905, and of the earlier foundation, God's House, 1448–1505*, ed. [J. A. Venn], 1 (1910), 41 · E. I. Fripp, *Shakespeare's Stratford* (1920), 55 · J. Merridew, *A catalogue of engraved portraits … connected with Warwickshire* (1848), 60 · T. H. Burbidge, ed., *Durham School register*, 3rd edn (1940), 2–3 · W. Prynne, *Canterburies doome, or, The first part of a compleat history of the commitment, charge, tryall, condemnation, execution of William Laud, late arch-bishop of Canterbury* (1646), 360, 493 · *Old Westminsters*, 2.855 · Foster, *Alum. Oxon.* · H. M. Wood, ed., *Durham protestations*, SurtS, 135 (1922), 43

Archives Bodl. Oxf., MS Rawlinson A441 · U. Durham L., papers relating to Durham dean and chapter library

Likenesses W. Hollar, etching, 1641, AM Oxf., BM, NPG

Wealth at death little wealth: Hunter, *An illustration*, 159

Smart, William (1853–1915), economist, was born at Barrhead, near Glasgow, on 10 April 1853, the eldest son of Alexander Smart JP and his wife, Elizabeth Duncan. At the time of William's birth, Alexander Smart ran an engineering business at Barrhead, but shortly afterwards he was persuaded by his uncle, the founder of John Clark & Co., to join the Mile End threadworks in Glasgow. He became a manager and senior partner before his retirement in 1879. William was educated at East End School and Glasgow high school. His father obtained a position for him in the thread mill but he showed an inclination to enter the church (his grandfather was a clergyman) and attempted to combine his commercial career with attendance at classes at Glasgow University, which he entered in 1867. The strain of both proved too great, and after giving up his studies to concentrate on his business career he eventually succeeded his father as partner. In 1876 he married Katharine Stewart, daughter of the Revd Dr William *Symington, of the Great Hamilton Street reformed presbyterian church, Glasgow.

During this period Smart became strongly attracted to John Ruskin's critique of industrialism; he belonged to the Guild of St George and became, in 1879, the first president of the Ruskin Society in Glasgow. His earliest publication was a study of Ruskin and his work (1880). His subsequent review of Ruskin's teaching, *A Disciple of Plato: a Critical Study of John Ruskin* (1883), was highly regarded, but its attempt to reconcile Ruskin to political economy was met with a scornful rebuff.

The sale of the Clark thread firm to an American company in 1884 left Smart free to pursue his true ambition: an academic career. He had completed his university course in 1882, when he graduated MA with first-class honours in philosophy. In his studies Smart came under the influence of Edward Caird, the professor of moral philosophy and leading idealist thinker in Scotland. Caird handed over to his former pupil the work of teaching political economy, which had been attached to the moral philosophy chair since the tenure of Gerschom Carmichael in the late 1720s and continued under Francis Hutcheson and Adam Smith. Smart also gave university extension lectures, taught for a year (1886–7) at University College, Dundee, and was appointed in 1886 a lecturer in political economy at Queen Margaret College, the women's college attached to Glasgow University. He was a strong supporter of the higher education of women and had helped to bring about the incorporation of Queen Margaret College in 1883. He made a pioneering study of the factors influencing the pay and conditions of women in industrial employment and became chairman of the Scottish Council for Women's Trades. With his wife he helped to run Toynbee House, the Glasgow branch of Toynbee Hall founded in 1886, where evening classes were organized.

In 1892 Smart was appointed by Glasgow University as the first 'independent', that is, specialized, lecturer in political economy, although still located within the department of moral philosophy. When the Adam Smith chair in political economy was endowed by the Glasgow ironmaster Andrew Stewart, Smart was appointed, in 1896, the first incumbent, although not without reservations among some of the electors, suspicious of his bimetallist views. As a teacher, he was known as an excellent, clear expositor of economics, generating enthusiasm among his students. His methods typified the trend among Glasgow professors of the period towards adopting more personal approaches to teaching. He received the degree of LLD from St Andrews in 1893 and DPhil from Glasgow in 1896. A photograph of him at this time reveals a large, bearded vigorous man, as befitted a keen golfer and cyclist.

This phase of Smart's career was marked by an interest in what was later known as the first Austrian school of economics, whose principal members were Carl Menger and Eugen von Böhm-Bawerk. At Caird's suggestion Smart brought out translations of Böhm-Bawerk's works in 1890 and 1891, having taught himself German for the purpose. But Smart, like Menger, was not a mathematical economist. Nor was he preoccupied with the theoretical dimension even if, as his pupil and teaching assistant Thomas Jones recalled, the theory of value provided the 'vertebral column' both of Smart's *An Introduction to the Theory of Value* (1891; 3rd edn, 1914) and of his lecture course (Jones, xxxiv). His preoccupation with the moral dimension to economic activity was evident in his last work, *Second Thoughts of an Economist* (1916), written with a real sense of urgency in the last year of his life. In it he drew attention to the fact that choices made by individuals and firms *should* have a moral dimension, calling for 'responsible' patterns of production and consumption. Nor did he (or Menger) neglect the institutional dimension; his lectures were markedly influenced by Alfred Marshall's *Industry and Trade*. In his lecture on *The Greatness of Adam Smith* (1901) he recognized that debt which is owed to Smith's system of social science.

Like his idealist mentors, Smart retained a close concern with social welfare and civic problems, although he avoided party politics. His attack on tariff reform in 1904, which revealed his 'ill-disguised contempt for politicians', was based on the belief that protection would lead to political corruption (Jones, xli). Regarding intemperance to be a major cause of poverty, he took part in attempts to regulate the drink trade in Glasgow. His major interest, however, was in housing reform: he became a founder of the Glasgow Workmen's Dwellings Company and a member of the housing commission appointed by the Glasgow presbytery (1888). He was a member of the municipal housing commission in Glasgow (1902–3), chaired by Sir Samuel Chisholm. He opposed the idea of taxing land values as a solution to housing shortages, and gave his views in an address on 'The Problem of Housing' as president of the economic science and statistics section of the British Association in 1904.

Smart was appointed in 1905 by Balfour as a member of the royal commission on the poor law, and he helped to draft large parts of the majority report (November 1909). He collaborated closely with Helen Bosanquet, and proved impervious to the views of Beatrice Webb, to the latter's annoyance as expressed in some unflattering comments on Smart in her diary (B. Webb, *Our Partnership*, 1948, 410). His work in preparing historical memoranda for the commission led him to embark on a massive programme of research, in which R. H. Tawney was one of his assistants, to gather data on the economic history of the nineteenth century. The first volume, *Economic Analysis of the Nineteenth Century, 1801–1820*, was published in 1910. The second volume, covering the years 1821–1830, was in the press at the time of his death, at his Glasgow home, Nunholm, Dowanhill Gardens, on 19 March 1915. His widow and their daughter survived him.   M. C. CURTHOYS

Sources T. Jones, Biographical sketch, in W. Smart, *Second thoughts of an economist* (1916), preface • E. Cannan, 'William Smart', *Economic Journal*, 25 (1915), 300–05 • private information (2004) [Professor Andrew S. Skinner] • M. Milgate, 'Smart, William', *The new Palgrave: a dictionary of economics*, ed. J. Eatwell, M. Milgate, and P. Newman, 4 vols. (1987) • A. M. McBriar, *An Edwardian mixed doubles: the Bosanquets versus the Webbs* (1987) • E. L. Ellis, *T. J. A life of Dr Thomas Jones, CH* (1992) • M. Moss, J. Forbes Munro, and R. H. Trainor, *University, City and State: the University of Glasgow since 1870* (2000)

Archives NL Wales, corresp. with Thomas Jones • University of Toronto Library, Thomas Fisher Rare Book Library, letters to James Mavor
Likenesses Messrs Annan, photograph, 1902, repro. in Smart, *Second thoughts*, frontispiece
Wealth at death £11,260 17s. 11d.: probate, 1915

Smart, William George [Billy] (1893–1966), circus proprietor, was born on 23 April 1893 at West Ealing, the son of Charles Smart and his wife, Susan. His was a fairground family, and he began work at the age of fifteen in charge of a hand-operated roundabout on his father's fairground at Slough, Buckinghamshire. After his marriage in 1914 to Nellie, daughter of Harry Digby, he set up his own business as a fairground proprietor, but met with little success. Facing considerable hardship, he bought a pony and cart, collected rags and bones, and again failed. He hired out the pony and cart for 3s. 6d. a week, sold winkles, and dug gardens, while his wife took in laundry. Gradually his fortunes improved, and he again began to build up a fairground business, this time with greater success. By 1939 it had become one of the largest in Britain, but was adversely affected by the wartime blackout.

Smart had always harboured an ambition to extend his business into the world of circus and in 1946, with the backing of his family, he staked all his resources on establishing a travelling circus. The circus grew rapidly to become one of the largest and most successful touring circuses in Britain, and was able to continue when other large circuses were being forced to disband because of steeply rising running costs. Smart's popularity was aided by the advent of television; his show was first screened by the BBC in 1957, and although all but two minutes were blacked out by a technical breakdown, the Smart circus became established as regular and popular television fare at holiday times.

Smart's circus grew to be one of the largest in the world, touring every part of the British Isles, and with permanent quarters and an associated zoo at Winkfield, Berkshire, not far from where Smart began his fairground career. The circus's popularity was greatly aided by the personality of its proprietor; he was a showman on the grand scale, weighed over 20 stone, constantly smoked large cigars, and on one occasion he rode an elephant through the streets of Mayfair and parked it at a meter before inserting a shilling. He owned a ciné camera and recorded new talent which he observed on tour in Britain or abroad (subsequently introducing new forms of bareback riding or trapeze artistry in his own circus). He performed extensive works for charity, and in recognition was made honorary mayor of Calgary, Canada.

In 1962 Smart made an offer to the town council of Blackpool to lay out and run a 150 acre replica of the Disneyland amusement park in California, but negotiations failed.

Smart and his wife had six daughters and four sons, and boasted an eldest grandson the same age as their youngest son. By maintaining regular television appearances, and combining the circus's winter quarters with a zoo, his family were able to continue the business successfully after his death. At its height the circus owned 150 horses and employed artistes of every nationality.

Smart collapsed and died on 25 September 1966 while conducting the band at his circus zoo at Ipswich, Suffolk. The funeral was of appropriate magnificence, the procession to his burial at Winkfield, on 2 October 1966, including a coffin weighing 7 hundredweight, three cars filled with flowers, and a large floral tribute in the shape of an elephant. ALAN HAMILTON, *rev.*

Sources P. MacGregor-Morris, *Spinners of the big top* (1960) · 'From a winkle-barrow to this', *Evening News* (8 Oct 1959) · *The Times* (26 Sept 1966), 10f · *The Times* (3 Oct 1966), 9e [funeral] · private information (1981)
Archives Sheffield University, National Fairground Archive
Likenesses photograph, repro. in *The Times* (26 Sept 1966), 10f
Wealth at death £18,330: probate, 25 Jan 1967, *CGPLA Eng. & Wales*

Smartt, Sir Thomas William (1858–1929), politician in South Africa, was born at Trim, co. Meath, Ireland, on 22 February 1858, the son of Thomas William Smartt, and his wife, Sarah Rerdon. He was educated in medicine at Trinity College, Dublin, qualifying LRCS, Ireland, and in 1880 went to South Africa and settled in Britstown, Cape Colony, where he practised as a doctor.

Smartt was popular and successful in his profession. He also gained a wide knowledge of agriculture, learned Dutch, and soon took up a political career, entering the house of assembly as member for Wodehouse in 1893. Smartt married in 1891 Sybil Anna, daughter of Edmond Lombard Swan, of Allworth, Abbeyleix, Ireland. They had one son, who died in infancy, and two daughters.

Smartt became a member of the Afrikaner Bond, which was allied with Cecil Rhodes until the Jameson raid, in 1895, although Smartt was personally sympathetic to Rhodes. Smartt became colonial secretary in the ministry of Sir Gordon Sprigg when Rhodes fell in 1896 but when the Sprigg cabinet fell in 1898 Smartt returned to parliament as member for Cathcart, in an opposition of which a section was in increasing sympathy with Rhodes, with Smartt its natural leader. Smartt and Rhodes became friends and political allies at the siege of Kimberley and when Rhodes died in March 1902 Smartt and Leander Starr Jameson took up his plans and ideals.

During the Second South African War, in June 1900, Sprigg again became prime minister, and Smartt held the portfolio of public works. They split over the suspension of the constitution, and Smartt led the Progressives in opposition to Sprigg. When the Sprigg ministry fell in 1904, Smartt realized that Jameson should be leader and, resigning his own claims, supported him. The Jameson cabinet lasted until 1908, with Smartt commissioner of crown lands and public works. He and Jameson attended the Imperial Conference held in London in 1907, supporting Alfred Deakin, prime minister of Australia, who urged the policy of imperial preference. At home they faced defeat but they had laid the foundations, together with General Louis Botha, of the 1909 union of the four states of South Africa. Jameson and Smartt were members of the national convention which drafted the South Africa Act,

and, at Botha's suggestion, Smartt was created KCMG in January 1911.

It was hoped that union would end Dutch and English antagonism but Botha could not form a cabinet on those lines. Jameson and Smartt then organized the Unionist Party, whose aim was to help Botha against the extremists on his side while supporting the policy of Cecil Rhodes. In 1912 Smartt succeeded Jameson as leader of the Unionists. The split between General Botha and General Hertzog, followed by the outbreak of the First World War, made Smartt's task one of great delicacy. When Botha died in 1919 and was succeeded by General Smuts, the Hertzog Nationalists gained political strength, and in 1920 Smuts was left without a majority. Labour had won seats from the Unionists, and Hertzog's Nationalists were the strongest single party. The combination in 1920 between the parties of Smuts and Smartt was essential to keep republican nationalists at bay. Smartt supported Smuts and held the office of secretary of agriculture from 1921 to 1924. Becoming ill, he retired in March 1929 and died a month later, on 17 April 1929, at Cape Town. He was buried on his farm, Glenban, in the Stellenbosch district. LYNN MILNE

Sources *The Times* (17 April 1929) · *Cape Times* (17 April 1929) · *DSAB* · T. R. H. Davenport, *South Africa: a modern history*, 2nd edn (1978) · L. M. Thompson, *The unification of South Africa, 1902–1910* (1960)
Archives priv. coll. | National Archives of Zimbabwe, Harare, corresp. with Francis Chaplin · Rhodes University, Grahamstown, South Africa, Cory Library for Historical Research, corresp. incl. J. G. Sprigg
Likenesses W. Stoneman, photograph, 1921, NPG · G. Goodman, portrait, Houses of Parliament, Cape Town · bust, Houses of Parliament, Cape Town · cartoon, priv. coll. · sketch, priv. coll.

Smeaton, Donald Mackenzie (1846–1910), administrator in India and Burma, was born at St Andrews on 9 September 1846, the eldest of the twelve children of David James Smeaton, schoolmaster of Letham House, Fife, and Abbey Park, St Andrews, and his wife, Elizabeth Charlotte, daughter of Captain Donald Mackenzie of the 42nd Black Watch, a veteran of Waterloo.

Smeaton was educated at his father's school at Abbey Park and at St Andrews University, where he graduated MA. In 1865 he came second in the open competition for the Indian Civil Service and in December 1867 was posted to Allahabad in the North-Western Provinces as an assistant magistrate. In the following May he began to specialize in revenue settlement work and in February 1877 attained the rank of settlement officer. In 1873, with Charles Haukes Todd Crosthwaite, he published *An Annotated Edition of the North-Western Provinces Revenue Act, XIX of 1873*, and, in 1877, a monograph entitled *The Currency of India*.

While engaged in settlement work in Mainpuri district in 1873, Smeaton married, on 2 February, Annette Louisa Lushington, daughter of Sir Henry Lushington, fourth baronet, with whom he had two sons, the first of whom died in infancy. In January 1880, ten days after giving birth to their second son, Arthur Lushington, Annette died of puerperal fever. She was buried in the Rangoon Presbyterian churchyard.

In April 1879 Smeaton was transferred to Burma as revenue and agriculture secretary, in which post he restructured virtually the entire revenue administration of Lower Burma. In August 1884 he returned to the North-Western Provinces as director of agriculture and commerce, but in April 1887, following the annexation of Upper Burma, he went back to Burma as chief secretary to the chief commissioner, initially Sir Charles Bernard and afterwards Sir Charles Crosthwaite. In addition to his official duties, Smeaton undertook a study of the hill peoples of the new territory, which he published in 1887 as *The Loyal Karens of Burma*. In June 1888 he was appointed commissioner of the central division of Upper Burma, where he helped crush the remaining resistance to the British occupation.

In March 1891 Smeaton was appointed financial commissioner of Burma, in which post he remained until his retirement in 1903. Many of his superiors praised his revenue work and recommended him for promotion, but he had early acquired a reputation for impetuosity which he was never able to shake off. As officers junior to him were promoted over his head, he began to suspect that there was a secret bar to his advancement. On 12 November 1894 he was married again, this time to Marion Henrietta Mary, daughter of Major Ansell of the 4th King's Own regiment, and with her had a daughter, and increasingly he worried about subjecting his new family to a long, unprofitable stay in Burma. He was gazetted CSI in 1895, officiated as chief commissioner in 1896, and served four times as Burma member on the central legislative council, from 1898–9 until 1901–2. All along, however, he was hoping to be made lieutenant-governor of Burma. Sir Frederick Fryer, the incumbent, was due to retire in May 1902, but rather than appoint Smeaton to the job Lord Curzon asked Fryer to stay on for another year, knowing that Smeaton would shortly complete his thirty-five years' service and be forced to retire. Furious at this 'betrayal', Smeaton launched a virulent letter-writing campaign against Fryer and Curzon. He returned to London in April 1902, vowing revenge, but had stirred up such embarrassment that the secretary of state refused to see him. In July 1903 Mrs Smeaton joined the fray with a letter to the *London Daily News*, alleging that Curzon had bullied the maharaja of Benares into parting with some priceless ivory furniture for his own use. The allegations, which sparked questions in the House of Commons, infuriated Curzon and reinforced his own sense of victimization.

Back in Britain, Smeaton immersed himself in politics, initially associating himself with the radical ex-civilians led by Henry Cotton who advocated political reform in India. At the general election of 1906 Smeaton was elected Liberal MP for Stirlingshire but, in spite of some attacks on the pomp and pageantry of Curzon's administration, proved to be more moderate in his politics than had been expected. He supported the government of India's crackdown on terrorism and sedition in 1907–8 and, in the debates on the Indian Councils Act, 1909, urged that the essentials of British authority remain intact. He followed Scottish questions closely and earned a reputation as a solid committee worker.

In poor health, Smeaton resigned his seat at the dissolution of 1910. He died on 19 April 1910 at his residence, Lawbrook, Gomshall, Surrey, and was buried at Peaslake, Surrey. He was survived by his second wife and their daughter. His son Arthur, a lieutenant in the 18th Tiwana lancers, had been killed at polo in July 1903.

KATHERINE PRIOR

Sources *The Times* (21 April 1910) · *DNB* · *WWBMP*, vol. 2 · *History of Services of Gazetted and Other Officers in Burma* (1902) · BL OIOC, Elgin MSS · BL OIOC, Curzon MSS · ecclesiastical records, BL OIOC · J. M. Anderson, ed., *The matriculation roll of the University of St Andrews, 1747–1897* (1905)
Archives BL OIOC, Elgin MSS
Likenesses H. J. C. Bryce, oils, priv. coll.
Wealth at death £16,611 15s. 2d.: probate, 22 June 1910, CGPLA Eng. & Wales

Smeaton, John (1724–1792), civil engineer, was born on 28 May 1724 at Austhorpe Lodge in Whitkirk, near Leeds, the eldest child of William Smeaton (1684–1749), attorney, and his wife, Mary, *née* Stones, (d. 1759). Smeaton attended Leeds grammar school from the age of ten, leaving at sixteen to become a pupil in his father's office in Leeds and moving to London in 1742 to continue his studies. However, while at home he devoted himself largely to mechanical pursuits, with a well-equipped workshop, and when only seventeen formed a friendship which lasted for thirty years, with Henry Hindley of York (1701–1771), a clock- and instrument-maker of genius. Finally recognizing that the legal profession was not for him, in 1744 Smeaton returned to Austhorpe and settled down to teach himself the skills required to become a maker of philosophical instruments. By 1748 he felt able to set up in London, first at Great Turnstile, off Holborn, and subsequently at Furnival's Inn Court where he employed three craftsmen and soon acquired a reputation in scientific circles as a young man of exceptional intelligence. There in 1752 he began his classic investigations on the power of water and wind. The paper describing the apparatus and results, presented in 1759, gained the Royal Society's Copley medal for original research; by then he had already published six papers in the *Philosophical Transactions* and been elected FRS in March 1753. He married Ann Jenkinson (1725–1784) of York on 7 June 1756 at St George's, Hanover Square, London. Two daughters, Ann (*b.* 1759) and Mary (*b.* 1761), survived into adulthood.

Consulting engineer There is evidence going back to 1748 of Smeaton's interest in engineering. His first commission in that line was for a watermill at Halton in Lancashire in 1753. During the next year another mill, at Wakefield, was built to his design; he prepared plans for a projected bridge over the Thames at Blackfriars, which were used as the basis for the enabling act of 1756, and he reported on a scheme for draining a large tract of peat land known as Lochar moss near Dumfries. His career as a consulting engineer had now been launched. In 1755 he spent five weeks in the Low Countries studying hydraulic

John Smeaton (1724–1792), by George Romney, c.1779 (after Rhodes)

works. On his return he reported on improvements of the Clyde navigation downstream of Glasgow and early in 1756 he was in Northumberland designing a bridge over the Tyne. Meanwhile in December 1755 the second Eddystone lighthouse, a timber structure, had been destroyed by fire. Advice was sought from the president of the Royal Society as to the best person to take charge of its rebuilding and on his recommendation Smeaton was appointed in February 1756. This demanding task he completed in a masterly and innovative manner, creating the prototype of all subsequent masonry lighthouses built in the open sea. It was erected on a rock in the channel 14 miles south of Plymouth, and the light, 80 ft above mean sea level, was permanently exhibited from 16 October 1759. When, after more than 120 years and due to progressive weakening of the rock, the lighthouse had to be replaced by a new one nearby Smeaton's structure was re-erected on Plymouth hoe in its creator's memory.

Building work out at sea was necessarily restricted to the summer months; preparation of the masonry went on in the winter. One of the early decisions to be made related to the choice of mortar, and it is characteristic of Smeaton that during the winter of 1756–7 he devoted many evenings to research on the nature of hydraulic limes (limes that can set under water), thereby taking the first steps in the chemistry of cements. The following winter he was free to undertake some other work, including a project for making the upper Calder navigable from Wakefield to Sowerby Bridge. He presented his report in November, accompanied by a large engraved plan, and in March 1758 gave evidence in parliament on the bill. A

month later he was in Scotland reporting on Dysart harbour before returning to Plymouth. In the following winter he reported again on the Clyde and in April 1759 gave parliamentary evidence on this scheme and also on a proposed extension of the River Wear navigation up to Durham. Shortly after completing the lighthouse he submitted revised designs for Blackfriars Bridge in an open competition eventually won by the young Robert Mylne, and towards the end of November returned to the Calder to direct the work due to start early next year.

Major construction works With a reputation firmly established by the Eddystone, Smeaton now embarked on a career of extraordinary distinction and breadth, producing a series of designs and plans unrivalled in clarity and logic and works ranging from mills (water and wind) and steam engines to bridges, harbours, river navigations, canals, and fen drainage, in addition to further contributions to engineering science. With regard to his professional practice, in 1760 he moved back to Austhorpe where he built his office and private workshop, and this remained his base. But he spent a few months in London every year: at Furnival's Inn to 1764, then with his relative by marriage the clockmaker John Holmes (1727–1797) in the Strand and, after various lodgings, in permanent chambers at Gray's Inn from 1783. He employed a clerk to make fair copies of reports for his clients and to enter copies of reports and of letters, sent and received, into report-books (seven of them dating from August 1760 to August 1787) and letter-books. From late 1759 William Jessop (1745–1814), whose father had been 'general assistant' on the Eddystone, was a pupil in residence. Jessop qualified as assistant engineer in 1767 and left in 1772, later to become, like his master, the foremost civil engineer in Britain. He was followed by Henry Eastburn (1753–1821) who stayed on until 1788, latterly perhaps in a part-time capacity.

Writing to a friend Smeaton said he regarded 'my profession as perfectly personal as that of a Phisician or councillor at Law' (Smeaton to Galton, 15 Jan 1783, letter-books, 1781–92). In that spirit all his drawings were in his own hands, to be copied by himself or an assistant when necessary. An almost complete collection of the drawings (about a thousand in number) is in the Royal Society library. Six of the letter-books survive, along with four diaries and original letters and reports (printed and manuscript) in many libraries and record offices. None of the report-books still exist but their entire contents plus seven post-1787 reports were published in 1812, and John Farey (1791–1851) made extensive use of now lost manuscripts on steam engines, mills, and hydraulics in articles in Rees's *Cyclopaedia* and elsewhere. As for fees, in the early 1760s Smeaton modestly charged 1 guinea a day plus expenses, the usual rate for consulting engineers at that time. It was not until 1767 that he raised his fees to 2 guineas when away from home; next year to be increased to 2½ guineas and 5 guineas while actually on site. This reflected the improved standing of the profession as well as Smeaton's personal status.

Construction of Smeaton's next big work after the Eddystone, the Calder navigation, was largely completed by the end of 1764. The river had an exceptionally steep gradient requiring 26 locks in a length of 24 miles, 12 new weirs, 5 miles of new cuts, floodgates on the cuts, and some new bridges. Smeaton made the working drawings and brought up from London Joseph Nickalls, a millwright skilled in sluice work, as assistant or 'resident engineer' to use the term introduced by Smeaton in 1768. Nickalls left in 1762 to be replaced by Matthias Scott and John Gwyn as superintendents under Smeaton's direction. Both were to continue as site engineers on his works until the end of their careers in 1783 and 1789 respectively.

Drainage projects The Calder required a great deal of Smeaton's attention. Nevertheless he found time to be involved on several other projects. In 1760 he first met and formed a lasting friendship with John Grundy of Spalding, a consulting engineer already established in Lincolnshire and east Yorkshire. Together with Langley Edwards they submitted a report in 1761 on improvements of the River Witham and drainage of adjacent low grounds. In 1762 Smeaton reported on Christchurch harbour, on the drainage of Potteric Carr near Doncaster and, with James Brindley, he made the first accurate calibration of a gauge to measure the flow of water in a stream, the results of which, along with later observations by the French engineer Du Buat, were still being quoted as the most reliable data available in the early nineteenth century. In February 1763 he responded to urgent calls for advice on securing the foundations of London Bridge, advice immediately acted upon. Also in 1763 a water-wheel and pumping engine at Stratford in east London were built by Nickalls to Smeaton's designs, and arising from a visit to Scotland came plans for his first two great bridges at Coldstream and Perth. Again in Scotland, Smeaton reported on the proposed Forth and Clyde Canal in March 1764; earlier he had reported jointly with John Grundy on the Holderness land drainage scheme, and later that year he produced reports on the drainage of Hatfield Chase and Adlingfleet Level.

All this planning proved fruitful. The Witham project was carried out 1763–7 with Langley Edwards as engineer in charge. Coldstream Bridge, a handsome five-arch structure over the River Tweed, was built in exactly the same period with Robert Reid as overseer. Smeaton made four site visits during construction. Work on Holderness drainage began 1765 under Grundy's direction, Smeaton having collaborated with him on design of the outfall sluice. Still in 1765 six large water-wheels and the associated blowing engines and hammers at Kilnhurst forge were built to his designs, and work started on draining the 4200 acres of low ground comprising Potteric Carr after a further report in May. Here Thomas Tofield acted as engineer in charge, with Matthias Scott as surveyor until 1772. This pattern of organization was followed in the drainage of Adlingfleet Level, an area of 5000 acres adjacent to the lower reaches of the Trent. Smeaton prepared the scheme, taking the levels himself, but John Grundy directed the work with David Buffery as surveyor (1767–72). Meanwhile, construction of Perth Bridge had started in

1766. Smeaton's drawings for this seven-arch structure over the Tay include details of the foundations, the parallel-wall hollow spandrels, and centering for the arches. The bridge was completed in 1770 with Gwyn as resident engineer.

Canals and harbours Of Smeaton's reports and works after 1765 only the principal ones can be mentioned; the others are too numerous to notice individually. In 1766 three sets of plans emerged: for a new pier 360 ft long forming St Ives harbour, built 1767–70 by Thomas Richardson who had been foreman mason on the Eddystone; for major improvements of the River Lea navigation, carried out 1767–71 by Thomas Yeoman; and for the River Ure navigation, linked by a short canal to Ripon (1767–72). On the latter scheme John Smith was resident engineer under Smeaton's direction, though Jessop may have acted at times as his deputy. Then in 1768 the pumping machinery and 32 ft diameter water-wheel for London Bridge waterworks were built to Smeaton's designs by Nickalls.

It was also in 1768 that work began on the Forth and Clyde Canal, Smeaton having provided two further planning reports and attended the bill in parliament. His largest single work, the canal was built to accommodate vessels of 20 ft beam. It had a water depth of 7 ft and a length of 28 miles from Grangemouth to Glasgow, with twenty locks, two sizeable aqueducts, and a 25 ft high earth dam impounding water to supply the summit level. Robert Mackell was resident engineer, with an assistant, working under Smeaton's direction for five years to 1773, after which Mackell took charge until completion in 1777 with Smeaton keeping in touch. Some measure of his involvement is given by 770 pages of letters sent and received, including progress reports, and fifty drawings from his hands. Close to the east end of the canal were the famous ironworks of the Carron Company, to whom Smeaton acted as consultant on several occasions, notably in 1769–70 when he designed a blowing engine for no. 2 furnace and a boring mill, both powered by water-wheels. Here, as elsewhere, he pioneered the use of cast iron in millwork.

The years 1755–70 saw a significant increase in the amount of civil engineering in Britain. This spirit of 'improvement' gave rise to what amounted practically to a new class of professional men in place of the somewhat isolated and relatively few practitioners of the early eighteenth century, and nothing signals more clearly the change taking place than the formation of the Society of Civil Engineers in 1771. The club, for such it was, has been known since 1830 as the Smeatonian Society in honour of its great founder member. Other members from the beginning included Thomas Yeoman (the first president), John Grundy, John Golborne, Robert Mylne, and Brindley's associates Hugh Henshall and Robert Whitworth, all first-class engineers. Almost every civil engineer of eminence up to the present time followed them in becoming a member.

After 1771, with work on the Forth and Clyde well under way, two other projects in Scotland were carried out to Smeaton's plans. First came a large masonry pier forming the harbour at Portpatrick on the west coast, built 1771–4 by John Gwyn, and then the bridge at Banff, a sturdy seven-arch structure replacing a bridge destroyed by floods in 1768. It was built 1772–9 by James Kyle and, like the bridges at Coldstream and Perth, remains little changed today. Meanwhile, in December 1771, Smeaton reported on improvements of the Aire and Calder navigation. The scheme was put into effect during 1775–9 with Jessop as engineer and John Gott as resident. Also in 1775 work began on the creation of Aberdeen harbour, one of Smeaton's finest achievements, the main component of which was the north pier, 1200 ft in length and projecting far beyond the mouth of the Dee. Gwyn again acted as resident engineer, and the pier was completed in 1780.

The measurement of energy Back in 1767 Smeaton had been asked to design a steam pumping engine for the New River Company at Islington, Middlesex. When tested in 1769 this proved to be a disappointment but with typical determination he set about finding why. To this end he made or caused to be made quantitative observations on the performance of fifteen of the best (Newcomen type) engines then in operation and, in the grounds at Austhorpe, he built an experimental engine with which all the variables could be studied systematically. The tests, over a hundred in number, lasted on and off for two years, and it was soon after drawing up his conclusions that he received a commission to design a new engine for Long Benton colliery in Northumberland. When put to work in 1774 the engine proved to have an efficiency 25 per cent greater than any previously built. His next engine, erected in 1775 at Chacewater mine in Cornwall, had the same high efficiency and at 72 hp was the most powerful then in existence. Nine more were built to his designs before 1783, though by that time the even more efficient engines of Boulton and Watt, incorporating the separate condenser, were beginning to dominate the scene.

The 'horsepower' of the Chacewater engine mentioned above is given in terms of Watt's definition, purposely set at a peak value of 33,000 ft-lb per min. However, the concept of horsepower, and indeed its practical measure as the work done by a horse in an eight-hour day (22,000 ft-lb per min.), had been introduced by Smeaton eighteen years earlier in 1765. But he went further, publishing in 1776 a paper on experiments to investigate the relationships between power, work done, momentum, and kinetic energy. Like his earlier paper of 1759, for which he had been awarded the Copley medal, this, together with a paper of 1782 in which he describes experiments to measure the loss of energy in non-elastic impact, became a classic in its field. The three papers were reprinted in book form no fewer than four times and twice in French translation. Nor were they Smeaton's only later contributions to engineering science. Responding to a query raised jointly by Tofield and Grundy in 1770 he stated clearly that for a given cross-sectional area and gradient the flow in an open channel increases with the ratio of area to wetted perimeter (the hydraulic radius), a concept which became generally recognized in the work of Du Buat (1786). He also made the first accurate measurements of the flow of water in pipes, before 1780, and expressed the relations

between head and velocity in a form identical with that published in 1804 by Riche de Prony. Moreover it is evident from a report of 1776 that Smeaton had a practical formula of the correct form for estimating the flow of water through a sluice.

Hydraulic projects This 1776 report, the second of Smeaton's on improving the drainage of Hatfield Chase, related chiefly to the provision of a better channel for the River Torne where it passes through this large area of low ground and a bigger sluice at its outfall into the Trent. Smeaton himself took the levels. Further improvements were proposed by Matthias Scott, who had been surveyor of the works at Hatfield Chase since leaving Potteric Carr. These were put into effect and extended after his retirement in 1783 by Samuel Foster, and the whole scheme when finished in 1789 may be considered the most important work of fen drainage in the eighteenth century, embodying the principle of complete separation of the living waters of the river from the land drains. Again in 1776 work began on a large sluicing basin at Ramsgate harbour. The idea of scouring a harbour by releasing at low tide water stored at high tide was not new but Ramsgate provides a particularly fine example, with six sluices in the cross wall forming the basin. These were designed by Smeaton with his customary attention to detail and he accepted a revised general layout suggested by the resident engineer Thomas Preston. When completed in 1781 the scheme proved very successful; the harbour as Smeaton said 'began to put off its forlorn appearance of a Repository of Mud' and after two years operation ships of 400 tons burden could be accommodated with ease.

Smeaton's next major work, however, ended in disaster. The bridge at Hexham had been destroyed by a flood of the River Tyne in 1771. After investigating the gravel river bed Smeaton selected what he judged to be a better site and designed a noble nine-arch structure, work on which started in 1777. Much difficulty was experienced with the foundations (at times a diving bell was used), but by 1779 they were finished and the piers surrounded by sheet piling with massive rubble masonry mounds as a protection against scour. Apart from site visits, Smeaton received and replied to frequent letters from the resident engineer Jonathan Pickernall, but despite all their care six of the eight piers were undermined by a violent flood in March 1782, two years after completion of the bridge. From the observed difference in water level upstream and downstream just before the collapse Smeaton calculated that the average velocity of flow between the piers reached the frightening figure of 17 ft per sec. 'All our Honours are now in the dust', he wrote to Pickernell. 'It cannot now be said, that in the course of thirty years practice and engaged in some of the most Difficult Enterprises, not one of Smeaton's works has failed. Hexham Bridge is a Melancholy witness to the contrary' (Smeaton to Pickernell, 6 June 1782, letter-books, 1781–92). The bridge was rebuilt by other hands to the same design but with the river bed between the piers and for some distance up and down stream covered, at great expense, by stone paving held down by timber piling.

Closing years Work had to go on, of course. Construction of Cromarty harbour was already under way, with Gwyn as resident engineer (1781–4); designs were needed for a new entrance gate and a dry dock at Ramsgate; evidence had to be prepared and given for a bill for the Birmingham Canal; the report on the Hexham Bridge failure took several weeks to write; and much time was spent on designs and site supervision of a steam engine and winding machinery at Walker colliery near Newcastle. Among this activity were few new commissions, Smeaton himself suffered a period of ill health in 1783, and his wife had become seriously ill. She died on 17 January 1784 aged fifty-nine.

Smeaton then retired from active work for almost three years. He began the lengthy task of writing his *Narrative of the Building … of the Edystone Lighthouse* and produced in 1785 an interesting paper on the history of precise circular graduation from the time of Tycho Brahe, but little else. Towards the end of 1786 he responded to a request for advice on lowering the Birmingham Canal summit level and in 1787 he resumed his consulting practice; further work at Aberdeen harbour, for instance, and at Ramsgate, where to reduce wave action within the outer harbour he proposed extending the east pier more than 300 ft into water 27 ft deep at high water springs. This, his last work, was carried out successfully under his direction from January 1788 and completed in 1792. It was also the last work of John Gwyn, who died in June 1789; 'a real loss to the public', Smeaton said, 'as well as lamented by his family and friends' (*Reports*, 3.121). He certainly counted himself among the latter.

During his career twenty-two of Smeaton's reports were printed, together with eighteen scientific papers. The Eddystone book, a magnificent folio volume, was published in January 1791 (2nd edn, 1793; repr. 1813) and his long historical account of Ramsgate harbour appeared later that year. In June he gave evidence in parliament on the proposed Worcester and Birmingham Canal and formally took leave of the profession in October. In London for the first six months of 1792 he was probably working on a treatise on hydraulic machinery before returning to Austhorpe. There, while walking in the garden, he suffered a stroke and died six weeks later on 28 October 1792. He was buried on 1 November at Whitkirk parish church where his daughters erected a tablet to him and their mother. Two hundred years later a memorial stone was placed in the floor of the nave of Westminster Abbey inscribed 'John Smeaton, Civil Engineer, 1724–1792'.

A. W. Skempton

Sources A. W. Skempton, ed., *John Smeaton, FRS* (1981) [incl. complete work list, references to primary sources and locations of MS material] · H. W. Dickinson and A. A. Gomme, eds., *A catalogue of the civil and mechanical engineering designs of John Smeaton* (1950) · *Reports of the late John Smeaton, FRS*, ed. M. Dixon (1812) · A. P. Woolrich, 'John Farey and the Smeaton manuscripts', *History of Technology*, 10 (1985), 181–216 · A. W. Skempton, *British civil engineering, 1640–1840: a bibliography of contemporary printed reports, plans, and books* (1987) · J. Smeaton, letter-books, 1764, 1781–92, Inst. CE · parish register (marriages), London, St George's, Hanover Square, 7 June 1756 · parish register (burials), Yorkshire, Whitkirk parish church, 1 Nov 1792

Archives California State Library, letter-book · Inst. CE, letters and reports · Inst. CE, letter-books · Inst. CE, report relating to Tyne Bridge · Mitchell L., Glas., Glasgow City Archives, contract with Glasgow for construction of lock and dam · NRA, diary · Ramsgate Public Library, reports and letters on Ramsgate Harbour · RIBA BAL, memorandum relating to wall and landing-steps at Greenwich · Trinity House, London, diaries · W. Yorks. AS, Halifax, corresp. relating to Aire and Calder Navigation | Birm. CA, letters to James Watt · BL, letters to Benjamin Wilson, Add. MS 30094 · NL Scot., reports and letters on Ramsgate Harbour

Likenesses attrib. J. Richardson, oils, *c.*1765, RS · G. Romney, oils, *c.*1770, Inst. CE · Rhodes, oils, *c.*1775, University of Strathclyde, Glasgow · G. Romney, oils, *c.*1779 (after Rhodes), NPG [*see illus.*] · T. Gainsborough, oils, 1783 (after Rhodes), priv. coll. · M. Brown, oils, *c.*1788, RS · T. R. Wildman, oils, 1834 (after T. Gainsborough), Inst. CE · H. C. Fahr, marble bust, *c.*1900 (after F. Chantrey), Inst. CE · W. Bromley, engraving (after M. Brown), repro. in M. Dixon, ed., *Reports*, frontispiece · W. Hull, engraving (after M. Brown), repro. in S. Smiles, *Lives of the engineers* (1861) · J. Richardson, oils, RS · engravings (after M. Brown) · lithograph (after T. Gainsborough), NPG

Smeaton [Smeton], **Thomas** (1536–1583), theologian, was born at Gask near Perth. Possibly educated at the school in Perth, in 1554 he was incorporated as a student in St Salvator's College, St Andrews. A promising scholar, he was a regent of the college in February 1558; and remained there until the reformers gained the ascendancy. He then refused to vote for John Rutherford as dean of the faculty of arts on the grounds that Rutherford was no priest, demanded St Salvator's share of the faculty's funds in June 1559, and departed with the rest of the college staff at the Reformation. With Provost William Cranston (who had removed the contents of the library) he went to the University of Paris, where he signed a deed in the cartulary of the German nation in December 1560 and acted as the nation's proctor in 1563 and 1564. With the appointment in 1564 of his former colleague Edmund Hay to be first principal of the Jesuit Collège de Clermont in Paris, Smeaton was himself attracted to the Jesuits, and after reading a course of rhetoric at the college travelled by way of Lyons to Rome, where he became a Jesuit novice on 22 September 1566. He may have met Andrew Melville in Paris before he left.

After his probation, during which he suffered from a tertian fever, Smeaton studied moral cases and theology for two years only, as his health gave continuous cause for concern. After returning to Paris he had a brief period of giving lectures at the Collège de Clermont, and he may have made a short visit to Scotland, but by 1570 he was back in Rome, on his way there passing through Geneva with Thomas Maitland, a younger brother of the secretary of state, William Maitland of Lethington. Maitland died in Italy, and thereby probably undermined Smeaton's Roman Catholicism and Jesuit vocation. In Rome, Smeaton visited prisons, guided by a Jesuit, Father Ledesma. He was proposed by Hay for Billom in the Auvergne in October 1571, before being sent from Rome to Paris in 1572. He was about to set out for a quiet retreat in Lorraine when he fell ill again. He consulted Hay, who advised him to go home and get married, and he finally decided to leave the

Roman Catholic church. The ill feeling against protestants, stirred up before the St Bartholomew's day massacres in August, forced him to take refuge with Sir Francis Walsingham, the English ambassador. On arriving in England he renounced Roman Catholicism and Walsingham settled him in Colchester as a schoolmaster.

In 1577 Smeaton returned to Scotland and was appointed minister of Paisley Abbey and dean of the faculty of arts to Glasgow University. He was soon playing a prominent part in church affairs. In October 1578 he was nominated as an assessor to the moderator in the general assembly, and in the following year he was himself chosen moderator. In 1579 he also engaged in theological controversy, publishing a Latin response to Archibald Hamilton's treatise (also in Latin) on the confusion of the Calvinist sect in Scotland, and prefacing this with a laudatory account of the death of John Knox. On 3 January 1580 he was appointed principal of Glasgow University, succeeding Andrew Melville, and drew up a new constitution affirming Melville's reforms. In April 1583 he was again chosen moderator of the general assembly. Melville was anxious that Smeaton should succeed him as principal of St Mary's College at St Andrews, but James VI (with the encouragement of the prior of St Andrews, who opposed the appointment) forbade his nomination, claiming it would damage the University of Glasgow. On his return to Glasgow, Smeaton was again seized with a high fever, and he died there on 13 December 1583. He had married before 1575 (the identity of his wife is unknown) and had a son named Thomas, who was connected with Glasgow University and who may have been the Thomas Smeaton who graduated MA in 1604 and died in 1657. The celebrated eighteenth-century civil engineer John Smeaton is said to have been his descendant.   JOHN DURKAN

Sources J. Durkan and J. Kirk, *The University of Glasgow, 1451–1577* (1977), appxs · H. M. B. Reid, *The divinity principals in the University of Glasgow, 1545–1654* (1917) · *The autobiography and diary of Mr James Melvill*, ed. R. Pitcairn, Wodrow Society (1842) · A. I. Dunlop, ed., *Acta facultatis artium universitatis Sanctiandree, 1413–1588*, 2, Scottish History Society, 3rd ser., 55 (1964), 408, 412, 414, 455 · Jesuit Archives, Rome, Germ. 106, fol. 128v; Gal. 81, fol. 33; Germ. 107, fol. 134v; Germ. 106, fols. 128v, 184v; Gal. 81, fol. 89v; Germ. 108, fol. 7, 107, fol. 189; Rom. 170, fol. 86; Rom. 78b, fol. 89; Rom. 78b, fol. 95v [1606] · Bibliothèque Nationale, Paris, nouvelles acquisitions, MS Lat. 535, fol. 170 [cartulary of German nation] · Archives Nationales, Paris, H3, 2583, fols. 108v and 11H [Smeaton as proctor] · J. M. Prat, *Maldonat et l'université de Paris au XVIe siècle* (1856), 115 · J. M. Anderson, ed., *Early records of the University of St Andrews*, Scottish History Society, 3rd ser., 8 (1926), 259 · J. Spottiswood, *The history of the Church of Scotland*, ed. M. Napier and M. Russell, 2, Bannatyne Club, 93 (1850), 319–20

Smedley [*married name* Armfield], (**Annie**) **Constance** (1876–1941), author and founder of the International Lyceum Clubs, was born in Trinity Road, Handsworth, Birmingham, on 20 June 1876, the elder daughter and first among the three children of William Thomas Smedley (1851–1934), a chartered accountant, and his wife, Annie Elizabeth (1851–1923), daughter of William Duckworth, a Birmingham coffee merchant, and his wife, Elizabeth Seaborn (1776–1854).

Smedley began her education at home before attending King Edward VI High School for Girls and Birmingham School of Art. Her severe physical disability, probably caused by childhood polio—which confined her to crutches, and, from her mid-thirties, to a wheelchair—rarely prevented her from pursuing her ambitions, or attracting admiring attention. She excelled at art school, publishing her first illustration, in *Pall Mall Magazine*, at sixteen, yet her interests shifted toward writing for the theatre. Through a combination of personal acquaintance and initiative, she attracted the attention of eminent theatrical figures, notably Sir Charles Wyndham, Mary Moore, and Mrs Patrick Campbell. While she was in her early twenties several of her plays were staged, including *Mrs Jordan*, with Campbell in the title role. Her family moved to London, where she mixed in artistic circles, associating with, among others, Richard Le Gallienne, Alice Meynell, and Gertrude Hudson. Her 'Princess' series in the *St James's Gazette*, dramatizing the dilemmas of modern womanhood, appeared as *The Boudoir Critic* in 1903, the same year as her first novel, *An April Princess*, about a young woman's rebellion against her philistine Victorian family. The works were, to an extent, self-referential. Smedley had two nicknames among her intimate circle: the Princess, a tribute to her benevolence and fantastical imagination; and Peter (the fairy-tale miller's third son), recognizing her longing for masculine freedom and adventure.

The books, the first of over forty, coincided with the beginning of Smedley's career as founder and honorary secretary of the International Lyceum Clubs for Women Artists and Writers, established to provide professional women with institutional support. In her vision the clubs were pioneering. She aspired, not only to enable women to compete equally with men, but to create a democratic, non-hierarchical, centre for worldwide cultural exchange, and travelled across Europe, helping women in Amsterdam (1904), Berlin (1905), Paris (1906), and Florence (1908) to open clubhouses.

Despite ambassadorial and administrative commitments Smedley continued to write for adults and children. Works published during her Lyceum years include *Conflict* (1907), a novel about the unsheltered lives of working women, and *Women: a Few Shrieks* (1907), a feminist polemic. Her encounters in the art world, through the Lyceum, eventually led her away from the institution. Meetings in Germany with Count Harry Kessler and Ruth St Denis were particularly important for the development of her beliefs and theatre practice. Kessler, the art patron who promoted Gordon Craig, encouraged her dedication to international peace and synthetic theatre. St Denis, the modernist dancer, identified rhythm as the basis of all art, and introduced Smedley to the Christian Science church, of which she became a lifelong member.

On 20 January 1909 Smedley married Maxwell Ashby *Armfield (1881–1972), painter, illustrator, and writer. They had an unconventional partnership: her handicap, and his sexual preference for men, precluded full marital relations, and thus children. Yet their intense working relationship, and romantic friendship, led to fertile collaboration in literature and theatre. Upon their marriage

Smedley resigned from the Lyceum, and they set up house at The Uplands, Minchinhampton (and from 1912 at Rodborough Common) in the Cotswolds, writing and illustrating books together. They founded the Cotswold Players, for which they both wrote plays, developing symbolist performance techniques, and a philosophy of communal, democratic art.

At the outbreak of the First World War the Armfields moved to Glebe Place, Chelsea, *en route* for America, where they hoped to participate in the 'little theatre' scene. They established a new drama company, the Greenleaf Theatre, promulgating their radical methods, and played a prominent part in an avant-garde, anti-war community centred on Margaret Morris's theatre on the King's Road, which included Morris herself, Hilda Spencer Watson, Geoffrey Whitworth, Vernon Lee, Haddon Squire, Henrietta Leslie, and McKnight Kauffer. At the end of 1915 they procured visas for America, where they directed and taught Greenleaf drama for seven years, basing themselves in New York and Berkeley. Armfield, however, wanted more seclusion, so, to Smedley's regret, they returned to England in 1922, setting up a Greenleaf studio at Mockbeggar Hill, Ibsley, the New Forest, and then at 8a Clareville Grove, South Kensington. Her publications during the 1920s included *Tales from Timbuktu* (1923, for children), *Justice Walk* (1924), *Greenleaf Rhythmic Plays* (1922–5), and *Greenleaf Theatre Elements* (1924–6, theatre textbooks). Her autobiography, *Crusaders* (1929), which unabashedly promotes herself and her work, captures her theatrical extravagance and warmth of character.

Deteriorating health and finances blighted Constance Smedley's last decade. The Greenleaf folded, and her publications dwindled. In 1939 she and Armfield moved to the Old Coaching Inn, 15a High Street, West Wycombe, where she died of heart failure on 9 March 1941. Her death may have been avoidable, but her Christian Scientist faith discouraged her from receiving treatment for her final illness, or for the cataracts that afflicted her towards the end of her life. She was buried on 14 March at St Lawrence's Church, West Wycombe. Her final obscurity has clouded her earlier achievements, yet her eloquence, inventiveness, and audacity, conveyed through all her projects, have made a lasting impact. Her writing remains fresh and persuasive, while the Cotswold Players and International Lyceum Clubs continue to thrive.

GRACE BROCKINGTON

Sources C. Smedley, *Crusaders: the reminiscences of Constance Smedley* (1929) · Tate collection, Maxwell Ashby Armfield archives [incl. memoirs, letters, visual material, publications, and journal articles by Smedley] · *Lyceum Club*, Association Internationale des Lyceum Clubs (1986) · *The Times* (13 March 1941) · *Mouvement Féministe* (12 July 1941) · Blain, Clements & Grundy, *Feminist comp.* · *Dictionary of British women's organizations, 1825–1860* (2001) · C. Purkis, 'Fin-de-siècle fantasy as performative memoir in Gertrude Hudson and Constance Smedley's writings on music', conference paper, 2000 · b. cert. · m. cert. · d. cert. · N. Gordon Bowe, 'Maxwell Armfield, 1881–1972: an account of his decorative arts', *Journal of the Decorative Arts Society*, 12 (1988), 26–37 · *WWW* · N. Gordon Bowe, 'Constance and Maxwell Armfield: an American interlude, 1915–1922', *Journal of Decorative and Propaganda Arts*, 14 (autumn 1989), 6–27 · B. D. Maclean, 'Some midland ancestors', 1997 [unpublished]
Archives Tate collection, papers of Maxwell Ashby Armfield, no. 976
Likenesses W. Smedley Aston, photograph, 1900?, repro. in Smedley, *Crusaders* · L. Caswell Smith, photograph, 1930?, repro. in Smedley, *Crusaders* · M. Armfield, portrait · W. Smedley Aston, photographs, Birm. CL

Smedley, Edward (1788–1836), writer, was born in the Sanctuary, Westminster, on 12 September 1788, the second son of the Revd Edward Smedley (d. 1825), fellow of Trinity College, Cambridge, usher of Westminster School, and latterly rector of North Bovey and of Powderham in Devon, and his wife, Hannah Bellas, fourth daughter of George Bellas of Willey in Surrey. He was sent to Westminster School as a home boarder in 1795 and became a king's scholar in 1800. He was elected head to Trinity College, Cambridge, in 1805. He obtained the wooden spoon in 1809, graduating BA in the same year and MA in 1812. As a middle bachelor he gained one of the members' prizes for Latin prose in 1810, and in the following year he gained a similar distinction as a senior bachelor. His first publication was a small volume, *A Few Verses, English and Latin*, published anonymously in 1812. He was elected to a fellowship of Sidney Sussex College in 1812, and won the Seatonian prize for English verse in 1813 for 'The Death of Saul and Jonathan', and in 1814 for 'Jephthah'.

Smedley was ordained deacon in September 1811 and took priest's orders in the following year. Through the kindness of his father's old friend Gerrard Andrewes, Smedley became preacher at St James's Chapel, Tottenham Court Road, and in July 1815 was appointed clerk in orders of St James's parish, Westminster. Smedley vacated his fellowship on his marriage on 8 January 1816 to Mary Hume, youngest daughter of James Hume of Wandsworth Common, a commissioner of the customs. They had five children, one of whom died in infancy. Among the surviving children was the writer Menella Bute *Smedley (1819–1877). Shortly after his marriage he became evening lecturer at St Giles's, Camberwell, a post which he held for a few years only. In the same year he completed *Prescience, or, The Secrets of Divination*. His next poem, *Religio clerici, or, A Churchman's Epistle* (1818), expressed his opposition to religious fanaticism and sectarianism. It met with sufficient success for him to publish *A Churchman's Second Epistle* in 1819, which was a more satirical piece. This was followed by *The Parson's Choice, or, Town and Country* (1821), an epistolary poem to a young divine taken to be autobiographical. In 1819 he resigned his appointment of clerk in orders of St James's parish, and moved to Wandsworth where he took to teaching in addition to his literary and clerical work.

In 1822 Smedley, who had written for the *British Critic* and the *Annual Register*, accepted the editorship of the *Encyclopaedia metropolitana* and held the post until his death. On the death of Dean Andrewes in 1823 he had lost his preachership at St James's Chapel but continued to preach at the chapel. To supplement his income he became a contributor to the Family Library, writing a history of Venice (2 vols., 1831–2). Owing to his increasing deafness (this was the first symptom of his fatal illness), he was compelled in 1826 to give up taking pupils, and in the following year he became totally deaf. To reduce his expenses Smedley moved to a small house in Dulwich and became reliant on his writing. He published *Lux renata: a protestant's epistle*, a historical poem influenced by Southey's *Book of the Church*. He won the Seatonian prize again in 1827 and 1828 for 'The Marriage of Cana' and 'Saul at Endor' respectively. The latter, composed in dramatic form in blank verse, was Smedley's last poem prepared for publication. In 1829 he was collated by the bishop of Lincoln to the prebend of Sleaford, and in 1831 he resigned his preachership at St James's Chapel after complaints were made about his delivery (caused by his deafness). He remarked that he had 'missed middle life, and stepped at once from youth to old age' (*Poems* 65). A projected edition of the *Faery Queen* was rejected by Murray, his publisher, in the same year. His illness took a stronger hold and his life became significantly restricted but he continued his literary labours until within a few months of his death. He published *History of the Reformed Religion in France* (1832–4), an account of the rise of the Huguenots, a history of France for the Society for the Diffusion of Useful Knowledge, and several biographical articles for the *Penny Cyclopaedia*. He took opium to relieve the pain of the neurological disease which was slowly killing him and he spoke of his illness in a number of remarkable 'dream songs', later collected in *Poems* (1837). He died on 29 June 1836 and was buried at Dulwich.

When Smedley was dying his friends solicited poems from Tennyson (who offered a piece which later became *Maud*), Lord John Russell, Wordsworth, and Southey for the benefit of Smedley's family. He died before it could be completed but *The Tribute* was published in 1837. His *Poems … with a Selection from his Correspondence and a Memoir of his Life* were published by his widow in the same year.

While Smedley was an eminent historian and churchman (and a 'witty apologist' for Anglicanism), and a gifted editor, he never truly fulfilled his promise as a poet. He was swept aside by Romanticism and did not venture to 'assimilate the new advances, even while showing signs of [the Romantic] influence' (McClatchy, 185).

G. F. R. BARKER, *rev.* CLARE L. TAYLOR

Sources *Poems by the late Rev. Edward Smedley, A.M.; with a selection from his correspondence and a memoir of his life* (1837) · J. D. McClatchy, 'Smedley and the death of Saul and Jonathan', *Yale University Library Gazette*, 47 (1973), 185–8
Archives BL, corresp. with Charles Babbage, Add. MSS 37183–37188, *passim* · UCL, letters to Society for the Diffusion of Useful Knowledge

Smedley, Francis Edward (1818–1864), novelist, was born on 4 October 1818 at Alfred House, Marlow High Street, Buckinghamshire (the home of his maternal grandfather), the only child of Francis Smedley (1791–1859), solicitor and high bailiff of Westminster, London, and his wife, Frances Sarah (*d.* 1876), daughter of George Ellison. After an illness in infancy his growth was restricted, his spine malformed, and his general health delicate. In adulthood, perhaps earlier, he wore a steel undercoat and

had no use of his legs. He was therefore educated at home until in 1834–5, aged fourteen, he spent a few months as one of the private pupils of the Revd Charles Millett at Brighton, Sussex, an experience which provided him with the material for his best book, *Frank Fairlegh*. He was later tutored by his second cousin, the Revd Edward Arthur Smedley (1804–1890), author of *Dramatic Poems on Scriptural Subjects* (1854), at Chesterton, near Cambridge, where he saw something of university life and country sports.

Smedley was encouraged to write by several girl cousins; Ellis hints that he loved hopelessly one of them, Millicent, later Mrs Crompton. Two other cousins, daughters of Smedley's uncle the Revd Edward *Smedley (1788–1836), were Menella Bute *Smedley (1819–1877) and Elizabeth Anna Smedley, later Hart, who published verse and prose. In May 1846 he contributed a sketch to *Sharpe's London Magazine* entitled 'Scenes from the life of a private pupil', and was encouraged to continue the story until May 1848. It was then issued in sixteen monthly numbers, with illustrations by George Cruikshank, and in one volume in 1850 as *Frank Fairlegh, or, Scenes from the Life of a Private Pupil*. The book was popular, and its early chapters are still fresh and funny, with stories of practical jokes and teasing. Smedley dedicated it to Menella and Millicent, describing it as 'mainly owing to your joint advice and encouragement', and himself as 'one, whose sphere, both of duties and of pleasures, Providence has seen fit to limit'.

Smedley became editor, at first unpaid, of *Sharpe's*, in which his next novel, *Lewis Arundel, or, The Railroad of Life*, ran from 1848 to 1851. Menella Smedley, as S. M., was also a frequent contributor. The first edition of *Lewis Arundel* (1852) had his name on the title-page for the first time; a preface comments on an American piracy which rewrote the ending. A dispute with the new owner of *Sharpe's*, resulting in the magazine's conclusion of *Harry Coverdale's Courtship* also being written by another hand, is mentioned in the preface to the first edition of that novel in 1855. But Smedley had evidently ceased editing *Sharpe's* by 1851, in which year he seems to have briefly contemplated taking on the editorship of *Leigh Hunt's Magazine*, trusting to his own experience in bringing *Sharpe's* into profit, though the project came to nothing. In 1854 he edited the short-lived *Cruikshank's Magazine*, for which he engaged in the thankless task of 'writing up to cuts', that is, providing text for illustrations. At this stage in his life Cuthbert Bede describes him as using 'a self-acting wheeled chair' (Jerrold, 2.192–3). *Harry Coverdale's Courtship* was completed although Smedley was suffering from severe headaches and had been forbidden to write by his doctor. The hero is good-looking, twenty-six, 6 feet 1 inch tall, and has £5000 a year and a country estate. He saves his best friend's sister from marriage to an elderly *nouveau riche* cotton spinner, after seeing off a bull and breaking in a dangerous horse with a heavy stick. In a pattern common in Smedley's fiction, the story then drifts into a tangled account of the (ultimately frustrated) attempts of villains to spoil the happiness and prosperity of the central characters. An incongruous episode in which Coverdale gets into a row with his prospective father-in-law by defending free trade is probably explained by the family connection with James Deacon Hume (1774–1842), whose sister was the mother of Menella Bute Smedley. Smedley also published a book of comic verse, *Mirth and Metre* (1855), with Edmund Yates, and contributed to the latter's periodical, *The Train*.

Several witnesses testify to Smedley's charm, and to the contrast between his depressing physical condition and the sprightliness of his works and his temper. Yates says 'his physical malady had kept his intercourse with the world so restricted, that while his mind was full, strong, and manly, his experiences of certain sides of life were as pure and unsullied as those of a young girl' (Yates, xiii). Brailsford mentions 'his many excellent and attaching qualities … his bright intellect, his kind heart, his quaint drollery' (Smedley, vi). What Yates calls 'manly' might be given a harsher description: there is a scene in *Lewis Arundel* in which several young gentlemen go out after dinner to break up a seditious meeting at a mechanics' institute by way of a spree, and generally Smedley's works have a distinct undercurrent which celebrates violence, some elements in his fiction looking forward to the vogue in the late 1850s of the novels of G. A. Lawrence. Though he wrote some lyrics, a few of which were set to music, most of his verse is facetious in the manner of R. H. Barham; some of it indicates that he was no friend either to the emancipation of women or to the emancipation of slaves.

After an accident in a pony carriage in 1856 Smedley's health deteriorated and his output almost ceased. In 1863 he bought himself a country house, Beechwood, near Marlow, Buckinghamshire, but he died at his mother's house, Grove Lodge, Regent's Park, London, on 1 May 1864, a series of epileptic fits having followed a stupor. He was buried in Marlow churchyard on 9 May 1864.

CHARLOTTE MITCHELL

Sources S. M. Ellis, *Mainly Victorian* (1924) • letter from Smedley to a friend of Leigh Hunt, 22/2/1851, BL, Add. MS 38/111, fol. 8 • B. Jerrold, *The life of George Cruikshank*, 2 vols. (1882) • E. Yates, 'Memorial preface', in *Gathered leaves: being a collection of the poetical writings of the late Frank E. Smedley*, ed. E. Yates (1865) • F. E. Smedley, *Last leaves from Beechwood*, ed. W. Brailsford (1867) • G. F. R. Barker and A. H. Stenning, eds., *The Westminster School register from 1764 to 1883* (1892) • will index, Principal Registry of the Family Division, London • *BL cat.*
Likenesses C. Combes, carte-de-visite, NPG
Wealth at death under £70,000: probate, 31 May 1864, *CGPLA Eng. & Wales*

Smedley, John (1803–1874), hydropathy practitioner and Free Methodist leader, was born on 12 June 1803 at Wirksworth, Derbyshire, the eldest son of John Smedley (*d.* 1840), mill owner, and his wife, Mary. On his mother's side he descended from a long line of Derbyshire landowning gentry. His father's family was involved in lead mining and textiles. The mill at Wirksworth, which Smedley claimed was first established by his great-grandfather, produced only modest profits. Soon after his father leased larger premises in 1818 (Lea Mills, at nearby Cromford Bridge), the business faced insolvency. About 1827, after

the sudden death of Smedley's younger brother George, his father withdrew from management.

Smedley left school at fifteen and began working at the mill. Realizing that the firm's long-term survival depended on his efforts and ingenuity, he laboured for years adapting the machinery to the manufacture of woollen knitwear. This proved exceedingly difficult. Eventually his various innovations, combined with his benevolent management style (which, in the 1820s during a time of acute labour unrest, proved invaluable), produced considerable profits in the manufacturing of merino hosiery. Smedley married on 24 June 1846 Caroline Ann Harward (*d.* 1892), second daughter of John Harward, vicar of Wirksworth. The marriage was childless. By the time of his marriage Smedley was able to retire from active management of the mill. The firm continued to prosper: incorporated as a limited company in 1893, by the beginning of the twenty-first century John Smedley (based at Lea Mills) had become Britain's longest-established knitwear manufacturer.

After their marriage Smedley and his wife left for Europe; there he contracted typhus, and he returned home in a state of great weakness. Traditional medical treatment proved ineffective, however, and he turned to Dr MacLeod's hydropathic establishment at Ben Rhydding, Yorkshire, where (despite the severity of the treatment) his health was restored. Smedley then devoted the remainder of his life to promoting hydropathy and—after his conversion about 1850—Christianity.

Smedley next established a free hydropathic hospital at Lea Mills for the benefit of his employees. In 1853 he acquired a small hydro on Matlock Bank which treated about a hundred patients a year; within twenty years he had increased the number of patients thirtyfold. To accommodate this demand he acquired adjoining properties and constructed (to his own design) a number of additional facilities. Smedley's Hydro (as it was known) quickly became one of the foremost hydropathic facilities in Europe. The daily routine at the hydro was frugal and regimented. No books, newspapers, or tracts of an irreligious nature were allowed, nor any newspapers (or visitors) on Sundays. Tobacco, alcohol, and snuff were banned, and meals were very simple. Periods of silence were enforced. Each day began and ended with family worship, and attendance was expected. Patients violating the rules were fined: 1d. for being late for a meal, and 10s. 10d. for men entering the ladies' sitting-room. The treatments were simple and mild, though occasionally unpleasant: combinations of hot and cold water were applied to various parts of the body. In a succession of publications, including *Hydropathy, or, The Water Cure* (1852), *Practical Hydropathy* (1858), and *The Ladies' Manual of Practical Hydropathy for Female Patients* (1861), Smedley and his wife detailed more than 200 separate procedures which claimed to cure such infirmities as venereal disease, diphtheria, and lockjaw. Each patient was treated personally by Smedley or his wife; in 1872 Smedley reluctantly engaged the first physician at the hydro, and this led to the introduction of new technology, including electricity.

Characteristically, Smedley's religious views were marked by individualism and certitude. After his conversion he crossed swords with both the Church of England and protestant nonconformity, denouncing them in a series of tracts. About 1850 he seceded from the established church. He then established his own connexion, built a number of Free Methodist chapels and schools around Matlock, and published a revised prayer book. An energetic itinerant preacher, he became known locally as the Prophet of the Peaks. His employees and patients were expected to toe the line religiously.

In 1862 Smedley began to build Riber Castle—an enormous medieval-style home overlooking Matlock, which cost approximately £70,000. He lived at Riber until his death there on 27 July 1874. He was buried on 1 August at the Free Methodist chapel, Holloway, near Matlock. His estate was valued for probate at under £70,000. The hydro (inherited by Smedley's cousin John Marsden) remained prosperous. Additional bedrooms were added, rules were relaxed, and luxuries were introduced; like a number of other similar establishments it came increasingly to resemble a fine hotel. The hydro continued to operate until the mid-1950s, when it became the home of Derbyshire county council.

Smedley's manufacturing success at Lea Mills, his promotion of hydropathy, his achievement at Smedley's Hydro, and his religious initiatives remain as his enduring legacies.   GRAYSON CARTER

Sources John Smedley memorial book, 1850–74, Derbys. RO, MS D763 · John Smedley/Smedley's Hydro/John Smedley Ltd of Lea Mills, Derbys. RO, MSS D1397, D3105, D3235/3, D3546 · parish register, Derbyshire, Wirksworth, Wirksworth parish church [baptism] · obituaries, Derbys. RO · obituaries, Derbyshire Local Studies Library, Matlock · J. Smedley and others, 'Strikes', *Manchester Guardian* (1872) [letters, with additional commentary by Smedley on the labour question at Lea Mills] · www.johnsmedley.co. uk · J. Buckley, *Recollections of the late John Smedley of Matlock* (1888) [repr. 1973] · L. du Garde Peach, *John Smedley of Matlock and his hydro* (1954) · A. Large, *John Smedley of Matlock. Mill-owner, hydrotherapist, preacher and philanthropist*, Derbyshire Heritage Series (1996) · H. Steer, *The Smedleys of Matlock Bank, being a review of the religious and philanthropic labours of Mr and Mrs John Smedley* (1897) · J. Knifton, 'The life and times of John Smedley', *Peak Advertiser* (11 Jan 1993) · E. Eisenberg, 'John Smedley', *Derbyshire Life and Countryside* (Jan 1978), 36, 44 · D. Fowkes, ed., *John Smedley, 1803–1874: centenary exhibition* (1974) [exhibition catalogue, Tawney House, Matlock Green, Matlock, Derbyshire] · J. Matthews, *Amos: Rev. Amos B. Matthews: Victorian Methodist traveller* (1992), 62–9 · 'The medicine man of Matlock', *Reflections Magazine* (Sept 1994), 24–5 · *Victorian vision: John Smedley and his influence on 19th-century Matlock*, Derbyshire Record Office [1995] · D. Thompson, *The 'British standard' and Mr Smedley's hydropathic establishment* (1864)

Archives Derbys. RO, memorial book, MS D763 | Derbys. RO, John Smedley/Smedley's Hydro/John Smedley Ltd of Lea Mills, MSS D1397, D3105, D3235/3, D3546

Likenesses photographs, Derbys. RO, Matlock MS D763, D3546/A3 · portrait, John Smedley Ltd, Lea Mills

Wealth at death under £70,000: probate, 1874

Smedley, Jonathan (1670/71–1729), Church of Ireland dean of Clogher and writer, was born in Dublin, the son of John Smedley. He entered Trinity College, Dublin, on 18 September 1689 at the age of eighteen; he graduated BA in 1695 and MA in 1698. In 1709 he was presented to the living of Rincurran, near Kinsale, in co. Cork; before that he may have served as a chaplain with the army. While at Rincurran he also officiated at the garrison in the nearby Charles Fort. Despite these duties he was able to spend time in Dublin; there he identified strongly with the whigs at a time of rising political partisanship. These affiliations, together with a literary rivalry, prompted him to attack Jonathan Swift's appointment as dean of St Patrick's by affixing mocking verses to the door of the cathedral. His place within the whig interest was confirmed when in 1715 he was chosen to preach to Irish protestants at St James's, Piccadilly, on the anniversary of the uprising of 1641. This occasion allowed him to descant on the need for unity among protestants in the face of Catholic designs. He accused the high-churchmen and tories of dividing the protestant interest and thereby, covertly at least, advancing Catholicism. Particular targets were the unlimited and arbitrary powers exercised alike by the Stuart monarchy (and potentially the pretender) and the Roman Catholic church. He returned to the same themes in *A Rational and Historical Account of the Principles which Gave Birth to the Late Rebellion* (1718). Staunch for the Hanoverians he championed the dissenters and disparaged the high-churchmen who had alleged that the established church was in danger. Such effusions provoked Swift in 1718 to decry 'a scoundrel sermon of that rascal Smedley' (*Correspondence of Jonathan Swift*, 2.234).

Smedley's manifestoes were calculated to strengthen his claims for further ecclesiastical preferment. Sir Richard Steele seconded these by writing of how Smedley had suffered for his loyalties before 1714. In 1718 Lord Townshend, the secretary of state, recommended him for the deanery of Killala, remote in the west of Ireland. In 1724 Smedley resigned the dignity; later in the same year, however, he was preferred to the more accessible and more remunerative deanery of Clogher. Even so he still pestered successive lords lieutenant Grafton and Carteret with requests for further advancement, couched sometimes in facile verse. Smedley now divided his time between Ireland and England; he had an address in Soho and schemed to exchange his Irish deanery for a London parish. In England he engaged in journalism on behalf of the government. In 1719 he published a collection of nine sermons, which was followed in 1721 by an anonymous volume of his verses; the latter was reissued and enlarged in 1723 and 1730. He also mortgaged part of the emoluments of the Clogher dignity to Bishop Benjamin Hoadly of Salisbury, which suggests that Smedley was financially embarrassed. The need to redeem his disordered finances probably led to his quitting Clogher and accepting a posting as chaplain at Fort Madras, a station of the East India Company. He died, unmarried, on 30 March 1729, shortly after embarking for India, and was buried at sea that day. Further allegations of venality attached to this appointment, it being rumoured that he had promptly sold his military chaplaincy in the colony for £500. It furnished the subject for number 20 of *The Intelligencer*: 'Dean Smedley gone to seek his fortune'; there he was dismissed as 'of Dullness, Pride, Conceit, a medley' (Swift and Sheridan, 220).

In part Smedley had provoked this ridicule with his continuing poetic exchanges with Swift. In 1728 he produced *Gulliveriana*, which traduced Pope and Swift. Smedley had somewhat grandiloquently styled himself 't'other Jonathan'; Swift retorted with 'The Duke's Answer'. Smedley had also contemplated an ambitious literary project, *An Universal View of All the Eminent Writers on the Holy Scriptures*. This seems to have been conceived principally for profit. A prospectus was issued and subscriptions sought but nothing resulted.   THOMAS SECCOMBE, *rev.* TOBY BARNARD

Sources Burtchaell & Sadleir, *Alum. Dubl.* · W. M. Brady, *Clerical and parochial records of Cork, Cloyne, and Ross*, 3 vols. (1863–4) · J. Swift and T. Sheridan, *The Intelligencer*, ed. J. Woolley (1992) · TCD, MS 1995–2008/1353 · J. B. Leslie, *Clogher clergy and parishes* (1929) · *The correspondence of Richard Steele*, ed. R. Blanchard (1941); repr. (1968) · *The poems of Jonathan Swift*, ed. H. Williams, 2nd edn, 3 vols. (1958) · *The correspondence of Jonathan Swift*, ed. H. Williams, 5 vols. (1963–5)
Likenesses J. Faber junior, mezzotint (after R. Dellon, 1723), BM

Smedley, Joseph (1784–1863), actor and theatre manager, was baptized on 8 February 1784 at Patrick Brompton, Yorkshire, probably the second child of Abraham Smedley, agent to the Dundas family, and his wife, Jane, *née* Close. His parents had married at Barton St Cuthbert on 25 August 1772, and a daughter, Elizabeth, was baptized at Hornby by Bedale on 20 February 1774. Smedley was destined for the bar but by 1803 he was married and both he and his wife, Melinda, *née* Boleyn or Bullen (1783/4–1870), were members of a stock company which, under the management of Thomas Shaftoe Robinson and Robert Henry Franklin, played in a circuit centred on Lincoln. By 1806, when he began an association with the newly built theatre in Burgess Street, Grimsby, that was to last for some thirty-five years, Smedley was himself the manager of a small company which in 1809–10 numbered twelve players, five of whom were women. In many places he utilized 'fit-ups': at Melton Mowbray performances were in auction rooms and at Gainsborough the 'theatre' was the great hall of a fourteenth-century manor house; at Rotherham it was a disused chapel. However, Smedley built theatres himself, at Sleaford (in 1824) and at March, and purchased others, at Southwell in 1814 and at Wakefield in 1836.

Smedley was a freemason, initiated in 1809 into St Matthew's Lodge, Barton upon Humber, and was a petitioner in 1812 for the formation of Apollo Lodge, Grimsby. Letters from fellow mason the Revd Dr George Oliver, covering a period of forty years, indicate the importance of masonic connections in ensuring Smedley's having both a licence to play and patronage for his performances. The correspondence also dwells on the threats from rival managers, the sub-letting of Grimsby theatre to supplement Smedley's income, the prospects for a winter season at Grimsby based on the number of vessels laid up in the docks, Methodist opposition to theatrical entertainment, the effect on Smedley's business of agricultural depression, and arrangements for Smedley to put on—anonymously—plays written by Oliver.

Smedley was praised for his 'uniform regularity and good conduct' (Lincolnshire County Archives, LLHS

38/9/3/2), and for his firm control over the members of his company. He was 'a tragedian on stage but off it a dandified gentleman, full of self-confidence and importance' (Scruton, 128). His playbills regularly included moralizing comments and his evening's entertainment, the conventional double bill of the period, was described in the *Wakefield and West Riding Herald* as 'unlikely to disturb the most fastidious puritan' (20 Nov 1835). Financially sound, but never greatly prosperous, he advised others on the money to be made from creating a billiard room under the stage and sub-letting theatre buildings for non-theatrical events.

Six of Smedley's children—four daughters and two sons—joined the company: he had at least two other sons. In the 1830s he concentrated increasingly on the growing towns of the industrial West Riding, including Barnsley, Bradford, Huddersfield, Rotherham, and Wakefield. He rarely engaged stars and had a repertory in which plays by Shakespeare, Sheridan, and Elizabeth Inchbald and adaptations of the novels of Dickens and Scott featured prominently. In 1841 Smedley gave up theatre management and settled in New Sleaford, Lincolnshire, where he set up in business as a printer and bookseller and where, in North Street, he died of typhus on 1 March 1863.

Between 1806 and 1841, in a period when evangelical opposition had a considerable effect on theatre audiences, Smedley had maintained what was perhaps the most extensive (in terms of both distance and the number of places where his companies performed) of provincial itineraries, having in 1833 the management of theatres in at least eighteen towns in Derbyshire, Cambridgeshire, Leicestershire, Lincolnshire, Nottinghamshire, and Yorkshire.   C. M. P. TAYLOR

Sources Lincs. Arch., Sumner papers · W. Senior, *The old Wakefield theatre* (1894) · W. Scruton, *Pen and pencil pictures of old Bradford* (1890) · A. Bates, *History of freemasonry in Grimsby* (1892) · C. M. P. Taylor, *Right royal: Wakefield theatre, 1776–1994* (1995) · A. Nicoll, *A history of English drama, 1660–1900*, 6 vols. (1952–9); repr. (1963) · A. Avison, 'History of the Lincolnshire theatres', Grimsby Library · priv. coll., letters from G. Oliver to J. Smedley · L. Warwick, *Drama that smelled* (1975) · G. Oliver, *A brief history of Witham lodge* (1841), 374 · W. White, *History, gazetteer, and directory of Lincolnshire*, 2nd edn (1856) · *Archivist's report*, 25, 1975, Lincs. Arch. · West Riding magistrates' quarter sessions order books, 1830–39 · *Wakefield and Halifax Journal* · *Bradford Observer* · History of Gainsborough theatre, Gainsborough Library · IGI [Yorkshire] · d. cert.
Archives Lincs. Arch., corresp. and papers, incl. account books of his theatre company · W. Yorks. AS, Leeds, Yorkshire Archaeological Society, playbills | Lincs. Arch., Sumner MSS · Wakefield Reference and Information Library, Cryer collection
Wealth at death under £1500: probate, 21 March 1863, CGPLA Eng. & Wales

Smedley, Menella Bute (1819–1877), poet and novelist, was born in Broad Street, Westminster, London, on 27 July 1819, the daughter of the Revd Edward *Smedley (1788–1836) and his wife, Mary, *née* Hume (1786–1868), and baptized on 28 July with the names Menella Elisa at St James's, Piccadilly, by her father, then a curate of the church. In September 1819 her father resigned his curacy owing to ill health and retired to Dulwich, where he acted as a private tutor. She was educated at home by her father, later working as his scribe when his health further declined. Following his death in 1836, her own frail health obliged her to spend a period of recuperation at Tenby. Her girlhood experience as housekeeper and amanuensis established the pattern of her domestic life. In January 1851 she assisted in the household of her maternal cousins, the Dodgsons, following the death of Archdeacon Dodgson's wife, Frances. She was later to act as the regular companion and literary assistant to another cousin, the novelist Francis (Frank) *Smedley, at his house in Regent's Park. In July 1855 she was instrumental in showing the early comic work of Charles Dodgson (Lewis Carroll) to her cousin Frank, through whose good offices it was published in the *Comic Times*. She was to remain the literary confidante of both men.

Menella Smedley's own literary career began in 1849 with the publication of *The Maiden Aunt* (reprinted in 1852) and 'A Very Woman' (included in *Seven Tales by Seven Authors*). Both were signed with the initials S. M. She employed the same signature for *The Uses of Sunshine: a Christmas Narrative* (1852), *Nina: a Tale for the Twilight* (1853), and for the collection of poems for children *Lays and Ballads from English History etc* (1856). As M. S. she published *The Story of Queen Isabel and other Verses* (1863). Her novel *Twice Lost*, the story of a 38-year-old woman forced into service as a lady's companion and set against a background of intrigue relating to Italian unification, was published in volume form in 1863 (reprinted 1866). *Linnet's Trial: a Tale in Two Volumes* appeared in 1864, *A Mere Story* in 1865, and *Other Folk's Lives* in 1869. Her much admired collection of *Poems*, containing 'Lady Grace', a five-act verse drama set in modern London, was published in 1868. With her sister Elizabeth Anna Hart, she co-wrote the verse collections *Poems Written for a Child* (1868) and *Child World* (1869) and in 1874 she published *Two Dramatic Poems* ('Blind Love' and 'Cyril: Four Scenes from a Life'). In the 1870s she was involved with Mrs Nassau W. Senior's campaigns for the improvement of girls' education in pauper schools, editing and reprinting Mrs Senior's *Reports on Pauper Education Blue Books of 1873-4* (1875) and publishing the article 'Workhouse schools for girls' in *Macmillans Magazine* in November 1874. Her essay 'The English girl's education' appeared in the *Contemporary Review* in April 1870. Menella Smedley died at her home, Grove Lodge (later Nuffield Lodge), Park Road, Regent's Park, on 25 May 1877.

ANDREW SANDERS

Sources BL cat. · d. cert. · register, St James's, Piccadilly, City Westm. AC [baptism] · Boase, *Mod. Eng. biog.*, vol. 6 · *Lewis Carroll's diaries: the private journal of Charles Lutwidge Dodgson*, ed. E. Wakeling, [6 vols.] (1993–) · *The letters of Lewis Carroll*, ed. M. N. Cohen and R. L. Green, 2 vols. (1979) · M. Reynolds, 'Menella Bute Smedley', *Victorian women poets: an anthology*, ed. A. Leighton and M. Reynolds (1995), 256–7 · Blain, Clements & Grundy, *Feminist comp.* · J. Sutherland, *The Longman companion to Victorian fiction* (1988) · DNB · H. B. Forman, *Our living poets* (1871), 71–85
Archives U. Reading, letters to George Bell & Sons

Smee, Alfred (1818–1877), chemist and surgeon, was baptized on 10 July 1818 at St Giles, Camberwell, Surrey, the second son of the four children of William Smee (1777–1858), accountant at the Bank of England, and his wife, Susanna (1790–1849), daughter of William Ray and his wife, Mary, of Tannington, Suffolk. He was educated in London at St Paul's School and later, studying medicine, at King's College and St Bartholomew's Hospital, where he was dresser to William Lawrence. Smee was awarded prizes for chemistry, anatomy, surgery, and physiology, and he became MRCS in 1840.

In 1829 Smee's father had been made chief accountant to the Bank of England and the family had moved from the new commuter suburbs south of the Thames to accommodation inside the bank buildings. There the demands of bank security restricted their social life in the evenings, and Smee spent a lot of time working in a small laboratory he set up in their apartment. His interest in chemistry and electricity, inspired by the physicist John Daniell (1790–1845), led him to develop a new battery cell. He described this in papers to the Royal Society, to the Royal Society of Arts, who awarded him the Isis gold medal in 1840, to the Royal Institution in 1841, and in his book *Elements of Electrometallurgy* (1840). The cell, made from plates of zinc, together with silver coated with platinum and an electrolyte of sulphuric acid, was found to be simple to operate, requiring little attention, and economical in use. It produced a steady current and, though less powerful than the cell developed by William R. Grove (1811–1896), it became very popular commercially for the production of electrotypes. In this, electroplating was used to coat small perishable objects in a metal, usually copper, forming an oversize copy or a mould for the manufacture of exact replicas. In 1853 the technique was adopted by the Bank of England for the production of bank notes. The finely engraved steel plates from which notes were printed became worn in use, affecting the quality of the printing. New plates were made which were cut in relief, and copper electrotypes were taken from them which reproduced every detail. The electrotypes were used for printing and replaced when necessary from the original steel master copy, thus ensuring constant production of high-quality notes. The long-lasting black printing ink was also developed by Smee in 1842.

On 2 June 1840 Smee married Elizabeth Hutchison at St Margaret, Lothbury, near the bank, and by early 1842 they had moved to 7 Finsbury Circus, which remained the family home. There were two children, Alfred Hutchison Smee (b. 1841) and Elizabeth Mary Smee (b. 1843). She married in 1872 William Odling (1829–1921), Waynflete professor of chemistry at Oxford. In 1841 Smee became surgeon-general to the Bank of England and was elected FRS.

In addition to his medical work Smee had considerable actuarial interests. Life assurance at this time was hampered by a lack of accurate statistical information on which to base assessments of risk. Encouraged by his father, Smee founded the Gresham Life Assurance and Accident Company and was medical officer for this and other companies. He encouraged the compilation and use of accurate mortality tables and promoted risk assessment.

Smee also had interests in horticulture—he used Wardian cases to grow plants in the City—and he wrote an impassioned letter to *The Times* in 1860 when it was planned to fell the trees in Finsbury Circus Gardens and build a railway station nearby; he opposed this on environmental grounds, citing the benefits to people of a green space in a crowded and smoky city. The plans were dropped and the trees survived. Smee planted a large ornamental and productive garden at his house, The Grange, by the River Wandle at Wallington, Surrey. His book *My Garden … * (1872) described not only the work of planting the site but also the natural history of the area. The damage done to his garden by untreated effluent from a nearby sewage works, and his concerns for public health, caused him to speak strongly in favour of proper legislation on sewage disposal in 1875 at the Royal Society of Arts. The next year he attended a conference organized by the RSA on health and sewage in towns.

Smee published books, lectures, pamphlets, and letters on a variety of medical topics, especially diseases of the eye; he also wrote about public health and disease and water supply; the causes of the potato blight in 1846; the chemistry underlying his battery; and mental philosophy. Smee died of diabetes, aged fifty-eight, on 11 January 1877, at 7 Finsbury Circus, London, and he was buried five days later at St Mary's Church, Beddington, Surrey, near his garden. His wife survived him.   P. D. Buchanan

Sources [E. Odling], *Memoir of the late Alfred Smee FRS by his daughter* (1878) • H. Willoughby Lyle, *King's and some King's men* (1935), 31 • C. Walford, *The insurance cyclopaedia*, 2 (1873) • D. McDonald and L. B. Hunt, *A history of platinum and its allied metals* (1982) • A. Smee, 'Proposed heads of legislation for the regulation of sewage grounds', *Journal of the Society of Arts*, 24 (1875–6), 34–43 • A. D. McKenzie, *The Bank of England note* (1953) • *BMJ* (20 Jan 1877), 79 • *The Lancet* (20 Jan 1877) • *JCS*, [31] (1877), 509–10 • V. G. Plarr, *Plarr's Lives of the fellows of the Royal College of Surgeons of England*, rev. D'A. Power, 2 vols. (1930) • E. Walford, *Greater London*, 3 (1883); repr. as *Village London* (1983), chap. 22 • R. B. Gardiner, ed., *The admission registers of St Paul's School, from 1748 to 1876* (1884) • private information (2004) • parish register, St Giles's Church, Camberwell, Surrey, 10 July 1818 [baptism] • parish register (marriage), St Margaret Lothbury, London, 2 June 1840 • *CGPLA Eng. & Wales* (1877)
Archives Sci. Mus. | RS, corresp. with Sir John Herschel
Likenesses C. H. Jeens, engraving (after engraving by Robertson), repro. in A. Smee, *The mind of man* (1875), frontispiece; photographic negative?, RCS Eng. • wood-engraving (after photograph by Grillet of Naples), NPG; repro. in *ILN* (27 Jan 1877)
Wealth at death under £7000: probate, 20 April 1877, *CGPLA Eng. & Wales*

Smeeton, George (*fl.* 1800–1828), printer and publisher, about whose early life little is known, became allied with James *Caulfield (1764–1826), an antiquarian print dealer, publisher, and compiler whose obituary Smeeton wrote for the *Gentleman's Magazine* (96/1, 1826, 569). About 1800 Smeeton compiled, under the pseudonym Guiniad Charfy, *The Fisherman*. The first edition is missing from the British Library, but in any case is judged to be 'of no value' by William Thomas Lowndes (Lowndes, 1.412). Some years later Smeeton witnessed the conflagration of Covent Garden Theatre on 20 September 1808 and dashed off a pamphlet describing the fire. That may have been the incident which brought Smeeton in touch with the Cruikshank family, for over the next twelve years he published more than a dozen books with illustrated coloured frontispieces by Isaac Cruikshank or his sons Isaac Robert and George. Smeeton issued the usual range of second-rate material—pamphlets about trials and funerals, songbooks, and the occasional illustrated broadside—first from 18 James Street, Covent Garden (1808–12?), then from 139, later 17 St Martin's Lane (1812–28). For Caulfield and Henry Lemoine, the editors, he printed and published the *Eccentric Magazine* (parts, 1812, 1813; 2 vols., 1814), containing lives and seventy-seven portraits of 'misers, dwarfs, idiots, and eccentrics'. During the same period he produced Pierce Egan's illustrated parts publication *Boxiana*. From 1817 Smeeton began producing reprints of seventeenth-century pamphlets; these—sixteen in most cases, seventeen in a few copies—were gathered in 1820 into two small quarto volumes, *Historical and Biographical Tracts*, embellished with reproductions of contemporary portraits and some notes. Most of the print run of 250 was destroyed in a fire; the remaining copies have always been prized by collectors (Lowndes, 3.2416). Following in Caulfield's footsteps, Smeeton also issued in 1820 his two-part, royal octavo *Biographia curiosa, or, Memoirs of Remarkable Characters of the Reign of George the Third*, incorporating thirty-nine portraits and an illustration, *The Beggar's Opera at St Giles's* (ibid.). He published three volumes of *The Unique* (1823–4), a series of engraved portraits of eminent persons, with brief memoirs. Smeeton moved in 1828 to Southwark, from which address he published *Doings in London, or, Day and night scenes of the frauds, frolics, manners and depravities of the metropolis*, illustrated with thirty-three designs by I. R. Cruikshank engraved by W. C. Bonner. Smeeton's last dated publication, which went into a fourteenth edition by the middle of the century, adapted the combination of rakish language, gossip, and scenes of high and low metropolitan life previously written by Egan and C. M. Westmacott; to some extent it anticipates depictions of the London underworld that appeared during the next decades in writings by Charles Dickens, Harrison Ainsworth, and Henry Mayhew.

The date of Smeeton's death is unknown.

ROBERT L. Patten

Sources W. T. Lowndes, *The bibliographer's manual of English literature*, ed. H. G. Bohn, [new edn], 6 vols. (1864) • A. M. Cohn, *George Cruikshank: a catalogue raisonné* (1924) • *DNB* • catalogue of printed books, BL • F. G. Stephens and M. D. George, eds., *Catalogue of political and personal satires preserved … in the British Museum*, 8–11 (1947–54) • Allibone, *Dict.* • *Annual Register* (1826), 246 • *GM*, 1st ser., 96/1 (1826), 569

Smellie, William (1697–1763), man-midwife, was born in the parish of Lesmahagow, Lanarkshire, on 5 February 1697, the son of Archibald Smellie (1663/4–1735) and Sara Kennedy (1657–1727). Little is known of his father, Archibald, except that he was sessions clerk to the parish church of Lesmahagow and therefore, as was customary at that time, a teacher in the local school. His mother, Sara, came from the family of Kennedys of Auchtyfardle,

William Smellie (1697–1763), self-portrait

landowners of some wealth. There is some evidence that a daughter, Beatrix, had been born prior to the birth of William and that she died in infancy, so that William was brought up as an only child in reasonably comfortable financial circumstances. He was educated at the grammar school in Lanark.

Smellie was apprenticed to William Inglis, an apothecary in Lanark in 1714. It is certain that he must have received some medical instruction from John Gordon, a Glasgow surgeon. It was through Gordon that Smellie met the novelist Tobias Smollett with whom he became lifelong friends. It seems certain that Smellie then spent a time serving as a naval surgeon (March 1720 – November 1721) on the *Sandwich* before setting up as an independent apothecary in Lanark in 1722. He may have supplemented his income by acting as a cloth merchant. In 1724 Smellie married Eupham Borland (1696/7–1769) and remained in practice for the next fifteen years in Lanark. The marriage was childless. During this time in Lanark, Smellie gained practical experience in midwifery, being called in by local midwives when complications arose which were beyond their competence. From 1737 he began to concentrate on midwifery, having become aware of the recently published forceps. His chief techniques were craniotomy and turning the child. Smellie always made a habit of keeping accurate and often extensive records of most of his cases

and this was to lay the foundations of his future career. On 5 May 1733 he became a member of the Faculty of Physicians and Surgeons of Glasgow. However, it was not until 18 February 1745 that he was awarded his MD degree by Glasgow University.

Stimulated by his desire for further education, Smellie moved to London in 1739 and spent a short time in Paris under Grégoire in order to gain further experience. Back in London the next year, he stayed at first with William Hunter and then set up in individual practice, first in St Albans Street, then in Gerrard Street, and finally in Wardour Street, where he stayed until his retirement in 1759.

Smellie began his career in London by setting himself up as a teacher, advertising the times and places of his teaching sessions and training methods at the cost of 3 guineas for a full course. Over the next ten years he taught over 900 male students and an unknown number of female ones. He soon began to augment his academic teaching by taking many of his pupils with him when he was attending poor women in their own homes during their confinements. These patients were not charged any fees and his pupils were able to observe not only the normal but the many abnormal cases they encountered. Most of his lectures, which dealt with all aspects of pregnancy and labour, both normal and abnormal, were combined with practical demonstrations on what were referred to as 'machines' that simulated the female pelvis and the unborn child. He obtained real bones, and covered them with leather as he did with most of the different forceps that he used and improved. In spite of his having no official appointments at any of the London teaching hospitals his reputation both as teacher and practitioner grew apace. Not surprisingly he attracted a considerable amount of criticism from some of his peers, notably John Douglas and the midwife Elizabeth Nihell who condemned Smellie's use of forceps, his 'machine', and his dress at deliveries. She also claimed that he possessed 'the delicate fist of a great-horse-godmother of a he-midwife' (Glaister, 304).

Having always kept exact records of his cases Smellie published in 1752 *A Treatise of the Theory and Practice of Midwifery*. This was supplemented two years later by a volume of illustrations entitled *A Set of Anatomical Tables, with Explanations*. The famous *Treatise* is divided into three volumes (the second appeared in 1752 and the third in 1764) in which he describes the physiology of pregnancy and the mechanisms of both normal and abnormal labour far more exactly than any previous writer had done. His description of the way the foetal head passes through the maternal pelvis was both accurate and original. The importance of the measurements of the pelvis is described as well as the influence that any variations of the maternal pelvis had on the course of labour. He devised many modifications of the obstetric forceps and describes their methods of application. He describes in detail the various methods to be applied in dealing with abnormalities in the presentation of the foetus. This monumental work was translated into French, German, and Dutch languages and became a classic in obstetric literature. The book made Smellie the best-known name in midwifery in Britain so that 'no-one could discuss the subject without referring to his book' (Wilson, 125).

In 1759 Smellie left London and returned to his native Lanark where he owned a small property. His health was deteriorating and he suffered particularly from asthma, so that in 1759 he drew up his will, to which he added four codicils. During his life Smellie had collected a very large library and this, together with all his own books, he left to his old school in Lanark with a bequest of £200. Unfortunately his library became neglected and fell into a state of disrepair. It was not until 1931 that a small group of obstetricians visited his library and were shocked by the state in which they found it. Professor Miles Phillips arranged for the books to be repaired and rebound and transferred to the Lindsay Institute in Lanark, where they remain under the care of a permanent librarian.

Smellie died at his home in Lanark on 5 March 1763 and was buried in the churchyard of St Kentigern's Church, Lanark. The tomb now lies in a chapel erected in 1931 by the Glasgow and Edinburgh obstetrical societies in tribute to Smellie. According to one historian 'Smellie's work took midwifery onto a new and higher plane' (Wilson, 125), and it was for this reason that he justly became known as the master of British midwifery.

JOHN PEEL

Sources J. Glaister, *Dr William Smellie and his contemporaries* (1894) • A. Wilson, *The making of man-midwifery: childbirth in England, 1660–1770* (1995) • J. Butterton, 'The education, naval service and early career of William Smellie', *Bulletin of the History of Medicine*, 60 (1986), 1–18 • H. Graham, *Eternal Eve* (1950) • R. W. Johnstone, *William Smellie master of British midwifery* (1952) • private information (2004) [R. Miller] • D. Guthrie, 'The travel journals of Peter Camper (1722–1784)', *Edinburgh Medical Journal*, 3rd ser., 55 (1948), 338–53 • P. J. Wallis and R. V. Wallis, *Eighteenth century medics*, 2nd edn (1988) • *GM*, 1st ser., 33 (1763), 146

Archives Lindsay Institute, Lanark, Lanark Library • Royal College of Physicians of Edinburgh, lecture notes • Wellcome L., lecture notes

Likenesses H. G. Hall, stipple (after G. Watson), Wellcome L. • W. Jardine, pen drawing, Wellcome L. • W. H. Lizars, line engraving (after G. Watson), Wellcome L. • W. Smellie, self-portrait, oils, Royal College of Surgeons, Edinburgh [*see illus.*]

Wealth at death large library and £200 to his old school, Lanark

Smellie, William (1740–1795), printer, editor, and author, was born in the Pleasance, a suburb of old Edinburgh, the second among six children of Alexander Smellie (1699–1752), a mason and master builder. His mother's identity is unknown and his own birth date uncertain because his father followed the Cameronians, an outlawed Presbyterian sect that eschewed record keeping for fear of persecution. His religious practices estranged Alexander from his family, and William Smellie's childhood was one of intense studies and regular attendance at secret Cameronian gatherings in the Pentland Hills outside Edinburgh. From such experiences Smellie derived the intellectual independence and disdain for authority that marked his career as printer and journalist.

Smellie's formal education began in the village school at Duddingston, continuing at Edinburgh's renowned high

William Smellie (1740–1795), by John Brown, 1783

school, where Smellie excelled in classical languages. In 1752 he entered an apprenticeship with the pre-eminent Edinburgh publishing firm Hamilton, Balfour, and Neill, and was appointed corrector to the press, winning the Edinburgh Society silver medal for printing (1757). By this time Smellie was an orphan and his master, Patrick Neill, took care to nurture his precocious intellect, permitting Smellie to absent himself from the printing house daily to attend Edinburgh University. Smellie completed courses in the arts and medicine but took no degree because he could not afford lecture fees. He became a favourite pupil of John Hope, professor of botany, and taught the class briefly when Hope was incapacitated, but it was John Gregory's medical lectures that encouraged Smellie to make the democratization of learning a lifelong vocation.

In 1759 Smellie left his indentures early to become corrector to the press for Sands, Murray, and Cochran, proprietors of the *Scots Magazine*. Smellie's contract called for him to compile and edit the magazine, a responsibility that aroused his passion for journalism. Smellie drew on his continuing medical studies to reshape the *Scots Magazine*, considerably extending its attention to medicine and natural history. When Smellie married Jean (1736–1823), daughter of John Robertson, army agent and sometime writer, on 27 March 1763, he intended to pursue a medical career, possibly as an apothecary, where his knowledge of materia medica could be applied. By 1765, however, these aspirations were gone and Smellie reluctantly decided 'to attempt something in the way of book-making, a poor shift indeed!' (Society of Antiquaries of Scotland, Smellie MSS, Charteris, 8). He left the *Scots Magazine* and entered a printing partnership with Robert and William Auld (1765–70); informal partnerships followed with John Balfour (1770–80) and William Creech (1780–90). Despite Smellie's self-confessed distaste for the book trade, he became Scotland's premier printer, favoured by Charles Elliot, John Murray, William Strahan, William Creech, Peter Hill, and Bell and Bradfute, the chief publishers of the day. Elliot declared Smellie the country's best Latinist, and Smellie printed the period's leading medical authors: William Cullen, John and James Gregory, Alexander Hamilton, Benjamin Bell, and his own distant relative, the midwife Dr William Smellie. He alone was trusted with printing Andrew Duncan's seminal periodical, the *Medical and Philosophical Commentaries*, and Smellie's intellectual reputation brought to his printing house works by David Hume, Adam Smith, William Robertson, Adam Fergusson, James Beattie, Joseph Black, James Hutton, lords Hailes, Kames, and Monboddo, and Robert Burns. Between 1765 and 1795, Smellie printed all the theses for Edinburgh University, supplying copies to the trade in London and Philadelphia. Eventually he conceived the *Thesaurus medicus* (1778–85), a four-volume compendium of Edinburgh medical theses, which he sold to Charles Elliot after completing the first two volumes on his own account.

Despite the formidable demands of his printing business, Smellie enjoyed remarkable success as the editor and author of works that helped to define the Edinburgh Enlightenment. Over a period of three years (1766–9), he edited and printed the first edition of William Buchan's *Domestic Medicine* (1769), a revolutionary layman's guide to maintaining good health which sold over 5000 copies in a matter of months. He was then hired to compile, edit, and write original essays for the first edition of the *Encyclopaedia Britannica* (1768–71). Both projects emphasize Smellie's commitment to the popular dissemination of knowledge. In the case of the *Britannica*, Smellie fought with the proprietors Andrew Bell and Colin Macfarquhar to expand the entries on medicine and the natural sciences and attempted to have the work issued in a cheaper octavo format. He lost the latter battle and was not offered subsequent editorships, although his biography of Lord Kames appears in the third edition. Smellie taught himself French in order to undertake a translation with original notes of Buffon; *Natural History* (8 vols., 1780; 9 vols., 1785) was still being reprinted in 1866. At the same time Smellie was active in editing, printing, and promoting popular works by lesser writers, including Malcolm McCoig's *Flora Edinburgensis* (1780), John Taylor's *Medical Treatise on St Bernard's Well* (1790), and Maria Riddell's *Voyages to the Madeira and Leeward Caribbean Isles* (1792). As an intellectual, Smellie courted controversy by defying systems and authorities: he contradicted Linnaeus on the sexuality of plants, proposed that human reason was only an extension of the

instincts common to all animals, promoted an early psychology of dreams, and made natural history accessible to women. Smellie's reputation as a natural historian was such that Charles Elliot paid £1000 for the copyright to volume one of Smellie's *Philosophy of Natural History*, which appeared in 1790, shortly after Elliot's death. Smellie was delayed in completing the work by the demands of business and most of his fee was tied up in Elliot's estate or lost to various arrestments for debt. As was often the case, financial success eluded Smellie, but he received international acclaim for the *Philosophy*, which became part of the new Harvard curriculum in an edition abridged by Dr John Ware that ran through over thirty impressions and was reissued at Boston as late as 1872. The second volume of the *Philosophy of Natural History* was published posthumously in 1799.

Although Smellie began his printing career under the patronage of Lord Kames, his scientific and political ventures moved him into radical whig circles. Throughout the 1770s he engaged in Edinburgh politics as the author and printer of numerous satirical pamphlets, notably his Scriblerian 'Behold yon pair' (1774) attacking the Dundas despotism. When the chair in natural history became vacant at Edinburgh University in 1775, Smellie, a founder of the Newtonian Club and member of the Philosophical (later the Royal) Society of Edinburgh, was nominated in opposition to the Revd Dr John Walker, noted for his natural history of the Scottish highlands and his close ties with Principal William Robertson's 'moderate party'. Walker ridiculed Smellie's theory of plant sexuality in Ruddiman's *Edinburgh Weekly Magazine*, Kames abandoned him, and the Dundases, who held the right to the appointment, blocked Smellie's ambitions. Never forgetting this academic disappointment, Smellie spent the rest of his life challenging the establishment. He confronted Walker and the university again in 1780 when David Stewart Erskine, Lord Buchan, invited Smellie to join the founders of the Society of Antiquaries of Scotland. Smellie was appointed the keeper and superintendent of natural history, became secretary (1793), wrote the *Account of the Society* (1782, 1784), and edited its *Transactions* (1792), but it was his proposal to deliver free public lectures which enraged Walker. Smellie reluctantly agreed to step down in order to secure a royal charter for his antiquaries.

Smellie was involved with at least six magazines and newspapers and was part owner of two: the *Edinburgh Weekly Journal* (1765–70) and the notorious *Edinburgh Magazine and Review* (1773–6). With Gilbert Stuart, Smellie made the *Magazine and Review* the most controversial periodical in Britain, writing about local politics and authoring over two dozen contentious reviews. Litigation and Smellie's poor management doomed the publication but not before it had established a Scottish style that set the standard for the *Edinburgh Review* (1802) and *Blackwood's* (1817). As a journalist Smellie took pride in 'pointing out in the strongest manner any act of mismanagement, littleness, dishonesty, or oppression' (NL Scot., Adv. MS, 29.5.8 (IV), fol. 34), something most apparent in his pamphlet *On the Nature, Powers, and Privileges of Juries* (1784), which was cited in the

1790s sedition trials and acknowledged by Fox in his call for judicial reform. Smellie's miscellaneous essays and biographies of Hume, Smith, Kames, and Gregory appeared posthumously (1800).

Still, it was conviviality not politics which derailed Smellie's ambitions and shortened his life. He enjoyed the tavern scene, spending most evenings in oyster bars and ale houses. His frequent haunt was Douglas's tavern in the Anchor Close, where Smellie kept his printing house and his lodgings. There Smellie founded the Crochallan Fencibles, a drinking club immortalized in the verse of his close friend and political ally Robert Burns, whose obscene *Merry Muses of Caledonia* was written for the club and printed by Alexander Smellie (1800). When Smellie died of stomach cancer in 1795, his printing firm was nearly insolvent, rescued only by £395 from Elliot's estate. Smellie was buried in Greyfriars kirkyard, Edinburgh. He was survived by nine of his thirteen children, his daughter Rebecca marrying the portrait painter George Watson, and his eldest son Alexander assuming the business, which was absorbed by Constable in 1846.

S. W. BROWN

Sources R. G. Cant, 'David Steuart Erskine, 11th earl of Buchan: founder of the Society of Antiquaries of Scotland', *The Scottish antiquarian tradition*, ed. A. S. Bell (1981), 1–30 · W. J. Couper, *The Edinburgh periodical press*, 2 vols. (1908) · M. E. Craig, *The Scottish periodical press, 1750–1789* (1931) · C. Hill, *Historical memorials of Stockbridge, the Dean, and Water of Leith* (1887) · W. Jardine, 'Memoir of William Smellie', *Naturalist's Library* (1843) · J. Kay, *A series of original portraits and caricature etchings … with biographical sketches and illustrative anecdotes*, ed. [H. Paton and others], 2 vols. in 4 (1837–8) · R. Kerr, *Memoirs of the life, writings and correspondence of William Smellie*, 2 vols. (1811) · A. G. Morton, *John Hope, 1725–1786: Scottish botanist* (1986) · W. Steven, *The history of the high school of Edinburgh* (1849) · R. B. K. Stevenson, 'The museum: its beginnings and its development', *The Scottish antiquarian tradition*, ed. A. S. Bell (1981), 31–85 · W. Zachs, *Without regard to good manners: a biography of Gilbert Stuart, 1743–1786* (1992)

Archives Society of Antiquaries of Scotland, Edinburgh, MSS · Society of Antiquaries of Scotland, Edinburgh, letter-books and minute books | John Murray, London, archives, Elliot papers · NL Scot., Watson MSS, Advocates MSS · Royal Botanic Garden, Edinburgh, John Hope MSS · Royal College of Physicians of Edinburgh, William Cullen MSS

Likenesses J. Brown, pencil drawing, 1783, National Museums of Scotland; on loan to Scot. NPG [*see illus.*] · J. Kay, double portrait, etching, 1789 (with Andrew Ball), BM; repro. in *Series of original portraits* (1837) · G. Watson, oils, 1793, National Museums of Scotland; on loan to Scot. NPG · J. Edgar, group portrait, wash drawing, c.1854 (*Robert Burns at an evening party of Lord Monboddo's, 1786*), Scot. NPG · R. Cummins, plaster bust, National Museums of Scotland; on loan to Scot. NPG · R. B. Hall, engraving (after G. Watson, 1793), repro. in Kerr, *Memoirs*, frontispiece

Wealth at death see Elliot papers, John Murray, London, archives

Smelt, Leonard (*bap.* 1725, *d.* 1800), military engineer and courtier, was baptized at Kirkby Fleetham, Yorkshire, on 2 May 1725, the son of William Smelt (1691–1755) of Leases, MP for Northallerton from 1740 to 1745 and afterwards 'receiver of His Majesty's casual revenue on the island of Barbados', and his wife, Dorothy, daughter of Cornelius Caley. An uncle, also Leonard Smelt (c.1683–1740), MP for Northallerton from 1713 to 1740, was clerk of deliveries of

Leonard Smelt (*bap.* 1725, *d.* 1800), by Sir Joshua Reynolds, 1755

the ordnance from 1722 and clerk of the ordnance from 1733, and probably secured Smelt his first position, as cadet gunner in the Tower of London (15 January 1739), where he attended the drawing office. He was trained by the best contemporary military engineers: the assistant draughtsman John Peter Desmaretz; Thomas Lascelles, chief engineer at Portsmouth, where Smelt was sent in 1741; and John Armstrong, chief engineer of Great Britain, to whom he became assistant clerk after returning to the Tower as a practitioner engineer on 13 August 1741.

In 1742–3 Smelt was extraordinary clerk to the Board of Ordnance at £60 per annum, and assistant recorder at £20 per annum. In Flanders from 1743 to 1745 he was present at the battles of Dettingen and Fontenoy, became engineer-extraordinary at £109 per annum, and worked on the repair and extension of the fortifications of Vilvorden. In 1748 he assisted Dougal Campbell with the survey of the military road from Newcastle upon Tyne to Carlisle, and took full charge of construction on 17 June 1750. He married Campbell's sister Jane (*d.* 1790) about this time. A daughter, Anne Jesia (or Anne Jesse), was baptized on 29 February 1748 and a son in 1750; the only children of the marriage to survive into adulthood were Dorothy, who married Thomas Goulton in York on 13 August 1770, and Anne Jesia, who may have been the Anne Jessie who married Nathaniel Cholmeley at St James's, Piccadilly, on 22 August 1774.

In 1751 Smelt was made engineer-in-ordinary and sent to Placentia, in Newfoundland, to report on its neglected fortifications. According to his report they had 'every defect of design, situation and execution … and are scarce capable of being made sufficient against a privateer' (BL, K TOP 119.101.C–F.). Smelt considered Placentia itself not worth fortifying, as Britain's interest was in the fishing grounds, which could be protected by the navy, but listed minimal repairs necessary for its defence. In 1753, disillusioned by the lack of esteem in which the corps of engineers was held, he joined fellow engineers in petitioning the duke of Cumberland over such grievances as the lack of travel allowances, the lack of promotion since 1750 (when the position of chief engineer had been vacated by the retirement of Thomas Lascelles), and most importantly the lack of military rank. This was finally granted in 1757, when Smelt was made captain and engineer in charge of the northern district. He was chief engineer at Plymouth when he resigned from the corps in 1758, having inherited both property and family obligations from his father in 1755, while his wife had inherited an annuity from her brother in 1757.

In 1770 Smelt's neighbour Robert D'Arcy, fourth earl of Holdernesse, introduced him to George III, who, taking a liking to him, despite his being a 'thorough revolutionary Whig' (*Last Journals of Horace Walpole*, 1.157), made him sub-governor to the prince of Wales and Prince Frederick in April 1771. However within the year Smelt tendered his resignation, feeling himself unsuited to the post; this George III refused, writing to Holdernesse on 25 July 1772 that he showed an 'excess of delicacy in wanting to retire from a post that every days experience adds to my conviction of your being most exactly calculated for' (BL, Add. MS 39168, fol. 116). Inspired with a zeal 'for their happiness and improvement' (ibid., fol. 114) Smelt subsequently wrote that 'for some time yet a retired education would be most calculated to give the children the fairest chance of calling out the powers of the mind of one and correcting the impetuosity of the other' (ibid., fol. 126). However when Holdernesse resigned as governor in May 1776 Smelt followed suit. With 'his usual incorruptible virtue' (*Last Journals of Horace Walpole*, 1.556) he refused a pension but did accept an allowance from George III's privy purse, and shortly before his death he was made deputy ranger of Richmond Park.

Smelt continued to dine with the prince of Wales thrice weekly until the prince took offence at reports of Smelt's speech to the meeting of the electors of Yorkshire at York on 30 December 1779. An edition of this speech was brought out by the Revd William Mason and other supporters of economical and political reform, who exaggerated and ridiculed Smelt's defence of the royal prerogative and the character of George III. He remained close to the king, however, who presented him with a house at Kew in 1787 and made several visits there. Of the king's acquaintance Fanny Burney considered Smelt 'perhaps the man in the world most to his taste of any person outside his own family' (*Diary and Letters*, 3.166).

After the death of his wife on 18 January 1790 Smelt retired to Langton, in Yorkshire, where he died on 2 September 1800; he had already sold Langton to his son-in-law Nathaniel Cholmeley. The birth of a grandson, Nathaniel, is recorded in 1779 but there is no further mention of him; a nephew, Cornelius, was lieutenant-governor of the Isle of Man from 1805 to 1832.

Smelt may seem a peripheral figure but he enjoyed a wide circle of friends and acquaintants, including Joshua Reynolds, Samuel Johnson, and Mary Delany. His engineering background and political views may have influenced the later interests of his royal pupils, as George IV had a lengthy affiliation with the whigs (which caused him to become estranged from Smelt) and an interest in the military, and Frederick, duke of York, when commander-in-chief of the army, established his own branch of engineers, the Royal Staff Corps.

SUSAN HOTS

Sources Royal Engineers Library, Chatham, Conolly papers · letters to Lord Holdernesse on the education of the king's children, BL, Add. MS 39168 · *Memoirs and portraits*, ed. M. Hodgart (1963), 240–42 · *The last journals of Horace Walpole*, ed. Dr Doran, rev. A. F. Steuart, 2 vols. (1910) · *DNB* · *N&Q*, 2nd ser., 7 (1859), 154, 246 · *Diary and letter of Madame D'Arblay*, ed. [C. Barrett], new edn, 7 vols. (1854) · *The autobiography and correspondence of Mary Granville, Mrs Delany*, ed. Lady Llanover, 2nd ser., 3 vols. (1862) · J. P. Proulx, *The military history of Placentia: a study of the French fortifications, Placentia, 1713–1811* (Ottawa, 1979) · D. W. Marshall, 'The British military engineers, 1741–1783', PhD diss., U. Mich., 1976 · *The system occasioned by the speech of Leonard Smelt Esq.* (1780) · L. Smelt, *An account of some particulars relative to the meeting held at York, Thursday 30 December 1779* (1780) · R. R. Sedgwick, 'Smelt, Leonard', HoP, *Commons, 1715–54* · R. R. Sedgwick, 'Smelt, William', HoP, *Commons, 1715–54* · IGI

Archives BL, maps, Placentia, Top 109.101.C–F [copies, NA Canada] · BL, maps, Vilvorden, Top 103.72.2B | BL, corresp. with Lord Holdernesse and George III, Add. MS 39168 · Yale U., Burney family collection, letters

Likenesses J. Reynolds, oils, 1755, priv. coll. [*see illus.*]

Wealth at death had already sold estate at Langton

Smetham, James (1821–1889), artist and writer, was born at Pateley Bridge, Yorkshire, on 9 September 1821 into a middle-class Methodist family. His father, also James Smetham, and some other family members were ministers, and Smetham was educated at Woodhouse Grove, a Wesleyan Methodist boarding-school. By the age of eight Smetham had resolved to become a painter; but at sixteen he began an apprenticeship in Lincoln with the architect E. J. Wilson. After release from his indenture in 1842, Smetham earned some money for a few years as a peripatetic portraitist, moving to London in the autumn of 1843 to obtain additional art training. However, his matriculation at the Royal Academy Schools proved ill-fated, and, beset by various health problems and family deaths, Smetham returned home where he remained between 1844 and 1847. In 1846 he began a close and lifelong friendship with William Davies, a minor poet and author who encouraged Smetham throughout his many periods of often severe mental depression and crisis.

In 1847 Smetham undertook initial efforts at what he called 'monumentalism', a system of writing that filled scores of books and journals with daily outpourings of his feelings, drawings, and thoughts. His letters, stream-of-consciousness 'ventilators' (openly 'ventilating' his emotions), and journals all conveyed his attempts to 'monumentalize' or enshrine individual moments and events in his life and also reflected his psychological obsessions with this process. Many entries were 'squared' with innumerable tiny, meticulously drawn compositions and private pictographs which formed part of the artist's unique visual and spiritual vocabulary. In addition, Smetham devised a strenuous daily regimen of painting, writing, Bible studies, walking, teaching, and other activities which he followed most of his adult life.

From 1851 to 1854 Smetham exhibited eight works at the Royal Academy (a total of eighteen were accepted there between 1851 and 1869; sixteen at the Society of British Artists; two at the British Institution; and numerous others at provincial venues). In 1851 he began teaching at Westminster College, a newly founded Methodist teacher training institution in London where he also met his future wife, Sarah Goble, that year. She was the daughter of John Goble, currier, and was herself a teacher and an aspiring artist; the couple married on 8 July 1854. Subsequently they settled in Stoke Newington and raised a family of six children. The year 1854 was, moreover, important because it was then that Smetham, attending classes at the Working Men's College, met John Ruskin. Ruskin's positive response to Smetham's work marked a turning point in his career, and Smetham sent Ruskin a detailed letter providing autobiographical information and other details about his artistic goals and influences. Although he praised Smetham's efforts, Ruskin none the less sensed the mental strain Smetham suffered and advised him to pursue less arduous work and subjects.

An associate of the Pre-Raphaelites, Smetham knew Ford Madox Brown and Frederic Shields well and was a weekly visitor to Dante Gabriel Rossetti's studio between the years 1863 and 1868. Like his close friend Rossetti, Smetham was a poet as well as a painter. Some of his criticism about artists as diverse as William Blake, John Linnell, and John Constable was published, and in his journals he also commented at length on the contemporary art and literary scene and on individuals such as Algernon Swinburne, Albert Moore, and Holman Hunt. Another subject he often addressed was his devout Methodism, which he believed to be in conflict with the reigning taste and values of the Victorian art market and the public.

Despite financial and health troubles, Smetham produced over four hundred paintings as well as numerous etchings and book illustrations. Most of the artist's paintings treated biblical themes and pastoral or Arcadian subjects, and many themes found in his poems—for example solitary travellers, pilgrims, and states of heightened communion with nature as well as psychological isolation and alienation—recurred in his paintings. Notable examples include a self-portrait of 1844 (AM Oxf.); *Naboth in the Vineyard* of 1856 (Tate collection); *The Dream* of 1856 (High Museum of Art, Atlanta, Georgia); *Evening Pasture* from the 1860s (Yale U. CBA); and *The Rose of Dawn* (c.1872–4; Forbes Magazine Collection, New York). His skill as a draughtsman is evident in works such as *The Flight of Porphyry* (*The Eve of St. Agnes*) (c.1858; Tate collection) and a series of twelve etchings he produced for *Studies from an Artist's Sketchbook* of 1861–2. Stylistically, Smetham moved from highly finished portraits and Pre-Raphaelite-

inspired works and techniques (done partly under the tutelage of Rossetti) to more personalized, imaginative landscapes executed with a looser, deliberately generalized handling.

In his writings Smetham frequently expressed his avid hopes and complicated theories about how audiences might understand the deeper meanings of his paintings and therefore might buy them, but he increasingly became disillusioned with their reactions to his art. While his own fate in the Victorian art market between 1850 and 1877 proved disappointing, he nevertheless codified his views on the subject both in words and in unique journal diagrams which represented patronage schematically, for example idiosyncratic associations of colour, the elements, and even 'trees of art'.

Plagued by bouts of mental illness and 'religious melancolia' throughout his life, Smetham experienced a final collapse in 1877 (possibly precipitated by debt to a patron). Various treatments and doctors were tried, including the Hydropathic Institution in Malvern, but Smetham none the less totally withdrew, rarely spoke, and became deluded. Despite the support of his family and friends, in his final years Smetham believed that God had abandoned him and that his paintings were worthless. He died on 5 February 1889, at Chipping Ongar, Essex, and was buried in Highgate cemetery.

RICHARD GARNETT, *rev.* SUSAN P. CASTERAS

Sources S. P. Casteras, *James Smetham: artist, author, Pre-Raphaelite associate* (1995) · *Letters of James Smetham, with an introductory memoir*, ed. S. Smetham and W. Davies (1891); 2nd edn (1892); repr. (1902) · *The literary works of James Smetham*, ed. W. Davies (1893) · J. Smetham, MS 'Daily journal', priv. coll. · J. Smetham, ed. S. Smetham, MS 'Family letters and memoranda, with some additional letters of J.S.', priv. coll. · J. Smetham, ed. S. Smetham, MS 'Letters and reminiscences', 2 vols., priv. coll. · J. Smetham, MS 'Studio notes', Dec 1871–Aug 1873, priv. coll. · m. cert. · d. cert.
Archives BL, literary notebook, Add. MS 50148 · priv. coll., MS daily journal, MS family papers and memoranda, MS letters and reminiscences, MS studio notes · Queen Mary College, London, corresp. and papers | Bodl. Oxf., letters from and concerning him, MSS Eng. c5315 · JRL, letters to Joseph Jones
Likenesses J. Smetham, self-portrait, oils, 1844, AM Oxf. · J. Smetham, self-portrait, chalk and wash, c.1845, NPG

Smethurst, Allan Francis (1927–2000), popular singer and songwriter, was born at 22 Pennington Street, Walshaw, Bury, Lancashire, on 18 November 1927, the son of Allan Smethurst, railway worker, and his wife, Gladys Mabel George, *née* Curson. He moved with his parents to Sheringham, Norfolk, as a boy, where he attended a local council school, and subsequently Paston grammar school, North Walsham.

Smethurst became a postman at Grimsby in 1953, and in his spare time began writing songs in Norfolk dialect which reflected the speech, mannerisms, and attitudes of the local people he had known or invented; sentiment was usually tinged with a perky but sad scepticism about human nature, which mirrored traditional East Anglian attitudes. The bespectacled and gap-toothed Smethurst sent a tape of some of his songs to the BBC at Norwich. From 1959 the performances of the Singing Postman, set to his own guitar accompaniment, were broadcast on local programmes, including *Wednesday Morning*. This was presented by the Lowestoft animal-feed merchant Ralph Tuck, who, faced in 1964 with lack of interest from the big recording companies, formed what he called The Smallest Recording Organisation in the World to record and release Smethurst's songs. Some publicity was organized by Tuck's friend, the local food manufacturer George W. Barker.

The first 7-inch vinyl extended play disc, issued in 1964, included 'Hev yew gotta loight, boy', Smethurst's best-remembered song. It concerned a Norfolk courtship which proceeded at a snail's pace because of the girl's repeated demands for lights for her cigarette. It became his greatest success, but the record also included three others: 'Come along a me', 'Moind yer hid, boy', and 'A miss from Diss'. Tuck at first cautiously ordered 100 copies of the disc. It sold more than 10,000 in four months, and outsold the Beatles in East Anglia. 'Hev yew gotta loight, boy' featured in the first LP, called *The Singing Postman's Year*, alongside drily bucolic musings with titles such as 'The Postman's Lament', 'January sales', 'Are yew alroight, boy', 'Followin' the boinder round', and 'Wass the bottom dropped owt'.

Smethurst's fame coincided with the 1960s satire boom, and to a limited extent drew upon it. The song called 'Moind yer hid, boy' was based on the drily mischievous theory that falling on to your head as a child could be beneficial in promoting a lifelong desire to 'moind yer hid', which might save you from all sorts of disasters, including wedlock (he himself never married). He was the supposed inspiration for Rambling Syd Rumpo, a character on the comedy radio programme *Round the Horne*, who sang cod-folk songs. Fame won him an engagement at the Windmill Theatre, Great Yarmouth, in 1965 and, after twelve years' service he left the Post Office. He was allowed to retain the postman's uniform which had become his stage costume and his trademark. He was a success with seaside audiences but a prey to stage fright. To counteract this, he began drinking whisky heavily. Though he appeared on television on the *Des O'Connor Show* and the BBC magazine programme *Nationwide*, and did a twelve-week show in Cardiff in 1966, his stage fright and drinking became an increasing problem, not lessened when 'Hev yew gotta loight, boy' won the Ivor Novello award for best novelty song of 1966. The version of the song later recorded by the Australian entertainer Rolf Harris took it back into the music charts, and in 1994 it was used in a television commercial for Ovaltine.

Smethurst gradually fell from public view and by 1970 arthritis had crippled his fingers so that he could no longer play the guitar. By then he depended on the dole: he confessed that he had made £20,000 from the eighty songs he had written, but had spent it all. In 1977 he recorded a little-regarded single, 'Fertilising Lisa'.

Smethurst died on 22 December 2000 in Grimsby where, dogged by his alcohol problems, he had been living since 1980 in a Salvation Army hostel. A seven-CD edition of his works was being issued by Anglian Music of Caister at the time of his death. There was something of the disorientated lost child in Smethurst's life and in much of his original and doleful work, which helped give it a sad charm. But he was virtually the only composer and performer of dialect songs to establish—even if only briefly—a national as well as a local reputation in the second half of the twentieth century. DENNIS BARKER

Sources personal knowledge (2004) · D. Barker, 'Local boy sings good', *The Guardian* (3 May 1965) · A. Smethurst, 'My early life', *East Anglian Magazine* (Jan 1976) · I. Walker, 'I've gotta loight again!', *The Sun* (15 Aug 1977) · *Eastern Daily Press* (23 Dec 2000) · *The Guardian* (27 Dec 2000) · *The Independent* (26 Dec 2000) · b. cert.
Wealth at death virtually nil; lived in Salvation Army hostel

Smethurst, John (1793–1859), Unitarian minister, was born at Failsworth, near Manchester, the son of a farmer. Having adopted Unitarian views, in 1814 he entered the academy at Hackney, Middlesex, which had been founded the year before by Robert Aspland to train popular Unitarian preachers. Having left Hackney in 1816, he acted as supply in vacant pulpits and for a time in a chapel at Dorchester. In July 1817 he became minister of the Unitarian congregation in Cross Street Chapel, Moretonhampstead, Devon. On the death on 2 December 1818 of Jacob Isaac, minister of the Fore Street General Baptist congregation, Smethurst succeeded him, holding both charges.

For some years the managers of the Unitarian Fund in London had tried in vain to get a missionary for the north of Ireland. At length Smethurst volunteered, and during the autumn of 1821 spent nine weeks in Ulster. His valuable report chronicles the mixed results of his efforts. He was warmly welcomed by some ministers, among them Fletcher Blakely at Moneyreagh and Andrew Craig (1754–1833) at Lisburn. At other places churches were closed against him, sometimes by the action of the committee overruling a well-disposed minister, but he was able to conduct some meetings in schoolrooms when churches were shut; on one such occasion he reported an attendance of a thousand. He thought that opposition to Unitarian ideas itself generated interest and that he had been able to encourage Christians who had come to Unitarian views by study of the Bible, 'almost the only Unitarian book of which they had ever heard' (J. Smethurst, 'Unitarian Fund report, 1822', *Christian Reformer*, 1st ser., 1822, 217–20), and even to open the minds of unbelievers who had been driven to that extreme position through rebellion against Calvinist orthodoxy. He was in fact the unwitting cause of the eventual separation, in 1829, of the remonstrant (Arian) party from the General Synod of Ulster by energizing the great controversial powers of Henry Cooke (1788–1868).

Returning to Moretonhampstead, Smethurst spent the rest of his life there. For some years he was scribe to the Exeter assembly, a periodic meeting of ministers that had survived from the seventeenth century. He devoted his leisure to Anglo-Saxon studies, and his fame as an angler led the minister and poet John Johns to style him the Walton of the moor. After a long illness he died, unmarried, on 27 June 1859 at Court Street, Moretonhampstead, and was buried on 3 July in the Cross Street burial-ground; the funeral sermon was preached by George Browne Brock (1805–1886) of Exeter. He has been confused with John Smethurst (1789–1820), educated at Manchester College, York, from 1805 to 1810, and minister at Knutsford, Cheshire, from 1810 to 1819.

ALEXANDER GORDON, *rev.* R. K. WEBB

Sources [G. B. Brock], 'Memoir of the late Rev. John Smethurst', *Christian Reformer, or, Unitarian Magazine and Review*, new ser., 15 (1859), 474–7 · A. Brockett, *Nonconformity in Exeter, 1650–1875* (1962) · d. cert.

Wealth at death under £200: probate, 20 July 1859, *CGPLA Eng. & Wales*

Smeton, Thomas. *See* Smeaton, Thomas (1536–1583).

Smibert, John (1688–1751), portrait painter, born at Edinburgh on 24 March 1688, was the second youngest of six children of Alison and John Smibert, a litster, or wool dyer. From 1702 to 1709 he was apprenticed to a house painter and plasterer in Edinburgh. In London by 1713 Smibert joined the Great Queen Street Academy, governed by Sir Godfrey Kneller, who greatly influenced his style. Two years later he returned to Edinburgh, where he found a patron in the Scottish judge Francis Grant, Lord Cullen of Monymusk. Smibert's half-length portrait, *Sir Francis Grant* (*c*.1720–26; Scot. NPG) and the ambitious eleven-figure group portrait *Sir Francis Grant and his Family* (1718; priv. coll.) are among his earliest surviving works.

In 1719 Smibert went to Italy, where he remained until 1722. During his stay he looked at and acquired works of art while painting portraits from life and copies after Raphael. On his return to London he opened a studio; his circle included the noted engraver and biographer George Vertue. He was an active member of the Rose and Crown Club, and about 1725 he joined the Society of Antiquaries, one of few artists to do so. His most notable portraits from these years are his full-length *Benjamin Morland* (1724; Yale U. CBA) and a three-quarters-length *Colonel James Otway* (1724; Royal Sussex Regiment, Chichester).

By 1728 George Berkeley (1685–1753), then dean of Derry (later bishop of Cloyne), persuaded Smibert to accompany him on his unsuccessful mission to establish a college in Bermuda, where Smibert was to teach painting. Smibert's masterpiece, the *Bermuda Group* (*c*.1729–31; Yale University Art Gallery, New Haven, Connecticut), commemorates those instrumental in the endeavour. It was the most sophisticated group portrait painted in the American colonies during the first half of the eighteenth century. While awaiting the fate of Berkeley's venture Smibert settled in Boston, where many of the leading citizens patronized him. On 30 July 1730 he married Mary Williams (*b*. *c*.1707/8, *d*. after 1760), the daughter of a local schoolmaster. Apart from a lucrative painting trip in 1740 to Philadelphia, New York, and Burlington, New Jersey, Smibert remained in Boston, where he painted 250 portraits.

Smibert painted landscapes for his own amusement, the only surviving example of which is his *View of Boston* (*c*.1738–41; Childs Gallery, Boston, Massachusetts), and completed the design for Faneuil Hall, Boston's first public market. During the 1740s his health became increasingly frail, and he ceased painting in 1746. He died in

Queen Street, Boston, on 2 April 1751 and was buried on 5 April in the Granary burying-ground. His son Nathaniel Smibert (1735–1756) briefly continued his father's profession.

RICHARD H. SAUNDERS

Sources R. H. Saunders, *John Smibert: colonial America's first portrait painter* (1995) · D. Evans, J. Kerslake, and A. Oliver, 'introduction', in *The notebook of John Smibert* (1969) · Vertue, *Note books*, 3.14, 24, 28–9, 36, 42–3, 161 · H. W. Foote, *John Smibert, painter* (1950) · J. Ingamells, ed., *A dictionary of British and Irish travellers in Italy, 1701–1800* (1997), 864–5

Archives Bolton Archive Service, corresp. · PRO, notebook

Likenesses J. Smibert, self-portrait, oils, *c*.1728, Montclair Art Museum, New Jersey · J. Smibert, group portrait, oils, *c*.1729–1731 (*Bermuda group*), Yale U.

Wealth at death £1387: Saunders, *John Smibert*, 263–4

Smibert, Thomas (1810–1854), poet and writer, was born on 8 February 1810 in Peebles, the son of Thomas Smibert, leather merchant and provost of the town (1808–11), and Janet Tait. Educated in Peebles, Smibert was apprenticed to a druggist, and afterwards qualified as a surgeon at Edinburgh University. He practised briefly in Innerleithen, near Peebles, but, disenchanted by his lack of success in both love and business, he left after a year. He settled in Peebles, where he was engaged by *Chambers's Edinburgh Journal*, of which he became sub-editor and editor between 1837 and 1842. During that time he wrote about 650 literary articles, tales, and biographical sketches for the periodical. He was also a major contributor to Chambers's *Information for the People* and latterly to *Hogg's Instructor*. In 1842 he became sub-editor of *The Scotsman*, but on receiving a legacy he soon afterwards abandoned journalism for literature.

In 1842 Smibert's historical play *Condé's Wife* had a run of nine nights in the Edinburgh Theatre Royal. His *Clans of the Highlands of Scotland* (1850) was admired for its authoritative nature. He collected his miscellaneous poems under the title *Io Anche! Poems Chiefly Lyrical* (1851). His most highly regarded poetry was that based on his early life, in particular 'The Scottish Widow's Lament', a portrait of life in the Tweedside glens written in dialect. Smibert died at Edinburgh on 16 January 1854.

T. W. BAYNE, *rev.* VICTORIA MILLAR

Sources private information (1897) · *The Scotsman* (17 Jan 1854) · C. Rogers, *The modern Scottish minstrel, or, The songs of Scotland of the past half-century*, 6 vols. (1855–7) · J. Hedderwick, *Backward glances, or, Some personal recollections* (1891), 98, 186, 269 · A. Williamson, *Glimpses of Peebles, or, Forgotten chapters in its history* (1895), chap. 5, pp. 221–3 · J. Veitch, *The history and poetry of the Scottish border* (1878), 530–35 · Irving, *Scots.* · R. Inglis, *The dramatic writers of Scotland* (1868), 105 · Boase, *Mod. Eng. biog.*

Likenesses attrib. T. Gibson, portrait

Smiles, Patricia. *See* Fisher, Patricia (1921–1995).

Smiles, Samuel (1812–1904), biographer and didact, born in a house on the High Street, Haddington, East Lothian, Scotland, on 23 December 1812, was one of eleven children of Samuel Smiles, at first a paper maker and afterwards a general merchant, who died of cholera early in 1832. His mother was Janet, daughter of Robert Wilson and Elizabeth, *née* Yellowlees, of Dalkeith. His paternal grandfather was an elder and field-preacher of the

Samuel Smiles (1812–1904), by Sir George Reid

Cameronians, the sect which suffered persecution in Charles II's reign, and his father was an Anti-Burgher. Childhood in this secessionist sect made a lasting impression on Samuel Smiles, though he soon abandoned the theological aspect of its extreme Calvinism.

After education at Patrick Hardie's school in Haddington and Haddington Academy, Smiles was bound apprentice for five years on 6 November 1826 to a firm of medical practitioners in the town. Dr Lewins, one of the partners, moved to Leith in 1829 and took Smiles with him. He matriculated at Edinburgh University in November 1829 and attended the medical classes there. John Brown, author of *Rab and his Friends*, was a fellow student. On the expiration of his apprenticeship he took lodgings in Edinburgh and, pursuing his medical education, obtained his medical diploma on 6 November 1832. Thereupon he set up as a surgeon and general practitioner in Haddington, though without a regular practice. His ambitions travelled beyond the routine of his profession, and he soon supplemented his narrow income by popular lectures on chemistry, physiology, and the conditions of health, as well as by contributions to the *Edinburgh Weekly Chronicle*. In 1837 he published at Edinburgh, at his own expense, 750 copies of *Physical Education, or, The Nurture and Management of Children* (2nd edn, 1868). The work was generally commended. A new edition with additions by Sir Hugh Beevor, bt, appeared in 1905. In the 1830s, Smiles's contacts with Unitarianism, and especially the influence of W. E. Channing, added rationalism to the dutiful morality

which he retained from Calvinism. Discontented with the prospects of his Haddington practice and anxious to widen his experience, in May 1838 he sold such property as he possessed and left Haddington for Hull, with a view to a foreign tour. From Rotterdam he went to Leiden, where he submitted himself to examination for a degree. A walking tour followed through the Netherlands and up the Rhine. In September 1838 he paid a first visit to London, lodging in the same boarding house (in Poland Street, Oxford Street) as Mazzini, and presenting introductions to Rowland Hill. On his way north he visited Ebenezer Elliott at Sheffield. Thence in answer to a newspaper advertisement, he went to Leeds to fulfil an engagement on the *Leeds Times*, a journal of advanced radicalism, from the editorship of which Robert Nicoll had just retired. In November 1838 Smiles became editor at a salary of £200 a year.

At Leeds, Smiles combined active, advanced radicalism with writing some 600 editorials for the *Leeds Times*. He was first secretary of the Leeds Household Suffrage Association for the redistribution and extension of the franchise. At public meetings in the city and its neighbourhood he advocated the anti-cornlaw movement and was markedly anti-aristocratic. He corresponded with Cobden and enthusiastically supported Joseph Hume's abortive candidature for Leeds at the general election of 1841. But his caution about Chartism softened his radicalism, and he came to look to individual improvement rather than structural change as the chief means of social advance. His many articles written in *Eliza Cook's Journal* between 1849 and 1854 reflected this change. In 1842 he resigned the editorship of the *Leeds Times*. Devoting himself to popular lecturing and literary hack work, he prepared guides to America and the colonies, and brought out in 1843, in monthly numbers, *A History of Ireland and the Irish People under the Government of England*, which was published collectively in 1844. On 7 December 1843 he married at Leeds Sarah Ann Holmes, daughter of a Leeds contractor. They had three daughters, one of whom, Janet, married into the Hartree family, and two sons.

In June 1840 Smiles had attended the opening of the North Midland Railway from Leeds to Derby, and met George Stephenson for the first time. When, at the end of 1845, the Leeds and Thirsk Railway was projected, Smiles was appointed assistant secretary. He was closely associated with railway enterprise for the next twenty-one years. The new Thirsk line was opened on 9 July 1849. In the same year Smiles published an essay on *Railway Property, its Conditions and Prospects*, which ran through two editions. He also acted as secretary of the board that managed the new Leeds Central Station, into which many companies ran their trains. He was prominent in the negotiations for the amalgamation of the Leeds and Thirsk Railway with the North Eastern, which was effected in 1854 and abolished his own office. Thereupon he left Leeds for London on being appointed secretary to the South Eastern Railway (11 November). He held the post for twelve years, in the course of which he successfully arranged for the extension of the line from Charing Cross to Cannon Street

(1858–9). He left the South Eastern Railway on 30 August 1866 and became president of the National Provident Institution.

Smiles continued writing and lecturing, but with a liberal rather than a radical tone. In *The Constitutional*, a Glasgow paper, he urged the transference of private bills to local legislatures. He wrote much on behalf of workmen's benefit societies in the *Leeds Mercury* and elsewhere, and for a time edited the *Oddfellows' Magazine*. He championed state education. The establishment of public libraries was one of his special interests, and he gave evidence in their favour before a House of Commons committee in 1849, welcoming the permissive Library and Museums Act of the following year. Between 1858 and 1869 Smiles wrote twelve articles on industrial subjects for the *Quarterly Review*; an article on 'Workmen's earnings, strikes, and savings' was reissued as a pamphlet in 1861. A speech at Huddersfield on the 'Industrial education of foreign and English workmen' was published in 1867.

While in Leeds, Smiles had developed his contacts with George Stephenson; after Stephenson's death in 1848 he wrote a memoir of him for *Eliza Cook's Journal* (1849) and then persuaded Stephenson's son, Robert, to allow him to write a full biography, which was published in June 1857, with a good sale and many reprints for the rest of the century. Smiles developed this interest with *Lives of the Engineers* (3 vols., 1861–2), *Industrial Biography: Iron Workers and Tool Makers* (1863), and *Lives of Boulton and Watt* (1865). A life of Robert Stephenson was included in the 1868 edition of his father's biography. This was a remarkable corpus. Smiles's biographies were carefully compiled, partly from interviews. He sometimes protected his subjects and used evidence partially, but his biographical studies represented a marked historiographical advance (though today they must be used with caution). He almost invented the subject of business history. His aim was to write about engineers within the tradition of exemplary biography, but his 'lives' transcended that genre. These 'lives' were those of men already famous, and were intended to show what character and application could achieve. But Smiles was also much interested in the education and improvement of ordinary people. One of his lectures, delivered as early as March 1845 to a mutual improvement society in Leeds, became especially popular with his audiences. Expanded for publication, it was rejected by Routledge in 1855 but was published by John Murray in 1859 as *Self-Help, with Illustrations of Character and Conduct*. The book, whose title quickly became a catch-phrase, caught the optimistic mood of its period; 20,000 copies were sold in the first year and 258,000 by 1905. It was widely translated, including into Dutch, German, Danish, Swedish, Spanish, Turkish, Arabic, and various Indian languages; it was especially popular in Japan and Italy (where by 1889 it had sold 75,000 copies in eighteen editions). The book later came to stand for the coarsest strain of Victorian materialism, but in fact it reflected an association of the moral aspects of the Calvinism Smiles had been taught as a child with the educational values of the Unitarians and the radicalism of the Anti-Corn Law League. The phrase 'self-help' came

perhaps from Carlyle and the book owed an explicit debt to G. L. Craik's *Pursuit of Knowledge under Difficulties* (2 vols., 1831–2). Smiles emphasized the importance of the application of good character to the problems of daily life as the key to individual and social improvement and illustrated his message with biographical examples. 'Character', he believed 'is the true antiseptic of society' (Travers, 256). Believing that his essential message was only partially accepted and cautious about the effect of the extension of the franchise in 1867, he developed his theme in *Character* (1871), *Thrift* (1875), *Duty* (1880), and *Life and Labour* (1887). By the 1890s, Smiles's individualism had lost its interest and in 1896 Murray turned down 'Conduct', the last of the series (Travers, 284).

Parallel to this series of national homilies, Smiles developed his skills as a biographer, accepting only subjects which appealed to him. From research in France into the Huguenots, which also produced *The Huguenots in France after the revocation of the edict of Nantes; with a visit to the Vandois* (1874), he published (1881) the life of Jacques Jasmin, the barber-poet of Agen. Self-taught Scots especially fitted the Smilesian mould and his lives of Thomas Edward of Banff, the naturalist (1876), and Robert Dick (1878), the Thurso baker who was also a botanist and geologist, are thorough as well as apologetic. His life (1878) of the philanthropist, George Moore, was the most popular of his later publications, but he disliked Moore's material success. *Josiah Wedgwood* (1894) was the last of these studies. Different in character, but an important work in the history of the publishing industry, was *A Publisher and his Friends: Memoir and Correspondence of the Late John Murray* (2 vols., 1891; abridged edn, 1911).

Smiles travelled widely in Europe, visiting Friesland in 1871 and 1881, Norway in 1884, and Italy three times, being, in 1879 on his second visit, received by Garibaldi and Queen Margherita. In 1880 he received the Italian order of St Maurice and St Lazarus and his fading radicalism was too weak to prevent him complaining at the rules which stopped him sporting it in Britain.

Smiles did not maintain the radicalism of his early years or a trust in middle- and working-class co-operation. In his later years he was a unionist on Ireland and an individualist with Conservative sympathies. But as his radicalism softened so did his edge, and his autobiography, which described his life to 1890, had a mellow, unpretentious tone. It was published posthumously by his friend and fellow individualist, Thomas Mackay. Smiles suffered from periodic bouts of illness, especially in 1871 and after, when he retired from the National Provident Institution. In 1874 he moved from Blackheath, in radical Greenwich, to 8 Pembroke Gardens, Kensington, where he died on 16 April 1904 after several years of failing powers. He was buried in Brompton cemetery.

Smiles became an almost burlesque figure in the early twentieth-century reaction against Victorianism, but historical interest in him developed in the 1950s, since which time he has been the subject of considerable research. A bowdlerized edition of *Self-Help*, abridged by George Bull with an introduction by Sir Keith Joseph (1986), did him little service. His business biographies retain their position as regularly consulted works.

H. C. G. MATTHEW

Sources T. Travers, *Samuel Smiles and the Victorian work ethic* (1987) · S. Smiles, *The autobiography of Samuel Smiles*, ed. T. Mackay (1905) · A. Smiles, *Samuel Smiles and his surroundings* (1956) · A. Briggs, *Victorian people* (1955) · J. F. C. Harrison, 'The Victorian gospel of success', *Victorian Studies*, 1 (1957–8) · K. Fielden, 'Samuel Smiles and self-help', *Victorian Studies*, 12 (1968–9), 155–76 · *The Times* (17 April 1904) · *CGPLA Eng. & Wales* (1904)

Archives BL, domestic and literary papers, Add. MSS 71070–71093 · Leeds Central Library · NL Scot., corresp. and copy of 'Life of a Scotch Naturalist' · W. Yorks. AS, Leeds, corresp. and papers | BL, Place MSS · FM Cam., Eva Hartree MSS · PRO, British Transport Historical Records · W. Sussex RO, Cobden MSS

Likenesses G. Reid, oils, 1879, Scot. NPG · A. Rossetti, bust, 1879 · G. de Sancto, sketch, 1889 · G. Reid, oils, 1891, Scot. NPG · L. Jopling-Rowe, chalk drawing, NPG · G. Reid, oils, NPG [*see illus.*] · Spy [L. Ward], chromolithograph caricature, NPG; repro. in *VF* (14 Jan 1882) · W. Walker & Sons, carte-de-visite, NPG

Wealth at death £79,964 10*s.* 11*d.*: administration, 6 July 1904, *CGPLA Eng. & Wales*

PICTURE CREDITS

Sharp, Abraham (*bap.* 1653, *d.* 1742)—Ashmolean Museum, Oxford

Sharp, Cecil James (1859-1924)—© National Portrait Gallery, London

Sharp, Clifford Dyce (1883-1935)—© reserved; New Statesman and Society; photograph National Portrait Gallery, London

Sharp, Evelyn Adelaide, Baroness Sharp (1903-1985)—© Yevonde Portrait Archive; collection National Portrait Gallery, London

Sharp, Granville (1735-1813)—© National Portrait Gallery, London

Sharp, James (1618-1679)—private collection

Sharp, John (1645?-1714)—reproduced by permission of His Grace the Lord Archbishop of York and the Church Commissioners

Sharp, William [Fiona MacLeod] (1855-1905)—Royal Photographic Society

Sharpe, Charles Kirkpatrick (1781-1851)—© National Portrait Gallery, London

Sharpe, Daniel (1806-1856)—© National Portrait Gallery, London

Sharpe, Richard Bowdler (1847-1909)—by permission of the Linnean Society of London

Sharples, Rolinda (1793-1838)—City Art Gallery, Bristol / Bridgeman Art Library

Shastri, Lal Bahadur (1904-1966)—Getty Images - Terry Fincher

Shaw, Alfred (1842-1907)—© National Portrait Gallery, London

Shaw, Charles James Dalrymple, Baron Kilbrandon (1906-1989)—© National Portrait Gallery, London

Shaw, Sir Eyre Massey (1828-1908)—© National Portrait Gallery, London

Shaw, George Bernard (1856-1950)—© Fitzwilliam Museum, University of Cambridge

Shaw, Glencairn Alexander Byam (1904-1986)—© National Portrait Gallery, London

Shaw, Helen Brown (1879-1964)—© National Portrait Gallery, London

Shaw, (George William) Hudson (1859-1944)—private collection

Shaw, Sir (William) Napier (1854-1945)—© National Portrait Gallery, London

Shaw, Percy (1890-1976)—Getty Images - Peter Laurie

Shaw, Richard Norman (1831-1912)—© National Portrait Gallery, London

Shaw, Robert Archibald (1927-1978)—© Bob Collins; collection National Portrait Gallery, London

Shaw, Thomas, first Baron Craigmyle (1850-1937)—© National Portrait Gallery, London

Shaw, Thomas (1872-1938)—© National Portrait Gallery, London

Sheares, John (1766-1798)—National Gallery of Ireland

Shee, Sir Martin Archer (1769-1850)—© National Portrait Gallery, London

Sheffield, Edmund, first earl of Mulgrave (1565-1646)—© National Portrait Gallery, London

Sheffield, John, first duke of Buckingham and Normanby (1647-1721)—© National Maritime Museum, London

Sheil, Richard Lalor (1791-1851)—National Gallery of Ireland

Sheldon, Gilbert (1598-1677)—University of Oxford: Curators of the Sheldonian Theatre; photograph: The Paul Mellon Centre for Studies in British Art

Sheldon, John (1752-1808)—© National Portrait Gallery, London

Shelley, Mary Wollstonecraft (1797-1851)—© National Portrait Gallery, London

Shelley, Percy Bysshe (1792-1822)—© National Portrait Gallery, London

Shelley, Sir Richard (*c.*1513-1587)—© Copyright The British Museum

Shelton, Anne (1923-1994)—V&A Images, The Victoria and Albert Museum; collection National Portrait Gallery, London

Shemza, Anwar Jalal (1928-1985)—private collection Mary Shemza

Shepard, Ernest Howard (1879-1976)—© National Portrait Gallery, London

Shepherd, Ian Douglas Dawson- (1915-1996)—Scope

Shepherd, Sir Samuel (1760-1840)—photograph by courtesy Sotheby's Picture Library, London

Sheppard, Sir Fleetwood (1634-1698)—private collection. Photograph: Photographic Survey, Courtauld Institute of Art, London

Sheppard, John [Jack] (1702-1724)—Collection Museum of London; © reserved in the photograph

Sheppard, Sir John Tressider (1881-1968)—© National Portrait Gallery, London

Sheppard, Katherine Wilson (1847-1934)—Alexander Turnbull Library, National Library of New Zealand, Te Puna Matauranga o Aotearoa (C-9028-1/2)

Shepstone, Sir Theophilus (1817-1893)—© National Portrait Gallery, London

Sheridan, Frances (1724-1766)—© National Portrait Gallery, London

Sheridan, Richard Brinsley (1751-1816)—© National Portrait Gallery, London

Sheridan, Thomas (1719?-1788)—National Gallery of Ireland

Sherley, Anthony, Count Sherley in the nobility of the Holy Roman empire (1565-1636?)—© National Portrait Gallery, London

Sherlock, Thomas (1677-1761)—© National Portrait Gallery, London

Sherriff, Robert Cedric (1896-1975)—© National Portrait Gallery, London

Sherrington, Helen Lemmens- (1834-1906)—© National Portrait Gallery, London

Sherwin, John Keyse (*bap.* 1751, *d.* 1790)—© National Portrait Gallery, London

Shield, William (*bap.* 1748/9, *d.* 1829)—© National Portrait Gallery, London

Shinwell, Emanuel, Baron Shinwell (1884-1986)—© National Portrait Gallery, London

Shipley, Sir Arthur Everett (1861-1927)—The de László Foundation; Witt Library, Courtauld Institute of Art, London

Shipley, Jonathan (1713-1788)—© National Portrait Gallery, London

Shipley, William (*bap.* 1715, *d.* 1803)—RSA London

Shipley, William Davies (1745-1826)—© National Portrait Gallery, London

Shipp, John (1785-1834)—© National Portrait Gallery, London

Shippen, William (*bap.* 1673, *d.* 1743)—reproduced by kind permission of His Grace the Duke of Beaufort. Photograph: Photographic Survey, Courtauld Institute of Art, London

Shipton, Eric Earle (1907-1977)—The Royal Geographical Society, London

Shirley, James (*bap.* 1596, *d.* 1666)—© Bodleian Library, University of Oxford

Shirley, Laurence, fourth Earl Ferrers (1720-1760)—© National Portrait Gallery, London

Shirley, William (1694-1771)—private collection. National Portrait Gallery, Smithsonian Institution

Shore, Elizabeth [Jane] (*d.* 1526/7?)—The Provost and Fellows of Eton College

Shore, (Margaret) Emily (1819-1839)—© National Portrait Gallery, London

Shore, John, first Baron Teignmouth (1751-1834)—© National Portrait Gallery, London

Short, Sir Francis Job (1857-1945)—© reserved; Garton & Co.

Short, (Hugh) Oswald (1883-1969)—Royal Aeronautical Society Library

Shorter, Dora Mary (1866-1918)—National Gallery of Ireland

Shorthouse, Joseph Henry (1834-1903)—© National Portrait Gallery, London

Shovell, Sir Cloudesley (*bap.* 1650, *d.* 1707)—© National Maritime Museum, London, Greenwich Hospital Collection

Showering, Francis Edwin (1912-1995)—© News International Newspapers Ltd

Shrapnel, Henry (1761-1842)—from the collection of The Royal Artillery Institution, Woolwich

Shuckburgh, Sir (Charles Arthur) Evelyn (1909-1994)—© National Portrait Gallery, London

Shuckburgh, Sir John Evelyn (1877-1953)—© National Portrait Gallery, London

Shudi, Burkat (1702-1773)—© National Portrait Gallery, London

Shuttleworth, Sir James Phillips Kay-, first baronet (1804-1877)—© National Portrait Gallery, London

Sibbald, James (1747-1803)—© Scottish National Portrait Gallery

Sibbald, Sir Robert (1641-1722)—Royal College of Physicians of Edinburgh

Sibbes, Richard (1577?-1635)—© National Portrait Gallery, London

Sibly, Sir (Thomas) Franklin (1883-1948)—by permission of the University of Reading

Sibthorp, Charles de Laet Waldo (1783-1855)—© National Portrait Gallery, London

Sibthorp, Richard Waldo (1792-1879)—© National Portrait Gallery, London

Sickert, Walter Richard (1860-1942)—© Estate of Walter R. Sickert 2004. All rights reserved, DACS; Collection Art Gallery of Hamilton, Gift of the Women's Committee, 1970

Siddal, Elizabeth Eleanor (1829-1862)—© Fitzwilliam Museum, University of Cambridge

Siddeley, John Davenport, first Baron Kenilworth (1866-1953)—Quadrant Picture Library

Siddiqui, Kalim (1933-1996)—© News International Newspapers Ltd

Siddons, Henry (1774-1815)—© National Portrait Gallery, London

Siddons, Sarah (1755-1831)—The Huntington Library, Art Collections and Botanical Gardens, San Marino, CA, USA

Sidgwick, Eleanor Mildred (1845-1936)—The Principal and Fellows, Newnham College, Cambridge

Sidgwick, Henry (1838-1900)—© National Portrait Gallery, London

Sidgwick, Nevil Vincent (1873-1952)—Lincoln College, Oxford

Sidney, Algernon (1623-1683)—Christie's Images Ltd. (2004)

Sidney, Sir Henry (1529-1586)—Petworth House, The Egremont Collection (The National Trust). Photograph: Photographic Survey, Courtauld Institute of Art, London

Sidney, Henry, first earl of Romney (1641-1704)—private collection

Sidney, Sir Philip (1554-1586)—reproduced by permission of the Marquess of Bath, Longleat House, Warminster, Wiltshire, Great Britain. Photograph: Photographic Survey, Courtauld Institute of Art, London

Sidney, Robert, second earl of Leicester (1595-1677)—private collection; photograph National Portrait Gallery, London

Sieff, Israel Moses, Baron Sieff (1889-1972)—© National Portrait Gallery, London

Siemens, Sir (Charles) William (1823-1883)—© National Portrait Gallery, London

Sieveking, Sir Edward Henry (1816-1904)—by permission of the Royal College of Physicians, London

Silcox, Lucy Mary (1862-1947)—© Estate of Stanley Spencer 2004. All rights reserved, DACS; private collection